CURRENT LAW

STATUTES

ANNOTATED

1985

VOLUME FOUR

EDITOR IN CHIEF

PETER ALLSOP, C.B.E., M.A.
Barrister

GENERAL EDITOR

KEVAN NORRIS, LL.B.
Solicitor

ASSISTANT GENERAL EDITOR

JULIE HARRIS, LL.B.

ADMINISTRATION

MARY GAZE, B.A.

LONDON

SWEET & MAXWELL   STEVENS & SONS

EDINBURGH

W. GREEN & SON

1986

Published by
SWEET & MAXWELL LIMITED
and STEVENS & SONS LIMITED
of 11 New Fetter Lane, London,
and W. GREEN & SON LIMITED
of St. Giles Street, Edinburgh,
and printed in Scotland.

ISBN This Volume only : 0 421 35010 5
As a set : 0 421 35020 2

CONTENTS

CHRONOLOGICAL TABLE

STATUTES 1985

VOLUME ONE

c. 1. Consolidated Fund Act 1985
    2. Elections (Northern Ireland) Act 1985
    3. Brunei and Maldives Act 1985
    4. Milk (Cessation of Production) Act 1985
    5. New Towns and Urban Development Corporations Act 1985
    6. Companies Act 1985
    7. Business Names Act 1985
    8. Company Securities (Insider Dealing) Act 1985
    9. Companies Consolidation (Consequential Provisions) Act 1985

VOLUME TWO

   10. London Regional Transport (Amendment) Act 1985
   11. Consolidated Fund (No. 2) Act 1985
   12. Mineral Workings Act 1985
   13. Cinemas Act 1985
   14. Shipbuilding Act 1985
   15. Hong Kong Act 1985
   16. National Heritage (Scotland) Act 1985
   17. Reserve Forces (Safeguard of Employment) Act 1985
   18. Betting, Gaming and Lotteries (Amendment) Act 1985
   19. Town and Country Planning (Compensation) Act 1985
   20. Charities Act 1985
   21. Films Act 1985
   22. Dangerous Vessels Act 1985
   23. Prosecution of Offences Act 1985
   24. Rent (Amendment) Act 1985
   25. Industrial Development Act 1985
   26. Intoxicating Substances Act 1985
   27. Coal Industry Act 1985
   28. Motor-Cycle Crash-Helmets (Restriction of Liability) Act 1985
   29. Enduring Powers of Attorney Act 1985
   30. Ports (Finance) Act 1985
   31. Wildlife and Countryside (Amendment) Act 1985
   32. Hill Farming Act 1985

INDEX OF SHORT TITLES

STATUTES 1985

References are to chapter numbers of 1985

Index of Short Titles

HOUSING ACT 1985*

(1985 c.68)

Tables of derivations and destinations can be found at the end of the Act.

ARRANGEMENT OF PARTS

ARRANGEMENT OF SECTIONS

PART I

INTRODUCTORY PROVISIONS

---

* Annotations by Andrew Arden, LL.B., Barrister.

PART II

PROVISION OF HOUSING ACCOMMODATION

PART V

THE RIGHT TO BUY

The right to buy

PART VII

IMPROVEMENT NOTICES

PART VIII

AREA IMPROVEMENT

PART IX

SLUM CLEARANCE

Part X

Overcrowding

Definition of overcrowding

Part XV

Grants for Works of Improvement, Repair and Conversion

PART XVI

ASSISTANCE FOR OWNERS OF DEFECTIVE HOUSING

Schedule 16—Local authority mortgage interest rates.
Schedule 17—Vesting of mortgaged house in authority entitled to exercise power of sale.
Schedule 18–Provisions with respect to advances under the Small Dwellings Acquisition Acts 1899 to 1923.
Schedule 19—Contributions under superseded enactments.
Schedule 20—Assistance by way of repurchase.
　　Part I—The agreement to repurchase.
　　Part II—Price payable and valuation.
　　Part III—Supplementary provisions.
Schedule 21—Dwellings included in more than one designation.
Schedule 22—Compulsory purchase orders under s.290.
Schedule 23—Payments in respect of well maintained houses.
Schedule 24—Payments in respect of houses which are owner-occupied or used for business purposes.
　　Part I—Payments in respect of owner-occupied houses.
　　Part II—Payments in respect of houses used for business purposes.

An Act to consolidate the Housing Acts (except those provisions consolidated in the Housing Associations Act 1985 and the Landlord and Tenant Act 1985), and certain related provisions, with amendments to give effect to recommendations of the Law Commission.

PARLIAMENTARY DEBATES
Hansard: H.L. Vol.463, col. 531; Vol. 464, col. 163; Vol. 466, cols. 321, 863; H.C. Vol. 84, cols. 116, 955.

PART I

INTRODUCTORY PROVISIONS

Local housing authorities

Local housing authorities

1. In this Act "local housing authority" means a district council, a London borough council, the Common Council of the City of London or the Council of the Isles of Scilly.

GENERAL NOTE
　This section introduces the "local housing authority", which is the principal authority for the purposes of this Act, but which must be distinguished from the "local authority", the "housing authority", the "public sector authority", the "purchasing authority", and so on, as they occur at different points in the legislation.
　As to district councils, and the Council of the Isles of Scilly, see Local Government Act 1972.
　As to London Borough Councils, and the Common Council of the City of London, see London Government Act 1963.
　As to land in more than one district, see s.3, below.

The district of a local housing authority

2.—(1) References in this Act to the district of a local housing authority are to the area of the council concerned, that is, to the district, London borough, the City of London or the Isles of Scilly, as the case may be.

(2) References in this Act to "the local housing authority", in relation to land, are to the local housing authority in whose district the land is situated.

DEFINITION
"local housing authority": s.1.

GENERAL NOTE
As to land in more than one district, see s.3, below.

Buildings situated in more than one district

3.—(1) Where a building is situated partly in the district of one local housing authority and partly in the district of another, the authorities may agree that—

(*a*) the building, or
(*b*) the building, its site and any yard, garden, outhouses and appurtenances belonging to the building or usually enjoyed with it,

shall be treated for the purposes of the enactments relating to housing as situated in such one of the districts as is specified in the agreement.

(2) Whilst the agreement is in force the enactments relating to housing have effect accordingly.

DEFINITIONS
"district": s.2.
"local housing authority": ss.1, 2.

GENERAL NOTE
Where a building is in the area of more than one local housing authority, they *may* agree that one of them should be the local housing authority for the purposes of those enactments (which can include a single section, see Interpretation Act 1978, s.1), as the agreement specifies. The agreement may extend to sites, yards, gardens, outhouses and appurtenances (*cf.* below, s.6), even if, *e.g.*, only the building is in two areas, and the added lands wholly in the area of one of the authorities. This could be germane where, *e.g.*, compulsory purchase was in issue. But if the building is in one area, while some other land is in more than one area, this section will not apply.

Other authorities and bodies

Other descriptions of authority

4. In this Act—

(*a*) "housing authority" means a local housing authority, a new town corporation or the Development Board for Rural Wales;
(*b*) "new town corporation" means a development corporation or the Commission for the New Towns;
(*c*) "development corporation" means a development corporation established by an order made, or having effect as if made, under the New Towns Act 1981;
(*d*) "urban development corporation" means an urban development corporation established under Part XVI of the Local Government, Planning and Land Act 1980;
(*e*) "local authority" means a county, district or London borough council, the Common Council of the City of London or the Council of the Isles of Scilly, and in sections 45(2)(*b*), 50(2), 51(6), 80(1), 157(1), 171(2), 438, 441, 442, 443, 444(4), 452(2), 453(2), 573(1), paragraph 2(1) of Schedule 1, grounds 7 and 12 in Schedule 2, ground 5 in Schedule 3, paragraph 7(1) of Schedule 4, paragraph 5(1)(*b*) of Schedule 5 and Schedule 16 includes the Inner London Education Authority and a joint authority established by Part IV of the Local Government Act 1985.

"local housing authority": ss.1, 2.

GENERAL NOTE
As to the bodies referred to in para. (*e*), see London Government Act 1963, and Local Government Act 1972.

Housing associations

5.—(1) In this Act "housing association" means a society, body of trustees or company—

(*a*) which is established for the purpose of, or amongst whose objects or powers are included those of, providing, constructing, improving or managing, or facilitating or encouraging the construction or improvement of, housing accommodation, and

(*b*) which does not trade for profit or whose constitution or rules prohibit the issue of capital with interest or dividend exceeding such rate as may be prescribed by the Treasury, whether with or without differentiation as between share and loan capital.

(2) In this Act "fully mutual", in relation to a housing association, means that the rules of the association—

(*a*) restrict membership to persons who are tenants or prospective tenants of the association, and

(*b*) preclude the granting or assignment of tenancies to persons other than members;

and "co-operative housing association" means a fully mutual housing association which is a society registered under the Industrial and Provident Societies Act 1965.

(3) In this Act "self-build society" means a housing association whose object is to provide, for sale to, or occupation by, its members, dwellings built or improved principally with the use of its members' own labour.

(4) References in this Act to registration in relation to a housing association are to registration under the Housing Associations Act 1985.

GENERAL NOTE
Housing associations are now governed by the Housing Associations Act 1985. However, there are many provisions of this Act which cross–refer to housing associations.
"*trading for profit*". This means trading for profit for use and enjoyment, as distinct from raising profits which have to be retained and/or re–employed for the purposes of the business or activity of the association, which latter class of profit accordingly does not take an association outside of this definition: *Goodman* v. *Dolphin Square Trust Ltd.* (1979) 38 P. & C.R. 257, C.A.

Housing trusts

6. In this Act "housing trust" means a corporation or body of persons which—

(*a*) is required by the terms of its constituent instrument to use the whole of its funds, including any surplus which may arise from its operations, for the purpose of providing housing accommodation, or

(*b*) is required by the terms of its constituent instrument to devote the whole, or substantially the whole, of its funds for charitable purposes and in fact uses the whole, or substantially the whole, of its funds for the purpose of providing housing accommodation.

GENERAL NOTE
The phrase "including any surplus which may arise from its operations" legislatively achieves the same effect as *Goodman* v. *Dolphin Square Trust Ltd.* (1979) 38 P. & C.R. 257, C.A. (see notes to s.5, above), *i.e.* the mere fact that a profit is made on one activity does not preclude qualification as a housing trust.

Supplementary provisions

Index of defined expressions: Part I

7. The following Table shows provisions defining or otherwise explaining expressions used in this Part (other than provisions defining or explaining an expression used in the same section or paragraph):—

district (of a local housing authority)	section 2(1)
local housing authority	section 1, 2(2)
tenancy and tenant	section 621

PART II

PROVISION OF HOUSING ACCOMMODATION

Main powers and duties of local housing authorities

Periodical review of housing needs

8.—(1) Every local housing authority shall consider housing conditions in their district and the needs of the district with respect to the provision of further housing accommodation.

(2) For that purpose the authority shall review any information which has been brought to their notice, including in particular information brought to their notice as a result of inspections and surveys carried out under section 605 (periodical review of housing conditions).

DEFINITIONS
"district": s.2.
"housing accommodation": s.56.
"local housing authority": ss.1, 2.

GENERAL NOTE
Until 1980, there was not only a duty to consider conditions and needs of a district, but also to provide new housing with which in effect to fulfil those needs. Now, conditions and needs alone have to be "considered." Provisions permitting authorities to provide housing have been available since 1851 (Labouring Classes Lodging Houses Act—see also, principally of the later 19th century legislation, the Housing of the Working Classes Acts, 1885 and 1890), although the (since 1980 defunct) requirement to provide housing dated only from 1919 (Housing, Town Planning, etc. Act).

The needs of the district are not, however, confined to the needs of people currently living in the district: *Re Havant and Waterloo Urban District Council, Compulsory Purchase Order (No. 4)* [1951] 2 K.B. 779. For example, an authority will commonly wish to consider housing needs in conjunction with economic development plans, *i.e.* new housing for new industry.

When considering the needs of the district, authorities are to have regard to the special needs of the chronically sick and disabled: s.3, Chronically Sick and Disabled Persons Act 1970.

As to conditions, there is a number of ways under this Act in which information as to the condition of housing stock in a district will come to the notice of an authority, additional to the periodic reviews required under s.605 which have to be carried out with a view to determining what action to take in respect of repairs notices under Part VI, area improvement under Part VIII, slum clearance under Part IX and houses in multiple occupation under Part XI. In particular, attention may be drawn to s.606(2), complaint by a justice of the peace of individual house unfitness or area unfitness.

Housing Accommodation
See notes to s.56, below.

Provision of housing accommodation

9.—(1) A local housing authority may provide housing accommodation—

(*a*) by erecting houses, or converting buildings into houses, on land acquired by them for the purposes of this Part, or

(*b*) by acquiring houses.

(2) The authority may alter, enlarge, repair or improve a house so erected, converted or acquired.

(3) These powers may equally be exercised in relation to land acquired for the purpose—

(*a*) of disposing of houses provided, or to be provided, on the land, or

(*b*) of disposing of the land to a person who intends to provide housing accommodation on it.

(4) A local housing authority may not under this Part provide a cottage with a garden of more than one acre.

DEFINITIONS

"house": s.56.

"housing accommodation": s.56.

"local housing authority": ss.1, 2.

GENERAL NOTE

This is the principal section conferring the powers to provide "housing accommodation," under which most local authority housing stock is provided and, accordingly, under which a substantial proportion of this country's housing has been provided. The principal means are by building houses on land acquired for the purpose, or by converting buildings into houses, or by purchase of houses. There is no express power to purchase houses for conversion into flats, but houses may be purchased to "provide housing accommodation" which by s.56 includes flats, and under subs. (2), property acquired under subs. (1) can be "altered." See s.610, below, for the powers of the court to discharge restrictive covenants which would otherwise prohibit conversion. Flats can be purchased, because they are "houses" under the extended definition in s.56, below.

Accommodation may be "provided" by the acquisition of housing for improvement, even although there may be no increase in the amount of accommodation available: *Andresier* v. *Minister of Housing and Local Government* (1965) 109 S.J. 594.

The power to purchase land is contained in s.15, below.

The powers in subs. (2) are important. Authorities may "alter, enlarge, repair or improve" a house "so erected, converted or acquired." There is no other *express* power to repair, or improve, *e.g.* planned maintenance, installation of central heating, etc., although powers under s.10 and the general management powers in s.21 are relevant and the latter perhaps wide enough in its own right.

Subs. (3)

Without this express provision, the powers in subss. (1) and (2) were probably wide enough to permit "acquisition and improvement for sale" (see *Meravale Builders Ltd.* v. *Secretary of State for the Environment* (1978) 36 P. & C.R. 87, but *cf. Victoria Square Property Co. Ltd.* v. *Southwark London Borough Council* [1978] 1 W.L.R. 463, C.A.), but it is now beyond doubt that authorities can buy in order to build, convert, alter, enlarge, repair or improve for sale, or buy to resell to someone else to provide the housing. See also s.15(2), below.

Provision of furnishings and fittings

10.—(1) A local housing authority may fit out, furnish and supply a house provided by them under this Part with all requisite furniture, fittings and conveniences.

(2) A local housing authority may sell, or supply under a hire-purchase agreement or a conditional sale agreement, furniture to the occupants of houses so provided, and may for that purpose buy furniture.

(3) In subsection (2) "conditional sale agreement" and "hire-purchase agreement" have the same meaning as in the Consumer Credit Act 1974.

DEFINITIONS
    "house": s.56.
    "local housing authority": ss.1, 2.

GENERAL NOTE
    Authorities can fit out their properties with fittings and conveniences, and may provide furniture. The latter can be sold to occupiers, outright or on hire-purchase or on a conditional sale agreement. "Fittings" may imply "fixtures and fittings" as at common law (see, *e.g.*, *Leigh* v. *Taylor* [1902] A.C. 157, H.L., *Spyer* v. *Phillipson* [1931] 2 Ch. 183, *Dibble* v. *Moore* [1970] 2 Q.B. 181), but in the light of the express inclusion of furniture would not seem here an important distinction.

Subs. (3)
    A "hire-purchase agreement" under the Consumer Credit Act 1974 is an agreement, other than a "conditional sale agreement," under which goods are "bailed . . . in return for periodical payments by the person to whom they are bailed . . . and . . . the property in the goods will pass to that person if the terms of the agreement are complied with and" either the person exercises an option to purchase, or he does, or there occurs, any other act or event specified in the agreement (s.189). A conditional sale agreement is any agreement for the sale of goods under which the purchase price or part of it is payable by instalments, and the ownership remains with the vendor (even though possession passes to purchaser) until the conditions of the agreement are fulfilled (*ibid.*).

Provision of board and laundry facilities

11.—(1) A local housing authority may provide in connection with the provision of housing accommodation by them under this Part—
    (*a*) facilities for obtaining meals and refreshments, and
    (*b*) facilities for doing laundry and laundry services,
such as accord with the needs of the persons for whom the housing accommodation is provided.
    (2) The authority may make reasonable charges for meals and refreshments provided by virtue of this section and for the use of laundry facilities or laundry services so provided.
    (3) A justices' licence under the Licensing Act 1964 for the sale of intoxicating liquor in connection with the provision of facilities for obtaining meals and refreshments under this section shall only authorise the sale of such liquor for consumption with a meal.
    (4) A local housing authority in carrying on activities under this section is subject to all relevant enactments and rules of law, including enactments relating to the sale of intoxicating liquor, in the same manner as other persons carrying on such activities.

DEFINITIONS
    "housing accommodation": s.56.
    "local housing authority": ss.1, 2.

GENERAL NOTE
    Authorities may provide facilities for obtaining "meals and refreshments": this clearly refers to "restaurant" facilities (or, *e.g.*, meals by delivery, for example to the elderly, infirm or disabled), because the power to provide and maintain *shops* is to be found in s.12, below. The second limb permits the provision of laundry *facilities* or *services, i.e.* either a laundry room with, for example, washing/drying machines, *or* an actual laundry service in which laundry is taken in by staff, etc. The services and facilities are to be those which "accord with" occupiers' "needs," although it is hardly likely that authorities would contemplate providing "luxury" services that did not do so.

Subs. (2)
    As the phrase "reasonable charges" occurs in the same Part, there would seem to be no greater reason why an authority who consider it proper to do so should not provide services and facilities under these powers at less than cost, *i.e.* subsidised services and facilities, than when determining accommodation charges under s.24, below. As to the principles to be applied, see notes thereto.

Provision of shops, recreation grounds, etc.

12.—(1) A local housing authority may, with the consent of the Secretary of State, provide and maintain in connection with housing accommodation provided by them under this Part—

(*a*) buildings adapted for use as shops,

(*b*) recreation grounds, and

(*c*) other buildings or land which, in the opinion of the Secretary of State, will serve a beneficial purpose in connection with the requirements of the persons for whom the housing accommodation is provided.

(2) The Secretary of State may, in giving his consent, by order apply, with any necessary modifications, any statutory provisions which would have been applicable if the land or buildings had been provided under any enactment giving a local authority powers for the purpose.

(3) The power conferred by subsection (1) may be exercised either by the local housing authority themselves or jointly with another person.

DEFINITIONS

"housing accommodation": s.56.

"local housing authority": ss.1, 2.

GENERAL NOTE

Either solely, or in partnership with someone else, *e.g.* a private company, in connection with housing accommodation provided by them, the authority may provide and maintain shops, recreation grounds, or other buildings or land which will serve a beneficial purpose "in connection with" the requirements of occupiers, but only with the consent of the Secretary of State. In *Conron* v. *London County Council* [1922] 2 Ch. 283, it was held that "a beer-house, to be conducted on the most improved lines" could be provided to meet the wants of people living on an estate.

The "beneficial purpose" in subs. (1)(*c*) may be one to be shared not only by those in the authority's own stock, but also by those in neighbouring areas: *Green & Sons* v. *Minister of Health* [1948] 1 K.B. 34, C.A. Where benefits are shared with the community as a whole, a credit from the authority's General Rate Fund to its Housing Revenue Account will be called for: see s.418 and Sched. 14, Part IV, para. 1, below.

The authority may make by-laws in relation to the use of land held under this section, other than land covered by buildings, within the curtilage of a building, or forming part of a highway: s.23(2), below.

Provision of streets, roads and open spaces and development generally

13.—(1) A local housing authority may lay out and construct public streets or roads and open spaces on land acquired by them for the purposes of this Part.

(2) Where they dispose of land to a person who intends to provide housing accommodation on it, they may contribute towards the expenses of the development of the land and the laying out and construction of streets on it, subject to the condition that the streets are dedicated to the public.

DEFINITIONS

"housing accommodation": s.56.

"local housing authority": ss.1, 2.

GENERAL NOTE

When land is acquired for the purposes of this Part, local housing authorities may lay out and construct streets, roads and open spaces on it. The breadth of subs. (1) suggests that this must be so whether they are intending to build on the land themselves, or to sell for someone else to build housing on it (see s.9, above, and s.15, below), so that the provisions of subs. (2) are additional, *i.e.* as an alternative to making a contribution to the laying out and construction of streets on land to be resold for private development, they could carry out those works themselves. Note that under subs. (2), they can also contribute to the development of housing by someone to whom they have sold the land.

Exercise of powers by authority outside district

14.—(1) A local housing authority may, for supplying the needs of their district, exercise outside their district the powers conferred by sections 9 to 13 (provision of housing accommodation and related powers).

(2) A district council shall before doing so give notice of their intention—

(*a*) to the council of the county in which their district is situated, and

(*b*) if they propose to exercise the power outside that county, to the council of the county in which they propose to exercise the power;

but failure to give notice does not invalidate the exercise of the power.

(3) Where housing operations under this Part are being carried out by a local housing authority outside their own district, the authority's power to execute works necessary for the purposes of, or incidental to the carrying out of, the operations, is subject to entering into an agreement with the council of the county, London borough or district in which the operations are being carried out, as to the terms and conditions on which the works are to be executed.

(4) Where housing operations under this Part have been carried out by a local housing authority outside their own district, and for the purposes of the operations public streets or roads have been constructed and completed by the authority, the liability to maintain the streets or roads vests in the council which is the local highway authority for the area in which the operations were carried out unless that council are satisfied that the streets or roads have not been properly constructed.

(5) Where a local housing authority carry out housing operations outside their own district, any difference arising between that authority and any authority in whose area the operations are carried out may be referred by either authority to the Secretary of State whose decision shall be final and binding on them.

Definitions
 "district": s.2.
 "housing accommodation": s.56.
 "local housing authority": ss.1, 2.

General Note
 The powers to provide housing are exercisable outside an authority's own district, subject to the conditions set out in this section. See s.16, below, for provisions governing London boroughs exercising powers outside Greater London. Powers to act outside the authority's own area date from the Housing of the Working Classes Act 1900.

Subs. (2)
 The first requirement is that notice is given to the *county* council of the authority's *own* district, regardless of whether or not the "external" housing is itself to be in their own county. If the housing *is* in the area of *another* county, then both the authority's *own* county council, *and* the county council for that *other* county, must be notified. Failure to give notice, however, is not to render the exercise of powers ultra vires.

Subs. (3)
 The authority's principal power to carry out works is that contained in s.9, but they enjoy incidental powers under ss.10–13, and a general incidental power under s.111, Local Government Act 1972, and indeed at common law (see *A.G.* v. *Great Eastern Railway* (1880) 5 App.Cas. 473). Under this subsection, the authority, in the exercise of these powers, must enter into an agreement with the council of the county, London borough or district in whose area the works are to be carried out, as to terms and conditions of execution of work. Under s.52, they are also bound to ensure that a fair wages clause is introduced into any building contract under this Act.

Subs. (4)

If the powers in s.13 have been used to construct streets or roads, liability to maintain them vests in the local highways authority (*i.e.* normally the county council—Highways Act 1980), *unless* that authority are satisfied that the streets or roads have not been properly constructed.

Subs. (5)

A difference may arise under either of the previous subsections, for the requirement to notify the county council in subs. (2) does not carry with it any right on the part of that council to refuse permission. Either authority may refer the matter to the Secretary of State for "final and binding" resolution. Even a decision reached by the Secretary of State which is impeachable on usual principles of administrative law (see notes to s.64, below) would not at first sight seem to be challengeable by the authority: see *Smith* v. *East Elloe Rural District Council* [1956] A.C. 736, H.L., applied in *R.* v. *Secretary of State for the Environment, ex parte Ostler* [1977] Q.B. 122, C.A., distinguishing *Anisminic Ltd.* v. *Foreign Compensation Commission* [1969] 2 A.C. 147, H.L.

However, the courts have shown less willing to accept diminution of their jurisdiction in cases such as *Pearlman* v. *Keepers & Governors of Harrow School* [1979] Q.B. 56, C.A. (in which the words "final and conclusive" did not prevent further challenge on the correct interpretation of the word "improvement" for the purposes of the Leasehold Reform Act 1967) and *Meade* v. *Haringey London Borough Council* [1979] 1 W.L.R. 637, C.A.

Powers of authorities in London

Additional powers of authorities in London

15.—(1) A London borough council may provide and maintain in connection with housing accommodation provided by them under this Part buildings or parts of buildings adapted for use for any commercial purpose.

(2) A local housing authority in Greater London may make arrangements for the rehousing of any person by another such authority; and the arrangements may include provision for the payment of contributions by the former authority to the latter.

(3) The council of an Inner London borough and the Common Council of the City of London may, for the purpose of facilitating the erection of houses in their district, suspend, alter or relax the provisions of any enactment or byelaw relating to the formation or laying out of new streets or the construction of sewers or of buildings intended for human habitation.

(4) The powers conferred by subsections (1) and (3) are exercisable only with the consent of the Secretary of State.

DEFINITIONS

"housing accommodation": s.56.

GENERAL NOTE

This and the next section contain the miscellaneous residual provisions derived initially from the London Government Act 1963, and scheduled for inclusion in this Act until the passage of the controversial Local Government Act 1985 abolished the Greater London Council (and the metropolitan county councils).

Subs. (2)

Following the abolition of the Greater London Council on April 1, 1986, the former Greater London Mobility Scheme has been replaced by the London Area Mobility Scheme, under which authorities provide "nomination rights" to one another, enabling a certain amount of "redistribution," often used—or, perhaps, misused, *cf.* notes to s.65, below—to discharge obligations under Part III to place the homeless other than in the area of the authority to which they have applied, *i.e.* in the "unpopular" areas.

Exercise of powers outside Greater London

16.—(1) A local housing authority in Greater London shall not exercise any powers under this Part outside Greater London unless it appears to the Secretary of State, on an application by the authority, expedient that the needs of the authority's district with respect to the provision of housing accommodation should be satisfied by the provision of such accommodation outside Greater London, and he consents to the exercise of the power.

(2) The power conferred by section 15(1) (provision of commercial buildings) shall not be exercised outside Greater London except with the consent of the Council of the district concerned.

DEFINITIONS
"housing association": s.5.
"local housing authority": ss.1, 2.

GENERAL NOTE
This section contains the remaining residual special provisions for London: see General Note to s.15, above.

Subs. (1)
The consent of the Secretary of State is needed to the provision of housing outside Greater London, by a London Borough Council or the Common Council, but *not* to the provision of accommodation merely in another London Borough (or the City). Such an exercise falls under s.14, above, and although the operations require agreement with the other Borough (or Common Council), under s.14(3), there is no county council to which notice must be given under s.14(2).

Acquisition of land, etc.

Acquisition of land for housing purposes

17.—(1) A local housing authority may for the purposes of this Part—
(*a*) acquire land as a site for the erection of houses,
(*b*) acquire houses, or buildings which may be made suitable as houses, together with any land occupied with the houses or buildings,
(*c*) acquire land proposed to be used for any purpose authorised by sections 11, 12 and 15(1) (facilities provided in connection with housing accommodation), and
(*d*) acquire land in order to carry out on it works for the purpose of, or connected with, the alteration, enlarging, repair or improvement of an adjoining house.

(2) The power conferred by subsection (1) includes power to acquire land for the purpose of disposing of houses provided, or to be provided, on the land or of disposing of the land to a person who intends to provide housing accommodation on it.

(3) Land may be acquired by a local housing authority for the purposes of this Part by agreement, or they may be authorised by the Secretary of State to acquire it compulsorily.

(4) A local housing authority may, with the consent of, and subject to any conditions imposed by, the Secretary of State, acquire land for the purposes of this Part notwithstanding that the land is not immediately required for those purposes; but an authority shall not be so authorised to acquire land compulsorily unless it appears to the Secretary of State that the land is likely to be required for those purposes within ten years from the date on which he confirms the compulsory purchase order.

DEFINITIONS
"house": s.56.
"housing accommodation": s.56.
"local housing authority": ss.1, 2.

GENERAL NOTE
This is the principal power to purchase land and housing, in order to provide housing by erection, or conversion, under s.9, or in order to sell the land to someone else to provide

housing on it (see also s.9(3)), or to provide facilities in connection with housing under ss.11 (board and laundry) and 12 (shops, recreation grounds or other beneficial purposes), or in order to carry out works of alteration, enlargement, repair or improvement to adjoining property in or to be in their ownership. Authorities may acquire by agreement, or compulsorily with the consent of the Secretary of State. Compulsory purchase—procedures and compensation—is dealt with in Part XVII and Scheds. 22–24, below.

The power itself is wide enough to include land partially developed with housing: *Green & Sons* v. *Minister of Health* [1948] 1 K.B. 34, C.A., and to acquire houses with a view to improvement only, *i.e.* even although there will be no increase in available accommodation—*Andresier* v. *Minister of Housing and Local Government* (1965) S.J. 594. "Land" includes "buildings and other structures, land covered with water, and any estate, interest, easement, servitude or right in or over land": Interpretation Act 1978, Sched. 1; it also includes rights over land which may not exist at the time of a compulsory purchase order—s.13, Local Government (Miscellaneous Provisions) Act 1976 (overturning the effect of *Sovmots* v. *Secretary of State for the Environment* [1979] A.C. 144, H.L.).

Where it is housing which is purchased, or a building for conversion to housing, local authorities are under obligations to bring the property into use, under s.16. Where land is to be purchased, however, the powers may be exercised even although there is no immediate need for the land, or perhaps plans for the housing to be built on it, *i.e.* a measure of land acquisition planning is permitted, but only if the land is *likely* to be required for Part II purposes within ten years, so that purely speculative purchasing is not permissible.

The need for the consent of the Secretary of State would at first blush appear to be a precondition to any prior purchase, whether or not the purchase is to be by agreement or compulsory, but the reference to "ten years from the date on which he confirms the compulsory purchase order" inclines towards the interpretation that his consent is only needed if the purchase is to be compulsory. It is submitted that this subsection is sufficiently ambiguous to merit reference back to the preceding legislation (s.97(2), Housing Act 1957), where it was clearly spelled out that consent was only needed where the purchase was to be compulsory. There is no corresponding Law Commission Recommendation (Cmnd. 9515) which justifies the alteration.

Government policy is, however, in favour of bringing land in urban areas into "full and effective use," and, more generally, local authorities "should aim to ensure that at all times land is or will become available within the next 5 years" (D.O.E. Circular 15/84), so that applications to purchase without a requirement in somewhat less than 10 years are unlikely to be viewed favourably. See also Part X, Local Government, Planning and Land Act 1980, governing registration of un- or under-used land and its s.98 power to direct its disposal.

Duties with respect to buildings acquired for housing purposes

18.—(1) Where a local housing authority acquire a building which may be made suitable as a house, they shall forthwith proceed to secure that the building is so made suitable either by themselves executing any necessary works or by leasing it or selling it to some person subject to conditions for securing that he will so make it suitable.

(2) Where a local housing authority—

   (*a*) acquire a house, or

   (*b*) acquire a building which may be made suitable as a house and themselves carry out any necessary work as mentioned in subsection (1),

they shall, as soon as practicable after the acquisition or, as the case may be, after the completion of the necessary works, secure that the house or building is used as housing accommodation.

DEFINITIONS

"house": s.56.
"housing accommodation": s.56.
"local housing authority": ss.1, 2.

GENERAL NOTE

This section contains two duties: (a) to ensure that a building purchased for housing is *forthwith* made suitable either by the authority carrying out works themselves, or by selling or leasing it to another subject to conditions for it to be made suitable; and (b) after the acquisition of a house for use as housing accommodation, or of works to a building to make it suitable for use as housing accommodation, to bring the property into use *as soon as practicable.*

The first of the two duties imposed by this section is directed to buildings, including houses, which are to be *converted* into accommodation, as distinct from a building or house purchased on land which is to be redeveloped as a whole, perhaps involving the demolition of the structure: *Uttoxeter Urban District Council* v. *Clarke* [1952] 1 All E.R. 1318. Nor does the duty contained in subs. (2) apply to a house purchased, not for re-use, but for demolition as part of a development, nor serve to prevent its demolition: *Attridge* v. *London County Council* [1954] 2 Q.B. 449.

The fact that the authority are in breach of the second duty does not prevent them including property in a clearance area under s.293, below, even though had they complied with subs. (2) the property might not have become unfit: *A.G., ex rel. Rivers-Moore* v. *Portsmouth City Council* (1978) 76 L.G.R. 643.

See also D.O.E. Circular 12/85 urging authorities to bring empty properties into use by, *inter alia*, better management of letting procedures and of their improvement programmes.

Appropriation of land

19.—(1) A local housing authority may appropriate for the purposes of this Part any land for the time being vested in them or at their disposal; and the authority have the same powers in relation to land so appropriated as they have in relation to land acquired by them for the purposes of this Part.

(2) Where a local housing authority have acquired or appropriated land for the purposes of this Part, they shall not, without the consent of the Secretary of State, appropriate any part of the land consisting of a house or part of a house for any other purpose.

(3) The Secretary of State's consent may be given—

(*a*) either generally to all local housing authorities or to a particular authority or description of authority, and

(*b*) either in relation to particular land or in relation to land of a particular description;

and it may be given subject to conditions.

DEFINITIONS
"house": s.56.
"local housing authority": ss.1, 2.

GENERAL NOTE
Under this section, any land owned by the authority, or at their disposal, may be appropriated to Part II use. However, the authority cannot without the consent of the Secretary of State appropriate "out" land, either acquired under this Part or formerly appropriated to the purposes of this Part, *to* any other purpose, so far as it consists of a house or part of a house.

The normal position, under s.122, Local Government Act 1972, is that an authority may appropriate land from one purpose to another, when it is no longer required for the purpose for which it was previously held.

If an appropriation is partly *intra vires*, and partly *ultra vires*, the courts may sever the appropriation, so as to sustain the *intra vires* part: *Thames Water Authority* v. *Elmbridge Borough Council* [1983] Q.B. 570.

Housing management

Application of housing management provisions

20.—(1) The following provisions of this Part down to section 26 (general provisions on housing management matters) apply in relation to all houses held by a local housing authority for housing purposes.

(2) References in those provisions to an authority's houses shall be construed accordingly.

"house": s.56.
"local housing authority": ss.1, 2.

GENERAL NOTE
The provisions of ss.21–26 inclusive apply only to housing held by a local housing authority "for housing purposes," *e.g.* they would not apply to a house held under non-housing powers, and perhaps in temporary use pending demolition. However, the expression used is "for housing purposes," as quite distinct from "for the purposes of this Part." If, therefore, housing is held by a local housing authority, under other powers, but to be retained in housing use by them, whether or not related to that other power, the provisions of ss.21–26 apply to that housing.

This application of the provisions is wider than that which has previously prevailed (variously: s.111, Housing Act 1957 [now, s.21, below] applied to houses provided under Part V of that Act, now this Part, s.112 [now s.23, below] generally to houses provided by the authority but arguably restricted to Part V houses, and s.113 of the 1957 Act [now split between ss.22 and 24, below], s.12, Prices and Income Act 1968 [now, s.25, below] and s.93, Housing Finance Act 1972 [now, s.26, below] to houses within the authority's Housing Revenue Account [as to which see, now, s.417, below]). The alteration is pursuant to Law Commission Recommendations (Cmnd. 9515), No. 2.

General powers of management

21.—(1) The general management, regulation and control of a local housing authority's houses is vested in and shall be exercised by the authority and the houses shall at all times be open to inspection by the authority.

(2) Subsection (1) has effect subject to section 27 (agreements for exercise of housing management functions by co-operative).

DEFINITIONS
"house": s.56.
"housing co-operative": s.27.
"local housing authority": ss.1, 2.

GENERAL NOTE
Although "general management" is conferred on local authorities, it is a discretion subject to considerable statutory intervention. Thus, though it includes the power to pick and choose tenants, this is governed by s.22, below. Similarly, although eviction is a feature of management, this is now extensively controlled by the security of tenure and succession provisions of Part IV, below.

Again, there is a number of housing management obligations imposed on authorities under Part IV, including the obligation to provide information about terms of tenancies (s.104), to consult on matters of housing management (s.105), and to provide information about allocation (s.106), while secure tenants enjoy a number of additional rights under the general heading of what might be termed housing management, including the right to exchange (s.92), to take in lodgers (s.93), to sublet part (ss.93, 94), to carry out repairs (s.96) and to improve (s.97) and to information about heating charges (s.108). In addition, there are housing management issues governed by the Landlord and Tenant Act 1985: repairing obligations, rent books, service charges.

As to regulation and control, see also s.23, below.
As to charges, see s.24, below.
As to obstruction of officers of the authority, see s.55, below.

Subs. (1)
Because the general management of their housing is conferred on the authority, it is not open to a court to derogate from that statutory power, by the appointment of a receiver: *Parker* v. *London Borough of Camden* (1985) 17 H.L.R. 380, C.A.

The general management provision has been held to extend to a scheme whereby the authority arranged for the insurance of occupiers' personal and household goods, and collected the premiums: *A.G., ex rel. Prudential Staff Union* v. *Crayford Urban District Council* [1962] Ch. 575, C.A.

Where occupiers are not within the security of tenure provisions of Part IV, eviction is a matter within the housing authority's general housing management powers. The authority have a common law right to recover possession: *Shelley* v. *London County Council* [1949] A.C. 56, H.L.

As public bodies, local housing authorities are, however, confined by the principles of administrative law (see notes to s.64, below), so that they must have regard to all relevant considerations, *e.g.* ministerial circulars, etc.: see *Bristol District Council* v. *Clark* [1975] 1 W.L.R. 1443, C.A. The same principles will be applicable whether an occupier is (or has been) a tenant or a licensee: see *Cleethorpes Borough Council* v. *Clarkson* [1978] L.A.G. Bulletin 166, C.A.

The burden of proving that the authority have not complied with the requirements of administrative law lies upon the person making the allegation, and the details of the authority's failure must be particularised, so that a general claim that the occupier "has done nothing wrong" will fail: see *Cannock Chase District Council* v. *Kelly* [1978] 1 W.L.R. 1, C.A.

The authority are under no duty to give reasons for their decision, nor is there a general duty to give an occupier concerned an opportunity to comment or make representations about matters brought to the attention of the authority, even where the matter might be considered as being to the discredit of the occupier—there is no duty to hold anything corresponding to a formal inquiry: see *Sevenoaks District Council* v. *Emmott* (1980) 130 New L.J. 139, C.A. However, the authority do have to stay within "the limits of fair dealing," or "comply with the requirements of fairness," and in an appropriate case this could require some sort of inquiry into the facts of, *e.g.*, an allegation against an occupier: *ibid.* See also *Hammersmith London Borough Council* v. *Ruddock* [1980] C.L.Y. 134, C.A., and *Hammersmith London Borough Council* v. *Jimenez* (1980) 130 New L.J. 139, C.A.

It should be noted that in *Emmott*, it was clear that the occupier enjoyed adequate opportunity to comment on what was being said against him, but had refused to avail himself of this opportunity. The decision in this respect is not dissimilar to that in *R.* v. *Southampton City Council, ex parte Ward* (1984) 14 H.L.R. 114, Q.B.D., under what is now Part III of this Act: see notes to s.60, below.

While the homelessness decisions—and, in particular, those on intentional homelessness (see notes to s.60, below)—will clearly have much relevance in an individual case, a distinction should be drawn between eviction decisions which *are* individual in their nature and those which are not. Thus, if a policy were to be applied to evict all those over a certain amount in arrears, or in arrears for more than a certain period, which policy was applied rigidly, *i.e.* without regard to individual circumstances (as distinct from a guideline, the application of which is reconsidered in each case, which would be permissible), that policy would seem to be impeachable: see, *e.g. British Oxygen Co. Ltd.* v. *Board of Trade* [1971] A.C. 610, H.L., *In Re Betts* [1983] 2 A.C. 613, 10 H.L.R. 97, H.L.

However, if a policy is adopted, *e.g.*, to sell off an estate, or to clear an area, or to knock down all buildings of a particular construction, or to bring short-life user to an end, this would seem available, and lawful, regardless of individual circumstances, although in adopting the policy it could be said that an authority would have to have regard to the hardship that might be caused, at the least in general terms.

Subs. (2)

The extent to which housing management functions may be transferred to a housing co-operative will depend on the terms of the agreement with the co-operative under s.27(1), below.

Allocation of housing

22. A local housing authority shall secure that in the selection of their tenants a reasonable preference is given to—

(*a*) persons occupying insanitary or overcrowded houses,
(*b*) persons having large families,
(*c*) persons living under unsatisfactory housing conditions, and
(*d*) persons towards whom the authority are subject to a duty under section 65 or 68 (persons found to be homeless).

DEFINITIONS

"house": s.56.
"local housing authority": ss.1, 2.

GENERAL NOTE

This is a most important section. Much is made of "local discretion" in the allocation of housing. In some areas allocation remains dependent entirely on time on waiting-list, or time in an area, and—relying on the popular concept of local discretion carried to an extreme—there may not even be to this day a "points system" or any other "system" or "method" for ensuring that the requirements of this section are discharged; authorities operating such "non-systems" may find themselves in this day and age and in the light of this section markedly more susceptible to intervention than others (who do operate a system properly so-called). It is, nonetheless, entirely correct to say that *how much* preference is to be given to those identified is a matter for local discretion, provided it is not so little that no reasonable authority could consider it a "preference" (let alone "reasonable preference") at all.

The reasonable preference applies in the selection of *tenants,* not all occupiers, and it would accordingly not apply in the allocation of accommodation on licence, *e.g.* short-life user pending demolition or redevelopment, nor in the selection of purchasers.

The terms used in (*a*) to (*c*) are vague. Overcrowded may be taken to mean overcrowding under Part X, below, and authorities which operate a points system will normally apply the same criterion, but it is the only term in these first three (and original—(*d*) represents that which was added by the Housing (Homeless Persons) Act 1977, s.6(2)) classes which is susceptible to direct statutory definition. Neither insanitary, nor large, nor unsatisfactory, are defined, in this Part, or elsewhere, though s.604 (definition of unfitness for human habitation) and the provisions of Parts VI and IX, or else of the Public Health Act 1936, will provide a useful *guide* to that which is "insanitary" and "unsatisfactory," although it is submitted not an exhaustive definition. Thus, for example, though of acceptable quality, housing conditions may yet be unsatisfactory because of the terms, *e.g.*. living with relatives in "unsatisfactory" circumstances.

The requirements contained in (*d*) are also important. Under ss.65 and 68, local authorities have obligations towards the homeless (as defined in s.58, below), *including* those who are *not* in priority need (as defined in s.59, below), and those who are homeless intentionally (as defined in s.60, below). The duty towards those who are homeless, in priority need and not homeless intentionally is to secure that accommodation is made available for his occupation, *i.e.* indefinitely, or "permanent accommodation": s.65(2); the duty to those not in priority need is to provide advice and such assistance as the authority consider appropriate: s.65(4); the duty to those in priority need but homeless intentionally is also to provide advice and assistance, and a period of "temporary" accommodation to give them an opportunity to find somewhere for themselves: s.65(3).

But *a* duty is owed to all of these people: "This section has effect as regards the duties owed by the local housing authority to an applicant where they are satisfied that he is homeless": s.65(1). *All* of the homeless (who have applied for assistance under Part III: see s.62) will be persons towards whom a duty is owed, either under s.65, or under s.68 if he is the subject of a "local connection reference" (see ss.61, 67 and 68), and are therefore those to whom a "reasonable preference" must be given in the allocation of Part II stock.

It is accordingly submitted that it is not open to a local authority to refuse to register on their waiting-lists the homeless not in priority need, or indeed even the homeless below a certain age, or the homeless intentionally. Nor, indeed, could an authority refuse to register an application from someone who had applied as—and was found to be—homeless merely because, *e.g.*, he had not spent long enough in the area. Of course, once registered, all of these people would gain only a "reasonable preference," which may make the benefit hardly worth pursuing although, again, it must be *a* preference.

Byelaws

23.—(1) A local housing authority may make byelaws for the management, use and regulation of their houses.

(2) A local housing authority may make byelaws with respect to the use of land held by them by virtue of section 12 (recreation grounds and other land provided in connection with housing), excluding land covered by buildings or included in the curtilage of a building or forming part of a highway.

(3) A local housing authority shall as respects their lodging-houses by byelaws make sufficient provision for the following purposes—

    (*a*) for securing that the lodging-houses are under the management and control of persons appointed or employed by them for the purpose,

    (*b*) for securing the due separation at night of men and boys above eight years old from women and girls, (*c*) for preventing damage, disturbance, interruption and indecent and offensive language and behaviour and nuisances, and

(*d*) for determining the duties of the persons appointed by them;
and a printed copy or a sufficient abstract of the byelaws relating to lodging-houses shall be put up and at all times kept in every room in the lodging-houses.

DEFINITIONS
  "house": s.56.
  "local housing authority": ss.1, 2.
  "lodging-house": s.56.

GENERAL NOTE
  These powers are commonly used on local authority estates. Byelaws may also be made under s.235, Local Government Act 1972, "for the good rule and government of the whole or any part of the district or borough . . . and for the prevention and suppression of nuisances therein," but subject to the confirmation of the Secretary of State, and *not* when there is authority to make the byelaws under any other enactment, *e.g.* this section. The provisions of s.236 of the 1972 Act, however, apply to byelaws whether made under s.235 or other enactments, and therefore including this section. Section 236 requires publicity for proposed byelaws. Under s.237, the limit of the penalty which may be imposed is level 2 on the standard scale, *i.e.* under s.37, Criminal Justice Act 1982, currently £100—see S.I. 1984 No. 447.

Subs. (3)
  The provisions may be compared to those regulating private sector common lodging-houses under Part XII: s.406, below.
  One cannot help wondering at the differences in ages specified for the purposes of what is here called "due separation" of men and boys from women and girls. Does life begin at 8 in a local authority lodging-house, 10 in a house under the overcrowding laws now to be found in Part X below (see s.325), 12 in a house in multiple occupation within Part XI below (see s.360), or whenever the authority consider appropriate to specify in a common lodging-house under Part XII below (see s.406).

Rents

24.—(1) A local housing authority may make such reasonable charges as they may determine for the tenancy or occupation of their houses.

(2) The authority shall from time to time review rents and make such changes, either of rents generally or of particular rents, as circumstances may require.

DEFINITIONS
  "house": s.56.
  "local housing authority": ss.1, 2.

GENERAL NOTE
  As with allocation (see notes to s.22, above), the "local discretion" of housing authorities to fix their own rents is well known. It has also long been upheld by the courts: see notes to subs. (1), below. As a matter of practice, however, it must be read subject to Part XIII, which governs housing finance and housing subsidy. Thus, while rents for Part II properties (see s.417) are a credit to the Housing Revenue Account (s.418 and Sched. 14), and outgoings a debit (*ibid*), subsidy to the H.R.A. is calculated not according to what authorities actually receive or spend, but according to what the government think they ought to be receiving or spending: see ss.422–425 and, in particular, s.425(2) defining reckonable income as "the amount which, in accordance with any determination made by the Secretary of State, the authority are assumed to receive for that year . . . "
  Rents are thus *influenced* by central government, as distinct from the central government *imposition* of higher rent levels under the Housing Finance Act 1972 (until frozen by the counter-inflation provisions of 1973, and repealed by the Housing Rents and Subsidies Act 1975), *i.e.* "fair rents," equivalent to those charged in the private sector under Rent Act 1977, fixed by Rent Officers and Rent Assessment Committees. Also relevant to rent determinations will be the availability of Housing Benefit under the Social Security and

Housing Benefits Act 1982, and the Housing Benefits Regulations 1985 (S.I. 1985 No. 677). Housing Benefits are available in principle to licensees as much as to tenants (subject in each case to exceptions), and the provisions of this section likewise apply to "tenancy or occupation" charges.

As to increase of rent, see ss.25 and 103, below. As to not increasing rent on account of a secure tenant's improvements, see s.101, below.

Subs. (1)

There has been a number of cases in which the ambit of the rents discretion has been considered. In only one case (*Backhouse* v. *Lambeth London Borough Council* (1972) 116 S.J. 802, which was a professed device to avoid certain provisions in the Housing Finance Act 1972) has a challenge been successful.

1. Statements of Principle

In *Belcher* v. *Reading Corporation* [1950] 1 Ch. 380, Romer J. said this of a challenge based on whether or not the charges were "reasonable":

> "The question, however, whether the Corporation's decision can be impeached . . . depends, in my judgment, not on whether it might have been preferable to charge this or that item against the ratepayers as a whole, or to have apportioned it in some manner between them and the tenants, but on whether the increased rents are 'reasonable' as the section requires them to be . . . I would, however, point out that the Corporation's tenants are not the only people whose interests they have to consider, for they have to bear the general body of ratepayers in mind as well."

> "It seems to me that in solving the economic problems with which local authorities are confronted today, and which derive mainly from the greatly increased cost of materials and labour, they are placed in a position of not inconsiderable difficulty. It is, of course, clear that they have to consider the welfare of people of small—sometimes of very small—means. On the other hand they have also to be mindful of the interests of the ratepayers as a whole—the majority of whom, in Reading, as I was informed, are people of comparable means with the tenants of the council houses. It is their duty, so far as possible, to maintain a balance between these two sections of the local community having due regard, of course, to any specific requirements of the Housing Acts. If the Council-house rents were much below those prevailing in the locality, then prima facie a local authority might be suspected of unduly favouring the tenants; while, if they were much in excess of such other rents, the presumption would be the other way round . . . "

The proposition that a balance must be struck between the interests of the beneficiaries of a service, and the ratepayers generally, has more recently been restated in a non-housing case, *R.* v. *Greater London Council, ex parte Bromley London Borough Council* [1982] 1 A.C. 768, H.L., in which the judgment of Diplock L.J. (as he then was) in *Luby* v. *Newcastle-under-Lyme Corporation* [1964] 2 Q.B. 64, C.A., was approved:

> "In determing the rent structure to be applied to houses provided by a local authority the local authority is applying what is, in effect, a social policy upon which reasonable men may hold different views. Since any deficit in the housing revenue account has to be made good from the general rate fund, the choice of rent structure involves weighing the interests of the tenants as a whole and of individual impoverished tenants against those of the general body of ratepayers. Since the passing of the National Assistance Act 1948, and the making of the National Assistance (Determination of Needs) Regulations 1948, which provide that the matters to be taken into consideration in assessing the relief to be granted to applicants shall include net rent payable or such a part thereof as is reasonable in the circumstances, there is also involved a choice as to whether the individual impoverished tenant should be assisted at the expense of the general body of ratepayers by a reduction in the rent or at the expense of the general body of taxpayers by way of National Assistance."

> "The evidence shows that the defendant Corporation has directed its mind to this problem and to the desirability or otherwise of applying a differential rent scheme. It has determined that the burden of assisting individual tenants who cannot afford to pay the rents which the Corporation has fixed as appropriate for the type of house which they occupy ought to fall upon the general body of taxpayers and not upon the general body of ratepayers in their district. It is in my view quite impossible for this court to say that this choice which is one of social policy, is one which no reasonable man could have made, and is therefore *ultra vires*, any more than it could be said that the opposite choice would be *ultra vires*. The policy which the defendant Corporation has adopted was, I think, within the discretion conferred upon them by section 111(1) of the

Housing Act 1957, [now, this section], that subsection being the statutory provision which confers the general power to determine the rent structure. . . . "

In *Evans* v. *Collins* [1965] 1 Q.B. 580, Widgery J. quoted the passage set out above in which Romer J. remarked on the comparison between council rents and private sector rents:

"That statement of principle, as it seems to me, although laid down in a case decided under the Act of 1936, is not dependent upon the statutory duty of considering other rentals which that Act imposed. As I see it, the judge is stating as a proposition of general application which has to be borne in mind by those examining the activities of a local authority in the conduct of its Housing Revenue Account.

"Before I leave that case I think it pertinent to point out that the decision was given in 1949 when, as is well known, the Rent Restriction Act 1939 was in full effect and was of very wide application throughout the country. It seems to me that in 1949 it may well have been that rents prevailing in private estates would not be significantly different from the rents which a council would be required to charge if they desired to recoup the entire cost of providing the houses in question. The rent which a council would be required to charge on that basis is conveniently referred to as the economic rent, but I am inclined to think that if Romer J. had been expressing his opinion at the present day he might have been minded to use the phrase 'economic rent' in that sense rather than rents prevailing in comparable estates. I say that because if in a period of inflation and complete relaxation of rent control the rents of private premises far outstripped the economic rent which a local authority might be minded to charge, it would, in my view, be unreal to suggest that the local authority is under any duty to charge market rents to its tenants.

"I can see no reason why a local authority should ever be under a duty to make a profit out of its tenants, and it seems to me that the proper basis of comparison at the present time is between rent charged by the authority and economic rents as I have sought to define them. Applying the dictum of Romer J. in this way one would consider whether the difference between the rents charged and the economic rent was so great as to indicate that the local authority were not holding the scales fairly between the two branches of the community to whom they owe a duty.

"Since *Belcher* v. *Reading Corporation*, there have been three other cases in which attacks have been made upon local authority rentals on the footing that those rentals are unreasonable . . . In each case the local authority has been successful in the sense that the attack made upon its rentals has failed. (The) cases cumulatively do emphasise to my mind the very wide discretion which local authorities have under section 111 of the Act of 1957 [now, this section] but also the reluctance which the courts have shown to interfere in matters which are very often matters of social policy and not really matters of law at all . . .

"I am quite satisfied that a . . . council, which has to consider the situation as between tenants and ratepayers, must have some regard to what I call the economic rental of its properties as a whole. A . . . council which sought to fix rents paid by its tenants with eyes entirely closed to the amount which it had to find for the provision of housing would run into grave danger of being unjust to the ratepayers and producing unreasonable rents. It seems quite clear that the housing authority must start its calculations from some point. It seems to me that the total cost of providing the houses is a perfectly proper starting point to choose, and there is no objection to the . . . council considering economic rentals in totum."

2. *Examples of Exercise of Discretion*

The cases have to be seen in the light of (a) the prevailing legislation, and (b) the nature of the challenge. In *Leeds Corporation* v. *Jenkinson* [1935] 1 K.B. 168, the authority were held to be permitted to charge different rent levels for similar houses in the same area, and in *Summerfield* v. *Hampstead Borough Council* [1957] 1 W.L.R. 167 the authority were allowed to charge different rents for identical accommodation. The provision is wide enough to permit authorities to charge differential rents based on the means of the tenants: *Smith* v. *Cardiff Corporation* (*No. 2*) [1955] Ch. 159.

In *Mandeville* v. *Greater London Council, The Times,* January 28, 1982, a differential rent scheme under which some tenants who had been admitted under a previous administration on the basis that they would subsequently purchase their homes was upheld even when the subsequent administration declined to permit the tenants to buy other than under what is now Part V. The court again referred to decisions on rents as matters of "social policy."

On the other hand, a decision to *not* operate a differential rent scheme is perfectly proper: *Luby* v. *Newcastle-under-Lyme Corporation* [1964] 2 Q.B. 64, C.A. In *R.* v. *Greater London Council, ex parte Royal Borough of Kensington and Chelsea, The Times*, April 7, 1982, decided in relation to stock transferred by the Greater London Council to the London boroughs, a social policy of "harmonisation," *i.e.* aiming at broadly similar rents within an area, was upheld.

Other cases in which (unsuccessful) challenges have been mounted are: *Taylor* v. *Munro* [1960] 1 W.L.R. 151, and *Giddens* v. *Harlow District Auditor* (1972) 70 L.G.R. 485. In *R.* v. *Secretary of State for Health and Social Services, ex parte Sheffield City Council* (1985) 18 H.L.R. 6, a scheme whereby tenants could pay a lower rent if taking upon themselves certain repairing obligations was held lawful, even although the operation of the scheme was such as to exclude those tenants on housing benefit, and was designed in this respect so as to maximise the authority's Housing Benefit Subsidy. (The authority did not, however, succeed in establishing that higher subsidy entitlement, on the terms of the relevant Housing Benefit Regulations.) Note that in *Smith* v. *Cardiff Corporation* [1954] 1 Q.B. 210 (*cf.* "No. 2," above), a group of tenants were held not to constitute a "class" capable of bringing a representative action under R.S.C., Order 15, rule 12. But *cf.*, now, s.105, below, where "classes" of (secure) tenants are given statutory recognition, although not in relation to rents.

3. Principles of Rent-Fixing In Practice

Taking the cases as a whole, it is submitted that the following will or may normally be relevant considerations:

1. *Governing Legislation.* The first thing which will always be relevant is the provision of this section to make "reasonable" charges, and to review them "from time to time."

2. *Expenditure.* What the housing actually costs is a relevant consideration, meaning both what it may have cost to provide, and management and maintenance expenditure. There is no requirement, however, to have regard to the cost (in either sense) of individual units: authorities are permitted to "pool" costs and, indeed, most authorities would find it too difficult to operate on any other basis.

3. *Inflation.* Inflation increases costs and will require an authority to *consider* increasing rents having regard to those increased costs. It is no part of the exercise of the discretion to use the rent fixing power as a general protection from inflation for local authority tenants. This is not to say that an authority need increase rents to the same extent as inflation, or necessarily at all; it merely requires the authority to consider an increase, and weigh up the effect of inflation against other factors.

4. *Exchequer Subsidy.* The extent to which exchequer subsidy under Part XIII is available, or is reduced or increased, will undoubtedly be a relevant consideration. Indeed, the method of fixing subsidy suggests that this is its precise purpose: to operate as a consideration and an influence, as distinct from a central government direction. To the extent that exchequer subsidy *is* available, it is for the authority to decide how much of this "taxpayer" contribution they consider it appropriate to rely on.

5. *The Cost of Tenancy.* It may be considered relevant to review how rents have risen, relevant to other housing tenure costs. Again, this says nothing of how the information is used: to justify increases, or reductions, or indeed to reach the conclusion that it is proper for tenants to pay more, or less. It is hard to say, however, that alternative tenure costs are irrelevant *per se.*

6. *Housing Benefit.* The fact that occupiers will or may benefit from assistance under the Housing Benefits Scheme, and the extent both as to level of assistance available to individual occupiers, and numbers qualifying, will be relevant. The extent of take-up, or non-take-up, may equally be a valid consideration. The Housing Benefits Scheme may also be relevant in so far as some authorities may be designated "high rent areas" which may result in higher levels of assistance, at no or a reduced cost to the authority: see Housing Benefits Regulations 1985, Regulation 22 and Schedule 4. A variation in the rent may affect designation.

7. *Harmonisation.* If there are substantial differences within an area between rents for similar properties, it will not be improper to adopt a policy of "harmonisation."

8. *Method of Imposing Increases.* The way in which an increase (or reduction) decision is implemented is for the authority. It is perfectly proper for an authority to determine that tenants should bear percentage or flat rate increases, alternatively that there should be differentials within rents, or within increases, as between classes of tenants, or classes of property, *e.g.* for different services.

9. *Balance between Ratepayers and Tenants.* This will invariably be relevant. On the one hand, a "fair" balance must be struck; on the other, just what is fair is pre-eminently a question of social policy of the sort courts will not interfere with.

10. *Rate Fund Consequences.* Under the Local Government, Planning and Land Act 1980, authorities suffer penalties if they spend beyond anticipated "targets." The cost of, *e.g.*, an

enhanced General Rate Fund subsidy to the Housing Revenue Account may well be in excess of the actual amount of that subsidy, because of such "overspending penalties." In addition, authorities who "overspend" are vulnerable to the provisions of the Rates Act 1984, *i.e.* "ratecapping." Such consequences, if any, must be taken into account.

11. *Institutionalising Decisions.* Because an authority will, under subs. (2), review rents, they must be careful not to "institutionalise" a previous decision in the sense that the consequences, *e.g.* under the Local Government, Planning and Land Act 1980, may continue in a subsequent year; the fact that a decision, and its consequences, were appropriate in one year does not mean that they are appropriate in another, or that "knock-on" consequences should not be taken into account anew in the subsequent year. No more than authorities are bound by their own previous decisions is it safe to take them for granted.

12. *Speed of Change.* However, if an authority wish to vary the levels of rent, set by a current or perhaps by a previous administration, they are entitled to do so at the speed they consider appropriate. For example, if a "cost rent" policy is replaced by a "subsidised rent" policy, it is on the one hand not necessary to reverse a process in one year, and on the other because the reversal does not take place within one year the option remains open to implement the new policy in a later year.

Each of these factors will or may be relevant. There may be other, local considerations. Each will have a different value in a different context, *i.e.* both as to geographical location, and time. This is not to say that authorities are constrained to carry out a detailed analysis of the operation of each factor in each context. Factors will *incline* in one direction or another, or may be neutral, and will mean something different to different authorities, and different members within each authority. Authorities are not expected to engage in a scientific or mathematical analysis or application of features.

Rather, this is exactly what is meant by "local democracy": authorities may take matters "in the round"; their task is to *reconcile* features (and some of the factors may in themselves be properly described as "reconciliating factors"), and the process of reconciliation is that which is the essentially political (*i.e.* application of policy) task.

Furthermore, in most cases, it is likely that decisions will be taken at a time when the operation of many of these factors will be uncertain. Indeed, in the last few years, the Secretary of State's "local contribution differential" under s.425 has only been available as a "consultation figure" rather than as a formal determination at the time most authorities have reached their rents decisions. Similarly, a rents decision will be taken in the course of budget-making as a whole, and for that reason, until the budget has been determined, and different and sometimes opposing bids decided, the exact rate-fund consequences will be unknown.

Again, as at the beginning of a financial year, when many authorities make their decisions, the Housing Benefit position through the year will be unknown: first of all, there are annual "upratings" which take effect in November; secondly, there are amendments to the scheme which may have considerably greater effect. Either class of change may be *anticipated*, perhaps by officers involved in a consultation process; authorities may have a good *sense* of what changes will take place. On the one hand, authorities are not bound to treat as law that which the government of the day indicate they propose to do; on the other hand, they are not bound to disregard anticipation, or its strength, or their evaluation of the likelihood of change. As with *any* other "budget" decision, authorities must, rather, do the best they can, working always with the most up-to-date information reasonably available, to reconcile possibly, if not probably, conflicting "interests" or "inclinations."

In the case of rents, at the end of the day, they must make a decision which stands up as an exercise of a *housing* power. To waive rent for some reason wholly extraneous to housing would be wrong in law; against that, a reason which is apparently wholly extraneous may conceal a good housing justification for a decision.

To take an apparently outrageous example, consider a "rent-free week" when, *e.g.*, the principal football team in an authority's area wins the Cup Final. At first blush, one would say that this was wholly extraneous, and "not housing management." But what if professional opinion had been advanced that the *benefits* of a gesture of this sort, and its identification of landlord with city-pride, would—or would probably—include a reduction in expensive vandalism, or a reduction in the extent of costly arrears?

Similarly, is it illegal to *raise* the rents of those who have been in arrears over a specified period (subject to review of individual cases and causes), as one London Borough recently decided? In this sort of case, the questions are, it is submitted: (a) is the decision one which a reasonable authority, which has had regard to all relevant considerations, acting fairly with regard not only to the beneficiaries of the service but also to the interests of the ratepayers, could consider within the ambit of what could be termed a "social policy"; and (b) has the decision been reached bona fide in pursuit of the *policy* of the legislation, *i.e.* a *housing* policy.

Subs. (2)

The duty to review rents from time to time, and to make such changes as circumstances may require, is usually applied by way of an annual review, commonly although not invariably at the time of an authority's overall budget review. So long as there are annual determinations under Part X111, and variations in the determinations (*i.e.* no national "freeze"), it is hard to argue that rents should not themselves be annually reviewed.

A scheme which provides for *ex post facto* adjustment of rents would have to do so in very clear language indeed: *Havant and Waterlooville Urban District Council* v. *Norum* [1958] 1 W.L.R. 721.

Increase of rent where tenancy not secure

25.—(1) This section applies where a house is let by a local housing authority on a weekly or other periodic tenancy which is not a secure tenancy.

(2) The rent payable under the tenancy may, without the tenancy being terminated, be increased with effect from the beginning of a rental period by a written notice of increase given by the authority to the tenant.

(3) The notice is not effective unless—

(*a*) it is given at least four weeks before the beginning of the rental period, or any earlier day on which the payment of rent in respect of that period falls to be made,

(*b*) it tells the tenant of his right to terminate the tenancy and of the steps to be taken by him if he wishes to do so, and

(*c*) it gives him the dates by which, if in accordance with subsection (4) the increase is not to be effective, a notice to quit must be received by the authority and the tenancy be made to terminate.

(4) Where the notice is given for the beginning of a rental period and the tenancy continues into that period, the notice shall not have effect if—

(*a*) the tenancy is terminated by notice to quit given by the tenant in accordance with the provisions (express or implied) of the tenancy,

(*b*) the notice to quit is given before the end of the period of two weeks following the date on which the notice of increase is given, or such longer period as may be allowed by the notice of increase, and

(*c*) the date on which the tenancy is made to terminate is not later than the earliest day on which the tenancy could be terminated by a notice to quit given by the tenant on the last day of that period.

(5) In this section "rental period" means a period in respect of which a payment of rent falls to be made.

DEFINITIONS

"house": s.56.
"local housing authority": ss.1, 2.
"secure tenancy": s.79.

GENERAL NOTE

This section permits increase of rent by notice of increase, in the case of a non-secure tenancy. Secure tenancies are governed by s.103, below. Without this provision, then unless the written agreement permitted variation, authorities would be obliged (as many used to do, and some still do), to terminate tenancies periodically, and regrant at higher rent levels: see *Bathavon Rural District Council* v. *Carlisle* [1958] 1 Q.B. 461. The provisions of this section apply also to a new town corporation: see s.30, below.

Rent can only be increased by this means with effect from the beginning of a rental period (subs. (2)), *i.e.* the period for which rent payments are made (subs. (5)). The notice must be given at least four weeks before the date when payment falls to be made, *i.e.* either the beginning of the rental period or, if rent is payable in advance of the first day of the period to which it relates, before that payment day: subs. (3)(*a*). The notice must inform the tenant of his right to bring the tenancy to an end, and of what steps he must take to do so: subs. (3)(*b*).

Service of a notice to quit will not *per se* prevent the notice of increase taking effect: there will commonly be less than four weeks between *receipt* of notice of increase and *service* of (tenant's) notice, so that there would be one or more weeks during the currency of the notice to quit, *i.e.* before its expiry, at the new and higher rent level. Even a *tenant's* notice to quit must comply with the legal minimum period of four weeks for notice to quit a dwelling: Protection From Eviction Act 1977, s.5.

However, this section provides a procedure for preventing the increase taking effect at all. The notice of increase must specify a date by which, if notice to quit is received by the authority, the increase will not take effect: subs. (3)(*c*). That date must be not less than two weeks: subs. (4)(*b*). The notice of increase must also specify the date by which the tenant's notice to quit must bring the tenancy to an end, *i.e.* a termination date for the tenancy: subs. (3)(*c*). That date must be not later than the *first* day on which the tenancy *could* be terminated by notice to quit given on the last day of the period during which the notice must be served: subs. (4)(*c*).

For example, notice of increase allows two weeks for service of notice to quit, notice to quit must be four weeks, earliest termination of tenancy will be six weeks after service of notice of increase, and *must* be for this date if the increase is not to take effect during the currency of the notice to quit. If the tenant's notice to quit goes beyond this date, it will not be effective to prevent the increase taking effect from the date it would have taken effect if no notice to quit in response is served, probably four weeks after it is served. It will, however, if otherwise valid (including if in writing—s.5, Protection From Eviction Act 1977) still be effective to determine the tenancy.

These provisions may be contrasted with those of s.103, which governs variation not only of rent, but of other terms of a secure tenancy, and which variations, including rent, can similarly be prevented from taking effect by response notice to quit: there is no provision in s.103, however, analogous to this requirement that the notice to quit determine the tenancy as at or by a specific date, which gives rise to the interesting argument whether or not a secure tenant could serve, *e.g.*, a five year notice to quit, thus preventing the variation taking place for five years, albeit subject to departure by that date—see notes to s.103, below.

A tenant who does not have certain plans for alternative, and adequate or "settled," accommodation, and who quits in response to a notice of increase because he does not believe that he can afford the increased rent, runs the very real risk of a finding of intentional homelessness under Part III, and a refusal of a further offer of accommodation from the authority: see notes to s.60, below. The tenant would do better to see what assistance or increased assistance is available attributable to the increase under the Housing Benefits Regulations 1985 (S.I. 1985, No. 677), and authorities have a general duty to publicise the availability of benefits under those Regulations, by s.31, Social Security and Housing Benefits Act 1982.

It should be noted that where there are joint tenants, notice to quit by just one of them will be effective to bring the tenancy to an end: *London Borough of Greenwich* v. *McGrady* [1982] 6 H.L.R. 36, C.A. If one joint tenant does so without the knowledge, assent or acquiescence of the other, then although the tenancy has been brought properly to an end, that other ought not to find himself vulnerable to a finding of intentional homelessness: see *R.* v. *North Devon District Council, ex parte Lewis* [1981] 1 W.L.R. 328, Q.B.D., and notes to ss.60, 62, below.

Financial assistance towards tenants' removal expenses

26.—(1) Where a tenant of one of the houses of a local housing authority moves to another house (whether or not that house is also one of theirs), the authority may—

(*a*) pay any expenses of the removal, and

(*b*) where the tenant is purchasing the house, pay any expenses incurred by him in connection with the purchase, other than the purchase price.

(2) If the house belongs to the same authority subsection (1)(*b*) only applies if the house has never been let and was built expressly with a view to sale or for letting.

(3) The Secretary of State may give directions to authorities in general or to any particular authority—

(*a*) as to the expenses which may be treated (whether generally or in any particular case) as incurred in connection with the purchase of a house, and

(*b*) limiting the amount which they may pay in respect of such expenses.

(4) An authority may make their payment of expenses subject to conditions.

DEFINITIONS
"house": s.56.
"local housing authority": ss.1, 2.

GENERAL NOTE
The provisions of this section apply both to local housing authorities, and to new town corporations: see s.30, below. The provisions apply only to tenants, *i.e.* not licensees.

This section permits payment of a removal grant to a tenant who moves, whether the property to which the tenant moves belongs to the landlord, another public landlord, a private landlord or, indeed, is to be owner-occupied. In the last case, the grant can extend beyond the expenses of the removal, to expenses other than purchase price incurred in connection with the purchase, *e.g.* legal or survey fees. Financial assistance towards the purchase price is governed by Part XIV, below. However, no "purchase grant" can be given if the purchase is from the landlord authority, unless the conditions of subs. (2) apply.

These conditions are first that the house was built expressly for sale or letting, and secondly, the house must never have been let. This means that in practice the purchase grant is available only if the property is new-build, whether originally expressly for sale or not, and the decision to sell has been taken before the house is ever occupied. However, also within the conditions would be a house sold without ever being let which has returned to the landlord, perhaps because of the inability of the "first buyer" to maintain the expense, *e.g.* under s.452, below.

The Secretary of State may identify what can qualify for, and/or may limit the amount of, a purchase grant: subs. (3). The Secretary of State has identified legal fees, search fees, other necessary disbursements, stamp duty, Land Registry fees and amounts relating to a mortgage as qualifying: Housing Subsidies and Accounting Manual (1981 Edition), App. H. There is, however, no fixed cash limit, *cf.* S.I. 1984 No. 1174, fixing £200 for analogous expenses under s.443, below, in connection with other classes of public sector purchase. The authority's power to make payments subject to conditions could include, *e.g.*, clearing arrears or remedying breaches before departure. The Secretary of State has suggested that authorities may wish to make payment of legal expenses under subs. (3) conditional on personal occupation by the tenant: Housing Subsidies and Accounting Manual (1981 Edition), para. 206.

Agreement with housing co-operatives

Agreements with housing co-operatives

27.—(1) A local housing authority may, with the approval of the Secretary of State, make an agreement with a housing co-operative—

(*a*) for the exercise by the co-operative, on such terms as may be provided in the agreement, of any of the authority's powers relating to land in which the authority has a legal estate and for the time being holds for the purposes of this Part, and the performance by the co-operative of any of the authority's duties relating to such land, or

(*b*) for the exercise by the co-operative, in connection with such land, of any of the authority's powers under section 10 or 11 (provision of furnishings and fittings or board and laundry facilities).

(2) In this section "housing co-operative" means a society, company or body of trustees for the time being approved by the Secretary of State for the purposes of this section.

(3) The Secretary of State's approval to the making of an agreement may be given either—

(a) generally to local housing authorities, or

(b) to particular authorities or descriptions of authority;

and may be given unconditionally or subject to conditions.

(4) The terms of the agreement may provide for the letting of land by the authority to the co-operative.

(5) Where an authority has entered into an agreement under this section, neither the agreement itself nor any letting of land in pursuance of it shall be taken into account—

(a) in determining the authority's reckonable income or expenditure for the purposes of housing subsidy under Part XIII, or

(b) as a ground for recovering, withholding or reducing any sum under section 427 (recoupment of housing subsidy);

but this applies where the letting is by way of a shared ownership lease only if, and to the extent that, the Secretary of State so determines.

(6) A housing association is not entitled to a housing association grant under the Housing Associations Act 1985, or to a revenue deficit grant or hostel deficit grant under that Act, in respect of land for the time being comprised in an agreement under this section.

DEFINITIONS
  "local housing authority": ss.1, 2.
  "shared ownership lease": s.622.

GENERAL NOTE

The term "housing co-operative" is widely used to denote a number of different forms of housing ownership. The only statutory use of the term is in this section, and denotes what is sometimes called a "management co-operative" (see also Final Report of the Working Party on Tenant Co-operatives (1976) and D.O.E. Circular 8/76).

In addition, the term is used to denote "non-equity" or "par value" co-operatives in the "quasi-public" sector, under which tenants collectively own—or seek to own (i.e. if formed while still seeking property)—housing through a housing association, membership of which is confined to tenants or prospective tenants, but have either no individual stake in the property, or a stake confined to a share repayable on leaving the co-operative at "par value" (i.e. the price paid for it, not, therefore, reflecting any increase in value). Finally, there are co-ownership societies, where the tenants collectively own and manage the property, but do share in the equity and its increase in value.

Under this section, the principal aim is to transfer management responsibilities to the co-operative: subs. (1). Both the agreement, and the co-operative, need the approval of the Secretary of State: subss. (1), (2). However, the agreement may include the letting of land by the authority to the co-operative, i.e. the agreement may extend to the grant of a lease: subs. (4). In either event, the co-operative does not qualify for (a) housing association grant, (b) revenue deficit grant, or (c) hostel deficit grant under Part II, Housing Associations Act 1985, in respect of the property comprised in the agreement: subs. (6). It can still, of course, so qualify in respect of other land it may hold, for the co-operative need not be confined to activity under one agreement with one authority under this section.

Instead of the grants available under the Housing Associations Act 1985, "subsidy" remains under this Act. The agreement, including any letting of land under it, is ignored for the purposes of calculating both the outgoings and income of the authority, and for the purpose of recoupment of subsidy, under Part XIII: subs. (5). In effect, subsidy to the authority continues irrespective of the management co-operative agreement. This leaves the authority in principal control, i.e. holding the purse-strings. However, if a related letting of land is by way of shared ownership lease, there may be a variation in subsidy on account of the agreement, in substance to the extent that the Secretary of State determines: subs. (5).

The provisions of this section apply to new town corporations, and the Development Board for Rural Wales: see s.30, below.

Powers of county councils

Reserve powers to provide housing accommodation

28.—(1) County councils have the following reserve powers in relation to the provision of housing accommodation.

(2) They may undertake any activity for the purposes of, or incidental to, establishing the needs of the whole or a part of the county with respect to the provision of housing accommodation.

(3) If requested to do so by one or more local housing authorities for districts within the county, they may, with the consent of the Secretary of State, undertake on behalf of the authority or authorities the provision of housing accommodation in any manner in which they might do so.

(4) With the approval of the Secretary of State given on an application made by them, they may undertake the provision of housing accommodation in any manner in which a local housing authority for a district within the county might do so.

(5) The Secretary of State shall not give his consent under subsection (3) or his approval under subsection (4) except after consultation with the local housing authorities who appear to him to be concerned; and his consent or approval may be made subject to such conditions and restrictions as he may from time to time specify and, in particular, may include conditions with respect to—

(*a*) the transfer of the ownership and management of housing accommodation provided by the county council to the local housing authority, and

(*b*) the recovery by the county council from local housing authorities of expenditure incurred by the county council in providing accommodation.

(6) Before a county council by virtue of subsection (3) or (4) exercise outside the county any power under this Part they shall give notice to the council of the county in which they propose to exercise the power; but failure to give notice does not invalidate the exercise of the power.

DEFINITIONS
    "housing accommodation": s.56.
    "local housing authority": ss.1, 2.

GENERAL NOTE
    This is the first of two express powers for county councils, rather than local housing authorities, to provide housing: see also s.29, below. The tenants of county councils may be secure tenants under Part IV, and enjoy the right to buy under Part V, although subject to qualifications.
    This section contains "reserve" powers, dating back to the Housing, Town Planning, etc. Act, 1919. Without anyone's consent, county councils are entitled to undertake activity designed to establish the needs for housing accommodation of the whole or any part of the county: subs. (2). On the request of a local housing authority within the county, and with the consent of the Secretary of State, they may exercise any local housing authority power concerning the provision of housing accommodation: subs. (3). On their own application, the Secretary of State may consent to them providing housing accommodation in any way that a local housing authority could do: subs. (4).
    In either of the latter two cases, however, the Secretary of State must consult with local housing authorities who appear to him to be concerned before giving his consent: subs. (5). This means he must provide such authorities with the opportunity to make informed comments, on a time-scale which, although prima facie for him to decide having regard to the urgency of the matter, must allow the authority to be consulted, time to consider proposals and respond to them, and himself time to consider their response: *R.* v. *Secretary of State for Social Services, ex parte Association of Metropolitan Authorities* (1985) 17 H.L.R. 487, Q.B.D., see further notes to s.420(4), below.
    Consent may be conditional, and the conditions and restrictions may be varied "from time to time," and in particular may make provision for the eventual transfer of ownership and

management to a local housing authority, and for a subsidy to be given by the local housing authority to the county council: subs. (5). If the county council wish to exercise powers outside their own council, they must give notice to the council of the county in which they propose to operate, although failure so to do does not invalidate the activity: subs. (6).

Provision of accommodation for employees of county councils

29.—(1) A county council may provide houses for persons employed or paid by, or by a statutory committee of, the council.

(2) For that purpose the council may acquire or appropriate land in the same way as a local housing authority may acquire or appropriate land for the purposes of this Part; and land so acquired or appropriated may be disposed of by them in the same way as land held for the purposes of this Part.

DEFINITIONS
"house": s.56.
"local housing authority": ss.1, 2.

GENERAL NOTE
Regardless of the reserve powers contained in the last section, county councils can also provide accommodation for their own employees. While within the security of Part IV, and the right to buy in Part V, below, the rights of these occupiers are that much more likely to be qualified: as to security, under Sched. 1, para. 2, as to grounds for possession, under Sched. 2, Grounds 7 and 12, as to exchange, under Sched. 3, Ground 5, and as to right to buy, under Sched. 5, para. 5.

The county council, in exercise of this power, will enjoy the same rights of acquisition and appropriation as local housing authorities under ss.15 and 17, above, and subject to the same constraints on disposal: see ss.32, *et seq.*, below.

A police superintendent is within the definition: *Rodwell* v. *Minister of Health* [1947] K.B. 404.

Miscellaneous powers of other authorities and bodies

Application of provisions to new town corporations, etc.

30.—(1) The following provisions apply in relation to a new town corporation as they apply in relation to a local housing authority—
    section 25 (increase of rent where tenancy not secure), and
    section 26 (financial assistance towards tenants' removal expenses).

(2) Section 27 (agreements with housing co-operatives) applies in relation to—
    (*a*) a new town corporation and the powers of the corporation under the New Towns Act 1981, and
    (*b*) the Development Board for Rural Wales and the powers of the Board under the Development of Rural Wales Act 1976,
as it applies in relation to a local housing authority and the functions of such an authority referred to in that section.

DEFINITIONS
"local housing authority": ss.1, 2.
"new town corporation": s.4.

GENERAL NOTE
New town corporations, and the Commission for the New Towns (see s.4, above), enjoy the powers in s.25 (to increase rent without notice to quit) and s.26 (removal expenses) as do local housing authorities, and to enter into management co-operative agreements under s.27, which latter power is also enjoyed by the Development Board for Rural Wales. The extension of the latter power to new town corporations and the Development Board is pursuant to Law Commissions Recommendations (Cmnd. 9515), No. 3.

Power of bodies corporate to sell or let land for housing purposes

31. A body corporate holding land may sell, exchange or lease the land for the purpose of providing housing of any description at such price, or for such consideration, or for such rent, as having regard to all the circumstances of the case is the best that can reasonably be obtained, notwithstanding that a higher price, consideration or rent might have been obtained if the land were sold, exchanged or leased for the purpose of providing housing of another description or for a purpose other than the provision of housing.

GENERAL NOTE

In general, local authorities owe a fiduciary duty to their ratepayers, analogous in some instances to that owed by trustees, and it is not normally open even to a limited company to be philanthropic to an unrestrained extent, at the expense of its shareholders. This section provides an exception to these general principles, where the disposal of land is involved: if it is for the purpose of providing housing, of any description, and to or by whomsoever, a better price need not be obtained by disposing of the land for an alternative use.

The cumbersome wording is attributable to the final demise of the expression "housing for the working classes" which had, despite its general abandonment under the Housing Act 1949, managed to survive in s.129, Housing Act 1957: Law Commission Recommendations (Cmnd. 9515), No. 4. Accordingly, land for the erection of housing for the working classes could be provided by any body corporate (whether a local authority or other public body or not) at the best price that could reasonably be obtained (*cf.* Local Government Act 1972, s.123) *having regard to that purpose and to all the circumstances of the case*, and even although a better price could be obtained if the land was sold, etc., for some other purpose. It is the passage emphasised in the last sentence which distinguishes the power from s.123 of the 1972 Act.

The redrafting has altered the wording of the purpose from "erection of houses" to "providing housing." In addition, the point is made that there could be differences in the price available for different types of housing, *e.g.* the difference is selling for single houses, and a block of flats. The power is available, therefore, to choose a less valuable sale even within housing options.

"Land" includes "buildings and other structures, land covered with water, and any estate, interest, easement, servitude or right in or over land": Interpretation Act 1978, Sched. 1.

Disposal of land held for housing purposes

Power to dispose of land held for purposes of this Part

32.—(1) Without prejudice to the provisions of Part V (the right to buy), a local authority have power by this section, and not otherwise, to dispose of land held by them for the purposes of this Part.

(2) A disposal under this section may be effected in any manner but, subject to subsection (3), shall not be made without the consent of the Secretary of State.

(3) No consent is required for the letting of land under a secure tenancy or under what would be a secure tenancy but for any of paragraphs 2 to 12 of Schedule 1 (tenancies, other than long leases, which are not secure).

(4) For the purposes of this section the grant of an option to purchase the freehold of, or any other interest in, land is a disposal and a consent given to such a disposal extends to a disposal made in pursuance of the option.

(5) Sections 128 to 132 of the Lands Clauses Consolidation Act 1845 (which require surplus land first to be offered to the original owner and to adjoining land-owners) do not apply to the sale by a local authority of land held by them for the purposes of this Part.

DEFINITIONS

"local authority": s.4.
"secure tenancy": s.79.

GENERAL NOTE

This section applies to land "held" for the purposes of Part II and accordingly includes land specifically purchased for Part II purposes, or to land appropriated under s.19, above. It does not apply to disposals under the right to buy, *i.e.* under Part V, below: subs. (1). See also s.43, below, for disposals of non-Part II housing.

No consent is required under this section for the grant of a secure tenancy under Part IV, *i.e.* "normal" lettings by local housing authorities: subs. (3). Nor is consent required for the grant of what would be a secure tenancy, but is not because of the provisions of Sched. 1, paras. 2 to 12 (exemptions from security): *ibid.* Consent *is* needed, however, for the grant of a lease for more than twenty-one years exempt from security by Sched. 1, para. 1: *ibid.* Consent is also needed in the case of any other disposal: subs. (2).

Consent is governed by s.34. See s.33, below, as to conditions of disposal. A disposal includes the grant of an option: subs. (4). If, however, consent is granted in connection with an option, no new consent is needed for the consequential disposal itself: *ibid.* See s.44, below, for the effect of disposal without consent.

Covenants and conditions which may be imposed

33.—(1) On a disposal under section 32 the local authority may impose such covenants and conditions as they think fit.

(2) But a condition of any of the following kinds may be imposed only with the consent of the Secretary of State—

(a) a condition limiting the price or premium which may be obtained on a further disposal of a house;

(b) in the case of a sale, a condition reserving a right of pre-emption;

(c) in the case of a lease, a condition precluding the lessee from assigning the lease or granting a sub-lease.

(3) In subsection (2)(b) a condition reserving a right of pre-emption means a condition precluding the purchaser from selling or leasing the land unless—

(a) he first notifies the authority of the proposed sale or lease and offers to sell or lease the land to them, and

(b) the authority refuse the offer or fail to accept it within one month after it is made.

(4) References in this section to the purchaser or lessee include references to his successors in title and any person deriving title under him or his successors in title.

DEFINITIONS

"house": s.56.
"local authority": s.4.

GENERAL NOTE

Local authorities may dispose on such conditions as they think fit, *save* that the consent of the Secretary of State is needed for the inclusion of any of the following terms:

(1) Condition limiting resale price (by way of conveyance of freehold, assignment of lease or indeed grant of lease or sublease);

(2) Condition on a *sale* reserving a right of pre-emption, *i.e.* a requirement that the purchaser cannot sell the property or grant a lease on it without first giving the vendor authority one month to refuse or fail to accept an offer of sale or lease back to the vendor authority;

(3) Condition on the grant of a *lease* which prohibits assignment or the grant of a sublease, *i.e.* restriction on alienation.

In each case, references to the purchaser or lessee include their successors in title, and persons deriving title under them or one such successor: subs. (4).

In substance, then, sales or grants of leases which are not secure tenancies (or what would be secure tenancies but for Sched. 1, paras. 2 to 12—see notes to s.32, above), cannot allow the vendor authority any real control on the use or occupation of the property beyond the immediate transaction, *save* to the extent that the Secretary of State permits. Note, however, that in some circumstances, a disposal in certain areas (national park, designated area of outstanding natural beauty, designated rural area) can contain a measure of future restriction: see notes to s.37, below.

Consents under ss.32 and 33

34.—(1) This section applies in relation to the giving of the Secretary of State's consent under section 32 or 33.

(2) Consent may be given—

   (*a*) either generally to all local authorities or to a particular authority or description of authority;

   (*b*) either in relation to particular land or in relation to land of a particular description.

(3) Consent may be given subject to conditions.

(4) Consent may, in particular, be given subject to conditions as to the price, premium or rent to be obtained on the disposal, including conditions as to the amount by which on the disposal of a house by way of sale or by the grant or assignment of a lease at a premium, the price or premium is to be, or may be, discounted by the local authority.

DEFINITIONS

   "house": s.56.

   "local authority": s.4.

GENERAL NOTE

   "General" consents are issued by Ministerial Letter, and by D.O.E. Circular: see, currently, Ministerial Letters of June 2, and June 4, 1981, (England and Wales respectively), as amended by Circular 21/84. Broadly, the general consents are designed to place voluntary disposals under these provisions on the same basis as disposals under the right to buy in Part V. When such analogous terms are included, *e.g.* discount, permitted pre-emption clause, the provisions of ss.35–42, below, apply. See s.44 for the effect of a disposal without consent.

Repayment of discount on early disposal

35.—(1) This section applies where, on a disposal of a house under section 32, a discount is given to the purchaser by the local authority in accordance with a consent given by the Secretary of State under subsection (2) of that section; but this section does not apply in any such case if the consent so provides.

(2) On the disposal the conveyance, grant or assignment shall contain a covenant binding on the purchaser and his successors in title to pay to the authority on demand, if within a period of five years there is a relevant disposal which is not an exempted disposal (but if there is more than one such disposal then only on the first of them), an amount equal to the discount, reduced by 20 per cent. for each complete year which has elapsed after the conveyance, grant or assignment and before the further disposal.

DEFINITIONS

   "exempted disposal": s.39.

   "house": s.56.

   "local authority": s.4.

   "relevant disposal": s.38.

GENERAL NOTE

   This is the first of a number of sections which create a statutory presumption in favour of treatment of purchasers under voluntary sales in the same way as those who purchase under the right to buy in Part V. That is to say, if a discount is allowed on a voluntary sale, under a consent to the sale granted by the Secretary of State under s.34, above, whether a general consent or a particular consent, there is to be a "clawback" of the discount, *unless* the consent provides that this section is not to apply.

   The clawback will operate over five years. There will be a clawback if there is a "relevant disposal" which is not an "exempted disposal." The clawback is to be of the whole discount, less 20 per cent. for every complete year following the original disposal (conveyance, grant or assignment) before the further—*i.e.* non-exempted relevant—disposal. In general terms, the purpose of the provisions are to permit what might be termed family or domestic rearrangements, compulsory or could-be compulsory purchases, and sales of curtilage lands, without activating the clawback.

"Relevant disposal" is defined in s.38 as a conveyance of the freehold, an assignment of a lease, or the grant of a lease or sublease (other than a mortgage term) for a term of more than 21 years *other* than at a rack rent. An option enabling a person to call for the grant of a relevant disposal which is not an exempted disposal is treated as a disposal: s.42, below.

"Rack rent" will be considered as at the grant: *London Corporation* v. *Cusack-Smith* [1955] A.C. 337, H.L. Time will run from when the tenant is legally entitled to take up occupation under the grant, not from delivery at a later date (*Brikom* v. *Seaford Investments Ltd.* [1981] 1 W.L.R. 863, 1 H.L.R. 21, C.A.), but conversely runs from the date of the grant, even if an earlier date is specified (*Roberts* v. *Church Commissioners for England* [1972] 1 Q.B. 278, C.A.); the reservation to the tenant under the lease of a right to determine the lease at an earlier time is disregarded both at common law (*Quinlan* v. *Avis* (1933) L.T. 214) and under s.38(2). In addition, it is to be assumed that an option to renew or extend will be exercised: s.38(2), below.

"Exempted disposal" is defined in s.39. There are five classes of exempted disposal.

(1) A conveyance of the freehold or the assignment of the lease of the whole of the property, to a person who is, or to a number of persons all of whom are, "qualifying persons," defined in s.39(2) as: (a) the person by whom the disposal is made, or one of the persons by whom the disposal is made (*e.g.* disposal by two joint owners to one of their number, or disposal by one joint owner to two persons, of whom he is one, and the other is also a qualifying person); (b) the spouse or former spouse of the person or one of the persons by whom the disposal is made; or (c) a member of the family of the person or one of the persons by whom the disposal is made, who has resided with him throughout the period of 12 months ending with the disposal. "Member of the family" is defined in s.56, by cross-reference to Part V, *i.e.* s.186. As to "residing with," see notes to s.87, below.

(2) A vesting of the whole of the house in a person taking under a will or on an intestacy.

(3) A disposal of the whole of the house pursuant to a property adjustment order under s.24, Matrimonial Causes Act 1973 or an order for financial provision from an estate under s.2, Inheritance (Provision for Family and Dependants) Act 1975.

(4) Compulsory disposal, as defined in s.40 to mean a disposal on a compulsory purchase, or by agreement to someone who has made or would have made a compulsory purchase order, or to someone on whose behalf a compulsory purchase order has been made or would have been made, *e.g.* a housing association for whom a local authority are prepared to make a compulsory purchase order.

(5) The property which is the subject of the disposal is land included with the house under s.56, below, *i.e.* "any yard, garden, outhouses and appurtenances belonging to the house or usually enjoyed with it": see notes to s.56.

In the case of the fourth and fifth exemptions, *i.e.* compulsory disposals and disposals of curtilage lands, the repayment covenant is not binding on the purchaser or his successor in title, and the covenant, and the charge, cease to apply in relation to the property disposed of, *i.e.* the whole property if that is what is subject to the compulsory purchase, or the curtilage lands. In addition, covenants applicable to property in National Parks, designated areas of outstanding natural beauty and designated rural areas, cease to apply: see notes to s.37, below. Otherwise, the covenant and charge bind the successor in title: see s.35(2), above.

Liability to repay is a charge on the premises

36.—(1) The liability that may arise under the covenant required by section 35 is a charge on the house, taking effect as if it had been created by deed expressed to be by way of legal mortgage.

(2) The charge has priority immediately after any legal charge securing an amount—

   (*a*) left outstanding by the purchaser, or

   (*b*) advanced to him by an approved lending institution for the purpose of enabling him to acquire the interest disposed of on the first disposal, or

   (*c*) further advanced to him by that institution;

but the local authority may at any time by written notice served on an approved lending institution postpone the charge taking effect by virtue of this section to a legal charge securing an amount advanced or further advanced to the purchaser by that institution.

(3) A charge taking effect by virtue of this section is a land charge for the purposes of section 59 of the Land Registration Act 1925 notwithstanding subsection (5) of that section (exclusion of mortgages), and subsection (2) of that section applies accordingly with respect to its protection and realisation.

(4) The approved lending institutions for the purposes of this section are—

     a building society,
     a bank,
     a trustee savings bank,
     an insurance company,
     a friendly society,

and any body specified, or of a class or description specified, in an order made under section 156 (which makes provision in relation to disposals in pursuance of the right to buy corresponding to that made by this section).

DEFINITIONS
   "house": s.56.
   "local authority": s.4.

GENERAL NOTE
   This section is ancillary to the last, *i.e.* if there is a covenant requiring repayment of discount it is to be a charge on the house, with priority immediately *after* any legal charge which secures an amount "left outstanding by the purchaser" (*i.e.* effectively, a mortgage from the vendor authority), or advanced for the purpose of the purchase by an "approved lending institution" as defined in subs. (4), or *further* advanced by *the same* approved lending institution, *e.g.* a further advance with which to carry out improvement works: subs. (2).

   However, the authority enjoy discretion to postpone the charge to a charge securing *any* amount advanced or further advanced by *any* approved lending institution, *e.g.* where a second mortgage is granted by a different lending institution for improvement works, or where there is a financial rearrangement by the owner under which one approved lending institution takes over the debt from another, but not merely by assignment of the original legal charge: subs. (2).

   As to approved lending institutions: see also notes to s.156, below.

Restriction on disposal of dwelling-houses in National Parks, etc.

37.—(1) Where a conveyance, grant or assignment executed under section 32 is of a house situated in—

   (a)   a National Park,
   (b)   an area designated under section 87 of the National Parks and Access to the Countryside Act 1949 as an area of outstanding natural beauty, or
   (c)   an area designated as a rural area by order under section 157 (which makes provision in relation to disposals in pursuance of the right to buy corresponding to that made by this section),

the conveyance, grant or assignment may (unless it contains a condition of a kind mentioned in section 33(2)(b) or (c) (right of pre-emption or restriction on assignment)) contain a covenant limiting the freedom of the purchaser (including any successor in title of his and any person deriving title under him or such a successor) to dispose of the house in the manner specified below.

(2) The limitation is that until such time (if any) as may be notified in writing by the local authority to the purchaser or a successor in title of his, there will be no relevant disposal which is not an exempted disposal without the written consent of the authority; but that consent shall not be withheld if the disposal is to a person satisfying the condition stated in subsection (3).

(3) The condition is that the person to whom the disposal is made (or, if it is made to more than one person, at least one of them) has,

throughout the period of three years immediately preceding the application for consent—

    (*a*) had his place of work in a region designated by order under section
          157(3) which, or part of which, is comprised in the National Park
          or area, or

    (*b*) had his only or principal home in such a region;

or has had the one in part or parts of that period and the other in the
remainder; but the region need not have been the same throughout the
period.

    (4) A disposal in breach of such a covenant as is mentioned in subsection
(1) is void.

    (5) The limitation imposed by such a covenant is a local land charge
and, if the land is registered under the Land Registration Act 1925, the
Chief Land Registrar shall enter the appropriate restriction on the register
of title as if application therefor had been made under section 58 of that
Act.

    (6) In this section "purchaser" means the person acquiring the interest
disposed of by the first disposal.

DEFINITIONS
    "exempted disposal": s.39.
    "house": s.56.
    "local authority": s.4.
    "relevant disposal": s.38.

GENERAL NOTE
    This is the third of the sections which aim to put voluntary sales on a par with sales under
the right to buy in Part V: see notes to s.157, below.
    Voluntary sales cannot normally include a pre-emption clause, or a restriction against
alienation, *i.e.* a covenant in a lease precluding the lessee from assignment or granting a
sub-lease: see s.33, above. However, such provisions *can* be included with the consent of the
Secretary of State: *ibid.* If consent is sought and obtained to either a pre-emption clause or
a restriction against alienation, the provisions of this section will not have effect: subs. (1).
    This section applies only to property in one of the three classes of area: National Parks,
designated areas of outstanding natural beauty, and designated rural areas (see notes to
s.157, below). As an alternative to permitted pre-emption clause or restriction on alienation,
the vendor authority may, without the consent of the Secretary of State, include the
limitation set out in subs. (2) on the freedom of the purchaser—and any successor in title of
his, or person deriving title under him or such successor—to dispose of the property. The
purpose is to prevent resale to persons looking for "second homes" in the country, and to
confine occupation to those who live or work in the country.
    The limitation is that until such time, if any, as the authority may notify the purchaser or
successor in title, in writing, there can be no "relevant disposal" which is not an "exempted
disposal" without the written consent of the authority. As to relevant and exempted
disposals, see notes to s.35, above. Consent cannot be withheld if the prospective purchaser,
assignee or lessee qualifies within subs. (3). If the initial disposal is by way of lease, and the
limitation is contained in the lease, it would also seem to be subject to s.19, Landlord and
Tenant Act 1927, that consent cannot unreasonably be withheld; see notes to s.94, below.
A disposal in breach of the limitation is void: subs. (4).
    The class qualifying under subs. (3) is of a person who has, for a period of three years
immediately preceding the application for consent, *either* had his place or work, *or* had his
only or principal home (as to which, see notes to s.81, below) in an area designated under
s.157(3). Such an area is *not* the same as a National Park, or designated area of outstanding
natural beauty, or designated rural area, but it or part of it must be in a National Park,
designated area of outstanding natural beauty or designated rural area. Qualification can be
made up by working for part of the period in a designated s.157(3) area, and having the only
or principal home in it for the remainder of the period. In no case, however, does the
designated s.157(3) area have to remain the same throughout the period.
    If the property is disposed of under an exempt disposal, the limitation will continue to
apply (subs. (2)), *save* in the case of a compulsory disposal, or if the disposal is only of
curtilage lands: see notes to s.35, above; see s.41.

Relevant disposals

38.—(1) A disposal, whether of the whole or part of the house, is a relevant disposal for the purposes of this Part if it is—

(*a*) a conveyance of the freehold or an assignment of the lease, or

(*b*) the grant of a lease or sub-lease (other than a mortgage term) for a term of more than 21 years otherwise than at a rack rent.

(2) For the purposes of subsection (1)(*b*) it shall be assumed—

(*a*) that any option to renew or extend a lease or sub-lease, whether or not forming part of a series of options, is exercised, and

(*b*) that any option to terminate a lease or sub-lease is not exercised.

GENERAL NOTE
See notes to s.35, above, and s.159, below.

Exempted disposals

39.—(1) A disposal is an exempted disposal for the purposes of this Part if—

(*a*) it is a disposal of the whole of the house and a conveyance of the freehold or an assignment of the lease and the person or each of the persons to whom it is made is a qualifying person (as defined in subsection (2));

(*b*) it is a vesting of the whole of the house in a person taking under a will or on an intestacy;

(*c*) it is a disposal of the whole of the house in pursuance of an order made under section 24 of the Matrimonial Causes Act 1973 (property adjustment orders in connection with matrimonial proceedings) or section 2 of the Inheritance (Provision for Family and Dependants) Act 1975 (orders as to financial provision to be made from estate);

(*d*) it is a compulsory disposal; or

(*e*) the property disposed of is property included with the house by virtue of the definition of "house" in section 56 (yard, garden, outhouses, &c.).

(2) For the purposes of subsection (1)(*a*), a person is a qualifying person in relation to a disposal if—

(*a*) he is the person or one of the persons by whom the disposal is made,

(*b*) he is the spouse or a former spouse of that person or one of those persons, or

(*c*) he is a member of the family of that person or one of those persons and has resided with him throughout the period of twelve months ending with the disposal.

DEFINITIONS
"compulsory disposal": s.40.
"house": s.56.
"member of the family": ss.56, 186.

GENERAL NOTE
See notes to s.35, above, and s.160, below.

Meaning of "compulsory disposal"

40. In this Part a "compulsory disposal" means a disposal of property which is acquired compulsorily, or is acquired by a person who has made or would have made, or for whom another person has made or would have made, a compulsory purchase order authorising its compulsory purchase for the purposes for which it is acquired.

GENERAL NOTE
See notes to s.35, above, and s.161, below.

Exempted disposals which end liability under covenants

41. Where there is a relevant disposal which is an exempted disposal by virtue of section 39(1)(*d*) or (*e*) (compulsory disposal or disposal of yard, garden, &c.)—

(*a*) the covenant required by section 35 (repayment of discount on early disposal) is not binding on the person to whom the disposal is made or any successor in title of his, and that covenant and the charge taking effect by virtue of section 36 (liability to repay a charge on the premises) cease to apply in relation to the property disposed of, and

(*b*) any such covenant as is mentioned in section 37 (restriction on disposal of houses in National Parks, etc.) ceases to apply in relation to the property disposed of.

DEFINITIONS
"compulsory disposal": s.40.
"exempted disposal": s.39.
"relevant disposal": s.38.

GENERAL NOTE
See notes to s.35, above, and s.162, below.

Treatment of options

42.—(1) For the purposes of this Part the grant of an option enabling a person to call for a relevant disposal which is not an exempted disposal shall be treated as such a disposal made to him.

(2) For the purposes of section 37(2) (requirement of consent to disposal of house in National Park, etc.) a consent to such a grant shall be treated as a consent to a disposal made in pursuance of the option.

DEFINITIONS
"exempted disposal": s.39.
"relevant disposal": s.38.

GENERAL NOTE
See notes to ss.35 and 36, above, and s.163, below.

Consent required for certain disposals not within s.32

43.—(1) The consent of the Secretary of State is required for the disposal by a local authority, otherwise than in pursuance of Part V (the right to buy), of a house belonging to the authority—

(*a*) which is let on a secure tenancy, or

(*b*) of which a lease has been granted in pursuance of Part V,

but which has not been acquired or appropriated by the authority for the purposes of this Part.

(2) Consent may be given—

(*a*) either generally to all local authorities or to any particular local authority or description of authority, and

(*b*) either generally in relation to all houses or in relation to any particular house or description of house.

(3) Consent may be given subject to conditions.

(4) Consent may, in particular, be given subject to conditions as to the price, premium or rent to be obtained on a disposal of the house, including conditions as to the amount by which, on a disposal of the house by way

of sale or by the grant or assignment of a lease at a premium, the price or premium is to be, or may be, discounted by the local authority.

(5) For the purposes of this section the grant of an option to purchase the freehold of, or any other interest in, a house to which this section applies is a disposal and a consent given under this section to such a disposal extends to a disposal made in pursuance of the option.

DEFINITIONS
"house": s.56.
"local authority": s.4.

GENERAL NOTE
The provisions considered since (and including) s.32 apply to land "held" for the purposes of Part II, *i.e.* acquired for or appropriated to those purposes. This *can* include land held by county councils: see. s.29(2). However, county councils also hold land for other purposes, and their tenants on such other land may well be secure: see s.79, below. They may also exercise the right to buy under Part V, below. Local authorities have a general freedom to dispose of property, albeit at the best price reasonably obtainable (see s.123, Local Government Act 1972, *cf.* notes to s.31, above), and of course provided the legislation under which the property is held does not restrict disposal (see 1972 Act, s.131), as does this Act where the property is held under this Part. There is an additional power to sell under s.26, Town and Country Planning Act 1959.

The purpose of this section is to prevent county councils, and other local authorities, who hold land *other* than under this Part, from disposing of it—or of an interest in it—without consent. The section applies only where the house is let on a secure tenancy, or in respect of which a lease has been granted under Part V, and does not of course apply to disposals under Part V.

Accordingly, it concerns disposals of interests in property subject to secure tenancies, which might prevent the tenancy remaining secure, or which has been the subject of a lease purchase under Part V, *i.e.* in substance it is designed to prevent avoidance of Parts IV and V. ("A local authority which is so minded is effectively in a position to frustrate a tenant's application to exercise his right to buy . . . by disposing of its interest in his home over his head to a third party who is not a right to buy landlord. . ." Mr. Gow, *Hansard*, H.C. Vol. 58, col. 611 [April 12, 1984]).

Property within this section cannot be disposed of without consent. Disposal includes the grant of an option: subs. (5). Consent to the grant of an option is, however, effective to cover the subsequent disposal itself: *ibid.*

Avoidance of certain disposals of houses without consent

44.—(1) A disposal of a house by a local authority made without the consent required by section 32 or 43 is void, unless—

(*a*) the disposal is to an individual (or to two or more individuals), and
(*b*) the disposal does not extend to any other house.

(2) Subsection (1) has effect notwithstanding section 29 of the Town and Country Planning Act 1959 and section 128(2) of the Local Government Act 1972 (protection of purchasers dealing with authority).

(3) In this section "house" does not have the extended meaning applicable by virtue of the definition of "housing accommodation" in section 56, but includes a flat.

DEFINITIONS
"house": s.56.
"local authority": s.4.

GENERAL NOTE
As a general proposition, an *ultra vires* disposal by a public authority is void: *Rhyl Urban District Council* v. *Rhyl Amusements Ltd.* [1959] 1 W.L.R. 465; consider also *Minister of Agriculture and Fisheries* v. *Matthews* [1950] 1 K.B. 148. Provisions designed to overturn this principle were introduced by s.29, Town and Country Planning Act 1959, and generally applied by s.128, Local Government Act 1972, under which purchasers are not required to investigate the powers of the authority and any necessary consents, and the disposal is valid notwithstanding any such flaw.

This section removes the protection of ss.29 and 128 of the 1959 and 1972 Acts respectively, and reinstates the *Rhyl* principle, where consent is needed but has not been obtained under either s.32 or s.43, *unless* the disposal is (a) of one house only, and (b) to an individual, or two or more individuals, *i.e.* not a corporate body. For this purpose "house" does not include a lodging-house or hostel.

Restriction on service charges payable after disposal of house

Disposals in relation to which ss.46 to 51 apply, etc.

45.—(1) The following provisions of this Part down to section 51 (restrictions on, and provision of information about, service charges) apply where—
- (*a*) a house has been disposed of by a public sector authority,
- (*b*) the conveyance or grant, or, in the case of an assignment of a lease, the lease, enabled the vendor or lessor to recover from the purchaser or lessee a service charge, and
- (*c*) the house is not a flat within the meaning of sections 18 to 30 of the Landlord and Tenant Act 1985 (which make provision for flats corresponding to that made by the following provisions of this Act).

(2) In subsection (1)(*a*)—
- (*a*) the reference to disposal is to the conveyance of the freehold or the grant or assignment of a long lease (that is, a lease creating a long tenancy as defined in section 115); and
- (*b*) "public sector authority" means—
  - a local authority,
  - a new town corporation,
  - an urban development corporation,
  - the Development Board for Rural Wales,
  - the Housing Corporation, or
  - a registered housing association.

(3) The following provisions—
  - section 170 (power of Secretary of State to give assistance in connection with legal proceedings), and
  - section 181 (jurisdiction of county court),

apply to proceedings and questions arising under this section and sections 46 to 51 as they apply to proceedings and questions arising under Part V (the right to buy).

DEFINITIONS
"house": s.56.
"local authority": s.4.
"new town corporation": s.4.
"registered housing association": s.5.
"service charge": s.46.
"urban development corporation": s.4.

GENERAL NOTE
Protection is available (including where the landlord is a public authority) to lessees of "flats," as defined in the Landlord and Tenant Act 1985, s.30, against unwarranted claims by landlords for "service charges," as defined for present purposes in s.46, in identical terms to those used in s.18, Landlord and Tenant Act: see ss.18–30, Landlord and Tenant Act 1985. This and the following sections make equivalent provision for those who take long leases of *houses*, under which a service charge is recoverable, or indeed who take a freehold of a house, and the conveyance reserves a service charge. For example, services may be provided to an estate of houses, one of which has been purchased either voluntarily under this Part, or under the right to buy in Part V.
Flat is defined in s.30, Landlord and Tenant Act 1985 as a separate set of premises, whether or not on the same floor, which (*a*) forms part of a building, and (*b*) is divided horizontally from some other part of that building, and (*c*) is constructed or adapted for use for the purpose of a dwelling and is occupied wholly or mainly as a private dwelling. A

service charge is an amount payable by a purchaser or lessee, directly or indirectly, for services, repairs, maintenance or insurance, or the vendor's or lessor's costs of management, and the whole or part of which varies or may vary according to the costs: s.46, below.

This section applies when the property is *not* a flat within the Landlord and Tenant Act 1985, and when a service charge *is* recoverable by the vendor or lessor, on a disposal by a public sector authority. For this purpose, disposal includes the conveyance of the freehold, or the grant or assignment of a long lease, *i.e.* a tenancy for a term of years certain exceeding 21 years (whether or not terminable before then by notice given by the tenant, or by re-entry or forfeiture), or a tenancy under a grant with a covenant or obligation for perpetual renewal, or a tenancy under Part V: see notes to s.115, below. Public sector authority is defined in subs. (2)(*b*).

Meaning of "service charge" and related expressions

46.—(1) In sections 45 to 51 "service charge" means an amount payable by the purchaser or lessee—

> (*a*) which is payable, directly or indirectly, for services, repairs, maintenance or insurance or the vendor's or lessor's costs of management, and
>
> (*b*) the whole or part of which varies or may vary according to the relevant costs.

(2) The relevant costs are the costs or estimated costs incurred or to be incurred by or on behalf of the payee, or (in the case of a lease) a superior landlord, in connection with the matters for which the service charge is payable.

(3) For this purpose—

> (*a*) "costs" includes overheads, and
>
> (*b*) costs are relevant costs in relation to a service charge whether they are incurred, or to be incurred, in the period for which the service charge is payable or in an earlier or later period.

(4) In relation to a service charge—

> (*a*) the "payee" means the person entitled to enforce payment of the charge, and
>
> (*b*) the "payer" means the person liable to pay it.

GENERAL NOTE

This section defines the service charges to which the provisions of ss.47–51, below, apply. The amount may be payable directly or indirectly, for services, repairs, maintenance or insurance, or the vendor's or lessor's costs of management, the whole or part of which varies or may vary according to the relevant costs. The relevant costs are either actual costs, or estimated costs incurred or to be incurred by or on behalf of the "payee" (*i.e.* the person entitled to enforce payment of the charges) or, in the case of a lease, by or on behalf of a superior landlord. "Costs" includes overheads. They may be relevant in relation to the service charge for one period even if they have been or are to be incurred during a different period.

In a different context (registered rents under the Rent Act 1977), it has been suggested that a service charge may include an element of profit: *Regis Property Co.* v. *Dudley* [1958] 1 Q.B. 346; see also *Perseus Property Co. Ltd.* v. *Burberry* (1984) 17 H.L.R. 243, Q.B.D. The wording of subs. (2) would not seem to permit this, although clearly "overheads" are permitted (subs. (3)(*a*)), and costs of management are admissible (subs. (1)(*a*)). In *Russell* v. *Laimond Properties Ltd.* (1983) 268 E.G. 49, C.A., it was said that "in my judgment . . . cost means cost; that is to say, money laid out and does not mean lost revenue or income, whether it be gross or net, which is foregone. But, cost, in the sense that I take it to mean, money laid out, might well include either interest paid or a reasonable return on the capital employed. . ."

The words in a lease or covenant "subject to payment of" a service charge does not mean that payment is a condition precedent to the landlord's obligations: *Yorkbrook Investments Ltd.* v. *Batten* (1985) 276 E.G. 545, 18 H.L.R., C.A.

Limitation of service charges

47.—(1) Relevant costs shall be taken into account in determining the amount of a service charge payable for a period—

(*a*) only to the extent that they are reasonably incurred, and

(*b*) where they are incurred on the provision of services or the carrying out of works, only if the services or works are of a reasonable standard;

and the amount payable shall be limited accordingly.

(2) Where the service charge is payable before the relevant costs are incurred, no greater amount than is reasonable is so payable and after the relevant costs have been incurred any necessary adjustment shall be made by repayment, reduction of subsequent charges or otherwise.

(3) An agreement by the payer (other than an arbitration agreement within the meaning of section 32 of the Arbitration Act 1950) is void in so far as it purports to provide for a determination in a particular manner or on particular evidence of any question—

(*a*) whether an amount payable before costs for services, repairs, maintenance, insurance or management are incurred is reasonable,

(*b*) whether such costs were reasonably incurred, or

(*c*) whether services or works for which costs were incurred are of a reasonable standard.

DEFINITIONS

"relevant costs": s.46.

"service charge": s.46.

GENERAL NOTE

Relevant costs are only to be taken into account to the extent that they are reasonably incurred, and when on the provision of services or the carrying out of works, only if the services or works are to a reasonable standard: subs. (1). Where the service charge is sought before the period for which it is payable, no greater amount than is reasonable is to be payable, and the amount paid is to be adjusted if needs be by repayment or reduction of subsequent charges: subs. (2). These two subsections are at the core of the protection which these sections serve to provide.

The requirement that works be to a reasonable standard incorporates the common law test discussed in *Re Davstone Estates Ltd.'s Leases* [1969] 2 Ch. 378 and *Finchbourne* v. *Rodrigues* [1976] 3 All E.R. 581, C.A. In *Parkside Knightsbridge Ltd.* v. *Horowitz* (1983) 268 E.G. 49, C.A., evidence was admitted of quotations for services from other agents: on the misunderstanding or misapplication of this evidence by the county court judge, the appeal was successful.

Only an arbitration agreement within s.32, Arbitration Act 1950, can be used to provide determination in a particular manner or on particular evidence of questions as to whether an amount payable before expenditure is reasonable, whether costs were reasonable incurred, and whether services or works are to a reasonable standard: subs. (3). An arbitration agreement under s.32 is one "a written agreement to submit present or future differences to arbitration, whether an arbitrator is named therein or not".

If not to a reasonable standard, a proportionate deduction may be applied; the wording does nor require an "all or nothing" approach: *Yorkbrook Investments Ltd.* v. *Batten* (1985) 276 E.G. 545, 18 H.L.R., C.A. Only in exceptional cases can a *de minimis* approach be adopted to inadequate or non-provision, for though such default may be small in quantum, it may be of considerable importance to the occupier: *ibid.*

Information as to relevant costs

48.—(1) The payer may require the payee in writing to supply him with a written summary of the costs incurred—

(*a*) if the relevant accounts are made up for periods of twelve months, in the last such period ending not later than the date of the request, or

(*b*) if the accounts are not so made up, in the period of twelve months ending with the date of the request,

and which are relevant to the service charges payable or demanded as payable in that or any other period.

(2) The payee shall comply with the request within one month of the request or within six months of the end of the period referred to in subsection (1)(*a*) or (*b*), whichever is the later.

(3) The summary shall set out those costs in a way showing how they are or will be reflected in demands for service charges and must be certified by a qualified accountant as in his opinion a fair summary complying with this requirement and as being sufficiently supported by accounts, receipts and other documents which have been produced to him.

(4) Where the payer has obtained such a summary as is referred to in subsection (1) (whether in pursuance of this section or otherwise), he may within six months of obtaining it require the payee in writing to afford him reasonable facilities—

(*a*) for inspecting the accounts, receipts and other documents supporting the summary, and

(*b*) for taking copies or extracts from them,

and the payee shall then make such facilities available to the payer for a period of two months beginning not later than one month after the request is made.

(5) A request under this section shall be deemed to be served on the payee if it is served on a person who receives the service charge on behalf of the payee; and a person on whom a request is so served shall forward it as soon as possible to the payee.

(6) A disposal of the house by the payer does not affect the validity of a request made under this section before the disposal; but a person is not obliged to provide a summary or make the facilities available more than once for the same house and for the same period.

DEFINITIONS
  "payee": s.46.
  "payer": s.46.
  "qualified accountant": s.51.
  "service charge": s.46.

GENERAL NOTE

This section entitles the payer to make a written request to the payee for a written summary of costs incurred relevant to service charges payable or demanded. The summary must be certified by a qualified accountant as in his opinion a fair summary and sufficiently supported by accounts, receipts and other documents which have been produced to him, and as reflecting how the costs are or will be reflected in demands. If accounts are made up for periods of twelve months at a time, the request relates to the last period of twelve months ending before the request; otherwise, the request relates to the period of twelve months preceding the request.

The request is to be complied with within one month of the request, or if accounts are made up for twelve months at a time, within six months of the end of the last twelve month period, whichever is the later: subs. (2). See s.49, below, where the costs are incurred by or on behalf of a superior landlord.

Within six months of receipt of the summary, or a summary voluntarily issued, the payer can demand "reasonable facilities" for inspection of accounts, receipts and other documents which support the summary, *and* for taking copies or extracts from them: subs. (4). This would certainly suggest that the payer can demand to photocopy documents, but also that the landlord can make a reasonable charge if he provides the photocopy facility. The facilities for inspection and copying must be made available for a period of two months, commencing no later than one month after the payer has asked for them. See s.49, below, where the necessary information is held by a superior landlord.

The request can be made by service on anyone by whom the service charge is receivable, who is under a corresponding obligation to forward the request to the payee as soon as possible: subs. (5). If there is a disposal of the property after either class of request (for written summary, or for inspection facilities), the request remains valid, although the landlord need only provide one summary, and facilities for only the one period: subs. (6).

Failure to comply with any of the duties imposed in this section—to provide summary, to make inspection facilities available, or on the recipient of a charge to forward a request to the payee as soon as possible—is a criminal offence: see s.50, below.

Information held by superior landlord

49.—(1) If a request under section 48(1) (information about costs incurred) relates in whole or in part to relevant costs incurred by or on behalf of a superior landlord and the payee is not in possession of the relevant information—

    (*a*) he shall in turn make a written request for the relevant information to the person who is his landlord (and so on if that person is not himself the superior landlord) and the superior landlord shall comply with that request within a reasonable time, and

    (*b*) the payee shall then comply with the payer's request, or that part of it which relates to the relevant costs incurred by or on behalf of the superior landlord, within the time allowed by section 48 or such further time, if any, as is reasonable in the circumstances.

(2) If a request made under section 48(4) (inspection of supporting accounts, receipts, etc.) relates to a summary of costs incurred by or on behalf of a superior landlord, the payee shall forthwith inform the payer of that fact and of the name and address of the superior landlord; and section 48(4) shall then apply as if the superior landlord were the payee.

DEFINITIONS
  "payee": s.46.
  "payer": s.46.
  "relevant costs": s.46.
  "summary of costs": s.48.

GENERAL NOTE
This section applies where a request is made for a summary of costs under s.48, above, and it relates in whole or in part to costs incurred by or on behalf of a superior landlord, and the payee, *i.e.* intermediate landlord, is not in possession of all the relevant information, *e.g.* where the obligation is to pay the whole or part of the charges made by superior landlord to intermediate landlord. In such a case, the intermediate landlord is obliged to make his own written request to the superior landlord ("and so on if that person is not himself the superior landlord").

There is no time limit within which the intermediate landlord must make this request "up", and the superior landlord is only obliged to respond "within a reasonable time", as distinct from the time limits imposed by s.48, above. Instead, compliance has to be within the s.48 limit "or such further time, if any, as is reasonable in the circumstances".

If the request is for inspection facilities under s.48(4), above, however, the intermediate landlord must inform the payer that it relates to a summary of costs incurred by or on behalf of a superior landlord, and provide the name and address of the superior landlord, "forthwith": subs. (2). In such a case, the duty to provide inspection facilities is imposed on the superior landlord.

It is a criminal offence to fail to comply with any of the obligations imposed by this section: see s.50, below.

Offences

50.—(1) If a person fails without reasonable excuse to perform a duty imposed on him by section 48 or 49 (provision of information, &c.), he commits a summary offence and is liable on conviction to a fine not exceeding level 4 on the standard scale.

(2) Subsection (1) does not apply where the payee is—

    a local authority,

    a new town corporation, or

    the Development Board for Rural Wales.

DEFINITIONS
"local authority": s.4.
"new town corporation": s.4.

GENERAL NOTE
It is a criminal offence, punishable by a fine not exceeding level 4 on the standard scale (*i.e.* under s.37, Criminal Justice Act 1982—currently £1,000, see S.I. 1984 No. 447), to fail without reasonable excuse to perform any duty imposed by either of the last two foregoing sections. However, as this does not apply when the payee is a local authority, or a new town corporation, or the Development Board for Rural Wales, those who are liable to be seen standing in the dock are confined to urban development corporations, the Housing Corporation and registered housing associations.

Meaning of "qualified accountant"

51.—(1) The reference to a "qualified accountant" in section 48(3) (certification of summary of information about relevant costs) is to a person who, in accordance with the following provisions, has the necessary qualification and is not disqualified from acting.

(2) A person has the necessary qualification if he is a member of one of the following bodies—

the Institute of Chartered Accountants in England and Wales,
the Institute of Chartered Accountants in Scotland,
the Association of Certified Accountants,
the Institute of Chartered Accountants in Ireland, or
any other body of accountants established in the United Kingdom and recognised by the Secretary of State for the purposes of section 389(1)(*a*) of the Companies Act 1985,

or if he is a person who is for the time being authorised by the Secretary of State under section 389(1)(*b*) of that Act (or the corresponding provision of the Companies Act 1948) as being a person with similar qualifications obtained outside the United Kingdom.

(3) A Scottish firm has the necessary qualification if each of the partners in it has the necessary qualification.

(4) The following are disqualified from acting—
(*a*) a body corporate, except a Scottish firm;
(*b*) an officer or employee of the payee or, where the payee is a company, of an associated company;
(*c*) a person who is a partner or employee of any such officer or employee.

(5) For the purposes of subsection (4)(*b*) a company is associated with the payee company if it is (within the meaning of section 736 of the Companies Act 1985) the payee's holding company or subsidiary or is a subsidiary of the payee's holding company.

(6) Where the payee is a local authority, a new town corporation or the Development Board for Rural Wales—
(*a*) the persons who have the necessary qualification include members of the Chartered Institute of Public Finance and Accountancy, and
(*b*) subsection (4)(*b*) (disqualification of officers and employees) does not apply.

DEFINITIONS
"local authority": s.4.
"new town corporation": s.4.
"payee": s.46.

GENERAL NOTE
This section defines the qualified accountants who may certify summaries under s.48, above. Note the inclusion of C.I.P.F.A. members where the payee is a local authority, new town corporation or the Development Board for Rural Wales. In this last class of case,

there is no "disqualification", but otherwise corporate bodies cannot qualify (except if a Scottish firm), officers or employees, or their partners or employees, cannot qualify, nor can an officer or employee of an associated company if the payee is itself a company: subs. (4), (5), (6).

Miscellaneous

Compliance with minimum standards in erection of houses

52. A local housing authority by whom a house is erected under the enactments relating to housing, whether with or without financial assistance from the government, shall secure—

(a) that a fair wages clause complying with the requirements of any resolution of the House of Commons for the time being in force with respect to contracts for government departments is inserted in all contracts for the erection of the house, and

(b) that, except in so far as the Secretary of State may, in a particular case, dispense with the observance of this paragraph, the house is provided with a fixed bath in a bathroom.

DEFINITIONS
"house": s.56.
"local housing authority": ss.1, 2.

GENERAL NOTE
The "fair wages" provision applies only in the case of a contract for the erection of a house. The Secretary of State may consent to the absence of a fixed bath in a bathroom.

Prefabs deemed to be houses provided under this Part

53.—(1) This section applies to prefabs, that is to say structures made available to a local authority under section 1 of the Housing (Temporary Accommodation) Act 1944 ("the 1944 Act").

(2) For the purposes of this Act prefabs shall be deemed to be houses provided by the local housing authority under this Part.

(3) A prefab and the land on which it is situated may, if immediately before the repeal of the 1944 Act (on 25th August 1972) it was deemed to be land acquired for the purposes of Part V of the Housing Act 1957, be appropriated or disposed of by the local housing authority in the same way as any other land acquired or deemed to be acquired for the purposes of this Part.

(4) The provisions of this section do not affect any obligation of a local housing authority to another person as respects the removal or demolition of a prefab.

(5) References in this section to a prefab include fittings forming part of it.

DEFINITIONS
"local housing authority": ss.1, 2.

GENERAL NOTE
"Part V of the Housing Act 1957", *i.e.* now, this Part.

Supplementary provisions

Powers of entry

54.—(1) A person authorised by a local housing authority or the Secretary of State may, at any reasonable time, on giving 24 hours' notice of his intention to the occupier, and to the owner if the owner is known, enter premises for the purpose of survey and examination—

(a) where it appears to the authority or Secretary of State that survey or examination is necessary in order to determine whether any powers under this Part should be exercised in respect of the premises, or

(*b*) in the case of premises which the authority are authorised by this Part to purchase compulsorily.

(2) An authorisation for the purposes of this section shall be in writing stating the particular purpose or purposes for which the entry is authorised.

DEFINITIONS
"local housing authority": ss.1, 2.

GENERAL NOTE
Either the local authority or the Secretary of State may authorise entry "at any reasonable time, on giving 24 hours' notice . . . to the occupier, and to the owner if the owner is known" to any premises—not just houses—for the purpose of survey and examination, in one of two cases. The authorisation must be in writing, and state the purpose or purposes for which the entry is authorised: subs. (2). The form of notice is prescribed under what is now s.614, below, (see currently The Housing (Prescribed Forms) Regulations 1972, S.I. 1972 No. 228, as amended by S.I. 1974 No. 1511, retained in force by s.2, Housing (Consequential Provisions) Act 1985), and as there is no power to dispense with the requirement for written authorisation, it must be strictly complied with: *Stroud* v. *Bradbury* [1952] 2 All E.R. 76.

The two cases are:

(1) Where it appears to the Secretary of State or the authority that survey or examination is necessary in order to determine whether any powers under this Part should be exercised in respect of the premises: this would include to consider housing conditions and needs in a district under s.8 (see also *Bedingfield* v. *Jones* (1957) 57 L.G.R. 319, D.C.), to consider purchase under s.15, to discharge the general housing management powers under s.21, to see if there has been a breach of bye-laws under s.23, and possibly to see if there is evidence of a disposal for the purposes of s.35.

(2) If the authority are already authorised to purchase compulsorily.

"Owner" is not defined for the purpose of this Part, although the definition of owner in s.189, Housing Act 1957, applied to s.159, 1957 Act, from which this section is derived.

It is a criminal offence to obstruct an officer of the authority or the Secretary of State, or another person authorised to enter premises under this section: see s.55, below.

Penalty for obstruction

55.—(1) It is a summary offence to obstruct an officer of the local housing authority, or of the Secretary of State, or any person authorised to enter premises in pursuance of this Part, in the performance of anything which he is by this Part required or authorised to do.

(2) A person who commits such an offence is liable on conviction to a fine not exceeding level 2 on the standard scale.

DEFINITIONS
"local housing authority": ss.1, 2.

GENERAL NOTE
It is a summary offence to obstruct an officer of, or person authorised by, a local housing authority or the Secretary of State in the performance of something he is authorised to do under this Part, including to enter under s.54, above. The offence is punishable by a fine not exceeding level 2 on the standard scale, *i.e.* under s.37, Criminal Justice Act 1982, currently £100—see S.I. 1984 No. 447.

Minor definitions

56. In this Part—

"house" includes any yard, garden, outhouses and appurtenances belonging to the house or usually enjoyed with it;

"housing accommodation" includes flats, lodging-houses and hostels, and "house" shall be similarly construed;

"lodging-houses" means houses not occupied as separate dwellings;

"member of family", in relation to a person, has the same meaning
    as in Part V (the right to buy);
"owner", in relation to premises—
    (*a*) means a person (other than a mortgagee not in possession)
        who is for the time being entitled to dispose of the fee simple
        in the premises, whether in possession or in reversion, and
    (*b*) includes also a person holding or entitled to the rents and
        profits of the premises under a lease of which the unexpired
        term exceeds three years.

DEFINITIONS
"hostel": s.622.

GENERAL NOTE
This section defines "housing accommodation" for the purposes of this Part, and "house"
is to be construed in accordance with it as, of course, as extended to yards, gardens,
outhouses and appurtenances belonging to the house (or, therefore, flat), or usually enjoyed
with it.

Flat
The term "flat" is not defined, although it is used elsewhere in the Act (see, *e.g.*, s.118,
in Part V, the "right to buy") to mean that which is not a house, *i.e.* that which overlaps or
"underlaps" another part of the structure of the building of which it forms a part (s.183).
See also s.374(2), "separate sets of premises, whether or not on the same floor, constructed
for use for the purpose of a dwelling and forming part of a building from some other part
of which they are divided."
Flats were also formerly recognised in Housing Act legislation in relation to housing
subsidies: see, *e.g.*, s.97, Housing Act 1935, s.188, Housing Act 1936, s.25, Housing
(Financial and Miscellaneous Provisions) Act 1946, s.58, Housing (Financial Provisions) Act
1958, using flat to mean a separate dwelling. The present subsidy provisions (Part XIII,
below) do not, however, refer to flats.

Lodging-Houses
Lodging-houses are "houses not occupied as separate dwellings." They should not be
confused with the "common lodging houses" which are the subject of Part XII (see s.401),
although of course a lodging-house may also be a common lodging-house. Rather, reference
should be made to s.79, and the notes thereto, as to what constitutes a letting "as a separate
dwelling." In essence, a letting must be capable of use on its own, as a dwelling, even if it
comprises no more than a single room, so that there is and needs be no sharing of "living
accommodation." This last term does not extend to a bathroom or a lavatory, but does
extent to cooking facilities.
Thus, if a room contains cooking facilities, and the only sharing is of bathroom/lavatory,
the room will be "let as a separate dwelling": see, *e.g.*, *Cole* v. *Harris* (1945) K.B. 474,
C.A., *Curl* v. *Angelo* (1948) 2 All E.R. 189, C.A., *Goodrich* v. *Paisner* (1957) A.C. 65,
H.L., *Marsh* v. *Cooper* (1969) 1 W.L.R. 803, C.A. If there is sharing of a kitchen (even a
kitchenette too small to eat in), or some other facility, however, there will be no letting as
a separate dwelling: see, *e.g.*, *Neale* v. *Del Soto* (1945) K.B. 144, C.A., *Winters* v. *Dance*
(1949) L.J.R. 165, C.A.

Hostel
Hostel is defined in s.622, as a building in which residential accommodation is provided,
other than in separate and self-contained premises, together with either board, or facilities
for the preparation of food.

Appurtenances
The extended definition, including appurtenances, dates as far back as the Artizans' and
Labourers' Dwellings Act 1868, and has been maintained since (see, *e.g.*, s.29, Housing of
the Working Classes Act 1890, s.135, Housing Act 1925, s.188, Housing Act 1936).
In *Trim* v. *Sturminster Rural District Council* [1938] 2 K.B. 508, decided under the last of
these provisions, 10 acres of grassland were let together with a cottage, and the question
arose whether they were appurtenant to the cottage. It was held, following *Bryan* v.
Wetherhead (1623) Cro. Cas. 17, that the word "appurtenances" was used in its well
established legal sense of including only such matters as outhouses, yards and gardens, but

not the land itself, although it might in certain cases be competent to pass incorporeal hereditaments. How much of the ten acres ought to be included depended on the facts of the case, which had to be a question for the county court judge, but it would certainly be less than the full ten acres in issue.

In *Clymo* v. *Shell-Mex & B.P. Ltd.* (1963) 10 R.R.C. 85, C.A., under the Rating and Valuation Act 1925, open land surrounded by depot buildings was held to be appurtenant to the buildings, on the basis that had there been a conveyance or demise it would have passed without specific mention:

> "The word 'appurtenance' is one of the oldest words in use in the history of English law, and we would not attempt to define it in any way; whether land is properly described as an appurtenance to one or more buildings must depend very much on the particular facts and circumstances of each case, and it does not seem possible to try to lay down any tests to determine whether land ought to be regarded as an appurtenance [for the purposes of the section]. Each case must be decided entirely on its own facts, and no doubt there may in practice be a number of difficult and borderline cases . . . "
>
> "It must be remembered that in law the grant of buildings automatically passes everything that can properly be described as an appurtenance belonging thereto. In strictness of law, it may be doubted whether the use of the word appurtenance [in the section] added anything to what would otherwise pass . . . but no doubt the words which follow were wisely added to prevent any argument on that matter." The same would seem applicable under this section. In *Methuen-Campbell* v. *Walters* [1979] Q.B. 525, under the Leasehold Reform Act 1967, it was held that land cannot ordinarily be appurtenant to land, but the ordinary and strict meaning of the word may yield to a wider meaning if the context so requires.

In *Hansford* v. *Jago* [1921] 1 Ch. 322, a right of way was held to pass with the word appurtenances. In *Sovmots Investments Ltd.* v. *Secretary of State for the Environment* [1979] A.C. 144, H.L., it was held that appurtenances could not include rights of way and other ancillary rights not yet defined or in some cases even in existence, although this decision was overturned by s.13, Local Government (Miscellaneous Provisions) Act 1976, so far as compulsory purchase by local authorities is concerned.

In *F.F.F. Estates Ltd.* v. *Hackney London Borough Council* [1981] Q.B. 503, 3 H.L.R. 107, C.A., the court, considering the meaning of dwelling under Part VII, below (see s.237, defining dwelling with this "appurtenant" extension), did not "find any real help" in caselaw considering right passing on a conveyance, and it would certainly seem at the least arguable that—as with the word "house" itself, see next note—the word should always be construed as a mixed question of fact and law, *i.e.* applying the relevant section or Part of the Act to the facts of each case: see in particular the quotation from *In Re Butler, Camberwell (Wingfield Mews) No. 2 Clearance Order* 1936 [1939] 1 K.B. 570, C.A., below.

House

The word "house" has fallen for consideration on a number of occasions, both under and not under Housing Acts. The approach of the courts is not merely to consider the word in relation to the Housing Acts, but, indeed, particular parts of the Housing Acts: "As usual, though the matter is so very clear to my mind on the facts and on the Act . . . , it has been embarrassed by a reference to a number of authorities . . . " (*per* Jessel M.R., *Duke of Bedford* v. *Dawson* (1875) L.R. 20 Eq. 353 at p357, cited by Browne L.J. in *Sovmots Investments Ltd.* v. *Secretary of State for the Environment* at the Court of Appeal, [1976] 3 All E.R. 720 at p728).

In *Quillotex Co. Ltd.* v. *Minister of Housing and Local Government* [1966] 1 Q.B. 704, Salmon L.J. adopted the view of Sir George Jessel M.R. in *Attorney-General* v. *Mutual Tontine Westminster Chambers Association Ltd.* (1876) 1 Ex. D. 469, C.A., that no real help can be gained as to the meaning of a word in Statute A by reference to its meaning in Statute B, C or D. "What is the ordinary natural meaning of the word within the context of the section in which it appears?" And: "In construing the language of any statutory enactment, it is important to look at it in its context and to consider, amongst other things, the mischief at which it is aimed . . . "

In *Annicola Investments Ltd.* v. *Minister of Housing and Local Government* [1968] 1 Q.B. 631, it was said "that the word has a distinct fluidity of meaning, and that it is best construed in relation to the context in which it is found, and in relation to the objects and purposes of the Act or of the section of the Act in which it is used." In *In Re Butler, Camberwell (Wingfield Mews) No. 2 Clearance Order* 1936 [1939] 1 K.B. 570, C.A., Sir Wilfred Greene M.R. said that "whether a particular building does or does not fall under that word is a mixed question of fact and law; fact in so far as it is necessary to ascertain all the relevant facts relating to the building, and law in so far as the application of the word 'houses' to those facts involves the construction of the Act.

"However, as so frequently happens in dealing with Acts of Parliament, words are found used—and very often the commoner the word is, the greater doubt it may raise—the application of which to individual cases can only be settled by the application of a sense of language in the context of the Act, and if I may say so, a certain amount of common sense in using and understanding the English language in a particular context . . . " In *Ashbridge Investments Ltd.* v. *Minister of Housing and Local Government* [1965] 1 W.L.R. 1320, C.A., it was held that it is left to the decision-maker, not the courts, to decide what is a house, and the courts could only interfere if the decision is perverse, *i.e.* on traditional principles of intervention. See also *Re South Shields (D'Arcy Street) Compulsory Purchase Order* 1937 [1939] 1 All E.R. 419.

It is also clear that the fact that there may be provisions in another part of the Act which treat issues differently will not be conclusive. . . . "It is dangerous to interpret one Part by reference to the provisions of another Part" (*per* Woolf J, in *R.* v. *Cardiff City Council, ex parte Cross* (1981) 1 H.L.R. 54, Q.B.D., upheld on appeal (1982) 6 H.L.R. 1, C.A.). This issue of "comparative" construction is considered in greater detail in *Okereke* v. *London Borough of Brent* [1967] 1 Q.B. 42, C.A., as to the effect of s.374, below, on the interpretation of "house" in s.345.

As, however, the word "house" in this section bears an already extended meaning, it is more appropriate to consider that issue elsewhere: see notes to s.345, below; see also notes to s.189 and s.289, considering the term for the purposes of (a) individual house unfitness and disrepair powers under Part VI, and (b) clearance area action under Part IX.

It has been said that "house" has no very precise meaning: the word can cover many types of building (*Quillotex* v. *Minister of Housing and Local Government* [1966] 1 Q.B. 704, C.A. See also *Critchell* v. *Lambeth Borough Council* [1957] 2 Q.B. 535, C.A.—a house means what is commonly called a house, *i.e.* a separate structure, but in this Part it of course includes flats by virtue of the definition in this section). In *Howard* v. *Ministry of Housing and Local Government* (1967) 65 L.G.R. 257, it was said that the word "house" in the 1957 legislation had the same meaning as "dwelling house" in the previous (1936) legislation.

A house is "a building for human habitation; especially a building that is the ordinary dwelling place of a family," according to the Oxford English Dictionary as quoted by Pearson L.J. in *Reed* v. *Hastings Corporation* (1964) 62 L.G.R. 588, C.A. In *Ashbridge Investments Ltd.* v. *Ministry of Housing and Local Government* [1965] 1 W.L.R. 1320, C.A., a greengrocer's shop with a rear living room and scullery, three first floor rooms and an outside lavatory, was considered within what could properly be held a house: "It is apparent that a 'house' . . . means a building which is constructed or adapted for use as or for the purposes of a dwelling" (per Lord Denning M.R. at p1324).

In *In Re Butler, Camberwell (Wingfield Mews) No. 2 Clearance Order* 1936 [1939] 1 K.B. 570, C.A. a structure consisting of a garage or workshop with a dwelling above was held to be a house (see also *Re Hammersmith (Bergham Mews) Clearance Order,* 1936 [1937] 3 All E.R. 539). Where a building is used partly for residential purposes, and partly for other purposes, the building has to be looked at as a whole to ascertain whether, as a question of degree, it can properly be described as a house: *Annicola Investments Ltd.* v. *Minister of Housing and Local Government* [1968] 1 Q.B. 631, C.A. It need not be shown that all of the rooms in a building are used for residential purposes: *Premier Garage Co.* v. *Ilkeston Corporation* (1933) 97 J.P. 786.

Although original construction of a building is an important consideration (*Re Butler, Camberwell (Wingfield Mews) No. 2 Clearance Order* 1936 [1939] 1 K.B. 570, C.A.) regard may be had to the use of a building at the time the question falls to be determined (*ibid;* see also *Grosvenor* v. *Hampstead Junction Railway* [1857] L.J. Ch. 731), so that something not built as a house but used as such may qualify. An unfinished house may qualify as a house: *Alexander* v. *Crystal Palace Railway* (1862) 30 Beav. 556. A building constructed as a house but used for other purposes has been held to remain a house: *Howard* v. *Ministry of Housing and Local Government* (1967) 65 L.G.R. 257.

A hostel or a building used for multiple occupation or as a lodging-house may itself qualify as a house, regardless of the extension effected by this section: see *London County Council* v. *Rowton Houses Ltd.* (1897) 62 J.P. 68; *Re Ross and Leicester Corporation* (1932) 96 J.P. 459; *R.* v. *London Borough of Southwark, ex parte Lewis Levy Ltd.* (1983) 8 H.L.R. 1, Q.B.D.; *R.* v. *London Borough of Camden, ex parte Rowton (Camden Town) Ltd.* (1983) 10 H.L.R. 28, Q.B.D.

Similarly, a building subdivided into flats can remain a house, whether so constructed or not: *Annicola Investments Ltd.* v. *Minister of Housing and Local Government* [1968] 1 Q.B.

631, *Quillotex Co. Ltd.* v. *Minister of Housing and Local Government* [1966] 1 Q.B. 704, *Benabo* v. *Wood Green Borough Council* [1946] 1 K.B. 38, *Critchell* v. *London Borough of Lambeth* [1957] 2 Q.B. 535, C.A., *Okereke* v. *London Borough of Brent* [1967] 1 Q.B., C.A.

In *Lake* v. *Bennett* [1970] 1 Q.B. 663, C.A., under the Leasehold Reform Act 1967, Lord Denning M.R. doubted that a tower block could reasonably be called a house, but Salmon L.J. emphasised that the decision did not necessarily affect the Housing Acts, and the wording of the 1967 Act refers to a house "reasonably so called." Note finally that for all the purposes of this Act "prefabs" are deemed to be houses: see s.53, above.

Member of the family
See notes to s.186, below.

Index of defined expressions: Part II

57. The following Table shows provisions defining or otherwise explaining expressions used in this Part (other than provisions defining or explaining an expression used in the same section or paragraph):—

bank	section 622
building society	section 622
compulsory disposal	section 40
development corporation	section 4(c)
district (of a local housing authority)	section 2(1)
exempted disposal	section 39
family (member of)	sections 56 and 186
friendly society	section 622
hostel	section 622
house	section 56
housing accommodation	section 56
housing association	section 5(1)
Housing Revenue Account	section 417
insurance company	section 622
lease	section 621
local authority	section 4(e)
local housing authority	sections 1, 2(2)
local housing authority's houses	section 20
lodging houses	section 56
new town corporation	section 4(b)
owner	section 56
payee and payer (in relation to a service charge)	section 46
qualified accountant (for the purposes of section 48(3))	section 51
registered (in relation to a housing association)	section 5(4)
relevant costs (in relation to a service charge)	section 46(2), (3)
relevant disposal	section 38 (and see section 452(3))
secure tenancy	section 79
service charge	section 46(1)
shared ownership lease	section 622
standard scale (in reference to the maximum fine on summary conviction)	section 622
street	section 622
tenancy and tenant	section 621
trustee savings bank	section 622
urban development corporation	section 4(d)

PART III

HOUSING THE HOMELESS

Main definitions

Homelessness and threatened homelessness

58.—(1) A person is homeless if he has no accommodation in England, Wales or Scotland.

(2) A person shall be treated as having no accommodation if there is no accommodation which he, together with any other person who normally resides with him as a member of his family or in circumstances in which it is reasonable for that person to reside with him—

(*a*) is entitled to occupy by virtue of an interest in it or by virtue of an order of a court, or

(*b*) has an express or implied licence to occupy, or in Scotland has a right or permission or an implied right or permission to occupy, or

(*c*) occupies as a residence by virtue of any enactment or rule of law giving him the right to remain in occupation or restricting the right of another person to recover possession.

(3) A person is also homeless if he has accommodation but—

(*a*) he cannot secure entry to it, or

(*b*) it is probable that occupation of it will lead to violence from some other person residing in it or to threats of violence from some other person residing in it and likely to carry out the threats, or

(*c*) it consists of a movable structure, vehicle or vessel designed or adapted for human habitation and there is no place where he is entitled or permitted both to place it and to reside in it.

(4) A person is threatened with homelessness if it is likely that he will become homeless within 28 days.

GENERAL NOTE

The term "homeless" is capable of sustaining a wide variety of meanings: at one extreme, it might be confined to those who lack a roof over their heads; at the other, it could include all those who lack a home that is in an acceptable condition, the right size and the right place, subject to adequate security. The *statutory* definition is at the "narrower" end of that spectrum, but it is important to bear in mind that it does not go so far as to consider the homeless only those without a roof. Rather, it defines homelessness initially by reference to *legal rights of occupation*. The statutory definition of homelessness is not apparently concerned with the *quality* of what is occupied.

There are, however, two qualifications on this restrictive proposition. First of all, the *case law* has assumed that some, albeit bare minimum, quality or standard must be applied before accommodation qualifies for consideration at all. Secondly, there should be no confusion between "becoming homeless," and "becoming homeless intentionally": see s.60, below. Thus, although a person may voluntarily give up accommodation which he has the right to occupy (and accordingly renders himself homeless), it does not automatically or legally follow from this that he has become homeless intentionally. It is only departure from a particular *class* of accommodation which can give rise to a finding of intentional homelessness, and at that stage questions of quality will come into greater prominence. And if there is no intentionality, the applicant will still be entitled to assistance under this Part.

This section is concerned only with the question of the class of accommodation a right to occupy which will prevent an applicant from being considered homeless for the purposes of Part III, and which, accordingly, means that there are no obligations on local authorities under Part III. *Being* homeless is the starting-point, without which the Part is inapplicable, unless or until the applicant *becomes* homeless.

Subs. (1)

It is only accommodation in England, Wales or Scotland which is to be taken into account. A person may be homeless for want of accommodation in England, Wales or Scotland, and yet own or have the right to occupy accommodation elsewhere. However, as departure from

68–65

accommodation abroad can qualify as intentional homelessness, this will not commonly lead to an unintended or unfair benefit: see, particularly, *de Falco, Silvestri* v. *Crawley Borough Council* [1980] Q.B. 460, C.A., and other cases cited on this point in the General Note to s.60, below.

Nonetheless, it will mean that an authority must consider an application, where they would not otherwise be obliged to do so, with the possibility that accommodation abroad, although theoretically available to the applicant, will have to be disregarded, because it cannot in practice be occupied, with the possible consequence that, *e.g.*, because of local political conditions, a finding of intentionality is not available: *R.* v. *Hillingdon Borough Council, ex parte Streeting* [1980] 1 W.L.R. 1425, D.C. and C.A. The predecessor legislation—the Housing (Homeless Persons) Act 1977—did not specify a want of accommodation in England, Wales or Scotland; however, (a) it had been accepted (albeit obiter) that only such accommodation should be taken into account (*Streeting*) and (b) in the absence of ambiguity, the courts will not consider the previous legislation and the limitation is accordingly now clearly stated: *Farrell* v. *Alexander* [1977] A.C. 59, H.L.

The first three cases on the meaning of homelessness were *Williams* v. *Cynon Valley Council*, January (1980) *L.A.G. Bulletin 16*, C.C., *R.* v. *London Borough of Ealing, ex parte Sidhu* (1982) 2 H.L.R. 45, Q.B.D. and *R.* v. *Waveney District Council, ex parte Bowers, The Times*, May 25, 1982, H.C. (not cross-appealed on this point—*cf.* [1983] Q.B. 238, 4 H.L.R. 118, C.A.). In each of these cases, the authority claimed that it was under no duty to applicants living in temporary accommodation. In *Cynon Valley*, and *Sidhu*, women were living in refuges. In *Bowers*, a man was staying in a night shelter, on a night by night basis, and he could be turned away if the hostel was full. Each of the occupiers was, of course, no more than a licensee, but occupation under licence is prima facie a sufficient right of occupation for the purposes of the definition (see subs. (2)).

The courts in each case held that there was no necessary inconsistency between being homeless, and having some temporary accommodation or shelter, even if it was occupied under what amounted to a licence. The proposition was first mooted in relation to the question of breaks in periods of intentional homelessness: *Din* v. *London Borough of Wandsworth* [1983] 1 A.C. 657, 1 H.L.R. 73, H.L. In *Sidhu*, the court adopted the words reported to have been spoken by the county court judge in *Cynon Valley*:

"It was important that refuges be seen as temporary crisis accommodation, and that women living in refuges were still homeless under the terms of the Act. If it was suggested that they were not homeless it would be necessary for voluntary organisations to issue immediate 28 days notice when women came in so that they would be under threat of homelessness. This would be totally undesirable and would simply add stress to stress. If living in crisis accommodation took women out of the 'homelessness' category then the Act was being watered down and its protection would be removed from a whole class of persons that it was set up to help and for whom it was extremely important."

The judge in *Sidhu* continued: " . . . I myself would be perfectly prepared to speak those words and I adopt them without hesitation. Did I need further support for what I think is plain beyond peradventure the correct construction of this Act, I find it in the speech of Lord Lowry in *Din* v. *Wandsworth London Borough Council*. I think all I need read are two short sentences from Lord Lowry's speech: 'I consider that to be homeless and to have found some temporary accommodation are not mutually inconsistent concepts. Nor does a person cease to be homeless merely by having a roof over his head or a lodging, however precarious.' "

These decisions might be considered to apply to the "quality of the arrangement". In other cases, attention has been directed to the "quality of the physical conditions", or to physical conditions and arrangement. These cases start with *R.* v. *South Herefordshire District Council, ex parte Miles* [1983] 17 H.L.R. 82, Q.B.D., in which it was held that the test is whether a reasonable housing authority, on the material made available to them as a result of carrying out their inquiries, could reasonably take the view that the applicant had accommodation which was capable of being described as such, for himself and those who normally reside with him: this proposition was approved by the Court of Appeal in *R.* v. *London Borough of Hillingdon, ex parte Puhlhofer* (1985) 17 H.L.R. 588, C.A. (N.B. a decision of the House of Lords is awaited in this case.)

A second proposition in *Miles*—that when determining what sort of accommodation qualifies within s.58, s.60 provides a guide, *i.e.* if the standard is lower than that which the applicant could leave without being regarded as homeless intentionally, the applicant may already be homeless—was, however, not approved in *Puhlhofer*. The accommodation need only be "habitable" (see also *City of Gloucester* v. *Miles* (1985) 17 H.L.R. 292, C.A.) or a "roof over his head", and there is no need to compare it with accommodation which could be quit without intentionality: *Puhlhofer*. It follows that a person may not be homeless, and may yet quit accommodation without becoming homeless intentionally, because although the accommodation is so bad that no reasonable authority could expect the occupier to remain in occupation, it is still habitable: *ibid.*

R. v. *South Herefordshire District Council, ex parte Miles* remains of interest on its facts, as a guide to the very low level of accommodation which will qualify as such for the purposes of this section. The accommodation in question was considered at two points in time. It consisted of a hut with no mains services. At the first date, the family comprised parents, and two children, and it was held that although the hut was on the borderline of what could in any circumstances be regarded as suitable for human habitation, it was not of such a bad standard that any reasonable authority would have to disregard it for the purposes of this section. As at the second date, however, a further child had been born, and from then on it was not reasonable of the authority to regard the hut as being any longer accommodation. Conditions, then, have to be considered in the light of who is to occupy them.

In *Puhlhofer,* a man and a woman were living together with two children, in a single room in a Guest House, containing a double bed and a single bed. They had no cooking facilities, although they were provided with breakfast. They had no facilities for washing clothes. They had to eat out at least twice a day, and virtually all their state benefits were used up in this way. They had practically no room to move in their bedroom since in addition to the beds, there was a baby's cradle and a dressing table. The room was also crowded with a pram, sterilised unit, toys, a baby-walker for the older child, and disposable nappies. The accommodation was overcrowded, within the meaning of Part X, below. The accommodation was nonetheless held to qualify as "a roof over the head" of the applicants, who were accordingly not homeless.

In *R.* v. *Dinefwr Borough Council, ex parte Marshall* (1985) 17 H.L.R. 310, Q.B.D., the applicant was occupying a farmhouse which was unfit for human habitation, within the meaning of s.604, below. The local authority served a repairs notice under s.189, below, requiring remedial works within 12 months, and also served notice on the occupier, advising him to boil water to be used for human consumption, because a water sample taken from the premises had proved to be unsatisfactory. The applicant both sought a decision from the local authority that he was homeless, and took proceedings against his landlady, seeking repairs. The court held that the applicant was not homeless for the purposes of this section. The court's further indication that he might be homeless shortly when the time for repairs had expired without their execution must be doubted, as the decision preceded that of the Court of Appeal in *Puhlhofer.*

The decision of the Court of Appeal in *R.* v. *Wyre Borough Council, ex parte Parr* (1982) 2 H.L.R. 71, C.A., see notes to s.65, below, that accommodation *provided* by an authority in discharge of duties under this Part must be appropriate (see also *R.* v. *Ryedale District Council, ex parte Smith* (1983) 16 H.L.R. 66, Q.B.D.) which was relied on in some of the earlier cases considered above was held in *Puhlhofer* inapplicable to the question of whether a person is already and actually homeless.

It follows that while accommodation under this section, occupation of which will prevent the applicant being homeless, has to be of "a" standard, it is a very low standard indeed, and entirely different from *either* the standard of accommodation which may be quit without intentionality under s.60, below, *or* the standard of accommodation which an authority must provide for an applicant under s.65.

The mere fact that person may—on some document—have identified an address as his "home", or "permanent address", does not necessarily mean that they have accommodation at that address. In *Tickner* v. *Mole Valley District Council*, August 1980 *L.A.G. Bulletin*, C.A., people living in mobile homes had given permanent addresses to the site manager, which led the local authority to conclude that they were not homeless:

"They made that finding because each couple gave their permanent address elsewhere. One gave a mother-in-law's address. Another gave a divorced husband's address. I think that was not sufficient. Enquiries should have been made at the addresses given as permanent addresses. If the mother-in-law was asked—or if the divorced husband was asked—the answer would have been: 'We are not going to have that person back.' So Mole Council should have found these couples were homeless."

Subs. (2)

Regardless of the factual state of affairs, a person is to be treated as having no accommodation if he has no accommodation which he is entitled to occupy, together with anyone else who normally resides with him either as a member of his family, or in circumstances in which it is reasonable for that person to reside with him, under one of the specified schedule of rights of occupation. Note that the wording has changed from "the authority consider reasonable" (1977 Act, s.1) to "it is reasonable".

This formulation is not easy to disentangle and has led to some confusion. Where other persons are to be taken into account, the relevant right to occupy must be such that *both* applicant *and* other person can reside in the accommodation in question. But the other person will be taken into account only if (a) he normally resides with the applicant, *and* (b) he does so *either* as a member of his family, *or* in circumstances in which it is reasonable for them to live together. Accordingly, a person who might reasonably be expected to reside with the applicant is *not* to be taken into account unless he normally resides with the applicant. The tests are alternative: a member of the family who normally resides with the applicant need not also be shown to do so reasonably: *cf. R.* v. *Hillingdon Homeless Persons Panel, ex parte Islam, The Times,* 24 February 1981, High Ct., not cross-appealed on the proposition, as it relates to priority need: see further notes to s.59, below.

Occupation Under Interest, Order or Licence
The legal entitlement must be in one of the ways specified. It may be by virtue of an "interest" in the accommodation: this would seem to mean a legal or equitable interest. Those with a legal interest would include owner-occupiers, and tenants, whether under long leases or on short, periodic tenancies. Those with an equitable interest commonly include the spouse of an owner-occupier. Spouses, whether of owner-occupiers or tenants, may also be given a right to occupy under an "order of the court" *i.e.* under matrimonial legislation.

The third way specified is licence. In England or Wales, there may be an express or implied licence; in Scotland, the equivalent is a right or permission, or an implied right or permission to occupy. Thus, lodgers will usually be classed as licensees rather than tenants, flatsharers may be only licensees rather than joint tenants, and a child in the home of his parents will almost certainly be a licensee rather than a tenant or sub-tenant: on the distinction between tenant and licensee, see most recently the important decision in *Street* v. *Mountford* [1985] A.C. 809; 17 H.L.R. 402, H.L., notes to s.93, below.

Occupation by Enactment or Restriction
The second basis on which a person may be deemed homeless is if he has no accommodation which he is occupying as a residence by virtue of any enactment or rule of law giving him the right to remain in occupation, or restricting the right of any other person to recover possession of it. Again, this must be accommodation which is being occupied together with the same class of person described above.

In this case the section refers to accommodation which *is* being so occupied, as distinct from the first approach, which concerns *rights* to occupy. Thus, a person who walks out of accommodation only occupied under this heading will accordingly be homeless, albeit, possibly, intentionally, while a person who walks out of a house in which he has an interest will, subject to the deemed homelessness provisions considered below (subs. (3)), not be homeless at all, until such time as he divests himself of that interest, *e.g.* by release or sale.

The definition itself closely follows the wording of the Protection from Eviction Act 1977, s.1(1). A tenant within the protection of the Rent Act 1977 (see notes to s.622, below) will occupy by virtue of an interest until the determination of the tenancy: thereafter, he is a statutory tenant. A statutory tenancy is not an interest in land: *Keeves* v. *Dean* [1924] 1 K.B. 685, C.A. However, it is a right of occupation by virtue of an enactment or rule of law, and, indeed, one which gives the tenant the right to remain in occupation and which restricts the right of another to recover possession.

A tenant within the security of Part IV, below, occupies by virtue of an interest until the date set by a court for him to give up possession: see s.82, below. An agricultural worker in tied accommodation, enjoying the benefit of the Rent (Agriculture) Act 1976 (see notes to s.622, below), will normally occupy by virtue of a licence before its determination, and thereafter in the same way as a Rent Act statutory tenant, while those who do not enjoy the benefit of that Act derive some temporary benefits under the Protection from Eviction Act 1977. Long leaseholders normally continue to occupy beyond what would otherwise contractually be the termination of their interests by virtue of a statutorily extended tenancy, and thus still an interest, and will subsequently become statutory tenants under the Rent Act 1977: Landlord and Tenant Act 1954, Part I.

The Protection from Eviction Act 1977 itself prohibits the eviction otherwise than by court proceedings of former unprotected tenants, those who have had licences granted on or after 28 November 1980 which qualify as restricted contracts within s.19, Rent Act 1977 (see notes to s.622, below), and certain service occupiers, so that all of these people will occupy by virtue of an interest or a licence until determination, and subsequently by virtue of an enactment restricting the right of another to recover possession. Matrimonial legislation will commonly protect spouses and sometimes cohabitants by giving them a right to remain in occupation, or restricting the right of another to recover possession.

Those who are left outside the definition altogether are (a) those who have been trespassers from the outset and remain so, and (b) those who have licences not within the Protection from Eviction Act 1977 (*i.e.* which are *not* restricted contracts granted on or after 28 November 1980) which have been brought to an end: see also *R.* v. *Portsmouth City Council, ex parte Knight* (1983) 10 H.L.R. 115, Q.B.D., and *R.* v. *Surrey Heath Borough Council, ex parte Li* (1984) 16 H.L.R. 79, Q.B.D. It follows that "squatters" properly so-called, as distinct from those to whom a licence to occupy has been granted, are statutorily homeless even although no possession order may yet have been made against them, for, even though they may have the benefit of a roof over their heads, they have no accommodation within any of the classes specified.

Subs. (3)

A person is also homeless even if he has accommodation of one of the classes specified, but "cannot secure entry to it". This provision is intended principally to benefit the illegally evicted tenant or occupier, or anyone else who for some reason cannot immediately be restored to occupation of a home to which he has a legal entitlement. This provision has not proved to be of as much practical use as was intended, because authorities have tended to consider that unless the applicant uses the legal remedies available to him, he will be considered intentionally homeless. Temporary accommodation pending the resolution of a legal dispute may be given. It is submitted that authorities should have no *policy* to this effect, for there must be circumstances in which, although legal redress exists, both the benefits to be gained from using it, and the circumstances generally, suggest that it would be inappropriate, *e.g.* illegal eviction by a resident landlord who will shortly recover possession in any event, and where tensions are such that it is impracticable for the tenant to remain in the property: see, *e.g. British Oxygen Co. Ltd.* v. *Board of Trade* [1971] A.C. 610, H.L., *Re Betts* [1983] 2 A.C. 613, 10 H.L.R. 97, H.L., *Att.-Gen., ex rel. Tilley* v. *London Borough of Wandsworth* [1981] 1 W.L.R. 854, C.A.

Again, even though there is a legal entitlement to occupy under one or other of the provisions considered, a person is to be considered homeless if it is "probable" that occupation of it will lead to violence from some other person residing in the accommodation, or to threats of violence from some other such person who is likely to carry out the threats: see *R.* v. *Purbeck District Council, ex parte Cadney* (1985) 17 H.L.R. 534, Q.B.D., where the authority's finding that the applicant was not homeless was upheld, in the absence of any evidence to show any attempt to occupy, and only the most indirect evidence that if she did attempt to occupy violence would result. This provision is confined to violence within the unit of accommodation, and is not, therefore, an alternative head for illegal eviction or harassment by a resident landlord occupying another unit of accommodation within the same building.

It is not necessary to show an actual history of violence, for the test may be satisfied by a lower standard, *viz.* threats of violence from a person likely to carry them out. Many authorities fail to observe this important distinction, and require a high standard of proof of actual violence in the past, as evidence of *both* probability *and* likelihood. As this section draws a careful distinction, so also must authorities, although it may be difficult to prove that they have failed to do so. The remarks made above about legal redress, and failure to use it, apply with possibly even greater force in this context.

Finally, a person is homeless if his accommodation consists of a movable structure, vehicle or vessel designed or adapted for human habitation, and there is no place where he is entitled or permitted both to place it and to reside in it. Thus, a mobile home, caravan, house-boat, etc., will qualify when there is nowhere both to put or moor it and live in it. In *Smith* v. *Wokingham District Council*, April 1980 *L.A.G. Bulletin* 92, C.C., a county court considered whether a family, once found to have become homeless in circumstances which might be construed as intentional, had been "housed" in the interim, in circumstances sufficiently settled that when it came to an end, they would not have become homeless intentionally (see further notes to s.60, below). The "interim" housing consisted of a caravan, parked on land belonging to a county council. The family had no permission to place their caravan on the land, but it was there, and they had lived in it for two-and-a-half years. The court found that the county council had acquiesced in their presence. This was enough to constitute permission for the purpose of s.58(3) which in turn meant that the family had ceased to be homeless and were not now homeless intentionally.

Subs. (4)

A person is threatened with homelessness for the purposes of Pt. III, if it is likely that he will become homeless within 28 days. This period of 28 days was clearly referable to the "normal" period granted by a court before a possession order would take effect. From

October 3, 1980, however, courts have been under an obligation to make orders take effect within 14 days, save where exceptional hardship would be caused: see Housing Act 1980, s.89, although this is applicable only where the court has no other discretion to suspend, for example under the Rent Act 1977, or this Act in relation to secure tenants (*cf.* notes to s.84, below).

Priority need for accommodation

59.—(1) The following have a priority need for accommodation—

(*a*) a pregnant woman or a person with whom a pregnant woman resides or might reasonably be expected to reside;

(*b*) a person with whom dependent children reside or might reasonably be expected to reside;

(*c*) a person who is vulnerable as a result of old age, mental illness or handicap or physical disability or other special reason, or with whom such a person resides or might reasonably be expected to reside;

(*d*) a person who is homeless or threatened with homelessness as a result of an emergency such as flood, fire or other disaster.

(2) The Secretary of State may by order made by statutory instrument—

(*a*) specify further descriptions of persons as having a priority need for accommodation, and

(*b*) amend or repeal any part of subsection (1).

(3) Before making such an order the Secretary of State shall consult such associations representing relevant authorities, and such other persons, as he considers appropriate.

(4) No order shall be made unless a draft of it has been approved by resolution of each House of Parliament.

DEFINITIONS
"homeless": s.58.
"threatened with homelessness": s.58.

GENERAL NOTE
Without a "priority need for accommodation" there are no *substantive* rights or duties under Part III: see ss.65, 66 and 70. Few of the reported cases have raised a dispute on this point. Even although a person does not fall within a category of priority need, however, he can still apply and it is suggested that a local authority cannot fetter their discretion by pre-determining that persons within specified groups, *e.g.* the single or childless homeless, should never be considered "vulnerable" within subs. (1)(c), above. See, *e.g. British Oxygen Co. Ltd.* v. *Board of Trade* [1971] A.C. 610, H.L., *Re Betts* [1983] 2 A.C. 613, 10 H.L.R. 97, H.L., *Att.-Gen., ex rel. Tilley* v. *London Borough of Wandsworth* [1981] 1 W.L.R. 854, C.A. Further, authorities are bound to provide advice and assistance even to those who are not in priority need: see s.65(4).

Subs. (1)
Pregnancy.
It cannot be stressed too strongly that *any* length of pregnancy qualifies as priority need. One of the objects of the 1977 Act was to eliminate the practice of some authorities, who refused to consider a woman's pregnancy as a factor until a given length of time into pregnancy. Once the pregnancy is established, the priority need exists.

Dependent Children
The first reported High Court decision on priority need was *R.* v. *Hillingdon Homeless Persons Panel, ex parte Islam, The Times,* February 24, 1981, Q.B.D., not cross-appealed by the authority on this point (*cf. Re Islam* [1983] 1 A.C. 688, C.A. and H.L., 1 H.L.R. 107, H.L.). The authority's unsuccessful contention was that if reliance was placed by an applicant on dependent children living with him, it was *also* necessary to show that such children might reasonably be expected to reside with him. The court held that the tests were alternative. If there were dependent children living with the applicant at the date of the

authority's decision, it was not relevant to consider whether or not they might reasonably be expected to do so.

In *R.* v. *Ealing London Borough Council, ex parte Sidhu* (1982) 2 H.L.R. 45, Q.B.D., the applicant was living in a women's refuge. She had an interim custody order from the county court, but the authority argued that they were entitled not to consider her in priority need until a full custody order was granted. The court held that a custody order was irrelevant to the question of priority need, nor indeed could the authority defer their decision in order to have time to assure themselves that no change would take place in the future, *i.e.* in this case, the remote prospect of the applicant losing custody at full hearing.

Although the court held that a custody order is irrelevant, this would not, of course, be so where an applicant's children are not currently residing with him, but might reasonably be expected to do so, *e.g.* where the applicant has won custody but cannot in practice take care of the children, for want of accommodation.

"Dependent" is not defined in Part III. The *Code of Guidance* issued under s.71, below, suggests that all children under the age of 16 should be treated as dependent, as well as those under the age of 19 who are either receiving full-time education or training or who are otherwise unable to support themselves. The *Code* points out that dependent children need not necessarily be children of the applicant, but may be related in some other way, or be adopted or foster children.

Vulnerability

Customarily, men and women at or past retirement age are considered vulnerable on account of old age. The *Code of Guidance* issued under s.71, below, suggests that in addition those who are approaching retirement age who are particularly frail or in poor health or vulnerable for any other reason, should also be treated as qualifying on account of old age.

The correct approach is to ask first whether there is vulnerability at all, and second whether the vulnerability is attributable to any of the factors set out in s.59, whether to one of them singly or to a combination of them: *R.* v. *Waveney District Council, ex parte Bowers* [1983] Q.B. 238, 4 H.L.R. 118, C.A. For this purpose, vulnerability means "less able to fend for oneself so that injury or detriment will result where a less vulnerable man will be able to copy without harmful effects" (*Bowers*) or vulnerability in housing terms or the context of housing (*R.* v. *Bath City Council, ex parte Sangermano* (1984) 17 H.L.R. 94, Q.B.D.). Cases of vulnerability due solely to the problems of drink will not *normally* be attributable to one of the specified causes (*Bowers*), although an extreme case may well still amount to a mental or physical handicap or disability.

In *Sangermano*, the court drew attention to the distinction between mental illness that is psychotic, and mental handicap. The latter is not concerned with illness, but with subnormality or severe subnormality. Not all subnormality will necessarily amount to vulnerability however. Where medical evidence of subnormality had been put before the authority, the authority ought either to have accepted it, or made their own further enquiries. When determining priority need, the applicant's earlier rent arrears were a wholly irrelevant consideration. The court also noted, with reference to one of the features of the case, that language difficulties on their own would not amount to a "special reason" within s.59(1)(c). The *Code* contains further guidance on the interpretation of the phrase "vulnerable as a result of . . . other special reason." Battered women, without children, who are at risk of violent pursuit or, if they return home, further violence, constitute one class who may qualify under this heading, and so are homeless young people at risk of sexual and financial exploitation. In *Kelly* v. *Monklands District Council*, July 12, 1985, Ct. of Session (O.H.), considering this passage of the *Code* and having regard to both *Bowers* and *Sangermano*, the court was "not persuaded that every 16 year old is vulnerable . . . However, when you find a girl of 16 who has no assets, no income and nowhere to go and who has apparently left home because of violence, I am of opinion that no reasonable authority could fail to conclude that she was vulnerable.

"A girl of that age and with that background is bound to be less able to fend for herself than a less vulnerable girl; being less able to cope, such a person is liable to injury or harm. For the respondents, it was contended strongly that there was no suggestion that the petitioner had been exploited financially or sexually, and that the police had advised the respondents that there had never been any question of exploitation of young people in their area. However, in my opinion, exploitation does not have to have occurred before exploitation can reasonably be apprehended. Having regard to the language used in the Code, 'at risk of sexual or financial exploitation', I am of opinion that the petitioner must be regarded as at risk even though the police have not encountered exploitation of this kind before . . . " (*per* Lord Ross).

Emergency

The event which causes the homelessness and the priority need must be *both* an emergency *and* a disaster. Fire and flood are not, of course, the only qualifying disasters. In *Noble* v. *South Herefordshire District Council* (1983) 17 H.L.R. 80, C.A., it was held that the words "or any other disaster" which appeared in Housing (Homeless Persons) Act 1977, s.2(1)(b), meant another disaster similar to flood or fire. The omission of the word "any" would not seem to affect this.

Noble was concerned with a demolition order under what is now s.265, below. A demolition order was held not to qualify as a disaster similar to flood or fire, although on the facts of the case the occupiers had moved in *after* the demolition order had been made and it may be distinguishable in the case of a dangerous structure notice under the Public Health Act 1936, s.58, or analogous powers, imposed without any real forewarning. Where a demolition order under s.265 is imposed, however, the prior procedural steps suggest that it would not qualify as an emergency, and an occupier will in any event normally be entitled to rehousing under s.39, Land Compensation Act 1973.

Subs.(3)

Consultation: See *R.* v. *Secretary of State for Social Services, ex parte Association of Metropolitan Authorities* (1985) 17 H.L.R. 487, Q.B.D. The period allowed for consultation should be sufficient to give the consultee time to make an informed response. For a full discussion of this case, and for other cases on consultation, see notes to s.420(4), below.

Becoming homeless intentionally

60.—(1) A person becomes homeless intentionally if he deliberately does or fails to do anything in consequence of which he ceases to occupy accommodation which is available for his occupation and which it would have been reasonable for him to continue to occupy.

(2) A person becomes threatened with homelessness intentionally if he deliberately does or fails to do anything the likely result of which is that he will be forced to leave accommodation which is available for his occupation and which it would have been reasonable for him to continue to occupy.

(3) For the purposes of subsection (1) or (2) an act or omission in good faith on the part of a person who was unaware of any relevant fact shall not be treated as deliberate.

(4) Regard may be had, in determining whether it would have been reasonable for a person to continue to occupy accommodation, to the general circumstances prevailing in relation to housing in the district of the local housing authority to whom he applied for accommodation or for assistance in obtaining accommodation.

DEFINITIONS

"available for his occupation": s.75.
"homeless": s.58.
"threatened with homelessness": s.58.

GENERAL NOTE

An overwhelming majority of homeless persons' cases have concerned this controversial issue of intentionality. Where a person is intentionally homeless the authority have no duty to secure permanent accommodation. The only substantive duty is to provide temporary accommodation for as long as the authority think is reasonable for the applicant to get his own accommodation: s.65(3), below.

There is no reason for drawing any distinction in principle between the operation of the two definitions: *Dyson* v. *Kerrier District Council* [1980] 1 W.L.R. 1205 at p.1212, C.A. This seems to be based on a concession by counsel, but must surely be correct.

The authority must satisfy themselves that *all* the elements of this definition apply to an applicant. For example, if the applicant left accommodation that was not available for his occupation there can be no finding of intentionality: *In Re Islam* [1983] 1 A.C. 688, C.A. and H.L., 1 H.L.R. 107, H.L.; see also, *e.g.*, *R.* v. *Eastleigh Borough Council, ex parte Beattie (No. 1)* (1983) 10 H.L.R. 134, Q.B.D.

The elements of the definition are:

(a) the applicant must *deliberately* have done something or failed to do something;

(b) the loss of accommodation must be *in consequence of* the act or omission;

(c) there must be a *cessation* of occupation as distinct from a failure to *take up* accommodation;

(d) the accommodation must have been *available for the occupation* of the homeless person; and

(e) it must have been *reasonable* for the homeless person *to continue to occupy* the accommodation.

Whose Conduct?

The question has now arisen in a number of cases as to how an authority should treat an application where one of the applicants, or a member of the applicant's household, has either already been adjudged homeless intentionally, or is susceptible to a finding of intentionality. The point tends to arouse strong passions for, as will be seen below (s.65), the duty to a homeless person will be to secure accommodation for himself *and* anyone who might reasonably be expected to reside with him, which may well include the putatively intentionally homeless household member.

The question first arose in *R.* v. *North Devon District Council, ex parte Lewis* [1981] 1 W.L.R. 328, Q.B.D., where a man quit his employment and lost his tied accommodation. He applied to the authority, who held that he had become homeless intentionally. Thereupon, the woman with whom he lived applied in her own name. The court rejected the authority's argument that they need only consider one application for the family unit as a whole. Each applicant was entitled to individual consideration.

The court did, however, uphold the authority's argument that, in considering whether or not she had become homeless intentionally, they could take into account conduct to which she had been a party, or in which she had acquiesced:

"In my view, the fact that the Act requires consideration of the family unit as a whole indicates that it would be perfectly proper in the ordinary case for the housing authority to look at the family as a whole and assume, in the absence of material which indicates to the contrary, where the conduct of one member of the family was such that he should be regarded as having become homeless intentionally, that was conduct to which the other members of the family were a party . . .

"If, however, at the end of the day because of material put before the housing authority by the wife, the housing authority are not satisfied that she was a party to the decision, they would have to regard her as not having become homeless intentionally. In argument the housing authority drew my attention to the difficulties which could arise in cases where the husband spent the rent on drink. If the wife acquiesced to his doing this then it seems to me it would be proper to regard her, as well as him, as having become homeless intentionally. If, on the other hand, she had done what she could to prevent the husband spending his money on drink instead of rent then she had not failed to do anything (the likely result of which would be that she would be forced to leave the accommodation) and it would not be right to regard her as having become homeless intentionally . . . "

Lewis was applied in *R.* v. *London Borough of Ealing, ex parte Sidhu* (1982) 2 H.L.R. 45, Q.B.D., where the authority additionally (*cf.* notes to s.59, above) sought to rely on an earlier finding of intentionality on account of rent arrears which had occurred while the applicant was still living with her husband, now that the couple had separated. It was also applied in *R.* v. *Eastleigh Borough Council, ex parte Beattie (No. 2)* (1984) 17 H.L.R. 168, Q.B.D., a case of non-payment of mortgage arrears, even though the couple were still living together, and in *R.* v. *West Dorset District Council, ex parte Phillips* (1985) 17 H.L.R. 336, Q.B.D., also a case of rent arrears, caused by the husband's drinking, again even though the couple were still living together.

It was applied again in *R.* v. *Penwith District Council, ex parte Trevena* (1984) 17 H.L.R. 526, Q.B.D., where a wife who was the sole tenant of a flat surrendered the tenancy in order to move in with another man in another town, leaving her husband in (unlawful) occupation: possession proceedings had to be taken for his eviction. Subsequently, the couple were reconciled, and he was able to rely on his lack of his acquiescence in (indeed, clear opposition to) the surrender, and notwithstanding the reconciliation. It was implicit in the *Lewis* decision that one partner may seek the benefit of the principle, even though continued cohabitation is intended.

In *R.* v. *Cardiff City Council, ex parte Thomas* (1983) 9 H.L.R. 64, Q.B.D., however, Woolf J, who had decided the *Lewis* case, although restating the principle, found "acquiescence" on the part of a male joint tenant, whose cohabitant had caused the loss of their council tenancy, by nuisance and annoyance, even although the man had been in prison at the time of the conduct, and at the time of the proceedings for possession. The factors which influenced the court were (a) that the man had been offered, but had declined, an opportunity to attend the hearing, and (b) that there was no evidence of attempts by him to persuade her to desist in the conduct, which had persisted up until the hearing.

The point is not confined to cohabitants. In *Smith* v. *Bristol City Council*, December 1981 L.A.G. Bulletin 287, C.A., a woman was held reponsible for acts of nuisance caused by her son and lodgers, which resulted in her eviction. Similarly, the basis for the order for possession which resulted in a finding of intentionality in *R.* v. *Salford City Council, ex parte Devenport* (1983) 8 H.L.R. 54, C.A., was conduct by the children of the family, and conduct by children was included in the reasons for the finding of intentionality in *R.* v. *Southampton City Council, ex parte Ward* (1984) 14 H.L.R. 114, Q.B.D. In *R.* v. *Cardiff City Council, ex parte John* (1982) 9 H.L.R. 56, Q.B.D., nuisance and annoyance by a lodger caused the eviction of the tenant, even though it occurred only when she was out of the flat, and he was both younger and considerably stronger than she, and she was unable to control his behaviour. Her "acquiescence" was the failure to evict him.

An attempt to raise a finding of intentionality against a wife, dating from before she met her husband, in relation to their subsequent joint application, was, unsurprisingly, rejected out of hand by the court in *R.* v. *London Borough of Hillingdon, ex parte Puhlhofer* (1985) 17 H.L.R. 278, Q.B.D., not appealed on this point—see (1985) 17 H.L.R. 588, C.A. (notes to s.58, above).

Deliberate Act or Omission

The provisions of subs. (3) have given rise to a number of cases, most (but not all) of which have concerned rent/mortgage arrears. It should be noted at once that it is ignorance of a relevant *fact* which is not deliberate, not ignorance of the *legal* consequences: *R.* v. *Eastleigh Borough Council, ex parte Beattie* (*No. 2*) (1984) 17 H.L.R. 168, Q.B.D.

(i) *Rent/Mortgage Arrears*: The *Code of Guidance* issued under s.71, below, gives as examples of those whose homelessness should not be treated as deliberate:

"Those who get into rent arrears, being unaware that they are entitled to rent allowances or rebates . . . or other welfare benefits; and those who left rented accommodation on receipt of notices to quit (or distraint warrants), being unaware of their legal rights as tenants."

"A person who chooses to sell his home, or who has lost it because of wilful and persistent refusal to pay rent, would in most cases be regarded as having become homeless intentionally. Authorities should in such cases be satisfied that the person has taken the action which has led to the loss of accommodation with full knowledge of the likely consequences. Where, however, a person was obliged to sell because he could not keep up the mortgage repayments, or got into rent arrears, because of real personal or financial difficulties or because he was incapable of managing his affairs on account of, *e.g.* old age or mental illness, his acts or omissions should not be regarded as having been deliberate."

A similar view was expressed by the Master of the Rolls, in *R.* v. *Slough Borough Council, ex parte L.B. Ealing* [1981] Q.B. 801, C.A., although the case concerned intentional homelessness only indirectly:

"They had a council house . . . but fell into arrears with their rent. In 1972 the council got an order for possession and payments of arrears . . . They did not keep up the instalments. So the order for possession was executed . . . They were housed by the Slough Council for a month. They were then granted a fresh tenancy of another council house . . . at a low rent of £2.89 a week. They did not pay this rent either. So another eviction order was made. It was executed on 12th April 1977. . . . The Slough Council found that the Lynch family was homeless intentionally . . . I should think their finding was debatable. Their non-payment of rent was deplorable, but it may not have been 'deliberate' in the sense required by s.17(1). The family did not do it deliberately so as to get turned out . . . "

In *Robinson* v. *Torbay Borough Council* [1982] 1 All E.R. 726, the High Court declined to follow Lord Denning's dictum, and, instead, adopted the view that the word deliberate governed only the act or omission. A person can be deemed homeless intentionally, if he "deliberately does an act the reasonable result of which is his eviction, and the act is in fact the cause of his eviction . . . even though he did not appreciate that it would be the cause. Similarly, if a person deliberately does an act and eviction is the likely result of what he deliberately does, then he becomes threatened with homelessness intentionally, even though he may not have appreciated that it would be the likely result."

Robinson was approved by the Court of Appeal in *R.* v. *Salford City Council, ex parte Devenport* (1983) 8 H.L.R. 54, C.A., and Lord Denning's dictum was not followed: "It is not necessary to show that the tenant deliberately did something intending to get himself turned out. That seems to me contrary to the language of s.17(1). The word 'deliberately,' in my opinion, governs only the act or omission . . . " In *R.* v. *Eastleigh Borough Council, ex parte Beattie* (*No. 2*) (1984) 17 H.L.R. 168, Q.B.D., persistent failure to pay mortgage arrears was upheld as deliberate, notwithstanding that the male applicant had been advised to the contrary by his solicitors: s.60(3) refers to ignorance of a material *fact*, which did not include ignorance as to a consequence of law.

In *White* v. *Exeter City Council*, December 1981 L.A.G. Bulletin 287, H.C., however, the applicant had occupied a freehold property, purchased with a mortgage from the authority. There were arrears, which increased during periods of sickness and unemployment. In October 1980, the applicant became unemployed through no fault of his own. As from January 1981, he believed that the Department of Health and Social Security were, or ought to be, paying the whole of the interest element on the mortgage instalments, by direct deduction from his benefit. In fact, his Supplementary Benefit entitlement was so low that the D.H.S.S. could not pay the full amount of the full amount of the interest, so that arrears continued to mount.

In June 1981, when the arrears totalled approximately £600, the authority, as mortgagees, obtained possession of the house. The applicant was held to have become homeless intentionally, because of non-payment of mortgage. In oral evidence, it emerged that the effective reason for the decision was non-payment of *interest* due under the mortgage, between November 1980 and June 1981, rather than arrears generally. The court found that for most of this period the applicant was under a genuine misapprehension as to the relevant fact—namely whether or not the D.H.S.S. were paying the whole of the interest payments—and that he had acted in good faith in failing himself to make the payments.

There was accordingly no deliberate omission and, in consequence, no intentional homelessness: knowing of the applicant's belief, at the time of its decision, the authority had acted unreasonably in reaching a decision of intentional homelessness at all. In *R.* v. *Wyre Borough Council, ex parte Joyce* (1983) 11 H.L.R. 73, Q.B.D., the authority did not even ask the applicant why mortgage arrears had arisen, and this failure was accordingly fatal to its decision for it had omitted to take something relevant into account, *i.e.* her explanation or answer.

(ii) Nuisance and Annoyance. Nuisance and annoyance can clearly be considered "deliberate" for this purpose: *R.* v. *Salford City Council, ex parte Devenport* (1983) 8 H.L.R. 54, C.A., *R.* v. *Cardiff City Council, ex parte John* (1982) 9 H.L.R. 56, Q.B.D.

(iii) Accommodation Arrangements. It will be seen below that leaving settled accommodation to move into unsettled accommodation can amount to intentional homelessness. Ignorance about the unsettled nature of intended accommodation, however, can amount to ignorance of a relevant fact, and as such may mean that the prior departure was not "deliberate", within s.60(3): *R.* v. *Wandsworth London Borough Council, ex parte Rose* (1983) 11 H.L.R. 105, Q.B.D.

(iv) Pregnancy. A person does not become homeless intentionally by becoming pregnant, for example, because accommodation is lost, whether on account of size (*R.* v. *Eastleigh Borough Council, ex parte Beattie* (*No. 1*) (1983) 10 H.L.R. 134, Q.B.D.), or for other reasons, such as terms of accommodation, or because it is in the family home and the family reject the pregnant woman. The point is made in the *Code*: "Nor would it be appropriate that a homeless pregnant woman be treated as intentionally homeless simply because she is pregnant." There is an alternative approach to the same point: in some cases, becoming pregnant will not so much have caused the loss of accommodation, as have rendered the accommodation unavailable for the applicant's occupation under s.75. To render accommodation unavailable in the statutory sense is not to commit an act which can be treated as intentional homelessness: *In Re Islam* [1983] 1 A.C. 688, 1 H.L.R. 107, H.L.

(v) Failure to Use Other Remedies. Two common examples of omission which are alleged to amount to intentional homelessness are (1) failure by an evicted private tenant to take civil proceedings to secure re-entry, and (2) failure by a cohabitant or spouse to use domestic remedies. Under s.58(3) "a person is also homeless if he has accommodation but . . . he cannot secure entry to it" (above). This defines as homeless a person who has been locked out of his home, and is generally taken to refer to the illegally evicted occupier: *Code of Guidance.* It seems that it is open to an authority to treat as intentionally homeless an occupier who does not use his civil remedies, although it is submitted that to adopt a policy that all such occupiers must use these remedies, would be illegal: see, *e.g. British Oxygen Co. Ltd.* v. *Board of Trade* [1971] A.C. 610, H.L., *In Re Betts* [1983] 2 A.C. 613, 10 H.L.R. 97, H.L., *Att.-Gen., ex rel. Tilley* v. *London Borough of Wandsworth* [1981] 1 W.L.R. 854, C.A.

"A person is also homeless if he has accommodation but . . . it is probable that occupation of it will lead to violence from some other person residing in it or to threats of violence from some other person residing in it and likely to carry out the threats" (s.58(3), above). Here, an authority must be much more careful, as it must be recognised that the chances of a landlord re-evicting after a court order requiring him to reinstate an occupier are smaller than the chances of a recurrence of domestic violence.

It is not possible to say that a reasonable authority could *never* require a woman to use her domestic remedies, for want of which she may be found to be intentionally homeless: see *R.* v. *Eastleigh Borough Council, ex parte Evans* (1984) 17 H.L.R. 515, Q.B.D.; see also *R.* v. *London Borough of Wandsworth, ex parte Nimako-Boateng* (1983) 11 H.L.R. 95, Q.B.D.; *cf. R.* v. *Purbeck District Council, ex parte Cadney* (1985) 17 H.L.R. 534, Q.B.D. However, it should be noted that (a) again, no *policy* that applicants should do so could be upheld, (b) in cases where there have been incidents of violence despite existing domestic court orders, it is less likely to be open to an authority to require such proceedings to be taken again, (c) there may be no domestic remedy for the threats of violence concerned, and (d) the authority risk a conflict between their decision on homelessness and their decision on intentional homelessness.

The *Code of Guidance* puts the propostion even higher: "A battered woman who has fled the marital home should never be regarded as having become homeless intentionally because it would clearly not be reasonable for her to remain . . . "

(vi) Loss of Tied Accommodation. Finally, there is the question of whether loss of tied accommodation is "deliberate." It was not merely accepted in the High Court in *R.* v. *North Devon District Council, ex parte Lewis* [1981] 1 W.L.R. 328, Q.B.D. (above), that the man's departure from his job, and consequent loss of accommodation, qualified as intentional, but an earlier (and otherwise unreported) challenge to that decision had been, albeit reluctantly, dismissed. Loss of tied accommodation also amounted to intentionality in *Goddard* v. *Torridge District Council,* December 1981 L.A.G. Bulletin 287, Q.B.D., and *Jennings* v. *Northavon District Council,* December 1981 L.A.G. Bulletin 287, Q.B.D., although the cases were fought on the meaning of "in consequence" and are, as such, considered below.

Detailed consideration was given to this common problem in *R.* v. *Thurrock Borough Council, ex parte Williams* (1982) 1 H.L.R. 129, Q.B.D., and the case is worth close study. The manager of a public house was dismissed for stock and profit irregularities, which he denied. In the course of an appeals procedure, which he pursued with the assistance of his union representative, his employers offered him the choice of resigning, or dismissal. He resigned and, while threatened with homelessness, applied to the local authority for accommodation.

The court accepted that "if an employee occupying tied accommodation loses it through his own wilful neglect or other wrong doing, the circumstances may be such that it is possible sensibly to say that he has deliberately done or failed to do something else the likely result of which would be that he would be forced to leave . . . So if the employers here were right in their complaints, and it was shown that as a result Mr. Williams lost his accommodation, one could see that it would be strongly arguable, and would probably be the case, that he was intentionally homeless or threatened with homelessness . . . "

But whether or not the applicant was guilty of the irregularities was in issue:

"The difficulty of local authorities . . . is that they do not have the machinery or the powers to carry out the kind of investigation that may be necesary to resolve a conflict of that kind. What they must do . . . is to carry out the necessary inquiries . . . It is a very difficult thing to do, because neither the powers nor the machinery exist, and applicants and employers resent it if local authorities become too deeply involved in matters which apparently are no concern of theirs. Still they must do the best they can . . . "

The court bore in mind the burden of proof in cases of intentional homelessness:

"It must, it seems to me, be the case that if there is doubt or uncertainty after making the necessary enquiries that uncertainty is to be resolved in favour of the applicant; which is not unreasonable, because it is an Act to provide for the homeless . . . ."

In this case, the authority wrote to the employers. Their letter set out their thinking:

"A person who defaults in his duties knowing full well what the consequences of his action would be might be said to be deliberately doing something in consequence of which he would cease to occupy his accommodation. However, a person who is incompetent in carrying out his duties, whether he is a sole employee or in a supervisory capacity over others, might not be said to be carrying out a 'deliberate' act. In this latter respect, I believe that Mr. Williams has been the manager of your house for about two years and presumably he was not found to be incompetent in any probationary period he may have served."

The court found this a clear and correct approach. The employer's answer described the circumstances of the applicant's departure, but concluded "for all intents and purposes he left the Company's employment of his own accord due to personal reasons." In their decision letter, the authority conceded that they appreciated the applicant's position:

"My understanding of the circumstances of your resignation lead me to the conclusion that, had you not resigned, the end result would be the same, *i.e.* that events leading up to your appeal against dismissal would be regarded as something the likely result of which is that you will be forced to leave accommodation which is available for your occupation and which it would have been reasonable for you to continue to occupy."

In substance, "that letter is primarily saying it was intentional because he resigned. It also seems to go on to say that in any event even if you had not resigned you would have been dismissed because of your own faults. In either event, it would have been an intentional homelesness."

In their affidavit, the authority elaborated:

"Although it was apparent that Mr. Williams would have been dismissed in any event and hence would appear to have been intentionally homeless even if he had not resigned, in my view it is no part of the Council's duty to have regard to hypothetical situations, and hence the Council's decision was made on the basis of Mr. Williams' resignation."

In argument, "the case for the respondent . . . is that once it is established that Mr. Wiliams resigned, then the consequential homelessness must have been intentional. I regard that as much too narrow a way of putting the matter. Everybody knows that a forced dismissal may be clothed in a resignation, and I do not think it can possibly be enough, when it comes to asking whether the necessary enquiries have been made, or what they reveal, to say 'well, since we discovered that he had resigned, it is unnecessary to pursue the matter further, and that is that, because inevitably it was his own doing and therefore intentional'."

The court's analysis is full and careful: in stages, the court asked why the applicant was homeless (because there had been a possession order against him); why a possession order (because his contract of employment came to an end); why did it end (because he resigned); why did he resign (because if he did not do so, he would be dismissed); why would he have been dismissed, was it his fault (this is in dispute).

The duty of the authority was to look into the matter "as best they could"; this was not to look into hypothetical situations. On their failure to do so, they had not acquired any information on the basis of which they could properly be satisfied that the applicant had become homeless intentionally.

During the course of the judgment, the court likened the position of the applicant to that of a person who has been constructively dismissed, for the purposes of employment law: "Had he gone to an Industrial Tribunal and complained that he had been unfairly dismissed, it would not have been open to the employers to say by way of answer . . . you resigned, because he would have been able to reply that he only resigned because he had been told that if he did not do so, he would be dismissed."

This is clearly one basis for distinguishing a resignation from dismissal. But what the authority were seeking to do was to say: either the applicant resigned (intentional homelessness) or he was dismissed (intentional homelessness), and they ignored the "grey area" of dispute, which had led to the compromise.

Much importance may be attached to what, it is submitted, was a careful, and as the court indicated, proper analysis of a job-departure case, in the letter quoted above—an act the consequences of which can be construed as a deliberate departure can qualify within the provisions; but someone who loses his job for incompetence, which will usually be a course of conduct spread over a period of time, cannot be said to be carrying out a deliberate act. He would lack the necessary intention, or state of mind, in the absence of clear proof that a course of incompetent conduct had been adopted in order to provoke dismissal.

R. v. *Thanet District Council, ex parte Reeve* (1981) 6 H.L.R. 31, Q.B.D., was also a case on loss of tied accommodation, although it is as much on the meaning of "in consequence" as "deliberate." A woman worked as a receptionist for a car hire firm, and lived above the office. She was living with a man. She told her employers that he was not disqualified from driving. In fact, he was, and when the employers found out they dismissed her. The authority found that she lost her accommodation, because of the misconduct leading to loss of employment, which misconduct was the statement made to the employers.

The allegation was, at the time of dismissal and indeed at the time of local authority decision and of hearing at the High Court, disputed. Nonetheless, the authority had investigated, and concluded that the dismissal was "for that deliberate act of misconduct." This distinguishes the case from *Williams.*

"Some acts which a person does will lead indirectly to their becoming homeless . . . Other acts will be sufficiently proximate to render the person within the category of those who become homeless intentionally . . . It is my view that this case probably comes close to the borderline. For it to fall on the right side so far as the local authority are concerned it seems to me that the termination of the employment . . . must be lawful. It must be some conduct on the part of the applicant which justifies the employer treating the contract as at an end . . . "

In Consequence. The homelessness must be "in consequence of" the deliberate act or omission. This is a question of "cause and effect" (*Dyson* v. *Kerrier District Council* [1980] 1 W.L.R. 1205, C.A., *Din* v. *London Borough of Wandsworth* [1983] 1 A.C. 657, 1 H.L.R. 73, H.L.) and the principal issue which has arisen is the attribution of *present* homelessness to *past* act or omission. That is to say, there is commonly an act which has been the subject of a finding of intentionality, or which is susceptible to such a finding, and the argument then becomes whether or not *it* (that act or omission) is the cause of *this* homelessness.

(i) Intervening Accommodation. The authority are entitled—and on occasion obliged (*R.* v. *Preseli District Council* (1984) 17 H.L.R. 147, Q.B.D.)—to look back to the start of the present period of homelessness (*Din* v. *London Borough of Wandsworth* [1983] 1 A.C. 657, 1 H.L.R. 73, H.L.). This is based on the wording of the provisions, and the distinction to be found between tenses in, *e.g.*, what are now ss.62, 64, 65, 67, and 74. The question, then, becomes one of whether the applicant has enjoyed a period of accommodation between act of intentionality and application: the phrase used is "settled accommodation", (*Din, per* Lord Wilberforce, adopting Ackner L.J. in the Court of Appeal) or "other than temporary accommodation" (*Din, per* Lord Lowry).

In respect of such accommodation,

"I consider that to be homeless and to have found some temporary accommodation are not mutually inconsistent concepts. Nor does a person cease to be homeless merely by having a roof over his head or a lodging, however precarious . . . There will be difficult questions of fact and law, but an obviously temporary letting or licence will not . . . cause homelessness to cease . . . It is also, in my view, still a matter for debate whether the terms 'occupation' and 'occupy' are appropriate to describe the position of a person sharing a house as a guest without having any portion of the accommodation definitely allotted to him" (*per* Lord Lowry).

In *de Falco, Silvestri* v. *Crawley Borough Council* [1980] Q.B. 460, C.A., the Court of Appeal held that it was permissible to look beyond a period of some months spent with relatives, to an earlier time when the families involved in the cases had quit their last permanent accommodation, in Italy. In *Smith* v. *Wokingham District Council*, 1980 L.A.G. Bulletin 92, C.C., a family spent some years in a caravan, parked on land belonging to another local authority. Though they had no formal right of occupation, sufficient to break their homelessness, the case was decided on the basis that a new period of not being homeless within s.58 (see subs. (3)(c) thereof, above), was necessarily sufficient to break the period.

That this may not necessarily be so was demonstrated in *Dyson* v. *Kerrier District Council* [1980] 1 W.L.R. 1205, C.A. A woman took an out-of-season, or winter, let, in order to be near her sister, and, *after* taking the winter let, surrendered her previous, local authority tenancy. At the termination of the winter let, she was held to have become threatened with homelessness intentionally, on account of the surrender of her previous accommodation. The principal point was that the new, and temporary, accommodation was secured *before* yielding up the earlier, and secure or permanent accommodation. Thus, the period in the winter let was a part of the act which had caused the loss of the earlier accommodation. In *Din*, however, Lord Lowry doubted this basis for the decision, inclining rather to the view that because the winter let was temporary, the woman never ceased to be homeless.

In *Davis* v. *Kingston-upon-Thames Royal London Borough, The Times,* March 27, 1981, C.A., a family who came from a travelling background, gave up secure council accommodation, as it were "to go back on the road". The caravan they acquired for this purpose subsequently became unusable. A replacement was found, but this, too, lasted for only a temporary period. The family were found by the authority to have become intentionally homeless when they left the earlier accommodation. It would appear that their first caravan had been purchased before quitting their council accommodation, which would put the case on the same basis as *Dyson*.

The Court of Appeal held that the date when intentional homelessness was caused was primarily a matter for the local authority, and the authority had not erred in treating it as at the date when they left their council accommodation, rather than either when their first or when their second caravan came to an end of its useful life:

"The evidence was such that the council could properly conclude that any accommodation which the Davises had, or might obtain, on leaving their council flat would only be precarious. Their decision was therefore reasonable in the circumstances of the case . . ."

In *Lambert* v. *London Borough of Ealing* [1981] 1 W.L.R. 550, 2 H.L.R. 41, C.A., a family gave up accommodation in Lyons, France, in circumstances which the authority could construe as intentional homelessness. They bought a caravan, in which they lived in this country for a while before they sold it. Then they took two holiday lettings, and on the expiry of the second applied to the authority. The Court of Appeal following *Dyson,* and *de*

Falco, held that the authority were entitled to link the family's present homelessness to the departure from accommodation in Lyons. In *R.* v. *London Borough of Harrow, ex parte Holland* (1980) 4 H.L.R. 108, C.A., a couple, one of whom was disabled, was similarly held to be intentionally homeless because they left a caravan site on which the authority decided they could have continued to live, despite a series of intervening accommodation arrangements, all of which were temporary.

An attempt by the couple to rely on an "intervening separation", so that intervening accommodation might be considered "settled", or adequate, for the purposes of their separate needs, was rejected on the basis that the separation had never been mentioned to the authority. This aspect of the case may be contrasted with the decision in *R.* v. *South Herefordshire District Council, ex parte Miles* (1983) 17 H.L.R. 82, Q.B.D., in which the authority wrongly "rubber-stamped" an earlier finding of intentionality by another authority, and thus failed to consider whether or not intervening accommodation might have been settled for the same reason, *i.e.* because it was adequate for the needs of the "two halves" of the family.

In *Goddard* v. *Torridge District Council*, December 1981 L.A.G. Bulletin 287, Q.B.D., a family quit tied accommodation in Hastings, in circumstances which had placed them under considerable pressure, and returned to Devon, where they had formerly lived. As in *Dyson*, the accommodation in Devon was an out-of-season, or a winter, letting, and, again, it had been arranged before the departure from Hastings. The decision of the authority that the applicant was homeless intentionally was upheld.

In *Jennings* v. *Northavon District Council*, December 1981 L.A.G. Bulletin 187, Q.B.D., a family quit secure council accommodation in order to move into a cottage belonging to the man's employers, to whom he subsequently gave notice determining his employment. Notwithstanding his belief that, regardless of how his employment ended, they would enjoy a further 9 months' rights of occupation, the authority decided that he had exchanged secure for insecure accommodation: in this case, though, the intentional homelessness was made up, as it were, of two elements—departing the earlier accommodation, and quitting the employment.

In *R.* v. *Purbeck District Council, ex parte Cadney* (1985) 17 H.L.R., Q.B.D., a woman sought to rely on a period of three months during which she had moved out of the matrimonial home and into the home of another man; their relationship was not successful, and she left. She sought to rely on this as a period of intervening accommodation, because she had intended to stay with him permanently. The court held that this was too subjective an approach, and that the authority were entitled to take the view that it was a transient or precarious arrangement, *i.e.* that an objective test could be applied.

(ii) Cause and Effect. The authority must clearly act reasonably in regarding present homelessness as being caused by a departure from earlier accommodation. In *Krishnan* v. *London Borough of Hillingdon*, January 1981 L.A.G. Bulletin 137, Q.B.D., a family moved out of accommodation it was sharing with relatives in Birmingham. The authority in Birmingham were putting pressure on the relatives to reduce overcrowding in the premises. There was a possibility of promotion if the family could move to London. Another relative offered accommodation in his home in Uxbridge, until such time as the family could afford to buy its own house.

Subsequently, the relative decided to sell his house and move to Canada, and it was then that the family's homelessness arose. The authority considered that the family could reasonably have gone on occupying the Birmingham property, on which point their decision was not upheld (see further below), and took the view that the Uxbridge arrangement was only temporary. On this, too, their decision was set aside by the court:

"I also hold that the Council's officers made insufficient enquiry as to the state of knowledge and expectations of the Plaintiff with regard to the availability of his accommodation at Uxbridge at the time when he moved here. Mrs Bates states in her note . . . that the Plaintiff did not deny that his accommodation at [Uxbridge] was temporary. That, however, was not the point. The word 'temporary' can aptly cover a considerable period. Thus, accommodation held on a tenancy for a year or more can rightly be described as temporary.

"As I have already indicated, the Plaintiff's expectation at the time when he moved . . . was that the accommodation there would be available for him for at least a year. It follows as it seems to me that if the Council's officers had been aware of that fact they might well have taken the view that the Plaintiff became homeless not because he moved to [Uxbridge] from . . . Birmingham, but because the Plaintiff's cousin changed his mind about the length of time for which he was willing to accommodate the Plaintiff and his family. . . ."

Similarly, in *R.* v. *London Borough of Wandsworth, ex parte Rose* (1983) 11 H.L.R. 105, Q.B.D., although decided on the meaning of the word "deliberate" (above), the point may as easily be made that the earlier departure did not *cause* the homelessness: what caused the homelessness was the loss of the intervening, temporary accommodation, which the applicant had not appreciated was—or was likely to be—temporary. In *R.* v. *Basingstoke & Deane Borough Council, ex parte Bassett* (1983) 10 H.L.R. 125, Q.B.D., temporary accommodation was lost not because of its temporary quality, but because it was accommodation with the applicant's sister-in-law, and the applicant separated from her husband.

In *R.* v. *Exeter City Council, ex parte Gliddon* (1984) 14 H.L.R. 103, Q.B.D., the applicants became homeless when they quit private sector accommodation. Initially, they had been granted a tenancy. The landlord alleged that they had obtained it by deception and compelled them to enter into a licence agreement in substitution. It was the loss of accommodation under licence which was the immediate cause of the homelessness. At first, the authority advised the applicants to await court proceedings for determination of their status: this was a valid approach, the court held (see further below).

On their failure to follow this advice, however, the authority reached a new decision, that the accommodation *had* been obtained by deception. Accordingly, it had been lost by the applicants' own fault. In the light of this finding of fact by the authority, it was no longer possible for the authority to conclude that the applicants could reasonably have remained in occupation, and the accommodation obtained by deception ought to have been ignored, with the authority required to look back instead to the applicants' previous accommodation.

In *R.* v. *Preseli District Council, ex parte Fisher* (1984) 17 H.L.R. 147, Q.B.D., it was held similarly that if the accommodation which was last occupied was temporary—or not "available and reasonable"—the authority *must* look back, even if necessary over several years, to the loss of the last permanent, or settled, accommodation which the applicant has occupied, if any. And in *City of Gloucester* v. *Miles* (1985) 17 H.L.R. 292, C.A., the authority erred in treating the loss of accommodation as causing homelessness on the basis of *Dyson* v. *Kerrier District Council* [1980] 1 W.L.R. 1205, C.A., when at the time when the applicant lost her accommodation, she was *already* homeless, because it had been vandalised by her husband.

The applicant had gone away for a time, but not clearly or certainly permanently quit, and during her absence her husband returned and caused the damage which rendered the premises uninhabitable. When they became uninhabitable, she became homeless: see notes to s.58, above. As she was not a party to the vandalisation, she had done nothing that could be classed as intentionality, even if she might subsequently have lost the property, either through failing to take up residence in it again, or because arrears had been accruing and there would have been a threat of possession proceedings.

In *R.* v. *Thanet District Council, ex parte Reeve* (1981) 6 H.L.R. 31, Q.B.D., the facts of which are set out above, the court said:

"It seems to me that the answer to the question of whether or not the council were entitled to take the view which they did of the applicant's conduct depends on the proper interpretation of s.17(1). It appears to me that the use of the words 'in consequence' in that subsection does raise problems of causation. Really, what is involved in deciding whether or not the applicant is right is a decision as to remoteness . . . "

(iii) No Settled Intervening Accommodation. The question posed in *Din* v. *London Borough of Wandsworth* [1983] 1 A.C. 657; 1 H.L.R. 73, H.L., was whether any circumstance *other* than a new period of housing or "settled residence" can break the chain of causation. Can an act which at its inception was one causing intentional homelessness cease to qualify as such? In *Din*, a family left accommodation under extremely trying circumstances, but they had been given advice from the local authority to remain in occupation until a court order was made against them.

It was common ground, at least on appeal, that if an application had been made immediately after their departure, the authority could have found them intentionally homeless, because at that date it would have been reasonable to remain in occupation. But on application at a later date, it was conceded by the authority that the family would by then almost certainly have become homeless in any event, and not intentionally. There was no defence to the landlord's proposed proceedings for possession and the order would have already taken effect.

During the interim period, the family had stayed with relatives, and it was not argued that there had, on that account, been a break in their homelessness. Rather, it was argued that the original *cause* of homelessness had ceased to be *effective*, for the family would now be unintentionally homeless regardless of their premature departure. The argument was upheld in the county court, but dismissed on appeal (by a majority). The House of Lords similarly failed to reach a unanimous decision: the majority upheld the result in the Court of Appeal: the question was whether the present period of homelessness had, at its inception, been intentional, so that the fact that the applicants would have become unintentionally homeless by date of application was irrelevant.

Cessation of Occupation. The accommodation which has been lost can be accommodation abroad, and the act causing its loss an act abroad: *de Falco, Silvestri* v. *Crawley Borough Council* [1980] Q.B. 460, C.A. In that case, the reasons given by the authority for finding intentional homelessness were that the families concerned had come to this country without arranging permanent accommodation. This reason was patently bad on its face. It was upheld by the Court of Appeal only by expanding it, against the factual background, to refer to the *departure* from accommodation in Italy. This point was made clear in *R.* v. *Reigate & Banstead Borough Council, ex parte Paris* (1984) 17 H.L.R. 103, Q.B.D., where the authority used the same wording as originally used in *de Falco*, and were held to have erred in failing to look at the accommodation which had been quit, and the circumstances of departure from it.

While it would seem probable that the accommodation lost must itself be such as to qualify as "settled," where the authorities are providing temporary housing pending a permanent allocation, sufficient that no allegation of failure of discharge (see notes to s.65, below) can be sustained, *i.e.* where they are discharging in stages, the loss of one such "stage" may lead to a finding of intentionality if on the facts what the applicant has been enjoying can properly be regarded as settled, *i.e.* there is no principle of law that all such arrangements are sufficiently unsettled to disbar the authority from a finding of intentionality: *R.* v. *East Hertfordshire District Council, ex parte Hunt* (1985) 18 H.L.R., Q.B.D.

An authority will sometimes seek to treat as intentionally homeless a person towards whom they, or another authority, have formerly acknowledged a full housing duty, but who has failed to take up an offer of accommodation under that duty. This is not a proper finding, because "ceasing to occupy" does not mean "failing to take up occupation."

One can well see why Parliament has adopted a definition which falls short of extending the principle of intentional homelessness to failure to take up accommodation. It would raise many questions which the homeless person would be unable to dispute, as to terms, conditions and quality of such accommodation, and matters of judgment, and, further, it is likely that most people at some time might have passed by the opportunity of poor quality accommodation, in circumstances which might be susceptible to a different interpretation later, or by a public authority.

However, although an authority cannot decide that homelessness is intentional because an offer has not been taken up, it can in appropriate circumstances (as to which, see notes to s.65, below) maintain that it has *discharged* its duties by making the offer: *R.* v. *Westminster City Council, ex parte Chambers* (1982) 6 H.L.R. 24, Q.B.D.; *R.* v. *London Borough of Hammersmith & Fulham, ex parte O'Brian* (1985) 17 H.L.R. 471, Q.B.D., although the applicant will be entitled to re-apply once there has been a material change of circumstances, and does not need to show "intervening settled accommodation": *R.* v. *London Borough of Ealing, ex parte McBain* [1985] 1 W.L.R. 1351; 18 H.L.R. 59, C.A. (see further notes to s.62, below).

Available for Occupation. The accommodation which has been lost must have been "available" for the applicant's accommodation. "Accommodation shall be regarded as available for a person's occupation only if it is available for occupation both by him and by any other person who might reasonably be expected to reside with him . . . " (s.75, below). If the applicant leaves accommodation which was available *only* to the applicant, and not to persons with whom he might reasonably be expected to reside, there cannot be a finding of intentional homelessness. In *In Re Islam* [1983] 1 A.C. 688, C.A. and H.L., 1 H.L.R. 107, H.L., the applicant had lost his right to a shared room, when—after a delay of 6 years awaiting entry clearance—his wife and four children flew from Bangladesh to join him in this country.

At no time had the man ever lived with his wife and children. He had lived and worked in Uxbridge for 16 years, paying five visits home, on the first of which he married, and on the subsequent of which his wife conceived. While awaiting clearance to join him in this country, his wife and children lived with his parents in Bangladesh. In the Court of Appeal, Lord Denning M.R. held that Mr. Islam had been in notional occupation, through his wife and children, of the family home in Bangladesh. So, when they left that property to come and join him here, he, albeit notionally, had also left and rendered himself (and them) intentionally homeless.

With this view, Sir Denys Buckley (who also dismissed Mr. Islam's challenge to the authority's decision) was unable to agree. Rather, he offered alternative explanations as to how Mr. Islam had become homeless intentionally: *either* the accommodation which had been quit was made up of the property in Bangladesh, plus Mr. Islam's shared room in

Uxbridge; *or*, by bringing his wife and children over, Mr. Islam had intentionally rendered his accommodation here unavailable for his occupation.

The House of Lords rejected all of these reasons, and allowed Mr. Islam's appeal. The basis for the decision was that at no time had Mr. Islam ever occupied accommodation which was "available" in the statutory sense under s.75. The shared room in this country was clearly not "available," and there was no evidence of availability in the family home in Bangladesh. Further, "I do not think that rooms in two separate continents can be combined" to make up "available accommodation" (*per* Lord Wilberforce).

As to occupation "through" the wife and children, "the Master of the Rolls was . . . using the word occupation in an artificial sense which, I very respectfully suggest, is quite inconsistent with its ordinary meaning and with the probably narrower sense in which it is used in the Act. When it speaks of occupying accommodation, the Act has in contemplation people who are residing in that accommodation . . . and residing in family units, where possible" (*per* Lord Lowry). Five visits over 12 years could not be construed as such occupation.

No decision was made on the position where, at some time, the family had been living together: "I do not deny that, in Great Britain or elsewhere, a husband who had set up house with his wife as a family unit could later leave his wife and children at home and continue to be the legal occupier . . . " (*per* Lord Lowry). In such cases, it would seem to be a question of fact whether—in Lord Lowry's example—the man could be said to have ceased to live in the family home, and to have acquired a home elsewhere in accommodation which is not available in the statutory sense, or whether he is, as it were, living in two homes. Further, "it can properly be decided that an applicant has become homeless intentionally whether the family moves as a unit or the husband, leaving suitable accommodation, comes first and then calls on the family to follow" *per* Lord Lowry (though see his qualification below, as to reasonableness to continue to occupy).

The true importance of the case probably concerns its application to a wholly different situation. Thus, two people get married. They have no accommodation. Each lives with her and his parents, who will not allow the spouse also to live in their houses. The woman becomes pregnant. At that point though neither is homeless, there is a priority need. Neither is occupying accommodation available for herself or himself *and* the other, who is a person with whom she or he might reasonably be expected to reside. To leave either house, accordingly, would not seem to amount to intentional homelessness.

This, at any rate, must be so if one accepts that a woman and a man who have or are shortly to have a child must reasonably be considered to be expected to reside together, and the contrary argument does not seem to be open to authorities:

"The only fact contradicting the conclusion that his family were persons who might reasonably be expected to reside with him was the lack of accommodation to enable them to live together: this is a circular argument because that lack is the very circumstance which section 16 [now s.75] and the Act are designed to relieve" (*per* Lord Lowry in *In Re Islam*).

The only way for an authority to get round this would be to fall back upon the approach of Sir Denys Buckley, that they had deliberately made the accommodation unavailable to them, by becoming pregnant. This conjures up a wholly distasteful picture—a concept of "lie back and think of the local authority" which is as unfounded in real behaviour as the original "coals in the bath" allegation against council tenants. Although the House of Lords did not directly consider this point, they wholeheartedly rejected Sir Denys Buckley's approach:

"Sir Denys Buckley . . . held that by bringing his family here the appellant deliberately did something which had the effect of rendering the shared room . . . accommodation no longer available for his accommodation. This, however, with respect, overlooked the provisions of section 16 [now, s.75] which was to be read into section 17 [now, this section]. The room . . . was never accommodation . . . available for occupation by him and his family—so section 17 could not be applied to it" (*per* Lord Wilberforce).

Lord Lowry similarly disposed of this approach by observing that as the accommodation was not available for occupation, "section 17(1) never came into play . . . " In *R.* v. *Eastleigh Borough Council, ex parte Beattie (No. 1)* (1983) 10 H.L.R. 134, Q.B.D., the court rejected out of hand a suggestion that pregnancy causing accommodation to cease to be reasonable to occupy could amount to intentionality. It appears, therefore, that the example is one in which no finding of intentional homelessness could follow, even where there was a voluntary departure from either parents' houses.

The want of availability in the statutory sense undermined a finding of intentionality in *R.* v. *Westminster City Council, ex parte Ali* (1983) 11 H.L.R. 83, Q.B.D., a case somewhat similar on its facts to *Islam*. The applicant occupied a series of rooms in a house, together with his wife and, as they were born, their five children. He first moved into one room in

1977, when there were only three children. Shortly afterwards, his wife and children went to Bangladesh, and the applicant moved into another room, shared with other lodgers. In 1979, his wife and children returned to this country, and took up occupation of two rooms in the same house.

After the birth of a fourth child, in 1980, his wife and three of the children returned again to Bangladesh. The man and his son remained in occupation of one room. A fifth child was born in Bangladesh in 1981. By the end of 1981, the applicant was again sharing with another man. At the beginning of 1982, he went out to Bangladesh, having vacated his accommodation. In May 1982, he returned, applying (not for the first time) to the authority, and notifying them that his family were due to follow him in eight weeks' time. In August 1982, the family applied as a whole, and the applicant was held to have become homeless intentionally, for voluntarily quitting the shared room he was occupying before he last visited Bangladesh. This was the decision which the court quashed.

In *R.* v. *Wimborne District Council, ex parte Curtis* (1985) 18 H.L.R., Q.B.D., the applicant was occupying her former matrimonial home under a separation agreement which contained a cohabitation clause to the effect that if she cohabited or remarried the property would be sold. The applicant did start to cohabit, and her husband enforced the power of sale. The authority found her homeless intentionally, a decision quashed by the court because they had not considered availability in the statutory sense, *i.e.* if it was reasonable for her and her cohabitant to live together, whether the property was (as it was not) available to both of them.

Reasonable to Continue to Occupy. The concept of "availability" clearly overlaps with that of whether it is "reasonable to continue to occupy" the accommodation, and if it is not so reasonable, there can be no finding of intentionality. However, while this would seem to open the way to departure from much inadequate accommodation, "regard may be had, in determining whether it would have been reasonable for a person to continue to occupy accommodation, to the general circumstances prevailing in relation to housing in the district of the local housing authority to whom he applied . . . " (subs. (4)). The comparison is between accommodation quit, wheresoever situated, and conditions in the area of the authority to which application is made.

(i) Physical Conditions. This "one ray of hope for the authorities" (*per* Lord Denning M.R. in *de Falco, Silvestri* v. *Crawley Borough Council* [1980] Q.B. 460, C.A.) allows the authority to consider, "*e.g.* whether there are many people in the area living in worse conditions than the applicants." (*Code of Guidance*). "If they are already overcrowded, they can say to the applicant if the facts warrant it: 'You ought to have stayed where you were before. You ought not to have landed yourself on us—when it would have been reasonable for you to stay where you were" (*per* Lord Denning M.R. in *de Falco*).

The decision in *Tickner* v. *Mole Valley District Council* August 1980 L.A.G. Bulletin, C.A., in which the applicants were evicted from a caravan site because they refused to pay increased rents which they thought excessive in view of the conditions on the site, turned on s.60(4):

"That is what influenced this authority here. They had long waiting lists for housing. On those lists there were young couples waiting to be married: or young married couples sometimes staying with their in-laws: or people in poor accommodation. All those people were on the housing waiting lists—people who had been waiting for housing for years. The council thought it would be extremely unfair to all those on the waiting lists if these caravan dwellers—by coming in in this way—jumped the queue, when they were well able to pay the rent for the caravans and stay on. Those were perfectly legitimate considerations for the local authority to consider."

In order to rely upon this provision, the authority need not set out in great detail all the information on housing conditions in their area, but may have regard to "the generally prevailing standard of accommodation in their area, with which people have to be satisfied" (*per* Lord Denning M.R. in *Tickner*). That is not to say that an authority can assume that a court will take judicial notice of these conditions, or need offer no evidence on the point, and more commonly than is popularly supposed it will be possible to dislodge judicial assumptions as to the availability of local authority accommodation in an area.

In *Tickner*, there was no dispute over whether or not there were deficiencies on the caravan site: a report had been prepared by the applicants' advisers, and by the local authority. However, the authority had agreed with the site owner that certain works would be executed, and decided that in view of this it was reasonable for the caravan dwellers to remain in occupation. In *Miller* v. *London Borough of Wandsworth, The Times*, March 19, 1980, D.C., a couple were advised to reoccupy fire-damaged premises once repairs had been carried out. Their failure to comply with this advice led to a finding of intentional homelessness.

In *R.* v. *Eastleigh Borough Council, ex parte Beattie (No. 1)* (1983) 10 H.L.R. 134, Q.B.D., the authority's failure to consider overcrowding meant that they had not considered whether or not it was reasonable for the family to remain in occupation of its accommodation. However, after the case was returned to the authority for reconsideration, the authority were held to be entitled to take into account that the property was *not* statutorily overcrowded, within Part X, below, when reaching the conclusion that it *would* have been reasonable for the family to remain: *R.* v. *Eastleigh Borough Council, ex parte Beattie (No. 2)* (1984) 17 H.L.R. 168, Q.B.D.

In *R.* v. *South Herefordshire District Council, ex parte Miles* (1983) 17 H.L.R. 82, Q.B.D., a hut which was approximately 20 feet by 10 feet, with two rooms, infested by rats, and with no mains services, although services were available in a nearby caravan occupied by relatives, was held to constitute accommodation an authority could consider it reasonable to remain in occupation of, at a time when there were two adults and two children living in it, albeit on the "borderline" of what was reasonable, but as crossing the borderline into what no authority could consider reasonable on the birth of a third child.

In *Krishnan* v. *London Borough of Hillingdon* January 1981 L.A.G. Bulletin 137, Q.B.D., the authority had failed to follow up the implications of what had been said to them, and their initial correspondence with the local authority in Birmingham, from which they would have learned that the Krishnan family would not have been able to remain in occupation in Birmingham, on account of over-crowding:

"I have little doubt that if the council's officers had made appropriate enquiries of the Housing Department in Birmingham, they would have ascertained that the Plaintiff was under pressure to leave his brother's house because of the overcrowding . . . If the Council's officers had obtained this information I cannot think that they would have taken the view that . . . it would have been reasonable for the Plaintiff to continue to occupy the accommodation there."

In *R.* v. *Westminster City Council, ex parte Ali* (1983) 11 H.L.R. 83, Q.B.D., even if accommodation had been "available," "that anyone should regard it as reasonable that a family of that size should live in one room 10ft x 12ft in size, or thereabouts, is something which I find astonishing. However, the matter has to be seen in the light of s.17(4) [now, subs. (4), above] which requires that reasonableness must take account of the general circumstances prevailing in relation to housing in the area. No evidence has been placed before me that accommodation in the area of the Westminster City Council is so desperately short that it is reasonable to accept overcrowding of this degree. In the absence of such evidence I am driven to the conclusion that this question could not properly have been determined against the applicant."

In *R.* v. *Preseli District Council, ex parte Fisher* (1984) 17 H.L.R. 147, Q.B.D., the applicant, and her children, had been living in temporary accommodation. For a period they lived in a caravan. Immediately before her application, they lived on a boat, without bath, shower, W.C., electricity, hot water system or kitchen with a sink. There was one cabin, which was kitchen, living room and bedroom combined, and she occupied it with her children and two friends. This was not accommodation which it was reasonable to remain in occupation of.

(ii) Legal Conditions. The fact that the accommodation in *R.* v. *Exeter City Council, ex parte Gliddon* (1984) 14 H.L.R. 103, Q.B.D. (above), had been obtained by deception meant that it would not have been reasonable to remain in occupation of it. In *R.* v. *Portsmouth City Council, ex parte Knight* (1983) 10 H.L.R. 115, Q.B.D., and in *R.* v. *Surrey Heath Borough Council, ex parte Li* (1984) 16 H.L.R. 79, Q.B.D., once service occupancies had been determined, and there could accordingly be no defence to an action for possession, the authorities could not consider that the occupiers should reasonably have remained in occupation pending proceedings. These cases should, however, be distinguished from those where the court has a power to suspend an order for possession, for example those with restricted contracts (Rent Act 1977, s.106A). In *R.* v. *Mole Valley District Council, ex parte Minnett* (1983) 12 H.L.R. 49, Q.B.D., the authority should have disregarded a departure one day before the date specified in a consent order for possession.

(iii) Other Conditions. Section 60(4) is not exhaustive of the matters to be taken into account in determining whether or not it is reasonable to remain in occupation: *R.* v. *London Borough of Hammersmith & Fulham, ex parte Duro-Rama* (1983) 9 H.L.R. 71, Q.B.D. In this case, issues of employment, and availability of benefits, were held relevant considerations which the authority had ignored by confining itself to the matters set out in s.60(4). In *In Re Islam* [1983] 1 A.C. 688, 1 H.L.R. 107, H.L., Lord Lowry commented:

"There will, of course, and in the interests of mobility of labour ought to be, cases where the housing authority will . . . accept that it would not have been reasonable in the circumstances for the applicant to continue to occupy the accommodation which he has left."

In *R.* v. *London Borough of Hillingdon, ex parte Wilson* (1983) 12 H.L.R. 61, Q.B.D., the court, with some hesitation, held that it was not reasonable for a woman to remain in accommodation in Australia, because (a) she had no legal permission to remain, and (b) she was pregnant and would shortly have reached the stage of pregnancy when airlines would not permit her to fly. In *R.* v. *Basingstoke & Deane Borough Council, ex parte Bassett* (1983) 10 H.L.R. 125, Q.B.D., the court held that a woman who followed her husband to Canada, notwithstanding the uncertainties of their prospects there, could not reasonably have remained in occupation of their secure council accommodation, because going to join him was her only chance of saving their marriage.

In *Islam*, again, the proposition that it would not have been reasonable for Mr. Islam's wife and children to remain in occupation of the Bangladesh home certainly influenced the dissenting judgment of Ackner L.J. at the Court of Appeal, and in the House of Lords, Lords Lowry and Bridge.

In *R.* v. *London Borough of Wandsworth, ex parte Nimako-Boateng* (1983) 11 H.L.R. 95, Q.B.D., however, the court upheld the decision of the authority that a woman could reasonably have remained in occupation of the matrimonial home in Ghana, even though her relationship with her husband had broken down. There is some difficulty with this decision: the court noted that it had been given no information about Ghanaian domestic law, and consequently assumed that the woman's rights would have been the same as under English law. On this basis, the decision is perhaps unsurprising. There was no complaint of domestic violence. *Nimako-Boateng* was followed in *R.* v. *Eastleigh Borough Council, ex parte Evans* (1984) 17 H.L.R. 515, Q.B.D.

Even if there had been domestic violence in *Nimako-Boateng*, although it would be contrary to the Code of Guidance (above), in an appropriate case (although not as a policy—see, *e.g. British Oxygen Co. Ltd.* v. *Board of Trade* [1971] A.C. 610, H.L., *In Re Betts* [1983] 2 A.C. 613, 10 H.L.R. 97, H.L., *Att.-Gen., ex rel. Tilley* v. *London Borough of Wandsworth* [1981] 1 W.L.R. 854, C.A.), the authority would appear to be able properly to advise a woman to seek redress from the courts, although probably less so if, for example, the violence was extreme, there have been previous, unobserved orders, the man is likely to harass her in other ways, or the damage already done—to applicant or perhaps the children—means that the woman cannot in any event be expected reasonably to continue to live in the property. (*cf. Adeoso* v. *Adeoso, The Times,* July 22, 1980, C.A., in which it was held that a couple living in a flat with only two rooms—*i.e.* bedroom and living-room—must be considered to be living together as husband and wife, albeit that for months the couple had not spoken, they had communicated only by notes, they each slept in one of the rooms and kept their rooms locked, but they shared the rent and the cost of the electricity).

If, however, there is no domestic redress available, for example because the couple is not married, and the right of occupation is the man's, and there is no reasonable prospect of even a limited ouster from the courts, then even if there is no violence it would seem surprising in this day and age if an authority could properly conclude that a woman should continue to live with a man with whom her relationship has broken down. Much may here depend on such factors as size of property.

(iv) Advice from the Authority. Questions such as burden of proof, the making of enquiries, accommodation duties even to the intentionally homeless, will be considered in the notes to ss.62, 64 and 65, below. The last issue to be raised here concerns the status of "advice" given by the authority, to the applicant, possibly at a time when he is not yet homeless. To what extent does failure to follow advice mean that someone who might otherwise not have been considered homeless intentionally become so, usually on this question of whether or not it was reasonable to remain in occupation.

In *Miller* v. *London Borough of Wandsworth, The Times,* March 19, 1980, Q.B.D., failure to follow advice to return to fire-damaged premises following repairs was central to the finding of intentionality. It is not uncommon for a person who fears homelessness, but is not yet technically threatened with it, to seek the authority's advice. The authority will usually suggest that if the applicant does not await a court order, he will be treated as intentionally homeless.

This is, in itself, contrary to the *Code of Guidance*:

"Where it is clear from the facts that tenants have no defence or counterlcaim to an application for possession, authorities should not insist that an order for possession is obtained, and a date for the eviction set, before agreeing to help the tenant. It will be counter-productive and may cause hardship to treat as intentionally homeless a tenant who is in such a position but who leaves before an order has actually been obtained.

For example, returning owner-occupiers may themselves seek temporary accommodation if they cannot recover their home promptly. Authorities should bear in mind that, quite apart from the expense of court proceedings, insistence on court orders, particularly in resident landlord and mandatory possession cases is likely to deter such landlords from re-letting and deter potential landlords from letting at all.

It is therefore suggested that, in cases where it appears that an occupier has no defence against a possession order, the landlord be asked to produce (or obtain from his solicitor) a letter of intent to seek possession, with suitable documentary backing and an explanation of the grounds on which he is proceeding; this letter could then be examined by the authority's solicitor, and if he so advises, the authority should accept the tenant as threatened with homelessness."

In some cases if the authority insist on an order it will clearly be wrong, because the applicant will already be statutorily homeless: see notes to s.58, above. For example, when a person is squatting, or has had a licence which has been brought to an end and which was not a restricted contract. In other cases, there will be some genuine doubt.

In *R.* v. *Penwith District Council, ex parte Hughes,* August 1980 L.A.G. Bulletin 187, Q.B.D., it appeared that an alleged winter letting might not fall within the provisions of Rent Act 1977, Sched 15, Case 13, so that there would be no mandatory ground for possession. The occupier was, accordingly, advised to await the outcome of proceedings but did not do so:

"The important point which this application raises . . . is the question as to what extent an authority exercising its powers under (the) Act is entitled to say to a person . . . 'You should remain in accommodation which you at present occupy and not leave that accommodation until there is a court order made against you requiring you to vacate the accommodation.'

"Under section 3 [now, s.62] . . . it is the authority's task to make the appropriate enquiries. The authority are not entitled to say merely because they find the case is a difficult one that the court should make the enquiries and not the authority. However, where there is a situation which is doubtful or difficult it is reasonable for the authority to give advice to a person who is a prospective candidate for assistance under the . . . Act . . . that they should not vacate the accommodation which they are at present occupying without the order of the court because otherwise they may be regarded as persons intentionally homeless.

"If after having given that advice and notwithstanding that advice the person concerned chooses not to follow the advice and leaves the accommodation, then the duty under the Act remains and there is the obligation upon the authority to do their best to decide the matter making the enquiries which they are required to make under the Act. If after having made those enquiries the authority comes to the conclusion that the person indeed was intentionally homeless, then an applicant cannot come before this court and say if this court were to investigate the matter they would come to a different conclusion and because of that the authority must have been in breach of their duty . . . "

The authority's enquiries should be directed towards whether it was possible for the applicant to remain in occupation. The *Hughes* decision, however, begs the question raised in *Din* v. *London Borough of Wandsworth* [1983] 1 A.C. 657, 1 H.L.R. 73, H.L. It will be recalled that in *Din*, a family left accommodation without waiting for a court order, despite the authority's advice. It was common ground that the authority were entitled to find them intentionally homeless at or about the time of, or shortly after, the departure, because at that time it was possible, and also reasonable in the authority's view, for them to remain in occupation until a court order was made. This point appears not to have been taken in *Hughes*.

If it had been, then the court in *Hughes* would have had to confront the same question as the House of Lords in *Din*: what is the import of the words "reasonable to continue to occupy" in this context? In the light of *Din* it seems that, while *Hughes* adds some refinement to the approach of the authority, it will commonly not be possible to go behind a decision based on failure to follow advice to await a court order. *Hughes* has not been overruled by *Din*, but it has been "marginalised," although it may be considered to have enjoyed some resurgence in *R.* v. *Portsmouth City Council, ex parte Knight* (1983) 10 H.L.R. 115, Q.B.D., and *R.* v. *Surrey Heath Borough Council, ex parte Li* (1984) 16 H.L.R. 79, Q.B.D.

Local connection

61.—(1) References in this Part to a person having a local connection with the district of a local housing authority are to his having a connection with that district—

(*a*) because he is, or in the past was, normally resident in that district, and that residence is or was of his own choice, or

(*b*) because he is employed in that district, or

(*c*) because of family associations, or

(*d*) because of special circumstances.

(2) For the purposes of this section—

(*a*) a person is not employed in a district if he is serving in the regular armed forces of the Crown;

(*b*) residence in a district is not of a person's own choice if he becomes resident in it because he, or a person who might reasonably be expected to reside with him, is serving in the regular armed forces of the Crown.

(3) Residence in a district is not of a person's own choice for the purpose of this section if he, or a person who might reasonably be expected to reside with him, became resident in it because he was detained under the authority of an Act of Parliament.

(4) The Secretary of State may by order specify other circumstances in which—

(*a*) a person is not to be treated for the purposes of this section as employed in a district, or

(*b*) residence in a district is not to be treated for those purposes as of a person's own choice.

(5) An order shall be made by statutory instrument which shall be subject to annulment in pursuance of a resolution of either House of Parliament.

DEFINITIONS

"local housing authority": ss.1, 2.

"regular armed forces of the Crown": s.622.

GENERAL NOTE

The local connection provisions of Part III allow one authority to pass on to another the burden of securing that permanent accommodation is made available to an applicant: ss.65, 67, 68. The provisions operate only in specified circumstances: it was one of the principal aims of the 1977 Act to end "shuttling" homeless persons between different local authorities, each alleging there was "greater" connection with the other.

It may be helpful to state, in outline, how and when these provisions operate, before proceeding to consider the meaning of local connection. The provisions exempt an authority to which application has been made (the "notifying" authority), from the duty to secure that permanent accommodation is made available, under s.64(2) (s.68(2)). This duty passes to the "notified" authority (*ibid.*). The circumstances in which this may occur are set out in some detail: there must be no local connection with the area of the notifying authority, there must be a local connection with the area of the notified authority, and there must be no risk of domestic violence in the area of the notified authority (s.67(2)).

In the event of a dispute between the two (or more) authorities, the first stage will be to try and resolve it by reference to the Local Authority Agreement (s.67(4)). In default of agreement, the matter must be referred to arbitration (*ibid.*, see also S.I.s 1978 Nos. 69 and 661, retained in force by the Housing (Consequential Provisions) Act 1985, s.2. For the position when Scottish connections are involved, see s.76, below). Pending the resolution of the dispute, principal responsibility for the homeless person or family rests with the authority to which application was initially made, *i.e.* the notifying authority (s.68(1)).

Subs. (1)

The four stated circumstances in which a local connection arises are but "grounds" of "local connection" and the latter remains the overriding consideration: see *In Re Betts* [1983] 2 A.C. 613, 10 H.L.R. 97, H.L., in which the House of Lords overturned the decision of the Court of Appeal ([1983] 1 W.L.R. 774, 8 H.L.R. 28). The applicant was living with his family in the district of Blaby D.C. between 1978 and 1980. In August 1980, he got a job in Southampton, and moved into a houseboat in the area, where he was joined by his family.

In October 1980, he was given a house by the Eastleigh B.C. Soon after, however, he lost his job through no fault of his own, fell into arrears with his rent, and was evicted. In

February 1981, shortly before the order for possession expired, he applied under the 1977 Act. Eastleigh referred the application to Blaby. The reason given for the decision was that the family had lived in Eastleigh's district for less than six months, and was not, accordingly, normally resident in their area. The applicant challenged this decision.

The Court of Appeal allowed this challenge. The only reason given for the finding that the family was not normally resident in its area was that it had lived in the area for less than six months, and this decision had been reached by rigid application of the Local Authority Agreement. Normal residence was where a person intended to settle not necessarily permanently or indefinitely, and a person may have more than one normal residence at different times. It requires consideration of many features of residence, not merely the application of a six month, or any other arbitrary, period.

Allowing the appeal, the House of Lords said that the fundamental question was whether or not the applicant had a local connection with the area. This meant more than "normal residence," and normal residence, or any of the other specified grounds of local connection, is a subsidiary component of the formula to be applied. It is governed by the proposition that residence of any sort will be irrelevant unless and until it is such as to establish a local connection.

The House of Lords did not dissent from the Court of Appeal's analysis of "residence," which was based on the decision in *R.* v. *Barnet London Borough Council, ex parte Shah* [1983] 2 A.C. 309, H.L., under the Education Act 1962. Nor did it dissent from the proposition that a rigid application of the Local Authority Agreement would constitute a fetter on the authority's discretion: see also, *British Oxygen Co. Ltd.* v. *Board of Trade* [1971] A.C. 610, H.L., *Att.-Gen., ex rel. Tilley* v. *London Borough of Wandsworth* [1981] 1 W.L.R. 854, C.A. However, the Agreement could certainly be taken into account, and applied as a guideline, provided the authority do not shut out the particular facts of the individual case, *i.e.* its *application* is given individual consideration. In the present case, the House of Lords found that the authority had not misdirected themselves in this respect.

Residence

Residence has to be "of choice." There is not residence of choice if the applicant, or a person who might reasonably be expected to reside with him, is serving in the regular armed forces (*i.e.* the Royal Navy, the regular armed forces as defined by the Army Act 1955, s.225, the regular air force as defined by the Air Force Act 1955, s.227, Queen Alexandra's Royal Nursing Service and the Women's Royal Naval Service—see s.622, below).

Nor is there residence of choice if the applicant or anyone who might reasonably be expected to reside with him is detained under the authority of any Act of Parliament. Thus, prisoners (whether or not convicted) and those detained under the Mental Health Act 1959 will not acquire a local connection with the area in which prison or hospital is situated. The Secretary of State has power to specify further circumstances in which residence is not to be considered "of choice" (subs. (4)).

Residence resulting from service in the armed forces was considered in *R.* v. *Vale of White Horse District Council, ex parte Smith and Hay* (1984) 17 H.L.R. 160, Q.B.D. Each of these two cases followed from the fact that the armed forces normally allow a period of time after the termination of service, before recovering possession of married quarters. It was held that the exclusion of residence as a result of service in the armed forces refers to the time residence commences. A fresh residence after leaving the armed forces can be established, even in the same premises, but it will not normally be established merely by holding over in married quarters after service has come to an end.

The Local Authority Agreement suggests a working (or extended) definition of "normal residence" as being established by 6 months in the area during the previous 12 months, or not less than 3 years during the previous 5 year period. In *In Re Betts* [1983] 2 A.C. 613, 10 H.L.R. 97, H.L., this was described as "eminently sensible and proper to have been included in the agreement." Residence of up to 6 months under one or more tenancies subject to Case 13, Sched. 15 Rent Act 1977 ("out-of-season holiday lettings,") is likely to be disregarded, and time spent in hospital, or time spent in an institution in which households are accepted only for a limited period (*e.g.* mother and baby homes, refuges, rehabilitation centres,) are described as further exceptions to the norm.

In *Smith and Hay*, a period of a few months some ten years before application, during which one of the spouses had been employed, and therefore resident, in an area was considered to be extremely short and not necessarily establishing a local connection.

Employment

A person is not regarded as being employed in an area if he is serving in the regular armed forces, or in such other circumstances as the Secretary of State may by order specify (subs.(4)). The Local Authority Agreement suggests that an authority should seek confirmation of employment from the employer, and that it is not of a casual nature. This implies that "employment" is to be given a restrictive meaning, *i.e.* one in the employ of another, but Part III does not suggest that the self-employed should be excluded, or that employment need be full-time. Given that employment is a subsidiary consideration, and merely one of the grounds for establishing a local connection, it is clearly open to an authority to exclude casual work, but not, it is submitted, the self-employed. In *R.* v. *Vale of White Horse District Council, ex parte Smith and Hay* (1984) 17 H.L.R. 160, Q.B.D., the same few months' employment (above), some ten years before the application, was described as limited and of short duration and the authority did not err in finding that it did not give rise to a local connection.

Family Associations

There is no statutory definition of this phrase, nor is any elaboration to be found in the *Code of Guidance* issued under s.71. The Local Authority Agreement suggests that it arises where an applicant or a member of his household, has parents, adult children, brothers or sisters currently residing in the area in question. The relatives must have been resident for a period of at least 5 years, and the applicant must indicate a wish to be near them. An applicant who objects to being referred to an area on account of family associations should not be so referred. (However, *cf. R.* v. *Mr. Referee McCall* (1981) 8 H.L.R. 48, Q.B.D., notes to s.67, below, in which it was observed that though the applicant's wishes are relevant where other factors are equally balanced, they cannot override the words of the statute).

Other Special Circumstances

This is likewise left undefined in both Part III and *Code*. The Local Authority Agreement states that "an authority is free to decide that an applicant has a local connection with its own area (but not in another authority's area without its agreement) for any reason it may decide . . . " It mentions families returning from abroad, those leaving the armed forces, or those who wish to return to an area where they were brought up or lived for a considerable length of time in the past. In *R.* v. *Vale of White Horse District Council, ex parte Smith and Hay* (1984) 17 H.L.R. 160, Q.B.D., one of the families attempted to place some reliance on their membership of an evangelical church, around the life of which their own lives revolved. Following *In Re Betts* [1983] 2 A.C. 613, 10 H.L.R. 97, that the fundamental test is whether or not there is a local connection, the authority had not erred in concluding as a matter of fact that this association did not amount to a special circumstance giving rise to a local connection in their case.

Duties of local housing authorities with respect to homelessness and threatened homelessness

Inquiry into cases of possible homelessness or threatened homelessness

62.—(1) If a person (an "applicant") applies to a local housing authority for accommodation, or for assistance in obtaining accommodation, and the authority have reason to believe that he may be homeless or threatened with homelessness, they shall make such inquiries as are necessary to satisfy themselves as to whether he is homeless or threatened with homelessness.

(2) If they are so satisfied, they shall make any further inquiries necessary to satisfy themselves as to—

(*a*) whether he has a priority need, and

(*b*) whether he became homeless or threatened with homelessness intentionally;

and if they think fit they may also make inquiries as to whether he has a local connection with the district of another local housing authority in England, Wales or Scotland.

DEFINITIONS

"homeless": s.58.

"intentionally": s.60.

"local connection": s.61.

"local housing authority": ss.1, 2.

"priority need": s.59.

"threatened with homelessness": s.58.

GENERAL NOTE

This is the first of the substantive provisions. Duties start with an application. There is no requirement that the application be in writing, or in any particular form. Further, "the Act does not place any express limitation on who can make an application or as to how many applications can be made . . . " (*R.* v. *North Devon District Council, ex parte Lewis* [1981] 1 W.L.R 328, Q.B.D.). Under s.12, Interpretation Act 1978, "where an Act confers a power or imposes a duty it is implied, unless the contrary intention appears, that the power may be exercised, or the duty is to be performed, from time to time as occasion requires."

Against this, it is quite clear that an applicant cannot simply make application after application, so that, even if homeless intentionally, as soon as one period of temporary accommodation (below, s.65(3)) comes to an end, he is entitled to another: *Delahaye* v. *Oswestry Borough Council, The Times*, July 29, 1980, Q.B.D.

There is a number of questions:

(a) is the right to re-apply dependent on a change in circumstances, or does it require an intervening period of settled accommodation, as where there has been intentionality?

(b) if the authority are exempt from a duty on account of an earlier application, does this mean that they do not have to entertain the new application, or does it mean that while they have to entertain the application, and accordingly engage in enquiries, etc., they can avoid the consequential duty by reference to their earlier discharge?

(c) if reliance is sought to be placed on "separate treatment," *i.e.* that although one member of a household is, or may be treated as, homeless intentionally, the other is not (see note on Whose Conduct, under s.60, above), does there have to be a *separate* application by this "innocent" party, or does a duty to consider this issue arise whoever makes the application?

(d) does the position change when there are applications to different authorities.

Before turning to these questions, however, it should be noted that if the authority have received new information, *i.e.* which might affect their decision, they are entitled to re-open their enquiries, of their own motion, when the decision has been adverse to the applicant: *R.* v. *Hambleton District Council, ex parte Geoghan* [1985] J.P.L. 394, Q.B.D. This will also serve to cure any defects in their earlier procedure, *e.g.* failure to consider relevant matters. If the authority have *power* to do so, then it is hard to see that any reasonable authority could refuse to *exercise* it, *i.e.* at the request of a disappointed applicant, provided at least that the new information could (if accepted) affect the decision.

The same would *not* appear to apply in the case of new information following a *successful* application, *i.e.* post-decision; it was doubted in *Geoghan*, and the criminal provisions of s.74 (a) would seem an adequate substitute (especially when coupled to the ground for possession based on securing accommodation by false information—see below, s.84 and Sched. 2, Ground 5), and (b) may not apply if the authority re-open their decision, on the basis that the duty is to supply the new information *before* decision.

Assuming therefore that new *information* is not available, the duty to entertain a new application will depend on the answers to the four questions referred to.

Change of Circumstances or Intervening Accommodation?

In *Wyness* v. *Poole Borough Council*, July 1979 L.A.G. Bulletin 166, C.C., on the first application, it was held that the family had no local connection with Poole, but there was a local connection with Hart, in Hampshire. The family declined to accept reference back to Hart, but made do in Poole until one member of the family had acquired employment and therefore a local connection with Poole. The local connection provisions then ceased to apply, and Poole was compelled to re-entertain the application. This was on the basis of change of circumstances, and the authority's argument that the one discharge (by reference back to Hart) was sufficient was rejected.

In *R.* v. *Westminster City Council, ex parte Chambers* (1982) 6 H.L.R. 15, Q.B.D., the applicants rejected an earlier offer of accommodation and returned, each to live with her and his parents. After a period of time, they reapplied, and the authority held that they had become homeless intentionally, because they had refused the earlier offer. This was clearly unsustainable, on the wording of s.60(1), with its reference to cessation of occupation. The court nonetheless refused relief, on the grounds that the authority had, by their earlier offer, discharged their duties:

> "The consequence is not to put housing authorities under an obligation to keep making offers of accommodation to a homeless person who unreasonably refuses to accept an appropriate offer. One such offer is enough. This is so even although the applicant's original state of unintentional homelessness subsists for a protracted period. If, in reality, he is experiencing one incidence of unintentional homelessness, one offer suffices. It will be otherwise with the person who experiences what can realistically be

regarded as two separate incidences of unintentional homelessness. The second inci-
dence will put the council under a fresh duty."

There was, however, no change of circumstances in *Chambers*, so that the *Wyness*
argument was not advanced. In *R.* v. *London Borough of Ealing, ex parte McBain* [1985] 1
W.L.R. 1351; 18 H.L.R. 59, C.A. a woman refused what she considered an inappropriate
offer. She was still challenging this offer in the county court, when she found she was
pregnant again and reapplied. The authority held that they had discharged their duty,
because there had been no change by way of intervening settled accommodation. In the
absence of a decision from the county court on the first offer, on judicial review it was
assumed, as it had to be, that the first offer had been adequate. The Court of Appeal
rejected the "intervening settled accommodation" approach and its equation of refusal with
intentionality, and held instead that re-application can be made when there has been a
"material change of circumstances." This means such a change that the earlier offer would
clearly no longer be suitable or that it would be an inadequate response to current need
(*e.g.* because of more children). In judging suitability, regard may be made to the general
circumstances of the area *i.e.* s.60(4).

No Need to Consider Application, or Reliance on Prior Discharge?

Most of the cases have not dealt expressly with the question whether no new duty means
that the authority do not even have to entertain a new application, or does it mean that
having received a new application, and decided that there has been no material change, the
authority discharge their duty by reference to the earlier offer. The same point may be made
in relation to intentionality cases (see notes to s.60, above), *i.e.* do the authority have to
entertain a new application at all, or do they make enquiries, and then rely on the earlier
finding?

This is, to some extent, a chicken-and-egg issue, for if the authority does not even enquire,
how can they establish that there has been no material change or intervening accommodation? But this could be a "non-statutory" enquiry, as distinct from an enquiry under s.62. In
the event, it would seem that the point is answered by *Delahaye* v. *Oswestry Borough
Council, The Times*, July 29, 1980, Q.B.D. for the purposes of re-application after a finding
of intentionality there can be no new application, for otherwise the applicant could continue
to enjoy new periods not only in s.65(3)(a) accommodation (for the homeless intentionally)
but also in s.63 accommodation (pending enquiries).

Whose Application?

It is now well-settled that a further application may be made by a member of the same
household, even although another member has been or could be found to have become
homeless intentionally: see notes to s.60, above. In *R.* v. *North Devon District Council, ex
parte Lewis* [1981] 1 W.L.R. 328, Q.B.D., the application was by the woman whose husband
had earlier been found homeless intentionally. In *R.* v. *London Borough of Ealing, ex parte
Sidhu* (1982) 2 H.L.R. 45, Q.B.D., *R.* v. *Cardiff City Council, ex parte John* (1982) 9
H.L.R. 56, Q.B.D., *R.* v. *Eastleigh Borough Council, ex parte Beattie (No. 2)* (1984) 17
H.L.R. 168, Q.B.D. and in *R.* v. *West Dorset District Council, ex parte Phillips* (1985) 17
H.L.R. 336, Q.B.D., the new application was also by the putatively "unintentionally
homeless" party. In *R.* v. *Penwith District Council, ex parte Trevena* (1985) 17 H.L.R.,
Q.B.D., the application was joint. However, the point of "whose application" was not
expressly taken, and in any event it is unclear that the court accepted the intentionalty of
the "other" party.

The section itself says that "if a person (an 'applicant') applies," and inquiries are whether
"he has" a priority need, "he became" homeless or threatened with homelessness intentionally, or whether "he has a local connection" with another authority. The wording, then,
suggests that it is "the applicant" who is to be considered. On the other hand, enquiries into
the local connection of the applicant alone would not suffice, for the local connections of a
person reasonably to be expected to reside with the applicant are relevant (see s.67(2)), and
priority need may arise by reference to non-applicants (see s.59). Similarly, if acquiescence
to, or participation in, the act of another causing loss of accommodation may result in a
finding of intentionality on the part of the applicant, the authority is at least entitled to
enquire into matters relating to that other.

Furthermore, accommodation provided under Part III has to be appropriate, and the
appropriateness is to be judged by reference to what is found out on enquiries, which must
themselves cover all questions relevant to priority need, so that again the circumstances of
a "non-applicant" have to be considered: see notes to s.65, below. It is accordingly submitted
that it would introduce a surprising—and inconsistent—degree of legality or formality into

Part III if anything turned on who actually signs an application form. It will be seen below that the burden of making enquiries to elicit relevant information is squarely on the authority, and this would seem to go far enough to include the issue of "separate" treatment.

Application to Different Authority

In *R.* v. *Slough Borough Council, ex parte L.B. Ealing* [1981] Q.B. 801, C.A., two applicants had been found homeless intentionally in Slough. One applicant then moved to Ealing, the other to Hillingdon, and both authorities concluded that the applicants were not homeless intentionally. In each case, however, the local connection provisions entitled Ealing and Hillingdon to refer the applicants back to Slough. While this approach may seem anomalous, it shows how different authorities can reach different conclusions on the same question.

In the event, it was held that Slough were bound by the decisions of Ealing and Hillingdon. There is nothing to stop an applicant, as it were, moving around until he finds an authority who will conclude that he is not homeless intentionally, and, provided that decision is not one which no reasonable authority could reach, there is no way in which the authority fixed with final responsibility for the applicants can defeat the decision, even although it conflicts with their own original decision.

There is, however, one anomaly. While this is the position in cases of intentionality, it does not apply in cases of "prior offer": *R.* v. *London Borough of Hammersmith & Fulham, ex parte O'Brian* (1985) 17 H.L.R. 471, Q.B.D. If Slough had not found intentionality, but had offered accommodation which the applicants had not accepted, and the applicants had similarly applied to Ealing and Hillingdon and had referred them back, Slough could rely on the prior discharge under s.65(2): the duty under s.68(2) has been held an extension or part of the duty under s.65(2): *O'Brian.*

Enquiries

The principal duty, if the application is to be entertained, is to make enquiries. The authority will be under a duty to make enquiries (a) if a person applies to them for accommodation or for assistance in obtaining accommodation, and (b) if they have reason to believe that he *may* be homeless or threatened with homelessness. These conditions arise relatively easily: the authority need only "have reason to believe," and this belief needs be no more than that the applicant *may* be homeless or threatened with homelessness.

The enquiries which the authority must make are: such enquiries as are necessary to satisfy the authority whether the applicant is homeless or threatened with homelessness, and, if the authority are so satisfied, such further enquiries as may be necessary to satisfy them whether he has a priority need for accommodation, and whether he has become homeless or threatened with homelessness intentionally. If the authority conclude that the applicant is neither homeless or threatened with homelessness, therefore, they need not proceed to any further enquiries, although they still have duties of notification: see s.64, below.

In addition, and if the authority think fit, they may make enquiries as to whether or not the applicant has a local connection with the area of another housing authority. Even if, at an early stage, they consider that there may be such local connection, they are still under a duty to make the preliminary enquiries as to homelessness, priority need and intentionality: *Delahaye* v. *Oswestry Borough Council, The Times,* July 29, 1980. Indeed, such enquiries are *exclusively* in the province of the authority to which application has been made: *R.* v. *Slough Borough Council, ex parte London Borough of Ealing* [1981] Q.B. 801, C.A.

There is no obligation to make enquiries into local connection at all; if local connection enquiries are made, the first such enquiry is whether the applicant has a local connection with the area of *another* authority. This is because, if there is no such local connection, it will be irrelevant to consider whether or not there is one with the authority to which application has been made, as persons without a connection elsewhere will remain the responsibility of that authority: *R.* v. *London Borough of Hillingdon, ex parte Streeting* [1980] 1 W.L.R. 1425, D.C. and C.A.; see also *Betts* v. *Eastleigh Borough Council* [1983] 1 W.L.R. 774, 8 H.L.R. 28, C.A., not overruled on this point by the House of Lords ([1983] 2 A.C. 613, 10 H.L.R 97).

The authority may request another relevant authority (see s.77, below) or a registered housing association (s.5, above), to assist in discharging the enquiry duty, and such body is obliged to co-operate in the discharge of the function to which the request relates, to the extent that is reasonable in the circumstances: s.72.

Enquiries will normally be connected with such matters as size and structure of household, nature and location of last accommodation, reasons for leaving it, prospects of return, alternative possibilities, such particular problems as illness or handicap or accommodation at a distance from a violent partner, and how long the applicant expects to stay in the area: *Code of Guidance.* The enquiries *must* cover all the factors relevant to questions of priority need, *i.e.* pregnancy, dependent children, vulnerability and emergency: *R.* v. *Ryedale District Council, ex parte Smith* (1983) 16 H.L.R. 66, Q.B.D. It may also be relevant to enquire into place and type of employment, family connection, or attendance at hospitals or schools. Authorities are asked to undertake these enquiries quickly and sympathetically: *Code.* In *R.* v. *West Dorset District Council, ex parte Phillips* (1985) 17 H.L.R. Q.B.D., the authority were criticised for failing to make their enquiries in the caring and sympathetic way required by the *Code.*

It is recognised that those seeking help may well be under considerable strain, may be confused, and may not find it easy to explain their position clearly and logically. They should be given the opportunity to explain their circumstances fully, and to be involved in discussing and understanding the options that are open to them. Authorities are asked to be ready to agree to the presence of someone the applicant knows and trusts, and an interpreter may be necessary: *Code.* Inconsistencies will very frequently be found when someone's native language is not English: *R.* v. *Surrey Heath Borough Council, ex parte Li* (1984) 16 H.L.R. 79, Q.B.D. It will usually be during the course of initial enquiries that an authority will be obliged to "administer the caution" about the applicant's duty to notify any material changes in his circumstances at any time prior to notification of decision: s.74(2), below. Authorities are reminded of the importance of doing this sensitively in the context of the interview, or the enquiries as a whole: *Code.*

It is clear that the sort of enquiries which need to be carried out are not so extensive as to amount to "CID-type" enquiries: *Lally* v. *Royal Borough of Kensington and Chelsea, The Times,* March 27, 1980, Ch.D., However, the burden of making enquiries is clearly and squarely on the authority: *R.* v. *Woodspring District Council, ex parte Walters* (1984) 16 H.L.R. 73, Q.B.D.; *R.* v. *Reigate & Banstead District Council, ex parte Paris* (1984) 17 H.L.R. 103, Q.B.D. In *Walters,* the applicant's solicitor gave the authority information which, if confirmed, would have led to a finding that the applicant was homeless. The authority took the view that the burden was on the applicant to prove her homelessness, with which approach the court strongly disagreed.

In *Paris,* it was held that enquiries into matters relevant to a finding of intentionality have to be made, whether or not the applicant provides information which suggests there may be something to follow up, *e.g.* whether or not the last accommodation occupied was available and reasonable to continue in occupation of. In *R.* v. *Preseli District Council, ex parte Fisher* (1985) 17 H.L.R. 147, Q.B.D., it was held that such enquiries may have to go back over several years, to the last accommodation occupied by the applicant (if any) which was available and reasonable.

In *R.* v. *Bath City Council, ex parte Sangermano* (1984) 17 H.L.R. 94, Q.B.D., it was held that the authority ought either to have accepted medical evidence which was sent in by advisers, or to have made their own further enquiries. In *R.* v. *Eastleigh Borough Council, ex parte Beattie (No.* 2) (1984) 17 H.L.R. 168, Q.B.D., affidavit evidence in earlier proceedings was material which the authority ought to have taken into account, even though not expressly referred to during the course of the second application which had been proposed by the court in place of reconsideration of the initial application (then some years old), and should have reasons for not accepting it, which they will subsequently have to put before a court if proceedings ensue.

Basic issues have to be put to an applicant, of course. In *R.* v. *Wyre Borough Council, ex parte Joyce* (1983) 11 H.L.R. 73, Q.B.D., the authority did not even ask why the applicant had fallen into mortgage arrears, which led them to leave something relevant out of account in their decision-making process, *i.e.* the answer she might have given. In *R.* v. *Wandsworth London Borough Council, ex parte Rose* (1983) 11 H.L.R. 105, Q.B.D., the authority should have enquired into the applicant's state of mind when she quit her previous accommodation, *i.e.* what she believed about the accommodation she was coming to, which turned out to be less than settled (*cf.* notes to s.60, above).

If an application arises through job-loss, the authority have to enquire into why the job was lost: *R.* v. *Thurrock District Council, ex parte Williams* (1981) 1 H.L.R. 128, Q.B.D., see notes to s.60, above. In *Krishnan* v. *London Borough of Hillingdon,* June 1981 L.A.G. Bulletin 137, Q.B.D., the authority were held to have made inadequate enquiries when they failed to chase up an unanswered letter to another authority, or to follow up the applicant's own description of pressure on him to leave his earlier accommodation because of overcrowding. In *Tickner* v. *Mole Valley District Council,* August 1980 L.A.G. Bulletin 187, C.A., Lord Denning M.R. criticised the inadequacy of enquiries as to homelessness itself: see notes to s.58(1), above.

The cases must all be seen in context. *Tickner* concerned mobile homes. When people are living in mobile homes, (and in this case under allegedly phony holiday lettings) it is to be expected (a) that they will be asked by the site owner to state a permanent address elsewhere, and (b) that the fact that they give one such permanent address is hardly evidence that they have a home elsewhere. All that Lord Denning M.R. was saying is that *in that case* the circumstances were such that the authority should not have drawn the inference of accommodation elsewhere with such ease.

It is not always easy to reconcile the decisions. They have to be taken on their own facts, and sometimes having regard to the evolution of the caselaw, and the arguments which have been raised at the time of a particular decision, which may even require consideration of when cases are reported, and sometimes they are affected by the type of hearing.

In *de Falco, Silvestri* v. *Crawley Borough Council* [1980] Q.B. 460, C.A., the applicants gave unemployment as the reason for leaving Naples, and did not put forward any material from which it might have been inferred that the accommodation that they had left was not accommodation suitable for their occupation. Accordingly, the authority did not err in drawing the inference that what they had left was suitable accommodation, even though they made no express enquiry to this effect. *De Falco*, however, was an interlocutory application, and treated as such in *R.* v. *Reigate and Banstead Borough Council, ex parte Paris* (1984) 17 H.L.R. 103, Q.B.D., where the express enquiry was held to be called for.

In *R.* v. *London Borough of Harrow, ex parte Holland* (1982) 4 H.L.R. 108, C.A., a couple applied as homeless. They had been living at a series of temporary addresses since leaving a caravan site, which the authority were satisfied had been left in circumstances amounting to intentional homelessness. At the Court of Appeal the couple sought to rely on a suggestion that the man had enjoyed an intervening period of what would have been permanent accommodation in a boarding-house but for reasons beyond his control, and so could not be treated as being intentionally homeless. The basis for this argument was that (a) the couple had at the relevant point in time separated following a quarrel, and (b) the room in which the man had been living (which was not available to the woman) would have remained available to him, had the boarding-house not shut down.

It was held that the authority had been given no reason for suspecting either that one of the addresses might be permanent, or that, even if it was, it would have been acceptable to the man. The separation between the couple had never been mentioned. Accordingly, they had not failed to make appropriate enquiries. The court, however, seems to have accepted that the case must be approached on the basis of what the authority knew or *ought* to have known, even though in the particular case there was no basis for saying that they ought to have known this *particular* additional information.

In conclusion on this point, it would seem that two points may be made. The burden is squarely on the authority to make enquiries, and this must be done in a way that elicits all the information relevant to the issues arising, *i.e.* homelessness, priority need, intentionality and, if appropriate, local connection. It must be done sympathetically, and not in a way that leads the applicant into a false position. The authority must apply common-sense and general knowledge in asking their questions.

Thus, if someone is homeless, he has normally left other accommodation. The authority must ask why, and whether it was available or reasonable. If someone has been evicted for arrears, it may well be that there is an explanation. In *R.* v. *West Dorset District Council, ex parte Phillips* (1985) 17 H.L.R. 336, Q.B.D., at interview, the applicant burst out at her husband that she had always told him his drinking would get them into trouble. This was not construable as acquiescence, even by the most hard-hearted of officers. It was astonishing that the officer had not made further enquiries. If he had, for example of social services, it would inevitably have led to the conclusion that she could not be blamed.

On the other hand, if reliance is sought to be placed on some eventuality which is not to be taken for granted, some peculiar circumstance which would alter the decision, and not even a suspicion of it has come to the authority, it is that much harder to complain of the failure to ask a relevant question. Advisers in particular should be careful to put *all* relevant matters before an authority. An authority will not be criticised for failing to make enquiries of someone they have no reason to believe will provide relevant information, for example a doctor or a school where health or education were not apparently in issue.

The questions of whether the enquiry duty has properly been discharged, and whether a decision has properly been reached will commonly overlap. Thus, lack of natural justice or fairness will usually found a challenge both to the enquiry process, and to the final decision. Indeed, it is unlikely that any attack will be made on the enquiry process alone—for no one will complain of the enquiry process if they do not also object to the decision to which it has led.

When conducting enquiries fairly, authorities are not, however, bound to treat the issue as if in a court of law: *R. v. Southampton City Council, ex parte Ward* (1984) 14 H.L.R. 114, Q.B.D. They act reasonably if they act on responsible material, from responsible people who might reasonably be expected to provide a reliant account. An authority can rely on hearsay, in the sense that they are not obliged to confine themselves to direct evidence, for example where an authority relied on evidence from a social worker's supervisor, rather than the social worker herself: *Ward.*

Nor, indeed, are the authority obliged to put *everything* to the applicant (*Ward*), although quite clearly the applicant must have an opportunity to deal at least with the generality of material which will adversely affect him, and this will normally mean matters of factual detail. In *Goddard* v. *Torridge District Council*, January 1982 L.A.G. Bulletin 9, Q.B.D., the authority discussed with the applicant's former employers the circumstances in which he had quit his job and, accordingly, lost his tied accommodation, but went into these matters fully with the applicant on three separate occasions, amounting to a sufficient investigation for these purposes.

In the Divisional Court hearing in *R. v. Hillingdon Homeless Persons Panel, ex parte Islam, The Times*, February 24, 1981, Q.B.D. (this issue did not form part of the subsequent appeals—see [1983] 1 A.C. 688, C.A. and H.L., 1 H.L.R. 107, H.L.), an allegation of want of natural justice failed as the authority had given the applicant, by the time of decision, not less than six interviews. Nonetheless, the judgment seems to assume that a want of natural justice will be fatal to an authority's decision. In *Jennings* v. *Northavon District Council*, 17 July 1981, unreported, Q.B.D., a want of natural justice was disclaimed by counsel for the applicant, but, again, it seems to be implied that had such an allegation been made and sustained, it would be an appropriate basis for setting the decision of the authority aside.

The final case to which reference should be made on enquiries is *R. v. Penwith District Council, ex parte Hughes*, August 1980 L.A.G. Bulletin 187, Q.B.D.: see facts and quote under heading "Advice from the Authority," in the notes to s.60, above.

Interim duty to accommodate in case of apparent priority need

63.—(1) If the local housing authority have reason to believe that an applicant may be homeless and have a priority need, they shall secure that accommodation is made available for his occupation pending a decision as a result of their inquiries under section 62.

(2) This duty arises irrespective of any local connection which the applicant may have with the district of another local housing authority.

DEFINITIONS
"applicant": s.62.
"available for his occupation": s.75.
"homeless": s.58.
"local connection": s.61.
"local housing authority": ss.1, 2.
"priority need": s.59.

GENERAL NOTE
If the authority have reason to believe that the applicant may be homeless and in priority need, they have to secure that accommodation is made available for his occupation pending any decision which they may make as a result of their enquiries. Again (*cf.* notes to s.62, above), a very low standard of belief is all that is necessary to establish the duty. This duty exists irrespective of questions of local connection. The requirement to make accommodation available for the applicant's occupation is, by definition, a requirement to make it available for the applicant *and* for any person who might reasonably be expected to reside with him: s.75.

In discharging this duty, the authority are entitled to call for co-operation from other bodies, including a registered housing association, or may arrange for social services or social work departments to discharge the duty on their behalf: s.72. The requirement calls for some action on the part of the authority. In *R. v. London Borough of Ealing, ex parte Sidhu* (1982) 2 H.L.R. 45, Q.B.D., a women's refuge, not even in the same area, provided accommodation, and the mere fact that such accommodation had been provided was unsuccessfully alleged by the authority to amount to a discharge of their duty.

The fact that the accommodation was in another area was not itself fundamental to the result, but it may not be without relevance. Many such refuges are funded by local authorities. In such circumstances, there are two reasons why accommodation provided voluntarily and other than at the arrangement of the authority may be less susceptible to challenge: (a) because as a matter of practice, the refuge is not entirely independent of the authority; and (b) because the provision of funds for the refuge may be held to denote active participation or assistance by the authority, if (but probably only if) linked to a positive nomination entitlement on the part of the authority.

The authority may require a person housed under this provision to pay such reasonable charges as they may determine, or to pay an amount towards the payment made by the authority to a third party for accommodation, for example a contribution towards the cost of private sector accommodation: s.69(2).

Security

Where the authority do provide the accommodation themselves, the applicant will not become a secure tenant, under the provisions of Part IV, until a year has expired from the date on which the applicant is notified of the authority's decision on his application (see Sched. 1, para 4, below). This exemption applies where the accommodation is arranged through another body whose tenants are or may be secure, for example a housing association: *Family Housing Association* v. *Miah* (1982) 5 H.L.R. 94, C.A.

In *Miah, Restormel District Council* v. *Buscombe* (1982) 14 H.L.R. 91, C.A., and in *Royal Borough of Kensington and Chelsea* v. *Hayden* (1984) 17 H.L.R 114, C.A., some doubt was cast on whether accommodation provided under the 1977 Act amounted to a tenancy or licence within the security provisions of what is now Part IV of this Act at all. This doubt, however, must be considered to have been resolved by *Eastleigh Borough Council* v. *Walsh* [1985] 1 W.L.R. 525; 17 H.L.R. 392, H.L., where express regard was paid to the provisions that are now Sched. 2, para. 4, and where accommodation provided under this temporary duty was held to amount to tenancy, notwithstanding the authority's attempt— successful at the Court of Appeal—to argue in substance that any temporary accommodation so provided had to be by way of licence.

In the light of this decision and of the decision of the House of Lords in *Street* v. *Mountford* [1985] A.C. 809; 17 H.L.R. 402, H.L. (see notes to s.93, below), it is submitted that even temporary accommodation under Part III will be considered held under tenancy, provided of course that other conventional requirements for tenancy, in particular exclusive possession, are met. Hostel temporary accommodation is still likely to be regarded as under licence, and if there is no letting "as a separate dwelling," for example because kitchen or other communal living accommodation (exclusive of bathroom/lavatory) is shared, there will be no secure tenancy: s.79.

Difficulty may arise if the authority do not get around to serving the notice of decision required by s.64. Notice is required of all decisions, including those which are favourable to the applicant, and although reasons must be provided if the decision is, or may be considered, unfavourable. If no notice is given of a decision, then the burden will lie on the applicant to show when it ought to have been given, *i.e.* when the authority's enquiries were complete: *Miah*.

Quality

There have been two decisions on the quality of temporary accommodation, and although they both relate to the temporary accommodation duty towards the intentionally homeless (see notes to s.65, below), the same principles would seem to apply. In *R.* v. *Exeter City Council, ex parte Gliddon* (1984) 14 H.L.R. 103, Q.B.D., the authority were alleged to have been in breach of their temporary duty because the accommodation provided was in substantial disrepair, requiring works to prevent it becoming unfit within s.190, below. It was held that an authority are entitled to have regard to the time for which accommodation is likely to be occupied when determining what quality of accommodation is appropriate. The court accepted that some quality of accommodation would fall below the line of acceptable discharge of even a temporary duty, but accommodation within s.190 did not do so. Accommodation which is so unfit that it is not even repairable at a reasonable expense within s.206, might well be inadequate even for a temporary purpose.

In *R.* v. *Southampton City Council, ex parte Ward* (1984) 14 H.L.R. 114, Q.B.D., accommodation on a caravan site that was described by a social worker as in appalling conditions was nonetheless upheld as an adequate discharge of the temporary duty, but having regard to the family's expressed wish to live on a site, rather than in a permanent structure.

The decision in *R.* v. *Ryedale District Council, ex parte Smith* (1983) 16 H.L.R. 66, Q.B.D., is at first sight one under this section. The applicants were placed in the accommodation—also a mobile home—immediately after application. However, as the court's ruling was that the sort of accommodation provided must be governed by what is learned during enquiries under s.62, although it is not clear that the authority had decided that it should be the applicants' permanent offer, it seems that it must be treated as a case on the duty under s.65(2).

Notification of decision and reasons

64.—(1) On completing their inquiries under section 62, the local housing authority shall notify the applicant of their decision on the question whether he is homeless or threatened with homelessness.

(2) If they notify him that their decision is that he is homeless or threatened with homelessness, they shall at the same time notify him of their decision on the question whether he has a priority need.

(3) If they notify him that their decision is that he has a priority need, they shall at the same time notify him—

(*a*) of their decision whether he became homeless or threatened with homelessness intentionally, and

(*b*) whether they have notified or propose to notify another local housing authority under section 67 (referral of application on grounds of local connection).

(4) If the local housing authority notify the applicant—

(*a*) that they are not satisfied that he is homeless or threatened with homelessness, or

(*b*) that they are not satisfied that he has a priority need, or

(*c*) that they are satisfied that he became homeless or threatened with homelessness intentionally, or

(*d*) that they have notified or propose to notify another local housing authority under section 67 (referral of application on grounds of local connection),

they shall at the same time notify him of their reasons.

(5) The notice required to be given to a person under this section shall be given in writing and shall, if not received by him, be treated as having been given to him only if it is made available at the authority's office for a reasonable period for collection by him or on his behalf.

DEFINITIONS
  "applicant": s.62.
  "homeless": s.58.
  "intentionally": s.60.
  "local connection": s.61.
  "local housing authority": ss.1, 2.
  "priority need": s.59.
  "threatened with homelessness": s.58.

GENERAL NOTE
  When the authority have completed their enquiries under s.62, they must notify their decision to the applicant. This should be done "as quickly as possible" (*Code of Guidance*). The first decision they must notify is, of course, whether or not they are satisfied that the applicant is homeless or threatened with homelessness. If they decide not, they are also bound to notify him of their reasons for this decision: subs. (4)(*a*).

  Where they are satisfied that there is homelessness or the threat of it then, at the same time, they must notify the applicant of their decision about priority need (subs. (2)) and also their reasons if they decide there is no priority need: subs. (4)(*b*). If they are satisfied that he has a priority need, then at the same time they are bound to notify him as to their decision on whether or not (a) they are satisfied that he became homeless intentionally, and (b) they intend to notify any other authority that the application has been made: subs. (3). If intentionally homeless, or there is to be a local connection referral, the notice must, again, be accompanied by the reasons for it: subs. (4)(*c*),(*d*).

  Where the local connection provisions are involved (s.67, below), the notifying authority are under the duty to notify the applicant of the final decision and the reasons for it: see s.68(3). There are also notification duties connected with the protection of property: see s.70.

The duties to notify and give reasons for decisions arise independently of the substantive duties to which they refer: *R.* v. *Beverley Borough Council, ex parte McPhee, The Times,* October 27, 1978, D.C. It is not open to an authority to claim that they have no duty under, for example, s.65 or s.68, on the ground that they have not yet given notice under s.64. To hold otherwise would, of course, permit an authority to rely upon their own wrong, *i.e.* failure to provide notice "on completion" of enquiries.

However, if an applicant seeks to rely upon a failure to give reasons, because he wishes to allege that he has become a secure tenant in accommodation provided under Pt. III, which is not secure until one year has elapsed from when the notice is given (see notes to s.63, above), the burden will lie on the applicant to show when the notice *ought* to have been given: *Family Housing Association* v. *Miah* (1982) 5 H.L.R. 94, C.A.

Notification, and reasons, must be given in writing, and if not received by the applicant will only be treated as having been given in writing if they were made available at the authority's office for a reasonable time for collection by him or on his behalf: subs. (5). This appears to be so even if a copy of the notice is sent by registered post, or to one of the authority's own hostels, or other property. The express requirement for writing was added pursuant to Law Commission Recommendations (Cmnd. 9515), No. 5.

Reasons

Reasons should be "sufficient and straightforward" (*Code of Guidance*). It has been suggested that the purpose of the requirement to give reasons is to enable the recipient to see whether they might be challengeable in law: *Thornton* v. *Kirklees Metropolitan Borough Council* [1979] Q.B. 626, C.A. (This appears to be a judicial summary of counsel's submission, rather than a judicial observation in its own right). However, it has been held that authorities are entitled to give their reasons quite simply: "their decision and their reasons are not to be analysed in minute detail. They are not to be gone through as it were with a toothcomb. They are not to be criticised by saying: 'They have not mentioned this or that' ": *Tickner* v. *Mole Valley D.C.* [1980] 2 April, C.A. Transcript.

However, in *City of Gloucester* v. *Miles* (1985) 17 H.L.R 292, C.A., the Court of Appeal considered that in order to comply with the requirement to state reasons, the notification of intentional homelessness ought to have stated: (a) that the authority are satisfied that the applicant for accommodation became homeless intentionally; (b) when he or she is considered to have become homeless; (c) why he or she is said to have become homeless at that time, *i.e.* what is the deliberate act or omission in consequence of which it is concluded that at that time he or she ceased to occupy accommodation which was available for his or her occupation; and, (d) that it would have been reasonable for him or her to continue to occupy it.

There is no reason why decisions under other provisions requiring reasons should not also apply, to the extent that an authority should deal with the substantive issues raised, by applicant or, perhaps, by an applicant's adviser: cf, *e.g., Re Poyser & Mills Arbitration* [1964] 2 Q.B. 467, *Givaudan* v. *Minister of Housing and Local Government* [1967] 1 W.L.R. 250, *Mountview Court Properties Ltd.* v. *Devlin* (1970) 21 P. & C.R. 689. In *Kelly* v. *Monklands District Council*, July 12, 1985, Ct. of Session (O.H.), however, a mere recital of the words of the Act was held sufficient on this point.

Further, the courts have not always held authorities to the words of their reasons when decisions are challenged. The wording of the decision in *de Falco, Silvestri* v. *Crawley Borough Council* [1980] Q.B. 460, C.A., was, so far as relevant, that "the council is of the opinion that you became homeless intentionally because you came to this country without having ensured that you had permanent accommodation to come to." This was clearly, and has since been expressly held to be, wrong: see notes to s.60, above. It was only upheld because the court was willing to go behind the wording used by the authority, and find that the applicants had left accommodation (in Italy) before coming to this country.

In *R.* v. *London Borough of Hillingdon, ex parte Islam* [1983] 1 A.C. 688, at the Court of Appeal, the court was similarly willing to disregard the express words used by the authority, and consider whether *in substance* there had been what could properly be called intentional homelessness. In *R.* v. *Cardiff City Council, ex parte John* (1982) 9 H.L.R. 56, Q.B.D., the court held that the fact that the decision letter may not itself disclose the proper reasons for the decision does not prevent the authority from relying on proper reasons and accordingly justifying their decision. In *R.* v. *City of Westminster, ex parte Chambers* (1982) 6 H.L.R. 15, Q.B.D., the decision that the applicants had become homeless intentionally could not be sustained (see notes to ss.60, 62, above), but no relief followed as the court held that the authority had discharged their duties to the applicants by an earlier offer.

Decisions

The authority must reach their own decision. Even although other authorities must co-operate if they request assistance (s.72), one authority cannot simply "rubber-stamp" the decision of another: *R.* v. *South Herefordshire District Council, ex parte Miles* (1983) 17 H.L.R. 82, Q.B.D. There may, for example, be information as to what has occurred between the two applications, for example a separation which means that intervening accommodation was "settled" for the purposes of the separated parts of a family: see notes to s.60, above.

A decision reached without proper enquiries will be invalid. For example, a decision reached pursuant to a policy to treat all those evicted for arrears will be void as a failure to exercise properly the duty to reach an individual decision: *Williams* v. *Cynon Valley Council,* January 1980 L.A.G. Bulletin 16, C.C. Nor can the authority treat as homeless intentionally all those who have been evicted from premises on grounds which reflect tenant default, for example nuisance and annoyance: *Devenport* v. *Salford City Council* (1983) 8 H.L.R. 54, C.A.; *R.* v. *Cardiff City Council, ex parte John* (1982) 9 H.L.R. 56, Q.B.D. An eviction will be relevant material for the authority to take into account, but they must look at the circumstances giving rise to the order: *ibid.*

An authority must bear in mind that possession orders are within the discretion of the county court judge, who may have taken into account matters for which the applicant has no responsibility. Thus in *Stubbs* v. *Slough Borough Council,* January 1980 L.A.G. Bulletin, C.C., a court ordered the authority to reconsider its decision on intentionality because one element in the decision to order possession on the ground of nuisance was the proximity of landlord and tenant, and their relationship, over which the tenant had no control.

If the enquiries suggest that the applicant may have become homeless intentionally, but any doubt or uncertainty remains, then the issue is to be resolved in favour of the applicant: *R.* v. *North Devon District Council, ex parte Lewis* [1981] 1 W.L.R. 328, Q.B.D.; see also *R.* v. *Thurrock Borough Council, ex parte Williams* (1982) 1 H.L.R. 71, Q.B.D. The same point is also made in the *Code of Guidance*. The authority are entitled to take the demeanour of an applicant into account when determining whether or not to believe him, but on application for judicial review the court is entitled to look at the factual basis for the authority's conclusion on this point, as relevant to the discretionary nature of relief: *R.* v. *Surrey Heath Borough Council, ex parte Li* (1984) 16 H.L.R. 79, Q.B.D. The fact that there are inconsistencies will very frequently occur, and as such is not a basis for finding dishonesty, when there are difficulties in communication, for example when the native language is not English: *ibid.*

Although the obligation to reach a decision is not spelled out in Part III, it is implicit: *R.* v. *London Borough of Ealing, ex parte Sidhu* (1982) 2 H.L.R. 45, Q.B.D. An authority may not defer the obligation in the hope or expectation of a change in circumstances such as might reduce their duties, for example by loss of priority need (*ibid.*), although it may be that in an appropriate case, a "de minimis" deferral, of perhaps just a few days, may be permissible where there is solid reason for the authority to anticipate a material change.

Otherwise, once the authority have completed their enquiries, they must make their decision. At first sight this might seem to impose a tight obligation on authorities. However, (a) it is consistent with some of the provisions of Part III, for example pregnancy, and some classes of vulnerability, where circumstances will change but it would be unthinkable for authorities to be permitted to delay until they had done so; and (b) at the time the 1977 Act was passed, local authority tenants had no security, so that in an appropriate case the authority could subsequently evict. Some measure of this liberty has been retained by the exclusion from security referred to above: notes to s.63.

The decision must be taken on the basis of the information known to the authority at the time it is made. Thus, an applicant could not complain of a decision which failed to take into account a matter which only came to the knowledge of the authority after they had made their decision: *R.* v. *Hillingdon Homeless Persons Panel, ex parte Islam, The Times,* February 24, 1981, Q.B.D. (This issue did not form part of the subsequent appeals—[1983] 1 A.C. 688, C.A. and H.L. 1 H.L.R. 107, H.L.) The proper course in such circumstances would appear to be to put the further information before the authority in order for them to re-open their enquiries, and to consider review of a refusal to do so: see note on *R.* v. *Hambleton District Council, ex parte Geoghan* [1985] J.P.L. 394, Q.B.D., in the notes to s.62, above.

But an authority also *must* take into account all that is relevant up to the date of their decision. It is clear that it is the date of the decision, not the date of application, because the applicant is under a positive duty to inform the authority of material changes which occur before notification, under criminal sanction for failure to do so (s.74(2)). The decisions in *Devenport* v. *Salford City Council* (1983) 8 H.L.R. 54, C.A., and in *R.* v. *Cardiff City*

Council, ex parte John (1982) 9 H.L.R. 56, Q.B.D., that while a possession order is relevant no finding of intentionality can automatically follow (see notes to s.62, above), similarly support the proposition that all circumstances up until decision must be taken into account.

Challenge

Challenging an adverse decision by a local authority under Pt. III is not a straightforward matter. It is not simply a question of knowing what rights and duties are set out in Pt. III, or of knowing what the *Code of Guidance* suggests is appropriate in a particular case. Where Pt. III imposes a duty on an authority, the duty arises *only* when the authority have "reason to believe," are "of the opinion," or are "satisfied" that a certain state of affairs exists: see ss.65–67, 70. A homeless person's rights arise and can be enforced only when the authority's satisfaction, belief or opinion can be established. At first glance, one might think that this assessment of the *subjective* qualities of the rights and duties would mean that an authority's decision cannot be challenged at all: "The section is framed in a 'subjective' form . . . This form of section is quite well-known and at first sight might seem to exclude judicial review . . . " per Lord Wilberforce, *Secretary of State for Education and Science* v. *Metropolitan Borough of Tameside* [1977] A.C. 1014, at H.L. 1047.

Reliance must, rather, be placed on what are sometimes known as "the principles of administrative law." It is sometimes said that this expression should not be used: but it is current usage, see *e.g.* per Lord Wilberforce, *R.* v. *Greater London Council, ex parte Bromley London Borough Council* [1983] 1 A.C. 768, H.L. At the heart of these principles is the proposition that Parliament intends that bodies such as local authorities should always act "reasonably." That is *not* to say that they would always arrive at "the" reasonable decision: one person's view of what is reasonable will often quite properly differ from that of another. And if Parliament has entrusted a decision to a local authority, it is that authority's view of what is reasonable which must prevail, rather than that of a court: *Associated Provincial Picture Houses Ltd.* v. *Wednesbury Corporation* [1948] 1 K.B. 223, C.A.

What the principle *does* involve is that authorities should always approach their decisions in a reasonable and lawful manner. If, then, it can be shown that a public body such as a local authority have improperly approached their decision, the decision will be void and the courts will not give effect to it. A decision improperly reached is "ultra vires," *i.e.* outside the (authority's) powers: de Smith, *Judicial Review of Administrative Action* (4th ed.), at pp. 151 *et seq.*; but consider *Ridge* v. *Baldwin* [1964] A.C. 40, H.L.

Where a decision is ultra vires the court can adopt one of two courses of action. First, it may quash the decision and compel the authority to approach it afresh. Second, although the court will not usually substitute its own decision for that of the authority, the findings of fact or law made by the court may on occasion be such that there is only one decision that the authority can properly make, *i.e.* with which they are left. In such cases either directly or indirectly, the court will (in effect) order the authority to come to that decision. In all of these cases, however, it is important to bear in mind that the court does not act as an appeal tribunal from the authority's decision; instead, it is undertaking an investigation into the way in which the decision has been reached: *Wednesbury*.

The "principles of administrative law" may be expressed, and classified, in a number of different ways. See, generally de Smith, *Judicial Review of Administrative Action*. In practice, they tend to overlap with each other. Most of them fall within one or more of the following headings:

(i) A statutory authority must take into account all the relevant factors before making their decision, and must disregard the irrelevant: *Wednesbury*. See also *Bristol District Council* v. *Clark* [1975] 1 W.L.R. 1443, C.A. For illustrations of this under Part III, see, *e.g.*, *Parr* v. *Wyre Borough Council* (1982) 2 H.L.R. 71, C.A., *R.* v. *London Borough of Hammersmith and Fulham, ex parte Duro-Rama* (1983) 9 H.L.R. 71, Q.B.D., *R.* v. *Eastleigh Borough Council, ex parte Beattie (No. 1)* (1983) 10 H.L.R. 134, Q.B.D., *R.* v. *Portsmouth City Council, ex parte Knight* (1983) 10 H.L.R. 115, Q.B.D., *R.* v. *Ryedale District Council, ex parte Smith* (1983) 16 H.L.R. 66, Q.B.D., *R.* v. *Surrey Heath Borough Council, ex parte Li* (1984) 16 H.L.R. 79, Q.B.D., *R.* v. *South Hertfordshire District Council, ex parte Miles* (1983) 17 H.L.R. 82, Q.B.D., *R.* v. *Bath City Council, ex parte Sangermano* (1984) 17 H.L.R. 94, Q.B.D., *R.* v. *Reigate and Banstead Borough Council, ex parte Paris* (1984) 17 H.L.R. 103, Q.B.D., and *R.* v. *Preseli District Council, ex parte Fisher* (1984) 17 H.L.R. 147, Q.B.D.

(ii) The decision must be based on the facts; a decision totally at variance with the facts or for which there is no factual basis cannot be sustained:

"If a judgment requires, before it can be made, the existence of some facts, then although the evaluation of those facts is for the Secretary of State alone, the courts must enquire whether those facts exist, and have been taken into account, whether the judgment has been made on a proper self-direction as to those facts, whether the judgment has not been made on other facts which ought not to have been taken into account . . . "

(*Per* Lord Wilberforce, *Secretary of State for Education and Science* v. *Metropolitan Borough of Tameside* [1977] A.C. 1014, H.L., at p. 1047), cited in *R.* v. *Bristol City Council, Ex parte Browne* [1979] 1 W.L.R. 1437, D.C. (see notes to ss.65, 67, below). The same substantive point—that there must be a factual basis for a decision or an element of a decision—will be found also in *R.* v. *Surrey Heath Borough Council, ex parte Li* (1984) 16 H.L.R. 79, Q.B.D., and *R.* v. *Eastleigh Borough Council, ex parte Beattie, (No.* 2) (1984) 17 H.L.R. 168, Q.B.D.

(iii)The authority must not act in bad faith or dishonestly: *Wednesbury.*

(iv) The authority must direct themselves properly in law, so that a decision based on a misunderstanding or misapplication of the law will not have been reached properly: *ibid.* See also, *e.g., In Re Islam* [1983] 1 A.C. 688, 1 H.L.R. 107, H.L., *R.* v. *Hillingdon London Borough Council, ex parte Streeting* [1980] 1 W.L.R. 1425, C.A., and *R.* v. *Slough Borough Council, ex parte London Borough of Ealing* [1981] Q.B. 801, C.A., *R.* v. *North Devon District Council, ex parte Lewis* [1981] 1 W.L.R. 328, Q.B.D., *R.* v. *Waveney District Council, ex parte Bowers* (1982) 4 H.L.R. 118, C.A., *Re Betts* [1983] 2 A.C. 613, 10 H.L.R. 97, H.L., for illustrations of homeless persons' cases turning on a legal interpretation of the provisions themselves.

(v) The authority must act so as to promote, and not to defeat, the objects or policy of the Act in question: *Padfield* v. *Minister of Agriculture, Fisheries & Food* [1968] A.C. 997, H.L.; see also *Meade* v. *Haringey London Borough Council* [1979] 1 W.L.R. 1, C.A.

(vi) The decision must not be one to which no reasonable authority could have come: this is conclusive evidence that the decision is improper: *Wednesbury.* The phrase "no reasonable authority" has occurred in a number of homeless persons' cases: *e.g., Slough, R.* v. *Westminster City Council, ex parte Ali* (1983) 9 H.L.R. 83, Q.B.D., *Sangermano and R.* v. *Penwith District Council, ex parte Trevena* (1984) 17 H.L.R. 526, Q.B.D.

(vii) The authority reach their own decision on each individual case; they must not fetter their discretion by approaching a decision with a predetermined policy as to how they will deal with any case falling within a particular class: de Smith, pp. 311 *et seq; R.* v. *Glamorganshire JJ.* (1850) 10 L.J.M.C. 172; see also *Sampson* v. *Supplementary Benefits Commission* [1979] J.S.W.L. 316, Q.B.D.. The leading case on this is now probably *British Oxygen Co. Ltd.* v. *Minister of Technology* [1971] A.C. 610, H.L. While a public authority can adopt a policy or limiting rule in order to guide the future exercise of their discretion if they think good administration requires it, they must consider its application individually in every case where it is sought to make an exception. *British Oxygen* was adopted and applied by the House of Lords in *In Re Betts.* Even the "guideline" approach was disapproved by Templeman L.J. in *Att.-Gen., ex rel. Tilley* v. *Wandsworth London Borough Council* [1981] 1 W.L.R.854, C.A., but the other two judges expressly reserved their positions on this and, of course, *British Oxygen* is the superior authority.

(viii) It is the authority who are entrusted with the decision-making power and must make the decision. They cannot avoid their duties by adopting the decision of another body: *Sampson.* See also *R.* v. *South Herefordshire District Council, ex parte Miles* (1983) 17 H.L.R. 82, Q.B.D. Moreover, as the full authority are prima facie entrusted with the decision-making power, the full authority must reach the decision unless they have, as they are empowered to do under Local Government Act 1972, s.101 delegated this power to a sub-committee or to an officer. Where a body or official without the power purports to reach a decision, then that decision is void and the authority are in the position of having reached no decision at all: de Smith, at pp.303 *et seq.*

(ix) In all cases, an authority must act fairly, or in accordance with natural justice: *Re HK* [1967] 2 Q.B. 617, C.A.; see also *Sevenoaks District Council* v. *Emmott* 30 November 1979, C.A., TR. The extent of this duty will depend upon circumstances, and the nature of the decision. See also *R.* v. *Hillingdon Homeless Persons Panel, ex parte Islam, The Times,* February 24, 1981, Q.B.D. (not appealed on this point—see [1983] 1 A.C. 688, C.A. and H.L., 1 H.L.R. 107, H.L.).

These propositions or principles are all, by and large, variations upon a theme. In *R.* v. *Greater London Council, ex parte Bromley London Borough Council* [1983] 1 A.C. 768, H.L., the propositions before the House of Lords were described as different ways of saying the same thing. Lack of natural justice or administrative fairness will usually mean that a public body have also failed to take something relevant into account, *i.e.* the views of the person affected, and what they might have told the authority. Similarly, the policy of an Act is a relevant consideration, and so also are the correct meaning of the law, and the correct facts. Bad faith or dishonesty would indicate consideration of irrelevant matters. Improper delegation, and the application of policy where an individual decision is required, both amount to a failure to consider the question (in the particular case) *at all*, which necessarily means that there has been a failure to take all that is relevant into account.

Whenever the decision of a public body is challenged on these principles, the burden of proof lies upon the person seeking to show that the decision is void: *Cannock Chase District Council* v. *Kelly* [1978] 1 W.L.R. 1, C.A. The allegations must be both substantiated, and particularised: *ibid.* For example, it is never enough to say simply that the applicant is a homeless person and in priority need, because this would not be enough to raise the inference of a duty: the duty arises only when the *authority are satisfied,* or have reason to believe etc., that the fact or state of affairs is as it is claimed to be. It must be alleged that they have refused or failed to reach a decision, or that such decision as has been reached must be treated by the courts as void, for want of compliance with specified principles of administrative law, and the factual basis for this allegation must be set out.

The traditional forum for challenging a local authority's decision is the Divisional Court of the Q.B.D., on application for judicial review (Rules of the Supreme Court—R.S.C.— Ord. 53). See also Supreme Court Act 1981, s.31. Leave should be sought without delay: see *R.* v. *Rochester City Council, ex parte Trotman, The Times,* May 9, 1983. However, delay in obtaining legal aid *may* constitute an acceptable reason for granting leave belatedly: *R.* v. *Stratford-on-Avon District Council, ex parte Jackson* [1985] 3 All E.R. 769, C.A. The fact that leave is granted to pursue an application is not final as to the question of whether an extension of time should be granted. That will be decided on the final hearing, when the respondent may still raise the issue of delay: *R.* v. *General Commissioners for Income Tax, ex parte Worth, The Times,* May 23, 1985, Q.B.D.

In the course of correspondence, an applicant or his adviser should always seek the information to which anyone who has applied for housing is entitled, under s.106(5), below, which consists of the "details of the particulars which he has given to the authority about himself and his family and which the authority has recorded as being relevant to his application for accommodation." This is not the same as "all" the information recorded, although some authorities will not try to conceal other information when answering a s.106 request, not least because discovery will be available once proceedings issue.

Proceedings *have* to be by way of judicial review, if the authority's basic decision is being challenged. This is because it will be necessary to apply the principles of administrative law described above in order to establish that the authority's decision is invalid. One cannot challenge by way of ordinary proceedings, whether in the county court or in the High Court, the authority's "state of mind," *i.e.* whether they are properly "satisfied," "of the opinion" etc: *Cocks* v. *Thanet District Council* [1983] A.C. 286, 6 H.L.R. 15, H.L.

If, however, the applicant is content with the nature of the decision, and wishes only to challenge the manner of their discharge, or if the authority simply decline to carry out their duty, then action may proceed for "breach of statutory duty": *Thornton* v. *Kirklees Metropolitan Borough Council* [1979] Q.B. 626, C.A. Action for breach of statutory duty was expressly approved in *Cocks*, subject to completion of the pre-conditional public law decisions. For example, it may be that an offer of accommodation is considered by the applicant so unsuitable that the authority has not discharged its duty under s.65(4): see *R.* v. *Wyre Borough Council, ex parte Parr* (1982) 2 H.L.R. 71, C.A.; see further notes to s.65, below.

Dicta in *R.* v. *London Borough of Hillingdon, ex parte Puhlhofer* (1985) 17 H.L.R. 588, C.A. describes the *Parr* decision in terms suggesting that the test would remain one of application of principles of administrative law; it is, however, submitted (a) that the remarks are obiter, because that question was not before the court, and (b) that they are descriptive of how the matter was being approached in *Parr*. Note also that a decision of the House of Lords is awaited in the *Puhlhofer* case.

In a case where it is only the manner of discharge that is in issue, it seems possible to bring proceedings for breach of statutory duty, in the county court, or in the High Court. Proceedings may only be brought in the county court, if a claim for damages can properly be added, and that claim is for damages within the county court jurisdiction for the time being (currently, £5,000). The county court's jurisdiction over property within its rateable value for the time being (under County Courts Act 1984, s.22), will not apply, because the court cannot order the authority to provide a *particular* unit of accommodation.

Breach of statutory duty is a tort: see, *e.g.* Salmond on the Law of Torts, Chapter 10; Clerk & Lindsell on Torts, Chapter 21. The general rule in tort is that damages are not usually awarded for minor inconvenience and discomfort, for example for mere personal suffering: *Constantine* v. *Imperial Hotels* [1944] K.B. 693; *Behrens* v. *Bertram Mills Circus* [1957] 2 Q.B. 1, although exceptions have been made in the case of certain, specified torts, not yet including breach of statutory duty. Damages for shock, physical inconvenience, mental harm or serious suffering, will be recoverable, and, of course, the applicant will be entitled to special damages, such as additional costs of eating out, or staying in more expensive accommodation.

The fact that such additional cost cannot easily be quantified—because it will usually be impossible to state exactly what local authority rent would have been payable had accommodation been provided—will not prevent an award of general damages as an estimate of what has been lost. If, however, no claim for damages can be made, then relief must be sought in the High Court.

Relief

The main relief sought will be housing. Two issues arise: interlocutory relief, and final orders.

(i) Interlocutory Relief. Interlocutory relief is available in the county court, or the High Court, in proceedings for breach of statutory duty. It is also available in the course of proceedings for judicial review (R.S.C. Ord. 53, r1). The normal position is that an interlocutory order will be granted if it can be shown that the balance of convenience is in favour of the order: *American Cyanamid* v. *Ethicon* [1975] A.C. 396, H.L., *Fellowes* v. *Fisher* [1976] Q.B. 122, C.A. In *de Falco, Silvestri* v. *Crawley Borough Council* [1980] Q.B. 460, C.A., however, Lord Denning M.R. held that in homeless persons' actions it was necessary to show that there was a strong prima facie case of breach by the authority. The justification for adopting a different approach was that, almost invariably, the applicant would be unable to give a worthwhile undertaking in damages should he eventually lose.

It must be said that the House of Lords in *Cyanamid* had included the ability of the applicant for interlocutory relief to give a meaningful undertaking in damages as just *one* of the factors to be weighed up in determining the balance of convenience. Furthermore, the *de Falco* approach would seem to conflict with Lord Denning's approach in *Allen v Jambo Holdings Ltd.* [1980] 1 W.L.R. 1252, C.A., a case in which the owners of an aircraft which was the subject of a *Mareva* injunction preventing its removal from the jurisdiction, at the instigation of a woman making a claim for the death of her husband, sought discharge of the order on the grounds that the woman, who was legally aided, could not give a valuable cross undertaking in damages. Lord Denning commented:

> "It is said that whenever a *Mareva* injunction is granted the plaintiff has to give the cross-undertaking in damages. Suppose the widow should lose this case altogether. She is legally aided. Her undertaking is worth nothing. I would not assent to that argument . . . A legally aided plaintiff is by our statutes not to be in any worse position by reason of being legally aided than any other plaintiff would be. I do not see why a poor plaintiff should be denied a *Mareva* injunction just because he is poor, whereas a rich plaintiff would get it . . ."

The other reason why Lord Denning's dictum in *de Falco* may not withstand close scrutiny is because it is unlikely that the authority will suffer any loss at all: either Housing Benefit under the Social Security and Housing Benefits Act 1982, and the Housing Benefits Regulation 1985 (S.I. 1985 No. 677) thereunder, or Supplementary Benefit (depending on the nature of the provision) will meet the authority's costs; it seems unlikely that damages for the loss incurred in providing housing temporarily to the applicant, as distinct from provision for someone else, was in mind, especially since most such accommodation would in any event be in Bed and Breakfast or a similar such establishment.

Interlocutory relief is discretionary, although the discretion is one that must be exercised in accordance with principles of law, not whimsically. In a clear case of breach there is likely to be no issue on whether or not such relief should be granted. In *de Falco*, however, in which an additional claim was made on the grounds that insufficient time under s.65(3) had been granted, it was held that as sufficient time had since elapsed, *i.e.* between notification and trial of the application for the injunction, no further time should be ordered.

The court will not expect that the evidence presented in the course of an interlocutory hearing will be as full as at trial and, in particular, it will not expect a local authority, presenting an affidavit in reply, to cross every t and dot every i, as it was put in *Tickner* v. *Mole Valley District Council*, August 1980, L.A.G. Bulletin 187, C.A. A reasonable summary will suffice.

(ii) Final Relief. There remains the question of final relief. It has already been noted that where the facts and circumstances are such that an authority can reach only one decision— one favourable to the applicant—the court has power to grant an order requiring the authority to provide accommodation, *i.e.* permanently or indefinitely. (See also *Barty-King* v. *Ministry of Defence* [1979] 2 All E.R. 80, Ch. D.). In other cases, the court will only quash the existing decision of the authority, because although this decision has been shown

to have been reached wrongfully, there is an alternative decision yet available to the authority, which *may* be adverse to the applicant. However, the structure of Part III is such that once a decision to refuse to house is quashed, the authority are, as it were, "back" under a duty to house, even if not permanently, *i.e.* back under a s.63 duty.

A court will not grant relief if the only purpose is because it *may* be of some vague or unidentified future benefit to the applicant: *R.* v. *Vale of White Horse District Council, ex parte Smith and Hay* (1984) 17 H.L.R. 160, Q.B.D., but the same principles will govern the grant of relief where the only purpose is in order to establish a breach of statutory duty upon which action may then issue in another court, as when housing itself is in issue: *R.* v. *South Herefordshire District Council, ex parte Miles* (1983) 17 H.L.R. 82, Q.B.D.

In the following homeless persons' cases already referred to in these notes, orders have been made—whether by declaration or mandamus—which have had the effect of placing the authority under a permanent duty within s.65(2), *i.e.* which have left the authority without any choice as to their final decision: *Re Islam, Krishnan* v. *London Borough of Hillingdon, Streeting, Slough, R.* v. *Beverley Borough Council, ex parte McPhee, R.* v. *Waveney District Council, ex parte Bowers, R.* v. *Thurrock Borough Council, ex parte Williams, R.* v. *Wyre Borough Council, ex parte Parr, R.* v. *Eastleigh Borough Council, ex parte Beattie (No.2),* and *R.* v. *West Dorset District Council, ex parte Phillips.* In *R.* v. *London Borough of Hammersmith and Fulham, ex parte Duro-Rama, R.* v. *Eastleigh Borough Council, ex parte Beattie (No.1) R.* v. *Portsmouth City Council, ex parte Knight, R.* v. *London Borough of Wandsworth, ex parte Rose, R.* v. *Wyre B.C., ex parte Joyce, R.* v. *Westminster City Council, ex parte Ali, R.* v. *London Borough of Hillingdon, ex parte Wilson, R.* v. *Mole Valley District Council, ex parte Minnett,* and *R.* v. *Exeter City Council, ex parte Gliddon,* certiorari has issued to quash the decision, but leaving the authority with a clear option as to its further decision.

Duties to persons found to be homeless

65.—(1) This section has effect as regards the duties owed by the local housing authority to an applicant where they are satisfied that he is homeless.

(2) Where they are satisfied that he has a priority need and are not satisfied that he became homeless intentionally, they shall, unless they notify another local housing authority in accordance with section 67 (referral of application on grounds of local connection), secure that accommodation becomes available for his occupation.

(3) Where they are satisfied that he has a priority need but are also satisfied that he became homeless intentionally, they shall—

(*a*) secure that accommodation is made available for his occupation for such period as they consider will give him a reasonable opportunity of securing accommodation for his occupation, and

(*b*) furnish him with advice and such assistance as they consider appropriate in the circumstances in any attempts he may make to secure that accommodation becomes available for his occupation.

(4) Where they are not satisfied that he has a priority need, they shall furnish him with advice and such assistance as they consider appropriate in the circumstances in any attempts he may make to secure that accommodation becomes available for his occupation.

DEFINITIONS
"applicant": s.62.
"available for his occupation": s.75.
"homeless": s.58.
"intentionally": s.60.
"local connection": s.61.
"local housing authority": ss.1, 2.
"priority need": s.59.

GENERAL NOTE
This section contains the principal duties towards the homeless under Part III. To the homeless in priority need who did not become homeless intentionally, a "full" housing duty is owed, under subs. (2). To the homeless in priority need who have been considered

homeless intentionally, a temporary housing duty is owed, for such period as the authority consider will give the applicant a reasonable opportunity to secure his own accommodation, and a duty is owed to provide advice and such assistance as the authority consider appropriate in his attempts to do so: subs. (3). To the homeless not in priority need, no more is owed than the advice and appropriate assistance duty: subs. (4).

This section is not concerned with those threatened with homelessness: see s.66, below. The full housing duty is subject to the local connection provisions of ss.67, 68, although the other duties are not. S.69 governs how the duties may be discharged, and s.70 imposes related obligations to protect the applicant's property. The duties are all within s.72, entitling the authority to seek the co-operation of another authority or a registered housing association in their discharge.

Subs. (2)

The obligation is to secure that accommodation becomes available for the applicant's occupation, which of definition means for him and any person with whom he is reasonably to be expected to reside: s.75. Accommodation may be secured by making available the authority's own accommodation, by securing that the applicant obtains accommodation from some other person, or by giving such advice and assistance that secures that accommodation is obtained from some other person: s.69 (1). Reasonable charges may be made for accommodation, or a contribution sought towards payments the authority make to another: s.69(2).

In the overwhelming majority of cases, authorities will be bound to find accommodation themselves. There is no right to be given a permanent home immediately: the authority take an indefinite responsibility, but it is clear that they must do no more than, as it were "the best they can" in the circumstances, *provided that which is offered or arranged qualifies as accommodation,* even although this may involve a series of temporary units before a permanent home is found: *R.* v. *Bristol City Council, ex parte Hendy* [1974] 1 W.L.R. 498, C.A.; see also *R.* v. *East Hertfordshire District Council, ex parte, Hunt* (1985) 18 H.L.R., Q.B.D., describing "discharge in stages".

Advice and assistance such that the applicant secures accommodation from another under s.69 seems wide enough to cover advice and assistance leading to house *purchase* by an applicant who is financially able to undertake such a step: *Code of Guidance.* Some other person, in the context of s.69, may be a person—or authority—abroad. In *R.* v. *Bristol City Council, ex parte Browne* [1979] 1 W.L.R. 1437, D.C., a woman with no local connection with Bristol, and no local connection with the area of any other housing authority in England, Wales or Scotland, was offered assistance to return to her home town of Tralee, Eire, where the authorities were prepared to ensure that she was housed.

It may be noted that in order to sustain this decision, Bristol did not need to know the exact details of the accommodation which was to be made available to her. The arrangement was, however, only appropriate once it was established by Bristol that, in their opinion, the woman ran no risk of domestic violence in Tralee: it would seem from the report that had there been a risk of domestic violence, the arrangement would not have been acceptable, for otherwise Bristol would have managed to circumvent the local connection provisions: see s.67, below.

In *Wyness* v. *Poole Borough Council*, July 1979 L.A.G. Bulletin 166, C.C., a county court rejected a similar attempt to house an applicant in the area of another authority, when the local connection provisions were inapplicable because of an employment connection, as housing in the area of the other authority would have meant that the employment would have to be given up: the court held that no reasonable authority could thus discharge the duty.

In *Parr* v. *Wyre Borough Council* (1982) 2 H.L.R. 71, C.A., an authority sought to discharge their duty by securing an offer of accommodation in Birmingham, an area with which the applicants had no connection at all. There were no details available of the accommodation to be provided, and the applicants had a limited time in which to accept. While it was common ground that discharge could be in another area, the Court of Appeal did not uphold this offer. The Court distinguished *Browne*. They held that the offer had to be of "appropriate accommodation." The house had to be appropriate for the size of the family, and in an appropriate area, and the applicant had to enjoy a reasonable opportunity to consider the offer.

In *R.* v. *Ryedale District Council, ex parte Smith* (1983) 16 H.L.R. 66, Q.B.D., accommodation was offered, apparently initially pending a decision, under s.63, above, consisting of a caravan on a site, served only by a toilet and outside tap some distance away. Although because of flawed enquiries the authority were not aware of all the details, the male applicant was 67 years of age, and according to his doctor suffered from acute exacerbation of bronchitis developing into pneumonia, chronic fibrosis of the lungs and emphysema.

The court held that the accommodation to be provided must be suitable or appropriate accommodation, the suitability of which is to be judged by reference to the outcome of enquiries, which enquiries must cover all the questions raised in s.59 (priority need), to which the state of health of the male applicant was a relevant consideration. It was by no means self-evident that the caravan was suitable for the male applicant, or that the authority would so have thought had his condition been known to them.

There has been no other court decision on "discharge" of the full duty, although in practice complaints of prejudicial treatment by authorities reluctant to recognise their obligations under Part III have been frequent. Thus, some authorities place the homeless in distinctly inferior accommodation. Undeniably, it will be *difficult* to show that accommodation offered is inadequate, but in appropriate circumstances it is clear that there is no reason why there should not be a challenge which, it is submitted, for the reasons considered in the notes to s.64, above, may be decided by a court as a question of fact, as distinct from exercising its limited "judicial review" role. Such a challenge may therefore be mounted by way of proceedings for breach of statutory duty, not only by judicial review: see notes to s.64.

Permanent accommodation should be secured as soon as possible: homeless people should not be obliged to spend a certain period in interim accommodation as a matter of policy: *Code.* Normally, self-contained accommodation will be appropriate, but occasionally more supportive or communal forms of accommodation are required, and authorities will wish to have regard in this respect to the personal circumstances and wishes of the people concerned: *Code.*

Subs. (3)

This class of applicant is the homeless intentionally, in priority need. The principal duty with which it will be concerned is that contained in sub-para. (*a*), *i.e.* the duty imposed on the authority, to secure that accommodation is made available for the applicant's occupation—which means (s.75) for the occupation of the applicant and of any person who might reasonably be expected to reside with her/him—"for such period as they consider will give him a reasonable opportunity of himself securing accommodation for his occupation."

This duty has given rise to a number of problems. The first question is: from when does the time run? In *Dyson* v. *Kerrier District Council* [1980] 1 W.L.R. 120, C.A., the applicant was told on May 21 that she would be provided with one month's accommodation from May 25 (the date when her homelessness would actually occur). This decision appears to have been taken by an official, and appears to have required ratification by a committee. In the event, the time was subsequently extended, to July 6, but it was not until July 3 that the committee's ratification was communicated to the applicant. It was held that time could run from the earlier notification, by the official, as the letter of July 3 was merely confirmation of that decision.

In *de Falco, Silvestri* v. *Crawley Borough Council* [1980] Q.B. 460, C.A., only four days had been allowed between notification of decision, and the expiry of what is now s.65(3)(*a*) accommodation. The Master of the Rolls thought that this period was probably adequate, having regard to the several weeks in accommodation provided by the authority, prior to their decision. However, he was also influenced by the time during which the applicants had been accommodated between the issue of proceedings and the hearing before the Court of Appeal. As *de Falco* was the hearing of an interlocutory appeal, for an interlocutory injunction to house until trial, that matter was conclusive on the exercise of judicial discretion.

The same point influenced Bridge L.J., although he was of the view that time prior to communication of the local authority's decision was wholly irrelevant, and that only time since that decision was communicated could be of relevance. As the purpose of the provisions was to give the applicant time to find somewhere else to live once it has been decided that the authority need not provide permanent assistance, this view seems preferable. Sir David Cairns thought that the decision was unreviewable.

The courts may, however, be less generous towards an applicant who lives with another person who has previously been found homeless intentionally, and already enjoyed a period of s.65(3)(*a*) accommodation, although it seems to be an irresistible inference from *R.* v. *North Devon District Council, ex parte Lewis* [1981] 1 W.L.R. 328, Q.B.D. and the other cases on this point (see notes to ss.60, 62, above), that such a person may, indeed, re-apply, and will be entitled to a new period of s.64(3) accommodation, and, further, could and should benefit from the reasoning of Bridge L.J. in *de Falco.* Some reconciliation of merits and principle will probably be found in the extent of acquiescence or participation in the act which results in the finding of intentionality, and the extent to which such finding should, accordingly, have been anticipated.

In *Smith* v. *Bristol City Council,* January 20, 1981, C.C., a county court judge held that even where a substantial period of warning had been given to the applicant, because the finding of intentionality preceded the homelessness, itself deferred by legal challenge, the authority were still obliged to give some time:

"I cannot accept that 'no time' can in any circumstances be a reasonable period . . . I find that a reasonable time must be given to the applicant after she actually becomes homeless . . ." The case went on appeal (1981 L.A.G. Bulletin 287, C.A.) but there was no cross-appeal on this point by the authority.

A further problem is posed by "policies." In particular, the frequency with which all kinds of applicants receive identical offers of 28 days' accommodation suggests that many authorities operate some sort of policy under this provision. If an inflexible policy can be demonstrated, it can be set aside: see, *e.g. British Oxygen Co. Ltd.* v. *Board of Trade* [1971] A.C. 610, H.L., *In Re Betts* [1983] 2 A.C. 613, 10 H.L.R. 97, H.L., *Att.-Gen., ex rel. Tilley* v. *L.B. Wandsworth* [1981] 1 W.L.R. 854, C.A. However, if the 28–day rule is merely a guideline, which is reconsidered in each case, it may not be possible to set it aside as *ultra vires.*

This much is clear: an applicant's circumstances must be individually considered, and if it can be shown that time allowed has been reached without regard to his circumstances or was such a short period that no authority could have considered that it gave the applicant a reasonable opportunity to find somewhere for himself, the courts will order sufficient time: *Lally* v. *Royal Borough of Kensington and Chelsea, The Times,* March 27, 1980, Ch.D.

An authority may discharge their duties under this provision not only by providing their own accommodation, but also by arranging for it to be provided by someone else, or by giving advice such as will secure that it is provided by someone else: s.69. The accommodation will not be secure under Part IV for a period of one year from notification of decision (Sched. 1, para. 4), whether provided by the authority or by another landlord whose tenants are or may be secure. This point has been considered in the notes to s.63, above, as has the quality of temporary accommodation.

The duty to provide advice and such assistance as the authority consider appropriate is the same duty as that owed to those not in priority need: see notes to subs. (4), below. However, in the case of those within this subsection, the *Code* also specifically reminds authorities that children should not be received into care for want of accommodation alone, and that they should take all possible steps to ensure that, even though homelessness is intentional, such people are not left without shelter.

Subs. (4)

If the authority are satisfied that an applicant is homeless or threatened with homelessness, but not in priority need, their only duty is to furnish him with advice and such assistance as they consider appropriate in the circumstances in any attempts he may make to secure his own accommodation. Obviously included in this is advice on rights of accommodation, for example in the private sector. This right to advice and assistance is not a significant right, nor one either that is likely commonly to be worth enforcing. The *Code,* however, asks authorities to respond helpfully and constructively, and where resources permit, to do all they can to ensure that accommodation is secured. When the authority's findings fall into this class, they also have a duty to notify the applicant of their decision and of the reasons for it: s.64(1), (2), (4)(*b*)).

The allocation provisions of s.22, above, apply to require authorities to give a reasonable preference to, among others, those towards whom they are subject to a duty under s.65, which includes the homeless not in priority need, and it is accordingly submitted that to decline even to register an applicant, for example single applicants, applicants without children, applicants below a certain age, applicants without a period of time in the area, who have been found to be homeless, will conflict with this obligation, although the *extent* of preference, for example number of points, will remain a subject of discretion, provided it is not such that no reasonable authority could conclude that it was "reasonable preference" at all.

Duties to persons found to be threatened with homelessness

66.—(1) This section has effect as regards the duties owed by the local housing authority to an applicant where they are satisfied that he is threatened with homelessness.

(2) Where they are satisfied that he has a priority need and are not satisfied that he became threatened with homelessness intentionally, they shall take reasonable steps to secure that accommodation does not cease to be available for his occupation.

(3) Where—

(*a*) they are not satisfied that he has a priority need, or

(*b*) they are satisfied that he has a priority need but are also satisfied that he became threatened with homelessness intentionally,

they shall furnish him with advice and such assistance as they consider appropriate in the circumstances in any attempts he may make to secure that accommodation does not cease to be available for his occupation.

(4) Subsection (2) does not affect any right of the local housing authority, whether by virtue of a contract, enactment or rule of law, to secure vacant possession of accommodation.

DEFINITIONS

"applicant": s.62.
"available for his occupation": s.75.
"homeless": s.58.
"intentionally": s.60.
"local housing authority": ss.1, 2.
"priority need": s.59.
"threatened with homelessness": s.58.

GENERAL NOTE

This section applies when the applicant is only threatened with homelessness by the time of a decision, *i.e.* it is likely that he will become homeless within 28 days: see s.58(4). The principal duty is that in subs. (2), to take reasonable steps to secure that accommodation does not cease to be available for his occupation which, of definition (s.75) means for his occupation and that of any person who is reasonably to be expected to reside with him. This duty, however, is subject to subs. (4), which means that it cannot be used as a defence by a person threatened with homelessness, to an action by an authority themselves for possession of current accommodation.

This duty is accordingly usually perceived as one requiring the authority to have accommodation available once homelessness itself actually occurs, as distinct from an obligation to take steps to defend the current home. As a person is not threatened with homelessness until 28 days before it is likely that he will become homeless proper, there will not commonly be much that authorities can at this stage do to avert homelessness. The proviso in subs. (4) also militates against another interpretation of the subs. (2) duty.

When the applicant is only threatened with homelessness when a finding of intentionality is made, the authority's duty is to "furnish him with advice and such assistance as they consider appropriate in any attempts he may make to secure that accommodation does not cease to be available for his occupation" which may obviously include financial advice, or advice on the powers of the court to suspend an order. It would seem that when homelessness itself occurs, the applicant is still entitled to a period of temporary accommodation under s.65(3)(a), although the point cannot be entirely free from doubt.

The duties in this section apply even although an issue of local connection may apply: it is only s.65(2) which is subject to s.67, not subs. (2) of this section. It has been held in the county court that the local connection provisions are not applicable when the authority's duty arises because of threatened homelessness under this section. In *Williams* v. *Exeter City Council*, September 1981 L.A.G. Bulletin 211, C.C., a woman was occupying army property let to her husband, a serviceman, in the Exeter area. As such, she had no connection with Exeter on the basis of residence of choice, nor on any other ground (*cf.* notes to s.61, above). The Ministry of Defence secured an order for possession against her, and before it was executed she applied to the authority.

The authority agreed that she was threatened with homelessness but referred her case to the East Devon D.C. As Ms Williams did not wish to leave the area, she challenged the decision and it was held that the local connection provisions applied only when the duty arose under s.65(2). It is unclear from the short report, however, whether the authority could have used the local connection provisions once actual homelessness occurred, or whether what was held is that the structure of the provisions implies that if a decision is made while the applicant is still only threatened with homelessness, the local connection provisions will remain irrelevant once actual homelessness occurs.

Referral of application to another local housing authority

67.—(1) If the local housing authority—

(*a*) are satisfied that an applicant is homeless and has a priority need, and are not satisfied that he became homeless intentionally, but

(*b*) are of opinion that the conditions are satisfied for referral of his application to another local housing authority in England, Wales or Scotland,

they may notify that other authority of the fact that his application has been made and that they are of that opinion.

(2) The conditions for referral of an application to another local housing authority are—

(*a*) that neither the applicant nor any person who might reasonably be expected to reside with him has a local connection with the district of the authority to whom his application was made,

(*b*) that the applicant or a person who might reasonably be expected to reside with him has a local connection with the district of that other authority, and

(*c*) that neither the applicant nor any person who might reasonably be expected to reside with him will run the risk of domestic violence in that other district.

(3) For this purpose a person runs the risk of domestic violence—

(*a*) if he runs the risk of violence from a person with whom, but for the risk of violence, he might reasonably be expected to reside, or from a person with whom he formerly resided, or

(*b*) if he runs the risk of threats of violence from such a person which are likely to be carried out.

(4) The question whether the conditions for referral of an application are satisfied shall be determined by agreement between the notifying authority and the notified authority or, in default of agreement, in accordance with such arrangements as the Secretary of State may direct by order made by statutory instrument.

(5) An order may direct that the arrangements shall be—

(*a*) those agreed by any relevant authorities or associations of relevant authorities, or

(*b*) in default of such agreement, such arrangements as appear to the Secretary of State to be suitable, after consultation with such associations representing relevant authorities, and such other persons, as he thinks appropriate.

(6) No order shall be made unless a draft of the order has been approved by resolution of each House of Parliament.

DEFINITIONS
 "applicant": s.62.
 "homeless": s.58.
 "intentionally": s.60.
 "local connection": s.61.
 "local housing authority": ss.1, 2.

GENERAL NOTE
 The local connection provisions exempt an authority from duties under s.62(5), *i.e.* the responsibility for permanent housing. They do not affect the provision of temporary accommodation provided for a person who is homeless, and in priority need, but who the authority to which application has been made have determined is homeless intentionally: s.65(3)(a). It has been held in the county court that the local connection provisions are not applicable when the authority's duty arises because of threatened homelessness under s.66(2): *Williams* v. *Exeter City Council*, September 1981 L.A.G. Bulletin 211, C.C., see notes to s.66, above.

An authority will be entitled to rely on the local connection provisions when they are satisfied that the applicant is homeless and in priority need, not satisfied that the applicant became homeless intentionally, and are of the opinion that the conditions for referral apply. The conditions are:

(a) neither the applicant nor any person who might reasonably be expected to reside with him has a local connection with their area; *and*

(b) the applicant or a person who might reasonably be expected to reside with him does have a local connection with the area of another housing authority; *and*

(c) neither the applicant nor any person who might reasonably be expected to reside with him will run the risk of domestic violence in that other authority's area.

It is clear that all three factors must be present: there must (i) be *no* local connection with the one area; *and* (ii) be *a* local connection with the other area; *and* (iii) be *no* risk of domestic violence. The procedure does not arise if there is a local connection with the area to which application has been made, but that authority are of the opinion that the applicant has a greater or closer local connection elsewhere: *Betts* v. *Eastleigh Borough Council* [1983] 1 W.L.R. 774, 8 H.L.R 28, C.A., not overruled on this point in the House of Lords (see [1983] 2 A.C. 613, 10 H.L.R. 97, H.L.): this was one of the mischiefs the 1977 Act was intended to end.

A person runs the risk of domestic violence for these purposes if (a) she (as it normally will be) runs the risk of violence from any person with whom, but for that risk, she might reasonably be expected to reside; *or* (b) she runs the risk of violence from any person with whom she formerly resided; *or* (c) she runs the risk of *threats* of violence from any such person, which are likely to be carried out: subs. (3). Note that the risk of domestic violence may be in the *area* of the other authority, which means that authorities cannot assume that the risk has been dissolved simply because, *e.g.*, the violent partner has moved out of the house, for Parliament has at least recognised the possibility (well-founded in experience) that the risk may still remain.

One point which may be made relates to the interaction of this part of the provisions with intentional homelessness. It is not uncommon for women not merely to leave home on account of domestic violence, but to leave or try to leave the area. Some authorities who find that a person in these circumstances is not homeless intentionally, will nonetheless seek to refer her back. It is true that there is no *necessary* conflict between finding that a woman is homeless (perhaps on account of the domestic violence) and *not* finding that she will run the risk of domestic violence in the area from which she has fled. An authority *can* take the view that while domestic violence drove her out, the risk is no longer present. Nonetheless, it is a relatively sophisticated distinction, for which there ought to be material reasons, and clear that automatically to refer her back without considering this distinction will be a bad decision in law.

In this connection, it may be noted that in *R.* v. *Bristol City Council, ex parte Browne* [1979] 1 W.L.R. 1437, D.C., which for these purposes and on this issue may be treated as if a local connection case (see notes to s.65(2), above), the authority had not found intentional homelessness, but appeared to have addressed themselves expressly to the point made in the last paragraph.

If a person has *no* local connection with any housing authority in England, Wales or Scotland, he will be entitled to housing from the authority to which the application has been made: *R.* v. *Hillingdon L.B.C., ex parte Streeting* [1980] 3 All E.R. 413, C.A.

Subss. (4), (5)

The first step is for authorities to seek to agree who has responsibility. If they cannot agree, the matter is to be resolved in accordance with arrangements made by the Secretary of State. Those arrangements are to be those agreed by the authorities, or associations of authorities, or in default of agreement such as appear to the Secretary of State to be suitable, after consultation with the local authority associations, and such other persons as he thinks appropriate: subs. (5).

Under these provisions, the local authority associations have agreed (a) the Local Authority Agreement, which serves as a guide to authorities wishing to reach agreement without resort to formal arbitration, and (b) appropriate arrangements which are embodied in an order made by the Secretary of State: S.I. 1978 No. 69, retained in force by the Housing (Consequential Provisions) Act 1985, s.2. A second such order has been made which governs arbitration when Scottish or cross-border disputes have to be resolved (as to which see also s.76, below): S.I. 1978, No. 661, also retained in force by the Consequential Provisions Act.

The present Local Authority Agreement was revised in June 1979 in the light of experience of the first 18 months of operation of the Act, and it may be reviewed subsequently. The substantive provisions of the Agreement in relation to the four grounds for local connections have been noted to s.61, above. The Agreement reminds the authorities that if there is any local connection with the area of the authority to which application is made, the local connection provisions will not be relevant, even though the household may have a greater local connection elsewhere. The authority are not concerned with the *degree* of connection with their own or any other area, but with whether or not the applicant has a local connection with them at all: *R. v. Mr. Referee McCall* (1981) 8 H.L.R. 48, Q.B.D.

The authority to which application has been made are urged to investigate all circumstances with the same thoroughness that they would use if they did not have it in mind to refer the application to another authority. These enquiries may be of another authority, one to which they may be making a referral, and such enquiries should be made as soon as possible. In some cases, of course, an applicant may have a local connection with a number of authorities. The Local Authority Agreement states that the notifying authority should weigh up all relevant factors in deciding which authority to notify, including as a relevant factor the views of the applicant and the degree of strength of local connection established by way of residence, family ties or employment.

In *McCall*, it was held that although an arbitrator will not normally be entitled to apply the criteria set out in the Local Authority Agreement, without the consent of the authorities, where issues are evenly balanced it is proper for him to have regard to the wishes of the applicant; indeed where all other considerations give no indication one way or another, the court described it as "perfectly reasonable and perfectly sensible, and within the spirit of the statutory provisions", to have regard to the wishes of the family. The *Code of Guidance* also specifies the wishes of the applicant as a matter to be taken into account when determining to which of more than one other authority with which there is a local connection the referral should be made.

Duties to persons whose applications are referred

68.—(1) Where, in accordance with section 67(1), a local housing authority notify another authority of an application, the notifying authority shall secure that accommodation is available for occupation by the applicant until it is determined whether the conditions for referral of his application to the other authority are satisfied.

(2) If it is determined that the conditions for referral are satisfied, the notified authority shall secure that accommodation becomes available for occupation by the applicant; if it is determined that the conditions are not satisfied, the notifying authority shall secure that accommodation becomes available for occupation by him.

(3) When the matter has been determined, the notifying authority shall notify the applicant—

(*a*) whether they or the notified authority are the authority whose duty it is to secure that accommodation becomes available for his occupation, and

(*b*) of the reasons why the authority subject to that duty are subject to it.

(4) The notice required to be given to a person under subsection (3) shall be given in writing and shall, if not received by him, be treated as having been given to him only if it is made available at the authority's office for a reasonable period for collection by him or on his behalf.

DEFINITIONS
"applicant": s.62.
"available for occupation": s.75.
"conditions for referral": s.67.
"local housing authority": ss.1, 2.

GENERAL NOTE
Pending resolution of a local connection issue, it is the authority to which application was made which must provide accommodation: subs. (1). This is temporary accommodation, and all the observations as to security, and its quality, which were made in relation to temporary accommodation under s.63 will apply here too. If the authority conclude that the applicant is homeless, in priority need, and has not become homeless intentionally, but they

intend to notify another authority of his application, they must notify the applicant of this and of their reasons for the decision: s.64(3), (4). So long as they remain under a duty towards the applicant, under either s.63 or s.68(1), the notifying authority also have duties in relation to the protection of the applicant's property: s.70(2).

The duty to make all preliminary enquiries into (a) homelessness, (b) priority need and (c) intentional homelessness lies upon the authority to which application is made: s.62. This is so even if it becomes apparent that the local connection provisions may apply (*Delahaye* v. *Oswestry Borough Council, The Times,* July 29, 1980, Q.B.D.), and even if the homeless person has already applied to the other authority and been rejected by it as intentionally homeless: *R.* v. *Slough Borough Council, ex parte London Borough of Ealing* [1981] Q.B. 801, C.A.

Furthermore, even if the notified authority have already made a previous, different decision, they will be bound by the decision arising on the new application to the notifying authority: *Slough*. This leads to the situation, described as a "merry-go-round" (*ibid.*), in which a person may apply to Authority A, be found homeless intentionally, move across to the area of Authority B, make a new application, be found unintentionally homeless and be referred back for permanent housing to Authority A.

If, however, an applicant applies to Authority A, is *not* found homeless intentionally, but rejects their offer, and then applies to Authority B who refer him back to Authority A, Authority A can still rely on their earlier offer, provided of course that offer was one sustainable by Authority A as a proper discharge of its duties (as to which, see notes to s.65(2), above): *R.* v. *London Borough of Hammersmith and Fulham, ex parte O'Brian* (1985) 17 H.L.R. 471, Q.B.D.

An authority who find an applicant homeless intentionally but wrongly refer the applicant to another authority, are not bound by their error, and the erroneous reference may simply be ignored, *i.e.* because the local connection provisions are inapplicable if there is intentionality, it does not follow that the erroneous subsequent referral "eradicates" or "eliminates" the intentionality decision: *Delahaye*.

Subss. (2), (3)

The obligation to house passes to the notified authority when the conditions for referral are fulfilled, but even when the resolution of the dispute results in the burden lying upon the notified authority, it is still the duty of the notifying authority to provide notification of the result of the reasons for it, to the applicant. If the burden of providing housing does not shift to the notified authority, it will remain with the notifying authority. The mere fact that an authority have unsuccessfully sought to shift the burden onto another authority is not, of course, any basis on which to alter the original decision that the applicant has not become homeless intentionally: *R.* v. *Beverley Borough Council, ex parte McPhee, The Times,* October 27, 1978, D.C.

The applicant will not become secure for one year from the date of notification of the outcome: see notes to s.63, above. All the remarks about discharge of the accommodation duty under s.65(2) will apply to accommodation provided under s.68(2), whether by notifying or notified authority.

Provisions supplementary to ss.63, 65 and 68

69.—(1) A local housing authority may perform any duty under section 65 or 68 (duties to persons found to be homeless) to secure that accommodation becomes available for the occupation of a person—

(a) by making available accommodation held by them under Part II (provision of housing) or under any other enactment,

(b) by securing that he obtains accommodation from some other person, or

(c) by giving him such advice and assistance as will secure that he obtains accommodation from some other person.

(2) A local housing authority may require a person to whom they were subject to a duty under section 63, 65 or 68 (interim duty to accommodate pending inquiries and duties to persons found to be homeless)—

(a) to pay such reasonable charges as they may determine in respect of accommodation which they secure for his occupation (either by making it available themselves or otherwise), or

(b) to pay such reasonable amount as they may determine in respect of sums payable by them for accommodation made available by another person.

DEFINITIONS
"available for occupation": s.75.
"local housing authority": ss.1, 2.

GENERAL NOTE
    The authority need not provide their own accommodation, but may provide it through another: see also s.72 (co-operation by other bodies). The wording is wide enough to suggest that in an appropriate case the advice or assistance may be towards home purchase: see *Code of Guidance* issued under s.71. Another person can include someone, or an authority, abroad: *R.* v. *Bristol City Council, ex parte Browne* [1979] 1 W.L.R. 1437, Q.B.D., although see notes to s.65(2) as to when and whether this will be appropriate. Again, it can include another local authority: *R.* v. *Wyre Borough Council, ex parte Parr* (1982) 2 H.L.R. 71, C.A., but again see notes to s.65(2) as to the appropriateness of so doing.

Subs. (2)
    If the authority provides their own accommodation, they can in any event make a reasonable charge under s.24, above. They may also call for a contribution towards costs paid by the authority to someone else, *e.g.* private sector accommodation.

Protection of property of homeless persons and persons threatened with homelessness

    70.—(1) This section applies where a local housing authority have reason to believe that an applicant is homeless or threatened with homelessness (or, in the case of an applicant to whom they owe a duty under section 63 (interim duty to accommodate pending inquiries), that he may be homeless) and that—
    (*a*) there is a danger of loss of, or damage to, any personal property of his by reason of his inability to protect it or deal with it, and
    (*b*) no other suitable arrangements have been or are being made.
    (2) If the authority have become subject to a duty towards the applicant under section 63, 65(2) or (3)(*a*), 66(2) or 68 (duty to accommodate during inquiries and duties to persons found to be homeless or threatened with homelessness), then, whether or not they are still subject to such a duty, they shall take reasonable steps to prevent the loss of the property or prevent or mitigate damage to it; and if they have not become subject to such a duty, they may take any steps they consider reasonable for that purpose.
    (3) The authority may for the purposes of this section—
    (*a*) enter, at all reasonable times, any premises which are the usual place of residence of the applicant or which were his last usual place of residence, and
    (*b*) deal with any personal property of his in any way which is reasonably necessary, in particular by storing it or arranging for its storage.
    (4) The authority may decline to take action under this section except upon such conditions as they consider appropriate in the particular case, which may include conditions as to—
    (*a*) the making and recovery by the authority of reasonable charges for the action taken, or
    (*b*) the disposal by the authority, in such circumstances as may be specified, of property in relation to which they have taken action.
    (5) When in the authority's opinion there is no longer any reason to believe that there is a danger of loss of or damage to a person's personal property by reason of his inability to protect it or deal with it, the authority cease to have any duty or power to take action under this section; but property stored by virtue of their having taken such action

may be kept in store and any conditions upon which it was taken into store continue to have effect, with any necessary modifications.

(6) Where the authority—
  (a) cease to be subject to a duty to take action under this section in respect of an applicant's property, or
  (b) cease to have power to take such action, having previously taken such action,
they shall notify the applicant of that fact and of the reason why they are of opinion that there is no longer any reason to believe that there is a danger of loss of or damage to his personal property by reason of his inability to protect it or deal with it.

(7) The notification shall be given to the applicant—
  (a) by delivering it to him, or
  (b) by leaving it, or sending it to him, at his last known address.

(8) References in this section to personal property of the applicant include personal property of any person who might reasonably be expected to reside with him.

DEFINITIONS
  "applicant": s.62.
  "homeless": s.58.
  "local housing authority": ss.1, 2.
  "threatened with homelessness": s.58.

GENERAL NOTE
Although these provisions have not yet been the subject of any court action they are nonetheless of considerable practical importance. Those who are homeless or threatened with it are likely to be from amongst the poorer sections of the community and failure to take steps to protect their belongings can only have the effect of prolonging or worsening their economic position. This section contains (a) a duty to protect property in some circumstances, and (b) a power to do so in others.

To whom is a duty owed?
The *duty* is owed to an applicant towards whom the authority has become subject to a housing duty under one of the following provisions: s.63(1) (accommodation pending enquiries), s.65(2) (permanent housing duty), s.65(3)(a) (temporary accommodation for the homeless intentionally in priority need), s.66(2) (accommodation for those threatened with homelessness, in priority need and not so threatened intentionally), and s.68 (accommodation for those who are or have been the subject of a local connection issue). The duty is also owed to someone who might reasonably be expected to reside with the applicant; *i.e.* for whom housing must also be provided—see ss.65, 66 and 75.

When is the duty owed?
The duty is owed when the authority have reason to believe (a) that by reason of his inability to protect or deal with it, there is a danger of loss of, or damage to, any personal property of the applicant, or other person to whom the duty is owed, and (b) that no other suitable arrangements have been or are being made: subs. (1). The duty continues until the authority are of the opinion that there is no longer any reason to believe that there is a danger of loss of, or damage to, that property by reason of the applicant's inability, or that of another to whom the duty is owed, to protect or deal with it: subs. (5).

The duty is owed not only when the authority *are* subject to one of the prescribed housing duties, but also when they *have been* so subject: subs. (2). For example, a person may be evicted from accommodation, and subsequently held to be homeless intentionally. The former landlord may have been willing to hold on to his property for a period of time. That period may be no longer than the period for which accommodation has been provided under 65(3)(a). If, after the expiry of s.65(3)(a) accommodation, the property duty has not expired application may yet be made for assistance under this section and if the relevant conditions are fulfilled, the authority will be obliged to provide that assistance.

Even when the property duty has expired, because the authority have formed the view that there is no further danger of loss of or damage to the property, or that the applicant is no longer unable to protect or deal with it, the authority have *power* to continue to protect that property: subs. (5). Property may be kept in store, and conditions on which it was taken into store will continue to have effect, with any necessary modifications (*ibid.*). The *Code of Guidance* illustrates as incapacity to protect property a person who is ill, mentally handicapped or personally inadequate, or who cannot afford to have it placed in store. Similarly, a person could be deemed capable of taking back responsiblity if no longer ill, or has obtained accommodation or a job.

What is the duty?
The duty is to take reasonable steps to prevent loss or prevent or mitigate damage to the property: subs. (2). In order to discharge the duty, the authority have a quite exceptional power of entry onto private property, which serves to underline the importance of these provisions. Such provisions were also to be found in legislation preceding the Housing (Homeless Persons) Act 1977—see s.48, National Assistance Act 1948. At all reasonable times, they may enter any premises which are "the usual place of residence of the applicant or which were his last usual place of residence," and deal with his property in any way which is reasonably necessary, including by storing or arranging to store the property: subs. (3).

Arranging storage is what the authority generally have to do. They may, however, refuse to exercise the duty, except upon appropriate conditions: subs. (4). This means such conditions as they consider appropriate in a particular case, and can include conditions empowering them (a) to charge for the discharge of the duty, and (b) to dispose of the property in respect of which they discharged the duty, in such circumstances as may be specified (*ibid*).

The *Code* suggests that the authority might dispose of the property if they lose touch with the person concerned and are unable to trace him after a specified period. Whether or not a charge is made or a duty to store exists the authority must, as bailees of the property, take reasonable care of it, and deliver it up when reasonably requested to do so: failure to do this will render them liable to damages, even if the failure to deliver up is accidental, albeit negligent accident: *Mitchell* v. *Ealing London Borough Council* [1979] Q.B. 1. The standard of care is high, and the burden of disproving negligence when damage has resulted from an accident lies upon the authority, as bailees: *Port Swettenham Authority* v. *T.W. Wu & Co.* [1979] A.C. 580, P.C. The *Code* suggests that authorities should arrange for insurance against loss or damage.

The position under this section may, however, have to be read subject to s.41, Local Government (Miscellaneous Provisions) Act 1982. That section applies wherever property comes into the possession of a local authority, after being found on premises owned or managed by them, or property has been deposited with the local authority and is not collected from them in accordance with the terms on which it was deposited. The section entitles the authority to give the owner or depositor of the property notice in writing that they require him to collect the property by a date specified in the notice, and that if he does not do so the property will vest in the authority as from that date. If the person notified then fails to comply with the notice, the property does vest in the authority on that date.

The date to be specified is to be not less than one month from the date of the notice. When an authority *find* property, as distinct from when it is deposited with them, and it appears to them that it is impossible to serve a notice, the property simply vests in them one month from the date when they so find it. In any other case, including deposit, when the authority are satisfied after reasonable enquiry that it is impossible to serve notice, the property simply vests in them six months after the property was deposited with them expired, whichever is the later.

Perishable property, and property the continued storage of which would involve the authority in unreasonable expense or inconvenience, may, in any event, be sold or otherwise disposed of by the authority as they think fit. In such a case, the proceeds of sale vest in the authority on the same date as the property itself would have done were it not perishable or inconvenient or too expensive to store. If property is claimed by its owner prior to the date when it vests in the authority, he can only collect it on payment to the authority of their costs in storing the property, and in making enquiries or carrying out any of the other steps referred to in this section.

There is no express reference in the 1982 Act to the provisions of the 1977 Act (or to this Part). The courts may therefore consider that references in the 1982 Act to "property deposited" with the authoriy do not include property taken into safe keeping under this section. If so these provisions only will apply. If not the 1982 Act makes it much easier for authorities to limit the effect of their duties.

The Power to Protect Property
The authority have *power* to take the identical steps to prevent loss of property, or to prevent or mitigate damage to it, as they are obliged to take when they are under the duty

described above, in any case where there is no duty to do so: subs. (2). This power might benefit those not in priority need of accommodation, and those who, though in priority need of accommodation, are only threatened with homelessness, and in respect of whom no decision on intentionality has yet been taken. Where the authority exercise this power, they have the same ancillary powers as in relation to the duty, *i.e.* entry into premises, imposing conditions, etc.

Notification of Cessation of Responsibility. When the authority consider that they no longer have a duty or a power to protect property, they are obliged to notify the person towards whom they were subject to the duty, or in relation to whose property they have exercised the power (a) that they have ceased to be subject to the duty, or to enjoy the power, and (b) why they are of the opinion that the duty or power has come to an end: subs. (6). The notification must be given by delivery to the person to be notified, or by leaving it, or sending it by post to, his last known address: subs. (7).

Administrative provisions

Guidance to authorities by the Secretary of State

71.—(1) In relation to homeless persons and persons threatened with homelessness, a relevant authority shall have regard in the exercise of their functions to such guidance as may from time to time be given by the Secretary of State.

(2) The Secretary of State may give guidance either generally or to specified descriptions of authorities.

DEFINITIONS
"homeless": s.58.
"relevant authority": s.77.
"threatened with homelessness": s.58.

GENERAL NOTE

The Secretary of State has issued the *Code of Guidance,* retained in force by s.2, Housing (Consequential Provisions) Act 1985, of which the current edition is that issued in 1983.

Authorities are not bound to follow the *Code* blindly. The authority may depart from its provisions, provided that they have first had regard to it: *de Falco, Silvestri* v. *Crawley Borough Council* [1980] Q.B. 460 C.A., *Miller* v. *Wandsworth London Borough Council, The Times,* March 19, 1980; *Lambert* v. *London Borough of Ealing* [1981] 1 W.L.R. 550, C.A. But it may remain useful in demonstrating policy (*Parr* v. *Wyre Borough Council* (1982) 2 H.L.R. 71, C.A.), and otherwise in interpretation of the provisions and in what may be called the correct approach: *R.* v. *West Dorset District Council, ex parte Phillips* [1985] 17 H.L.R. 336, Q.B.D., in which the court held that the authority had failed to conduct their enquiries in the caring and sympathetic manner required by the *Code.*

As Parliament has imposed an express requirement on authorities to have regard to the *Code,* deviation from its provisions may amount to a prima facie case that it has not been taken into account. In practice, if not in law, the authority may then have to justify this departure: *Padfield* v. *Minister of Agriculture, Fisheries & Food* [1968] A.C. 997, H.L.; see also per Lord Denning M.R. in *de Falco, Parr.* Part III is, however, the governing instrument: the *Code* must be read in its context, and it will govern if there is a conflict between them: *R.* v. *Waveney District Council, ex parte Bowers* (1982) 4 H.L.R. 118, C.A.

Co-operation between authorities

72. Where a local housing authority—
  (*a*) request another local housing authority in England, Wales or Scotland, a new town corporation, a registered housing association or the Scottish Special Housing Association to assist them in the discharge of their functions under sections 62, 63, 65 to 67 and 68(1) and (2) (which relate to homelessness and threatened homelessness as such),
  (*b*) request a social services authority in England, Wales or Scotland to exercise any of their functions in relation to a case which the local housing authority are dealing with under those provisions, or
  (*c*) request another local housing authority in England, Wales or

Scotland to assist them in the discharge of their functions under section 70 (protection of property of homeless persons and persons threatened with homelessness),
the authority to whom the request is made shall co-operate in rendering such assistance in the discharge of the functions to which the request relates as is reasonable in the circumstances.

DEFINITIONS
"homelessness": s.58.
"local housing authority": ss.1, 2.
"new town corporation": s.4.
"registered housing association": s.5.
"threatened with homelessness": s.58.

GENERAL NOTE
Where housing duties of any class arise, or when enquiry duties arise, the authority may seek co-operation from one of the specified bodies, or may even request a social services authority to take over their functions, and that authority shall co-operate to the extent "as is reasonable in the circumstances." A request for assistance may also be made to another housing authority in relation to the property functions (*i.e.* duty or power) under s.70.

Assistance for voluntary organisations

Financial and other assistance for voluntary organisations concerned with homelessness

73.—(1) The Secretary of State, with the consent of the Treasury, may, upon such terms and subject to such conditions as he may determine, give to a voluntary organisation concerned with homelessness, or with matters relating to homelessness, assistance by way of grant or loan.

(2) A local housing authority may, upon such terms and subject to such conditions as they may determine, give to such a voluntary organisation such assistance as is mentioned in subsection (1), and may also assist such an organisation by—

(a) permitting them to use premises belonging to the authority upon such terms and subject to such conditions as may be agreed,

(b) making available furniture or other goods, whether by way of gift, loan or otherwise, and

(c) making available the services of staff employed by the authority.

(3) No assistance shall be given under subsection (1) or (2) unless the voluntary organisation first give an undertaking—

(a) that they will use the money, furniture or other goods or premises made available to them for a specified purpose, and

(b) that they will, if the person giving the assistance serves notice on them requiring them to do so, furnish, within the period of 21 days beginning with the date on which the notice is served, a certificate giving such information as may reasonably be required by the notice with respect to the manner in which the assistance given to them is being used.

(4) The conditions subject to which assistance is given under this section shall in all cases include, in addition to any conditions determined or agreed under subsection (1) or (2), conditions requiring the voluntary organisation to—

(a) keep proper books of account and have them audited in such manner as may be specified,

(b) keep records indicating how they have used the money, furniture or other goods or premises made available to them, and

(c) submit the books of account and records for inspection by the person giving the assistance.

(5) If it appears to the person giving the assistance that the voluntary organisation have failed to carry out their undertaking as to the purpose for which the assistance was to be used, he shall take all reasonable steps to recover from the organisation an amount equal to the amount of the assistance; but no sum is so recoverable unless he has first served on the voluntary organisation a notice specifying the amount which in his opinion is recoverable and the basis on which that amount has been calculated.

DEFINITIONS

"homelessness": s.58.
"local housing authority": ss.1, 2.
"voluntary organisation": s.77.

GENERAL NOTE

Voluntary organisations have long played an important role in assisting the homeless. Bodies such as housing associations have provided significant assistance to local authorities in the discharge of their obligations towards the homeless, especially the homeless in "special categories."

A voluntary organisation is, for the purposes of Part III, a body whose activities are carried on otherwise than for profit, but not including a public or local authority. This definition is clearly wide enough to include housing associations: *Goodman* v. *Dolphin Square Trust Ltd.* (1979) 38 P. & C.R. 257, C.A. The powers permit the Secretary of State, with the consent of the Treasury, to give money by way of grant or loan, to such voluntary organisations, on such terms and conditions as he may determine: subs. (1). In addition, local housing authorities may provide funds to such voluntary organisations by way of grant or loan, and subject to such terms and conditions as they may determine: subs. (2). They may also assist them by letting them use premises belonging to them, on such terms and conditions as may be agreed, and by making available furniture or other goods—by way of gift, loan or otherwise—and even the services of staff employed by them: *ibid.*

No assistance of any kind is, however, to be given unless the voluntary organisation first gives an undertaking (a) to use the money, furniture or other goods or premises made available to them, for a purpose to be specified in the undertaking, and (b) that if required to do so by the body providing such assistance, they will, within 21 days of notice served upon them, certify such information as to the manner in which assistance given to them is being used, as may reasonably be required by the notice: subs. (3).

In every case in which assistance is provided, the conditions must include a requirement that the voluntary organisation keep proper books of account and have them audited in a specified manner, keep records indicating how the assistance has been used and submit accounts and records for inspection by the body providing the assistance: subs. (4).

If it appears to the body providing the assistance that the voluntary organisation is not using it for the purposes specified in the undertaking, the assisting body is obliged to take all reasonable steps to recover from the organisation an amount equal to the amount of the assistance, although no such amount is recoverable unless there has first been served on the voluntary organisation a notice specifying the amount alleged to be recoverable, and the basis upon which it has been calculated: subs. (5).

Particular care should be taken when providing assistance to voluntary organisations for which no satisfactory registration process (*e.g.* under Charities Act 1960, Industrial and Provident Societies Act 1965 or Housing Associations Act 1985) exists. In general, it is suggested that authorities should not commit assistance for more than three years ahead, without adequate provision for reappraisal: D.O.E. Circular 116/77.

Authorities may co-operate in providing assistance to organisations or projects whose work is relevant to the area of more than one authority, although it is such projects or organisations which are to operate in a wider context than the area of one authority who are most likely to secure assistance from the Secretary of State directly (*ibid.*). Generally, assistance under these provisions will not commonly be for the provision of accommodation, for which assistance under the alternative provisions is available, or which are innovative. The use of voluntary organisations is, as a general principle, to be encouraged (*ibid*).

Supplementary provisions

False statements, withholding information and failure to disclose change of circumstances

74.—(1) If a person, with intent to induce a local housing authority to believe, in connection with the exercise of their functions under this Part, that he or another person—

(*a*) is homeless or threatened with homelessness, or

(*b*) has a priority need, or

(*c*) did not become homeless or threatened with homelessness intentionally,

knowingly or recklessly makes a statement which is false in a material particular, or knowingly withholds information which the authority have reasonably required him to give in connection with the exercise of those functions, he commits a summary offence.

(2) If before an applicant receives notification of the local housing authority's decision on his application there is any change of facts material to his case, he shall notify the authority as soon as possible; and the authority shall explain to every applicant, in ordinary language, the duty imposed on him by this subsection and the effect of subsection (3).

(3) A person who fails to comply with subsection (2) commits a summary offence unless he shows that he was not given the explanation required by that subsection or that he had some other reasonable excuse for non-compliance.

(4) A person guilty of an offence under this section is liable on conviction to a fine not exceeding level 4 on the standard scale.

DEFINITIONS

"homeless": s.58.

"intentionally": s.60.

"local housing authority": ss.1, 2.

"priority need": s.59.

"threatened with homelessness": s.58.

GENERAL NOTE

To prevent abuse of Part III, certain attempts to obtain accommodation are made criminal offences. There are three such offences: (i) making a false statement; (ii) withholding information; and (iii) failing to notify of changes. Offences under these provisions are prosecuted in the magistrates' court, and carry a maximum fine of level 4 on the standard scale, which means the standard scale under the Criminal Justice Act 1982, s.37, currently £2,000 (S.I. 1984, No. 447).

Making a False Statement

This offence is committed by anyone, not just an applicant, who knowingly or recklessly makes a statement which is false in a material particular, with intent to induce an authority, in connection with the exercise of their functions under Part III to believe that the person making the statement, or any other person, is homeless, or threatened with homelessness, or has a priority need, or did not become homeless or threatened with homelessness intentionally.

The offence is sufficiently widely drafted to catch *e.g.* an adviser who makes representations on behalf of an applicant, but the offence clearly requires proof of intent to induce the authority to believe something which is not true, and the prosecutor must accordingly include proof of such intent as part of the prosecution.

Withholding Information

This offence is committed by anyone, again not just an applicant, who knowingly withholds information which the authority have reasonably required him to give in connection with the exercise of their functions under Part III. This is a surprisingly widely drafted provision, enabling an authority to *require* information from, for example, a relative or a former landlord. However, an intent must be shown to induce the authority, in connection with the exercise of their Part III functions, to believe that the person withholding the information, or any other person, is homeless or is threatened with homelessness intentionally.

Failure to Notify Changes

This offence may be committed only by an applicant. An applicant is under a positive duty to inform the authority as soon as possible of any change of facts material to his application, which occurs before the receipt of notification under s.64 of their decision on his application. This is less straightforward than the two offences previously considered. Of particular difficulty is the issue of what constitutes a "material change of facts." In accordance with the usual principles of criminal law, the courts should interpret the provisions narrowly, in favour of the accused.

A related duty is imposed upon authorities—to explain to an applicant, in ordinary language, the nature of his duty to notify them of material changes and that failure to do so is a criminal offence. It is a defence for the applicant to show that he was not given such an explanation, and it is also a defence to show that he had a reasonable excuse for non-compliance: subs. (3). "Because it may not be obvious to those concerned what changes are material or that they ought to be disclosed, the Act requires the authority to explain to them the obligation to notify the authority of such changes. Authorities will appreciate the importance of doing this clearly and sensitively in the context of the interview or the inquiries as a whole." (*Code of Guidance*).

Meaning of accommodation available for occupation

75. For the purposes of this Part accommodation shall be regarded as available for a person's occupation only if it is available for occupation both by him and by any other person who might reasonably be expected to reside with him; and references to securing accommodation for a person's occupation shall be construed accordingly.

GENERAL NOTE

This is a most important provision. Accommodation is only available for a person's occupation if it is available for occupation both by him and by any other person who might reasonably be expected to reside with him. In *In Re Islam* [1983] 1 A.C. 688, C.A. and H.L., 1 H.L.R. 107, H.L., the applicant had lost his right to a shared room, when his wife and four children flew from Bangladesh to join him in this country. In the Court of Appeal, Sir Denys Buckley suggested that the accommodation which was available for his occupation was made up of the property which the family had been occupying in Bangladesh, plus Mr. Islam's shared room in Uxbridge.

The House of Lords rejected this. The shared room in this country was clearly not "available." Furthermore, "I do not think that rooms in two separate continents can be combined" to make up "available accommodation" (*per* Lord Wilberforce). As to an argument that Mr. Islam had made the accommodation unavailable by bringing his family over, "this is a circular argument because that lack is the very circumstance which section 16 [now, this section] and the Act are designed to relieve."

In *R.* v. *Eastleigh Borough Council, ex parte Beattie* (*No.* 1) (1983) 10 H.L.R. 134, Q.B.D., the court rejected out of hand a suggestion that pregnancy causing accommodation to cease to be reasonable to occupy could amount to intentionality: see notes to s.60, above. See also *R.* v. *Westminster City Council, ex parte Ali* (1983) 11 H.L.R. 83, Q.B.D., for an illustration of another case in which the court found the proposition that a small room was "available" for a large family "quite extraordinary": see notes to s.60, above. And, again, see *R.* v. *Preseli District Council, ex parte Fisher* (1984) 17 H.L.R. 147, Q.B.D., notes to s.60, for a case of accommodation likely not to be held available.

Application of this Part to cases arising in Scotland

76.—(1) Sections 67 and 68 (referral of application to another local housing authority and duties to persons whose applications are referred) apply—

    (*a*) to applications referred by a housing authority in Scotland in pursuance of section 5(1) of the Housing (Homeless Persons) Act 1977, and

    (*b*) to persons whose applications are so transferred,

as they apply to cases arising under this Part.

(2) Section 72 (duty of other authorities to co-operate with local housing authority) applies to a request by a housing authority in Scotland under

section 9(1) of the Housing (Homeless Persons) Act 1977 as it applies to a request by a local housing authority in England or Wales.

(3) In this Part, in relation to Scotland—

(*a*) "local housing authority" means a district or islands council and references to the district of such an authority are to the area of that council,

(*b*) "social services authority" means a local authority for the purposes of the Social Work (Scotland) Act 1968, that is to say, a regional or islands council;

and in section 72(*a*) (requests for co-operation) "new town corporation" includes a development corporation established under the New Towns (Scotland) Act 1968.

DEFINITIONS
"local housing authority": ss.1, 2.

GENERAL NOTE
This section "reapplies" the Housing (Homeless Persons) Act 1977, where Scottish accommodation or connections are involved.

Minor definitions

77. In this Part—

"relevant authority" means a local housing authority or social services authority;

"social services authority" means a local authority for the purposes of the Local Authority Social Services Act 1970, as defined in section 1 of that Act;

"voluntary organisation" means a body, not being a public or local authority, whose activities are carried on otherwise than for profit.

Index of defined expressions: Part III

78. The following Table shows provisions defining or otherwise explaining expressions used in this Part (other than provisions defining or explaining an expression used in the same section):—

accommodation available for occupation	section 75.
applicant (for housing accommodation)	section 62(1).
district (of a local housing authority)	sections 2(1) and 76(3).
homeless	sections 58(1) to (3).
housing association	section 5(1).
intentionally homeless or threatened with homelessness	section 60.
local connection (in relation to the district of a local housing authority)	section 61.
local housing authority (in England and Wales)	section 1, 2(2).
(in Scotland)	section 76(3).
new town corporation	sections 4(*b*) and 76(3).
priority need (for accommodation)	section 59.
registered (in relation to a housing association)	section 5(4).
regular armed forces of the Crown	section 622.
relevant authority	section 77.
securing accommodation for a person's occupation	section 75.

social services authority	sections 76(3) and 77.
standard scale (in reference to the maximum fine on summary conviction)	section 622.
threatened with homelessness	section 58(4).
voluntary organisation	section 77.

PART IV

SECURE TENANCIES AND RIGHTS OF SECURE TENANTS

Security of tenure

Secure tenancies

79.—(1) A tenancy under which a dwelling-house is let as a separate dwelling is a secure tenancy at any time when the conditions described in sections 80 and 81 as the landlord condition and the tenant condition are satisfied.

(2) Subsection (1) has effect subject to—

(*a*) the exceptions in Schedule 1 (tenancies which are not secure tenancies),

(*b*) sections 89(3) and (4) and 90(3) and (4) (tenancies ceasing to be secure after death of tenant), and

(*c*) sections 91(2) and 93(2) (tenancies ceasing to be secure in consequence of assignment or subletting).

(3) The provisions of this Part apply in relation to a licence to occupy a dwelling-house (whether or not granted for a consideration) as they apply in relation to a tenancy.

(4) Subsection (3) does not apply to a licence granted as a temporary expedient to a person who entered the dwelling-house or any other land as a trespasser (whether or not, before the grant of that licence, another licence to occupy that or another dwelling-house had been granted to him).

DEFINITIONS
"dwelling-house": s.112.
"landlord condition": s.80.
"tenant condition": s.81.

GENERAL NOTE

This section defines those who are within the "security of tenure" provisions initially introduced as Part I, Chapter II, Housing Act 1980. Chapter I of Part I of the 1980 Act contained the other element of "the tenants' charter," *i.e.* the "right to buy" now contained in Part V, below. One major innovation in housing law was the extension of the provisions of the tenants' charter to licensees under what is now subs. (3), subject to subs. (4) (see further below), although in the light of the recent decisions of the House of Lords in *Street* v. *Mountford* [1985] A.C. 809, 17 H.L.R. 402, and *Eastleigh Borough Council* v. *Walsh* [1985] 1 W.L.R. 525; 17 H.L.R. 392, that distinction has taken on somewhat less importance than hitherto: see further notes to s.93, below.

In this Part, save where an express distinction is drawn, all references to tenants includes licensees.

In outline, the tenants of local authorities, housing associations and trusts, new town corporations, urban development corporations and the Development Board for Rural Wales are prima facie to enjoy security of tenure and other rights under this Part, but (a) many are excluded by Sched. 1, (b) s.109 expressly excludes a co-operative housing association from some of the provisions, and (c) there is power for the Secretary of State to exclude development corporations from other provisions, under s.114. In addition, security may be lost (i) on grounds for possession under s.84, (ii) on second succession under ss.87–90, (iii) on assignment under s.91, or (iv) on subletting of whole under s.93. It would also be wrong to assume that all secure tenants will enjoy the right to buy under Part V: see ss.118–121 and Sched. 5, below.

In addition, note the important residential qualification contained in s.81, below.

Subs (1)
Dwelling-house
"Dwelling-house" is defined in s.112, below, to mean "a house or part of a house." As to "house," see notes to s.56, above. A purpose-built hotel has been held to be a house for the purposes of what is now s.19, Rent Act 1977 (restricted contracts), in which the word "dwelling" is given the same meaning: *Luganda* v. *Service Hotels Ltd.* [1969] 2 Ch. 209, C.A. The same meaning is also applied for the purposes of full protection under that Act. "It must be a question of fact whether premises are a house or not . . . ": *per* Scarman L.J. in *Horford Investments Ltd.* v. *Lambert* [1976] Ch. 39 at p.51, C.A.

In *Makins* v. *Elson* [1977] 1 W.L.R. 221, it was held that a caravan can constitute a "house" for tax purposes, where the wheels had been raised and permanent services connected; see also *R.* v. *Guildford Area Rent Tribunal, ex parte Grubey* (1951) (unreported), April 19, D.C.); see further *Norton* v. *Knowles* [1969] 1 Q.B. 572, as to qualification under the Protection From Eviction Act 1977, where, however, what is in issue is residential occupation of "any premises," not statutorily defined.

In *R.* v. *Rent Officer of Nottingham Registration Area, ex parte Allen* (1985) 17 H.L.R. 481, Q.B.D., it was said that just because what is let is a caravan it is not necessarily outside the Rent Acts; whether or not it qualifies depends on the circumstances of the letting; if the caravan is let as a moveable chattel, it cannot be a house; where it is rendered completely immobile, either by the removal of its wheels, or permanently blocked in, then it is more likely to be regarded as a house much as a prefabricated dwelling or bungalow would be. The difficulties arise between these extremes: it is necessary to look at those features revealing elements of permanence on site, and those features revealing mobility. If the caravan is used by the tenant as his permanent home, there is a greater likelihood of it being permanently in place than if it is being used as a temporary expedient.

Unless the land is agricultural land (as defined in s.26(3)(*a*), General Rate Act 1967), in excess of two acres, land let together with the dwelling-house is to be treated as part of the dwelling-house: s.112(2), below. This, too, is based on the Rent Act 1977, see s.26 thereof. In *Bradshaw* v. *Smith* (1980) 255 E.G. 699, C.A., it was held that a field of more than two acres was not agricultural land within the meaning of s.26, 1977 Act, as it was not *used* only as a meadow or pasture within s.26, General Rate Act 1967, but was used mainly or exclusively for the purposes of recreation; therefore, the field was part of the letting and enjoyed protection.

For land to be let together with the dwelling-house, it is not necessary that land and house should be let under the one tenancy or agreement: *Mann* v. *Merrill* [1945] 1 All E.R. 705, C.A.; see also *Wimbush* v. *Cibulia* [1949] 2 K.B. 564, C.A. Nor need the land and the dwelling be contiguous, provided they are within the same vicinity: *Langford Property Co.* v. *Batten* [1951] A.C. 223, H.L. Nor, indeed, need the landlord be the same or payment be under one rent: *Jelley* v. *Buckman* [1974] 2 Q.B. 488, C.A.; but *cf. Cumbes* v. *Robinson* [1951] 2 K.B. 83, C.A., and *Lewis* v. *Purvis* (1947) 177 L.T. 267, C.A. But there must *be* a dwelling-house for any land to be let together with it: *Ellis & Sons Amalgamated Properties* v. *Sisman* [1948] 1 K.B. 653, C.A. The issue is to be decided at the date when it arises, not the date of letting: *Mann* v. *Merrill.*

Let
The phrase "let as a separate dwelling" is also modelled on the Rent Act 1977, s.1. Under that Act, the term "let" has generated considerable case-law, based on the distinction between tenancy and licence; indeed, much of the case-law on that issue derives from the proposition that only tenancies, not licences, are Rent Act protected: see, *e.g., Oakley* v. *Wilson* [1927] 2 K.B. 279, *Fordree* v. *Barrell* [1933] 2 K.B. 257, C.A., *Marcroft Waggons Ltd.* v. *Smith* [1951] 2 K.B. 496, C.A., and *Marchant* v. *Charters* [1977] 1 W.L.R. 1181, C.A. Because of the provisions of subs. (3), subject to subs. (4), this is not a live issue under this Act.

However, there has been some case law independent of the question of licence. A tenancy at sufferance is within the term (*Artizans, Labourers & General Dwelling Co. Ltd.* v. *Whitaker* [1919] 2 K.B. 301, *Dobson* v. *Richards* (1919) 63 S.J. 663; [1919] W.N. 166, K.B., *Remon* v. *City of London Real Property Co. Ltd.* [1921] 1 K.B. 49, C.A.) and so is a tenancy at will (*Chamberlain* v. *Farr* (1942) 112 L.J.K.B. 206, C.A.) and a tenancy by estoppel (*Mackley* v. *Nutting* [1949] 2 K.B. 55, C.A., *Whitmore* v. *Lambert* [1955] 1 W.L.R. 495, C.A., *Stratford* v. *Syrett* [1958] 1 Q.B. 107, C.A.).

As

The letting has to be "as" a separate dwelling. This word imports consideration of the purpose of the letting: *Horford Investments* v. *Lambert* [1976] Ch. 39, C.A. The terms of the letting, so far as they indicate purpose, are the "primary consideration" (*Wolfe* v. *Hogan* [1949] 2 K.B. 194, C.A., *Horford*), but they are not conclusive, for a court may conclude that there has been a sufficient consensual variation to bring security into play, although something more than mere payment of rent in knowledge of changed user is probably called for, *i.e.* a positive statement or act of affirmation: see *Wolfe, Court* v. *Robinson* [1951] 2 K.B. 60, C.A., *Whitty* v. *Scott-Russell* [1950] 2 K.B. 32, C.A., *Williams* v. *Perry* [1924] 1 K.B. 936, D.C., *Levermore* v. *Jobey* [1956] 1 W.L.R. 697, C.A.

What is contemplated by the agreement may be a matter of construction. Thus, a letting of a shop with living accommodation above it is likely to be construed as a letting for use as a dwelling: *R.* v. *Folkestone Rent Tribunal, ex parte Webb* [1954] 1 Q.B. 454n., *Rolfe* v. *Sidney McFarlane Ltd.* (1957) 168 E.G. 584, C.A., *R.* v. *Brighton and Area Rent Tribunal, ex parte Slaughter* [1954] 1 Q.B. 446, D.C., *Levermore* v. *Jobey* [1956] 1 W.L.R. 697, C.A. And where no specific user is contemplated by the agreement, then *de facto* user as at the time possession is sought or the question is otherwise raised, will govern whether or not the premises are let as a separate dwelling: *Gidden* v. *Mills* [1925] 2 K.B. 713, D.C.

In *Russell* v. *Booker* (1982) 5 H.L.R. 10, C.A., a property had been let as an agricultural holding, but over the years the agricultural use had been abandoned. The court did not uphold the claim to a Rent Act protected tenancy, applying the following principles:

(i) Where the terms of a tenancy agreement provide for or contemplate the use of the premises for some particular purposes, then, subject to the qualification in (ii), below, that purpose is the essential factor in deciding whether or not the property has been let "as" a dwelling;

(ii) Nevertheless, where the original tenancy agreement provided for or contemplated the use of the premises for some particular purpose, but, by the time possession proceedings are commenced, that agreement has been superseded by a subsequent contract providing for a different user, the subsequent contract may be looked at in deciding purpose;

(iii) If a tenant changes the user of the premises and the fact of the change is fully known to, and accepted by, the landlord, it may be possible for the court to infer a subsequent contract to let "as" a dwelling, although this would be a contract different in essentials from the original tenancy agreement;

(iv) However, unless such a contract can be spelled out, a mere unilateral change of user will not enable a tenant to claim protection (or security) in a case where the terms of the tenancy agreement itself provide for and contemplate the use of the premises for some particular purpose which does not attract protection;

(v) Where the tenancy agreement itself does not provide for or contemplate the use of the premises for any particular purpose, actual subsequent use has to be looked at in determining the purpose of the letting.

A

The purpose must be to let as "a" separate dwelling. In *St. Catherine's College* v. *Dorling* [1980] 1 W.L.R. 66, C.A., a college took the tenancy of a flat, already subdivided into separate living units, for sub-leasing to their own students. As against the college, the students could not enjoy full Rent Act protection (*cf.* 1977 Act, s.8), and as against the landlord, the college could not avail itself of a statutory tenancy following the contractual arrangement, for a corporate body cannot as such "reside" (*cf.* notes to s.81, below). The college sought, however, to avail itself of the provisions of Pt. IV of the 1977 Act, governing the registration of rents.

It was held that the letting was not as *a* separate dwelling but, indeed, as several separate dwellings: see also *Whitty* v. *Scott-Russell* [1950] 2 K.B. 32, C.A., *Horford Investments* v. *Lambert* [1976] Ch. 39, C.A., *Regalian Securities Ltd.* v. *Ramsden* (1980) 254 E.G. 1191, C.A.

But two or more dwellings may be let for use as one: *Langford Property Co. Ltd.* v. *Goldrich* [1949] 1 K.B. 511, C.A., *Whitty* v. *Scott-Russell* [1950] 2 K.B. 32, C.A., *Lower* v. *Porter* [1956] 1 Q.B. 325, C.A. Similarly, several lettings at different times may add up to one letting, as one dwelling: *Verity* v. *Waring* [1953] C.P.L. 423, C.A. And while a letting of a unit already subdivided into several separate living units for use as such, will not be let as *a* dwelling, a letting of one unit subsequently subdivided into living units, *e.g.* into bedsitting rooms, does not cease to be a letting as a separate dwelling on that account: *Sissons Cafe Ltd.* v. *Barber* (1929) E.G.D. 117, D.C.

Separate

The essence of "separate" dwelling is that the premises in question must be capable of use on their own, as a dwelling, even if they comprise no more than a single room (see, *e.g. Curl v. Angelo* [1948] 2 All E.R. 189, C.A.), so that there is and needs be no sharing with another of "living accommodation." The term "living accommodation" is a judicial creation, and does not extend to the sharing of a bathroom or lavatory: *Cole v. Harris* [1945] K.B. 474, C.A. A bathroom or lavatory is accommodation not used for living in, but merely visited for occasional, specific purposes, as distinct from a room used for the primary purposes of living, or one in which a person spends a significant part of his time: see also *Curl, Goodrich v. Paisner* [1957] A.C. 65, H.L., *Marsh v. Cooper* [1969] 1 W.L.R. 803, C.A.

For these purposes, the primary living purposes may be considered as sleeping, cooking and feeding (*Wright v. Howell* (1947) 92 S.J. 26, C.A., *Curl v. Angelo* [1948] 2 All E.R. 189, C.A., but *not*, as noted, sanitary activities.

But a kitchenette, even though too small to eat in and only available to cook or wash up in, has been held to constitute living accommodation (*Winters v. Dance* [1949] L.J.R. 165, C.A.), as also has a normal kitchen: *Neale v. Del Soto* [1945] K.B. 144, C.A., *Sharpe v. Nicholls* (1945) 147 E.G. 177, C.A. So if the letting comprises premises together with shared user of such living accommodation, there is, prima facie, no use as a "separate dwelling": *Winters v. Dance, Neale v. Del Soto, Goodrich v. Paisner* [1957] A.C. 65, H.L.

Sharing with one's own sub-tenant, or sub-licensee (see 93, below), does not prevent use as a separate dwelling: *Baker v. Turner* [1950] A.C. 401, H.L. And sharing living accommodation must be distinguished from a letting which leaves someone else, *e.g.* another occupier or even the landlord, with a defined or limited right merely to *use* part of the accommodation which has been let, *e.g.* the right to come in and make a morning cup of tea as in *James v. James* [1952] C.L.Y. 2948, C.C., a right of passage as in *James v. Coleman* [1949] E.G.D. 122, C.C., a right to use a bath sited in a kitchen as in *Trustees of the Waltham Abbey Baptist Church v. Stevens* (1950) E.G. 294, C.C., and a right to draw and boil water weekly as in *Hayward v. Marshall* [1952] 2 Q.B. 89, C.A.

In each case, the whole of the circumstances must be looked at in order to ascertain whether a person has the right to use a separate dwelling, or something less: *Goodrich v. Paisner* [1957] A.C. 65, H.L. In Rent Act law, the fact that a sharing right is not exercised does not bring the tenant back into full protection (*Stanley v. Compton* [1951] 1 All E.R. 859, C.A., *Kenyon v. Walker* [1946] 2 All E.R. 595, C.A.) although it has been thought that a clear abandonment of the right might do so: *Stanley v. Compton.*

The question is to be determined as at the date when it is relevant, rather than as at the date of letting: *Baker v. Turner* [1950] A.C. 401, H.L.

Dwelling

"Dwelling" itself has been defined as something in which all the major activities of life, such as sleeping, cooking and feeding, are carried out: *Wright v. Howell* (1947) 92 S.J. 26, C.A., *Curl v. Angelo* [1948] 2 All E.R. 189, C.A., *Metropolitan Properties v. Barder* [1968] 1 All E.R. 536. Premises not used for sleeping cannot be in use as a dwelling: *Wimbush v. Cibulia* [1949] 2 K.B. 564, C.A. But use need not be by the person to whom the premises are let: *Whitty v. Scott-Russell* [1950] 2 K.B. 32, C.A., *Edgware Estates Ltd. v. Coblentz* [1949] 2 K.B. 717, C.A., *Carter v. S.U. Carburetter Co.* [1942] 2 K.B. 288, C.A., *Watson v. Saunders-Roe Ltd.* [1947] K.B. 437, C.A., *Anspach v. Charlton SS Co. Ltd.* [1955] 2 Q.B. 21, C.A.

"At Any Time When"

A tenancy is a secure tenancy "at any time when" both the "landlord conditions" (s.80) and the "tenant condition" (s.81) are fulfilled. The phrase "at any time when" is to be found in the 1977 Act, ss.13–16. It is clear that if the landlord's interest changes hands, and a new landlord does not fulfil the criteria described as the "landlord condition," the tenancy will cease to be secure, and, conversely, if the landlord ceases to be exempt from these provisions, the tenancy will be brought within security.

Subs. (2)

"*Subject to the Exceptions in Schedule 1:* The exceptions in brief are:
1. Long leases (see also s.115, below);
2. Tied accommodation as specified;
3. Land acquired for development;
4. Accommodation for homeless persons for a limited period;
5. Temporary accommodation to encourage job mobility;

6. Sub-leasing schemes;
7. Temporary rehousing during works;
8. Agricultural holdings;
9. Licensed premises;
10. Specified student lettings;
11. Business or assured tenancies;
12. Almshouses. See further, notes to Sched. 1, below.

Subss. (3), (4)

By subs. (3), the difficult (see notes to s.93, below) question of tenancy or licence is rendered largely irrelevant for the purposes of this Part, subject to subs. (4). Note, however, that a person occupying pending determination of right of occupation and court proceedings for possession does not have a "licence" for the purposes of this provision: *Harrison* v. *London Borough of Hammersmith & Fulham* [1981] 1 W.L.R. 650, C.A. See also *Restormel Borough Council* v. *Buscombe* (1982) 14 H.L.R. 91, C.A., in which the phrase used is "tolerated trespassers."

There is no need to show that rent or other consideration is paid for the licence (and no "low rent" exemption from security, analogous to that to be found in the Rent Act 1977, s. 5). But the occupation as licensee must be in such circumstances that if the licence were a tenancy, it would be a secure tenancy. This does not only refer to the exemptions in Sched. 1, but to the landlord conditions of s.80, the tenant condition of s.81, and, above all, the requirement that there be a letting "as a separate dwelling" (see notes above).

Thus, a *genuine* non-exclusive occupation agreement (*cf. Somma* v. *Hazlehurst* [1978] 1 W.L.R. 1014; 7 H.L.R. 30, C.A.; *Aldrington Garages* v. *Fielder* (1978) 7 H.L.R. 51, C.A., *Sturolson & Co.* v. *Weniz* (1984) 17 H.L.R. 140, C.A.), will still be excluded from protection, although it will not be possible to use this as a device to defeat the Act, unless the arrangement is wholly genuine (*cf. Street* v. *Mountford* [1985] A.C. 809, 17 H.L.R. 402, H.L. disapproving the above-mentioned three cases, see also *O'Malley* v. *Seymour* (1978) 7 H.L.R. 70, C.A.; *Demuren* v. *Seal Estates Ltd.* (1978) 7 H.L.R. 83, C.A.).

But excluded from this general extension to licences are licensees granted as a temporary expedient to persons who entered the dwelling-house in question, or any other land, as a trespasser, whether or not, before the grant of the current licence, another licence to occupy that or another dwelling-house had been granted to the licensee. This concerns former squatters, who may have subsequently been granted short-life licences of the properties originally squatted, or of other properties eventually intended for improvement, conversion, redevelopment, etc.

The licence must have been granted as a temporary expedient. It must have been granted to a person who entered the dwelling-house as a trespasser. It follows that an allegation of licence *ab initio* will raise a most serious issue and, if upheld, will provide an absolute defence to a claim for possession based only on this subsection. The phrase "any other land" is very broad indeed, but it seems tolerably clear that there must be some nexus between original squat and current licence, even if there has been a series of intervening licences. Land includes buildings on land and parts of buildings: Interpretation Act 1978, Sched. 1.

The landlord condition

80.—(1) The landlord condition is that the interest of the landlord belongs to one of the following authorities or bodies—

a local authority,

a new town corporation,

an urban development corporation,

the Development Board for Rural Wales,

the Housing Corporation,

a housing trust which is a charity, or

a housing association or housing co-operative to which this section applies.

(2) This section applies to—

(*a*) a registered housing association other than a co-operative housing association, and

(*b*) an unregistered housing association which is a co-operative housing association.

(3) If a co-operative housing association ceases to be registered, it shall, within the period of 21 days beginning with the date on which it ceases to

be registered, notify each of its tenants who thereby becomes a secure tenant, in writing, that he has become a secure tenant.

(4) This section applies to a housing co-operative within the meaning of section 27 (agreements for exercise of authority's housing management functions by co-operative) where the dwelling-house is comprised in an agreement under that section.

DEFINITIONS
"co-operative housing association": s.5.
"housing association": s.5.
"housing co-operative": s.27.
"housing trust": s.5.
"local authority": s.4.
"new town corporation": s.4.
"registered": s.5.
"secure tenant": s.79.
"urban development corporation": s.4.

GENERAL NOTE
This section defines the public and quasi-public landlords who are affected by the provisions of this and the next Parts.

Subs. (2)
A co-operative housing association is a fully mutual housing association registered under the Industrial and Provident Societies Act 1965, and a fully mutual association is one the membership of which is restricted to tenants or prospective tenants, and the rules of which confine the grant or assignment of tenancies to members: s.5, above. Accordingly, a housing co-operative in the most common use of that term, registered *both* with the Housing Corporation under the Housing Associations Act 1985 *and* with the registrar of Friendly Societies under the 1965 Act, are *not* landlords whose tenants are secure. But the tenants of such an association which is *not* registered with the Corporation *are* secure.

Subs. (4)
Housing *management* co-operatives, as they are commonly called, included by reason of this subsection are associations which, under an approved agreement, discharge housing functions on behalf of a local authority or new town development corporation: see s.27. The tenancy is, however, only a secure tenancy if it is of a dwelling-house within the terms of the approved agreement. This recognises that some such housing co-operatives are also housing associations, and may manage or own *other* property. Whether or not that other property is within these security provisions will depend on the status of the co-operative as an association. In turn, that depends upon qualification within subs. (2).

The tenant condition

81. The tenant condition is that the tenant is an individual and occupies the dwelling-house as his only or principal home; or, where the tenancy is a joint tenancy, that each of the joint tenants is an individual and at least one of them occupies the dwelling-house as his only or principal home.

DEFINITIONS
"dwelling-house": s.112.

GENERAL NOTE
This section details the "tenant condition." The tenant must be an individual, *i.e.* as distinct from a corporate body or association. This specific provision enacts what had been held to be the law under the Rent Acts once, but only from when, a protected tenancy thereunder had been determined and had thus become a statutory tenancy: see, *e.g. Hiller* v. *United Dairies (London) Ltd.* [1934] 1 K.B. 57 C.A., *Firstcross Ltd.* v. *East West Ltd.* (1980) 7 H.L.R. 98, C.A.

The most important requirement is that the tenant must occupy the premises as his only or principal home: see below. If the tenancy is a joint tenancy, each of the joint tenants must be an individual, but only one of them need occupy as an only or principal home. But note, too, the possibility of determination of the joint tenancy by one only of the joint tenants by notice to quit served *on* the landlord: *Greenwich L.B.C.* v. *McGrady,* (1982) 6 H.L.R. 36, C.A.—see further notes to s.103, below.

"his only or principal home"

This important phrase is not defined in the Act. It is similar to that used in the Leasehold Reform Act 1967, s.1(2): "only or main residence." By analogy, it would accordingly include a tenant who occupies part, but sublets the remainder of his home: see *Harris* v. *Swick Securities* [1969] 1 W.L.R. 1604. In *Poland* v. *Cadogan* [1980] 3 All E.R. 544, C.A., it was held that while long absences from a house may not prevent occupation, a long absence abroad with the premises sublet may indicate a lack of intention to occupy, sufficient to defeat the meaning of occupation for the purposes of that Act. In *Fowell* v. *Radford* (1970) 21 P. & C.R. 99, C.A., a claim by a husband and wife each to be occupying a different house as the main home, although considered unusual, was upheld.

The phrase "only or main residence" also occurs in relation to taxation. In *Frost* v. *Feltham* [1981] 1 W.L.R. 452, Ch.D., it was held that a publican who lived above his pub, which was rented, and who spent two or three days a month in a house he owned in Wales—the only property he actually owned—was entitled to claim the house in Wales as his only or main residence.

What is absolutely clear is that reliance cannot be placed on case law decided under the closest equivalent Rent Act phrase: "if and so long as he occupies the dwelling-house as his residence" (Rent Act 1977, s.2). This has been generously interpreted by the courts, in effect to mean occupation as *a* residence: see, *e.g.* *Bevington* v. *Crawford* (1974) 232 E.G. 191, C.A., *Gofor Investments* v. *Roberts* (1975) 119 S.J. 320, C.A.; see also *Langford Property Co. Ltd.* v. *Tureman* [1949] 1 K.B. 29, C.A., and *Beck* v. *Scholtz* [1953] 1 Q.B. 570, C.A., for two cases which usefully illustrate where the line is drawn. It would quite clearly be contrary to the intention of Parliament under this Part, to permit a person to qualify in more than one property.

Security of tenure

82.—(1) A secure tenancy which is either—

(*a*) a weekly or other periodic tenancy, or

(*b*) a tenancy for a term certain but subject to termination by the landlord,

cannot be brought to an end by the landlord except by obtaining an order of the court for the possession of the dwelling-house or an order under subsection (3).

(2) Where the landlord obtains an order for the possession of the dwelling-house, the tenancy ends on the date on which the tenant is to give up possession in pursuance of the order.

(3) Where a secure tenancy is a tenancy for a term certain but with a provision for re-entry or forfeiture, the court shall not order possession of the dwelling-house in pursuance of that provision, but in a case where the court would have made such an order it shall instead make an order terminating the tenancy on a date specified in the order and section 86 (periodic tenancy arising on termination of fixed term) shall apply.

(4) Section 146 of the Law of Property Act 1925 (restriction on and relief against forfeiture), except subsection (4) (vesting in under-lessee), and any other enactment or rule of law relating to forfeiture, shall apply in relation to proceedings for an order under subsection (3) of this section as if they were proceedings to enforce a right of re-entry or forfeiture.

DEFINITIONS

"dwelling'house": s.112.

"secure tenancy": s.79.

GENERAL NOTE

This is an important section and, conceptually, most attractive. What it says is that the secure tenancy cannot be brought to an end by the landlord until a date when the tenant is ordered to give up possession. Thus, all the private sector problems of notice to quit, new tenancy, distinction between contractual and statutory periods of occupation, mesne profits, status of tenant, etc., have been avoided.

But it only prevents termination *by the landlord*. A tenant may determine his tenancy in the usual way: if periodic, by notice to quit or surrender; if fixed-term, and unless the contract otherwise provides, only by surrender. See *Harrison* v. *London Borough of Hammersmith & Fulham* [1981] 1 W.L.R. 650, C.A., and *London Borough of Greenwich* v. *McGrady* (1982) 6 H.L.R. 36, C.A., as to the continuation of the common law other than as specified in this section.

The requirement for a court order before *eviction* is not new: since 1964, it has been obligatory to use court proceedings before evicting former tenants, and in some cases (extended in 1980) former licensees: see Protection From Eviction Act 1977. It is the requirement for a court order before termination of the *tenancy* itself which was the innovatory element of the security provisions of this Part when first introduced in 1980.

The circumstances in which a court may order possession—and thus termination of tenancy—are set out in s.84, and Sched. 2. The court's powers are fettered by s.83, which sets out the procedure which must be followed before it will be able to make an order for possession, but are extended by s.85, which gives the court powers in relation to secure tenants similar to those which it has long enjoyed in relation to statutory tenants under the Rent Acts (see now Rent Act 1977, s. 100), *i.e.* to adjourn proceedings, or suspend or postpone orders: see notes to s.85, below.

Subs. (1).

This subsection sets out the fundamental proposition. Whether a periodic tenancy (and whether weekly or of any other periods) or whether a term certain (but subject to termination by the landlord) a secure tenancy cannot be brought to an end by the landlord, save by obtaining an order for possession from the court, *and*, in the case of term certain, an order determining the term certain (under subs. (2)). Even if a term certain is brought to an end, then unless the court orders *both* termination *and* possession to take effect on the same date, a periodic tenancy will follow: subs.(3).

Subs. (2)

The tenancy as thus brought to an end by the court ends on the date the court specifies, not, *e.g.* the date of hearing, but nor at any later date when the tenant is actually evicted. Between date ordered to give up possession, and date when evicted (usually by bailiffs), the tenant will normally be a trespasser.

Even if rent is accepted during such a period, it would seem unlikely that any new tenancy *or licence* sufficient to justify the argument that a new arrangement attracting security has come into being: see *Street* v. *Mountford* [1985] A.C. 809; 17 H.L.R. 402, H.L., upholding *Marcroft Waggons Ltd.* v. *Smith* [1951] 2 K.B. 496, C.A. See also, *e.g. Clarke* v. *Grant* [1950] 1 K.B. 104, C.A., *Baron* v. *Phillips* (1978) 38 P. & C.R. 91, C.A., *Longrigg, Burrough & Trounson* v. *Smith* (1979) 251 E.G. 847, C.A. See also the decisions in *Harrison* v. *London Borough of Hammersmith* [1981] 1 W.L.R. 650, C.A., and *Restormel Borough Council* v. *Buscombe* (1982) 14 H.L.R. 91, C.A., see notes to s.79, above.

Subs. (3).

This section deals with terms certain (see also subs. (4)). If there is a proviso for re-entry for forfeiture, the court is not to order possession in consequence of an upheld claim to have re-entered or forfeited, but is instead to make an order determining the term certain. In such circumstances, and unless the court contemporaneously orders the tenant to give up possession, the term certain will be followed by a periodic tenancy. In effect, the tenant will have lost the security of his fixed term, with such consequential benefits as assignability or disposition on death, non-determinability, or fixed rent for the remainder of the term, and will thereinafter enjoy no more than the same security as that enjoyed by a periodic tenant.

The power may be viewed as a cautionary "shot across the bows," and arguably only in the severest cases should the first exercise of the power to determine the term be accompanied by an outright order for possession. The court is, of course, only to determine the term if it would normally have ordered possession on a re-entry or forfeiture, and the specific application of the rules governing restriction on and relief from forfeiture, re-applied by subs. (4), below, reinforce the view that determination of term certain and an order to give up possession altogether will rarely and are intended rarely to be ordered at the same time, for almost all of the substantive powers exercisable on relief could anyway otherwise have been exercised under s.84.

Subs. (4).

The effect of this subsection is to apply the rules governing restriction on and relief from forfeiture to an application under the last subsection to determine a fixed-term secure tenancy. In normal circumstances a right of re-entry or a right to forfeit will not entitle the landlord to recover possession of premises let as a dwelling without a court order in any event: Protection from Eviction Act 1977, s.2.

Note that reference is to a term certain, rather than a term of years certain, thus avoiding any argument over whether or not a fixed term letting need be for at least one year (*cf. Re Land and Premises at Liss, Hants* [1971] Ch. 986, *Gladstone* v. *Bower* [1960] 2 Q.B. 384, but see, in any event, Rent Act 1977, Sched. 15, Case 13, referring to "a term of years certain not exceeding 8 months . . . ")

Unless a right to forfeit for breach of covenant is expressly reserved, there is only a right to forfeit if the breach is of an express condition in the lease, or an implied condition fundamental to the nature of the agreement: see, generally, Woodfall, *Landlord and Tenant* (28th ed., 1978), Vol. 1, paras. 1–1880 *et seq.* A right of re-entry for a forfeiture has to be exercised within 12 years after the right has accrued: Limitation Act 1980, s.15(1) and Sched. 1, para. 7. The right must also still be extant, *i.e.* it must not have been waived.

The most common form of waiver is acceptance of rent, in knowledge of the breach giving rise to the right to forfeit. While on the one hand, a mere single acceptance of rent may not suffice (especially where, as under this Part, the tenant would be entitled to remain in occupation until a court orders him out, *cf. Oak Property Co.* v. *Chapman* [1947] K.B. 886, C.A.), on the other hand a landlord cannot have the best of both worlds by continuing to accept rent and "reserving" for future use, as it best suits him, his right to forfeit: *Carter* v. *Green* [1950] 2 K.B. 76, C.A., *Oak Property Co.* v. *Chapman* (above).

To establish that there has been a waiver, it is necessary to show that the landlord knew of the breach, and has so conducted himself, by words or action, as to affirm the continuation of the term, in spite of the breach. Such knowledge may, however, be the knowledge of an employee or agent, attributed to the landlord: see, *e.g. Ace Parade Ltd.* v. *Barrow* [1957] E.G.D. 176, C.C., *Gailinski* v. *Wheatley* (1955) 165 E.G. 724, C.A., *Metropolitan Properties Co. Ltd.* v. *Cordery* (1979) 251 E.G. 567, C.A. But *cf. Swallow Securities Ltd.* v. *Isenberg* (1985) 274 E.G. 1028, C.A.

But although it is said that courts of law always lean against a forfeiture (*Goodright Walter* v. *Davids* (1778) 2 Cowp. 803) it is clear that mere knowledge of a breach is not enough, and some positive action of affirmation of tenancy is called for: *Doe d. Sheppard* v. *Allen* (1810) 3 Taunt. 78. The state of the landlord's knowledge is important: he must be (or be deemed to be) aware of the facts which give rise to the exercise of his right to forfeit, before he can be deemed to have waived those rights: *David Blackstone* v. *Burnetts* (*West End*) [1973] 1 W.L.R. 1487.

Whether or not money is tendered and accepted *as rent*, for the purposes of waiver, is a question of fact, but once decided that it was, whether or not the consequence *is* waiver is one of law: *Windmill Investments* (*London*) *Ltd.* v. *Milano Restaurant Ltd.* [1962] 2 Q.B. 373.

Even a demand for rent expressed to be "without prejudice" can operate as a waiver of forfeiture: *Segal Securities Ltd.* v. *Thoseby* [1963] 1 Q.B. 887. But in the same case it was held that a demand for rent payable in advance operates only as a waiver of such breaches as are known to the landlord at the time of the demand, *i.e.* past breaches, and of those which it is known to the landlord will continue during such period as he knows they will continue for, *i.e.* it does not operate as a blanket waiver for the whole of the period paid for in advance. And an act of waiver in relation to a covenant prohibiting a particular user of premises only waives past breaches, because a breach of such a covenant is a continuing breach: *Cooper* v. *Henderson* (1982) 5 H.L.R. 1, C.A.

Save when the forfeiture is for rent arrears the Law of Property Act 1925, s.146, requires that preliminary notice be given a tenant before a forfeiture, to give the tenant an opportunity to remedy a breach, provided the breach is remediable, and to give him an opportunity of applying to the court for relief from forfeiture. S.146(4) permits application for relief from a sub-tenant, but this subsection is expressly excluded where what is in question is determination of a secure tenant's term certain.

The s.146 notice must comply with the formal requirements of s.196 of the 1925 Act. Where the basis of the claim to forfeit is dilapidations, the provisions of the Landlord and Tenant Act 1927, s.18(2), add to the requirements of s.146, and in some cases, the Leasehold Property (Repairs) Act 1938, as extended by s.51 of the Landlord and Tenant Act 1954, will impose additional restrictions (but the 1938 Act only applies to tenancies for a term certain of not less than seven years, of which three or more years remain unexpired).

A s.146 notice should be served on the assignee (not the assignor) of the leasehold interest, for he is the person concerned to avoid the forfeiture: *Old Grovebury Manor Farm Ltd.* v. *W. Seymour Plant Sales Ltd.* [1979] 1 W.L.R. 1397. All joint tenants must be served: *Blewett* v. *Blewett* [1936] 2 All E.R. 188. Service of the notice may be by delivery at the premises: *Newborough (Lord)* v. *Jones* [1975] Ch. 90.

Relief may be granted in respect of part only property comprised in lease: *G.M.S. Syndicate* v. *Gary Elliott Ltd.* [1982] Ch. 1. In general, the courts are unwilling to specify rules or principles for the grant of relief: *Rose* v. *Hyman* [1912] A.C. 623, H.L. If a breach has been remedied, relief will commonly but not invariably be granted: see, *e.g. Bathurst (Earl)* v. *Fine* [1974] 1 W.L.R. 905. Remedy of breach is normally required as a condition of relief, although, again, not invariably: see, *e.g. Belgravia Insurance Co.* v. *Meah* [1964] 1 Q.B. 436, *Central Estates Ltd* v. *Woolgar (No.* 2) [1972] 1 Q.B. 48, C.A., *Scala* v. *Forbes* [1974] Q.B. 575. Although the tenant will normally have to bear the costs of an application for relief *(Belgravia)*, this will not be so if the landlord's claim to forfeit is wholly unmeritorious: see, *e.g. Woodtrek Ltd.* v. *Jezek* (1982) 261 E.G. 571.

While an application for relief is pending, the tenant may still enforce, or seek to enforce, the covenants in the lease: *Peninsular Maritime Ltd.* v. *Padseal Ltd.* (1981) 259 E.G. 860, C.A.

Where arrears are concerned, relief is governed by the Supreme Court Act 1981, s.38, and the County Courts Act 1984, s.138, under the provisions of which latter Act a tenant can acquire automatic relief in the course of proceedings issued by the landlord in the county court, by paying into court, at least five clear days before the date specified for the hearing, the whole of the arrears together with the costs of the action. A court will, in any event, invariably order payment of arrears as a condition of relief, within a time specified if not forthwith: *Barton, Thompson & Co.* v. *Stapling Machines Co.* [1966] Ch. 499.

Under s.138, however, if its terms are not complied with, the right to relief is entirely lost, and it has been held that this means relief is not otherwise available in county court or High Court: *Di Palma* v. *Victoria Square Property Co Ltd.* (1985) 17 H.L.R. 448, C.A.

Notice of proceedings for possession or termination

83.—(1) The court shall not entertain—

(*a*) proceedings for the possession of a dwelling-house let under a secure tenancy, or

(*b*) proceedings for the termination of a secure tenancy,

unless the landlord has served on the tenant a notice complying with the provisions of this section.

(2) The notice shall—

(*a*) be in a form prescribed by regulations made by the Secretary of State,

(*b*) specify the ground on which the court will be asked to make an order for the possession of the dwelling-house or for the termination of the tenancy, and

(*c*) give particulars of that ground.

(3) Where the tenancy is a periodic tenancy the notice—

(*a*) shall also specify a date after which proceedings for the possession of the dwelling-house may be begun, and

(*b*) ceases to be in force twelve months after the date so specified;

and the date so specified must not be earlier than the date on which the tenancy could, apart from this Part, be brought to an end by notice to quit given by the landlord on the same date as the notice under this section.

(4) Where the tenancy is a periodic tenancy, the court shall not entertain any such proceedings unless they are begun after the date specified in the notice and at a time when the notice is still in force.

(5) Where a notice under this section is served with respect to a secure tenancy for a term certain, it has effect also with respect to any periodic tenancy arising on the termination of that tenancy by virtue of section 86; and subsections (3) and (4) of this section do not apply to the notice.

(6) Regulations under this section shall be made by statutory instrument and may make different provision with respect to different cases or descriptions of case, including different provision for different areas.

DEFINITIONS

"dwelling-house": s.112.
"secure tenancy": s.79.

GENERAL NOTE

This section governs the pre-eviction procedure. The section introduces, in place of notice to quit, a notice of seeking possession. The circumstances in which possession may be ordered are set out in s.84 and Sched. 2; the court's powers on application for possession, in s.85. This section concerns both periodic, and fixed term, secure tenancies.

The court cannot entertain proceedings for possession, or to determine a secure term certain, unless there has been a prior notice complying with the provisions of this section. Forms prescribed are contained in the Secure Tenancies (Notices) Regulations 1980 (S.I. 1980 No. 1339), as amended by the Secure Tenancies (Notices) (Amendment) Regulations 1984, (S.I. 1984 No. 1224), retained in force by s.2, Housing (Consequential Provisions) Act 1985.

By subs. (3), when the tenancy is a periodic tenancy, the notice must specify a date after which the proceedings may be begun, which date must not be earlier than the date on which the tenancy could otherwise have been brought to an end by notice to quit served on the same date as the notice of intended proceedings. Apart from this Act, a notice to quit a periodic tenancy of a dwelling must be served at least four weeks before it is due to take effect: Protection From Eviction Act 1977, s.5 (which also requires (a) that the notice be in writing, and (b) in certain cases, that it contain prescribed information).

The four weeks need not be four clear weeks: *Schnabel* v. *Allard* [1967] 1 Q.B. 627, C.A. But if the periods of the tenancy are longer than four weeks, *e.g.* a monthly or quarterly tenancy, then the notice to quit must be of at least one period of the tenancy (save where the tenancy is of periods of one year, in which case it need be of no more than six months' duration): *Doe d. Peacock* v. *Raffan* (1806) 6 Esp. 4. The notice must expire on the first or the last day of a period: *Crate* v. *Miller* [1947] K.B. 946.

The notice of seeking possession under this section lapses 12 months after the date specified in it when proceedings may first be brought. The proceedings must accordingly be commenced *after* date specified, but *within* the following year. This is not so, however, of a notice to determine a fixed term tenancy, which requires no earliest date on which proceedings might be commenced, and which does not lapse after any particular time (although a notice left in force for a lengthy time would suggest that the possibility of waiver is greatly increased: see notes to s.82(4), above). A notice to determine a fixed term suffices as notice of intended proceedings in relation to the periodic tenancy which would otherwise, and might yet, arise under s.82(3), and no separate notice need be served.

The notice—of either class—must state the ground on which the court will be asked to make the order for possession, or the order determining the fixed term, and give particulars of that ground, in sufficient detail to enable the tenant to know and to meet the case against him: *Torridge District Council* v. *Jones* (1985) 18 H.L.R., C.A., in which a mere statement that "the reasons for taking this action are non-payment of rent" was held insufficient. The court held that the notice of seeking possession is a "warning shot across the bows" with the object of enabling the tenant to know what he has to do to put matters right before proceedings are commenced. The court has power (s.84(3)) to allow alteration of or addition to grounds stated on which possession is to be sought.

Grounds and orders for possession

84.—(1) The court shall not make an order for the possession of a dwelling-house let under a secure tenancy except on one or more of the grounds set out in Schedule 2.

(2) The court shall not make an order for possession—

(a) on the grounds set out in Part I of that Schedule (grounds 1 to 8), unless it considers it reasonable to make the order,

(b) on the grounds set out in Part II of that Schedule (grounds 9 to 11), unless it is satisfied that suitable accommodation will be available for the tenant when the order takes effect,

(c) on the grounds set out in Part III of that Schedule (grounds 12 to

16), unless it both considers it reasonable to make the order and is satisfied that suitable accommodation will be available for the tenant when the order takes effect;

and Part IV of that Schedule has effect for determining whether suitable accommodation will be available for a tenant.

(3) The court shall not make such an order on any of those grounds unless the ground is specified in the notice in pursuance of which proceedings for possession are begun; but the grounds so specified may be altered or added to with the leave of the court.

DEFINITIONS
    "dwelling-house": s.112.
    "notice": s.83.
    "secure tenancy": s.79.

GENERAL NOTE
    Analogous to Rent Act 1977, s.98, this section imposes a fetter on the court's power to grant an order for possession, to which the landlord has shown his common law entitlement: see, *e.g. Goldthorpe* v. *Bain* [1952] 2 Q.B. 455, C.A., *Moses* v. *Lovegrove* [1952] 2 Q.B. 533, C.A. The landlord is bound to prove all of the elements necessary before the court has power to make an order: see, *e.g. Smith* v. *McGoldrick* (1976) 242 E.G. 1047, C.A., *Mann* v. *Cornella* (1980) 254 E.G. 403, C.A. As to the court's extended powers once it is shown that an order may be made, see s.85. Note that a Registrar may exercise powers under this section (*a*) with the leave of the judge, *and* (*b*) where the defendant does not object: Practice Direction, October 10, 1985.
    The provisions of this section, taken together with Sched. 2, work in this way: a Sched. 2 ground for possession must be specified, and particularised, in the notice of seeking possession under s.83(2): the court has power to allow these grounds to be added to, or altered, with leave. While this would seem broad enough to permit substitution of a wholly new ground, the policy of this Part, as reflected in s.83(2), is to enable the tenant to know and to meet the case against him and, indeed, in the case of a remediable breach, perhaps to give him an opportunity to remedy the breach. This suggests that it would be wrong for a court to grant leave permitting a landlord to vary a case, without also giving the tenant an opportunity to take fresh advice and perhaps call different evidence.
    Indeed, save in a case where no tenant could possibly be considered to have been taken by surprise by ground *and* particulars relied upon, it may even be that a refusal of an adjournment would be appealable: see, *e.g. Jantzen Investments Ltd.* v. *Correger* [1974] *L.A.G. Bulletin* 87, C.A. It might even be appealable if a court were to fail to advise an unrepresented tenant of the possibility of adjournment, *e.g.* to obtain legal advice.
    Having overcome the notice, grounds and particulars hurdle, the landlord must then show:
    (a) that one of Sched. 2, Grounds 1–8 applies, *and* that it is reasonable to make the order; *or*
    (b) that one of Sched. 2, Grounds 9–11 applies, *and* suitable alternative accommodation as defined in Sched. 2, Pt. IV, will be available for the tenant; *or*
    (c) that one of Sched. 2, Grounds 12–16 applies, *and* suitable alternative accommodation will be available for the tenant, *and* it is reasonable to make the order.
    Even if there is an element of reasonableness required in the body of one of the Grounds (*e.g.* Grounds 10, 16), then if reasonableness is an overriding consideration, the court must proceed to consider overall reasonableness in its own right (*Shrimpton* v. *Rabbits* (1942) 131 L.T. 478, D.C., *Hensman* v. *McIntosh* (1954) 163 E.G. 322, C.A., *Peachey Property Corporation* v. *Robinson* [1967] 2 Q.B. 543, C.A.), although if reasonableness has been considered in relation to a specific element of the Ground, the Court of Appeal will, in the absence of a case to the contrary, be inclined to presume that the county court judge has both considered reasonableness overall and considered it properly: *Rhodes* v. *Cornford* [1947] 2 All E.R. 601, C.A., *Tendler* v. *Sproule* [1947] 1 All E.R. 193, C.A.
    The Court of Appeal will rarely intervene in the question of reasonableness, even if it might itself have come to a different view, for it is primarily a question for the trial judge: *Cresswell* v. *Hodgson* [1951] 2 K.B. 92, C.A. There is no general restriction, save relevance, as to what the court can take into account under this general heading of reasonableness (see *Cresswell* v. *Hodgson*) which is to be considered as at the date of the hearing (*Rhodes* v. *Cornford*). Nonetheless, an order may be made even if conduct leading to an order has abated by the date of hearing: see, *e.g. Florent* v. *Horez* (1983) 12 H.L.R. 1, C.A.

"Reasonable" means reasonable having regard to the interests of the parties, and also reasonable having regard to the interests of the public: *ibid*; see also *Battlespring* v. *Gates* (1983) 11 H.L.R. 6, C.A. In *Gladyric Ltd.* v. *Collinson* (1983) 11 H.L.R. 12, C.A., it was considered proper in that case to take into account when determining reasonableness that the tenant had been told at the beginning of the tenancy that it would only be for a short period, on account of the landlord's development plans.

Conduct in a general sense is relevant to reasonableness: *Yelland* v. *Taylor* [1957] 1 W.L.R. 459, C.A., *Abrahams* v. *Wilson* [1971] 2 Q.B. 88, C.A. However, where neglect of a garden led to an order in the county court, the Court of Appeal allowed the appeal on the grounds that for some part of the period of neglect the tenant did not have *legal* (as distinct from moral) responsibility for the garden as tenant, *i.e.* he had become tenant by succession during the (latter part of the) period of neglect: *Holloway* v. *Povey* (1984) 15 H.L.R. 104, C.A.

The Grounds in brief are:
1. Rent arrears or breach of obligation of tenancy;
2. Nuisance and annoyance, or conviction for use of premises for immoral or illegal purposes;
3. Deterioration of premises or common parts;
4. Deterioration of furniture;
5. Grant of tenancy induced by false statement;
6. Premium paid in connection with assignment;
7. Premises let in connection with employment, related to non-housing purposes and conduct inconsistent with those purposes;
8. Temporary rehousing during works, and former premises now available;
9. Overcrowding;
10. Demolition or other works to premises;
11. Conflict with purposes of a charity landlord;
12. Premises let in connection with employment, related to non-housing purposes, and required for new employee;
13. Premises adapted for disabled;
14. Conflict with purposes of specialised housing association or trust;
15. Sheltered accommodation;
16. Underoccupation on death of tenant.

These Grounds, and the definition of suitable alternative accommodation, are considered in the notes to Sched. 2.

There is no such thing as a "consent order" in the light of the wording of the section ("shall not make . . . except"): *R.* v. *Bloomsbury and Marylebone County Court, ex parte Blackburne* (1984) 14 H.L.R. 56, Q.B.D. This is consistent with the general proposition that protective legislation of this order cannot be "contracted out" of: *Barton* v. *Fincham* [1921] 2 K.B. 291, C.A., *R.M.R. Housing Society Ltd.* v. *Combs* [1951] 1 K.B. 486. The term "consent order" ought to be avoided: *Thorne* v. *Smith* [1947] 1 K.B. 307, C.A.; *Barton;* see also *Plashkes* v. *Jones* (1982) 9 H.L.R. 110, C.A.

But although there is, accordingly, properly no such entity as the consent order, it may be that the court can in appropriate circumstances imply an admission, *e.g.* that the tenant is in arrears and that it is reasonable to make the order: *Thorne*. However, *Blackburne* seems to suggest that an *express* admission is required. Furthermore, implied admission will not be available when more than one Ground, or more than one set of facts within one Ground, is pleaded.

Public Law Defences

Where public authorities are concerned, there is the additional issue of "public law," *i.e.* "*Wednesbury* principles" (*Associated Provincial Picture Houses* v. *Wednesbury Corporation* [1948] 1 K.B. 223, C.A.). See, generally, as to these principles, notes to s.64, above.

A number of public law decisions may well lie behind the circumstances leading to an attempted eviction, *e.g.* a decision to improve (see Sched. 2, Ground 10), or to impose a rent increase, for non-payment of which possession is sought (Sched. 2, Ground 1). It is, of course, well settled that rents decisions are vulnerable to public law challenge: (see notes to s.24, above). Have the authority taken everything relevant into account, and ignored the irrelevant? Have they reached a decision within the ambit of what a reasonable authority could decide? Have they had regard to their fiduciary duties to the ratepayers?

In *O'Reilly* v. *Mackman* [1983] 2 A.C. 237, and *Cocks* v. *Thanet District Council* [1983] 2 A.C. 286, 6 H.L.R. 15, the House of Lords held that issues of public law must be raised by way of proceedings for judicial review (R.S.C. Order 53), rather than by way of High Court action for a declaration, or action for breach of statutory duty. Proceedings for judicial review begin, of course, with an application for leave, which serves to protect public authorities against frivolous challenges.

A distinction was drawn in *Cocks* between public law challenges, and private law rights (against public authorities). Thus, under the Housing (Homeless Persons) Act 1977, (now Part III, above) with which the House of Lords was concerned in *Cocks* v. *Thanet D.C.*, if the challenge is to the propriety of an authority's decision that an applicant is, *e.g.* homeless intentionally (see above, s.60 and the large number of cases decided thereunder), that challenge must be mounted by way of judicial review, whereas if the authority have reached a decision in consequence of which housing, or another facility (*e.g.* property protection, see above, s.70), is to be provided, but fail to provide the applicant with his entitlement, the challenge can still be mounted by way of action for breach of statutory duty.

O'Reilly, and *Cocks*, were concerned with proceedings initiated by the person seeking to challenge the authority. In *Wandsworth London Borough Council* v. *Winder* [1985] A.C. 461, 17 H.L.R. 196, H.L., however, the proceedings were proceedings for possession under this section, and the public law challenge was raised by way of defence. The facts are relatively straightforward. In 1981 and 1982, the authority raised rents. The defendant objected to the increases because he considered them excessive and *ultra vires* (on the basis that circumstances did not reasonably require the rent to be increased to the extent to which the authority had resolved). He paid his former rent only, and the authority sought possession for the consequential arrears.

The tenant's defence was struck out in the county court, as an abuse of the process, following *O'Reilly*, and *Cocks*. It was held on appeal that a distinction could be drawn with those cases. The distinction rested upon the tenant's vested—or preexisting—private law right, *i.e.* to his tenancy at the previously established rent he was obliged to pay. To limit challenge to judicial review would adversely affect the tenant's private law rights.

Licensees

It will not be possible to use summary proceedings (R.S.C. Order 113, C.C.R. Order 24) against secure *licensees* (*cf.* s.79(3), above), because those proceedings are available only against *former* licensees (*G.L.C.* v. *Jenkins* [1975] 1 W.L.R. 155, C.A.), and the effect of s.82, above, is that the licence will continue until the date set by the court for possession. However, if it is not clear that the licensee is secure, and the landlord's case is that he is not, those proceedings may be used, but should only proceed on affidavit evidence if the issue is clear and straightforward: *Shah* v. *Givert* (1980) 124 S.J. 513, C.A.

If it is apparent that a serious issue is bound to arise, the use of summary proceedings will be inappropriate and may even constitute an abuse of the process of the court: *Henderson* v. *Law* (1984) 17 H.L.R. 237, C.A. If an unexpected issue arises, the court must exercise its discretion to decide whether it is wiser to continue the summary hearing or adjourn it for a further hearing, or dismiss the application and leave the landlord to issue anew: *ibid.*

Power of Court of Appeal

In *Pollock* v. *Kumar* (1976) 242 E.G. 371, C.A., a possession order was set aside on appeal, but after the tenant had been obliged to go out of occupation for failure to comply with the terms of a stay of execution ordered by the county court (*i.e.* payment pending appeal). The premises had been relet. The Court of Appeal held that its powers under R.S.C. Order 59, rule 10(4)—"the Court of Appeal may make any order, on such terms as the court thinks just, to ensure the determination on the merits of the real question in controversy between the parties"—were wide enough to remit the case to the county court for the assessment of compensation.

Compensation was to be assessed on the basis of financial loss shown to have been suffered by reason of the eviction, not including any element of mental suffering or anything of that sort. It should be a purely financial calculation. However, this was not to be taken as the only basis that would ever be appropriate. Although it is not clear, it may be that in so limiting the compensation, the Court of Appeal was influenced by the appellant's loss of the premises due to his failure to comply with the (financial) terms of the stay.

Extended discretion of court in certain proceedings for possession

85.—(1) Where proceedings are brought for possession of a dwelling-house let under a secure tenancy on any of the grounds set out in Part I or Part III of Schedule 2 (grounds 1 to 8 and 12 to 16: cases in which the court must be satisfied that it is reasonable to make a possession order), the court may adjourn the proceedings for such period or periods as it thinks fit.

(2) On the making of an order for possession of such a dwelling-house on any of those grounds, or at any time before the execution of the order, the court may—

(*a*) stay or suspend the execution of the order, or

(*b*) postpone the date of possession,

for such period or periods as the court thinks fit.

(3) On such an adjournment, stay, suspension or postponement the court—

(*a*) shall impose conditions with respect to the payment by the tenant of arrears of rent (if any) and rent or payments in respect of occupation after the termination of the tenancy (mesne profits), unless it considers that to do so would cause exceptional hardship to the tenant or would otherwise be unreasonable, and

(*b*) may impose such other conditions as it thinks fit.

(4) If the conditions are complied with, the court may, if it thinks fit, discharge or rescind the order for possession.

(5) Where proceedings are brought for possession of a dwelling-house which is let under a secure tenancy and—

(*a*) the tenant's spouse or former spouse, having rights of occupation under the Matrimonial Homes Act 1983, is then in occupation of the dwelling-house, and

(*b*) the tenancy is terminated as a result of those proceedings,

the spouse or former spouse shall, so long as he or she remains in occupation, have the same rights in relation to, or in connection with, any adjournment, stay, suspension or postponement in pursuance of this section as he or she would have if those rights of occupation were not affected by the termination of the tenancy.

DEFINITIONS

"dwelling-house": s.112.

"secure tenancy": s.79.

GENERAL NOTE

This section provides the county court with the powers in relation to secure tenants when the claim for possession is made under the grounds specified (see notes to s.84 and Sched.2) as it enjoys in relation to protected and statutory tenants under Rent Act 1977, s.100, when a claim is brought on one of the discretionary grounds for possession under that Act (see s.98 and Sched. 15 thereof).

Where no specific legislation or inherent jurisdiction (*i.e.* on forfeiture proceedings—*cf.* notes to s.82, above) of the court permits suspension or postponement of the operation of a possession order, the court's powers on an application for possession will normally be subject to the restrictions imposed by Housing Act 1980, s.89, *i.e.* to make the order take effect within 14 days or, in a case of exceptional hardship, such longer period as it considers appropriate to a maximum of 6 weeks.

Subs. (1)

The grounds for possession in relation to which these powers are exercisable are those where the element of reasonableness must also be shown: see notes to s.84 and Sched. 2.

Subs. (2)

The power to stay or suspend or postpone eviction is available on subsequent application, *i.e.* prior to execution, even if the initial order was an outright or absolute order for possession: *Birtwistle* v. *Tweedale* [1954] 1 W.L.R. 190, C.A., *Yates* v. *Morris* [1951] 1 K.B. 77, C.A., *Vandermolen* v. *Toma* (1981) 9 H.L.R. 91, C.A. The court has power to make more than one order, but only prior to execution; a mere application for a stay or suspension does not operate as a stay in itself—*Moore* v. *Registrar of Lambeth County Court* [1969] 1 All E.R. 782, C.A.

When an order for possession is made for a fixed time, or for so long as a condition, commonly payment off arrears, is fulfilled, it is not to read as an order enabling the landlord to execute as soon as the condition is not complied with; accordingly, the court still has power to entertain an application by the tenant to suspend the warrant for possession when the landlord seeks to execute it: *R.* v. *Ilkeston County Court, ex parte Kruza* (1985) 17 H.L.R. 539, Q.B.D.

If an outright order is made, a successor (see ss.87 *et seq.*, below), will take subject to it: *American Economic Laundry* v. *Little* [1951] 1 K.B. 400, C.A. If a suspended order has been made, the successor will take subject to its terms: *Sherrin* v. *Brand* [1956] 1 Q.B. 403, C.A. A court should not make an order producing an indefinite suspension: *Vandermolen* v. *Toma* (1981) 9 H.L.R. 91, C.A.; even an order likely to last for a lengthy period is not desirable, especially where questions of succession may arise—rather, no order for possession should be made, but the tenant warned, and the landlord advised, that on further default, an outright order will follow: *Mills* v. *Allen* [1953] 2 Q.B. 341, C.A.

If the court does order a date on which possession must be given up, that date determines the secure tenancy: see notes to s.82, above.

Subs. (3)

Where arrears are continuing, and there is a likelihood that the tenant will dissipate any housing benefit unless an order is made, it may be possible for a landlord to obtain an interlocutory order to require the tenant to pay his housing benefit towards the rent: *Berg* v. *Markhill* (1985) 17 H.L.R. 455, C.A.

Subs. (4)

This might be applicable when an order had been suspended on payment of current rent plus an amount off the arrears, which arrears have now been cleared, or on terms that there be no further nuisance to neighbours, an order might be discharged after a period of "good behaviour."

Subs. (5)

See also notes to s.91, below.

Periodic tenancy arising on termination of fixed term

86.—(1) Where a secure tenancy ("the first tenancy") is a tenancy for a term certain and comes to an end—

(*a*) by effluxion of time, or

(*b*) by an order of the court under section 82(3) (termination in pursuance of provision for re-entry or forfeiture),

a periodic tenancy of the same dwelling-house arises by virtue of this section, unless the tenant is granted another secure tenancy of the same dwelling-house (whether a tenancy for a term certain or a periodic tenancy) to begin on the coming to an end of the first tenancy.

(2) Where a periodic tenancy arises by virtue of this section—

(*a*) the periods of the tenancy are the same as those for which rent was last payable under the first tenancy, and

(*b*) the parties and the terms of the tenancy are the same as those of the first tenancy at the end of it;

except that the terms are confined to those which are compatible with a periodic tenancy and do not include any provision for re-entry or forfeiture.

DEFINITIONS

"dwelling-house": s.112.

"secure tenancy": s.79.

GENERAL NOTE

Under the provisions of s.82, a periodic tenancy which is a secure tenancy does not come to an end by notice, but by order of the court requiring the tenant to give up possession, the tenancy continuing until the date so ordered. A tenancy for a term certain normally ends by effluxion of time: *secure* tenancies for a term certain instead are to continue periodically under the provisions of this section.

Of course, a fixed-term tenancy may also be brought to an end before the expiry of the term, by re-entry or forfeiture: under s.82, such a termination must be by court order, but the court order will not necessarily order the tenant to give up possession, or not necessarily at the same time as the term is brought to an end, in which case the periodic tenancy specified by this section will still come into existence. The landlord may, however, seek an order both determining the term certain, and requiring the tenant to give up possession, in one and the same proceedings, in which case, if successful, no such periodic tenancy will come into existence.

Note, too, that the provisions of this section apply only to *secure* tenancies: a fixed term tenancy may cease to be secure before the expiry of the term certain. In such a case, the normal course of events will follow: either a new contractual agreement, or eviction, in which latter case a court order must still be sought (Protection From Eviction Act 1977, ss.1–3). A new contractual arrangement may, however, pre-empt the periodic tenancy otherwise automatically arising, even if the tenancy is secure at its determination.

Subs. (1)

The section applies only to tenancies for a term certain.

There will be no automatic periodic tenancy, if the tenant is granted a new secure tenancy of the same dwelling-house (whether another term certain or a periodic tenancy), to commence on the coming to an end of the original term. This will almost invariably mean a prior grant, for any hiatus between term certain and new tenancy will mean that in the meantime, the tenant has become a periodic tenant. Any new tenancy designed to pre-empt the otherwise automatic periodic tenancy, must be a new *secure* tenancy.

Subs. (2)

This subsection settles the terms of the periodic tenancy which will normally arise on the coming to an end of the secure term certain, under subs. (1). The periods of the tenancy are to be the same as those for which rent was last payable under the term certain.

The parties are to be the same as the parties at the end of the term certain. So also are the terms, save that the terms are confined to those compatible with a periodic tenancy and do not include any provision for re-entry or forfeiture. An example of a term not compatible with a periodic tenancy might be one requiring decoration or painting within a fixed time before expiry of term certain, or one requiring the tenant to permit prospective purchasers or tenants to inspect prior to the expiry of the term certain. As to variation of terms once the tenancy becomes a periodic tenancy, see s.102.

Succession on death of tenant

Persons qualified to succeed tenant

87. A person is qualified to succeed the tenant under a secure tenancy if he occupies the dwelling-house as his only or principal home at the time of the tenant's death and either—

(*a*) he is the tenant's spouse, or

(*b*) he is another member of the tenant's family and has resided with the tenant throughout the period of twelve months ending with the tenant's death;

unless, in either case, the tenant was himself a successor, as defined in section 88.

DEFINITIONS

"dwelling-house": s.112.
"member of . . . family": s.113.
"secure tenancy": s.79.
"successor": s.88.

GENERAL NOTE

This and the next three sections govern the question of succession to the tenancy under statute. Under the Rent Act 1977, there can be two "statutory successions" (*cf.* 1977 Act, Sched. 1). But under this Act there is only one: the provisions of this section only apply if the secure tenant who has died was not already a successor, as defined in the next section. The definition of successor is also somewhat wider than under the Rent Acts. Another point of distinction is that where there is a choice of potential successors, and no statutory priority (*cf.* (*a*)), nor agreement as to who shall succeed, the choice lies with landlord, rather than, as under the Rent Acts, by determination of the county court.

A person is only qualified to succeed if he occupied the dwelling-house at the time of the tenant's death, as his only or principal home, as to the meaning of which, see notes to s.81, above. If the would-be successor is not the deceased tenant's spouse, then he must additionally show that he has been residing with the deceased tenant: *Peabody Donation*

Fund Governors v. *Grant* (1982) 6 H.L.R. 41, C.A. A spouse succeeding does not have to show residence with the deceased: the requirement is confined to other members of the family who may succeed.

The question of whether or not the would-be successor has been residing with the deceased is one of fact: *Middleton* v. *Bull* (1951) 2 T.L.R. 1010, C.A. A member of the family residing with the deceased *as a sub-tenant* might not be considered to be residing with him, although otherwise the fact that the deceased and the member of the family were living largely separate lives would not affect the question: *Edmunds* v. *Jones* [1957] 1 W.L.R. 118n, C.A., *Collier* v. *Stoneman* [1957] 1 W.L.R. 1108, C.A. The fact that the tenant was in hospital at the time of death will not prevent residence "with" the deceased, for to reside does not necessarily require immediate presence: *Tompkins* v. *Rowley* [1949] E.G.D. 314, C.A. But where a would-be successor moved into the tenant's home when she was already in hospital, where she died, and never lived with her beforehand, he was not residing with her for this purpose: *Foreman* v. *Beagley* [1969] 1 W.L.R. 1387, C.A.

As to the meaning of "member of the family," see notes to s.113, below.

Cases where the tenant is a successor

88.—(1) The tenant is himself a successor if—

(*a*) the tenancy vested in him by virtue of section 89 (succession to a periodic tenancy), or

(*b*) he was a joint tenant and has become the sole tenant, or

(*c*) the tenancy arose by virtue of section 86 (periodic tenancy arising on ending of term certain) and the first tenancy there mentioned was granted to another person or jointly to him and another person, or

(*d*) he became the tenant on the tenancy being assigned to him (but subject to subsections (2) and (3)), or

(*e*) he became the tenant on the tenancy being vested in him on the death of the previous tenant.

(2) A tenant to whom the tenancy was assigned in pursuance of an order under section 24 of the Matrimonial Causes Act 1973 (property adjustment orders in connection with matrimonial proceedings) is a successor only if the other party to the marriage was a successor.

(3) A tenant to whom the tenancy was assigned by virtue of section 92 (assignments by way of exchange) is a successor only if he was a successor in relation to the tenancy which he himself assigned by virtue of that section.

(4) Where within six months of the coming to an end of a secure tenancy which is a periodic tenancy ("the former tenancy") the tenant becomes a tenant under another secure tenancy which is a periodic tenancy, and—

(*a*) the tenant was a successor in relation to the former tenancy, and

(*b*) under the other tenancy either the dwelling-house or the landlord, or both, are the same as under the former tenancy,

the tenant is also a successor in relation to the other tenancy unless the agreement creating that tenancy otherwise provides.

DEFINITIONS
"dwelling-house": s.112.
"secure tenancy": s.79.

GENERAL NOTE
This section defines who is already a successor, for there will be no succession if the deceased tenant was himself a successor, *i.e.* there can only be one succession: see notes to s.87, above. Furthermore, the definition of successor is somewhat wider than might at first be imagined, *i.e.* it includes surviving joint tenants.

Subss. (1), (2), (3)
A person is a successor secure tenant, if:
(a) he succeeded under the provisions of s.89; *or*

(b) he was a joint tenant and has become sole tenant (in the private sector, such occupation would not qualify as succession, for the occupation would be in the surviving joint tenant's own right—*cf. Lloyd* v. *Sadler* [1978] Q.B. 774, C.A.); *or*

(c) the periodic tenancy is one which arose automatically under s.86, and the prior term certain was granted to some other person, or to the present tenant together with another person; *or*

(d) he became the tenant on the tenancy being assigned to him; *or*

(e) he became the tenant on its being vested in him on the death of the previous tenant.

An assignee tenant is a successor only if, (i) on an assignment under the 1973 Act, the spouse from whom the tenancy was assigned was a successor, or (ii) on an assignment under the "right to exchange," he was a successor under the tenancy he exchanged, *i.e.* the assigning tenant is the one who remains a successor or non-successor, or, by way of illustration, if Tenant A is a successor and exchanges with Tenant B, a non-successor, Tenant A remains a successor in his new property, while Tenant B remains a non-successor.

Subs. (4)

On its face, this is an odd provision, explicable in part by reference to Sched. 2, Ground 16, governing the recovery of possession after the decease of a secure tenant, for reasons of under-occupation. Unless the tenancy agreement otherwise provides, when a successor is offered a new tenancy of the same dwelling-house, or of another dwelling-house from the same landlord, to commence within six months of the determination of the earlier tenancy—which itself was a periodic tenancy—the successor remains a successor even in relation to the new tenancy.

This provision might also be capable of use if two persons each of whom could succeed to a secure tenancy wished to succeed jointly: this cannot be achieved under s.89, below, but could be achieved by the grant of a new tenancy to the would-be joint successors, in which case this could be done without the joint successors gaining the opportunity of passing on the tenancy one more time.

Succession to periodic tenancy

89.—(1) This section applies where a secure tenant dies and the tenancy is a periodic tenancy.

(2) Where there is a person qualified to succeed the tenant, the tenancy vests by virtue of this section in that person, or if there is more than one such person in the one to be preferred in accordance with the following rules—

(*a*) the tenant's spouse is to be preferred to another member of the tenant's family;

(*b*) of two or more other members of the tenant's family such of them is to be preferred as may be agreed between them or as may, where there is no such agreement, be selected by the landlord.

(3) Where there is no person qualified to succeed the tenant and the tenancy is vested or otherwise disposed of in the course of the administration of the tenant's estate, the tenancy ceases to be a secure tenancy unless the vesting or other disposal is in pursuance of an order made under section 24 of the Matrimonial Causes Act 1973 (property adjustment orders in connection with matrimonial proceedings).

(4) A tenancy which ceases to be a secure tenancy by virtue of this section cannot subsequently become a secure tenancy.

DEFINITIONS

"member of . . . family": s.113.

"qualified to succeed": s.87.

"secure tenancy": s.79.

GENERAL NOTE

This section applies only to periodic tenancies, whether originally so, or arising under s.86. When the tenancy is still fixed-term, the succession will be governed by s.90, below.

The present provisions, governing periodic tenancies, do not abolish normal rules as to succession in relation to a periodic secure tenancy, but any such devolution will certainly take second place to these statutory provisions (*cf. Moodie* v. *Hosegood* [1952] A.C. 61). If there is no statutory succession under this section—either because no one qualifies, or because the deceased was himself a successor—the contract will devolve in the normal way, but also subject to termination in the normal way, rather than in the manner prescribed for secure tenancies (see s.83) for the tenancy will have ceased to be secure: see subs. (3).

If an order for possession has been made, the successor will take effect subject to its terms and conditions, if conditional (*Sherrrin* v. *Brand* [1956] 1 Q.B. 403, C.A.), or, indeed, if outright (*American Economic Laundry* v. *Little* [1951] 1 K.B. 400, C.A.).

The section only operates: (a) where there is a periodic secure tenancy; and (b) where there is a person qualified to succeed the tenant under the provisions of s.87. But the provisions do not apply at all if the tenant was himself a successor: see s.87. If there is more than one qualifying successor, subs. (2) governs the choice of who is to succeed.

The statute is silent as to what happens between death and succession, should a conflict cause there to be a delay: presumably, the person upon whom the contract devolves (see subs. (3)) will hold the contractual tenancy upon trust for whomsoever is statutorily to succeed, but in the intervening period it would seem that the tenancy is not a *secure* tenancy, although any attempt by a public authority to avail themselves of this technical proposition by determining the tenancy in the intervening period would undoubtedly be overcome by the courts.

The section governs the choice of successor, when there are more than one who might qualify. The spouse of the deceased tenant has priority over any other member of the family. This repeats the Rent Act rule, to give equality to surviving spouses of both sexes. But, unlike under the Rent Acts, where a dispute between other potential successors is referred to the county court (*cf. Williams* v. *Williams* [1970] 1 W.L.R. 1530, C.A.) under this Act, the landlord chooses.

If there *is* agreement as to who shall succeed, there is no necessity that the agreement should be notified to the landlord before it is treated as valid: *General Management Ltd.* v. *Locke* (1980) 255 E.G. 155, C.A.

The wording of the section clearly precludes any question of joint succession (see also *Dealex Properties* v. *Brooks* [1966] 1 Q.B. 542, C.A.). It would, of course, theoretically be possible for a landlord to grant a new joint tenancy, although this is likely to be impracticable if the parties have already had to refer the matter to the landlord for resolution of a dispute.

Devolution of term certain

90.—(1) This section applies where a secure tenant dies and the tenancy is a tenancy for a term certain.

(2) The tenancy remains a secure tenancy until—
(*a*) it is vested or otherwise disposed of in the course of the administration of the tenant's estate, as mentioned in subsection (3), or
(*b*) it is known that when it is so vested or disposed of it will not be a secure tenancy.

(3) The tenancy ceases to be a secure tenancy on being vested or otherwise disposed of in the course of administration of the tenant's estate, unless—
(*a*) the vesting or other disposal is in pursuance of an order made under section 24 of the Matrimonial Causes Act 1973 (property adjustment orders in connection with matrimonial proceedings), or
(*b*) the vesting or other disposal is to a person qualified to succeed the tenant.

(4) A tenancy which ceases to be a secure tenancy by virtue of this section cannot subsequently become a secure tenancy.

DEFINITIONS
"qualified to succeed": s.87.
"secure tenancy": s.79.

GENERAL NOTE
This section makes provisions corresponding to the last, but for fixed term tenants. If the devolution is such that it passes to a person who qualifies as a successor, then that person becomes not merely the tenant, but the secure tenant. If, on the other hand, it passes to a person who does not so qualify, or it is known that when the tenancy passes it will be to such a person, the fixed-term tenancy ceases to be a secure tenancy, and the new tenant has only his contractual security, determinable as and when the contract provides.

Assignment, lodgers and subletting

Assignment in general prohibited

91.—(1) A secure tenancy which is—

(*a*) a periodic tenancy, or

(*b*) a tenancy for a term certain granted on or after 5th November 1982,

is not capable of being assigned except in the cases mentioned in subsection (3).

(2) If a secure tenancy for a term certain granted before 5th November 1982 is assigned, then, except in the cases mentioned in subsection (3), it ceases to be a secure tenancy and cannot subsequently become a secure tenancy.

(3) The exceptions are—

(*a*) an assignment in accordance with section 92 (assignment by way of exchange);

(*b*) an assignment in pursuance of an order made under section 24 of the Matrimonial Causes Act 1973 (property adjustment orders in connection with matrimonial proceedings);

(*c*) an assignment to a person who would be qualified to succeed the tenant if the tenant died immediately before the assignment.

DEFINITIONS

"qualified to succeed": s.87.

"secure tenancy": s.79.

GENERAL NOTE

This section provides that most secure tenancies are simply incapable of assignment, other than (*a*) by a court order under s.24, Matrimonial Causes Act 1973, ("property transfer order"), (*b*) an assignment to a person who could have succeeded to the tenancy if the tenant had died immediately before the assignment, and (*c*) under the "right to exchange," see notes to s.92, below. This section is not applicable to a secure tenancy from a co-operative housing association (within the meaning of s.5, above, *cf.* notes to s.80, above): s.109, below.

The provision does not apply to fixed-term secure tenancies granted before November 5, 1982, when an amendment was introduced into the then Housing and Building Control Bill, and these continue to be subject to the former provisions: see Housing (Consequential Provisions) Act 1985, Sched. 4, para. 9.

If there is a purported assignment of a tenancy, or in the case of a pre-November 5, 1982 fixed-term tenancy, an assignment leading to loss of security, the tenancy cannot subsequently become a secure tenancy: subs. (2).

Assignment to Potential Successor

The provision permitting assignment to a potential successor may be used, *e.g.* where the tenant wishes to prevent a dispute between one of two potential successors (*cf.* notes to s.89, above), or else to permit a tenant to assign to a potential successor, and then leave the premises, perhaps to retire to another town or even country (as in *Peabody Donation Fund* v. *Higgins* [1983] 1 W.L.R. 1091, 10 H.L.R. 82, C.A.)

In *Higgins*, the tenancy agreement contained an absolute prohibition on assignment. The tenant, intending to retire to Ireland and wishing to permit his daughter to remain in their home, executed an assignment by deed. As such, it was an effective assignment, albeit one contrary to the terms of the tenancy. The daughter would, however, be vulnerable to an action for possession on the ground of breach of term of tenancy (requiring proof of reasonableness—Sched. 2, Ground 1).

Note that an assignment, to be effective, must be by deed, even if the tenancy under assignment did not itself require to be in writing: see Law of Property Act 1925, s.52, *Botting* v. *Martin* (1808) 1 Camp. 317. However, in some circumstances, this requirement may be avoided if the assignment is evidenced in writing, or if there is sufficient part performance of the assignment, in which case the assignment may take effect as an enforceable contract for the assignment: see Law of Property Act 1925, s.40, *Butcher* v. *Stapeley* (1685) 1 Vern. 363, *Montacute* v. *Maxwell* (1720) 1 P.Wms. 616, *Walsh* v. *Lonsdale* (1882) 21 Ch. 9; see also Woodfall, *Landlord and Tenant* (28th ed., 1978), Vol. 1 Chap. 16.

Property Transfer Order

For the purpose of a property transfer order under the 1973 Act, property includes a weekly or any other periodic tenancy, as well as a tenancy for a term certain: *Hale* v. *Hale* [1975] 1 W.L.R. 931, C.A. This applies just as much when the tenancy is of a local authority property: *Thompson* v. *Thompson* [1976] Fam. 25, C.A. The caveat expressed in *Regan* v. *Regan* [1977] 1 W.L.R. 84, concerned the prohibition on assignment without consent formerly incorporated into local authority lettings, but this may now be disregarded as that prohibition was repealed in 1980.

In *Rodewald* v. *Rodewald* [1977] Fam. 192; [1977] 2 W.L.R. 191; [1977] 2 All E.R. 609, C.A., the court expressed a similar reluctance to intervene in local authority allocation discretion, but this, too, may be disregarded, as the policy of this Part is overwhelmingly clearly to leave such dispositions to the court: see also *Hansard,* H.L., June 30, 1980, col. 177.

Some doubt has been expressed over the court's powers to order a transfer of tenancy under s.24, where there is a prohibition (absolute or qualified) on assignment under the tenancy: see *Thompson* v. *Thompson* [1976] Fam. 25; *Hale* v. *Hale* [1975] 1 W.L.R. 931, and *Hutchings* v. *Hutchings* (1975) 237 E.G. 571, C.A., discussed at (1979) 129 New L.J., 1069.

None of this affects the power of the court to order a transfer of a secure tenancy— whether joint into one name, or from one name into another—under the Matrimonial Homes Act 1983, which power is exercisable on or after grant of decree, although not once the spouse applying for the transfer has remarried.

There is, however, one problem with this power, which arises (a) in the case of a sole tenancy only, (b) if the tenant is no longer living in the premises, and (c) application under the 1983 Act is not made until after decree absolute. Until decree absolute, even if the tenant is no longer living in the premises, it is likely that his tenancy will still be treated as secure, by way of occupation "through" his spouse; but such notional occupation will determine with decree absolute: see *Brown* v. *Draper* [1944] K.B. 309, C.A., *Robson* v. *Headland* (1948) 64 T.L.R. 596, C.A., *Old Gate Estates* v. *Alexander* [1950] 1 K.B. 311, C.A., *Middleton* v. *Baldock* [1950] 1 K.B. 657, C.A., and *Wabe* v. *Taylor* [1952] 2 Q.B. 735, C.A.

In *Lewis* v. *Lewis* [1985] A.C. 459, 17 H.L.R. 459, H.L., the House of Lords considered the right to transfer after divorce, as it had been introduced under the Matrimonial Homes and Property Act 1981. In that case, the attempt was to apply the Act retrospectively, which was dismissed. Part of the reasoning, however, was that the Act could not be used to revive a statutory (or, here, secure) tenancy which had ceased to exist before the application for transfer. But that is exactly the position which will have arisen in the circumstances set out in the last paragraph, once a decree has become absolute without application for transfer.

Their Lordships did leave the point open, as unnecessary to decide in *Lewis,* but unless or until there is a decision which undoes the effect of the case law cited in the last paragraph, secure tenants and their advisers will have to be careful to apply for a 1983 transfer before decree absolute, for they might otherwise be reliant upon the 1973 Act, with its attendant difficulties.

Assignments by way of exchange

92.—(1) It is a term of every secure tenancy that the tenant may, with the written consent of the landlord, assign the tenancy to another secure tenant who satisfies the condition in subsection (2).

(2) The condition is that the other secure tenant has the written consent of his landlord to an assignment of his tenancy either to the first-mentioned tenant or to another secure tenant who satisfies the condition in this subsection.

(3) The consent required by virtue of this section shall not be withheld except on one or more of the grounds set out in Schedule 3, and if withheld otherwise than on one of those grounds shall be treated as given.

(4) The landlord may not rely on any of the grounds set out in Schedule 3 unless he has, within 42 days of the tenant's application for the consent, served on the tenant a notice specifying the ground and giving particulars of it.

(5) Where rent lawfully due from the tenant has not been paid or an obligation of the tenancy has been broken or not performed, the consent required by virtue of this section may be given subject to a condition

requiring the tenant to pay the outstanding rent, remedy the breach or perform the obligation.

(6) Except as provided by subsection (5), a consent required by virtue of this section cannot be given subject to a condition, and a condition imposed otherwise than as so provided shall be disregarded.

DEFINITIONS
"secure tenancy": s.79.
"term": s.116.

GENERAL NOTE

This section introduces a "right to exchange" (see also Sched. 2, Ground 6, constituting a ground for possession if a premium is charged in connection with the exercise). This section is not applicable to a secure tenancy from a co-operative housing association (within the meaning of s.5, above, *cf.* notes to s.80, above): s.109, below.

An exchange operates by way of an assignment, with written consent of the landlord, within subs. (1). Subs. (1) applies to any other secure tenant—not necessarily of the same landlord—who has the written consent of his landlord to assign to *the* or *an* other secure tenant. The extension to "an" other is designed to permit three-way, or multiple, exchanges. Everyone involved must have permission to assign to another secure tenant, who himself has permission to assign to a secure tenant.

Consent is not to be withheld save on specified grounds. These are set out in Schedule 3, and cover a range of circumstances: In brief, they are:

1. Tenant or assignee obliged to give up possession under a court order;
2. Proceedings commenced for possession against tenant or assignee under Sched. 2, Grounds 1–6, or notice of seeking possession on one or more of those Grounds served under s.83;
3. Accommodation substantially more extensive than reasonably required by assignee;
4. Extent of accommodation not reasonably suitable to needs of assignee and family;
5. Accommodation let to tenant in consequence of employment, related to non-housing purposes;
6. Conflict with purposes of charity landlord;
7. Adapted for disabled person;
8. Conflict with purposes of specialist housing association or trust;
9. Sheltered accommodation.

See, further, notes to Sched. 3, below.

If consent is withheld on any ground other than one of the specified grounds, the consent is to be treated as given. Furthermore, the landlord can only withhold consent if reply is given within 42 days' of application, specifying the Ground and "giving particulars of it." It seems likely that this would be held to mean more than merely setting out the words of the Schedule, *i.e.* a landlord ought to apply the Ground to the particular circumstances in issue.

In addition to the specified grounds of *objection*, however, the landlord is entitled to require payment of any rent arrears, or the remedying of any other breach of an obligation of the tenancy, as a *condition* of consent, and this entitlement is not limited by failure to reply within 42 days. No other conditions may be attached, however, and if such is specified it is to be disregarded.

The possibility of a conditional consent of this latter class—arrears or breach of obligation of tenancy—suggests that a failure by the landlord to reply within 42 days is *not* to be treated as the giving of consent (and the Act is noticeably silent on any "deemed consent" in this case—*cf.* s.94(5), below, treating improperly conditional consent to subletting as unconditionally given).

It follows that if the landlord fails to reply at all, the tenant will need to take action, *e.g.* for an injunction or a declaration in the county court, under s.110, below, to compel a reply, and cannot simply proceed to assign in default. Such an assignment would be a non-assignment, by reason of s.91, above.

Note that on an exchange, an assign*ee* who is a successor (as defined in s.88), remains a successor. In other words, the status of successor goes with the person of the tenant, rather than the tenancy, or the property, in question. Thus, if Tenant A, a successor, exchanges with Tenant B, a non-successor, Tenant A remains a successor in his new property, while Tenant B remains a non-successor in his. See s.88(3).

Lodgers and subletting

93.—(1) It is a term of every secure tenancy that the tenant—
  (*a*) may allow any persons to reside as lodgers in the dwelling-house, but
  (*b*) will not, without the written consent of the landlord, sublet or part with possession of part of the dwelling-house.
  (2) If the tenant under a secure tenancy parts with the possession of the dwelling-house or sublets the whole of it (or sublets first part of it and then the remainder), the tenancy ceases to be a secure tenancy and cannot subsequently become a secure tenancy.

DEFINITIONS
  "dwelling-house": s.112.
  "secure tenant": s.79.

GENERAL NOTE
  Under the Housing Act 1957, as amended on the introduction of this provison by the Housing Act 1980, local authorities were bound to make it a term of every letting that the tenant should not assign, sub-let or otherwise part with possession of the premises or any part of them, without the written consent of the authority, which consent was not to be given unless the authority were satisfied about the rents to be charged to sub-tenant or assignee. Instead, as a significant part of the "tenant's charter," there was introduced the provisions that are now this section, *i.e.* unconditional right to take in lodgers, and the right to sublet with consent not unreasonably to be withheld and not to be subject to conditions (see s.94(5), below).
  This section is not applicable to a secure tenancy from a co-operative housing association (within the meaning of s.5, above, *cf.* notes to s.80, above): s.109, below.

Lodgers
  A secure tenant has an absolute right to permit "lodgers" to reside in the premises. There is no statutory definition of "lodger," although the term is well-known in popular usage and not unknown in law: see, *e.g. Douglas* v. *Smith* [1907] 2 K.B. 568, C.A. see also Woodfall, *Landlord and Tenant* (28th ed. 1978), Vol. 1, para. 1–0021, wherein it is suggested that the test of whether or not a person is lodger or sub-tenant is determined by the degree of control retained by the householder over the rooms which the lodger occupies (see also *Appah* v. *Parncliffe Investments* [1964] 1 W.L.R. 1064).
  The term has recently been given attention by the House of Lords, in *Street* v. *Mountford* [1985] A.C. 809, 17 H.L.R. 402. Save in exceptional circumstances, *i.e.* where the parties do not intend to enter into legal relationships at all, or where the relationship is that of vendor and purchaser, master and service occupier, or where the owner (a public landlord) had no power to grant a tenancy, an arrangement whereby one person takes exclusive occupation of residential accommodation at a rent will invariably be *tenancy, unless* it is one of "lodging." For this purpose, lodging was defined to mean where the landlord provides attendance and services which require the landlord or his employees to exercise unrestricted access to and use of the premises.
  Where the lodger is a relative, or an elderly person to whom some assistance is provided, or where the lodger uses cooking facilities, it is likely that there will be no problem arising from the distinction: see, *e.g.*, *Booker* v. *Palmer* [1942] 2 All E.R. 674, C.A., *Marcroft Waggons Ltd.* v. *Smith* [1951] 2 K.B. 496, C.A., *Abbeyfield (Harpenden) Society Ltd.* v. *Woods* [1968] 1 W.L.R. 374, C.A., *Barnes* v. *Barratt* [1970] 2 Q.B. 657, C.A. The decision in *Marchant* v. *Charters* [1971] 1 W.L.R. 1181, C.A., was one described by the House of Lords in *Street* as one of lodging.
  Note that a lodger may have a restricted contract within s.19 of the Rent Act 1977, which means that he will be able to refer his rent to the Rent Tribunal under the Rent Act 1977, Part V, and he will enjoy a small degree of security against eviction, under the Rent Act 1977, s.106A: *cf. Luganda* v. *Service Hotels Ltd.* [1969] 2 Ch. 209, C.A., *R* v. *South Middlesex Rent Tribunal, ex p. Beswick The Times* March 25, 1976, D.C., *Marchant* v. *Charters* (above).

Subletting
  The qualified prohibition on subletting amounts to a positive entitlement to sublet, *with consent.* Consent is governed by s.94, below. The right is, however, only to sublet *part*, not the whole. The distinction between the absolute right to take in lodgers, and subletting,

means that the difference between licence and tenancy—generally not relevant under this Part (see s.79, above), and rarely of any other relevance under the Act as a whole, is more important in this context than anywhere else in the Act.

All of the recent law on the subject has to be reconsidered in the light of the two decisions of the House of Lords: *Street* v. *Mountford* [1985] A.C. 809, 17 H.L.R. 402, and *Eastleigh Borough Council* v. *Walsh* [1985] 17 H.L.R. 392. The first-mentioned case, even although the later judgment, is the more important, but the cases have in common that the courts are now not to be concerned with the "intention of the parties" *other* than as derived from the key circumstances: *i.e.* has exclusive occupation or possession of residential occupation, at a rent, been passed as a result of an arrangement, which arrangement does not amount to one of "lodging" or one of the other exceptional circumstances described above.

The House of Lords held that, save in those circumstances (exceptional cases and lodging), an occupier of residential accommodation at a rent will be a tenant if the occupier is granted exclusive possession for a fixed or periodic term certain in consideration of a premium or periodical payments; unless these three hallmarks are decisive, it becomes impossible to distinguish contractual tenancy from contractual licence; the grant may be express, or may be inferred where the owner or landlord accepts weekly or other periodical payments from the occupier; exclusive possession is of the first importance in considering whether an occupier is a tenant; in order to ascertain the nature and quality of an occupancy, the court must decide whether upon its true construction the agreement confers on the occupier exclusive possession in fact.

The consequences in law of an agreement can only be determined by consideration of its effect, having regard to the circumstances and the conduct of the parties; if the agreement satisfies all the requirements of a tenancy, then the agreement produces a tenancy and the parties cannot alter the effect of the agreement by insisting that they only created a licence; the only intention relevant is the intention demonstrated by the agreement to grant exclusive possession for a term at a rent; observations of Lord Greene M.R. in *Booker* v. *Palmer* [1942] 2 All E.R. 674, C.A., were not directed to the distinction between a contractual tenancy and a contractual licence, but to whether or not the conduct of the parties (not their professed intentions) indicated that they intended to contract at all. For a recent case in which *Street* was applied, see *Royal Philanthropic Society* v. *County, The Times*, November 9, 1985; (1985) 18 H.L.R., C.A., in which a former service occupier (see notes to Sched. 1, para. 2, below) was held to be a tenant when moved to alternative accommodation, on the basis that (a) he was not a lodger, and (b) as he was not a service occupier in the new premises, his occupation no longer fell within the "exceptional circumstances" described above.

A sub-letting in contravention of the term, even though it will constitute an illegal sub-letting and, for the tenant, a breach of a term of his tenancy (*cf.* s.84 and Sched. 2, Ground 1) will still be valid as between tenant and sub-tenant, for the illegality will be that of the tenant, who cannot take advantage of his own wrong: *Critchley* v. *Clifford* [1962] 1 Q.B. 131, C.A.

The sub-tenant—whether legal or illegal—will usually not be a protected sub-tenant under the Rent Act 1977, because he will have a resident landlord (*cf.* 1977 Act, s.12) but he will have a restricted contract within s.19 of the 1977 Act which, as for a lodger, will provide him with a slight degree of security against eviction, by the 1977 Act, s.106A. He will also be able to refer his rent to the Rent Tribunal under Pt. V, Rent Act 1977 (although *cf.* the self-evident danger of retaliatory eviction involved). The fact that the *superior* landlord will be exempt from the Rent Acts will not affect the matter at all, for the position must be viewed as between sub-tenant and tenant, if only by estoppel: *Lewis* v. *Morelli* [1948] 2 All E.R. 1021, *Stratford* v. *Syrett* [1958] 1 Q.B. 107.

Note, however, that even an illegal sub-tenant may in some circumstances come to hold a tenancy of the landlord direct. This Part contains no provisions analogous to those to be found in the Rent Act 1977, s.137, which, in effect, elevate a legal sub-tenant into the position of a tenant of the superior landlord on the determination of the mesne tenancy, although this provision in any event is thought only to apply when both mesne tenant, and sub-tenant, enjoy protected or statutory tenancies under that Act.

What this Part does provide is that if a tenancy ceases to be secure on account of sub-letting of the whole of the premises, the tenancy cannot become a secure tenancy (subs. (2)). This, it would seem, refers only to the mesne tenancy, which is thus prevented from reattaining security should the tenancy be assigned back, or the sub-letting determined.

In this statutory silence, we must, therefore, revert to the common law. The normal rule is that with the determination of a tenancy, all inferior interests also determine: thus, on determination of mesne tenancy, sub-tenancy will come to an end, even without notice to quit. But exceptionally, if mesne tenant surrenders, or if mesne tenant gives notice to quit to the landlord, then there is considered to be a merger of landlord and mesne tenant's interest, with the result that interests binding on the mesne tenant, come to bind the landlord, *whether legal or illegal interests*, so that in such cicumstances, both an illegal, and a legal, sub-tenant will become the tenant of the landlord direct and, all other things being equal, will become a secure tenant: *Mellor* v. *Watkins* (1874) L.R. 9 (Q.B.), 400, *Parker* v. *Jones* [1910] 2 K.B. 32. Note, however, that this will not apply to lodgers who, as licensees, have no interest at law in any part of the premises.

Finally, it may be noted that a periodic tenant may sub-let either for periods similar to his own, or may even grant a fixed term sub-tenancy for a period in excess of his own periods of tenancy: *Curteis* v. *Corcoran* (1947) 150 E.G. 44. A letting to a lodger will not constitute a parting with possession: *Edwards* v. *Barrington* [1901] 85 L.T. 650 H.L., *Segal Securities Ltd.* v. *Segal* [1963] 1 Q.B. 887.

Subs. (2)

" . . . cannot subsequently become . . . ": *i.e.* security is not regained by evicting one or all of the sub-tenants, or the sole sub-tenant of the whole.

Consent to subletting

94.—(1) This section applies to the consent required by virtue of section 93(1)(*b*) (landlord's consent to subletting of part of dwelling-house).

(2) Consent shall not be unreasonably withheld (and if unreasonably withheld shall be treated as given), and if a question arises whether the withholding of consent was unreasonable it is for the landlord to show that it was not.

(3) In determining that question the following matters, if shown by the landlord, are among those to be taken into account—

   (*a*) that the consent would lead to overcrowding of the dwelling-house within the meaning of Part X (overcrowding);

   (*b*) that the landlord proposes to carry out works on the dwelling-house, or on the building of which it forms part, and that the proposed works will affect the accommodation likely to be used by the sub-tenant who would reside in the dwelling-house as a result of the consent.

(4) Consent may be validly given notwithstanding that it follows, instead of preceding, the action requiring it.

(5) Consent cannot be given subject to a condition (and if purporting to be given subject to a condition shall be treated as given unconditionally).

(6) Where the tenant has applied in writing for consent, then—

   (*a*) if the landlord refuses to give consent, it shall give the tenant a written statement of the reasons why consent was refused, and

   (*b*) if the landlord neither gives nor refuses to give consent within a reasonable time, consent shall be taken to have been withheld.

DEFINITIONS

"dwelling-house": s.112.
"overcrowding": s.324.

GENERAL NOTE

This section replaces, but to some extent reproduces, the existing law on the subject of qualified covenants, *i.e.* a covenant not to do something—in this case not to sub-let—without the consent of the landlord (which consent, in this case, must, under s.93(1)(*b*), above, be in writing). Indeed, to some extent it is superfluous, for s.19(1) of the Landlord and Tenant Act 1927 would in any event insert the requirement that such consent is not unreasonably to be withheld, now to be found in this subsection.

The statement that if consent is unreasonably withheld it is treated as given also reproduces the existing law: see *Balls Brothers Ltd.* v. *Sinclair* [1931] 2 Ch. 325. It is, however, quite clear that, as under s.19(1) of the 1927 Act, a tenant cannot rely on a withheld consent in defence to an action based upon illegal sub-letting, unless consent has actually been sought, no matter how unreasonable *any* withholding might be, or how well-founded the anticipation of (unreasonable) withholding: see *Barrow* v. *Isaacs* [1891] 1 Q.B. 417, *Eastern Telegraph Co.* v. *Dent* [1899] 1 Q.B. 835.

It is unreasonable withholding that is prohibited by the section, not unreasonable refusal, so that a failure to reply to a request for consent amounts to unreasonable withholding, on failure to respond within a reasonable time: see subs. (6)(*b*), and *Wilson* v. *Fynn* [1948] W.N. 242; [1948] 2 All E.R. 40. But in case of failure to seek consent, consent may be sought and validly given after the sub-letting: subs. (4).

The county court has jurisdiction to declare that a consent has unreasonably been withheld, even if no relief other than a declaration is sought: s.110. It is theoretically open to a tenant from whom consent has unreasonably been withheld to carry on with the letting, and subsequently defend any proceedings on the ground that an unreasonably withheld consent is to be treated as given, but a tenant is well-advised to seek a declaration even if confident of the outcome of any such subsequent proceedings: *Mills* v. *Cannon Brewery Co.* [1920] 2 Ch. 38. But if proceedings are commenced on the mere failure to seek consent, when it could not unreasonably have been withheld, no order for possession will follow: *cf. Leeward Securities Ltd.* v. *Lilyheath Properties Ltd.* (1983) 17 H.L.R. 35, C.A.

Subs. (2)

Under this subsection, there is a statutory presumption that a withholding of consent is unreasonable (*cf.* the existing law on this topic: *Shanley* v. *Ward* (1913) 29 T.L.R. 714, *Pimms* v. *Tallow Chandlers Co.* [1964] 2 Q.B. 547, *Lambert* v. *F. W. Woolworth & Co.* (*No. 2*) [1938] Ch. 883, *Frederick Berry Ltd.* v. *Royal Bank of Scotland* [1949] 1 K.B. 619). Subs. (3) also specifies factors which are to be taken into account, if shown to be relevant by the landlord, but these factors are certainly not exhaustive and the existing law will retain importance on this subject, at least so far as it does not conflict with the words of the section.

Consent may not be given conditionally, and if granted subject to a condition is treated as given unconditionally: subs. (5). Under subs. (6)(a), the landlord refusing consent is bound to give his reasons in writing, and withholding of consent is deemed to amount to a refusal, once a reasonable time has elapsed.

Subs. (3)

In addition to the usual considerations which may be taken into account, the statute specifies two, which are, however, only applicable if shown by the landlord, upon whom lies the burden of showing a reasonable withholding of consent: (a) that the consent would lead to overcrowding under Part X; and (b) that the landlord proposes to carry out works on the dwelling-house, or on the building of which it forms part, and the proposed works will affect the accommodation likely to be used by the sub-tenant for whose benefit consent is sought. This would seem to envisage works of alteration reducing the size of, or altering the layout of, the premises, and would appear to indicate actual proposals, not just vague, generalistic intention.

It is, however, the reasonableness of the particular landlord that is to be taken into account: in order to establish reasonable withholding, it is sufficient to show (a) that "any" reasonable landlord could withhold consent, and (b) that the particular landlord does so; but if no reasonable landlord could withhold consent, then the withholding will be unreasonable—see *Re Town Investments Underlease* [1954] Ch. 301, *Pimms* v. *Tallow Chandlers* [1964] 2 Q.B. 547, *Lovelock* v. *Margo* [1963] 2 Q.B. 786.

Although prima facie it is such matters as the identity of the proposed sub-tenant, or the use to which the premises will be put, which dominate the issue (*Houlder Bros. & Co. Ltd* v. *Gibbs* [1925] Ch. 575, *Swanson* v. *Forton* [1949] Ch. 143) it is reasonable to take into account matters affecting other property belonging to the landlord, *e.g.* the use of facilities on an estate or in a block of flats: *Tredegar* v. *Harwood* [1929] A.C. 72, H.L. *Houlder Bros. & Co. Ltd.* v. *Gibbs* (above).

Consent cannot be withheld in order to obtain for the landlord a windfall benefit wholly outside the contemplation of the agreement or simply because the landlord's policy or practice dictates a withholding: *Bromley Park Garden Estates Ltd.* v. *Moss* [1982] 1 W.L.R. 1019, 4 H.L.R. 61, C.A. A landlord cannot set out in advance, *e.g.* in a tenancy agreement, in what circumstances consent will or will not be withheld: *Creery* v. *Summersell and Flowerdew & Co. Ltd.* [1949] Ch. 751, *Re Smith's Lease, Smith* v. *Richards* [1951] 1 T.L.R. 254.

It would be unreasonable to refuse consent because the would-be sub-tenant was the landlord's tenant elsewhere, and the property it was intended to quit would be hard to let again: *Houlder Brothers & Co. Ltd.* v. *Gibbs* (above).

If a sub-tenant's references are taken up, and are inadequate, this may be sufficient to justify a refusal of consent: *Shanley* v. *Ward* (1913) 29 T.L.R. 714. A landlord may take into account breaches of other covenants by the tenant, although just how relevant this will be in relation to a would-be sub-letting will be a question of fact in each set of circumstances, and may be affected by the severity of the tenant's breach: *Farr* v. *Cummings* (1928) 44 T.L.R. 249, *Goldstein* v. *Sanders* [1915] 1 Ch. 549, *Cosh* v. *Fraser* (1964) 108 S.J. 116.

If the landlord has grounds for fearing that the new tenant or sub-tenant will cause breaches of covenant, refusal may be reasonable (*Granada TV Network* v. *Great Universal Stores* (1963) 187 E.G. 391) although this is not decisive, because the landlord will still have recourse to other remedies: *Killick* v. *Second Covent Garden Property Co.* [1973] 1 W.L.R. 658. The question will always turn on the facts of each case: see *Houlder Bros. & Co. Ltd.* v. *Gibbs* (above), see also *Lee* v. *K. Carter Ltd.* [1949] 1 K.B. 85 and *Bickel* v. *Duke of Westminster* [1977] Q.B. 517, C.A. This will be so even if questions of statutory protection under this, or the 1977 (or another) Act, will arise: *West Layton Ltd.* v. *Joseph* [1979] Q.B. 593, C.A., *Leeward Securities Ltd.* v. *Lilyheath* (1983) 17 H.L.R. 35, C.A.

A refusal based on illegal discrimination, whether sex or race, will, however, itself be illegal and, as such, inescapably unreasonable: see Sex Discrimination Act 1975, s. 31, Race Relations Act 1976, s. 24.

Subs. (4)
This provides that a consent may validly be given, even although it follows the action which requires it. It does not interfere with the proposition that consent must be sought before it can be deemed to have been unreasonably withheld, but it provides tenants with a further opportunity to rely upon the provisions of these two sections, to seek consent after the action, and then to apply to the county court (s.110) if it is unreasonably withheld.

Subs. (5)
This prohibits conditional consents. The sanction against the landlord is severe: while one might have anticipated that a conditional consent would be treated as a withheld consent, rather the condition is simply treated as non-existent. This provision would pre-empt use of the device used in *Adler* v. *Upper Grosvenor Street Investments* [1957] 1 W.L.R. 227, and *Bocardo S.A.* v. *S. & M. Hotels Ltd.* [1980] 1 W.L.R. 17, C.A., under which cases it was held that a contractual covenant requiring a tenant to offer to surrender instead of exercising a right to sub-let or to assign did not offend the prohibition on unreasonable withholding of consent.

Subs. (6)
This subsection incorporates the rule that if consent is sought, and there is no reply within a reasonable time, the consent is treated as having been withheld: see *Wilson* v. *Flynn* [1948] 2 All E.R. 40. If consent is refused, the landlord is bound to give the tenant a written statement of the reasons for such refusal. Clearly, this must go beyond an opaque statement that the landlord does not consider it reasonable to consent, but must give the tenant a sufficient basis to understand why the landlord is refusing consent, and to know, and perhaps to seek advice upon, the basis for challenge, if any.

Assignment or subletting where tenant condition not satisfied

95.—(1) This section applies to a tenancy which is not a secure tenancy but would be if the tenant condition referred to in section 81 (occupation by the tenant) were satisfied.

(2) Sections 91 and 93(2) (restrictions on assignment or subletting of whole dwelling-house) apply to such a tenancy as they apply to a secure tenancy, except that—

(*a*) section 91(3)(*b*) and (*c*) (assignments expected from restrictions) do not apply to such a tenancy for a term certain granted before 5th November 1982, and

(*b*) references to the tenancy ceasing to be secure shall be disregarded, without prejudice to the application of the remainder of the provisions in which those references occur.

DEFINITIONS
"secure tenancy": s.79.

GENERAL NOTE
This is a section which shows the value of consolidation, for the point made now clearly was formerly well-obscured. If a tenant ceases to reside, the tenancy ceases to be secure:

s.81. Therefore, if the agreement itself does not prohibit assignment or subletting, the limited permissions to assign (s.91) and the restriction on subletting other than of part (s.93) would cease to "bite" and the tenant (no longer secure, but still a tenant at law), would be able to do one or the other, possibly with the effect of imposing a new tenant on the landlord, perhaps to become secure.

Essentially, this section contains the same law as applies when the tenancy *is* secure, to prevent non-occupation opening the door to evasion of ss.91 and 93.

This section is not applicable to a secure tenancy from a co-operative housing association (within the meaning of s.5, above, *cf.* notes to s.80, above): s.109, below.

Repairs and improvements

Right to carry out repairs

96.—(1) The Secretary of State may by regulations make a scheme for entitling secure tenants, subject to and in accordance with the provisions of the scheme—

    (*a*) to carry out to the dwelling-houses of which they are secure tenants repairs which their landlords are obliged by repairing covenants to carry out, and

    (*b*) after carrying out the repairs, to recover from their landlords such sums as may be determined by or under the scheme.

(2) The regulations may make such procedural, incidental, supplementary and transitional provision as may appear to the Secretary of State to be necessary or expedient, and may in particular—

    (*a*) provide for questions arising under the scheme to be referred to and determined by the county court;

    (*b*) provide that where a secure tenant makes application under the scheme his landlord's obligation under the repairing covenants shall cease to apply for such period and to such extent as may be determined by or under the scheme.

(3) The regulations may make different provision with respect to different cases or descriptions of case, including different provision for different areas.

(4) Regulations under this section shall be made by statutory instrument which shall be subject to annulment in pursuance of a resolution of either House of Parliament.

(5) In this section "repairing covenant", in relation to a dwelling-house, means a covenant, whether express or implied, obliging the landlord to keep in repair the dwelling-house or any part of the dwelling-house.

DEFINITIONS

"dwelling-house": s.112.

"secure tenants": s.79.

GENERAL NOTE

This section is an enabling section, permitting the creation of a "right to repair." "There is general agreement that tenants on the whole suffer from an unsatisfactory repairs service from their landlords." (Standing Committee B, November 8, 1983, col. 523.) It was introduced by the Housing and Building Control Act 1984. This section is not applicable to a secure tenancy from a co-operative housing association (within the meaning of s.5, above, *cf.* notes to s.80, above): s.109, below.

The section applies to works within a landlord's repairing covenant, whether an express or implied covenant (subs. (5)). It accordingly applies to the provisions of s.11, Landlord and Tenant Act 1985, under which the landlord is responsible for repairs to the structure and exterior of a dwelling-house, and for specified utility installations (water, gas, electricity, for sanitation, and for heating, whether space or water). (See, further, notes to s.104, and to Sched. 6, para. 14, below).

The regulations may provide for the suspension of the landlord's obligations "for such period and to such extent as may be determined by or under the scheme" (subs. (2)(*b*)). The scheme can, however, apply only to covenants to repair the dwelling itself not, *e.g.* common parts (consider *Campden Hill Towers* v. *Gardner* [1977] Q.B. 823, 13 H.L.R. 64,

C.A.). A roof of a top floor flat, while not in the possession of the top floor tenant, may yet fall within s.11, in an appropriate case and, consequently, may fall within a scheme: *Douglas-Scott* v. *Scorgie* [1984] 1 W.L.R. 716, 13 H.L.R. 97, C.A.

The essence of the section is to permit secure tenants to execute works for which the landlord is responsible, recouping the cost from the landlord. It recognises the considerable dissatisfaction that has been caused in many areas by delays in execution of repairs. The legislation is silent, however, on questions of "quality control", and ignores the legal and practical difficulties that may follow from negligent works (consider, *e.g.*, *Sleafer* v. *Lambeth Borough Council* [1960] 1 Q.B. 43, C.A.).

The point was not missed in 1984 Act Committee. "In respect of insurance cover, who will meet the difficulties that may arise if there are safety or health problems or if accidents occur? Who will cover the tenant? We need a clear exposition . . . about what precisely would happen in respect of insurance cover. I understand that insurance companies have certain worries in this respect." (Mr Heffer, Standing Committee B, November 10, 1983, cols. 560 *et seq.*)

The first scheme was introduced by S.I. 1985 No. 1493 retained in force by Housing (Consequential Provisions) Act 1985, s.2, with effect from January 1, 1986. See also D.O.E. Circular 23/85. The scheme is limited to "qualifying repairs", meaning any repairs for which the landlord is responsible, *other than* repairs to the structure and exterior of a flat (Reg. 1(2)).

The scheme starts with a notice from the tenant to the landlord describing the proposed works, why they are needed and the materials to be used. The landlord is required to respond within 21 days either granting or refusing the tenant's repair claim (Reg. 4). Annex B sets out two sets of circumstances in which consent may be refused: those where the landlord *may* withhold consent and those where it *must*.

The discretionary grounds for refusal are:

    (a) The landlord's costs would be more than £200.

    (b) The landlord intends to carry out the works within 28 days of the claim.

    (c) The works are not reasonably necessary for the personal comfort or safety of the tenant and those living with him and the landlord intends to carry them out within one year as part of a planned programme of repair.

    (d) The works would infringe the terms of any guarantee of which the landlord has the benefit.

    (e) The tenant has unreasonably failed to provide the landlord with access to inspect the site for the works.

The mandatory grounds for refusal are:

    (a) The landlord's costs would be less than £20.

    (b) The works do not constitute a qualifying repair.

    (c) The works if carried out using the materials specified would not in the landlord's opinion satsifactorily remedy the lack of repair.

If the landlord accepts the claim then it must serve a notice in reply specifying: the date by which a claim for compensation must be made following completion of the works (which must allow at least 3 months); the amount of the landlord's costs (*i.e.* those it would incur if it were to carry out the works); the percentage of those costs it is willing to pay (which must be at least 75 per cent. and may be up to 100 per cent.); and any modifications of the works and or materials (Reg. 8). Where the landlord fails to serve a notice in reply or fails to carry out works within the time limit specified in the notice in reply the tenant may serve a default notice if the estimate for the works is less than £200. The landlord must respond to this within seven days again either approving or refusing with grounds (Reg. 10).

Between consent and notification of completion of the works (or withdrawal of application to repair) the landlord's repairing obligations in respect of the notified defect are held in abeyance. The landlord's notice informs the tenant of this and also advises the tenant of the possibility of his liability for damage in this intervening period and suggests he consider the insurance position.

Once the landlord has approved the works or failed to respond to the default notice the tenant may carry out the works. After completion the next stage is for the tenant to make a claim for payment to which the landlord must reply within 21 days (Regs. 12 and 13). The landlord *must* refuse to pay if it is not satisfied with the works and *may* refuse if the authorised materials have not been used, access has unreasonably been refused, conditions have not been complied with or the claim for payment was not made within the specified time. If the claim is refused due to lack of satisfaction with the works the tenant may carry out further works and make a further claim, for which the landlord has a discretion to allow further costs to be claimed (Regs. 16 and 17).

In the case of the tenant carrying out the works because of the landlord's failure to respond to a default notice the tenant can claim 100 per cent. of the cost, up to the maximum of £200 and must submit the claim within four months of service of the default notice (Reg. 12(3)(*b*)).

When the claim for payment has been accepted the landlord must make payment within 14 days. If the tenant is in arrears the payment may be credited to the tenant's rent account (Reg. 23(1)).

Any disputes may be referred by either party to the county court for determination.

Tenant's improvements require consent

97.—(1) It is a term of every secure tenancy that the tenant will not make any improvement without the written consent of the landlord.

(2) In this Part "improvement" means any alteration in, or addition to, a dwelling-house, and includes—

(*a*) any addition to or alteration in landlord's fixtures and fittings,

(*b*) any addition or alteration connected with the provision of services to the dwelling-house,

(*c*) the erection of a wireless or television aerial, and

(*d*) the carrying out of external decoration.

(3) The consent required by virtue of subsection (1) shall not be unreasonably withheld, and if unreasonably withheld shall be treated as given.

(4) The provisions of this section have effect, in relation to secure tenancies, in place of section 19(2) of the Landlord and Tenant Act 1927 (general provisions as to covenants, &c. not to make improvements without consent).

DEFINITIONS

"secure tenancy": s.79.
"term": s.116.

GENERAL NOTE

This provision relates substantively to s.463, below, enabling tenants who benefit from this relatively new power to improve (it dates from Housing Act 1980) to apply for grant-aid under Part XV, below. See also: s.98, below, governing the issue of reasonable withholding of consent, s.99, below on conditional consents, s.100, below for reimbursement on departure, and s.101, below, governing rents after improvements.

This section is not applicable to a secure tenancy from a co-operative housing association (within the meaning of s.5, above, *cf.* notes to s.80, above): s.109, below.

Subs. (1)

The covenant is cast in a negative form: the tenant will not improve without consent. This is because at common law, a tenant can improve, unless the lease or tenancy agreement prohibits it. However, when read together with subs. (3)—that the landlord cannot withhold consent unreasonably—the implied term becomes positive in substance. But consent from the landlord does not, of course, obviate any need there may be for planning consent, or under the Building Act 1984 and Building Regulations 1985: see, generally, notes to s.460, below.

Thus in *Tromans* v. *Secretary of State for the Environment and the Wye Forest D.C.* [1983] J.P.L. 474, a granny flat extension was held to constitute a building within the meaning of the concept of development in the Town and Country Planning Act 1971, s.22. Such an extension also came within the concept of "new construction," which was prohibited under the local structure plan as being contrary to Green Belt policy.

In addition, it is important to appreciate that those who improve or renovate their dwellings, using independent contractor labour, must not be negligent towards such workers: see *Kealey* v. *Heard* [1983] 1 W.L.R. 573; Q.B.

Subs. (2)

This subsection defines improvement for the purposes of this Part. The reference to the provision of services incorporates the decision in *Pearlman* v. *Governors and Keepers of Harrow School* [1979] Q.B. 56, C.A., that the installation of central heating constitutes an improvement within the Housing Act 1974, Sched. 8. As to the distinction between improvement and repair, see notes to s.471, below.

Subs. (3)

Note that consent may be given subsequent to the improvement, as well as before it: s. 98(3). *Semble* too consent may be constituted by waiver of breach, *e.g.* by acceptance of rent with knowledge of the improvement (*cf. Metropolitan Properties Co.* v. *Cordery* (1979) 251 E.G. 576, C.A., as to knowledge of an agent or employee sufficing, but *cf. Swallow Securities Ltd.* v. *Isenberg* (1985) 274 E.G. 1028, C.A.). Breach of the term may give rise to an order for possession, although it will be one subject to the overriding requirement of reasonableness in any event, under Ground 1 of Schedule 2, below.

What constitutes reasonable withholding is considered in the notes to s. 98, below.

Subs. (4)

The "replaced" provisions of s.19(2), Landlord and Tenant Act 1927 applied only where the lease or tenancy agreement permitted the tenant to improve or alter, *i.e.* s.19(2) did not grant such permission. Furthermore, s.19(2) applied only to "qualified" covenants, *i.e.* those which permitted improvement or alteration with the landlord's consent as distinct from "absolute" covenants prohibiting such works outright. The present provisions (this section and ss.98 and 99, below), go much further: they actually introduce a qualified covenant into all secure tenancies.

Provisions as to consents required by s.97

98.—(1) If a question arises whether the withholding of a consent required by virtue of section 97 (landlord's consent to improvements) was unreasonable, it is for the landlord to show that it was not.

(2) In determining that question the court shall, in particular, have regard to the extent to which the improvement would be likely—

    (*a*) to make the dwelling-house, or any other premises, less safe for occupiers,

    (*b*) to cause the landlord to incur expenditure which it would be unlikely to incur if the improvement were not made, or

    (*c*) to reduce the price which the dwelling-house would fetch if sold on the open market or the rent which the landlord would be able to charge on letting the dwelling-house.

(3) A consent required by virtue of section 97 may be validly given notwithstanding that it follows, instead of preceding, the action requiring it.

(4) Where a tenant has applied in writing for a consent which is required by virtue of section 97—

    (*a*) the landlord shall if it refuses consent give the tenant a written statement of the reason why consent was refused, and

    (*b*) if the landlord neither gives nor refuses to give consent within a reasonable time, consent shall be taken to have been withheld.

DEFINITIONS

    "dwelling-house s.112.

    "improvement": s.97.

GENERAL NOTE

This section governs consents to improvement under s.97, above. See also s.99, below, as to conditional consents.

Subs. (1)

This shifts the normal burden (*Shanly* v. *Ward* (1913) 29 T.L.R. 714, *Premier Confectionery (London) Co.* v. *London Commercial Sale Rooms* [1933] Ch 904, *Re Town Investments Underlease* [1954] Ch 301, *Pimms* v. *Tallow Chandlers Co* [1964] 2 Q.B. 547) under which the burden is on the tenant to show reasonableness. However, even at common law, if the landlord has given reasons which are on their face patently unreasonable, the burden would probably shift anyway (*Berry* v. *Royal Bank of Scotland* [1949] 1 K.B. 619, *Lovelock* v. *Margo* [1963] 2 Q.B. 786)).

See also notes to s.460, below.

Subs. (2)

It is generally said that whether or not an alteration amounts to an improvement must be viewed from the point of view of the tenant: *Balls Bros.* v. *Sinclair* [1931] 2 Ch. 325; *Lambert* v. *F. W. Woolworth & Co. Ltd.* (*No.* 2) [1938] Ch. 883. But this proposition must be viewed as slightly qualified, given the overriding considerations specified in this subsection. For the same reason, other cases decided under the Landlord and Tenant Act 1927, s.19(2), must be treated with care, but reference may be made to *Tideway Investment and Property Holdings Ltd.* v. *Wellwood* [1952] Ch. 791; *Lilley & Skinner Ltd.* v. *Crump* (1929) 73 S.J. 366, and *James* v. *Hutton & J. Cook Ltd.* [1950] 1 K.B. 9.

A landlord is entitled to ask the purpose for which consent to improve is sought: *Fuller's Theatres* v. *Rofe* [1923] A.C. 435, H.L., and consent may reasonably be refused if to grant it would inevitably lead to a breach of other covenants, *e.g.* to use the premises as a private dwelling-house only (*Day* v. *Waldron* (1919) 88 L.J.K.B. 937; *Dobbs* v. *Linford* [1953] 1 Q.B. 48), or not to engage in business user (*Thorn* v. *Madden* [1925] Ch. 847; *Barton* v. *Reed* [1932] 1 Ch. 362). The reasonableness to be considered is that of the landlord in question, so that unreasonableness cannot be established by showing that "a" reasonable landlord would consent. *Tredegar* v. *Harwood* (1929) A.C. 72.

Aesthetic, artistic or even sentimental considerations have been considered by the Court of Appeal to fall within the ambit of what might contribute to a reasonable refusal: *F. W. Woolworth & Co. Ltd* (*No.* 2) (above).

It has been suggested that "if a reasonable man in the landlord's position might regard the proposed improvement as detrimental to his property interests or as conflicting with the proper management of his estate in some respect that cannot be said to be unfounded", he cannot be said to be acting unreasonably in withholding consent: See Woodfall, para 1–1266, and see *Re Town Investments Underlease* [1954] Ch. 301.

See also notes to s.460, below.

Subs. (4)

A landlord is not normally confined to any reasons he may have given before a dispute calls for judicial resolution, but may advance further reasons for refusal at a hearing. *Somenthal* v. *Newton* (1965) 109 S.J. 333 (C.A.); *Welch* v. *Birrane* (1974) 29 P & C.R. 102. This may be in doubt in view of the express requirements for a written statement of reasons. The Court of Appeal, however, is confined to consideration of matters raised in the county court: *Lovelock* v. *Margo* [1963] 2 Q.B. 786.

Conditional consent to improvements

99.—(1) Consent required by virtue of section 97 (landlord's consent to improvements) may be given subject to conditions.

(2) If the tenant has applied in writing for consent and the landlord gives consent subject to an unreasonable condition, consent shall be taken to have been unreasonably withheld.

(3) If a question arises whether a condition was reasonable, it is for the landlord to show that it was.

(4) A failure by a secure tenant to satisfy a reasonable condition imposed by his landlord in giving consent to an improvement which the tenant proposes to make, or has made, shall be treated for the purposes of this Part as a breach by the tenant of an obligation of his tenancy.

DEFINITIONS

"improvement": s.97.
"secure tenant": s.79.

GENERAL NOTE

Consent to improve may be conditional. However, imposition of an unreasonable condition is treated as deemed withholding: subs. (2). And, the burden remains on the landlord—should the question arise—to show that a condition is reasonable: subs. (3).

Subs. (4)

The landlord will still have to establish that it is reasonable to make the order sought even though it will have had to be considered whether the condition was reasonably attached:

Shrimpton v. *Rabbits* (1924) 131 L.T. 478, D.C.; *Hensman* v. *McIntosh* (1954) 163 E.G. 322, C. A.; *Peachey Property Corporation* v. *Robinson* [1967] 2 Q.B. 543, C.A. See notes to s.84, above.

A tenant who considers a condition to have been unreasonably imposed is well-advised to seek a declaration to that effect from the county court. For much the same reasons, a tenant is well-advised to seek consent even after the improvement has been carried out, under s.98(3), above, if he failed to do so before, and to seek a declaration under s.110, below, that consent has unreasonably been withheld.

Power to reimburse cost of tenant's improvements

100.—(1) Where a secure tenant has made an improvement and—
  (*a*) the work on the improvement was begun on or after 3rd October 1980,
  (*b*) the landlord, or a predecessor in title of the landlord, has given its written consent to the improvement or is treated as having given its consent, and
  (*c*) the improvement has materially added to the price which the dwelling-house may be expected to fetch if sold on the open market, or the rent which the landlord may be expected to be able to charge on letting the dwelling-house,
the landlord may, at or after the end of the tenancy, make to the tenant (or his personal representatives) such payment in respect of the improvement as the landlord considers to be appropriate.

(2) The amount which a landlord may pay under this section in respect of an improvement shall not exceed the cost, or likely cost, of the improvement after deducting the amount of any improvement grant, intermediate grant, special grant or repairs grant under Part XV in respect of the improvement.

(3) The power conferred by this section to make such payments as are mentioned in subsection (1) is in addition to any other power of the landlord to make such payments.

DEFINITIONS
  "dwelling-house": s.112.
  "improvement": s.97.
  "secure tenant": s.79.

GENERAL NOTE
This section provides a discretionary power to landlords to make a payment to tenants who have improved their properties, with or without the assistance of grant-aid under Part XV. This section is not applicable to a secure tenancy from a co-operative housing association (within the meaning of s.5, above, *cf.* notes to s.80, above): s.109, below.

The right to improve is governed by the last three sections, above. See also s.101, below, restricting the landlord's right to increase rent on account of tenant's improvements.

Subs. (1)
The section applies where a secure tenant has made an improvement to which improvement the landlord or its predecessor in title has given written consent, or is treated as having given such consent, *and* work on the improvement has materially added to the price which the property may be expected to fetch if sold on the open market, or the rent which the landlord may be expected to be able to charge on letting the property. Improvement, for these purposes, has the meaning given it by s.97(2): it means any alteration in, or addition to, the property, and includes any addition or alteration connected with the provision of any services to the property, the erection of a wireless or television aerial, and the carrying out of external decorations.

Subss. (2), (3)
It is these subsections which provide the landlord with the power to make payments—at or after the end of the tenancy—to the tenant or to his personal representatives. The amount of the payment is discretionary: such amount in respect of the improvement as the landlord considers appropriate, but to a maximum of the cost or likely cost of the improvement (*i.e.*

if figures are no longer available) after deducting any of the specified grants that were given under Pt. XV, but *not* a home insulation grant (under s.521).

Rent not to be increased on account of tenant's improvements

101.—(1) This section applies where a person (the "improving tenant") who is or was the secure tenant of a dwelling-house has lawfully made an improvement and has borne the whole or part of its cost; and for the purposes of this section a person shall be treated as having borne any cost which he would have borne but for an improvement grant, intermediate grant, special grant or repairs grant under Part XV.

(2) In determining, at any time whilst the improving tenant or his qualifying successor is a secure tenant of the dwelling-house, whether or to what extent to increase the rent, the landlord shall treat the improvement as justifying only such part of an increase which would otherwise be attributable to the improvement as corresponds to the part of the cost which was not borne by the tenant (and accordingly as not justifying an increase if he bore the whole cost).

(3) The following are qualifying successors of an improving tenant—

(*a*) a person in whom the tenancy vested under section 89 (succession to periodic tenancy) on the death of the tenant:

(*b*) a person to whom the tenancy was assigned by the tenant and who would have been qualified to succeed him if he had died immediately before the assignment;

(*c*) a person to whom the tenancy was assigned by the tenant in pursuance of an order made under section 24 of the Matrimonial Causes Act 1973 (property adjustment orders in connection with matrimonial proceedings);

(*d*) a spouse or former spouse of the tenant to whom the tenancy has been transferred by an order under paragraph 2 of Schedule 1 to the Matrimonial Homes Act 1983.

(4) This section does not apply to an increase of rent attributable to rates.

DEFINITIONS
    "dwelling-house": s.112.
    "improvement": s.97.
    "secure tenant": s.79.

GENERAL NOTE
    This section restricts the extent to which the landlord can recover a rent increase, on account of improvements for which the tenant has paid. This section is not applicable to a secure tenancy from a co-operative housing association (within the meaning of s.5, above, *cf.* notes to s.80, above): s.109, below.
    Rent is not to be increased on account of expenditure on improvements (as defined in s.97(2)) so long as the secure tenant who carried out the improvements is still the secure tenant of the dwelling-house in question, or one of his qualifying successors is the tenant.
    Rent may not be increased while *anyone* who succeeds under the statutory succession provisions of s.89 is a secure tenant of the property. Also protected is someone to whom the tenancy is assigned or on whom it devolves, under s.91 (not, therefore, including an "exchange-assignment"—see s.92 above). Finally, it covers a spouse to whom the tenancy is transferred under either the Matrimonial Homes Act 1983 (*cf.* notes to s.91, above) or under s.24, Matrimonial Causes Act 1973. In each case, the change of tenant is, therefore, to another member of the family.
    Note that the protection remains as long as the protected occupier remains *a* secure tenant. Thus if B succeeds to A's secure tenancy, but is subsequently granted a wholly new secure tenancy, the rent still cannot be increased on account of the improvements.
    Only lawful improvements are to be disregarded. It matters not at all whether the tenant received grant-aid under Part XV, for the whole of the cost of the improvement is to be disregarded unless and only unless the tenant has received a contribution to the cost *other* than under the specified provisions of Part XV, *e.g.* under s.521, or under provisions

permitting grants to be made in relation to noise, fire, smoke control, etc. Note, too, that it is only *improvements* which are disregarded: if a property is *repaired*, either independently or in connection with one of the specified Part XV grants, the *repairs* will not be disregarded, and could well enhance the value of the property.

Subs. (4)

The section does not preclude an increase in the rates attributable to the improvement, whether the rates are payable or calculated separately, or whether an inclusive rent is paid, in which latter case the rates "element" is normally—but not for the purposes of this restriction—treated as part of the rent: see, *e.g. Sidney Trading Co.* v. *Finsbury Corporation* [1952] 1 All E.R. 460, D.C., *Wilkes* v. *Goodwin* [1923] 2 K.B. 86, C.A., *Artillery Mansions Ltd.* v. *Macartney* [1947] 1 K.B. 594, approved in *Property Holding Co. Ltd.* v. *Clark* [1948] 1 K.B. 630, H.L. A payment of rates separate from the rent to a landlord authority *qua* rating authority will not be considered rent in any event.

Variation of terms of tenancy

Variation of terms of secure tenancy

102.—(1) The terms of a secure tenancy may be varied in the following ways, and not otherwise—

   (*a*) by agreement between the landlord and the tenant;

   (*b*) to the extent that the variation relates to rent or to payments in respect of rates or services, by the landlord or the tenant in accordance with a provision in the lease or agreement creating the tenancy, or in an agreement varying it;

   (*c*) in accordance with section 103 (notice of variation of periodic tenancy).

(2) References in this section and section 103 to variation include addition and deletion; and for the purposes of this section the conversion of a monthly tenancy into a weekly tenancy, or a weekly tenancy into a monthly tenancy, is a variation of a term of the tenancy, but a variation of the premises let under a tenancy is not.

(3) This section and section 103 do not apply to a term of a tenancy which—

   (*a*) is implied by an enactment, or

   (*b*) may be varied under section 93 of the Rent Act 1977 (housing association and other tenancies: increase of rent without notice to quit).

(4) This section and section 103 apply in relation to the terms of a periodic tenancy arising by virtue of section 86 (periodic tenancy arising on termination of a fixed term) as they would have applied to the terms of the first tenancy mentioned in that section had that tenancy been a periodic tenancy.

DEFINITIONS

   "secure tenancy": s.79.

   "term": s.116.

GENERAL NOTE

This section, read together with the next, governs changes in terms and conditions of secure tenancies. This section is not applicable to a secure tenancy from a co-operative housing association (within the meaning of s.5, above, *cf.* notes to s.80, above): s.109, below. Where changes constitute a change in a matter of housing management, consultation may be also required under s.105, below. The provisions apply whether the secure tenancy has always been periodic, or has become such following determination of a fixed-term tenancy (by effluxion of time, or a court order: see s.86).

In outline, the section provides for variation of any term, *other than* one implied by statute (including this Act—Interpretation Act 1978, s.1) as permitted under the letting agreement, or a subsequent agreement, or, in the case of a periodic tenancy only, by "notice of variation". But no variation is permitted other than in accordance with the provisions of the section (subs. (1)).

The section does not apply to terms implied by statute, including this Act: *e.g.* the repairing covenant implied by the Landlord and Tenant Act 1985, s.110; s.93, above (subletting and lodgers); s.97, above (tenant's improvements). Nor does it apply to a notice by a housing association within Pt.VI of the Rent Act 1977, permitting increase of rent without notice to quit. See also s.25, above, as to increase of rent without notice to quit where non-secure tenancies are involved.

The section preserves the power of the landlord and the tenant to agree to a variation without complying with these statutory provisions. A term permitting variation may also be written into the lease or tenancy agreement, but only in so far as it relates to rent or to payments for rates or services.

Subs. (2)

Expressly excluded from variation is any change in the premises the subject of the tenancy.

Notice of variation of periodic tenancy

103.—(1) The terms of a secure tenancy which is a periodic tenancy may be varied by the landlord by a notice of variation served on the tenant.

(2) Before serving a notice of variation on the tenant the landlord shall serve on him a preliminary notice—

(a) informing the tenant of the landlord's intention to serve a notice of variation,

(b) specifying the proposed variation and its effect, and

(c) inviting the tenant to comment on the proposed variation within such time, specified in the notice, as the landlord considers reasonable;

and the landlord shall consider any comments made by the tenant within the specified time.

(3) Subsection (2) does not apply to a variation of the rent, or of payments in respect of services or facilities provided by the landlord or of payments in respect of rates.

(4) The notice of variation shall specify—

(a) the variation effected by it, and

(b) the date on which it takes effect;

and the period between the date on which it is served and the date on which it takes effect must be at least four weeks or the rental period, whichever is the longer.

(5) The notice of variation, when served, shall be accompanied by such information as the landlord considers necessary to inform the tenant of the nature and effect of the variation.

(6) If after the service of a notice of variation the tenant, before the date on which the variation is to take effect, gives a valid notice to quit, the notice of variation shall not take effect unless the tenant, with the written agreement of the landlord, withdraws his notice to quit before that date.

DEFINITIONS

"rental period": s.116.

"secure tenancy": s.79.

GENERAL NOTE

This section governs variation (as defined in the last section) of terms of a periodic secure tenancy. This section is not applicable to a secure tenancy from a co-operative housing association (within the meaning of s.5, above, *cf.* notes to s.80, above): s.109, below.

Subss. (2), (3), (4)

The notice of variation must specify the variation it is intended to effect and the date on which it is to take effect (subject to subs. (6)). The period between service and date on which variation takes effect must be no less than four weeks, or one rental period of the tenancy (as to which, see s.116, below), whichever is longer.

The notice of variation must, by subs. (5), below, be accompanied by such information as the landlord considers necessary to inform the tenant of the nature and effect of the variation.

The subsections import a degree of prior consultation before notice of variation may be served (see also ss.104, 105, below). Such prior consultation is not required if the variation applies only to variation of rent, or payments for services or facilities provided by the landlord, or payment for or in respect of rates. Otherwise, the landlord must serve a preliminary notice, informing the tenant of its intention to serve notice, as the landlord considers reasonable.

Clearly, a reasonable time must indeed be given, and a time such that no tenant could reasonably respond would render the preliminary notice, and in consequence the notice of variation, void or, at the least, voidable: *cf.* notes to s.420(4), below. Failure to consider a tenant's comments in response to the preliminary notice would also void the subsequent process, as a failure to take a relevant consideration into account: see notes to s.64, above.

Subs. (6)

At any time before the date specified in the notice of variation as being when the variation is to take effect, the tenant may serve notice to quit which, if valid, prevents the notice of variation taking effect at all, unless the tenant, with the written agreement of the landlord, withdraws the notice to quit. A notice to quit to be valid must comply with the provisions of the Protection From Eviction Act 1977, s.5, which means that it must be in writing, and must be of at least four weeks' duration, and must otherwise comply with common law requirements of notice to quit.

The continuation of the common law notwithstanding the general effect of this Part was restated in this context in *Greenwich L.B.C.* v. *McGrady* (1982) 6 H.L.R. 36, C.A., in which notice to quit served by one only of two joint tenants was held valid to bring the tenancy to an end.

The provisions of this subsection may be compared with those of s.25, above, where notice of increase of rent is served on a non-secure tenant; such notice can be avoided by the tenant also by serving a notice to quit in response. However, under that section, the notice to quit has to take effect within a specified time limit. There is no such requirement in this subsection, so that a notice to quit for a *longer* period than that required at common law or under the Protection From Eviction Act 1977, could be considered valid, both as notice to quit, and to pre-empt the effect of the notice of variation. However, a notice to quit served for a very long period indeed—*e.g.* several years—*might* be considered a sham by a court.

A tenant disliking the effect of a notice of variation should think very carefully indeed before responding with notice to quit, for he may not be able to secure further accommodation, on the grounds that he is considered homeless intentionally under s.60, above.

Provision of information and consultation

Provision of information about tenancies

104.—(1) Every body which lets dwelling-houses under secure tenancies shall from time to time publish information about its secure tenancies, in such form as it considers best suited to explain in simple terms, and so far as it considers it appropriate, the effect of—

(*a*) the express terms of its secure tenancies,

(*b*) the provisions of this Part and Part V (the right to buy), and

(*c*) the provisions of sections 11 to 16 of the Landlord and Tenant Act 1985 (landlord's repairing obligations),

and shall ensure that so far as is reasonably practicable the information so published is kept up to date.

(2) The landlord under a secure tenancy shall supply the tenant with—

(*a*) a copy of the information for secure tenants published by it under subsection (1), and

(*b*) a written statement of the terms of the tenancy, so far as they are neither expressed in the lease or written tenancy agreement (if any) nor implied by law;

and the statement required by paragraph (*b*) shall be supplied on the grant of the tenancy or as soon as practicable afterwards.

DEFINITIONS
  "dwelling-houses": s.112.
  "secure tenancy": s.79.
  "term": s.116.

GENERAL NOTE

This section requires landlords under secure tenancies to produce information, in simple terms, to explain the effects of the express terms of its secure tenancies, the provisions of Pts. IV and V of this Act, and the terms of the Landlord and Tenant Act 1985, ss.11–16. This section is not applicable to a secure tenancy from a co-operative housing association (within the meaning of s.5, above, *cf.* notes to s.80, above): s.109, below.

All secure tenants are to be provided with a copy of the information, and with a written statement governing any other terms of the tenancy that are neither contained in the tenancy agreement, nor implied by law.

The landlord is to ensure that so far as it is reasonably practicable to do so, the information is kept up to date, *i.e.* to incorporate changes in the terms of its secure tenancies.

At the commencement of the tenancy or as soon as practicable thereafter, the landlord is bound to provide the tenant with a written statement of the terms of his tenancy, *other than* those which are expressed in any lease or written tenancy agreement, *and other than* those implied by law, which will, of course, be described in the information published under subs. (1) , a copy of which is to be provided to the tenant.

In effect, even an oral tenancy will now have some written evidence of its terms: this statement, or the published information. While the section does not go so far as to require every tenancy to be by written agreement, or to set out the terms of the Landlord and Tenant Act 1985, ss.11–16, or terms implied by this Part, it will probably be a great deal simpler for landlords to embody all of the information they are now required, in one form or another, to provide to their tenants, in one document or, as some authorities are already doing, in a "package" of tenants' information.

*Landlord and Tenant Act 1985, ss.*11–16

These sections contain the principal repairing obligations imposed on landlords in relation to tenancies for less than seven years, including of course periodic tenancies even although they may have lasted for more than that period, but provided the tenancy was granted on or after October 24, 1961 (commencement of Housing Act 1961): Landlord and Tenant Act 1985, s.13. The obligation also does not apply to a tenancy granted to an existing tenant, or a former tenant still in possession, if the previous tenancy was not within the provisions: *ibid.*, s.14. Nor does it apply to a tenancy which is an agricultural holding, nor to tenancies *to* specified public bodies (*i.e.* to permit subleasing of short-life property scheduled for development): *ibid.* The obligation in s.11 cannot be contracted out of, without the consent of the county court: *ibid.*, s.12.

The covenant itself is to keep in repair the structure and exterior of the property, including its drains, gutters and external pipes, and to keep in repair and proper working order its installations for water-supply, gas-supply and electricity-supply, and for sanitation (including basins, sinks, baths and sanitary conveniences, but not other fixtures, fittings and appliances for making use of the water, gas or electricity supplies), and to keep in repair and proper working order its installations for water and space heating: *ibid*, s.11.

The covenant does not require the landlord to do works for which the tenant is liable under a duty to use premises in a tenant-like manner, nor to rebuild or reinstate in case of fire, tempest, floor or other inevitable accident, nor to keep the tenant's fixtures in repair: *ibid*. The covenant includes a right of inspection to view the condition and state of repair: *ibid*. Similar language is to be found in Sched. 6, para. 14, below, governing the terms of a lease under the right to buy in Part V, below: see notes thereto. See also the notes to ss.11–16, Landlord and Tenant Act 1985, in this series.

Consultation on matters of housing management

105.—(1) A landlord authority shall maintain such arrangements as it considers appropriate to enable those of its secure tenants who are likely to be substantially affected by a matter of housing management to which this section applies—

    (*a*) to be informed of the authority's proposals in respect of the matter, and

    (*b*) to make their views known to the authority within a specified period;

and the authority shall, before making any decision on the matter, consider any representations made to it in accordance with those arrangements.

(2) For the purposes of this section, a matter is one of housing management if, in the opinion of the landlord authority, it relates to—

(*a*) the management, maintenance, improvement or demolition of dwelling-houses let by the authority under secure tenancies, or

(*b*) the provision of services or amenities in connection with such dwelling-houses;

but not so far as it relates to the rent payable under a secure tenancy or to charges for services or facilities provided by the authority.

(3) This section applies to matters of housing management which, in the opinion of the landlord authority, represent—

(*a*) a new programme of maintenance, improvement or demolition, or

(*b*) a change in the practice or policy of the authority,

and are likely substantially to affect either its secure tenants as a whole or a group of them who form a distinct social group or occupy dwelling-houses which constitute a distinct class (whether by reference to the kind of dwelling-house, or the housing estate or other larger area in which they are situated).

(4) In the case of a landlord authority which is a local housing authority, the reference in subsection (2) to the provision of services or amenities is a reference only to the provision of services or amenities by the authority acting in its capacity as landlord of the dwelling-houses concerned.

(5) A landlord authority shall publish details of the arrangements which it makes under this section, and a copy of the documents published under this subsection shall—

(*a*) be made available at the authority's principal office for inspection at all reasonable hours, without charge, by members of the public, and

(*b*) be given, on payment of a reasonable fee, to any member of the public who asks for one.

(6) A landlord authority which is a registered housing association shall, instead of complying with paragraph (*a*) of subsection (5), send a copy of any document published under that subsection—

(*a*) to the Housing Corporation, and

(*b*) to the council of any district or London borough in which there are dwelling-houses let by the association under secure tenancies;

and a council to whom a copy is sent under this subsection shall make it available at its principal office for inspection at all reasonable hours, without charge, by members of the public.

DEFINITIONS

"dwelling-house": s.112.
"landlord authority": s.114.
"secure tenancy": s.79.
"local housing authority": ss.1, 2.
"registered housing association": s.5.

GENERAL NOTE

Landlords bound by this section are obliged to make and maintain arrangements to secure a degree of consultation with their secure tenants on matters of housing management, as defined in subs. (2). They must publish details of these arrangements, and make them available to members of the public. Special provision is made, governing the availability of these details where a landlord authority is a housing association, which may have its offices a long way from—perhaps even in a different town to—the houses subject to its secure tenancies.

As to landlords within this section, see s.114, below, and note the possibility of exemption certificated by the Secretary of State under *ibid.*, subs. (2). This section is not applicable to a secure tenancy from a co-operative housing association (within the meaning of s.5, above, *cf.* notes to s.80, above): s.109, below.

Subs. (1)

A landlord authority within the provisions (*cf.* s.114) must make and thereafter maintain such arrangements as it considers appropriate to consult with its secure tenants matters of housing management (as defined in subs. (2)). The arrangements must enable the secure tenants likely to be affected to be informed of the authority's proposals, and to make their views known to the authority within a specified period (see also s.103, above, where a degree of individual consultation may also be required if the housing management proposals will also involve variation of terms of secure tenancies).

The period set must clearly be sufficient to enable secure tenants to make their views known. The greatest difficulty in enforcing this provision is likely to lie in the apparent discretion which a landlord authority enjoys to make and maintain such arrangements as it considers appropriate. But there must be *some* arrangements, and such that "a" reasonable authority could consider appropriate: see further notes to s.420(4), below, on consultation generally.

There is no reason in principle why the duty should not be enforced by injunction, even in the county court under s.110, perhaps by way of representative action under C.C.R., Ord. 5, r.8.

The landlord must consider any representations made to it in accordance with the arrangements, before reaching a decision on a matter of housing management. This duty would, in any event, be implied from the duty to make and maintain arrangements: see further notes to s.64, above.

Subs. (2)–(4)

A matter is not a matter of housing management so far as it relates to the rent payable under a secure tenancy, or to any charge for services or facilities provided by the landlord authority. A matter is otherwise one of housing management if, in the opinion of the landlord authority, it fulfils three conditions:

(i) it relates to the management, maintenance, improvement or demolition of dwelling-houses let by the authority under secure tenancies, or to the provision of services or amenities in connection with such dwellings (although only in so far as these are provided by a landlord authority as landlord, as distinct from the landlord authority as local authority—subs. (4));

(ii) it represents a new programme of maintenance, improvement or demolition, or a change in the practice or policy of the landlord authority; and

(iii) it is likely substantially to affect its secure tenants as a whole, or a group of them. A group is defined as a group of secure tenants who form a distinct social group, or who occupy dwelling-houses which constitute a distinct class, whether by reference to the kind of dwelling-house, to an estate, or to some larger area in which the houses are located.

The three criteria must be fulfilled "in the opinion of the landlord authority," which means that a court can only intervene on limited grounds, *e.g.* if the opinion is one that no reasonable authority could form, or if it has been reached without regard to relevant considerations, or having regard to the irrelevant, other than in good faith, or in pursuit of a policy conflicting with the policy of the Act: see, generally, *Associated Provincial Picture Houses* v. *Wednesbury Corporation* [1948] 1 K.B. 223, C.A.; *Meade* v. *L.B. Haringey* [1979] 1 W.L.R. 637, C.A., and cases cited to s.64, above.

If the landlord authority is a housing association or trust, even these grounds for intervention may not be available: *Peabody Housing Association Ltd.* v. *Green* (1979) 38 P. & C.R. 644, C.A. But it would seem that a challenge could be launched by way of application for declaration in the county court (*cf.* s.110), in which case there would seem to be no reason, if a declaration is all that is to be sought, why such should not be sought by way of representative action: see C.C.R. Ord. 5, r.8. Certainly, it was within the contemplation of Parliament that in the final analysis it would be for the courts to determine the meaning of the less than precise phraseology used in these provisions: see 1980 Act, Standing Committee F, col. 898.

Subs. (5)

The landlord authority must publish details of the arrangements it makes, and a copy of the publication is (a) to be made available at the principal office of the landlord authority, for inspection at all reasonable hours, without charge, by any member of the public—not only its secure tenants—and, (b) shall be provided on demand to any member of the public who asks for a copy, on payment of a reasonable fee.

Subs. (6)

When the landlord authority is a registered housing association, while it retains the duty to provide a copy of its published consultation arrangements on payment of a reasonable fee, its duty to make a copy available without charge for inspection is discharged by sending a copy to the Housing Corporation, and to the council for an area where it has dwelling-houses let under secure tenancies, which council is then bound to make the publication available for inspection in the same way as it must keep its own publication available.

Information about housing allocation

106.—(1) A landlord authority shall publish a summary of its rules—

(*a*) for determining priority as between applicants in the allocation of its housing accommodation, and

(*b*) governing cases where secure tenants wish to move (whether or not by way of exchange of dwelling-houses) to other dwelling-houses let under secure tenancies by that authority or another body.

(2) A landlord authority shall—

(*a*) maintain a set of the rules referred to in subsection (1) and of the rules which it has laid down governing the procedure to be followed in allocating its housing accommodation, and

(*b*) make them available at its principal office for inspection at all reasonable hours, without charge, by members of the public.

(3) A landlord authority which is a registered housing association shall, instead of complying with paragraph (*b*) of subsection (2), send a set of the rules referred to in paragraph (*a*) of that subsection—

(*a*) to the Housing Corporation, and

(*b*) to the council of any district or London borough in which there are dwelling-houses let or to be let by the association under secure tenancies;

and a council to whom a set of rules is sent under this subsection shall make it available at its principal office for inspection at all reasonable hours, without charge, by members of the public.

(4) A copy of the summary published under subsection (1) shall be given without charge, and a copy of the set of rules maintained under subsection (2) shall be given on payment of a reasonable fee, to any member of the public who asks for one.

(5) At the request of a person who has applied to it for housing accommodation, a landlord authority shall make available to him, at all reasonable times and without charge, details of the particulars which he has given to the authority about himself and his family and which the authority has recorded as being relevant to his application for accommodation.

D<small>EFINITIONS</small>

"dwelling-house": s.112.

"landlord authority": s.114.

"registered housing association": s.5.

"secure tenant": s.79.

G<small>ENERAL</small> N<small>OTE</small>

This section makes limited provision obliging landlord authorities to make public their allocation priorities, and their rules for exchanges and transfers, and entitles an applicant on the waiting list to check on the accuracy of the information the landlord has recorded about his application. It is important to note that this last right concerns only the information *which the applicant has provided* to the landlord.

Landlord authority is defined in s.114, below, but note the possibility of exemption certificated by the Secretary of State under *ibid.*, subs. (2). This section is not applicable to a secure tenancy from a co-operative housing association (within the meaning of s.5, above, *cf.* notes to s.80, above): s.109, below.

It is unclear to what extent these rights may be enforced: could an applicant who qualifies under a priority policy but is nonetheless denied housing, for no apparent cause, take action to force the landlord to provide him with housing, even throwing the burden on the landlord to show why, notwithstanding apparent entitlement, housing has not been provided? A right without any means of enforcement is no real right at all: consider *Thornton* v. *Kirklees M.B.C.* [1979] Q.B. 626, C.A., see also *Padfield* v. *Minister of Agriculture, Fisheries & Food* [1968] A.C. 997, H.L.

More straightforwardly, action to compel the landlord to rectify the recorded information would seem a possibility whether the landlord is a public authority, or a housing association or trust.

Subs. (1)

A landlord authority is bound to publish a *summary* of its rules governing priority, exchanges and transfers. Note that local authorities do not have a completely unfettered allocation discretion: they are bound to afford a reasonable preference to those who are overcrowded, who live in insanitary accommodation, who have large families or are otherwise living in unsatisfactory housing conditions, and to those towards whom they owe duties under Part III: see s.22, above.

Subs. (2)

The landlord authority must also maintain a set of the rules which are to be summarised under subs. (1), *and* a set of rules governing procedure on application. Local authority and other public landlords are to make these *rules* available at all reasonable hours at their principal office, for inspection without charge by any member of the public, not just one who is an applicant on the waiting-list, or who wishes to consider an exchange or transfer.

Subs. (3)

A registered housing association landlord must send a copy of its rules to the Housing Corporation, and to a council in whose area as it has dwelling-houses let or to be let under secure tenancies, in which case it is for the council to make the rules available in the same way as they must do their own.

Subs. (4)

Copies of the *summary* are to be made available without charge, and copies of the rules are to be provided on payment of a reasonable fee, to any member of the public who asks for one.

Subs. (5)

This provision applies only to a person who has actually applied for housing accommodation. The landlord authority must make available to him, at all reasonable times and without charge, those details which the authority have recorded as being relevant to his application for accommodation, being details of particulars about himself and his family, *which he has provided to the authority.* It does not cover other particulars which may have been recorded.

Miscellaneous

Contributions towards costs of transfers and exchanges

107.—(1) The Secretary of State may with the consent of the Treasury make grants or loans towards the cost of arrangements for facilitating moves to and from homes by which—

    (*a*) a secure tenant becomes, at his request, the secure tenant of a different landlord, or

    (*b*) each of two or more tenants of dwelling-houses, one at least of which is let under a secure tenancy, becomes the tenant of the other or one of the others.

(2) The grants or loans may be made subject to such conditions as the Secretary of State may determine, and may be made so as to be repayable, or as the case may be repayable earlier, if there is a breach of such a condition.

DEFINITIONS
  "dwelling-house": s.112.
  "secure tenancy": s.79.

GENERAL NOTE

This section provides the Secretary of State with power to contribute towards the costs of exchanges and transfers. The local authority associations have adopted new proposals and have put forward a scheme to operate nationally, under which a proportion of the stock will be kept free as a mobility factor, additional to existing arrangements for transfers and exchanges, and this section is designed to permit the government to contribute towards the cost of this scheme: see 1980 Act, Standing Committee F, cols. 949–950, *Hansard,* H.L., June 9, 1980, col. 22.

The scheme started on April 1, 1981, sponsored by the A.D.C., A.M.A., L.B.A., G.L.C., N.T.A., N.F.A. and the D.O.E. There is also a Tenants Exchange Scheme which produces lists of tenants wanting exchanges, who may send a registration form available from local authorities, CABx. and housing advice centres, to P.O. Box 170, London, SW1P 3PX, for free inclusion on a monthly list.

On June 1, 1984, the scheme was extended to Scotland. "Certain operational changes have been made to coincide with the extension. The main changes are that, to help keep the Scheme's lists more up to date, the registration period, during which tenants remain on these lists, is being reduced from one year to six months; tenants will be sent a letter inviting renewal of their registration about a month before it is due to expire. The space on the Scheme's monthly lists for a tenant's comments will be doubled so that tenants may include information about the type of property and the area to which they want to move, in addition to further details about their present home . . . " (D.O.E. Press Notice 275, June 8, 1984).

This section is not applicable to a secure tenancy from a co-operative housing association (within the meaning of s.5, above, *cf.* notes to s.80, above): s.109, below.

Heating charges

108.—(1) This section applies to secure tenants of dwelling-houses to which a heating authority supply heat produced at a heating installation.

(2) The Secretary of State may by regulations require heating authorities to adopt such methods for determining heating charges payable by such tenants as will secure that the proportion of heating costs borne by each of those tenants is no greater than is reasonable.

(3) The Secretary of State may by regulations make provision for entitling such tenants, subject to and in accordance with the regulations, to require the heating authority—

(*a*) to give them, in such form as may be prescribed by the regulations, such information as to heating charges and heating costs as may be so prescribed, and

(*b*) where such information has been given, to afford them reasonable facilities for inspecting the accounts, receipts and other documents supporting the information and for taking copies or extracts from them.

(4) Regulations under this section—

(*a*) may make different provision with respect to different cases or descriptions of case, including different provision for different areas;

(*b*) may make such procedural, incidental, supplementary and transitional provision as appears to the Secretary of State to be necessary or expedient, and may in particular provide for any question arising under the regulations to be referred to and determined by the county court; and

(*c*) shall be made by statutory instrument which shall be subject to annulment in pursuance of a resolution of either House of Parliament.

(5) In this section—

(*a*) "heating authority" means a housing authority who operate a heating installation and supply to premises heat produced at the installation;

(*b*) "heating installation" means a generating station or other installation for producing heat;

(*c*) references to heat produced at an installation include steam produced from, and air and water heated by, heat so produced;

(*d*) "heating charge" means an amount payable to a heating authority in respect of heat produced at a heating installation and supplied to premises, including in the case of heat supplied to premises let by the authority such an amount payable as part of the rent;

(*e*) "heating costs" means expenses incurred by a heating authority in operating a heating installation.

Definitions
"dwelling-house": s.112.
"secure tenants": s.79.

General Note
This section is an enabling section, introduced in 1984, but under which a scheme has yet to be made. This section is not applicable to a secure tenancy from a co-operative housing association (within the meaning of s.5, above, *cf.* notes to s.80, above): s.109, below.

This right meets a common complaint, of inadequate explanation for apparently high heating charges payable by tenants to their own authorities, under district, or "communal" (Mr Wyn Roberts, 1984 Act, Standing Committee B, November 10, 1983, col. 610) heating schemes (which may be confined to a single estate, or may cover a wider geographical area). "We all agree that communal heating charges are a source of complaint by many tenants." (*ibid.*)

Whether or not payment is made as a part of the rent, a heating charge is a payment by a tenant of the authority's own property, to that authority, for heat both produced by them and supplied by them. The heating cost is the actual expenditure incurred in the operating of the generating station or other installation at which the heat is produced.

The Secretary of State may by regulation require heating authorities to adopt particular methods for determining heating charges, payable by secure tenants, in order to ensure that each tenant bears no greater proportion of the heating costs than is reasonable. Regulations may also provide for secure tenants to require the provision of information about heating charges and costs, in a prescribed form and to afford reasonable facilities for inspecting accounts, receipts and other documents supporting the information, and for taking copies or extracts from them.

In substance, this is a "service charge" protection, similar to that available (in private and public sectors) to leaseholders and other tenants of flats, under ss.18–30, Landlord and Tenant Act 1985, and leaseholders or even freeholders of some houses under ss.45–51, above.

Provisions not applying to tenancies of co-operative housing associations

109. Sections 91 to 108 (assignment and subletting, repairs and improvements, variation of terms, provision of information and consultation, contributions to costs of transfers and heating charges) do not apply to a tenancy when the interest of the landlord belongs to a co-operative housing association.

Definitions
"co-operative housing association": s.5.

General Note
See notes to ss.5 and 80, above.

Supplementary provisions

Jurisdiction of county court

110.—(1) A county court has jurisdiction to determine questions arising under this Part and to entertain proceedings brought under this Part and claims, for whatever amount, in connection with a secure tenancy.

(2) That jurisdiction includes jurisdiction to entertain proceedings on the following questions—

(*a*) whether a consent required by section 92 (assignment by way of exchange) was withheld otherwise than on one or more of the grounds set out in Schedule 3,

(*b*) whether a consent required by section 93(1)(*b*) or 97(1) (landlord's consent to subletting of part of dwelling-house or to carrying out of improvements) was withheld or unreasonably withheld, or

(*c*) whether a statement supplied in pursuance of section 104(2)(*b*) (written statement of certain terms of tenancy) is accurate,

notwithstanding that no other relief is sought than a declaration.

(3) If a person takes proceedings in the High Court which, by virtue of this section, he could have taken in the county court, he is not entitled to recover any costs.

DEFINITIONS
"secure tenant": s.79.

GENERAL NOTE
This section confers a broad, general jurisdiction on the county court, wider than, and additional to, its jurisdiction under the County Courts Act 1984. In particular, any claim brought in connection with a secure tenancy may be brought in the county court, regardless of amount: *cf.* the general monetary limits imposed by the County Courts Act 1984, ss.145, 147 as set by the County Courts Jurisdiction Order 1981, S.I. 1981 No. 1123, at £5,000. Compare generally the jurisdiction conferred on the county court by the Rent Act 1977, s. 141. It is clear that a declaration may be sought, even if no other relief within the jurisdiction is claimed, on any question arising under this part and on the other questions specified.

Any question within this Part will normally be capable of being referred to the county court in any event, and notwithstanding that no relief other than a declaration—or injunction—is sought, under the County Courts Act 1984, s.22, provided the property is within the county court rateable value limits, and the declaration or injunction is sought in respect of, or relating to "any land, or the possession, occupation, use of enjoyment of any land . . . "

County court rules and directions

111.—(1) The Lord Chancellor may make such rules and give such directions as he thinks fit for the purpose of giving effect to—

(*a*) section 85 (extended discretion of court in certain proceedings for possession), and

(*b*) section 110 (jurisdiction of county court to determine questions arising under this Part).

(2) The rules and directions may provide—

(*a*) for the exercise by a registrar of a county court of any jurisdiction exercisable under the provisions mentioned in subsection (1), and

(*b*) for the conduct of proceedings in private.

(3) The power to make rules is exercisable by statutory instrument which shall be subject to annulment in pursuance of a resolution of either House of Parliament.

Meaning of "dwelling-house"

112.—(1) For the purposes of this Part a dwelling-house may be a house or a part of a house.

(2) Land let together with a dwelling-house shall be treated for the purposes of this Part as part of the dwelling-house unless the land is agricultural land (as defined in section 26(3)(*a*) of the General Rate Act 1967) exceeding two acres.

GENERAL NOTE
See notes to s.79, above.

Members of a person's family

113.—(1) A person is a member of another's family within the meaning of this Part if—

    (*a*) he is the spouse of that person, or he and that person live together as husband and wife, or

    (*b*) he is that person's parent, grandparent, child, grandchild, brother, sister, uncle, aunt, nephew or niece.

(2) For the purpose of subsection (1)(*b*)—

    (*a*) a relationship by marriage shall be treated as a relationship by blood,

    (*b*) a relationship of the half-blood shall be treated as a relationship of the whole blood,

    (*c*) the stepchild of a person shall be treated as his child, and

    (*d*) an illegitimate child shall be treated as the legitimate child of his mother and reputed father.

GENERAL NOTE

This codification was, on its introduction in the Housing Act 1980, specifically designed to supplant Rent Act law, decided under what is now the Rent Act 1977, Sched. 1, for the purposes of statutory succession.

Cohabitation

The separate treatment of "spouse" and persons living together "as husband and wife" does suggest that a common law relationship, no matter how long-standing, will qualify only under the latter phrase and not the former, an important consideration when it comes to such questions as priority in succession (s.87, above), and grounds for possession (Sched. 2, Ground 16).

The phrase "living together as husband and wife", or variations upon it, is to be found in other legislation: see, *e.g.* Social Security (Miscellaneous Provisions) Act 1977, Domestic Violence and Matrimonial Proceedings Act 1976, Matrimonial Causes Act 1973. In accordance with the normal rule, words and phrases are construed in context. Little assistance can, therefore, be derived from the rather different contexts of these other Acts, and were the phrase as applied in the law relating to social security (the so-called "co-habitation rule") to be applied in this context, very little connection would have to be shown before a person qualified as a member of the other's family. However, in most of the cases where the phrase is relevant in this Part, an additional residential qualification must be shown by the putative member of the family, and it would clearly be quite artificial to read the words in isolation.

One decision under the 1976 Act which may be of assistance, however, is that in *Adeoso* v. *Adeoso, The Times*, July 22, 1980, C.A., in which it was held that a couple living in a flat with only two rooms (*i.e.* bedroom and living room), must be considered to be living together as husband and wife, albeit that for months the couple had not spoken, they had communicated only by notes, they each slept in one of the rooms and kept their rooms locked, but they shared the rent and the cost of the electricity.

Under the Rent Acts, and clearly applicable here, it had become clear that a cohabitant could, in appropriate circumstances, succeed to the tenancy of a deceased partner, as a member of his or her family, though not as his or her spouse.

In *Gammans* v. *Ekins* [1950] 2 K.B. 328 C.A., following *Brock* v. *Wollams* [1949] 2 K.B. 388, C.A., the Court of Appeal had rejected this proposition: the submission was said to be an abuse of the English language.

By *Hawes* v. *Evenden* [1953] 1 W.L.R. 1169, C.A., however, a woman who had lived with a man for 12 years without taking his name, and who had two children by him, was held to be a member of his family. In *Dyson Holdings Ltd.* v. *Fox* [1976] 1 Q.B. 503, C.A., it was held that although relationships of a casual and intermittent character could not qualify as family, a stable relationship could do so, so that 20 years' cohabitation without marriage, where the woman had taken the man's name, should be regarded as a family relationship, having regard to the changing popular meaning of the word family.

However, in *Helby* v. *Rafferty* [1979] 1 W.L.R. 13, C.A., the Court of Appeal rejected the idea that the meaning of the word "family" could change with time, stated that it should have the meaning applicable when first used by Parliament, and rejected a claim to succeed by a man who had lived with the deceased tenant for approximately five years, as her lover, sharing expenses, caring for her while she was dying, but not having taken her name, nor she having taken his. In *Watson* v. *Lucas* [1980] 1 W.L.R. 1493, C.A., a man was held to be a member of the family of the deceased tenant, who was a woman with whom he had lived for nearly 20 years, even though he remained undivorced from his lawful wife. The Court of Appeal considered that they were bound by *Dyson*.

Against this background, it may be said that it was inevitable that at some point in time the courts would have to decide whether one partner of a lesbian or homosexual couple could qualify as a member of the family of another, who had died. It would have seemed, however, that this question could only logically be raised under the Rent Act 1977, where the sole question would be the meaning of the phrase "member of family," rather than under this Part, where the question would have to be posed under what would seem to be the only available definition limb, *i.e.* "living together as husband and wife."

In the event, in *Harrogate Borough Council* v. *Simpson* (1984) 17 H.L.R. 205, the Court of Appeal held that the expression "living together as husband and wife" in what is now this section, is not apt to include a lesbian or homosexual relationship. The point may remain open under the Rent Acts, *sed dubitante*.

Children
The definition of children does not expressly include adopted children, as an adopted child is to be treated as if a natural child under the Children Act 1975, s.8 and Sched.1.

Less clear is whether a *de facto* (but not *de jure*) adopted child comes within the definition: see *Brock* v. *Wollams* [1949] 2 K.B. 388, C.A., where this was allowed under the Rent Acts, even although by the time the question arose, the child had achieved his majority. But as there can be no *de jure* adoption between adults, there can likewise be no *de facto* adoption between adults: *Carega Properties S.A.* v. *Sharratt* [1979] 1 W.L.R. 928, H.L. Note too the specific inclusion of step-children: there is no specific inclusion of step-*parents*, although "any relationship by marriage (is) a relationship by blood," and it seems likely that step-parents were simply overlooked and should not be treated as excluded merely on account of the specific inclusion of step-children.

Meaning of "landlord authority"

114.—(1) In this Part "landlord authority" means—
   a local housing authority,
   a registered housing association other than a co-operative housing association,
   a housing trust which is a charity,
   a development corporation,
   an urban development corporation, or
   the Development Board for Rural Wales,
other than an authority in respect of which an exemption certificate has been issued.

(2) The Secretary of State may, on an application duly made by the authority concerned, issue an exemption certificate to—
   a development corporation,
   an urban development corporation, or
   the Development Board for Rural Wales,
if he is satisfied that it has transferred, or otherwise disposed of, at least three-quarters of the dwellings which have at any time before the making of the application been vested in it.

(3) The application shall be in such form and shall be accompanied by such information as the Secretary of State may, either generally or in relation to a particular case, direct.

DEFINITIONS
   "development corporation": s.4.
   "housing trust": s.6.
   "local housing authority": ss.1, 2.
   "registered housing association": s.5.
   "urban development corporation": s.4.

GENERAL NOTE
   This section defines the public and quasi-public landlords for the purposes of ss.105–106, above.

Subs. (2), (3)

These subsections permit the Secretary of State to issue an exemption certificate to a limited class of landlord who would otherwise qualify as a landlord authority. The authorities who may here qualify are the Development Board for Rural Wales, the development corporation of a new town, and an urban development corporation.

Under this section, on application by development corporation or Board, the Secretary of State may issue an exemption certificate if satisfied that they have transferred or otherwise disposed of at least three-quarters of their housing stock.

Meaning of "long tenancy"

115.—(1) The following are long tenancies for the purposes of this Part, subject to subsection (2)—

(*a*) a tenancy granted for a term certain exceeding 21 years, whether or not it is (or may become) terminable before the end of that term by notice given by the tenant or by re-entry or forfeiture;

(*b*) a tenancy for a term fixed by law under a grant with a covenant or obligation for perpetual renewal, other than a tenancy by sub-demise from one which is not a long tenancy;

(*c*) any tenancy granted in pursuance of Part V (the right to buy).

(2) A tenancy granted so as to become terminable by notice after a death is not a long tenancy for the purposes of this Part, unless—

(*a*) it is granted by a housing association which at the time of the grant is registered,

(*b*) it is granted at a premium calculated by reference to a percentage of the value of the dwelling-house or of the cost of providing it, and

(*c*) at the time it is granted it complies with the requirements of the regulations then in force under section 140(4)(*b*) of the Housing Act 1980 (conditions for exclusion of shared ownership leases from Part I of the Leasehold Reform Act 1967) or, in the case of a tenancy granted before any such regulations were brought into force, with the first such regulations to be in force.

DEFINITIONS

"dwelling-house": s.112.
"housing association": s.5.
"registered": s.5.

GENERAL NOTE

A tenancy is not a secure tenancy if it is a long tenancy, (see Sched. 1, para. 1) which means a tenancy granted for a term certain exceeding 21 years. The fact that the lease may be determinable before the period of 21 years has expired, by re-entry or forfeiture, or by notice given *by* the tenant, does not prevent the lease being a long lease (incorporating the common law rule, see *Quinlan* v. *Avis* (1933) 149 L.T.214): see also *Eton College* v. *Bard* [1983] Ch. 321, C.A.

The term will run from the date of its grant. Thus, a term of twenty-one and a quarter years from March 25, 1950, not granted until October 29, 1952, was held not a long tenancy in *Roberts* v. *Church Commissioners for England* [1972] 1 Q.B. 278, C.A. On the other hand, time will run from when the tenant first takes up occupation under a legal right to remain in occupation for more than 21 years, *e.g.* if occupation is allowed from before grant, under a binding contract for the grant—see *Brikom Investments Ltd.* v. *Seaford* [1981] 1 W.L.R. 863, 1 H.L.R. 21, C.A.

The definition includes a tenancy for a term fixed by law under a grant with a convenant or obligation for perpetual renewal, unless it is a tenancy by way of sub-demise from one which is not itself a long tenancy. A grant for a covenant or obligation for permanent renewal takes effect as a lease for 2,000 years (Law of Property Act 1922, s.145, Sched. 15; Law of Property Act 1925, s.202), although if granted by way of sub-lease it takes effect as a grant for a term one day less than the term out of which it was granted (Law of Property Act 1922, s.145 and Sched. 15). The effect in this Act is that all grants with a covenant or obligation for perpetual renewal are long leases, save where the grant is of a sub-lease and the superior lease is not a long lease.

But a tenancy determinable by notice after death is expressly not a long lease, *unless* the lease constitutes a shared ownership tenancy: subs. (2).

A shared ownership tenancy is one (a) granted by a registered housing association (see s.5, above), (b) is granted at a premium calculated by reference to a percentage of the value of the dwelling-house or of the cost of providing it (*cf.* ss.143 *et seq.*, below); and (c) at the time of the grant it complies with the regulations in force under s.140, Housing Act 1980, or, if granted before such regulations are brought into force, it complies with the first such regulation brought into force.

Section 140 governs the exclusion of certain long leases, under shared ownership tenancies, from the provisions of the Leasehold Reform Act 1967. Unless thus excluded, a long tenancy at a low rent will normally qualify within the 1967 Act, so that the tenant may be able to enfranchise or extend his lease, if the property the subject of the tenancy is a house within the 1967 Act.

Minor definitions

116. In this Part—
"common parts", in relation to a dwelling-house let under a tenancy, means any part of a building comprising the dwelling-house and any other premises which the tenant is entitled under the terms of the tenancy to use in common with the occupiers of other dwelling-houses let by the landlord;
"housing purposes" means the purposes for which dwelling-houses are held by local housing authorities under Part II (provision of housing) or purposes corresponding to those purposes;
"rental period" means a period in respect of which a payment of rent falls to be made;
"term", in relation to a secure tenancy, includes a condition of the tenancy.

Index of defined expressions: Part IV

117. The following Table shows provisions defining or otherwise explaining expressions used in this Part (other than provisions defining or explaining an expression in the same section or paragraph):—

cemetery	section 622
charity	section 622
common parts (in relation to a dwelling-house let under a tenancy)	section 116
co-operative housing association	section 5(2)
development corporation	section 4(*c*)
dwelling-house	section 112
family (member of)	section 113
housing association	section 5(1)
housing authority	section 4(*a*)
housing purposes	section 116
housing trust	section 6
improvement	section 97(2)
landlord authority	section 114
local authority	section 4(*e*)
local housing authority	section 1, 2(2)
long tenancy	section 115
new town corporation	section 4(*b*)
qualified to succeed (on the death of a secure tenant)	section 87
registered and unregistered (in relation to a housing association)	section 5(4)
rental period	section 116
secure tenancy	section 79
term (in relation to a secure tenancy)	section 116

urban development corporation   section 4(*d*)
variation (of the terms of a secure tenancy)   section 102(2)

Part V

The Right to Buy

The right to buy

The right to buy

118.—(1) A secure tenant has the right to buy, that is to say, the right, in the circumstances and subject to the conditions and exceptions stated in the following provisions of this Part—

    (*a*) if the dwelling-house is a house and the landlord owns the freehold, to acquire the freehold of the dwelling-house;

    (*b*) if the landlord does not own the freehold or if the dwelling-house is a flat (whether or not the landlord owns the freehold), to be granted a lease of the dwelling-house.

(2) Where a secure tenancy is a joint tenancy then, whether or not each of the joint tenants occupies the dwelling-house as his only or principal home, the right to buy belongs jointly to all of them or to such one or more of them as may be agreed between them; but such an agreement is not valid unless the person or at least one of the persons to whom the right to buy is to belong occupies the dwelling-house as his only or principal home.

Definitions

"dwelling-house": ss.183, 184.
"flat": s.183.
"house": s.183.
"secure tenant": ss.79, 185.

General Note

This section introduces the "right to buy", *i.e.* the right to acquire the freehold of a house of which the landlord has a freehold interest, or the lease of a flat, or a house where the landlord's interest is only leasehold. The right prima facie belongs to secure tenants, *i.e.* as defined for the purposes of Part IV, in ss.79–81, above, subject to the Sched. 1 exceptions, and accordingly includes most licensees (above, s.79), but under this Part subject to (a) the residential qualification requirements of s.119, (b) the exceptions in Sched. 5 (by virtue of s.120) and (c) the limitations in s.121. If the secure tenant ceases to be such before completion of purchase, *e.g.* moves out after starting the procedure, the right to buy is no longer available: see *Sutton L.B.C.* v. *Swann, The Times,* November 30, 1985; (1985) 18 H.L.R., C.A.

The purchase is to be at a discount (ss.129), reflecting years of public sector tenancy (*not* exclusively time as a secure tenant—Sched. 4), and is accompanied by a "right to a mortgage" (s.132). If the tenant still cannot afford to purchase, he then has a choice, of "freezing" the price for two years (*i.e.* the right to defer—s.142), or to take a shared ownership lease instead (s.143), *i.e.* to purchase part of the equity, and continue paying rent on the balance.

Not least because of unconcealed opposition to the concept, this Part is replete with procedural provisions, and contains what have been referred to (*R.* v. *Secretary of State for the Environment, ex parte Norwich City Council* [1982] Q.B. 808, 2 H.L.R. 1, C.A.) as "draconian" powers of intervention on the part of the Secretary of State. The right to buy was introduced in the Housing Act 1980, and extended—and its procedural provisions and powers of intervention tightened or strengthened—by the Housing and Building Control Act 1984.

Subs. (1)

If the home is a house (as defined in s.183) then the right is the right to acquire a largely unencumbered freehold interest (see s.139 and Sched. 6), unless the landlord does not own the freehold, in which case the right is to a lease. If the home is a flat (as defined in s.137) then the right is to acquire a long leasehold interest. As for the lease, s.139 sets out that the grant shall conform with the provisions of Sched. 6, para. 11, requires that the grant shall be at a rent of not more than £10 per annum, for a minimum term of 125 years, save where there has already been a grant of a lease under these provisions, in respect of another flat in the same building, in which case the lease may be for a lesser period, designed to come to an end at the same time as the first lease.

If the lease is of a house or flat of which the landlord does not own the freehold, it will still be for 125 years, *unless* either (a) the landlord's interest is of less than 125 years and five days, in which case the grant is to be for a period expiring five days before the landlord's interest, or (b) the lease is of a flat in a building in which a previous long lease under the right to buy has already been granted, in which case the grant may be for a shorter period, coterminous with the earlier grant.

Under Sched. 5, para. 4, however, if the landlord's lease is for not more than (a) 21 years in the case of a house, or (b) 50 years in the case of a flat, in each case dating from when the tenant serves notice claiming the right to buy (see s.122, below), the right to buy is simply inapplicable.

Note, too, that under sss.172–174, the purchaser of a *house* (but not a flat), of which the landlord does not own the freehold, will normally acquire the right, after three years as leaseholder under the right to buy, to enfranchise under the Leasehold Reform Act 1967.

The right will be exercisable not merely against the (public sector) landlord, but also against the (possibly—indeed, probably—private sector) freeholder: see 1967 Act, s.5 and Sched. 1. Landlords affected by the present Act could not themselves enfranchise because—as legal, corporate or "artificial" persons—they cannot fulfil the residential qualifications of the 1967 Act, s.1 (see, *e.g. Duke of Westminster* v. *Oddy* (1984) 15 H.L.R. 80, C.A.).

Another intervention in the private sector is effected by s.179, below, which voids provisions in leases (*i.e.* including those granted by private landlords) which would prevent or limit the grant of subleases under the right to buy, or which would prevent or limit the sublessee's rights to further dispose of the sublease.

The entitlement to a lease where the landlord does not own the freehold does not necessarily include cases where the interest superior to that of the authority is the Crown: see Sched. 5, para. 12. In outline, the exemption will *not* apply (and the right will therefore be available) if either the Crown consents to the grant, or no consent to the grant is or would be required under the terms of the lease.

Save in the case of property in areas of natural beauty or specially designated for the purposes of this Part (s.157), there is no power to include a pre-emption clause in conveyance or grant. Even on a resale within a relatively short time after exercise of the right to buy, the only protection for the former landlord is the entitlement to recoup a part of the discount that is allowed to the purchaser under s.129 (see s.155).

Subs. (2)

When there is a joint tenancy, the right to buy belongs to all of the joint tenants jointly, even if one or more of those joint tenants does not occupy the dwelling-house as his only or principal home (or indeed, at all). Alternatively, it may be exercised by such one—or less than all—of the joint tenants as may be agreed with the other, non-purchasing joint tenant or tenants. But an agreement must be a "valid" agreement and this means that at least one of the purchasing joint tenants must occupy the dwelling-house as his only or principal home (as to the meaning of which phrase, see notes to s.81, above). Section 123, below, contains power in some circumstances for a secure tenant or joint tenants to purchase together with non-tenants.

There is a number of problems not dealt with expressly in the legislation. For example, does joint tenancy here mean joint tenancy in law only, or in law or equity? The point may be important, for if an equitable joint tenant wished to purchase and could only otherwise be added under s.123, below, he would also have to prove an added residential qualification. At law, there can be no more than four legal joint tenants: Trustee Act 1925, s.34. Where more than four are named as joint tenants, then the first four named are the legal joint tenants, holding on trust for themselves and the fifth and subsequent named persons: Law of Property Act 1925, s.34. If the four named joint tenants wished to purchase, they would presumably acquire ownership itself for themselves *and* the others. But if one of the four named did not wish to exercise the right, or to be named as an owner, could, *e.g.* a fifth named joint tenant, whose interest is in equity alone, claim to be added as of right, even if not in residence, or perhaps against the will of the legal joint tenants?

No equivalent problem arises *merely* on account of a joint tenant's minority: until majority, the adult will hold as sole tenant, on trust for himself, and minor, for, of course, the minor cannot hold a legal interest in his own right: Law of Property Act 1925, ss.1(6), 19(2). He can no more exercise the right to buy during his minority, while if he had achieved his majority, he would have become a legal joint tenant. If the adult tenant exercised the right to buy during the other's minority, he would acquire ownership for himself *and* minor, as with a fifth named joint tenant. It may be noted that these problems are not necessarily academic, certainly where minors are involved: consider the couple, married or living together as husband and wife, one of whom was under age, who might qualify for mandatory housing under Part III.

And what of others who allege that a legal tenancy was taken on trust—for such other alone, or for the named tenant together with such other? Such an equitable joint tenancy is at least theoretically possible, and a common-place claim under matrimonial law. The difficulty may be to find the basis for the claim: *subsequent* contributions to, *e.g.* improvement costs (*cf.* ss.97 *et seq.*) will not qualify, *unless* the contributor is married or engaged to the tenant: see Matrimonial Proceedings and Property Act 1970, s.37, and Law Reform (Miscellaneous Provisions) Act 1970, s.2. And it has been held that contributions to *rent* go to the use of the premises, not to the acquisition of an equitable interest in the title: *Savage* v. *Dunningham* [1974] Ch. 181 (which may, however, be distinguishable, given that time spent as a *secure* tenant—as distinct from as a protected tenant as in that case—clearly sounds in money, *i.e.* the amount of discount available).

It is submitted that, especially given the value of the right to buy, and the value of the discount, it will be open to someone other than a named tenant to allege that there is a joint tenancy in equity, but it will be extremely difficult to establish. The examples given in the last few paragraphs should support the availability of the argument, but application will clearly vary from case to case. In the event, no similar problems are likely to arise in the case of a claim to be an undisclosed principal, for unless there is evidence within the letting agreement that the tenancy is taken as agent for another, such evidence will not be admitted: *Hanstown Properties Ltd.* v. *Green* (1977) 246 E.G. 917, C.A.

A further problem may arise on the exercise—by agreement—of the right to buy by less than all the joint tenants. On such a purchase, the secure tenancy will itself determine: s.139. If there is a subtenant, Law of Property Act 1925, s.139 applies *as* on a merger or surrender: s.139(2). But there is no reason in *law* why the *joint* tenancy should be treated as having merged with the interest acquired by exercise of the right to buy, for there will be no absolute community of identity between new owner of superior interest, and the joint tenants. While, as a general proposition, one person cannot grant a tenancy to himself (*Rye* v. *Rye* [1962] A.C. 496, H.L.), this rule does not extend so far as to prohibit one person taking a tenancy from himself *and* others: *Cowper* v. *Fletcher* (1865) 6 B. & S. 464, Law of Property Act 1925, s.72(4).

The fact that there is agreement to the purchase by less than all may well be sufficient, *i.e.* and notwithstanding any subsequent falling out, at the time the non-purchasing joint tenant must surely have been aware that the tenancy itself would come to an end, as s.139 provides. This will be sufficient, it would seem, for the courts to interpret the agreement between the joint tenants which allows less than all of them to purchase so to extend to a release of the interest of the non-purchasing joint tenant but, where appropriate, will be equally ready to imply the grant of an irrevocable licence, or a licence revocable only in appropriate circumstances: see, *e.g. Foster* v. *Robinson* [1951] 1 K.B. 149, C.A., *Errington* v. *Errington & Woods* [1952] 1 K.B. 290, C.A., *Binions* v. *Evans* [1972] 1 Ch. 359, C.A., *Tanner* v. *Tanner* [1975] 1 W.L.R. 1346, *Williams* v. *Staite* (1977) L.S.Gaz. 1129, C.A., *Hardwick* v. *Johnson* [1978] 1 W.L.R. 683, C.A., *Chandler* v. *Kerley* [1978] 1 W.L.R. 693, C.A., *Piquet* v. *Tyler* [1980] L.A.G.Bulletin 93, C.A., and *Greasley* v. *Cooke* (1980) 124 S.J. 629, C.A.

But note the possibility that if the joint tenants "fall out" *before* completion, one only of them can effectively bring the tenancy to an end by notice served *on* the landlord: *Greenwich L.B.C.* v. *McGrady,* (1982) 6 H.L.R. 36, C.A.—see, further, notes to s.103, above.

Qualifying period for right to buy

119.—(1) The right to buy does not arise unless the period which, in accordance with Schedule 4, is to be taken into account for the purposes of this section is at least two years.

(2) Where the secure tenancy is a joint tenancy the condition in subsection (1) need be satisfied with respect to one only of the joint tenants.

Definitions
"secure tenancy": ss.79, 185.

General Note

This section introduces Sched. 4, which determines the time to be taken into account for the purposes of establishing the residential precondition to right to buy, initially (1980) three years, since 1984, only two. The period of qualification is as a "public sector tenant," not necessarily a secure tenant, and includes, *e.g.*, time in armed forces accommodation, and times with other public or quasi-public landlords. Note, too, that under s.185, time before the introduction of either the 1980 or the 1984 Acts which would have been secure if those Acts had been in force is treated as secure, *i.e.* allowing the addition of pre-security time (without which provision, on introduction of the right to buy in 1980, no exercise of it could have occurred until 1983). Qualifying periods are calculated in the same way for the purposes of discount under s.129, below.

The important point is that the residential qualification need not be established in the same premises, or with the same landlord; it is time *as* a public sector tenant (which, of course, include secure tenant) which qualifies—see further the notes to Sched. 4, below.

Subs. (2).

Only one of more than one purchasing joint tenants needs fulfil the residential qualification. If there are two joint tenants, one of whom fulfils the residential qualification and the other of whom does not, then provided the purchasing joint tenant occupies as an only or principal home an agreement under s.118(2), above, for less than all to purchase will still be valid even though the purchasing joint tenant is not the joint tenant with the residential qualification. Thus, A is a secure tenant with at least two years residential qualification. She marries B, who has no public sector time of his own. They are granted a new, joint tenancy, whether or not of the same property. A then leaves B, and home. Provided A agrees to B buying, and B is in occupation as an only or principal home, B will have the right to buy.

Exceptions to the right to buy

120. The right to buy does not arise in the cases specified in Schedule 5 (exceptions to the right to buy).

Definitions

"right to buy": s.118.

General Note

This section brings in Sched. 5—see also s.121, below. Under Sched. 5, the following exceptions exist in relation to the right to buy, described here in outline—see further notes to Sched. 5, below:

1. Charitable housing association or housing trust landlord.
2. Co-operative housing association (see s.5, above) landlord.
3. Housing association landlord which has at no time received public funds, as defined in Sched. 5, para. 3.
4. Landlord with insufficient leasehold interest: see also notes to s.118, above.
5. Certain dwelling-houses let in connection with employment, in relation to non-housing purposes.
6. Three classes of dwelling for the disabled—designed and constructed or converted with special features, subsequently adapted in specified ways, and sheltered accommodation.
7. Sheltered accommodation for the mentally disordered.
8. Two classes of accommodation for the elderly—single dwellings certified by the Secretary of State, and sheltered accommodation.
9. Dwelling-houses in which a superior interest belongs to the Crown (subject to exceptions).

Circumstances in which the right to buy cannot be exercised

121.—(1) The right to buy cannot be exercised if the tenant is obliged to give up possession of the dwelling-house in pursuance of an order of the court or will be so obliged at a date specified in the order.

(2) The right to buy cannot be exercised if the person, or one of the persons, to whom the right to buy belongs—

(*a*) has a bankruptcy petition pending against him,
(*b*) has a receiving order in force against him,
(*c*) is an undischarged bankrupt, or

(*d*) has made a composition or arrangement with his creditors the terms of which remain to be fulfilled.

DEFINITIONS
   "dwelling-house": ss.183, 184.
   "right to buy": s.118.

GENERAL NOTE
   The right to buy cannot be exercised if the tenant is in occupation following a court order. Under s.82, a secure tenancy lasts until the date when the secure tenant is ordered to give up possession. There is no notice to quit as such, but a notice of seeking possession, and grounds for commencing proceedings. There is, thus, no "statutory tenancy," or a period of occupation between termination of notice to quit and court order, during which the occupant is a former tenant holding over, *i.e.* a trespasser.
   The wording of this section, and the provisions of s.82, mean that a tenant who is the subject of a suspended possession order, *e.g.* subject to conditions, will still be able to exercise the right to buy, and only excluded therefrom are former tenants who are already under an obligation to give up possession (but who have not left, *e.g.* because they are awaiting the bailiffs), and tenants against whom a *fixed* date for possession has been ordered (and who are, accordingly, occupying between court order and that date): see, generally, s.84. But note that if there are arrears of rent, the landlord can refuse to complete until they are cleared: s.138, below.
   The other circumstances in which the right cannot be exercised is if the tenant, or any one of the persons to whom the right to buy belongs, is an undischarged bankrupt, or has made a composition or arrangement with his creditors, the terms of which remain to be fulfilled, or has a bankruptcy petition or a receiving order pending against him.
   The exclusion of undischarged bankrupts would seem only to be relevant where there is a joint tenancy, and only one (or less than all) of the joint tenants is bankrupt, for a bankrupt sole tenant will have ceased to be tenant at all, as the tenancy will have vested in the trustee in bankruptcy or the official receiver: see Bankruptcy Act 1914. Under the same Act, the undischarged bankrupt will be prohibited from dealing in property. The trustee or the receiver could not exercise the right to buy, for he will not be occupying the property as his only or principal home—or at all—and so will not be a *secure* tenant (s.81).

Claim to exercise right to buy

Tenant's notice claiming to exercise right to buy

   122.—(1) A secure tenant claims to exercise the right to buy by written notice to that effect served on the landlord.
   (2) In this Part "the relevant time", in relation to an exercise of the right to buy, means the date on which that notice is served.
   (3) The notice may be withdrawn at any time by notice in writing served on the landlord.

DEFINITIONS
   "right to buy": s.118.
   "secure tenant": ss.79, 185.

GENERAL NOTE
   The notice claiming to exercise the right to buy activates the process which the following provisions of this Part detail. Once the notice has been given, it runs with the landlord's interest (notwithstanding the absence of any provision requiring registration of the notice): s.137. The effect of a transfer of the landlord's interest is that the notice takes effect as if the new landlord had been the landlord at the time of service, so that in the event of a transfer to a landlord whose tenants are not entitled to exercise the right to buy, the notice would simply be rendered ineffective.
   The Secretary of State has power to prescribe forms of notice for the purposes of this Part: s.176(1). A tenant is entitled to require an appropriate form from the landlord: s.176(2). Notice under this Part may be served by sending it by post: s.176(3). As to the form of notices, see Housing (Right to Buy) (Prescribed Forms) Regulations 1984 (S.I. 1984 No. 1175), retained in force by s.2, Housing (Consequential Provisions) Act 1984. The form required under this section is form RTB1. The date when it is served is of considerable

importance, for it will be relevant to questions of entitlement to buy, discount, valuation, etc. It is known as the "relevant time."

Under s.177, omissions from, or errors in, forms or particulars, are to be adjusted on discovery prior to completion, to the extent of withdrawal of admission or denial of right to buy.

If there is a change of secure tenant, by succession or in the other circumstances in which this is permitted (see ss.87–91, above), other than under the right to exchange (s.92), the new secure tenant steps into the shoes of the former secure tenant, and is treated as if he had served the notice, although the qualification of any added purchaser (s.123) would have to be re-established in relation to the new tenant, and the new tenant will have to establish his own entitlement to mortgage (s.132): s.136.

Claim to share right to buy with members of family

123.—(1) A secure tenant may in his notice under section 122 require that not more than three members of his family who are not joint tenants but occupy the dwelling-house as their only or principal home should share the right to buy with him.

(2) He may validly do so in the case of any such member only if—

(*a*) that member is his spouse or has been residing with him throughout the period of twelve months ending with the giving of the notice, or

(*b*) the landlord consents.

(3) Where by such a notice any members of the tenant's family are validly required to share the right to buy with the tenant, the right to buy belongs to the tenant and those members jointly and he and they shall be treated for the purposes of this Part as joint tenants.

DEFINITIONS
  "dwelling-house": ss.183, 184.
  "member of family": s.186.
  "right to buy": s.118.
  "secure tenant": ss.79, 185.

GENERAL NOTE
  This section provides for the addition of joint purchasers, *i.e.* "deemed joint tenants" in contradistinction to the "actual joint tenants" who share the right to buy under s.118, above.

If this power is used, it would seem that the *tenant's* discount under s.129, below, will represent a contribution to the purchase price. Furthermore, it may be that if the parties subsequently fall out, the added purchasers will be unable to secure an order for sale. Thus, in *Charlton* v. *Lester* (1976) 238 E.G. 115, a woman was a protected tenant under the Rent Acts; her daughter and husband came to live with her; subsequently the freeholder offered to sell the house to the tenant at a price of £2,000, clearly reflecting a sitting-tenant's discount. The daughter and her husband persuaded the tenant to purchase, with the aid of a G.L.C. mortgage, subject to terms as to repairs; both the payments under the mortgage, the repairs, and legal fees, were paid for by the daughter and her husband. The property was put into joint names.

The open-market value of the house was £5,200, so that the former tenant's contribution by way of the discount was worth £3,200. To the open-market valuation of the house, the court added the cost of the repairs, and legal fees, to make a total of £5,585. On that analysis, the discount proved to be worth 200/349 of the total cost of the transaction, and this accordingly represented the former tenant's share.

The application of the daughter and her husband for an order for sale was refused. They were buying a new house, and had been prepared to build an extension for the former tenant. They were now paying a mortgage on two properties. They were under a great burden of debt. However, even though the house was now worth £15,000 or £16,000, a sale would mean that the former tenant lost her home. She had been reluctant to buy, because she knew she was safe as a protected tenant, had only agreed because she was persuaded that she could keep the house. She was of slender means. Her son was in a nearby hospital and she wanted to remain near to him, so that he could visit her. Relationships had deteriorated, and it was no longer realistic to expect the parties to live in the same house. Nonetheless, the former tenant should not be turned out.

Subs. (1)

The limitation to three allows for the 1925 legislation referred to in the notes to s.118, above. If the added members qualify, they are then to be deemed joint tenants for the purposes of this Part, but only for the purposes of this Part, not, *e.g.* also for the security of tenure provisions of Part IV: subs. (3). The purpose of such an election will usually be to increase amount of mortgage (s.133) and in some circumstances it may also increase entitlement to discount (s.129). Where there is a change of secure tenant after RTB1 has been served (s.122) the qualification of added purchasers must be re-established in relation to the new tenant, although save for entitlement to mortgage the new tenant will otherwise be in the same position as the secure tenant who served the notice (s.136).

Subs. (2)

To add purchasers it must be shown: (i) that the added purchasers qualify under subs. (2)(*a*); *or* (ii) that the landlord consents. The personal qualifications are: (a) that each would be added purchaser occupies the dwelling-house as his only or principal home (as to the meaning of which phrase, see notes to s.81, above); (b) that each is a member of the tenant's family (as to the meaning of which, see s.186, below, referring back to the notes to s.113, above); *and* (c) *either* that the added purchaser is the tenant's spouse (which, given the definition of member of the family means legal spouse, not common law spouse) *or* that another member of the family has been residing with (as to which, see notes to s.87, above) the secure tenant throughout the period of 12 months ending with the relevant date (*i.e.* under s.122, service of RTB1).

The last consideration is whether the consent of the landlord can be secured, where this is necessary. This is cast as an absolute discretion, a proposition reinforced by the absence of any suggestion that consent should not unreasonably be withheld (*cf.* ss.94, 97, above). It would be wrong for a local authority landlord to adopt a fixed policy of never granting consent to add further purchasers, although there would be nothing wrong with a general indication that this is the likely outcome of any application, provided that each application will be—as it must be—considered on its merits and a decision taken whether or not to apply or deviate from the policy: see, *e.g., British Oxygen Co.* v. *Ministry of Technology* [1971] A.C. 610, H.L., *In Re Betts* [1983] 2 A.C. 613, 10 H.L.R. 97, H.L.

Accordingly, where the landlord will not consent, it will be necessary to impeach the decisions on usual principles of administrative law, *e.g.* such wrongful binding by policy, or that something relevant has been left out of account, etc.—see generally notes to s.64, above. But a housing association landord is not vulnerable to these principles of judicial review and intervention, so that even a rigid policy would seem not to be illegal: *Peabody Housing Association Ltd.* v. *Housing Association Ltd.* v. *Green* (1979) 38 P. & C.R. 644 C.A.

Landlord's notice admitting or denying right to buy

124.—(1) Where a notice under section 122 (notice claiming to exercise right to buy) has been served by the tenant, the landlord shall, unless the notice is withdrawn, serve on the tenant within the period specified in subsection (2) a written notice either—

(*a*) admitting his right, or

(*b*) denying it and stating the reasons why, in the opinion of the landlord, the tenant does not have the right to buy.

(2) The period for serving a notice under this section is four weeks where the requirement of section 119 (qualifying period for the right to buy) is satisfied by a period or periods during which the landlord was the landlord on which the tenant's notice under section 122 was served, and eight weeks in any other case.

(3) A landlord's notice under this section shall inform the tenant of any application for a determination under paragraph 11 of Schedule 5 (determination that right to buy not to be capable of exercise) and, in the case of a notice admitting the tenant's right to buy, is without prejudice to any determination made on such an application.

Definitions

"right to buy": s.118.

GENERAL NOTE

In normal circumstances, the landlord is bound to serve a counter-notice either admitting or denying the tenant's right to buy within four weeks. But an eight week period is allowed where reliance is placed in establishing the two-year minimum period of qualification to exercise the right to buy (s.119, above), on time spent as the secure tenant of another landlord. This allows more time to a landlord who may have to make inquiries to establish the validity of a claim with another landlord, possibly another local authority, perhaps in relation to a period of time long before the date when the notice is served (see also s.185).

But landlords may avail themselves of this extension even if the property, and the tenancy, were the same throughout, *i.e.* the greater time is allowed if there is a different *landlord.* "The Secretaries of State . . . look to authorities to adhere strictly to the statutory time limits for the issue of notices under" what is now this section. (D.O.E. Circular 21/84).

Where application has been made to the Secretary of State for exemption of an elderly person's dwelling (*cf.* Sched. 5, para. 11, below), the tenant should be so informed, and admission of the right to buy is without prejudice to the Secretary of State's determination: subs. (3).

If the landlord denies the tenant's right to buy, reasons must be given why, in their opinion, the tenant has failed to qualify. As to reasons, see notes to s.64, above.

This raises the subject of tenants' remedies for refusal. *Completion* under the right to buy is specifically enforceable by injunction: s.138(3). One remedy would be to invite the Secretary of State to exercise his powers of intervention under s.164. But it is unlikely that the existence of this possibility would be sufficient to cause the courts to decline jurisdiction altogether (*cf. Pasmore* v. *Oswaldtwistle U.D.C.* [1898] A.C. 387, J.L., *Meade* v. *L.B. Haringey* [1979] 1 W.L.R. 637, C.A.).

Notwithstanding the use of the words "in (the landlord's) opinion", entitlement to buy is a factual question, not dependent (save as to such matters as discretionarily added purchasers—see notes to s.123, above) on opinion-making by landlords, and it accordingly seems clear that a wrongful refusal can be challenged, *e.g.* by way of proceedings in-the county court, under s.181, below.

Where relevant facts are obscure, it is open to a landlord to accept a statutory declaration as sufficient evidence of the facts stated in it: s.180, below. But this is an indisputably discretionary power, for the landlord need only accept such a declaration "if it thinks fit".

Notice

The Secretary of State has power to prescribe forms of notice for the purposes of this Part: s.176(1). Notice under this Part may be served by sending it by post: s.176(3). As to the form of notices, see Housing (Right to Buy) (Prescribed Forms) Regulations 1984 (S.I. 1984 No. 1175), retained in force by s.2, Housing (Consequential Provisions) Act 1984. The form required under this section is form RTB2. Under s.177, omissions from, or errors in, forms or particulars, are to be adjusted on discovery prior to completion, to the extent of withdrawal of admission or denial of right to buy.

Landlord's notice of purchase price and other matters

125.—(1) Where a secure tenant has claimed to exercise the right to buy and that right has been established (whether by the landlord's admission or otherwise), the landlord shall—

(*a*) within eight weeks where the right is that mentioned in section 118(1)(*a*) (right to acquire freehold), and

(*b*) within twelve weeks where the right is that mentioned in section 118(1)(*b*) (right to acquire leasehold interest),

serve on the tenant a notice complying with this section.

(2) The notice shall describe the dwelling-house, shall state the price at which, in the opinion of the landlord, the tenant is entitled to have the freehold conveyed or, as the case may be, the lease granted to him and shall, for the purpose of showing how the price has been arrived at, state—

(*a*) the value at the relevant time,

(*b*) the improvements disregarded in pursuance of section 127 (improvements to be disregarded in determining value), and

(*c*) the discount to which the tenant is entitled, stating the period to be taken into account under section 129 (discount) and, where applicable, the amount mentioned in section 130(1) (reduction for previous discount) or section 131(1) or (2) (limits on amount of discount).

(3) The notice shall state the provisions which, in the opinion of the landlord, should be contained in the conveyance or grant.

(4) Where the notice states provisions which would enable the landlord to recover from the tenant service charges (within the meaning of section 18 of the Landlord and Tenant Act 1985 or section 46 of this Act), the notice shall also state—

(a) the landlord's estimate of the average annual amount (at current prices) which would be payable in respect of each head of charge, and

(b) the aggregate of those estimated amounts.

(5) The notice shall also inform the tenant of—

(a) his right under section 128 to have the value of the dwelling-house at the relevant time determined or re-determined by the district valuer,

(b) the right to a mortgage and the effect of sections 134 and 135 (procedure for claiming to exercise that right),

(c) the effect of sections 140, 141(1), (2) and (4) and 142(1) and (2) (landlord's notices to complete, effect of failure to comply and right to defer completion), and

(d) the effect of the provisions of this Part relating to the right to be granted a shared ownership lease;

and the notice shall be accompanied by a form for use by the tenant in claiming to exercise the right to a mortgage.

DEFINITIONS

"dwelling-house": ss.183, 184.
"improvements": s.187.
"relevant time": s.122.
"right to buy": s.118.
"right to mortgage": s.132.
"secure tenant": ss.79, 185.
"shared ownership lease": s.622.

GENERAL NOTE

An offer notice:

(a) has to be served within eight weeks, save where the right is to a lease (see s.118, above), in which case it must be served within twelve weeks,

(b) must state the price payable, supported by a statement of value calculated under s.127, discount under s.129 and improvements disregarded under s.127,

(c) must provide an estimate relating to service charges which will be payable—if any, but whether in respect of flats or houses (*cf.* s.46, above, and Sched. 6, para. 18, below, but note that under Sched. 6, para. 18, the charge attributable to the rectification of structural defects is not here included),

(d) must inform the tenant about the right to redetermination of value under s.128, below,

(e) must inform the tenant about the right to a mortgage under s.132,

(f) must inform the tenant about the right to defer completion,

(g) must inform the tenant about the right to a shared ownership lease (ss.143 *et seq.*), and

(h) must be accompanied by a form on which to claim a mortgage.

There is no corresponding requirement to provide forms for deferral or on which to claim shared ownership, because the entitlement to either of these options depends on the outcome of a mortgage claim: ss.142, 143.

"The Secretaries of State . . . look to authorities to adhere strictly to the statutory time limits for the issue of notices under" what is now this section. (D.O.E. Circular 21/84).

The requirement to describe the dwelling-house means not merely that the address must be stated, but particulars of what is to be the subject of the conveyance or grant, including land to be included under s.184.

Purchase price

Purchase price

126.—(1) The price payable for a dwelling-house on a conveyance or grant in pursuance of this Part is—
   (*a*) the amount which under section 127 is to be taken as its value at the relevant time, less
   (*b*) the discount to which the purchaser is entitled under this Part.
(2) References in this Part to the purchase price include references to the consideration for the grant of a lease.

DEFINITIONS
   "dwelling-house": ss.183, 184.
   "relevant time": s.122.

GENERAL NOTE
   The effect of this section is merely to state that the price payable will be value calculated under s.127, as at the relevant time, *i.e.* date of service of RTB1 under s.122, above, less discount under ss.129–131, below.

Value of dwelling-house

127.—(1) The value of a dwelling-house at the relevant time shall be taken to be the price which at that time it would realise if sold on the open market by a willing vendor—
   (*a*) on the assumptions stated for a conveyance in subsection (2) and for a grant in subsection (3), and
   (*b*) disregarding any improvements made by any of the persons specified in subsection (4) and any failure by any of those persons to keep the dwelling-house in good internal repair.
(2) For a conveyance the assumptions are—
   (*a*) that the vendor was selling for an estate in fee simple with vacant possession,
   (*b*) that neither the tenant nor a member of his family residing with him wanted to buy, and
   (*c*) that the dwelling-house was to be conveyed with the same rights and subject to the same burdens as it would be in pursuance of this Part.
(3) For the grant of a lease the assumptions are—
   (*a*) that the vendor was granting a lease with vacant possession for the appropriate term defined in paragraph 12 of Schedule 6 (but subject to sub-paragraph (3) of that paragraph),
   (*b*) that neither the tenant nor a member of his family residing with him wanted to take the lease,
   (*c*) that the ground rent would not exceed £10 per annum, and
   (*d*) that the grant was to be made with the same rights and subject to the same burdens as it would be in pursuance of this Part.
(4) The persons referred to in subsection (1)(*b*) are—
   (*a*) the secure tenant,
   (*b*) any person who under the same tenancy was a secure tenant before him, and
   (*c*) any member of his family who, immediately before the secure tenancy was granted, was a secure tenant of the same dwelling-house under another tenancy,
but do not include, in a case where the secure tenant's tenancy has at any time been assigned by virtue of section 92 (assignments by way of exchange), a person who under that tenancy was a secure tenant before the assignment.

DEFINITIONS
"dwelling-house": ss.183, 184.
"improvements": s.187.
"member of family": s.186
"relevant time": s.122.
"secure tenant": ss.79, 185.

GENERAL NOTE
This section dictates the principles upon which the purchase price of the property is to be calculated. In default of agreement, valuation will be determined by the district valuer: s.128, below.
The value is to be calculated as at the relevant time, which will be the date when RTB1 is served under s.122: s.126, above.

Subss. (1), (2), (3)
The valuation is to be an open market value, subject to the following assumptions:
(a) the vendor is a willing vendor;
(b) if a freehold, the vendor is selling an estate in fee simple with vacant possession;
(c) if a leasehold, the vendor is selling a lease for 125 years or such shorter period as is permitted under Sched. 6, para. 11, at a ground rent of not more than £10 per year;
(d) the conveyance or grant will be subject to the same rights and burdens set out in this Part; and
(e) neither the tenant nor a member of his family residing with him wanted to buy or take the lease.
In addition, there are to be disregarded both (i) improvements, and (ii) failure to keep in good internal repair, by any of the persons specified in subs. (4).

Subs. (4)
The person whose improvements, and whose failure to keep in good internal repair, are to be disregarded are: (a) the secure tenant himself; (b) a person who was the secure tenant under the same tenancy before him, *i.e.* a person to whom tenancy the present secure tenant has succeeded (ss.87 *et seq.*) or a person from whom the tenancy has been assigned, in the limited circumstances in which this is permitted (s.91—but *not* including an exchange-assignment under s.92); and (c) a member of the tenant's family who was a secure tenant of the same property under *another* tenancy immediately before the grant of the present secure tenancy. This last class is designed to permit the benefit of improvements to be carried over, when a landlord permits the tenancy to change hands between members of the family, other than by assignment, which will mean by surrender and new grant, for, even with consent, and save in the limited circumstances in which this is permitted, the secure tenancy is not assignable: s.91.
As to the right to carry out improvements, and the possibility of grant-aid to pay for them, see ss.97, above, and 463, below.

Determination of value by district valuer

128.—(1) Any question arising under this Part as to the value of a dwelling-house at the relevant time shall be determined by the district valuer in accordance with this section.
(2) A tenant may require that value to be determined, or as the case may be re-determined, by a notice in writing served on the landlord not later than three months after the service on him of the notice under section 125 (landlord's notice of purchase price and other matters) or, if proceedings are then pending between the landlord and the tenant for the determination of any other question arising under this Part, within three months of the final determination of the proceedings.
(3) If such proceedings are begun after a previous determination under this section—
(*a*) the tenant may, by notice in writing served on the landlord within four weeks of the final determination of the proceedings, require the value of the dwelling-house at the relevant time to be re-determined, and
(*b*) the landlord may at any time within those four weeks, whether or

not a notice under paragraph (*a*) is served, require the district
  valuer to re-determine that value;
and where the landlord requires a re-determination to be made in
pursuance of this subsection, it shall serve on the tenant a notice stating
that the requirement is being or has been made.

(4) Before making a determination or re-determination in pursuance of
this section, the district valuer shall consider any representation made to
him by the landlord or the tenant within four weeks from the service of
the tenant's notice under this section or, as the case may be, from the
service of the landlord's notice under subsection (3).

(5) As soon as practicable after a determination or re-determination
has been made in pursuance of this section, the landlord shall serve on
the tenant a notice stating the effect of the determination or re-determination and the matters mentioned in section 125(2) and (3) (terms for
exercise of right to buy).

(6) A notice under subsection (5) shall inform the tenant of the right to
a mortgage and of the effect of sections 134 and 135 (procedure for
claiming to exercise that right) and shall be accompanied by a form for
use by the tenant in claiming to exercise that right.

DEFINITIONS
  "district valuer": s.622.
  "dwelling-house": ss.183, 184.
  "relevant time": s.122.

GENERAL NOTE
  Although a general jurisdiction is conferred upon the county court to determine any
question arising under this Part (s.181) that jurisdiction is expressed to be subject to the
provisions of this section. This section, accordingly, confers exclusive jurisdiction on the
district valuer to determine the value of the property the subject of a conveyance or grant,
as at the relevant time (s.126).
  The district valuer is "an officer of the Commission of Inland Revenue who is for the time
being appointed by the Commissioners to be, in relation to the valuation list for the area in
which the dwelling-house is situated, the valuation officer or deputy valuation officer or one
of the valuation officers, or deputy valuation officers": s.622. The district valuer is,
accordingly, a valuation officer or deputy valuation officer: General Rate Act 1967, s.115(1).

Subss. (2), (3)
  A tenant is entitled to call for a determination or redetermination by notice in writing
served on the landlord within three months of service upon him of the landlord's offer
notice under s.125. This period may be extended: (a) if proceedings are pending for the
determination of any other question, up to three months after the final determination of
such proceedings; or (b) to four weeks after the final determination of proceedings begun
after an earlier determination by the district valuer, in which latter case the landlord also has
the right to require a redetermination.
  Examples of the first class of proceedings may be if there is a dispute as to what property
is included in the right to buy, or who may be added as a purchaser, or whether a property
is a house or a flat. Examples of the second class of proceedings may be if there is a dispute
as to a tenant's right to complete, following a deferred completion under s.142, or if there
is a dispute as to entitlement to mortgage, or to add purchasers, where there has been a
change of tenant (s.136).

Subs. (4)
  The district valuer is bound to take into account any representations made by either
landlord or tenant, made within four weeks of the notice requiring determination or
redetermination, whether served by tenant or landlord. Save as to the time limit for
submissions, this provision does no more than the courts would certainly in any event have
required in accordance with natural justice or administrative fairness.

Subss. (5), (6)
  Once there has been a determination or redetermination by the district valuer, the burden
is on the landlord to inform the tenant of the result of it. The notice must state the effect of

the determination or redetermination and specifically deal with the matters raised by s.125 (2), (3): price, provisions of conveyance or grant, value at relevant time, discount, period taken into account, minimum purchase price (if any), and improvements disregarded.

Further, the notice must reinform the tenant of his right to a mortgage (s.132), and the time limits thereon (ss.134, 135) and must be accompanied by a form for claiming a mortgage. There is, however, no obligation to re-inform the tenant of the right to defer completion (s.142), but this will have to be restated in the counter-notice served by the landlord or Housing Corporation in response to the notice claiming a mortgage (s.135).

Discount

129.—(1) Subject to the following provisions of this Part, a person exercising the right to buy is entitled to a discount equal to the following percentage of the price before discount—

> (*a*) if the period which, in accordance with Schedule 4, is to be taken into account for the purposes of discount is less than three years, 32 per cent.;
> (*b*) if that period is three years or more, 32 per cent. plus one per cent. for each complete year by which that period exceeds two years.

(2) The discount shall not exceed 60 per cent.

(3) Where joint tenants exercise the right to buy, Schedule 4 shall be construed as if for the secure tenant there were substituted that one of the joint tenants whose substitution will produce the largest discount.

DEFINITIONS
"right to buy": s.118.
"secure tenant": ss.79, 185.

GENERAL NOTE
This important section details the discount to which the purchaser is entitled. If less than three years, the discount is 32 per cent., plus 1 per cent. for each further year, to a maximum of 60 per cent. The discount may be reduced for a "second-time purchaser", under s.130, below, and the Secretary of State has power to set a "discount ceiling" under s.131, below.

The section rests upon Sched. 4, below, *i.e.* the periods to be taken into account are qualifying periods as a public sector tenant (not the same as secure tenant, but of course including secure tenant—see also s.185, below, counting time before the introduction of the 1980 and 1984 Acts as secure, for otherwise it would still be many years before the higher discounts were achieved).

Subs. (3)
Where joint tenants buy, they cannot add their discounts together (for otherwise, in every case, once the two-year minimum had been achieved, the maximum 60 per cent. would be achieved and, indeed, passed). Instead, the one whose period according to Sched. 4 would produce the highest discount will govern the amount. For this purpose, "added purchasers" under s.123, above, will qualify as joint tenants: s.123(3).

Reduction of discount where previous discount given

130.—(1) There shall be deducted from the discount an amount equal to any previous discount qualifying, or the aggregate of previous discounts qualifying, under the provisions of this section.

(2) A "previous discount" means a discount given before the relevant time—

> (*a*) on conveyance of the freehold, or a grant or assignment of a long lease, of a dwelling-house by a person within paragraph 7 of Schedule 4 (public sector landlords) or, in such circumstances as may be prescribed by order of the Secretary of State, by a person so prescribed, or
> (*b*) in pursuance of the provision required by paragraph 1 of Schedule 8 (terms of shared ownership lease: right to acquire additional shares), or any other provision to the like effect.

(3) A previous discount qualifies for the purposes of this section if it was given—

(*a*) to the person or one of the persons exercising the right to buy, or

(*b*) to the spouse of that person or one of those persons (if they are living together at the relevant time), or

(*c*) to a deceased spouse of that person or one of those persons (if they were living together at the time of the death);

and where a previous discount was given to two or more persons jointly, this section has effect as if each of them had been given an equal proportion of the discount.

(4) Where the whole or part of a previous discount has been recovered by the person by whom it was given (or a successor in title of his)—

(*a*) by the receipt of a payment determined by reference to the discount, or

(*b*) by a reduction so determined of any consideration given by that person (or a successor in title of his), or

(*c*) in any other way,

then, so much of the discount as has been so recovered shall be disregarded for the purposes of this section.

(5) An order under this section—

(*a*) may make different provision with respect to different cases or descriptions of case, including different provision for different areas, and

(*b*) shall be made by statutory instrument which shall be subject to annulment in pursuance of a resolution of either House of Parliament.

(6) In this section "dwelling-house" includes any yard, garden, out-houses and appurtenances belonging to the dwelling-house or usually enjoyed with it.

DEFINITIONS

"dwelling-house": ss.183, 184.
"long lease": s.187.
"relevant time": s.122.
"shared ownership lease": s.622.

GENERAL NOTE

The principle governing discount for second-time purchasers is to deduct actual discounts previously allowed, rather than excluding periods of time prior to the previous purchase (as was the case between the 1980 and 1984 Acts). All qualifying "previous discounts" are to be deducted.

Subs. (3)

A previous discount qualifies if it was given to the purchaser, or one of the purchasers, or the spouse of purchaser or one of purchasers, or the deceased spouse of purchaser or one of the purchasers. However, a previous discount given to a spouse is not to count unless purchaser (or one of purchasers) and spouse were living together at date of notice claiming right to buy (*e.g.* the relevant time—see s.122). Similarly, unless purchaser (or one of purchasers) and deceased spouse were living together at time of death, the deceased spouse's previous discount is not to count.

If a previous discount was given to joint purchasers, only one or less than all of whom is or are now the subject of reduced discount, the previous discount is to be treated as having been allowed in equal portions.

Subs. (4)

If the previous discount was the subject of a repayment under s.155, below, the "deduction" is to be reduced by the amount of the repayment.

Subs. (6)

See notes to s.56, above.

Limits on amount of discount

131.—(1) Except where the Secretary of State so determines, the discount shall not reduce the price below the amount which, in accordance with a determination made by him, is to be taken as representing so much of the costs incurred in respect of the dwelling-house as, in accordance with the determination—

(*a*) is to be treated as incurred after 31st March 1974 (or such later date as may be specified in an order made by the Secretary of State), and

(*b*) is to be treated as relevant for the purposes of this subsection; and if the price before discount is below that amount, there shall be no discount.

(2) The discount shall not in any case reduce the price by more than such sum as the Secretary of State may by order prescribe.

(3) An order or determination under this section may make different provision for different cases or descriptions of case, including different provision for different areas.

(4) An order under this section shall be made by statutory instrument which shall be subject to annulment in pursuance of a resolution of either House of Parliament.

DEFINITIONS
"dwelling-house": ss.183, 184.

GENERAL NOTE
This section imposes maximum discounts: (a) by means of a minimum sale price, and (b) by order of the Secretary of State. The minimum sale price safeguards the amount which represents what has been spent on the dwelling-house after March 31, 1974 (or such later date as the Secretary of State may determine). If the price before discount is below that price, there is no discount allowed at all.

The shut-off date of March 31, 1974, refers to local government reorganisation under the Local Government Act 1972 (which took effect on April 1, 1974). It was thought difficult if not impossible to ascertain all costs prior to that date. It was originally intended to set the floor at the cost of *providing a* dwelling after the shut-off date, but this would not have allowed for expenditure on dwellings since that date, particularly when that expenditure was on improvement or conversion of dwellings purchased from the private sector.

It is for the Secretary of State to say how such expenditure is to be calculated, what is to be treated as incurred after the shut-off date, and what is relevant expenditure for these purposes. As to maximum discount by order of the Secretary of State, this has been set at £25,000: see Housing (Right to Buy) (Maximum Discount) Order 1980 (S.I. 1980 No. 1342), retained in force by s.2, Housing (Consequential Provisions) Act 1985. See also the Cost Floor Determinations 1984.

The right to a mortgage

The right to a mortgage

132.—(1) A secure tenant who has the right to buy has the right, subject to the following provisions of this Part—

(*a*) to leave the whole or part of the aggregate amount mentioned in section 133(1) outstanding on the security of a first mortgage of the dwelling-house, or

(*b*) if the landlord is a housing association, to have the whole or part of that amount advanced to him on that security by the Housing Corporation;

and in this Act that right is referred to as "the right to a mortgage".

(2) Where the right to buy belongs jointly to two or more persons, the right to a mortgage also belongs to them jointly.

Definitions
"dwelling-house": ss.183, 184.
"housing association": s.5.
"right to buy": s.118.
"secure tenant": ss.79, 185.

General Note
This is the parallel "right to a mortgage", with which to exercise the right to buy, *e.g.* the right to leave the purchase price outstanding (on a mortgage), or in the case of a housing association to have the purchase price advanced by the Housing Corporation. Section 133 governs its amount; ss.134–135 contain its procedural provisions.

The amount to be secured

133.—(1) The amount which a secure tenant exercising the right to a mortgage is entitled to leave outstanding, or have advanced to him, on the security of the dwelling-house is, subject to the limit imposed by this section, the aggregate of—

(*a*) the purchase price,

(*b*) so much of the costs incurred by the landlord or the Housing Corporation as is chargeable to the tenant under section 178(2) (costs), and

(*c*) any costs incurred by the tenant and defrayed on his behalf by the landlord or the Housing Corporation.

(2) The limit is that the amount which the tenant is entitled to leave outstanding or have advanced to him on the security of the dwelling-house may not exceed—

(*a*) where the right to a mortgage belongs to one person, the amount to be taken into account, in accordance with regulations under this section, as his available annual income multiplied by such factor as, under the regulations, is appropriate to it;

(*b*) where the right to a mortgage belongs to more than one person, the aggregate of the amounts to be taken into account in accordance with the regulations as the available annual income of each of them, after multiplying each of those amounts by the factor appropriate to it under the regulations.

(3) The Secretary of State may by regulations make provision for calculating the amount which is to be taken into account under this section as a person's available annual income and for specifying a factor appropriate to it; and the regulations—

(*a*) may provide for arriving at a person's available annual income by deducting from the sums taken into account as his annual income sums related to his needs and commitments, and may exclude sums from those to be taken into account as a person's annual income, and

(*b*) may specify different amounts and different factors for different circumstances.

(4) Where the amount which a secure tenant is entitled to leave outstanding on the security of the dwelling-house is reduced by the limit imposed by this section, the landlord may, if it thinks fit and the tenant agrees, treat him as entitled to leave outstanding on that security such amount exceeding the limit, but not exceeding the aggregate mentioned in subsection (1), as the landlord may determine.

(5) References in this Part to a secure tenant being entitled, or treated as entitled, to a "full mortgage" are to his being entitled, or treated as entitled, to leave outstanding or have advanced to him on the security of the dwelling-house an amount equal to the aggregate mentioned in subsection (1).

(6) Regulations under this section—

(*a*) may make different provision with respect to different cases or descriptions of case, including different provision for different areas, and

(*b*) shall be made by statutory instrument which shall be subject to annulment in pursuance of a resolution of either House of Parliament.

DEFINITIONS
"dwelling-house": ss.183, 184.
"right to mortgage": s.132.
"secure tenant": ss.79, 185.

GENERAL NOTE
This section concerns the right to a mortgage: by s.132 that means the right to leave an amount of money outstanding on the security of the dwelling-house, if the vendor is a local authority landlord, and the right to have the amount advanced on the security of the dwelling-house by the Housing Corporation, if the vendor is a housing association. The amount is that calculated in accordance with subs. (1), subject to the ceiling calculated under subs. (2). Claim is under s.134, below, and the landlord's or Corporation's duties in response under s.135, below.

Subs. (1)
The principal amount of mortgage is: (a) the purchase price, which means (s.126) the value (s.127) less the discount (s.129); *plus* (b) that part of the costs which, under s.178, the landlord or Housing Corporation is permitted to charge to the purchasing tenant, which is only their costs incurred in relation to the grant of the mortgage (to a maximum of £200, see notes to s.178); *plus* (c) any other costs which the tenant has incurred, but which the landlord or Housing Corporation has agreed to defray on his behalf, *e.g.* legal costs. This sum is known as a "full mortgage" (subs. (5)).

Subss. (2)–(4)
The amount calculated in accordance with subs. (1) will, however, be reduced if the tenant's available annual income ascertained in accordance with regulations made by the Secretary of State, multiplied by the appropriate factor specified in such regulations, produces a lower entitlement. When there are joint purchasers (*i.e.* including added purchaser under s.123) their available annual incomes, multiplied by the appropriate factor, are to be added together for these purposes. It is clear that the Secretary of State's powers are wide enough to specify different appropriate factors when a purchaser is a sole purchaser, and when there are joint purchasers, which would be in accordance with usual building society practice.

A landlord may, however, agree to grant a mortgage up to a full mortgage, if the mortgage would otherwise be reduced, but only "if it thinks fit." It is not entirely clear whether this power is confined to local authority vendors, or whether it is open to a housing association vendor so to agree, notwithstanding that the amount will be advanced not by the association, but by the Housing Corporation.

See S.I. 1980 No. 1423, retained in force by s.2, Housing (Consequential Provisions) Act 1985, for the relevant calculations.

Tenant's notice claiming to exercise right to a mortgage

134.—(1) A secure tenant cannot exercise his right to a mortgage unless he claims to exercise it by notice in writing served on the landlord, or, if the landlord is a housing association, on the Housing Corporation.

(2) The notice must be served within the period of three months beginning with the service on the tenant of—

(*a*) where he exercises his right under section 128 (determination of value by district valuer), the notice under subsection (5) of that section (further notice by landlord after determination) or,

(*b*) where he does not exercise that right, the notice under section 125 (landlord's notice of purchase price and other matters),

or within that period as extended under the following provisions.

(3) Where there are reasonable grounds for doing so, the landlord or, as the case may be, the Housing Corporation shall by notice in writing

served on the tenant extend (or further extend) the period within which the tenant's notice claiming to exercise his right to a mortgage must be served.

(4) If in such a case the landlord or Housing Corporation fails to do so, the county court may by order extend or further extend that period until such date as may be specified in the order.

GENERAL NOTE

This section governs the claim to a mortgage, which may be the right to leave an amount outstanding on the security of the dwelling-house, if the vendor is a local authority, or to have the amount advanced on the security of the dwelling-house by the Housing Corporation, if the vendor is a housing association: s.132. Section 135 deals with the landlord's response thereto.

Unless the period is extended, the tenant has three months to serve notice claiming a mortgage, running from *either* (a) the landlord's offer notice under s.125, *or* (b) if the tenant exercises the right to valuation by the district valuer under s.128, the landlord's notice informing the tenant of the results thereof. The landlord or the Housing Corporation may extend the three-month period, if there are reasonable grounds for so doing, which extension must be granted in writing. If no extension is granted, the tenant may apply to the county court for an order extending or further extending his time to claim a mortgage. It would seem that such an application may be made outside the three-month limit: see *Arieli* v. *Duke of Westminster* (1983) 269 E.G. 535, C.A., *Johnson* v. *Duke of Westminster* (1984) 17 H.L.R. 136, C.A.

No guidance as to reasonable grounds is provided: an example of a reasonable ground might be that the tenant was seeking finance elsewhere, and had good cause to believe it would be forthcoming, notwithstanding which, for reasons not attributable to the tenant's default, such finance is not going to be available after all. Another example might be unexpected, and blameless, loss of job.

A further extension to the time in which to claim mortgage is always provided if there is a change of secure tenant, in which case the new secure tenant has three months from the time he becomes the secure tenant in which to claim, with a possibility of further extension on reasonable grounds, including if necessary by way of application to the county court: s.136.

Landlord's notice of amount and terms of mortgage

135.—(1) As soon as practicable after the service on it of a notice under section 134, the landlord or Housing Corporation shall serve on the tenant a notice in writing stating—

    (*a*) the amount which, in the opinion of the landlord or Housing Corporation, the tenant is entitled to leave outstanding or have advanced on the security of the dwelling-house,

    (*b*) how that amount has been arrived at, and

    (*c*) the provisions which, in the opinion of the landlord or Housing Corporation, should be contained in the deed by which the mortgage is to be effected.

(2) The notice shall be accompanied by a form for use by the tenant in claiming, in accordance with section 142(1), to be entitled to defer completion and shall also inform the tenant of the effect of subsection (4) of that section (right to serve further notice claiming mortgage).

(3) Where, in the opinion of the landlord or Housing Corporation, the tenant is not entitled to a full mortgage, the notice shall also inform the tenant of the effect of the provisions of this Part relating to the right to be granted a shared ownership lease and shall be accompanied by a form for use by the tenant in claiming to exercise that right in accordance with section 144(1).

(4) The Housing Corporation shall send to the landlord a copy of any notice served by it on the tenant under this section.

GENERAL NOTE
   As soon as practicable after service of the tenant's notice, the landlord or the Housing Corporation must serve a counter-notice stating: (a) the provisions which the landlord, or the Housing Corporation, consider should be included in the mortgage deed (see s.139 and Sched. 7); (b) the amount of mortgage to which the tenant is entitled, and how that amount has been arrived at (s.133); and (c) that the tenant has the right to defer completion for up to two years from date of RTB1 under s.123 on payment of a £100 deposit (s.142).
   The notice must also inform the tenant of the right to a shared ownership lease under ss.143 *et seq.*, below, where the amount to which the tenant is entitled is less than the full amount needed to purchase outright. It is to be accompanied by a form for use in connection with the right. The Housing Corporation must serve a copy of its notice on the landlord, *i.e.* the housing association.

Change of tenant or landlord after service of notice claiming right to buy

Change of secure tenant after notice claiming right to buy

136.—(1) Where, after a secure tenant ("the former tenant") has given a notice claiming the right to buy, another person ("the new tenant")—
   (*a*) becomes the secure tenant under the same secure tenancy, otherwise than on an assignment made by virtue of section 92 (assignments by way of exchange), or
   (*b*) becomes the secure tenant under a periodic tenancy arising by virtue of section 86 (periodic tenancy arising on termination of fixed term) on the coming to an end of the secure tenancy,
the new tenant shall be in the same position as if the notice had been given by him and he had been the secure tenant at the time it was given.
   (2) If a notice under section 125 (landlord's notice of purchase price and other matters) has been served on the former tenant, the landlord shall serve on the new tenant a further form for his use in claiming to exercise the right to a mortgage.
   (3) The new tenant may then serve a notice under section 134 (tenant's notice claiming to exercise right to a mortgage) within the period of three months beginning with the service on him of that form or within that period as extended under the following provisions.
   (4) Where there are reasonable grounds for doing so, the landlord or, as the case may be, the Housing Corporation shall by notice in writing served on the new tenant extend (or further extend) the period within which his notice claiming to exercise the right to a mortgage may be served.
   (5) If in such a case the landlord or Housing Corporation fails to do so, the county court may by order extend or further extend that period until such date as may be specified in the order.
   (6) The preceding provisions of this section do not confer any right on a person required in pursuance of section 123 (claim to share right to buy with members of family) to share the right to buy, unless he could have been validly so required had the notice claiming to exercise the right to buy been given by the new tenant.
   (7) The preceding provisions of this section apply with the necessary modifications if there is a further change in the person who is the secure tenant.

DEFINITIONS
  "member of family": s.186.
  "right to buy" s.118.
  "right to mortgage": s.132.
  "secure tenant": ss.79, 185.

GENERAL NOTE
  On the determination of a fixed-term secure tenancy, there will normally automatically arise a periodic tenancy: s.86. The present provisions govern a change of tenant under the same secure tenancy, or under one such periodic tenancy. Such a change will usually be as a result of succession (s.87) although in limited circumstances it may be in consequence of an assignment (s.91), but *not* an assignment under the "right to exchange" in s.92. The present provisions occur on a first or subsequent change, although it will not normally be possible for there to be more than one change (s.88). The new tenant is put in the same position as the former tenant, and is treated as if he had himself served the RTB1 under s.122, save in two respects: mortgage entitlement, and added purchasers.
  If the proceedings have already reached the stage of the landlord's offer notice under s.125, which, among other things, sets out at what price the landlord believes the tenant is entitled to buy, and the tenant's right to refer the matter to the district valuer, then regardless of whether or not there has been a reference to the district valuer, leading to the service of a further notice under s.128(5), and regardless of whether or not the former tenant has served notice claiming to exercise the right to a mortgage or the landlord a counter-notice thereto (ss.134, 135), the landlord must serve a further form on the new tenant, entitling the new tenant to claim to exercise the right to a mortgage within three months of service of this claim form upon him.

Subs. (6)
  There must also be a reassessment of the qualification of any added purchasers. The new secure tenant will usually be amongst those who might, in any event, have been added by the former secure tenant, but it does not follow that those who qualified in relation to the former secure tenant, will also qualify in relation to the new: s.123.

Change of landlord after notice claiming right to buy or right to a mortgage

137. Where the interest of the landlord in the dwelling-house passes from the landlord to another body after a secure tenant has given a notice claiming to exercise the right to buy or the right to a mortgage, all parties shall be in the same position as if the other body had become the landlord before the notice was given and had been given that notice and any further notice given by the tenant to the landlord and had taken all steps which the landlord had taken.

DEFINITIONS
  "dwelling-house": ss.183, 184.
  "right to buy": s.118.
  "right to mortgage": s.132.
  "secure tenant": ss.79, 185.

GENERAL NOTE
  A change of landlord will have little effect on the tenant. It will, in any event, be an uncommon occurrence, given the requirement for consent to disposals: s.32. The tenant will be treated as if the new landlord had been the landlord at the time of RTB1 under s.122, above, which means that if the new landlord is a landlord exempt from the right to buy, the notice will simply be rendered nugatory.

Completion of purchase in pursuance of right to buy

Duty of landlord to convey freehold or grant lease

138.—(1) Where a secure tenant has claimed to exercise the right to buy and that right has been established, then, as soon as all matters relating to the grant and to the amount to be left outstanding or advanced on the security of the dwelling-house have been agreed or determined, the landlord shall make to the tenant—

    (*a*) if the dwelling-house is a house and the landlord owns the freehold, a grant of the dwelling-house for an estate in fee simple absolute, or

    (*b*) if the landlord does not own the freehold or if the dwelling-house is a flat (whether or not the landlord owns the freehold), a grant of a lease of the dwelling-house,

in accordance with the following provisions of this Part.

(2) If the tenant has failed to pay the rent or any other payment due from him as a tenant for a period of four weeks after it has been lawfully demanded from him, the landlord is not bound to comply with subsection (1) while the whole or part of that payment remains outstanding.

(3) The duty imposed on the landlord by subsection (1) is enforceable by injunction.

DEFINITIONS

    "dwelling-house": ss.183, 184.
    "flat": s.183.
    "house": s.183.
    "right to buy": s.118.
    "secure tenant": ss.79, 185.

GENERAL NOTE

    This section takes forward the process of purchase to its final stage: completion. "The Secretaries of State . . . expect that, *provided tenants and their solicitors act expeditiously*, they should be in a position to complete sales in most cases within three or four months of the right to buy being admitted; and they invite landlords to ensure that arrangements are made to enable this to happen . . . " (D.O.E. Circular 21/84).

    The statutory provisions, which are noticeably lacking in any provision for exchange of contract, would seem to supplant the normal rules governing the stages leading to a completion, and in particular, it would seem that the right to withdraw at any stage before completion suggests that no binding contract to buy will arise independently of the provisions (*cf. Gibson* v. *Manchester City Council* [1979] 1 W.L.R. 294; *cf.* also the provisions of s.5, Leasehold Reform Act 1967—"Where . . . a tenant . . . gives notice of his desire to have (the freehold or an extended lease), the rights and obligations of the landlord and the tenant arising from the notice shall inure . . . as rights and obligations arising under a contract for a sale or lease freely entered into . . . ").

    Note, however, that a delay in completion could render the party at fault liable in damages for consequential loss: see *Phillips* v. *Lamdin* [1949] 2 K.B. 33, *Raineri* v. *Miles* [1981] A.C. 1050, H.L. Such an action would seem to be available for a period of 12 years, under Limitation Act 1980, s.8, as an action on a specialty, not six years under *ibid*, s.5, as an action founded on simple contract, nor 15 years under *ibid*, s.15., as an action for the recovery of land: *cf. Collin* v. *Duke of Westminster* [1985] Q.B. 581, 17 H.L.R. 246, C.A. However, as this Part makes provision for the landlord to require the tenant to complete (see ss.140, 141, below), failure to use those powers would seem (a) to limit damage to that arising before the landlord *could* have nullified the notice thereunder, and (b) to make available the argument that as the statute has provided that period of time, any loss is not actionable.

    It is noticeable, too, that, just as there is no provision for registration of a notice claiming to exercise the right to buy (s.122) there is also no provision for registration of other notices, up to and including the notice which permits the tenant to defer completion for up to two years (*cf.* s.142, below). But although these notices—and perhaps even a secure tenant's inchoate right to buy—would otherwise be registerable, it would again seem that the express provisions of the Act override such requirements, and in particular, s.137 renders registration unnecessary. In practice, of course, given the need for consent to other disposals (s.32), these problems are unlikely to be of any real relevance.

Subss. (1)–(3)

    Once the right to buy has been claimed and established, and all outstanding matters agreed or determined, the landlord is bound to convey a freehold interest, or grant a lease for 125 years, or such shorter time as may be permitted under Sched. 6, para. 11. If the landlord does not do so, he may be compelled so to do by injunction: subs. (3).

But under subs. (2), the tenant is not entitled to complete if during a period of four weeks after it is demanded from him, he fails to pay the landlord any arrears of rent or other sums due *as tenant, e.g.* service charge. Thus, a rates debt would only qualify to disbar the tenant, if the rates are paid, with the rent, to a local authority as landlord, rather than as rating authority. As to what constitutes arrears of rent, see notes to Sched. 2, Ground 1.

If the tenant does not comply with the demand within the four weeks specified, the tenant is deemed not to be complying with a notice requiring completion, which means that if he does not clear the debt and complete within the time allowed under the notice requiring completion, he will lose the right to buy: s.141(4), below. The tenant can recommence proceedings to buy, forthwith if he wishes, although there is, of course, the prospect of a rise in the value of the property.

If the purchasing tenant is no longer a *secure* tenant, *e.g.* because he has moved out, the landlord is under no obligation to make the grant: *Sutton L.B.C.* v. *Swann, The Times,* November 30, 1985; (1985) 18 H.L.R., C.A.

Terms and effect of conveyance or grant and mortgage

139.—(1) A conveyance of the freehold executed in pursuance of the right to buy shall conform with Parts I and II of Schedule 6; a grant of a lease so executed shall conform with Parts I and III of that Schedule; and Part IV of that Schedule has effect in relation to certain charges.

(2) The secure tenancy comes to an end on the grant to the tenant of an estate in fee simple, or of a lease, in pursuance of the provisions of this Part relating to the right to buy; and if there is then a subtenancy section 139 of the Law of Property Act 1925 (effect of extinguishment of reversion) applies as on a merger or surrender.

(3) The deed by which a mortgage is effected in pursuance of the right to a mortgage shall, unless otherwise agreed between the parties, conform with the provisions of Schedule 7.

DEFINITIONS
   "right to buy": s.118.
   "right to mortgage": s.132.
   "secure tenancy": ss.79, 185.

GENERAL NOTE
   This subsection does no more, and no less, than incorporate Sched. 6, which sets out the terms of a conveyance or grant in accordance with an exercise of the right to buy under this Part, and Sched. 7, dealing with the terms of the mortgage.
   Sched. 6, Pt. I sets out provisions common to both conveyance and grant; Pt. II sets out provisions peculiar to freehold; Pt. III, provisions peculiar to lease; and Pt. IV deals with the redemption of any outstanding charges on the land. The extent to which these provisions may be varied is governed by the Schedule: see notes thereto.

Subs. (2)
   The purchase determines the secure tenancy, presumably even if the purchase is by only one—or less than all—of a number of joint tenants (*cf.* notes to s.118, above). If there are any sub-tenants, they become the tenants of the new owner, as if there had been a proper merger or surrender of a mesne tenancy with a landlord's interest: Law of Property Act 1925, s.139.

Landlord's first notice to complete

140.—(1) The landlord may, subject to the provisions of this section, serve on the tenant at any time a written notice requiring him—
   (a) if all relevant matters have been agreed or determined, to complete the transaction within a period stated in the notice, or
   (b) if any relevant matters are outstanding, to serve on the landlord within that period a written notice to that effect specifying the matters,
and informing the tenant of the effect of this section and of section 141(1), (2) and (4) (landlord's second notice to complete).

(2) The period stated in a notice under this section shall be such period (of at least 56 days) as may be reasonable in the circumstances.

(3) A notice under this section shall not be served earlier than whichever of the following is applicable—

(*a*) if the tenant has not claimed to exercise the right to a mortgage, nine months after the end of the period within which a notice claiming it could have been served by him;

(*b*) if he has claimed the right to a mortgage, but is not entitled to defer completion, nine months after the service of the notice under section 135 (landlord's notice of terms and amount of mortgage);

(*c*) if he is entitled to defer completion, two years after the service of his notice under section 122 claiming to exercise the right to buy or, if later, nine months after the service of the notice under section 135 (landlord's notice of terms and amount of mortgage).

(4) A notice under this section shall not be served if—

(*a*) a requirement for the determination or re-determination of the value of the dwelling-house by the district valuer has not been complied with,

(*b*) proceedings for the determination of any other relevant matter have not been disposed of, or

(*c*) any relevant matter stated to be outstanding in a written notice served on the landlord by the tenant has not been agreed in writing or determined.

(5) In this section "relevant matters" means matters relating to the grant and to the amount to be left outstanding or advanced on the security of the dwelling-house

DEFINITIONS
"dwelling-house": ss.183, 184.
"right to mortgage": s.132.

GENERAL NOTE
At any time, the landlord may serve a preliminary notice requiring either completion, if all relevant matters (defined in subs. (5)), have been agreed or determined (whether by court, or under s.128 by district valuer,) or notification back to the landlord, in writing, of what matters are considered outstanding, *i.e.* not agreed or determined.

It would seem that the question of whether or not all relevant matters have been agreed or determined is one for tenant, not landlord. The notice is to tell the tenant to complete, or specify reasons (unagreed or undetermined relevant matters) why not, as distinct from the landlord choosing which class of notice is appropriate (completion or statement of unagreed or undetermined relevant matters).

The notice must specify a period for "response"—*i.e.* completion or statement, which period is to be not less than 56 days: subs. (2). The notice must also inform the tenant of its "effect," and of the "effect" of s.141, below.

Subs. (3)
A preliminary notice cannot be served earlier than specified dates: (*a*) nine months after the tenant's time to exercise the right to a mortgage (see s.134), has elapsed, without the right being sought; (*b*) if the tenant is not entitled to defer completion (see s.142, below), nine months after notification of mortgage rights under s.135; or (*c*) if the tenant is entitled to defer completion, either two years after RTB1 under s.122, above, or three months after notification of mortgage rights under s.135, whichever is the later.

Subs. (4)
No preliminary notice may be served if one of three sets of circumstances applies. First of all, no notice may be served if there is a requirement for determination or redetermination of value by district valuer, which has not been complied with. Determinations and redeterminations are dealt with in s.128. Secondly, no preliminary notice may be served if proceedings for the determination of any other relevant matter have not been disposed of. Thirdly, no preliminary notice may be served if a relevant matter considered by the tenant

to be unagreed or undetermined has been the subject of a written notice served by him on the landlord.

Landlord's second notice to complete

141.—(1) If the tenant does not comply with a notice under section 140 (landlord's first notice to complete), the landlord may serve on him a further written notice—

(a) requiring him to complete the transaction within a period stated in the notice, and.

(b) informing him of the effect of this section in the event of his failing to comply.

(2) The period stated in a notice under this section shall be such period (of at least 56 days) as may be reasonable in the circumstances.

(3) At any time before the end of that period (or that period as previously extended) the landlord may by a written notice served on the tenant extend it (or further extend it).

(4) If the tenant does not comply with a notice under this section the notice claiming to exercise the right to buy shall be deemed to be withdrawn at the end of that period (or, as the case may require, that period as extended under subsection (3)).

(5) If a notice under this section has been served on the tenant and by virtue of section 138(2) (failure of tenant to pay rent, etc.) the landlord is not bound to complete, the tenant shall be deemed not to comply with the notice.

DEFINITIONS
"right to buy": s.118.

GENERAL NOTE
If the tenant does not comply with the preliminary notice, *i.e.* within the time specified (not less than 56 days), and neither completes nor states in writing what the outstanding relevant matters are, the landlord can serve a further, and final notice, requiring completion, also in a time to be specified, being not less than 56 days. This notice must warn the tenant of the effect of non-compliance.

The effect of non-compliance is contained in subss. (4) and (5), but is no more than that the notice claiming to exercise the right to buy is deemed to have been withdrawn. The tenant can recommence the process at once, albeit at risk of an increased price (attributable to a later "relevant time," *i.e.* date of [new] notice claiming right to buy: see s.122). Under subs. (3) the landlord has and retains the power to extend the time specified in this notice.

If the landlord does not utilise the completion notices in this and the last section, it would seem that the notice will remain in force for 12 years, under s. 8, Limitation Act 1980, as an action on a specialty, rather than six years under *ibid.* s.5, as an action found on simple contract, or 15 years, under *ibid.* s.15, as an action for recovery of land; furthermore, abandonment will not be inferred unless either the landlord can show a contract for mutual release, or mutual promises not to proceed, or words or conduct of the tenant on which the landlord has relied to his detriment to the extent of an estoppel—*cf. Collin* v. *Duke of Westminster* [1985] Q.B. 581, 17 H.L.R. 246, C.A.

When tenant is entitled to defer completion

142.—(1) A tenant is entitled to defer completion if—

(a) he has claimed the right to a mortgage but is not entitled, or treated as entitled, to a full mortgage,

(b) he has, within the period mentioned below, served on the landlord a notice claiming to be entitled to defer completion, and

(c) he has, within the same period, deposited the sum of £100 with the landlord.

(2) The period within which the notice must be served and the sum of £100 deposited is the period of three months beginning with the service

on the tenant of the notice under section 135 (notice of terms and amount of mortgage), or that period as extended under subsection (3).

(3) If there are reasonable grounds for doing so the landlord shall extend (or further extend) that period; and if it fails to do so the county court may by order extend or further extend that period until such date as may be specified in the order.

(4) A tenant who is entitled to defer completion may at any time before the service on him of a notice under section 140 (landlord's first notice to complete), serve a further notice under section 134(1) (notice claiming to exercise right to a mortgage); and if he does, section 135(1) and (4) (notice of terms and amount of mortgage) apply accordingly.

(5) If in pursuance of a notice under this section the tenant deposits the sum of £100 with the landlord, then—

    (*a*) if he completes the transaction, the sum shall be treated as having been paid towards the purchase price, and

    (*b*) if he does not complete the transaction but withdraws his notice claiming to exercise the right to buy, or is deemed to have withdrawn it by virtue of section 141(4) (effect of failure to comply with landlord's second notice to complete), the sum shall be returned to him.

DEFINITIONS
"right to mortgage": s.132.

GENERAL NOTE
The right to defer completion arises if the right to a mortgage (see s.132), has been claimed (s.134), and the tenant's personal entitlement means that he will receive less than a full mortgage, *i.e.* 100 per cent. plus related costs, *and*, within three months of the service of the s.135 notification of mortgage rights, he has claimed the right to defer completion and paid a £100 deposit in pursuance thereof. The three month period may be extended under subs. (3), and extension may be sought from the county court on refusal of landlord: it would seem that such an application may be made outside the three-month limit: see *Arieli* v. *Duke of Westminster* (1983) 269 E.G. 535, C.A., *Johnson* v. *Duke of Westminster* (1984) 17 H.L.R. 136, C.A.

Those with the right to defer completion may opt for shared ownership: see ss. 143 *et seq.*, below.

Subs. (4)
At any time before a landlord's preliminary notice to complete, the tenant may re-apply for a mortgage, *i.e.* in order to find out how much he qualifies for and, therefore, whether he is yet in a position to proceed.

Subs. (5)
If a deposit is lodged pursuant to the right to defer completion, and subsequently the purchase is completed, the amount is put towards the purchase price. This price is the original purchase price. If the tenant does not complete, or is deemed to have withdrawn his notice claiming to exercise the right to buy, the sum is to be returned to him.

The right to a shared ownership lease

Right to be granted a shared ownership lease

143.—(1) Where a secure tenant has claimed to exercise the right to buy and—

    (*a*) his right has been established and his notice claiming to exercise it remains in force,

    (*b*) he has claimed the right to a mortgage but is not entitled, or treated as entitled, to a full mortgage, and

    (*c*) he is entitled to defer completion,

he also has the right to be granted a shared ownership lease of the dwelling-house in accordance with the following provisions of this Part.

(2) Where the right to buy belongs to two or more persons jointly, the right to be granted a shared ownership lease also belongs to them jointly.

DEFINITIONS
  "dwelling-house": ss.183, 184.
  "right to buy": s.118.
  "right to mortgage": s.132.
  "secure tenant": ss.79, 185.
  "shared ownership lease": s.622.

GENERAL NOTE
   This is the first of eleven sections introducing the "right to a shared ownership lease". See also Scheds. 8 and 9, governing terms of shared ownership lease, and the right to further advances. See also s.173 for *dis*qualification to enfranchise under Leasehold Reform Act 1967, so long as any of the equity remains unpurchased, but s.174, for the acquisition of residential time under that Act even when the rent payable is *not* less than two-thirds of the rateable value.
   A shared ownership lease is one granted on payment of a premium calculated by reference to a *percentage* of the value of the property or its cost of provision, or under the terms of which a tenant may on departure receive a sum of money calculated by reference to its value: s.622.
   Shared ownership was described as "a new concept which I believe is not widely understood although I understand it is now proving quite popular, especially under the do-it-yourself shared ownership scheme. A recent parliamentary answer revealed that some 2,156 people had taken advantage of the scheme so far, quite apart from the shared ownership arrangements entered into by housing associations." (Mr John Fraser, 1984 Act, Standing Committee B, November 1, 1983, col. 370.) (D.I.Y. shared ownership is a housing association scheme under which the would-be purchaser finds the property to be the subject of a shared ownership lease.)
   In outline, a shared ownership lease is one under which the tenant purchases a "tranche" or "slice" of a long lease, with the right to purchase successive tranches until the whole has been acquired. Pending acquisition of the whole, the tenant will pay a rent reduced according to the slice of the interest acquired by the tenant. There will additionally be a balance to pay where the landlord is also mortgagee of the portion acquired.
   The right to a shared ownership lease arises only where (*a*) the tenant has claimed the right to buy *and* (*b*) the notice remains in force, *i.e.* has not been the subject of completion procedures resulting in it being deemed withdrawn, *and* (c) the tenant has claimed the right to a mortgage, *and* (d) the tenant is not entitled to a full mortgage, *i.e.* 100 per cent. plus costs, under s.134, above, *and* (e) is entitled to defer completion under s.142, above, which means that he will have had to pay £100 deposit under s.142(1)(c). It is, then, an alternative to deferral under s.142, above. The following sections adapt full right to buy procedures to the procedure for claiming a shared ownership lease.

Tenant's notice claiming to exercise right to shared ownership lease

   144.—(1) A secure tenant claims to exercise the right to be granted a shared ownership lease by written notice to that effect served on the landlord stating the initial share which he proposes to acquire.
   (2) The notice may be withdrawn or varied at any time by notice in writing served on the landlord.
   (3) On the service of a notice under this section, any notice served by the landlord under section 140 or 141 (landlord's notices to complete purchase in pursuance of right to buy) shall be deemed to have been withdrawn; and no such notice may be served by the landlord whilst a notice under this section remains in force.
   (4) If on the service by the tenant of a further notice under section 134 (claim to exercise right to a mortgage) he becomes entitled, or treated as entitled, to a full mortgage, he ceases to be entitled to exercise the right to be granted a shared ownership lease; and any notice of his under this section shall be deemed to have been withdrawn.
   (5) Where a notice under this section is withdrawn, or deemed to have been withdrawn, the tenant may complete the transaction in accordance with the provisions of this Part relating to the right to buy.

DEFINITIONS
"initial share": s.145.
"right to buy": s.118.
"right to mortgage": s.132.
"secure tenant": ss.79, 185.
"shared ownership lease": s.622.

GENERAL NOTE

This section sets out the procedure to be followed on the exercise of the right to a shared ownership lease (see notes to s.143 above). It is the equivalent of s.122, above, in normal right to buy cases.

Subs. (1)

The notice claiming the right to a shared ownership lease must state the initial share which the tenant proposes to buy. It may be varied under subs. (2), at any time (*i.e.* before completion). "Initial share" is defined in s.145, below.

Subs. (2)

The notice may be withdrawn, *or varied, e.g.* to claim a different initial share.

Subs. (3)

If a tenant serves notice claiming the right to a shared ownership lease, a landlord's notice to complete under ss.140 or 141, *i.e.* whether preliminary or final, is deemed to have been withdrawn, and no further such notice may be served so long as the notice claiming a shared ownership lease remains in force.

Subs. (4)

At any time before notice to complete, a tenant who has exercised the right to defer completion can serve a new notice claiming the right to a mortgage: see s.142(4), above. If the result of that application is to establish an entitlement to a full mortgage, the right to a shared ownership lease is lost. In other words, once the full amount is available from public funds, full ownership is to be acquired, in preference to and to the exclusion of the right to shared ownership.

Subs. (5)

Once a notice claiming the right to a shared ownership lease either has actually been withdrawn, or is deemed to have been withdrawn (under subs. (4)) the tenant may proceed to full purchase.

Tenant's initial share

145.—(1) The tenant's initial share in the dwelling-house shall be a multiple of the prescribed percentage and shall not be less than the minimum initial share.

(2) The prescribed percentage is 12.5 per cent. or such other percentage as the Secretary of State may by order prescribe.

(3) The minimum initial share is 50 per cent. or such other percentage as the Secretary of State may by order prescribe.

(4) An order under this section—

(*a*) may make different provision with respect to different cases or descriptions of case, including different provision for different areas, and

(*b*) may contain such transitional provisions as appear to the Secretary of State to be necessary or expedient.

(5) An order under this section shall be made by statutory instrument which shall be subject to annulment in pursuance of a resolution of either House of Parliament.

DEFINITIONS
"dwelling-house": ss.183, 184.

GENERAL NOTE

When claiming the right to a shared ownership lease, the tenant must state how much equity he seeks to acquire. This must be a multiple of 12.5 per cent., and not less than 50 per cent.: it must, accordingly, be 50 per cent., 62.5 per cent., 75 per cent. or 87.5 per cent. However, the Secretary of State may by order prescribe different percentages for 50 per cent. and 12.5 per cent. The 50 per cent. minimum is called the "minimum initial share", and the 12.5 per cent. factor is the "prescribed percentage". That which the tenant opts for is the "tenant's initial share."

Landlord's notice admitting or denying right

146. Where a notice under section 144 (notice claiming to exercise right to shared ownership lease) has been served by the tenant, the landlord shall, unless the notice is withdrawn, serve on the tenant within four weeks a written notice either—

(*a*) admitting the tenant's right, or
(*b*) denying it and stating the reasons why, in the opinion of the landlord, the tenant does not have the right to be granted a shared ownership lease.

DEFINITIONS
"shared ownership lease": s.622.

GENERAL NOTE

This is analogous to s.124, above, save that there is no extension to eight weeks because, of course, preliminary issues as to qualification under this Part have already been determined, or the right to shared ownership would not have arisen at all.

Landlord's notice of initial contribution, etc.

147.—(1) Where a secure tenant has claimed to exercise the right to be granted a shared ownership lease and that right has been established (whether by the landlord's admission or otherwise), the landlord shall, within eight weeks, serve on the tenant a written notice complying with this section.

(2) The notice shall state—

(*a*) the amount which, in the opinion of the landlord, should be the amount of the consideration for the grant of the lease on the assumption that the tenant's initial share is that stated in the notice under section 144; and
(*b*) the effective discount on an acquisition of that share for that consideration,

determined in each case, in accordance with section 148.

(3) The notice shall state the provisions which, in the opinion of the landlord, should be included in the lease.

(4) Where the landlord is not a housing association, the notice shall state any variation in the provisions which, in the opinion of the landlord, should be contained in the deed by which the mortgage is to be effected.

(5) Where the landlord is a housing association, the landlord shall send a copy of the notice to the Housing Corporation, and the Housing Corporation shall, as soon as practicable after receiving the notice, serve on the tenant a written notice stating any variation in the provisions which, in the opinion of the Housing Corporation, should be contained in the deed by which the mortgage is to be effected.

DEFINITIONS
"housing association": s.5.
"initial share": s.145.
"secure tenant": ss.79, 185.
"shared ownership lease": s.622.

GENERAL NOTE

This section takes the procedure for the grant of a shared ownership lease into the next stage and is the equivalent of a s.125 offer notice.

Once (and howsoever, *i.e.* including by legal proceedings) the right to a shared ownership lease has been established, the landlord has eight weeks to serve a notice stating: (*a*) how much it considers the tenant's payment is to be for a share of the proportion stated in the tenant's notice (see s.145, above); (*b*) the amount of tenant's discount reflected in that payment; (*c*) what provisions are to be contained in the lease; and (*d*) what variations are to be contained in the provisions of the mortgage deed. (In the case of a housing association, the last statement is not to be included: instead, a copy of the notice is to be sent to the Housing Corporation, which, "as soon as practicable" must serve its own notice: subs. (5)).

The purchase price is determined under s.148, below. The need to specify the discount separately is (*a*) so that the tenant can know that the correct amount has been allowed, and (*b*) so that the tenant can know what amount is vulnerable to repayment on early disposal—provision for recoupment of which is made in s.155, below.

The provisions which are to be included in the lease are to conform with Sched. 8, below; the provisions of the mortgage are to be agreed, or otherwise are as under Sched. 9, below. The reference to a *variation* in the provisions which should be contained in the mortgage deed arises in the following way:

In relation to the full right to buy, the terms of the mortgage deed are to conform with Sched. 7 "unless otherwise agreed by the parties" (s.139(3)). The provisions to be contained in the mortgage are to be stated in the notice under s.135, in response to the tenant's claim to a mortgage. Such a notice will necessarily have been served prior to any claim to a shared ownership lease. Accordingly, the notice at this stage will be "varying" the provisions as earlier stated, to reflect the changed nature of the transaction.

The procedure does not require a new notice claiming the right to a mortgage, or therefore a new notice dealing with mortgage alone. This equivalent of the s.125 offer notice accordingly subsumes the s.135 mortgage offer.

Tenant's initial contribution and effective discount

148.—(1) The consideration for the grant of a shared ownership lease (the tenant's "initial contribution") shall be determined by the formula—

$$C = \frac{S\,(V - D)}{100}$$

and the effective discount shall be determined by the formula—

$$E = \frac{S \times D}{100}$$

where—

    C= the tenant's initial contribution,

    E= the effective discount,

    S= the tenant's initial share expressed as a percentage,

    V= the value of the dwelling-house at the relevant time, determined in accordance with section 127, and

    D= the discount which if the tenant were exercising the right to buy would be applicable under sections 129 to 131.

(2) In determining the value of the dwelling-house for the purposes of this section, the assumptions to be made under section 127 (which vary according to whether it is the freehold or a lease which is to be acquired) are those applicable in relation to the dwelling-house for the purposes of the right to buy.

DEFINITIONS

    "dwelling-house": ss.183, 184.

    "initial share": s.145.

    "shared ownership lease": s.622.

GENERAL NOTE

The "tenant's initial contribution" is the price which the tenant must pay for the initial share. The contribution is to be the same percentage of what the tenant would have to pay were the full right to buy exercised, calculated (and determined) in all other respects as if it was a full exercise. See notes to s. 127, above.

Change of landlord after notice claiming to exercise right to shared ownership lease

149. Where the interest of the landlord in the dwelling-house passes from the landlord to another body after a secure tenant has given notice claiming to exercise the right to be granted a shared ownership lease, all parties shall be in the same position as if the other body had become the landlord before the notice was given and had been given that notice and any further notice given by the tenant to the landlord and had taken all steps which the landlord had taken.

DEFINITIONS
   "dwelling-house": ss.183, 184.
   "secure tenant": ss.79, 185.
   "shared ownership lease": s.622.

GENERAL NOTE
   This section is substantively the same provision as applies to the full right to buy, following a notice claiming to exercise the right to a mortgage: s.137, above.

Duty of landlord to grant shared ownership lease

150.—(1) Where a secure tenant has claimed to exercise the right to be granted a shared ownership lease and that right has been established, then, as soon as all matters relating to the grant and to the amount to be left outstanding or advanced on the security of the dwelling-house have been agreed or determined, the landlord shall grant the tenant a shared ownership lease of the dwelling-house in accordance with the following provisions of this Part.

(2) If the tenant has failed to pay the rent or any other payment due from him as a tenant for a period of four weeks after it has been lawfully demanded from him, the landlord is not bound to comply with subsection (1) while the whole or part of that payment remains outstanding.

(3) The duty imposed on the landlord by subsection (1) is enforceable by injunction.

DEFINITIONS
   "dwelling-house": ss.183, 184.
   "secure tenant": ss.79, 185.
   "shared ownership lease": s.622.

GENERAL NOTE
   See notes to s.138, above.

Terms and effect of grant and mortgage

151.—(1) A grant of a shared ownership lease in pursuance of this Part shall conform—
   (*a*) with Schedule 8 (terms of shared ownership lease), and
   (*b*) subject to that, with Parts I and III of Schedule 6 (terms of lease granted in pursuance of right to buy);
and Part IV of Schedule 6 (charges) applies to a shared ownership lease as it applies to a lease granted in pursuance of the right to buy.

(2) The secure tenancy comes to an end on the grant of the shared ownership lease, and if there is then a sub-tenancy section 139 of the Law of Property Act 1925 (effect of extinguishment of reversion) applies as on a merger or surrender.

(3) Where the transaction is duly completed the sum of £100 deposited by the tenant with the landlord in pursuance of section 142 (deferment of completion) shall be treated as having been paid towards the tenant's initial contribution.

(4) A deed by which a mortgage is effected where the tenant exercises both the right to a mortgage and the right to be granted a shared ownership lease shall, unless otherwise agreed between the parties, conform with—

(a) Schedule 7 (terms of mortgage granted in pursuance of right to a mortgage), and

(b) without prejudice to that, with Schedule 9 (right to further advances).

DEFINITIONS
"initial contribution": s.148.
"right to buy": s.118.
"right to mortgage": s.132.
"secure tenancy": ss.79, 185.
"shared ownership lease": s.622.

GENERAL NOTE
See notes to s.139, above, and to Scheds. 8 and 9, below. Note that the £100 deferral deposit is applied to the initial contribution under s.148, above.

Landlord's first notice to complete

152.—(1) The landlord may, subject to the provisions of this section, serve on the tenant at any time a written notice requiring him—

(a) if all relevant matters have been agreed or determined, to complete the transaction within a period stated in the notice, or

(b) if any relevant matters are outstanding, to serve on the landlord within that period a written notice to that effect specifying the matters,

and informing the tenant of the effect of this section and of section 153(1), (2) and (4) (landlord's second notice to complete and its effect).

(2) The period stated in a notice under this section shall be such period (of at least 56 days) as may be reasonable in the circumstances.

(3) A notice under this section shall not be served before the end of the period of two years after the service of the tenant's notice under section 122 (notice claiming to exercise right to buy) or, if later, nine months after the service of the notice under section 135 (landlord's notice of terms and amount of mortgage).

(4) A notice under this section shall not be served if—

(a) a requirement for the determination or re-determination of the value of the dwelling-house by the district valuer has not been complied with,

(b) proceedings for the determination of any other relevant matter have not been disposed of, or

(c) any relevant matter stated to be outstanding in a written notice served on the landlord by the tenant has not been agreed in writing or determined.

(5) In this section "relevant matters" means matters relating to the grant and to the amount to be left outstanding or advanced on the security of the dwelling-house.

DEFINITIONS
"dwelling-house": ss.183, 184.
"right to buy": s.118.

GENERAL NOTE
See notes to s.140, above.

Landlord's second notice to complete

153.—(1) If the tenant does not comply with a notice under section 152 landlord's first notice to complete), the landlord may serve on him a further written notice—

(*a*) requiring him to complete the transaction within a period stated in the notice, and

(*b*) informing him of the effect of this section in the event of his failing to comply.

(2) The period stated in a notice under this section shall be such period (of at least 56 days) as may be reasonable in the circumstances.

(3) At any time before the end of that period (or that period as previously extended) the landlord may by a written notice served on the tenant extend it (or further extend it).

(4) If the tenant does not comply with a notice under this section, the notice claiming to exercise the right to be granted a shared ownership lease and the notice claiming to exercise the right to buy shall be deemed to have been withdrawn at the end of that period (or, as the case may require, that period as extended under subsection (3)).

(5) If a notice under this section has been served on the tenant and by virtue of section 150(2) (failure of tenant to pay rent, etc.) the landlord is not bound to complete, the tenant shall be deemed not to comply with the notice.

DEFINITIONS
    "right to buy": s.118.
    "shared ownership lease": s.622.

GENERAL NOTE
    See notes to s.141, above.
    Note that deemed withdrawal on non-compliance is of *both* claim to shared-ownership lease, *and* claim to right to buy.

Registration of title

Registration of title

154.—(1) Where the landlord's title to the dwelling-house is not registered, section 123 of the Land Registration Act 1925 (compulsory registration of title) applies in relation to—

(*a*) the conveyance of the freehold or the grant of a lease in pursuance of this Part, or

(*b*) the conveyance of the freehold in pursuance of such a right as is mentioned in paragraph 2(1) or 8(1) of Schedule 8 (terms of shared ownership lease; right to freehold on acquiring 100 per cent. interest),

whether or not the dwelling-house is in an area in which an Order in Council under section 120 of that Act is for the time being in force (areas of compulsory registration) and, in the case of a lease, whether or not the lease is granted for a term of not less than 40 years.

(2) Where the landlord's title to the dwelling-house is not registered, the landlord shall give the tenant a certificate stating that the landlord is entitled to convey the freehold or make the grant subject only to such incumbrances, rights and interests as are stated in the conveyance or grant or summarised in the certificate.

(3) Where the landlord's interest in the dwelling-house is a lease, the certificate under subsection (2) shall also state particulars of that lease and, with respect to each superior title—

(*a*) where it is registered, the title number;

(*b*) where it is not registered, whether it was investigated in the usual way on the grant of the landlord's lease.

(4) A certificate under subsection (2) shall be—

(*a*) in a form approved by the Chief Land Registrar, and

(*b*) signed by such officer of the landlord or such other person as may be approved by the Chief Land Registrar.

(5) The Chief Land Registrar shall, for the purpose of the registration of title, accept such a certificate as sufficient evidence of the facts stated in it; but if as a result he has to meet a claim against him under the Land Registration Acts 1925 to 1971 the landlord is liable to indemnify him.

(6) Sections 8 and 22 of the Land Registration Act 1925 (application for registration of leasehold land and registration of dispositions of leasehold) apply in relation to a lease granted in pursuance of this Part notwithstanding that it is a lease for a term of which not more than 21 years are unexpired or, as the case may be, a lease granted for a term not exceeding 21 years.

DEFINITIONS

"dwelling-house": ss.183, 184.

"shared ownership lease": s.622.

GENERAL NOTE

This section requires that on exercise of the right to buy, the title shall be registered, whether or not the land is in an area of compulsory registration under Land Registration Act 1925, s.120. It follows that, once the title has been so registered, the land is for all subsequent purposes treated as registered land: *ibid.* s.3(xxiv). Compulsory registration does not normally apply to leases of less than 40 years (*ibid,*) but as a result of this section, will apply to such leases granted under the right to buy.

Where the land is not, as at the time of sale, already registered land, the landlord is required to provide the tenant with a certificate stating its entitlement to convey the freehold or make the grant, subject to such incumbrances, rights and interests as are stated in the conveyance or grant, or summarised in the certificate. The certificate is to be in a form approved by the Chief Land Registrar, and to be signed by such officer of the landlord or other person as he may approve.

This certificate is to be accepted by the Chief Land Registrar as sufficient evidence of the facts stated in it. If in consequence of accepting such a certificate, the Chief Land Registrar subsequently has to meet a claim against him under the Land Registration Act 1925, s.83, and the Land Registration and Land Charges Act 1971, ss.1, 2, he is entitled to be indemnified in turn by the landlord: see, in any event, 1925 Act, s.83(9)(10).

These provisions are not applicable or necessary in the case of land which is already registered land.

Provisions affecting future disposals

Repayment of discount on early disposal

155.—(1) A conveyance of the freehold or grant of a lease in pursuance of this Part shall contain (unless, in the case of a conveyance or grant in pursuance of the right to buy, there is no discount) a covenant binding on the secure tenant and his successors in title to the following effect.

(2) In the case of a conveyance or grant in pursuance of the right to buy, the covenant shall be to pay to the landlord on demand, if within a period of five years there is a relevant disposal which is not an exempted disposal (but if there is more than one such disposal, then only on the first of them), the discount to which the secure tenant was entitled, reduced by 20 per cent. for each complete year which has elapsed after the conveyance or grant and before the disposal.

(3) In the case of a grant in pursuance of the right to be granted a shared ownership lease, the covenant shall be to pay to the landlord on demand, if within a period of five years commencing with the acquisition by the tenant of his initial share or the acquisition by him of an additional

share there is a relevant disposal which is not an exempted disposal (but
if there is more than one such disposal, then only on the first of them),
the aggregate of—
  (*a*) the effective discount (if any) to which the tenant was entitled on
       the acquisition of his initial share, and
  (*b*) for each additional share, the effective discount (if any) to which
       the tenant was entitled on the acquisition of that share,
reduced, in each case, by 20 per cent. for each complete year which has
elapsed after the acquisition and before the disposal.

DEFINITIONS
  "exempted disposal": s.160.
  "relevant disposal": s.159.
  "right to buy": s.118.
  "secure tenant": ss.79, 185.
  "shared ownership lease": s.622.

GENERAL NOTE
  The central intention of this section is to ensure that the purchaser will have to repay 20
per cent of his discount (s.129) for each year less than five years, if he sells the property
within that time. The purpose is obvious: as in most cases there will be no pre-emption
clause (but *cf.* s.157, below, for the limited circumstances in which such may be inserted)
there is no other way of at the least slowing down the loss of the property onto the open
market. The requirement to repay discount, or a proportion of it, is only a requirement to
repay it on demand.
  The covenant is only inserted if there is a discount at all. But if there is a discount, then
the covenant must be inserted into every conveyance or grant under this Part, including a
shared ownership lease. The covenant is to bind the purchaser, and his successors in title
and those claiming under them, *e.g.* mortgagees or sublessees. But the obligation only arises
in respect of certain classes of disposal: *i.e.* relevant disposals under s.159, below, which are
not exempted disposals under s.160, below. Repayment is, however, only required on the
first non-exempt disposal.
  In the case of a shared ownership lease, the covenant runs not merely for five years from
the initial grant, but for five years from the acquisition of each subsequent tranche of equity
in relation to which there is an effective discount, and with the repayment amount running
independently in relation to initial, and subsequent, purchases. Accordingly, if discount is
(as it usually will be—see Sched. 8, below) available until the acquisition of the last tranche,
that much of the discount will still remain vulnerable to repayment for a further five years,
even though, *e.g.* repayment of discount on initial acquisition is itself now outside the five
year period.

Liability to repay is a charge on the premises

  156.—(1) The liability that may arise under the covenant required by
section 155 is a charge on the dwelling-house, taking effect as if it had
been created by deed expressed to be by way of legal mortgage.
  (2) The charge has priority immediately after any legal charge securing
an amount—
  (*a*) left outstanding by the tenant in exercising the right to buy or the
       right to be granted a shared ownership lease, or
  (*b*) advanced to him by an approved lending institution for the purpose
       of enabling him to exercise that right, or
  (*c*) further advanced to him by that institution;
but the landlord may at any time by written notice served on an approved
lending institution postpone the charge taking effect by virtue of this
section to a legal charge securing an amount advanced or further advanced
to the tenant by that institution.
  (3) A charge taking effect by virtue of this section is a land charge for
the purposes of section 59 of the Land Registration Act 1925 notwithstanding subsection (5) of that section (exclusion of mortgages), and subsection
(2) of that section applies accordingly with respect to its protection and
realisation.

(4) The approved lending institutions for the purposes of this section are—

the Housing Corporation,
a building society,
a bank,
a trustee savings bank,
an insurance company,
a friendly society,

and any body specified, or of a class or description specified, in an order made by the Secretary of State with the consent of the Treasury.

(5) An order under subsection (4)—

(*a*) shall be made by statutory instrument, and

(*b*) may make different provision with respect to different cases or descriptions of case, including different provision for different areas.

(6) Before making an order varying or revoking a previous order, the Secretary of State shall give an opportunity for representations to be made on behalf of any body which, if the order were made, would cease to be an approved lending institution for the purposes of this section.

DEFINITIONS
"bank": s.622.
"building society": s.622.
"dwelling-house": ss.183, 184.
"friendly society": s.622.
"right to buy": s.118.
"shared ownership lease": s.622.
"trustee savings bank": s.622.

GENERAL NOTE
The repayment covenant is to be a charge on the property. Under s.154, even if the property is not in a compulsory registration area, the conveyance or grant should be followed by application for registration in compliance with the Land Registration Act 1925, s.123. Once registered the land will be treated as registered land for all subsequent purposes: Land Registration Act 1925, s.3(xxiv). Failure to apply for registration in due course will render the conveyance void at law, but otherwise fully effective in equity, creating enforceable equitable interests in unregistered land. In practice, one would expect the vendor or lessor, *i.e.* the former landlord, to lodge the application for registration, for they will also normally be the mortgagee and as such will retain the title deeds. The repayment covenant is protected as a land charge, under the Land Registration Act 1925, s.59(2), by entry of a notice or caution.

The charge is to take effect as if it had been created by deed expressed to be by way of legal mortgage, and it will have priority immediately following the priority of the mortgage with which the property is itself purchased, or a further advance from *any* of the bodies within subs. (4). This means that a mortgage created by leaving an amount outstanding (*i.e.* a mortgage under the right to a mortgage, from the former landlord—see s.132, above), may be taken over by a body within subs. (4) without loss of priority, or that further advances by the same mortgagee may be granted, *e.g.* for improvement purposes, or even, although this will be uncommon in practice, that a second mortgage may be granted by one of the bodies within subs. (4), even if it did not grant the first mortgage.

A purchase effected with a loan by someone other than one of the bodies specified in subs. (4) will accordingly mean that the lender's charge on the property takes priority behind the repayment covenant.

The Secretary of State may specify bodies or classes of body for this purpose (and may subsequently vary or revoke such an order, although only after giving any body affected an opportunity to make representations): subs. (4). By the Housing (Right to Buy) (Priority of Charges) Order 1984, S.I. 1984 No. 1554, retained in force by s.2, Housing (Consequential Provisions) Act 1985, the Secretary of State has specified further bodies, some of whom have now been taken into the list in subs. (4).

Restriction on disposal of dwelling-houses in National Parks, etc.

157.—(1) Where in pursuance of this Part a conveyance or grant is executed by a local authority, the Development Board for Rural Wales or a housing association ("the landlord") of a dwelling-house situated in—

(*a*) a National Park,

(*b*) an area designated under section 87 of the National Parks and Access to the Countryside Act 1949 as an area of outstanding natural beauty, or

(*c*) an area designated by order of the Secretary of State as a rural area,

the conveyance or grant may contain a covenant limiting the freedom of the tenant (including any successor in title of his and any person deriving title under him or such a successor) to dispose of the dwelling-house in the manner specified below.

(2) The limitation is, subject to subsection (4), that until such time (if any) as may be notified in writing by the landlord to the tenant or a successor in title of his, there will be no relevant disposal which is not an exempted disposal without the written consent of the landlord; but that consent shall not be withheld if the disposal is to a person satisfying the condition stated in subsection (3).

(3) The condition is that the person to whom the disposal is made (or, if it is made to more than one person, at least one of them) has, throughout the period of three years immediately preceding the application for consent—

(*a*) had his place of work in a region designated by order of the Secretary of State which, or part of which, is comprised in the National Park or area, or

(*b*) had his only or principal home in such a region;

or has had the one in part or parts of that period and the other in the remainder; but the region need not have been the same throughout the period.

(4) If the Secretary of State or, where the landlord is a housing association, the Housing Corporation, consents, the limitation specified in subsection (2) may be replaced by the following limitation, that is to say, that until the end of the period of ten years beginning with the conveyance or grant there will be no relevant disposal which is not an exempted disposal, unless in relation to that or a previous such disposal—

(*a*) the tenant (or his successor in title or the person deriving title under him or his successor) has offered to reconvey the dwelling-house, or as the case may be surrender the lease, to the landlord for such consideration as is mentioned in section 158, and

(*b*) the landlord has refused the offer or has failed to accept it within one month after it was made.

(5) The consent of the Secretary of State or the Housing Corporation under subsection (4) may be given subject to such conditions as he or, as the case may be, the Corporation, thinks fit.

(6) A disposal in breach of such a covenant as is mentioned in subsection (1) is void.

(7) Where such a covenant imposes the limitation specified in subsection (2), the limitation is a local land charge and the Chief Land Registrar shall enter the appropriate restriction on the register of title as if application thereof had been made under section 58 of the Land Registration Act 1925.

(8) An order under this section—

(*a*) may make different provision with respect to different cases or descriptions of case, including different provision for different areas, and (*b*) shall be made by statutory instrument which shall be subject to annulment in pursuance of a resolution of either House of Parliament.

DEFINITIONS
"dwelling-house": ss.183, 184.
"exempted disposal": s.160.
"housing association": s.5.
"relevant disposal": s.159.

GENERAL NOTE
The purpose of this section is to provide some limited protection for landlords in rural areas, areas of natural beauty and national parks. They have, subject to the consent of the Secretary of State, an option to include one of two types of restrictive covenant in the conveyance or grant: either they may limit the class of person to whom a relevant property can be resold (which will, of course, have a corresponding effect on value under s.127) or they may insert a pre-emption clause entitling the landlord to repurchase the property on a further disposal within 10 years from the date of sale. A disposal in breach of either class of covenant is wholly void: subs. (6).

A restrictive covenant of the classes prescribed by this section may be inserted into a conveyance or grant of property under this Part if the property is situated in: (a) a National Park; or (b) an area designated as of outstanding natural beauty under the National Parks and Access to the Countryside Act 1949, s.87; or (c) it is in an area designated by the Secretary of State, as a rural area. In any case, the provisions apply only to local authorities (as defined in s.4), the Development Board for Rural Wales or a housing association (see s.5). Excluded, therefore, are new town and urban development corporations. The Secretary of State has designated rural areas in Wales for these purposes: see S.I. 1980 No. 1375, and in England see S.I. 1981 No.397, S.I. 1981 No. 940, S.I. 1982 No. 21 and S.I. 1982 No. 187, all retained in force by s.2, Housing (Consequential Provisions) Act 1985.

A covenant under subs. (2) is a local land charge, subs. (7). It is to be protected under Land Registration Act 1925, s.58, by entry of a restriction, which means that the landlord will receive notification prior to any further transfer. This is an "interesting" innovation as local land charges are not normally protected on the register, and never by restriction under s.58. They do not require registration, for they qualify as overriding interests under Land Registration Act 1925, s.70(1)(i) in any event. That the land will have become registered land assumes compliance with s.154, the requirement to register on completion under the right to buy, even when the land is not otherwise registered land.

A covenant under subs. (4) will be an estate contract, registerable under the Land Charges Act 1972, if there is no compliance with s.154 and the land remains unregistered (see *Greene* v. *Church Commissioners for England* [1974] Ch. 467, C.A.) and in the case of registered land as it will usually have become, to be protected by entry of a notice or caution in the register under Land Registration Act 1925, s.59. The covenants are, in any event, binding on the tenant's successors in title, under subs.(1).

Subss. (2), (3)
The first class of restrictive covenant, which the landlord may insert without the consent of the Secretary of State, is a prohibition on disposal without consent of the landlord until such time as the landlord may notify the purchaser that it is waiving its rights under the covenant, if the landlord ever does choose to waive these rights. Both notification of waiver, and notification of consent must be in writing. Disposals are relevant disposals under s.159, which are not exempted disposals under s.160: see notes thereto.

Consent is not, however, to be withheld if the disposal is to a person who has, throughout three years preceding the application for consent, either (a) had his place of work in a region designated for these purposes under subs. (3), which region, or part of which region, is comprised in the National Park, area of outstanding natural beauty, or designated rural area, or (b) had his only or principal home (as to the meaning of which, see notes to s.81, above) in such a designated region. Regions have been designated for these purposes, for Wales, under S.I. 1980 No. 1375, and for England, by S.I. 1980 No. 1345, S.I. 1981 No. 397, S.I. 1982 No. 21 and S.I. 1982 No. 187, all retained in force by s.2, Housing (Consequential Provisions) Act 1985.

The three-year period may be made up in part by residence, and in part by workplace, and the designated region need not have been the same throughout the period, although it would appear that if more than one designated region is to be relied upon each such designated region must have at the least an overlapping area with the National Park, area of outstanding natural beauty or designated rural area in which the property the subject of the application for consent is situated. A distinction is, of course, drawn between designated rural areas, and designated regions: the latter will be defined so as to permit sales to persons living and/or working around, not just in, the areas in which the property is situated.

Subss. (4) (5)
The second class of covenant may only be inserted with the consent of the Secretary of State or the Housing Corporation, depending upon whether the vendor landlord is a local or other public authority, or a housing association. Such consent may be given subject to such conditions as Secretary of State or Housing Corporation thinks fit. The covenant is in place of, not in addition to, that considered in the notes to subss. (2), (3) above, and is a pre-emption clause, lasting for a period of 10 years from the date of conveyance or grant. The pre-emption clause is only activated by a relevant disposal under s.159, which is not an exempt disposal under s.160: see notes thereto, below.
Prior to such a disposal, there must be an offer to reconvey to the former landlord the property in question, at a price determined in accordance with s.158, below, which means to be agreed or to be determined by the district valuer, as at the date on which the offer to reconvey is made. If the landlord declines the offer, or fails to accept it within one month after it is made, the former tenant may go ahead and sell to whomsoever he may please. A general consent to the substitution of the pre-emption (subs. (4)) clause, is to be found in Ministerial Letter, September 22, 1980, para. 28.

Consideration for reconveyance or surrender under s. 157

158.—(1) The consideration for the offer by a tenant, referred to in section 157(4)(*a*), to reconvey or surrender his interest to the landlord shall be such amount as may be agreed between the parties or determined by the district valuer as being the amount which is to be taken as the value of the dwelling-house at the time the offer is made.

(2) That value shall be taken to be the price which, at that time, the interest to be reconveyed or surrendered would realise if sold on the open market by a willing vendor, on the assumption that any liability under—

    (*a*) the covenant required by section 155 (repayment of discount on early disposal), and

    (*b*) any covenant required by paragraph 6 of Schedule 8 (payment for outstanding share on disposal of dwelling-house subject to shared ownership lease),

would be discharged by the vendor.

(3) If the landlord accepts the offer, no payment shall be required in pursuance of any such covenant as is mentioned in subsection (2), but the consideration shall be reduced by such amount (if any) as, on a disposal made at the time the offer was made, being a relevant disposal which is not an exempted disposal, would fall to be paid under that covenant.

DEFINITIONS
"dwelling-house": ss.183, 184.
"exempted disposal": s.160.
"relevant disposal": s.159.
"shared ownership lease": s.622.

GENERAL NOTE
The provisions of this section are designed (a) to settle the repurchase price, as at the time of offer to reconvey, which will be based on the same principles as those governing the original sale price, save that there will be no disregard of tenant's improvements, and (b) to ensure that if the landlord would otherwise be entitled to reclaim a proportion of discount, under s.155, that sum is knocked off the resale price, although no further claim to recoup discount is then to be made.

Relevant disposals

159.—(1) A disposal, whether of the whole or part of the dwelling-house, is a relevant disposal for the purposes of this Part if it is—

    (*a*) a further conveyance of the freehold or an assignment of the lease, or

    (*b*) the grant of a lease (other than a mortgage term) for a term of more than 21 years otherwise than at a rack rent.

(2) For the purposes of subsection (1)(*b*) it shall be assumed—

    (*a*) that any option to renew or extend a lease or sub-lease, whether or not forming part of a series of options, is exercised, and

    (*b*) that any option to terminate a lease or sub-lease is not exercised.

DEFINITIONS
"dwelling-house": ss.183, 184.

GENERAL NOTE
Repayment is required on the *first* non-exempt disposal, *whether of the whole or part of the property*: conveyance of freehold, assignment of lease, or grant of lease or sub-lease for a term of more than 21 years otherwise than at a rack-rent. Note that for this purpose a grant for less than 21 years, with an option to renew which will or may take the period over 21 years, qualifies as a grant for more than 21 years, by assumption that the option will be exercised. It will be assumed that an option to determine a lease for more than 21 years in a period of less than 21 years will not be exercised. Furthermore, by s.163, the grant of an option enabling a person to call for such a disposal is itself to be treated as a disposal, which also serves to slow down the process of putting the property onto the private market by preventing tenants buying with a commitment to resell and even, perhaps, purchasing with funds provided by the prospective next purchaser.

Note that a sub-tenancy for the whole of the unexpired period of a lease will take effect as an assignment at law, and is likely, therefore, to attract repayment: *Milmo* v. *Carrerras* [1946] K.B. 306. The fact that there is a right of re-entry or to forfeit will not prevent a lease being a lease for more than 21 years: *Quinlan* v. *Avis* (1933) 149 L.T. 214. The term "rack-rent" means a rent of, or near, the full annual value of a property (*Re Sawyer and Withall* [1919] 2 Ch. 333) determined as at the date of the grant (*London Corporation* v. *Cusack-Smith* [1955] A.C. 337). It has been defined as "the full amount which a landlord can reasonably be expected to get from a tenant," so that where property is subject to Rent Act control of rents, the maximum permitted rent is the rack-rent: *Rawlance* v. *Croydon Corporation* [1952] 2 Q.B. 803, C.A. A lease or sub-lease by way of mortgage term is not, however, a lease or sub-lease for these purposes, and so not a disposal: subs. (1)(b).

The word "conveyance" itself means "an instrument that transfers property from one person to another" (*Eastbourne Corporation* v. *Att.-Gen.* [1904] A.C. 155). It is defined somewhat more broadly under the Law of Property Act 1925, s.205(1)(ii), but as this definition is not imported into this Part, the common law definition will prevail. In the event, an instrument which does not pass a legal estate will not qualify as a conveyance, even if it is sufficient to amount to an enforceable contract for the conveyance and so pass an equitable interest in the property under the rule in *Walsh* v. *Lonsdale* (1882) 21 Ch.D. 9, *Rodger* v. *Harrison* (1893) 1 Q.B. 161, *I.R.C.* v. *Angus* (1889) 23 Q.B.D. 579.

Subs. (2)
The purpose was described thus: " . . . it would be possible for a tenant who has bought his home under the right to buy to get round the discount clawback provisions by granting a lease for less than 21 years with an option to renew, which would take the total period above 21 years.

"The object of these amendments is to stop that loophole which they do, in effect, by providing that for the purpose of asserting whether a lease is for more than 21 years, it shall be assumed that any option to extend or renew the lease is exercised, and that any option to terminate the lease is not exercised. Anyone granting a lease for less than 21 years with an option to extend or renew will therefore be caught by the discount clawback provisions." (Lord Bellwin, *Hansard*, H.L. Vol. 450, col. 804 (April 5, 1984)).

Exempted disposals

160.—(1) A disposal is an exempted disposal for the purposes of this Part if—

    (*a*) it is a disposal of the whole of the dwelling-house and a further conveyance of the freehold or an assignment of the lease and the person or each of the persons to whom it is made is a qualifying person (as defined in subsection (2));

(*b*) it is a vesting of the whole of the dwelling-house in a person taking under a will or on an intestacy;

(*c*) it is a disposal of the whole of the dwelling-house in pursuance of an order made under section 24 of the Matrimonial Causes Act 1973 (property adjustment orders in connection with matrimonial proceedings) or section 2 of the Inheritance (Provision for Family and Dependants) Act 1975 (orders as to financial provision to be made from estate);

(*d*) it is a compulsory disposal (as defined in section 161); or

(*e*) it is a disposal of property consisting of land included in the dwelling-house by virtue of section 184 (land let with or used for the purposes of the dwelling-house).

(2) For the purposes of subsection (1)(*a*), a person is a qualifying person in relation to a disposal if—

(*a*) he is the person, or one of the persons, by whom the disposal is made,

(*b*) he is the spouse or a former spouse of that person, or one of those persons, or

(*c*) he is a member of the family of that person, or one of those persons, and has resided with him throughout the period of twelve months ending with the disposal.

DEFINITIONS

"compulsory disposal": s.161.
"dwelling-house": ss.183, 184.
"member of family": s.186.

GENERAL NOTE

Specifically excepted from the repayment provisions are disposals in pursuance of an order under the Matrimonial Causes Act 1973, s.24 (see notes to s.91, above), a disposal under the Inheritance (Provision for Family Dependants) Act 1975, s.2, or a vesting in a person taking under a will or on intestacy. In other words, disposals in the course of a domestic breakdown or on death are not such disposals as to attract repayment of discount.

In addition, other family disposals are permitted: *e.g.* where several joint owners dispose to one or less than all of their number, voluntary disposals between spouses or former spouses, and disposals to members of the family who would qualify as joint purchasers.

There are two further groups of exempt disposal, *i.e.* disposals not attracting repayment of discount. First, there is the "compulsory disposal" within s.161, below, which permits purchase without repayment of discount, when the purchase is by a public authority, enjoying compulsory purchase powers, whether or not the purchase is in fact compulsory or by agreement, and whether or not the purchase is for the authority themselves or on behalf of another body, *e.g.* a local authority buying for a housing association.

Secondly, while the repayment requirement is normally activated by a disposal of all or part only of the dwelling-house (see s.159(1)), it is permitted to dispose of "land included" under s.184, below, *i.e.* land let together with the dwelling-house, or land used with it which is reasonably included. These added lands may be disposed of, without requiring repayment of discount.

In either of these last two classes of case, the repayment covenant itself will not bind the purchaser, or a later successor in title, and the covenant and the consequential charge ceases to apply in relation to the property disposed of: see s.162, below.

Meaning of "compulsory disposal"

161. In this Part a "compulsory disposal" means a disposal of property which is acquired compulsorily, or is acquired by a person who has made or would have made, or for whom another person has made or would have made, a compulsory purchase order authorising its compulsory purchase for the purposes for which it is acquired.

GENERAL NOTE

This section defines the "compulsory disposal" for the purposes of s.160, above, *i.e.* a disposal which although "relevant" under s.159, above, will qualify as exempted from the discount clawback requirement of s.155, above. Note that the purchase may be for the purchasing authority themselves, or on behalf of another, *e.g.* a local authority purchasing on behalf of a housing association. Note, too, that the compulsory powers do not need to be exercised, *i.e.* it is sufficient if the purchase is by an authority with compulsory powers.

Exempted disposals which end liability under covenants

162. Where there is a relevant disposal which is an exempted disposal by virtue of section 160(1)(*d*) or (*e*) (compulsory disposals or disposals of land let with or used for purposes of dwelling-house)—

(*a*) the covenant required by section 155 (repayment of discount on early disposal) is not binding on the person to whom the disposal is made or any successor in title of his, and that covenant and the charge taking effect by virtue of section 156 cease to apply in relation to the property disposed of, and

(*b*) any such covenant as is mentioned in section 157 (restriction on disposal of dwelling-houses in National Parks, etc.) ceases to apply in relation to the property disposed of.

DEFINITIONS

"compulsory disposal": s.161.
"dwelling-house": ss.183, 184.
"exempted disposal": s.160.
"relevant disposal": s.159.

GENERAL NOTE

On a relevant disposal under s.159, which is exempted under s.160(1)(d), *i.e.* a compulsory disposal under s.161, or under s.160(1)(e), either of which may be of part only of the land, the normal rule that the repayment covenant under s.155 binds successors in title is inapplicable and so far as the land involved is concerned, ceases to apply, as does either class of the covenants permitted under s.157.

Treatment of options

163.—(1) For the purposes of this Part the grant of an option enabling a person to call for a relevant disposal which is not an exempted disposal shall be treated as such a disposal made to him.

(2) For the purposes of section 157(2) (requirement of consent to disposal of dwelling-house in National Park, etc.) a consent to such a grant shall be treated as a consent to a disposal in pursuance of the option.

DEFINITIONS

"dwelling-house": ss.183, 184.
"exempted disposal": s.160.
"relevant disposal": s.159.

GENERAL NOTE

The grant of an option entitling a person to call for a relevant disposal under s.159 which is not an exempted disposal under s.160 is treated as a relevant disposal, so as to prevent such a grant before the five year period for repayment under s.155 expires, or such a grant in contravention of the s.157(2) covenant, but if consent to such a grant is obtained under s.157(2), it is an effective consent to the subsequent disposal.

Powers of Secretary of State

Secretary of State's general power to intervene

164.—(1) The Secretary of State may use his powers under this section where it appears to him that tenants generally, a tenant or tenants of a particular landlord, or tenants of a description of landlords, have or may have difficulty in exercising effectively and expeditiously the right to buy or the right to be granted a shared ownership lease.

(2) The powers may be exercised only after he has given the landlord or landlords notice in writing of his intention to do so and while the notice is in force.

(3) Such a notice shall be deemed to be given 72 hours after it has been sent.

(4) Where a notice under this section has been given to a landlord or landlords, no step taken by the landlord or any of the landlords while the notice is in force or before it was given has any effect in relation to the exercise by a secure tenant of the right to buy, the right to a mortgage or the right to be granted a shared ownership lease, except in so far as the notice otherwise provides.

(5) While a notice under this section is in force the Secretary of State may do all such things as appear to him necessary or expedient to enable secure tenants of the landlord or landlords to which the notice was given to exercise the right to buy, the right to a mortgage and the right to be granted a shared ownership lease; and he is not bound to take the steps which the landlord would have been bound to take under this Part.

(6) Where in consequence of the exercise by a secure tenant of the right to a mortgage a landlord becomes a mortgagee of a dwelling-house whilst a notice under this section is in force in relation to the landlord and to the dwelling-house, then, while the notice remains in force—

(*a*) the Secretary of State may, on behalf of the mortgagee, receive any sums due to it and exercise all powers and do all things which the mortgagee could have exercised or done, and

(*b*) the mortgagee shall not receive any such sum, exercise any such power or do any such thing, except with the consent of the Secretary of State, which may be given subject to such conditions as the Secretary of State thinks fit.

DEFINITIONS
    "dwelling-house": ss.183, 184.
    "right to buy": s.118.
    "right to mortgage": s.132.
    "secure tenant": ss.79, 185.
    "shared ownership lease": s.622.

GENERAL NOTE
    This section introduces "draconian" powers enabling the Secretary of State to step in and administer this Part, in relation to the tenants of any landlord bound to sell to its tenants: see, generally, *R.* v. *Secretary of State for the Environment, ex p. Norwich City Council* [1982] Q.B. 808, 2 H.L.R. 1, C.A. See also the powers contained in ss.165–170, below.

Subss. (1), (2), (3)
    The principal precondition of the exercise of these powers is that *it appears to* the Secretary of State that tenants generally, or a tenant or tenants of a particular landlord have *or may have* difficulty in exercising the right to buy effectively or expeditiously. There must be some basis for the Secretary of State's intervention: see the *Norwich* case, above, see also, *e.g. Secretary of State for Employment* v. *ASLEF (No.* 2) [1972] 2 Q.B. 455, 949, C.A., *Laker Airways* v. *Department of Trade* [1977] Q.B. 643, C.A. and, especially, *Secretary of State for Education and Science* v. *M. B. Tameside* [1977] A.C. 1014, H.L. ("If a judgment requires, before it can be made, the existence of some facts, then, although the evaluation of those facts is for the Secretary of State alone, the court must inquire whether those facts exist, and have been taken into account, whether the judgment has been made on a proper self direction as to those facts, whether the judgment has not been made on other facts which ought not to have been taken into account. If these requirements are not met, then the exercise of judgment, however bona fide it may be, becomes capable of challenge . . . " *per* Lord Wilberforce). See, also, generally, notes to s.64, above.

The financial consequences to the ratepayers of an authority, and the direct loss to a housing association (*cf.* subs. (6)), are such that the Secretary of State must comply with the requirements of natural justice, or at least of fair administration, before exercising these powers: see the *Norwich* case, above, see also, for example, *Secretary of State for Education and Science* v. *M. B. Tameside*, in the Court of Appeal, but same reference as above; see also *Fairmount Investments Ltd.* v. *Secretary of State for the Environment* [1976] 1 W.L.R. 1255, H.L.

Clearly, the notice requirement in subs. (2) is not itself notice designed to comply with such requirements, for 72 hours under subs. (3) is insufficient to permit representations, to have them taken into account, and fully considered. It is submitted, therefore, that a landlord must be given an opportunity to know and to comment on the Secretary of State's reasons or basis for action, *before* service of the "72-hour notice".

In the *Norwich* case (above), there were seven complaints against the City Council: (i) delay in issuing s.125 offer notices; (ii) delay caused by a requirement introduced by the authority that all would-be purchasers attend counselling interviews; (iii) over-high initial valuations; (iv) onerous and unreasonable covenants; (v) poor performance compared with other authorities; (vi) refusal to use the services of the District Valuer at the initial valuation stage (*cf.* s.128); (vii) where tenants applied to exchange properties, the council would insist on assignments instead of agreeing the grant of new tenancies, which would (at that date, see now s.92 above, introduced by Housing and Building Control Act 1984) cause the loss of security and, consequently, loss of right to buy.

It was held that the more extensive the powers of the Secretary of State, the more carefully will the courts scrutinise their exercise. Lord Denning M.R. held that these powers should not be used other than in accordance with the rules of natural justice, while Lord Justice Kerr held that they should be used fairly, and Lord Justice May fairly and reasonably. On any test, however, the Secretary of State had complied with the requirements.

Lord Denning M.R. also held that the Secretary of State should only intervene if the authority's default was unreasonable or inexcusable, but the remainder of the Court held that he can intervene whenever it appears to him that tenants have or may have difficulty in exercising the right to buy effectively or expeditiously, regardless of whether or not the authority's behaviour was reasonable, provided the Secretary of State's own decision was one to which a reasonable man might come, in accordance with normal administrative law principles: see s.64, above. Finally, it was held appropriate for the Secretary of State to consider the situation in Norwich in relation to other authorities, and he would have been criticised had he failed to do so.

The notice may be withdrawn at any time: s.166, below.

Subss. (4)–(5)

The first effect of a notice is to void any steps taken by the landlord, before the notice was served, or while it is in force, but only in relation to the exercise of the right to buy, or the right to a mortgage, and save in so far as the notice may otherwise provide. The powers cannot, accordingly, be used to affect any steps taken by, *e.g.* a local authority in respect of other housing powers. It does seem clear, however, that the Secretary of State can reconsider any of the vital steps considered above, as to the addition of purchasers (s.123) qualification (s.121), discount (s.129) or inclusion of time of parents (Sched. 4, para. 4), etc.

The notice also gives the Secretary of State power to do all that appears to him necessary or expedient to enable secure tenants to exercise the rights to buy, to a mortgage, and to a shared ownership lease, but he is not bound to take all of the steps which a landlord would have been bound to take under this Part.

Subs. (6)

So long as the notice remains in force (*cf.* s.166, below) the Secretary of State will receive any moneys due to the landlord as mortgagee, *i.e.* after the property has been sold. This only relates to mortgages arising after the notice has come into effect. The Secretary of State enjoys all the usual powers of a mortgagee. The landlord/mortgagee is prohibited from receiving any moneys due under the mortgage, and from exercising any other powers, or doing anything as mortgagee, save with the consent of the Secretary of State, which consent may be given subject to conditions. No equivalent prohibition applies to the Housing Corporation, for the Housing Corporation is not a landlord who has become a mortgagee.

Vesting orders for purposes of s.164

165.—(1) For the purpose of conveying a freehold or granting a lease in the exercise of his powers under section 164 the Secretary of State may execute a document, to be known as a vesting order, containing such provisions as he may determine; and for the purposes of stamp duty the vesting order shall be treated as a document executed by the landlord.

(2) A vesting order has the like effect, except so far as it otherwise provides, as a conveyance or grant duly executed in pursuance of this Part, and, in particular, binds both the landlord and its successors in title and the tenant and his successors in title (including any person deriving title under him or them) to the same extent as if the covenants contained in it and expressed to be made on their behalf had been entered into by them.

(3) If the landlord's title to the dwelling-house in respect of which a vesting order is made is not registered, the vesting order shall contain a certificate stating that the freehold conveyed or grant made by it is subject only to such incumbrances, rights and interests as are stated elsewhere in the vesting order or summarised in the certificate.

(4) The Chief Land Registrar shall, on a vesting order being presented to him, register the tenant as proprietor of the title concerned; and if the title has not previously been registered—

(a) he shall so register him with an absolute title, or as the case may require a good leasehold title, and

(b) he shall, for the purpose of the registration, accept any such certificate as is mentioned in subsection (3) as sufficient evidence of the facts stated in it.

(5) Where the landlord's title to a dwelling-house with respect to which the right to buy, or the right to be granted a shared ownership lease, is exercised is registered, the Chief Land Registrar shall—

(a) if so requested by the Secretary of State, supply him (on payment of the appropriate fee) with an office copy of any document required by the Secretary of State for the purpose of executing a vesting order with respect to the dwelling-house, and

(b) notwithstanding section 112 of the Land Registration Act 1925 (authority of proprietor required for inspection of register, etc.), allow any person authorised by the Secretary of State to inspect and make copies of and extracts from any register or document which is in the custody of the Chief Land Registrar and relates to the dwelling-house.

(6) If a person suffers loss in consequence of a registration under this section in circumstances in which he would have been entitled to be indemnified under section 83 of the Land Registration Act 1925 by the Chief Land Registrar had the registration of the tenant as proprietor of the title been effected otherwise than under this section, he is instead entitled to be indemnified by the Secretary of State and section 166(4) of this Act (recovery of Secretary of State's costs from landlord) applies accordingly.

DEFINITIONS
   "dwelling-house": ss.183, 184.
   "right to buy": s.118.
   "shared ownership lease": s.622.

GENERAL NOTE
   This section is ancillary to the last.

Subss. (1), (2)
   As the Secretary of State is not, of course, the landlord, he cannot per se convey or grant a legal interest in the property. These subsections provide for a vesting order, containing such provisions as the Secretary of State may determine, subject to stamp duty as if it were a conveyance or grant executed by the landlord, to have the same effect, save as it may provide, as if it were a conveyance or grant duly executed under this Part. It binds the landlord, the tenant, and their successors in title, and persons claiming title under them, just as if the terms had been contained in a document agreed by the landlord and the tenant.

Subss. (3)–(6)

Where the dwelling-house is not already registered land, the vesting order is to contain a certificate analogous to that which the landlord provides under s.154, and which is to be accepted as sufficient evidence of the facts stated therein. The Chief Land Registrar is to register the tenant as proprietor of the title concerned, with an absolute title thereof (see Land Registration Act 1925, ss.5, 9) unless, of course, there has been an earlier registration with a lesser title (see *ibid.* ss.6, 7, 10–12).

Where the land is already registered land, the Chief Land Registrar is placed under a duty to provide the Secretary of State with office copies of any document which he requires in order to execute the vesting order, *i.e.* an office copy of the register: *ibid.* s.112. He is also to permit anyone authorised by the Secretary of State to inspect and make copies of and extracts from any register or document which is in his custody and which relates to the dwelling-house, notwithstanding *ibid.* s.111 governing confidentiality of the register and documents in his custody. He may, however, charge for this privilege. Note that whereas under s.154, the landlord indemnifies the Chief Land Registrar against any claims he must meet in consequence of registration based upon the landlord's certificate, in the case of a registration following a vesting order, the Secretary of State indemnifies a person who could otherwise have claimed against the Chief Land Registrar under the Land Registration Act 1925, s.83, although the Secretary of State may recover such moneys from the landlord.

Other provisions supplementary to s.164

166.—(1) A notice under section 164 may be withdrawn by a further notice in writing, either completely or in relation to a particular landlord or a particular case or description of case.

(2) The further notice may give such directions as the Secretary of State may think fit for the completion of a transaction begun before the further notice was given; and such directions are binding on the landlord, and may require the taking of steps different from those which the landlord would have been required to take if the Secretary of State's powers under section 164 had not been used.

(3) Where in consequence of the exercise of his powers under section 164 the Secretary of State receives sums due to a landlord, he may retain them while a notice under that section is in force in relation to the landlord and is not bound to account to the landlord for interest accruing on them.

(4) Where the Secretary of State exercises his powers under section 164 with respect to secure tenants of a landlord, he may—

    (*a*) calculate, in such manner and on such assumptions as he may determine, the costs incurred by him in doing so, and

    (*b*) certify a sum as representing those costs;

and a sum so certified is a debt from the landlord to the Secretary of State payable on a date specified in the certificate, together with interest from that date at a rate so specified.

(5) Sums payable under subsection (4) may, without prejudice to any other method of recovery, be recovered from the landlord by the withholding of sums due from the Secretary of State, including sums payable to the landlord and received by the Secretary of State in consequence of his exercise of his powers under section 164.

(6) In this section the references to a landlord include references to a body which has become a mortgagee in consequence of the exercise by a secure tenant of the right to a mortgage, and the references to the powers of the Secretary of State with respect to the secure tenants of a landlord include references to the powers of the Secretary of State to act on behalf of such a mortgagee.

DEFINITIONS

    "right to mortgage": s.132.

    "secure tenant": ss.79, 185.

GENERAL NOTE
A notice under s.164 may be withdrawn, by a further notice in writing, wholly or in relation to a particular landlord, or in relation to a particular case or class of case, and may be subject to such directions as the Secretary of State may think fit for the completion of transactions commenced prior to the further notice, *i.e.* usually, but not necessarily, transactions commenced while the s.164 notice was in force. Such directions are binding on the landlord, and may include different steps from those which the landlord would have been required to take if the Secretary of State had at no time intervened, *i.e.* steps which the Secretary of State, released from the obligations imposed on a landlord by s.164(5), above, could take.

Subss. (4), (5)
These subsections contain the ancillary financial provisions, enabling the Secretary of State to pass on the costs of taking over an authority's or a housing association's duties, and dealing with the recovery of moneys due to central government from the landlord. Under s.164, the Secretary of State is entitled to retain moneys received, so long as the notice is in force. He is not obliged to account to the landlord for interest on such retained moneys. Under subs. (4) of this section, he may also calculate, in such manner as he may determine, how much the exercise has cost him, and certify such sums as representing those costs, in which case that amount together with interest at such rate as he may prescribe, represents a debt from landlord to Secretary of State, payable on demand. Interest runs only from the date of certification.

What the Secretary of State had in mind here was not his own administrative costs, but, *e.g.* the cost of outside solicitors or use of the Department of the Environment: 1980 Act, Standing Committee F, col. 1506. Finally, and without prejudice to any other method of recovery, the Secretary of State may simply deduct such monies owing from moneys received by him in the exercise of these powers, or by withholding any other sum due to the landlord: subs. (5).

Power to give directions as to covenants and conditions

167.—(1) Where it appears to the Secretary of State that, if covenants or conditions of any kind were included in conveyances or grants of dwelling-houses of any description executed in pursuance of this Part—

(*a*) the conveyances would not conform with Parts I and II of Schedule 6, or

(*b*) the grants would not conform with Parts I and III of that Schedule, he may direct landlords generally, landlords of a particular description or particular landlords not to include covenants or conditions of that kind in such conveyances or grants executed on or after a date specified in the direction.

(2) A direction under this section may be varied or withdrawn by a subsequent direction.

DEFINITIONS
"dwelling-house": ss.183, 184.

GENERAL NOTE
This section permits the Secretary of State to issue a direction, to landlords generally, landlords of a particular description, or to a particular landlord, which falls short of s.164 intervention. The provision permits the Secretary of State to specify covenants or conditions which are not to be included in a conveyance or grant. The power may be exercised when it appears that conveyances or grants would not conform with Sched. 6 were covenants or conditions of a particular kind to be included.

There is clearly validity in the proposition that "we have a clause which will put the Secretary of State in a position in which he will be interpreting legislation" (Standing Committee B, October 27, 1983, col. 335, Mr. Kaufman). The government response was that "the direction cannot be made unless the conveyance or grant is in breach of the 1980 Act" (*ibid.* col. 337, Sir George Young). This, however, ignores the breadth of the words "where it appears to the Secretary of State," which will of course be interpreted in line with the *Norwich* decision, (see notes to s.164, above). *i.e.* if a covenant or condition "could reasonably be considered to fall outside Sched. 6," an exercise of the power is unlikely to be challengeable, even though this is a lower test than "is in breach . . . ".

Against this, it might be said that if the covenant is *not* in breach of Sched. 6, there is no factual basis for the Secretary of State's opinion, alternatively that by construing the covenant as in such breach he has made an error of law, or left out of account the correct interpretation: see notes to s.64, above, and s.164, above. It must surely be the case that in the absence of express limitation, as, *e.g.*, under s.181, below, the county court is not to engage in issues reserved to the District Valuer under s.128, above, the courts will be extremely hesitant to allow the Secretary of State a power of interpreting statutes which overrides, or must even be given equal status with, their own. The notion flies in the face of the power and role of the judiciary.

This section and the next permit the Secretary of State to intervene in terms of conveyance or grant, without actually intervening in the sales programme itself. The next section permits such limited intervention to apply retrospectively.

Effect of direction under s.167 on existing covenants and conditions

168.—(1) If a direction under section 167 so provides, the provisions of this section shall apply in relation to a covenant or condition which—

    (*a*) was included in a conveyance or grant executed before the date specified in the direction, and

    (*b*) could not have been so included if the conveyance or grant had been executed on or after that date.

(2) The covenant or condition shall be discharged or (if the direction so provides) modified, as from the specified date, to such extent or in such manner as may be provided by the direction; and the discharge or modification is binding on all persons entitled or capable of becoming entitled to the benefit of the covenant or condition.

(3) The landlord by whom the conveyance or grant was executed shall, within such period as may be specified in the direction—

    (*a*) serve on the person registered as the proprietor of the dwelling-house and on any person registered as the proprietor of a charge affecting the dwelling-house, a written notice informing him of the discharge or modification, and

    (*b*) on behalf of the person registered as the proprietor of the dwelling-house, apply to the Chief Land Registrar (and pay the appropriate fee) for notice of the discharge or modification to be entered in the register.

(4) For the purposes of enabling the landlord to comply with the requirements of subsection (3) the Chief Land Registrar shall, notwithstanding section 112 of the Land Registration Act 1925 (authority of proprietor required for inspection of register, etc.), allow any person authorised by the landlord to inspect and make copies of and extracts from any register or document which is in the custody of the Chief Land Registrar and relates to the dwelling-house.

(5) Notwithstanding anything in section 64 of the Land Registration Act 1925 (certificates to be produced and noted on dealings), notice of the discharge or modification may be entered in the register without the production of any land certificate outstanding in respect of the dwelling-house, but without prejudice to the power of the Chief Land Registrar to compel production of the certificate for the purposes mentioned in that section.

DEFINITIONS

"dwelling-house": ss.183, 184.

GENERAL NOTE

The section permits extension of a s.167 direction to include covenants or conditions which would have been prohibited by the s.167 direction had the conveyance or grant been executed after the date specified in the direction, but which were included in prior conveyances or grants. The direction permits discharge or modification of such covenants or conditions, to an extent or in a manner which it is to specify. The direction is also to state a time during which the landlord affected is to serve on (*a*) the registered proprietor of the property, and (*b*) any person registered as the proprietor of a charge affecting the property, notice of the discharge or modification, and during which the landlord is to apply to the Chief Land Registrar for notice of discharge or modification to be entered into the register.

Land Registration Act 1925, s.112
   Under normal circumstances, inspection of, and copying from, the registers in the custody of the Chief Land Registrar, are accessible only to the registered proprietor of land or charge, persons authorised by such registered proprietor, court order and, otherwise, government departments and local authorities as authorised under the Land Registration Act 1925: *ibid*, s.112.

Land Registration Act 1925, s.64
   Under normal circumstances, on every entry in the register of a disposition by the proprietor of registered land or charge, and on every registered transmission, and in every case other than as specifically mentioned in s.64, Land Registration Act 1925, where notice of any estate right or claim, or a restriction, is entered or placed on the register, the land certificate or charge certificate must be produced to the Chief Land Registrar: *ibid*.

Power to obtain information, etc.

169.—(1) Where it appears to the Secretary of State necessary or expedient for the purpose of determining whether his powers under section 164 or 166 (general power to intervene) or section 167 or 168 (power to give directions as to covenants and conditions) are exercisable, or for or in connection with the exercise of those powers, he may by notice in writing to a landlord require it—

  (*a*) at such time and at such place as may be specified in the notice, to produce any document, or

  (*b*) within such period as may be so specified or such longer period as the Secretary of State may allow, to furnish a copy of any document or supply any information.

(2) Any officer of the landlord designated in the notice for that purpose or having custody or control of the document or in a position to give that information shall, without instructions from the landlord, take all reasonable steps to ensure that the notice is complied with.

(3) In this section references to a landlord include—

  (*a*) a landlord by whom a conveyance or grant was executed in pursuance of this Part, and

  (*b*) a body which has become a mortgagee in consequence of the exercise by a secure tenant of the right to a mortgage.

DEFINITIONS
   "right to mortgage": s.132.
   "secure tenant": ss.79, 185.

GENERAL NOTE
   Under 1980 Act powers of intervention, the Secretary of State "where it appears . . . necessary or expedient for the exercise of his powers . . . " under what is now s.164, above, could serve written notice on the landlord requiring the production of documentation, or the supply of information. An officer, designated as such in the notice, or who had custody or control of documentation, or was in a position to provide the information, was bound to take all reasonable steps to ensure that the notice was complied with, regardless of instructions from the landlord. The wording quoted at the beginning of this paragraph suggested that the powers described arose only *after* service of notice of intervention, *i.e.* as distinct from in order to find out whether or not to intervene.
   The present power, introduced in 1984, is broader: it clearly permits use of the power "for the purpose of determining whether his powers . . . are exercisable;" it also permits specification of a time and place at which documentation is to be produced; it also permits the Secretary of State to require the production of copies, not merely original documentation; finally, it extends the power as thus defined to mortgagees under the right to buy, which will include (*a*) the Housing Corporation on behalf of a housing association, or (*b*) a body which

has taken over a local authority's mortgage. It would not seem, however, that a "private mortgagee" would have "become a mortgagee in consequence of the exercise by a secure tenant of the right to a mortgage," for when a private mortgage is granted, the need to rely on the right to a mortgage is averted.

Power to give assistance in connection with legal proceedings

170.—(1) This section applies to—

(*a*) proceedings under this Part or to determine a question arising under or in connection with this Part, and

(*b*) proceedings to determine a question arising under or in connection with a conveyance or grant executed in pursuance of this Part,

other than proceedings to determine a question as to the value of a dwelling-house (or part of a dwelling-house).

(2) A party or prospective party to proceedings or prospective proceedings to which this section applies, who—

(*a*) has claimed to exercise or has exercised the right to buy or the right to be granted a shared ownership lease, or

(*b*) is a successor in title of a person who has exercised either of those rights,

may apply to the Secretary of State for assistance under this section.

(3) The Secretary of State may grant the application if he thinks fit to do so on the ground—

(*a*) that the case raises a question of principle, or

(*b*) that it is unreasonable having regard to the complexity of the case, or to any other matter, to expect the applicant to deal with it without such assistance,

or by reason of any other special consideration.

(4) Assistance by the Secretary of State under this section may include—

(*a*) giving advice,

(*b*) procuring or attempting to procure the settlement of the matter in dispute,

(*c*) arranging for the giving of advice or assistance by a solicitor or counsel,

(*d*) arranging for representation by a solicitor or counsel, including such assistance as is usually given by a solicitor or counsel in the steps preliminary or incidental to any proceedings, or in arriving at or giving effect to a compromise to avoid or bring to an end any proceedings, and

(*e*) any other form of assistance which the Secretary of State may consider appropriate;

but paragraph (*d*) does not affect the law and practice regulating the descriptions of persons who may appear in, conduct, defend and address the court in any proceedings.

(5) In so far as expenses are incurred by the Secretary of State in providing the applicant with assistance under this section, the recovery of those expenses (as taxed or assessed in such manner as may be prescribed by rules of court) shall constitute a first charge for the benefit of the Secretary of State—

(*a*) on any costs which (whether by virtue of a judgment or order of a court or an agreement or otherwise) are payable to the applicant by any other person in respect of the matter in connection with which the assistance was given, and

(*b*) so far as relates to any costs, on his rights under any compromise or settlement arrived at in connection with that matter to avoid or bring to an end any proceedings;

but subject to any charge under the Legal Aid Act 1974 and to any provision of that Act for payment of any sum into the legal aid fund.

(6) References in this section to a solicitor include the Treasury Solicitor.

    "dwelling-house": ss.183, 184.
    "right to buy": s.118.
    "shared ownership lease": s.622.

GENERAL NOTE

This section was described as a right for the Secretary of State to grant "free and open-ended legal aid" (Standing Committee B, November 1, 1983, Col. 365, Mr. Kaufman), to individuals engaged in proceedings—actual or prospective—to determine any question arising under or in relation to the exercise of the right to buy (other than a question as to the value of the dwelling-house in issue).

The grant of this new form of legal aid is entirely in the discretion of the Secretary of State, save that the power is only exercisable by him if (i) the case raises a question of principle, or (ii) it is unreasonable to expect the applicant for assistance to deal with the case without this special class of assistance, having regard to the complexity of the case, or having regard to "any other matter," or (iii) on account of any other special consideration.

"A number of matters could arise between a landlord and a tenant when the Secretary of State might intervene. For example, there might be a dispute over whether a dwelling was part of a sheltered scheme . . . There could be a dispute over whether a garage was land let together with the dwelling-house . . . There could be disputes about whether specific covenants were reasonable in the circumstances . . . There could be a dispute about the discount entitlement and about whether the dwelling was a house or a flat . . .

"In all such cases, the Secretary of State might take the view that the tenant had a strong case and he might consider that there was an important point of principle that could benefit from clarification by the courts. In each of those contexts, issues might be raised which a tenant could not reasonably be expected to tackle alone. We would not want to assist in every such case that came our way because that would be unrealistic. But those are the types of issues on which we might want to consider the case for assistance." (Standing Committee B, November 1, 1983, Col. 368, Sir George Young).

The "aid" available is described in subs. (4) and includes advice, negotiations towards settlement, arranging for advice, assistance or representation by solicitor or counsel, or any other form of assistance which the Secretary of State considers appropriate. The assistance may include representation by Treasury Solicitor, or may be by way of paying for private (legal) sector assistance.

Whereas under the Legal Aid Act 1974, legal aid is means-tested, there is no suggestion of means-testing aid under this section.

Finally, the Secretary of State's charge is subject to any Law Society charge under the 1974 Act, *i.e.* takes effect following a 1974 Act charge. It is presumably envisaged that this might arise where either a person has formerly been on legal aid, but subsequently secures Secretary of State assistance, or where the Secretary of State uses his powers to pay a legally-aided person's contribution.

Power to extend right to buy, etc.

Power to extend right to buy, etc.

171.—(1) The Secretary of State may by order provide that, where there are in a dwelling-house let on a secure tenancy one or more interests to which this section applies, this Part and Part IV (secure tenancies) have effect with such modifications as are specified in the order.

(2) This section applies to an interest held by—
    a local authority,
    a new town corporation,
    an urban development corporation,
    the Development Board for Rural Wales,
    the Housing Corporation, or
    a registered housing association,
which is immediately superior to the interest of the landlord or to another interest to which this section applies.

(3) An order under this section—

(*a*) may make different provision with respect to different cases or descriptions of case;

(*b*) may contain such consequential, supplementary or transitional provisions as appear to the Secretary of State to be necessary or expedient; and

(*c*) shall be made by statutory instrument which shall be subject to annulment in pursuance of a resolution of either House of Parliament.

DEFINITIONS
"dwelling-house": ss.183, 184.
"local authority": s.4.
"new town corporation": s.4.
"registered housing association": s.5.
"secure tenant": ss.79, 185.
"urban development corporation": s.4.

GENERAL NOTE
This section applies to property in respect of which there is a number of interests. The property must be let on a secure tenancy. In addition to the interest of the landlord, there must be an interest belonging to a local authority (as defined in s.4, above), a new town or urban development corporation, the Housing Corporation, a registered housing association, or the Development Board for Rural Wales.

In relation to such a property, the Secretary of State may modify this Part. The purpose would seem to be to permit the Part to be amended so as to enable tenants to purchase freeholds, where on the face of the Part at present only a leasehold would be available, in cases where the superior interests belong to public landlords.

Modifications of Leasehold Reform Act 1967 in relation to leases granted under this Part

Exclusion of leases where landlord is housing association and freeholder is a charity

172.—(1) Part I of the Leasehold Reform Act 1967 (enfranchisement and extension of long leaseholds) does not apply where, in the case of a tenancy or sub-tenancy to which this section applies, the landlord is a housing association and the freehold is owned by a body of persons or trust established for charitable purposes only.

(2) This section applies to a tenancy created by the grant of a lease in pursuance of this Part of a dwelling-house which is a house.

(3) Where Part I of the 1967 Act applies as if there had been a single tenancy granted for a term beginning at the same time as the term under a tenancy falling within subsection (2) and expiring at the same time as the term under a later tenancy, this section also applies to that later tenancy.

(4) This section applies to any sub-tenancy directly or indirectly derived out of a tenancy falling within subsection (2) or (3).

DEFINITIONS
"dwelling-house": ss.183, 184.
"house": s.183.
"housing association": s.5.

GENERAL NOTE
The Leasehold Reform Act 1967 enables long leaseholders of *houses*, not flats, to "enfranchise", *i.e.* buy out all superior interests, or "extend" their leases for an additional fifty years. A long lease for this purpose is, as under this and the last Part (*cf.* notes to s.115, above) one for more than 21 years (but *cf.* s.174, below, treating all leases under the right to buy as long leases for this purpose, even if they are not for more than 21 years). The long

lease has to be at a low rent (meaning less than two-thirds of the rateable value, but *cf.* ss.173 and 174, below).

Initially (1980), the right to buy simply did not apply if the landlord did not own the freehold. The only leases, therefore, were of flats, to which the 1967 Act is inapplicable. In 1984, however, the right to buy was extended to houses where the landlord did not own the freehold: see s.118, above. As rent under the lease could not be more than £10 per annum, and as most such leases would be in excess of 21 years, this meant that public tenants would acquire the right to enfranchise. This section represents a compromise on that principle, *i.e.* that such rights are not available when (a) the landlord is a housing association, and (b) the freehold is owned by a body or trust established for charitable purposes only.

Exclusion of shared ownership leases granted under this Part

173.—(1) Where a tenancy of a dwelling-house which is a house is created by the grant of a lease in pursuance of the right to be granted a shared ownership lease, then, so long as the rent payable under the lease exceeds £10 per annum, neither the tenant nor the tenant under a sub-tenancy directly or indirectly derived out of the tenancy shall be entitled the acquire the freehold or an extended lease of the dwelling-house under Part I of the Leasehold Reform Act 1967.

(2) Subsection (1) applies notwithstanding the provisions of section 174 (leases granted under this Part to be treated as long leases at a low rent).

DEFINITIONS
 "dwelling-house": ss.183, 184.
 "shared ownership lease": s.622.

GENERAL NOTE
 A shared ownership lease is prima facie within the Leasehold Reform Act 1967 (as to which, see notes to s.172, above). If the tenant buys only 50 per cent. of the equity, it is fairly unlikely that the rent would fall below two-thirds of the rateable value, but by the time the tenant owns 87.5 per cent., it could well do so. This section in effect says that the shared owner cannot enfranchise or extend unless and until the rent payable under the lease has fallen to no more than £10, *i.e.* the time when he will have acquired 100 per cent. of the equity (*cf.* Sched. 8, para. 4, below).

Leases granted under this Part to be treated as long leases at a low rent

174. For the purposes of Part I of the Leasehold Reform Act 1967 (enfranchisement and extension of long leaseholds)—

 (*a*) a tenancy created by the grant of a lease in pursuance of this Part of a dwelling-house which is a house shall be treated as being a long tenancy notwithstanding that it is granted for a term of 21 years or less, and

 (*b*) a tenancy created by the grant of such a lease in pursuance of the right to be granted a shared ownership lease shall be treated as being a tenancy at a low rent notwithstanding that rent is payable under the tenancy at a yearly rate equal to or more than two-thirds of the rateable value of the dwelling-house on the first day of the term.

DEFINITIONS
 "dwelling-house": ss.183, 184.
 "house": s.183.
 "long tenancy": s.187.
 "shared ownership lease": s.622.

GENERAL NOTE
 This penultimate provision dealing with the Leasehold Reform Act 1967 deals with two points arising thereunder. First of all, to enfranchise or extend, a lease must be a long lease, *i.e.* more than 21 years. Leases under the right to buy could be for less. Thus, a lease under the right to buy will be available if at the date of RTB1 under s.122, above, the landlord's

own leasehold interest in the house (for we are concerned here only with houses—see notes to s.172, above) is itself only 21 years: see Sched. 5, para. 4). But the lease to be granted will itself only be for five days less than the landlord's interest: see Sched. 6, para. 12.

By the time of the actual grant, therefore, the landlord's lease could be several months or even a year or two (consider deferral under s.142, above) less than 21 years, and the tenant's entitlement correspondingly less. By this section, for the purposes of the 1967 Act, the lease remains a long lease, *i.e.* the tenant will, once residential qualification under that Act (three years) has been established, be able to enfranchise or extend.

The second point arises in this way. The residential qualification under the 1967 Act requires three years' occupation, *as* a long leaseholder at a low rent: s.1. A shared ownership lease is not likely to be at a low rent until most or perhaps the whole of the equity has been purchased: see notes to s.173, above. The shared owner cannot enfranchise or extend until he has acquired 100 per cent.: *ibid.* But the shared owner's residential qualification will be running, even at a time when he has not acquired 100 per cent., or his rent has not yet fallen to a low rent, *i.e.* less than two-thirds of the rateable value.

Determination of price payable

175.—(1) Where, in the case of a tenancy or sub-tenancy to which this section applies, the tenant exercises his right to acquire the freehold under Part I of the Leasehold Reform Act 1967, the price payable for the dwelling-house shall be determined in accordance with section 9(1A) of that Act notwithstanding that the rateable value of the dwelling-house does not exceed £1,000 in Greater London or £500 elsewhere.

(2) This section applies to a tenancy created by the grant of a lease in pursuance of this Part of a dwelling-house which is a house.

(3) Where Part I of the 1967 Act applies as if there had been a single tenancy granted for a term beginning at the same time as the term under a tenancy falling within subsection (2) and expiring at the same time as the term under a later tenancy, this section also applies to that later tenancy.

(4) This section applies to any sub-tenancy directly or indirectly derived out of a tenancy falling within subsection (2) or (3).

(5) This section also applies to a tenancy granted in substitution for a tenancy or sub-tenancy falling within subsections (2) to (4) in pursuance of Part I of the 1967 Act.

DEFINITIONS
"dwelling-house": ss.183, 184.

GENERAL NOTE
Different provisions apply in the determination of price payable for enfranchisement under the Leasehold Reform Act 1967 (*cf.* notes to last three sections), depending on the rateable value of the property. In a normal case, lower rated housing is to be valued according to a set of presumptions in 1967, s.9(1) (which assumes in the tenant's favour the alternative right under the 1967 Act of 50-year extension of lease) and only higher rated housing is valued in accordance with s.9(1A), added by Housing Act 1974, s.118(4), and which does not presume the 50-year extension. By this section, s.9(1A) of the 1967 Act applies regardless of rateable value.

Supplementary provisions

Notices

176.—(1) The Secretary of State may by regulations prescribe the form of any notice under this Part and the particulars to be contained in the notice.

(2) Where the form of, and the particulars to be contained in, a notice under this Part are so prescribed, a tenant who proposes to claim, or has claimed, to exercise the right to buy may request the landlord to supply him with a form for use in giving such notice; and the landlord shall do so within seven days of the request.

(3) A notice under this Part may be served by sending it by post.

(4) Where the landlord is a housing association, a notice to be served by the tenant on the landlord under this Part may be served by leaving it at, or sending it to, the principal office of the association or the office of the association with which the tenant usually deals.

(5) Regulations under this section—

(*a*) may make different provision with respect to different cases or descriptions of case, including different provision for different areas, and

(*b*) shall be made by statutory instrument.

DEFINITIONS

"housing association": s.5.

"right to buy": s.118.

GENERAL NOTE

Forms have been prescribed for the purposes of ss.122 and 124, above: see Housing (Right to Buy) (Prescribed Forms) Regulations 1984 (S.I. 1984 No. 1175), retained in force by s.2, Housing (Consequential Provisions) Act 1985.

Note the provisions of s.177, below, governing the correction of errors, omissions, etc., in forms under regulations made under this section.

Subs. (2)

Yet another right: this time, the right to a form from the landlord! And within 7 days of request!

Errors and omissions in notices

177.—(1) A notice served by a tenant under this Part is not invalidated by an error in, or omission from, the particulars which are required by regulations under section 176 to be contained in the notice.

(2) Where as a result of such an error or omission—

(*a*) the landlord has mistakenly admitted or denied the right to buy or the right to be granted a shared ownership lease in a notice under section 124 or 146, or

(*b*) the landlord or the Housing Corporation has formed a mistaken opinion as to any matter required to be stated in a notice by any of the provisions mentioned in subsection (3) and has stated that opinion in the notice,

the parties shall, as soon as practicable after they become aware of the mistake, take all such steps (whether by way of amending, withdrawing or re-serving any notice or extending any period or otherwise) as may be requisite for the purpose of securing that all parties are, as nearly as may be, in the same position as they would have been if the mistake had not been made.

(3) The provisions referred to in subsection (2)(*b*) are—

section 125 (notice of purchase price, etc.),

section 135 (notice of mortgage entitlement),

section 147 (notice of initial contribution),

paragraph 1(3) of Schedule 8 (notice of additional contribution), and

paragraph 5 of Schedule 9 (notice of entitlement to further advance).

(4) Subsection (2) does not apply where the tenant has exercised the right to which the notice relates before the parties become aware of the mistake.

DEFINITIONS

"right to buy": s.118.

"shared ownership lease": s.622.

GENERAL NOTE

An error in, or omission from, particulars required in connection with the exercise of right to buy, right to shared ownership lease, or right to mortgage, is not to invalidate the relevant notice. Instead, the parties are to take such steps as may be needed in order to put them all in the same position as if the mistake had not been made, or in a position as nearly the same as may be. This may lead to withdrawal of admission of right to buy, or right to a shared ownership lease, or denial, or variation of price, mortgage entitlement, initial contribution, additional contribution or further advance. However, this section ceases to apply once the tenant has exercised the right in issue.

Costs

178.—(1) An agreement between—

(*a*) the landlord and a tenant claiming to exercise the right to buy, the right to be granted a shared ownership lease, or any such right as is mentioned in paragraphs 1(1), 2 or 8 of Schedule 8 (terms of shared ownership lease: right to acquire additional shares or call for conveyance of freehold), or

(*b*) the landlord or, as the case may be, the Housing Corporation and a tenant claiming to exercise the right to a mortgage, or such a right as is mentioned in paragraph 1 of Schedule 9 (right to further advances),

is void in so far as it purports to oblige the tenant to bear any part of the costs incurred by the landlord or Housing Corporation in connection with the tenant's exercise of that right.

(2) Where a tenant exercises the right to a mortgage, or such a right as is mentioned in paragraph 1 of Schedule 9 (right to further advances), the landlord or, as the case may be, the Housing Corporation may charge to him the costs incurred by it in connection with his exercise of that right, but only—

(*a*) on the execution of the deed by which the mortgage is effected, and

(*b*) to the extent that the costs do not exceed such amount as the Secretary of State may by order specify.

(3) An order under this section—

(*a*) may make different provision with respect to different cases or descriptions of case, including different provision for different areas, and

(*b*) shall be made by statutory instrument which shall be subject to annulment in pursuance of a resolution of either House of Parliament.

DEFINITIONS

"right to buy": s.118.
"right to mortgage": s.132.
"shared ownership lease": s.622.

GENERAL NOTE

This is a relatively straightforward provision, designed to prevent a landlord from passing on to the tenant any costs which it has incurred in relation to the tenant's exercise of the right to buy, but permitting the landlord—or the Housing Corporation—to charge the tenant for the costs they have incurred in connection with the exercise of the right to a mortgage, although *only* those "on the execution of the deed by which the mortgage is effected . . .", *i.e.* only legal costs. The Secretary of State has power to specify a maximum amount which may be charged for this. He has set an amount, by way of maximum, of £200: see Housing (Local Authority Contributions towards Mortgage Costs) Order 1984 S.I. 1984 No. 1174, retained in force by s.2, Housing (Consequential Provisions) Act 1985.

Provisions restricting right to buy etc. of no effect

179.—(1) A provision of a lease held by the landlord or a superior landlord, or of an agreement (whenever made), is void in so far as it purports to prohibit or restrict—

(a) the grant of a lease in pursuance of the right to buy or the right to be granted a shared ownership lease, or

(b) the subsequent disposal (whether by way of assignment, sub-lease or otherwise) of a lease so granted,

or to authorise a forfeiture, or impose on the landlord or superior landlord a penalty or disability, in the event of such a grant or disposal.

(2) Where a dwelling-house let on a secure tenancy is land held—

(a) for the purposes of section 164 of the Public Health Act 1875 (pleasure grounds), or

(b) in accordance with section 10 of the Open Spaces Act 1906 (duty of local authority to maintain open spaces and burial grounds),

then, for the purposes of this Part, the dwelling-house shall be deemed to be freed from any trust arising solely by virtue of its being land held in trust for enjoyment by the public in accordance with section 164 or, as the case may be, section 10.

DEFINITIONS
   "dwelling-house": ss.183, 184.
   "secure tenant": ss.79, 185.
   "shared ownership lease": s.622.

GENERAL NOTE
   This is a private sector intervention. Subs. (1) voids any provision in the mesne tenant/landlord's lease which would otherwise prevent or limit the grant of a sub-lease under the right to buy, or interfere with the terms of such a sub-lease by limiting the sub-tenant's further rights of disposal (by assignment or subleasing) or penalise the mesne tenant/landlord for granting a sub-lease under the right to buy or for a subsequent disposal of such a sub-lease.

Subs. (2)
   The purpose of this sub-section is to enable public trust land to be sold under the right to buy; see also s.123 of the Local Government Act 1972, as amended by Sched. 23 of the Local Government, Planning and Land Act 1980.

Statutory declarations

180. A landlord, the Housing Corporation or the Secretary of State may, if the landlord, Corporation or Secretary of State thinks fit, accept a statutory declaration made for the purposes of this Part as sufficient evidence of the matters declared in it.

GENERAL NOTE
   A statutory declaration is a declaration made by virtue of the Statutory Declarations Act 1835: see Interpretation Act 1978, s.5, Sched. 1. It is a declaration made before a magistrate, or commissioner for oaths, in the prescribed form, and a false statutory declaration constitutes an act of perjury: Perjury Act 1911, s.5.

Jurisdiction of county court

181.—(1) A county court has jurisdiction—

(a) to entertain any proceedings brought under this Part, and

(b) to determine any question arising under this Part or under a shared ownership lease granted in pursuance of this Part;

but subject to sections 128 and 158 and paragraph 11 of Schedule 8 (which provide for matters of valuation to be determined by the district valuer).

(2) The jurisdiction conferred by this section includes jurisdiction to entertain proceedings on any such question as is mentioned in subsection (1)(*b*) notwithstanding that no other relief is sought than a declaration.

(3) If a person takes proceedings in the High Court which, by virtue of this section, he could have taken in the county court, he is not entitled to recover any costs.

(4) The Lord Chancellor may make such rules and give such directions as he thinks fit for the purpose of giving effect to this section; and such rules or directions may provide—

(*a*) for the exercise by a registrar of a county court of any jurisdiction exercisable under this section, and

(*b*) for the conduct of proceedings in private.

(5) The power to make rules under this section is exercisable by statutory instrument which shall be subject to annulment in pursuance of a resolution of either House of Parliament.

DEFINITIONS
"shared ownership lease": s.622.

GENERAL NOTE
See notes to s.110, above, but note the reservation of valuation issues to the District Valuer.

Power to repeal or amend local Acts

182.—(1) The Secretary of State may by order repeal or amend a provision of a local Act passed before 8th August 1980 where it appears to him that the provision is inconsistent with a provision of this Part relating to the right to buy or the right to a mortgage.

(2) Before making an order under this section the Secretary of State shall consult any local housing authority appearing to him to be concerned.

(3) An order made under this section may contain such transitional, incidental or supplementary provisions as the Secretary of State considers appropriate.

(4) An order under this section—

(*a*) may make different provision with respect to different cases or descriptions of case, including different provision for different areas, and

(*b*) shall be made by statutory instrument which shall be subject to annulment in pursuance of a resolution of either House of Parliament.

DEFINITIONS
"local housing authority": ss.1, 2.
"right to buy": s.118.
"right to mortgage": s.132.

GENERAL NOTE
As to consultation, see notes to s.420(4), below.

Meaning of "house", "flat" and "dwelling-house"

183.—(1) The following provisions apply to the interpretation of "house", "flat" and "dwelling-house" when used in this Part.

(2) A dwelling-house is a house if, and only if, it (or so much of it as does not consist of land included by virtue of section 184) is a structure reasonably so called; so that—

(*a*) where a building is divided horizontally, the flats or other units into which it is divided are not houses;

(*b*) where a building is divided vertically, the units into which it is divided may be houses;

(*c*) where a building is not structurally detached, it is not a house if a material part of it lies above or below the remainder of the structure.

(3) A dwelling-house which is not a house is a flat.

GENERAL NOTE

The section distinguishes what constitutes a house, and what a flat, for the purposes of exercising the right to buy. A tenant buying a house will usually be entitled to acquire a freehold interest, while a tenant buying a flat will acquire only a leasehold interest: see notes to s.118, above.

A dispute on the question of whether a dwelling-house is a house or a flat could be referred to a county court, notwithstanding that no relief other than a declaration is sought: s.181, see also County Courts Act 1984, s.22.

Subss. (2)(3)

Any dwelling-house which is not a house is a flat. The key definition, therefore, is of house. A dwelling-house is a house if and only if it is a structure reasonably so-called. The phrase "reasonably so-called" is, like much other language in this section, derived from the Leasehold Reform Act 1967, s.2. What is a house reasonably so-called is a question of fact and law, although a house of which part is used as a shop may be a house reasonably so-called: *Lake* v. *Bennett* [1970] 1 Q.B. 663, C.A. *Cf. Tandon* v. *Trustees of Spurgeon's Homes* [1982] A.C. 755, 4 H.L.R. 1, H.L., in which a part of a parade of shops, consisting of a shop, yard and "modest" living accommodation above of which 75 per cent. of the unit was used for the purposes of the shop, was held to constitute a house for the purposes of that Act.

See also, generally, *Levermore* v. *Jobey* [1956] 1 W.L.R. 697, *Peck* v. *Anicar Properties* [1971] 1 All E.R. 517, *Wolf* v. *Critchley* [1971] 1 W.L.R. 99, C.A. The provisions of subs. (2)(*b*) put beyond doubt that each of a row of terraced houses can qualify as a house in its own right, even although the houses are not structurally detached from each other.

This will not be so, however, if any material part of the building lies above or below the remainder of the structure (subs. (2)(*c*)). This last phrase, too, is derived from the 1967 Act, s.2. What is material is a matter of fact for a court: *Parsons* v. *Trustees of Smith's Charity* [1974] 1 W.L.R. 435 (in which it was also held that the words "structurally detached" meant detached from any other structure). In *Gaidowski* v. *Gonville and Caius College, Cambridge* [1975] 1 W.L.R. 1066, C.A., it was held that the mere fact that a person used a storeroom in an adjoining house did not mean that part of the house in which he lived lay above or below a part of the structure not comprised in the house, *i.e.* the court was prepared to discount use of the storeroom altogether.

Land let with or used for purposes of dwelling-house

184.—(1) For the purpose of this Part land let together with a dwelling-house shall be treated as part of the dwelling-house, unless the land is agricultural land (within the meaning set out in section 26(3)(*a*) of the General Rate Act 1967) exceeding two acres.

(2) There shall be treated as included in a dwelling-house any land which is not within subsection (1) but is or has been used for the purpose of the dwelling-house if—

(*a*) the tenant, by a written notice served on the landlord at any time before he exercises the right to buy or the right to be granted a shared ownership lease, requires the land to be included in the dwelling-house, and

(*b*) it is reasonable in all the circumstances for the land to be so included.

(3) A notice under subsection (2) may be withdrawn by a written notice served on the landlord at any time before the tenant exercises the right to buy or the right to be granted a shared ownership lease.

(4) Where a notice under subsection (2) is served or withdrawn after the service of the notice under section 125 (landlord's notice of purchase price, etc.), the parties shall, as soon as practicable after the service or

withdrawal, take all such steps (whether by way of amending, withdrawing or re-serving any notice or extending any period or otherwise) as may be requisite for the purpose of securing that all parties are, as nearly as may be, in the same position as they would have been in if the notice under subsection (2) had been served or withdrawn before the service of the notice under section 125.

DEFINITIONS
  "dwelling-house": ss.183, 184.
  "right to buy": s.118.
  "shared ownership lease": s.622.

GENERAL NOTE
  There are two potential additions to the dwelling-house—(*a*) land used for the purposes of the dwelling-house which the landlord and the tenant agree to include; and (*b*) land let together with the dwelling-house unless it is agricultural land exceeding two acres. As to the latter, see notes to s.79, above.
  As to land used for the purposes of the dwelling-house, this is to be included if it is or has been so used, and if the tenant requests its inclusion, and it is reasonable in all the circumstances for the land to be so included. A request may be made—or withdrawn—at any time before exercise of the right to buy, *i.e.* completion, and if the request is made or withdrawn after the s.125 offer notice has been served, the parties are to take such steps as are necessary to put themselves in the same position as if request or withdrawal had taken place before service of s.125.
  A dispute on reasonableness of request for inclusion can be resolved by reference to the county court: see s.181.

Meaning of "secure tenancy" and "secure tenant"

185.—(1) References in this Part to a secure tenancy or a secure tenant in relation to a time before 26th August 1984 are to a tenancy which would have been a secure tenancy if Chapter II of Part I of the Housing Act 1980 and Part I of the Housing and Building Control Act 1984 had then been in force or to a person who would then have been a secure tenant.
  (2) For the purpose of determining whether a person would have been a secure tenant and his tenancy a secure tenancy—
  (*a*) a predecessor of a local authority shall be deemed to have been such an authority, and
  (*b*) a housing association shall be deemed to have been registered if it is or was so registered at any later time.

GENERAL NOTE
  This is a most important provision. Without it, no tenant could add time spent in public and quasi-public sector accommodation prior to the commencement of the 1980 and 1984 Acts. This section extends the meaning of secure tenant further for the purposes of this Part, to include a period when, if the relevant Act had been in force, a person would have qualified as a secure tenant, and a tenancy as a secure tenancy.

Members of a person's family

186.—(1) A person is a member of another's family within the meaning of this Part if—
  (*a*) he is the spouse of that person, or he and that person live together as husband and wife, or
  (*b*) he is that person's parent, grandparent, child, grandchild, brother, sister, uncle, aunt, nephew or niece.
  (2) For the purposes of subsection (1)(*b*)—
  (*a*) a relationship by marriage shall be treated as a relationship by blood,

(b) a relationship of the half-blood shall be treated as a relationship of the whole blood,

(c) the stepchild of a person shall be treated as his child, and

(d) an illegitimate child shall be treated as the legitimate child of his mother and reputed father.

GENERAL NOTE
See notes to s.113, above.

Minor definitions

187. In this Part—
"improvement" means any alteration in, or addition to, a dwelling-house and includes—
    (a) any addition to, or alteration in, landlord's fixtures and fittings and any addition or alteration connected with the provision of services to a dwelling-house,
    (b) the erection of a wireless or television aerial, and
    (c) the carrying out of external decoration;
"long tenancy" means—
    (a) a long tenancy within the meaning of Part IV,
    (b) a tenancy falling within paragraph 1 of Schedule 1 to the Tenants' Rights, Etc. (Scotland) Act 1980, or
    (c) a tenancy falling within paragraph 1 of Schedule 2 to the Housing (Northern Ireland) Order 1983;
    and "long lease" shall be construed accordingly;
"total share", in relation to the interest of a tenant under a shared ownership lease, means his initial share plus any additional share or shares in the dwelling-house acquired by him.

DEFINITIONS
"dwelling-house": ss.183, 184.
"initial share": s.145.
"shared ownership lease": s.622.

GENERAL NOTE
"improvement": see also notes to s.97, above, and s.471, below.
"long tenancy": see also notes to s.115, above.
"total share": see also notes to s.145, above; see further, Sched. 8, para. 1, below.

Index of defined expressions: Part V

188. The following Table shows provisions defining or otherwise explaining expressions used in this Part (other than provisions defining or explaining an expression used in the same section or paragraph):—

additional share and additional contribution (in relation to a tenant under a shared ownership lease)	paragraphs 1 and 3 of Schedule 8
bank	section 622
building society	section 622
cemetery	section 622
charity	section 622
compulsory disposal	section 161
co-operative housing association	section 5(2)
dwelling-house	sections 183 and 184
effective discount (in relation to shares under a shared ownership lease)	section 148 and paragraph 3 of Schedule 8
exempted disposal	section 160
family (member of)	section 186
flat	section 183

friendly society	section 622
full mortgage	section 133(5)
house	section 183
housing association	section 5(1)
housing trust	section 6
improvement	section 187
incumbrances	paragraph 7 of Schedule 6
initial share and initial contribution (in relation to a shared ownership lease)	section 147 and 148
insurance company	section 622
lease	section 621
local authority	section 4(*e*)
local housing authority	section 1, 2(2)
long tenancy (and long lease)	section 187
new town corporation	section 4(*b*)
prescribed percentage (in relation to shares in a shared ownership lease)	section 145
public sector tenancy (and public sector tenant)	paragraphs 6 to 10 of Schedule 4
purchase price	section 126
registered (in relation a housing association)	section 5(4)
regular armed forces of the Crown	section 622
relevant disposal	section 159 and see section 452(3)
relevant time	section 122(2)
right to be granted a shared ownership lease	section 143
right to buy	section 118(1)
right to further advances	paragraph 1 of Schedule 9
right to a mortgage	section 132
secure tenancy and secure tenant	sections 79 and 185
tenant's incumbrance	paragraph 7 of Schedule 6
total share (of a tenant under a shared ownership lease)	section 187
trustee savings bank	section 622
urban development corporation	section 4(*d*)

PART VI

REPAIR NOTICES

Repair Notices

Repair notice in respect of unfit house

189.—(1) Where the local housing authority are satisfied that a house is unfit for human habitation, they shall serve a repair notice on the person having control of the house, unless they are satisfied that the house is not capable of being rendered so fit at reasonable expense.

(2) A repair notice under this section shall—

(*a*) require the person on whom it is served to execute the works specified in the notice within such reasonable time, not being less than 21 days, as is specified in the notice, and

(*b*) state that in the opinion of the authority the works specified in the notice will render the house fit for human habitation.

(3) The authority, in addition to serving the notice on the person having control of the house, may serve a copy of the notice on any other person having an interest in the house, whether as freeholder, mortgagee, lessee or otherwise.

(4) The notice becomes operative, if no appeal is brought, on the expiration of 21 days from the date of the service of the notice and is final and conclusive as to matters which could have been raised on an appeal.

DEFINITIONS
  "house": s.207.
  "local housing authority": ss.1, 2.
  "person having control": s.207.
  "reasonable expense": s.206.
  "unfit for human habitation": s.604.

GENERAL NOTE
  This is a most important section. Historically, it dates back to the Artizans' and Labourers' Dwellings Act 1868, ss.7–9 of which contain provisions for notices, and appeals, which bear a continuing similarity to the provisions of this Act.
  In outline, the powers of the authority to intervene in relation to individual unfit houses operate in this way: there is a presumption in favour of serving a repairs notice under this section; that presumption is shifted only if the authority are satisfied that the house is not repairable at a reasonable expense; in such a case, the authority then turn to the provisions now contained in Part IX, below, and, in particular, to s.264 which requires service of a "time-and-place" notice, which will lead either to voluntarily undertaken works to render the property fit, or to the cessation of its use for human habitation.
  There are two important points which must be made, even in relation to such an outline, which derive from case law. First of all, it was held in *R.* v. *Kerrier District Council, ex parte Guppys (Bridport) Ltd. (No. 1)* (1977) 32 P. & C.R. 411, C.A., that the provisions of this section and s.264, below, taken together are mandatory, *i.e.* one or the other *must* be applied, even if, *e.g.*, alternative action under Part III, Public Health Act 1936 (statutory nuisance), is proposed or taken. However, if action is being taken under the clearance area provisions (ss.289 *et seq.*) of Part IX, below, there is no need to take action under this Part as well: *Holmes* v. *Ministry of Housing and Local Government* (1960) 12 P. & C.R. 72.
  Secondly, if the person to be served, *i.e.* person having control, is the local housing authority themselves, the provisions of this section are inapplicable, even if there is someone else with a relevant interest under subs. (3), although if the authority have the relevant interest and someone else is the person having control, the provisions remain applicable: see *R.* v. *Cardiff City Council, ex parte Cross* (1981) 1 H.L.R. 54, Q.B.D., upheld on appeal (1982) 6 H.L.R. 6, C.A.
  Attention may be drawn to some related provisions: where the property is not unfit but is in disrepair, action may be available under s.190, below; and, where an area of housing is unfit, action may be taken under Part IX, below. In addition, note that complaint of unfitness may be made to a magistrate, who may in turn complain to the authority, under s.606, below; and, the authority are bound to inspect their district from time to time, with the provisions of this Part in mind, under s.605, below.
  That much said by way of opening, a great deal remains to be said on closer examination of this section. Subs. (1) contains no less than four central issues: (a) house, (b) unfit for human habitation, (c) person having control, and (d) reasonable expense. In view of the length of consideration required in relation to the last three of these, reference is made to the notes to s.604 for the meaning of unfitness, to s.207 for the person having control, and to s.206 for reasonable expense.

House
  "House" is defined in s.207 as including "any yard, garden, outhouses and appurtenances belonging to the house or usually enjoyed with it." This is the "usual" and "extended" definition, considered in the notes to s.56, above, and as equally uninformative as to application of the "basic" word, *i.e.* what is the "house" which may be thus extended?
  Relatively *few* of the cases cited in the discussion on this aspect of the question in the notes to s.56, or at all, have concerned application under what is now this Part: *Critchell* v. *Lambeth Borough Council* [1957] 2 Q.B. 535, C.A., did so—a house means what is commonly called a house, *i.e.* a separate structure. The cases on "mixed user" cited in the notes to s.56 above would appear applicable under this Part: see *Ashbridge Investments Ltd.*

v. *Ministry of Housing and Local Government* [1965] 1 W.L.R. 1320, C.A. (greengrocer's shop with a rear living room and scullery, three first floor rooms and an outside lavatory); *Re Butler, Camberwell (Wingfield Mews) No. 2 Clearance Order 1936* [1939] 1 K.B. 570, C.A. (structure consisting of a garage or workshop with a dwelling above; see also *Re Hammersmith (Bergham Mews) Clearance Order*, 1936 [1937] 3 All E.R. 539).

Where a building is used partly for residential purposes, and partly for other purposes, the building has to be looked at as a whole to ascertain whether, as a question of degree, it can properly be described as a house: *Annicola Investments Ltd.* v. *Minister of Housing and Local Government* [1968] 1 Q.B. 631, C.A. It need not be shown that all of the rooms in a building are used for residential purposes: *Premier Garage Co.* v. *Ilkeston Corporation* (1933) 97 J.P. 786.

Although original construction of a building is an important consideration (*In Re Butler, Camberwell (Wingfield Mews) No. 2 Clearance Order 1936* [1939] 1 K.B. 570, C.A.) regard may be had to the use of a building at the time the question falls to be determined (*ibid.* see also *Grosvenor* v. *Hampstead Junction Railway* [1857] L.J. Ch. 731), so that something not built as a house but used as such may qualify. An unfinished house may qualify as a house: *Alexander* v. *Crystal Palace Railway* (1862) 30 Beav. 556. A building constructed as a house but used for other purposes has been held to remain a house: *Howard* v. *Ministry of Housing and Local Government* (1967) 65 L.G.R. 257.

Part of the reason why there is so little direct case law under this Part is because the most obvious forum for argument—flats and single room lettings—is covered by the legislation itself: under s.205, below, "the local housing authority may take the like proceedings under this Part in relation to—

"(a) any part of a building which is used, or is suitable for use, as a dwelling . . . as they are empowered to take in relation to a house." ((b) adds: "hut, tent, caravan or other temporary or movable structure which is used for human habitation and has been in the same enclosure for a period of two years next before action is taken.")

The other *main* arena for argument is whether or not the term "house" is apt to include a block of flats. In *Pollway Nominees Ltd.* v. *London Borough of Croydon* (1984) 16 H.L.R. 41, Ch.D., Harman J described this as "the wider question," with "very far-reaching effects," calling for a "radical review," which the court did not need to engage in in the light of its finding on the question it took first, who was the "person having control"—see notes to s.207, below; the Court of Appeal was similarly not called on to consider this aspect when *Pollway* was upheld—see (1985) 17 H.L.R. 503, C.A.

The proper approach to this important question in practice must start with the statements of principle set out in the notes to s.56, above, *i.e.* that the word "house" must be construed as a mixed question of fact and law in the context of the Part or provisions of the Act, and that definitions under other legislation are not of assistance: see *per* Jessel M.R., in *Duke of Bedford* v. *Dawson* (1875) L.R. 20 Eq. 353 at p.357, cited by Browne L.J. in *Sovmots Investments Ltd.* v. *Secretary of State for the Environment* at the Court of Appeal, [1976] 3 All E.R. 720 at p.728.

See further *Quillotex Co. Ltd.* v. *Minister of Housing and Local Government* [1966] 1 Q.B. 704, adopting *Attorney-General* v. *Mutual Tontine Westminster Chambers Association Ltd.* (1876) 1 Ex.D. 469, C.A.; *Annicola Investments Ltd.* v. *Minister of Housing and Local Government* [1968] 1 Q.B. 631; *Re Butler, Camberwell (Wingfield Mews) No. 2 Clearance Order 1936* [1939] 1 K.B. 570, C.A.; *Ashbridge Investments Ltd.* v. *Minister of Housing and Local Government* [1965] 1 W.L.R. 1320, C.A.; *Re South Shields (D'Arcy Street) Compulsory Purchase Order 1937* [1939] 1 All E.R. 419.

See also *R.* v. *London Borough of Camden, ex parte Rowton (Camden Town) Ltd.* (1983) 17 H.L.R. 28, Q.B.D.: "In my judgment one must start with the Acts; one must have regard to their subject-matter and the object which Parliament would appear to have desired to achieve. If it can be shown that, prior to the passing of these Acts, the courts had interpreted the word 'house' when used in this field as bearing a meaning other than that ordinarily understood by the citizen, then Parliament may be presumed to have been aware of this interpretation and, unless the contrary appears, to have intended to perpetuate it."

It is also clear that the fact that there may be provisions in another part of the Act which treat issues differently will not be conclusive. " . . . It is dangerous to interpret one Part by reference to the provisions of another Part" (*per* Woolf J. in *R.* v. *Cardiff City Council, ex parte Cross* (1981) 1 H.L.R. 54, Q.B.D., upheld on appeal (1982) 6 H.L.R. 1, C.A.). This issue of "comparative" construction is considered in greater detail in *Okereke* v. *London Borough of Brent* [1967] 1 Q.B. 42, C.A., as to the effect of s.374, below, on the interpretation of "house" in s.345.

It has been said that "house" has no very precise meaning: the word can cover many types of building (*Quillotex* v. *Minister of Housing and Local Government* [1966] 1 Q.B. 704,

C.A.). In *Howard* v. *Ministry of Housing and Local Government* (1967) 65 L.G.R. 257, it was said that the word "house" in the 1957 legislation had the same meaning as "dwelling-house" in the previous (1936) legislation. "It is apparent that a 'house' . . . means a building which is constructed or adapted for use as or for the purposes of a dwelling": *Ashbridge Investments Ltd.* v. *Ministry of Housing and Local Government* [1965] 1 W.L.R. 1320, C.A., per Lord Denning M.R. at p.1324.

A hostel or a building used for multiple occupation or as a lodging-house may qualify as a house for the purposes of Pt. XI, below: *London County Council* v. *Rowton Houses Ltd.* (1897) 62 J.P. 68; *Re Ross and Leicester Corporation* (1932) 96 J.P. 459; *R.* v. *London Borough of Southwark, ex parte Lewis Levy Ltd.* (1983) 8 H.L.R. 1, Q.B.D.; *R.* v. *London Borough of Camden, ex parte Rowton (Camden Town) Ltd.* (1983) 10 H.L.R. 28, Q.B.D.

Similarly, a building subdivided into flats has been held a house under the clearance area provisions (ss.289 *et seq.*) of Pt. IX, below: *Annicola Investments Ltd.* v. *Minister of Housing and Local Government* [1968] 1 Q.B. 631 (large purpose-built block of tenement flats and shops); *Quillotex Co. Ltd.* v. *Minister of Housing and Local Government* [1966] 1 Q.B. 704 (series of eight buildings each containing tenement flats). Under this Part, in *Benabo* v. *Wood Green Borough Council* [1946] 1 K.B. 38, a house let off in flats was held still a house, and in *Critchell* v. *London Borough of Lambeth* [1957] 2 Q.B. 535, C.A., the fact that a house had a separate, self-contained basement flat did not prevent it being a house. In *Okereke* v. *London Borough of Brent* [1967] 1 Q.B., C.A., under Part XI, below, conversion did not prevent the house remaining such.

In *Lake* v. *Bennett* [1970] 1 Q.B. 663, C.A., under the Leasehold Reform Act 1967, Lord Denning M.R. doubted that a tower block could reasonably be called a house, but Salmon L.J. emphasised that the decision did not necessarily affect the Housing Acts, and the wording of the 1967 Act refers to a house "reasonably so called." In *Weatheritt* v. *Cantlay* [1901] 2 K.B. 285, it was suggested that a tenement block could not be a house for purposes analogous to those in Part XI, below, but this was limited almost immediately afterwards in *Kyffin* v. *Simmons* [1903] J.P. 227, and more recently in *Okereke* v. *Brent London Borough* *Council* [1967] 1 Q.B. 42, C.A. See, further notes to s.345, below.

The issue appears, therefore, to be open. Little can be added, other than by further reference to the notes to s.56, above, and to s.345, below. In the final analysis, it may be that one has to accept that Parts dealing with different procedures, and accordingly utilising language somewhat differently (*cf. Holmes* v. *Minister of Housing and Local Government* (1960) 12 P. & C.R. 72), are all theoretically susceptible of application to a range of types of structure, but with the authority susceptible to intervention if their choice of application is such that no reasonable authority could so have acted, on "usual" principles of administrative law, *cf.* notes to s.64, above.

Satisfied

The authority act on the information which has come into their possession, whether by virtue of a report under s.606(1), or a complaint under s.606(2), below, or as a result of the periodic inspection the authority are obliged to carry out under s.605, below. Prima facie satisfaction is sufficient to justify service of a repairs notice: *Hall* v. *Manchester Corporation* (1915) 84 L.J. Ch. 732, H.L.

They do not need to set a high standard of satisfaction, or give forewarning of their intentions and an opportunity to be heard: see *Fletcher* v. *Ilkeston Corporation* (1931) 96 J.P. 7, C.A.; see also *Cohen* v. *West Ham Corporation* [1933] Ch. 814, C.A., *Critchell* v. *Lambeth London Borough Council* [1957] 2 Q.B. 535, C.A., *Hillbank Properties Ltd.* v. *Hackney London Borough Council* [1978] Q.B. 998, 3 H.L.R. 73, C.A. They do not need to make a detailed prior study of estimates: *Bacon* v. *Grimsby Corporation* [1950] 1 K.B. 272, 3 H.L.R. 1, C.A. The fact that there is an appeal procedure under s.191, below, may be taken into account.

Notice

The Secretary of State has power to prescribe forms for use under any provision of this Act which requires or authorises notice, advertisement, statement or other document, under s.614, below. The current forms are those to be found in the Housing (Prescribed Forms) Regulations 1972 (S.I. 1972 No. 228), as amended (S.I. 1974 No. 1511, 1975 No. 500, 1981 No. 1347), retained in force by s.2, Housing (Consequential Provisions) Act 1985, but these are expected to be replaced in the near future to reflect this consolidation.

Under subs. (2), not less than 21 days from service must be allowed, and specified. As to service, see notes to s.617, below. But the time allowed must *also* be "reasonable," which may therefore be longer, although what *is* reasonable is a question of fact, primarily for the authority: *Ryall* v. *Cubitt Heath* [1922] 1 K.B. 275. The notice must specify the works to be done; the actual works should be specified, not merely their *effect*: *cf. Canterbury City Council* v. *Bern* [1981] J.P.L. 749, D.C. The specification must be reasonably precise, sufficient to enable the person served to obtain an estimate from a builder: *Cohen* v. *West Ham Corporation* [1933] Ch. 814, C.A.

However, phrases such as "thoroughly overhaul the roof," "properly examine," and "as necessary," may not be too vague in context: *Church of Our Lady of Hal* v. *Camden London Borough Council* (1980) 255 E.G. 991, C.A. A notice which covers works under a number of statutory provisions, including a local Act, need not allocate each job to each provision: *Benabo* v. *Wood Green Borough Council* [1946] K.B. 38, *Leslie Maurice* v. *Willesden Corporation* [1953] 2 Q.B. 1, C.A.

The notice must specify that in the opinion of the authority, once the works have been completed, the property will be fit for human habitation: subs. (2)(*b*).

The authority have a discretion to serve a copy of the notice on anyone else with an interest in the property, including a tenant, but not a statutory tenant (*cf.* notes to s.622, below), who has no legal "interest" as such: *Keeves* v. *Dean* [1924] 1 K.B. 685, C.A. A copy of the notice *must*, however, be served on an owner (as defined in s.207, below), who has served notice on the authority registering his interest, under s.202, below.

Subs. (4)

Appeal lies to the county court, under s.191, below. The possibility of appeal would suggest that it is the more appropriate course than application for judicial review: see *R.* v. *Hackney London Borough Council, ex parte Teepee Estates (1956) Ltd.* (1967) 19 P. & C.R. 87, D.C. See also *Minford Properties Ltd.* v. *London Borough of Hammersmith* (1978) 247 E.G. 561, D.C.; but *cf. R.* v. *London Borough of Southwark, ex parte Lewis Levy Ltd.* [1983] 8 H.L.R. 1, Q.B.D., in which the court considered that if an issue is one which goes to *vires,* including whether or not a property is a house within the applicable provisions, it is appropriately raised by way of application for judicial review.

The *vires* of the authority in reaching their decision, *i.e.* on normal principles of administrative law (*cf.* notes to s.64, above), are challengeable even on an appeal in the county court, for the effect of the notice is to seek to take away a vested right to which the appellant would otherwise be entitled, *i.e.* to leave the property as he wishes: see *London Borough of Wandsworth* v. *Winder* [1985] A.C. 461, 17 H.L.R. 196, H.L., with the effect that it would seem to be exempt from the principle in *Cocks* v. *Thanet District Council* [1983] A.C. 286; 6 H.L.R. 15, H.L., that judicial review is the only way to impeach a decision of the authority which is a precondition to the acquisition of a right. See also *Elliott* v. *Brighton Borough Council* (1980) 258 E.G. 441, C.A.

This view would in this case help to support the approach of *Smith* v. *East Elloe Rural District Council* [1956] A.C. 736, H.L., applied in *R.* v. *Secretary of State for the Environment* [1976] 3 All E.R. 90, C.A., distinguishing *Anisminic Ltd.* v. *Foreign Compensation Commission* [1969] 2 A.C. 147, H.L., *i.e.* that a matter which is to be treated as "final and conclusive" is to be so treated to the extent of excluding application for judicial review. However, the courts have shown less willing to accept diminution of their jurisdiction in cases such as *Pearlman* v. *Keepers & Governors of Harrow School* [1979] Q.B. 56, C.A. (in which the words "final and conclusive" did not prevent further challenge on the correct interpretation of the word "improvement" for the purposes of the Leasehold Reform Act 1967) and *Meade* v. *Haringey London Borough Council* [1979] 1 W.L.R. 637, C.A.

The last-mentioned case went so far as to suggest that if want of vires is the basis of challenge it is not even necessary to show that "domestic" remedies (*i.e.* an Act's own statutory procedures for redress or complaint including appeals) have been exhausted, contrary to the "usual" rule (see *Doe d. Bishop of Rochester* v. *Bridges* (1831) 1 B. & Ad. 847; *Pasmore* v. *Oswaldtwistle Urban District Council* [1898] A.C. 387, H.L.; *Barraclough* v. *Brown* [1897] A.C. 615, H.L.; *Watt* v. *Kesteven County Council* [1955] 1 Q.B. 408; *Wyatt* v. *London Borough of Hillingdon* (1978) 76 L.G.R. 727; *London Borough of Southwark* v. *Williams* [1971] Ch. 734, and *Kensington and Chelsea Royal London Borough Council* v. *Wells* (1974) 72 L.G.R. 289, C.A.).

If a notice is served on the wrong person, *i.e.* not the person having control, it is simply invalid and can be ignored, and there is no need to appeal it to the county court under s.191, below: *Pollway Nominees Ltd.* v. *London Borough of Croydon* (1985) 17 H.L.R. 503, C.A. See also *Graddage* v. *London Borough of Haringey* [1975] 1 W.L.R. 241, Ch.D.

Repair notice in respect of house in state of disrepair but not unfit

190.—(1) Where the local housing authority—

    (*a*) are satisfied that a house is in such a state of disrepair that,

although not unfit for human habitation, substantial repairs are
necessary to bring it up to a reasonable standard, having regard to
its age, character and locality, or

(*b*) are satisfied on a representation made by an occupying tenant that
a house is in such a state of disrepair that, although not unfit for
human habitation, its condition is such as to interfere materially
with the personal comfort of the occupying tenant,

they may serve a repair notice on the person having control of the house.

(2) A repair notice under this section shall require the person on whom
it is served, within such reasonable time, not being less than 21 days, as
is specified in the notice, to execute the works specified in the notice, not
being works of internal decorative repair.

(3) The authority, in addition to serving the notice on the person having
control of the house, may serve a copy of the notice on any other person
having an interest in the house, whether as freeholder, mortgagee, lessee
or otherwise.

(4) The notice becomes operative, if no appeal is brought, on the expiry
of 21 days from the date of service of the notice and is final and conclusive
as to matters which could have been raised on an appeal.

DEFINITIONS
  "house": s.207.
  "local housing authority": ss.1, 2.
  "occupying tenant": s.236.
  "person having control": s.207.
  "unfit for human habitation": s.604.

GENERAL NOTE
  The three main points of distinction between this section and the last are: (a) the powers
are discretionary; (b) there is no express requirement that the works be capable of execution
at a reasonable expense; and (c) that different standards apply, *i.e.* it is not necessary that
the property be unfit for human habitation (within s.604, below). As to application to
"house", and to an authority's own property, see notes to last section. As to person having
control, see notes to s.207, below.

Reasonable Expense?
  The absence of reference to repairability at a reasonable expense in the preceding
legislation was clearly deliberate, for that which is now s.191(3) (Housing Act 1957, s.11(3))
needed express amendment to restrict its operation to what is now s.189, above. Nonetheless,
in *Hillbank Properties Ltd.* v. *Hackney London Borough Council* [1978] Q.B. 998, 3 H.L.R.
73, C.A., it was held that the same considerations which will determine the issue under
s.206, below, will remain relevant.
  In *Kenny* v. *Kingston Upon Thames Royal London Borough Council* (1985) 17 H.L.R.
344, C.A., the applicability of the s.206 test of reasonable expense was considered in greater
detail. The county court judge set out seven propositions, which were approved by the
Court of Appeal, noting that what is now this section does not expressly incorporate the
s.206 formulation:
  (1) As long as they are relevant to the issue, there is no limit to the matters to which the
judge can have regard when considering an appeal under s.191, below;
  (2) The means or financial position of the owner are among the relevant matters; (but *cf.*
Hillbank, in which the Court of Appeal held that the county court should have "torn off the
corporate veil" of a one-house company relying on its want of finance);
  (3) The cost of repairs to the house as compared to the value of the house when repaired
is relevant;
  (4) A comparison between the value of the house unrepaired and the value of the house
repaired, *i.e.* the increase in value by reason of the repairs, as compared with the cost of the
repairs, is relevant—*i.e.* s.206, below;
  (5) For the purposes of the previous considerations the relevant value is the realistic value
of the "house" as a saleable asset in the hands of the landlord. In a case where there is a
protected tenant there may be evidence as to whether or not the tenancy is likely to come
to an end for one reason or another in the foreseeable future. If there is no evidence one
way or another the court may conclude that the true value of the house is too uncertain for

it to base any conclusion on it at all, or it may take the mean figure between the two extremes of "vacant possession" and "sitting tenant" value (*cf.* notes to s.206, below);

(6) The fact that if the repairs are not done the "house" and indeed the property as a whole will sink into greater disrepair to the point where it becomes unfit for human habitation within s.604, below, so that a protected tenant can be evicted to the landlord's ultimate profit, with the undesirable social consequences of such a course of events, is relevant;

(7) The fact that a property is unsafe or may become so while a tenant is still in occupation, if the repairs are not done, is a valid consideration.

The county court took into account what it concluded was a deliberate policy of neglect by the owner, which would mean that the tenant and his family would have to live for a long period in deteriorating, and unsafe, conditions, and that this was socially undesirable. These policy considerations outweighed a difference between cost of compliance, and increase in value (as to which, see further notes to s.206, below). The Court of Appeal upheld the decision: whether or not the policy considerations did outweigh the financial considerations was essentially a matter for the judge.

While the decision is one on an appeal, it is of course equally one on what the authority may properly have regard to when reaching their own decision on whether or not to exercise their discretion under this section.

Standards

Subs. (1)(*a*). The purpose of this provision is to prevent the landlord allowing a property to fall into such disrepair that not only does it become unfit but it may even become so unfit that it is not repairable at a reasonable expense, with the consequence (see Part IX, ss.264–279, below), that the tenant has to vacate: *Hillbank Properties Ltd.* v. *Hackney London Borough Council* [1978] Q.B. 998, 3 H.L.R. 73, C.A. It is now well recognised that the value to a property owner of an unfit house with vacant possession is greater than a fit house with a sitting (and protected) tenant: *ibid*; see also *Buswell* v. *Goodwin* [1971] 1 W.L.R. 92, C.A.

The words "substantial repairs" are thought to be capable of referring to one or more larger items, or to a combination of smaller ones; the provision is designed to cope with cumulative deterioration of a property rather than the rectification of inevitable minor defects—M.H.L.G. Circular 64/69. The provision does not apply to "improvements": see the distinction in the notes to s.471, below; see also Part VII, below (compulsory improvement).

The words "age, character and locality" are drawn from *Proudfoot* v. *Hart* (1890) 25 Q.B.D. 42; see also *Jaquin* v. *Holland* [1960] 1 W.L.R. 258. There has not been much judicial consideration of what the words actually mean, beyond the oft-cited observation in *Proudfoot* that different standards will apply by reference to "the occupation of a reasonable minded tenant of the class who would be likely to take" a property, so that different standards would be expected in Grosvenor Square than in Spitalfields. (Probably still true—but Islington?)

Subs. (1)(*b*). This sort of notice concerns the personal comfort of an occupying tenant. An occupying tenant is someone other than an owner-occupier who is entitled to occupy under a tenancy, or is a statutory tenant (under either the Rent Act 1977 or the Rent (Agriculture) Act 1976—see notes to s.622, below) or occupies under a restricted contract (under s.19, Rent Act 1977—see notes to s.622, below), or is employed in agriculture, and occupies as part of his terms of employment: s.236, below. (On the complaint of such in writing, procedure for compulsory *improvement* may be commenced under Part VII—see s.212, below).

The condition of the property must be such that, although it is not unfit, it materially interferes with the occupying tenant's personal comfort. Neither material interference nor personal comfort is defined. When it was introduced, the provision was said to be sufficiently widely drafted to cover electric wiring in poor or dangerous condition, and to have been intended to reverse the decision in *National Coal Board* v. *Thorpe* [1976] 1 W.L.R. 543, D.C., a case under Part III, Public Health Act 1936, in which it was held that if the condition of premises was not injurious to the health of an occupier, to constitute a statutory nuisance within s.92(1)(*a*) of the 1936 Act there had to be a nuisance at common law, *i.e.* originating in premises *other than* in the tenant's possession—*Hansard*, H.C. Deb., Vol. 985, col. 93.

Notice

While the remarks under this heading in the notes to the last section are generally applicable, it may be noted that there is no requirement that the notice specify that the house will be fit on completion of works for, of course, it presumably already is. Note, too, the express exclusion of works of internal decoration from the authority's notice: however, if the disrepair itself constituted a breach of the landlord's repairing obligations to the tenant under contract, or under s.11, Landlord and Tenant Act 1985, the landlord will be obliged to make good the decorative repair, and liable in damages for failure to do so—see *McGreal* v. *Wake* (1984) 13 H.L.R. 107, C.A., *Bradley* v. *Chorley Borough Council* (1985) 17 H.L.R. 305, C.A.

Subs. (4)
See notes to s.189(4), above.

Appeals against repair notices

191.—(1) A person aggrieved by a repair notice may within 21 days after the date of service of the notice, appeal to the county court.

(2) On an appeal the court may make such order either confirming, quashing or varying the notice as it thinks fit.

(3) Where the appeal is allowed against a repair notice under section 189 (repair notice in respect of unfit house), the judge shall, if requested to do so by the local housing authority, include in his judgment a finding whether the house can or cannot be rendered fit for human habitation at a reasonable expense.

(4) If an appeal is brought the notice does not become operative until—

(*a*) a decision on the appeal confirming the notice (with or without variation) is given and the period within which an appeal to the Court of Appeal may be brought expires without any such appeal having been brought, or

(*b*) if a further appeal to the Court of Appeal is brought, a decision on that appeal is given confirming the notice (with or without variation);

and for this purpose the withdrawal of an appeal has the same effect as a decision confirming the notice or decision appealed against.

DEFINITIONS
"house": s.207.
"local housing authority": ss.1, 2.
"reasonable expense": s.206.
"repair notice": ss.189, 190.
"unfit for human habitation": s.604.

GENERAL NOTE
This section provides for appeals against a repairs notice under either of the last sections.

Person Aggrieved
Appeal lies at the instance of a "person aggrieved" by the notice. This means someone who has been deprived of a legal entitlement, or subjected to a legal burden, but does not necessarily mean pecuniary grievance: *Ex parte Sidebotham* (1880) 14 Ch. D. 458, and *R.* v. *London Quarter Sessions, ex parte Westminster Corporation* [1951] 2 K.B. 508. (The more relaxed approach evidenced in, *e.g.*, *Turner* v. *Secretary of State for the Environment* (1973) 28 P. & C.R. 123, *Nicholson* v. *Secretary of State for Energy* (1977) 76 L.G.R. 693, *Buxton* v. *Minister of Housing and Local Government* [1961] 1 Q.B. 278, would not seem likely to be applied in this sort of case).

Reasonable Expense
Special provision is made for *successful* appeals against a s.189 notice: the authority may ask the court to, and the court if asked must, include in its judgment a finding as to whether or not the property is repairable at a reasonable expense: subs. (3). The request must be made at the hearing, in time for the judge to include the finding in his judgment (which will be at any time before judgment is *entered*, in the sense of a minute of the judgment recorded in the books of the court—see *Millinsted* v. *Grosvenor House (Park Lane) Ltd.* [1937] 1 K.B. 736, C.A., *Moons Motors* v. *Kiuan Wou* [1952] Lloyd's Rep. 80).

Once judgment has been entered, if the authority have not asked for the specific finding, *e.g.* by oversight, it will be too late: *Victoria Square Property Co. Ltd.* v. *Southwark London Borough Council* [1978] 1 W.L.R. 463, C.A. The importance of this is because under s.192, below, the authority have power to purchase a property which has (a) been the subject of a s.189 notice, and (b) been the subject of such a finding; without the finding, there is no power of purchase and an alternative purchase, such as under s.300, below, will not be available: *ibid*.

Time for Appeal

Appeal must be brought within 21 days: subs. (1). This does not include the day of service: *Goldsmith's Co.* v. *West Metropolitan Railway Co.* [1904] 1 K.B. 1, C.A.; *Stewart* v. *Chapman* [1951] 2 All E.R. 613. Although the county court has a general power to enlarge time (C.C.R. Ord. 13, r. 4), it would seem that the general power cannot be used to override the statutory time limit: see *Honig* v. *Lewisham Borough Council* (1958) 122 J.P.J. 302.

Grounds of Appeal

No grounds for appeal are specified, and can include validity of the notice itself: *Elliott* v. *Brighton Borough Council* (1980) 258 E.G. 441, C.A.

The *vires* of the authority in reaching their decision, *i.e.* on normal principles of administrative law (*cf.* notes to s.64, above), are challengeable even on an appeal in the county court, for the effect of the repairs notice is to seek to take away a vested right to which the appellant would otherwise be entitled, *i.e.* to leave the property as he wishes: see *London Borough of Wandsworth* v. *Winder* [1985] A.C. 461, 17 H.L.R. 196, H.L., with the effect that it would seem to be exempt from the principle in *Cocks* v. *Thanet District Council* [1983] A.C. 286, 6 H.L.R. 15, H.L., that judicial review is the only way to impeach a decision of the authority which is a precondition to the acquisition of a right.

The possibility of appeal would suggest that it is the more appropriate course than application for judicial review: see *R.* v. *Hackney London Borough Council, ex parte Teepee Estates (1956) Ltd.* (1967) 19 P. & C.R. 87, D.C. See also *Minford Properties Ltd.* v. *London Borough of Hammersmith* (1978) 247 E.G. 561, D.C.; but *cf. R.* v. *London Borough of Southwark, ex parte Lewis Levy Ltd.* [1983] 8 H.L.R. 1, Q.B.D. in which the court considered that if an issue is one which goes to *vires*, including whether or not a property is a house within the applicable provisions, it is appropriately raised by way of application for judicial review.

Note that no question which can be raised on an appeal against the notice will subsequently be admitted as a ground for appeal against recovery of costs of works in default under s.193, below: Sched. 10, para. 6. However, as objection to carrying out works in default cannot be raised on an appeal against the notice, it can be raised on an appeal against the demand for payment: *Elliott* v. *Brighton Borough Council* (1980) 258 E.G. 441, C.A.

If a notice is served on the wrong person, *i.e.* not the person having control, it is simply invalid and can be ignored, and there is no need to appeal it to the county court under this section: *Pollway Nominees Ltd.* v. *London Borough of Croydon* (1985) 17 H.L.R. 503, C.A., *Graddage* v. *London Borough of Haringey* [1975] 1 W.L.R. 241, Ch. D.

County Court

Formerly, appeal had to be brought to the county court with jurisdiction over the area where the premises are situated: Housing Act 1957, s.11. Pursuant to Law Commission Recommendations (Cmnd. 9515), No. 9(ii), appeal lies now simply "to the county court" which means, under the County Court Rules (S.I. 1981 No. 1687), Ord. 4, rule 9, the court for the district in which the decision appeal against was made.

Powers of Court

Apart from the obligation to make a finding as to reasonable expense if asked to do so by the authority, the court may make such order as it thinks fit, confirming, quashing, or varying the notice: subs. (2). It may make findings of fact: *Fletcher* v. *Ilkeston Corporation* (1932) 96 J.P. 7. Instead of varying a notice, a court which thinks that some works are necessary, but those required are excessive, is entitled (not, of course, obliged), to quash the notice, and leave it to the authority to serve a new notice: *Cochrane* v. *Chanctonbury Rural District Council* [1950] 2 All E.R. 1134, C.A.

Subs. (4)

The notice does not become operative if an appeal is brought within the 21 days allowed, until the confirmation of the notice by the county court together with the passing of time to appeal to the Court of Appeal (four weeks—R.S.C. Ord. 59, rule 19). If appeal *is* brought to the Court of Appeal, then the notice does not become operative until the decision of that court; if an appeal is brought, but withdrawn, the withdrawal has the effect of a decision dismissing the appeal, *i.e.* at whichsoever level, to or from county court.

Power to purchase house found on appeal to be unfit and beyond repair at reasonable expense

192.—(1) Where a person has appealed against a repair notice under section 189 (repair notice in respect of unfit house) and the court in allowing the appeal has found that the house cannot be rendered fit for human habitation at a reasonable expense, the local housing authority may purchase the house by agreement or be authorised by the Secretary of State to purchase it compulsorily.

(2) The Secretary of State shall not confirm an order for the compulsory purchase of a house under this section unless the order is submitted to him within six months after the determination of the appeal.

(3) If an owner or mortgagee of the house undertakes to carry out to the satisfaction of the Secretary of State, within such period as the Secretary of State may fix, the works specified in the notice against which the appeal was brought, the Secretary of State shall not confirm the compulsory purchase order unless that person has failed to fulfil his undertaking.

(4) If the local housing authority purchase the house compulsorily they shall forthwith execute all the works specified in the notice against which the appeal was brought.

Definitions
"house": s.207.
"local housing authority": ss.1, 2.
"owner": s.207.
"person having control": s.207.
"reasonable expense": s.206.
"repair notice": s.189.
"unfit for human habitation": s.604.

General Note
If the authority ask the county court on an appeal against a notice under s.189, above, to make a finding as to whether or not the property is repairable at a reasonable expense, the court is bound to make such a finding: s.191(3). If the court finds that it is *not* so repairable, the authority can nonetheless purchase the property—by agreement or compulsorily—themselves: subs. (1). However, submission of the order to the Secretary of State for confirmation must be within six months of the final determination of the appeal, *i.e.* under s.191(4), above: subs. (2).

If the authority do purchase the property, they must *forthwith* carry out all the works specified in the s.189 notice: subs. (4). The Secretary of State is not, however, to confirm a compulsory purchase order if an owner (as defined in s.207, below), or a mortgagee, gives (and keeps to) an undertaking to the Secretary of State to complete the works to his satisfaction, and within a time he specifies: subs. (3).

Compulsory purchase—procedure and compensation—is dealt with in Part XVII, below; note the provisions of s.582, giving the court extended powers to protect tenants against eviction pending confirmation and entry. The cost of the purchase and subsequent works is debited to the Housing Revenue Account (maintained under s.418, below; see Sched. 14, para. 1).

The purpose of the provision is for the authority to add the property as part of their permanent, Part II stock. If they fail to seek the appropriate ruling from the county court, they cannot fall back on the use of powers under s.300, below, *i.e.* to purchase for temporary use: *Victoria Square Property Co. Ltd.* v. *Southwark London Borough Council* [1978] 1 W.L.R. 463, C.A.

Enforcement

Power of local housing authority to execute works

193.—(1) If a repair notice is not complied with the local housing authority may themselves do the work required to be done by the notice.

(2) For this purpose compliance with the notice means the completion of the works specified in the notice within—

(*a*) the period specified in the notice, or,

(*b*) if an appeal is brought against the notice, the period of 21 days, or such longer period as the court in determining the appeal may fix,

from the date on which the notice becomes operative.

(3) The provisions of Schedule 10 apply with respect to the recovery by the local housing authority of expenses incurred by them under this section.

DEFINITIONS

"local housing authority": ss.1, 2.
"operative": s.191.
"repair notice": ss.189, 190.

GENERAL NOTE

This section gives the authority power to carry out works in default in relation to either class of notice. The power is discretionary and the authority cannot adopt a fixed policy of always exercising it, although they can have a policy by way of guideline, *i.e.* that they will normally exercise the power but will consider application in every case: *Elliott* v. *Brighton Borough Council* (1980) 258 E.G. 441, C.A.; see, also, *e.g. British Oxygen Co. Ltd.* v. *Board of Trade* [1971] A.C. 610, H.L., *In Re Betts* [1983] 2 A.C. 613, 10 H.L.R. 97, H.L., *Att.-Gen.* v. *L.B. Wandsworth, ex rel. Tilley* [1981] 1 W.L.R. 854, C.A.

The power does not arise until non-compliance, *i.e.* within the period specified in the notice itself, or if an appeal is brought within 21 days from the end of the appeal, or such longer period as the court may decide: subs. (2). Ancillary provisions governing obstruction and the powers of the court, are to be found in ss.194–198, below.

Schedule 10

This Schedule governs the recovery of the cost of works in default, and is applicable under this, and a number of other, sections. The expenses are prima facie recoverable from the person served with the appropriate notice: para. 2. However, they are *also* recoverable from a person on behalf of whom the person served was acting as agent or trustee: *ibid.* If the person served was acting as agent or trustee, his own liability is limited to the moneys he has had in his hands since the service of the demand for the expenses: *ibid.*

The demand itself is served on the person from whom the money is sought: para. 3. Under para. 4, it will be recoverable with interest, at the reasonable rate determined by the authority, from date of service until payment. When the demand is served, a copy is also to be served on anyone else who the authority know to be an owner, lessee or mortgagee of the premises: para. 3. Unless the demand is appealed, it will become operative 21 days from date of service, and is "final and conclusive" as to matters which could have been raised on an appeal (as to which, see notes to s.189(4), above).

If no appeal is brought, the person served cannot subsequently allege that the demand is inaccurate or excessive: *Benabo* v. *Wood Green Borough Council* [1946] 1 K.B. 38. The demand must, however, be a valid demand. If the demand is invalid, *e.g.* procedurally, the person served can ignore it, and raise the invalidity in any subsequent proceedings for its recovery: *West Ham Corporation* v. *Benabo* [1934] 2 K.B. 253.

The authority can by order declare the amount to be payable by weekly or other periodic instalments over a maximum 30 year period, together with interest: para. 5. An instalment order becomes operative 21 days after service, unless an appeal is brought, and is, again, final and conclusive as to matters which could have been raised on an appeal. If an attempt is made to recover by action, which does not result in payment, the authority's right to make an instalment order has not been lost, or "merged" in the judgment: see *Salford Corporation* v. *Hale* [1925] 1 K.B. 253. Similarly, the authority's right to interest does not end with judgment: *Ealing London Borough Council* v. *El Isaacs* [1980] 1 W.L.R. 932, C.A.

Appeal lies within 21 days to the county court: para. 6. Formerly, appeal had to be brought to the county court with jurisdiction over the area where the premises are situated: Housing Act 1957, s.11. Pursuant to Law Commission Recommendations (Cmnd. 9515), No. 9(ii), appeal lies now simply "to the county court" which means, under the County Court Rules (S.I. 1981 No. 1687), Ord. 4, rule 9, the court for the district in which the decision appealed against was made.

The 21 days do not include the day of service: *Goldsmith's Co.* v. *West Metropolitan Railway Co.* [1904] 1 K.B. 1, C.A.; *Stewart* v. *Chapman* [1951] 2 All E.R. 613. Although

the county court has a general power to enlarge time (C.C.R. Ord. 13, r. 4), it has been
suggested that the general power cannot be used to override the statutory time limit: see
Honig v. *Lewisham Borough Council* (1958) 122 J.P.J. 302. But see *Arieli* v. *Duke of
Westminster* (1983) 269 E.G. 535, C.A., and *Johnston* v. *Duke of Devonshire* (1984) 17
H.L.R. 136, C.A., under Leasehold Reform Act 1967 and Housing Act 1974, Sched. 8.

The demand or order does not become operative if an appeal is brought within the 21
days allowed, until the confirmation of the demand or order on final determination of the
appeal: para. 6. Note that a question which could have been raised on an appeal against the
notice itself cannot be raised on an appeal against a demand for the expenses: *ibid*. However,
as objection to carrying out works in default cannot be raised on an appeal against the
notice, it can be raised on an appeal against the demand: *Elliott* v. *Brighton Borough
Council* (1980) 258 E.G. 441, C.A.

The expenses and interest are a charge on the property, giving the authority the powers
and remedies of a mortgagee, including the power to appoint a receiver from one month
after the charge takes effect, which is when the demand becomes operative: para. 7.

Notice of authority's intention to execute works

194.—(1) Where the local housing authority are about to enter upon a
house under the provisions of section 193 for the purpose of doing any
work, they may give notice in writing of their intention to do so to the
person having control of the house and, if they think fit, to any owner of
the house.

(2) If at any time after the expiration of seven days from the service of
the notice on him and whilst any workman or contractor employed by the
local housing authority is carrying out works in the house—

(*a*) the person on whom the notice was served is in the house for the
purpose of carrying out any works, or

(*b*) any workman employed by him or by any contractor employed by
him is in the house for such purpose,

the person on whom the notice was served shall be deemed for the
purpose of section 198 (penalty for obstruction) to be obstructing the
authority in the execution of this Part unless he shows that there was
urgent necessity to carry out the works in order to obviate danger to
occupants of the house.

DEFINITIONS
"house": s.207.
"local housing authority": ss.1, 2.
"owner": s.207.
"person having control": s.207.

GENERAL NOTE
Notice of entry to execute works in default is not obligatory: subs. (1). However, it is
necessary if entry is to be backed-up by the possibility of offences under this or the next
section.

Under this section, notice may be given in writing, to the person having control, and to
an owner: if the owner has given notice under s.202, below, an authority giving notice to the
person having control will accordingly be obliged to give the owner a copy of the notice
under this section.

Once seven days have passed, an offence is committed by any person who has been served
with the notice if either (a) he, or (b) any workman or contractor of his, is in the house in
order to carry out works, at the same time as the authority's work people are in the
property, unless he can show that the works were needed to obviate danger to occupants:
subs. (2). The purpose is clearly to avoid a clash of workforces, and for the offence to be
committed it is not necessary that the works the person served is seeking to carry out are
those the authority are carrying out, *i.e.* works under the notice. The offence is obstruction
under s.198, below.

There is no offence if the authority are acting outside their powers, *e.g.* if the original
notice was invalid: *Canterbury City Council* v. *Bern* [1981] J.P.L. 749, D.C.

Power of court to order occupier or owner to permit things to be done

195.—(1) If a person, after receiving notice of the intended action—

(*a*) being the occupier of premises, prevents the owner or person having control of the premises, or his officers, servants or agents, from carrying into effect with respect to the premises any of the provisions of this Part, or

(*b*) being the occupier, owner or person having control of premises, prevents an officer, servant or agent of the local housing authority from so doing,

a magistrates' court may order him to permit to be done on the premises all things requisite for carrying into effect those provisions.

(2) A person who fails to comply with an order of the court under this section commits a summary offence and is liable on conviction to a fine not exceeding £20 in respect of each day during which the failure continues.

DEFINITIONS
   "local housing authority": ss.1, 2.
   "owner": s.207.
   "person having control": s.207.

GENERAL NOTE
   The magistrates' court may order an occupier to co-operate with an owner or person having control, or the authority, seeking to carry into effect a repairs notice under ss.189 or 190, or carrying out works in default under s.193; an owner, or a person having control, may also be ordered to co-operate with the authority under this section: subs. (1). Failure to comply with the order is an offence punishable by a fine of up to £20 per day on which it continues.

Power of court to authorise owner to execute works on default of another owner

196.—(1) If it appears to a magistrates' court, on the application of an owner of premises in respect of which a repair notice has been served, that owing to the default of another owner of the premises in executing works required to be executed, the interests of the applicant will be prejudiced, the court may make an order empowering the applicant forthwith to enter on the premises and execute the works within a period fixed by the order.

(2) Where the court makes such an order, the court may, where it seems to the court just to do so, make a like order in favour of any other owner.

(3) Before an order is made under this section, notice of the application shall be given to the local housing authority.

DEFINITIONS
   "local housing authority": ss.1, 2.
   "owner": s.207.

GENERAL NOTE
   Any owner may apply to the magistrates' court for an order permitting him to execute works in default of compliance by another owner: subs. (1). Notice must be given to the authority before the court makes such an order: subs. (3). The power only arises, however, if the owner can show that his interests will be prejudiced if there is non-compliance.

Powers of entry

197.—(1) A person authorised by the local housing authority or the Secretary of State may at any reasonable time, on giving 24 hours' notice of his intention to the occupier, and to the owner if the owner is known, enter premises for the purpose of survey and examination—

(*a*) where it appears to the authority that survey or examination is necessary in order to determine whether any powers under this Part should be exercised in respect of the premises,

(*b*) where a repair notice has been served in respect of the premises, or

(*c*) in the case of premises which the authority are authorised by this Part to purchase compulsorily.

(2) An authorisation for the purposes of this section shall be in writing stating the particular purpose or purposes for which the entry is authorised.

DEFINITIONS
"local housing authority": ss.1, 2.
"owner": s.207.

GENERAL NOTE
This section confers power of entry on the authority, and on the Secretary of State, for the purposes and subject to the notice specified: subs. (1). The requirements of subs. (2) are mandatory, and entry without compliance will not be pursuant to this power, with the consequence that no offence of obstruction (on this account) will be committed under s.198, below: *Stroud* v. *Bradbury* [1952] 2 All E.R. 76, D.C.

Penalty for obstruction

198.—(1) It is a summary offence to obstruct an officer of the local housing authority or of the Secretary of State, or a person authorised in pursuance of this Part to enter premises, in the performance of anything which that officer, authority or person is required or authorised by this Part to do.

(2) A person who commits such an offence is liable on conviction to a fine not exceeding level 2 on the standard scale.

DEFINITION
"local housing authority": ss.1, 2.

GENERAL NOTE
It is a criminal offence to obstruct an officer of the authority or of the Secretary of State under s.197, above, or an owner authorised under s.196, above, when exercising a power of entry under this Part: subs. (1). Note that this will include the presence of workmen at the same time as those of the authority, under s.194, above. The offence is punishable by a fine of up to level 2 on the standard scale under s.37, Criminal Justice Act 1982, currently £100, by S.I. 1984 No. 447.

If a person is not properly authorised, no offence will be committed: *Stroud* v. *Bradbury* [1952] 2 All E.R. 76, D.C.

Provisions for protection of owner and others

Recovery by lessee of proportion of cost of works

199.—(1) A lessee of a house who, or whose agent, incurs expenditure—

(*a*) in complying with a repair notice, or

(*b*) in defraying expenses incurred by the local housing authority under section 193 (execution of works by authority),

may recover from the lessor under the lease such part (if any) of the expenditure as may be agreed between the parties or, in default of agreement, is determined by the county court to be just.

(2) The county court in making the determination shall have regard in particular to—

(*a*) the obligations of the lessor and the lessee under the lease with respect to the repair of the house,

(*b*) the length of the unexpired term of the lease, and

(*c*) the rent payable under the lease.

(3) Where a person from whom a sum is recoverable under this section is himself a lessee of the house, the provisions of this section apply to that sum as they apply to expenditure of the kind mentioned in subsection (1).

(4) This section does not apply to expenditure in respect of which a charging order is in force under section 200 (charging order in favour of owner executing works) or in respect of which an application for such an order is pending.

DEFINITIONS
   "house": s.207.
   "lease": s.621.
   "lessee": s.621.
   "lessor": s.621.
   "local housing authority": ss.1, 2.
   "person having control": s.207.
   "repair notice": ss.189, 190.

GENERAL NOTE
   When an owner completes works under a repairs notice, he may secure a charging order on the property under s.200, below. When a *lessee* does so, or if he has to make payments to the authority for works in default (see notes to s.193, above), he may seek to recover from the lessor a "just" proportion, by action in the county court, under subs. (1) of this section. When making its decision, the court must have regard to respective repairing obligations, how long the lease has to run (*i.e.* who will derive the long-term benefit, or for how long each party will derive a benefit), and the rent payable: subs. (2). If the lessor is himself only the holder of a lease, then he can proceed to seek a contribution from *his* lessor: subs. (3).

Charging order in favour of owner executing works

200.—(1) Where an owner has completed, in respect of a house, works required to be executed by a repair notice, he may apply to the local housing authority for a charging order.

(2) An applicant for a charging order shall produce to the authority—

   (*a*) the certificate of the proper officer of the authority that the works have been executed to his satisfaction, and

   (*b*) the accounts of and vouchers for the expenses of the works.

(3) The authority, when satisfied that the owner has duly executed the required works and of the amount of the expenses, shall make an order accordingly charging on the premises an annuity to repay that amount together with the amount of the costs properly incurred in obtaining the charging order.

(4) The annuity charged shall be at the rate of £6 for every £100 of the aggregate amount charged, shall commence from the date of the order and shall be payable for a term of 30 years to the owner named in the order, his executors, administrators or assigns.

(5) A person aggrieved by the charging order may, within 21 days after notice of the order has been served upon him, appeal to the county court; and where notice of appeal has been given no proceedings shall be taken under the order until the appeal is determined or ceases to be prosecuted.

(6) The proper officer of the local housing authority shall file and record copies, certified by him to be true copies, of any charging order made under this section, the certificate given under subsection (2)(*a*) and the accounts as passed by the authority.

DEFINITIONS
   "house": s.207.
   "local housing authority": ss.1, 2.
   "owner": s.207.
   "repair notice": ss.189, 190.

GENERAL NOTE

When an owner complies with a repairs notice, he will, of course, improve the house, which may be to the benefit of others with an interest in it. This section permits him to apply to the authority to place a charging order on the property, so as to secure his expenditure: subs. (1). The application must be supported by a certificate from the authority's officer that the works have satisfactorily been completed, and the accounts and vouchers relating to the costs: subs. (2). The authority, once satisfied as to works and cost, must make an order charging the property with those costs (plus the costs properly incurred in applying for the charging order), to produce an annuity over 30 years of 6 per cent.: subs. (3), (4).

There is no power to make an order charging different interests, *i.e.* apportioning the burden of the charge: *Holborn and Frascati Ltd.* v. *London County Council* (1916) 80 J.P. 225. See also *Paddington Borough Council* v. *Finucane* [1928] Ch. 567.

Appeal against the charging order lies now to the county court: subs. (5). This is pursuant to Law Commission Recommendations (Cmnd. 9515), No. 9(i); appeal lay formerly to the magistrates' court. Appeal must be brought within 21 days: subs. (1). This does not include the day of service: *Goldsmith's Co.* v. *West Metropolitan Railway Co.* [1904] 1 K.B. 1, C.A.; *Stewart* v. *Chapman* [1951] 2 All E.R. 613. Although the county court has a general power to enlarge time (C.C.R. Ord. 13, r. 4), it has been suggested that the general power cannot be used to override the statutory time limit: see *Honig* v. *Lewisham Borough Council* (1958) 122 J.P.J. 302. But see *Arieli* v. *Duke of Westminster* (1983) 269 E.G. 535, C.A., and *Johnston* v. *Duke of Devonshire* (1984) 17 H.L.R. 136, C.A., under the Leasehold Reform Act 1967 and the Housing Act 1974, Sched. 8.

The express obligation on authorities in subs. (6) is pursuant to Law Commission Recommendations (Cmnd. 9515), No. 10. The form of the charging order, and its priority, is pursuant to s.201, below; under s.201(6), the order is redeemable by another owner, or someone else interested in the premises. The powers of the person entitled to the charge are under s.201(4), (5), below.

Form, effect, &c. of charging orders

201.—(1) A charging order under section 200 shall be in such form as the Secretary of State may prescribe.

(2) The charge created by such a charging order is a charge on the premises specified in the order having priority over all existing and future estates, interests and incumbrances, with the exception of—

(*a*) charges under section 229 (charge in favour of person executing works required by improvement notice);

(*b*) tithe rentcharge;

(*c*) charges within section 1(1)(*a*) of the Local Land Charges Act 1975 (statutory charges in favour of public authorities); and

(*d*) charges created under any Act authorising advances of public money.

(3) Charges under section 200 and section 229 (the corresponding provision in relation to improvement notices) take order as between themselves according to their respective dates.

(4) The annuity created by a charging order may be recovered by the person for the time being entitled to it by the same means and in the like manner in all respects as if it were a rentcharge granted by deed out of the premises by the owner of the premises.

(5) The benefit of the charge may be from time to time transferred in like manner as a mortgage or rentcharge may be transferred, and the transfer shall be in such form as the Secretary of State may prescribe.

(6) An owner of, or other person interested in, premises on which an annuity has been charged by a charging order under section 200 may at any time redeem the annuity on payment to the person entitled to the annuity of such sum as may be agreed upon, or in default of agreement, determined by the Secretary of State.

GENERAL NOTE

This makes ancillary provision to the charging order power under s.200, above.

Subs. (2)

The express statement of priorities is now pursuant to Law Commission Recommendations (Cmnd. 9515), No. 11.

Subs. (4)

If there is a lessee in possession, the annuity under s.200(3), (4), above, is recoverable from him, rather than from the freeholder: *Hyde* v. *Berners* (1889) 53 J.P. 453. Arrears of the annuity may be sued for: *Re Herbage Rents, Greenwich* [1896] 2 Ch. 811.

Owner not in receipt of rents, &c. to receive notice of proceedings

202. If an owner of premises who is not the person in receipt of the rents and profits gives notice to the local housing authority of his interest in the premises, the authority shall give him notice of any proceedings taken by them in pursuance of this Part.

DEFINITIONS
"local housing authority": ss.1, 2.
"owner": s.207.

GENERAL NOTE
Notices under ss.189 and 190 *may* be served on an owner, but *must* be served on the person having control; similarly, service of a demand notice under Sched. 10 for works in default under s.193, will be on the person from whom the authority seek to recover. An owner under s.207, below, includes a person holding or entitled to the rents and profits of the premises under a lease of which at least three years remains unexpired, and accordingly may be the person having control; on the other hand, he may be a freeholder not having control. An owner of this last class is entitled to serve notice on the authority under this section, which will oblige the authority to serve him with notice of any proceedings taken by them under this Part.

Saving for rights arising from breach of covenant, &c.

203.—(1) Nothing in this Part prejudices or interferes with the rights or remedies of an owner for breach of any covenant or contract entered into by a lessee in reference to premises in respect of which a repair notice is served.

(2) If an owner is obliged to take possession of premises in order to comply with a repair notice the taking possession does not affect his right to avail himself of any such breach which occurred before he took possession.

(3) No action taken under this Part prejudices or affects any remedy available to the tenant of a house against his landlord, either at common law or otherwise.

DEFINITIONS
"house": s.207.
"lessee": s.621.
"owner": s.207.
"repair notice": ss.189, 190.

GENERAL NOTE
Even although the authority may take action under this Part, an owner will retain his rights for contractual breach by his lessee: subs. (1). Similarly, if the owner takes possession in order to comply (*cf.* s.196, above), this is without prejudice to action on a prior breach, *i.e.* if the breach is not waived by the owner utilising his powers to do the works in default himself: subs. (2). Finally, action taken under this Part does not prejudice the tenant's remedies against his landlord.

Thus, even though an authority cannot include works of internal repair in a s.190 notice, a landlord under a repairing obligation to his tenant which includes the works the subject of that notice will still be under a duty to the tenant to make good the internal decorations, or liable for damages in lieu: see *McGreal* v. *Wake* (1984) 13 H.L.R. 107, C.A.; see also *Bradley* v. *Chorley Borough Council* (1985) 17 H.L.R. 305, C.A.

Effect of approved proposals for re-development

204. Where the local housing authority have under section 308 (owner's re-development proposals) approved proposals for the re-development of land, no action shall be taken in relation to the land under this Part if and so long as the re-development is being proceeded with in accordance with the proposals and within the time limits specified by the authority, subject to any variation or extension approved by the authority.

DEFINITIONS
"local housing authority": ss.1, 2.
"owner": s.207.

GENERAL NOTE
Section 308 permits an owner to put forward "re-development proposals", during the course of which no action is to be taken under this Part.

Supplementary provisions

Application of provisions to parts of buildings and temporary or movable structures

205. The local housing authority may take the like proceedings under this Part in relation to—
 (*a*) any part of a building which is used, or is suitable for use as, a dwelling, or
 (*b*) a hut, tent, caravan or other temporary or movable structure which is used for human habitation and has been in the same enclosure for a period of two years next before action is taken,
as they are empowered to take in relation to a house.

DEFINITIONS
"house": s.207.
"local housing authority": ss.1, 2.

GENERAL NOTE
See notes to s.189, above.

Repair at reasonable expense

206. In determining for the purposes of this Part whether premises can be rendered fit for human habitation at a reasonable expense, regard shall be had to the estimated cost of the works necessary to render them so fit and the value which it is estimated they will have when the works are completed.

DEFINITION
"fit for human habitation": s.604.

GENERAL NOTE
In the notes to s.189, above, this was described as one of the "key" issues. Under s.189, a repair notice can only be served to render premises fit for human habitation if the works can be carried out at a reasonable expense; there is no such express requirement in relation to s.190, but the same considerations are considered "relevant" when reaching a decision as to whether or not to serve a repairs notice under that section: see *Hillbank Properties Ltd.* v. *Hackney London Borough Council* [1978] Q.B. 998, 3 H.L.R. 73, C.A., *Kenny* v. *Kingston Upon Thames Royal London Borough Council* (1985) 17 H.L.R. 344, C.A., see notes to s.190, above. If action cannot be taken under this Part, and the premises are unfit for human habitation, action has to follow under Part IX, below, leading commonly to the loss of the property as rented accommodation.
 This section does not purport exhaustively to define reasonable expense, so that valuation is not necessarily conclusive (see *per* Megaw L.J., in *Inworth* v. *Southwark London Borough Council* (1977) 3 H.L.R. 67, 76 L.G.R. 263, C.A.), but there is no doubt that this is the

single element in the formulation which has received the greatest attention, and that it is the principal criterion (*Kimsey* v. *London Borough of Barnet* (1976) 3 H.L.R. 45, C.A.), which will only be displaced by other factors in cases of doubt: *Inworth*. (But this would seem to be less true in the case of a notice under s.190: see further, note on *Kenny*, below.)

Where a court has regard to the financial position of an owner (*e.g.* an owner-occupier), which will usually be irrelevant in the case of tenanted property, it is entitled to "tear off" the "corporate veil" of a one-house company, and investigate its true financial strength: *Hillbank Properties Ltd.* v. *Hackney London Borough Council* [1978] Q.B. 998, 3 H.L.R. 73, C.A.

Provided it is clear that a judge has taken everything relevant into account, he is not bound to set out his arithmetical reasoning: *Dudlow Estates Ltd.* v. *Sefton Metropolitan Borough Council* (1978) 3 H.L.R. 91, C.A. Valuation will be as at the date of a court hearing, *i.e.* on appeal under s.191, above, *not* as at the date of service of the notice under ss.189, 190: *Leslie Maurice & Co. Ltd.* v. *Willesden Corporation* [1953] 2 Q.B. 1, 3 H.L.R. 12, C.A.

The Court of Appeal can only intervene on an error of law: *Victoria Square Property Co. Ltd.* v. *Southwark London Borough Council* [1978] 1 W.L.R. 463, *Dudlow Estates*, *Bacon* v. *Grimsby Corporation* [1950] 1 K.B. 272, 3 H.L.R. 1, C.A., *Kimsey* v. *London Borough of Barnet* (1976) 3 H.L.R. 45, C.A. *Ellis Copp & Co. Ltd.* v. *Richmond Upon Thames London Borough Council* (1976) 3 H.L.R. 55, C.A., *F.F.F. Estates* v. *London Borough of Hackney* [1981] Q.B. 503, 3 H.L.R. 107, C.A., *Phillips* v. *London Borough of Newham* (1981) 3 H.L.R. 136, C.A.

The following seems the appropriate approach to valuation based on the decisions of the courts:

(1) The cost of the works needed to render the house fit, or remedy the disrepair or interference with comfort, should be calculated. A notice under ss.189 or 190 will not be rendered invalid because there have been no detailed prior estimates: *Bacon* v. *Grimsby Corporation* [1950] 1 K.B. 272, 3 H.L.R. 1, C.A.; see also *Hillbank Properties* v. *Hackney London Borough Council* [1978] Q.B. 998, 3 H.L.R. 73, C.A., and *Johnson* v. *Leicester Corporation* [1934] 1 K.B. 638.

The cost will be of the works specified in the notice, but it should be recognised that other works may be "opened up" during the execution of the specified works, that there will be redecorating costs (*cf.* notes to s.203, above), and that rental income may be lost and interest payable on capital: *Ellis Copp* v. *Richmond Upon Thames London Borough Council* (1976) 3 H.L.R. 55, C.A. See also *Kimsey* v. *London Borough of Barnet* (1976) 3 H.L.R. 45, C.A., and *F.F.F. Estates Ltd.* v. *Hackney London Borough Council* [1981] Q.B. 503, 3 H.L.R. 107, C.A.

However, against the cost of interest may be set the increased rental: *Ellis Copp*. In the case of a Rent Act protected or statutory tenant (see notes to s.622, below), this may mean that the landlord is entitled to a rent re-registration at an earlier time than hitherto, covering not only the new works but any other even unrelated reasons for an increase: *London Housing and Commercial Properties Ltd.* v. *Cowan* [1977] Q.B. 148, D.C.

In addition, and of considerable importance, grant-aid under Part XV, below, is to be deducted, bearing in mind that a *mandatory* repairs grant will be available (see s.494, below): *Harrington* v. *Croydon Corporation* [1968] 1 Q.B. 856, 3 H.L.R. 24, C.A., *Kenny* v. *Kingston Upon Thames Royal London Borough Council* (1983) 17 H.L.R. 344, C.A. If the alternative is demolition, then from the works cost can be deducted the cost of demolition: *Dudlow* v. *Sefton Metropolitan Borough Council* (1978) 3 H.L.R. 91, C.A.

(2) To the cost of the works should be added the value of the house *unrepaired*. In *Kimsey* v. *London Borough of Barnet* (1976) 3 H.L.R. 45, C.A., the Court of Appeal suggested that *no* value should be attached to the house unrepaired, because there could be no continuing expectation of its use as a house *unless* repaired. This, clearly, is inapplicable under s.190, and in other cases on this subject *some* value has been attached to the house even unrepaired—see, *e.g.*, *Ellis Copp & Co. Ltd.* v. *Richmond Upon Thames London Borough Council* (1976) 3 H.L.R. 55, C.A., *Inworth* v. *London Borough of Southwark* (1977) 3 H.L.R. 67, 76 L.G.R. 263, C.A. A *nominal* value was applied, and approved by the Court of Appeal, in *Dudlow Estates Ltd.* v. *Sefton Metropolitan Borough Council* (1979) 3 H.L.R. 91, C.A.

(3) The total of works (as reduced) and value unrepaired are to be compared to the post-works value. Regardless of the interest of the person served, the property will be valued as a freehold property: *Bacon* v. *Grimsby Corporation* [1950] 1 K.B. 272, 3 H.L.R. 1, C.A., *Harrington* v. *Croydon Corporation* [1968] 1 Q.B. 856, 3 H.L.R. 24, C.A. The value is to be open-market, not investment: *Inworth Property Co. Ltd.* v. *London Borough of Southwark* (1977) 3 H.L.R. 67, 76 L.G.R. 263, C.A.

There is no fixed rule as to whether the open-market value of a freehold estate in the property is to be taken with vacant possession or not. The question is: what are the factors which will influence the minds of a willing vendor and a willing purchaser, approached realistically, of which the presence or otherwise of tenants will be one such factor, as will the extent of their security and the real likelihood of their remaining: see *Bacon* v. *Grimsby Corporation* [1950] 1 K.B. 272, 3 H.L.R. 1, C.A., *Hillbank Properties Ltd.* v. *Hackney London Borough Council* [1978] Q.B. 998, 3 H.L.R. 73, *Dudlow Estates* v. *Sefton Metropolitan Borough Council* (1978) 3 H.L.R. 91, C.A., *F.F.F. Estates Ltd.* v. *Hackney London Borough Council* [1981] Q.B. 503, 3 H.L.R. 107, *Phillips* v. *London Borough of Newham* (1981) 3 H.L.R. 136, C.A.

In *Hillbank,* Lord Denning M.R. inclined to the view that the value should always be vacant possession, on the ground that Parliament cannot have intended different treatment to depend on occupation. However, Geoffrey Lane L.J. thought that the open-market value would depend on the evidence before the court, *i.e.* as to the likelihood of vacant possession, and this was adopted in *Dudlow*—"all the factors which would influence the mind of the willing seller and the willing purchaser, and obviously the possibility of getting vacant possession and the strength of that possibility is one of such factors . . . "

In *F.F.F.*, Stephenson L.J. summarised the cases as agreeing "in requiring . . . a realistic approach to the value . . . as a saleable asset in the hands of the landlord when considering the reasonableness of the expense required to improve it and therefore, to have regard to the presence of tenants and their rights of continued occupation and the effect that they have on the market value . . . " Finally, in *Phillips*, the Court of Appeal, including Lord Denning M.R., preferred the approach of Geoffrey Lane L.J. in *Hillbank*, as summarised by Stephenson L.J., and Lord Denning M.R. accepted that he may have caused some difficulty with his decision in *Hillbank*. The approach of Geoffrey Lane L.J. was also adopted in *R.* v. *London Borough of Ealing, ex parte Richardson* (1982) 4 H.L.R. 125, C.A.

In *Kenny* v. *Kingston Upon Thames Royal London Borough Council* (1985) 17 H.L.R. 344, C.A., the "realistic value" as a "saleable asset in the hands of the landlord" test was similarly applied. It was held that in a case where there is a protected tenant there may be evidence as to whether or not the tenancy is likely to come to an end for one reason or another in the foreseeable future. If there is no evidence one way or another the court may conclude that the true value of the house is too uncertain for it to base any conclusion on it at all, or it may take the mean figure between the two extremes of "vacant possession" and "sitting tenant" value.

Kenny raised a number of other points; however, the notice was under what is now s.190, and it is unclear to what extent the same considerations could allow the mathematical calculation to be overriden in the case of a notice under s.189, above. It was held that as long as they are relevant to the issue, there is no limit to the matters to which the judge can have regard when considering an appeal. The means or financial position of the owner are among the relevant matters, although no point was made on this by the appellant in that case.

In addition, it was held relevant that if the repairs were not done the "house" and indeed the property as a whole would sink into greater disrepair to the point where it became unfit for human habitation so that a protected tenant could be evicted to the landlord's ultimate profit, and the undesirable social consequences of such a course of events. The fact that a property is unsafe or may become so while a tenant is still in occupation, if the repairs are not done, was held a valid consideration.

In *Kenny,* the cost of repairs was estimated at £20,400, but with grant-aid this would be reduced to £14,000 or £15,000, while the increase in value of the property would be £8,000 to £9,000. The cost of repairs accordingly greatly exceeded the increase in value, although the court took note that the value of the property repaired would still exceed the cost of repairs so that it would not be "one of those glaring cases where the excess of cost of repairs over the increase in value was so pronounced as to make it a case where it would be financial folly to incur the expenditure necessary to comply with the notice."

The county court took into account what it concluded was a deliberate policy of neglect by the owner, which would mean that the tenant and his family would have to live for a long period in deteriorating, and unsafe, conditions, and that this was socially undesirable. These policy considerations outweighed the difference between cost of compliance, and increase in value. The Court of Appeal upheld the decision: whether or not the policy considerations did outweigh the financial considerations was essentially a matter for the judge. The Court of Appeal also agreed that the judge had been correct to compare the cost of repairs to the value of the whole property (less a ground floor shop which could have been sold off separately), because the works affected not only the maisonette at which they were principally aimed, but other flats and common parts of the building.

Minor definitions

207. In this Part—

"house" includes any yard, garden, outhouses and appurtenances belonging to the house or usually enjoyed with it;

"occupying tenant" has the same meaning, in relation to a dwelling which consists of, or forms part of, the house concerned, as it has in Part VII (improvement notices);

"owner" in relation to premises—

    (*a*) means a person (other than a mortgagee not in possession) who is for the time being entitled to dispose of the fee simple in the premises, whether in possession or reversion, and

    (*b*) includes also a person holding or entitled to the rents and profits of the premises under a lease of which the unexpired term exceeds three years;

"person having control", in relation to premises, means the person who receives the rack-rent of the premises (that is to say, a rent which is not less than 2/3rds of the full net annual value of the premises), whether on his own account or as agent or trustee for another person, or who would so receive it if the house were let at such a rack-rent.

DEFINITION:
"lease": s.621.

GENERAL NOTE
"House": see notes to s.189, above.
"Occupying tenant": see notes to s.190, above.
"Owner": therefore, a freeholder, and a leaseholder whose lease has at least three years to run.

Person Having Control
This was also identified as a key definition in the notes to s.189, above. There are two possibilities, or limbs of the definition: when let at a rack-rent, and when not. The fact that there are statutory controls on rents will not affect whether what is charged is a rack-rent or not: rack-rent means "the full amount which a landlord can reasonably be expected to get from a tenant," having regard to rent restrictions—*Rawlance* v. *Croydon Corporation* [1952] 2 Q.B. 803, C.A. Whether or not premises are let at a rack-rent is to be determined to the value of the land at the time of *letting*, not (relevant) action: *London Corporation* v. *Cusack-Smith* [1955] A.C. 337, H.L.

The definition is similar to that in use in relation to the term "owner" in the Public Health Act 1936. *Kensington Borough Council* v. *Allen* (1926) 1 K.B. 576, was concerned with the Public Health Act definition, and was decided on the first limb, where the lessee of a house sublet at a rack-rent. The subtenant occupied a part of the house himself, but further sublet other parts of the house, and received more than a rack-rent therefrom. The lessee was served with notice, as the "owner." The court held that where there was in fact a letting at a rack-rent, "it is otiose to look further to see if there is somebody else who, in certain circumstances, might let the premises at a rack-rent."

Truman, Hanbury, Buxton & Co. Ltd. v. *Kerslake* (1894) 2 Q.B. 774, decided under the Public Health Acts, concerned the second limb: there were a lease and a sub-lease, both at rents less than rack-rents. The sub-lease was for the whole of the term of the lease, less a few days. It was held that the sub-lessee was the "owner" under the Public Health Acts, as the only person in a position to let the premises at, and receive, a rack-rent:

"His interest as assignee of that sub-lease gives him the power of so letting; and if the premises were so let, he is the person who would receive the rack-rent. He chooses, it is true, to occupy the premises himself: but we see nothing to prevent the same person being both occupier of the premises and 'owner' within the meaning of this section."

Truman was applied in *London Corporation* v. *Cusack-Smith* (1955) A.C. 337. In this case, the House of Lords considered the definition of "owner" under s.119, Town and Country Planning Act 1959, again in very similar terms:

"In this Act, except so far as . . . the context otherwise requires . . . 'owner', in relation to land, means . . . a person . . . who . . . is entitled to receive the rack-rent of the land or, where the land is not let at a rack-rent, would be so entitled if it were so let . . . "

A derelict site had been let on a long (75 year) lease at a rent of £750 per annum, which was less than a rack-rent. The freeholders nonetheless sought to serve a purchase notice on the local authority, as "owner." The House of Lords held unanimously that the question whether or not a rent is a rack-rent is to be determined according to the value of the land at the time of letting: the land does not cease to be a rack-rent when during the currency of a lease its value increases.

By a majority, it was also held that the freeholders were not the "owner," within s.119:

"The definition has two limbs, the first dealing with the case where a person is entitled to receive the rack-rent and the second with the case where the land is not let at a rack-rent. I do not find much difficulty about the first limb. There may be only one lease or there may be a chain of lease and subleases: if any one of the lessors is entitled to receive a rack-rent then the first limb of the definition applies, and if only one is entitled to receive a rack-rent than he and he alone is the 'owner' . . .

"The second limb of the definition appears to me to be more obscure. It must deal with two cases: the one where the land is not let at all, the freeholder being the occupier, and the other where the land is let but the rents payable by the tenant and the subtenant, if there is one, are not rack-rents. In each case it requires one to find a person who would be entitled to receive the rack-rent if the land were let at a rack-rent. In the case where the land is not let at all, this can only mean that one must suppose that there is in existence a lease by the freeholder to a hypothetical tenant under which the rent is a rack-rent.

"But where, as in the present case, the land is let but for less than a rack-rent the second limb is ambiguous. What has to be supposed is that the land is let at a rack-rent and one could suppose either that the rent of £750 under the existing lease was increased to what would have been a rack-rent at the date of that lease, or that the land was let by the appellants," ie the leaseholders, "to a new hypothetical tenant at what is now a rack-rent . . . The two would produce diametrically opposite results . . .

"The second limb of the definition must have the one meaning or the other: it cannot have both . . . I am of the opinion that the latter is the supposition which the definition requires to be made . . . One looks for the person who at the relevant date would be entitled to make a new lease at a rack-rent and supposes that he does so, and the only person entitled to make a new lease is the person in possession, in this case the appellants . . . In my judgment, a freeholder who lets at less than a rack-rent is excluded by the definition both in cases where his tenant does not sublet and in cases where he does sublet either at a rack-rent or at less than a rack-rent . . . "

Lords Tucker and Keith came to the same conclusions: under the alternative definition, there can be but one owner under the alternative limb, and that owner is the person who is actually in a position to grant a lease at a rack-rent.

Neither *Truman,* nor *Cusack-Smith,* was concerned with flats. The *Kensington* case was. In the course of judgment, Lord Hewart C.J. said: "It is true in a sense that if rent issues out of a part of the premises, it issues out of 'the premises'. It is another thing to say that because rent is received out of the premises, although only for some parts of them, it is the rack-rent of 'the premises' . . . (The subtenant) did not receive the rent of the premises, that is to say of this house: he received various subsidiary rents of various parts of these premises . . . "

Lord Hewart was followed by Branson J, who agreed with the judgment but added:

"I do not mean that if a sub-tenant let off the whole of the premises to separate tenants of his own and the rents he so received were in the sum the rents of the whole of the premises, that would not amount to a receipt by him of the rack-rent of the whole of the premises. My judgment is founded upon the fact that the mesne tenant in this case did not receive the rent of the whole of the premises, he having been in occupation of a part of them himself . . . "

In consequence, Lord Hewart added to his judgment: "In contemplating a tenant who was subletting or had sublet, I certainly was not speaking of a tenant who had sublet the whole. I was speaking of a sub-tenant who, although he had power to sublet the whole, had in fact sublet something less than the whole."

The question of a block of, or house converted into, flats was, then, left open; the first sentence quoted of Branson J. read in isolation would seem to tackle the issue, although leaving obscure whether or not he had in mind a case in which the landlord still retained the common parts; taken together with the second sentence, however, not only was the first sentence clearly *obiter,* but seems rather to have been no more than illustration of what he was *not* deciding; the addition by Lord Hewart C.J., similarly, left the issue open, rather than decided the point, and suggests that what was in mind was a subletting of the whole of the premises.

Flats fell to be considered in detail in *Pollway Nominees Ltd.* v. *London Borough of Croydon* (1985) 17 H.L.R. 503, C.A. It concerned the issue of central practical application, of the operation of the definition of "person having control" in relation to a block of—or any other property let out in—flats, on long leases at low rents.

The respondents were the freehold owners of a block of 42 flats. 32 of them were let out on individual, 99 year leases, and 10 were demised on a block lease of the same length. Under the terms of the lease, the respondents remained in possession of the whole structure, internal and external, of the building. The total ground rent receivable was substantially less than two-thirds of the full net annual value. The respondents also received service charges. The local authority served on the respondents a notice under what is now s.189, above, requiring works to the roof of the block. The respondents contended that they were not the person having control of the house. They issued an originating summons for declarations to this effect.

Harman J. in the Chancery Division ((1984) 14 H.L.R. 41) upheld the respondents' contention. As the property had already been let at rents totalling less than two-thirds of the full net annual value, it could not be deemed to be lettable again by the freeholders. The local authority appealed. It was assumed for the purposes of the appeal that a block of purpose-built flats can properly as a whole be considered a single house (*cf.* notes to s.189, above).

The Court of Appeal upheld the decision of Harman J. If a house is let at a rack-rent then the only inquiry is who is in receipt of that rent; where the house is let in flats, under which less than a rack-rent is paid, one has to look at the alternative formulation in this section, and find who, if the whole house was let at a rack-rent, would be in receipt of that rent.

In determining this question, a rack-rent paid by the occupying tenant is in contemplation; the existing outstanding terms under the leases are to be taken into account; in no circumstances were the respondents capable of granting a lease of the block to an occupying tenant at a rack-rent and they could not, accordingly, be the person having control. It follows that in some circumstances there may accordingly be no one person having control.

The implication of the decision seems to be that a notice may have to be addressed to and served on *all* the persons with control of each of the individual flats, *i.e.* the freeholders so far as tenanted flats are concerned, the individual leaseholders on long leases, as it were collectively constituting the person having control; the alternative implication is that no one has control.

Index of defined expressions: Part VI

208. The following Table shows provisions defining or otherwise explaining expressions used in this Part (other than provisions defining or explaining an expression used in the same section or paragraph):—

district (of a local housing authority)	section 2(1)
fit for human habitation	section 604
house	sections 205 and 207
lease, lessee and lessor	section 621
local housing authority	section 1, 2(2)
occupying tenant	sections 207, 236(2)
owner	section 207
person having control	section 207
reasonable expense (in relation to repair)	section 206
repair notice	sections 189 and 190
standard scale (in reference to the maximum fine on summary conviction)	section 622
unfit for human habitation	section 604

PART VII

IMPROVEMENT NOTICES

Improvement notices

General conditions for service of improvement notice

209. The general conditions for service of an improvement notice in respect of a dwelling are that the dwelling—

(*a*) is without one or more of the standard amenities (whether or not it is also in a state of disrepair),

(*b*) is capable at reasonable expense of improvement to the full standard or, failing that, to the reduced standard, and

(*c*) was provided (by erection or by the conversion or a building already in existence) before 3rd October 1961.

DEFINITIONS

"dwelling": s.237.
"full standard": s.234.
"improvement": s.237.
"improvement notice": s.216.
"reduced standard": s.234.
"standard amenities": s.508.

GENERAL NOTE

"Compulsory improvement" was introduced by Part II, Housing Act 1964, and was most recently contained in Part VIII, Housing Act 1974. It is, of course, the provisions of the latter which are here reproduced.

It is attractive to see compulsory improvement brought back into such prominence by this relatively early location of the provisions, and logically located given the layout of the Act; that said, this Part is extensively dependent on (a) Part XV, below, *i.e.* housing improvement grants, and (b) to a lesser but still significant extent Part VIII, area improvement. It is accordingly difficult to understand at this stage, without extensive forward reference: the alternative, of locating the substantive material to be found in those Parts in the notes to this, and then referring back, would be unrealistic given the relative uses in practice. (See, particularly, s.227 below, entitling a person subject to these powers to serve a counter-notice requiring purchase of the property: a strong disincentive to use of the powers at all.)

Furthermore, the recent Green Paper, Home Improvement—A New Approach, Cmnd. 9513, May 1985, suggests that the provisions of this Part may not be with us much longer: "Apart from housing below the fitness standard, compulsory improvement powers against private housing (other than H.M.O.s) are not justified except where a nuisance is being caused to neighbouring property or to passers-by . . . " (para. 74).

Dwelling

Compulsory improvement is concerned with "dwellings," defined in s.237 to mean "a building or part of a building occupied or intended to be occupied as a separate dwelling, together with any yard, garden, outhouses and appurtenances belonging to it or usually enjoyed with it." As to "separate dwelling," see notes to s.79, above, and to s.460, below. As to appurtenances, see notes to s.56, above.

"Dwelling" was recently considered, in the context of "housing accommodation" for the purposes of Part VIII, below, in *R.* v. *Camden London Borough Council, ex parte Comyn Ching & Co. (London) Ltd.* [1984] J.P.L. 661, Q.B.D. The question is to be answered by asking whether occupation as a dwelling is intended by the person in control of the property as at the date when the issue arises (in this case, service of a provisional notice under ss.210 or 213, below).

Accordingly, buildings constructed as housing, but used for warehousing, *might* not be dwellings at the relevant date, even though it was the authority's intention that they should subsequently be used as a such. If property was already occupied as housing, then there is no difficulty determining whether or not it constitutes a dwelling; otherwise, it is largely a question of fact. Planning use might be some indication of the use to which it is intended to put a property, but no more than an indication.

Standard Amenities

The "standard amenities" are, by virtue of s.237, below, as defined in s.508, below: fixed bath or shower, hot and cold water supply at fixed bath or shower, wash-hand basin, hot and cold water supply at wash-hand basin, sink, hot and cold water supply at sink, water closet. It has been held that standard amenities in this Part mean standard amenities for the *exclusive* use of the occupiers of the dwelling in question, as distinct from shared amenities: see *F.F.F. Estates Ltd.* v. *Hackney London Borough Council* [1981] Q.B. 503, 3 H.L.R. 107, C.A.

Reasonable Expense?

"Reasonable expense" is not defined in this Part (*cf.* s.206, above). Although the cases noted to s.206 would nonetheless seem to be relevant, bearing especially in mind that some of them were decided under what is now s.190, above, where, as here, the express criterion of s.206 was not applied, it may be noted that under the 1964 Act (above), express regard was required, in an appeal against an improvement notice, "to the estimated cost of the works and the value which it is estimated that the dwelling or other premises will have when the works are completed" (s.27(2)(a)), and it may fairly be said that as Parliament did not reproduce this requirement in the 1974 Act (see s.91 thereof, see now s.217, below), the same criteria should not be too quickly applied.

In *F.F.F. Estates Ltd.* v. *Hackney London Borough Council* [1981] Q.B. 503, 3 H.L.R. 107, C.A., however, the Court of Appeal was clearly aware of the distinction, for reference was made to *Harrington* v. *Croydon Corporation* [1968] 1 Q.B. 856, 3 H.L.R. 24, C.A., which applied the 1964 Act criterion; reliance was, nonetheless, placed on *Hillbank Properties Ltd. Hackney London Borough Council* [1978] Q.B. 998, 3 H.L.R. 73, C.A., in which it was considered by Geoffrey Lane L.J. (as he then was) that the omission from what is now s.190, above, of the reference to reasonable expense under what is now s.206, above, was attributable to the fact that s.190 was added (as s.9(1A)) to the Housing Act 1957, as "an afterthought".

This was taken in *F.F.F.* as sufficient authority to include the same criteria as under s.206: "There is no fetter (apart from admissibility and relevance) upon those matters which the local authority or the judge can take into account. The estimated cost of the required repairs compared with the value of the premises is obviously an important consideration . . . " The costs of decorating, and financing the improvement works, together with professional fees, are to be included: *ibid.* In *Harrington*, however, it was held that grant-aid should be deducted from the assessment of cost, and that will clearly remain correct. See, further, notes to s.206, above.

Improvement

"Improvement" includes "alteration and enlargement and, so far as also necessary to enable a dwelling to reach the full standard or the reduced standard, repair": s.237, below. Accordingly, the common law distinction between improvement and repair is of much less importance in this Part than elsewhere: see notes to s.471, below. It is thought that, if needed in order to reach the required standard (below), an extension can be required under this terminology—*Harrington* v. *Croydon Corporation* [1968] 1 Q.B. 856, 3 H.L.R. 24, C.A.

Full and Reduced Standard

"Full standard" means that the dwelling will be provided with all the standard amenities, for the exclusive use of its occupants, is in reasonable repair (disregarding internal decorative repair), having regard to age, character and locality (see also notes to s.190, above), that it conforms with the Secretary of State's requirements for thermal insulation (see D.O.E. Circular 11/82, Appendix E, para. 2), is in all other respects fit for human habitation within the meaning of s.604, below, and is likely to be available for use as a dwelling for a period of 15 years or such other period as may be specified by the Secretary of State for this purpose: s.234(1), below.

"Reduced standard" is the full standard as reduced by the authority, under its discretion in s.234(2), below, to "dispense wholly or in part with any of the conditions in subsection (1)," subject, however, to this qualification: the authority cannot dispense with the standard amenities' requirement if the property is a house in multiple occupation in relation to which the authority could serve notice under s.352, below (see notes thereto): s.234(3).

A class of "public" or "quasi-public" owner is exempt from these provisions altogether: see s.232, below.

Service of provisional notice: dwellings in general improvement area or housing action area

210.—(1) The local housing authority may serve a provisional notice on the person having control of a dwelling in—

(*a*) a general improvement area, or

(*b*) a housing action area,

if it appears to the authority that the general conditions for service of an improvement notice are met, but subject to subsection (2) if the dwelling is owner-occupied.

(2) The authority may only serve a provisional notice in respect of a dwelling which is owner-occupied if it appears to them that the circumstances are such that it is not reasonably practicable for another dwelling—

(*a*) which is in the same building as, or is adjacent to, the owner-occupied dwelling, and

(*b*) which is not owner-occupied or in respect of which an application for an improvement grant, intermediate grant, special grant or repairs grant has been approved,

to be improved to the full standard or, as the case may be, to the reduced standard without affecting the improvement to one of those standards of the owner-occupied dwelling.

DEFINITIONS
"dwelling": s.237.
"full standard": s.234.
"general conditions for service": s.209.
"general improvement area": s.253.
"housing action area": s.239.
"improvement": s.237.
"improvement grant": s.467.
"improvement notice": s.216.
"intermediate grant": s.474.
"local housing authority": ss.1, 2.
"owner-occupied": s.237.
"person having control": s.236.
"provisional notice": s.213.
"reduced standard": s.234.
"repairs grant": s.491.
"special grant": s.483.

GENERAL NOTE
The first class of action the authority may take is in respect of dwellings in a housing action area ("H.A.A.") and a general improvement area ("G.I.A.")—see Part VIII, below. The initatory step of serving a "provisional notice" under this section is available to the authority, of their own motion (*cf.* s.212, below), *save* if the dwelling is "owner-occupied": subs. (1). If the dwelling *is* owner-occupied, then no provisional notice may be served, unless the provisions of subs. (2) are fulfilled.

For the purposes of this Part, an owner-occupier is the owner, *i.e.* freeholder (see definition of "owner" in s.237, below), or leaseholder under a long tenancy (which is defined in s.237 by cross-reference to the Leasehold Reform Act 1967, s.3), and under which the freeholder or leaseholder occupies or is entitled to occupy: s.237, below. Section 3 of the 1967 Act defines "long tenancy" as a lease for a term certain exceeding 21 years, excluding specified leases terminable by notice after death or marriage, and with additional provision for renewable shorter leases, shorter leases succeeding long leases, leases as extended under Part 1, Landlord and Tenant Act 1954. Note that the lease runs from *when* it is actually granted, not an earlier date that might be entered in it: *Roberts* v. *Church Commissioners for England* [1972] 1 Q.B. 278, C.A. See, further, notes to s.115, above.

To serve a provisional notice at all under this section, the "general conditions" for service set out in s.209, above, must be applicable. To serve a notice on an owner-occupier, the conditions of subs. (2) must be fulfilled, *i.e.* the property must be adjacent to, or in the same building as, another property which it is not reasonably practicable to improve to either the full or reduced standard (see notes to s.209, above) without improving those standards in the owner-occupied dwelling, *and* either (i) that dwelling is itself *not* owner-occupied, or (ii) one of the range of main Part XV grants has been approved in respect of it—see Part XV, below. As to service generally see notes to s.617 below.

In any event, the person to be served is the "person having control" of the dwelling, defined in s.236 in the following ways:

(1) If owner-occupied, the owner-occupier;

(2) If there is an "occupying tenant" (also defined in s.236, but see notes to s.212, below), who is employed in agriculture and who occupies the dwelling as part of the terms of his employment, his employer or other person by whose authority he so occupies; or

(3) In any other case, the person who is the owner, *i.e.* freeholder, or long leaseholder (each as defined in s.237, and see note above), whose interest is not in reversion on that of another person with a long tenancy, *i.e.* one stops at the first person with a long lease.

A provisional notice is defined in s.213, below. There is no appeal against it, but if the person served does not wish to offer an undertaking under s.211, below, the authority will serve a full improvement notice under s.214, appeal against which lies under s.217, below. On non-compliance with an effective improvement notice, the authority enjoy power to carry out works in default under s.220, with the right to recover their expenses under Sched. 10, below.

The principal reasons why these powers are not much used is because the person served has the right to serve a notice on the authority requiring them to purchase the property, under s.227, below, and otherwise to require a loan from the authority with which to comply, under s.228, below. Note also that some of the conditions normally applicable to intermediate grants under s.474, below, are disapplied if in order to execute works under an improvement notice (or undertaking): see s.477, below.

Section 233 governs the continuation of powers should a dwelling cease to be in an H.A.A. or G.I.A. during the course of proceedings under this Part.

A class of "public" or "quasi-public" owner is exempt from these provisions altogether: see s.232, below.

Acceptance of undertaking to do works

211.—(1) In any case where an improvement notice has not yet been served in respect of a dwelling falling within section 210 (certain dwellings in general improvement areas or housing action areas), the local housing authority may accept an undertaking from—

(*a*) the person having control of the dwelling, or

(*b*) any other person having an estate or interest in the dwelling,

to improve the dwelling to the full standard or, if in the opinion of the authority it is not practicable at reasonable expense for the dwelling to be improved to the full standard, to the reduced standard.

(2) The undertaking shall be in writing and shall specify the works agreed to be carried out and the period, being a period ending not more than nine months after the date on which the undertaking is accepted, within which the works are to be carried out.

(3) Before accepting an undertaking, the authority shall satisfy themselves that, if there is an occupying tenant—

(*a*) the housing arrangements are satisfactory or none are required, and

(*b*) the undertaking incorporates the written consent of the occupying tenant signed by him to the carrying out of the works specified in the undertaking,

and that the person giving the undertaking has a right to carry out the works specified in the undertaking as against all other persons having an estate or interest in the dwelling.

(4) Where the authority accept an undertaking, they shall serve a notice to that effect on the person by whom the undertaking was given and shall not thereafter serve an improvement notice with respect to that dwelling unless—

(*a*) the works specified in the undertaking are not carried out within the period so specified or such longer period as the authority may in writing allow, or

(*b*) the authority are satisfied that, owing to a change of circumstances since the undertaking was accepted by them, the undertaking is unlikely to be fulfilled.

(5) An authority who have accepted an undertaking may discharge it by serving notice of the discharge on the person by whom the undertaking was given, and they shall do so if at any time they consider that the general conditions for service of an improvement notice in respect of the dwelling are no longer met.

(6) Where an authority serve a notice under subsection (4) or (5) on the person by whom an undertaking was given, they shall at the same time serve a copy of the notice on the person (if any) who is the occupying tenant of the dwelling at that time and on every other person who, to the

knowledge of the authority, is an owner, lessee or mortgagee of the dwelling.

DEFINITIONS
  "dwelling": s.237.
  "full standard": s.234.
  "general conditions for service": s.209.
  "general improvement area": s.253.
  "housing action area": s.239.
  "housing arrangements": s.235.
  "improvement": s.237.
  "improvement notice": s.216.
  "local housing authority": ss.1, 2.
  "occupying tenant": s.236.
  "person having control": s.236.
  "reduced standard": s.234.

GENERAL NOTE
  Following from the last section, if a person served with the provisional notice, *i.e.* the person having control of the dwelling as defined in s.236, below (see notes to s.210, above), *or* someone else with an estate or interest in it, wishes to improve, the authority may accept an undertaking from him, to improve to either full or reduced standard (see notes to s.209, above). The authority's discretion to accept a reduced standard is only exercisable if the full standard cannot be achieved at a reasonable expense: see s.209, above.
  The undertaking has to be in writing, and identify both the works to be carried out, and the time for their completion (not more than nine months): subs. (2). The *effect* of the undertaking is to prevent the service of a full improvement notice under s.214, below, unless the conditions of subs. (4) are fulfilled, *i.e.* non-compliance within time allowed or as in writing extended, or likely non-compliance. The authority may, however, discharge the undertaking at any time, and must do so if the general conditions in s.209 are no longer applicable, *e.g.* because an increase in costs means that the works can no longer be carried out at a reasonable expense: subs. (5). At the request and expense of the person giving the undertaking, the authority can carry out the works on his behalf: s.225, below.
  Before accepting an undertaking, however, the authority have to satisfy themselves (a) that the person offering the undertaking has the right to do the works as against all others with an estate or interest in the dwelling, and (b) as to the arrangements for, and consent of, an "occupying tenant": subs. (3). An occupying tenant is defined in s.236 as someone other than an owner-occupier (see notes to s.210, above), who:
  (1) Occupies or is entitled to occupy under a lease or tenancy; or
  (2) Is a statutory tenant of the dwelling, *i.e.* under the Rent Act 1977 or the Rent (Agriculture) Act 1976, see notes to s.622, below; or
  (3) Occupies under a restricted contract within s.19, Rent Act 1977—see notes to s.622, below; or
  (4) Is employed in agriculture and occupies as part of his terms of employment.
  "Housing arrangements" means (s.235, below) arrangements for the occupying tenant and his household, either during, or after, or both during and after works, and includes any incidental or ancillary matters, *e.g.* furniture storage, removal costs, costs of alternative accommodation, etc. The arrangements must be in writing, and signed by the occupying tenant, and either the landlord or the local authority or both must be a party to them: *ibid.*
  "In most cases the tenant concerned will probably be temporarily rehoused, either by the local authority or the landlord, while works are being carried out, and will return to his original home after it has been improved. But the housing arrangements could provide for the tenant to move permanently into another property in the landlord's ownership, or into local authority housing. The situation could also be covered in which, although the tenant returns to his original home, the improvement works would have altered the dwelling in such a way that a legal change of identity has occurred and a new tenancy is necessary . . .
  "The written agreement containing the housing arrangements will give the tenant the power of recourse to an action in the courts for breach of contract if the landlord or the local authority fail to fulfil the terms . . . if, for example, the landlord does not allow the tenant to return . . . " (D.O.E. Circular 21/80, App. E, paras 4, 6).
  If the tenant is permanently displaced, *e.g.* because the installation of standard amenities will reduce the property to a size at which he could no longer satisfactorily occupy, he will normally be entitled to home loss payment and/or disturbance payment, and to rehousing, under ss.29–39, Land Compensation Act 1973.

If a Rent Act 1977 statutory tenant (see notes to s.622, below) is not willing to allow the works to be carried out, and either the authority issue a certificate stating that if application is made by the landlord for an improvement or intermediate grant under s.467 or s.474, below, it is likely to be approved, or application for such has been made and approved, the landlord may be able to obtain a court order requiring the tenant to permit execution of the works, under s.116, Rent Act 1977. The court will, however, consider all the circumstances, including disadvantage to the tenant, his age and health, and his housing arrangements during the works: *ibid*.

Note also that some of the conditions normally applicable to intermediate grants under s.474, below, are disapplied if in order to execute works under an improvement notice (or undertaking): see s.477, below. The rights of entry of the person having control are as set out in s.224, below.

If no undertaking is offered, the authority may serve a full improvement notice under s.214, appeal against which lies under s.217, below. On non-compliance with an effective improvement notice, the authority enjoy power to carry out works in default under s.220, with the right to recover their expenses under Sched. 10, below. The occupying tenant will be aware of developments, because he must be served with the provisional notice, by s.213, below.

A class of "public" or "quasi-public" owner is exempt from these provisions altogether: see s.232, below.

Service of provisional notice: other dwellings

212.—(1) An occupying tenant of a dwelling which—

(a) is not in a general improvement area or housing action area, and

(b) is without one or more of the standard amenities (whether or not it is also in a state of disrepair), and

(c) was provided (by erection or by the conversion of a building already in existence) before 3rd October 1961,

may make representations in writing to the local housing authority with a view to the exercise by the authority of their powers under this section.

(2) The authority shall notify the person having control of the dwelling of any such representations made to them.

(3) If on taking the representations into consideration the authority are satisfied that—

(a) the person making the representations is an occupying tenant of the dwelling in question,

(b) the general conditions for service of an improvement notice are met, and

(c) the dwelling ought to be improved to the full standard or, as the case may be, to the reduced standard and is unlikely to be so improved unless they exercise their powers under this section,

they shall either serve a provisional notice on the person having control of the dwelling or notify the occupying tenant of their decision not to do so and give him a written statement of their reasons for that decision.

(4) The authority may serve a provisional notice under this section and take any further steps authorised under the following provisions of this Part notwithstanding that—

(a) the occupying tenant quits the dwelling, or

(b) the authority pass a resolution declaring an area in which the dwelling is situated to be a general improvement area or housing action area.

Definitions
"dwelling": s.237.
"full standard": s.234.
"general conditions for service": s.209.
"general improvement area": s.253.
"housing action area": s.239.
"improvement": s.237.

"local housing authority": ss.1, 2.
"occupying tenant": s.236.
"person having control": s.236.
"provisional notice": s.213.
"reduced standard": s.234.
"standard amenities": s.508.

GENERAL NOTE

This section deals with provisional notices *outside* H.A.A.s and G.I.A.s (*cf.* s.210, above) (but continues to govern if subsequent to service an area is declared, *or* if the occupying tenant quits: see subs. (4)). Apart from the "area condition" (subs. (1)(*a*)), the conditions for service are (subs. (1)(*b*)(*c*)) the same as under s.209, above, *save* that there is no express reference to reasonable expense: *cf.* notes to s.209, above. The absence is because (a) the authority have to be satisfied of this in any event, under subs. (3)(*b*), and (b) inability to execute at a reasonable expense is a ground for appeal under s.217, below. As to service generally se notes to s.617 below.

The procedure starts with a representation *in writing* by an occupying tenant (as to which, see notes to s.211, above): subs. (1). The authority must notify the person having control (as to which, see notes to s.210, above) of its receipt: subs. (2). The conditions for service are set out in subs. (3): (a) the person making the representation *is* an occupying tenant, and (b) the general conditions of s.209 are met, and (c) the dwelling ought to be improved to either the full or reduced standard (as to which, see notes to s.209, above) and (d) is unlikely to be unless these powers are exercised.

But even if wholly satisfied of all these features, the authority retain an absolute discretion not to serve a notice: subs. (3). If they decide not to proceed, they must give the tenant a statement in writing of their reasons; this, however, only applies once satisfied of the relevant features, *i.e.* it is inapplicable if one of the conditions is not met.

There is no provision for undertakings analogous to that under s.211, above. The provisional notice itself is, however, the same as that which will be served in an H.A.A. or G.I.A.: see s.213, below.

A class of "public" or "quasi-public" owner is exempt from these provisions altogether: see s.232, below.

Provisional notice: contents and matters arising

213.—(1) A provisional notice is a notice—

(*a*) specifying the works which in the opinion of the local housing authority are required for the dwelling to be improved to the full standard or, as the case may be, to the reduced standard, and

(*b*) stating a date, not less than 21 days after the service of the notice, and time and place at which the authority's proposals for the carrying out of the works, any alternative proposals, any proposed housing arrangements, the views and interests of any occupying tenant and any other matters may be discussed.

(2) The authority shall, not less than 21 days before the date so stated, in addition to serving the notice on the person having control of the dwelling, serve a copy of the notice on—

(*a*) any occupying tenant of the dwelling, and

(*b*) every other person who to the knowledge of the authority is an owner, lessee or mortgagee of the dwelling.

(3) The person having control of the dwelling, any occupying tenant and every other person who is an owner, lessee or mortgagee of the dwelling are entitled to be heard when the authority's proposals are discussed in accordance with the notice.

(4) After the service of a provisional notice and before taking any other action under the following provisions of this Part, the authority shall take into consideration all representations made on or before the occasion when their proposals with respect to the dwelling are discussed in accordance with the notice, and in particular any representations with respect to the nature of the works proposed by them for improving the dwelling or with respect to any proposed housing arrangements.

DEFINITIONS
"dwelling": s.237.
"full standard": s.234.
"housing arrangements": s.235.
"improvement": s.237.
"local housing authority" ss.1, 2.
"occupying tenant": s.236.
"owner": s.237.
"person having control": s.236.
"reduced standard": s.234.

GENERAL NOTE
This section governs the content of a provisional notice, under either s.210 or s.212, above. Like a slum clearance notice under Part IX, below, it operates by way of a "time-and-place notice" (*cf.* s.264, below), not less than 21 days after the provisional notice is served: subs. (1)(*b*). The provisional notice must specify the works required to improve the dwelling to either the full or the reduced standard (as to which, see notes to s.209, above): subs. (1)(*a*). The actual works should be specified, not merely their *effect*: *cf. Canterbury City Council* v. *Bern* [1981] J.P.L. 749, D.C.

The purpose of the time-and-place meeting is to consider housing arrangements (see notes to s.211, above), the authority's works proposals, any alternative proposals, *and* the views of the occupying tenant (as to whom, see notes to s.211, above).

The occupying tenant must be served, if not at the same time as the person having control, then no less than 21 days before the meeting (subs. (2)(*a*)); so also must be any owner, lessee or mortgagee (subs. (2)(*b*)). Owner means freeholder (other than a mortgagee): s.237, below. If not served with a copy, anyone else who has an estate or interest in the dwelling is also entitled to require a copy: s.226, below. The person having control (see notes to s.210, above), and all of those required to be served—including the occupying tenant—are entitled to be heard at the meeting, and their views and proposals taken into account: subss. (3), (4).

Service of improvement notice: dwellings in general improvement area or housing action area

214.—(1) If a local housing authority have served a provisional notice in respect of a dwelling under section 210(1) (dwellings in general improvement area or housing action area) and—

(*a*) no undertaking has yet been accepted in respect of the dwelling under section 211, or

(*b*) such an undertaking has been accepted but the case falls within subsection (4)(*a*) or (*b*) of that section (undertaking not carried out within allotted period or unlikely to be fulfilled),

the authority may, subject to the following provisions of this section, serve an improvement notice on the person having control of the dwelling.

(2) Before serving an improvement notice under this section the authority shall satisfy themselves—

(*a*) that the dwelling continues to be in a general improvement area or a housing action area,

(*b*) that the general conditions for service of an improvement notice in respect of the dwelling are still met,

(*c*) that the dwelling is not for the time being owner-occupied or that the circumstances specified in section 210(2) apply or still apply in relation to it (circumstances in which provisional order may be served in respect of owner-occupied dwelling), and

(*d*) that, if there is an occupying tenant, the housing arrangements are satisfactory or none are required or the tenant has unreasonably refused to enter into any such arrangements.

(3) An improvement notice may not be served—

(*a*) by virtue of subsection (1)(*a*) (no undertaking accepted) more than nine months after the service of the provisional notice, or

(*b*) by virtue of subsection (1)(*b*)(undertaking not fulfilled) more than six months after the expiry of the period specified in the undertaking, or such longer period as has been duly allowed by the authority, for the completion of the works.

(4) Where an authority serve an improvement notice under this section on the person having control of a dwelling, they shall at the time serve a copy of the notice on any occupying tenant of the dwelling and on every other person who, to the knowledge of the authority, is an owner, lessee or mortgagee of the dwelling.

(5) An improvement notice served under this section is a local land charge.

DEFINITIONS
"dwelling": s.237.
"general conditions for service": s.209.
"general improvement area": s.253.
"housing action area": s.239.
"housing arrangements": s.235.
"improvement": s.237.
"improvement notice": s.216.
"local housing authority" ss.1, 2.
"occupying tenant": s.236.
"owner-occupied": s.237.
"person having control": s.236.
"provisional notice": s.213.

GENERAL NOTE
The improvement notice which will result from a provisional notice which relates to a dwelling in an H.A.A. or G.I.A. may be served in the absence of an undertaking under s.211, or in those circumstances when the giving of an undertaking no longer inhibits service of a full improvement notice (*i.e.* non-compliance within time allowed including as extended, or likely non-compliance), at any time within *either* in a case where no undertaking has been accepted, nine months of service of the provisional notice, *or* if an undertaking is not fulfilled, six months of the period allowed for compliance with the undertaking: subss. (1), (3).

The authority are not obliged to proceed: *cf. Elliott* v. *Brighton Borough Council* (1980) 258 E.G. 441, C.A., notes to s.193, above; indeed, they may not even have a *fixed* policy of doing so, although they are entitled to have a policy of doing so, by way of guideline the application of which they consider in each case: see, *e.g. British Oxygen Co. Ltd.* v. *Board of Trade* [1971] A.C. 610, H.L., *In Re Betts* [1983] 2 A.C. 613, 10 H.L.R. 97, H.L., *Att.-Gen.* v. *L.B. Wandsworth, ex rel. Tilley* [1981] 1 W.L.R. 854, C.A.

Before proceeding, the authority have to satisfy themselves in terms of subs. (2):
(1) Dwelling still in H.A.A. or G.I.A.;
(2) General conditions still met—see notes to s.209, above;
(3) Dwelling still not owner-occupied or otherwise the exception to the owner-occupier exemption remains applicable—see notes to s.210, above;
(4) Housing arrangements for occupying tenant (see notes to s.211, above) are satisfactory, or not required, or have been unreasonably refused by occupying tenant.

The full improvement notice is served on the person having control: see notes to s.210, above and s.617 below; however, copies must be served on all those on whom the time-and-place notice was served under s.213, above, with the same consequence as to entitlement to copy on the part of anyone else with an estate or interest, under s.226, below. The content of the improvement notice is governed by s.216, below.

A class of "public" or "quasi-public" owner is exempt from these provisions altogether: see s.232, below.

Service of improvement notice: other dwellings

215.—(1) Where the local housing authority have served a provisional notice in respect of a dwelling under section 212(1) (dwelling not in general improvement area or housing action area), they may, at any time before the expiry of the period of twelve months beginning with the date on which the representations of the occupying tenant were received by them under that section, serve an improvement notice on the person having control of the dwelling.

(2) Before serving an improvement notice under this section the authority shall satisfy themselves that—

> (*a*) the general conditions for service of an improvement notice in respect of the dwelling are still met,
>
> (*b*) the dwelling ought to be improved to the full standard or, as the case may be, to the reduced standard and is unlikely to be so improved unless the authority exercise their compulsory improvement powers, and
>
> (*c*) the housing arrangements are satisfactory or none are required or the occupying tenant has unreasonably refused to enter into any housing arrangements.

(3) Where an authority serve an improvement notice under this section on the person having control of a dwelling, they shall at the same time serve a copy of the notice on any occupying tenant of the dwelling and on every other person who, to the knowledge of the authority, is an owner, lessee or mortgagee of the dwelling.

(4) An improvement notice served under this section is a local land charge.

DEFINITIONS
"dwelling": s.237.
"full standard": s.234.
"general conditions for service": s.209.
"general improvement area": s.253.
"housing action area": s.239.
"housing arrangements": s.235.
"improvement": s.237.
"improvement notice": s.216.
"local housing authority" ss.1, 2.
"occupying tenant": s.236.
"person having control": s.236.
"provisional notice": s.213.
"reduced standard": s.234.

GENERAL NOTE
This section governs an improvement notice when the dwelling is not in an H.A.A. or G.I.A. (*cf*. s.214, above). Within 12 months of receipt of the representations under s.212, above, a full improvement notice may be served: subs. (1). See s.216, below, as to contents of the improvement notice.

The observations in the notes to s.214, above, as to discretion and policy in relation to exercise of this power are as applicable under this section. Similarly, service of the full improvement notice is required on all those on whom the time-and-place notice had to be served under s.213 (subs. (3)), with the same consequence for others with an estate or interest (s.226, below) as under s.214, above.

Subs. (2) contains the matters as to which the authority must remain satisfied before proceeding:

(1) Conditions for service under s.209, above;

(2) Dwelling still ought to be improved to appropriate standard and is unlikely to be so unless they proceed—see notes to ss.209 and 212, above;

(3) Satisfactory housing arrangements for occupying tenant—see s.211, above—or none needed, or occupying tenant has unreasonably refused to enter into any such arrangements.

A class of "public" or "quasi-public" owner is exempt from these provisions altogether: see s.232, below.

Improvement notice: contents

216.—(1) An improvement notice shall—

> (*a*) specify the works which in the opinion of the local housing authority are required to improve the dwelling to the full standard or, as the case may be, to the reduced standard,

(*b*) state the authority's estimate of the cost of carrying out the works, and

(*c*) require the person having control of the dwelling to carry out the works to the authority's satisfaction within the period of twelve months beginning with the date on which the notice becomes operative or such longer period as the authority may by permission in writing from time to time allow.

(2) The works specified in the improvement notice may be different from the works specified in the provisional notice but shall not require the improvement of a dwelling to the full standard if the provisional notice specified works for improving the dwelling only to the reduced standard.

(3) In an improvement notice which requires the improvement of a dwelling only to the reduced standard the authority may, if they think fit, substitute for the period of twelve months specified in subsection (1)(*c*) such shorter period as appears to them to be appropriate.

Definitions
"dwelling": s.237.
"full standard": s.234.
"improvement": s.237.
"local housing authority": ss.1, 2.
"operative date": s.218.
"person having control": s.236.
"provisional notice": s.213.
"reduced standard": s.234.

General Note
The improvement notice, under whichever of the foregoing two sections is applicable, must specify the works required to achieve the appropriate standard (see notes to s.209, above): subs. (1)(*a*). The actual works should be specified, not merely their *effect*: *cf. Canterbury City Council* v. *Bern* [1981] J.P.L. 749, D.C. The works can be different from those specified in the provisional notice (because, of course, the authority will between times have taken into account representations under s.213, above), but not so as to substitute the full standard for the reduced standard: subs. (2).

The notice must include an estimate of costs: subs. (1)(*b*). This will be relevant on any appeal under s.217, below. The notice must specify a time for completion, of not less than 12 months or such longer period as the authority may in writing allow (subs. (1)(*c*)), unless only the reduced standard is involved, in which case a shorter period is permitted under subs. (3). Time runs from the "operative date" (subs. (1)(*c*)), *i.e.* the end of the period during which an appeal can be brought under s.217, below or, if such an appeal is brought, its final determination: see s.218, below.

Appeals against improvement notices

217.—(1) Within six weeks from the service of an improvement notice on the person having control of the dwelling—

(*a*) that person,

(*b*) any occupying tenant of the dwelling, or

(*c*) any other person having an estate or interest in the dwelling,

may appeal against the notice to the county court

(2) The grounds on which an appeal may be brought by any of those persons are—

(*a*) that it is not practicable to comply with the requirements of the notice at reasonable expense;

(*b*) that the local housing authority have refused unreasonably to approve the execution of alternative works, or that the works specified in the notice are otherwise unreasonable in character or extent;

(*c*) that the dwelling is in a clearance area and it would be unreasonable for the authority to require the works specified in the notice to be carried out;

(*d*) that the dwelling is not, or is no longer, without one or more of the standard amenities;

(*e*) that, in a case where the notice requires the improvement of the dwelling to the full standard, the works specified in the notice are inadequate to secure that the dwelling will attain that standard;

(*f*) that some person other than the appellant will, as the holder of an estate or interest in the dwelling (whether or not that estate or interest entitles him to occupation), derive a benefit from the execution of the works and ought to pay the whole or part of the cost of executing the works;

(*g*) that the notice is invalid on the ground that a requirement of this Part has not been complied with or on the ground of some informality, defect or error in or in connection with the notice.

(3) An appeal may also be brought—

(*a*) by an owner-occupier on the ground that the local housing authority are in error in considering that the circumstances specified in section 210(2) (circumstances in which notice may be served in respect of owner-occupied dwelling) exist in relation to the dwelling;

(*b*) by an occupying tenant on the ground that the condition in section 214(2)(*d*) or 215(2)(*c*) (housing arrangements) is not fulfilled.

(4) An improvement notice shall not be varied on appeal—

(*a*) so as to extend the period within which the works specified in the notice are to be carried out, or

(*b*) so as to require the carrying out of works to improve a dwelling to the full standard if the works specified in the notice were works to improve the dwelling to the reduced standard, or

(*c*) so as to require the carrying out of works to improve a dwelling to the reduced standard if the works specified in the notice were works to improve the dwelling to the full standard;

but, subject to that, on an appeal the court may make such order either confirming, quashing or varying the improvement notice as the court thinks fit.

(5) Where an appeal is brought on the ground specified in subsection (2)(*f*) (other person benefiting from execution of works), the court may make such order as it thinks fit with respect to the payment to be made by the other person referred to in that paragraph to the appellant or, where by virtue of section 220 the works are carried out by the local housing authority, to the authority.

(6) In so far as an appeal is based on the ground that the improvement notice is invalid, the court shall confirm the notice unless satisfied that the interests of the appellant have been substantially prejudiced by the facts relied on by him.

DEFINITIONS

"clearance area": s.289.
"dwelling": s.237.
"full standard": s.234.
"general conditions for service": s.209.
"housing arrangements": s.235.
"improvement": s.237.
"improvement notice": s.216.
"local housing authority": ss.1, 2.
"occupying tenant": s.236.
"owner-occupied": s.237.
"person having control": s.236.
"reduced standard": s.234.
"standard amenities": s.508.

GENERAL NOTE
Six weeks are allowed for appeal to the county court, which may be brought by the person having control (see notes to s.210, above), an occupying tenant (see notes to s.211, above) or any other person with an estate or interest in the dwelling: subs. (1). Any of them may appeal on the grounds set out in subs. (2):

(1) Not capable of compliance at a reasonable expense—see notes to ss.209, 206, above;

(2) Authority have unreasonably refused an alternative specification, or the works are in themselves unreasonable in character or extent;

(3) Dwelling in a clearance area and therefore unreasonably required—see notes to s.289, below;

(4) No absent standard amenities—see notes to s.209, above;

(5) Although full standard (see notes to s.209, above) specified, the works will not achieve that effect;

(6) Someone other than the appellant will, as the holder of an estate or interest, derive a benefit from the execution of the works and ought to pay all or part of the costs; this will not include a statutory tenant (*Harrington* v. *Croydon Corporation* [1968] 1 Q.B. 856, 3 H.L.R. 24, C.A.; see also notes to s.622, below); when an appeal is brought on this ground, the court enjoys power to order another person to contribute or pay the costs (subs. (5)), and although there is no express requirement to give such person notice of the appeal and an opportunity to be heard, this will be absolutely required in any event, for the order would otherwise be void for want of natural justice;

(7) Notice invalid on ground of informality, defect or error—but the court is not to allow an appeal on this ground unless the appellant has been substantially prejudiced by the facts relied on (subs. (6)); there is such substantial prejudice when an owner has been required to carry out works by the authority for which he has no other legal liability—*De Rothschild* v. *Wing* [1967] 1 W.L.R. 470, C.A.

In addition, an owner-occupier can bring an appeal on the ground that the exemption to the normal prohibition against notice under s.210 is not applicable (see notes to s.210, above): subs. (3)(*a*). An occupying tenant can also bring an appeal on the grounds that suitable housing arrangements have not been made (see notes to s.211, above): subs. (3)(*b*).

Subs. (4)
The court's powers are not unfettered: it cannot extend the period for the execution of works; it cannot order works to the full standard if the improvement notice specified only reduced standard; and, it cannot specify reduced standard if the improvement notice required full standard—subs. (4). Otherwise, its discretion is to confirm, quash or vary: *ibid.*

Operative date and effect of improvement notice

218.—(1) If no appeal is brought an improvement notice becomes operative at the expiration of the period within which an appeal might have been brought.

(2) If an appeal is brought, an improvement notice becomes operative, if and so far as it is confirmed by the county court on appeal or on appeal from the county court, on the final determination of the appeal.

(3) For the purposes of subsection (2) the withdrawal of an appeal shall be deemed to be the final determination thereof, having the like effect as a decision confirming the notice or the decision appealed against.

(4) An improvement notice is, subject to the right of appeal conferred by section 217, final and conclusive as to matters which could have been raised on such an appeal.

DEFINITION
"improvement notice": s.216.

GENERAL NOTE
An appeal must be brought within six weeks: s.217, above. If no appeal is brought, it becomes operative at the end of that period: subs. (1). If an appeal is brought, it becomes operative on the final determination of the appeal, at county court or Court of Appeal (subs. (2)), treating withdrawal of an appeal as a decision confirming the notice: subs. (3).

The possibility of appeal would suggest that it is the more appropriate course than application for judicial review: see *R.* v. *Hackney London Borough Council, ex parte Teepee Estates* (1956) *Ltd.* (1967) 19 P. & C.R. 87, D.C. See also *Minford Properties Ltd.* v.

London Borough of Hammersmith (1978) 247 E.G. 561, D.C.; but *cf. R.* v. *London Borough of Southwark, ex parte Lewis Levy Ltd.* [1983] 8 H.L.R. 1, Q.B.D. in which the court considered that if an issue is one which goes to *vires*, including whether or not a property is a house within the provisions, it is appropriately raised by way of application for judicial review.

The *vires* of the authority in reaching their decision, *i.e.* on normal principles of administrative law (*cf.* notes to s.64, above), remains available even on an appeal, for the effect of the improvement notice is to seek to take away a vested right to which the appellant would otherwise be entitled, *i.e.* to leave his property as is: *cf. London Borough of Wandsworth* v. *Winder* [1985] A.C. 461, 17 H.L.R. 196, H.L. so that it would seem to be exempt from the principle in *Cocks* v. *Thanet District Council* [1983] A.C. 286, 6 H.L.R. 15, H.L., that judicial review is the only way to impeach a decision of the authority which is a precondition to the acquisition of a right.

Subs. (4)

Nonetheless, if want of *vires* is alleged, and notwithstanding this subsection, it would seem that judicial review will still be available: see, *e.g.*, *Pearlman* v. *Keepers & Governors of Harrow School* [1979] Q.B. 56, C.A. and *Meade* v. *Haringey London Borough Council* [1979] 1 W.L.R. 637, C.A.

The last-mentioned case went so far as to suggest that if want of *vires* is the basis of challenge it is not even necessary to show that "domestic" remedies (*i.e.* an Act's own statutory procedures for redress or complaint including appeals) have been exhausted, contrary to the "usual" rule (see *Doe d. Bishop of Rochester* v. *Bridges* (1831) 1 B. & Ad. 847, *Pasmore* v. *Oswaldtwistle Urban District Council* [1898] A.C. 387, H.L., *Barraclough* v. *Brown* [1897] A.C. 615, H.L., *Watt* v. *Kesteven County Council* [1955] 1 Q.B. 408, *Wyatt* v. *London Borough of Hillingdon* (1978) 76 L.G.R. 727, *London Borough of Southwark* v. *Williams* [1971] Ch. 734, and *Kensington and Chelsea Royal London Borough Council* v. *Wells* (1974) 72 L.G.R. 289, C.A.).

This view may be contrasted with the approach in *Smith* v. *East Elloe Rural District Council* [1956] A.C. 736, H.L., applied in *R.* v. *Secretary of State for the Environment, ex parte Ostler* [1977] Q.B. 122, C.A., distinguishing *Anisminic Ltd.* v. *Foreign Compensation Commission* [1969] 2 A.C. 147, H.L., *i.e.* that the matter would be treated as "final and conclusive", so as to exclude application for judicial review, as distinct from the approach of greater willingness to intervene (or reluctance to see jurisdiction diminished), reflected in the cases cited in the penultimate paragraph.

Withdrawal of improvement notice

219.—(1) The local housing authority may, if they think fit, at any time withdraw an improvement notice by serving notice of the withdrawal on the person having control of the dwelling.

(2) The authority shall serve a copy of any such notice on the occupier of the dwelling (if different from the person having control of it) and on every other person who, to the knowledge of the authority, is an owner, lessee or mortgagee of the dwelling.

DEFINITIONS
   "dwelling": s.237.
   "improvement notice": s.216.
   "local housing authority": ss.1, 2.
   "owner": s.237.
   "person having control": s.236.

GENERAL NOTE
   The authority have a discretion to withdraw an improvement notice at any time by service on the person having control (see notes to s.210, above), with a copy to any occupier and every other known owner, lessee or mortgagee, with the consequence (s.226, below), that anyone else with an estate or interest in the dwelling is entitled to a copy of the notice of withdrawal.

Enforcement

Power of local housing authority to execute works

220.—(1) If the works to be carried out in compliance with an improvement notice have not been carried out in whole or in part within the period for compliance, the local housing authority may themselves carry out so much of the works as has not been completed.

(2) If before the expiry of the period for compliance the person who is for the time being the person having control of the dwelling notifies the local housing authority in writing that he does not intend, or is unable to do the works in question, the authority may, if they think fit, do the works before the expiry of that period.

(3) If the local housing authority have reason to believe that the person who is for the time being the person having control of the dwelling does not intend or is unable to do the works in question in compliance with the notice—

(*a*) they may before the expiry of the period for compliance, but not earlier than six months after the date on which the notice becomes operative, serve on him a notice requiring him to furnish them, within 21 days of the service of the notice, with evidence of his intentions with respect to the carrying out of the works, and

(*b*) if, from evidence so furnished to them or otherwise, the authority are not satisfied that that person intends to carry out the works in compliance with the notice, they may, if they think fit, do the works before the expiry of the period for compliance.

(4) Not less than 21 days before beginning to do the works the local housing authority shall serve notice of their intention on the occupier of the dwelling, the person having control of the dwelling and on every other person who, to the knowledge of the authority, is an owner, lessee or mortgagee of the dwelling.

(5) In this section the "period for compliance" with an improvement notice is the period specified in the notice or such longer period as the local housing authority may by permission in writing have allowed.

(6) The provisions of Schedule 10 apply with respect to the recovery by the local housing authority of expenses incurred by them under this section.

DEFINITIONS
   "dwelling": s.237.
   "improvement": s.237.
   "improvement notice": s.216.
   "local housing authority": ss.1, 2.
   "owner": s.237.
   "person having control": s.236.

GENERAL NOTE
   This section entitles the authority to engage in works in default for non-compliance with the full notice ("in whole or part") within the period allowed: subs. (1). Period permitted means the time specified in the notice, as extended in writing by the authority if applicable: subs. (5). The authority need not await the expiry of the period permitted if the person having control (see notes to s.210, above) notifies them in writing that he does not intend to do, or is incapable of doing, the works in question: subs. (2).
   Indeed, if the authority have reason to believe (*cf.* notes to s.64, above) that he does not intend to comply, or is incapable of complying, they can serve notice requiring evidence of intent under subs. (3)(*a*). However, they cannot do this any earlier than six months after the notice became operative (see notes to s.218, above). If the response to the request for evidence is unsatisfactory, then again they need not await the end of the time permitted; subs. (3)(*b*).
   Before commencing works in default, the authority must serve prior notice of intention under subs. (4). If an occupier, owner or person having control obstructs the authority in these works, the authority may obtain an order of the magistrates' court to restrain obstruction, failure to comply with which order is a criminal offence: see s.221, below. Recovery of the authority's expenses is governed by Schedule 10: subs. (6).
   The authority cannot adopt a fixed policy of executing works in default; *cf. Elliott* v. *Brighton Borough Council* (1980) 258 E.G. 441, C.A., but *cf.* notes to s.214 above, as to

policies which are no more than guidelines the application of which is reconsidered in each case.

Power of court to order occupier or owner to permit things to be done

221.—(1) If a person, after receiving an improvement notice or a copy of an improvement notice—

    (*a*) being the occupier of the premises, prevents the owner or person having control of the premises, or his officers, servants or agents, from carrying into effect with respect to the premises any of the provisions of this Part, or

    (*b*) being the occupier, owner or person having control of the premises, prevents an officer, servant or agent of the local housing authority from so doing,

a magistrates' court may order him to permit to be done on the premises all things requisite for carrying into effect those provisions.

(2) A person who fails to comply with an order of the court under this section commits a summary offence and is liable on conviction to a fine not exceeding £20 in respect of each day during which the failure continues.

DEFINITIONS
"dwelling": s.237.
"improvement notice": s.216.
"local housing authority": ss.1, 2.
"owner": s.237.
"person having control": s.236.

GENERAL NOTE
If an occupier prevents (a) an owner, or (b) a person having control, or (c) the agent of either, or (d) an officer, servant or agent of the authority, from carrying into effect any of the provisions of this Part, he can be ordered to co–operate by a magistrate's court, failure to comply with which order is punishable by a fine of up to £20 for each day on which the offence continues. Similarly, if an owner or the person having control obstructs the authority, he too can be so ordered, subject to the same penalty.

Powers of entry

222.—(1) A person authorised by the local housing authority may at any reasonable time, on giving 24 hours' notice of his intention to the occupier, and to the owner if the owner is known, enter premises for the purpose of survey and examination with a view to ascertaining whether the requirements of an improvement notice served, or undertaking accepted, under this Part has been complied with.

(2) An authorisation for the purposes of this section shall be in writing stating the particular purpose for which the entry is authorised.

DEFINITIONS
"improvement notice": s.216.
"local housing authority": ss.1, 2.
"owner": s.237.

GENERAL NOTE
The power of entry is for the purpose of seeing whether the requirements of an improvement notice, *or* an undertaking under s.211 above, have been complied with: failure to comply with the requirements of subs. (2) will mean that the entry is unauthorised—see *Stroud* v. *Bradbury* [1952] 2 All E.R. 76, D.C. Obstruction of a properly authorised officer is an offence under s.223, below.

Penalty for obstruction

223.—(1) It is a summary offence to obstruct a person authorised in pursuance of section 222 to enter premises in the performance of anything which he is required or authorised under that section to do.

(2) A person who commits such an offence is liable on conviction to a fine not exceeding level 2 on the standard scale.

<small>GENERAL NOTE</small>
Obstruction of an officer properly authorised under s.222, above, is a criminal offence punishable by a fine of up level 2 on the standard scale, *i.e.* under s.37, Criminal Justice Act 1982, currently £100, by S.I. 1984 No. 447.

Right of person having control as against others to carry out works

224.—(1) The person having control of any premises which consist of or include—

    (*a*) a dwelling in a general improvement area or housing action area which is without all or any of the standard amenities, or

    (*b*) a dwelling in respect of which representations have been made by an occupying tenant under section 212 (representations to local housing authority with view to exercise of compulsory improvement powers),

has, as against the occupying tenant of the dwelling and any other person having an estate or interest in the premises, the right to enter the premises in order to carry out any survey or examination required with a view to providing the dwelling with any of the standard amenities and, where appropriate, of putting it in good repair (disregarding internal decorative repair) having regard to its age and character and the locality in which it is situated.

(2) On and after the date on which an improvement notice becomes operative, the person having control of the dwelling has the right, as against any occupying tenant of the dwelling and any other person having an estate or interest in the premises which consist of or include the dwelling, to take any reasonable steps for the purpose of complying with the improvement notice.

(3) A person bound by an undertaking accepted under this Part has the right as against any occupying tenant of the dwelling to take any reasonable steps for the purpose of complying with the undertaking.

(4) The carrying out of works in pursuance of an improvement notice or an undertaking accepted under this Part shall not give rise to any liability on the part of a lessee to reinstate any premises at any time in the condition in which they were before the works were carried out, or to any liability for failure so to reinstate the premises.

<small>DEFINITIONS</small>
    "dwelling": s.237.
    "general improvement area": s.253.
    "housing action area": s.239.
    "improvement": s.237.
    "improvement notice": s.216.
    "local housing authority": ss.1, 2.
    "occupying tenant": s.236.
    "person having control": s.236.
    "standard amenities": s.508.

<small>GENERAL NOTE</small>
This section confers two powers of entry on the person having control (see notes to s.210, above), one power of entry upon a person who is bound by an undertaking under s.211, above, and a general exemption on a lessee, from civil liability (whether or not under contract) for carrying out works under an improvement notice or pursuant to a s.211 undertaking. An authority executing works at the request of a person having control or with an estate or interest, under s.225, below, will enjoy the same powers: s.225(2), below.

Subs. (1)
The first power of entry is for the purposes of survey and examination only, and arises either on the motion of a person having control of a dwelling in an H.A.A. or G.I.A. which

is lacking in standard amenities (see notes to s.209, above), or as a result of a representation under s.212, above, by an occupying tenant (as to whom, see notes to s.211, above). It does *not* confer a power to enter to *do* the respective works. The power of entry is good not only against an occupying tenant, but against anyone else with an estate or interest in the premises.

Subs. (2)

Once an improvement notice under s.216 has become operative (as to which see notes to s.218, above), the person having control has power of entry to take any steps reasonably required to comply with the notice, again as against occupying tenant or person with estate or interest.

Subs. (3)

A person who has given an undertaking under s.211, above, also has power of entry to comply with it, good against an occupying tenant.

Subs. (4)

A lessee incurs neither liability nor obligation to reinstate, regardless of the terms of his lease, in respect of works carried out under a s.216 improvement notice, or pursuant to a s.211 undertaking. This exemption will extend to liability for (ameliorating) waste, *i.e.* is not confined to *contractual* liability.

Execution of works by local housing authority by agreement

225.—(1) The local housing authority may by agreement with a person having control of a dwelling or any other person having an estate or interest in a dwelling execute at his expense any works which he is required to carry out in the dwelling in pursuance of an improvement notice served or undertaking accepted under this Part.

(2) For that purpose the authority have all such rights as that person would have as against any occupying tenant of the dwelling and any other person having an interest in the dwelling.

DEFINITIONS
"dwelling": s.237.
"improvement notice": s.216.
"local housing authority": ss.1, 2.
"occupying tenant": s.236.
"person having control": s.236.

GENERAL NOTE

This section authorises an agency agreement, with the authority, to carry out works under a s.216 improvement notice, or under a s.211 undertaking: see also s.514, below. In exercise of such an agreement, the authority are entitled to the rights of entry as against an occupying tenant, or anyone else with an interest in the dwelling, including—but not confined to—under s.224, above.

Provisions for protection of owners and others

Owners, etc. not known to local housing authority may obtain copy of notices

226. Where under this Part a local housing authority are required to serve a copy of a notice on any person who, to their knowledge, is an owner, lessee or mortgagee of a dwelling, any person having an estate or interest in the dwelling who is not served with a copy of the notice is entitled, on application in writing to the authority, to obtain a copy of the notice.

DEFINITIONS
"dwelling": s.237.
"local housing authority": ss.1, 2.
"owner": s.237.

GENERAL NOTE
    Anyone with an estate or interest in the dwelling is entitled to apply in writing for a copy of any notice which the authority are bound to serve on an owner, lessee or mortgagee, *e.g.* under ss.211, 213, 214, 215, 219, 220, above, or s.227, below.

Right to serve counter-notice requiring purchase

227.—(1) Where a local housing authority have served an improvement notice, the person having control of the dwelling may, by notice in writing served on the authority at any time within the period of six months beginning with the date on which the improvement notice becomes operative, require the authority to purchase his interest in the dwelling in accordance with this section.

(2) Where the person having control of a dwelling serves a notice on the authority under subsection (1), the authority shall be deemed—

(a) to be authorised under and for the purposes of Part II (provision of housing) to acquire his interest in the dwelling compulsorily, and

(b) to have served a notice to treat in respect of that interest on the date of the service of the notice under subsection (1);

and the power conferred by section 31 of the Land Compensation Act 1961 to withdraw a notice to treat is not exercisable in the case of a notice to treat deemed to have been so served.

(3) Within 21 days of the receipt of a notice under subsection (1) served by the person having control of a dwelling, the local housing authority shall notify every other person who, to their knowledge, is an owner, lessee or mortgagee of the dwelling or who is the occupier of it.

DEFINITIONS
    "dwelling": s.237.
    "improvement notice": s.216.
    "local housing authority": ss.1, 2.
    "operative date": s.218.
    "person having control": s.236.

GENERAL NOTE
    In some ways, this is the "catch", and the reason (or one of the reasons—see also s.228, below) why these powers have been relatively little used by authorities. The person having control has six months from when an improvement notice becomes operative (as to which, see notes to s.218, above), to serve a counter–notice, in writing, requiring the purchase of the property by the authority: subs. (1). On so doing, the authority are treated as if authorised compulsorily to purchase under Part II, above, and to have served notice to treat under s.5, Compulsory Purchase Act 1965, on the date of the counter–notice, without the right to withdraw the notice under s.31, Land Compensation Act 1961: subs. (2). (See, generally, Part XVII, below). The authority must notify those specified in subs. (3) or receipt of the notice, within 21 days: subs. (3).

Duty of local housing authority to offer loan to meet expenses of compulsory improvement

228.—(1) If a person who is liable—

(a) to incur expenditure in complying with an improvement notice served, or undertaking accepted, under this Part, or

(b) to make a payment as directed by a court under section 217(5) (contribution from third party deriving benefit from execution of works),

applies to the local housing authority for a loan, the authority shall, subject to the following provisions of this section, offer to enter into a contract with him for a loan by them to be secured by a mortgage of his interest in the dwelling concerned.

(2) The application shall be made in writing within the period of three months beginning with the date on which the improvement notice becomes operative or the undertaking is accepted or the payment is to be made as directed by the court, or such longer period as the authority by permission given in writing may allow.

(3) The authority shall not make an offer unless they are satisfied that the applicant can reasonably be expected to meet the obligations assumed by him in pursuance of this section in respect of the loan; and if the authority are not so satisfied as regards a loan of the amount applied for, they may, if they think fit, offer a loan of a smaller amount as regards which they are so satisfied.

(4) The authority shall not make an offer unless they are satisfied—

    (*a*) that the applicant's interest in the dwelling concerned is an estate in fee simple absolute in possession or an estate for a term of years which will not expire before the date for final repayment of the loan, and

    (*b*) that, according to a valuation made on their behalf, the amount of the principal of the loan does not exceed the value which it is estimated that the mortgaged security will bear after improvement of the dwelling to the full standard or, as the case may be, to the reduced standard.

(5) The contract shall contain a condition to the effect that if—

    (*a*) an improvement grant or intermediate grant becomes payable in respect of the expenditure in question, or

    (*b*) such a grant becomes payable partly in respect of that expenditure and partly in respect of other expenditure or another payment,

the authority shall not be required to lend more than the amount of the expenditure or payment remaining after deducting the grant or, as the case may be, that part of the grant which in the opinion of the authority is attributable to that expenditure or payment.

(6) The contract offered by the authority shall require proof of title and contain such other reasonable terms as the authority may specify in their offer, and in particular may provide for the advance to be made by instalments as the works progress.

(7) The rate of interest payable on the loan shall be such as the Secretary of State may direct, either generally or in any particular case; and the Secretary of State may, if he thinks fit, give directions, either generally or in any particular case, as to the time within which a loan under this section, or any part of such a loan, is to be repaid.

DEFINITIONS

  "dwelling": s.237.
  "full standard": s.234.
  "improvement grant": s.467.
  "improvement notice": s.216.
  "intermediate grant": s.474.
  "local housing authority": ss.1, 2.
  "operative date": s.218.
  "reduced standard": s.234.

GENERAL NOTE

  This is the other (*cf.* notes to s.227, above) main reason why authorities do not use these powers as extensively as they might otherwise do; those with a sufficient interest (see subs. (4)) are entitled to a loan with which to meet the costs of (a) complying with a s.216 improvement notice, or (b) a s.211 undertaking, or (c) an order of the court under s.217 to make a payment in respect of works: subs. (1). The loan is to be secured by a mortgage (subs. (1)). The loan must be sought in writing, within three months of when the notice becomes operative (see notes to s.216, above), the undertaking is accepted, or the court order is made, or such longer period as the authority may permit: subs. (2).

The authority are entitled to refuse a loan, or pay less than the whole of the amount sought, if not satisfied that the applicant can reasonably be expected to meet his obligations: subs. (3). The provisions of Part XIV, below, would seem to apply to loans under this section: see ss.435, 436 and 438. However, the loan contract must contain a term the effect of which is to reduce the loan by any amount attributable to the relevant works under an improvement or intermediate grant under Part XV, below: subs. (5). In other respects, the authority are obliged to require proof of title, and entitled to add such terms as they consider reasonable, including as to stage payments: subs. (6).

Charging order in favour of person executing works

229.—(1) Where the person having control of a dwelling has completed in respect of the dwelling works required to be executed by an improvement notice, he may apply to the local housing authority for a charging order.

(2) An applicant for a charging order shall produce to the authority—

(*a*) the certificate of the proper officer of the authority that the works have been executed to his satisfaction, and

(*b*) the accounts of and vouchers for the expenses of the works.

(3) The authority, when satisfied that the applicant has duly executed the required works and of the amount of the expenses, shall make an order accordingly charging on the premises an annuity to repay that amount together with the amount of the costs properly incurred in obtaining the charging order.

(4) The annuity charged shall be at the rate of £6 for every £100 of the aggregate amount charged, shall commence from the date of the order and shall be payable for a term of 30 years to the person named in the order, his executors, administrators or assigns.

(5) A person aggrieved by a charging order may, within 21 days after notice of the order has been served on him, appeal to the county court; and where notice of such an appeal has been given no proceedings shall be taken under the order until the appeal is determined or ceases to be prosecuted.

(6) The proper officer of the local housing authority shall file and record copies, certified by him to be true copies, of any charging order made under this section, the certificate given under subsection (2)(*a*) and the accounts as passed by the authority.

DEFINITIONS
  "dwelling": s.237.
  "improvement notice": s.216.
  "local housing authority": ss.1, 2.
  "person having control": s.236.

GENERAL NOTE
  This section applies to permit a person having control who has executed works under a s.216 improvement notice (but *not* under a s.211 undertaking) to apply for a charging order against the premises, *i.e.* to secure his costs in relation to other interests in the premises: subs. (1). Anyone aggrieved—in substance, anyone whose interest is thus affected—can appeal to the county court: the transfer of jurisdiction to the county court is pursuant to Law Commission Recommendations (Cmnd. 9515), No. 9(i). The obligation to maintain records expressly imposed on the local housing authority by subs. (6) is pursuant to *ibid*, No. 10.

Form, effect, etc. of charging order

230.—(1) A charging order under section 229 shall be in such form as the Secretary of State may prescribe.

(2) The charge created by such a charging order shall be a charge on the premises specified in the order having priority over all existing and future estates, interests and incumbrances, with the exception of—

(*a*) charges under section 200 (charge in favour of person executing works required by repair notice),
(*b*) tithe rentcharge.
(*c*) charges within section 1(1)(*a*) of the Local Land Charges Act 1975 (statutory charges in favour of public authorities), and
(*d*) charges created under any Act authorising advances of public money.

(3) Charges under section 229 and section 200 (the corresponding provision in relation to repair notices) take order as between themselves according to their respective dates.

(4) The annuity created by a charging order may be recovered by the person for the time being entitled to it by the same means and in the like manner in all respects as if it were a rentcharge granted by deed out of the premises by the owner of the premises.

(5) The benefit of the charge may be from time to time transferred in like manner as a mortgage or rentcharge may be transferred, and the transfer shall be in such form as the Secretary of State may prescribe.

(6) An owner of, or other person interested in, premises on which an annuity has been charged by a charging order under section 229 may at any time redeem the annuity on payment to the person entitled to the annuity of such sum as may be agreed upon, or in default of agreement determined by the Secretary of State.

DEFINITION
"owner": s.237.

GENERAL NOTE
This makes provision ancillary to the right of the person having control of the premises to secure a charging order on the premises under s.229, above, against his expenditure complying with a s.216 improvement notice. The order of priority under subs. (2) is as amended pursuant to Law Commission Recommendations (Cmnd. 9515), No. 11. See also notes to s.201 above (2).

Miscellaneous

Modifications of the Agricultural Holdings Act 1948

231.—(1) Section 9 of the Agricultural Holdings Act 1948 (increase of rent for improvements carried out by landlord) applies to improvements carried out in compliance with an improvement notice or an undertaking accepted under this Part as it applies to improvements carried out at the request of the tenant; but where a tenant has contributed to the cost incurred by his landlord in carrying out the improvement, the increase in rent provided for by that section shall be reduced proportionately.

(2) Works carried out in compliance with an improvement notice or an undertaking accepted under this Part shall be included among the improvements specified in paragraph 8 of Schedule 3 to the Agricultural Holdings Act 1948 (tenant's right to compensation for erection, alteration or enlargement of buildings); but subject to the power conferred by section 78 of that Act to amend that Schedule.

(3) Section 49 of the Agricultural Holdings Act 1948 (tenant's right to compensation conditional on landlord consenting to the carrying out of the improvements) does not apply to works carried out in compliance with an improvement notice or an undertaking accepted under this Part.

(4) Where a person other than the tenant claiming compensation has contributed to the cost of carrying out works in compliance with an improvement notice or an undertaking accepted under this Part, compensation in respect of the works, as assessed under section 48 of the Agricultural Holdings Act 1948, shall be reduced proportionately.

DEFINITIONS
"improvement": s.237.
"improvement notice": s.216.

GENERAL NOTE
This section allocates the benefit of improvements under this Part, in relation to the Agricultural Holdings Act 1948 (as amended by the Agricultural Holdings Act 1984).

Exclusion of dwellings controlled by Crown or a public authority

232.—(1) No provisional notice or improvement notice may be served in respect of a dwelling in which there is a Crown or Duchy interest except with the consent of the appropriate authority; but if that consent is given this Part applies as to a dwelling in which there is no such interest.

(2) No provisional notice or improvement notice may be served in respect of a dwelling if the person having control of the dwelling is—

    a local authority,

    a new town corporation,

    the Development Board for Rural Wales,

    the Housing Corporation,

    a registered housing association, or

    a housing trust which is a charity.

(3) If after a provisional notice or improvement notice has been served in respect of a dwelling—

(a) in the case of a dwelling in which there is a Crown or Duchy interest, the appropriate authority becomes the person having control of the dwelling, or

(b) any such body as is mentioned in subsection (2) becomes the person having control of the dwelling,

the notice, and any undertaking accepted under this Part with respect to the dwelling, shall cease to have effect.

(4) Where an improvement notice ceases to have effect by virtue of subsection (3), the body which or person who has become the person having control of the dwelling shall notify the officer who registered the notice in the register of local land charges and furnish him with all information required by him for the purpose of cancelling the registration.

(5) In this section "Crown or Duchy interest" means an interest belonging to Her Majesty in right of the Crown or of the Duchy of Lancaster, or belonging to the Duchy of Cornwall or belonging to a government department, or held in trust for Her Majesty for the purposes of a government department, and "the appropriate authority" means—

(a) in relation to land belonging to Her Majesty in right of the Crown and forming part of the Crown Estate, the Crown Estate Commissioners;

(b) in relation to land belonging to Her Majesty in right of the Crown and not forming part of the Crown Estate, the government department having the management of the land;

(c) in relation to land belonging to Her Majesty in right of the Duchy of Lancaster, the Chancellor of the Duchy;

(d) in relation to land belonging to the Duchy of Cornwall, such person as the Duke of Cornwall, or the possessor for the time being of the Duchy of Cornwall, appoints;

(e) in relation to land belonging to a government department or held in trust for Her Majesty for the purposes of a government department, that department;

and if any question arises as to what authority is the appropriate authority in relation to any land, the question shall be referred to the Treasury whose decision shall be final

(6) In this section "local authority" includes—

a parish or community council,
the trustees of the Honourable Society of the Inner Temple,
the trustees of the Honourable Society of the Middle Temple, and
the police authority for any police area,
and any joint board or joint committee all the constituent members of
which are local authorities for the purposes of this section.

DEFINITIONS
"dwelling": s.237.
"housing trust": s.6.
"improvement notice": s.216.
"local authority": s.4.
"local housing authority": ss.1, 2.
"new town corporation": s.4.
"person having control": s.236.
"provisional notice": s.213.
"registered housing assocation": s.5.

GENERAL NOTE
This section excludes the operation of this Part where the public or quasi–public authorities
specified in subs. (2) are the person having control (as to whom, see notes to s.210, above),
and stops the procedure if at any time after a provisional or improvement notice has been
served, or an undertaking accepted, one such body becomes the person having control:
subs. (3). For the purpose of this section, local authority bears the extended meaning under
subs. (6).
    The section also disapplies this Part where the Crown or Duchy of Cornwall have any
interest in the dwelling (whether or not the person having control), unless the "appropriate
authority" (as defined in subs. (5)) consents, in which case the Part operates as normal:
subs. (1).

Effect of area ceasing to be general improvement area or housing action area

233. If, after an undertaking has been accepted under this Part in
respect of a dwelling or an improvement notice has been served in respect
of a dwelling under section 214 (dwelling in general improvement area or
housing action area)—

(*a*) the general improvement area or housing action area in which the
dwelling is situated ceases to be such an area, or

(*b*) the land on which the dwelling is situated is excluded from such an
area,

the provisions of this Part continue to apply in relation to the undertaking
or notice as if the dwelling continued to be in a general improvement area
or housing action area declared by the authority by whom the undertaking
was accepted or the notice served.

DEFINITIONS
"dwelling": s.237.
"general improvement area": s.253.
"housing action area": s.239.
"improvement notice": s.216.

GENERAL NOTE
    Land may cease to be an H.A.A., or excluded from an H.A.A., under ss.239, 241, 250
or 251, below; land may cease to be within a G.I.A. under s.258, below. In any such case,
if a s.211 undertaking has been accepted, or a s.216 improvement notice served, the
respective provisions continue to apply as if the dwelling remained in an H.A.A. or G.I.A.

Supplementary provisions

Meaning of "full standard" and "reduced standard"

234.—(1) For the purposes of this Part a dwelling shall be taken to
attain the full standard if the following conditions are met—

(*a*) it is provided with all the standard amenities for the exclusive use
of its occupants;

(*b*) it is in reasonable repair (disregarding the state of internal decorative repair) having regard to its age and character and the locality
in which it is situated;

(*c*) it conforms with such requirements with respect to thermal insulation as may be specified by the Secretary of State for the purposes
of this section;

(*d*) it is in all other respects fit for human habitation;

(*e*) it is likely to be available for use as a dwelling for a period of 15
years or such other period as may be specified by the Secretary of
State for the purposes of this section.

(2) The local housing authority may (subject to subsection (3)) dispense
wholly or in part with any of the conditions in subsection (1), and a
dwelling shall be taken to attain the reduced standard if those conditions
are met so far as not dispensed with.

(3) The authority shall not dispense with the condition specified in
subsection (1)(*a*) (standard amenities) where they are satisfied that the
dwelling is, or forms part of, a house or building in respect of which they
could by notice under section 352 (houses in multiple occupation: power
to require execution of works to render premises fit for number of
occupants) require the execution of such works as are referred to in that
section.

DEFINITIONS
"dwelling": s.237.
"fit for human habitation": s.604.
"house in multiple occupation": s.345.
"local housing authority": ss.1, 2.
"standard amenities": s.508.

GENERAL NOTE
See notes to s.209, above.

Meaning of "housing arrangements"

235. In this Part "housing arrangements" means arrangements—

(*a*) making provision for the housing of an occupying tenant of a
dwelling and his household during the period when improvement
works are being carried out, or after the completion of the works,
or during that period and after completion of the works (and for
any incidental or ancillary matters), and

(*b*) contained in a written agreement to which the occupying tenant
and either his landlord or the local housing authority, or both, are
parties.

DEFINITIONS
"dwelling": s.237.
"local housing authority": ss.1, 2.

GENERAL NOTE
See notes to s.211, above.

Meaning of "person having control" and "occupying tenant"

236.—(1) References in this Part to the person having control of a
dwelling shall be construed as follows–

(*a*) if the dwelling is owner-occupied, the person having control of it
is the owner-occupier;

(*b*) if there is an occupying tenant of the dwelling who is a person employed in agriculture (as defined in section 17(1) of the Agricultural Wages Act 1948) and who occupies or resides in the dwelling as part of the terms of his employment, the person having control of the dwelling is the employer or other person by whose authority the occupying tenant occupies or resides in the dwelling;

(c) in any other case, the person having control of the dwelling is the person who is either the owner of it or the lessee of it under a long tenancy and whose interest in the dwelling is not in reversion on that of another person who has a long tenancy.

(2) In this Part "occupying tenant", in relation to a dwelling, means a person (other than an owner-occupier) who—

(a) occupies or is entitled to occupy the dwelling as a lessee; or

(b) is a statutory tenant of the dwelling; or

(c) occupies the dwelling as a residence under a restricted contract; or

(d) is employed in agriculture (as defined in section 17(1) of the Agricultural Wages Act 1948) and occupies or resides in the dwelling as part of his terms of employment.

DEFINITIONS
  "dwelling": s.237.
  "long tenancy": s.237.
  "owner": s.237.
  "restricted contract": s.622.
  "statutory tenant": s.622.

GENERAL NOTE
  See notes to ss.210, 211, above.

Minor definitions

237. In this Part—

"dwelling" means a building or part of a building occupied or intended to be occupied as a separate dwelling, together with any yard, garden, outhouses and appurtenances belonging to it or usually enjoyed with it;

"improvement" includes alteration and enlargement and, so far as also necessary to enable a dwelling to reach the full standard or the reduced standard, repair, and "improved" shall be construed accordingly;

"long tenancy" has the same meaning as in Part I of the Leasehold Reform Act 1967;

"owner", in relation to a dwelling, means the person who otherwise than as a mortgagee in possession, is for the time being entitled to dispose of the fee simple in the dwelling;

"owner-occupier", in relation to a dwelling, means the person who, as owner or as lessee under a long tenancy, occupies or is entitled to occupy the dwelling, and "owner-occupied" shall be construed accordingly;

"standard amenities" has the same meaning as in Part XV (improvement grants, &c.).

GENERAL NOTE
  See notes to ss.209, 210, above.

Index of defined expressions: Part VII

238. The following Table shows provisions defining or otherwise explaining expressions used in this Part (other than provisions defining or explaining an expression used in the same section or paragraph):—

charity	section 622
clearance area	section 289(1)
dwelling	section 237
full standard	section 234(1)
general conditions for service of improvement notice	section 209
general improvement area	section 253
housing action area	section 239
housing arrangements	section 235
housing association	section 5(1)
housing trust	section 6
improvement (and improved)	section 237
improvement notice	section 216
lessee	section 621
local authority	section 4(*e*)
local housing authority	sections 1, 2(2)
long tenancy	section 237
new town corporation	section 4(*b*)
occupying tenant	section 236(2)
owner	section 237
owner-occupier (and owner-occupied)	section 237
person having control	section 236(1)
provisional notice	section 213
reduced standard	section 234
registered (in relation to a housing association)	section 5(4)
restricted contract	section 622
standard amenities	sections 237 and 508
standard scale (in reference to the maximum fine on summary conviction)	section 622
statutory tenant	section 622

PART VIII

AREA IMPROVEMENT

Housing action areas

Declaration of housing action area

239.—(1) Where a report with respect to an area within their district consisting primarily of housing accommodation is submitted to the local housing authority by a person appearing to the authority to be suitably qualified (who may be an officer of the authority), and the authority, upon consideration of the report and of any other information in their possession, are satisfied, having regard to—

    (*a*) the physical state of the housing accommodation in the area as a whole, and

    (*b*) social conditions in the area,

that the requirement mentioned in subsection (2) is fulfilled with respect to the area, they may cause the area to be defined on a map and by resolution declare it to be a housing action area.

    (2) The requirement is that the living conditions in the area are unsatisfactory and can most effectively be dealt with within a period of five years so as to secure—

    (*a*) the improvement of the housing accommodation in the area as a whole, (*b*) the well-being of the persons for the time being resident in the area, and

(*c*) the proper and effective management and use of that accommodation,

by declaring the area to be a housing action area.

(3) In considering whether to take action under this section the local housing authority shall have regard to such guidance as may from time to time be given by the Secretary of State, either generally or with respect to a particular authority or description of authority or in any particular case, with regard to the identification of areas suitable to be declared housing action areas.

(4) An area which is declared to be a housing action area shall be such an area for the period of five years beginning with the date on which the resolution is passed, subject to—

(*a*) section 241(2)(*a*) (power of Secretary of State to overrule declaration),

(*b*) section 250(1)(*b*) (power of local housing authority to terminate housing action area), and

(*c*) section 251 (extension of duration of housing action area).

(5) A resolution declaring an area to be a housing action area is a local land charge.

DEFINITIONS
"district": s.2.
"housing accommodation": s.252.
"local housing authority": ss.1, 2.

GENERAL NOTE
"The housing activity of many urban local authorities was, for many years, dominated by the need to clear and redevelop areas of old housing for which no other solution was available, a process which often enabled extra homes to be built for families on the waiting-list. Not unnaturally run-down areas not already in the clearance programme were often assumed to be suitable for demolition and redevelopment in due course. Residents of privately rented dwellings were usually believed to be content to change their tenancy for that of a council house or flat; adverse blighting effects of clearance and the dispersal of communities were seen as being more than outweighed by the benefits conferred by the improvement in housing standards. Within the last few years, however, the position has altered significantly. Except in a few cities the programme of large-scale slum clearance should now be drawing to a close . . . . Alternative courses of action in older neighbourhoods have become increasingly possible". (D.O.E. Circular 13/75).

This section introduces the "housing action area" ("H.A.A."). It is an area of poor housing, usually inner–city, in relation to which the authority have the powers set out in the first series of section in this Part (down to and including s.252), and, of considerable practical importance, in relation to which substantially higher levels of grant-aid are available under Part XV, below—see ss.473, 482, 490, 498, below.

In addition to the H.A.A., there is the "general improvement area" ("G.I.A.") introduced by s.253, below, in relation to which the authority have somewhat fewer powers, and a lower level of grant-aid is available (see the same sections). The G.I.A. was introduced by the Housing Act 1969; it was joined in 1974 by the H.A.A., and substantially strengthened; in addition there were "priority neighbourhoods", *i.e.* areas marked out for future action as H.A.A. or G.I.A. In 1980, priority neighbourhoods "disappeared" from the legislation, and G.I.A.s returned to substantially their 1969 Act form—which is accordingly that reproduced in this Part, below. Improvement areas as we now know them date generally only from Part II, Housing Act 1964.

The government are considering significant amendments to improvement programmes: see the Green Paper, Home Improvement—A New Approach, Cmnd. 9513, of May 1985, although an initial consultation date of July 9, 1985, was subsequently set back to September, so that it is uncertain whether and when, and how much of, these proposals will be pursued. "Area action has an important role as part of a strategy for improving the condition of the housing stock; it will continue as a central plank in the Government's policy. The declaration of an area can do a great deal to increase private spending by reassuring the inhabitants and others, such as the lending institutions, that its future is secure. Areas also provide a way of concentrating public sector help so that it has the maximum effect.

"There are at present 617,000 houses in 1,927 statutory improvement areas in England— 311 Housing Action Areas . . . and 1,616 General Improvement Areas . . . In Wales there are 48,000 houses in 130 areas. The number of houses in potential areas is even greater 1.4m in 1981 . . . The Government proposes that in future the main purpose of areas will be to increase local confidence and attract private funding . . . The arrangements for declaring areas will be drastically simplified. It is not necessary to have two types of areas . . . There will therefore be a single type of area—a Housing Improvement Area . . . The rules governing local authority assistance to householders will be the same there as elsewhere . . ." (*Ibid*, paras. 49–51).

Taken together with the Green Papers' proposals to change the grant-aid system in Part XV, it is clearly necessary to remain aware of the possibility of substantial changes in this (and that) Part.

The Report

The starting-point for declaration is a "report", which need not be by an officer of the authority (but may be), provided the authors (as it will usually be), appear to the authority to be "suitably qualified": subs. (1). "Reports may thus be prepared by: (a) officers of an authority with power to declare an H.A.A.; (b) neighbourhood councils, residents' associations, housing associations or other voluntary bodies; (c) consultants; or (d) other persons with the relevant knowledge or experience". (D.O.E. Circular 14/75, Memorandum A, para. 3). "Authorities should welcome the contribution that housing associations or other persons can make in identifying an H.A.A . . . ." (*Ibid*, para. 4).

"A report need not be an elaborate document nor involve sophisticated presentational devices. It is a working document, and a basis for decision . . . A report should . . . contain information . . . on:

"(a) the number of dwellings, houses in multiple occupation, and hostels in the area, categorised by age; unfitness; absence of standard amenities; state of disrepair; rateable values; and tenure;

"(b) the number of households in the area, categorised by tenure; those who share or lack access to amenities; and overcrowding;

"(c) the presence in the area of significant numbers of families, groups, or individuals with special housing needs or problems, including large families, one-parent families, households whose head is unemployed, old people, and those people likely to suffer deprivation, for instance ethnic minorities;

"(d) special housing problems in the area, as indicated, for instance, by harassment, evictions, homelessness, and the number of children taken into care because of housing problems;

"(e) recent changes in housing conditions as indicated, for instance, by improvement grants applied for or made, planning permissions for conversions or redevelopment and changes in the average levels of recorded rents". (D.O.E. Circular 14/75, Memorandum A, paras. 5–6).

Other Information

Under s.8, above, and ss.334, 605, below, the authority have duties of inspection, which would result in information relevant to be taken into account: see also D.O.E. Circular 13/75, para. 7. The authority and the Secretary of State enjoy powers of entry for the purpose of deciding whether or not powers under this Part ought to be exercised (s.260, below), obstruction of which constitutes an offence under s.261, below.

Housing Accommodation

The report must concern an area within the district of the authority, which consists primarily of "housing accommodation": subs. (1). This is defined (s.252) to mean "dwellings, houses in multiple occupation and hostels". "Dwelling" is itself defined in *ibid.* as "a building or part of a building occupied or intended to be occupied as a separate dwelling, together with any yard, garden, outhouses and appurtenances belonging to or usually enjoyed with that building or part". As to "separate dwelling", see notes to s.79, above, and s.525, below. As to "appurtenances", see s.56, above.

"Dwelling" in the context of "housing accommodation" for the purposes of this Part was considered in *R. v. Camden London Borough Council, ex parte Comyn Ching & Co. (London) Ltd.* [1984] J.P.L. 661, Q.B.D. The question is to be answered by asking whether occupation as a dwelling is intended by the person in control of the property as at the date when the issue arises (see further, s.243, below).

Accordingly, buildings constructed as housing, but used for warehousing, *might* not be dwellings at the relevant date, even though it was the authority's intention that they should subsequently be used as such. If property is already occupied as housing, then there is no difficulty determining whether or not it constitutes a dwelling; otherwise, it is largely a question of fact. Planning use might be some indication of the use to which it is intended to put a property, but no more than an indication.

"House in multiple occupation" ("H.M.O.") means "a house which is occupied by persons who do not form a single household, exclusive of any part of the house which is occupied as a separate dwelling by persons who do form a single household": s.252. As to house, and household, see notes to s.345, below; this definition, however, is the basic definition of H.M.O. for the purposes of Pt. XI below *as adapted* to the purposes of grant-aid under Pt. XV, below, *i.e.* for special grants (see ss.483, *et seq.*, below), meaning an H.M.O. *exclusive* of those parts of the property in occupation as a separate dwelling: see notes to s.525, below.

A building formerly in conventional multiple-occupation (*e.g.* bedsitting rooms), vacated for conversion to self-contained flats, ceases to be an H.M.O. when it is emptied with the intention that it should not return to that class of occupation: *R.* v. *Kerrier District Council, ex parte Guppys (Bridport) Ltd.*, (*No. 2*) [1985] 17 H.L.R. 426, C.A. This decision would seem consistent with the approach adopted in *Comyn Ching*, in relation to "dwelling" (above).

Physical and Social
In addition to the pre-existence of relevant conditions, *i.e.* those set out in subs. (1), the authority must *also* be satisfied that the requirements of subs. (2) are fulfilled:

(1) That living conditions in the area are unsatisfactory;
(2) That H.A.A. treatment can deal with them effectively;
(3) That they can secure the objectives within five years;
(4) That they can secure the improvement of the housing in the area as a whole within that period;
(5) That they can secure the well-being of the current residents within that period;
(6) That they can secure the proper and effective management and use of accommodation within that period.

"The area should not be declared an H.A.A. unless the means are available not only to improve the housing there within a reasonably short time but also to do so without prejudicing the interests of the residents". (D.O.E. Circular 14/75, Memorandum A, para. 9).

Guidance
Authorities are required to have regard to the guidance of the Secretary of State as to what sort of areas are suitable to be declared as H.A.A.s: subs. (3). The Secretary of State has issued guidance for this purpose in D.O.E. Circular, Memorandum A, paras. 11–16, of which the following represents the key aspects (but full regard must be had to the Circular itself when a particular area is to be considered):

"In assessing the *physical condition* . . . regard should principally be had to the proportion of houses which lack the standard amenities [see, now, s.508, below] . . . Secondarily, regard should be had to the proportion of houses which are unfit in the sense of [now, s.604, below] and to bad external layout (*e.g.* cramped backyards, back alleys) and other adverse features of the surroundings . . .

"In assessing *social conditions* . . . regard should principally be had to . . . the proportion of households sharing cooking facilities, a bath, a water closet or other facilities . . . density . . . the proportion . . . in privately-rented accommodation . . . the concentration of households likely to have special housing problems . . .

"Local authorities should have regard to the *extent to which physical and social factors combine and interact* to create unsatisfactory living conditions . . . An area in which the physical condition of the housing stock is the sole cause of bad housing conditions or where improvement could effectively be secured without the H.A.A. provisions is not appropriate for declaration as an H.A.A.

"Authorities should have particular regard to *whether sufficient resources will be available* to secure a significant improvement . . . within five years . . . By 'resources' is here meant . . . financial resources . . . staff . . . resources, of money and staff, available to registered housing associations working in the area . . . the local capacity of the building industry . . . rehousing or 'decanting' space . . .

"*The size of an H.A.A. will depend on particular circumstances in the localities* . . . An H.A.A. should not, however, be so large that significant progress . . . cannot be secured within the first five years. Where housing stress exists over an extensive area, the authority should initially declare only part and thereafter . . . proceed by stages as resources are released or become available . . .

"The H.A.A. provisions are not designed to deal with social or physical problems arising in *property already owned by a local authority* and it would not be appropriate for an H.A.A. to be declared which, at the time of declaration, contained estates, or a significant number of houses, already owned by a local authority . . . "

Map
"An H.A.A. map will need to be drawn to such a scale and in sufficient detail to make clear beyond reasonable doubt which buildings are included . . . " (D.O.E. Circular 14/74, Memorandum A, para. 8). Land in a G.I.A. proposed for inclusion in an H.A.A. has to be specifically identified on the map: s.242, below.

Declaration
It is for the authority to make the declaration, by resolution (subs. (1)), and prima facie it will be effective for five years: subs. (4). The Secretary of State's power to control declarations (with their grant-aid consequences not only to the authority, but also to the government on account of subsidies—see ss.516, 517, below) is to 'overrule' a declaration—in whole or part—under s.241, below; the authority may themselves bring an H.A.A. prematurely to an end—in whole or part—under s.250, below; they may also extend the duration of the area under s.251 (again subject to being overruled by the Secretary of State).

Steps to be taken after declaration of housing action area

240.—(1) As soon as may be after passing a resolution declaring an area to be a housing action area the local housing authority shall take the following steps.

(2) They shall publish in two or more newspapers circulating in the locality (of which one at least shall, if practicable, be a local newspaper) a notice of the resolution—

(*a*) identifying the area, and

(*b*) naming a place where a copy of the resolution, a map on which the area is defined and of the report referred to in section 239 may be inspected at all reasonable times.

(3) They shall take such further steps as appear to them best designed to secure—

(*a*) that the resolution and the obligations imposed by section 247 (duty to notify local housing authority of changes of ownership or occupation of land) are brought to the attention of persons residing or owning property in the area, and

(*b*) that those persons are informed of the name and address of the person to whom should be addressed inquiries and representations concerning action to be taken with respect to the area or concerning the obligations imposed by that section.

(4) They shall send to the Secretary of State—

(*a*) a copy of the resolution, the map and a copy of the report mentioned in section 239(1),

(*b*) a statement of the numbers of dwellings, houses in multiple occupation and hostels in the area, and

(*c*) a statement, containing such information as the Secretary of State may for the time being require, either generally or with respect to a particular authority or description of authority or in any particular case, showing the basis on which the authority satisfied themselves, having regard to the matters mentioned in section 239(1) and any relevant guidance under section 239(3), that the area was suitable to be a housing action area.

(5) They shall also send to the Secretary of State a statement of their proposals, whether general or specific, for the participation of registered housing associations in dealing with living conditions in the area.

GENERAL NOTE

The first steps after declaration are those set out in this section. They must publicise the declaration in two newspapers, one of which is if practicable to be a local paper: subs. (2). They must take further steps to bring the declaration to the attention of residents, including the notification duties of s.247, which cover not only *sales* (excluding certain sales, *e.g.* by owner-occupiers) but *notice to quit* (see notes below), and to tell them where they may obtain further information: subs. (3).

They must also send the information specified in subss. (4) and (5) to the Secretary of State. The Secretary of State has required information as to physical and social factors, and other matters to which the authority have had regard, information as to the housing function of the area at time of declaration and under the authority's proposals, general nature of proposed improvements, reasoned statement as to why living conditions are considered unsatisfactory and why declaration is considered the most effective way of dealing with them, information as to available resources, an account of the steps taken under subs. (3), and an account of consultation by the authority with other authorities or agencies: see D.O.E. Circular 14/75, Memorandum A, para. 24.

As to subs. (5), "Minister have made it clear . . . that registered housing associations can and should play an important role in supporting authorities, particularly tackling areas of housing stress and meeting the housing needs of special groups of people . . . The Secretary of State . . . attaches importance to the housing association statement . . . Authorities who have not hitherto made a practice of working with housing associations, or in whose districts there has been little housing association activity, should not hesitate to consult the Housing Corporation . . . In a district where more than one association is active, their involvement should be zoned so that in any particular H.A.A. only one association is used. This will enable associations to concentrate their efforts and eliminate the risk of their competing with each other.

"Local authorities will wish to bear in mind the possibility of using not only general housing associations . . . but also . . . housing co-operatives . . . " (D.O.E. Circular 14/75, Memorandum A, paras. 26–27). As to the functions of the Secretary of State, see s.241, below.

Functions of Secretary of State with respect to declaration of housing action area

241.—(1) When a local housing authority have declared an area to be a housing action area and have sent to the Secretary of State the documents referred to in section 240(4), he shall send them a written acknowledgement of the receipt of those documents.

(2) If it appears to the Secretary of State appropriate to do so, he may, at any time within the period of 28 days beginning with the day on which he sent the acknowledgement, notify the authority—

  (*a*) that the area declared by them to be a housing action area is no longer to be such an area, or

  (*b*) that land defined on a map accompanying the notification is to be excluded from the area,

or notify them that he requires more time to consider their declaration of the area as a housing action area.

(3) Where the Secretary of State notifies an authority that he requires more time, he may direct the authority to send him such further information and documents as are specified in the direction; and on completion of his consideration of the matter, he shall either—

  (*a*) notify the authority as mentioned in subsection (2)(*a*) or (*b*), or

  (*b*) notify them that he proposes to take no further action with respect to their declaration.

(4) Where the Secretary of State notifies the authority as mentioned in subsection (2)(*a*) or (*b*) (whether under that subsection or under subsection (3)), the area concerned shall cease to be a housing action area or, as the case may be, the land concerned shall be excluded from the housing action area, with effect from the date on which the authority is so notified.

(5) The authority shall, as soon as may be after the receipt of the notification, publish in two or more newspapers circulating in the locality (of which one at least shall, if practicable, be a local newspaper) a notice—

(*a*) stating the effect of the Secretary of State's notification, and

(*b*) naming a place where a copy of the notification and, in the case of a notification excluding land from the area, a copy of the amended map of the housing action area, may be inspected at all reasonable times,

and take such further steps as may appear to them best designed to secure that the effect of the notification is brought to the attention of persons residing or owning property in the area declared by them to be a housing action area.

DEFINITIONS
"housing action area": s.239.
"local housing authority": ss.1, 2.
"owner": s.262.

GENERAL NOTE
Prima facie, the Secretary of State must respond within tight time-limits. This, however, is a misleading impression. Time runs from when the Secretary of State acknowledges the s.240 submissions in writing: subs. (2). But there is no time attached to the Secretary of State's duty to send the written acknowledgment: subs. (1).

Once the acknowledgment *has* been sent, the Secretary of State can take any one of the following courses of action:

(1) He does nothing—the declaration stands as is;
(2) Within 28 days, he overrules the H.A.A. (subs. (2)(*a*))—the H.A.A. ceases to be such (subs. (4));
(3) Within 28 days, he excludes part of the area from the declaration (subs. (2)(*b*))—that part comes out of the H.A.A. (subs. (4));
(4) Within 28 days, he notifies the authority that he requires more time to consider the declaration (subs. (2))—in this case, he may also require more information (subs. (3)); on completion of his consideration, he is then bound to notify them either that he proposes to take no further action, in which case the H.A.A. stands as is, or in the same terms as (2) or (3): subs. (3).

The authority's duty to republicise arises under (2), (3) or (4), but not (1): subs. (5). The wording results in the imposition of a republicisation obligation even if the Secretary of State, having taken more time to consider, notifies the authority that he proposes to take no further action: this is contrary to the former provisions of s.37, Housing Act 1974, and appears to be a slip—*cf.* s.251(6), below. Further publicity duties arise in relation to a continuing H.A.A. under s.246, below.

Incorporation into housing action area of land comprised in general improvement area

242.—(1) If a local housing authority propose to declare as a housing action area an area which consists of or includes land which is comprised in a general improvement area, they shall indicate on the map referred to in section 239(1) the land which is so comprised.

(2) With effect from the date on which the resolution is passed declaring such an area to be a housing action area, the land so indicated shall be deemed to have been excluded from the general improvement area or, as the case may be, to have ceased to be such an area by virtue of a resolution under section 258 passed on that date, but subject to the following provisions.

(3) If the Secretary of State notifies the local housing authority in accordance with section 241 that the area declared by them to be a housing action area is no longer to be such an area, subsection (2) shall be treated as never having applied in relation to land in that area.

(4) If the Secretary of State notifies the local housing authority in accordance with section 241 that any land within the area declared by the authority to be a housing action area is to be excluded from the housing action area, subsection (2) shall be treated as never having applied in relation to land so excluded.

DEFINITIONS
"general improvement area": s.253.
"housing action area": s.239.
"local housing authority": ss.1, 2.

GENERAL NOTE
Land in a G.I.A. has to be identified on the map required by s.239(1), above: subs. (1). From the date of declaration of the H.A.A., the G.I.A. ceases to exist as such, as if it had been excluded from a G.I.A. or declared to have ceased to be a G.I.A. under s.258, below, and is of course H.A.A. instead: subs. (2). However, if the Secretary of State uses his powers under s.241 to overrule the H.A.A. in whole or in the relevant part, not only does the former G.I.A. revert to G.I.A. status, but it is treated as if it had never (even temporarily) become H.A.A. (subss. (3), (4)); the importance of this lies in levels of grant-aid (*cf.* ss.473, 482, 490, 498, below, but see also s.516, below on subsidies), *i.e.* even if applied for or approved between declaration as H.A.A. and reversion to G.I.A., G.I.A. levels will apply.

General powers of local housing authority

243.—(1) Where a local housing authority have declared an area to be a housing action area, they may, for the purpose of securing or assisting in securing all or any of the objectives specified in section 239(2)(*a*) to (*c*) exercise the following powers.

(2) They may acquire by agreement, or be authorised by the Secretary of State to acquire compulsorily, land in the area on which there are premises consisting of or including housing accommodation.

(3) They may undertake on land so acquired all or any of the following activities—
(*a*) the provision of housing accommodation (by the construction, conversion or improvement of buildings, or otherwise);
(*b*) the carrying out of works for the improvement or repair of housing accommodation (including works to the exterior, or on land within the curtilage, of buildings containing housing accommodation);
(*c*) the management of housing accommodation;
(*d*) the provision of furniture, fittings or services in or in relation to housing accommodation.

(4) If after—
(*a*) the authority have entered into a contract for the acquisition of land under subsection (2), or
(*b*) a compulsory purchase order authorising the acquisition of land under that subsection has been confirmed,
the housing action area concerned ceases to be such an area or the land is excluded from the area, the provisions of that subsection continue to apply as if the land continued to be in a housing action area.

DEFINITIONS
"housing accommodation": s.252.
"housing action area": s.239.
"local housing authority": ss.1, 2.

GENERAL NOTE

This section contains the principal powers of the authority in a declared (but not necessarily yet *approved, i.e.* within the meaning of s.241, above) H.A.A., all of which are *only* exercisable in order to secure, or to assist in securing, any of the principal objectives set out in s.239(2)(*a*) to (*c*), above: subs. (1). They also enjoy "environmental" powers under s.244, below.

Purchase Power

The first power is to acquire land on which there are premises consisting of or including housing accommodation, as defined in s.252 (see notes to s.239, above): subs. (2). "Land" includes "buildings and other structures, land covered with water, and any estate, interest, easement, servitude or right in or over land": Interpretation Act 1978, Schedule 1. But there must *be* premises consisting of or including housing accommodation, for the purchase to go ahead at all.

As to compulsory purchase, see generally Part XVII, below. The relevant date for determining whether or not something is housing accommodation for the purpose of exercising this power of acquisition is the date when the issue arises, so that the intentions of the authority, *e.g.* to use as housing accommodation that which might in fact *not* be housing accommodation, are irrelevant: see *R.* v. *Camden London Borough Council, ex parte Comyn Ching & Co. (London) Ltd.* [1984] J.P.L. 661, Q.B.D. (see further notes to s.239, above).

An authority can seek, and the Secretary of State can authorise, a compulsory purchase order under this provision, even though the authority at the time know that they will not, or are willing to not, proceed with the purchase if the owner of the property himself executes satisfactory proposals for repair and improvement, *i.e.* they can "hold" the powers pending the outcome of a negotiated improvement package: *Varsani* v. *Secretary of State for the Environment* (1980) 40 P. & C.R. 354, Q.B.D.

The authority and the Secretary of State enjoy powers of entry for the purpose of survey or valuation under this section (s.260, below), obstruction of which constitutes an offence under s.261, below.

Works

Once the property has been purchased, the authority enjoy the powers of subs. (3), to carry out works on the land acquired, to provide housing accommodation, to improve or repair such accommodation—including external and curtilage works to a building containing housing accommodation—and to manage it, including by the provisions of furniture, fittings or services. The conversion power must, of definition, relate to the conversion of what is already housing accommodation of one sort, to housing accommodation of another, for if the property is not housing accommodation to begin with, the purchase power will not itself exist: *R.* v. *Camden London Borough Council, ex parte Comyn Ching & Co. (London) Ltd.* [1984] J.P.L. 661, Q.B.D.

Subs. (4)

This subsection deals with the situation which arises if the authority have contracted to purchase, or actually purchased, or their compulsory purchase order has arrived at the stage of confirmation, and the land then ceases to be in an H.A.A. The latter two illustrations are only likely to arise where the H.A.A.—or relevant part of it—has not been overruled by the Secretary of State under s.241, above; but the former might arise between declaration and overruling. The provisions will also of course apply in the other cases when land ceases to be in an H.A.A.: see ss.250, 251, below.

Environmental works

244.—(1) For the purpose of improving the amenities in a housing action area, the local housing authority may—

    (*a*) carry out environmental works on land belonging to them, and

    (*b*) give assistance towards the carrying out of environmental works by others.

(2) Assistance under subsection (1)(*b*) may be given to any person having an interest in the land in question and may consist of all or any of the following—

    (*a*) a grant in respect of expenditure which appears to the authority to have been properly incurred in carrying out the works;

(*b*) the provision of materials for the carrying out of the works;

(*c*) the execution of the works, by agreement with the person concerned, either at his expense or at the authority's expense or partly at his expense and partly at the authority's expense.

(3) No such assistance shall be given towards works in respect of which an application for an improvement grant, intermediate grant, special grant or repairs grant has been approved.

(4) Where the assistance takes the form of a grant, it may be paid—

(*a*) after completion of the works, or

(*b*) in part by instalments as the works progress and the balance after completion of the works;

but where part is paid by instalments the aggregate amount of the instalments paid at any time whilst the works are in progress shall not exceed one-half of the cost of the works executed up to that time.

(5) In this section "environmental works" means any works other than works to the interior of housing accommodation.

DEFINITIONS

"housing accommodation": s.252.
"housing action area": s.239.
"improvement grant": s.467.
"intermediate grant": s.474.
"local housing authority": ss.1, 2.
"repairs grant": s.491.
"special grant": s.483.

GENERAL NOTE

Under Part XV, a range of principal grants is available:

(1) Improvement Grant—for the provision of dwellings by conversion, or for works of improvement to a dwelling more extensive than works within the Intermediate Grant (s.467);

(2) Intermediate Grant—for the improvement of a dwelling lacking standard amenities (within s.508) (or standard amenities accessible to a disabled occupant) by their provision, together with works needed to ensure that the dwelling is on completion of works fit for human habitation with s.604, below (s.474);

(3) Repairs Grant—for repairs works of a substantial and structural character in "old dwellings" as defined under s.492 (s.491);

(4) Special Grants—for works either for the provision of standard amenities, or for the provision of means of escape from fire in an H.M.O. (s.483).

This section confers power to add to these forms of assistance (but not to replace them if actually approved—see subs. (3)), by the execution of "environmental works", *i.e.* any works *other than* to the interior of housing accommodation. The authority's *subsidised* expenditure as a whole under this section is limited by s.245, below, but although that limit will comprise a powerful practical inhibition on any greater such expenditure, it does not constitute a legal bar on unsubsidised expenditure (although *cf.* notes to s.421, below, for the limits imposed on all capital expenditure—as which these works will qualify—under Local Government, Planning and Land Act 1980).

Earlier practices using these powers involved street works, landscaping, exteriors and curtilages of buildings, community facilities, and miscellaneous works, excluding not only grant-aidable works and works to the interior of accommodation (which are statutorily excluded), but also works to provide or improve facilities which would be expected to produce revenue for the authority, works to commercial and industrial premises likely to increase significantly the profits of those occupying the premises, and works of routine maintenance which the authority or any other public body have a duty to carry out, or to private property: see D.O.E. Circular 21/80, Appendix F, para. 14, determining in respect of which matters the Secretary of State would provide assistance under what is now s.245, below.

These general practices have more recently tended to give way to the much-favoured policy of "enveloping": this "is the renovation of the external fabric and curtilage of dwellings which have deteriorated beyond the scope of routine maintenance. It is carried out at the instigation of the local authority but with the consent of the owners of the properties concerned and at no cost to those owners. It includes such items as repair or renewal of roof and chimneys, rainwater goods, work to external walls, repair or replacement of doors and windows and improvements to the curtilages. Whole terraces or blocks are dealt with simultaneously with consequent economies through the use of standard components and materials and the involvement of major building contractors who might not otherwise be attracted to housing rehabilitation work . . . " (D.O.E. Circular 29/82, para. 2).

The importance of this policy has been reasserted in D.O.E. Circular 26/84 ("a mainstream housing policy"): "It is a way of tackling the worst economically improvable elements of the housing stock by achieving maximum effect rapidly at reasonable public sector cost. It reduces the unit costs of repair through the economies of scale which result from carrying out standardised works to the exterior of whole blocks or terraces of housing . . . " The Green Paper, Home Improvement—A New Approach, Cmnd. 9513, May 1985, see notes to s.239, above, proposes legislation to extend powers to carry out enveloping, but subject to contribution from owners.

The statutory powers are (a) to carry out works on their own land, and (b) to provide assistance towards the execution of environmental works by others: subs. (1). "Land" includes "buildings and other structures, land covered with water, and any estate, interest, easement, servitude or right in or over land": Interpretation Act 1978, Schedule 1. Enveloping "schemes that include local authority dwellings will not be approved unless the local authority dwellings are small in number . . . " (D.O.E. Circular 29/82, para. 8).

Assistance to others is confined to someone with an interest in the land: subs. (2). However, in contrast to the provisions of Part XV (see s.463, below), there is no requirement as to particular class of interest, so that any contractual tenant (but *not* a statutory tenant—*cf.* notes to s.622, below), leaseholder or owner, will qualify, although a licensee will not. Assistance can consist of any mix of the powers in subs. (2): outright grant, provision of materials, execution of works by the authority (or sub-contracted by them), with either the person assisted or the authority or both bearing or sharing the expense.

There is no limit to the amount of grant-aid, equivalent to the eligible expense and appropriate percentage limits of Part XV, below, but if "stage payments" (*cf.* s.511, below) are made, they are to be limited to 50 per cent. of the works to date: subs. (4).

Contributions by Secretary of State

245.—(1) The Secretary of State may pay contributions to a local housing authority towards such expenditure incurred by them under section 244 (environmental works) as he may determine.

(2) The contributions shall be annual sums—

(*a*) payable in respect of a period of 20 years beginning with the financial year in which the expenditure towards which the contribution is made is incurred, and

(*b*) equal to one-half of the annual loan charges referable to that expenditure, that is to say, the annual sum that, in the opinion of the Secretary of State, would fall to be paid by the local housing authority for the repayment of principal and the payment of interest on a loan of an amount equal to the expenditure repayable over that period.

(3) The aggregate of the expenditure towards which such contributions may be made with respect to a housing action area shall not exceed the sum arrived at by multiplying—

(*a*) £400, by

(*b*) the number of dwellings, houses in multiple occupation and hostels stated by the local housing authority under section 240(4)(*b*) to be in the area;

but two adjoining housing action areas may for this purpose be treated as one.

(4) The Secretary of State may, with the consent of the Treasury—

(*a*) by order substitute in subsections (2) and (3) another fraction for one-half and another amount for £400;

(*b*) direct that those subsections shall have effect, in the case of a housing action area specified in the direction or of a description so specified, with the substitution of a higher fraction or a greater amount than that for the time being specified in the subsection.

(5) An order under subsection (4)(*a*)—
  (*a*) may make different provision with respect to different cases or descriptions of case, including different provision for different areas, and
  (*b*) shall be made by statutory instrument which shall be subject to annulment in pursuance of a resolution of the House of Commons.

DEFINITIONS
  "dwelling": s.252.
  "hostel": s.622.
  "house in multiple occupation": s.252.
  "housing action area": s.239.
  "local housing authority": ss.1, 2.

GENERAL NOTE
This section governs the subsidy available to the authority under s.244, above, *i.e.* environmental works. It does not constitute a legal maximum on their expenditure, but on the expenditure which will qualify for subsidy, although this, of course, constitutes a powerful practical inhibition on any larger such expenditure, especially when taken together with the provisions of the Local Government, Planning and Land Act 1980 (see notes to s.421, below).

Qualifying expenditure is such as the Secretary of State determines: subs. (1); see D.O.E. Circulars 21/80, 29/82 and 26/84 (*cf.* notes to s.244, above). However, it is to a limit of £400 (or such other sum as the Secretary of State may specify—see subs. (4)) multiplied by the number of dwellings, H.M.O.s and hostels within the H.A.A. As "dwelling" includes part of a building occupied or intended to be occupied as a separate dwelling, it is the actual units of accommodation which provides the multiplier.

In view of the definition of "separate dwelling", and the definition of H.M.O. excluding separate dwellings (s.252 and notes to s.460, below), it could seem that a house occupied in bed-sitting rooms may give rise to a number of units, *i.e.* each separately occupied bed-sitting room, plus one for the house itself. However, as this is a legal analysis, based not least on the recent decision in *Street* v. *Mountford* [1985] A.C. 809, 17 H.L.R. 402, H.L., (see notes to s.93, above), *i.e.* because those who are not lodgers will be tenants and should therefore be treated as the "occupiers" of their individual rooms, some caution should be adopted in this respect, bearing in mind that the issue of subsidy is discretionary (subs. (1)).

The actual subsidy is half the loan charges over a period of 20 years: subs. (2). The Secretary of State may vary this proportion (subs. (4)), and has done so for "enveloping" schemes (*cf.* notes to s.244, above), to a proportion of 75 per cent.—see now D.O.E. Circular 26/84. It should be noted that the D.O.E.'s approval must be sought before contracts are let under a proposed enveloping scheme, if it is to be eligible for the 75 per cent. subsidy: ibid, para. 2. "In evaluating proposals, the Secretary of State will require to be satisfied that enveloping is cost-effective. In general, houses should be sufficiently beyond the scope of routine maintenance to warrant the special attention that enveloping affords but sound enough to justify the investment". (Ibid, para. 5).

The criteria which the D.O.E. will use to evaluate the value and costs of projects are set out in *ibid*, App. C. In general, the D.O.E. expects that at least 20–25 dwellings should be involved: *ibid*, para. 9.

Duty to publish information

246. Where a local housing authority have declared an area to be a housing action area, they shall bring to the attention of persons residing or owning property in the area—
  (*a*) the action they propose to take in relation to the housing action area, and
  (*b*) the assistance available for the improvement of the housing accommodation in the area,
by publishing from time to time, in such manner as appears to them appropriate, such information as is in their opinion best designed to further the purpose for which the area was declared a housing action area.

"housing accommodation": s.252.
"housing action area": s.239.
"local housing authority": ss.1, 2.
"owner": s.262.

GENERAL NOTE
Under this section, the authority have a continuing duty to publicise, from time to time and in the manner that seems to them appropriate, such information as they consider is best designed to further the purposes of the H.A.A., to bring to the attention of residents and owners (*a*) their own proposals for action, and (*b*) what assistance is available, *i.e.* under Part XV, below, and perhaps under s.244, above (if applicable).

Changes of ownership or occupation of land to be notified to local housing authority

247.—(1) This section—

(*a*) applies to land in a housing action area which consists of or includes housing accommodation, and

(*b*) comes into operation in relation to a housing action area at the end of the period of four weeks beginning with the date on which the housing action area is declared.

(2) Where notice to quit is served in respect of land to which this section applies on a tenant who occupies as a dwelling the whole or part of the land, the landlord by whom, or on whose behalf, the notice was served shall, within the period of seven days beginning with the date on which the notice was served, notify the local housing authority that the notice has been served.

(3) Where a tenancy of land to which this section applies is about to expire by effluxion of time, the person who is the landlord under the tenancy shall, not less than four weeks before the tenancy does so expire, notify the local housing authority that the tenancy is about to expire.

(4) A person who carries out a disposal of land to which this section applies, other than a disposal excepted by subsection (5), shall notify the local housing authority, not less than four weeks or more than six months before the date of the disposal, that the disposal is about to take place.

(5) Subsection (4) does not apply to—

(*a*) a disposal by a person who, throughout the period of six months ending on the date of the disposal has been continuously in exclusive occupation (with or without members of his household) of the land to which the disposal relates;

(*b*) a disposal to which the local housing authority are a party;

(*c*) the grant of a protected tenancy or protected occupancy or the entering into of a restricted contract;

(*d*) the grant or assignment of a lease (of land or an interest in land) for a term which expires within the period of five years and three months beginning on the date of the grant of the lease, where neither the lease nor any other instrument or contract confers on the lessor or the lessee an option (however expressed) to renew or extend the term so that the new or extended term would continue beyond the end of that period;

(*e*) the grant of an estate or interest by way of security for a loan;

(*f*) a conveyance of an estate or interest which gives effect to a contract to convey that estate or interest which was duly notified to the local housing authority in accordance with subsection (4).

(6) When the local housing authority receive notification from a person under this section with respect to any land they shall—

(*a*) send him, as soon as practicable, written acknowledgement of the receipt of the notification, stating the date on which it was received, and (*b*) inform him, within the period of four weeks beginning with that date, of what action, if any, they propose to take with respect to that land as a result of the notification.

DEFINITIONS
"disposal": s.262.
"dwelling": s.252.
"housing accommodation": s.252.
"housing action area": s.239.
"local housing authority": ss.1, 2.
"owner": s.262.
"protected occupancy": s.622.
"protected tenancy": s.622.
"restricted contract": s.622.

GENERAL NOTE

The duties imposed on landlords and owners under this section are those to which attention must be drawn under s.240(3), above. They are duties of notification which, in substance, exist in order to permit the authority to exercise their powers of purchase under ss.243(2), above, bearing in mind that the *purpose* of the H.A.A. (whether or not it has been achieved in practice) is to improve conditions for benefit of *current* residents, *i.e.* "persons for the time being resident in the area" (s.239(2)(*b*), above; see notes thereto).

The section applies to land in an H.A.A., which consists of or includes housing accommodation: see notes to s.239, above (subs. (1)(*a*)). It is operative four weeks after the date of the declaration under s.239: subs. (1)(*b*). It is, accordingly, likely to become operative before it is known whether or not the Secretary of State will use his powers of overruling under s.241, above. The authority's duties in relation to notifications are set out in subs. (6), below. The form and content of notification is described in s.248, below. Penalties for failure to comply with the requirement to give notification is under s.249, below. Failure to give notification as required does not, however, affect the validity of the transaction in question: s.249(2), below.

There are two broad classes of obligation: termination of tenancies, and disposals.

Termination of Tenancies

The first class relates to tenants: not licensees, but *cf.* notes to s.93, above, and consider the impact of *Street* v. *Mountford* [1985] A.C. 809, 17 H.L.R. 402, H.L., especially on, *e.g.*, rooms in H.M.O.s (*cf.* notes to s.245, above). Under this class, the landlord must give the authority notification (a) of notice to quit, within seven days of its service, whether he served it or it was served on his behalf (subs. (2)), and (b) expiry of fixed-term tenancy, no later than four weeks before it is due to expire (subs. (3)).

The provisions do not seem to apply to forfeiture proceedings: *cf.* notes to s.82, above. Nor do they apply on a tenant's notice to quit, or surrender: *cf.* notes to ss.93, 103, above. However, it has been held that they *do* apply, even although the notice to quit may itself not have been valid (*e.g.* at common law, or under s.5, Protection from Eviction Act 1977): *Fawcett* v. *Newcastle-upon-Tyne City Council* (1977) 242 E.G. 695, D.C.

The provisions apply to protected tenancies and occupancies, and restricted contracts: the exemption in subs. (5) relates to *grants* of such rights of occupation.

Disposals

"Disposal" includes a conveyance of, or a contract to convey, an estate or interest not previously in existence: s.262, below. Accordingly, the *creation* of a tenancy will *prima facie* qualify as a disposal under subs. (4), but will be exempt by subs. (5)(*c*), if it is the grant of a protected tenancy (*i.e.* Rent Act 1977), a protected occupancy (*i.e.* Rent (Agriculture) Act 1976), or a restricted contract (*i.e.* letting by resident landlord): see, as to the meaning of each of these terms, notes to s.622, below. The extension to protected occupancies is pursuant to Law Commission Recommendations (Cmnd. 9515), No. 14(ii).

As disposal is not defined further than as *extended* by s.262, below, it *may* be taken to include the creation of a licence: support for this may be found in the extension last referred to, as most agricultural tied occupiers are licensees (see, *e.g.*, *Crane* v. *Morris* [1965] 1 W.L.R. 1104, C.A.; see further notes to Sched. 1, para. 2, below). It may also be assisted by the purposive interpretation given to the section in the *Fawcett* decision. The reference to restricted contract would not seem to assist, as this could be a tenancy from a resident landlord (Rent Act 1977, s.12) as much as a licence within s.19, 1977 Act: see further notes to s.622, below.

Whether or not the provisions extend to licences, disposals by any occupiers who have been in *exclusive* occupation, *i.e.* without subletting (*cf.* notes to s.93, above), but disregarding occupation shared by members of an occupiers' household, are exempt, provided the exclusive occupation has been sustained for at least six months, and has been continuous (*cf.* unbroken occupation for the purposes of the owner-occupier's supplementary compensation under Sched. 24, below, see cases in notes thereto); an owner-occupier thus defined as genuine will accordingly be exempt: subs. (5)(*a*).

Disposals to which the authority are a party will also be exempt: subs. (3)(*b*). This will not include where the authority purchase an interest under s.243(2), above, but where a "housing arrangement" is made in connection with compulsory improvement powers—see notes to s.214, above. Grants of tenancies for relatively short periods (*i.e.* five years and three months from grant, and without option to renew or extend beyond that limit) are exempt: subs. (3)(*d*).

Assignments of such leases are also exempt: *ibid.* Note that that which is assigned must itself be a short lease as defined, for time runs from *grant* of lease in either event, so that assignment of the residue of a longer lease will not be exempt. However, if the assignment is by someone who has been in occupation within subs. (5)(*a*) for a long enough period, that provision will exempt the disposal, whether the lease is long or short. Mortgages are exempt: subs. (5)(*e*). Finally, a conveyance pursuant to a contract to convey which has itself been notified is also exempt.

Subs. (6)

The authority's corresponding duty is to acknowledge the notification in writing, identifying the date of receipt of the notification, and to inform the notifying person—within four weeks of the date stated to be that of receipt of notification—what if any action they propose to take, *i.e.* purchase under s.243(2), or not.

Form and contents of notification under s.247

248.—(1) A notification under section 247 shall be in writing and contain the information required by this section.

(2) Every notification shall contain—

(*a*) the name and address of the person by whom it is given,

(*b*) the address of, and any further information necessary to identify, the land to which it relates, and

(*c*) the estate or interest in that land which the person by whom it is given has at the time it is given.

(3) The reference in subsection (2)(*a*) to a person's address is to his place of abode or place of business or, in the case of a company, to its registered office.

(4) To the extent that it is capable of being given by reference to a plan accompanying the notification, the information required by subsection (2)(*b*) may be so given.

(5) A notification required by section 247(2) or (3) (notice to quit or impending expiry of tenancy) shall specify—

(*a*) whether the tenancy concerned is periodic or for a term certain,

(*b*) the length of the period or term, and

(*c*) the date on which the tenancy will come to an end (by virtue of the service of the notice to quit or by effluxion of time);

and in the case of a notification required by section 247(2) the landlord may also, if he considers it appropriate, give his reason for serving notice to quit.

(6) A notification required by section 247(4) (disposal of land) shall specify—

(*a*) whether at the time the notification is given the person giving it intends to retain an estate or interest in the land, and

(*b*) if he does, the nature of that estate or interest and the land in which he intends that it should subsist.

GENERAL NOTE

This section governs the content of a notification under the last. For service on authorities, see notes to s.617, below. Knowingly or recklessly omitting information required by this section is an offence under s.249, below. However, failure to give notification, or giving a notification which is wrong or incomplete, will not invalidate the transaction in question: s.249(2), below.

Penalty for failure to notify, &c.

249.—(1) A person who—

(*a*) fails without reasonable excuse to comply with an obligation imposed on him by section 247(2) or (3), or

(*b*) without reasonable excuse carries out a disposal of land without having complied with the obligation imposed on him by section 247(4), or

(*c*) in purporting to comply with an obligation imposed on him by section 247 knowingly or recklessly furnishes a notification which is false in a material particular, or

(*d*) knowingly or recklessly omits from any such notification any information required to be contained in it by virtue of any provision of section 248,

commits a summary offence and is liable on conviction to a fine not exceeding level 5 on the standard scale.

(2) The commission by a person of an offence under subsection (1) does not affect—

(*a*) in the case of a notification required by section 247(2) or (3) (notice to quit or expiry of tenancy), the date on which the tenancy expires;

(*b*) in the case of a notification required by section 247(4) (disposal of land), the validity of the disposal.

DEFINITION.
"disposal": s.262.

GENERAL NOTE
This section has two parts. The first deals with criminal penalties for non-compliance with either of the last two sections; the second, with the civil (non-)consequences of non-compliance.

Subs. (1)
The four offences carry a fine of up to level 5 on the standard scale, *i.e.* under s.37, Criminal Justice Act 1982, currently £2,000, by S.I. 1984 No. 447.

Subs. (2)
Commission of an offence does not invalidate the transaction in question. The former wording referred to "conviction" of an offence; the change is pursuant to Law Commission Recommendations (Cmnd. 9515), No. 15.

Exclusion of land from, or termination of, housing action area

250.—(1) The local housing authority may by resolution—

(*a*) exclude land from a housing action area, or

(*b*) declare that an area shall cease to be a housing action area on the date on which the resolution is passed;

and as soon as may be after passing such a resolution the authority shall take the following steps.

(2) They shall send a copy of the resolution to the Secretary of State.

(3) They shall publish in two or more newspapers circulating in the locality (of which one at least shall, if practicable, be a local newspaper) a notice of the resolution—

(*a*) in the case of a resolution excluding land from a housing action area, identifying the housing action area concerned and the land excluded from it,

(*b*) in the case of a resolution declaring that an area is no longer to be a housing action area, naming a place at which a copy of the resolution may be inspected at all reasonable times.

(4) They shall take such further steps as may appear to the authority best designed to secure that the resolution is brought to the attention of persons residing or owning property in the housing action area.

DEFINITIONS
"housing action area": s.239.
"local housing authority": ss.1, 2.
"owner": s.262.

GENERAL NOTE
It is within the discretion of the authority at any time to resolve to discontinue the H.A.A., or to exclude land from it, and the Secretary of State enjoys nothing more than the right to a copy of the resolution (subss. (1), (2)), *i.e.* he has no power to overrule the authority (*cf.* s.241, above, and s.251, below). Subss. (3), (4), contain publicity duties corresponding to those on declaration (s.240(2), (3)) and on a variation or overruling of the declaration by the Secretary of State (or, indeed, notification of confirmation after his extended consideration): see s.241(5).

Extension of duration of housing action area

251.—(1) The local housing authority may by resolution extend the duration of a housing action area by a period of two years, and may do so more than once.

(2) Written notification of the passing of the resolution must be given by the authority to the Secretary of State at least three months before the date on which the housing action area would otherwise cease to exist.

(3) On receipt of a notification under subsection (2) the Secretary of State shall send a written acknowledgement to the authority.

(4) If it appears to the Secretary of State appropriate to do so, he may, at any time within the period of 28 days beginning with the day on which he sent the acknowledgement, notify the authority—

(*a*) that the duration of the housing action area is not to be extended in accordance with their resolution, or

(*b*) that he requires more time to consider their extension of the duration of the housing action area.

(5) Where the Secretary of State notifies an authority that he requires more time, he shall on completion of his consideration of the matter notify the authority—

(*a*) that the duration of the housing action area is not to be extended in accordance with their resolution,

(*b*) where the extension has already begun to run, that the area is to cease to be a housing action on such date as may be specified in the notification, or

(*c*) that he proposes to take no further action with respect to their resolution.

(6) As soon as may be after passing a resolution or receiving a notification from the Secretary of State under this section (other than a notification that he proposes to take no further action), the local housing authority shall—

(*a*) publish in two or more newspapers circulating in the locality (of which at least one shall, if practicable, be a local newspaper) a notice of the resolution or, as the case may be, stating the effect of the notification, naming a place where a copy of the resolution or notification may be inspected at all reasonable times, and

(*b*) take such further steps as appear to the authority best designed to secure that the resolution or notification is brought to the attention of persons residing or owning property in the housing action areas concerned.

"housing action area": s.239.
"local housing authority": ss.1, 2.
"owner": s.262.

GENERAL NOTE
The authority can extend an H.A.A. for up to two years at a time, without limit: subs. (1). However, they must send a copy of the resolution to the Secretary of State, no later than three months before the H.A.A. would otherwise expire: subs. (2). At this point, the position is exactly the same as under s.241, above, with the exceptions (a) that there is no power to require further information (*cf.* s.241(3), but if the authority does not want the extension to be overruled, it will of course wish to comply with his reasonable requests for such in any event as a matter of practice), and (b) that unlike under s.241(5), there is no duty to republicise after the decision of the Secretary of State if he proposes to permit the extension.

"It may sometimes be necessary for the duration of a Housing Action Area to be extended to accommodate an enveloping scheme . . . " (D.O.E. Circular 26/84, para. 14; *cf.* notes to ss.244, 245, above).

Meaning of "housing accommodation" and related expressions

252. In the provisions of this Part relating to housing action areas—
  (*a*) "housing accommodation" means dwellings, houses in multiple occupation and hostels;
  (*b*) "dwelling" means a building or part of a building occupied or intended to be occupied as a separate dwelling, together with any yard, garden, outhouses and appurtenances belonging to or usually enjoyed with that building or part; and
  (*c*) "house in multiple occupation" means a house which is occupied by persons who do not form a single household, exclusive of any part of the house which is occupied as a separate dwelling by persons who do form a single household.

GENERAL NOTE
See notes to s.239, above.

General improvement areas

Declaration of general improvement area

253.—(1) Where a report with respect to a predominantly residential area within their district is submitted to the local housing authority by a person appearing to the authority to be suitably qualified (who may be an officer of the authority), and it appears to the authority, upon consideration of the report and of any other information in their possession—
  (*a*) that living conditions in the area can most appropriately be improved by the improvement of the amenities of the area or of dwellings in the area, or both, and
  (*b*) that such an improvement may be effected or assisted by the exercise of their powers under the provisions of this Part relating to general improvement areas,
the authority may cause the area to be defined on a map and by resolution declare it to be a general improvement area.

(2) A general improvement area may not be defined so as to include, but may be defined so as to surround, land which is comprised in a housing action area.

(3) A general improvement area may not (unless the land has been cleared of buildings) be so defined as to include, but may be so defined as to surround—
  (*a*) land comprised in a clearance area,

(*b*) land purchased by the local housing authority under section 290(2) (land surrounded by or adjoining clearance area), or

(*c*) land included in a clearance area under section 293(1) (local housing authority's own property);

and where the Secretary of State on confirming a compulsory purchase order under Schedule 22 (acquisition of land for clearance) modifies the order by excluding from a clearance area land adjoining a general improvement area, the land shall, unless the Secretary of State otherwise directs, be taken to be included in the general improvement area.

DEFINITIONS
  "district": s.2.
  "housing action area": s.239.
  "local housing authority": ss.1, 2.
  "owner": s.262.

GENERAL NOTE
  This section introduces the G.I.A.: see also notes to s.239, above. Note that a G.I.A. is concerned with living conditions which can be improved by the improvement of amenities, and/or dwellings: subs. (1)(*a*). These sections do not, accordingly, deal in "housing accommodation". "Dwelling" is not defined: s.263, which contains the now familiar, but nonetheless novel, schedule of cross-references, defines it in terms of s.252, but that section is expressly confined to the provisions relating to H.A.A.s. The distinction is, however, unlikely to prove of any practical importance.
  "The word amenity still connotes in a statute what Scrutton L.J. thought it did on its first appearance in the Housing, Town Planning, etc. Act 1909; 'pleasant circumstances or features, advantages': *Ellis* v. *Ruislip-Northwood Urban Council* [1920] 1 K.B. 343, 370". (*per* Stephenson L.J., in *F.F.F. Estates Ltd.* v. *Hackney London Borough Council* [1981] Q.B. 503, 3 H.L.R. 107, C.A.).
  The observations in the notes to s.239 as to "suitably qualified persons" would appear to apply in relation to G.I.A.s, as will those under the headings "other information" and "map". The powers of entry available under s.260, below, subject to the criminal provisions of s.261, below, are also applicable to G.I.A.s. See also the caution about forthcoming changes in the introductory remarks to s.239.
  G.I.A.s are concerned with areas which are "predominantly residential": subs. (1). This term is not defined. Guidance provided in 1975 (D.O.E. Circulars 13/75 and 14/75) must be treated with some caution in view of the general reinstatement of the 1969 Act provisions under the Housing Act 1980; similarly, that in 1969 must be considered with caution as following the 1980 Act there was no "reinstatement of circulars". Nonetheless, it probably seems correct still to say that in general a G.I.A. will be in a better condition than an H.A.A., and may well be true that it will have a higher proportion of owner-occupiers to tenants: D.O.E. Circular 13/75, para. 18.
  The lack of guidance is not surprising, for the essence of the G.I.A. is that it is largely in the discretion of authorities, who enjoy powers which are few relative to H.A.A.s, reflected in the absence of any "overruling" powers of the Secretary of State, analogous to those to be found in either s.241 or s.251, above: "In future local authorities will have full control over the declaration of G.I.A.s". (D.O.E. Circular 21/80, Appendix F, para. 4). Their general powers are set out in s.255, below; levels of grant-aid under Part XV are not as high as in H.A.A.s and in some cases outside H.A.A.s, but are higher than other "non-priority" cases: see notes to ss.473, 482, 490, and 498, below; see also notes to s.516, below, with reference to subsidy.
  The G.I.A. cannot include H.A.A. land: subs. (2). See also s.242, above, under which an H.A.A. effectively supersedes a G.I.A. It also cannot include land within a clearance area, or added, under Part IX, below. There is no preordained life-span for the G.I.A.: it is up to the authority when they use their powers of determination under s.258, below.

Steps to be taken after declaration

254.—(1) As soon as may be after passing a resolution declaring an area to be a general improvement area the local housing authority shall take the following steps.

(2) They shall publish in two or more newspapers circulating in the
locality (of which one at least shall, if practicable, be a local newspaper)
a notice of the resolution—
   (*a*) identifying the area, and
   (*b*) naming a place where a copy of the resolution, of the map on
       which the area is defined and of the report mentioned in section
       253(1) may be inspected at all reasonable times.
(3) They shall take such further steps as appear to them best designed
to secure—
   (*a*) that the resolution is brought to the attention of persons residing
       or owning property in the area, and
   (*b*) that those persons are informed of the name and address of the
       person to whom enquiries and representations should be addressed
       concerning action to be taken in the exercise of the authority's
       powers under the provisions of this Part relating to general improve-
       ment areas.
(4) They shall send to the Secretary of State a copy of the resolution,
of the report and of the map and a statement of the number of dwellings
in the area.

DEFINITIONS
   "general improvement area": s.253.
   "local housing authority": ss.1, 2.
   "owner": s.262.

GENERAL NOTE
   This makes provision equivalent to that following declaration of an H.A.A. under s.240,
above, save, of course (*cf.* notes to s.253, above), that there is no requirement for submission
of statements to the Secretary of State and so, accordingly, no requirement to settle such
statements. A copy of the resolution and map under s.253 must, however, be sent to the
Secretary of State.

General powers of local housing authority

255.—(1) Where a local housing authority have declared an area to be
a general improvement area, they may, for the purpose of effecting or
assisting the improvement of the amenities of the area, or of the dwellings
in the area, or both—
   (*a*) carry out works on land owned by them and assist (by grants, loans
       or otherwise) in the carrying out of works on land not owned by
       them,
   (*b*) acquire any land by agreement, and
   (*c*) let or otherwise dispose of land for the time being owned by them;
and may be authorised by the Secretary of State to acquire compulsorily
land within the general improvement area or adjoining it.
(2) The authority may not under this section—
   (*a*) improve a dwelling which has not been acquired or provided by
       them in pursuance of this section, or
   (*b*) make a grant towards the cost of works in a case where an
       improvement grant, intermediate grant, special grant or repairs
       grant might be made under Part XV.

DEFINITIONS
   "general improvement area": s.253.
   "improvement grant": s.467.
   "intermediate grant": s.474.
   "local housing authority": ss.1, 2.
   "repairs grant": s.491.
   "special grant": s.483.

GENERAL NOTE
This section prescribes the powers of an authority in a G.I.A.: the powers, though expressed much more briefly than under ss.243 and 244 for H.A.A.s, include compulsory purchase (see notes to s.243, above), and the carrying out of works, not confined to but including environmental works (see notes to s.244, above). The most important difference is that works which are *capable of* being included in one of the specified grants cannot be the subject of assistance, whereas in relation to H.A.A.s, such works are only excluded if grant-aid has been *approved*. The terminology of subs. (1)(*a*) ("or otherwise") seems wide enough to cover carrying out works on behalf of an owner, as does the combination of subs. (1)(*b*) and (*c*) with subs. (2)(*a*) appear to cover as many powers as are more expressly spelled out in s.243(3), above.

Subsidy is dealt with in respect of all of the costs of this Part, by s.259, below.

Power to apply for orders extinguishing right to use vehicles on highway

256.—(1) A local housing authority who have declared a general improvement area may exercise the powers of a local planning authority under section 212 of the Town and Country Planning Act 1971 (extinguishment of right to use vehicles on certain highways) with respect to a highway in that area notwithstanding that they are not the local planning authority, but subject to the following provisions.

(2) The local housing authority shall not make an application under subsection (2) or (8) of that section (application to Secretary of State to make or revoke order extinguishing right to use vehicles) except with the consent of the local planning authority.

(3) If the local housing authority are not also the highway authority, any such application made by them shall in the first place be sent to the highway authority who shall transmit it to the Secretary of State.

(4) Where an order under subsection (2) of that section (order extinguishing right to use vehicles) has been made on an application made by a local housing authority by virtue of this section—

(*a*) any compensation under subsection (5) of that section (compensation for loss of access to highway) is payable by them instead of by the local planning authority, and

(*b*) they may exercise their powers as the competent authority under section 213 of that Act (provision of amenities for highway reserved to pedestrians) without the consent to the local planning authority.

DEFINITIONS
"general improvement area": s.253.
"local housing authority": ss.1, 2.

GENERAL NOTE
The purpose of this application of the powers of s.212, Town and Country Planning Act 1971 is to facilitate the "amenities" emphasis of the G.I.A.
"Highways authority": see Highways Act 1980.

Duty to publish information

257. Where a local housing authority have declared an area to be a general improvement area, they shall bring to the attention of persons residing in the area or owning property in it—

(*a*) the action they propose to take in the exercise of their powers under the provisions of this Part relating to general improvement areas, and

(*b*) the assistance available for the improvement of the amenities of the area or of the dwellings in the area,

by publishing from time to time, in such manner as appears to them appropriate, such information as is in their opinion best designed to further the objects of those provisions.

DEFINITIONS
　"general improvement area": s.253.
　"local housing authority": ss.1, 2.
　"owner": s.262.

GENERAL NOTE
　This is analogous to s.246, above: see notes thereto.

Exclusion of land from, or termination of, general improvement area

258.—(1) The local housing authority may by resolution—
(*a*) exclude land from a general improvement area, or
(*b*) declare an area to be no longer a general improvement area.
　(2) The resolution does not affect the continued operation of the provisions of this Part relating to general improvement areas, or any other provision so relating, in relation to works begun before the date on which the resolution takes effect; but the exclusion or cessation does apply with respect to works which have not been begun before that date, notwithstanding that expenditure in respect of the works has been approved before that date.

DEFINITIONS
　"general improvement area": s.253.
　"local housing authority": ss.1, 2.

GENERAL NOTE
　This is analogous to s.250, above, save that there is no express "depublicisation" obligation, and the provisions of subs. (2) serve to divide continued application where works have begun, from works not yet begun. Subs. (2) will apply to grant-aid under Part XV.

Contributions by Secretary of State

259.—(1) The Secretary of State may pay contributions to a local housing authority towards such expenditure incurred by them under the provisions of this Part relating to general improvement areas as he may determine.
　(2) The contributions shall be annual sums—
(*a*) payable in respect of a period of 20 years beginning with the financial year in which the expenditure towards which the contribution is made is incurred, and
(*b*) equal to one-half of the annual loan charges referable to that expenditure, that is to say, the annual sum that, in the opinion of the Secretary of State, would fall to be paid by the local housing authority for the repayment of principal and the payment of interest on a loan of an amount equal to the expenditure repayable over that period.
　(3) The aggregate of the expenditure towards which such contributions may be made with respect to a general improvement area shall not exceed the sum arrived at by multiplying—
(*a*) £400, by
(*b*) the number of dwellings stated by the local housing authority under section 254(4) to be in the area;
but two adjoining general improvement areas may for this purpose be treated as one.
　(4) The Secretary of State may, with the consent of the Treasury—
(*a*) by order substitute in subsections (2) and (3) another fraction for one-half and another amount for £400;
(*b*) direct that those subsections shall have effect, in the case of a general improvement area specified in the direction or of a description so specified, with the substitution of a higher fraction or a

greater amount than that for the time being specified in the subsection.

(5) An order under subsection (4)(*a*)—

(*a*) may make different provision for different cases or descriptions of case, including different provision for different areas, and

(*b*) shall be made by statutory instrument which shall be subject to annulment in pursuance of a resolution of the House of Commons.

(6) For the purposes of this section—

(*a*) the cost of acquiring an estate or interest in a case where periodical payments fall to be made in connection with the acquisition shall be taken to include such sum as the Secretary of State may determine to be the capital equivalent of those payments; and

(*b*) the cost of works shall be taken to include the cost of the employment in connection with the works of an architect, engineer, surveyor, land-agent or other person in an advisory or supervisory capacity.

(7) In the case of contributions payable in respect of—

(*a*) works to which the Housing Act 1971 applied (works in certain areas completed before 23rd June 1974), or

(*b*) expenditure on providing land treated as expenditure on such works by virtue of section 2(4) of that Act,

subsection (2)(*b*) above has effect with the substitution of "75 per cent." for "one-half".

DEFINITIONS
  "dwelling": s.252.
  "general improvement area": s.253.
  "local housing authority": ss.1, 2.

GENERAL NOTE
  This makes provision analogous to s.245, above (see notes thereto), save that it is not confined to environmental works, but is extended to all activity under these G.I.A. provisions, with the corresponding addition of subs. (6).

Supplementary provisions

Powers of entry

260.—(1) A person authorised by the local housing authority or the Secretary of State may at any reasonable time, on giving 24 hours' notice of his intention to the occupier, and to the owner if the owner is known, enter premises—

(*a*) for the purpose of survey and examination where it appears to the authority or the Secretary of State that survey or examination is necessary in order to determine whether any powers under this Part should be exercised; or

(*b*) for the purpose of survey or valuation where the authority are authorised by this Part to purchase the premises compulsorily.

(2) An authorisation for the purposes of this section shall be in writing stating the particular purpose or purposes for which the entry is authorised.

DEFINITIONS
  "local housing authority": ss.1, 2.
  "owner": s.262.

GENERAL NOTE
  The power of entry is similar to that to be found in ss.197 and 222, above, and ss.319, 340 and 395, below; see notes thereto. The requirements of subs. (2) are obligatory, and failure to comply will mean that entry is not pursuant to the statutory permission: see *Stroud* v. *Bradbury* [1952] 2 All E.R. 76, D.C. Obstruction of entry is an offence under s.261, below.

Penalty for obstruction

261.—(1) It is a summary offence to obstruct an officer of the local housing authority, or of the Secretary of State, or a person authorised to enter premises in pursuance of this Part, in the performance of anything which that officer, authority or person is by this Part required or authorised to do.

(2) A person who commits such an offence is liable on conviction to a fine not exceeding level 2 on the standard scale.

DEFINITION
"local housing authority": ss.1, 2.

GENERAL NOTE
The offence is punishable by a fine of up level 2 on the standard scale, *i.e.* under s.37, Criminal Justice Act 1982, currently £100, by S.I. 1984 No. 447.

Minor definitions

262. In this Part—
    "disposal", in relation to land, includes a conveyance of, or contract to convey, an estate or interest not previously in existence;
    "owner", in relation to premises—
        (*a*) means a person (other than a mortgagee not in possession) who is for the time being entitled to dispose of the fee simple in the premises, whether in possession or reversion, and
        (*b*) includes also a person holding or entitled to the rents and profits of the premises under a lease of which the unexpired term exceeds three years.

GENERAL NOTE
"Disposal": see also notes to s.247, above.

Index of defined expressions: Part VIII

263. The following Table shows provisions defining or otherwise explaining expressions used in this Part (other than provisions defining or explaining an expression used in the same section):—

clearance area	section 289
disposal (of land)	section 262
district (of a local housing authority)	section 2(1)
dwelling (in provisions relating to housing action areas)	section 252
general improvement area	section 253
hostel	section 622
house in multiple occupation	section 252
housing accommodation	section 252
housing action area	section 239
lease, lessee and lessor	section 621
local housing authority	section 1, 2(2)
owner (of premises)	section 262
protected occupancy	section 622
protected tenancy	section 622
restricted contract	section 622
standard scale (in reference to the maximum fine on summary conviction)	section 622
tenancy and tenant	section 621

Part IX

Slum Clearance

Demolition or closing of unfit premises beyond repair at reasonable cost

Power to accept undertaking as to reconstruction or use of unfit house

264.—(1) Where the local housing authority are satisfied that a house is unfit for human habitation and not capable of being rendered so fit at reasonable expense, they shall serve on—

(a) the person having control of the house,

(b) any other person who is an owner of the house, and

(c) every mortgagee of the house whom it is reasonably practicable to ascertain,

notice of a time (at least 21 days after the service of the notice) and place at which the condition of the house and any offer which he may wish to submit with respect to the carrying out of works, or the future user of the premises, will be considered by the authority.

(2) Every person on whom such a notice is served is entitled to be heard when the matter is so taken into consideration.

(3) A person on whom such a notice is served shall, if he intends to submit an offer with respect to the carrying out of works—

(a) within 21 days from the date of the service of the notice on him, serve on the authority notice in writing of his intention to make such an offer, and

(b) within such reasonable period as the authority may allow, submit to them a list of the works which he offers to carry out.

(4) The local housing authority may, if after consultation with an owner or mortgagee of the house they think fit to do so, accept an undertaking from him, either—

(a) that he will within a specified period carry out such works as will, in the opinion of the authority, render the house fit for human habitation, or

(b) that the house will not be used for human habitation until the authority, on being satisfied that it has been rendered fit for that purpose, cancel the undertaking.

(5) Nothing in the Rent Acts prevents possession being obtained by an owner of premises in a case where an undertaking has been given under this section that the premises will not be used for human habitation.

(6) A person who, knowing that an undertaking has been given under this section that premises will not be used for human habitation, uses the premises in contravention of the undertaking or permits them to be so used, commits a summary offence and is liable on conviction to a fine not exceeding level 5 on the standard scale and to a further fine not exceeding £5 for every day or part of a day on which he so uses them or permits them to be used after conviction.

(7) In this section references to a house include a hut, tent, caravan or other temporary or movable form of shelter which is used for human habitation and has been in the same enclosure for a period of two years next before action is taken.

Definitions

  "house": s.322.

  "local housing authority": ss.1, 2.

  "owner": s.322.

  "person having control": s.322.

  "reasonable expense": s.321.

  "Rent Acts": s.622.

  "unfit for human habitation": s.604.

GENERAL NOTE

This Part contains a number of provisions, formerly contained in Parts II and III, Housing Act 1957; the provisions of Part VI of this Act (repairs notices) were formerly contained in Part II of the 1957 Act, together with the provisions which start with this section and continue until and including s.282, and comprise the code for dealing with *individual* unfit housing, as distinct from the clearance of *obstructive* buildings (whether or not housing) to be found in ss.283–288, and the clearance of *areas* of unfit housing, to be found in ss.289–299, formerly contained in Part III of the 1957 Act, the latter dating back to the Artisans and Labourers' Dwellings Improvement Act 1875. The principal separation of unfitness powers that is now observed, therefore, is between repair and slum clearance, rather than between individual and area action.

This first series of sections concerns unfit housing *not* capable of being rendered fit at a reasonable expense. Such housing will either be the subject of voluntary fitness works or closing under this section, a demolition or a closing order under ss.265 *et seq.*, or purchase by the authority for temporary housing accommodation under s.300. The series has its principal origins in the Artizans' and Labourers' Dwellings Act 1868, ss.7–9, which dealt in repairs notices and demolition orders; closing orders were initially a part of the public health code, ancillary to "nuisance orders" (and remain in that code: see now s.94(2), Public Health Act 1936), but were given a "life of their own" in Housing Acts from the Housing of the Working Classes Act 1903, s.8.

Reasonable expense has the meaning given it by s.321, which is in identical terms to, and is accordingly described in the notes to, s.206, above. Unfitness itself is discussed in the notes to s.604, below. "House" is, for the purposes of this first series of sections, as discussed in the notes to s.189, above; see also subs. (7).

Proceedings in relation to a part of a building are, however, confined to a choice between undertakings to render fit or not to use for human habitation under this section, and a closing order under the provisions of ss.265 *et seq.*, and do not (of course) include demolition: s.266, below. Demolition orders are also prohibited when a building is a listed building: see s.304, below. In addition, closing order procedure may be used in relation to an underground room, which is *deemed* to be unfit for human habitation, under s.282, below.

All of these provisions save a voluntary undertaking under this section to do the works needed to render the property fit (subs. (3), (4)(a)), will lead to loss of Rent Act protection to Rent Act 1977 protected or statutory tenants, and to Rent (Agriculture) Act 1976 protected occupants or statutory tenants, and even to those with a restricted contract under s.19, Rent Act 1977: see notes to s.622, below. Occupiers will normally, however, be entitled to rehousing under s.39, home loss payment under s.29, and/or disturbance payment under s.37, Land Compensation Act 1973.

Ancillary provisions governing the rights of owners are to be found at ss.307–311, below, and governing powers of entry, obstruction, and rights and liabilities as between parties to leases, are to be found at ss.315–320, below.

Notice

Once satisfied of unfitness, the authority *must* take action, *either* under Part VI, *or* under this Part: *R.* v. *Kerrier District Council, ex parte Guppys (Bridport) Ltd., (No.* 1) (1977) 32 P. & C.R. 411, C.A. This is so even if, *e.g.* alternative action under Part III, Public Health Act 1936 (statutory nuisance) is proposed or taken. However, if action is being taken under the clearance area provisions of ss.289 *et seq.*, below, there is no need *also* to take action under Part VI/this series of sections: *Holmes* v. *Ministry of Housing and Local Government* (1960) 12 P. & C.R. 72.

Notices under this section are commonly known as "time-and-place notices" (*cf.* wording of subs. (1)). Notice *must* be served on the person having control, *and* any other person who is an owner of the property, *and* every mortgagee who it is practicable to ascertain: subs. (1). This obligation may be contrasted with the provisions of s.189, which *requires* service only on the person having control, but *permits* service on these others.

This distinction gives rise to the following position where the local authority have an interest in the property themselves. If they are the person having control, and action is to be taken under s.189, the provisions of Part VI are inapplicable, even if there is someone else who is an owner; if they are the owner, and someone else has control, and action is available under Part VI, the action has to be taken; if Part VI is inapplicable, then these sections will not apply where the property is exclusively in the ownership of the authority, but *will* apply if anyone else has a "controller's", owner's or mortgagee's interest—*R.* v. *Cardiff City Council, ex parte Cross* (1981) 1 H.L.R. 54, Q.B.D., affirmed on appeal (1982) 6 H.L.R. 6, C.A.

"Person having control" and "owner" are defined in s.322 in the same terms as in s.207 for the purposes of Part VI, see notes to s.207. A periodic tenant and a fixed term tenant with less than three years to run (or a tenant of part only) will not qualify for service of notice under this section; nor will a statutory tenant (of all or part). (See also *Brown* v. *Ministry of Housing and Local Government* [1953] 1 W.L.R. 1370). There is, however, no legal reason why the authority should not voluntarily serve a copy on any such tenant, and every practical reason why the authority should do so.

While appeal is not confined to persons served, it is not available to someone in occupation under a lease of agreement of three years or less or, probably, a statutory tenant (*Brown*): ss.269, below. However, such a person is entitled to take proceedings for judicial review, if the circumstances are appropriate, *e.g.* because action under this section is being taken when premises *are* repairable at a reasonable expense: *R.* v. *London Borough of Ealing, ex parte Richardson* (1982) 4 H.L.R. 125, C.A.

The Secretary of State has power to prescribe forms for use under any provision of this Act which requires or authorises notice, advertisement, statement or other document: s.614, below. The current forms are those to be found in the Housing (Prescribed Forms) Regulations 1972 (S.I. 1972 No. 228), as amended (S.I. 1974 No. 1511, 1975 No. 500, 1981 No. 1347), retained in force by s.2, Housing (Consequential Provisions) Act 1985, but these are expected to be replaced in the near future to reflect this consolidation. As to service, see notes to s.617, below.

Time-and-Place Meeting

The notice is to set a time-and-place meeting at which in effect the future of the house will be considered, including, of course, any offer which any of the persons served might feel inclined to make. Any such person is entitled to be heard at the meeting: subs. (2). The authority ought not to have made up their mind before the meeting: *Fletcher* v. *Ilkeston Corporation* (1931) 96 J.P. 7.

If an offer is to be made to do works to render the property fit, within 21 days of service of the notice under subs. (1) the person must notify the authority in writing of his intention to do so, and must follow this up with a list of proposed works within such period as the authority permit: subs. (2). It is in the discretion of the authority whether or not to accept the undertaking, but they are not at this point concerned with the reasonableness of the expense, so that this should not be their sole reason for rejecting it: *Stidworthy* v. *Brixham Urban District Council* (1935) 2 L.J.C.C.R. 41, *Coleman* v. *Dorchester Rural District Council* (1935) 2 L.J.C.C.R. 113.

The undertakings appear to be alternative: the wording of subs. (4)(*b*) suggests that if the landlord wishes to repair, but without the tenant, the appropriate undertaking is not to use the premises until cancellation on satisfaction of the authority that the property has been rendered fit. If a works undertaking is offered, it should be in writing, and specify the period in which the works are to be carried out: *Johnson* v. *Leicester Corporation* [1934] 1 K.B. 638.

Undertaking Not To Use For Human Habitation

Rent Act protection is lost to protected and statutory tenants under the Rent Act 1977, to occupiers under the Rent (Agriculture) Act 1976, and to those with a restricted contract under s.19, Rent Act 1977—see notes to s.622, below: subs. (5). They will, however, normally be entitled to rehousing and compensation under ss.29–39, Land Compensation Act 1973. Note that no provision is made to remove security under Part IV, above, *e.g.* in respect of a housing association tenant, but *cf.* Sched. 2, Ground 10, below, for an appropriate (although not synonymous) ground for possession.

Use or permitting use of premises knowingly in contravention of an undertaking is a criminal offence punishable by a fine of up to level 5 on the standard scale under s.37, Criminal Justice Act 1982, currently £2,000, by S.I. 1984 No. 447, with up to a further £5 per day for continuation after conviction.

Breach of Undertaking

If the undertaking is not complied with, either in the sense of not completing works within the specified period, or in the sense of using the premises in contravention of its terms, the authority acquire the powers they will enjoy if no undertaking is accepted: s.265(1), below.

Securing Premises Against Unauthorised Entry or Health Danger

Under the provisions of s.8, Local Government (Miscellaneous Provisions) Act 1976, the authority can take steps to secure premises subject to an undertaking against unauthorised entry, or in order to prevent them from being a danger to public health. They may take such steps as they consider necessary, but must first give not less than 48 hours' notice to anyone who is an owner of the premises of their intention to do the works.

Undertaking Refused
The correct course of action is to do nothing until the authority have made a closing or demolition order, and appeal that order under s.269, below. Note, however, that no appeal can be based on an offer of a works undertaking, unless the procedure for offering such an undertaking to the authority before the time-and-place meeting was complied with: s.269(4).

Demolition or closing order to be made where no undertaking accepted or undertaking broken

265.—(1) If no undertaking under section 264 is accepted by the local housing authority or if, where they have accepted such an undertaking—
    (*a*) any work to which the undertaking relates is not carried out within the specified period, or
    (*b*) the house is at any time used in contravention of the terms of the undertaking,
the authority shall forthwith make a demolition or closing order in respect of the premises to which the notice under that section relates.
    (2) The authority shall make a demolition order unless—
    (*a*) they consider it inexpedient to make a demolition order having regard to the effect of the demolition on another building, or
    (*b*) section 304(1) applies (listed buildings and buildings protected by notice pending listing),
in which case they shall make a closing order.
    (3) The provisions of this section have effect subject to section 300 (power to purchase for temporary housing use houses liable to be demolished or closed).

DEFINITIONS
    "closing order": s.267.
    "demolition order": s.267.
    "house": s.322.
    "local housing authority": ss.1, 2.

GENERAL NOTE
    If no undertaking is accepted, or if an undertaking which has been accepted is breached, the authority shall forthwith make either a demolition or a closing order. "Forthwith" means within a reasonable time: *London Borough of Hillingdon* v. *Cutler* [1968] 1 Q.B. 124, C.A. The presumption is in favour of demolition, save where either the premises are or are in a listed building (see s.304, below), or it is "inexpedient" having regard to the effect of the demolition on another building, *i.e.* where the house is not detached: subs. (2). In these cases, as under the next section, the authority must make a closing order.
    The authority enjoy, however, power under s.300 to buy the property for temporary housing use, as an alternative to demolition/closing.

Power to make closing order as to part of building

266. A local housing authority may under sections 264 and 265 take the like proceedings in relation to—
    (*a*) any part of a building which is used, or is suitable for use, as a dwelling, or
    (*b*) an underground room which is deemed to be unfit for the purposes of this section in accordance with section 282,
as they are empowered to take in relation to a house, subject, however, to the qualification that instead of a demolition order they shall make a closing order.

DEFINITIONS
    "closing order": s.267.
    "demolition order": s.267.

"house": s.322.
"local housing authority": ss.1, 2.

This section applies where *either* the premises the subject of action under ss.264, 265 above, are only part of a building, or an underground room *deemed* unfit by s.282, below: in such a case, if no undertaking is accepted under s.264, only a closing order is available under s.265.

Content of demolition and closing orders

267.—(1) A demolition order is an order requiring that the premises—

(*a*) be vacated within a specified period (of at least 28 days) from the date on which the order becomes operative, and

(*b*) be demolished within six weeks after the end of that period or, if it is not vacated before the end of that period, after the date on which it is vacated or, in either case, within such longer period as in the circumstances the local housing authority consider it reasonable to specify.

(2) A closing order is an order prohibiting the use of the premises to which it relates for any purpose not approved by the local housing authority.

(3) The approval of the local housing authority shall not be unreasonably withheld, and a person aggrieved by the withholding of such approval by the authority may, within 21 days of the refusal, appeal to the county court.

DEFINITIONS
"closing order": s.267.
"demolition order": s.267.
"local housing authority": ss.1, 2.

GENERAL NOTE
This section defines demolition and closing order.

Demolition Order
A demolition order is an order that the premises be vacated within a specified period (not less than 28 days) from the date when the order becomes operative, *and* that it be demolished within six weeks thereafter or, if later, six weeks from when the premises are vacated, or (in either case) such longer period as the authority specify: subs. (1). The order becomes operative 21 days from service, unless an appeal is brought: s.268(2). If an appeal is brought, it becomes operative after final confirmation of the order on appeal: s.269(6).

Service is governed by s.268; appeals by s.269; recovery of possession and demolition by ss.270–273; the submission of reconstruction proposals by s.274; substitution of a closing order by s.275.

Closing Order
A closing order prohibits the use of the property for any purpose not approved by the authority: subs. (2). Application may be made for a particular use, and the authority shall not unreasonably refuse permission; a person aggrieved by the authority's refusal can appeal to the county court within 21 days—subs. (3). As to person aggrieved, and appeal against refusal, see also notes to s.269, below.

Formerly, appeal had to be brought to the county court with jurisdiction over the area where the premises are situated: Housing Act 1957, s.27. Pursuant to Law Commission Recommendations (Cmnd. 9515), No. 9(ii), appeal lies now simply "to the county court" which means, under the County Court Rules (S.I. 1981 No. 1687), Order 4, rule 9, the court for the district in which the decision appealed against was made.

Service is governed by s.268; appeals by s.269; possession, and use in contravention of a closing order, are dealt with in ss.276–277; determination of closing orders in s.278; substitution of a demolition order in s.279.

Under the provisions of s.8, Local Government (Miscellaneous Provisions) Act 1976, the authority can take steps to secure premises subject to a closing order against unauthorised entry, or in order to prevent them from being a danger to public health. They may take such steps as they consider necessary, but must first give not less than 48 hours' notice to anyone who is an owner of the premises of their intention to do the works.

Forms of Orders

The Secretary of State has power to prescribe forms for use under any provision of this Act which requires or authorises notice, advertisement, statement or other document: s.614, below. The current forms are those to be found in the Housing (Prescribed Forms) Regulations 1972 (S.I. 1972 No. 228), as amended (S.I. 1974 No. 1511, 1975 No. 500, 1981 No. 1347), retained in force by s.2, Housing (Consequential Provisions) Act 1985, but these are expected to be replaced in the near future to reflect this consolidation.

As to service, see s.268, below.

Service of notice of order

268.—(1) Where a local housing authority have made a demolition or closing order, they shall serve a copy of the order on—

(*a*) the person having control of the premises,

(*b*) any other person who is an owner of the premises, and

(*c*) every mortgagee of the premises whom it is reasonably practicable to ascertain.

(2) An order against which no appeal is brought becomes operative at the end of the period of 21 days from the date of service of the order and is final and conclusive as to matters which could have been raised on an appeal.

DEFINITIONS

"closing order": s.267.

"demolition order": s.267.

"local housing authority": ss.1, 2.

"owner": s.322.

"person having control": s.322.

GENERAL NOTE

Under subs. (1), the order (demolition or closing) made under the last section is to be served on the person having control, owner and any ascertainable mortgagee—see notes to s.207, above. As to service, see notes to s.617, below.

Under subs. (2), the order becomes operative 21 days after service, unless appealed under s.269, below, and if no appeal is brought it is final and conclusive as to matters which could have been raised on an appeal.

Appeal lies to the county court, under s.269, below. The possibility of appeal would suggest that it is the more appropriate course than application for judicial review: see *R.* v. *Hackney London Borough Council, ex parte Teepee Estates (1956) Ltd.* (1967) 19 P. & C.R. 87, D.C. See also *Minford Properties Ltd.* v. *London Borough of Hammersmith* (1978) 247 E.G. 561, D.C.; but *cf. R.* v. *London Borough of Southwark, ex parte Lewis Levy Ltd.* [1983] 8 H.L.R. 1, Q.B.D. in which the court considered that if an issue is one which goes to *vires*, including whether or not a property is a house within the applicable provisions, it is appropriately raised by way of application for judicial review.

The *vires* of the authority in reaching their decision, *i.e.* on normal principles of administrative law (*cf.* notes to s.64, above), are challengeable even on an appeal in the county court, for the effect of the notice is to seek to take away a vested right to which the appellant would otherwise be entitled, *i.e.* to leave the property as he wishes: see *London Borough of Wandsworth* v. *Winder* [1985] A.C. 461, 17 H.L.R. 196, H.L., with the effect that it would seem to be exempt from the principle in *Cocks* v. *Thanet District Council* [1983] A.C. 286, 6 H.L.R. 15, H.L., that judicial review is the only way to impeach a decision of the authority which is a precondition to the acquisition of a right. See also *R.* v. *Brighton Borough Council* (1980) 258 E.G. 441, C.A.

This view would in this case help to support the approach of *Smith* v. *East Elloe Rural District Council* [1956] A.C. 736, H.L., applied in *R.* v. *Secretary of State for the Environment, ex parte Ostler* [1977] Q.B. 122, C.A., distinguishing *Anisminic Ltd.* v. *Foreign Compensation Commission* [1969] 2 A.C. 147, H.L., *i.e.* that a matter which is to be treated as "final and conclusive" is to be so treated to the extent of excluding application for judicial review. However, the courts have shown less willing to accept diminution of their jurisdiction in cases such as *Pearlman* v. *Keepers & Governors of Harrow School* [1979] Q.B. 56, C.A. (in which the words "final and conclusive" did not prevent further challenge on the correct interpretation of the word "improvement" for the purposes of the Leasehold Reform Act 1967) and *Meade* v. *Haringey London Borough Council* [1979] 1 W.L.R. 637, C.A.

The last-mentioned case went so far as to suggest that if want of *vires* is the basis of challenge it is not even necessary to show that "domestic" remedies (*i.e.* an Act's own statutory procedures for redress or complaint including appeals) have been exhausted, contrary to the "usual" rule (see *Doe d. Bishop of Rochester* v. *Bridges* (1831) 1 B. & Ad. 847, *Pasmore* v. *Oswaldtwistle Urban District Council* [1898] A.C. 387, H.L., *Barraclough* v. *Brown* [1897] A.C. 615, H.L., *Watt* v. *Kesteven County Council* [1955] 1 Q.B. 408, *Wyatt* v. *London Borough of Hillingdon* (1978) 76 L.G.R. 727, *London Borough of Southwark* v. *Williams* [1971] Ch. 734, and *Kensington and Chelsea Royal London Borough Council* v. *Wells* (1974) 72 L.G.R. 289, C.A.).

Right of appeal against order

269.—(1) A person aggrieved by a demolition or closing order may, within 21 days after the date of the service of the order, appeal to the county court.

(2) No appeal lies at the instance of a person who is in occupation of the premises under a lease or agreement with an unexpired term of three years or less.

(3) On an appeal the court—

(*a*) may make such order either confirming or quashing or varying the order as it thinks fit, and

(*b*) may, if it thinks fit, accept from an appellant any undertaking which might have been accepted by the local housing authority.

(4) The court shall not accept an undertaking to carry out works from an appellant on whom a notice was served under section 264(1) (notice of appointment to consider condition of premises) unless the appellant complied with the requirements of section 264(3) (duty to give notice of intention to offer undertaking and to supply list of works).

(5) An undertaking accepted by the court has the same effect as an undertaking given to and accepted by the local housing authority under section 264.

(6) If an appeal is brought the order does not become operative until—

(*a*) a decision on the appeal confirming the order (with or without variation) is given and the period within which an appeal to the Court of Appeal may be brought expires without any such appeal having been brought, or

(*b*) if a further appeal to the Court of Appeal is brought, a decision on that appeal is given confirming the order (with or without variation);

and for this purpose the withdrawal of an appeal has the same effect as a decision confirming the order or decision appealed against.

DEFINITIONS
"closing order": s.267.
"demolition order": s.267.
"local housing authority": ss.1, 2.

GENERAL NOTE
Appeal lies only at the instance of a "person aggrieved", *not* including someone in occupation under a lease or agreement of which there is less than three years to run, which include a periodic tenant and, probably, a statutory tenant: *cf. Brown* v. *Ministry of Housing and Local Government* [1953] 1 W.L.R. 1370—subs. (1), (2). A tenant thus excluded from appeal may yet take proceedings for judicial review, if the circumstances are appropriate, *e.g.* because the authority have erred in considering that the property is not repairable at a reasonable expense and ought, therefore, to have taken action under Part VI instead (with

the consequence of allowing the tenant to remain in occupation): see *R*. v. *London Borough of Ealing, ex parte Richardson* (1982) 4 H.L.R. 125, C.A.

Person Aggrieved

This means someone who has been deprived of a legal entitlement, or subjected to a legal burden: *Ex parte Sidebotham* (1880) 14 Ch. D. 458, *R*. v. *London Quarter Sessions, ex parte Westminster Corporation* [1951] 2 K.B. 508.

Appeal Against Undertaking Refused

If an undertaking under s.264 is not accepted, the appropriate course is to wait for the authority to make a demolition or closing order under s.265, and appeal under this section: the court has power to accept any undertaking which might have been accepted by the authority (subs. (3)(*b*)), although *not* a works undertaking unless the requirement in s.264(3) to give notice of intention, and a list of works, was complied with (subs. (4)), *i.e.* unless the authority were themselves in a position to receive such an offer. An undertaking accepted by the court has the same effect as if accepted by the authority: subs. (5). See, generally, notes to s.264, above.

Appeal Against Orders

The court may confirm, quash or vary the order: subs. (3)(*a*). Where there has been a change of circumstances between service of the time-and-place notice, or the holding of the meeting, the court should consider facts as they exist on the appeal: *Leslie Maurice & Co. Ltd*. v. *Willesden Corporation* [1953] 2 Q.B. 1, C.A. The court can only extend the time for vacating the premises (*cf.* s.267, above), to the extent necessary to allow the rehousing of the occupiers: *Pocklington* v. *Melksham Urban District Council* [1964] 2 Q.B. 673. (This case preceded rehousing rights under the Land Compensation Act 1973, s.39, and therefore refers to time for the occupiers to find their own alternative accommodation.)

Appeal must be brought within 21 days: subs. (1). This does not include the day of service: *Goldsmith's Co*. v. *West Metropolitan Railway Co*. [1904] 1 K.B. 1, C.A.; *Stewart* v. *Chapman* [1951] 2 All E.R. 613. Although the county court has a general power to enlarge time (C.C.R. Ord. 13, r. 4), it has been suggested that the general power cannot be used to override the statutory time limit: see *Honig* v. *Lewisham Borough Council* (1958) 122 J.P.J. 302. But *cf. Arieli* v. *Duke of Westminster* (1983) E.G. 535, C.A., and *Johnston* v. *Duke of Devonshire* (1984) 17 H.L.R. 136, C.A., under Leasehold Reform Act 1967 and Housing Act 1974, Sched. 8.

Formerly, appeal had to be brought to the county court with jurisdiction over the area where the premises are situated: Housing Act 1957, s.20. Pursuant to Law Commission Recommendations (Cmnd. 9515), No. 9(ii), appeal lies now simply "to the county court" which means, under the County Court Rules (S.I. 1981 No. 1687), Order 4, rule 9, the court for the district in which the decision appealed against was made.

The notice does not become operative if an appeal is brought within the 21 days allowed, until the confirmation of the notice by the county court together with the passing of time to appeal to the Court of Appeal (four weeks—R.S.C. Order 59, rule 19): subs. (6). If appeal *is* brought to the Court of Appeal, then the notice does not become operative until the decision of that court; if an appeal is brought, but withdrawn, the withdrawal has the effect of a decision dismissing the appeal, *i.e.* at whichsoever level, to or from county court: *ibid*.

Demolition orders

Demolition orders: recovery of possession of building to be demolished

270.—(1) Where a demolition order has become operative, the local housing authority shall serve on the occupier of any building, or part of a building, to which the order relates a notice—

  (*a*) stating the effect of the order,

  (*b*) specifying the date by which the order requires the building to be vacated, and

  (*c*) requiring him to quit the building before that date or before the expiration of 28 days from the service of the notice, whichever may be the later.

(2) If any person is in occupation of the building, or any part of it, at any time after the date on which the notice requires the building to be vacated, the local housing authority or an owner of the building may apply to the county court which shall thereupon order vacant possession of the

building or part to be given to the applicant within such period, of not less than two or more than four weeks, as the court may determine.

(3) Nothing in the Rent Acts affects the provisions of this section relating to the obtaining possession of a building.

(4) Expenses incurred by the local housing authority under this section in obtaining possession of a building, or part of a building, may be recovered by them by action from the owner, or from any of the owners, of the building.

(5) A person who, knowing that a demolition order has become operative and applies to a building—

    (*a*) enters into occupation of the building, or a part of it, after the date by which the order requires it to be vacated, or

    (*b*) permits another person to enter into such occupation after that date,

commits a summary offence and is liable on conviction to a fine not exceeding level 5 on the standard scale and to a further fine not exceeding £5 for every day or part of a day on which the occupation continues after conviction.

DEFINITIONS

"demolition order": s.267.
"local housing authority": ss.1, 2.
"owner": s.322.
"Rent Acts": s.622.

GENERAL NOTE

The demolition order becomes operative 21 days after service, unless an appeal is brought, in which case it does not become operative until after its final confirmation on appeal: see ss.268, 269, and notes thereto, above. The order requires the premises to be vacated within a time specified, but not less than 28 days after service, and to be demolished within a further six weeks or such longer period as the authority may specify in the order: see s.267, above.

Recovery of Possession

Once the demolition order has become operative, the *authority* shall serve on the *occupier* of the whole or any part of the building in question, a notice which sets out the effect of the order, the date by which the property is to be vacated, and requiring him to quit before that date or 28 days (whichever is the later): subs. (1). The appropriate form (see notes to s.267, above) is Form 10. If an occupier remains in occupation after time has run out, the *authority* or an *owner* (not necessarily the landlord, see s.322, defining owner as distinct from the person having control, see also notes to s.207, above), can apply to the county court for a possession order: subs. (2).

Neither the Rent Act 1977 nor the Rent (Agriculture) Act 1976 applies so as to protect a protected or statutory tenant or occupier, or even someone with a restricted contract under s.19, Rent Act 1977—see notes to s.622, below: subs. (3). Such occupiers will, however, normally be entitled to rehousing and compensation under the provisions of the Land Compensation Act 1973, ss.29–39. This "lifting" of Rent Act protection does not occur until service of the notice under subs. (1), as distinct from the date when the demolition order becomes operative: *Marela* v. *Machorowski* [1953] 1 Q.B. 565. No direct provision is made to deal with secure tenants, *e.g.* of housing associations, under Part IV, above, but an appropriate ground for possession is to be found at Sched. 2, Ground 10, below.

There is no discretion to delay service and implementation in order to secure time for finding alternative accommodation for the occupiers: *R.* v. *Epsom and Ewell Corporation, ex parte R.B. Property Investments (Eastern)* [1964] 1 W.L.R. 1060, D.C.

Owner-occupiers are also entitled to rehousing under the Land Compensation Act 1973, s.39, and may be entitled to compensation under either ss.29–38 of that Act, or under the provisions of ss.586, 587, and Scheds. 23 and 24, below.

Recovery of Expenses

The authority can reclaim the expenses of recovering possession from any owner of the building: subs. (4). Transfer of jurisdiction from the magistrates' court to the county court on this issue is pursuant to Law Commission Recommendations (Cmnd. 9515), No. 9(i).

Occupation After Order

Knowingly occupying, or permitting occupation, after the date when the demolition order requires the premises to be vacated is a criminal offence, punishable by a fine of up to level 5 on the standard scale under s.37, Criminal Justice Act 1982, currently £2,000, by S.I. 1984 No. 447, with an addition £5 for each day on which the offence continues after conviction. The mere fact that the demolition order is registered in the Local Land Charges Registry is *not* sufficient to prove notice for the purposes of this section: *Barber* v. *Shah* (1985) 17 H.L.R. 584, D.C.

Demolition orders: execution of order

271.—(1) When a demolition order has become operative, the owner of the premises to which it applies shall demolish the premises within the time limited by the order, and if the premises are not demolished within that time the local housing authority shall enter and demolish them and sell the materials.

(2) Subsection (1) has effect subject to—
   section 273 (cleansing before demolition),
   section 274 (power to permit reconstruction), and
   section 275 (use otherwise than for human habitation).

DEFINITIONS
   "demolition order": s.267.
   "local housing authority": ss.1, 2.
   "owner": s.322.

GENERAL NOTE

The demolition order becomes operative 21 days after service, unless an appeal is brought, in which case it does not become operative until after its final confirmation on appeal: see ss.268, 269, and notes thereto, above. The order requires the premises to be vacated within a time specified, but not less than 28 days after service, and to be demolished within a further six weeks or such longer period as the authority may specify in the order: see s.267, above.

This section requires the owner to comply with the obligation to demolish. However, under s.274, below, he may apply for an extension of time, to fit in with reconstruction proposals, and under s.275 he can seek the substitution of a closing order, to permit user other than for human habitation. See also s.273, below, for the possibility of a "cleansing order" before demolition. Note that if the property is "listed" before execution of the demolition order, a closing order is to be substituted: see s.304, below.

Subject to this, if the owner does not demolish, the authority *must* enter, demolish and sell the materials: subs. (1). As to recovery of expenses by the authority, see s.272, below. The authority's failure to comply with this requirement does not operate so as to render the demolition order invalid through lapse of time: *Martin* v. *Downham Rural District Council* [1953] C.L.Y. 1604, C.A.

Demolition orders: expenses of local housing authority, &c.

272.—(1) Expenses incurred by the local housing authority under section 271 (execution of demolition order), after giving credit for any amount realised by the sale of materials, may be recovered by them from the owner of the premises.

(2) If there is more than one owner—
   (*a*) the expenses may be recovered by the local housing authority from the owners in such shares as the court may determine to be just and equitable, and
   (*b*) an owner who pays to the authority the full amount of their claim may recover from any other owner such contribution, if any, as the court may determine to be just and equitable.

(3) A surplus in the hands of the authority shall be paid by them to the owner of the premises or, if there is more than one owner, as the owners may agree.

(4) If there is more than one owner and the owners do not agree as to the division of the surplus, the authority shall, by virtue of this subsection, be trustees of the surplus for the owners of the premises and section 63 of the Trustee Act 1925 (which relates to payment into court by trustees) has effect accordingly.

(5) The county court has jurisdiction to hear and determine proceedings under subsection (1) or (2), and has jurisdiction under section 63 of the Trustee Act 1925 in relation to such a surplus as is referred to in subsection (4).

(6) In determining for the purposes of this section the shares in which expenses are to be paid or contributed by, or a surplus divided between, two or more owners of premises, the court shall have regard to all the circumstances of the case, including—

(*a*) their respective interests in the premises, and

(*b*) their respective obligations and liabilities in respect of maintenance and repair under any covenant or agreement, whether express or implied.

DEFINITIONS

   "demolition order": s.267.
   "local housing authority": ss.1, 2.
   "owner": s.322.

GENERAL NOTE

   If the authority carry out the demolition, because the owner does not do so, under s.271, above, this section governs the costs. The amount received on sale is to be set-off against the costs, but the authority comply with this duty by granting one contract, allowing the contractor to keep or resell the materials—see *London Borough of Hillingdon* v. *Cutler* [1968] 1 Q.B. 124, C.A. An owner is *not*, however, under a positive obligation to *clear* the site, so that the costs of clearing the site, *i.e. removal* of the materials, is not to be included: *Wigan Corporation* v. *Hartley* [1963] C.L.Y. 1664.

   Where there is more than one owner, the authority can claim against them all, and unless agreement is reached a court will decide the apportionment: subs. (2)(*a*). Alternatively, one owner can meet the full claim, and then claim a contribution from another: subs. (2)(*b*). When determining such an issue, the court will have regard to respective interests, obligations and liabilities: subs. (6).

Treatment of Surplus

   If there is a surplus on the demolition exercise, *i.e.* because the value of the materials exceeded the authority's costs, it is to be paid to the owner or, if more than one, as they may agree between them: subs. (3). If they fail to agree, the authority are trustees of the money, and enjoy the right to pay it into court under s.63, Trustee Act 1925, which will discharge their obligations: subs. (4). Payment into court is governed by County Court Rules 1981 (S.I. 1981 No. 1687), Ord. 11.

   Thereafter, any owner can make application to the court as to the application of the money under s.63(1) of the 1925 Act (subs. (5)), and the court will again reach its determination having regard to respective interests, obligations and liabilities: subs. (6).

Demolition orders: cleansing before demolition

273.—(1) If it appears to the local housing authority that premises to which a demolition order applies require to be cleansed from vermin, they may, at any time between the date on which the order is made and the date on which it becomes operative, serve notice in writing on the owner or owners of the premises that they intend to cleanse the premises before they are demolished.

(2) Where the authority have served such a notice—

(*a*) they may, at any time after the order has become operative and the premises have been vacated, enter and carry out such work as they may think requisite for the purpose of destroying or removing vermin, and

(b) the demolition shall not be begun or continued by an owner after service of the notice on him, except as mentioned in subsection (3), until the authority have served on him a further notice authorising him to proceed with the demolition.

(3) An owner on whom a notice has been served under subsection (1) may, at any time after the premises have been vacated, serve notice in writing on the authority requiring them to carry out the work within 14 days from the receipt of the notice served by him, and at the end of that period shall be at liberty to proceed with the demolition whether the work has been completed or not.

(4) Where the local housing authority serve a notice under subsection (1), they shall not take action under section 271 (under which they are to demolish the house if the owners do not) until the expiration of six weeks from the date on which the owner or owners become entitled by virtue of subsection (2) or (3) to proceed with the demolition.

DEFINITIONS
"demolition order": s.267.
"house": s.322.
"local housing authority": ss.1, 2.
"owner": s.322.

GENERAL NOTE
If the property needs cleansing of vermin before demolition, *i.e.* to prevent spread to other properties, at any time between making the demolition order and the date when it becomes operative (see notes to s.270, above), the authority may inform the owner or owners that they intend to cleanse before demolition: subs. (1). Once the order has become operative, and the premises have been vacated, the authority can enter and carry out the necessary cleansing works and the demolition is not to commence until the owner or owners are authorised to do so by the authority: subs. (2).

If an owner wishes to proceed with the demolition, he can serve notice requiring the authority within 14 days to complete their cleansing works, and is then entitled to proceed whether or not they have done so: subs. (3). As to service on the authority, see notes to s.617, below.

If this cleansing power is invoked, the authority's power to demolish in default under s.271, above, does not arise until six weeks from the date either of their notice to proceed, or from 14 days after they have been served with notice to complete cleansing by the owner: subs. (4).

Demolition orders: power to permit reconstruction of condemned house

274.—(1) Where a demolition order has become operative—
(a) the owner of the house, or
(b) any other person who in the opinion of the local housing authority is or will be in a position to put his proposals into effect,
may submit proposals to the authority for the execution by him of works designed to secure the reconstruction, enlargement or improvement of the house, or of buildings including the house.

(2) If the authority are satisfied that the result of the works will be the provision of one or more houses fit for human habitation, they may, in order that the person submitting the proposals may have an opportunity of carrying out the works, extend for such period as they may specify the time within which the owner of the house is required under section 271 to demolish it.

(3) That time may be further extended by the authority, once or more often as the case may require, if—
(a) the works have begun and appear to the authority to be making satisfactory progress, or
(b) though they have not begun, the authority think there has been no unreasonable delay.

(4) Where the authority determine to extend, or further extend, the time within which the owner of a house is required under section 271 to demolish it, notice of the determination shall be served by the authority on every person having an interest in the house, whether as freeholder, mortgagee or otherwise.

(5) If the works are completed to the satisfaction of the authority they shall revoke the demolition order (but without prejudice to any subsequent proceedings under this Part).

DEFINITIONS
"demolition order" s.267.
"fit for human habitation" s.604.
"house" s.322.
"local housing authority" ss.1, 2.
"owner" s.322.

GENERAL NOTE
Without prejudice to their power to start proceedings under this Part anew at any subsequent time, the authority can revoke the demolition order on completion of approved works of reconstruction under this section: subs. (5). This section applies to reconstruction for *housing* only (subs. (2)); see s.275, below, for the substitution of a closing order when non-housing user is proposed.

A reconstruction submission can only be made once the order has become operative (subs. (1)), as to the meaning of which see notes to s.270, above. The submission can be made not only by an owner, but also by anyone else the authority consider is or will be in a position to carry it through, *e.g.* a prospective purchaser: subs. (1). If the submission will result in housing fit for human habitation, the authority can extend time for demolition under s.271, above, to give the person making the submission the opportunity to carry out the works: subs. (2). Time can be subsequently extended if works have begun and are progressing satisfactorily, or if although not begun, there has been no unreasonable delay: subs. (3).

Notice of a decision to extend time (initially or subsequently) has to be given to everyone with an interest in the property: subs. (4).

If revocation of demolition order does follow, s.590 below governs repayment of any compensation paid under Scheds. 23 or 24, below.

Demolition orders: substitution of closing order to permit use otherwise than for human habitation

275.—(1) If an owner of a house in respect of which a demolition order has become operative, or any other person who has an interest in the house, submits proposals to the local housing authority for the use of the house for a purpose other than human habitation, the authority may if they think fit to do so determine the demolition order and make a closing order as respects the house.

(2) The authority shall serve notice that the demolition order has been determined, and a copy of the closing order, on—
  (*a*) the person having control of the house, and
  (*b*) any other person who is an owner of the house, and
  (*c*) every mortgagee of the house whom it is reasonably practicable to ascertain.

DEFINITIONS
"closing order": s.267.
"demolition order": s.267.
"house": s.322.
"local housing authority": ss.1, 2.
"owner": s.322.
"person having control": s.322.

GENERAL NOTE
The last of the provisions specific to demolition orders is the power to substitute a closing order if an owner or anyone else with an interest submits proposals for a non-housing user:

subs. (1). Notice of determination and a copy of the closing order has to be served on the person having control, any other owner, and reasonably ascertainable mortgagees (subs. (2)), *i.e.* those on whom the notice under s.264, above, had to be served.

A closing order will also have to be substituted under s.304, below, if the building is "listed" before it is demolished.

Closing orders

Closing orders: recovery of possession of house

276. Nothing in the Rent Acts prevents possession being obtained by the owner of premises in respect of which a closing order is in force.

DEFINITIONS
"closing order": s.267.
"owner": s.322.
"Rent Acts": s.622.

GENERAL NOTE
If a closing order is in force (*i.e.* is operative), the Rent Acts (*i.e.* Rent Act 1977, Rent (Agriculture) Act 1976—see s.622, below) cease to apply to prevent possession being obtained by an owner (*n.b.* not necessarily the person having control—see s.322, below—so that if the landlord has been the person having control, *not* also being an owner, the owner must first "exclude" the right to possession of the person having control, *e.g.* by determination of *his* interest). Those who will thus lose protection are protected and statutory tenants and occupiers under the 1977 and 1976 Acts, and those with restricted contracts under s.19, 1977 Act: see notes to s.622, below. Normally, these people will, however, be entitled to rehousing and compensation under the Land Compensation Act 1973, ss.29–39.

The Rent Acts only cease to apply as to *possession*, not in other respects, *e.g.* rents. Notwithstanding that the premises will of definition be unfit for human habitation, while a Rent Officer fixing a fair rent within the meaning of s.70, Rent Act 1977, must take this into account, it does not have the *necessary* consequence that a nil or nominal rent must be fixed: *Williams* v. *Khan* (1981) 258 E.G. 554, C.A. As this case was decided at a time when rent registrations were backdated to application, whereas they are now effective only from actual registration (see s.72, 1977 Act, as introduced by Housing Act 1980, s.61), the position where a closing order precedes registration may today be different. As this section is now applied, it covers a closing order in relation to a listed building under s.304, below, pursuant to Law Commission Recommendations (Cmnd. 9515), No. 16(i).

Note that owner-occupiers may also be entitled to rehousing under s.39, Land Compensation Act 1973, and either to compensation under ss.29–38 of that Act, or under the provisions of ss.586, 587, and Scheds. 23 and 24, below.

Closing orders: enforcement

277. If a person, knowing that a closing order has become operative and applies to premises, uses the premises in contravention of the order, or permits them to be so used, he commits a summary offence and is liable on conviction to a fine not exceeding level 5 on the standard scale and to a further fine not exceeding £20 for every day or part of a day on which he so uses them or permits them to be so used after conviction.

DEFINITION
"closing order": s.267.

GENERAL NOTE
The closing order becomes operative 21 days after service, unless an appeal is brought, in which case it does not become operative until after its final confirmation on appeal: see ss.268, 269, and notes thereto, above.

Knowingly to use, or permit the use of, premises in contravention of a closing order is a criminal offence punishable by a fine of up to level 5 on the standard scale under s.37, Criminal Justice Act 1982, currently £2,000, by S.I. 1984 No. 447, with an additional fine of up to £20 per day for continuation after conviction.

The mere fact that the closing order is registered in the Local Land Charges Registry is *not* sufficient to prove notice for the purposes of this section: *Barber* v. *Shah* (1985) 17 H.L.R. 584, D.C.

Closing orders: determination of order on premises being rendered fit

278.—(1) The local housing authority shall determine a closing order on being satisfied that the premises have been rendered fit for human habitation, and if so satisfied as respects part of the premises they shall determine the order so far as it relates to that part.

(2) A person aggrieved by a refusal by the local housing authority to determine a closing order, either wholly or as respects part of the premises to which it relates, may, within 21 days after the refusal, appeal to the county court.

(3) No appeal lies at the instance of a person who is in occupation of the premises, or a relevant part of the premises, under a lease or agreement of which the unexpired term is three years or less.

DEFINITIONS
"closing order": s.267.
"fit for human habitation": s.604.
"local housing authority": ss.1, 2.

GENERAL NOTE
If the authority are satisfied that premises have been rendered fit for human habitation, they must determine the closing order; alternatively, if satisfied that part of the premises have been rendered so fit, they must determine the order as respects that part—subs. (1). Appeal against a refusal lies to the county court, at the instigation of a person aggrieved, not including someone with a lease with less than three years to run: see notes to s.269, above, as to appeals, person aggrieved, tenants.

If a closing order is determined, s.590 below governs repayment of compensation which may have been paid under Scheds. 23 or 24, below.

Closing orders: substitution of demolition order

279.—(1) Where a local housing authority have made a closing order, they may, subject to subsection (2), at any time revoke it and make a demolition order.

(2) The power conferred by subsection (1) is not exercisable in relation to a closing order made under or by virtue of—

section 266 (parts of buildings and underground rooms),
section 304(1) (listed buildings), or
section 304(2) (building subject to demolition order becoming listed),

or where the closing order has been determined under section 278 as respects part of the premises to which it relates.

(3) The provisions of this Part relating to demolition orders, including the provisions relating to service of copies of the order and appeals, apply to an order under this section as they apply to a demolition order under section 265.

DEFINITIONS
"closing order": s.267.
"demolition order": s.267.
"local housing authority": ss.1, 2.

GENERAL NOTE
Subject to the limitations in subs. (2), the authority can at any time revoke a closing order, and substitute a demolition order (subs. (1)), with the duties and consequences which follow if a demolition order is made in the first place: subs. (3). This power is inapplicable to parts of buildings, underground rooms, and listed buildings: subs. (2)—*cf.* ss.280–282 and 304, below.

Closing of underground rooms

Meaning of "underground room"

280. In this Part "underground room" means a room the surface of the floor of which is more than three feet below—

    (*a*) the surface of the part of the street adjoining or nearest to the room, or

    (*b*) the surface of any ground within nine feet of the room.

GENERAL NOTE

This section defines an "underground room" for the purposes of this Part, *i.e.* for the purposes of s.281, below, permitting the authority to make regulations as to their condition, and of s.282, below, deeming them in certain circumstances to be unfit for human habitation. An underground room means that the surface of the floor is more than three feet below either the surface of the part of the street nearest to the room or the surface of any ground within nine feet of the room. If, therefore, there is a *lowered* street or walkway, less than nine feet across, and to less than three feet above the room, between room and ground, a room may yet be underground; put another way, the provisions cannot be avoided by digging a shallow trench adjoining the room.

Regulations as to ventilation, lighting, etc. of underground rooms

281.—(1) A local housing authority may, with the consent of the Secretary of State, make regulations for securing the proper ventilation and lighting of underground rooms and the protection of such rooms against dampness, effluvia or exhalation.

(2) If a local housing authority, after being required to do so by the Secretary of State, fail to make regulations under subsection (1), or to make such regulation as he approves, the Secretary of State may himself by statutory instrument make regulations which shall have effect as if made by the authority under that subsection.

DEFINITIONS

    "local housing authority": ss.1, 2.
    "underground room": s.280.

GENERAL NOTE

The authority can, with consent, make regulations to secure proper ventilation and lighting of underground rooms and their protection from dampness, effluvia or exhalation (*i.e.* the consequence of condensation resulting from inadequate ventilation): subs. (1). The authority can be obliged to make such regulations by the Secretary of State and, if they still do not do so, he can make regulations in default: subs. (2).

Non-compliance with the regulations results in the room being deemed unfit under s.282, below.

Closing of underground room deemed to be unfit for human habitation

282.—(1) An underground room shall be deemed for the purposes of section 266 (closing orders) to be unfit for human habitation if—

    (*a*) the average height of the room from floor to ceiling is not at least seven feet, or

    (*b*) the room does not comply with regulations made by the local housing authority under section 281.

(2) Nothing in this section affects the taking of action in respect of premises consisting of or including an underground room on the ground that they are unfit for human habitation in accordance with section 604 (fitness for human habitation: general provisions).

DEFINITIONS

    "closing order": s.267.
    "local housing authority": ss.1, 2.

"underground room": s.280.
"unfit for human habitation": s.604.

GENERAL NOTE
An underground room is deemed to be unfit for human habitation (and therefore within the provisions of s.266, above, *i.e.* permitting closing order action) if *either* its average height from floor to ceiling is not at least seven feet, *or* it does not comply with s.281 regulations: subs. (1). However, this is an *additional* means of finding unfitness, without prejudice to the definition in s.604: subs. (2).

Demolition of obstructive buildings

Buildings liable to be demolished as "obstructive buildings"

283.—(1) In this Part "obstructive building" means a building which, by virtue only of its contact with or proximity to other buildings, is dangerous or injurious to health.
(2) A building is not liable to be demolished as an obstructive building under the following provisions of this Part if it is—
(*a*) the property of statutory undertakers (unless the building is used for the purposes of a dwelling, showroom or office), or
(*b*) the property of a local authority.
(3) In subsection (2) "statutory undertakers" means persons authorised by an enactment, or by an order, rule or regulation made under an enactment, to construct, work or carry on a railway, canal, inland navigation, dock, harbour, tramway, gas, electricity, water or other public undertaking.

DEFINITION
"local authority": s.4.

GENERAL NOTE
This section introduces a new series of powers, formerly contained in Part III, Housing Act 1957, even although they apply to individual buildings (*cf.* notes to s.264, above).
With the exception of property belonging to (a) *any* local authority, as defined in s.4, above, and (b) the property of a statutory undertaker as defined in subs. (3), the provisions of ss.284–288, below, apply to "obstructive buildings", as defined in subs. (1), *i.e.* a building (not necessarily a house, nor even necessarily a building used for human habitation or as a dwelling) which is dangerous or injurious to health, by virtue *only* of its contact with or proximity to another building.
If the building is dangerous or injurious to health for any other reason, it will qualify as a statutory nuisance under s.92, Public Health Act 1936. If a house (as that term is used in this Part—*cf.* notes to s.264, above, referring back to s.189, above, and notes to s.289, below), it may of course qualify for treatment either under Part II or the preceding provisions of this Part, or may be included in (or if a building containing flats, actually comprise—*cf.* notes to s.289, below) a clearance area within s.289, below.
If the building is obstructive for some reason other than its contact with or proximity to another building, it will not be an obstructive building for the purposes of this series of sections. Building is a wide phrase, capable of applying to "buildings of all descriptions, dwelling-houses, manufactories, places of worship, and even statues and monuments": *Jackson* v. *Knutford Urban District Council* [1914] 2 Ch. 686 at p.695, referring to s.38, Housing of the Working Classes Act 1890.
The provisions constitute a code in their own right, without reliance either on the preceding provisions of this Part, or the clearance area provisions of ss.289 *et seq.*: s.284 contains an equivalent of the "time-and-place" notice under s.264, above, and contains power to make its own demolition order; appeal is under s.285, below; recovery of possession is governed by s.286, and execution of the order by an owner or the authority under s.287, with recovery of the authority's expenses dealt with under s.288, below.

Obstructive building order

284.—(1) The local housing authority may serve upon every owner of a building which appears to them to be an obstructive building, notice of a time (not being less than 21 days after the service of the notice) and place at which the question of ordering the building to be demolished will be considered by the authority.

(2) Every owner of the building is entitled to be heard when the matter is so taken into consideration.

(3) If, after so taking the matter into consideration, the authority are satisfied that the building is an obstructive building and that the building, or a part of it, ought to be demolished, they shall make an obstructive building order, that is to say, an order requiring—

(*a*) that the building, or part of it, be demolished, and

(*b*) that the building, or such part of it as is required to be vacated for the purposes of the demolition, be vacated within two months from the date on which the order becomes operative.

(4) The authority shall serve a copy of the order on every owner of the building.

(5) The order becomes operative, if no appeal is brought against it, on the expiration of 21 days from the date of the service of the order and is final and conclusive as to matters which could have been raised on such an appeal.

DEFINITIONS

    "local housing authority": ss.1, 2.
    "obstructive building": s.283.
    "owner": s.322.

GENERAL NOTE

    This section makes provision analogous to that under s.264, above, for service of a time-and-place notice on owners of obstructive buildings; however, the only question to be considered at the meeting is whether or not the building ought to be demolished: subs. (1). Every owner is entitled to be heard at the meeting: subs. (2). The demolition order may be as to part of the building only: subs. (3)(*a*), and will include an order for the building or part of it to be vacated within two months from when the order becomes operative: subs. (3)(*b*). Every owner is to be served with a copy of the order: subs. (4).

Subs. (4)

    See notes to s.268(2), above.

Right of appeal against obstructive building order

    285.—(1) A person aggrieved by an obstructive building order may, within 21 days after the date of the service of the order, appeal to the county court.

    (2) No appeal lies at the instance of a person who is in occupation of the building to which the order relates under a lease or agreement of which the unexpired term is three years or less.

    (3) On an appeal the court may make such order either confirming, quashing or varying the order as it thinks fit.

    (4) If an appeal is brought, the order does not become operative until—

(*a*) a decision on the appeal confirming the order (with or without variation) is given and the period within which an appeal to the Court of Appeal may be brought expires without any such appeal having been brought, or

(*b*) if a further appeal to the Court of Appeal is brought, a decision on that appeal is given confirming the order (with or without variation);

and for this purpose the withdrawal of an appeal has the same effect as a decision confirming the order or decision appealed against.

"local housing authority": ss.1, 2.
"obstructive building": s.283.
"obstructive building order": s.284.

GENERAL NOTE
Save as regards the power to accept an undertaking, this section is in identical terms to s.269, above: see notes thereto.

Obstructive building order: recovery of possession of building to be demolished

286.—(1) Where an obstructive building order has become operative, the local housing authority shall serve on the occupier of the building, or part of a building, to which the order relates a notice—

(*a*) stating the effect of the order,

(*b*) specifying the date by which the order requires the building to be vacated, and

(*c*) requiring him to quit the building before that date or before the expiration of 28 days from the service of the notice, whichever may be the later.

(2) If at any time after the date on which the notice requires the building to be vacated a person is in occupation of the building, or part of it, the local housing authority or an owner of the building may apply to the county court which shall order vacant possession of the building, or of the part of it, to be given to the applicant within such period, of not less than two or more than four weeks, as the court may determine.

(3) Nothing in the Rent Acts affects the provisions of this section relating to the obtaining of possession of a building.

(4) A person who, knowing that an obstructive building order has become operative and applies to a building—

(*a*) enters into occupation of the building, or of a part of it, after the date by which the order requires the building to be vacated, or

(*b*) permits another person to enter into such occupation after that date,

commits a summary offence and is liable on conviction to a fine not exceeding level 2 on the standard scale and to a further fine not exceeding £5 a day for every day or part of a day on which the occupation continues after conviction.

DEFINITIONS
"local housing authority": ss.1, 2.
"obstructive building": s.283.
"obstructive building order": s.284.
"owner": s.322.

GENERAL NOTE
This section is in identical terms to s.270, above (see notes thereto), with two exceptions: (a) there is no provision for the local authority to recover from the owner their costs of evicting an occupier; and, (b) the penalty is not at level 5, but level 2 on the standard scale under s.37, Criminal Justice Act 1982, currently £100, by S.I. 1984 No. 447.

Execution of obstructive building order

287.—(1) If before the end of the period within which a building in respect of which an obstructive building order is made is required by the order to be vacated—

(*a*) an owner whose estate or interest in the building and its site is such that its acquisition by the local housing authority would enable the authority to carry out the demolition provided for by the order, or

(*b*) owners whose combined estates or interests in the building and its

site are such that their acquisition by the authority would enable
the authority to carry out the demolition provided by the order,
make to the authority an offer for the sale of that interest, or of those
interests, at a price to be assessed as if it were compensation for a
compulsory purchase under section 290 (acquisition of land for clearance),
the authority shall accept the offer and shall, as soon as possible after
obtaining possession, carry out the demolition.

(2) If no such offer is made before the end of the period within which
the building is required by the order to be vacated, the owner or owners
shall carry out the demolition provided for by the order before the
expiration of six weeks from—

(*a*) the last day of that period, or

(*b*) if the building, or such part of it as is required to be vacated, is not
vacated until after that day, the day on which it is vacated,

or, in either case, such longer period as in the circumstances the local
housing authority deem reasonable.

(3) If the demolition is not so carried out, the local housing authority
shall enter and carry out the demolition and sell the materials rendered
available by the demolition.

DEFINITIONS

"local housing authority": ss.1, 2.
"obstructive building": s.283.
"obstructive building order": s.284.
"owner": s.322.

GENERAL NOTE

Until the end of the period for vacation of the property (*i.e.* two months from operative
date of order—see s.284, above), an owner, or all the owners between them, whose estate
or combined estates will permit demolition, can require the local authority to purchase their
interests at a price to be assessed as if a compulsory purchase under s.290, below: subs. (1).
If this occurs, the authority must demolish as soon as possible after obtaining possession:
ibid.

If no purchase offer is made, the provisions of subss. (2), (3), analogous to those in s.271,
above, will apply: see notes to s.271, above. Recovery of expenses by the authority is under
s.288, below.

Obstructive buildings: expenses of local housing authority, &c.

288.—(1) Expenses incurred by the local housing authority under
section 287(3) (execution of obstructive building order) after giving credit
for any amount realised by the sale of materials, may be recovered by
them from the owner of the building.

(2) If there is more than one owner—

(*a*) the expenses may be recovered by the authority from the owners
in such shares as the court may determine to be just and equitable,
and

(*b*) an owner who pays to the authority the full amount of their claim
may recover from any other owner such contribution, if any, as the
court may determine to be just and equitable.

(3) A surplus in the hands of the authority shall be paid by them to the
owner of the building or, if there is more than one owner, as the owners
may agree.

(4) If there is more than one owner and the owners do not agree as to
the division of the surplus, the authority shall, by virtue of this subsection,
be trustees of the surplus for the owners of the premises and section 63 of
the Trustee Act 1925 (which relates to payment into court by trustees)
has effect accordingly.

(5) The county court has jurisdiction to hear and determine proceedings
under subsection (1) or (2), and has jurisdiction under section 63 of the

Trustee Act 1925 in relation to such a surplus as is referred to in subsection (4).

(6) In determining for the purposes of this section the shares in which expenses are to be paid or contributed by, or a surplus divided between, two or more owners of a building, the court shall have regard to all the circumstances of the case, including—

(a) their respective interests in the building, and

(b) their respective obligations and liabilities in respect of maintenance and repair under any covenant or agreement, whether express or implied.

DEFINITIONS
"local housing authority": ss.1, 2.
"obstructive building": s.283.
"obstructive building order": s.284.
"owner": s.322.

GENERAL NOTE
This section is in identical terms to s.272, above: see notes thereto.

Clearance areas

Declaration of clearance area

289.—(1) A clearance area is an area which is to be cleared of all buildings in accordance with the following provisions of this Part.

(2) The local housing authority shall declare an area to be a clearance area if they are satisfied—

(a) that the houses in the area are unfit for human habitation or are by reason of their bad arrangement, or the narrowness or bad arrangement of the streets, dangerous or injurious to the health of the inhabitants of the area, and

(b) that the other buildings, if any, in the area are for a like reason dangerous or injurious to the health of the inhabitants of the area,

and that the most satisfactory method of dealing with the conditions in the area is the demolition of all the buildings in the area.

(3) If the authority are so satisfied they shall—

(a) cause the area to be defined on a map in such manner as to exclude from the area any building which is not unfit for human habitation or dangerous or injurious to health, and

(b) pass a resolution declaring the area so defined to be a clearance area.

(4) Before passing such a resolution the authority shall satisfy themselves—

(a) that, in so far as suitable accommodation does not already exist for the persons who will be displaced by the clearance of the area, the authority can provide, or secure the provision of, such accommodation in advance of the displacements which will from time to time become necessary as the demolition of the buildings in the area, or in different parts of it, proceeds, and

(b) that the resources of the authority are sufficient for the purposes of carrying the resolution into effect.

(5) The authority shall forthwith transmit to the Secretary of State a copy of any resolution passed by them under this section, together with a statement of the number of persons who on a day specified in the statement were occupying the buildings comprised in the clearance area.

(6) A clearance area shall not be so defined as to include land in a general improvement area.

DEFINITIONS
"general improvement area": s.253.
"house": s.322.
"local housing authority": ss.1, 2.
"unfit for human habitation": s.604.

GENERAL NOTE
This section is the first in the series, formerly contained in Part III, Housing Act 1957, down to and including s.299, which concerns "clearance areas", *i.e.* areas predominantly of housing which is unfit for human habitation within s.604, below, or otherwise dangerous or injurious to health to the inhabitants of the area.

The code is alternative to that in the first series of sections in this Part, *i.e.* ss.264–282, for dealing with individual unfit housing by means of undertaking, or closing or demolition order: *Holmes* v. *Ministry of Housing and Local Government* (1960) 12 P. & C.R. 72, see also *Lewington, Newland and Eckersley* v. *Secretary of State for the Environment and London Borough of Southwark* [1976] J.P.L. 425. The fact that a clearance area is declared does not preclude action under Part III, Public Health Act 1936 (statutory nuisance), although it may affect the extent of an order made under those provisions: *Nottingham Corporation* v. *Newton* [1974] 1 W.L.R. 923, D.C., *Salford City Council* v. *McNally* [1976] A.C. 379, H.L.

The core of the provisions is the acquisition and clearance of land under s.290, below: see notes thereto.

Houses
Many of the cases noted to s.56, above, analysing what constitutes a "house", concerned clearance areas: see particularly, *Ashbridge Investments Ltd.* v. *Ministry of Housing and Local Government* [1965] 1 W.L.R. 1320, C.A., *In Re Butler Camberwell (Wingfield Mews) No. 2 Clearance Order, 1936* [1939] 1 K.B. 570, C.A., and *Re Hammersmith (Bergham Mews) Clearance Order, 1936* [1937] 3 All E.R. 539, concerning "mixed user" buildings (*i.e.* dwellings above shops or other non-housing units), and *Annicola Investments Ltd.* v. *Minister of Housing and Local Government* [1968] 1 Q.B. 631, in which it was held that a purpose-built block containing both flats and other units could properly be treated as a clearance area in itself.

A hostel or a building used for multiple occupation or as a lodging-house would seem to qualify as a house for this purpose: see *London County Council* v. *Rowton Houses Ltd.* (1897) 62 J.P. 68; *Re Ross and Leicester Corporation* (1932) 96 J.P. 459; *R.* v. *London Borough of Southwark, ex parte Lewis Levy Ltd.* (1983) 8 H.L.R. 1, Q.B.D.; *R.* v. *London Borough of Camden, ex parte Rowton (Camden Town) Ltd.* (1983) 10 H.L.R. 28, Q.B.D.

Similarly, a building subdivided into flats can remain a house, whether so constructed or not: *Annicola Investments Ltd.* v. *Minister of Housing and Local Government* [1968] 1 Q.B. 631, *Quillotex Co. Ltd.* v. *Minister of Housing and Local Government* [1966] 1 Q.B. 704, *Benabo* v. *Wood Green Borough Council* [1946] 1 K.B. 38, *Critchell* v. *London Borough of Lambeth* [1957] 2 Q.B 535, C.A., *Okereke* v. *London Borough of Brent* [1967] 1 Q.B., C.A.

In *Lake* v. *Bennett* [1970] 1 Q.B. 663, C.A., under the Leasehold Reform Act 1967, Lord Denning M.R. doubted that a tower block could reasonably be called a house, but Salmon L.J. emphasised that the decision did not necessarily affect the Housing Acts, and the wording of the 1967 Act refers to a house "reasonably so called".

See further notes to ss.56, 189, above, and s.345, below.

The houses do not *have* to be unfit within the meaning of s.604, for they may be included in a clearance area if they are dangerous or injurious to the health of the inhabitants of the area by reason of their bad arrangement, *or* the narrowness or bad arrangement of the streets: subs. (2)(*a*). Clearance by reason of bad arrangement only has, however, become increasingly rare: see D.O.E. Circular 77/75, paras. 12–13, requiring "grounds" for their inclusion in a clearance area. "Bad arrangement" land will receive full compensation on purchase under s.290, below, rather than the site value from which compensation for unfit housing starts: see ss.585–589 and Scheds. 23, 24, below.

Other Buildings
Other buildings can be included if they are dangerous or injurious because of their bad arrangement, or the narrowness or bad arrangement of the streets, to the extent that they are dangerous or injurious to the health of the inhabitants of the area: subs. (2)(*b*). But an area cannot consist of such buildings *only*; there must be housing within subs. (2)(*a*) for there to be a clearance area at all, before other buildings can then be included. Such

buildings will also be admissible for full compensation on acquisition, rather than site value, under s.585, below.

Preconditions
The first precondition is in subs. (2), *i.e.* that the authority are satisfied that the most satisfactory method of dealing with the conditions of the area is demolition. Note that the area cannot include land in a general improvement area under s.253: subs. (6). There is no equivalent provision excluding land in a housing action area under s.239.

Before declaration, however, the authority must satisfy themselves that to the extent that suitable accommodation is not available to those who will be displaced, they can provide or secure the provision of such accommodation before it is needed (not necessarily before the whole programme is effected, but as it progresses): subs. (4)(*a*). This duty does not include suitable *business* accommodation: *Re Gateshead County Borough (Burn Close) Clearance Order 1931* [1933] 1 K.B. 429, *Byrne* v. *Glasgow Corporation* [1955] C.L.Y. 1213.

The authority must also satisfy themselves that they will have the resources to carry the programme through: subs. (4)(*b*). The authority are not, however, bound to consider specific figures, *i.e.* a general satisfaction may be sufficient: *Goddard* v. *Minister of Housing and Local Government* [1958] 1 W.L.R. 1151. Nor are they bound to hear objections from owners before the initial resolution: *Fredman* v. *Minister of Health* (1935) 154 L.T. 240.

Procedure
The procedural requirements for declaration are (a) to define by means of a map the extent of the area, so far as it concerns buildings unfit for human habitation or dangerous or injurious to health *only*, and (b) to pass a resolution declaring that area to be a clearance area: subs. (3). The authority's power to acquire *additional* land for the purposes of redevelopment arises under s.290, below, and such land is *not* to be included in the initial map. They can, however, include land which already belongs to them (s.293), even if the reason for the unfitness of its housing is its own failure to comply with their obligations under s.16, above, *i.e.* to bring housing acquired under Part II up to standard and into use: *Att.-Gen., ex rel. Rivers-Moore* v. *Portsmouth City Council* (1978) 76 L.G.R. 643.

The authority have to send a copy of the resolution to the Secretary of State under subs. (5), together with a statement of the number of people occupying the buildings in the area defined on a date stated in the statement. The Secretary of State has no direct power to overrule the declaration: his powers arise on the pursuit of the programme by purchase, compulsory if necessary, under s.290. If the Secretary of State does decline to confirm compulsory purchase, the clearance area ceases to exist so far as that land is concerned (which may, of course, mean the whole area): see *R.* v. *Secretary of State for the Environment, ex parte Wellingborough Council* (1982) 80 L.G.R. 603, D.C.

Acquisition of land for clearance

290.—(1) So soon as may be after the local housing authority have declared an area to be a clearance area, they shall proceed to secure the clearance of the area (subject to and in accordance with the provisions of this Part) by purchasing the land comprised in the area and themselves undertaking, or otherwise securing, the demolition of the buildings on the land.

(2) Where the authority determine to purchase land comprised in a clearance area, they may also purchase—

(*a*) land which is surrounded by the clearance area and the acquisition of which is reasonably necessary for the purpose of securing a cleared area of convenient shape and dimensions, and

(*b*) adjoining land the acquisition of which is reasonably necessary for the satisfactory development or use of the cleared area.

(3) Where the authority have determined to purchase land under this section, they may purchase the land by agreement or be authorised by the Secretary of State to purchase the land compulsorily.

(4) The powers conferred by subsection (3) are exercisable notwithstanding that any of the buildings within the area have been demolished since the area was declared to be a clearance area.

DEFINITIONS
"clearance area": s.289.
"local housing authority": ss.1, 2.

GENERAL NOTE
This is really the core section of the clearance area provisions, for the authority's duty is to purchase the land and demolish, or secure the demolition of, the buildings on it: subs. (1). If there is opposition, therefore, from owners, the authority will not be able to purchase by agreement, and will be dependent on compulsory purchase powers under subs. (3), *i.e.* with the consent of the Secretary of State. If the Secretary of State does not consent to compulsory purchase, the clearance area will cease to exist, so far as that land is concerned (which may, of course, mean the whole area): *R.* v. *Secretary of State for the Environment, ex parte Wellingborough Council* (1982) 80 L.G.R. 603, D.C.

"Land" includes "buildings and other structures, land covered with water, and any estate, interest, easement, servitude or right in or over land": Interpretation Act 1978, Schedule 1. *Procedures* for compulsory purchase are governed by s.579 and Schedule 22, below: see notes thereto. Procedures *following* compulsory purchase are governed by s.584, below. Compulsory purchase *compensation* is governed by ss.585–589, and Scheds. 23 and 24, below: see notes thereto.

Tenants displaced by clearance area action will normally be entitled to rehousing under s.39, and home loss payment under s.29 and/or disturbance payment under s.37, Land Compensation Act 1973. Owner-occupiers may also be entitled to rehousing and compensation under that Act, or under the provisions of ss.586, 587, and Scheds. 23 and 24, below.

The need to purchase may be averted if the Secretary of State consents, on the joint application of owner or owners and local authority, to demolition by owner or owners, and is satisfied that the authority can secure the proper clearance of the remainder of the area without buying that land: s.292, below.

Added Land
In addition to the property within the map under s.289(3), above, the authority may purchase land (a) surrounded *by* the clearance area, which is reasonably necessary to secure a cleared area of convenient shape and dimensions, and (b) *adjoining* the area, which is reasonably necessary for the satisfactory redevelopment or use of the area. Any land contiguous with the clearance area can properly be described as adjoining land: *Bass Charrington Ltd.* v. *Minister of Housing and Local Government* (1971) 22 P. & C.R. 31.

A court can inquire into whether there is *any* material upon which it can be concluded that added lands are reasonably necessary, and a mere statement to that effect by the authority will not be sufficient: *Sheffield Burgesses* v. *Minister of Health* (1935) 100 J.P. 99, *Coleen Properties* v. *Minister of Housing and Local Government* [1971] 1 W.L.R. 433, C.A. And a question as to convenience of shape or dimensions addressed to land added for the purposes of satisfactory development or use will constitute an error: *Gosling* v. *Secretary of State for the Environment* [1975] J.P.L. 406.

The fact that the authority may be *considering* changing their plans, without having already actually done so, will not undermine the power of the Secretary of State to confirm an order, for he is entitled to proceed on an assumption that the authority will continue to act in accordance with law, *i.e.* in accordance with the provisions of this Part. *Wahiwala* v. *Secretary of State for the Environment and Peterborough City Council* [1976] J.P.L. 366; see also *Migdal Investments* v. *Secretary of State for the Environment* [1976] J.P.L. 365.

Method of dealing with land acquired for clearance

291.—(1) A local housing authority who have purchased land under section 290 shall, so soon as may be, cause every building on the land to be vacated and deal with the land in one or other of the following ways, or partly in one of those ways and partly in the other, that is to say—

    (*a*) themselves demolish every building on the land within the period mentioned in subsection (2) and thereafter appropriate or dispose of the land, subject to such restrictions and conditions (if any) as they think fit, or

    (*b*) dispose of the land as soon as may be subject to a condition that the buildings on it be demolished forthwith, and subject to such restrictions and other conditions (if any) as they think fit.

(2) The period within which the authority is to demolish a building under paragraph (*a*) of subsection (1) is six weeks from the date on which the building is vacated or such longer period as in the circumstances they consider reasonable.

(3) This section has effect subject to—

section 301 (retention of premises for temporary housing use),

sections 305 and 306 (suspension of clearance procedure on building becoming listed), and

Schedule 11 (rehabilitation orders).

(4) The references in subsection (1) to appropriation or disposal are to appropriation or disposal under the general powers conferred by section 122 or 123 of the Local Government Act 1972.

DEFINITION

"local housing authority": ss.1, 2.

GENERAL NOTE

The procedure following purchase under s.290 is to cause all the buildings to be vacated and *either* demolish the buildings themselves within six weeks from when each is vacated or such longer period as they consider reasonable (*e.g.* to allow for block demolition), followed by disposal of the land or appropriation to another use, *or* dispose of the land without demolition, but subject to a demolition condition and such other restrictions and conditions as they think fit: subs. (1). As to the authority's power to enforce conditions, see also s.609, below.

The duty is not applicable if the authority decide to retain the building for temporary housing use, or if the buildings are listed, and the procedures are suspended or have to be abandoned, or if the rehabilitation order provisions of Sched. 11 are applicable—see s.299, below. Appropriation is under s.122, Local Government Act 1972; disposal is under s.123, Local Government Act 1972 which requires, save in the case of a short (*i.e.* not exceeding seven year) lease, that unless the Secretary of State otherwise consents, the authority must obtain the best consideration reasonably obtainable. See also *London and Westcliff Properties* v. *Ministry of Housing and Local Government* [1961] 1 W.L.R. 519.

This part of the procedure will be averted if the Secretary of State has consented, on the joint application of owner or owners and local authority, to demolition by owner or owners, and is satisfied that the authority can secure the proper clearance of the remainder of the area without buying that land: s.292, below.

Power to discontinue proceedings if acquisition of land proves unnecessary

292. Where the local housing authority have submitted to the Secretary of State an order for the compulsory purchase of land in a clearance area and the Secretary of State, on an application being made to him by the owner or owners of the land and the authority, is satisfied—

(*a*) that the owner or owners of the land, with the concurrence of any mortgagee of the land, agree to the demolition of the buildings on the land, and

(*b*) that the authority can secure the proper clearance of the area without acquiring the land,

the Secretary of State may authorise the authority to discontinue proceedings for the purchase of the land on their being satisfied that such covenants have been or will be entered into by all necessary parties as may be requisite for securing that the buildings will be demolished, and the land become subject to the like restrictions and conditions, as if the authority had dealt with the land in accordance with the provisions of section 291.

DEFINITIONS

"clearance area": s.289.

"local housing authority": ss.1, 2.

"owner": s.322.

GENERAL NOTE
This section applies to permit purchase to be by-passed if the owner or owners and the local authority make joint application to the Secretary of State, on the basis that the owner or owners will themselves demolish, and the authority can clear the remainder of the area without needing to buy their land. The Secretary of State must also be satisfied that adequate covenants have been or will be entered into so as to secure the position as if the procedure under s.291 had been followed—see notes thereto.

Property belonging to the local housing authority

293.—(1) The local housing authority may include in a clearance area land belonging to them which they might have included in the area if it had not belonged to them, and the provisions of this Part apply to land so included as they apply to land purchased by the authority as being comprised in the clearance area.

(2) Where land belonging to the local housing authority is surrounded by or adjoins a clearance area and might, had it not previously been acquired by them, have been purchased by the authority under section 290(2), the provisions of this Part apply to that land as they apply to land purchased by the authority as being surrounded by or adjoining the clearance area.

DEFINITIONS
"clearance area": s.289.
"local housing authority": ss.1, 2.

GENERAL NOTE
This section permits the authority to include their own land in a clearance area, *i.e.* under s.289 (subs. (1)), or to add land under s.290 (subs. (2)). Land can be included even although the only reason for its unfitness is that the authority have failed to comply with their obligations under s.18, above, to bring property acquired for Part II purposes up to standard and into use: *A.G., ex rel. Rivers-Moore* v. *Portsmouth City Council* (1978) 76 L.G.R. 643. The authority are also entitled to *exclude* land included (in either way), without the consent of the Secretary of State: *Frost* v. *Minister of Health* [1935] 1 K.B. 286.

Extinguishment of public rights of way over land acquired

294.—(1) The local housing authority may, with the approval of the Secretary of State, by order extinguish any public right of way over land acquired by them under section 290 (land acquired for clearance).

(2) Where the authority have resolved to purchase under that section land over which a public right of way exists, they may make and the Secretary of State may approve, in advance of the purchase, an order extinguishing that right as from the date on which the buildings on the land are vacated, or at the end of such period after that date as may be specified in the order or as the Secretary of State in approving the order may direct.

(3) The order shall be published in such manner as may be prescribed and if objection to the order is made to the Secretary of State before the expiration of six weeks from its publication, he shall not approve the order until he has caused a public local inquiry to be held into the matter.

DEFINITIONS
"clearance area": s.289.
"local housing authority": ss.1, 2.

GENERAL NOTE
This section permits the authority, with the consent of the Secretary of State, to make an order existinguishing a public right of way over any of the land they have acquired under s.290, above. If there is an objection to the order, the Secretary of State has to hold a public local inquiry. See also s.298, below, for the position of telecommunications apparatus under, in, on, over, along or across the public right of way.

Extinguishment of other rights over land acquired

295.—(1) Upon the completion by the local housing authority of the purchase by them under section 290 (land acquired for clearance)—
- (a) all private rights of way over the land,
- (b) all rights of laying down, erecting, continuing or maintaining apparatus on, under or over the land, and
- (c) all other rights or easements in or relating to the land,

shall be extinguished and any such apparatus shall vest in the authority.

(2) Subsection (1) has effect subject to—
- (a) any agreement which may be made between the local housing authority and the person in or to whom the right or apparatus is vested or belongs, and
- (b) sections 296 and 298 (which relate to the rights and apparatus of statutory undertakers and certain operators of telecommunication systems).

(3) A person who suffers loss by the extinguishment of any right or the vesting of any apparatus under subsection (1) is entitled to be paid by the local housing authority compensation to be determined under and in accordance with the Land Compensation Act 1961.

DEFINITIONS
"apparatus": s.296.
"local housing authority": ss.1, 2.
"statutory undertakers": s.296.

GENERAL NOTE
Subject to agreement to the contrary, and to the provisions of ss.296–298, below, governing statutory undertakers and telecommunications apparatus (subs. (2)), on completion of purchase private rights of way, rights relating to apparatus on, under or over the land, and other rights or easements, are extinguished: subs. (1). A person suffering loss is, however, entitled to compensation: subs. (3).

The wording of subs. (1)(c) has been held wide enough to cover a right to light, so that compensation was payable: *Badham* v. *Morris* (1881) 52 L.J.Ch. 237n, under s.20, Artizans' and Labourers' Dwellings Improvement Act 1875. See also *Barlow* v. *Ross* (1890) 24 Q.B.D. 381, C.A. It covers a right to support, so that the authority cannot be restrained from their duty to demolish under s.291: *Swainston* v. *Finn and Metropolitan Board of Works* (1883) 52 L.J.Ch. 235.

Apparatus of statutory undertakers

296.—(1) Section 295(1) (extinguishment of rights over land acquired for clearance and vesting of apparatus in local housing authority) does not apply to—
- (a) any right vested in statutory undertakers of laying down, erecting, continuing or maintaining any apparatus, or
- (b) any apparatus belonging to statutory undertakers.

(2) Where the removal or alteration of apparatus belonging to statutory undertakers—
- (a) on, under or over land purchased by a local housing authority under section 290 (land acquired for clearance), or
- (b) on, under or over a street running over, or through, or adjoining any such land,

is reasonably necessary for the purpose of enabling the authority to exercise any of the powers conferred on them by the provisions of this Part relating to clearance areas, the authority may execute works for the removal or alteration of the apparatus, subject to and in accordance with the provisions of section 297 (procedure for removal or alteration of apparatus).

(3) The local housing authority shall make reasonable compensation to statutory undertakers for any damage sustained by the undertakers by

reason of the execution by the authority of works under this section and not made good by the provision of substituted apparatus; and any question as to the right of undertakers to recover such compensation or as to its amount shall be referred to and determined by the Lands Tribunal.

(4) In this section—

(a) "statutory undertakers" means persons authorised by an enactment, or by an order, rule or regulation made under an enactment, to construct, work or carry on a railway, canal, inland navigation, dock, harbour, tramway, gas, electricity, water or other public undertaking;

(b) "apparatus" means sewers, drains, culverts, water-courses, mains, pipes, valves, tubes, cables, wires, transformers and other apparatus laid down or used for or in connection with the carrying, conveying or supplying to any premises of a supply of water, water for hydraulic power, gas or electricity, and standards and brackets carrying street lamps;

(c) references to the alteration of apparatus include references to diversion and to the alteration of position or level.

DEFINITION
"local housing authority": ss.1, 2.

GENERAL NOTE
The apparatus of statutory undertakers as defined in subs. (4) is exempt from the automatic extinguishment of rights under s.295, above, but may be subject to removal or alteration under s.297, below, with the consequence that "reasonable" compensation is payable and referable to the Lands Tribunal, under subs. (3).

Procedure for removal or alteration of apparatus under s.296

297.—(1) A local housing authority who intend to remove or alter apparatus in exercise of the power conferred by section 296—

(a) shall serve on the undertakers notice in writing of their intention with particulars of the proposed works and of the manner in which they are to be executed and plans and sections of them, and

(b) shall not commence any works until the expiration of the period of 28 days from the date of service of that notice;

and within that period the undertakers may, by notice in writing served on the authority, make objections to, or state requirements with respect to, the proposed works as follows.

(2) The undertakers may object to the execution of the works, or any of them, on the ground that they are not reasonably necessary for the purpose mentioned in section 296(2); and if objection is so made to any works and not withdrawn, the authority shall not execute the works unless they are determined by arbitration to be so necessary.

(3) The undertakers may state requirements to which, in their opinion, effect ought to be given as to—

(a) the manner of, or the conditions to be observed in, the execution of the works, or

(b) the execution of other works for the protection of other apparatus belonging to the undertakers or for the provision of substituted apparatus, whether permanent or temporary;

and if any such requirement is so made and not withdrawn, the authority shall give effect to it unless it is determined by arbitration to be unreasonable.

(4) At least seven days before commencing any works which they are authorised by section 296, or required by subsection (3), to execute, the local housing authority shall, except in case of emergency, serve on the undertakers notice in writing of their intention to do so; and the works

shall be executed by the authority under the superintendence (at the expense of the authority) and to the reasonable satisfaction of the undertakers.

(5) If within seven days from the date of service on them of such a notice the undertakers so elect, they shall themselves execute the works in accordance with the reasonable directions and to the reasonable satisfaction of the authority; and the reasonable costs of the works shall be repaid to the undertakers by the authority.

(6) Any matter which by virtue of subsection (2) or (3) is to be determined by arbitration, and any difference arising between statutory undertakers and a local housing authority under subsection (4) or (5), shall be referred to and determined by an arbitrator to be appointed, in default of agreement, by the Secretary of State.

DEFINITION
"local housing authority": ss.1, 2.

GENERAL NOTE
This section governs the procedure to be followed when the authority want to remove or alter the apparatus of statutory undertakers under s.296, above. Note that disputes are referable to an arbitrator, who may be appointed by the Secretary of State if the parties cannot agree: subs. (6).

Telecommunications apparatus

298.—(1) In this section—
(a) "the telecommunications code" means the code contained in Schedule 2 to the Telecommunications Act 1984,
(b) "telecommunications code system" means a telecommunication system to which that code applies, and
(c) expressions which are defined for the purposes of that code by paragraph 1 of that Schedule, or are defined in that Act for the purposes of that Act, have the same meaning in this section.

(2) Where a public right of way over land is extinguished by an order under section 294 and immediately before the order comes into operation there is under, in, on, over, along or across the land telecommunication apparatus kept installed for the purposes of a telecommunications code system, the powers of the operator of the system in respect of the apparatus are not affected by the order, but any person entitled to the land over which the right of way subsisted may require the alteration of the apparatus, and paragraph 21 of the telecommunications code (procedure for exercise of right to require removal of apparatus) applies.

(3) Section 295(1) (extinguishment of other rights over land acquired for clearance and vesting of apparatus in local housing authority) does not apply to—
(a) any right conferred by or in accordance with the telecommunications code on the operator of a telecommunications code system, or
(b) telecommunication apparatus kept installed for the purposes of such a system;
but the local housing authority may, where it is reasonably necessary for the purpose of enabling the authority to exercise any of the powers conferred on them by the provisions of this Act relating to clearance areas, execute works for the alteration of such apparatus, and paragraph 23 of the telecommunications code (procedure for works involving alteration of apparatus) applies.

DEFINITIONS
"local housing authority": ss.1, 2.

GENERAL NOTE
This section governs telecommunications apparatus both on the extinguishment by order of a public right of way under s.295, above, and on the extinguishment of other rights under s.296.

Rehabilitation orders

Rehabilitation orders in respect of houses in clearance areas

299.—(1) Schedule 11 has effect with respect to rehabilitation orders in respect of houses acquired for clearance, or which it was resolved to acquire, before 2nd December 1974 (when the provisions of the Housing Act 1974 with respect to housing action areas and improvement notices came into force), as follows:—

Part I—The making of the order and its effect.

Part II—Procedural matters.

(2) References in that Schedule to improvement to "the full standard" have the same meaning as in Part VII (improvement notices).

DEFINITIONS
"full standard": s.234.
"housing action area": s.239.
"improvement notice": s.216.

GENERAL NOTE
This section and Schedule 11 contain transitional provisions, governing "rehabilitation orders" which could be made in relation to property within a clearance area, purchased before December 2, 1974, or subject to a confirmed compulsory purchase order made before December 2, 1974, and confirmed before March 2, 1975, in order to substitute the housing action area provisions of Part VIII above, or to use the compulsory improvement procedures of Part VII. If an owner asks the authority to use this power, the authority must consider doing so, and give reasons for refusing: *Elliott* v. *Southwark London Borough Council* [1976] 1 W.L.R. 499, C.A. However, a wish to demolish and provide new housing will be sufficient reason for the refusal: *ibid*. The power to make a rehabilitation order is applicable only to unfit housing, which can be brought up to the "full standard" within s.234, above.

Use of condemned houses for temporary housing accommodation

Purchase of houses liable to be demolished or closed

300.—(1) Where the local housing authority would be required under section 265 to make a demolition or closing order in respect of a house, they may, if it appears to them that the house is or can be rendered capable of providing accommodation of a standard which is adequate for the time being, purchase it instead.

(2) Where an authority have determined to purchase a house under this section—

(*a*) they shall serve a notice of their determination on the persons on whom they would have been required by section 268(1) to serve a copy of a demolition or closing order, and

(*b*) sections 268(2) and 269 (operative date and right of appeal) apply to such a notice as they apply to a demolition or closing order.

(3) At any time after the notice has become operative the authority may purchase the house by agreement or be authorised by the Secretary of State to purchase it compulsorily.

(4) In this section "house"—

(*a*) does not have the extended meaning given by section 264(7) (temporary or movable structures), and

(*b*) does not include premises against which action is taken by virtue of section 266 (parts of buildings and underground rooms).

(5) This section does not apply where section 304(1) applies (listed building or building protected pending listing).

Definitions
"closing order": s.267.
"demolition order": s.267.
"house": s.322.
"local housing authority": ss.1, 2.
"underground room": s.280.

General Note
This section provides an alternative to s.265, above, *i.e.* where the authority have not accepted an undertaking under s.264, and would otherwise make a demolition or closing order, they may instead purchase the property for temporary housing use: subs. (1). The power is not available, however, in relation to tents and other movable structures within s.264(7), nor is it available in relation to parts of buildings and underground rooms (subs. (4)), nor is it available in relation to a listed building within the protection (permanent or temporary) of s.304, below (subs. (5)).

Temporary Accommodation
The power is for the provision of providing accommodation "for the time being": subs. (1). The authority are not bound to decide in advance for how long they propose to use the property, and in relation to s.301, below, it has been held that a period of 24 years was not so long that no reasonable authority could defer clearance in order to keep a property in analogous "temporary" use: *R.* v. *City of Birmingham Corporation, ex parte Sale* (1983) 9 H.L.R. 33, Q.B.D. The authority cannot use this power in order to add to their *permanent, i.e.* Part II, stock: *Victoria Square Property Co.* v. *Southwark London Borough Council* [1978] 1 W.L.R. 463, C.A.

Standard
The standard need only be "adequate", and under s.302, below, the provisions of s.8, Landlord and Tenant Act 1985, which imply a term into a letting at a very low rent that the property will be and will be kept fit for human habitation with the meaning of s.10 of that Act, s.604 of this Act, are expressly disapplied. It seems self-evident that the standard can be less than fitness, and in any event neither Part VI, nor ss.264 *et seq.*, above, will apply: see notes to ss.189, 264, with reference to the decision in *R.* v. *Cardiff City Council, ex parte Cross* (1981) 1 H.L.R. 54, Q.B.D., affirmed on appeal (1982) 6 H.L.R. 1, C.A. Nonetheless, the statutory nuisance provisions of Part III, Public Health Act 1936 will continue to apply: *Nottingham Corporation* v. *Newton* [1974] 1 W.L.R. 923, D.C., *Salford City Council* v. *McNally* [1976] A.C. 379, H.L.

Procedure
A purchase notice is served on the same persons as would be the demolition or closing order, and the same provisions governing operative dates and appeals are applicable: subs. (2). See notes to ss.268, 269, above. The purchase under subs. (3) will be at site value under s.585, below, but subject to the possibility of additional compensation under Scheds. 23 and 24. Previous occupiers will normally qualify for rehousing and compensation under ss.29–39, Land Compensation Act 1973.

Retention of houses acquired for clearance

301.—(1) The local housing authority, having declared an area to be a clearance area, may postpone for such period as they may determine the demolition of houses on land purchased by them within the area if, in their opinion, the houses are or can be rendered capable of providing accommodation of a standard which is adequate for the time being.

(2) Where the local housing authority are satisfied that a house on land purchased by them within a clearance area which is not retained by them for temporary use for housing purposes—
   (*a*) is required for the support of a house which is so retained, or
   (*b*) should not be demolished for the time being for some other special reason connected with the exercise in relation to the clearance area of the authority's powers under subsection (1),

they may retain the house for the time being and are not required to demolish it so long as it is required for that purpose or, as the case may be, so long as those powers are being exercised by the authority in relation to that area.

(3) Where the demolition of any houses in a clearance area is postponed under this section, the local housing authority may also postpone the taking of proceedings under section 290(1) (acquisition of land for clearance) in respect of buildings other than houses within the area.

DEFINITIONS
"clearance area": s.289.
"house": s.322.
"local housing authority": ss.1, 2.

GENERAL NOTE
This section is analogous to the last, but relates to property purchased under s.290, above, within a clearance area under s.289. Note that only housing within the clearance area, not added lands under s.289, falls within the section.

The first power is to postpone the demolition duty arising under s.291, above, for the purpose of providing accommodation of a standard which is "adequate for the time being": subs. (1). See further the headings Temporary Accommodation and Standard in the notes to s.300, above. The case of *R.* v. *City of Birmingham Corporation, ex parte Sale* (1983) 9 H.L.R. 33, Q.B.D., concerned this power: the additional point to be made here is that it was held that the authority cannot retain accommodation in use under this power *merely* because there is housing need in their area; some reason *additional* to the fact that there is a need for housing and that the property can be maintained to a standard adequate for the time being by the expenditure of money (*cf.* s.302, below), is called for.

The second power is to postpone demolition either as ancillary to the first power, *i.e.* to support retained property, or for some other special reason: subs. (2).

Management and repair of houses acquired under s.300 or retained under s.301

302. Where a house is acquired by a local housing authority under section 300 or retained by a local housing authority under section 301 for temporary use for housing purposes—

(*a*) the authority have the like powers in respect of the house as they have in respect of dwellings provided by them under Part II (provision of housing accommodation);

(*b*) the authority may carry out such works as may from time to time be required for rendering and keeping the house capable of providing accommodation of a standard which is adequate for the time being pending its demolition;

(*c*) section 8 of the Landlord and Tenant Act 1985 (implied condition of fitness for human habitation) does not apply to a contract for the letting of the house by the authority.

DEFINITIONS
"house": s.322.
"local housing authority": ss.1, 2.

GENERAL NOTE
The authority can exercise their general management powers under Part II in relation to housing retained under the last two sections: see notes to ss.20 *et seq.*, above.

The authority can spend money rendering and keeping such property to a standard which is adequate for the time being.

However, the provisions of s.8, Landlord and Tenant Act 1985 are inapplicable. That section implies into lettings at very low rents (which may well be appropriate to property retained under the last two sections) that the house will be and will be kept fit throughout the letting. Fitness is defined in s.10 of that Act, in identical terms to s.604, below.

Listed buildings

Meaning of "listed building"

303. In this Part "listed building" means a building included in a list of buildings of special architectural or historic interest under section 54 of the Town and Country Planning Act 1971.

GENERAL NOTE

This series of sections, down to and including s.306, deals with the special position of buildings which are (or may become—*cf.* s.304(3), below), "listed" as of special architectural or historic interest, under s.54, Town and Country Planning Act 1971.

Closing order to be made in respect of listed building subject to s.265

304.—(1) A local housing authority shall not make a demolition order under section 265 (unfit premises beyond repair at reasonable cost) in respect of a listed building but shall instead make a closing order under that section.

(2) Where a house in respect of which a demolition order has been made becomes a listed building, the local housing authority shall determine the order, whether or not it has become operative, and make a closing order in respect of the house; and they shall serve—

(*a*) notice that the demolition order has been determined, and

(*b*) a copy of the closing order,

on every person on whom they would be required by section 268 to serve a copy of a closing order made under section 265.

(3) The Secretary of State may give notice in respect of a house to the local housing authority stating that its architectural or historic interest is sufficient to render it inexpedient that it should be demolished pending determination of the question whether it should be a listed building; and the provisions of this section apply to a house in respect of which such a notice is in force as they apply to a listed building.

DEFINITIONS

"closing order": s.267.
"demolition order": s.267.
"house": s.322.
"listed building": s.303.
"local housing authority": ss.1, 2.
"reasonable expense": s.321.

GENERAL NOTE

For the purposes of this section, a building is a listed building whether it is already listed, or the Secretary of State has given the authority notice under subs. (3), *i.e.* in effect notice of possible impending listing.

If a building has been listed before action falls to be considered following a time-and-place notice under s.264, above, no demolition order is to be made under s.265: subs. (1). If such an order has already been made, but has not yet been executed (*i.e.* demolished), regardless of whether or not the order has become operative (*cf.* notes to ss.268, 269, above), the order is to be determined, and a closing order substituted, and all those on whom the closing order would have to have been served under s.268 are to be reserved: subs. (2).

Building becoming listed when subject to compulsory purchase for clearance

305.—(1) Where a building to which a compulsory purchase order under section 290 applies (acquisition of land for clearance) becomes a listed building at any time after the making of the order, the authority making the order may, within the period of three months beginning with the date on which the building becomes a listed building, apply to the

Secretary of State (and only to him) under section 55 of the Town and Country Planning Act 1971 (listed building consent) for his consent to the demolition of the building.

(2) If the authority have not served notice to treat in respect of the building under section 5 of the Compulsory Purchase Act 1965, they shall not do so unless and until the Secretary of State gives that consent.

(3) The following provisions of this section have effect where—

(*a*) an application for such consent is made and refused, or

(*b*) the period for making an application expires without the authority having made an application;

and in those provisions "the relevant date" means the date of the refusal or, as the case may be, the expiry of that period.

(4) If at the relevant date—

(*a*) the building has not vested in the authority, and

(*b*) no notice to treat has been served by the authority under section 5 of the Compulsory Purchase Act 1965 in respect of an interest in the building,

the compulsory purchase order shall cease to have effect in relation to the building and, where applicable, the building shall cease to be comprised in a clearance area.

(5) Where a building which was included in a clearance area solely by reason of its being unfit for human habitation ceases to be comprised in the area by virtue of subsection (4), the authority concerned shall forthwith take whichever of the following steps is appropriate—

(*a*) serve a notice in respect of the building under section 189 (repair notice), or

(*b*) make a closing order in respect of the building under section 265.

(6) Where subsection (4) does not apply, the authority shall cease to be subject to the duty imposed by section 291 (method of dealing with land acquired for clearance) to demolish the building, and—

(*a*) if the building or an interest in it is vested in the authority at the relevant date, it shall be treated in the case of a house as appropriated to the purposes of Part II of this Act (provision of housing accommodation) and in any other case as appropriated to the purposes of Part VI of the Town and Country Planning Act 1971 (planning purposes);

(*b*) in relation to an interest in the building which has not at the relevant date vested in the authority, the compulsory purchase order has effect in the case of a house as if made and confirmed under Part II of this Act and in any other case as if made and confirmed under Part VI of the Town and Country Planning Act 1971.

(7) No account shall be taken for the purposes of section 4 of the Compulsory Purchase Act 1965 (time limit for completing compulsory purchase) of any period during which an authority are prevented by this section from serving a notice to treat under section 5 of that Act.

DEFINITIONS

"clearance area": s.289.

"closing order": s.267.

"house": s.322.

"listed building": s.303.

"local housing authority": ss.1, 2.

"unfit for human habitation": s.604.

GENERAL NOTE

If a building within a compulsory purchase order made under s.290, *i.e.* land for the purposes of a clearance area (and therefore including both land within the area under s.289, and added lands under s.290(2)), is listed (not merely may be listed: the provisions of s.304(3) are not here applicable), the authority can apply for consent within three months of listing to continue with the demolition notwithstanding: subs. (1). Pending the determination of the issue, notice to treat under s.5, Compulsory Purchase Act 1965 (see notes to s.583, below) is not to be served (subs. (2)), and time does not begin to run under that Act until this prohibition on service ends: subs. (7).

If the application for consent is refused, or no consent is sought, then as at the date of refusal, or the end of the period for seeking consent, if the notice to treat has still not been served, *and* the building has not yet vested in the authority (*i.e.* they have not purchased by agreement—*cf.* s.306, below), the compulsory purchase order ceases to have effect and the building ceases to be a part of the clearance area (if it was, *i.e.* if it was not added lands): subss. (3), (4). If the property was included in the clearance area solely because it was unfit for human habitation within s.604, below (*cf.* notes to s.289, above), the authority can either serve a repairs notice under s.189, or make a closing order under s.265, as appropriate, *i.e.* depending on reasonable cost: subs. (5).

In other cases, the duty to demolish under s.291 also comes to an end and *either*, if the authority have acquired an interest in the property, if a house it is treated as appropriated to Part II, above, and if not a house, to planning purposes, *or* if no interest has yet vested in the authority, the compulsory purchase order continues, either under Part II or the Town and Country Planning Act 1971, Part VI: subs. (6).

Building becoming listed when acquired by agreement for clearance

306.—(1) Where section 291 (method of dealing with land acquired for clearance) applies to a building purchased by the local housing authority by agreement and the building becomes a listed building, the authority may, within the period of three months beginning with the date on which the building becomes a listed building, apply to the Secretary of State (and only to him) under section 55 of the Town and Country Planning Act 1971 for his consent to the demolition of the building.

(2) Where such an application is made and is refused, or the period for making such an application expires without the authority making an application—

(*a*) the authority shall cease to be subject to the duty imposed by section 291 to demolish the building, and

(*b*) the building shall be treated in the case of a house as appropriated to the purposes of Part II of this Act (provision of housing accommodation) and in any other case as appropriated to the purposes of Part VI of the Town and Country Planning Act 1971 (planning purposes).

DEFINITIONS
"house": s.322.
"listed building": s.303.
"local housing authority": ss.1, 2.

GENERAL NOTE
If property has been purchased by agreement in relation to a clearance area (whether within the area under s.289, or added lands under s.290(2), above), and becomes listed (actually, not prospectively: s.304(3) has no application), the authority may as under the last section apply for consent within three months of the listing to continuing with demolition: subs. (1). Consent can only be obtained from the Secretary of State: *ibid.* If no application is made, or it is refused, then the authority cease to be under a duty to demolish under s.291, and instead are treated as having appropriated the property, if a house to Part II, above, and if not a house to Part VI, Town and Country Planning Act 1971.

Provisions for protection or assistance of owners

Saving for rights arising from breach of covenant, &c.

307.—(1) Nothing in the provisions of this Part relating to—
(*a*) the demolition, closing or purchase of unfit premises, or
(*b*) the demolition of obstructive buildings,

prejudices or interferes with the rights or remedies of an owner for breach of any covenant or contract entered into by a lessee in reference to premises in respect of which an order is made by the local housing authority under those provisions.

(2) If an owner is obliged to take possession of premises in order to comply with such an order, the taking possession does not affect his right to avail himself of any such breach which occurred before he so took possession.

DEFINITIONS

"obstructive building": s.283.
"owner": s.322.

GENERAL NOTE

See notes to s.203, above. The extension to parts of buildings and movable or temporary structures is pursuant to Law Commission Recommendations (Cmnd. 9515), No. 16(ii).

Approval of owner's proposals for re-development

308.—(1) A person proposing to undertake the re-development of land may submit particulars of his proposals to the local housing authority for approval under this section.

(2) The authority shall consider the proposals and if they appear to the authority to be satisfactory, the authority shall give notice to that effect to the person by whom they were submitted, specifying times within which the several parts of the re-development are to be carried out.

(3) Where the authority have so given notice of their satisfaction with proposals, no action shall be taken in relation to the land under any of the powers conferred by the provisions of this Part relating to—

(*a*) the demolition, closing or purchase of unfit premises, or
(*b*) clearance areas,

if and so long as the re-development is being proceeded with in accordance with the proposals and within the specified time limits, subject to any variation or extension approved by the authority.

(4) This section does not apply to premises—

(*a*) in respect of which a demolition order has become operative, or
(*b*) comprised in a compulsory purchase order under section 290 (acquisition of land for clearance) which has been confirmed by the Secretary of State;

and has effect subject to section 311 in a case where proposals are submitted under this section with respect to premises in a clearance area.

DEFINITIONS

"clearance area": s.289.
"demolition order": s.267.
"local housing authority": ss.1, 2.

GENERAL NOTE

This is the first of four sections governing action by owners or others to redevelop land themselves. See also s.610, below, enabling application to court for permission to carry out conversions contrary to the terms of a restrictive covenant or a lease.

This first power may be exercised regardless of whether action has been taken under this Part, *save* if a demolition order has already become operative (as to which, see notes to ss.268, 269, above), *or* the premises are comprised in a confirmed compulsory purchase order under s.290, above: subs. (4). If the premises are within a clearance area (see notes to s.289, above), then the provisions of this section are subject to s.311, below.

Anyone who is proposing to undertake redevelopment of land can submit his proposals to the authority for approval: subs. (1). No particular interest is called for but as the benefit will last only so long as time-conditions for redevelopment are complied with, the person will in substance have to be in a position to put his proposals into effect.

The authority are bound to consider the proposals and, if satisfactory, approve them, specifying times for completion: subs. (2). If the premises are in a clearance area, however, the authority can decline to reach a decision but instead send the proposals on to the Secretary of State for consideration under s.311, below. Consideration is in substance as an objection to the compulsory purchase order proposed under s.290, above. If the Secretary of State when confirming the order excludes the premises, the matter then returns to the authority for decision under this section.

The authority are not obliged to follow this procedure, but they must do one or the other, *i.e.* consider and reach a decision themselves, or send the proposals on: *Menachem Schleider* v. *Secretary of State for the Environment and Gateshead Metropolitan Borough Council* [1983] J.P.L. 382, Q.B.D. There is no time limit for reaching a decision, so that an application must merely be dealt with in what is in all the circumstances a reasonable time, but the decision cannot be deferred generally, *i.e.* until after a decision on a proposed compulsory purchase order: *ibid.*

If satisfied with the proposal, the authority can issue to a landlord a certificate that suitable alternative accommodation will be available for a protected or statutory tenant within the Rent Act 1977, which certificate will be conclusive evidence that such is or will be available, although *not* that it is reasonable to make the order for possession under s.98, Rent Act 1977 (*cf.* notes to s.84, above): see s.309, below.

The effect of approval is that so long as redevelopment continues in accordance with the times specified, subject to any variation or extension agreed by the authority, no action is to be taken under any of the specified powers of this Part: subs. (3). Disregard of this prohibition would be judicially reviewable: *R.* v. *Minister of Health, ex parte Davis* [1929] 1 K.B. 619. In addition, application can be made for an order of the court permitting the works to be carried out, under s.318, below.

Recovery of possession of premises for purposes of approved re-development

309.—(1) Where the local housing authority have given notice of their satisfaction with proposals submitted to them under section 308 and are satisfied—

(*a*) that it is necessary for the purpose of enabling re-development to be carried out in accordance with the proposals that a dwelling-house let on or subject to a protected tenancy or statutory tenancy (within the meaning of the Rent Act 1977) should be vacated, and

(*b*) that alternative accommodation complying with the requirements of this section is available for the tenant or will be available for him at a future date,

they may issue to the landlord a certificate, which shall be conclusive evidence for the purposes of section 98(1)(*a*) of the Rent Act 1977 (grounds for possession), that suitable alternative accommodation is available for the tenant or will be available for him by that future date.

(2) The requirements with which the alternative accommodation must comply are—

(*a*) that it must be a house in which the tenant and his family can live without causing it to be overcrowded within the meaning of Part X;

(*b*) that it must be certified by the local housing authority to be suitable to the needs of the tenant and his family as respects security of tenure, proximity to place of work and otherwise, and to be suitable in relation to his means; and

(*c*) that if the house belongs to the local housing authority it must be certified by them to be suitable to the needs of the tenant and his family as regards accommodation, for this purpose treating a house containing two bedrooms as providing accommodation for four persons, a house containing three bedrooms as providing accommodation for five persons and a house containing four bedrooms as providing accommodation for seven persons.

DEFINITIONS
  "house": s.322.
  "local housing authority": ss.1, 2.

GENERAL NOTE
  This section is ancillary to the last. If there is a Rent Act 1977 protected or statutory tenant in occupation, who needs to be moved for the redevelopment proposals to be put into effect, the authority can issue a certificate to the landlord under the tenancy that suitable alternative accommodation will be available. Unlike under Part IV, above, it is a ground for possession under s.98, Rent Act 1977, that suitable alternative accommodation (as defined in *ibid*, Sched. 15, Part IV) will be available, without proof of any other ground (*cf.* notes to s.84, above), although subject to the overriding requirement that it is reasonable to make the order sought: again, see notes to s.84, above.
  What this section does in effect is to substitute for the criteria in subs. (2) for the definition in Sched. 15, Part IV, Rent Act 1977. Sched. 15, Part IV, para. 3, already provides that a certificate from the authority that they will provide suitable alternative accommodation for the purposes of that Act shall be conclusive evidence that it will be available.
  The provisions of this section differ in that (a) such a certificate may be issued in relation to accommodation to be provided by someone other than the authority, and (b) that if they do provide the accommodation themselves the standard has to comply with subs. (2)(c), which is the same standard as is applicable to suitable alternative accommodation for the purposes of the overcrowding provisions of Part X, below: see s.342, below. In other respects, the criteria are similar, and similar to those applicable in relation to the provision of suitable alternative accommodation under Part IV: see Sched. 2, Part IV, below.

Certificate of fitness resulting from owner's improvements or alterations

310.—(1) An owner of a house in respect of which works of improvement or structural alteration are proposed to be executed may submit a list of the proposed works to the local housing authority with a request in writing that the authority inform him whether in their opinion the house would, after the execution of those works, or of those works together with additional works, be fit for human habitation and, with reasonable care and maintenance, remain so fit for a period of at least five years.

(2) As soon as may be after the receipt of such a list and request, the authority shall take the list into consideration and shall inform the owner whether they are of that opinion, and, if they are, furnish him with a list of any additional works appearing to them to be required.

(3) Where the authority have stated that they are of that opinion and the works specified in the list, together with any additional works specified in a list furnished by them, have been executed to their satisfaction, they shall, on the application of the owner and on payment by him of a fee of five pence, issue to him a certificate that the house is fit for human habitation and will with reasonable care and maintenance remain so fit for such period (not being less than five nor more than 15 years) as may be specified in the certificate.

(4) During the period specified in a certificate given under this section—

  (*a*) no action shall be taken in relation to the house under the provisions of this Part relating to the demolition, closing or purchase of unfit premises, and

  (*b*) no action shall be taken under the provisions of this Part relating to clearance areas with a view to the demolition of the house as being unfit for human habitation.

(5) For the purposes of this section "works of improvement" includes the provision of additional or improved fixtures or fittings but not works by way of decoration or repair.

(6) This section does not apply to premises—

  (*a*) in respect of which a demolition order has become operative, or

  (*b*) comprised in a compulsory purchase order under section 290

(acquisition of land for clearance) which has been confirmed by the
    Secretary of State;
and has effect subject to section 311 in a case where proposals are
submitted under this section with respect to premises in a clearance area.

DEFINITIONS
    "clearance area": s.289.
    "house": s.322.
    "local housing authority": ss.1, 2.
    "owner": s.322.
    "unfit for human habitation": s.604.

GENERAL NOTE
    This section is only applicable in the same circumstances as a redevelopment proposal
under s.308, above: see notes thereto. It is also subject to s.311, below: see notes on
Menachem Schleider v. *Secretary of State for the Environment and Gateshead Metropolitan
Borough Council* [1983] J.P.L. 382, Q.B.D., in the notes to s.308, above, and s.311, below.
    Unlike s.308, however, application can only be made under this section by an owner: see
s.322, below. The owner may make a request in writing for the authority to inform him
whether a schedule of proposed works of improvement or structural alteration would—on
their own, or with other works specified by the authority—render a house fit for human
habitation within the meaning of s.604, below: subs. (1). Improvement or alteration does
not include decorative works, or repairs, but can include the provision of additional or
improved fixtures or fittings: subs. (5). As to the distinction between repair and improvement,
see notes to s.471, below.
    Subject to transmission to the Secretary of State under s.311, below, the authority are
bound to consider the list and reach a decision, with additional works if necessary: subs. (2).
If the authority state that they are satisfied as to future fitness, they shall also, on request,
provide a certificate to that effect, on payment of a fee of 5p, specifying a period for which
it lasts, of between five and 15 years: subs. (3). During that period no action shall be taken
under the provisions of this Part specified in subs. (4), and the authority could be prevented
by judicial review from disregarding this prohibition: *R.* v. *Minister of Health, ex parte Davis*
[1929] 1 K.B. 619.
    If the application has been approved, application can be made for an order of the court
permitting the works to be carried out, under s.318, below. See also s.610, below, enabling
application to court for permission to carry out conversions contrary to the terms of a
restrictive covenant or a lease.

Consideration of proposals under s.308 or s.310 with respect to premises in clearance area

311.—(1) Where proposals as respects premises in a clearance area are
submitted to the local housing authority under section 308 (owner's re-
development) or section 310 (owner's improvements or alterations), the
authority may, instead of proceeding under that section, transmit the
proposals to the Secretary of State.
    (2) The Secretary of State shall deal with the proposals in connection
with the consideration by him of the compulsory purchase order relating
to the premises as if the proposals had been objections to the order made
on the date on which they were submitted to the authority.
    (3) If in confirming the order the Secretary of State excludes the
premises from the clearance area, the authority shall then proceed in
relation to the proposals under section 308 or 310, as the case may be.

DEFINITIONS
    "clearance area": s.289.
    "local housing authority": ss.1, 2.
    "owner": s.322.

GENERAL NOTE
    When application is made under either s.308 or s.310 in respect of premises in a clearance
area, the authority have a discretion to forward the proposals to the Secretary of State for

them to be treated as if they were objections to the compulsory purchase order which will follow declaration—see notes to s.290, above: subss. (1), (2). The authority are not obliged to do this, but they must either do so, or determine the applications themselves, and cannot merely defer their decision until the compulsory purchase order has been confirmed: *Menachem Schleider* v. *Secretary of State for the Environment and Gateshead Metropolitan Borough Council* [1983] J.P.L. 382, Q.B.D. On the inquiry (see notes to Sched. 22, below), the inspector should consider the proposals, even if they are on their face not financially viable: *ibid.*

If the Secretary of State excludes the property from the clearance area, the authority must still then reach their own decision: subs. (3).

Slum clearance subsidy

Slum clearance subsidy

312.—(1) Slum clearance subsidy is payable to a local housing authority (for the credit of their general rate fund) for any year in which the authority incur a loss in connection with the exercise of their slum clearance functions.

(2) For this purpose "slum clearance functions" means functions under the provisions of this Part relating to—

(*a*) the demolition, closing or purchase of unfit premises,

(*b*) the demolition of obstructive buildings, or

(*c*) clearance areas,

but does not include functions under section 308 to 311 (owner's re-development or improvements); and no account shall be taken of expenditure resulting from an order under paragraph 9(1) of Schedule 22 (expenses of owner in opposing compulsory purchase order).

(3) The amount of the subsidy is 75 per cent. of the loss.

(4) Payment of the subsidy is subject to the making of a claim for it in such form, and containing such particulars, as the Secretary of State may from time to time determine.

(5) The subsidy shall be paid by the Secretary of State at such times and in such manner as the Treasury may direct and subject to such conditions as to records, certificates, audit or otherwise as the Secretary of State may, with the approval of the Treasury, impose.

(6) In the provisions of this Part relating to slum clearance subsidy "year" means financial year.

DEFINITION·
"local housing authority": ss.1, 2.

GENERAL NOTE
This section provides for a 75 per cent. central government subsidy for the slum clearance functions specified under this Part. Slum clearance costs, and therefore the subsidy, are not within the Housing Revenue Account: see notes to s.418, below. The subsidy is accordingly credited to the general rate fund: subs. (1).

Determination of entitlement to subsidy and amount

313.—(1) The method of determining whether an authority have incurred a loss in connection with the exercise of their slum clearance functions, and the amount of the loss, shall be prescribed by regulations made by the Secretary of State with the concurrence of the Treasury.

(2) Schedule 12 has effect with respect to the provision which may be made by the regulations.

(3) The regulations shall be made by statutory instrument which shall be subject to annulment in pursuance of a resolution of either House of Parliament.

(4) The amount of subsidy payable to an authority for a year shall be calculated to the nearest pound, by disregarding an odd amount of 50

pence or less and treating an odd amount exceeding 50 pence as a whole pound.

GENERAL NOTE
See the Slum Clearance Subsidy Regulations 1974, S.I. 1974 No. 618, as qualified as to by whom certain valuations may be carried out by S.I. 1984 No. 244, both retained in force by s.2, Housing (Consequential Provisions) Act 1985.

Power to modify application of subsidy provisions

314.—(1) The Secretary of State may direct that the provisions of this Part relating to slum clearance subsidy apply to a local housing authority subject to modifications.

(2) The modifications may not increase the sums payable to the authority by way of slum clearance subsidy.

(3) A direction may be a general direction or a direction for a particular case, and may be given for a period or subject to conditions.

(4) The modifications, and where applicable the period for which the direction is given and any conditions subject to which it is given, shall be specified in the direction.

(5) A direction may be revoked by the Secretary of State or varied by a further direction.

DEFINITION
"local housing authority": ss.1, 2.

Miscellaneous

Power of court to order occupier or owner to permit things to be done

315.—(1) If a person, after receiving notice of the intended action—

(*a*) being the occupier of premises, prevents the owner or person having control of the premises, or his officers, servants or agents, from carrying into effect with respect to the premises any of the provisions of this Part, or

(*b*) being the occupier, owner or person having control of premises, prevents an officer, servant or agent of the local housing authority from so doing,

a magistrates' court may order him to permit to be done on the premises all things requisite for carrying into effect those provisions.

(2) A person who fails to comply with an order of the court under this section commits a summary offence and is liable on conviction to a fine not exceeding £20 in respect of each day during which the failure continues.

DEFINITIONS
"local housing authority": ss.1, 2.
"owner": s.322.

GENERAL NOTE
See notes to s.195, above.

Power of court to authorise owner to demolish premises on default of another owner

316.—(1) If it appears to a magistrates' court on the application of an owner of premises in respect of which a demolition order, or obstructive building order has been made, that owing to the default of another owner of the premises in demolishing the premises, the interests of the applicant will be prejudiced, the court may make an order empowering the applicant forthwith to enter on the premises, and, within a period fixed by the order, demolish them.

(2) Where the court makes an order under subsection (1), the court may, where it seems to the court just to do so, make a like order in favour of any other owner.

(3) Before an order is made under this section, notice of the application shall be given to the local housing authority.

DEFINITIONS
"demolition order": s.267.
"local housing authority": ss.1, 2.
"obstructive building": s.283.
"obstructive building order": s.284.
"owner": s.322.

GENERAL NOTE
If one owner is defaulting on compliance with either a demolition order under s.265 above or an obstructive building order under s.284, above, to the prejudice of another owner, *e.g.* because he will fall under a legal liability to the authority resulting from the failure or their execution of the order in default, the magistrates' court may make an order permitting him to enter and demolish within a specified time. Notice of the application must be given to the authority: subs. (3).

Power of court to determine lease where premises demolished or closed

317.—(1) Where premises in respect of which a demolition or closing order under this Part has become operative form the subject matter of a lease, the lessor or the lessee may apply to the county court for an order determining or varying the lease.

(2) On the application the court may make such an order if it thinks fit, after giving any sub-lessee an opportunity of being heard.

(3) The order may be unconditional or subject to such terms and conditions (including conditions with respect to the payment of money by one party to the proceedings to another by way of compensation, damages or otherwise) as the court may think just and equitable to impose, having regard to the respective rights, obligations and liabilities of the parties under the lease and to all the other circumstances of the case.

(4) In this section "lessor" and "lessee" include a person deriving title under a lessor or lessee.

DEFINITIONS
"closing order": s.267.
"demolition order": s.267.

GENERAL NOTE
This section permits application to the county court for an order varying the terms of, or determining, a lease of premises in respect of which a demolition or closing order has become operative (as to which see notes to ss.268, 269, above): subs. (1). When considering what order to make, *particular* regard will be had to the respective rights, obligations and liabilities under the lease: *Malik* v. *Politi* [1964] C.L.Y. 1703.

The extension to closing orders of parts of buildings is pursuant to Law Commission Recommendations (Cmnd. 9515), No. 16(iv).

Power of court to authorise execution of works on unfit premises or for improvement

318.—(1) Where on an application made by a person entitled to any interest in land used in whole or in part as a site for houses the court is satisfied—

(*a*) that the premises on the land are, or are likely to become, dangerous or injurious to health or unfit for human habitation and the interests of the applicant are thereby prejudiced, or (*b*) that the applicant should be entrusted with the carrying out of a scheme of improvement or reconstruction approved by the local housing authority,

the court may make an order empowering the applicant forthwith to enter on the land and within a period fixed by the order execute such works as may be necessary.

(2) Where the court makes such an order, it may order that any lease held from the applicant and any derivative lease shall be determined, subject to such conditions and the payment of such compensation as the court may think just.

(3) The court shall include in its order provisions to secure that the proposed works are carried out and may authorise the local housing authority to exercise such supervision or take such action as may be necessary for the purpose.

(4) In this section "the court" means the High Court or the county court, where those courts respectively have jurisdiction.

DEFINITIONS
"house": s.322.
"local housing authority": ss.1, 2.
"unfit for human habitation": s.604.

GENERAL NOTE
Application may be made to court, for an order empowering anyone with an interest in the whole or part of premises to enter and execute such works of improvement or reconstruction (not necessarily, but including, those approved under ss.308 and 310, above), within a time specified by the court, if the applicant's interests are prejudiced because the premises are or are likely to become dangerous or injurious to health or unfit for human habitation within s.604, below: subs. (1). The power of the court extends to determining leases, subject to such conditions and payment of compensation as the court thinks just: subs. (2). The authority can be authorised to supervise the works, and the court shall in any event include provision in the order to ensure that the works actually are carried out: subs. (3).

Subs. (4)
The application is to the county court or the High Court, depending on jurisdiction, *i.e.* the rateable value of the premises: the county court jurisdiction under s.21, County Courts Act 1984, is currently limited to £1,000.

Supplementary provisions

Powers of entry

319.—(1) A person authorised by the local housing authority or the Secretary of State may at any reasonable time, on giving 24 hours' notice of his intention to the occupier, and to the owner if the owner is known, enter premises—

(*a*) for the purpose of survey and examination where it appears to the authority or the Secretary of State that survey or examination is necessary in order to determine whether any powers under this Part should be exercised in respect of the premises; or

(*b*) for the purpose of survey and examination where a demolition or closing order, or an obstructive building order, has been made in respect of the premises; or

(*c*) for the purpose of survey or valuation where the authority are authorised by this Part to purchase the premises compulsorily.

(2) An authorisation for the purposes of this section shall be in writing stating the particular purpose or purposes for which the entry is authorised.

DEFINITIONS
"local housing authority": ss.1, 2.
"owner": s.322.

GENERAL NOTE
See notes to s.197, above. The extension of this power to all classes of closing order is pursuant to Law Commission Recommendations (Cmnd. 9515), No. 16(iii).

Penalty for obstruction

320.—(1) It is a summary offence to obstruct an officer of the local housing authority or of the Secretary of State, or any person authorised to enter premises in pursuance of this Part, in the performance of anything which he is by this Part required or authorised to do.

(2) A person committing such an offence is liable on conviction to a fine not exceeding level 2 on the standard scale.

DEFINITION
"local housing authority": ss.1, 2.

GENERAL NOTE
See notes to s.198, above.

Repair at reasonable expense

321. In determining for the purpose of this Part whether premises can be rendered fit for human habitation at a reasonable expense, regard shall be had to the estimated cost of the works necessary to render them so fit and the value which it is estimated they will have when the works are completed.

DEFINITION
"fit for human habitation": s.604.

GENERAL NOTE
See notes to s.206, above.

Minor definitions

322. In this Part—
"house" includes any yard, garden, outhouses and appurtenances belonging to the house or usually enjoyed with it;
"owner", in relation to premises—
(*a*) means a person (other than a mortgagee not in possession) who is for the time being entitled to dispose of the fee simple in premises, whether in possession or in reversion, and
(*b*) includes also a person holding or entitled to the rents and profits of the premises under a lease of which the unexpired term exceeds three years;
"person having control", in relation to premises, means the person who receives the rack-rent of the premises (that is, a rent which is not less than two-thirds of the full net annual value of the premises), whether on his own account or as agent or trustee for another person, or who would so receive it if the house were let at such a rack-rent.

DEFINITION
"lease": s.621.

GENERAL NOTE
See notes to s.207, above.

Index of defined expressions: Part IX

323. The following Table shows provisions defining or otherwise explaining expressions used in this Part (other than provisions defining or explaining an expression used in the same section or paragraph):—

clearance order	section 289(1)
closing order	section 267(2)
demolition order	section 267(1)
district (of a local housing authority)	section 2(1)
fit (or unfit) for human habitation	sections 282 and 604
the full standard (in relation to rehabilitation orders)	section 234(1) and 299(2)
general improvement area	section 253
house	section 322
land liable to be cleared (in Schedule 11)	paragraph 1(3) of Schedule 11
lease, lessee and lessor	section 621
listed building	section 303
local housing authority	section 1, 2(2)
obstructive building	section 283
obstructive building order	section 284
owner (of premises)	section 322
person having control (of premises)	section 322
prescribed	section 614
reasonable expense	section 321
rehabilitation order	Schedule 11
the Rent Acts	section 622
slum clearance functions (for purposes of slum clearance subsidy)	section 312(2)
slum clearance subsidy	section 312(1)
standard scale (in reference to the maximum fine on summary conviction)	section 622
underground room	section 280
unfit (or fit) for human habitation	sections 282 and 604
year (for purposes of slum clearance subsidy)	section 312(6)

PART X

OVERCROWDING

Definition of overcrowding

Definition of overcrowding

324. A dwelling is overcrowded for the purposes of this Part when the number of persons sleeping in the dwelling is such as to contravene—
  (*a*) the standard specified in section 325 (the room standard), or
  (*b*) the standard specified in section 326 (the space standard).

DEFINITION
  "dwelling": s.343.

GENERAL NOTE
  This Part concerns overcrowding in "dwellings", meaning "premises used or suitable for use as a separate dwelling": s.343. The provisions date back to the Housing Act 1935. They may be distinguished from the provisions of ss.358 *et seq.*, below, concerning overcrowding in houses in multiple occupation. The two definitions overlap, however, for clearly a single room may be used "as a separate dwelling", and yet it may be a part of a house in multiple occupation (see notes to s.345, below).
  Under this Part, we are not concerned with the legal classification of the letting: use may be as a result of tenancy, or licence (*cf.* notes to s.93, above). Accordingly, a letting of

anything from as much as a whole house, through a flat (self-contained or not) to as little as a single room, may be "overcrowded", provided always it fulfils this criterion of use "as a separate dwelling".

The term "separate dwelling" has received most attention under the Rent Acts, now Rent Act 1977. Under s.1, the 1977 Act is concerned with "let as a separate dwelling", which has been interpreted to import a requirement of tenancy (inapplicable here), and consideration of the purpose of the letting ("as"); as this Part is concerned with *use*, the case-law on purpose of letting would equally seem to be inapplicable.

The essence of "separate dwelling" is that the premises in question must be capable of use on their own, as a dwelling, even if they comprise no more than a single room (see, *e.g.* *Curl* v. *Angelo* [1948] 2 All E.R. 189, C.A.), so that there is and needs be no sharing with another of "living accommodation". The term "living accommodation" is a judicial creation, and does not extend to the sharing of a bathroom or lavatory: *Cole* v. *Harris* [1945] K.B. 474, C.A. A bathroom or lavatory is accommodation not used for living in, but merely visited for occasional, specific purposes, as distinct from a room used for the primary purposes of living, or one in which a person spends a significant part of his time.

But a kitchenette, even though too small to eat in and only available to cook or wash up in, has been held to constitute living accommodation (*Winters* v. *Dance* [1949] L.J.R. 165, C.A.), as also has a normal kitchen: *Neale* v. *Del Soto* [1945] K.B. 144, C.A., *Sharpe* v. *Nicholls* (1945) 147 E.G. 177, C.A. So if the letting comprises premises together with shared user of such living accommodation, there is, prima facie, no use as a "separate dwelling": *Winters* v. *Dance*, *Neale* v. *Del Soto*, *Goodrich* v. *Paisner* [1957] A.C. 65, H.L. (Such lettings are brought back within Rent Act protection if the sharing is with someone other than the landlord, by Rent Act 1977, s.22, and treated as a restricted contract under *ibid.* s.19, if with the landlord: *ibid.* s.21).

Sharing with one's own sub-tenant, or sub-licensee, does not prevent use as a separate dwelling: *Baker* v. *Turner* [1950] A.C. 401, H.L. And sharing living accommodation must be distinguished from a letting which leaves someone else, *e.g.* another occupier or even the landlord, with a defined or limited right merely to *use* part of the accommodation which has been let, *e.g.* the right to come in and make a morning cup of tea as in *James* v. *James* [1952] C.L.Y. 2948, C.C., a right of passage as in *James* v. *Coleman* [1949] E.G.D. 122, C.C., a right to use a bath sited in a kitchen as in *Trustees of the Waltham Abbey Baptist Church* v. *Stevens* (1950) E.G. 294, C.C., and a right to draw and boil water weekly as in *Hayward* v. *Marshall* [1952] 2 Q.B. 89, C.A.

In each case, the whole of the circumstances must be looked at in order to ascertain whether a person has the right to use a separate dwelling, or something less: *Goodrich* v. *Paisner* [1957] A.C. 65, H.L. In Rent Act law, the fact that a sharing right is not exercised does not bring the tenant back into full protection (*Stanley* v. *Compton* [1951] 1 All E.R. 859, C.A., *Kenyon* v. *Walker* [1946] 2 All E.R. 595, C.A.) although it has been thought that a clear abandonment of the right might do so: *Stanley* v. *Compton*. But where as in this section "use" is all that is in question, it would seem probable that a much lower standard of "abandonment" would suffice.

"Dwelling" itself has been defined as something in which all the major activities of life, such as sleeping, cooking and feeding, are carried out: *Wright* v. *Howell* (1947) 92 S.J. 26, C.A., *Curl* v. *Angelo* [1948] 2 All E.R. 189, C.A., *Metropolitan Properties* v. *Barder* [1968] 1 All E.R. 536. Premises not used for sleeping cannot be in use as a dwelling: *Wimbush* v. *Cibulia* [1949] 2 K.B. 564, C.A. But use need not be by the person to whom the premises are let: *Whitty* v. *Scott-Russell* [1950] 2 K.B. 32, C.A., *Edgware Estates Ltd.* v. *Coblentz* [1949] 2 K.B. 717, C.A., *Carter* v. *S.U. Carburetter Co.* [1942] 2 K.B. 288, C.A., *Watson* v. *Saunders-Roe Ltd.* [1947] K.B. 437, C.A., *Anspach* v. *Charlton SS Co. Ltd.* [1955] 2 Q.B. 21, C.A.

Under this Part, however, it is enough to show that premises are *suitable* for use as a separate dwelling, so that if what is let is part of a larger whole which is itself suitable for use as a separate dwelling, *e.g.* single rooms in a house or flat, the overcrowding laws to be considered can be applied (as can the provisions of Part XI, *i.e.* houses in multiple occupation) to that larger "dwelling"; but if there is no one unit which either *is* in use as a separate dwelling, nor which would be *suitable* for such use, the provisions of this Part would not seem applicable, and reliance must instead be placed on Part XI (see, especially, ss.358 *et seq.*, governing overcrowding in houses in multiple occupation).

The question is whether the number of people *sleeping* in the dwelling contravenes either of the standards. The standards themselves contribute to define "people", for under the room standard children under the age of ten are not taken into account (see s.325(2)(*a*), below), while under the space standard children under the age of one are not taken into account, but children of one or over and under ten count as a half-person (see s.326(2)(*a*), below). A daughter away at boarding-school has been held to live at home and therefore to be taken into account: *Zaitzeff* v. *Olmi* (1952) 102 L.J. 416, C.C. But in the same case it was held that a nephew who only slept in the house on occasional visits did not qualify.

Note that a landlord can recover possession of a dwelling which is otherwise protected under the Rent Act 1977 if the occupation is in such circumstances as to render the occupier guilty of an offence under this Part: Rent Act 1977, s.101. The offence must subsist at the date of the hearing of the claim: *Zbytniewski* v. *Broughton* [1956] 2 Q.B. 673, C.A. This entitlement would seem to be available even where the landlord is himself at fault: *cf. Buswell* v. *Goodwin* [1971] 1 W.L.R. 92, C.A.

In addition, the authority can themselves take proceedings for possession where occupation is such that the occupier is guilty of an overcrowding offence under this Part, under s.338, below.

The room standard

325.—(1) The room standard is contravened when the number of persons sleeping in a dwelling and the number of rooms available as sleeping accommodation is such that two persons of opposite sexes who are not living together as husband and wife must sleep in the same room.
(2) For this purpose—
  (*a*) children under the age of ten shall be left out of account, and
  (*b*) a room is available as sleeping accommodation if it is of a type normally used in the locality either as a bedroom or as a living room.

DEFINITION
  "dwelling": s.343.

GENERAL NOTE
  The first of the two standards is "the room standard", sometimes called "sexual overcrowding" because of its clear intent to prevent people of opposite sexes having to share a room, other of course than when they live together "as husband and wife" (as to which, see notes to s.113, above). Children under the age of ten are left out of account altogether (*cf.* s.23, above, setting eight as the age in local authority lodging-houses, s.360, below, setting 12 as the age in a house in multiple occupation, and s.406, below, giving the local authority a discretion to separate sexes in a common lodging-house).
  The standard is set in relation to "the number of rooms available as sleeping accommodation" (subs. (1)), which means a room "of a type normally used in the locality either as a bedroom or as a living room" (subs. (2)(*b*)). A kitchen furnished with six chairs, a table and a folding bed has been held to qualify, in *Zaitzeff* v. *Olmi* (1952) 102 L.J. 416, C.C., but a room unfit for human habitation not to do so in *Patel* v. *Godal* [1979] 12 C.L.Y. 1620, C.C. Clearly, it is a question of fact whether a room *is* "of a type . . . ", but it may be a type normally used as a bedroom *or* as a "living room", which would seem to exclude those rooms described in the notes to s.324, above, as not "living accommodation".
  The key point to note, however, is that the standard is *only* offended when the number of people is such that they *must* sleep in the same room. This means that the standard is very low indeed. The fact that *in practice* people no longer sleep in a living room does not mean that premises will not be overcrowded, for the room is available. Thus, a unit with three qualifying rooms (bedrooms *or* living rooms), in the occupation of parents living together as husband and wife, will not be overcrowded on this standard regardless of the number of children, because all the male children and all the female children *can be* separated. In such a case, reliance must be placed on the next section.
  When the overcrowded accommodation comprises a secure tenancy within the meaning of s.79, above, the landlord can recover possession under s.84, above, and Sched. 2, Ground 9, below, without proof of reasonableness, but on the provision of suitable alternative accommodation as defined in Schedule 2, Part IV, for which purpose the alternative accommodation is not to be treated as unsuitable merely because it will itself be overcrowded under the space standard in s.326, below.

The space standard

326.—(1) The space standard is contravened when the number of persons sleeping in a dwelling is in excess of the permitted number, having regard to the number and floor area of the rooms of the dwelling available as sleeping accommodation.

(2) For this purpose—

(*a*) no account shall be taken of a child under the age of one and a child aged one or over but under ten shall be reckoned as one-half of a unit, and

(*b*) a room is available as sleeping accommodation if it is of a type normally used in the locality either as a living room or as a bedroom,

(3) The permitted number of persons in relation to a dwelling is whichever is the less of—

(*a*) the number specified in Table I in relation to the number of rooms in the dwelling available as sleeping accommodation, and

(*b*) the aggregate for all such rooms in the dwelling of the numbers specified in column 2 of Table II in relation to each room of the floor area specified in column 1.

No account shall be taken for the purposes of either Table of a room having a floor area of less than 50 square feet.

TABLE I

Number of rooms	Number of persons
1	2
2	3
3	5
4	$7\frac{1}{2}$
5 or more	2 for each room

TABLE II

Floor area of room	Number of persons
110 sq. ft. or more	2
90 sq. ft. or more but less than 110 sq.ft.	$1\frac{1}{2}$
70 sq. ft. or more by less than 90 sq. ft.	1
50 sq. ft. or more but less than 70 sq. ft.	$\frac{1}{2}$

(4) The Secretary of State may by regulations prescribe the manner in which the floor area of a room is to be ascertained for the purposes of this section; and the regulations may provide for the exclusion from computation, or the bringing into computation at a reduced figure, of floor space in a part of the room which is of less than a specified height not exceeding eight feet.

(5) Regulations under subsection (4) shall be made by statutory instrument which shall be subject to annulment in pursuance of a resolution of either House of Parliament.

(6) A certificate of the local housing authority stating the number and floor areas of the rooms in a dwelling, and that the floor areas have been ascertained in the prescribed manner, is prima facie evidence for the purposes of legal proceedings of the facts stated in it.

DEFINITIONS
"dwelling": s.343.
"local housing authority": ss.1, 2.

GENERAL NOTE

The alternative standard is the space standard. This, too, is concerned with numbers of persons related to rooms available as sleeping accommodation, *i.e.* "of a type normally used in the locality either as a living room or as a bedroom": see notes to s.325, above.

In relation to this standard, children simply do not count at all until one year after birth (*Zbytniewski* v. *Broughton* [1956] 2 Q.B. 673, C.A.), and children of one but under the age of ten count as a half-person.

The question is whether the permitted number is exceeded. This is calculated in two ways. First of all, by a simple counting of the qualifying rooms. Secondly, by measurement of those rooms, setting a maximum number per room according to its size. The *lower* number of persons thus produced sets the permitted number for the dwelling (as to which, see notes to s.324, above). Authorities have power of entry to determine permitted numbers, under s.337, below.

One may start with the easier calculation—Table 1. If there is only one room available, the permitted number is two persons; two rooms, three persons; three rooms, five persons; four rooms, seven-and-a-half persons; five or more, add two for each room. If the number sleeping in the dwelling exceeds these figures, the dwelling is overcrowded and it is unnecessary to look to Table 2. If it does not, then each of the rooms must be measured, and the number permitted in each according to its size aggregated. Thus, two people can sleep in a room of 110 square feet or more; one-and-a-half in a room of 90 square feet but less than 110 square feet; one in a room of 70 square feet but less than 90 square feet; a half person in a room of 50 square feet but less than 70 square feet; no one (but a child of less than one) in a room of less than 50 square feet.

Measurement is still governed by the Housing Act (Overcrowding and Miscellaneous Forms) Regulations 1937, S.R.& O. 1937 No. 80, retained in force formerly by s.191(4), Housing Act 1957, now by s.2, Housing (Consequential Provisions) Act 1985. These regulations require the *exclusion* of any part of the floor space of a room over which the vertical height is reduced to less than five feet, because of a sloping roof or ceiling; but the *inclusion* of floor space in a bay window extension, an area covered by fitted cupboards, or an area overhung by projecting chimney breasts (Regulation 4). All measurements are to be at floor level and are to be taken to the back of all projecting skirtings: *ibid*.

Responsibility of occupier

Penalty for occupier causing or permitting overcrowding

327.—(1) The occupier of a dwelling who causes or permits it to be overcrowded commits a summary offence, subject to subsection (2).

(2) The occupier is not guilty of an offence—

(*a*) if the overcrowding is within the exceptions specified in section 328 or 329 (children attaining age of 10 or visiting relatives), or

(*b*) by reason of anything done under the authority of, and in accordance with any conditions specified in, a licence granted by the local housing authority under section 330.

(3) A person committing an offence under this section is liable on conviction to a fine not exceeding level 1 on the standard scale and to a further fine not exceeding £2 in respect of every day subsequent to the date on which he is convicted on which the offence continues.

DEFINITIONS
"dwelling": s.343.
"local housing authority": ss.1, 2.
"overcrowded": s.324.

GENERAL NOTE

An offence is committed by the occupier of the dwelling if, subject to the exceptions, he permits it to be overcrowded. There is no definition of occupier, but clearly the occupier must be of the whole dwelling under consideration so that if the dwelling to which the overcrowding provisions is applied is a house let off in rooms in such a way that none of the units let is, or is suitable for use as, a separate dwelling (see notes to s.324, above), none of the occupiers of the individual units will be guilty of an offence, but the person "occupying", *i.e.* who has created the lettings, the dwelling will be.

There are three classes of permissible overcrowding: under s.328, when a child attains a "relevant age" (*cf.* notes to ss.325, 326, above, *i.e.* "natural growth"); overcrowding resulting from temporary use by a member of the occupier's family under s.329; and, licensed overcrowding under s.330. In none of these cases will the occupier commit any offence. A fourth class relating to overcrowding dating from the application of these provisions under the Housing Act 1935 has been omitted, pursuant to Law Commission Recommendations (Cmnd. 9515), No. 17, but is preserved by the general saving provision of s.5 and Schedule 4, Housing (Consequential Provisions) Act 1985.

Otherwise, the offence is punishable on level 1 on the standard scale under s.37, Criminal Justice Act 1982, currently £50, by S.I. 1984 No. 447, with an additional fine of £2 *per diem* following conviction. It is hard to see, however, that an offence could be committed if the overcrowding is under the space standard in s.326, above, resulting from an order for possession on account of overcrowding (on either standard) in earlier accommodation under a secure tenancy (within the meaning of s.79, above), which may be made under s.84, above, and Sched. 2, Ground 9, below, without proof of reasonableness, but on the provision of suitable alternative accommodation within the meaning of Sched. 2, Part IV, which is not to be considered unsuitable merely because it offends the s.326 space standard. The problem would not seem to be capable of avoidance by licensing under s.330, below (see notes thereto).

Note that a landlord can recover possession of a dwelling which is otherwise protected under the Rent Act 1977 if the occupation is in such circumstances as to render the occupier guilty of an offence under this Part: Rent Act 1977, s.101. The offence must subsist at the date of the hearing of the claim: *Zbytniewski* v. *Broughton* [1956] 2 Q.B. 673, C.A. This entitlement would seem to be available even where the landlord is himself at fault: *cf. Buswell* v. *Goodwin* [1971] 1 W.L.R. 92, C.A.

As to landlord's offences, see ss.331–333, below; as to further offences by the occupier, relevant to providing information to the local authority, see ss.335–6, below; as to obstruction of an officer of the authority, see s.341, below; as to the power of the authority themselves to seek possession, see s.338, below.

Exception: children attaining age of 1 or 10

328.—(1) Where a dwelling which would not otherwise be overcrowded becomes overcrowded by reason of a child attaining the age of one or ten, then if the occupier—

(*a*) applies to the local housing authority for suitable alternative accommodation, or

(*b*) has so applied before the date when the child attained the age in question,

he does not commit an offence under section 327 (occupier causing or permitting overcrowding), so long as the condition in subsection (2) is met and the occupier does not fail to take action in the circumstances specified in subsection (3).

(2) The condition is that all the persons sleeping in the dwelling are persons who were living there when the child attained that age and thereafter continuously live there, or children born after that date of any of those persons.

(3) The exception provided by this section ceases to apply if—

(*a*) suitable alternative accommodation is offered to the occupier on or after the date on which the child attains that age, or, if he has applied before that date, is offered at any time after the application, and he fails to accept it, or

(*b*) the removal from the dwelling of some person not a member of the occupier's family is on that date or thereafter becomes reasonably practicable having regard to all the circumstances (including the availability of suitable alternative accommodation for that person), and the occupier fails to require his removal.

DEFINITIONS

"dwelling": s.343.

"local housing authority": ss.1, 2.

"overcrowded": s.324.

"suitable alternative accommodation": s.342.

General Note
     The first circumstance in which although there is overcrowding by reason of s.325 or
s.326, above, there is no offence under s.327, above, is when a child achieves a relevant age,
i.e. one or ten—"natural growth". To avail himself of this exemption, the applicant must
apply to the local authority for suitable alternative accommodation, as defined in s.342.
There are two limbs to the application condition: the occupier applies, or the occupier has
applied before the date in question. It follows that if no application is made until after the
date in question, exemption can be "re-acquired", although there may be an intervening
period when the occupier was guilty of an offence, *i.e.* from date in question to date of
application.
     The standard of suitable alternative accommodation in s.342 is high. The accommodation
must be such that it can be occupied without overcrowding; and, must be certified by the
authority to be suitable to the needs of the occupier and his family as regards security of
tenure, proximity to work and otherwise, and suitable as regards means (as to these criteria,
see notes to Sched. 2, Part IV, below); and, where the accommodation belongs to the
authority, it must be certified by them as suitable to needs as respects accommodation
(again, see notes to Sched. 2, Part IV, below). For this last purpose, a dwelling containing
two bedrooms is to be treated as providing accommodation for four persons, containing
three bedrooms as accommodation for five persons, and containing four bedrooms as for
seven persons. The requirement is for *bedrooms*, not living rooms. Accordingly, the
accommodation, to be suitable, may have to be considerably better than the overcrowded
family is used to.
     The provisions may be contrasted with those to be found in s.84, above, and Sched. 2,
Ground 9, below, under which a possession order may be made against a person on account
of overcrowding, without proof of reasonableness, but on the provision of suitable alternative
accommodation under Sched. 2, Part IV, under which accommodation is not to be treated
as unsuitable *even although* the occupier will still be overcrowded on the "space standard"
in s.326, above.
     Although the application has strictly to be *for* suitable alternative accommodation *as thus
defined*, presumably any application to the authority for rehousing will qualify: the occupier
is hardly likely to be familiar with the express requirements of this section. The wording
reproduces the former wording but, in subs. (1), might have been more suitably phrased as
"applies for accommodation" or even "for alternative accommodation".
     There are further conditions. First of all, by subs. (2), those who are sleeping in the
dwelling must be people who were sleeping in it at the date in question, so that if anyone
is added after that date, the exemption will not apply. Secondly, the exemption ceases to
apply by subs. (3)(*a*), if after either the date of application to the authority by the occupier,
or after the date in question, suitable alternative accommodation as specifically defined is
offered and not accepted; similarly, under subs. (3)(*b*), if on or after the date in question
the removal of someone who is not a member of the occupier's family becomes reasonably
practicable and the occupier does not require his removal.
     This latter limb only applies, however, if it becomes reasonably practicable having regard
to all the circumstances, including the availability of suitable alternative accommodation.
For this purpose, the special definition of suitable alternative accommodation in s.342 does
not apply, as it only relates to the occupier of the dwelling: see s.342(1).

Exception; visiting member of family

329. Where the persons sleeping in an overcrowded dwelling include a
member of the occupier's family who does not live there but is sleeping
there temporarily, the occupier is not guilty of an offence under section
327 (occupier causing or permitting overcrowding) unless the circumstances are such that he would be so guilty if that member of his family
were not sleeping there.

Definitions
     "dwelling": s.343.
     "overcrowded": s.324.

General Note
     Temporary use of the dwelling by a member of the family does not result in illegal
overcrowding, unless of course the premises would in any event be illegally overcrowded.
Member of the family is not defined (but *cf.* notes to s.113, above).

Licence of local housing authority

330.—(1) The occupier or intending occupier of a dwelling may apply to the local housing authority for a licence authorising him to permit a number of persons in excess of the permitted number to sleep in the dwelling.

(2) The authority may grant such a licence if it appears to them that there are exceptional circumstances (which may include a seasonal increase of population) and that it is expedient to do so; and they shall specify in the licence the number of persons authorised in excess of the permitted number.

(3) The licence shall be in the prescribed form and may be granted either unconditionally or subject to conditions specified in it.

(4) The local housing authority may revoke the licence at their discretion by notice in writing served on the occupier and specifying a period (at least one month from the date of service) at the end of which the licence will cease to be in force.

(5) Unless previously revoked, the licence continues in force for such period not exceeding twelve months as may be specified in it.

(6) A copy of the licence and of any notice of revocation shall, within seven days of the issue of the licence or the service of the notice on the occupier, be served by the local housing authority on the landlord (if any) of the dwelling.

DEFINITIONS
   "dwelling": s.343.
   "landlord": s.343.
   "local housing authority": ss.1, 2.
   "permitted number": s.326.

GENERAL NOTE
   This section permits *licensed* overcrowding, but *only* so far as the space standard (*i.e.* not the room standard) is concerned. There can be no licensing of a contravention of the room standard.

   The power is only available *on the application of the occupier* (or an intending occupier): subs. (1). Accordingly, unless an occupier co-operates, this would not seem to be a means of averting the problem described in the notes to s.327, above, *i.e.* of occupation of premises overcrowded under the s.326 space standard, following from an order for possession made under Sched. 2, Ground 9, against a former secure tenant within the meaning of s.79, above, on the ground of illegal overcrowding, and the provision of suitable alternative accommodation within the meaning of Sched. 2, Part IV, which is not to be considered unsuitable because it is overcrowded under the space standard.

   Furthermore, the licence may only be granted (a) for a specified period (subs. (4), not exceeding twelve months (subs. (5)), and (b) if it appears to the authority that there are "exceptional circumstances", with specific reference to "seasonal overcrowding", *e.g.* holiday season, or a season during which there is an influx of workers for an agricultural purpose: subs. (2). It must also be expedient to grant the licence: *ibid.*

   The licence must specify the excess number permitted (subs. (2)), and may be conditional or unconditional and must be in prescribed form (subs. (3)). The prescribed form is Form E, of the Housing Act (Overcrowding and Miscellaneous Forms) Regulations 1937, S.R. & O. 1937, No. 80, retained in force initially by s.191(4), Housing Act 1957, and now by s.2, Housing (Consequential Provisions) Act 1985.

   The licence may be revoked at any time, on at least one month's written notice: subs. (4). Form F of the Miscellaneous Forms Regulations 1937 contains notice of revocation, although there is no requirement that it be in prescribed form. Both licence, and revocation, must be served on the landlord within seven days of issue; subs. (6). The landlord is (s.343, below), the immediate landlord of an occupier and includes an employer in the case of a dwelling occupied under a contract of employment if such occupation forms part of the employee's remuneration.

Responsibilities of landlord

Penalty for landlord causing or permitting overcrowding

331.—(1) The landlord of a dwelling commits a summary offence if he causes or permits it to be overcrowded.

(2) He shall be deemed to cause or permit it to be overcrowded in the following circumstances, and not otherwise—

(*a*) if he or a person effecting the letting on his behalf had reasonable cause to believe that the dwelling would become overcrowded in circumstances rendering the occupier guilty of an offence;

(*b*) if he or a person effecting the letting on his behalf failed to make inquiries of the proposed occupier as to the number, age and sex of the persons who would be allowed to sleep in the dwelling;

(*c*) if notice is served on him or his agent by the local housing authority that the dwelling is overcrowded in such circumstances as to render the occupier guilty of an offence and he fails to take steps as are reasonably open to him for securing the abatement of the overcrowding, including if necessary legal proceedings for possession of the dwelling.

(3) A person committing an offence under this section is liable on conviction to a fine not exceeding level 1 on the standard scale and to a further fine not exceeding £2 in respect of every day subsequent to the day on which he is convicted on which the offence continues.

DEFINITIONS
"agent": s.343.
"dwelling": s.343.
"landlord": s.343.
"local housing authority": ss.1, 2.
"overcrowded": s.324.

GENERAL NOTE
The principal offence committed by a landlord (*i.e.*, by s.343, below, the immediate landlord of an occupier, including an employer in the case of a dwelling occupied under a contract of employment if such occupation forms part of the employee's remuneration) is that of "causing or permitting" overcrowding: subs. (1). This offence is exhaustively defined in subs. (2):

(1) He or a person effecting the letting on his behalf had reasonable cause to believe that the dwelling would become overcrowded in circumstances rendering the occupier guilty of an offence—see notes to s.327, above, as to occupation constituting an offence by the occupier;

(2) He or a person effecting the letting on his behalf failed to make inquiries of the proposed occupier as to the number, age and sex of those who would be allowed to sleep in the dwelling;

(3) He fails to take such steps as are reasonably open to him for securing the abatement of the overcrowding, including proceedings for possession, following service on him or his agent that the dwelling is illegally overcrowded. An agent is (s.343, below), a person who collects rent in respect of the dwelling on his behalf, or is authorised to do so, and in the case of a landlord/employer includes the person who pays or is authorised to pay the employee.

The landlord can recover possession of a dwelling which is otherwise protected under the Rent Act 1977 if the occupation is in such circumstances as to render the occupier guilty of an offence under this Part: Rent Act 1977, s.101. The offence must subsist at the date of the hearing of the claim: *Zbytniewski* v. *Broughton* [1956] 2 Q.B. 673, C.A. This entitlement would seem to be available even where the landlord is himself at fault: *cf. Buswell* v. *Goodwin* [1971] 1 W.L.R. 92, C.A.

The authority can themselves take proceedings for possession, under s.338, below.

An offence under this section is punishable by a fine of up to level 1 on the standard scale under s.37, Criminal Justice Act 1982, currently £50, by S.I. 1984 No. 447, and £2 per day for each day following conviction on which the offence continues. No prosecution can, however, be brought against the authority themselves without the consent of the Attorney-

General, and otherwise the prosecution can only be brought by the local housing authority: s.339, below.

Information to be contained in rent book

332.—(1) Every rent book or similar document used in relation to a dwelling by or on behalf of the landlord shall contain—

(*a*) a summary in the prescribed form of the preceding provisions of this Part, and

(*b*) a statement of the permitted number of persons in relation to the dwelling.

(2) If a rent book or similar document not containing such a summary and statement is used by or on behalf of the landlord, the landlord is guilty of a summary offence and liable on conviction to a fine not exceeding level 1 on the standard scale.

(3) The local housing authority shall on the application of the landlord or the occupier of a dwelling inform him in writing of the permitted number of persons in relation to the dwelling; and a statement inserted in a rent book or similar document which agrees with information so given shall be deemed to be a sufficient and correct statement.

DEFINITIONS

"dwelling": s.343.
"landlord": s.343.
"local housing authority": ss.1, 2.
"permitted number": s.326.

GENERAL NOTE

By s.4, Landlord and Tenant Act 1985, where a tenant or licensee has a right to occupy premises as a residence in consideration of a rent payable weekly (and, therefore, including a rent so *payable* but calculated on another basis, but excluding a rent calculated on a weekly basis but *payable* at less frequent intervals), "the landlord shall provide a rent book or other similar document for use in respect of the premises". This is not, however, applicable where the payment includes an amount in respect of board, and the value of that board to the tenant forms a substantial proportion of the whole rent (as to the meaning of which, see notes to s.622, below, under the heading Restricted Contract). Section 5 of the Landlord and Tenant Act 1985 governs the information which is to be contained in such rent book or similar document.

This section contains an additional requirement, applicable whenever a rent book or similar document (*e.g.* Giro paying-in book) is used in connection with a dwelling, *i.e.* regardless of whether or not such is *required* under s.4, Landlord and Tenant Act 1985. Each such book or document must contain a summary in the prescribed form of the preceding provisions of this Part, *and* a statement of the permitted number under s.326, above. The prescribed form is in Part I of the Schedule to the Housing (Overcrowding and Miscellaneous Provisions) Regulations 1937, S.R. & O. 1937 No. 80, retained in force initially by s.191(4), Housing Act 1957, and now by s.2, Housing (Consequential Provisions) Act 1985.

In connection with this requirement, the authority are bound to respond to a request from either the landlord or the occupier, with a statement in writing of the permitted number, and provided the rent book or other document uses the same figure, no offence will be committed, *i.e.* even if the authority are wrong: subs. (3). The authority enjoy powers of entry to determine the permitted number, under s.337, below.

Subject to subs. (3), it is an offence to provide a rent book or similar document without complying with the requirement, punishable by a fine of up to level 1 on the standard scale under s.37, Criminal Justice Act 1982, currently £50, by S.I. 1984 No. 447. No prosecution can, however, be brought against the authority themselves without the consent of the Attorney-General, and otherwise the prosecution can only be brought by the local housing authority: s.339, below. The authority have power to require the production of a rent book or similar document, under s.336, below.

The wording of the requirement is changed so as to reflect omission of the former "original overcrowding" exemption, dating back to the application of the Housing Act 1935, pursuant to Law Commission Recommendations (Cmnd. 9515), No. 17.

Duty to inform local housing authority of overcrowding

333.—(1) Where it comes to the knowledge of the landlord of a dwelling, or of his agent, that the dwelling is overcrowded, then, except in the cases mentioned in subsection (2), the landlord or, as the case may be, the agent shall give notice of the fact of overcrowding to the local housing authority within seven days after that fact first comes to his knowledge.

(2) The obligation to notify does not arise in the case of overcrowding which—

(*a*) has already been notified to the local housing authority,

(*b*) has been notified to the landlord or his agent by the local housing authority, or

(*c*) is constituted by the use of the dwelling for sleeping by such number of persons as the occupier is authorised to permit to sleep there by a licence in force under section 330 (licence of local housing authority).

(3) A landlord or agent who fails to give notice in accordance with this section commits a summary offence and is liable on conviction to a fine not exceeding level 1 on the standard scale.

DEFINITIONS
"agent": s.343.
"dwelling": s.343.
"landlord": s.343.
"local housing authority": ss.1, 2.
"overcrowded": s.324.

GENERAL NOTE
Yet another offence by landlords (*i.e.* the immediate landlord of an occupier and including an employer in the case of a dwelling occupied under a contract of employment if such occupation forms part of the employee's remuneration—see s.343, below), and, this time, their agents (*i.e.* a person who collects, or who is authorised to collect, rent on behalf of the landlord, including the person who pays or is authorised to pay an employee where applicable—*ibid.*). The offence is failure to notify the authority of overcrowding which has come to the knowledge of landlord or agent, other than in a case within subs. (2):

(1) Where the overcrowding has already been notified to the authority; or

(2) The landlord or agent was notified of it by the authority; or

(3) Is licensed overcrowding under s.330, above.

Accordingly, the fact that the overcrowding may not be illegal by reason of ss.328, 329, above, does not excuse the landlord or agent from the obligation to notify the authority.

The offence is punishable by a fine of up to level 1 on the standard scale under s.37, Criminal Justice Act 1982, currently £50, by S.I. 1984 No. 447. The prosecution can only be brought by the local housing authority: s.339, below. (The authority would seem to be exempt from the obligation altogether, for they cannot be required to notify themselves, or accused—even with the consent of the Attorney-General—of failing to do so: *cf. R. v. Cardiff City Council, ex parte Cross* (1981) 1 H.L.R. 1, Q.B.D., and (1982) 6 H.L.R. 1, C.A.).

Powers and duties of local housing authority

Duty to inspect, report and prepare proposals

334.—(1) If it appears to the local housing authority that occasion has arisen for a report on overcrowding in their district or part of it, or if the Secretary of State so directs, the authority shall—

(*a*) cause an inspection to be made,

(*b*) prepare and submit to the Secretary of State a report showing the result of the inspection and the number of new dwellings required in order to abate the overcrowding, and

(*c*) unless they are satisfied that the dwellings will be otherwise provided, prepare and submit to the Secretary of State proposals for providing the required number of new dwellings.

(2) Where the Secretary of State gives a direction under subsection (1), he may after consultation with the local housing authority fix dates before which the performance of their functions under that subsection is to be completed.

DEFINITIONS
    "district": s.2.
    "dwellings": s.343.
    "local housing authority": ss.1, 2.
    "overcrowding": s.324.

GENERAL NOTE
    The obligation to prepare plans for fulfilling the housing needs of the district, formerly coupled to what is now the s.8, above, obligation to consider housing conditions in the district, was removed under the Housing Act 1980: see notes to s.8, above. The present section, however, conserves a similar requirement where an overcrowding report is undertaken.
    The authority are *obliged* to undertake the process described in this section if *either* it appears to them that occasion has arisen for a report on overcrowding in their district, *or* the Secretary of State directs them to: subs. (1). If the Secretary of State directs the authority to do so, he may even fix times for completion, albeit after consultation with the authority (as to the meaning of which, see notes to s.420(4), below).
    The process starts with an inspection: authorities have powers of entry appropriate to the fulfilment of this exercise, under s.340, below, in addition to those for determining permitted numbers under s.337, below. The next stage is a report showing the results of the inspection, which also shows the number of *new* dwellings, *i.e.* property which needs to be built, needed to abate the overcrowding. This report must be submitted to the Secretary of State. The third stage only arises if the authority are not satisfied that the dwellings will be "otherwise provided", *i.e.* by others. In this case, they must provide, prepare and submit to the Secretary of State proposals for providing the requisite number of dwellings.

Power to require information about persons sleeping in dwelling

335.—(1) The local housing authority may, for the purpose of enabling them to discharge their duties under this Part, serve notice on the occupier of a dwelling requiring him to give them within 14 days a written statement of the number, ages and sexes of the persons sleeping in the dwelling.

(2) The occupier commits a summary offence if—
    (*a*) he makes default in complying with the requirement, or
    (*b*) he gives a statement which to his knowledge is false in a material
        particular,
and is liable on conviction to a fine not exceeding level 1 on the standard scale.

DEFINITIONS
    "dwelling": s.343.
    "local housing authority": ss.1, 2.

GENERAL NOTE
    A further occupier's offence is committed by failure to comply with the requirement of the authority to provide a written statement within 14 days of numbers, ages and sexes of people sleeping in a dwelling, or providing a statement which to his knowledge is false in a material particular. The offence carries a fine of up to level 1 on the standard scale under s.37, Criminal Justice Act 1982, currently £50, by S.I. 1984 No. 447.

Power to require production of rent book

336.—(1) A duly authorised officer of the local housing authority may require an occupier of a dwelling to produce for inspection any rent book or similar document which is being used in relation to the house and is in his custody or under his control.

(2) On being so required, or within seven days thereafter, the occupier shall produce any such book or document to the officer or at the offices of the authority.

(3) An occupier who fails to do so commits a summary offence and is liable on conviction to a fine not exceeding level 1 on the standard scale.

DEFINITIONS
"dwelling": s.343.
"local housing authority": ss.1, 2.

GENERAL NOTE
Yet another offence by an occupier, this time of failing to produce for inspection on demand a rent book or similar document, used in relation to the property, *and* in his custody or under his control: subs. (1). The occupier has seven days in which to comply: subs. (2). Failure to produce the book or document is an offence, punishable by a fine of up to level 1 on the standard scale under s.37, Criminal Justice Act 1982, currently £50, by S.I. 1984 No. 447.

This offence is related to the obligation imposed on a landlord to include information concerning overcrowding, under s.332, above.

Power of entry to determine permitted number of persons

337.—(1) A person authorised by the local housing authority may at any reasonable time, on giving 24 hours' notice of his intention to the occupier, and to the owner if the owner is known, enter premises for the purpose of measuring the rooms of a dwelling in order to ascertain for the purposes of this Part the number of persons permitted to use the dwelling for sleeping.

(2) An authorisation for the purposes of this section shall be in writing stating the particular purpose for which the entry is authorised.

DEFINITIONS
"dwelling": s.343.
"local housing authority": ss.1, 2.
"owner": s.343.
"number of persons permitted": s.326.

GENERAL NOTE
The authority can enter in order to measure the rooms for the purposes of Table 2 of the space standard under s.326, above, on 24 hours' notice to occupier, *and* owner, if owner is known. The owner for this purpose means someone other than a mortgagee not in possession who is for the time being entitled to dispose of the freehold of the premises, but includes a person holding or entitled to the rents and profits of the premises under a lease of which at least three years remain unexpired: s.343, below. The authority may be able to find out who the owner is by using their powers of enquiry under s.16, Local Government (Miscellaneous Provisions) Act 1976.

It is an offence to obstruct an officer of the authority in the exercise of this power: see s.341, below.

Notice to abate overcrowding

338.—(1) Where a dwelling is overcrowded in circumstances such as to render the occupier guilty of an offence, the local housing authority may serve on the occupier notice in writing requiring him to abate the overcrowding within 14 days from the date of service of the notice.

(2) If at any time within three months from the end of that period—

(*a*) the dwelling is in the occupation of the person on whom the notice was served or of a member of his family, and

(*b*) it is overcrowded in circumstances such as to render the occupier guilty of an offence, the local housing authority may apply to the county court which shall order vacant possession of that dwelling to be given to the landlord within such period, not less than 14 or more than 28 days, as the court may determine.

(3) Expenses incurred by the local housing authority under this section in securing the giving of possession of a dwelling to the landlord may be recovered by them from him by action.

DEFINITIONS
"dwelling": s.343.
"landlord": s.343.
"local housing authority": ss.1, 2.
"overcrowded": s.324.

GENERAL NOTE
The authority can take direct action to prevent the continuation of overcrowding, by using this abatement procedure, although an alternative is available, by means of a notice served on the landlord which will have the effect requiring him to take eviction proceedings, if he is not to commit an offence under s.331(2)(c), above.

Under this section, the authority can serve an abatement notice requiring the occupier to bring the overcrowding to an end within 14 days. This only applies when the occupation constitutes illegal overcrowding, *i.e.* is not exempt from illegality under ss.328–330, above.

If the occupier fails to comply, then three months from the expiry of the 14 days, if the offence persists, and the dwelling is still in the occupation of the same occupier or a member of his family, the authority can issue their own proceedings in the county court for possession to be yielded up to the landlord (within 14–28 days at the court's discretion) (subs. (2)) and recover their costs in so doing from the landlord, by direct action under subs. (3).

"The procedure contemplated . . . appears to be: first a 14 days' notice requiring the overcrowding to be abated; then a period of three months allowed from the date of the service of the notice with a view to the overcrowding being abated, and failing such abatement, then, if the house is in occupation of the persons upon whom the notice was served, or the members of his family, the local authority may" take the proceedings for possession. "So . . . it may be said that the position crystallises at the end of the period of three months, and, provided the house is still overcrowded at the date when the" proceedings are issued, a possession order must be made: *per* Jenkins L.J., *Zbytniewski* v. *Broughton* [1956] 2 Q.B. 673, at 688.

Costs were formerly recoverable summarily as a civil debt in the magistrates' court: they are now recoverable as an ordinary civil debt, *i.e.* in the county court (assuming they do not exceed the county court limits for the time being in force), pursuant to Law Commission Recommendations (Cmnd. 9515), No. 9.

Supplementary provisions

Enforcement of this Part

339.—(1) The local housing authority shall enforce the provisions of this Part.

(2) A prosecution for an offence against those provisions may be brought only—

(*a*) by the local housing authority, or

(*b*) in the case of a prosecution against the authority themselves, with the consent of the Attorney General.

DEFINITION
"local housing authority": ss.1, 2.

GENERAL NOTE
Enforcement of this Part lies with the local housing authority, who are the sole prosecuting authority, save when they are the ones alleged to have committed an offence, in which case prosecution may be brought against them, but only with the consent of the Attorney-General.

Powers of entry

340.—(1) A person authorised by the local housing authority may at all reasonable times, on giving 24 hours' notice to the occupier, and to the owner if the owner is known, enter any premises for the purpose of survey and examination where it appears to the authority that survey or examination is necessary in order to determine whether any powers under this Part should be exercised.

(2) An authorisation for the purposes of this section shall be in writing stating the particular purpose for which it is given.

DEFINITIONS
"local housing authority": ss.1, 2.
"owner": s.343.

GENERAL NOTE
This is a general power of entry, on 24 hours' notice to occupier, and to owner if owner is known, comparable to that applicable specifically to entry for measurement of rooms—see notes to s.337, above. It may be used in connection with a s.334 inspection.

Penalty for obstruction

341.—(1) It is a summary offence to obstruct an officer of the local housing authority, or any person authorised to enter premises in pursuance of this Part, in the performance of anything which he is by this Part required or authorised to do.

(2) A person committing such an offence is liable on conviction to a fine not exceeding level 2 on the standard scale.

DEFINITIONS
"local housing authority": ss.1, 2.

GENERAL NOTE
Obstruction of an officer of the authority under this Part is an offence punishable by a fine of up to level 2 on the standard scale under s.37, Criminal Justice Act 1982, currently £100, by S.I. 1984 No. 447.

Meaning of "suitable alternative accommodation"

342.—(1) In this Part "suitable alternative accommodation", in relation to the occupier of a dwelling, means a dwelling as to which the following conditions are satisfied—

(*a*) he and his family can live in it without causing it to be overcrowded;
(*b*) it is certified by the local housing authority to be suitable to his needs and those of his family as respects security of tenure, proximity to place of work and otherwise, and to be suitable in relation to his means;
(*c*) where the dwelling belongs to the local housing authority, it is certified by them to be suitable to his needs and those of his family as respects accommodation.

(2) For the purpose of subsection (1)(*c*) a dwelling containing two bedrooms shall be treated as providing accommodation for four persons, a dwelling containing three bedrooms shall be treated as providing accommodation for five persons and a dwelling containing four bedrooms shall be treated as providing accommodation for seven persons.

DEFINITIONS
"dwelling": s.343.
"local housing authority": ss.1, 2.

GENERAL NOTE
See notes to s.328, above.

Minor definitions

343. In this Part—

"agent", in relation to the landlord of a dwelling—

(*a*) means a person who collects rent in respect of the dwelling on behalf of the landlord, or is authorised by him to do so, and

(*b*) in the case of a dwelling occupied under a contract of employment under which the provision of the dwelling for his occupation forms part of the occupier's remuneration, includes a person who pays remuneration on behalf of the employer, or is authorised by him to do so;

"dwelling" means premises used or suitable for use as a separate dwelling;

"landlord", in relation to a dwelling—

(*a*) means the immediate landlord of an occupier of the dwelling, and

(*b*) in the case of a dwelling occupied under a contract of employment under which the provision of the dwelling for his occupation forms part of the occupier's remuneration, includes the occupier's employer;

"owner", in relation to premises—

(*a*) means a person (other than a mortgagee not in possession) who is for the time being entitled to dispose of the fee simple, whether in possession or in reversion, and

(*b*) includes also a person holding or entitled to the rents and profits of the premises under a lease of which the unexpired term exceeds three years.

GENERAL NOTE

"Dwelling". See notes to s.324, above.

Index of defined expressions: Part X

344. The following Table shows provisions defining or otherwise explaining expressions used in this Part (other than provisions defining or explaining an expression used in the same section or paragraph):—

agent (in relation to the landlord of a dwelling)	section 343
district (of a local housing authority)	section 2(1)
dwelling	section 343
landlord	sections 343 and 621
local housing authority	section 1, 2(2)
overcrowding (and related expressions)	section 324
owner	section 343
permitted number (of persons sleeping in a dwelling)	section 326
prescribed	section 614
standard scale (in reference to the maximum fine on summary conviction)	section 622
suitable alternative accommodation	section 342

PART XI

HOUSES IN MULTIPLE OCCUPATION

Introductory

Meaning of "multiple occupation"

345. In this Part "house in multiple occupation" means a house which is occupied by persons who do not form a single household.

DEFINITION
  "house": s.399.

GENERAL NOTE
  This is the key definition section for the purposes of this Part; it should be distinguished from "house in multiple occupation" (hereinafter, "H.M.O." in accordance with common usage) for the purposes of Part XV (housing improvement grants), under which H.M.O. "means a house which is occupied by persons who do not form a single household," as here, *but* "exclusive of any part of the house which is occupied as a separate dwelling by persons who form a single household" (s.525, below), *i.e.* having defined a property as an H.M.O. one then "removes" those parts of the house which are not multiply-occupied—see notes to s.525, below.
  There are three parts of the definition: "house", "occupied" and "by persons who do not form a single household".

House
  In many ways, this is the key question: can the property be treated as a house at all? If it can, it is likely to be relatively easy to resolve whether or not it is in single household occupation: see notes, below. "House" is defined in s.399, below, in now familiar terms: it "includes any yard, garden, outhouses and appurtenances belonging to the house or usually enjoyed with it" (see further notes to s.56, above). With the exception—likely to be rare in practice—of a house occupied by one person or household, with a structure in the yard, garden or outhouse occupied by another person or household, the extension would seem to have little practical application, and to be of no assistance at all on what are more likely to be the contentious cases.
  Some of the problems of application may be resolved by s.374, below, which applies ss.369–373 (management powers) to "a building which is not a house but comprises separate dwellings two or more of which are occupied by persons who do not form a single household", and to "a building which is not a house but comprises separate dwellings two or more of which do not have a sanitary convenience and personal washing facilities accessible only to those living in the dwelling", and to "a tenement block in which all or any of the flats are without one or more of the standard amenities".
  For this purpose, "tenement block" is defined to mean "a building or a part of a building which was constructed in the form of, and consists of, two or more flats . . . " (s.374(2)). Similarly, an amenities' notice under s.352 can be served in relation to "a building which is not a house but comprises separate dwellings two or more of which" are occupied other than in single household occupation, or which do not have certain amenities: s.352(6), below. This last class is also within the registration scheme provisions of s.346(1)(a), below.
  Prima facie, the existence of these provisions might appear to imply that a building (*house or block of flats*) cannot itself be a "house". This has been held not to be so, in relation to a converted house, in *Okereke* v. *London Borough of Brent* [1967] 1 Q.B., C.A., under what is now this Part. Rather, these provisions were held to be extensions of the term "house in multiple occupation" as defined, *i.e.* now as defined in this section, and possibly as intended to dispell doubt caused by the decision in *Weatheritt* v. *Cantlay* [1901] 2 K.B. 285, decided under s.94, Public Health (London) Act 1891, in which it had been held for analogous purposes that each of the flats in a tenement block was a house in itself, and that the block could not be called a house. This decision was limited shortly afterwards, in *Kyffin* v. *Simmons* (1901) 67 J.P. 227, and doubted in *Okereke* itself.
  Accordingly, the "normal" principles discussed in the notes to ss.56, 189, above, would seem to be applicable. The starting-point, therefore, remains the statements of principle set out in the notes to s.56, above, *i.e.* that the word "house" must be construed as a mixed question of fact and law in the context of the Part or provisions of the Act, and that definitions under other legislation are not of assistance: see *per* Jessel M.R., in *Duke of Bedford* v. *Dawson* (1875) L.R. 20 Eq. 353 at p357, cited by Browne L.J. in *Sovmots Investments Ltd.* v. *Secretary of State for the Environment at the Court of Appeal,* [1976] 3 All E.R. 720 at p728.
  See further *Quillotex Co. Ltd.* v. *Minister of Housing and Local Government* [1966] 1 Q.B. 704, adopting *Attorney-General* v. *Mutual Tontine Westminster Chambers Association Ltd.* (1876) 1 Ex. D. 469, C.A., *Annicola Investments Ltd.* v. *Minister of Housing and Local Government* [1968] 1 Q.B. 631, *In Re Butler, Camberwell (Wingfield Mews) No. 2 Clearance Order 1936* [1939] 1 K.B. 570, C.A., *Ashbridge Investments Ltd.* v. *Minister of Housing and Local Government* [1965] 1 W.L.R. 1320, C.A., *Re South Shields (D'Arcy Street) Compulsory Purchase Order 1937* [1939] 1 All E.R. 419.

See also *R.* v. *London Borough of Camden, ex parte Rowton (Camden Town) Ltd.* (1983) 17 H.L.R. 28, Q.B.D., decided under what is now this Part: "In my judgment one must start with the Acts; one must have regard to their subject-matter and the object which Parliament would appear to have desired to achieve. If it can be shown that, prior to the passing of these Acts, the courts had interpreted the word 'house' when used in this field as bearing a meaning other than that ordinarily understood by the citizen, then Parliament may be presumed to have been aware of this interpretation and, unless the contrary appears, to have intended to perpetuate it".

"House" has no very precise meaning: the word can cover many types of building (*Quillotex* v. *Minister of Housing and Local Government* [1966] 1 Q.B. 704, C.A.). In *Howard* v. *Ministry of Housing and Local Government* (1967) 65 L.G.R. 257, it was said that the word "house" in the 1957 legislation had the same meaning as "dwelling house" in the previous (1936) legislation. "It is apparent that a 'house' . . . means a building which is constructed or adapted for use as or for the purposes of a dwelling": *Ashbridge Investments Ltd.* v. *Ministry of Housing and Local Government* [1965] 1 W.L.R. 1320, C.A., per Lord Denning M.R. at p1324.

A hostel or a building used for multiple occupation or as a lodging-house may qualify as a house for the purposes of this Part: *London County Council* v. *Rowton Houses Ltd.* (1897) 62 J.P. 68; *Re Ross and Leicester Corporation* (1932) 96 J.P. 459; *R.* v. *London Borough of Southwark, ex parte Lewis Levy Ltd.* (1983) 8 H.L.R. 1, Q.B.D.; *R.* v. *London Borough of Camden, ex parte Rowton (Camden Town) Ltd.* (1983) 10 H.L.R. 28, Q.B.D. See also *Breachberry Ltd.* v. *Secretary of State for the Environment and Shepway District Council* [1985] J.P.L. 180, Q.B.D. under the Town and Country Planning Act 1971.

Similarly, a building subdivided into flats has been held a house under the clearance area provisions (ss.289 *et seq.*) of Part IX, above: *Annicola Investments Ltd.* v. *Minister of Housing and Local Government* [1968] 1 Q.B. 631 (large purpose-built block of tenement flats and shops), *Quillotex Co. Ltd.* v. *Minister of Housing and Local Government* [1966] 1 Q.B. 704 (series of eight buildings each containing tenement flats).

Under Part VI, in *Benabo* v. *Wood Green Borough Council* [1946] 1 K.B. 38, a house let off in flats was held still a house, and in *Critchell* v. *London Borough of Lambeth* [1957] 2 Q.B. 535, C.A., the fact that a house had a separate, self-contained basement flat did not prevent it being a house.

In *Lake* v. *Bennett* [1970] 1 Q.B. 663, C.A., under the Leasehold Reform Act 1967, Lord Denning M.R. doubted that a tower block could reasonably be called a house, but Salmon L.J. emphasised that the decision did not necessarily affect the Housing Acts, and the wording of the 1967 Act refers to a house "reasonably so called".

The issue appears, therefore, to be open. Little can be added, other than by further reference to the notes to ss.56, 189, above. In the final analysis, it may be that one has to accept that Parts dealing with different procedures, and accordingly utilising language somewhat differently (*cf. Holmes* v. *Minister of Housing and Local Government* (1960) 12 P. & C.R. 72) are all theoretically susceptible of application to a range of types of structure, but with the authority susceptible to intervention if their choice of application is such that no reasonable authority could so have acted, on "usual" principles of administrative law, *cf.* notes to s.64, above.

Okereke itself puts *converted* houses beyond doubt (whether or not into self-contained flats): see also *Kyffin* v. *Simmons* (1901) 67 J.P. 227. In *Guppys (Bridport) Ltd.* v. *Kerrier District Council (No. 2)* (1985) 17 H.L.R. 426, C.A., it was said that a house converted into flats is not an H.M.O. at all: however, this case concerned the definition of H.M.O. in s.525, below, where parts of the building let in separate dwellings have to be excluded, and the point was not considered whether the common parts might have remained an H.M.O. or not. Indeed, the very exclusion of parts of a house let off in separate dwellings in the context of Part XV supports the proposition that such properties otherwise would or at least could be H.M.O.s.

The cases on "mixed user" cited in the notes to s.56 above would appear applicable under this Part: see *Ashbridge Investments Ltd.* v. *Ministry of Housing and Local Government* [1965] 1 W.L.R. 1320, C.A. (greengrocer's shop with a rear living room and scullery, three first floor rooms and an outside lavatory), *Re Butler, Camberwell (Wingfield Mews) No. 2 Clearance Order 1936* [1939] 1 K.B. 570, C.A. (structure consisting of a garage or workshop with a dwelling above, see also *Re Hammersmith (Bergham Mews) Clearance Order, 1936* [1937] 3 All E.R. 539).

Where a building is used partly for residential purposes, and partly for other purposes, the building has to be looked at as a whole to ascertain whether, as a question of degree, it can properly be described as a house: *Annicola Investments Ltd.* v. *Minister of Housing and Local Government* [1968] 1 Q.B. 631, C.A. It need not be shown that all of the rooms in a building are used for residential purposes: *Premier Garage Co.* v. *Ilkeston Corporation* (1933) 97 J.P. 786.

Although original construction of a building is an important consideration (*In Re Butler, Camberwell (Wingfield Mews) No. 2 Clearance Order 1936* [1939] 1 K.B. 570, C.A.) regard may be had to the use of a building at the time the question falls to be determined (*ibid*; see also *Grosvenor* v. *Hampstead Junction Railway* [1857] L.J. Ch. 731), so that something not built as a house but used as such may qualify. An unfinished house may qualify as a house: *Alexander* v. *Crystal Palace Railway* (1862) 30 Beav. 556. A building constructed as a house but used for other purposes has been held to remain a house: *Howard* v. *Ministry of Housing and Local Government* (1967) 65 L.G.R. 257.

Occupied By

This does not necessarily mean under any particular legal arrangement: in *Minford Properties* v. *London Borough of Hammersmith* (1978) 247 E.G. 561, D.C., it was held that a former tenant occupying premises pending expiry of a suspended possession order which had already been made is probably still to be considered as a person in occupation. In *Silbers* v. *Southwark London Borough Council* (1977) 76 L.G.R. 421, C.A., it was said that "occupied" merely meant, broadly, "lived in".

Persons Not Forming A Single Household

In earlier legislation, the reference was to letting in lodgings, or in occupation by persons being members of more than one family: see also now Housing (Consequential Provisions) Act 1985, s.5 and Sched. 4, para. 13, retaining the amendment introduced by s.58, Housing Act 1969 that (as it reads in para. 13) "any statutory provision passed or made before 25th August 1969 referring (in whatever terms) to a house which, or part of which, is let in lodgings or which is occupied by members of more than one family shall continue to have effect as if it referred to a house which is occupied by persons who do not form a single household".

The 1969 Act reversed the decision in *Holme* v. *Royal Borough of Kensington and Chelsea* [1968] 1 Q.B. 646, in which it was decided that a son and daughter-in-law living on one floor of a house occupied by the father and mother were members of the same family, although not of the same household, with the consequence that it did not qualify as multiple occupation.

Occupation as a single household is not defined. Clearly, case-law on the pre-1969 definition must be treated with some caution in any attempt to apply it, as a change was certainly intended. It has been said that "both the expression 'household' and membership of it is a question of fact and degree, there being no certain indicia the presence or absence of which is by itself conclusive . . . " (*per* Lord Hailsham, *Simmons* v. *Pizzey* [1979] A.C. 37, H.L.) In that case, some 75 people were in occupation of a refuge for the victims of domestic violence. It was not intended that they should live indefinitely at the refuge; some might move on to permanent accommodation of their own, while others might return to the homes from which they had fled.

As no occupant had any special part of the house to herself, there could be no concept of separate households. Rather, the women organised the business of the house collectively, eating and undertaking the arrangements of the house together. It was held that this could not, however, amount to occupation as a single household. In *Silbers* v. *Southwark London Borough Council* (1977) 76, L.G.R. 421, C.A., a house (at one time registered as a common lodging house under what is now Part XII, below) used as a hostel for women, including alcoholics and the mentally disturbed, who stayed for varying periods of time and lived in dormitories, was similarly not in single household occupation.

In *London Borough of Hackney* v. *Ezedinma* [1981] 3 All E.R. 438, D.C., however, it was held that lettings of rooms in "groups", the members of each group sharing a separate kitchen from the other groups, could "just" be called occupation in three "households" (for the purposes of a direction under s.354, below). However, the case must be seen in context: a prosecutor's appeal from the dismissal of a charge of allowing more households than the number specified in the s.354 direction to occupy the house in question. The rooms had been let to the individual members of each "group": "It would have been open to the justices . . . had they been so minded, to hold that each of the separate rooms, singly let, constituted a household on its own and that, accordingly, the direction had been breached . . . "

The justices had not taken this approach: "The substantial question which we have to consider . . . is whether there was any evidence on which justices, properly directing themselves on the facts and the law, could have come to the conclusion that this house contained any less than six, seven or eight single households . . . The only evidence on which the justices could so have acted was . . . that to the effect that the single tenants . . . lived in groups, at least to this extent, that each group occupied a separate floor or . . . two floors forming a single unit, and each such group shared only one particular kitchen of the three . . . in the house.

"I do not find this altogether compelling evidence that the tenants of the rooms in this house comprised three 'households' . . . Nevertheless, if, as I think it is, the question is a matter of fact and degree for the justices, I think that this evidence was just sufficient for them to conclude, as they did, that the appellants had not proved beyond a reasonable doubt that there were more than three households in the premises . . . " (*per* May J.). "For myself, I am very doubtful if, on the material before the justices, I would have concluded that these students were living as three households . . . However, I feel unable to say that there was no evidence on which any bench could reasonably have come to the conclusion that these magistrates did . . . " (*per* Griffiths LJ).

These decisions are consistent with earlier ministerial guidance: "a number of persons where the relationships between the various individuals resident at any one time are so tenuous as to support the view that they can neither singly nor collectively be regarded as forming a single household" (M.H.L.G. Circular 67/69). The Circular suggests that a distinction may be drawn when there are one two lodgers "living in" as part of the family, which might be treated as single household occupation, and a house where there is catering for lodgers on a substantial scale as a business enterprise, which will constitute multiple occupation.

The references here to "lodgers" should not be confused with the use of this term as a licence distinct from tenancy: see notes to s.93, above. It is quite clear that the mere fact that occupiers may live in bed-sitting rooms which will qualify as "let as a separate dwelling" for Rent Act purposes (see notes to ss.79, 324, above) or indeed whole flats will not necessarily prevent the house being an H.M.O. for otherwise the definition in s.525, below, would be otiose.

Registration schemes

Registration schemes

346.—(1) The local housing authority may make and submit to the Secretary of State for confirmation by him a registration scheme authorising the authority to compile and maintain a register for their district of—

(*a*) houses in multiple occupation, and

(*b*) buildings which comprise separate dwellings, two or more of which do not have a sanitary convenience and personal washing facilities accessible only to those living in the dwelling;

and the Secretary of State may if he thinks fit confirm the scheme, with or without modification.

(2) A registration scheme need not be for the whole of the authority's district and need not be for every description of house or building falling within paragraphs (*a*) and (*b*) of subsection (1).

(3) A registration scheme may—

(*a*) specify the particulars to be inserted in the register,

(*b*) make it the duty of such persons as may be specified by the scheme to notify the authority of the fact that a house or building appears to be registrable and to give the authority as regards such a house or building all or any of the particulars specified in the scheme,

(*c*) make it the duty of such persons as may be specified by the scheme to notify the authority of any change which makes it necessary to alter the particulars inserted in the register as regards a house or building.

(4) A registration scheme shall not come into force before it has been confirmed but subject to that comes into force on such date as may be fixed by the scheme or, if no date is so fixed, at the expiration of one month after it is confirmed.

(5) A registration scheme may vary or revoke a previous registration scheme; and the local housing authority may at any time, with the consent of the Secretary of State, by order revoke a registration scheme.

(6) A person who contravenes or fails to comply with a provision of a registration scheme commits a summary offence and is liable on conviction to a fine not exceeding, except in a case within section 347(4) (which relates to the contravention of certain control provisions), level 2 on the standard scale.

<small>DEFINITIONS</small>
"district": s.2.
"house": s.399.
"house in multiple occupation": s.345.
"local housing authority": ss.1, 2.

<small>GENERAL NOTE</small>
The first of the series of powers applicable to H.M.O.s (see notes to s.345, above) is the "registration scheme", applicable not only to H.M.O.s as conventionally defined, but also as extended to buildings which comprise separate dwellings, two or more of which lack specified facilities: subs. (1)(b). "Personal washing facilities" can include a hot water supply: *McPhail* v. *Islington London Borough Council* [1970] 2 Q.B. 197. As to "separate dwelling", see notes to ss.79, 324, above, and s.525, below. The scheme may be selective, as to area, and classes of property: subs. (2).

The scheme must, however, be confirmed by the Secretary of State (subs. (1)), and does not come into force until after confirmation: subs. (4). The scheme may fix a date for its commencement, but if it does not do so, it will come into force one month after confirmation: *ibid.* The scheme may be varied or revoked with the consent of the Secretary of State. Before submitting a scheme—including a scheme which varies or revokes a previous scheme—the authority must publicise it, as they must do once the scheme is confirmed: s.349, below. If a scheme is revoked by order, rather than revoked by a new scheme, the order, too, must be publicised: *ibid.* Copies of a scheme have to be made available: *ibid.*

Ministerial guidance (M.H.L.G. Circular 51/64, paras 9–15) is in favour of schemes which are limited, to those wards "in which squalid conditions are known to be most prevalent. A limited scheme of this nature will be more readily publicised, brought into operation and followed up by inspection than one applied indiscriminately to the whole of an authority's area . . . The power to make an amending scheme . . . enables the area covered . . . to be extended once the 'black spots' have been dealt with. The Minister will not refuse to consider a scheme covering the whole of an authority's area; but in such a case he will expect the authority . . . to provide an indication of their reasons for so deciding".

The provisions of subs. (3) specify the substance of the scheme, but see also s.347, below, enabling extension to, and in some respects the alternative of, "control provisions", not to be confused with the much more drastic—and individually applicable – "control orders" of ss.379, *et seq.*

The basic aim of this section is to secure information about multiple occupation. The scheme may specify particulars to be inserted in a register, and identify those who are to be under a duty to notify the authority that a property appears to be registrable under the scheme, and provide particulars about it, and identify those who are to be under a duty to notify the authority about material changes in occupation. The authority have an ancillary power to require information, for the purposes of establishing whether a property is registrable and ascertaining relevant particulars, under s.350, below.

Note that the section contains no limitations on *who* can be made the subject of the requirements; it would seem (*cf.* s.348, below) that persons having control (as defined in s.398, below) and "managers" (defined in *ibid*) are clearly within the intention of the provisions, and there would seem to be no reason why an owner (as defined in *ibid*) should not, although on conventional principles of administrative law, imposing the requirement on anyone who could not in any way put himself in a position to comply would be wrong.

Model Registration Schemes were drafted by the Ministry of Housing and Local Government (now the Department of the Environment), which are of three types—"informatory" (without s.347 control provisions), "regulatory" (with) and "combined": M.H.L.G. Circular 67/69. "Local authorities may not in every case wish to conform precisely to a model, but Ministers will be reluctant to give approval to a scheme which involves undue elaboration of the particulars to be supplied and recorded" (*ibid*, para. 12).

It is an offence to fail to notify the authority that a property is registrable, or to fail to provide the material particulars, or to fail to notify the authority of changes, so far as these are required by the scheme, punishable by a fine of up to level 2 on the standard scale under s.37, Criminal Justice Act 1982, currently £100, by S.I. 1984 No. 447: subs. (6). Section 347(4), however, carries a different (and higher) penalty. An authority may inspect to see if an offence under this section has been committed, without prior warning: see s.395, below.

Control provisions

347.—(1) A registration scheme may contain control provisions, that is to say, provisions for preventing multiple occupation of a house unless—
  (a) the house is registered, and
  (b) the number of households or persons occupying it does not exceed the number registered for it.

(2) Control provisions may prohibit persons from permitting others to take up residence in a house or part of a house but shall not prohibit a person from taking up or remaining in residence in the house.

(3) Control provisions shall not apply—
  (a) where the persons occupying the house form only two households, or
  (b) where, apart from one household (if any), the house is occupied by no more than four persons;
and shall not affect the continued occupation of a house by the number of households or persons occupying it when the provisions come into force.

(4) A person convicted of an offence under section 346(6) (contravention or failure to comply with provisions of registration scheme) consisting of a contravention of so much of control provisions as relates—
  (a) to occupation to a greater extent than permitted under those provisions of a house which is not registered, or
  (b) to occupation of a house which is registered by more households or persons than the registration permits,
is liable to a fine not exceeding level 4 on the standard scale.

DEFINITIONS
  "house": s.399.
  "house in multiple occupation": s.345.

GENERAL NOTE
    This section and the next contain the most active elements permissible under a registration scheme—"control provisions". The "regulatory" Model Scheme referred to in M.H.L.G. Circular 67/69 (see notes to s.346, above), incorporates these provisions, and a "combined" scheme also does so. The point may be made: these provisions can be used as an alternative to information requirements under s.346(3)(b) and (c), although as registration itself remains an essential under this section, some particulars must presumably still be provided under s.346(3)(a).
    The essence of the difference is that while s.346 requires only that information be provided, this section permits the authority to impose limits on households or persons in occupation: subs. (1). The limits must be related to specific numbers (subs. (1)(b)), which would appear to mean by "type" of property, or by specific application to individual properties, and may prohibit *people from permitting* others to take up residence in the house, or even a part of it: subs. (2). However, they cannot prohibit *people from taking up residence* (*ibid.*), *i.e.* they cannot be addressed to individual would be occupiers; nor can they require someone to leave a property (*ibid.*). (As to "residence", *cf.* notes to s.87, above: a distinction may validly be drawn between "residing" and "occasional visits".)
    The minimum numbers to which the control provisions can be applied are those set out in subs. (3): where there are no more than two households, or no more than one house plus four individuals. In either case, they cannot operate in respect of those in occupation when the provisions come into force: *ibid.* (The same point as in the last paragraph may be made about "occupation" and "occasional visits"). As to the meaning of "household", see notes to s.345, above. The provisions of the next section enable the extension of control provisions to permit the authority to *refuse* registration, on specified grounds, or to impose a condition

of works. There is, again, no reference to who can be placed under a duty by the provisions: see notes to s.346, above.

The two offences specified carry a fine of up to level 4 on the standard scale under s.37, Criminal Justice Act 1982, currently £1,000, by S.I. 1984 No. 447.

Control provisions: decisions and appeals

348.—(1) Control provisions may enable the local housing authority—

(*a*) to refuse to register or to vary the registration of a house on the ground that the house is unsuitable and incapable of being made suitable for such occupation as would be permitted by virtue of the registration or variation;

(*b*) to refuse to register a house on the ground that the person having control of the house or the person intended to be the person managing the house is not a fit and proper person;

(*c*) to require as a condition of registration or of varying the registration of a house that such works are executed as will make the house suitable for such occupation as will be permitted by virtue of the registration or variation.

(2) Control provisions shall provide that where the local housing authority refuse to register or vary the registration of a house, or require the execution of works as a condition of doing so, they shall give the applicant a written statement of their reasons.

(3) Where a person has applied for the registration or the variation of the registration of a house in pursuance of control provisions and the local housing authority—

(*a*) notify him that they refuse to register the house or to vary the registration in accordance with the application, or

(*b*) notify him that they require the execution of works as a condition of registering the house or varying the registration in accordance with the application, or

(*c*) do not within five weeks after receiving the application, or such longer period as may be agreed in writing between the authority and the applicant, register the house or vary the registration in accordance with the application,

the applicant may, within 21 days of being so notified or of the end of the period mentioned in paragraph (*c*), or such longer period as the authority may in writing allow, appeal to the county court.

(4) On such an appeal the court may confirm, reverse or vary the decision of the authority; and where the decision of the authority was a refusal to register or vary the registration of a house, the court may direct them to register or vary the registration either in accordance with the application as made or in accordance with that application as varied in such manner as the court may direct.

DEFINITIONS
"house": s.399.
"local housing authority": ss.1, 2.
"person having control": s.398.
"person managing": s.398.

GENERAL NOTE
This is the last of the provisions governing the substance of a registration scheme. When the authority adopt control provisions within the last section, they may enable the authority to refuse registration on specified grounds (subs. (1)): house unsuitable and incapable of being made suitable; and, person having control or intended manager not a fit and proper person (*cf.* s.404, permitting refusal of registration as a common lodging-house on similar grounds). Alternatively, the provisions may permit the authority to require works to be carried out to render the house suitable for as many as will occupy under the registration (*ibid.*). As to person having control, and person managing, see notes to s.398, below.

If the authority exercise any of these powers in respect of a particular property, they have to provide a statement in writing of reasons (subs. (2)), which may be used as the basis for appeal to the county court: subs. (3). There can also be an appeal if the authority do not reply to a request for registration (or variation) within five weeks, or such longer period as the applicant agrees in writing: *ibid*. Appeal must be brought within 21 days of notification, or 21 days of the five week (or that period as extended) failure to respond, unless the authority agrees a longer period in writing: *ibid*. On appeal, the court may confirm, reverse or vary the decision of the authority, and can issue directions to the authority as to how to deal with the application: subs. (4).

Steps required to inform public about scheme

349.—(1) The local housing authority shall publish notice of their intention to submit a registration scheme to the Secretary of State for confirmation in one or more newspapers circulating in their district at least one month before the scheme is submitted for confirmation.

(2) As soon as a registration scheme is confirmed by the Secretary of State, the local housing authority shall publish in one or more newspapers circulating in their district a notice—

(*a*) stating the fact that a registration scheme has been confirmed, and

(*b*) describing any steps which will have to be taken under the scheme by those concerned with registrable houses and buildings (other than steps which have only to be taken after a notice from the authority), and

(*c*) naming a place where a copy of the scheme may be seen at all reasonable hours.

(3) A copy of a registration scheme confirmed by the Secretary of State—

(*a*) shall be printed and deposited at the offices of the local housing authority by whom it was made, and

(*b*) shall at all reasonable hours be open to public inspection without payment;

and a copy of the scheme shall on application be furnished to any person on payment of such sum, not exceeding 5p for every copy, as the authority may determine.

(4) If the local housing authority revoke a registration scheme by order they shall publish notice of the order in one or more newspapers circulating in their district.

DEFINITIONS
"house": s.399.
"local housing authority": ss.1, 2.

GENERAL NOTE
This section contains the publicity duties imposed on local authorities in relation to registration schemes. The publicity must extend to describing the steps which those placed under duties by the scheme have to take. The scheme must also be available for inspection, free of charge, and a copy must be made available, at a maximum cost of 5p.

Power to require information for purposes of scheme

350.—(1) The local housing authority may—

(*a*) for the purpose of ascertaining whether a house or building is registrable, and

(*b*) for the purpose of ascertaining the particulars to be entered in the register as regards a house or building,

require a person who has an estate or interest in, or who lives in, the house or building to state in writing any information in his possession which the authority may reasonably require for that purpose.

(2) A person who, having been required in pursuance of this section to give information to a local housing authority; fails to give the information,

or knowingly makes a mis-statement in respect of it, commits a summary offence and is liable on conviction to a fine not exceeding level 2 on the standard scale.

DEFINITIONS
  "house": s.399.
  "local housing authority": ss.1, 2.
  "person having an estate or interest": s.398.

GENERAL NOTE
  This section provides the authority with power to require information from anyone who lives in a property, or anyone with an estate or interest in it (which includes for this purpose a statutory tenant—see s.398, below), in order *either* to ascertain whether it is registerable, *or* to ascertain what particulars need to be entered: subs. (1). Failure to provide the information, or knowingly making a mis-statement, is an offence punishable by a fine of up to level 2 on the standard scale under s.37, Criminal Justice Act 1982, currently £100, by S.I. 1984 No. 447.

Proof of scheme and contents of register

351.—(1) If there is produced a printed copy of a registration scheme purporting to be made by a local housing authority, upon which there is endorsed a certificate purporting to be signed by the proper officer of the authority stating—

  (*a*) that the scheme was made by the authority,
  (*b*) that the copy is a true copy of the scheme, and
  (*c*) that on a specified date the scheme was confirmed by the Secretary of State,

the certificate is prima facie evidence of the facts so stated without proof of the handwriting or official position of the person by whom it purports to be signed.

  (2) A document purporting to be a copy of an entry in a register kept under a registration scheme and to be certified as a true copy by the proper officer of the authority is prima facie evidence of the entry without proof of the handwriting or official position of the person by whom it purports to be signed.

DEFINITION
  "local housing authority": ss.1, 2.

Fitness for the number of occupants

Power to require execution of works to render premises fit for number of occupants

352.—(1) The local housing authority may serve a notice under this section where the condition of a house in multiple occupation is, in the opinion of the authority, so far defective with respect to any of the following matters—

  natural and artificial lighting,
  ventilation,
  water supply,
  personal washing facilities,
  drainage and sanitary conveniences,
  facilities for the storage, preparation and cooking of food, and for the disposal of waste water, or
  installations for space heating or for the use of space heating appliances,

having regard to the number of individuals or households, or both, accommodated for the time being on the premises, as not to be reasonably suitable for occupation by those individuals or households.

(2) The notice shall specify the works which in the opinion of the authority are required for rendering the premises reasonably suitable—

> (a) for occupation by the individuals or households for the time being accommodated there, or
>
> (b) for a smaller number of individuals or households and the number of individuals or households, or both, which, in the opinion of the authority, the premises could reasonably accommodate if the works were carried out.

(3) The notice may be served—

> (a) on the person having control of the house, or
>
> (b) on a person to whom the house is let at a rack-rent or who, as agent or trustee of a person to whom the house is so let, receives rents or other payments from tenants of parts of the house or lodgers in the house;

and the authority shall inform any other person who is to their knowledge an owner, lessee or mortgagee of the house of the fact that the notice has been served.

(4) The notice shall require the person on whom it is served to execute the works specified in the notice within such period (of at least 21 days from the service of the notice) as may be so specified; but that period may from time to time be extended by written permission of the authority.

(5) If the authority are satisfied that—

> (a) after the service of a notice under this section the number of individuals living on the premises has been reduced to a level which will make the works specified in the notice unnecessary, and
>
> (b) that number will be maintained at or below that level, whether in consequence of the exercise of the authority's powers under section 354 (power to limit number of occupants of house) or otherwise,

they may withdraw the notice by notifying that fact in writing to the person on whom the notice was served, but without prejudice to the issue of a further notice.

(6) This section applies to a building which is not a house but comprises separate dwellings two or more of which—

> (a) are occupied by persons who do not form a single household, or
>
> (b) do not have a sanitary convenience and personal washing facilities accessible only to those living in the dwelling,

as it applies to a house in multiple occupation, but not so as to authorise the service in relation to such a building of such a notice as is mentioned in subsection (2)(b) (notice requiring works to make premises fit for smaller numbers of occupants).

DEFINITIONS
"house": s.399.
"house in multiple occupation": s.345.
"local housing authority": ss.1, 2.
"person having control": s.398.

GENERAL NOTE
This section applies to H.M.O.s as conventionally defined (see notes to s.345, above), and to buildings which are not houses, but comprise separate dwellings two or more of which are in multiple occupation, or do not have a sanitary convenience and personal washing facilities for the exclusive use of those living in the separate dwelling: subs. (6). This is the provision formerly contained in s.21, Housing Act 1961, and considered in the case of *Okereke* v. *Brent London Borough Council* [1967] 1 Q.B. 42, C.A. discussed in the notes to s.345, above. Personal washing facilities includes a hot water supply: *McPhail* v. *Islington London Borough Council* [1970] 2 Q.B. 197. As to separate dwelling, see notes to ss.79, 324, above, and s.525, below.

Subsection (1) in some ways resembles s.604, below, defining unfitness: see notes thereto. Of the propositions and cases set out therein, the following seem of direct relevance:

(1) That an authority's *own* housing is not within the provisions, on the basis that they cannot normally be compelled to apply enforcement provisions to themselves (see *R.* v. *Cardiff City Council, ex parte Cross* (1982) 6 H.L.R. 1, C.A., affirming (1981) 1 H.L.R. 54, Q.B.D., which contains a more detailed analysis and reasoning than is to be found in the judgment of the Court of Appeal; see further notes to s.189, above);

(2) That the question to be asked is whether the property suffers from any one or more of the specified defects, and then whether or not the totality of the defects, taken in the round, means that the property is not reasonably suitable for occupation: *E.A. Wyse* v. *Secretary of State for the Environment and Borough of Newcastle-under-Lyme* [1984] J.P.L. 256, Q.B.D.

(3) That no high standard of proof is required—see, *e.g.*, *Jones* v. *Green* [1925] 1 K.B. 659, D.C.: "it is only required that the place must be decently fit for human beings to live in"; in *Hall* v. *Manchester Corporation* (1915) L.J. Ch. 732, H.L., it was said that the standard was that of the "ordinary reasonable man";

(4) That it is the effect of the defects which matters: *Summers* v. *Salford Corporation* [1943] A.C. 283—"such that by ordinary user damage may naturally be caused to the occupier, either in respect of personal injury to life or limb or injury to health".

"The extent of works which it would be reasonable to require in a particular house is essentially a matter for judgment by the local authority. Ideally, each family should have its own kitchen, bathroom and w.c. in self-contained accommodation, but for some time to come standards short of the ideal will have to be accepted in many areas and some sharing of facilities by families will be unavoidable in many houses. Standards of provision which it would be reasonable to require will depend not only on the age, character and physical limitations of individual houses but also on the general housing situation in a particular district.

"Where some sharing is unavoidable, authorities should, however, endeavour to ensure that family sharing of kitchens is kept to a minimum and that the facilities provided in the kitchen are adequate for the number of persons for whom they have to cater. Even in shared kitchens each family should have its own cooking facilities wherever possible". (M.H.L.G. Circular 16/61, Memorandum, paras. 34 and 35).

But at the core is the issue of for how many households (see notes to s.345, above) and individuals the amenities must cater: "The powers . . . do not stand in isolation. They can be supported, where the local authority consider it appropriate, by the powers [now, s.354, below] which may be applied to limit the occupancy of a house either before or after additional facilities have been provided, or to secure a progressive reduction in the number of occupants to a level more in accord with the facilities in the house". (*Ibid.* para. 29.)

This section does not permit the authority to set occupation levels, even although under subs. (2)(*b*), the authority can determine reasonable suitability by reference not to the number of individuals and households actually in occupation, but by a smaller number who *could* be accommodated once the works are carried out. The intention is that a related notice is served under s.354, below, which fixes a limit (*cf.* s.354(6)), which does not require evictions, but does require "natural decline", *i.e.* if lower than existing occupation, as people leave not to replace them. (See notes to s.354, below.)

The notice must specify the works required (subs. (2), not merely the effect that unspecified works are to achieve: *Canterbury City Council* v. *Bern* [1981] J.P.L. 749, D.C. It must specify a time for completion, of not less than 21 days, subject to written extensions from time to time: subs. (4). The notice is to be served on either the person having control of the house, or on a person to whom the house is let at a rack-rent, or on a person who receives rents or other payments from tenants or lodgers on behalf of a person to whom it is let at a rack-rent: subs. (3). As to "person having control", and "rack-rent", see s.398, below.

There is no express requirement that the notice specify the subs. (2) number, but the necessity to do so is implied in a subs. (2)(*b*), case: see also s.353(2)(*b*), below. If the notice does specify a number (of necessity under subs. (2)(*b*), optionally under subs. (2)(*a*)), that number may be taken into account when determining an occupation level under s.354, below. The works notice may be withdrawn under subs. (5), because of reduction in numbers, if the authority are additionally satisfied (whether or not because of the service of a s.354 notice) that numbers will be maintained at or below the level which will make the works unnecessary. The withdrawal is without prejudice to a further notice: *ibid.*

As to appeal, see s.353, below; as to consequences of default in compliance (criminal and civil, *i.e.* works in default), see ss.375 *et seq.*, below. As to the availability of grant-aid to assist with the cost of the works, see ss.483 *et seq.*, below. As to service of notice, see notes to s.617, below.

Appeal against notice under s.352

353.—(1) A person on whom a notice is served under section 352 (notice requiring works to render premises fit for number of occupants), or any other person who is an owner, lessee or mortgagee of the premises to which the notice relates, may, within 21 days from the service of the notice, or such longer period as the local housing authority may in writing allow, appeal to the county court.

(2) The appeal may be on any of the following grounds—

(*a*) that the condition of the premises did not justify the authority, having regard to the considerations set out in subsection (1) of that section, in requiring the execution of the works specified in the notice;

(*b*) in the case of a notice under subsection (2)(*b*) of that section (notice requiring works to render premises fit for smaller number of occupants), that the number of individuals or households, or both, specified in the notice is unreasonably low;

(*c*) that there has been some informality, defect or error in, or in connection with, the notice;

(*d*) that the authority have refused unreasonably to approve the execution of alternative works, or that the works required by the notice to be executed are otherwise unreasonable in character or extent, or are unnecessary;

(*e*) that the time within which the works are to be executed is not reasonably sufficient for the purpose; or

(*f*) that some other person is wholly or partly responsible for the state of affairs calling for the execution of the works, or will as holder of an estate or interest in the premises derive a benefit from their execution, and ought to pay the whole or a part of the expenses of executing them.

(3) In so far as an appeal is based on the ground mentioned in subsection (2)(*c*), the court shall dismiss the appeal if it is satisfied that the informality, defect or error was not a material one.

(4) If on an appeal the court is satisfied that—

(*a*) the number of persons living in the premises has been reduced, and

(*b*) adequate steps have been taken (by the exercise of the local housing authority's powers under section 354 (power to limit number of occupants of house) or otherwise) to prevent that number being again increased,

the court may if it thinks fit revoke the notice or vary the list or works specified in the notice.

(5) Where the grounds on which an appeal is brought include the ground mentioned in subsection (2)(*f*), the court, if satisfied that the other person referred to in the notice of appeal has had proper notice of the appeal, may on the hearing of the appeal make such order as it thinks fit with respect to the payment to be made by him to the appellant or, where the works are executed by the local housing authority, to the authority.

DEFINITIONS
"house": s.399.
"lessee": s.398.
"local housing authority": ss.1, 2.
"owner": s.398.
"person having an estate or interest": s.398.

GENERAL NOTE
This section sets out the grounds of appeal against a works notice under s.352, above. Where reliance is placed on ground (*c*), if the informality, defect or error is not material, the court is bound to dismiss the appeal (subs. (3)); where reliance is placed on ground (*f*), the court may make an order for some other person to contribute to the costs, provided that such other person has had proper notice of the appeal: subs. (5). However, only someone (regardless of their interest in the premises) who is wholly or partly responsible can be called on to meet all or part of the cost, or someone who will derive a benefit, as holder of an estate or interest, defined in s.398, below, to include a statutory tenant.

If by the time of the appeal the number of occupiers has been reduced, and adequate steps have been taken (*e.g.*, but not confined to, notice under s.354, below) to prevent a subsequent increase in numbers, the court may revoke or vary the notice (subs. (4)): otherwise, the court does not have power to vary a notice, so that the court must either allow or dismiss the appeal.

Appeal must be brought, whether by person on whom the notice was served (*cf.* notes to s.352, above), or by an owner (see notes to s.398, below), lessee (see s.398, below—this includes a statutory tenant) or mortgagee, within 21 days or such longer period as the authority may in writing allow: subs. (1).

The possibility of appeal would suggest that it is the more appropriate course than application for judicial review: see *R.* v. *Hackney London Borough Council, ex parte Teepee Estates (1956) Ltd.* (1967) 19 P. & C.R. 87, D.C.). See also *Minford Properties Ltd.* v. *London Borough of Hammersmith* (1978) 247 E.G. 561, D.C.; but *cf. R.* v. *London Borough of Southwark, ex parte Lewis Levy Ltd.* (1983) 8 H.L.R. 1, Q.B.D. in which the court considered that if an issue is one which goes to *vires*, including whether or not a property is a house within the provisions, it is appropriately raised by way of application for judicial review.

Power to limit number of occupants of house

354.—(1) The local housing authority may, for the purpose of preventing the occurrence of, or remedying, a state of affairs calling for the service of a notice or further notice under section 352 (notice requiring execution of works to render house fit for number of occupants)—

(*a*) fix as a limit for the house what is in their opinion the highest number of individuals or households, or both, who should, having regard to the considerations set out in subsection (1) of that section, occupy the house in its existing condition, and

(*b*) give a direction applying that limit to the house.

(2) The authority may also exercise the powers conferred by subsection (1) in relation to a part of a house; and the authority shall have regard to the desirability of applying separate limits where different parts of a house are, or are likely to be, occupied by different persons.

(3) Not less than seven days before giving a direction under this section, the authority shall—

(*a*) serve on an owner of the house, and on every person who is to their knowledge a lessee of the house, notice of their intention to give the direction, and

(*b*) post such a notice in some position in the house where it is accessible to those living in the house,

and shall afford to any person on whom a notice is so served an opportunity of making representations regarding their proposal to give the direction.

(4) The authority shall within seven days from the giving of the direction—

(*a*) serve a copy of the direction on an owner of the house and on every person who is to their knowledge a lessee of the house, and

(*b*) post a copy of the direction in some position in the house where it is accessible to those living in the house.

(5) A direction may be given notwithstanding the existence of a previous direction laying down a higher maximum for the same house or part of a house.

(6) Where the local housing authority have in pursuance of section 352 served a notice specifying the number of individuals or households, or both, which in the opinion of the the authority the house could reasonably accommodate if the works specified in the notice were carried out, the authority may adopt that number in fixing a limit under subsection (1) as respects the house.

(7) The powers conferred by this section—

    (*a*) are exercisable whether or not a notice has been given under section 352, and

    (*b*) are without prejudice to the powers conferred by section 358 (overcrowding notices).

DEFINITIONS
"house": s.399.
"lessee": s.398.
"local housing authority": ss.1, 2.
"owner": s.398.

GENERAL NOTE
This section gives the authority power to issue "directions", for the specific purposes of remedying a state of affairs sufficient to justify a notice under s.352, above, *i.e.* inadequate amenities for number of occupiers, or of preventing such a state of affairs arising: subs. (1). The discretion, then, is very wide: see also subs. (7). The directions may relate to an H.M.O. as ordinarily defined, or as extended under s.352(6), above: see notes to s.345, above. The house must be in multiple occupation at the date when directions are given, although need not reach or exceed the number of occupants specified in the directions: *Simmons* v. *Pizzey* [1979] A.C. 37, H.L., *i.e.* the power can be used to pre-empt increased occupation.

Directions can apply a limit of households (see notes to s.345, above), or individuals, or both, who ought to occupy having regard to the same matters identified in s.352(1), above. Directions can be applied to part only of a house, and the authority are obliged to *consider* applying different limits to different parts: subs. (2). Directions may in substance replace earlier, higher limits: subs. (5). The number selected may expressly be referable to the number taken into account for the purposes of deciding whether or not to serve a notice under s.352, above.

The powers are intended to be used in support of s.352, *e.g.* "in order to forestall the necessity for works . . . where the number of people already living in a house is such that any increase would require the installation of additional facilities. Alternatively, a direction may follow the carrying out of works . . . where the local authority consider it necessary to ensure that the position does not again deteriorate. Where rehousing from a multi-occupied house has been carried out by the local authority it would be open to the authority to apply a direction so as to prevent any further overcrowding". (M.H.L.G. Circular 16/62, Memorandum, para. 46).

Before issuing directions, the authority are bound to serve notice of their intentions on owners and lessees (including a statutory tenant), as defined in s.398,below, and to post a copy in the house in a position which is accessible to those actually in occupation: subs. (3). Those *served* must be given an opportunity to make representations, of course before the directions are imposed. After directions are made, a copy must be served and posted in the same way: subs. (4). As to service of notices, see notes to s.617, below.

The effect of the directions is set out in s.355, below; directions may be varied or revoked on application under s.357. There is no direct appeal against directions, so that the proper course is to apply for variation or revocation under s.357, and appeal its refusal.

Effect of direction under s.354

355.—(1) Where a direction under section 354 is given (direction limiting number of occupants), it is the duty of—

    (*a*) the occupier for the time being of the house, or part of a house, to which the direction relates, and

    (*b*) any other person who is for the time being entitled or authorised to permit individuals to take up residence in that house or part,

not to permit the number of individuals or households occupying that house or part to which the direction relates to increase to a number above the limit specified in the direction or, if it is for the time being above that number, not to permit it to increase further.

(2) A person who knowingly fails to comply with the requirements imposed on him by subsection (1) commits a summary offence and is liable on conviction to a fine not exceeding level 4 on the standard scale.

DEFINITION
"house": s.399.

GENERAL NOTE
The directions under s.354, above, impose duties on two classes of person: (a) the occupier of the house or part of the house to which the directions relate—this means the occupier of the whole house, or the occupier of the whole part, not the individual occupiers of less than house or whole part; and (b) anyone else, *e.g.* an agent or manager, who is entitled or authorised to permit people to take up occupation of house, or part.

The duties are: (i) not to permit the number to increase beyond the levels set under the directions; or (ii) if the number is already in excess, not to permit it to increase further. It would seem that (i) is sufficiently widely drafted to include a case where the number in occupation is higher than the current limit, people leave so as to bring the number down, and then new occupiers replace them: there will be, or will be deemed to be, a period of time, even if so little as a scintilla of time or a notional period (*cf.* by analogy, *Church of England Building Society* v. *Piskor* [1954] 1 Ch. 553, C.A.), during which the occupation level drops, and is then "increased" (beyond limit). The second limb would not "prevent" breach of the duty because, for that moment in time, the level would not "for the time being" be above the level.

This construction is supported by M.H.L.G. Circular 16/62, Memorandum, para. 45: "Its purpose is to enable a limit to be set on the number of occupants who should live in a house having regard to the availability of the basic facilities and services specified . . . and to ensure that the number of occupants does not exceed that limit or that where it does there are no relettings when vacancies occur". The alternative construction would permit continued occupation at the same level, but this would seem to leave the directions virtually without any effect where—as they plainly can be (*cf.* s.352(2)(*b*), s.354(6), and the wording of subs. (1) in this section)—they set a lower limit than current occupation.

Knowingly failing to comply with either of these requirements is punishable by a fine of up to level 4 on the standard scale under s.37, Criminal Justice Act 1982, currently £1,000, by S.I. 1984 No. 447.

Authorities have power to obtain information under s.356, below, which may be used to establish whether or not an offence has been committed under this section. In addition, an authority may inspect to see if an offence under this section has been committed, without prior warning: see s.395, below.

Power to require information about occupation of house

356.—(1) The local housing authority may from time to time serve on the occupier of a house or part of a house in respect of which there is in force a direction under section 354 (direction limiting number of occupants) a notice requiring him to furnish them within seven days with a statement in writing giving all or any of the following particulars—

(*a*) the number of individuals who are, on a date specified in the notice, living in the house or part of the house, as the case may be;

(*b*) the number of families or households to which those individuals belong;

(*c*) the names of those individuals and of the heads of each of those families or households;

(*d*) the rooms used by those individuals and families or households respectively.

(2) An occupier who makes default in complying with the requirements of a notice under this section, or furnishes a statement which to his knowledge is false in a material particular, commits a summary offence and is liable on conviction to a fine not exceeding level 2 on the standard scale.

DEFINITIONS
"house": s.399.
"local housing authority": ss.1, 2.

GENERAL NOTE
This section permits the authority to require information about occupation. Notice may be served on the occupier of a house, or on part of a house, to which the directions relate (subs. (1)), *i.e.* the occupier of the whole house, or the whole part to which the directions relate—see notes to s.355, above. The notice must provide at least seven days for compliance: subs. (1).

Failure to comply, or providing a statement knowingly false in a material particular is punishable by a fine of up to level 2 on the standard scale under s.37, Criminal Justice Act 1982, currently £100, by S.I. 1984 No. 447.

Revocation or variation of direction under s.354

357.—(1) The local housing authority may, on the application of a person having an estate or interest in a house in respect of which a direction is in force under section 354 (direction limiting number of occupants), having regard to any works which have been executed in the house or any other change of circumstances, revoke the direction or vary it so as to allow more people to be accommodated in the house.

(2) If the authority refuse such an application or do not within 35 days from the making of such an application, or such further period as the applicant may in writing allow, notify the applicant of their decision, the applicant may appeal to the county court.

(3) On an appeal the court may revoke the direction or vary it in any manner in which it might have been varied by the authority.

DEFINITIONS
"house": s.399.
"local housing authority": ss.1, 2.
"person having estate or interest": s.398.

GENERAL NOTE
Anyone with an estate or interest (which includes a statutory tenant), as defined in s.398, below, may apply to the authority for variation of directions, or revocation, and the authority may vary or revoke the directions, having had regard to works executed, or any other change of circumstances: subs. (1).

If the authority refuse the application, or fail to notify their decision within 35 days or such further period as the applicant may in writing allow, the applicant can apply to the county court (subs. (2)), which enjoys the same powers as the authority to vary or evoke the directions: subs. (3). This procedure is the only means of "appealing" directions under s.354, above.

Overcrowding

Service of overcrowding notice

358.—(1) Where it appears to the local housing authority in the case of a house in multiple occupation—

(*a*) that an excessive number of persons is being accommodated on the premises, having regard to the rooms available, or

(*b*) that it is likely that an excessive number of persons will be accommodated on the premises, having regard to the rooms available,

they may serve an overcrowding notice on the occupier of the premises or on the person managing the premises, or on both.

(2) At least seven days before serving an overcrowding notice, the local housing authority shall—

(*a*) inform the occupier of the premises and any person appearing to them to be managing the premises, in writing, of their intention to do so, and

(*b*) ensure that, so far as is reasonably possible, every person living in the premises is informed of that intention;

and they shall afford those persons an opportunity of making representations regarding their proposal to serve the notice.

(3) If no appeal is brought under section 362, the overcrowding notice becomes operative at the end of the period of 21 days from the date of service, and is final and conclusive as to matters which could have been raised on such an appeal.

(4) A person who contravenes an overcrowding notice commits a summary offence and is liable on conviction to a fine not exceeding level 1 on the standard scale.

DEFINITIONS

"house": s.399.
"house in multiple occupation": s.345.
"local housing authority": ss.1, 2.
"person managing": s.398.

GENERAL NOTE

This procedure is separate from, and may be used additionally to, the directions procedure under s.354, above: see s.354(7)(*b*). Its genesis is different: whereas the provisions considered to date emanated from parts of the Housing Acts 1961–1969 specifically concerned with H.M.O.s, this series of sections (down to and including s.364, below) has its origin in Part IV, Housing Act 1957 (albeit as substituted by s.146, Housing Act 1980), *i.e.* the general overcrowding laws now to be found in Part X, above.

The provisions apply to H.M.O.s as conventionally defined, not as extended (*cf.* notes to s.345, above). A large house used as a holiday home for children has been held within the provision: see *Reed* v. *Hastings Borough Council* (1964) 62 L.G.R. 318, D.C., see also further notes to s.345, above. The provisions only continue to apply so long as the house remains in multiple occupation; where a notice had been served under s.360, below, but after the arrival of his family, the owner ceased to use the property as a lodging-house, no offence was committed by the way the house was occupied *by* his family—*Ali* v. *Wolkind* [1975] 1 W.L.R. 171, D.C.

The provisions apply when it appears to the authority *either* that there is already an excessive number of persons on the premises as a whole, *or* that it is likely that an excessive number will be on the premises as a whole, in each case of course having regard to the rooms available: subs. (1). Note, however, that the authority may deem a room unsuitable for use as sleeping accommodation: s.359(1)(*b*), below. The authority must specify the maximum number for each room: s.359(1)(*a*). The authority must make their choice between two classes of prohibition, not to permit an excessive number to sleep on the premises within s.360, or not to admit new residents within s.361—s.359(2), below.

Notice may be served either on the occupier of the premises (*i.e.* the occupier of the whole of the premises in question) or on the person managing the premises as defined in s.398, below, or on both: subs. (1). As to service of notices, see s.617, below. Service on the manager, rather than on a person having *both* control (see s.398, below) *and* management, is pursuant to Law Commission Recommendations (Cmnd. 9515), No. 18(i).

Notice of intention must be given at least seven days before service of the overcrowding notice itself, and must be served on the occupier of the premises and any person appearing to them to be a person managing the premises, *and* must be drawn to the attention of all the occupiers: subs. (2). All of these people must have the opportunity to make representations: *ibid.* The notice becomes operative after 21 days from service and unless there is an appeal under s.362, below, is "final and conclusive as to matters which could have been raised on such an appeal": subs. (3).

The *vires* of the authority in reaching their decision, *i.e.* on normal principles of administrative law (*cf.* notes to s.64, above), would seem to be available even on an appeal, for the effect of the overcrowding notice is to seek to take away a vested right to which the appellant would otherwise be entitled, *i.e.* to let to as many as he wishes: *cf. London Borough of Wandsworth* v. *Winder* [1985] A.C. 461, 17 H.L.R. 196, H.L. so that it would seem to be exempt from the principle in *Cocks* v. *Thanet District Council* [1983] A.C. 286, 6 H.L.R. 15, H.L., that judicial review is the only way to impeach a decision of the authority which is a precondition to the acquisition of a right.

This view would in this case support the approach in *Smith* v. *East Elloe Rural District Council* [1956] A.C. 736, H.L., applied in *R.* v. *Secretary of State for the Environment, ex parte Ostler* [1977] Q.B. 122, C.A., distinguishing *Anisminic Ltd.* v. *Foreign Compensation Commission* [1969] 2 A.C. 147, H.L., *i.e.* that the matter would be treated as "final and conclusive", so as to exclude application for judicial review, as distinct from the approach of greater willingness to intervene (or reluctance to see jurisdiction diminished), reflected in cases such as *Pearlman* v. *Keepers & Governors of Harrow School* [1979] Q.B. 56, C.A. and *Meade* v. *Haringey London Borough Council* [1979] 1 W.L.R. 637, C.A.

The last-mentioned case went so far as to suggest that if want of *vires* is the basis of challenge it is not even necessary to show that "domestic" remedies (*i.e.* an Act's own statutory procedures for redress or complaint including appeals) have been exhausted, contrary to the "usual" rule (see *Doe d. Bishop of Rochester* v. *Bridges* (1831) 1 B. & Ad. 847, *Pasmore* v. *Oswaldtwistle Urban District Council* [1898] A.C. 387, H.L., *Barraclough* v. *Brown* [1897] A.C. 615, H.L., *Watt* v. *Kesteven County Council* [1955] 1 Q.B. 408, *Wyatt* v. *London Borough of Hillingdon* (1978) 76 L.G.R. 727, *London Borough of Southwark* v. *Williams* [1971] Ch. 734, and *Kensington and Chelsea Royal London Borough Council* v. *Wells* (1974) 72 L.G.R. 289, C.A.).

Contravention of an overcrowding notice is punishable by a fine of up to level 1 on the standard scale under s.37, Criminal Justice Act 1982, currently £50, by S.I. 1984 No. 447. An authority may inspect to see if an offence under this section has been committed, without prior warning: see s.395, below.

As to appeals, see s.362, below; as to revocation and variation, see s.363, below; as to the authority's power to obtain information, see s.364, below.

Contents of overcrowding notice

359.—(1) An overcrowding notice shall state in relation to every room on the premises—

   (*a*) what in the opinion of the local housing authority is the maximum number of persons by whom the room is suitable to be occupied as sleeping accommodation at any one time, or

   (*b*) that the room is in their opinion unsuitable to be occupied as sleeping accommodation;

and the notice may specify special maxima applicable where some or all of the persons occupying the room are under such age as may be specified in the notice.

(2) An overcrowding notice shall contain either—

   (*a*) the requirement set out in section 360 (not to permit excessive number of persons to sleep on premises), or

   (*b*) the requirement set out in section 361 (not to admit new residents if number of persons is excessive);

and where the local housing authority have served on a person an overcrowding notice containing the latter requirement, they may at any time withdraw the notice and serve on him in its place an overcrowding notice containing the former requirement.

DEFINITIONS
"local housing authority": ss.1, 2.
"overcrowding notice": s.358.

GENERAL NOTE
This section contains two important provisions governing an overcrowding notice under s.358, above. First of all, the notice must specify in relation to every room what is the maximum number who may sleep in it, save in so far as the authority consider some rooms to be wholly unsuitable as sleeping accommodation: subs. (1). In so specifying, the authority can specify ages: *ibid.* Secondly, the notice has to opt between a requirement not to permit excessive numbers to sleep on the premises within s.360, and not to admit new residents within s.361—subs. (2). However, a requirement of the latter class may be withdrawn and replaced with a requirement of the former class, at any time: *ibid.*

As to appeals, see s.362, below; as to revocation and variation, see s.363, below; as to the authority's power to obtain information, see s.364, below.

Requirement as to overcrowding generally

360.—(1) The first requirement referred to in section 359(2) is that the person on whom the notice is served must refrain from knowingly—

(*a*) permitting a room to be occupied as sleeping accommodation otherwise than in accordance with the notice, or

(*b*) permitting persons to occupy the premises as sleeping accommodation in such numbers that it is not possible to avoid persons of opposite sexes who are not living together as husband and wife sleeping in the same room.

(2) For the purposes of subsection (1)(*b*)—

(*a*) children under the age of 12 shall be left out of account, and

(*b*) it shall be assumed that the persons occupying the premises as sleeping accommodation sleep only in rooms for which a maximum is set by the notice and that the maximum set for each room is not exceeded.

GENERAL NOTE

This is the first class of overcrowding notice: either it, or the second class under s.361, below, must be selected by the authority, but if the authority impose this requirement they cannot subsequently withdraw it and replace it with a requirement under s.362, below: s.359(2). Although there are alternative bases for serving an overcrowding notice in the first place, *i.e.* existing overcrowding or anticipated overcrowding (see s.358(1), above), the choice of requirement is not linked to the actual basis on which the authority have proceeded.

The distinction between the two requirements is that the requirement in this section is the more stringent, because an offence is committed by continuing overcrowding, even with current residents: *cf.* s.354, above, and s.361, below. It is obviously most suitable for use in connection with existing overcrowding under s.358(1)(*a*), above, but otherwise might be chosen when coupled to rehousing by the authority of some of the occupants, and the s.361 requirement when the authority are not prepared to rehouse.

Under this requirement, the person on whom the notice is served (see notes to s.358, above) must refrain from knowingly doing one of two things: *either* permitting a room to be occupied as sleeping accommodation other than in accordance with the notice, *or* permitting people to occupy the premises in such numbers that it is not possible to avoid people of the opposite sex not living together as husband and wife (see notes to s.113, above), sleeping in the same room: subs. (1). Those under the age of 12 are left entirely out of account: subs. (2)(*a*); *cf.* s.23, above, setting an age of eight in local authority lodging houses, s.325, above, setting 10 as the appropriate age for the purposes of Part X, and s.406, below, leaving the authority with a discretion to determine sexual separation in a common lodging-house.

The principal proposition is that the person served must not permit such *numbers* of people to occupy in such a way that it is *not possible to avoid* sexual overcrowding: *cf.* notes to s.325, above. The prohibition is not on *actual* such overcrowding. In working this out, however, (a) only sleeping rooms identified in the notice are to be taken into account, and (b) only to the maximum specified for each room in the notice: subs. (2)(*b*).

Requirement as to new residents

361.—(1) The second requirement referred to in section 359(2) is that the person on whom the notice is served must refrain from knowingly—

(*a*) permitting a room to be occupied by a new resident as sleeping accommodation otherwise than in accordance with the notice, or

(*b*) permitting a new resident to occupy any part of the premises as sleeping accommodation if that is not possible without persons of opposite sexes who are not living together as husband and wife sleeping in the same room;

and for this purpose "new resident" means a person who was not living in the premises immediately before the notice was served.

(2) For the purposes of subsection (1)(*b*)—

(*a*) children under the age of 12 shall be left out of account, and

(*b*) it shall be assumed that the persons occupying any part of the premises as sleeping accommodation sleep only in rooms for which a maximum is set by the notice and that the maximum set for each room is not exceeded.

GENERAL NOTE

The alternative to the more stringent requirement of s.360 (see notes thereto) is that which prohibits the creation or exacerbation of overcrowding with new residents. It may be used as a result of a decision to serve a notice at all based on anticipated rather than actual overcrowding under s.358, although it is not specifically tied to such a decision, and could be used when there is actual overcrowding but the authority do not wish to cause homelessness, *e.g.* of people without a priority need under Part III, above (see s.59). If the authority choose this requirement, however, it may at any time be withdrawn and replaced with a requirement under s.360, above.

The requirement prohibits the person on whom the notice was served under s.358 (see notes thereto, above) from doing one of two things: *either* permitting a room to be occupied by a new resident as sleeping accommodation other than in accordance with the notice, *or* admitting a new resident in such circumstances that occupation cannot continue without people of the opposite sex not living together as husband and wife sleeping in the same room (subs. (1))—*cf.* notes to s.360, above. The ancillary provisions as to ages and assumptions which applied under s.360 apply again here and, indeed, the only distinction is the introduction of the "new resident element", defined to mean someone not living in the premises immediately before the notice was served: subs. (1).

Appeal against overcrowding notice

362.—(1) A person aggrieved by an overcrowding notice may, within 21 days after the date of service of the notice, appeal to the county court, which may make such order either confirming, quashing or varying the notice as it thinks fit.

(2) If an appeal is brought the notice does not become operative until—

(*a*) a decision on the appeal confirming the order (with or without variation) is given and the period within which an appeal to the Court of Appeal may be brought expires without any such appeal having been brought, or

(*b*) if a further appeal to the Court of Appeal is brought, a decision on that appeal is given confirming the order (with or without variation);

and for this purpose the withdrawal of an appeal has the same effect as a decision confirming the notice or decision appealed against.

DEFINITION

"overcrowding notice": s.358.

GENERAL NOTE

Appeal against an overcrowding notice lies at the instance of any person aggrieved, which would seem to include an occupier who will suffer eviction as a result of a notice under s.360 (but not, of course, as a result of a notice under s.361); a potential occupier would not seem to be a person aggrieved by a notice under either section, because he has no existing right which is being affected, unless, of course and in this type of property unusually, there is a prior agreement already entered into. Consider *Ex parte Sidebotham* (1880) 14 Ch. D. 458, and *R.* v. *London Quarter Sessions, ex parte Westminster Corporation* [1951] 2 K.B. 508.

On an appeal, the court may make such order as it thinks fit, either confirming, quashing or varying the notice: these words seem wide enough to substitute a s.361 for a s.360 requirement, as an authority can do, but perhaps even to substitute a s.360 for a s.361 requirement, *i.e.* the more stringent for the less stringent, as even the authority cannot do: *cf.* s.357(3), above, and s.363(3), below—"the court may revoke . . . or vary . . . in any manner *in which it might have been varied by the authority*" (emphasis added).

If an appeal is brought within the 21 days permitted, the notice does not take effect until the decision of the county court, *plus* the time allowed for appeal to the Court of Appeal, and if further appeal is lodged until the decision of the higher court: subs. (2). Withdrawal of an appeal has the effect of a decision confirming the notice: *ibid.* Under R.S.C. Ord. 59, r.19, the period for appeal to the Court of Appeal is four weeks.

Revocation and variation of notice

363.—(1) The local housing authority may at any time, on the application of a person having an estate or interest in the premises—

(*a*) revoke an overcrowding notice, or

(*b*) vary it so as to allow more people to be accommodated on the premises.

(2) If the authority refuse such an application, or do not within 35 days from the making of the application (or such further period as the applicant may in writing allow) notify the applicant of their decision, the applicant may appeal to the county court.

(3) On an appeal the court may revoke the notice or vary it in any manner in which it might have been varied by the local housing authority.

DEFINITIONS

"local housing authority": ss.1, 2.

"overcrowding notice": s.358.

"person having estate or interest": s.398.

GENERAL NOTE

Any person with an estate or interest in the premises (which includes a statutory tenant), as defined in s.398, below, may apply for variation or revocation of an overcrowding notice under s.358, above: subs. (1). If the authority refuse, or fail to give a decision within 35 days or such longer period as the applicant may in writing permit, the applicant can appeal to the county court (subs. (2)), which may make such order revoking or varying the order as the local housing authority might have made: subs. (3).

Power to require information where notice in force

364.—(1) The local housing authority may from time to time serve on the occupier of premises in respect of which an overcrowding notice is in force a notice requiring him to furnish them within seven days with a statement in writing giving any of the following particulars—

(*a*) the number of individuals who are, on a date specified in the notice, occupying any part of the premises as sleeping accommodation;

(*b*) the number of families or households to which those individuals belong;

(*c*) the names of those individuals and of the heads of each of those families or households;

(*d*) the rooms used by those individuals and families or households respectively.

(2) A person who—

(*a*) knowingly fails to comply with the requirements of such a notice, or

(*b*) furnishes a statement which he knows to be false in a material particular,

commits a summary offence and is liable on conviction to a fine not exceeding level 2 on the standard scale.

DEFINITIONS

"local housing authority": ss.1, 2.

"overcrowding notice": s.385.

GENERAL NOTE

The occupier of the premises the subject of an overcrowding notice under s.358, above, may be served with a notice requiring information about occupation: subs. (1). The notice must allow seven days for reply: *ibid.* Knowingly failing to comply, or furnishing a statement false in a material particular, is punishable by a fine of up to level 2 on the standard scale under s.37, Criminal Justice Act 1982, currently £100, by S.I. 1984 No. 447: subs. (2).

Means of escape from fire

Means of escape from fire: general provisions as to exercise of powers

365.—(1) If it appears to the local housing authority that a house in multiple occupation is not provided with such means of escape from fire as the authority consider necessary, the authority may exercise such of their powers under—

    section 366 (power to require execution of works), and

    section 368 (power to secure that part of house not used for human habitation),

as appear to them to be most appropriate.

(2) The authority shall so exercise those powers if the house is of such description or is occupied in such manner as the Secretary of State may specify by order.

(3) Before serving a notice under section 366 or accepting an undertaking or making a closing order under section 368, the local housing authority shall consult with the fire authority concerned.

(4) An order under subsection (2)—

    (*a*) may make different provision with respect to different cases or descriptions of case, including different provision for different areas, and

    (*b*) shall be made by statutory instrument which shall be subject to annulment in pursuance of a resolution of either House of Parliament.

DEFINITIONS

    "house": s.399.

    "house in multiple occupation": s.345.

    "local housing authority": ss.1, 2.

GENERAL NOTE

This series of sections (to and including s.368, below), concerns most important powers—means of escape from fire. The powers are to require works (s.366) or to impose a closing order on part of a house (s.368). The powers are applicable in relation to H.M.O.s as conventionally defined only: see notes to s.345, above.

It may be said that unless H.M.O. includes purpose-built blocks of flats, the *only* provisions available are those now to be found in s.72, Building Act 1984, which applies only to buildings (including blocks of flats) which exceed two storeys in height, of which the floor of an upper storey is more than twenty feet from the surface of the street or ground—*i.e.* it excludes low-rise apartment buildings,—and only in respect of means of escape from such upper storeys, *i.e.* it does not include means of escape from the lower storeys. Section 72 provision does not include the power to make a partial closing order available under these provisions.

It has been held that means of escape from fire includes the provision of precautions such as a smoke screen at the top of a flight of stairs: *Horgan* v. *Birmingham Corporation* (1964) 63 L.G.R. 33, C.A. It has also been held that in considering what is necessary, the authority may have regard to the age and character—*i.e.* type—of people living in the house, and to whether there is supervision in the property: *Kingston-Upon-Hull District Council* v. *University of Hull* [1979] L.A.G. Bulletin 191, C.A. It is sometimes suggested by owners that "means of escape" does not include notices, but it may be noted that under the Building Act 1984, a distinction is drawn between means of escape *including* execution of works, and *other than* execution of works (s.72(3), Building Act 1984).

The powers are prima facie discretionary, but become mandatory if the Secretary of State orders. The Housing (Means of Escape from Fire in Houses in Multiple Occupation) Order 1981, S.I. 1981 No. 1576, retained in force by s.2, Housing (Consequential Provisions) Act 1985, require the application of the powers to houses of at least three storeys (excluding basements) and in which the combined floor area, including any staircases *and* basements, exceeds 500 square metres. It may be said that there is continuous pressure for greater application of the provisions, or the provision of wider powers, resulting not least from a series of recent tragedies in multiply-occupied properties.

Means of escape from fire: power to require execution of works

366.—(1) The local housing authority may serve a notice specifying—

(*a*) the works which in the opinion of the local housing authority are required as respects the house to provide the necessary means of escape from fire, or

(*b*) where the authority exercise their powers under section 368 to secure that part of the house is not used for human habitation, such work only as in their opinion is required to provide the means of escape from fire which will be necessary if that part is not so used.

(2) The notice may be served—

(*a*) on the person having control of the house, or

(*b*) on a person to whom the house is let at a rackrent or who as agent or trustee of a person to whom the house is so let, receives rents or other payments from tenants of parts of the house or lodgers in the house;

and the authority shall inform any other person who is to their knowledge an owner, lessee or mortgagee of the house of the fact that the notice has been served.

(3) The notice shall require the person on whom it is served to execute the works specified in the notice within such period, not being less than 21 days from the service of the notice, as may be so specified; but that period may from time to time be extended by written permission of the authority.

DEFINITIONS
"house": s.399.
"lessee": s.398.
"local housing authority": ss.1, 2.
"owner": s.398.
"person having control": s.398.

GENERAL NOTE
The first power—or duty in an appropriate case: see notes to s.365, above,—is to serve a notice requiring works, such as the authority consider necessary to provide means of escape from fire (see notes to s.365, above) to the whole house, or to that part of the house which will remain occupied if the authority exercise their power under s.368, below, to impose a partial closing order.

The notice is to be served (see notes to s.617, below) on the person having control (as defined in s.398, below) or on a person to whom the house is let at a rack-rent (see notes to s.398, below) or his agent or trustee in receipt of rents from tenants or lodgers (as to the distinction between which, see notes to s.93, above): subs. (2). The fact that the notice has been served is information which the authority must give to anyone who is to the knowledge of the authority an owner, mortgagee or lessee of the house: owner and lessee are defined in s.398, below, the latter to include a statutory tenant. An owner may ensure that he is informed of any action by prior service of a notice of his interest under s.378, below.

The notice should specify the works, not merely their effect: *cf. Canterbury City Council* v. *Bern* [1981] J.P.L. 749, D.C. The notice must provide at least 21 days for completion, which period may, however, subsequently be extended in writing by the authority: subs. (3). The express power to extend time was added pursuant to Law Commission Recommendations (Cmnd. 9515), No. 19. As to appeals, see s.367, below; as to consequences of non-compliance (both criminal and civil, *i.e.* works in default) see ss.375 *et seq.*, below.

Appeal against notice under s.366

367.—(1) A person on whom a notice is served under section 366 (means of escape from fire: notice requiring execution of works), or any other person who is an owner, lessee or mortgagee of the house to which the notice relates, may, within 21 days from the service of the notice, or such longer period as the local housing authority may in writing allow, appeal to the county court.

(2) The appeal may be on any of the following grounds—

(*a*) that the notice is not justified by the terms of that section;

(*b*) that there has been some informality, defect or error in, or in connection with, the notice;

(*c*) that the authority have refused unreasonably to approve the execution of alternative works, or that the works required by the notice to be executed are otherwise unreasonable in character or extent, or are unnecessary;

(*d*) that the time within which the works are to be executed is not reasonably sufficient for the purpose;

(*e*) that some other person is wholly or partly responsible for the state of affairs calling for the execution of the works, or will as the holder of an estate or interest in the premises derive a benefit from their execution, and ought to pay the whole or a part of the expenses of executing them.

(3) In so far as an appeal is based on the ground mentioned in subsection (2)(*b*), the court shall dismiss the appeal if it is satisfied that the informality, defect or error was not a material one.

(4) Where the grounds on which an appeal is brought include the ground mentioned in subsection (2)(*e*), the court, if satisfied that the other person referred to in the notice of appeal has had proper notice of the appeal, may on the hearing of the appeal make such order as it thinks fit with respect to the payment to be made by that other person to the appellant or, where the works are executed by the local housing authority, to the authority.

DEFINITIONS

"lessee": s.398.

"local housing authority": ss.1, 2.

"owner": s.398.

GENERAL NOTE

This section provides an appeal procedure analogous to that under s.353, above—see notes thereto. In *Kingston-Upon-Hull City Council* v. *University of Hull* [1979] L.A.G. Bulletin 191, C.A. (see notes to s.365, above), it was held proper to balance requirements, and their cost, against benefit.

Means of escape from fire: power to secure that part of house not used for human habitation

368.—(1) If it appears to the local housing authority that the means of escape from fire would be adequate if part of the house were not used for human habitation, they may secure that that part is not so used.

(2) For that purpose, the authority may, if after consultation with any owner or mortgagee they think fit to do so, accept an undertaking from him that that part will not be used for human habitation without the permission of the authority.

(3) A person who, knowing that such an undertaking has been accepted—

(*a*) uses the part of the house to which the undertaking relates in contravention of the undertaking, or

(*b*) permits that part of the house to be so used,

commits a summary offence and is liable on conviction to a fine not exceeding level 5 on the standard scale; and if he so uses it or permits it to be so used after conviction, he commits a further summary offence and is liable on conviction to a fine not exceeding £5 for every day or part of a day on which he so uses it or permits it to be so used.

(4) If the local housing authority do not accept an undertaking under subsection (2) with respect to a part of a house, or where they have

accepted such an undertaking and that part of the house is at any time used in contravention of the undertaking, the authority may make a closing order with respect to that part of the house.

(5) The provisions of Part IX apply to a closing order under subsection (4) as they apply to a closing order made under section 265 by virtue of section 266(*a*) (closing order in respect of part of building unfit for human habitation), but with the modification that the ground on which the authority are required to determine the order under section 278(1) (premises rendered fit) shall be that the authority are satisfied that the means of escape from fire with which the house is provided is adequate (owing to a change of circumstances) and will remain adequate if the part of the house with respect to which the order was made is again used for human habitation.

(6) Nothing in the Rent Acts prevents possession being obtained of a part of a house which in accordance with an undertaking in pursuance of this section cannot for the time being be used for human habitation.

DEFINITIONS
  "house": s.399.
  "local housing authority": ss.1, 2.
  "owner": s.398.
  "Rent Acts": s.622.

GENERAL NOTE
An ancillary power to the power (or in some cases duty—see notes to s.365, above) to serve a notice requiring the provision of means of escape from fire, is the power conferred by this section to make a part closing order, so that the means of escape from fire either already are adequate, or those required by a notice under s.366 would be. The authority may take action under this section, without taking action under s.366.

The powers are analogous to the closing order provisions of Part IX: see notes to s.265, above. In particular, note that while Rent Act protection is lost (subs. (6)), an occupier displaced by a closing order or undertaking under this section will normally be entitled to rehousing under s.39, and home loss payment under s.29 and/or disturbance payment under s.37, Land Compensation Act 1973. The removal of protection of the Rent Acts means (s.622, below) protection under the Rent Act 1977, or the Rent (Agriculture) Act 1976: the latter was added pursuant to Law Commission Recommendations (Cmnd. 9515), No. 14.

An undertaking can only be accepted under this section after consultation (as to the meaning of which, see notes to s.420(4), below) with any owner (as defined in s.398) and mortgagee of the property: subs. (2). Subs. (5) incorporates the provisions of Part IX in their entirety (save as adapted), which means that the time-and-place procedure in s.264 must be followed. It is hard to see that much less in any event comply either with the consultation requirement, or indeed natural justice.

The incorporation of Part IX means that there is a right of appeal under s.269, and the criminal penalty for using premises in contravention of a closing order under s.277 will apply. The provision for determination of a closing order under s.278 applies as adapted by subs. (5), to replace fitness with adequacy of means of escape from fire (both existing adequacy, and future adequacy).

Subs. (3) is analogous to s.264(6), above. The offence is punishable by a fine of up to level 5 on the standard scale under s.37, Criminal Justice Act 1982, currently £2,000, by S.I. 1984 No. 447. An authority may inspect to see if an offence under this section has been committed, without prior warning: see s.395, below.

The authority may substitute closing order for undertaking on breach of the undertaking: subs. (4).

Standards of management

The management code

369.—(1) The Secretary of State may, with a view to providing a code for the management of houses in multiple occupation, by regulations make provision for ensuring that the person managing a house in multiple occupation observes proper standards of management.

(2) The regulations may, in particular, require the person managing the house to ensure the repair, maintenance, cleansing and good order of—
> all means of water supply and drainage in the house,
> kitchens, bathrooms and water closets in common use,
> sinks and wash-basins in common use,
> common staircases, corridors and passage ways, and
> outbuildings, yards and gardens in common use,

and to make satisfactory arrangements for the disposal of refuse and litter from the house.

(3) The regulations may—

(a) make different provision for different types of house;

(b) provide for keeping a register of the names and addresses of those who are persons managing houses;

(c) impose duties on persons who have an estate or interest in a house or part of a house to which the regulations apply as to the giving of information to the local housing authority, and in particular make it the duty of a person who acquires or ceases to hold an estate or interest in the house to notify the authority;

(d) impose duties on persons who live in the house for the purpose of ensuring that the person managing the house can effectively carry out the duties imposed on him by the regulations;

(e) authorise the local housing authority to obtain information as to the number of individuals or households accommodated in the house;

(f) make it the duty of the person managing the house to cause a copy of the order under section 370 applying the regulations to the house, and of the regulations, to be displayed in a suitable position in the house;

(g) contain such other incidental and supplementary provisions as may appear to the Secretary of State to be expedient.

(4) Regulations under this section may vary or replace for the purposes of this section and of the regulations made under it the definition given in section 398 of the "person managing" a house.

(5) A person who knowingly contravenes or without reasonable excuse fails to comply with a regulation under this section as applied under section 370 in relation to a house commits a summary offence and is liable on conviction to a fine not exceeding level 3 on the standard scale.

(6) Regulations under this section shall be made by statutory instrument which shall be subject to annulment in pursuance of a resolution of either House of Parliament.

DEFINITIONS
"house": s.399.
"house in multiple occupation": ss.345, 374.
"local housing authority": ss.1, 2.
"person having estate or interest": s.398.
"person managing": s.398.

GENERAL NOTE
This section introduces the power to make a management order, *i.e.* to apply the provisions of the code of management determined by the Secretary of State, to an H.M.O. (as to which, see notes to s.345, above). This series of provisions (down to and including s.373) is applied to additional properties by s.374, below: see also notes to s.345, above. The provisions are not exclusive of the use of other powers (save that a control order will bring the application of the provisions to an end—see s.381(4), below).

Use by local authority is governed by s.370, below, which also requires reconsideration on application by someone with an estate or interest in the property; appeal against the making of an order, or failure to revoke, is governed by s.371, below (and is the proper approach, rather than judicial review—see *R.* v. *Hackney London Borough Council, ex parte Teepee Estates* (1956) Ltd. (1967) 19 P. & C.R. 87, D.C.) See also *Minford Properties Ltd.* v.

London Borough of Hammersmith (1978) 247 E.G. 561, D.C.; but *cf. R.* v. *London Borough of Southwark, ex parte Lewis Levy Ltd.* (1983) 8 H.L.R. 1, Q.B.D. in which the court considered that if an issue is one which goes to *vires*, including whether or not a property is a house within the provisions, it is appropriately raised by way of application for judicial review). Under s.372, below, the authority can serve a notice requiring works to an H.M.O. to which the management code has been applied, appeal against which is governed by s.373, below. Ancillary powers of entry are to be found in ss.395, *et seq.*, below.

This section is concerned with the content of the management code, and penalty for non-compliance. Subs. (2) identifies the principal objects of the code, and subs. (3) permits the inclusion of related obligations—as to the keeping of a register of "managers" (by the local housing authority), requiring those with an estate or interest to provide information to the authority, imposing duties on residents to enable the manager to carry out his duties, authorising the authority to obtain information, for display of the regulations, and the order under s.370 which applies them to the property, and otherwise as appears expedient to the Secretary of State.

"Managers" are as defined in s.398, below; persons having an estate or interest (which includes statutory tenancy) in *ibid.*

The Secretary of State has made the Housing (Management of Houses in Multiple Occupation) Regulations 1962, S.I. 1962 No. 668, retained in force by s.2, Housing (Consequential Provisions) Act 1985. Their contents are a mixture of the statutory requirement of this section, and discretion. They are extremely detailed. Their provisions include:

(1) Duties on non-resident managers to ensure proper discharge of the requirements of the Regulations;

(2) Further duties in relation to the discharge of the requirements imposed on trustee-managers or agent-managers (*cf.* notes to s.398, below);

(3) Requirements in relation to the repair, clean condition, good order and continuity of water supplies and drainage;

(4) Requirements in relation to the repair, working order and continuity of gas and electricity supplies and installations for their use, lighting, space and water heating, in the parts of the house in common use;

(5) Repair, condition and cleanliness of certain common rooms and parts;

(6) Requirements in relation to the repair and condition of rooms when let, or when the regulations are first applied to the house, and for their maintenance;

(7) Requiring windows and other means of ventilation to be put and kept in good order and repair;

(8) Repair, good order, and freedom from obstruction of means of escape from fire, and display of notices related to fire escapes such as the authority may require;

(9) Repair, condition and order of outbuildings, yards, areas and forecourts in common use;

(10) Keeping the garden in a tidy condition;

(11) Provision for refuse and litter;

(12) General precautions to protect occupiers from injury as a result of structural conditions in the house;

(13) Display of information, including the management order, in a suitable position in the house;

(14) Provision of information by managers to the authority;

(15) Requiring the co-operation of occupiers;

(16) Requiring the authority to keep a register of managers of H.M.O.s to which the regulations have been applied.

Subs. (5)

There are two limbs to the offence: (a) knowingly contravening the regulations, and (b) without reasonable excuse failing to comply. Under the second limb, there is no requirement of knowledge of failure on the part of the defendant, although the burden of proof (under either limb) lies on the prosecution, so that, under the second limb, they must prove absence of reasonable excuse: *City of Westminster* v. *Mavroghenis* [1983] 11 H.L.R. 56, D.C. An authority may inspect to see if an offence under this section has been committed, without prior warning: see s.395, below.

Application of management code to particular houses

370.—(1) If it appears to the local housing authority that a house in multiple occupation is in an unsatisfactory state in consequence of failure to maintain proper standards of management and, accordingly, that it is necessary that the regulations made under section 369 should apply to the house, the authority may by order direct that those regulations shall so apply.

(2) The order comes into force when it is made.

(3) The local housing authority shall within seven days from the making of the order—

(*a*) serve a copy of it on an owner of the house and on every person who is to the knowledge of the authority a lessee of the house, and

(*b*) post a copy of it in some position in the house where it is accessible to those living in the house.

(4) The local housing authority may at any time revoke the order on the application of a person having an estate or interest in the house.

(5) An order under this section is a local land charge.

DEFINITIONS
"house": s.399.
"house in multiple occupation": s.345, 374.
"lessee": s.398.
"local housing authority": ss.1, 2.
"owner": s.398.
"person having estate or interest": s.398.

GENERAL NOTE
This section governs application of the management code or regulations under s.369, above. The precondition is that it must appear to the authority that an H.M.O. (see notes to s.345, above), is in an unsatisfactory state as a result of failure to maintain proper standards of management, in respect of which decision, the substance of the regulations themselves will clearly be a relevant consideration, and provide useful guidance (see also s.372(1)(*b*), below). As a result of these conditions, it must appear necessary to apply the regulations.

An order comes into force as soon as it is made: there is no requirement for prior notification, or discussion with either the owner, or manager, or even the occupiers. This aspect may be compared with s.379, below, similarly applying a control order without forewarning. A former requirement of notice was repealed by the Housing Act 1969. The purpose is obvious: if forewarning is given of action, there is a real risk of either pre-emptive evictions, *i.e.* so that the property is no longer in multiple occupation, or retaliatory evictions, *i.e.* because an individual is believed to have been responsible by complaint to the authority.

The authority do, however, have powers of entry under s.395, below, in order to ascertain whether any of the powers of this Part, including the management powers, ought to be exercised, and an inspection will be necessary in order to fulfil the preconditions of subs. (1).

Within seven days of making the order, the authority have to serve a copy of it on every owner and lessee of the house (as to each of which, see s.398, below—lessee includes statutory tenant), and post a copy in some position in the house where it is accessible to those living in it: subs. (3). Anyone with an estate or interest (see s.398, below, again including a statutory tenant), may apply for the order to be revoked: subs. (4). Alternatively, he may appeal to the county court against the making of the order: s.371(1), below. He may also appeal a refusal to revoke under s.371(1).

Appeal is the correct redress, rather than judicial review: *R.* v. *Hackney London Borough Council, ex parte Teepee Estates (1956) Ltd.* (1967) 19 P. & C.R. 87, D.C. See also *Minford Properties Ltd.* v. *London Borough of Hammersmith* (1978) 247 E.G. 561, D.C.; but *cf. R.* v. *London Borough of Southwark, ex parte Lewis Levy Ltd.* (1983) 8 H.L.R. 1, Q.B.D. in which the court considered that if an issue is one which goes to *vires*, including whether or not a property is a house within the provisions, it is appropriately raised by way of application for judicial review.

As to service, see notes to s.617, below.

Appeal against making of, or failure to revoke, order under s.370

371.—(1) A person who is served with a copy of an order under section 370 (order applying management code to house), and any other person who is a lessee of the house in respect of which the order is made, may, within 21 days from the service of the notice, or such longer period as the local housing authority may in writing allow, appeal to the county court on the ground that the making of the order was unnecessary.

(2) On the appeal the court shall take into account the state of the house at the time of the making of the order as well as at the time the appeal was instituted and shall disregard any improvement in the state of the house between those times unless the court is satisfied that effective steps have been taken to ensure that the house will in future be kept in a satisfactory state.

(3) If the court allows the appeal it shall revoke the order, but without prejudice to the operation of the order prior to its revocation or to the making of a further order.

(4) If the local housing authority—

   (*a*) refuse an application for the revocation of an order under section 370, or

   (*b*) do not within 35 days from the making of such an application, or such further period as the applicant may in writing allow, notify the applicant of their decision,

the applicant may appeal to the county court which may, if of opinion that there has been a substantial change in the circumstances since the making of the order, and that it is in other respects just to do so, revoke the order.

DEFINITIONS
   "house": s.399.
   "lessee": s.398.
   "local housing authority": ss.1, 2.
   "management code": s.369.

GENERAL NOTE
   Anyone served with a copy of the notice, or any lessee, has a right of appeal against the making of the order: subs. (1). The limitation to persons served excludes individual occupiers who merely benefited from the posting of the notice: *cf.* s.362, above—"person aggrieved"; see also s.353, which limits appeal to persons served and others with a legal interest, as does this section. Appeal must be brought within 21 days, or such longer period as the authority in writing allow: subs. (1). Appeal lies now to the county court, rather than the magistrates' court, pursuant to Law Commission Recommendations (Cmnd. 9515), No. 9.

   The ground of the appeal is that it was not necessary to make the order applying the management code: *ibid.* On such an appeal, the court is to take into account the state of the house at the time the order was made *and* at the date of issue of the appeal, but is to disregard improvements between those dates (and, of course, thereafter): subs. (2). The court need not disregard the improvements if satisfied that effective steps have been taken to ensure that the house will be kept in a satisfactory state in the future: *ibid.* Revocation of the order on appeal is without prejudice to the operation of the order before revocation, and without prejudice to the making of a further order: subs. (3).

   Appeal also lies to the county court (again pursuant to Law Commission Recommendation No. 9), against refusal to allow a revocation application under s.371(4), above. The appeal arises on refusal or after 35 days or such longer period as the applicant may in writing allow, if the authority fail to give a decision: subs. (4). The county court may allow the appeal if it considers that there has been a substantial change of circumstances since the order was made, and that it is just to do so in other respects: *ibid.*

Power to require execution of works to remedy neglect of management

372.—(1) If in the opinion of the local housing authority the condition of a house to which an order under section 370 applies (order applying management code) is defective in consequence of—

   (*a*) neglect to comply with the requirements imposed by regulations under section 369 (regulations prescribing management code), or

   (*b*) in respect of a period falling wholly or partly before the regulations

applied to the house, neglect to comply with standards corresponding to the requirements imposed by the regulations,
the authority may serve on the person managing the house a notice
specifying the works which, in the opinion of the authority, are required
to make good the neglect.

(2) If it is not practicable after reasonable inquiry to ascertain the name
or address of the person managing the house, the notice may be served by
addressing it to him by the description of "manager of the house" (naming
the house to which it relates) and delivering it to some person on the
premises.

(3) The notice shall require the person on whom it is served to execute
the works specified in the notice within such period, not less than 21 days
from the service of the notice, as may be so specified; but that period may
from time to time be extended by written permission of the authority.

(4) Where the authority serve a notice under this section on the person
managing a house, they shall inform any other person who is to their
knowledge an owner, lessee or mortgagee of the house of the fact that the
notice has been served.

(5) References in this section to the person managing a house have the
same meaning as in section 369 (and accordingly are subject to amendment
by regulations under that section).

DEFINITIONS
"house": s.399.
"lessee": s.398.
"local housing authority": ss.1, 2.
"management code": s.369.
"owner": s.398.
"person managing": s.369.

GENERAL NOTE
The management code requires standards to be achieved and maintained: see notes to
s.369, above. However, the defects which led to the making of the order applying the code
to an H.M.O. may be such that they cannot be achieved by the mere requirements of the
regulations themselves; alternatively, the requirements of the regulations as to conditions
may not be complied with. In *either* case, the authority may serve a works notice under this
section: subs. (1). The substantive content of the works is such in effect as will bring the
property up to the standards of the management code. A notice should specify the works,
not merely their effect: *cf. Canterbury City Council* v. *Bern* [1981] J.P.L. 749, D.C.
The notice is to be served (as to which, see notes to s.617, below), on the person managing
the house who is, for this purpose, the manager as defined by the management regulations
under s.369, above, currently the Housing (Management of Houses in Multiple Occupation)
Regulations 1962, S.I. 1962 No. 668, retained in force by s.2, Housing (Consequential
Provisions) Act 1985: subs. (5). The notice must allow at least 21 days for compliance, but
may subsequently be extended in writing by the authority; subs. (3). The consequences of
non-compliance (criminal and civil, *i.e.* works in default) are dealt with in ss.375, *et seq.*,
below.
The authority must also tell any owner, lessee (each as defined in s.398, below, and
including a statutory tenant), or mortgagee of the fact that the notice has been served: subs.
(4). An owner may protect his interests by registering his details with the authority under
s.378. below.
Appeal against the notice is under s.373, below.

Appeal against notice under s.372

373.—(1) A person on whom a notice is served under section 372
(notice requiring works to remedy neglect of management), or any other
person who is an owner, lessee or mortgagee of the house to which the
notice relates, may, within 21 days from the service of the notice, or such
longer period as the local housing authority may in writing allow, appeal
to the county court.

(2) The appeal may be on any of the following grounds—

(*a*) that the condition of the house did not justify the local housing authority in requiring the execution of the works specified in the notice;

(*b*) that there has been some informality, defect or error in, or in connection with, the notice;

(*c*) that the authority have refused unreasonably to approve the execution of alternative works, or that the works required by the notice to be executed are otherwise unreasonable in character or extent, or are unnecessary;

(*d*) that the time within which the works are to be executed is not reasonably sufficient for the purpose;

(*e*) that some other person is wholly or partly responsible for the state of affairs calling for the execution of the works, or will as the holder of an estate or interest in the premises derive a benefit from their execution and ought to pay the whole or a part of the expenses of executing them.

(3) In so far as an appeal is based on the ground mentioned in subsection (2)(*b*), the court shall dismiss the appeal if it is satisfied that the informality, defect or error was not a material one.

(4) Where the grounds on which an appeal is brought include the ground specified in subsection (2)(*e*), the appellant shall serve a copy of his notice of appeal on each other person referred to, and on the hearing of the appeal the court may make such order as it thinks fit with respect to the payment to be made by any such other person to the appellant or, where the works are executed by the local housing authority, to the authority.

DEFINITIONS
  "house": s.399.
  "lessee": s.398.
  "local housing authority": ss.1, 2.
  "owner": s.398.
  "person having estate or interest": s.398.

GENERAL NOTE
  This makes identical provision to that in ss.353 and 367, above, see notes to the former. The appeal now lies to the county court, rather than the magistrates' court, pursuant to Law Commission Recommendations (Cmnd. 9515), No. 9.

Application of ss.369 to 373 to buildings other than houses

374.—(1) The provisions of section 369 to 373 (provisions for remedying inadequate management) apply to—

(*a*) a building which is not a house but comprises separate dwellings two or more of which are occupied by persons who do not form a single household,

(*b*) a building which is not a house but comprises separate dwellings two or more of which do not have a sanitary convenience and personal washing facilities accessible only to those living in the dwelling, and

(*c*) a tenement block in which all or any of the flats are without one or more of the standard amenities,

as they apply to a house in multiple occupation.

(2) In this section—

  "tenement block" means a building or a part of a building which was constructed in the form of, and consists of, two or more flats, that is to say, separate sets of premises, whether or not on the same floor, constructed for use for the purpose of a dwelling and forming part of a building from some other part of which they are divided horizontally; and

"the standard amenities" has the same meaning as in Part XV (improvement grants, &c.).

(3) If the local housing authority make an order under section 370 (order applying management code) as respects a building or tenement block by virtue of this section at a time when another such order is in force as respects one of the dwellings in the building or block, they shall revoke the other order.

DEFINITIONS
"house": s.399.
"local housing authority": ss.1, 2.
"standard amenities": s.508.

GENERAL NOTE
This section adds to the definition of H.M.O. for the purposes of the management order provisions of ss.369–373, above. For this purpose, personal washing facilities can include a supply of hot water: *McPhail* v. *Islington London Borough Council* [1970] 2 Q.B. 197. The standard amenities are: fixed bath or shower, hot and cold water supply at fixed bath or shower, wash-hand basin, hot and cold water supply at wash-hand basin, sink, hot and cold water supply at sink, and a water closet: see s.508, below.

The first two limbs of the addition are identical to those to be found in s.352(6), above. These limbs were considered in *Okereke* v. *Brent London Borough Council* [1967] 1 Q.B. 42, C.A. in which it was held that they were intended to widen the scope of powers, and possibly to have been intended to undo the effect of *Weatheritt* v. *Cantlay* [1901] 2 K.B. 285, D.C., in which it had been held that analogous earlier provisions did not apply to blocks of flats.

As to the third limb, the origin of the different terminology is to be found in Part II, Housing Act 1964, which contained compulsory improvement provisions preceding those now to be found in Part VII, above. Those provisions, and the provisions in Part VII, dealt in "dwellings". Special provision was made for "dwellings" in "tenement blocks" as defined in s.44 of the 1964 Act.

Part IV of the 1964 Act concerned H.M.O.s. The management powers were introduced by the Housing Act 1961, and were within s.21 thereof (now s.352(6), above). However, their application was limited: "Section 69 extends the applicability to tenement blocks of the management powers in sections 12 to 14 of the Act of 1961. Section 21 of the Act of 1961 applied these powers to such blocks if, *inter alia*, washing or sanitary facilities were shared between dwellings. Since there have come to light cases in which the supervision of matters within the management code continued to be necessary even after the installation of separate washing and sanitary facilities, the management code is now to continue applicable to tenement blocks in which dwellings lacked standard amenities (as defined for improvement grant purposes) on November 13, 1963" (M.H.L.G. Circular 51/64, App. 1, para. 7).

The means of the extension was to adopt the more modern term "tenement block" to be found in Part II of the 1964 Act (and not—contrary to the impression given by this quote—in the 1961 Act). It may be seen, therefore, that the difference in wording between s.352(6) and s.374 is historical: the latter was substantively intended to apply to the same class of property as the former, but by use of the then more modern description of the specific properties.

As to household, see also notes to s.345, above.

Subs. (3) governs the situation which arises when by virtue of this section the management code is applied to a block, when the management code has already been applied to one of the units in it: the earlier order is to be revoked.

Supplementary provisions as to works notices

Carrying out of works by local housing authority

375.—(1) If a notice under section 352, 366 or 372 (notices requiring the execution of works) is not complied with, the local housing authority may themselves do the work required to be done by the notice.

(2) Compliance with a notice means the completion of the works specified in the notice within the period for compliance, which is—

(a) if no appeal is brought against the notice, the period specified in the notice with any extension duly permitted by the local housing authority;

(b) if an appeal is brought against the notice, and the notice is confirmed in whole or in part on the appeal, the period of 28 days from the final determination of the appeal or such longer period as the court in determining the appeal may fix.

(3) If, before the expiration of the period for compliance with the notice, the person on whom the notice was served notifies the local housing authority that he is not able to do the work in question, the authority may, if they think fit, themselves do the work forthwith.

(4) The provisions of Schedule 10 apply with respect to the recovery by the local housing authority of expenses incurred by them under this section.

DEFINITIONS
   "final determination": s.399.
   "local housing authority": ss.1, 2.

GENERAL NOTE
   This section permits the authority to do works in default in relation to an amenities notice under s.352, a means of escape notice under s.366, or a management works notice under s.372, in the event of non-compliance: subs. (1). For this purpose, non-compliance means completion within the period specified by the notice (as possibly extended—see notes to ss.352, 366 and s.372, above), or within 28 days from the final determination of an appeal, or such longer period as the court on appeal may allow: subs. (2). Final determination includes withdrawal, and withdrawal takes effect as a decision dismissing the appeal: s.399, below.
   The authority's power to execute works in default will arise at an earlier time if the person served notifies them that he is unable to comply: subs. (3). If the authority reply stating that they do intend to carry out the works in default, the person served is no longer liable for the offence of non-compliance under s.376, below: see s.376(4).
   The authority have a discretion whether or not to exercise the power to do works in default, and must consider each case individually on its merits: *cf. Elliott* v. *Brighton Borough Council* (1980) 258 E.G. 441, C.A., even though they may lawfully adopt a policy of intending to do works in default, subject to consideration of application of policy in each case: see, *e.g. British Oxygen Co. Ltd.* v. *Board of Trade* [1971] A.C. 610, H.L., *Re Betts* [1983] 2 A.C. 613, 10 H.L.R. 97, H.L., *Att.-Gen.* v. *L.B. Wandsworth, ex rel. Tilley* [1981] 1 W.L.R. 854, C.A.
   The provisions of Sched. 10, considered in the notes to s.193, above, govern recovery of expenses incurred by the authority in executing works in default: subs. (4). A magistrates' court can order an owner or occupier not to prevent the authority carrying out works in default, under s.377, below.
   Note that non-compliance may also be a criminal offence under s.376, below.

Penalty for failure to execute works

376.—(1) A person on whom a notice has been served under section 352, 366 or 372 (notices requiring the execution of works) who wilfully fails to comply with the notice commits a summary offence and is liable on conviction to a fine not exceeding level 4 on the standard scale.

(2) The obligation to execute the works specified in the notice continues notwithstanding that the period for compliance has expired; and a person who wilfully fails to comply with that obligation, after being convicted of an offence in relation to the notice under subsection (1) or this subsection, commits a further summary offence and is liable on conviction to a fine not exceeding level 4 on the standard scale.

(3) References in this section to compliance with a notice and to the period for compliance shall be construed in accordance with section 375(2).

(4) No liability arises under subsection (1) if the local housing authority, on being notified in accordance with section 375(3) that the person on whom the notice was served is not able to do the work in question, serve notice that they propose to do the work and relieve him from liability under subsection (1).

(5) The provisions of this section are without prejudice to the exercise by the local housing authority of their power under section 375 to carry out the works themselves.

DEFINITION

"local housing authority": ss.1, 2.

GENERAL NOTE

It is an offence, punishable by a fine of up to level 4 on the standard scale under s.37, Criminal Justice Act 1982, currently £1,000, by S.I. 1984 No. 447, to fail to comply with a notice under s.352 (amenities), s.366 (means of escape from fire) or s.372 (management works): see also s.375, above, for the authority's power to execute works in default (which is unaffected by this section: subs. (5)). Compliance has the same meaning as under s.375, above. The obligation to comply is not discharged by the conviction, and a continuation of the failure to comply constitutes a further offence: subs. (2). However, if the authority serve notice that they propose to do the works in default, following a notice from the person served that he is unable to comply under s.375(3), above, no offence is committed: subs. (4).

An authority may inspect to see if an offence under this section has been committed, without prior warning: see s.395, below.

Powers of court to facilitate execution of works, &c.

377.—(1) Where—

(a) a person is required by a notice under section 352, 366 or 372 to execute works and

(b) another person having an estate or interest in the premises unreasonably refuses to give a consent required to enable the works to be executed,

the person required to execute the works may apply to the county court and the court may give the necessary consent in place of that other person.

(2) If a person, after receiving notice of the intended action—

(a) being the occupier of premises, prevents the owner or his officers, agents, servants or workmen, from carrying into effect with respect to the premises any of the preceding provisions of this Part, or

(b) being the owner or occupier of premises, prevents an officer, agent, servant or workman of the local housing authority from so doing,

a magistrates' court may order him to permit to be done on the premises all things requisite for carrying into effect those provisions.

(3) A person who fails to comply with an order of the court under subsection (2) commits a summary offence and is liable on conviction to a fine not exceeding level 3 on the standard scale; and if the failure continues, he commits a further summary offence and is liable on conviction to a fine not exceeding £20 for every day or part of a day during which the failure continues.

DEFINITIONS

"local housing authority": ss.1, 2.

"owner": s.398.

"person having estate or interest": s.398.

GENERAL NOTE

Where one person has been served with a works notice under s.352 (amenities), s.366 (means of escape from fire) or s.372 (management works), and someone else with an estate or interest (including a statutory tenant—see s.398, below) unreasonably refuses a consent needed for the works to be carried out, the person served may apply for an order from the county court: subs. (1).

In addition, a *magistrates'* court may order an occupier not to prevent an *owner* (see s.398, below), or his representatives, from carrying out works under these provisions, or can order an *owner or occupier* not to prevent the authority from carrying out works, *i.e.* in default under s.375, above: subs. (2). Failure to comply with a magistrate's order under this section is punishable by a fine of up to level 3 on the standard scale under s.37, Criminal Justice Act 1982, currently £400, by S.I. 1984 No. 447, with an additional fine of up to £20 per day for continuation of the failure after conviction: subs. (3).

Provisions for protection of owners

378.—(1) If an owner of premises who is not the person in receipt of the rents and profits gives notice to the local housing authority of his interest in the premises, the authority shall give to him notice of any proceedings taken by them in relation to the premises under any of the preceding provisions of this Part.

(2) Nothing in the preceding provisions of this Part prejudices or interferes with the rights or remedies of an owner for breach, non-observance or non-performance of a covenant or contract entered into by a lessee in reference to premises—

    (*a*) in respect of which a notice requiring the execution of works is served by the local housing authority under 352, 366 or 372, or

    (*b*) as respects which an order under section 370 (order applying management code) is for the time being in force;

and if an owner is obliged to take possession of premises in order to comply with such a notice, the taking possession does not affect his right to avail himself of any such breach, non-observance or non-performance which occurred before he took possession.

DEFINITIONS
"lessee": s.398.
"local housing authority": ss.1, 2.
"owner": s.398.

GENERAL NOTE
Owner is defined in s.398, below, in two ways: a freeholder, and a person holding or entitled to the rents and profits of the premises under a lease of which more than three years remains unexpired. An owner of the first class, *i.e.* a freeholder, may protect his interests by giving notice to the authority under subs. (1), which requires the authority to give him notice—as well as anyone else served—of any proceedings they take under the preceding provisions of this Part.

Where action is taken under this Part, it is without prejudice to the right of the owner to take proceedings for breach of covenant or contract, *i.e.* the fact that works are done in default under s.375, or that they are only done because of one of the specified notices, does not deprive the owner of his rights to rely on any breach: subs. (2). Similarly, if the owner takes possession in order to comply with a notice, he may still take civil action for breaches before he takes possession (*ibid.*), *i.e.* he is not deemed to have waived those breaches by taking possession.

Control orders

Making of control order

379.—(1) The local housing authority may make a control order in respect of a house in multiple occupation if—

    (*a*) a notice has been served in respect of the house under section 352 or 372 (notices requiring the execution of works),

    (*b*) a direction has been given in respect of the house under section 354 (direction limiting number of occupants),

    (*c*) an order under section 370 is in force in respect of the house (order applying management code), or (*d*) it appears to the authority that the state or condition of the house is such as to call for the taking of action under any of those sections,

and it appears to the authority that the living conditions in the house are such that it is necessary to make the order in order to protect the safety, welfare or health of persons living in the house.

(2) A control order comes into force when it is made, and as soon as practicable after making a control order the local housing authority shall, in exercise of the powers conferred by the following provisions of this Part and having regard to the duties imposed on them by those provisions, enter on the premises and take all such immediate steps as appear to them to be required to protect the safety, welfare or health of persons living in the house.

(3) As soon as practicable after making a control order the local housing authority shall—

(*a*) post a copy of the order, together with a notice as described in subsection (4), in some position in the house where it is accessible to those living in the house, and

(*b*) serve a copy of the order, together with such a notice, on every person who, to the knowledge of the authority, was immediately before the coming into force of the order a person managing or having control of the house or is an owner, lessee or mortgagee of the house.

(4) The notice mentioned above shall set out the effect of the order in general terms, referring to the rights of appeal against control orders conferred by this Part and stating the principal grounds on which the local housing authority consider it necessary to make a control order.

DEFINITIONS
"house": s.399.
"house in multiple occupation": s.345.
"lessee": s.398.
"local housing authority": ss.1, 2.
"owner": s.398.
"person having control": s.398.
"person managing": s.398.

GENERAL NOTE
This is the most drastic power in relation to an H.M.O., and amounts to virtually complete take-over of the property by the local authority. Until relatively recently, it was a little-used power: less than double figures throughout the country by 1982 since introduction in 1964; however, two circumstances combined to bring the power into prominence. First of all, there was a series of deaths by fire in H.M.O.s and similar properties; secondly, large, purpose-built hostels were the subject of considerable attention. The applicability of the provisions to such properties was upheld in *R.* v. *London Borough of Southwark, ex parte Lewis Levy Ltd.* (1983) 8 H.L.R. 1, Q.B.D., and *R.* v. *London Borough of Camden, ex parte Rowton (Camden Town) Ltd.* (1983) 10 H.L.R. 28, Q.B.D.

The provisions were introduced by the Housing Act 1964, although amendments and extensions were contained in the Housing Act 1969. They were described as "an entirely new power to take over the control and management of a multi-occupied house summarily if the living conditions are so bad that immediate intervention by the local authority, rather than the more protracted process of requiring the proprietor to ameliorate the conditions, is necessary for the protection of the residents' safety, welfare or health", and "a drastic new means of dealing with the worst cases of squalor". (M.H.L.G. Circular 51/64, paras. 2 and 4).

They were not intended to replace other provisions, either under the Housing Acts, or under the Public Health Acts: *ibid.* There was some caution: "So strong a power, if misused, can readily come into discredit. But where a local authority find conditions which, in their view, can only satisfactorily be dealt with by taking over the property, (the Minister) trusts that they will act promptly. If the new powers are used judiciously and responsibly the

beneficial results will extend far beyond the property in respect of which they are exercised".
(*Ibid*).

A control order comes into force as soon as it is made: subs. (2) (see also s.370(2),
above). "The procedure for making a control order is designedly peremptory. It has been
said that, in some of the worst cases of squalor, the taking of action under Part II of the Act
of 1961 [now, ss.346–357 and 365–374, above] has been inhibited by the residents' fear that
they will lose the benefit of the inadequate shelter they have if they invoke action by the
local authority . . . A control order may be made without prior notice . . . Authorities
should so arrange their procedures that they are able to make control orders without prior
notice or warning where they consider this necessary". (*Ibid*., para. 5).

The preconditions to the making of an order are set out in subs. (1):

(1) A notice has been served under s.352 (amenities) or s.372 (means of escape from fire);
or

(2) A direction has been given under s.354 (limiting occupation); or

(3) A management order under s.371 *is in force*; or

(4) *It appears to the authority* that the state or condition of the house is such that action
under any of those sections *is called for*.

In other words, the authority may go direct to control order, without "passing through"
the alternative procedures, provided those procedures would be available to them, *i.e.* the
preconditions to each of them are present. But in *each* case, it must *also* appear to the
authority that *living* conditions (as distinct from the physical conditions which had given or
could give rise to a notice under the alternative procedures) are such that it is *necessary* to
make the order to protect the safety, welfare or health of occupiers.

In *R.* v. *London Borough of Southwark, ex parte Lewis Levy Ltd.* (1983) 8 H.L.R. 1,
Q.B.D., a threat to close a hostel and evict the residents was considered proper to take into
account as protection of the welfare of the occupiers. In M.H.L.G. Circular 51/64, it was
"not thought that the words 'living conditions' will restrict the authority to considering only
the existence, in an exaggerated form, of defects which could be regulated under the 1961
Act [now, ss.346–357 and 365–374, above]. Plainly the authority will wish to record as much
evidence of this kind as is available, but in forming a picture of the living conditions they
would appear to be entitled to add such other evidence of the environment in which the
residents live (for example noise, bad smells, rowdyism or other openly anti-social behaviour
within the house) as is capable of being established by direct observation". (App. 1, para.
12).

The Circular goes on to the emphasise that "the authority should not rely upon any
rumour or hearsay but base their decision on reports of living conditions actually observed
by responsible officers, or other evidence such that the existence of bad living conditions at
the time of making the order can be substantiated to their satisfaction and in any subsequent
appeal proceedings . . . " This must rather overstate the case: there will often be little
occasion for "direct observation" without giving the person in control of the property the
sort of warning that the "designedly peremptory" provisions of subs. (2) exist to avert.

Clearly, the authority should not act on "rumour", but "hearsay" cannot be read in this
context in a legal sense; rather, it is submitted, the authority are entitled—and will often be
obliged—to rely on evidence other than from their own officers, and will not err by
precipitate action if those on whose evidence they rely are people they are entitled to
consider responsible: *cf. R.* v. *Southampton City Council, ex parte Ward* (1984) 14 H.L.R.
124, Q.B.D., a case on what is now Part III of this Act (homelessness)—see notes to s.60,
above. It may be noted that as from the moment the order comes into force (*i.e.*
immediately), the authority enjoy their powers to revoke the order of their own initiative,
under s.392(2), below.

There is no requirement to estimate the costs of the "scheme" which the authority will
normally be obliged to undertake in the property under s.386, below, before making the
control order, and indeed they would not be able to prepare a realistic estimate until they
found themselves in a position to carry out a detailed inspection: *R.* v. *London Borough of
Southwark, ex parte Lewis Levy Ltd.* (1983) 8 H.L.R. 1, Q.B.D.

Once the order has been made, the authority are bound to enter on to the premises and
take such immediate steps as appear to them to be needed to protect the residents' safety,
welfare or health: subs. (2). The authority must also post a copy of the order in some
position in the house where it is accessible to those living in it (subs. (3)(*a*)), and post with
it a notice setting out the effect of the order in general terms, including reference to the
rights of appeal under ss.384, 386, and 393, below, and the main grounds on which the
authority took the decision to make the order: subs. (4).

A copy of the order and the notice must also be served on everyone who the authority
know to have been, until the order came into force, a person managing the house, a person

having control of the house, an owner or a lessee (including a statutory) tenant, or a mortgagee of the house: subs. (3)(*b*), and see s.398, below.

Modification of control order where proprietor resides in part of house

380.—(1) The local housing authority may exclude from the provisions of a control order a part of the house which, when the control order comes into force, is occupied by a person who has an estate or interest in the whole of the house.

(2) Except where a contrary intention appears, references in this Part to the house to which a control order relates do not include a part of the house so excluded from the provisions of the order.

DEFINITIONS
"control order": s.379.
"house": s.399.
"local housing authority": ss.1, 2.
"person having estate or interest": s.398.

GENERAL NOTE
The authority are not obliged to exercise the power contained in this section, but are entitled to exclude from the effect of the control order a part of the house which is occupied by a person with an estate or interest in the *whole* of the house: subs. (1). As to estate or interest, see s.398 below, including statutory tenant. Note, however, that the relevant estate or interest must be in the *whole* of the property.

Refusal to exercise the power is appealable to the county court under s.384, below. The authority will still enjoy rights of entry in relation to a part excluded under this section: see s.387, below.

General effect of control order

381.—(1) While a control order is in force the local housing authority—
  (*a*) have the right to possession of the premises,
  (*b*) have the right to do (and authorise others to do) in relation to the premises anything which a person having an estate or interest in the premises would, but for the making of the order, be entitled to do, without incurring any liability to any such person except as expressly provided by this Part, and
  (*c*) may, notwithstanding that they do not, under this section, have an interest amounting to an estate in law in the premises, create an interest in the premises which, as near as may be, has the incidents of a leasehold;
but subject to section 382 as regards the rights of persons occupying parts of the house under existing tenancies or agreements.

(2) The local housing authority shall not, without the consent in writing of the person or persons who would have power to create the right if the control order were not in force, create in exercise of the powers conferred by this section any right in the nature of a lease or licence which is for a fixed term exceeding one month or is terminable by notice to quit (or an equivalent notice) of more than four weeks.

(3) Any enactment or rule of law relating to landlords and tenants or leases applies in relation to—
  (*a*) an interest created under this section, or
  (*b*) a lease to which the authority become a party under section 382,
as if the authority were the legal owner of the premises; but subject to the provisions of section 382 relating to the Rent Acts.

(4) On the coming into force of a control order any notice, direction or order under section 352, 354, 366, 370 or 372 shall cease to have effect as respects the house to which the control order applies, but without prejudice to any criminal liability incurred before the coming into force of

the control order, or to the right of the local housing authority to recover any expenses incurred in carrying out works.

(5) A control order is a local land charge.

(6) References in any enactment to housing accommodation provided or managed by the local housing authority do not include a house which is subject to a control order.

DEFINITIONS
"control order": s.379.
"house": s.399.
"local housing authority": ss.1, 2.
"person having estate or interest": s.398. .;.
"Rent Acts": s.622.

GENERAL NOTE

The "general effect" of the order is to give the local authority the right to possession of the premises, to give them the right to do anything in relation to the premises which someone with an estate or interest could do, and to create interests which equate with tenancies: subs. (1). However, this is qualified in a number of ways:

(1) The power is subject to the provisions of s.382, below, as to the rights of those already in occupation (*ibid.*);

(2) The authority cannot incur liabilities on behalf of someone with an estate or interest, save as the provisions otherwise permit (*ibid.*);

(3) The interests created must not—without the consent in writing of the person who would otherwise have the right to create the right of occupation—amount to tenancies or licences for a fixed term of more than one month, or which are periodic on more than four weeks' notice (and, therefore, does not include a monthly tenancy, which requires a full month's notice) (subs. (2)).

The general law—including an enactment (which includes another provision of this Act: Interpretation Act 1978, s.1)—applicable to landlord/tenant will apply to rights created under this section, and indeed to those to which the authority become a party under s.382, below, *i.e.* pre-existing rights: subs. (3). This means that by virtue of ss.14–16, Rent Act 1977, no right created by the authority will amount to a protected tenancy (under the Rent Act 1977 or, by extension, under the Rent (Agriculture) Act 1976); however, those Acts continue to apply to prior lettings—see s.382(3), below. The provisions of the Landlord and Tenant Act 1985 governing rent books (ss.4 *et seq.*), repairs (ss.11 *et seq.*) and service charges (ss.18 *et seq.*, and if applicable, which will not be common in an H.M.O. subject to a control order), will therefore apply.

Subs. (4)

Without prejudice to liability already incurred for non-compliance, notices, directions and orders under the specified foregoing provisions of this Part cease to have effect when the order is made. Note, however, that *occupiers*' duties under the management regulations (see notes to s.369, above) apply to an occupier of a house when it is subject to a control order; it would seem that this is so *even if* the management regulations were never applied to the property by s.370, above.

Subs. (5)

Property managed under a control order is not part of the authority's Part II stock, nor subject to Part II powers and provisions.

Effect of control order on persons occupying house

382.—(1) This section applies to a person who, at the time when a control order comes into force, is occupying part of the house and does not have an estate or interest in the whole of the house.

(2) Section 381 (general effect of control order) does not affect the rights or liabilities of such a person under a lease, licence or agreement (whether in writing or not) under which he is occupying part of the house at the time when the control order comes into force; and—

(*a*) such a lease, licence or agreement has effect while the control order is in force as if the local housing authority were substituted in it for any party to it who has an estate or interest in the house and is not a person to whom this section applies, and

(*b*) such a lease continues to have effect as near as may be as a lease notwithstanding that the rights of the local housing authority, as substituted for the lessor, do not amount to an estate in law in the premises.

(3) The provisions which exclude local authority lettings from the Rent Acts, that is—

(*a*) sections 14 to 16 of the Rent Act 1977, and

(*b*) those sections as applied by Schedule 2 to the Rent (Agriculture) Act 1976 and section 5(2) to (4) of that Act,

do not apply to a lease or agreement under which a person to whom this section applies is occupying part of the house.

(4) If immediately before the control order came into force a person to whom this section applies was occupying part of the house under—

(*a*) a protected or statutory tenancy within the meaning of the Rent Act 1977, or

(*b*) a protected occupancy or statutory tenancy within the meaning of the Rent (Agriculture) Act 1976,

nothing in this Part prevents the continuance of that tenancy or occupancy or affects the continued operation of either of those Acts in relation to the tenancy or occupancy after the coming into force of the control order.

(5) So much of the regulations made under section 369 (regulations prescribing management code) as imposes duties on persons who live in a house to which the regulations apply also applies to persons who live in a house as respects which a control order is in force.

DEFINITIONS
"control order": s.379.
"house": s.399.
"local housing authority": ss.1, 2.
"person having estate or interest": s.398.
"protected tenancy": s.622.
"protected occupancy": s.622.
"Rent Acts": s.622.
"statutory tenancy": s.622.

GENERAL NOTE
This section governs the position of occupiers of part, who do not have an estate or interest (including statutory tenancy—see s.398, below) in the *whole*: subs. (1). See s.380, above, for the position of an occupant of part who *does* have an estate or interest in the whole.

Occupiers within this section are not to lose any rights; the authority step into the shoes of the "lessor" under any lease, tenancy or licence, which will continue as before (subs. (2)), even to the extent that the provisions excluding local authorities from the Rent Acts (*i.e.* Rent Act 1977 and Rent (Agriculture) Act 1976—see s.622, below) are inapplicable (subs. (3)), with the consequence that occupiers already protected by those Acts remain so (subs. (4)). There is no equivalent provision, however, "re-including" those with restricted contracts under the Rent Act 1977: see notes to s.622. For an outline of all of these classes of occupation, see notes to s.622, below.

Subs. (5)
See notes to s.381(4), above.

Effect of control order in relation to furniture in case of furnished letting

383.—(1) If on the date on which the control order comes into force there is furniture in the house which a resident in the house has the right to use in consideration of periodical payments to the dispossessed proprietor, whether included in the rent payable by the resident or not, the right to possession of the furniture as against all persons other than the resident vests in the local housing authority on that date and remains vested in the authority while the control order remains in force.

(2) The authority may, on the application in writing of the person owning such furniture, by notice in writing served on that person not less than two weeks before the notice takes effect, renounce the right to possession of the furniture conferred by subsection (1).

(3) If the local housing authority's right to possession of furniture conferred by subsection (1) is a right exercisable as against more than one person interested in the furniture, any of those persons may apply to the county court for an adjustment of their respective rights and liabilities as regards the furniture.

(4) On such an application the county court may make an order for such an adjustment of rights and liabilities either unconditionally or subject to such terms and conditions (including terms or conditions with respect to the payment of money by a party to the proceedings to another party to the proceedings by way of compensation, damages or otherwise) as it thinks just and equitable.

(5) In this section "furniture" includes fittings and other articles.

DEFINITIONS
"control order": s.379.
"dispossessed proprietor": s.399.
"house": s.399.
"local housing authority": ss.1, 2.

GENERAL NOTE
This section governs what happens to furniture (including fittings and other articles—see subs. (5)) for the use of which residents are paying (whether in the rent or by separate payment) the "dispossessed proprietor". The dispossessed proprietor is the person who would have been receiving the rents and other payments for the house, but for the intervention by the authority, and his successors in title: s.399.

Regardless of what arrangements the dispossessed proprietor has—*e.g.* hire–purchase— possession of the furniture vests in the authority and remains with them so long as the control order remains in force: subs. (1). However, an owner of the furniture can apply to the authority (in writing) for the authority to give up this right, and the authority may do so, under subs. (2), also by notice in writing containing not less than two weeks' notice of their intention to comply. Refusal is not appealable.

But if there is more than one person with an interest in the furniture, any such person can apply to the county court under subs. (3) for an "adjustment of rights and liabilities", on which application the county court may make such order as it thinks just and equitable under subs. (4).

As to accounting for furniture charges, see s.389, below.

Appeal against control order

384.—(1) A person having an estate or interest in a house to which a control order relates or, subject to subsection (3), any other person may appeal to the county court against the control order on any of the following grounds—

(*a*) that, whether or not the local housing authority have made an order or issued a notice or direction under any of the provisions of this Part mentioned in section 379(1)(*a*) to (*c*) the state or condition of the house was not such as to call for the taking of action under any of those provisions;

(*b*) that it was not necessary to make the control order in order to protect the safety, welfare or health of persons living in the house;

(*c*) where part of the house was occupied by the dispossessed proprietor when the control order came into force, that it was practicable and reasonable for the local housing authority to exercise their powers under section 380 so as to exclude from the provisions of the control order a part of the house (or a greater part than has been excluded);

(*d*) that the control order is invalid on the ground that a requirement of this Part has not been complied with or on the ground of some informality, defect or error in, or in connection with the control order.

(2) An appeal may be brought at any time after the making of the control order but not later than the expiration of a period of six weeks from the date on which the local housing authority serve a copy of a management scheme relating to the house in accordance with section 386, or such longer period as the authority may in writing allow.

(3) The court may, before entertaining an appeal brought by a person who had not, when he brought an appeal, an estate or interest in the house, require the appellant to satisfy the court that he may be prejudiced by the making of the order.

(4) In so far as an appeal is based on the ground that the control order is invalid, the court shall confirm the order unless satisfied that the interests of the appellant have been substantially prejudiced by the facts relied on by him.

(5) Further provisions as to certain matters arising on the revocation of a control order on appeal are contained in Part III of Schedule 13.

(6) Subject to the right of appeal conferred by this section, a control order is final and conclusive as to any matter which would have been raised on such an appeal.

DEFINITIONS
"control order": s.379.
"dispossessed proprietor": s.399.
"house": s.399.
"local housing authority": ss.1, 2.
"person having estate or interest": s.398.

GENERAL NOTE
This section provides for appeals to the county court against (1) the making of the control order (grounds (a), (b) and (d)), and (2) a refusal to exercise the power in s.380, above, to exclude from the control order a part of the house occupied by the dispossessed proprietor (ground (c)): subs. (1).

The appeal must be brought within six weeks of the date on which the authority comply with the "scheme" provisions of s.386, below, or such period as extended by the authority in writing: subs. (2). The addition of a power to extend time is pursuant to Law Commissions Recommendations (Cmnd. 9515), No. 19.

Appeal lies at the instance of anyone with an estate or interest in a house—not necessarily the whole house, and therefore including a tenant or statutory tenant of part; appeal may also be brought by "any" person, but if the person does not have an estate or interest, the court is entitled to require him to satisfy it that he may be prejudiced by the making of the order: subs. (3). The cases on "person aggrieved" would seem relevant here: consider *Ex parte Sidebotham* (1880) 14 Ch.D. 458, and *R.* v. *London Quarter Sessions, ex parte Westminster Corporation* [1951] 2 K.B. 508.

The possibility of appeal would suggest that it is the more appropriate course than application for judicial review: see *R.* v. *Hackney London Borough Council, ex parte Teepee Estates (1956) Ltd.* (1967) 19 P. & C.R. 87, D.C. See also *Minford Properties Ltd.* v. *London Borough of Hammersmith* (1978) 247 E.G. 561, D.C.; but in *R.* v. *London Borough of Southwark, ex parte Lewis Levy Ltd.* (1983) 8 H.L.R. 1, Q.B.D. it was held that if an issue is one which goes to *vires* including whether or not a property is a house within the provisions, it is appropriately raised by way of application for judicial review.

Subs. (5)
Part III of Schedule 13 governs the "undoing" of a control order, *i.e.* what is to happen when it comes to an end; para. 17 expressly deals with revocation on appeal by the county court. In such a case, the court is to consider whether action ought to be taken under the following previous provisions of this Part: s.352 (amenities), s.354 (limit on number of

occupants), s.366 (means of escape from fire), s.370 (application of management code) and s.372 (management works). The court may approve action under any of these provisions and if it does so, no appeal lies against the action under its own appeal procedures.

If at the time of the decision the authority are carrying out works of a class which they could, had they not made the control order, require someone else to do under any provision of this Part, or any other enactment relating to housing or public health (including other provisions of this Act—see Interpretation Act 1978, s.1), and on the hearing the court is satisfied that the works cannot be postponed because of their urgent necessity for the sake of the safety, welfare or health of residents or others (*e.g.* neighbours, if they are works under Part III, Public Health Act 1936, *i.e.* statutory nuisance), the court can suspend revocation until the works are completed.

The county court is to fix the date for termination of the order, even if the authority propose to appeal its order. The court can also authorise the authority to create tenancies, terminable up to six months after the order is to come to an end, notwithstanding the limitation in s.381, above; in effect, the authority can give the residents six additional months' security, beyond termination.

Under Sched. 13, Part III, para. 18, on termination the authority are also to pay to the dispossessed proprietor any balances which have accrued to them, after deducting from receipts their expenditure (not including capital expenditure), and compensation payments they may have made to the dispossessed proprietor: see further, s.389, below. The court has power to increase the balance offered, if they are satisfied that it is unduly low for any reason within the control of the authority, having regard to the management code standards of s.369, above, and the standards as to occupation numbers and rents which the authority ought to have applied. The limit of the court's power is the amount the dispossessed proprietor may have lost by reason of the order. If there is more than one dispossessed proprietor, the district valuer has jurisdiction to allocate the balance between them: Sched. 13, para. 14.

Under Sched. 13, para. 19, provision is made for the recovery by the authority of their capital expenditure on the house prior to revocation on appeal. The authority can apply to the court for approval of the works they have carried out on the ground that the authority could have required to be carried out under the powers of this Act or Public Health Act powers in any event, and that they could not be postponed for the sake of the safety, welfare or health of residents or others. The approved expenditure can be deducted from the para. 18 balance and to the extent that a sum is outstanding, is a charge on the premises and all estates and interests in them, including any part excluded from the order under s.380, above. The charge takes effect from the date of revocation, and carries interest; if not repaid within one month, a receiver may be appointed.

Under Sched. 13, para. 20, on an unsuccessful appeal the appellant can indicate that he proposes to appeal further, *i.e.* to the Court of Appeal, and seek an order that works will not subsequently be chargeable by the authority if carried out before confirmation of the control order by the Court of Appeal. If the decision of the county court is appealed, and the Court of Appeal revoke the order, they may also postpone the date of revocation on the same "works in progress" ground as the county court.

Subs. (6)

Although the vires of the authority in reaching their decision, *i.e.* on normal principles of administrative law (*cf.* notes to s.64, above), would seem to be available even on an appeal, for the effect of the control order is to take away a vested right to which the appellant would otherwise be entitled: *cf. London Borough of Wandsworth* v. *Winder* [1985] A.C. 461, 17 H.L.R. 196, H.L. so that it would seem to be exempt from the principle in *Cocks* v. *Thanet District Council* [1983] A.C. 286, 6 H.L.R. 15, H.L., that judicial review is the only way to impeach a decision of the authority which is a precondition to the acquisition of a right, the decision in *R.* v. *London Borough of Southwark, ex parte Lewis Levy Ltd.* (1983) 8 H.L.R. 1, Q.B.D., means that this subsection does not have quite the final effect that it seeks.

General duties of local housing authority when control order is in force

385.—(1) The local housing authority shall—

    (*a*) exercise the powers conferred on them by a control order so as to maintain proper standards of management in the house,

    (*b*) take such action as is needed to remedy all the matters which they would have considered it necessary to remedy by the taking of action under any other provision of this Act if they had not made a control order, and

(c) make reasonable provision for insurance of the premises subject to the control order against destruction or damage by fire or other cause.

(2) The reference in subsection (1)(c) to the premises subject to the control order includes any part of the premises excluded from the provisions of the order under section 380 (modification of order where proprietor resides in part of the house).

(3) Premiums paid for the insurance of the premises shall be treated for the purposes of this Part as expenditure incurred by the authority in respect of the premises.

DEFINITIONS
"control order": s.379.
"house": s.399.
"local housing authority": ss.1, 2.

GENERAL NOTE
This section contains the general obligation imposed on authorities under a control order, to maintain proper standards of management (*cf.* the management code under s.369, above), to remedy all matters which they would have considered needed remedying by action under any other provision of the Act, and make reasonable provision for insuring the premises (including a part excluded under s.380, above), the premiums for which insurance are deductible as part of their costs (see further s.390 and Sched. 13, below).

Duty to prepare management scheme

386.—(1) After a control order has been made, the local housing authority shall prepare a management scheme and shall, not later than eight weeks after the date on which the control order comes into force, serve a copy of the scheme on—

(a) every person who is, to the knowledge of the authority, a dispossessed proprietor or an owner, lessee or mortgagee of the house, and

(b) any other person on whom the authority served a copy of the control order.

(2) Part I of Schedule 13 has effect with respect to the matters to be provided for in a management scheme and for appeals against such schemes and related matters.

(3) This section does not affect the powers conferred on the local housing authority by section 381 (general effect of control order), and accordingly the authority may carry out works in a house which is subject to a control order whether or not particulars of the works have been included in a management scheme.

DEFINITIONS
"control order": s.379.
"dispossessed proprietor": s.399.
"house": s.399.
"lessee": s.398.
"local housing authority": ss.1, 2.
"owner": s.398.

GENERAL NOTE
Under s.394, "Part IV (of Sched. 13) provides for the case where a control order is followed by a compulsory purchase order"; under Schedule 13, Part IV, the duties comprised in this section are deferred if, within 28 days of making the control order, the authority make a compulsory purchase order under Part II, above, until after the outcome of the C.P.O. procedure. As, in practice, such C.P.O.s are common when related to control orders, it is suprising that there is not at the least a reference ("Subject to the provisions of . . .") at the commencement of this section. See further notes to s.394, below.

The substance of this section is the obligation to prepare a "management scheme", a copy of which must be served within eight weeks of the making of the control order on (1) everyone who is a dispossessed proprietor (see s.399) an owner or lessee (see s.398) or a mortgagee of the house, and (2) anyone else on whom the authority served a copy of the notice of control order under s.379(3), above. The phraseology does not seem to confine owners, lessees and mortgagees to the *whole* house, *i.e.* an owner, lessee or mortgagee of part only would seem to be included—*cf.* ss.380, 382, above.

The management scheme is without prejudice to the general duty in s.381—"and accordingly the authority may carry out works . . . whether or not particulars of the works have been included in a management scheme". The substance of the management scheme itself is described in Sched. 13, Part I.

The Management Scheme

Under para. 1 of Sched. 13, the scheme has to give particulars of all works which the authority would have required under this Act or Public Health Act powers, or any other enactment relating to housing or public health, and which the authority consider to amount to "works of capital expenditure", a term not otherwise defined, but in the analysis of which the authority will undoubtedly have regard to their usual practices, and to the Housing Subsidies and Accounting Manual (1981 Edition), see notes to s.421, below.

The scheme has to include:

(1) An estimate of the costs of these works;

(2) A specification of maximum number of occupants who should live in the property from time to time, having regard to the amenities referred to in s.352, above, and the existing condition, and its future condition, *i.e.* from time to time as works progress;

(3) An estimate of the balance which will accrue to the authority, *i.e.* excess of receipts over (i) compensation payable under s.389 and Sched. 13, Part II, plus (ii) all non–capital expenditure (if any).

This last amount is known as the surpluses on revenue account. It is only an estimate: see also Sched. 13, para. 5, below. The authority have power, as does the court (see further below), to vary the scheme, and this may have an effect on the surpluses (*i.e.* because it may increase or decrease them, *e.g.* because there are fewer occupants with lesser works, or lesser revenue outgoings, with greater capital works, or greater revenue outgoings with lesser capital works): Sched. 13, para 2. But a variation of the surpluses which will result in a decrease in surplus has to be reviewed by the court under Sched. 13, para. 6, below.

When calculating the income, payments for furniture (see s.383, above) are taken together with the rents from occupiers. When calculating expenditure, the authority include not only the insurance premium costs under s.385, above, but may also include the costs of temporarily rehousing people while works are in progress (including removal and return costs).

The scheme is appealable under Sched. 13, para. 3, within six weeks from the date on which it is served, or such longer time as the authority may in writing allow. The power to extend was added pursuant to Law Commission Recommendations (Cmnd. 9515), No. 19. Appeal lies to the county court, and is on any of the following grounds: works unreasonable in character or extent or unnecessary; the works ought not to be treated as capital expenditure; number of occupiers specified in the scheme unreasonably low; estimate of surpluses unduly low on account of assumptions made by the authority as to matters within their control, *e.g.* rents to be charged. The court may confirm or vary the scheme as it thinks fit. If there is a joint appeal against order under s.384, and scheme under this paragraph, and the court allows the appeal against order, it is not to proceed with the appeal against scheme.

The authority have to keep an account during the period of the control order, under Sched. 13, para. 4: see also s.390, below. It must show the surpluses on revenue as settled by the scheme, and the capital expenditure on the scheme. The balance is to be struck at half-yearly intervals. So far as expenditure exceeds revenue, as it commonly will, the deficit carries interest until it can be set off by receipts, or until the control order ceases to have effect, in which case it will carry forward as a charge on interests in the same way as if the control order is revoked on appeal under s.384, above. Future surpluses can also be applied to interest accrued on earlier deficits.

The authority are entitled to vary the scheme at any time so as to increase the surplus, under Sched. 13, para. 5. They are also entitled to apply to the court for a review of the scheme, including the surpluses, and the scheme is entitled to vary the scheme so far as it relates to any matter *other* than the capital works, *i.e.* may vary it so as to reflect a decrease in surplus. Someone with an estate or interest (see s.398, below) may also apply for such a review of the scheme. The court will take into account whether the actual balances have been greater or lesser than the estimate in the original scheme, and whether there has been any change of circumstances in the property, *e.g.* number of occupiers, rents and other payments, and whether either ought to be greater or lesser than originally estimated.

Right of entry for inspection and carrying out of works

387.—(1) The local housing authority, and any person authorised in writing by the authority, have, as against a person having an estate or interest in a house which is subject to a control order, the right at all reasonable times to enter any part of the house for the purpose of survey and examination or of carrying out works.

(2) The right conferred by subsection (1) is without prejudice to the rights conferred on the authority by section 381 (general effect of control order).

(3) Where part of a house is excluded from the provisions of a control order under section 380 (modification of order where dispossessed proprietor resides in part of the house), the right conferred by subsection (1) is exercisable as respects that part so far as is reasonably required for the purpose of survey and examination of, or carrying out works in, the part of the house which is subject to the control order.

(4) If the occupier of part of a house subject to a control order, after receiving notice of the intended action, prevents any officers, agents, servants, or workmen of the local housing authority from carrying out work in the house a magistrates' court may order him to permit to be done on the premises anything which the authority consider necessary.

(5) A person who fails to comply with an order of the court under subsection (4) commits a summary offence and is liable to a fine not exceeding level 3 on the standard scale and to a further fine not exceeding £20 for every day or part of a day during which the failure continues.

DEFINITIONS
  "control order": s.379.
  "house": s.399.
  "local housing authority": ss.1, 2.

GENERAL NOTE
  This provides the authority with power of entry, not only in relation to the property the subject of the control order, but including of a part which has been excluded under s.380, above. If an occupier obstructs entry, the authority may seek an order for co-operation from the magistrates' court, failure to comply with which is a criminal offence punishable by a fine of up to level 3 on the standard scale under s.37, Criminal Justice Act 1982, currently £400, by S.I. 1984 No. 447, with an additional fine of up to £20 per day on which the failure continues.

Power to supply furniture and fittings

388. The local housing authority may fit out, furnish and supply a house subject to a control order with such furniture, fittings and conveniences as appear to them to be required.

DEFINITIONS
  "control order": s.379.
  "house": s.399.
  "local housing authority": ss.1, 2.

Compensation payable to dispossessed proprietor

389.—(1) The local housing authority shall pay compensation to the dispossessed proprietor—
    (*a*) in respect of the period during which the control order is in force, at a rate calculated in accordance with Part II of Schedule 13 by reference to the rateable value of the house;

(*b*) in respect of a period during which the authority have the right to possession of furniture in pursuance of section 383 (house subject to furnished letting when control order made), at such rate as the parties agree or is determined in default of agreement by the rent tribunal for the district in which the house is situated.

(2) Compensation accrues from day to day (and is apportionable in respect of time accordingly) and is payable by quarterly instalments, the first instalment being payable three months after the date when the control order comes into force.

(3) If at the time when compensation accrues due the estate or interest of the dispossessed proprietor or, as the case may be, the furniture in question is subject to a mortgage or charge, the compensation is also comprised in the mortgage or charge.

<small>DEFINITIONS</small>
"control order": s.379.
"dispossessed proprietor": s.399.
"house": s.399.
"local housing authority": ss.1, 2.

<small>GENERAL NOTE</small>
The dispossessed proprietor is entitled to compensation at a rate calculated under Sched. 13, Part II: subs. (1). In addition, payment must be made for use of furniture retained by the authority under s.383, above, at the rate that is agreed or, in default of agreement, as is determined by the Rent Tribunal for the area: *ibid*. The Rent Tribunal is the same as the Rent Assessment Committee established under s.65 and Sched. 10, Rent Act 1977, by virtue of s.72, Housing Act 1980. The Rent Tribunal traditionally had jurisdiction over furnished lettings, prior to the Rent Act 1974 which brought such lettings into full Rent Act protection, save where there is a resident landlord. The Tribunal also has jurisdiction over furnished licences.

Compensation of either class accrues daily, and is payable quarterly: subs. (2). If the estate or interest of the dispossessed proprietor, or the furniture, is subject to a mortgage or charge, the mortgage or charge attaches to the compensation: subs. (3).

Under Sched. 13, Part II, para. 7, the compensation is at an annual rate equal to one half of the gross value of the property, multiplied by the appropriate multiplier. The appropriate multiplier is three–and–one–fifth, by S.I. 1984 No. 1629, retained in force by s.2, Housing (Consequential Provisions) Act 1985. Paras. 8–12 of Sched. 13 govern calculation of gross value. Under *ibid.*, para. 14, if more than one person qualifies as a dispossessed proprietor, compensation is to be apportioned between them according to the gross values of the parts of the property in which each is interested, and in the absence of agreement between them, the matter is to be resolved by the district valuer.

Facilities to be afforded to dispossessed proprietor and others

390.—(1) The local housing authority shall—
(*a*) keep full accounts of their income and expenditure in respect of a house which is subject to a control order, and
(*b*) afford to the dispossessed proprietor, or any other person having an estate or interest in the house, all reasonable facilities for inspecting, taking copies of and verifying those accounts.

(2) While a control order is in force the local housing authority shall afford to the dispossessed proprietor, or any other person having an estate or interest in the house, any reasonable facilities requested by him for inspecting and examining the house.

<small>DEFINITIONS</small>
"control order": s.379.
"dispossessed proprietor": s.399.
"house": s.399.
"local housing authority": ss.1, 2.
"person having estate or interest": s.398.

GENERAL NOTE
  See also notes to s.386, above.

Power of court to modify or determine lease

391.—(1) Either the lessor or lessee under a lease of premises which consist of or include a house which is subject to a control order, other than a lease to which section 382(2) applies (leases under which persons are occupying parts of the house and which have effect as if the local housing authority were substituted as landlord), may apply to the county court for an order for the determination of the lease or for its variation.
  (2) If on such an application the court is satisfied that—
  (*a*) if the lease is determined and the control order is revoked, the lessor will be in a position, and intends, to take all such action to remedy the condition of the house as the local housing authority consider they would, if a control order had not been in force, have required to be carried out under any provision of this Part, and
  (*b*) that the authority intend, if the lease is determined, to revoke the control order,
the court shall exercise the jurisdiction conferred by this section so as to determine the lease.
  (3) An order under this section may be unconditional or subject to such terms and conditions as the court thinks just and equitable to impose having regard to the respective rights, obligations and liabilities of the parties under the lease and to the other circumstances.
  (4) The terms and conditions may include terms or conditions with respect to the payment of money by a party to the proceedings to another party to the proceedings, by way of compensation, damages or otherwise.
  (5) An order under this section may include provisions for modifying in relation to the lease the effect of the provisions of paragraph 15 of Schedule 13 (re-transfer of the landlord's interest on the cessation of control order).

DEFINITIONS
  "control order": s.379.
  "house": s.399.
  "lessee": s.398.
  "local housing authority": ss.1, 2.

GENERAL NOTE
  This section applies to leases of the property subject to the control order, other than leases of parts of the premises to an occupier without an interest in the whole house, under s.382(1). It applies, therefore, to a lease to an occupying dispossessed proprietor, or to a superior lease. Either party under such a lease may apply to the county court for determination of the lease: subs. (1).
  The court is only to determine the lease if (1) satisfied that on determination the authority will revoke the control order, and (2) that on revocation of control order, the lessor will be in a position to take all such action as the authority would require under any provision in this Part, and intends to do so: subs. (2). The power exists to permit a superior landlord to step in and remedy the position created or permitted by the person who has been in charge of the premises, which has resulted in the control order—although either landlord or tenant under such a lease may make the application.
  The court may impose conditions (subs. (3)), including payment of compensation or damages (subs. (4)), and may vary the operation of Sched. 13, para. 15 (see notes to s.384, above), *i.e.* the provisions governing transfer back to landlord on determination of control order.

Expiry or revocation of control order

392.—(1) A control order ceases to have effect at the expiry of the period of five years beginning with the date on which it came into force.

(2) The local housing authority may at any earlier time, either on application or on their own initiative, by order revoke a control order.

(3) The authority shall, at least 21 days before revoking a control order, serve notice of their intention to do so on—

(*a*) the persons occupying any part of the house, and

(*b*) every person who is to the knowledge of the authority an owner, lessee or mortgagee of the house.

(4) If a person applies to the local authority requesting the authority to revoke a control order and giving the grounds on which the application is made, the authority shall if they refuse the application inform the applicant of their decision and of their reasons for rejecting the grounds advanced by him.

(5) Where the local housing authority propose to revoke a control order under this section on their own initiative and apply to the county court under this subsection, the court may approve the taking of any of the following steps to take effect on the revocation of the control order, that is—

(*a*) the serving of a notice under section 352, 366 or 372 (notices requiring the execution of works),

(*b*) the giving of a direction under section 354 (direction limiting number of occupants of house), or

(*c*) the making of an order under section 370 (order applying management code to house);

and no appeal lies against a notice or order so approved.

DEFINITIONS

"control order": s.379.

"house": s.399.

"lessee": s.398.

"local housing authority": ss.1, 2.

"owner": s.398.

GENERAL NOTE

In addition to revocation of order by court on appeal under s.384, above, there are three additional ways in which the control order can come to an end:

(1) After five years, by effluxion of time; or

(2) On the authority's own initiative, at any time (*e.g.* if conditions on entry do not seem as bad as they had appeared when it was decided to make the order—see notes to s.379, above); in such a case, the authority can apply to the county court under subs. (5), for authority to serve specified notices, and if that authority is given by the court, no appeal will lie from such notices under their own appeal procedures;

(3) On application of any person (*cf.* notes to s.384, above). If an application for revocation is refused it shall be accompanied by a statement of reasons: subs. (4). Appeal against refusal—or failure to notify of a decision within 42 days or such period as the applicant may in writing allow—is governed by s.393, below.

Whether of their own motion, or on application, the authority have to serve at least 21 days' notice of intention to revoke, on all occupiers, and on owners, lessees (see s.398, below) and mortgagees: subs. (4).

By s.394, below, Part III of Sched. 13 applies to cessation of control orders, including by revocation under this section. Under Sched. 13, para. 15, the general consequence of cessation is to put an original party (or his successor in title) back into the position of landlord under a lease, licence or other agreement which pre-existed the control order, and into whose place the authority stepped under s.382, above, and the dispossessed proprietor into the position of the authority under rights of occupation created by the authority under s.381, above, *i.e.* new rights. If the dispossessed proprietor thus assumes liabilities he could not have assumed under his own lease, he is exempt from liability to the superior landlord, *i.e.* the creation of rights in contravention of his own lease.

On the cessation of the order, a final balance in the accounts is to be struck, and expenditure incurred by the authority on the management scheme, together with interest on it, and including as the scheme has been varied, (see notes to s.386, above), so far as unmet by income, is to be a charge on the premises: Sched. 13, para. 16. The premises subject to the charge include a part excluded from the order under s.380, above. After one month from determination, a receiver may be appointed. If variation proceedings are still pending at date of termination, they may be continued, and if the charge is enforced before final determination of such variation proceedings, the authority will have to account for any excess they have thus recovered.

Appeal against refusal to revoke control order

393.—(1) If the local housing authority—
> (*a*) refuse an application under section 392 for the revocation of a control order, or
> (*b*) do not within 42 days from the making of such an application or such further period as the applicant may in writing allow, inform him of their decision,

the applicant may appeal to the county court and the county court may revoke the order.

(2) The court shall revoke the control order if—
> (*a*) the appellant has an estate or interest in the house which, apart from the rights conferred on the local housing authority by section 381 (general effect of control order) and the rights of persons occupying any part of the house, would give him the right to possession of the house,
> (*b*) that estate or interest was, when the control order came into force, subject to a lease for a term of years which has subsequently expired, and
> (*c*) the appellant satisfies the court that he is in a position, and intends, if the control order is revoked, to demolish or reconstruct the house or to carry out substantial work of construction on the site of the house;

and if the court is not so satisfied but would be so satisfied if the date of revocation of the control order were a date later than the hearing of the appeal, the court shall, if the appellant so requires, make an order for the revocation of the control order on that later date.

(3) If an appeal is brought under this section, the leave of the court is required for the bringing of another appeal against the same order, whether by the same or a different appellant, within the period of six months beginning with the final determination of the previous appeal.

(4) Further provisions as to certain matters arising on the revocation of a control order on appeal are contained in Part III of Schedule 13.

DEFINITIONS
> "control order": s.379.
> "final determination": s.399.
> "house": s.399.
> "local housing authority": ss.1, 2.
> "person having estate or interest": s.398.

GENERAL NOTE
There is a general discretion in the court to revoke an order on appeal from a refusal to revoke, or on application if the authority do not notify a decision within 42 days or such longer period as the applicant may in writing allow: subs. (1). If an appeal is brought, and does not result in revocation, no further appeal may be brought by the same *or a different* applicant within six months of the final determination of the first appeal (as to which, see s.399, below), without the leave of the court: subs. (4).

The court is *bound* to revoke the order if satisfied of the circumstances set out in subs. (2):
> (1) The appellant has an estate or interest (see s.398, below), which was subject to a lease at the time the order came into force, which interest has since expired; and,
> (2) Apart from the control order and the rights of occupiers, he would now be entitled to possession; and,

(3) He satisfies the court that he is in a position to demolish or reconstruct the property, or carry out substantial works of construction on the site of the property, and intends to do so.

If the court is satisfied that these conditions are not yet, but will by a certain date, be fulfilled, it can order revocation as of that later date.

On revocation, the provisions of Part III, Sched. 13 apply. The general provisions described in the notes to s.392, above, apply. In addition, under para. 21, the court may postpone revocation to permit the authority to complete works within the management scheme under s.386, above, which they have already commenced. The court can also stay the revocation to permit the authority to appeal against revocation.

The court can authorise service of specified notices on determination of the order, and if it does so, there is no appeal under their own procedures: these are the same notices described in the notes to s.384, above. If on revocation the authority will be entitled to a charge under para. 16 of the Schedule (see notes to s.392, above), the court can make revocation conditional on all or part of the debt. The court can also authorise the creation of the same class of interests it may authorise on a successful appeal against the control order: see notes to s.384, above.

Cessation of control order

394. Further provisions as to matters arising on the cessation of a control order are contained in Parts III and IV of Schedule 13—

Part III relates to the cessation of control orders generally, and

Part IV provides for the case where a control order is followed by a compulsory purchase order.

DEFINITION
"control order": s.379.

GENERAL NOTE
The provisions of Sched. 13, Part III, have been described in the notes to ss.384, 392 and 393, above.

The provisions of Sched. 13, Part IV, apply if the authority make a compulsory purchase order within 28 days of the making of the control order, so as to defer the operation of the obligation to prepare a management scheme under s.386, above. The C.P.O. will be a purchase under Part II, above (see Sched. 13, para. 22).

The obligation to make a management scheme is deferred until the Secretary of State has notified the authority of the outcome of the proposed C.P.O. If he decides not to confirm the order, the management scheme must be served within eight weeks; if he does confirm the order, the scheme must still be served, but within eight weeks of when the C.P.O. becomes operative.

The control order itself will cease to have effect if the C.P.O. is confirmed on the date when the authority contract to purchase the property, or else on the date when they serve notice of entry under s.11, Compulsory Purchase Act 1965, or notice under s.583 below: see notes to s.583, below. If this is done within eight weeks of the C.P.O. becoming operative, there will be no obligation to serve the management scheme (see also M.H.L.G. Circular 67/69, App., para. 11): Sched. 13, para. 24.

Under Sched. 13, para. 25, a balance is to be struck when the control order ceases to have effect, *i.e.* the excess of income over outgoings and compensation (*cf.* s.389, above). Notice of the proposed payment must be given to the dispossessed proprietor (see s.398), who within 21 days or such longer time as the authority may in writing permit, may appeal to the county court. The court may order the balance to be increased in the same circumstances as it can do on revocation on appeal, and subject to the same limit and provision for apportionment between more than dispossessed proprietor: see notes to s.384, above.

Under Sched. 13, para. 26, if the authority have carried out capital works (*cf.* notes to s.386, above) before the control order ceases to have effect, they may serve notice on the dispossessed proprietor, specifying those works which they could have required under this Act or Public Health Act powers, and which could not have been postponed for the sake of the safety, welfare or health of residents or others (*cf.* notes to s.384, above). The notice must inform the dispossessed proprietor of his right to appeal, which lies, within 21 days or such longer time as the authority may in writing permit, to the county court, which may confirm, vary or quash the notice. The amount still owing to the authority is deductible first from any balance owing under para. 25, and secondly, together with interest, from compulsory purchase compensation.

General supplementary provisions

Powers of entry

395.—(1) Where it appears to the local housing authority that survey or examination of any premises is necessary in order to determine whether any powers under this Part should be exercised in respect of the premises, a person authorised by the authority may at any reasonable time, on giving 24 hours' notice of his intention to the occupier, and to the owner if the owner is known, enter the premises for the purpose of such a survey and examination.

(2) A person authorised by the local housing authority may at any reasonable time, without any such prior notice as is mentioned in subsection (1), enter any premises for the purpose of ascertaining whether an offence has been committed under any of the following provisions of this Part—

> section 346(6) (contravention of or failure to comply with provision of registration scheme),
>
> section 355(2) (failure to comply with requirements of direction limiting number of occupants of house),
>
> section 358(4) (contravention of overcrowding notice),
>
> section 368(3) (use or permitting use of part of house with inadequate means of escape from fire in contravention of undertaking),
>
> section 369(5) (contravention of or failure to comply with regulations prescribing management code),
>
> section 376(1) or (2) (failure to comply with notice requiring execution of works).

(3) An authorisation for the purposes of this section shall be in writing stating the particular purpose or purposes for which the entry is authorised.

DEFINITIONS
"local housing authority": ss.1, 2.
"owner": s.398.

GENERAL NOTE
This section gives the authority power to enter, on 24 hours' notice to the occupier and, if known (*e.g.* by virtue of a notice under s.378, above), an owner, in order to inspect to see whether any of the powers in this Part should be exercised: subs. (1). The authority's representative must be authorised in writing, and the authority must state the purpose of the entry: subs. (3). Failure to comply with these requirements means that the entry will be unauthorised: *Stroud* v. *Bradbury* [1952] 2 All E.R. 76, D.C.

No prior notice need be given, however, if the purpose of the inspection is to see whether there has been an offence under any of the stated provisions: subs. (2). Some of this Schedule was added pursuant to Law Commission Recommendations (Cmnd. 9515), No. 20: s.346(6), s.358(4), s.368(3).

If entry is refused, or where warning is not required, a request for entry would defeat the purpose of the entry, an officer of the authority can obtain a warrant for entry from a justice of the peace under s.397, below. Obstruction of an officer of the authority is a criminal offence under s.396, below.

Penalty for obstruction

396.—(1) It is a summary offence to obstruct an officer of the local housing authority, or any person authorised to enter premises in pursuance of this Part, in the performance of anything which he is by this Part required or authorised to do.

(2) A person committing such an offence is liable on conviction to a fine not exceeding level 2 on the standard scale.

DEFINITION
"local housing authority": ss.1, 2.

GENERAL NOTE

Provided the officer of the authority is properly authorised (see *Stroud* v. *Bradbury* [1952] 2 All E.R. 76, D.C., above, notes to s.395), it is an offence to obstruct an officer of the authority, or anyone else authorised to enter (*e.g.* authorised under s.377, above), in the execution of this Part, punishable by a fine of up to level 2 on the standard scale under s.37, Criminal Justice Act 1982, currently £100, by S.I. 1984 No. 447.

Warrant to authorise entry

397.—(1) Where it is shown to the satisfaction of a justice of the peace, on sworn information in writing, that admission to premises specified in the information is reasonably required by a person employed by, or acting on the instructions of, the local housing authority—

(*a*) for the purpose of survey and examination to determine whether any powers under this Part should be exercised in respect of the premises, or

(*b*) for the purpose of ascertaining whether an offence has been committed under any of the provisions of this Part listed in section 395(2),

the justice may by warrant under his hand authorise that person to enter on the premises for those purposes or for such of those purposes as may be specified in the warrant.

(2) The justice shall not grant the warrant unless he is satisfied—

(*a*) that admission to the premises has been refused and, except where the purpose specified in the information is that mentioned in subsection (1)(*b*), that admission was sought after not less than 24 hours' notice of the intended entry had been given to the occupier, or

(*b*) that application for admission would defeat the purpose of the entry.

(3) The power of entry conferred by the warrant includes power to enter by force, if need be, and may be exercised by the person on whom it is conferred either alone or together with other persons.

(4) If the premises are unoccupied or the occupier is temporarily absent, a person entering under the authority of the warrant shall leave the premises as effectively secured against trespassers as he found them.

(5) The warrant continues in force until the purpose for which the entry is required is satisfied.

DEFINITION

"local housing authority": ss.1, 2.

GENERAL NOTE

If entry cannot be obtained under s.395, a justice of the peace can issue a warrant permitting an officer of the authority to enter premises, where entry is reasonably required for the purposes specified in subs. (1)—see also s.395(2), above. The information seeking the warrant must be sworn, and in writing: subs. (1). The J.P. is not to grant the warrant unless satisfied that admission has been refused and in a case within s.395(2), where no prior warning has to be given, either that notice of intended entry *was* given, or else that a request to enter would defeat the purpose of the entry: subs. (2). The power of entry extends to entry by force, and if necessary the officer may be accompanied: subs. (3). The warrant continues in force until its purpose is discharged: subs. (5). If premises are unoccupied, or the occupier is temporarily absent, premises shall be left as secure against trespassers as found; subs. (4).

These powers have been extended to the same cases as the powers under s.395(2), above, were extended, *plus* to enforcement of control order powers, by Law Commission Recommendations (Cmnd. 9515), No. 20, but also amended pursuant to *ibid.*, to bring them into line with the division in s.395 between entry for the purpose of survey and examination, and entry in order to see if an offence has been committed.

Meaning of "lessee", "owner", "person having control" and similar expressions

398.—(1) In this Part the expressions "lessee", "owner", "person having an estate or interest", "person having control", and "person managing" shall be construed as follows.

(2) "Lessee" includes a statutory tenant of the premises, and references to a lease or to a person to whom premises are let shall be construed accordingly.

(3) "Owner"—

(*a*) means a person (other than a mortgagee not in possession) who is for the time being entitled to dispose of the fee simple of the premises whether in possession or in reversion, and

(*b*) includes also a person holding or entitled to the rents and profits of the premises under a lease having an unexpired term exceeding three years.

(4) "Person having an estate or interest" includes a statutory tenant of the premises.

(5) "Person having control" means the person who receives the rack-rent of the premises, whether on his own account or as agent or trustee of another person, or who would so receive it if the premises were let at a rack-rent (and for this purpose a "rack-rent" means a rent which is not less than $\frac{2}{3}$ of the full net annual value of the premises).

(6) "Person managing"—

(*a*) means the person who, being an owner or lessee of the premises, receives, directly or through an agent or trustee, rents or other payments from persons who are tenants of parts of the premises, or who are lodgers, and

(*b*) includes, where those rents or other payments are received through another person as agent or trustee, that other person.

GENERAL NOTE

"Lessee": Statutory tenants, *i.e.* under the Rent Act 1977 and the Rent (Agriculture) Act 1976 (see notes to s.622, below), are included, but not, of course, licensees (*cf.* notes to s.93, above); the uniform treatment in this Part of statutory tenants under 1977 and 1976 Acts is pursuant to Law Commission Recommendations (Cmnd. 9515), No. 14(i).

"Person having estate or interest": the uniform application of this definition is pursuant to *ibid.*, No. 18(ii). Again, statutory tenants are included: see notes to s.622, below.

"Person having control": see notes to s.207, above.

"Person managing": as to the distinction between tenants and lodgers, see notes to s.93, above.

Minor definitions

399. In this Part—

"dispossessed proprietor", in relation to a house subject to a control order, means the person by whom the rent or other periodical payments to which the local housing authority become entitled on the coming into force of the order would have been receivable but for the making of the order, and the successors in title of that person;

"final determination", in relation to an appeal, includes the withdrawal of the appeal, which has the same effect for the purposes of this Part as a decision dismissing the appeal;

"house" includes any yard, garden, outhouses and appurtenances belonging to the house or usually enjoyed with it.

DEFINITION

"House": see notes to s.345, above.

Index of defined expressions: Part XI

400. The following Table shows provisions defining or otherwise explaining expressions used in this Part (other than provisions defining or explaining an expression used in the same section or paragraph):—

appropriate multiplier	Schedule 13, paragraph 13
control order	section 379(1)
control provisions	section 347(1)
dispossessed proprietor	section 399
district (of a local housing authority)	section 2(1)
district valuer	section 622
expenditure incurred (in respect of a house subject to a control order)	section 385(3) and Schedule 13, paragraph 2(3)
final determination (in relation to an appeal)	section 399
gross value	Schedule 13, paragraphs 8 to 12
house	section 399
house in multiple occupation	section 345
lessee (and "lease" and "let")	sections 398 and 621
local housing authority	section 1, 2(2)
management code	section 369
management scheme	section 386
overcrowding notice	section 358(1)
owner	section 398(3)
person having control	section 398(5)
person having an estate or interest	section 398(4)
person managing	sections 369(4), 372(5) and 398(6)
registration scheme	section 346
the Rent Acts	section 622
rents or other payments	Schedule 13, paragraph 2(2)
standard scale (in reference to the maximum fine on summary conviction)	section 622
statutory tenant	section 622
surpluses on revenue account as settled by the scheme (in Schedule 13)	Schedule 13, paragraph 2(1)
tenant	section 621

Part XII

Common Lodging Houses

Introductory

Meaning of "common lodging house"

401. In this Part "common lodging house" means a house (other than a public assistance institution) provided for the purpose of accommodating by night poor persons, not being members of the same family, who resort to it and are allowed to occupy one common room for the purpose of sleeping or eating, and includes, where part only of a house is so used, the part so used.

GENERAL NOTE

This Part has been, in its entirety, transported from the nether regions of the Public Health Act 1936 (Part IX). Its origins are to be found in the first principal (and nationally available) Public Health Act, 1848.

The principal terms used in this section are not defined: "house", "public assistance institution", "poor persons", "members of the family", "common room". The statutory definition, albeit thus unelaborated, is exhaustive: *People's Hostels Ltd.* v. *Turley* [1939] 1 K.B. 149.

Public Assistance Institution

This may refer to premises established under the Public Assistance Order 1930. It is probably an inheritance from days when the several functions under related "social welfare" legislation were spread amongst a number of different authorities within a geographical area, and would have been intended to disapply the provisions to, *e.g.*, accommodation provided under Part III, National Assistance Act 1948 (which could still be with another authority) or what is now Part III of this Act, *i.e.* accommodation for homeless persons. The fact that the house is maintained by a charity is irrelevant: *Logsdon* v. *Booth* [1900] 1 Q.B. 401.

House

This includes part of a house where that is all which is used as a common lodging-house. It has been suggested that a purpose-built hostel would be likely to fall outside the definition, while a house converted to the relevant use would fall within: *Re Ross and Leicester Corporation* (1932) J.P. 459, *London County Council* v. *Rowton Houses Ltd.* (1897) 62 J.P. 68. However, in the light of *R.* v. *London Borough of Southwark, ex parte Lewis Levy Ltd.* [1983] 8 H.L.R. 1, Q.B.D., and *R.* v. *London Borough of Camden, ex parte Rowton (Camden Town) Ltd.* [1983] 10 H.L.R. 28, Q.B.D., and the analyses therein of the earlier cases, it would now seem more likely that even a purpose-built hostel would qualify as a common lodging-house if put to the appropriate use. See, generally, notes to ss.56, 189, 345, above.

Accommodating by night

The fact that lettings may be by the week will not prevent a house being a common lodging-house: *People's Hostels Ltd.* v. *Turley* [1939] 1 K.B. 149.

Members of the same family

The definitions at s.113, above, and s.520, below, are clearly not applicable. If a keeper of a lodging-house wishes to rely on the proposition that persons are members of the same family, the burden lies on him to do so, even if this arises in the course of a criminal prosecution under s.408, *i.e.* contrary to the normal principle that the prosecutor must prove all elements of an offence: s.414.

One Common Room

There must be an element of community, *i.e.* a common room for sleeping *or* eating. Thus, while single sleeping rooms with a shared dining room could qualify, the mere fact that rooms are let out by the night, *without* any element of community, does not turn the use into that of common lodging house: *London County Council* v. *Hankins* [1914] 1 K.B. 490.

Regulation of common lodging houses

No person to keep a common lodging house unless registered

402. No person shall keep a common lodging house, or receive a lodger in a common lodging house, unless he is registered as the keeper of the house under this Part.

Provided that, when the registered keeper of a common lodging house dies, his widow or any other member of his family may, for a period not exceeding four weeks from his death or such longer period as the local housing authority may sanction, keep the common lodging house without being registered as the keeper.

<small>DEFINITIONS</small>
"common lodging house": s.401.
"local housing authority": ss.1, 2, 619.

<small>GENERAL NOTE</small>
Registration is governed by ss.403–405, and 408–409, below. With the temporary exception in the proviso to this section, no one shall keep a common lodging-house unless a registered keeper. It is a criminal offence to breach this requirement: s.408, below.

The term "keeper" is not defined. Clearly there is no requirement for a particular—or indeed a—legal interest. This is emphasised by the alternative prohibition: "receiving" lodgers.

The Sub-Treasurer of the Inner Temple and the Under-Treasurer of the Middle Temple are "the local housing authority" in respect of their Inns, for the purposes of this Part: s.619.

Register of common lodging house keepers and their houses

403. The local housing authority shall keep a register in which shall be entered—
(*a*) the full names and the place of residence of every person registered as the keeper of a common lodging house;
(*b*) the situation of every such lodging house;
(*c*) the number of persons authorised to be received in the lodging house; and
(*d*) the full names and places of residence of any persons who are to act as deputies of the keeper of the lodging house.

<small>DEFINITIONS</small>
"common lodging house": s.401.
"local housing authority": ss.1, 2, 619.

<small>GENERAL NOTE</small>
The authority are under a duty to maintain a register of both keepers (names and residences) and common lodging-houses. The authorised number of occupants is under bye-laws under s.406, below. The register extends to the keeper's deputies.

The Secretary of State enjoys default powers under ss.322–326, Public Health Act 1936, which continue to apply to these provisions; s.410, below.

Provisions with respect to registration

404.—(1) Subject to the following provisions of this section, a local housing authority, on receiving from a person an application in writing—
(*a*) for registration as a keeper of a common lodging house, or
(*b*) for the renewal of his registration,
shall register the applicant in respect of the common lodging house named in the application, or renew his registration in respect of it, and issue to him a certificate of registration or renewal.

(2) The authority shall not register an applicant until an officer of the authority has inspected the premises named in the application and has made a report on them.

(3) The authority may refuse to register, or renew the registration of, an applicant if they are satisfied that—
(*a*) he, or a person employed or proposed to be employed by him at the common lodging house, as a deputy or otherwise, is not a fit person, whether by reason of his age or otherwise, to keep or to be employed at a common lodging house; or
(*b*) the premises are not suitable for use as a common lodging house

or are not, as regards sanitation and water supply and in other respects, including means of escape in case of fire, suitably equipped for such use; or

(*c*) the use of the premises as a common lodging house is likely to occasion inconvenience or annoyance to persons residing in the neighbourhood.

(4) The registration of a person as a keeper of a common lodging house remains in force for such period, not exceeding 13 months, as may be fixed by the authority, but may be renewed by them for a period not exceeding 13 months at any one time.

(5) If a local housing authority refuse to grant or renew registration, they shall, if required by the applicant, give him a statement in writing of the grounds on which his application is refused.

(6) A local housing authority shall at any time, on the application of a person registered as the keeper of a common lodging house—

(*a*) remove from the register the name of any person entered in it as a deputy of the keeper, or

(*b*) insert the name of any other person (being a person approved by the authority) whom the keeper proposes to employ as a deputy,

and shall make any consequential alterations in the certificate of registration.

DEFINITIONS
"common lodging house": s.401.
"local housing authority": ss.1, 2, 619.

GENERAL NOTE
Anyone wishing to be registered as the keeper of a common lodging-house may apply for registration. The authority are bound to consider the application, even if, at the date of application, the premises to which the application relates are not in use as a common lodging-house: *R.* v. *Hounslow London Borough Council, ex parte Pizzey* [1977] 1 W.L.R. 58, D.C. Registration lasts for the period fixed by the authority, but to a maximum of 13 months at one time: subs. (4). If registration is allowed, then the authority cannot subsequently revoke the registration, although they can of course prosecute an offence under s.408, and this can lead to cancellation by a court, and/or disqualification from further registration for a period under s.409: *Blake* v. *Kelly* (1887) 52 J.P. 263. A registered keeper can, however, apply at any time for a change of deputy to be registered.

The authority enjoy wide powers of refusal of registration. There is to be no registration until there has been an inspection and report by an officer of the authority: subs. (2). This clearly applies on re-registration as much as on an initial registration. The grounds for refusal are:

(1) The applicant, or someone employed or proposed to be employed by him as a deputy, is not a fit person, whether by reason of age or otherwise, to keep or be employed at a common lodging-house; or

(2) The premises are not suitable for use as a common lodging-house, or are not suitably equipped for use as such, as regards sanitation, water supply, means of escape in case of fire, or otherwise; or

(3) The use of the premises as a common lodging-house is likely to cause inconvenience or annoyance to people living in the neighbourhood (*n.b.* not people with shops, businesses, etc., only).

It is a criminal offence for a person disqualified under s.409, below, to apply for registration. It is also a criminal offence to make a statement knowingly false in an application for registration: *ibid.*

If an application is refused, the applicant is entitled to ask for a statement of reasons in writing (subs. (5)), perhaps to consider appeal under s.405. As to reasons, see notes to s.64, above. In any event, when notifying a refusal, the authority must inform the applicant of his right of appeal: s.405(3).

If an application is granted by resolution of the authority, or, presumably, a properly authorised officer under delegated powers (s.101, Local Government Act 1972), but the authority fail to enter the registration in the register maintained under s.403, above, or perhaps fail to issue the certificate of registration, the registration is still effective: *Coles* v. *Fibbens* (1884) 52 L.J. 358.

Appeals against refusal of registration

405.—(1) A person aggrieved by the refusal of a local housing authority under section 404 to grant or renew registration may appeal to a magistrates' court.

(2) The time within which an appeal may be brought is 21 days from the date on which notice of the authority's refusal was served on the person desiring to appeal; and for the purposes of this subsection the making of the complaint shall be deemed to be the bringing of the appeal.

(3) Where such an appeal lies, the document notifying to the person concerned the decision of the authority in the matter shall state the right of appeal to a magistrates' court and the time within which such an appeal may be brought.

(4) A person aggrieved by a decision of a magistrates' court on such an appeal may appeal to the Crown Court.

(5) Where on an appeal under this section a court varies or reverses the authority's decision, the authority shall make any necessary entry in the register and issue any necessary certificate.

DEFINITION
"local housing authority": ss.1, 2, 619.

GENERAL NOTE
It would seem that a person aggrieved by a refusal could include a proposed deputy who has been found not fit, or even a person with a legal interest in the premises who wishes to let it to a proposed keeper whose application has been refused. Appeal is to the magistrates' court, by complaint, which is to be issued within 21 days from service of notice of refusal, and from the magistrates' court to the Crown Court.

Byelaws as to common lodging houses

406. A local housing authority may, and if so required by the Secretary of State shall, make byelaws—

(*a*) for fixing the number of persons who may be received into a common lodging house, and for the separation of the sexes in it;

(*b*) for promoting cleanliness and ventilation in common lodging houses, and requiring the walls and ceilings of such lodging houses to be limewashed, or treated with some other suitable preparation, at specified intervals;

(*c*) with respect to the taking of precautions when any case of infectious disease occurs in such a lodging house; and

(*d*) generally for the well-ordering of such lodging houses.

DEFINITIONS
"common lodging-house": s.401.
"local housing authority": ss.1, 2, 619.

GENERAL NOTE
Where an enactment authorises the making of byelaws, the general power to make byelaws under s.235, Local Government Act 1972, is inapplicable. However, the procedural requirements of *ibid.* s.236, and the limits of penalty in *ibid.* s.237, still apply: see also notes to s.23, above. The limit is level 2 on the standard scale, *i.e.* under s.37, Criminal Justice Act 1982, currently £100—see S.I. 1984 No. 447.

The authority are bound to make byelaws if required to do so by the Secretary of State (*cf.* s.410, default powers), which must cover the specified matters. Additional provisions concerning infectious disease are to be found in the Public Health (Control of Disease) Act 1984, ss.39–42. As to "well-ordering" of the lodging house, see also the requirements of s.407, below.

Management and control of common lodging houses

407.—(1) The keeper of a common lodging house shall, if required by the local housing authority to do so, affix, and keep affixed and undefaced and legible, a notice with the words "Registered Common Lodging-house" in some conspicuous place on the outside of the house.

(2) Either the keeper of the lodging house, or a deputy registered under this Part, shall manage the lodging house and exercise supervision over persons using it, and either the keeper or a deputy so registered shall be at the lodging house continuously between the hours of nine o'clock in the evening and six o'clock in the morning of the following day.

(3) The local housing authority may by notice require the keeper of a common lodging house in which beggars or vagrants are received to report daily to them, or to such persons as they may direct, every lodger who resorted to the house during the preceding day or night.

(4) An authority who require such reports to be made shall supply to the keeper of the lodging house schedules to be filled up by him with the information required and to be transmitted by him in accordance with their notice.

(5) The keeper of a common lodging house, and every other person having the care or taking part in the management of it, shall at all times, if required by an authorised officer of the local housing authority, allow him to have free access to all parts of the house.

DEFINITIONS
"common lodging house": s.401.
"local housing authority": ss.1, 2, 619.

GENERAL NOTE
The notice described in subs. (1) only has to be displayed if the authority require the keeper to do so. The authority can also require the keeper to file a daily report, on schedules to be provided by them, on lodgers in a house "in which beggars or vagrants are received": subss. (3), (4).

The requirement that the keeper or a *registered* deputy be present between nine in the evening and six the following morning, and manage and exercise supervision over people in the lodging-house, is effective without notice from the authority: subs. (2). The authority may enter on request and have free access to any part of the property: subs. (5). See also s.411, below.

Offences

408.—(1) It is a summary offence for a person—

(*a*) to contravene or fail to comply with any of the provisions of this Part;

(*b*) being the registered keeper of a common lodging house, to fail to keep the premises suitably equipped for use as such;

(*c*) to apply to be registered as the keeper of a common lodging house at a time when he is, under section 409, disqualified from being so registered; or

(*d*) in an application for registration, or for the renewal of his registration, as the keeper of a common lodging house, to make a statement which he knows to be false.

(2) A person committing such an offence is liable on conviction to a fine not exceeding level 1 on the standard scale and, subject to subsection (3), to a further fine not exceeding £2 for each day on which the offence continues after conviction.

(3) The court by which a person is convicted of the original offence may fix a reasonable period from the date of conviction for compliance by the defendant with any directions given by the court and, where a court has fixed such a period, the daily penalty is not recoverable in respect of any day before the period expires.

DEFINITION
"common lodging house": s.401.

The criminal offences set out in this section are:

(1) Contravening or failing to comply with any of the provisions of this Part, *e.g.* s.407(2), above;

(2) Failing to keep the premises suitably equipped as a common lodging house—*cf.* s.404(3)(*b*) for the meaning of "suitably equipped";

(3) To apply for registration at a time when he is disqualified under s.409, below, *i.e.* in the course of a previous conviction;

(4) To make a statement knowingly false in the course of an application for registration under s.404, above.

A conviction carries a penalty not exceeding level 1 on the standard scale, *i.e.* under s.37, Criminal Justice Act 1982—currently £50, see S.I. 1984 No. 447. There is also a daily penalty of up to £2 per day for continuation of the offence past conviction, although the court may defer the coming into effect of the added daily penalty by allowing time for compliance with any directions it may give, *i.e.* as to rectifying the matters which gave rise to the offence. See also s.409, below, as to the power of the court to cancel registration, or to disqualify the keeper from further registration for a period. See also s.412, below, for the offence of obstruction.

Note that only a person aggrieved, or the local housing authority, can take proceedings for an offence under this Part without the written consent of the Att.-Gen.: s.412, below.

Power of court on conviction to cancel registration and to disqualify for re-registration

409. Where the registered keeper of a common lodging house is convicted of—

(*a*) an offence under this Part or a byelaw made under it, or

(*b*) an offence under section 39(2) or 49(2) of the Public Health (Control of Disease) Act 1984 (failure to notify case of infectious disease or failure to comply with closing order made on account of notifiable disease),

the court by which he is convicted may cancel his registration as a common lodging house keeper and may order that he be disqualified for such period as the court thinks fit from being again registered as such a keeper.

DEFINITION
"common lodging house": s.401.

GENERAL NOTE
On conviction for an offence under this Part—s.408, above, s.412, below—or under a byelaw under s.406, above, or on an offence of failure to notify the authority of an infectious disease in the lodging-house, or on an offence of failing to comply with a closing order resulting from a notifiable disease (both under the Public Health (Control of Disease) Act 1984), the court can cancel an existing registration, and disqualify the keeper from further registration—for any common lodging house—for a specified period. It is an offence to apply for registration while disqualifed: s.408(1)(*c*).

Enforcement

Duty of local housing authority to enforce this Part

410.—(1) The local housing authority shall carry this Part into execution.

(2) Sections 322 to 326 of the Public Health Act 1936 (default powers of Secretary of State and related provisions) apply in relation to failure by a local housing authority to discharge their functions under this Part.

DEFINITION
"local housing authority": ss.1, 2, 619.

GENERAL NOTE
This preserves the applicability of the Secretary of State's Public Health Act 1936 default powers to the provisions governing common lodging houses now transferred to this Act. The powers include: declaration of default and directions as to discharge (Public Health Act

1936, s.322(2)); transfer of functions to himself (*ibid.* s.322(3)); and, recovery of costs of carrying out their functions (*ibid.* s.324). Section 326 contains ancillary provisions concerning the position of staff.

Powers of entry

411.—(1) An authorised officer of a local housing authority may at any reasonable time, on giving 24 hours' notice of his intention to the occupier and producing, if so required, some duly authenticated document showing his authority, enter premises for the purpose—

(a) of ascertaining whether there is, or has been, on or in connection with the premises, any contravention of the provisions of this Part or of any byelaw made under it;

(b) of ascertaining whether circumstances exist which would authorise or require the authority to take any action under this Part or any such byelaws;

(c) for the purpose of taking any action authorised or required by this Part or any such byelaws to be taken by the authority; or

(d) generally, for the purpose of the performance by the authority of their functions under this Part or any such byelaws.

(2) If it is shown to the satisfaction of a justice of the peace on sworn information in writing that there is reasonable ground for entry into premises for any of the purposes mentioned in subsection (1) and—

(a) that admission to premises has been refused, or that refusal is apprehended,

(b) that the premises are unoccupied or the occupier is temporarily absent, or

(c) that the case is one of urgency or that an application for admission would defeat the object of the entry,

he may, by warrant under his hand, authorise the authority by any authorised officer to enter the premises, by force if need be.

(3) A warrant shall not be issued unless the justice is satisfied either—

(a) that notice of the intention to apply for a warrant has been given to the occupier, or

(b) that the premises are unoccupied, the occupier is temporarily absent, the case is one of urgency, or the giving of such notice would defeat the object of the entry.

(4) An authorised officer entering premises by virtue of this section, or of a warrant issued under this section, may take with him such other persons as may be necessary; and on leaving any unoccupied premises which he has entered by virtue of such a warrant shall leave them as effectually secured against trespassers as he found them.

(5) A warrant granted under this section continues in force until the purpose for which the entry is necessary has been satisfied.

DEFINITION
"local housing authority": ss.1, 2, 619.

GENERAL NOTE
The authority may authorise an officer to enter *any* premises to see whether there is, or has been, any contravention of the provisions of this Part, including byelaws made under it: this would include the requirement for registration of a common lodging-house and its keeper, *i.e.* premises which *may* be in use as such without registration. The purposes can include to see whether any action needs to be taken, *e.g.* prosecution under s.408, or an additional requirement by notice under s.407, or under the byelaws. The purposes can include entry in order to take such action. Finally, the purposes can include the general performance of duties under this Part or byelaws, *e.g.* the general requirement to carry this Part into execution under s.410(1).

The entry must normally be on 24 hours' notice. However, if admission is refused, or a refusal is anticipated, or the premises are unoccupied, or the occupier is temporarily absent, or the case is urgent, or applying would defeat the object of the entry, *i.e.* because the breach would be remedied, a single justice of the peace can authorise entry, if needs be by force: subss. (2), (3). A warrant continues in force until the entry has been effected: subs. (5).

In the case of either class of entry, the officer can be accompanied by whoever else may be necessary, and on leaving unoccupied premises entered by warrant they shall be left as secure as found: subs. (4).

It is a criminal offence to obstruct a person acting in the execution of this Part, or a byelaw or warrant made or issued under it; s.412, below.

Penalty for obstruction

412.—(1) It is a summary offence for a person wilfully to obstruct a person acting in the execution of this Part or of any byelaw or warrant made or issued under it.

(2) A person committing such an offence is liable on conviction to a fine not exceeding level 1 on the standard scale.

GENERAL NOTE

This contains an additional offence of wilfully obstructing a person in the execution of this Part of the Act, or a byelaw made under it (s.406, above), or a warrant issued under s.411(2), (3), above. The offence carries a penalty not exceeding level 1 on the standard scale, *i.e.* under s.37, Criminal Justice Act 1982—currently £50, see S.I. 1984 No. 447. See also s.409, above, as to the power of the court to cancel registration, or to disqualify the keeper from further registration for a period.

Restriction on right to prosecute

413. Proceedings in respect of an offence created by or under this Part shall not, without the written consent of the Attorney General, be taken by any person other than a party aggrieved or the local housing authority.

DEFINITION

"local housing authority": ss.1, 2, 619.

GENERAL NOTE

Only a person aggrieved by an offence, or the local housing authority, can prosecute an offence under ss.408 or s.12, above, without the written consent of the Att.-Gen.

Supplementary provisions

Evidence in legal proceedings

414.—(1) If in proceedings under this Part it is alleged that the inmates of a house or part of a house are members of the same family, the burden of proving that allegation rests on the person by whom it is made.

(2) In proceedings under this Part a document purporting to be a copy of an entry in the register of common lodging houses and purporting to be certified as such by the proper officer of the local housing authority shall be prima facie evidence of the matters recorded in the entry.

(3) The proper officer of the local housing authority shall supply such a certified copy free of charge to any person who applies for it at a reasonable hour.

DEFINITIONS

"common lodging house": s.401.
"local housing authority": ss.1, 2, 619.

GENERAL NOTE

Contrary to the normal requirement that a prosecutor must prove all relevant elements of an offence, if the defence to a prosecution involves the proposition that occupation was by members of the same family, the person raising the proposition must prove it.

Power to apply provisions to Crown property

415. Section 341 of the Public Health Act 1936 (power to apply provisions to Crown property) applies to the provisions of this Part as it applies to provisions of that Act.

GENERAL NOTE

The provisions of this Part will apply to Crown property if the local authority agree with the "appropriate authority" for the purposes of s.341, Public Health Act 1936, that they, or specified provisions, should do so.

Index of defined expressions: Part XII

416. The following Table shows provisions defining or otherwise explaining expressions used in this Part (other than provisions defining or explaining an expression used in the same section):—

common lodging house	section 401
local housing authority	section 1, 2(2)
standard scale (in reference to the maximum fine on summary conviction)	section 622

PART XIII

GENERAL FINANCIAL PROVISIONS

Housing accounts of local housing authorities

The Housing Revenue Account

417.—(1) A local housing authority shall keep an account, called the "Housing Revenue Account", of the income and expenditure of the authority in respect of—

(a) all houses and other buildings which have been provided under Part II (provision of housing),

(b) all houses purchased under section 192 (purchase of house found on appeal against repair notice to be unfit and beyond repair at reasonable cost),

(c) all dwellings in respect of which a local authority have received assistance under section 1 or section 4(2A) of the Housing (Rural Workers) Act 1926, and

(d) all land which has been acquired or appropriated for the purposes of Part II,

and such land, houses or other buildings not within the preceding paragraphs as the authority may determine from time to time with the consent of the Secretary of State.

(2) The consent of the Secretary of State for the purposes of subsection (1) may be given either generally to local housing authorities or to a particular authority or description of authority or in a particular case.

(3) References in this Part to the houses or other property of an authority within the authority's Housing Revenue Account are to the houses, dwellings or other property falling within subsection (1).

(4) A local housing authority not possessing property falling within subsection (1) shall nevertheless keep a Housing Revenue Account if they are entitled to receive income arising from the investment or other use of money borrowed by them for the purpose of—

(a) the provision of housing accommodation under Part II, or

(b) the purchase of houses under section 192 (houses found on appeal against repair notice to be beyond repair at reasonable cost) or the carrying out of works on houses purchased under that section, or if they are entitled to receive income arising from the investment or other use of money derived from the sale or other disposal of dwellings or other property which has at any time been within their Housing Revenue Account.

DEFINITION
"local housing authority": ss.1, 2.

GENERAL NOTE
This section contains the requirement that local housing authorities maintain a Housing Revenue Account ("H.R.A.") if either they hold property within subs. (1), or they fulfill the conditions of subs. (4). The provisions of Sched. 14, govern what is to be credited to the account, and what is to be debited to it: see notes to s.418 and to Sched. 14, below. Section 419 governs the *optional* Housing Repairs Account, which may be considered in many respects a sub-account of the H.R.A. Under s.420, the Secretary of State has reserve powers to issue "accounting directions".

Subs. (1)
The H.R.A. is to be maintained in respect of—potentially—five classes of property (see also subs. (3), below):
(1) All houses and other buildings provided under Part II. This, accordingly, covers the principal stock-holding of a local housing authority, and extends not only to the units of housing, but any additional property, *e.g.* under s.11 (board and laundry facilities), or s.12 (shops, recreation grounds or other buildings with a beneficial purpose). It also covers buildings or housing purchased but not yet improved or converted for use.
However, in exercise of his powers now contained in s.420, below, the Secretary of State has excluded from the H.R.A. dwellings in a scheme of repair, improvement or conversion for sale under s.429, below, save where the disposal is on a shared ownership lease (*cf.* s.143, above) in which latter case the dwelling is only treated as within the H.R.A. at and after the date of the disposal: Housing Subsidies and Accounting Manual (1981 Edition, issued under cover of D.O.E. Circular 5/82, App. I.
(2) In addition, all land which has been acquired or appropriated for Part II purposes is within the H.R.A., *e.g.* common parts of an estate, land with a beneficial purpose under s.12, or land bought for or appropriated to development which has not yet taken place. "Land" includes "buildings and other structures, land covered with water, and any estate, interest, easement, servitude or right in or over land": Interpretation Act 1978, Sched. 1.
This provision includes land deemed to have been acquired for Part V, Housing Act 1957 purposes (*i.e.* now, Part II purposes) under 1957, s.57(6)—land acquired for redevelopment in pursuance of a redevelopment plan—before the repeal of s.57(6) on August 15, 1969, and any structures on such land which were made available to the authority under s.1, Housing (Temporary Accommodation) Act 1944, *i.e.* "prefabs" (see also s.53, above): Sched. 14, Part III, para. 1, below.
(3) Houses purchased under s.192: under Part VI, above, where a house is unfit, but repairable at a reasonable expense, the authority can serve a repairs notice: see s.189, above. Under s.191, a person aggrieved by a repair notice can appeal to the county court: see notes thereto, above. No particular grounds are specified, but one basis for allowing an appeal is if the house is *not* repairable at a reasonable expense: see also notes to s.206, above.
If an appeal is allowed, then at the request of the authority, the court is bound to include in its judgment an express finding on this issue of whether or not it is repairable at a reasonable expense: s.191(3). If the court finds that it is *not*, the authority are entitled to purchase the property, either by agreement or, with the consent of the Secretary of State, compulsorily, and if they do buy it, they are bound then to carry out forthwith all the works specified in the initial repairs notice: s.192. Property thus purchased falls within the H.R.A.
(4) Property in respect of which the authority received assistance under ss.1 or 4(2A) of the Housing (Rural Workers) Act 1926.
(5) Any land which the authority wish to include in the H.R.A., to the inclusion of which the Secretary of State consents. Such consent may be given either generally, or particularly: subs. (2). As to applications for consent, see the Housing Subsidies and Accounting Manual, paras. 188–190.

Subs. (3)

In addition to the property in subs. (1), above, property brought within the H.R.A. before August 10, 1972, either under s.50(1)(e), Housing (Financial Provisions) Act 1958, with the consent of the Minister, or under s.50(2) of the 1958 Act, is to be treated as within the H.R.A.: Sched. 14, Part III, para. 2, below. However, *prima facie* excluded from the H.R.A. is property provided on or before February 1, 1919 (Sched. 14, Part III, para. 4); under his powers now contained in s.420, below, the Secretary of State has given permission for the inclusion of such properties if provided under provisions corresponding to Part II in previous legislation—see the Housing Subsidies and Accounting Manual, App. E.

Subs. (4)

Even if the authority have no property within subs. (1), they may yet be obliged to maintain a H.R.A. if *either* they have borrowed money in order to provide Part II accommodation or to purchase or carry out works on housing under s.192, and have put the money to some other purpose from which they derive an income, *or* they have an income from the proceeds of the disposal of property formerly within the H.R.A.

The keeping of the Housing Revenue Account

418. The provisions of Schedule 14 have effect with respect to the keeping of an authority's Housing Revenue Account, as follows—

Part I—Credits to the account.

Part II—Debits to the account.

Part III—Supplementary provisions as to matters arising before 1972.

Part IV—Rate fund contributions.

Part V—Other supplementary provisions.

DEFINITION

"Housing Revenue Account": s.417.

GENERAL NOTE

There are five Parts to Sched. 14. Part I specifies what money is to be credited to the Housing Revenue Account ("H.R.A.") which the authority are obliged to maintain under s.417, above. Part II governs what is to be debited to the H.R.A. Part III contains a number of supplementary provisions relating to "matters arising before 1972", *i.e.* prior to the major change in subsidy systems introduced by the Housing Finance Act 1972 (before they were changed again in 1975 and again in 1980). Part IV deals with rate fund contributions to the H.R.A. Part V contains supplementary provisions. In addition, see s.420, below, as to the Secretary of State's power (and exercise thereof) to give directions as to credits and debits to the H.R.A. See s.430 for the application of capital monies received on disposal.

Part I

The first and most obvious item which the authority must credit to the H.R.A. is "rents and charges" in respect of houses and other property within the account: Sched. 14, Part I, para. 1. As to what property is within the account, see s.417(3) referring back to s.417(1), see notes thereto, above. The main block of property will be land, houses and other buildings within Part II, above.

Where a rent (or licence fee) is remitted by way of rebate under the Social Security and Housing Benefits Act 1982, and the Housing Benefits Regulations 1985 (S.I. 1985 No. 677) thereunder, only the net amount actually paid by the tenant is credited to the account, but both the rent rebate supplement payable under the 1982 Act, and any balance made up out of the general rate fund will also be credited: Sched. 14, Part I, paras. 4 and 5, and Part II, para. 3.

Most local authority rents are paid, on a weekly or other periodic basis, inclusive of rates. The amount attributable to the rates is not to be credited to the H.R.A., *save* in the case of a lodging-house or hostel. In such cases, for the purposes of s.16, General Rate Act 1967, the occupier would be unlikely to be considered in rateable occupation.

Charges for services, *e.g.* central heating, are credited to the H.R.A. under Sched. 14, Part I, para. 2. The paragraph includes income from a board or laundry service under s.11.

Housing subsidy payable under this Part (see notes to ss.421–425, below), is credited to the H.R.A.: Sched. 14, Part I, para. 3.

Contributions to the cost of any amount falling to be *debited* to the H.R.A. under Sched. 14, Part II, are to be credited to the H.R.A.: Sched. 14, Part I, para. 5. This will include contributions from the general rate fund under Sched. 14, Part IV. It should also include income from social services authorities towards the cost of special facilities for old people's housing: Housing Subsidies and Accounting Manual (1981 Edition, issued under cover of D.O.E. Circular 5/82), para. 168.

Under Sched. 14, Part I, para. 6, certain investment income is to be credited. This may arise from money within the H.R.A. It may also arise if an authority borrow for Part II purposes, but because it is not immediately used for its purpose, it is reinvested—in which case its income is also to be credited to the H.R.A. under this paragraph. Under Sched. 14, Part III, para. 5, investment income in respect of money borrowed for works in respect of which, before August 10, 1972, the Minister made a contribution or the local authority gave assistance under the Housing (Rural Workers) Act 1926 is to be credited to the H.R.A.

Under Sched. 14, Part I, para. 7, when property is sold, authorities may invest the proceeds, and the income from such investment is to be carried to the H.R.A. However, the Secretary of State may direct that the income is not to be credited to the H.R.A. Instalments of principal received from purchasers of Part II housing, and lump sums on outright sale of such, are not to be credited to the H.R.A., but to a Housing Capital Receipts Account: Housing Subsidies and Accounting Manual, para. 194. However, income from sale of housing built for sale (see s.9, above) goes to the H.R.A., either as a capital receipt or by investment and credit of the income: *ibid*, para. 195. The requirement to credit does not apply if the capital was carried to a fund under para. 16 of Schedule 13 to the Local Government Act 1972.

Finally, under Sched. 14, Part I, para. 8, if the authority maintain a Housing Repairs Account under s.419, they are entitled to carry a credit in the account to the H.R.A., if they consider that it will not be required for the purposes of the Housing Repairs Account: s.419(5). If they cease to maintain a Housing Repairs Account, the balance is to be carried to the H.R.A.: s.419(6).

Two further credits are identified in Sched. 14, Part III. Para. 3 thereof deals with the Housing Equalisation Accounts which authorities maintained prior to the Housing Finance Act 1972. On the abolition of the account by that Act, the balance was to be treated as a capital receipt by the authority, and income generated by it is still to be credited to the H.R.A. Secondly, on demolition, the authority may derive a sum of money, *e.g.* from sale of materials or scrap. The proceeds therefrom which arise on demolition of properties under one of three specified provisions are to be credited to the H.R.A. annually: Sched. 14, Part III, para. 7.

Part II

Loan charges (as defined in para. 2 of Part V of Sched. 14, below) for (a) providing housing under Part II, (b) purchasing houses under s.192 (see notes thereto, and to s.417, above), and (c) improvement of any property within the H.R.A. (see notes to s.417, above) are to be debited to the H.R.A. In addition, loan charges in respect of works to which, before August 10, 1972, the Minister made a contribution, or the local authority gave assistance, under the Housing (Rural Workers) Act 1926, are to be debited: Sched. 14, Part III, para. 5.

Also to be debited are the authority's outgoings by way of rent, rates, taxes or other charges which they have to pay for property within the H.R.A. (as to which, see notes to s.417, above), *e.g.* if they lease property and have to pay rent and/or other charges to a superior landlord, if they are not the rating authority, water rates, etc.: Sched. 14, Part II, para. 2. However, rates and charges *except* water rates or charges and owner's land drainage rates, are *not* to be debited to the H.R.A. so far as they relate to houses (not other buildings) within the H.R.A., *except* lodging-houses and hostels, and property occupied by caretakers and residential managers, *i.e.* if the rates are not to be credited to the H.R.A. under para. 1 of Part I of Sched. 14, nor are they to be debited.

The next, and obvious, debit is the cost of repair, maintenance, supervision and management of both the housing and other property within the H.R.A. (as to which, see notes to s.417, above): Sched. 14, Part II, para. 3. Repairs and maintenance will not be paid for from the H.R.A. however, if the authority maintain a Housing Repairs Account under s.419, below. Finally, authorities may debit to the H.R.A. sums paid to the optional Housing Repairs Account maintained under s.419: *ibid*. para. 4.

Part III

The effect of paras. 1, 2, and 4 of Sched. 14, Part III, have been noted to s.417, above. The effect of para. 5 has been noted under the last two sub-headings in this General Note. Paras. 3 and 7 have also been described in the note to Part I, above.

Under Sched. 14, Part III, para. 6, the power of the authority to make adjustments (credit or debit) to the H.R.A. which would have been made in 1972/73 or subsequent years had the Housing Finance Act 1972 not been passed is retained. Similarly, an adjustment on appropriation which has been required under s.24, Town and Country Planning Act 1959 but the time for effecting which has not yet arrived, remains in force.

Part IV

Sched. 14, Part IV, para. 1 expresses an important principle. When an authority exercise powers under s.12 (shops, recreation and beneficial purposes), the benefit may be shared by the community as a whole, *i.e.* not only the tenants or occupiers of an estate: see also notes to s.24, above; see also *Green & Sons* v. *Minister of Health* [1948] 1 K.B. 34, C.A. Such benefits and amenities may be reflected in the rates paid by those people. Whether or not they are, an amount which "properly reflects the community's share" is to be paid from the general rate fund to the H.R.A. The Secretary of State has a reserve power to enforce this requirement, subject to prior consultation (as to the meaning of which, see notes to s.420, below).

Under the Local Government Act 1972, s.123, local authorities may dispose of land at the best price reasonably obtainable, or at a lesser price with the consent of the Secretary of State. Similar powers are to be found in the Town and Country Planning Acts. If the property to be disposed of is from within the H.R.A. (see also ss.32 *et seq.*, above), the Secretary of State may require a contribution from the general rate fund over a number of years: Sched. 14, Part IV, para. 2. See the Housing Subsidies and Accounting Manual, para. 186.

Finally, under *ibid.* para. 4, the authority may make a voluntary transfer from the general rate fund to the H.R.A., and *must* do so if there is a deficit shown in the account for any year, *i.e.* the account must be kept out of deficit.

Part V

Conversely, if the H.R.A. is in credit, any part of that credit *may* be carried to the general rate fund, *i.e.* the housing may subsidise the rates, rather than the more traditional assumption that housing is subsidised by the rates: Sched. 14, Part V, para. 1. If no such transfer is made, the credit is carried forward to the next year: *ibid.*

Much public housing accounting is of necessity achieved by way of estimate, and later adjustment: *ibid.*, para. 3 authorises this approach.

Ibid., para. 4 contains additional provisions on appropriation to or from Part II purposes. Adjustment of accounts on appropriation is normally governed by s.24, Town and Country Planning Act 1959. In the case of an appropriation to or from Part II purposes, adjustment is, under this paragraph, as the Secretary of State may direct, either generally or particularly. See paragraph 187 and the general directions at App. F of the Housing Subsidies and Accounting Manual. See also s.27(5) of the 1959 Act, which permits the Secretary of State to direct an adjustment when a housing capital receipt is used for a non-Part II function, and paras. 191–193 and the general direction at App. G of the Manual.

The Secretary of State is entitled to review the "state of the Housing Revenue Account", and to require an authority, *or* an officer or employee of the authority, to provide him with such information as he may specify, generally or particularly, for that purpose: Sched. 14, Part V, para. 5. He can require such information to be supported by certificates: *ibid.*

The Secretary of State can permit an authority to disapply or modify any of the provisions of Sched. 14 to property within Part II, either by general or particular direction, and conditionally or unconditionally: *ibid.*, para. 6. This is available when the Secretary of State is satisfied that any of the provisions are "inappropriate".

The Housing Repairs Account

419.—(1) A local housing authority who are required to keep a Housing Revenue Account may also keep, in accordance with this section, an account called the "Housing Repairs Account".

(2) An authority who keep a Housing Repairs Account shall credit to the account—

(a) contributions from their Housing Revenue Account,

(b) sums received by the authority in connection with the repair or maintenance of houses or other property within the authority's Housing Revenue Account (either from their tenants or from the sale of scrapped or salvaged materials), and

(c) income arising from the investment or other use of money credited to the account.

(3) The authority shall debit to the account—

(*a*) all expenditure incurred by them in connection with the repair or maintenance of houses or other property within their Housing Revenue Account,

(*b*) such expenditure incurred by them in connection with the improvement or replacement of houses or other property within their Housing Revenue Account as may from time to time be determined by the Secretary of State, and

(*c*) any amount which is carried to the credit of the Housing Revenue Account in accordance with subsection (5);

and in this subsection "expenditure" includes loan charges.

(4) The authority shall secure that sufficient credits are carried to the account to secure that it never shows a debit balance.

(5) If the authority consider that a credit balance in the account at the end of a year will not be required for the purposes of the account, they may carry some or all of the balance to the credit of their Housing Revenue Account.

(6) If an authority who have opened a Housing Repairs Account cease to maintain the account, any balance shall be carried to their Housing Revenue Account.

(7) A determination of the Secretary of State under subsection (3)(*b*) may be made to apply to local housing authorities generally or to a particular authority or group of authorities and may make different provision in respect of different cases or descriptions of case.

DEFINITIONS
"Housing Revenue Account": s.417.
"local housing authority": ss.1, 2.

GENERAL NOTE
This section permits—but does not oblige—an authority to keep a Housing Repairs Account, effectively a sub-account of the Housing Revenue Account ("H.R.A."). They may pay money to it from the H.R.A. (subs. (2)(*a*), and indeed must do so to ensure that the Housing Repairs Account never shows a deficit (subs. (4)). They may also pay to it money received in connection with repairs and maintenance, *e.g.* a charge to a tenant, or on sale of scrap or salvage (subs. (2)(*b*)), and income derived from investing money in the account (subs. (2)(*c*)). This permits the authority to use the Housing Repairs Account to establish a fund from which the cost of future repairs and maintenance may be met.

If the authority maintain a Housing Repairs Account they must debit all the repairs and maintenance costs of property within the H.R.A. to it (*cf.* Sched. 14, Part II, para. 3, under which such costs are otherwise debited direct to the H.R.A. itself): subs. (3)(*a*). The authority must also debit to the Housing Repairs Account such improvement and replacement costs as the Secretary of State may determine (subs. (3)(*b*)); such a determination may be general or particular (subs. (7)).

Finally, the authority must debit to the Housing Repairs Account any money they transfer to the H.R.A. under subs. (5) (subs. (3)(*c*)), *i.e.* a credit balance which will not be required for the purposes of the account. This does not mean required in the forthcoming year, for the power is permissive, and they need only carry some if they wish. It would also contradict the investment provision, and, indeed, much of the purpose of the Housing Repairs Account. If, however, they choose to close the Housing Repairs Account, then the whole of the balance must be carried to the H.R.A.: subs. (6).

Directions to secure proper accounting

420.—(1) Where it appears to the Secretary of State, as regards a Housing Revenue Account or Housing Repairs Account—

(*a*) that amounts in respect of incomings and outgoings provided for in this Part have not been properly credited or debited to the account, or

(*b*) that amounts in respect of incomings and outgoings not so provided for ought properly to be credited or debited to the account, or (*c*) that amounts have been improperly credited or debited to the account,

he may give directions for the appropriate credits or debits to be made, or for the rectification of the account, as the case may require.

(2) In the case of incomings and outgoings not provided for in this Part the direction may, instead of directing particular amounts to be credited or debited, direct generally that credits or debits shall be made in respect of incomings and outgoings of a kind specified in the direction.

(3) Without prejudice to the generality of the preceding provisions, the Secretary of State may give such directions (which may be general directions or directions for a particular case) as to the amounts to be credited or debited to a Housing Revenue Account or Housing Repairs Account as in his opinion will ensure that the account reflects a proper system of internal accounting of the authority.

(4) Before giving a direction the Secretary of State shall consult—

(*a*) such associations of local authorities as appear to him to be concerned, and

(*b*) any local authority with whom consultation appears to him to be desirable,

except where the authorities who are to comply with the direction are all named in it, in which case the Secretary of State shall consult each of those authorities and need not consult any association of local authorities.

DEFINITIONS
"Housing Repairs Account": s.419.
"Housing Revenue Account": s.417.
"local authority": s.4.

GENERAL NOTE
This is the last of the sections governing the Housing Revenue Account ("H.R.A.") and the Housing Repairs Account. In some ways, it is the most important, for under its provisions, and certain of the provisions in Sched. 14 (see also notes to preceding three sections), is issued the Housing Subsidies and Accounting Manual (now, 1981 Edition, issued under cover of D.O.E. Circular 5/82) in which are to be found the financial details which take the law into financial practice.

Subs. (1) is concerned with improper credits or debits, and permits the Secretary of State to issue directions, or order rectification. This is the "control" power. Under subs. (2), where incomings and outgoings are not subject to any particular provision in this Part (*i.e.* the last foregoing sections and Sched. 14), the Secretary of State may issue a general direction covering such items. Under subs. (3), he may issue general or particular directions as to the amounts to be credited or debited as ensure that the account reflects "a proper system of internal accounting of the authority".

Under App. D of the Housing Subsidies and Accounting Manual, the Secretary of State has issued a general direction dealing with: (a) treatment of instalments on purchase price or premium of a house built expressly for disposal under s.9, above; (b) net loss of the demolition of certain buildings; and (c) treatment of interest on working balances in the H.R.A. or surpluses within the H.R.A.

Subs. (4)
Consultation. Before giving any direction under this section, the Secretary of State must "consult" with local authority associations, and any particular authority with whom consultation appears to him to be desirable. However, if the direction names all the affected authorities, then he must instead consult with those authorities named.

There has been a number of cases on the meaning of consultation: see, *e.g., Rollo* v. *Minister of Town and Country Planning* [1948] L.J.R. 817, 1 All E.R. 13, *Re. Union of Benefices of Whippingham and East Cowes, St. James* [1954] A.C. 245, H.L., *Sinfield* v. *London Transport Executive* [1970] 1 Ch. 550, and *R.* v. *Sheffield City Council, ex parte Mansfield* (1978) 37 P. & C.R. 1. Most recently, the question was considered in relation to consultation on amendments to the Housing Benefits Regulations, as required by s.36, Social Security and Housing Benefits Act 1982, in *R.* v. *Secretary of State for Social Services, ex parte Association of Metropolitan Authorities* (1985) 17 H.L.R. 487, Q.B.D. The importance of the case, and its apparent applicability to a number of instances in which consultation is required under this Act, suggest that it is worth considering the judgment in some detail.

(1) The essence of consultation is the communication of a genuine invitation to give advice and a genuine receipt of that advice; to achieve consultation, sufficient information must be supplied by the consulting to the consulted party to enable it to tender helpful advice; sufficient time must be given by the consulting to the consulted party to enable it to do so, and sufficient time must be available for such advice to be considered by the consulting party; sufficient in this context does not mean ample, but at least enough to enable the relevant purpose to be fulfilled; helpful advice in this context means sufficiently informed and considered information or advice about aspects of the form or substance of the proposals, or their implication for the consulted party, being aspects material to the implementation of the proposal as to which the consulting party might not be fully informed or advised and as to which the party consulted might have relevant information or advice to offer.

(2) Where insufficient consultation is alleged, the challenge is to the vires of the subordinate legislation; accordingly, the correct test is whether there has been sufficient consultation, rather than whether the consultation process fails to satisfy the test known as "rationality", or the "unreasonable" test in *Associated Provincial Pictures Houses Ltd.* v. *Wednesbury Corporation* [1948] 1 K.B. 223, C.A.

(3) The power to make the Regulations was conferred on the Secretary of State, and his is the duty to consult; both the form or substance of new Regulations and the time allowed for consulting before making them, may well depend in whole or in part on matters of a political nature, as to the force or implications of which the Secretary of State rather than the court is the best judge; when considering whether or not consultation has in substance been carried out, the court should have regard not so much to the actual facts which preceded the making of the Regulations as to the material before the Secretary of State when he made the Regulations, which material includes facts or information as it appeared or must have appeared to the Secretary of State acting in good faith, and any judgments made or opinions expressed to him before the making of the Regulations about those facts which appeared or could have appeared to him to be reasonable.

(4) The urgency of the need for the Regulations as seen by the Secretary of State *was* such, taking into account the nature of the amendments proposed, that the Department was entitled to require that views in response to its invitation for comments should be expressed quickly; the urgency of the need for the Regulations, as seen by the Secretary of State, taking into account the nature of the amendments proposed, *was not* such that the Department was entitled to require views to be expressed within such a short period that those views would or might be insufficiently informed or insufficiently considered so that the applicants would or might be unable to tender helpful advice.

(5) Taking into account both the urgency of the matter, as seen by the Department, and the material features of the Regulations, and bearing in mind that the applicants had no knowledge until after the Regulations were made of one of their features, the Secretary of State failed to fulfil his obligation to consult before making the Regulations; the time allowed was so short, and the failure to provide amendments was such that, as the Department must have known even without imputing to them precise knowledge of the applicants' internal arrangements for formulating a response, only piecemeal, and then only partial, assistance could be given.

(6) In the ordinary case, a decision made *ultra vires* is likely to be set aside; in the present case the applicants sought to strike down Regulations which had become part of the public law of the land; it may be that when delegated legislation is held to be *ultra vires*, it is not necessarily to be regarded as normal practice to revoke the instrument. As a matter of pure discretion, the Statutory Instrument would not be revoked for the following reasons: only one of the six associations which had been and habitually were consulted had applied for revocation, and that one applied only on the ground that it was not properly consulted; the Regulations had been in force for about six months and authorities must have adapted themselves as best they could to the difficulties which had been imposed on them; if the Regulations were revoked, all those who had been refused benefit because of them would be entitled to make fresh claims, and all authorities would be required to consider each such claim; the Amendment Regulations had been consolidated into the Housing Benefit Regulations 1985 (S.I. 1985, No. 677) and which had come into operation, which Regulations were not challenged.

Housing subsidy

Housing subsidy

421.—(1) Housing subsidy is payable for each year to housing authorities.

(2) Housing subsidy shall be credited—

    (*a*) if paid to a local housing authority, to the authority's Housing Revenue Account, and

    (*b*) if paid to another body, to that body's housing account or appropriate housing account.

(3) Housing subsidy shall be paid by the Secretary of State at such times, in such manner and subject to such conditions as to records, certificates, audit or otherwise as he may, with the agreement of the Treasury, determine.

(4) Payment of housing subsidy is subject to the making of a claim for it in such form, and containing such particulars, as the Secretary of State may from time to time determine.

DEFINITIONS

    "housing authority": s.4.

    "Housing Revenue Account": s.417.

    "local housing authority": ss.1, 2.

    "year": s.433.

GENERAL NOTE

If the authority to which subsidy is payable is a local housing authority, it is to be credited to their Housing Revenue Account ("H.R.A."): subs. (2)(*a*); see also s.418 and Sched. 14, Part I, para. 3. If it is paid to another body (see s.426, below), to that body's housing or appropriate housing account: subs. (2)(*b*). Subsidy is payable for each year, which means a period of twelve months beginning on April 1: s.433. It is paid at such times, in such manner and subject to such conditions as to records, certificates, audit or otherwise as the Secretary of State may, with the agreement of the Treasury, determine: subs. (4). It is subject to claim in such form, containing such particulars, as the Secretary of State may determine: subs. (5).

App. B of the Housing Subsidies and Accounting Manual (1981 Edition, issued under cover of D.O.E. Circular 5/82), contains the current determination under subs. (4). Forms under subs. (5) are issued annually. They are the Housing Investment Programme ("H.I.P.") Application forms, and contain information as to the authority's past expenditure, existing commitments, and aspirations for the next financial year. Subsequently, the Secretary of State issues the authority's H.I.P. Allocation, which is the authority's share of what the government consider that the country can afford to spend on housing nationally: "These new arrangements will represent a major change in the system of the determination of priorities between different categories of spending within the national total of capital expenditure available for public housing". (D.O.E. Circular 63/77, para. 4, on the introduction of the system).

The H.I.P. system is not confined to housing subsidy under this Part. What the H.I.P. application is for, and what the H.I.P. allocation permits, is the amount of *borrowing* by local authorities to meet their capital expenditure under the many provisions of this Act. What housing subsidies are for is to meet, or to help meet, the loan charges on such borrowing. To the extent that the activity is within Part II, above, the subsidy is under ss.422–425, below; to the extent that it is under ss.244 and 253–258, in Part VIII, the subsidy is under ss.245 and 259, above; Part IX slum clearance subsidy is under ss.312–314, above; subsidy under Part XV (housing improvement grants) is under ss.516–517, below, save that "homes insulation grants" is under s.522, below; subsidy under Part XVI (defective houses) is under ss.569–570, below.

Borrowing above the amount permitted in the H.I.P. Allocation is not *per se* illegal (indeed, much local authority housing borrowing does not appear to require consent as such: see notes to s.428, below); however, the loan charges will not be admitted for subsidy under this Part, and additional borrowing will accordingly be very expensive indeed. It is at this point that "housing finance" meets local government finance as a whole, and a short note of how local government finance now operates may assist in identifying and locating the controls that now exist on housing spending.

A Note On Local Government Finance

The amount of the H.I.P. allocation will normally be the same as the amount specified for borrowing within the housing block of the "prescribed expenditure" levels set under Part VIII, Local Government, Planning and Land Act 1980. "True" control lies in *that* Act.

Under Part VIII of that Act, *capital* spending (whether on housing or otherwise) is restricted, or "prescribed". The items which qualify as capital spending for this purpose are defined in Sched. 12 of the Act, as further qualified by statutory instrument. They include most public housing capital expenditure. Levels are annually adjusted. The allowances can be "vired" between the different blocks in which permission is granted. It is subject to a 10 per cent. "tolerance" between years. The prescribed expenditure level is not a fixed amount, but related to income from sales (to extents specified by statutory instrument) and even source of money, *e.g.* some capital expenditure on Part II stock will not count as prescribed to the extent that it is met by income from rents.

It is, accordingly, a severe control on capital spending, for the effect of overspending is that the excess is deducted from future years' permitted levels, with the consequence that an authority could soon find it had no capital spending capacity left at all. The Secretary of State enjoys reserve powers to issue directions to prohibit capital overspending under these provisions. To the extent that authorities do spend on capital, or have so spent in past years before the 1980 Act, the loan charges generated are or become a revenue expenditure— perhaps reduced by housing subsidy under the following sections, perhaps not (see notes to ss.422–425, below).

Revenue expenditure, too, is controlled. This is achieved under Part VI, 1980 Act, under which the authority will (or may) receive Rate Support Grant, for its General Rate Fund, based on an annual "target" Grant Related Expenditure Assessment (G.R.E.A.). To the extent that their global expenditure exceeds their annual G.R.E.A. under Part VI, their Rate Support Grant is *reduced*, at levels that exceed the amount of the overspend, so that in substance the more that is spent above the G.R.E.A., the less Rate Support Grant that will be paid, to the point that a number of authorities now receive no Rate Support Grant at all, and have to meet their full General Rate Fund costs out of rates.

This is where the general controls meet housing spending. As already noted (above, s.418), the Housing Revenue Account *must* be kept out of deficit. If an authority's spending—including its loan charges—is above the total of its income from subsidy (under ss.422–425, below), if any, and its income from other sources, *i.e.* principally rents (see notes to s.418), but also from sales, the General Rate Fund will *have* to make a contribution to meet the shortfall. That contribution is part of the authority's global expenditure. That contribution may cause global expenditure to exceed G.R.E.A., and in turn generate an additional cost by way of lost Rate Support Grant, *i.e.* must be made up out of the rates. To complete the picture, the Rates Act 1984 permits the government to set limits on the rates ("ratecapping") which an authority can raise.

Local authority spending, then, is now highly constrained by central government controls, principally under the 1980 Act (with the threat of the 1984 Act in the background—and, it is well known, in annual use). To summarise: housing capital expenditure is restrained by (a) Part VIII, 1980 Act, (b) the extent to which it will qualify for housing subsidy under this Act, and (c) the fact that the revenue cost (loan charges) so far as unmet by subsidy must be met from income (rents and other) to the Housing Revenue Account, and if that is not sufficient from the General Rate Fund, with the consequence (d) that the authority may overspend its 1980 Act G.R.E.A. "target", with (e) loss of 1980 Act Rate Support Grant, so that reliance is increasingly on (f) income from rates, with the final threat of (g) "ratecapping" under the 1984 Act.

Calculation of housing subsidy for local housing authorities

422.—(1) The amount of the housing subsidy payable to a local housing authority for a year (the year of account) shall be calculated from the amounts which, in accordance with sections 423 to 425, are the authority's—

(*a*) base amount (BA),

(*b*) housing costs differential (HCD), and

(*c*) local contribution differential (LCD),

for the year, and shall be so calculated by using the formula BA + HCD − LCD.

(2) If the amount so calculated is nil or a negative amount, no housing subsidy is payable to the authority for that year.

DEFINITIONS
"base amount": s.423.
"housing costs differential": s.424.
"local contribution differential": s.425.
"local housing authority": ss.1, 2.

GENERAL NOTE
This section defines the amount of housing subsidy. The formula is relatively simple: base amount plus housing costs differential less local contribution differential. No subsidy is payable if, as is now not uncommon, the amount is nil or a negative amount. But a nil or negative amount will continue to count: for it will be the starting-point of the next year's calculation—see s.423, below.

Note that an alteration of accounting practices by an authority will not be taken into account when determining subsidy, unless the consent of the Department of the Environment has been secured: Housing Subsidies and Accounting Manual (1981 Edition, issued under cover of D.O.E. Circular 5/82), para. 22.

Note, too, that if subsidy is not spent on the purpose for which it was paid, it may be "recouped" under s.427, below.

The base amount

423.—(1) A local housing authority's base amount for a year of account is, subject to any adjustment under subsection (2), the amount calculated for the preceding year under section 422, that is to say, the amount of the housing subsidy payable to the authority for that year or, if none was payable, nil or a negative amount, as the case may be.

(2) If the Secretary of State is of opinion that particular circumstances require it, he may adjust the base amount for any year by increasing or decreasing it, either generally or in relation to any description of authority or any particular authority.

DEFINITIONS
"local housing authority": ss.1, 2.
"year": s.433.

GENERAL NOTE
The base amount was the amount calculated for the previous year, which can be a nil or negative amount. The important point to make is that the provisions were introduced by s.97, Housing Act 1980, and under s.98 thereof the "first" base amount was the amount of subsidy payable in 1981–82, which was calculated by reference to the amount payable under previous legislation in 1980–81. The "base" then refers in substance to 1980–81, subject only to adjustment under subs. (2).

There is no express requirement for consultation before adjustment, although such is assumed in the Housing Subsidies and Accounting Manual (1981 Edition, issued under cover of D.O.E. Circular 5/82), para. 15, where it is also noted that "it is expected that the need for such adjustments will be infrequent". It would seem, however, wholly impossible for the Secretary of State to decrease the base amount without consultation with the authority affected, without risk of challenge for want of natural justice or administrative fairness, or failure to take something relevant (*i.e.* the views of the authority affected) into account, unless, of course, the cause and consequence were well-known to the authority, and wholly within their control. See, generally, the cases noted to s.64, above. Consider also, *e.g.*, *McInnes* v. *Onslow Fane* [1978] 1 W.L.R. 1520.

Clearly, there must be some basis for adjustment, and if the reason is inadequate, or based on false information, a decision to adjust may be impeachable: see, *e.g.*, *Secretary of State for Employment* v. *A.S.L.E.F. (No. 2)* [1972] 2 Q.B. 455, C.A., *Secretary of State for Education and Science* v. *Metropolitan Borough of Tameside* [1977] A.C. 1014, H.L. (see the quotation in the notes to s.64, above), and *Laker Airways Ltd.* v. *Department of Trade* [1977] Q.B. 643, C.A.

The housing costs differential

424.—(1) A local housing authority's housing costs differential for a year of account is the amount by which their reckonable expenditure for

that year exceeds their reckonable expenditure for the preceding year
(and accordingly is nil or, as the case may be, a negative amount if the
reckonable expenditure for the year is the same as or less than that for
the preceding year).

(2) A local housing authority's reckonable expenditure for a year is the
aggregate of—

  (a) so much of the expenditure incurred by the authority in that year
      and falling to be debited to the authority's Housing Revenue
      Account as the Secretary of State may determine, and

  (b) so much of any other expenditure incurred by the authority in that
      year, or treated as so incurred in accordance with a determination
      made by the Secretary of State, as the Secretary of State may
      determine to be taken into account for the purposes of housing
      subsidy.

(3) A determination may be made for all local housing authorities or
different determinations may be made—

  (a) for authorities of different descriptions, or

  (b) for authorities in England and authorities in Wales, or in different
      parts of England or Wales; or

  (c) for individual authorities;

and a determination may be varied or revoked in relation to all or any of
the authorities for which it was made.

(4) Before making a determination for all local housing authorities the
Secretary of State shall consult organisations appearing to him to be
representative of local housing authorities.

DEFINITIONS
  "Housing Revenue Account": s.417.
  "local housing authority": ss.1, 2.
  "year": s.433.

GENERAL NOTE
  This is the amount by which the base amount (see s.423, above) *may* be increased, *if* the
reckonable expenditure increases: subs. (1). That which will be added to the base amount
is the increase in reckonable expenditure. However, to achieve an increase in reckonable
expenditure effectively requires the consent of the Secretary of State, for that which is
reckonable is only so much of the expenditure falling to be debited to the Housing Revenue
Account ("H.R.A.") (above, ss.417, 418) as the Secretary of State determines, plus so much
other expenditure actually or deemed to have been incurred as the Secretary of State
determines to be taken into account for the purpose of subsidy. Note that if the reckonable
expenditure is *less* than the previous year, the decrease is *deducted* from the base amount.
  If the authority maintain a Housing Repairs Account (above, s.419) expenditure therefrom
on repair and maintenance can be included in reckonable expenditure: Housing Subsidies
and Accounting Manual (1981 Edition, issued under cover of D.O.E. Circular 5/82), para.
19. The principal items admitted to reckonable expenditure are those specified in App. A
to the Manual, expanded in paras. 23 to 150. However, App. A does not deal with
expenditure on repairs, maintenance, management and supervision of H.R.A. dwellings:
this is covered by an annual "M. & M." determination by the Secretary of State: Manual,
para. 37.

Subs. (3)
  Determinations may be general, or applicable to particular authorities, or by areas.

Subs. (4)
  As to consultation, see note to s.420(4), above.

The local contribution differential

425.—(1) A local housing authority's local contribution differential for
a year of account is the amount by which their reckonable income for that
year exceeds their reckonable income for the preceding year (and accord-

ingly is nil or, as the case may be, a negative amount if their reckonable income for the year is the same as or less than that for the preceding year).

(2) An authority's reckonable income for a year is the amount which, in accordance with any determination made by the Secretary of State, the authority are assumed to receive for that year as income which they are required to carry to their Housing Revenue Account including—

(a) any contribution made by the authority out of their general rate fund, and

(b) any rent rebate subsidy payable under section 32 of the Social Security and Housing Benefit Act 1982,

but excluding any other subsidy, grant or contribution.

(3) A determination shall state the assumptions on which it is based and the method of calculation used in it, and in making it the Secretary of State shall have regard, amongst other things, to past and expected movements in incomes, costs and prices.

(4) A determination may be made for all local housing authorities or different determinations may be made—

(a) for authorities of different descriptions, or

(b) for authorities in England and authorities in Wales, or in different parts of England and Wales, or

(c) for individual authorities.

(5) Before making a determination for all local housing authorities the Secretary of State shall consult organisations appearing to him to be representative of local housing authorities.

(6) A determination shall be made known to the authorities for which it is made in the year preceding the year of account for which it is to have effect.

DEFINITIONS

"Housing Revenue Account": s.417.

"local housing authority": ss.1, 2.

"year": s.433.

GENERAL NOTE

This is the third, and in some respects the most critical element in the calculation of subsidy. The Secretary of State determines the reckonable income of an authority, and to the extent that it is higher than the reckonable income in a previous year the subsidy to which the authority would otherwise be entitled (base amount under s.423 plus housing costs differential under s.424) is reduced: subs. (1). Conversely, although only when an authority have a significant stock reduction is this in the current climate of public expenditure anything other than theoretical, if the reckonable income reduces, subsidy could be increased.

The principal element is rents. The Secretary of State makes an annual determination of by how much rents are expected to increase. Local contribution differential is not dealt with at all in the Housing Subsidies and Accounting Manual (1981 Edition, issued under cover of D.O.E. Circular 5/82): see para. 151 thereof. In addition, however, the Secretary of State's calculation covers what he assumes the authority will pay to their H.R.A. from the general rate fund, and how much will be paid (by the Department of Health and Social Security) by way of rent rebate subsidy under s.32, Social Security and Housing Benefits Act 1982.

The determination, which must be made known at the latest by March 31 in the year before that to which it is to apply (subs. (6) and s.433), has to state the assumptions on which it is based, and the method of calculation which it uses, and in making it the Secretary of State has to have regard to "past and expected movements in incomes, costs and prices". Before making the determination, the Secretary of State must consult: see notes to s.420(4), above.

Of central if unstated relevance will be the Secretary of State's own assessment of the authority's G.R.E.A. "target" for spending under the Local Government, Planning and Land Act 1980, Part VI (see notes to s.421, above), for the Secretary of State cannot in practice assume an amount from the general rate fund which is inconsistent with the amount to which he has related the authority's Rate Support Grant (under threat of penalty if it is exceeded).

As to rent-fixing by authorities, including in the light of these provisions, see notes to s.24, above.

Subs. (4)
Determinations may be general, for a particular authority, or by areas.

Calculation of housing subsidy for other authorities

426.—(1) Sections 422 to 425 (calculation of housing subsidy) apply in relation to new town corporations and the Development Board for Rural Wales as they apply in relation to local housing authorities, but subject to the following provisions of this section.

(2) In relation to a new town corporation—

(*a*) sections 424(2) and 425(2) (reckonable expenditure and income) have effect with the substitution for references to the authority's Housing Revenue Account of references to the corporation's housing account, and

(*b*) section 425(2)(*a*) (reckonable income to include rate fund contributions) has effect with the substitution for the reference to the authority's general rate fund of a reference to the corporation's general revenue account.

(3) In relation to the Board—

(*a*) sections 424(2) and 425(2) (reckonable expenditure and income) have effect with the substitution for references to the authority's Housing Revenue Account of references to the Board's housing account, and

(*b*) section 425(2)(*a*) (reckonable income to include rate fund contributions) has effect with the substitution for the reference to any contribution made by the authority out of their general rate fund of a reference to any contribution made by the Board out of revenue.

(4) The consultation required by section 424(4) or 425(5) (consultation before making general determinations) shall be with organisations appearing to the Secretary of State to be representative of new town corporations or, as the case may be, with the Development Board for Rural Wales.

(5) The Commission for the New Towns shall be treated as a separate body in respect of each of its new towns.

DEFINITIONS
"local housing authority": ss.1, 2.
"new town corporation": s.4.

GENERAL NOTE
This adapts the subsidy provisions to the accounting procedures and requirements of new town corporations, the Development Board for Rural Wales, and the Commission for the New Towns: see New Towns Act 1981, and Development of Rural Wales Act 1976.

Recoupment of subsidy in certain cases

427.—(1) Where housing subsidy has been paid to a local housing authority or other body and it appears to the Secretary of State that—

(*a*) the purpose for which it was paid has not been fulfilled or not completely or adequately or not without unreasonable delay, and

(*b*) that the case falls within rules published by him,

he may recover from the authority or other body the whole or such part of the payment as he may determine in accordance with the rules, with interest from such time and at such rates as he may so determine.

(2) A sum recoverable under this section may, without prejudice to other methods of recovery, be recovered by withholding or reducing housing subsidy.

(3) The withholding or reduction under this section of housing subsidy for a year does not affect the base amount for the following year.

<small>DEFINITION</small>
"local housing authority": ss.1, 2.

<small>GENERAL NOTE</small>
Subsidy may be "recouped", by withholding or reduction of future subsidy (subs. (2)) or otherwise, if it appears to the Secretary of State (a) that the purpose for which it was paid has not been fulfilled, or not completely fulfilled, or not adequately fulfilled, or not fulfilled without unreasonable delay, *and* (b) that the case falls within rules published by him. The rules are to set out how recoupment (and interest thereon) is to be calculated.

The rules are in App. C of the Housing Subsidies and Accounting Manual (1981 Edition, issued under cover of D.O.E. Circular 5/82). The extent of detail suggests that additional prior notice and opportunity to comment will not be required: indeed, the requirement is for the authority to notify the Secretary of State that recoupment is to be effected—App. C, para. 8.

Borrowing powers

Continuance of certain powers to borrow for housing purposes

428.—(1) A local authority may borrow for any of the purposes for which borrowing was, before the commencement of this Act, authorised by—

section 136(1) of the Housing Act 1957,
section 54(1) of the Housing (Financial Provisions) Act 1958, or
paragraph 19 of Schedule 8 to the Housing Act 1969.

(2) The maximum period which may be sanctioned as the period for which money may be borrowed for any of those purposes by the Common Council of the City of London is 80 years, notwithstanding the provisions of any Act of Parliament.

<small>DEFINITION</small>
"local authority": s.4.

<small>GENERAL NOTE</small>
Section 136(1), Housing Act 1957, authorised borrowing for the following purposes:

(a) Part II of the 1957 Act so far as it related to the execution of repairs and works by local authorities—now, works in default under Parts VI and IX (so far as individual houses, rather than clearance areas, are concerned) of this Act;

(b) Part III of the 1957 Act—now, Part IX of this Act so far as clearance areas are concerned;

(c) Part IV of the 1957 Act—now, Part X of this Act;

(d) Part V of the 1957 Act—now, Part II of this Act, together with s.58, Housing Associations Act 1985 (grants and loans to registered housing associations), except ss.25–28.

Section 54(1) of the Housing (Financial Provisions) Act 1958 permitted borrowing for any of the purposes of the 1958 Act—now, ss.435–440, below.

Sched. 8, para. 19, Housing Act 1969 permitted borrowing for any of the purposes of the 1969 Act—now, the General Improvement Area provisions of Part VIII of this Act, certain of the provisions of Part XI of this Act relating to houses in multiple occupation, and certain of the provisions of Part XVII of this Act relating to payments for well-maintained housing.

The importance of the continuation of these powers is that no ministerial consent appears to be required for the borrowing. The provisions of s.172 and Sched. 13, Local Government Act 1972, would not appear to be applicable to borrowing under another statute (compare the wording of Sched. 13, paras. 1 and 2, and s.111).

This is *not* to say that the cost of loan charges on such borrowing will qualify for subsidy, because under App. A to the Housing Subsidies and Accounting Manual (1981 Edition, issued under cover of D.O.E. Circular 5/82,—see also notes to ss.417–420, above) in order to be admissible loan charges must be within borrowing consents (even though that consent may not be needed), nor is it to say that the cost of loan charges will not offend the spending targets in Part VI, Local Government, Planning and Land Act 1980 (*cf.* notes to s.421, above). Nor, of course, will the fact that no consent is needed legitimise the spending in relation to the prescribed expenditure levels in Part VIII of that Act (see *ibid.*).

The sole value of the provision would accordingly seem to be where (perhaps on account of rate support grant "penalties" in Part VI of the 1980 Act, see notes to s.421, above) borrowing for current (or "revenue") expenditure is considered (by the proper officer of the authority for the purposes of s.151, Local Government Act 1972) "proper administration" within that section. Even then all the borrowing must also comply with the requirements of the Borrowing (Control and Guarantees) Act 1946, and orders thereunder. The Control of Borrowing Order of January 1, 1968, however, provides a general consent to local authority borrowing subject to only limited exceptions, so that this should not prove an insuperable fetter.

Miscellaneous

The improvement for sale scheme

429.—(1) The Secretary of State may, with the consent of the Treasury, make schemes for making contributions to the net cost (as determined under the schemes) to local housing authorities of disposing of dwellings where the authority—

(*a*) disposes of a house as one dwelling,

(*b*) divides a house into two or more separate dwellings and disposes of them, or

(*c*) combines two houses to form one dwelling and disposes of it,

after carrying out works of repair, improvement or conversion.

(2) The cost towards which contributions may be made under such a scheme shall not exceed, for any one dwelling—

(*a*) in respect of a dwelling in Greater London, £10,000,

(*b*) elsewhere, £7,500,

or such other amount as may be prescribed by order of the Secretary of State made with the consent of the Treasury.

(3) An order under this section—

(*a*) may make different provision in respect of different cases or descriptions of case, including different provision for different areas, and

(*b*) shall be made by statutory instrument which shall be subject to annulment in pursuance of a resolution of either House of Parliament.

(4) In this section "house" includes a flat.

DEFINITION
"local housing authority": ss.1, 2.

GENERAL NOTE
Under s.9, above, an authority may provide housing by purchase of houses or buildings, and by erection or conversion, and they may exercise these powers even if it is intended to dispose of them for sale. Under ss.32 *et seq.*, they may sell Part II housing, subject to consent. Under this section, the Secretary of State may provide assistance to local authorities who sell after carrying out works of repair, improvement or conversion, whether the sale is as one house, or by dividing a house into flats, or by combining houses to form a single dwelling. The sections taken together permit authorities to purchase expressly for the purpose of taking advantage of such a scheme (in which case it is known as "A.I.M.S."—acquisition and improvement for sale), or else to use the scheme in connection with property they already own. Properties should not be included in the Housing Revenue Account: see notes to s.417, above.

The grant is available only for voluntary sales, not for disposals under the right to buy in Part V: see D.O.E. Circular 20/80, Annex A, para. 2.4. The figures in subs. (2) reflect those which have been in force since June 8, 1981: see S.I. 1981 No. 723. They are maxima of the amounts *towards which a contribution may be made*, and the Secretary of State in fact meets only a proportion of the cost: see D.O.E. Circular 18/21, Annex. The maximum actual *contribution* is £6,500 per dwelling in Greater London and £4,875 elsewhere under the Circular. The cost relates to the dwelling provided, not the property or properties from which it or they have been converted. The requirement of project approval in s.431, below, is not applicable: see Annex A to Circular 20/80.

Application of capital money received on disposal of land

430.—(1) Capital money received by a local authority in respect of a disposal of, or other dealing with, land held for any of the purposes of this Act shall be applied either in the repayment of debt or for any other purpose for which capital money may properly be applied.

(2) Where section 27 of the Town and Country Planning Act 1959 (general power to apply capital money without consent) does not apply, the application of capital money in accordance with subsection (1) shall be effected only with the consent of the Secretary of State, except that capital money received in respect of the disposal of, or other dealing with, land held for the purposes of Part II (provision of housing) may, without such consent, be applied by the authority in or towards the purchase of other land for the purposes of Part II.

DEFINITION
"local authority": s.4.

GENERAL NOTE
"Land" includes "buildings and other structures, land covered with water, and any estate, interest, easement, servitude or right in or over land": Interpretation Act 1978, Sched. 1.

If the authority dispose of land—whether under Part II or under the last foregoing section or otherwise—they are to apply the receipt either in repayment of the outstanding debt or to any other purpose for which capital moneys may properly be applied: subs. (1). However, under subs. (2), if the disposal does not fall within s.27, Town and Country Planning Act 1959, the consent of the Secretary of State is required for the application of a disposal of property held for the purposes of Part II, above, unless it is applied in or towards the purchase of other land.

Section 27 of the 1959 Act permits disposal without consent, even if such is otherwise required, if one of the following conditions is fulfilled. In such a case, therefore, the consent of the Secretary of State is not needed, even if the disposal is of Part II land or property.

(1) In the case of a county council, the sum involved is less than £1,000;

(2) In the case of a district council either £1,000 or, if less, the product of a 0.4p rate;

(3) The money is to be applied in repayment of a debt wholly or in part incurred for the purpose of acquiring or developing the land in question, or otherwise in connection with that land;

(4) The money is to be applied towards the repayment of any debt repayable within the next fifteen years;

(5) The money is to be applied to a purpose authorised by paragraph 1(b), Sched. 13, Local Government Act 1972;

(6) The money is to be applied from a capital fund under para. 16, Sched. 13, Local Government Act 1972, or established under a local enactment which includes a provision requiring money derived from the sale of land bought from a fund to be repaid to the same fund.

Control of expenditure by housing authorities on works of conversion or improvement

431.—(1) A local authority or new town corporation may not incur expenses in—

(*a*) providing dwellings by the conversion of houses or other buildings, or

(*b*) carrying out works required for the improvement of dwellings, with or without associated works of repair,

except in accordance with proposals submitted by the authority or corporation to the Secretary of State and for the time being approved by him.

(2) The Secretary of State's approval may be given subject to such conditions, and may be varied in such circumstances, as appear to him to be appropriate; but before varying the terms of an approval he shall consult the authority or corporation concerned.

(3) In this section "dwelling" has the same meaning as in Part XV (grants for works of improvement, repair and conversion).

DEFINITIONS
"local authority": s.4.
"new town corporation": s.4.

GENERAL NOTE
This section contains the requirement for prior "project control" on works of conversion and improvement. It is aimed at renovation of the authority's own stock, and municipalisation: see D.O.E. Circular 23/82. It does not cover improvement for sale under s.429, above: see D.O.E. Circular 20/80. The details of project control (in Circular 23/82) are an important part of the control of costs qualifying for subsidy, under s.422, above.

Subs. (2)
"Consult". See notes to s.420(4), above.

Subs. (3)
See notes to s.460, below.

Superseded contributions, subsidies, grants, and other financial matters

432. The provisions of Schedule 15 have effect with respect to superseded contributions, subsidies, grants and other financial matters, as follows—

Part I—Loans under the Housing (Rural Workers) Acts 1926 to 1942.

Part II—Exchequer contributions for agricultural housing.

Part III—Contributions for improvement of dwellings by housing authorities.

Part IV—Town development subsidy.

GENERAL NOTE
Sched. 15 contains the continuation provisions in relation to a number of miscellaneous subordinate subsidies under previous legislation, *i.e.* those not taken into the base amount by s.423, above, and before that s.98, Housing Act 1980.

Supplementary

Minor definitions

433. In this Part—
"year" means a period of twelve months beginning on a 1st April.

Index of defined expressions: Part XIII

434. The following Table shows provisions defining or otherwise explaining expressions used in this Part (other than provisions defining or explaining an expression used in the same section or paragraph):—

base amount	section 423
development corporation	section 4(*c*)
general rate fund	section 622
hostel	section 622
houses or other property within the account (in reference to the Housing Revenue Account)	section 417(3)
housing authority	section 4(*a*)
housing costs differential	section 424

Housing Repairs Account	section 419(1)
Housing Revenue Account	section 417(1)
housing subsidy	section 421(1)
loan charges (in relation to the keeping of the Housing Revenue Account)	paragraph 2 of Part V of Schedule 14
local authority	section 4(*e*)
local contribution differential	section 425
local housing authority	section 1, 2(2)
new town corporation	section 4(*b*)
receiving authority (in Part IV of Schedule 15)	paragraph 6 of that Part
year	section 433
year of account (in relation to housing subsidy)	section 422

PART XIV

LOANS FOR ACQUISITION OR IMPROVEMENT OF HOUSING

Local authority mortgages

Power of local authorities to advance money

435.—(1) A local authority may advance money to a person for the purpose of—

(*a*) acquiring a house,

(*b*) constructing a house,

(*c*) converting another building into a house or acquiring another building and converting it into a house, or

(*d*) altering, enlarging, repairing or improving a house,

or for the purpose of facilitating the repayment of an amount outstanding on a previous loan made for any of those purposes.

(2) The authority may make an advance notwithstanding that it is intended that some part of the premises will be used, or continue to be used, otherwise than as a dwelling if it appears to the authority that the principal effect of making the advance would be to meet the applicant's housing needs; and in such a case the premises shall be treated as a building to be converted into a house.

(3) The authority may make advances whether or not the houses or buildings are in the authority's area.

(4) An advance may be made in addition to assistance given by the authority in respect of the same house under any other Act or any other provision of this Act

DEFINITIONS

"house": s.457.

"local authority": s.4.

GENERAL NOTE

This is the general power of local authorities to advance money for house purchase, exercisable in or outside of their own area (subs. (3)), and additional to assistance under any other Act, or any other provision of this Act, *e.g.* right to a mortgage under Part V, or in connection with improvements under Part XV, below. Loan powers have been available since the Small Dwellings Acquisition Act 1899 (now repealed but subject to savings for existing advances: see s.456 and Sched. 18).

For the purposes of this Part, "house" not only includes "any yard, garden, outhouses and appurtenances belonging to the house or usually enjoyed with it" (*cf.* notes to s.56, above), but also "any part of a building which is occupied or intended to be occupied as a separate dwelling including, in particular, a flat": s.457. As to separate dwelling: see notes to ss.79,

324, above. The powers are, however, available even if part of the premises is used other than as a dwelling, if the principal purpose of the advance is to meet the applicant's housing needs: subs. (2). In so far as the powers are exercised in relation to shared ownership leases (as to which, see s.143, above), they extend to further advances: see s.453.

There are six purposes:
(1) Acquisition;
(2) Construction;
(3) Acquisition of a building for conversion into a house;
(4) Conversion of a building into a house;
(5) Alteration, enlargement, repair or improvement;
(6) Repayment of an outstanding loan for any of these purposes.

The purpose of the last of these is to enable the authority to take over an existing mortgage, and perhaps enlarge available capital for the execution of works, *e.g.* for the applicant to find the additional resources with which to accept an offer of grant-aid under Part XV, below. Similarly, a loan for the latter purpose can be given on its own. This last power *cannot* be used unless the authority satisfy themselves that the primary effect of the advance will be to meet the housing needs of the applicant in one of two ways: (a) by enabling him to retain an interest in the property, or (b) by enabling him to carry out works of conversion, alteration, enlargement, repair or improvement under heads (4) and (5): s.439(3), below. Payments under heads (2)–(5) may be in stages as works proceed: s.436(4), below.

None of these provisions is for the purpose of exercising the right to buy under Part V (including the right to a shared ownership lease under the right to buy, as distinct from a voluntary shared ownership lease), for Part V contains its own (and mandatory) provisions. These provisions can apply, however, in the case of a voluntary disposal by an authority (*cf.* ss.32 *et seq.*, above, and s.437, below), or, if the finance is available to the authority, to fund purchase in the private sector. Additional assistance is available for "first-time buyers" under ss.445–450, below.

Loans for house purchase under these provisions are classified as capital expenditure under the Local Government, Planning and Land Act 1980, s.71 and Schedule 12, paragraph 1 (*cf.* above, notes to s.421). The provisions of Sched. 16, below, governing interest, mean that the borrower will always be paying more either than the loan actually costs the authority (*i.e.* than the authority are paying to borrow the money to lend him), or than the cost of the fund from which the borrowing by the authority originated: see further notes to s.438, below.

In theory, the loan can be to any "person", which by s.5 and Sched. 1, Interpretation Act 1978, includes any body of persons corporate or incorporate. However, in practice loans will only be available for the "priority groups" identified from time to time by the government for the purposes of Housing Investment Programme Allocations (*cf.* notes to s.421, above), who are individuals wanting homes for their own occupation.

Before advancing money under this section, the authority must satisfy themselves that the property is or will be fit for human habitation (as defined in s.604, below) in all respects: s.439. The authority have power instead of lending money themselves to offer a guarantee or indemnity to specified institutions: s.442, below. To encourage use of private sector mortgages, they may make a grant for the related costs: s.443, below. As to terms of the advance, see s.436, below; as to rates of interest, see s.438 and Sched. 16, below; as to vesting in the authority on default, see s.452, below.

Terms of advance

436.—(1) The provisions of this section have effect with respect to the terms of advances under section 435.

(2) The advance, together with the interest on it, shall be secured by a mortgage of the land concerned; and an advance shall not be made unless the estate proposed to be mortgaged is either—

(*a*) an estate in fee simple absolute in possession, or
(*b*) an estate for a term of years absolute of which a period of not less than ten years in excess of the period fixed for the repayment of the advance remains unexpired on the date on which the mortgage is executed.

(3) The amount of the principal of the advance shall not exceed the value of the mortgaged security or, as the case may be, the value which it is estimated the mortgaged security will bear when the construction,

conversion, alteration, enlargement, repair or improvement has been carried out; and the advance shall not be made except after a valuation duly made on behalf of the authority.

(4) Where the advance is for any of the purposes specified in section 435(1)(*b*) to (*d*) (construction, conversion, alteration, enlargement, repair or improvement), it may be made by instalments from time to time as the works progress.

(5) The mortgage deed shall provide—

(*a*) for repayments of the principal either by instalments of equal or unequal amounts, beginning on the date of the advance or at a later date, or at the end of a fixed period (with or without a provision allowing the authority to extend the period) or on the happening of a specified event before the end of that period, and

(*b*) for the payment of instalments of interest throughout the period beginning on the date of the advance and ending when the whole of the principal is repaid;

but subject to section 441 (waiver or reduction of payments in case of property requiring repair or improvement) and to section 446(1)(*b*) (assistance for first-time buyers: part of loan interest-free for up to five years).

(6) The mortgage deed shall also provide that, notwithstanding the provisions referred to in subsection (5), the balance for the time being unpaid—

(*a*) shall become repayable on demand by the authority in the event of any of the conditions subject to which the advance is made not being complied with, and

(*b*) may, in any event, be repaid on one of the usual quarterdays by the person for the time being entitled to the equity of redemption after one month's written notice of intention to repay has been given to the authority.

GENERAL NOTE

This section governs the terms of an advance under s.435, above; as to rates of interest, see s.438 and Sched. 16, below; as to vesting in the authority on default, see s.452, below. See also s.440, below, for deposit or retention against maintenance or repair.

Subs. (2)

The advance is to be secured by a mortgage. A mortgage is a conveyance or transfer of a legal or equitable interest in property by the mortgagor to the mortgagee which contains a provison for redemption, *i.e.* that on repayment of the loan the interest will be reconveyed to the mortgagor: *Santley* v. *Wilde* [1899] 2 Ch. 474, C.A.

A legal mortgage must be of a legal estate in land, *i.e.* freehold or leasehold under Law of Property Act 1925, s.1(1). If the land is unregistered and freehold, the mortgage must be either a charge by deed expressed to be by way of legal mortgage, or a demise (lease) for a term of years absolute, subject to a provision for termination of the lease on redemption: Law of Property Act 1925, s.85(2). If unregistered and leasehold, the same applies save that the demise may be by way of sub-lease, for a term at least one day shorter than that vested in the mortgagor: *ibid.*, s.86(1). Most commonly, the first method is used, *i.e.* charge expressed to be by way of legal mortgage, under which the mortgagee does not take a legal estate but is protected as if he had done so: Law of Property Act 1925, s.87(1); see also *Grand Junction Co. Ltd.* v. *Bates* [1954] 2 Q.B. 160.

In the case of registered land, the methods are basically the same: a legal mortgage may be in any form (Land Registration Act 1925, s.25) including by demise or sub-demise; unless the latter is expressly provided for in the deed, it takes effect as a legal mortgage: Land Registration Act 1925, s.27. The words "by way of legal mortgage", although in common use, and although necessary in the case of unregistered land, are not strictly required: *Cityland & Property (Holdings) Ltd.* v. *Dabrah* [1968] Ch. 166. The charge must, to be completely effective, be registered, and is not completely effective until registered: Land Registration Act 1925, 26; see also *Lever Finance* v. *Needleman's Trustee* [1956] Ch. 375.

The charge will take effect subject to the interests existing at the date of registration (*Re Boyle's Claim* [1961] 1 W.L.R. 339) which are overriding interests (Land Registration Act

1925, s.70(1)), including the interests of those in actual occupation of the land: *ibid.* s.70(1)(g); see also *Grace Rymer Investments* v. *Waite* [1958] Ch. 831; see also *Williams & Glyn's Bank Ltd.* v. *Boland* [1981] A.C. 487, H.L. (but *cf. Bristol & West Building Society* v. *Henning* [1985] 1 W.L.R. 778, 17 H.L.R. 442, C.A.).

Where the mortgage is of a lease, the mortgagee is entitled to apply for relief against forfeiture under s.146, Law of Property Act 1925, (*Grand Junction Co. Ltd.* v. *Bates* [1954] 2 Q.B. 160), sought before recovery of possession, or under the court's inherent jurisdiction: see *Abbey National Building Society* v. *Maybeech Ltd.* [1984] 3 All E.R. 262, Ch. D.

The mortgage is to be secured against land: "land" includes "buildings and other structures, land covered with water, and any estate, interest, easement, servitude or right in or over land": Interpretation Act 1978, Sched. 1. The interest to be mortgaged must be either estate in fee simple absolute in possession, or estate for a term of years absolute, of which at least ten years will remain beyond the period fixed for repayment—*i.e.* on default towards the end of the lease, there will remain a ten year interest for sale as protection of the mortgagee.

Subs. (3)

The amount advanced must not exceed the value of the security, or the value which the security will have once any proposed works have been carried out. An advance which is for the purpose of refinancing an existing loan, *e.g.* in order to consolidate and provide funds for improvement, etc. (see notes to s.435, above), was not formerly subject to this requirement, but is now so subject pursuant to Law Commission Recommendations (Cmnd. 9515), No. 21.

The authority must have the security valued. Note that a valuer can owe a duty of care to the mortgag*or*, and there is no "contributory negligence" on the part of a mortgagor in failing to have his own survey: *Yianni* v. *Edwin Evans* [1982] Q.B. 438. Although not specified in the legislation, it is envisaged that the borrower will pay the cost of the valuation: see M.H.L.G. Circular 42/54.

Subs. (4)

When the advance is for construction, conversion, alteration, enlargement, repair or improvement, it may be by way of stage payments. See also s.440, below, for retention against maintenance or repair.

Subs. (5)

Subject to the special provisions for "homesteading schemes" under s.441, below, and first-time buyers under ss.445–446, below, the mortgage *must* require the payment of interest throughout the period of the mortgage. However, capital repayment may be in virtually any way—equal or unequal instalments, postponed or even on the happening of an event. The *rate* of interest is governed by s.438, and Sched. 16, below.

Subs. (6)

The mortgage deed is also required to provide (a) for repayment on demand for breach of condition, and (b) for voluntary repayment by one month's written notice given on one of the usual quarter days. The courts have long held that there can in any event be "no clog on the equity of redemption": see, *e.g.*, *Vernon* v. *Bethell* (1762) 2 Eden 110. As to the power of the authority to vest the property in themselves: see s.452, below.

In addition to repayment for breach of condition, mortgagees will of course also have the right to seek possession: indeed, the legal interest which is acquired as a result of a mortgage *is* a right to possession, even although it is of course the mortgagor who remains in actual occupation: Law of Property Act 1925, ss.87(1), 95(4), Land Registration Act 1925, s.34(1); *Alliance Perpetual Building Society* v. *Belrum Investments* [1957] 1 W.L.R. 720. Many mortgages now contain a clause under which the mortgagee undertakes not to enforce the right to possession except in the case of default by the mortgagor.

But mortgagors of dwelling-houses are entitled to seek the protection of the Administration of Justice Act 1970, ss.36–38 and the Administration of Justice Act 1973, s.8. Under these provisions, if it appears to the court that the mortgagor is likely to be able within a reasonable period to pay any sums due under the mortgage, or to remedy a default consisting of a breach of any other obligation arising under or by virtue of the mortgage, the court may adjourn proceedings for possession, or, on giving judgment or making an order for delivery of possession of the mortgaged property or at any time before execution of such judgment or order, stay or suspend execution of the judgment or order, or postpone the date for delivery of possession for such period or periods as the court thinks reasonable.

Likelihood is a question of fact for the judge or registrar, to be decided on the evidence before him, whether or not on affidavit: *Royal Trust Co. of Canada* v. *Markham* [1975] 1 W.L.R. 1416, C.A., *Western Bank Ltd.* v. *Schindler* [1977] Ch. 1, C.A.

As to what constitutes repayment within a reasonable period, in *Centrax Trustees Ltd.* v. *Ross* [1979] 2 All E.R. 952, Goulding J. remarked that the court "must bear in mind the rights and obligations of both parties, including the (mortgagee's) right to recover their money by selling the property, if necessary, and the whole past history of the security". In *First Middlesborough Trading and Mortgage Co. Ltd.* v. *Cunningham* (1974) 28 P. & C.R. 69, C.A., Scarman L.J. suggested that there was a presumption in favour of the whole period of the mortgage being the reasonable period, although in practice much shorter periods are commonly considered reasonable by the courts.

Decisions of the court under these provisions may be made subject to such conditions regarding payment by the mortgagor or remedy of default, as the court thinks fit: Administration of Justice Act 1970, s.36(3).

In addition to claiming possession, mortgagees will enjoy a power of sale, whether expressly included in the mortgage deed, or under statute (Law of Property Act 1925, ss.101–107). The statutory power arises when (a) the mortgage is made by deed, (b) the mortgage repayment is due (which will in effect mean as soon as any instalment is in arrears—under this subsection, see also *Payne* v. *Cardiff Rural District Council* [1932] 1 K.B. 241), and (c) there is nothing in the mortgage deed which excludes, expressly or by implication, the statutory power.

However, although the power of sale may have arisen, it is not exercisable unless either (i) notice has been served on the mortgagor, requiring repayment and has not been complied with for three months after service, or (ii) interest under the mortgage is in arrears for more than two months after becoming due, or (iii) there has been a breach of a provision—other than for payment of principal or interest—contained in the mortgage deed (or in the Law of Property Act 1925 itself).

On a sale, the mortgagee owes a duty to the mortgagor to take reasonable care to obtain a proper price, or "the true market value of the mortgaged property" (per Salmon L.J., *Cuckmere Brick Co. Ltd.* v. *Mutual Finance Ltd.* [1971] Ch. 949 at p.966); see also *Reliance Permanent Building Society* v. *Harwood-Stamper* [1944] Ch. 362. The burden of proof that this duty has not been fulfilled is on the mortgagor (*Haddington Island Quarry Co. Ltd.* v. *Huson* [1911] A.C. 727, P.C.) and will not easily be discharged: *Palmer* v. *Barclays Bank* (1972) 23 P. & C.R. 30. The mortgagee is not bound to wait until the market is in a favourable state, but can sell at his own convenience: *Farrar* v. *Farrars Ltd.* (1888) 40 Ch. D. 395, *Reliance Permanent Building Society* v. *Harwood-Stamper, Cuckmere Brick*.

When selling a tenanted property (*e.g.* if an owner-occupier has someone living in the house with him), the mortgagee should secure vacant possession prior to sale: *Holohan* v. *Friends Provident and Century Life Office* [1966] I.R. 1.

The sale must normally be a "true sale", not including a sale (direct or indirect) to the mortgagee: *Farrar* v. *Farrars Ltd., Downes* v. *Grazebrook* (1817) 3 Mer. 200, but *cf. Tse Kwong Lam* v. *Wong Chit Sen* [1983] 1 W.L.R. 1349, P.C. This is so even if the mortgagee has reserved a right of pre-emption to himself, which could arise on a disposal by a local authority which also allows an amount to be left outstanding by way of mortgage: *Williams* v. *Wellingborough Borough Council* [1975] 1 W.L.R. 1327. However, in the case of a sale by a local authority there is now an express power in some circumstances to vest the property in themselves: see s.452 and Sched. 17, below.

Foreclosure is not now a commonly used remedy. It involves the total destruction of the mortgagor's equity of redemption and the transfer of his title to the mortgagee (Law of Property Act 1925, ss.88(2), 89(2)), and is hedged about with procedural restrictions; in particular, foreclosure can only take place by court order (*Re Farnol, Eades, Irvine & Co.* [1915] 1 Ch. 22) and the courts have been generally reluctant to grant such decrees. If foreclosure proceedings are started, the court may at the request of the mortgagee or any other person with an interest, including the mortgagor, order a sale instead of foreclosure: Law of Property Act 1925, s.91(2).

In the same circumstances as the power of sale arises and is exercisable, another remedy available, but not commonly used, is the appointment of a receiver: *ibid.* s.101(1)(iii); see also *ibid.*, s.109. Finally, most mortgages contain an express covenant under which the mortgagor is personally liable for the debt. The value of this to the mortgagee is if the sale does not raise sufficient to clear the debt, then the mortgagor may still be sued for the outstanding balance: *Rude* v. *Richens* (1873) L.R. 8 C.P. 358, *Gordon Grant & Co.* v. *Boos* [1926] A.C. 781, P.C.

Power of local authority on disposal to leave amount outstanding on mortgage

437. On the disposal of a house under section 32 (disposal by local authority of land held for purposes of Part II)—

(*a*) by way of sale, or

(*b*) by the grant or assignment of a lease at a premium,

the local authority may agree to the price or premium, or part of it, and any expenses incurred by the purchaser, being secured by a mortgage of the premises.

<small>DEFINITION</small>
"local authority": s.4.

<small>GENERAL NOTE</small>
This expressly applies the power to grant a mortgage to an authority's disposal of its own property under s.32: see notes thereto, above. The mortgage is effected in practice by leaving an amount outstanding on the disposal.

Local authority mortgage interest rates

438.—(1) Where after 3rd October 1980 a local authority—

(*a*) advance money for any of the purposes mentioned in section 435, or

(*b*) on the disposal of a house allow, or have to allow, a sum to be left outstanding on the security of the house, or

(*c*) take a transfer of a mortgage in pursuance of section 442 (agreement by local authority to indemnify mortgagee),

the provision made by them with respect to interest on the sum advanced or remaining outstanding shall comply with the provisions of Schedule 16.

(2) This section does not prevent a local authority from giving assistance in the manner provided by—

section 441 (waiver or reduction of payments in case of property requiring repair or improvement), or

section 446(1)(*b*) (assistance for first-time buyers: part of loan interest-free for up to five years).

(3) This section does not apply to loans made by local authorities under—

section 228 (duty to make loans for improvements required by improvement notice), or

section 58(2) of the Housing Associations Act 1985 (financial assistance for housing associations).

<small>DEFINITION</small>
"local authority": s.4.

<small>GENERAL NOTE</small>
Under s.442, below, the authority may enter into an indemnity agreement with a specified lending institution, in consequence of which the mortgage may be transferred to them. Whether in this way, or whether a "direct" mortgage under s.435 or a mortgage by leaving an amount outstanding under s.437, interest is governed by Sched. 16, below. This, however, does not inhibit the provisions governing "homesteading schemes" under s.441, below, or assistance for first-time buyers under ss.445–446, below, nor do the provisions apply to *mandatory* improvement-related loans under s.228, above, or loans to housing associations under s.58, Housing Associations Act 1985.

Sched. 16 operates on the basis of two concepts: a "standard national rate", and an "applicable local average rate", the higher of which is the rate payable: para. 1. The mortgage must provide for a variable rate of interest: *ibid*. The Secretary of State has, however, power to direct that one or other rate is to be treated as the higher, *i.e.* even if it is not: para. 7.

If variation is possible under the Schedule, it is mandatory: para. 5. Notice of change must be served no later than two months after the change in rate: *ibid*. The notice must set a date for the variation to take effect, no later than one month after the change if a reduction, and no earlier than one month but not later than three months after service of the notice if an increase: *ibid*. The maximum period for which the authority can, accordingly, defer the effect of an increase is for five months.

The authority can also vary the actual periodic payments if the rate of interest is varied, and are obliged to do so if the effect of the variation would otherwise be to reduce the repayment period, *i.e.* if there is a decrease in the rate of interest they must reduce the periodic payments for otherwise the payments would start to reduce the capital quicker than was originally intended: para. 6. Variation of payments is to be at the same time as variation of the rate of interest: *ibid*.

The standard national rate is set by the Secretary of State, after taking into account interest rates being charged by building societies, and movement in those rates: para. 2. Two local average rates have to be set by each authority, twice a year, in the month before the half-year to which they will apply: para. 3.

The two local average rates are: (a) a rate for mortgages granted by them under s.435 and for mortgages transferred to them under a s.442 indemnity scheme; and (b) a rate for mortgages on their own former property under s.437, *i.e.* voluntary sales (*ibid.*). The first of these is to be one-quarter per cent. above the amount the authority have to pay, *i.e.* borrow the money at: para. 4. The second is to be one-quarter per cent. above the average cost of the loan charges across one of two accounts—if former Part II property, the Housing Revenue Account (as to which, see s.421, above), or otherwise the general rate fund: *ibid*. Loan charges include notional loan charges, *i.e.* internal accounting loan charges: *ibid*.

Requirements as to fitness of premises, &c.

439.—(1) Before advancing money under section 435 for the purpose specified in subsection (1)(*a*) (acquisition of a house), the authority shall satisfy themselves that the house to be acquired is, or will be made, in all respects fit for human habitation.

(2) Before advancing money for any of the purposes specified in subsection (1)(*b*) to (*d*) of that section (construction, conversion, alteration, enlargement, repair or improvement), the authority shall satisfy themselves that the house concerned will when the relevant works have been completed be in all respects fit for human habitation.

(3) An advance shall not be made for the purpose specified in the closing words of section 435(1) (repayment of previous loan), unless the authority satisfy themselves that the primary effect of the advance will be to meet the housing needs of the applicant by enabling him either—

(*a*) to retain an interest in the house concerned, or

(*b*) to carry out such works in relation to the building or house concerned as would be eligible for an advance under paragraph (*c*) or (*d*) of that subsection (conversion, alteration, enlargement, repair or improvement).

DEFINITIONS
"fit for human habitation": s.604.
"house": s.457.

GENERAL NOTE
If a loan is for acquisition, the property must already be, or after works must become, fit for human habitation, as defined in s.604 (see notes thereto, below). Similarly, if the loan is for construction, conversion, alteration, enlargement, repair or improvement, the property must be fit once the works are completed. Note that the authority can accept a deposit from the mortgagor (in substance, impose a retention) against the completion of repairs: s.440, below. Under s.436(4), above, the mortgage may be paid in instalments against progress of works for construction, conversion, alteration, enlargement, repair or improvement.

Subs. (2)
This confines the purposes for which a refinancing loan may be granted: see notes to s.435, above.

Deposits in respect of maintenance or repair of mortgaged premises

440. A local authority by whom money has been advanced on the mortgage of a house in pursuance of any enactment may accept the deposit by the mortgagor of the sums estimated to be required for the maintenance or repair of the mortgaged premises, and may pay interest on sums so deposited.

DEFINITIONS
"house": s.457.
"local authority": s.4.

GENERAL NOTE
This power of general application permits the authority to require payment of a sum—or in practice effect a retention—on which interest may be paid, against sums required for maintenance or repair. See also s.436(4), above, for stage payments of mortgage on construction, conversion, alteration, enlargement, repair or improvement.
"Enactment" includes another provision of this Act: Interpretation Act 1978, s.1.

Waiver or reduction of payments in case of property requiring repair or improvement

441.—(1) Where a local authority—
  (*a*) advance money for the acquisition of a house which is in need of repair or improvement, or
  (*b*) on the disposal of a house which is in need of repair or improvement allow, or have to allow, a sum to be left outstanding on the security of the house,
they may, if the conditions stated in subsection (2) are satisfied, give assistance in accordance with this section to the person acquiring the house.
  (2) The conditions are—
    (*a*) that the assistance is given in accordance with a scheme which either has been approved by the Secretary of State or conforms with such requirements as may be prescribed, and
    (*b*) that the person acquiring the house has entered into an agreement with the local authority to carry out, within a period specified in the agreement, such works of repair or improvement as are so specified.
  (3) The assistance shall take the form of making provision—
    (*a*) for waiving or reducing the interest payable on the sum advanced or remaining outstanding, and
    (*b*) for dispensing with the repayment of principal,
for a period ending not later than five years after the date of the advance or, as the case may be, the date of the disposal.
  (4) In this section "prescribed" means prescribed by order of the Secretary of State made with the consent of the Treasury.
  (5) An order—
    (*a*) may make different provision with respect to different cases or descriptions of case, including different provision for different areas, and
    (*b*) shall be made by statutory instrument which shall be subject to annulment in pursuance of a resolution of either House of Parliament.

DEFINITIONS
"house": s.457.
"local authority": s.4.

GENERAL NOTE
This is a limited power, applicable only in relation to a scheme approved by the Secretary of State or conforming with specified requirements, and known generally as "homesteading"

(see D.O.E. Circular 20/80). It is intended to permit authorities to provide people with an incentive to buy and improve older property, by way of waiving interest and/or repayment of principal, for up to five years from the date of the mortgage: subs. (3). While repayment of principal can be deferred under s.436(5), above, interest must normally be paid over the whole of the period of the mortgage, *i.e.* from commencement, save for this section and s.446, below (first-time buyers).

The power is available only in two circumstances:

(1) the loan is for acquisition of a house (or flat—see s.457, below) which is in need of repair or improvement; or

(2) the loan is by way of leaving an amount outstanding, *i.e.* is a disposal by the authority, either voluntarily under s.437, above, or under the right to a mortgage in Part V, above.

The power may be exercised only when both of the conditions in subs. (2) are fulfilled:

(a) The assistance conforms with a scheme or requirements; and

(b) There is an agreement between the borrower and the authority to carry out specified works of repair or improvement within a specified time.

When considering authority for a homesteading scheme, the Secretary of State will include the following considerations: (i) that the dwelling is in need of significant improvement or repair; (ii) that the purchaser enters into an agreement with the authority to carry out specified works within a specified period (this reproduces the other statutory requirement); and (iii) that the extent to which interest is reduced, and the length of the reduction or waiver within the maximum five-year period permitted, will depend on the inducement needed in the particular circumstances of the scheme—D.O.E. Circular 20/80, para. 26.

Local authority assistance in connection with mortgages

Agreement by local authority to indemnify mortgagee

442.—(1) A local authority may, with the approval of the Secretary of State, enter into an agreement with—

(*a*) a building society lending on the security of a house, or

(*b*) a recognised body making a relevant advance on the security of a house,

whereby, in the event of default by the mortgagor, and in the circumstances and subject to conditions specified in the agreement, the authority binds itself to indemnify the society or body in respect of the whole or part of the mortgagor's outstanding indebtedness and any loss or expense falling on the society or body in consequence of the mortgagor's default.

(2) The agreement may also, if the mortgagor is made party to it, enable or require the authority in specified circumstances to take a transfer of the mortgage and assume rights and liabilities under it, the building society or recognised body being then discharged in respect of them.

(3) The transfer may be made to take effect—

(*a*) on terms provided for by the agreement (including terms involving the substitution of a new mortgage agreement or modification of the existing one), and

(*b*) so that the authority is treated as acquiring (for and in relation to the purposes of the mortgage) the benefit and burden of all preceding acts, omissions and events.

(4) The Secretary of State may approve particular agreements or give notice that particular forms of agreement have his approval, and in either case may make his approval subject to conditions.

(5) The Secretary of State shall before giving notice that a particular form of agreement has his approval consult—

(*a*) in the case of a form of agreement with a building society, the Chief Registrar of Friendly Societies and such organisations representative of building societies and local authorities as the Secretary of State thinks expedient;

(*b*) in the case of a form of agreement with a recognised body, such organisations representative of recognised bodies and local authorities as he thinks expedient.

Definitions
DEFINITIONS
"building society": s.622.
"house": s.457.
"local authority": s.4.
"recognised body": s.444.
"relevant advance": s.444.

GENERAL NOTE
As an alternative to lending money themselves, local authorities can—with the consent of the Secretary of State—enter into "indemnity" agreements with either a building society lending on the security of a house (or flat, see s.457), or a "recognised body making a relevant advance" on the security of a house. The powers are designed to be particularly valuable for loans on unimproved housing: the indemnity might, for example, justify a building society lending on the improved value of an unimproved house: D.O.E. Circular 5/81, paras. 7–10.

A recognised body means a body specified—or of a class or description specified—by the Secretary of State: s.444(1). A relevant advance is one under which the purchaser has acquired the freehold or a long lease from a local authority, a new town corporation, an urban development corporation, the Development Board for Rural Wales, the Housing Corporation or a registered housing association: s.444(4). A long lease is a long tenancy within s.115, above, see notes thereto: s.458.

The powers permit the authority to agree with the building society or other body that if the mortgagor defaults, they will, subject to the conditions of the agreement, indemnify the society or other body in respect of the whole or part of the outstanding liability, and any loss or expense falling on the society or other body in consequence of the default: subs. (1). The agreement may, if the mortgagor is made a party to it, enable or require the authority to take a transfer of the mortgage, and the rights and liabilities of the mortgagee under it: subs. (2).

The Secretary of State can give consent by means of approval of particular types of agreement, and three different such models are to be found in D.O.E. Circular 5/81. Note that the agreement must provide that on transfer the Sched. 16 provisions as to interest will apply: see notes to s.438, above. The authority can contribute to the mortgagor's costs under a scheme such as this: see s.443, below.

Subs. (5)
"Consultation". See notes to s.420(4), above.

Local authority contributions to mortgage costs

443.—(1) A local authority may contribute towards costs incurred by a person in connection with a legal charge which secures, or a proposed legal charge which is intended to secure, a relevant advance made or proposed to be made to him by a building society or recognised body.

(2) The contribution shall not exceed such amount as may be specified by order of the Secretary of State.

(3) An order shall be made by statutory instrument which shall be subject to annulment in pursuance of a resolution of either House of Parliament.

DEFINITIONS
"building society": s.622.
"local authority": s.4.
"recognised body": s.444.
"relevant advance": s.444.

GENERAL NOTE
In order to encourage people to borrow from the private sector—whether in connection with an indemnity scheme under s.442, or indeed in connection with the right to buy under Part V, *i.e.* without reliance on the right to a mortgage therein (see Hansard, H.C. Deb. Standing Committee B, November 3, 1983, col. 488)—local authorities can give a grant towards the mortgagor's costs in connection with a mortgage which is a relevant advance by a building society or recognised body, to a limit specified by the Secretary of State, *e.g.* for survey or legal fees. The current limit is £200 under S.I. 1984 No. 117 (retained in force by

s.2, Housing (Consequential Provisions) Act 1985). See also the powers in s.26, above, where applicable.

Recognised bodies and relevant advances for purposes of ss.442 and 443

444.—(1) The expression "recognised body" in sections 442 and 443 (agreements to indemnify mortgagees and contributions to mortgage costs) means a body specified, or of a class or description specified, by order of the Secretary of State made with the consent of the Treasury.

(2) An order shall be made by statutory instrument.

(3) Before making an order varying or revoking a previous order the Secretary of State shall give an opportunity for representations to be made on behalf of a body which, if the order were made, would cease to be a recognised body.

(4) The expression "relevant advance" in those sections means an advance made to a person whose interest in the house on the security of which the advance is made is, or was, acquired by virtue of a conveyance of the freehold, or a grant or assignment of a long lease, by—

    a local authority,
    a new town corporation,
    an urban development corporation,
    the Development Board for Rural Wales,
    the Housing Corporation, or
    a registered housing association.

DEFINITIONS
    "local authority": s.4.
    "new town corporation": s.4.
    "registered housing association": s.5.
    "urban development corporation": s.4.

GENERAL NOTE
    This section defines the recognised bodies whose lending on relevant advances may be indemnified by local authorities under s.442, above, and whose borrowers may be able to obtain a grant towards their costs (*e.g.* legal fees, survey fees) under s.443, above. The section also defines relevant advances for these purposes; they are confined to purchases from the public or quasi-public sectors.

Assistance for first-time buyers

Advances to recognised lending institutions to assist first-time buyers

445.—(1) The Secretary of State may make advances to recognised lending institutions enabling them to provide assistance to first-time purchasers of house property in Great Britain where—

    (*a*) the purchaser intends to make his home in the property,
    (*b*) finance for the purchase of the property (and improvements, if any) is obtained by means of a secured loan from the lending institution, and
    (*c*) the purchase price is within the prescribed limits.

(2) In this section "prescribed" means prescribed by order of the Secretary of State.

(3) An order—

    (*a*) may prescribe different limits for properties in different areas, and
    (*b*) shall be made by statutory instrument which shall be subject to annulment in pursuance of a resolution of the House of Commons.

DEFINITION
    "recognised lending institutions": s.447.

GENERAL NOTE

This section concerns "first-time buyers". The term "first-time purchaser" is not defined, but under the House Purchase Assistance Directions 1978 issued under what is now s.449(2), below, retained in force by s.2, Housing (Consequential Provisions) Act 1985, a first-time purchaser is someone who has not previously been the beneficial owner (whether individually or jointly or in common with others) of a relevant interest in house property in the United Kingdom in which he made his home. "Relevant interest" means the freehold or the interest of the tenant under a lease granted for a term of more than 21 years. "House property" includes any building or part of a building used or intended to be used in whole or in part as a dwelling, but not a mobile home or a houseboat.

The section permits the Secretary of State to make advances to recognised lending institutions as defined in s.447, to enable them to provide assistance as defined in s.446. The assistance is by way of a sum of up to £600, on which both interest and capital repayment is deferred for up to five years, and possibly a bonus of up to £120. Three conditions have to be fulfilled before the scheme can be applied:

(1) The purchaser intends to make his home in the property (under the Directions, within 12 months of the purchase); and

(2) Finance for the purchase (and improvement if any) is obtained by means of a secured loan (defined in the Directions as by legal mortgage) from the lending institution; and

(3) The purchase price is within the limits prescribed under subss. (2) and (3).

The purpose of this last provision is to ensure that the money is directed towards the lower end of the market, rather than an additional or windfall benefit to those purchasing more expensive property.

Under the Home Purchase Assistance (Price Limits) Order 1985 (S.I. 1985 No. 937, retained in force by s.2, Housing (Consequential Provisions) Act 1985), the limits are:

Counties of Cleveland, Cumbria, Durham, Northumberland and Tyne and Wear £21,500
Counties of Humberside, North Yorkshire, South Yorkshire and West Yorkshire £20,400
Counties of Derbyshire, Leicestershire, Lincolnshire, Northamptonshire and Nottinghamshire £22,100
Counties of Cambridgeshire, Norfolk and Suffolk £26,000
Greater London £38,000
Counties of Bedfordshire, Berkshire, Buckinghamshire, East Sussex, Essex, Hampshire, Hertfordshire, Isle of Wight, Kent, Oxfordshire, Surrey and West Sussex £33,500
Counties of Avon, Cornwall, Devon, Dorset, Gloucestershire, Somerset and Wiltshire, and the Isles of Scilly £28,200
Counties of Hereford and Worcester, Shropshire, Staffordshire, Warwickshire and West Midland £21,900
Counties of Cheshire, Greater Manchester, Lancashire and Merseyside £21,700
Wales £22,700
Scotland £26,000

Under s.446(4), there is, however, also an effective *minimum* price: no assistance is to be given unless the amount of the secured loan is at least £1,600 and amounts to not less than 25 per cent. of the purchase price, therefore assistance is not available in respect of property worth less than £6,400.

Forms of assistance and qualifying conditions

446.—(1) Assistance under section 445 (assistance for first-time buyers) may be given in the following ways—

(a) the secured loan may be financed by the Secretary of State to the extent of £600 (that amount being normally additional to that which the institution would otherwise have lent, but not so that the total loan exceeds the loan value of the property);

(b) £600 of the total loan may be made free of interest, and of any obligation to repay principal, for up to five years from the date of purchase; and

(c) the institution may provide the purchaser with a bonus on his savings (which bonus shall be tax-exempt) up to a maximum of £110, payable towards the purchase or expenses arising in connection with it.

(2) The purchaser qualifies for assistance under subsection (1)(a) and (b) (interest-free loan) by satisfying the following conditions with respect to his own savings—

(*a*) that he has been saving with a recognised savings institution for at least two years preceding the date of his application for assistance,

(*b*) that throughout the twelve months preceding that date he had at least £300 of such savings, and

(*c*) that by that date he has accumulated at least £600 of such savings;

and he qualifies for assistance under subsection (1)(*c*) (bonus on savings) by satisfying the conditions specified in paragraphs (*a*) and (*b*) above.

(3) The Secretary of State may allow for the conditions to be relaxed or modified in particular classes of case.

(4) No assistance shall be given in any case unless the amount of the secured loan is at least £1,600 and amounts to not less than 25 per cent. of the purchase price of the property.

(5) The Secretary of State may by order made with the consent of the Treasury—

(*a*) alter any of the money sums specified in this section;

(*b*) substitute a longer or shorter period for either or both of the periods mentioned in subsection (2)(*a*) and (*b*) (conditions as to savings);

(*c*) alter the condition in subsection (2)(*c*) so as to enable the purchaser to satisfy it with lesser amounts of savings and to enable assistance to be given in such a case according to reduced scales specified in the order;

(*d*) alter the percentage mentioned in subsection (4) (minimum secured loan).

(6) An order shall be made by statutory instrument which shall be subject to annulment in pursuance of a resolution of the House of Commons.

DEFINITION

"recognised savings institution": s.448.

GENERAL NOTE

This section defines (a) the assistance available, and (b) the qualifying conditions under a s.445 scheme. In each case, the Home Purchase Directions 1978, retained in force by s.2, Housing (Consequential Provisions) Act 1985, provide elaboration. The assistance is encouraged by way of a loan from the Secretary of State to the lending institution (as defined in s.447, below) to an amount of £600, which is to be additional to the amount which the institution would otherwise have lent. As this is not to increase the total loan above the loan value of the property (subs. (1)(*a*)), this is designed to add to the limits which would otherwise be available by reference to the purchaser's income: *cf.* s.450, below.

The assistance to the purchaser is that this £600 will be free of interest for up to five years, and of any requirement to repay principal, *i.e.* this much of the principal (subs. (1)(*b*). In addition, the institution may give the purchaser a (tax-exempt) "bonus" up to a maximum of £110, which may be applied either towards the purchase price, or expenses arising in connection with it.

To qualify for the £600 deferred interest and repayment assistance, the purchaser must have been saving with a recognised savings institution (as defined in s.448, below) for at least two years before he applies for assistance, have saved at least £600 of his own by that date, and have had at least £300 of such savings throughout the year before he so applies: subs. (2). He qualifies for the bonus if he has been saving for two years, and had at least £300 of such savings during the last year. In effect, if he does not achieve the £600 which qualifies him for deferred interest and repayment assistance, he can still qualify for the bonus. Those who do achieve the £600 will qualify for *both* classes of assistance.

The amount of the bonus is, under the Home Purchase Directions 1978, related to the amount of savings, with £110 only available to those who had at least £1,000 saved during the year before application for assistance.

Subs. (3)

The Secretary of State may relax or modify the conditions in subs. (2).

Subs. (4)
In effect, therefore, the minimum purchase price must be £6,400; as to maximum purchase prices, see notes to s.445, above.

Recognised lending institutions

447.—(1) The lending institutions recognised for the purposes of section 445 (assistance for first-time buyers) are—
    designated building societies,
    local authorities,
    new town corporations,
    the Development Board for Rural Wales,
    trustee savings banks,
    banks,
    insurance companies, and
    friendly societies.
(2) The Secretary of State may by order made with the consent of the Treasury—
    (*a*) add to the list in subsection (1), or
    (*b*) direct that a named body shall no longer be a recognised lending institution;
but before making an order under paragraph (*b*) he shall give an opportunity for representations to be made on behalf of the body concerned.
(3) An order shall be made by statutory instrument.

DEFINITIONS
    "bank": s.622.
    "designated building societies": s.458.
    "friendly societies": s.622.
    "insurance companies": s.622.
    "local authority": s.4.
    "new town corporation": s.4.
    "trustee savings bank": s.622.

GENERAL NOTE
In addition to those specified as recognised lending institutions for the purpose of the first-time buyers' scheme under the last two sections, the Secretary of State can designate further bodies, or direct that a particular body (whether in subs. (1) or added by designation) shall no longer qualify as a recognised lending institution.

Recognised savings institutions

448.—(1) The savings institutions recognised for the purposes of section 446 (qualifying conditions as to savings) are—
    designated building societies
    local authorities
    trustee savings banks,
    banks,
    friendly societies,
    the Director of Savings, and
    the Post Office,
and savings institutions recognised for the purposes of the corresponding provisions in force in Scotland or Northern Ireland.
(2) The Secretary of State may by order made with the consent of the Treasury—
    (*a*) add to the list in subsection (1), or
    (*b*) direct that a named body shall no longer be a recognised savings institution;

but before making an order under paragraph (*b*) he shall give an opportunity for representations to be made on behalf of the body concerned.

(3) An order shall be made by statutory instrument.

DEFINITIONS
   "bank": s.622.
   "corresponding Scottish or Northern Ireland provisions": s.458.
   "designated building societies": s.458.
   "friendly societies": s.622.
   "local authority": s.4.
   "trustee savings bank": s.622.

GENERAL NOTE
   These are the savings institutions, saving with whom can qualify an applicant for assistance under ss.445–446. The Secretary of State can add to the list, or direct that a named body shall no longer be recognised as a savings institution for this purpose. The Secretary of State has added to the subs. (1) list: see S.I. 1978 No. 1785, retained in force by s.2, Housing (Consequential Provisions) Act 1985.

Terms of advances and administration

449.—(1) Advances to lending institutions under section 445 (assistance for first-time buyers) shall be on such terms as to repayment and otherwise as may be settled by the Secretary of State, with the consent of the Treasury, after consultation with lending and savings institutions or organisations representative of them; and the terms shall be embodied in directions issued by the Secretary of State.

(2) The following matters, among others, may be dealt with in directions issued by the Secretary of State—

  (*a*) the cases in which assistance is to be provided;
  (*b*) the method of determining the loan value of property for the purpose of section 446(1)(*a*) (limit on total loan);
  (*c*) the method of quantifying bonus by reference to savings;
  (*d*) the considerations by reference to which a person is or is not to be treated as a first-time purchaser of house property;
  (*e*) the steps which must be taken with a view to satisfying the conditions in section 446(2) (conditions as to purchaser's own savings), and the circumstances in which those conditions are or are not to be treated as satisfied;
  (*f*) the supporting evidence and declarations which must be furnished by a person applying for assistance, in order to establish his qualification for it, and the means of ensuring that restitution is made in the event of it being obtained by false representations;
  (*g*) the way in which amounts paid over by way of assistance are to be repaid to the lending institutions and to the Secretary of State.

(3) The Secretary of State may, to the extent that he thinks proper for safeguarding the lending institutions, include in the terms an undertaking to indemnify the institutions in respect of loss suffered in cases where assistance has been given.

DEFINITIONS
   "lending institutions": s.447.
   "savings institutions": s.448.

GENERAL NOTE
   Under this section, the Secretary of State has made the Home Purchase Assistance Directions 1978, retained in force by s.2, Housing (Consequential Provisions) Act 1978. The Directions include exercise of the subs. (3) power to indemnify against loss. The subs. (2) schedule of items is "among others", *i.e.* it is not exhaustive.
   "Consultation". See notes to s.420(4), above.

Modifications of building society law

450.—(1) The following provisions apply with respect to an advance by a building society which is partly financed under section 445 (assistance for first-time buyers) or the corresponding Scottish or Northern Ireland provisions—

(*a*) so much of the advance as is so financed shall be treated as not forming part of the advance for the purpose of determining whether the advance, or any further advance made within two years of the date of purchase, is beyond the powers of the society,

(*b*) the society, in complying with section 28(3) of the Building Societies Act 1962 (statutory notice to borrower where security taken from third party), shall state the amount of the basic advance without including the amount so financed, and

(*c*) section 41 of the Building Societies Act 1962 (statutory provisions to be set out in society's acknowledgement of loan) does not apply to an acknowledgement for such an advance.

(2) The following provisions apply with respect to an undertaking of indemnity under section 449(3) or the corresponding Scottish or Northern Ireland provisions—

(*a*) the undertaking shall not be treated for any purpose of the Building Societies Act 1962 as additional security for the advance, and

(*b*) section 28 of the Building Societies Act 1962 (statutory notice to borrower where security taken from third party) does not apply by reason only of such an undertaking having been given.

DEFINITIONS
"building society": s.622.
"corresponding Scottish or Northern Ireland provisions": s.458.

GENERAL NOTE
This section makes provisions relating these comparatively unusual transactions to the law governing building societies: Building Societies Act 1962.

Subs. (1)(a)
Under a building society's own rules, the amount of a loan is likely to be restricted by the income of the borrower, and a loan in excess thereof would, on normal principles, accordingly be *ultra vires*, but for this provision.

Subs. (1)(b)
Under s.28, Building Societies Act 1962, a building society must normally provide statutory notice to the borrower if additional security (other than a purely personal guarantee) for the loan is taken from another person. This may arise where more is lent than the amount the society would consider proper to advance on the security of the property alone (the "basic advance"—1962, s.129) and additional security is taken for an "excess advance" (*ibid.*). Under s.28(3), notice must be given which sets out both basic advance and excess advance, but the excess advance statement need not be fulfilled so far as it is attributable to the addition available under s.446, above. See also subs. (2).

Subs. (1)(c)
Section 41 of the Building Societies Act 1962 requires that specified other provisions of that Act be set out in writing and in full in or upon every deposit book or acknowledgment or security of any kind. If the acknowledgment in question relates to a loan partly financed under s.446, the requirement of s.41 need not be complied with.

Subs. (2)
An indemnity under s.449(3) (see also the Home Purchase Directions 1978) does not class as additional security (as defined in Building Societies Act 1962) for any purpose of the 1962 Act, nor does the requirement of statutory notice in s.28 of that Act (see also note to subs. (1)(*b*), above) apply merely because such an indemnity has been given.

Miscellaneous

Loans by Public Works Loan Commissioners

451.—(1) The Public Works Loan Commissioners may lend money for the purpose of constructing or improving houses, or facilitating or encouraging the construction or improvement of houses, to any person entitled to land for an estate in fee simple absolute in possession or for a term of years absolute of which not less than 50 years remains unexpired.

(2) A loan for any of those purposes, and interest on the loan, shall be secured by a mortgage of—

(*a*) the land in respect of which the purpose is to be carried out, and

(*b*) such other land, if any, as may be offered as security for the loan; and the money lent shall not exceed three-quarters of the value, to be ascertained to the satisfaction of the Public Works Loan Commissioners, of the estate or interest in the land proposed to be so mortgaged.

(3) Loans may be made by instalments from time to time as the building or other work on land mortgaged under subsection (2) progresses (so, however, that the total amount lent does not at any time exceed the amount specified in that subsection); and a mortgage may be accordingly made to secure such loans so made.

(4) If the loan exceeds two-thirds of the value referred to in subsection (2), the Public Works Loan Commissioners shall require, in addition to such a mortgage as is mentioned in that subsection, such further security as they may think fit.

(5) The period for repayment of the loan shall not exceed 40 years, and no money shall be lent on a mortgage of land or houses unless the estate proposed to be mortgaged is either a fee simple absolute in possession or an estate for a term of years absolute of which not less than 50 years are unexpired at the date of the loan.

(6) This section does not apply to housing associations; but corresponding provision is made by section 67 of the Housing Associations Act 1985.

Definition
  "house": s.458.

General Note
  This preserves the power of the Public Works Loan Commissioners to lend for house-building or improvement. It is available only in respect of freehold property, or leases in excess of 50 years. The maximum loan is of 75 per cent. of the value, and if the loan is to be more than sixty-six and two-thirds of the value security additional to a mortgage on the property in question is required: subs. (4). Security may in any event be on the land in question or any other land. "Land" includes "buildings and other structures, land covered with water, and any estate, interest, easement, servitude or right in or over land": Interpretation Act 1978, Sched. 1.
  Loans may be in instalments, as work progresses (subs. (3)). The maximum repayment period is 40 years (subs. (5)).

Vesting of house in authority entitled to exercise power of sale

452.—(1) Where there has been a disposal of a house by a housing authority and—

(*a*) the authority is a mortgagee of the house,

(*b*) the conveyance or grant contains a pre-emption provision in favour of the authority, and

(*c*) within the period during which the pre-emption provision has effect the authority becomes entitled as mortgagee to exercise the power of sale conferred by section 101 of the Law of Property Act 1925 or the mortgage deed, the provisions of Schedule 17 apply with respect to the vesting of the house in the authority.

(2) In subsection (1)—

"disposal" means a conveyance of the freehold or a grant or assignment of a long lease;

"housing authority" means—

a local authority,

a new town corporation,

an urban development corporation,

the Development Board for Rural Wales,

the Housing Corporation, or

a registered housing association;

"pre-emption provision" means a covenant imposing a condition of the kind mentioned in section 33(2)(*b*) or (*c*) (right of pre-emption or prohibition of assignment), the limitation specified in section 157(4) (restriction on disposal of dwellings in National Parks, etc.), or any other provision to the like effect.

(3) The vesting of a house under Schedule 17 shall be treated as a relevant disposal for the purposes of—

(*a*) the provisions of Parts II and V relating to the covenant required by section 35 or 155 (repayment of discount on early disposal), and

(*b*) any provision of the conveyance or grant to the like effect as the covenant required by those sections.

(4) Where a conveyance or grant executed before 26th August 1984 contains both—

(*a*) a pre-emption provision within the meaning of subsection (1), and

(*b*) the covenant required by section 35 or 155 (repayment of discount on early disposal) or any other provision to the like effect,

the latter covenant or provision has effect as from that date with such modifications as may be necessary to bring it into conformity with the provisions of this section.

(5) The preceding provisions of this section do not apply where the conveyance or grant was executed before 8th August 1980.

(6) Where before 8th August 1980 a local authority sold property under the powers of section 104(1) of the Housing Act 1957 (disposal of houses provided under Part V of that Act) and—

(*a*) part of the price was secured by a mortgage of the property,

(*b*) such a condition was imposed on the sale as was mentioned in section 104(3)(*c*) of that Act, and

(*c*) within the period during which the authority has the right to re-acquire the property they become entitled to exercise the power of sale conferred by section 101 of the Law of Property Act 1925 or by the mortgage deed,

the provisions of Schedule 17 apply with respect to the vesting of the property in the authority, but subject to the modifications specified in paragraph 4 of that Schedule.

DEFINITIONS

"house": s.458.

"local authority": s.4.

"new town corporation": s.4.

"registered housing association": s.5.

"urban development corporation": s.4.

GENERAL NOTE

When a mortgagee, on the default of the mortgagor, acquires a power of sale under s.101, Law of Property Act 1925, exercise of the power is subject to a duty to obtain the market value for the property: see notes to s.436(6), above.

This had caused something of a contradiction when local authorities sold property, subject to a mortgage granted by them, prior to the passage of the Housing Act 1980 (August 8, 1980), when pre-emption clauses were relatively common and freely available at least for a period of five years from completion, under s.104(3)(c), Housing Act 1957. The sale has to be a true sale: see notes to s.436(6), above. See also *Williams* v. *Wellingborough Borough Council* [1975] 1 W.L.R. 1327.

If the mortgagor defaulted during the life of the pre-emption clause, what were the duties of the authority as mortgagee, in relation to the duty to get the best price obtainable, given that the right of pre-emption would, of course, depress the sale price? (See Wutzburg & Mills, *Building Society Law* (14th. ed., 1976), pp. 211–212). This section and Sched. 17 now make provision permitting the re-vesting of the property in the authority.

The power is only exercisable with the leave of the county court: Sched. 17, para. 1. The county court may authorise the vesting in the authority of that which it could sell on exercise of the power of sale, freed from all estates, interests and rights to which they, as mortgagee, have priority, *i.e* subsequent interests, etc., created by the mortgagor: *ibid.*

On an application, the court can adjourn the proceedings or postpone the date of vesting in the authority, for such periods as the court thinks reasonable, and subject to such terms governing payments or the remedying of default as the court thinks fit: *ibid.* Note that there is no requirement that it appear to the court that the mortgagor is likely to be able within a reasonable period to pay sums due under the mortgage, or remedy a default, analogous to ss.36–38, Administration of Justice Act 1970 and s.8, Administration of Justice Act 1973: see notes to s.436(6), above. This would seem to be intentional, and to place the discretion on the same wide footing as, *e.g.*, is available when a secure tenant is in arrears—see notes to s.84, above.

Sched. 17, para. 2 governs the effect of the vesting. If the authority are a local housing authority, and retain the land, the property is treated as acquired under Part II; if they sell on to someone else, that person's title will not be defeasible on the grounds that the provisions of the Schedule have not been complied with. If the house has appreciated in value between vesting in the authority and subsequent sale, it would seem that the fiduciary duty of the authority to their ratepayers may prevent any additional payment to the former owner: *Re Brown's Mortgage, Wallasey Corporation* v. *Att.-Gen.* [1945] Ch. 166.

Sched. 17, para. 3 deals with the financial consequences of vesting. The authority must set up a fund equal to the amount which they would have had to pay in exercise of their right of pre-emption, together with interest thereon; the money is to be applied in discharge of any interests *prior* to the mortgage which are discharged by the vesting, next in recovering the costs, charges and expenses incidental to the vesting, thirdly in recovering principal, interest, costs and any other money due under the mortgage, fourthly in recoupment of discount (see notes to ss.36, 156, above), or payment of outstanding share on a shared ownership disposal (see notes to Sched. 8, below), and finally the remainder—if any—is to be paid to the person entitled to the mortgaged property, or who whould have been entitled to the receipts had the property been sold.

Subss. (1), (2)

The section applies only where there has been the conveyance of a freehold or a grant or assignment of a long lease by a local authority, new town corporation, urban development corporation, the Development Board for Rural Wales, the Housing Corporation or a registered housing association, which conveyance or grant contains a pre-emption provision in favour of the vendor, which pre-emption provision is still operative at the time when the authority become entitled as mortgagee to exercise the power of sale under s.101, Law of Property Act 1925, or under an express power contained in the mortgage deed.

A pre-emption provision is:

(1) A condition precluding the purchaser of a freehold from selling or leasing the land unless he first notifies the authority of the proposed sale or lease and offers to sell or lease the land to them, and the authority refuse the offer or fail to accept it within one month after it is made: s.33(2)(b) and (3), above; or

(2) A condition in a lease precluding the lessee from assigning the lease or granting a sub-lease: s.33(2)(c), above; or

(3) A condition in a conveyance or grant of property in a National Park, a designated area of outstanding natural beauty or a designated rural area, included with the consent of the Secretary of State or the Housing Corporation, which prevents a non-exempt relevant disposal for a period of ten years from conveyance or grant without an offer to reconvey or surrender, which offer has been refused by the landlord or not accepted within one month: s.157(4), above; or

(4) Any other provision to the like effect as heads (1)–(3).

It is clear, therefore, that a relevant pre-emption provision can arise under a voluntary sale, or a right to buy sale.

Subss. (3), (4)
A vesting under Sched. 17 counts as a relevant disposal for the purposes of repayment of discount under a Part II voluntary sale (see notes to s.35, above) or a Part V right to buy sale (see notes to s.155, above), or a provision of the conveyance or grant to like effect. Repayment of discount covenants in conveyances and grants before August 26, 1984, are modified so far as necessary to bring them into conformity with these provisions, *i.e.* if needs be to ensure that the vesting will qualify as a disposal for the purpose of repayment of discount.

Further advances in case of disposal on shared ownership lease

453.—(1) Where—
  (*a*) a lease of a house, granted otherwise than in pursuance of the provisions of Part V (the right to buy) relating to shared ownership leases, contains a provision to the like effect as that required by paragraph 1 of Schedule 8 (terms of shared ownership lease: right of tenant to acquire additional shares), and
  (*b*) a housing authority has, in the exercise of any of its powers, left outstanding or advanced any amount on the security of the house,
that power includes power to advance further amounts for the purpose of assisting the tenant to make payments in pursuance of that provision.
  (2) In subsection (1) "housing authority" means—
    a local authority,
    a new town corporation,
    an urban development corporation,
    the Development Board for Rural Wales, or
    a registered housing association.

DEFINITIONS
  "house": s.458.
  "local authority": s.4.
  "new town corporation": s.4.
  "registered housing association": s.5.
  "urban development corporation": s.4.

GENERAL NOTE
  This section applies to *voluntary* shared ownership leases. It provides that power to lend on the *initial* sale (*cf.* notes to s.435, above) or to leave money outstanding (see s.437, above) includes power to advance monies (or leave further sums outstanding) with which to purchase subsequent tranches of equity, in the same way as a purchaser under the statutory shared ownership scheme (see notes to s.143, above, and Sched. 8, below) can obtain further advances.

Exclusion of Restrictive Trade Practices Act: recommendations as to implementation of this Part

454. Section 16(3) and (5) of the Restrictive Trade Practices Act 1976 (recommendations by services supply associations to members) do not apply to—
  (*a*) recommendations made to building societies or recognised bodies about the making of agreements under section 442 (local authority agreements to indemnify mortgagees) or the corresponding Northern Ireland provision, or
  (*b*) recommendations made to lending institutions and savings institutions about the manner of implementing sections 445 to 449 (assistance for first-time buyers) or the corresponding Scottish or Northern Ireland provisions,

provided that the recommendations are made with the approval of the Secretary of State or, as the case may be, the Department of the Environment for Northern Ireland, which may be withdrawn at any time on one month's notice.

DEFINITION
    "building society": s.622.

GENERAL NOTE
    The Building Societies Association and similar financial associations of other relevant institutions under ss.447, 448, above, are not affected by the provisions of an order under s.11, Restrictive Trade Practices Act 1976 governing restrictive agreements as to services, in relation to the first-time buyer scheme under ss.445, 446, above, so far as they concern recommendations made with the approval of the Secretary of State.
    See also s.455, below.

Exclusion of Restrictive Trade Practices Act: agreements as to loans on security of new houses

455.—(1) In determining for the purposes of the Restrictive Trade Practices Act 1976 whether an agreement between building societies is one to which that Act applies by virtue of an order made, or having effect as if made, under section 11 of that Act (restrictive agreements as to services), no account shall be taken of any term (whether or not subject to exceptions) by which the parties or any of them agree not to grant loans on the security of new houses unless they have been built by or at the direction of a person who is registered with, or has agreed to comply with the standards of house building laid down or approved by, an appropriate body.
    (2) In subsection (1)—
        "appropriate body" means a body concerned with the specification and control of standards of house building which—
            (*a*) has its chairman, or the chairman of its board of directors or other governing body, appointed by the Secretary of State, and
            (*b*) promotes or administers a scheme conferring rights in respect of defects in the condition of houses on persons having or acquiring interest in them; and
        "new house" means a building or part of a building intended for use as a private dwelling and not previously occupied as such.
    (3) The reference in subsection (1) to a term agreed to by the parties or any of them includes a term to which the parties or any of them are deemed to have agreed by virtue of section 16 of the Restrictive Trade Practices Act 1976 (recommendations of services supply associations).

DEFINITION
    "building society": s.622.

GENERAL NOTE
    Since 1966, the Building Societies Association have recommended that mortgage finance should only be forthcoming for new-build housing where the builder is registered with the National House-Builders Registration Council, unless its construction is supervised by a qualified architect or surveyor employed by the purchaser. This section exempts a recommendation of this or a similar kind from an order under s.11, Restrictive Trades Practices Act 1976 (see also s.454, above). The section applies to "new houses", defined to mean a building or part or a building intended for use as a private dwelling and not previously occupied as such, and could accordingly include conversion of a non-housing building to housing: subs. (2).

Advances under the Small Dwellings Acquisition Acts

456. The provisions of Schedule 18 have effect with respect to advances made under the Small Dwellings Acquisition Acts 1899 to 1923 before the repeal of those Acts by the Housing (Consequential Provisions) Act 1985.

GENERAL NOTE
The Small Dwellings Acquisition Act 1899 was the earliest general power under which local authorities lent money on mortgage. Even as amended (last by s.44(1), Housing Act 1949), it never applied to property above £5,000. Nonetheless, even although use of the powers had long since declined, it is possible that there are some mortgages still in existence under the Acts, and Sched. 18 preserves the special provisions which govern them. The Schedule governs such matters as rate of interest, repayment method, residence by proprietor, insurance, maintenance on good sanitary condition and repair, use of the house, powers of entry by authority, person liability, repossession and disposal.

Supplementary provisions

Meaning of "house" and "house property"

457. In this Part "house" includes—
(a) any yard, garden, outhouses and appurtenances belonging to the house or usually enjoyed with it, and
(b) any part of a building which is occupied or intended to be occupied as a separate dwelling including, in particular, a flat;
and "house property" shall be construed accordingly.

GENERAL NOTE
See also notes to s.56, above.

Minor definitions

458. In this Part—
"the corresponding Northern Ireland provisions," means—
(a) in relation to section 442 (local authority agreements to indemnify mortgagees), Article 156 of the Housing (Northern Ireland) Order 1981;
(b) in relation to sections 445 to 449 (assistance for first-time buyers), Part IX of that Order;
"the corresponding Scottish provisions", in relation to sections 445 to 449 (assistance for first-time buyers), means the Home Purchase Assistance and Housing Corporation Guarantee Act 1978;
"designated building society" means a building society designated for the purposes of the Trustee Investments Act 1961;
"long lease" means a lease creating a long tenancy within the meaning of section 115.

Index of defined expressions: Part XIV

459. The following Table shows provisions defining or otherwise explaining expressions used in this Part (other than provisions defining or explaining an expression used in the same section or paragraph):—

bank	section 622
building society	section 622
corresponding Northern Ireland provisions	section 458
corresponding Scottish provisions	section 458
designated building society	section 458
district valuer	section 622
first time purchaser	section 449(2)(*d*)

fit for human habitation	section 604
friendly society	section 622
house	section 457
house property	section 457
housing association	section 5(1)
Housing Revenue Account	section 417
insurance company	section 622
local authority	section 4(*e*)
long lease	sections 115 and 458
new town corporation	section 4(*b*)
ownership and proprietor (in relation to an advance under the Small Dwellings Acquisition Acts)	paragraphs 9(2) and (3) of Schedule 18
recognised body	section 444(1)
recognised lending institution	section 447
recognised savings institution	section 448
registered housing asssociation	section 5(4)
residence (in relation to an advance under the Small Dwellings Acquisition Acts)	paragraph 9(1) of Schedule 18
statutory conditions (in relation to an advance under the Small Dwellings Acquisition Acts)	paragraph 2 of Schedule 18
trustee savings bank	section 622
urban development corporation	section 4(*d*)

PART XV

GRANTS FOR WORKS OF IMPROVEMENT, REPAIR AND CONVERSION

Main forms of grant assistance

General description of the main grants

460.—(1) The following grants are payable by local housing authorities in accordance with the following provisions of this Part—
    improvement grants (sections 467 to 473),
    intermediate grants (sections 474 to 482),
    special grants (sections 483 to 490), and
    repairs grants (sections 491 to 498);
and references in this Part to grants, without more, are to those grants.
  (2) The grants are payable towards the cost of works required for—
   (*a*) the provision of dwellings by the conversion of houses or other buildings,
   (*b*) the improvement of dwellings,
   (*c*) the repair of dwellings, and
   (*d*) the improvement of houses in multiple occupation.
  (3) The grants are not payable where the provision, improvement or repair is by—
    a local authority,
    a new town corporation, or
    the Development Board for Rural Wales.

DEFINITIONS
  "dwelling": s.525.
  "house in multiple occupation": s.525.
  "improvement": s.525.

"improvement grant": s.467.
"intermediate grant": s.474.
"local authority": s.4.
"new town corporation": s.4.
"local housing authority": ss.1, 2.
"repairs grant": s.491.
"special grant": s.483.

GENERAL NOTE

There are four basic or "main" grants: the improvement grant, for the conversion of premises into dwellings, or for "major" works of improvement, above and beyond the intermediate grant (see s.467, below); the intermediate grant, for the improvement of dwellings lacking standard amenities, principally by their provision (see s.474, below); the repairs grant, for works of repair or replacement not associated with conversion or major improvements, or the provision of standard amenities (see s.491, below); and, the special grant, for works (including means of escape from fire) to a house in multiple occupation (as defined in s.525, below) (see s.483, below).

In addition, "homes insulation grants" may be available under a somewhat different scheme, now to be found in ss.521-522, below. See also Part XVI, below, as to the alternative scheme for system-built housing, including Airey Houses formerly dealt with under what is now this Part.

The Health and Safety at Work etc. Act 1974 also contains useful additional powers, which apply to "non-domestic premises," which have been held to include lifts and electrical installations in a block of flats: *Westminster City Council* v. *Select Management Ltd.* [1985] 1 W.L.R. 576, C.A.

Note that the government have recently issued a Green Paper, "Home Improvement—A New Approach," Cmnd. 9513, in which significant changes are proposed to the entire structure of this Part, including the possibility of the replacement of grants by loans in some circumstances, and "means-testing." An initial response date in July 1985 was subsequently postponed to September 1985, and it is not yet known when or if change will follow, or to what extent.

Amongst the proposals are: mandatory assistance for works to bring dwellings up to a new fitness standard, regardless of whether notice had been served under ss.189, 190, above; a single discretionary repairs/improvement grant for whatever works are needed to bring property up to a reasonable standard of repair and give them a 30-year life, and available in respect of all dwellings built before 1940; loan assistance only where aid is discretionary, possibly interest-free but equity-sharing, but grants for mandatory assistance, with power to "top up" mandatory grant with discretionary loan; a separate scheme for "development," *i.e.* building or conversion for sale; and, greater powers for the authority to satisfy themselves as to quality of works resulting, and limiting assistance to where the builder employed is the one who has provided the estimate (other than change for good reason).

The Main Grants

Modern housing improvement grants as we know them were introduced in 1949 (Housing Act 1949, s.20). At that time, they were purely discretionary. In 1959 (House Purchase and Housing Act 1959, s.4), however, the forerunner of the intermediate grant was made mandatory, *i.e.* if all the relevant statutory conditions were fulfilled, an applicant was entitled to the grant as of right (see now s.479, below). The overwhelming bulk of grant activity remained, however, discretionary.

The present range of "main grants" was introduced in 1974. The intermediate grant was mandatory (see s.479), but the remaining grants were all discretionary. In 1980, however, amendment to the Housing Act 1974 by the Housing Act 1980 "elevated" both the repairs grant and the special grant to mandatory status, when (but only when) the application for grant-aid followed a repairs notice under what is now Part VI (see now s.494, below) or an equivalent notice under what is now Part XI (H.M.O.s, including a notice requiring means of escape from fire under what is now s.366, above) (see now s.486, below).

The range of main grants is not available when the works in respect of which they are payable are carried out by local authorities, new town corporations or the Development Board for Rural Wales: subs. (3). They are, however, available to housing associations, as well as to private owners and, in some circumstances, to tenants: see s.463, below. The provisions of this Part should be read together with Part VIII (area improvement), and Part VII (improvement notices).

The principal influences on the grant policies which local authorities will adopt are: (a) that some grants are mandatory and authorities accordingly will have no option but to approve them, and (b) the extent to which they have finance available (after budgeting and paying for mandatory grants). This is governed by the provisions of the Local Government Act 1980 (see notes to s.421, above), and by the subsidy provisions applicable to this Part (ss.516-517, below): see notes thereto, below. As to the extent to which individual applications need to be considered, in the light of policies, see notes to s.470, below. The grants are payable for:

(1) Provision of dwellings by conversion; this is the improvement grant itself (see s.467, below); the building to be converted cannot be one erected after October 2, 1961 (see s.462, below);

(2) Improvement of dwellings; improvement includes alteration and enlargement (s.525, below); this will either be under an improvement grant (see s.467, below) or an intermediate grant (see s.474, below);

(3) Repair of dwellings; repairs works will often be required in connection or association with either improvement grant activity (see s.467, below) or intermediate grant activity (see s.474, below), but may be carried out on their own under s.491, below;

(4) Improvement of H.M.O.s, under s.483, below.

Dwelling

"Dwelling" means a building or part of a building occupied or intended to be occupied as a separate dwelling, together with any yard, garden, outhouses and appurtenances belonging to it or usually enjoyed with it: s.525. "House" is not defined for the purposes of this Part, but is of little significance on its own because the principal object is the dwelling as thus defined.

As to occupation "as a separate dwelling", see notes to ss.79, 324, above. The dwelling, to be "separate", must contain all the facilities for normal living activity, *e.g.* a kitchen (see, *e.g.*, *Neale* v. *Del Soto* [1945] K.B. 144, C.A., *Winters* v. *Dance* [1949] L.J.R. 165, C.A.) although not necessarily its own bathroom/lavatory (see, *e.g.*, *Cole* v. *Harris* [1945] K.B. 474, C.A., *Curl* v. *Angelo* [1948] 2 All E.R. 189, C.A., *Goodrich* v. *Paisner* [1957] A.C. 65, H.L., *Marsh* v. *Cooper* [1969] 1 W.L.R. 803, C.A.). The latter will, however, be required in the case of an improvement grant or an intermediate grant, as "standard amenities" under s.508, below.

The definition of dwelling is not wholly free from practical difficulty in one, important, respect, *i.e.* its application to flats. Grants are available for "parts of a building", which of course includes a flat. In each of the three main cases, works concern "a dwelling" (improvement grants—s.467, intermediate grants—s.474, repairs grants—s.491). Prima facie, therefore, works to, *e.g.*, the roof of a block of flats (whether or not purpose built) could not be considered part of any dwelling other than a top-floor flat, and then only in an appropriate case (*e.g.* where the roof is demised to the lessee of the top floor flat).

Even where in practice the roof forms part of the top floor flat (consider *Douglas-Scott* v. *Scorgie* [1984] 13 H.L.R. 1397, C.A.), the problem is exacerbated by the requirement in s.463(1), below, that "the applicant has, or proposes to acquire, an owner's interest in every parcel of land on which the relevant works are to be or have been carried out". Again, unless a roof (or, perhaps, part of a roof) is demised to the lessee of the top floor flat (or, in theory, the lessee of another flat, so as to bring it within his dwelling by what would be an unusual but not apparently impossible device), lessees of flats will not normally have the appropriate interest (as defined in s.463(2), below), in the roof.

Similar remarks will commonly apply in relation to foundations, and the position governing, *e.g.* external and common pipes or gutters, is also far from clear. A special grant may be available to the freeholder, or superior lessor with an interest in these "common parts" (*cf. Dunster* v. *Hollis* [1918] 2 K.B. 795, *Cockburn* v. *Smith* [1924] 2 K.B. 119), for the special grant is available in relation to an H.M.O., defined to mean those parts of a house *exclusive of* those parts occupied as a separate dwelling: s.525.

One "answer" to these problems *might* lie in the word "appurtenances" in the definition of dwelling, but (a) this would not seem apt to cover the "interest" of a leaseholder in a roof (see notes to s.56, above), and (b) would not overcome the problem of the requirement for a specific legal interest to be found in s.463.

However, these problems would not seem to arise in the case of a mandatory repairs grant, under s.494, below, *i.e.* where notice has been served under ss.189, 190, above. The first point to note is that the application for a repairs grant does not have to be by the person served. The second point is that in such cases, the requirement of specific legal interest in s.463 is disapplied. Finally, note that under s.491(1), repairs grant work is defined as "relating to" a dwelling, not "to" the dwelling.

In addition, no certificate of future occupation under s.464 is called for in the case of a mandatory repairs grant. As the repairs grant may relate to more than one dwelling (see s.493(1), below), it would accordingly seem not only that works to the roof (or foundations, etc.) are within the works available to the leaseholders or indeed tenants of individual flats, provided the other conditions for repairs grant (see particularly s.493, below) are fulfilled, but that the person served with the notice, or other person in a position to cause the works to be executed, can also apply for a grant. As the amount of grant is limited per grant, *i.e.* rather than per dwelling involved (see s.497, below), this may produce a useful additional amount.

These problems are canvassed in D.O.E. Circular 26/85, paras. 11–16.

House in Multiple Occupation

The definition of H.M.O. (s.525) also gives rise to one practical problem: the definition is clearly deliberately different from that to be found in Part XI (see s.345, above), with the result that, although notice may have been served under s.352 (general works) or s.366 (means of escape from fire), and as such give rise to a claim for a mandatory special grant under s.486 below, there is likely to be a substantial difference between the works the subject of the notice, and the works which will qualify as works to an H.M.O. as defined for the purpose of this Part, *i.e.* the latter will exclude those works which are to parts of the house *not* in separate occupation, which may well have been included in one of the former class of notice.

In *R.* v. *Kerrier District Council, ex parte Guppys (Bridport) Ltd. (No.* 2) (1985) 17 H.L.R. 426, the Court of Appeal considered the definition of "house in multiple occupation" for the purposes of application for mandatory special grant under s.486, below. What was in issue was a large building, with shops at street level, and a number of rooms from the first floor upwards. The property was initially being used as what the Court of Appeal in the present case describe as a "lodging house", in single rooms, and with the occupiers as "probably" licensees. (This aspect of the decision conflicts with the decision of the Court of Appeal in *Guppys (Bridport) Ltd.* v. *Brookling and James* (1983) 14 H.L.R. 1, where two of the occupiers in the same house were held to be tenants.)

In the event, notices were served under what are now ss.352 and 356, above. The landlords, after their purchase of the property in September 1980, applied for planning permission to convert the upper floors into self-contained flats, which works would cater for all the requirements of the notices. During 1981, the landlords set about conversion works. There were still two occupiers, and the works carried out by the landlords led to action by these occupiers, resulting in an award of exemplary damages, upheld in the Court of Appeal (above). The two occupiers had left by October 1981.

In April 1982, the landlords applied to the authority for a special grant. In June 1982, the application was refused, on the grounds that in the circumstances of the case then known to the authority, and in particular because the landlords did not intend complying with the 1961 Act notices for the purpose of improving a house in multiple occupation, they were not entitled to special grant. The landlords challenged this decision.

The Court of Appeal held that the authority had to ask whether the works were for the improvement of an H.M.O., at the date of application for the grant. At that date, and at the date when the authority gave their decision, there was no one in occupation, and no intention to let the house as an H.M.O. again, but to turn it into a block of self-contained flats, which was outwith the intention of Parliament as reflected in this definition. If what would emerge from the works was not an H.M.O., the works could not be for the improvement of an H.M.O. It was accepted that in some cases a house, even although empty, may still qualify as an H.M.O., *e.g.* where the occupiers have temporarily removed during works.

See also D.O.E. Circular 26/85.

Additional Constraints

The fact that grants may be available under this Part does not, of course, obviate the need to secure appropriate permissions for the work to be executed. Thus, building regulations (now, the Building Regulations 1985, S.I. 1985, No. 1065) under the Building Act 1984, will commonly have to be complied with. Similarly, and especially in the case of conversions of non-housing buildings to housing, and in the case of a house into flats, approval may need to be secured under the Town and Country Planning Act 1971.

Planning Law

The 1971 Act deals in "development", not "improvement" or "alteration": 1971, s.23. Development means "the carrying out of building, engineering, mining or other operations in, on, over or under land, or the making of any material change in the use of any building or other land": 1971, s.22(1). Normally exempt, however, is the "carrying out of works for the maintenance, improvement or other alteration of any building, being works which affect only the interior of the building or which do not materially affect the external appearance of the building": 1971, s.22(2).

Nonetheless, even without change in external appearance, conversion of a non-housing building to housing use is a material change of use amounting to development (*Birmingham Corporation* v. *Ministry of Housing and Local Government* [1964] 1 Q.B. 178, D.C.), and conversion of a single dwelling into two or more separate dwellings, or a house in multiple occupation, can be a change of use, amounting to development: 1971, s.22(3); see also *Birmingham Corporation, Borg* v. *Khan* (1965) 17 P. & C.R. 144, D.C.; *Clarke* v. *Minister of Housing and Local Government* (1966) 64 L.G.R. 346, D.C.; *London Borough of Hammersmith* v. *Secretary of State for the Environment* (1975) 73 L.G.R. 288; *Mayflower (Cambridge) Ltd.* v. *Secretary of State for the Environment* (1975) 30 P. & C.R. 28; *Duffy* v. *Pilling* (1977) 33 P. & C.R. 85, and *Backer* v. *Secretary of State for the Environment* (1982) 264 E.G. 536, Q.B.D.

A "granny-flat extension" is development under 1971, s.22: *Tromans* v. *Secretary of State for the Environment and the Wye Forest District Council* [1983] J.P.L. 474. Mere intensification of use can be sufficiently substantial to amount to a change of use: *Brooks & Burton* v. *Secretary of State for the Environment* [1977] 1 W.L.R. 1294, C.A.; see also *Wakelin* v. *Secretary of State for the Environment* (1983) 46 P. & C.R. 214, C.A., and *Winton* v. *Secretary of State for the Environment* (1983) 46 P. & C.R. 205, Q.B.D., but *cf. Royal Borough of Kensington and Chelsea* v. *Secretary of State for the Environment* [1981] J.P.L. 50.

There is no change of use from one use to another within the same Use Classes Order (currently, S.I. 1972 No. 1385, as amended), although there is no Class which includes housing with other uses. It will also be unnecessary to obtain planning permission if the development is within a General Development Order: 1971, s.24. S.I. 1977 No. 289, as amended, makes it unnecessary to obtain planning permission in relation to much private housing improvement—see Class 1 of the Order, allowing a specified extent of enlargement, improvement or other alteration, subject to conditions, of dwelling-houses.

Whether or not something qualifies as a dwelling-house for the purposes of Class 1 is a question of fact: see *Scurlock* v. *Secretary of State for Wales* (1976) 33 P. & C.R. 202; *Gravesham Borough Council* v. *Secretary of State for the Environment and O'Brian* [1973] J.P.L. 306, Q.B.D. See also *Backer* v. *Secretary of State for the Environment* [1983] 1 W.L.R. 1485, and *Macmillan & Co. Ltd.* v. *Rees* [1946] 1 All E.R. 675.

There are also special provisions applicable to listed buildings under 1971, s.54 (and, indeed, special levels of grant aid available in some circumstances for listed buildings—see notes to ss.472 and 497, below). These special provisions apply also to buildings within a conservation area (as defined in 1971, s.277, as amended), and those subject to a building preservation order imposed by a local authority pending a decision on listing by the Secretary of State under 1971, s.54 (1971, s.58). Planning permission is always required for any works to a listed building, if the works include works for the alteration or extension of the building in any manner which would affect its character as a building of special architectural or historic interest: 1971, s.55.

Private Law Constraints

Finally, there may of course be private law constraints on improvements, *e.g.* a covenant against improvement in a long lease. If there is an "absolute" covenant against improvement, *i.e.* which does not even permit improvement with consent, then it can only be discharged by application to the county court under s.610, below, or by application to the Lands Tribunal under Law of Property Act 1925, s.84, as substantially amended by Law of Property Act 1969, s.28.

However, no such application can be made in the case of a lease unless the lease is of a minimum of 40 years, of which at least 25 years have already expired: 1925, s.84(12) as amended by Landlord and Tenant Act 1954, s.52. A qualified covenant can also theoretically be discharged in either of these ways, although it is probably easier to apply to the landlord for consent: see further below.

Application to the county court under s.610, below, or the Lands Tribunal may also be made by a freeholder suffering the burden of a restrictive covenant, or a leaseholder (subject to the same restrictions as to the length of lease and time expired) in respect of another restrictive covenant which prevents improvement, *i.e.* not one imposed by the landlord.

The jurisdiction of the Lands Tribunal is to discharge or modify a restrictive covenant, on payment of compensation if appropriate, where:

(1) There have been changes in the character of the property affected or of the neighbourhood; or

(2) There have been changes in other material circumstances; or

(3) The restriction is obsolete; or

(4) The continued application of the covenant would prevent some reasonable use of the land without giving any material benefit to anyone; or

(5) All persons of full age and legal capacity who are entitled to the benefit of the covenant agree to discharge or modification, expressly or by implication of conduct; or

(6) The discharge or modification would not harm anyone so entitled; or

(7) Reasonable use of the land is prevented and either there is no practical benefit to anyone entitled to enforce it, or the covenant is contrary to the public interest, and in either event monetary compensation could meet the loss of benefit of the covenant (1925, s.84 as amended).

In *Re Hughes' Application* [1983] J.P.L. 318, the Lands Tribunal held that if a restrictive covenant afforded a high degree of privacy, this was certainly a practical benefit and one which could not be compensated in money terms. "Benefit" under head (4) means benefit affecting the locality, and it is not necessary for an objector to show that he personally takes advantage of that benefit: *Gilbert* v. *Spoor* [1983] Ch. 87, C.A.; see also *Re Speakman's Application* [1983] J.P.L. 680, L.T. In reaching their decision, the Lands Tribunal must have regard to planning policies, as declared or ascertained: 1925, s.84, as amended; however, the grant of planning permission will not be decisive—*Gilbert* v. *Spoor*.

Where a lease with a qualified covenant is involved, *i.e.* a covenant not to improve or alter without consent, then whether or not the covenant so states, such consent cannot unreasonably be withheld: s.19, Landlord and Tenant Act 1927. What constitutes an improvement for this purpose is to be considered from the point of view of the tenant: *Lambert* v. *Woolworth & Co. (No. 2)* [1938] Ch. 883.

It is usually the tenant who must assume the burden of showing that a refusal of consent is unreasonable: *Shanly* v. *Ward* (1913) 29 T.L.R. 714, *Premier Confectionery (London) Co.* v. *London Commercial Sale Rooms* [1933] Ch. 904, *Re Town Investments Underlease* [1954] Ch. 301, *Pimms* v. *Tallow Chandlers Co.* [1964] 2 Q.B. 547. In practice, however, if a landlord gives reasons which are patently unreasonable, the burden may move on to him: *Berry* v. *Royal Bank of Scotland* [1949] 1 K.B. 619, *Lovelock* v. *Margo* [1963] 2 Q.B. 786. However, the landlord is not then confined to the reasons given, on a challenge: *Sonnenthal* v. *Newton* (1965) 109 S.J. 333, C.A., *Welch* v. *Birrane* (1974) 29 P. & C.R. 102.

The landlord is not obliged to give reasons: *Young* v. *Ashley Gardens Properties* [1903] 1 Ch. 112, *Goldstein* v. *Sanders* [1915] 1 Ch. 549, *Parker* v. *Boggon* [1947] K.B. 346, *Berry* v. *Royal Bank of Scotland* [1949] 1 K.B. 619. However, in such a case, again, the burden may shift to the landlord to show reasonable refusal: *Lambert* v. *F. W. Woolworth & Co. (No. 2)* [1938] Ch. 883.

The reasonableness is prima facie that of the landlord in question, not just "a" reasonable landlord: *Tredegar* v. *Harwood* [1929] A.C. 72, H.L., although it may be that the test is neither wholly objective nor wholly subjective: see *Lovelock* v. *Margo* [1963] 2 Q.B. 786, and *Searle* v. *Burroughs* (1966) S.J. 248, C.A. The Law Commission Report No. 141 on Covenants Restricting Dispositions, Alterations and Change of User, H.C. 278, put it in this way: "the courts seem generally to ask whether a *reasonable* person in the same position as the *actual* landlord *might* regard the thing in question as damaging to his interests; and they will not normally find his refusal unreasonable merely because other people might have taken a different view" (para 3.69).

The landlord is entitled to ask the purpose of the consent: *Fuller's Theatres* v. *Rolfe* [1923] A.C. 435, H.L. Future letting potential as improved or altered is clearly relevant: *Premier Confectionery (London) Co.* v. *London Commercial Sale Rooms* (above), *Re Town Investments Underlease* (above). The reasons must not be wholly extraneous: *Houlder Brothers & Co.* v. *Gibbs* [1925] Ch. 575. The cases on withholding of consent to subletting considered in the notes to s.93, above, will be of general relevance and some applicability.

A refusal may be challenged (by application for declaration, see *Mills* v. *Cannon Brewery Co. Ltd.* [1920] 2 Ch. 38) in the county court: Landlord and Tenant Act 1954, s.53. However, consent must be sought, however well-founded is anticipation of refusal, or however unreasonable any refusal would be: *Barrow* v. *Isaacs* [1891] 1 Q.B. 417; *Eastern Telegraph Co.* v. *Dent* [1889] 1 Q.B. 835.

Alternatively, and provided consent has been sought, the leaseholder may proceed and await and defend action for breach on the grounds that consent was unreasonably refused: *Treloar* v. *Bigge* (1874) L.R. 9 Ex. 151; *Sear* v. *House Property and Investment Society* (1880) 16 Ch. D. 387; *Lewis & Allenby* v. *Pegge* [1914] 1 Ch. 782, *Mills* v. *Cannon Brewery* [1920] 2 Ch. 38; *Ideal Film Renting Co.* v. *Nielsen* [1921] 1 Ch. 575.

If works are carried out without asking for consent but in circumstances in which consent could not reasonably have been withheld, the breach is largely technical and the landlord will only be entitled to nominal damages: *Graystone Property Investments Ltd.* v. *Margolies* (1984) 269 E.G. 538, C.A.

If the landlord withholds consent unreasonably, resulting in loss to the tenant, the tenant has no claim for the loss from the landlord: *Treloar* v. *Bigge* (1874) L.R. 9 Ex. 151. The Law Commission (*op. cit.*) recommend that such a remedy should be available: paragraphs 8.65 and 8.112.

See further on this subject, notes to s.97, above.

Tenanted Property

Where property is tenanted, and the applicant is the landlord, he will not be able to proceed unless he can do so under the terms of the tenancy, without bringing the tenancy to an end. Where the tenancy is protected under the Rent Act 1977, and on termination accordingly becomes statutory, he can seek an order of the county court to permit works under an improvement grant or an intermediate grant within this Part, provided the application has been approved or the authority issue a certificate that it is likely to be approved, under Rent Act 1977, s.116.

The county court can make a conditional order, governing accommodation of the tenant and household, and storage of his property, during works, and when determining whether or not to grant the order, or attach conditions, the court must have regard to all the circumstances and in particular to the age and health of the tenant, and the possible disadvantage to the tenant (*e.g.* both the fact that there will be a rent increase when the rent is next registered, under 1977 Act, s.70, and that the landlord may be able to apply for re-registration sooner than otherwise under *ibid.*, s.67, with the effect that not only will the landlord get an increased rent attributable to the improvement, but also commonly an increase attributable to inflation—see *London Housing and Commercial Properties* v. *Cowan* [1977] Q.B. 148).

Grant applications

461.—(1) A grant shall be paid by a local housing authority only if an application for it is made to the authority in accordance with the provisions of this Part and is approved by them.

(2) The application shall specify the premises to which the application relates and contain—

(*a*) particulars of the works in respect of which the grant is sought (referred to in this Part as "the relevant works") and an estimate of their cost, and

(*b*) such other particulars as may be specified by the Secretary of State.

(3) A local housing authority may not entertain an application for a grant if—

(*a*) the relevant works are or include works which were the relevant works in relation to an application previously approved under this Part, and

(*b*) the applicant is, or is the personal representative of, the person who made the earlier application,

except in the circumstances specified in subsection (4).

(4) Such an application may be entertained if the relevant works have not been begun and either—

(*a*) more than two years have elapsed since the date on which the previous application was approved, or

(*b*) the application is made with a view to taking advantage of an order under section 509 (orders varying appropriate percentage for purposes of determining amount of grant).

Definitions

"appropriate percentage": s.509.
"grant": s.460.
"local housing authority": ss.1, 2.

GENERAL NOTE

An application must comply with the requirements of this section, and the authority cannot pay a grant unless it does so. Note also the requirements of s.462 (recently constructed or converted dwellings), s.463 (the applicant's interest in the premises), s.464 (certificate of future occupation), and s.465 (prior works). Note, too, that additional requirements will be found in s.464 (improvement, intermediate and repairs), s.475 (intermediate), and s.484 (special).

Subs. (2)

The application must specify:

 (1) The premises to which the application relates;
 (2) Particulars of the "relevant works", *i.e.* the works for which grant-aid is sought;
 (3) An estimate of the cost of the relevant works;
 (4) Such further particulars as the Secretary of State may specify.

The Secretary of State has specified additional particulars in para. 3 of App. A to D.O.E. Circular 21/80:

(i) *Improvement grants*:

 (a) in the case of improvement works, "before-and-after" plans of the dwelling;
 (b) in the case of conversion works, "before-and-after" plans of the building or buildings;
 (c) a statement saying whether the dwelling to be improved, or the building to be converted, was provided before October 2, 1961 (*cf.* s.462, below);
 (d) a statement of rateable value or values.

(ii) *Intermediate grants*:

 (a) a plan of the dwelling to which the application relates showing the local of proposed works;
 (b) a statement saying whether the dwelling was provided before October 2, 1961 (*cf.* s.462, below).

(iii) *Repairs grant*:

 (a) a statement of rateable value;
 (b) a statement saying whether the dwelling is, or forms part of, a building erected before January 1, 1919 (*cf.* s.492, below);
 (c) a statement saying whether the dwelling was provided before October 2, 1961 (*cf.* s.462, below);
 (d) a statement as to whether the works are necessary for compliance with a notice under ss.189 or 190, above, and the date and reference of any such notice.

(iv) *Special grant*:

 (a) "before-and-after" plans of the house in multiple occupation;
 (b) a statement as to whether the works are necessary for compliance with a notice under ss.352 or 366, above, and the date and reference of any such notice.

Neither the section nor the Secretary of State requires that plans be professionally prepared. The section requires only that "an" estimate of cost be included, which could mean a professional (independent) estimate, more commonly is taken to mean a builder's estimate, but can include the applicant's own estimate of materials' costs if he intends to do the works himself. The Secretary of State has suggested that "rather than insisting on more than one estimate, local authorities may wish to consider a single estimate and to rely on their officers to assess its reasonableness. This would be particularly appropriate for relatively minor works . . . ": D.O.E. Circular 21/80, App. B, para. 34.

Neither the section nor the Secretary of State *requires* that the application be in any particular *form*, although "Model Forms" are to be found in App. C of D.O.E. Circular 21/80.

Authorities in practice commonly insist (a) on application by a particular form, and (b) on more than one estimate. Less commonly, but not unknown, authorities may insist on professionally prepared plans. These are issues of considerable practical, and sometimes legal, importance. Obtaining more than one estimate can be difficult, and within an area it can lead to builders treating with scepticism requests for estimates, and a correspondingly casual attitude to when he will actually be in a position to commence works—with a knock-on effect for local authority budgeting (*cf.* notes to s.516, below) and at risk of offending a completion condition under s.512, below.

A requirement for professionally prepared plans involves the applicant in *prior* expenditure (although not "prior works" within s.465, below), perhaps at a time when grant availability is uncertain, so that although the cost may be available for grant *if* approved, it will be lost if not approved. Finally, if applications are not treated as "made" until the authority's own requirements are fulfilled, the date may have a legal effect, under subs. (4) of this section, or if different levels of grant-aid are dependent on when an application is made, *e.g.*, as occurred in 1982–84 (see notes to ss.482, 498, below), and in a number of other circumstances under, *e.g.* s.469, below.

The question which arises is whether local authorities are *entitled* to impose *any* actual *requirements* as to the form or content of an application, *other* than as specified in, or under the authority of, this Part. In practice, there are so many features—*e.g.* post-works standards, propriety of expenditure—as to which the authority must be "satisfied", that refusal to provide all the information which the authority require is likely to lead to a refusal of grant, even a mandatory grant. But provision of information between application and approval is different from the question of whether or not an application has been *made* at a particular date.

Prior to this Act, it was relatively clear that if the requirements of and under what is now this Part were fulfilled, the application had to be *entertained*, and treated as *made*: see Housing Act 1974, ss.61(1), 65(1), 69(1) and 71(1) ("A local authority shall pay [the relevant] grant if an application for such a grant, *made in accordance with this Part of this Act*, is approved by them, and the conditions for the payment of the grant are fulfilled". Emphasis added.)

Today, the position is less clear, although there is no Law Commission Recommendation (Cmnd. 9515) which suggests that any alteration was intended. The Part proceeds by way of negative injunctions save in the mandatory cases under ss.479 (intermediate), 486 (special) and 494 (repairs). The principal difference is that the word "only" in subs. (1) of this section, which confirms that this section is negative in intent (as in Housing Act 1974, s.57(1)) is not accompanied by the equivalent positive injunctions formerly contained in the sections referred to in the last paragraph. It is submitted that there is sufficient material in this Part to suggest that it is a complete code, and sufficient ambiguity to permit the courts to have reference to the previous legislation as an aid to construction: *cf. Farrell* v. *Alexander* [1977] A.C. 59, H.L.

Subss. (3), (4)

The authority cannot entertain an application for a grant if *any* of the works for which grant-aid is sought have been the subject of a previous *approval* under this Part (or the predecessor legislation—see Housing (Consequential Provisions) Act 1985, s.2(3)), which was issued to the same applicant, or the personal representative of the former, successful applicant.

There are three points to note: this prohibition does not apply merely because there was an earlier *application*, *i.e.* it applies only to former *approvals*; it *does* apply even if notwithstanding the approval the applicant did not do any of the relevant works, but in such a case only for a period of two years from the prior approval (subs. (4)); and, it will also *not* apply if no works were carried out *and* the purpose of the application is to take advantage of an increase in the appropriate percentage of grant-aid available.

Preliminary condition: the age of the property

462.—(1) A local housing authority shall not entertain an application for—

(*a*) an improvement grant in respect of works required for the provision of a dwelling by the conversion of a house or other building which was erected after 2nd October 1961, or

(*b*) any grant for the improvement or repair of a dwelling which was provided after 2nd October 1961,

unless they consider it appropriate to do so.

(2) The authority's discretion to entertain such applications is subject to such general or special directions as may be given by the Secretary of State.

DEFINITIONS
　"dwelling": s.525.
　"grant": s.460.
　"improvement": s.525.
　"improvement grant": s.467.
　"local housing authority": ss.1, 2.

GENERAL NOTE

There is a presumption against grants for the conversion of new property, *i.e.* newly built, and against grants generally for property newly converted to residential occupation. The authority are not to entertain an application for an improvement grant if it is a conversion grant under s.467(1)(*a*) if the building to be converted was erected after October 2, 1961. Nor is any grant to be entertained for improvement or repair of a dwelling which was itself provided after the same date. The significance of the date is that it is since then that authorities have had power under s.33, Public Health Act 1936 (now Building Act 1984, s.27), to reject plans for dwellings without a bath or shower and hot and cold water supplies thereto.

In either case, however, the application may be entertained if the authority consider it appropriate to do so, but subject to general or special directions from the Secretary of State under subs. (2). The Secretary of State has directed (D.O.E. Circular 21/80, App. A, para. 2) that no applications relating to such properties shall be entertained unless:

(1) Where the application is to provide a dwelling by conversion of a house or other building which lacked one or more of the standard amenities (as to which, see s.508, below) immediately after its erection, but the plans for the erection were deposited with the local authority and passed by them before October 2, 1961;

(2) Similarly, where the application is for the improvement or repair of a dwelling provided after that date, which lacked one of the standard amenities, but the plans for the provision of the dwelling were deposited with and passed by the local authority before October 2, 1961;

(3) The application is for an improvement grant under s.467, and the works are to meet a requirement for a disabled occupant;

(4) Similarly, if the application is for an intermediate grant under s.474(1)(*b*), *i.e.* where a standard amenity exists, but is inaccessible to a disabled occupant by reason of his disability;

(5) The application is for a repairs grant under s.491, *cf.* s.492, below.

Preliminary condition: the interest of the applicant in the property

463.—(1) A local housing authority may entertain an application for a grant only if they are satisfied that—

(*a*) the applicant has, or proposes to acquire, an owner's interest in every parcel of land on which the relevant works are to be or have been carried out, or

(*b*) the applicant is a tenant of the dwelling;

and references in this Part to an "owner's application" or a "tenant's application" shall be construed accordingly.

(2) In subsection (1)(*a*) an "owner's interest" means an interest which is either—

(*a*) an estate in fee simple absolute in possession, or

(*b*) a term of years absolute of which not less than five years remain unexpired at the date of the application;

and where an authority entertain an owner's application by a person who proposes to acquire the necessary interest, they shall not approve the application until they are satisfied that he has done so.

(3) In subsection (1)(*b*) a "tenant" means a person who has in relation to the dwelling—

(*a*) a protected tenancy, protected occupancy or statutory tenancy,

(*b*) a secure tenancy,

(*c*) a tenancy to which section 1 of the Landlord and Tenant Act 1954 applies (long tenancies at low rents) and of which less than five years remain unexpired at the date of the application, or

(*d*) a tenancy which satisfies such conditions as may be prescribed by order of the Secretary of State.

(4) An authority shall not entertain a tenant's application for an improvement grant in respect of works required for the provision of a dwelling.

(5) An order under this section—

(*a*) may make different provision with respect to different cases or descriptions of case, including different provision for different areas, and

(b) shall be made by statutory instrument which shall be subject to annulment in pursuance of a resolution of either House of Parliament.

(6) This section has effect subject to—

sections 486 and 494 (works required by statutory notice), and section 513 (parsonages, applications by charities, etc.).

DEFINITIONS

"appropriate percentage": s.509.
"dwelling": s.525.
"grant": s.460.
"improvement grant": s.467.
"local housing authority": ss.1, 2.
"protected occupancy": s.622.
"protected tenancy": s.622.
"relevant works": s.461.
"repairs grant": s.491.
"secure tenancy": s.79.
"statutory tenancy": s.622.

GENERAL NOTE

The applicant for a grant has to have—or be intending to have—an appropriate interest in the property. This is not so, however, if the application is as a result of a notice under Parts VI or XI, above, giving rise to a mandatory grant under ss.486 or 494, below, or if it is an application by the sequestrator of the profits of a benefice in respect of glebe land or the residence house of an ecclesiastical benefice made at a time when the benefice is vacant, or an application by charity trustees by or on behalf of a charity, under s.513, below.

There are two classes of application: owner's applications, and tenant's applications. An owner has to have—or be proposing to acquire—a relevant interest in *every parcel of land* on which the relevant works are to be or have been (but *cf.* s.465, below) carried out (see notes to s.460, above): subs. (1). Relevant interest means freehold, or leasehold with at least five years unexpired (but *cf.* subs. (3), below) at the date of the application: subs. (2). Where the application is from a prospective owner, approval must await acquisition of relevant interest: *ibid.* "Land" includes "buildings and other structures, land covered with water, and any estate, interest, easement, servitude or right in or over land": Interpretation Act 1978, Sched. 1.

Owners' applications have to be accompanied by a certificate of future occupation under s.464, below. Related to this certificate are the grant conditions as to future occupation to be found in ss.499–505, below, for breach of which grant-aid may be recoverable under s.506, below.

Only certain classes of tenant qualify: Rent Act 1977 protected and statutory tenants, Rent (Agriculture) Act 1976 protected occupants, secure tenants under Part IV, above, those leaseholders with less than five years to run who will become statutory tenants under the Rent Act 1977 by operation of Part I, Landlord and Tenant Act 1954, and those within conditions prescribed by the Secretary of State: see, further, as to these classes of occupation, notes to s.622, below. Under S.I. 1982 No. 1039 (retained in force by s.2, Housing (Consequential Provisions) Act 1985), tenants of agricultural holdings within the meaning of s.1, Agricultural Holdings Act 1948 (as now amended by s.10 and Sched. 3, para. 1, Agricultural Holdings Act 1984), have been specified provided that, if they are leaseholders, they have less than five years to run (because otherwise they will qualify as owners in any event).

In the case of a tenant's application, the authority may refuse to entertain the grant if it is not accompanied by a certificate of availability for letting from a person from whom an owner's application could have been entertained: s.464(2), below. Unless such is sought, the authority will subsequently be unable to impose additional conditions as to future occupation under ss.503–504, below, and even the general condition as to future occupation in s.501 will be inapplicable.

Tenants may not apply for an improvement grant for the provision of a dwelling by conversion under s.467(1)(a), below. Secure tenants enjoy a "right to improve" under ss.97–99, above, and *may* be reimbursed for their share of the cost under s.100 (see notes thereto). Their rent cannot be increased on account of the improvements, even if or to the extent that they are grant-aided: see s.101, above.

Protected and statutory tenants enjoy a similar right to improve under Housing Act 1980, Part III (unrepealed so far as it concerns them), but without any similar express inhibition on rent increase or, of course, power to reimburse. Not all protected or statutory tenants enjoy this right to improve: those under notices related to the "mandatory" grounds for possession (Rent Act 1977, s.98 and Sched. 15, Part II) including protected shorthold tenants under Housing Act 1980, s.52 do not qualify "unless the tenant proves that, at the time the landlord gave the notice, it was unreasonable for the landlord to expect to be able in due course to recover possession of the dwelling-house under" the relevant provision (Housing Act 1980, s.81(4)). There is no analogous inhibition on application for grant-aid under this Part.

Local authorities should accordingly be careful before accepting such applications. A landlord may be happy to *agree* to the improvement, even if the tenant *is* under a mandatory notice. It may well enhance the value of the property. After five years, there will be no condition requiring the landlord to relet, even if a certificate is sought under s.464(2), below: see s.464(5). If the improvement is under Housing Act 1980, s.81 it is at least arguably under the terms of the tenancy and as such something which a rent officer is *not* bound to disregard (*i.e.* may take into account) when determining a fair rent under Rent Act 1977, s.70 so that there will be a risk that the tenant will pay twice over—once for his balance of the works' cost under this Part, and once on a rent increase: see also *Ponsford* v. *H.M.S. Aerosols Ltd.* [1979] A.C. 63, H.L. And with no obligation to reimburse the tenant, the landlord has an added incentive to evict.

Preliminary condition: certificate as to future occupation

464.—(1) A local housing authority shall not entertain an owner's application, other than an application for a special grant, unless it is accompanied by—

(*a*) a certificate of owner-occupation, or
(*b*) a certificate of availability for letting,

in respect of the dwelling, or each of the dwellings for the provision, improvement or repair of which the application is made.

(2) A local housing authority may refuse to entertain a tenant's application unless it is accompanied by a certificate of availability for letting given by a person from whom the authority could have approved an owner's application.

(3) A "certificate of owner-occupation" is (except where it is given by personal representatives or trustees) a certificate stating that the applicant intends that, on or before the first anniversary of the certified date and throughout the period of four years beginning on that first anniversary, the dwelling will be the only or main residence of, and will be occupied exclusively by, either—

(*a*) the applicant himself and members of his household (if any), or
(*b*) a person who is a member of the applicant's family, or a grandparent or grandchild of the applicant or his spouse, and members of that person's household (if any).

(4) Where the application for grant is made by the personal representatives of a deceased person or by trustees, a "certificate of owner-occupation" is a certificate stating that the applicants are personal representatives or trustees and intend that, on or before the first anniversary of the certified date and throughout the period of four years beginning with that first anniversary, the dwelling will be the only or main residence of, and exclusively occupied by, either—

(*a*) a beneficiary and members of his household (if any), or
(*b*) a person related to a beneficiary by being a member of his family or a grandparent or grandchild of the beneficiary or his spouse, and members of that person's household (if any);

and in this subsection "beneficiary" means a person who, under the will or intestacy, or, as the case may require, under the terms of the trust, is beneficially entitled to an interest in the dwelling or the proceeds of sale of it.

(5) A "certificate of availability for letting" is a certificate stating that the person giving the certificate intends that, throughout the period of five years beginning with the certified date—

    (*a*) the dwelling will be let or available for letting as a residence, and not for a holiday, to a person other than a member of the family of the person giving the certificate, or

    (*b*) the dwelling will be occupied or available for occupation by a member of the agricultural population in pursuance of a contract of service and otherwise than as a tenant,

(disregarding any part of that period in which neither of the above paragraphs applies but the dwelling is occupied by a protected occupier under the Rent (Agriculture) Act 1976).

DEFINITIONS
    "agricultural population": s.525.
    "certified date": s.499.
    "dwelling": s.525.
    "grant": s.460.
    "local housing authority": ss.1, 2.
    "member of family": s.520.
    "owner's application": s.463.
    "special grant": s.483.
    "tenant's application": s.463.

GENERAL NOTE
This section governs future occupation. It is concerned with *intentions* at the time of application, and must be distinguished from *conditions* as to future occupation, and *breach* of such conditions. The conditions are set out in ss.499–505, and recovery for breach is governed by s.506. The intentions which have to be stated in consequence of this section are *not* identical to the *conditions* in ss.500–501, below. If, therefore, non-compliance with the intentions set out in this section does not also amount to breach of condition as set out in ss.500–501, there will be no breach on the basis of which to exercise the power of recovery in s.506.

In such a case, there would seem to be only two remedies open to the authority, and only occasionally available: (a) in a particularly blatant case, to invite investigation and possible prosecution by the police, and/or (b) to take civil action for recovery not under s.506, but for the tort of deceit. Action for deceit can be founded on a statement of intentions: "The state of a man's mind is as much a fact as the state of his digestion. It is true that it is very difficult to prove what the state of a man's mind at a particular time is, but if it can be ascertained it is as much a fact as anything else": *Edginton* v. *Fitzmorris* (1885) 29 Ch. D. 459.

This section is inapplicable in a case within s.513, below, *i.e.* glebe lands, etc.

Subs. (2)
The authority may refuse to entertain a tenant's application unless it is accompanied by a certificate of availability for letting (as to the meaning of which, see notes to subs. (5), below) from a person whose owner's application could have been approved: see the notes to s.463, above.

Subs. (3)
If the application is an owner's application (as to which, see notes to s.463, above), it must be accompanied by *either* a certificate of owner-occupation *or* a certificate of availability for letting (as to which, see subs. (5)).

A certificate of owner-occupation is normally (*cf.* subs. (4)) one stating that the applicant intends that the dwelling will, for a stated period, be the only or main residence of *and* in the *exclusive* occupation of, *either* the applicant and members of his own household, *or* a member of his family as defined in s.520, below, extended for this purpose to include the applicant's grandparents or grandchildren and those of his spouse, together of course with members of their households: subs. (3). Parents and children of spouses are already covered by the definition in s.520(2), which defines relationships by marriage as by blood, and stepchildren as actual.

Household is not defined. One distinction may be between tenants and lodgers: see notes to s.93, above. If a lodger eats with the family, then there is no reason why he should not be regarded as a member of the household. However, if the lodger is not provided with board, he is likely to have a restricted contract under Rent Act 1977, s.19 and as the classification of occupancy as restricted contract is recognised in s.504, below, this would suggest that something *other* than a restricted contract is in mind when a different term such as "household" is used.

The period of occupation is "not exactly" five years. It extends to a point in time five years from the date when the authority certify the property as fit for reoccupation following works: see s.499, below. However, the applicant need only intend that occupation should commence *during* the year following this "certified date", and continue until five years from the certified date, so that the "occupation intention" could in theory be for as little as the last four years and one day of the five year period.

The two principal distinctions between intention and condition (see General Note, above), are: (a) that the occupation condition can be fulfilled by a person deriving title to the property through or under the applicant—*i.e.* the applicant can sell, assign or lease; and (b) that the occupation condition is fulfilled if the intended occupation continues for only one year, but thereafter is let, in whole or part—see s.500, below. The latter is of the greater importance, for many authorities seek to confine grant-aid, where they have a discretion, to those who want the property for their own occupation, *i.e.* so as to exclude landlords (prospective or actual), yet may find that, notwithstanding the certified intention, their policy has been achieved for only the first year following fitness for reoccupation.

Subs. (4)

Application for grant-aid may be made by personal representatives or trustees. In such a case, the certificate of owner-occupation must so say, and is otherwise adapted to reflect occupation by "a" beneficiary and members of his household, or a member of the family of the beneficiary as extended (see notes to subs. (3), above) and members of his household. It follows that where the property is held under the estate or trust for more than one beneficiary, intended occupation by one beneficiary will be sufficient.

Subs. (5)

A certificate of availability for letting is the owner's alternative to a certificate of owner-occupation, or may be sought in connection with a tenant's application (under subs. (2), above). The certificate must state the intention that the dwelling will be let or available for letting or occupation *throughout* the five years beginning on the "certified date", *i.e.* the date when the property is certified by the authority as fit for reoccupation following works (s.499, below)—*cf.* the "almost" five years applicable in the case of a certificate of owner-occupation, see notes to subs. (3), above.

The dwelling must be let or available for letting as a residence, and other than for the purposes of a holiday, to someone other than a member of the family of the person giving the certificate. Member of the family does not include spouse's children or parents: s.520 and see notes to subs. (3), above.

The person giving the certificate could be a personal representative or trustee, in which case if the beneficiary is not a member of his family, and consents (if the trust so requires) to the letting to himself, it would seem that the certificate of availability for letting could be fulfilled by occupation by someone otherwise intended to be dealt with under a certificate of owner-occupation. This may not be without benefit, where a grant has been given to a landlord, perhaps in a Housing Action Area or General Improvement Area, under a deliberate policy which will, of course, only be achieved by tenanted occupation.

There is no specification as to the type of letting. Local authorities are, however, entitled—and in housing action areas and general improvement areas obliged—to add *conditions* as to grants which deal with the terms of tenancies, and their qualification under protective legislation: see ss.503, 504, below.

The key practical problem is whether letting *the* dwelling as *a* residence to *a* person can include the letting of *parts* to different occupiers. The normal rule is that the singular includes the plural, unless the context otherwise requires: Interpretation Act 1978, s.6. It is submitted that this presumption does not apply. If a property is, or is to be, a house in multiple occupation, it is intended to be dealt with by way of special grant, and conversely the provisions with which this section is concerned (*i.e.* improvement, intermediate and repairs grants) are aimed at individual units (*cf.* note on *R.* v. *Kerrier District Council, ex parte Guppys (Bridport) Ltd.* (*No.* 2) [1985] 17 H.L.R. 426, C.A. in notes to s.460, above).

Thus, the standard amenity requirements of s.468 (improvement grants) and s.474 (intermediate grants) are concerned with individual dwellings (defined so as to be let as a separate dwelling—see notes to s.460, above). It would be wholly contrary to the intention of the legislation if an improvement or intermediate grant could be awarded, occupation subdivided, and the authority then find themselves in a position of taking enforcement action under Part XI, with the consequence that a mandatory grant under s.486 has to be made available to bring the available amenities up to the number required because of multiple occupation.

Restriction on grants for works already begun

465.—(1) A local housing authority may not approve an application for a grant if the relevant works have been begun unless they are satisfied that there were good reasons for beginning the works before the application was approved.

(2) Subsection (1) has effect subject to sections 486 and 494 (works required by statutory notice).

DEFINITIONS
"dwelling": s.525.
"grant": s.460.
"local housing authority": ss.1, 2.
"relevant works": s.461.

GENERAL NOTE
"Prior works" will prevent approval, unless the authority are satisfied that there were good reasons for commencing works before approval, *e.g.* urgency. The model application forms at App. C of D.O.E. Circular 21/80 contain prominent warnings to this effect. But the requirement is not applicable in the case of mandatory special (s.486) and repairs (s.494) grants: subs. (2).

Grants requiring consent of Secretary of State

466.—(1) The Secretary of State may direct that applications for an improvement grant or intermediate grant of a specified description shall not be approved without his consent.

(2) Such directions may be given to local housing authorities generally or to a particular local housing authority.

(3) The Secretary of State's consent may be given generally or with respect to a particular authority or particular description of application.

DEFINITIONS
"improvement grant": s.467.
"intermediate grant": s.474.
"local housing authority": ss.1, 2.

GENERAL NOTE
By para. 4 of App. A to D.O.E. Circular 21/80, retained in force by s.2, Housing (Consequential Provisions) Act 1985, improvement grants of the following description may not be approved without the consent of the Secretary of State:

(1) The grant is for the provision of a dwelling or dwellings by conversion (*i.e.* under s.467(1)(*a*)) of a house or houses which is accompanied by a certificate of owner-occupation (under s.464, above) (and even if where more than one house is involved, the certificate relates to only one of them); and

(2) On the date of application the rateable value of the house or where the conversion is of more than one house of all the houses involved, exceeds £400 in Greater London or £225 elsewhere; and

(3) The number of dwellings (as defined in s.525, see notes to s.460, above) to be provided is *less* than the number of dwellings in the house or houses involved as at the date of the application.

Notwithstanding this general bar, the Secretary of State will be "favourably disposed towards any request for consent" to consider such applications in Housing Action Areas (under Part VIII, above): D.O.E. Circular 5/81, para. 35.

Improvement grants

Works for which improvement grants may be given

467.—(1) The works for which an improvement grant may be given are—

    (*a*) works required for the provision of a dwelling by the conversion of a house or other building, or

    (*b*) works required for the improvement of a dwelling,

other than works falling entirely within section 474 (works for which intermediate grant may be given).

(2) The references in subsection (1) to works required for the provision or improvement of a dwelling include any works of repair or replacement needed, in the opinion of the local housing authority, for the purpose of enabling the dwelling concerned to attain the required standard referred to in section 468.

DEFINITIONS

    "dwelling": s.525.
    "house in multiple occupation": s.525.
    "improvement": s.525.
    "intermediate grant": s.474.
    "local housing authority": ss.1, 2.
    "relevant works": s.461.

GENERAL NOTE

This section defines the works for which the *improvement* grant is available. In general terms, an improvement grant is available for works of conversion to produce dwellings, or for works of improvement to an existing dwelling which go beyond those works covered by an intermediate grant: subs. (1). In either case, the works include those works of repair or replacement, *i.e.* not in themselves works of improvement, which the authority consider are needed to ensure that the dwelling or dwellings concerned will reach the required standard: subs. (2). However, an improvement grant will only allow up to 50 per cent. of the total estimated expense in respect of such works of repair or replacement: see s.471(2), below.

The required standard is that the dwelling or each of the dwellings to be provided:

(a) is provided with all the standard amenities (see s.508, below,) for the exclusive use of its occupants—s.468(2)(*a*), below;

(b) is in reasonable repair (defined in s.519, below, to mean disregarding internal decorative repair, but having regard to its age, character and locality)—s.468(2)(*b*), below;

(c) conforms with such additional requirements concerning construction, physical conditions, services and amenities as the Secretary of State for the Environment may have specified—s.468(2)(*c*); and

(d) is likely to provide satisfactory housing accommodation for a period of 30 years—s.468(2)(*d*).

The authority may, however, reduce any of these requirements *other* than the 30 year requirement, if they are satisfied that it is not practicable at a reasonable expense to satisfy them all, to the extent that will enable them to approve the application, *i.e.* to the extent that the works can be brought within a reasonable expense—s.468(3). They may also dispense with any of these three requirements (*i.e.* other than the 30 year requirement), to the extent they think fit, if satisfied the works could not be financed without undue financial hardship to the applicant—s.468(4). They may additionally reduce the 30 year rule to a minimum of 10 years, if they think it reasonable to do so in a particular case—s.468(5).

Improvement grants are discretionary (s.470, below) but are not available in respect of properties above specified rateable values, although subject to specified exceptions: see s.469, below. The amount of an improvement grant is governed by ss.471–473, below.

Required standard to be attained

468.—(1) A local housing authority shall not approve an application for an improvement grant unless they are satisfied that, on completion of the relevant works, the dwelling or, as the case may be, each of the dwellings to which the application relates will attain the required standard.

(2) A dwelling attains the required standard if—

(*a*) it is provided with all the standard amenities for the exclusive use of its occupants,

(*b*) it is in reasonable repair,

(*c*) it conforms with such requirements with respect to construction and physical conditions and the provision of services and amenities as may for the time being be specified by the Secretary of State for the purposes of this section, and

(*d*) it is likely to provide satisfactory housing accommodation for a period of 30 years.

(3) If it appears to the authority that it is not practicable at reasonable expense for a dwelling—

(*a*) to be provided with all the standard amenities, or

(*b*) to be put into a state of reasonable repair, or

(*c*) to conform in every respect with the requirements referred to in subsection (2)(*c*),

the authority may, for that dwelling, reduce the required standard by dispensing with the condition in question to such extent as will enable them, if they think fit, to approve the application.

(4) The authority may also, to the extent that they think fit, dispense with any of the conditions specified in subsection (2)(*a*) to (*c*) if they are satisfied that the applicant could not, without undue hardship, finance the cost of the works without the assistance of a grant.

(5) The authority may, if it appears to them reasonable to do so in any case, reduce the required standard by substituting for the period specified in subsection (2)(*d*) such shorter period of not less than 10 years as appears to them to be appropriate in the circumstances.

DEFINITIONS

"dwelling": s.525.

"improvement grant": s.467.

"local housing authority": ss.1, 2.

"reasonable repair": s.519.

"relevant works": s.461.

"standard amenities": s.508.

GENERAL NOTE

This section sets the standard which is to be attained under an improvement grant: unless satisfied that the standard will be attained on completion of the relevant works, the grant is not to be approved.

The required standard is (subs. (2)) that the dwelling or each of the dwellings to be provided:

(a) is provided with all the standard amenities (see s.508, below,) for the exclusive use of its occupants;

(b) is in reasonable repair (defined in s.519, below, to mean disregarding internal decorative repair, but having regard to its age, character and locality);

(c) conforms with such additional requirements concerning construction, physical conditions, services and amenities as the Secretary of State for the Environment may have specified; and

(d) is likely to provide satisfactory housing accommodation for a period of 30 years.

The authority may, however, reduce any of these requirements *other* than the 30 year requirement, if they are satisfied that it is not practicable at a reasonable expense to satisfy them all, to the extent that will enable them to approve the application, *i.e.* to the extent that the works can be brought within a reasonable expense: subs. (3).

They may also dispense with any of these three requirements (*i.e.* other than the 30 year requirement), to the extent they think fit, if satisfied the works could not be financed without undue financial hardship to the applicant: subs. (4). They may additionally reduce the 30 year rule to a minimum of 10 years, if they think it reasonable to do so in a particular case: subs. (5).

The Secretary of State has specified requirements under subs. (2)(c) in D.O.E. Circular 21/80, App. A, para. 5 (retained in force by s.2, Housing (Consequential Provisions) Act 1985). The dwelling must:

(1) be substantially free from damp;
(2) have adequate natural lighting and ventilation in each habitable room;
(3) have adequate and safe provision throughout for artificial lighting, and have sufficient electric socket outlets for the safe and proper functioning of domestic appliances;
(4) be provided with adequate drainage facilities;
(5) be in a stable structural condition;
(6) have satisfactory internal arrangement;
(7) have satisfactory facilities for preparing and cooking food;
(8) be provided with adequate facilities for heating;
(9) have proper provision for the storage of fuel (where necessary) and for the storage of refuse;
(10) fulfil defined requirements for thermal insulation in a roof space (as defined). The requirements for thermal insulation were altered by D.O.E. Circular 11/82, App. E.

"Reasonable expense" is not defined in this Part, and it does not therefore call for the application of the formula to be found at s.206, above, although it would seem that the principles discussed in the cases and noted thereto will be of relevance, *i.e.* pre- and post-works values.

"Undue hardship" is not defined either, but those in financial hardship may be able to benefit from higher levels of grant-aid than others: see notes to s.473, below.

Rateable value limit for owner-occupied dwellings

469.—(1) This section applies where an application for an improvement grant in respect of works required for—
(*a*) the improvement of a dwelling or dwellings, or
(*b*) the provision of a dwelling or dwellings by the conversion of premises which consist of a house or two or more houses,
is accompanied by a certificate of owner-occupation relating to that dwelling or, as the case may be, one of those dwellings.

(2) In a case within subsection (1)(*a*) the local housing authority shall not approve the application if, on the date of the application, the rateable value of the dwelling to which the certificate relates is in excess of the limit specified under this section.

(3) In a case within subsection (1)(*b*) the local housing authority shall not approve the application if, on the date of the application—
(*a*) the rateable value of the house or, as the case may be, any of the houses referred to in that paragraph, or
(*b*) where the certificate relates to a dwelling to be provided by the conversion of premises consisting of or including two or more houses, the aggregate of the rateable values of those houses,
is in excess of the limit specified under this section.

(4) The Secretary of State may by order made with the consent of the Treasury specify the rateable value limits for the purposes of this section.

(5) An order—
(*a*) may make different provision with respect to different cases or descriptions of case, including different provision for different areas, and
(*b*) shall be made by statutory instrument which shall be subject to annulment in pursuance of a resolution of either House of Parliament.

(6) For the purposes of this section the rateable value on any day of a dwelling or house is—
(*a*) if the dwelling or house is a hereditament for which a rateable value is then shown in the valuation list, that rateable value;
(*b*) if the dwelling or house forms part only of such a hereditament, or consists of or forms part of more than one such hereditament, such value as the local housing authority, after consultation with the applicant as to an appropriate apportionment or aggregation, shall determine.

(7) This section does not apply—

(*a*) to dwellings in housing action areas, or
(*b*) where the application for an improvement grant is made in respect of a dwelling for a disabled occupant and it appears to the local housing authority that the works are needed to meet a requirement arising from the particular disability from which the disabled occupant suffers.

DEFINITIONS
"certificate of owner-occupation": s.464.
"dwelling": s.525.
"improvement": s.525.
"improvement grant": s.467.
"local housing authority": ss.1, 2.

GENERAL NOTE
This section sets rateable value limits so that "high value" properties will not qualify for an improvement grant. The provisions do not apply at all in a Housing Action Area (see Part VIII, above), or where the application is in respect of a dwelling for a disabled occupant and it appears to the authority that the works are needed to meet a requirement arising from the disability from which the occupant suffers: see also s.518, below. The section is only applicable where the application is accompanied by a certificate of owner-occupation (see notes to s.464, above): subs. (1).
The rateable values (as defined in subs. (6)) are applied as at the date of application (*cf.* notes to s.461, above), and are applied either to individual house improvements, or to the provision of dwellings by conversion, in which case the rateable value applies to the house to be converted or, if there is more than one, their aggregate rateable values: subs. (3).
The rateable value limits have remained unchanged for some years. They are, by S.I. 1977 No. 1213, retained in force by s.2, Housing (Consequential Provisions) Act 1985, in the case of an individual house improvement, £400 in Greater London and £225 elsewhere, and in the case of conversions £600 in Greater London and £350 elsewhere.

Improvement grants are discretionary

470.—(1) A local housing authority may approve an application for an improvement grant in such circumstances as they think fit.
(2) Subsection (1) has effect subject to the following provisions (which restrict the cases in which applications may be approved)—
section 463(2) (person who proposes to acquire but has not yet acquired an owner's interest),
section 465 (works already begun),
section 466 (cases in which consent of Secretary of State is required),
section 468 (standard of repair to be attained), and
section 469 (rateable value limit for owner-occupied dwellings).

DEFINITIONS
"improvement grant": s.467.
"local housing authority": ss.1, 2.

GENERAL NOTE
Provided the authority are not prevented from approving the application for an improvement grant by one of the specified provisions, approval or refusal is entirely in their discretion. As anyone can make an application, it would seem that the authority are bound to consider each application, on its merits, but are perfectly entitled to formulate and adopt policies which will normally be applied: see, *e.g. British Oxygen Co. Ltd.* v. *Board of Trade* [1971] A.C. 610, H.L., *Re Betts* [1983] 2 A.C. 613, 10 H.L.R. 97, H.L.
The proper procedure will be for the authority to formulate their policies, which will usually be by a committee of the authority under Local Government Act 1972, s.101 and delegate to officers the power to refuse those outwith their policies, as well as, of course, if they wish, to approve those within. This will be sufficient to constitute consideration of an individual's application, but if the authority or a committee reserve to themselves the function of refusal, officers will—if an applicant cannot be persuaded to withdraw the application—be obliged to put even applications outwith the policies to the committee. (This

would arguably even be so if the legislation prohibits approval, if the officers do not enjoy appropriate powers, although as relief will be discretionary the point is entirely academic.)

In addition to their own policies, and the law, as improvement grant spending is prescribed expenditure under s.71 and Sched. 12, para. 1, Local Government, Planning and Land Act 1980, the authority will have to have regard to the provisions of that Act, both as to the restraints on capital spending under Part VIII, and as to the continuing consequences on the rate fund under Part VI: see notes to s.421, above, and to s.516, below.

The provisions governing the amount of the grant are contained in ss.471–473, below.

Improvement grants: estimated expense of works

471.—(1) Where a local housing authority approve an application for an improvement grant, they shall determine the amount of the expenses which in their opinion are proper to be incurred for the execution of the relevant works, and shall notify the applicant of that amount.

(2) Not more than 50 per cent., or such other percentage as may be prescribed, of the estimated expense of any works shall be allowed for works of repair and replacement.

(3) If, after an application for a grant has been approved, the authority are satisfied that owing to circumstances beyond the control of the applicant the relevant works will not be carried out on the basis of the estimate contained in the application, they may, on receiving a further estimate, redetermine the estimated expense in relation to the grant.

(4) If the applicant satisfies the authority that—

(*a*) the relevant works cannot be, or could not have been, carried out without carrying out additional works, and

(*b*) this could not have been reasonably foreseen at the time the application was made,

the authority may determine a higher amount as the amount of the estimated expense.

(5) In this section "prescribed" means prescribed by order of the Secretary of State.

(6) An order—

(*a*) may make different provision for different cases or descriptions of case, including different provision for different areas, and

(*b*) shall be made by statutory instrument which shall be subject to annulment in pursuance of a resolution of either House of Parliament.

DEFINITIONS
"improvement grant": s.467.
"local housing authority": ss.1, 2.
"relevant works": s.461.

GENERAL NOTE
The first stage in the calculation of an improvement grant is to establish the expense of the works. Not the whole of this expense will be eligible for grant-aid: s.472, below, governs the limits to be taken into account. Even then, only a proportion of this eligible expense will be provided by way of grant: see s.473, below. Where works have to be financed privately, *i.e.* because those required to achieve the relevant standard are in excess of those which are eligible, or to meet the part of the eligible expense not covered by the grant, a loan may be available from the authority under s.435, above.

The expenses to be taken into account are those which the authority consider "proper to be incurred", which clearly permits the authority to exclude estimates which in their experience are exorbitant: see also notes to s.461, above. Insofar as works consist of "associated" works of repair or replacement under s.467(2), above, as distinct from works for the provision of dwellings or of improvement, they are only admissible to a total of 50 per cent. of the estimated expense, or such other amount as may be prescribed. Under S.I. 1982 No. 1205 (retained in force by s.2, Housing (Consequential Provisions) Act 1985), 70 per cent. has been prescribed "where the dwelling is, or is to be provided by the conversion of a dwelling which is, in need of works of repair of a substantial and structural character".

D.O.E. Circular 21/80 suggests that "as a broad guide, where a house is being improved to the '30 year life' standard, it would be reasonable to allow for grant all repairs that would be likely to arise within a few years of the improvement if not carried out as part of the major scheme. These could include re-roofing, replacement of ineffective damp-proof courses, suspect electrical wiring and defective rainwater pipes and guttering. In all cases, the cost of repairs and redecorations to make good damage occurring as a result of carrying out improvements would normally attract grant as being incidental to those improvements, but any other internal decorative repair ought . . . generally to be excluded" (para. 53).

Repair or Improvement?

The distinction between repair and improvement accordingly has some importance in this context. That which is alteration and enlargement is of definition improvement: s.525, below. Otherwise, it would seem that the distinction is to be regarded as a question of fact and degree, having regard in particular to the cost of a particular job, relative to the value of the property: *Ravenseft Properties Ltd.* v. *Davstone Holdings Ltd.* [1980] Q.B. 12; see also *Smedley* v. *Chumley & Hawkes Ltd.* (1981) 261 E.G. 775, C.A., *Halliard Property Co. Ltd.* v. *Nicholas Clarke Investments Ltd.* (1983) 269 E.G. 1257, Q.B., and *Elmcroft Developments Ltd.* v. *Tankersley-Sawyer* (1984) 15 H.L.R. 63, C.A.

These recent cases have made a considerable impact in this area of the law. Until *Ravenseft*, it was thought that repair must always be distinguished from improvement, using the latter term to mean the provision of something different in quality, or in kind, from that which was demised under a lease or tenancy, and this was sometimes accompanied by, and sometimes assimilated into, another proposition, that to cure an inherent (*e.g.* design, construction) meant improvement rather than repair. Thus, classically, while damp might have to be treated as a repair, if premises lack a damp-proof course only a right to require improvement could be used to secure its installation, even where installation is the most modern, convenient, efficient or even economic means of treating the damp: *Pembery* v. *Lamdin* [1940] 2 All E.R. 434, C.A.

Similarly, it had been thought that if underpinning was needed to save an old house from falling down, and was the only means of preventing destruction of the house, such works would be works of improvement, and as such not qualifying as repair: *Sotheby* v. *Grundy* [1947] 2 All E.R. 761, *Collins* v. *Flynn* [1963] 2 All E.R. 1068, *Lurcott* v. *Wakeley* [1911] 1 K.B. 905, *Brew Brothers* v. *Snax (Ross) Ltd.* [1970] 1 Q.B. 612.

All of these older cases were reviewed in *Ravenseft Properties Ltd.* v. *Davstone Holdings Ltd.* [1980] Q.B. 12. Tenants were under an obligation to repair a block of flats, clad in stone, mounted on a concrete frame. As built, the construction lacked expansion joints, to retain the stone cladding once the frame expanded. In consequence, when expansion started, the stone cladding threatened to tumble from the frame. The fault was clearly a design fault.

As a professional proposition, no competent engineer would permit rectification of the fault without the introduction of expansion joints, even though to do so meant to introduce a modern method of construction. The court held that such works *could* be required by the repairing covenant. The court rejected the concept of "inherent defect" constituting improvement, or that works of construction could not fall within a repairing covenant. Each one of the earlier cases could be construed as a decision as to fact and degree. Of particular relevance is the question of cost of works, relative to value of property. Even if the works were down, it could not be said that the landlord's reversion was now in something different from that which had been demised.

It would now seem to be open, to refer back to the earlier cases, to consider the modern costs of a damp-proof course, or underpinning, and current value of premises. This line of argument derives much support from the second of the recent cases, *Smedley* v. *Chumley & Hawkes Ltd.* (1981) 261 E.G. 775, C.A. This case concerned a restaurant constructed at a river's edge. The restaurant was built on a raft, or pier. The pier lacked adequate underpinning. The restaurant was beginning to sink. The question was whether works could be required within the landlord's repairing obligation, and the Court of Appeal held that they could be.

A distinction was here drawn between old houses, and new properties, and the approach adopted was that of construction of covenant in the lease, which will not be relevant under this Part (but can be substituted with the question of construction of section, *i.e.* intention). In *Elmcroft Developments Ltd.* v. *Tankersley-Sawyer* (1984) 15 H.L.R. 63, C.A., a county court finding that rising damp attributable to an ineffectual damp-proof course constituted a breach of a covenant to repair was upheld, even though the remedy found by the court to be necessary was replacement of the course by a different and modern method of protection.

The Court of Appeal followed *Ravenseft* in approaching the issue as one of fact and degree. Referring to *Pembery* v. *Lamdin* [1940] 2 All E.R. 434, the Court of Appeal considered it to be "of no assistance at all. It does not involve the letting of a flat. It involved a letting of premises that contained this cellar in a building which was built some 100 years before the court considered the problems. That must be round about 1840. We are concerned with a letting a few years ago of what was built as a separate self-contained flat and a flat in a high-class fashionable residential area in the centre of London. I entirely agree with what Forbes J. said in the *Ravenseft* case—'that this was a decision arrived at by considering the question as one of degree . . . ' "

Ravenseft was also followed in *Halliard Property Co. Ltd.* v. *Nicholas Clarke Investments Ltd.* (1983) 269 E.G. 1257, Q.B.D. It was held, as a question of fact and degree, that a repairing obligation did not extend to a requirement to rebuild a back-addition warehouse or storehouse, at a cost representing more than a third of the cost of rebuilding the whole premises, although still a cost less than that for which the premises could be sold. The rebuilding of what was described as an "unstable jerry-built structure" would involve handing back on the expiry of the lease an entirely different edifice.

In another recent decision, however, *Pembery* was still being applied: *Wainwright* v. *Leeds City Council* (1984) 13 H.L.R. 117, C.A. That case concerned a back-to-back terraced house in a poor part of Leeds, built in the early part of the century. It suffered from damp, some of which was attributable to the absence of a damp-proof course. The Court of Appeal decided that a house with a damp-proof course was a different "thing" from a house without, following *Pembery* as binding *as to* facts (as distinct from as to degree), and that accordingly the introduction of a damp-proof course did not fall within the principal modern repairing obligation, now to be found in s.11, Landlord and Tenant Act 1985 (see notes to s.104, above, and to Sched. 6, para. 14, below).

Neither *Ravenseft*, nor *Smedley*, nor *Halliard* was cited in *Wainwright*; nor, most relevantly, was *Elmcroft*, not only similar on its facts, but also a *prior* decision of the Court of Appeal (unlike *Ravenseft*, in the High Court)—*Elmcroft* was not, however, reported until shortly after judgment in *Wainwright*. *Wainwright* appears to have proceeded on an argument—which was unsurprisingly rejected—that in the construction of the s.11 covenant, local authority landlords should be held to apply a higher standard than others. It was, accordingly, distinguished in *Quick* v. *Taff Ely District Council* [1985] 3 All E.R. 34; 18 H.L.R., C.A., in which the *Ravenseft* line of cases was approved.

Subs. (3)

This meets the case where the applicant has to obtain a new estimate, *e.g.* if the builder who has provided the estimate withdraws (*cf.* notes to s.461, above). This can and does commonly occur if the authority take a very long time to approve an application. Periods in excess of a year are not unknown in authorities which have not been able to develop appropriate systems. If a new estimate is used—which suggests a new builder, whether the amount is higher *or lower*—the authority must recalculate the estimated expense. Note the powers of the authority to carry out works under an "agency" agreement: s.514, below.

Subs. (4)

Normally, the expense is estimated as at the date the grant is approved. However, an applicant can apply for an increase on the grounds of "unforeseeable additional works", in which case the authority can increase the estimated expense, with consequential increase of the amount of grant under s.473(3).

Improvement grants: limit on expense eligible for grant

472.—(1) Except in a case or description of case in which the Secretary of State approves a higher eligible expense, the eligible expense for the purposes of an improvement grant is so much of the estimated expense as does not exceed the limit determined under this section.

(2) The limit is the amount for the dwelling or, if the application relates to more than one dwelling, the total of the amounts for each of the dwellings applicable under the following paragraphs—

(a) for a dwelling which is provided by the conversion of a house or other building consisting of three or more storeys (counting the basement as a storey if all or part of the dwelling is in the basement), £2,400 or such other sum as may be prescribed, and

(b) for a dwelling which is improved by the relevant works or is provided by them otherwise than as mentioned in paragraph (a), £2,000 or such other sum as may be prescribed.

(3) In subsection (2) "prescribed" means prescribed by order of the Secretary of State.

(4) An order—

(*a*) may make different provision for different cases or descriptions of case, including different provision for different areas, and

(*b*) shall be made by statutory instrument which shall be subject to annulment in pursuance of a resolution of the House of Commons.

(5) If the local housing authority are satisfied in a particular case that there are good reasons for increasing the amount of the limit, they may substitute such higher amount as the Secretary of State may approve; and his approval may be given either with respect to a particular case or with respect to a description of case.

DEFINITIONS

"dwelling": s.525.
"estimated expense": s.471.
"improvement grant": s.467.
"local housing authority": ss.1, 2.

GENERAL NOTE

Not the whole of the estimated expense, or even the whole of what would be the estimated expense but for the limitation to 50–70 per cent. in respect of works of repair or replacement under s.471(2), above, is admitted for the purpose of grant calculation: the expense so admitted must not exceed the eligible expense as defined in this section. Even so, it will not be the whole of the eligible expense which will be met by grant-aid: see s.473, below. Where the balance has to be financed privately, a loan may be available from the authority under s.435, above.

The eligible expense is that set out in subs. (2), unless varied by the Secretary of State, or unless the authority seek special consent to allow a higher eligible expense under subs. (5). The "basic" figures are £2,400 per dwelling provided by conversion of a house or other building consisting of three or more storeys, or £2,000 per dwelling provided by conversion of a building or house with less than three storeys, or improvement of a single dwelling.

The Secretary of State has increased these figures by S.I. 1983 No. 613 (retained in force by Housing (Consequential Provisions) Act 1985, s.2). The increase operates by reference to two categories of dwelling:

Category A: on the date the application is approved—

(a) the dwelling is in a Housing Action Area (under Part VIII, above);

(b) it is or forms part of a house in relation to which the authority have served a notice under ss.189 or 264, above, and the works consist of or include works which if executed would contribute towards making the house fit for human habitation within the meaning of s.604, below;

(c) dwellings which lack, or are provided by conversion from dwellings which lack, one or more of the standard amenities (within s.508, below), and have so lacked each of the absent standard amenities for at least 12 months before application, and the works consist of or include the provision of the absent standard amenities;

(d) the dwelling is in need of works of repair of a substantial and structural character, and the works consist of or include such works (*cf.* notes to s.471(2), above); or

(e) the dwelling is for a disabled occupant, and the works consist of or include works needed to meet a requirement arising from his particular disability.

Category B is all other dwellings.

The amounts available are:

(1) For works of provision of dwellings by conversion of three-storey plus buildings or houses, which are not listed buildings under Town and Country Planning Act 1971, s.54—

Category A, Greater London, £16,000, elsewhere, £11,800
Category B, Greater London, £10,400, elsewhere, £7,700;

(2) For works of provision of dwellings by conversion of three-storey plus listed buildings or houses—

Category A, Grade I listing, Greater London, £17,700, elsewhere £13,500
Category A, Grade II starred listing, Greater London, £17,000, elsewhere £12,800
Category A, Grade II unstarred listing, Greater London, £16,490, elsewhere £12,290
Category B, Grade I listing, Greater London, £12,180, elsewhere, £9,420
Category B, Grade II starred listing, Greater London, £11,480, elsewhere, £8,720
Category B, Grade II unstarred listing, Greater London, £10,970, elsewhere, £8,210;

(3) For works of improvement of an individual dwelling, or provision by conversion of a building or house of less than three storeys, which is not a listed building—
Category A, Greater London, £13,800, elsewhere, £10,200
Category B, Greater London, £9,000, elsewhere, £6,600;
(4) For works of improvement of an individual dwelling, or provision by conversion of a building or house of less than three storeys, which is a listed building—
Category A, Grade I listing, Greater London, £15,540, elsewhere, £11,940
Category A, Grade II starred listing, Greater London, £14,840, elsewhere, £11,240
Category A, Grade II unstarred listing, Greater London, £14,320, elsewhere, £10,720
Category B, Grade I listing, Greater London, £10,740, elsewhere, £8,340
Category B, Grade II starred listing, Greater London, £10,040, elsewhere, £7,640
Category B, Grade II unstarred listing, Greater London, £9,520, elsewhere, £7,120.

Improvement grants: determination of amount

473.—(1) The amount of an improvement grant shall be fixed by the local housing authority when they approve the application, and shall not exceed the appropriate percentage of the eligible expense.

(2) The authority shall notify the applicant of the amount of the grant together with the notification under section 471(1) (notification of estimated expense of relevant works).

(3) Where the authority redetermine the amount of the estimated expense under section 471(3) (new estimate where works cannot be carried out in accordance with original estimate), they shall make such other adjustments relating to the amount of the grant as appear to them to be appropriate; but the amount of the grant shall not be increased beyond the amount which could have been notified when the application was approved if the estimate contained in the application had been of the same amount as the further estimate.

(4) Where the authority redetermine the amount of the estimated expense under section 471(4) (re-determination where additional works prove necessary), the eligible expense under section 472 shall be re-calculated and if on the re-calculation the amount of the eligible expense is greater than it was at the time when the application was approved, the amount of the grant shall be increased and the applicant notified accordingly.

DEFINITIONS
    "appropriate percentage": s.509.
    "eligible expense": s.472.
    "improvement grant": s.467.
    "local housing authority": ss.1, 2.

GENERAL NOTE
    This is the last limb in the calculation. Note that the amount payable is not to exceed the amount stated, so that authorities have a discretion (*cf.* ss.482(1), 490(1)(*a*) and 498(1)(*a*)) to pay as little as they wish: see s.510, below, but note its requirement for a statement in writing of the reasons for paying less than the appropriate percentage of the eligible expense. The maximum is the "appropriate percentage" of the eligible expense as calculated under s.472, above. Appropriate percentage is defined in s.509, below, and is a percentage prescribed by the Secretary of State. Where the balance has to be financed privately, a loan may be available from the authority under s.435, above.
    In relation to improvement grants, the appropriate percentage is, by S.I. 1980 No. 1735, as amended by S.I. 1981 No. 1712, retained in force by Housing (Consequential Provisions) Act 1985, s.2 as follows:
    (1) 75 per cent. in the cases of an application which falls within Category A in the notes to s.472, above, as at the date of application;
    (2) 60 per cent. if not within the Category A group but in a General Improvement Area within Part VIII, above, on date of approval of application;
    (3) 50 per cent. in all other cases.
    However, a 75 per cent. grant can be increased to 90 per cent., and a 50 per cent. grant to 65 per cent., if it appears to the authority that the applicant would not be able to finance without undue hardship so much of the cost as is not to be met by the grant.

It has been suggested (D.O.E. Circular 21/80, App. B, para. 10) that favourable consideration should be given to those who qualify for supplementary benefit or family income supplement, even if neither has been claimed, and that many of those who qualify for rate rebate (now under the Social Security and Housing Benefits Act 1982) are unlikely to have adequate savings to meet their normal share of the costs, or sufficient income to bear without stress the loan charges that will arise if they resort to borrowing; very sympathetic consideration is urged for those whose principal source of income consists of a state retirement or disability pension.

The authority have to notify the applicant of the amount which is to be paid together with the notification of estimated expense under s.471, above. In the case of an addition or reduction because the applicant could not proceed on the original estimate (s.471(3), or an increase for unforeseeable works under s.471(4)), the grant is to be recalculated, but only to the maximum which would in any event have been payable, *i.e.* the appropriate percentage of the eligible expense.

As to payment of grant, see s.511, below. As to completion of works, see s.512, below.

Intermediate grants

Works for which intermediate grants may be given

474.—(1) The works for which an intermediate grant may be given are—

(*a*) works required for the improvement of a dwelling by the provision of a standard amenity where the dwelling lacks an amenity of that description (including works such as are referred to in section 475(3)(*b*) (works for provision of amenity affected by other relevant works)), or

(*b*) works required for the improvement of a dwelling by the provision of a standard amenity where, in the case of a dwelling for a disabled occupant, an existing amenity of the same description is not readily accessible to him by reason of his disability.

(2) The references in subsection (1) to works required for the improvement of a dwelling by the provision of a standard amenity include any works of repair or replacement which, in the opinion of the local housing authority, are needed for the purpose of putting the dwelling into a state of reasonable repair.

DEFINITIONS
"dwelling": s.525.
"improvement": s.525.
"intermediate grant": s.474.
"local housing authority": ss.1, 2.
"reasonable repair": s.519.
"relevant works": s.461.
"standard amenities": s.508.

GENERAL NOTE
The second of the "main" grants is the intermediate grant. At the core of the intermediate grant is the concept of the standard amenity. This is defined in s.508:
(1) A fixed bath or shower;
(2) A hot and cold water supply to the fixed bath or shower;
N.B. The fixed bath or shower should be in a bathroom; however, if it is (a) not reasonably practicable to provide it in a bathroom, but (b) is reasonably practicable for it to be supplied with a hot and cold water supply, it can be in any other part of the dwelling which is not a bedroom;
(3) A wash-hand basin;
(4) A hot and cold water supply at a wash-hand basin;
(5) A sink;
(6) A hot and cold water supply at a sink;
(7) A water closet, which, if reasonably practicable, is to be in and accessible from within the dwelling or, if the dwelling is part of a larger building, is to be readily accessible from the dwelling.

The works which qualify for an intermediate grant are works required for the improvement of the dwelling, by the provision of an absent standard amenity, including, where necessary, for the provision of an amenity which is present but which will be interfered with by other works (*cf.* s.475, below), and works for the provision of a standard amenity which is not lacking but which is not readily accessible to a disabled occupant (not necessarily the applicant) by reason of his disability: subs. (1); see also s.518, below. Note the limitation in s.475, below, on for how long standard amenities must have been lacking. Only one standard amenity of each kind is admissible per dwelling: s.480(2).

In addition, however, works of repair or replacement which the authority consider are needed to put the dwelling into a state of reasonable repair qualify for an intermediate grant: subs. (2). The express addition of this last is pursuant to Law Commission Recommendations (Cmnd. 9515), No. 24(i).

Notwithstanding the wording of subs. (2), it would not, however, seem that works of repair or replacement could be carried out under an intermediate grant unless there is *an* absent or inaccessible standard amenity, albeit possibly not works of repair or replacement connected with *the* particular amenity to be introduced, for works elsewhere in the property or otherwise unconnected may be needed in order to meet the standard in s.485, below.

As to "reasonable repair", see s.519, below, and notes to s.471, above. The related works of repair and replacement must, however, *only* be those needed to achieve a standard of reasonable repair. This is related to, but not synonymous with, the minimum requirement that the dwelling must, at the end of the works, be fit for human habitation within the meaning of s.604: see s.476, below. If the works of repair or replacement go beyond those needed to put the dwelling into reasonable repair, with the applicant's consent the authority can vary the application so as to eliminate such added works, or so as to limit them: see s.478, below.

Requirements as to standard amenities provided or to be provided

475.—(1) An application for an intermediate grant shall specify the standard amenity or amenities which it is intended to provide by the relevant works, and if some only of the standard amenities are to be so provided shall state whether the dwelling is already provided with the remainder.

(2) An application for a grant for such works as are mentioned in section 474(1)(*a*) (works for provision of standard amenity which is lacking) shall state with respect to each standard amenity to be provided whether to the best of the knowledge and belief of the applicant the dwelling has been without that amenity for a period of at least twelve months ending with the date on which the application is made.

(3) The local housing authority shall not approve such an application unless they are satisfied, with respect to each of the standard amenities to be provided—

(*a*) that the dwelling concerned has been without that amenity for a period of at least twelve months ending with the date on which the application is made, or

(*b*) that the dwelling is provided with that amenity on the date of the application but relevant works (other than those for the provision of the amenity) involve, and it would not be reasonably practicable to avoid, interference with or replacement of that amenity.

(4) An application for an intermediate grant for such works as are mentioned in section 474(1)(*b*) (works for provision of standard amenity in place of amenity not readily accessible to disabled occupant) shall state that the dwelling possesses the standard amenity in question but that it is not or will not be readily accessible to the disabled occupant by reason of his disability.

(5) The local housing authority shall not approve such an application unless they are satisfied that the existing amenity in question is not or will not be readily accessible to the disabled person by reason of his disability.

DEFINITIONS
"dwelling": s.525.
"house in multiple occupation": s.525.

"intermediate grant": s.474.
"local housing authority": ss.1, 2.
"reasonable repair": s.519.
"relevant works": s.461.
"standard amenities": s.508.

GENERAL NOTE

The application must specify the standard amenities (see notes to s.474, above) which are lacking and which it is intended to provide under the grant-aided works, and if only some of them are to be provided must confirm that the dwelling is already provided with the remainder: subs. (1). It is the *dwelling* which must be provided with the remainder, *i.e.* they will, save possibly in the case of a water closet (*cf.* s.508(1), Note 3), have to be in the dwelling, not in a building of which the dwelling may be part. See also *F.F.F. Estates Ltd.* v. *Hackney London Borough Council* [1981] Q.B. 503, 3 H.L.R. 107, C.A.

The application shall also state that to the best of the knowledge and belief of the applicant the amenity or amenities has or have been lacking for at least the previous twelve months: subs. (2). If they have not been, then unless it is an application for the benefit of a disabled occupant, the intermediate grant will not be approved (subs. (3)(*a*)) *save* for the exception in subs. (3)(*b*), *i.e.* because other works will disrupt an existing amenity. This provision does not apply if the application is pursuant to an improvement notice consisting solely of works under an improvement notice or undertaking within Part VII, above: see s.477, below.

If the purpose of the provision is to provide for a disabled occupant a standard amenity which exists but is inaccessible to him, this must be stated in the application and, again, the application is not to be approved unless the authority are satisfied that this is the case: subss. (4), (5). See further, s.518, below.

Subs. (3)(*b*)
This covers the case where works will disrupt an existing amenity.

Standard of fitness to be attained

476. A local housing authority shall not approve an application for an intermediate grant unless—
  (*a*) they are satisfied that on completion of the relevant works the dwelling or, as the case may be, each of the dwellings to which the application relates will be fit for human habitation, or
  (*b*) it seems reasonable in all the circumstances to approve the application even though the dwelling or dwellings will not reach that standard on completion of the relevant works.

DEFINITIONS
"dwelling": s.525.
"intermediate grant": s.474.
"local housing authority": ss.1, 2.
"reasonable repair": s.519.
"relevant works": s.461.

GENERAL NOTE

Although it is the provision of accessible standard amenities which the intermediate grant is intended to secure (see notes to s.474, above), and although the grant is available for related works of repair or replacement (see s.474(2)), the minimum standard which has to be attained is that of fitness for human habitation, within the meaning of s.604, below: subs. (1). Even so, the authority can approve the application without achieving fitness in the dwelling, if "it seems reasonable in all the circumstances": subs. (2). Furthermore, the standard need not be attained if the application is pursuant to an improvement notice or undertaking under Part VII, above: s.477, below.

These are "curious" provisions, since under s.189, above, the authority *must* serve a repairs notice requiring works to remedy unfitness unless satisfied that the dwelling cannot be rendered fit at a reasonable expense within the meaning of s.206, to which the availability of grant will be relevant (see *Harrington* v. *Croydon Corporation* [1968] 1 Q.B. 856, 3 H.L.R. 24, C.A.), in which event they *must* take action under s.264, leading to the closing of the property: *R.* v. *Kerrier District Council, ex parte Guppys (Bridport) Ltd. (No. 1)*

[1976] 32 P. & C.R. 411, C.A. Furthermore, authorities must act on the basis of any information in their possession that a property is unfit: see s.606(1), below.

The only analogous legislative sanction for illegality is to be found in s.84 and Sched. 2, Ground 9, which permits a court to make an order for possession against a secure tenant (within s.79, above) whose accommodation is overcrowded, on the basis of the availability of alternative accommodation, *which may itself be overcrowded* under the "space standard" in s.326, above: see Sched. 2, Part IV, para. 3. If Parliament recognises illegal inactivity in this way, are the courts bound to do so, or might it not just as easily be open to a court to refuse to adopt such a legal nonsense?

Works required by improvement notice or undertaking

477. The following provisions do not apply to an application for an intermediate grant, duly made in accordance with this Part, where the relevant works consist solely of works which the applicant is required to carry out by an improvement notice served or an undertaking accepted under Part VII (improvement notices)—

> section 463 (preliminary condition: interest of applicant in the property),
> section 464 (preliminary condition: certificate of future occupation),
> section 465 (application not to be approved if works already begun),
> section 466 (approval requiring consent of Secretary of State),
> section 475 (requirements as to standard amenities provided or to be provided),
> section 476 (standard of fitness to be attained by dwelling).

DEFINITIONS
"grant": s.460.
"improvement notice": s.209.
"intermediate grant": s.474.
"relevant works": s.461.
"undertaking": s.211.

GENERAL NOTE
The specified provisions do not apply to an application for an intermediate grant if the application is for works consisting *solely* of works within a compulsory improvement notice under s.209, above, or an improvement undertaking accepted under s.211, above.

Restriction on works of repair or replacement

478. Where the relevant works specified in an application for an intermediate grant include works of repair or replacement which go beyond those needed, in the opinion of the local housing authority, to put the dwelling into reasonable repair, the authority may with the consent of the applicant treat the application as varied so that the relevant works—

> (*a*) are confined to works other than works of repair or replacement, or
> (*b*) include only such works of repair and replacement as (taken with the rest of the relevant works) will, in the opinion of the authority, put the dwelling into reasonable repair,

and may approve the application as so varied.

DEFINITIONS
"dwelling": s.525.
"intermediate grant": s.474.
"local housing authority": ss.1, 2.
"reasonable repair": s.519.
"relevant works": s.461.

GENERAL NOTE
If the application includes works of repair or replacement (see s.474(2), above), and those works in the opinion of the authority go beyond those needed to put the dwelling into

reasonable repair (within the meaning of s.519, below, see also notes to s.471, above), the authority can, with the applicant's consent, vary the application so as to eliminate works of repair or replacement, or limit them to those needed to put the dwelling into reasonable repair.

As the intermediate grant is mandatory (see s.479, below), there is some obscurity about how this works if the applicant does *not* consent to the variation. The answer seems to lie in s.480(1)(*a*), under which the authority have to determine the amount of expenses which *in the opinion of the authority* are proper to be incurred, which in turn refers to s.474(2), being works of repair or replacement which *in the opinion of the authority* are *needed* to put the dwelling into a state of reasonable repair. Furthermore, only the works which will *in the opinion of the authority* put the dwelling into reasonable repair will be admitted as *eligible* expense under s.481(2), below. In other words, if the applicant persists, the authority simply deduct the contentious works from the estimated expense under s.480 and/or the eligible expense under s.481.

Intermediate grants are mandatory

479.—(1) A local housing authority shall approve an application for an intermediate grant which is duly made in accordance with the provisions of this Part.

(2) Subsection (1) has effect subject to the following provisions (which restrict the cases in which applications may be approved)—

> section 463(2) (person who proposes to acquire but has not yet acquired an owner's interest),
>
> section 465 (works already begun),
>
> section 466 (cases in which consent of Secretary of State is required),
>
> section 475(3) and (5) (requirements as to amenities provided), and
>
> section 476 (standard of fitness to be attained).

DEFINITIONS
"intermediate grant": s.474.
"local housing authority": ss.1, 2.

GENERAL NOTE
This section contains the straightforward proposition that intermediate grants are mandatory, subject to the specified provisions containing the various qualifying conditions described in the notes to previous sections.

Intermediate grant: estimated expense of works

480.—(1) Where a local housing authority approve an application for an intermediate grant, they shall determine separately the amount of the expenses which in their opinion are proper to be incurred—

(*a*) for the execution of those of the relevant works which relate solely to the provision of standard amenities, and

(*b*) for the execution of those of the relevant works which consist of works of repair and replacement;

and they shall notify the applicant of the amounts so determined by them.

(2) Where the relevant works make provision for more than one standard amenity of the same description, only one amenity of that description shall be taken into account.

(3) If, after an application for a grant has been approved, the authority are satisfied that owing to circumstances beyond the control of the applicant the relevant works will not be carried out on the basis of the estimate contained in the application, they may, on receiving a further estimate, redetermine the estimated expense in relation to the grant.

(4) If the applicant satisfies the authority that—

(*a*) the relevant works cannot be, or could not have been, carried out without carrying out additional works, and

(*b*) that this could not have been reasonably foreseen at the time the application was made, the authority may determine a higher amount under either or both of paragraphs (*a*) and (*b*) of subsection (1).

DEFINITIONS
    "intermediate grant": s.474.
    "local housing authority": ss.1, 2.
    "relevant works": s.461.
    "standard amenities": s.508.

GENERAL NOTE
    The determination of estimated expense is to be in two parts: (a) the standard amenity provisions, and (b) the added works of repair and replacement. Each has to be notified to the applicant. Only one standard amenity is admissible per dwelling. The amounts to be admitted for grant-aid are as specified in s.481, below; the amounts *payable* are as specified in s.482, below. Where a balance has to be financed privately, *i.e.* because the works required to achieve the relevant standard are in excess of those which are eligible, or to meet the part of the eligible expense not covered by the grant, a loan may be available from the authority under s.435, above.
    The section makes provision analogous to that to be found in s.471(3) and (4) for works which proceed on a different estimate to that on which the application was based, and unforeseeable works: see notes thereto, above. Note the powers of the authority to carry out works under an "agency" agreement: s.514, below.

Intermediate grants: limit on expense eligible for grant

481.—(1) Except in a case or description of case in which the Secretary of State approves a higher eligible expense, the eligible expense for the purpose of an intermediate grant is the aggregate of—
    (*a*) so much of the estimated expense determined under section 480(1)(*a*) (expense of provision of standard amenities) as does not exceed the total of the amounts specified in column 2 of the Table in section 508(1) (standard amenities and maximum eligible amounts) in relation to each of the standard amenities to be provided by the relevant works, and
    (*b*) so much of the estimated expense determined under section 480(1)(*b*) (expense of works of repair and replacement) as does not exceed the limit determined under the following provisions of this section.
    (2) The limit referred to in subsection (1)(*b*) in a case where either—
    (*a*) the dwelling will in the opinion of the local housing authority be put on completion of the relevant works into reasonable repair, or
    (*b*) it appears to the authority that the applicant could not without undue hardship finance the cost of the works necessary to put the dwelling into reasonable repair,
is £2,000 or such other amount as may be prescribed.
    (3) In any other case the limit referred to in subsection (1)(*b*) is £200, or such other amount as may be prescribed, multiplied by the number of standard amenities to be provided on completion of the relevant works, subject to a maximum of £800 (or such other amount as may be prescribed).
    (4) In this section "prescribed" means prescribed by order of the Secretary of State.
    (5) An order—
    (*a*) may make different provision for different cases or descriptions of case, including different provision for different areas, and.
    (*b*) shall be made by statutory instrument which shall be subject to annulment in pursuance of a resolution of the House of Commons.

DEFINITIONS
    "dwelling": s.525.
    "estimated expense": s.480.

"intermediate grant": s.474.
"local housing authority": ss.1, 2.
"reasonable repair": s.519.
"relevant works": s.461.
"standard amenities": s.508.

GENERAL NOTE

As with the improvement grant (see notes to s.472) it is not the whole of the estimated expense which is to be taken into account. Rather, the *eligible* expense is the basis on which grant is calculated and even then only a percentage of that eligible expense will be payable: see s.482, below. Where a balance has to be financed privately, a loan may be available from the authority under s.435, above.

The calculation of eligible expense depends on the break-down into two parts of the estimated expense, *i.e.* provision of standard amenities, and works of repair or replacement: see s.480(1). The amount to be allowed for standard amenities is *not more than* (*i.e.* could be less than if a lower estimate is obtained) the amount specified for each in Column 2 of the Table in s.508(1), below, as potentially varied from time to time by the Secretary of State: subs. (1)(*a*). Those amounts differentiate between Greater London and elsewhere, but no useful purpose is served by setting them out here: see s.508(1), Table, below.

The amounts for each are added together, and it follows that if an estimate is obtained under which *one* amenity to be provided is in excess of the amount in Column 2, while *another* is lower, the *total* in the estimate is compared to the *total* of the relevant parts of Column 2 and some of the "first" excess may be cancelled out by the "second" reduction.

In addition, the eligible expense will include a limited amount of the related or associated works of repair or replacement. That limit is, prima facie, £2,000, where the dwelling will be put into reasonable repair on completion of the works (*cf.* notes to s.478, above), *or* the applicant could not finance the works necessary to put the dwelling into reasonable repair without undue hardship. The £2,000 limit may be varied by the Secretary of State, and has been varied under S.I. 1983 No. 613, retained in force by Housing (Consequential Provisions) Act 1985, s.2 to the higher amounts of £4,200 in Greater London and £3,000 elsewhere.

If the conditions for these limits do not apply, the limit is, prima facie, £200 or such other amount that may be prescribed, multiplied by the number of standard amenities to be provided, to a maximum of £800 or other prescribed amount: subs. (3). By S.I. 1983 No. 613, these figures are increased to, respectively, £420 and £1,680 in Greater London, and £300 and £1,200 elsewhere (thus perpetuating the maximum multiplication by four).

As to financial hardship, see notes to s.473, above.

Intermediate grants: determination of amount

482.—(1) The amount of an intermediate grant shall be the appropriate percentage of the eligible expense.

(2) The authority shall notify the applicant of the amount of the grant together with the notification under section 480(1) (notification of estimated expense of relevant works).

(3) Where the authority redetermine the amount of the estimated expense under section 480(3) (new estimate where works cannot be carried out in accordance with original estimate), they shall make such other adjustments relating to the amount of the grant as appear to them to be appropriate; but the amount of the grant shall not be increased beyond the amount which could have been notified when the application was approved if the estimate contained in the application had been of the same amount as the further estimate.

(4) Where the authority redetermine the amount of the estimated expense under section 480(4) (redetermination where additional works prove necessary), the eligible expense shall be re-calculated under section 481 and if on the recalculation the amount of the eligible expense is greater than it was at the time that the application was approved, the amount of the grant shall be increased, and the applicant notified, accordingly.

DEFINITIONS

"appropriate percentage": s.509.
"eligible expense": s.481.

"estimated expense": s.480.
"intermediate grant": s.474.
"local housing authority": ss.1, 2.
"relevant works": s.461.

GENERAL NOTE

It is only the appropriate percentage of the eligible part of the estimated expense which is payable: subs. (1). It must be notified to the applicant together with the notification of estimated expense under s.480(1), above: subs. (2). The notification may subsequently be varied under subss. (3) or (4), in the same way as in relation to improvement grants under s.473(3) and (4): see notes thereto, above. Where a balance has to be financed privately, a loan may be available from the authority under s.435, above.

The appropriate percentage depends on a number of factors. If the dwelling falls within what was described as Category A of S.I. 1983 No. 613 in relation to improvement grants in the notes to s.472, above, the appropriate percentage will be 75 per cent.; otherwise, if in a General Improvement Area under Part VIII, above, 65 per cent.; otherwise 50 per cent.: S.I. 1980 No. 1735. However, 75 per cent. may be increased to 90 per cent. and 50 per cent. to 65 per cent. in cases of undue financial hardship: see notes to s.473, above.

Where the application was received on or before, initially, December 31, 1982, and approved after April 12, 1982 (S.I. 1982 No. 581), subsequently extended to applications received on or before March 31, 1984, approved after December 31, 1982 (S.I. 1982 No. 1763), the appropriate percentage was increased to 90 per cent. in all cases, but this "incentive" scheme has now terminated.

As to payment of grant, see s.511, below. As to completion of works, see s.512, below.

Special grants

Works for which special grants may be made

483.—(1) The works for which a special grant may be made are works required for the improvement of a house in multiple occupation by the provision of—
  (*a*) standard amenities, or
  (*b*) means of escape from fire.
  (2) The reference in subsection (1) to works required for the improvement of a house in multiple occupation in the respects mentioned includes any works of repair or replacement which, in the opinion of the local housing authority, are needed for the purpose of enabling the house to attain the standard of repair required by section 485.

DEFINITIONS

"house in multiple occupation": s.525.
"improvement": s.525.
"local housing authority": ss.1, 2.
"standard amenities": s.508.

GENERAL NOTE

The works for which a special grant is available are those which will secure the provision of standard amenities (see s.508, below), and means of escape from fire (not defined, but see notes to s.365, above), in a house in multiple occupation: subs. (1). H.M.O. bears the special meaning to be found in s.525, *i.e.* it is a house which is occupied by people who do not form a single household (as to which, see notes to s.345, above), *excluding* all those parts of the house which are occupied by persons who do form a single household— the house in multiple occupation, then, for these purposes, is what is left, *e.g.* the common parts, the roof, etc. See also notes to s.460, above.

In *R.* v. *Kerrier District Council, ex parte Guppys (Bridport) Ltd.* (*No.* 2) (1985) 17 H.L.R. 426, the Court of Appeal considered a large building, with shops at street level, and a number of rooms from the first floor upwards, at a time when it was being converted into self-contained flats. The Court of Appeal held that the authority had to ask whether the works were for the improvement of an H.M.O., at the date of application for the grant.

At that date, and at the date when the authority gave their decision, there was no one in occupation, and no intention to let the house as a house in multiple occupation again, but to turn it into a block of self-contained flats, which was outwith the intention of Parliament as reflected in this definition. If what would emerge from the works was not an H.M.O., the works could not be for the improvement of an H.M.O. It was accepted that in some cases a house, even although empty, may still qualify as an H.M.O., *e.g.* where the occupiers have temporarily removed during works.

The court did not consider, however, whether or not the building was an H.M.O. so far as the residual common parts were concerned, or whether grant-aid would have been available for (means of escape) works thereto.

The standard amenities, then, are for the benefit of people *not* in, *e.g.*, self-contained flats. Under s.484, below, the application has to state by how many households and individuals the house concerned is occupied, the standard amenities with which it is already provided, and the means of escape from fire already available.

Additionally qualifying for the special grant are associated works of repair or replacement such as the authority consider are needed to bring the house up to the standard of repair required by s.485: subs. (2). This express inclusion of these added works is also (*cf.* notes to s.474, above) pursuant to Law Commission Recommendations (Cmnd. 9515), No. 24(ii). The authority cannot approve the application unless on completion the house will be in reasonable repair (disregarding internal decorative repair, but having regard to age, character and locality—s.519, below): s.485(1). If the application contains more extensive works than the authority consider necessary to attain this standard, then—with the consent of the applicant—the application may be treated as varied so as to eliminate unnecessary works: s.485(2).

The special grant is mandatory so far as it relates to the provision of standard amenities required to comply with a notice under s.352, above: s.486(1)(*a*). It is also mandatory so far as it relates to the provision of means of escape from fire required by a notice under s.366, above: s.486(1)(*b*). The special grant is otherwise discretionary: s.487. The calculation of special grant is under ss.488–490, below.

Particulars to be stated in application

484. An application for a special grant shall state by how many households and individuals the house concerned is occupied and, as applicable—

    (*a*) the standard amenities with which it is already provided, and

    (*b*) the means of escape from fire which are already available.

DEFINITIONS

    "special grant": s.483.

    "standard amenities": s.508.

GENERAL NOTE

    An application for a special grant must state by how many households and individuals the house in multiple occupation is occupied, the standard amenities (below, s.508) with which the house is already provided, and the means of escape from fire (see notes to s.365 above), which are already available.

Standard of repair to be attained

485.—(1) The local housing authority shall not approve an application for a special grant unless they are satisfied that on completion of the relevant works the house will be in reasonable repair.

(2) If in the opinion of the authority the relevant works are more extensive than is necessary for the purpose of securing that the house will attain that standard, the authority may, with the consent of the applicant, treat the application as varied so that the relevant works include only such works as seem to the authority necessary for that purpose; and they may then approve the application as so varied.

DEFINITIONS

    "local housing authority": ss.1, 2.

    "reasonable repair": s.519.

    "relevant works": s.461.

    "special grant": s.483.

GENERAL NOTE
    As to reasonable repair, see notes to s.471, above.
    This section makes analogous provision to that made under s.476, above, for intermediate grants. The house must achieve reasonable repair, and the grant is not otherwise to be approved: subs. (1). If works to a higher standard are included, then with the consent of the applicant, the authority can treat the application as varied: subs. (2).
    If the applicant's consent cannot be secured, then (a) the special grant is in any event only mandatory so far as it relates to the standard amenities and means of escape from fire which are subject to the relevant notices (see s.486, below), and (b) only those works which are *needed* in the *opinion of the authority* qualify under s.483(2), above.

Mandatory grants for works required by notice under Part XI

    486.—(1) The local housing authority shall not refuse an application, duly made, for a special grant—
    (*a*) in so far as it relates to the provision of standard amenities and the authority are satisfied that the relevant works are necessary for compliance with so much of a notice under section 352 (works required to render house fit for number of occupants) as relates to standard amenities;
    (*b*) in so far as it relates to the provision of means of escape from fire and the authority are satisfied that the relevant works are necessary for compliance with a notice under section 366 (works required for provision of means of escape from fire).
    (2) So far as this section applies to an application, the following provisions do not apply—
        section 463 (preliminary conditions: interest of applicant in the property),
        section 465 (restriction on grants for works already begun), and
        section 485(1) (standard of repair to be attained).

DEFINITIONS
    "local housing authority": ss.1, 2.
    "relevant works": s.461.
    "special grant": s.483.
    "standard amenities": s.508.

GENERAL NOTE
    The special grant is mandatory, but *only* to the extent specified, *i.e.* so far as it concerns the provision of standard amenities within a notice under s.352, above, and means of escape from fire within a notice under s.366, above: subs. (1). There is no requirement that the person served with the relevant notice should be the applicant for grant-aid: the question is whether the *works* are required for compliance.
    Grant-aid for the associated works of repair or replacement (s.483(2)) is not mandatory, even when these "basic" elements are, and the normal requirement of s.485(1), above, that a standard of reasonable repair be achieved is expressly disapplied: subs.(2). Similarly, there is no requirement as to the interest of the applicant in the property under s.463, above, or a restriction on prior works under s.465, above: *ibid.* The requirement for a certificate of future occupation is also not applicable: s.464(1), above. The special grant is otherwise discretionary: s.487, below.

Special grants not within s.486 are discretionary

    487.—(1) To the extent that the application does not fall within section 486 (mandatory grants for works required by notice under Part XI) the local housing authority may approve an application for a special grant in such circumstances as they think fit.
    (2) Subsection (1) has effect subject to the following provisions (which restrict the cases in which applications may be approved)—
        section 463(2) (person who proposes to acquire but has not yet acquired an owner's interest),
        section 465 (works already begun), and
        section 485 (standard of repair to be attained).

DEFINITIONS
"local housing authority": ss.1, 2.
"special grant": s.483.
"standard amenities": s.508.

GENERAL NOTE
The special grant is discretionary when it is not mandatory: subs. (1). The discretion is limited by the specified provisions, but note that no certificate of future occupation is required under s.464, above: see s.464(1). The amount of special grant is as calculated under ss.488–490, below; to the extent that the grant is discretionary (*e.g.* if a discretionary amount is allowed for associated works of repair or replacement under s.483(2), necessary to achieve the standard in s.485(1), above), the authority also have a discretion as to *how much* to allow, below the limits calculated under the following sections, although if they exercise this part of their discretion they must provide the applicant with a statement of reasons for so doing: s.510, below. See also notes to s.470, above, as to the proper approach to discretionary grants.
Payment of grant is dealt with in s.511, below.

Special grants: estimated expense of works

488.—(1) Where a local authority approve an application for a special grant, they shall determine separately the amounts of the expenses which they think proper to be incurred for those of the relevant works which—
    (*a*) consist in providing standard amenities,
    (*b*) relate to the provision of means of escape from fire, and
    (*c*) consist of works of repair and replacement;
and they shall notify the applicant of the amounts so determined by them.
    (2) If, after the application for the grant has been approved, the authority are satisfied that owing to circumstances beyond the control of the applicant the relevant works will not be carried out on the basis of the estimate contained in the application, they may, on receiving a further estimate, redetermine the estimate expense in relation to the grant.
    (3) If the applicant satisfies the authority that—
    (*a*) the relevant works cannot be, or could not have been, carried out without carrying out additional works, and
    (*b*) that this could not have been reasonably foreseen at the time the application was made,
the authority may determine a higher amount under any of paragraphs (*a*) to (*c*) of subsection (1).

DEFINITIONS
"local housing authority": ss.1, 2.
"relevant works": s.461.
"special grant": s.483.
"standard amenities": s.508.

GENERAL NOTE
This is the first stage in the calculation of grant, analogous to that to be found in s.471, above, for the improvement grant, and s.480, above, for the intermediate grant. The amounts which the authority consider proper to be incurred are to be calculated in three separate heads—standard amenities (see also s.508, below), means of escape from fire and works of repair and replacement (under s.484(2), above): subs. (1). They have to notify the applicant of these amounts on approval (together with the actual amount of grant-aid under s.490, below): *ibid.* Where a balance has to be financed privately, *i.e.* because works required to achieve the relevant standard are in excess of those which are eligible, or to meet the part of the eligible expense not covered by the grant, a loan may be available from the authority under s.435, above.
    Subss. (2) and (3) contain the analogous provisions to ss.471 and 480, above, governing (a) proceeding on a different estimate (see also notes to s.461, above), which is likely to

mean an increase but could mean a reduction, and (b) unforeseeable extra works. Note the powers of the authority to carry out works under an "agency" agreement: s.514, below.

Only the eligible part of the estimated expense will be admissible for grant-aid, calculated under s.489, below, and only the proportion calculated under s.490 will actually be paid. Payment of grant itself is covered by s.511, below; completion of works by s.512, below.

Special grants: limit on expense eligible for grant

489.—(1) Except in a case or description of case in which the Secretary of State approves a higher eligible expense, the eligible expense for the purposes of a special grant is the aggregate of the contributory elements specified in the following subsections.

(2) As regards the provision of standard amenities, the contributory element is so much of the amount determined under section 488(1)(*a*) as does not exceed the aggregate of the amounts specified in the second column of the Table in section 508(1) (standard amenities and maximum eligible amounts) in relation to each of the standard amenities to be provided by the relevant works (so that, where the relevant works make provision for more than one standard amenity of the same description, a separate amount shall be aggregated for each of those amenities).

(3) As regards the provision of means of escape from fire, the contributory element is so much of the amount determined under section 488(1)(*b*) as does not exceed £6,750 or such other amount as may be prescribed.

(4) As regards works of repair and replacement, the contributory element is so much of the amount determined under section 488(1)(*c*) as does not exceed £2,000 or such other amount as may be prescribed.

(5) In this section "prescribed" means prescribed by order of the Secretary of State.

(6) An order—

(*a*) may make different provision with respect to different cases or descriptions of case, including different provision for different areas, and

(*b*) shall be made by statutory instrument which shall be subject to annulment in pursuance of a resolution of the House of Commons.

DEFINITIONS
  "relevant works": s.461.
  "special grant": s.483.
  "standard amenities": s.508.

GENERAL NOTE
After establishing the estimated expense under s.488, above, the authority calculate the eligible expense, also in three parts, under this section. Where a balance has to be financed privately, a loan may be available from the authority under s.435, above.

The first part is the calculation of standard amenities. There may be more than one standard amenity of each type (in contrast to the position under the intermediate grant—see s.474, above). The aggregate of the amounts specified in Column 2 of the Table in s.508(1) below, forms the maximum allowable for the standard amenities and, as with the intermediate grant, if one standard amenity is costing more than allowed, while another is costing less, the saving will offset the excess: see notes to s.481, above.

Means of escape from fire are admissible to a maximum of £6,750 or such other amount as may be prescribed by the Secretary of State.

Works of repair or replacement are admissible to a maximum of £2,000 or such other amount as the Secretary of State may prescribe.

The Secretary of State has exercised his powers of prescribing higher amounts by S.I. 1983 No. 613, retained in force by s.2, Housing (Consequential Provisions) Act 1985. Means of escape from fire are admissible to a limit of £10,800 in Greater London and £8,100 elsewhere; works of repair or replacement are admissible to a limit of £4,200 in Greater London, and £3,000 elsewhere.

Special grants: determination of amount

490.—(1) The amount of a special grant—

(*a*) so far as the grant is made in pursuance of section 486(1) (mandatory grants for works required by notice under Part XI), is the appropriate percentage of the eligible expense, and

(*b*) otherwise, is such as may be fixed by the local housing authority when they approve the application for the grant but shall not exceed the appropriate percentage of the eligible expense.

(2) The authority shall notify the applicant of the amount of the grant together with the notification under section 488(1) (notification of estimated expense of relevant works).

(3) Where the authority redetermine the amount of the estimated expense under section 488(2) (new estimate where works cannot be carried out in accordance with original estimate), they shall make such other adjustments relating to the amount of the grant as appear to them to be appropriate; but the amount of the grant shall not be increased beyond the amount which could have been notified when the application was approved if the estimate contained in the application had been of the same amount as the further estimate.

(4) Where the authority redetermine the amount of the estimated expense under section 488(3) (redetermination where additional works prove necessary), the eligible expense shall be recalculated under section 489 and if on the recalculation the amount is greater than when the application was approved, the amount of the grant shall be increased, and the applicant notified, accordingly.

DEFINITIONS

"appropriate percentage": s.509.
"eligible expense": s.489.
"estimated expense": s.488.
"local housing authority": ss.1, 2.
"relevant works": s.461.
"special grant": s.483.

GENERAL NOTE

The final element of the grant calculation is to apply the appropriate percentage to the eligible part calculated in accordance with s.489, above, of the estimated expense calculated in accordance with s.488, above. To the extent that the grant is mandatory (see s.486, above), the full amount thus calculated must be paid; to the extent that it is discretionary (see s.487, above), the full amount forms a maximum, and the authority may pay less, although if they do so they must provide the applicant with a statement in writing of their reasons for doing so: s.510, below. Where a balance has to be financed privately, a loan may be available from the authority under s.435, above.

The applicant is to be notified of the amount of grant at the same time as he is notified of the amount of the estimated expense under s.488(1). Provision is made in subss. (3) and (4) for revision of the grant in the event of the applicant proceeding on a different estimate, or unforeseeable added works: see s.488(2), (3).

The appropriate percentage starts with what was described as Category A under S.I. 1983 No. 613 in relation to the eligible expense for an improvement grant in the notes to s.472, above, which is substantively the same as the class qualifying for a 75 per cent. grant under S.I. 1980 No. 1735—see also notes to ss.473, and 482, above. These orders are retained in force by Housing (Consequential Provisions) Act 1985, s.2.

In the case of a special grant, the following *additional* observations may be made:

(1) notice may have been served under ss.189 or 264, above, because the house is unfit, even although it is a house in multiple occupation, in which case the grant still qualifies for a 90 per cent. appropriate percentage if the relevant works will contribute towards rendering the house fit for human habitation within the meaning of s.604, below; and,

(2) a special grant also qualifies for a 75 per cent. grant if the works consist of or include the provision of standard amenities which the authority consider necessary to make the house reasonably suitable for occupation by the number of people for the time being in occupation, or if the house is not provided with necessary means of escape from fire for such

people, *even if the grant is not a mandatory grant*, *i.e.* even if the authority have not served notice under ss.352 or s.366, above.

Where the grant does not fall within the 75 per cent. class, the grant payable is 65 per cent. if the premises are in a General Improvement Area within Part VIII, above, and otherwise 50 per cent., with the proviso that 75 per cent. can be raised to 90 per cent., and 50 per cent. to 65 per cent., in a case of financial hardship: see notes to s.473, above.

Repairs grants

Works for which repairs grants may be made

491.—(1) The works for which a repairs grant may be given are works of repair or replacement relating to a dwelling, not being works associated with other works required for the provision of the dwelling by conversion of a house or other building or for the improvement of the dwelling.

(2) A local housing authority shall not approve an application for a repairs grant unless—

(*a*) they are satisfied that the relevant works are of a substantial and structural character, or

(*b*) the relevant works satisfy such requirements as may be prescribed for the purposes of this section by order of the Secretary of State made with the consent of the Treasury.

(3) An order—

(*a*) may make different provision with respect to different cases or descriptions of case, including different provision for different areas, and

(*b*) shall be made by statutory instrument which shall be subject to annulment in pursuance of a resolution of either House of Parliament.

DEFINITIONS
  "dwelling": s.525.
  "improvement": s.525.
  "local housing authority": ss.1, 2.
  "relevant works": s.461.

GENERAL NOTE
  This is the last of the "main" grants available under this Part. The repairs grant is a discretionary grant, save when it is in order to satisfy a repairs notice under ss.189 or 190, above, *i.e.* unfit but repairable at a reasonable expense, or not unfit but in need of works to prevent the property becoming unfit or to prevent interference with the comfort of an occupying tenant: s.494, below.
  A repairs grant is only available in relation to an "old dwelling" as defined in s.492(1), below, and if (a) *not* within a housing action area within Part VIII, above, *and* (b) accompanied by a certificate of owner-occupation within s.464, above, not if the rateable value is above the limit specified under s.492(2), below. (A mandatory grant will not be accompanied by a certificate of owner-occupation: see s.494, below).
  The amount of the repairs grant is calculated in accordance with ss.496–498, below; payment is governed by s.511, below; completion of works by s.512, below.
  Repairs grants are for works of repair or replacement (as to which, see notes to s.471, above), which are *not* associated with works for the provision of a dwelling by conversion (which qualifies for the discretionary improvement grant, see notes to s.467, above) or for the improvement (as defined in s.520, below) of the dwelling, which could mean either an improvement grant or an intermediate grant under s.474, above: subs. (1). The grant is not to be approved, however, unless the dwelling will achieve a standard of reasonable repair under s.493, below.
  The principal conditions are those in subs. (2). The works must be of a "substantial and structural character", a term not otherwise defined, but one which clearly includes such items of common disrepair as roofs, windows (see *Boswell* v. *Crucible Steel Co.* [1925] 1 K.B. 119), and foundations.
  Depending on cost, the term could include the insertion of a damp-proof course: see notes to s.471, above; see also *Pearlman* v. *Governors and Keepers of Harrow School* [1979]

Q.B. 56, C.A. (works to the structure include works to those subsidiary parts of the property which are vital to normal use and part of its complex whole, as well as the obvious parts such as walls, roofs and foundations).

D.O.E. Circular 20/81, App. B, para. 68, contains details of "the main type of structural repair for which the Secretary of State envisages that grant might be considered:

Roofs
—replacing or repairing defective roofs and timbers and associated renewal of gutters and rainwater pipes;
—rebuilding, removal or repointing of defective chimney stacks;

External Walls
—renewing or repairing defective walls;
—replacing defective doors and/or frames;
—replacing defective window frames and/or sills;
—replacing defective damp-proof course;

Foundations
—repair or renewal of defective foundations;
—underpinning substandard foundations;

Floors
—replacement of defective ground floor;
—replacement of defective upper floor timbers and boarding;
—strengthening or replacing defective floor joists;

Internal
—replacing or repairing defective internal walls and ceilings;
—replacing or repairing defective staircase".

Under *ibid.*, para. 70, "Local authorities will note that electrical rewiring is not included in the list . . . The Secretary of State considers that repairs grant should not be given for such work, either on its own or in association with other works. More generally, the grant is not intended to cover works of routine repair".

The works must also satisfy the requirements of the Secretary of State. These are to be found in S.I. 1982 No. 1205, retained in force by Housing (Consequential Provisions) Act 1985, s.2. "The requirements are . . . that the relevant works shall consist of the replacement of the whole or part of a pipe which is made of lead and which connects, or forms part of a pipe which connects, the tap in the dwelling mainly used for supplying drinking water directly or indirectly to the main, by such a pipe not made of lead" (Art. 3). In the case of works which satisfy this requirement, the definition of "old dwelling" in s.492(1), below, is varied.

Former special provisions governing "Airey Houses" ceased to be available in relation to applications on or after December 1, 1984, after which time the provisions of what is now Part XVI, below, came into operation.

Dwellings in respect of which repairs grants may be made

492.—(1) An application for a repairs grant shall only be approved if it is made in respect of an old dwelling, as defined by order of the Secretary of State.

(2) Where an application for a repairs grant is accompanied by a certificate of owner-occupation, and the dwelling is not situated in a housing action area, the application shall only be approved if the rateable value at the date of the application is within the limits specified by order of the Secretary of State made with the consent of the Treasury.

(3) An order under subsection (1) or (2)—

(a) may make different provision with respect to different cases or descriptions of case, including different provision for different areas, and

(b) shall be made by statutory instrument which shall be subject to annulment in pursuance of a resolution of either House of Parliament.

DEFINITIONS
   "certificate of owner-occupation": s.464.
   "dwelling": s.525.

"housing action area": s.239.
"repairs grant": s.491.

GENERAL NOTE
There are two statutory limitations on repairs grants, which relate to the premises. First of all, the dwelling must be an "old dwelling" as defined by the Secretary of State. Under S.I. 1982 No. 1205, retained in force by Housing (Consequential Provisions) Act 1985, s.2, this means "a dwelling which is, or forms part of, a building which was erected before . . . 1st January 1919" in most cases, but "before . . . 3rd October 1961, if the relevant works satisfy the requirements prescribed by article 3 above" (Art. 4), *i.e.* include the replacement of lead piping: see notes to s.491, above.

This first limitation applies even if the grant is a mandatory grant within s.494, below. The second limitation does not apply if the premises are within a Housing Action Area within Part VIII, above, but does apply if the application is accompanied by a certificate of owner-occupation within s.464, above, which will not include mandatory grants within s.494, below: see notes to s.494. In a case where it does apply, the property has to be within the rateable value limits specified, as at the date of application (*cf.* notes to s.461, above).

The rateable value limits are also set out in S.I. 1982 No. 1205: in Greater London, £400; elsewhere, £225.

Standard of repair to be attained

493.—(1) The local housing authority shall not approve an application for a repairs grant unless they are satisfied that on completion of the relevant works the dwelling or, as the case may be, each of the dwellings to which the application relates will be in reasonable repair.

(2) If in the opinion of the authority the relevant works are more extensive than is necessary for the purpose of securing that the dwelling or dwellings attain that standard, the authority may, with the consent of the applicant, treat the application as varied so that the relevant works include only such works as seem to the authority to be necessary for that purpose; and they may then approve the application as so varied.

DEFINITIONS
"dwelling": s.525.
"local housing authority": ss.1, 2.
"reasonable repair": s.519.
"relevant works": s.461.
"repairs grant": s.491.

GENERAL NOTE
This makes analogous provision as is made by s.468 for improvement grants, s.476 for intermediate grants, and s.485 for special grants. The dwelling must be in reasonable repair, as defined in s.519, (see notes to s.471), above, after the completion of works: subs. (1). If more works are included than are needed to achieve this standard, the authority can treat the application as varied so as to exclude the superfluous works, with the consent of the applicant: subs. (2). If the applicant does not consent, then (a) to the extent that the grant is discretionary it may be refused or reduced (see also notes to s.495, below), and (b) only properly incurred expenditure is admissible under s.496, below.

Mandatory grants for works required by repairs notice

494.—(1) The local housing authority shall not refuse an application, duly made, for a repairs grant so far as it relates to the execution of works required by a notice under section 189 or 190 (repair notices) and the authority are satisfied that the works are necessary for compliance with the notice.

(2) So far as this section applies to an application, the following provisions do not apply—

  section 463 (preliminary condition: interest of applicant in the
      property),

section 464 (preliminary condition: certificate as to future occupation), and

section 465 (restriction on grants for works already begun).

DEFINITIONS
"local housing authority": ss.1, 2.
"relevant works": s.461.
"repairs grant": s.491.

GENERAL NOTE
This makes analogous provision to that made by s.486, above, for mandatory special grants. To the extent that the application for repairs grant relates to works within a notice under either s.189 or s.190, above, the grant must be approved: subs. (1). Again, there is no requirement that application be made by person served with notice: it is the *works* which must be required by the notice.

In such circumstances, the specified conditions (interest of applicant, certificate of future occupation, and prior works) do not apply: subs. (2). In such circumstances, the amount of the grant will be the full appropriate percentage of the eligible part (s.497) of the estimated expense (s.496), attributable to such works, *i.e.* the authority will not have any discretion to pay a lower amount: see s.498, below.

A notice under s.189 is a repairs notice requiring the remedying of unfitness where the works can be carried out at a reasonable expense as defined in s.206, above; a notice under s.190 may be either in respect of substantial works needed to bring the property up to a reasonable standard, even although it is not unfit, or in respect of works needed to prevent material interference with the comfort of the occupying tenant, again, even although the property is not unfit. See notes to ss.189, 190, above.

Repairs grants not within s.494 are discretionary

495.—(1) To the extent that the application does not fall within section 494 (mandatory grants for works required by repairs notice), the local housing authority may approve an application for a repairs grant in such circumstances as they think fit.

(2) Subsection (1) has effect subject to the following provisions (which restrict the cases in which applications may be approved)—

section 463(2) (person who proposes to acquire but has not yet acquired an owner's interest),

section 465 (works already begun),

section 491(2) (nature of works for which repairs grants may be given),

section 492 (dwelling in respect of which repairs grants may be given), and

section 493 (standard of repair to be attained).

DEFINITIONS
"dwelling": s.525.
"local housing authority": ss.1, 2.
"repairs grant": s.491.

GENERAL NOTE
Where the grant is not mandatory under s.494, above, it is discretionary, albeit subject to the requirements of the specified sections. When the grant is discretionary, the authority can pay any amount up to the appropriate percentage of the eligible part (s.497) of the estimated expense (s.496): s.498, below. If they use this discretion, however, then they must notify the applicant in writing of their reasons for paying a lesser amount: s.510, below. See the notes to s.470, above, as to the proper approach to discretionary grants.

Repairs grants: estimated expense of works

496.—(1) Where a local housing authority approve an application for a repairs grant, they shall determine the amount of the expenses which in their opinion are proper to be incurred for the execution of the relevant works and shall notify the applicant of that amount.

(2) If, after an application for a grant has been approved, the authority are satisfied that owing to circumstances beyond the control of the applicant the relevant works will not be carried out on the basis of the estimate contained in the application, they may, on receiving a further estimate, redetermine the estimated expense in relation to the grant.

(3) If the applicant satisfies the authority that—

(a) the relevant works cannot be, or could not have been, carried out without carrying out additional works, and

(b) this could not have been reasonably foreseen at the time the application was made,

the authority may determine a higher amount under subsection (1).

DEFINITIONS

"local housing authority": ss.1, 2.
"relevant works": s.461.
"repairs grant": s.491.

GENERAL NOTE

As with the improvement grant (s.471), the intermediate grant (s.480) and the special grant (s.488), the calculation of grant starts with the calculation of the estimated expense under this section. Only the eligible part of it will qualify: see s.497, below. Only up to the appropriate percentage under s.498 will actually be payable. Payment is dealt with in s.511, below; completion of works in s.512, below. Where a balance has to be financed privately, *i.e.* because the works required to achieve the relevant standard are in excess of those which are eligible, or to meet the part of the eligible expense not covered by the grant, a loan may be available from the authority under s.435, above.

Subject to the provisions of subss. (2) and (3), which permit revision if the applicant proceeds on an estimate other than that on which the grant was approved (*cf.* notes to s.461, above), and increase for unforeseeable added works (see also notes to s.471, above), the estimated expense, which is to be notified to the applicant (together with notification of the amount of grant—see s.498(2), below), is simply that amount which the authority consider proper to be incurred.

Note the powers of the authority to carry out works under an "agency" agreement: s.514, below.

Repairs grants: limit on expense eligible for grant

497.—(1) Except in a case or description of case in respect of which the Secretary of State approves a higher eligible expense, the eligible expense for the purpose of a repairs grant is so much of the estimated expense as does not exceed £800 or such other amount as may be prescribed.

(2) In subsection (1) "prescribed" means prescribed by order of the Secretary of State.

(3) An order—

(a) may make different provision with respect to different cases or descriptions of case, including different provision for different areas, and

(b) shall be made by statutory instrument which shall be subject to annulment in pursuance of a resolution of the House of Commons.

DEFINITIONS

"estimated expense": s.496.
"local housing authority": ss.1, 2.
"repairs grant": s.491.

GENERAL NOTE

A repairs grant is only available in respect of £800 or such other amount as may be prescribed. Where a balance has to be financed privately, a loan may be available from the authority under s.435, above.

By S.I. 1983 No. 613, retained in force by s.2, Housing (Consequential Provisions) Act 1985, much higher amounts are specified:

(1) In the case of a Grade I listed building, under Town and Country Planning Act 1971, s.54, in Greater London £7,480, elsewhere £5,680;

(2) In the case of a Grade II starred listed building, in Greater London £7,130, elsewhere £5,330;

(3) In the case of a Grade II unstarred listed building, in Greater London £6,860, elsewhere £5,060;

(4) In the case of an unlisted building, in Greater London £6,600, elsewhere £4,800.

Repairs grants: determination of amount

498.—(1) The amount of a repairs grant—

(a) so far as the grant is made in pursuance of section 494(1) (mandatory grants for works required by repairs notice), is the appropriate percentage of the eligible expense, and

(b) otherwise, is such as may be fixed by the local housing authority when they approve the application for the grant but shall not exceed the appropriate percentage of the eligible expense.

(2) The authority shall notify the applicant of the amount of the grant together with the notification under section 496(1) (notification of estimated expense of works).

(3) Where the authority redetermine the amount of the estimated expense under section 496(2) (new estimate where works cannot be carried out in accordance with original estimate), they shall make such other adjustments relating to the amount of the grant as appear to them to be appropriate; but the amount of the grant shall not be increased beyond the amount which could have been notified when the application was approved if the estimate contained in the application had been of the same amount as the further estimate.

(4) Where the authority redetermine the amount of the estimated expense under section 496(3) (redetermination where additional works prove necessary), the eligible expense shall be recalculated under section 497, and if on the re-calculation the amount is greater than when the application was approved the amount of the grant shall be increased, and the applicant notified, accordingly.

DEFINITIONS

"appropriate percentage": s.509.
"eligible expense": s.497.
"estimated expense": s.496.
"local housing authority": ss.1, 2.
"repairs grant": s.491.

GENERAL NOTE

It is only the appropriate percentage of the eligible part of the estimated expense which is payable: subs. (1). It must be notified to the applicant together with the notification of estimated expense under s.496(1), above: subs.(2). The notification may subsequently be varied under subss. (3) or (4): cf. s.496(2), (3), above. Where a balance has to be financed privately, a loan may be available from the authority under s.435, above.

The appropriate percentage depends on a number of factors. If the dwelling falls within what was described as Category A of S.I. 1983 No. 613 in relation to improvement grants in the notes to s.472, above, the appropriate percentage will be 75 per cent.; otherwise, if in a General Improvement Area under Part VIII, above, 65 per cent.; otherwise 50 per cent.: S.I. 1980 No. 1735, retained in force by Housing (Consequential Provisions) Act 1985 s.2. However, 75 per cent. may be increased to 90 per cent. and 50 per cent. to 65 per cent. in cases of undue financial hardship: see notes to s.473, above.

Where the application was received on or before, initially, December 31, 1982, and approved after April 12, 1982 (S.I. 1982 No. 581), subsequently extended to applications received on or before March 31, 1984, approved after December 31, 1982 (S.I. 1982 No. 1763), the appropriate percentage was increased to 90 per cent. in all cases, but this "incentive" scheme has now, of course, terminated.

As to payment of grant, see s.511, below. As to completion of works, see s.512, below.

Grant conditions

Conditions as to future occupation: introductory

499.—(1) Where an application for a grant (other than a special grant) has been approved by a local housing authority, the provisions of—

section 500 (condition as to owner-occupation),

section 501 (condition as to availability for letting), and

section 502 (conditions as to provision of information about occupation),

apply during the initial period as to the occupation of the dwelling or, as the case may be, each of the dwellings to which the grant relates.

(2) The "initial period" means the period of five years beginning with the date certified by the authority as the date on which the dwelling first becomes fit for occupation after the completion of the relevant works to the satisfaction of the authority.

(3) That date is referred to in this Part as "the certified date".

DEFINITIONS

"dwelling": s.525.

"grant": s.460.

"local housing authority": ss.1, 2.

"special grant": s.483.

GENERAL NOTE

This identifies the "initial period" during which grant conditions will apply. Sections 500–502 will apply in all cases; additional conditions may and in some cases must be imposed under ss.503–504, below. Grant conditions normally remain in force for five years: see s.505, below. Section 506 governs repayment of grant for breach of condition, although a condition may be "lifted" by voluntary repayment under s.507, below.

The three conditions (ss.500–502) governed by this section apply to the dwelling, or each of the dwellings to which the grant relates, including of course dwellings provided by conversion under s.467, above.

The initial period is five years from the certified date, which is the date on which the dwelling first becomes fit for occupation after completion of the relevant works to the satisfaction of the authority: where the property remains fit for occupation throughout the works, therefore, the certified date will be the date when the authority certify the works as complete to their satisfaction.

As to completion of works, see s.512, below.

Condition as to owner-occupation

500.—(1) This section applies where the application for the grant was accompanied by a certificate of owner-occupation.

(2) It is a condition of the grant that—

(*a*) throughout the first year of the initial period the dwelling will, as a residence, be occupied exclusively by, or be available for the exclusive occupation of, a qualifying person and the members of his household (if any), and

(*b*) if at any time after that first year (but during the initial period) the dwelling is not occupied exclusively as his only or main residence by a qualifying person and members of his household (if any), it will be let or available for letting by a qualifying person as a residence, and not for a holiday, to persons other than members of that person's family.

(3) The following persons are "qualifying persons" for the purposes of this section—

(*a*) the applicant and any person deriving title to the dwelling through or under him;

(*b*) a member of the applicant's family or a grandparent or grandchild of the applicant or his spouse;

(*c*) at a time when personal representatives or trustees are the qualifying persons by virtue of paragraph (*a*), a person who under the will or intestacy or, as the case may be, under the terms of the trusts concerned is beneficially entitled to an interest in the dwelling or the proceeds of sale of the dwelling;

(*d*) a person related to one who qualifies under paragraph (*c*) by being a member of his family or a grandparent or grandchild of his or of his spouse.

(4) In determining whether there is a breach of the condition specified in subsection (2), a period of not more than twelve months during which the condition was not fulfilled shall be disregarded if—

(*a*) the period began on the death of a qualifying person who immediately before his death was occupying the dwelling as his residence, and

(*b*) throughout the period an interest in the dwelling (or in the proceeds of sale of the dwelling), being either the interest which belonged to the deceased or an interest which arose or fell into possession on his death, is vested in his personal representatives (acting in that capacity), or in trustees as such, or by virtue of section 9 of the Administration of Estates Act 1925 (vesting of estate of intestate between death and grant of administration) in the Probate Judge within the meaning of that Act.

DEFINITIONS
"certificate of owner-occupation": s.464.
"dwelling": s.525.
"grant": s.460.
"initial period": s.499.
"member of the family": s.520.

GENERAL NOTE
The first of the grant conditions applies when the application was accompanied by a certificate of *owner*-occupation, under s.464, above; where accompanied by a certificate of availability for letting, see s.501, below; the condition to provide information as to occupation in s.502, below, applies to both this section and s.501. As to repayment for breach, see s.506, below; as to voluntary repayment in order to get a condition lifted, see s.507, below. As to further conditions which may, and in some cases must, be imposed by local authorities, see ss.503–504, below. As to duration of grant conditions, see s.505, below. As to cessation of interest *before* (complete) payment of grant, see s.515, below.

This section will not apply in the case of a special grant, because there is no certificate of owner-occupation: see s.464(1), above; nor will it apply in the case of an intermediate grant for works under an improvement notice within Part VII, above: see s.477; nor will it apply in the case of a mandatory repairs grant: see s.494, above.

During the first year of the initial period as defined in s.499, above, the dwelling must be in—or available for—the exclusive occupation as a residence of a qualifying person and members of his household. For the remaining four years of the initial period, if not so occupied, it must be let or available for letting by a qualifying person, as a residence and not under a holiday letting (see Rent Act 1977, ss.9 and 19(7)), to someone other than the member of the family of a qualifying person.

There is a discrepancy between subs. (2)(*a*) and subs. (2)(*b*). Subs. (2)(*a*) refers only to exclusive occupation as a residence, while subs. (2)(*b*) as an *only or main* residence. This is not necessarily an error, or irreconcilable. As to the difference between the two terms, see notes to s.81, above. It is possible to be moving in during the first year, to the extent that occupation is as a residence, and provided no one else is in occupation so that occupation is exclusive, while still in partial residence elsewhere; by the second year, occupation must be "only or main".

The condition is not the same as the statement in the certificate of owner-occupation within s.464, above: it is, of course, for breach of this *condition*, not non-compliance with the certificate of owner-occupation, that grant may be reclaimed under s.506, below.

The definition of "member of the family" is in s.520 below, and includes spouses, parents and children, step-relationships and relationships by marriage: see notes to s.464, above.

Qualifying persons are defined in subs. (3). They include the applicant, *and* any person deriving title to the dwelling through or under him. This clearly includes a purchaser of the whole of his interest, and a sublessee of the whole of the dwelling (but not a sublessee of part—"title to *the* dwelling"). A member of the applicant's family is a qualifying person, as is his grandparent or grandchildren, and the grandparent or grandchild of his spouse.

If the applicant or someone deriving title through or under him is a personal representative or trustee, a beneficiary under the will, on intestacy, or under the terms of the trust, who is entitled to *an* interest in the property or the proceeds of sale of the property is a qualifying person: this includes someone who is only entitled to a beneficial interest along with another. See also *Chetwynd* v. *Boughey* (1979) C.A., Transcript, unreported but misleadingly noted at [1981] C.L. 17. The same extension to members of the family, and grandparents and grandchildren, as applies where there is no estate or trust applies where there is.

Subs. (4)

There is no breach of the condition for one year following the death of a qualifying person who was in occupation immediately before his death. (*cf. Tomkins* v. *Rowley* [1949] E.G.D. 314, C.A.—the fact that the qualifying person may have spent his last period in hospital, and died there, will not preclude "residence" in the dwelling). However, throughout this year, the deceased's interest, or an interest which arose on his death, is vested in his personal representatives or in trustees (or in the President of the Family Division on intestacy, under Administration of Estates Act 1925, s.9).

Condition as to availability for letting

501.—(1) This section applies where the application for the grant was accompanied by a certificate of availability for letting.

(2) It is a condition of the grant that throughout the initial period—

(*a*) the dwelling will be let or available for letting as a residence, and not for a holiday, by a qualifying person to persons other than members of the family of that qualifying person or of any other person who is for the time being a qualifying person in relation to the dwelling, or

(*b*) the dwelling will be occupied or available for occupation by a member of the agricultural population in pursuance of a contract of service and otherwise than as a tenant,

(disregarding any part of that period in which neither of the above paragraphs applies but the dwelling is occupied by a person who is a protected occupier under the Rent (Agriculture) Act 1976).

(3) The following persons are "qualifying persons" for the purposes of this section—

(*a*) the applicant and any person who derives title to the dwelling through or under him otherwise than by a conveyance for value;

(*b*) a member of the applicant's family or a grandparent or grandchild of the applicant or his spouse;

(*c*) at a time when personal representatives or trustees are the qualifying persons by virtue of paragraph (*a*), a person who under the will or intestacy or, as the case may require, under the terms of the trusts concerned is beneficially entitled to an interest in the dwelling or the proceeds of sale of the dwelling;

(*d*) a person related to one who qualifies under paragraph (*c*) by being a member of his family or a grandparent or grandchild of his or of his spouse.

(4) Where the application was accompanied by a certificate under section 464(2) (tenants' applications: certificate to be given by owner or landlord), subsection (3) has effect with the substitution for the references to the applicant of references to the person who gave the certificate.

DEFINITIONS

"agricultural population": s.525.
"certificate of availability for letting": s.464.

"dwelling": s.525.
"grant": s.460.
"initial period": s.499.

GENERAL NOTE

If the application was accompanied by a certificate of availability for letting under s.464, rather than a certificate of owner-occupation, this section applies rather than s.500, above; the condition to provide information as to occupation in s.502, below, applies to both this section and s.500. As to repayment for breach, see s.506, below; as to voluntary repayment in order to get a condition lifted, see s.507, below. As to further conditions which may, and in some cases must, be imposed by local authorities, see ss.503–504, below. As to duration of condition, see s.505, below. As to cessation of interest *before* (complete) payment of grant, see s.515, below.

This section will not apply in the case of a special grant, because there is no certificate of future occupation: see s.464(1), above; nor will it apply in the case of an intermediate grant for works under an improvement notice within Part VII, above: see s.477; nor will it apply in the case of a mandatory repairs grant: see s.494, above.

The provisions of this section are far closer to the contents of the certificate of availability for letting under s.464, above, than are the conditions in s.500 to a certificate of owner-occupation. It remains the case, nonetheless, that it is breach of this section which gives rise to repayment under s.506, rather than non-compliance with the certificate under s.464. Note that unless conditions as to class of letting are imposed under ss.503–504 below, this section is silent as to what kind of letting must be granted, in terms of protective legislation.

However, the letting must not be as a holiday: see ss.9, 19(7), Rent Act 1977, excluding such lettings from protection under that Act, whether full or restricted protection. The requirement seems to be for *tenancy* as distinct from *licence* (*cf.* the provisions of subs. (2)(*b*)), see most recently *Street* v. *Mountford* [1985] A.C. 809, 17 H.L.R. 402, H.L., see notes to s.93, above. As to "agricultural population", see s.525, below.

The letting must be *by* a qualifying person, and to someone who is not a member of the family of a qualifying person. As to member of the family, see s.520, below. The applicant is a qualifying person, and so is someone who derives title to the dwelling through or under him, *i.e.* successor in title or sublessee of the whole ("title to *the* dwelling . . . "), *other* than by way of a conveyance for value (as to which, see most recently *Midland Bank Trust Co.* v. *Green* [1981] A.C. 513, H.L.) A commercial transaction between landlords is, accordingly, prohibited during the initial period.

A member of the family of a qualifying person is a qualifying person in his own right. If the applicant or person deriving title through or under him (but not for value) is a personal representative or trustee, then any beneficiary entitled to *an* (*cf.* notes to s.500, above) interest in the property or the proceeds of sale is also a qualifying person, as are his members of the family as extended to grandparents and grandchildren.

Subs. (4)

When the certificate of availability for letting was required by the authority under s.464(2), above, from someone from whom they could have entertained an application, but when the application was by a tenant qualifying under s.463, above, the provisions as to qualifying persons are adapted to the person who provided the certificate.

Conditions as to provision of information about occupation

502. It is a condition of the grant—

(*a*) that if, at any time within the initial period, the authority by whom the grant was paid serve notice on the owner of the dwelling requiring him to do so, he shall, within the period of 21 days beginning with the date on which the notice is served, furnish to the authority a certificate giving such information as the authority may reasonably require with respect to the occupation of the dwelling, and

(*b*) that, if required to do so by the owner of the dwelling, any tenant of the dwelling will furnish the owner with such information as he may reasonably require to enable him to furnish the certificate to the authority.

DEFINITIONS
  "dwelling": s.525.
  "grant": s.460.
  "initial period": s.499.
  "owner": s.525.

GENERAL NOTE
  Throughout the initial period (as defined in s.499, above), the owner of the dwelling is liable to be served with notice by the authority requiring him to provide a certificate as to occupation. The information in the certificate is to be such as the authority reasonably require. The owner has 21 days to reply. In addition, any *tenant* must furnish the owner with such information as the owner may require to enable the owner to comply with the requirements of the authority.
  The owner may be liable to reimbursement of grant for breach, under s.506, below, but there is no sanction on the part of the authority against the tenant. However, as a grant condition is enforceable against anyone with an interest as if it were a term of a lease or tenancy (including statutory tenancy), by s.505(2)(*b*), below, the owner will be able to take proceedings for breach against a tenant. The authority can in any event find the information out themselves, under Local Government (Miscellaneous Provisions) Act 1976, s.16.
  "Owner" is defined in s.525 below, "in relation to a dwelling", which is itself defined in s.525 as a building or part of a building occupied or intended to be occupied as a separate dwelling: *cf.* notes to s.460, above. Where the grant was a special grant, and the house is a house in multiple occupation, this definition would seem wholly inappropriate, and accordingly so would this condition.
  A person who is entitled to receive from a lessee of the dwelling a rent of not less than two-thirds of the net annual value is an owner, as is a person who would be so entitled if the dwelling were so let: see s.207, above. As the reference is to "dwelling", there is not the problem disclosed in *Pollway Nominees Ltd.* v. *London Borough of Croydon* (1985) 17 H.L.R. 503, C.A., of the "owner" of a block of flats let on leases at low rents—see notes to s.207, above. If the grant-aid produced low rent leases, the condition will attach to each such dwelling (see s.499), the freeholder or superior lessee will neither be in receipt of a sufficient rent, nor will he qualify under the "if so let" limb. This will be the low rent leaseholder: see *London Corporation* v. *Cusack-Smith* [1955] 1 A.C. 337, H.L., *Truman, Hanbury & Co.* v. *Kerslake* [1894] 2 Q.B. 774, *Walford* v. *Hackney Board of Works* (1894) 43 W.R. 110.
  Where, however, the letting is not at a low rent, the person who receives the rent will still not be the owner under the definition in s.525, below, if he himself is only an intermediate lessee and has to pay rent to a superior landlord, not itself a low rent: see s.525, definition of "owner", limb (*b*). In such a case, the superior landlord will be the "owner", until a landlord is reached who does pay only a low rent.

Imposition of further conditions by local housing authority

  503.—(1) Where an application for an improvement grant, intermediate grant or repairs grant is approved by a local housing authority, then, subject to subsection (2), the authority—
  (*a*) may impose with respect to the dwelling or, as the case may be, each of the dwellings to which the grant relates the further conditions specified in section 504 (further conditions as to letting of dwellings), and
  (*b*) shall do so, subject to subsection (3), in the case of a dwelling situated in an area which on the date on which the application is approved is a housing action area or general improvement area;
but the authority may impose no other condition in relation to the approval or making of the grant, whether purporting to operate by way of a condition of the grant, a personal covenant or otherwise.
  (2) The further conditions specified in section 504 may not be imposed to the extent that the grant relates to—
  (*a*) a dwelling in which a registered housing association or co-operative housing association has an estate or interest on the date on which the application is approved, or
  (*b*) a dwelling in respect of which a certificate of owner-occupation has

been given and which has not been let in whole or in part for residential purposes at any time during the period of twelve months immediately preceding the date on which the application is approved (disregarding for this purpose any letting to the applicant, to a member of his family or to a grandparent or grandchild of the applicant or his spouse), or

(c) a dwelling which is occupied by or available for occupation by a member of the agricultural population in pursuance of a contract of service and otherwise than as a tenant, or

(d) a dwelling which is occupied by a person who is a protected occupier or statutory tenant under the Rent (Agriculture) Act 1976,

or where the application is a tenant's application and is not accompanied by a certificate of availability for letting.

(3) In the case of a dwelling within subsection (1)(b) in respect of which a certificate of owner-occupation has been given, the local housing authority need not impose the further conditions specified in section 504 if it appears to them that in the special circumstances of the case it would be reasonable to dispense with them.

DEFINITIONS
   "agricultural population": s.525.
   "certificate of availability for letting": s.464.
   "certificate of owner-occupation": s.464.
   "co-operative housing association": s.5.
   "dwelling": s.525.
   "general improvement area": s.253.
   "grant": s.460.
   "housing action area": s.239.
   "improvement grant": s.467.
   "intermediate grant": s.474.
   "local housing authority": ss.1, 2.
   "registered housing association": s.5.
   "repairs grant": s.491.

GENERAL NOTE
Conditions on future occupation are defined in s.504, below, and operate for the time specified in s.505, below. Breach of such a condition may result in a repayment requirement under s.506, below, and the condition may be "lifted" by voluntary repayment under s.507, below. These conditions are inapplicable in the case of a special grant: subs. (1). As to grant conditions not related to future occupation, see s.512, below.

Apart from the conditions in ss.504 and 512, the authority "may impose no other condition in relation to the approval or making of the grant, whether purporting to operate by way of a condition of the grant, a personal covenant or otherwise". Where discretionary grants are involved, it would accordingly not seem improper for the authority to ask for a "voluntary" statement of intentions, whether as to future occupation or, in relation to works (cf. s.512) commencement or completion of works, and would seem proper to be taken into account when determining whether or not to approve the grant.

This is clearly not an option available in the case of a mandatory grant, and failure to comply with the stated intention could not result in recovery of grant—certainly under s.506, below—except perhaps in a particularly blatant case where deceit might be used (cf. notes to s.464, above).

The conditions *may* be imposed in relation to the dwellings subject to the grant, and *must* be if the property was in a Housing Action Area or General Improvement Area under Part VIII, above, on the date of *approval*. However, the further conditions *cannot* be imposed in any of the cases specified in subs. (3):

(1) A registered or co-operative housing association (see s.5, above) has *any* estate or interest on date of approval;

(2) A certificate of owner-occupation under s.464, above, was provided, and the dwelling has not been let out in whole or part for residential purposes during the year before the approval, other than to the applicant, a member of his family—see s.525, below—or a grandparent or grandchild of the applicant or his spouse.

The purpose of this is to exclude the further conditions in cases of genuine owner-occupation, as distinct from a case where someone purchases recently tenanted property (other than which he or a relative has been occupying *as* a tenant—"any letting *to* . . . "), files a certificate of owner-occupation, but then sells, given the sale potential in s.500, above); even where this condition can be applied, or must be applied, in a Housing Action Area or General Improvement Area, the authority may dispense with it if it appears reasonable to do so in the special circumstances of the case—see subs. (3); "a local authority may wish to use this discretion, for example, where a dwelling which was formerly rented is sold to someone other than a sitting tenant under a homesteading [see notes to s.441, above] scheme, or in particular cases where the previous tenant has been satisfactorily rehoused" (D.O.E. Circular 21/80, App. B, para. 19);

(3) Occupied under a contract of service otherwise than as a tenant by a member of the agricultural population (see s.525, below), or occupied under the Rent (Agriculture) Act 1976, by a protected occupier or statutory tenant thereunder, which includes *both* tenants and licensees (see, generally, as to these classes, notes to s.622, below);

(4) The grant was on a tenant's application (*cf.* s.463, above), and the authority did not require a certificate of availability for letting under s.464(2), above.

Further conditions as to letting of dwelling

504.—(1) The conditions referred to in section 503(1) (power of local housing authority to impose further conditions) are—

(*a*) that the dwelling will be let or available for letting on a regulated tenancy or a restricted contract;

(*b*) that the owner of the dwelling will, if the authority serve notice requiring him to do so, give the authority, within the period of 21 days beginning with the date on which the notice is served, a certificate that the condition set out in paragraph (*a*) is being fulfilled;

(*c*) that any tenant of the dwelling will, if required to do so by the owner, give him such information as he may reasonably require for the purpose of enabling him to comply with the condition set out in paragraph (*b*);

(*d*) that, if on the certified date there is no registered rent for the dwelling and no application or reference is pending, an application or reference will be made before the expiry of the period of 14 days beginning with the first day, not being earlier than the certified date, on which the dwelling is or becomes subject to a regulated tenancy or let on a restricted contract;

(*e*) that any such application or reference, either pending or made as mentioned in paragraph (*d*), will be diligently proceeded with and not withdrawn; and

(*f*) that no premium (within the meaning of Part IX of the Rent Act 1977) will be required as a condition of the grant, renewal or continuance, on or after the certified date of a lease or agreement for a lease of, or restricted contract relating to, the dwelling.

(2) In subsection (1)—

(*a*) "regulated tenancy" has the same meaning as in the Rent Act 1977,

(*b*) "registered rent", in relation to a dwelling subject to, or available for letting on, a regulated tenancy, means a rent registered under Part IV of that Act, and in relation to a dwelling let or available for letting on a restricted contract, means a rent registered in the register kept under section 79 of that Act, and

(*c*) "application" and "reference", in relation to the registration of a rent, mean, respectively, an application to the rent officer and a reference of the restricted contract to the rent tribunal.

DEFINITIONS
  "certified date": s.499.
  "dwelling": s.525.

"grant": s.460.
"local housing authority": ss.1, 2.
"owner": s.525.
"restricted contract": s.622.

GENERAL NOTE

These are the conditions which authorities may, and in some instances must, impose in the circumstances set out in s.503, above, which last for the period specified in s.505, below, breach of which can give rise to a repayment requirement under s.506, below, and which can be lifted by voluntary repayment under s.507, below. They are additional to the conditions on future occupation to be found in ss.499–502, but are the *only* additional conditions which the authority may impose (see s.503(1), and notes thereto), other than a condition on completion of works under s.512, below.

Type of Letting

The main conditions are that the dwelling will be let or available for letting on a regulated tenancy or a restricted contract: see notes to s.622, below.

Information

There are conditions as to the provision of information that are similar to those to be found in s.502, above, save that the information to be required is more specific, *viz.* that the dwelling is let on a regulated tenancy or restricted contract.

Registration of Rent

Rents may be registered either under Part IV, Rent Act 1977, for a regulated tenancy, or under s.79, if a restricted contract. The registration of a rent for a regulated tenancy is by the Rent Officer, and on appeal therefrom by a Rent Assessment Committee. The registration of rent for a restricted contract is by a Rent Tribunal, which is drawn from the same panel as the Rent Assessment Committee: see Housing Act 1980, s.72.

Regulated rents are "fair rents" under s.70, Rent Act 1977, *i.e.* rents which disregard "scarcity", as well as tenant's disrepair and improvements, but otherwise having regard to the age, character and locality and state of repair of the dwelling and any furniture provided. Restricted contract rents are "reasonable rents" under *ibid.*, s.78.

In either case, if there is no rent registered for the dwelling on the certified date, *i.e.* the date the dwelling is fit for occupation following the completion to the satisfaction of the authority of the works under the grant (see s.499, above), it is a condition that the applicant will apply for registration (or "refer" the contract to the Rent Tribunal) within 14 days from the start of the regulated tenancy or restricted contract, and that any application or reference will be diligently proceeded with and not withdrawn.

Premiums

Premiums are prohibited in connection with the grant, renewal or continuance of a protected (*i.e.* contractual, regulated) tenancy: Rent Act 1977, s.119. They are also prohibited in relation to restricted contracts if, but only if, a rent is already registered for the premises: *ibid.*, s.122. The condition in this section prohibits premiums in any event, for the purposes of breach of grant condition, and if needs be recovery under s.506, below.

An excessive purchase price for furniture classes as a premium: 1977, s.123. (It is not only a criminal offence to seek a premium in this or any other way in which it is prohibited under the 1977 Act, but also to ask a price for furniture, as a condition of the grant, renewal or continuance of a protected tenancy or a restricted contract of which the rent is registered with the Rent Tribunal, without providing a written inventory, specifying the price sought for each item, *i.e.* even if it is not exorbitant or excessive: 1977, s.124). Unlawful premiums are recoverable by the persons by whom they are paid: 1977, s.125.

Premium is defined in 1977, s.128, as "any fine or other like sum, any other pecuniary consideration in addition to rent, and any sum paid by way of a deposit, other than one which does not exceed one-sixth of the annual rent and is reasonable in relation to the potential liability in respect of which it is paid."

An actual payment of money may not be required. In *Elmdene Estates Ltd.* v. *White* [1960] A.C. 528, H.L., an agency agreed to secure a tenancy for vendors of a house, on terms that they would pay a lower sum on the purchase, so that the reduction in purchase price qualified as a premium on the grant of the tenancy: "The phrase 'any other pecuniary consideration' is apt to cover any other consideration that sounds in money to the tenant, either in the way of involving him in a payment of money or of foregoing a receipt of money" (*per* Lord Keith of Avonholm, at p. 543).

Duration and enforceability of grant conditions

505.—(1) A grant condition is in force—
(*a*) in the case of a condition imposed under section 503 (further conditions) with respect to a dwelling which on the date on which the application is approved is in a housing action area, for the period of seven years beginning with the certified date, and
(*b*) in any other case, for the period of five years beginning with that date;
but subject to the provisions of sections 506 and 507 (repayment of grant).
(2) So long as a grant condition remains in force—
(*a*) it is binding on any person, other than a housing authority or registered housing association, who is for the time being the owner of the dwelling to which the grant relates, and
(*b*) it is enforceable against all other persons having an interest in the dwelling as if it were a condition of the terms of every lease, agreement for a lease or statutory tenancy of, or of property including, the dwelling.
(3) A grant condition is a local land charge.

DEFINITIONS
"certified date": s.499.
"dwelling": s.525.
"grant": s.460.
"housing action area": s.239.
"housing authority": s.4.
"owner": s.525.
"registered housing association": s.5.

GENERAL NOTE
Grant conditions normally remain in force for five years from the certified date, but if the property was in a Housing Action Area under Part VIII, above, on the date the grant was approved, a condition under ss.503–504, above, *i.e.* further conditions governing, particularly, types of letting, will remain in force for seven years: subs. (1).

So long as the grant condition is in force, it binds any owner for the time being, other than a registered housing association, or a housing authority (see s.4, above, *i.e.* a local housing authority under ss.1, 2, above, a new town corporation or the Development Board for Rural Wales): subs. (2). As to "owner", see s.525, below. The grant condition is enforceable against anyone else with any interest in the dwelling: under this provision, an owner can enforce the tenant's requirement to provide him with information in order to enable him to answer the authority's request for information under ss.502 or 504, above, *i.e.* by way of proceedings for breach of a term of the tenancy.

Repayment of grant for breach of condition

506.—(1) In the event of a breach of a grant condition, the local housing authority may demand that the owner for the time being of the dwelling repay the grant forthwith.
(2) The amount payable is—
(*a*) where the grant related to a single dwelling, the amount of the grant, or
(*b*) where the grant related to two or more dwellings, such part of the grant as appears to the authority to be referable to the dwelling to which the breach relates,
together with compound interest on that amount or part as from the certified date, calculated at such reasonable rate as the local housing authority may determine and with yearly rests.
(3) The authority may determine not to make such a demand or may demand a lesser amount.
(4) On satisfaction of the liability arising from a demand under this section, all conditions of the grant cease to be in force with respect to the dwelling in question.

DEFINITIONS
 "certified date": s.499.
 "dwelling": s.525.
 "local housing authority": ss.1, 2.
 "owner": s.525.

GENERAL NOTE
 On breach, the authority are entitled (but not obliged) to demand repayment of the whole of the grant paid, together with *compound* interest at the *reasonable* rate the authority determine. There is no reduction for "years of compliance" (*cf.* repayment of discount under Parts II and V, ss.35 and 155, above). If the grant related to more than one dwelling, the authority are to apportion it. Once the money has been repaid, all grant conditions cease to be in force: subs. (4). The entitlement to interest continues until payment, and does not end with (by merger in) the judgment: *Ealing London Borough Council v. El Isaacs* [1980] 1 W.L.R. 932, C.A.
 Note that the whole of the money can be reclaimed from "the owner for the time being": see notes to s.502, above. The owner for the time being will have been on notice because of the registration as the condition as a local land charge under s.505, above.
 As to voluntary repayment, see s.507, below. As to repayment for breach of completion of works condition, see s.512, below. As to "breach", *e.g.* by cessation of interest, before payment or before complete payment, see s.515, below.

Voluntary repayment of grant

 507.—(1) If at any time while a condition of a grant remains in force—
    (*a*) the owner of the dwelling to which the condition relates pays to the local housing authority by whom the grant was made the amount specified in section 506(2) (amount repayable for breach of condition), or
    (*b*) a mortgagee of the interest of the owner in that dwelling, being a mortgagee entitled to exercise a power of sale, makes such a payment,
all conditions of the grant cease to be in force with respect to that dwelling.
 (2) An amount paid under subsection (1) by a mortgagee shall be treated as part of the sums secured by the mortgage and may be discharged accordingly.
 (3) The purposes authorised for the application of capital money by—
    section 73 of the Settled Land Act 1925,
       that section as applied by section 28 of the Law of Property Act 1925 in relation to trusts for sale, and
    section 26 of the Universities & College Estates Act 1925,
include the making of payments under subsection (1).

DEFINITIONS
 "dwelling": s.525.
 "grant": s.460.
 "local housing authority": ss.1, 2.
 "owner": s.525.

GENERAL NOTE
 An owner can voluntarily repay the grant, to the same amount as is recoverable on breach under s.506, *i.e.* up to the whole grant, plus compound interest at the reasonable rate determined by the authority, calculated on an annual basis. Repayment may be made by a mortgagee entitled to exercise the power of sale: see notes to s.436, above. The amount so repaid is treated as part of the sum secured by the mortgage, *i.e.* may be repaid out of the proceeds of the sale: subs. (2). On repayment, all grant conditions cease to have effect.

Main grants: supplementary provisions

Standard amenities and maximum eligible amounts

508.—(1) The standard amenities for the purposes of this Part are those described in column 1 of the following Table (subject to the Notes below); and the maximum eligible amounts for each description of amenity are those shown in column 2 of the Table.

TABLE

Description of amenity	Maximum eligible amount	
	Premises in Greater London	Premises elsewhere
A fixed bath or shower (see Notes 1 and 2)	450	340
A hot and cold water supply at a fixed bath or shower (see Notes 1 and 2)	570	430
A wash-hand basin	175	130
A hot and cold water supply at a wash-hand basin	300	230
A sink	450	340
A hot and cold water supply at a sink	380	290
A water closet (see Note 3)	680	515

NOTES

1. A fixed bath or shower shall be in a bathroom, unless Note 2 applies.

2. If it is not reasonably practicable for the fixed bath or shower to be in a bathroom but it is reasonably practicable for it to be provided with a hot and cold water supply, it need not be in a bathroom but may be in any part of the dwelling which is not a bedroom.

3. A water closet shall, if reasonably practicable, be in, and accessible from within, the dwelling or, where the dwelling is part of a larger building, in such a position in that building as to be readily accessible from the dwelling.

4. Notes 2 and 3 do not apply for the purposes of special grants.

(2) The Secretary of State may by order vary the provisions of the above Table and Notes.

(3) An order—

(*a*) may make different provision with respect to different cases or descriptions of case, including different provision for different areas,

(*b*) may contain such transitional or other supplementary provisions as appear to the Secretary of State to be expedient, and

(*c*) shall be made by statutory instrument which shall be subject to annulment in pursuance of a resolution of the House of Commons.

GENERAL NOTE

See ss.468, 474 and 483, as to when these are required; see ss.480 and 488 for application of the amounts. The text reflects the most recent variation, under S.I. 1983 No. 613.

Meaning of "the appropriate percentage"

509.—(1) The "appropriate percentage" for the purpose of determining the amount or maximum amount of a grant shall be prescribed by order of the Secretary of State made with the consent of the Treasury.

(2) An order—

(*a*) may make different provision with respect to different cases or descriptions of case, including different provision for different areas, and

(*b*) shall be made by statutory instrument and shall not be made unless a draft of it has been laid before and approved by resolution of the House of Commons.

(3) An order has effect with respect to applications for grants approved after such date as may be specified in the order, and the specified date shall not be earlier than the date of the laying of the draft.

GENERAL NOTE

This is applicable to each of the main grants, and is described in the greatest details in the notes to s.473, above; see also notes to ss.482, 490 and 498, above. Where a balance has to be financed privately, *i.e.* because works required to achieve the relevant standard are in excess of those which are eligible, or to meet the part of the eligible expense not covered by the appropriate percentage of the grant under this section, a loan may be available from the authority under s.435, above.

Statement of reasons for refusing application or giving less than maximum grant

510. If the local housing authority—

(a) do not approve an application for a grant, or

(b) where the amount of the grant is discretionary, fix the amount at less than the appropriate percentage of the eligible expense,

they shall give the applicant a statement in writing of their reasons for doing so.

DEFINITIONS

"appropriate percentage": s.509.

"grant": s.460.

"local housing authority": ss.1, 2.

GENERAL NOTE

The authority must provide a statement of their reasons for (a) refusing a grant, or (b) paying less than the full amount available, where the grant is discretionary. In the case of mandatory grants, there can be no refusal, and no reduction on the maximum available (*i.e.* estimated cost, limited by eligible expense, reduced to appropriate percentage); otherwise, a grant may be refused, or less than the maximum paid. The discretionary grants are: improvement grants under s.467, above; special grants not within s.486, above (s.483, above); and, repairs grants not within s.494, above (s.491, above). As to the proper approach to exercise of discretion, see notes to s.470, above.

Payment of grants: general

511.—(1) Where the local housing authority have approved an application for a grant, they shall pay the grant, subject to section 512 (conditions as to completion of works).

(2) The grant may be paid—

(a) after the completion of the works towards the cost of which it is payable, or

(b) in part by instalments as the works progress and the balance after completion of the works.

(3) Where a grant is paid in instalments, the aggregate of the instalments paid before the completion of the works shall not at any time exceed—

(a) in the case of an intermediate grant, the appropriate percentage of the total cost of the works so far executed;

(b) in the case of an improvement grant, special grant or repairs grant, an amount bearing to that total cost the same proportion as the amount of the grant fixed by the authority bears to the eligible expense.

DEFINITIONS

"grant": s.460.

"improvement grant": s.467.

"intermediate grant": s.474.

"local housing authority": ss.1, 2.
"repairs grant": s.491.
"special grant": s.483.

GENERAL NOTE

This governs payment of grant. It is, however, subject to s.515, below, if the applicant ceases to have a relevant interest before payment (of whole or part of grant).

The basic proposition is in subs. (1), that grant *shall be paid*, subject to completion under s.512. There is no discretion to withhold payment, even of a discretionary grant, once all the works have satisfactorily been completed. Assuming inspection and satisfaction, then subject to a normal, but minimal, period following claim for administration of payment, the money is a statutory debt and recoverable as such, if needs be by action (which, in turn, would carry with it the right to recover interest—in the county court, under County Courts Act 1974; in the High Court, under R.S.C., Ord. 42, in each case at the prescribed statutory rate).

If the authority are not in funds, they would accordingly be entitled to pay interest on the debt of their own motion: *e.g.* under Local Government Act 1972, s.111.

Grant may be paid after satisfactory completion of works, or in instalments. Instalments, or "stage payments" as they are sometimes called, are entirely discretionary. However, they are subject to the limits set out in subs. (3). In the case of the mandatory intermediate grant, the appropriate percentage (see s.482, above) of the *total* cost of works thus far executed (not scaled down by reference to eligible expense under s.481, above, although of course to no more than that amount). In the case of the predominantly discretionary grants, the more complex formula in subs. (3)(*b*) applies, *i.e.* the stage payments are scaled down in relation to the total actually payable.

As to non-completion of works *following* a stage payment, see s.512(4), below.

Payment of grants: conditions as to completion of works

512.—(1) The payment of a grant, or part of a grant, is conditional upon the works or the corresponding part being executed to the satisfaction of the local housing authority.

(2) In approving an application for a grant the authority may require as a condition of paying the grant that the relevant works are carried out within such time, not being less than twelve months, as the authority may specify or such further time as they may allow.

(3) In particular, where the authority are satisfied that the relevant works cannot or could not have been carried out without the carrying out of additional works, they may allow further time as the time within which the relevant works and the additional works are to be carried out.

(4) If an instalment of a grant is paid before the completion of the works and the works are not completed within—

(*a*) the time specified by the authority under subsection (2) or such further time as they may allow, or

(*b*) if no time was so specified, twelve months from the date on which the instalment is paid or such further time as the authority may allow,

the authority may demand the repayment forthwith by the applicant or his personal representatives of that instalment, and any further sums paid by the authority, together with interest at such reasonable rate as the authority may determine from the date of payment until repayment.

DEFINITIONS

"grant": s.460.
"local housing authority": ss.1, 2.
"relevant works": s.461.

GENERAL NOTE

Payment is entirely dependent on the execution of works to the satisfaction of the authority. No time for completion is necessarily implied, *save* in a case where the authority have not expressly specified a time *and* have made stage payments under s.511, above, in which case twelve months is implied by subs. (4)(*b*). The authority are, however, entitled to impose a *completion* condition, but not of less than twelve months. This time may be extended periodically, and in particular may be extended if the works cannot or could not have been carried out without unforeseeable additional works: subs. (3).

The limitation to a 12-month minimum is arduous for authorities and in the case of many minor grants (*i.e.* grants for relatively small amounts of work), generous to applicants. There is no provision for a "commencement" condition, which would undoubtedly act as an incentive to applicants to see work through to its end as fast as practicable. As authorities are on annual budgets (*cf.* notes to s.421, above), the constraints mean in effect that relatively little can be "turned around" within a current financial year. Although the burden of what they will have "committed forward" is noted in their Housing Investment Programme Applications, they will not know for certain how much is to be allowed until shortly before the start of a financial year: see notes to s.421, above.

A statement of commencement intention may be permissible in the case of a discretionary grant: see notes to s.503, above.

Subs. (4)

If stage payments are made under s.511, above, and the works are not completed within a time specified under subs. (2) (perhaps as extended) or twelve months if no such time is specified, repayment, with *simple* interest (*cf.* s.506, above), from date of payment to repayment, may be demanded by the authority.

Special cases: parsonages, applications by charities, &c.

513.—(1) This section applies to—

(a) an application for a grant in respect of glebe land or the residence house of an ecclesiastical benefice made, during a period when the benefice is vacant, by a sequestrator of the profits of the benefice, and

(b) an application for a grant made by a charity or on behalf of a charity by the charity trustees of the charity.

(2) The following provisions do not apply to an application to which this section applies—

section 463(1) (preliminary condition: interest of applicant in the property),

section 464 (preliminary condition: certificate as to future occupation), and

sections 499 to 504 (grant conditions as to future occupation, &c.).

DEFINITIONS
"charity": s.622.
"charity trustees": s.622.
"grant": s.460.

GENERAL NOTE
This section disapplies occupation certificates and conditions in the cases stated. As to charity, and charity trustees, see s.622, below.

Power of local housing authority to carry out works which would attract grant

514.—(1) The local housing authority may by agreement with a person having the requisite interest execute at his expense—

(a) any works towards the cost of which a grant under this Part is payable or might be paid on an application duly made and approved, and

(b) any further works which it is in their opinion necessary or desirable to execute together with the works mentioned in paragraph (a).

(2) The "requisite interest" means an interest in every parcel of land on which the works are to be carried out which is either—

(a) an estate in fee simple absolute in possession, or

(b) a term of years absolute of which not less than five years remains unexpired.

(3) The works with respect to which an agreement may be made under this section include, if the works are to be carried out in a general improvement area—

  (*a*) any works the carrying out of which will or might be assisted under section 255(1)(*a*) (improvement of amenities or dwellings), or

  (*b*) any works of external repair (including decorative repair) or replacement.

DEFINITIONS
  "dwelling" s.525.
  "general improvement area": s.253.
  "grant": s.460.
  "local housing authority": ss.1, 2.

GENERAL NOTE
  This section permits "agency arrangements", under which the authority "execute" grant-aided works, or works which could have been grant-aided, and any additional works they consider necessary or desirable to carry out together with such works (subs. (1)(*b*)) and, if the property is within a general improvement area under Part VIII, above, external works or works under s.255(1)(*a*), above: subs. (3). Note that external works include repair, replacement and decorative repair: the purpose is to encourage "enveloping": see notes to s.244, above; see also D.O.E. Circulars 29/82 and 26/84.
  The person for whom the authority carry out the works must have a requisite interest as defined in subs. (2). A tenant's application under s.463, above, may still lead to agency works provided the person with whom the arrangement is made has a requisite interest, for the works will still be grant-aided or grant-aidable.
  "Execution" seems amply wide to cover not only doing the works themselves, *e.g.* by a Direct Labour Organisation (but *cf.* the provisions of Local Government, Planning and Land Act 1980, Part III), but also commissioning and supervising works: "Many owners have been deterred from improving their houses because they do not know how to set about it, or because they do not relish making the detailed arrangements . . . The local authority would be in a position to supervise the improvement works; and to make sure that the work was well done at reasonable cost . . . " (D.O.E. Circular 63/69, para. 9).

Grants restricted to applicant and his personal representatives

  515.—(1) In relation to a grant or an application for a grant, references in the preceding provisions of this Part, and in subsection (2) below, to the applicant shall be construed in relation to any time after his death as a reference to his personal representatives.

  (2) If, before the certified date, the applicant ceases to have an owner's interest or ceases to be a tenant of the dwelling—

  (*a*) no grant shall be paid or, as the case may be, no further instalments shall be paid, and

  (*b*) the local housing authority may demand that any instalment of the grant which has been paid, be repaid forthwith, together with interest from the date on which it was paid until repayment at such reasonable rate as the authority may determine.

  (3) In subsection (2) "owner's interest" and "tenant" have the same meaning as in section 463(1) (preliminary condition: interest of applicant in the property).

DEFINITIONS
  "certified date": s.499.
  "dwelling": s.525.
  "grant": s.460.
  "local housing authority": ss.1, 2.
  "owner": s.525.

GENERAL NOTE
  Under subs. (1), "applicant" is to be taken as including his personal representatives in any of the preceding provisions of this Part, *i.e.* including recovery, and for the purposes of the rest of this section.

Subsection (2) applies if before the date when the authority certify the dwelling as fit for occupation following satisfactory completion of works (s.499, above), the applicant ceases to have the appropriate interest, the grant is not to be paid, or no further stage payments are to be made, and the authority are entitled to recover instalments already paid, together with simple interest thereon (*cf.* s.506, above).

Contributions by Secretary of State

516.—(1) The Secretary of State may make contributions towards the expense incurred by a local housing authority in making a grant.

(2) The contributions shall be annual sums—

(*a*) payable in respect of a period of 20 years beginning with the financial year in which the works towards the cost of which the grant was made were completed, and

(*b*) equal to a percentage of the annual loan charges referable to the amount of the grant.

(3) Subject to any order under section 517 (power to vary percentages), the percentage is—

(*a*) 90 per cent. in a case where the premises to which the application relates are in a general improvement area or housing action area, and

(*b*) 75 per cent. in any other case;

and, subject to subsection (4), the applicable percentage shall be determined by reference to the state of affairs at the date when the application is approved.

(4) Where on that date the premises are in an area declared to be a housing action area and the Secretary of State subsequently notifies the local housing authority—

(*a*) that the area is no longer to be such an area, or

(*b*) that land on which the premises are situated is to be excluded from the area,

he may (without prejudice to his discretion under subsection (1) not to make a contribution) make a contribution on the basis that the applicable percentage is 75 per cent.

(5) The annual loan charges referable to the amount of a grant are the annual sums which, in the opinion of the Secretary of State, would fall to be provided by a housing authority for the payment of interest on, and the repayment of, a loan of that amount repayable over a period of 20 years.

(6) Contributions under this section are payable subject to such conditions as to records, certificates, audit or otherwise as the Secretary of State may, with the approval of the Treasury, impose.

DEFINITIONS
"general improvement area": s.253.
"grant": s.460.
"housing action area": s.239.
"local housing authority": ss.1, 2.

GENERAL NOTE
In many ways the key provision, from the point of view of authorities, and in terms of how well this Part of the Act is implemented, this section deals with central government subsidy for the exercise. Subsidy takes the form, as it does under Part XVI, below, of payment of a proportion of the loan charges (assessed by the Secretary of State and therefore notional rather than actual—subs. (5)) over a 20 year period: subs. (2).

Payment is within the discretion of the Secretary of State: subs. (1). He may impose conditions as to records, certificates, audit or otherwise: subs. (6). Authorities include their expenditure under this Part in their Housing Investment Programme Applications (see notes to s.421, above), both as to past expenditure and expenditure committed by a date specified in the annual notes for guidance for completion of that Application, and as to their aspirations for the following year. A number of circumstances when the Secretary of State will not normally pay subsidy are identified in D.O.E. Circular 26/85.

The Secretary of State does not normally specify the expenditure under this Part in the H.I.P. Allocation, although he can do so and has done so in the past, for the purposes of Part VIII, Local Government, Planning and Land Act 1980 (see *ibid.*, Sched. 12, para. 1, defining grants as "prescribed expenditure" for the purposes of that Act). Authorities' spending on housing improvement grants is accordingly confined by Part VIII, within their housing capital expenditure as a whole (see notes to s.421, above), subject only to virement from other blocks of prescribed expenditure, and a 10 per cent. virement "either way", *i.e.* unspent from a past year, or from the next year's allowance. There is no express power to borrow, so that permission is needed under Local Government Act 1972, s.172 and Sched. 13 and para. 1, but the amounts allowed for the purposes of the 1980 Act will also be allowed for that purpose.

The proportion of the loan charges is as set out in subs. (3), but is variable by order under s.517, below. Where on the date of approval the premises are in a Housing Action Area or General Improvement Area under Part VIII, above, the higher level is applicable. In the case of a Housing Action Area, declaration of which is rescinded, or in a part of the area which is excluded, by the Secretary of State under s.241, above, the Secretary of State may nonetheless pay the higher level of grant-aid: subs. (4).

Subsidy starts with the year in which the grant-aided work is completed (therefore not on discretionary stage payments under s.511): subs. (2). In a year of intense activity, this can cause a distorted impression of the *residual* amount which remains to be borne by the general rate fund, itself confined by the threat of penalty under Part VI, Local Government Planning and Land Act 1980, if spending targets under that Part are exceeded: see notes to s.421, above.

The distortion works in this way. Assuming no stage payments, the authority will not have borne loan charges for the whole of the year in which the grant is paid, *i.e.* a minimal amount will have been paid on the first day of the financial year. Yet the support is *as if* a full year's loan charges had been paid. It is at a relatively high level. Accordingly, the authority could theoretically *receive* more than they have to *pay out*.

In practice, stage payments are made. Nonetheless, the level of support remains such that a much higher proportion than the proportions stated in subs. (3) will in practice be received. Correspondingly, the burden left to the general rate fund is diminished. This distortion may remain so long as activity is at the same, or an increased, general level, for the imbalance on new grants will persist. However, once the level of activity falls off, there is no new corresponding imbalanced income, and the residual cost to the general rate fund will suddenly shoot up.

Power to vary percentages mentioned in s.516

517.—(1) The Secretary of State may by order made with the consent of the Treasury vary either or both of the percentages mentioned in section 516 (contributions by Secretary of State to expense of making grants).

(2) An order—

(*a*) may make different provision with respect to different cases or descriptions of case, including different provision for different areas, and

(*b*) shall be made by statutory instrument and shall not be made unless a draft of it has been laid before and approved by resolution of the House of Commons.

(3) An order has effect with respect to applications for grants approved after such date as may be specified in the order, and the specified date shall not be earlier than the date of the laying of the draft.

DEFINITION
"grant": s.460.

GENERAL NOTE
The levels specified in s.516(3), above, have been varied. Under S.I. 1980 No. 1735, retained in force by Housing (Consequential Provisions) Act 1985, s.2, if the appropriate percentage is 75 per cent. or 90 per cent., the Secretary of State pays 90 per cent. of the loan charges, and if it is 65 per cent. (*i.e.* not within a priority category, nor a case of undue

hardship, but within a general improvement area), the Secretary of State pays 75 per cent. of the loan charges, while in all other cases (*i.e.* 50 per cent. appropriate percentage) it is also 75 per cent., under s.516(3), above: see notes to ss.473, 482, 490, 498, above.

During the period when higher levels of grant-aid were available for intermediate and repairs grants, higher levels of subsidy (95 per cent.) were also available (S.I. 1982 Nos.581 and 1763): see notes to ss.482 and 498, above.

Meaning of "dwelling for a disabled occupant" and related expressions

518.—(1) In this Part "dwelling for a disabled occupant" means a dwelling which—

(*a*) is a disabled occupant's only or main residence when an application for a grant in respect of it is made, or

(*b*) is likely in the opinion of the local housing authority to become a disabled occupant's only or main residence within a reasonable period after the completion of the relevant works,

and "disabled occupant" means a disabled person for whose benefit it is proposed to carry out any of the relevant works.

(2) In subsection (1) "disabled person" means—

(*a*) a person who is registered in pursuance of arrangements made under section 29(1) of the National Assistance Act 1948 (handicapped persons' welfare), or

(*b*) any other person for whose welfare arrangements have been made under that provision or, in the opinion of the welfare authority, might be made under it;

and for this purpose "welfare authority" means the council which is the local authority for the purposes of the Local Authority Social Services Act 1970 for the area in which the dwelling is situated.

(3) In this Part "improvement", in relation to a dwelling for a disabled occupant, includes the doing of works required for making it suitable for his accommodation, welfare or employment.

DEFINITIONS
"dwelling": s.525.
"local housing authority": ss.1, 2.
"relevant works": s.461.

GENERAL NOTE
This section adapts the provisions to the needs of the disabled. Note that the disabled occupant need not be the applicant, but will have to be in occupation as "an only or main residence", see notes to s.81, above. Note, too, that the adaptation may be for the purposes of the accommodation, welfare *or employment* of the disabled occupant: subs. (3).

Meaning of "reasonable repair"

519. In determining what is "reasonable repair", in relation to a dwelling or house, a local housing authority—

(*a*) shall have regard to the age and character of the dwelling or house and locality in which it is situated,

(*b*) for the purposes of an intermediate grant, shall also have regard to the period during which the dwelling is likely to be available for use as a dwelling, and

(*c*) shall disregard the state of internal decorative repair.

DEFINITIONS
"dwelling": s.525.
"intermediate grant": s.474.
"local housing authority": ss.1, 2.

GENERAL NOTE
The formula in subs. (*a*) for determining reasonable repair is the relatively common formula applicable to repair: see Landlord and Tenant Act 1985, s.11; see also Rent Act

1977, s.70. The expression derives from *Calthorpe* v. *McOscar* [1924] 1 K.B. 716: "such repair as, having regard to the age, character and locality of the house, would make it reasonably fit for the occupation of a reasonably minded tenant of the class who would be likely to take it". Likely life of the dwelling is also a consideration in the case of an intermediate grant: it is an express requirement of the standard for an improvement grant in any event, see notes to s.468, above.

The state of internal decorative repair is to be disregarded.

Members of a person's family

520.—(1) A person is a member of another's family within the meaning of this Part if—
  (*a*) he is the spouse of that person, or
  (*b*) he is that person's parent or child.
(2) For the purposes of subsection (1)(*b*)—
  (*a*) a relationship by marriage shall be treated as a relationship by blood,
  (*b*) the stepchild of a person shall be treated as his child, and
  (*c*) an illegitimate child shall be treated as the legitimate child of his mother and reputed father.

Grants for thermal insulation

Schemes for grants for thermal insulation

521.—(1) Local housing authorities shall make grants, in accordance with such schemes as may be prepared and published by the Secretary of State and laid by him before Parliament, towards the cost of works undertaken to improve the thermal insulation of dwellings in their district.
(2) Schemes under this section shall specify—
  (*a*) the descriptions of dwelling and the insulation works qualifying for grants, and
  (*b*) the persons from whom applications may be entertained in respect of different descriptions of dwelling.
(3) The grant shall be such percentage of the cost of the works qualifying for grant, as may be prescribed, or such money sum as may be prescribed, whichever is the less.
(4) A scheme may provide for grants to be made only to those applying on grounds of special need or to be made in those cases on a prescribed higher scale; and for this purpose "special need" shall be determined by reference to such matters personal to the applicant (such as age, disability, bad health and inability without undue hardship to finance the cost of the works) as may be specified in the scheme.
(5) In this section "prescribed" means prescribed by order of the Secretary of State made with the approval of the Treasury.
(6) An order shall be made by statutory instrument which shall be subject to annulment in pursuance of a resolution of the House of Commons.

DEFINITIONS
  "dwelling": s.525.
  "local housing authority": ss.1, 2.

GENERAL NOTE
  This section is the first of the two which restate the Homes Insulation Act 1978, which was conceived as part of a national "energy conservation drive". The schemes are settled by the Secretary of State, and local authorities can only pay grants under them to the financial limits set by the Secretary of State under s.522(2), below.
  The schemes must, by subs. (2), specify *both* the dwellings and works for which a grant is to be available, *and* the potential beneficiaries. The beneficiaries may be defined by reference to special needs within subs. (4). A grant is to be limited by a percentage of the

cost of works, or a fixed amount (subs. (3)), whichever is the less, and may make different provision for persons with different needs (subs. (4)).

The most recent Order under these provisions is S.I. 1983 No. 285, retained in force by Housing (Consequential Provisions) Act 1985, s.2, which specifies percentages and fixed amounts: cases of special need, 90 per cent. or £95; others, 66 per cent. or £69.

The Homes Insulation Scheme 1984, D.O.E. Circular 13/84, as amended, defines "special need" as applications by an applicant who, or whose spouse, is in receipt of supplementary pension, supplementary allowance, or housing benefit, and who, or whose spouse, has attained the age of 65, if a man, or the age of 60, if a woman, or an applicant who, or whose spouse, is in receipt of supplementary allowance or housing benefit, and who, or whose spouse or one of whose dependants, is severely disabled. Severely disabled is itself further defined in the Directions.

Dwellings which qualify for the grant are those constructed or converted before January 1, 1976, except: those without any roof space, those which have already received a grant under what is now this Part, and those in which at any time during the applicant's interest in the property there has been in any part of the roof space insulation material of at least 30mm thickness. This therefore prevents people *replacing* already adequate insulation with the assistance of a grant under the Scheme. However, there are defined exceptions to this "existing insulation exemption", *i.e.* where the insulation is only of a water tank, cylinder, water supply pipe or overflow or expansion pipe, and where it is confined to the roof space in a part of the dwelling which has been added to the original construction.

An application may be entertained from anyone in occupation of the dwelling, or anyone entitled to occupy an unoccupied dwellings, or a landlord or a licensor. However, there can be no application by a local authority, police authority, Commission for the New Towns, development corporation, Housing Corporation, Development Board for Rural Wales, registered housing association, or a housing co-operative under s.27, above: see ss.4, 5, above.

Both location of the insulation to be provided, and the materials which may be used, are defined, together with thickness. To qualify, at the end of the works insulation must be provided throughout the roof space, other than a part access to which cannot reasonably practicably be obtained, or where absence of insulation is needed for adequate ventilation of the roof space, or below a water tank, or which is already insulated additional roof space; in addition, hot water tanks or cylinders, and water supply overflow and expansion pipes, must be insulated.

Finance and administration of schemes under s.521

522.—(1) Finance for the making of grants under section 521 shall be provided to local housing authorities from time to time by the Secretary of State.

(2) A local housing authority is not required, nor has power, to make grants under section 521 in any year beyond those for which the Secretary of State has notified them that finance is committed for that year in respect of the authority's district.

(3) In the administration of grants under section 521 local housing authorities shall comply with any directions given to them by the Secretary of State after consultation with their representative organisations.

(4) The Secretary of State may, in particular, give direction as to—

(a) the way in which applications for grants are to be dealt with, and the priorities to be observed between applicants and different categories of applicant, and

(b) the means of authenticating applications, so that grants are only given in proper cases, and of ensuring that the works are carried out to any standard specified in the applicable scheme.

(5) The Secretary of State shall, with the approval of the Treasury, pay such sums as he thinks reasonable in respect of the administrative expenses incurred by local housing authorities in operating schemes under section 521.

DEFINITION
"local housing authority": ss.1, 2.

GENERAL NOTE

This governs the administration of the Scheme under s.521, above. Each year, the Secretary of State expressly notifies the authority how much is available, and the authority cannot pay grants beyond that limit: subs. (2). The Directions govern such matters as how to prioritise applicants, authentication of claims and the Secretary of State's administration allowance (currently, £2.50 for each application accepted, and £5 for each grant paid: see D.O.E. Circular 13/84, para. 20).

Miscellaneous

Assistance for provision of separate service pipe for water supply

523.—(1) The local housing authority may, if they think fit, give assistance in respect of the provision of a separate service pipe for a house which has a piped supply of water from a water main but no separate service pipe.

(2) The assistance shall be by way of a grant in respect of all or part of the expenses incurred in the provision of the separate service pipe.

(3) The reference in subsection (2) to the expenses incurred in the provision of the separate service pipe includes, in a case where all or part of the works are carried out by statutory water undertakers (whether in exercise of default powers or otherwise), sums payable to the undertakers by the owner of the house, or any other person, for carrying out the works.

DEFINITION

"local housing authority": ss.1, 2.

GENERAL NOTE

This is a wholly discretionary power to make grants, up to the full cost, in the provision of separate service pipes. It is often used in connection with area action under Part VIII, but is not confined to such areas.

Contributions under superseded enactments

524. Schedule 19 has effect with respect to contributions payable under superseded enactments

GENERAL NOTE

Sched. 19 maintains payments under pre-1974 grant legislation.

General supplementary provisions

Minor definitions

525. In this Part—

"agricultural population" means—

(*a*) persons whose employment or latest employment is or was employment in agriculture or in an industry mainly dependent on agriculture, and

(*b*) the dependents of those persons;

and for this purpose "agriculture" includes dairy-farming and poultry-farming and the use of land as grazing, meadow or pasture land, or orchard or osier land or woodland, or for market gardens or nursery grounds;

"charity trustees" has the same meaning as in the Charities Act 1960;

"dwelling" means a building or part of a building occupied or intended to be occupied as a separate dwelling, together with any yard, garden, outhouses and appurtenances belonging to it or usually enjoyed with it;

"house in multiple occupation" means a house which is occupied by persons who do not form a single household, exclusive of any part of the house which is occupied as a separate dwelling by persons who form a single household;

"improvement" includes alteration and enlargement;

"owner", in relation to a dwelling, means the person who—

(*a*) is for the time being entitled to receive from a lessee of the dwelling (or would be so entitled if the dwelling were let) a rent of not less than two-thirds of the net annual value of the dwelling; and

(*b*) is not himself liable as lessee of the dwelling, or of property which includes the dwelling, to pay such a rent to a superior landlord.

GENERAL NOTE

"Charity trustees": see s.622, below.

"Dwelling": see notes to s.460, above.

"House in multiple occupation": see notes to s.460, above.

"Improvement": see notes to s.471, above.

Index of defined expressions: Part XV

526. The following Table shows provisions defining or otherwise explaining expressions used in this Part (other than provisions defining or explaining an expression in the same section):—

agricultural population	section 525
applicant	section 515(1)
appropriate percentage	section 509
certificate of availability for letting	section 464(5)
certificate of owner-occupation	section 464(3), (4)
certified date	section 499(3)
charity	section 622
charity trustees	section 525
co-operative housing association	section 5(2)
district (of a local housing authority)	section 2(1)
dwelling	section 525
dwelling for a disabled occupant	section 518
eligible expense	sections 472, 481, 489 and 497
fit for human habitation	section 604
general improvement area	section 253
grant (without more)	section 460(1)
house in multiple occupation	section 525
housing action area	section 239
housing association	section 5(1)
housing authority	section 4(*a*)
improvement	sections 518(3) and 525
improvement grant	sections 460 and 467
initial period	section 499(2)
intermediate grant	sections 460 and 474
lessee and let	section 621
local housing authority	section 1, 2(2)
member of family	section 520
owner	section 525

protected occupancy	section 622
protected tenancy	section 622
reasonable repair	section 519
registered and unregistered (in relation to a housing association)	section 5(4)
relevant works	section 461(2)
repairs grant	sections 460 and 491
restricted contract	section 622
secure tenancy	section 79
special grant	sections 460 and 483
standard amenity	section 508(1)
statutory tenancy	section 622
tenancy and tenant	section 621

PART XVI

ASSISTANCE FOR OWNERS OF DEFECTIVE HOUSING

Eligibility for assistance

Eligibility for assistance

527. A person is eligible for assistance under this Part in respect of a dwelling if—
(*a*) he is an individual who is not a trustee, a trustee for beneficiaries who are all individuals or a personal representative,
(*b*) the dwelling is a defective dwelling within the meaning of this Part by virtue of a designation under section 528 (designation by Secretary of State) or section 559 (designation under local scheme),
(*c*) he holds a relevant interest in the dwelling, as defined in section 530, and
(*d*) the conditions specified in section 531 (conditions of eligibility: disposal by public sector authority, etc.) are satisfied;
but subject to section 533 (exceptions to eligibility).

DEFINITIONS
"designation": ss.528, 559.
"dwelling": s.575.
"relevant interest": s.530.

GENERAL NOTE
The purpose of this Part of the Act is to make provision for those who purchased "system-built" housing from local or public authorities, which housing is defective, and which, because the defective nature of the housing is generally known, has been substantially reduced in value. The buildings in question have been constructed since 1945 (see *Hansard* H.C. Vol. 56, col. 52). System-building was predominantly to be found in the public sector, but the right to buy provisions of Part V, above, and voluntary sales programmes, have meant that some of it has found its way into private ownership.
A limited scheme, to assist those who had purchased Airey Houses, was first introduced in 1982, and then extended, by means of what are now Part XV grants, until replaced by the Housing Defects Act 1984, now this Part. The Part applies only to "individuals", *i.e.* not corporate bodies, not including trustees unless all the beneficiaries are individuals, and to personal representatives.

Designation of defective dwellings by Secretary of State

528.—(1) The Secretary of State may designate as a class buildings each of which consists of or includes one or more dwellings if it appears to him that—

(*a*) buildings in the proposed class are defective by reason of their design or construction, and

(*b*) by virtue of the circumstances mentioned in paragraph (*a*) having become generally known, the value of some or all of the dwellings concerned has been substantially reduced.

(2) A dwelling which is, or is included in, a building in a class so designated is referred to in this Part as a "defective dwelling"; and in this Part, in relation to such a dwelling—

(*a*) "the qualifying defect" means what, in the opinion of the Secretary of State, is wrong with the buildings in that class, and

(*b*) "the cut-off date" means the date by which, in the opinion of the Secretary of State, the circumstances mentioned in subsection (1)(*a*) became generally known.

(3) A designation shall describe the qualifying defect and specify—

(*a*) the cut-off date,

(*b*) the date (being a date falling on or after the cut-off date) on which the designation is to come into operation, and

(*c*) the period within which persons may seek assistance under this Part in respect of the defective dwellings concerned.

(4) A designation may make different provision in relation to England and Wales; subject to that, a designated class shall not be described by reference to the area in which the buildings concerned are situated.

(5) Notice of a designation shall be published in the London Gazette.

(6) Any question arising as to whether a building is or was at any time in a class designated under this section shall be determined by the Secretary of State.

DEFINITION

"dwellings": s.575.

GENERAL NOTE

This section provides for designation by the Secretary of State: *cf.* local designations by local authorities, see s.559, below. The criteria are that the dwelling, or if the dwelling is part of a larger building, *e.g.* a block of flats, the building in which the dwelling is situated, is of defective design or construction, and that this circumstance has become generally known, resulting in reduction in value of some or all of the dwellings of that class. Subject to local authority designation (see s.559, below), it is for the Secretary of State to decide whether a building is or was at any time within a designated class: see subs. (6). Once designated, the dwelling is known as a "defective dwelling", whether it is the dwelling which has been designated, or the building of which the dwelling is a part: see subs. (2).

A designation must describe the "qualifying defect", *i.e.* that which the Secretary of State considers to be wrong with the design or construction of the class in question (see subs. (2)(*a*)), the "cut-off date", *i.e.* the date by which the defective nature of the class became generally known (see subs. (2)(*b*)), the date when the designation is to come into operation, and the period during which assistance may be sought: see subs. (3). A designation may only distinguish as between England and Wales, and not otherwise between areas: see subs. (4). Notice of designation is to be published in the *London Gazette*: see subs. (5). There are analogous provisions covering local designations: see ss.559–561, below. Local authorities are also under a publicity duty, whether a designation is national or local: see s.562.

The Housing Defects (Prefabricated Concrete Dwellings) (England and Wales) Designations 1984 (October 31 and November 1, 1984—Department of the Environment/Welsh Office), which remain in force by Housing (Consequential Provisions) Act 1985, s.2, incorporate 22 designations of classes of dwelling, each defined (in part) by diagram, but each of which suffers from the same qualifying defect (*viz.* "Ineffective protection of the embedded steel in the reinforced concrete loadbearing parts of the buildings"), all with the cut-off date of April 26, 1984 save for Airey Houses (September 8, 1982) and each with the same period for seeking assistance, (*viz.* 10 years from December 1, 1984, on which date the designations came into operation):

(1) Airey; (2) Boot; (3) Cornish; (4) Dorran; (5) Dyke; (6) Gregory; (7) Myton; (8) Newland; (9) Orlit; (10) Parkinson; (11) Reema Hollow Panel; (12) Schindler and Hawksley SGS; (13) Stent; (14) Stonecrete; (15) Tarran; (16) Underdown; (17) Unity and Butterley; (18) Waller; (19) Wates; (20) Wessex; (21) Winget; (22) Woolaway.

Variation or revocation of designation

529.—(1) The Secretary of State may—

(*a*) vary a designation under section 528, but not so as to vary the cut-off date, or

(*b*) revoke such a designation.

(2) The Secretary of State may by a variation of the designation extend the period referred to in section 528(3)(*c*) (period within which assistance must be applied for) whether or not it has expired.

(3) The variation or revocation of a designation does not affect the operation of the provisions of this Part in relation to a dwelling if, before the variation or revocation comes into operation, the dwelling is a defective dwelling by virtue of the designation in question and an application for assistance under this Part has been made.

(4) Notice of the variation or revocation of a designation shall be published in the London Gazette.

DEFINITIONS
"cut-off date": ss.528, 559.
"designation": ss.528, 559.

GENERAL NOTE
The Secretary of State may vary or revoke a designation, including by extending the period during which assistance may be sought (currently 10 years from December 1, 1984, see notes to s.528, above), but not so as to vary the cut-off date (April 26, 1984, for all the classes currently designated except Airey, which is September 8, 1982, see notes to s.528, above), nor so as to affect the operation of the provisions of this Part retrospectively, *i.e.* if an application for assistance has already been made. Notice of the variation or revocation must, like notice of designation itself, be published in the *London Gazette* (*cf.* notes to s.528, above): subs. (4).

Meaning of "relevant interest"

530.—(1) In this Part "relevant interest", in relation to a dwelling, means the freehold or a long tenancy, not being in either case subject to a long tenancy.

(2) A tenancy is a long tenancy for this purpose, subject to subsection (3), if it is—

(*a*) a tenancy granted for a term certain exceeding 21 years, whether or not it is (or may become) terminable before the end of that term by notice given by or to the tenant or by re-entry, forfeiture or otherwise,

(*b*) a tenancy granted in pursuance of Part V (the right to buy), or

(*c*) a tenancy for a term fixed by law under a grant with a covenant or obligation for perpetual renewal, unless it is a tenancy by sub-demise from one which is not a long tenancy.

(3) A tenancy is not a long tenancy for this purpose if it is—

(*a*) an interest created by way of security and liable to termination by the exercise of a right of redemption or otherwise, or

(*b*) a secure tenancy.

(4) References in this Part to an interest in a dwelling are to an interest in land which is or includes the dwelling.

DEFINITION
"dwelling": s.575.

GENERAL NOTE
This section defines the "relevant interest" which an applicant for assistance under this Part must enjoy. The applicant must be an individual, not a corporate body, not including trustees unless all the beneficiaries are individuals, but including personal representatives:

see s.527(2), above. The relevant interest must be a freehold, or a long tenancy. As to shared ownership leases (see above, s.143), see s.567, below; as to assistance for mortgagees, see s.568, below.

Long tenancy for the purpose of this Part means (1) a term certain for more than 21 years (whether or not terminable by landlord or tenant), (2) a tenancy granted pursuant to Part V, right to buy, which can include a tenancy for less than 21 years (*cf.* notes to s.115, above), or (3) a tenancy for a term fixed by law under a grant with a covenant or obligation for perpetual renewal (*i.e.* 2,000 years under s.145 and Sched. 15, Law of Property Act 1922), unless it is a sub-tenancy from a tenancy which is not itself a long tenancy. The first of these is a lease which will not be a secure tenancy: see s.79 and Sched. 1. Neither secure tenancies, nor leases created by way of mortgage, qualify: subs. (3).

Note that under s.563, a local authority may give notice to a prospective purchaser of a defective dwelling, in effect that if he proceeds he will not be within the provisions of this Part.

Conditions of eligibility: disposal by public sector authority, etc.

531.—(1) The conditions referred to in section 527(*d*) (eligibility for assistance) are that there has been a disposal by a public sector authority of a relevant interest in the dwelling and that either of the following sets of conditions is satisfied.

(2) The first set of conditions is that—

(*a*) the disposal by a public sector authority was made before the cut-off date, and

(*b*) there has been no disposal for value by any person of a relevant interest in the dwelling on or after that date.

(3) The second set of conditions is that—

(*a*) a person to whom section 527 applies acquired a relevant interest in the dwelling on a disposal for value occurring within the period of twelve months beginning with the cut-off date,

(*b*) he was unaware on the date of the disposal of the association of the dwelling with the qualifying defect,

(*c*) the value by reference to which the price for the disposal was calculated did not take any, or any adequate, account of the qualifying defect, and

(*d*) if the cut-off date had fallen immediately after the date of the disposal, the first set of conditions would have been satisfied.

(4) For the purposes of this section where a public sector authority hold an interest in a dwelling a disposal of the interest by or under an enactment shall be treated as a disposal by the authority.

DEFINITIONS

"cut-off date": ss.528, 559.
"disposal": s.532.
"dwelling": s.575.
"public sector authority": ss.573, 574.
"relevant interest": s.530.

GENERAL NOTE

This section defines the conditions for qualification for assistance under a national scheme (*cf.* s.559, below, for local schemes), referable to the applicant as distinct from to the dwelling itself (*cf.* ss.528, 529) or to the nature of the applicant's interest (*cf.* s.530). Subject to the exceptions in s.533, below, there must have been a disposal (see s.532, below) by a public sector authority, which includes local authorities, new town corporations, housing associations (see s.573, below), and the Crown (see s.574, below). In addition, the applicant must fulfil one of two additional conditions.

(1) The disposal by the public sector authority must have been before the cut-off date (currently, April 26, 1984 for all designations except Airey, which is September 8, 1984—see notes to s.528, above); and, there has been no disposal for value (see s.532, below) of a relevant interest (see s.530, above) on or after that date.

(2) The applicant did acquire a relevant interest (see s.530, above) on a disposal for value (see s.532, below) within the twelve months beginning with the cut-off date (see notes to

s.528, above); *and* as a matter of fact he was unaware on the date of the disposal that the dwelling contained the qualifying defect (as to which, see s.528, above); *and* the value of the disposal did not take account, or adequate account, of the qualifying defect; and if the cut-off date had occurred *after* the disposal, the first set of conditions would have been satisfied, *i.e.* the dwelling would have been within a designated class and there has been no *other* disposal of a relevant interest.

There are two issues of fact which may be in issue. First of all, was the applicant aware when he bought the property that the dwelling contained the qualifying defect? Note that it is not a question of whether or not the applicant knew that the dwelling was within a designated class, but whether or not the defect was known of. This relates to one of the problems with this class of dwelling, *viz.* that the defect may well not show up on survey, and indeed nothing may be known or identified (other than by general knowledge or designation itself) until deterioration sets in.

Secondly, did the purchase price reflect the defect (at all or adequately)? For example, the vendor may have known of the defect, but not revealed it to the purchaser. He may, accordingly, have set the price low in any event, in order to make a sale. The purchaser may have believed he was "getting a bargain" without knowing he was buying instead a major headache. A challenge to a decision of the local authority (*cf.* notification of determination, s.540, below) on either of these questions may be brought in the county court: s.572, below.

Although the authority have to give a decision on an application, the criteria are set out as matters of fact, rather than matters of opinion, *i.e.* it is not the case that the authority must be "satisfied" or "of opinion" or "have reason to believe" that one or other of the relevant conditions apply, but simply whether or not they do apply (*cf. e.g.* Pt. III, above). The county court will accordingly consider these and other questions as facts, not applying an administrative law/judicial review approach: see notes to s.64, above.

Note that it is *not* a condition of assistance that the owner is in actual occupation, *save* if occupation is by a protected occupier or statutory tenant under the Rent (Agriculture) Act 1976 (below, s.533), or, of course, if the owner as freeholder or long leaseholder has granted a long lease. Note, too, that assistance will not be available to those who have, before application, already carried out works which have in the opinion of the authority already cured the defect: see s.533, below.

Under s.563, a local authority may give notice to a prospective purchaser of a defective dwelling, in effect that if he proceeds he will not be within the provisions of this Part.

Subs. (4)

This covers transfers between public authorities, *e.g.* New Towns Act 1981, or s.19, above, which would not otherwise be disposals for the purposes of this Part.

Construction of references to disposal, etc.

532.—(1) References in this Part to a disposal include a part disposal; but for the purposes of this Part a disposal of an interest in a dwelling is a disposal of a relevant interest in the dwelling only if on the disposal the person to whom it is made acquires a relevant interest in the dwelling.

(2) Where an interest in land is disposed of under a contract, the time at which the disposal is made is, for the purposes of this Part—

    (*a*) if the contract is unconditional, the time at which the contract is made, and

    (*b*) if the contract is conditional (and in particular if it is conditional on the exercise of an option), the time when the condition is satisfied;

and not, if different, the time at which the interest is conveyed.

(3) Reference in this Part to a disposal of an interest for value are to a disposal for money or money's worth, whether or not representing full value for the interest disposed of.

(4) In relation to a person holding an interest in a dwelling formed by the conversion of another dwelling, references in this Part to a previous disposal of an interest in the dwelling include a previous disposal on which an interest in land which included that part of the original dwelling in which his interest subsists was acquired.

Definitions

    "dwelling": s.575.

    "relevant interest": s.530.

GENERAL NOTE

Disposals are relevant to conditions of eligibility for assistance: see s.531, above. A disposal includes disposal of part of a dwelling: subs. (1). An application for assistance may, of course, be made by someone who has a flat in a building within a designated class (see s.528, above), which could include a flat produced by conversion. In the case of an application for assistance by the owner of a flat produced by conversion, references to prior disposals include prior disposal of the house as a whole: subs. (4).

A disposal is for value if it is for money or money's worth: see most recently *Midland Bank Trust Co.* v. *Green* [1981] A.C. 513, H.L. This is so "whether or not representing full value for the interest disposed of", but *cf.* s.531(3)(c), above. The time taken for the disposal is to be the date of the contract for the disposal, rather than the actual conveyance, although if the contract is conditional, it is the time when the condition is satisfied: subs. (2).

Under s.563, a local authority may give notice to a prospective purchaser of a defective dwelling, in effect that if he proceeds he will not be within the provisions of this Part.

Exceptions to eligibility

533.—(1) A person who holds a relevant interest in a defective dwelling is not eligible for assistance in respect of the dwelling at any time when that interest is subject to the rights of a person who is a protected occupier or statutory tenant within the meaning of the Rent (Agriculture) Act 1976.

(2) A person is not eligible for assistance in respect of defective dwelling if the local housing authority are of the opinion—

(*a*) that work to the building which consists of or includes the dwelling has been carried out in order to deal with the qualifying defect, and

(*b*) that on the completion of the work, no further work relating to the dwelling was required to be done to the building in order to deal satisfactorily with the qualifying defect.

DEFINITIONS

"defective dwelling": ss.528, 559.
"dwelling": s.575.
"eligible for assistance": s.531.
"qualifying defect": ss.528, 559.
"relevant interest": s.530.

GENERAL NOTE

There are two, very different, exclusions from the principles of eligibility for assistance described in s.531, above. First of all, although there is no general requirement that the dwelling be not let (apart, of course, from not let on a long lease—*cf.* s.530, above), if the dwelling is in occupation by a protected occupier or statutory tenant under the Rent (Agriculture) Act 1976 (see notes to s.622, below), no claim may be made for assistance.

Secondly, no claim may be made if *the local housing authority are of the opinion* that work to the building has been carried out in order to deal with the defect, and that no further work was required to deal satisfactorily with the defect on completion of those works (see also s.535, below, as to grant-aid under Part XV). It follows that if works were started but never completed, the owner is not precluded from applying. Note, however, that this is a matter for the local authority, so that provided there is some factual basis for their opinion, *i.e.* it is not an opinion which no reasonable authority could maintain, it will not be open to challenge in the courts (*i.e.* unless the case can be brought within the principle of *Associated Provincial Picture Houses Ltd.* v. *Wednesbury Corporation* [1948] 1 K.B. 223, C.A.): see, generally, notes to s.64, above.

Furthermore, although the county court has general jurisdiction to make declarations under this Part (see s.572, below), it will not have jurisdiction to entertain the argument that no reasonable authority could reach that opinion. Such an argument can only be raised by proceedings for judicial review under R.S.C., Ord. 53: see *Cocks* v. *Thanet D.C.* [1983] A.C. 286, 6 H.L.R. 15, H.L.

Under s.563, a local authority may give notice to a prospective purchaser of a defective dwelling, in effect that if he proceeds he will not be within the provisions of this Part.

Determination of entitlement

Application for assistance

534. A person seeking assistance under this Part in respect of a defective dwelling shall make a written application to the local housing authority within the period specified in the relevant designation.

Definitions
  "defective dwelling": ss.528, 559.
  "dwelling": s.575.
  "period": s.528.

General Note
  Applications must be in writing. There is no provision requiring local authorities to make application forms available (*cf.* s.176, above), and although authorities can provide their own forms, it will not be lawful to require applicants to complete those forms as a precondition of assistance.

Application not to be entertained where grant application pending or approved

535.—(1) The local housing authority shall not entertain an application for assistance under this Part if—

(*a*) an application has been made in respect of the defective dwelling (whether before or after the relevant designation came into operation) for an improvement grant, intermediate grant, special grant or repairs grant under Part XV, and

(*b*) the relevant works in relation to that grant include the whole or part of the work required to reinstate the dwelling,

unless the grant application has been refused or has been withdrawn under subsection (2) or the relevant works have been completed.

(2) Where a person has applied for such a grant in respect of a dwelling and—

(*a*) the dwelling is a defective dwelling, and

(*b*) the relevant works include the whole or part of the work required to reinstate it,

he may withdraw his application, whether or not it has been approved, if the relevant works have not been begun.

(3) In this section "relevant works", in relation to a grant, has the same meaning as in Part XV.

Definitions
  "defective dwelling": ss.528, 559.
  "designation": ss.528, 559.
  "dwelling": s.575.
  "improvement grant": s.467.
  "intermediate grant": s.474.
  "local housing authority": ss.1, 2.
  "relevant works": s.461.
  "repairs grant": s.491.
  "special grant": s.483.

General Note
  This section deals with the relationship between this Part, and grant-aid under Pt. XV. Prior to the commencement of the Housing Defects Act 1984, which this Part replaces, grant-aid under what is now Pt. XV was the only assistance available. This Part provides two forms of assistance: reinstatement grant or repurchase—see notes to s.537, below. In some circumstances, it will be preferable to proceed under this Part, but in others it may remain preferable to proceed under Pt. XV, *e.g.* if the applicant wishes to remain in occupation, but in addition to works needed to remedy the specific qualifying defect (see

notes to s.528, above) has to carry out further works so that the property will have a 30-year life (see notes to s.538, below).

If application has been made for one of the range of principal grants under Pt. XV, and the works for which grant-aid has been sought include the whole, or indeed only part, of the works needed to deal with the defect, the authority may not entertain an application under this Part, unless and until the grant application has been determined, by withdrawal by applicant or by refusal by authority.

Of course, if aid under this Part would be greater than under Pt. XV, it is intended that authorities should advise the applicant to withdraw the application for a Pt. XV grant. Nonetheless, there is no obligation on authorities so to do: applicants should be careful to consider the alternative schemes of assistance. In the event, even if the authority have proceeded to approve the application for a Pt. XV grant, the applicant may still withdraw the application, provided the grant-aided works have not begun. If works have been performed under a Pt. XV grant, then the applicant is entitled to apply under this Part, in which case the test which will apply is that contained in s.533(2), above, *i.e.* whether or not, in the opinion of the authority, the defect has been satisfactorily dealt with.

Determination of eligibility

536.—(1) A local housing authority receiving an application for assistance under this Part shall as soon as reasonably practicable give notice in writing to the applicant stating whether in their opinion he is eligible for assistance in respect of the defective dwelling.

(2) If they are of opinion that he is not so eligible, the notice shall state the reasons for their view.

(3) If they are of opinion that he is so eligible, the notice shall inform him of his right to make such a claim as is mentioned in section 537(2) (claim that assistance by way of reinstatement grant is inappropriate in his case).

DEFINITIONS

"defective dwelling": ss.528, 559.
"dwelling": s.575.
"eligible for assistance": ss.531, 533.
"local housing authority": ss.1, 2.

GENERAL NOTE

"As soon as reasonably practicable" after receiving an application (in writing, see s.534, above) for assistance, the authority must reply in writing stating whether or not the applicant is eligible for assistance (as to which, see ss.531, 533, above). Non-eligibility may be because the dwelling is not a designated defective dwelling, or because the applicant does not have a relevant interest, or because works have been carried out which in the opinion of the authority have dealt satisfactorily with the defect, or because the applicant acquired his interest after the cut-off date and does not qualify under the alternative limb in s.531, or because there is a protected occupier or statutory tenant under the 1976 Act in occupation, or because the relevant period was not still running at the date of application.

The reply must also be in writing. No form is prescribed. Reasons must be stated if the authority's conclusion is that the applicant is not eligible. The reasons clearly have to be more than a mere statement of non-eligibility, and it is submitted that they have to go beyond mere statement of the words of the relevant provision, but extend to explain the factual elements: see, *e.g.*, *Gloucester City Council* v. *Miles* (1985) 17 H.L.R. 292, C.A., notes to s.64, above. A refusal of assistance which the applicant considers ill-founded may normally be referred to the county court under s.572, below, although not if the reason for refusal is that the authority are of the opinion that the defect has been cured by prior works, in which case the challenge will have to be by way of judicial review: see notes to s.533, above.

If the applicant is considered eligible, then the authority must in the same notice move on to the next stage, by informing him whether or not assistance by way of reinstatement grant is available: see notes to ss.537–539. below.

Determination of form of assistance to which applicant is entitled

537.—(1) A local housing authority receiving an application for assistance under this Part shall, if the applicant is eligible for assistance, determine whether he is entitled to assistance by way of reinstatement grant or by way of repurchase.

(2) If the authority are satisfied, on a claim by the applicant to that effect, that it would be unreasonable to expect him to secure or await the carrying out of the work required to reinstate the defective dwelling, the applicant is entitled to assistance by way of repurchase.

(3) Subject to subsection (2), the applicant is entitled to assistance by way of reinstatement grant if the authority are satisfied that the conditions for such assistance set out in section 538 are met, and otherwise to assistance by way of repurchase.

DEFINITIONS
  "defective dwelling": ss.528, 559.
  "dwelling": s.575.
  "eligible for assistance": ss.531, 533.
  "local housing authority": ss.1, 2.
  "reinstatement grant": s.541.
  "repurchase": s.547.

GENERAL NOTE
  There are two forms of assistance provided for under this Part of the Act: *either* a reinstatement grant (see s.541, below), *or* repurchase (see s.547, below). The presumption is in favour of reinstatement. There are two circumstances only in which repurchase will apply: (a) if the conditions for reinstatement grant are not fulfilled (subs. (3)—see s.538, below); or (b) if *the authority are satisfied* that it would be unreasonable to expect the applicant either to arrange, or to await, the execution of works required to reinstate the dwelling (as to which, see s.539, below). Note that, as with whether prior works have satisfactorily dealt with the defect (above, s.533(2)), the question of whether or not it is reasonable for the applicant to remain in occupation is one for the authority, susceptible only to judicial review, not reference to the county court under s.572.

  Local authorities may enter into "agency agreements" to carry out work on behalf of the applicant: see s.564, below.

  Note that it is for the applicant to *claim* repurchase instead of reinstatement grant, under subs. (2), *i.e.* on the ground that it is not reasonable for him to secure or await the works.

Conditions for assistance by way of reinstatement grant

538.—(1) The conditions for assistance by way of reinstatement grant are, subject to any order under subsection (2)—
  (*a*) that the dwelling is a house (as defined in section 575);
  (*b*) that if the work required to reinstate the dwelling (together with any other work which the local housing authority are satisfied the applicant proposes to carry out) were carried out—
        (i) the dwelling would be likely to provide satisfactory housing accommodation for a period of at least 30 years, and
        (ii) an individual acquiring the freehold of the dwelling with vacant possession would be likely to be able to arrange a mortgage on satisfactory terms with a lending institution;
  (*c*) that giving assistance by way of reinstatement grant is justified having regard, on the one hand, to the amount of reinstatement grant that would be payable in respect of the dwelling and, on the other hand, to the likely value of the freehold of the dwelling with vacant possession after the work required to reinstate it has been carried out; and
  (*d*) that the amount of reinstatement grant would not be likely to exceed the aggregate of the price payable on the acquisition of the applicant's interest in the dwelling in pursuance of this Part and the amount to be reimbursed under section 552 (reimbursement of expenses incidental to repurchase).

(2) The Secretary of State may by order amend the conditions set out in subsection (1) so as to modify or omit any of the conditions or to add or substitute for any of the conditions other conditions.

(3) An order—

(*a*) may make different provision for different classes of case,

(*b*) shall be made by statutory instrument, and

(*c*) shall not be made unless a draft of it has been laid before and approved by a resolution of each House of Parliament.

(4) An order does not affect an application for assistance made before the order comes into force.

DEFINITIONS

"dwelling": s.575.

"house": s.575.

"reinstatement grant": s.541.

"work required to reinstate": s.539.

GENERAL NOTE

The principal means of providing assistance under this Part is by way of reinstatement grant, with repurchase only available if either the authority are satisfied that it would be unreasonable to expect the applicant to secure or await the carrying out of the work required for reinstatement of the dwelling, or if one of the conditions set out in this section is not met: see notes to s.537, above.

The first condition is that the dwelling is a house: see notes to s.575. A reinstatement grant is not available for a flat, because, of course, there would be no necessary right to carry out works to the building as a whole. Secondly, the works have to produce something which is "mortgageable" and with a prospective life of at least 30 years. The latter is the same as the requirement for improvement grants under Pt. XV: see s.468, above. It will not necessarily be achieved by remedial works directed at the qualifying defect alone, but may be achieved if taken together with additional works which *the authority are satisfied* the applicant proposes to carry out. Again, this is a point for the authority, not a court other than on judicial review: see notes to s.533, above.

Because a Pt. XV grant is not available at the same time as a reinstatement grant under this Part, the applicant will presumably have to find the cost of such additional works himself, which may be one circumstance when assistance under Pt. XV may be more advantageous than assistance under this Part.

The third condition is that giving assistance by way of reinstatement grant is justified "having regard . . . to the amount of reinstatement grant that would be payable . . . and . . . to the likely value of the freehold with vacant possession after . . . works . . ." This is superficially similar to the "repairable at reasonable expense" test to be found in s.206, above. It operates differently, however, in so far as (a) it is the amount of the grant which is to be compared to post-works value, as distinct from the residual or owner-borne cost, and (b) the section specifies that it is freehold, vacant possession value which is to be taken into account.

This condition is not subject to qualification by reference to the opinion or satisfaction of the authority (*cf.* notes to s.533, above), and is therefore open to review by the county court under s.572. Where the amount of the grant would exceed the post-works value it will, of course, not be justifiable—indeed, it would be "financial folly", see *Kenny* v. *Royal London Borough of Kingston Upon Thames* (1985) 17 H.L.R. 344, C.A.; see, further, notes to s.206, above.

Finally, the fourth condition ties up with the alternative assistance available under this Part, *viz.* repurchase (see s.547 and Sched. 20, below). The amount of the reinstatement grant (see s.543, below) must not be likely to exceed the price payable on repurchase (see Sched. 20, Part II, below) together with the "reimbursement of expenses incidental to repurchase" (see s.552, below). Reinstatement, then, is not available if it is the more expensive option for the authority.

Any or all of these conditions may be amended, modified, omitted, added to, or substituted for, by the Secretary of State, by order (under affirmative resolution procedure) which may make different provision for different classes of case, although not so as retrospectively to affect an application. It would not seem that the "fetter" on differences contained in s.528(4), above, would apply to an order under this section, though *cf.* below, s.543(4), expressly permitting different levels of maximum expenditure under a reinstatement grant in different areas.

Meaning of "work required for reinstatement" and "associated arrangement"

539.—(1) For the purposes of this Part the work required to reinstate a defective dwelling is the work relating to the dwelling that is required to be done to the building that consists of or includes the dwelling in order to deal satisfactorily with the qualifying defect, together with any further work—

(*a*) required to be done, in order to deal satisfactorily with the qualifying defect, to any garage or outhouse designed or constructed as that building is designed or constructed, being a garage or outhouse in which the interest of the person eligible for assistance subsists and which is occupied with and used for the purposes of the dwelling or any part of it, or

(*b*) reasonably required in connection with other work falling within this subsection.

(2) In this Part "associated arrangement" means an arrangement which is entered into in connection with the execution of the work required to reinstate a defective dwelling and is likely to contribute towards the dwelling being regarded as an acceptable security by a lending institution.

DEFINITIONS
"defective dwelling": ss.528, 559.
"dwelling": s.575.
"qualifying defect": ss.528, 559.

GENERAL NOTE
The work for which aid is available under a reinstatement grant is the "work required to reinstate a defective dwelling". This is work to remedy the qualifying defect (see notes to s.528, above) in the dwelling itself, and in any garage or outhouse which was designed or constructed in the same way, provided that the applicant has an interest (not necessarily a relevant interest, *cf.* s.530, above) in the garage or outhouse and occupies it with and uses it for the purposes of the dwelling, not, *e.g.* for a business or some other purpose. Included within the work required to reinstate a defective dwelling is work "reasonably required" in connection with other work within subs. (1), *e.g.* because non-related features have to be altered or removed or replaced. It does *not* include *other* works, *e.g.* to ensure that the property has a 30-year life, or that it is mortgageable, under s.538(1), above.

Local authorities may enter into "agency agreements" to carry out work on behalf of the applicant: see s.564, below.

Assistance is also available (see ss. 540, 543, below), for the cost of an "associated arrangement". This means an arrangement, *e.g.* a warranty or an insurance policy, "likely to contribute towards the dwelling being regarded as acceptable security by a lending institution". It would not seem to cover further *works* which would aid mortgageability.

Notice of determination

540.—(1) Where an applicant is eligible for assistance, the authority to whom the application was made shall as soon as reasonably practicable give him notice in writing (a "notice of determination") stating the form of assistance to which he is entitled.

(2) If, on such a claim by the applicant as is mentioned in section 537(2) (claim that assistance by way of reinstatement grant is inappropriate in his case), the authority are not satisfied that it would be unreasonable to expect him to secure or await the carrying out of the work required to reinstate the defective dwelling, the notice shall state the reasons for their view.

(3) A notice stating that the applicant is entitled to assistance by way of reinstatement grant shall also state—

(*a*) the grounds for the authority's determination;

(*b*) the work which, in their opinion, is required to reinstate the defective dwelling;

(c) the amount of expenditure which, in their opinion, may properly be incurred in executing the work;

(d) the amount of expenditure which, in their opinion, may properly be incurred in entering into an associated arrangement;

(e) the condition required by section 542 (execution of work to satisfaction of authority within specified period), including the period within which the work is to be carried out; and

(f) their estimate of the amount of grant payable in respect of the dwelling in pursuance of this Part.

(4) A notice stating that the applicant is entitled to assistance by way of repurchase shall also state the grounds for the authority's determination and the effect of—

(a) paragraphs 1 to 3 of Schedule 20 (request for notice of proposed terms of repurchase), and

(b) sections 554, 556 and 557(1) (provisions for grant of tenancy to former owner-occupier of repurchased dwelling).

(5) References in the following provisions of this Part to a person entitled to assistance by way of reinstatement grant or, as the case may be, by way of repurchase are to a person who is eligible for assistance in respect of the dwelling and on whom a notice of determination has been served stating that he is entitled to that form of assistance.

DEFINITIONS

"associated arrangement": s.539.
"defective dwelling": ss.528, 559.
"dwelling": s.575.
"qualifying work": s.541.
"reinstatement grant": s.541.
"repurchase": s.547.
"work required to reinstate": s.539.

GENERAL NOTE

Again, "as soon as reasonably practicable" (*cf.* s.536, above), the authority must send a written notice of determination stating whether assistance is to be by way of reinstatement grant, or repurchase. If the applicant has made a claim for repurchase on the grounds that it would be unreasonable to secure or await the execution of works, and the authority are not satisfied that this is so, they have to state their reasons (*cf.* notes to s.536, above).

Where the notice states that the applicant is to receive a reinstatement grant, it must also state:

(a) on what grounds to authority have so decided;

(b) what works they consider are required to reinstate the dwelling (*cf.* notes to s.539, above);

(c) how much may properly be incurred in executing these works (which will not be the same as the grant available—see (f), below, and notes to s.543, below);

(d) how much may properly be spent on an associated arrangement (*cf.* notes to s.539, above);

(e) the condition specified in s.542, below, together with the period for completion of the works (not less than 12 months—see notes to s.542, below); and,

(f) their estimate of the grant.

It does not *have to*, but doubtless can in an accompanying document, inform the applicant that the authority may enter into "agency agreements" to carry out work on his behalf: see s.564, below.

Where the notice states that the applicant is entitled to repurchase, it must also state:

(i) the grounds for the decision;

(ii) the effect of Sched. 20, paras. 1–3—see notes thereto, below; and

(iii) the effect of ss.553, 555 and 556(1)—see notes thereto, below. This requirement is of crucial importance, because claims for a "replacement" tenancy have to be made by specified dates, or are lost.

Assistance by way of reinstatement grant

Reinstatement grant

541.—(1) Where a person is entitled to assistance by way of reinstatement grant, the local housing authority shall pay reinstatement grant to him in respect of—

(*a*) the qualifying work, and

(*b*) any associated arrangement,

subject to and in accordance with the following provisions of this Part.

(2) The "qualifying work" means the work stated in the notice of determination, or in a notice under section 544 (notice of change of work required), to be the work which in the opinion of the local housing authority is required to reinstate the dwelling.

DEFINITIONS

"associated arrangement": s.539.
"local housing authority": ss.1, 2.
"notice of determination": s.540.
"person entitled to assistance": s.540.

GENERAL NOTE

Payment of the reinstatement grant is to be subject to the provisions which follow: see ss.542, 544, 545, 546, below. Section 542 details "conditions" attached to payment (works to a satisfactory standard, period for completion of works); s.544 concerns adjustment of amounts stated in the s.540 notice of determination; s.545 provides for payment in a single sum on completion, or by way of interim or stage payments; s.546 concerns repayment for breach of condition. All of these provisions are modelled on those applicable to grants under Part XV. Payment is in respect of an "associated arrangement" (see notes to s.539, above) or otherwise "qualifying work" which means (subs. (2)) the work stated in the notice of determination under s.540, as extended by a notice under s.544, *i.e.* "added works".

Local authorities may enter into "agency agreements" to carry out work on behalf of the applicant: see s.564, below.

Conditions of payment of reinstatement grant

542.—(1) It is a condition of payment of reinstatement grant that the qualifying work is carried out—

(*a*) to the satisfaction of the local housing authority, and

(*b*) within the period specified in the notice of determination, or that period as extended.

(2) The period so specified shall be such reasonable period (of at least twelve months), beginning with service of the notice, as the authority may determine.

(3) The authority shall, if there are reasonable grounds for doing so, by notice in writing served on the person entitled to assistance, extend or further extend the period for carrying out the qualifying work (whether or not the period has expired).

(4) Payment of reinstatement grant shall not be subject to any other condition, however expressed.

DEFINITIONS

"local housing authority": ss.1, 2.
"notice of determination": s.540.
"qualifying work": s.541.
"reinstatement grant": s.541.

GENERAL NOTE

As with grants under Pt. XV, work must be completed to the satisfaction of the authority. Furthermore, work is to be completed within the period specified in the s.540 notice of determination, which must be "such reasonable period . . . as the authority may determine", but not less than 12 months, although provision is made (subs. (3)) for extending that period "if there are reasonable grounds for doing so". An extension must be in writing, and there can be more than one extension. An extension may well be permitted when and if "added works" are allowed under s.544. The authority can attach no other condition.

Thus, for example, they cannot at present specify the builder by whom the works are to be carried out, or indeed that the builder on whose estimate a grant was calculated shall be used: permission to attach either or both of such conditions is being considered in relation to Pt. XV grants (Home Improvement —A New Approach, 1985, Cmnd. 9513) and if legislation follows, might reasonably be expected to be permitted under this Part as well. Local authorities may enter into "agency agreements" to carry out work on behalf of the applicant: see s.564, below.

Amount of reinstatement grant

543.—(1) The amount of reinstatement grant payable is the appropriate percentage of whichever is the least of—

    (*a*) the amount stated in the notice of determination, or in a notice under section 544 (notice of change in work required or expenditure permitted), to be the amount of expenditure which, in the opinion of the local housing authority, may properly be incurred in executing the qualifying work and entering into any associated arrangement,

    (*b*) the expenditure actually incurred in executing the qualifying work and entering into any associated arrangement, and

    (*c*) the expenditure which is the maximum amount permitted to be taken into account for the purposes of this section.

(2) The appropriate percentage is 90 per cent. or, in a case where the authority are satisfied that the person entitled to assistance would suffer financial hardship unless a higher percentage of the expenditure referred to in subsection (1) were paid to him, 100 per cent.

(3) The Secretary of State may by order vary either or both of the percentages mentioned in subsection (2).

(4) The maximum amount of expenditure permitted to be taken into account for the purposes of this section is the amount specified as the expenditure limit by order made by the Secretary of State, except in a case or description of case in which the Secretary of State, on the application of a local housing authority, approves a higher amount.

(5) An order under subsection (4) may make different provision for different areas, different designated classes and different categories of dwelling.

(6) An order under this section shall be made by statutory instrument which shall be subject to annulment in pursuance of a resolution of the House of Commons.

DEFINITIONS
    "associated arrangement": s.539.
    "local housing authority": ss.1, 2.
    "notice of determination": s.540.
    "person entitled to assistance": s.540.
    "qualifying work": s.541.
    "reinstatement grant": s.541.

GENERAL NOTE
    This section details the amount of the reinstatement grant. It follows the format for calculation of Pt. XV grants, *i.e.* an appropriate percentage of a maximum amount. As under Pt. XV, therefore, while generous appropriate percentages may be available, they can be deceptive, if the actual amount on which the appropriate percentage is based is less than the cost of all the works necessary to remedy the defect. In such a case, the applicant must find not only the balance of the appropriate percentage, but also the additional amount in full, for all the works specified in the notice of determination under s.540, plus any further or "added works" under s.544, have to be completed to the satisfaction of the authority as a condition of payment at all: see s.542(1), above. Note that the government are considering "means-testing" grants under Pt. XV (see Home Improvement—A New Approach, 1985,

Cmnd. 9513), but have said nothing about whether the same might be adopted under this Part.

The amount of the appropriate percentage is specified as 90 per cent., unless the authority are satisfied that the person entitled to assistance would suffer financial hardship, in which case 100 per cent. may be paid. The appropriate percentage is of whichever is the *less* of one of three amounts: (a) the amount stated in the s.540 notice of determination, or as varied under s.544, or (b) the expenditure actually incurred in carrying out the works and entering into an associated arrangement, or (c) the maximum amount specified for the purposes of this section (called in Part XV but not here "eligible expense"). The maximum amount is currently specified in the Housing Defects (Expenditure Limit) Order 1984 (S.I. 1984 No. 1705), retained in force by s.2, Housing (Consequential Provisions) Act 1985, as £14,000. Note the effect of Sched. 21, para. 3, where a dwelling is "dually designated" under both a local, and a national, scheme.

The authority may, however, apply to the Secretary of State to approve a higher maximum, although the order itself may make different provisions for different areas, different designated classes and different categories of dwelling, and the Secretary of State may by order vary the appropriate percentage. In either case, the order is subject to negative resolution procedure.

Changes in work or expenditure

544. Where the local housing authority are satisfied that—

(*a*) the work required to reinstate the defective dwelling is more extensive than that stated in the notice of determination or in a previous notice under this section, or

(*b*) the amount of the expenditure which may properly be incurred in executing that work is greater than that so stated, or

(*c*) there is an amount of expenditure which may properly be incurred in entering into an associated arrangement but no such amount is stated in the notice of determination or a previous notice under this section, or

(*d*) where such an amount is so stated, the amount of expenditure which may be properly so incurred is greater than that amount,

they shall by notice in writing served on the person entitled to assistance state their opinion as to that amount or, as the case may be, that work and that amount; and the amount of reinstatement grant shall be adjusted accordingly.

DEFINITIONS
"associated arrangement": s.539.
"defective dwelling": ss.528, 559.
"dwelling": s.575.
"local housing authority": ss.1, 2.
"notice of determination": s.540.
"person entitled to assistance": s.540.
"reinstatement grant": s.541.

GENERAL NOTE
This section permits the authority to adjust the amount of reinstatement grant, in one of four circumstances: (a) the works needed prove to be greater than already notified ("added works"); (b) proper increase in costs; (c) associated arrangement, for which no previous allowance has been made; or (d) increased cost of associated arrangement.

Payment of reinstatement grant

545.—(1) The local housing authority may pay reinstatement grant in respect of the qualifying work in a single sum on completion of the work or by instalments.

(2) No instalment shall be paid if the instalment, together with any amount previously paid, would exceed the appropriate percentage of the cost of so much of the qualifying work as has been executed at that time.

(3) The authority shall pay reinstatement grant in respect of an associated arrangement when payment in respect of the expenditure incurred in entering into the arrangement falls to be made.

DEFINITIONS
"appropriate percentage": s.543.
"associated arrangement": s.539.
"local housing authority": ss.1, 2.
"qualifying work": s.541.
"reinstatement grant": s.541

GENERAL NOTE
Payment may be in a single sum on completion, or it may be by way of interim, or stage, payments. There is no discretion to not pay once works are satisfactorily completed, so that the grant is due and payable as a statutory debt, although doubtless subject to a minimal time for administration of payment. If stage payments are made, they are to a limit, *viz.* the appropriate percentage (currently, 90 per cent., see notes to s.543, above) of the *cost* of the qualifying works (see notes to s.541, above) executed by the time of the payment, *not* the appropriate percentage of any of the other bases for calculating appropriate percentage set out in s.543, above. But payment for an associated arrangement is as and when due under that arrangement. The authority's control over that payment is in approving or not its terms.

Repayment of grant for breach of condition

546.—(1) Where an amount of reinstatement grant has been paid in one or more instalments and the qualifying work is not completed within the period for carrying out the work, the local housing authority may, if they think fit, require the person who was entitled to assistance to repay that amount to them forthwith.

(2) The amount required to be repaid (or, if it was paid in more than one instalment, the amount of each instalment) shall carry interest, at such reasonable rate as the authority may determine, from the date on which it was paid until repayment.

DEFINITIONS
"local housing authority": ss.1, 2.
"person entitled to assistance": s.540.
"qualifying work": s.541.
"reinstatement grant": s.541.

GENERAL NOTE
On failure to complete works within the period allowed (including any extension, see notes to s.542, above), presumably to the satisfaction of the authority (*cf.* s.542, above), the authority may demand immediate repayment, together with interest from the date of payment (*not* date of demand for repayment).

Assistance by way of repurchase

Repurchase

547. The provisions of Schedule 20 have effect with respect to assistance by way of repurchase, as follows—
Part I—The agreement to repurchase.
Part II—Price payable and valuation.
Part III—Supplementary provisions

GENERAL NOTE
When repurchase is the redress which is to be made available (as to which, see notes to s.537, above, but see also s.549, below), Sched. 20 governs: (a) the agreement to repurchase (Part I), (b) the price payable and valuation (Part II), and (c) a number of supplementary provisions (Part III).
The agreement to purchase will cover the owner's interest, in both defective dwelling (as to the meaning of which, see s.528), and any garage, or outhouse (see s.539), *and* yard and

appurtenance (see notes to s.56, above), but in these "additional" cases only if "used for the purposes of the dwelling or a part of it", which would suggest only if used for the purposes of the dwelling *as* a dwelling not, *e.g.*, a related business use (*cf.* notes to s.539, above). But subject to this, the interest of the person entitled to assistance need not be a "relevant interest" (see s.530) in the added cases.

Within three months of the notice of determination (see s.540), or that period if extended, the owner may request the authority in writing to notify him of the proposed terms and conditions of acquisition of interest. An extension is to be granted in writing by the authority, if there are reasonable grounds for so doing, even if the initial three months has expired; a refusal to extend is expressly challengeable in the county court under s.572(3), and in that connection it may be noted that the question is whether there *are* reasonable grounds for doing so, not whether there are reasonable grounds for doing so "in the opinion of the authority" or "if the authority are so satisfied", etc. See notes to s.533.

The authority then have a further three months to serve a first notice in writing stating their opinion as to the value of the interest to be acquired, and the effect of the remaining provisions of Part I of Sched. 20. The provisions for repurchase, other than as to price payable and valuation are to be those agreed, or are otherwise those which are reasonable as determined in accordance with this Part, *i.e.* under s.572 county court jurisdiction.

Within three months of agreement or determination, the authority have to draw up an agreement embodying the terms and conditions of the repurchase, and serve a copy on the owner. The authority cannot pass on the cost of this work: see s.552, below. The last stage is for the owner to notify the authority in writing within six months of service of this agreement that he requires them to enter into an agreement embodying the terms and conditions agreed or determined, and the authority shall comply with that requirement. If there are reasonable grounds for so doing, the authority shall in writing extend or further extend that period, and if they do not do so a dispute may be referred to the county court under s.572(3).

The price payable is 95 per cent. of the value at the time when the authority's notice of proposed terms of acquisition is served. The 5 per cent. reduction presumably reflects the fact that the owner, or a tenant, may have to be rehoused by the authority: see ss.554–557. Value means open market value, without the qualifying defect (as to which see s.528, above), and without liability to repay discount which will arise if the initial purchase was from a local authority under Part II, or if under the right to buy under Part V, and five years have not elapsed since purchase. Also disregarded are the fact that authority are obliged to buy, and that the authority may be under a rehousing obligation (see ss.554–557).

The initial valuation will be by the authority when serving the first notice. It is only if this is not accepted by the owner that there is a further or later valuation. In that case, there will be a valuation by the district valuer, *i.e.* a valuation at a later time, but referable to an earlier date. In such a case, it is expressly provided that later material changes of circumstance which have an effect on value are to be treated as if they had occurred *before* the date when the first notice was served. There is no such express provision in relation to the right to buy (*cf.* s.127, above).

Valuation disputes are referable to the district valuer, *not* the county court (see s.572(2)). There can only be a reference to the district valuer between service of the first notice, and the copy of terms and conditions, unless there has been a change of circumstances such as affects value, in which case the reference—or a further reference—can be made at any time before the parties enter into the agreement. Reference is made by either party—owner or authority—serving notice on the district valuer, with a copy to the other party. Once notice has been served on the district valuer, the parties have four weeks to make representations to the district valuer. Once the district valuer has determined or redetermined the value, the authority have to "re-comply" with the duty to serve a copy of the agreement within three months, and the six months begin to run anew.

Repurchase by authority other than local housing authority

548.—(1) Where the local housing authority give a notice of determination to a person stating that he is entitled to assistance by way of repurchase and they are of opinion that—

  (*a*) a relevant interest in the dwelling was disposed of by a public sector authority mentioned in column 1 of the following Table (or a predecessor mentioned there of such an authority),

  (*b*) there has been no disposal within paragraph (*a*) since the time of that disposal, and (*c*) any conditions mentioned in column 2 of the Table in relation to the authority are met,

they shall forthwith give that other authority a notice in writing, together with a copy of the notice of determination, stating that the authority may acquire, in accordance with this Part, the interest of the person entitled to assistance.

TABLE

Public sector authority	*Conditions*
1. A registered housing association (other than a co-operative housing association) or a predecessor housing association of that association.	None.
2. A development corporation.	No interests have at any time been transferred from the corporation in pursuance of a scheme made or having effect as if made under section 42 of the New Towns Act 1981 (transfer of housing to district council).
3. The Development Board for Rural Wales.	None.
4. Another local housing authority or a predecessor of that authority.	The local housing authority provide housing accommodation in the vicinity of the defective dwelling with which the dwelling may conveniently be managed.
5. Any other public sector authority prescribed by order of the Secretary of State, or a predecessor so prescribed.	Any conditions prescribed in the order.

(2) The other authority may, within the period of four weeks beginning with the service of the notice on them, give notice in writing to the local housing authority—

(*a*) stating that they wish to acquire the interest, and

(*b*) specifying the address of the principal office of the authority and any other address which may also be used as an address for service;

and the local housing authority shall forthwith give to the person entitled to assistance a transfer notice, that is, a notice in writing of the contents of the notice received by them and the effect of subsection (3).

(3) After a transfer notice has been given to the person entitled to assistance, the other authority shall be treated as the appropriate authority for the purposes of anything done or falling to be done under this Part, except that—

(*a*) a request under paragraph 2 of Schedule 20 (request for notice of proposed terms of acquisition) may be made either to the local housing authority or to the other authority, and

(*b*) any such request given to the local housing authority (whether before or after the notice) shall be forwarded by them to the other authority;

and references in this Part to "the purchasing authority" shall be construed accordingly.

(4) An order under this section shall be made by statutory instrument.

DEFINITIONS

"disposal": s.532.
"dwelling": s.575.

"local housing authority": ss.1, 2.
"notice of determination": s.540.
"person entitled to assistance": s.540.
"public sector authority": ss.573, 574.
"relevant interest": s.530.

GENERAL NOTE

If the authority are of the opinion that a relevant interest (see notes to s.530, above) was disposed of by a public sector authority (as to which see notes to ss.573, 574), *and* that there has been no intervening disposal of a relevant interest, *and* that the conditions in Column 2 of the Table are met, they must give that authority the option of carrying out the repurchase themselves. The authority then have four weeks in which to give notice in writing to the local housing authority saying that they do wish to repurchase the dwelling, in which case the local housing authority give the public sector authority a "transfer notice" which has the effect of placing the public sector authority in the shoes of the local housing authority, in all respects, including as to Sched. 20, and as to rehousing (see ss.554–557, below).

Interest subject to right of pre-emption &c.

549.—(1) This section applies where a person ("the owner") is entitled to assistance by way of repurchase in respect of a defective dwelling and there is a covenant relating to his interest in the dwelling whereby—

(*a*) before disposing of the interest he must offer to dispose of it to a public sector authority, or

(*b*) in the case of a leasehold interest, he may require a public sector authority who are his landlord to accept a surrender of the lease but is otherwise prohibited from disposing of it.

(2) If the public sector authority are the local housing authority, the covenant shall be disregarded for the purposes of Schedule 20 (repurchase).

(3) If the public sector authority are not the local housing authority, the provisions of this Part as to repurchase do not apply so long as there is such a covenant; but if—

(*a*) the owner disposes of his interest to the public sector authority in pursuance of the covenant or lease, and

(*b*) the interest acquired by that authority on the disposal subsists only in the land affected, that is to say, the defective dwelling and any garage, outhouse, garden, yard and appurtenances occupied with and used for the purposes of the dwelling or part of it,

the owner is entitled to be paid by the local housing authority the amount (if any) by which 95 per cent. of the defect-free value exceeds the consideration for the disposal.

(4) For the purposes of this section—

(*a*) the "consideration for the disposal" means the amount before any reduction required by section 158(3) (reduction corresponding to amount of discount repayable or amount payable for outstanding share under shared ownership lease) or any provision to the like effect, and

(*b*) the "defect-free value" means the amount that would have been the consideration for the disposal if none of the defective dwellings to which the designation in question related had been affected by the qualifying defect.

DEFINITIONS
"defective dwelling": ss.528, 559.
"disposal": s.532.
"dwelling": s.575.
"local housing authority": ss.1, 2.
"public sector authority": ss.573, 574.
"qualifying defect": ss.528, 559.
"repurchase": s.547.

GENERAL NOTE

Dwellings in specified areas (*e.g.* rural areas, areas of natural beauty) sold under the right to buy may contain a pre-emption clause: see s.157, above. Other dwellings sold by public sector authorities may also contain such clauses. Further, a lease may contain a requirement that the landlord is bound to accept a surrender, although and because the tenant is otherwise prohibited from disposing of it.

If the public sector authority is also the local housing authority, any such covenant or clause is simply to be disregarded for the purposes of repurchase (see notes to s.547, above). If, on the other hand, it is another authority, the repurchase provisions are inapplicable but on disposal under the covenant, the owner is entitled to receive the balance between the price payable to him by the public sector authority and the price he would have received on repurchase under Sched. 20. If on resale to the public sector authority the price payable is reduced (under s.158, above), by discount clawback, the discount is added to the price before the balance is calculated, *i.e.* the owner does not make an additional windfall gain.

A claim must be made within two years of the disposal back to the public sector authority: see s.551, below.

Compulsory purchase compensation to be made up to 95 per cent. of defect-free value

550.—(1) Where a person ("the owner") has disposed of an interest in a defective dwelling, otherwise than in pursuance of Schedule 20 (repurchase), to an authority possessing compulsory purchase powers and—

(a) immediately before the time of the disposal he was eligible for assistance under this Part in respect of the dwelling,

(b) the amount paid as consideration for the disposal did not include any amount attributable to his right to apply for such assistance, and

(c) on the disposal the authority acquired an interest in any of the affected land, that is to say, the defective dwelling and any garage, outhouse, garden, yard and appurtenances occupied with and used for the purposes of the dwelling or part of it,

he is entitled, subject to the following provisions of this section, to be paid by the local housing authority the amount (if any) by which 95 per cent. of the defect-free value exceeds the amount of the compensation for the disposal.

(2) For the purposes of this section—

(a) the "amount of compensation for the disposal" means the amount that would have been the proper amount of compensation for the disposal (having regard to any relevant determination of the Lands Tribunal) or, if greater, the amount paid as the consideration for the disposal, and

(b) the "defect-free value" means the amount that would have been the proper amount of compensation for the disposal if none of the defective dwellings to which the designation in question related had been affected by the qualifying defect;

but excluding, in either case, any amount payable for disturbance or for any other matter not directly based on the value of land.

(3) For the purposes of this section, it shall be assumed that the disposal occurred on a compulsory acquisition (in cases where it did not in fact do so).

(4) Where the compensation for the disposal fell to be assessed by reference to the value of the land as a site cleared of buildings and available for development, it shall be assumed for the purposes of determining the defect-free value that it did not fall to be so assessed.

(5) The amount payable by the local housing authority under this section shall be reduced by the amount of any payment made in respect

of the defective dwelling under Schedule 23 (payments for well-maintained houses).

(6) In this section "authority possessing compulsory purchase powers" has the same meaning as in the Land Compensation Act 1961.

DEFINITIONS
"defective dwelling": ss.528, 559.
"disposal": s.532.
"dwelling": s.575.
"eligible for assistance": s.527.
"local housing authority": ss.1, 2.
"qualifying defect": ss.528, 559.

GENERAL NOTE
This section allows an owner to claim the balance between what he has in fact been paid on a compulsory purchase and what he could have received on a repurchase under this Part. Indeed, the wording of the provision is such that even if a person is entitled to a reinstatement grant rather than repurchase, then he may claim this amount, although presumably only until such time as the works have been completed and the grant paid, because at that point he ceases to be a "person eligible for assistance" within s.527. A claim must be made within two years of the "disposal", *i.e.* the compulsory purchase: see s.551, below.

The provision does not apply if the amount paid for the disposal reflected his rights under this Part. Note, however, that although any provision which would have restricted the amount payable on the compulsory purchase to site value (see s.585), is not to be applied, a well-maintained payment (see s.586) is to be subtracted from the payable balance (if any).

Supplementary provisions as to payments under s.549 or 550

551.—(1) The local housing authority are not required to make a payment to a person under—
   (*a*) section 549 (making-up of consideration on disposal in pursuance of right of pre-emption, &c.), or
   (*b*) section 550 (making up of compulsory purchase compensation),
unless he makes a written application to them for payment before the end of the period of two years beginning with the time of the disposal.

(2) Where the authority—
   (*a*) refuse an application for payment under section 549 on any grounds, or
   (*b*) refuse an application for payment under section 550 on the grounds that the owner was not eligible for assistance in respect of the defective dwelling,
they shall give the applicant written notice of the reasons for their decision.

(3) Any question arising—
   (*a*) under section 549 or 550 as to the defect-free value, or
   (*b*) under section 550 as to the amount of compensation for the disposal,
shall be determined by the district valuer if the owner or the local housing authority so require by notice in writing served on the district valuer.

(4) A person serving a notice on the district valuer in pursuance of subsection (3) shall serve notice in writing of that fact on the other party.

(5) Before making a determination in pursuance of subsection (3), the district valuer shall consider any representation by the owner or the authority made to him within four weeks from the service of the notice under that subsection.

DEFINITIONS
"disposal": s.532.
"district valuer": s.622.
"eligible for assistance": s.527.
"local housing authority": ss.1, 2.

GENERAL NOTE
To claim "making-up" payments under either of the last two sections, the owner must make a claim in writing within two years of the relevant disposal, which will include acquisition under a compulsory purchase (above, s.550(3)). If the claim is refused, the authority have to give reasons (*cf.* notes to s.536, above). Questions relating to value, or compensation, go to the district valuer, in much the same way as under Sched. 20, *i.e.* by written notice from either party, with a copy to the other party, and with four weeks in which to make additional representations.

Reimbursement of expenses incidental to repurchase

552.—(1) A person whose interest in a defective dwelling is acquired by the purchasing authority in pursuance of Schedule 20 (repurchase) is entitled to be reimbursed by the purchasing authority the proper amount of—

    (*a*) expenses in respect of legal services provided in connection with the authority's acquisition, and

    (*b*) other expenses in connection with negotiating the terms of that acquisition,

being in each case expenses which are reasonably incurred by him after receipt of a notice under paragraph 3 of that Schedule (authority's notice of proposed terms of acquisition).

(2) An agreement between a person and the purchasing authority is void in so far as it purports to oblige him to bear any part of the costs or expenses incurred by the authority in connection with the exercise by him of his rights under this Part.

DEFINITIONS
    "defective dwelling": ss.528, 559.
    "dwelling": s.575.

GENERAL NOTE
This provision permits the owner to claim the costs incurred in relation to the terms of the repurchase, from but only from the first notice given to him by the authority under Sched. 20. The wording covers not only legal costs, but also professional costs incurred in respect of the valuation, and does not assume that there has to be a dispute, referred to county court or district valuer, before they can be claimed. They are only to be reimbursed to the extent that they are "reasonably incurred". Presumably a dispute as to this can also be resolved by reference to the county court under s.572. Any agreement to the contrary is void, *e.g.* a term of the proposed conveyance. Self-evidently, the authority cannot pass on *their* costs, legal or technical, because they would then become the owner's costs and, as such, claimable under this section.

Effect of repurchase on occupier

Effect of repurchase on certain existing tenancies

553.—(1) Where an authority mentioned in section 80 (authorities satisfying the landlord condition for secure tenancy) acquire an interest in a defective dwelling in pursuance of Schedule 20 (repurchase) and—

    (*a*) the land in which the interest subsists is or includes a dwelling-house occupied as a separate dwelling, and

    (*b*) the interest of the person entitled to assistance by way of repurchase is, immediately before the completion of the authority's acquisition, subject to a tenancy of the dwelling-house,

the tenancy shall not, on or after the acquisition, become a secure tenancy unless the conditions specified in subsection (2) are met.

(2) The conditions are—

    (*a*) that the tenancy was a protected tenancy throughout the period beginning with the making of an application for assistance under

this Part in respect of the defective dwelling and ending immediately
before the authority's acquisition; and

(*b*) no notice was given in respect of the tenancy in accordance with
any of Cases 11 to 18 and 20 in Schedule 15 to the Rent Act 1977
(notice that possession might be recovered under that Case) or
under section 52(1)(*b*) of the Housing Act 1980 (notice that tenancy
is to be a protected shorthold tenancy).

DEFINITIONS
  "defective dwelling": ss.528, 559.
  "dwelling": s.575.
  "dwelling-house": s.558.
  "person entitled to assistance": s.540.
  "protected tenancy": s.622.
  "secure tenancy": ss.79, 558.

GENERAL NOTE
  This section is concerned only with defective dwellings which have been tenanted. When
the house is repurchased, if the purchasing authority is one of the landlords whose tenants
are normally secure tenants (see Part IV, above), the tenant would normally become
immediately secure, provided the "tenant condition" in s.81 is fulfilled, and the letting is
both a dwelling-house and let as a separate dwelling (above, s.79). There is no need to *claim*
a tenancy, let alone a secure tenancy, because the tenancy will continue, *i.e.* this Part does
not provide for termination of contractual tenancies.
  Because the tenancy will continue, it will normally become secure (see s.79, above). This
section, however, limits the circumstances in which tenants become secure tenants. Only
those tenants who have Rent Act protected tenancies (see notes to s.622, below) from the
period beginning with the application for assistance under this Part and until the repurchase
will become secure, and not even then if the tenancy is subject to notice under the specified
"mandatory" grounds, including lettings by former owner-occupiers, lettings of a prospective
retirement home, out-of-season holiday and student lettings, miscellaneous lettings in
agriculture and of church property, lettings by servicemen and shorthold tenancies. The
section does not apply to Rent Act *statutory* tenants (see notes to s.622, below), whose
position is governed by s.555, below.

Grant of tenancy to former owner-occupier

  554.—(1) Where an authority acquire an interest in a defective dwelling
in pursuance of Schedule 20 (repurchase), or in the circumstances
described in section 549(3) (exercise of right of pre-emption &c.), and—

(*a*) the land in which the interest subsists is or includes a dwelling-
house occupied as a separate dwelling, and

(*b*) an individual is an occupier of the dwelling-house throughout the
period beginning with the making of an application for assistance
under this Part in respect of the dwelling and ending immediately
before the completion of the authority's acquisition, and

(*c*) he is a person entitled to assistance by way of repurchase in respect
of the defective dwelling, or the persons so entitled are in relation
to the interest concerned his trustees,

the authority shall, in accordance with this section, either grant or arrange
for him to be granted a tenancy (of that dwelling-house or another: see
section 556) on the completion of their acquisition of the interest
concerned.

  (2) If the authority are among those mentioned in section 80(1) (public
sector authorities capable of granting secure tenancies) their obligation is
to grant a secure tenancy.

  (3) In any other case their obligation is to grant or arrange for the grant
of either—

(*a*) a secure tenancy, or

(*b*) a protected tenancy other than one under which the landlord might
recover possession under one of the cases in Part II of Schedule 15

to the Rent Act 1977 (cases in which the court must order possession).

(4) Where two or more persons qualify for the grant of a tenancy under this section in respect of the same dwelling-house, the authority shall grant the tenancy, or arrange for it to be granted, to such one or more of them as they may agree among themselves or (if there is no such agreement) to all of them.

DEFINITIONS
"defective dwelling": ss.528, 559.
"dwelling": s.575.
"dwelling-house": s.558.
"person entitled to assistance": s.540.
"protected tenancy": s.622.
"secure tenancy": ss.79, 558.

GENERAL NOTE
On repurchase, provided the property is (a) a dwelling-house, (b) occupied as a separate dwelling (see s.79, above), (c) the property has been occupied by an individual (not a corporate body) from the time when the application for assistance was made under this Part until repurchase, and (d) that individual is the person entitled to assistance under this Part (or the persons so entitled are his trustees), the authority have to either grant him, or arrange for him to be granted, a tenancy, which may be of the same property (subject to s.556, below) or of another property, from the date of the repurchase. As to claim for secure tenancy, see s.557, below. Notice of right to secure tenancy will have been given in the s.540 notification.

If the authority are amongst those whose tenants are normally secure (above, s.80), they must grant a secure tenancy, again of either the same (subject to s.556, below) or another property. If they are not, then they can grant a protected tenancy, or arrange for the grant of a secure tenancy. In the case of a protected tenancy, however, they cannot grant one subject to the "mandatory" grounds for possession, see notes to s.554, above. If there are two or more persons entitled to assistance, they can agree that one of them, or less than all of them, shall become the tenant or joint tenants, but in default of agreement, the tenancy must be a joint tenancy for all of them.

Grant of tenancy to former statutory tenant

555.—(1) Where an authority mentioned in section 80(1) (public sector authorities capable of granting secure tenancies) acquire an interest in a defective dwelling in pursuance of Schedule 20 (repurchase) and—

    (*a*) the land in which the interest subsists is or includes a dwelling-house occupied as a separate dwelling, and

    (*b*) an individual is an occupier of a dwelling-house throughout the period beginning with the making of an application for assistance under this Part in respect of the dwelling and ending immediately before the completion of the authority's acquisition, and

    (*c*) he is a statutory tenant of the dwelling-house at the end of that period, and

    (*d*) no notice was given in respect of the original tenancy in accordance with any of Cases 11 to 18 and 20 in Schedule 15 to the Rent Act 1977 (notice that possession might be recovered under that Case) or under section 52(1)(*b*) of the Housing Act 1980 (notice that tenancy is to be a protected shorthold tenancy), and

    (*e*) the interest of the person entitled to assistance would, if the statutory tenancy were a contractual tenancy, be subject to the tenancy at the end of the period mentioned in paragraph (*b*),

the authority shall grant him a secure tenancy (of that dwelling-house or another: see section 556) on the completion of their acquisition of the interest concerned.

(2) Where two or more persons qualify for the grant of a tenancy under this section in respect of the same dwelling-house, the authority shall

grant the tenancy to such one or more of them as they may agree among themselves or (if there is no such agreement) to all of them.

(3) If at any time after the service of a notice of determination it appears to the purchasing authority that a person may be entitled to request them to grant him a secure tenancy under this section, they shall forthwith give him notice in writing of that fact.

DEFINITIONS
"dwelling": s.575.
"dwelling-house": s.558.
"secure tenancy": ss.79, 558.
"statutory tenant": s.622.

GENERAL NOTE
Whereas s.553 dealt with contractual, Rent Act protected tenants, this section deals with statutory tenants, *i.e.* those whose contractual tenancy has ended, but who remain in residence at the property. They, too, are entitled to a tenancy from the authority, provided the authority are one whose tenants are normally secure (see s.80, above). (If the public sector landlord is *not* one whose tenants are normally secure, the tenant will on acquisition become *its* statutory tenant, because the purchase will be subject to the tenancy). The statutory tenant has to have been in occupation (whether or not as statutory tenant or indeed whether or not as tenant) throughout the period from claim to repurchase, and the tenancy must not be one subject to one of the "mandatory" grounds for possession, see notes to s.553, above.

The secure tenancy must be claimed: see s.557, below. If after the service of the notice of determination under s.540 it appears to the authority that someone might be entitled under this section, they are bound to give him notice in writing of his prospective entitlement. The secure tenancy granted may be of the same property (subject to s.556, below), or another property, and if there are two or more joint statutory tenants must be in the name of such one or more of them as they agree or, in default, in all of their names.

Alternative accommodation under s.554 or 555

556.—(1) The dwelling-house to be let under the tenancy granted to a person—
   (*a*) under section 554 or 555 (grant of tenancy to former owner-occupier or statutory tenant of defective dwelling-house acquired by authority), or
   (*b*) under arrangements made for the purposes of section 554,
shall be the dwelling-house of which he is the occupier immediately before the completion of the authority's acquisition (the "current dwelling-house"), except in the following Cases.

Case 1

By reason of the condition of any building of which the current dwelling-house consists or of which it forms part, the dwelling-house may not safely be occupied for residential purposes.

Case 2

The authority intend, within a reasonable time of the completion of their acquisition of the interest concerned—
   (*a*) to demolish or reconstruct the building which consists of or includes the defective dwelling in question, or
   (*b*) to carry out work on any building or land in which the interest concerned subsists,
and cannot reasonably do so if the current dwelling-house remains in residential occupation.

(2) In those Cases the dwelling-house to be let shall be another dwelling-house which, so far as is reasonably practicable in the case of that authority, affords accommodation which is—

(a) similar as regards extent and character to the accommodation afforded by the current dwelling-house,

(b) reasonably suitable to the means of the prospective tenant and his family, and

(c) reasonably suitable to the needs of the prospective tenant and his family as regards proximity to place of work and place of education.

DEFINITIONS
"defective dwelling": ss.528, 559.
"dwelling": s.575.
"dwelling-house": s.558.
"statutory tenant": s.622.

GENERAL NOTE
The presumption is in favour of a tenancy—whether to a former owner-occupier, or to a statutory tenant,—in the same (the "current") property, *save* in the circumstances specified. Case 2 is similar to one of the grounds for possession against secure tenants: see Sched. 2, Ground 2. The criteria for alternative accommodation are similar to those applicable to secure tenants under Sched. 2, see Part IV thereof.

Request for tenancy under s.554 or 555

557.—(1) An authority are not required to grant, or arrange for the grant of, a tenancy to a person under section 554 or 555 unless he requests them to do so in writing before—

(a) in the case of an acquisition under Schedule 20 (repurchase), the service on the person entitled to assistance of a copy of the agreement drawn up under paragraph 5 of that Schedule, or

(b) in the case of an acquisition in the circumstances described in section 549(3) (acquisition in pursuance of right of pre-emption, &c.), the time of the disposal.

(2) An authority receiving a request under subsection (1) shall, as soon as reasonably practicable, give notice in writing to the person making the request stating whether in their opinion either of the Cases in section 556(1) applies (cases in which tenancy may be of a dwelling-house other than the current dwelling-house).

(3) If their opinion is that either Case does apply, the notice shall also state which of the Cases is applicable and the effect of section 556.

DEFINITION
"person entitled to assistance": s.540.

GENERAL NOTE
This is a most important section. A former owner-occupier will have been advised of the entitlement to claim a tenancy from the authority in the notice of determination: see s.540(4), above. A statutory tenant will have been advised by the authority direct, under s.555(3), above. There is no provision for an extension of time, *e.g.* by the county court.

Interpretation of ss.553 to 557

558. In sections 553 to 557 (effect of repurchase on occupier)—

(a) "dwelling-house" has the same meaning as in Part IV (secure tenancies);

(b) "occupier", in relation to a dwelling-house, means a person who occupies the dwelling-house as his only or principal home or (in the case of a statutory tenant) as his residence;

(c) references to the grant of a secure tenancy are to the grant of a tenancy which would be a secure tenancy assuming that the tenant under the tenancy occupies the dwelling-house as his only or principal home

GENERAL NOTE
  "dwelling-house". See notes to s.79, above.
  "only or principal home", "residence". See notes to s.81, above.

Local schemes

Designation of defective dwellings under local schemes

559.—(1) A local housing authority may by resolution designate as a class buildings in their district each of which consists of or includes one or more dwellings if it appears to them that—

   (*a*) buildings in the proposed class are defective by reason of their design or construction, and

   (*b*) by virtue of the circumstances mentioned in paragraph (*a*) having become generally known, the value of some or all of the dwellings concerned has been substantially reduced.

(2) Subsection (1) does not apply to a building in a class designated under section 528 (designation by Secretary of State); but a building does not cease to be included in a class designated under this section by virtue of its inclusion in a class designated under that section.

(3) A dwelling which is, or is included in, a building in a class so designated is referred to in this Part as a "defective dwelling"; and in this Part, in relation to such a dwelling—

   (*a*) "the qualifying defect" means what, in the opinion of the authority, is wrong with the buildings in that class, and

   (*b*) "the cut-off date" means the date by which, in the opinion of the authority, the circumstances mentioned in subsection (1)(*a*) became generally known.

(4) A designation shall describe the qualifying defect and specify—

   (*a*) the cut-off date,

   (*b*) the date (being a date falling on or after the cut-off date) on which the designation is to come into operation, and

   (*c*) the period within which persons may seek assistance under this Part in respect of the defective dwellings concerned.

(5) A designation may not describe a designated class by reference to the area (other than the authority's district) in which the buildings concerned are situated; but a designated class may be so described that within the authority's district there is only one building in the class.

(6) Any question arising as to whether a building is or was at any time in a class designated under this section shall be determined by the local housing authority concerned.

DEFINITIONS
  "dwellings": s.575.
  "local housing authority": ss.1, 2.

GENERAL NOTE
  This section makes parallel provisions permitting local authorities themselves to designate dwellings (or merely in substance one dwelling: see subs. (5)) in their areas as defective dwellings, setting their own "cut-off date" and describing the "qualifying defect" for themselves: see s.528, above. A local designation cannot include property of the class designated by the Secretary of State, although if the Secretary of State subsequently designates a dwelling that is within a local designation, the dwelling remains designated and, indeed, dually designated, in which case the provisions of Sched. 21 will apply: see notes thereto, and to s.566, below.
  The resolution of designation cannot define by references to an area *within* an authority's area, *i.e.* it must refer to the whole of the authority's area, but can be defined so that there is in fact only one dwelling which qualifies. It is for the authority to resolve any question as

to whether or not a dwelling fell within a designation at a relevant time, which would seem to confine challenge to judicial review: see notes to ss.528, 533. Provision is made for variation or revocation by the authority (s.560, below), and local designations are within the provisions for publicity (s.562, below).

A resolution must allow at least two months to elapse before it comes into effect, and notice must be given to the Secretary of State who may, in effect, overrule the resolution: see s.561.

Variation or revocation of designation under local scheme

560.—(1) The local housing authority may by resolution—

(*a*) vary a designation under section 559, but not so as to vary the cut-off date, or

(*b*) revoke such a designation.

(2) The authority may by a variation of the designation extend the period referred to in section 559(4)(*c*) (period within which assistance must be applied for) whether or not it has expired.

(3) The variation or revocation of a designation does not affect the operation of the provisions of this Part in relation to a dwelling if, before the variation or revocation comes into operation, the dwelling is a defective dwelling by virtue of the designation in question and application for assistance under this Part has been made.

DEFINITIONS
"cut-off date": s.559.
"designation": s.559.
"dwelling": s.575.
"local housing authority": ss.1, 2.

GENERAL NOTE
This section is analogous to s.529, above, *i.e.* the authority may vary or revoke a designation, but not so as retrospectively to affect qualification. Note that variation or revocation, as designation, is subject to the veto of the Secretary of State: see s.561, below.

Secretary of State's control over designation, variation or revocation

561.—(1) Where a local housing authority have passed a resolution under—

(*a*) section 559 (designation under local scheme) or,

(*b*) section 560 (variation or revocation of designation under local scheme),

they shall give written notice to the Secretary of State of the resolution before the expiry of the period of 28 days beginning with the date on which it is passed.

(2) The designation, variation or revocation shall not come into operation before the expiry of the period of two months beginning with the receipt by the Secretary of State of the notice under subsection (1).

(3) If within that period the Secretary of State serves notice in writing to that effect on the authority, the designation, revocation or variation shall not come into operation.

DEFINITIONS
"designation": s.559.
"local housing authority": ss.1, 2.

GENERAL NOTE
There must be a lapse of at least two months between designation under a local scheme, or variation or revocation of a local designation, in order to permit the Secretary of State an effective one month to consider exercising his subsection (3) power of veto, *i.e.* two months less the up to 28 days which the authority have for notifying the Secretary of State of the resolution.

Miscellaneous

Duty of local housing authority to publicise availability of assistance

562.—(1) A local housing authority shall, within the period of three months beginning with the coming into operation of—

(*a*) a designation under section 528 (designation of defective dwellings by Secretary of State) or section 559 (designation of defective dwellings under local scheme), or,

(*b*) a variation of such a designation,

publish in a newspaper circulating in their district notice suitable for the purpose of bringing the effect of the designation or variation to the attention of persons who may be eligible for assistance in respect of such of the dwellings concerned as are situated within their district.

(2) No such notice need be published by a local housing authority who are of opinion—

(*a*) that none of the dwellings concerned are situated in their district, or

(*b*) that no-one is likely to be eligible for assistance in respect of the dwellings concerned which are situated in their district.

(3) If at any time it becomes apparent to a local housing authority that a person is likely to be eligible for assistance in respect of a defective dwelling within their district, they shall forthwith take such steps as are reasonably practicable to inform him of the fact that assistance is available.

DEFINITIONS
"designation": ss.528, 559.
"defective dwelling": ss.529, 559.
"dwelling": s.575.
"eligible for assistance": s.527.
"local housing authority": ss.1, 2.
"variation": ss.526, 561.

GENERAL NOTE
This section contains the principal duty to publicise the provisions of this Part of the Act, whether a designation is national or local. Any local housing authority will prima facie be under a duty by virtue of this section if there "may" be people who are eligible. That said, if they are "of the opinion" that there are no designated dwellings in their area, or that no one is likely to be eligible (which will, of course, be wholly inconsistent with a local designation), they are exempt. It follows that an authority *must* consider publication, and of course that there must be some basis, *e.g.* an officer report, that one of the two exemption conditions applies. Publication is to be within three months of designation.

In addition, however, there is the "individual" duty under subsection (3), arising when "it becomes apparent to" the authority that a person "is likely to be eligible", to take such steps as are "reasonably practicable" to inform him of the fact that assistance is available.

Duties of public sector authority disposing of defective dwelling

563.—(1) A public sector authority shall, where a person is to acquire a relevant interest in a defective dwelling on a disposal by the authority, give him notice in writing before the time of the disposal—

(*a*) specifying the qualifying defect, and

(*b*) stating that he will not be eligible for assistance under this Part in respect of the dwelling.

(2) A public sector authority shall, before they convey a relevant interest in a defective dwelling in pursuance of a contract to a person on whom a notice under subsection (1) has not been served, give him notice in writing—

(*a*) specifying the qualifying defect,

(*b*) stating, where the time of disposal of the interest falls after the cut-off date, that he will not be eligible for assistance under this Part, and

(*c*) stating the effect of subsection (3).

(3) A person on whom a notice under subsection (2) is served—

(*a*) is not obliged to complete the conveyance before the expiry of the period of six months beginning with the service of that notice on him, and

(*b*) may within that period withdraw from the transaction by notice in writing to the authority to that effect;

and upon such a notice of withdrawal being given to the authority the parties to the contract are discharged from any obligations in connection with it and any deposit paid shall be repaid.

(4) Where a public sector authority are required to serve a notice under section 124 (landlord's response to notice claiming to exercise right to buy) in respect of a defective dwelling, the notice under subsection (1) shall be served with that notice.

(5) A notice under subsection (1) or (2) shall, (except in the case of a notice under subsection (1) which is served in accordance with subsection (4)), be served at the earliest date at which it is reasonably practicable to do so.

DEFINITIONS

"cut-off date": ss.528, 559.
"defective dwelling": ss.528, 559.
"disposal": s.532.
"dwelling": s.575.
"public sector authority": ss.573, 574.
"qualifying defect": ss.528, 559.
"relevant interest": s.530.

GENERAL NOTE

Where a public sector authority are selling a property, which will in these cases commonly be under the right to buy (above, Part V), before the disposal takes place, they are bound to give the purchaser notice in writing which identifies the qualifying defect, and advises the purchaser that if he continues with the purchase, he will not benefit from this Part of the Act. This duty should be complied with "at the earliest date at which it is reasonably practicable to do so": subs. (5). The duty arises regardless of whether the cut-off date is likely to fall before the sale, *i.e.* so that the purchaser would not benefit in any event. The purchaser may still, of course, apply for grant-aid under Part XV. The notice is to be served together with a notice responding to the right to buy under s.124, if the purchase is under Part V: subsection (4).

If exchange of contracts has been reached before a subsection (1) notice has been served, the authority are to serve a slightly different notice, again "at the earliest date at which it is reasonably practicable to do so" (subs. (5)), also identifying the qualifying defect, and stating non-qualification for assistance, specifying the cut-off date if that will be after the conveyance (so that, in effect, the purchaser would not in any event have qualified), and stating the effect of subsection (3). (N.B. Not setting out the words of it, but "stating its effect", which is different: *cf.* s.104, above).

The effect of subsection (3) is that the prospective purchaser may take up to six months to decide whether or not to complete, and may withdraw at any time during that period. This will be of particular importance where there has been an exchange of contracts, and will override the requirements of the contract, to the extent, if the purchaser decides not to proceed, of discharging the contract and entitling the purchaser to receive back any deposit.

It will rarely have any effect under the right to buy, because (a) contracts are not usually used under Part V, above, therefore (b) purchasers can always withdraw, and (c) the time limits for serving notices requiring completion are longer than those applicable here. Nonetheless, should a notice under subsection (2) be served on a right to buy purchaser (because Part V does not prohibit exchange of contracts), at a late stage, when final notice to complete under s.141, above, has less than six months to run, it should override (*i.e.* extend) that notice.

Subs. (5)

Of course, it will not be practicable to serve a notice prior to designation—national or local—although the wording is wide enough to suggest that the section should be complied with at a time between designation (or resolution) and coming into operation: see ss.528(3)(*b*), 559 and 561.

Reinstatement of defective dwelling by local housing authority

564.—(1) Where a relevant interest in a defective dwelling has been disposed of by a public sector authority, the local housing authority may, before the end of the period within which a person may seek assistance under this Part in respect of the dwelling, enter into an agreement with—

(*a*) any person holding an interest in the dwelling, or

(*b*) any person who is a statutory tenant of it,

to execute at his expense any of the work required to reinstate the dwelling.

(2) For the purposes of this section a disposal by or under an enactment of an interest in a dwelling held by a public sector authority shall be treated as a disposal of the interest by the authority.

DEFINITIONS

"defective dwelling": ss.528, 559.

"disposal": s.532.

"dwelling": s.575.

"public sector authority": ss.573, 574.

"statutory tenant": s.622.

GENERAL NOTE

Part of this section is straightforward: it permits "agency agreements" which will allow the authority to carry out the works on behalf of the owner, which is widely enough worded to permit the authority to sub-contract the work. If the works are to be carried out by the authority's own work-force, the Direct Labour Organisation provisions of the Local Government, Planning and Land Act 1980 may apply. The section may be compared with s.514, above. The owner with a relevant interest will, of course, still qualify for the reinstatement grant, hence "at his expense".

Less straightforward are the references to person with "any" interest and "statutory tenant", for *unless* there is a relevant interest they will *not* qualify for reinstatement grant, and one must wonder why, through this backdoor, they are suddenly being invited to bear the whole or any of the cost. What can be understood is that the authority or the owner may well need a tenant to be a party to an agreement, in order to secure access, etc.

The answer would seem to be that the latter was what was *intended*. In the previous section (Housing Defects Act 1984, s.16) the relevant part of the wording is the same, but not set out in sub-paragraphs. Read thus, it is not so difficult to see that what was intended was for the words "at his expense" to refer back to the "person who may seek assistance". That was still arcane, if the intention has been properly comprehended, and split up as it now is, the difficulty has been exacerbated. The difficulty is unlikely to raise real problems of practice, however, provided no local authority seek to abuse it by seeking contributions or indeed full burden of costs from protected or statutory tenants, instead of the owner (with the assistance of reinstatement grant).

Death of person eligible for assistance, &c.

565.—(1) Where a person who is eligible for assistance in respect of a defective dwelling—

(*a*) dies, or

(*b*) disposes of his interest in the dwelling (otherwise than on a disposal for value) to such a person as is mentioned in section 527(*a*) (persons qualifying for assistance: individuals, trustees for individuals and personal representatives),

this Part applies as if anything done (or treated by virtue of this subsection as done) by or in relation to the person so eligible had been done by or in relation to his personal representatives or, as the case may be, the person acquiring his interest.

(2) In sections 549 to 551 (subsidiary forms of financial assistance) references to the owner of an interest in a defective dwelling include his personal representatives.

DEFINITIONS
"defective dwelling": ss.528, 559.
"disposal": s.532.
"dwelling": s.575.
"eligible for assistance": s.527.

GENERAL NOTE
This section is straightforward. On the death of a person who is eligible for assistance, or who disposes of his interest in such a way that entitlement to assistance is not lost (see s.531(1), *i.e.* loss of entitlement on disposal for value), the previous actions, *e.g.* notices, under this Part become those of the successor.

Dwellings included in more than one designation

566. The provisions of Schedule 21 have effect with respect to dwellings included in more than one designation.

DEFINITIONS
"designation": ss.528, 559.
"dwelling": s.575.

GENERAL NOTE
Provided designations by the Secretary of State continue to refer not only to defect, but also manufacturer, it would seem impossible for a dwelling to be defective within two such national designations: see notes to s.528. However, if the Secretary of State designates a dwelling that is already within a local designation (see s.559), the dwelling will fall into two categories: see s.559(2). In such circumstances the provisions of Sched. 21 will apply. There can be no local designation of dwellings already within a national designation: s.559(2).

Under Sched. 21, if a person is already eligible for assistance under a local designation, and there is subsequently a national designation, the potential applicant stays under the local designation if, *but only if* (a) he is not eligible for assistance under the national designation, or (b) the entitlement under the local designation is to repurchase. Accordingly, a national designation supplants a local designation when the applicant was eligible under local and is now eligible under national, unless local would lead to repurchase. Where national does *not* supplant local, *both* will apply: see next paragraphs.

Where *both* designations apply, references to designation, qualifying defect, and period within which a person may seek assistance, mean under either designation, while the maximum amount to be taken into account for the purpose of calculating grant-aid means the maximum under *both*, added together: see s.543, above. If a national scheme which also applies to a local scheme does come into operation, the authority must give the applicant notice stating whether or not the national designation is to be disregarded. If it is, they must state their reasons: *cf.* s.533. If the notice states that the national designation is not to be disregarded, and accordingly the applicant is, as it were, dually designated, the authority have to tell the applicant so, telling him what the effect of the new, national designation is, and of the effect of being dually designated.

They must also refer the applicant to s.537, *i.e.* the right to seek repurchase instead of reinstatement grant. This is aimed at those cases where dual designation works against the interests of the applicant. The authority thereafter make a new determination of the form of assistance to which the applicant is entitled, taking the new designation into account. Where the effect is repurchase, they must address the applicant to the further provisions, which deal with the circumstance of the applicant who has already contracted for, or started, works under the reinstatement grant, and which provisions will ensure that he still receives the grant, to the amount appropriate to the commitment he has already undertaken, although he will still lose his part of the expenditure.

Modifications of this Part in relation to shared ownership leases

567.—(1) The Secretary of State may by regulations provide for this Part to have effect, in its application to a case in which the interest of a person eligible for assistance in respect of a defective dwelling is—

(*a*) a shared ownership lease, or

(*b*) the freehold acquired under the terms of a shared ownership lease,

subject to such modifications as may be specified in the regulations.

(2) The regulations may, in particular, in relation to such a case—

(*a*) make any provision that may be made by an order under section 538(2) (modification of conditions for assistance by way of reinstatement grant), or

(*b*) require an authority receiving an application for assistance to determine under section 537 that the person is entitled to assistance by way of repurchase.

(3) An authority shall not entertain an application for assistance by a person whose interest in the defective dwelling is such as is mentioned in subsection (1)(*a*) or (*b*) unless regulations under this section are in force at the time of application in respect of that interest.

(4) In this section "shared ownership lease" means—

(*a*) a shared ownership lease granted in pursuance of Part V (the right to buy),

(*b*) a lease of a dwelling-house granted otherwise than in pursuance of that Part which contains provision to the like effect as that required by paragraphs 1 and 2 of Schedule 9 (terms of shared ownership lease: right to acquire additional shares and to acquire freehold),

(*c*) a lease of a description specified by regulations made by the Secretary of State, or

(*d*) a lease determined, or of a class determined, by the Secretary of State to be a shared ownership lease.

(5) The fact that a lease becomes a shared ownership lease by virtue of regulations under subsection (4)(*c*) or a determination under subsection (4)(*d*) does not affect the operation of the provisions of this Part in relation to a case where an application for assistance under this Part has previously been made.

(6) Regulations under this section—

(*a*) may make different provision for England and Wales and for different descriptions of shared ownership lease, and

(*b*) shall be made by statutory instrument which shall be subject to annulment in pursuance of a resolution of either House of Parliament.

DEFINITIONS

"defective dwelling": ss.528, 559.

"dwelling": s.575.

"eligible for assistance": s.528.

"repurchase": s.547.

GENERAL NOTE

The Secretary of State may make regulations, and which may be different for England and Wales (but, presumably, therefore not for different areas within England or Wales, *cf.* s.528(4), above), concerning the applicability of this Part to "shared ownership leases", or for different types of shared ownership lease. Shared ownership leases may be under Part V (the right to buy), or similar such leases, or leases specified by the Secretary of State: see subs. (4). The regulations may "in particular" modify the conditions under which reinstatement grant is payable (see s.538, referable particular no doubt to the cost of works comparison with value after works) and correspondingly the conditions under which repurchase will be the assistance available: see s.537.

Extension of assistance to mortgagees

568.—(1) The Secretary of State may by regulations make provision for conferring rights and obligations on a mortgagee of a defective dwelling where—

    (*a*) a power of sale (whether conferred by section 101 of the Law of Property Act 1925 or otherwise) is exercisable by the mortgagee, and

    (*b*) the mortgagor is eligible for assistance in respect of the defective dwelling.

(2) The rights that may be so conferred are—

    (*a*) rights corresponding to those conferred by this Part on a person holding a relevant interest in the defective dwelling,

    (*b*) the right to require the purchasing authority to acquire in accordance with the regulations any interest in the defective dwelling to be disposed of in exercise of the power of sale, and

    (*c*) where the mortgagee is the purchasing authority, the right by deed to vest the dwelling in themselves;

and those rights may be conferred in place of rights conferred by this Part on any other person.

(3) The regulations may provide that where the conditions in subsection (1)(*a*) and (*b*) are or have been satisfied, this Part, the power of sale in question and any enactment relating to the power of sale shall have effect subject to such modifications as may be specified in the regulations.

(4) Where a defective dwelling is vested in a mortgagee in pursuance of—

    (*a*) regulations under this section, or

    (*b*) section 452 and Schedule 17 (vesting of dwelling-house in authority entitled to exercise power of sale),

the regulations may provide for the payment in respect of the vesting of an amount calculated on the assumption that none of the defective dwellings to which the designation in question relates is affected by the qualifying defect; and those enactments shall have effect subject to any such provisions.

(5) Regulations under this section—

    (*a*) may make different provision for different cases and may make incidental and consequential provision; and

    (*b*) shall be made by statutory instrument which shall be subject to annulment in pursuance of a resolution of either House of Parliament.

(6) In this section "mortgagee" and "mortgagor" have the same meaning as in the Law of Property Act 1925.

DEFINITIONS

    "defective dwelling": ss.528, 559.

    "dwelling": s.575.

    "eligible for assistance": s.527.

    "purchasing authority": s.548.

    "qualifying defect": ss.528, 559.

    "relevant interest": s.530.

GENERAL NOTE

    This is an enabling provision, permitting the Secretary of State by regulations (which may make different provisions for different cases, and include incidental and consequential provisions, to replace the rights of owners with equivalent rights on the part of a mortgagee, either to reinstatement grant or repurchase within this Part, or to require purchase under this section. The regulations are limited to cases where the mortgagee's power of sale is exercisable, and the mortgagor is eligible for assistance.

Contributions by Secretary of State

Contributions by Secretary of State

569.—(1) The Secretary of State may, if he thinks fit in any case, contribute towards the expense incurred by a local housing authority—

(*a*) in giving assistance by way of reinstatement grant,

(*b*) in giving assistance by way of repurchase of a dwelling which is a defective dwelling by virtue of a designation under section 528 (designation by Secretary of State), or

(*c*) in making payments under section 549 (making up of consideration on disposal in pursuance of right of pre-emption, &c.) or section 550 (making up of compulsory purchase compensation).

(2) The contributions shall be annual payments—

(*a*) in respect of a period of 20 years beginning with the financial year in which, as the case may be, the work in respect of which the grant was payable was completed, the acquisition of the interest concerned was completed or the payment was made, and

(*b*) of a sum equal to the relevant percentage of the annual loan charges referable to the amount of the expense incurred.

(3) The relevant percentage is—

(*a*) 90 per cent. in the case of reinstatement grant,

(*b*) 75 per cent. in the case of repurchase or a payment under section 549 or 550 where there has at any time been a disposal of a relevant interest in the defective dwelling by the local housing authority or a predecessor of that authority, and

(*c*) 100 per cent. in the case of repurchase or a payment under those sections not within paragraph (*b*);

or such other percentage as, in any of those cases, may be provided by order under section 570.

(4) The amount of the expense incurred is—

(*a*) in the case of reinstatement grant, the amount of the grant,

(*b*) in the case of repurchase, the price paid for the acquisition, together with any amount reimbursed under section 552 (incidental expenses), less the value of the interest at the relevant time determined in accordance with paragraph 8 of Schedule 20 (value for purposes of repurchase) but without the assumption required by paragraph 8(1)(*a*) (assumption that dwelling is defect free),

(*c*) in the case of a payment under section 549 or 550, the amount of the payment.

(5) The annual loan charges referable to the amount of the expense incurred means the annual sum which, in the opinion of the Secretary of State, would fall to be provided by a local housing authority for the payment of interest on, and the repayment of, a loan of that amount repayable over a period of 20 years.

(6) Payment of contributions under this section is subject to the making of a claim in such form, and containing such particulars, as the Secretary of State may determine; and the contributions are payable at such times, in such manner and subject to such conditions, as to records, certificates, audit or otherwise, as the Secretary of State may, with the agreement of the Treasury, determine.

DEFINITIONS

"defective dwelling": ss.528, 559.

"designation": ss.528, 559.

"disposal": s.532.

"dwelling": s.575.

"local housing authority": ss.1, 2.

"reinstatement grant": s.541.

"relevant interest": s.530.

"repurchase": s.547.

GENERAL NOTE

In many ways the key provision, from the point of view of local authorities, and in terms of how well this Part of the Act is implemented, and how likely it is that there will be local designations, this section deals with central government subsidy for the exercise. Subsidy takes the form, as it does under Part XV, of payment of a proportion of the loan charges over a 20 year period.

Subsidy is available in relation to any reinstatement grants, but repurchase only under a national scheme, and "making up" payments (under ss.549, 550). Subsidy starts with the year in which the reinstatement grant-aided work is completed (therefore not on discretionary stage payments under s.545), completion of repurchase, or the making up payment was made.

Note that in a year of intense activity, there can be a distortion arising out of the principle that an annual payment is made in the year in which reinstatement grant-aided work is payable. If there have been no stage payments, it is unlikely to be the case that the authority have themselves had to bear loan charges for the whole of the year. Applying the relevant percentages available under subsection (3), they may have paid out *less* in a year than the relevant percentage of a *full year's* payments amount to. Accordingly, the revenue consequences, *i.e.* the rate fund burden of the balance which the authority must find for themselves (see notes to s.421, above), may be deceptively low or even non-existent in that first year.

This apparent windfall gain will, of course, certainly catch up with the authority in 20 years' time, but few authorities in current financial conditions plan that far ahead. But the distortion effect will not operate "cleanly", *i.e.* for one year after the Housing Defects Act 1984 came into force. It will *also* obscure the true revenue consequences in latter years. This is the real danger: as long as activity remains at a consistent or increasing level, the distortion or extent of rate fund burden will be concealed; it will come suddenly, and potentially painfully, to light if there is a sudden decline in activity.

The relevant percentages are as specified: note that the Secretary of State may vary them by Order (as to which, see s.570, below); note, too, that under subs. (3)(b) a lower repurchase subsidy is available where the property has at some time been in the ownership of the authority themselves. As with reinstatement grant itself (*cf.* s.543, above), the relevant percentage is not necessarily on actual expenditure, but on "expense incurred" as defined in subs. (4). This bites on repurchase: see subs. (4)(b).

Power to vary relevant percentage

570.—(1) The Secretary of State may by order made with the consent of the Treasury vary all or any of the percentages specified in section 569(3) (relevant percentages for purposes of contribution to expenditure of local housing authority) in respect of assistance or payments, or a class of assistance or payments, specified in the order.

(2) An order—

(*a*) may make different provision for assistance given or payments made in respect of defective dwellings in different areas or under different provisions or for different purposes of the same provision;

(*b*) shall be made by statutory instrument; and

(*c*) shall not be made unless a draft of it has been laid before and approved by a resolution of the House of Commons.

(3) An order applies to assistance given or payments made in pursuance of applications made after such date as may be specified in the order, and the specified date shall not be earlier than the date of the laying of the draft.

DEFINITIONS

"defective dwellings": ss.529, 559.
"dwelling": s.575.
"local housing authority": ss.1, 2.

GENERAL NOTE

This section is ancillary to s.569, above, dealing with Orders to vary the relevant percentages applicable to subsidies for implementation of this Part. Procedure is affirmative (see subs. (2)(c)). Orders may make different provisions, including for different areas (subs. (2)(a), *cf.* s.528(4)).

Supplementary provisions

Service of notices

571.—(1) A notice or other document under this Part may be given to or served on a person, and an application or written request under this Part may be made to a person—

(*a*) by delivering it to him or leaving it at his proper address, or

(*b*) by sending it to him by post,

and also, where the person concerned is a body corporate, by giving or making it to or serving it on the secretary of that body.

(2) For the purposes of this section, and of section 7 of the Interpretation Act 1978 as it applies for the purposes of this section, the proper address of a person is—

(*a*) in the case of a body corporate or its secretary, the address of the principal office of the body,

(*b*) in any other case, his last known address,

and also, where an additional address for service has been specified by that person in a notice under section 548(2) (notice of intention to assume responsibility for repurchase), that address.

DEFINITION
"repurchase": s.547.

Jurisdiction of county court

572.—(1) The county court has jurisdiction—

(*a*) to determine any question arising under this Part notwithstanding that a declaration is the only relief sought, and

(*b*) to entertain any proceedings brought in connection with the performance or discharge of obligations arising under this Part, including proceedings for the recovery of damages in the event of the obligations not being performed.

(2) Subsection (1) has effect subject to—

sections 528(6) and 559(6) (questions of designation to be decided by designating authority), and

section 551(3) and paragraph 9 of Schedule 20 (questions of valuation to be determined by district valuer).

(3) Where an authority fail to extend or further extend a period when required to do so by—

(*a*) section 542(3) (reinstatement grant: period within which work is to be completed), or

(*b*) paragraph 2(2) or 6(2) of Schedule 20 (repurchase: period for service of request or notice by person entitled to assistance),

the county court may by order extend or further extend that period until such date as may be specified in the order.

(4) The Lord Chancellor may make such rules and give such directions as he thinks fit for the purpose of giving effect to this section.

(5) The rules and directions may provide for the exercise by a registrar of the county court of any jurisdiction exercisable under this section.

(6) Rules under this section shall be made by statutory instrument which shall be subject to annulment in pursuance of a resolution of either House of Parliament.

GENERAL NOTE

The county court has jurisdiction to determine any question arising under this Part, even if a declaration is the only relief sought. (Questions under this Part would not seem to fall within County Courts Act 1984, s.22, even if, as is probable, the property is within the rateable values for the time being applicable under that Act, as it is hard to define them as relating to the "use, occupation, enjoyment or possession" of the property, without some stretching of the imagination or language.) In the event, this jurisdiction does *not* include issues of whether or not a property is within a designation, which is with the designating authority, *i.e.* Secretary of State or local authority, so that an argument on that point will have to be by way of judicial review: see notes to s.533, above). Nor does it include the questions of valuation reserved to the district valuer: see Sched. 20.

Meaning of "public sector authority"

573.—(1) In this Part "public sector authority" means—
a local authority (or a predecessor of a local authority),
a joint board of which every constituent member is, or is appointed
by, a local authority (or a predecessor of a local authority),
the Peak Park Joint Planning Board,
the Lake District Special Planning Board,
a water authority,
the Housing Corporation,
a registered housing association other than a co-operative housing
association (or a predecessor housing association of such an
association),
a new town corporation,
the Development Board for Rural Wales,
the National Coal Board, or
the United Kingdom Atomic Energy Authority,
or a body corporate or housing association specified by order of the Secretary of State in accordance with the following provisions.

(2) The Secretary of State may provide that a body corporate shall be treated as a public sector authority if he is satisfied—
(*a*) that the affairs of the body are managed by its members, and
(*b*) that its members hold office by virtue of appointment (to that or
another office) by a Minister of the Crown under an enactment,
or if he is satisfied that it is a subsidiary of such a body.

(3) The Secretary of State may provide that a housing association shall be treated as a public sector authority if he is satisfied that the objects or powers of the association include the provision of housing accommodation for individuals employed at any time by a public sector authority or dependants of such individuals.

(4) Where the Secretary of State is satisfied that a body or association met the requirements of subsection (2) or (3) during any period, he may, whether or not he makes an order in respect of the body or association under that subsection, provide that it shall be treated as having been a public sector authority during that period.

(5) If the Secretary of State is satisfied that a body or association specified in an order under subsection (2) or (3) has ceased to meet the requirements of that subsection on any date, he may by order provide that it shall be treated as having ceased to be a public sector authority on that date.

(6) An order under this section shall be made by statutory instrument.

DEFINITIONS
"co-operative housing association": s.5.
"local authority": s.4.
"new town corporation": s.4.
"registered housing association": s.5.

GENERAL NOTE
This defines the public sector authorities affected by this Part, to which list the Secretary of State may add under subss. (2), (3).

Disposal of certain Crown interests in land treated as disposal by public sector authority

574. References in this Part to a disposal of an interest in a dwelling by a public sector authority include a disposal of—

    (a) an interest belonging to Her Majesty in right of the Crown,

    (b) an interest belonging to, or held in trust for Her Majesty for the purposes of, a government department or Minister of the Crown, or

    (c) an interest belonging to Her Majesty in right of the Duchy of Lancaster or belonging to the Duchy of Cornwall.

DEFINITIONS
  "disposal": s.532.
  "dwelling": s.575.
  "public sector authority": s.573.

GENERAL NOTE
  This section adds Crown property to references to a public sector authority where, but only where, the issue is whether there has been a disposal "by a public sector authority", see, *e.g.* ss.531, 549, but *not* s.548, above.

Meaning of "dwelling" and "house"

575.—(1) In this Part "dwelling" means any house, flat or other unit designed or adapted for living in.

(2) For the purposes of this Part a building so designed or adapted is a "house" if it is a structure reasonably so called; so that where a building is divided into units so designed or adapted—

    (a) if it is so divided horizontally, or a material part of a unit lies above or below another unit, the units are not houses (though the building as a whole may be), and

    (b) if it is so divided vertically, the units may be houses.

(3) Where a house which is divided into flats or other units is a defective dwelling in respect of which a person is eligible for assistance, the fact that it is so divided shall be disregarded for the purposes of section 538(1)(a) (first condition for assistance by way of reinstatement: that the dwelling is a house).

DEFINITIONS
  "defective dwelling": ss.528, 559.
  "eligible for assistance": s.527.

GENERAL NOTE
  See notes to s.183, above.

Meaning of "lending institution"

576. In this Part "lending institution" means—

  a building society,
  a bank,
  a trustee savings bank, or
  an insurance company.

Index of defined expressions: Part XVI

577. The following Table shows provisions defining or otherwise explaining expressions used in this Part (other than provisions defining or explaining an expression used in the same section or paragraph):—

the agreement (in Part III of Schedule 20)	paragraph 11(1) of Schedule 20
appropriate percentage (in relation to rein-statement grant)	section 543(2)
associated arrangement	section 539(2)
the authority (in Part III of Schedule 20)	paragraph 11(1) of Schedule 20
bank	section 622
building society	section 622
charge (in Part III of Schedule 20)	paragraph 11(2)(*a*) of Schedule 20
the conveyance (in Part III of Schedule 20)	paragraph 11(1) of Schedule 20
co-operative housing association	section 5(2)
cut-off date	sections 528(2)(*b*) and 559(3)(*b*)
defective dwelling	sections 528(2) and 559(3)
development corporation	section 4(*c*)
disposal	section 532(1)
disposal for value	section 532(3)
district (of a local housing authority)	section 2(1)
district valuer	section 622
dwelling	section 575(1)
dwelling-house (in sections 553 to 557)	section 558(*a*)
eligible for assistance	sections 527 and 533
house	section 575(2)
housing association	section 5(1)
insurance company	section 622
the interest acquired (in Part III of Schedule 20)	paragraph 11(1) of Schedule 20
interest in a dwelling	section 530(4)
interest to be acquired (in relation to repurchase)	paragraph 1 of Schedule 20
lending institution	section 576
local authority	section 4(*e*)
local housing authority	sections 1, 2(2)
new town corporation	section 4(*b*)
notice of determination	section 540(1)
occupier (in sections 553 to 557)	section 558(*b*)
person entitled to assistance (by way of reinstatement grant or repurchase)	section 540(5)
previous disposal	section 532(4)
protected tenancy	section 622
public sector authority	section 573 (and see section 574)
the purchase price (in Part III of Schedule 20)	paragraph 11(1) of Schedule 20
purchasing authority	section 548(3)
qualifying defect	sections 528(2)(*a*) and 559(3)(*a*)
qualifying work	section 541(2)
registered (in relation to a housing association)	section 5(4)
reinstatement grant	section 541(1)
relevant charge (in Part III of Schedule 20)	paragraph 7(2) of Schedule 20
relevant interest	section 530(1)

the relevant time (in relation to valuation for repurchase)	paragraph 7(2) of Schedule 20
repurchase	section 547
secure tenancy	section 79 (and see section 558(*c*))
statutory tenancy and statutory tenant	section 622
subsidiary	section 622
time of disposal	section 532(2)
trustee savings bank	section 622
the vendor (in Part III of Schedule 20)	paragraph 11(1) of Schedule 20
work required to reinstate a defective dwelling	section 539(1)

PART XVII

COMPULSORY PURCHASE AND LAND COMPENSATION

Introductory

General enactments relating to compulsory purchase, &c., apply subject to this Part

578. The Acquisition of Land Act 1981, the Compulsory Purchase Act 1965 and the Land Compensation Act 1961 apply to the compulsory purchase of land under this Act subject to the following provisions of this Part.

GENERAL NOTE

The purpose of this Part is to make the ancillary provisions for compulsory purchase and land compensation applicable to the Act as a whole. The starting-point is that the "normal" provisions of the three principal compulsory purchase Acts are applied, *as adapted*—and added to—by the remainder of this Part.

The 1981 Act is the general provision which applies to *procedures* on compulsory purchase, if and to the extent that it is adopted by a particular or "special" Act—*i.e.* as under this section. The 1965 Act governs *post-confirmation procedures*. The 1961 Act governs the *amount and assessment* of compensation.

Special provision as regards acquisition of land for clearance

579.—(1) The Acquisition of Land Act 1981 does not apply (except so far as expressly applied) to the compulsory purchase of land under section 290 (acquisition of land for clearance); instead, the provisions of Schedule 22 apply with respect to the making, confirmation, validity and operation of a compulsory purchase order under that section.

(2) However, in relation to a compulsory purchase order under that section—

(*a*) the provisions of Part I of the Compulsory Purchase Act 1965 apply as they apply to a compulsory purchase order under the Acquisition of Land Act 1981 (references to "the special Act" being read as references to this Act and the order); and

(*b*) the compensation payable shall be assessed in accordance with the Land Compensation Act 1961,

subject to the following provisions of this Part.

GENERAL NOTE

The Acquisition of Land Act 1981 is *not* to apply to compulsory purchase orders under s.290, *i.e.* Part IX "slum clearance" areas. Instead, the provisions of Sched. 22 apply: see notes thereto.

Once the order is made, however, Part I of the Compulsory Purchase Act 1965 applies to post-confirmation procedures, and compensation is assessed in accordance with the Land Compensation Act 1961, subject to the other provisions of this Part: see ss.583 and 584, below, as to adaptation of post-confirmation procedures; see ss.585–589 as to additional compensation provisions.

Compulsory purchase

Incorporation of enactments relating to mineral rights

580. A compulsory purchase order under section 290 (acquisition of land for clearance) shall incorporate Parts II and III of Schedule 2 to the Acquisition of Land Act 1981 (mineral rights).

GENERAL NOTE

An order will not carry with it the rights to mines under the land, unless it expressly so provides and identifies and conveys them: Part II, Sched. 2, 1981 Act. Part III of Schedule 2 details how the owner may proceed to work such mines, or be compensated by the authority for refusal of permission to do so, as well as providing for compensation for the added costs of working mines as extended beyond the purchased land. However, the mine-owner must also work mines, under or as extended beyond the purchased land, so as to avoid damage to the land itself.

Acquisition of commons, open spaces, &c.

581.—(1) In so far as a compulsory purchase order under section 290 (acquisition of land for clearance) authorises the purchase of land forming part of a common, open space or allotment, the order shall be subject to special parliamentary procedure except where it provides for giving in exchange for such land other land, not being less in area, certified by the Secretary of State to be equally advantageous to the persons, if any, entitled to commonable or other rights and to the public.

(2) Before giving a certificate the Secretary of State shall give public notice of the proposed exchange, shall afford opportunities to all persons interested to make representations and objections in relation to it and shall, if necessary, hold a local inquiry on the subject.

(3) An order which authorises such an exchange shall provide for—

(*a*) vesting the land given in exchange in the persons in whom the common, open space or allotment was vested, subject to the same rights, trusts and incidents as attached to the common, open space or allotment, and

(*b*) discharging the land acquired from all rights, trusts and incidents to which it was previously subject.

(3) In this section—

"common" includes any land subject to be enclosed under the Inclosure Acts 1845 to 1882, and any town or village green;

"open space" means any land laid out as a public garden or used for the purposes of public recreation, or land which is a disused burial ground;

"allotment" means any allotment set out as a fuel or field garden allotment under an Inclosure Act.

GENERAL NOTE

Because they are needed to ensure a reasonably satisfactory area, commons, open spaces or allotments may be included in an order under s.290: see notes thereto. Unless the order provides for lands in exchange certified by the Secretary of State to be equally advantageous to those entitled to rights and to the public, the order is to be subject to the special parliamentary procedure to be found in the Statutory Orders (Special Procedure) Act 1945: the requirements of this Act do not come into effect until the normal steps for confirmation of the order have been completed—1945, s.2. .

The Secretary of State shall, if necessary, hold a local inquiry on a proposed exchange, and must both give notice of it, and afford opportunities to all persons interested to make representations and objections.

This section does not operate by implication so as to repeal the provisions of a relevant local Act: *R.* v. *Minister of Health, ex parte Villiers* [1936] 2 K.B. 29.

Restriction on recovery of possession after making of compulsory purchase order

582.—(1) This section applies where a local housing authority have made a compulsory purchase order authorising—

    (*a*) the acquisition of a house in multiple occupation under—

        section 17 (provision of housing),

        section 192 (house subject to repair order found to be beyond repair) or

        section 300 (purchase of condemned house for temporary housing use), or

    (*b*) the acquisition of land under section 243(2) (land in housing action area on which there are premises consisting of or including housing accommodation),

and within the period specified in subsection (2) proceedings for possession of premises forming part of the house or land in question are brought in the county court against a person who was the lessee of the premises when the order was made, or became the lessee after the order was made, but is no longer the lessee.

(2) The period referred to in subsection (1) is the period beginning with the making of the compulsory purchase order and ending with—

    (*a*) the third anniversary of the date on which the order became operative, or

    (*b*) any earlier date on which the Secretary of State notifies the authority that he declines to confirm the order or the order is quashed by a court.

(3) Where this section applies the court may suspend the execution of any order for possession for such period, and subject to such conditions, as it thinks fit.

(4) The period of suspension ordered by the court shall not extend beyond the end of the period of three years beginning with the date on which the court makes its order or, if earlier, the date on which the compulsory purchase order became operative.

(5) The court may from time to time vary the period of suspension (but not so as to enlarge it beyond the end of the period of three years referred to in subsection (4)), or terminate it, or vary the terms of the order in other respects.

(6) If at any time—

    (*a*) the Secretary of State notifies the authority that he declines to confirm the compulsory purchase order, or the order is quashed by a court, or

    (*b*) the authority decide, whether before or after the order has been submitted to the Secretary of State for confirmation, not to proceed with it,

the authority shall notify the person entitled to the benefit of the order for possession and that person shall be entitled, on applying to the court, to obtain an order terminating the period of suspension, but subject to the exercise of the same discretion in fixing the date on which possession is to be given as the court might exercise if it were then making an order for possession for the first time.

(7) This section does not apply—

    (*a*) where the person entitled to possession of the premises is the local housing authority;

(*b*) where the net annual value for rating of the premises exceeds the county court limit for the purposes of section 21(1) of the County Courts Act 1984 (actions for the recovery of land).

(8) In this section "house in multiple occupation" has the same meaning as in Part XI.

DEFINITIONS
"house": s.602.
"house in multiple occupation": s.345.
"lessee": s.621.
"local housing authority": ss.1, 2.

GENERAL NOTE
When a compulsory purchase order is *made, i.e.* by the authority, prior to confirmation by the Secretary of State, the owner may wish to evict those in occupation, *e.g.* so as to seek increased compensation, or so as to be able to put forward viable alternative proposals at an inquiry. This section provides a protection for those who *were* lessees (which includes subtenants and those holding under an agreement for a lease or tenancy or sub-lease or sub-tenancy—see s.621, below) whether or not from before the order was made, but who are no longer lessees, *i.e.* because their tenancy has been determined.

In such circumstances, there will commonly be alternative protective legislation: under the Landlord and Tenant Act 1954, Part I, in relation to long leases which will qualify as statutory tenancies on determination (not common in houses in multiple occupation), under Rent Act 1977 if the tenancy is a statutory tenancy, or if a restricted contract, or under the Rent (Agriculture) Act 1976 (also not very common in H.M.O.s, given the provisions of s.23 of that Act excluding workers' hostels): see, generally, notes to s.662, below.

However, those who have had restricted contracts can obtain security for only three months from a court order on an application for possession (Rent Act 1977, s.106A, added by Housing Act 1980, s.69, unless the contract pre-dated the commencement of that amendment [November 28, 1980], in which case the former power of reference to the Rent Tribunal for security of up to six months at a time without theoretical limitation on number of applications or, correspondingly, protection, continues to apply—see 1977 Act, s.102A, added by 1980 Act s.69).

Those who do not fall within any of these protective provisions will be subject to the "normal" rule in Housing Act 1980, s.89, that an order for possession will take effect in 14 days, unless it appears to the court that exceptional hardship would be caused by requiring possession by then, in which case the court has a discretion to postpone possession for up to six weeks. The period of four to six weeks was in any event the norm at common law: *McPhail* v. *Persons Unknown* [1973] Ch. 447, see also *Sheffield Corporation* v. *Luxford* [1929] 2 K.B. 180.

This section provides an additional protection in two cases:

(1) H.M.O.s only, and only where the purchase is under one of the specified provisions; and,

(2) Housing Action Area powers of purchase.

Note in the latter connection that notification of notice to quit or expiry of tenancy must be given to the authority under s.247, in which circumstances the authority may wish to advise the occupiers of their rights under this section.

The basic right is in subs. (3), for the court to suspend the execution of an order for possession, for such periods and subject to such conditions as it thinks fit. There is no requirement, analogous to that to be found in Rent Act 1977, s.100 or s.85, above, that conditions be imposed as to payment, and arrears (if any). Suspension is not to extend beyond the period of three years starting with either the date of the court order, or the date when the compulsory purchase order becomes operative: subs. (4). Subject to this limit, the court may extend or reduce the period of suspension, or otherwise vary the order, *i.e.* as to conditions: subs. (5).

A compulsory purchase order will usually become operative on the date on which notice of confirmation is published in accordance with the requirements of Land Acquisition Act 1981, s.15: see *ibid.* s.26. However, under *ibid.* s.24, the court has a power to suspend operation pending challenge, in the same way as is permitted under Sched. 22, para. 7, below.

If the confirmation is refused, or the order quashed by a court, or the authority decide not to proceed, the authority have to notify anyone entitled to the benefit of the order for possession, who may apply for termination of the suspension, at which point the court's "usual" or "other" appropriate powers are exercisable: subs. (6).

Subs. (7).

The section has no application at all if the local housing authority are the person entitled to possession, or if the net annual value for rating exceeds the county court limit for the time being in force under s.21, County Courts Act 1984, currently £1,000.

Continuance of tenancies of houses compulsorily acquired and to be used for housing purposes

583.—(1) Where a local housing authority—

(*a*) are authorised to purchase compulsorily a house which is to be used for housing purposes, and

(*b*) have acquired the right to enter on and take possession of the house by virtue of having served a notice under section 11 of the Compulsory Purchase Act 1965,

they may, instead of exercising that right by taking actual possession of the house, proceed by serving notice on any person then in occupation of the house, or part of it, authorising him to continue in occupation upon terms specified in the notice or on such other terms as may be agreed.

(2) Where the authority proceed in accordance with subsection (1)—

(*a*) the like consequences follow with respect to the determination of the rights and liabilities of any person arising out of any interest of his in the house, or a part of it, and

(*b*) the authority may deal with the premises in all respects,

as if they had taken actual possession on the date of the notice.

(3) A person who by virtue of this section ceases to be entitled to receive rent in respect of the premises shall be deemed for the purposes of section 20 of the Compulsory Purchase Act 1965 (compensation of tenants, &c.) to have been required to give up possession of the premises.

(4) In this section "house" includes—

(*a*) any part of a building which is occupied as a separate dwelling, and

(*b*) any yard, garden, outhouses and appurtenances belonging to the house or usually enjoyed with it.

DEFINITION

"local housing authority": ss.1, 2.

GENERAL NOTE

Post-confirmation procedure under the Compulsory Purchase Act 1965 starts with a "notice to treat" under s.5 thereof. It must be served within three years of the operative date (see notes to last section) of the order: *ibid.*, s.4. Notice to treat is served on all those the authority know to have an interest in, or power to sell, convey or release, the land in question: *ibid.*, s.5. This includes tenants, other than those whose interests are from year to year or for a lesser period: *ibid.*, s.20. Licensees (see notes to s.93, above) are not, accordingly, included: *Frank Warr & Co. Ltd.* v. *London County Council* [1904] 1 K.B. 713.

Once notice to treat has been served, the owner cannot create new interests so as to increase the amount of compensation payable: *Birmingham City Corporation* v. *West Midland Baptist Trust* [1970] A.C. 874. He can, however, continue to deal with the property, and thereby transfer the right to compensation: *Cardiff Corporation* v. *Cook* [1923] 2 Ch. 115. Notice to treat also initiates the proceedings towards the assessment or agreement of compensation; it also allows the authority serve "notice of entry", under s.11 of the Act of 1965.

Notice of entry must be of at least 14 days: *ibid.*, s.11. There is no prescribed form, but the notice must state exactly when the entry is proposed. Once the time specified has arrived, the authority may enter on the land and take possession of it, just as if they had purchased it. A backdated notice of entry will be treated as valid from the day on which it was actually served, and will accordingly regularise an otherwise unauthorised entry from 14 days after service: *Cohen* v. *London Borough of Haringey* (1980) 42 P. & C.R. 6, C.A.

By this section, instead of entry pursuant to a s.11 notice of entry, the authority can serve notice on anyone in occupation of the house or part of the house, which permits him to remain in occupation, on terms specified: subs. (1). They are then in the same position as if the authority had taken actual possession, and compensation consequences follow as if actual possession had been taken: subss. (2), (3).

This procedure will not be needed where the provisions of the next section apply.

Power to enter and determine short tenancies of land acquired or appropriated

584.—(1) This section applies where a local housing authority have agreed to purchase or have determined to appropriate land for the purposes of—

Part II (provision of housing),

Part VIII (area improvement), or

the provisions of Part IX relating to clearance areas,

subject to the interest of the person in possession of the land.

(2) If that person's interest is not greater than that of a tenant for a year, or from year to year, the authority may, after giving him not less than 14 days' notice, enter on and take possession of the land, or such part of the land as is specified in the notice, without previous consent.

(3) The power conferred by subsection (2) may be exercised at any time after the making of the agreement or determination, except where the appropriation requires Ministerial consent in which case the power is not exercisable until that consent has been given.

(4) The exercise of the local housing authority's power under subsection (2) is subject to the payment to the person in possession of the like compensation, and interest on the compensation awarded, as would be payable if—

(a) the authority had been authorised to acquire the land compulsorily, and

(b) that person had been required in pursuance of their powers in that behalf to quit possession before the expiry of his term or interest in the land;

but without any necessity for compliance with section 11 of the Compulsory Purchase Act 1965 (which prohibits entry on the land acquired before the compensation has been ascertained and paid or secured).

DEFINITIONS

"clearance area": s.289.

"local housing authority": ss.1, 2.

GENERAL NOTE

Where the authority have *agreed* to purchase land subject to existing interests, under Pt. II, or under Pt. VIII (area action), or under Pt. IX so far as it concerns clearance areas (s.289 *et seq.*, above), they can take possession by notice of not less than 14 days served on the person in possession: subss. (1), (2). However, this is only applicable where the person in possession is a tenant with no greater interest than that of a fixed tenancy for a year, or a periodic tenancy from year to year, *i.e.* it will include fixed-term tenancies for lesser periods, or shorter periodic tenancies: subs. (2). The power is also exercisable on an appropriation, unless the appropriation requires consent (see notes to s.17, above), in which case it is exercisable once consent to appropriation has been obtained: subs. (3).

The powers previously applied in the cases of Pt. II and clearance areas under Pt. IX, and General Improvement Areas under Pt. VIII, but not to Housing Action Areas under Pt. VIII: the extension to Housing Action Areas is pursuant to Law Commissions Recommendations (Cmnd. 9515), No. 25.

Subs. (4)

Use of this provision will only be available when the same compensation is payable as if the purchase was compulsory and the person in possession was required to quit before the expiry of his interest under the tenancy, although there is no need for compliance with s.11, Compulsory Purchase Act 1965: see notes to s.583, above.

Site value compensation for unfit houses and related matters

Site value compensation for unfit houses

585.—(1) The compensation payable for—

(*a*) a house purchased compulsorily under section 192 (unfit house found to be beyond repair at reasonable cost),

(*b*) land purchased under section 290 as being comprised in a clearance area, except as mentioned in subsection (2), or

(*c*) a house purchased compulsorily under section 300 (purchase of condemned houses for temporary housing use),

is the value at the time when the valuation is made of the site as a cleared site available for development in accordance with the requirements of the building regulations in force in the district.

(2) Subsection (1)(*b*) does not apply to the site of a house or other building properly included in a clearance area only on the ground that it is dangerous or injurious to the health of the inhabitants of the area by reason of its bad arrangement in relation to other buildings or the narrowness or bad arrangement of the streets, unless—

(*a*) it is a building constructed or adapted as, or for the purposes of, a dwelling, or partly for those purposes and partly for other purposes, and

(*b*) part of it (not being a part used for other purposes) is unfit for human habitation.

(3) The provisions of this section as to site value compensation are without prejudice to any further payment falling to be made under—

section 586 and Schedule 23 (well maintained houses),

section 587 and Schedule 24 (houses which are owner-occupied or used for business purposes), or

section 589(2) (minimum compensation in certain cases),

and have effect subject to section 589(1) (maximum compensation in certain cases).

DEFINITIONS

"building regulations": s.622.
"clearance area": s.289.
"house": s.602.
"unfit for human habitation": s.604.

GENERAL NOTE

As discouragement to owners to allow property to fall into disrepair, compensation is in certain cases limited to "site value". However, protection is reintroduced, for those in actual occupation, under either s.586 (well-maintained payments—recognising that with the best efforts in the world property *will* fall into such disrepair that it qualifies for the description "slum"), or s.587 (owner-occupier's supplement—recognising that some owner-occupiers have only been able to afford to buy slum property for their own homes, and supplement for housing with a business use).

This section applies to three categories of property:

(1) A house purchased compulsorily under s.192, above; this is the case of a house which has been the subject of a repairs notice because the authority considered that it could be repaired at a reasonable expense, but which, on appeal to the county court, has been found not repairable at a reasonable expense; in such a case, the authority may themselves purchase the property, do the works in the original notice, and add it to their Part II stock—see notes to s.192, above;

(2) A house within a clearance area purchased under s.290; however, this does not extend to property included in the area on the grounds specified in subs. (2) (see also s.289(2)), *i.e.* other than those included as houses unfit for human habitation within s.604, below, *unless* it is a building constructed as a dwelling or for mixed user, or adapted to housing use or mixed use, a part of which is not used for non-housing purposes, and is unfit for human habitation, as it were in its own right;

(3) A house otherwise to be subject to a closing or demolition order under s.265, which has been compulsorily purchased under s.300; this is the case of an unfit property, which is

or can be rendered capable of providing accommodation "of a standard which is adequate for the time being".

"Site value" means the value as a cleared site available for development in accordance with the requirements of the building regulations in force in the district, as to which see s.622, below. It would be wrong to assume that this is always a small amount: consider, *e.g.* a house the demolition of which will make it an attractive proposition to someone with land behind, to which access may now be available—this could easily be in excess of the value of the house as it stands. Section 589, below, however, places both minimum and maximum limits.

Note that occupiers displaced by these classes of action by the authority will normally be entitled to payments under Land Compensation Act 1973, ss.29–38, and to rehousing under *ibid.*, s.39. See also s.591, below, for the discharge or modification of mortgages when no more than site value is payable, as a result of this section.

Payments in respect of well maintained houses

586. The provisions of Schedule 23 have effect as regards payments in respect of well maintained houses purchased at site value or demolished or closed under this Act.

GENERAL NOTE

Even although housing may qualify as "slum", to the extent that it is purchased under one of the provisions referred to in the last section, so that of definition it must be unfit for human habitation within the meaning of s.604, below, it may yet be "well-maintained", *i.e.* the owner has done the best he can to keep it in a good state. "Well-maintained" is not defined, here or in Sched. 23, below, but its meaning is relatively clear, having regard to the context set by Sched. 23.

Note that payments are available under s.587, and Sched. 24, below, for owner-occupied houses, or houses with a business use: by s.588, below, well-maintained payments and Sched. 24 supplements are mutually exclusive, save if the Sched. 24 payment relates to only part of a house, in which case the well-maintained payment remains payable in part. Note also that occupiers affected by the relevant action of the authority will normally be entitled to compensation under Land Compensation Act 1973, ss.29–38 and to rehousing under *ibid.*, s.39.

This section is *not* only applicable on compulsory purchase, but also on closing or demolition of a house: see the notes to Sched. 23, below. See also s.591, below, for the discharge or modification of mortgages in circumstances which may coincide with those when a payment is made under Sched. 23.

Payments in respect of houses which are owner-occupied or used for business purposes

587. The provisions of Schedule 24 have effect as regards payments in respect of houses purchased at site value or demolished or closed under this Act, as follows—

Part I: Payments in respect of owner-occupied houses.
Part II: Payments in respect of houses used for business purposes.

GENERAL NOTE

As with the last section, even although housing may qualify as "slum", to the extent that it is purchased under one of the provisions referred to in s.585, above, so that of definition it must be unfit for human habitation within the meaning of s.604, below, there may be qualification for a supplement under Sched. 24, Part I of which concerns owner-occupiers, and Part II of which concerns premises with a business use. This section is *not* only applicable on compulsory purchase, but also on the closing or demolition of a property: see notes to Sched. 24, below.

Note that payments are available under s.586, and Sched. 23, for housing which is well-maintained. By s.588, below, Sched. 24 supplements and well-maintained payments under Sched. 23 are mutually exclusive, save if the supplement under this section and Sched. 24 relates to only part of a house, in which case the well-maintained payment under Sched. 23 remains payable in part. Note also that occupiers affected by the relevant action of the authority will normally be entitled to compensation under ss.29–38, Land Compensation Act 1973, and to rehousing under *ibid.*, s.39.

See also s.591, below, for the discharge or modification of mortgages when a payment is made under Part I of Sched. 24.

Avoidance of double compensation

588.—(1) Where a payment falls to be made in respect of an interest in a house under Schedule 24 (payments in respect of houses which are owner-occupied or used for business purposes), no payment shall be made in respect of that house under Schedule 23 (payments for well maintained houses) unless the other payment relates to part only of the house, and in that case such part only of the amount which would otherwise be payable in accordance with Schedule 23 shall be payable as may reasonably be attributable to the remainder of the house.

(2) In Schedules 23 and 24 references to a demolition order do not include such an order in respect of a house already subject to a closing order so far as it affects any part of the house in relation to which a payment under either of those Schedules has fallen to be made in respect of the closing order.

DEFINITION
"house": s.602.

GENERAL NOTE
This governs the mutual exclusivity of well-maintained payments under Sched. 23 and the owner-occupier's supplement under Sched. 24, and prevents double payments under either where a demolition order follows a closing order.

Maximum and minimum compensation where s.585 applies

589.—(1) Subject to the following provisions of this section, the compensation payable in respect of a compulsory acquisition in relation to which section 585 applies (site value compensation) shall not in any event exceed the amount which would have been payable if—

(*a*) that section did not apply, and

(*b*) in a case where any of the relevant land is in a clearance area, that area had not been declared to be a clearance area,

but in all other respects the acquisition had been effected in the circumstances in which it actually is effected.

(2) Where section 585 applies in relation to a compulsory acquisition of land which consists of or includes the whole or part of a house and—

(*a*) on the date of the making of the compulsory purchase order the person then entitled to the relevant interest was, in right of that interest, in occupation of the house, or part of it, as a private dwelling, and

(*b*) that person either continues, on the date of service of the notice to treat, to be entitled to the relevant interest, or if he has died before that date, continued to be entitled to that interest immediately before his death,

the amount of the compensation payable in respect of the acquisition of that interest, together with any amount payable under Schedules 23 or 24 (payments for well maintained houses and houses which are owner-occupied or used for business purposes), shall not in any event be less than the gross value of the dwelling.

(3) The gross value of the dwelling for this purpose shall be determined as follows—

(*a*) if the dwelling constitutes the whole of the house, its gross value is that shown in the valuation list in force on the date of service of the notice to treat as the gross value of the house for rating purposes;

(*b*) if the dwelling is only part of the house, its gross value is the amount certified by the district valuer as being properly attributable to the dwelling on an apportionment of the gross value of the house as determined under paragraph (*a*).

(4) The gross value of a dwelling whose rateable value is by virtue of subsection (1) of section 19 of the General Rate Act 1967 to be taken to be its net annual value, as ascertained in accordance with subsections (2) to (4) of that section, shall be taken to be its corresponding gross value.

(5) The corresponding gross value means a gross value which would be equivalent to the net annual value of the dwelling as shown in the valuation list if there were deducted any amount that by virtue of an order made or falling to be treated as made under section 19(2) of the General Rate Act 1967 would be deducted from the gross value of the dwelling if it had been required to be assessed to its gross value instead of its net annual value.

(6) If more than one value is so ascertained to be the corresponding gross value, the highest value so ascertained shall be taken.

DEFINITIONS
"demolition order": s.265.
"house": s.602.

GENERAL NOTE
Where payment is to be under s.585, *i.e.* site value only, this section sets a maximum, and a minimum. The compensation is not to exceed what would be normally payable, *i.e.* full value assessed in accordance with the Land Compensation Act 1961, with the added assumption that if the land is in a clearance area, the fact that it is a clearance area is to be disregarded: subs. (1).

On the other hand, the compensation is not to be less than under subs. (2), if the precondition is fulfilled of occupation of all or part as a private dwelling by the person entitled to the relevant interest, who was still entitled to that interest at the date of notice to treat (*cf.* s.583, above) or, if earlier, his death. In such a case, the site value compensation is added to anything payable under either Sched. 23 (well-maintained payments) or Sched. 24 (owner-occupier's or business supplement) and they are together not to be less than the gross value calculated in accordance with subss. (3)–(6).

Repayment on revocation of demolition or closing order

590.—(1) Where a payment in respect of a house has been made by a local housing authority under Schedule 23 or 24 in connection with a demolition or closing order and—
  (*a*) the demolition order is revoked under section 274 (revocation of demolition order to permit reconstruction of house), or
  (*b*) the closing order is determined under section 278 (determination of closing order on premises being rendered fit),
then, if at that time, the person to whom the payment was made is entitled to an interest in the house, he shall on demand repay the payment to the authority.

(2) In subsection (1) "interest" in a house does not include the interest of a tenant for a year or any less period or of a statutory tenant.

(3) Where by virtue of section 278 a closing order is determined as respects part of the premises to which it relates and—
  (*a*) a payment has been made by the local housing authority in respect of the premises in pursuance of Schedule 23 or 24, and
  (*b*) if the order and payment had related only to that part of the premises any person would by virtue of subsection (1) have been liable on demand to repay the payment to the authority,
that person shall on demand pay to the authority an amount equal to the appropriate fraction of the payment.

(4) The appropriate fraction of the payment is, except where subsection (5) applies, the fraction obtained by dividing the rateable value of the part of the premises in question by the rateable value of the premises.

(5) If the payment was reduced in pursuance of paragraph 4(3) of Part I of Schedule 24 (reduction where part of premises not occupied for purposes of private dwelling), the appropriate fraction is the fraction obtained by dividing the rateable value of so much of the part of the premises in question as was used for the purposes of a private dwelling by the rateable value of so much of the premises as was so used.

(6) For the purposes of subsections (4) and (5) the rateable value of premises or a portion of them is—

(a) if the premises or portion are a hereditament for which a rateable value is shown in the valuation list in force on the date on which the closing order was made, that rateable value;

(b) if the premises or portion form part only of such a hereditament, or consist of or form part of more than one such hereditament, such value as is found by a proper apportionment or aggregation of the rateable value or values shown;

and any question arising as to the proper apportionment or aggregation of any value or values shall be referred to and determined by the district valuer.

DEFINITION
"closing order": s.265.
"demolition order": s.265.
"local housing authority" ss.1, 2.

GENERAL NOTE
Either a well-maintained payment under Sched. 23 or an owner-occupier's or business supplement under Sched. 24 is repayable on demand if the payment was in connection with a demolition or closing order which is revoked or determined under either of the provisions specified in subs. (1). Calculation of the repayment is governed by subss. (3)–(6).

Modifications of obligations under mortgages etc.

591.—(1) This section applies where—

(a) a house is purchased at site value in accordance with section 585 (site value compensation for unfit houses), or

(b) is vacated in pursuance of a demolition or closing order under section 265 (unfit houses beyond repair at reasonable cost), or

(c) might have been the subject of such a demolition order but is vacated and demolished in pursuance of an undertaking for its demolition given to the local housing authority.

(2) Where this section applies and a relevant interest in the house is subject to a mortgage or charge, or to an agreement to purchase by instalments, either party to the mortgage, charge or agreement may apply to the county court which may, after giving the other party an opportunity to be heard, make an order—

(a) in the case of a house which has been purchased compulsorily, discharging or modifying any outstanding liabilities of the holder of the interest by virtue of any bond, covenant or other obligation with respect to the debt secured by the mortgage or charge or by virtue of the agreement, or

(b) in the case of a house vacated in pursuance of a demolition or closing order, or of an undertaking, discharging or modifying the terms of the mortgage, charge or agreement,

and in either case either unconditionally or subject to such terms and conditions, including conditions with respect to the payment of money, as the court may think just and equitable to impose.

(3) An interest is a relevant interest for the purposes of this section if—

(a) a payment in respect of it falls to be made under Part I of Schedule 24 (payments in respect of owner-occupied houses), and (*b*) it is subject to the mortgage, charge or agreement, at the date when the house is purchased compulsorily or, as the case may be, vacated.

(4) An interest is also a relevant interest for the purposes of this section if—

     (*a*) it is an interest in right of which, at the date of the making of the compulsory purchase or other order, or the giving of the undertaking, a person occupies the whole or part of the house as a private dwelling, and

     (*b*) that person continues to own the interest until the end of the period mentioned in subsection (5), and

     (*c*) the interest is subject to the mortgage, charge or agreement throughout that period.

(5) The period referred to in subsection (4) is the period from the date of the making of the compulsory purchase or other order, or the giving of the undertaking to—

     (*a*) in the case of a compulsory purchase order, the date of service of notice to treat (or deemed notice to treat) for purchase of the interest or, if the purchase is effected without service of notice to treat, the date of completion of the purchase, and

     (*b*) in the case of any other order, or of an undertaking, the date of vacation of the house in pursuance of the order or undertaking,

or, if the owner of the interest died before the date specified in paragraph (*a*) or (*b*), to the date of death.

(6) In this section—

     "house" includes any building constructed or adapted wholly or partly as, or for the purposes of, a dwelling; and

     "interest" in a house does not include the interest of a tenant for a year or any less period or of a statutory tenant.

DEFINITIONS

     "closing order": s.265.
     "demolition order": s.265.
     "house": s.602.

GENERAL NOTE

     This section applies to property subject to site value compensation under s.585, or is vacated pursuant to a demolition or closing order, or is demolished pursuant to an undertaking under s.264, above. It applies only where a "relevant interest" is subject to a mortgage or charge, or a rental purchase agreement. Relevant interest is defined in subs. (3): the house must be subject to the mortgage, charge or agreement at the date of compulsory purchase or being vacated, and a payment falls to be made under Part I of Sched. 24, *i.e.* an owner-occupier's supplement.

     If disqualified from Pt. I of Sched. 24, an interest will also be a relevant interest if there is residential occupation by the person entitled to an interest, who continues to own that interest throughout the period in subs. (5), *and* the interest is subject to the mortgage, charge or agreement throughout that period: subs. (4). The subs. (5) period starts with the date on which the compulsory purchase or other relevant order is made and ends on the date of service of notice to treat (*cf.* notes to s.583, above) (or if none, date of completion) on a compulsory purchase, or date of vacation in the case of another order, or if earlier in either case, date of owner's death.

     The provisions entitle either party to the mortgage, charge or agreement to apply to the county court which may, after giving the other party an opportunity to be heard, make such order, unconditionally or subject to terms and conditions, including financial conditions, as it may think just and equitable, discharge or modify any outstanding liability (including a personal covenant on the mortgage), on a compulsory purchase, or discharge or modify the mortgage in the case of another class of order. However, the power is to be exercised subject to the considerations set out in the next section.

Factors to be considered in proceedings under s.591

592.—(1) In determining what order, if any, to make under section 591 (modification of obligations under mortgage, &c.) the court shall have regard to all the circumstances of the case, and in particular to the following matters.

(2) In the case of a mortgage or charge the court shall have regard to whether the mortgagee or person entitled to the benefit of the charge acted reasonably in advancing the principal sum on the terms of the mortgage or charge; and that person shall be deemed to have acted unreasonably if, at the time when the mortgage or charge was made, he knew or ought to have known that in all the circumstances of the case the terms of the mortgage or charge did not afford sufficient security for the principal sum advanced.

(3) In the case of a mortgage or charge the court shall have regard to the extent to which the house may have become unfit for human habitation owing to default on the part of the mortgagor or person entitled to the interest charged in carrying out any obligation under the terms of the mortgage or charge with respect to the repair of the house.

(4) In the case of a mortgage or charge securing a sum which represents all or any part of the purchase price payable for the interest, the court shall have regard to whether the purchase price was excessive.

(5) In the case of an agreement to purchase by instalments the court shall have regard to how far—

(a) the amount already paid by way of principal, or

(b) where the house has been purchased compulsorily the aggregate of that amount and so much, if any, of the compensation in respect of the compulsory purchase as falls to be paid to the vendor,

represents an adequate price for the purchase.

GENERAL NOTE

This section sets out the considerations to which the court shall have regard when determining how to exercise its powers under the last section to discharge or modify an outstanding liability on a compulsory purchase, or a mortgage in the case of vacation of a house pursuant to a demolition order or undertaking, or a closing order. The behaviour of the mortgagee or chargee will be taken into account: did he behave reasonably in advancing the money; he is to be deemed to have acted unreasonably if at the time the mortgage or charge was made, he knew or in all the circumstances ought to have known that insufficient security was afforded by the purchase; in the case of unfitness within s.604, the default of the mortgagor will be taken into account; whether or not the purchase price was excessive will be taken into account.

In the case of a rental purchase agreement, the court will have regard to the amounts of principal already paid, and how much the vendor will receive by way of compensation, and the extent to which these taken together represent an adequate price for the purchase.

Other land compensation matters

Compensation where compulsory purchase order deemed to be made under different provision

593. Where a compulsory purchase order under section 290 (acquisition of land for clearance) is to be treated as made under Part II of this Act (provision of housing) or Part VI of the Town and Country Planning Act 1971 (planning purposes) by virtue of—

section 305(6)(b) (building becoming listed when subject to compulsory purchase for clearance), or

paragraph 5(3) of Schedule 11 (building in clearance area in respect of which rehabilitation order is made),

compensation for the compulsory acquisition of the land comprised in the compulsory purchase order shall be assessed in accordance with the provisions applying to a compulsory acquisition under Part II of this Act or Part VI of the 1971 Act, as the case may be.

GENERAL NOTE

Additional compensation will be payable in the circumstances specified in this and the next section: see the Slum Clearance (Retention of Buildings) Order 1975, S.I. 1975 No. 1108, retained in force by Housing (Consequential Provisions) Act 1985, s.2.

Compensation where land deemed to be appropriated for purposes of Part II

594.—(1) This section applies where an interest in land in a clearance area is, by virtue of—

> section 305(6)(*a*) (building becoming listed when subject to compulsory purchase for clearance),
>
> section 306(2) (building becoming listed when acquired by agreement for clearance), or
>
> paragraph 6 of Schedule 11 (building in respect of which rehabilitation order is made),

to be treated as appropriated for the purposes of Part II (provision of housing).

(2) Compensation for the compulsory acquisition of the interest shall, where it increases the amount, be assessed or reassessed in accordance with the provisions applying to a compulsory acquisition under Part II.

(3) Where the interest is acquired by agreement (after the declaration of the clearance area), compensation shall, where subsection (2) would have increased the amount, be assessed and paid as if the acquisition were a compulsory acquisition under section 290 (acquisition of land for clearance) to which subsection (2) above applied; but there shall be deducted from the amount of compensation so payable any amount previously paid in respect of the acquisition of that interest by the authority.

(4) Where subsection (2) or (3) applies, the local housing authority shall not later than six month after (as the case may be)—

> (*a*) the relevant date as defined in section 305(3), or
>
> (*b*) the date on which the rehabilitation order becomes operative in accordance with paragraph 14 of Schedule 11,

serve on the person entitled to the compensation a notice in the prescribed form giving particulars of the amount of compensation payable in accordance with the provisions applying to a compulsory acquisition under Part II.

(5) If the person served does not, within 21 days from service of the notice, accept the particulars, or if he disputes the amount stated, the question of disputed compensation shall be referred to the Lands Tribunal.

(6) References in this section to an increase in compensation shall be read as if payments under—

> Schedule 23 (payments for well maintained houses),
>
> Schedule 24 (payments in respect of houses which are owner-occupied or used for business purposes), and
>
> section 37 of the Land Compensation Act 1973 (disturbance payments for persons without compensatable interests),

and any extra-statutory payments by way of additional compensation were, to the extent that they were made to the person holding the interest in question, compensation in respect of the compulsory purchase.

GENERAL NOTE

See note to last section. In the circumstances set out in this section, however, the authority have to serve notice on the person entitled to the increased compensation. Any payments under Scheds. 23 and 24 (and Land Compensation Act 1973, s.37) are treated as compulsory purchase payments, for the purpose of calculating what additional sum has to be paid: subs. (6). Adaptation of the Land Compensation Act 1961 and the Compulsory Purchase Act 1965 to the particular circumstances arising under this section is to be found in s.595, below.

Application of other enactments where s.594 applies

595.—(1) Section 30 of the Compulsory Purchase Act 1965 (service of notices) applies to the notice to be served under section 594(4) (notice of particulars of compensation).

(2) Section 594(2) shall be left out of account in considering whether under section 22 of the Compulsory Purchase Act 1965 (procedure for acquiring interest mistakenly omitted from purchase) compensation has been properly paid for the land, and accordingly does not prevent an acquiring authority from remaining in undisputed possession of the land.

(3) Where section 594(2) makes an increase in compensation to be assessed in accordance with Schedule 2 to the Compulsory Purchase Act 1965 (absent and untraced owners)—

(*a*) a deed poll executed under paragraph 2(2) of that Schedule before the latest date for service of a notice under section 594(4) is not invalid because the increase in compensation has not been paid, and

(*b*) the local housing authority, shall not later than six months after that date, proceed under that Schedule to pay the proper additional amount into court.

(4) A sum payable by virtue of section 594 carries interest at the rate prescribed under section 32 of the Land Compensation Act 1961 from the time of entry on the land by the local housing authority, or from vesting of the land or interest, whichever is the earlier, until payment.

GENERAL NOTE
In the circumstances of the last section, when additional compensation may be payable, the provisions of the Land Compensation Act 1961 and the Compulsory Purchase Act 1965 are adapted by this section.

Power to compensate shop-keepers in areas affected by clearance

596. Where, as a result of action taken by a local housing authority under the provisions of Part IX relating to clearance areas, the population of the locality is materially decreased, the authority may pay to any person carrying on a retail shop in the locality such reasonable allowance as they think fit towards any loss involving personal hardship which in their opinion he will thereby sustain, but in estimating any such loss they shall have regard to the probable future development of the locality.

DEFINITIONS
"clearance area": s.289.
"local housing authority": ss.1, 2.

GENERAL NOTE
This is a discretionary power to compensate retail traders for personal hardship resulting from the diminution in clientele caused by clearance action under Pt. IX, but subject to the probable future development of the locality.

Compensation payable on demolition of obstructive building

597.—(1) Where a building is demolished under section 287 (execution of obstructive building order), whether by the owner or by the local housing authority, compensation shall be paid by the authority to the owner in respect of loss arising from the demolition.

(2) The compensation shall be assessed in accordance with Part I of the Land Compensation Act 1961 (determination of questions of disputed compensation).

(3) In assessing the compensation no allowance shall be made on account of the demolition being compulsory.

DEFINITION
"local housing authority": ss.1, 2.

GENERAL NOTE
The owner of an obstructive building demolished under s.288 receives compensation on normal principles, under Part I, Land Compensation Act 1961, referable to the Lands Tribunal under s.1, thereof, rather than compensation as reduced or limited as under s.585, above.

Disregard of things done to obtain increased compensation

598. Section 4 of the Acquisition of Land Act 1981 (disregard to things done to obtain increased compensation) applies in relation to compulsory purchase under section 290 (acquisition of land for clearance).

GENERAL NOTE
Under Land Acquisition Act 1981, s.4 the Lands Tribunal is not to "take into account any interest in land, or any enhancement of the value of any interest in land, by reason of any building erected, work done or improvement or alteration made, whether on the land purchased or on any other land with which the claimaint is, or was at the time of the erection, doing or making of the building, works, improvement or alteration, directly or indirectly concerned, if the Lands Tribunal is satisfied that the creation of the interest, the erection of the building, the doing of the work, the making of the improvement or the alteration, as the case may be, was not reasonably necessary and was undertaken with a view to obtaining compensation or increased compensation".

A similar provision appeared in Sched. 3 to the Housing Act 1957 (now, Sched. 22 to this Act), and the more modern form of the 1981 Act is applied pursuant to Law Commission Recommendations (Cmnd. 9515), No. 26. Otiose provisions in the 1957 Act governing the exclusion of compensation for overcrowded premises or illegal user, and the reduction of compensation for the increased value of other land in the same ownership attributable to the authority's actions, are not reproduced pursuant to *ibid.*, as adequately represented in any event by Land Compensation Act 1961, ss.5, 6.

Application of compensation due to another local authority

599. Compensation payable in respect of land of another local authority in pursuance of a compulsory purchase under—
    section 17 (provision of housing),
    section 192 (house subject to repair notice found to be beyond repair),
    section 290 (acquisition of land for clearance), or
    section 300 (purchase of condemned house for temporary housing use)
which would otherwise be paid into court in accordance with Schedule 1 to the Compulsory Purchase Act 1965 (purchase from persons not having power to dispose) may, if the Secretary of State consents, instead be paid and applied as he may determine.

Supplementary provisions

Powers of entry

600.—(1) A person authorised by the local housing authority or the Secretary of State may at any reasonable time, on giving 24 hours' notice of his intention to the occupier, and to the owner if the owner is known, enter premises for the purpose of survey and examination where it appears to the authority or the Secretary of State that survey or examination is necessary in order to determine whether any powers under this Part should be exercised in respect of the premises.

(2) An authorisation for the purposes of this section shall be in writing stating the particular purpose or purposes for which the entry is authorised.

<small>DEFINITIONS</small>
"local housing authority": ss.1, 2.
"owner": s.602.

<small>GENERAL NOTE</small>
Cf. ss.54, 197, 222, 260, 319, 340 and 395, above, and notes thereto.

Penalty for obstruction

601.—(1) It is a summary offence to obstruct an officer of the local housing authority or of the Secretary of State, or any person authorised to enter premises in pursuance of this Part, in the performance of anything which he is by this Part required or authorised to do.

(2) A person committing such an offence is liable on conviction to a fine not exceeding level 2 on the standard scale.

<small>DEFINITION</small>
"local housing authority": ss.1, 2.

<small>GENERAL NOTE</small>
Cf. ss.55, 198, 223, 261, 320, 341 and 396, above, and notes thereto.

Minor definitions

602. In this Part—
"house" includes any yard, garden, outhouses and appurtenances belonging to the house or usually enjoyed with it;
"owner", in relation to premises—
 (*a*) means a person (other than a mortgagee not in possession) who is for the time being entitled to dispose of the fee simple in the premises, whether in possession or in reversion, and
 (*b*) includes also a person holding or entitled to the rents and profits of the premises under a lease of which the unexpired term exceeds three years.

<small>GENERAL NOTE</small>
"House": see notes to s.56, above.

Index of defined expressions: Part XVII

603. The following Table shows provisions defining or otherwise explaining expressions used in this Part (other than provisions defining or otherwise explaining an expression used in the same section or paragraph):—

building regulations	section 622
business (in Part II of Schedule 24)	paragraph 5 of that Part
clearance area	section 289
closing order	section 267(2)
demolition order	
(generally)	section 267(1)
(in Schedules 23 and 24)	section 588(2)
district valuer	section 622

house	
(generally)	section 602
(in Part I of Schedule 24)	paragraph 5(1) of that Part
(in Part II of Schedule 24)	paragraph 5 of that Part
interest in a house	
(in Part I of Schedule 24)	paragraph 5(1) of that Part
(in Part II of Schedule 24)	paragraph 5 of that Part
lease and lessee	section 621
local housing authority	section 1, 2(2)
member of family (in Part I of Schedule 24)	paragraph 6 of that Part
owner	section 602
prescribed	section 614
site value	section 585
relevant date (in Part I or II of Schedule 24)	paragraph 1(2) of that Part
statutory tenant	section 622
unfit for human habitation	section 604

Part XVIII

Miscellaneous and General Provisions

General provisions relating to housing conditions

Fitness for human habitation

604.—(1) In determining for any of the purposes of this Act whether premises are unfit for human habitation, regard shall be had to their condition in respect of the following matters—

> repair,
> stability,
> freedom from damp,
> internal arrangement,
> natural lighting,
> ventilation,
> water supply,
> drainage and sanitary conveniences,
> facilities for the preparation and cooking of food and for the disposal of waste water;

and the premises shall be deemed to be unfit if, and only if, they are so far defective in one or more of those matters that they are not reasonably suitable for occupation in that condition.

(2) Subsection (1) does not affect the operation of sections 266 and 282 (special powers to close underground rooms deemed to be unfit for human habitation).

GENERAL NOTE

One of the most important provisions of the Act, this Section defines "unfit for human habitation". The identical provision is to be found in Landlord and Tenant Act 1985, s.10, where it is relevant to *contractual* terms of certain tenancies. In this Act, it is relevant to most Parts, for at the core of local government intervention in private housing conditions is the idea that housing ought to be fit.

Ironically, an authority's *own* housing need not be fit, for they cannot normally be compelled to apply enforcement provisions to themselves (see *R.* v. *Cardiff City Council, ex parte Cross* (1982) 6 H.L.R. 1, C.A., affirming (1981) 1 H.L.R. 54, Q.B.D., which contains a more detailed analysis and reasoning than is to be found in the judgment of the Court of Appeal; see further notes to s.189, above).

Notwithstanding *Cross*, a tenant is left with contractual remedies under the Landlord and Tenant Act 1985, but (a) very few tenancies will be subject to the express contractual application of the unfitness criteria to be found in s.8 of that Act (which are limited to lettings at very low rents indeed), and (b) it is not necessarily right to assume that if a house is unfit, there is automatically a breach of the more modern contractual term to be found in *ibid.*, s.11 (structure and exterior, etc., see notes to s.104, above, and to Sched. 6, para. 14, below), for having regard to age, character, locality and prospective life under *ibid.*, s.11(3), it does not automatically follow that the landlord is in breach even if the premises are statutorily unfit: *London Borough of Newham* v. *Patel* (1978) 13 H.L.R. 77, C.A.

Common Law

At common law, there is no implied term that premises will either be fit for human habitation at the commencement of a term, or rendered so fit (see *Hart* v. *Windsor* (1844) 12 M. & W. 68, *Cruse* v. *Mount* [1933] Ch. 278, *Sleafer* v. *London Borough of Lambeth* [1960] 1 Q.B. 43), save (a) in the case of a furnished letting (*Wilson* v. *Finch Hatton* (1877) 2 Ex. D. 336), and (b) in the case of a lease or agreement for a lease entered into while a house or other premises is still under construction. In such a case it is implied that the house will be fit at the commencement of the lease (*Perry* v. *Sharon Development Co.* [1937] All E.R. 390).

In each of these cases, the term does not extend to an undertaking to *keep* the premises fit for human habitation throughout the letting, but is confined to their state at the outset: *Hart* v. *Windsor* (1844) 12 M. & W. 68, *Sarsons* v. *Roberts* [1895] 2 Q.B. 395. The proposition as it related to furnished accommodation was that "every person who undertakes to let a ready-furnished house or apartment is bound to take care that the premises are free from nuisance . . . If a man lets a house, he does so under an implied contract that it is fit for the receiption of a family; and it is his duty to take care that it is so, and that it is in a comfortable and tenantable state . . . " (*Smith* v. *Marrable* (1983) 11 M. & W. 5.)

On appeal, Lord Abinger C.B. added: "It is plain good common sense, that if a man lets a house, it shall be fit for the purposes of occupation . . . " (*ibid.*). The apparent applicability of this to *all* lettings for residential accommodation was restricted to *furnished* lettings in a series of later cases: see *Sutton* v. *Temple* (1843) 12 M. & W. 52, *Hart* v. *Windsor* (1844) 12 M. & W. 68, *Cruse* v. *Mount* [1933] Ch. 278, *Sleafer* v. *London Borough of Lambeth* [1960] 1 Q.B. 43. Further, while it has been held that the furniture restriction is as applicable to flats as houses (*Cruse* v. *Mount*), this decision was without reference to an earlier, conflicting authority: *Sarsons* v. *Roberts* [1895] 2 Q.B. 395.

Amongst the matters which were considered to amount to unfitness for human habitation at common law are: inadequate drainage (*Wilson* v. *Finch Hatton* (1877) 2 Ex. D. 336), infestation by bugs or pests (*Smith* v. *Marrable* (1843) 11 M. & W. 5), infection (*Bird* v. *Greville* (1844) C. & E. 317, *Collins* v. *Hopkins* [1923] 2 K.B. 617, *Hart* v. *Windsor* (1844) 12 M. & W. 68, *Sutton* v. *Temple* (1843) 12 M. & W. 52), premises unsafe for occupation (*Edwards* v. *Etherington* (1825) 7 Dow. & Ry. K.B. 117, *Cruse* v. *Mount* [1933] Ch. 278), and insufficiency of water supplies (*Chester* v. *Powell* (1885) 52 L.T. (n.s.) 722).

Statute

Housing Act use of the term "unfit for human habitation" dates back to the Artizans and Labourers Dwellings Act 1868, which introduced what are now repairs notices under s.189, or demolition orders under s.265, above; in the Artizans and Labourers Dwellings Improvement Act 1887, it was used in relation to what are now known as clearance areas under s.289, above; by Housing of the Working Classes Act 1885, s.12, the condition was introduced that "in any contract made after the passing of this Act for letting for habitation by persons of the working classes a house or part of a house, there shall be implied a condition that the house is at the commencement of the holding in all respects reasonably fit for human habitation". (This is, of course, the predecessor of the contractual requirement now to be found in Landlord and Tenant Act 1985, s.8.)

Letting for the working classes meant lettings below specified rent levels. By Housing of the Working Classes Act 1903, s.12, the condition was to take effect "notwithstanding any agreement to the contrary, and any such agreement made after the passing of this Act shall be void". The rent limits were extended by Housing, Town Planning etc. Act 1909, s.14, and by *ibid.*, s.15, the condition was extended to cover *keeping* in repair throughout the letting.

The term "unfit for human habitation" meant "in all respects reasonably fit for human habitation", otherwise unqualified, until the Housing Repairs and Rents Act 1954 when, by s.9, the present definition was introduced, without "internal arrangement" but with facilities for "storage" as well as for preparation and cooking of food. The addition of internal arrangement, and the elimination of food storage facilities (the latter on account of powers now to be found in Building Act 1984, s.70 permitting the authority to require their introduction in existing dwellings, *i.e.* not just in new properties), were effected by Housing Act 1969, s.71.

The earlier cases on the statutory definition must accordingly be read subject to the "all respects reasonably fit" general definition, as distinct from the present requirement that premises are not "reasonably suitable for occupation", having regard to whether or not "they are so far defective in one or more of" the specified schedule: *Critchell* v. *Lambeth Borough Council* [1957] 2 Q.B. 535, C.A. But this does not mean that unfitness must be attributable to each of the matters specified, as it were in turn and in isolation. The question to be asked is whether the property suffers from any one or more of those defects, and then whether or not the totality of the defects, taken in the round, means that the property is not reasonably suitable for occupation: *E.A. Wyse* v. *Secretary of State for the Environment and Borough of Newcastle-under-Lyme* [1984] J.P.L. 256, Q.B.D.

Nonetheless, the earlier cases remain relevant. Thus, in *Jones* v. *Green* [1925] 1 K.B. 659, D.C., it was said that a high standard of proof is not required: "it is only required that the place must be decently fit for human beings to live in". It is a standard of repair lower than that of "good and tenantable repair": *ibid.* In *Hall* v. *Manchester Corporation* [1915] L.J. Ch. 732, H.L., it was said that the standard was that of the "ordinary reasonable man". In *Summers* v. *Salford Corporation* [1943] A.C. 283, the House of Lords adopted the minority judgment of Atkin L.J. (as he then was) in *Morgan* v. *Liverpool Corporation* [1927] 2 K.B. 131, C.A.: "If the state of repair of a house is such that by ordinary user damage may naturally be caused to the occupier, either in respect of personal injury to life or limb or injury to health, then the house is not in all respects reasonably fit for human habitation".

Repair remains, of course, one of the defects which may mean that premises are not "reasonably suitable for occupation", and it is difficult to see a basis for distinguishing the proposition. Similarly, *Summers* was a case of a broken sash-cord to the window of one of two bedrooms in the house, out of a total of four rooms. The House of Lords was in no doubt that this rendered the whole house unfit, because it would be difficult to confine the effects of inadequate ventilation to one room alone. Ventilation remains a specified defect. The question of unfitness has been said to be one of fact, to be determined in a judicial spirit: *Hall* v. *Manchester* [1915] L.J. Ch. 732, H.L.

It is the *effect* of the defect which matters: "One is rather inclined to associate the idea of a house being unfit for human habitation with its being in such a condition, structurally or otherwise, as to call for demolition . . . At the first blush it seemed to me difficult to say that the existence of a broken sash-cord in the window of one of the four rooms of the appellant's house caused the house not to be 'in all respects reasonably fit for human habitation', but a closer consideration has convinced me that the respondents have committed a breach of the undertaking . . . " (*i.e.* the statutorily implied condition—at that time, under Housing Act 1936, s.2, now Landlord and Tenant Act 1985, s.8). "The result of such a state of affairs was that the window could not be put to its normal use, namely, being opened and shut for the purpose of ventilation or cleaning, without danger to the operator" (*per* Lord Russell of Killowen, in *Summers*).

The proposition that unfitness can arise even though the defect does not suggest demolition is in any event clear from the first statutory context in which this section now applies, *i.e.* the presumption in favour of a repairs notice under s.189, above, unless the property cannot be rendered fit at a reasonable expense within the meaning of s.206, above: see notes thereto. The effect of the defect must be measured in terms of the whole of the property in question: *Hall* v. *Manchester Corporation* (1915) 84 L.J.Ch. 732, H.L.; see also *Estate and Trust Agencies (1927) Ltd.* v. *Singapore Improvement Trust* [1937] A.C. 898, P.C.; *Summers* v. *Salford Corporation* [1943] A.C. 283, H.L. But it is only the property, not, *e.g.* common parts, such as stairs: *Dunster* v. *Hollis* [1918] 2 K.B. 795.

A fall of plaster from the ceiling has been held to be a breach of the implied condition to keep premises fit: *Walker* v. *Hobbs & Co.* (1889) 23 Q.B.D. 458, *Fisher* v. *Walters* [1926] 2 K.B. 315, *Porter* v. *Jones* (1942) 112 L.J.K.B. 173; so has a defective lavatory and guttering: *Horrex* v. *Pidwell* [1958] C.L.Y. 1461. *Infestation* with rats, as distinct from an *occasional* (*i.e.* from time to time) invasion, was considered a breach in *Stanton* v. *Southwick* [1920] 2 K.B. 642 (but it is hard to imagine that this distinction would now be applied, at least once the number of times on which the "visits" occurred were sufficient to make clear that it is the property which is the attraction). Where a tenant and his wife were driven from their bed by fleas, the house was held not to be reasonably fit for human habitation: *Thompson* v. *Arkell* (1949) 99 L.J. 597, C.C. Defective stairs were held to make a house unfit in *McCarrick* v. *Liverpool Corporation* [1947] A.C. 219, H.L.

Principal government guidance on the provisions is still that to be found in M.H.L.G. Circular 69/67:

(1) Repair. "To be satisfactory, any part of the structure must function in the manner in which it was intended. Any disrepair that may exist in the house and its curtilage should not be a threat to the health of, or cause any serious inconvenience to the occupants. A multiplicity of items may well cause serious inconvenience.

"Consideration must be given to the condition of all parts of the fabric of the house and to the fixtures normally provided by a landlord. It is not expected that disrepair of outbuildings, of boundary walls and of the surfaces of yards and paths will be sufficient, in the absence of defects in the house itself, to render it unfit but disrepair of these items should be taken into account in assessing the unfitness of the whole house". (M.H.L.G. Circular 69/67, App., para. 2).

Internal decorative conditions will not normally be taken into account: *ibid*; see also *Ellis Copp* v. *Richmond London Borough Council* (1978) 245 E.G. 931, C.A., and *Adams* v. *Tuer* (1923) 130 L.T. 218. However, these can be a valid indicator of structural conditions. See also notes to s.471, above, as to the distinction between repair and improvement.

(2) Stability. "Evidence of instability is only significant if it indicates the probability of further movement which would constitute a threat to the occupants of the house". (M.H.L.G. Circular 69/67, App., para. 2).

(3) Freedom from Damp. "Any dampness should not be so extensive or so pervasive as to be a threat to the health of the occupants. Such items as a small patch of damp caused by defective pointings around window reveals or door jambs or by a defective rain water pipe are due to disrepair rather than inherent dampness. Care must also be taken not to be misled by temporary condensation". (M.H.L.G. Circular 69/67, App., para. 2).

Nonetheless, in cases under Part III, Public Health Act 1936 (statutory nuisances) it has been established that condensation dampness can be dangerous to health, and further that this may be attributable to the construction (original or by adaptation) of the property: see *Dover District Council* v. *Farrar* (1980) 2 H.L.R. 32, D.C., explained in *Greater London Council* v. *London Borough of Tower Hamlets* (1983) 15 H.L.R. 54, D.C. Indeed, given that ventilation is a consideration under this section, and that condensation dampness is closely related to the degree of ventilation available, there is all the more reason to treat condensation as a symptom of statutory unfitness.

In *Tower Hamlets*, the flat had been constructed with an open solid fuel fire in the living room. Subsequently, because the flues were found to be defective, they were blocked up, and the open fireplace removed and replaced with an electric heater. The result was that the advantages of a fire which would have been kept in for most of the day, and its considerable ventilating effect, were lost. The Greater London Council put in one storage heater, which was insufficient to combat the condensation that might be anticipated following the blocking up of the flues. Subsequently, even this storage heater was removed by them. Griffiths L.J. said:

"If the construction of a building is so unusual that there has to be some special form of heating to combat condensation, it is reasonable that the landlord should be expected to instal items such as storage heaters to provide that warmth. Of course, if the tenant does not choose to use the facilities provided, he will have no cause for complaint if the result is that condensation makes the place uninhabitable.

"A landlord is required to apply his mind to the necessity of ventilation and, if need be, to insulation and heating. The landlord must provide a combination of these factors to make a house habitable for the tenant. However, once the landlord has provided the facilities, the tenant must use them. If it is shown in any further inquiry into condensation in this flat that the landlord has done everything reasonable and the cause of the continuing condensation is that the tenant is unwilling to use the applicances or any reasonable alternative means of heating the flat, then the landlord cannot be held responsible for the ensuing state of the premises".

While the issues of liability to which Griffiths L.J. was addressing himself are not apparently relevant to the question of whether or not *premises* are so far defective as regards freedom from damp, or ventilation, as to be unfit, it is submitted that the test will serve equally well to determine whether or not premises are defective, as distinct from a *use* of premises which results in a defect. Dicta in *Quick* v. *Taff Ely District Council* [1985] 3 All

E.R. 321, 18 H.L.R., C.A., a decision on what is now s.11, Landlord and Tenant Act 1985, suggests that ordinary use of premises which lead to condensation would constitute unfitness.

(4) Internal Arrangements. M.H.L.G. Circular 68/69, App., para. 23, suggests that "internal bad arrangement is any feature which prohibits the safe or unhampered passage of the occupants in the dwelling, *e.g.* narrow, steep or winding staircases, absence of hand rails, inadequate landings outside bedrooms, ill-defined changes in floor levels, a bedroom entered only through another bedroom, and also includes a W.C. opening directly from a living room or kitchen".

(5) Natural Lighting. "There should be sufficient natural lighting in all rooms intended for sleeping, sitting or the consumption of meals to enable domestic work to be done without the use of artificial light under good weather conditions". (M.H.L.G. Circular, App., para. 2).

(6) Ventilation. "There should be adequate ventilation of all habitable rooms and working kitchens to the external air. For example, windows should be capable of being opened to such an extent that fresh air can readily circulate to all parts of the room. Windows, satisfactory in themselves, may be made unsatisfactory by external obstructions". (*Ibid*). See also the comments on ventilation and condensation, under (3) Dampness, above.

(7) Water Supply. "There must be an adequate and wholesome water supply within the house. Whilst one tap may be adequate a polluted supply would, and an intermittent supply could alone be a sufficiently serious defect to render the house unfit". (*Ibid*). The supply need only be judged, however, for the purposes of domestic use: *Re Willesden Corporation and Municipal Mutual Insurance Ltd.'s Arbitration* [1944] 2 All E.R. 600. Authorities may give grants for the provision of separate service pipes, to ensure an adequate supply, under s.523, above.

(8) Drainage and Sanitary Conveniences. "There should be a readily accessible water closet for the exclusive use of the occupants of the dwelling in a properly lighted and ventilated compartment . . . The water closet and bath or shower (if any) should be connected to an efficient disposal system, *i.e.* a public sewerage system, septic tank or cesspool capable of dealing with the normal discharge. There should be adequate means for the disposal of water from roof surfaces and yard pavings. Gutter and disposal pipes should be of a capacity capable of dealing with the normal discharge". (M.H.L.G. Circular 67/69, App., para. 2).

(9) Facilities for Preparation and Cooking of Food and Disposal of Waste Water. "There should be a sink, with an impervious surface, located beneath the piped water supply and connected to a suitable disposal system. There should be either a suitable fixed solid fuel or oil fired cooking appliance or provision for the installation of a gas or electric cooker. Generally the disposition of these facilities should make the preparation and cooking of food capable of being carried out in a convenient and hygienic manner". (*Ibid*). The repeal by Housing Act 1969, s.71 of the former reference to food storage facilities was considered not to make any substantial difference to the operation of the provisions, in M.H.L.G. Circular 68/69, App., para. 11

Underground Rooms

Subs. (2) preserves the deemed unfitness of "underground rooms" as defined in s.282, for the purposes of action to close such a room under s.266; s.282(2) expressly provides that this deemed unfitness is not to affect or preclude the taking of action in respect of an underground room which is unfit by reason of this section.

Periodic inspection of district by local housing authority

605.—(1) The local housing authority shall cause an inspection of their district to be made from time to time with a view to determining what action to take in the performance of their functions under—

     Part VI (repair notices),

     Part VIII (area improvement),

     Part IX (slum clearance), and

     Part XI (houses in multiple occupation).

(2) For the purpose of carrying out that duty the authority and their officers shall comply with any directions the Secretary of State may give and shall keep such records and supply him with such information as he may specify.

DEFINITIONS
"district": s.2.
"local housing authority": ss.1, 2.

GENERAL NOTE

This section had its origins in the Housing Act 1969, s.70; it may be read together with the duty in s.8, above, to consider the needs of a district for housing.

In view of the phrase "from time to time", and the power of the Secretary of State to issue directions, which is not limited to the keeping of records, etc., it would be difficult to succeed in an application for judicial review for failure to perform this duty, although not impossible: see, *e.g. Meade* v. *Haringey London Borough Council* [1979] 1 W.L.R. 637, C.A.

The duty is exercisable "as occasion requires": s.12, Interpretation Act 1978.

Reports on particular houses or areas

606.—(1) The proper officer of the local housing authority shall make a report in writing to the authority whenever he is of the opinion—

(*a*) that a house in their district is unfit for human habitation, or

(*b*) that an area in their district should be dealt with as a clearance area;

and the authority shall take into consideration as soon as may be any such report made to them.

(2) If a complaint in writing that a house is unfit for human habitation, or that an area should be dealt with as a clearance area, is made to the proper officer of the local housing authority by—

(*a*) a justice of the peace having jurisdiction in any part of their district, or

(*b*) a parish or community council for a parish or community within their district,

the officer shall forthwith inspect the house or area and make a report to the authority stating the facts of the case and whether in his opinion the house is unfit for human habitation or the area should be dealt with as a clearance area.

(3) The absence of a complaint under subsection (2) does not excuse the proper officer of the authority from inspecting a house or area or making a report on it under subsection (1).

DEFINITIONS
"clearance area": s.289.
"district": s.2.
"local housing authority": ss.1, 2.
"unfit for human habitation": s.604.

GENERAL NOTE

This section now imposes a duty on "the proper officer of the local authority" (appointed under Local Government Act 1972, s.112), but used to refer to the Medical Officer of Health, an officer with statutorily protected independence, the specific duty to appoint whom, and whose protection, disappeared under the 1972 Act pursuant to the Interim Report of the Working Group of the Study Group on Local Authority Management Structures (see *The New Local Authorities, Management and Structure*, H.M.S.O. 1972, popularly referred to as "Bains"). The obligation to report on unfitness itself dates back to Artizans and Labourers Dwellings Act 1868, s.5, although did not include what are now clearance areas (see, now, ss.289 *et seq.*, above) until s.4, Artizans and Labourers Dwellings Improvement Act 1875. Powers for householders (formerly) and justices of the peace to complain to the Medical Officer of Health similarly date back to the 1868 and 1875 Acts: see now subs. (2).

Notwithstanding the obligation to report to the authority, if the proper officer with responsibility for housing conditions also enjoys delegated power under Local Government Act 1972, s.101 to decide whether or not action should be taken, the report may, in effect, be to himself, *i.e.* this statutory requirement does not operate so as to prevent delegation of

the power to *receive* the report: *R.* v. *Cardiff City Council, ex parte Cross* (1981) 1 H.L.R. 54, Q.B.D., not appealed on this point (see (1982) 6 H.L.R. 1, C.A.).
"Parish or community council": see Local Government Act 1972, ss.9, 27.

Environmental considerations

Local housing authority to have regard to environmental considerations

607. A local housing authority in preparing any proposals for the provision of housing accommodation, or in taking any action under this Act, shall have regard to—
  (*a*) the beauty of the landscape or countryside,
  (*b*) the other amenities of the locality, and
  (*c*) the desirability of preserving existing works of architectural, historic or artistic interest;
and they shall comply with such directions in that behalf as may be given to them by the Secretary of State.

DEFINITION
  "local housing authority": ss.1, 2.

GENERAL NOTE
  Hitherto, this obligation has not been applied uniformly throughout housing legislation. The extension to all of the provisions of this Act is pursuant to Law Commission Recommendations (Cmnd. 9515), No. 27.
  "Amenities": "The word 'amenity' still connotes in a statute what Scrutton L.J. thought it did on its first appearance in the Housing, Town Planning, etc. Act, 1909; 'pleasant circumstances or features, advantages': *Ellis* v. *Ruislip-Northwood Urban Council* [1920] 1 K.B. 343, 370"—*F.F.F. Estates Ltd.* v. *Hackney London Borough Council* [1981] Q.B. 503, 3 H.L.R. 107, C.A.

Acquisition of ancient monuments, &c.

608. Land which is the site of an ancient monument or other object of archaeological interest—
  (*a*) may not be acquired for the purposes of section 192 (unfit house subject to repair notice found to be beyond repair) or Part IX (slum clearance), and
  (*b*) may be acquired for the purposes of Part II (provision of housing) only by compulsory purchase order.

GENERAL NOTE
  Note that the prohibition on acquisition under Part II is only, in effect, against acquisition by agreement, *i.e.* the acquisition *must* be by way of compulsory purchase, which of definition means that it will require consent and may result in an inquiry.
  "Ancient Monument": see the Ancient Monuments and Archaeological Areas Act, 1979.

Enforceability of covenants, &c.

Enforcement of covenants against owner for the time being

609. Where—
  (*a*) a local housing authority have disposed of land held by them for any of the purposes of this Act and the person to whom the disposal was made has entered into a covenant with the authority concerning the land, or
  (*b*) an owner of any land has entered into a covenant with the local housing authority concerning the land for the purposes of any of the provisions of this Act,
the authority may enforce the covenant against the persons deriving title under the covenantor, notwithstanding that the authority are not in possession of or interested in any land for the benefit of which the

covenant was entered into, in like manner and to the like extent as if they had been possessed of or interested in such land.

DEFINITIONS
"local housing authority": ss.1, 2.
"owner": s.623.

GENERAL NOTE
While a covenant will remain enforceable as between the parties to it, to be enforceable against a third party, it must as a rule be negative, or restrictive, in quality: *Tulk* v. *Moxhay* (1848) 2 Ph. 774, *Haywood* v. *Brunswick Permanent Benefit Building Society* (1881) 8 Q.B.D. 403. Furthermore, the covenant must be for the benefit of land, not simply for "personal" benefit (which in this context will of course include the benefit of an authority): see, *e.g. London County Council* v. *Allen* [1914] 3 K.B. 642. On a disposal of land, *e.g.* under Part II, a local authority may wish to include covenants, *e.g.* to carry out works, perhaps in connection with the requirement that property for which they provide a mortgage is to be made fit, under s.439, above. This section ensures the enforceability of covenants which would not otherwise be enforceable at common law.

The applicability of this section is also (*cf.* notes to s.608, above) now general, rather than selective, pursuant to Law Commission Recommendations (Cmnd. 9515), No. 27. See also *ibid.*, No. 1, pointing out that hitherto it applied on a sale or exchange, whereas the wording of the general disposal power in what is now Part II (s.32, above), means that a disposal may be in any manner, even gratuitous.

Power of court to authorise conversion of house into flats

610.—(1) The local housing authority or a person interested in a house may apply to the county court where—
  (*a*) owing to changes in the character of the neighbourhood in which the house is situated, it cannot readily be let as a single tenement but could readily be let for occupation if converted into two or more tenements, or
  (*b*) planning permission has been granted under Part III of the Town and Country Planning Act 1971 (general planning control) for the use of the house as converted into two or more separate dwelling-houses instead of as a single dwelling-house,
and the conversion is prohibited or restricted by the provisions of the lease of the house, or by a restrictive covenant affecting the house, or otherwise.

(2) The court may, after giving any person interested an opportunity of being heard, vary the terms of the lease or other instrument imposing the prohibition or restriction, subject to such conditions and upon such terms as the court may think just.

DEFINITIONS
"house": s.623.
"local housing authority": ss.1, 2.

GENERAL NOTE
This section adds to the circumstances in which a covenant—whether in a lease, or otherwise—restricting conversion of single houses into flats can be overriden: see also the provisions of (a) Law of Property Act 1925, s.84 as amended, and (b) Landlord and Tenant Act 1927, s.19 where one or other is applicable, in the notes to s.460, above. The requirements are (1) the property cannot readily be let as a single unit, but could be readily let if converted, owing to changes in the character of the neighbourhood, or (2) that planning permission for the change of use has been granted. As to the need for planning permission for such a change of use, see notes to s.460, above.

"House" for this purpose is to be interpreted widely: "I can see no reason for confining the word 'house' . . . to dwelling-house. It might well include a block of offices suitable for conversion into dwelling-houses", and regardless of class of tenants for whom the housing would be suitable—*Johnston* v. *Maconochie* [1921] 1 K.B. 239, C.A., *per* Atkin L.J. However, the conversion need not be into self-contained dwellings, or indeed involve any structural alterations at all (if under the first limb—*cf.* subs. (1)(*b*), where reliance is placed on the grant of planning permission): *Stack* v. *Church Commissioners for England* [1952] 1 All E.R. 136.

Where reliance is placed on subs. (1)(*b*), there is no jurisdiction when the conversion for which permission has been obtained would divide the house into a number of "half-dwellings", the other "halves" lying in an adjoining property: *Josephine Trust Ltd.* v. *Champagne* [1963] 2 Q.B. 160. Planning permission is alternative to proof of changes in the character of the neighbourhood, but the court retains its discretion whether or not to grant the application: *Sarum Trust* v. *Duke of Westminster* [1953] C.P.L. 86. When subs. (1)(*a*) is relied on, the court must ask (1) whether the house is not readily lettable as a single unit, (2) whether it is readily lettable in more than one unit, (3) whether this is attributable to changes in the character of the neighbourhood, and (4) what those changes are: *Alliance Economic Investment Co.* v. *Berton* (1923) 92 L.J.K.B. 750, C.A.

Notwithstanding the similarity with Law of Property Act 1925 s.84 (see notes to s.460), the Law Commission earlier concluded (L.C. No. 141, Covenants Restricting Disposals, Alterations and Change of User—H.C, 278, para. 9.7.) that this separate jurisdiction should be retained. They also recommended (*ibid.*, para 9.14.) that the word "tenement" in subs. (1)(*a*) should be replaced with the word "dwelling-houses"—"being less Victorian in character", and to correspond with subs. (1)(*b*). Presumably, this was thought too contentious for a consolidating Act. Similarly, in *ibid.*, para 9.15., they recommended overruling the effect of *Josephine Trust* (above), and (*ibid.*, para 9.17.) an express power to include compensation under what is now subs. (2); again, neither has been adopted in the course of the current exercise.

Miscellaneous powers of local housing authorities

Removal or alteration of apparatus of statutory undertakers

611.—(1) Where by reason of the stopping up, diversion or alteration of the level or width of a street by a local housing authority under powers exercisable by them by virtue of this Act—

(*a*) the removal or alteration of apparatus belonging to statutory undertakers, or

(*b*) the execution of works for the provision of substituted apparatus, whether permanent or temporary,

is reasonably necessary for the purposes of their undertaking, the statutory undertakers may by notice in writing served on the authority require them to remove or alter the apparatus or to execute the works.

(2) Where such a requirement is made and not withdrawn, the authority shall give effect to it unless—

(*a*) they serve notice in writing on the undertakers of their objection to the requirement within 28 days of the service of the notice upon them, and

(*b*) the requirement is determined by arbitration to be unreasonable.

(3) At least seven days before commencing any works which they are required under this section to execute, the authority shall, except in case of emergency, serve on the undertakers notice in writing of their intention to do so; and if the undertakers so elect within seven days from the date of service of the notice on them, they shall themselves execute the works.

(4) If the works are executed by the authority, they shall be executed at the authority's expense and under the superintendence (also at the authority's expense) and to the reasonable satisfaction of the undertakers; and if the works are executed by the undertakers, they shall be executed in accordance with the reasonable directions and to the reasonable satisfaction of the authority, and the reasonable costs of the works shall be repaid to the undertakers by the authority.

(5) Any difference arising between statutory undertakers and a local housing authority under subsection (3) or (4), and any matter which by virtue of subsection (2)(*b*) is to be determined by arbitration, shall be referred to and determined by an arbitrator to be appointed, in default of agreement, by the Secretary of State.

(6) In this section—
(*a*) "statutory undertakers" means any person authorised by an enactment, or by an order, rule or regulation made under an enactment, to construct, work or carry on a railway, canal, inland navigation, dock, harbour, tramway, gas, electricity, water or other public undertaking;
(*b*) "apparatus" means sewers, drains, culverts, water-courses, mains, pipes, valves, tubes, cables, wires, transformers and other apparatus laid down or used for or in connection with the carrying, conveying or supplying to premises of a supply of water, water for hydraulic power, gas or electricity, and standards and brackets carrying street lamps;
(*c*) references to the alteration of apparatus include diversion and the alteration of position or level.

DEFINITION
"local housing authority": ss.1, 2.

GENERAL NOTE
A local authority may want either the removal or alteration of apparatus of statutory undertakers, or works for the provision of substituted apparatus, permanent or temporary, in connection with their powers to do works to streets under Pts. II and IX. For this purpose the statutory undertakers and their apparatus are as defined in subs. (6).

The undertakers may require the authority to do the works themselves, by serving notice under subs. (1) and if it is not withdrawn, the authority *have* to do so unless they object by notice in writing within 28 days (subs. (2)). Objection is followed by reference to arbitration, and the authority will still have to do the works, unless on arbitration it is found that the undertakers' requirement is unreasonable. The undertakers and the authority are to agree on the arbitrator and, in default, he will be appointed by the Secretary of State: subs. (5).

If the authority are to do the works, then save in the case of emergency, the authority must serve at least seven days' notice on the undertakers who, under subs. (3), then have an option to do the work themselves. If the authority do the works, they pay for them, and pay for their superintendence by the undertakers, and must do them to the satisfaction of the undertakers: subs. (4). If the undertakers do the works, they are to be executed at the cost of the authority, but to the reasonable directions and satisfaction of the authority: *ibid.* A difference on these matters is also to be determined by arbitration, by an arbitrator appointed by agreement or in default by the Secretary of State: subs. (5).

General provisions

Exclusion of Rent Act protection

612. Nothing in the Rent Acts prevents possession being obtained of a house of which possession is required for the purpose of enabling a local housing authority to exercise their powers under any enactment relating to housing.

DEFINITIONS
"house": s.623.
"local housing authority": ss.1, 2.
"Rent Acts": s.622.

GENERAL NOTE
Rent Act protection is expressly removed when a property is subject to a closing or demolition order: see ss.264, 270, 276, above. By this section, it may be removed whenever possession is needed to enable the authority to exercise powers under any enactment relating to housing.

A number of points may be made. First of all, possession must be needed: if, therefore, the exercise will not prevent reoccupation, and the tenant consents to move elsewhere, granting the authority a licence to enter, etc., *possession* will not be required—see notes to s.84, above, and Sched. 2, Ground 10, below. Secondly, the purpose of the provision is to enable the *authority* to exercise powers, not the landlord: *cf.* notes to s.460, above, where the power of the landlord to apply to the county court for an order permitting works within an improvement or intermediate grant (within Pt. XV, above) under Rent Act 1977, s.116 is described.

Thirdly, it appears to be the *enactment* not the *exercise* which must relate to housing, so that the provision would not seem to apply in the case of, *e.g.* action by the authority under Part III, Public Health Act 1936 (statutory nuisance—but in *any* premises, including but not confined to or expressly referring to housing).

The section does not confer a right to recover possession, but prevents a tenant relying on the Rent Acts, against whomsoever is entitled to claim possession, if the purpose is to enable the authority to exercise powers under a relevant enactment: *cf.* ss.270, 286, 338, above, conferring an express power to recover possession, not available in other circumstances. In *Guppys (Bridport) Ltd.* v. *Brookling, James* (1983) 14 H.L.R. 1, however, the Court of Appeal did suggest that this section *might* permit a local authority to recover possession against tenants, in order to carry out works in default under what is now s.375, above. The point was not taken further and would not appear to have been at the forefront of the decision, so much as an ancillary observation.

Liability of directors, etc. in case of offence by body corporate

613.—(1) Where an offence under this Act committed by a body corporate is proved to have been committed with the consent or connivance of, or to be attributable to any neglect on the part of, a director, manager, secretary or other similar officer of the body corporate, or a person purporting to act in any such capacity, he, as well as the body corporate, is guilty of an offence and liable to be proceeded against and punished accordingly.

(2) Where the affairs of a body corporate are managed by its members, subsection (1) applies in relation to the acts and defaults of a member in connection with his functions of management as if he were a director of the body corporate.

GENERAL NOTE

"Most of the offences in Housing Acts since 1961 have the benefit of the common form provision expressly imposing liability on the officers of a company where the body commits an offence . . . The absence of such a provision in relation to the offences in the Housing Act 1957 is due to the fact that the Act reproduced legislation, much of it from the 1930s, dating from a time before such provisions were regularly included . . . " Law Commission Recommendations (Cmnd. 9515), No. 28. Accordingly, the present provision now applies through the offences created by this Act.

The provision applies when the offence is proved to have been committed with the consent or connivance of an officer of the class specified, *or* is attributable to any neglect on his part.

Power to prescribe forms etc.

614.—(1) The Secretary of State may by regulations prescribe—

(*a*) anything which by this Act is to be prescribed; or

(*b*) the form of any notice, advertisement, statement or other document which is required or authorised to be used under or for the purposes of this Act.

(2) The regulations shall be made by statutory instrument which shall be subject to annulment in pursuance of a resolution of either House of Parliament.

(3) The power conferred by this section is not exercisable where specific provision for prescribing a thing, or the form of a document, is made elsewhere.

GENERAL NOTE

This is also (*cf.* notes to ss.607, 609, 613, above) now a provision of general applicability, formerly of selective application, pursuant to Law Commission Recommendations (Cmnd. 9515), No. 27.

Earlier regulations are retained in force by Housing (Consequential Provisions) Act 1985 s.2.

Dispensation with advertisements and notices

615.—(1) The Secretary of State may dispense with the publication of advertisements or the service of notices required to be published or served by a local authority under this Act if he is satisfied that there is reasonable cause for dispensing with the publication or service.

(2) A dispensation may be given by the Secretary of State—

(*a*) either before or after the time at which the advertisement is required to be published or the notice is required to be served, and

(*b*) either unconditionally or upon such conditions, as to the publication of other advertisements or the service of other notices or otherwise, as the Secretary of State thinks fit,

due care being taken by him to prevent the interests of any persons being prejudiced by the dispensation.

GENERAL NOTE

This is also (*cf.* notes to ss.607, 609, 613, 614, above) now a provision of general applicability, formerly of selective application, pursuant to Law Commission Recommendations (Cmnd. 9515), No. 27.

Note that dispensation may be given *after* publication or service was required, provided due care is taken to prevent prejudice to the interests of anyone prejudiced by the dispensation.

Local inquiries

616. For the purposes of the execution of his powers and duties under this Act, the Secretary of State may cause such local inquiries to be held as he may think fit.

GENERAL NOTE

This is also (*cf.* notes to ss.607, 609, 613–615, above) now a provision of general applicability, formerly of selective application, pursuant to Law Commission Recommendations (Cmnd. 9515), No. 27.

As to local inquiry, see notes to Sched. 22, below. See also Tribunals and Inquiries Act 1971.

Service of notices

617.—(1) Where under any provision of this Act it is the duty of a local housing authority to serve a document on a person who is to the knowledge of the authority—

(*a*) a person having control of premises, however defined, or

(*b*) a person managing premises, however defined, or

(*c*) a person having an estate or interest in premises, whether or not restricted to persons who are owners or lessees or mortgagees or to any other class of those having an estate or interest in premises,

the authority shall take reasonable steps to identify the person or persons coming within the description in that provision.

(2) A person having an estate or interest in premises may for the purposes of any provision to which subsection (1) applies give notice to the local housing authority of his interest in the premises and they shall enter the notice in their records.

(3) A document required or authorised by this Act to be served on a person as being a person having control of premises (however defined) may, if it is not practicable after reasonable enquiry to ascertain the name or address of that person, be served by—

(*a*) addressing it to him by the description of "person having control of" the premises (naming them) to which it relates, and

(*b*) delivering it to some person on the premises or, if there is no person on the premises to whom it can be delivered, by affixing it, or a copy of it, to some conspicuous part of the premises.

(4) Where under any provision of this Act a document is to be served on—

    (*a*) the person having control of premises, however defined, or
    (*b*) the person managing premises, however defined, or
    (*c*) the owner of premises, however defined,

and more than one person comes within the description in the enactment, the document may be served on more than one of those persons.

DEFINITIONS
"local housing authority": ss.1, 2.
"owner": s.623.

GENERAL NOTE
Earlier provisions governing the authentication of orders, notices and certificates, service on an authority, service of documents *on* authorities, and general provisions as to service, have been repealed, pursuant to Law Commission Recommendations (Cmnd. 9515), No. 37(vii), in favour of reliance on Local Government Act 1972 corresponding provisions:
"The only practical difference appears to be that section 166(2) [of the Housing Act 1957] requires certain orders, in particular demolition orders and most closing orders, to be given under the seal of the authority. It seems unlikely that this additional formality adds significantly to the protection afforded to the individual affected".
Service *on* authorities is governed by 1972 Act, s.231, which requires that a notice, order or other document be given or served by addressing it to the local authority and leaving it at, or sending it by post to, the principal office of the authority or any other office of the authority specified by them as one at which they accept documents of a particular description. This is not applicable to documents in the course of court proceedings.
Section s.233, 1972 Act, permits service *by* authorities by delivery of a document to the person to be served, or by posting it to him at his proper address, or by leaving it at his proper address. In the case of a body corporate, service may be on the secretary or clerk of that body, and in the case of a partnership, on a partner or on a person having control or management of the partnership business. The "proper" address of a person is his last known address, save that in the case of a body corporate it is the registered or principal office, and in the case of a partnership, the principal office of the partnership. Use of a misnomer will not invalidate service if it does not mislead or cause confusion: *Malkin's Bank Estates Ltd.* v. *Kirkham* [1966] L.G.R. 361.
Section 234, 1972 Act, requires authentication by signature by the proper officer of the authority. Signature includes facsimile "by whatever process reproduced". A document, etc., not signed by the proper officer will be invalid: *West Ham Corporation* v. *Benabo* [1934] 2 K.B. 253, *Becker* v. *Crosby Corporation* [1952] 1 All E.R. 1350, *Graddage* v. *Haringey London Borough Council* [1975] 1 W.L.R. 241. However, an authorised assistant can sign, "pp" or "for and on behalf of": *Tennant* v. *London County Council* (1957) 121 J.P. 428.
The purpose of this section is to govern the case where the authority cannot find out upon whom to serve a notice: it starts with an obligation to "take reasonable steps to identify" the person with the relevant description: subs. (1). This will include use of their powers to require information from occupants and others with an interest, under Local Government (Miscellaneous Provisions) Act 1976, s.16. For their own protection, those with an estate or interest can give notice to the authority, even if no action has been taken, which information the authority must record: subs. (2).
Where the name or address of a person having control of premises cannot be ascertained, authorities may fall back upon their long-standing powers (similar powers date back to the Public Health Act 1948, s.150, and were also included in Housing Acts from the Artizans and Labourers Dwellings Act 1868, s.16) to serve in the manner set out in subs. (3). What is a conspicuous part of premises is a question of fact: *West Ham Corporation* v. *Thomas* (1908) 73 J.P. 65.

The Common Council of the City of London

    618.—(1) The Common Council of the City of London may appoint a committee, consisting of so many persons as they think fit, for any purposes of this Act or the Housing Associations Act 1985 which in their opinion may be better regulated and managed by means of a committee.
    (2) A committee so appointed—

(*a*) shall consist as to a majority of its members of members of the Common Council, and

(*b*) shall not be authorised to borrow money or to make a rate,

and shall be subject to any regulations and restrictions which may be imposed by the Common Council.

(3) A person is not, by reason only of the fact that he occupies a house at a rental from the Common Council, disqualified from being elected or being a member of that Council or any committee of that Council; but no person shall vote as a member of that Council, or any such committee, on a resolution or question which is proposed or arises in pursuance of this Act or the Housing Associations Act 1985 and relates to land in which he is beneficially interested.

(4) A person who votes in contravention of subsection (1) commits a summary offence and is liable on conviction to a fine not exceeding level 2 on the standard scale; but the fact of his giving the vote does not invalidate any resolution or proceeding of the authority.

DEFINITION

"house": s.623.

GENERAL NOTE

Under Local Government Act 1972, ss.93–97, restrictions are imposed on all local councillors relating to voting on matters in which they are interested. Under s.97, the Secretary of State has power to remove a disability, if "the number of members of the local authority disabled . . . at any one time would be so great a proportion of the whole as to impede the transaction of business, or in any other case in which it appears to the . . . Secretary of State in the interests of the inhabitants of the area that the disability should be removed". This power has been used in order to permit unfurnished tenants who are councillors to speak and vote on matters of general housing policy: D.O.E. Circular 105/73.

Local authority for this purpose does not include the Common Council of the City of London. Nor are they within 1972 Act, s.101 permitting delegation to a committee, sub-committee or officer. By this section, the Common Council are entitled to appoint a committee for any of the purposes of this (or the Housing Associations) Act. Council tenants of the Corporation are entitled to be a member of the Council or a committee of the Council, but not to vote on an issue which relates to land in which he is beneficially interested. Contravention of this provision constitutes a criminal offence, punishable by a fine of up to level 2 on the standard scale under Criminal Justice Act 1982, s.37, currently £100 by S.I. 1984 No. 447, but does not invalidate the vote: subs. (3).

This is also (*cf.* notes to ss.607, 609, 613–616, above) now a provision of general applicability, formerly of selective application, pursuant to Law Commission Recommendations (Cmnd. 9515), No. 27.

The Inner and Middle Temples

619.—(1) For the purposes of Part XII (common lodging houses) the local housing authority—

(*a*) for the Inner Temple is the Sub-Treasurer of the Inner Temple, and

(*b*) for the Middle Temple is the Under-Treasurer of the Middle Temple.

(2) The other provisions of this Act are among those for which provision may be made by Order in Council under section 94 of the Local Government Act 1985 (general power to provide for exercise of local authority functions as respects the Temples).

The Isles of Scilly

620.—(1) This Act applies to the Isles of Scilly subject to such exceptions, adaptations and modifications as the Secretary of State may by order direct.

(2) An order shall be made by statutory instrument which shall be subject to annulment in pursuance of a resolution of either House of Parliament.

GENERAL NOTE

Since 1975, housing legislation has applied to the Isles of Scilly. Previous legislation applied, but by specific orders. During consolidation of the Rent Acts in 1977, the solution to inconsistent treatment advanced (Law Commission Recommendations (Cmnd. 6751), No. 13) and adopted (Rent Act 1977, s.153) was to apply the provisions, subject to a power to make exceptions. That is what has been done here, pursuant to Law Commission Recommendations (Cmnd. 9515), No. 29.

Meaning of "lease" and "tenancy" and related expressions

621.—(1) In this Act "lease" and "tenancy" have the same meaning.

(2) Both expressions include—

(*a*) a sub-lease or sub-tenancy, and

(*b*) an agreement for a lease or tenancy (or sub-lease or sub-tenancy).

(3) The expressions "lessor" and "lessee" and "landlord" and "tenant", and references to letting, to the grant of a lease or to covenants or terms, shall be construed accordingly.

Minor definitions: general

622. In this Act—

"bank" means—

(*a*) a recognised bank within the meaning of the Banking Act 1979, or

(*b*) a company as to which the Secretary of State was satisfied immediately before the repeal of the Protection of Depositors Act 1963 that it ought to be treated as a banking company or discount company for the purposes of that Act;

"building regulations" means—

(*a*) building regulations made under Part I of the Building Act 1984,

(*b*) new street byelaws made under Part X of the Highways Act 1980, or

(*c*) any provision of a local Act, or of a byelaw made under a local Act, dealing with the construction and drainage of new buildings and the laying out and construction of new streets;

"building society" means a building society within the meaning of the Building Societies Act 1962 or the Building Societies Act (Northern Ireland) 1967;

"cemetery" has the same meaning as in section 214 of the Local Government Act 1972;

"charity" has the same meaning as in the Charities Act 1960;

"district valuer" means an officer of the Commissioners of Inland Revenue appointed to be, in relation to the valuation list for the area in which the land in question is situated, the valuation or deputy valuation officer or one of the valuation officers or deputy valuation officers;

"friendly society" means a friendly society, or a branch of a friendly society, registered under the Friendly Societies Act 1974 or earlier legislation;

"general rate fund" means—

(*a*) in relation to the Council of the Isles of Scilly, the general fund of that council;

(*b*) in relation to the Common Council of the City of London, that council's general rate;

"hostel" means a building in which is provided, for persons generally or for a class or classes of persons—

(*a*) residential accommodation otherwise than in separate and self-contained sets of premises, and

(*b*) either board or facilities for the preparation of food adequate to the needs of those persons, or both;

"insurance company" means an insurance company to which Part II of the Insurance Companies Act 1982 applies;

"protected occupancy" and "protected occupier" have the same meaning as in the Rent (Agriculture) Act 1976;

"protected tenancy" has the same meaning as in the Rent Act 1977;

"regular armed forces of the Crown" means the Royal Navy, the regular forces as defined by section 225 of the Army Act 1955, the regular air force as defined by section 223 of the Air Force Act 1955, Queen Alexandra's Royal Naval Nursing Service and the Women's Royal Naval Service;

"the Rent Acts" means the Rent Act 1977 and the Rent (Agriculture) Act 1976;

"restricted contract" has the same meaning as in the Rent Act 1977;

"shared ownership lease" means a lease—

(*a*) granted on payment of a premium calculated by reference to a percentage of the value of the dwelling or of the cost of providing it, or

(*b*) under which the tenant (or his personal representatives) will or may be entitled to a sum calculated by reference, directly or indirectly, to the value of the dwelling;

"standard scale", in reference to the maximum fine on conviction of a summary offence, has the meaning given by section 75 of the Criminal Justice Act 1982;

"statutory maximum", in reference to the maximum fine on summary conviction of an offence triable either summarily or on indictment, has the meaning given by section 74 of the Criminal Justice Act 1982;

"statutory tenancy" and "statutory tenant" mean a statutory tenancy or statutory tenant within the meaning of the Rent Act 1977 or the Rent (Agriculture) Act 1976;

"street" includes any court, alley, passage, square or row of houses, whether a thoroughfare or not;

"subsidiary" has the same meaning as in the Companies Act 1985;

"trustee savings bank" means a trustee savings bank registered under the Trustee Savings Bank Act 1981 or earlier legislation.

GENERAL NOTE

"Building Regulations". See currently the Building Regulations 1985, S.I. 1985 No. 1065.

"Cemetery". This "includes a burial ground or any other place for the interment of the dead (including any part of any such place set aside for the interment of a dead person's ashes)": Local Government Act 1972, s.214.

"Hostel". See also notes to s.56, above.

"Protected Occupancy", "Protected Occupier". Under the Rent (Agriculture) Act 1976, a person is a protected occupier, and therefore has a protected occupancy, if he has

(1) A relevant licence or tenancy of a dwelling-house or part of a house; and

(2) At some time during the subsistence of the relevant licence or tenancy the house has been in qualifying ownership; and

(3) The occupier is, or at any time during the subsistence of the licence or tenancy has been, a qualifying worker (Rent (Agriculture) Act 1976, ss.2(1), 34(3)).

A relevant licence is one which, whether or not for any consideration, confers exclusive occupation of premises for use as a residence (*ibid.*, s.34(1)) and which, if it had been a tenancy, would have been a protected tenancy under the Rent Act 1977 given certain modifications of those Acts (*ibid.*, Sched. 2, para. 1).

A relevant tenancy is one which, not being a tenancy to which the Landlord and Tenant Act 1954 applies (as to which, see Sched. 1, para. 11, below), and not being a tenancy of an agricultural holding within the Agricultural Holdings Act 1948, as amended by the Agricultural Holdings Act 1984 (see Sched. 1, para. 8, below), would be a protected tenancy under the Rent Act 1977, again given modification (Rent (Agriculture) Act 1976, Sched. 2, para. 2). Tenancy includes sub-tenancy (*ibid.*, s.34(1)).

The modifications of the Rent Act 1977 (*cf.* notes to "protected tenancy", below) are:

(i) Occupation will be included even though the occupier pays no rent or pays only a low rent, or even although the tenancy or licence is of a dwelling-house comprised in an agricultural holding;

(ii) Occupation will be excluded from protection if it is a bona fide term of the letting that the landlord provides the occupier with board or attendance, *excluding* meals given in the course of employment, and attendances where the value to the occupier is not substantial (*cf.* notes, below).

Note that where a tenant/licensee has the right to exclusive occupation of some part of his accommodation, but shares another part (with someone other than his landlord, for he will be excluded from protection if there is a resident landlord, *i.e.* because he would not be protected under the Rent Act 1977—see notes, below), a protected occupancy is still available on the basis of the separate accommodation (*ibid.*, ss.23(1), 34(1),(2)), unless the separate accommodation consists of only one room and, at the time of the grant, at least three other similar rooms were let or available for letting (*ibid.*, s.23(2)), *i.e.* hostels for agricultural workers are excluded.

Qualifying ownership means that either the occupier's employer is the landlord under the letting, or that the dwelling has been let by some person with whom the occupier's employer has made arrangements for the premises in question to be used for persons employed by him in agriculture: Rent (Agriculture) Act 1976, Sched. 3, para. 3(1). Employer includes one of a number of joint employers: *ibid.*, para. 3(2). Employment in agriculture includes dairy farming, livestock keeping and breeding, arable farming, market gardening and forestry: *ibid.*, s.1(1). Gamekeepers have been held outside this definition: *Glendyne* v. *Rapley* (1978) E.G. 573, C.A.; *Earl of Normanton* v. *Giles* [1980] 1 W.L.R. 28, H.L.

A qualifying worker is a person who has worked whole-time in agriculture, or has worked in agriculture as a permit-worker for not less than 91 out of the previous 104 weeks: Rent (Agriculture) Act 1976, Sched. 3, para. 1. A person works whole-time if he works not less than the standard number of hours in agriculture: *ibid.*, para. 4. A permit-worker is one who has been granted a permit under Agricultural Wages Act 1948, s.5: *ibid.*, paras. 5, 7. There are provisions to protect a worker against loss of qualifying time by reason of injury or disease, holiday entitlement, or if the worker is absent with the consent of his employer: *ibid.*, para. 4(3)–(5), para. 5(3)–(4).

"Protected Tenancy". A protected tenancy is a regulated (*i.e.* contractual) tenancy within the full protection of the Rent Act 1977: see s.1 thereof. In outline, it is the letting as a separate dwelling (see notes to s.79, above) under a tenancy (not licence, see *Street* v. *Mountford* [1985] A.C. 809, 17 H.L.R. 402, H.L., see notes to s.93, above) which is not excluded from protection under any of the provisions of Part I of the 1977 Act. The exclusions are:

(1) High rated property—1977, s.4;

(2) Low rented tenancies—1977, s.5;

(3) Lettings together with land exceeding 2 acres (other than agricultural land)—1977, ss.6 and 26 (*cf.* s.184, above);

(4) Tenancies under which board to any value, or attendances to a value which represents a substantial proportion of the rent, are provided—1977, s.7; as to substantial proportion, see note to Restricted Contract, below;

(5) Specified student lettings—1977, s.8 (*cf.* the different specifications for the purposes of Sched. 1, para. 10, below);

(6) Holiday lettings—1977, s.9;

(7) Agricultural holdings—1977, s.10 (*cf.* Sched. 1, para. 8, below);

(8) Licensed premises—1977, s.11 (*cf.* Sched. 1, para. 9, below);

(9) Tenancies from a resident landlord—1977, s.12 (*cf.* notes to s.93, above);

(10) Crown tenancies not under the management of the Crown Estate Commissioners—1977, s.13;

(11) Tenancies from local authorities and development corporations—1977, s.14 (*cf.* s.4, above);

(12) Tenancies from registered housing associations and housing trusts—1977, s.15 (*cf.* s.5, above);

(13) Tenancies from a housing co-operative under s.27, above—1977, s.16;

(14) Assured tenancies under Part II, Housing Act 1980—1977, s.16A (*cf.* notes to Sched. 1, para. 11, below);
(15) Business tenancies—1977, s.24 (*cf.* Sched. 1, para. 11, below).
Notwithstanding that the premises are not let as a separate dwelling, they may be the subject of a protected or statutory tenancy if the only sharing is with other tenants (1977, s.22), although if the sharing is with the landlord, the tenancy will be a restricted contract, even if it would not otherwise so qualify (1977, s.21). A tenancy from a resident landlord is similarly a restricted contract, even if it would not otherwise so qualify: 1977, s.20.

"Restricted Contract". A restricted contract is a tenancy *or licence* under which one person grants to another, in consideration for a rent which includes payment for rent or services, the right to occupy a dwelling as a residence: 1977, s.19(2). Services for this purpose includes attendances (*e.g.* room cleaning, changing sheets, porterage), provision of heating or lighting, supply of hot water, and any other privilege or facility connected with the occupation, *other* than those merely of access, or cold water supply or sanitary accommodation: 1977, s.19(8). There must be exclusive occupation of some part of the dwelling, but the letting can still be a restricted contract even if, in addition to an exclusive part, there is sharing of other accommodation: 1977, s.19(6).

Holiday lettings are excluded: s.19(7). So are high rated dwellings (s.19(3), (4)), regulated tenancies (above), lettings from local authorities and development corporations, lettings from the Crown other than when the property is under the management of the Crown Estate Commissioners, a protected occupancy under the Rent (Agriculture) Act 1976, a *tenancy* (but not a licence) from a registered housing association, housing trust or the Housing Corporation within Rent Act 1977, s.86, and a letting under which the rent includes payment for board, and the value of the board to the occupier forms a substantial proportion of the whole rent (1977, s.19(5)).

"Substantial proportion" is usually taken as from 15 per cent. or 20 per cent. of the rent: see *Palser* v. *Grinling* [1948] A.C. 291, H.L.; see also *Woodward* v. *Docherty* [1974] 1 W.L.R. 966, C.A.; "board" means more than a mere early morning cup of tea—see *Wilkes* v. *Goodwin* [1923] 2 K.B. 86, C.A.

"Shared Ownership Lease". See notes to s.143 above.

"Statutory Tenancy", "Statutory Tenant". Under either Act, this means a former protected tenant or occupier—see notes, above—*i.e.* after the termination of the contractual arrangement. In each case, however, a statutory tenancy will last only so long as the premises are occupied as a residence: see notes to s.81, above, distinguishing occupation as *a* residence from occupation as an only or principal home.

Minor definitions: Part XVIII

623. In this Part—
"house" includes any yard, garden, outhouses and appurtenances belonging to the house or usually enjoyed with it;
"owner", in relation to premises—
(*a*) means a person (other than a mortgagee not in possession) who is for the time being entitled to dispose of the fee simple absolute in the premises, whether in possession or in reversion, and
(*b*) includes also a person holding or entitled to the rents and profits of the premises under a lease of which the unexpired term exceeds three years.

GENERAL NOTE
"House". See notes to s.56, above.

Index of defined expressions: Part XVIII

624. The following Table shows provisions defining or otherwise explaining expressions used in this Part (other than provisions defining or explaining an expression used in the same section):—

owner	section 623
Rent Acts	section 622
standard scale (in reference to the maximum fine	
on summary conviction	section 622
street	section 622
unfit for human habitation	section 604

GENERAL NOTE
"House". See notes to s.56, above.

Final provisions

Short title, commencement and extent

625.—(1) This Act may be cited as the Housing Act 1985.

(2) This Act comes into force on 1st April 1986.

(3) This Act extends to England and Wales only.   ·

SCHEDULES

Section 79   SCHEDULE 1

TENANCIES WHICH ARE NOT SECURE TENANCIES

Long leases

1. A tenancy is not a secure tenancy if it is a long tenancy.

Premises occupied in connection with employment

2.—(1) A tenancy is not a secure tenancy if the tenant is an employee of the landlord or of—

     a local authority,

     a new town corporation,

     an urban development corporation,

     the Development Board for Rural Wales, or

     the governors of an aided school,

and his contract of employment requires him to occupy the dwelling-house for the better performance of his duties.

(2) A tenancy is not a secure tenancy if the tenant is a member of a police force and the dwelling-house is provided for him free of rent and rates in pursuance of regulations made under section 33 of the Police Act 1964 (general regulations as to government, administration and conditions of service of police forces).

(3) A tenancy is not a secure tenancy if the tenant is an employee of a fire authority (within the meaning of the Fire Services Acts 1947 to 1959) and—

     (*a*) his contract of employment requires him to live in close proximity to a particular fire station, and

     (*b*) the dwelling-house was let to him by the authority in consequence of that requirement.

(4) A tenancy is not a secure tenancy if—

     (*a*) within the period of three years immediately preceding the grant the conditions mentioned in sub-paragraph (1), (2) or (3) have been satisfied with respect to a tenancy of the dwelling-house, and

     (*b*) before the grant the landlord notified the tenant in writing of the circumstances in which this exception applies and that in its opinion the proposed tenancy would fall within this exception,

until the periods during which those conditions are not satisfied with respect to the tenancy amount in aggregate to more than three years.

(5) In this paragraph "contract of employment" means a contract of service or apprenticeship, whether express or implied and (if express) whether oral or in writing.

Land acquired for development

3.—(1) A tenancy is not a secure tenancy if the dwelling-house is on land which has been acquired for development and the dwelling-house is used by the landlord, pending development of the land, as temporary housing accommodation.

(2) In this paragraph "development" has the meaning given by section 22 of the Town and Country Planning Act 1971 (general definition of development for purposes of that Act).

Accommodation for homeless persons

4.—(1) A tenancy granted in pursuance of—

(*a*) section 63 (duty to house pending inquiries in case of apparent priority need),

(*b*) section 65(3) (duty to house temporarily person found to have priority need but to have become homeless intentionally), or

(*c*) section 68(1) (duty to house pending determination whether conditions for referral of application are satisfied),

is not a secure tenancy before the expiry of the period of twelve months beginning with the date specified in sub-paragraph (2), unless before the expiry of that period the tenant is notified by the landlord that the tenancy is to be regarded as a secure tenancy.

(2) The date referred to in sub-paragraph (1) is the date on which the tenant received the notification required by section 64(1) (notification of decision on question of homelessness or threatened homelessness) or, if he received a notification under section 68(3) (notification of which authority has duty to house), the date on which he received that notification.

Temporary accommodation for persons taking up employment

5.—(1) A tenancy is not a secure tenancy before the expiry of one year from the grant if—

(*a*) the person to whom the tenancy was granted was not, immediately before the grant, resident in the district in which the dwelling-house is situated,

(*b*) before the grant of the tenancy, he obtained employment, or an offer of employment, in the district or its surrounding area,

(*c*) the tenancy was granted to him for the purpose of meeting his need for temporary accommodation in the district or its surrounding area in order to work there, and of enabling him to find permanent accommodation there, and

(*d*) the landlord notified him in writing of the circumstances in which this exception applies and that in its opinion the proposed tenancy would fall within this exception;

unless before the expiry of that year the tenant has been notified by the landlord that the tenancy is to be regarded as a secure tenancy.

(2) In this paragraph—

"district" means district of a local housing authority; and

"surrounding area", in relation to a district, means the area consisting of each district that adjoins it.

Short-term arrangements

6. A tenancy is not a secure tenancy if—

(*a*) the dwelling-house has been leased to the landlord with vacant possession for use as temporary housing accommodation,

(*b*) the terms on which it has been leased include provision for the lessor to obtain vacant possession from the landlord on the expiry of a specified period or when required by the lessor,

(*c*) the lessor is not a body which is capable of granting secure tenancies, and

(*d*) the landlord has no interest in the dwelling-house other than under the lease in question or as a mortgagee.

Temporary accommodation during works

7. A tenancy is not a secure tenancy if—

(*a*) the dwelling-house has been made available for occupation by the tenant (or a predecessor in title of his) while works are carried out on the dwelling-house which he previously occupied as his home, and

(*b*) the tenant or predecessor was not a secure tenant of that other dwelling-house at the time when he ceased to occupy it as his home.

Agricultural holdings

8. A tenancy is not a secure tenancy if the dwelling-house is comprised in an agricultural holding (within the meaning of the Agricultural Holdings Act 1948) and is occupied by the person responsible for the control (whether as tenant or as servant or agent of the tenant) of the farming of the holding.

Licensed premises

9. A tenancy is not a secure tenancy if the dwelling-house consists of or includes premises licensed for the sale of intoxicating liquor for consumption on the premises.

Student lettings

10.—(1) A tenancy of a dwelling-house is not a secure tenancy before the expiry of the period specified in sub-paragraph (3) if—
    (*a*) it is granted for the purpose of enabling the tenant to attend a designated course at an educational establishment, and
    (*b*) before the grant of the tenancy the landlord notified him in writing of the circumstances in which this exception applies and that in its opinion the proposed tenancy would fall within this exception;
unless the tenant has before the expiry of that period been notified by the landlord that the tenancy is to be regarded as a secure tenancy.

(2) A landlord's notice under sub-paragraph (1)(*b*) shall specify the educational establishment which the person concerned proposes to attend.

(3) The period referred to in sub-paragraph (1) is—
    (*a*) in a case where the tenant attends a designated course at the educational establishment specified in the landlord's notice, the period ending six months after the tenant ceases to attend that (or any other) designated course at that establishment;
    (*b*) in any other case, the period ending six months after the grant of the tenancy.

(4) In this paragraph—
    "designated course" means a course of any kind designated by regulations made by the Secretary of State for the purposes of this paragraph;
    "educational establishment" means a university or establishment of further education.

(5) Regulations under sub-paragraph (4) shall be made by statutory instrument and may make different provision with respect to different cases or descriptions of case, including different provision for different areas.

1954 Act tenancies

11. A tenancy is not a secure tenancy if it is one to which Part II of the Landlord and Tenant Act 1954 applies (tenancies of premises occupied for business purposes).

Almshouses

12.—(1) A licence to occupy a dwelling-house is not a secure tenancy if—
    (*a*) the licence was granted by an almshouse charity, and
    (*b*) any sum payable by the licensee under the licence does not exceed the maximum contribution that the Charity Commissioners have from time to time authorised or approved for the almshouse charity as a contribution towards the cost of maintaining its almshouses and essential services in them.

(2) In this paragraph "almshouse charity" means a corporation or body of persons which is a charity and is prevented by its rules or constituent instrument from granting a tenancy of the dwelling-house.

GENERAL NOTE

This Schedule defines the tenancies and licences (*cf.* notes to s.79, above) of the landlords defined in s.80, above, who are not secure.

Para. 1

See notes to s.115, above.

Para. 2

A tenancy is not a secure tenancy if (a) the tenant is an employee of the landlord, or, if not the employee of the landlord is the employee of a local authority (as defined in s.4), a development corporation of a new town, an urban development corporation, the Development Board for Rural Wales or the governors of an aided school; *and* (b) his contract of employment requires him to occupy the dwelling-house for the better performance of his duties. A contract of employment for these purposes includes a contract of service or of apprenticeship, whether express or implied, and if express, whether oral or in writing.

The phrase "better performance of duties" is not peculiar to this Act. It is commonly to be found in lettings of tied accommodation. It is derived from the case law distinguishing a service tenant and a service occupant. The former is a true tenant, but the latter qualifies only as a licensee. In the event, having brought licensees generally into security (see s.79) this paragraph effectively re-excludes many service occupants.

That the requirement to occupy the dwelling-house need only be expressed in the contract of employment would not seem sufficient to override the common law proposition that such a requirement cannot be inserted as an arbitrary whim: see, *e.g. Gray* v. *Holmes* (1949) 30 T.C. 467, *per* Croom-Johnson J. Nor can it be introduced as a mere device to defeat security, or as a means of establishing greater control over the employee. Only "strictly tied accommodation" is intended to be covered by this paragraph (1980 Act, *Hansard,* H.L., Vol. 412, col. 115).

It would seem, therefore, that the cases on the distinction between service tenant and service occupant will apply much as they normally apply, even under this paragraph. In *Smith* v. *Seghill Overseers* (1875) L.R. 10 Q.B. 422, it was said that "where the occupation is necessary for the performance of services and the occupier is required to reside in the house in order to perform those services, the occupation being strictly ancillary to the performance of the duties which the occupier has to perform, the occupation is that of the servant.

"Required means more than the master saying you must reside in one of my houses if you come into my service. The residence must be ancillary and necessary to the performance of the servant's duty and unless he is required for that purpose to reside in the house and not merely as an arbitrary regulation on the part of the master, I do not think he is prevented from occupying as tenant. Unless the men are required to live in the houses for the better performance of their duties, it does not convert the occupation of a tenant into that of a servant. The governing principle is that in order to constitute an occupation as a servant it must be an occupation ancillary to the performance of the duties which the occupier has engaged to perform".

In *Fox* v. *Dalby* (1874) L.R. 10 C.P. 285, however, it was held that there was a true service occupancy if *either* it was necessary for the purposes of the employment to live in the premises in question, *or* the employer imposed the requirement in the contract of employment. In *Glasgow Corporation* v. *Johnstone* [1965] A.C. 609, H.L., it was said that "if the servant is given the privilege of residing in the house of the master as part of his emoluments the occupation is that of the servant . . . . If on the other hand the servant is genuinely obliged by his master for the purposes of his master's business or if it is necessary for the servant to reside in the house for the performance of his services, the occupation will be that of the master . . . ".

But in *Hirst* v. *Sargent* (1967) 65 L.G.R. 127, Widgery J. added the following qualification: "The only additional reference I need to make is point out that the word necessary used in that test is clearly to be applied strictly. Once it is accepted, as I feel bound to accept, that these were part of his duties under his contract of service and once it is recognised as obvious as it seems to me to be obvious that these functions could not possibly have been performed otherwise than by a man living in this hereditament or house similarly situated it seems to me clear that the second limb of . . . [that] test is satisfied."

The fact that it is merely convenient for the employee to live in the premises in question would therefore not seem sufficient to make it "for the better performance of his duties": see also *Chapman* v. *Freeman* [1978] 1 W.L.R. 1298; and *Ford* v. *Langford* [1949] W.N. 87; L.J.R. 586, C.A. In *Street* v. *Mountford* [1985] A.C. 809, 17 H.L.R. 402, H.L., the House of Lords adopted the test stated in *Smith* v. *Seghill Overseers, i.e.* the more strict approach, as adopted by Widgery J in *Hirst*, rather than the alternatives posited in *Fox* v. *Dalby*. See also, *Royal Philanthropic Society* v. *County* (1985) 18 H.L.R. 83, C.A., for a recent case of a former service occupier whose occupation of alternative accommodation was held to amount to tenancy, not licence, applying *Street* v. *Mountford*. See notes to s.93, above.

Sub-paras. (2) and (3) take out of security a number of occupiers who would otherwise have been brought within it by the extension of security in 1984 to tenants of county councils, *i.e.* police and fire officers.

Property occupied under any limb of this para. may also be kept out of security for a period of three years, following occupation under sub-paras (1)–(3), by sub-para. (4). This operates by the grant of a tenancy or licence to a new occupier. The exemption only lasts for three years, so that the period of grace cannot be extended by the grant of, *e.g.* a six year lease. In either eventuality, written notice must be given not later than the grant.

Para. 3

A tenancy is not a secure tenancy if the dwelling-house is on land which has been acquired for development and the dwelling-house is being used by the landlord, pending development of the land, as temporary housing accommodation. The paragraph permits short-life user of property which is intended for redevelopment. As to the meaning of development, see notes to s.460, above.

Para. 4

A tenancy granted in pursuance of ss.63, 65(3) or 68(1) of this Act, (Part III—Housing the Homeless) is not a secure tenancy before the expiry of a period of 12 months commencing with the date when the tenant has received notification required by s.64(1), or, if he receives notification under s.68(3), commencing with the date when he receives that notification. This exemption is, however, subject to an overriding provision, that the landlord may at any time before the expiry of the period notify the tenant that the tenancy is to be treated as a secure tenancy.

The purpose of the provision is to leave out of security a tenancy (or, of definition, and perhaps more relevantly, a licence, see s.79) granted to a person under any one of the following three provisions: (a) s.63, duty to accommodate pending completion of inquiries a person who the authority have reason to believe may be homeless, and in priority need of accommodation: (b) s.65(3), duty to accommodate for such period as will give the person a reasonable opportunity of securing accommodation for his own occupation, someone who is homeless, and in priority need, but who has been found to be intentionally homeless; (c) s.68(1), duty to provide accommodation to a person who is homeless, has a priority need for accommodation, has not become homeless intentionally, but who is alleged to have a local connection with the area of another housing authority in Great Britain, pending resolution of a dispute between the two authorities as to who shall provide permanent accommodation to the homeless person.

So far as the first two classes are concerned, on the completion of inquiries, the authority are bound to give notice in writing of their decision and, save where they are prepared to admit to a full housing obligation, of their reasons for it. The duty arises independently of the duty to provide accommodation: see *R.* v. *Beverley Borough Council, ex p. McPhee* [1979] J.P.L. 94. In these two cases, the 12 months run from the date of notification. So far as the third class is concerned, if the notification informs the applicant that another authority is to be notified of their application, then once the matter has been resolved between the two authorities involved, the authority must give a further notice, informing the applicant of the outcome of the reference to the other authority. If, in the event, the homeless person remains with the authority to which he applied, then the 12 months run from the date of that later notification.

The effect of the provision in relation to persons who are found to be entitled to permanent accommodation, after a period of temporary housing under s.63, appears to be this: while in the s.63 accommodation they are not secure; once notification is given, stating the entitlement to housing, the year starts to run and so long as the homeless person is left in the *same accommodation* as that in which he was housed under s.63, he is not secure during that year; if, however, he is rehoused *after* notification, he would seem to become secure at once (in the new accommodation), because this housing will not be under s.63 *at all* but under s.65 (*i.e.* s.65(2)).

The exemption applies to a temporary letting by a housing association discharging the authority's duty by arrangement: *Family Housing Association* v. *Miah* (1982) 5 H.L.R. 94. If *no* notification of decision was given, the burden is likely to rest on the tenant to show that it *ought* to have been given more than a year ago, and therefore ought to be treated *as if* given: *ibid.* In *Restormel Borough Council* v. *Buscombe* (1982) 14 H.L.R. 91, and in *Royal Borough of Kensington & Chelsea* v. *Hayden* (1984) 17 H.L.R. 114, the Court of Appeal expressed some doubts about whether temporary accommodation pending long-term resolution of the position of a homeless person constituted accommodation under tenancy or licence capable of attracting security in any event.

But this doubt was removed by the decision of the House of Lords in *Eastleigh Borough Council* v. *Walsh* [1985] 1 W.L.R. 525, 17 H.L.R. 392, in which express regard was paid to what is now this paragraph, and it was held that normal principles of construction of an arrangement (*cf.* notes to s.93, above) are to be applied, so that where the homeless person had been granted rights of occupation, at a rent, with exclusive occupation, and indeed a number of references to tenancy, there was no room for arguing that the arrangement constituted licence merely because it had been provided under what is now Part III. (The relevance of the argument was not security in itself, but arose because the notice determining the right of occupation before the one year expired was insufficient to determine tenancy, but sufficient to determine a licence).

Para. 5
The purpose of this provision is to provide temporary accommodation for people moving jobs. Note that the need for accommodation, and the job, may be within the area of the landlord, *or* adjoining district or London Borough. But there is a need for a coincidence between district or London borough where dwelling-house is situated, and where place of employment is situated. Note, too, that the landlord may waive this exception before the one year period has expired.

Para. 6
This provision is designed to preserve "North Wiltshire" type schemes: see, also, "Leasing Schemes" (1977) 127 New L.J. 667. The provisions of sub-paras. (*c*) and (*d*) are designed to pre-empt any evasive use of this paragraph. As originally employed—and, indeed, as continued by this paragraph—the scheme was designed to avert the effects of the Rent Act 1977. The letting to the local authority or housing association intermediate landlord would itself be outside Rent Act *security* provisions, while the tenancy between intermediate landlord and occupant would not be protected at all, because of ss.13–16 of the 1977 Act. The effect of the paragraph is to ensure that the occupant will not be secure under this Act, either.

Para. 7
This paragraph is designed to permit a landlord to move a tenant who is not, on some other count, a secure tenant, while works are carried out to his home, without the tenant acquiring security in the temporary accommodation. It might be used, *e.g.*, in connection with housing arrangements on compulsory improvement: see Part VII, above.

Para. 8
This paragraph is derived from s.10 of the Rent Act 1977. It is designed to exclude from security farm-managers, whether they work for the landlord, or for a tenant of the land.

Para. 9
This provision is derived from s.11 of the Rent Act 1977 and governs only on-licensed premises, *e.g.* a pub or club.

Para. 10
This is the equivalent of the provisions of s.8 of the Rent Act 1977, but is drafted somewhat differently. The landlord may waive the exception by notice. The key definition is of period of exemption: it lasts until six months after the tenant ceases to attend the designated course—or any other designated course—at the educational establishment which the landlord specified in the notification that, in its opinion, the tenancy would fall within the provisions. If the tenant fails to take up any designated course at the educational establish-ment, the period of exemption expires six months after the date of the grant. The order designating courses is the Secure Tenancies (Designated Courses) Regulations 1980 (S.I. 1980 No.1407), retained in force by s.2, Housing (Consequential Provisions) Act 1985.

Para. 11
This provision is derived from s.24 of the Rent Act 1977. A tenancy is not a secure tenancy if it is one to which Part II of the Landlord and Tenant Act 1954 applies. Note that in addition to business tenancies, this will also exclude from security an assured tenant: Housing Act 1980, ss. 56–58. Under s.23(1) of the 1954 Act, Part II applies "to any tenancy where the property comprised in the tenancy is or includes premises which are occupied by the tenant and are so occupied for the purposes of a business carried on by him or for those and other purposes." "Business" includes "a trade, profession or employment and includes any activity carried on by a body of persons, whether corporate or unincorporate" (s.23(2) of the 1954 Act). Part II does not apply to a tenancy for a fixed period of not more than six months, unless the tenancy contains provisions for renewal beyond that time, or the tenant or his predecessor in the business has been in occupation for more than 12 months: s.43 of the 1954 Act.
Of particular relevance are the cases determining when sub-letting and keeping lodgers or engaging in other activities amounts to such a business user as to take the letting into Part II. Where the whole of the premises are sub-let, the letting clearly cannot come within Part II, for the tenant cannot still be in occupation (*Ebner* v. *Lascelles* [1928] 2 K.B. 486, D.C.,

Carter v. *S.U. Carburetter Co.* [1942] 2 K.B. 288, C.A.), but in such circumstances security under the present Act will in any event be lost by s.81, *i.e.* non-residence.

In order to attract the provisions of Part II the business user must be of some significance, and where there is insignificant business or professional user, the present Act may still continue to apply: compare *Cheryl Investments Ltd.* v. *Saldanha,* and *Royal Life Saving Society* v. *Page,* reported together at [1978] 1 W.L.R. 1329, C.A. Whether the degrees of business user is significant enough is a question of fact for the judge: *Pulleng* v. *Curran* (1980) 44 P. & C.R. 58, C.A., in which it was also held that a lease extended by Part II, 1954 Act cannot subsequently become residential.

As to lodgers, keeping lodgers does not necessarily imply business user: all of the circumstances must be looked at, *e.g.* commercial advantage, number of lodgers, size of house, money charged. Spare-time activities, even if there is a minor financial element involved, do not necessarily change the character of the user from residential to business: *Lewis* v. *Weldcrest* [1978] 1 W.L.R. 1107, C.A., *Abernethie* v. *Kleiman Ltd.* [1970] 1 Q.B. 10, C.A.

The four cases last cited provide a useful study of the principles. Thus, in *Cheryl Investments Ltd.,* a businessman rented residential premises, but almost immediately began to use them for the purposes of his business. The business had no other offices, and both stationery and telephone user were based at the premises. It was held that this user was business user within the 1954 Act, rather than residential within the Rent Act 1977. On the other hand, in *Royal Life Saving Society,* a doctor took an assignment of a lease of residential premises and, with the landlord's consent, installed a consulting room, in which he saw the occasional patient, although his principal consulting rooms and practice were elsewhere. It was held that the degress of business user was insufficient to attract the 1954 Act, the principal purpose of his occupation being residential.

In *Lewis,* an elderly lady took in lodgers, for whom she provided breakfast and Sunday lunch. Having regard to the income she derived from this alleged "business" and to all of the circumstances of the case a patently sympathetic Court of Appeal, remarking that she no doubt took in lodgers because she liked it and was good at it, held that this was not a business user within the 1954 Act. In *Abernethie,* a man used a loft in his premises to conduct Sunday School classes for about 30 children. He made no charge, but kept a subcription box for donations to a scripture mission. Again, such a spare-time activity was held not to amount to a "trade, profession or employment" within s.23 of the 1954 Act, and so the letting remained residential.

A letting of premises for sub–occupation by students may be a letting within the provisions of Part II: *Groveside Properties Ltd.* v. *Westminster Medical School* (1983) 9 H.L.R. 118, C.A.

Para. 12

This paragraph was necessitated by the specific inclusion of licensees generally: s.79. Note the inhibition on licence fees charged, contained in sub-para. (*b*).

Section 84   SCHEDULE 2

GROUNDS FOR POSSESSION OF DWELLING-HOUSES LET UNDER SECURE TENANCIES

PART I

GROUNDS ON WHICH COURT MAY ORDER POSSESSION IF IT CONSIDERS IT REASONABLE

Ground 1

Rent lawfully due from the tenant has not been paid or an obligation of the tenancy has been broken or not performed.

Ground 2

The tenant or a person residing in the dwelling-house has been guilty of conduct which is a nuisance or annoyance to neighbours, or has been convicted of using the dwelling-house or allowing it to be used for immoral or illegal purposes.

Ground 3

The condition of the dwelling-house or of any of the common parts has deteriorated owing to acts of waste by, or the neglect or default of, the tenant or a person residing in the dwelling-house and, in the case of an act of waste by, or the neglect or default of, a person lodging with the tenant or a sub-tenant of his, the tenant has not taken such steps as he ought reasonably to have taken for the removal of the lodger or sub-tenant.

Ground 4

The condition of furniture provided by the landlord for use under the tenancy, or for use in the common parts, has deteriorated owing to ill-treatment by the tenant or a person residing in the dwelling-house and, in the case of ill-treatment by a person lodging with the tenant or a sub-tenant of his, the tenant has not taken such steps as he ought reasonably to have taken for the removal of the lodger or sub-tenant.

Ground 5

The tenant is the person, or one of the persons, to whom the tenancy was granted and the landlord was induced to grant the tenancy by a false statement made knowingly or recklessly by the tenant.

Ground 6

The tenancy was assigned to the tenant, or to a predecessor in title of his who is a member of his family and is residing in the dwelling-house, by an assignment made by virtue of section 92 (assignments by way of exchange) and a premium was paid either in connection with that assignment or the assignment which the tenant or predecessor himself made by virtue of that section.

In this paragraph "premium" means any fine or other like sum and any other pecuniary consideration in addition to rent.

Ground 7

The dwelling-house forms part of, or is within the curtilage of, a building which, or so much of it as is held by the landlord, is held mainly for purposes other than housing purposes and consists mainly of accommodation other than housing accommodation, and—

(a) the dwelling-house was let to the tenant or a predecessor in title of his in consequence of the tenant or predecessor being in the employment of the landlord, or of—
a local authority,
a new town corporation,
an urban development corporation,
the Development Board for Rural Wales, or
the governors of an aided school,
and
(b) the tenant or a person residing in the dwelling-house has been guilty of conduct such that, having regard to the purpose for which the building is used, it would not be right for him to continue in occupation of the dwelling-house.

Ground 8

The dwelling-house was made available for occupation by the tenant (or a predecessor in title of his) while works were carried out on the dwelling-house which he previously occupied as his only or principal home and—

(a) the tenant (or predecessor) was a secure tenant of the other dwelling-house at the time when he ceased to occupy it as his home,
(b) the tenant (or predecessor) accepted the tenancy of the dwelling-house of which possession is sought on the understanding that he would give up occupation when, on completion of the works, the other dwelling-house was again available for occupation by him under a secure tenancy, and
(c) the works have been completed and the other dwelling-house is so available.

PART II

GROUNDS ON WHICH THE COURT MAY ORDER POSSESSION IF SUITABLE ALTERNATIVE ACCOMMODATION IS AVAILABLE

Ground 9

The dwelling-house is overcrowded, within the meaning of Part X, in such circumstances as to render the occupier guilty of an offence.

Ground 10

The landlord intends, within a reasonable time of obtaining possession of the dwelling-house—

(*a*) to demolish or reconstruct the building or part of the building comprising the dwelling-house, or

(*b*) to carry out work on that building or on land let together with, and thus treated as part of, the dwelling-house,

and cannot reasonably do so without obtaining possession of the dwelling-house.

Ground 11

The landlord is a charity and the tenant's continued occupation of the dwelling-house would conflict with the objects of the charity.

Part III

Grounds on which the Court may Order Possession if it Considers it Reasonable and Suitable Alternative Accommodation is Available

Ground 12

The dwelling-house forms part of, or is within the curtilage of, a building which, or so much of it as is held by the landlord, is held mainly for purposes other than housing purposes and consists mainly of accommodation other than housing accommodation, or is situated in a cemetery, and—

(*a*) the dwelling-house was let to the tenant or a predecessor in title of his in consequence of the tenant or predecessor being in the employment of the landlord or of—

a local authority,

a new town corporation,

an urban development corporation,

the Development Board for Rural Wales, or

the governors of an aided school,

and that employment has ceased, and

(*b*) the landlord reasonably requires the dwelling-house for occupation as a residence for some person either engaged in the employment of the landlord, or of such a body, or with whom a contract for such employment has been entered into conditional on housing being provided.

Ground 13

The dwelling-house has features which are substantially different from those of ordinary dwelling-houses and which are designed to make it suitable for occupation by a physically disabled person who requires accommodation of a kind provided by the dwelling-house and—

(*a*) there is no longer such a person residing in the dwelling-house, and

(*b*) the landlord requires it for occupation (whether alone or with members of his family) by such a person.

Ground 14

The landlord is a housing association or housing trust which lets dwelling-houses only for occupation (whether alone or with others) by persons whose circumstances (other than merely financial circumstances) make it especially difficult for them to satisfy their need for housing, and—

(*a*) either there is no longer such a person residing in the dwelling-house or the tenant has received from a local housing authority an offer of accommodation in premises which are to be let as a separate dwelling under a secure tenancy, and

(*b*) the landlord requires the dwelling-house for occupation (whether alone or with members of his family) by such a person.

Ground 15

The dwelling-house is one of a group of dwelling-houses which it is the practice of the landlord to let for occupation by persons with special needs and—

(*a*) a social service or special facility is provided in close proximity to the group of dwelling-houses in order to assist persons with those special needs,

(b) there is no longer a person with those special needs residing in the dwelling-house, and

(c) the landlord requires the dwelling-house for occupation (whether alone or with members of his family) by a person who has those special needs.

Ground 16

The accommodation afforded by the dwelling-house is more extensive than is reasonably required by the tenant and—

(a) the tenancy vested in the tenant by virtue of section 89 (succession to periodic tenancy), the tenant being qualified to succeed by virtue of section 87(b) (members of family other than spouse), and

(b) notice of the proceedings for possession was served under section 83 more than six months but less than twelve months after the date of the previous tenant's death.

The matters to be taken into account by the court in determining whether it is reasonable to make an order on this ground include—

(a) the age of the tenant,

(b) the period during which the tenant has occupied the dwelling-house as his only or principal home, and

(c) any financial or other support given by the tenant to the previous tenant.

Part IV

Suitability of Accommodation

1. For the purposes of section 84(2)(b) and (c) (case in which court is not to make an order for possession unless satisfied that suitable accommodation will be available) accommodation is suitable if it consists of premises—

(a) which are to be let as a separate dwelling under a secure tenancy, or

(b) which are to be let as a separate dwelling under a protected tenancy, not being a tenancy under which the landlord might recover possession under one of the Cases in Part II of Schedule 15 to the Rent Act 1977 (cases where court must order possession),

and, in the opinion of the court, the accommodation is reasonably suitable to the needs of the tenant and his family.

2. In determining whether the accommodation is reasonably suitable to the needs of the tenant and his family, regard shall be had to—

(a) the nature of the accommodation which it is the practice of the landlord to allocate to persons with similar needs;

(b) the distance of the accommodation available from the place of work or education of the tenant and of any members of his family;

(c) its distance from the home of any member of the tenant's family if proximity to it is essential to that member's or the tenant's well-being;

(d) the needs (as regards extent of accommodation) and means of the tenant and his family;

(e) the terms on which the accommodation is available and the terms of the secure tenancy;

(f) if furniture was provided by the landlord for use under the secure tenancy, whether furniture is to be provided for use in the other accommodation, and if so the nature of the furniture to be provided.

3. Where possession of a dwelling-house is sought on ground 9 (overcrowding such as to render occupier guilty of offence), other accommodation may be reasonably suitable to the needs of the tenant and his family notwithstanding that the permitted number of persons for that accommodation, as defined in section 326(3) (overcrowding: the space standard), is less than the number of persons living in the dwelling-house of which possession is sought.

4.—(1) A certificate of the appropriate local housing authority that they will provide suitable accommodation for the tenant by a date specified in the certificate is conclusive evidence that suitable accommodation will be available for him by that date.

(2) The appropriate local housing authority is the authority for the district in which the dwelling-house of which possession is sought is situated.

(3) This paragraph does not apply where the landlord is a local housing authority.

GENERAL NOTE

This Schedule contains the grounds for possession against a secure tenant, in three classes—(a) ground plus reasonable to make the order sought, (b) ground plus suitable alternative accommodation, and (c) ground plus reasonable to make the order sought, plus suitable alternative accommodation. As to reasonableness, see notes to s.84, above; as to suitable alternative accommodation, see Part IV of this Schedule, and notes below.

Part I: 1–8; Ground Plus Reasonableness
Ground 1

This may be compared with Rent Act 1977, Sched. 15, Case 1. This is one of the most common Grounds, not only because arrears of rent are common, but also because where another Ground is alleged (*e.g.* Grounds 2, 3 or 4, below), there may *also* be a breach of the term of the tenancy, so that landlords are inclined to plead Ground 1 in the alternative: see, for example, *Heglibiston Establishment* v. *Heyman* (1977) 76 P. & C.R. 351, C.A. In the case of a breach of a term which does *not* also amount to a further Ground, the courts will be less inclined to make an order, for these Grounds constitute a form of "code of eviction" in their own right. It should be noted that even where a breach is to continue, the court is entitled to decline to make the order sought: *Tideway Investments & Property Holdings* v. *Wellwood* [1952] Ch. 791.

Arrears must exist as at the date of commencement of proceedings: *Bird* v. *Hildage* [1948] 1 K.B. 91, C.A. If rent has been tendered, but refused, then there will be no arrears for the purposes of Ground 1: *ibid.* If rent is tendered between commencement and hearing, the court still has power to make an order for possession (*Brewer* v. *Jacobs* [1923] 1 K.B. 528, D.C.; *Dellenty* v. *Pellow* [1951] 2 K.B. 858), but it will be extremely unusual for it to do so if arrears have in fact been cleared. In such circumstances it is unlikely to be reasonable to make the order sought, unless there has been a long history of arrears, or unless the landlord has repeatedly had to issue proceedings in order to get paid: *Heyman* v. *Rowlands* [1957] 1 W.L.R. 317, C.A.; *Dellenty* v. *Pellow*, above; *Grimshaw* v. *Dunbar* [1953] 1 Q.B. 408, C.A.

In *Woodspring District Council* v. *Taylor* (1982) 4 H.L.R. 95, C.A., the court dismissed an appeal against the refusal of the court below to make an outright order against tenants with a long history of good payment, who had only recently fallen into arrears on account of unemployment and illness, even though the arrears had amounted to more than £550 by the date of hearing.

No order should be made if the reason for the arrears is that there has been a genuine dispute as to the amount owing (*Dun Laoghaire U.D.C.* v. *Moran* (1921) 2 I.R. 404), and it may be inappropriate or even impossible if the reason the rent has been withheld is because of a genuine complaint of disrepair attributable to the landlord's default: see *Lal* v. *Nakum* (1981) 1 H.L.R. 50, C.A.

Indeed, in such circumstances no rent at all may be owing. Once the landlord's repairing liability has arisen (*cf.* the requirement of notice, *O'Brien* v. *Robinson* [1973] A.C. 912, H.L.) a tenant may expend moneys on the discharge of his landlord's repairing obligations (*Lee-Parker* v. *Izzett* [1971] 1 W.L.R. 1688), whether future rents or rent arrears (*Asco Developments Ltd.* v. *Lowes, Lewis & Gordon* (1978) 248 E.G. 683), and may also be able to set-off an amount by way of claim to general damages (*British Anzani (Felixstowe) Ltd.* v. *International Marine Management (U.K.) Ltd.* [1980] 1 Q.B. 137, C.A.).

The same principles apply on a landlord's undertaking (rather than covenant) to repair: *Melville* v. *Grapelodge Developments Ltd.* (1978) 254 E.G. 1193. As a set-off, such moneys would not actually be due as rent. It is thought, however, and especially as the developments in this area are so recent (*cf.* earlier authorities to the contrary, such as *Taylor* v. *Beal* (1591) Cro.Eliz. 222; *Waters* v. *Weigall* (1795) 2 Anst. 575), that a tenant may be obliged, and is certainly well-advised, to give a landlord plenty of opportunity to repair, to consider an estimate before the tenant commissions a repair, and to agree a claim for general damages, before exercising this right (see, especially, *Lee-Parker* v. *Izzett*, above, on this point). See further, by way of comparison *Woodtrek Ltd.* v. *Jezek* (1981) 261 E.G. 571, where non-payment of an irrecoverable service charge could not found a forfeiture.

For an order to be based on arrears, the arrears must be those of the tenant himself, not those of a predecessor in title: *Tickner* v. *Clifton* [1929] 1 K.B. 207. However, it should be noted that the obligation to pay rent remains, notwithstanding the failure of the landlord to provide a rent book, under the provisions of the Landlord and Tenant Act 1985, s.4: *Shaw* v. *Groom* [1970] 2 Q.B. 504, C.A.

Where the tenant is still in occupation, and arrears are continuing, and there is a likelihood that the tenant will dissipate any housing benefit unless an order is made, it may be possible for a landlord to obtain an interlocutory order to require the tenant to pay the housing benefit towards the rent: *Berg* v. *Markhill* (1985) 17 H.L.R. 455, C.A.

An obligation of the tenancy does not include a personal undertaking by the tenant (*R.M.R. Housing Society* v. *Combs* [1951] 1 K.B. 486, C.A.), although it does extend to implied, as well as express, obligations: see *William Deacons Bank* v. *Catlow* [1928] E.G.D.

286; *Chapman* v. *Hughes* (1923) 129 L.T. 223. Covenants are not, of course, easily implied into a tenancy, even if they seem reasonable and desirable: *Liverpool County Council* v. *Irwin* [1977] A.C. 239, H.L. However, some terms are implied by statute, breach of which will qualify under this Ground: see ss.93, 97, and note that failure to comply with a condition attached to a consent to improve is expressly included as a breach of an obligation of the tenancy: s.99(4).

A tenant must use premises in a tenant-like manner (*Warren* v. *Keen* [1954] 1 Q.B. 15, C.A.), failure to do which will, in any event, usually constitute a ground under Ground 3, below. Breach of a covenant in a term certain incompatible with Part IV, *e.g.* to yield up possession at expiry of the term, would not, of course, constitute a breach of obligation for these purposes: *Artizans Dwellings Co.* v. *Whittaker* [1919] 2 K.B. 301; *R.M.R. Housing Society* v. *Combs* (above).

Ground 2

This is based on the Rent Act 1977, Sched. 15, Case 2, but the word "neighbours" has been substituted for "adjoining occupiers" in the 1977 Act. In *Cobstone Investments Ltd.* v. *Maxim* [1985] Q.B. 140, 15 H.L.R. 113, C.A., it was held under the Rent Act that "adjoining" was wider than contiguous, as one meaning of the word is "neighbouring" and all that the context requires is that the premises of the adjoining occupiers should be near enough to be affected by the tenant's conduct in his premises. There may, accordingly, now be no practical difference between that provision and this.

Nuisance is not here used in a technical sense, but is given a natural meaning: indeed, even if a nuisance under statute is established, it does not follow that there is necessarily a nuisance for these purposes: *Timmis* v. *Pearson* (1934) 1 L.J.N.C.C.R. 115. Annoyance is wider than nuisance, although it must be annoyance such as would annoy a reasonable occupier, not one who is ultra-sensitive: *Todd-Heatly* v. *Benham* (1888) 40 Ch.D. 80, C.A.

Use of the premises for prostitution is a common example of nuisance and annoyance (*Frederick Platts Co. Ltd.* v. *Grigor* (1950) 66 T.L.R. (Pt. 1) 859, C.A.; *Yates* v. *Morris* [1950] 2 All E.R. 577, C.A.), as is private immorality (*Benton* v. *Chapman* [1953] C.L.Y. 3099, Cty.Ct.), although cohabitation by an unmarried couple is no longer to be considered immoral for these purposes: *Heglibiston Establishment* v. *Heyman* (1977) 76 P. & C.R. 351, C.A. The use of the word "guilty" of such conduct, and the express provision for persons convicted of immoral user, suggest that a court should rarely use immorality as a basis for an order for possession, where there is no such conviction. A single act of annoyance or nuisance may, strictly, qualify, but is unlikely to prove sufficient under the Ground, and where the last act complained of had taken place some nine months before the hearing, with no more recent acts, a court refused to make an order, although costs were awarded against the defendant: *Ottway* v. *Jones* [1955] 1 W.L.R. 706, C.A.

The second limb, obviously, requires an actual conviction of a criminal court. It is not enough that a person has been convicted of committing a crime in the premises, although it need not be shown that user was a specific element of the criminal offence, it is a question of showing sufficient nexus between crime and user of the premises: *Abrahams* v. *Wilson* [1971] 2 Q.B. 88, C.A. In that case, the tenant was convicted of possessing a small amount of cannabis found in one of the rooms she occupied. The Court of Appeal held that conviction for such an offence could fall within the Ground, but, as the county court judge had held, considering reasonableness, "the chairman of the quarter sessions, having considered the evidence, could not have been more lenient. The suggestion now is that the additional very severe penalty of eviction should be imposed."

The point is clear: the tenant had been convicted, and punished, once, and the court should think very carefully before imposing a further penalty, especially, *e.g.* where the offence has not, as it were, brought the premises themselves into disrepute: see also *Schneiders & Sons Ltd.* v. *Abrahams* [1925] 1 K.B. 301, C.A.; *Hodson* v. *Jones* [1951] W.N. 127, C.A.; *Waller* v. *Thomas* [1921] 1 K.B. 541.

The nuisance, annoyance, or act leading to conviction for immoral or illegal user, need not be committed by the tenant, but may be committed by a person residing with him. A man living away from home, but visiting at the weekends, has, for these purposes, been held to be residing with his wife: *Green* v. *Lewis* [1951] C.L.Y. 2860.

Ground 3

This Ground is based on Rent Act 1977, Sched. 15, Case 3. However, it is here extended to cover deterioration not only in the dwelling-house but also in any of the common parts (as defined in s.116 above). Given the difficulty of proving by whose act deterioration in the common parts has occurred, and the potential for abuse by unfriendly neighbours, this extended limb should clearly be applied with care. The Ground may, however, apply even although there is no actual breach of obligation by the tenant: *Lowe* v. *Lendrun* (1950) E.G. 423, C.A.

Waste includes pulling down part of the premises, making unauthorised alterations, and the like: *Marsden* v. *Heyes* [1927] 2 K.B. 1, but *cf.* the right to improve, s.97, and the specific provisions for failure to comply with a condition attached to a consent to improve, s.99(4). Not every waste will, in any event, qualify: there must be deterioration by waste (neglect or default).

Ground 4

This, too, is based on a Rent Act ground. See 1977 Act, Sched. 15, Case 4. Originally introduced by the Rent Act 1974 when security was conferred on furnished tenants, it has here, as with the last Ground, been extended to the common parts, as defined. It is not likely to have substantial use for, although local authorities have power to provide furniture (s.10, above), it is little used.

Ground 5

This is a wholly new ground. It may, perhaps, be considered in connection with the criminal provisions of s.74, above (homelessness). Note that the landlord must be *induced* to grant the tenancy by the false statement, so that a statement patently false or which any reasonable landlord would have disregarded is unlikely to qualify. Clearly, an attempt to recover possession on this ground implies a most serious charge and, given the quasi-criminal language of the provision, it is submitted that a burden of proof analogous to that applicable in criminal proceedings would be appropriate.

Ground 6

Ground 6 cross-refers to s.92, which confers the right to assign, although only as between secure tenants, *i.e.* a right to exchange.

Ground 6 is designed to prevent the charging of premiums on an "exchange assignment" under s.92. It is offended if either the tenant has charged an assignment, for the tenancy he "gave" in exchange, or has paid one for his present tenancy. The ground is available against a successor in title of the tenant who charged or paid one such offending premium, but only so long as the predecessor is still living in the dwelling-house. It must, of course, be reasonable to make the order sought.

Ground 7

This is a ground for possession against certain tied occupiers. It applies, however, only to property within the curtilage of a building, which may not include property in a cemetery (see the distinction observed in Sched. 4, Ground 5, and Sched. 5, para. 5. See also Ground 12, below). Note the requirement that the conduct of which the occupier is guilty must relate to the purpose for which the building is used.

Ground 8

This is a quasi-management ground, for it enables landlords to move tenants around while works are done to their premises, with the tenant's consent, of course, without the tenant necessarily gaining security in the temporary property. But it remains within the class in relation to which the landlord must demonstrate reasonableness, for if the works in question have taken a long time, it may indeed be unreasonable to expect a tenant and his family to uproot themselves all over again. The expression "works" is not defined, but was amended from its original form, in which it referred to improvements, so as to cover, *e.g.* mere (*but* presumably extensive) repairs: 1980 Act, Standing Committee F, col. 2409.

Part II: 9–11; Ground Plus Suitable Alternative Accommodation
Ground 9

Overcrowding is dealt with in Pt. X, above. It is defined (s.324) in alternative ways: there is overcrowding if the permitted number of persons sleeping in the house is in excess of the number calculated in accordance with s.326 (the "space" standard); and it is overcrowded whenever two or more persons, being persons 10 years old or more, of opposite sexes, and not being persons living together as husband and wife, must sleep in the same room (the "room" standard): s.325. See notes to these sections.

But this Ground for possession only arises if the overcrowding is such that an offence is committed: see s.327, above. There are three classes of permissible, or legal, overcrowding: (a) natural growth, under s.328; (b) visiting member of family, under s.329; and, (c) licensed overcrowding, under s.330. See notes to these sections.

Extraordinarily, although providing a Ground in relation to overcrowding, the definition of suitable alternative accommodation to be considered below, is varied, specifically and exclusively for the purposes of this Ground: accommodation is not to be considered unsuitable to the needs of the tenant and his family only because it offends the space standard, considered above: Part IV, para. 3, below. The only analogous housing legislation is that to be found in s.476, above, permitting an authority to waive the requirement that premises be fit for human habitation when works under an intermediate grant have been completed, even although under s.189, above, they will then be bound to take unfitness action under that section, or under ss.264 *et seq.*

Ground 10

Note that *possession* must reasonably be required of the dwelling-house in order to carry out the works in question. Thus, where only "works" are involved, if a tenant is keen to remain, he may wish to consider offering a licence to the landlord to enter and carry out the works. Of course, that will generate the problem of temporary accommodation during works. The tenant will want the landlord to provide somewhere temporarily. The landlord may then seek to say: that is too difficult, administratively. But could the landlord maintain that response in the light of the wording of this Ground?

Ground 11

This ground might apply when a change in the tenant's circumstances means that he is no longer within the class intended to benefit from the charity. See also Ground 15, below.

Part III: 12–16; *Ground Plus Reasonableness Plus Suitable Alternative Accommodation*
Ground 12

This is also a ground for possession against tied occupiers (*cf.* Ground 7, above). It does, however, include property situated in a cemetery: see also Sched. 5, para. 5, below.

The first element of the ground is that the landlord reasonably requires the property for someone in its employment, or the employment of one of the other bodies specified, or with whom there is a contract of employment conditional on housing being provided. This part of the ground is modelled on Rent Act 1977, Sched. 15, Case 8, although note that, unlike under Case 8, the incoming occupier's employment need not be "whole-time."

The landlord's requirement must itself be reasonable (*cf. Kennealy* v. *Dunne* [1977] 1 Q.B. 837, C.A., under Rent Act 1977, Sched. 15, Case 11, where the ground refers only to the landlord "requiring"—*i.e.* not "reasonably requiring"—the property), which is a separate consideration from overall reasonableness (*R. F. Fuggle* v. *Gadsden* [1948] 2 K.B. 236, C.A.).

The second element of the ground is that the dwelling-house was let in consequence of employment with the landlord, or one of the other specified landlords, and the tenant or predecessor has ceased to be in that employment. The occupier need not have known the landlord's motive in granting the right of occupation (*Royal Crown Derby Porcelain Co.* v. *Russell* [1949] 2 K.B. 417, C.A.).

Ground 13

This Ground is aimed primarily at successors to physically disabled tenants, or at tenants who have formerly had a physically disabled person living with them. Note that the landlord must actually require the property for occupation by such a person. As to "features substantially different . . . designed" for a disabled person, see notes to Sched. 5, para. 6, below.

Ground 14

This Ground may be compared with, and supplements, Ground 11, above. Note, again, that the property must be required for the occupation of a person intended to benefit from the activities of the association or trust. But note, too, the alternative circumstances in which it can apply. The intention is that the ground should be available if *either* there is no one intended to benefit from the activities of the association, *or*, in substance, that such a "beneficiary" has been "filtered through" into local authority accommodation.

Ground 15

This Ground concerns persons with special needs not necessarily related to age. There must be a social service or special facility provided in close proximity to the group of dwelling-houses, for the benefit of such persons and, again, the landlord must need the property for occupation by a person with special need of the class in question.

Ground 16

This last Ground has been cast with some consideration. It concerns under-occupation, in consequence of a succession on death under s.89. It does *not* apply if the successor is the spouse of the deceased tenant. It will also *not* apply if the tenancy is a fixed term tenancy at the time of succession, for such succession will be under s.90, not under s.89. Notice must be given no earlier than six months after death—presumably to avoid adding to grief—but no later than 12 months after death—presumably so as not to lull the family into a false sense of being resettled in the property. A successor moved under these provisions will normally remain a successor: see s.88(4), above.

Part IV
Note the provisions of para. 4, which may override all other considerations: where the landlord seeking possession is not the local housing authority themselves, a certificate of the local housing authority for the area in which the dwelling-house of which possession is sought (as opposed to that to be offered) that they will provide suitable alternative accommodation is to be taken as conclusive evidence that such will be available by the date specified in the certificate, to the exclusion of the considerations specified in paras. 1 and 2.

Otherwise, accommodation is suitable only if it consists of premises which are to be let as a separate dwelling (see notes to s.79) on a secure tenancy, or on a protected tenancy within the meaning of the Rent Act 1977 (see notes to s.622, above), *other* than one which is liable to repossession on any of the grounds set out in Sched. 15, Pt. II to the 1977 Act, *i.e.* the so-called "mandatory grounds for possession," which include the shorthold ground introduced by s.52 of the Housing Act 1980 Act, lettings by servicemen, such other grounds as lettings by absentee owner-occupiers and lettings of prospective retirement homes, out-of-season holiday lettings, and off-season student lettings. When any of these grounds (called Cases under the 1977 Act) apply, there is no requirement that the landlord prove reasonableness in addition to proof of the elements of the case. Hence, their exclusion from this definition.

The alternative accommodation must also be reasonably suitable to the needs of the tenant and his family. While this conceptually leans upon the Rent Act, so that cases decided thereunder will still be of relevance, this Schedule spells out to what the court is to have regard in somewhat greater detail than is to be found in the 1977 Act (see Sched. 15, Pt. IV). Under the Rent Act 1977 it was not clear whether the matters specified would be treated as exhaustive, or as indicative only: *cf.. Barnard* v. *Towers* [1953] 1 W.L.R. 1203, C.A., and *Standingford* v. *Probert* [1950] 1 K.B. 377, C.A. But under this Schedule, it has been held that the list of matters is not exhaustive: *Enfield London Borough Council* v. *French* (1984) 17 H.L.R. 211, C.A.

Notably absent from the schedule of considerations in this Schedule is the provision to be found in the private sector, that the premises be suitable as to character (1977, Sched. 15, Pt. IV, para. 5 (*b*)). This has been held to be a deliberate omission: *French*. As such, it overrides the decision in *Redspring Ltd.* v. *Francis* [1973] 1 W.L.R. 134, C.A., in which the court held that environmental factors fell within the meaning of the word "character," and allowed an appeal against a possession order which would cause the tenant to be moved from a quiet residential street to a noisy main road with a fish and chip shop next door. Where reasonableness needs still be shown, such a factor could in any event be taken into account under that heading.

In *French*, the distinction was explained by reference to the requirement to have regard to something which is no concern of the tenant, *i.e.* the nature of the accommodation which it is the practice of the landlord to allocate to people of similar needs. In that case, the court considered the need of a tenant for a garden. It concluded that although a garden *can* qualify as one of the needs of a tenant, some of a tenant's needs may be more important than others; the weight to be given to needs is a matter of degree in each case, and in all the circumstances of a case accommodation may be regarded as reasonably suitable even if one particular need cannot be met.

"Place of work" can include voluntary work (*Dakyns* v. *Pace* [1948] 1 K.B. 22) and a person may work in several places, *e.g.* a salesman, in which case no one place forms the place of work for these purposes, but the whole area to which the tenant must travel is to be taken into account: *Yewbright Properties Ltd.* v. *Stone* (1980) 254 E.G. 863, C.A., in which it was also held that distance incorporated questions of travelling facilities and times.

Although there is authority for the proposition that new premises insufficient for the tenant's furniture may yet be suitable, this must surely be of dubious weight if the tenant reasonably requires all of the furniture, and would seem not to apply when what is in issue is suitability as regards *extent*: *cf. Mykolyshyn* v. *Noah* [1970] 1 W.L.R. 1271, C.A. Similarly, there is authority for the proposition that premises without a garage are a suitable alternative to premises with a garage (*Briddon* v. *George* [1946] 1 All E.R. 609, C.A.), which authority has, however, been doubted by the Court of Appeal (in *MacDonnell* v. *Daly* [1969] 1 W.L.R. 1482, C.A.).

The last-mentioned decision is also authority for the proposition that where what is to be given up is for mixed residential and professional user (but not such as to take the letting out of security altogether: see notes to Sched. 1, para. 11), in that case an artist's studio, the alternative accommodation must also be sufficient for the professional user.

Courts tend not to pay much attention to the ability to meet a new rent, inclining, rather, to assume that housing benefit will make up any difference that the tenant cannot afford. This, with respect, is wrong, both in practice and in law. It is wrong in practice, because under standard housing benefit (those not on supplementary benefit), the tenant is left with a substantial sum to pay, and under recent proposals it may soon be the case that even those on certificated benefit (supplementary benefit cases) will have to pay a proportion of the *rates*. It is wrong in law, for it amounts to declining to exercise jurisdiction to make a decision in the face of the requirement to consider means, and it clearly remains open to a court to take the view that, notwithstanding the benefit system, the rent of the premises is not "reasonably suitable" to the means of the tenant and his family.

As to para. 3, see notes to Ground 9, above.

Section 92   SCHEDULE 3

GROUNDS FOR WITHHOLDING CONSENT TO ASSIGNMENT BY WAY OF EXCHANGE

Ground 1

The tenant or the proposed assignee is obliged to give up possession of the dwelling-house of which he is the secure tenant in pursuance of an order of the court, or will be so obliged at a date specified in such an order.

Ground 2

Proceedings have been begun for possession of the dwelling-house of which the tenant or the proposed assignee is the secure tenant on one or more of grounds 1 to 6 in Part I of Schedule 2 (grounds on which possession may be ordered despite absence of suitable alternative accommodation), or there has been served on the tenant or the proposed assignee a notice under section 83 (notice of proceedings for possession) which specifies one or more of those grounds and is still in force.

Ground 3

The accommodation afforded by the dwelling-house is substantially more extensive than is reasonably required by the proposed assignee.

Ground 4

The extent of the accommodation afforded by the dwelling-house is not reasonably suitable to the needs of the proposed assignee and his family.

Ground 5

The dwelling-house—
(a) forms part of or is within the curtilage of a building which, or so much of it as is held by the landlord, is held mainly for purposes other than housing purposes and consists mainly of accommodation other than housing accommodation, or is situated in a cemetery, and
(b) was let to the tenant or a predecessor in title of his in consequence of the tenant or predecessor being in the employment of—
the landlord,
a local authority,
a new town corporation,
the Development Board for Rural Wales,
an urban development corporation, or
the governors of an aided school.

Ground 6

The landlord is a charity and the proposed assignee's occupation of the dwelling-house would conflict with the objects of the charity.

Ground 7

The dwelling-house has features which are substantially different from those of ordinary dwelling-houses and which are designed to make it suitable for occupation by a physically disabled person who requires accommodation of the kind provided by the dwelling-house and if the assignment were made there would no longer be such a person residing in the dwelling-house.

Ground 8

The landlord is a housing association or housing trust which lets dwelling-houses only for occupation (alone or with others) by persons whose circumstances (other than merely financial circumstances) make it especially difficult for them to satisfy their need for housing and if the assignment were made there would no longer be such a person residing in the dwelling-house.

Ground 9

The dwelling-house is one of a group of dwelling-houses which it is the practice of the landlord to let for occupation by persons with special needs and a social service or special facility is provided in close proximity to the group of dwelling-houses in order to assist persons with those special needs and if the assignment were made there would no longer be a person with those special needs residing in the dwelling-house.

GENERAL NOTE

This Schedule contains the grounds on which a landlord may object to an assignment under the "right to exchange": see s.92, above. Many of the grounds cross-refer to grounds for possession, or to circumstances in which the right to buy cannot be exercised.

Ground 1

Cf. notes to s.84, above.

Ground 2

Possession proceedings begin with a notice of seeking possession, which must specify the Ground (under Sched. 2), on which possession is sought: s.83. Grounds 1–6 are grounds on which possession may be ordered if it is reasonable to do so. This Ground applies whether proceedings have actually been commenced, or a mere notice of seeking possession has been served. (Such a notice may survive for more than a year: see s.83.)

Ground 3

Note that the accommodation afforded by the property must be *substantially* more extensive than reasonably required by proposed assignee.

Ground 4

This Ground would appear to cover the case where a family seek to move into accommodation which is too *small* for them, *e.g.* for reasons of economy.

It is the word "extent" to which attention must be paid. If it was not present, the Ground might be construed as permitting refusal of, *e.g.* a flat, to a family with young children, or a property with difficult access to an elderly or disabled person. ("Special" accommodation—for the physically handicapped—is covered by Ground 7, below; sheltered for the elderly is covered by Ground 9, but adapted for the elderly is left wholly uncovered but might have been within the present Ground, again were it not for the word "extent.") But "extent" clearly refers to the *amount* of accommodation, as distinct from its nature or quality, or indeed its special facilities.

Ground 5

Cf. Sched. 1, Ground 12, above, and Sched. 5, para. 5, below.

Ground 6

Cf. Sched. 2, Ground 11, which would be available if the assignment took place.

Ground 7

Cf. Sched. 2, Ground 13, which would be available if the assignment took place.

Ground 8

Cf. Sched. 2, Ground 14, which would be available if the assignment took place.

Ground 9
   Cf. Sched. 2, Ground 15, which would be available if the assignment took place.

———————

Sections 119 and 129   SCHEDULE 4

QUALIFYING PERIOD FOR RIGHT TO BUY AND DISCOUNT

Introductory

1. The period to be taken into account—
  (*a*) for the purposes of section 119 (qualification for right to buy), and
  (*b*) for the purposes of section 129 (discount),
is the period qualifying, or the aggregate of the periods qualifying, under the following provisions of this Schedule.

Periods occupying accommodation subject to public sector tenancy

2. A period qualifies under this paragraph if it is a period during which, before the relevant time—
  (*a*) the secure tenant, or
  (*b*) his spouse (if they are living together at the relevant time), or
  (*c*) a deceased spouse of his (if they were living together at the time of the death),
was a public sector tenant or was the spouse of a public sector tenant and occupied as his only or principal home the dwelling-house of which the spouse was such a tenant.

3. For the purposes of paragraph 2 a person who, as a joint tenant under a public sector tenancy, occupied a dwelling-house as his only or principal home shall be treated as having been the public sector tenant under that tenancy.

4.—(1) This paragraph applies where the public sector tenant of a dwelling-house died or otherwise ceased to be a public sector tenant of the dwelling-house, and thereupon a child of his who occupied the dwelling-house as his only or principal home (the "new tenant") became the public sector tenant of the dwelling-house (whether under the same or under another public sector tenancy).

(2) A period during which the new tenant, since reaching the age of 16, occupied as his only or principal home a dwelling-house of which a parent of his was the public sector tenant or one of joint tenants under a public sector tenancy, being either—
  (*a*) the period at the end of which he became the public sector tenant, or
  (*b*) an earlier period ending two years or less before the period mentioned in paragraph
      (*a*) or before another period within this paragraph,
shall be treated for the purposes of paragraph 2 as a period during which he was a public sector tenant.

(3) For the purposes of this paragraph two persons shall be treated as parent and child if they would be so treated under section 186(2) (members of a person's family: relationships other than those of the whole blood).

Periods occupying forces accommodation

5. A period qualifies under this paragraph if it is a period during which, before the relevant time—
  (*a*) the secure tenant, or
  (*b*) his spouse (if they are living together at the relevant time), or
  (*c*) a deceased spouse of his (if they were living together at the time of the death),
occupied accommodation provided for him as a member of the regular armed forces of the Crown or was the spouse of a person occupying accommodation so provided and also occupied that accommodation.

Meaning of "public sector tenant"

6.—(1) In this Schedule a "public sector tenant" means a tenant under a public sector tenancy.

(2) For the purposes of this Schedule, a tenancy, other than a long tenancy, under which a dwelling-house was let as a separate dwelling was a public sector tenancy at any time when the conditions described below as the landlord condition and the tenant condition were satisfied.

(3) The provisions of this Schedule apply in relation to a licence to occupy a dwelling-house (whether or not granted for a consideration) as they apply in relation to a tenancy.

(4) Sub-paragraph (3) does not apply to a licence granted as a temporary expedient to a person who entered the dwelling-house or any other land as a trespasser (whether or not, before the grant of that licence, another licence to occupy that or another dwelling-house had been granted to him).

The landlord condition

7.—(1) The landlord condition is, subject to any order under paragraph 8, that the interest of the landlord belonged to, or to a predecessor of—

    a local authority,

    a new town corporation,

    the Development Board for Rural Wales,

    an urban development corporation,

    the Housing Corporation,

    a registered housing association which is not a co-operative housing association,

    a housing co-operative within the meaning of section 27 (co-operatives exercising authority's management functions),

or to, or to a predecessor of, an authority or other body falling within sub-paragraph (2) or (3) (corresponding authorities and bodies in Scotland and Northern Ireland),

    (2) The corresponding authorities and bodies in Scotland are—

    a regional, islands or district council,

    a joint board or joint committee of such a council,

    the common good of such a council or a trust under its control,

    a development corporation established by an order made or having effect as if made under the New Towns (Scotland) Act 1968,

    the Scottish Special Housing Association,

    a housing association which falls within paragraph (*e*) of section 10(2) of the Tenants' Rights, Etc. (Scotland) Act 1980 but is not a registered society within the meaning of section 11 of that Act, and

    a housing co-operative within the meaning of section 5 of the Housing Rents and Subsidies (Scotland) Act 1975.

    (3) The corresponding authorities and bodies in Northern Ireland are—

    a district council within the meaning of the Local Government Act (Northern Ireland) 1972,

    the Northern Ireland Housing Executive, and

    a registered housing association within the meaning of Chapter II of Part II of the Housing (Northern Ireland) Order 1983.

8.—(1) The landlord condition shall also be treated as having been satisfied, in such circumstances as may be prescribed for the purposes of this paragraph by order of the Secretary of State, if the interest of the landlord belonged to a person who is so prescribed.

    (2) An order under this paragraph—

    (*a*) may make different provision with respect to different cases or descriptions of case, including different provision for different areas, and

    (*b*) shall be made by statutory instrument which shall be subject to annulment in pursuance of a resolution of either House of Parliament.

The tenant condition

9. The tenant condition is that the tenant was an individual and occupied the dwelling-house as his only or principal home; or, where the tenancy was a joint tenancy, that each of the joint tenants was an individual and at least one of them occupied the dwelling-house as his only or principal home.

Application to certain housing association tenancies

10. For the purpose of determining whether at any time a tenant of a housing association was a public sector tenant and his tenancy a public sector tenancy, the association shall be deemed to have been registered at that time, under the Housing Associations Act 1985 or the corresponding Northern Ireland legislation, if it was so registered at any later time.

GENERAL NOTE

This Schedule governs periods of public sector occupation, for the purposes of qualification to buy, and discount, under Pt. V. The key to the provisions is to be found in the concept of the "public sector tenancy," as defined in para. 6. Broadly it is time spent as a public sector tenant which serves as qualifying time, either for the purposes of right to buy or for discount.

Para. 1

The periods identified in the following paragraphs are to be added together to constitute entitlement, either to buy or to discount.

Paras. 2, 3

The first period to be taken into account is a period of time in which (*a*) the secure tenant, or (*b*) his or her spouse, or (*c*) his or her deceased spouse, was (i) a public sector tenant, or (ii) the spouse of a public sector tenant. The period ceases at date of service of notice claiming right to buy ("the relevant time"—s.122).

However, certain periods apparently qualifying are excluded. The first is that time spent by tenant, tenant's spouse or tenant's deceased spouse, as the spouse of a public sector tenant does not qualify unless at the time he or she was occupying the property as an only or principal home, as to which see notes to s.81, above.

Thus, if ex-H was public sector tenant of property A, and the parties separated, and W is the secure tenant now seeking to establish the right to buy at property B, or count a period for discount, she will only be able to count the time she spent in property A as her only or principal home. If, therefore, on separation, *she* left the former home, she also abandoned the acquisition of a further period at property A. If ex-H left, however, then even though he remained the secure tenant of property A, and was not living with her, she can continue to acquire more time.

Reliance may only be placed on a period of public sector tenancy of a spouse, if secure tenant and spouse are living together at the time right to buy is claimed. Similarly, reliance may only be placed on a period of public sector tenancy of a deceased spouse, if secure tenant and deceased spouse were living together at time of death. However, occupation as a joint public sector tenant classes as occupation as a sole public sector tenant, provided the property in question was occupied as an only or principal home: para. 3.

Para. 4

The child of a public sector tenant, who becomes a secure tenant (whether or not because of statutory succession—see notes to s.91, above, under the provisions of which a secure tenant may assign to a child who could have qualified under the statutory succession provisions had the tenant died—and whether or not under the same tenancy), will be able to count time spent in the property, provided such time was occupation as an only or principal home, as to which, see notes to s.81, above.

Only time from the age of 16 is to be taken into account. Furthermore, the time to be taken into account must be immediately before the date when the new tenant took over, or a period ending not more than two years before that date. There will have to be *some* period immediately before taking over, because there could otherwise be no succession (see s.87), and if no capacity for succession, no right to take an assignment (and remain secure): see s.91, above. The alternative limb, therefore, permits the addition of a continuous period (of however long), ending within the previous two years.

Para. 5

Additional to the period or periods to be taken into account under the last paragraph is a period or periods prior to service of notice claiming right to buy, during which the secure tenant or a spouse or deceased spouse occupied armed forces accommodation. Such periods may only be added, however, if both (then) spouses occupied the armed forces accommodation. Further, the time of a spouse or deceased spouse can only be added if secure tenant was living with spouse at time of right to buy claim, or time of death.

Paras. 6–7

These paras. and paras. 8 to 10 below, define the "public sector tenant" who, when he acquires a secure tenancy, will be able to claim time for the purposes of qualification to buy, and to discount. The definition proceeds through the key elements of the definition of secure tenancy itself, although expanded as necessary to reflect the wider class of landlord, and types of occupation, to be taken into account.

See ss.79, 80, above. See also ss.115, 187, above.

Para. 8

The Secretary of State has power to prescribe further landlords for the purposes of this Schedule. See the Housing (Right to Buy) (Prescribed Persons) Order 1984 (S.I. 1984 No. 1173), retained in force by Housing (Consequential Provisions) Act 1985, s.2.

Para. 9

See s.81, above.

Para. 10

If a housing association subsequently secures registration, the effect is to turn the earlier time of tenants—or former tenants—into public sector tenancy time.

Section 120   SCHEDULE 5

EXCEPTIONS TO THE RIGHT TO BUY

Charities

1. The right to buy does not arise if the landlord is a housing trust or a housing association and is a charity.

Certain housing associations

2. The right to buy does not arise if the landlord is a co-operative housing association.

3. The right to buy does not arise if the landlord is a housing association which at no time received a grant under—

> any enactment mentioned in paragraph 2 of Schedule 1 to the Housing Associations Act 1985 (grants under enactments superseded by the Housing Act 1974),
>
> section 31 of the Housing Act 1974 (management grants),
>
> section 41 of the Housing Associations Act 1985 (housing association grants),
>
> section 54 of that Act (revenue deficit grants),
>
> section 55 of that Act (hostel deficit grants), or
>
> section 58(2) of that Act (grants by local authorities).

Landlord with insufficient interest in the property

4. The right to buy does not arise unless the landlord owns the freehold or has an interest sufficient to grant a lease in pursuance of this Part for—

(*a*) where the dwelling-house is a house, a term exceeding 21 years, or

(*b*) where the dwelling-house is a flat, a term of not less than 50 years,

commencing, in either case, with the date on which the tenant's notice claiming to exercise the right to buy is served.

Dwelling-houses let in connection with employment

5.—(1) The right to buy does not arise if the dwelling-house—

(*a*) forms part of, or is within the curtilage of, a building which, or so much of it as is held by the landlord, is held mainly for purposes other than housing purposes and consists mainly of accommodation other than housing accommodation, or is situated in a cemetery, and

(*b*) was let to the tenant or a predecessor in title of his in consequence of the tenant or predecessor being in the employment of the landlord or of—

> a local authority,
>
> a new town corporation,
>
> the Development Board for Rural Wales,
>
> an urban development corporation, or
>
> the governors of an aided school.

(2) In sub-paragraph (1)(*a*) "housing purposes" means the purposes for which dwelling-houses are held by local housing authorities under Part II (provision of housing) or purposes corresponding to those purposes.

Certain dwelling-houses for the disabled

6. The right to buy does not arise if—

(*a*) the dwelling-house has features which are substantially different from those of ordinary dwelling-houses and are designed to make it suitable for occupation by physically disabled persons, and

(*b*) it has had those features since it was constructed or, where it was provided by means of the conversion of a building, since it was so provided.

7. The right to buy does not arise if the dwelling-house has features which are substantially different from those of ordinary dwelling-houses and are designed to make it suitable for occupation by physically disabled persons, and—

(*a*) it is one of a group of dwelling-houses which it is the practice of the landlord to let for occupation by physically disabled persons, and

(*b*) a social service or special facilities are provided in close proximity to the group of dwelling-houses wholly or partly for the purpose of assisting those persons.

8. The right to buy does not arise if the landlord or a predecessor of the landlord has carried out, for the purpose of making the dwelling-house suitable for occupation by physically disabled persons, one or more of the following alterations—

(*a*) the provision of not less than 7.5 square metres of additional floor space;

(*b*) the provision of an additional bathroom or shower-room;

(*c*) the installation of a vertical lift.

9.—(1) The right to buy does not arise if—

(*a*) the dwelling-house is one of a group of dwelling-houses which it is the practice of the landlord to let for occupation by persons who are suffering or have suffered from a mental disorder, and

(*b*) a social service or special facilities are provided wholly or partly for the purpose of assisting those persons.

(2) In sub-paragraph (1)(*a*) "mental disorder" has the same meaning as in the Mental Health Act 1983.

Certain dwelling-houses for persons of pensionable age

10.—(1) The right to buy does not arise if the dwelling-house is one of a group of dwelling-houses—

(*a*) which are particularly suitable, having regard to their location, size, design, heating systems and other features, for occupation by persons of pensionable age, and

(*b*) which it is the practice of the landlord to let for occupation by persons of pensionable age, or for occupation by such persons and physically disabled persons,

and special facilities such as are mentioned in sub-paragraph (2) are provided wholly or mainly for the purposes of assisting those persons.

(2) The facilities referred to above are facilities which consist of or include—

(*a*) the services of a resident warden, or

(*b*) the services of a non-resident warden, a system for calling him and the use of a common room in close proximity to the group of dwelling-houses.

11.—(1) The right to buy does not arise if the Secretary of State has determined, on the application of the landlord, that it is not to be capable of being exercised with respect to the dwelling-house.

(2) The Secretary of State shall so determine if, and only if, he is satisfied that the dwelling-house—

(*a*) is particularly suitable, having regard to its location, size, design, heating system and other features, for occupation by persons of pensionable age, and

(*b*) was let to the tenant or a predecessor in title of his for occupation by a person of pensionable age or a physically disabled person (whether the tenant or predecessor or another person).

(3) An application for a determination under this paragraph shall be made within the period for service of the landlord's notice under section 124 (notice admitting or denying right to buy).

Dwelling-houses held on Crown tenancies

12.—(1) The right to buy does not arise if the dwelling-house is held by the landlord on a tenancy from the Crown, unless—

(*a*) the landlord is entitled to grant a lease in pursuance of this Part without the concurrence of the appropriate authority, or

(*b*) the appropriate authority notifies the landlord that as regards any Crown interest affected the authority will give its consent to the granting of such a lease.

(2) In this paragraph "tenancy from the Crown" means a tenancy of land in which there is a Crown interest superior to the tenancy, and "Crown interest" and "appropriate authority" mean respectively—

(*a*) an interest comprised in the Crown Estate, and the Crown Estate Commissioners or other government department having the management of the land in question;

(*b*) an interest belonging to Her Majesty in right of the Duchy of Lancaster, and the Chancellor of the Duchy;

(*c*) an interest belonging to the Duchy of Cornwall, and such person as the Duke of Cornwall or the possessor for the time being of the Duchy appoints;

(*d*) any other interest belonging to a government department or held on behalf of Her Majesty for the purposes of a government department, and that department.

(3) Section 179(1) (which renders ineffective certain provisions restricting the grant of leases under this Part) shall be disregarded for the purposes of sub-paragraph (1)(*a*).

GENERAL NOTE

This Schedule defines those circumstances when the right to buy is not available. See also ss. 119 (minimum qualifying period of tenancy) and 121 (existing order for possession or bankruptcy related orders).

Para. 1

The tenants of housing trusts and associations which are also charities within the meaning of the Charities Act 1960 are excluded from the right to buy.

Para. 2

This excludes the tenant of co–operative housing associations from the right to buy: see s.5, above.

Para. 3

The class of association excluded by this para. is the association which has at no time received public funds for its activities, under the statutory provisions listed. Those provisions include grants by local authorities to housing associations, now under Housing Associations Act 1985, s.58, formerly Housing Act 1957 s.119. An association which has benefited from local authority support by way of subscription to share or loan capital will not on that account be brought within the right to buy, for it will still not have received a grant.

The enactments specified in Housing Associations Act 1985, Sched. 1, para. 2, are the principal predecessor provisions enabling grants to be made to housing associations, before the introduction of new provisions in 1974. Basic residual subsidy received under the Housing Finance Act 1972 amounts to a "grant" within those provisions: *Wood* v. *South Western Co-Operative Housing Society* (1982) 4 H.L.R. 101, C.A.

Para. 4

Part V excludes from the right to a lease (s.118) those cases where the landlord does not have a sufficient interest to grant a lease. *Sufficient interest* means, in the case of a house, an interest sufficient to grant a term exceeding 21 years commencing with the relevant time; in the case of a flat the term is to be of not less than 50 years commencing with the relevant time.

Para. 5

This paragraph leaves out of the right to buy the occupiers of property forming part of, or within the curtilage of, a building held by the landlord mainly for non-housing purposes, *i.e.* not the purposes for which local authorities hold accommodation under Part II. The building must be one which consists mainly of non-housing accommodation. However, the exclusion will only apply if the dwelling-house was let to the tenant, or his predecessor in title, in consequence of employment with the landlord, or with one of the other landlords who benefit from this provision (thus permitting landlords to house one another's employees). The same exemption applies where what is occupied is a dwelling-house in a cemetery (within the meaning of Local Government Act 1972 s.214).

Paras. 6 to 8

These paras. concern property for the physically disabled. The words "features substantially different from those of ordinary dwelling-houses and which are designed to make . . . suitable for occupation by physically disabled persons", which appear in the first two of these paras. were considered in *Freeman* v. *Wansbeck District Council* (1983) 10 H.L.R. 54, C.A., in which it was held that the introduction of an indoor, downstairs lavatory was not a feature substantially different from the features of ordinary dwelling-houses, even although introduced by use of powers contained in the Chronically Sick and Disabled Persons Act 1970 for the benefit of the daughter of the tenants, who suffered from spina bifida. The word "designed" was held to refer to the architectural process, and does not mean "intended."

The Court of Appeal also held that when determining what constitutes the features of ordinary dwelling-houses, comparison should not be limited to other dwelling-houses in the same locality. Illustrations of appropriate special features included ramps, widened doors, lifts, and cooking surfaces at special heights.

The exclusions, however, require more than that there are features substantially different from those of ordinary dwelling-houses. There are further conditions, in each of the three paras. The first and third paras. concern single dwellings (*i.e.* not in groups of sheltered accommodation for the disabled, see further below,) and the second concerns dwellings which are in groups. (In addition, attention may be drawn to paras. 10 and 11, below, concerning occupation of dwelling for the *elderly*, by a *disabled* person).

To deal first with single dwellings, they may be excluded from right to buy in two different ways. First of all, under para 6. the property is excluded if the dwelling was *constructed* with those features, including as construction for this purpose a dwelling produced by conversion. This limb, then, does not include *alterations* to existing dwellings. The features will, of course, have to be those of the order discussed in *Freeman*.

Secondly, however, under para. 8, single dwellings will be excluded if the landlord, or a predecessor to the landlord, has carried out one or more of the specified three alterations, *i.e.* additional floor space, additional bathroom or shower-room, or installation of a lift.

Dwellings for the disabled may, nonetheless, be excluded, even if they do not fall within these single dwelling "construction or alteration" classes, if they are within the para. 7 class of disabled persons' dwellings, that is to say they are part of a group of "sheltered" dwellings with "*Freeman*" features.

To qualify, (*a*) the individual unit must be one of a group, (*b*) the dwelling must have features of the class discussed in *Freeman*, designed to make suitable for occupation by the physically disabled (whether by construction or subsequent alteration,) (*c*) it must be the practice of the landlord to let the group for occupation by the physically disabled, and (*d*) a "social service or special" facility must be provided "in close proximity to the group of dwelling-houses." Furthermore, that facility must be "wholly or partly for the purpose of assisting" the disabled occupants.

The allocation and adaptation of a single unit on an estate, or even one unit in each block on an estate, will not qualify as "one of a group" of dwelling-houses. Such properties would only be excluded if they qualify as "constructed" with, or altered to incorporate, special features, *i.e.* as if single units. But it is not necessary that an entire estate, or block, be for the disabled, so that the physically disabled persons units in developments for a range of special purposes will not necessarily fail to qualify under this heading. There must be something, however, susceptible to description as a "group," of which the property in issue is one.

Para. 9

This paragraph deals with accommodation for the mentally handicapped. There is, of course, no requirement for physical adaptation of property, nor for warden facilities, although only grouped accommodation will qualify, and there must be a social service or special facility provided "wholly or partly" to assist the occupants (*cf.* notes to paras. 6 to 8, above).

Para. 10

This paragraph requires that a *group* of dwelling-houses (*a*) is "particularly suitable" for occupation by the elderly, having regard to location, size, design, heating systems and other features, (*b*) it is the practice of the landlord to let the accommodation to the elderly or to the elderly together with physically handicapped, and (*c*) there are special facilities which must include either a resident warden or, in the absence of a resident warden, a non-resident warden, *plus* a system for calling him, plus, the use of a common room in close proximity to the group of houses. A small number of houses designed or adapted for the elderly, but on an otherwise conventional estate, would seem unlikely to qualify, because of the need for the warden facility.

Para. 11

Note that, although concerned with the elderly, this paragraph, like paras. 6 to 8, is also concerned, though to a lesser extent, with the physically disabled. The dwelling has to be particularly suitable, having regard to location, size, design, heating system and other features, for persons of pensionable age, *and* must have been let to the tenant or a predecessor for occupation by one such, *or* by a physically disabled person.

The landlord must make application within whichever time-scale applies to determine by when it must acknowledge or deny the tenant's application under s.124, *i.e.* 4 or 8 weeks, but if such an application is made, the notice in reply to the tenant is without prejudice to the outcome of the application: s.124(3).

As to challenging refusal by the Secretary of State to certify, see generally notes to s.64, above.

Para. 12

Exempt from the general right to a lease in cases where the landlord does not own the freehold (see s.118), are cases where the interest superior to that of the landlord is the

Crown. However, the exemption does not apply (and therefore the right to a lease *is* available), if *either* (i) (without the benefit of s.179, above), under the terms of the lease the landlord would be entitled to grant the sub-lease claimed by the tenant without the permission of the Crown, *or* (ii) the Crown consents to the grant of the sub-lease, through the offices of the specified bodies.

Sections 139 and 151   SCHEDULE 6

CONVEYANCE OF FREEHOLD AND GRANT OF LEASE IN PURSUANCE OF RIGHT TO BUY

PART I

COMMON PROVISIONS

Rights to be conveyed or granted—general

1. The conveyance or grant shall not exclude or restrict the general words implied under section 62 of the Law of Property Act 1925, unless the tenant consents or the exclusion or restriction is made for the purpose of preserving or recognising an existing interest of the landlord in tenant's incumbrances or an existing right or interest of another person.

Rights of support, passage of water, etc.

2.—(1) The conveyance or grant shall, by virtue of this Schedule, have the effect stated in sub-paragraph (2) as regards—
  (*a*) rights of support for a building or part of a building;
  (*b*) rights to the access of light and air to a building or part of a building;
  (*c*) rights to the passage of water or of gas or other piped fuel, or to the drainage or disposal of water, sewage, smoke or fumes, or to the use or maintenance of pipes or other installations for such passage, drainage or disposal;
  (*d*) rights to the use or maintenance of cables or other installations for the supply of electricity, for the telephone or for the receipt directly or by landline of visual or other wireless transmissions.
(2) The effect is—
  (*a*) to grant with the dwelling-house all such easements and rights over other property, so far as the landlord is capable of granting them, as are necessary to secure to the tenant as nearly as may be the same rights as at the relevant time were available to him under or by virtue of the secure tenancy or an agreement collateral to it, or under or by virtue of a grant, reservation or agreement made on the severance of the dwelling-house from other property then comprised in the same tenancy; and
  (*b*) to make the dwelling-house subject to all such easements and rights for the benefit of other property as are capable of existing in law and are necessary to secure to the person interested in the other property as nearly as may be the same rights as at the relevant time were available against the tenant under or by virtue of the secure tenancy or an agreement collateral to it, or under or by virtue of a grant, reservation or agreement made as mentioned in paragraph (*a*).
(3) This paragraph—
  (*a*) does not restrict any wider operation which the conveyance or grant may have apart from this paragraph; but
  (*b*) is subject to any provision to the contrary that may be included in the conveyance or grant with the consent of the tenant.

Rights of way

3. The conveyance or grant shall include—
  (*a*) such provisions (if any) as the tenant may require for the purpose of securing to him rights of way over land not comprised in the dwelling-house, so far as the landlord is capable of granting them, being rights of way that are necessary for the reasonable enjoyment of the dwelling-house; and
  (*b*) such provisions (if any) as the landlord may require for the purpose of making the dwelling-house subject to rights of way necessary for the reasonable enjoyment of other property, being property in which at the relevant time the landlord has an interest, or to rights of way granted or agreed to be granted before the relevant time by the landlord or by the person then entitled to the reversion on the tenancy.

Covenants and conditions

4. The conveyance or grant shall include such provisions (if any) as the landlord may require to secure that a tenant is bound by, or to indemnify the landlord against breaches of, restrictive covenants (that is to say, covenants or agreements restrictive of the use of any land or premises) which affect the dwelling-house otherwise than by virtue of the secure tenancy or an agreement collateral to it and are enforceable for the benefit of other property.

5. Subject to paragraph 6, and to Parts II and III of this Schedule, the conveyance or grant may include such covenants and conditions as are reasonable in the circumstances.

No charge to be made for landlord's consent or approval

6. A provision of the conveyance or lease is void in so far as it purports to enable the landlord to charge the tenant a sum for or in connection with the giving of a consent or approval.

Meaning of "incumbrances" and "tenant's incumbrance"

7. In this Schedule—
    "incumbrances" includes personal liabilities attaching in respect of the ownership of land or an interest in land though not charged on the land or interest; and
    "tenant's incumbrance" means—
        (*a*) an incumbrance on the secure tenancy which is also an incumbrance on the reversion, and
        (*b*) an interest derived, directly or indirectly, out of the secure tenancy.

PART II

CONVEYANCE OF FREEHOLD

General

8. The conveyance shall not exclude or restrict the all estate clause implied under section 63 of the Law of Property Act 1925, unless the tenant consents or the exclusion or restriction is made for the purpose of preserving or recognising an existing interest of the landlord in tenant's incumbrances or an existing right or interest of another person.

9.—(1) The conveyance shall be of an estate in fee simple absolute, subject to—
    (*a*) tenant's incumbrances,
    (*b*) burdens (other than burdens created by the conveyance) in respect of the upkeep or regulation for the benefit of any locality of any land, building, structure, works, ways or watercourses;
but otherwise free from incumbrances.

(2) Nothing in sub-paragraph (1) shall be taken as affecting the operation of paragraph 5 of this Schedule (reasonable covenants and conditions).

Covenants

10. The conveyance shall be expressed to be made by the landlord as beneficial owner (thereby implying the covenant set out in Part I of Schedule 2 to the Law of Property Act 1925 (covenant for title)).

PART III

LEASES

General

11. A lease shall be for the appropriate term defined in paragraph 12 (but subject to sub-paragraph (3) of that paragraph) and at a rent not exceeding £10 per annum, and the following provisions have effect with respect to the other terms of the lease.

The appropriate term

12.—(1) If at the time the grant is made the landlord's interest in the dwelling-house is not less than a lease for a term of which more than 125 years and five days are unexpired, the appropriate term is a term of not less than 125 years.

(2) In any other case the appropriate term is a term expiring five days before the term of the landlord's lease of the dwelling-house (or, as the case may require, five days before the

first date on which the term of any lease under which the landlord holds any part of the dwelling-house) is to expire.

(3) If the dwelling-house is a flat contained in a building which also contains one or more other flats and the landlord has, since 8th August 1980, granted a lease of one or more of them for the appropriate term, the lease of the dwelling-house may be for a term expiring at the end of the term for which the other lease (or one of the other leases) was granted.

Common use of premises and facilities

13. Where the dwelling-house is a flat and the tenant enjoyed, during the secure tenancy, the use in common with others of any premises, facilities or services, the lease shall include rights to the like enjoyment, so far as the landlord is capable of granting them, unless otherwise agreed between the landlord and the tenant.

Covenants by the landlord

14.—(1) This paragraph applies where the dwelling-house is a flat.

(2) There are implied covenants by the landlord—

(*a*) to keep in repair the structure and exterior of the dwelling-house and of the building in which it is situated (including drains, gutters and external pipes) and to make good any defect affecting that structure;

(*b*) to keep in repair any other property over or in respect of which the tenant has rights by virtue of this Schedule;

(*c*) to ensure, so far as practicable, that services which are to be provided by the landlord and to which the tenant is entitled (whether by himself or in common with others) are maintained at a reasonable level and to keep in repair any installation connected with the provision of those services;

but subject to paragraph 15(3) (restrictions where landlord's interest is leasehold).

(3) The covenant to keep in repair implied by sub-paragraph (2)(*a*) includes a requirement that the landlord shall rebuild or reinstate the dwelling-house and the building in which it is situated in the case of destruction or damage by fire, tempest, flood or any other cause against the risk of which it is normal practice to insure.

(4) The county court may, by order made with the consent of the parties, authorise the inclusion in the lease or in an agreement collateral to it of provisions excluding or modifying the obligations of the landlord under the covenants implied by this paragraph, if it appears to the court that it is reasonable to do so.

15.—(1) This paragraph applies where the landlord's interest in the dwelling-house is leasehold.

(2) There is implied a covenant by the landlord to pay the rent reserved by the landlord's lease and, except in so far as they fall to be discharged by the tenant, to discharge its obligations under the covenants contained in that lease.

(3) A covenant implied by virtue of paragraph 14 (implied covenants where dwelling-house is a flat) shall not impose on the landlord an obligation which the landlord is not entitled to discharge under the provisions of the landlord's lease or a superior lease.

(4) Where the landlord's lease or a superior lease or an agreement collateral to the landlord's lease or a superior lease, contains a covenant by a person imposing obligations which, but for sub-paragraph (3), would be imposed by a covenant implied by virtue of paragraph 14, there is implied a covenant by the landlord to use its best endeavours to secure that that person's obligations under the first-mentioned covenant are discharged.

Covenant by tenant

16. Unless otherwise agreed between the landlord and the tenant, there is implied a covenant by the tenant—

(*a*) where the dwelling-house is a house, to keep the dwelling-house in good repair (including decorative repair);

(*b*) where the dwelling-house is a flat, to keep the interior of the dwelling-house in such repair.

Avoidance of certain provisions

17.—(1) A provision of the lease, or of an agreement collateral to it, is void in so far as it purports to prohibit or restrict the assignment of the lease or the subletting, wholly or in part, of the dwelling-house.

(2) Sub-paragraph (1) has effect subject to section 157 (restriction on disposal of dwelling-houses in National Parks, etc.).

18.—(1) Subject to the following provisions of this paragraph, where the dwelling-house is a flat, a provision of the lease or of an agreement collateral to it is void in so far as it purports—

(*a*) to enable the landlord to recover from the tenant any part of costs incurred by the landlord in discharging or insuring against the obligations imposed by the covenants implied by virtue of paragraph 14(2)(*a*) or (*b*) (landlord's obligations with respect to repair of dwelling-house, etc.), or

(*b*) to enable any person to recover from the tenant any part of costs incurred, whether by him or by another person, in discharging or insuring against any obligations to the like effect as the obligations which would be so imposed but for paragraph 15(3) (obligations not to be implied which landlord would not be entitled to discharge).

(2) A provision is not void by virtue of sub-paragraph (1) in so far as it requires the tenant to bear a reasonable part of the costs of carrying out repairs not amounting to the making good of structural defects.

(3) A provision is not void by virtue of sub-paragraph (1) in so far as it requires the tenant to bear a reasonable part of costs incurred in respect of a structural defect—

(*a*) of the existence of which the landlord informed the tenant in the notice under section 125 (landlord's notice of purchase price, etc.), stating the landlord's estimate of the amount (at current prices) which would be payable by the tenant towards the cost of making it good, or

(*b*) of the existence of which the landlord becomes aware ten years or more after the grant of the lease.

(4) Where the lease acknowledges the right of the tenant and his successors in title to production of the relevant policy, a provision is not void by virtue of sub-paragraph (1) in so far as it requires the tenant to bear a reasonable part of the costs of insuring against risks involving such repairs or the making good of such defects.

(5) Any estimated amount stated as mentioned in sub-paragraph (3)(*a*) (estimate of costs to be borne by tenant in respect of structural defect) shall be disregarded for the purposes of any statement under section 125(4) (estimate of service charges payable).

19. A provision of the lease, or of an agreement collateral to it, is void in so far as it purports to authorise a forfeiture, or to impose on the tenant a penalty or disability, in the event of his enforcing or relying on the preceding provisions of this Schedule.

Part IV

Charges

Grant of lease

20. A charge (however created or arising) on the interest of the landlord which is not a tenant's incumbrance does not affect a lease granted in pursuance of the right to buy.

Conveyance of freehold

21.—(1) This paragraph applies to a charge (however created or arising) on the freehold where the freehold is conveyed in pursuance of the right to buy.

(2) If the charge is not a tenant's incumbrance and is not a rentcharge the conveyance is effective to release the freehold from the charge; but the release does not affect the personal liability of the landlord or any other person in respect of any obligation which the charge was created to secure.

(3) If the charge is a rentcharge the conveyance shall be made subject to the charge; but if the rentcharge also affects other land—

(*a*) the conveyance shall contain a covenant by the landlord to indemnify the tenant and his successors in title in respect of any liability arising under the rentcharge, and

(*b*) if the rentcharge is of a kind which may be redeemed under the Rentcharges Act 1977 the landlord shall immediately after the conveyance take such steps as are necessary to redeem the rentcharge so far as it affects land owned by him.

(4) In this paragraph "rentcharge" has the same meaning as in the Rentcharges Act 1977; and—

(*a*) for the purposes of sub-paragraph (3) land is owned by a person if he is the owner of it within the meaning of section 13(1) of that Act, and

(*b*) for the purposes of that sub-paragraph and that Act land which has been conveyed by the landlord in pursuance of the right to buy but subject to the rentcharge shall be treated as if it had not been so conveyed but had continued to be owned by him.

This Schedule governs the terms of a conveyance or grant under the right to buy, *i.e.* whether freehold or leasehold.

Part I: Applicable to Freehold and Leasehold
Para. 1
The Law of Property Act 1925, s. 62, sets out the principle that unless a contrary intention is expressed in the conveyance, the purchaser takes together with all buildings, fences, rights, easements, etc., appertaining or reputed to appertain to the land or any part of it, or demised, occupied or enjoyed with the land at the time of conveyance, or known as part or parcel of or appurtenant to the land or any part of it. Under para. 1 of this Schedule, there can be no exclusion or restriction of this principle, save with the consent of the purchaser, unless the exclusion or restriction is for the purpose of preserving or recognising an existing interest of the landlord in tenant's incumbrances (as defined in para. 7), or any existing right or interest of any other person.

Para. 2
The purpose of this provision is to leave the tenant with the benefit of the same rights of support, access of light and air, passage of water, sewage, drainage, gas, etc., use or maintenance of cables, etc., as he enjoyed as a tenant at the date the notice claiming the right to buy was served (s.122), while also subject to the burden of the same rights for the benefit of others as he enjoyed while he was a tenant. The provision may be varied with consent.

Para. 3
Similarly, the intention is to provide the tenant with all necessary rights of way to the dwelling-house, but also to ensure that existing rights of way for the benefit of others, or rights of way which are necessary for the reasonable enjoyment of other property in which the landlord has an interest, follow the conveyance or grant.

Para. 4
The conveyance or grant is to require the tenant to be bound by restrictive covenants, or indemnify the landlord against breaches of restrictive covenants, affecting the property, other than have arisen out of the secure tenancy or an agreement collateral to it, and only so far as they are enforceable for the benefit of other property.

Paras. 5, 6
Subject to the more detailed provisions of the Schedule, a conveyance or grant "may include such covenants and conditions as are reasonable in the circumstances". However, any attempt to incorporate in the conveyance or lease a provision which enables the landlord to charge the tenant for consents or approvals that might be needed in connection with its terms is void.

Part II: Applicable to Freehold Only
Para. 8
The Law of Property Act 1925, s.63, implies, save where a contrary intention is expressed in the conveyance, that the conveyance is effective to pass all the estate, right, title, interest, claim and demand which the conveying parties respectively have in, to, or on the property conveyed, or expressed or intended so to be, or which they respectively have power to convey in, to, or on the same. In other words, the conveyance passes the whole of the vendor's title in relation to the property. This provision can only be excluded or restricted if the tenant consents or the exclusion or restriction is for the purpose of preserving or recognising an existing interest of the landlord in tenant's incumbrances (as defined in para. 7) or any existing right or interest of any other person.

Para. 9
Note (*a*) the "declaration" in sub-para. (2), that nothing in this para. is to be taken as affecting the operation of para. 5, above, and (*b*) that the burdens do not include burdens created by the conveyance. The purpose of this 'declaration' is to prevent any argument that (i) para. 9, limits the general requirement that conveyance or grant may include such covenants and conditions as are reasonable in the circumstances, or (ii) that para. 9 permits the creation by the conveyance of *new* burdens in relation to upkeep or regulation for the benefit of any locality of any land, buildings, structure, works, ways or watercourse, outside the para. 5 requirement.

Part III: Applicable to Leasehold
Paras. 11, 12
There is a presumption in favour of a lease of 125 years whether in relation to houses or flats. However, where a lease has been granted of one flat in a building, later grants can be for a shorter period, coterminous with the first grant. Where the landlord does not own the freehold of a house or flat, sub-leases are to be for five days less than the landlord's lease.

Where the landlord holds more than one lease in respect of a property, *e.g.* of different parts, then the sub-lease is to expire five days before the earliest expiry date of any of the landlord's leases. (For example: landlord takes lease on one flat in sub-divided house; subsequently, landlord takes lease for same length, on the other; lease of first flat will expire before lease of second; landlord removes sub-division and sublets to secure tenant as one house, to which tenant has right to sublease, expiring five days before landlord's first lease.)

No *minimum* period is prescribed in this paragraph, but the right to buy (including a sub-lease) does not arise unless the landlord has a lease of at least 21 years in respect of a house, and 50 years in respect of a flat, as at date of service of notice claiming right: see Sched. 5, para. 4, above.

Para. 13
This paragraph requires the inclusion in leases of rights to the same use of facilities and services, in common with other occupants of a block, as the tenant enjoyed before purchase. It applies *only* in the case of flats, not to a lease of houses.

Para. 14
This provision is based in part upon some of Landlord and Tenant Act 1985, s.11, (see notes to s.104, above), *i.e.* the principal modern repairing obligation which is likely to have applied to the former secure tenancy. In some respects, however, it goes further, for s.11 does not extend to the whole of a building in which a dwelling-house is situated (*Campden Hill Towers* v. *Gardner* [1977] Q.B. 823, 13 H.L.R. 64, C.A.). The para. also incorporates the result in *Liverpool C.C.* v. *Irwin* [1977] A.C. 239, 13 H.L.R. 38, H.L., that there was an implied covenant to keep the common parts of the building in that case in repair.

A partition wall between two properties qualifies as exterior (*Green* v. *Eales* (1841) 2 Q.B. 225, *Pembery* v. *Lamdin* [1940] 2 All E.R. 434), and so also do windows (*Boswell* v. *Crucible Steel Co.* [1925] 1 K.B. 119, but *cf. Holiday Fellowship* v. *Hereford* [1959] 1 W.L.R. 211). Windows were assumed to be part of the structure or exterior in *Quick* v. *Taff Ely Borough Council* (1985) 18 H.L.R. 9, C.A. A blocked pipe is a pipe out of repair: *Bishop* v. *Consolidated London Properties* (1933) 102 L.J.K.B. 257. But the disrepair must be *to* the structure or exterior, not resulting *from* their condition, so that condensation caused by design, but not leaving the structure or exterior in physical disrepair itself was held not to fall within the s.11 covenant (or, therefore, this) in *Quick.*

A landlord's liability under a repairing covenant arises only once he has notice of a defect (*O'Brien* v. *Robinson* [1973] A.C. 912, 13 H.L.R. 7, H.L., *McGreal* v. *Wake* (1984) 13 H.L.R. 107, C.A.), although not necessarily notice *from* tenant, *i.e.* actual notice will suffice—*ibid.*, see also *Sheldon* v. *West Bromwich Corporation* (1973) 13 H.L.R. 23, C.A. The notice requirement is in any event inapplicable in relation to common parts and parts in the landlord's possession and control: *Melles & Co.* v. *Holme* [1918] 2 K.B. 100; *Bishop* v. *Consolidated London Properties* (1933) 102 L.J.K.B. 257.

There are other ways in which the covenant goes beyond s.11. Thus, the covenant extends to ensuring so far as practicable that any services provided by landlord to tenant, *e.g.* central heating, are maintained at a reasonable level, and to keeping in repair any installations connected with the provision of those services. This avoids the problem in *Campden Hill Towers* v. *Gardner,* above, in which it was held that central heating installations not sited in any one flat were not within the terms of s.11, so that the cost of repairs thereto could be imposed on the tenants notwithstanding that section. Under these provisions, the landlord is bound to keep them in repair, but may charge the tenants if so permitted under the lease: see para. 18.

The covenant also extends to rebuilding and reinstatement of dwelling-house and building in which it is situated in the case of destruction or damage by fire or other disaster of the class against which it is normal practice to insure.

As under s.12 of the Landlord and Tenant Act 1985, the lease may incorporate provisions excluding or modifying these terms, but only by consent of the parties, *and* with the approval of the county court, which approval is only to be granted if it appears to the court that it is reasonable so to do. The provision applies only to flats: leases of houses are dealt within para. 15, below; note, though, that para. 15 applies to both flats and houses, and may exempt the landlord from the provisions of this para.

Para. 15

This paragraph deals with both houses and flats. If the landlord has only a lease, para. 14 will not apply so as to require it to do anything which it is not permitted to do under its lease. However, where the superior landlord retains obligations which under para. 14 would otherwise be on the landlord, the landlord is placed under an obligation to use its best endeavours to ensure that the superior landlord complies with those duties, and in any event the landlord is obliged to carry out its obligations under the lease (which may coincide with para. 14 obligations) and pay its rent.

Para. 16

This paragraph governs the tenant's obligations which, in relation to a flat, are confined to interior repairs, including decorative repairs, but in relation to a house include the structure and exterior.

Para. 17

Subject to s.157, above, the lease cannot prohibit or restrict the assignment or sub-letting, whether of the whole or in part, of the dwelling-house.

Para. 18

Prima facie, the lease cannot require the tenant to pay even a part of the landlord's costs of discharging or insuring against its para. 14 obligations, or to enable anyone, *e.g.* a superior landlord, to recover from the tenant the costs of discharging or insuring against the discharge of any similar functions which would be the landlord's obligation, but for the exemption in para. 15.

That said, sub-para. (2) reinstates the right of the landlord to require the tenant to bear a reasonable part of the costs of carrying out repairs, *other than* repairs to make good a structural defect. And even repairs to make good a structural defect can be the subject of a requirement that the tenant bear a reasonable part of the costs, if the requirements of sub-para. (4) have been complied with, *i.e.* either the landlord notified the tenant of their existence when serving notice under s.125, together with its estimate of what the tenant's part of its remedial costs would be (at then current prices), or the landlord did not learn of the structural defects until at least ten years after the grant.

In addition, sub-para. (4) enables insurance charges to be passed on if the lease, in turn, permits the tenant to call for production of the insurance policy. With access to such policy, the tenant will usually be able to persuade a mortgagee not to require further insurance; without it, mortgagees will usually require further insurance, so that the tenant has to pay for two lots of insurance, (*a*) that required by their own mortgagee, and (*b*) that required by the landlord.

All of these charges will be service charges within Landlord and Tenant Act 1985, ss.18-30 and it will accordingly be possible for the leaseholder to utilise the protection afforded by those sections to secure details of how costs have been worked out, and to ensure that (a) no more than is reasonably incurred is passed on, and (b) the charge relates only to works or services to a reasonable standard. In some circumstances, that Act requires prior estimates, and consultation with tenants or tenants association.

Para. 19

The lease cannot authorise a forfeiture, penalty or disability for reliance upon on enforcement of the provisions of the Schedule by the tenant. Any such condition or covenant is wholly void, whether contained in the lease, or in a collateral agreement.

Part IV: Applicable to Freehold or Leasehold

The landlord is bound to convey a freehold free of all charges, other than tenant's incumbrances (as defined in para. 7): para. 9, above. However, a rentcharge within the meaning of the Rentcharges Act 1977 will pass. The conveyance otherwise has the effect of extinguishing any such disallowed charge, while leaving the former landlord personally liable in respect of that which the charge was designed to protect. A leasehold must be granted free even of a rentcharge.

A rentcharge is any annual or other periodic sum charged on or issuing out of land *other* than rent reserved by lease or tenancy, or a sum payable by way of interest: 1977, s.1. The owner of the land subject to the rentcharge is a person, other than a mortgagee not in possession, who is for the time being entitled to dispose of the fee simple, whether in possession or in reversion, and includes a person holding or entitled to the rents and profits of the land under a lease or agreement: 1977, s.13(1).

A rentcharge affecting only the land the subject of the conveyance passes to the purchaser. A rentcharge affecting that and other land also passes, but subject to an indemnity against any claim thereunder, and subject to a duty upon the landlord to redeem the charge, provided it is redeemable under the Rentcharges Act 1977. This duty remains even if the landlord has conveyed all of the land subject to the rentcharge, in separate parcels.

Rentcharges which are *not* redeemable under the 1977 Act include: a rentcharge which is, by enactment, agreement or custom, charged on or otherwise payable in relation to land wholly or partly in lieu of tithes; a rentcharge designed to ensure that land becomes settled land in consideration of marriage or by way of family arrangement (under s.1(1)(*v*) of the Settled Land Act 1925); an estate rentcharge; a rentcharge by Act of Parliament in connection with the execution of works; or a rentcharge by court order (1977 Act, ss.2(3), 3(3)(*a*)).

An estate rentcharge is one created in order to render covenants over servient land enforceable by the owner of the rentcharge, or for meeting or contributing towards the cost of the performance by the rent owner of covenants for the provisions of services, the carrying out of maintenance or repairs, the effecting of insurance, or the payment of moneys for the benefit of the land affected by the rentcharge: 1977, s.2(4).

Sections 139 and 151   SCHEDULE 7

MORTGAGE IN PURSUANCE OF RIGHT TO A MORTGAGE

1. The deed shall provide for repayment of the amount secured in equal instalments of principal and interest combined.

2.—(1) The period over which repayment is to be made shall be—

(*a*) 25 years, or

(*b*) where the mortgagor's interest in the dwelling-house is leasehold and the term of the lease is less than 25 years, a period equal to the term of the lease,

or, at the option of the mortgagor, a shorter period.

(2) The period mentioned in sub-paragraph (1) may be extended by the mortgagee.

3.—(1) The Secretary of State may by order—

(*a*) vary the preceding provisions of this Schedule, or

(*b*) prescribe additional terms to be contained in the deed,

but only in relation to deeds executed after the order comes into force.

(2) An order under this paragraph—

(*a*) may make different provision with respect to different cases or descriptions of case, including different provision for different areas, and

(*b*) shall be made by statutory instrument which shall be subject to annulment in pursuance of a resolution of either House of Parliament.

4. The deed may contain such other provisions as may be—

(*a*) agreed between the mortgagor and the mortgagee, or

(*b*) determined by the county court to be reasonably required by the mortgagor or the mortgagee.

GENERAL NOTE

This Schedule deals with the terms of the mortgage. As to interest rates under local authority mortgages, see Sched. 16, below. The Schedule is not mandatory, and applies only where the parties fail otherwise to agree: para. 4. If the parties do so fail to agree, the terms of the deed will require repayment in equal instalments of principal and interest: para. 1. The repayment period is 25 years, unless the mortgagor opts for a shorter term, or the mortgagee permits a longer term, or the lease itself is for less than 25 years: para. 2. Further terms may be determined by the county court as reasonably required by either mortgagor or mortgagee: para. 4. The Secretary of State may, however, prescribe additional mandatory provisions, and may vary the terms of repayment, as to balance between capital and interest, and as to period, although in all cases only in relation to deeds executed after the order comes into force: para. 3.

Section 151   SCHEDULE 8

TERMS OF SHARED OWNERSHIP LEASE

Additional shares

1.—(1) The lease shall state the tenant's initial share of the dwelling-house and shall contain provision enabling the tenant to acquire additional shares in the dwelling-house, which shall be either the prescribed percentage (within the meaning of section 145) or a multiple of that percentage.

(2) The right so conferred is exercisable at any time during the term of the lease on the tenant serving written notice on the landlord, stating the additional share he proposes to acquire.

(3) Where the tenant claims to exercise the right to acquire an additional share, the landlord shall, as soon as practicable, serve on the tenant a written notice stating—

(*a*) the amount which in the opinion of the landlord should be the amount of the consideration for that share on the assumption that the share is as stated in the tenant's notice, and

(*b*) the effective discount on an acquisition of that share, determined in each case, in accordance with paragraph 3(1).

(4) A notice required by this paragraph may be withdrawn at any time by notice in writing served on the landlord.

2.—(1) Where the dwelling-house is a house and the landlord owns the freehold, the lease shall provide that, on his acquiring an additional share such that his total share will be 100 per cent., the tenant is entitled to require the freehold to be conveyed either to himself or to such other person as he may direct.

(2) The right so conferred is exercisable at any time during the term of the lease on the tenant serving written notice on the landlord.

(3) As soon as practicable after the right mentioned in sub-paragraph (1) has become exercisable, the landlord shall serve on the tenant a written notice—

(*a*) informing him of the right, and

(*b*) stating the provisions which, in the opinion of the landlord, should be contained in the conveyance.

(4) A conveyance executed in pursuance of that right—

(*a*) shall conform with Parts I and II of Schedule 6 (terms of conveyance in pursuance of right to buy), and

(*b*) shall preserve the effect of the covenant required by section 155 (repayment of discount on early disposal), and

(*c*) where the lease contains any such covenant as is mentioned in section 157 (restriction on disposal of dwelling-houses in National Parks, etc.), shall preserve the effect of that covenant;

and Part IV of Schedule 6 (charges) applies to such a conveyance as it applies to a conveyance of the freehold in pursuance of the right to buy.

(5) A notice required by this paragraph may be withdrawn at any time by notice in writing served on the landlord.

Additional contributions

3.—(1) The consideration for an additional share (referred to in this Part as an "additional contribution") shall be determined by the formula—

$$C = \frac{S\,(V-D)}{100}$$

and the effective discount to which the tenant is entitled on the acquisition of an additional share shall be determined by the formula—

$$E = \frac{S \times D}{100}$$

where—

C = the additional contribution,

E = the effective discount,

S = the additional share expressed as a percentage,

V = the value of the dwelling-house (determined in accordance with paragraph 11) at the time when the notice under paragraph 1 is served, and

D = the discount which on the assumptions stated in sub-paragraph (2) below would be applicable under sections 129 to 131 (discount on exercise of right to buy).

(2) The assumptions are that—

(*a*) the shared ownership lease had not been granted and the secure tenancy had not come to an end, and

(*b*) the tenant was exercising the right to buy and his notice under paragraph 1 was a notice claiming to exercise that right.

Rent

4.—(1) The lease shall provide that, for any period for which the tenant's total share is less than 100 per cent., the rent payable under the lease shall be determined by the formula—

$$R = \frac{F\,(100-S)}{100}$$

where—

    R = the rent payable,
    F = the amount determined by the landlord as the rent which would be payable for that period if the shared ownership lease had not been granted and the secure tenancy had not come to an end, but excluding any element attributable to rates or to services provided by the landlord, and
    S = the tenant's total share expressed as a percentage.

(2) In making a determination under sub-paragraph (1) the landlord shall take into account all matters which appear to it to be relevant including, in particular, where comparable dwelling-houses in the locality are let on secure tenancies, the rents payable under those tenancies.

(3) The lease shall also provide that, for any such period, if the Secretary of State by order so provides—

(*a*) the rent payable under the lease as so determined, or
(*b*) any amount payable by the tenant under the lease which is payable, directly or indirectly, for repairs, maintenance, or insurance,

shall be adjusted in such manner as may be provided by the order.

(4) The Secretary of State may by order under sub-paragraph (3) provide for such adjustment as he considers appropriate having regard to the differing responsibilities for repairs, maintenance and insurance of a tenant under a shared ownership lease and a secure tenant.

(5) An order under this paragraph—

(*a*) may make different provision with respect to different cases or descriptions of case, including different provision for different areas, and
(*b*) may contain such transitional provisions as appear to the Secretary of State to be necessary or expedient,

and shall be made by statutory instrument which shall be subject to annulment in pursuance of a resolution of either House of Parliament.

(6) In this paragraph "rates" includes charges for services performed, facilities provided or rights made available by a water authority.

5. The lease shall provide that, for any period for which the tenant's total share is 100 per cent., the rent payable under the lease shall be £10 per annum.

Payment for outstanding share on disposal

6.—(1) The lease shall contain a covenant binding on the tenant and his successors in title to pay to the landlord on demand for the outstanding share an amount determined in accordance with sub-paragraph (2) if, at a time when the tenant's total share is less than 100 per cent., there is—

(*a*) a relevant disposal which is not an exempted disposal, or
(*b*) a compulsory disposal.

(2) The amount payable under the covenant shall be determined by the formula—

$$P = \frac{V\,(100-S)}{100}$$

where—

    P = the amount payable under the covenant,
    V = the value at the time of the disposal (determined in accordance with paragraph 11) of the dwelling-house or, in the case of a compulsory disposal of a part of the dwelling-house, of the part disposed of, and
    S = the tenant's total share expressed as a percentage.

(3) Section 156 (liability to repay discount a charge on the premises) applies in relation to the liability that may arise under the covenant required by this paragraph as it applies in

relation to the liability that may arise under the covenant required by section 155 (repayment of discount on early disposal).

7. The lease shall provide that, on the discharge of a liability arising under the covenant required by paragraph 6—

(*a*) the rent payable under the lease, or

(*b*) in the case of a compulsory disposal of a part of the dwelling-house, the rent payable under the lease so far as relating to that part,

shall be £10 per annum.

8.—(1) Where the dwelling-house is a house and the landlord owns the freehold, the lease shall provide that on the discharge of a liability arising under the covenant required by paragraph 6—

(*a*) any person in whom the tenant's interest in the dwelling-house is vested, or

(*b*) in the case of a compulsory disposal of a part of the dwelling-house, any person in whom that part is vested,

is entitled to require the freehold of the dwelling-house, or as the case may be that part of the dwelling-house, to be conveyed either to himself or to such other person as he may direct.

(2) The right so conferred is exercisable at any time during the term of the lease on the person referred to in sub-paragraph (1) (*a*) or (*b*) serving written notice on the landlord.

(3) As soon as practicable after such a right as is mentioned in sub-paragraph (1) has become exercisable by any person, the landlord shall serve on him a written notice—

(*a*) informing him of the right, and

(*b*) stating the provisions which, in the opinion of the landlord, should be contained in the conveyance

(4) A conveyance executed in pursuance of such a right—

(*a*) shall conform with Parts I and II of Schedule 6 (terms of conveyance in pursuance of right to buy), and

(*b*) where the lease contains any such covenant as is mentioned in section 157 (restriction on disposal of dwelling-houses in National Parks, etc.), shall preserve the effect of that covenant;

and Part IV of Schedule 6 (charges) applies to such a conveyance as it applies to a conveyance of the freehold in pursuance of the right to buy.

(5) A notice required by this paragraph may be withdrawn at any time by notice in writing served on the landlord.

No disposals of part while share outstanding

9.—(1) The lease shall contain a covenant binding on the tenant and his successors in title that there will be no relevant disposal of part of the dwelling-house, other than a compulsory disposal, at any time when the tenant's total share is less than 100 per cent.

(2) A disposal in breach of the covenant required by sub-paragraph (1) is void.

Applications of provisions after disposal

10.—(1) The lease shall provide that in the event of a relevant disposal which is an exempted disposal by virtue of—

section 160(1) (*a*) (a disposal of whole dwelling-house to member of family),

section 160(1) (*b*) (vesting on death of tenant), or

section 160(1) (*c*) (matrimonial property adjustment or family provision order),

references to the tenant in the provisions of the lease required by this Schedule or by section 155 (repayment of discount on early disposal) shall include references to the person to whom the disposal is made.

(2) The lease shall also provide that, in the event of a compulsory disposal of a part of the dwelling-house, references in those provisions to the dwelling-house shall be construed as references to the remaining part of the dwelling-house.

Value of dwelling-house or part

11.—(1) For the purposes of paragraph 3 (additional contributions) and paragraph 6 (payment for outstanding share on disposal) the value of the dwelling-house, or a part of the dwelling-house, at any time is the amount agreed between the parties or determined by the district valuer as the amount which, in accordance with this paragraph, is to be taken as its value at that time.

(2) That value shall be taken to be the price which the interest of the tenant in the dwelling-house or part would realise if sold on the open market by a willing vendor—

(*a*) on the assumption that the liabilities mentioned in sub-paragraph (3) would be discharged by the vendor, and

(*b*) disregarding the matters specified in sub-paragraph (4).

(3) The liabilities referred to in sub-paragraph (2) (*a*) are—

(*a*) any mortgages of the tenant's interest,

(*b*) any liability under the covenant required by paragraph 6 (payment for outstanding share on disposal), and

(*c*) any liability under the covenant required by section 155 (repayment of discount on early disposal).

(4) The matters to be disregarded in pursuance of sub-paragraph (2) (*b*) are any interests or rights over the dwelling-house created by the tenant, any improvements made by the tenant or any of the persons mentioned in section 127(4) (certain predecessors as secure tenant) and any failure by the tenant or any of those persons—

(*a*) where the dwelling-house is a house, to keep the dwelling-house in good repair (including decorative repair);

(*b*) where the dwelling-house is a flat, to keep the interior of the dwelling-house in such repair.

GENERAL NOTE

This Schedule governs the terms of a shared ownership lease, *cf.* ss.143 *et seq.*, above, designed to secure that shared owners are in no worse, but also no better, position than those exercising full right to buy.

Para. 1

The shared ownership lease is to contain a provision enabling the tenant to acquire further shares—in tranches of the prescribed percentage or a multiple thereof. The right is to be exercisable on written notice, stating how much more of the equity the tenant wants (his "additional share"). The landlord is to respond with a notice stating consideration due, and how much discount has been allowed for in that calculation.

Para. 2

The lease is also to contain a provision entitling conveyance to a tenant who has acquired 100 per cent. of the equity of the freehold of a house of which the landlord owns the freehold. This right is exercisable at any time, also by service of notice. The conveyance may be to the tenant, or to a person nominated by the tenant.

Para. 3

The price for additional shares is calculated on the same basis as the initial share, *save* that the valuation of the property is as at the date when the notice seeking an additional share is served. The tenant thus buys subsequent tranches at later valuations, which will normally mean at a higher price. Discount entitlement also continues, however, to the date of the notice seeking the subsequent slice. This is at the full rate, rather than "further discounted" to reflect the fact that occupation since the initial grant has been as shared owner. That is to say, the tenant continues to acquire a full discount for each year of occupation, even though he is occupying "half" (for example) as owner. The discount is, though, only a percentage, and of course is now to be applied to a share that will be at most 50 per cent.

Para. 4

Rent is to be the appropriate proportion of what would otherwise be a "normal" secure tenant's rent. The purpose of this sub-para. (2) is clearly to prevent penally high rents being set in respect of properties subject to an exercise of the right to a shared ownership lease, given authorities' broad discretion to determine their rent levels—see notes to s.24, above. Sub-para. (2) does not *prohibit* the use of rent differentials where shared ownership leases are involved, but it does *require* consideration of other rent levels, and this, in effect, places a burden on authorities to show that their decision to use the rent-differential discretion has been properly reached.

The "rent base" is to exclude rates (including water rates) and services, which will of course be charged separately under the lease. But the Secretary of State may prescribe appropriate adjustments to reflect differing responsibilities as between shared owners and secure tenants. See the Housing (Right to a Shared Ownership Lease) (Repairs Etc. Adjustment) Order 1984 (S.I. 1984 No. 1280), retained in force by Housing (Consequential Provisions) Act 1985, s.2.

Para. 5

Once the tenant acquires 100 per cent. of the equity, the rent is to become £10 per annum, as with a conventional lease under the right to buy (see Sched. 6, para 11, above).

Paras. 6 to 8

Both on the acquisition of an initial share, and on the acquisition of additional shares, the landlord's notice stating the contribution has to identify the "effective discount" to which the tenant was entitled. These paras. provide for repayment of the discount on early disposal, in line with the provisions governing a full exercise.

The requirement lasts for five years from the initial acquisition, *or* from the acquisition of additional shares. 20 per cent. is deducted from (a) the initial effective discount, for each year of occupation following the initial acquisition, and (b) subsequent effective discounts, for each year of occupation following each subsequent acquisition.

Once discount has been repaid, the right to conveyance of the freehold arises.

Paras. 9, 10

These provisions serve to prohibit disposals other than exempt disposals—*i.e.* those on which discount is repayable—unless or until the tenant has acquired a 100 per cent. share.

Para. 11

This "adapts" the normal assumptions for calculation of value of a lease to the particular circumstance of the "shared owner" seeking a further tranche of the equity, *i.e.* a circumstance which is neither wholly future (as on a normal grant of a lease) nor wholly past (as under, *e.g.*, an option to purchase a superior interest). The amount payable will not be affected, *i.e.* reduced, either by a mortgage, or by rights over or interests in the property which have been created by the shared owner.

Section 151   SCHEDULE 9

RIGHT TO FURTHER ADVANCES

Right to further advances

1.—(1) The deed shall enable the tenant to require further sums to be advanced to him in the circumstances and subject to the limits stated in this Schedule.

(2) The right so conferred is exercisable, within three months of the tenant claiming to exercise his right to acquire an additional share, on the tenant serving written notice on the landlord or Housing Corporation.

(3) Such a notice may be withdrawn at any time by notice in writing served on the landlord or Housing Corporation.

Amount of further advance

2. The amount which a tenant exercising the right to a further advance is entitled to have advanced to him is, subject to the limit imposed by paragraph 3, the amount of his additional contribution.

3.—(1) The limit is that the aggregate of that amount and the amount for the time being secured by the mortgage shall not exceed—

(a) where the right to a further advance belongs to one person, the amount to be taken into account, in accordance with regulations under paragraph 4, as his available annual income multiplied by such factor as, under the regulations, is appropriate to it;

(b) where the right to a further advance belongs to more than one person, the aggregate of the amounts to be taken into account in accordance with the regulations as the available annual income of each of them, after multiplying each of those amounts by the factor appropriate to it under the regulations.

(2) Where the amount which a tenant is entitled to have advanced to him is reduced by the limit imposed by this paragraph, the landlord may, if it thinks fit and the tenant agrees, treat him as entitled to have advanced to him such amount exceeding that limit, but not exceeding the amount of his additional contribution, as the landlord may determine.

4.—(1) The Secretary of State may by regulations make provision for calculating the amount which is to be taken into account as a person's available annual income and for specifying a factor appropriate to it.

(2) The regulations may—

(*a*) provide for arriving at a person's available annual income by deducting from the sums taken into account as his annual income sums related to his needs and commitments, and may exclude sums from those to be taken into account as a person's annual income, and

(*b*) specify different amounts and different factors for different circumstances.

(3) Regulations under this paragraph—

(*a*) may make different provision with respect to different cases or descriptions of case, including different provision for different areas, and

(*b*) shall be made by statutory instrument which shall be subject to annulment in pursuance of a resolution of either House of Parliament.

Notice of amount and terms of further advance

5. As soon as practicable after the service on it of a notice required by paragraph 1, the landlord or Housing Corporation shall serve on the tenant a written notice stating—

(*a*) the amount which, in the opinion of the landlord or Housing Corporation, the tenant is entitled to have advanced to him on the assumption that the additional share is as stated in the tenant's notice under paragraph 1 of Schedule 8 (claim to exercise right to acquire additional shares),

(*b*) if greater than that amount, the amount which, in the opinion of the landlord or Housing Corporation, the tenant would be entitled to have advanced to him if the additional share were such that his total share would be 100 per cent.,

(*c*) how that amount, or those amounts, have been arrived at, and

(*d*) the provisions which, in the opinion of the landlord or Housing Corporation, should be contained in the deed by which the further mortgage is effected.

Terms of deed by which further mortgage is effected

6. Schedule 7 (terms of mortgage granted in pursuance of right to a mortgage) applies to the deed by which the further mortgage is effected, but with the substitution for any reference to the term of the lease of a reference to the unexpired term of the lease.

GENERAL NOTE

This Schedule contains the adaptations to shared ownership of the right to a mortgage, in relation to further advances.

Unless otherwise agreed by the parties, the mortgage deed is to contain provision enabling the tenant to obtain further advances, on three months' notice. The purpose is to fund the purchase of further tranches of equity. The price applicable to such further tranches is recalculated on notice of wish to make a further purchase: see Sched. 8, above.

The tenant is entitled to further advances equal to the full amount of the additional amount payable for the further tranche of equity, subject to the total amount thus secured not exceeding the tenant's "personal limit": *i.e.* the amount available having regard to income, in accordance with regulations to be made under para. 4. See the Housing (Right to a Shared Ownership Lease) (Further Advances Limit) Regulations 1985, S.I. 1985 No. 758, retained in force by Housing (Consequential Provisions) Act 1985, s.2.

Sections 193, 220 and 375   SCHEDULE 10

RECOVERY OF EXPENSES INCURRED BY LOCAL HOUSING AUTHORITY

Introductory

1. The provisions of this Schedule have effect for enabling the local authority to recover expenses reasonably incurred by them in carrying out, in default of the person on whom the notice was served, works required to be carried out by a notice under—

section 189 or 190 (repair notices),

section 214 or 215 (improvement notices), or

section 352, 366 or 372 (notices relating to houses in multiple occupation).

Recovery of expenses

2.—(1) The expenses are recoverable by the authority from the person on whom the notice was served.

(2) Where the person on whom the notice was served—

(*a*) in the case of a notice under section 189 or 190 (repair notices), receives the rent of the premises as agent or trustee for some other person, or

(*b*) in the case of a notice under section 352, 366 or 372 (notices relating to houses in multiple occupation), was only properly served with that notice as being an agent or trustee for some other person,

the expenses are also recoverable by the authority from that other person, or partly from him and partly from the person on whom the notice was served.

(3) Where the person on whom the notice was served proves—

(*a*) that sub-paragraph (2) applies, and

(*b*) that he has not, and since the date of the service on him of the demand has not had, in his hands on behalf of that other person sufficient money to discharge the whole demand of the authority,

his liability is limited to the total amount of the money which he has, or has had, in his hands as mentioned in paragraph (*b*).

(4) Expenses are not recoverable under this paragraph to the extent that they are by any direction of the court on appeal recoverable under an order of the court.

Service of demand

3.—(1) A demand for the expenses, together with interest in accordance with paragraph 4, shall be served on the person from whom the authority seek to recover them.

(2) On the date on which the demand is served, the authority shall serve a copy of it on every other person who, to the knowledge of the authority, is an owner, lessee or mortgagee of the premises.

(3) The demand becomes operative, if no appeal is brought, on the expiry of 21 days from the date of service of the demand and is final and conclusive as to matters which could have been raised on an appeal.

Interest

4. Expenses in respect of which a demand is served carry interest, at such reasonable rate as the authority may determine, from the date of service until payment of all sums due under the demand.

Order for payment by instalments

5.—(1) The authority may by order declare the expenses to be payable by weekly or other instalments within a period not exceeding 30 years, with interest at such reasonable rate as the authority may determine until the whole amount is paid.

(2) The order becomes operative, if no appeal is brought, on the expiry of 21 days from the date of service of the order and is final and conclusive as to matters which could have been raised on an appeal.

(3) The instalments and interest, or any part of them, may be recovered from any owner or occupier of the house and if recovered from an occupier may be deducted by him from the rent of the house.

Appeals

6.—(1) A person aggrieved by a demand for the recovery of expenses or by an order of the local housing authority with respect to such expenses, may within 21 days of the service of the demand or copy, or of the order appeal to the county court.

(2) On an appeal the court may make such order either confirming, quashing or varying the demand or order as it thinks fit.

(3) A demand or order against which an appeal is brought becomes operative, so far as it is confirmed on appeal, on the final determination of the appeal; and the withdrawal of an appeal has for this purpose the same effect as a decision dismissing the appeal.

(4) No question may be raised on appeal under this paragraph which might have been raised on an appeal against the relevant notice.

Expenses and interest to be a charge on the premises

7.—(1) The expenses recoverable by the authority, together with the interest accrued due, are, until recovered, a charge on the premises to which the notice related.

(2) The charge takes effect when the demand for the expenses and interest becomes operative.

(3) The authority have for the purpose of enforcing the charge the same powers and remedies, under the Law of Property Act 1925 and otherwise, as if they were mortgagees by deed having powers of sale and lease, of accepting surrenders of leases and of appointing a receiver.

(4) The power of appointing a receiver is exercisable at any time after the expiration of one month from the date when the charge takes effect.

Recovery of expenses and interest from other persons profiting from execution of works

8.—(1) This paragraph applies only to notices under section 352, 366 or 372 (notices relating to houses in multiple occupation).

(2) If the authority apply to the county court and satisfy the court that—

(*a*) the expenses and interest have not been and are unlikely to be recovered, and

(*b*) some person is profiting by the execution of the works in respect of which the expenses were incurred to obtain rents or other payments which would not have been obtainable if the number of persons living in the premises was limited to that appropriate for the premises in their state before the works were executed,

the court may, if satisfied that that person has had proper notice of the application, order him to make such payments to the authority as may appear to the court to be just.

GENERAL NOTE

This Schedule governs the recovery of the cost of works in default, and is applicable under a number of sections.

Para. 2

Expenses are prima facie recoverable from the person served with the appropriate notice. However, they are *also* recoverable from a person on behalf of whom the person served was acting as agent or trustee. If the person served was acting as agent or trustee, his own liability is limited to the monies he has had in his hands since the service of the demand for the expenses.

Para. 3

The demand itself is served on the person from whom the money is sought. Under para. 4, it will be recoverable with interest, at the reasonable rate determined by the authority, from date of service until payment. When the demand is served, a copy is also to be served on anyone else whom the authority know to be an owner, lessee or mortgagee of the premises. Unless the demand is appealed under para. 6 of the Schedule, it will become operative 21 days from date of service, and is "final and conclusive" as to matters which could have been raised on an appeal.

As to final and conclusive, see notes to s.189(4), above. If no appeal is brought, the person served cannot subsequently allege that the demand is inaccurate or excessive: *Benabo* v. *Wood Green Borough Council* [1946] K.B. 38. The demand must, however, be a valid demand. If the demand is invalid, the person served can ignore it, and raise the invalidity in any subsequent proceedings for its recovery: *West Ham Corporation* v. *Benabo* [1934] 2 K.B. 253. See also *Pollway Nominees Ltd.* v. *London Borough of Croydon* (1985) 17 H.L.R. 503, C.A., and *Graddage* v. *London Borough of Haringey* [1975] 1 W.L.R. 241, Ch.D.

Para. 4

Similarly, the authority's right to interest does not end with (or merge in) judgment for the money, *i.e.* it continues so long as the money is unpaid: *Ealing London Borough Council* v. *El Isaacs* [1980] 1 W.L.R. 932, C.A.

Para. 5

The authority can by order declare the amount to be payable by weekly or other periodic instalments over a maximum 30-year period, together with interest. An instalment order becomes operative 21 days after service, unless an appeal is brought under para. 6, and is, again, final and conclusive as to matters which could have been raised on an appeal: see notes to s.189(4), above. If an attempt is made to recover by action, which does not result in payment, the authority's right to make an instalment order has not been lost, or "merged" in the judgment: see *Salford Corporation* v. *Hale* [1925] 1 K.B. 253.

Para. 6

Appeal must be brought within 21 days. This does not include the day of service: *Goldsmith's Co.* v. *West Metropolitan Railway Co.* [1904] 1 K.B. 1, C.A.; *Stewart* v.

Chapman [1951] K.B. 792. Although the county court has a general power to enlarge time (C.C.R., Ord. 13, r.4), it has been suggested that the general power cannot be used to override the statutory time limit: see *Honig* v. *Lewisham Borough Council* (1958) 122 J.P.J. 302. But *cf. Arieli* v. *Duke of Westminster* (1983) 269 E.G. 535, C.A., and *Johnston* v. *Duke of Westminster* (1984) 17 H.L.R. 136, C.A., under the Leasehold Reform Act 1967 and the Housing Act 1974, Sched. 8.

Formerly, appeal had to be brought to the county court with jurisdiction over the area where the premises are situated: Housing Act 1957, s.11. Pursuant to Law Commission Recommendations (Cmnd. 9515), No. 9(ii), appeal lies now simply "to the county court," which means, under the County Court Rules (S.I. 1981 No. 1687), Order 4, rule 9, the court for the district in which the decision appealed against was made.

The demand or order does not become operative if an appeal is brought within the 21 days allowed, until the confirmation of the demand or order on final determination of the appeal. Note that a question which could have been raised on an appeal against the notice itself cannot be raised on an appeal against a demand for the expenses. However, as objection to carrying out works in default cannot be raised on an appeal against the notice, it can be raised on an appeal against the demand: *Elliott* v. *Brighton Borough Council* (1980) 258 E.G. 441, C.A.

Para. 7

The expenses and interest are a charge on the property, giving the authority the powers and remedies of a mortgagee, including the power to appoint a receiver from one month after the charge takes effect, which is when the demand becomes operative.

Para. 8

This paragraph is particular to H.M.O.s and permits the authority to apply to the court for an order that someone other than the person served, who is profiting by the works because the works have permitted a larger number of people to live in the property, should make payments to the authority. That person must be given notice of the application, and the power can only be used if the expenses and interest have not been and are not likely to be recovered.

Section 299   SCHEDULE 11

Rehabilitation Orders

Part I

The Making of the Order and its Effect

Introductory

1.—(1) This Schedule applies to a house comprised in a clearance area which—
(a) was purchased under section 290 (acquisition of land for clearance), by agreement or compulsorily, before 2nd December 1974, or
(b) is subject to a compulsory purchase order made under that section before that date and confirmed before 2nd March 1975

(2) In the case of a clearance area comprising houses within sub-paragraph (1) (a) or (b), this Schedule also applies to houses included in it by virtue of section 293 (local housing authority's own property).

(3) In this Schedule "land liable to be cleared", in relation to a clearance area, means—
(a) land in the clearance area,
(b) land surrounded by or adjoining the clearance area for whose purchase a resolution under section 290(2) has been passed (whether or not it has been so purchased), and
(c) land to which the provisions of this Part relating to clearance areas apply by virtue of section 293 (local housing authority's own property),
but does not include land subject to a clearance order made and confirmed under section 44 of the Housing Act 1957 before the repeal of that provision on 9th October 1979.

Power to make rehabilitation order

2.—(1) Where a house to which this Schedule applies—
(a) was included in the clearance area by reason of its being unfit for human habitation, and

(*b*) in the opinion of the local housing authority is capable of being, and ought to be, improved to the full standard,

the authority may make and submit to the Secretary of State a rehabilitation order in relation to the house.

(2) In addition to applying to such a house, the order may, if the authority think fit, be made to apply to other land liable to be cleared.

(3) Where the owner of a house to which this Schedule applies and which was included in the clearance area by reason of its being unfit for human habitation requests the local housing authority to make a rehabilitation order in respect of the house and they refuse to do so, they shall give him in writing the reasons for their refusal.

Clearance procedure suspended on making of order

3.—(1) Where the local housing authority have made a rehabilitation order they shall not—

(*a*) serve notice to treat under section 5 of the Compulsory Purchase Act 1965 in respect of land included in a compulsory purchase order made and confirmed by virtue of section 290 which includes land in relation to which a notice is required to be served under paragraph 10 below (notice of intention to submit order for confirmation), or

(*b*) demolish, without the consent of the Secretary of State, any building on land in relation to which such a notice is required to be served,

until after the date on which the notice becomes operative or, as the case may be, on which confirmation of the order is refused.

(2) No account shall be taken for the purposes of section 4 of the Compulsory Purchase Act 1965 (time limit for completing compulsory purchase) of any period during which an authority are prevented by sub-paragraph (1) from serving a notice to treat under section 5 of that Act.

Principal effects of rehabilitation order

4.—(1) On the date on which a rehabilitation order becomes operative, the local housing authority cease to be subject to any duty under this Part to demolish or secure the demolition of buildings on the land.

(2) The authority shall then take such steps as are necessary—

(*a*) to restore the house so as to provide one or more dwellings to the full standard, or

(*b*) where the house is not vested in the authority, to ensure that the house is restored with that object.

(3) The authority may accept undertakings for the purposes of sub-paragraph (2) (*b*) from the owner of the house, or any other person who has or will have an interest in it, concerning the works to be carried out to restore the house and the time within which the works are to be carried out.

Other effects of rehabilitation order

5.—(1) This paragraph applies where a rehabilitation order becomes operative in respect of land included in a compulsory purchase order made and confirmed by virtue of section 290 (acquisition of land for clearance).

(2) If at the date on which the rehabilitation order becomes operative—

(*a*) no interest in the land has vested in the local housing authority, and

(*b*) they have not served a notice to treat under section 5 of the Compulsory Purchase Act 1965 in respect of any interest in the land,

the compulsory purchase order ceases to have effect in relation to the land and if the land is included in a clearance area it ceases to be so included.

(3) Where sub-paragraph (1) does not apply the compulsory purchase order has effect in relation to any interest in the land which has not vested in the authority at the date on which the rehabilitation order becomes operative—

(*a*) in so far as it relates to a house, as if made and confirmed under Part II (provision of housing), and

(*b*) in so far as it relates to land other than a house, as if made and confirmed under Part VI of the Town and Country Planning Act 1971 (planning purposes).

6. Where a rehabilitation order becomes operative in respect of land and an interest in the land comprised in the order is vested in the local housing authority, the interest shall be treated—

(*a*) in the case of an interest in a house, as appropriated to the purposes of Part II (provision of housing), and (*b*) in the case of any other interest, as appropriated to the purposes of Part VI of the Town and Country Planning Act 1971.

7.—(1) A rehabilitation order may be made and confirmed notwithstanding that the effect of the order in excluding land from a clearance area is to sever the area into two or more separate and distinct areas.

(2) In such a case the provisions of this Act relating to the effect of a compulsory purchase order when confirmed, and to the proceedings to be taken after confirmation of such an order, apply as if those areas formed one clearance area.

8. Where a rehabilitation order becomes operative in respect of land and its effect is to exclude from the clearance area land adjoining a general improvement area, the land shall be included in the general improvement area unless the Secretary of State otherwise directs.

PART II

PROCEDURAL MATTERS

The form of the order

9. A rehabilitation order shall be made in the prescribed form and shall describe, by reference to a map—
  (*a*) the houses to which it applies and which were included in the clearance area by reason of their being unfit for human habitation,
  (*b*) any other land to which it applies, and
  (*c*) any land not within paragraph (*a*) or (*b*) in respect of which notice is required to be served under paragraph 10.

Notices to be given

10.—(1) Before submitting a rehabilitation order to the Secretary of State the local housing authority shall, except so far as the Secretary of State directs otherwise, comply with the following provisions.

(2) They shall publish in one or more newspapers circulating in their district a notice in the prescribed form—
  (*a*) stating that the rehabilitation order has been made,
  (*b*) describing the land to which it applies, and
  (*c*) naming a place where a copy of the order and its accompanying map may be seen at all reasonable hours.

(3) They shall serve on every person mentioned in sub-paragraph (4) a notice in the prescribed form stating—
  (*a*) the effect of the rehabilitation order,
  (*b*) that it is about to be submitted to the Secretary of State for confirmation, and
  (*c*) the time within which and the manner in which objections to the order can be made.

(4) The persons to whom notice must be given are—
  (*a*) every person on whom notice was served of the making under this Part of a compulsory purchase order which at the date of its confirmation included land subsequently comprised in the rehabilitation order;
  (*b*) every successor in title of such a person;
  (*c*) every owner, lessee and occupier of land liable to be cleared, other than a tenant for a month or a period less than a month;
  (*d*) mortgagees of such land, so far as it is reasonably practicable to ascertain them; and
  (*e*) every person on whom notice would have been required to be served under paragraph (*c*) or (*d*) but whose interest has been acquired under section 290 (acquisition of land for clearance) since the clearance area was declared.

(5) A notice under this paragraph shall be accompanied by a statement of the grounds on which the authority are seeking confirmation of the order.

Confirmation of the order

11.—(1) If no objection is duly made by any of the persons on whom notices are required to be served under paragraph 10, or if all objections so made are withdrawn, the Secretary of State may confirm the order with or without modifications.

(2) If an objection duly made is not withdrawn, the Secretary of State shall, before confirming the order, either—
  (*a*) cause a public local inquiry to be held, or
  (*b*) afford to every person by whom an objection has been duly made and not withdrawn

an opportunity of appearing before and being heard by a person appointed by the Secretary of State for the purpose.

(3) After considering any objection not withdrawn and the report of the person who held the inquiry or was appointed under sub-paragraph (2), the Secretary of State may confirm the order with or without modifications.

(4) The Secretary of State may require a person who has made an objection to state the grounds of the objection in writing, and may disregard the objection if he is satisfied that it relates exclusively to matters which can be dealt with by the tribunal by whom any compensation is to be assessed.

(5) The Secretary of State's power to modify a rehabilitation order includes power, subject to sub-paragraph (6), to extend it to any land liable to be cleared.

(6) The Secretary of State shall not extend the application of a rehabilitation order to any land unless he has served on the following persons—

(*a*) the authority who make the order,

(*b*) every owner, lessee and occupier of the land, except a tenant for a month or a period less than a month, and

(*c*) every mortgagee of any of the land whom it is reasonably practicable to ascertain, a notice stating the effect of his proposals, and has afforded them an opportunity to make their views known.

Notice of confirmation of the order

12.—(1) So soon as may be after the order has been confirmed by the Secretary of State, the local housing authority shall comply with the following provisions.

(2) They shall publish in a newspaper circulating in their district a notice in the prescribed form—

(*a*) stating that the order has been confirmed, and

(*b*) naming a place where a copy of the order as confirmed and of the map referred to in the order may be seen at all reasonable hours.

(3) They shall serve a like notice on—

(*a*) every person who, having given notice to the Secretary of State of his objection to the order, appeared at the public local inquiry or before the appointed person in support of his objection, and

(*b*) every person on whom the Secretary of State served notice under paragraph 11(6) (notice of proposal to confirm order with modification extending its operation).

Challenge to validity of order

13.—(1) If a person aggrieved by the order desires to question its validity on the ground—

(*a*) that it is not within the powers of this Act, or

(*b*) that any requirement of this Act has not been complied with,

he may within six weeks after publication of the notice of confirmation make an application for the purpose to the High Court.

(2) Where such an application is duly made, the court may by interim order suspend the operation of the order, either generally or in so far as it affects property of the applicant, until the final determination of the proceedings.

(3) If on the hearing of the application the court is satisfied—

(*a*) that the order is not within the powers of this Act, or

(*b*) that the interests of the applicant have been substantially prejudiced by any requirement of this Act not having been complied with,

the court may quash the order, either generally or in so far as it affects property of the applicant.

(4) No appeal lies to the House of Lords from a decision of the Court of Appeal in proceedings under this paragraph except by leave of the Court of Appeal.

(5) Subject to the provisions of this paragraph, the order shall not be questioned in any legal proceedings whatsoever, either before or after the order is confirmed.

Notice of order having become operative

14.—(1) The order becomes operative (subject to any order under paragraph 13) at the expiration of six weeks from the date on which notice of confirmation of the order is published in accordance with paragraph 12.

(2) So soon as may be after the order has become operative the local housing authority shall serve a copy of the notice on every person on whom a notice was served by them of their intention to submit the order to the Secretary of State for confirmation.

Section 313   SCHEDULE 12

SLUM CLEARANCE SUBSIDY REGULATIONS

Introductory

1. This Schedule has effect with respect to the provision which may be made by regulations under section 313 prescribing the method of determining whether a local authority have incurred a loss in connection with the exercise of their slum clearance functions and the amount of the loss.

Treatment of expenditure or receipts of a capital nature

2.—(1) The regulations may require expenditure or receipts to be treated, or not to be treated, as of a capital nature.

(2) The regulations may, in the case of an item of a capital nature, determine the method of arriving at the appropriate equivalent annual amounts to be taken into account, and their number, or may specify classes of case in which an item of a capital nature is to be taken into account for a single year.

(3) The number of equivalent annual amounts prescribed under sub-paragraph (2) shall not in any case exceed 60.

(4) The regulations may provide that, where the prescribed number of equivalent annual amounts in respect of an item exceeds 15, all equivalent annual amounts in respect of that item shall be left out of account from such year, not being less than 15 years after the year in which the item arises and not earlier than 1986–87, as may be specified in the regulations.

Approval of expenditure by Secretary of State

3. The regulations may provide that expenditure of any class or description shall not be taken into account unless, and except so far as, the Secretary of State has approved the expenditure.

Avoidance of double payment of subsidy, &c.

4. The regulations may, in order to prevent subsidy or other payments out of money provided by Parliament being made in respect of the same loss or expenditure, or in respect of the same land, both under section 312 (slum clearance subsidy) and under—

    (*a*) section 7 of the Local Government Act 1966 or section 250 of the Town and Country Planning Act 1971 (grants for development and re-development), or

    (*b*) any other enactment, including any other provision of this Act,

provide for the exclusion of any item of expenditure or the making of any other adjustment.

Expenditure of receipts in connection with land acquired before 1st April 1965

5. The regulations shall not take into account expenditure or receipts (whether capital or not, and whether incurred or due before 1st April 1971 or later) in connection with land acquired by the authority before 1st April 1965.

Expenditure or receipts incurred or due before 1st April 1971

6.—(1) Except as mentioned in sub-paragraph (2), the regulations shall not take into account expenditure or receipts incurred or due before 1st April 1971.

(2) Where in the period of six years beginning on 1st April 1965 and ending on 31st March 1971 the authority have acquired land for the purposes of their slum clearance functions and continue to hold that land for those purposes until the end of that period, the regulations may take into account the equivalent annual amounts in respect of capital expenditure incurred, or capital receipts becoming due, in that period in connection with that land.

Miscellaneous

7. The regulations may—

    (*a*) make different provision for different classes of authorities, or special provision for particular authorities;

(*b*) contain such transitional and other supplementary or incidental provisions as appear to the Secretary of State to be necessary or expedient.

8. Nothing in paragraphs 3, 4 or 7 of this Schedule prejudices the generality of the regulation-making power conferred by section 313.

GENERAL NOTE

See the Slum Clearance Subsidy Regulations 1974, S.I. 1974 No. 618, qualified as to by whom certain valuations may be carried out by S.I. 1984 No. 244, both retained in force by Housing (Consequential Provisions) Act 1985, s.2.

Sections 384, 386,
389, 393 and 394   SCHEDULE 13

FURTHER PROVISIONS RELATING TO CONTROL ORDERS UNDER PART XI

PART I

MANAGEMENT SCHEMES

Contents of management scheme

1.—(1) The scheme shall give particulars of all works which, in the opinion of the local housing authority, they would, if a control order were not in force, have required to be carried out under any provision of this Part, or under any other enactment relating to housing or public health, and which, in their opinion, constitute works of capital expenditure.

(2) The scheme shall include an estimate of the costs of carrying out the works of which particulars are given in the scheme.

(3) The scheme shall specify what, in the opinion of the authority, is the highest number of individuals or households who should live in the house from time to time, having regard to—

(*a*) the considerations set out in section 352(1) matters relevant to fitness of house for number of occupants), and

(*b*) the existing condition of the house and its future condition as the works progress which the authority carry out in the house.

(4) The scheme shall include an estimate of the balance which will from time to time accrue to the authority after deducting from the rent or other payments received by the authority from persons occupying the house—

(*a*) the compensation payable by the authority to the dispossessed proprietor under section 389 and Part II of this Schedule, and

(*b*) all expenditure, other than that of which particulars are given under sub-paragraph (2), incurred by the authority in respect of the house while the control order is in force.

The estimate in the scheme of surpluses on revenue account

2.—(1) References in this Schedule to the surpluses on revenue account as settled by the scheme are to the amount included in the scheme by way of an estimate under paragraph 1(4), subject to any variation of the scheme made by the local housing authority or on an appeal or application to the court.

(2) In paragraph 1(4), and elsewhere in this Schedule, "rent or other payments", in relation to payments received by the local housing authority from persons occupying a house subject to a control order, means rent or other payments so received—

(*a*) under leases or licences, or

(*b*) in respect of furniture to which section 383(1) applies (furniture comprised in furnished letting of which right to possession vests in authority).

(3) In paragraph 1(4), and elsewhere in this Schedule, references to expenditure incurred by the local housing authority in respect of a house subject to a control order include, in a case where the authority—

(*a*) require persons living in the house to vacate their accommodation for a period while the authority are carrying out works in the house, and

(*b*) provide housing accommodation for those persons for any part of that period or defray all or any part of the expenses incurred by or on behalf of those persons removing from and returning to the house,

the net cost to the authority in so providing housing accommodation and the sums so defrayed by the authority.

Appeal against scheme

3.—(1) A person having an estate or interest in a house to which a control order relates may, within six weeks from the date on which a management scheme relating to the house was served in accordance with section 386, or such longer period as the local housing authority may in writing allow, appeal to the county court against the scheme.

(2) The appeal may be on any of the following grounds—

(a) that, having regard to the condition of the house and to the other circumstances, any of the works of which particulars are given in the scheme (whether already carried out or not) are unreasonable in character or extent, or are unnecessary;

(b) that any of the works do not involve expenditure which ought to be regarded as capital expenditure;

(c) that the number of individuals or households living in the house, as specified by the local housing authority in the scheme, is unreasonably low;

(d) that the estimate of the surpluses on revenue account in the scheme is unduly low on account of assumptions made by the authority as to matters within their control (for example, as to the rents charged by them).

(3) On an appeal the court may, as it thinks fit, confirm or vary the scheme.

(4) Proceedings on an appeal against a scheme shall, so far as practicable, be combined with proceedings on any appeal under section 384 against the control order itself; and if on such an appeal the court decides to revoke the control order, the court shall not proceed with any appeal against the scheme.

Expenditure on works to be set against surpluses on revenue account

4.—(1) An account shall be kept by the local housing authority for the period during which the control order is in force showing—

(a) the surpluses on revenue account as settled by the scheme, and

(b) the expenditure incurred by the authority in carrying out works of which particulars were given in the scheme;

and balances shall be struck in the account at half-yearly intervals so as to ascertain the amount of that expenditure which cannot be set off against those surpluses.

(2) So far as, at the end of a half-yearly period, the expenditure is not so set off, it shall carry interest, at such reasonable rate as the authority may determine, until it is so set off or until the charge arising under paragraph 16 of this Schedule (recovery of expenditure when control order ceases to have effect) is satisfied.

(3) So far as there is a sum out of the surpluses on revenue account not required to meet expenditure incurred by the authority, it shall go to meet interest under sub-paragraph (2).

Variation or review of surpluses on revenue account as settled by the scheme

5. The local housing authority may at any time vary a scheme in such a way as to increase the amount of the surpluses on revenue account as settled by the scheme for all or any periods, including past periods.

6.—(1) The local housing authority, or a person having an estate or interest in the house, may at any time apply to the county court for a review of the surpluses on revenue account as settled by the scheme.

(2) On such an application the court shall take into consideration—

(a) whether in the period since the control order came into force the actual balances mentioned on paragraph 1(4) have exceeded, or been less than, the surpluses on revenue account as settled by the scheme, and

(b) whether there has been any change in circumstances such that the number of persons or households who should live in the house, or the amount of the rents and other payments receivable by the local housing authority from persons occupying the house, ought to be greater or less than was originally estimated.

(3) The court may on such an application, as it thinks fit, confirm or vary the scheme (but not so as to affect the provisions of the scheme relating to the works), and may vary the surpluses on revenue account as settled by the scheme for all or any period, including past periods.

PART II

COMPENSATION PAYABLE TO DISPOSSESSED PROPRIETOR

Rate of compensation

7. The compensation payable by the local housing authority to the dispossessed proprietor in pursuance of section 389(1)(*a*) shall be at an annual rate equal to one half of the gross value of the house multiplied by the appropriate multiplier.

Ascertainment of gross value of house

8. Subject to the following provisions, the gross value of a house for the purposes of this Part of this Schedule is its gross value for rating purposes as shown in the valuation list on the date when the control order comes into force.

9.—(1) If the house forms part only of a hereditament, the gross value of the house is such proportion of the gross value shown in the valuation list for that hereditament as may be agreed in writing between the local housing authority and the person claiming compensation.

(2) If any dispute arises under sub-paragraph (1), the authority or the person claiming compensation may by means of a reference in writing submit the dispute for decision by the district valuer.

10. If the house consists or forms part of more than one hereditament, the gross value shall be ascertained by determining the gross value of each hereditament or part as if it were a separate house and aggregating the gross values so determined.

11.—(1) The gross value of a hereditament whose rateable value is by virtue of subsection (1) of section 19 of the General Rate Act 1967 to be taken to be its net annual value ascertained in accordance with subsections (2) to (4) of that section shall be taken to be its corresponding gross value, that is to say, the gross value which would be equivalent to the net annual value shown in the valuation list if there were deducted any amounts which by virtue of an order made or falling to be treated as made under section 19(2) of the General Rate Act 1967 would be deducted from the gross value of the hereditament if it had been required to be assessed to its gross value instead of its net annual value.

(2) If more than one value is so ascertained to be the corresponding gross value, the highest value so ascertained shall be taken.

12. Where after the date on which the control order comes into force—

(*a*) the valuation list is altered so as to vary the gross value (or where paragraph 11 applies the net annual value) of the house or of the hereditament of which the house forms part, and

(*b*) the alteration has effect from a date before, or from the same date as, the control order came into force,

compensation is payable as if the value shown in the list on the date when the control order came into force had been that shown in the list as altered.

The appropriate multiplier

13.—(1) The appropriate multiplier for the purposes of this Part of this Schedule is that specified by order of the Secretary of State.

(2) An order under this paragraph shall be made by statutory instrument which shall be subject to annulment in pursuance of a resolution of either House of Parliament.

Apportionment of compensation between proprietors of different parts of house

14.—(1) If different persons are the dispossessed proprietors of different parts of the house, the compensation payable shall be apportioned between them according to the proportions of the gross value of the house properly attributable to the parts of the house in which they are respectively interested.

(2) If they do not agree on the apportionment they shall refer the matter, in writing, for determination by the district valuer.

PART III

CESSATION OF CONTROL ORDER

General consequences of cessation of control order

15.—(1) On and after the date on which a control order ceases to have effect—

(*a*) a lease, licence or agreement in which the local housing authority were substituted for another party by virtue of section 382 (effect of order on persons occupying house) has effect with the substitution of the original party, or his successor in title, for the authority,

(b) an agreement in the nature of a lease or licence created by the local housing authority has effect with the substitution of the dispossessed proprietor for the authority.

(2) If the dispossessed proprietor is a lessee, nothing in a superior lease imposes liability on him, or on a superior lessee, in respect of anything done in pursuance of the terms of an agreement in which the dispossessed proprietor is substituted for the local housing authority by virtue of this paragraph.

(3) This paragraph applies in all circumstances in which a control order ceases to have effect.

16.—(1) When a control order ceases to have effect, a final balance shall be struck in the account mentioned in paragraph 4(1) and the expenditure reasonably incurred by the local housing authority in carrying out works of which particulars were given in the management scheme, together with interest at such reasonable rate as the authority may determine is, so far as not set off against the surpluses on revenue account as settled by the scheme, a charge on the premises.

(2) The premises subject to the charge include any part of the premises excluded from the provisions of the order under section 380 (modification of order where proprietor resides in part of the house).

(3) The local housing authority have for the purposes of enforcing the charge all the same powers and remedies, under the Law of Property Act 1925 and otherwise, as if they were mortgagees by deed having powers of sale and lease, of accepting surrender of leases and of appointing a receiver.

(4) The power of appointing a receiver is exercisable at any time after the expiration of one month from the date when the charge takes effect.

(5) References in this paragraph to the provisions of the management scheme include reference to the provisions as varied; and if, when the control order ceases to have effect, proceedings are pending which may result in a variation of the scheme—

(a) those proceedings may be continued until finally determined, and

(b) if the charge under this paragraph is enforced before the final determination of those proceedings, the local housing authority shall account for any money recovered by enforcing the charge which, having regard to the decision in the proceedings as finally determined, they ought not to have recovered.

(6) This paragraph does not apply—

(a) where a control order is revoked by the county court on an appeal against the order, or

(b) where a control order ceases to have effect under Part IV of this Schedule (control order followed by compulsory purchase order),

but applies in every other case where a control order ceases to have effect (including the case where the order is revoked by a court on appeal from the county court).

Revocation of order by county court on appeal against making of order

17.—(1) The provisions of this paragraph apply where a control order is revoked by the county court on an appeal against the control order.

(2) The court shall take into consideration whether the state or condition of the house is such that action ought to be taken by the local housing authority under any other provision of this Part, and shall approve the taking of any of the following steps accordingly, that is—

(a) the serving of a notice under section 352, 366 or 372 (notices requiring the execution of works),

(b) the giving of a direction under section 354 (direction limiting number of occupants of house), or

(c) the making of an order under section 370 (order applying management code to house);

and no appeal lies against a notice or order so approved.

(3) If the local housing authority are in the course of carrying out works in the house which, if a control order were not in force, the authority would have power to require some other person to carry out under any provision of this Part or under any other enactment relating to housing or public health, and on the hearing of the appeal the court is satisfied that the carrying out of the works could not be postponed until after the determination of the appeal by the county court because the works were urgently required for the sake of the safety, welfare or health of persons living in the house, or of other persons, the court may suspend the revocation of the control order until the works have been completed.

(4) The county court shall fix the date on which the control order is to be revoked without regard to whether an appeal has been or may be brought against the decision of the county court; but that does not prevent the local housing authority from bringing such an appeal.

(5) The court may authorise the local housing authority to create under section 381(1)(c) (power to create interests akin to leases) interests which expire, or which the dispossessed proprietor can terminate, within six months from the time when the control order ceases to have effect, being interests which, notwithstanding section 381(2), are for a fixed term exceeding one month or are terminable by notice to quit (or an equivalent notice) of more than four weeks.

18.—(1) If a control order is revoked by the county court on an appeal against the order, the local housing authority shall pay to the dispossessed proprietor the balances which from time to time accrued to the authority after deducting from the rent or other payments received by the authority from persons occupying the house—

(a) the compensation payable by the authority to the dispossessed proprietor, and

(b) all expenditure (other than capital expenditure) incurred by the authority in respect of the house while the control order was in force.

(2) If the court is satisfied that the balances which the local housing authority are under sub-paragraph (1) liable to pay to the dispossessed proprietor are unduly low for any reason within the control of the authority, having regard to—

(a) the desirability of observing the standards of management contained in regulations made under section 369 (the management code), and

(b) the other standards which the authority ought to observe as to the number of persons living in the house and the rents which they ought to charge,

the court shall direct that, for the purposes of the authority's liability to the dispossessed proprietor under this paragraph, the balances under sub-paragraph (1) shall be deemed to be such greater sums as the court may direct.

(3) The court shall not under sub-paragraph (2) give a direction which will afford to the dispossessed proprietor a sum greater than what he may, in the opinion of the court, have lost by the making of the control order.

(4) If different persons are dispossessed proprietors of different parts of the house, sums payable under this paragraph by the local housing authority shall be apportioned between them in the manner provided by paragraph 14.

19.—(1) The provisions of this paragraph have effect for the purpose of enabling the local housing authority to recover capital expenditure incurred in carrying out works in the house in the period before the control order is revoked on an appeal against the order.

(2) On the hearing of the appeal the authority may apply to the court for the approval of those works on the ground that—

(a) they were works which, if a control order had not been in force, the authority could have required some person to carry out under any provision of this Part or under any other enactment relating to housing or public health, and

(b) the works could not be postponed until after the determination of the appeal by the county court because they were urgently required for the sake of the safety, welfare or health of persons living in the house, or other persons.

(3) Expenditure reasonably incurred by the authority in carrying out works so approved—

(a) may be deducted by the authority out of the balances which they are liable to pay to the dispossessed proprietor under paragraph 18, and

(b) so far as not so deducted, is a charge on the premises and on all estates and interests in the premises;

and the premises subject to the charge include any part of the premises which was excluded from the provisions of the order under section 380 (modification of order where proprietor resides in part of the house).

(4) The charge takes effect as from the date when the control order is revoked and the expenditure so charged carries interest from that date at such reasonable rate as the authority may determine.

(5) The local housing authority have for the purposes of enforcing the charge all the same powers and remedies, under the Law of Property Act 1925 and otherwise, as if they were mortgagees by deed having powers of sale and lease, of accepting surrenders of leases and of appointing a receiver.

(6) The power of appointing a receiver is exercisable at any time after the expiration of one month from the date when the charge takes effect.

Revocation of control order on further appeal

20.—(1) If on an appeal from a decision of the county court confirming a control order it is determined that the control order should be revoked, but the local housing authority satisfy the court hearing the appeal—

(*a*) that they are in the course of carrying out works in the house which, if a control order were not in force, they would have power to require some person to carry out under any provision of this Part of this Act or under any other enactment relating to housing or public health, and

(*b*) that the carrying out of the works could not be postponed until the time when the control order could no longer be revoked by order of any court on an appeal against the order because the works were urgently required for the sake of safety, welfare or health of persons living in the house, or other persons,

the court may suspend the revocation of the control order until the works have been completed.

(2) If on the hearing by the county court of an appeal against a control order the appellant indicates—

(*a*) that an appeal may be brought against any decision of the county court confirming the order, and

(*b*) that certain works ought not, unless the control order is confirmed on the further appeal, to be works the cost of which can be recovered by the local housing authority under paragraph 4 or 16,

the county court may direct that those works shall not be works of which the cost may be so recovered if they are begun before the time when the further appeal is finally determined and the control order is not confirmed on that appeal.

Revocation of control order by county court on appeal against refusal to revoke

21.—(1) The provisions of this paragraph apply where a control order is revoked by the county court on an appeal under section 393 (appeal against refusal of local housing authority to revoke order).

(2) If the local housing authority represent to the court that revocation of the control order would unreasonably delay completion of works of which particulars were given in the management scheme, and which the authority have begun to carry out, the court shall take the representations into account and may, if it thinks fit, revoke the control order as from the time when the works are completed.

(3) The court may make an order under which the revocation does not take effect until the time for appealing against the decision of the county court has expired and any appeal brought within that time has been finally determined.

(4) The court may approve the taking of any of the following steps, to take effect on the revocation of the control order, that is—

(*a*) the serving of a notice under section 352, 366 or 372 (notices requiring the execution of works),

(*b*) the giving of a direction under section 354 (direction limiting number of occupants of house), or

(*c*) the making of an order under section 370 (order applying management code to house);

and no appeal lies against a notice or order so approved.

(5) Where the house will on the revocation of the control order be charged with any sum in favour of the local housing authority by virtue of any provision of this Schedule, the court may make it a condition of the revocation of the order that the appellant first pays off to the authority that sum, or such part of that sum as the court may specify.

(6) The court may authorise the local housing authority to create under section 381(1)(*c*) (power to create interests akin to leases) interests which expire, or which the dispossessed proprietor can terminate, within six months from the time when the control order ceases to have effect, being interests which, notwithstanding section 381(2), are for a fixed term exceeding one month or are terminable by notice to quit (or an equivalent notice) of more than four weeks.

PART IV

CONTROL ORDER FOLLOWED BY COMPULSORY PURCHASE ORDER

Introductory

22. The provisions of this Part of this Schedule apply where the local housing authority make a control order with respect to a house and within 28 days of the making of that order

make a compulsory purchase order for the acquisition of the house under Part II of this Act (provision of housing accommodation).

Preparation and service of management scheme

23.—(1) The local housing authority need not prepare or serve a management scheme under section 386 until they are notified by the Secretary of State of his decision to confirm or not to confirm the compulsory purchase order.

(2) The time within which copies of the scheme are to be served under section 386 is—

(*a*) if the Secretary of State's decision is not to confirm the compulsory purchase order, eight weeks from the date on which that decision is notified to the authority;

(*b*) if the Secretary of State's decision is to confirm the compulsory purchase order, eight weeks from the time at which the compulsory purchase order becomes operative.

Control order ceases to have effect on acquisition of house

24. Where the compulsory purchase order is confirmed by the Secretary of State, the control order ceases to have effect—

(*a*) if the local housing authority enter into a contract to purchase the house, on the date when the contract is made;

(*b*) if the local housing authority, in pursuance of a notice served under section 11 of the Compulsory Purchase Act 1965, enter and take possession of the house or serve a notice under section 583 of this Act (power to take possession without displacing tenant), on the date when the notice under section 11 is served.

Balances payable to dispossessed proprietor

25.—(1) Where a control order ceases to have effect by virtue of paragraph 24, the local housing authority shall pay to the dispossessed proprietor the balance which from time to time accrued to the authority after deducting from the rent or other payments received by them from persons occupying the house—

(*a*) the compensation payable to him by the authority, and

(*b*) all expenditure (other than capital expenditure) incurred by the authority in respect of the house while the control order was in force.

(2) The local housing authority shall give notice to the dispossessed proprietor informing him of the balances which they propose to pay him under this paragraph and of his right to appeal.

(3) The dispossessed proprietor may, within 21 days of the service of the notice or such longer period as the local housing authority may in writing allow, appeal to the county court.

(4) If on such an appeal the court is of opinion that the balances are unduly low for any reason within the control of the local housing authority, having regard to—

(*a*) the desirability of observing the standards of management contained in regulations made under section 369 (the management code), and

(*b*) the other standards which the authority ought to observe as to the number of persons living in the house and the rents which they ought to charge,

the court shall direct that for the purposes of the authority's liability to the dispossessed proprietor under this paragraph the balances shall be deemed to be such greater amount as the court may direct.

(5) The court shall not under sub-paragraph (4) give a direction which will afford to the dispossessed proprietor a sum greater than the amount which, in the opinion of the court, he may have lost by the making of the control order.

(6) If different persons are dispossessed proprietors of different parts of the house, sums payable under this paragraph shall be apportioned between them in the manner provided by paragraph 14.

Recovery of capital expenditure incurred by local housing authority

26.—(1) The provisions of this paragraph have effect for the purpose of enabling the local housing authority to recover capital expenditure incurred in carrying out works in the house in the period before the control order ceases to have effect.

(2) The local housing authority may, by a notice served on the dispossessed proprietor, specify such works as being works—

(*a*) which the authority could, if the control order were not in force, have required some person to carry out under any provision of this Part of this Act or under any other enactment relating to housing or public health, and (*b*) which could not be postponed because they were urgently required for the sake of the safety, welfare or health of persons living in the house, or other persons;

and such a notice shall inform the dispossessed proprietor of his right to appeal.

(3) The dispossessed proprietor may, within 21 days of the service of the notice or such longer period as the local housing authority may in writing allow, appeal to the county court which may confirm, vary or quash the notice.

(4) Expenditure reasonably incurred by the local housing authority in carrying out the works specified in a notice under this paragraph (or specified in such a notice as varied on appeal) may be deducted by the authority from the balances which they are liable to pay to the dispossessed proprietor under paragraph 25.

(5) So far as that expenditure exceeds those balances, it may, if the house is purchased compulsorily, be deducted from the amount payable as compensation, and accordingly any interest payable on that amount shall be calculated after allowing for the deduction.

GENERAL NOTE

This Schedule contains a number of detailed provisions governing control orders under Part XI, above.

Part I

Para. 1

The management scheme under s.386 has to give particulars of all works which the authority would have required under this Act or Public Health Act powers, or any other enactment relating to housing or public health, and which the authority consider to amount to "works of capital expenditure", a term not otherwise defined, but in the analysis of which the authority will undoubtedly have regard to their usual practices, and to the Housing Subsidies and Accounting Manual (1981 Edition).

The scheme has to include:

(1) An estimate of the costs of these works;

(2) A specification of maximum number of occupants who should live in the property from time to time, having regard to the amenities referred to in s.352, above, and the existing condition, and its future condition, *i.e.* from time to time as works progress;

(3) An estimate of the balance which will accrue to the authority, *i.e.* excess of receipts over (i) compensation payable under s.389 and Part II of this Schedule, below, plus (ii) all non-capital expenditure (if any).

Para. 2

The last amount mentioned in para. 1 is known as the surpluses on revenue account. It is only an estimate: see also para. 5, below. The authority have power, as does the court (see further below), to vary the scheme, and this may have an effect on the surpluses (*i.e.* because it may increase or decrease them, *e.g.* because there are fewer occupants with lesser works, or lesser revenue outgoings, with greater capital works, or greater revenue outgoings with lesser capital works). But a variation of the surpluses which will result in a decrease in surplus has to be reviewed by the court under para. 6, below.

When calculating the income, payments for furniture (see s.383, above) are taken together with the rents from occupiers. When calculating expenditure, the authority include not only the insurance premium costs under s.385, above, but may also include the costs of temporarily rehousing people while works are in progress (including removal and return costs).

Para. 3

This paragraph provides for appeal against the scheme. It must be brought within six weeks from the date on which it is served, or such longer time as the authority may in writing allow. The power to extend was added pursuant to Law Commission Recommendations (Cmnd. 9515), No. 19. Appeal lies to the county court, and is on any of the following grounds: works unreasonable in character or extent or unnecessary; the works ought not to be treated as capital expenditure; number of occupiers specified in the scheme is unreasonably low; estimate of surpluses unduly low on account of assumptions made by the authority as to matters within their control, *e.g.* rents to be charged. The court may confirm or vary the scheme as it thinks fit. If there is a joint appeal against order under s.384, and scheme under this paragraph, and the court allows the appeal against order, it is not to proceed with the appeal against scheme.

Para. 4

The authority have to keep an account during the period of the control order: see also s.390, above. It must show the surpluses on revenue as settled by the scheme, and the capital expenditure on the scheme. The balance is to be struck at half-yearly intervals. So far as expenditure exceeds revenue, as it commonly will, the deficit carries interest until it can be set off by receipts, or until the control order ceases to have effect, in which case it will carry forward as a charge on interests in the same way as if the control order is revoked on appeal under s.384, above. Future surpluses can also be applied to interest accrued on earlier deficits.

Para. 5
The authority are entitled to vary the scheme at any time so as to increase the surplus.

Para. 6
The authority are also entitled to apply to the court for a review of the scheme, including the surpluses, and the scheme may be varied so far as it relates to any matter *other* than the capital works, *i.e.* so as to reflect a decrease in surplus. Someone with an estate or interest (see s.398, above) may also apply for such a review of the scheme. The court will take into account whether the actual balances have been greater or lesser than the estimate in the original scheme, and whether there has been any change of circumstances in the property, *e.g.* number of occupiers, rents and other payments, and whether either ought to be greater or lesser than originally estimated.

Part II

Compensation is at an annual rate equal to one-half of the gross value of the property, multiplied by the appropriate multiplier. The appropriate multiplier is three-and-one-fifth, by S.I. 1984 No. 1629, retained in force by Housing (Consequential Provisions) Act 1985, s.2. Paras. 8–12 govern calculation of gross value. Under para. 14, if more than one person qualifies as a dispossessed proprietor, compensation is to be apportioned between them according to the gross values of the parts of the property in which each is interested, and in the absence of agreement between them, the matter is to be resolved by the district valuer.

Part III

Para. 15
The general consequence of cessation is to put an original party (or his successor in title) back into the position of landlord under a lease, licence or other agreement which pre-existed the control order, and into whose place the authority stepped under s.382, above, and the dispossessed proprietor into the position of the authority under rights of occupation created by the authority under s.381, above, *i.e.* new rights. If the dispossessed proprietor thus assumes liabilities he could not have assumed under his own lease, he is exempt from liability to the superior landlord, *i.e.* the creation of rights in contravention of his own lease.

Para. 16
On the cessation of the order, a final balance in the accounts is to be struck, and expenditure incurred by the authority on the management scheme, together with interest on it, and including if the scheme has been varied, (see notes to Part I, above), so far as unmet by income, is to be a charge on the premises. The premises subject to the charge include a part excluded from the order under s.380, above. After one month from determination, a receiver may be appointed. If variation proceedings are still pending at date of termination, they may be continued, and if the charge is enforced before final determination of such variation proceedings, the authority will have to account for any excess they have thus recovered.

Para. 17
This paragraph expressly deals with revocation on appeal by the county court. In such a case, the court is to consider whether action ought to be taken under the following previous provisions of Part XI: s.352 (amenities), s.354 (limit on number of occupants), s.366 (means of escape from fire), s.370 (application of management code) and s.372 (management works). The court may approve action under any of these provisions and if it does so, no appeal lies against the action under its own appeal procedures.
If at the time of the decision the authority are carrying out works of a class which they could, had they not made the control order, require someone else to do under any provision of Part XI, or any other enactment relating to housing or public health (including other provisions of this Act—see Interpretation Act 1978, s.1), and on the hearing the court is satisfied that the works cannot be postponed because of their urgent necessity for the sake of the safety, welfare or health of residents or others (*e.g.* neighbours, if they are works

under Part III, Public Health Act 1936, *i.e.* statutory nuisance), the court can suspend revocation until the works are completed.

The county court is to fix the date for termination of the order, even if the authority propose to appeal its order. The court can also authorise the authority to create tenancies, terminable up to six months after the order is to come to an end, notwithstanding the limitation in s.381, above; in effect, the authority can give the residents six additional months' security, beyond termination.

Para. 18

On termination the authority are also to pay to the dispossessed proprietor any balances which have accrued to them, after deducting from receipts their expenditure (not including capital expenditure), and compensation payments they may have made to the dispossessed proprietor: see Part II, above. The court has power to increase the balance offered, if they are satisfied that it is unduly low for any reason within the control of the authority, having regard to the management code standards of s.369, above, and the standards as to occupation numbers and rents which the authority ought to have applied. The limit of the court's power is the amount the dispossessed proprietor may have lost by reason of the order. If there is more than one dispossessed proprietor, the district valuer has jurisdiction to allocate the balance between them: *cf.* para. 14, above.

Para. 19

This makes provision for the recovery by the authority of their capital expenditure on the house prior to revocation on appeal. The authority can apply to the court for approval of the works they have carried out on the ground that the authority could have required to be carried out under Housing Act or Public Health Act powers in any event, and that they could not be postponed for the sake of the safety, welfare or health of residents or others. The approved expenditure can be deducted from the para. 18 balance and to the extent that a sum is outstanding, is a charge on the premises and all estates and interests in them, including any part excluded from the order under s.380, above. The charge takes effect from the date of revocation, and carries interest; if not repaid within one month, a receiver may be appointed.

Para. 20

On an unsuccessful appeal the appellant can indicate that he proposes to appeal further, *i.e.* to the Court of Appeal, and seek an order that works will not subsequently be chargeable by the authority if carried out before confirmation of the control order by the Court of Appeal. If the decision of the county court is appealed, and the Court of Appeal revoke the order, they may also postpone the date of revocation on the same 'works in progress' ground as the county court.

Para. 21

On revocation, the general provisions described above apply. In addition, the court may postpone revocation to permit the authority to complete works within the management scheme under Part I, above, which they have already commenced. The court can also stay the revocation to permit the authority to appeal against revocation.

The court can authorise service of specified notices on determination of the order, and if it does so, there is no appeal under their own procedures: these are the same notices described in the notes to para. 17, above. If on revocation the authority will be entitled to a charge under para. 16, the court can make revocation conditional on all or part of the debt. The court can also authorise the creation of the same class of interests it may authorise on a successful appeal against the control order: see notes to para. 17, above.

Part IV

Para. 23

The obligation to make a management scheme under s.386, above, is deferred until the Secretary of State has notified the authority of the outcome of the proposed C.P.O. If he decides not to confirm the order, the management scheme must be served within eight weeks; if he does confirm the order, the scheme must still be served, but within eight weeks of when the C.P.O. becomes operative.

Para. 24

The control order itself will cease to have effect if the C.P.O. is confirmed on the date when the authority contract to purchase the property, or else on the date when they serve notice of entry under Compulsory Purchase Act 1965, s.11 or notice under s.583 above: see notes to s.583, above. If this is done within eight weeks of the C.P.O. becoming operative, there will be no obligation to serve the management scheme (see also M.H.L.G. Circular 67/69, App., para. 11).

Para. 25

A balance is to be struck when the control order ceases to have effect, *i.e.* the excess of income over outgoings and compensation (*cf.* s.389, above). Notice of the proposed payment must be given to the dispossessed proprietor (see s.398), who within 21 days or such longer time as the authority may in writing permit, appeal to the county court. The court may order the balance to be increased in the same circumstances as it can do on revocation on appeal, and subject to the same limit and provision for apportionment between more than dispossessed proprietor: see notes to para. 18, above.

Para. 26

If the authority have carried out capital works (*cf.* notes to para. 1, above) before the control order ceases to have effect, they may serve notice on the dispossessed proprietor, specifying those works which they could have required under this Act or Public Health Act powers, and which could not have been postponed for the sake of the safety, welfare or health of residents or others (*cf.* notes to para. 19, above). The notice must inform the dispossessed proprietor of his right to appeal, which lies, within 21 days or such longer time as the authority may in writing permit, to the county court, which may confirm, vary or quash the notice. The amount still owing to the authority is deductible first from any balance owing under para. 25, and secondly, together with interest, from compulsory purchase compensation.

Section 418   SCHEDULE 14

The Keeping of the Housing Revenue Account

Part I

Credits to the Account

For each year a local housing authority who are required to keep a Housing Revenue Account shall carry to the credit of the account amounts equal to the items listed in this Part of this Schedule.

Item 1: rents

The income of the authority for the year from rents and charges in respect of houses and other property within the account.

This item does not include—
(*a*) rent remitted by way of rebate, or
(*b*) except in the case of lodging-houses and hostels, amounts included in the rents and charges in respect of rates.

Item 2: charges for services and facilities

The income of the authority for the year in respect of services or facilities provided by them in connection with the provision by them of houses and other property within the account.

This item includes, in particular, income in respect of services or facilities provided under sections 10 and 11 (power to provide furniture, board and laundry facilities), but not payments for the purchase of furniture or hire-purchase instalments for furniture.

Item 3: housing subsidy

Housing subsidy payable to the authority for the year.

Item 4: rent rebate subsidy

Rent rebate subsidy payable to the authority for the year under Part II of the Social Security and Housing Benefits Act 1982, to the extent that it is calculated by reference to Housing Revenue Account rebates within the meaning of that Part, or the cost of administering such rebates.

Item 5: certain contributions

Contributions of any description paid to the authority for the year towards expenditure falling to be debited to the account (for that or any other year).

Item 6: investment income

Income, and receipts in the nature of income, arising to the authority for the year from the investment or other use of—

(*a*) money carried to the account, or

(*b*) borrowed money in respect of which the authority are required by Part II of this Schedule to debit loan charges to the account.

Item 7: income from proceeds of disposals

Income of the authority arising from the investment or other use of capital money received by the authority in respect of the sale or other disposal of houses or other property within the account.

This item does not apply—

(*a*) where the Secretary of State otherwise directs, which he may do as respects the whole or part of any such income, or

(*b*) as respects income from capital money carried to a fund established under paragraph 16 of Schedule 13 to the Local Government Act 1972 (general power of authorities to establish such funds as they think appropriate).

Any such direction may be varied or revoked by a further direction.

Item 8: sums transferred from the Housing Repairs Account

Sums transferred from the Housing Repairs Account in accordance with section 419(5) or (6) (credit balance at end of year or on ceasing to maintain account).

PART II

DEBITS TO THE ACCOUNT

For each year the authority shall debit to the account amounts equal to the items listed in this Part of this Schedule.

Item 1: loan charges

The loan charges which the authority are liable to pay for the year in respect of money borrowed for any of the following purposes—

(*a*) the provision of housing accommodation under Part II,

(*b*) the purchase of, or the carrying out of works on, houses purchased under section 192 (unfit houses found to be beyond repair at reasonable cost), or

(*c*) the improvement of houses and other property within the account.

Item 2: rents, rates, taxes and other charges

The rents, rates, taxes and other charges which the authority are liable to pay for the year in respect of houses and other property within the account.

This item does not include, as respects occupied houses within the account other than mentioned below, rates and charges other than water rates or charges or owner's drainage rates (within the meaning of section 63(2)(*a*) of the Land Drainage Act 1976).

The houses to which the above exception does not apply are—

(*a*) lodging-houses and hostels, and

(*b*) houses occupied, pursuant to a contract of service, by persons employed by the authority on the maintenance, supervision and management of houses and other property within the account.

Item 3: expenditure on repairs, maintenance and management

The expenditure (including loan charges) of the authority for the year in respect of the repair, maintenance, supervision and management of houses and other property within the account.

This item does not include expenditure properly debited to the authority's Housing Repairs Account.

Item 4: contributions to Housing Repairs Account

Contributions from the account to the Housing Repairs Account.

PART III

SUPPLEMENTARY PROVISIONS WITH RESPECT TO MATTERS ARISING BEFORE 1972

Land acquired for re-development

1. The reference in section 417(1)(*d*) to land acquired for the purposes of Part II includes—

(*a*) land which a local authority were deemed to have acquired under Part V of the Housing Act 1957 by virtue of section 57(6) of that Act (land acquired for re-development in pursuance of re-development plan) before the repeal of that section on 25th August 1969, and

(*b*) any structures on such land which were made available to a local authority under section 1 of the Housing (Temporary Accommodation) Act 1944 (prefabs).

Houses and other property brought within the account under s.50 of the Housing (Financial Provisions) Act 1958

2. The houses and other property within an authority's Housing Revenue Account include any property brought within the account before 10th August 1972—

(*a*) with the consent of a Minister given under section 50(1)(*e*) of the Housing (Financial Provisions) Act 1958, or

(*b*) by virtue of section 50(2) of that Act (houses vesting in local authority on default of another person).

Income arising from balance left on abolition of Housing Equalisation Account

3.—(1) For each year the authority shall carry to the credit of the Housing Revenue Account amounts equal to any income, and receipts in the nature of income, arising to the authority for the year from the investment or other use of money representing a sum treated as a capital receipt in pursuance of paragraph 4 of Schedule 10 to the Housing Finance Act 1972 (balance left at 31st March 1972 on abolition of Housing Equalisation Account).

(2) In complying with the requirements of this paragraph the authority shall act in accordance with any directions which may be given by the Secretary of State.

(3) Any such directions may be varied or revoked by further directions.

Housing provided on or before 6th February 1919

4. References in section 417 (the Housing Revenue Account) or this Schedule to property provided under Part II (provision of housing) do not include property provided on or before 6th February 1919.

Money borrowed for the execution of works assisted under the Housing (Rural Workers) Act 1926

5. Section 417(4) (investment income to be carried to Housing Revenue Account), and item 1 of Part II of this Schedule (loan charges to be debited to the account) apply to money borrowed for the execution of works in respect of which, before 10th August 1972—

(*a*) a Minister made a contribution under section 4(2A) of the Housing (Rural Workers) Act 1926, or

(*b*) the local authority for the purposes of that Act gave assistance under that Act, as they apply to money borrowed for the provision of housing accommodation under Part II.

Adjustments affecting the account

6.—(1) Where, but for the coming into force of the Housing Finance Act 1972, a correction of a Housing Revenue Account for the year 1971–72 or any earlier year would have been effected by entering a credit or debit in the account for the year 1972–73 or any later year, the correction shall be made notwithstanding the provisions of this Act as to the nature of the credits or debits to be entered in the account.

(2) Any direction given under section 24 of the Town and Country Planning Act 1959 (adjustment of accounts on appropriation of land) concerning the Housing Revenue Account of a local authority shall apply in relation to the account to be kept under this Act as it

would have applied to the account to be kept under the Housing (Financial Provisions) Act 1958.

Proceeds from certain demolitions

7.—(1) The authority shall credit to the account an amount equal to the net proceeds for the year derived by the authority from any demolition of—

    (*a*) structures made available to a local authority under section 1 of the Housing (Temporary Accommodation) Act 1944 (prefabs),

    (*b*) buildings demolished upon ceasing to be used for the purpose of providing housing accommodation in pursuance of arrangements approved before 10th August 1972 under section 16 of the Housing (Financial Provisions) Act 1958 (use of war buildings for temporary housing accommodation), or

    (*c*) houses to which section 92 of the Housing Act 1964 applied before its repeal on 10th August 1972 (aluminium 'B.2' houses).

(2) In this paragraph "net proceeds" means the sum realised by the authority by the disposal of materials derived from the demolished building or structure, after deducting the cost of the demolition and any cost incurred in reinstating the site of the building or structure.

Part IV

Rate Fund Contributions to the Account

Amenities shared by the whole community

1.—(1) Where benefits or amenities arising from the exercise of a local housing authority's functions under Part II (provision of housing) and provided for the persons housed by the authority are shared by the community as a whole, the authority shall make such contributions from their general rate fund to their Housing Revenue Account as, in their opinion and having regard to the amounts of the contributions and the period over which they are made, will properly reflect the community's share of the benefits or amenities.

(2) Where it appears to the Secretary of State that an authority have failed to comply with sub-paragraph (1), either generally or in a particular case, he may give them such directions as appear to him appropriate to ensure compliance.

(3) The direction may contain particulars as to the amounts of the contributions and the years for which they are to be made.

(4) Before giving a direction the Secretary of State shall consult with the authority.

Land disposed of at less than market value

2. The Secretary of State in giving his consent under any enactment for the disposal at less than market value of land within the account may impose a condition requiring the authority to make a contribution from their general rate fund for such years and of such amount, or of any amount calculated in such manner, as he may determine.

Rent rebates in excess of subsidy

3. There shall be credited to the account any contribution made under section 34(1) of the Social Security and Housing Benefits Act 1982 (housing benefits: contribution from general rate fund representing excess of rent rebates over subsidy).

Deficits in the account

4.—(1) If for any year a deficit is shown in the account, the authority shall carry to the credit of the account a contribution from their general rate fund of an amount equal to the deficit.

(2) The authority may also carry to the credit of the account, in addition to any amount required by sub-paragraph (1), such further amounts, if any, as they may think fit.

Part V

Other Supplementary Provisions

Credit balances in the account

1.—(1) An authority who keep a Housing Revenue Account may from time to time carry to the credit of their general rate fund the whole or part of any balance in the account.

(2) Subject to sub-paragraph (1), if at the end of a year a credit balance is shown in an authority's Housing Revenue Account it shall be carried forward and credited to the account for the next following year.

Ascertainment of loan charges

2.—(1) In this Schedule "loan charges"—

(a) in relation to money borrowed, means the sums required for the payment of interest on the money and for its repayment (either by instalments or by means of a sinking fund) and the expenses of managing the debt, and

(b) includes loan charges made by an authority as a matter of internal accounting (including charges for debt management), whether in respect of borrowing from a capital fund kept by the authority or in respect of borrowing between accounts kept by the authority for different purposes or otherwise.

(2) Where money borrowed by a local authority for different purposes is carried to a common fund or account, the loan charges in respect of money borrowed for any one of those purposes shall be ascertained by reference to the accounting practice of the authority and the manner in which loan charges are ascertained for the purposes of their internal accounting.

(3) Sub-paragraph (2) has effect subject to any direction under section 420 (directions by Secretary of State to secure proper accounting).

Use of estimated figures

3. Any requirement of this Schedule as to the crediting or debiting of an amount to the Housing Revenue Account may be met by taking in the first instance an estimate of the amount and making adjustments in the account for a later year when the amount is more accurately known or is finally ascertained.

Adjustment of accounts on appropriation of land

4.—(1) Where land is appropriated by a local housing authority for the purposes of Part II (provision of housing), or on the discontinuance of use for those purposes, such adjustment shall be made in the accounts of the authority as the Secretary of State may direct.

(2) A direction may be either a general direction or a direction for a particular case and may be varied or revoked by a further direction.

(3) Where this paragraph applies section 24 of the Town and Country Planning Act 1959 (which also relates to the adjustment of accounts on the appropriation of land) does not apply.

Duty to supply information

5.—(1) A local housing authority, and any officer or employee of a local housing authority concerned with their housing functions, shall supply the Secretary of State with such information as he may specify, either generally or in any particular case, for the purpose of enabling the Secretary of State to ascertain the state of the authority's Housing Revenue Account for any year.

(2) A local housing authority shall supply the Secretary of State with such certificates supporting the information required by him as he may specify.

Directions excluding or modifying statutory provisions

6.—(1) Where the Secretary of State is satisfied, on the application of a local housing authority, that any of the provisions of this Part relating to the Housing Revenue Account are inappropriate for any housing accommodation or other property provided by the authority under Part II, he may direct that all or any of those provisions shall not apply to that property, or shall apply subject to such modifications as are specified in the direction.

(2) The Secretary of State may direct that the provisions of this Part relating to the Housing Revenue Account shall apply to a local authority subject to such modifications as are specified in the direction.

(3) A direction may be a general direction or a direction for a particular case, and may be given for such period and subject to such conditions as may be specified in the direction.

(4) A direction may be varied or revoked by a further direction.

Transfers of housing stock between authorities in London

7.—(1) Where houses and other property within the account have been transferred from one authority to another under section 23(3) of the London Government Act 1963 (orders transferring land held by London borough council or Common Council of City of London), the Secretary of State may by order direct, for any of the purposes of this Part—

    (*a*) within whose Housing Revenue Account the transferred houses and property are to be treated as falling, and

    (*b*) how relevant expenditure and income are to be treated in the Housing Revenue Accounts of the authorities to whom the order applies.

(2) The order may be made to apply to a description of local authorities specified in the order or to a specified local authority, and may make different provision in respect of different years or for different purposes in relation to the same year.

(3) An order under this paragraph may amend an order made under section 23(3) of the London Government Act 1963 and may provide that one authority shall pay to another in respect of houses and property to which it relates such amounts calculated by such methods and in respect of such items and such years as appear to the Secretary of State to be appropriate.

(4) An order under this paragraph—

    (*a*) shall be made by the Secretary of State with the concurrence of the Treasury, and

    (*b*) shall be made by statutory instrument which shall be subject to annulment in pursuance of a resolution of either House of Parliament.

(5) Before making an order the Secretary of State shall consult such associations of local authorities as appear to him to be concerned, and with any local authority with whom consultation appears to be desirable.

Contributions in respect of land in general improvement area

8. Where a contribution under section 259 (contributions by Secretary of State towards expenditure on general improvement area) has been paid towards expenditure incurred by a local housing authority in relation to land held by them for the purposes of Part II (provision of housing), neither the expenditure nor the contribution shall be carried to the Housing Revenue Account except with the consent of the Secretary of State.

GENERAL NOTE

There are five Parts to this Schedule. Part I specifies what money is to be credited to the Housing Revenue Account ("H.R.A.") which the authority are obliged to maintain under s.417, above. Part II governs what is to be debited to the H.R.A. Part III contains a number of supplementary provisions relating to "matters arising before 1972", *i.e.* prior to the major change in subsidy systems introduced by the Housing Finance Act 1972. Part IV deals with rate fund contributions to the H.R.A. Part V contains supplementary provisions.

PART I

Para. 1

The first and most obvious item which the authority must credit to the H.R.A. is "rents and charges" in respect of houses and other property within the account. As to what property is within the account, see s.417(3) referring back to s.417(1), see notes thereto, above. The main block of property will be land, houses and other buildings within Part II, above.

The reference to "rents and charges" is the same as that appearing in s.24, *i.e.* because some occupiers may be licensees and so their payments are not strictly "rent". It could not seem to cover additional payments, such as for central heating, or laundry or board, as these are within para. 2, below. However, it could include a garage charge. Where a rent (or licence fee) is remitted by way of rebate under the Social Security and Housing Benefits Act 1982, and the Housing Benefits Regulations 1985 (S.I. 1985 No. 677) thereunder, only the net amount actually paid by the tenant is credited to the account under this paragraph: see also para. 4, below.

Most local authority rents are paid, on a weekly or other periodic basis, inclusive of rates. The amount attributable to the rates is not to be credited to the H.R.A., *save* in the case of a lodging-house or hostel. In such cases, for the purposes of General Rate Act 1967, s.16 the occupier would be unlikely to be considered in rateable occupation.

See also para. 117, Housing Subsidies and Accounting Manual (1981 Edition, issued under cover of D.O.E. Circular 5/82), excluding from this provision, in addition to hostels and lodging-houses, dwellings occupied under a contract of service by persons employed by the authority for maintenance or management, other property where the authority is the rateable occupier (*e.g.* buildings used in connection with repair or management), vacant dwellings so far as empty rates are concerned, all drainage rates, and charges under General Rate Act 1967. ss.36 or 56 See also Part II, para. 2, below.

Para. 2

The authority may provide services, such as central heating, for which a charge is made. Even although it is possibly payable with the rent, if it can be identified with or attributed to the service, it is credited to the H.R.A. under this paragraph. The paragraph includes income from a board or laundry service under s.11.

Para. 3

Housing subsidy payable under Pt. XIII is credited to the H.R.A.: see notes to ss.421–425, above.

Para. 4

Under the Social Security and Housing Benefits Act 1982, s.32, local authorities receive subsidies for (a) the rate rebates they grant, (b) the rent rebate they grant, and (c) the rent allowances they grant. Subsidy currently includes an amount for administration of the scheme: s.32(2). (However, the recent Review of Social Security suggests that this element may be withdrawn). Under s.32(4), rent rebate subsidy is to be credited to the H.R.A. to the extent that it is calculated by reference to "Housing Revenue Account rebates and the costs of administering such rebates", *i.e.* rebates on H.R.A. dwellings (see s.35 of the 1982 Act).

Para. 5

This would include contributions under Pt. IV, para. 1, below, *i.e.* contributions from the general rate fund where benefits or amenities provided under Pt. II are shared by the community as a whole, contributions required by the Secretary of State under Pt. IV, para. 2, contributions from the general rate fund for the balance of rent rebates granted under Pt. IV, para. 3, and a contribution under Pt. IV, para. 4 from the general rate fund, to make up a deficit in the H.R.A.

It would also include contributions from a social services authority towards the cost of providing special facilities for the elderly, refund of cost of tenant's repairs by tenant (but *cf.* s.419, above, if there is a Housing Repairs Account), and payments by displacing authorities under s.42, Land Compensation Act 1973: Housing Subsidies and Accounting Manual (1981 Edition), para. 168.

Para. 6

Investment income may arise from money within the H.R.A. If an authority borrow for Part II purposes, then the loan charges have to be carried to the H.R.A. under Pt. II of this Schedule, para. 1; if it is not immediately used for its purpose, then it may be reinvested— in which case its income is also to be credited to the H.R.A. under this paragraph.

Para. 7

When property is sold, authorities may invest the proceeds, and the income from such investment is to be carried to the H.R.A. However, the Secretary of State may direct that the income is not to be credited to the H.R.A. Nor does it apply if the capital was carried to a fund under para. 16 of Sched. 13 to the Local Government Act 1972. See also para. 2 of Pt. IV of this Schedule, below.

Payments, whether outright or in instalments, on sale of Part II property is to be treated as capital, and not credited to the H.R.A.: Housing Subsidies and Accounting Manual, para. 194. However, instalments and/or lump sums payable on disposal of housing built expressly for sale under s.429, above, may be credited to the H.R.A., either as a capital sum or by way of reinvestment and use of income: *ibid.*, para. 195.

Para. 8

Under s.419, authorities may maintain a Housing Repairs Account. They are bound to keep it out of debit: s.419(4). They are entitled to carry a credit in the account to the H.R.A., if they consider that it will not be required for the purposes of the Housing Repairs Account: s.419(5). If they cease to maintain a Housing Repairs Account, the balance is to be carried to the H.R.A.: s.419(6).

PART II

Para. 1

Housing capital expenditure is principally financed by borrowing money. This will include not only initial provision of accommodation, but also major works. The loan charges (as defined in para 2 of Part V of this Schedule, below) for (a) providing housing under Pt. II,

(b) purchasing houses under s.192 (see notes thereto, and to s.417, above), and (c) improvement of any property within the H.R.A. (see notes to s.417, above) are to be debited to the H.R.A. See also para. 5 of Pt. III of this Schedule, below.

Para. 2

Also to be debited are the authority's outgoings by way of rent, rates, taxes or other charges which they have to pay for property within the H.R.A. (as to which, see notes to s.417, above), *e.g.* if they lease property and have to pay rent and/or other charges to a superior landlord, if they are not the rating authority, water rates, etc. However, rates and charges *except* water rates or charges and owner's land drainage rates, are *not* to be debited to the H.R.A. so far as they relate to houses (not other buildings) within the H.R.A., *except* lodging-houses and hostels, and property occupied by caretakers and residential managers, *i.e.* if the rates are not to be credited to the H.R.A. under para. 1 of Part I of this Schedule, nor are they to be debited.

Para. 3

The next, and obvious, debit is the cost of repair, maintenance, supervision and management of both the housing and other property within the H.R.A. (as to which, see notes to s.417, above). However, this does not include monies debited to the optional Housing Repairs Account under s.419 (but see next paragraph).

Para. 4

Finally, authorities may debit to the H.R.A. sums paid to the optional Housing Repairs Account maintained under s.419.

PART III

Para. 1

See notes to s.417, above.

Para. 2

See notes to s.417, above.

Para. 3

Prior to the Housing Finance Act 1972, local authorities maintained a Housing Equalisation Account. On the abolition of the account by that Act, the balance was to be treated as a capital receipt by the authority, and income generated by it is still to be credited to the H.R.A.

Para. 4

See notes to s.417, above.

Para. 5

See notes to s.417, above.

Para. 6

This continues the power of the authority to make adjustments (credit or debit) to the H.R.A. which would have been made in 1972/73 or subsequent years had the Housing Finance Act 1972 not been passed. Similarly, an adjustment on appropriation which has been required under Town and Country Planning Act 1959, s.24 but the time for effecting which has not yet arrived, remains in force. See also para. 4 of Pt. V of this Schedule, below.

Para. 7

On demolition, the authority may derive a sum of money, *e.g.* from sale of materials or scrap. The proceeds therefrom which arise on demolition of properties under any of these specified provisions are to be credited to the H.R.A. annually.

PART IV

Para. 1

This is an important principle. When an authority exercise powers under s.12 (shops, recreation and beneficial purposes), the benefit may be shared by the community as a whole, *i.e.* not only the tenants or occupiers of an estate: see also notes to s.12, above; see also *Green & Sons* v. *Minister of Health* [1948] 1 K.B. 34, C.A. Such benefits and amenities may be reflected in the rates paid by those people. Whether or not they are, an amount which "properly reflects the community's share" is to be paid from the general rate fund to the H.R.A. The Secretary of State has a reserve power to enforce this requirement, subject to prior consultation (as to the meaning of which, see notes to s.420(4), above).

Para. 2

Under the Local Government Act 1972, s.123, local authorities may dispose of land at the best price reasonably obtainable, or at a lesser price with the consent of the Secretary of State. Similar powers are to be found in the Town and Country Planning Acts. If the property to be disposed of is within the H.R.A. (see also ss.32 *et seq.*, above), the Secretary of State may require a contribution from the general rate fund over a number of years. This paragraph may be read together with para. 7 of Part I of this Schedule, above. See the Housing Subsidies and Accounting Manual (1981 Edition), para. 186.

Para. 3

Government subsidy under the Social Security and Housing Benefits Act 1982 will not meet the whole cost of the rent rebates granted by the authority; there may also be additional costs if the authority exercise their discretion under s.30 of that Act to increase benefits by means of a "local scheme", or exercise their discretion to make an "exceptional" payment under Regulation 25 of the Housing Benefits Regulations 1982 (S.I. 1985 No. 677), neither of which is admissible for subsidy purposes. The balance is to be paid from the general rate fund, and credited to the H.R.A.

Para. 4

The H.R.A. is to be kept out of debit, by transfer from the general rate fund if needs be. Such a transfer may voluntarily put the H.R.A. into credit, if the authority wish.

PART V

Para. 1

If the H.R.A. is in credit, any part of that credit may be carried to the general rate fund, *i.e.* the housing may subsidise the rates, rather than the more traditional assumption that housing is subsidised by the rates. If no such transfer is made, the credit is carried forward to the next year.

Para. 2

This defines loan charges for the purposes of this Schedule. Note that authorities are not entitled to vary their accounting practices for the purposes of calculating housing subsidy, without the approval of the Department of the Environment: Housing Subsidies and Accounting Manual (1981 Edition), para. 22. See also notes to s.420, above.

Para. 3

Much public housing accounting is of necessity achieved by way of estimate, and later adjustment.

Para. 4

Adjustment of accounts on appropriation is governed by Town and Country Planning Act 1959, s.24 (see also para. 6 of Pt. III of this Schedule, above), but in the case of an appropriation to or from Part II purposes, adjustment is under this paragraph, *i.e.* as the Secretary of State may direct, either generally or particularly. See para. 187 and the general directions at App. F of the Housing Subsidies and Accounting Manual (1981 Edition). See also s.27 of the 1959 Act, which permits the Secretary of State to direct an adjustment when a housing capital receipt is used for a non-Pt. II function, and paras. 191–193 and the general direction at App. G of the Manual.

Para. 5

The Secretary of State is entitled to review the "state of the Housing Revenue Account", and to require an authority, *or* an officer or employee of the authority, to provide him with such information as he may specify, generally or particularly, for that purpose. He can require such information to be supported by certificates.

Para. 6

The Secretary of State can permit an authority to disapply or modify any of the provisions of this Schedule to property within Pt. II, either by general or particular direction, and conditionally or unconditionally. This is available when the Secretary of State is satisfied that the provisions or any of the provisions are "inappropriate".

Para. 7

This is ancillary to the power to order transfer of stock between authorities under s.19, above.

Para. 8

In a General Improvement Area, "curtilage" grants are available for improving the amenities or the dwellings of an area (but not including works for which a grant under Part XV is available—s.255), the calculation and use of which can in some circumstances include property owned by the authority: ss.255, 259. This paragraph prevents the authority carrying the cost or the contribution to the H.R.A. without the consent of the Secretary of State.

Section 432   SCHEDULE 15

SUPERSEDED CONTRIBUTIONS, GRANTS, SUBSIDIES, &c.

PART I

LOANS UNDER THE HOUSING (RURAL WORKERS) ACTS 1926 TO 1942

The Housing (Rural Workers) Acts 1926 to 1942, and any enactment so far as it relates to the rate of interest payable on a loan under those Acts, continue to have effect in relation to a loan made under section 2 of the Housing (Rural Workers) Act 1926 before 10th August 1972.

PART II

EXCHEQUER CONTRIBUTIONS FOR AGRICULTURAL HOUSING

(*s.46 of the Housing (Financial Provisions) Act 1958*)

Contributions by Secretary of State to local housing authority

1.—(1) Contributions by the Secretary of State to a local housing authority remain payable under section 46 of the Housing (Financial Provisions) Act 1958 (contributions payable over a period of 40 years for agricultural housing provided under arrangements made with the authority) in pursuance of an undertaking made before 10th August 1972.

(2) The contributions are payable at such times and in such manner as the Treasury may direct, and subject to such conditions as to records, certificates, audit or otherwise as the Secretary of State may, with the approval of the Treasury, impose.

Conditions of payment of contributions

2.—(1) It is a condition of the payment of a contribution in respect of a house in any year that throughout the year the house—

(*a*) is reserved for members of the agricultural population, and

(*b*) if let, is let at rent not exceeding the limit applicable in accordance with the following provisions of this paragraph,

and that the local housing authority certify to the Secretary of State that all reasonable steps have been taken to secure the maintenance of the house in a proper state of repair during the year.

(2) The condition specified in sub-paragraph (1)(*a*) shall be deemed to be observed at any time if the house is let on or subject to a protected or statutory tenancy to which section 99 of the Rent Act 1977 applies (dwelling-houses let to agricultural workers, etc.) or is subject to a protected occupancy or statutory tenancy within the meaning of the Rent (Agriculture) Act 1976.

(3) The limit referred to in sub-paragraph (1)(*b*) is in the case of a condition imposed before 8th December 1965—

(*a*) if the tenancy is a regulated tenancy (other than a converted tenancy within the meaning of Schedule 17 to the Rent Act 1977), the rent which would be recoverable if the tenancy had been converted from being a controlled tenancy on the commencement of section 64 of the Housing Act 1980 and accordingly as if it were a converted tenancy;

(*b*) if the tenancy is a converted tenancy, or a housing association tenancy within the meaning of Part VI of the Rent Act 1977, the rent recoverable under that Act;

(*c*) if the tenancy is a protected occupancy or statutory tenancy within the meaning of the Rent (Agriculture) Act 1976, the rent recoverable in accordance with that Act;

(*d*) in any other case, such rent as may from time to time be, or have been, agreed between the landlord and the local housing authority or as may, in default of agreement, be or have been determined by the Secretary of State.

(4) The limit referred to in sub-paragraph (1)(*b*) is in the case of a condition imposed on or after 8th December 1965 such rent as the local housing authority may from time to time determine as being in their opinion the rent which would have been appropriate for them to charge if the house had been provided by them.

(5) Where the house is let together with other land at a single rent, such proportion of that rent as the local housing authority may determine shall be deemed for the purposes of the condition specified in sub-paragraph (1)(*b*) to be the rent at which the house is let.

3.—(1) In the case of a house completed on or after 18th April 1946 the payment of a contribution for any year during which the house is at any time occupied by a member of the agricultural population in pursuance of a contract of service and otherwise than as a tenant is also subject to the following condition.

(2) The condition is that if the contract of service is terminated—

(*a*) by less than four weeks' notice given by the employer, or

(*b*) by dismissal of the employee without notice, or

(*c*) by the death of either party,

the employer or his personal representatives will permit the employee (or, in the case of his death, any person residing with him at his death) to continue to occupy the house free of charge from the determination of the contract until the expiration of a period of four weeks beginning with the date on which the notice is given, or, if the contract is determined otherwise than by notice, with the date on which it is determined.

Grants payable to owners by local housing authority

4.—(1) Where a contribution is paid to a local housing authority, the authority shall pay by way of annual grant to the owner of the house an amount not less than the contribution paid by the Secretary of State.

(2) No such grant shall be made if before it is made the Secretary of State is satisfied that during the whole or the greater part of the period to which the payment of the grant is referable the house has not been available as a dwelling fit for habitation, unless he is satisfied that that could not with reasonable diligence have been achieved.

(3) Any question as to the period to which a payment is referable shall be determined for the purposes of this paragraph by the Secretary of State.

(4) Where the duty of a local housing authority to make a grant is wholly or partly discharged by virtue of this paragraph, the Secretary of State shall make such consequential reductions as he thinks fit in any sum payable by him to the authority.

No further payments if house vests in local housing authority

5. Where a house which has been provided under arrangements under section 46 of the Housing (Financial Provisions) Act 1958 becomes vested in the local housing authority making the arrangements, no further sums are payable by the Secretary of State or the authority in respect of the house under this Part of this Schedule.

PART III

CONTRIBUTIONS FOR IMPROVEMENT OF DWELLINGS BY HOUSING AUTHORITIES

(*s.9 of the Housing (Financial Provisions) Act 1958; s.13 of the House Purchase and Housing Act 1959*)

1.—(1) Subject to sub-paragraph (2), contributions by the Secretary of State to a local authority remain payable—

(*a*) under section 9 of the Housing (Financial Provisions) Act 1958 (contributions over a period of 20 years towards the cost to local authorities of works of conversion or improvement) in pursuance of proposals approved before 25th August 1969, and

(*b*) under section 13 of the House Purchase and Housing Act 1959 (contributions over a period of 20 years in respect of standard amenities provided by local authorities), in pursuance of applications approved before 25th August 1969.

(2) No contribution is payable under this paragraph in respect of a dwelling within a local housing authority's Housing Revenue Account or a new town corporation's housing account.

(3) The contributions are payable at such times and in such manner as the Treasury may direct, and subject to such conditions as to records, certificates, audit or otherwise as the Secretary of State may, with the approval of the Treasury, impose.

(4) The amount or duration of any contribution payable under this paragraph to which section 25(2) of the Housing (Financial Provisions) Act 1958 applied immediately before the commencement of this Act (payments arising out of the exercise of housing powers by county councils) may be reduced by the Secretary of State at his discretion.

(*ss.17 to 20 of the Housing Act 1969*)

2.—(1) Contributions by the Secretary of State to a housing authority remain payable under section 18 or 19 of the Housing Act 1969 (improvement contributions or standard contributions payable over a period of 20 years for dwellings converted or improved by the authority) in pursuance of applications approved before 2nd December 1974.

(2) The contributions are payable at such times and in such manner as the Treasury may direct, and subject to such conditions as to records, certificates, audit or otherwise as the Secretary of State may, with the approval of the Treasury, impose.

(3) No contribution is payable under this paragraph in respect of a dwelling within a local housing authority's Housing Revenue Account or a new town corporation's housing account.

(4) The amount or duration of any contribution payable under this paragraph to which section 25(2) of the Housing (Financial Provisions) Act 1958 Act applied immediately before the commencement of this Act (payments arising out of the exercise of housing powers by county councils) may be reduced by the Secretary of State at his discretion.

(*s.79 of the Housing Act 1974*)

3.—(1) Subject to sub-paragraph (2), contributions by the Secretary of State to a housing authority remain payable under section 79 of the Housing Act 1974 (improvement contributions payable over a period of 20 years) in pursuance of applications approved before 8th August 1980.

(2) No contribution is payable under this paragraph in respect of dwellings within a local housing authority's Housing Revenue Account or a new town corporation's housing account.

(3) The contributions are payable subject to such conditions as to records, certificates, audit or otherwise as the Secretary of State may, with the approval of the Treasury, impose.

PART IV

TOWN DEVELOPMENT SUBSIDY

(*s.9 of the Housing Finance Act 1972; s.5 of the Housing Rents and Subsidies Act 1975*)

Transitional town development subsidy

1.—(1) Transitional town development subsidy is payable each year, subject to the following provisions of this Part of this Schedule, to a sending authority to whom town development subsidy under section 9 of the Housing Finance Act 1972 was payable for the year 1974–75; and the amount of the subsidy, subject to the following provisions of this Schedule, is the amount of town development subsidy payable to the authority for the year 1974–75.

(2) The subsidy is payable for the credit of the sending authority's general rate fund.

2.—(1) The subsidy is payable by the Secretary of State at such times and in such manner as the Treasury may direct, and subject to such conditions as to records, certificates, audit or otherwise as the Secretary of State may, with the approval of the Treasury, impose.

(2) The payment of subsidy is subject to the making of a claim for it in such form and containing such particulars as the Secretary of State may from time to time determine.

(3) The amount of the subsidy for any year shall be calculated to the nearest pound, by disregarding an odd amount of £0·50, or less, and by treating an odd amount exceeding £0·50 as a whole pound.

(4) A direction or determination under this paragraph may contain supplementary or incidental provisions and may be made to apply to a specified description of authorities or to a specified authority.

Reduction or discontinuance of subsidy

3.—(1) The Secretary of State may reduce or discontinue a sending authority's transitional town development subsidy if a dwelling in respect of which it is payable—

(*a*) has been demolished,
(*b*) has been disposed of by the receiving authority,
(*c*) is not fit to be used, or is not being used, for letting as a dwelling, or
(*d*) in any other circumstances he considers relevant.

(2) The Secretary of State may from time to time determine for the purposes of sub-paragraph (1)—

    (*a*) the circumstances in which a dwelling is to be treated as having been demolished or disposed of,

    (*b*) the circumstances in which a dwelling is to be treated as not fit to be used, or as not being used, for letting as a dwelling,

    (*c*) in which circumstances other than those mentioned in sub-paragraph (1)(*a*) to (*c*) an authority's transitional town development subsidy is to be reduced or discontinued, and

    (*d*) the method by which any calculation is to be made;

and the power conferred by paragraph (*b*) above also includes power to determine what constitutes letting as a dwelling.

(3) A determination under this paragraph may contain supplementary or incidental provisions and may be made to apply to a specified description of authorities or dwellings or to a specified authority.

Payments to receiving authority

4.—(1) Where transitional town development subsidy is payable, the sending authority shall for each year pay to the receiving authority four times the amount of the sending authority's transitional town development subsidy attributable to dwellings of the receiving authority which are available in that year for tenants from the sending authority.

(2) The payments are for the credit of the receiving authority's general rate fund.

Commutation of subsidy and payments to receiving authority

5.—(1) The Secretary of State may, with the agreement of the sending authority and the receiving authority, determine—

    (*a*) to commute further payments of transitional town development subsidy into a single payment of an amount to be determined by him or calculated in a manner determined by him, and

    (*b*) to commute the corresponding payments by the sending authority to the receiving authority under paragraph 4 into a single payment of four times that payable under paragraph (*a*).

(2) In making a determination the Secretary of State shall make such allowance, if any, as appears to him appropriate for circumstances in which, if there were no commutation, his power under paragraph 3 to reduce or discontinue the sending authority's transitional town development subsidy might be exercised.

Meaning of "receiving authority"

6. In this part of this Schedule "receiving authority" means the council of a receiving district within the meaning of the Town Development Act 1952.

GENERAL NOTE

This Schedule contains the continuation provisions relating to miscellaneous subordinate subsidies under previous legislation, *i.e.* those not taken into the "principal" housing subsidy as part of the base amount under s.423, above (previously Housing Act 1980 s.98).

Section 438   SCHEDULE 16

LOCAL AUTHORITY MORTGAGE INTEREST RATES

The rate of interest

1.—(1) The rate of interest shall be whichever is for the time being the higher of—

    (*a*) the standard national rate, or

    (*b*) the applicable local average rate.

(2) The rate shall be capable of being varied by the local authority whenever a change in either or both of those rates requires it; and the amount of the periodic payments shall be capable of being changed accordingly.

The standard national rate

2. The standard national rate is the rate for the time being declared as such by the Secretary of State after taking into account interest rates charged by building societies in the United Kingdom and any movement in those rates.

The local average rate

3. A local authority shall for every period of six months declare, on a date falling within the month immediately preceding that period—

(*a*) a rate applicable to the advances and transfers mentioned in section 438(1)(*a*) and (*c*) (advances under section 435 and transfers of mortgages under section 442), and

(*b*) a rate applicable to sums left outstanding as mentioned in section 438(1)(*b*) (sums left outstanding on disposal of house).

4.—(1) The rate declared under paragraph 3(*a*) shall be a rate exceeding by ¼ per cent. that which the authority estimate they have to charge in order to service the loan charges on money borrowed or to be borrowed by them for the purpose of the advances and transfers referred to.

(2) The rate declared under paragraph 3(*b*) shall be a rate exceeding by ¼ per cent. the average, on the date the rate is declared, of the rates at which all loan charges debited to the authority's appropriate account are serviced.

(3) The appropriate account is—

(*a*) for sums left outstanding on the disposal of a house held by a local authority under Part II (provision of housing), the authority's Housing Revenue Account, and

(*b*) for other sums left outstanding, the county fund in the case of a county council and the general rate fund or general fund in any other case.

(4) For the purposes of this paragraph loan charges include loan charges made by the authority as a matter of internal accounting (including charges for debt management), whether in respect of borrowing from a capital fund kept by the authority, or in respect of borrowing between accounts kept by the authority for different functions, or otherwise.

Variation of rate of interest

5.—(1) Where on a change of the standard national rate or the applicable local average rate a rate of interest is capable of being varied, the local authority shall vary it.

(2) The authority shall serve on the person liable to pay the interest notice in writing of the variation not later than two months after the change.

(3) The variation shall take effect with the first payment of interest due after a date specified in the notice, which—

(*a*) if the variation is a reduction, shall be not later than one month after the change, and

(*b*) if the variation is an increase, shall not be earlier than one month nor later than three months after the service of the notice.

6.—(1) On a variation of the rate of interest, the local authority may make a corresponding variation of the periodic payments.

(2) The authority shall do so if the period over which the repayment of principal is to be made would otherwise be reduced below the period fixed when the mortgage was effected.

(3) The variation shall be notified and take effect together with the variation of the rate of interest.

Directions by Secretary of State

7.—(1) The Secretary of State may by notice in writing to a local authority direct it to treat a rate specified in the notice as being the higher of the two rates mentioned in paragraph 1, either for a period specified in the notice or until further notice; and the preceding provisions of this Schedule have effect accordingly.

(2) A direction so given may be varied or withdrawn by a further notice in writing.

GENERAL NOTE

This Schedule governs the rate of interest on mortgages under ss.435, 437 and 442. It does not, however, inhibit the provisions governing "homesteading schemes" under s.441, or assistance for first-time buyers under ss.445–446, nor do the provisions apply to *mandatory* improvement-related loans under s.228, or loans to housing associations under Housing Associations Act 1985 s.58.

Para. 1

The Schedule operates on the basis of two concepts: the standard national rate, and the applicable local average rate, the higher of which is the rate payable. The mortgage must provide for a variable rate of interest. The Secretary of State has, however, power under para. 7, below, to direct that one or other rate is to be treated as the higher, *i.e.* even if it is not. If variation is possible under this Schedule, it is mandatory: see para. 5, below.

Para. 2

The Secretary of State determines the standard national rate.

Para. 3

Twice a year, the authority are under a duty to declare two local average rates, in the month before the half-year to which they will apply. The two local average rates are: (a) a rate for mortgages granted by them under s.435 and for mortgages transferred to them under a s.442 indemnity scheme; and (b) a rate for mortgages on their own former property, *i.e.* voluntary sales.

Para. 4

The first of the two local average rates in para. 3 (granted under s.435 or transferred under s.442) is one-quarter per cent. above the amount the authority have to pay, *i.e.* borrow the money at. The second of the two local average rates in para. 3 (voluntary sales) is one-quarter per cent. above the average cost of the loan charges across one of two accounts—if former Part II property, the Housing Revenue Account (as to which, see s.417, above), or otherwise the general rate fund. To some extent, then, the borrower will pay that which reflects the authority's standards of financial management and investment. Note that loan charges include notional loan charges, *i.e.* internal accounting loan charges.

Para. 5

The authority are obliged to vary the rate of interest payable whenever it can be varied under the provisions of this Schedule. Notice of change must be served no later than two months after the change in rate. The notice must set a date for the variation to take effect, no later than one month after the change if a reduction, and no earlier than one month but not later than three months after service of the notice if an increase. The maximum period for which the authority can, accordingly, defer the effect of an increase is for five months.

Para. 6

If the rate of interest is varied, the authority can vary the periodic payments, and is obliged to do so if the effect of the variation would otherwise be to reduce the repayment period, *i.e.* if there is a decrease in the rate of interest they must reduce the periodic payments for otherwise the payments would start to reduce the capital quicker than was intended. Variation of payments is to be at the same time as variation of the rate of interest.

Para. 7

This permits the Secretary of State to order the authority to treat as the higher rate a different rate than would otherwise be the case.

Section 452 SCHEDULE 17

VESTING OF MORTGAGED HOUSE IN AUTHORITY ENTITLED TO EXERCISE POWER OF SALE

Vesting of house with leave of court

1.—(1) The authority may, if the county court gives it leave to do so, by deed vest the house in itself—

(*a*) for the estate and interest in the house which is the subject of the mortgage and which the authority would be authorised to sell or convey on exercising its power of sale, and

(*b*) freed from all estates, interests and rights to which the mortgage has priority,

but subject to all estates, interests and rights which have priority to the mortgage.

(2) Where application for leave under this paragraph is made to the county court, the court may adjourn the proceedings or postpone the date for the execution of the authority's deed for such period as the court thinks reasonable.

(3) An adjournment or postponement may be made subject to such conditions with regard to payment by the mortgagor of any sum secured by the mortgage or the remedy of any default as the court thinks fit; and the court may from time to time vary or revoke any such conditions.

Effect of vesting

2.—(1) On the vesting of the house the authority's mortgage term or charge by way of legal mortgage, and any subsequent mortgage term or charge, shall merge or be extinguished as respects the house.

(2) Where the house is registered under the Land Registration Acts 1925 to 1971, the Chief Land Registrar shall, on application being made to him by the authority, register the authority as the proprietor of the house free from all estates, interests and rights to which its mortgage had priority, and he shall not be concerned to inquire whether any of the requirements of this Schedule were complied with.

(3) Where the authority conveys the house, or part of it, to a person—

(a) he shall not be concerned to inquire whether any of the provisions of this Schedule were complied with, and

(b) his title shall not be impeachable on the ground that the house was not properly vested in the authority or that those provisions were not complied with.

(4) A house which is vested under this Schedule in a local housing authority shall be treated as acquired under Part II (provision of housing).

Compensation and accounting

3.—(1) Where the authority has vested the house in itself under paragraph 1, it shall appropriate a fund equal to the aggregate of—

(a) the amount agreed between the authority and the mortgagor or determined by the district valuer as being the amount which under sub-paragraph (2) is to be taken as the value of the house at the time of the vesting, and

(b) interest on that amount, for the period beginning with the vesting and ending with the appropriation, at the rate prescribed for that period under section 32 of the Land Compensation Act 1961 (rate prescribed for compulsory purchase cases where entry is made before compensation is paid).

(2) The value of the house at the time of the vesting shall be taken to be the price which, at that time, the interest vested in the authority would realise if sold on the open market by a willing vendor on the assumption that any prior incumbrances to which the vesting is not made subject would be discharged by the vendor.

(3) The fund shall be applied in the following order—

(a) in discharging, or paying sums into court for meeting, any prior incumbrances to which the vesting is not made subject;

(b) in recovering the costs, charges, and expenses properly incurred by the authority as incidental to the vesting of the house;

(c) in recovering the mortgage money, interest, costs and other money (if any) due under the mortgage;

(d) in recovering any amount which falls to be paid under the covenant required by section 35 or 155 (repayment of discount, etc. on disposal) or paragraph 6 of Schedule 8 (terms of shared ownership lease: payment for outstanding share on disposal) or any provision of the conveyance or grant to the like effect;

and any residue then remaining in the fund shall be paid to the person entitled to the mortgaged house, or who would have been entitled to give receipts for the proceeds of sale of the house if it had been sold in the exercise of the power of sale.

(4) Section 107(1) of the Law of Property Act 1925 (mortgagee's written receipt sufficient discharge for money arising under power of sale) applies to money payable under this Schedule as it applies to money arising under the power of sale conferred by that Act.

Modifications in case of conveyance or grant before 8th August 1980

4. In a case to which this Schedule applies by virtue of section 452(6) (disposals before 8th August 1980 of property held by local authorities for housing purposes), the preceding paragraphs have effect with the following modifications—

(a) for "house" substitute "property";

(b) for paragraph (a) of paragraph 3(1) (value of house) substitute—

"(a) the price at which the authority could have re-acquired the property by virtue of the condition mentioned in section 452(6)(b),"

and omit paragraph 3(2) (which provides for ascertaining the value of the house);

(*c*) omit paragraph (*d*) of paragraph 3(3) (which relates to repayment of discount and similar matters).

GENERAL NOTE

This Schedule governs the vesting in an authority of a property in relation to which there is both an extant pre-emption condition and default by their mortgagor to the extent that the authority are in a position to exercise their power of sale as mortgagees: see notes to s.452, above.

Para. 1

The power of vesting is only exercisable with the leave of the county court. The county court may authorise the vesting in the authority of that which it could sell on exercise of the power of sale, freed from all estates, interests and rights to which they, as mortgagee, have priority, *i.e.* subsequent interests, etc., created by the mortgagor.

On an application, the court can adjourn the proceedings or postpone the date of vesting in the authority, for such periods as the court thinks reasonable, and subject to such terms governing payments or the remedying of default as the court thinks fit. Note that there is no requirement that it appear to the court that the mortgagor is likely to be able within a reasonable period to pay sums due under the mortgage, or remedy a default, analogous to Administration of Justice Act 1970, ss.36–38 and Administration of Justice Act 1973, s.8: see notes to s.436(6), above. This would seem to be intentional, and to place the discretion on the same wide footing as, *e.g.* is available when a secure tenant is in arrears—see notes to s.84, above.

Para. 2

This paragraph governs the effect of the vesting. If the authority are a local housing authority, and retain the land, the property is treated as acquired under Part II; if they sell on to someone else, that person's title will not be defeasible on the grounds that the provisions of the Schedule have not been complied with. If the house has appreciated in value between vesting in the authority and subsequent sale, it would seem that the fiduciary duty of the authority may prevent any additional payment to the former owner: *Re Brown's Mortgage, Wallasey Corporation* v. *Att.-Gen.* [1945] Ch. 166.

Para. 3

This paragraph deals with the financial consequences of vesting. The authority must set up a fund equal to the amount which they would have had to pay in exercise of their right of pre-emption, together with interest thereon; the money is to be applied in discharge of any interests *prior* to the mortgage which are discharged by the vesting, next in recovering the costs, charges and expenses incidental to the vesting, thirdly in recovering principal, interest, costs and any other money due under the mortgage, fourthly in recoupment of discount (see notes to ss.36, 156, above), or payment of outstanding share on a shared ownership disposal (see notes to Sched. 8, above), and finally the remainder—if any—is to be paid to the person entitled to the mortgaged property, or who would have been entitled to the receipts had the property been sold.

Section 456   SCHEDULE 18

PROVISIONS WITH RESPECT TO ADVANCES UNDER THE SMALL DWELLINGS ACQUISITION ACTS 1899 TO 1923

Repayment of advance

1.—(1) The advance shall be repaid with interest within such period not exceeding 30 years as may be agreed upon.

(2) The rate of interest is ¼ per cent. in excess of the rate of interest which, one month before the date on which the terms of the advance were settled, was the rate fixed by the Treasury in respect of loans to local authorities for the purposes of Part V of the Housing Act 1957 (provision of housing), as follows—

(*a*) where the time referred to is before 27th February 1964, the rate so fixed under section 1 of the Public Works Loans Act 1897;

(*b*) where the time referred to is on or after 27th February 1964 and before 1st April 1968, the rate so fixed under section 2 of the Public Works Loans Act 1964 in respect of loans made on the security of local rates, or, where there was more than one rate so fixed, such of those rates as the Treasury have directed in that behalf under that section;

(c) where the time referred to is on or after 1st April 1968, the rate determined under section 6(2) of the National Loans Act 1968 in respect of local loans of that class made on the security of local rates, subject to any relevant direction given by the Treasury under that subsection.

(3) The repayment may be made either by equal instalments of principal or by an annuity of principal and interest combined; and all payments on account of principal or interest shall be made either weekly or at such other periods not exceeding half a year as may be agreed.

(4) The proprietor of a house in respect of which an advance has been made may at any of the usual quarter days, after one month's written notice, and on paying all sums due on account of interest, repay to the local authority—

(a) the whole of the outstanding principal of the advance, or

(b) any part of it, being £10 or a multiple of £10;

and where the repayment is made by an annuity of principal and interest combined, the amount so outstanding, and the amount by which the annuity will be reduced where a part of the advance is paid off, shall be determined by a table annexed to the instrument securing the repayment of the advance.

The statutory conditions

2.—(1) The house of which the ownership was acquired by means of the advance shall be held subject to the following conditions (in this Schedule referred to as "the statutory conditions"):—

(a) Every sum for the time being due in respect of principal or interest of the advance shall be punctually paid:

(b) The proprietor shall reside in the house:

(c) The house shall be kept insured against fire to the satisfaction of the local authority, and the receipts for the premiums produced when required by them:

(d) The house shall be kept in good sanitary condition and good repair:

(e) The house shall not be used for the sale of intoxicating liquors, or in such a manner as to be a nuisance to adjacent houses:

(f) The local authority shall have power to enter the house by any person, authorised by them in writing for the purpose, at all reasonable times for the purpose of ascertaining whether the statutory conditions are complied with.

(2) The statutory condition as to residence has effect for a period of three years from the date when the advance is made, or from the date on which the house is completed, whichever is the later.

(3) The other statutory conditions have effect until the advance has been fully repaid, with interest, or the local authority have taken possession or ordered a sale under this Schedule.

Condition as to residence may be dispensed with or suspended

3.—(1) The statutory condition as to residence may at any time be dispensed with by the local authority.

(2) The local authority may allow a proprietor to permit, by letting or otherwise, a house to be occupied as a furnished house by some other person—

(a) during a period not exceeding four months in all in any twelve months, or

(b) during his absence from the house in the performance of any duty arising from or incidental to any office, service or employment held or undertaken by him;

and the statutory condition as to residence is suspended while the permission continues.

(3) Where the proprietor of a house subject to the statutory conditions dies, the condition requiring residence is suspended until the expiration of twelve months from the death, or any earlier date at which the personal representatives transfer the ownership or interest of the proprietor in the course of administration.

(4) Where the proprietor of any such house becomes bankrupt, or his estate is administered in bankruptcy under section 130 of the Bankruptcy Act 1914, and in either case an arrangement under this Schedule is made with the trustee in bankruptcy, the local authority may, if they think fit, suspend the condition as to residence during the continuance of the arrangement.

(5) Where an advance has been made in pursuance of section 7(1) of the Small Dwellings Acquisition Act 1899 (power to make advance on strength of undertaking to begin residence), the statutory condition requiring residence is suspended during the period allowed before residence must be begun.

Personal liability and powers of the proprietor

4.—(1) The proprietor of the house of which the ownership was acquired by means of the advance is personally liable for the repayment of any sum due in respect of the advance until he ceases to be proprietor by reason of a transfer made in accordance with this paragraph.

(2) The proprietor of the house may with the permission of the local authority (which shall not be unreasonably withheld) at any time transfer his interest in the house, but any such transfer shall be made subject to the statutory conditions.

(3) The provisions of sub-paragraph (2) requiring the consent of the local authority to the transfer of the proprietor's interest in the house do not apply to a charge on that interest made by the proprietor, so far as the charge does not affect any rights or powers of the local authority under this Schedule.

Circumstances in which local authority may take possession or order sale

5.—(1) Where default is made in complying with the statutory condition as to residence, the local authority may take possession of the house, and where default is made in complying with any of the other statutory conditions, whether the statutory condition as to residence has or has not been complied with, the local authority may either take possession of the house or order the sale of the house without taking possession.

(2) In the case of the breach of any condition other than that of punctual payment of the principal and interest of the advance, the authority shall, previously to taking possession or ordering a sale, by notice in writing delivered at the house and addressed to the proprietor, call on the proprietor to comply with the condition, and if the proprietor—

(*a*) within 14 days after the delivery of the notice gives an undertaking in writing to the authority to comply with the notice, and

(*b*) within two months after the delivery of the notice complies with it,

the authority shall not take possession or, as the case may be, order a sale.

(3) In the case of the bankruptcy of the proprietor of the house, or in the case of a deceased proprietor's estate being administered in bankruptcy under section 130 of the Bankruptcy Act 1914, the local authority may either take possession of the house or order the sale of the house without taking possession, and shall do so except in pursuance of some arrangement to the contrary with the trustee in bankruptcy.

Recovery of possession and disposal of house

6.—(1) Where a local authority take possession of a house, all the estate, right, interest and claim of the proprietor in or to the house shall vest in and become the property of the local authority, and the authority may either retain the house under their own management or sell or otherwise dispose of it as they think expedient.

(2) Where a local authority take possession of a house, they shall pay to the proprietor either—

(*a*) such sum as may be agreed upon, or

(*b*) a sum equal to the value of the interest in the house at the disposal of the local authority, after deducting the amount of the advance then remaining unpaid and any sum due for interest;

and that value, in the absence of a sale and in default of agreement, shall be settled by a county court judge as arbitrator or, if the Lord Chancellor so authorises, by a single arbitrator appointed by the county court judge, and the Arbitration Act 1950 shall apply to any such arbitration.

(3) The sum so payable to the proprietor if not paid within three months after the date of taking possession shall carry interest at the rate of three per cent. per annum from the date of taking possession.

(4) All costs of or incidental to the taking possession, sale or other disposal of the house (including the costs of the arbitration, if any) incurred by the local authority, before the amount payable to the proprietor has been settled either by agreement or arbitration, shall be deducted from the amount otherwise payable to the proprietor.

(5) Where the local authority are entitled under this Schedule to take possession of a house, possession may be recovered in a county court whatever the annual value of the house for rating.

Procedure as to ordering sale

7.—(1) Where a local authority order the sale of a house without taking possession, they shall cause it to be put up for sale by auction and shall retain out of the proceeds of sale—

(*a*) any sum due to them on account of the interest or principal of the advance, and (*b*) all costs, charges and expenses properly incurred by them in or about the sale of the house,

and shall pay over the balance (if any) to the proprietor.

(2) If the local authority are unable at the auction to sell the house for such a sum as will allow of the payment out of the proceeds of sale of the interest and principal of the advance then due to the authority, and the costs, charges and expenses referred to above, they may take possession of the house in manner provided by this Schedule, but shall not be liable to pay any sum to the proprietor.

List of advances and accounts to be kept

8.—(1) A local authority shall keep at their offices a book containing a list of the advances made by them containing—

(*a*) a description of the house in respect of which the advance was made, and

(*b*) the amount advanced.

(2) The authority shall enter in the book with regard to each advance—

(*a*) the amount for the time being repaid,

(*b*) the name of the proprietor for the time being of the house, and

(*c*) such other particulars as the authority think fit to enter.

(3) The book shall be open to inspection at the office of the local authority during office hours free of charge.

(4) Separate accounts shall be kept by every local authority of their receipts and expenditure in relation to advances to which this Schedule applies.

Meaning of "residence", "ownership" and "proprietor"

9.—(1) A person shall not be treated for the purposes of this Schedule as resident in a house unless he is both the occupier of and resident in the house.

(2) In this Schedule "ownership" means such interest, or combination of interests, in a house as, together with the interest of the purchaser of the ownership, will constitute either—

(*a*) a fee simple in possession, or

(*b*) a leasehold interest in possession of which at least 60 years are unexpired at the date of the purchase.

(3) Where the ownership of a house is acquired by means of an advance to which this Schedule applies, the purchaser of the ownership or, in the case of any devolution or transfer, the person in whom the interest of the purchaser is for the time being vested, is the proprietor of the house for the purposes of this Schedule.

Date of advance

10. For the purposes of this Schedule an advance shall be deemed to have been made on the date on which the instrument securing the repayment of the advance was executed.

GENERAL NOTE

This Schedule continues the specific, detailed provisions governing mortgages granted under the Small Dwellings Acquisition Acts 1899–1923. Even when last amended, under Housing Act 1949, s.44(1) the provisions never applied to housing the market value of which exceeded £5,000, the provisions had long fallen into disuse for new loans, and replaced by the general, and much broader, powers now to be found in s.435, above. Nonetheless, as loans could be for up to 30 years (Small Dwellings Acquisition Act 1899 s.1(2)), it is possible that some mortgages are still unredeemed. The Schedule governs such matters as rate of interest, repayment method, residence by proprietor, insurance, maintenance in good sanitary condition and repair, use of the house, powers of entry by authority, person liability, repossession and disposal.

Section 524   SCHEDULE 19

CONTRIBUTIONS UNDER SUPERSEDED ENACTMENTS

(Section 36 of the Housing (Financial Provisions) Act 1958)

1.—(1) Contributions remain payable by the Secretary of State under section 36 of the Housing (Financial Provisions) Act 1958 (contributions over a period of 20 years towards certain grants under Part II of that Act, Part II of the House Purchase and Housing Act

1959 or Part III of the Housing Act 1964) in pursuance of applications made before 25th August 1969.

(2) The contributions are payable at such times and in such manner as the Treasury may direct and subject to such conditions as to records, certificates, audit or otherwise as the Secretary of State may, with the approval of the Treasury, impose.

(Section 16 of the Housing Act 1969)

2.—(1) Contributions remain payable by the Secretary of State under section 16 of the Housing Act 1969 (contributions over a period of 20 years towards grants paid under Part I of that Act) in pursuance of applications made before 12th December 1974.

(2) The contributions are payable at such times and in such manner as the Treasury may direct, and subject to such conditions as to records, certificates, audit or otherwise as the Secretary of State may, with the approval of the Treasury, impose.

GENERAL NOTE

This Schedule maintains payments under pre-1974 grant legislation, now replaced by Pt. XV, above.

Section 547

SCHEDULE 20

ASSISTANCE BY WAY OF REPURCHASE

PART I

THE AGREEMENT TO REPURCHASE

The interest to be acquired

1. In this Schedule "the interest to be acquired" means the interest of the person entitled to assistance by way of repurchase, so far as subsisting in—
   (*a*) the defective dwelling, and
   (*b*) any garage, outhouse, garden, yard and appurtenances occupied and used for the purposes of the dwelling or a part of it.

Request for notice of proposed terms of acquisition

2.—(1) A person who is entitled to assistance by way of repurchase may, within the period of three months beginning with the service of the notice of determination, or that period as extended, request the purchasing authority in writing to notify him of the proposed terms and conditions for their acquisition of the interest to be acquired.

(2) The authority shall, if there are reasonable grounds for doing so, by notice in writing served on the person so entitled, extend, or further extend, the period within which he may make a request under this paragraph (whether or not the period has expired).

Authority's notice of proposed terms

3. The purchasing authority shall, within the period of three months beginning with the making of a request under paragraph 2, serve on the person so entitled a notice in writing specifying the proposed terms and conditions and stating—
   (*a*) their opinion as to the value of the interest to be acquired, and
   (*b*) the effect of the following provisions of this Part of this Schedule.

Settlement of terms

4. Subject to the provisions of Part II of this Schedule (price payable and valuation), an agreement for the acquisition by the purchasing authority of the interest to be acquired shall contain such provisions as the parties agree or, in default of agreement, are determined in accordance with this Part of this Act to be reasonable.

Service of draft agreement

5. The authority shall, within three months of all the provisions to be included in the agreement being agreed or determined—
   (*a*) draw up for execution by the parties an agreement embodying those provisions, and
   (*b*) serve a copy of the agreement on the person entitled to assistance.

Notice to enter into agreement

6.—(1) The person entitled to assistance may, at any time within the period of six months beginning with the service of the copy of the agreement, or within that period as extended, notify the authority in writing that he requires them to enter into an agreement embodying those provisions and the authority shall comply with the requirement.

(2) The authority shall, if there are reasonable grounds for doing so, by notice in writing served on the person so entitled extend, or further extend, the period within which a notice under this paragraph may be given (whether or not the period has expired).

Part II

Price Payable and Valuation

The price

7.—(1) The price payable for the acquisition of an interest in pursuance of this Part of this Act is 95 per cent. of the value of the interest at the relevant time.

(2) In this Schedule "the relevant time" means the time at which the notice under paragraph 3 above (authority's notice of proposed terms of acquisition) is served on the person entitled to assistance.

The value

8.—(1) For the purposes of this Schedule, the value of an interest at the relevant time is the amount which, at that time, would be realised by a disposal of the interest on the open market by a willing seller to a person other than the purchasing authority on the following assumptions—

(a) that none of the defective dwellings to which the designation in question relates is affected by the qualifying defect;

(b) that no liability has arisen or will arise under a covenant required by section 35 or 155 (covenant to repay discount) or paragraph 6(1) of Schedule 8 (terms of shared ownership lease: covenant to pay for outstanding share), or any covenant to the like effect;

(c) that no obligation to acquire the interest arises under this Part of this Act; and

(d) that (subject to the preceding paragraphs) the seller is selling with and subject to the rights and burdens with and subject to which the disposal is to be made.

(2) Where the value of an interest falls to be considered at a time later than the relevant time and there has been since the relevant time a material change in the circumstances affecting the value of the interest, the value at the relevant time shall be determined on the further assumption that the change had occurred before the relevant time.

(3) In determining the value of an interest no account shall be taken of any right to the grant of a tenancy under section 554 (former owner-occupier) or section 555 (former statutory tenant).

Determination of value

9.—(1) Any question arising under this Schedule as to the value of an interest in a defective dwelling shall be determined by the district valuer in accordance with this paragraph.

(2) The person entitled to assistance or the purchasing authority may require that value to be determined or redetermined by notice in writing served on the district valuer—

(a) within the period beginning with the service on the person entitled to assistance of a notice under paragraph 3 above (authority's notice of proposed terms of acquisition) and ending with the service under paragraph 5 above of the copy of the agreement drawn up for execution by the parties, or

(b) after the end of that period but before the parties enter into an agreement for the acquisition of the interest of the person so entitled, if there is a material change in the circumstances affecting the value of the interest.

(3) A person serving notice on the district valuer under this paragraph shall serve notice in writing of that fact on the other party.

(4) Before making a determination in pursuance of this paragraph, the district valuer shall consider any representation made to him, within four weeks of the service of the notice under this paragraph, by the person entitled to assistance or the purchasing authority.

Service of amended draft agreement

10. Where the value of an interest is determined, or redetermined, in pursuance of a notice served under paragraph 9(2)(*b*) (notice given after service of draft agreement)—

   (*a*) the purchasing authority shall comply again with paragraph 5 (service of draft agreement within three months of terms being settled), and

   (*b*) paragraph 6 (notice to enter into agreement) shall apply in relation to that agreement instead of the earlier one.

PART III

SUPPLEMENTARY PROVISIONS

Introductory

11.—(1) In this Part of this Schedule "the agreement" means the agreement entered into in pursuance of Parts I and II of this Schedule, and—

   "the authority" means the authority acquiring an interest in a defective dwelling under the agreement;

   "the conveyance" means the conveyance executed under the agreement;

   "the interest acquired" means the interest in the dwelling concerned of which the vendor disposes under the agreement;

   "the purchase price" means the price which the agreement requires the authority to pay for the interest acquired; and

   "the vendor" means the person with whom the authority enter into the agreement.

(2) In this Part of this Schedule—

   (*a*) references to a charge include a mortgage or lien, but not a rentcharge within the meaning of the Rentcharges Act 1977, and

   (*b*) references to a relevant charge are to a charge to which the interest acquired is subject immediately before the conveyance and which secures the performance of an obligation but is not either a local land charge or a charge which is, or would be, overreached by the conveyance apart from this Schedule.

Conveyance frees interest acquired from relevant charges

12.—(1) The conveyance is effective—

   (*a*) to discharge the interest acquired from any relevant charge,

   (*b*) to discharge the interest acquired from the operation of any order made by a court for the enforcement of such a charge, and

   (*c*) to extinguish any term of years created for the purposes of such a charge,

without the persons entitled to or interested in such a charge, order or term of years becoming parties to or executing the conveyance.

(2) The effect of this paragraph is restricted to discharging the interest acquired from the charge and does not affect personal liabilities.

(3) This paragraph does not prevent a person from joining in the conveyance for the purpose of discharging the interest acquired from a charge.

(4) The operation of this paragraph is subject to paragraph 14 (effect of failure to apply purchase price in or towards satisfaction of charge).

Application of purchase price in satisfaction of relevant charges

13.—(1) The authority shall apply the purchase price in the first instance in or towards the redemption of any relevant charge securing the payment of money (if there is more than one, then according to their priorities), subject to the provisions of this paragraph.

(2) For the purposes of this paragraph—

   (*a*) a person entitled to a charge may not exercise a right to consolidate the charge with a separate charge on other property;

   (*b*) a person may be required to accept three months' or longer notice of the intention to repay the principal or any part of it secured by the charge, together with interest to the date of payment, notwithstanding that this differs from the terms of the security as to the time and manner of payment;

   (*c*) a charge to which the vendor or the authority themselves are entitled ranks for payment as it would if another person were entitled to it; and

   (*d*) where a person, without payment or for less payment than he would otherwise be entitled to, joins in the conveyance for the purpose of discharging the interest acquired from a charge, the persons to whom the purchase price ought to be paid shall be determined accordingly.

(3) This paragraph does not apply to—

(*a*) a charge in favour of the holders of a series of debentures issued by a body, or

(*b*) a charge in favour of trustees for such debenture holders which at the date of the conveyance is a floating charge;

and the authority shall disregard such charges in performing their duty under this paragraph.

14. If the authority do not apply an amount which under paragraph 13 they are required to apply in or towards the redemption of a charge (and do not pay that amount into court in accordance with paragraph 15), the charge is not discharged by virtue of paragraph 12 and the interest acquired remains subject to the charge as security for that amount.

Power to make payment into court in case of difficulty

15.—(1) Where a person is or may be entitled by virtue of paragraph 13 to receive, in respect of a relevant charge, the whole or part of the purchase price and—

(*a*) for any reason difficulty arises in ascertaining how much is payable in respect of the charge, or

(*b*) for any reason mentioned in sub-paragraph (2) difficulty arises in making a payment in respect of the charge,

the authority may pay into court on account of the purchase price the amount, if known, of the payment to be made in respect of the charge or, if the amount is not known, the whole of the purchase price or such lesser amount as the authority think right in order to provide for that payment.

(2) The reasons referred to in sub-paragraph (1)(*b*) are—

(*a*) that a person who is or may be entitled to receive payment cannot be found or ascertained;

(*b*) that any such person refuses or fails to make out a title, or to accept payment and give a proper discharge, or to take any step reasonably required of him to enable the sum payable to be ascertained and paid; or

(*c*) that a tender of the sum payable cannot, by reason of complications in the entitlement to payment or the want of two or more trustees or for other reasons, be effected, or not without incurring or involving unreasonable cost or delay.

Duty to pay into court in certain cases

16.—(1) The authority shall pay the purchase price into court if, before the execution of the conveyance, written notice is given to them—

(*a*) that the vendor, or a person entitled to a charge on the interest to be acquired, so requires either for the purpose of protecting the rights of persons so entitled or for reasons related to the bankruptcy or winding up of the vendor, or

(*b*) that steps have been taken to enforce a charge on the interest to be acquired by the bringing of proceedings in a court, by the appointment of a receiver or otherwise.

(2) Where a payment into court is made by reason only of a notice under this paragraph and the notice is given with reference to proceedings in a specified court (other than the county court), payment shall be made into that court.

Registration of title

17.—(1) Section 123 of the Land Registration Act 1925 (compulsory registration of title) applies in relation to the conveyance whether or not the dwelling concerned is in an area in which an Order in Council under section 120 of that Act is in force (areas of compulsory registration).

(2) For the purposes of registration of title to the land acquired by the authority—

(*a*) the authority shall give to the Chief Land Registrar a certificate stating that the person from whom the relevant interest was acquired was entitled to convey the interest subject only to such incumbrances, rights and interests as are stated in the conveyance or summarised in the certificate, and

(*b*) the Chief Land Registrar shall accept the certificate as sufficient evidence of the facts stated in it;

but if, as a result, he has to meet a claim against him under the Land Registration Acts 1925 to 1971, the authority shall indemnify him

(3) A certificate under sub-paragraph (2) shall be in a form approved by the Chief Land Registrar and shall be signed by such officer of the authority, or such other person, as may be approved by the Chief Land Registrar.

Interest acquired by local housing authority treated as acquired under Part II

18. If the authority are a local housing authority, the interest acquired by them shall be treated as acquired by them under section 17 (acquisition of land for purposes of Part II (provision of housing)).

Certain grant conditions cease to have effect

19.—(1) Where the interest acquired is or includes a dwelling in relation to which an improvement grant, intermediate grant, special grant or repairs grant has been paid under Part XV—
  (a) any grant condition imposed under or by virtue of that Part ceases to be in force with respect to the dwelling with effect from the time of disposal of the interest, and
  (b) the owner for the time being of the dwelling is not liable to make in relation to the grant any payment under section 506 (repayment of grant for breach of condition) except in pursuance of a demand made before the time of disposal of the interest.

(2) In this paragraph "dwelling" and "owner" have the same meaning as in Part XV.

Overreaching effect of conveyance

20. The conveyance has effect under section 2(1) of the Law of Property Act 1925 (conveyances overreaching certain equitable interests and powers) to overreach any incumbrance capable of being overreached under that section—
  (a) as if the requirements to which that section refers as to the payment of capital money allowed any part of the purchase price paid under paragraph 13, 15 or 16 (payment in satisfaction of charge or into court) to be so paid, and
  (b) where the interest conveyed is settled land, as if the conveyance were made under the powers of the Settled Land Act 1925.

GENERAL NOTE

When repurchase is the redress which is to be made available (as to which, see notes to s.537, above), this Schedule governs: (a) the agreement to repurchase (Pt. I), (b) the price payable and valuation (Pt. II), and (c) a number of supplementary provisions (Pt. III). Note, however, that in certain circumstances repurchase may not follow, when the property is subject to a pre-emption or surrender clause within s.549, although this Schedule will still be relevant as to price and value, so as to ensure that the owner does not suffer a loss because of it.

Part I
Para. 1
"Person entitled to assistance". See s.540. Note that the agreement is to cover that person's interest, in both defective dwelling (as to the meaning of which, see s.528), but also any garage, or outhouse (see s.539), *and* yard and appurtenance (see s.56), but in these "additional" cases only if "used for the purposes of the dwelling or a part of it", which would suggest only if used for the purposes of the dwelling *as* a dwelling not, *e.g.* a related business use (*cf.* notes to s.539, above). But subject to this, the interest of the person entitled to assistance need not be a "relevant interest" (see s.530) in the added cases.

Para. 2
"A person . . . entitled to assistance by way of repurchase . . . " See notes to s.537, above. Within three months of the notice of determination (see s.540), or that period if extended, the owner may request the authority in writing to notify him of the proposed terms and conditions of acquisition of interest. An extension is to be granted in writing by the authority, if there *are* reasonable grounds for so doing, even if the initial three months has expired; a refusal to extend is expressly challengeable in the county court under s.572(3), and in that connection it may be noted that the question is whether there *are* reasonable grounds for doing so, not whether there are reasonable grounds for doing so "in the opinion of the authority" or "if the authority are so satisfied", etc. See notes to s.533.

Para. 3
The authority then have a further three months to serve notice in writing stating their opinion as to the value of the interest to be acquired (as to which, see Pt. II, below), and the effect of the remaining provisions of Pt. I, *i.e.* this Part, of the Schedule.

Para. 4

The provisions for repurchase, other than as to price payable and valuation (see Part II, below), are to be those agreed, or are otherwise those which are reasonable as determined in accordance with Part XVI, *i.e.* s.572 county court jurisdiction.

Para. 5

Within three months of agreement or determination (see para 4, above), the authority have to draw up an agreement embodying the terms and conditions of the repurchase, and serve a copy on the owner. The authority cannot pass on the cost of this work: see s.552, above.

Para. 6

The last stage is for the owner to notify the authority in writing within six months of service of the paragraph 5 agreement that he requires them to enter into an agreement embodying the terms and conditions agreed or determined, and the authority shall comply with that requirement. If there are reasonable grounds for so doing, the authority shall in writing extend or further extend that period, and if they do not do so a dispute may be referred to the county court under s.572(3), see also notes to paragraph 2, above.

Part II
Para. 7

The price payable is 95 per cent. of the value at the time when the authority's notice of proposed terms of acquisition is served, under paragraph 3, above. The five per cent. reduction presumably reflects the fact that the owner, or a tenant, may have to be rehoused by the authority: see ss.554–557.

Para. 8

Value means open market value, without the qualifying defect (as to which see s.528, above), and without liability to repay discount which will arise if the initial purchase was from a local authority under Pt. II, or if under the right to buy under Pt. V, and five years have not elapsed since purchase. Also disregarded are the fact that authority are obliged to buy, and that the authority may be under a rehousing obligation (see ss.554–557), see also note to para. 7, above.

Sub-para. 2 would seem to refer to consideration of value by the district valuer (see notes to para 9, below). The initial valuation will be by the authority when serving the para. 3 notice. It is only if this is not accepted by the owner so that there is a further or later valuation, that the circumstances referred to in this sub-paragraph will occur, *i.e.* a valuation at a later time, but referable to an earlier date. There is no such express provision in relation to the right to buy (*cf.* s.127, above), as here: any change of circumstances affecting the value is to be taken into account.

Para. 9

Valuation disputes are referable to the district valuer, *not* the county court (see s.572(2)). There can only be a reference to the district valuer between service of the para. 3 notice, and the para. 5 copy of terms and conditions, unless there has been a change of circumstances such as affects value, in which case the reference—or a further reference—can be made at any time before the parties enter into the agreement. Reference is made by either party— owner or authority—serving notice on the district valuer, with a copy to the other party. Once notice has been served on the district valuer, the parties have four weeks to make representations to the district valuer.

Para. 10

Once the district valuer has determined or redetermined the value, the authority have to "re-comply" with para. 5, *viz.* serve a copy of the agreement within three months, and the para. 6 six months begins to run anew.

Part III
Para. 11

This paragraph defines the terms used in the remaining paragraphs of this Schedule. Note the reference to "relevant charge", which will normally mean a mortgage, but will not include minor charges or local land charges.

Para. 12

The authority take the premises free of a relevant charge (see para. 11) even if, *e.g.* there has been an order for possession not yet executed, in favour of the mortgagee, and extinguishes a mortgage by way of lease, and even though the mortgagee will not be a party to the conveyance. However, this does not release the former owner from the customary personal warranty contained in a mortgage. See, further, notes to para. 14, below.

Para. 13

The authority first pay off any relevant charge (see para. 11), subject to the provisions of this paragraph, which excludes the right of a mortgagee first to consolidate the charge with a charge on other property, or to insist on any period of notice other than that chosen by the authority, which is to be three months' or longer.

Para. 14

The para. 12 discharge only takes effect if the authority do not comply with the para. 13 obligation.

Para. 15

Where there are difficulties arranging for payment of the purchase money to discharge of a mortgage, the authority may pay the money into court.

Para. 16

The authority are obliged to make a payment into court in the circumstances specified in this paragraph.

Para. 17

Whether or not the land is in an area for registration, the conveyance to the authority is to be registered.

Para. 18

The property is, if the authority are a local housing authority, treated as acquired under Pt. II of this Act, *i.e.* the principal powers under which the local authority hold their housing stock.

Para. 19

This paragraph overrides conditions on a grant under Pt. XV, including a repayment of grant on disposal condition.

Para. 20

The conveyance overreaches equitable interests in the property, *e.g.* an interest of a spouse, and the interests will transfer to the money.

Section 566   SCHEDULE 21

Dwellings Included in More Than One Designation

Introductory

1. This Schedule applies in relation to a defective dwelling where the building that the dwelling consists of or includes falls within two or more designations under section 528 (designation by Secretary of State) or 559 (designation under local scheme).

Cases in which later designation to be disregarded

2. Where a person is already eligible for assistance in respect of a defective dwelling at a time when another designation comes into operation, the later designation shall be disregarded if—
   (*a*) he would not be eligible for assistance in respect of the dwelling by virtue of that designation, or
   (*b*) he is by virtue of an earlier designation entitled to assistance by way of repurchase in respect of the dwelling.

In other cases any applicable designation may be relied on

3. Where a person is eligible for assistance in respect of a defective dwelling and there are two or more applicable designations, this Part has effect in relation to the dwelling as if—
   (*a*) references to the designation were to any applicable designation;
   (*b*) references to the provision by virtue of which it is a defective dwelling were to any provision under which an applicable designation was made;

(c) references to the qualifying defect were to any qualifying defect described in an applicable designation;

(d) references to the period within which persons may seek assistance under this Part were to any period specified for that purpose in any applicable designation; and

(e) the reference in section 543(1)(c) (amount of reinstatement grant) to the maximum amount permitted to be taken into account for the purposes of that section were to the aggregate of the maximum amounts for each applicable designation.

Procedure to be followed where later designation comes into operation

4. The following provisions of this Schedule apply where—

(a) notice has been given to a person under section 536 (determination of eligibility) stating that he is in the opinion of the local housing authority eligible for assistance in respect of a defective dwelling, and

(b) after the notice has been given another designation comes into operation designating a class within which the building that consists of or includes the dwelling falls.

5.—(1) The local housing authority shall, as soon as reasonably practicable, give him notice in writing stating whether in their opinion the new designation falls to be disregarded in accordance with paragraph 2.

(2) If in their opinion, it is to be disregarded the notice shall state the reasons for their view.

6.—(1) This paragraph applies where it appears to the authority that the new designation does not fall to be disregarded.

(2) They shall forthwith give him notice in writing—

(a) stating the effect of the new designation and of paragraph 3 (new designation may be relied on) and sub-paragraph (3) below (entitlement to be redetermined), and

(b) informing him that he has the right to make a claim under section 537(2) (claim that assistance by way of reinstatement grant is inappropriate in his case).

(3) They shall as soon as reasonably practicable—

(a) make a further determination under section 537(1) (determination of form of assistance to which person is entitled), taking account of the new designation, and

(b) give a further notice of determination in place of the previous notice;

and where the determination is that he is entitled to assistance by way of repurchase, the notice shall state the effect of paragraph 7 (cases where reinstatement work already begun or contracted for).

7.—(1) This paragraph applies where a person entitled to assistance by way of reinstatement grant is given a further notice of entitlement under paragraph 6 stating that he is entitled to assistance by way of repurchase; and "the reinstatement work" means the work stated in the previous notice or in a notice under section 544 (change of work required).

(2) Where in such a case—

(a) he satisfies the authority that he has, before the further notice was received, entered into a contract for the provision of services or materials for any of the reinstatement work, or

(b) any such work has been carried out before the further notice was received, and has been carried out to the satisfaction of the appropriate authority,

the previous notice (and any notice under section 544 (change of work required)) continues to have effect for the purposes of reinstatement grant in relation to the reinstatement work or, in a case within paragraph (b), such of that work as has been carried out as mentioned in that paragraph, and the authority shall pay reinstatement grant accordingly.

(3) Where in a case within sub-paragraph (2) the reinstatement work is not completed but part of the work is carried out to the satisfaction of the appropriate authority within the period stated in the notice in question—

(a) the amount of reinstatement grant payable in respect of that part of the work shall be an amount equal to the maximum instalment of grant payable under section 545(2) (instalments not to exceed appropriate percentage of cost of work completed), and

(b) section 546 (repayment of grant in event of failure to complete work) does not apply in relation to reinstatement grant paid in respect of that part of the work.

GENERAL NOTE

Provided designations by the Secretary of State continue to refer not only to defect, but also manufacturer, it would seem impossible for a dwelling to be defective within two such national designations: see notes to s.528. However, if the Secretary of State designates a dwelling that is already within a local designation (see s.559), the dwelling will fall into two categories: see s.559(2). In such circumstances the provisions of this Schedule will apply. There can be no local designation of dwellings already within a national designation: *ibid*.

Para. 2

If a person is already eligible for assistance under a local designation, and there is subsequently a national designation, the potential applicant stays under the local designation if, *but only if* (a) he is not eligible for assistance under the national designation, or (b) the entitlement under the local designation is to repurchase. Accordingly, and notwithstanding the inversion, a national designation supplants a local designation when the applicant was eligible under local and is now eligible under national, unless local would lead to repurchase. Thus, although prima facie within both, he may not qualify under the latter because there has been a disqualifying intervening disposal for value (s.531(1), but *cf.* s.531(3)). Note, however, that where national does *not* supplant local, *both* will apply: see next paragraphs.

Para. 3

Where *both* designations apply (see last paragraph), references to designation, qualifying defect, and period within which a person may seek assistance, mean under either designation, while the maximum amount to be taken into account for the purpose of calculating grant-aid means the maximum under *both*, added together.

Para. 4

If after an applicant has been notified of eligibility under a local scheme, a national scheme comes into operation, the following paragraphs apply.

Para. 5

In the circumstances referred to in the last paragraph, the authority must give the applicant notice stating whether or not the national designation is to be disregarded under para. 2, above. If it is, they must state their reasons: see s.533.

Para. 6

If the para. 5 notice states that the national designation is not to be disregarded, and accordingly the applicant is, as it were, dually designated, the authority have to tell the applicant so, telling him what the effect of the new, national designation is, and of the para. 3 effect of being dually designated, and referring him to s.537, *i.e.* the right to seek repurchase instead of reinstatement grant, which is aimed at those cases where dual designation works against the interests of the applicant. The authority thereafter make a new determination of the form of assistance to which the applicant is entitled, taking the new designation into account, and where the effect is repurchase, address the applicant to para. 7, below.

Para. 7

This paragraph applies where repurchase is the effect of dual designation, but has entered into a contract for reinstatement work, or such work has been carried out before the paragraph 6 notice was received, the authority still pay the appropriate amount of reinstatement grant. What the applicant will lose, therefore, is his part of the expenditure.

Section 579   SCHEDULE 22

COMPULSORY PURCHASE ORDERS UNDER SECTION 290

Introductory

1. This Schedule applies to compulsory purchase orders under section 290 (acquisition of land comprised in, surrounded by or adjoining a clearance area).

Form of order

2. The order shall be in the prescribed form, shall describe by reference to a map the land to which it applies and shall show in the prescribed manner—

   (*a*) what parts, if any, of the land to be purchased compulsorily are outside the clearance area, and
   (*b*) what buildings, if any, to be purchased compulsorily are included in the clearance area only on the ground that they are by reason of their bad arrangement in relation to other buildings, or the narrowness or bad arrangement of the streets, dangerous or injurious to the health of the inhabitants of the area.

Notice of making an order

3.—(1) Before submitting the order to the Secretary of State the local housing authority shall comply with the following requirements.

(2) They shall publish in one or more newspapers circulating in their district a notice in the prescribed form stating the fact of such an order having been made, describing the area comprised in it, and naming a place where a copy of the order and of the map referred to in it may be seen at all reasonable hours.

(3) They shall serve on—

(a)　every owner of the land to which the order relates,

(b)　every lessee or occupier of the land, other than a tenant for a month or less than a month or a statutory tenant, and

(c)　every mortgagee of the land whom it is reasonably practicable to ascertain,

a notice in the prescribed form stating the effect of the order and that it is about to be submitted to the Secretary of State for confirmation and specifying the time within and the manner in which objections to it can be made.

(4) A notice which under sub-paragraph (3) is to be served on an owner, lessee or occupier may be served by addressing it to him by the description of "owner" or "lessee" or "occupier" of the land (describing it) to which it relates and delivering it to some person on the premises or, if there is no person on the premises to whom it may be delivered, by fixing it, or a copy of it, to some conspicuous part of the premises.

Hearing of objections

4.—(1) If an objection duly made by a person on whom a notice is required to be served under paragraph 3 is not withdrawn, the Secretary of State shall before confirming the order either—

(a)　cause a public local inquiry to be held, or

(b)　afford to every such person by whom an objection has been made and not withdrawn an opportunity of appearing before and being heard by a person appointed by the Secretary of State for the purpose,

and shall consider any objection not withdrawn and the report of the person who held the inquiry or was so appointed.

(2) Where an objection not withdrawn has been made on the ground that a building included in the order is not unfit for human habitation, the local housing authority shall, at least 28 days before the date of the inquiry or hearing—

(a)　serve on the objector a notice in writing stating what facts have emerged as their principal grounds for being satisfied that the building is so unfit, and

(b)　send a copy of the notice to the Secretary of State.

(3) A person who objects to the order on the grounds that a building included in the order (being a building in which he is interested) is not unfit for human habitation and who appears at the public local inquiry or hearing in support of his objection shall, if the building is included in the order as confirmed as being unfit for human habitation, be entitled, on making a request in writing, to be furnished by the Secretary of State with a statement in writing of his reasons for deciding that the building is so unfit.

(4) Notwithstanding anything in the foregoing provisions of this paragraph, the Secretary of State may require a person who has made an objection to state in writing the grounds of his objection and may disregard the objection for the purposes of this paragraph if he is satisfied that it relates exclusively to matters which can be dealt with by the tribunal by whom the compensation is to be assessed.

Confirmation of order

5.—(1) The Secretary of State may confirm the order, with or without modification—

(a)　if no objection is duly made by any of the persons on whom notices are required to be served or if all objections so made are withdrawn; or

(b)　after considering any objection made which is not withdrawn and the report of the person who held the inquiry or of the appointed person.

(2) His power to confirm the order with modifications is not exercisable so as to authorise the local housing authority—

(a)　to purchase land which the order as submitted would not have authorised them to purchase, or

(b)　to purchase as land comprised in the clearance area land shown in the order as submitted as being outside the area, or

(c)　to purchase a building compulsorily on terms less favourable as to compensation than those which would have applied if the order had been confirmed as submitted.

(3) If the Secretary of State is of opinion that land included by the local housing authority in the clearance area should not have been so included, he shall in confirming the order modify it so as to exclude the land for all purposes from the clearance area; but if in such a case he is of opinion that the land might properly be purchased by the authority under section 290(2) (land surrounded by or adjoining clearance area), he shall further modify the order so as to authorise them to purchase the land under that provision.

(4) The Secretary of State may confirm the order notwithstanding that the effect of the modifications made by him in excluding a building from the clearance area is to sever the area into two or more separate and distinct areas; and in such a case the provisions of this Act relating to the effect of the order when confirmed and to the proceedings to be taken subsequent to its confirmation apply to those areas as one clearance area.

Notice of confirmation of order

6. So soon as may be after the order has been confirmed by the Secretary of State, the local housing authority shall—

(*a*) publish in a newspaper circulating in their district a notice in the prescribed form stating that the order has been confirmed and naming a place where a copy of the order as confirmed and of the map referred to in the order may be seen at all reasonable hours, and

(*b*) serve a like notice on every person who, having given notice to the Secretary of State of his objection to the order, appeared at the public local inquiry or before the appointed person in support of his objection.

Challenge to validity of order

7.—(1) If a person aggrieved by the order desires to question its validity on the ground—

(*a*) that it is not within the powers of this Act, or

(*b*) that any requirement of this Act has not been complied with,

he may within six weeks after publication of the notice of confirmation of the order make an application for the purpose to the High Court.

(2) Where such an application is duly made, the court may by interim order suspend the operation of the order, either generally or in so far as it affects property of the applicant, until the final determination of the proceedings.

(3) If on the hearing of the application the court is satisfied—

(*a*) that the order is not within the powers of this Act, or

(*b*) that the interests of the applicant have been substantially prejudiced by any requirement of this Act not having been complied with,

the court may quash the order, either generally or in so far as it affects property of the applicant.

(4) No appeal lies to the House of Lords from a decision of the Court of Appeal in proceedings under this paragraph except by leave of the Court of Appeal.

(5) Subject to the provisions of this paragraph, the order shall not be questioned in any legal proceedings whatsoever, either before or after the order is confirmed.

Notice of order having become operative

8.—(1) Subject to the provisions of paragraph 7, the order becomes operative at the expiration of six weeks from the date on which notice of confirmation of the order is published in accordance with paragraph 6.

(2) So soon as may be after the order has become operative the local housing authority shall serve a copy of the notice on every person on whom a notice was served by them under paragraph 3 of their intention to submit the order to the Secretary of State for confirmation.

Costs of opposing orders, &c.

9.—(1) The Secretary of State may make such order as he thinks fit in favour of an owner of lands included in the compulsory purchase order for the allowance of reasonable expenses properly incurred by the owner in opposing the order.

(2) The following shall be deemed to be expenses of the local housing authority under this Part—

(*a*) expenses allowed to a person under sub-paragraph (1), and

(*b*) expenses incurred by the Secretary of State in relation to a compulsory purchase order, to such amount as he thinks proper to direct, and shall be paid to that person and to the Secretary of State in such manner and at such times, either in one sum or by instalments, as the Secretary of State may order.

(3) The Secretary of State may order interest to be paid, at such rate not exceeding 5 per cent. per annum as he thinks fit, upon any sum for the time being due in respect of expenses under sub-paragraph (2).

(4) An order made by the Secretary of State in pursuance of this paragraph may be made a rule of the High Court, and be enforced accordingly.

GENERAL NOTE

This Schedule contains the compulsory purchase procedures which are applicable to purchases under s.290, *i.e.* clearance areas within Pt. IX, in place of the procedures of the Acquisition of Land Act 1981.

Para. 2

In addition to the requirement that the order be in prescribed form (see, S.I. 1972 No. 228, Form 24, retained in force by Housing (Consequential Provisions) Act 1985, s.2), the order must include incorporate a map showing the land to which it applies. The map must show what land is incorporated in the clearance area by reason only of bad arrangement *between* buildings, or narrowness or bad arrangement of streets—see s.289,—and what land is outside the area proper but "added" for reasons of convenient redevelopment or clearance under s.290.

Para. 3

The draft order must be publicised, and notice in prescribed form (S.I. 1972 No. 228) must be served on every owner, lessee and occupier, other than a periodic tenant whose tenancy is for periods of less than a month, and with the exception of a statutory tenant under the Rent Act 1977 or the rent (Agriculture) Act 1976. In addition, every mortgagee of any land affected insofar as it is reasonably practicable to ascertain who they may be must be served.

Although a time must be specified during which objections can be made, no time is specified by the statute, so that the question is one for the authority, subject to the elementary proposition that a time too short to enable objections to be properly formulated would certainly not be upheld by the courts.

The notice has to state what the effect of the order will be, not also the authority's reasons for believing that it may be made: *Wyse* v. *Secretary of State for the Environment and Borough of Newcastle-under-Lyme* [1984] J.P.L. 256.

Para. 4

If there is an objection, which is not withdrawn, the Secretary of State must either cause a public local inquiry to be held, or arrange a hearing into the objection. The distinction between the two is not important, although the former is considered to be somewhat more formal than the latter (Ministry of Health Circular 104/46), and whereas notice of the latter is given only to the authority and objectors, notice of the former is also advertised locally: Compulsory Purchase by Public Authorities (Inquiries Procedure) Rules 1976 (S.I. 1976 No. 74).

If the basis of the objection is not clear, the Secretary of State is entitled to call for a written statement of grounds, and if those grounds relate only to matters of compensation, may disregard the objection. Where an objection is on the basis that the property is not unfit for human habitation, at least 28 days before the inquiry the authority must provide a written statement of the facts on which the finding of unfitness was based.

Under the Inquiry Rules, Rule 7, at least 42 days' notice of the inquiry must be given. No less than 28 days before the inquiry, the authority must serve on objectors a statement of reasons for making the order, together with a list of documents on which the authority propose to rely at the hearing, and details of how these may be inspected by an objector: Rule 4. Failure to provide a complete list, so that new material is introduced in the course of the hearing, could lead to an adjournment: Rule 7. The length of any such adjournment will depend on the amount of new material submitted: *Performance Cars Ltd.* v. *Secretary of State for the Environment* [1977] J.P.L. 585, C.A.

Once there are objections to a proposed order, the Secretary of State's function becomes quasi-judicial: *Johnson* v. *Minister of Health* [1947] 2 All E.R. 395, C.A. He cannot thereafter have any consultations with the authority on a relevant matter without giving the objector an opportunity to be present: *Steele* v. *Minister of Housing and Local Government* (1956) 6 P. & C.R. 386; see also *Errington* v. *Ministry of Health* [1935] 1 K.B. 249, C.A., but *cf. Ackerman* v. *Secretary of State for the Environment* (1980) 257 E.G. 1037, C.A., where on the facts it was held that there had been no such denial of opportunity to be heard.

In *Ostreicher* v. *Secretary of State for the Environment* [1978] 1 W.L.R. 810, C.A., a refusal of an adjournment of an inquiry set for a religious holiday was upheld, where the application for the adjournment was made only two weeks before the due date, written submissions from surveyors had already been received, and the objectors could be represented at the inquiry.

The Secretary of State's Inspector must also act judicially: "He must only hear evidence and inspect the property when both sides are present. He must not take into consideration extrinsic information which comes to his knowledge in the absence of one party or the other. The Minister . . . must only consider the report and the material properly before him. He must not act on extrinsic evidence which the houseowner has no opportunity of contradicting": *Steele.*

Thus, when an Inspector went back to a site after an inquiry had finished and noticed something which he took into account in reaching his decision, there was a breach of the rules of natural justice: *Fairmount Investments Ltd.* v. *Secretary of State for the Environment* [1976] 1 W.L.R. 1255, H.L.; see also *Hibernian Property Co. Ltd.* v. *Secretary of State for the Environment* (1973) 27 P. & C.R. 197. However, an Inspector is bound to visit a site if asked to do so by authority or objector (Inquiry Rules, Rule 8); both may accompany him, but if the appointed time ceases to be convenient, he is not bound to adjourn to another time or date: *ibid.* He may also visit a site before or during the inquiry, unaccompanied: *ibid.*

There is no rule against hearsay evidence, but an Inspector should not allow anything at all to be put in evidence: *French Kier Developments* v. *Secretary of State for the Environment* [1977] 1 All E.R. 296. See also *Re London (Hammersmith) Housing Order* [1936] 2 All E.R. 1063, in which an Inspector's decision to refuse to allow a statement by counsel which it was not intended to support with evidence was upheld.

Although the Inspector is not obliged to allow cross-examination (*Miller* v. *Minister of Housing and Local Government* [1968] 1 W.L.R. 922, C.A., *Bushell and Brunt* v. *Secretary of State for the Environment* [1981] A.C. 75, H.L.), as a general principle, cross-examination should be permitted on relevant matters: *Wednesbury Corporation* v. *Ministry of Housing and Local Government (No. 2)* [1966] 2 Q.B. 275, C.A., *Errington* v. *Minister of Health* [1935] 1 K.B. 249, C.A., *Nicholson* v. *Secretary of State for Energy* (1977) 76 L.G.R. 693.

A common ground for objection is an owner's alternative proposals. Even if these are not on their face financially viable, an Inspector ought to consider their genuiness: *Menachem Schleider* v. *Secretary of State and Gateshead Metropolitan Borough Council* [1983] J.P.L. 382, Q.B.D. An owner's alternative proposals should always be dealt with: *London Welsh Association Ltd* v. *Secretary of State for the Environment* (1980) 255 E.G. 1095, C.A. If the issue is raised before an Inspector, it would be wrong to exclude consideration of the respective costs of clearance and rehabilitation: *Eckersley* v. *Secretary of State for the Environment* (1977) 244 E.G. 299, C.A.

If the Secretary of State differs from an Inspector's findings of fact, he is bound to provide an opportunity for representations to be made on the point: Inquiry Rules 1976, Rule 9. However, the Secretary of State is entitled to take the view as a matter of policy that it is more satisfactory to allow an owner's proposals to be put into effect than for the authority to acquire land, even at some sacrifice of efficiency or certainty, and in accepting the likelihood of an owner carrying out his proposals he may be exercising a judgment or expressing an opinion as distinct from differing from the Inspector on a finding of fact: *Islington London Borough Council* v. *Secretary of State* (1982) 43 P. & C.R. 300, Q.B.D.

Para. 5

This paragraph contains the power to confirm the order, which may be subject to modifications, although not such as to authorise the authority to purchase land not within the original draft, or to purchase as clearance area land that which was originally identified as added lands (*i.e.* confirmation of added lands must be on the original grounds), or to purchase on terms which would lead to less compensation than as submitted. The Secretary of State can, however, permit the authority to purchase as added lands that which was initially included as clearance area land.

If the Secretary of State declines to confirm the order, the clearance area will cease to exist as such so far as those lands are concerned: *R.* v. *Secretary of State for the Environment, ex parte Wellingborough Council* (1982) 80 L.G.R. 603, Q.B.D. There is no reason in principle why an authority should not challenge the Secretary of State's *refusal* to confirm: *London Borough of Islington, Stockport Metropolitan Borough Council* v. *Secretary of State for the Environment* (1982) 43 P. & C.R. 300, Q.B.D.

Para. 6

Once an order has been confirmed, with or without modification, the authority must publicise (in prescribed form—see S.I. 1972 No. 228, Form 27) the confirmation, providing information as to where the order, and the map under para. 2, may be inspected, *and* serve notice on every objector who appeared at the inquiry or before the Inspector.

Under the Inquiry Rules (above), Rule 10, the Secretary of State is bound to give his reasons for his decision. The Secretary of State is not bound to provide a copy of the Inspector's report, but one may be sought within the month after notification of the decision: *ibid.* The duty to give reasons means that proper and adequate reasons dealing with the substantive issues raised must be given: *Re Poyser & Mills Arbitration* [1964] 2 Q.B. 467; see also *Givaudan* v. *Minister of Housing and Local Government* [1967] 1 W.L.R. 250. However, the decision-letter and report are not to be read as if a statute, to be scrutinised for errors, but in a "common-sense" way: *Parker* v. *Secretary of State* (1980) 257 E.G. 718, C.A.

Para. 7

There are two grounds of challenge which may be subject to appeal to the High Court within six weeks of publication of notice of confirmation under para. 6, above: that the order is not within the powers of the Act, or that any requirement of the Act has not been complied with: see *Re Bowman, South Shields (Thames Street) Clearance Order, 1931* [1932] 2 K.B. 621; *Re Falmouth (Well Lane, Sedgmond's Court and Smithwick Hill) Clearance Order, 1936* [1937] 3 All E.R. 308, *Re London County Council (Riley Street, Chelsea No. 1) Order, 1938* [1945] 2 All E.R. 484.

However, an order will only be quashed for non-compliance with the requirement of that Act if the interests of the applicant have been substantially prejudiced by the failure: sub-para. (3)(*b*). Appeal may be by any person aggrieved, which will include the "statutory objectors", *i.e.* those who had to be served with notice of the draft order, *and* anyone who in the discretion of the Inspector was given a right of audience at the inquiry: *Turner* v. *Secretary of State for the Environment* (1973) 28 P. & C.R. 123.

A breach of the Inquiry Rules (above) will constitute a failure to comply with a requirement of the Act. It is hard to generalise on what constitutes "substantial prejudice", although it has been said that a person will be substantially prejudiced by a defect in procedure if he loses a chance of being "better off in relation to the proposed order": *Hibernian Property Co.* v. *Secretary of State for the Environment* (1973) 27 P. & C.R. 197; see also *McMeechan* v. *Secretary of State for the Environment* [1974] J.P.L. 411, C.A. A failure either to approve proposals under ss.308 or 310, above, (redevelopment proposals by owner), or to comply with the requirement that they be transmitted to the Secretary of State under s.311, above, is a requirement of the Act for this purpose: *Menachem Schleider* v. *Secretary of State for the Environment* [1983] J.P.L. 383.

Although the appeal must be brought within six weeks (which means that the notice of motion under R.S.C., Order 94 must be entered at the Crown Office of the High Court and served—see *Summers* v. *Minister of Health* [1947] 1 All E.R. 184), the court may subsequently allow an amendment: *Hanily* v. *Minister of Local Government and Planning* [1951] 2 K.B. 917. If both the authority and the Secretary of State are made parties to a challenge, the appellant need only pay one set of costs, and the authority and the Secretary of State should arrange conduct of the proceedings between them: *Re Bowman, South Shields (Thames Street) Clearance Order, 1931* [1932] 2 K.B. 621; *Re Mason* (1934) 50 T.L.R. 392.

The courts will intervene when conclusions are not supported by evidence: *Coleen Properties* v. *Minister of Housing and Local Government* [1971] 1 W.L.R. 433, C.A. They will also intervene when the Secretary of State has left something material out of account (see *Brinklow & Croft Brothers Ltd.* v. *Secretary of State for the Environment* [1976] J.P.L. 299, *Eckersley* v. *Secretary of State for the Environment* (1977) 244 E.G. 299, C.A.) or has misdirected himself in law or wrongfully fettered his discretion: *Lavender* v. *Minister of Housing and Local Government* [1970] 1 W.L.R. 1231.

However, fettering by policy must be distinguished from the Secretary of State's freedom to maintain a prior policy, which he chooses to apply after considering an individual issue: *Stringer* v. *Minister of Housing and Local Government* [1970] 1 W.L.R. 1281. See, also, *e.g.* *British Oxygen Co. Ltd.* v. *Board of Trade* [1971] A.C. 610, H.L., and *Re Betts* [1983] 2 A.C. 613, 10 H.L.R. 97, H.L.

The provisions of this paragraph do not apply to a decision to *not* confirm an order: *Islington London Borough Council, Stockport Metropolitan Borough Council* v. *Secretary of State for the Environment* (1982) 43 P. & C.R. 300, Q.B.D; nor do they apply if someone seeks to challenge the resolution of the authority to make the order in the first place: *R.* v.

London Borough of Camden, ex parte Comyn Ching & Co. (London) Ltd. [1984] J.P.L. 661, Q.B.D.

The "ouster" clause in sub-para. (5) excludes judicial review even on such grounds as bad faith or fraud: see *Smith* v. *East Elloe Rural District Council* [1956] A.C. 736, H.L., applied in *R.* v. *Secretary of State for the Environment, ex parte Ostler* [1977] Q.B. 122, C.A., distinguishing *Anisminic Ltd.* v. *Foreign Compensation Commission* [1969] 2 A.C. 147, H.L.

Para. 8

The order is operative six weeks' from publication of notice of confirmation and service of notice under paragraph 6, above, subject to any express order of the court deferring its operation under para. 7(2), above.

Para. 9

The Secretary of State may make an order as to the costs of opposing an order.

Section 586   SCHEDULE 23

PAYMENTS IN RESPECT OF WELL-MAINTAINED HOUSES

Well-maintained houses subject to demolition or closing orders

1.—(1) Where a house—
(a) is vacated in pursuance of a demolition or closing order under section 265 (unfit houses beyond repair at reasonable cost), or
(b) might have been the subject of such a demolition order but is vacated and demolished in pursuance of an undertaking for its demolition given to the local housing authority,
a person may represent to the local housing authority that the house in question has been well maintained and that the good maintenance of the house is attributable wholly or partly to work carried out by him or at his expense

(2) The representation must be made within three months of the service by the local housing authority of a copy of the order or, as the case may be, of the date of the undertaking.

(3) If the authority are satisfied that the representation is correct, they shall make to the person by whom the representation was made such payment, if any, as is authorised by the following provisions of this Schedule; and if they are not so satisfied they shall serve on him notice that no such payment falls to be made.

(4) In reaching that decision the authority shall leave out of account any defects in the house in respect of the matters listed in section 604 (standard of fitness for human habitation) other than repair.

(5) A person aggrieved by a notice under sub-paragraph (3) may, within 21 days after the date of the service of the notice, appeal to the county court and on the appeal the court may make such order confirming, quashing or varying the notice as it thinks fit.

(6) If the persons who would be entitled to appear and be heard on such an appeal so agree in writing, any matter which might have been the subject of an appeal shall instead be submitted to arbitration.

Well-maintained houses purchased under s.192 or 300

2.—(1) Where a house is purchased compulsorily under—
        section 192 (unfit house subject to repair notice found to be beyond repair), or
        section 300 (purchase of condemned house for temporary housing use),
a person may represent to the local housing authority that the house in question has been well maintained and that the good maintenance of the house is attributable wholly or partly to work carried out by him or at his expense.

(2) The representation must be made within three months of the service by the local housing authority of—
(a) in the case of a purchase under section 192, the notice of the compulsory purchase order;
(b) in the case of a purchase under section 300, the notice of their determination to purchase under that section.

(3) If the authority are satisfied that the representation is correct, they shall make to the person by whom the representation was made such payment, if any, as is authorised by the following provisions of this Schedule; and if they are not so satisfied, they shall serve on him notice that no such payment falls to be made.

[B. 9]

(4) In reaching that decision the authority shall leave out of account any defects in the house in respect of the matters listed in section 604 (standard of fitness for human habitation), other than repair.

(5) A person aggrieved by a notice under sub-paragraph (3) may, within 21 days after the date of the service of the notice, appeal to the county court and on the appeal the court may make such order confirming, quashing or varying the notice as it thinks fit.

(6) If the persons who would be entitled to appear and be heard on such an appeal so agree in writing, any matter in dispute which might have been the subject of an appeal shall instead be submitted to arbitration.

Well-maintained house subject to clearance

3.—(1) Where a house—
   (*a*) is made the subject of a compulsory purchase order under section 290 (acquisition of land for clearance) as being unfit for human habitation, and
   (*b*) is on that ground included in the order as confirmed by the Secretary of State,
the local housing authority shall if they are satisfied that the house has been well maintained make a payment of such amount, if any, as is authorised by the following provisions of this Schedule.

(2) The payment shall be made—
   (*a*) if the house is occupied by an owner, to him;
   (*b*) if the house is not so occupied, to the person or persons liable under any enactment, covenant or agreement to maintain and repair the house (and, if more than one person is so liable, in such shares as the authority think equitable in the circumstances);
unless some other person satisfies the authority that the good maintenance is attributable to a material extent to the work carried out by him or at his expense, in which case the authority may, if it appears to them to be equitable in the circumstances, make the payment, in whole or in part, to him.

Amount of payment for well-maintained house

4.—(1) The amount of the payment to be made under paragraph 1, 2 or 3 is an amount equal to the rateable value of the house multiplied by four or such other multiplier as may be prescribed by order of the Secretary of State; but subject to the limit that the amount shall not exceed the amount, if any, by which the full value of the house exceeds its site value.

(2) For this purpose the rateable value of a house is—
   (*a*) if the house is a hereditament for which a rateable value is shown in the valuation list in force on the relevant date, that rateable value;
   (*b*) if the house forms part only of such a hereditament, or consists of or forms part of more than one such hereditament, such value as is found by a proper apportionment or aggregation of the rateable value or values shown;
and any question arising as to the proper apportionment or aggregation of any value or values shall be referred to and determined by the district valuer.

(3) The "relevant date" is—
   (*a*) if the house was purchased compulsorily under section 192 (house subject to repair notice found to be beyond repair), the date when the notice mentioned in that section was served;
   (*b*) if the house was vacated in pursuance of a demolition or closing order, the date when the order was made;
   (*c*) if the house was vacated and demolished in pursuance of an undertaking for its demolition given to the local housing authority, the date on which the undertaking was given;
   (*d*) if the house was comprised in an area declared a clearance area, the date on which the area was so declared;
   (*e*) if the house was purchased compulsorily in pursuance of a notice served under section 300 (purchase of condemned house for temporary housing use), the date on which the notice was served.

(4) An order of the Secretary of State prescribing a multiplier for the purposes of this paragraph shall be made by statutory instrument which shall be of no effect unless approved by a resolution of each House of Parliament.

(5) In this paragraph—
      "full value" means the amount which would have been payable as compensation if the house had been purchased compulsorily but not as being unfit for human habitation, and

"site value" means the amount which is payable as compensation by virtue of its being purchased compulsorily as being unfit for human habitation, or which would have been so payable if it had been so purchased;

and any question as to such value shall be determined, in default of agreement, in the same way as a question of disputed compensation arising on such a purchase.

Partially well-maintained houses

5.—(1) A house which apart from this paragraph would not fall to be treated as well maintained for the purposes of paragraphs 1 to 3 shall be so treated if either the exterior or the interior of the house has been well maintained.

(2) A payment made under paragraph 1, 2 or 3 by virtue of this paragraph shall be one half of the amount ascertained in accordance with paragraph 4.

Well maintained flats and parts of buildings

6.—(1) Where—

(*a*) a house comprises more than one dwelling, or

(*b*) a house is occupied partly for the purposes of a dwelling or dwellings and partly for other purposes,

the dwellings or each of the dwellings shall be deemed to be a house for the purposes of the provisions of this Schedule so far as they relate to the maintenance of the interior of a house, but not so far as they relate to the maintenance of the exterior of the house.

(2) For this purpose the exterior of such a house includes any part of the house which is not included in the interior of a dwelling.

(3) Where a closing order is made by virtue of section 266(*a*) (part of building used, or suitable for use, as a dwelling) with respect to a part of a building the interior of which is well maintained, that part shall be deemed to be a house for the purposes of the provisions of this Schedule.

Notification required in case of house acquired for clearance

7.—(1) Where a house is made the subject of a compulsory purchase order under section 290 (acquisition of land for clearance) as being unfit for human habitation, the local housing authority shall serve notice in accordance with this paragraph as regards payments under this Schedule.

(2) Notice shall be served—

(*a*) with respect to the house, on every owner, lessee, mortgagee and occupier of the house, and

(*b*) with respect to each dwelling in the case of a house falling within paragraph 6(1) (houses comprising more than one dwelling or occupied partly for the purposes of a dwelling and partly for other purposes), on every owner, lessee, mortgagee and occupier of the dwelling,

so far as it is reasonably practicable to ascertain those persons.

(3) The notice shall be served not later than the date, or if there is more than one the last date, on which the authority serve notice of the effect of the compulsory purchase order under paragraph 3(3) of Schedule 22 (notice that order about to be submitted for confirmation).

(4) The notice shall be in the prescribed form and shall state that the authority are satisfied—

(*a*) that, in the case of a house which does not fall within paragraph 5 or 6(1) (payments in respect of partially well maintained house or parts of buildings), both the interior and exterior of the house have been well maintained,

(*b*) that, in the case of a house which would not be treated as well maintained apart from paragraph 5 or 6(1), either the interior or the exterior of the house has been well maintained,

(*c*) that in the case of a house falling within paragraph 6(1), the exterior of the house (as defined in that paragraph) has been well maintained,

(*d*) that in the case of a dwelling falling within paragraph 6(1), the interior of the dwelling has been well maintained, or

(*e*) that no part of the house or dwelling has been well maintained.

(5) A notice stating that the authority are satisfied—

(*a*) as mentioned in sub-paragraph (4)(*b*) shall also state the reasons why the authority are not satisfied that the interior or, as the case may be, the exterior of the house concerned has been well maintained;

(*b*) as mentioned in sub-paragraph (4)(*e*) shall state the reasons why the authority are satisfied that no part of the house or dwelling has been well maintained.

Appeal against notification under paragraph 7

8.—(1) An owner, lessee, mortgagee or occupier of a house or dwelling in respect of which a notice is served to which paragraph 7(5) applies (duty to state reasons for adverse decision) who is aggrieved at the decision of the local housing authority may make a written representation to that effect to the Secretary of State.

(2) The representation shall be made in the prescribed manner and within the period within which an objection may be made to the compulsory purchase order concerned.

(3) The Secretary of State may if he thinks it appropriate to do so and (if he considers it necessary) after causing the house or dwelling concerned to be inspected by an officer of his, give directions for the making by the local housing authority of a payment (or, as the case may be, a further payment) in respect of the house or dwelling concerned, of the amount ascertained in accordance with paragraph 4 or, as the case may require, one-half of that amount.

GENERAL NOTE

Where slum housing is purchased under ss.192, 290 or 300, above, normally only the cleared site value is payable: s.585, subject to the maxima and minima specified in s.589. By s.587 and Sched. 24, additional payments are available for owner-occupied housing, or houses with a business use. By s.586 and this Schedule, payments are available where houses have, notwithstanding that under one or other of the relevant provisions they are unfit for human habitation as defined in s.604, been "well-maintained", a term that is not defined otherwise by than the context of this Schedule. By s.588, well-maintained payments and Sched. 24 supplements are mutually exclusive, save if the latter applies to only part of a house, in which case a well-maintained payment under this Schedule remains available, but in part only.

Para. 1

This defines the first class qualifying for payment of a well-maintained payment. This paragraph applies to a property which is vacated (not necessarily purchased) pursuant to a demolition or closing order under s.265, above. However, for this purpose, a demolition order does not qualify if it relates to any part of a house, or the house as a whole, which has already been subject to a closing order in respect of which a payment has previously been made under this Schedule or Sched. 24, below. The provisions also apply if the property is vacated and demolished under an undertaking: see s.264, above.

There must be a representation that the house has been well-maintained, and that the good maintenance is attributable wholly or partly to work which he has carried out, or paid for the execution of. Authorities should inform tenants of this possibility: M.H.L.G. Circulars 69/67, para. 5, and 68/69, para. 9. Provision is made for the case of a partially well-maintained house, where *either* the exterior, *or* the interior, of the house is well-maintained: below, para. 5.

There is no requirement as to the interest of the person making the claim: a licensee or a statutory tenant could qualify. The claim must be made within three months of service by the authority of a copy of the closing or demolition order, or the date of acceptance of the undertaking. The authority must either make a payment, or serve notice that no such payment is to be made: the payment is mandatory, if the authority are satisfied as to the correctness of the representation. When reaching their decision, the authority are to ignore all the matters specified in s.604 *except* state of repair. Appeal lies to the county court at the instance of anyone aggrieved by the decision, which may make whatsoever order it thinks fit. If all the parties to the appeal agree, the matter may instead be referred to arbitration.

For the application of these provisions to flats, or parts of buildings also used for non-housing purposes, see para. 6, below.

Para. 2

This second class concerns houses bought compulsorily under ss.192 and 300, above. The same representation as under para. 1 must be made, but within three months of the authority's notice of compulsory purchase under s.192, or notice of decision to purchase under s.300. The ancillary provisions as to response, considerations and appeal or arbitration are the same as under para. 1, above. See also para. 5, below, for partially well-maintained houses; see para. 6, below, for flats and parts of buildings used also for non-housing purposes.

Para. 3
The third class applies to houses the subject of a compulsory purchase order as unfit for human habitation, within an order confirmed by the Secretary of State on that ground (*cf.* Notes to Sched. 22, above). The precondition is simply that the authority are satisfied that the house has been well-maintained, but this is payable prima facie to an owner-occupier, or otherwise to anyone liable under an enactment, covenant or agreement to maintain and repair the house (divided between them if there is more than one such, *e.g.* a leaseholder with an obligation to the freeholder to maintain, and a sub-leaseholder with an obligation to an occupying tenant under s.11, Landlord and Tenant Act 1985, *i.e.* the principal repairing obligation in short leases and tenancies).

However, if someone else, *e.g.* an occupying tenant or even a licensee, can satisfy the authority that the good maintenance is attributable *to a material extent* to work he has carried out or paid for, the whole or part of the payment may be made to him instead. If a tenant makes a claim, the authority should not agree to pay it without submitting to the landlord the tenant's documents purporting to establish his entitlement: *Hoggard* v. *Worsborough Urban District Council* [1962] 2 Q.B. 93. The authority's decision is quasi-judicial and can be challenged if there is no material before them on which the merits of two competing claims can be assessed: *ibid.*

There is no precondition for representation under this provision: instead, the burden lies on the authority to make a determination, and issue notification of it, under para. 7, below, and for representations from the decision of the authority to the Secretary of State under para. 8, below.

See also para. 5, below, for partially well-maintained houses. See para. 6, below, for the application to flats, and parts of buildings which also have a non-housing use.

Para. 4
This paragraph determines the amount of a well-maintained payment. It is to be a multiplier of the rateable value of the property: the current multiplier is 14 by S.I. 1982 No. 1112, retained in force by Housing (Consequential Provisions) Act 1985, s.2. But the payment is subject to an additional limit: it must not be more than the *difference* between site value (which will be payable under s.585) and the full value of the house, defined to mean that which would have been payable if the house had not been purchased as unfit. (It may, of course, "happen" to be unfit, but not purchased *as* an unfit house). A dispute on value is treated as a question of disputed compensation, *i.e.* is referable to the Lands Tribunal, under Land Compensation Act 1961, s.1.

Rateable value is to be determined as at the specified different "relevant dates", and if an apportionment of rateable value is called for, *i.e.* where there is no separate rateable value for a part of a building, the matter is determinable by the district valuer.

Half the amount otherwise payable is available in the case of a partially well-maintained house under para. 5, below.

Para. 5
If a property is excluded from a well-maintained payment because only the interior, or only the exterior, is well-maintained, then half the amount under para. 4 is payable. "The most common example is where the tenant has done his best to maintain the interior of his house": M.H.L.G. Circular 68/69, para. 8.

Para. 6
This paragraph deems flats, or parts of buildings, to be "a house" for the purposes of this Schedule, so far as the interior of the dwelling is concerned, but not so far as the exterior is concerned. In effect, therefore, the authority look only to the state of interior maintenance so far as those qualifying for payment on account of their residence of part of the building are concerned, although they will still look to the exterior in the case of someone concerned with the building as a whole.

Para. 7
Where the provisions are activated by compulsory purchase under s.290, there is no need for a representation to be made by a would-be claimant for payment under this Schedule. Instead, the authority have to notify every owner, lessee, mortgagee and occupier, of the house or indeed of part of the house or building within para. 6, above, so far as it is reasonably practicable to ascertain those persons. Local authorities have powers to obtain information as to interests in and occupation of a dwelling, under Local Government (Miscellaneous Provisions) Act 1976, s.16.

Notification has to be in prescribed form: see S.I. 1974 No. 1511, retained in force by Housing (Consequential Provisions) Act 1985, s.2. It must be served no later than the last date on which notice has to be served under para. 3 of Sched. 22. The notification has to specify their decision under whichever of the five heads is applicable, *i.e.* not well-maintained, well-maintained interior and exterior, well-maintained interior or exterior. Where the decision contains an element of not being satisfied as to good maintenance, the notice has to give reasons.

"Appeal" lies to the Secretary of State, under para. 8, below.

Para. 8

In a case to which the last paragraph applies, anyone aggrieved by the authority's decision can make representations in writing to the Secretary of State in the same way and time as objection can be made to the compulsory purchase order itself: see Notes to Sched. 22, above. The Secretary of State can direct the authority to make the appropriate payment. Provided the Secretary of State is not acting *ultra vires*, there is no further appeal: *Re Housing Act, 1936, London County Council (Riley Street, Chelsea, No. 1) Order, 1938* [1945] 2 All E.R. 484.

Section 587   SCHEDULE 24

PAYMENTS IN RESPECT OF HOUSES WHICH ARE OWNER-OCCUPIED OR USED FOR BUSINESS PURPOSES

PART I

PAYMENTS IN RESPECT OF OWNER-OCCUPIED HOUSES

Introductory

1.—(1) This Part of this Schedule applies where a house—

(a) has been acquired at site value in accordance with section 585 (site value compensation for unfit houses acquired), or

(b) has been vacated in pursuance of a demolition order or closing order under section 265 (unfit houses beyond repair at reasonable cost), or

(c) might have been the subject of such a demolition order but is vacated and demolished in pursuance of an undertaking for its demolition given to the local housing authority.

(2) The "relevant date" for the purposes of this Part of this Schedule is—

(a) if the house was purchased compulsorily under section 192 (house subject to repair notice found to be beyond repair), the date when the notice mentioned in that section was served;

(b) if the house was vacated in pursuance of a demolition order or closing order, the date when the order was made;

(c) if the house was demolished in pursuance of an undertaking given in accordance with section 264, the date when the undertaking was given;

(d) if the house was comprised in an area declared as a clearance area under section 289, the date when the area was so declared;

(e) if the house was purchased compulsorily in pursuance of a notice served under section 300 (purchase of condemned house for temporary housing use), the date when the notice was served.

Right to payment: main cases

2.—(1) Where this Part of this Schedule applies and—

(a) on the relevant date and throughout the period of two years ending with that date the house was wholly or partly occupied as a private dwelling, and

(b) the person so occupying it (or, if during that period it was so occupied by two or more persons in succession, each of those persons) was a person entitled to an interest in the house or a member of the family of a person so entitled,

the local housing authority shall make in respect of that interest a payment of an amount determined in accordance with the following provisions of this Part of this Schedule.

(2) The authority shall also make such a payment where an interest in the house was acquired by a person less than two years before the relevant date if—

(a) the conditions specified in sub-paragraph (1) were met for the period beginning with the acquisition and ending with the relevant date,

(b) the authority are satisfied that before acquiring the interest he made all reasonable inquiries to ascertain whether it was likely that the notice, order, undertaking or declaration in question would be served, made or given within two years of the acquisition, and that he had no reason to believe that it was likely, and

(c) the person entitled to the interest when the house is purchased or vacated is the person mentioned above or a member of his family.

(3) For the purposes of this paragraph a person previously in occupation of the whole or part of the house who, during a part of the qualifying period amounting (or parts together amounting) to not more than one year, was not in occupation by reason only of—

(a) a posting in the course of his duties as a member of the armed forces of the Crown, or

(b) a change in the place of his employment or occupation,

shall be deemed to have continued in occupation during that part or those parts.

Right to payment: occupation before 13th December 1955

3.—(1) Where this Part of this Schedule applies and—

(a) on 13th December 1955 the house was wholly or partly occupied as a private dwelling,

(b) the person so occupying it was (or was a member of the family of) a person who acquired an interest in the house by purchase for value on or after 1st September 1939 and either before 13th December 1955 or before the relevant date, and

(c) at the date when the house was purchased or vacated that person or a member of his family was entitled to an interest in the house,

the local housing authority shall make in respect of that interest a payment of an amount determined in accordance with the following provisions of this Part of this Schedule.

(2) Where a person ceased to occupy a house or part of a house not more than one year before 13th December 1955 by reason only of—

(a) a posting in the course of his duties as member of the armed forces of the Crown, or

(b) a change in the place of his employment or occupation,

sub-paragraph (1) has effect as if he had occupied the house or part on that day in like manner as immediately before he ceased to occupy it.

(3) This paragraph applies only where no payment falls to be made under paragraph 2.

Amount of payment

4.—(1) The amount of the payment to be made in respect of an interest is its full compulsory purchase value less the compensation which was or would have been payable in respect of the interest in connection with the compulsory purchase of the house at site value.

(2) For this purpose—

(a) "full compulsory purchase value" means the compensation which would be payable in respect of the compulsory purchase of that interest if it fell to be assessed in accordance with the Land Compensation Act 1961, and

(b) "site value" means compensation assessed in accordance with section 585.

(3) The amount payable shall be reduced by so much, if any, of the amount as may reasonably be attributed to any part of the house occupied, at the date of the making of the order in question or the giving of the undertaking, for any purposes other than those of a private dwelling.

(4) Any question as to the purposes for which any part of a house was occupied shall be determined by the Secretary of State; subject to that, the amount of any payment under this Part of this Schedule shall be determined (in default of agreement) as if it were compensation payable in respect of the compulsory purchase of the interest and shall be dealt with accordingly.

Supplementary provisions

5.—(1) In this Part of this Schedule—

"house" includes any building constructed or adapted wholly or partly for use as a dwelling, and

"interest" in a house does not include the interest of a tenant for a year or any less period or of a statutory tenant.

(2) For the purposes of this Part of this Schedule a person who on the death of another became entitled to an interest of his shall be deemed to have been entitled to that interest as from the date of death.

(3) A payment under this Part of this Schedule in respect of an interest which, at the date when the house was purchased compulsorily or, as the case may be, vacated, was held by virtue of an agreement to purchase by instalments shall be made to the person entitled to the interest at that date.

6.—(1) For the purposes of this Part of this Schedule a person is a member of another's family if that person is—

(*a*) the other's wife or husband, or

(*b*) a son or daughter or a son-in-law or daughter-in-law of the other, or of the other's wife or husband, or

(*c*) the father or mother of the other, or of the other's wife or husband.

(2) In sub-paragraph (1)(*b*) any reference to a person's son or daughter includes a step-son or step-daughter and any illegitimate son or daughter of that person, and "son-in-law" and "daughter-in-law" shall be construed accordingly.

PART II

PAYMENTS IN RESPECT OF HOUSES USED FOR BUSINESS PURPOSES

Introductory

1.—(1) This Part of this Schedule applies where a house—

(*a*) has been purchased at site value in pursuance of section 585,

(*b*) has been vacated in pursuance of a demolition order under section 265 (unfit houses beyond repair at reasonable cost), or

(*c*) might have been the subject of such a demolition order but is vacated and demolished in pursuance of an undertaking for its demolition given to the local housing authority.

(2) The "relevant date" for the purpose of this Part of this Schedule is—

(*a*) if the house was purchased compulsorily, the date of making of the compulsory purchase order;

(*b*) if the house was vacated in pursuance of a demolition order, the date when the order was made;

(*c*) if the house was vacated in pursuance of an undertaking for its demolition, the date when the undertaking was given.

Right to payment: main case

2. If at the relevant date and at all times during the two years preceding that date—

(*a*) the house was occupied wholly or partly for the purposes of a business, and

(*b*) the person entitled to the receipts of the business held an interest in the house,

the local housing authority shall make in respect of that interest a payment of the amount specified in the following provisions of this Part of this Schedule.

Right to payment: business use on 13th December 1955

3. The authority shall also make such a payment if no payment falls to be made under paragraph 2 but the conditions specified in sub-paragraphs (*a*) and (*b*) of that paragraph were satisfied at the relevant date and on 13th December 1955.

Amount of payment

4.—(1) The amount of the payment to be made in respect of an interest is its full compulsory purchase value less the compensation which was or would have been payable in respect of the interest in connection with the compulsory purchase of the house at site value.

(2) For this purpose—

(*a*) "full compulsory purchase value" means the compensation which would be payable in respect of the compulsory purchase of that interest if it fell to be assessed in accordance with the Land Compensation Act 1961, and

(*b*) "site value" means compensation assessed in accordance with section 585.

(3) The amount payable shall be reduced by so much, if any, of the amount as may reasonably be attributed to any part of the house not occupied at the relevant date for the purposes of the business.

(4) Any question arising under sub-paragraph (3) as to the purposes for which any part of a house was occupied shall be determined by the Secretary of State; subject to that, the amount of any payment under this Part of this Schedule shall be determined (in default of agreement) as if it were compensation payable in respect of the compulsory purchase of the interest and shall be dealt with accordingly.

Supplementary provisions

5. In this Part of this Schedule—

"business," in relation to the purposes for which a house was occupied, does not include the letting of accommodation in the house, whether with or without service;

"house" includes any building constructed or adapted wholly or partly for use as a
    dwelling;
"interest" in a house does not include the interest of a tenant for a year or any less
    period or of a statutory tenant.

GENERAL NOTE
Part I of this Schedule makes provision for an "owner-occupier's supplement" so as to
place owner-occupiers in unfit housing in a position, in effect, to purchase elsewhere and
remain an owner-occupier (although there is no obligation so to use the payment). Part II
makes analogous provision for property with a business use.
  Note that payments are available under s.586, and Sched. 23, above, for housing which
is well-maintained. By s.588, Sched. 23 well-maintained payments and supplements under
this Schedule are mutually exclusive, save if the payment under this Schedule relates to only
part of a house, in which case the Sched. 23 well-maintained payment remains payable in
part. Note also that occupiers affected by the relevant action of the authority may be entitled
to compensation under Land Compensation Act 1973, ss.29–38, and to rehousing under
ibid., s.39. See also s.591 for the modification or discharge of mortgages when a payment is
made under this section.

Part I
Para. 1
  Part 1 applies to a house—defined by para. 5, below, to include any building constructed
or adapted wholly or partly for use as a dwelling—which has been purchased at site value
under s.585, above, *i.e.* as unfit for human habitation within the meaning of s.604, above,
or which has been vacated pursuant to a closing or demolition order or demolition
undertaking: see ss.264, 287, above. There is, then, no need that the property actually be
compulsorily purchased.

Para. 2
  The main cases covered by the Schedule are where the conditions of sub-paras. (1) or (2)
apply:
  (1) On the relevant date as defined in paragraph 1(2), and throughout the preceding two
years, the house was wholly or partly occupied as a private dwelling, *and* the occupier was
a person with an interest in the house or a member of the family of a person with an
interest. "Interest" means any interest, except that of a tenant for a year or any lesser
period, or a statutory tenant, *i.e.* under the Rent Act 1977 or the Rent (Agriculture) Act
1976, see notes to s.622, above, and therefore excludes a periodic tenant (other than one
with periods of a year or more) even if he has been in occupation for more than a year:
para. 5.
  A person retains his interest, however, even where he has contracted to sell it: *Pilling* v.
Hucknall Urban District Council (1964) 15 P. & C.R. 43, L.T. But interest does not include
a claim under an unadministered estate, or the right of a surety who has been called upon
to pay a mortgage debt: *Eastbourne Mutual Building Society* v. *Hastings Corporation* [1965]
1 All E.R. 779. An equitable interest is sufficient: *Heron* v. *Sandwell Metropolitan Borough
Council* (1980) 40 P. & C.R. 232, L.T. But an interest which is only in the proceeds of sale
of the property is not: *Mohammed Niaz* v. *Metropolitan Borough of Rochdale* (1980) 41 P.
& C.R. 113, L.T. An interest qualifies even if it has not been registered: *Blamires* v.
Bradford Corporation [1964] 2 All E.R. 603.
  "Member of the family" is defined in para. 6. Occupation "through" a member of the
family has been held to include even a 12-year-old child: *Singh* v. *Derby City Council* (1981)
(1982) 44 P. & C.R. 258, C.A. See also *Lahney & Lahney* v. *Hartlepool Borough Council*
(1983) 48 P. & C.R. 331, L.T.
  There is no requirement that the person having the interest shall be the same person
throughout, *i.e.* transmission by sale is permitted, but it *is* a requirement that occupation has
been sustained throughout the two year period, *by* the person holding the interest (or a
member of his family) so as to discourage "collusive sales from landlord to tenant in
anticipation of clearance merely for the purpose of obtaining higher compensation":
M.H.L.G. Circular 68/69, para. 4.
  Continuous occupation is not broken by a posting arising out of service in the armed
forces, or indeed a change in employment or occupation: sub-para. (3).
  Otherwise, the continuous occupation requirement has been construed strictly. In *Laundon*
v. *Hartlepool Borough Council* [1979] Q.B. 252, C.A., it was held that while a break of
seven to ten days for removal and changeover might be considered de minimis, longer
breaks, *e.g.* a month, will destroy the continuous occupation requirement. This would not

apply in the case of a break in established occupation, *e.g.* on holiday, in hospital, etc.: see *Mohammed Niaz* v. *Metropolitan Borough of Rochdale* (1980) 41 P. & C.R. 113, L.T. But see *Westerman* v. *St. Helen's Metropolitan Borough Council* (1983) 46 P. & C.R. 236, L.T., in which a person went from hospital to an old person's home, where she died, and was held to have gone out of occupation for these purposes because it could not be said that she had any genuine intention to return to her home.

Occupation can be very rough indeed—living in one room, not eating in the house because electricity and gas were cut off, no bath—"pigging it"; if the occupation is residential in quality, it is qualifying occupation: *Singh* v. *Derby City Council* (1982) 44 P. & C.R. 258, C.A.; see also *Patel* v. *Leicester City Council* (1982) 43 P. & C.R. 278, L.T. A corporate body cannot occupy at all (*cf.* notes to s.81, above): *G. E. Stevens (High Wycombe)* v. *High Wycombe Corporation* [1962] 2 Q.B. 547.

Occupation can be through furniture, or a caretaker, and constructively through control of a house: *Reeve* v. *Hartlepool Borough Council* (1975) 30 P. & C.R. 517, L.T., not disapproved in the Court of Appeal, sub. nom. *Laundon* v. *Hartlepool Borough Council* [1979] Q.B. 252, C.A. See also *Mohammed Niaz* v. *Metropolitan Borough of Rochdale* (1980) 41 P. & C.R. 113, L.T., *Abdul Aziz* v. *Tameside Metropolitan Borough Council* (1981) 43 P. & C.R. 436, and *Manzur Hussain* v. *Tameside Metropolitan Borough Council* (1981) 43 P. & C.R. 441, L.T.

In *Heron* v. *Sandwell Metropolitan Borough Council* (1980) 40 P. & C.R. 232, L.T., a woman had a half-share in a house, but subsequently married and worked in another town, although returning to what she regarded as her permanent home most weekends, and spending holiday periods there. She left her furniture in the house of which she was part owner, and was held to be in occupation. In *Panchal* v. *Preston Borough Council* (1978) 36 P. & C.R. 281, L.T., a man bought a house shortly before the declaration of a clearance area which would include his existing home. He was advised by council officials to remain in occupation until declaration, and followed the advice, by sleeping in the old house, and by keeping a bed, chest of drawers, carpet and cupboard there, while eating at the new house where his wife and children were living; he was held in occupation.

Whether or not there is occupation at the relevant time or for the relevant period is a question of fact. In *Sohbat Ali* v. *Leeds City Council* (1983) J.P.L. 680, declaration of a clearance area was on November 7, 1979. The claimant had determined to purchase a house in the area in October 1977 and paid the deposit then; he obtained keys by the beginning of November 1977 in order to carry out roof repairs, but the contract of sale was not signed until June 29, 1978, and the claimant did not move in until July or August 1978. The Lands Tribunal held that he could not be regarded as an owner-occupier until the last of these dates, and had therefore not been an occupier for two years preceding the relevant date (November 7, 1979).

The requirement is for occupation as a private dwelling, "wholly or partly." However, the amount of compensation is reduced under para. 4, on account of non-housing user. But mere subletting as a private dwelling retains qualification, provided the "owner" is living in some part of the property: *Hunter* v. *Manchester City Council* [1975] Q.B. 877, C.A., or that a member of his family is doing so—see *Lahney & Lahney* v. *Hartlepool Borough Council* (1983) 48 P. & C.R. 331, L.T. The fact that he may be sharing with people who are not members of his family does not prevent a finding that the whole of the dwelling is used as a private home: *Aziz* v. *Tameside Metropolitan Borough Council* (1982) 43 P. & C.R. 436, L.T.

(2) In some cases, however, occupation for two years cannot be shown. Also provisionally qualifying under this paragraph is someone who on the relevant date and throughout the period since his acquisition fulfils the residential qualifications, *i.e.* wholly or partly occupied as a private dwelling by the person with an interest or a member of his family. "Cases may arise of purchases within the qualifying period of owner-occupation where the purchaser was genuinely unaware of the likelihood of slum clearance action within the near future": M.H.L.G. Circular 68/69, para. 4.

The provisional nature of this additional qualification lies in sub-para. (2)(b), *i.e.* that "the authority are satisfied that before acquiring the interest he made all reasonable inquiries to ascertain whether it was likely that the notice, order, undertaking or declaration in question would be served, made or given within two years of the acquisition, and that he had no reason to believe that it was likely."

The key words are "the authority are satisfied," which places the matter squarely within the decision-making power of the authority, subject only to "normal" principles of administrative law as to the correctness of the approach to the decision (see notes to s.64, above). A challenge on such grounds cannot be raised in the Lands Tribunal: see *Ebadat Ali* v. *Nottingham City Council* (1979) 38 P. & C.R. 229, L.T,; *Mohammed Saghir* v. *City of*

Birmingham (1980) 39 P. & C.R. 602, L.T. Instead, the applicant would need to take proceedings for judicial review in order to establish the precondition for payment: see also *Cocks* v. *Thanet District Council* [1983] A.C. 286, 6 H.L.R. 15, H.L.

In this connection, it may be noted that the forms for enquiries of local authorities do not contain an appropriate query; the form asks, rather, whether any relevant action *has* been taken, not whether it is likely that it will be taken. It is submitted that a more appropriate enquiry should be added (by an adviser) in each case, so that the question has at least been *asked*, even although it is highly unlikely to be *answered*.

The requirement in sub-para. (2)(*c*) means that this "exemption" from the normal two-year rule can only be used in relation to one uninformed purchase.

Para. 3

This paragraph contains analogous but not identical provisions to those in the last paragraph, concerning purchases after September 1, 1939, applicable where qualification cannot be sustained under the last paragraph, *e.g.* for want of continuous occupation.

Para. 4

This paragraph determines the amount of the supplement. It is the difference between site value and full value, reduced by an amount attributable to any part of the property not occupied as a private dwelling. Disputes as to apportionment are to be determined by the Secretary of State, but disputes as to value are otherwise to be determined by the Lands Tribunal, as if a dispute as to compensation for compulsory purchase, under s.1, Land Compensation Act, 1961. There is no exclusion for residential occupation by tenants: *Hunter* v. *Manchester City Council* [1975] Q.B. 877, C.A.

Part II
Para. 1

This paragraph is analogous to para. 1 of Part I, save that closing orders are not included.

Para. 2

The only conditions are that at the relevant date as defined in para. 1(2), and for the two years preceding that date, the house has been occupied wholly or partly for the purposes of a business, and the person entitled to the receipts of the business held an interest in the house. There is no occupation for the purpose of a business if it is held for occupation by an employee; *G.E. Stevens (High Wycombe)* v. *High Wycombe Corporation* [1962] 2 Q.B. 547. Nor does the business of letting of accommodation qualify: para. 5, below. Interest is defined in *ibid.*

Para. 3

This makes analogous provision to that made in para. 3 of Pt. I.

Para. 4

This governs the amount of compensation, and corresponds to para. 4 of Pt. I.

TABLE OF DERIVATIONS

1. The following abbreviations are used in this Table:—

Acts of Parliament

1899	=	The Small Dwellings Acquisition Act 1899 (c.44).
1923 (c.24)	=	The Housing, &c. Act 1923.
1935 (c.40)	=	The Housing Act 1935.
1936 (c.49)	=	The Public Health Act 1936.
1957	=	The Housing Act 1957 (c.56).
1958	=	The Housing (Financial Provisions) Act 1958 (c.42).
1959 (H)	=	The House Purchase and Housing Act 1959 (c.33).
1959 (U)	=	The Housing (Underground Rooms) Act 1959 (c.34).
1959 (c.53)	=	The Town and Country Planning Act 1959.
1961 (c.33)	=	The Land Compensation Act 1961.
1961	=	The Housing Act 1961 (c.65).
1961 (c.64)	=	The Public Health Act 1961.
1963 (c.33)	=	The London Government Act 1963.
1964 (c.9)	=	The Public Works Loans Act 1964.
1964	=	The Housing Act 1964 (c.56).
1965 (c.56)	=	The Compulsory Purchase Act 1965.
1965 (c.75)	=	The Rent Act 1965.
1965	=	The Housing (Slum Clearance Compensation) Act 1965 (c.81).
1967 (c.9)	=	The General Rate Act 1967.
1967 (c.80)	=	The Criminal Justice Act 1967.
1968 (c.13)	=	The National Loans Act 1968.
1968 (c.23)	=	The Rent Act 1968.
1968 (c.42)	=	The Prices and Incomes Act 1968.
1969 (c.19)	=	The Decimal Currency Act 1969.
1969	=	The Housing Act 1969 (c.33).
1971 (c.23)	=	The Courts Act 1971.
1971	=	The Housing Act 1971 (c.76).
1971 (c.78)	=	The Town and Country Planning Act 1971.
1972	=	The Housing Finance Act 1972 (c.47).
1972 (c.70)	=	The Local Government Act 1972.
1972 (c.71)	=	The Criminal Justice Act 1972.
1973 (H)	=	The Housing Amendment Act 1973 (c.5).
1974 (c.7)	=	The Local Government Act 1974.
1974 (c.39)	=	The Consumer Credit Act 1974.
1974	=	The Housing Act 1974 (c.44).
1975	=	The Housing Rents and Subsidies Act 1975 (c.6).
1975 (c.24)	=	The House of Commons Disqualification Act 1975.
1975 (c.72)	=	The Children Act 1975.
1975 (c.76)	=	The Local Land Charges Act 1975.
1976 (c.52)	=	The Armed Forces Act 1976.
1976 (c.57)	=	The Local Government (Miscellaneous Provisions) Act 1976.
1976 (c.75)	=	The Development of Rural Wales Act 1976.
1976 (c.80)	=	The Rent (Agriculture) Act 1976.
1977 (c.42)	=	The Rent Act 1977.
1977 (c.43)	=	The Protection from Eviction Act 1977.
1977 (c.45)	=	The Criminal Law Act 1977.
1977	=	The Housing (Homeless Persons) Act 1977 (c.48).
1978	=	The Home Purchase Assistance and Housing Corporation Guarantee Act 1978 (c.27).
1978 (c.30)	=	The Interpretation Act 1978.
1978 (I)	=	The Home Insulation Act 1978 (c.48).
1980 (c.43)	=	The Magistrates' Courts Act 1980.
1980	=	The Housing Act 1980 (c.51).
1980 (c.65)	=	The Local Government, Planning and Land Act 1980.
1981 (c.54)	=	The Supreme Court Act 1981.
1981 (c.64)	=	The New Towns Act 1981.
1981 (c.67)	=	The Acquisition of Land Act 1981.

1982 (c.24)	=	The Social Security and Housing Benefits Act 1982.
1982 (c.48)	=	The Criminal Justice Act 1982.
1984 (c.12)	=	The Telecommunication Act 1984.
1984 (c.22)	=	The Public Health (Control of Disease) Act 1984.
1984 (c.28)	=	The County Courts Act 1984.
1984	=	The Housing and Building Control Act 1984 (c.29).
1984 (D)	=	The Housing Defects Act 1984 (c.50).
1985 (c.9)	=	The Companies Consolidation (Consequential Provisions) Act 1985.
1985 (c.51)	=	The Local Government Act 1985.

Subordinate legislation

S.I. 1972/1204	=	The Isles of Scilly (Housing) Order 1972.
S.I. 1973/886	=	The Isles of Scilly (Housing) (No. 2) Order 1973.
S.I. 1975/512	=	The Isles of Scilly (Housing) Order 1975.
S.I. 1979/72	=	The Isles of Scilly (Functions) Order 1979.
S.I. 1981/723	=	The Local Authority Contributions (Disposal of Dwellings) Order 1981.
S.I. 1982/1109	=	The Crown Court Rules 1982.
S.I. 1983/613	=	The Grants by Local Authorities (Eligible Expense Limits) Order 1983.
S.I. 1983/1122	=	The Housing (Northern Ireland Consequential Amendments) Order 1983.

2. The Table does not show the effect of Transfer of Functions Orders.

3. The letter R followed by a number indicates that the provision gives effect to the Recommendation bearing that number in the Law Commission's Report on the Consolidation of the Housing Act (Cmnd. 9515).

4. A reference followed by "*passim*" indicates that the provision of the consolidation derives from passages within those referred to which it is not convenient, and does not appear necessary, to itemise.

5. The entry "drafting" indicates a provision of a mechanical or editorial nature affecting the arrangement of the consolidation; for instance, a provision introducing a Schedule or introducing a definition to avoid undue repetition of the defining words.

Provision	Derivation
Part I	
1	1936 (c.49) s.1(2) "local authority"; 1957 s.1(1), (2); 1963 (c.33) s.21(1), (2); 1969 s.39; 1972 (c.70) ss.180(1), 193(1); 1977 s.19(1) "housing authority"; S.I. 1972/1204; S.I. 1973/886; S.I. 1975/512; S.I. 1979/72; 1980 ss.29(1), 50(1) "local authority", 105(1) "local authority".
2(1), (2)	drafting.
3(1), (2)	1957 s.155(1), (2).
4	drafting.
5(1)	1957 s.189(1) "housing association".
(2)	drafting.
(3)	1974 s.12 "self-build society".
(4)	drafting.
6	1977 (c.42) s.15(5); 1980 s.74(2).
7	drafting.
Part II	
8(1), (2)	1957 s.91; 1969 Sch. 8 para 8.
9(1)	1957 ss.92(1).
(2)	1957 s.92(2).
(3)	1980 s.93(*b*).
(4)	1957 s.92(4).
10(1)–(3)	1957 s.94; 1974 (c.39) Sch. 4 para. 18.
11(1), (2)	1957 s.95(1).
(3), (4)	1957 s.95(2).
12(1)	1957 s.93(1).
(2)	1957 s.93(2).
(3)	1957 s.93(1).

Provision	Derivation
13(1)	1957 s.107.
(2)	1957 s.107; R.1(i).
14(1)	1957 s.92(1) and *passim*.
(2)	1972 (c.70) s.193(2).
(3)	1957 s.108(1); 1972 (c.70) Sch. 22 para. 4(1).
(4)	1957 s.109(1); 1972 (c.70) Sch. 22 para. 5(1).
(5)	1957 s.110.
15(1)	1957 s.93(3); 1963 (c.33) Sch. 8 para. 3(*a*).
(2)	1963 (c.33) s.21(10).
(3)	1957 s.146; 1985 (c.51) Sch. 8 para. 14(3).
(4)	1957 ss.93(3), 146.
16(1)	1963 (c.33) s.21(3).
(2)	1957 s.93(3) proviso; 1963 (c.33) Sch. 8 para. 3(*b*).
17(1)	1957 s.96.
(2)	1980 s.93(*a*).
(3)	1957 s.97(1).
(4)	1957 s.97(2).
18(1)	1957 s.105(4).
(2)	1957 s.105(4A); 1974 Sch. 13 para. 4.
19(1)	1957 s.99; drafting.
(2)	1957 s.110A(1); 1980 s.95.
(3)	1957 s.110A(2), (3); 1980 s.95.
20(1), (2)	R.2.
21(1)	1957 s.111(1), (2).
(2)	drafting.
22	1957 s.113(2); 1977 s.6(2).
23(1)	1957 s.112(1).
(2)	1976 (c.57) s.9.
(3)	1957 s.112(2).
24(1)	1957 s.111(1).
(2)	1957 s.113(1), (1A); 1975 s.1(2).
25(1)	1968 (c.42) s.12(1); 1980 Sch. 25 para. 20
(2)	1968 (c.42) s.12(1).
(3)	1968 (c.42) s.12(1), (3).
(4)	1968 (c.42) s.12(2).
(5)	1968 (c.42) s.12(1).
26(1)	1972 s.93(1), (2).
(2)	1972 s.93(3).
(4)	1972 s.93(4).
27(1)	1980 Sch. 20 para. 2(1), 3; R.3.
(2)	1980 Sch. 20 para. 1.
(3)	1980 Sch. 20 para. 4.
(4)	1980 Sch. 20 para. 5.
(5)	1980 Sch. 20 para. 2(1), (2).
(6)	1980 Sch. 20 para. 6.
28(1)	1972 (c.70) s.194(1).
(2)	1972 (c.70) s.194(6).
(3)	1972 (c.70) s.194(2).
(4)	1972 (c.70) s.194(3).
(5)	1972 (c.70) s.194(4).
(6)	1972 (c.70) s.194(5).
29(1), (2)	1957 s.126; 1980 Sch. 25 para. 7.
30(1)	1972 ss.93, 106 *passim*, Sch. 9 para. 14.
(2)	1980 Sch. 20 *passim*; 1981 (c.64) Sch. 12 para. 27(*d*); R.3.
31	1957 s.129; R.4(iii).
32(1)	1957 s.104(1); 1980 s.91(1).
(2)	1957 s.104(2); 1980 s.91(1).
(3)	1957 s.104(3); 1980 s.91(1).
(4)	1957 s.104(9); 1980 s.91(1).
(5)	1957 s.104(8); 1980 s.91(1).
33(1)	1957 s.104(5); 1980 s.91(1).
(2)–(4)	1957 s.104(5), (6); 1980 s.91(1).

Provision	Derivation
34(1)	drafting.
(2)	1957 s.104A(1); 1980 s.92.
(3)	1957 s.104A(2); 1980 s.92.
(4)	1957 s.104A(3); 1980 s.92.
35(1)	1957 s.104B(1); 1980 s.92.
(2)	1957 s.104B(2), (3); 1980 s.92; 1984 Sch. 6 para. 1(1).
36(1)	1957 s.104B(5)(*a*); 1980 s.92; 1984 Sch. 6 para. 1(3).
(2)	1957 s.104B(5)(*b*), (5A); 1980 s.92; 1984 Sch. 6 para. 1(4).
(3)	1957 s.104B(7); 1980 s.92.
(4)	1957 s.104B(6); 1978 Sch. paras. 6–9; 1984 Sch. 6 para. 1(5).
37(1)	1957 s.104C(1), (9); 1980 s.92; 1984 Sch. 6 para. 2(1), (5).
(2)	1957 s.104C(2); 1980 s.92; 1984 Sch. 6 para. 2(2).
(3)	1957 s.104C(3); 1980 s.92.
(4)	1957 s.104C(5); 1980 s.92.
(5)	1957 s.104C(6); 1980 s.92.
(6)	1957 s.104C(8); 1980 s.92.
38	1957 ss.104B(4), 104C(7A); 1984 Sch. 6 paras. 1(2), 2(4).
39(1)	1957 s.104B(4A); 1984 Sch. 6 para. 1(2).
(2)	1957 s.104B(4B); 1984 Sch. 6 para. 1(2).
40	1957 s.104B(4A)(*d*); 1984 Sch. 6 para. 1(2); drafting.
41	1957 ss.104B(4C), 104C(7); 1984 Sch. 6 paras. 1(2), 2(4).
42(1)	1957 ss.104B(9), 104C(10); 1980 s.92; 1984 Sch. 6 para. 1(6), 2(6).
(2)	1957 s.104C(10); 1980 s.92.
43(1)	1984 s.22(1), (2).
(2)	1984 s.22(3).
(3)	1984 s.22(4).
(4)	1984 s.22(5).
(5)	1984 s.22(8).
44(1), (2)	1980 s.137(1); 1984 s.22(7), Sch. 11 para. 28.
(3)	1980 s.137(2); drafting.
45(1)	1984 s.18(1).
(2)	1984 s.18(1), (3), (4) "conveyance", "grant", "long lease".
(3)	1984 Sch. 11 paras. 21, 25(2).
46(1)	1984 s.18(1)(*b*).
(2), (3)	1984 Sch. 4 para. 1(2).
(4)	1984 Sch. 4 paras. 12, 13.
47(1)	1984 Sch. 4 paras. 2, 3.
(2)	1984 Sch. 4 para. 2.
(3)	1984 Sch. 4 para. 8.
48(1)	1984 Sch. 4 para. 4(1), (4).
(2)	1984 Sch. 4 para. 4(1).
(3), (4)	1984 Sch. 4 para. 4(2), (3).
(5)	1984 Sch. 4 para. 6.
(6)	1984 Sch. 4 para. 7.
49(1), (2)	1984 Sch. 4 para. 5(1), (2).
50(1)	1984 Sch. 4 para. 9(1).
(2)	1984 Sch. 4 para. 10(1)(*a*), (2).
51(1)	1984 Sch. 4 para. 11 *passim*; drafting.
(2)	1984 Sch. 4 para. 11(1); 1985 (c.9) Sch. 2.
(3), (4)	1984 Sch. 4 para. 11(2), (3).
(5)	1984 Sch. 4 para. 11(2)(*b*); 1985 (c.9) Sch. 2.
(6)	1984 Sch. 4 para. 10(1)(*b*), (2).
52	1957 s.92(3).
53(1)	drafting.
(2)	1972 Sch. 8 para. 4(5).
(3)	1972 Sch. 8 para. 4(5) proviso.
(4)	1972 Sch. 8 para. 4(6).
(5)	1972 Sch. 8 para. 4(8).
54(1), (2)	1957 s.159(*a*), (*c*).
55(1)	1957 s.160.
(2)	1957 s.160; 1977 (c.45) s.31(6); 1982 (c.48) ss.37, 46(1).

Provision	Derivation
56	
"house"	1957 s.189(1) "house" para. (*a*).
"housing accommodation"	1957 ss.92(4), 189(1) "house" para. (*b*); 1974 s.106(3).
"lodging-houses"	1957 s.112(2).
"member of family"	1957 s.104B(4B)(*c*); 1984 Sch. 6 para. 1(2).
"owner"	1957 s.189(1) "owner".
57	drafting.
Part III	
58(1), (2)	1977 s.1(1).
(3)	1977 s.1(2).
(4)	1977 s.1(3).
59(1)	1977 s.2(1), (2).
(2)	1977 ss.2(3), 15(1).
(3)	1977 ss.2(3), 19(1) "appropriate consultations".
(4)	1977 s.2(4).
60(1)	1977 s.17(1).
(2)	1977 s.17(2).
(3)	1977 s.17(3).
(4)	1977 s.17(4).
61(1)	1977 s.18(1).
(2)	1977 s.18(2)(*a*)(i), (3)(*a*).
(3)	1977 s.18(2)(*a*)(ii).
(4)	1977 s.18(2)(*b*), (3)(*b*).
(5)	1977 s.15(1), (3).
62(1)	1977 s.3(1), (2)(*a*).
(2)	1977 s.3(2)(*b*), (3).
63(1), (2)	1977 s.3(4).
64(1)	1977 s.8(1).
(2)	1977 s.8(2).
(3)	1977 s.8(3).
(4)	1977 s.8(4).
(5)	1977 s.8(8), (9); R.5.
65(1)	1977 s.4(1).
(2)	1977 s.4(5).
(3)	1977 ss.4(2)(*b*), (3), 19(1) "appropriate assistance".
(4)	1977 ss.4(2)(*a*), 19(1) "appropriate assistance".
66(1)	1977 s.4(1).
(2)	1977 s.4(4).
(3)	1977 ss.4(2), 19(1) "appropriate assistance".
(4)	1977 s.4(6).
67(1), (2)	1977 ss.4(5), 5(1).
(3)	1977 s.5(11).
(4)	1977 s.5(7), (8).
(5)	1977 ss.5(9), 19(1) "appropriate consultations", "relevant authorities".
(6)	1977 s.5(10).
68(1)	1977 s.5(6).
(2)	1977 s.5(3), (4).
(3)	1977 s.8(5).
(4)	1977 s.8(8), (9); R.5.
69(1)	1977 s.6(1).
(2)	1977 s.10.
70(1)	1977 s.7(1), (11).
(2)	1977 s.7(1), (2), (3).
(3)	1977 s.7(4), (5).
(4)	1977 s.7(6), (7).
(5)	1977 s.7(8)–(10).
(6)	1977 s.8(6), (7).
(7)	1977 s.8(10), (11).
(8)	1977 s.7(1), (3); drafting.

Provision	Derivation
71(1)	1977 s.12(1).
(2)	1977 s.12(2).
72	1977 s.9(1), (2).
73(1)	1977 s.13(1).
(2)	1977 s.13(2), (3).
(3)	1977 s.13(4).
(4)	1977 s.13(7).
(5)	1977 s.13(5), (6).
74(1)	1977 s.11(1), (5).
(2)	1977 s.11(2), (3).
(3)	1977 s.11(4), (5).
(4)	1977 s.11(5); 1982 (c.48) ss.37, 46(1).
75	1977 s.16.
76(1)	1977 s.5(1); drafting.
(2)	1977 s.5(3); drafting.
(3)	1977 s.19(1) "development corporation", "housing authority", "social work authority"; drafting.
77	
"relevant authority"	1977 s.19(1) "relevant authority".
"social services authority"	1977 s.19(1) "social services authority".
"voluntary organisation"	1977 s.19(1) "voluntary organisation".
78	drafting.
Part IV	
79(1), (2)	1980 s.28(1).
(3)	1980 s.48(1).
(4)	1980 s.48(2).
80(1)	1980 s.28(2), (4); 1980 (c.65) s.156(2)(*a*); 1984 s.36(1).
(2)	1977 (c.42) s.15(3); 1980 ss.28(2), 49(1), (2).
(3)	1980 s.49(4), (5).
(4)	1980 ss.28(2)(*c*), 50(1) "housing co-operative", "housing co-operative agreement".
81	1980 s.28(3).
82(1), (2)	1980 s.32(1).
(3)	1980 ss.29(1), 32(2).
(4)	1980 s.32(3).
83(1)	1980 s.33(1).
(2)	1980 s.33(2).
(3)	1980 s.33(3).
(4)	1980 s.33(1).
(5)	1980 s.33(4).
(6)	1980 s.151(1), (3).
84(1)	1980 s.34(1).
(2)	1980 s.34(2), (3), (4); 1984 s.25(2).
(3)	1980 s.34(1).
85(1)	1980 s.87(1); R.6.
(2)	1980 s.87(2).
(3)	1980 s.87(3).
(4)	1980 s.87(4).
(5)	1980 s.87(5), (6).
86(1)	1980 s.29(1).
(2)	1980 s.29(2).
87	1980 ss.30(1), (2), 37B(2)(*b*); 1984 s.26(1).
88(1)	1980 s.31(1).
(2), (3)	1980 s.31(1A); 1984 Sch. 11 para. 23.
(4)	1980 s.31(2).

Provision	Derivation
89(1), (2)	1980 s.30(1), (3).
(3)	1980 s.37B(2); 1984 s.26(1).
(4)	1980 s.37B(3)(*a*); 1984 s.26(1).
90(1)	drafting.
(2)	1980 s.28(5).
(3)	1980 s.37B(2); 1984 s.26(1).
(4)	1980 s.37B(3)(*a*); 1984 s.26(1).
91(1), (2)	1980 s.37(1), (2)(*a*), (3), (4)(*a*); 1984 s.26(1).
(3)	1980 s.37(1); 1984 s.26(1).
92(1), (2)	1980 s.37A(1); 1984 s.26(1).
(3)	1980 s.37A(2); 1984 s.26(1).
(4)	1980 s.37A(3); 1984 s.26(1).
(5)	1980 s.37A(4); 1984 s.26(1).
(6)	1980 s.37A(5); 1984 s.26(1).
93(1)	1980 s.35(1), (2).
(2)	1980 s.37B(1), (3)(*a*); 1984 s.26(1).
94(1)	1980 s.36(5).
(2), (3)	1980 ss.35(3), 36(1).
(4)	1980 s.36(2).
(5)	1980 s.36(3).
(6)	1980 s.36(4).
95(1), (2)	1980 ss.37(1), (2)(*b*), (3), (4)(*b*), 37B(3)(*b*); 1984 s.26(1).
96(1)	1980 s.41A(1); 1984 s.28.
(2)	1980 s.41A(2), (3); 1984 s.28.
(3)	1980 s.151(3).
(4)	1980 s.151(1).
(5)	1980 s.41A(4); 1984 s.28.
97(1)	1980 s.81(1), (2).
(2)	1980 s.81(5).
98(1), (2)	1980 ss.81(3), 82(1).
(3)	1980 s.82(2).
(4)	1980 s.82(3).
99(1)	drafting.
(2)	1980 s.82(2).
(3)	1980 s.82(3)(*b*).
(4)	1980 s.82(4).
(5)	1980 s.83.
100(1)	1980 s.38(1), (2).
(2)	1980 s.38(3).
(3)	1980 s.38(2).
101(1)–(4)	1980 s.39; 1984 s.27.
102(1)	1980 s.40(1), (3), (4).
(2)	1980 s.40(9).
(3)	1980 s.40(2).
(4)	1980 s.40(10).
103(1)	1980 s.40(4).
(2)	1980 s.40(6).
(3)	1980 s.40(7).
(4)	1980 s.40(5).
(5)	1980 s.40(6).
(6)	1980 s.40(8).
104(1)	1980 s.41(1), (2).
(2)	1980 s.41(3), (4).
105(1)	1980 s.43(1), (2).
(2)	1980 s.42(2)(*a*), (3).
(3)	1980 s.42(2)(*b*), (*c*), (4).
(4)	1980 s.42(5).

Provision	Derivation
105(5)	1980 s.43(3).
(6)	1977 (c.42) s.15(3)(*a*); 1980 s.43(4), (5).
106(1)	1980 s.44(1).
(2)	1980 s.44(2).
(3)	1980 s.44(3), (4).
(4)	1980 s.44(5).
(5)	1980 s.44(6).
107(1)	1980 s.46(1).
(2)	1980 s.46(2).
108(1)	1980 s.41B(1); 1984 s.29.
(2)	1980 s.41B(2); 1984 s.29.
(3)	1980 s.41B(3); 1984 s.29.
(4)	1980 ss.41B(4), (5), 151(1), (3); 1984 s.29.
(5)	1980 s.41B(1), (6); 1984 s.29.
109	1980 ss.49(3), 84.
110(1)	1980 s.86(1).
(2)	1980 s.86(2); 1984 Sch. 11 para. 25(1).
(3)	1980 s.86(3).
111(1)	1980 s.86(4).
(2)	1980 s.86(5).
(3)	1980 s.86(6).
112(1), (2)	1980 s.50(2).
113(1), (2)	1980 s.50(3).
114(1)	1977 (c.42) s.15(3); 1980 ss.42(1), 49(3); 1980 (c.65) s.156(2)(*b*).
(2)	1980 s.45(1).
(3)	1980 s.45(2).
115(1)	1980 Sch. 3 para. 1(2), (2A); 1984 Sch. 1 para. 12, Sch. 11 para. 33(1).
(2)	1980 Sch. 3 para. 1(2), (3).
116	
"common parts"	1980 Sch. 4 Part I, grounds 3, 4.
"housing purposes"	1980 Sch. 1 para. 1(2); 1984 s.2(1).
"rental period"	1980 s.50(1).
"term"	1980 s.50(1).
117	drafting.
Part V	
118(1)	1980 s.1(1), (2); 1984 s.1(2).
(2)	1980 s.4(1).
119(1)	1980 s.1(3); 1984 s.3(1).
(2)	1980 s.19(4); 1984 s.3(2).
120	drafting.
121(1), (2)	1980 Sch. 1 Pt. II paras. 1, 2.
122(1)	1980 s.5(1).
(2)	1980 s.3(5).
(3)	1980 s.5(3).
123(1), (2)	1980 s.4(2).
(3)	1980 s.4(3).
124(1)	1980 s.5(1).
(2)	1980 s.5(1A); 1984 Sch. 11 para. 8(1).
(3)	1980 s.5(2); 1984 Sch. 11 para. 8(2).
125(1)	1980 s.10(1); 1984 Sch. 11 para. 10(1).
(2)	1980 s.10(1), (2); 1984 Sch. 11 para. 10(2).
(3)	1980 s.10(1)(*b*).
(4)	1980 s.10(2A); 1984 Sch. 11 para. 10(3).
(5)	1980 s.10(3); 1984 Sch. 11 para. 10(4).

Provision	Derivation
126(1)	1980 s.6(1).
(2)	1980 s.1(8); 1984 Sch. 1 para. 1.
127(1), (2)	1980 s.6(2), (3).
(3)	1980 s.6(4); 1984 Sch. 1 para. 2.
(4)	1980 s.6(5), (6); 1984 Sch. 11 para. 9.
128(1), (2)	1980 s.11(1), (2).
(3)	1980 s.11(2), (3).
(4), (5)	1980 s.11(4), (5).
(6)	1980 s.11(6); 1984 Sch. 11 para. 11.
129(1)	1980 s.7(1); 1984 s.3(2).
(2)	1980 s.7(1)(*b*); 1983 s.3(2).
(3)	1980 s.7(1); 1984 s.3(2).
130(1)	1980 s.7(1A), Sch. 1A Pt. II para. 5; 1984 s.3(2), (5), Sch. 2.
(2)	1980 Sch. 1A Pt. III para. 10(1) "conveyance", "grant", "previous discount", (2); 1984 s.3(5), Sch. 2, Sch. 11 para. 31.
(3)	1980 Sch. 1A Pt. II paras. 6(1)–(3), 8; 1984 s.3(5), Sch. 2.
(4)	1980 Sch. 1A Pt II para. 7(1), (2); 1984 s.3(5), Sch. 2.
(5)	1980 s.151(1), (3).
(6)	1957 s.189(1) "house"; 1980 Sch. 1A Pt. III para. 10(1) "dwelling-house"; 1984 s.3(5), Sch. 2.
131(1)	1980 s.7(2), (3); 1984 s.3(3).
(2)	1980 s.7(4).
(3)	1980 ss.7(3), 151(1), (3).
132(1)	1980 s.1(1), (2).
(2)	1980 s.4(1), (3).
133(1)	1980 s.9(1).
(2)	1980 s.9(2), (3).
(3), (4)	1980 s.9(4), (5).
(5)	drafting.
(6)	1980 s.151(1), (3).
134(1)	1980 s.12(1).
(2)	1980 s.12(1), (3).
(3), (4)	1980 s.12(2).
135(1), (2)	1980 s.12(4), (5).
(3)	1980 s.12(5A); 1984 Sch. 11 para. 12.
(4)	1980 s.12(6).
136(1), (2)	1980 s.13(1), (2); 1984 Sch. 11 para. 13(1), (2).
(3)	1980 s.13(2).
(4), (5)	1980 s.13(3).
(6)	1980 s.13(4).
(7)	1980 s.13(5).
137	1980 s.14; 1984 Sch. 1 para. 3.
138(1)	1980 s.16(1), (12); 1984 s.6(1), Sch. 1 para. 4.
(2), (3)	1980 s.16(9), (10).
139(1)	1980 s.17; 1984 Sch. 1 para. 5.
(2)	1980 s.16(11).
(3)	1980 s.18(1).
140(1), (2)	1980 s.16(2); 1984 s.6(2).
(3)	1980 s.16(3); 1984 s.6(3).
(4)	1980 s.16(2A); 1984 s.6(2).
(5)	1980 s.16(12); 1984 s.6(6).
141(1), (2)	1980 s.16(6); 1984 s.6(4).
(3), (4)	1980 s.16(6A), (6B); 1984 s.6(4).
(5)	1980 s.16(9)(*b*); 1984 s.6(5).
142(1), (2)	1980 s.16(4).
(3)	1980 s.16(5).
(4)	1980 s.16(8).

Provision	Derivation
142(5)	1980 s.6(7); 1984 s.6(5).
143(1)	1984 s.12(1), (2).
(2)	1980 s.4(3); 1984 Sch. 11 para. 7.
144(1)	1984 s.13(1), (2)(a), Sch. 3 para. 1(1).
(2)	1984 s.13(2)(b).
(3)–(5)	1984 s.13(3)–(5).
145(1)	1984 Sch. 3 para. 1(2).
(2)	1984 Sch. 3 para. 1(5).
(3)	1984 Sch. 3 para. 1(4).
(4), (5)	1984 Sch. 3 para. 10(1), (2).
146	1984 s.13(1).
147(1)	1984 s.14(1).
(2)	1984 s.14(1)(a), (b).
(3)	1984 s.14(1)(c).
(4)	1984 s.14(1)(d).
(5)	1984 s.14(2).
148(1)	1984 Sch. 3 paras. 2(1), 6(3).
(2)	1984 Sch. 3 para. 2(2).
149	1984 s.15.
150(1)	1984 s.17(1).
(2)	1984 s.17(9)(a).
(3)	1984 s.17(10).
151(1)	1984 ss.12(1), 17(1), Sch. 11 para. 32.
(2)	1984 s.17(11).
(3)	1984 s.17(2).
(4)	1984 s.16(1).
152(1), (2)	1984 s.17(3).
(3)	1980 s.16(3)(c); 1984 ss.6(3), 17(5).
(4)	1984 s.17(4).
(5)	1984 s.17(12).
153(1), (2)	1984 s.17(6).
(3), (4)	1984 s.17(7), (8).
(5)	1984 s.17(9)(b).
154(1)	1980 s.20(1)(a); 1984 Sch. 1 para. 7, Sch. 11 para. 16(a).
(2)	1980 s.20(1)(b); 1984 Sch. 1 para. 7.
(3)	1980 s.20(1A); 1984 Sch. 1 para. 7.
(4)	1980 s.20(3); 1984 Sch. 1 para. 7.
(5)	1980 s.20(4).
(6)	1980 s.20(1)(c), (2); 1984 Sch. 1 para. 7, Sch. 11 para. 16(b).
155(1)	1980 s.8(1); 1984 Sch. 3 para. 6(1).
(2)	1980 s.8(1), (2); 1984 s.5(1).
(3)	1984 Sch. 3 para. 6(1), (2).
156(1)	1980 s.8(4); 1984 Sch. 3 para. 6(10); R.7.
(2)	1980 s.8(4), (4A); 1984 s.5(4), Sch. 3 para. 6(10).
(3)	1980 s.8(6); 1984 Sch. 3 para. 6(10).
(4)	1980 s.8(5); 1984 s.5(5), Sch. 3 para. 6(10).
(5)	1980 s.151(1), (3); 1984 Sch. 11 para. 30.
(6)	1980 s.8(5A); 1984 s.5(5), Sch. 3 para. 6(10).
157(1)	1980 s.19(1); 1984 s.8(1), Sch. 11 para. 15(1).
(2)	1980 s.19(2); 1984 s.8(2).
(3)	1980 s.19(3).
(4)	1980 s.19(4); 1984 s.8(3).
(5)	1980 s.19(5).
(6)	1980 s.19(9).
(7)	1980 s.19(10).
(8)	1980 s.151(1), (3).
158(1)	1980 s.19(4)(a); 1984 s.8(3).
(2)	1980 s.19(6); 1984 s.8(4), Sch. 11 para. 15(2)(b).
(3)	1980 s.19(7); 1984 s.8(5), Sch. 11 para. 15(2)(c).
159	1980 ss.8(3), (7), 19(12); 1984 ss.5(2), 8(8), Sch. 3 para. 6(4), (8), Sch. 11 para. 15(2)(e).
160(1)	1980 ss.8(3A), 19(12); 1984 ss.5(2), 8(8), Sch. 3 para. 6(5), Sch. 11 para. 15(2)(a).

Provision	Derivation
160(2)	1980 s.8(3B); 1984 s.5(2), Sch. 3 para. 6(6).
161	1980 s.8(3A)(*d*); 1984 s.5(2), Sch. 3 paras. 6(5)(*d*), 7(1)(*b*) and *passim;* drafting.
162	1980 ss.8(3C), 19(11); 1984 ss.5(2), 8(7), Sch. 3 para. 6(7), Sch. 11 para. 15(2)(*d*).
163(1)	1980 ss.8(8), 19(12); 1984 ss.5(6), 8(8), Sch. 3 para. 6(9).
(2)	1980 s.19(12).
164(1)–(3)	1980 s.23(1); 1984 Sch. 11 para. 19(4).
(4)	1980 s.23(2); 1984 Sch. 11 para. 19(4).
(5)	1980 s.23(3); 1984 Sch. 11 para. 19(4).
(6)	1980 s.23(4).
165(1)	1980 s.24(1).
(2)	1980 s.24(2); 1984 Sch. 11 para. 20(1), (2).
(3)	1980 s.24(3); 1984 Sch. 1 para. 8(*a*).
(4)	1980 s.24(4); 1984 Sch. 1 para. 8(*b*).
(5)	1980 s.24(5); 1984 Sch. 1 para. 8(*c*); R.7.
(6)	1980 s.24(6).
166(1)	1980 s.23(6).
(2)	1980 s.23(6), (7).
(3)	1980 s.23(8).
(4)	1980 s.23(9); 1984 Sch. 11 para. 19(2).
(5)	1980 s.23(10).
(6)	1980 s.23(11); 1984 Sch. 11 para. 19(3).
167(1)	1980 s.24A(1), (3); 1984 s.9, Sch. 11 para. 21.
(2)	1980 s.24A(2); 1984 s.9.
168(1)	1980 s.24B(1); 1984 s.9. Sch. 11 para. 21.
(2)	1980 s.24B(2); 1984 s.9.
(3), (4)	1980 s.24B(3); 1984 s.9.
(5)	1980 s.24B(4); 1984 s.9.
169(1), (2)	1980 s.24C(1); 1984 s.10.
(3)	1980 s.24C(2); 1984 s.10, Sch. 11 para. 21.
170(1)	1980 s.24D(2); 1984 s.11, Sch. 11 para. 21; R.8.
(2), (3)	1980 s.24D(1); 1984 s.11, Sch. 11 para. 21.
(4)	1980 s.24D(3); 1984 s.11.
(5)	1980 s.24D(4), (5); 1984 s.11.
(6)	1980 s.24D(7); 1984 s.11.
171(1)	1984 s.30(1), (2).
(2)	1984 ss.18(3), 30(2).
(3)	1984 s.30(3), (4).
172(1)	1984 Sch. 11 para. 2(1).
(2)–(4)	1984 Sch. 11 para. 2(6).
173(1), (2)	1984 Sch. 11 para. 2(4).
174	1984 Sch. 11 para. 2(2), (3).
175(1)	1984 Sch. 11 para. 2(5).
(2)–(5)	1984 Sch. 11 para. 2(6).
176(1)	1980 s.22(1); 1984 Sch. 11 para. 18(2).
(2)	1980 s.22(1A); 1984 Sch. 11 para. 18(1).
(3)	1980 s.22(2); 1984 Sch. 11 para. 18(2).
(4)	1980 s.22(3); 1984 Sch. 11 para. 18(2).
(5)	1980 s.151(1), (3).
177(1)–(4)	1984 s.32(1)–(4).
178(1)	1980 s.21(1); 1984 Sch. 11 para. 17(1), (2)(*a*), (*b*).
(2)	1980 s.21(2); 1984 Sch. 11 para. 17(1), (2)(*b*).
(3)	1980 s.151(1), (3).
179(1)	1980 Sch. 2 para. 19A; 1984 Sch. 1 para. 11(3), Sch. 11 para. 32.
(2)	1984 s.31.
180	1980 s.25; 1984 Sch. 11 para. 21.
181(1)	1980 s.86(1); 1984 Sch. 11 para. 25(2).
(2), (3)	1980 s.86(2), (3).
(4)	1980 s.86(4), (5).
(5)	1980 s.86(6).
182(1)–(3)	1980 s.26(1)–(3).

Provision	Derivation
182(4)	1980 s.151(1), (3).
183(1)	1980 s.3(1); 1984 s.38(1).
(2), (3)	1980 s.3(2), (3); 1984 s.4(2).
184(1)	1980 ss.27(1), 50(2)(*b*); 1984 s.38(1).
(2)	1980 s.3(4); 1984 s.4(3), Sch. 11 para. 6.
(3)	1980 s.3(4A); 1984 s.4(3), Sch. 11 para. 6.
(4)	1984 s.4(4).
185(1), (2)	1980 s.27(3); 1984 Sch. 11 para. 22.
186(1), (2)	1980 ss.27(1), 50(3); 1984 s.38(1).
187	
"improvement"	1980 s.81(5).
"long tenancy"	1980 Sch. 1A Pt. III para. 10(1) "long lease"; 1984 s.3(5), Sch. 2.
"total share"	1984 Sch. 3 para. 3(9).
188	drafting.
Part VI	
189(1), (2)	1957 s.9(1)
(3)	1957 s.9(2).
(4)	1957 s.37(1).
190(1), (2)	1957 s.9(1A), (1B); 1969 s.72; 1980 s.149.
(3)	1957 s.9(2).
(4)	1957 s.37(1).
191(1)	1957 s.11(1); R.9(ii).
(2)	1957 s.11(3).
(3)	1957 s.11(3); 1969 Sch. 8 para. 6.
(4)	1957 s.37(1), (2).
192(1)	1957 s.12(1).
(2), (3)	1957 s.12(2).
(4)	1957 s.12(3).
193(1), (2)	1957 s.10(1).
(3)	drafting.
194(1), (2)	1957 s.10(2).
195(1)	1957 s.161; 1964 s.103(4).
(2)	1957 s.161.
196(1), (2)	1957 s.163(1).
(3)	1957 s.163(2).
197(1), (2)	1957 s.159.
198(1), (2)	1957 s.160; 1977 (c.45) s.31(6); 1982 (c.48) ss.37(2), 46.
199(1), (2)	1957 s.13(1).
(3), (4)	1957 s.13(2), (3).
200(1)	1957 s.14(1).
(2)	1957 s.14(2); 1972 (c.70) Sch. 29 paras. 1(1), 4(*a*).
(3)	1957 s.14(2).
(4)	1957 s.14(3).
(5)	1957 s.14(5); 1971 (c.23) Sch. 9; S.I. 1982/1109 Sch. 3 Pt. II para. 1; R.9(i).
(6)	1957 s.14(4); 1971 (c.23) Sch. 8 para. 1; 1972 (c.70) Sch. 29 paras. 1(1), 4(*a*); R.10.
201(1)–(3)	1957 s.15(1); R.11.
(4)–(6)	1957 s.15(3)–(5).
202	1957 s.33(1); R.12.
203(1), (2)	1957 s.33(2).
(3)	1957 s.10(9).
204	1957 ss.40, 68(1).
205	1957 s.9(3); R.13.
206	1957 s.39(1).
207	
"house"	1957 s.189(1) "house".
"occupying tenant"	1957 s.9(1C); 1980 s.149.
"owner"	1957 s.189(1) "owner".
"person having control"	1957 s.39(2).

Provision	Derivation
208	drafting.
Part VII	
209	1974 s.85(1), 86–89 *passim*.
210(1)	1974 s.85(1).
(2)	1974 s.85(3).
211(1)	1974 s.87(1).
(2)	1974 s.87(1), (2).
(3)	1974 s.87(3); 1975 Sch. 5 para. 20.
(4)–(6)	1974 s.87(4)–(6).
212(1), (2)	1974 s.89(1), (2).
(3)	1974 s.89(3), (4).
(4)	1974 s.89(7).
213(1)	1974 s.85(2).
(2), (3)	1974 ss.85(4), 89(4).
(4)	1974 ss.85(5), 89(4).
214(1)–(4)	1974 s.88(1)–(4).
(5)	1974 s.90(4); 1975 (c.76) Sch. 1.
215(1)	1974 s.89(5).
(2)	1974 s.89(1), (3), (6).
(3)	1974 ss.88(4), 89(5).
(4)	1974 s.90(4); 1974 (c.76) Sch. 1.
216(1)–(3)	1974 s.90(1)–(3).
217(1)–(3)	1974 s.91(1)–(3).
(4)	1974 s.91(4), (5).
(5)	1974 s.91(6).
(6)	1974 s.91(7).
218(1), (2)	1974 s.92(1).
(3), (4)	1974 s.92(2), (3).
219(1), (2)	1974 s.92(4).
220(1)–(4)	1974 s.93(1)–(4).
(5)	1974 s.93 *passim*.
(6)	drafting.
221(1), (2)	1957 s.161; 1974 s.96(3).
222(1), (2)	1957 s.159; 1974 s.97(1).
223(1)	1957 s.160; 1972 s.97(1).
(2)	1957 s.160; 1977 (c.45) s.31(6); 1982 (c.48) ss.37(2), 46.
224(1)	1974 s.96(1).
(2), (3)	1974 s.96(2).
(4)	1974 s.96(4).
225(1), (2)	1974 s.97(2).
226	1974 s.97(3).
227(1)–(3)	1974 s.101(1)–(3).
228(1)	1974 s.100(1), (2).
(2)	1974 s.100(8).
(3)	1974 s.100(2), (3).
(4)	1974 s.100(5).
(5)	1974 s.100(4), (9).
(6)	1974 s.100(7).
(7)	1974 s.100(6).
229(1)	1957 s.14(1); 1974 s.95.
(2)	1957 s.14(2); 1972 (c.70) Sch. 29 paras. 1(1), 4(*a*); 1974 s.95.
(3)	1957 s.14(2); 1974 s.95.
(4)	1957 s.14(3); 1974 s.95.
(5)	1957 s.14(5); 1971 (c.23) Sch. 9; 1974 s.95; R.9(i).
(6)	1957 s.14(4); 1971 (c.23) Sch. 8 para. 1; 1972 (c.70) Sch. 29 paras. 1(1), 4(*a*); 1974 s.95; R.10.
230(1)	1957 s.15(1).
(2)	1957 s.15(1); R.11.
(3)	1957 s.15(1).
(4)–(6)	1957 s.15(3)–(5).
231(1)–(4)	1974 s.98(1)–(4).

Provision	Derivation
232(1)	1974 s.99(1).
(2)	1974 s.99(2); 1976 (c.75) Sch. 7 para. 14; 1977 (c.42) Sch. 23 para. 64; 1981 (c.64) Sch. 12 para. 13(*c*).
(3)–(5)	1974 s.99(3)–(5).
(6)	1974 ss.84 "local authority", 99(6), 104(1) "local authority".
233	1974 s.102.
234(1)–(3)	1974 s.103A(1)–(3); 1980 Sch. 25 para. 26.
235	1974 ss.86(1), (2), 89(4).
236(1)	1974 s.104(2).
(2)	1974 s.104(1) "occupying tenant".
237	
"dwelling"	1974 s.129(1) "dwelling".
"improvement"	1974 s.104(1) "improvement".
"long tenancy"	1974 s.104(3).
"owner"	1974 s.104(1) "owner".
"owner-occupier"	1974 s.104(1) "owner-occupier".
"standard amenities"	1974 s.104(1) "standard amenities".
238	drafting.
Part VIII	
239(1)–(3)	1974 s.36(1)–(3).
(4)	1974 s.39(1).
(5)	1974 s.36(5); 1975 (c.76) Sch. 1.
240(1)	1974 s.36(4).
(2)	1974 s.36(4)(*a*).
(3)	1974 s.36(4)(*b*).
(4)	1974 s.36(4)(*c*).
(5)	1974 s.36(4)(*d*).
241(1), (2)	1974 s.37(1), (2).
(3)	1974 s.37(3), (4).
(4)	1974 s.37(5).
(5)	1974 s.37(6).
242(1)–(4)	1974 s.38(1)–(4).
243(1)	1974 ss.43(1), 44(1), (2).
(2)	1974 s.43(1).
(3)	1974 s.44(1), (2).
(4)	1974 s.43(3).
244(1)	1974 s.45(1); 1980 Sch. 13 para. 9(2).
(2)	1974 s.45(2).
(3)	1974 s.45(3); 1980 Sch. 13 para. 9(3).
(4)	1974 s.45(4).
(5)	1974 s.45(1); 1980 Sch. 13 para. 9(2).
245(1)	1974 s.46(1); 1980 Sch. 13 para. 10.
(2)	1974 s.46(2), (3); 1980 Sch. 13 para. 10.
(3)	1974 s.46(4); 1980 Sch. 13 para. 10.
(4)	1974 s.46(5); 1980 Sch. 13 para. 10.
(5)	1974 ss.46(6); 128(1), (1A), (3); 1980 Sch. 13 para. 10, Sch. 25 para. 30.
246	1974 s.41.
247(1)	1974 s.47(4) and *passim*.
(2)–(4)	1974 s.47(1)–(3).
(5)	1974 s.47(6); R.14(ii).
(6)	1974 s.47(5).
248(1)	1974 Sch. 4 para. 1.
(2)–(4)	1974 Sch. 4 para. 2(1)–(3).
(5)	1974 Sch. 4 para. 3(1), (2).
(6)	1974 Sch. 4 para. 4.
249(1)	1974 s.47(7); 1982 (c.48) ss.37, 38(9), 46(1).
(2)	1974 s.47(10); R.15.
250(1)–(3)	1974 ss.39(3), (7), 40(1), (2).
251(1), (2)	1974 s.39(2).

Provision	Derivation
251(3), (4)	1974 s.39(4).
(5)	1974 s.39(5).
(6)	1974 s.39(7).
252	
"housing accommodation"	1974 s.36(6).
"dwelling"	1974 s.129(1).
"house in multiple occupation"	1974 s.129(1).
253(1)	1969 s.28(1); 1980 Sch. 13 para. 1(1).
(2)	1969 s.29A; 1974 Sch. 5 Pt. II.
(3)	1969 s.29(1), (2).
254(1)–(4)	1969 s.28(2).
255(1)	1969 s.32(1).
(2)	1969 s.32(5); 1974 Sch. 13 para. 3.
256(1)–(3)	1969 s.33(1); 1971 (c.78) Sch. 23 Pt. II.
(4)	1969 s.33(2); 1971 (c.78) Sch. 23 Pt. II.
257	1969 s.31.
258(1)	1969 s.30(1).
(2)	1969 s.30(1A); 1974 Sch. 5 para. 2(1).
259	1969 s.37(1); 1980 Sch. 13 para. 5.
(2)	1969 ss.37(2), 86(5); 1980 Sch. 13 para. 5.
(3), (4)	1969 s.37(3), (4); 1980 Sch. 13 para. 5.
(5)	1969 ss.37(5), 85(1A); 1980 Sch. 13 para. 5, Sch. 25 para. 21.
(6)	1969 ss.84, 86(4).
(7)	1971 ss.1, 2(4); 1973 (H) s.1(1).
260	1957 s.159; 1969 Sch. 8 para. 11; 1974 ss.48(1)(*a*), 54(1)(*g*).
261	1957 s.160; 1969 Sch. 8 para. 11; 1974 ss.48(1)(*b*), 54(1)(*g*); 1977 (c.45) s.31(6); 1982 (c.48) ss.37, 46(1).
262	
"disposal"	1974 s.47(3).
"owner"	1957 s.189(1).
263	drafting.
Part IX	
264(1)–(4)	1957 s.16(1)–(4).
(5)	1957 s.16(5); 1976 (c.80) Sch. 8 para. 4; 1977 (c.42) Sch. 23 para. 22.
(6)	1957 s.16(6); 1982 (c.48) ss.37, 39, 46(1), Sch. 3.
(7)	1957 s.16(7).
265(1)	1957 s.17(1).
(2)	1957 s.17(1) proviso, (3)(*b*), (*c*).
(3)	drafting.
266	1957 s.18(1).
267(1)	1957 s.21.
(2)	1957 s.27(1).
(3)	1957 s.27(2), (3); R.9(ii).
268(1)	1957 ss.16(1), 19.
(2)	1957 s.37(1).
269(1)–(3)	1957 s.20(1)–(3); R.9(ii).
(4)	1957 s.20(3) proviso.
(5)	1957 s.20(3).
(6)	1957 s.37(1), (2).
270(1)	1957 s.22(1).
(2)	1957 s.22(2); 1965 (c.75) Sch. 6 para. 10(2); 1977 (c.43) Sch. 2 para. 2.
(3)	1957 s.22(5); 1976 (c.80) Sch. 8 para. 4; 1977 (c.42) Sch. 23 para. 22.
(4)	1957 s.22(3); R.9(i).
(5)	1957 s.22(4); 1982 (c.48) ss.37, 39, 46(1), Sch. 3.
271(1), (2)	1957 s.23(1).
272(1), (2)	1957 s.23(2).
(3), (4)	1957 s.23(3).

Provision	Derivation
272(5)	1957 s.23(4); R.9(ii).
(6)	1957 s.23(5).
273(1)	1957 s.25(1).
(2)	1957 s.25(2).
(3)	1957 s.25(2) proviso.
(4)	1957 s.25(3).
274(1), (2)	1957 s.24(1); 1961 s.25.
(3)	1957 s.24(2).
(4)	1957 s.24(3).
(5)	1957 s.24(2).
275(1)	1961 s.26(1).
(2)	1957 s.16(1); 1961 s.26(2).
276	1957 s.27(5); 1961 s.26(3); 1976 (c.80) Sch. 8 para. 4; 1977 (c.42) Sch. 23 para. 22; R.16(i).
277	1957 s.27(1); 1972 (c.71) s.32; 1982 (c.48) ss.37, 39, 46(1), Sch. 3.
278(1)	1957 s.27(2); 1976 (c.57) s.10(1)(*a*).
(2)	1957 s.27(3); 1976 (c.57) s.10(1)(*b*); R.9(ii).
(3)	1957 s.27(4); 1976 (c.57) s.10(1)(*c*).
279(1)	1957 s.28; 1961 s.26(3).
(2)	1957 s.28; 1976 (c.57) s.10(2).
(3)	1957 s.28; 1961 s.26(3).
280	1957 s.18(2).
281(1)	1957 s.18(2)(*b*).
(2)	1957 s.18(2) proviso.
282(1)	1957 s.18(2).
(2)	drafting.
283(1)	1957 s.72(4).
(2)	1957 s.72(5).
(3)	1957 s.189(1).
284(1), (2)	1957 s.72(1).
(3), (4)	1957 s.72(2).
(5)	1957 ss.37(1), 72(3).
285(1), (2)	1957 s.72(3); R.9(ii).
(3)	1957 ss.37(1), (2), 72(3).
(4)	1957 s.72(3).
286(1)	1957 s.73(1).
(2)	1957 s.73(2); 1965 (c.75) Sch. 6 para. 10; 1977 (c.43) Sch. 2 para. 2.
(3)	1957 s.73(3); 1977 (c.45) s.31(6); 1982 (c.48) ss.37, 46(1).
(4)	1957 s.73(4); 1976 (c.80) Sch. 8 para. 4; 1977 (c.42) Sch. 23 para. 24.
287(1)	1957 s.74(1).
(2), (3)	1957 s.74(2).
288(1), (2)	1957 ss.23(2), 74(3).
(3), (4)	1957 ss.23(3), 74(3).
(5)	1957 ss.23(4), 74(3).
(6)	1957 ss.23(5), 74(3).
289(1)–(3)	1957 s.42(1).
(4)	1957 s.42(1) proviso.
(5)	1957 s.42(2).
(6)	1957 s.29(3).
290(1)	1957 s.43(1).
(2)	1957 s.43(2).
(3), (4)	1957 s.43(3).
291(1), (2)	1957 s.47(1), R.37(i)
(3)	drafting.
(4)	drafting: R.37(i).
292	1957 s.50.
293(1), (2)	1957 s.49.
294(1)	1957 s.64(1).
(2)	1957 s.64(2).
(3)	1957 s.64(1).

Provision	Derivation
295(1), (2)	1957 s.64(3).
(3)	1957 s.64(3); 1961 (c.33) Sch. 4 para. 9.
296(1)	1957 s.64(3) proviso.
(2)	1957 s.65(1).
(3)	1957 s.65(3), (6)(*a*).
(4)	1957 ss.65(7), 189(1).
297(1)–(3)	1957 s.65(2).
(4)	1957 s.65(5).
(5)	1957 s.65(5) proviso.
(6)	1957 s.65(6)(*b*).
298(1)	1957 s.74A(4); 1984 (c.12) Sch. 4 paras. 1, 35(1).
(2)	1957 s.74A(2), (5); 1984 (c.12) Sch. 4 para. 35.
(3)	1957 s.74A(1), (3); 1984 (c.12) Sch. 4 para. 35(1).
299(1)	drafting.
(2)	1974 s.114(8) "full standard"; 1975 Sch. 5 para. 21; 1980 Sch. 25 para. 28(3)(*a*).
300(1)	1957 s.17(2).
(2)	1957 ss.19, 20, 37; R.9(ii).
(3)	1957 s.29(1).
(4)	1957 s.18(1); drafting.
(5)	1957 s.17(3).
301(1)	1957 s.48(1).
(2)	1957 s.48(3).
(3)	1957 s.48(2).
302	1957 ss.29(3), (4), 48(1), (4).
303	1957 s.17(3); 1974 ss.110, 111; 1978 (c.30) s.17(2)(*a*).
304(1)	1957 s.17(3).
(2)	1957 s.26.
(3)	1957 s.17(3).
305(1)	1974 s.110(1), (2), (3).
(2)	1974 s.110(9).
(3)	1974 s.110(4).
(4)	1974 s.110(5).
(5)	1974 s.110(6).
(6)	1974 s.110(7), (8).
(7)	1965 (c.56) s.4; 1974 s.116.
306(1)	1974 s.111(1), (2).
(2)	1974 s.111(3).
307(1), (2)	1957 ss.33(2), 74(6); R.16(ii).
308(1)–(3)	1957 s.68(1).
(4)	1957 s.70(1), (2); 1974 Sch. 13 para. 3.
309(1)	1957 s.68(2); 1968 (c.23) Sch. 15; 1977 (c.42) Sch. 15 para. 3, Sch. 23 para. 23, Sch. 24 para. 30.
(2)	1957 ss.68(2), 87.
310(1)–(5)	1957 s.69(1)–(5).
(6)	1957 s.70(1), (2).
311(1)–(3)	1957 s.70(2).
312(1)	1972 s.11(1).
(2)	1972 s.11(2).
(3)	1972 s.11(7).
(4)	1972 s.15(2).
(5)	1972 s.15(1).
(6)	1972 s.104(1).
313(1)	1972 s.11(3), (10)(*a*).
(2)	drafting.
(3)	1972 s.11(10)(*b*).
(4)	1972 s.15(5).
314(1), (2)	1972 s.105(3); 1975 Sch. 1 para. 13(1).
(3)	1972 s.105(4).
(4)	1972 s.105(3), (4); 1975 Sch. 1 para. 13(1).
(5)	1972 s.104(4).
315(1), (2)	1957 s.161

Provision	Derivation
316(1), (2)	1957 s.163(1).
(3)	1957 s.163(2).
317(1)	1957 s.162(1); R.9(ii); R.16(iv).
(2), (3)	1957 s.162(2).
(4)	1957 s.162(3).
318(1), (2)	1957 s.164(1).
(3), (4)	1957 s.164(2), (3).
319(1), (2)	1957 s.159; R.16(iii).
320	1957 s.160; 1977 (c.45) s.31(6); 1982 (c.48) ss.37, 46(1).
321	1957 s.39(1).
322	
"house"	1957 s.189(1) "house".
"owner"	1957 s.189(1) "owner".
"person having control"	1957 s.39(2).
323	drafting.
Part X	
324	1957 s.77(1).
325(1)	1957 s.77(1)(*a*).
(2)	1957 s.77(1)(*a*), 87 "room".
326(1)	1957 s.77(1)(*b*).
(2)	1957 ss.77(2), 87 "room".
(3)	1957 Sch. 6.
(4)	1957 s.81(3).
(5)	1957 s.178(1), (2).
(6)	1957 s.81(4).
327(1)–(3)	1957 ss.78(1)–(4), 80(5); 1977 (c.45) s.31(5), (6); 1982 (c.48) ss.37, 46(1).
328(1)–(3)	1957 s.78(3).
329	1957 s.78(4).
330(1)	1957 s.80(1).
(2)	1957 s.80(1), (6).
(3)	1957 s.80(2).
(4), (5)	1957 s.80(3).
(6)	1957 s.80(4).
331(1)	1957 s.78(1).
(2)	1957 s.78(5).
(3)	1957 s.78(1); 1977 (c.45) s.31(5), (6); 1982 (c.48) ss.37, 46(1).
332(1), (2)	1957 s.81(1); R.17.
(3)	1957 s.81(2).
333(1), (2)	1957 s.83.
(3)	1957 s.83; 1977 (c.45) s.31(5), (6); 1982 (c.48) ss.37, 46(1).
334(1), (2)	1957 s.76.
335(1)	1957 s.85(3).
(2)	1957 s.85(3); 1977 (c.45) s.31(5), (6); 1982 (c.48) ss.37, 46(1).
336(1), (2)	1957 s.81(1).
(3)	1957 s.81(1); 1977 (c.45) s.31(6); 1982 (c.48) ss.37, 46(1).
337(1), (2)	1957 s.159.
338(1)	1957 s.85(2).
(2)	1957 s.85(2); 1965 (c.75) Sch. 6 para. 10; 1977 (c.43) Sch. 2 para. 2.
(3)	1957 s.85(2); R.9(i).
339(1), (2)	1957 s.85(1).
340(1), (2)	1957 s.159(*c*).
341(1)	1957 s.160.
(2)	1957 s.160; 1977 (c.45) s.31(6); 1982 (c.48) ss.37, 46(1).
342(1), (2)	1957 s.87 "suitable alternative accommodation".
343	
"agent"	1957 s.87
"dwelling"	1957 s.87; R.4(i).
"landlord"	1957 s.87.
"owner"	1957 s.189(1).

Provision	Derivation
344	drafting.
Part XI	
345	1969 s.58(1).
346(1)	1961 s.22(1); 1969 Sch. 8 para. 4.
(2), (3)	1961 s.22(3).
(4)	1961 s.22(2).
(5)	1961 s.22(9).
(6)	1969 s.64(7); 1980 Sch. 23 para. 9; 1982 (c.48) ss.37, 46(1).
347(1)	1969 s.64(1), (2).
(2)	1969 s.64(1).
(3)	1969 s.64(3).
(4)	1969 s.64(7); 1980 Sch. 23 para. 9; 1982 (c.48) ss.37, 46(1).
348(1)	1969 s.64(4).
(2)	1969 s.64(5).
(3), (4)	1969 s.64(6).
349(1)	1961 s.22(6).
(2)	1961 s.22(7).
(3)	1961 s.22(8); 1969 (c.19) s.10(1).
(4)	1961 s.22(9).
350(1)	1961 s.22(4).
(2)	1961 s.22(4); 1980 Sch. 23 para. 4; 1982 (c.48) ss.37, 46(1).
351(1), (2)	1961 s.22(10); 1969 s.64(8); 1972 (c.70) Sch. 29 para. 4.
352(1)	1961 s.15(1); 1969 Sch. 8 para. 2.
(2)	1961 s.15(1); 1964 s.67(1), (2).
(3)	1961 s.15(1), (4); 1964 s.64(6).
(4)	1961 s.15(3).
(5)	1961 s.15(2).
(6)	1961 s.21(1); 1964 s.67(4); 1969 Sch. 8 para. 3.
353(1), (2)	1961 ss.17(1), 21(3); 1964 ss.64(7), 67(2).
(3)	1961 s.17(2).
(4)	1961 ss.17(4), 21(3).
(5)	1961 s.17(3).
354(1)	1961 s.19(1); 1969 s.62(1)(*a*).
(2)	1961 s.19(3).
(3)	1961 s.19(4).
(4)	1961 s.19(5).
(5)	1961 s.19(6).
(6)	1964 s.67(3).
(7)	1961 s.19(12).
355(1)	1961 s.19(2), (3); 1964 s.67(5); 1969 s.62(1)(*b*).
(2)	1961 s.19(10), (11); 1980 Sch. 23(3)(*b*); 1982 (c.48) ss.37, 46(1).
356(1)	1961 s.19(9).
(2)	1961 s.19(10); 1980 Sch. 23 para. 23(3)(*a*); 1982 (c.48) ss.37, 46(1).
357(1)	1961 s.19(7).
(2), (3)	1961 s.19(8).
358(1)	1957 s.90(1); 1980 s.146; R.18(i).
(2)	1957 s.90(8); 1980 s.146.
(3)	1957 ss.37(1), 90(10)(*b*); 1980 s.146.
(4)	1957 s.90(13); 1980 s.146; 1982 (c.48) ss.37, 46(1).
359(1)	1957 s.90(2), (3); 1980 s.146.
(2)	1957 s.90(1), (7); 1980 s.146.
360(1), (2)	1957 s.90(4); 1980 s.146.
361(1), (2)	1957 s.90(5), (6); 1980 s.146.
362(1)	1957 s.90(10); 1980 s.146.
(2)	1957 ss.37(1), (2); 90(10)(*b*); 1980 s.146.
363(1)	1957 s.90(11); 1980 s.146.
(2), (3)	1957 s.90(12); 1980 s.146.
364(1)	1957 s.90(9); 1980 s.146.
(2)	1957 s.90(14); 1980 s.146; 1982 (c.48) ss.37, 46(1).
365(1), (2)	1980 Sch. 24 para. 1.
(3)	1980 Sch. 24 para. 8.
(4)	1980 s.151(1), (3).

Provision	Derivation
366(1)	1980 Sch. 24 paras. 2(1), 4.
(2)	1980 Sch. 24 para. 2(1), (3).
(3)	1980 Sch. 24 para. 2(1), (2); R.19.
367(1)	1961 s.17(1); 1964 s.64(7); 1980 Sch. 24 para. 12.
(2)	1961 s.17(2); 1980 Sch. 24 para. 12.
(3)	1961 s.17(3); 1980 Sch. 24 para. 12.
368(1)	1980 Sch. 24 para. 3.
(2)	1980 Sch. 24 para. 5.
(3)	1980 (c.43) s.34(1); 1980 Sch. 24 para. 7; 1982 (c.48) ss.37, 39, 46(1), Sch. 3.
(4)	1980 Sch. 24 para. 6.
(5)	1980 Sch. 24 para. 11.
(6)	1980 Sch. 24 para. 9; R.14(ii).
369(1)	1961 s.13(1); 1969 Sch. 8 para. 2.
(2)	1961 s.13(1).
(3)	1961 s.13(3).
(4)	1961 s.13(2).
(5)	1961 s.13(4); 1980 Sch. 23 para. 2; 1982 (c.48) ss.37, 46(1).
(6)	1961 s.13(1), (5).
370(1)	1961 s.12(1); 1969 Sch. 8 para. 2.
(2), (3)	1961 s.12(3).
(4)	1961 s.12(6).
(5)	1961 s.12(7); 1975 (c.76) Sch. 1.
371(1)	1961 s.12(4); 1969 s.59(2).
(2)	1961 s.12(5); 1969 s.59(3).
(3)	1961 s.12(5).
(4)	1961 s.12(6).
372(1)	1961 s.14(1).
(2)	1961 s.14(2).
(3)	1961 s.14(3).
(4)	1961 s.14(4); 1964 s.64(6).
(5)	1961 s.14(1).
373(1), (2)	1961 s.14(5); 1964 s.64(7); R.9(i).
(3)	1961 s.14(6).
(4)	1961 s.14(7).
374(1)	1961 s.21(1), (3); 1964 s.69(1); 1969 Sch. 8 paras. 5, 29.
(2)	1964 ss.43, 44(1), 69(4); 1969 Sch. 8 para. 29; 1978 (c.30) s.17(2)(*a*).
(3)	1961 s.21(2); 1964 s.69(2).
375(1)	1961 s.18(1); 1980 Sch. 24 para. 12.
(2)	1964 s.65(5).
(3)	1961 s.18(2); 1964 s.65(2).
(4)	drafting.
376(1)	1964 s.65(1); 1980 Sch. 23 para. 6(1), Sch. 24 para. 12; 1982 (c.48) ss.37, 46(1).
(2)	1969 s.61(1), (2); 1980 Sch. 23 para. 8(1), Sch. 24 para. 12; 1982 (c.48) ss.37, 46(1).
(3)	1964 s.65(5); 1969 s.61(1).
(4)	1964 s.65(2).
(5)	1964 s.65(3); 1969 s.61(4).
377(1)	1961 s.23(1).
(2)	1961 s.26A; 1980 Sch. 23 para. 5.
(3)	1961 s.26A; 1980 Sch. 23 para. 5; 1982 (c.48) ss.37, 46(1).
378(1)	1957 s.33(1); 1961 s.23(2); 1980 Sch. 24 para. 12.
(2)	1961 s.23(3); 1980 Sch. 24 para. 12.
379(1)	1964 s.73(1); 1969 Sch. 8 para. 5.
(2)	1964 s.73(2).
(3)	1964 s.73(3).
(4)	1964 s.73(4).
380(1), (2)	1964 s.76(1).
381(1)	1964 s.74(1), (2).
(2)	1964 s.74(3).

Provision	Derivation
381(3)	1964 s.74(2).
(4)	1964 s.74(4); 1980 Sch. 24 para. 12.
(5)	1964 s.73(5); 1975 (c.76) Sch. 1.
(6)	1964 s.74(5).
382(1)	1964 s.75(1).
(2)	1964 s.75(2).
(3)	1964 s.75(3); 1976 (c.80) Sch. 8 para. 11; 1977 (c.42) Sch. 23 para. 35.
(4)	1964 s.75(3A); 1976 (c.80) Sch. 8 para. 11; 1977 (c.42) Sch. 23 para. 35.
(5)	1964 s.75(4).
383(1)	1964 s.81(1).
(2)	1964 s.81(2).
(3), (4)	1964 s.81(4).
(5)	1964 s.81(6).
384(1)	1964 s.82(1), (3).
(2)	1964 s.82(1); R.19.
(3)	1964 s.82(2).
(4)	1964 s.82(4).
(5)	drafting.
(6)	1964 s.82(5).
385(1)	1964 s.77(1), (2).
(2), (3)	1964 s.77(2).
386(1)	1964 s.79(1).
(2)	drafting.
(3)	1964 s.79(6).
387(1), (2)	1964 s.75(5).
(3)	1964 s.76(2).
(4)	1964 s.75(6).
(5)	1964 s.75(6); 1980 Sch. 23 para. 7; 1982 (c.48) ss.37, 46(1).
388	1964 s.90.
389(1)	1964 ss.78(1), 81(3); 1977 (c.42) Sch. 23 para. 36; 1980 s.72.
(2)	1964 ss.78(2), (3), 81(5).
(3)	1964 ss.78(4), 81(5).
390(1)	1964 s.89(1).
(2)	1964 s.89(2).
391(1)	1964 s.88(1), (2).
(2)	1964 s.88(3).
(3), (4)	1964 s.88(2).
(5)	1964 Sch. 4 para. 3.
392(1)	1964 s.86(1).
(2)	1964 s.86(2).
(3)	1964 s.86(3).
(4)	1964 s.86(4).
(5)	1964 s.86(9).
393(1)	1964 s.86(4).
(2)	1964 s.86(6), (7).
(3)	1964 s.86(4).
(4)	drafting.
394	drafting.
395(1)	1957 s.159(c); 1961 s.28(2); 1964 s.91(5); R.20(i).
(2)	1957 s.159; 1961 s.23(6); 1964 s.65(4); 1969 s.61(5); 1980 Sch. 24 para. 12; R.20(i).
(3)	1957 s.159.
396(1)	1957 s.160.
(2)	1957 s.160; 1977 (c.45) s.31(6); 1982 (c.48) ss.37, 4
397(1)	1964 s.68(1); 1969 s.61(5); 1980 Sch. 24 para.
(2)	1964 s.68(2); 1980 Sch. 24 para. 12; R.20
(3)	1964 s.68(5).
(4)	1964 s.68(4).
(5)	1964 s.68(3).

Provision	Derivation
398(1)	drafting.
(2)	1961 s.23(7); R.18(ii).
(3)	1957 s.189(1); 1961 s.28(2); 1964 s.91(5); 1980 Sch. 24 para. 10.
(4)	1961 s.23(7).
(5)	1957 s.39(2); 1961 s.15(1)(*a*); 1964 s.91(1).
(6)	1961 s.13(2); 1964 s.91(1).
399	
"dispossessed proprietor"	1964 s.78(6).
"final determination"	1964 s.91(4).
"house"	1957 s.189(1); 1961 s.28(2); 1964 s.91(5); 1969 s.63(11); 1980 Sch. 24 para. 10.
400	drafting.
Part XII	
401	1936 (c.49) s.235.
402	1936 (c.49) s.236.
403	1936 (c.49) s.237.
404(1)	1936 (c.49) ss.238(1), 283(1).
(2), (3)	1936 (c.49) s.238(1).
(4)–(6)	1936 (c.49) s.238(2)–(4).
405(1)	1936 (c.49) s.239.
(2), (3)	1936 (c.49) s.300(2), (3).
(4)	1936 (c.49) s.301; 1971 (c.23) s.56(2), Sch. 9 Pt. I.
(5)	1936 (c.49) s.302.
406	1936 (c.49) s.240.
407(1), (2)	1936 (c.49) s.241(1), (2).
(3), (4)	1936 (c.49) s.241(3).
(5)	1936 (c.49) s.241(4).
408(1)	1936 (c.49) ss.246, 296.
(2)	1936 (c.49) s.246; 1967 (c.80) s.92, Sch. 3 Pt. I; 1982 (c.48) ss.37, 46(1).
(3)	1936 (c.49) s.297.
409	1936 (c.49) s.247; 1984 (c.22) Sch. 2 para. 2.
410(1)	1936 (c.49) s.1(1).
(2)	1936 (c.49) ss.322–326.
411(1)	1936 (c.49) s.287(1).
(2), (3)	1936 (c.49) s.287(2).
(4), (5)	1936 (c.49) s.287(3), (4).
412(1)	1936 (c.49) ss.288, 296.
(2)	1936 (c.49) s.288; 1967 (c.80) s.92, Sch. 3 Pt. I; 1982 (c.48) ss.37, 46(1).
413	1936 (c.49) s.298.
414(1)	1936 (c.49) s.248(1).
(2), (3)	1936 (c.49) s.248(2), (3); 1972 (c.70) Sch. 29 Pt. para. 4(1)(*a*).
415	1936 (c.49) s.341.
416	drafting.
Part XIII	
417(1)	1972 s.12(1); 1974 s.106(1), Sch. 13 para. 24.
(2)	1972 s.12(1)(*e*); 1974 Sch. 13 para. 24.
(3)	1972 s.104(1) "houses and other property within the account".
(4)	1972 s.12(3).
	drafting.
	1980 s.135(1).
	1980 s.135(2), (10) "housing stock".
	1980 s.135(3), (10) "expenditure", "housing stock".
	1980 s.135(4)–(6).
	1980 s.135(9).
	1972 Sch. 1 para. 5(1); 1980 s.135(8).
	1972 Sch. 1 para. 5(2).

Provision	Derivation
420(3)	1972 Sch. 1 para. 5(3).
(4)	1972 Sch. 1 para. 5(4).
421(1)	1980 s.96(1)(*a*).
(2)–(4)	1980 s.103(1)–(3).
422(1), (2)	1980 s.97(1), (2).
423(1), (2)	1980 s.98(1), (2).
424(1)–(4)	1980 s.99(1)–(4).
425(1)	1980 s.100(1).
(2)	1980 s.100(2); 1978 (c.30) s.17(2)(*a*).
(3)–(5)	1980 s.100(3)–(5).
(6)	1980 ss.100(4), 105 "year of account".
426(1)	1980 s.101(1).
(2)	1980 s.101(2)(*b*).
(3)	1980 s.101(3)(*b*).
(4), (5)	1980 s.101(4), (5).
427(1)–(3)	1980 s.102(1)–(3).
428(1)	1957 s.136(1); 1958 s.54(1); 1969 Sch. 8 para. 19.
(2)	1957 s.136(3); 1958 s.54(3); 1969 Sch. 8 para. 19.
429(1)	1980 s.108(1), (2), (4) "local authority".
(2)	1980 s.108(3); S.I. 1981/723.
(3)	1980 s.151(1), (3).
(4)	1980 s.108(4) "house".
430(1)	1957 s.142; 1972 (c.70) s.153(1).
(2)	1957 s.142; 1959 (c.53) s.27(1)–(3); 1972 (c.70) s.153(2).
431(1)	1974 ss.84 "housing authority", 105(1), (3); 1976 (c.75) Sch. 7 para. 15.
(2)	1974 s.105(2).
(3)	1974 s.105(3).
432	drafting.
433	
"year"	1972 s.104(1) "year"; 1975 s.16(1) "year"; 1978 (c.30) Sch. 1 "financial year"; 1980 s.105 "year".
434	drafting.
Part XIV	
435(1)	1958 s.43(1); 1974 (c.7) s.37(2).
(2)	1958 s.43(5); 1974 (c.7) s.37(5).
(3)	1958 s.43(1).
(4)	1958 s.43(4).
436(1)	1958 s.43(3).
(2)	1958 s.43(3)(*a*), (*f*).
(3)	1958 s.43(3)(*b*), (*e*); R.21.
(4)	1958 s.43(3)(*d*).
(5), (6)	1958 s.43(3)(*c*); 1974 (c.7) s.37(4); R.22.
437	1957 s.104(4); 1980 s.91.
438(1)	1980 s.110(1), (2); 1984 Sch. 11 para. 26.
(2)	1980 s.110(11)–(13).
(3)	1980 s.110(14); drafting.
439(1), (2)	1958 s.43(2).
(3)	1958 s.43(2A); 1974 (c.7) s.37(3).
440	1958 s.44.
441(1)–(3)	1980 s.110(1), (2), (11), (12); R.22.
(4)	1980 s.110(12).
(5)	1980 s.151(1), (3).
442(1)	1980 s.111(1); 1984 s.20(1).
(2)–(4)	1980 s.111(3)–(5); 1984 s.20(2)–(4).
(5)	1980 s.111(5)(*b*); 1984 s.20(4)(*b*).
443(1), (2)	1984 s.21(1), (2), (4).
(3)	1984 s.21(3).
444(1), (2)	1984 s.20(5) "recognised body".
(3)	1984 s.20(6).

Provision	Derivation
444(4)	1984 ss.18(3), (4) "conveyance", "grant", 20(5) "relevant advance".
445(1), (2)	1978 s.1(1), (2).
(3)	1978 s.1(2).
(4)	1978 s.2(7).
446(1)	1978 s.1(4).
(2)	1978 s.1(3), (5).
(3)	1978 s.1(3).
(4)	1978 s.1(5).
(5)	1978 s.1(6).
(6)	1978 s.2(7).
447(1)	1978 Sch. 1 Part I.
(2)	1978 s.2(1).
(3)	1978 s.2(7).
448(1)	1978 Sch. 1 Part II.
(2)	1978 s.2(1).
(3)	1978 s.2(7).
449(1)	1978 s.2(2).
(2)	1978 s.2(3).
(3)	1978 s.2(4).
450(1)	1978 ss.3(1), (3), (4), 4(2); drafting.
(2)	1978 ss.3(2), (3), 4(2); drafting.
451(1)	1958 s.47(1), (2).
(2)	1958 s.47(3), (5)(c), (6).
(3)	1958 s.47(5)(c).
(4)	1958 s.47(6) proviso (b).
(5)	1958 s.47(5)(a), (b).
(6)	1958 s.47(2)(c); drafting.
452(1), (2)	1984 ss.18(3), (4) "conveyance", "grant", 19(1).
(3)	1984 s.19(3).
(4)	1984 s.19(4).
(5)	1984 s.19(2).
(6)	1980 s.112(1), (2).
453(1)	1984 s.24(1).
(2)	1984 s.18(3).
454	1978 s.2(5); 1980 s.111(8); 1984 s.20(7); S.I. 1983/1122 Art. 2(2).
455(1)	1984(D) s.28(1).
(2)	1984(D) s.28(2).
(3)	1984(D) s.28(4).
456	drafting.
457	1958 s.58(1) "house".
458	
"the corresponding Northern Ireland provisions"	1978 ss. 2(5), 4(2); S.I. 1983/1122, Art. 2(2); drafting.
"the corresponding Scottish provisions"	1978 *passim*; drafting.
"designated building society"	1978 Sch. 1 Part I.
"long lease"	1984 s.18(4) "long lease".
459	drafting.
Part XV	
460(1)	1974 s.56(1), (2); drafting.
(2)	1974 s.56(1).
(3)	1974 ss.56(1), 84, "housing authority"; 1976 (c.75) Sch. 7 para. 13.
461(1)	1974 ss.57(1), 61(1)(a), 65(1)(a), 69(1)(a), 71(1)(a).
(2)	1974 s.57(2).
(3)	1974 s.57(6).
(4)	1974 s.57(6A); 1980 Sch. 12 para. 2.

Provision	Derivation
462(1)	1974 s.56(3), (4).
(2)	1974 s.56(4).
463(1)	1974 s.57(3); 1980 s.106(1), Sch. 12 paras. 1, 26(1), 28; R.23.
(2)	1974 s.57(3); R.23.
(3), (4)	1980 s.106(1).
(5)	1974 s.84 "prescribed"; 1980 ss.106(5), 151(1), (3).
(6)	1974 s.57(3).
464(1)	1974 s.60(1), (1A), (2); 1980 Sch. 12 para. 29.
(2)	1980 s.106(2), (3); R.23.
(3)	1974 s.60(3); 1980 Sch. 12 para. 5.
(4)	1974 s.60(4); 1980 Sch. 12 para. 5.
(5)	1974 s.60(5); 1980 s.106(2), Sch. 12 para. 6.
465(1), (2)	1974 s.57(5); 1980 Sch. 12 para. 26(2).
466(1)–(3)	1974 s.57(4).
467(1)	1974 s.56(2)(*a*).
(2)	1974 s.84 "improvement", "relevant standard".
468(1)	1974 s.61(2).
(2)	1974 s.61(3); 1980 Sch. 12 para. 20(1).
(3)	1974 s.61(4).
(4)	1974 s.61(4A); 1980 Sch. 12 para. 20(2).
(5)	1974 s.61(5).
469(1)–(3)	1974 s.62(1), (2).
(4)	1974 s.62(3).
(5)	1974 s.128(1), (1A), (3); 1980 Sch. 25 para. 30.
(6)	1974 s.62(4).
(7)	1974 s.62(5), (6); 1980 Sch. 12 para. 7.
470(1), (2)	1974 s.61(1).
471(1)	1974 s.63(1).
(2)	1974 s.63(2).
(3)	1974 s.57(7).
(4)	1974 s.63(3).
(5)	1974 s.84 "prescribed".
(6)	1974 s.128(1), (1A), (3); 1980 Sch. 25 para. 30.
472(1)	1974 s.64(3).
(2)	1974 s.64(3), (8).
(3)	drafting.
(4)	1974 s.64(4), 128(1A); 1980 Sch. 25 para. 30.
(5)	1974 s.64(5).
473(1)	1974 s.64(1).
(2)	1974 s.64(2).
(3)	1974 s.57(7).
(4)	1974 s.64(6).
474(1)	1974 ss.56(2)(*b*), 65(3)(*b*).
(2)	1974 s.84 "improvement"; R.24(i).
475(1)	1974 s.65(2).
(2)	1974 s.65(2); 1975 Sch. 5 para. 16(1).
(3)	1974 s.65(3); 1975 Sch. 5 para. 16(3).
(4)	1974 s.65(2A); 1975 Sch. 5 para. 16(2).
(5)	1974 s.65(4); 1975 Sch. 5 para. 16(4).
476	1974 s.66; 1980 Sch. 12 para. 9.
477	1974 s.67(2).
478	1974 s.67(3); 1980 Sch. 12 para. 10(2).
479(1), (2)	1974 s.67(1).
480(1)	1974 s.68(1).
(2)	1974 s.68(4).
(3)	1974 s.57(7).
(4)	1974 s.68(2).
481(1)	1974 s.68(3); 1980 Sch. 12 para. 11.
(2), (3)	1974 s.68(3A); 1980 Sch. 12 para. 11.
(4)	1974 s.84 "prescribed".
(5)	1974 ss.68(3B), 128(1), (1A); 1980 Sch. 12 para. 11, Sch. 25 para. 30.

Provision	Derivation
482(1), (2)	1974 s.68(5).
(3)	1974 s.57(7).
(4)	1974 s.68(6).
483(1)	1974 s.56(2)(*c*); 1980 Sch. 12 para. 15.
(2)	1974 s.84 "improvement", "relevant standard"; 1980 Sch. 12 para. 16(2); R.24(ii).
484	1974 s.69(2); 1980 Sch. 12 para. 16.
485(1)	1974 s.69(2A), (2C); 1980 Sch. 12 para. 16.
(2)	1974 s.69(2B); 1980 Sch. 12 para. 16.
486(1)	1974 s.69A(1), (2); 1980 Sch. 12 para. 17.
(2)	1974 ss.57(3), (5), 69(2)(*a*), 69A(1), (2); 1980 Sch. 12 paras. 16, 17, 26(1), (2)
487(1), (2)	1974 s.69(1).
488(1)	1974 s.70(1); 1980 Sch. 12 para. 18(1).
(2)	1974 s.57(7).
(3)	1974 s.70(2); 1980 Sch. 12 para. 18(1).
489(1)–(4)	1974 s.70A(1)–(4); 1980 Sch. 12 para. 19.
(5)	1974 s.84 "prescribed".
(6)	1974 ss.70A(5), 128(1), (1A); 1980 Sch. 12 para. 19, Sch. 25 para. 30.
490(1), (2)	1974 s.70(3), (4); 1980 Sch. 12 para. 18(1).
(3)	1974 s.57(7).
(4)	1974 s.70(5); 1980 Sch. 12 para. 18(1).
491(1)	1974 s.56(2)(*d*).
(2)	1974 s.71(2); 1980 Sch. 12 para. 12(1).
(3)	1974 ss.84 "prescribed", 128(1), (1A), (3); 1980 Sch. 25 para. 30.
492(1)	1974 s.71(3A)(*a*); 1980 Sch. 12 para. 12(2).
(2)	1974 s.71(3A)(*b*), (3B); 1980 Sch. 12 para. 12(2).
(3)	1974 s.128(1), (1A), (3); 1980 Sch. 25 para. 30.
493(1)	1974 s.71(3), (5); 1980 Sch. 12 para. 20(3).
(2)	1974 s.71(4).
494(1)	1974 s.71A; 1980 Sch. 12 para. 13.
(2)	1974 ss.57(3), (5), 71A; 1980 Sch. 12 paras. 13, 26(1), (2).
495(1), (2)	1974 s.71(1).
496(1)	1974 s.72(1).
(2)	1974 s.57(7).
(3)	1974 s.72(2).
497(1)	1974 s.72(3).
(2)	1974 s.84 "prescribed".
(3)	1974 ss.72(3A), 128(1A); 1980 Sch. 12 para. 14(1), Sch. 25 para. 30.
498(1)	1974 s.72(4); 1980 Sch. 12 para. 14(2).
(2)	1974 s.72(4A); 1980 Sch. 12 para. 14(2).
(3)	1974 s.57(7).
(4)	1974 s.72(5); 1980 Sch. 12 para. 14(3).
499(1)	1974 s.73(1).
(2)	1974 ss.73(1), 75(6).
(3)	1974 s.75(6).
500(1), (2)	1974 s.73(2).
(3)	1974 s.73(3); 1980 Sch. 12 para. 21.
(4)	1974 s.73(5).
501(1)	1974 s.73(4).
(2)	1974 s.73(4); 1980 Sch. 12 para. 22.
(3)	1974 s.73(3); 1980 Sch. 12 para. 21.
(4)	1974 s.73(3); 1980 Sch. 12 para. 30.
502	1974 s.73(6).
503(1)	1974 s.74(1); 1980 Sch. 12 para. 23.
(2)	1974 s.74(3), (3A); 1980 s.106(4), Sch. 12 para. 24.
(3)	1974 s.74(2A); 1980 Sch. 12 para. 23.
504(1)	1974 s.74(2); 1977 (c.42) Sch. 23 para. 62.
(2)	1974 s.74(4); 1977 (c.42) Sch. 23 para. 63.

Provision	Derivation
505(1)	1974 s.75(3), (4).
(2)	1974 s.75(2).
(3)	1974 s.75(5); 1975 (c.76) Sch. 1.
506(1), (2)	1974 s.76(1), (2), (3); 1980 (c.65) Sch. 6 para. 17.
(3)	1974 s.76(4).
(4)	1974 s.76(5); 1975 Sch. 5 para. 17.
507(1)	1974 s.77(1).
(2)	1974 s.77(2).
(3)	1974 s.77(3).
508(1)	1974 ss.58(1), 69(3), Sch. 6; S.I. 1983/613 Art. 6.
(2)	1974 s.58(2).
(3)	1974 ss.58(2), (3), 128(1), (1A); 1980 Sch. 12 para. 3, Sch. 25 para. 30.
509(1)	1974 s.59(1); 1980 Sch. 12 para. 4.
(2)	1974 ss.59(2), 128(1), (1A); 1980 Sch. 12 para. 4, Sch. 25 para. 30.
510	1974 s.80.
511(1)	1974 ss.61(1), 65(1), 69(1), 71(1).
(2)	1974 s.82(3).
(3)	1974 s.82(4); 1980 Sch. 12 para. 25.
512(1)	1974 s.82(5).
(2)	1974 s.82(1).
(3)	1974 s.82(2).
(4)	1974 s.82(6), (7); 1980 (c.65) Sch. 6 para. 19.
513(1), (2)	1974 s.83(1).
514(1)	1969 s.75(1); 1974 Sch. 13 para. 20(1).
(2)	1969 s.75(3).
(3)	1969 s.75(2); 1974 Sch. 13 para. 20(2).
515(1)	1974 s.81(1).
(2)	1974 s.81(2); 1980 Sch. 12 para. 32; 1980 (c.65) Sch. 6 para. 18.
516(1)–(3)	1974 s.78(1)–(3).
(4)	1974 s.78(7).
(5)	1974 s.78(6).
(6)	1974 s.127(2).
517(1)	1974 s.78(4).
(2)	1974 s.78(5)(*a*), 128(1), (1A); 1980 Sch. 25 para. 30.
(3)	1974 s.78(4), (5)(*b*).
518(1)	1974 s.84 "dwelling for disabled occupant", "disabled occupant"; 1975 Sch. 5 para. 19(2).
(2)	1974 s.84 "disabled person", "welfare authority"; 1975 Sch. 5 para. 19(2).
(3)	1974 s.84 "improvement"; 1975 Sch. 5 para. 19(1).
519	1974 ss.61(3)(*b*), 67(3), 68(3A), 69(2C), 71(5); 1980 Sch. 12 paras. 10(2), 11, 16, 20(1), (3).
520(1), (2)	1974 s.129(3), (4).
521(1), (2)	1978(I) s.1(1), (2).
(3)	1978(I) s.1(4).
(4)	1978(I) s.1(5), (6).
(5)	1978(I) s.1(4), (5)(*b*), (9).
(6)	1978(I) s.1(9).
522(1), (2)	1978(I) s.2(1).
(3), (4)	1978(I) s.1(7).
(5)	1978(I) s.2(2).
523(1)	1964 s.96(1), (5).
(2)	1964 s.96(2).
(3)	1964 s.96(4).
524	drafting.

Provision	Derivation
525	
"agricultural population"	1974 s.84 "agricultural population".
"charity trustees"	1974 s.84 "charity trustees".
"dwelling"	1974 s.129(1) "dwelling".
"house in multiple occupation"	1974 s.129(1) "house in multiple occupation".
"improvement"	1974 s.84 "improvement".
"owner"	1974 s.84 "owner".
526	drafting.
Part XVI	
527	1984(D) s.2(1), (7).
528(1)–(3)	1984(D) s.1(1)–(3).
(4)	1984(D) s.1(7).
(5), (6)	1984(D) s.1(5), (6).
529(1)–(3)	1984(D) s.1(4).
(4)	1984(D) s.1(5).
530(1)	1984(D) s.2(8)(*a*).
(2), (3)	1984(D) s.2(9), (10).
(4)	1984(D) s.2(8)(*b*).
531(1)–(4)	1984(D) s.2(2), (3).
532(1)	1984(D) s.2(6).
(2)	1984(D) s.27(5), (6).
(3)	1984(D) s.2(8)(*d*).
(4)	1984(D) s.2(8)(*c*).
533(1), (2)	1984(D) s.2(4), (5).
534	1984(D) s.3(1).
535(1)	1984(D) s.3(8).
(2)	1984(D) s.3(9).
(3)	1984(D) s.3(8), (9).
536(1)–(3)	1984(D) s.4(1).
537(1)	1984(D) s.3(2).
(2), (3)	1984(D) s.3(3), (5).
538(1)	1984(D) s.3(4).
(2)	1984(D) s.3(6).
(3)	1984(D) ss.3(6)(*a*), 24(1), (2).
(4)	1984(D) s.3(6)(*b*).
539(1)	1984(D) s.3(7).
(2)	1984(D) s.4(6).
540(1), (2)	1984(D) s.4(2).
(3)–(5)	1984(D) s.4(3)–(5).
541(1), (2)	1984(D) s.5(1), (2).
542(1)–(3)	1984(D) s.5(3)–(5).
(4)	1984(D) s.5(3).
543(1)–(3)	1984(D) Sch. 1 para. 1(1)–(3).
(4), (5)	1984(D) Sch. 1 para. 2(1), (2).
(6)	1984(D) s.24(1), (5).
544	1984(D) Sch. 1 para. 3.
545(1)–(3)	1984(D) Sch. 1 para. 4(1)–(3).
546(1), (2)	1984(D) Sch. 1 para. 5(1), (2).
547	drafting.
548(1)	1984(D) s.26(2).
(2)	1984(D) s.26(3), (4).
(3)	1984(D) s.26(5), (6).
(4)	1984(D) s.24(1).
549(1)–(4)	1984(D) s.9(1)–(4).
550(1), (2)	1984(D) s.8(1), (2).
(3)–(5)	1984(D) s.8(3).
(6)	1984(D) s.8(9).
551(1)	1984(D) ss.8(4), 9(6).
(2)	1984(D) ss.8(5), 9(7).

Provision	Derivation
551(3)	1984(D) ss.8(6), 9(8).
(4)	1984(D) ss.8(8), 9(10).
(5)	1984(D) ss.8(7), 9(9).
552(1), (2)	1984(D) s.11(1), (2).
553(1)	1984(D) ss.9(5), 10(1), (10), 26(7), (8).
(2)	1984(D) s.10(10), (11).
554(1)	1984(D) ss.9(5), 10(1), (3), 26(7), (8)(*a*).
(2)	1984(D) ss.9(5), 10(3).
(3)	1984(D) ss.10(3), 26(7), (8)(*b*).
(4)	1984(D) ss.10(5), 26(8)(*d*).
555(1)	1984(D) ss.9(5), 10(1), (4), 26(7)(*a*).
(2)	1984(D) s.10(5).
(3)	1984(D) s.10(9).
556(1)	1984(D) ss.10(1), (6), 26(8)(*e*) Sch. 3 para. 1 "current dwelling-house", 2.
(2)	1984(D) s.10(6), Sch. 3 para. 3.
557(1), (2)	1984(D) ss.9(5)(*b*), 10(7), (8), 26(8) (*c*), (*f*).
(3)	1984(D) s.10(8).
558	1984(D) s.10(1)(*b*), (2), Sch. 3 para. 1 "dwelling-house".
559(1)	1984(D) s.12(1), (5).
(2)–(4)	1984(D) s.12(2)–(4).
(5)	1984(D) s.12(9).
(6)	1984(D) s.12(8).
560(1)–(3)	1984(D) s.12(5).
561(1)	1984(D) s.12(6)(*a*).
(2)	1984(D) s.12(6)(*b*).
(3)	1984(D) s.12(7).
562(1), (2)	1984(D) s.14(1).
(3)	1984(D) s.14(2).
563(1)–(5)	1984(D) s.14(3)–(7).
564(1), (2)	1984(D) s.16(1), (2).
565(1)	1984(D) s.3(10).
(2)	1984(D) ss.8(10)(*a*), 9(11).
566	drafting.
567(1)–(3)	1984(D) s.21(1)–(3).
(4), (5)	1984(D) s.21(4).
(6)	1984(D) ss.21(5), 24(1), (4).
568(1)–(4)	1984(D) s.22(1)–(4).
(5)	1984(D) ss.22(5), 24(1), (4).
(6)	1984(D) s.22(6).
569(1)–(3)	1984(D) s.19(1)–(3).
(4)	1984(D) s.19(5).
(5)	1984(D) s.19(6).
(6)	1984(D) s.19(7), (8).
570(1)	1984(D) s.19(3).
(2)	1984(D) ss.19(4), 24(1).
(3)	1984(D) s.19(3), (4)(*c*).
571(1), (2)	1984(D) s.15(1), (2).
572(1)	1984(D) s.17(1), (2).
(2)	1984(D) s.17(1).
(3)	1984(D) s.17(3).
(4), (5)	1984(D) s.17(4), (5).
(6)	1984(D) s.24(3).
573(1)	1984(D) Sch. 4 para. 1 and *passim*.
(2)	1984(D) Sch. 4 para. 2(1)(*a*), (3).
(3)	1984(D) Sch. 4 para. 3(1)(*a*), (3).
(4)	1984(D) Sch. 4 paras. 2(1)(*b*), 3(1)(*b*).
(5)	1984(D) Sch. 4 paras. 2(2), 3(2).
(6)	1984(D) s.24(1).
574	1984(D) s.27(4).
575(1), (2)	1984(D) s.27(2).
(3)	1984(D) s.27(3).

Provision	Derivation
576	1978 Sch. paras. 6, 7, 8; 1984(D) s.27(1) "lending institution".
577	drafting.
Part XVII	
578	1957 Sch. 1 para. 1(1), Sch. 7 para. 1(1); 1961 (c.33) s.1; 1965 (c.56) s.1(1); 1969 s.32(2); 1974 s.43(2); 1981 (c.67) Sch. 4 para. 1.
579(1)	1957 s.43(3); drafting.
(2)	1957 s.59(1); 1965 (c.56) s.34(1).
580	1957 Sch. 3 para. 7(1), (2).
581(1)–(4)	1957 s.150(1)–(4).
582(1)	1964 s.72(1), (2); 1969 Sch. 8 para. 5; 1974 s.43(5).
(2)	1964 s.72(1); 1974 Sch. 13 para. 10(5)(*a*).
(3)	1964 s.72(2)(*a*).
(4)	1964 s.72(2)(*a*), (2A); 1974 Sch. 13 para. 10(5)(*b*)(*c*).
(5)	1964 s.72(2)(*b*); 1974 Sch. 13 para. 10(5)(*b*).
(6)	1964 s.72(2).
(7)	1964 s.72(4)(4A); 1984 (c.28) Sch. 2 para. 27.
(8)	drafting.
583(1)–(3)	1957 s.98, Sch. 1 para. 3, Sch. 3 para. 10; 1965 (c.56) Sch. 7; 1969 Sch. 8 para. 10.
(4)	1957 s.189(1) "house".
584(1)–(3)	1957 ss.62(1), 101(1); 1969 Sch. 8 para. 11; R.25.
(4)	1957 ss.62(2), 101(2); 1965 (c.56) Sch. 7; 1978 (c.30) s.17(2)(*a*).
585(1)	1957 ss.12(4), 29(2), 59(2); 1961 (c.64) Sch. 1 Pt. III.
(2)	1957 s.59(2) proviso.
(3)	1957 ss.12(4), 29(2); drafting.
586	drafting.
587	drafting.
588(1)	1957 Sch. 2 para. 1(3); 1969 Sch. 4.
(2)	1957 s.30(7), Sch. 2 para. 7(3); 1969 Sch. 5 para. 5(4), Sch. 6 para. 4, Sch. 8 para. 7.
589(1)	1961 (c.33) Sch. 2 paras. 1(2), 6(2); 1969 Sch. 8 para. 24.
(2)	1961 (c.33) Sch. 2 paras. 3(1), (2), (4), 6(2); 1969 Sch. 8 paras. 23, 24.
(3)	1961 (c.33) Sch. 2 para. 3(3), (5).
(4)–(6)	1961 (c.33) Sch. 2 para. 3(3A)–(3C); 1980 (c.65) Sch. 33 para. 6(3).
590(1)	1969 s.69; 1974 Sch. 13 para. 19.
(2)	1969 s.69, Sch. 5 para. 5(2) "interest"; 1976 (c.80) Sch. 8 para. 28; 1977 (c.42) Sch. 23 para. 48.
(3)	1976 (c.57) s.10(3).
(4), (5)	1976 (c.57) s.10(4).
(6)	1957 Sch. 2 para. 3(1), (2); 1969 Sch. 4; 1976 (c.57) s.10(5).
591(1)	1957 Sch. 2 paras. 4(1), 5(1), 7(1); 1965 s.2(1), (2), (6); 1974 Sch. 13 para. 11.
(2)	1957 Sch. 2 para. 5(1); drafting.
(3)	1957 Sch. 2 para. 5(1); 1969 Sch. 5 para. 4.
(4)	1965 s.2(2).
(5)	1965 s.2(5).
(6)	1957 Sch. para. 7 "house", "interest"; 1965 s.2(6); 1976 (c.80) Sch. 8 para. 28; 1977 (c.42) Sch. 23 para. 48.
592(1)–(3)	1957 Sch. 2 para. 5(2).
(4)	1965 s.2(3).
(5)	1957 Sch. 2 para. 5(2).
593	1974 s.115(1).
594(1)	1974 s.115(2), (3).
(2)	1974 s.115(2).
(3)	1974 s.115(3).
(4)	1974 ss.114(8) "effective date", 115(4), (5); 1975 Sch. 5 paras. 21, 22.

Provision	Derivation
594(5)	1974 s.115(4).
(6)	1974 s.115(10).
595(1)	1974 s.115(5); 1975 Sch. 5 para. 22.
(2), (3)	1974 s.115(6), (7).
(4)	1974 s.115(9).
596	1957 s.63(2).
597(1)	1957 s.74(4).
(2)	1957 s.74(4); 1961 (c.33) Sch. 4 para. 10.
(3)	1957 s.74(4); 1961 (c.33) s.5 rule (1), Sch. 4 para. 10.
598	1957 Sch. 3 para. 8(5); R.26(i).
599	1957 Sch. 1 para. 1(3), Sch. 3 para. 8(7), Sch. 7 para. 1(3); 1978 (c.30) s.17(2)(a).
600(1), (2)	1957 s.159(c).
601(1), (2)	1957 s.160; 1977 (c.45) s.31(6); 1982 (c.48) ss.37, 46(1).
602	
"house"	1957 s.189(1) "house" para. (a).
"owner"	1957 s.189(1) "owner".
603	drafting.
Part XVIII	
604(1)	1957 s.4(1); 1958 s.58(3); 1969 s.71.
(2)	1959(U) s.1(1).
605(1), (2)	1969 s.70; 1974 s.48(3).
606(1)	1957 s.157(1), (3), (5); 1972 (c.70) Sch. 29 paras. 1(1), 4(a).
(2), (3)	1957 s.157(2); 1972 (c.70) Sch. 22 para. 14(1).
607	1957 s.149(1); R.27.
608	1957 s.149(2).
609	1957 s.151; R.1(ii); R.27.
610(1), (2)	1957 s.165; 1978 (c.30) s.17(2)(a).
611(1)–(5)	1957 s.65(4)–(6).
(6)	1957 ss.65(7), 189(1) "apparatus", "statutory undertakers".
612	1957 s.158(1); 1976 (c.80) Sch. 8 para. 4; 1977 (c.42) Sch. 23 para. 26.
613(1), (2)	1961 s.23(4), (5); 1964 s.65(6); 1969 s.61(3); 1974 s.47(8), (9); 1984 Sch. 4 para. 9(2), (3); R.28.
614(1), (2)	1936 (c.49) s.283(2); 1957 s.178; 1974 s.104(4)(c), Sch. 10 para. 1(2); 1975 Sch. 25 para. 25; R.27.
(3)	drafting.
615(1), (2)	1957 s.179; 1969 Sch. 8 para. 13; 1974 s.104(4)(d); R.27.
616	1936 (c.49) s.318; 1957 s.181; 1969 Sch. 8 para. 14; R.27.
617(1)	1964 s.102(1); 1974 s.103(1).
(2)	1964 s.102(2).
(3)	1964 s.103(1); 1974 s.103(2).
(4)	1964 s.103(2); 1974 s.103(3).
618(1)–(3)	1957 s.187(1), (2); R.27.
(4)	1957 s.187(3); 1982 (c.48) ss.37, 46(1).
619(1)	1972 (c.70) s.180(1)(d).
(2)	1985 (c.51) s.94(1).
620(1), (2)	1972 s.103; 1975 Sch. 5 para. 7(1); S.I. 1972/1204; S.I. 1974/886; S.I. 1975/512; R.29.
621(1)–(3)	drafting.
622	
"bank"	1978 Sch. 1 para. 7; 1979 (c.37) Sch. 6 para. 11; and *passim*; R.
"building regulations"	1957 ss.12(4), 29(2), 59(2), 189(1) "building byelaws"; 1961 (c.64) Sch. 1 Pt. III; 1978 (c.30) s.17(2)(a); 1984 (c.55) s.89(2), Sch. 5 para. 2.
"building society"	drafting.
"cemetery"	1980 ss.27(1), 50(1) "cemetery"; 1984 Sch. 11 para. 24.
"charity"	1980 ss.2(1), (2)(a), 28(4)(e).
"district valuer"	1957 Sch. 2 para. 3(2); 1967 (c.9) s.115(1) "valuation officer"; 1980 s.27(2) "district valuer"; 1984(D) s.9(11), Sch. 2 para. 3(7); and *passim*.

Provision	Derivation
"friendly society"	1978 Sch. 1 para. 9; and *passim*.
"general rate fund"	1972 s.104(1) "general rate fund"; 1975 s.16(1) "general rate fund".
"hostel"	1974 s.129(1) "hostel".
"insurance company"	1978 Sch. 1 para. 8; 1978 (c.30) s.17(2)(*a*); and *passim*.
"protected occupancy"	drafting.
"protected tenancy"	drafting.
"regular armed forces of the Crown"	1977 s.18(4); 1975 (c.24) s.1(3) "regular armed forces of the Crown"; 1976 (c.52) s.20(6); 1980 Sch. 1A para. 10(1) "regular armed forces of the Crown"; 1984 s.3(5), Sch. 2.
"the Rent Acts"	drafting.
"restricted contract"	drafting.
"shared ownership lease"	drafting.
"standard scale"	1982 (c.48) s.75(*a*).
"statutory maximum"	1982 (c.48) s.74(1).
"statutory tenancy"	drafting; R.14(i).
"street"	1957 s.189(1) "street".
"subsidiary"	drafting.
"trustee savings bank"	1978 Sch. 1 para. 6; 1978 (c.30) s.17(2)(*a*); and *passim*.
623	
"house"	1957 s.189(1) "house" para. (*a*).
"owner"	1957 s.189(1) "owner".
624(1)–(3)	drafting.
625	drafting.
Schedules	
Sch. 1	
para. 1	1980 Sch. 3 para. 1(1).
2(1)	1980 Sch. 1 para. 1(3), Sch. 3 para. 2(1); 1984 s.2(2), Sch. 11 para. 33(2).
(2)	1980 Sch. 3 para. 2A; 1984 s.36(2).
(3)	1980 Sch. 3 para. 2B(1); 1984 s.36(2).
(4)	1980 Sch. 3 para. 2C; 1984 s.36(2).
(5)	1980 Sch. 3 paras. 2(2), 2B(2); 1984 s.36(2).
3	1980 Sch. 3 para. 4.
4	1980 Sch. 3 para. 5.
5	1980 Sch. 3 para. 6; 1984 s.36(3).
6	1980 Sch. 3 para. 7.
7	1980 Sch. 3 para. 9.
8	1980 Sch. 3 para. 8; 1984 Sch. 11 para. 33(3).
9	1980 Sch. 3 para. 10.
10(1)–(4)	1980 Sch. 3 para. 11.
(5)	1980 s.151(1), (3).
11	1980 Sch. 3 para. 12.
12	1980 Sch. 3 para. 13.
Sch. 2	
Pt. I	
Ground 1	1980 Sch. 4 Pt. I ground 1.
Ground 2	1980 Sch. 4 Pt. I ground 2.
Ground 3	1980 Sch. 4 Pt. I ground 3.
Ground 4	1980 Sch. 4 Pt. I ground 4.
Ground 5	1980 Sch. 4 Pt. I ground 5.
Ground 6	1980 Sch. 4 Pt. I ground 5A; 1984 s.25(1).
Ground 7	1980 Sch. 1 para. 1(2), (3), Sch. 4 Pt. I ground 5B; 1984 ss.2(1), 25(1).
Ground 8	1980 Sch. 4 Pt. I ground 6; 1984 Sch. 11 para. 34.

68

Provision	Derivation
Sch. 2	
Pt. II	
Ground 9	1980 Sch. 4 Pt. I ground 7.
Ground 10	1980 Sch. 4 Pt. I ground 8.
Ground 11	1980 Sch. 4 Pt. I ground 9.
Pt. III	
Ground 12	1980 Sch. 1 para. 1(2), (3), Sch. 4 Pt. I ground 9A; 1984 ss.2(1), 25(2).
Ground 13	1980 Sch. 4 Pt. I ground 10.
Ground 14	1980 Sch. 4 Pt. I ground 11.
Ground 15	1980 Sch. 4 Pt. I ground 12.
Ground 16	1980 s.34(3A), Sch. 4 Pt. I ground 13; 1984 s.25(3).
Pt. IV	
para. 1	1980 Sch. 4 Pt. II paras. 1(1), (2).
2, 3	1980 Sch. 4 Pt. II para. 2.
4(1)–(3)	1980 Sch. 4 Pt. II para. 3.
Sch. 3	1980 Sch. 1, para. 1, Sch. 4A; 1984 s.26(2), Sch. 7.
Sch. 4	
para. 1	1980 Sch. 1A para. 1; 1984 s.3(5), Sch. 2.
2	1980 Sch. 1A para. 2(1)–(4); 1984 s.3(5), Sch. 2.
3	1980 Sch. 1A para. 2(5); 1984 s.3(5), Sch. 2.
4(1)–(3)	1980 Sch. 1A para. 4(1)–(3); 1984 s.3(5), Sch. 2.
5	1980 Sch. 1A paras. 3(1)–(4), 10(1) "armed forces occupier"; 1984 s.3(5), Sch. 2.
6(1)	1980 Sch. 1A para. 10(1) "public sector tenant"; 1984 s.3(5), Sch. 2.
(2)	1980 Sch. 1A para. 9(1); 1984 s.3(5), Sch. 2.
(3), (4)	1980 Sch. 1A para. 9(5), (6); 1984 s.3(5), Sch. 2.
7(1)–(3)	1980 Sch. 1A para. 9(2); 1984 s.3(5), Sch. 2.
8(1)	1980 Sch. 1A para. 9(2); 1984 s.3(5), Sch. 2.
(2)	1980 s.151(1).
9	1980 Sch. 1A para. 9(3); 1984 s.3(5), Sch. 2.
10	1980 Sch. 1A para. 9(4); 1984 s.3(5), Sch. 2; R.
Sch. 5	
para. 1	1980 s.2(1), (2)(*a*).
2	1977 (c.42) s.15(3)(*d*); 1980 s.2(2)(*b*).
3	1980 s.2(2)(*c*).
4	1980 s.2(3); 1984 s.1(3).
5(1), (2)	1980 Sch. 1 Pt. I para. 1(1)–(3); 1984 s.2(1).
6, 7	1980 Sch. 1 Pt. I para. 3; 1984 s.2(2).
8	1980 Sch. 1 Pt. I para. 3A; 1984 s.2(2).
9(1), (2)	1980 Sch. 1 Pt. I para. 3B; 1984 s.2(2).
10(1), (2)	1980 Sch. 1 Pt. I para. 4; 1984 s.2(2).
11(1)	1980 Sch. 1 Pt. I para. 5(1); 1984 s.2(3).
(2)	1980 s.5(2), Sch. 1 Pt. I para. 5(2); 1984 s.2(3).
12(1)	1980 Sch. 1 Pt. I para. 6(1), (2); 1984 Sch. 1 para. 9.
(2)	1980 Sch. 1 Pt. I para. 6(3); 1984 Sch. 1 para. 9.
(3)	1980 Sch. 1 Pt. I para. 6(2)(*a*); 1984 Sch. 1 para. 9.
Sch. 6	
Pt. I	
paras. 1–4	1980 Sch. 2 paras. 1–4.
5	1980 Sch. 2 para. 5; 1984 s.7(1).
6	1980 Sch. 2 para. 5A; 1984 s.7(1).
7	1980 Sch. 2 para. 6(*a*), (*b*).
Pt. II	
para. 8	1980 Sch. 2 para. 7.
9(1), (2)	1980 Sch. 2 paras. 8, 9; 1984 s.7(2)(*a*), (*b*).
10	1980 Sch. 2 para. 10.
Pt. III	
para. 11	1980 Sch. 2 para. 11(1); 1984 Sch. 1 para. 10(1).
12(1), (2)	1980 Sch. 2 para. 11(2); 1984 Sch. 1 para. 10(1).
(3)	1980 Sch. 2 para. 11(3); 1984 Sch. 1 para. 10(1).

Provision	Derivation
Sch. 6	
Pt. III	
para. 13	1980 Sch. 2 para. 12; 1984 Sch. 1 para. 10(2).
14(1)	1980 Sch. 2 para. 13(1); 1984 Sch. 1 para. 10(3)(*c*).
(2)	1980 Sch. 2 para. 13(1A); 1984 Sch. 1 para. 10(3)(*a*), (*b*).
(3)	1980 Sch. 2 para. 13(2); 1984 Sch. 1 para. 10(3)(*d*).
(4)	1980 Sch. 2 para. 13(3).
15(1)–(4)	1980 Sch. 2 para. 13A(1)–(4); 1984 Sch. 1 para. 10(4).
16	1980 Sch. 2 para. 14; 1984 Sch. 1 para. 10(5).
17(1), (2)	1980 Sch. 2 para. 15(1)(*a*); 1984 Sch. 1 para. 10(6).
18(1)	1980 Sch. 2 para. 15(2); 1984 Sch. 1 para. 10(6).
(2)	1980 Sch. 2 para. 16(*a*); 1984 s.7(3).
(3)	1980 Sch. 2 paras. 16(*b*), 17(1), (2); 1984 s.7(3).
(4)	1980 Sch. 2 para. 16(*c*); 1984 s.7(3).
(5)	1980 s.10(2A); 1984 Sch. 11 para. 10(3).
19	1980 Sch. 2 para. 15(1)(*c*); 1984 Sch. 1 para. 10(6).
Pt. IV	
para. 20	1980 Sch. 2 para. 18(*b*); 1984 Sch. 1 para. 11(2).
21(1)	1980 Sch. 2 paras. 18(*a*), 19.
(2)	1980 Sch. 2 para. 18(*a*).
(3)	1980 Sch. 2 para. 19(1)–(3).
(4)	1980 Sch. 2 paras. 19(4), 20.
Sch. 7	
para. 1	1980 s.18(1)(*a*).
2(1), (2)	1980 s.18(1)(*b*), (2); 1984 Sch. 1 para. 6.
3(1)	1980 s.18(3); 1984 Sch. 1 para. 6.
(2)	1980 s.151(1), (3).
4	1980 s.18(1)(*c*).
Sch. 8	
para. 1(1)	1984 Sch. 3 paras. 1(3), 3(1), (3).
(2)	1984 Sch. 3 para. 3(1), (2).
(3)	1984 Sch. 3 para. 3(4).
(4)	1984 Sch. 3 para. 3(8).
2(1), (2)	1984 Sch. 3 para. 3(5).
(3)	1984 Sch. 3 para. 3(6).
(4)	1984 Sch. 3 para. 3(7), Sch. 11 para. 32.
(5)	1984 Sch. 3 para. 3(8).
3(1)	1984 Sch. 3 paras. 4(1), 6(3).
(2)	1984 Sch. 3 para. 4(2).
4(1)	1984 Sch. 3 para. 5(1).
(2)	1984 Sch. 3 para. 5(4).
(3)	1984 Sch. 3 para. 5(2).
(4)	1984 Sch. 3 para. 5(5).
(5)	1984 Sch. 3 para. 10(1), (2).
(6)	1984 Sch. 3 para. 5(6).
5	1984 Sch. 3 para. 5(3).
6(1), (2)	1984 Sch. 3 para. 7(1), (2).
(3)	1984 Sch. 3 para. 6(10).
7	1984 Sch. 3 para. 7(4).
8(1), (2)	1984 Sch. 3 para. 7(5).
(3)–(5)	1984 Sch. 3 para. 7(6)–(8).
9(1), (2)	1984 Sch. 3 para. 8(1), (2).
10(1), (2)	1984 Sch. 3 para. 9(1), (2)
11(1)	1984 Sch. 3 paras. 4(1), 7(2).
(2)–(4)	1984 Sch. 3 paras. 4(3), 7(3).
Sch. 9	
para. 1(1), (2)	1984 s.16(1).
(3)	1984 s.16(2).
2	1984 s.16(3).
3(1)	1984 s.16(4), (5).
(2)	1984 s.16(7).
4(1), (2)	1984 s.16(6).

Provision	Derivation
Sch. 9	
para. 4(3)	1984 s.16(9), (10).
5	1984 s.16(8).
6	1984 Sch. 11 para. 14(1), (2).
Sch. 10	
para. 1	1957 s.10(3); 1961 s.18(3); 1974 s.94(1); drafting.
2(1)–(4)	1957 s.10(3); 1961 s.18(3); 1974 s.94(1); R.9(i); R.30(i).
3(1)–(2)	1957 s.10 *passim*; 1961 s.18 *passim*; 1964 s.64(2); 1974 s.94(2); R.30(ii).
(3)	1957 s.37(1).
4	1957 s.10(3); 1961 s.18(3); 1974 s.94(3); 1980 (c.65) Sch. 6 paras. 7(*a*)(i), 8, 20.
5(1)	1957 s.10(5); R.30(iii).
(2)	1957 s.37(1).
(3)	1957 s.10(5); R.9(i).
6(1)–(4)	1957 ss.11(1)–(3); 37(1), (2); 1964 ss.64(2), (4), (5), 91(4); 1974 s.94(5)–(7); R.9(ii); R.30(iv), (v).
7(1)–(4)	1957 s.10(7), (8); 1961 s.18(5); 1964 s.64(1), (3); 1974 s.94(4); R.30(iv).
8(1), (2)	1961 s.18(6).
Sch. 11	
Pt. I	
para. 1(1), (2)	1974 s.114(1), (1A); 1975 Sch. 5 para. 21; 1980 Sch. 25 para. 28(1).
(3)	1974 s.114(8) "Part III land"; 1975 Sch. 5 para. 21.
2(1)	1974 s.114(2); 1975 Sch. 5 para. 21.
(2)	1974 Sch. 10 para. 3(2); 1975 Sch. 5 para. 25.
3(1)	1974 Sch. 10 para. 3(1); 1975 Sch. 5 para. 25.
(2)	1965 (c.56) s.4; 1974 s.116.
4(1)	1974 s.114(5); 1975 Sch. 5 para. 21.
(2)	1974 s.114A(1); 1980 Sch. 25 para. 29.
(3)	1974 s.114A(2); 1980 Sch. 25 para. 29.
5(1)	1974 Sch. 10 para. 4(1), (2); 1975 Sch. 5 para. 25.
(2)	1974 Sch. 10 para. 4(1); 1975 Sch. 5 para. 25.
(3)	1974 Sch. 10 para. 4(2); 1975 Sch. 5 para. 25.
6	1974 Sch. 10 para. 4(3); 1975 Sch. 5 para. 25.
7(1), (2)	1974 Sch. 10 para. 2; 1975 Sch. 5 para. 25.
8	1974 Sch. 10 para. 5; 1975 Sch. 5 para. 25.
Pt. II	
para. 9	1974 Sch. 10 paras. 1 "notice land", 6; 1975 Sch. 5 para. 21; 1980 Sch. 25 para. 31.
10(1)–(3)	1974 Sch. 10 para. 7(1); 1975 Sch. 5 para. 21.
(4)	1974 Sch. 10 para. 7(2); 1975 Sch. 5 para. 21.
(5)	1974 Sch. 10 para. 7(3); 1975 Sch. 5 para. 21.
11(1)–(6)	1974 Sch. 10 para. 8(1)–(6); 1975 Sch. 5 para. 21.
12(1)–(3)	1957 Sch. 4 para. 1; 1974 s.114(4), Sch. 10 para. 9; 1975 Sch. 5 paras. 21, 25; R.31.
13(1)–(3)	1957 Sch. 4 para. 2; 1974 s.114(4), Sch. 10 para. 9(*a*); 1975 Sch. 5 paras. 21, 25.
(4)	1957 Sch. 4 para. 4; 1974 s.114(4); 1975 Sch. 5 para. 21.
(5)	1957 Sch. 4 para. 3; 1974 s.114(4); 1975 Sch. 5 para. 21.
14(1)	1957 Sch. 4 para. 3; 1974 s.114(4); 1975 Sch. 5 para. 21.
(2)	1957 Sch. 4 para. 5; 1974 s.114(4); 1975 Sch. 5 para. 21.
Sch. 12	
para. 1	drafting.
2(1), (2)	1972 s.11(4).
(3), (4)	1972 s.11(5).
3	1973 s.11(6)(*a*).
4	1972 s.11(6)(*b*).
5	1972 s.11(9)(*a*).
6(1)	1972 s.11(9)(*b*).
(2)	1972 s.11(8).
7(1)	1972 s.11(6)(*d*).

Provision	Derivation
Sch. 12	
para. 7(2)	1972 s.11(6)(*c*).
8	1972 s.11(6).
Sch. 13	
Pt. I	
para. 1(1)	1964 s.79(2).
(2)–(4)	1964 s.79(3).
2(1)	1964 s.79(4).
(2)	1964 s.91(2).
(3)	1964 s.91(3).
3(1)	1964 s.83(1); R.19.
(2)	1964 s.83(1).
(3)	1964 s.83(3).
(4)	1964 s.83(4), (5).
4(1)	1964 s.80(1), (2).
(2)	1964 s.80(3); 1980 (c.65) Sch. 6 para. 9.
(3)	1964 s.80(3).
5	1964 s.79(5).
6(1)	1964 s.83(2).
(2)	1964 s.83(6).
(3)	1964 s.83(3), (6).
Pt. II	
para. 7	1964 s.78(1); 1980 (c.65) Sch. 33 para. 8(1).
8	1964 s.78(1); 1980 (c.65) Sch. 33 para. 8(1).
9(1)	1964 s.78(5)(*b*).
(2)	1964 s.78(5).
10	1964 s.78(5)(*c*).
11(1)	1964 s.78(5A), (5B); 1980 (c.65) Sch. 33 para. 8(2), (3).
(2)	1964 s.78(5C); 1980 (c.65) Sch. 33 para. 8(3).
12	1964 s.78(5)(*a*); 1980 (c.65) Sch. 33 para. 8(2).
13(1)	1964 s.78(5D); 1980 (c.65) Sch. 33 para. 8(3).
(2)	1964 s.78(5D), (5E); 1980 (c.65) Sch. 33 para. 8(3).
14	1964 s.78(6).
Pt. III	
para. 15(1)	1964 Sch. 4 para. 1(1), (2).
(2)	1964 Sch. 4 para. 1(3).
(3)	1964 Sch. 4 para. 4.
16(1), (2)	1964 s.80(2), (4).
(3)	1964 s.80(5).
(4)	1964 s.80(6).
(5)	1964 s.80(7).
(6)	1964 s.80(4).
17(1)–(3)	1964 ss.84(1)–(3).
(4)	1964 s.84(9); 1984 (c.28) Sch. 2 para. 28.
(5)	1964 s.87(2).
18(1)	1964 s.84(4).
(2), (3)	1964 s.84(8).
(4)	1964 s.84(10).
19(1), (2)	1964 s.84(5).
(3)	1964 s.84(6).
(4)	1964 s.84(7).
(5), (6)	1964 ss.80(5), (6), 84(7).
20(1)	1964 s.85(1).
(2)	1964 s.85(2).
21(1)	drafting.
(2)	1964 s.86(5).
(3)	1964 s.86(8).
(4)	1964 s.86(9).
(5)	1964 s.86(10).
(6)	1964 s.87(2).

Provision	Derivation
Sch. 13	
Pt. IV	
para. 22	1969 s.63(1).
23(1), (2)	1969 s.63(2).
24	1969 s.63(3).
25(1)	1969 s.63(4).
(2)	1969 s.63(8), (10).
(3)–(5)	1969 s.63(8).
(6)	1969 s.63(9).
26(1)	1969 s.63(5).
(2)	1969 s.63(5), (10).
(3)	1969 s.63(6).
(4), (5)	1969 s.63(7).
Sch. 14	
Pt. I	
opening	1972 Sch. 1 para. 1.
item 1	1972 Sch. 1 para. 1(1)(*a*); 1974 Sch. 7 para. 1; 1975 Sch. 5 para. 8(2).
item 2	1972 Sch. 1 para. 1(1)(*b*).
item 3	1980 s.103(1).
item 4	1972 Sch. 1 para. 1(1)(*c*); 1982 (c.24) s.32(4)(*a*)(i).
item 5	1972 Sch. 1 para. 1(1)(*e*).
item 6	1972 Sch. 1(1)(*f*), (4).
item 7	1972 s.104(4), Sch. 1 para. 1(2), (3).
item 8	1980 s.135(6), (9).
Pt. II	
opening	1972 Sch. 1 para. 3(1).
item 1	1972 Sch. 1 para. 3(1)(*a*); 1975 Sch. 5 para. 8(4)(*a*).
item 2	1972 Sch. 1 para. 3(1)(*b*), (2)–(4); 1975 Sch. 5 para. 8(4)(*b*), (*c*); 1978 (c.30) s.17(2)(*a*).
item 3	1972 Sch. 1 para. 3(1)(*c*); 1980 s.135(7)(*a*).
item 4	1972 Sch. 1 para. 3(1)(*d*); 1980 s.135(7)(*b*).
Pt. III	
para. 1	1972 s.12(1)(*d*).
2	1972 Sch. 10 para. 5(1).
3	1972 s.104(4), Sch. 10 para. 4(3), (4).
4	1972 Sch. 10 para. 5(2).
5	1972 s.12(3)(*c*), Sch. 1 para. 3(1)(*a*)(iii).
6	1972 Sch. 10 para. 5(3), (4).
7	1972 Sch. 1 para. 2.
Pt. IV	
para. 1(1)	1972 Sch. 1 para. 10(1).
(2), (3)	1972 Sch. 1 para. 10(2).
(4)	1972 Sch. 1 para. 10(3).
2	1972 Sch. 1 para. 8.
3	1972 Sch. 1 para. 6(*a*); 1975 Sch. 5 para. 5; 1982 Sch. 4 para. 6(4).
4(1)	1972 Sch. 1 para. 14(2); 1975 Sch. 5 para. 8(6).
(2)	1972 Sch. 1 para. 14(3); 1975 Sch. 5 para. 8(6).
Pt. V	
para. 1(1)	1980 s.134(2).
(2)	1972 Sch. 1 para. 14(1); 1975 Sch. 5 para. 6.
2(1)	1972 s.104(3).
(2), (3)	1972 Sch. 1 para. 4(1).
3	1972 Sch. 1 para. 4(2).
4(1)	1972 s.101(1).
(2)	1972 ss.101(2), 104(4).
(3)	1972 s.101(3).
5(1), (2)	1972 s.104(1) "officer", Sch. 1 para. 20.
6(1)	1972 s.105(2).
(2)	1972 s.105(3); 1975 Sch. 1 para. 13(1).
(3)	1972 s.105(4).
(4)	1972 s.104(4).

Provision	Derivation
Sch. 14	
Pt. V	
para. 7(1)	1972 Sch. 1 para. 22(1); 1975 Sch. 5 para. 8(7).
(2)	1972 s.16(4), Sch. 1 para. 22(2), (5).
(3)	1972 Sch. 1 para. 22(3).
(4)	1972 s.16(3), Sch. 1 para. 22(5).
(5)	1972 s.16(5), Sch. 1 para. 22(5).
8	1969 s.38; 1972 Sch. 9 para. 15.
Sch. 15	
Pt. I	1972 Sch. 8 para. 2D.
Pt. II	
para. 1(1)	1958 s.46(1); 1972 Sch. 8 para. 7(1).
(2)	1958 s.28.
2(1)	1958 s.46(2).
(2)	1958 s.46(2A); 1976 (c.80) Sch. 8 para. 6; 1977 (c.42) Sch. 23 para. 28(*b*).
(3), (4)	1958 s.46(1)(*b*); 1968 (c.23) Sch. 15; 1977 (c.42) s.145(1)–(4), Sch. 23 para. 28(*a*), Sch. 24 para. 30; 1980 Sch. 25 para. 52.
(5)	1958 s.46(6).
3(1), (2)	1958 s.46(3).
4(1)–(4)	1958 s.46(4).
5	1958 s.46(5).
Pt. III	
para. 1(1)	1958 s.9; 1959 ss.13–17; 1969 Sch. 9 para. 1.
(2)	1974 s.79(2A); 1975 Sch. 5 para. 18(1).
(3)	1958 s.28; 1959 Sch. 1 para. 4.
(4)	1958 s.25(2) proviso; 1959 Sch. 1 para. 3.
2(1)	1969 ss.17–20; 1974 Sch. 14 para. 5.
(2)	1958 s.28; 1969 Sch. 8 para. 17.
(3)	1980 s.96(1)(*c*), Sch. 11 Pt. II.
(4)	1958 s.25(2) proviso; 1969 Sch. 8 para. 16.
3(1)	1974 s.79; 1978 (c.30) s.16(1)(*c*); 1980 s.108(5).
(2)	1980 s.96(1)(*c*), Sch. 11 Pt. II.
(3)	1974 s.127(2).
Pt. IV	
para. 1(1)	1975 s.5(1), (3).
(2)	1975 s.5(2).
2(1)	1975 Sch. 1 para. 12(1).
(2)	1975 Sch. 1 para. 12(3).
(3)	1975 Sch. 1 para. 12(4).
(4)	1975 s.15(5), (6).
3(1)	1975 s.5(4).
(2)	1975 ss.5(5), 15(4).
(3)	1975 s.15(5), (6).
4(1), (2)	1975 s.5(6).
5(1), (2)	1980 s.104(1), (2).
6	1975 s.16(1) "receiving authority", "receiving district".
Sch. 16	
para. 1(1), (2)	1980 s.110(3).
2	1980 s.110(4).
3	1980 s.110(6).
4(1)	1980 s.110(6)(*a*).
(2)	1980 s.110(6)(*b*).
(3)	1972 s.129(3)(*b*); 1980 s.110(7); 1985 (c.51) Sch. 14 para. 58(*c*)(i).
(4)	1980 s.110(7).
5(1)–(3)	1980 s.110(8).
6(1)–(3)	1980 s.110(9).
7(1), (2)	1980 s.110(10).
Sch. 17	
para. 1(1)	1980 s.112(2); 1984 Sch. 5 para. 1(1).
(2)	1980 s.112(6); 1984 Sch. 5 para. 1(2).
(3)	1980 s.112(7); 1984 Sch. 5 para. 1(3).

Provision	Derivation
Sch. 17	
para. 2(1)–(3)	1980 s.112(3)–(5); 1984 Sch. 5 para. 2(1)–(3).
(4)	1980 s.112(8); 1984 Sch. 5 para. 2(4).
3(1)	1980 s.113(1); 1984 Sch. 5 para. 3(1).
(2)	1984 Sch. 5 para. 3(2).
(3)	1980 s.113(2); 1984 Sch. 5 para. 3(3).
(4)	1980 s.113(3); 1984 Sch. 5 para. 3(4).
4	1980 ss.112, 113 *passim.*
Sch. 18	
para. 1(1)	1899 s.1(2).
(2)	1935 (c.40) s.92(2); 1964 (c.9) s.2(3); 1968 (c.13) s.6(1), (2); 1978 (c.30) s.17(2)(*a*).
(3)	1899 s.1(4).
(4)	1899 s.1(5).
2(1)	1899 s.3(1).
(2)	1923 (c.24) s.22(*c*).
(3)	1899 s.3(1).
3(1)	1923 (c.24) s.22(*c*).
(2)	1899 s.7(2).
(3), (4)	1899 s.7(3); 1978 (c.30) s.17(2)(*a*).
(5)	1899 s.7(1).
4(1)	1899 s.4(1).
(2)	1899 s.3(2).
(3)	1899 s.4(2).
5(1)	1899 s.3(3).
(2)	1899 s.3(4).
(3)	1899 s.3(5); 1978 (c.30) s.17(2)(*a*).
6(1)	1899 s.5(1).
(2)	1899 s.5(2); 1978 (c.30) s.17(2)(*a*).
(3)	1899 s.5(3).
(4)	1899 s.5(4).
(5)	1899 s.5(5); 1981 (c.54) Sch. 5.
7(1), (2)	1899 s.6(1), (2).
8(1), (2)	1899 s.8(1).
(3)	1899 s.8(2).
(4)	1899 s.9(9).
9(1)–(3)	1899 s.10(1)–(3).
10	1935 (c.40) s.92(3).
Sch. 19	
para. 1(1)	1969 s.91(4), Sch. 9 para. 1.
(2)	1958 s.28.
2(1)	1974 Sch. 14 para. 7(1); S.I. 1974/1791.
(2)	1958 s.28; 1969 Sch. 8 para. 17.
Sch. 20	
Pt. I	
para. 1	1984(D) s.6(1).
2(1)	1984(D) s.6(1).
(2)	1984(D) s.6(6)(*a*).
3	1984(D) s.6(2).
4	1984(D) s.6(3).
5	1984(D) s.6(4).
6(1)	1984(D) s.6(5).
(2)	1984(D) s.6(6)(*b*).
Pt. II	
para. 7(1), (2)	1984(D) Sch. 2 para. 1(1), (2).
8(1)	1984(D) Sch. 2 para. 2(1), (2)(*a*)–(*c*), (*e*).
(2)	1984(D) Sch. 2 para. 2(2)(*d*).
(3)	1984(D) Sch. 2 para. 2(1).
9(1)	1984(D) Sch. 2 para. 3(1).
(2)	1984(D) Sch. 2 para. 3(2), (3).
(3)	1984(D) Sch. 2 para. 3(6).
(4)	1984(D) Sch. 2 para. 3(5).

Provision	Derivation
Sch. 20	
Pt. II	
para. 10	1984(D) Sch. 2 para. 3(4).
Pt. III	
para. 11(1)	1984(D) Sch. 2 para. 7(*a*); drafting.
(2)	1984(D) Sch. 2 paras. 7(*b*), 8(3).
12(1), (2)	1984(D) Sch. 2 para. 8(1), (2).
(3)	1984(D) Sch. 2 para. 10.
(4)	1984(D) Sch. 2 para. 8(1).
13(1)	1984(D) Sch. 2 para. 9(1).
(2)	1984(D) Sch. 2 paras. 9(4)–(6), 10.
(3)	1984(D) Sch. 2 para. 9(2).
14	1984(D) Sch. 2 para. 9(3).
15(1), (2)	1984(D) Sch. 2 para. 11(1), (2).
16(1), (2)	1984(D) Sch. 2 para. 11(3).
17(1)–(3)	1984(D) Sch. 2 para. 12(1)–(3).
18	1984(D) s.6(7).
19	1984(D) Sch. 2 para. 4.
20	1984(D) Sch. 2 para. 6.
Sch. 21	
para. 1	1984(D) s.13(1)–(4) *passim*.
2	1984(D) s.13(1).
3	1984(D) s.13(2).
4	1984(D) s.13(3), (4)(*a*).
5(1), (2)	1984(D) s.13(3).
6(1)	1984(D) s.13(4)(*b*), (5), (6).
(2)	1984(D) s.13(5).
(3)	1984(D) s.13(6).
7(1), (2)	1984(D) s.13(7).
(3)	1984(D) s.13(8).
Sch. 22	
para. 1	drafting.
2	1957 Sch. 3 Pt. I para. 1(1), (2).
3(1), (2)	1957 Sch. 3 Pt. I para. 2(1).
(3)	1957 Sch. 3 Pt. I para. 2(1), (3); 1978 (c.30) s.17(2)(*a*); R.14(i).
(4)	1957 Sch. 3 Pt. I para. 2(2).
4(1)	1957 Sch. 3 Pt. I para 3(3).
(2)	1957 Sch. 3 Pt. I para. 3(4); 1980 Sch. 25 para. 8.
(3), (4)	1957 Sch. 3 Pt. I para. 3(5), (6).
5(1)	1957 Sch. 3 Pt. I para. 3(2), (3).
(2)	1957 Sch. 3 Pt. I para. 4(1), (2).
(3), (4)	1957 Sch. 3 Pt. I para. 4(3), (4).
6	1957 Sch. 4 para. 1; R.31.
7(1)–(3)	1957 Sch. 4 para. 2.
(4)	1957 Sch. 4 para. 4.
(5)	1957 Sch. 4 para. 3.
8(1)	1957 Sch. 4 para. 3.
(2)	1957 Sch. 4 para. 5.
9(1)	1957 s.67(1).
(2), (3)	1957 s.67(2).
(4)	1957 s.67(3).
Sch. 23	
para. 1(1), (2)	1957 s.30(1)–(3), (6).
(3)	1957 s.30(3), (4).
(4)	1957 s.30(3)(*b*).
(5), (6)	1957 s.30(5); R.
2(1), (2)	1957 s.30(1), (3); 1969 s.65(1), (2).
(3)	1957 s.30(3), (4).
(4)	1957 s.30(3)(*b*).
(5), (6)	1957 s.30(5); R.
3(1)	1957 s.60(1), (1C); 1974 Sch. 9.
(2)	1957 s.60(2).

Provision	Derivation
Sch. 23	
para. 4(1)	1957 Sch. 2 Pt. I para. 1(1), (2); 1969 Sch. 4.
(2)	1957 Sch. 2 Pt. I para. 3(1), (2); 1969 Sch. 4.
(3)	1957 Sch. 2 Pt. I para. 3(3); 1969 Sch. 4.
(4)	1957 Sch. 2 Pt. I paras. 1(1), 2; 1969 Sch. 4.
(5)	1957 Sch. 2 Pt. I para. 1(2); 1969 Sch. 4.
5(1)	1969 s.67(1).
(2)	1969 s.67(4).
6(1), (2)	1969 s.67(2), (5).
(3)	1969 s.67(3).
7(1)–(3)	1957 s.60(1); 1974 Sch. 9.
(4)	1957 s.60(1A); 1974 Sch. 9.
(5)	1957 s.60(1B); 1974 Sch. 9.
8(1)–(3)	1957 s.60(1D); 1974 Sch. 9.
Sch. 24	
Pt. I	
para. 1(1)	1957 Sch. 2 paras. 4(1), 7(1); 1969 Sch. 5 paras. 1(1), 5(3); 1974 Sch. 13 para. 21.
(2)	1957 Sch. 2 para. 4(2)(*b*), (6); 1969 Sch. 5 para. 5(1) "relevant date".
2(1)	1969 Sch. 5 paras. 1(1)(*b*), 5(1) "qualifying period"; 1974 Sch. 13 para. 21.
(2)	1969 Sch. 5 paras. 1(2), 5(1) "qualifying period".
(3)	1969 Sch. 5 para. 1(3).
3(1)	1957 Sch. 2 para. 4(2).
(2)	1957 Sch. 3 para. 4(3).
(3)	1969 s.68(1).
4(1)	1957 Sch. 2 para. 4(4); 1969 Sch. 5 para. 2.
(2)	1957 Sch. 2 para. 7(2) "full compulsory purchase value", "site value"; 1969 Sch. 5 para. 5(2) "full compulsory purchase value", "site value".
(3)	1957 Sch. 2 para. 4(4) proviso; 1969 Sch. 5 para. 3(1); 1974 Sch. 13 para. 7.
(4)	1957 Sch. 2 para. 4(5); 1969 Sch. 5 para. 3(2).
5(1)	1957 Sch. 2 para. 7(2) "house", "interest"; 1969 Sch. 5 para. 5(2) "house", "interest"; 1976 (c.80) Sch. 8 paras. 5, 28; 1977 (c.42) Sch. 23 paras. 27, 48.
(2)	1969 Sch. 5 para. 5(5).
(3)	1957 Sch. 2 para. 4(5) proviso; 1969 Sch. 5 para. 3(3).
6(1), (2)	1957 Sch. 2 para. 4(7); 1969 s.86(2), Sch. 6 para. 2; 1975 (c.72) Sch. 3 paras. 15, 66.
Pt II	
para. 1(1)	1957 Sch. 2 paras. 6(1), 7(1).
(2)	1957 Sch. 2 paras. 6(2), 7(1).
2	1957 Sch. 2 para. 6(2); 1969 Sch. 6 para. 3.
3	1957 Sch. 2 para. 6(2).
4(1)	1957 Sch. 2 para. 6(3).
(2)	1957 Sch. 2 para. 7(2) "full compulsory purchase value", "site value".
(3)	1957 Sch. 2 para. 6(3) proviso.
(4)	1957 Sch. 2 para. 6(4).
5	1957 Sch. 2 paras. 6(5), 7(2) "house ", "interest"; 1976 (c.80) Sch. 8 para. 5; 1977 (c.42) Sch. 23 para. 27.

TABLE OF DESTINATIONS

Small Dwellings Acquisition Act 1899

1899	1985	1899	1985	1899	1985
s.1(2)	Sch. 18, para. 1(1)	s.3(5)	Sch. 18, para. 5(3)	s.7(1)	Sch. 18, para. 3(5)
(4)	Sch. 18, para. 1(3)	4(1)	Sch. 18, para. 4(1)	(2)	Sch. 18, para. 3(2)
(5)	Sch. 18, para. 1(4)	(2)	Sch. 18, para. 4(3)	(3)	Sch. 18, para. 3(3)(4)
3(1)	Sch. 18, para. 2(1), (3)	5(1)	Sch. 18 para. 6(1)	8(1)	Sch. 18, para. 8(1)(2)
(2)	Sch. 18, para. 4(2)	(2)	Sch. 18, para. 6(2)	(2)	Sch. 18, para. 8(3)
(3)	Sch. 18, para. 5(1)	(3)	Sch. 18 para. 6(3)	9(9)	Sch. 18, para. 8(3), (4)
(4)	Sch. 18, para. 5(2)	(4)	Sch. 18, para. 6(4)	10(1)–(3)	Sch. 18, para. 9(1) to (3)
		(5)	Sch. 18, para. 6(5)		
		6(1)(2)	Sch. 18, para. 7(1)(2)		

Housing &c. Act 1923

1923	1985
s.22(c)	Sch. 18, paras. 2(2), 3(1)

Housing Act 1935

1935	1985
s.92(2)	Sch. 18, para. 1(2)
(3)	Sch. 18, para. 10

Public Health Act 1936

1936	1985	1936	1985	1936	1985
s.1(1)	s.410(1)	s.241(4)	s.407(5)	s.296	s.408(1), 412(1)
(2)	1	246	408(1)(2)	297	408(3)
235	401	247	409	298	413
236	402	248(1)	414(1)	300(2), (3)	405(2), (3)
237	403	(2), (3)	414(2), (3)	301	405(4)
238(1)	404(1)–(3)	283(1)	404(1)	302	405(5)
(2) to (4)	404(4)–(6)	(2)	614(1), (2)	318	616
239	405(1)	287(1)	411(1)	322–326	410(2)
240	406	(2)	411(2), (3)	341	415
241(1), (2)	407(1), (2)	(3), (4)	411(4), (5)		
(3)	407(3), (4)	288	412(1)		

Housing Act 1957

1957	1985	1957	1985	1957	1985
s.1(1)	s.1	s.9(3)	s.205	s.10(5)	Sch. 10, para. 5(1), (3)
(2)	1	10 *passim*	Sch. 10, para. 3(1) to (2)	(7), (8)	Sch. 10, para. 7(1) to (4)
4(1)	604(1)	10(1)	s.193(1), (2)	(9)	s.203(3)
9(1)	189(1), (2)	(2)	194(1), (2)	s.11(1)	191(1)
(1A)	190(1), (2)	(3)	Sch. 101, paras. 1, 2(1)–(4), 4		
(1B)	190(1), (2)				
(1C)	207				
(2)	189(3), 190(3)				

HOUSING ACT 1957—*continued*

1957	1985
s.11(1)–(3)	...Sch. 10, para. 6(1)–(4)
(3)	s.191(2), (3)
12(1)	192(1)
(2)	192(2), (3)
(3)	192(4)
(4)	585(1)(3), 622 "building regulations"
13(1)	199(1), (2)
(2)	199(3), (4)
(3)	199(3), (4)
14(1)	200(1), 229(1)
(2)	200(2), (3), 229(2), (3)
(3)	200(4), 229(4)
(4)	200(6), 229(6)
(5)	200(5), 229(5)
15(1)	201(1)–(3), 230(1)–(3)
(3)–(5)	201(4)–(6), 230(4)–(6)
16(1)	264(1)–(4), 268(1), 275(2)
(2)–(4)	264(1)–(4)
(5)	264(5)
(6)	264(6)
(7)	264(7)
(1)	265(1), (2)
(2)	300(1)
(3)	300(5), 303, 304(1)(3)
(3)(b)	265(2)
(3)(c)	265(2)
18(1)	266, 300(4)
(2)	280, 282(1)
proviso	281(2)
(2)(b)	281(1)
19	268(1), 300(2)
20	300(2)
(1)–(3)	269(1)–(3)
(3)	269(5)
proviso	269(4)
21	267(1)
22(1)	270(1)
(2)	270(2)
(3)	270(4)
(4)	270(5)
(5)	270(3)
23(1)	271(1), (2)
(2)	272(1), (2), 288(1)(2)
(3)	272(3), (4), 288(3)(4)
(4)	272(5), 288(5)
(5)	272(6), 288(6)
24(1)	274(1), (2)
(2)	274(3)(5)
(3)	274(4)

1957	1985
s.25(1)	s.273(1)
(2)	273(2)
proviso	273(3)
25(3)	273(4)
26	304(2)
27(1)	267(2), 277
(2)	267(3), 278(1)
(3)	267(3), 278(2)
(4)	278(3)
(5)	276
28	279(1)–(3)
29(1)	300(3)
(2)	585(1)(3), 622 "building regulations"
(3), (4)	302
33(1)	378(1)
(2)	307(1), (2)
30(1)(3)	Sch. 23, para. 2(1)(2)
(1)–(3),	
(6)	Sch. 23, para. 1(1)(2)
(3)(b)	Sch. 23, paras. 1(4), 2(4)
(3)(4)	Sch. 23, paras. 1(3), 2(3)
(5)	Sch. 23, paras. 1(5)(6), 2(5)(6)
(7)	588(2)
33(1)	202
(2)	203(1), (2)
37(1)	189(4), 190(4), 191(4), 268(2), 269(6), 284(5), 285(3), 358(3), 362(2), Sch. 10, paras. 3(3), 5(2), 6(1)–(4)
(2)	191(4), 269(6), 285(3), 362(2), Sch. 10, para. 6 (1)–(4)
39(1)	206, 321
(2)	207, 322 "person having control", 398
40	204
42(1)	289(1)–(3)
proviso	289(4)
42(2)	289(5)
43(1)	290(1)
(2)	290(2)
(3)	290(3), (4), 579(1)
47(1)	291(1), (2)
48(1)	301(1), 302
(2)	301(3)
(3)	301(2)
(4)	302
49	293(1), (2)

1957	1985
s.50	s.292
59(1)	579(2), 585(1)
(2)	585(1), 622 "building regulations"
proviso	585(2)
60(1)	Sch. 23, para. 7(1)–(3)
60(1)(1C)	Sch. 23, para. 3(1)
(1A)	Sch. 23, para. 7(4)
(1B)	Sch. 23, para. 7(5)
(1D)	Sch. 23, para. 8(1)–(3)
(2)	Sch. 23, para. 3(2)
62(1)	s.584(1)–(3)
(2)	584(4)
63(2)	596
64(1)	294(1)(3)
(2)	294(2)
(3)	295(1)–(3)
proviso	296(1)
65(1)	296(2)
(2)	297(1)–(3)
(3), (6)(a)	296(3)
(4)–(6)	611(1)–(5)
(5)	297(4)
(5)	
proviso	297(5)
65(6)(b)	297(6)
(7)	296(4), 611(6)
67(1)	Scheds. 22, para. 9(1), Sch. 23, para. 5(1)
(2)	Sch. 22, para. 9(2)(3)
(3)	Sch. 22, para. 9(4)
68(1)	s.204, 308(1)–(3)
(2)	309(1)(2)
69(1)–(5)	310(1)–(5)
70(1), (2)	308(4), 310(6)
(2)	311(1)–(3)
72(1)	284(1), (2)
(2)	284(3), (4)
(3)	284(5), 285(1)–(4)
(4)	283(1)
(5)	283(2)
73(1)	286(1)
(2)	286(2)
(3)	286(3)
(4)	286(4)
74(1)	287(1)
(2)	287(2), (3)
(3)	288(1)–(6)
(4)	597(1)–(3)
(6)	307(1), (2)

HOUSING ACT 1957—*continued*

HOUSING ACT 1957—*continued*

1957	1985
s.189(i) "house" para.	
(b)	s.56 "housing accommodation"
189(i) "owner"	56 "owner", 322 "owner", 602 "owner", 623 "owner"
189(i) "statutory undertakers" .	611(6)
189(i) "street"	622 "street"
Sch. para. 7 "house", "interest"	591(6)
Sch. 1,	
(1) ..	578
(3) ..	599
para. 3	583(1)–(3)
Sch. 2, Pt. 1,	
para. 1(1) ..	Sch. 23, para. 4(1)(4)
(2) ..	Sch. 23, para. 4(1)(5)
2	Sch. 23, para. 4(4)
3(1)(2)	Sch. 23, para. 4(2)
(3) ..	Sch. 23, para. 4(3)
Sch. 2,	
para. 1(3) ..	s.588(1)
3(1) ..	590(6)
(2) ..	590(6), 622 "district valuer"
para. 4(1) ..	591(1), Sch. 24, Pt. 1, para. 1(1)
(2) ..	Sch. 24, Pt. 1, para. 3(1)
(b), (6) ...	Sch. 24, Pt. I, para. 1(2)
(3) ..	Sch. 24, Pt. I, para. 3(2)
(4) ..	Sch. 24, para. 4(2)
proviso	Sch. 24, Pt. I, para. 4(3)

1957	1985
Sch. 2,	
para. 4(5) ..	Sch. 24, Pt. I, para. 4(4)
proviso	Sch. 24, Pt. 1, para. 5(3)
(7) ..	Sch. 24, Pt. I, para. 6(1)(2)
para. 5(1) ..	s.591(1)–(3)
(2) ..	592(1)–(3), (5)
6(1) ..	Sch. 24, Pt. II, para. 1(1)
(2) ..	Sch. 24, Pt. II, paras. 1(2), 2, 3
(3) ..	Sch. 24, Pt. II, para. 4(1)
proviso	Sch. 24, Pt. II, para. 4(3)
para. 6(4) ..	Sch. 24, Pt. II, para. 4(4)
(5) ..	Sch. 24, Pt. II, para. 5
7(1) ..	s.591(1) Sch. 24, Pt. I, para. 1(1), Pt. II, para. 1(1)(2)
(2) "full compulsory purchase value", "site value"	Sch. 24, Pt. I, para. 4(2), Pt. II, para. 4(2)
s.7(2) "house", "interest"	Sch. 24, Pt. I, para. 5(1) Pt. II, para. 5.
para. 7(3) ..	s.588(2)
Sch. 3	264(6)
Sch. 3, Pt. 1,	
para. 1(1)(2)	Sch. 22, para. 2
Sch. 3, Pt. I,	
para. 2(1) ..	Sch. 22, para. 3(1)(3)
(2) ..	Sch. 22, para. 3(4)
(3) ..	Sch. 22, para. 3(3)
3(2) ..	Sch. 22, para. 5(1)

1957	1985
Sch. 3, Pt. I,	
para. 3(3) ..	Sch. 22, paras 4(1), 5(1)
(4) ..	Sch. 22, para. 4(2)
(5)(6)	Sch. 22, para. 4(3)(4)
4(1)(2)	Sch. 22, para. 5(2)
(3)(4)	Sch. 22, para. 5(3)(4)
Sch. 3,	
para. 7(1),	
(2)	s.580
8(5) ..	598
(7) ..	599
10	583(1)–(3)
Sch. 4,	
para. 1	Sch. 11, para. 12(1) to (3), Sch. 22, para. 6
2	Sch. 11, para. 13(1) to (3), Sch. 22, para. 7(1) to (3)
3	Sch. 11, paras. 13(5), 14(1), Sch. 22, paras. 7(5), 8(1)
4	Sch. 11, para. 13(4), Sch. 22, para. 7(4)
5	Sch. 11, para. 14(2), Sch. 22, para. 8(2)
Sch. 6	s.326(3)
Sch. 7,	
para. 1(1) ..	578
(3) ..	599

HOUSING (FINANCIAL PROVISIONS) ACT 1958

1958	1985
s.9	Sch. 15, Pt. III, para. 1(1)
25(2) proviso	Sch. 15, Pt. III, paras. 1(4), 2(4)
28	Sch. 15, Pt. II, para. 1(2), Pt. III, paras. 1(3), 2(2), Sch. 19, paras. 1(2), 2(2)
43(1)	s.435(1)(3)
(2)	439(1), (2)
(2A)	439(3)

1958	1985
s.43(3)	s.436(1)
(a),(f)	436(2)
(b),(e)	436(3)
(c)	436(5), (6)
(d)	436(4)
(4)	435(4)
(5)	435(2)
44	440
46(1)	Sch. 15, Pt. II, para. 1(1)
(b)	Sch. 15, Pt. II, para. 2(3)(4)
(2)	Sch. 15, Pt. II, para. 2(1)
(2A)	Sch. 15, Pt. II, para. 2(2)
(3)	Sch. 15, Pt. II, para. 3(1), (2)

1958	1985
s.46(4)	Sch. 15, Pt. II, para. 4(1) to (4)
(5)	Sch. 15, Pt. II, para. 5
(6)	Sch. 15, Pt. II, para. 2(5)
47(1), (2)	s.451(1)
(2)(c)	451(6)
(5)(a),(b)	451(5)
(c)	451(3)
(3), (5)(c), (6)	451(2)
(6) proviso (b)	451(4)
54(1)	428(1)
(3)	428(2)
58(1)	
"house"	457
58(3)	604(1)

HOUSE PURCHASE AND HOUSING ACT 1959

1959	1985
ss.13 to 17	Sch. 15, Pt. III, para. 1(1)

1959	1985
Sch. 1, para. 3	Sch. 15, Pt. III, para. 1(4)

1959	1985
Sch. 1, para. 4	Sch. 15, Pt. III, para. 1(3)

HOUSING (UNDERGROUND ROOMS) ACT 1959

1959	1985
s.1(1)	s.604(2)

TOWN AND COUNTRY PLANNING ACT 1959

1959	1985
s.27(1) to (3)	s.430(2)

LAND COMPENSATION ACT 1961

1961	1985
s.1	s.578
5 rule (1)	597(3)
Sch. 2, para. 1(2)	589(1)
3(1), (2), (4)	589(2)

1961	1985
Sch. 2, para. 3(3), (5)	s.589(3)
para. 3(3A) to (3C)	589(4)–(6)

1961	1985
Sch. 2, para. 6(2)	s.589(1)(2)
Sch. 4, para. 9	295(3)
10	597(2)(3)

HOUSING ACT 1961

1961	1985
s.12(1)	s.370(1)
(3)	370(2), (3)
(4)	371(1)
(5)	371(2)(3)
(6)	370(4), 371(4)
(7)	370(5)
13(1)	369(1)(2)(6)

1961	1985
s.13(2)	s.369(4), 398(6)
(3)	369(3)
(4)	369(5)
(5)	369(6)
14(1)	372(1)(5)
(2)	372(2)
(3)	372(3)

1961	1985
s.14(4)	s.372(4)
(5)	373(1), (2)
(6)	373(3)
(7)	373(4)
15(1)	352(1)–(3)
(1)(a)	398(5)
(2)	352(5)
(3)	352(4)

HOUSING ACT 1961—*continued*

1961	1985	1961	1985	1961	1985
s.15(4)	s.352(3)	s.19(1)	s.354(1)	s.22(6)	s.349(1)
17	353(1)(2)	(2)	355(1)	(7)	349(2)
(1)	367(1)	(3)	354(2),	(8)	349(3)
(2)	353(3),		355(1)	(9)	346(5),
	367(1)	(4)	354(3)		349(4)
(3)	353(5),	(5)	354(4)	(10)	351(1), (2)
	367(3)	(6)	354(5)	23(1)	377(1)
(4)	353(4)	(7)	357(1)	(2)	378(1)
18 *passim* ..	Sch. 10,	(8)	357(2), (3)	(3)	378(2)
	para. 3(1)(2)	(9)	356(1)	(4), (5) ...	613(1), (2)
(1)	s.375(1)	(10)	355(2),	(6)	395(2)
(2)	375(3)		356(2)	(7)	398(2)(4)
(3)	Sch. 10,	(11)	355(2)	25	274(1), (2)
	paras. 1,	(12)	354(7)	26(1)	275(1)
	2(1)–(4), 4	21(1)	352(6),	(2)	275(2)
(5)	Sch. 10,		374(1)	(3)	276,
	para. 7(1) to	(2)	374(3)		279(1)(3)
	(4)	(3)	353(1), (2),	26A	377(2)(3)
(6)	Sch. 10,		(4), 374(1)	28(2)	395(1),
	para. 18(1),	22(1)	346(1)		398(3), 399
	(2)	(2)	346(4)		"house"
		(3)	346(2), (3)		
		(4)	350(1)(2)		

PUBLIC HEALTH ACT 1961

1961	1985
Sch. 1, Pt. III	ss.585(1), 622
	"building
	regulations"

LONDON GOVERNMENT ACT 1963

1963	1985
s.21(1)	s.1
(2)	1
(3)	16(1)
(10)	15(2)
Sch. 8,	
para. 3(*a*) ..	15(1)
(*b*) ..	16(2)

PUBLIC WORKS LOANS ACT 1964

1964	1985
s.2(3)	Sched. 18,
	para. 1(2)

HOUSING ACT 1964

1964	1985	1964	1985	1964	1985
s.43	s.374(2)	s.64(6)	ss.352(3),	s.65(6)	s.613(1)(2)
44(1)	374(2)		372(4)	67(1), (2) ...	352(2)
64(1), (3) ...	Sched. 10,	(7)	353(1), (2),	(2)	353(1), (2)
	para. 7(1) to		367(1),	(3)	354(6)
	(4)		373(1)(2)	(4)	352(6)
(2)	Sched. 10,	65(1)	376(1)	(5)	355(1)
	paras. 3(1)	(2)	375(3),	68(1)	397(1)
	to (2),		376(4)	(2)	397(2)
	6(1)–(4)	(3)	376(5)	(3)	397(5)
(4), (5) ...	Sched. 10,	(4)	395(2)	(4)	397(4)
	para. 6(1) to	(5)	375(2),	(5)	397(3)
	(4)		376(3)	69(1)	374(1)

HOUSING ACT 1964—*continued*

COMPULSORY PURCHASE ACT 1965

1965	1985
s.1(1)	s.578
4	305(7),
	Sched. 11,
	para. 3(2)
34(1)	s.579(2)
Sched. 7	ss.583(1) to
	(3), 584(4)

RENT ACT 1965

1965	1985
Sched. 6, para.	
10	s.286(2),
	338(2)
para. 10(2) .	270(2)

HOUSING (SLUM CLEARANCE COMPENSATION) ACT 1965

1965	1985
s.2(1)	s.591(1)
(2)	591(1)(4)
(3)	592(4)
(5)	591(5)
(6)	591(1)(6)

GENERAL RATE ACT 1967

1967	1985
s.115(1)	
"valuation	
officer"	s.622
	"district
	valuer"

CRIMINAL JUSTICE ACT 1967

1967	1985
s.92,	
Sched. 3, Pt. 1	ss.408(2),
	412(2)

NATIONAL LOANS ACT 1968

1968	1985
s.6(1)(2) ......Sched. 18,	
	para. 1(2)

RENT ACT 1968

1968	1985
Sched. 15	s.309(1),
	Sched. 15,
	Pt. II,
	para. 2(3)(4)

PRICES AND INCOMES ACT 1968

1968	1985
s.12(1)	s.25(1) to
	(3)(5)
(2)	25(4)
(3)	25(3)

DECIMAL CURRENCY ACT 1969

1969	1985
s.10(1)	.... s.349(3)

HOUSING ACT 1969

1969	1985	1969	1985	1969	1985
ss.17–20	........Sched. 15, Pt. III, para. 2(1)	s.63(11)	.... s.399 "house"	Sched. 5, para. 2	......Sched. 24, Pt. I, para. 4(1)
s.28(1)	.... s.253(1)	64(1)	.... 347(2)		
(2)	.... 254(1)–(4)	(1), (2) ...	347(1)	3(1)	..Sched. 24, Pt. I, para. 4(3)
29(1)	.... 253(3)	(3)	.... 347(3)		
(2)	.... 253(3)	(4)	.... 348(1)	(2)	..Sched. 24, Pt. I, para. 4(4)
(3)	.... 289(6)	(5)	.... 348(2)		
29A	.... 253(2)	(6)	.... 348(3), (4)	(3)	..Sched. 24, Pt. I, para. 5(3)
30(1)	.... 258(1)	(7)	.... 346(6), 347(4)		
(1A)	..... 258(2)	(8)	.... s.351(1), (2)	4	...... s.591(3)
31	 257	65(1)(2)	.....Sched. 23, para. 2(1)(2)	5(1) "qualifying period"	........Sched. 24, Pt. I, para. 2(1)(2)
32(1)	.... 255(1)	67(2)(5)	.....Sched. 23, para. 6(1)(2)		
(2)	 578				
(5)	.... 255(2)	(3)	........Sched. 23, para. 6(3)		
33(1)	.... 256(1)–(3)	(4)	........Sched. 23, para. 5(2)	Sched. 5, para. 5(1) "relevant date"	...........Sched. 24, Pt. I, para. 1(2)
(2)	.... 256(4)	68(1)	........Sched. 24, Pt. I, para. 3(3)		
37(1)	 259				
(2)	.... 259(2)	69	.... s.590(1)(2)		
(3)	.... 259(3), (4)	70	.... 605(1), (2)	Sched. 5, para. 5(2) "full compulsory purchase value", "site value"	..........Sched. 24, Pt. I, para. 4(2)
(4)	.... 259(3), (4)	71	.... 604(1)		
(5)	.... 259(5)	72	.... 190(1), (2)		
38	...........Sched. 14, Pt. V, para. 8	75(1)	.... 514(1)		
		(2)	.... 514(3)		
39	.... s.1	(3)	.... 514(2)	Sched. 5, para. 5(2) "house"	........Sched. 24, Pt. I, para. 5(1)
58(1)	 345	84	.... 259(6)		
59(2)	.... 371(1)	85(1A)	...... 259(5)		
(3)	.... 371(2)	86(2)	........Sched. 24, Pt. I, para. 6(1)(2)	Sched. 5, para. 5(2) "interest"	...... s.590(2),
61(1)	.... 376(2)(3)			Sched. 24,	.....Pt. I, para. 5(1)
(2)	.... 376(2)	(4)	.... s.259(6)		
(3)	.... 613(1), (2)	(5)	.... 259(2)		
(4)	.... 376(5)	91(4)	........Sched. 19, para. 1(1)	Sched. 5, para. 5(4)	.. 588(2)
(5)	.... 395(2), 397(1)			5(5)	..Sched. 24, Pt. I, para. 5(2)
62(1)(*a*)	..... 354(1)	Sched. 4	......ss.588(1), 590(6), Sched. 23, para. 4(1) to (5)		
(*b*)	.... 355(1)			Sched. 6, para. 2	......Sched. 24, Pt. I, para. 6(1)(2)
63(1)	........Sched. 13, para. 22	Sched. 5, paras. 1(1), 5(3)	.........Sched. 24, Pt. I, para. 1(1)		
(2)	........Sched. 13, para. 23(1)(2)			Sched. 6, para. 3	......Sched. 24, Pt. II, para. 2
(3)	........Sched. 13, para. 24	Sched. 5, para. 1(1)(*b*)	.........Sched. 24, Pt. I, para. 2(1)		
(4)	........Sched. 13, para. 25(1)			4	...... s.588(2)
(5)	........Sched. 13, para. 26(1)(2)	Sched. 5, para. 1(2)	..Sched. 24, para. 2(2)		
(6)	........Sched. 13, para. 26(3)				
(7)	........Sched. 13, para. 26(4)(5)	para. 1(3)	..Sched. 24, Pt. I, para. 1(3)		
(8)	........Sched. 13, paras. 22, (3)–(5), 25(2)				
(9)	........Sched. 13, para. 25(6)				
(10)	.......Sched. 13, paras. 25(2), 26(2)				

HOUSING ACT 1969—*continued*

1969	1985
Sched. 8,	
para. 2 ......ss.352(1),	
	369(1), 370(1)
3 ...... s.352(6)	
4 ...... 346(1)	
5 ......ss.374(1),	
	379(1), 582(1)
6 ...... s.191(3)	
7 ...... 588(2)	
8 ...... 8(1), (2)	
10 ..... 583(1) to (3)	

1969	1985
Sched. 8,	
para. 11 .....ss.260, 261,	
	584(1) to (3)
13 ..... s.615(1), (2)	
14 616	
16 .....Sched. 2,	
	para. 2(4)
17 .....Sched. 15,	
	Pt. III,
	para. 2(2),
	Sched. 19,
	para. 2(2)

1969	1985
Sched. 8,	
para. 19 ..... s.428(1)(2)	
23 ..... 589(2)	
24 ..... 589(1)(2)	
29 ..... 374(2)	
Sched. 9,	
para. 1 ......Sched. 15,	
	Pt. III,
	para. 1(1),
	Sched. 19,
	para. 1(1)

COURTS ACT 1971

1971	1985
s.56(2),	
Sched. 9,	
Pt. 1 .... s.405(4)	
Sched. 8	
para. 1 ......ss.200(6),	
	229(6)
Sched. 9 .... 200(5),	
	229(5)

HOUSING ACT 1971

1971	1985
s.1 .... s.259(7)	
2(4) .... 259(7)	

TOWN AND COUNTRY PLANNING ACT 1971

1971	1985
Sched. 23	
Pt. II .... s.256(1)–(3),	
	(4)

HOUSING FINANCE ACT 1972

1972	1985
s.11(1) .... s.312(1)	
(2) .... 312(2)	
(3) .... 313(1)	
(4) ....Sched. 12,	
	para. 2(1)(2)
(5) ....Sched. 12,	
	para. 2(3)(4)
(6) ....Sched. 12,	
	para. 8
(c) .....Sched. 12,	
	para. 7(2)
(d) ....Sched. 12,	
	para. 7(1)
(7) .... s.312(3)	
(8) ....Sched. 12,	
	para. 6(2)
(9)(a) .....Sched. 12,	
	para. 5
(b) ....Sched. 12,	
	para. 6(1)
(10)(a) ... s.313(1)	
(b) ... s.313(3)	

1972	1985
s.12(1) .... s.417(1)	
(d) ....Sched. 14,	
	Pt. III,
	para. 1
(e) ..... s.417(2)	
(3) .... 417(4)	
(c) .....Sched. 14,	
	Pt. III,
	para. 5
15(1) .... s.312(5)	
(2) .... 312(4)	
(5) .... 313(4)	
16(3) ....Sched. 14,	
	Pt. V,
	para. 7(4)
(4) ....Sched. 14,	
	Pt. V,
	para. 7(2)
(5) ....Sched. 14,	
	Pt. V,
	para. 7(5)

1972	1985
s.93 .... s.30(1)	
(1) .... 26(1)	
(3) .... 26(2)	
(4) .... 26(4)	
97(1) .... 223(1)	
101(1) ....Sched. 14,	
	Pt. V,
	para. 4(1)
(2) ....Sched. 14,	
	Pt. V,
	para. 4(2)
(3) ....Sched. 14, Pt.	
	V,
	para. 4(3)
103 .... s.620(1)(2)	
104(1) .... 312(6)	
(1)	
"general rate	
fund" 622	
	"general rate
	fund"

HOUSING FINANCE ACT 1972—*continued*

1972	1985
s.104(1)	
"houses and other property within the account"	417(3)
104(1)	
"officer", ...Sched. 14, Pt. V, para. 5(1)(2)	
104(1)	
"year"	s.433 "year"
104(3) ....Sched. 14, Pt. V, para. 2(1)	
(4)	s.314(5) Sched. 14, Pt. I, item 7, Pt. III, para. 3, Pt. V, paras. 4(2), 6(4)
105(2) ....Sched. 14, Pt. V, para. 6(1)	
(3)	s.314(1)(2), (4), Sched. 14, Pt. V, para. 6(2)
(4)	s.314(3)(4), Sched. 14, Pt. V, para. 6(3)
106	s.30(1)
129(3)(*b*) ...Sched. 16, para. 4(3)	
Sched. 1,	
para. 1 ......Sched. 14, Pt. I opening	
(1)(*a*)Sched. 14, Pt. I, item 1	
(*b*)Sched. 14, Pt. I item 2	
(*c*)Sched. 14, Pt. I item 4	
(*e*)Sched. 14, Pt. I item 5	

1972	1985
Sched. 1,	
(*f*) Sched. 14, Pt. I item 6	
(2),	
(3) .. Sched. 14, Pt. I, item 7	
para. 1(4) ..Sched. 14, Pt. 1, item 6	
para. 2 ......Sched. 14, Pt. III, para. 7	
para. 3(1) ..Sched. 14, Pt. II opening	
(*a*)Sched. 14, Pt. II, item 1	
3(1)(*a*)(iii) Sched. 14, Pt. III, para. 5	
(*b*),	
(2)–(4) ....Sched. 14, Pt. II, item 2	
(*c*)Sched. 14, Pt. II, item 3	
4(1) ..Sched. 14, Pt. V, para. 1(2)(3)	
(2) ..Sched. 14, Pt. V, para. 3	
5(1) ..	s.420(1)
(2) ..	420(2)
(3) ..	420(3)
(4) ..	420(4)
6(*a*) ..Sched. 14, Pt. IV, para. 3	
8 ......Sched. 14, Pt. IV, para. 2	
10(1) .Sched. 14, Pt. IV, para. 1(1)	
(2) .Sched. 14, Pt. IV, para. 1(2)(3)	

1972	1985
Sched. 1,	
para. 10(3) .Sched. 14, Pt. IV, para. 1(4)	
14(1) .Sched. 14, Pt. V, para. 1(2)	
(2) .Sched. 14, Pt. IV, para. 4(1)	
(3) .Sched. 14, Pt. IV, para. 4(2)	
20 .....Sched. 14, Pt. V, para. 5(1)(2	
22(1) .Sched. 14, Pt. V, para. 7(1)	
(2) .Sched. 14, Pt. V, para. 7(2)	
(3) .Sched. 14, Pt. V, para. 7(3)	
(5) .Sched. 14, Pt. V, para. 7(2), (5)	
Sched. 8,	
para. 2D ....Sched. 15, Pt. I	
4(5) ..	s.53(2)(3)
(6) ..	53(4)
(8) ..	53(5)
7(1) ..Sched. 15, Pt. II, para. 1(1)	
Sched. 9,	
para. 14	30(1)
Sched. 10,	
para. 4(3)(4)Sched. 14, Pt. III, para. 3	
5(1) ..Sched. 14, Pt. III,para. 2	
(2) ..Sched. 14, Pt. III, para. 4	
(3)(4)Sched. 14, Pt. III, para. 6	

LOCAL GOVERNMENT ACT 1972

1972	1985
s.153(1)	s.430(1)
(2)	430(2)
180(1)	1
(1)(*d*) ...	619(1)
193(1)	1
(2)	14(2)
194(1)	28(1)
(2)	28(3)
(3)	28(4)
(4)	28(5)
(5)	28(6)

1972	1985
s.194(6)	s.28(2)
Sched. 22,	
para. 4(1) ..	14(3)
Sched. 22,	
para. 5(1) ..	14(4)
5(1) ..	606(2), (3)
Sched. 29,	
para. 1(1) ..	200(2)(6), 229(2), (6), 606(1)

1972	1985
Sched. 29,	
para. 4	s.351(1), (2)
(*a*) ..	200(2), (6), 229(2), (6), 606(1)
Sched. 29, Pt.,	
para. 4(1)(*a*)	414(2), (3)

Housing Act 1985

CRIMINAL JUSTICE ACT 1972

1972	1985
s.32	.... s.277

HOUSING AMENDMENT ACT 1973

1973	1985
s.1(1)	.... s.259(7)
11(6)(a)	.....Sched. 12, para. 3
)(b)	....Sched. 12, para. 4

LOCAL GOVERNMENT ACT 1974

1974	1985
s.37(2)	.... s.435(1)
(3)	.... 439(3)
(4)	.... 436(5), (6)
(5)	.... 435(2)

CONSUMER CREDIT ACT 1974

1974	1985
Sched. 4, para. 18	..... s.10(1) to (3)

HOUSING ACT 1974

1974	1985	1974	1985	1974	1985
s.12	.... s.5(3)	s.46(1)	.... s.245(1)	s.57(7)	.... s.471(3), 473(3), 480(3), 482(3), 488(2), 490(3), 496(2), 498(3)
36(1)–(3)	... 239(1)–(3)	46(3)	.... 245(2)		
(4)	.... 240(1)	(4)	.... 245(3)		
(a)	.... 240(2)	(5)	.... 245(4)		
(b)	.... 240(3)	(6)	.... 245(5)		
(c)	.... 240(4)	47(1)–(3)	... 247(2)–(4)	58(1)	.... 508(1)
(d)	.... 240(5)	(3)	 262	(2)	.... 508(2), (3)
(5)	.... 239(5)	(4)	.... 247(1)	(3)	.... 508(3)
(6)	 252	(5)	.... 247(6)	59(1)	.... 509(1)
37(1)	.... 241(1), (2)	(6)	.... 247(5)	(2)	.... 509(2)
(2)	.... 241(1), (2)	(7)	.... 249(1)	60(1), (1A),	
7(3)	.... 241(3)	(8), (9)	... 613(1), (2)	(2)	.... 464(1)
(4)	.... 241(3)	(10)	...... 249(2)	(3)	.... 464(3)
(5)	.... 241(4)	48(1)(a)	 260	(4)	.... 464(4)
(6)	.... 241(5)	(b)	 261	(5)	.... 464(5)
38(1)–(4)	... 242(1)–(4)	(3)	.... 605(1), (2)	61(1)	.... 470(1), (2), 511(1)
39(1)	.... 239(4)	54(1)(g)	..... 260, 261		
(2)	.... 251(1), (2)	56(1)	.... 460(1)–(3)	(a)	..... 461(1)
(3)	.... 250(1)–(3)	(2)	.... 460(1)	(2)	.... 468(1)
s.39(4)	...... s.251(3), (4)	(a)	.... 467(1)	(3)	.... 468(2)
(5)	.... 251(5)	(b)	.... 474(1)	(b)	 519
(7)	.... 250(1)–(3), 251(6)	(c)	.... 483(1)	(4)	.... 468(3)
		(d)	.... 491(1)	(4A)	...... 468(4)
40(1)	.... 250(1)–(3)	(3)	.... 462(1)	(5)	.... 468(5)
(2)	.... 250(1)–(3)	(4)	.... 462(1),(2)	62(1), (2)	... 469(1)–(3)
41	 246	57(1)	.... 461(1)	(3)	.... 469(4)
43(1)	.... 243(1), (2)	(2)	.... 461(2)	(4)	.... 469(6)
(2)	 578	(3)	.... 463(1)(2)(6), 486(2), 494(2)	(5), (6)	... 469(7)
(3)	.... 243(4)			63(1)	.... 471(1)
(5)	.... 582(1)	(4)	.... 466(1)–(3)	(2)	.... 471(2)
44(1)	.... 243(1), (3)	(5), 71A	. 494(2)	(3)	.... 471(4)
(2)	.... 243(1), (3)	(5)	.... 465(1), (2), 486(2), 494(2)	64(1)	.... 473(1)
45(1)	.... 244(1), (5)			(2)	.... 473(2)
(2)	.... 244(2)	(6)	.... 461(3)	(3)	.... 472(1)
(3)	.... 244(3)	(6A)	...... 461(4)	(3)	.... 472(2)
(4)	.... 244(4)			(4)	.... 472(4)

HOUSING ACT 1974—*continued*

HOUSING ACT 1974—*continued*

1974	1985
s.99(3)–(5)	... s.232(3)–(5)
(6)	.... 232(6)
100(1)	.... 228(1)
(2)	...... 228(1), (3)
(3)	...... 228(3)
(4)	...... 228(5)
(5)	...... 228(4)
(6)	...... 228(7)
(7)	...... 228(6)
(8)	...... 228(2)
(9)	...... 228(5)
101(1)–(3)	.. 227(1)–(3)
102	 233
103(1)	.... 617(1)
(2)	...... 617(3)
(3)	...... 617(4)
103A(1)–(3)	234(1)–(3)
104(1)	...... 232(6),
	236(2),237
(2)	...... 236(1)
(3)	 237
(4)(*c*)	... 614(1), (2)
(4)(*d*)	... 615(1), (2)
105(1)	.... 431(1)
(2)	...... 431(2)
(3)	...... 431(1)(3)
106(1)	.... 417(1)
(3)	 56
	"housing
	accommo
	dation"
110	 303
(1), (2),	
(3)	.... 305(1)
(4)	...... 305(3)
(5)	...... 305(4)
(6)	...... 305(5)
(7), (8)	. 305(6)
(9)	...... 305(2)
111	 303
(1), (2)	. 306(1)
(3)	...... 306(2)
114(1), (1A)	Sched. 11,
	para. 1(1),
	(2)
(2)	.......Sched. 11,
	para. 2(1)
(4)	.......Sched. 11,
	paras. 12(1)
	(3), 13(1)–(5),
	14(1)(2)
(5)	.......Sched. 11,
	para. 4(1)
(8)	
"effective	
date"	.... 594(4)
114(8)	
"full standard"	299(2)
114(8)	
"Part III land"	Sched. 11,
	para. 1(3)
114A(1)	....Sched. 11,
	para. 4(2)
(2)	....Sched. 11,
	para. 4(3)

1974	1985
s.115(1)	.... s.593
(2)	...... 594(1)(2)
(3)	...... 594(1)(3)
(4)	...... 594(4)(5)
(5)	...... 594(4),
	595(1)
(6), (7)	. 595(2), (3)
(9)	...... 595(4)
(10)	.... 594(6)
116	.... 305(7),
	Sched. 11,
	para. 3(2)
127(2)	...... 516(6),
	Sched. 15, Pt.
	III para.
	3(3)
128(1)	...... 245(5)
(1A)	. 481(5),
	489(6),
	508(3), 509(2),
	517(2)
128(1),	
(1A), (3)	...... 469(5),
	471(6),
	491(3), 492(3)
128(1A)	.... 245(5),
	472(4),
	497(3)
(3)	...... 245(5)
129(1)	.......ss.237, 252
129(1)	
"dwelling"	..... s.525
	"dwelling"
129(1)	
"hostel"	 622
	"hostel"
129(1)	
"house in	
multiple	
occupation"	... 525
	"house in
	multiple
	occupation"
129(3), (4)	. 520(1), (2)
Sched. 4,	
para. 1	...... 248(1)
22(1)–(3)	... 248(2)–(4)
3(1)	.. 248(5)
(2)	.. 248(5)
4	...... 248(6)
Sched. 5,	
para. 2(1)	.. 258(2)
Pt. II	.... 253(2)
Sched. 6	.... 508(1)
Sched. 7,	
para. 1	......Sched. 14,
	Pt. I item 1
Sched. 9	.......Sched. 23,
	paras. 3(1),
	7(1)–(5)
	8(1)–(3)
Sched. 10,	
paras. 1	
"notice land",	
6	.................Sched. 11,
	para. 9

1974	1985
Sched. 10,	
paras. 1(2)	. 614(1)(2)
2	......Sched. 11,
	para. 7(1),
	(2)
3(1)	..Sched. 11,
	para. 3(1)
Sched. 10,	
para. 3(2)	..Sched. 11,
	para. 2(2)
4(1)	..Sched. 11,
	para. 5(1)(2)
(2)	..Sched. 11,
	para. 5(1),
	(3)
(3)	..Sched. 11,
	para. 6
5	......Sched. 11,
	para. 8
7(1)	..Sched. 11,
	para. 10(1)–
	(3)
(2)	..Sched. 11,
	para. 10(4)
(3)	..Sched. 11,
	para. 10(5)
Sched. 10	
para.	
8(1)–(6)	........Sched. 11,
	para. 11(1)–
	(6)
9(*a*)	..Sched. 11,
	paras.
	12(1)–(3),
	13(1)–(3)
Sched. 13	...... s.255(2),
	308(4)
para. 7	......Sched. 24, Pt.
	I,
	para. 4(3)
10(5)(*a*)	..... s.582(2)
(*b*)	..... 582(5)
(6)(*c*)	. 582(4)
Sched. 13	
para. 11	..... 591(1)
4	...... 18(2)
19	..... 590(1)
20(1)	. 514(1)
(2)	. 514(3)
para. 21	.....Sched. 24, Pt.
	I,
	paras. 1(1),
	2(1)
24	..... s.417(1) (2)
Sched. 14,	
para. 5	......Sched. 15, Pt.
	III,
	para. 2(1)
7(1)	..Sched. 19,
	para. 2(1)
Sched. 25,	
para. 30	..... s.245(5)

HOUSING RENTS AND SUBSIDIES ACT 1975

1975	1985
s.1(2)	.... s.24(2)
5(1), (3)	....Sched. 15, Pt. IV, para. 1(1)
(2)	..........Sched. 15, Pt. IV, para. 1(2)
(4)	..........Sched. 15, Pt. IV, para. 3(1)
(5)	..........Sched. 15, Pt. IV, para. 3(2)
(6)	..........Sched. 15, Pt. IV, para. 4(1)(2)
15(4)	........Sched. 15, Pt. IV, para. 3(2)
(5)(6)	.....Sched. 15, Pt. IV, paras. 2(4), 3(3)
16(1) "general rate fund"	.... s.622 "general rate fund"
16(1) "receiving authority", "receiving district"	........Sched. 15, Pt. IV, para. 6
16(1) "year"	.... s.433 "year"

1975	1985
Sched. 1, para. 12(1)	.Sched. 15, Pt. IV, para. 2(1)
(3)	.Sched. 15, Pt. IV, para. 2(2)
(4)	.Sched. 15, Pt. IV, para. 2(3)
para. 13(1)	. s.314(1)(2), (4)
	Sched. 14, Pt. V, para. 6(2)
Sched. 5, para. 5	......Sched. 14, Pt. IV, para. 3
6	......Sched. 14, Pt. V, para. 1(2)
7(1)	.. s.620(1), (2)
8(2)	..Sched. 14, Pt. I, item 1
(4)(a)	Sched. 14, Pt. II, item 1
(b)(c)	...Sched. 14, Pt. II, item 2
(6)	..Sched. 14, Pt. IV, para. 4(1)(2)
(7)	..Sched. 14, Pt. V, para. 7(1)

1975	1985
Sched. 5, para. 16(1)	. s.475(2)
(2)	. 475(4)
(3)	. 475(3)
(4)	. 475(5)
17	..... 506(4)
18(1)	.Sched. 15, Pt. III, para. 1(2)
19(1)	. 518(3)
(2)	. 518(1)(2)
20	..... 211(3)
21	.....ss.299(2), 594(4),
Sched. 11,	paras. 1(1)–(3), 2(1), 4(1), 9, 10(1)–(5), 11(1)–(6), 12(1)–(3), 13(1)–(5), 14(1)(2)
para. 22	..... 594(4), 595(1)
25	.....Sched. 11, paras. 2(2), 3(1), 5(1) to(3), 6, 7(1)(2), 8, 12(1)–(3), 13(1)–(3)
Sched. 25, para. 25	..... s.614(1), (2)

HOUSE OF COMMONS DISQUALIFICATION ACT 1975

1975	1985
s.1(3) "regular armed forces of the Crown"	.... s.622 "regular armed forces of the Crown"

CHILDREN ACT 1975

1975	1985
Sched. 3, paras. 15, 66	Sched. 24, Pt. I, para. 6(1)(2)

LOCAL LAND CHARGES ACT 1975

1975	1985
Sched. 1	.......ss.214(5), 215(4),239(5), 370(5), 381(5),505(3)

ARMED FORCES ACT 1976

1976	1985
s.20(6)	.... s.622 "regular armed forces of the Crown"

LOCAL GOVERNMENT (MISCELLANEOUS PROVISIONS) ACT 1976

1976	1985
s.9	s.23(2)
10(1)(a)	278(1)
(b)	278(2)
(c)	278(3)
10(2)	279(2)
10(3)	590(3)
10(4)	590(4), (5)
10(5)	590(6)

DEVELOPMENT OF RURAL WALES ACT 1976

1976	1985
Sch. 7,	
para. 13	s.460(3)
14	232(2)
15	431(1)

RENT (AGRICULTURE) ACT 1976

1976	1985	1976	1985	1976	1985
Sch. 8,		Sch. 8,		Sch. 8,	
para. 4 ......ss.264(5),		para. 5 ......Sch. 24, Pt. I,		para. 11 ..... s.382(3)(4)	
	270(3), 276,		para. 5(1)		28 ..... 590(2),
	286(3), 612		6 ......Sch. 15,		591(6), Sch.
......Sch. 24,			para. 2(2)		24, Pt. I,
Pt. II,					para. 5(1)
para. 5					

RENT ACT 1977

1977	1985	1977	1985	1977	1985
s.15(3) ....ss.80(2), 114(1)		Sch. 23,		para. 28(a) .Sch. 15, Pt. II,	
(a) ..... s.105(6)		para. 23 ..... s.309(1)		para. 2(3)(4)	
(d) ....Sch. 5,		Sch. 23,		28(b) .Sch. 18, Pt. II,	
para. 2		para. 24 .... 286(4)		para. 2(2)	
(5) s.6		35 ..... 382(3), (4)		48 ..... 590(2),	
145(1)–(4) ..Sch. 15, Pt. II,		36 ..... 389(1)		591(6),	
para.		64 ..... 232(2)		Sch. 24,	
2(3),(4)		26 612		Pt. I,	
Sch. 15,		27 .....Sch. 24, Pt. I,		para. 5(1)	
para. 3 ...... s.309(1)		para. 5(1),		62 ..... s.504(1)	
Sch. 23,		Pt. II,		63 ..... 504(2)	
para. 22 .....ss.264(5),		para. 5		Sch. 24,	
270(3), 276				para. 30 .....Sch. 15, Pt. II,	
				para. 2(3), (4)	

PROTECTION FROM EVICTION ACT 1977

1977	1985
Sch. 2,	
para. 2 ......ss.270(2),	
286(2), 338(2)	

CRIMINAL LAW ACT 1977

1977	1985
s.31(5) .... ss.327(1)–(3),	
331(3), 333(3),	
335(2)	
(6) .... 55(2),	
198(1)(2),	
223(2), 261,	
286(3), 320,	
327(1)–(3),	
331(3), 333(3),	
335(2), 336(3),	
341(2), 396(2),	
601(1)(2)	

HOUSING (HOMELESS PERSONS) ACT 1977

1977	1985	1977	1985	1977	1985
s.1(1)	s.58(1), (2)	s.5(7)	s.67(4)	s.8(9)	s.68(4),(5)
(2)	58(3)	(8)	67(4)	(10)	70(7)
(3)	58(4)	(9)	67(5)	(11)	70(7)
2(1)	59(1)	(10)	67(6)	9(1)	72
(2)	59(1)	(11)	67(3)	(2)	72
(3)	59(2), (3)	6(1)	69(1)	10	69(2)
(4)	59(4)	(2)	22	11(1)	74(1)
3(1)	62(1)	7(1)	70(1)(2)	(2)	74(2)
(2)(*a*)	62(1)	(1)	70(8)	(3)	74(2)
(2)(*b*)	62(2)	(2)	70(2)	(4)	74(3)
(3)	62(2)	(3)	70(2)(8)	(5)	74(1), (3),
(4)	63(1), (2)	(4)	70(3)		(4)
4(1)	ss.65(1), 66(1)	(5)	70(3)	12(1)	71(1)
(2)	s.66(3)	(6)	70(4)	(2)	71(2)
(2)(*a*)	65(4)	(7)	70(4)	13(1)	73(1)
(2)(*b*)	65(3)	(8)–(10)	70(5)	(2)	73(2)
(3)	65(3)	(11)	70(1)	(3)	73(2)
(4)	66(2)	8(1)	64(1)	(4)	73(3)
(5)	65(2)	(2)	64(2)	(5)	73(5)
(5)	67(1), (2)	(3)	64(3)	13(6)	73(5)
(6)	66(4)	(4)	64(4)	(7)	73(4)
5(1)	ss.67(2), 76(1)	(5)	68(3)	15(1)	ss.59(2), 61(5)
(3)	68(2), 76(2)	(6)	70(6)	(3)	s.61(5)
(4)	s.68(2)	(7)	70(6)	16	75
(6)	68(1)	(8)	ss.64(5), 68(4)	17(1)	60(1)

HOUSING (HOMELESS PERSONS) ACT 1977

1977	1985	1977	1985	1977	1985
s.17(2)	s.60(2)	s.18(2)(*b*)	s.61(4)	s.19(1)	ss.1, 59(3),
(3)	60(3)	(3)(*a*)	61(2)		66(3), 65(3)(4),
(4)	60(4)	(3)(*b*)	61(4)		67(5), 76(3),
18(1)	61(1)	(4)	622 "regular		77
(2)(*a*)(i)	61(2)		armed forces	Sch. 24,	
(2)(*a*)(iii)	61(3)		of the Crown"	para. 30	s.309(1)

HOMES PURCHASE ASSISTANCE AND HOUSING CORPORATION GUARANTEE ACT 1978

1978	1985	1978	1985	1978	1985
s.1(1)	s.445(1), (2)	s.2(7)	s.445(4),	Sch. 1, Pt. I	ss.447(1), 458
(2)	445(1)–(3)		446(6), 447(3),		"designated
(3)	446(2)(3)		448(3)		building
(4)	446(1)	3(1), (3)(4)	s.450(1)		society"
(5)	446(2)(4)	(2), (3)	450(2)	Sch. 1, Pt. II	s.448(1)
(6)	446(5)	4(2)	ss.450, 450(2)	Sch. 1,	
2(1)	ss.447(2),		458 "the	para. 6	622 "trustee
	448(2), 449		Corresponding		savings bank"
(2)	449(1)		Northern	Sch. 1,	
(3)	449(2)		Ireland	para. 7	622 "bank"
(4)	449(3)		provisions"	Sch. 1,	
(5)	ss.454, 458	68(1)	s.480(1)	para. 8	622
	"the	Sch.			"insurance
	corresponding	paras. 6, 7,			company"
	Northern	8	ss.36(4), 576	Sch. 1,	
	Ireland	Sch.		para. 9	622 "friendly
	provisions"	para. 9	s.36(4)		society"

Housing Act 1985

INTERPRETATION ACT 1978

1978	1985
s.16(1)(c) .....Sch. 15, Pt. III, para. 3(1)	

1978	1985
17(2)(a) .....ss.303, 374(2), 425(2), 584(4), 599, 610(1)(2), 622 "building regulations", "insurance company", "trustee savings bank", Sch. 14, Pt. II, item 2, Sch. 18, paras. 1(2), 3(3)(4), 5(3), 6(2), Sch. 22, para. 3(3)	

1978	1985
Sch. 1 "financial year" .... s.433 "year"	

HOME INSULATION ACT 1978

1978	1985
s.1(1), (2) .... s.521(1)(2)	
(4) .... 521(3)(5)	
(5), (6) .... 521(4)	
(5)(b) ...... 521(5)	

1978	1985
s.1(7) .... s.522(3), (4)	
(9) .... 521(5)(6)	
2(1) .... 522(1), (2)	
(2) .... 522(5)	

BANKING ACT 1979

1979	1985
Sch. 6, para. 11 ..... s.622 "bank"	

MAGISTRATES' COURTS ACT 1980

1980	1985
s.34(1) .... s.368(3)	

HOUSING ACT 1980

1980	1985
s.1(1) ....ss.118(1), 132(1)	
(2) .... 117(1), 132(1)	
(3) .... s.119(1)	
(8) .... 126(2)	
s.2(1), (2)(a) s.622 "charity", Sch. 5, para. 1	
(2)(b) ......Sch. 5, para. 2	
s.2(2)(c) ......Sch. 5, para. 3	
(3) ....Sch. 5, para. 4	
3(1) .... s.183(1)	
(2) .... 183(2), (3)	
(3) .... 183(2), (3)	
s.3(4) .... s.184(2)	
(4A) ...... 184(3)	
(5) .... 122(2)	

1980	1985
s.4(1) .... s.118(2), 132(2)	
(2) .... 123(1), (2)	
(3) .... 123(3), 132(3)	
(3) .... 143(2)	
5(1) .... 122(1), 124(1)	
(1A) ...... 124(2)	
(2) .... 124(3)	
	Sch. 5, para. 11(2)
(3) .... 122(3)	
6(1) .... 126(1)	
(2) .... 127(1), (2)	
(3) .... 127(1), (2)	
(4) .... 127(3)	
(5) .... 127(4)	
(6) .... 127(4)	
(7) .... 142(5)	
7(1) .... 129(1)(3)	
(1)(b) ...... 129(2)	

1980	1985
s.7(1A) ...... s.130(1)	
(2) .... 131(1)	
(3) .... 131(1)(3)	
(4) .... 131(2)	
8(1) .... 155(1), (2)	
(2) .... 155(2)	
(3) 159	
(3A) ...... 160(1)	
(d) ... 161	
(3B) ...... 160(2)	
(3C) 161	
(4) .... 156(1), (2)	
(4A) ...... 156(2)	
(5) .... 156(4)	
(5A) ...... 156(6)	
(6) .... 156(3)	
(7) 159	
(8) .... 163(1)	
9(1) .... 133(1)	
(2) .... 133(2)	
(3) .... 133(2)	
(4) .... 133(3), (4)	

HOUSING ACT 1980—*continued*

Housing Act 1980—*continued*

1980	1985
s.41B(5)	s.108(4)
(6)	108(5)
42(1)	114(1)
(2)(a)	105(2)
(b)	105(3)
(c)	105(3)
(3)	105(2)
(4)	105(3)
(5)	105(4)
43(1)	105(1)
(2)	105(1)
(3)	105(5)
(4)	105(6)
(5)	105(6)
44(1)	106(1)
(2)	106(2)
(3)	106(3)
(4)	106(3)
(5)	106(4)
(6)	106(5)
45(1)	114(2)
(2)	114(3)
46(1)	107(1)
(2)	107(2)
48(1)	79(3)
(2)	79(4)
49(1)	80(2)
(2)	80(2)
(3)	109, 114(1)
(4)	80(3)
(5)	80(3)
50(1)	1, 80(4), 116
(1)	
"cemetery"	622
	"cemetery"
50(2)	112(1), (2)
(b)	184(1)
(3)	113(1), (2),
	186(1)(2)
72	s.389(1)
74(2)	6
81(1)	97(1)
(2)	97(1)
(3)	98(1), (2)
82(1)	98(1), (2)
81(5)	97(2), 187
82(2)	98(3), 99(2)
(3)	s.98(4)
(b)	99(3)
(4)	99(4)
83	99(5)
84	109
86(1)	110(1),
	181(1)
(2)	110(2),
	181(2)(3)
(3)	110(3),
	181(2)(3)
(4)	111(1),
	181(4)
(5)	111(2),
	181(4)
(6)	111(3),
	181(5)
87(1)	85(1)
(2)	85(2)
(3)	85(3)
(4)	85(4)
(5)	85(5)
(6)	85(5)

1980	1985
s.91(1)	ss.32(2)–(5),
	33(1)–(4), 437
92	34(2)–(4),
	35(1) (2),
	36(1)–(3),
	37(1)–(6),
	42(1)(2)
93(a)	17(2)
(b)	9(3)
95	19(2)(3)
96(1)(a)	421(1)
(c)	Sch. 15,
	Pt. III,
	paras. 2(3),
	3(2)
97(1), (2)	s.422(1), (2)
98(1), (2)	423(1), (2)
99(1)–(4)	424(1)–(4)
100(1)	425(1)
(2)	425(2)
(3)–(5)	425(3)–(5)
100(4), 105	
"year of	
account"	425(6)
s.101(1)	426(1)
(2)(b)	426(2)
s.101(3)(b)	s.426(3)
102(1)–(3)	427(1)–(3)
103(1)	Sch. 14,
	Pt. I,
	item 3
(1)–(3)	s.421(2)–(4)
104(1)(2)	Sch. 15,
	Pt. IV,
	para. 5(1)(2)
(4), (5)	426(4), (5)
105	
"year"	433
	"year"
105	
"year of	
account"	425(6)
105(1)	1
106(1)	463(3), (4)
(1)	463(1)
(2)	464(2)(5)
(3)	464(2)
(4)	503(2)
(5)	463(5)
108(1),	
(2), (4)	
"local	
authority"	429(1)
108(3)	429(2)
(4)	
"house"	429(4)
108(5)	Sch. 15,
	Pt. III,
	para. 3(1)
110(1), (2)	438(1),
	441(1)–(3)
(3)	Sch. 16,
	para. 1(1)(2)
(4)	Sch. 16,
	para. 2
(6)	Sch. 16,
	para. 3
(a)	Sch. 16,
	para. 4(1)

1980	1985
s.110(6)(b)	Sch. 16,
	para. 4(2)
(7)	Sch. 16,
	para. 4(3)(4)
(8)	Sch. 16,
	para.
	5(1)–(3)
(9)	Sch. 16,
	para.
	6(1)–(3)
(10)	Sch. 16,
	para.
	17(1)(2)
(11)	ss.438(2),
	441(1)–(3)
(12)	438(2),
	441(1)–(4)
(13)	s.438(2)
(14)	438(3)
111(1)	442(1)
(3)–(5)	442(2)–(4)
(5)(b)	442(5)
(8)	454
112, 113	
passim	Sch. 17,
	para. 4
112(1)	s.452(6)
112(2)	452(6),
	Sch. 17,
	para. 1(1)
(3)–(5)	Sch. 17,
	para.
	2(1)–(3)
(6)	Sch. 17,
	para. 1(2)
(7)	Sch. 17,
	para. 1(3)
(8)	Sch. 17,
	para. 2(4)
113(1)	Sch. 17,
	para. 3(1)
(2)	Sch. 17,
	para. 3(3)
(3)	Sch. 17,
	para. 3(4)
134(2)	Sch. 14, Pt. V,
	para. 1(1)
135(1)	419(1)
(2), (10)	
"housing	
stock"	419(2)
135(3), (10)	
"expenditure",	
"housing	
stock"	419(3)
135(4)–(6)	419(4)–(6)
(6)(9)	Sch. 14, Pt. I,
	item 8
(7)(a)	Sch. 14, Pt. II,
	item 3
(b)	Sch. 14, Pt. II,
	item 4
(8)	s.420(1)
(9)	419(7)
137(1)	44(1), (2)
(2)	44(3)

HOUSING ACT 1980—*continued*

Column 1

1980	1985
s.146	ss.358(1)–(4), 359(1)(2), 360(1)(2), 361(1)(2), 362(1), (2), 363(1)–(3), 364(1)(2)
149	190(1), (2), 207
151(1)	83(6), 96(4), 108(4), 130(5), 131(3), 133(6), 156(5), 157(8), 176(5), 178(3), 182(4), 365(4), 429(3), 441(5), 463(5), Sch. 1, para. 10, Sch. 4, para. 8(2), Sch. 7, para. 3(2)
(3)	83(6), 96(3), 108(4), 130(5), 131(3), 133(6), 156(5), 157(8), 176(5), 178(3), 182(4), 365(4), 429(3), 441(5), 463(5), Sch. 1, para. 10(5), Sch. 7, para. 3(2)
Sch. 1, Pt. I, para. 1(1)–(3)	Sch. 5, para. 5(1), (2)
para. 3	Sch. 5, para. 6, 7
3A	Sch. 5, para. 8
3B	Sch. 5, para. 9(1), (2)
4	Sch. 5, para. 10(1), (2)
5(1)	Sch. 5, para. 11(1)
5(2)	Sch. 5, para. 11(2)
6(1), (2)	Sch. 5, para. 12(1)
6(2)(a)	Sch. 5, para. 12(3)
6(3)	Sch. 5, para. 12(2)
Sch. 1, Pt. II, para. 1	s.121(1), (2)
2	121(1), (2)
Sch. 1A, Pt. II, para. 5	130(1)
6(1)	130(3)
(2)	130(3)

Column 2

1980	1985
Sch. 1A, Pt. II, para. 6(3)	s.130(3)
7(1)	130(4)
(2)	130(4)
8	130(3)
Pt. III, para. 10(1)	187, 130(2)(6)
(2)	130(2)
Sch. 1, para. 1	Sch. 3
(2)	s.116 "housing purposes"
(2), (3)	Sch. 2, Pt. I, ground 7, Pt. III, ground 12
(3)	Sch. 1, para. 2(1)
Sch. 1A, para. 1	Sch. 4, para. 1
para. 2(1)–(4)	Sch. 4, para. 2
(5)	Sch. 4, para. 3
Sch. 1A, para. 3(1)–(4)	Sch. 4, para. 5
para. 4(1)–(3)	Sch. 4, para. 4(1)–(3)
para. 9(1)	Sch. 4, para. 6(2)
(2)	Sch. 4, paras. 7(1)–(3), 8(1)
(3)	Sch. 4, para. 9
(4)	Sch. 4, para. 10
(5), (6)	Sch. 4, para. 6(3)(4)
para. 10(1) "armed forces occupier"	Sch. 4, para. 5
Sch. 1A, para. 10(1) "public sector tenant"	Sch. 4, para. 6(1)
Sch. 1A, para. 10(1) "regular armed forces of the Crown"	622 "regular armed forces of the Crown"

Column 3

1980	1985
Sch. 2	s.130(1)
paras. 1–4	Sch. 6, Pt. I, paras. 1–4
5	Sch. 6, Pt. I, para. 5
5A	Sch. 6, Pt. I, para. 6
6 (a)(b)	Sch. 6, Pt. I, para. 7
7	Sch. 6, Pt. II, para. 8
paras. 8, 9	Sch. 6, Pt. II, para. 9(1), (2)
para. 10	Sch. 6, Pt. II, para. 10
Sch. 2, para. 11(1)	Sch. 6, Pt. III, para. 11
(2)	Sch. 6, Pt. III, para. 12(1), (2)
(3)	Sch. 6, Pt. III, para. 12(3)
12	Sch. 6, Pt. III, para. 13
13(1)	Sch. 6, Pt. III, para. 14(1)
13(1A)	Sch. 6, Pt. III, para. 14(2)
(2)	Sch. 6, Pt. III, para. 14(3)
(3)	Sch. 6, Pt. III, para. 14(4)
para. 13A(1)–(4)	Sch. 6, Pt. III, para. 15(1)–(4)
14	Sch. 6, Pt. III, para. 16
para. 15(1)(a)	Sch. 6, Pt. III, para. 17(1)(2)
para. 15(1)(c)	Sch. 6, Pt. III, para. 19
(2)	Sch. 6, Pt. III, para. 18(1)
16(a)	Sch. 6, Pt. III, para. 18(2)
(c)	Sch. 6, Pt. III, para. 18(4)
paras. 16(b), 17(1), (2)	Sch. 6, Pt. III, para. 18(3)
para. 18(a)	Sch. 6, para. 21(2)
paras. 18(a), 19	Sch. 6, para. 21(1)
para. 18(b)	Sch. 6, para. 20
para. 19(4)	Sch. 6, para. 21(4)
Sch. 2, para. 19(1)–(3)	Sch. 6, para. 21(3)

HOUSING ACT 1980—*continued*

1980	1985
Sch. 2,	
para. 19A	.. s.179(1)
20	.....Sch. 6,
	para. 21(4)
Sch. 3,	
para. 1(1)	..Sch. 1,
	para. 1
(2)	.. s.115(1)(2)
(2A)	115(1)
(3)	.. 115(2)
2(1)	..Sch. 1,
	para. 2(1)
(2),	
2B(2)	..........Sch. 1,
	para. 2(5)
2A	....Sch. 1,
	para. 2(2)
2B(1)	Sch. 1,
	para. 2(3)
2C	....Sch. 3,
	para. 2(4)
4	......Sch. 1,
	para. 3
5	......Sch. 1,
	para. 4
6	......Sch. 1,
	para. 5
7	......Sch. 1,
	para. 6
8	......Sch. 1,
	para. 8
9	......Sch. 1,
	para. 7
10	.....Sch. 1,
	para. 9
11	.....Sch. 1,
	para.
	10(1)–(4)
12	.....Sch. 1,
	para. 11
13	.....Sch. 1,
	para. 12
Sch. 4, Pt. I,	
ground 1	....Sch. 2, Pt. I,
	ground 1
2	....Sch. 2, Pt. I,
	ground 2
3	.... s.116,
	Sch. 2, Pt. I,
	ground 3
4	 116,
	Sch. 2, Pt. I,
	ground 4
5	....Sch. 2, Pt. I,
	ground 5
5A	.Sch. 2, Pt. I,
	ground 6
5B	..Sch. 2, Pt. I,
	ground 7
6	....Sch. 2, para. I,
	ground 8
7	....Sch. 2, Pt. II,
	ground 9
8	....Sch. 2, Pt. II,
	ground 10
9	....Sch. 2, Pt. II,
	ground

1980	1985
Sch. 4, Pt. I,	
ground 9A	.Sch. 2, Pt. III,
	ground 12
10	..Sch. 2, Pt. III,
	ground 13
11	..Sch. 2, Pt. III,
	ground 14
12	..Sch. 2, Pt. III,
	ground 15
13	..Sch. 2, Pt. III,
	ground 16
Sch. 4, Pt. II,	
paras. 1(1),	
(2)	...............Sch. 2, Pt. IV,
	para. 1
para. 2	......Sch. 2, Pt. IV,
	paras. 2, 3
3	......Sch. 2, Pt. IV,
	para.
	4(1)–(3)
Sch. 4A	........Sch. 3
Sch. 11, Pt. II	Sch. 15, Pt. III,
	paras. 2(3),
	3(2)
Sch. 12,	
para. 1	...... s.463(1)
2	...... 461(4)
3	...... 508(3)
4	...... s.509(1)(2)
5	...... 464(3)(4)
6	...... 464(5)
7	...... 469(7)
9	 476
10(2)	. 478, 519
11	.... 481(1)–(3)
	(5), 519
12(1)	. 491(2)
(2)	. 492(1)(2)
13	.... 494(1)(2)
14(1)	. 497(3)
(2)	. 498(1)(2)
(3)	. 498(4)
15	..... 483(1)
16	 484,
	485(1)(2),
	486(2), 519
(2)	. 483(2)
17	..... 486(1)(2)
18(1)	. 488(1), (3),
	490(1)(2)(4)
19	..... s.489(1)–(4),
	(6)
20(1)	. 468(2), 519
(2)	. s.468(4)
(3)	. 493(1), 519
21	..... 500(3),
	501(3)
22	..... s.501(2)
23	..... 503(1)(3)
24	..... 503(2)
25	..... 511(3)
26(1)	. 463(1),
	486(2),
	494(2)

1980	1985
Sch. 12,	
para. 26(2)	. 465(1), (2),
	486(2), 494(2)
28	..... s.463(1)
29	..... 464(1)
30	..... 501(4)
32	..... 515(2)
Sch. 13,	
para. 1(1)	.. 253(1)
5	 259,
	259(2), (3),
	(4), (5)
9(2)	.. s.244(1), (5)
(3)	.. 244(3)
10	..... 245(2),
	245(3), (4), (5)
Sch. 20	.... s.30(2)
para. 1	...... 27(2)
2(1)	.. 27(1)
2(1)	.. 27(5)
2(2)	.. 27(5)
3	...... 27(1)
4	...... 27(3)
5	...... 27(4)
6	...... 27(6)
Sch. 23(3)(*b*)	. 355(2)
para. 2	...... 369(5)
4	...... 350(2)
5	...... 377(2)
5	...... 377(3)
6(1)	.. 376(1)
para. 7	...... s.387(5)
8(1)	.. 376(2)
9	...... 346(6),
	347(4)
para.	
33(3)(*a*)	.... s.356(2)
Sch. 24,	
para. 1	...... 365(1), (2)
2(1)	.. 366(1)–(3)
(2)	.. 366(3)
(3)	.. 366(2)
3	...... 368(1)
4	...... 366(1)
5	...... 368(2)
6	...... 368(4)
7	...... 368(3)
8	...... 365(3)
9	...... 368(6)
10	..... 398(3),
	399 "house"
11	..... s.368(5)
12	..... 367(1)–(3),
	375(1) 376(1),
	(2),
	378(1)(2),
	381(4), 395(2),
	397(1)(2)
Sch. 25,	
para. 7	...... s.29(1), (2)
8	......Sch. 22,
	para. 4(2)
20	..... s.25(1)
21	..... 259(5)
26	..... 234(1)–(3)
28(1)	.Sch. 11,
	para. 1(1),
	(2)
. (3)(*a*)	... s.299(2)

HOUSING ACT 1980—*continued*

1980	1985
Sch. 25,	
para. 29	.....Sch. 11,
	para. 4(2)(3)

1980	1985
Sch. 12,	
para. 30	..... 469(5),
	471(6),
	472(4), 481(5),
	489(6), 491(3),
	492(3), 497(3),
	508(3), 509(2),
	517(2)

1980	1985
Sch. 12,	
para. 31	.....Sch. 11,
	9
52	.....Sch. 15, Pt. II,
	para. 2(3)(4)

LOCAL GOVERNMENT PLANNING AND LAND ACT 1980

1980	1985
s.156(2)(*a*)	... s.80(1)
156(2)(*b*)	... 114(1)
Sch. 6,	
paras.	
7(*a*)(i), 8	.......Sch. 10,
	para. 4
Sch. 6,	
para. 9	......Sch. 13,
	para. 4(2)
17	..... s.506(1), (2)

1980	1985
Sch. 6,	
para. 18	..... s.515(2)
19	..... 512(4)
20	.....Sch. 10,
	para. 4
Sch. 33,	
para. 6(3)	.. s.589(4)–(6)
8(1)	..Sch. 13,
	paras. 7, 8

1980	1985
Sch. 33,	
para. 8(2)	..Sch. 13,
	paras. 11(1),
	12
(3)	..Sch. 13,
	paras.
	11(1)(2),
	13(1)(2)

SUPREME COURT ACT 1981

1981	1985
Sch. 5	..........Sch. 18,
	para. 6(5)

NEW TOWNS ACT 1981

1981	1985
Sch. 12,	
para. 13(*c*)	. s.232(2)
27(*d*)	. 30(2)

ACQUISITION OF LAND ACT 1981

1981	1985
Sch. 4,	
para. 1	...... s.578

SOCIAL SECURITY AND HOUSING BENEFITS ACT 1982

1982	1985
s.32(4)(*a*)(i)	.Sch. 14, Pt. I,
	item 4
Sch. 4,	
para. 6(4)	..Sch. 14, Pt.
	IV,
	para. 3

CRIMINAL JUSTICE ACT 1982

1982	1985
s.37	............ss.55(2), 74(4),
	249(1), 249(1),
	261, 264(6),
	270(5), 277,
	286(3), 320,
	327(1) to (3),
	331(3), 333(3),
	335(2), 336(3),
	341(2), 346(6),
	347(4), 350(2),
	355(2), 356(2),
	358(4), 364(2),
	368(3), 369(5),
	376(1)(2),
	377(3), 387,
	396(2), 408(2)
	412(2),
	601(1)(2),
	618(4)

1982	1985
s.37(2)	........ss.198(1), (2),
	223(2)
38(9)	.... s.249(1)
39	............ss.264(6),
	270(5), 277,
	368(3)
46	.... 198(1), (2),
	223(2)
(1)	.... 55(2), 74(4),
	249(1), 261,
	264(6), 270(5),
	277, 286(3),
	320, 327(1)
	to (3), 331(3),
	333(3), 335(2),
	336(3), 341(2),
	346(6), 347(4),
	350(2), 355(2),
	356(2), 358(4),

1982	1985
s.46(1)	.... s.364(2),
	368(3), 369(5),
	376(1)(2),
	377(3), 387(5),
	396(2), 408(2),
	412(2),
	601(1)(2),
	618(4)
74(1)	.... s.622
	"statutory
	maximum"
75(*a*)	.... s.622
	"standard
	scale"
Sch. 3	..........ss.270(5),
	277, 368(3)

TELECOMMUNICATIONS ACT 1984

1984	1985
Sch. 4,	
para. 1	s.298(1)
para. 35	s.298(2)
para. 35(1) .	s.298(1)(3)

PUBLIC HEALTH (CONTROL OF DISEASES) ACT 1984

1984	1985
Sch. 2,	
para. 2	s.409

COUNTY COURTS ACT 1984

1984	1985
Sch. 2,	
para. 27	s.582(7)
28	Sch. 13,
	para. 17(4)

HOUSING AND BUILDING CONTROL ACT 1984

1984	1985
s.1(2)	s.118(1)
(3)	Sch. 5, para. 4
2(1)	s.116, Sch. 2, Pt. I, ground 7, Pt. III, ground 12, Sch. 5, para. 5(1)(2)
(2)	Sch. 1, para. 2(1), Sch. 5, para. 6, 7, 8, 9(1)(2), 10(1)(2)
(3)	Sch. 5, para. 11(1)(2)
3(1)	s.119(1)
(2)	ss.119(2), 129(1)(3), 130(1)
(3)	s.131(1)
(3)(5), ...	130(1) to (4), (6), 187, 622 "regular armed forces of the Crown", Sch. 4, paras. 1 to 3, 4(1) to (3), 5, 6(1) to (4), 7(1) to (3), 8(1), 9
4(2)	s.183(2), (3)
(3)	184(2), (3)
(4)	184(4)
5(1)	155(2)
(2)	ss.159, 160(1), 160(2), 161, 162
(4)	s.156(2)
(5)	156(4), (6)
(6)	163(1)
6(1)	138(1)
(2)	140(1)(2)(4)
(3)	ss.140(3), 152(3)
(4)	s.141(1)–(4)
(5)	ss.141(5), 142(5)

1984	1985
s.6(6)	s.140(5)
7(1)	Sch. 6, Pt. I, para. 5, 6
(2)(a), (b)	Sch. 6, Pt. II, para. 9(1), (2)
(3)	Sch. 6, Pt. III, para. 18(2) to (4)
8(1)	s.157(1)
(2)	157(2)
(3)	157(4), 158(1)
(4)	158(2)
(5)	158(3)
(7)	162
(8)	159, 160(1), 163(1)
9	167(1), (2), 168(1)–(5)
10	169(1), (2), (3)
11	170(1)–(6)
12(1)	143(1), 151(1)
(2)	143(1)
13(1)	144(1), 146
(2)(a)	144(1)
(2)(b)	144(2)
(3)–(5) ...	144(3)–(5)
14(1)	147(1)
(1)(a)	147(2)
(1)(b)	147(2)
(1)(c)	147(3)
(1)(d)	147(4)
(2)	147(5)
15	149
16(1)	151(4), Sch. 9, para. 1(1)(2)
(2)	Sch. 9, para. 1(3)
(3)	Sch. 9, para. 2
(4), (5) ...	Sch. 9, para. 3(1)
(6)	Sch. 9, para. 4(1), (2)

1984	1985
s.16(7)	Sch. 3(2)
(8)	Sch. 9, para. 5
(9), (10) .	Sch. 9, para. 4(3)
17(1)	ss.150(1), 151(1)
(2)	151(3)
(3)	152(1), (2)
(4)	152(4)
(5)	152(3)
(6)	153(1), (2)
(7)	153(3), (4)
(8)	153(3), (4)
(9)(a)	150(2)
(9)(b)	153(5)
(10)	150(3)
(11)	151(2)
(12)	152(5)
18(1)	45(1)(2)
(1)(b)	46(1)
(3)	45(2), 171(2), 444(4), 452(1)(2), 453(2)
18(4)	45(2)
"conveyance", "grant", 20(5)	
"relevant advice"	444(4), 452(1)(2)
"long lease" ..	458
	"long lease"
19(1)	452(1)(2)
(2)	452(5)
(3)	452(3)
(4)	452(4)
20(1)	442(1)
(2)–(4) ...	442(2)–(4)
(4)(b)	442(5)
(5)	
"recognised body"	444(1)(2)
"relevant advice"	444(4)
20(6)	444(3)
(7)	454

Housing and Building Control Act 1984—*continued*

1984	1985
s.22(1)	.... s.43(1)
(2)	.... 43(1)
(3)	.... 43(2)
(4)	.... 43(3)
(5)	.... 43(4)
(7)	.... 44(1), (2)
(8)	.... 43(5)
24(1)	.... 453(1)
25(1)	........Sch. 2, Pt. I, grounds 6, 7
25(2)	........Sch. 2, Pt. III, ground 12
25(3)	........Sch. 2, Pt. III, ground 16
26(1)	........ss.89(3)(4), 90(3)(4), 91(1) to (3), 92(1) to (6), 93(2), 95(1)(2)
(2),	
Sch. 7	..........Sch. 3
s.27	.... 101(1)–(4)
(5), (6)	... 532(2)
28	.... 96(1)(2)(5)
29	.... 108(1)–(5)
30(1)	.... 171(1)
(2)	.... 171(1), (2)
(3)	.... 171(3)
(4)	.... 171(3)
31	.... 179(2)
32(1)–(4)	... 177(1)–(4)
36(1)	.... 80(1)
(2)	........Sch. 1, para. 2(2)–(5)
(3)	........Sch. 1, para. 5
38(1)	........ss.183(1), 184(1), 186(1), (2)
Sch. 1,	
para. 1	...... 126(2)
2	...... 127(3)
3	 137
4	...... 138(1)
5	...... 139(1)
6	......Sch. 7, paras. 2(1), (2),3(1)
7	...... s.154(1), (2), (3), (4), (6)
8(*a*)	.. 165(3)
(*b*)	.. 165(4)
(*c*)	... 165(5)
9	......Sch. 5, para. 12(3)
10(1)	.Sch. 6, Pt. III, paras. 11, 12(1) to (3), 13
10(2)	.Sch. 6, Pt. III, para. 14(1)
10(3)	
(*c*)	....Sch. 6, Pt. III, para. 14(2)
10(3)	
(*d*)	....Sch. 6, Pt. III, para. 14(3)

1984	1985
Sch. 1,	
para. 10(4)	.Sch. 6, Pt. III, para. 15(1) to (4)
10(5)	.Sch. 2, para. 16
10(6)	.Sch. 6, Pt. I, para. 17(1)(2), Pt. III, paras. 18(1), 19
11	..... s.128(6)
(2)	.Sch. 6, para. 20
(3)	. s.179(1)
12	..... 115(1)
Sch. 2	..........ss.130(2) to (4)(6),187, 622 "regular armed forces of the Crown", Sch. 4, paras. 1 to 3, 4(1) to)3), 5, 6(1) to (4), 7(1) to (3), 8(1), 9
Sch. 3,	
para. 1(1)	.. s.144(1)
(2)	.. 145(1)
(3)	..Sch. 8, para. 1(1)
(4)	.. s.145(3)
(5)	.. 145(2)
2(1)	.. 148(1)
(2)	.. 148(2)
3(1)	..Sch. 8, para. 1(1)(2)
(2)	..Sch. 8, para. 1(2)
(3)	..Sch. 8, para. 1(1)
(4)	..Sch. 8, para. 1(3)
(5)	..Sch. 8, para. 2(1), (2)
(6)	..Sch. 8, para. 2(3)
(7)	..Sch. 8, para. 2(4)
(8)	..Sch. 8, paras. 1(4), 2(5)
(9)	
"total share"	.. s.187
4(1)	..Sch. 8, paras. 3(1), 11(1)
(2)	..Sch. 8, para. 3(2)
Sch. 3,	
para. 4(3)	..Sch. 8, para. 11(2)– (4)
5(1)	..Sch. 8, para. 4(1)
(2)	..Sch. 8, para. 4(3)
(3)	..Sch. 8, para. 5

1984	1985
Sch. 3,	
para. 5(4)	..Sch. 8, para. 4(2)
(5)	..Sch. 8, para. 4(4)
(6)	..Sch. 8, para. 4(6)
6(1)	.. 155(1), (3)
(2)	.. 155(3)
(3)	.. s.148(1), Sch. 8, para. 3(1)
(4)	.. 159
(5)	.. 160(1)
(*d*)	.. 161
(6)	.. 160(2)
(7)	.. 162
(8)	.. 159
(9)	.. 163(1)
(10)	156(1)–(6), Sch. 6, para. 6(3)
7(1)	..Sch. 8, para. 6(1), (2)
(1)(*b*	161
(2)	..Sch. 8, paras. 6(1) (2), 11(1)
(3)	..Sch. 8, para. 11(2) to (4)
(4)	..Sch. 6, para. 7
(5)	..Sch. 6, para. 8(1), (2)
(6)–(8)	..Sch. 6, para. 8(3)– (5)
8(1),	
(2)	..Sch. 8, para. 9(1), (2)
9(1),	
(2)	..Sch. 8, para. 10(1), (2)
10(1)	. 145(4), (5), Sch. 8, para. 4(5)
(2)	. 145(4), (5), Sch. 8, para. 4(5)
Sch. 4,	
para. 1(2)	.. s.46(2), (3)
2	...... 47(1)(2)
3	...... 47(1)
4(1)	.. 48(1)
(1)	.. s.48(2)
(2)	.. 48(3), (4)
(3)	.. 48(3), (4)
(4)	.. 48(1)
5(1)	.. 49(1), (2)
(2)	.. 49(1), (2)
6	...... 48(5)
7	...... 48(6)
8	...... 47(3)

HOUSING AND BUILDING CONTROL ACT 1984—*continued*

1984	1985
Sch. 4,	
para. 9(1)	.. s.50(1)
(2),	
(3)	.. 613(1), (2)
10(1)	
(a)	. 50(2)
10(1)	
(b)	. 51(6)
(2)	.ss.50(2), 51(6)
11	..... s.51(1)
(1)	. 51(2)
(2)	. 51(3), (4)
11(2)	
(b)	. 51(5)
11(3)	. 51(3), (4)
12	..... 46(4)
13	..... 46(4)
Sch. 5,	
1(1)	Sch. 17,
	para. 1(1)
(2)	..Sch. 17,
	para. 1(2)
(3)	..Sch. 17,
	para. 1(3)
2(1)–	
(3)	..Sch. 17,
	para. 2(1)–
	(3)
(4)	..Sch. 17,
	para. 2(4)
3(1)	..Sch. 17,
	para. 3(1)
(2)	..Sch. 17,
	para. 3(2)
(3)	..Sch. 17,
	para. 3(3)
(4)	..Sch. 17,
	para. 3(4)
Sch. 6,	
para. 1(1)	.. s.35(2)
(2)	..ss.38, 39(1)(2),
	40, 41, 56
	"member of
	family"
(3)	.. 36(1)

1984	1985
Sch. 6,	
para. (4)	.. s.36(2)
(5)	.. 36(4)
(6)	.. 42(1)
2(1)	.. 37(1)
(2)	.. 37(2)
(4)	..ss.38, 41
(5)	.. s.37(1)
(6)	.. 42(1)
Sch. 11,	
para. 2(1)	.. 172(1)
(2)	.. 174
(3)	.. 174
(4)	.. 173(1), (2)
(5)	.. 175(1)
(6)	..ss.172(2)–(4),
	175(2)–(5)
6	...... s.184(2), (3)
7	...... 143(2)
8(1)	.. 124(2)
(2)	.. 124(3)
9	...... 127(4),
	Sch. 5,
	para. 12(2)
10(1)	. 125(1)
(2)	. 125(2)
(3)	. 125(4),
	Sch. 6, Pt. III,
	para. 18(5)
(4)	. 125(5)
12	..... 135(3)
13(1)	. 136(1), (2)
(2)	. 136(1), (2)
14(1),	
(2)	..Sch. 9,
	para. 6
15(1)	. 157(1)
15(2)	
(a)	. 160(1)
15(2)	
(b)	. 158(2)
(2)	
(c)	.ss.158(3), 159
15(2)	
(d)	. 162

1984	1985
Sch. 11,	
para. 16(a)	. s.154(1)
(b)	. 154(6)
17(1)	. 178(1), (2)
17(2)	
(a)	. 178(1)
17(2)	
(b)	. 178(1), (2)
18(1)	. 176(2)
(2)	. 176(1), (3),
	(4)
19(2)	. 166(4)
(3)	. 166(6)
(4)	. 164(1)–(5)
20(1)	. 165(2)
(2)	. 165(2)
21	.....ss.45(3),
	167(1),
	168(1), 169(3),
	170(1), (2),
	(3), 180
22	..... s.185(1), (2)
23	..... 88(2), (3)
24	 622
	"cemetery"
25(1)	. 110(2)
25(2)	.ss.45(3), 181(1)
26	..... s.438(1)
28	..... 44(1), (2)
30	..... 156(5)
31	..... 130(2)
32	.....ss.151(1),
	179(1),
	Sch. 8,
	para. 2(4)
33(1)	. s.115(1)
(2)	.Sch. 1,
	para. 2(1)
(3)	.Sch. 1,
	para. 8
34	.....Sch. 2, Pt. I,
	ground 8

HOUSING DEFECTS ACT 1984

1984	1985
s.1(1)–(3)	.. s.528(1)–(3)
(4)	.... 529(1)–(3)
(5)	..........ss.528(5)(6),
	529(4)
(6)	.... s.528(5), (6)
(7)	.... 528(4)
2(1)	 527
(2), (3)	.... 531(1)–(4)
(4), (5)	.... 533(1), (2)
(6)	.... 532(1)
(7)	 527
(8)(a)	...... 530(1)
(b)	...... 530(4)
(c)	...... 532(4)
(d)	...... 532(3)
(9), (10)	... 530(2), (3)
3(1)	 534
(2)	.... 537(1)
(3)	.... 537(2), (3)
(4)	.... 538(1)
(5)	.... 537(2)(3)
(6)	.... 538(2)

1984	1985
s.3(6)(a)	...... s.583(3)
(b)	...... 538(4)
(7)	.... 539(1)
(8)	.... 535(1)(3)
(9)	.... 535(2)(3)
(10)	.... 565(1)
4(1)	.... 536(1)–(3)
(2)	.... 540(1), (2)
(3)–(5)	..... 540(3)–(5)
(6)	.... 539(2)
5(1), (2)	.... 541(1), (2)
(3)	.... 542(4)
(3)–(5)	..... 542(1)–(3)
6(1)	..........Sch. 20, Pt. I,
	paras. 1,
	2(1)
(2)	..........Sch. 20, Pt. I,
	para. 3
(3)	..........Sch. 20, Pt. I,
	para. 4
(4)	..........Sch. 20, Pt. I,
	para. 5

1984	1985
s.6(5)	..........Sch. 20,
	para. 6(1)
(6)(a)	......Sch. 20, Pt. I,
	para. 2(2)
(b)	......Sch. 20, Pt. I,
	para. 6(2)
(7)	..........Sch. 20
	para. 18
8(1), (2)	.... s.550(1), (2)
(3)	.... 550(3)–(5)
(4)	.... 551(1)
(5)	.... 551(2)
(6)	.... 551(3)
(7)	.... 551(5)
(8)	.... 551(4)
(9)	.... 550(6)
(10)(a),	
9(11)	.... 565(2)
(1)–(4)	..... 549(1)–(4)
(5)	..........ss.553(1),
	554(1)(2),
	555(1)

HOUSING DEFECTS ACT 1984—*continued*

Building Act 1984
1984	1985

s.89(2), Sch.
5,
para. 2 .... s.622
"building
regulations"

Companies Consolidation (Consequential Provisions) Act 1985
1985	1985

Sch. 2 .... s.51(2)(5)

Local Government Act 1985
1985	1985

s.94(1) .... s.619(2)
Sch. 8,
  para. 14(3) . 15(3)
Sch. 14,
  para.
58(*c*)(*i*) ....Sch. 16,
                  para. 4(3)

Destinations for Statutory Instruments

Isles of Scilly (Housing) Order 1972
1972	1985

S.I. 1972
  No. 1204 ....ss.1, 620(1)(2)

Isles of Scilly (Housing) (No. 2) Order 1973
1973	1985

S.I. 1983
  No. 886 .....ss.1, 620(1),
                  (2)

Order 1974
1974	1985

S.I. 1974
  No. 1791 ....Sch. 19,
                  para. 2(1)

Isles of Scilly (Housing) Order 1975
1975	1985

S.I. 1975
  No. 512 .....ss.1, 620(1),
                  (2)

Isles of Scilly (Functions) Order 1985
1979	1985

S.I. 1972
  No. 72 .... s.1

Local Authority Contributions (Disposal of Dwellings) Order 1981
1981	1985

S.I. 1981
  No. 723 ..... s.429(2)

the Crown Court Rules 1982
1982	1985

S.I. 1982
  No. 1109
Sch. 3, Pt. II,
  para. 1 ...... s.200(5)

Grants by Local Authorities (Eligible Expense Limits) Order 1983
1983	1985

S.I. 1983
  No.   613,
Art. 6 .... s.508(1)

1985 *c.* 68 **68**

Housing (Northern Ireland Consequential Amendments) Order 1983

1983   **1985**

S.I. 1983
No.   1122,
Art. 2(2) ss.454, 458
"the
corresponding
Northern
Ireland
provisions"

Consolidation of the Housing Acts (Cmnd. 9515) Recommendations

R. .... s.622 "bank"
R. ....Sch. 4,
              para. 10
R. ....Sch. 23,
              para. 1(5)(6)
R. ....Sch. 23,
              para. 2(5)(6)
R.1(i) .... s.13(2)
R.1(ii) 609
R.2 .... 20(1)(2)
R.3 ....ss.27(1), 30(2)
R.4(i) s.343
              "dwelling"
R.4(iii) 31
R.5 ....ss.64(5), 68(4)
R.6 .... 85(1)
R.7 ....ss.156(1),
              165(5)
R.8 .... 170(1)
R.9(i) ....ss.229(5),
              270(4), 338(3),
              373(1)(2),
              Sch. 10,
              para.
              2(1)–(4),
              para. 5(3)
R.9(iii) .... 191(1),
              267(3),
              269(1)–(3),
              272(5), 278(2),
              285(1)(2),
              300(2), 317(1),
              Sch. 10,
              para.
              6(1)–(4)

R.10 .... s.200(6),
              229(6)
R.11 .... 201(1)–(3),
              230 (2)
R.12 .... s.202
R.13 205
R.14(i) 622
              "statutory
              tenancy",
              Sch. 22,
              para. 3(3)
R.14(ii) ....ss.247(5),
              368(6)
R.15 .... s.249(2)
R.16(i) s.276
R.16(ii) .... 307(1), (2)
R.16(iii) .... 319(1), (2)
R.16(iv) .... 317(1)
R.17 .... 332(1), (2)
R.18(i) .... 358(1)
R.18(ii) .... 398(2)
R.19 ....ss.366(3),
              384(2),
              Sch. 13,
              para. 3(1)
R.20(i) .... s.395(1)
R.20(i) .... 395(2)
R.20(ii) .... 397(1)
R.20(ii) .... 397(2)
R.21 .... 436(3)
R.22 .... 436(5), (6)
R.22 .... 441(1)–(3)
R.23 .... 463(1)
R.23 .... 463(2)
R.23 .... 464(2)

R.24(i) .... s.474(2)
R.24(ii) .... 483(2)
R.25 .... 584(1)–(3)
R.26(ii) 598
R.27 609
R.27 607
R.27 .... 614(1), (2)
R.27 .... 615(1), (2)
R.27 616
R.27 .... 617(1)–(3)
R.28 .... 613(1), (2)
R.29 .... 620(1), (2)
R.30(i) ....Sch. 10,
              para.
              2(1)–(4)
R.30(ii) ....Sch. 10,
              para.
              3(1)–(2)
R.30(iii) ....Sch. 10,
              para. 5(1)
R.30(iv) ....Sch. 10,
              para.
              7(1)–(4)
R.30(iv), (v) ..Sch. 10,
              para.
              6(1)–(4)
R.31 ....Sch. 11,
              para.
              12(1)–(3)
R.31 ....Sch. 22,
              para. 6
R.37(i) .... s.291(1),
              (2)(4)

68–779

HOUSING ASSOCIATIONS ACT 1985*

(1985 *c.* 69)

Tables of derivations and destinations can be found at the end of the Act.

ARRANGEMENT OF SECTIONS

PART I

REGULATION OF HOUSING ASSOCIATIONS

---

* Annotations by Andrew Arden, LL.B., Barrister, and James Ramage, B.A., Barrister.

An Act to consolidate certain provisions of the Housing Acts relating to housing associations, with amendments to give effect to recommendations of the Law Commission and of the Scottish Law Commission.

PARLIAMENTARY DEBATES

Hansard: H.L. Vol. 463, col. 531; Vol. 464, col. 170; Vol. 466, col. 322, 864; Vol. 467, cols. 1560 to 1569; H.C. Vol. 84, cols. 116, 966.

PART I

REGULATION OF HOUSING ASSOCIATIONS

Introductory

Meaning of "housing association" and related expressions

1.—(1) In this Act "housing association" means a society, body of trustees or company—

    (*a*) which is established for the purpose of, or amongst whose objects or powers are included those of, providing, constructing, improving or managing, or facilitating or encouraging the construction or improvement of, housing accommodation, and

    (*b*) which does not trade for profit or whose constitution or rules prohibit the issue of capital with interest or dividend exceeding such rate as may be prescribed by the Treasury, whether with or without differentiation as between share and loan capital.

(2) In this Act "fully mutual", in relation to a housing association, means that the rules of the association—

    (*a*) restrict membership to persons who are tenants or prospective tenants of the association, and

    (*b*) preclude the granting or assignment of tenancies to persons other than members;

and "co-operative housing association" means a fully mutual housing association which is a society registered under the Industrial and Provident Societies Act 1965 (in this Part referred to as "the 1965 Act").

(3) In this Act "self-build society" means a housing association whose object is to provide, for sale to, or occupation by, its members, dwellings built or improved principally with the use of its members' own labour.

DEFINITIONS
"dwelling": s.106.
"hostel": s.106.

GENERAL NOTE
This section defines the principal organisations with which this Act is concerned, *i.e.* "housing associations" as described.

The term "housing association" is commonly used loosely, to refer to a number of different organisations: conventional "landlord/tenant" associations and trusts (see also s.2, below), co-ownership societies (meaning those where the tenants have an interest in the equity of the association's property), co-operatives (meaning those where the tenants' interest is limited to a "par value" share, usually £1, so that they do not benefit from increase in values), and "management co-operatives", being those to whom local authorities, new town corporations or the Development Board for Rural Wales, may pass management responsibilities for housing, *e.g.*, an estate, under ss.27, 30, Housing Act 1985.

The legal definition of housing association in subs. (1) was first contained in the Housing Act 1935 and remained in the same form until amended by the Housing Act 1974. Housing associations are not legal bodies as such: the term is of generic application to a number of legal entities engaged in common activities. It is the definition of activity, under sub-paras. (*a*) and (*b*) which govern whether or not one of the three specified bodies is properly a housing association for the purposes of this Act, and also the Housing Act 1985 which contains the provisions governing security of tenure and the "right to buy", so far as they apply to housing association tenants.

The three classes of body specified are: society, body of trustees or company. A "society" is not further defined by this subsection, but note that only societies which are registered under the Industrial and Provident Societies Act 1965 can be registered as a housing association with the Housing Corporation, under s.4, below. The reference to "trustees" covers charities, which will commonly be established by trust deed. Charities are subject to the jurisdiction of the Charity Commissioners, and governed by the provisions of the Charities Act 1960. The Commissioners maintain a register of charities and charity trustees are obliged to apply for registration. The third class of body is a "company" *i.e.* a body which is incorporated under the Companies Act 1985. Incorporation carries with it a number of obligations, and places the company under the jurisdiction of the Registrar of Companies in relation to compliance with them.

The qualifying purpose, objects and powers of a specified body are provided by subs. (1)(*a*): a housing association may be a body providing housing, improving housing or managing housing or hostels. It may also be a body which serves to facilitate or encourage the construction or improvement of housing (*i.e.* a "secondary association"). The definition is not limited to bodies engaged exclusively in these tasks. Note however the more restrictive requirements imposed on associations wishing to register with the Housing Corporation, *i.e.* in order to qualify for funding assistance: s.4, below. Under subs. (1)(*b*) the association must not trade for profit, or if it does, must not issue capital with interest or dividend exceeding the Treasury prescribed rate. The rate referred to is 5 per cent. per annum: Statutory Rules and Orders of 1934 No. 913, applying to "public utility societies" and, *semble*, including housing associations.

Subs. (2)
This subsection introduces two additional qualifications for subsequent use in this Act: a housing association the rules of which restrict membership to tenants or prospective tenants and preclude the grant or assignment of property to non-members is "fully mutual", and if registered under the 1965 Act becomes a "co-operative housing association".

Subs. (3)
This subsection defines a particular species of collectively oriented housing association which may receive assistance by way of Housing Corporation loans, under s.79, below. This is an exception to the normal scheme of funding assistance to housing associations, where

registration with the Corporation is a prerequisite. Although a "self-build" association may be able to qualify for registration under the Industrial and Provident Societies Act 1965 (and be entitled thereby to apply for registration with the Corporation, under s.4, below), many such associations will not be so eligible. Associations falling within this subsection may nevertheless receive loan assistance (but not Housing Association Grant: see s.41) notwithstanding that they are not registered with the Housing Corporation.

Meaning of "housing trust"

2. In this Act "housing trust" means a corporation or body of persons which—
   (a) is required by the terms of its constituent instrument to use the whole of its funds, including any surplus which may arise from its operations, for the purpose of providing housing accommodation, or
   (b) is required by the terms of its constituent instrument to devote the whole, or substantially the whole, of its funds to charitable purposes and in fact uses the whole, or substantially the whole, of its funds for the purpose of providing housing accommodation.

GENERAL NOTE
   This section defines a "housing trust" for the purposes of the Act. Many housing trusts are registered charities under the Charities Act 1960, and thereby qualify for registration with the Housing Corporation, under s.4, below. Since a housing trust, as defined, will necessarily qualify as a housing association under s.1, above, the need for this further definition is at first sight unclear. However, there are residual distinctions: see, *e.g.*, ss.35, 36, below.

Registration

The register

3.—(1) A register of housing associations shall be maintained by the Housing Corporation and shall be open to inspection at the head office of the Corporation at all reasonable times.
   (2) In this Act "registered" and "unregistered", and other references to registration, in relation to a housing association, refer to registration in the register of housing associations maintained under this section.

DEFINITION
   "housing association": s.1.

GENERAL NOTE
   The Housing Act 1974 introduced the now all-important concept of "registration" of housing associations with the Housing Corporation. The Corporation was itself established by the Housing Act 1964, but with a much more limited role than it now enjoys. With the exception of "self-build societies" as defined in s.1, registration with the Corporation is a prerequisite to an association obtaining central and local government funding, under Pt. II, below, and is the lynch pin of the system of Housing Corporation regulation and control of housing associations provided by the following sections in this part of the Act. In 1985 a total of 2,642 housing associations were on the Corporation's register: H.C. Annual Report 1984/5. Ss.4, 5, below, set out the conditions of eligibility and criteria to be satisfied by associations seeking registration.

Eligibility for registration

4.—(1) A housing association is eligible for registration if it is—
   (a) a registered charity, or
   (b) a society registered under the 1965 Act which fulfils the following conditions.

(2) The conditions are that the association does not trade for profit and is established for the purpose of, or has among its objects or powers, the provision, construction, improvement or management of—

(*a*) houses to be kept available for letting, or

(*b*) houses for occupation by members of the association, where the rules of the association restrict membership to persons entitled or prospectively entitled (as tenants or otherwise) to occupy a house provided or managed by the association, or

(*c*) hostels,

and that any additional purposes or objects are among the following.

(3) The permissible additional purposes or objects are—

(*a*) providing land or buildings for purposes connected with the requirements of the persons occupying the houses or hostels provided or managed by the association;

(*b*) providing amenities or services for the benefit of those persons, either exclusively or together with other persons;

(*c*) acquiring, or repairing and improving, or creating by the conversion of houses or other property, houses to be disposed of on sale or on lease;

(*d*) building houses to be disposed of on shared ownership leases;

(*e*) encouraging and giving advice on the formation of other housing associations which would be eligible for registration by the Corporation;

(*f*) providing services for, and giving advice on the running of, registered housing associations;

(*g*) effecting transactions falling within section 45(1) (acquisition and disposal of house at discount to tenant of charitable body).

DEFINITIONS

"hostel": s.106.

"house": s.106.

"housing association": s.1.

"1965 Act": s.37.

"registered": s.3.

"registered charity": s.38.

"shared ownership lease": s.106.

GENERAL NOTE

This section sets out the requirements for eligibility for registration with the Housing Corporation under s.5, below. Unconditional eligibility is conferred on associations which are registered charities (*i.e.* charities which are registered under s.4, Charities Act 1960, and not "exempt charities" within the meaning of that Act: s.38, below). Registration of associations which are 1965 Act societies is conditional upon compliance with the provisions of subs. (2) and (3).

Subs. (2)

This subsection restricts eligibility to non-profit making associations existing for a primary purpose of housing provision, improvement or management of dwellings for letting; for occupation by the association's own members where the association is fully mutual; and hostel provision. If the association has other purposes or objects, they must qualify under subs. (3).

"Trading for profit". The fact that an activity of an association produces a profit does not mean that it trades for profit; the term means trading for profit in the sense of profit which may be extracted from the organisation, to be used and enjoyed by its proprietors, as distinct from profits which must be kept within, or ploughed back into, the activities of the organisation: *Goodman* v. *Dolphin Square Trust Ltd.* (1979) 38 P. & C.R. 257, C.A.

Subs. (3)

The list of additional permissible purposes or objects is exhaustive. Note the inclusion (from s.127, Housing Act 1980), to include the acquisition and development (other than by new building) of housing for disposal by sale or lease, and the building of housing for disposal on shared ownership ("equity share") leases; see note to s.43, below, for an explanation of the scheme of acquisition and disposal of housing to tenants of charitable housing associations, referred to at sub-para. (*g*).

"Land" includes "buildings and other structures, land covered with water, and any estate, interest, easement, servitude or right in or over land": Interpretation Act 1978, Sched.1.

Registration

5.—(1) The Housing Corporation may register any housing association which is eligible for registration but—

(*a*) the Corporation shall establish criteria which should be satisfied by a housing association seeking registration, and

(*b*) in deciding whether to register an association the Corporation shall have regard to whether it satisfies those criteria.

(2) The Corporation may vary the criteria established by them under subsection (1).

(3) As soon as may be after registering a housing association the Corporation shall give notice of the registration—

(*a*) if the association is a registered charity, to the Charity Commissioners, or

(*b*) if the association is a society registered under the 1965 Act, to the appropriate registrar,

who shall record the registration.

(4) For all purposes other than rectification of the register a body shall be conclusively presumed to be, or to have been, a housing association eligible for registration at any time when it is, or was, on the register.

DEFINITIONS

"appropriate register": s.37.
"housing association": s.1.
"1965 Act": s.37.
"registered charity": s.3.
"registration": s.3.

GENERAL NOTE

This section provides for the discretionary registration of associations which comply with the criteria of eligibility set out under s.4, and with their own additional criteria.

The Housing Corporation, after consultation with the Housing Associations Registration Advisory Committee appointed by the Secretary of State has issued a document HAR 1/2 which sets out the criteria. The main requirements relate to proper control of the association by its managing body, a sound financial basis, adequate standards of development and housing management skills, and the intended role of the association in relation to housing needs within the area where it proposes to operate.

Subs. (4)

The only way to challenge registration is by means of a prerogative order compelling the Housing Corporation to use its powers under ss.6, 16, 17 or 22, below, and *not* by way of action for a declaration by an individual aggrieved that the housing association does not fulfil the statutory criteria: *Goodman* v. *Dolphin Square Trust Ltd.* (1979) 38 P. & C.R. 257, C.A.

Removal from the register

6.—(1) A body which has been registered shall not be removed from the register except in accordance with this section.

(2) If it appears to the Housing Corporation that a body which is on the register—

(*a*) is no longer a housing association eligible for registration, or

(*b*) has ceased to exist or does not operate.

the Corporation shall, after giving the body at least 14 days' notice, remove it from the register.

(3) In the case of a body which appears to the Corporation to have ceased to exist or not to operate, notice under subsection (2) shall be deemed to be given to the body if it is served at the address last known to the Corporation to be the principal place of business of the body.

(4) A body which is registered may request the Corporation to remove it from the register if it has not at any time received—

(*a*) a housing association grant,

(*b*) a revenue deficit grant, or

(*c*) any such payment or loan as is mentioned in paragraph 2 or 3 of Schedule 1 (grant-aided land),

and the Corporation may, if it thinks fit, do so.

(5) As soon as may be after removing a body from the register the Corporation shall give notice of the removal—

(*a*) if the body is a registered charity, to the Charity Commissioners,

(*b*) if the body is a society registered under the 1965 Act, to the appropriate registrar,

who shall record the removal.

DEFINITIONS

"appropriate register": s.37.
"eligible for registration": s.4.
"housing association grant": s.41.
"1965 Act": s.37.
"register, registered": s.3.
"revenue deficit grant": s.54.

GENERAL NOTE

This section provides the grounds and procedure for the removal of an association from the Housing Corporation register, either at its own request under subs. (3), if the association has never received any of the central or local government funding referred to, or on the initiative of the Corporation if it appears that an association is no longer eligible for registration. For conditions of eligibility see ss.4 and 5, above. For the powers of the Corporation to inquire into the affairs of an association see s.28, below. Although funding assistance will not be available to an association removed from the register, it will remain subject to Corporation control in respect of any disposal of grant-aided land: s.9(4), below. For the right of appeal against removal from the register see s.7, below.

Appeal against removal

7.—(1) A body which is aggrieved by a decision of the Housing Corporation to remove it from the register may appeal against the decision to the High Court or, as the case may be, to the Court of Session.

(2) If an appeal is brought the Corporation shall not remove the body concerned from the register until the appeal has been finally determined or is withdrawn.

(3) As soon as may be after an appeal is brought the Corporation shall give notice of the appeal—

(*a*) if the body concerned is a registered charity, to the Charity Commissioners, or

(*b*) if the body concerned is a society registered under the 1965 Act, to the appropriate registrar.

DEFINITIONS

"appropriate register": s.37.
"1965 Act": s.37.
"register": s.3.
"registered charity": s.38.

GENERAL NOTE

This section provides for a right of appeal against a decision under s.6 to remove an association from the Housing Corporation register. The Housing Corporation is a corporate body established under the Housing Act 1964, and is required to exercise its functions in accordance with the statutory provisions now contained in this Act: see s.75, below. There can be no doubt that the exercise of the Corporation's powers would be subject to the controlling jurisdiction of the High Court on application for judicial review by a person interested, under R.S.C. Order 53. The specific provision for an appeal, under this section, ensures that an appeal may be brought as of right, *i.e.* without the necessity of first seeking leave or, it seems, complying with the restricted time limit for applications for judicial review under Order 53. Otherwise, the grounds for appeal and the remedies available must, it is suggested, be identical to those on an application for judicial review, *i.e.* certiorari and mandamus will be available, at the court's discretion, to remedy any decision to remove an association which has been made *ultra vires* the Corporation's powers, *e.g.* on the basis of bad faith, or unreasonableness in accordance with established administrative law principles.

Disposal of land

Power of registered housing associations to dispose of land

8.—(1) Without prejudice to the provisions of Part V of the Housing Act 1985 (the right to buy), every registered housing association has power, subject to section 9 (control by Housing Corporation of land transactions), by virtue of this section but not otherwise, to dispose, in such manner as it thinks fit, of land held by it.

(2) Section 39 of the Settled Land Act 1925 (disposal of land by trustees) does not apply to the disposal of land by a registered housing association; and accordingly the disposal need not be for the best consideration in money that can reasonably be obtained.

(3) Nothing in subsection (2) shall be taken to authorise any action on the part of a charity which would conflict with the trusts of the charity.

DEFINITIONS
"charity": s.38.
"housing association": s.1.
"registered": s.3.

GENERAL NOTE
This and the following three sections govern the disposal of housing association property. The powers are without prejudice to the right to buy provisions now contained in Pt. V of the Housing Act 1985, which correspondingly impose an obligation on an association bound by them a duty to sell.
Subs. (1) gives associations a general power to dispose of land as they think fit, but subject to the restriction in subs. (3) and, further, subject to Housing Corporation consent in respect of disposals caught by the provisions of s.9, below. See also s.11 and Sched. 2 which make special provisions in the case of houses sold at a discount (*i.e.* under the "right to buy" scheme, referred to above), and houses situated in National Parks and other protected rural areas.
"Land" includes "buildings and other structures, land covered with water, and any estate, interest, easement, servitude or right in or over land": Interpretation Act 1978, Schedule 1.

Subss. (2), (3)
Section 39, Settled Land Act 1925, governs the powers of a tenant for life and the trustees of a settlement, in relation to land qualifying as settled land, and limits the conditions on which settled land can be sold. The same powers are enjoyed by trustees for sale: Law of Property Act 1925, ss.28, 205(1). Under s.29, Settled Land Act 1925, they also apply to the trustees of a charity or a public trust. As many housing associations are also registered charities they would, but for subs. (2), be bound to comply with s.39, which includes a general requirement to obtain the best consideration in money that can reasonably be obtained.
The liberty conferred by subs. (2) is not to be interpreted as authorising any action on the part of a charity which would conflict with the trusts of a charity: subs. (3). Note that where land forms part of the permanent endowment of a charity, as opposed to land given to a charity for its use and disposal, it is subject to the restrictions contained in the Charities Act 1960, s.29 (see note to s.10(1), below).

Control by Housing Corporation of dispositions of land by housing associations

9.—(1) The consent of the Housing Corporation, by order under the seal of the Corporation, is required for—

(*a*) any disposition of land by a registered housing association, and

(*b*) a disposition of grant-aided land (as defined in Schedule 1) by an unregistered housing association,

except where the disposition is one excepted from this section by section 10.

(2) The consent of the Corporation may be so given—

(*a*) generally to all housing associations or to a particular housing association or description of association;

(*b*) in relation to particular land or in relation to a particular description of land;

and may be given subject to conditions.

(3) A disposition by a housing association which requires the consent of the Corporation under this section is valid in favour of a person claiming under the association notwithstanding that the consent of the Corporation has not been given; and a person dealing with the association, or with a person claiming under the association, shall not be concerned to see or inquire whether any such consent has been given.

This subsection has effect subject to section 12 (avoidance of certain dispositions of houses without consent).

(4) Where at the time of its removal from the register under section 6(2) (removal of bodies no longer eligible for registration or defunct) a body owns land, this section continues to apply to that land after the removal as if the body concerned continued to be a registered housing association.

(5) For the purposes of this section "disposition" means sale, lease, mortgage, charge or any other disposal.

DEFINITIONS
"housing association": s.1.
"register, registered": s.3.

GENERAL NOTE
Housing Corporation consent is needed for the disposal of any land by a registered housing association, and any land in respect of which central or local government funding has been received, in the case of an association not registered with the Corporation. Sched. 1, below, defines "grant-aided land". The grants referred to in that schedule are those made under the provisions of various statutes pre-dating the Housing Act 1974, which brought into operation the present scheme of housing association funding, with its prerequisite of registration with the Housing Corporation.

S.10, below, contains exceptions in respect of certain disposals by associations which are registered charities, lettings under secure tenancies, and certain other periodic tenancies and short leases. Consent is not required for disposals to purchasers under the "right to buy" scheme: s.8(1), above.

"Land" includes "buildings and other structures, land covered with water, and any estate, interest, easement, servitude or right in or over land": Interpretation Act 1978, Sched. 1.

Subs. (2)
This specifies the manner in which consent may be given, effectively giving the Corporation similar powers to those enjoyed by the Secretary of State in relation to local authorities, under s.34, Housing Act 1985. Circulars P.C. 13/23 and P.C. 21/84, set out the Corporation's policy and procedure on consent to disposals, and give details of general consents to disposals of various kinds, including properties in low-cost home ownership projects. The Housing Corporation has also issued a general consent to cover disposals under the home ownership scheme for tenants of charitable housing associations, set up originally under s.35 of the Housing and Building Control Act 1984: see Circular H.C. 16/84. But see Circular H.C. 35/85, which gives details of a current stop on applications for this scheme received by the Corporation on or after August 23, 1985.

Subs. (3)

This protects a purchaser of property from a housing association where consent is absent, but does not apply where the property is a house, unless the purchaser is an individual (or two or more individuals) and the transaction involves one house only: see s.12, below.

Subs. (4)

For the provisions as to removal of an association from the Corporation register, see s.6 above and note thereto.

Dispositions excepted from s.9

10.—(1) A disposition by an unregistered housing association which is a charity is not within section 9 if by virtue of section 29 of the Charities Act 1960 it cannot be made without an order of the court or the Charity Commissioners; but the Charity Commissioners shall consult the Housing Corporation before making an order in such a case.

(2) A letting by a registered housing association, or by an unregistered housing association which is a housing trust, is not within section 9 if it is—

(*a*) a letting of land under a secure tenancy, or

(*b*) a letting of land under what would be a secure tenancy but for any of paragraphs 2 to 12 of Schedule 3 of the Housing Act 1985 or paragraphs 2 to 7 of Schedule 1 to the Tenants' Rights &c. (Scotland) Act 1980 (tenancies excepted from being secure tenancies for reasons other than that they are long leases).

(3) The grant by an unregistered housing association which does not satisfy the landlord condition in section 80 of the Housing Act 1985 (bodies which are capable of granting secure tenancies) of a lease for a term ending within the period of seven years and three months beginning on the date of the grant is not within section 9 unless—

(*a*) there is conferred on the lessee (by the lease or otherwise) an option for renewal for a term which, together with the original term, would expire outside that period, or

(*b*) the lease is granted wholly or partly in consideration of a fine.

(4) In subsection (3) the expression "lease" includes an agreement for a lease and a licence to occupy, and the expressions "grant" and "term" shall be construed accordingly.

DEFINITIONS

"housing association": s.1.
"housing trust": s.2.
"registered": s.3.
"secure tenancy": s.39.

GENERAL NOTE

S.9 restricts the powers of a registered housing association, and, in respect of grant-aided land, an unregistered association, to dispose of land without Housing Corporation consent. This section provides exceptions to the requirement of consent.

Subs. (1)

Under s.29 of the Charities Act 1960, land which forms part of the permanent endowment of a charity, as opposed to land given to a charity for its use and disposal, cannot be disposed of without an order of the court or the consent of the Charity Commissioner or, where appropriate, the Secretary of State for Education and Science, except on a disposal for a term of years of not more than 22 years, granted without taking a fine. Under this subsection *unregistered* associations which are registered charities do not require Corporation consent in addition to the restrictions imposed by s.29 of the Charities Act 1960, where that section applies. However, where consent is being sought from the Charity Commissioners, this subsection requires the Commissioners to consult the Corporation.

Subs. (2)
Corporation consent is not required for a letting by a registered housing association, or by any unregistered housing *trust* (as defined in s.2, above), which either creates a secure tenancy or which would create a secure tenancy but for the fact that the nature of the tenancy is such that it is excluded from being a secure tenancy, *e.g.* because it is an employee occupancy, or a student letting, under the exceptions listed in Sched. 3 of the Housing Act 1985 or the corresponding Scottish legislation. See, generally, Pt. IV, Housing Act 1985.

Subs. (3)
The exemption under this subsection is confined to those unregistered housing associations which do not grant secure tenancies because they do not fulfil the "landlord condition" of s.80 of the Housing Act 1985, *i.e.*, an unregistered housing association which is a co-operative housing assocation (*cf.* s.1, above). The exemption is confined to leases of less than seven years three months, and does not include shorter leases with a tenant's option to renew for a period which would in total exceed that period. Neither does the exemption apply to leases granted in consideration of a fine: see s.205(1) of the Law of Property Act 1925 for the definition of "fine".

Further provisions as to certain disposals of houses

11. Schedule 2 applies in relation to a disposal of a house under section 8 where—
  (*a*) a discount is given to the purchaser, or
  (*b*) the house is situated in a National Park, an area designated under section 87 of the National Parks and Access to the Countryside Act 1949 as an area of outstanding beauty, or an area designated as a rural area by order under section 157 of the Housing Act 1985.

DEFINITION
  "house": s.106.

GENERAL NOTE
This section applies the provisions of Sched. 2 to any disposal of a house by a housing association when either a *voluntary* discount is given to the purchaser (because the "right to buy" provisions of Pt. V of the Housing Act 1985 contain analogous provisions for a compulsory discount), or the house in question is situated in a National Park or one of the other protected rural areas referred to under sub-para. (*b*). Sched. 2 contains (i) provisions for repayment of discount on early sale of the property, *i.e.* before the expiry of five years from date of sale, and (ii) restrictions on the further disposal of houses situated in the areas referred to in sub-para. (*b*).

Avoidance of certain disposals of houses without consent

12. A disposal of a house by a housing association made without the consent required by section 9 is void, unless—
  (*a*) the disposal is to an individual (or to two or more individuals), and
  (*b*) the disposal does not extend to any other house.

DEFINITIONS
  "house": s.106.
  "housing association": s.1.

GENERAL NOTE
This section substantially qualifies the protection afforded to purchasers of properties from a housing association where that association lacks the necessary Housing Corporation consent to a disposal, under s.9(3), above. The rather misleading sub-division of the relevant provisions into two sections, originating from the Housing Act 1980, is continued in this Act.
In the case of a *house*, any disposal other than to an individual purchaser, or group of individual purchasers, is void in the absence of the requisite Housing Corporation consent to the disposal. The disposal of more than one house to the same individual, or group of individuals, is not however protected by this section. Note that the section applies only to

houses; the disposal of other land remains within the sole ambit of s.9(3) so that any purchaser is protected thereby.

Control of payments to members, etc.

Payments by way of gift, dividend or bonus

13.—(1) A registered housing association shall not make a gift or pay a sum by way of dividend or bonus to—

    (*a*) a person who is or has been a member of the association, or

    (*b*) a person who is a member of the family of a person within paragraph (*a*), or

    (*c*) a company of which a person within paragraph (*a*) or (*b*) is a director, or

    (*d*) a Scottish firm of which a person within paragraph (*a*) or (*b*) is a member,

except as permitted by this section.

(2) The following are permitted—

    (*a*) the payment of a sum which, in accordance with the rules of the association concerned, is paid as interest on capital lent to the association or subscribed by way of shares in the association;

    (*b*) the payment by a fully mutual housing association to a person who has ceased to be a member of the association, of a sum which is due to him either under his tenancy agreement with the association or under the terms of the agreement under which he became a member of the association.

(3) Where an association which is a society registered under the 1965 Act pays a sum or makes a gift in contravention of this section the association may recover the sum or the value of the gift, and proceedings for its recovery shall be taken by the association if the Housing Corporation so directs.

DEFINITIONS
    "fully mutual": s.1.
    "housing association": s.1.
    "member of family": s.105.
    "1965 Act": s.37.
    "registered": s.3.

GENERAL NOTE
    This section prohibits the payment of money or the making of gifts, dividends or bonuses to members of registered housing associations or to members of their families, as defined by s.105, below, except in the circumstances prescribed by subs. (2). Sections 14, 15, below, deal with permitted payments by way of expenses and under contracts of employment to members, officers and employees of the association where the association is registered under the Industrial and Provident Societies Act 1965.

Subs. (2)(*b*)
    This protects the position of co-operative and co-ownership associations whose members may be entitled either to repayment of a share at par value, or to a lump sum payment reflecting an equity share, on quitting the association: *cf.* notes to s.1, above.

Subs. (3)
    This subsection provides for recovery by the association of any sum or gift transferred in breach of subs. (1), and an association is obliged to make recovery where the Housing Corporation requires it to do so.

Maximum amounts payable by way of fees, expenses, etc.

14.—(1) The Housing Corporation may from time to time specify the maximum amounts which may be paid by a registered housing association which is a society registered under the 1965 Act—

(*a*) by way of fees or other remuneration, or by way of expenses, to a member of the association who is not a member of its committee or an officer or employee of the association,

(*b*) by way of expenses to a member of its committee (including a co-opted member) who is not an officer or employee of the association, or

(*c*) by way of expenses to an officer of the association who does not have a contract of employment with the association;

and different amounts may be so specified for different purposes.

(2) Where such an association makes a payment in excess of the specified maximum, the association may recover the excess and proceedings for its recovery shall be taken by the association if the Corporation so directs.

DEFINITIONS
"committee": s.37.
"housing association": s.1.
"1965 Act": s.37.
"registered": s.3.

GENERAL NOTE
This section enables the Housing Corporation to set maximum amounts which an association which is a 1965 Act registered society may pay, by way of remuneration or expenses to members of the association who are *not* committee members, officers or employees. Expenses payments to officers of the association who are not employees are also within this section.

Payments and benefits to committee members, etc.

15.—(1) A registered housing association which is a society registered under the 1965 Act shall not make a payment or grant a benefit to—

(*a*) a committee member (including a co-opted member), officer or employee of the association, or

(*b*) a person who at any time within the preceding twelve months has been a person within paragraph (*a*), or

(*c*) a close relative of a person within paragraph (*a*) or (*b*), or

(*d*) a business trading for profit of which a person falling within paragraph (*a*), (*b*) or (*c*) is a principal proprietor or in the management of which such a person is directly concerned,

except as permitted by this section.

(2) The following are permitted—

(*a*) payments made or benefits granted to an officer or employee under his contract of employment with the association;

(*b*) the payment of expenses to a committee member (including a co-opted member) or to an officer of the association who does not have a contract of employment with the association;

(*c*) any such payment as may be made in accordance with section 13(2) (interest payable in accordance with the rules and certain sums payable by a fully mutual housing association to a person who has ceased to be a member);

(*d*) the grant or renewal of a tenancy by a co-operative housing association;

(*e*) where a tenancy of a house has been granted to, or to a close relative of, a person who later became a committee member (including a co-opted member), officer or employee, the grant to that tenant of a new tenancy, whether of the same or another house.

(3) Where an association pays a sum or grants a benefit in contravention of this section, the association may recover the sum or the value of the

benefit, and proceedings for its recovery shall be taken by the association if the Housing Corporation so directs.

DEFINITIONS
    "committee": s.37.
    "co-operative housing association": s.1.
    "co-opted member": s.37.
    "fully mutual": s.1.
    "housing association": s.1.
    "1965 Act": s.37.
    "registered": s.3.

GENERAL NOTE
This section prohibits the payment of any amount, or the grant of any benefit (clearly including the grant of a tenancy) to a person who is, or during the preceding 12 months has been, a committee member, officer or employee of the association, or to a close relative of such, or to a business trading for profit in which the committee member, officer or employee has a personal interest, but all save as excepted. As to "trading for profit", with reference to subs. (1)(*d*), *cf.* note on *Goodman* v. *Dolphin Square Trust Ltd.* (1979) 38 P. & C.R. 257, C.A. in notes to s.4, above. Note also the inclusion of payments or benefits given to a "close relative". The restriction on payments or gifts under s.13, above extends to a "member of the family", as defined under s.105. Clearly, "close relative" is a narrower definition, but this somewhat loose expression is not defined in the Act.

Subs. (2)
The provisions do not apply to payments made or benefits granted to an officer or employee under his contract of employment, or to the payment of expenses to a member of the committee, or to payments permitted under s.13(2), above. Nor do the provisions apply to the payment of expenses to an officer who does not have a contract of employment with the association. While the expression "grant (of) a benefit", in subs. (1), clearly includes the grant of a tenancy, nothing in the section is to prevent the grant or renewal of tenancies by a co-operative association. The provisions do not prevent the grant of a new tenancy to a person who was already a tenant of the association prior to becoming a committee member, officer or employee of the association, or to a close relative of such who was already a tenant.

Subs. (3)
As under s.13, above, the association may take proceedings for recovery of sums illegally paid, and must do so if so required by the Housing Corporation.

Constitution, change of rules, amalgamation and dissolution

General power to remove committee member

16.—(1) The Housing Corporation may by order remove a committee member of a registered housing association if—
  (*a*) in England and Wales, he has been adjudged bankrupt or he has made an arrangement with his creditors,
  (*b*) in Scotland, he has become notour bankrupt or he has executed a trust deed for behoof of, or has made a composition contract or arrangement with, his creditors,
  (*c*) he is incapable of acting by reason of mental disorder,
  (*d*) he has not acted, or
  (*e*) he cannot be found or does not act and his absence or failure to act is impeding the proper management of the association's affairs.
  (2) Before making an order the Corporation shall give at least 14 days' notice of its intention to do so to the person whom it intends to remove, and to the association concerned.
  (3) Notice under subsection (2) may be given by post, and if so given to the person whom the Corporation intend to remove may be addressed to his last known address in the United Kingdom.

(4) A person who is ordered to be removed under this section may appeal against the order to the High Court or, as the case may be, the Court of Session.

DEFINITIONS
"housing association": s.1.
"mental disorder": s.39.
"registered": s.3.

GENERAL NOTE
This section enables the Housing Corporation to remove individual committee members or trustees of a registered housing association for any of the reasons set out in subs. (1). Note however the provisions of s.18, below, in respect of associations which are registered charities under the Charities Act 1960. A person intended for removal must be given 14 days notice of that intention, and has a right of appeal to the High Court, or in Scotland to the Court of Session. As to appeals, see note to s.7, above. See also s.30, below, for the Corporation's powers of removal of committee members, trustees and others after an inquiry into or audit of a registered housing association.
    The reference in subs. (1)(*a*) to being adjudged bankrupt brings the provisions as they apply in England into line with those as they have applied in Scotland, pursuant to Law Commission Recommendations (Cmnd. 9515), No. 32.

Power to appoint new committee member

17.—(1) The Housing Corporation may by order appoint a person to be a committee member of a registered housing association—
    (*a*) in place of a person removed by the Corporation,
    (*b*) where there are no members of the committee, or
    (*c*) where the Corporation is of opinion that it is necessary for the proper management of the association's affairs to have an additional committee member.
    (2) A person may be so appointed whether or not he is a member of the association and, if he is not, notwithstanding that the rules of the association restrict appointment to members.
    (3) A person appointed under this section shall hold office for such period and on such terms as the Corporation may specify and on the expiry of the appointment the Corporation may renew the appointment for such period as it may specify; but this does not prevent a person appointed under this section from retiring in accordance with the rules of the association.
    (4) A person appointed under this section is entitled—
    (*a*) to attend, speak and vote at any general meeting of the association and to receive all notices of and other communications relating to any general meeting which a member of the association is entitled to receive, and
    (*b*) to require a general meeting of the association to be convened within 21 days of a request to that effect made in writing to the committee of the association.

DEFINITIONS
"housing association": s.1.
"registered": s.3.

GENERAL NOTE
This section enables the Housing Corporation to appoint a committee member or trustee to replace a person removed from the management of a registered housing association in the exercise of the Corporation's powers of removal under s.16, above or s.30, below. The Corporation may also appoint an additional member or trustee where it considers this necessary for the proper management of the association's affairs. Note however the special provisions applying to associations which are registered charities s.18, below.

A person appointed by the Corporation holds office for such period, or periods, and on such terms, as the Corporation may specify. The rights of an appointed member or trustee are set out in subs. (4). In the year 1984/5 the Corporation appointed members to the committees of 6 housing associations, "to strengthen their management and to ensure that public money was being fully safeguarded": Housing Corporation Annual Report 1984/5.

Exercise of powers under ss.16 and 17 in relation to registered charities

18.—(1) The Housing Corporation may exercise its powers under sections 16 and 17 (removal or appointment of committee member) in relation to an association which is a registered charity only if the association has, at any time before the powers are exercised, received a grant or loan under—

section 41 (housing association grants),
section 54 or 55 (revenue deficit grants or hostel deficit grants),
section 58(2) (grants or loans by local authorities),
section 79 (loans by Housing Corporation),
section 31 of the Housing Act 1974 (management grants), or
any enactment mentioned in paragraph 2 or 3 of Schedule 1 (pre-1974 grants and certain loans).

(2) Sections 16 and 17 apply in relation to a trustee of such an association as they apply in relation to a committee member.

(3) Before exercising its powers under section 17 (appointment of committee member or trustee) in relation to such an association the Corporation shall consult the Charity Commissioners; and the Corporation may not under that section appoint a trustee in excess of the maximum number permissible under the association's constitution.

DEFINITION
"registered charity": s.38.

GENERAL NOTE
This section restricts the Housing Corporation's powers of removal and appointment of trustees, under ss.16, 17 above, in respect of housing associations which are registered charities under the Charities Act 1960: only charitable associations which have received grants or loans under the principal provisions specified are liable to have trustees removed under the foregoing sections.

Subs. (3)
This applies to the appointment of trustees only, and requires the Housing Corporation to consult the Charity Commissioners before making an appointment under s.17. The Corporation cannot appoint additional trustees to exceed the maximum of trustees permitted by the association's constitution.

Change of rules under the 1965 Act

19.—(1) This section applies to a registered housing association—
 (*a*) which is a society registered under the 1965 Act, and
 (*b*) whose registration under this Part has been recorded by the appropriate registrar in accordance with section 5(3).

(2) Notice shall be sent to the Housing Corporation of a change of the association's name or of the situation of its registered office.

(3) Any other amendment of the association's rules is not valid without the Corporation's consent, given by order under the seal of the Corporation; and a copy of such consent shall be sent with the copies of the amendment required by section 10(1) of the 1965 Act to be sent to the appropriate registrar.

(4) The 1965 Act applies in relation to the provisions of this section as if they were contained in section 10 of that Act (amendment of registered rules).

Definitions
    "appropriate register": s.37.
    "housing association": s.1.
    "the 1965 Act": s.37.
    "registered": s.3.

General Note
    Under s.10 of the Industrial and Provident Societies Act 1965, no variation of the rules of a registered society is valid, without registration under that Act. This section adds the requirement of Housing Corporation consent to such a variation if the association is also a registered housing association, and a copy of the consent must be lodged with the Registrar of Friendly Societies in the course of registration of the variation. Under s.10(2) of the 1965 Act, notice of any change in the situation of the society's registered office or its name must be forwarded to the Registrar and, under subs. (2) of this section, to the Housing Corporation, also, if the society is a registered housing association.

Change of objects by certain charities

20.—(1) This section applies to a registered housing association—
    (*a*) which is a registered charity and is not a company incorporated under the Companies Act, and
    (*b*) whose registration under this Part has been recorded by the Charity Commissioners in accordance with section 5(3).

(2) No power contained in the provisions establishing the association as a charity, or regulating its purposes and administration, to vary or add to its objects may be exercised without the consent of the Charity Commissioners, and before giving their consent the Charity Commissioners shall consult the Housing Corporation.

Definitions
    "housing association": s.1.
    "registered": s.3
    "registered charity": s.38.

General Note
    This section applies to registered housing associations which are also registered charities, but are not exempt charities or companies registered under the Companies Acts. It prohibits them from changing the objects of the charity without consent of the Charity Commissioners, who must consult the Housing Corporation.

Amalgamation and dissolution under the 1965 Act

21.—(1) This section applies to a registered housing association—
    (*a*) which is a society registered under the 1965 Act, and
    (*b*) whose registration under this Part has been recorded by the appropriate registrar in accordance with section 5(3).

(2) The appropriate registrar shall not register a special resolution which is passed for the purposes of—
    (*a*) section 50 of the 1965 Act (amalgamation of societies), or
    (*b*) section 51 of that Act (transfer of engagements between societies), unless, together with the copy of the resolution, there is sent to him a copy of the Housing Corporation's consent to the amalgamation or transfer concerned.

(3) Section 52 of the 1965 Act (power of society to convert itself into, amalgamate with or transfer its engagements to a company registered under the Companies Act) does not apply.

(4) If the association resolves by special resolution that it be wound up voluntarily under the Companies Act, the resolution has no effect unless—
    (*a*) before the resolution was passed the Corporation gave its consent to its passing, and

(*b*) a copy of the consent is forwarded to the appropriate registrar together with the copy of the resolution required to be so forwarded in accordance with the Companies Act.

(5) If the association is to be dissolved by instrument of dissolution, the appropriate registrar shall not—

(*a*) register the instrument in accordance with section 58(5) of the 1965 Act, or

(*b*) cause notice of the dissolution to be advertised in accordance with section 58(6) of that Act,

unless together with the instrument there is sent to him a copy of the Corporation's consent to its making.

(6) The references in this section to the Corporation's consent are to an order under the seal of the Corporation giving its consent.

DEFINITIONS
"appropriate register": s.37.
"Companies Act": s.106.
"housing association": s.1.
"the 1965 Act": s.37.

GENERAL NOTE
This section prevents a housing association registered under the Industrial and Provident Societies Act and under s.5 of this Act from exercising powers to amalgamate with or transfer engagements to another society or to a company registered under the Companies Acts, or to become such a company, or to dissolve itself, without the consent of the Corporation, by prohibiting the appropriate registrar from registering the resolution or instrument concerned.

Housing Corporation's power to petition for winding up

22.—(1) The Housing Corporation may present a petition for the winding up under the Companies Act of a registered housing association to which this section applies on the ground that the association is failing properly to carry out its purposes or objects.

(2) This section applies to a registered housing association which is—

(*a*) a company incorporated under the Companies Act, or

(*b*) a society registered under the 1965 Act (to which the winding up provisions of the Companies Act apply in accordance with section 55(*a*) of the 1965 Act).

DEFINITIONS
"Companies Act": s.106.
"housing association": s.1.
"registered": s.3.

GENERAL NOTE
This section gives power to the Housing Corporation to petition for the winding-up of a housing association which is registered either under the Companies Acts or the Industrial and Provident Societies Acts, 1965 on the ground that the association is failing properly to carry out its purposes or objects.

Transfer of net assets on dissolution

23.—(1) Where a registered housing association which is a society registered under the 1965 Act is dissolved under that Act, so much of the property of the association as remains after meeting the claims of its creditors and any other liabilities arising on or before the dissolution shall be transferred—

(*a*) to the Housing Corporation, or

(*b*) if the Corporation so directs, to such registered housing association as may be specified in the direction, notwithstanding anything in the 1965 Act or in the rules of the association.

(2) In order to avoid the necessity for the sale of land belonging to the association, and thereby secure the transfer of the land under this section, the Corporation may, if it appears to it appropriate to do so, make payments to discharge such claims or liabilities as are referred to in subsection (1).

(3) Where the association which is dissolved is a charity, the Corporation may dispose of property transferred to it by virtue of this section only to another registered housing association—

(*a*) which is also a charity, and

(*b*) the objects of which appear to the Corporation to be, as nearly as practicable, akin to those of the dissolved association.

(4) In any other case the Corporation may dispose of property transferred to it by virtue of this section to a registered housing association or to a subsidiary of the Corporation.

(5) Where property transferred to the Corporation by virtue of this section includes land subject to an existing mortgage or charge (whether in favour of the Corporation or not), the Corporation may, in exercise of its powers under Part III, dispose of the land either—

(*a*) subject to that mortgage or charge, or

(*b*) subject to a new mortgage or charge in favour of the Corporation securing such amount as appears to the Corporation to be appropriate in the circumstances.

DEFINITIONS
  "charity": s.38.
  "housing association": s.1.
  "1965 Act": s.37.
  "registered": s.3.

GENERAL NOTE

This section enables the Housing Corporation to secure the transfer to itself or to another housing association of any of the property of a housing association registered under the Industrial and Provident Societies Act 1965 which is being dissolved, after its liabilities have been met, and to meet such liabilities in order to prevent the sale of any land to meet the liabilities.

The Corporation may not dispose of property transferred in this way other than to one of its subsidiaries or to a registered housing association, and if the dissolved association was a charity may only dispose of it to a registered association which is also a charity and one whose objects are as near as practicable, in the Corporation's view, to those of the dissolved association.

Subs. (1)

S.55 of the Act of 1965 provides that a society may be dissolved either on being wound up in a similar manner to that prescribed for companies under the Companies Acts, or by an instrument of dissolution signed by threequarters of the members.

"Property" does not appear to be limited to land, since both words are used in subs. (5).

Subs. (3)

The question whether the objects of the transferee charity are akin to those of the dissolved association appears to be entirely in the discretion of the Corporation.

Subs. (5)

"Land" includes "buildings and other structures, land covered with water, and any estate, interest, easement, servitude or right in or over land": Interpretation Act 1978, Sched. 1.

Accounts and audit

General requirements as to accounts and audit

24.—(1) The Secretary of State may by order lay down accounting requirements for registered housing associations with a view to ensuring that the accounts of every registered housing association—

    (*a*) are prepared in the requisite form, and

    (*b*) give a true and fair view of the state of affairs of the association, so far as its housing activities are concerned, and of the disposition of funds and assets which are, or at any time have been, in its hands in connection with those activities.

(2) The method by which an association shall distinguish in its accounts between its housing activities and other activities shall be laid down by orders under subsection (1).

(3) The accounts of every registered housing association shall comply with the requirements laid down under this section; and the auditor's report shall state, in addition to any other matters which it is required to state, whether in the auditor's opinion the accounts do so comply.

(4) Every registered housing association shall furnish to the Housing Corporation a copy of its accounts and auditor's report within six months of the end of the period to which they relate.

(5) An order under this section—

    (*a*) may make different provision with respect to different cases or descriptions of case, including different provision for different areas, and

    (*b*) shall be made by statutory instrument which shall be subject to annulment in pursuance of a resolution of either House of Parliament;

and the provisions of such an order shall not apply in relation to a period beginning before the day on which the order comes into force.

DEFINITIONS

    "housing activities": s.106.

    "housing association": s.1.

    "registered": s.3.

GENERAL NOTE

    This section permits the Secretary of State to introduce accounting requirements governing all registered housing associations. As to penalties for non-compliance, see s.27, below. The obligation to give a true and fair view of the state of affairs of an association is already imposed on associations which are societies registered under the Industrial and Provident Societies Act 1965 by s.3 of the Friendly and Industrial and Provident Societies Act 1968. Registered associations which are registered charities are placed under a similar obligation by s.26 and Sched. 3, below. The purpose of this section is to impose uniform requirements in relation to all registered housing associations, in relation to their housing activities: housing activities are those activities which qualify an association as such under s.1, above, and provide eligibility for registration with the Corporation under s.5.

Subs. (5)

    The Registered Housing Associations (Accounting Requirements) Order 1982 S.I. 1982 No. 828, retained in force by s.2, Housing (Consequential Provisions) Act 1985, sets out requirements as to the financial statements and balance sheet to be prepared by registered housing associations, and the information to be provided therein. The Order further provides for the method of inclusion of surplus rental income, under a Grant Redemption Fund: see s.80, below, into the accounts. Housing Corporation guidance to housing associations is contained in its publication "Recommended Form of Published Accounts for Housing Associations", and in Circular H.C. 8/82.

    S.I. 1983 No. 207 makes special provision for housing associations which are almshouses, and removes the obligation to provide statements of the source and application of funds, as required by S.I. 1982 No. 828, above. See also H.C. 6/83. S.I. 1984 No. 1833 amends the accounting requirements in case of certain small housing associations (as defined in that Order): see Circular H.C. 9/85.

Appointment of auditors by associations registered under the 1965 Act

25. Section 4(1) of the Friendly and Industrial and Provident Societies Act 1968 (obligation to appoint qualified auditors to audit accounts and balance sheet for each year of account) applies to every registered housing association which is a society registered under the 1965 Act, without regard to the volume of its receipts and payments, the number of its members or the value of its assets.

DEFINITIONS
"housing association": s.1.
"1965 Act": s.37.
"registered": s.3.

GENERAL NOTE
Societies registered under the Industrial and Provident Societies Act 1965 are obliged, by s.4 of the Friendly and Industrial and Provident Societies Act 1968, to appoint a qualified auditor, or qualified auditors, to audit their accounts. But the obligation does not arise in relation to societies with membership below a specified number, of which the assets, receipts and payments fall below specified amounts, in a given year. This section requires all such societies which are registered housing associations to appoint a qualified auditor or qualified auditors, notwithstanding volume of receipts, payments, assets or number of members. As to the general requirements for accounts and audit, see s.24 above, and notes thereto.

Accounting requirements for registered housing associations not within the 1965 Act

26.—(1) A registered housing association which is a registered charity shall, in respect of its housing activities (and separately from its other activities, if any) be subject to the provisions of Schedule 3 (which impose accounting and audit requirements corresponding to those imposed by the Friendly and Industrial and Provident Societies Act 1968).

(2) But this does not affect any obligation of the charity under section 8 of the Charities Act 1960 (statement of accounts to be transmitted to Charity Commissioners).

DEFINITIONS
"housing association": s.1.
"registered": s.3.
"registered charity": s.38.

GENERAL NOTE
Under s.8 of the Charities Act 1960, registered charities other than "exempt charities" within the meaning s.4 of that Act are required to provide accounts properly audited by a member of one of a number of specified bodies, on demand by the Charity Commissioners, or, in the case of a charity having a permanent endowment, annually without demand in relation to that endowment. This section introduces a further requirement for a registered housing association which is a registered charity, but only in relation to its housing activities (as defined in s.106, below, with reference to ss.1, 4, above).
An association is required to comply with the provisions of Sched. 3, which correspond to the accounting and audit requirements imposed on an association registered under the 1965 Act.

Responsibility for securing compliance with accounting requirements

27.—(1) Every responsible person, that is to say, every person who—
   (*a*) is directly concerned with the conduct and management of the affairs of a registered housing association, and
   (*b*) is in that capacity responsible for the preparation and audit of accounts,

shall ensure that section 24 (general requirements as to accounts and audit) and, where applicable, Schedule 3 (accounting requirements for associations not within 1965 Act) are complied with by the association.

(2) If—

(a) section 24(4) (furnishing of accounts and auditor's report) is not complied with, or

(b) the accounts furnished to the Housing Corporation under that provision do not comply with the accounting requirements laid down under section 24(1), or

(c) Schedule 3, where applicable, is not complied with,

every responsible person, and the association itself, commits a summary offence and is liable on conviction to a fine not exceeding level 3 on the standard scale.

(3) It is a defence—

(a) for a responsible person to prove that he did everything that could reasonably have been expected of him by way of discharging the duty imposed by subsection (1);

(b) for an association to prove that every responsible person did everything that could reasonably have been expected of him by way of discharging the duty imposed by subsection (1) in relation to the association.

(4) Proceedings for an offence under this section may in England and Wales be brought only by or with the consent of the Corporation or the Director of Public Prosecutions.

DEFINITIONS
"housing association": s.1.
"1965 Act": s.37.
"registered": s.3.
"standard scale": s.39.

GENERAL NOTE
This section imposes liability on the "responsible person", as defined in subs. (1), and also on the association itself, in the event of a failure to comply with the accounting and audit requirements set out in ss.24, 26, above, and Sched. 3, below. The offence carried a penalty not exceeding level 3 on the standard scale under s.37, Criminal Justice Act 1982, currently £400, 4– by S.I. 1984 No. 447.

Inquiries into affairs of housing associations

Inquiry

28.—(1) The Housing Corporation may appoint a person (not a person who is, or at any time has been, a member of the Corporation's staff) to conduct an inquiry into the affairs of a registered housing association.

(2) The appointed person may by notice in writing served on—

(a) the association concerned, or

(b) any person who is, or has been, an officer, agent or member of the association,

require the association or person to produce to him such books, accounts and other documents relating to the association's business and to give him such other information so relating, as he considers necessary for the purposes of the inquiry.

(3) An association or other person who fails without reasonable excuse to comply with the requirements of a notice under subsection (2) commits a summary offence and is liable on conviction to a fine not exceeding level 5 on the standard scale.

(4) On completion of the inquiry the appointed person shall make a report to the Corporation on such matters and in such form as the Corporation may specify.

(5) In this section "agent" includes banker, solicitor and auditor; but nothing in this section requires the disclosure—

(*a*) by a solicitor, of a privileged communication made to him in his capacity as solicitor, or

(*b*) by a housing association's banker, of information as to the affairs of any of their other customers.

DEFINITIONS
"housing association": s.1.
"registered": s.3.
"standard scale": s.39.

GENERAL NOTE
This section permits the Housing Corporation to appoint a person to hold an inquiry into the affairs of any registered housing association (but as to its application to associations which are also registered charities, see s.31, below). Note the prohibition on appointment of any member or former member of the Corporation's staff. Subs. (2) confers wide powers on a person so appointed: to require production of documents relating to the association's business, and other such related information as he considers necessary for the purposes of the inquiry.

Such a person cannot, however, seek to enforce these powers by way of court order, in his own name. In the event that a person refuses to provide the information required, the only redress available to the person appointed is to ask the Attorney-General to make an application to court for compliance: *Ashby* v. *Ebdon* [1984] 17 H.L.R. 1, Ch.D.

Subs. (3)
Non-compliance is a criminal offence, punishable by a fine of up to level 5 on the standard scale under s.37, Criminal Justice Act 1982, currently £2,000, by S.I. 1984 No. 447.

Subs. (5)
This subsection confirms the solicitor/client privilege attaching to communications between an association and a solicitor acting in his professional capacity. A housing association's bank cannot be required to disclose information relating to the affairs of its other customers, *e.g.* an officer of the association in his own name.

Extraordinary audit for purposes of inquiry

29.—(1) For the purposes of an inquiry under section 28 the Housing Corporation may require the accounts and balance sheet of the association concerned, or such of them as the Corporation may specify, to be audited by a qualified auditor appointed by the Corporation.

(2) A person is a qualified auditor for this purpose if he is under section 7(1) of the Friendly and Industrial and Provident Societies Act 1968 a qualified auditor for the purposes of that Act, or is under section 7(2) of that Act a qualified auditor in relation to the association concerned.

(3) On completion of the audit the appointed auditor shall make a report to the Corporation on such matters and in such form as the Corporation may specify.

(4) The expenses of the audit, including the remuneration of the auditor, shall be paid by the Corporation.

(5) An audit under this section is additional to, and does not affect, any audit made or to be made under any other enactment.

GENERAL NOTE
This section enables the Housing Corporation, at its own expense, to arrange for the accounts of a registered housing association to be audited by an appointed auditor, for the purposes of an inquiry under s.28, above.

Subs. (2)
The persons qualified under the 1968 Act are: members of the Institute of Chartered Accountants in England and Wales, or of Scotland, and certain other persons recognised,

or belonging to a body of accountants recognised, by the Secretary of State under s.389 of the Companies Act 1985.

General powers exercisable as a result of inquiry or audit

30.—(1) Where the Housing Corporation is satisfied, as the result of an inquiry under section 28 or an audit under section 29, that there has been misconduct or mismanagement in the affairs of a registered housing association, it may—

    (*a*) by order remove any member of the committee of the association, or any officer, agent or employee of the association, who has been responsible for or privy to the misconduct or mismanagement or has by his conduct contributed to it or facilitated it;

    (*b*) by order suspend such a person for up to six months, pending determination whether he should be removed;

    (*c*) order any bank or other person who holds money or securities on behalf of the association not to part with the money or securities without the approval of the Corporation;

    (*d*) by order restrict the transactions which may be entered into, or the nature or amount of the payments which may be made, in the administration of the association without the approval of the Corporation.

(2) Before making an order under subsection (1)(*a*) the Corporation shall give at least 14 days' notice of its intention to do so—

    (*a*) to the person it intends to remove, and

    (*b*) to the association concerned.

(3) Notice under subsection (2) may be given by post, and if so given to the person whom the Corporation intends to remove may be addressed to his last known address in the United Kingdom.

(4) A person who is ordered to be removed under subsection (1)(*a*) or suspended under subsection (1)(*b*) may appeal against the order to the High Court or, as the case may be, the Court of Session.

(5) Where a person is suspended under subsection (1)(*b*), the Corporation may give directions with respect to the performance of his functions and otherwise as to matters arising from the suspension.

(6) A person who contravenes an order under subsection (1)(*c*) commits a summary offence and is liable on conviction to a fine not exceeding level 5 on the standard scale or imprisonment for a term not exceeding three months or both; but proceedings for such an offence may be brought in England and Wales only by or with the consent of the Corporation or the Director of Public Prosecutions.

DEFINITIONS
    "bank": s.106.
    "housing association": s.1.
    "registered": s.3.
    "standard scale": s.39.

GENERAL NOTE
    This section enables the Housing Corporation to suspend and/or remove committee members, officers, trustees, agents or employees of a registered housing association where misconduct or mismanagement is revealed after an inquiry or audit under ss.28, 29, above. As to the application of this section to associations which are registered charities, see s.31, below, and note thereto. Note that under s.17, above, the Corporation may appoint a committee member or trustee (but not an officer, agent or employee) to replace a person removed under this section if it is considered necessary to do so.

Subs. (1)
    In addition to its powers of suspension and removal of individuals, the Corporation may "freeze" money or securities belonging to the association wherever they are held, and may

restrict administrative transactions by the association concerned. The power of suspension is not an independent power, *i.e.* a temporary penalty, but can only be exercised pending a decision on removal.

Subs. (2)
Before removing or suspending an individual, under subs. (1), the Corporation must give at least 14 days' notice of that intention, both to the individual and the housing association concerned.

Subs. (4)
For the right of appeal, see also notes to s.7, above.

Subs. (6)
Contravention of an order to a bank or other person holding money on or other securities on behalf of the association not to part with either without Corporation approval is a criminal offence punishable by imprisonment for up to three months and/or a fine not exceeding level 5 on the standard scale under s.37, Criminal Justice Act 1982, currently £2,000, by S.I. 1984 No. 447.

Exercise of powers under ss. 28 to 30 in relation to registered charities

31.—(1) The Housing Corporation may exercise its powers under sections 28 to 30 (inquiry, audit, etc.) in relation to an association which is a registered charity only if the association has, at any time before the powers are exercised, received a grant or loan under—
  section 41 (housing association grants),
  section 54 or 55 (revenue deficit grants or hostel deficit grants),
  section 58(2) (grants or loans by local authorities),
  section 79 (loans by Housing Corporation),
  section 31 of the Housing Act 1974 (management grants), or
  any enactments mentioned in paragraph 2 or 3 of Schedule 1 (pre-1974 grants and certain loans).
(2) In relation to such an association sections 28 to 30 have effect with the following adaptations—
  (*a*) references to an officer, agent or member, or to a member of the committee, include a trustee of the association;
  (*b*) references to the association's business are confined to its housing activities;
  (*c*) references to the association's accounts do not include revenue accounts which do not relate to its housing activities, except so far as such accounts are necessary for the auditing of revenue accounts which do so relate or of the association's balance sheet;
  (*d*) a person is a qualified auditor for the purposes of section 29 (extraordinary audit) only if he is an auditor qualified for the purposes of paragraph 3 of Schedule 3.
(3) In relation to such an association the powers conferred on the Corporation by—
  section 28(1) (appointment of person to inquire into association's affairs), and
  section 30(1)(*a*) and (*b*) (removal of person in connection with misconduct or mismanagement and suspension with a view to removal),
are exercisable only after consultation with the Charity Commissioners.

DEFINITIONS
  "housing activities": s.106.
  "registered charity": s.38.

GENERAL NOTE
Subs. (1)
This subsection restricts the Corporation's powers under s.28 and s.30, above, in respect of housing associations which are registered charities. The Corporation's powers under those

sections apply only to registered charities which have received grants or loans under the principal support provisions, as listed in this subsection.

Subs. (2)

"housing activities" are all those activities carried out by an association in pursuance of those purposes or objects which confer eligibility for registration with the Housing Corporation: see s.4, above.

Subs. (3)

This requires the Corporation to consult the Charity Commissioners prior to instituting an inquiry, under s.28, or removing or suspending a person, under s.30.

Power to direct transfer of land to another housing association or the Housing Corporation

32.—(1) Where, as the result of an inquiry under section 28 or an audit under section 29, the Housing Corporation is satisfied as regards a registered housing association which is a society registered under the 1965 Act—

(a) that there has been misconduct or mismanagement in the administration of the association, or

(b) that the management of the land belonging to the association would be improved if the land belonging to the association were transferred in accordance with the provisions of this section,

the Corporation may, with the consent of the Secretary of State, direct the association to make such a transfer.

(2) Where the association concerned is a charity, the Housing Corporation may only direct a transfer to be made to another registered housing association—

(a) which is also a charity, and

(b) the objects of which appear to the Corporation to be, as nearly as practicable, akin to those of the association concerned.

(3) In any other case the Corporation may direct a transfer to be made to the Corporation or to another registered housing association.

(4) A transfer in pursuance of a direction under this section shall be made on the terms that the transferee will pay or undertake to pay to the association concerned such sum (if any) as will be necessary to defray all its proper debts and liabilities (including debts and liabilities secured on the land) after taking into account any money or other assets belonging to the association.

(5) If it appears to the Corporation likely that the association concerned will as a result of the transfer be dissolved under the 1965 Act, the Corporation shall secure that the costs of the dissolution are taken into account in determining the sum payable to the association under subsection (4).

DEFINITIONS

"charity": s.38.

"dissolved under the 1965 Act": s.37.

"housing association": s.1.

"1965 Act": s.37.

"registered": s.3.

GENERAL NOTE

This section gives power to the Housing Corporation, with the consent of the Secretary of State, to direct the transfer of an association's land to itself or to another registered association if misconduct or mismanagement of a housing association registered under the Industrial and Provident Societies Act 1965 is revealed as the result of an inquiry or audit under s.28 or s.30, above. See also notes to s.23, above.

Subs. (1)
"Land" includes "buildings and other structures, land covered with water, and any estate, interest, easement, servitude or right in or over land": Interpretation Act 1978, Sched. 1.

Subs. (2)
This applies to any charity, whether registered under the Charities Act 1960 or not, and prevents the Corporation from transferring the land of any such association other than to a charity having objects which are as nearly as practicable akin to those of the first association.

Subs. (4)
This provides for the terms of transfer to include a payment by the transferee association to the association concerned, of a sum needed to meet that association's outstanding debts and liabilities including charges on the land in question, after taking into account any assets held by the association. The object of this provision is to ensure that an association is in a position to satisfy its creditors after the transfer of what is likely to be its principal assets.

Subs. (5)
If, as is likely, an association is to be dissolved following a transfer of its land, the costs of that dissolution are to be included in the determination of any sum payable under subs. (4).

Miscellaneous

Recognition of central association

33.—(1) The Secretary of State may, if he thinks fit, recognise for the purposes of this section a central association or other body established for the purposes of promoting the formation and extension of housing associations and of giving them advice and assistance.

(2) The Secretary of State may make a grant in aid of the expenses of the association or body of such amount as he may, with the approval of the Treasury, determine.

DEFINITION
"housing association": s.1.

GENERAL NOTE
The central agency recognised under this section is the National Federation of Housing Associations, 175, Gray's Inn Road London W.C.1X 8UP
Formed in 1935, the N.F.H.A. has a membership of some 2000 housing associations, trusts and societies. Although it receives financial assistance from the Department of the Environment, under subs. (2), the N.F.H.A. is a wholly independent body controlled by a National Council elected by its membership. A principal activity of the N.F.H.A. is the representation of its members' interests to central and local government and the Housing Corporation in relation to existing and proposed legislation and administrative procedures. To this end it maintains a number of liaison groups and working parties comprising experts in particular fields such as finance and development.
In addition the N.F.H.A. has an important advisory role, and provides information and assistance to existing and prospective members on a wide range of matters, in respect of both day to day problems and substantial questions of policy. It publishes a series of guides on the common areas of difficulty such as tenancy agreements and tenant consultation, and provides an advisory service to deal with inquiries by telephone as well as by letter. The N.F.H.A. arranges frequent training courses and other conferences, and produces a monthly magazine "Voluntary Housing," as well as carrying out research into particular aspects of housing association activity. An Annual Report, giving details of the N.F.H.A.'s operations and a financial summary, can be obtained from its offices at the above address.

Provision of land by county councils

34.—(1) Where a housing association wishes to erect houses which in the opinion of the Secretary of State are required and the local housing authority in whose district the houses are proposed to be built are unwilling to acquire land with a view to selling or leasing it to the association, the county council, on the application of the association, may acquire land for that purpose.

(2) For that purpose the county council may exercise all the powers of a local housing authority under Part II of the Housing Act 1985 (provision of housing) in regard to the acquisition and disposal of land; and the provisions of that Act as to the acquisition of land by local housing authorities for the purposes of that Part apply accordingly.

DEFINITIONS

"housing association": s.1.
"local housing authority": s.104.

GENERAL NOTE

A local housing authority, *i.e.* a district council or London borough council, has wide powers of acquisition of land, including any houses or buildings thereon, for the purpose of providing housing accommodation under the provisions of Pt. II, Housing Act 1985. These powers can be exercised for the benefit of an association. However, where they are unwilling to do so, the Secretary of State can in substance authorise a county council to exercise the like powers on behalf of the association.

Housing trusts: power to transfer housing to local housing authority

35.—(1) A housing trust may—

(*a*) sell or lease to the local housing authority the houses provided by the trust, or

(*b*) make over to the authority the management of the houses.

(2) So far as subsection (1) confers power to dispose of land—

(*a*) it does not apply to registered housing associations (on whom power to dispose of land is conferred by section 8);

(*b*) it has effect subject to section 9 (dispositions requiring consent of Housing Corporation) where the housing trust is an unregistered housing association and the land is grant-aided land (as defined in Schedule 1); and

(*c*) it has effect subject to section 29 of the Charities Act 1960 (dispositions which cannot be made without an order of the court or the Charity Commissioners) where the housing trust is a charity.

DEFINITIONS

"charity": s.38.
"housing association": s.1.
"housing trust": s.2.
"local housing authority": s.104.
"registered": s.3.

GENERAL NOTE

There has long been power for trustees of a housing trust to transfer its property to the local authority. The original provision, most recently contained in s.128(1) of the Housing Act 1957, referred to "the trustees of any houses for the working classes for the time being provided by private subscriptions or otherwise . . . ," and this terminology reflects the origins of the present-day housing association movement in the philanthropic private housing societies established in the 19th century for the provision of housing for urban workers. Intended to operate on a self-financing basis, many of these societies were unable to obtain sufficient return from rental income to remain viable, and the provisions of what is now this section enabled the property and/or the management of a society's housing stock to be transferred to a local authority.

Pursuant to Law Commissions Recommendations (Cmnd. 9515), No. 4, the wording now omits the anachronistic reference to "houses for the working classes." The exceptions to disposal of property in subsection (2) reflect the fact that for the great majority of housing associations, which are registered with the Housing Corporation under s.5, above, the section is of no application at all, and disposal is regulated by the Corporation under s.8. In the case of unregistered housing trusts, Housing Corporation consent to disposal is required in the case of land upon which one of the principal types of grant assistance has been paid.

Trusts which are registered charities are subject to the requirement of the consent of the Charity Commissoners to disposals of land falling within s.29 of the Charities Act 1960.

Housing trusts: functions of Secretary of State with respect to legal proceedings

36.—(1) If it appears to the Secretary of State—

(*a*) that the institution of legal proceedings is requisite or desirable with respect to any property belonging to a housing trust, or

(*b*) that the expediting of any such legal proceedings is requisite or desirable,

he may certify the case to the Attorney-General who may institute legal proceedings or intervene in legal proceedings already instituted in such manner as he thinks proper in the circumstances.

(2) Before preparing a scheme with reference to property belonging to a housing trust, the court or body which is responsible for making the scheme shall communicate with the Secretary of State and consider any recommendations made by him with reference to the proposed scheme.

DEFINITION
"housing trust": s.2.

GENERAL NOTE
This section enables the Secretary of State, where it appears that legal proceedings with respect to housing trust property is necessary or desirable, to refer a case to the Attorney-General who may then institute legal proceedings, or intervene in legal proceedings already commenced. The court or an appointed body may prepare a scheme for the administration of the trust property: subs. (2) requires consultation with the Secretary of State in the preparation of such a scheme, and any recommendations made must be considered, though not necessarily implemented.

Supplementary

Definitions relating to the 1965 Act and societies registered under it

37. In this Part "the 1965 Act" means the Industrial and Provident Societies Act 1965, and in relation to a society registered under that Act—

"appropriate registrar" has the same meaning as in that Act (where it is defined in section 73(1)(*c*) by reference to the situation of the society's registered office);

"committee" means the committee of management or other directing body of the society;

"co-opted member", in relation to the committee, includes any person co-opted to serve on the committee, whether he is a member of the society or not;

"dissolved under the 1965 Act" means dissolved either as mentioned in section 55(*a*) of that Act (winding up under the Companies Act) or as mentioned in section 55(*b*) of that Act (instrument of dissolution).

Definitions relating to charities

38. In this Part—

(*a*) "charity" has the same meaning as in the Charities Act 1960; and

(*b*) "registered charity" means a charity which is registered under section 4 of that Act and is not an exempt charity within the meaning of that Act.

Minor definitions

39. In this Part—

"mental disorder" has the same meaning as in the Mental Health Act 1983 or the Mental Health (Scotland) Act 1984;

"secure tenancy" has the same meaning as in section 79 of the Housing Act 1985 or section 10 of the Tenants' Rights &c. (Scotland) Act 1980;

"standard scale" has the meaning given by section 75 of the Criminal Justice Act 1982.

Index of defined expressions: Part I

40. The following Table shows provisions defining or explaining expressions used in this Part (other than provisions defining or explaining an expression used only in the same section or paragraph):—

appropriate register (in relation to a society registered under the 1965 Act)	section 37
bank	section 106
charge (in relation to Scotland)	section 106
charity	section 38(*a*)
committee (in relation to a society registered under the 1965 Act)	section 37
compulsory disposal (in Schedule 2)	paragraph 6 of that Schedule
co-operative housing association	section 1(2)
co-opted member (in relation to the committee of a society registered under the 1965 Act)	section 37
the Companies Act	section 106
dissolved under the 1965 Act (in relation to a society registered under that Act)	section 37
district (of a local housing authority)	section 104(2)
dwelling	section 106
eligible for registration (in relation to a housing association)	section 4
exempted disposal (in Schedule 2)	paragraph 5 of that Schedule
friendly society	section 106
fully mutual (in relation to a housing association)	section 1(2)
hostel	section 106
house	section 106
housing activities	section 106
housing association	section 1(1)
housing association grant	section 41
housing trust	section 2
insurance company	section 106
local housing authority	section 104
member of family	section 105
mental disorder	section 39
mortgage (in relation to Scotland)	section 106
the 1965 Act	section 37
register, registered, registration and unregistered (in relation to a housing association)	section 3(2)
registered charity	section 38(*b*)
relevant disposal (in Schedule 2)	paragraph 4 of that Schedule
revenue deficit grant	section 54
secure tenancy	section 39

shared ownership lease section 106
standard scale section 39
trustee savings bank section 106.

PART II

HOUSING ASSOCIATION FINANCE

Housing association grants

Housing association grants

41.—(1) The Secretary of State may make grants ("housing association grants") to registered housing associations in respect of their expenditure in connection with housing projects which are approved by him or fall within an approved development programme.

(2) An approved development programme is a programme for the development of housing by registered housing associations prepared by the Housing Corporation or a local authority and for the time being approved by the Secretary of State for the purposes of this section.

DEFINITIONS
"housing association": s.1.
"housing project": ss. 42–45.
"local authority": s.106.
"registered": s.3.

GENERAL NOTE
This and ss.42 to 57 govern the principal provision of central government funding to housing associations registered with the Housing Corporation. There are three grants: Housing Association Grant (ss.41–52), known as H.A.G., Revenue Deficit Grant ("R.D.G.") (ss.54, 56–57) and Hostel Deficit Grant (ss.55–57). This "set" of grants was introduced by the Housing Act 1974. This section introduces the first, *i.e.* H.A.G.

Subs. (2)
Sched. 18 of the Housing Act 1980 gave powers to the Secretary of State, now contained in this subsection, to replace approval of individual housing projects proposed by a housing association with approval of a programme of housing developments by a housing association, or associations, prepared by the Corporation or a local housing authority: see D.O.E. Circular No. 14/83.

Projects qualifying for grant: accommodation for letting, hostels

42.—(1) A project is a housing project for the purposes of housing association grant if it is undertaken for the purpose of—
(*a*) providing dwellings for letting,
(*b*) providing a building for use as a hostel,
(*c*) improving or repairing such accommodation, or
(*d*) providing land or buildings which, in the opinion of the Secretary of State, will be for the benefit of persons for whom such accommodation is provided, or improving or repairing such buildings.
(2) In subsection (1)—
(*a*) "letting" in paragraph (*a*) includes the grant of a shared ownership lease, and
(*b*) in paragraph (*b*) "building" includes part of a building and "hostel" includes part of a hostel.
(3) References in this section to letting or the grant of a lease include the grant of a licence to occupy.

DEFINITIONS
   "dwelling": s.106.
   "hostel": s.106.
   "housing association grant": s.41.

GENERAL NOTE
   This section defines the projects which qualify as "housing projects" for the purposes of H.A.G. under s.41, above.

Subs. (1)
   Included are the provision, improvement or repair of dwellings, and hostel accommodation, and also the provision of ancilliary facilities, *e.g.* communal play areas, car parking spaces, clothes drying rooms, and which the Secretary of State considers are for the benefit of persons for whom the accommodation is provided.

Subs. (2)
   Sub-para. (a) ensures that the definition of "housing project" includes dwellings provided for the purpose of disposal to tenants under a shared ownership lease. For the definition of this now statutorily recognised equity-shared leasehold interest, see s.106, below.

Subs. (3)
   This provision is necessitated by the inclusion of hostels, the occupiers of which will normally be licensees rather than tenants.

Projects qualifying for grant: improvement for sale

43. A project where a registered housing association, after carrying out works of repair, improvement or conversion—
   (*a*) disposes of a house as one dwelling,
   (*b*) divides a house into two or more separate dwellings and disposes of them, or
   (*c*) combines two houses to form one dwelling and disposes of it,
is a housing project for the purposes of housing association grant.

DEFINITIONS
   "dwelling": s.106.
   "house": s.106.
   "housing association": s.1.
   "registered": s.3.

GENERAL NOTE
   The provisions of this section, first introduced by s.130 of the Housing Act 1980, extend H.A.G. to include housing projects of repairing, improving or converting (but, n.b. not new-buildings) of houses or flats for sale. S.4(3)(*c*), above, empowers a housing association to repair, improve or convert properties for sale as one of its permissible additional purposes or objects. Guidance on policy and practice for associations carrying out Improvements For Sale (I.F.S.) projects is contained in the Housing Corporation's Schemework Procedure Guide, approved for this purpose by the Department of the Environment, and in Circulars H.C. 22/84 and 16/85.

Projects qualifying for grant: repair or improvement after exercise of right to buy etc.

44.—(1) A project where a registered housing association carries out works of repair or improvement to a dwelling-house, or to the building in which a dwelling-house is situated, after the tenant has exercised, or claimed to exercise, the right to buy or the right to a shared ownership lease under Part V of the Housing Act 1985 is a housing project for the purposes of housing association grant.
   (2) Where in such a case a housing association grant is made after the tenant has exercised the right to buy or the right to be granted a shared ownership lease, the Secretary of State may reduce the amount of the grant.

(3) In this section "dwelling-house" has the same meaning as in Part V of the Housing Act 1985.

GENERAL NOTE
This section makes it clear that H.A.G. is payable for works carried out after a tenant has exercised the right to buy, or right to a shared ownership lease, under what is now Pt. V of the Housing Act 1985.

Subs. (2)
This provides for a reduction in allowable H.A.G. to take account of sales completed, and therefore purchase monies received, before a grant is paid over. The wording is not considered to be wide enough to require *repayment* by an association of H.A.G. already received. Provisions for repayment of H.A.G., in total or in part, after disposal of property under the right to buy or shared ownership schemes are, however, set out in s.52(1),(2), below.

Projects qualifying for grant: disposal to tenant of charitable housing association etc.

45.—(1) A project where a registered housing association first acquires a house and then disposes of it at a discount to a tenant to whom this section applies is a housing project for the purposes of housing association grant.

(2) This section applies to a tenant of a publicly-funded dwelling who, but for paragraph 1 of Schedule 5 to the Housing Act 1985 (exceptions to the right to buy: landlord a charitable housing trust or housing association) would have the right to buy.

(3) A dwelling is publicly-funded for this purpose if housing association grant has been paid in respect of a project which included—

(*a*) the acquisition of the dwelling,
(*b*) the acquisition of a building and the provision of the dwelling by means of the conversion of the building, or
(*c*) the acquisition of land and the construction of the dwelling on the land.

(4) Where a registered housing association contracts for the acquisition of a house and, without taking the conveyance, grant or assignment, disposes of its interest to a tenant to whom this section applies, subsection (1) and the following provisions have effect as if the association first acquired the house and then disposed of it to the tenant—

section 8 (disposal of land by registered housing associations),
section 9 (consent of Housing Corporation to disposals),
Schedule 2 (covenants for repayment of discount on early disposal and restricting disposal of houses in National Parks, &c.),
section 79(2) (power of Housing Corporation to lend to person acquiring interest from registered housing association), and
section 130 of the Housing Act 1985 (reduction of discount on exercise of right to buy where previous discount given).

GENERAL NOTE

Tenants of housing trusts and associations which are charities within the meaning of the Charities Act 1960 have always been excluded from the "right to buy" scheme introduced under the Housing Act 1980: see now para. 1 of Sched. 5, Housing Act 1985. The Housing and Building Control Act 1984 introduced the scheme which is now provided for by this section, enabling a charitable housing trust or association to arrange the acquisition of an alternative dwelling for the purpose of immediate onward disposal to a tenant who, but for the charitable landlord exception, would have had the right to buy the property he lived in. The rationale for the provisions of this section was explained during debate of the Bill which became the Housing and Building Control Act 1984:

"This Bill does not contain a clause that would give the tenants of charitable housing associations the right to buy the homes they live in, much as I myself, frankly, would have liked to included it.

"Your Lordships will, however, be aware of the proposals for a new home ownership scheme for tenants of charitable housing associations . . . This scheme, in outline, would offer the chance of home ownership to tenants of charitable dwellings provided with housing association grant through a purchase on the open market with a discount similar to what they would have had under the right to buy. For every tenant who was able to take advantage of the scheme, a charitable dwelling would be vacated and become available for re-letting to a person or a family with acute housing needs in line with the objects of the charitable landlord . . . " (Lord Belwin, *Hansard*, H.L. Vol. 447, col. 457, January 30, 1984.)

Conceptually the section contains a certain, if arcane, theoretical consistency. For many years now, private sector landlords have made substantial cash payments to persuade their tenants to go, either in order to convert and sell the converted property, or to relet on an unprotected or unregulated letting. In recent years, such ex-tenants will commonly have used these payments in order to make up the deposit on a house purchase. Housing associations are sometimes described as the "quasi-public sector" (the phrase appears first to have been used in the Report of the Select Committee on Artisans' and Labourers' Dwellings [1881] in relation to the Peabody Trust.) This "premium" may be described as one more of the many ways in which they straddle the sectors.

The details of the scheme now operating in England and Wales are set out in Circular H.C. 16/84. Note however, that there is currently a temporary "stop" on applications under the scheme received by the Corporation on or after August 23, 1985: Circular H.C. 35/85 refers. In summary, a tenant wishing to participate in the scheme makes an initial approach to the landlord charitable association to establish eligibility. Thereafter, the tenant identifies an available property on the open market, within the cost limits provided by the scheme, and then approaches a participating non-charitable registered housing association. This association will in turn, subject to Housing Corporation approval, arrange either for the conveyance of the property from the vendor to the tenant direct or, if the arrangement is to be for acquisition on a shared ownership basis, the participating association will itself acquire the necessary interest in the property concerned.

Subs. (1)

H.A.G. may be claimed by the participating non-charitable housing association in respect of allowable costs of arranging for acquisition of a property under the scheme.

Subss. (2), (3)

The provisions apply only to tenants of "publicly-funded" dwellings who would, but for the "charitable landlord" exception (see note above) have had the right to buy the dwellings which they occupy. "Publicly-funded" is defined as the payment of Housing Association Grant for either the acquisition, construction or conversion of the dwelling which the tenant currently occupies.

Subs. (4)

This subsection makes it clear that H.A.G. may be paid where the participating, non-charitable association arranges for the purchase of a dwelling between the vendor and tenant direct, *e.g.* by way of an exchange of contract between vendor and association, and immediate assignment of the option to purchase to the tenant, so that the association never takes title in its own name. Other provisions applied are those requiring repayment of discount on early disposal, Housing Corporation consent to disposal, and Housing Corporation house-purchased lending powers, all in the same way as if the association had completed purchase before resale.

Applications for housing association grant

46.—(1) A housing association grant is not payable in respect of a project unless an application for it is submitted to the appropriate body.

(2) The appropriate body in England and Wales is—

(*a*) where the housing association concerned makes an application to a local authority for a loan under section 58(2) in connection with the project, that authority, and

(*b*) in any other case, the Housing Corporation.

(3) The appropriate body in Scotland is a local authority, the Housing Corporation or the Secretary of State.

(4) Where a local authority or the Housing Corporation receive an application under this section, they shall forward it to the Secretary of State together with their own assessment of the project.

DEFINITIONS
"housing association": s.1.
"housing association grant": s.1.
"local authority": s.106.

GENERAL NOTE
A housing project will normally be financed initially by a loan advance to the association concerned, either from the local authority or from the Housing Corporation. H.A.G. is paid subsequently, on completion of the project. H.A.G. must be applied for, from the "appropriate body", *i.e.* a lending local authority, or the Corporation itself. In Scotland, application may be directly to the Secretary of State. The authority or Corporation is merely the agent of the Secretary of State, and does not approve the project, although they must "scrutinise" the claim themselves, to reach their own assessment of the costs.

D.O.E. Circulars Nos. 52/75, 103/77 and 14/83 set out the arrangements for the administration of housing project approval and payment of grant as regards local authorities. In particular, associations are required to submit a claim for the payment of grant to the lending authority not later than the end of the month after the month in which the project reaches practical completion: Circular 103/77, para. 4, Appendix A. As regards applications to the Housing Corporation, the Corporation has produced a H.A.G. Manual which sets out the basis of the administration of grants: See also Circulars P.C. 2/82 and P.C. 19/83.

Subs. (4)
The local authority, or the Housing Corporation, must forward an application for H.A.G. to the Department of the Environment for its approval. The H.A.G. application form completed by the association makes provision for the certification of calculations and amounts claimed, and for certification of satisfactory completion of the project, by the local authority or the Housing Corporation as the case may be.

Amount of housing association grant: net cost

47.—(1) The housing association grant payable in respect of a project is equal to the net cost of the project to the association, determined in accordance with the following provisions, but subject to section 48 (maximum levels of cost and grant).

(2) The net cost of a project to the association is the difference between—

(*a*) the estimated expenditure of the association which is, in the opinion of the Secretary of State, attributable to the project and is reasonable and appropriate having regard to all the circumstances, and

(*b*) the estimated income which, in the opinion of the Secretary of State, the association might reasonably be expected to receive in respect of the project, including sums received or to be received by way of grant or subsidy, other than sums received or to be received by way of housing association grant.

(3) Estimated expenditure and estimated income for this purpose shall be calculated in such manner as the Secretary of State may, with the consent of the Treasury, from time to time determine, and the calculation

may take account of expenditure and income likely to be incurred or received in connection with the premises to which the project relates after the completion of the project.

(4) Before making a general determination under subsection (3) the Secretary of State shall consult such bodies appearing to him to be representative of housing associations as he considers appropriate.

(5) In determining the net cost of a project the Secretary of State may adopt the assessment of the body forwarding the grant application to him under section 46.

(6) If in the case of an application for a housing association grant in respect of a particular project it appears to the Secretary of State appropriate to do so, he may determine the net cost in such manner as he considers appropriate instead of in accordance with the preceding provisions.

DEFINITIONS
"housing association": s.1.
"housing association grant": s.41.

GENERAL NOTE
This section sets out the basis upon which H.A.G. is to be assessed.

Subs. (1)
H.A.G. is a sum equal to the net cost of the project for which H.A.G. is claimed, so that, at least in theory, the association concerned will thereafter be in a position to meet continuing liabilities in respect of the project from revenue received, *i.e.* rental income. In fact, many associations experience serious difficulty in meeting ongoing costs of management, maintenance and loan charges, and provision has been made for further subsidy where required, by means of a Revenue Deficit Grant under s.54, below.
For current levels of allowable costs and grants, see s.48, below.

Subss. (2), (3)
The determination of the manner in which the estimated income and estimated expenditure attributable to an approved housing project shall be calculated is contained in D.O.E. Circular No. 52/75, as reviewed in subsequent circulars the most recent of which is Circular No. 14/83. As to administration allowances currently in operation, see Circular H.C. 13/85.

Subs. (4)
The body recognised by the Secretary of State under this subsection is the National Federation of Housing Associations: see s.33 and note thereto, above.
There has been a number of cases on the meaning of consultation: see, *e.g., Rollo* v. *Minister of Town and Country Planning* [1948] L.J.R. 817, 1 All E.R. 13, *Re Union of Benefices of Whippingham and East Cowes, St. James* [1954] A.C. 245, H.L., *Sinfield* v. *London Transport Executive* [1970] 1 Ch. 550, and *R.* v. *Sheffield City Council, ex parte Mansfield* (1978) 37 P. & C.R. 1. Most recently, the question was considered in relation to consultation on amendments to the Housing Benefits Regulations, as required by s.36, Social Security and Housing Benefits Act 1982, in *R.* v. *Secretary of State for Social Services, ex parte Association of Metropolitan Authorities* [1985] 17 H.L.R. 487, Q.B.D., in which it was held as follows:

(1) The essence of consultation is the communication of a genuine invitation to give advice and a genuine receipt of that advice; to achieve consultation, sufficient information must be supplied by the consulting to the consulted party to enable it to tender helpful advice; sufficient time must be given by the consulting to the consulted party to enable it to do so, and sufficient time must be available for such advice to be considered by the consulting party; sufficient in this context does not mean ample, but at least enough to enable the relevant purpose to be fulfilled; helpful advice in this context means sufficiently informed and considered information or advice about aspects of the form or substance of the proposals, or their implication for the consulted party, being aspects material to the implementation of the proposal as to which the consulting party might not be fully informed or advised and as to which the party consulted might have relevant information or advice to offer.

(2) Where insufficient consultation is alleged, the challenge is to the *vires* of the subordinate legislation; accordingly, the correct test is whether there has been sufficient

consultation, rather than whether the consultation process fails to satisfy the test now known as "rationality", formerly the "unreasonable" test in *Associated Provincial Picture Houses Ltd.* v. *Wednesbury Corporation* [1948] 1 K.B. 223, C.A.

(3) The power to make the Regulations was conferred on the Secretary of State, and his is the duty to consult; both the form or substance of new Regulations and the time allowed for consulting before making them, may well depend in whole or in part on matters of a political nature, as to the force or implications of which the Secretary of State rather than the court is the best judge; when considering whether or not consultation has in substance been carried out, the court should have regard not so much to the actual facts which preceded the making of the Regulations as to the material before the Secretary of State when he made the Regulations, which material includes facts or information as it appeared or must have appeared to the Secretary of State acting in good faith, and any judgments made or opinions expressed to him before the making of the Regulations about those facts which appeared or could have appeared to him to be reasonable.

(4) The urgency of the need for the Regulations as seen by the Secretary of State was such, taking into account the nature of the amendments proposed, that the Department was entitled to require that views in response to its invitation for comments should be expressed quickly; the urgency of the need for the Regulations, as seen by the Secretary of State, taking into account the nature of the amendments proposed, was not such that the Department was entitled to require views to be expressed within such a short period that those views would or might be insufficiently informed or insufficiently considered so that the applicants would or might be unable to tender helpful advice.

(5) Taking into account both the urgency of the matter, as seen by the Department, and the material features of the Regulations, and bearing in mind that the applicants had no knowledge until after the Regulations were made of one of their features, the Secretary of State failed to fulfil his obligation to consult before making the Regulations; the time allowed was so short, and the failure to provide amendments was such that, as the Department must have known even without imputing to them precise knowledge of the applicants' internal arrangements, only piecemeal, and then only partial, assistance could be given.

(6) In the ordinary case, a decision made *ultra vires* is likely to be set aside, in the present case the applicants sought to strike down Regulations which had become part of the public law of the land; it may be that when delegated legislation is held to be *ultra vires*, it is not necessarily to be regarded as normal practice to revoke the instrument. As a matter of pure discretion, the Statutory Instrument would not be revoked for the following reasons: only one of the six associations which had been and habitually were consulted had applied for revocation, and that one applied only on the ground that it was not properly consulted; the Regulations had been in force for about six months and authorities must have adapted themselves as best they could to the difficulties which they imposed on them; if the Regulations were revoked, all those who had been refused benefit because of them would be entitled to make fresh claims, and all authorities would be required to consider each such claim; the Amendment Regulations had been consolidated into the Housing Benefit Regulations 1985 (S.I. 1985, No. 677) and which had come into operation, which Regulations were not challenged.

Amount of housing association grant: maximum levels of cost and grant

48.—(1) The Secretary of State may, with the consent of the Treasury, determine maximum levels of cost or of housing association grant applicable to—

(*a*) housing projects generally,

(*b*) any description of housing project, or

(*c*) a particular housing project,

and the amount of grant payable shall be limited in accordance with any such determination.

(2) Before making a general determination under subsection (1) the Secretary of State shall consult such bodies appearing to him to be representative of housing associations as he considers appropriate.

(3) The maximum grant which may be paid for any one dwelling in a case of the kind mentioned in section 43 (where dwelling disposed of after conversion, &c.) is—

(*a*) in respect of a dwelling in Greater London or the City of Glasgow district, £12,500,

(*b*) in respect of a dwelling elsewhere, £9,500,
or such other sum as the Secretary of State may prescribe by order made
with the consent of the Treasury.

(4) An order—

(*a*) may make different provision for different cases or descriptions of
case, including different provision for different areas;

(*b*) shall be made by statutory instrument which shall be subject to
annulment in pursuance of a resolution of either House of
Parliament.

DEFINITIONS

"housing association": s.1.
"housing association grant": s.41.
"housing project": ss.42–45.

GENERAL NOTE

This section provides for the determination by the Secretary of State of the maximum
levels of costs of housing projects, and the level of H.A.G. payable, either generally or in
respect of particular projects, or projects falling within a specified description or class. Since
May 16, 1983 the new cost criteria originally applicable to Housing Corporation projects
only has extended to all funded schemes. The new criteria of Total Indicative Costs (T.I.C.)
are intended to serve as "guide-lines" rather than cost limits, and to provide indicia of the
level of costs which would normally be expected for the kind of accommodation to be
provided. Projects submitted for D.O.E. approval which are within the T.I.C. cost criteria
will receive automatic approval, whereas projects submitted with greater forecast costs are
required to be supported by recommendations for approval by the local authority or by the
Housing Corporation (for submission of applications, see s.46, above), and will be critically
considered by the Department: see D.O.E. Circular 14/83.

The cost criteria are reviewed annually, and the current amounts are set out in Circular
H.C. 11/85, as amended in part by H.C. 37/85.

Subs. (2)

See note to s.47(4), above.

Subs. (3)

Note the limitation on H.A.G. payable for I.F.S. dwellings: see notes to s.43, above.

Payment of housing association grants

49.—(1) A housing association grant in respect of a project is payable
either in a single sum or in annual instalments, as the Secretary of State
may determine.

(2) A grant payable in a single sum is payable when in the opinion of
the Secretary of State the project is completed or its completion has
become impossible.

(3) A grant payable in annual instalments is payable in instalments—

(*a*) beginning in the financial year in which, in the opinion of the
Secretary of State, the project is completed or its completion has
become impossible, and

(*b*) continuing over such number of years as he may determine, either
generally or in relation to the particular project.

(4) The Secretary of State may, if he considers it appropriate to do so,
make payments on account of the grant at a time earlier than indicated by
subsection (2) or (3).

(5) The Secretary of State may, on such terms as he may with the
approval of the Treasury specify, appoint the Housing Corporation or a
local housing authority to act as his agent in connection with the making,
in such cases as he may specify, of payments in respect of housing
association grant; and, where such an appointment is made, the Corporation or authority shall act as such an agent in accordance with the terms
of their appointment.

(6) No sum shall be paid in respect of a housing association grant to a body which has been removed from the register of housing associations under section 6.

DEFINITIONS
  "housing association grant": s.41.
  "local authority": s.104.

GENERAL NOTE
  This section provides that H.A.G. may be paid either in a single lump sum or in annual instalments, either on completion of a project or after its completion has become impossible. D.O.E. Circular No. 103/77, sets out the scheme for payment of H.A.G. In respect of projects which have become impossible to complete, see P.C. 16/83, which supersedes certain provisions of D.O.E. Circular No. 103/77 in respect of "abortive projects", and explains the procedure and policy considerations applicable to the grant of H.A.G. in these circumstances.

Subs. (5)
  For the agency arrangements currently in operation see para. 59 and Appendix F. to D.O.E. Circular No. 52/75.

Grant conditions

50.—(1) The Secretary of State may provide—
  (*a*) where the project is approved by him for the purposes of housing association grant, in giving his approval, or
  (*b*) where the project falls within an approved development programme (and thus does not require separate approval), before first making a payment of grant in respect of the project,
that the payment of a housing association grant is conditional on compliance by the housing association concerned with such conditions as he may specify.

(2) The conditions may include, in a case where the project has not yet been completed, conditions as to the period within which it is to be completed.

DEFINITIONS
  "approved development programme": s.41.
  "housing association": s.1.
  "housing association grant": s.41.

GENERAL NOTE
  The main conditions for the payment of Housing Association Grant are set out in D.O.E. Circular No. 14/83. For the reference in subs. (1)(*b*) to "approved development programme", see s.41(2) above, and note thereto. Conditions can only be attached on approval (if not within an approved development programme), or before first payment of H.A.G. (if within).

Payment of grant to another association on transfer of property

51.—(1) The Secretary of State may, where at any time—
  (*a*) a housing association grant is payable in respect of a project, and
  (*b*) a dwelling or hostel to which the project relates, or part of such a dwelling or hostel, becomes vested in, or is leased for a term exceeding seven years to, a registered housing association other than the association by whom the grant application was made, or trustees for such an association,
pay to that other association the whole or part of the housing association grant, or any instalment of it, which would otherwise have been paid after that time to the association by whom the grant application was made.

(2) For the purposes of subsection (1) a lease shall be treated as being for a term exceeding seven years where the original term is for a lesser

period but the lease confers on the lessee an option for renewal for a term which, together with the original term, exceeds seven years.

GENERAL NOTE
This section provides for the payment of H.A.G. to a registered housing association which acquires a dwelling or hostel developed by another housing association, where H.A.G. payable in respect of that dwelling or hostel project has not been paid to the transferring association. The provision applies to all acquisitions where the property in question becomes vested in the acquiring association, other than under a lease for a period of seven years or less. Under subs. (2), a lease of less than seven years with an option for the acquiring association to renew which would, if exercised, create a term exceeding seven years, is within the qualifying definition.

Section 52, below, contains provisions for discontinuance of the whole or any part of H.A.G. payable to the transferring association, upon such a disposal.

The provisions for a voluntary disposal of land by a housing association are contained in s.8, 9, above. For the powers of the Housing Corporation to direct a transfer of land to another housing association, see s.32, above.

Circumstances in which grant may be reduced, suspended or reclaimed

52.—(1) This section applies where a housing association grant has been made to an association and—

(*a*) a condition imposed under section 50 is not complied with, or

(*b*) the Secretary of State is satisfied that land to which the grant relates has ceased to be used, or to be available for use, for the purpose for which, at the time the project concerned was approved, it was intended that it should be used, or

(*c*) land to which the grant relates is disposed of (in any manner) by the association, or

(*d*) there is paid to the association, in respect of land to which the grant relates, an amount payable in pursuance of the covenant required by paragraph 1 of Schedule 2 to this Act or section 155 of the Housing Act 1985 (repayment of discount on early disposal) or any other covenant or provision to the like effect, or

(*e*) there is paid to the association, in respect of land to which the grant relates, an amount payable in pursuance of the provision required by paragraph 1 or 6 of Schedule 8 to the Housing Act 1985 (terms of shared ownership lease: acquisition of additional shares or payment for outstanding share on disposal) or any other provision to the like effect.

(2) Where this section applies, the Secretary of State may—

(*a*) reduce the amount of, or of any payment in respect of, the grant,

(*b*) suspend or discontinue any instalment of the grant, or

(*c*) if a payment has been made to the association in respect of the grant, direct the association to pay to him an amount equal to the whole, or such proportion as he may determine, of the amount paid to the association.

(3) Where, after a housing association grant has been made to an association, there is—

(*a*) such a disposal as is mentioned in subsection (1)(*c*), or

(*b*) such a payment as is mentioned in subsection (1)(*d*) or (*e*),

the association shall notify the Secretary of State, and if so required by written notice of the Secretary of State, shall furnish him with such particulars of and information relating to the disposal or payment as are specified in the notice.

(4) Where a housing association grant has been made to an association, the Chief Land Registrar may furnish the Secretary of State with such particulars and information as he may reasonably require for the purpose of determining—

(*a*) whether there has been such a disposal as is mentioned in subsection (1)(*c*), or

(*b*) whether there has been made such a payment as is mentioned in subsection (1)(*d*) or (*e*).

DEFINITIONS
"housing association grant": s.41.
"shared ownership lease": s.106.

GENERAL NOTE
This section provides for the reduction, suspension, or discontinuance of H.A.G. in the circumstances set out in subs. (1), or recoupment of already paid H.A.G.

Subs. (1)(*a*)
Section 50 requires a housing association to comply with conditions specified by the Secretary of State relating to the payment of H.A.G. The main conditions are set out in D.O.E. Circular No. 14/83, retained in force by s.2, Housing (Consequential Provisions) Act 1985. This sub-paragraph makes it clear that payment of grant is conditional upon compliance with those conditions.

Subs. (1)(*b*)
H.A.G. may be withheld or withdrawn, or required to be repaid, if land to which the grant relates becomes unavailable to be used for the provision of housing accommodation.

Subs. (1)(*c*)
For the provision for transfer of outstanding H.A.G. to a housing association taking a disposal of the land and housing project upon which H.A.G. has been assessed, see s.51, above. In the case of land disposed of to a tenant under the "right to buy" or "shared ownership" schemes contained in Pt. V of the Housing Act 1985, or following a voluntary disposition, the capital receipt may be insufficient to cover all H.A.G. attributable to the property, *e.g.* because of the percentage discount allowed to tenants exercising their right to buy the dwelling they occupy. In this circumstance the Secretary of State will not seek to recover the full amount of any H.A.G. paid if this would result in the housing association making a loss after paying approved costs: see Circular H.C. 15/80.

Subs. (1)(*d*)(*e*)
These provisions allow for adjustment of H.A.G. to take account of repayment to an association of purchase discounts, following early disposal of the property in question, and any further capital receipt resulting from a shared-ownership leaseholder's acquisition of additional tranches of the equity in the property. A housing association receiving such a further capital receipt may now be required, effectively, to pay the sum over to the D.O.E. to offset any H.A.G. paid, or payable, on the dwelling.

Subs. (3)
This requires an association to notify the D.O.E. of *any* disposal of land, and any capital receipt, of the types referred to in subs. (1)(*d*) and (*e*), above.

Subs. (4)
This enables the Secretary of State to obtain land registry information concerning disposals of property, and repayments of discounts, which are registerable as land charges.

Recoupment of surplus rental income

53.—(1) A registered housing association which has at any time received a housing association grant shall show separately in its accounts for any period the surpluses arising from increased rental income during that period from housing projects in connection with which the grant was made.

(2) The surpluses shall be shown by each association in a fund to be known as the Grant Redemption Fund; and the method of constituting the Fund and of showing it in the association's accounts shall be as required by order of the Secretary of State under section 24 (general requirements as to accounts).

(3) The surpluses in respect of a period shall be calculated in such manner as the Secretary of State may determine for housing associations generally.

(4) In making that determination the Secretary of State may take account of—

(*a*) the rental income received or capable of being received by an association, and

(*b*) the management and maintenance costs and loan charges incurred or likely to be incurred by it;

and surpluses may be calculated differently for housing associations of different kinds or dwellings in different parts of Great Britain.

(5) The manner of calculating surpluses shall be determined after consultation with organisations appearing to the Secretary of State to be representative of registered housing associations, and shall be made known to the associations.

(6) The Secretary of State may from time to time give notice to a registered housing association requiring it to pay to him, with interest if demanded, or to apply or appropriate for purposes he specifies, any sums standing in its Grant Redemption Fund at the end of a period of account.

(7) Interest demanded by such a notice is payable—

(*a*) at the rate or rates previously determined by the Secretary of State, with the consent of the Treasury, for housing associations generally and published by him, or, if no such determination has been made, at the rate or rates specified with the consent of the Treasury in the notice;

(*b*) either from the date of the notice or from such earlier date, not earlier than the end of the period of account, as may be specified in the notice.

DEFINITIONS
"housing association": s.1.
"housing project": ss.42–45.
"registered": s.3.

GENERAL NOTE
In respect of housing projects for letting, registered housing associations apply for and charge rents registered by the Rent Officer Service, under Part VI, Rent Act 1977. Registered rents may be re-assessed, and may therefore increase, every two years. This section provides for the identification of any surplus increased rent, *i.e.* that element of the rent not taken into account in the original housing association grant assessment, with a view to recoupment of that element by the D.O.E.

Grant Redemption Fund is assessed by deducting from the sum of fair rents and service charges, the sum of net debt charges, relevant management and maintenance allowances, service costs and certain miscellaneous expenditure. The method of calculating any surplus is as prescribed by the Secretary of State. Thus, for example, the Secretary of State may have regard not merely to actual income received, but to the rental income which could have been received.

It may be noted that the G.R.F. provisions effectively deprive a housing association of the financial advantages enjoyed by other organisations to benefit from the surplus actually flowing from fixed price assets acquired in earlier years, thus reducing the scope for development of those independent initiatives which are said to be the hallmark of non-government activity. Furthermore, while associations are left with many risks relating to the housing development process, they are deprived of the opportunity to balance risk with profit when a project is developed and managed successfully.

Subss. (2) *to* (5)

The Registered Housing Associations (Accounting Requirements) Order 1982, S.I. 1982 No. 828, retained in force by s.2, Housing (Consequential Provisions) Act 1985, provides for the manner of inclusion of surplus rental income, under the Grant Redemption Fund, in the association's accounts. See note to s.24, above, on accounting requirements and the relevant Housing Corporation Circulars. See also Circulars H.C. 15/83 and 24/85 for the manner of calculating surpluses.

The recognised body for consultative purposes, under subs. (5), is the National Federation of Housing Associations: see note to s.30. As to consultation, see note to s.47(4), above.

Subs. (6)

Current policy on the use of G.R.F. surpluses is explained in Circular H.C. 12/85: surpluses are to be used in the first instance to offset an association's assessed and approved revenue deficit (for revenue deficit provisions see s.54, below.) Thereafter, most associations will be required to pay any remaining sum, with interest, to the D.O.E.

Subs. (7)

The Grant Redemption Fund (Rate of Interest) Determination 1982, retained in force by s.2, Housing (Consequential Provisions) Act 1985, specifies that the rate of interest which the Secretary of State will require is the rate that can be obtained on deposit at a major clearing bank.

Deficit grants

Revenue deficit grants

54.—(1) The Secretary of State may pay a grant (a "revenue deficit grant") to a registered housing association which incurs a deficit on its revenue account for any period.

(2) An association incurs such a deficit if its relevant expenditure exceeds its relevant income.

(3) For this purpose—

    (*a*) its relevant expenditure is its expenditure for the period which, in the opinion of the Secretary of State, is attributable to its housing activities and is reasonable and appropriate having regard to all the circumstances, and

    (*b*) its relevant income is the income which, in the opinion of the Secretary of State, it might reasonably be expected to receive for the period in respect of its housing activities, including sums by way of grant or subsidy,

and income and expenditure shall be calculated in such manner as the Secretary of State may, with the consent of the Treasury, determine.

(4) The revenue deficit grant payable to an association in respect of a period shall be of such amount as the Secretary of State may determine in relation to that association, but shall not be greater than the amount of the excess determined under subsection (3).

(5) For the purposes of this section the housing activities of an association do not include activities relating to hostels.

DEFINITIONS

"hostel": s.106.
"housing activities": s.106.
"housing association": s.1.
"registered": s.3.

GENERAL NOTE

This section introduces Revenue Deficit Grant—R.D.G. It is payable, at the discretion of the Secretary of State, if a registered association incurs a deficit between income and expenditure in any accounting period.

The existence of a "deficit" is dependent on the Secretary of State's determination of what expenditure is, in his opinion, attributable to dwellings provided by the association and is reasonable and appropriate, and what income the association might reasonably expect to receive, *i.e.* it is a wholly discretionary grant. If H.A.G. proves in any particular case, and for an acceptable reason, to be inadequate to enable an association to meet its expenses out of income, the deficit may be met out of R.D.G.

Subss. (2)(3)
For the principles applied by the D.O.E. in assessing R.D.G. applications, see H.C. 14/83 and 11/84.

Subs. (5)
For similar provisions relating to hostel projects, see s.55, below.

Hostel deficit grants

55.—(1) The Secretary of State may pay a grant (a "hostel deficit grant") to a registered housing association which, in relation to a hostel managed by it, incurs a revenue deficit in respect of any period.

(2) An association incurs such a deficit if its relevant expenditure exceeds its relevant income.

(3) For this purpose—

    (*a*) its relevant expenditure is its expenditure for the period which, in the opinion of the Secretary of State, is attributable to the hostel and is reasonable and appropriate having regard to all the circumstances, and

    (*b*) its relevant income is the income which, in the opinion of the Secretary of State, it might reasonably be expected to receive in respect of the hostel for that period, including sums received or to be received in respect of that period by way of grant or subsidy,

and income and expenditure shall be calculated in such manner as the Secretary of State may, with the consent of the Treasury, determine.

(4) The reference in subsection (3)(*b*) to the income which an association might reasonably be expected to receive in respect of a hostel in a period includes so much as is reasonably attributable to the hostel of sums received or to be received by the association in respect of that period otherwise than by reference to a specific hostel or purpose.

(5) Where an association which applies for a hostel deficit grant manages more than one hostel, the Secretary of State may, if he considers it appropriate to do so, treat all the hostels managed by the association, or any two or more of them, as a single hostel for the purpose of determining whether the association has incurred a revenue deficit.

(6) The hostel deficit grant payable to an association in respect of a period shall be such amount as the Secretary of State may determine in relation to that association, but shall not be greater than the amount of the excess determined under subsection (3).

DEFINITIONS
    "hostel": s.106.
    "housing association": s.1.
    "registered": s.3.

GENERAL NOTE
    This section provides for the payment of a Hostel Deficit Grant on principles similar to those applicable to the payment of Revenue Deficit Grant under s.54. The scheme recognises the particular difficulties of low income and high running costs applicable to hostels, and affords some encouragement to associations to provide this type of accommodation. Where an association provides more than one hostel, however, subs. (5) states that all the hostels provided can be treated together as a single hostel for the purpose of assessing the association's eligibility to H.D.G.

Subss. (2)(3)
These subsections confer a wide discretion on the Secretary of State as to the assessment of H.D.G. eligibility in a particular case: see the note to s.54, above, which contains similar provisions for the assessment of Revenue Deficit Grant.

Subs. (4)
This casts the net of "likely receivable income," under subs. (3), somewhat wider, to include sums received, or likely to be received which are not directly referable to a specific hostel, to the extent that such a sum or part thereof is "reasonably attributable" to the hostel in question.

Subs. (6)
For the principles used in assessing applications for H.D.G., see Circulars H.C. 1/84 and H.C. 11/84.

Applications for deficit grants

56.—(1) A revenue deficit grant or hostel deficit grant is payable to an association in respect of a period only if an application complying with this section is made by the association to the Secretary of State and is approved by him.

(2) An application for either description of grant—
   (*a*) shall be made within 15 months after the end of the period to which it relates, and
   (*b*) shall be in such form and contain such information as the Secretary of State may determine.

(3) An application for a revenue deficit grant shall be accompanied by the audited accounts of the association for the period to which the application relates.

DEFINITIONS
   "hostel deficit grant": s.55.
   "revenue deficit grant": s.54.

GENERAL NOTE
This section requires housing associations wishing to claim R.D.G. or H.D.G, under ss.54, 55, above, to make an application in the form specified by the Secretary of State, within the time limits set out in subs. (2). Subs. (3) provides that such an application must be accompanied by a set of audited accounts for the period to which the application relates. The D.O.E. has produced application forms for R.D.G. and H.D.G., and applications must be submitted on these forms: see Circulars H.C. 14/83 [R.D.G.] and H.C. 1/84 [H.D.G.]

Payment of deficit grants

57.—(1) A revenue deficit grant shall be paid in a single sum in respect of the period to which it relates.

(2) A hostel deficit grant shall be paid either in a single sum or in instalments, as the Secretary of State may determine; and if payable by instalments shall be paid at such times and in such manner as the Treasury may direct.

(3) The Secretary of State may, if he considers it appropriate to do so, make payments on account of a revenue deficit grant or hostel deficit grant which he considers is likely to become payable to an association for any period.

(4) No sum shall be paid in respect of a revenue deficit grant or hostel deficit grant to a body which has been removed under section 6 from the register of housing associations.

DEFINITIONS
   "hostel deficit grant": s.55.
   "revenue deficit grant": s.54.

GENERAL NOTE
For the provisions for the payment of revenue deficit grants and hostel deficit grants to registered housing associations, see ss.54, 55, above. This section provides that R.D.G. shall be paid to an association in a single lump sum in respect of the period to which it relates, and that H.D.G. may be paid either in a lump sum or in instalments. Under subs. (3) there is provision for payments on account. In respect of both R.D.G. and H.D.G., any association which is experiencing cash-flow difficulties can apply for an on-account payment of grant. Any payment thus made will be based on a maximum of 80 per cent. of the eligible deficit incurred over a preceding period of not less than three months: see Circulars H.C. 14/83 [R.D.G.] and H.C. 1/84 [H.D.G.]

Arrangements with local authorities

Powers of local authorities to promote and assist housing associations: England and Wales

58.—(1) A local authority may promote the formation or extension of or, subject to the provisions of this Act, assist a housing association.

(2) A local authority may, subject to section 60 (assistance restricted to registered housing associations), for the assistance of a housing association—

(*a*) make grants or loans to the association,

(*b*) subscribe for share or loan capital of the association, or

(*c*) guarantee or join in guaranteeing the payment of the principal of, and interest on, money borrowed by the association (including money borrowed by the issue of loan capital) or of interest on share capital issued by the association,

on such terms and conditions as to rate of interest and repayment or otherwise and on such security as the local authority think fit.

(3) A term of an agreement for such a grant or loan is void if it purports—

(*a*) to limit the aggregate amount of rents payable in respect of dwellings to which the agreement relates or contributions towards the cost of maintaining such dwellings, or

(*b*) to specify a limit which the rent of a dwelling is not to exceed.

DEFINITIONS
"dwelling": s.106.
"housing association": s.1.
"local authority": s.106.
"registered": s.1.

GENERAL NOTE
This section enables local authorities, consistently with their function of promoting housing provision within their areas, under Part 11, Housing Act 1985, to promote the formation of housing associations and assist their activities by the provision of grants or loans, subscriptions to shares or loan capital, and by guaranteeing sums borrowed by a housing association and interest thereon. Under s.60(1), below, assistance by way of grants, loans, or guarantees may only be extended to associations which are registered with the Housing Corporation, unregistered self-build societies, and certain other unregistered associations which received grant assistance for housing schemes prior to 1974.

For the powers of the Secretary of State to vary or terminate a loan or grant agreement under this section, see s.69, below.

This section does not apply to Scotland: see s.59, below.

Subs. (3)

This prevents a local authority imposing restrictions on the rent payable on the housing association's dwellings. To qualify for housing association grant (see s.44 and subsequent sections, above), an association will, as regards non-hostel accommodation, have to arrange for rents to be registered by the Rent Officer, and for the purpose of H.A.G. calculation this is the rent payable on the dwelling: see D.O.E. Circular No. 14/83. This subsection prevents a local authority from taking it upon itself to arrange subsidisation of local housing association rents by expressly limiting the rents chargeable, as a term of a grant or loan agreement.

Powers of local authorities to promote and assist housing associations: Scotland

59.—(1) A local authority or regional council may promote the formation or extension of or, subject to section 60 (assistance restricted to registered housing associations), assist a housing association whose objects include the erection, improvement or management of housing accommodation.

(2) A local authority or regional council may, with the consent of and subject to any regulations or conditions made or imposed by the Secretary of State, for the assistance of such an association–

(*a*) make grants or loans to the association,

(*b*) subscribe for share or loan capital of the association, or

(*c*) guarantee or join in guaranteeing the payment of the principal of, and interest on, money borrowed by the association (including money borrowed by the issue of loan capital) or of interest on share capital issued by the association,

on such terms and conditions as to rate of interest and repayment or otherwise and on such security as the local authority or regional council think fit.

(3) A term of an agreement for such a grant or loan is void if it purports to relate to the rent payable in respect of a house to which the agreement relates or the contributions payable towards the cost of maintaining such a house.

(4) Regulations under this section shall be made by statutory instrument which shall be subject to annulment in pursuance of a resolution of either House of Parliament.

DEFINITIONS
    "house": s.106.
    "housing association": s.1.
    "local authority": s.106.
    "registered": s.3.

GENERAL NOTE
    This section gives Scottish local authorities and regional councils analogous powers to those given to local authorities in England and Wales, under s.58, above, to promote and assist housing associations. See note to s.58, above.

Certain assistance restricted to registered housing associations

60.—(1) Subject to the following provisions of this section, grants, loans and guarantees may be made or given under sections 58(2)(*a*) and (*c*) and 59(2)(*a*) and (*c*) only if the association is at the time the grant or loan is made, or the guarantee is given, a registered housing association.

(2) Subsection (1) does not apply in relation to the making of a loan to an unregistered self-build society for the purpose of enabling it to meet the whole or part of the expenditure incurred, or to be incurred, by it in carrying out its objects.

(3) Nothing in subsection (1) prevents the making of a loan to an unregistered association for the assistance of the association—

(*a*) in connection with works required to be carried out in pursuance of, or the acquisition of an estate or interest in a dwelling or other building for the purposes of, arrangements under section 121 of the Housing Act 1957 or section 155 of the Housing (Scotland) Act 1966 (arrangements with local authorities for the improvement of housing) which were approved by the Secretary of State before 1st April 1975;

(b) in connection with dwellings which were relevant dwellings for the purposes of section 73 of the Housing Finance Act 1972 (certain dwellings approved for purposes of subsidy before 10th August 1972);

(c) in connection with the provision of works which are relevant works, approved for subsidy, within the meaning of section 53 of the Housing (Financial Provisions) (Scotland) Act 1972;

(d) in connection with a building scheme within the meaning of section 75 of the Housing Finance Act 1972 (new building subsidy) which was approved by the Secretary of State for the purposes of that section before 1st April 1975;

(e) in connection with a building scheme or improvement scheme, within the meaning of sections 55 and 57 of the Housing (Financial Provisions) (Scotland) Act 1972 which was approved by the Secretary of State for the purposes of those sections before 1st April 1975.

DEFINITIONS
"dwelling": s.106.
"housing association": s.1.
"registered": s.3.
"self-build society": s.1.

GENERAL NOTE
Subs. (1)
This subsection provides that local authority, and regional council loans, grants and guarantees to housing associations under ss.58, 59, above, can only be made to housing associations which are registered with the Housing Corporation, *i.e.* under s.5, (but note the exceptions to this provision, contained in subss. (2)(3)).

Subs. (2)
This provides an exception to the registration requirement in the case of self-build societies. This particular species of society is defined in s.1(3), above.

Subs. (3)
This subsection contains a list of exceptions to the registration requirement in respect of housing associations with certain housing projects approved before the coming into force of the Housing Act 1974, which introduced the prerequisite of registration as a condition of receipt of central or local government finance in the case of associations other than self-build societies.

Power of local housing authority to supply furniture to housing association tenants

61.—(1) A local housing authority may sell, or supply under a hire-purchase agreement, furniture to the occupants of houses provided by a housing association under arrangements made with the authority, and may buy furniture for the purpose.

(2) In this section "hire-purchase agreement" means a hire-purchase agreement or conditional sale agreement within the meaning of the Consumer Credit Act 1974.

DEFINITIONS
"house": s.106.
"housing association": s.1.
"local housing authority": s.104.

GENERAL NOTE
This section provides that, in line with similar powers under s.10, Housing Act 1985 in respect of its own tenants, a local housing authority may sell, or supply under a hire-

purchase agreement, furniture to housing association tenants. The provision however only applies to the occupants of houses provided under arrangements with the local authority *i.e.* financial arrangements involving local authority assistance to the housing association under s.58 or 59.

Grants for affording tax relief

Grants for affording tax relief

62.—(1) If a housing association makes a claim to the Secretary of State in respect of a period and satisfies him that throughout the period it was a housing association to which this section applies and its functions either—

(a) consisted exclusively of the function of providing or maintaining housing accommodation for letting or hostels and activities incidental to that function, or

(b) included that function and activities incidental to that function,

the Secretary of State may make grants to the association for affording relief from tax chargeable on the association.

(2) This section applies to a housing association if—

(a) it does not trade for profit, and

(b) it is or was registered throughout the period in respect of which the claim is made,

and it is not for the time being approved for the purposes of section 341 of the Income and Corporation Taxes Act 1970 (tax treatment of co-operative housing associations).

(3) References in this section to tax chargeable on an association are to income tax (other than income tax which the association is entitled to deduct on making any payment) and corporation tax.

(4) A grant under this section may be made—

(a) in a case falling within subsection (1)(a), for affording relief from any tax chargeable on the association for the period in respect of which the claim is made, and

(b) in a case falling within subsection (1)(b), for affording relief from such part of any tax so chargeable as the Secretary of State considers appropriate having regard to the functions of the association;

and in any case shall be of such amount, shall be made at such times and shall be subject to such conditions as the Secretary of State thinks fit.

(5) The conditions may include conditions for securing the repayment in whole or in part of a grant made to an association in the event of tax in respect of which it was made subsequently being found not to be chargeable or in such other events (including the association subsequently beginning to trade for profit) as the Secretary of State may determine.

(6) A claim under this section shall be made in such manner and shall be supported by such evidence as the Secretary of State may direct.

(7) The Commissioners of Inland Revenue and their officers may disclose to the Secretary of State such particulars as he may reasonably require for determining whether a grant should be made on a claim or whether a grant should be repaid or the amount of such a grant or repayment.

DEFINITIONS
"hostel": s.106.
"housing association": s.1.

GENERAL NOTE
This section enables the Secretary of State to make grants to reimburse payments of income tax and corporation tax by an association which is registered with the Housing

Corporation and which does not trade for profit (as to the meaning of which, see notes to s.4, above), provided that during the period of taxation in question, the association was engaged wholly or mainly in providing housing or hostel accommodation and activities incidental thereto.

A housing association is not *per se* exempt from corporation tax,' and although an association's income from rents may exactly match its outgoings, so that there is no excess income over expenditure, nevertheless corporation tax may be chargeable. This is because corporation tax legislation does not recognise as a legitimate deduction from expenditure that element of an association's repayment of annual loan charges which goes to repayment of *capital*, *i.e.* which represents acquisition of property assets.

Housing associations which are registered charities are exempt from liability to pay corporation tax, under s.360, Income and Corporation Taxes Act 1970. So also are "fully mutual" co-operative societies (*see* s.1, above), under *ibid*, s.341, in respect of chargeable gains. As regards other associations, the re-imbursement provisions of this section are of considerable importance: the disposal of a housing association property under the Right to Buy scheme now contained in Part V, Housing Act 1985, or on a voluntary disposal under s.8, above, will give rise to corporation tax liability on any surplus arising from the sale. Circular H.C. 17/83 contains advice to associations on liability to pay corporation tax, and details of the policy of the Secretary of State as regards re-imbursement of tax chargeable, under this section.

Building society advances

Building society advances: certain advances not special advances but subject to their own limit

63.—(1) An advance to which this section applies is one made by a building society to a housing association on the security of a freehold or leasehold estate by means of a mortgage where—

(*a*) immediately before the execution of the mortgage, the Housing Corporation has an interest in the same freehold or leasehold estate under a mortgage entered into by the housing association, and

(*b*) the security represented by the last-mentioned mortgage is, with the agreement of the Corporation, postponed to the building society's security under the first-mentioned mortgage.

(2) The following advances—

(*a*) an advance to which this section applies, and

(*b*) an advance which in accordance with section 21(7) of the Building Societies Act 1962 a building society is treated as having made by reason of a transfer from one housing association to another, or from a housing association to the Housing Corporation, or from the Housing Corporation to a housing association, of the mortgagor's interest under a mortgage securing an advance made by the building society,

do not constitute special advances as defined by section 21 of the Building Societies Act 1962 and shall not be brought into account under section 22(2)(*b*) of that Act (ordinary limits on special advances).

(3) A building society shall not in the first financial year in which it makes advances on the security of freehold or leasehold estate make any advances to which this section applies.

(4) In any subsequent financial year a building society shall not, except in accordance with a permission under subsection (5), make advances to which this section applies of a total amount which exceeds 15 per cent. of the total of the advances of all descriptions made by the building society in the last preceding financial year on the security of freehold or leasehold estate.

(5) The Chief Registrar may, if he thinks fit, grant to a building society permission in writing to make advances to which this section applies in excess of the limit imposed by subsection (4), but subject to such other limits as may be specified in the permission.

(6) For the purposes of this section—

    (*a*) "financial year" has the meaning given by section 128 of, and paragraph 11 of Schedule 8 to, the Building Societies Act 1962, subject to paragraph (*b*) below;

    (*b*) for the purposes of subsection (4) if a financial year is shorter or longer than the last preceding financial year, a corresponding reduction or increase shall be made in the figure of 15 per cent. mentioned in that subsection; and

    (*c*) section 21(7) of the Building Societies Act 1962 (deemed advance on transfer of mortgage) applies for the purpose of ascertaining what advances a building society has made in a financial year.

DEFINITIONS
"building society": s.72.
"housing association": s.1.

GENERAL NOTE
This section applies to building society advances in respect of property for which there is also an advance from, and mortgage in favour of, the Housing Corporation, which Corporation mortgage has been postponed to the building society mortgage. The purpose is to limit the amount of advances by the building society.

Subs. (1)
Under this subsection the Housing Corporation must first have made a mortgage advance to the association concerned, and must then agree to that security being postponed to that of the building society's security, thereby giving the building society a first charge on the freehold or leasehold.

Subs. (2)
Any advances made by a building society in accordance with this section are not to be treated as special advances for the purposes of ss.21–24 of the Building Societies Act 1962, and are therefore not subject to the limitations on the amount which may be advanced by a building society, which those sections provide for. Consequently, the sole limitation on advances are those contained in this section.

Subss. (3), (4)
A building society may not make any advances of this class in its first year, and in any subsequent year may not make advances amounting to more than 15 per cent. of its total advances of all descriptions during the prior year, without the consent of the Chief Registrar. For the penalties for non-compliance with these provisions, see s.64, below.

Failure to comply with limit on advances an offence

64.—(1) If a building society does not comply with the requirements of section 63(3), (4) and (5) (limits on advances to which that section applies)—

    (*a*) the society and

    (*b*) every officer of the society who knowingly or wilfully authorises or permits the failure to comply,

commits an offence which is triable either way.

(2) A society which is convicted of an offence under this section is liable—

    (*a*) on conviction on indictment, to a fine, and

    (*b*) on summary conviction, to a fine not exceeding the statutory maximum.

(3) An officer who is convicted of an offence under this section is liable—

    (*a*) on conviction on indictment, to imprisonment for a term not exceeding two years, or a fine, or both;

    (*b*) on summary conviction, to imprisonment for a term not exceeding three months, or a fine not exceeding the statutory maximum, or both.

(4) In this section "statutory maximum" has the meaning given by section 74 of the Criminal Justice Act 1982.

DEFINITION
"building society": s.72.

GENERAL NOTE
This section makes it a criminal offence to fail to comply with the provisions of s.64(3)(4)(5), above, which limit a building society's powers to make mortgage advances to housing associations. Both the society itself and any officer who knowingly or wilfully authorises or permits the failure to comply are liable to prosecution. Fines may be imposed on the building society and any officer who is convicted, and an officer may also be sentenced to a term of imprisonment not exceeding two years, on indictment, or three months if tried summarily.

Building society advances: advances by more than one building society

65. A building society may make an advance to which section 63 applies by means of a mortgage under which the same freehold or leasehold estate constitutes the security both for that advance and for advances made to the same housing association by one or more other persons by means of the same mortgage, but only if—

    (*a*) every other person making an advance by means of that mortgage is another building society, and

    (*b*) the mortgagees in the mortgage all covenant with each other not to transfer their interests as mortgagees to a person who is not a building society.

DEFINITIONS
"building society": s.72.
"housing association": s.1.

GENERAL NOTE
This section enables building societies to grant second mortgages to housing associations on the security of a freehold or leasehold estate, being one to which s.63 applies, provided the existing or prior other mortgages are from building societies, and they have all agreed not to allow the mortgage to pass to a non-building society.

Application of ss.63 to 65 to Scotland

66. In the application to Scotland of sections 63 to 65 (building society advances)—

    (*a*) for the references to freehold or leasehold estate, substitute references to an estate or interest in land;

    (*b*) for the references to an advance on the security of freehold or leasehold estate, or to an advance by means of a mortgage, and similar references, substitute references to an advance upon a heritable security;

    (*c*) for the references to a mortgage, mortgagor or mortgagee substitute, respectively, references to a heritable security, a debtor in a heritable security and the creditor in a heritable security;

    (*d*) for the reference to an offence triable either way substitute a reference to an offence triable either summarily or on indictment.

GENERAL NOTE
This section applies the provisions of ss.63–65, above, which relate to building society mortgage advances for housing associations, to Scotland, and makes the necessary amendments to those sections to incorporate the relevant estates and interests recognised in Scotland.

Loans by Public Works Loan Commissioners

Loans by Public Works Loan Commissioners: England and Wales

67.—(1) The Public Works Loan Commissioners may lend money to a housing association—

   (*a*) for the purpose of constructing or improving, or facilitating or encouraging the construction or improvement, of houses,

   (*b*) for the purchase of houses which the association desires to purchase with a view to their improvement, and

   (*c*) for the purchase and development of land.

(2) A loan for any of those purposes, and interest on the loan, shall be secured by mortgage of—

   (*a*) the land in respect of which that purpose is to be carried out, and

   (*b*) such other lands, if any, as may be offered as security for the loan;

and the money lent shall not exceed three-quarters (or, if the payment of the principal of, and interest on, the loan is guaranteed by a local authority, nine-tenths) of the value, to be ascertained to the satisfaction of the Public Works Loan Commissioners, of the estate or interest in the land proposed to be so mortgaged.

(3) Loans may be made by instalments as the building of houses or other work on land mortgaged under subsection (2) progresses (so, however, that the total amount lent does not at any time exceed the amount specified in that subsection); and a mortgage may be accordingly made to secure such loans so to be made.

(4) If the loan exceeds two-thirds of the value referred to in subsection (2), and is not guaranteed as to principal and interest by a local authority, the Public Works Loan Commissioners shall require, in addition to such a mortgage as is mentioned in that subsection, such further security as they may think fit.

(5) Subject to subsection (6), the period for repayment of a loan under this section shall not exceed 40 years, and no money shall be lent on mortgage of any land unless the estate proposed to be mortgaged is either an estate in fee simple absolute in possession or an estate for a term of years absolute of which not less than 50 years are unexpired at the date of the loan.

(6) Where a loan under this section is made for the purpose of carrying out a scheme for the provision of houses approved by the Secretary of State, the maximum period for the repayment of the loan is 50 instead of 40 years, and money may be lent on the mortgage of an estate for a term of years absolute of which a period of not less than ten years in excess of the period fixed for the repayment of the sums advanced remains unexpired at the date of the loan.

DEFINITIONS
   "house": s.106.
   "housing association": s.1.

GENERAL NOTE
   This section preserves the discretionary power of the Public Works Loan Board Commissioners to lend money to housing associations.

Loans by Public Works Loan Commissioners: Scotland.

68.—(1) The Public Works Loan Commissioners may lend money to a housing association—

   (*a*) for the purpose of constructing or improving, or facilitating or encouraging the construction or improvement of, houses,

   (*b*) for the purchase of houses, and

   (*c*) for the purchase and development of land.

(2) A loan for any of those purposes shall be secured with interest by a heritable security over—

    (*a*) the land in respect of which that purpose is to be carried out, and

    (*b*) such other land, if any, as may be offered as security for the loan;

and the money lent shall not exceed three-quarters (or, if the payment of the principal of and interest on the loan is guaranteed by a local authority, nine-tenths) of the value, to be ascertained to the satisfaction of the Public Works Loan Commissioners, of the estate or interest in the land proposed to be burdened.

(3) Loans may be made by instalments as the building of houses or other work on the land burdened under subsection (2) progresses (so, however, that the total loans do not at any time exceed the amount specified in that subsection); and the heritable security may be granted accordingly to secure such loans so to be made.

(4) If the loan exceeds two-thirds of the value referred to in subsection (2), and is not guaranteed as to principal and interest by a local authority, the Public Works Loan Commissioners shall require, in addition to such a heritable security as is mentioned in that subsection, such further security as they may think fit.

(5) Subject to subsection (6), the period for repayment of a loan under this section shall not exceed 40 years, and no money shall be lent on the security of any land unless the estate or interest proposed to be burdened is either ownership or a lease of which a period of not less than 50 years remains unexpired at the date of the loan.

(6) Where a loan under this section is made for the purposes of carrying out a scheme, for the provision of houses approved by the Secretary of State, the maximum period for the repayment of the loan is 50 instead of 40 years, and money may be lent on heritable security over a lease recorded under the Registration of Leases (Scotland) Act 1857 of which a period of not less than ten years in excess of the period fixed for the repayment of the loan remains unexpired at the date of the loan.

DEFINITIONS
    "house": s.106.
    "housing association": s.1.

GENERAL NOTE
    This section repeats the provisions of s.67, above, for loans to housing associations by the Public Works Loan Commissioners, in Scotland, with the necessary amendments to reflect the estates and interests recognised in Scotland.

Miscellaneous

Power to vary or terminate certain agreements with housing associations

69.—(1) This section applies to agreements of the following descriptions—

    (*a*) an agreement for a loan to a housing association by the Housing Corporation under section 2 of the Housing Act 1964;

    (*b*) an agreement which continues in force under Part I of Schedule 4 (arrangements with local authority for the provision or improvement of housing);

    (*c*) an agreement to which Part II of Schedule 4 applies (subsidy agreements with local authorities);

    (*d*) an agreement which continues in force under Part III of Schedule 4 (special arrangements with the Secretary of State);

    (*e*) an agreement for a loan or grant to a housing association under section 58(2) or 59(2) (financial assistance by local authorities);

(*f*) a scheme which continues in force under Part V of Schedule 5 (schemes for unification of grant conditions).

(2) On the application of a party to an agreement to which this section applies, the Secretary of State may, if he thinks fit, direct—

(*a*) that the agreement shall have effect with such variations, determined by him or agreed by the parties, as may be specified in the direction, or

(*b*) that the agreement shall be terminated.

(3) No variation shall be directed under subsection (2) which would have the effect of including in an agreement a term—

(*a*) limiting the aggregate amount of rents payable in respect of dwellings to which the agreement relates or contributions towards the cost of maintaining such dwellings, or

(*b*) specifying a limit which the rent of a dwelling is not to exceed.

This subsection does not extend to Scotland.

(4) No variation shall be directed under subsection (2) which would have the effect of including in an agreement a term relating to the rent payable in respect of a house to which the agreement relates or contributions towards the cost of maintaining such a house.

This subsection extends to Scotland only.

DEFINITIONS
"dwelling": s.106.
"house": s.106.
"housing association": s.1.
"local authority": s.106.

GENERAL NOTE
This section enables a party to an agreement specified in subs. (1) to apply to the Secretary of State to vary or terminate that agreement. The Secretary of State has a wide discretion, under subs. (2), to act, or refuse to act, as he thinks fit. The agreements referred to are loans made by the Housing Corporation to a housing association prior to the introduction of Housing Association Grant under the Housing Act 1974, and other loans and subsidies made to housing associations by local authorities. Subss. (3), (4), prevent any such variation by the Secretary of State which purports to include a term restricting the rents or maintenance charges payable for housing association dwellings (*cf.* s.58(3), above).

Continuation of arrangements under repealed enactments

70. The provisions of Schedule 4 have effect in relation to certain arrangements affecting housing associations which continue in force despite the repeal of the enactments under or by reference to which they were made, as follows—

Part I—Arrangements with local authorities for the provision or improvement of housing.

Part II—Subsidy agreements with local authorities.

Part III—Special arrangements with the Secretary of State in Scotland.

DEFINITIONS
"hostel": s.106.
"housing association": s.1.
"local authority": s.106.

GENERAL NOTE
By their nature, funding arrangements in respect of housing association dwellings are commonly of long duration, *e.g.* repayments of secured loans may run over a period of thirty years. This section and Sched. 4, below, preserve the continuity of loan and subsidy agreements made between housing associations and local authorities under statutory provisions since repealed.

Superseded contributions, subsidies and grants

71. The provisions of Schedule 5 have effect with respect to superseded subsidies, contributions and grants, as follows—
Part I—Residual subsidies: England and Wales.
Part II—Residual subsidies: Scotland.
Part III—Contributions and grants under arrangements with local authorities.
Part IV—Contributions under arrangements with the Secretary of State in Scotland.
Part V—Schemes for the unification of grant conditions.
Part VI—New building subsidy and improvement subsidy.
Part VII—Payments in respect of hostels under pre-1974 enactments.

Supplementary provisions

GENERAL NOTE
This section and Sched. 5, below, provide for the continuation of payments of subsidies and grants by the D.O.E. to housing associations, which were originally arranged under provisions since repealed in the Housing Finance Act 1972, and subsidies and grants to local authorities under other repealed legislation: see Sched. 5, below.

Minor definitions

72. In this Part—
"building society" has the same meaning as in the Building Societies Act 1962;
"Chief Registrar", in relation to a building society, means the Chief Registrar of Friendly Societies;
"officer", in relation to a building society, has the same meaning as in the Building Societies Act 1962;
"registered charity" has the same meaning as in Part I.

Index of defined expressions: Part II

73. The following Table shows provisions defining or explaining expressions used in this Part (other than provisions defining or explaining an expression in the same section):—

approved development programme	section 41(2)
building society	section 72
Chief Registrar (in relation to a building society)	section 72
co-operative housing association	section 1(2)
dwelling	section 106
fully mutual (in relation to a housing association)	section 1(2)
heritable security	section 106
hostel	section 106
hostel deficit grant	section 55
house	section 106
housing activities	section 106
housing association	section 1(1)
housing association grant	section 41(1)
housing project	sections 42 to 45
local authority	section 106
local housing authority	section 104
officer (in relation to a building society)	section 72
registered and related expressions (in relation to a housing association)	section 3(2)
registered charity	section 72
revenue deficit grant	section 54

self-build society   section 1(3)
shared ownership lease   section 106

PART III

THE HOUSING CORPORATION

Constitution and other general matters

The Housing Corporation

74.—(1) This Part has effect with respect to the Housing Corporation, which is referred to in this Part as "the Corporation".

(2) The provisions of Schedule 6 have effect with respect to the constitution and proceedings of, and other matters relating to, the Corporation.

GENERAL NOTE

This Part deals with the Housing Corporation, and Schedule 6 governs its constitution and proceedings.

The Corporation was established under Pt. 1, Housing Act 1964, for the purpose of promoting and assisting the development of housing societies registered under the Industrial and Provident Act 1893. The Corporation is a body corporate, and is a public body for the purposes of the Prevention of Corruption Acts 1889 to 1916. It is not a servant or agent of the Crown, and its property is not to be regarded as being held for or on behalf of the Crown.

The maximum membership of the Corporation is limited to fifteen persons, who are appointed by and may be removed by the Secretary of State. A Chairman and Deputy Chairman must be appointed from the members, by the Secretary of State. Provision is made for the payment of remuneration, allowances and pensions to members, subject to Treasury approval. The Corporation determines its quorum and arrangements for its meetings subject to directions of the Secretary of State. Any member directly or indirectly interested in a contract made, or proposed to be made, by the Corporation is required to disclose the nature of that interest and is prevented from taking any part in the Corporation's decisions relating to that contract.

The headquarters of the Corporation are at 149 Tottenham Court Road, London W1P 0BN. The Corporation maintains twelve regional offices throughout Great Britain, each dealing with the Corporation's day to day activities in the area which it serves. For the functions of the Housing Corporation, see s.75, below, and note thereto.

General functions of the Corporation

75.—(1) The Corporation has the following general functions—

    (*a*) to promote and assist the development of registered housing associations and unregistered self-build societies;

    (*b*) to facilitate the proper performance of the functions, and to publicise the aims and principles, of registered housing associations and unregistered self-build societies;

    (*c*) to maintain a register of housing associations and to exercise supervision and control over registered housing associations;

    (*d*) to act as the Secretary of State's agent, to such extent as he may require, with respect to the consideration of applications for, and the payment of grants to, registered housing associations;

    (*e*) to undertake, to such extent as the Corporation considers necessary, the provision (by construction, acquisition, conversion, improvement or otherwise) of dwellings for letting or for sale and of hostels, and the management of dwellings or hostels so provided.

(2) The Corporation shall exercise its general functions subject to and in accordance with the provisions of this Act.

(3) Subsection (1) is without prejudice to specific functions conferred on the Corporation by or under this Act.

(4) The Corporation may do such things and enter into such transactions as are incidental to or conducive to the exercise of any of its functions, general or specific, under this Act.

DEFINITIONS
"dwelling": s.106.
"hostel": s.106.
"housing association": s.1.
"registered": s.3.
"self-build society": s.1.
"unregistered": s.3.

GENERAL NOTE
The evolution of the Housing Corporation is in itself an important part of the recent history of housing associations. It was established under the Housing Act 1964, when increased funds were made available for housing society activity, meaning at that stage unsubsidised, or cost rent societies. Until 1972, its powers were substantively unchanged. Its general duties were to "promote and assist the development of the housing societies, to facilitate the proper exercise and performance of the functions of such societies, and to publicise, in the case of societies providing houses for their own members no less than in the case of those providing houses for letting, the aims and principles of such societies." (Housing Act 1964, s.1).

Progress towards a larger role for the Corporation was suggested in the Working Paper of the Central Housing Advisory Committee on Housing Associations (D.O.E. 1971). A first step was taken in 1972 when its funding powers were extended to housing associations, in relation to new-build projects. In 1973, the government intimated their intention to expand the role of the Corporation, and appointed a new Chairman both to the Corporation and to the National Building Agency, with closer working links in mind. The role for which the Corporation has subsequently become well known—that of policeman to the housing association movement—was advanced in the Housing and Planning Bill 1973. This Bill fell with the government, in early 1974, but the relevant provisions were adopted by the incoming administration, and became the Housing Act 1974.

From then on the Corporation has enjoyed co-extensively with local authorities full (*i.e.* housing association as well as society, conversion as well as new-build,) funding powers and financial resources which—with the growth of restrictions on local authority spending—have increasingly left it as the main source of funding for housing associations, and extensive supervisory powers and duties.

The first Chairman of the expanded Corporation indicated how he *hoped* the role of the Corporation would develop, in the Corporation's Annual Report for 1974: "The Housing Corporation might well be an organisation that could go some way towards rectifying the delays and complications of an excessive administrative control. We are in the most valid sense a government organisation and our money comes from government: but we are run by chairman, board, chief executive and others who are not government officials, are not inured or sympathetic to governmental procedures or tempo and who can be expected to inject innovations and accelerations . . . "

Subs. (1)
Sub-paras. (*a*), (*b*) and (*c*) set out the twin roles of the Corporation in promoting and assisting, and at the same time supervising and controlling, registered housing associations. The Corporation maintains a policy of continuing monitoring of registered housing associations. Current monitoring arrangements are set out in Circular H.C. 19/85. The provision of advice and assistance also extends to unregistered self-build societies. This species of housing association, defined under s.1(3), above, is unlikely to be registerable as a charity, or under the Industrial and Provident Societies Act 1965, and consequently will not be eligible for registration with the Corporation (*cf.* s.5, above).

Sub-para. (*d*) confirms the Corporation's role as agent to the D.O.E. for the purposes of the receipt and consideration of applications for housing association grant. Sub-para. (*e*) enables the Corporation to undertake the provision of houses and hostels, and management of the same, in its own right.

Subss. (2), (3)

Specific provisions for the exercise of the Corporation's powers in relation to its promotional role are set out in subsequent sections, as follows:

Section 77 provides for an advisory service to housing associations, and prospective associations and self-build societies.

Sections 79–86 confer lending powers and loan guarantee provisions in respect of registered housing associations, and self-build societies.

Section 87 enables the Corporation to make grants to registered housing associations and other voluntary organisations, for the formation of, and provision of services and advice to, registered housing association.

Sections 88–90 set out the Corporation's powers to acquire and dispose of land in connection with housing provision, and to build and improve houses and hostels itself.

The regulatory powers and functions of the Corporation in relation to housing associations are contained in Pt. I.

Subs. (4)

This subsection confirms the Corporation's wide general powers, consistent with its status as an independent corporate body, to enter into such transactions as are appropriate to the carrying out of its specific or general functions under this Act.

Directions by the Secretary of State

76.—(1) The Secretary of State may give directions to the Corporation as to the exercise of its functions.

(2) A direction as to the terms of loans made under section 79 (lending powers of Corporation) requires the consent of the Treasury.

(3) Directions may be of a general or particular character and may be varied or revoked by subsequent directions.

(4) Non-compliance with a direction does not invalidate a transaction between a person and the Corporation unless the person had actual notice of the direction.

GENERAL NOTE

This section confirms that the Secretary of State, through the D.O.E., may give directions to the Corporation as to the exercise of its functions. The terms of loans by the Corporation to associations, the power to issue which is to be found in s.79, below, are expressly stated to be subject to directions made under this section, and subs. (2) provides that any such directions given by the Secretary of State must be approved by the Treasury. Subs. (3) makes it clear that there is a wide power conferred on the Secretary of State to issue directions of specific or general application. Under subs. (4), the position of a person dealing with the Corporation is protected in the event of a transaction made in breach of a direction of the Secretary of State, provided that person did not have actual notice of the direction (*cf. Rhyl U.D.C.* v. *Rhyl Amusements Ltd.* [1959] 1 W.L.R. 465, where it was held that a lease made by a local authority without a necessary consent was *ultra vires* and void).

Advisory service

77.—(1) The Corporation may provide an advisory service for the purpose of giving advice on legal, architectural and other technical matters to housing associations (whether registered or unregistered) and to persons who are forming a housing association or are interested in the possibility of doing so.

(2) The Corporation may make charges for the service.

DEFINITIONS

"housing association": s.1.
"registered": s.3.
"unregistered": s.3.

GENERAL NOTE

The Corporation provides general guidance to registered housing associations by means of Circulars—designated "H.C." and "P.C." (*i.e.* Practice Circulars)—which are distributed to associations, and by a variety of publications explaining procedures and criteria to be satisfied by associations.

This section enables the Corporation to provide a technical and advisory service to all housing associations, prospective associations and self-build societies, and to make a charge for services provided. For this purpose the Corporation has set up the Housing Association Consultancy and Advisory Service Ltd., an associated company limited by guarantee, which provides specific advice, and in conjunction with the National Federation of Housing Associations has arranged for the establishment of the Insurance Service for Housing Associations Ltd., an associated company providing advice on insurance matters and arranging insurance cover for housing associations.

Annual report

78.—(1) The Corporation shall, as soon as possible after the end of each financial year, make a report to the Secretary of State on the exercise of its functions during the year.

(2) It shall include in the report a copy of its audited accounts and shall set out in the report any directions given to it by the Secretary of State during the year.

(3) The Secretary of State shall lay a copy of the report before each House of Parliament.

GENERAL NOTE

This section requires the Housing Corporation to prepare an annual report, including its audited accounts, for presentation to the Secretary of State after the close of each financial year. Copies of the report are available to interested persons, directly from the Corporation.

Corporation's powers with respect to grants and loans

Lending powers

79.—(1) The Corporation may lend to—
a registered housing association,
an unregistered self-build society,
a subsidiary of the Corporation, or
any other body in which the Corporation holds an interest,
for the purpose of enabling the body to meet the whole or part of expenditure incurred or to be incurred by it in carrying out its objects.

(2) The Corporation may lend to an individual for the purpose of assisting him to acquire from the Corporation, or from any such body as is mentioned in subsection (1), a legal estate or interest in a dwelling which he intends to occupy.

(3) A loan under this section may be by way of temporary loan or otherwise, and the terms of a loan made under subsection (1) may include (though the terms of a loan made under subsection (2) may not) terms for preventing repayment of the loan or part of it before a specified date without the consent of the Corporation.

(4) The terms of a loan under this section shall, subject to subsection (3) and to any direction under section 76 (general power of Secretary of State to give directions), be such as the Corporation may determine, either generally or in a particular case.

DEFINITIONS
"housing association": s.1.
"registered": s.3.
"self-build society": s.1.
"subsidary": s.101.
"unregistered": s.3.

GENERAL NOTE
A housing association will rarely be in a position to finance housing development or improvement schemes from its own resources. This section enables the Housing Corporation

to make loans to a registered housing association, or an unregistered self-build society, to provide the necessary development capital for a housing project, or other purposes related to the carrying out of an association's or society's objects. Repayment of the loan principal and interest is deferred until completion of the project in question, and the capital cost and deferred interest is then eligible, in the case of subsidised schemes, for inclusion in housing association grant assessment under s.41, above. Loans to housing associations and self-build societies in the year ending March 31, 1985 amounted to £822 million: Housing Corporation Annual Report 1984/85.

Subs. (2)

This enables the Corporation to make loans to individuals, *e.g.* housing association tenants, to assist in their acquisition of a dwelling which they intend to occupy. The provision applies to acquisitions from the Corporation itself, a registered housing association, or a self-build society, or from a subsidiary of the Corporation or some other body in which the Corporation holds an interest. Note that these provisions are in addition to, and do not affect, the right of housing association and certain other tenants exercising the right to buy the dwellings which they occupy, to be granted a mortgage by the Corporation, under the provisions of Pt. V of the Housing Act 1985.

Subs. (3)

The Corporation may not include a condition in any mortgage agreement made with an individual, under subs. (2), which prevents an early repayment of the loan.

Security for loans to unregistered self-build societies

80.—(1) Where the Corporation—

(*a*) makes a loan to an unregistered self-build society under section 79(1); and

(*b*) under a mortgage or heritable security entered into by the society to secure the loan has an interest as mortgagee or creditor in land belonging to the society,

it may, with the written consent of the Secretary of State, give the society directions with respect to the disposal of the land.

(2) The society shall comply with directions so given so long as the Corporation continues to have such an interest in the land.

(3) Directions so given may be varied or revoked by subsequent directions given with the like consent.

(4) The Secretary of State shall not consent to the Corporation's giving directions under this section requiring a society to transfer its interest in land to the Corporation, or to any other person, unless he is satisfied that arrangements have been made which will secure that the members of the society receive fair treatment in connection with the transfer.

DEFINITIONS

"heritable security": s.106.
"self-build society": s.1.
"unregistered": s.3.

GENERAL NOTE

This section applies to unregistered housing associations which are "self-build societies", as defined by s.1(3), above, and in respect of which the Housing Corporation has an interest under a mortgage or security advanced to the society. The Corporation, with the written consent of the Secretary of State, may give directions to the society with respect to the disposal of land subject to the Corporation's interest. This includes a direction that the land in question be transferred to the Corporation, or to some other person, but subject to the requirement, under subs. (4), that the Secretary of State is satisfied that arrangements have been made which will secure the fair treatment of members of the society in connection with the transfer.

Further advances in case of disposal on shared ownership lease

81. Where—

(*a*) a lease of a dwelling, granted otherwise than in pursuance of the provisions of Part V of the Housing Act 1985 (the right to buy) relating to shared ownership leases, contains a provision to the like effect as that required by paragraph 1 of Schedule 8 to that Act (terms of shared ownership lease: right of tenant to acquire additional shares), and

(*b*) the Corporation has, in exercise of any of its powers, left outstanding or advanced any amount on the security of the dwelling,

that power includes power to advance further amounts for the purpose of assisting the tenant to make payments in pursuance of that provision.

GENERAL NOTE
The power to grant a mortgage on a shared ownership scheme (not within Pt. V, Housing Act 1985), includes power to grant a further mortgage on subsequent purchases of successive tranches of the equity.

Loans made under s.2 of the Housing Act 1964

82. Schedule 7 (further powers of Corporation with respect to land of certain housing associations) applies where a loan has been made to a housing association under section 2 of the Housing Act 1964 and the loan has not been repaid.

DEFINITION
"housing association": s.1.

GENERAL NOTE
Sched. 7 enables the Housing Corporation, with the consent of the Secretary of State, to give directions for the disposal of land which remains subject to an unrepaid Housing Corporation loan, and allows the Corporation to establish a scheme for the provision of housing accommodation in place of that provided by a housing association which is experiencing difficulties in continuing its operations.

Power to guarantee loans

83.—(1) The Corporation may, with the consent of the Secretary of State given with the approval of the Treasury, guarantee the repayment of the principal of, and the payment of interest on, sums borrowed by—

registered housing associations,

unregistered self-build societies, or

other bodies in which the Corporation holds an interest.

(2) Where the Corporation gives such a guarantee, it may impose such terms and conditions as it thinks fit.

(3) The aggregate amount outstanding in respect of—

(*a*) loans for which the Corporation has given a guarantee under this section, and

(*b*) payments made by the Corporation in meeting an obligation arising by virtue of such a guarantee and not repaid to the Corporation,

shall not exceed £300 million or such greater sum not exceeding £500 million as the Secretary of State may specify by order made with the approval of the Treasury.

(4) An order under subsection (3) shall be made by statutory instrument and no such order shall be made unless a draft of it has been laid before and approved by the House of Commons.

DEFINITIONS
"housing association": s.1.
"registered": s.3.
"self-build society": s.1.
"unregistered": s.3.

GENERAL NOTE

This section enables the Housing Corporation to guarantee borrowing by registered housing associations, self-build societies and bodies in which it has an interest, to a limit of £300 million, with a reserve power in the Secretary of State to increase it, by order with Treasury consent, to £500 million.

Agreements to indemnify certain lenders: England and Wales

84.—(1) The Corporation may, with the approval of the Secretary of State, enter into an agreement with—

(*a*) a building society lending on the security of a house, or

(*b*) a recognised body making a relevant advance on the security of a house,

whereby, in the event of default by the mortgagor, and in circumstances and subject to conditions specified in the agreement, the Corporation binds itself to indemnify the society or body in respect of the whole or part of the mortgagor's outstanding indebtc dness and any loss or expense falling on the society or body in consequence of the mortgagor's default.

(2) The agreement may also, if the mortgagor is made party to it, enable or require the Corporation in specified circumstances to take a transfer of the mortgage and assume rights and liabilities under it, the building society or recognised body being then discharged in respect of them.

(3) The transfer may be made to take effect—

(*a*) on terms provided for by the agreement (including terms involving substitution of a new mortgage agreement or modification of the existing one), and

(*b*) so that the Corporation is treated as acquiring (for and in relation to the purposes of the mortgage) the benefit and burden of all preceding acts, omissions and events.

(4) The Secretary of State may approve particular agreements or give notice that particular forms of agreement have his approval, and in either case may make his approval subject to conditions.

(5) The Secretary of State shall, before giving notice that a particular form of agreement has his approval, consult—

(*a*) in the case of a form of agreement with a building society, the Chief Registrar of Friendly Societies and such organisations representative of building societies and local authorities as he thinks expedient, and

(*b*) in the case of a form of agreement with a recognised body, such organisations representative of such bodies and local authorities as he thinks expedient.

(6) Section 16(3) and (5) of the Restrictive Trade Practices Act 1976 (recommendations by services supply associations to members) does not apply to recommendations made to building societies or recognised bodies about the making of agreements under this section, provided that the recommendations are made with the approval of the Secretary of State, which may be withdrawn at any time on one month's notice.

DEFINITIONS

"building society": s.101.

"house": s.106.

"recognised body": s.85.

GENERAL NOTE

Building societies commonly will not lend on property in areas well-known to be run-down or declining. This section is designed to permit the Housing Corporation to enter into indemnity agreements with building societies to help persuade them away from this practice principally, of course, in connection with purchases from or through associations. The section applies not only to building societies in England and Wales, but also to other financial bodies as may be specified in an order made under s.85, below. For provisions relating to Scotland, see s.86, below.

An agreement under this section must be approved by the Secretary of State, but such approval may be issued generally as well as specifically. A general approval must follow consultation with the Chief Registrar of Friendly Societies, and such representatives of building societies or other financial bodies as may be specified by an order under subs. (1)(*b*). As to consultation, see notes to s.47(4), above. An approval is specifically exempt from the provisions of the Restrictive Trade Practices Act 1976, s.16, which concerns recommendations by "service supply associations" to its members, and which would otherwise be subject to regulation under that Act. The Secretary of State may withdraw his approval of an agreement on one month's notice: subs. (6).

The agreement is an indemnity agreement, in respect of the whole or part of a defaulting mortgagor's liability, and consequential losses or expenses, falling on the building society (subs. (1)). The agreement may provide for the Housing Corporation to take a transfer of the mortgage, and assume rights and liabilities thereunder, to the future exclusion of the building society (subs. (2)), and may include the grant of a new mortgage by the Corporation, so as to give the Corporation the benefit and burden of all proceeding acts, including omissions and events (subs. (3)), *i.e.* they may step wholly into the shoes of the mortgagee building society, even if the agreement operates by way of a new mortgage.

Meaning of "recognised body" and "relevant advance"

85.—(1) The expressions "recognised body" and "relevant advance" in section 84 (agreements to indemnify certain lenders) shall be construed in accordance with the following provisions.

(2) A "recognised body" means a body specified, or of a class or description specified, in an order made by statutory instrument by the Secretary of State with the consent of the Treasury.

(3) Before making such an order varying or revoking an order previously made, the Secretary of State shall give an opportunity for representations to be made on behalf of a recognised body which, if the order were made, would cease to be such a body.

(4) A "relevant advance" means an advance made to a person whose interest in the dwelling is or was acquired by virtue of a conveyance of the freehold or an assignment of a long lease, or a grant of a long lease by—

> a local authority,
> a new town corporation,
> an urban development corporation,
> the Development Board for Rural Wales,
> the Corporation, and
> a registered housing association.

(5) In subsection (4) "long lease" has the same meaning as in Part V of the Housing Act 1985 (the right to buy).

DEFINITIONS
> "dwelling": s.106.
> "housing association": s.1.
> "local authority": s.106.
> "new town corporation": s.106.
> "registered": s.3.
> "urban development corporation": s.106.

GENERAL NOTE
This section permits the Secretary of State to specify bodies or classes of bodies other than building societies, with which the Housing Corporation may enter into such similar indemnity agreements as apply in the case of building societies, under s.84, above. Indemnities may however only be given in respect of conveyances of the freehold interest, or grants of long leases by the bodies specified in subs. (4), *i.e.* public authorities and corporations, and registered housing associations.

Agreements to indemnify building societies: Scotland

86.—(1) The Corporation may, with the approval of the Secretary of State, enter into an agreement with a building society under which the Corporation binds itself to indemnify the building society in respect of—

(*a*) the whole or part of any outstanding indebtedness of a borrower; and

(*b*) loss or expense to the building society resulting from the failure of the borrower duly to perform any obligation imposed on him by the heritable security.

(2) The agreement may also, where the borrower is made party to it, enable or require the Corporation in specified circumstances to take an assignation of the rights and liabilities of the building society under the heritable security.

(3) Approval of the Secretary of State under subsection (1) may be given generally in relation to agreements which satisfy specified requirements, or in relation to individual agreements, and with or without conditions, as he thinks fit, and such approval may be withdrawn at any time on one month's notice.

(4) Before issuing any general approval under subsection (1) the Secretary of State shall consult with such bodies as appear to him to be representative of islands and district councils, and of building societies, and also with the Corporation and with the Chief Registrar of Friendly Societies.

(5) Section 16(3) and (5) of the Restrictive Trade Practices Act 1976 (recommendations by services supply associations to members) does not apply to recommendations made to building societies about the making of agreements under this section provided that the recommendations are made with the approval of the Secretary of State.

DEFINITIONS
"building society": s.101.
"heritable security": s.106.

GENERAL NOTE
This section enables the Housing Corporation to indemnify building societies in Scotland, on similar principles to those contained in s.84, above, applying to England and Wales, with appropriate amendment to reflect the estates and interests recognised in Scotland. Note, however, that there is no provision to include any body other than a building society: *cf.* ss.84, 85, in England and Wales. See further, note to s.84.

Grants towards expenses in promoting or assisting registered housing associations

87.—(1) The Corporation may make grants to registered housing associations and other voluntary organisations towards expenses incurred by them—

(*a*) in encouraging and giving advice on the formation of housing associations which would be eligible for registration under Part I, and

(*b*) in providing services for, and giving advice on the running of, registered housing associations.

(2) Any such grant may be made subject to such conditions as the Corporation may determine.

(3) The exercise of the Corporation's powers under subsection (1) or (2) requires the consent of the Secretary of State and the Treasury.

(4) In this section "voluntary organisation" means an organisation whose activities are not carried on for profit.

DEFINITIONS
"housing association": s.1.
"registered": s.3.

GENERAL NOTE
The permissible additional objects of a housing association in relation to its eligibility for registration with the Housing Corporation under s.4, above, include the functions specified in subs. (1)(*a*), (*b*), of this section. An association which is concerned with the promotion of other associations, *e.g.* co-operatives or co-ownerships, is sometimes known as a "secondary association".

It has in the past been the practice of the Corporation to make grants for these purposes, presumably under the general power to "promote and assist the development of registered housing associations", now contained in s.75, above. The provisions of this section, previously contained in s.121 of the Housing Act 1980, provide explicitly for the making of grants for the purposes specified, but that power is, however, expressed to be subject to the approval of the Secretary of State and the Treasury.

Subs. (4)
The bodies who may receive grants under this section are registered housing associations and "other voluntary organisations". This subsection defines the latter term. Note that the fact that an activity of an association produces a profit does not necessarily mean that it "trades for profit". The term means trading for the profit in the sense of profit which may be extracted from the organisation, and used and enjoyed by its proprietors, as distinct from profits which must be kept within, or ploughed back into, the activities of the organisation: *Goodman* v. *Dolphin Square Trust Ltd.* (1979) 38 P. & C.R. 257, C.A.

Corporation's powers with respect to land and works

Acquisition of land

88.—(1) The Corporation may acquire land by agreement for the purpose of—
    (*a*) selling or leasing it to a registered housing association or an unregistered self-build society, or
    (*b*) providing dwellings (for letting or for sale) or hostels,
and may be authorised by the Secretary of State to acquire land compulsorily for any such purpose.

(2) Land may be so acquired by the Corporation notwithstanding that it is not immediately required for any such purpose.

(3) In relation to a compulsory purchase of land by the Corporation under this section—
    (*a*) in England and Wales, the Acquisition of Land Act 1981 applies;
    (*b*) in Scotland, the Acquisition of Land (Authorisation Procedure) (Scotland) Act 1947 applies as if the Corporation were a local authority and as if this section were contained in an Act in force immediately before the commencment of that Act.

(4) For the purposes of the purchase of land in Scotland by agreement by the Corporation—
    (*a*) the Lands Clauses Acts (except so much of them as relates to the acquisition of land otherwise than by agreement, the provisions relating to access to the special Act and sections 120 to 125 of the Lands Clauses Consolidation (Scotland) Act 1845), and
    (*b*) sections 6 and 70 to 78 of the Railways Clauses Consolidation (Scotland) Act 1845 (as originally enacted and not as amended by section 15 of the Mines (Working Facilities and Support) Act 1923),
are hereby incorporated with this section, and in construing those Acts for the purposes of this section this section shall be deemed to be the special Act and the Corporation shall be deemed to be the promotors of the undertaking or company, as the case may require.

(5) In Scotland the Corporation may (without prejudice to their own power to acquire land compulsorily) request the Scottish Special Housing

Association to acquire land compulsorily on its behalf (as provided in section 175(2) of the Housing (Scotland) Act 1966) for any purpose for which the Corporation may purchase land compulsorily.

DEFINITIONS
  "hostel": s.106.
  "housing association": s.1.
  "registered": s.3.
  "self-build society": s.1.
  "unregistered": s.3.

GENERAL NOTE
  This and the following two sections set out the Housing Corporation's powers of acquisition, development and disposal of land. Under subs. (1), the Corporation may acquire land by agreement for the purpose of future disposal to a housing association or self-build society, and also for the purpose of providing dwellings or hostels by its own development, under s.89, below. In addition to acquisition by agreement, the Corporation is given powers of compulsory purchase of land, subject in each case to the authorisation of the Secretary of State.

Subs. (2)
  This subsection enables the Corporation to acquire a stock of land for future housing development purposes.

Subs. (3)
  The statutes referred to in this subsection contain the general powers and provisions relating to compulsory purchase in England and Wales, and Scotland.

Subs. (5)
  The Scottish Special Housing Association is a government sponsored housing association enjoying compulsory purchase powers in its own right. This subsection enables the Housing Corporation to make arrangements with the S.S.H.A. for compulsory purchase of land on the Corporation's behalf.

Provision of dwellings or hostels and clearance, management and development of land

89.—(1) The Corporation may provide or improve dwellings or hostels on land belonging to it.

(2) The Corporation may clear land belonging to it and carry out other work on the land to prepare it as a building site or estate, including—

(*a*) the laying out and construction of streets or roads and open spaces, and

(*b*) the provision of sewerage facilities and supplies of gas, electricity and water.

(3) The Corporation may repair, maintain and insure buildings or works on land belonging to it, may generally deal in the proper course of management with such land and buildings or works on it, and may charge for the tenancy or occupation of such land, buildings or works.

(4) The Corporation may carry out such operations on, and do such other things in relation to, land belonging to it as appear to it to be conducive to facilitating the provision or improvement of dwellings or hostels on the land—

(*a*) by the Corporation itself, or

(*b*) by a registered housing association or unregistered self-build society.

(5) In the exercise of its powers under subsection (4) the Corporation may carry out any development ancillary to or in connection with the provision of dwellings or hostels, including development which makes provision for buildings or land to be used for commercial, recreational or other non-domestic purposes.

DEFINITIONS
  "dwelling": s.106.
  "hostel": s.106.
  "housing association": s.1.
  "registered": s.3.
  "self-build society": s.1.
  "unregistered": s.3.

GENERAL NOTE
This section confers wide powers on the Housing Corporation to carry out development in its own right, either for the provision or improvement of housing or hostels as a completed scheme, or for the preparation of a cleared, laid out site with services and facilities, *i.e.* suitable to be transferred to a housing association for the construction of dwellings on the site, under the powers of disposal conferred on the Corporation by s.90, below.

Disposal of land

90.—(1) The Corporation may dispose of land in respect of which it has not exercised its powers under section 89(1) (provision or improvement of dwellings or hostels) and on which it has not carried out any such development as is mentioned in section 89(5) (ancillary development) to—

    a registered housing association,
    an unregistered self-build society,
    a subsidiary of the Corporation, or
    any other body in which the Corporation holds an interest.

(2) The Corporation may dispose of land on which dwellings or hostels have been provided or improved in exercise of its powers under section 89 to—

    a registered housing association,
    a local authority,
    a new town corporation,
    the Scottish Special Housing Association,
    the Development Board for Rural Wales, or
    a subsidiary of the Corporation.

(3) The Corporation may sell or lease individual dwellings to persons for their own occupation; but where the dwelling concerned was acquired by compulsory purchase under section 88(1), it shall not be disposed of under this subsection without the written consent of the Secretary of State.

(4) The Corporation may dispose of a building or land intended for use for commercial, recreational or other non-domestic purposes in respect of which development has been carried out by virtue of section 89; but no such building or land shall be disposed of for less than the best consideration it commands except with the written consent of the Secretary of State.

(5) The Corporation may dispose of land which is not required for the purposes for which it was acquired; but where the land—

  (*a*) was acquired compulsorily by, or on behalf of, the Corporation or by a local housing authority who transferred it to the Corporation, or

  (*b*) is disposed of (otherwise than for use as, or in connection with, a highway or street) for less than the best consideration it commands,

the Corporation shall not dispose of the land except with the written consent of the Secretary of State.

(6) The Corporation may not dispose of land except in accordance with the provisions of this section.

DEFINITIONS
  "dwelling": s.106.
  "hostel": s.106.

"local authority": s.106.
"local housing authority": s.104.
"new town corporation": s.106.
"registered": s.3.
"subsidiary": s.101.
"unregistered": s.3.

GENERAL NOTE
This section defines the Housing Corporation's powers to dispose of land.
"Land" includes "buildings and other structures, land covered with water, and any estate, interest, easement, servitude or right in or over land": Interpretation Act 1978, Sched. 1.

Subs. (1)
Land on which no improvement or provision of dwellings or hostels has been made, and on which no ancillary development, under s.89(5), has taken place (*i.e.* undeveloped land), may only be transferred to a registered housing association, a "self-build society", or subsidiaries of the Corporation or a body in which the Corporation holds an interest.

Subs. (2)
In the case of developed land, on which dwellings or hostels have been built or improved, in addition to disposal to a registered housing association the Corporation may make a disposal to a local authority or the development agencies specified in this subsection, or to a subsidiary of the Corporation.

Subss. (3) *to* (6)
These subsections specify the circumstances in which the consent of the Secretary of State is required to a disposal of land by the Corporation, and make it clear that no such disposal shall be made other than in compliance with the provisions of this section.

Protection of persons deriving title under transactions requiring consent

91. Where the Corporation purport to acquire or dispose of land—

(*a*) in favour of a person claiming under the Corporation the transaction is not invalid by reason that any consent of the Secretary of State which is required has not been given, and

(*b*) a person dealing with the Corporation, or with a person claiming under the Corporation, shall not be concerned to see or inquire whether any such consent has been given.

GENERAL NOTE
Disposals of land by the Housing Corporation, under s.89, require the consent of the Secretary of State. This section absolves a person deriving title from the Corporation under a transaction requiring this consent from the need to make enquiry that the necessary consent has been given, and prevents the transaction from being invalidated if in fact that consent has not been given (*cf. Rhyl U.D.C.* v. *Rhyl Amusements Ltd.* [1959] 1 W.L.R. 465, where it was held that a lease made by a local authority without a necessary consent was *ultra vires* and void).

The Corporation's finances

Borrowing powers

92.—(1) The Corporation may borrow from the Secretary of State, and the Secretary of State may lend to the Corporation, by way of temporary loan or otherwise, such sums in sterling as the Corporation may require.

(2) The Corporation may, with the consent of the Secretary of State or in accordance with a general authorisation given by him, borrow temporarily by overdraft or otherwise such sums in sterling as the Corporation may require.

(3) The Corporation may, with the consent of the Secretary of State, borrow—

(a) from the European Investment Bank or the Commission of the European Communities, sums in any currency, and

(b) from any other person, sums in a currency other than sterling.

(4) A loan made to the Corporation by the Secretary of State shall be repaid to him at such times and by such methods, and interest on the loan shall be paid to him at such rates and at such times, as he may from time to time determine.

(5) The Treasury may issue to the Secretary of State out of the National Loans Fund such sums as are necessary to enable him to make loans to the Corporation in pursuance of this section; and sums received by the Secretary of State in pursuance of subsection (4) shall be paid into that Fund.

(6) The Secretary of State may act under this section only with the approval of the Treasury.

GENERAL NOTE

This section contains the provisions enabling the Housing Corporation to obtain loans from the Secretary of State, or from other sources on the conditions set out in subs. (3). Loans agreed by the Secretary of State are advanced to the Corporation from the National Loans Fund, and are repayable on such terms as the Secretary of State directs. Financial limits on Housing Corporation borrowing are contained in s.93, below.

Limit on borrowing

93.—(1) The Corporation has only the borrowing powers conferred by section 92 and those powers are exercisable subject to the following limit.

(2) The aggregate amount outstanding by way of principal of—

(a) advances made to the Corporation under section 9 of the Housing Act 1964 before 18th September 1974 (when that section was repealed),

(b) advances made to housing associations before 1st April 1975 in respect of which the rights and obligations of the Secretary of State were then transferred to the Corporation by section 34 of the Housing Act 1974,

(c) money borrowed by the Corporation under section 92, and

(d) money borrowed by a subsidiary of the Corporation otherwise than from the Corporation,

shall not exceed £2,500 million or such greater sum not exceeding £3,000 million as the Secretary of State may specify by order made with the consent of the Treasury.

(3) An order under subsection (2) shall be made by statutory instrument and no such order shall be made unless a draft of it has been laid before and approved by the House of Commons.

(4) In ascertaining the limit imposed by subsection (2), interest payable on a loan made by the Secretary of State to the Corporation which, with the approval of the Treasury, is deferred and treated as part of the loan, shall, so far as outstanding, be treated as outstanding by way of principal.

(5) The power of the Corporation to borrow from a subsidiary of the Corporation is not affected by subsection (1) and borrowing from such a subsidiary shall be left out of account for the purposes of subsection (2).

DEFINITION

"housing association": s.1.

GENERAL NOTE

This section limits the borrowing powers of the Housing Corporation which are set out in s.92. The limit of £2,500 million, previously provided by the Housing Corporation Advances (Increase of Limit Order) 1983 S.I. 1983 No. 664, remains unchanged, but may be increased by an order made under subs. (2).

Subs. (4)

This subsection makes it clear that in determining whether or not the Corporation is within its borrowing ceiling, deferred capitalised interest payments are to be regarded as part of the principal outstanding.

Treasury guarantees of borrowing

94.—(1) The Treasury may guarantee, in such manner and on such conditions as they think fit, the repayment of the principal of and the payment of interest on and the discharge of any other financial obligation in connection with sums which the Corporation borrows from a person other than the Secretary of State.

(2) Immediately after a guarantee is given the Treasury shall lay a statement of the guarantee before each House of Parliament.

(3) Any sums required by the Treasury for fulfilling the guarantee shall be charged on and issued out of the Consolidated Fund.

(4) If any sums are so issued, the Corporation shall make to the Treasury, at such times and in such manner as the Treasury may from time to time direct—

(*a*) payments of such amounts as the Treasury so direct in or towards repayment of the sums so issued, and

(*b*) payments of interest, at such rate as the Treasury so direct, on what is outstanding for the time being in respect of sums so issued.

(5) Sums received by the Treasury in pursuance of subsection (4) shall be paid into the Consolidated Fund.

(6) Where a sum is issued for fulfilling a guarantee given under this section, the Treasury shall, as soon as possible after the end of each financial year, beginning with that in which the sum is issued and ending with that in which all liability in respect of the principal of the sum and in respect of interest on it is finally discharged, lay before each House of Parliament a statement relating to the sum.

General Note

Under s.92, the Housing Corporation is able to borrow sums from the European Community or from private sources as an alternative to obtaining loans from the National Loans Fund, with the consent of the Secretary of State. This section enables the Treasury to guarantee the repayment of loans, together with interest and any connected financial liabilities, made to the Corporation by persons other than the Secretary of State.

Grants to the Corporation

95.—(1) The Secretary of State may make such grants to the Corporation as appear to him to be required to enable the Corporation to meet the expenses incurred by it in the exercise of its functions.

(2) A grant may be made subject to such conditions as the Secretary of State may determine.

(3) The Secretary of State may act under this section only with the consent of the Treasury.

General Note

This section provides for direct grants to be made to the Housing Corporation to meet expenses incurred in carrying out its functions. In the year ended 31 March 1985, the total grant-in-aid for administration expenses paid to the Housing Corporation amounted to some £14 million. S.96, below, contains provision for repayment of any part of the grant assistance which is held in reserve by the Corporation and is not for the time being required for the exercise of its functions.

General financial provisions

96.—(1) The Corporation may turn its resources to account so far as they are not required for the exercise of its functions.

(2) If for an accounting year the revenues of the Corporation exceed the total sums properly chargeable to revenue account, the Corporation shall apply the excess in such manner as the Secretary of State may, after consultation with the Corporation, direct; and the Secretary of State may direct that the whole or part of the excess be paid to him.

(3) The Secretary of State may give directions to the Corporation as to matters relating to—

(*a*) the establishment or management of reserves,

(*b*) the carrying of sums to the credit of reserves, or

(*c*) the application of reserves for the purposes of the Corporation's functions.

(4) The Secretary of State may, after consultation with the Corporation, direct the Corporation to pay to him the whole or part of any sums for the time being standing to the credit of reserves of the Corporation or being of a capital nature and not required for the exercise of the Corporation's functions.

(5) The Secretary of State may act under this section only with the approval of the Treasury.

GENERAL NOTE

This section gives a general power to the Housing Corporation to make investments in relation to sums not for the time being required for its operations, subject to directions which the Secretary of State may give as to the application of any surpluses shown on its revenue account, or as to the establishment and operation of a reserve fund. Surpluses (under subs. (2)), and any sums standing to credit in a reserve fund (subs. (4)), may be required to be paid over to the Secretary of State. Treasury approval is required for any direction given by the Secretary of State under this section: subs. (4).

Accounts and audit

97.—(1) The Corporation shall keep proper accounts and proper records in relation to the accounts and shall prepare in respect of each financial year annual accounts in such form as the Secretary of State may, with the approval of the Treasury, direct.

(2) The accounts of the Corporation for each financial year shall be audited by a qualified accountant appointed for the purpose by the Secretary of State.

(3) As soon as the annual accounts of the Corporation for a financial year have been audited, the Corporation shall send to the Secretary of State a copy of the accounts prepared by it for the year in accordance with this section, together with a copy of any report made on them by the auditor.

(4) The Secretary of State shall prepare in respect of each financial year, in such form and manner as the Treasury may direct, an account of—

(*a*) the sums issued to him and lent to the Corporation, and

(*b*) sums received by him from the Corporation and paid into the National Loans Fund in respect of the principal and interest on sums so lent, or on sums advanced to the Corporation under section 9 of the Housing Act 1964,

and shall transmit the accounts so prepared by him to the Comptroller and Auditor General on or before 30th November in the following financial year.

(5) The Comptroller and Auditor General shall examine and certify the accounts prepared by the Secretary of State and lay before each House of Parliament copies of the accounts together with his report on them.

(6) In this section "qualified accountant" means a person who is a member, or a firm all the partners in which are members, of one or more of the following bodies—

(*a*) the Institute of Chartered Accountants in England and Wales;
(*b*) the Institute of Chartered Accountants in Scotland;
(*c*) the Association of Certified Accountants;
(*d*) the Institute of Chartered Accountants in Ireland;
(*e*) any other body of accountants established in the United Kingdom and recognised for the purposes of section 389(1)(*a*) of the Companies Act 1985.

DEFINITION
"financial year": s.101.

GENERAL NOTE
This section deals with the presentation and auditing of the accounts of the Housing Corporation, and also for the preparation of accounts by the Secretary of State in respect of sums lent to, or received from, the Corporation. The Corporation's annual accounts are annexed to the Annual Report prepared by the Corporation in accordance with the requirements of s.78: see note to s.78.

Acquisition of securities and control of subsidiaries

Acquisition of securities and promotion of body corporate

98.—(1) The Corporation may with the consent of the Secretary of State—
(*a*) subscribe for or acquire securities of a body corporate, and
(*b*) promote or participate in the promotion of a body corporate.
(2) In this section "securities" means shares, stock, debenture stock and other securities of a like nature.

GENERAL NOTE
This section enables the Housing Corporation to acquire shares and other securities in other corporate bodies. For provisions in relation to bodies which are subsidiaries of the Corporation, see s.99, below.

Control of subsidiaries

99.—(1) The Corporation shall exercise its control over its subsidiaries so as to secure that no subsidiary—
(*a*) engages in an activity which the Corporation is not empowered to carry on, or
(*b*) engages in an activity in a manner in which the Corporation itself could not engage by reason of a direction given to it under section 76 (directions by Secretary of State).
(2) The Corporation shall also exercise its control over its subsidiaries so as to secure that no subsidiary of its—
(*a*) borrows money from a person other than the Corporation, or
(*b*) raises money by the issue of shares or stock to a person other than the Corporation,
without the consent of the Secretary of State.

DEFINITION
"subsidiary": s.101.

GENERAL NOTE
This section limits the manner in which subsidiary bodies controlled by the Housing Corporation may operate, by imposing the same limitations as apply to the Corporation itself under directions given by the Secretary of State, either in respect of its functions generally, under s.76, above, or by specific consent in relation to the borrowing and financing activities set out in subs. (2).

Supplementary provisions

Scottish Special Housing Association may act as agents for Corporation in Scotland

100. The Corporation may, on such terms and conditions as may be agreed between it and the Scottish Special Housing Association, authorise the Association to act in Scotland as the agents of the Corporation for the purpose of carrying out any of the functions vested in the Corporation under—

    (*a*) section 77 (advisory service);
    (*b*) sections 88 and 89 (powers with respect to land and works), or
    (*c*) paragraph 5 of Schedule 7 (schemes for provision of housing accommodation in place of a housing association).

DEFINITION
"housing association": s.1.

GENERAL NOTE
This section enables the Housing Corporation to authorise the Scottish Special Housing Association to act as its agent in Scotland, for the purpose of carrying out the wide range of activities set out in sub-paras. (*a*), (*b*) and (*c*). The S.S.H.A. is a government sponsored housing association with extensive powers in its own right. For particular provisions for the S.S.H.A. to act as agent of the Corporation in respect of compulsory acquisition of land in Scotland, see s.88.

Minor definitions

101. In this Part—
    "building society" means a building society within the meaning of the Building Societies Act 1962 or the Building Societies Act (Northern Ireland) 1967;
    "financial year" means the period of 12 months ending with the 31st March;
    "highway", in relation to Scotland, includes a public right of way;
    "subsidiary" has the same meaning as in the Companies Act.

Index of defined expressions: Part III

102. The following Table shows provisions defining or explaining expressions used in this Part (other than provisions defining or explaining an expression in the same section or paragraph)—

building society	section 101
the Companies Act	section 106
dwelling	section 106
financial year	section 101
heritable security	section 106
highway (in relation to Scotland)	section 101
hostel	section 106
housing association	section 1(1)
local authority	section 106
local housing authority	section 104
new town corporation	section 106
recognised body	section 85(2)
registered (in relation to a housing association)	section 3(2)
relevant advance	section 85(4)
self-build society	section 1(3)
subsidiary	section 101
unregistered (in relation to a housing association)	section 3(2)
urban development corporation	section 106

PART IV

GENERAL PROVISIONS

General provisions

Application to Isles of Scilly

103.—(1) This Act applies to the Isles of Scilly subject to such exceptions, adaptations and modifications as the Secretary of State may by order direct.

(2) An order shall be made by statutory instrument which shall be subject to annulment in pursuance of a resolution of either House of Parliament.

GENERAL NOTE

This section implements Law Commission Recommendations (Cmnd. 9515) No. 29, that the traditional method of applying the provisions of enactments to the Isles of Scilly by order under statutory instrument should be dispensed with, and that instead, adopting the more modern form, provision should be made for any necessary exceptions, adaptations and modifications to be implemented by such an order.

Local housing authorities

104.—(1) In this Act "local housing authority"—
   (*a*) in relation to England and Wales, has the meaning given by section 1 of the Housing Act 1985, and
   (*b*) in relation to Scotland, means an islands or district council.
(2) References in this Act to the district of a local housing authority—
   (*a*) in England and Wales shall be construed in accordance with section 2 of the Housing Act 1985, and
   (*b*) in Scotland are to the islands area or the district, as the case may be.

GENERAL NOTE

Section 1 of the Housing Act 1985 defines a "local housing authority" to be a district council, a London borough council, the Common Council of the City of London or the Council of the Isles of Scilly.

Members of a person's family

105.—(1) A person is a member of another's family if—
   (*a*) he is the spouse of that person, or he and that person live together as husband and wife, or
   (*b*) he is that person's parent, grandparent, child, grandchild, brother, sister, uncle, aunt, nephew or niece.
(2) For the purposes of subsection (1)(*b*)—
   (*a*) a relationship by marriage shall be treated as a relationship by blood,
   (*b*) a relationship of the half-blood shall be treated as a relationship of the whole blood,
   (*c*) the stepchild of a person shall be treated as his child, and
   (*d*) an illegitimate child shall be treated as the legitimate child of his mother and reputed father.

GENERAL NOTE

This section defines "member of family" for the purposes of s.13, above, which makes restrictions on gifts and payments by registered housing associations to their members, and to members' families.

Minor definitions—general

106.—(1) In the application of this Act in England and Wales—
"bank" means—

(*a*) a recognised bank within the meaning of the Banking Act 1979, or

(*b*) a company as to which the Secretary of State was satisfied immediately before the repeal of the Protection of Depositors Act 1963 that it ought to be treated as a banking company or discount company for the purposes of that Act;

"the Companies Act" means the Companies Act 1985;

"dwelling" means a building or part of a building occupied or intended to be occupied as a separate dwelling, together with any yard, garden, outhouses and appurtenances belonging to it or usually enjoyed with it;

"friendly society" means a friendly society or branch of a friendly society registered under the Friendly Societies Act 1974 or earlier legislation;

"hostel" means a building in which is provided for persons generally or for a class or classes of persons—

(*a*) residential accommodation otherwise than in separate and self-contained sets of premises, and

(*b*) either board or facilities for the preparation of food adequate to the needs of those persons, or both;

"house" includes—

(*a*) any part of a building which is occupied or intended to be occupied as a separate dwelling;

(*b*) any yard, garden, outhouses and appurtenances belonging to the house or usually enjoyed with it;

"housing activities", in relation to a registered housing association, means all its activities in pursuance of the objects, powers or purposes by reference to which it is to be regarded as a housing association and as eligible for registration;

"insurance company" means an insurance company to which Part II of the Insurance Companies Act 1982 applies;

"local authority" means a county, district, or London borough council, the Common Council of the City of London or the Council of the Isles of Scilly and in sections 84(5) and 85(4) includes the Inner London Education Authority and a joint authority established by Part IV of the Local Government Act 1985;

"new town corporation" means the Commission for the New Towns or a development corporation within the meaning of the New Towns Act 1981;

"shared ownership lease" means a lease—

(*a*) granted on payment of a premium calculated by reference to a percentage of the value of the house or dwelling or of the cost of providing it, or

(*b*) under which the tenant (or his personal representatives) will or may be entitled to a sum calculated by reference directly or indirectly to the value of the house or dwelling;

"trustee savings bank" means a trustee savings bank registered under the Trustee Savings Banks Act 1981 or earlier legislation;

"urban development corporation" means an urban development corporation established under Part XVI of the Local Government, Planning and Land Act 1980.

(2) In the application of this Act in Scotland—
"bank" has the same meaning as in subsection (1);

"charge" includes a heritable security;

"the Companies Act" has the same meaning as in subsection (1);

"dwelling" means a house;

"friendly society" has the same meaning as in subsection (1);

"heritable security" means any security capable of being constituted over any interest in land by disposition or assignation of that interest in security of any debt and of being recorded in the Register of Sasines or, as the case may be, registered in the Land Register of Scotland and which includes a security constituted by an ex facie absolute disposition or assignation or by a standard security;

"hostel" means—

(*a*) in relation to a building provided or converted before 3rd January 1962, a building in which is provided, for persons generally or for any class or classes of persons residential accommodation (otherwise than in separate and self-contained dwellings) and board, and

(*b*) in relation to a building provided or converted on or after that date, a building in which is provided for persons generally or for any class or classes of persons, residential accommodation (otherwise than in houses) and either board or common facilities for the preparation of adequate food to the needs of those persons, or both;

"house" includes—

(*a*) any part of a building, being a part which is occupied or intended to be occupied as a separate dwelling, and in particular includes a flat, and

(*b*) includes also any yard, garden, outhouses and pertinents belonging to the house or usually enjoyed with it;

"housing activities" has the same meaning as in subsection (1);

"insurance company" has the same meaning as in subsection (1);

"local authority" means an islands council or district council;

"mortgage" means a heritable security and "mortgagee" means a creditor in such a security;

"new town corporation" means a development corporation within the meaning of the New Towns (Scotland) Act 1968;

"shared ownership lease" has the same meaning as in subsection (1);

"trustee savings bank" has the same meaning as in subsection (1).

GENERAL NOTE

"Dwelling". Any building—not only a house (*cf.* notes below)—qualifies. However, the dwelling must be occupied or intended to be occupied as a separate dwelling. Because of the inclusion of actual occupation, case law on the purpose of a letting will be less relevant here than under s.1, Rent Act 1977, or s.79, Housing Act 1985, when defining protected or secure tenancies. But the letting must still be as "a" separate dwelling. In *St. Catherine's College* v. *Dorling* [1980] 1 W.L.R. 66, C.A., a college took the tenancy of a flat, already subdivided into separate living units, for sub-leasing to their own students. As against the college, the students could not enjoy full Rent Act protection (*cf.* 1977 Act, s.8, below), and as against the landlord, the college could not avail itself of a statutory tenancy following the contractual arrangement, for a corporate body cannot as such "reside". The college sought, however, to avail itself of the provisions of Pt. IV of the 1977 Act, governing the registration of rents.

It was held that the letting was not as *a* separate dwelling but, indeed, as several separate dwellings: see also *Whitty* v. *Scott-Russell* [1950] 2 K.B. 32, C.A., *Horford Investments* v. *Lambert* [1976] Ch. 39, C.A., *Regalian Securities Ltd.* v. *Ramsden* (1980) 254 E.G. 1191, C.A.

But two or more dwellings may be let for use as one: *Langford Property Co. Ltd.* v. *Goldrich* [1949] 1 K.B. 511, C.A., *Whitty* v. *Scott-Russell* [1950] 2 K.B. 32, C.A., *Lower* v. *Porter* [1956] 1 Q.B. 325, C.A. Similarly, several lettings at different times may add up to one letting, as one dwelling: *Verity* v. *Waring* [1953] C.P.L. 423, C.A. And while a letting of a unit already subdivided into several separate living units for use as such, will not be let as *a* dwelling, a letting of one unit subsequently subdivided into living units, *e.g.* into bedsitting rooms, does not cease to be a letting as a separate dwelling on that account: *Sissons Cafe Ltd.* v. *Barber* (1929) E.G.D. 117, D.C.

The essence of "separate" is that the premises in question must be capable of use on their own, as a dwelling, even if they comprise no more than a single room (see, *e.g. Curl* v. *Angelo* [1948] 2 All E.R. 189, C.A.), so that there is and needs be no sharing with another of "living accommodation". The term "living accommodation" is a judicial creation, and does not extend to the sharing of a bathroom or lavatory: *Cole* v. *Harris* [1945] K.B. 474, C.A. A bathroom or lavatory is accommodation not used for living in, but merely visited for occasional, specific purposes, as distinct from a room used for the primary purposes of living, or one in which a person spends a significant part of his time: see also *Curl, Goodrich* v. *Paisner* [1957] A.C. 65, H.L., *Marsh* v. *Cooper* [1969] 1 W.L.R. 803, C.A.

For these purposes, the primary living purposes may be considered as sleeping, cooking and feeding (*Wright* v. *Howell* (1947) 92 S.J. 26, C.A., *Curl* v. *Angelo* [1948] 2 All E.R. 189, C.A.), but *not*, as noted, sanitary activities.

But a kitchenette, even though too small to eat in and only available to cook or wash up in, has been held to constitute living accommodation (*Winters* v. *Dance* [1949] L.J.R. 165, C.A.), as also has a normal kitchen: *Neale* v. *Del Soto* [1945] K.B. 144, C.A., *Sharpe* v. *Nicholls* (1945) 147 E.G. 177, C.A. So if the letting comprises premises together with shared user of such living accommodation, there is, prima facie, no use as a "separate dwelling": *Winters* v. *Dance, Neale* v. *Del Soto, Goodrich* v. *Paisner* [1957] A.C. 65, H.L.

Sharing with one's own sub-tenant, or sub-licensee, does not prevent use as a separate dwelling: *Baker* v. *Turner* [1950] A.C. 401, H.L. And sharing living accommodation must be distinguished from a letting which leaves someone else, *e.g.* another occupier, with a defined or limited right merely to *use* part of the accommodation which has been let, *e.g.* the right to come in and make a morning cup of tea as in *James* v. *James* [1952] C.L.Y. 2948, C.C., a right of passage as in *James* v. *Coleman* [1949] E.G.D. 122, C.C., a right to use a bath sited in a kitchen as in *Trustees of the Waltham Abbey Baptist Church* v. *Stevens* (1950) E.G. 294, C.C., and a right to draw and boil water weekly as in *Hayward* v. *Marshall* [1952] 2 Q.B. 89, C.A.

In each case, the whole of the circumstances must be looked at in order to ascertain whether a person has the right to use a separate dwelling, or something less: *Goodrich* v. *Paisner* [1957] A.C. 65, H.L. In Rent Act law, the fact that a sharing right is not exercised does not bring the tenant back into full protection (*Stanley* v. *Compton* [1951] 1 All E.R. 859, C.A., *Kenyon* v. *Walker* [1946] 2 All E.R. 595, C.A.) although it has been thought that a clear abandonment of the right might do so: *Stanley* v. *Compton*.

The question is to be determined as at the date when it is relevant, rather than as at the date of letting: *Baker* v. *Turner* [1950] A.C. 401, H.L.

Finally, there is the word dwelling itself, *i.e.* within the definition. This has been defined as something in which all the major activities of life, such as sleeping, cooking and feeding, are carried out: *Wright* v. *Howell* (1947) 92 S.J. 26, C.A., *Curl* v. *Angelo* [1948] 2 All E.R. 189, C.A., *Metropolitan Properties* v. *Barder* [1968] 1 All E.R. 536. Premises not used for sleeping cannot be in use as a dwelling: *Wimbush* v. *Cibulia* [1949] 2 K.B. 564, C.A. But use need not be by the person to whom the premises are let: *Whitty* v. *Scott-Russell* [1950] 2 K.B. 32, C.A., *Edgware Estates Ltd.* v. *Coblentz* [1949] 2 K.B. 717, C.A., *Carter* v. *S.U. Carburetter Co.* [1942] 2 K.B. 288, C.A., *Watson* v. *Saunders-Roe Ltd.* [1947] K.B. 437, C.A., *Anspach* v. *Charlton SS Co. Ltd.* [1955] 2 Q.B. 21, C.A.

"House". The word "house" has fallen for consideration on a number of occasions, both under and not under Housing Acts. The approach of the courts is not merely to consider the word in relation to the Housing Acts, but, indeed, particular parts of the Housing Acts: "As usual, though the matter is so very clear to my mind on the facts and on the Act . . ., it has been embarrassed by a reference to a number of authorities. . ." (*per* Jessel M.R., *Duke of Bedford* v. *Dawson* (1875) L.R. 20 Eq. 353 at p.357, cited by Browne L.J. in *Sovmots Investments Ltd.* v. *Secretary of State for the Environment* at the Court of Appeal, [1979] A.C. 144, C.A. and H.L.)

In *Quillotex Co. Ltd.* v. *Minister of Housing and Local Government* [1966] 1 Q.B. 704, Salmon L.J. adopted the view of Sir George Jessel M.R. in *Attorney-General* v. *Mutual Tontine Westminster Chambers Association Ltd.* (1876) 1 Ex. D. 469, C.A., that no real help can be gained as to the meaning of a word in Statute A by reference to its meaning in Statute B, C or D. "What is the ordinary natural meaning of the word within the context of the section in which it appears?" And: "In construing the language of any statutory enactment, it is important to look at it in its context and to consider, amongst other things, the mischief at which it is aimed. . ."

In *Annicola Investments Ltd.* v. *Minister of Housing and Local Government* [1968] 1 Q.B. 631, it was said "that the word has a distinct fluidity of meaning, and that it is best construed in relation to the context in which it is found, and in relation to the objects and purposes of the Act or of the section of the Act in which it is used". In *In Re Butler, Camberwell (Wingfield Mews) No. 2 Clearance Order 1936* [1939] 1 K.B. 570, C.A., Sir Wilfred Greene M.R. said that "whether a particular building does or does not fall under that word is a mixed question of fact and law; fact in so far as it is necessary to ascertain all the relevant facts relating to the building, and law in so far as the application of the word "houses" to those facts involves the construction of the Act.

"However, as so frequently happens in dealing with Acts of Parliament, words are found used—and very often the commoner the word is, the greater doubt it may raise—the application of which to individual cases can only be settled by the application of a sense of language in the context of the Act, and if I may say so, a certain amount of common sense in using and understanding the English language in a particular context. . ."

It is also clear that the fact that there may be provisions in another part of the Act which treat issues differently will not be conclusive. ". . . It is dangerous to interpret one Part by reference to the provisions of another Part" (*per* Woolf J, in *R.* v. *Cardiff City Council, ex parte Cross* (1981) 1 H.L.R. 54, Q.B.D., upheld on appeal (1982) 6 H.L.R. 1, C.A.). "Comparative" construction was also considered and rejected in *Okereke* v. *London Borough of Brent* [1967] 1 Q.B. 42, C.A.

It has been said that "house" has no very precise meaning: the word can cover many types of building (*Quillotex* v. *Minister of Housing and Local Government* [1966] 1 Q.B. 704, C.A. See also *Critchell* v. *Lambeth Borough Council* [1957] 2 Q.B. 535, C.A.—a house means what is commonly called a house, *i.e.* a separate structure, but in this Act it of course includes flats by virtue of the definition in this section). In *Howard* v. *Ministry of Housing and Local Government* (1967) 65 L.G.R. 257, it was said that the word "house" in the Housing Act 1957 from which this section is derived had the same meaning as "dwelling house" in the previous (1936) legislation.

A house is "a building for human habitation; especially a building that is the ordinary dwelling place of a family", according to the Oxford English Dictionary as quoted by Pearson L.J. in *Reed* v. *Hastings Corporation* (1964) 62 L.G.R. 588, C.A. In *Ashbridge Investments Ltd.* v. *Ministry of Housing and Local Government* [1965] 1 W.L.R. 1320, C.A., a greengrocer's shop with a rear living room and scullery, three first floor rooms and an outside lavatory, was considered within what could properly be held a house: "It is apparent that a "house". . . means a building which is constructed or adapted for use as or for the purposes of a dwelling" (*per* Lord Denning M.R. at p1324).

In *Re Butler, Camberwell (Wingfield Mews) No. 2 Clearance Order 1936* [1939] 1 K.B. 570, C.A. a structure consisting of a garage or workshop with a dwelling above was held to be a house (see also *Re Hammersmith (Bergham Mews) Clearance Order, 1936* [1937] 3 All E.R. 539). Where a building is used partly for residential purposes, and partly for other purposes, the building has to be looked at as a whole to ascertain whether, as a question of degree, it can properly be described as a house: *Annicola Investments Ltd.* v. *Minister of Housing and Local Government* [1968] 1 Q.B. 631, C.A. It need not be shown that all of the rooms in a building are used for residential purposes: *Premier Garage Co.* v. *Ilkeston Corporation* (1933) 97 J.P. 786.

Although original construction of a building is an important consideration (*In Re Butler, Camberwell (Wingfield Mews) No. 2 Clearance Order 1936* [1939] 1 K.B. 570, C.A.) regard may be had to the use of a building at the time the question falls to be determined (*ibid.*; see also *Grosvenor* v. *Hampstead Junction Railway* [1857] L.J. Ch. 731), so that something not built as a house but used as such may qualify. An unfinished house may qualify as a house: *Alexander* v. *Crystal Palace Railway* (1862) 30 Beav. 556. A building constructed as a house but used for other purposes has been held to remain a house: *Howard* v. *Ministry of Housing and Local Government* (1967) 65 L.G.R. 257.

A hostel or a building used for multiple occupation or as a lodging-house may itself qualify as a house, *i.e.* independently of the definition above: *London County Council* v. *Rowton Houses Ltd.* (1897) 62 J.P. 68; *Re Ross and Leicester Corporation* (1932) 96 J.P. 459; *R.* v. *London Borough of Southwark, ex parte Lewis Levy Ltd.* (1983) 8 H.L.R. 1, Q.B.D.; *R.* v. *London Borough of Camden, ex parte Rowton (Camden Town) Ltd.* (1983) 10 H.L.R. 28, Q.B.D.

Similarly, a building subdivided into flats can remain a house, whether so constructed or not: *Annicola Investments Ltd.* v. *Minister of Housing and Local Government* [1968] 1 Q.B. 631, *Quillotex Co. Ltd.* v. *Minister of Housing and Local Government* [1966] 1 Q.B. 704, *Benabo* v. *Wood Green Borough Council* [1946] 1 K.B. 38, *Critchell* v. *London Borough of*

Lambeth [1957] 2 Q.B. 535, C.A., *Okereke* v. *London Borough of Brent* [1967] 1 Q.B., C.A.

In *Lake* v. *Bennett* [1970] 1 Q.B. 663, C.A., under the Leasehold Reform Act 1967, Lord Denning M.R. doubted that a tower block could reasonably be called a house, but Salmon L.J. emphasised that the decision did not necessarily affect the Housing Acts, and the wording of the 1967 Act refers to a house "reasonably so called".

"Appurtenances". In addition, "any yard, garden, outhouses and appurtenances belonging to. . . or usually enjoyed with" the house are to be considered part of the house. In *Trim* v. *Sturminster Rural District Council* [1938] 2 K.B. 508, 10 acres of grassland were let together with a cottage, and the question arose whether they were appurtenant to the cottage. It was held, following *Bryan* v. *Wetherhead* (1623) Cro.Cas. 17, that the word "appurtenances" was used in its well established legal sense of including only such matters as outhouses, yards and gardens, but not the land itself, although it might in certain cases be competent to pass incorporeal hereditaments. How much of the ten acres ought to be included depended on the facts of the case, which had to be a question for the county court judge, but it would certainly be less than the full ten acres in issue.

In *Clymo* v. *Shell-Mex & B.P. Ltd.* (1963) 10 R.R.C. 85, C.A., under the Rating and Valuation Act 1925, open land surrounded by depot buildings was held to be appurtenant to the buildings, on the basis that had there been a conveyance or demise it would have passed without specific mention:

"The word 'appurtenance' is one of the oldest words in use in the history of English law, and we would not attempt to define it in any way; whether land is properly described as an appurtenance to one or more buildings must depend very much on the particular facts and circumstances of each case, and it does not seem possible to try to lay down any tests to determine whether land ought to be regarded as an appurtenance [for the purposes of the section]. Each case must be decided entirely on its own facts, and no doubt there may in practice be a number of difficult and borderline cases. . .

"It must be remembered that in law the grant of buildings automatically passes everything that can properly be described as an appurtenance belonging thereto. In strictness of law, it may be doubted whether the use of the word appurtenance [in the section] added anything to what would otherwise pass . . . but no doubt the words which follow were wisely added to prevent any argument on that matter". The same would seem applicable under this definition. In *Methuen-Campbell* v. *Walters* [1979] Q.B. 525, under the Leasehold Reform Act 1967, it was held that land cannot ordinarily be appurtenant to land, but the ordinary and strict meaning of the word may yield to a wider meaning if the context so requires.

In *Hansford* v. *Jago* [1921] 1 Ch. 322, a right of way was held to pass with the word appurtenances. In *Sovmots Investments Ltd.* v. *Secretary of State for the Environment* [1979] A.C. 144, H.L., it was held that appurtenances could not include rights of way and other ancillary rights not yet defined or in some cases even in existence, although this decision was overturned by s.13, Local Government (Miscellaneous Provisions) Act 1976, so far as compulsory purchase by local authorities is concerned.

In *F.F.F. Estates Ltd.* v. *Hackney London Borough Council* [1981] Q.B. 503, 3 H.L.R. 107, C.A., the court, considering the meaning of dwelling under what is now Part VII, Housing Act 1985, defining dwelling with this "appurtenant" extension), did not "find any real help" in caselaw considering rights passing on a conveyance, and it would certainly seem at the least arguable that—as with the word "house" itself—the word should always be construed as a mixed question of fact and law, *i.e.* applying the relevant section to the facts of each case: see in particular the quotation from *Re Butler, Camberwell (Wingfield Mews) No. 2 Clearance Order 1936* [1939] 1 K.B. 570, C.A., above.

Final provisions

Short title, commencement and extent

107.—(1) This Act may be cited as the Housing Associations Act 1985.
(2) This Act comes into force on 1st April 1986.
(3) The following provisions of this Act apply to England and Wales only—

    section 2,
    section 4(3)(*g*),
    section 8(2) and (3),
    sections 11 and 12,
    section 17(4),

section 18,
section 20,
section 31,
sections 34 to 36,
section 38,
sections 44 and 45,
section 52(1)(*d*) and (*e*), (3) and (4),
section 58,
section 67,
section 69(3),
section 81,
sections 84 and 85,
section 103,
section 105,
Schedules 2 and 3,
In Schedule 4, Part I,
In Schedule 5, Part I, paragraphs 1 and 2 of Part III and paragraph 1 of Part V.

(4) The following provisions of this Act apply to Scotland only—
section 59,
section 66,
section 68,
section 69(4),
section 86,
In Schedule 4, Part III,
In Schedule 5, Part II, paragraphs 3 and 4 of Part III, Part IV and Part VII.

(5) This Act does not extend to Northern Ireland.

SCHEDULES

Sections 6, 9.   SCHEDULE 1

GRANT-AIDED LAND

Definition of "grant-aided land"

1. For the purposes of section 9(1)(*b*) (control by Corporation of dispositions of land by unregistered housing associations) "grant-aided land" means land—
   (*a*) in respect of which a payment of a description specified in paragraph 2 falls or fell to be made in respect of a period ending after 24th January 1974, or
   (*b*) on which is, or has been, secured a loan of a description specified in paragraph 3 in respect of which a repayment (by way of principal or interest or both) falls or fell to be made after 24th January 1974.

Payments

2. The payments referred to in paragraph 1(*a*) are—
   (*a*) payments by way of annual grants or exchequer contributions under—
      section 31(3) of the Housing Act 1949,
      section 19(3) of the Housing (Scotland) Act 1949, or
      section 121(3) of the Housing (Scotland) Act 1950
      (arrangements by local authorities for improvement of housing accommodation);
   (*b*) payments by way of annual grants or exchequer contributions under—
      section 12(1) or 15 of the Housing (Financial Provisions) Act 1958,
      section 89(1) of the Housing (Scotland) Act 1950,
      section 12 of the Housing (Scotland) Act 1962, or
      section 21 of the Housing (Financial Provisions) (Scotland) Act 1968
      (contributions for dwellings improved under arrangements with local authorities or grants for hostels);

    (*c*) payments by way of annual grant or exchequer contributions under—
          section 12(6) of the Housing Subsidies Act 1967,
          section 121 of the Housing (Scotland) Act 1950,
          section 62 of the Housing Act 1964, or
          section 17 of the Housing (Financial Provisions) (Scotland) Act 1968
          (subsidies for conversions or improvements by housing associations);
    (*d*) payments by way of annual grant under—
          section 21(8) of the Housing Act 1969 (contributions for dwellings provided or
          improved by housing associations under arrangements with local authorities);
    (*e*) payments by way of subsidy under—
          section 72, 73, 75 or 92 of the Housing Finance Act 1972,
          section 52, 53, 55 or 57 of the Housing (Financial Provisions) (Scotland) Act
          1972, or
          Parts I, II, VI and VII of Schedule 5 to this Act (basic or special residual
          subsidy, new building or improvement subsidy, hostel subsidy).

Loans

3. The loans referred to in paragraph 1(*b*) are—
    (*a*) loans under—
          section 119 of the Housing Act 1957,
          section 152 of the Housing (Scotland) Act 1966,
          section 58 of this Act, or
          section 59 of this Act
          (powers of certain local authorities to promote and assist housing associations);
    (*b*) loans to housing associations under—
          section 47 of the Housing (Financial Provisions) Act 1958,
          section 78 of the Housing (Scotland) Act 1950,
          section 24 of the Housing (Financial Provisions) (Scotland) Act 1968,
          section 67 of this Act, or
          section 68 of this Act
          (loans by Public Works Loan Commissioners to certain bodies);
    (*c*) advances made under—
          section 7 of the Housing Act 1961,
          section 11 of the Housing (Scotland) Act 1962, or
          section 23 of the Housing (Financial Provisions) (Scotland) Act 1968
          (advances to housing associations providing housing accommodation for letting);
    (*d*) loans under—
          section 2 of the Housing Act 1964
          (loans by Housing Corporation to housing associations).

NOTES

This Schedule defines "grant-aided land" for the purposes of s.9, above, which provides for the requirement of Housing Corporation consent to a disposal of such land even by an unregistered housing association: see notes to s.9.

Section 11   SCHEDULE 2

FURTHER PROVISIONS AS TO CERTAIN DISPOSALS OF HOUSES

Repayment of discount on early disposal

1.—(1) This paragraph applies where, on a disposal of a house under section 8, in accordance with a consent given by the Housing Corporation under section 9, a discount has been given to the purchaser by the housing association; but this paragraph does not apply in any such case if the consent so provides.

(2) On the disposal the conveyance, grant or assignment shall contain a covenant binding on the purchaser and his successors in title to pay to the housing association on demand, if within a period of five years there is a relevant disposal which is not an exempted disposal (but if there is more than one such disposal then only on the first of them), an amount equal

to the discount reduced by 20 per cent. for each complete year which has elapsed after the conveyance, grant or assignment and before the further disposal.

Liability to repay is a charge on the premises

2.—(1) The liability that may arise under the covenant required by paragraph 1 is a charge on the house, taking effect as if it had been created by deed expressed to be by way of legal mortgage.

(2) The charge has priority immediately after any legal charge securing an amount—
    (a) left outstanding by the purchaser, or
    (b) advanced to him by an approved lending institution for the purpose of enabling him to acquire the interest disposed of on the first disposal, or
    (c) further advanced to him by that institution;
but the housing association may at any time by written notice served on an approved lending institution postpone the charge taking effect by virtue of this paragraph to a legal charge securing an amount advanced or further advanced to the purchaser by that institution.

(3) A charge taking effect by virtue of this section is a land charge for the purposes of section 59 of the Land Registration Act 1925 notwithstanding subsection (5) of that section (exclusion of mortgages), and subsection (2) of that section applies accordingly with respect to its protection and realisation.

(4) The approved lending institutions for the purposes of this paragraph are—
    a building society,
    a bank,
    a trustee savings bank,
    an insurance company,
    a friendly society,
    the Housing Corporation
and any body specified, or of a class or description specified, in an order made under section 156 of the Housing Act 1985 (which makes provision in relation to disposals in pursuance of the right to buy corresponding to that made by this paragraph).

Restriction on disposal of houses in National Parks, etc.

3.—(1) Where a conveyance, grant or assignment executed under section 8 is of a house situated in—
    (a) a National Park,
    (b) an area designated under section 87 of the National Parks and Access to the Countryside Act 1949 as an area of outstanding natural beauty, or
    (c) an area designated as a rural area by order under section 157 of the Housing Act 1985 (which makes provision in relation to disposals in pursuance of the right to buy corresponding to that made by this paragraph),
the conveyance, grant or assignment may (unless it contains a condition of a kind mentioned in section 33(2)(b) or (c) of the Housing Act 1985 (right of pre-emption or restriction on assignment)) contain a covenant limiting the freedom of the purchaser (including any successor in title of his and any person deriving title under him or such a successor) to dispose of the house in the manner specified below.

(2) The limitation is that until such time (if any) as may be notified in writing by the housing association to the purchaser or a successor in title of his, there will be no relevant disposal which is not an exempted disposal without the written consent of the housing association; but that consent shall not be withheld if the disposal is to a person satisfying the condition stated in sub-paragraph (3).

(3) The condition is that the person to whom the disposal is made (or, if it is made to more than one person, at least one of them) has, throughout the period of three years immediately preceding the application for consent—
    (a) had his place of work in a region designated by order under section 157(3) of the Housing Act 1985 which, or part of which, is comprised in the National Park or area, or
    (b) had his only or principal home in such a region;
or has had the one in part or parts of that period and the other in the remainder; but the region need not have been the same throughout the period.

(4) A disposal in breach of such a covenant as is mentioned in sub-paragraph (1) is void.

(5) The limitation imposed by such a covenant is a local land charge and, if the land is registered under the Land Registration Act 1925, the Chief Land Registrar shall enter the appropriate restriction on the register of title as if application therefor had been made under section 58 of that Act.

(6) In this paragraph "purchaser" means the person acquiring the interest disposed of by the first disposal.

Relevant disposals

4.—(1) A disposal, whether of the whole or part of the house, is a relevant disposal for the purposes of this Schedule if it is—
(a) a conveyance of the freehold or an assignment of the lease, or
(b) the grant of a lease or sub-lease (other than a mortgage term) for a term of more than 21 years otherwise than at a rack rent.
(2) For the purposes of sub-paragraph (1)(b) it shall be assumed—
    (a) that any option to renew or extend a lease or sub-lease, whether or not forming part of a series of options, is exercised, and
    (b) that any option to terminate a lease or sub-lease is not exercised.

Exempted disposals

5.—(1) A disposal is an exempted disposal for the purposes of this Schedule if—
    (a) it is a disposal of the whole of the house and a conveyance of the freehold or an assignment of the lease and the person or each of the persons to whom it is made is a qualifying person (as defined in sub-paragraph (2));
    (b) it is a vesting of the whole of the house in a person taking under a will or on an intestacy;
    (c) it is a disposal of the whole of the house in pursuance of an order made under section 24 of the Matrimonial Causes Act 1973 (property adjustment orders in connection with matrimonial proceedings) or section 2 of the Inheritance (Provision for Family and Dependants) Act 1975 (orders as to financial provision to be made from estate);
    (d) it is a compulsory disposal; or
    (e) the property disposed of is property included with the house by virtue of paragraph (b) of the definition of "house" in section 106(1) (yard, garden, outhouses, &c.).
(2) For the purposes of sub-paragraph (1)(a), a person is a qualifying person in relation to a disposal if—
(a) he is the person or one of the persons by whom the disposal is made,
(b) he is the spouse or a former spouse of that person or one of those persons, or
(c) he is a member of the family of that person or one of those persons and has resided with him throughout the period of twelve months ending with the disposal.

Meaning of "compulsory disposal"

6. In this Schedule a "compulsory disposal" means a disposal of property which is acquired compulsorily, or is acquired by a person who has made or would have made, or for whom another person has made or would have made, a compulsory purchase order authorising its compulsory purchase for the purposes for which it is acquired.

Exempted disposals which end liability under covenants

7. Where there is a relevant disposal which is an exempted disposal by virtue of paragraph 5(1)(d) or (e) (compulsory disposal or disposal of yard, garden etc.)—
(a) the covenant required by paragraph 1 (repayment of discount on early disposal) is not binding on the person to whom the disposal is made or any successor in title of his, and that covenant and the charge taking effect by virtue of paragraph 2 cease to apply in relation to the property disposed of, and
(b) any such covenant as is mentioned in paragraph 3 (restriction on disposal of houses in National Parks, etc.) ceases to apply in relation to the property disposed of.

Treatment of options

8.—(1) For the purposes of this Schedule the grant of an option enabling a person to call for a relevant disposal which is not an exempted disposal shall be treated as such a disposal made to him.
(2) For the purposes of paragraph 3(2) (requirement of consent to disposal of house in National Park, etc.) a consent to such a grant shall be treated as a consent to a disposal made in pursuance of the option.

NOTES
Paras. 1, 2

Registered housing associations may, if consent so provides, grant discounts when selling dwellings voluntarily to their sitting tenants. The discount scheme is equivalent to that operating in respect of disposals to sitting tenants under the "right to buy" provisions contained in Pt. V of the Housing Act 1985. These paragraphs introduce identical provisions to those in that Act, for the repayment of discount on a relevant "early disposal" of the dwelling after a voluntary, discounted sale.

What amounts to a "relevant" disposal is set out in para. 4. The purchaser, and his successors in title, are bound to repay to the vendor housing association an amount equal to the full discount less 20 per cent. for each full year of occupation between conveyance (or grant of lease) *i.e.*, after occupation for a full five years no discount is repayable. The housing association's right to repayment of discount is protected under para. 2, which provides that the covenant to repay is to take effect as a legal charge on the dwelling. The charge has immediate priority subject only to a charge securing any amount left outstanding by the purchaser to the association itself, or a mortgage charge advanced to the purchaser by one of the approved lending institutions specified in sub-para. (4), for the purpose of his acquiring an interest in the property, either on an initial, or on a further, advance.

The housing association may however postpone the charge under this paragraph to an approved lending institution.

Para. 3

The purpose of this paragraph is to provide some protection for the existing population, and housing associations operating in their interests, in rural areas, areas of natural beauty, and National Parks. A housing association may include in a conveyance, grant or assignment of a house situated in one of the above areas, a restrictive covenant preventing a future disposal of the property without the association's consent. It, too, is equivalent to "right to buy" provisions under Pt. V, Housing Act 1985.

Section 26   SCHEDULE 3

ACCOUNTING REQUIREMENTS FOR CHARITABLE HOUSING ASSOCIATIONS

Books of account, &c.

1.—(1) The association shall in respect of its housing activities—
    (*a*) cause to be kept proper books of account showing its transactions and its assets and liabilities, and
    (*b*) establish and maintain a satisfactory system of control of its books of account, its cash holdings and all its receipts and remittances.

(2) The books of account must be such as to enable a true and fair view to be given of the state of affairs of the association in respect of its housing activities, and to explain its transactions in the course of those activities.

Accounts and balance sheets

2.—(1) The association shall for each period of account prepare—
    (*a*) a revenue account giving a true and fair view of the association's income and expenditure in the period, so far as arising in connection with its housing activities, and
    (*b*) a balance sheet giving a true and fair view as at the end of the period of the state of the association's affairs.

(2) The revenue account and balance sheet must be signed by at least two trustees of the association.

Appointment of auditor

3.—(1) The association shall in each period of account appoint a qualified auditor to audit the accounts prepared in accordance with paragraph 2.

(2) A person is qualified for the purposes of this paragraph if he is either a member of one of the following bodies—
    the Institute of Chartered Accountants in England and Wales,

the Institute of Chartered Accountants in Scotland,
the Association of Certified Accountants,
the Institute of Chartered Accountants in Ireland, or
any other body of accountants established in the United Kingdom and recognised by
    the Secretary of State for the purposes of section 389(1)(*a*) of the Companies
    Act 1985,
or is a person who is for the time being authorised by the Secretary of State under section
389(1)(*b*) of that Act or any corresponding earlier legislation as being a person with similar
qualifications obtained outside the United Kingdom.

(3) But none of the following shall be appointed—
    (*a*) a trustee, officer or employee of the association or of an associated body,
    (*b*) a person who is a partner of, or in the employment of, or who employs a person
        within paragraph (*a*), or
    (*c*) a body corporate;
and a body of persons (whether corporate or unincorporate and whether or not itself a
charity) is for this purpose an associated body if it is essentially under the same management
or control as the association.

(4) A Scottish firm is qualified for appointment as auditor, notwithstanding sub-paragraph
(3)(*c*), if each of the partners in it is qualified for appointment.

Auditor's report

4.—(1) The association's auditor appointed under this Schedule shall make a report to the
association on the accounts audited by him.

(2) The report shall state whether in the auditor's opinion—
    (*a*) the revenue account gives a true and fair view of the state of income and
        expenditure of the association in respect of its housing activities and of any other
        matters to which it relates, and
    (*b*) the balance sheet gives a true and fair view of the state of affairs of the
        association as at the end of the period of account.

Duties of auditor

5. The auditor in preparing his report shall carry out such investigations as will enable him
to form an opinion as to the following matters—
    (*a*) whether the association has kept, in respect of its housing activities, proper books of
        account in accordance with the requirements of this Schedule;
    (*b*) whether the association has maintained a satisfactory system of control over its
        transactions in accordance with those requirements, and
    (*c*) whether the accounts are in agreement with the association's books;
and if he is of opinion that the association has failed in any respect to comply with this
Schedule, or if the accounts are not in agreement with the books, he shall state that fact in
his report.

Auditor's right of access to books, etc.

6. The auditor—
    (*a*) has a right of access at all times to the books, deeds and accounts of the
        association, so far as relating to its housing activities, and to all other documents
        relating to those activities, and
    (*b*) is entitled to require from the trustees or officers of the association such
        information and explanations as he thinks necessary for the performance of his
        duties;
and if he fails to obtain all the information and explanations which, to the best of his
knowledge and belief, are necessary for the purposes of his audit, he shall state that fact in
his report.

Periods of account

7. A period of account for the purposes of this Schedule is twelve months or such other
period not less than six months or more than 18 months as the association may, with the
consent of the Corporation, determine.

NOTES

This Schedule sets out the accounting requirements for registered housing associations
which are also registered as charities under the Charities Act 1960. The requirements, which

reproduce those imposed on associations registered under the Industrial and Provident Societies Act 1965, relate only to an association's housing activities as defined under s.106, above: see s.26, above. The requirements of this Schedule are in addition, and without prejudice to, any accounting requirements imposed by the Secretary of State on registered housing associations generally, under s.24, above: see notes to that section.

Sections 69, 70   SCHEDULE 4

HOUSING ASSOCIATIONS: CONTINUATION OF ARRANGEMENTS UNDER REPEALED ENACTMENTS

PART I

ARRANGEMENTS WITH LOCAL AUTHORITIES FOR PROVISION OR IMPROVEMENT OF HOUSING

(*ss. 120 and 121 of the Housing Act 1957*)

1. Arrangements between a local authority and a housing association under section 120 of the Housing Act 1957 (arrangements for provision of housing) which were made before 10th August 1972 and are in force immediately before the commencement of this Act remain in force under this paragraph.

2. Arrangements between a local authority and a housing association under section 121 of the Housing Act 1957 (arrangements for improvement or conversion of housing) which were made before 1st April 1975 and are in force immediately before the commencement of this Act remain in force under this paragraph.

PART II

SUBSIDY AGREEMENTS WITH LOCAL AUTHORITIES

(*s. 79 of the Housing Finance Act 1972 and s. 59 of the Housing (Financial Provisions) (Scotland) Act 1972*)

1. In this Part "subsidy agreement" means an agreement made between a local authority and a housing association which provides for payments to be made under or by reference to any of the following enactments—

    section 2 of the Housing (Financial Provisions) Act 1924,

    section 29(1) of the Housing Act 1930,

    section 27(3) of the Housing Act 1935,

    section 26 of the Housing (Scotland) Act 1935,

    section 94(3) of the Housing Act 1936,

    section 87(1) of the Housing (Scotland) Act 1950,

    section 1(2)(*b*) of the Housing Subsidies Act 1956,

    section 2, 3 or 4 of the Housing and Town Development (Scotland) Act 1957,

    section 1(2)(*b*) of the Housing (Financial Provisions) Act 1958,

    section 1(2) of the Housing Act 1961,

    section 2, 4, 5, 6 or 7 of the Housing (Scotland) Act 1962,

    section 1(5) or 9(4) of the Housing Subsidies Act 1967,

    section 2, 4, 6, 7, 9 or 10 of the Housing (Financial Provisions) (Scotland) Act 1968,

(being enactments with respect to which it was provided by the Housing Finance Act 1972 or the Housing (Financial Provisions) (Scotland) Act 1972 that no further payments were to be made for 1972–73 or any subsequent year).

2. Where a subsidy agreement provides for the payment of greater amounts than those which the authority would have been obliged to pay under the relevant enactment, the authority shall continue to pay to the housing association sums equal to the difference between the amounts for the payment of which the agreement provides and the amounts which they would have been obliged to pay by that enactment.

PART III

SPECIAL ARRANGEMENTS WITH THE SECRETARY OF STATE IN SCOTLAND

(s.1(1)(d) of the Housing (Scotland) Act 1962; s.1(2)(d) of the Housing (Financial Provisions)
(Scotland) Act 1968)

Arrangements made between the Secretary of State and a housing association under section 1(1)(d) of the Housing (Scotland) Act 1962 or section 1(2)(d) of the Housing (Financial Provisions) (Scotland) Act 1968 (special arrangements for provision of housing) which were made before 3rd August 1972 and are in force immediately before the commencement of this Act remain in force under this paragraph.

NOTES

This Schedule specifies the arrangements and subsidy agreements made between housing associations and local authorities, and the Secretary of State in Scotland, under enactments which have since been repealed, and provides that they remain in force after the coming into operation of this Act.

Sections 69, 71   SCHEDULE 5

HOUSING ASSOCIATION FINANCE: SUPERSEDED SUBSIDIES, CONTRIBUTIONS AND GRANTS

PART I

RESIDUAL SUBSIDIES: ENGLAND AND WALES

(ss.72 and 73 of the Housing Finance Act 1972)
Entitlement to residual subsidies

1.—(1) Basic residual subsidy is payable to a housing association in accordance with the following provisions where the association received payments from the Secretary of State for the financial year 1971–72 under certain enactments under which, in accordance with the Housing Finance Act 1972, no payments were to be made for 1972–73 or any subsequent year.

(2) A housing association is entitled to basic residual subsidy for a financial year if—
    (a) it was entitled to basic residual subsidy under section 72 of the Housing Finance Act 1972 for the financial year 1972–73, and
    (b) it has continued to be entitled to basic residual subsidy, under that section or this Schedule, for each succeeding financial year up to and including that immediately before the year in question.

(3) The amount of basic residual subsidy payable to an association for any year is the amount (if any) by which the basic residual subsidy payable for the previous year exceeds the withdrawal factor.

(4) Subject to any direction of the Secretary of State under paragraph 4(2), the withdrawal factor is the sum produced by multiplying £20 by the number of dwellings as at 31st March 1972 in respect of which the association's subsidies for 1971–72 (as defined in section 72(4) of the Housing Finance Act 1972) were payable.

2.—(1) Special residual subsidy is payable to a housing association in accordance with the following provisions in respect of dwellings which—
    (a) were approved by the Secretary of State for the purposes of Part I of the Housing Subsidies Act 1967 before 10th August 1972, and
    (b) were completed during the year 1972–73, 1973–74 or 1974–75.

(2) A housing association is entitled to special residual subsidy for a financial year if—
    (a) it was entitled by virtue of section 73 of the Housing Finance Act 1972 to special residual subsidy for any of the years 1972–73, 1973–74 or 1974–75, and
    (b) it has continued to be entitled to special residual subsidy, under that section or this Schedule, for each succeeding financial year up to and including that immediately before the year in question.

(3) The amount of special residual subsidy payable to an association for any year is the amount (if any) by which the special residual subsidy payable for the previous year exceeds the reduction factor.

(4) Subject to any direction of the Secretary of State under paragraph 4(2), the reduction factor is the sum produced by multiplying £20 by the number of dwellings satisfying the description in sub-paragraph (1).

3. No basic or special residual subsidy is payable to a co-operative housing association.

Power to vary withdrawal factor or reduction factor

4.—(1) This paragraph applies where a housing association, by furnishing to the Secretary of State such information as to its financial position as he may require, satisfies him as regards any financial year that its income for its dwellings, will be, or was, inadequate having regard to its normal sources of income to meet such expenditure (including loan charges) as in his opinion it would be, or was, reasonable for the association to incur for that financial year in the exercise of its housing functions.

(2) Where this paragraph applies, the Secretary of State may direct that the amount of basic residual subsidy or special residual subsidy payable to the association for the financial year in question shall be determined—

(a) by reference to a withdrawal factor or reduction factor calculated by reference to a smaller sum of money per dwelling than that mentioned in paragraph 1(4) or 2(4), or

(b) by reference to a withdrawal factor or reduction factor of zero.

(3) A direction under this paragraph may be varied or revoked by the Secretary of State by a further direction.

(4) In sub-paragraph (1) "housing functions" means—

(a) constructing or improving, or facilitating or encouraging the construction or improvement, of dwellings,

(b) managing dwellings,

(c) the provision of dwellings by conversion, and

(d) the acquisition of dwellings;

and includes functions which are supplementary or incidental to any of those functions.

(5) For the purposes of this paragraph "loan charges", in relation to money borrowed by an association, means–

(a) the sums required for the payment of interest on the money and for its repayment, either by instalments or by means of a sinking fund, and

(b) the expenses of managing the debt,

and includes any such charges made by the association itself, whether in respect of borrowing from a capital fund kept by the association or in respect of borrowing between accounts kept by the association for different functions, or otherwise.

Administrative provisions

5.—(1) Payment of basic or special residual subsidy is subject to the making of a claim for the payment in such form, and containing such particulars, as the Secretary of State may from time to time determine.

(2) The amount of basic or special residual subsidy payable to a housing association for a financial year shall be calculated to the nearest pound by rounding up any odd amount of 50p or more and rounding down any lesser amount.

(3) Basic or special residual subsidy is payable at such times and in such manner as the Treasury may direct, and subject to such conditions as to records, certificates, audit or otherwise as the Secretary of State may, with the approval of the Treasury, impose.

Powers exercisable in case of disposal of dwellings by association

6.—(1) The Secretary of State may reduce, suspend or discontinue the payment of basic or special residual subsidy to an association if the association leases for a term exceeding seven years or otherwise disposes of any of the dwellings in respect of which the association is entitled to the payment.

(2) If any dwellings of an association are leased for a term exceeding seven years to, or become vested in—

(a) another housing association, or trustees for another housing association, or

(b) the Housing Corporation,

the Secretary of State may pay to them any basic or special residual subsidy which he would otherwise have paid to the former association for any financial year, beginning with that in which the dwellings are so leased or become so vested.

(3) For the purposes of this paragraph a lease shall be treated as being for a term exceeding seven years where the original term is for a lesser period but the lease confers on the lessee an option for renewal for a term which, together with the original term, exceeds seven years.

Saving for financial years beginning before the commencement of this Act

7.—(1) The preceding provisions apply in relation to the financial year 1986–87 and subsequent financial years.

(2) The repeal by the Housing (Consequential Provisions) Act 1985 of the provisions of the Housing Finance Act 1972 relating to basic and special residual subsidies does not affect the operation of those provisions in relation to previous financial years.

PART II

RESIDUAL SUBSIDIES: SCOTLAND

(ss. 52 and 53 of the Housing (Financial Provisions) (Scotland) Act 1972)

Entitlement to residual subsidies

1.—(1) Basic residual subsidy is payable to a housing association in accordance with the following provisions where the association received payments from the Secretary of State for the financial year 1971–72 under certain enactments under which, in accordance with the Housing (Financial Provisions) (Scotland) Act 1972, no payments were to be made for 1972–73 or any subsequent year.

(2) A housing association is entitled to basic residual subsidy for a financial year if—
- (*a*) it was entitled to basic residual subsidy under section 52 of the Housing (Financial Provisions) (Scotland) Act 1972 for the financial year 1972–73, and
- (*b*) it has continued to be entitled to basic residual subsidy, under that section or this Schedule, for each succeeding financial year up to and including that immediately before the year in question.

(3) The amount of basic residual subsidy payable to an association for any year is the amount (if any) by which the basic residual subsidy payable for the previous year exceeds the withdrawal factor.

(4) Subject to any direction of the Secretary of State under paragraph 4(2), the withdrawal factor is the sum produced by multiplying £20 by the number of houses as at 31st March 1972 in respect of which the association's subsidies for 1971–72 (as defined in section 52(4) of the Housing (Financial Provisions) (Scotland) Act 1972) were payable.

2.—(1) Special residual subsidy is payable to a housing association in accordance with the following provisions in respect of houses—
- (*a*) the erection of which was approved by the Secretary of State for the purposes of sections 1 to 12 of the Housing (Financial Provisions) (Scotland) Act 1968 before 3rd August 1972, and
- (*b*) which were completed by the association during the year 1972–73, 1973–74 or 1974–75.

(2) A housing association is entitled to special residual subsidy for a financial year if—
- (*a*) it was entitled by virtue of section 53 of the Housing (Financial Provisions) (Scotland) Act 1972 to special residual subsidy for any of the years 1972–73, 1973–74 or 1974–75, and
- (*b*) it has continued to be entitled to special residual subsidy, under that section or this Schedule, for each succeeding financial year up to and including that immediately before the year in question.

(3) The amount of special residual subsidy payable to an association for any year is the amount (if any) by which the special residual subsidy payable for the previous year exceeds the reduction factor.

(4) Subject to any direction of the Secretary of State under paragraph 4(2), the reduction factor is the sum produced by multiplying £20 by the number of houses satisfying the description in sub-paragraph (1).

3. No basic or special residual subsidy is payable to a co-operative housing association.

Power to vary withdrawal factor or reduction factor

4.—(1) This paragraph applies where a housing association, by furnishing to the Secretary of State such information as to its financial position as he may require, satisfies him as regards any financial year that its income from its houses will be, or was, inadequate having regard to its normal sources of income to meet such expenditure (including loan charges) as in his opinion it would be, or was, reasonable for the association to incur for that financial year in the exercise of its housing functions.

(2) Where this paragraph applies, the Secretary of State may direct that the amount of basic residual subsidy or special residual subsidy payable to the association for the financial year in question shall be determined—

(*a*) by reference to a withdrawal factor or reduction factor calculated by reference to a smaller sum of money per house than that mentioned in paragraph 1(4) or 2(4), or

(*b*) by reference to a withdrawal factor or reduction factor of zero.

(3) A direction under this paragraph may be varied or revoked by the Secretary of State by a further direction.

(4) In sub-paragraph (1) "housing functions" means—

(*a*) constructing or improving, or facilitating the construction or improvement, of houses,

(*b*) managing houses,

(*c*) the provision of houses by conversion, and

(*d*) the acquisition of houses;

and includes functions which are supplementary or incidental to any of those functions.

(5) For the purposes of this paragraph "loan charges", in relation to money borrowed by an association includes loan charges made by the association itself (including charges for debt management), whether in respect of borrowing from a capital fund kept by the association or in respect of borrowing between accounts kept by the association for different functions, or otherwise.

Administrative provisions

5.—(1) Payment of basic or special residual subsidy is subject to the making of a claim for the payment in such form, and containing such particulars, as the Secretary of State may from time to time determine.

(2) The amount of basic or special residual subsidy payable to a housing association for a financial year shall be calculated to the nearest pound by rounding up any odd amount of 50p or more and rounding down any lesser amount.

(3) Basic or special residual subsidy is payable at such times and in such manner as the Treasury may direct, and subject to such conditions as to records, certificates, audit or otherwise as the Secretary of State may, with the approval of the Treasury, impose.

Powers exercisable in case of disposal of houses by association

6.—(1) The Secretary of State may reduce, suspend or discontinue the payment of basic or special residual subsidy to a housing association if the association leases for a term exceeding seven years or otherwise disposes of any of the houses in respect of which the association is entitled to the payment.

(2) If any houses of an association are leased for a term exceeding seven years to, or become vested in—

(*a*) another housing association, or trustees for another housing association, or

(*b*) the Housing Corporation,

the Secretary of State may pay to that association or to the Corporation any basic or special residual subsidy which he would otherwise have paid to the former association for any financial year, beginning with that in which the houses are so leased or become so vested.

(3) For the purposes of this paragraph a lease shall be treated as being for a term exceeding seven years where the original term is for a lesser period but the lease confers on the lessee an option for renewal for a term which, together with the original term, exceeds seven years.

Saving for financial years beginning before the commencement of this Act

7.—(1) The preceding provisions apply in relation to the financial year 1986–87 and subsequent financial years.

(2) The repeal by the Housing (Consequential Provisions) Act 1985 of the provisions of the Housing (Financial Provisions) (Scotland) Act 1972 relating to basic and special residual subsidies does not affect the operation of those provisions in relation to previous financial years.

Part III

CONTRIBUTIONS AND GRANTS UNDER ARRANGEMENTS WITH LOCAL AUTHORITIES

(s. 12 of the Housing (Financial Provisions) Act 1958; s. 12 of the Housing Subsidies Act 1967; s. 21 of the Housing Act 1969)

1.—(1) Contributions by the Secretary of State in connection with arrangements made under section 121 of the Housing Act 1957 (arrangements between housing associations and local authorities for improvement of housing) remain payable—

(a) under section 12 of the Housing (Financial Provisions) Act 1958 and section 12 of the Housing Subsidies Act 1967 as regards arrangements made before 25th August 1969, and

(b) under section 21 of the Housing Act 1969 as regards arrangements made on or after that date and approved under subsection (2) of that section before 1st April 1975.

(2) The contributions are payable at such times and in such manner as the Treasury may direct, and subject to such conditions, as to records, certificates, audit or otherwise as the Secretary of State may, with the approval of the Treasury, impose.

(3) Where such a contribution is paid to a local authority, the authority shall pay to the housing association by way of annual grant an amount not less than the contribution.

2. If the Secretary of State is satisfied, in the case of contributions payable under section 12 of the Housing (Financial Provisions) Act 1958, that the housing association have made default in giving effect to the terms of the arrangements, he may, as he thinks just—

(a) reduce the amount of the contribution payable to the local authority, or

(b) suspend or discontinue the payment;

and the local authority may reduce to a proportionate or any less extent the annual grant payable by them to the association or, as the case may be, suspend the payment for a corresponding period or discontinue the payment.

(s. 17 of the Housing (Financial Provisions) (Scotland) Act 1968)

3.—(1) Contributions by the Secretary of State under section 17 of the Housing (Financial Provisions) (Scotland) Act 1968 remain payable in connection with arrangements made under section 121 of the Housing (Scotland) Act 1950 or section 155 of the Housing (Scotland) Act 1966 (arrangements between housing associations and local authorities for improvement of housing) and approved on or after 16th August 1964 and before 1st April 1975.

(2) The contributions are payable at such times and in such manner as the Treasury may direct, and subject to such conditions as to records, certificates, audit or otherwise as the Secretary of State may, with the approval of the Treasury, impose.

(3) Where such a contribution is paid to a local authority, the authority shall pay to the housing association by way of annual grant an amount not less than the contribution.

4.—(1) The Secretary of State may, in any of the circumstances mentioned in sub-paragraph (2), reduce the amount of the contributions in respect of a particular subsidised unit, or suspend or discontinue the payment of the contributions, or part of them, as he thinks just in the circumstances.

(2) The circumstances referred to in sub-paragraph (1) are—

(a) that the housing association has made default in giving effect to the terms of the arrangements with the local authority, or

(b) that the subsidised unit has been converted, demolished or destroyed, is not fit to be used or has ceased to be used for the purpose for which it was intended, has been sold or leased for a stipulated duration exceeding twelve months or has been transferred, whether by sale or otherwise,

(3) The local authority may reduce to a corresponding or less extent the annual grant payable by them to the association, or, as the case may be, suspend payment of the whole or a corresponding part of the payment for a corresponding period, or discontinue the payment or a corresponding part.

Part IV

CONTRIBUTIONS UNDER ARRANGEMENTS WITH THE
SECRETARY OF STATE IN SCOTLAND

(s.16 of the Housing (Financial Provisions) (Scotland) Act 1968)

1.—(1) Contributions by the Secretary of State under section 16 of the Housing (Financial Provisions) (Scotland) Act 1968 remain payable in connection with arrangements made under—

section 14 of the Housing (Scotland) Act 1962, or

section 154 of the Housing (Scotland) Act 1966.

(arrangement between Secretary of State and housing associations) and approved before 1st April 1975.

(2) The Secretary of State may, in any of the circumstances mentioned in sub-paragraph (3), reduce the amount of the contributions in respect of a particular subsidised unit, or suspend or discontinue the payment of the contributions, or part of them, as he thinks just in the circumstances.

(3) The circumstances referred to in sub-paragraph (2) are—

    (*a*)   that the housing association has made default in giving effect to the terms of the arrangements, or

    (*b*)   the subsidised unit has been converted, demolished or destroyed, is not fit to be used or has ceased to be used for the purpose for which it was intended, has been sold or leased for a stipulated duration exceeding twelve months or has been transferred, whether by sale or otherwise.

PART V

SCHEMES FOR THE UNIFICATION OF GRANT CONDITIONS

(s. 123 of the Housing Act 1957; s. 157 of the Housing (Scotland) Act 1966)

1. A scheme under section 123 of the Housing Act 1957 (schemes for the unification of divergent grant conditions affecting the management of a housing association's houses) which was made before 10th August 1972 and is in force immediately before the commencement of this Act remains in force under this paragraph.

2. A scheme under section 157 of the Housing (Scotland) Act 1966 (schemes for the unification of divergent grant conditions affecting the management of a housing association's houses) which was made before 3rd August 1972 and is in force immediately before the commencement of this Act remains in force under this paragraph.

PART VI

NEW BUILDING SUBSIDY AND IMPROVEMENT SUBSIDY

(s.75 of the Housing Finance Act 1972; ss.55 and 57 of the Housing (Financial Provisions) (Scotland) Act 1972)

1.—(1) The following subsidies remain payable in respect of building schemes or improvement schemes approved by the Secretary of State before 1st April 1975—

    (*a*)   new building subsidy under section 75 of the Housing Finance Act 1972 or section 55 of the Housing (Financial Provisions) (Scotland) Act 1972, and

    (*b*)   improvement subsidy under section 57 of the Housing (Financial Provisions) (Scotland) Act 1972.

(2) Payment of the subsidy is subject to the making of a claim for the payment in such form, and containing such particulars as the Secretary of State may from time to time determine.

(3) The amount of the subsidy payable for a financial year shall be calculated to the nearest pound by rounding up any odd amount of 50p or more and rounding down any lesser amount.

(4) The subsidy is payable at such times and in such manner as the Treasury may direct, and subject to such conditions as to records, certificates, audit or otherwise as the Secretary of State may, with the approval of the Treasury, impose.

2.—(1) The Secretary of State may make reduced payments of subsidy, or suspend or discontinue such payments, if—

    (*a*)   he made his approval of the scheme subject to conditions and is satisfied that any of the conditions has not been complied with, or

    (*b*)   he is satisfied that a dwelling comprised in the scheme has been converted, demolished or destroyed, is not fit to be used or is not being used for the purpose for which it was intended, has been sold or leased for a term exceeding seven years or has ceased for any reason whatsoever to be vested in the association or trustees for the association.

(2) If any of the dwellings comprised in the scheme become vested in, or are leased for a term exceeding seven years to—

    (*a*)   a housing association, or trustees for a housing association other than the association which received approval for the scheme, or

    (*b*)   the Housing Corporation,

the Secretary of State may, for any year beginning with that in which they come to be so vested or are so leased, pay them the whole or any part of the subsidy which he would otherwise have paid to the association which received approval for the scheme.

(3) For the purposes of this paragraph a dwelling shall be treated as leased for a term exceeding seven years if it is leased for a lesser term by a lease which confers on the lessee an option for renewal for a term which, together with the original term, exceeds seven years.

3.—(1) Where a housing association satisfies the Secretary of State, by furnishing him with such information as to its financial position as he may require, that the amount of new building subsidy for a year will be, or was, inadequate having regard to its normal sources of income to enable it to meet such expenditure (including loan charges) as in his opinion it would be, or was, reasonable for it to incur for that year in the exercise of its housing functions, he may direct that for that year the percentage of the initial deficit to be met by subsidy shall be greater than that otherwise applicable.

(2) The percentage shall not, however, be greater than 90 per cent. or the percentage met by subsidy for the immediately preceding year, whichever is less.

(3) This paragraph does not apply in relation to the year of completion or the second or third year for which new building subsidy is payable.

(4) In this paragraph—

"housing functions" means constructing, improving or managing, or facilitating or encouraging the construction or improvement of dwellings, the provision of dwellings by conversion and the acquisition of dwellings, and includes functions which are supplementary or incidental to any of those functions;

"loan charges" includes any loan charges made by a housing association (including charges for debt management) whether in respect of borrowing from a capital fund kept by the association or in respect of borrowing between accounts kept by the association for different functions or otherwise.

4.—(1) Where before 1st April 1976 a registered housing association made an application for housing association grant in respect of a housing project which was or included a building scheme or improvement scheme which had been previously approved for the purposes of any of the provisions mentioned in paragraph 1 and the Secretary of State gave his approval to that project for the purposes of housing association grant, no further payments of new building subsidy or improvement subsidy shall be made in respect of that approved scheme.

(2) A condition imposed by the Secretary of State in such a case by virtue of section 35(2)(b) of the Housing Act 1974, requiring the repayment of all or any of the payments of new building subsidy or improvement subsidy already paid, if in force immediately before the commencement of this Act, remains in force under this sub-paragraph.

(3) No account shall be taken under section 47(2)(b) (estimation of net cost of project for purposes of housing association grant; income to include subsidies) of payments of subsidy received which are required to be repaid in pursuance of such a condition.

PART VII

PAYMENTS IN RESPECT OF HOSTELS UNDER PRE-1974 ENACTMENTS

(s.21 of the Housing (Financial Provisions) (Scotland) Act 1968)

1.—(1) Section 21 of the Housing (Financial Provisions) (Scotland) Act 1968 (exchequer contributions for hostels) continues to have effect in relation to buildings provided or converted by a housing association which were approved by the Secretary of State for the purposes of subsection (1) of that section before 1st April 1975.

(2) A registered housing association may not make an application for housing association grant in respect of a housing project which consists of or includes the carrying out of works for the provision of hostels if before 1st April 1975 any contribution has been made under section 21 of the Housing (Financial Provisions) (Scotland) Act 1968.

(3) If in a case where sub-paragraph (2) does not prevent the making of such an application a registered housing association makes an application for housing association grant in respect of a housing project falling within that sub-paragraph and the Secretary of State gives his approval to the project for the purposes of housing association grant, section 21 of the Housing (Financial Provisions) (Scotland) Act 1968 shall cease to have effect with respect to the provision of hostels referred to in that sub-paragraph.

NOTES
This schedule provides for the continuation of central government grants and subsidies to housing associations and to local authorities, under enactments which have since been repealed but which have continued to be payable under previous saving provisions in the repealing enactments. The saving provisions are now consolidated by, and continued within, this Schedule.

Section 74   SCHEDULE 6

CONSTITUTION OF HOUSING CORPORATION

Status of Corporation

1.—(1) The Housing Corporation is a body corporate.
(2) It is a public body for the purposes of the Prevention of Corruption Acts 1889 to 1916.
(3) It shall not be regarded—
    (*a*) as the servant or agent of the Crown, or
    (*b*) as enjoying any status, immunity or privilege of the Crown, or
    (*c*) as exempt from any tax, duty, rate, levy or other charge whatsoever, whether general or local;
and its property shall not be regarded as property of, or held on behalf of, the Crown.

Membership of Corporation

2.—(1) The members of the Housing Corporation, of whom there shall not be more than fifteen, shall be appointed by the Secretary of State.
(2) Before appointing a person to be a member of the Corporation the Secretary of State shall satisfy himself that he will have no financial or other interest likely to affect prejudicially the exercise of his functions as member; and the Secretary of State may require a person whom he proposes to appoint to give him such information as he considers necessary for that purpose.
3.—(1) The members of the Housing Corporation shall hold and vacate office in accordance with the terms of their appointment, subject to the following provisions.
(2) A member may resign his membership by notice in writing addressed to the Secretary of State.
(3) The Secretary of State may remove a member from office if he is satisfied that—
    (*a*) he has been adjudged bankrupt or made an arrangement with his creditors or (in Scotland) has had his estate sequestrated or has made a trust deed for behoof of his creditors or a composition contract,
    (*b*) he is incapacitated by physical or mental illness,
    (*c*) he has been absent from meetings of the Corporation for a period longer than three consecutive months without the permission of the Corporation, or
    (*d*) he is otherwise unable or unfit to discharge the functions of a member, or is unsuitable to continue as a member.
(4) The Secretary of State shall satisfy himself from time to time with respect to every member that he has no financial or other interest likely to affect prejudicially the exercise of his functions as a member; and he may require a member to give him such information as he considers necessary for that purpose.

Chairman and Deputy Chairman

4.—(1) The Secretary of State shall appoint one of the members to be Chairman and one to be Deputy Chairman; and the members so appointed shall hold and vacate those offices in accordance with the terms of their appointment, subject to the following provisions.
(2) The Chairman or Deputy Chairman may resign his office by notice in writing addressed to the Secretary of State.
(3) If the Chairman or Deputy Chairman ceases to be a member of the Corporation, he also ceases to be Chairman or Deputy Chairman.

Remuneration and allowances

5.—(1) The Secretary of State may pay the Chairman, Deputy Chairman and members such remuneration as he may, with the consent of the Treasury, determine.

(2) The Housing Corporation may pay them such reasonable allowances as may be so determined in respect of expenses properly incurred by them in the performance of their duties.

Pensions

6.—(1) The Secretary of State may, with the consent of the Treasury, determine to pay in respect of a person's office as Chairman, Deputy Chairman or member—

(a) such pension, allowance or gratuity to or in respect of that person on his retirement or death as may be so determined, or

(b) such contributions or other payments towards provision for such pension, allowance or gratuity as may be so determined.

(2) As soon as may be after the making of such a determination the Secretary of State shall lay before each House of Parliament a statement of the amount payable in pursuance of the determination.

(3) Sub-paragraph (1) does not apply in the case of a member who has been admitted in pursuance of regulations under section 7 of the Superannuation Act 1972 to participate in the benefits of a superannuation fund maintained by a local authority.

(4) In such a case the Secretary of State shall make any payments required to be made to the fund in respect of the member by the employing authority and may make such deductions from his remuneration as the employing authority might make in respect of his contributions to the fund.

Proceedings of the Corporation

7.—(1) The quorum of the Housing Corporation and the arrangements relating to its meetings shall, subject to any directions given by the Secretary of State, be such as the Corporation may determine.

(2) The validity of proceedings of the Corporation is not affected by any defect in the appointment of any of its members.

8.—(1) Where a member of the Housing Corporation is in any way directly or indirectly interested in a contract made or proposed to be made by the Corporation—

(a) he shall disclose the nature of his interest at a meeting of the Corporation, and the disclosure shall be recorded in the minutes of the Corporation, and

(b) he shall not take any part in any decision of the Corporation with respect to the contract.

(2) A general notice given by a member at a meeting of the Corporation to the effect that he is a member of a specified company or firm and is to be regarded as interested in any contract which may be made with the company or firm is a sufficient disclosure of his interest for the purposes of this paragraph in relation to a contract made after the date of the notice.

(3) A member need not attend in person at a meeting of the Corporation in order to make any disclosure which he is required to make under this paragraph provided he takes reasonable steps to secure that the disclosure is brought up and read at the meeting.

9.—(1) The fixing of the Housing Corporation's seal may be authenticated by the signature of the Chairman or of any other person authorised for the purpose.

(2) A document purporting to be duly executed under the seal of the Corporation shall be received in evidence and be deemed to be so executed unless the contrary is proved.

NOTES

This schedule sets out the constitution of the Housing Corporation, and provides for the appointment of members, Chairman and Deputy Chairman, the payment of remuneration, allowances and pensions, and regulates its proceedings. See further, note to s.74.

Section 82   SCHEDULE 7

POWERS EXERCISABLE WHERE LOAN OUTSTANDING UNDER SECTION 2 OF
THE HOUSING ACT 1964

Introductory

1. This Schedule applies where the Housing Corporation has made a loan to a housing association under section 2 of the Housing Act 1964 before the repeal of that section by the Housing (Consequential Provisions) Act 1985 and the loan has not been repaid.

Directions as to disposal of land securing loan

2.—(1) The Corporation may, with the consent in writing of the Secretary of State, give the association directions with respect to the disposal of land belonging to the association in which the Corporation has an interest as mortgagee under a mortgage, or as creditor in a heritable security, entered into by the association to secure the loan.

(2) Directions so given may be varied or revoked by subsequent directions given with the like consent.

3. Where the Corporation proposes to give a housing association directions under paragraph 2 requiring the association to transfer to the Corporation the association's interest in any land, the Secretary of State shall not consent to the giving of the directions unless he at the same time approves, or has previously approved, a scheme under paragraph 5 with respect to that land.

4. Where the Corporation proposes to give directions under paragraph 2 to an association whose rules restrict membership to persons entitled or prospectively entitled (whether as tenants or otherwise) to occupy a dwelling provided or managed by the association requiring the association to transfer its interest in any such land to the Corporation, or to any other person, the Secretary of State shall not consent to the giving of the directions unless he is satisfied that arrangements have been made which, if the directions are given, will secure that the members of the association receive fair treatment in connection with the transfer.

Schemes for Corporation to provide housing accommodation in place of association

5.—(1) If it appears to the Corporation—
   (a) that the association is experiencing difficulty in providing housing accommodation on any land which it has acquired or in managing housing accommodation provided by it on any land, or is in any way failing to perform its functions as a housing association in relation to any land, and that accordingly it is undesirable for the land in question to remain in the hands of the association,
   (b) that there is no other housing association, whether in existence or about to be formed, to which the association's interest in the land in question can suitably be transferred, and
   (c) that the land is capable of being, or continuing to be, used to provide housing accommodation for letting,
the Corporation may prepare and submit to the Secretary of State a scheme.

(2) The scheme shall be for the Corporation—
   (a) to acquire the association's interest in the land,
   (b) to undertake all such operations as may be required for the provision or continued provision on the land of housing accommodation for letting (including any operation which might have been carried out by a housing association in connection with the provision of housing accommodation), and
   (c) to retain the accommodation and keep it available for letting so long as the scheme has not been terminated in any manner provided for in the scheme.

(3) Where such a scheme is submitted to the Secretary of State by the Corporation, the Secretary of State, on being satisfied of—
   (a) the undesirability of the land remaining in the hands of the association, and
   (b) the lack of any housing association to which it can suitably be transferred,
may, if he thinks fit, approve the scheme.

(4) If he does so the Corporation shall have power to acquire for the purposes of the scheme the association's interest in the land and to carry through the provisions of the scheme.

(5) A scheme approved by the Secretary of State under this paragraph may be varied from time to time in accordance with proposals in that behalf made by the Corporation and approved by the Secretary of State.

NOTES
   This Schedule sets out the Housing Corporation's supervisory function in respect of housing associations which have received Corporation loans under the provisions of s.2 of the Housing Act 1964. Loans under that section were advanced to "housing societies", as defined in s.1 of the 1964 Act, in conjunction with building society mortgages, for the purpose of cost-rent (*i.e.*unsubsidised) housing schemes provided by those societies. The reference to "housing society" was amended to "housing association" by the Housing Finance Act 1972, s.77(2).

Paras. 2–4

The Corporation may, subject to the consent of the Secretary of State, direct the housing association to transfer land in respect of which the Corporation has an interest under an outstanding loan charge, to the Corporation itself, or to any other person. However, no such direction may be made for the Corporation itself to acquire housing association land unless a scheme, under para. 5, is or has been approved by the Secretary of State: para. 3. Where the association in question is a co-operative, *i.e.* as described in para. 4, that paragraph requires the Secretary of State to be satisfied that arrangements have been made which will secure that members of the association will receive fair treatment.

Para. 5

This paragraph sets out the powers of the Housing Corporation to prepare a scheme for the acquisition of housing association land and dwellings, and to step into the shoes of the association for the purpose of providing, or continuing to provide, accommodation for letting. A proposed scheme must be submitted to the Secretary of State for approval, and he may approve the scheme if he is satisfied that it is undesirable for the land in question to remain in the hands of the association, and, that there is no other housing association to which it could be transferred. Any scheme which is approved may subsequently be varied by the Corporation in accordance with any proposals which have been approved by the Secretary of State.

TABLE OF DERIVATIONS

1. The following abbreviations are used in this Table:—

Acts of Parliament

1957	=	The Housing Act 1957 (c.56).
1958 (c.42)	=	The Housing (Financial Provisions) Act 1958.
1959 (c.53)	=	The Town and Country Planning Act 1959.
1959 (c.70)	=	The Town and Country Planning (Scotland) Act 1959.
1960 (c.58)	=	The Charities Act 1960.
1961	=	The Housing Act 1961 (c.65).
1963 (c.33)	=	The London Government Act 1963.
1964	=	The Housing Act 1964 (c.56).
1965 (c.12)	=	The Industrial and Provident Societies Act 1965.
1965 (c.25)	=	The Finance Act 1965.
1966 (S.)	=	The Housing (Scotland) Act 1966 (c.49).
1968 (c.13)	=	The National Loans Act 1968.
1968 (S.)	=	The Housing (Financial Provisions) (Scotland) Act 1968 (c.31).
1969	=	The Housing Act 1969 (c.33).
1970 (c.10)	=	The Income and Corporation Taxes Act 1970.
1970 (c.35)	=	The Conveyancing and Feudal Reform (Scotland) Act 1970.
1972 (S.)	=	The Housing (Financial Provisions) (Scotland) Act 1972 (c.46).
1972	=	The Housing Finance Act 1972 (c.47).
1972 (c.70)	=	The Local Government Act 1972.
1973 (c.65)	=	The Local Government (Scotland) Act 1973.
1974	=	The Housing Act 1974 (c.44).
1975	=	The Housing Rents and Subsidies Act 1975 (c.6).
1975 (c.28)	=	The Housing Rents and Subsidies (Scotland) Act 1975.
1975 (c.55)	=	The Statutory Corporations (Financial Provisions) Act 1975.
1976 (c.75)	=	The Development of Rural Wales Act 1976.
1977 (c.42)	=	The Rent Act 1977.
1978	=	The Home Purchase Assistance and Housing Guarantee Act 1978 (c.27).
1980 (c.43)	=	The Magistrates' Courts Act 1980.
1980	=	The Housing Act 1980 (c.51).
1980 (S.)	=	The Tenants Rights etc. (Scotland) Act 1980 (c.52).
1981 (c.64)	=	The New Towns Act 1981.
1981 (c.67)	=	The Acquisition of Land Act 1981.
1982 (c.48)	=	The Criminal Justice Act 1982.
1983 (c.29)	=	The Miscellaneous Financial Provisions Act 1983.
1984	=	The Housing and Building Control Act 1984 (c.29).
1985 (c.9)	=	The Companies Consolidation (Consequential Provisions) Act 1985.
1985 (c.51)	=	The Local Government Act 1985.

Subordinate legislation

S.I. 1972/1204	=	The Isles of Scilly (Housing) Order 1972.
S.I. 1973/886	=	The Isles of Scilly (Housing) (No. 2) Order 1973.
S.I. 1975/374	=	The Housing Act 1974 (Commencement No. 4) Order 1975.
S.I. 1975/512	=	The Isles of Scilly (Housing) Order 1975.
S.I. 1983/664	=	The Housing Corporation Advances (Increase of Limit) Order 1983.
S.I. 1984/1803	=	The Housing Association Grant (Disposal of Dwellings) Order 1984.

2. The Table does not show the effect of Transfer of Functions Orders.

3. The letter R followed by a number indicates that the provision gives effect to the Recommendation bearing that number in the Law Commission's Report on the Consolidation of the Housing Acts (Cmnd. 9515).

4. A reference followed by "*passim*" indicates that the provision of the consolidation derives from passages within those referred to which it is not convenient, and does not appear necessary, to itemise.

5. The entry "drafting" indicates a provision of a mechanical or editorial nature affecting the arrangement of the consolidation; for instance, a provision introducing a Schedule or introducing a definition to avoid undue repetition of the defining words.

Provision	Derivation
1(1)	1957 s.189(1); 1964 s.12(1); 1966 (S.) s.208(1); 1974 s.129(1), (2), Sch. 13 para. 6
(2)	drafting.
(3)	1974 s.12.
2	1977 s.2(6A); 1977 (c.42) s.15(5); 1980 ss.74(2), 123(7).
3	1974 s.13(1), (7).
4(1)	1974 s.13(1).
(2)	1974 s.13(2).
(3)	1974 s.13(3); 1980 s.127(1)–(3); 1984 s.35(4); Sch. 11 para. 27.
5(1)	1974 s.13(1), (4), (5).
(2)	1974 s.13(4).
(3)	1974 s.16(1), (2).
(4)	1974 s.13(6).
6(1)	1974 s.15(1).
(2), (3)	1974 s.15(2).
(4)	1974 s.15(2A); 1980 s.128(1)(*a*), (2).
(5)	1974 s.16(1), (2).
7(1)	1974 s.15(3).
(2)	1974 s.15(4).
(3)	1974 s.16(3).
8(1)–(3)	1980 s.122(1)–(3).
9(1)	1974 s.2(1), (6).
(2)	1974 s.2(1A), (1B); 1980 s.123(2).
(3)	1974 s.2(5A); 1980 s.123(6), 137(1).
(4)	1974 s.15(6); 1980 s.128.
(5)	1974 s.2(1).
10(1)	1974 s.2(2), (3); 1980 s.123(3).
(2)	1974 s.2(3A); 1980 s.123(4).
(3)	1974 s.2(4); 1980 s.123(5).
(4)	1974 s.2(3).
11	drafting.
12	1980 s.137(1), (2); 1984 Sch. 11 para. 28.
13(1)	1974 s.26(1).
(2)	1974 s.26(2); 1980 Sch. 25 para. 25.
(3)	1974 s.26(5); 1980 Sch. 11 Part II.
14(1)	1974 s.26(3), (4), (6); 1980 Sch. 16 Part II.
(2)	1974 s.26(5); 1980 Sch. 16 Part II.
15(1)	1974 s.27(1)–(3); 1980 Sch. 16 Part II.
(2)	1974 s.27(5)–(7); 1980 Sch. 16 Part II.
(3)	1974 s.27(4); 1980 Sch. 16 Part II.
16(1)	1974 s.20(2); 1970 (c.35) Sch. 3 para. 9(2); R.32.
(2), (3)	1974 s.20(6).
(4)	1974 s.20(6).
17(1), (2)	1974 s.20(3).
(3)	1974 s.20(4).
(4)	1980 Sch. 17 para. 8.
18(1)	1980 Sch. 17 paras. 4, 5.
(2)	1980 Sch. 17 para. 6(*b*).
(3)	1980 Sch. 17 para. 7.
19(1)	1974 s.24(1).
(2)–(4)	1965 (c.12) s.10; 1974 s.24(5A); 1980 s.132.
20(1)	1974 s.25(1).
(2)	1960 (c.58) s.46; 1974 s.25(1)–(3).
21(1)–(6)	1974 s.24(1)–(5), (6).
22(1), (2)	1974 s.22(1), (2).
23(1)	1974 s.23(1).
(2)	1974 s.23(2).
(3)	1974 s.23(3).
(4)	1974 s.23(4).
(5)	1974 s.23(3).

Provision	Derivation
24(1)	1980 s.124(1).
(2)	1980 s.124(6).
(3)	1980 s.124(2).
(4)	1980 s.124(3).
(5)	1980 s.124(7), 151(1), (3).
25	1980 s.124(4).
26	1980 s.124(5).
27(1)	1980 s.125(1).
(2)	1980 s.125(2); 1982 (c.48) ss.37(1), 46(2).
(3)	1980 s.125(3).
(4)	1980 s.125(4).
28(1)	1974 s.19(1), (1A); 1980 Sch. 17 para. 1.
(2)	1974 s.19(2); 1980 Sch. 17 paras. 2, 6(*b*).
(3)	1974 s.19(3); 1975 (c.21) ss.289F, 289G; 1982 (c.48) ss.37, 46(1), 54.
(4)	1974 s.19(5).
(5)	1974 s.19(8); 1980 Sch. 17 para. 2.
(6)	1980 s.155(2).
29(1)	1974 s.19(4).
(2)	1974 s.19(4); 1980 Sch. 17 para. 6(*e*).
(3)	1974 s.19(5).
(4)	1974 s.19(6).
(5)	1974 s.19(7).
30(1)	1974 s.20(1); 1980 Sch. 17 paras. 3(*a*), 6(*b*).
(2), (3)	1974 s.20(6).
(4)	1974 s.20(5); 1980 Sch. 17 para. 3(*c*).
(5)	1974 s.20(1A); 1980 Sch. 17 para. 3(*b*).
(6)	1974 s.20(7); 1975 (c.21) ss.289F, 289G; 1980 Sch. 17 para. 9; 1982 (c.48) ss.37, 46(1), 54.
31(1)	1974 ss.19, 20 *passim*; 1980 Sch. 17 paras. 4, 5, 6(*a*).
(2)	1980 Sch. 17 para. 7.
(3)	1980 Sch. 17 para. 6(*c*)(*d*).
32(1)	1974 s.21(1).
(2)	1974 s.21(2)(*a*).
(3)	1974 s.21(2)(*b*).
(4)	1974 s.21(3).
(5)	1974 s.21(4).
33(1)	1957 s.124; 1966 (S.) s.158(1).
(2)	1957 s.124; 1966 (S.) s.158(2).
34(1), (2)	1957 s.119(2).
35(1)	1957 s.128(1); R.4(ii).
(2)	drafting.
36(1)	1957 s.128(2); R.4(ii).
(2)	1957 s.128(3); R.4(ii).
37	"appropriate registrar" 1974 s.28; "committee" 1965 s.74, 1974 s.28; "co-opted member" 1974 s.26(6), 1980 Sch. 16 Part II; drafting.
38	1974 ss.28, 129(1); 1980 s.133(1).
39	"mental disorder" 1974 s.20(2)(*a*); "secure tenancy" 1974 s.2(6A), 1980 s.123(7).
40	drafting.
41(1)	1974 ss.29(1), 29A(2); 1975 s.6; 1975 (S.) s.12; 1980 Sch. 18 para. 3.
(2)	1974 s.29A(1); 1980 Sch. 18 para. 3.
42(1)	1974 s.29(2).
(2), (3)	1974 s.29(2), (2A); 1980 Sch. 18 para. 1.
43	1980 s.130(1).
44(1)	1984 s.33(1).
(2)	1984 s.33(2).
(3)	drafting.

Provision	Derivation
45(1), (2)	1984 s.35(1).
(3)	1984 s.35(2).
(4)	1984 s.35(3).
46	1974 s.29(3).
47(1)	1974 s.29(4).
(2), (3)	1974 s.29(6).
(4)	1974 s.29(8).
(5)	1974 s.29(6A); 1980 Sch. 18 para. 2.
(6)	1974 s.29(7).
48(1)	1974 s.29(5).
(2)	1974 s.29(8).
(3)	1980 s.130(2); S.I. 1984/1803.
(4)	1980 s.151(1), (3).
49(1)–(4)	1974 s.30(1); 1980 Sch. 18 para. 4.
(5)	1974 s.30(8).
(6)	1974 s.15(5).
50(1), (2)	1974 s.30(2), (2A); 1980 Sch. 18 para. 5.
51(1), (2)	1974 s.30(4), (6).
52(1)	1974 s.30(3); 1980 Sch. 18 para. 6; 1984 s.34(1).
(2)	1974 s.30(3);. 1980 Sch. 18 para. 6.
(3)	1984 s.34(2).
(4)	1984 s.34(3).
53(1)	1980 s.131(1).
(2)	1980 s.131(2).
(3)	1980 s.131(3).
(4)	1980 s.131(3), (4).
(5)	1980 s.131(4).
(6)	1980 s.131(5).
(7)	1980 s.131(6).
54(1)	1974 s.32(1); 1975 s.6; 1975 (S.) s.12; 1980 Sch. 18 para. 9(*a*).
(2), (3)	1974 s.32(3); 1980 Sch. 18 para. 9(*c*).
(4)	1976 s.32(5); 1980 Sch. 18 para. 9(*e*).
(5)	1974 s.32(3); 1980 s.133(2), Sch. 18 para. 9(*c*).
55(1)	1974 s.33(1); 1980 Sch. 18 para. 10(*a*).
(2)–(4)	1974 s.33(3); 1980 Sch. 18 para. 10(*c*).
(5)	1974 s.33(4); 1980 Sch. 18 para. 10(*d*).
(6)	1974 s.33(5); 1980 Sch. 18 para. 10(*e*).
56(1)	1974 ss.32(2), 33(2); 1980 Sch. 18 paras. 9(*b*)(i), 10(*b*).
(2)	1974 ss.32(2)(*a*), (*b*), 33(2), (7); 1980 Sch. 18 paras. 9(*b*)(ii), 10(*b*).
(3)	1974 s.32(2)(*c*); 1980 Sch. 18 para. 9(*b*)(iii).
57(1)–(3)	1974 ss.32(6), 33(6); 1980 Sch. 18 paras. 9(*f*), 10(*f*).
(4)	1974 s.15(5).
58(1)	1957 s.119(1).
(2)	1957 s.119(3).
(3)	1972 s.78(1), (2)(*a*), (4).
59(1)	1966 (S.) s.152(1), (3); 1973 (c.65) Sch. 12 para. 10.
(2)	1966 (S.) s.152(2), (3); 1973 (c.65) Sch. 12 para. 10.
(3)	1972 (S.) s.58(1), (2)(*b*), (3).
(4)	1966 (S.) ss.152(2), 198.
60(1)	1974 s.17(1)(*b*).
(2)	1974 s.17(3), (5); 1975 Sch. 5 para. 13; 1975 (S.) Sch. 3 para. 13.
(3)	1974 s.17(4).
61(1)	1957 s.122; 1966 (S.) s.156(1).
(2)	1957 s.122; 1966 (S.) s.156(2); R.33.
62(1)	1965 (c.25) s.93(1).
(2)	1965 (c.25) s.93(6); 1970 (c.10) Sch. 15 para. 11 Table Pt. II; 1974 s.17(2), (3).
(3)	1965 (c.25) s.93(4).
(4)	1965 (c.25) s.93(1), (2).
(5)	1965 (c.25) s.93(2).
(6), (7)	1965 (c.25) s.93(3).

Provision	Derivation
63(1)	1964 s.8(1); 1974 Sch. 13 para. 10(2).
(2)	1964 s.8(2); 1974 Sch. 13 para. 10(2).
(3)	1964 s.8(10); 1974 Sch. 13 para. 10(2).
(4)	1964 s.8(3).
(5)	1964 s.8(4).
(6)	1964 s.8(3), (10).
64	1964 s.8(8); 1975 (c.21) s.298(1); 1977 Sch. 11; 1980 (c.44) s.32(2); 1982 (c.48) s.74(1).
65	1964 s.8(5); 1974 Sch. 13 para. 10(2).
66(1)(*a*), (*b*)	1964 s.8(12).
(*c*)	1964 s.107.
(*d*)	drafting.
(2)	1964 s.107.
67(1)	1958 s.47(1), (2)(*b*).
(2)	1958 s.47(3), (5)(*c*), (6).
(3)	1958 s.47(5)(*c*).
(4)	1958 s.47(6) proviso (*b*).
(5)	1958 s.47(5)(*a*), (*b*) proviso.
68(1)	1968 (S.) s.24(1).
(2)	1968 (S.) s.24(2), (4)(*c*), (5).
(3)	1968 (S.) s.24(4)(*c*).
(4)	1968 (S.) s.24(5) proviso (*b*).
(5), (6)	1968 (S.) s.24(4)(*a*), (*b*) proviso.
69(1)	1972 (S.) ss.58(2), 59(1); 1972 ss.78(2), 79(1).
(2)	1972 (S.) ss.58(5), 59(2); 1972 ss.78(6), 79(2).
(3)	1972 ss.78(1), 79(2).
(4)	1972 (S.) ss.58(1), (5), 59(2).
70	drafting.
71	drafting.
72	"building society" 1964 s.8(11); "Chief Registrar" 1964 s.8(11); "officer" 1964 s.8(11); "registered charity" drafting see 1974 s.32(3)(1).
73	drafting.
74(1), (2)	drafting.
75(1)	1974 s.1(2).
(2)	1974 s.1(3).
(3)	1974 s.1(2).
(4)	1964 Sch. 1 para. 5; 1974 Sch. 1 para. 3.
76(1)	1964 s.1(2); R.34(i).
(2)	1974 s.9(3).
(3)	1964 s.1(2).
(4)	1959 (c.53) s.29; 1959 (c.70) s.29; 1964 s.1(4), (9).
77	1964 s.7; R.35.
78	1964 s.10(6).
79(1)	1974 s.9(1).
(2)	1974 s.9(2).
(3)	1974 s.9(1), (2), (4).
(4)	1974 s.9(3).
80(1)–(3)	1974 s.9(5).
(4)	1974 s.9(6).
81	1984 s.24(1).
82	drafting.
83(1), (2)	1974 s.10(1).
(3), (4)	1974 s.10(2); 1978 s.5(1), (2).
84(1)	1980 s.111(1); 1984 s.20(1).
(2)	1980 s.111(3); 1984 s.20(2).
(3)	1980 s.111(4); 1984 s.20(3).
(4)	1980 s.111(1), (5); 1984 s.20(4)(*a*).
(5)	1980 s.111(5), (6); 1984 s.20(4)(*b*).
(6)	1980 s.111(8); 1984 s.20(7).

Provision	Derivation
85(1)	drafting.
(2)	1984 s.20(5); "recognised body".
(3)	1984 s.20(6).
(4)	1984 ss.18(3), (4), 20(5) "relevant advance".
(5)	1984 s.18(4) "long lease".
86	1980 (S.) s.31.
87(1)–(3)	1980 s.121(2).
(4)	1980 s.121(3).
88(1)	1974 ss.1(2)(*d*), 3(1), (3).
(2)	1974 s.3(6).
(3)	1974 s.3(4); 1981 Sch. 4 para. 1.
(4)	1974 s.3(2).
(5)	1974 s.3(5).
89	1974 s.4.
90(1)	1974 s.5(2).
(2)	1974 s.5(3); 1976 (c.75) Sch. 7 para. 12; 1981 (c.64) Sch. 12 para. 13(*a*).
(3)	1974 s.5(3A); 1980 Sch. 25 para. 24.
(4)	1974 s.5(4).
(5)	1974 s.5(5)–(7).
(6)	1974 s.5(1).
91	1959 (c.53) s.29(1); 1959 (c.70) s.29(1); 1964 s.1(4), (9).
92(1)	1974 s.7(2).
(2)	1974 s.7(3).
(3)	1974 s.7(4); 1975 (c.55) Sch. 4 para. 8.
(4)	1974 s.7(6).
(5)	1974 s.7(8).
(6)	1974 s.7(7).
93(1)	1974 s.7(1).
(2)	1974 s.7(5); 1975 Sch. 5 para. 12; S.I. 1975/374; 1980 s.120(1); S.I. 1983/664.
(3)	1974 ss.7(5), 128(1).
(4)	1980 s.120(2).
(5)	1974 s.7(9).
94(1)	1974 s.8(1); 1983 (c.29) s.4.
(2)	1974 s.8(2).
(3)	1974 s.8(3).
(4)	1974 s.8(4).
(5)	1974 s.8(5).
(6)	1974 s.8(2).
95	1980 s.121(1).
96(1)	1974 s.10(3).
(2)	1974 s.10(4).
(3)	1974 s.10(5).
(4)	1974 s.10(6).
(5)	1974 s.10(4), (5), (6).
97(1)	1964 s.10(1).
(2)	1964 s.10(2).
(3)	1964 s.10(3).
(4)	1964 s.10(4), (5); 1968 (c.13) Sch. 1; 1974 Sch. 13 para. 10(3).
(5)	1964 s.10(5); 1985 (c.9) Sch. 2.
(6)	1964 s.10(7).
98(1)	1974 s.6(1).
(2)	1974 s.6(3).
99	1974 s.6(2).
100	1964 s.11; 1974 Sch. 13 para. 10(4).
101	"building society" 1980 s.111(7); "financial year" 1964 s.10(7); 1978 (c.30) Sch. 1; "highway" 1974 s.12; "subsidiary" 1974 s.12; 1985 (c.9) Sch. 2.
102	drafting.
103	1972 s.103; 1975 Sch. 5 para. 7(1); S.I. 1972/1204; S.I. 1975/512; R.29.

Provision	Derivation
104(1)	1963 (c.33) s.21(1), (2); 1972 (c.70) s.193(1); 1966 (S.) s.1; 1973 (c.65) s.130(3), Sch. 12 para. 6; S.I. 1972/1204; S.I. 1973/886; S.I. 1975/512.
(2)	drafting.
105	1957 s.104B(4B)(*c*); 1984 Sch. 6 para. 1(2).
106(1), (2)	"bank" 1957 s.104B(6), 1978 Sch. para. 7, 1984 Sch. 6 para. 1(5); "building society" *passim*; "dwelling" 1966 (S.) s.208(1), 1972 s.104(1), 1974 s.129(1)(2); "friendly society" *passim*; "hostel" 1974 s.129(1)(2), 1966 (S.) s.208(1); "house" 1957 s.189(1); 1966 (S.) s.208(1), 1980 s.130(3); "housing activities" 1980 s.133(2), Sch. 18 para. 9, 1984 Sch. 6 para. 1(5); "insurance company" 1957 s.104B(6), 1978 Sch. para. 8, 1984 Sch. 6 para. 1(5); "local authority" 1957 s.1, 1974 ss.5, 129, 1980 s.111, 1980 (c.52) s.31, 1984 ss.18(3), 20(5); 1985 (c.51) Sch. 14 para. 64(*a*), (*b*); "new town corporation" 1972 (S.) s.78(1), 1974 s.5(3)(*c*)(*d*), 1981 (c.64) Sch. 12 para. 13(*a*); "shared ownership lease" drafting; "trustee savings bank" 1957 s.104B(6), 1978 Sch. para. 6, 1984 Sch. para. 1(5); "urban development corporation" 1984 s.18(3).
107	drafting.
Schedules	
Sch. 1	
para. 1	1974 Sch. 2 para. 1.
2	1974 Sch. 2 para. 2.
3	1974 Sch. 2 para. 3.
Sch. 2	1980 s.122(4), (5), (6).
para. 1(1)	1957 s.104B(1); 1980 s.92.
(2)	1957 s.104B(2), (3); 1980 s.92; 1984 Sch. 6 para. 1(1).
2(1)	1957 s.104B(5); 1980 s.92; 1984 Sch. 6 para. 1(3).
(2)	1957 s.104B(5A); 1984 Sch. 6 para. 1(4).
(3)	1957 s.104B(7); 1980 s.92.
(4)	1957 s.104B(6); 1978 Sch. paras. 6–9; 1984 Sch. 6 para. 1(5).
3(1)	1957 s.104C(1), (9); 1980 s.92; 1984 Sch. 6 para. 2(1), (5).
(2)	1957 s.104C(2); 1980 s.92; 1984 Sch. 6 para. 2(2).
(3)	1957 s.104C(3); 1980 s.92.
(4)	1957 s.104C(5); 1980 s.92.
(5)	1957 s.104C(6); 1980 s.92.
(6)	1957 s.104C(8); 1980 s.92.
4	1957 s.104B(4), 104C(7A); 1984 Sch. 6 para. 1(2), 2(4).
5(1)	1957 s.104B(4A); 1984 Sch. 6 para. 1(2).
(2)	1957 s.104B(4B), (8); 1984 Sch. 6 para. 1(2).
6	1957 s.104B(4A)(*d*); 1984 Sch. 6 para. 1(2); drafting.
7	1957 ss.104B(4C), 104C(7); 1984 Sch. 6 paras. 1(2), 2(4).
8(1)	1957 ss.104B(9), 104C(10); 1980 s.92; 1984 Sch. 6 para. 1(6), 2(6).
(2)	1957 s.104C(10); 1980 s.92.
Sch. 3	
para. 1(1), (2)	1980 Sch. 16 Part I para. 1(1), (2).
2(1), (2)	1980 Sch. 16 Part I para. 2(1), (2).
3(1)–(4)	1980 Sch. 16 Part I para. 3(1)–(4).
4(1), (2)	1980 Sch. 16 Part I para. 4(1), (2).
5	1980 Sch. 16 Part I para. 5(1), (2).
6	1980 Sch. 16 Part I para. 5(3), (4).
7	1980 Sch. 16 Part I para. 6.
Sch. 4.	
Pt. I	
para. 1	1972 s.78(2), (3), (5).
2	1974 Sch. 13 para. 5.
Pt. II	
para. 1	1972 Sch. 7 Pt. III; 1972 (S.) Sch. 1 Pts. IV, VI.
2	1972 s.79(1); 1972 (S.) s.59(1).
Pt. III	1972 (S.) s.58(2)(*a*), (*g*), (4).

Provision	Derivation
Sch. 5	
Pt. I	
para. 1	1972 s.72(1)–(7), (9).
2	1972 s.73(1)–(7).
3	1972 s.104(1) "housing association".
4	1972 ss.74(1), (5), 104(4).
5	1972 ss.15(1), (2), (5), 71(4).
6	1972 s.74(2)–(4).
7	drafting.
Pt. II	
para. 1	1972 (S.) s.52(1)–(6), 8.
2	1972 (S.) s.53(1)–(3), (8), (9).
3	1972 (S.) s.78(1) "housing association".
4	1972 (S.) ss.54(1), 68(1).
5	1972 (S.) ss.13, 51(4).
6	1972 (S.) s.54(2)–(4).
7	drafting. .
Pt. III	
para. 1(1)	1969 Sch. 9 para. 1; 1974 Sch. 14 para. 6.
(2)	1958 s.28; 1967 Sch. 3 para. 6; 1969 Sch. 8 para. 17.
(3)	1958 s.12(1); 1967 s.12(6); 1969 s.21(8); Sch. 9 para. 1; 1974 Sch. 14 para. 6.
2	1958 s.12(2); 1969 Sch. 9 para. 1.
3(1)	1968 (S.) s.17(3); 1974 Sch. 14 para. 6.
(2)	1968 (S.) s.57(1).
(3)	1968 (S.) s.17(2); 1974 Sch. 14 para. 6.
4(1)	1968 (S.) s.58(1).
(2)	1968 (S.) s.58(3).
(3)	1968 (S.) s.58(2).
Pt. IV	
para. 1(1)	1968 (S.) s.16(2); 1974 Sch. 14 para. 6.
(2)	1968 (S.) s.58(1).
(3)	1968 (S.) s.58(3).
Pt. V	
para. 1	1972 s.78(2)(*d*), (5).
2	1972 (S.) s.58(2)(*f*), (4).
Pt. VI	
para. 1(1)	1974 s.35(1).
(2)–(4)	1972 ss.15(1), (2), (5), 71(4); 1972 (S.) ss.13(1)–(3), 51(4).
2(1)	1972 (S.) ss.56(2), 57(4); 1972 s.76(2).
(2)	1972 (S.) ss.56(3), 57(4); 1972 s.76(3).
(3)	1972 (S.) ss.56(4), 57(4); 1972 s.76(4).
3(1)–(3)	1972 (S.) s.55(12); 1972 s.75(12); 1974 Sch. 13 paras. 23(4), 32.
(4)	1972 (S.) s.57(4); 1972 s.74(5).
4	1974 s.35(2).
Pt. VII	
para. 1(1)	1974 s.35(1).
(2)	1974 s.35(4).
(3)	1974 s.35(5).
Sch. 6	
para. 1(1)	1964 Sch. 1 para. 1.
(2)	1964 Sch. 1 para. 6; 1974 Sch. 1 para. 4.
(3)	1964 s.1(3).
2(1)	1964 Sch. 1 para. 2(1); 1974 Sch. 1 para. 1.
(2)	1964 Sch. 1 para. 2A(1); 1974 Sch. 1 para. 2.
3(1)	1964 Sch. 1 para. 2(2).
(2)	1964 Sch. 1 para. 2(4).
(3)	1964 Sch. 1 para. 2(5).
(4)	1964 Sch. 1 para. 2A(1); 1974 Sch. 1 para. 2.
4(1)	1964 Sch. 1 para. 2(1), (2).
(2)	1964 Sch. 1 para. 2(4).
(3)	1964 Sch. 1 para. 2(3).

Provision	Derivation
Sch. 6—*cont.*	
para. 5(1), (2)	1964 Sch. 1 para. 2(7).
6(1), (2)	1964 Sch. 1 para. 2(8).
(3), (4)	1964 Sch. 1 para. 2(9); 1972 (c.11) Sch. 6 para. 47.
7(1)	1964 Sch. 1 para 3(1).
(2)	1964 Sch. 1 para. 3(2).
8(1)	1964 Sch. 1 para. 2A(2); 1974 Sch. 1 para. 2.
(2)	1964 Sch. 1 para. 2A(3); 1974 Sch. 1 para. 2.
(3)	1964 Sch. 1 para. 2A(4); 1974 Sch. 1 para. 2.
9(1)	1964 Sch. 1 para. 4(1); 1980 Sch. 25 para. 13.
(2)	1964 Sch. 1 para. 4(2).
Sch. 7	
para. 1	R.36.
2(1)	1964 s.2(3); 1972 s.77(2); 1974 Sch. 14 para. 1; R.36.
(2)	1964 s.2(3).
3	1964 s.5(3); R.36.
4	1964 s.2(4); R.36.
5(1), (2)	1964 s.5(1); R.36.
(3), (4)	1964 s.5(2); R.36.
(5)	1964 s.5(4).

TABLE OF DESTINATIONS

The Housing Act 1957

1957	1985
s.1	s.106(1), (2)
"local authority" ..	
104B(1)	.....Sch. 2, para. 1(1)
(2)(3) .	para. 1(2)
(4)	para. 4
(4A) ..	para. 5(1)
(d) ...	para. 6
(4B) ...	para. 5(2)
(c) ...	s.105
(4C) ...	para. 7
(5)	para. 2(1)
(5A) ..	para. 2(2)

1957	1985
s.104B(6)	.....Sch. 2, para. 2(4)
"bank"	s.106(1)(2)
"insurance company" ..	106(1)(2)
"trustee savings bank"	106(1)(2)
s.104B(7)	.....Sch. 2, para. 2(3)
(8)	para. 5(2)
(9)	para. 8(1)
104C(1)	para. 3(1)
(2)	para. 3(2)
(3)	para. 3(3)
(5)	para. 3(4)

1957	1985
s.104C(6)	.....Sch. 2, para. 3(5)
(7)	para. 7
(7A) ..	para. 4
(8)	para. 3(6)
(9)	para. 3(1)
(10) ...	para. 8(1)(2)
124	s.33(1)(2)
119(1)	58(1)
(2)	34(1)(2)
(3)	58(2)
122	61(1)(2)
128(1)	35(1)
(2)	36(1)
(3)	36(2)
189(1)	1(1)
"house"	106(1)(2)

The Housing (Financial Provisions) Act 1958

1958	1985
s.12(1)	Sch. 5, Pt. III, para. 1(3)
(2)	para. 2
28	para. 1(2)
47(1)(2)(b) .	s.67(1)

1957	1985
s.47(3)	s.67(2)
(5)(a)(b)	
proviso	67(5)
(5)(c)	67(2)(3)
(6)	67(2)
(6)	
proviso (b) .	(4)

The Town and Country Planning Act 1959

1959	1985
s.29	s.76(4)
(1)	91

The Town and Country Planning (Scotland) Act 1959

1959	1985
s.29	s.76(4)
(1)	91

The Charities Act 1960

1960	1985
s.46	s.20(2)

The London Government Act 1963

1963	1985
s.21(1)(2)	s.104(1)

THE HOUSING ACT 1964

1964	1985
s.1(2)	.... s.76(1)(3)
(3)	..........Sch. 6,
	para. 1(3)
(4)	..........ss.76(4), 91
(9)	.... 76(4), 91
2(3)	..........Sch. 7,
	paras.
	2(1)(2)
(4)	..........Sch. 7,
	para. 4
5(1)	..........Sch. 7,
	para. 5(1)(2)
(2)	..........Sch. 7,
	para. 5(3)(4)
(3)	..........Sch. 7,
	para. 3
(4)	..........Sch. 7,
	para. 5(5)
7	.... s.77
8(1)	.... 63(1)
(2)	.... (2)
(3)	.... (4)(6)
(4)	.... (5)
(5)	 65
(8)	 64
(10)	.... 63(3)
(11)	
"building society"	 72
(11)	 72

1964	1985
"Chief Registrar"	..
s.8(11)	.... s.72
"officer"	....
(12)	.... 66(1)(a)(b)
10	.... 63(6)
(1)	.... 97(1)
(2)	.... 97(2)
(3)	.... 97(3)
(4)	.... 97(4)
(5)	.... 97(4)(5)
(6)	 78
(7)	.... 97(6)
(7)	
"financial year"	 101
11	 100
12(1)	.... 1(1)
107	.... 66(1)(c), (2)
Sch. 1,	
para. 1	......Sch. 6,
	para. 1(1)
2(1)	.. paras. 2(1),
	4(1)
(2)	.. paras. 3(1),
	4(1)
(3)	.. para. 4(3)

1964	1985
para. 2(4)	..Sch. 6,
	paras. 3(2),
	4(2)
2(5)	.. para. 3(3)
(7)	.. para. 5(1)(2)
(8)	.. para. 6(1)(2)
(9)	.. para. 6(3)(4)
2A(1)	paras. 2(2),
	3(4)
(2)	para. 8(1)
(3)	para. 8(2)
(4)	para. 8(3)
3(1)	..Sch. 5,
	para. 7(1)
(2)	..Sch. 6,
	para. 7(2)
4(1)	.. para. 9(1)
(2)	.. para. 9(2)
5	...... s.75(4)
6	......Sch. 6,
	para. 1(2)

THE INDUSTRIAL AND PROVIDENT SOCIETIES ACT 1965

1965	1985
s.10	.... s.19(2) to (4)
74	
"committee"	37

THE FINANCE ACT 1965

1965	1985
s.93(1)	.... s.62(1)(4)
(2)	.... (4)(5)
(3)	.... (6)(7)
(4)	.... (3)
(6)	.... (2)

THE HOUSING (SCOTLAND) ACT 1966

1966	1985	1966	1985
s.1	.... s.104(1)	s.158(2)	.... s.33(2)
152(1)	...... 59(1)	198	.... 59(4)
(2)	...... (2)(4)	208(1)	.... 1(1),
(3)	...... (1)(2)(4)		106(1)(2)
156(1)	...... 61(1)	"dwelling"	..... 106(1)(2)
(2)	...... (2)	"hostel"	.... 106(1)(2)
158(1)	.... 33(1)		

THE HOUSING SUBSIDIES ACT 1967

1967	1985
s.12(6)	........Sch. 5, Pt. III,
	para. 1(3)
Sch. 3,	
para. 6	...... para. 1(2)

THE NATIONAL LOANS ACT 1968

1968	1985
Sch. 1	.... s.97(4)

The Housing (Financial Provisions) (Scotland) Act 1968

1968	1985
s.16(2)	........Sch. 5, Pt. IV, para. 1(1)
17(2)	........Sch. 5, Pt. III, para. 3(3)
(3)	........Sch. 5, Pt. III, para. 3(1)
24(1)	.... s.68(1)
(2)(5)	..... 68(2)
(4)(*a*)(*b*)	
proviso	...... 68(5)(6)

1968	1985
s.24(4) (*c*)	.... s.68(2)(3)
(5)	
proviso (*b*)	. 68(4)
57(1)	........Sch. 5, Pt. III, para. 3(2)

1968	1985
s.58(1)	........Sch. 5, Pt. III, para. 4(1), Pt. IV, para. 1(2)
(2)	.... Pt. III, para. 4(3)
(3)	.... para. 4(2), Pt. IV, para. 1(3)

The Housing Act 1969

1969	1985
s.21(8)	........Sch. 5, Pt. III, para. 1(3)
Sch. 8, para. 17	.....Sch. 5, Pt. III, para. 1(2)

1969	1985
Sch. 9, para. 1	......Sch. 5, Pt. III, paras. 1(1)(3), 2

The Income and Corporation Taxes Act 1970

1970	1985
Sch. 15, para. 11, Table Pt. II	... s.62(2)

The Conveyancing and Feudal Reform (Scotland) Act 1970

1970	1985
Sch. 3, para. 9(2)	.. s.16(1)

The Superannuation Act 1972

1972	1985
Sch. 6, para. 47	.....Sch. 6, para. 6(3)(4)

The Housing (Financial Provisions) (Scotland) Act 1972

1972	1985
s.13	............Sch. 5, Pt. II, para. 5
(1) to (3)	Pt. VI, para. 1(2)–(4)
51(4)	.... Pt. II, para. 5, Pt. VI, para. 1(2)–(4)
52(1) to (6), (8)	.... Pt. II, para. 1
53(1) to (3), (8)(9)	...... para. 2
54(1)	.... para. 4
(2) to (4)	para. 6

1972	1985
s.55(12)	.......Sch. 5, Pt. VI, para. 3(1)–(3)
56(3)	........Sch. 5, Pt. VI, para. 2(2)
(4)	........Sch. 5, Pt. VI, para. 2(3)
57(4)	........Sch. 5, Pt. VI, paras. 2(1)–(3), 3(4)
58(1)	........ss.59(3), 69(4)
(2),	.... s.69(1)
(2)(*a*) (*g*)	
(4)	......Sch. 4, Pt. III
(2) (*b*)	... 59(3)
(2)(*f*) (4)	Sch. 5, Pt. V, para. 2

1972	1985
s.58	.... s.59(3)
(5)	.... 69(2)(4)
59(1)	.... 69(1), Sch. 4, Pt. II, para. 2
(2)	.... s.69(2)(4)
68(1)	........Sch. 5, Pt. II, para. 4
78(1)	.... para. 3
"housing association"	
78(1)	.... s.106 (1)(2)
"new town corporation"	
Sch. 1, Pts. IV, VI	..............Sch. 4, Pt. II, para. 1

The Housing Finance Act 1972

1972	1985
s.15(1)(2)(5)	.Sch. 5, Pt. I, para. 5, Pt. VI, para. 1(2)–(4)
56(2)	........Sch. 5, Pt. VI, para. 2(1)

1972	1985
s.71(4)	........Sch. 5,Pt. I, para. 5, Pt. VI, para. 1(2)–(4)
72(1) to (7)	
(9)	..........Sch. 5, Pt. I, para. 1

THE HOUSING FINANCE ACT 1972—*continued*

1972	1985
s.73(1) to (7)	Sch. 5, Pt. I, para. 2
74(1)	para. 4
(2)–(4) ...	para. 6
(5)	Pt. VI, paras. 3(4), 4
75(12)	para. 3(1)–(3)
76(2)	para. 2(1)

1972	1985
s.76(3)	Sch. 5, Pt. VI, para. 76(3)
(4)	para. 2(3)
77(2)	Sch. 7, para. 2(1)
78(1)	s.69(3)
(1)(2)(a), (4)	58(3)
8(2)	69(1)
(2)(d)(5) .Sch. V,	para. 1
(2)(3)(5) .Sch. 4, Pt. I,	para. 1
(6)	s.69(2)

1972	1985
s.79(1)	Sch. 4, Pt. II, para. 2
(2)	s.69(2)(3)
103	103
104(1)	106(1)(2)
"dwelling" .. 104(1)	.......Sch. 5, Pt. I, para. 3
"housing association" 104(4)	para. 4
Sch. 7, Pt. III	Sch. 4, Pt. II, para. 1

THE LOCAL GOVERNMENT ACT 1972

1972	1985
s.193(1)	s.104(1)

THE LOCAL GOVERNMENT (SCOTLAND) ACT 1973

1973	1985	1973	1985
s.130(3), Sch. 12, para. 6 ... s.104(1)		Sch. 12, para. 10	59(1)(2)

THE HOUSING ACT 1974

1974	1985
s.1(2)	s.75(1)(3)
(2)(d)	88(1)
(3)	75(2)
2(1)	9(1)(5)
(1A), (1B)	(2)
(2)	10(1)
(3)	(1)(4)
(3A)	(2)
(4)	(3)
(5A)	9(3)
(6)	(1)
(6A)	
"secure tenancy"	39
3(1)(3)	88(1)
(2)	(4)
(4)	(3)
(5)	(5)
(6)	(2)
4	89
5(1)	90(6)
(2)	(1)
(3)	(2)
(3A)	(3)
(4)	(4)
(5) to (7) .	(5)
5	106(1)(2)
(3)(c)(d) ..	(1)(2)
6(1)	98(1)
(2)	99
(3)	98(2)
7(1)	93(1)
(2)	92(1)
(3)	(2)
(4)	(3)
(5)	93(2)
(5)	(3)
(6)	92(4)

1974	1985
s.7(7)	s.92(6)
(8)	92(5)
(9)	93(5)
8(1)	94(1)
(2)	94(2)(6)
(3)	94(3)
(4)	94(4)
(5)	94(5)
9(1)	79(1)(3)
(2)	79(2)(3)
(3)	76(2), 79(4)
(4)	79(3)
(5)	80(1) to (3)
(6)	80(4)
10(1)	83(1)(2)
(2)	83(3)(4)
(3)	96(1)
(4)	96(2)(5)
(5)	96(3)(5)
(6)	96(4)(5)
12	1(3)
"highway" ..	101
"subsidiary"	101
13(1)	3, 4(1), 5(1)
(2)	4(2)
(3)	4(3)
(4)	5(1)(2)
(5)	5(1)(2)
(6)	5(4)
(7)	3
15(1)	6(1)
(2)	6(2), (3)
(2A)	6(4)
(3)	7(1)
(4)	7(2)
(5)	49(6), 57(4)

1974	1985
s.15(6)	s.9(4)
16(1), (2) ...	5(3), 6(5)
(3)	7(3)
17(1)(b)	60(1)
(2)	62(2)
(3)	60(2), 62(2)
(4)	60(3)
(5)	(2)
19	31(1)
(1), (1A)	28(1)
(2)	(2)
(3)	(3)
(4)	29(1)(2)
(5)	28(4), 29(3)
(6)	29(4)
(7)	9(5)
(8)	28(5)
20 *passim* ..	31(1)
(1)	30(1)
(1A)	(5)
(2)	16(1)
(2)(a)	
"mental disorder" ...	39
(3)	17(1), (2)
(4)	(3)
(5)	30(4)
(6)	16(2)–(4), 30(2)(3)
(7)	30(6)
21(1)	32(1)
(2)(a)	(2)
(b)	(3)
(3)	(4)
(4)	(5)
22(1), (2) ..	22(1), (2)
23(1)	23(1)

THE HOUSING ACT 1974—*continued*

1974	1985
s.23(2)	s.23(2)
(3)	23(3)(5)
(4)	23(4)
24(1)	19(1), 21(1)–(6)
(2) to (6)	21(1)–(6)
(5A)	19(2)–(4)
25(1)	20(1)(2)
(2)(3)	(2)
26(1)	13(1)
(2)	(2)
(3), (4), (6)	14(1)
(5)	13(3), 14(2)
(6)	
"co-opted member"	37
27(1) to (3)	15(1)
(4)	(3)
(5) to (7)	(2)
28	
"appropriate registrar"	37
28	
"committee"	37
28	38
29(1)	41(1)
(2)	42(1)–(3)
(2A)	(2), (3)
(3)	46
(4)	47(1)
(5)	48(1)
(6)	47(2), (3)
(6A)	45(5)
(7)	47(6)
(8)	47(4), 48(2)
29A(1)	41(2)
(2)	(1)
30(1)	49(1)–(4)
(2), (2A)	50(1), (2)

1974	1985
s.30(3)	s.52(1)(2)
(4), (6)	51(1), (2)
(8)	49(5)
32(1)	54(1)
(2)	56(1)
(2)(a), (b)	(2)
(2)(c)	(3)
(3)	54(2), (3)(5)
(3)(1)	
"registered charity"	72
32(6)	57(1)–(3)
33(1)	55(1)
(2)	56(1)(2)
(3)	55(2)–(4)
(5)	(6)
(6)	57(1)–(3)
(7)	56(2)
35(1)	Sch. 5, Pt. VI, para. 1(1), Pt. VII, para. 1(1)
(2)	Pt. VI, para. 4
(4)	Pt. VII, para. 1(2)
(5)	Pt. VII, para. 1(3)
128(1)	s.93(3)
129	
"local authority"	106(1)(2)
(1)	38
(1)(2)	
"dwelling hostel"	
(1), (2)	1(1)

1974	1985
Sch. 1,	
para. 1	Sch. 6, para. 2(1)
para. 2	paras. 2(2), 3(4), 8(1)–(3)
para. 3	s.75(4)
para. 4	Sch. 6, para. 1(2)
Sch. 2,	
para. 1	Sch. 1, para. 1
para. 2	para. 2
para. 3	para. 3
Sch. 13,	
para. 5	Sch. 4, Pt. I, para. 2
para. 6	s.1(1)
para. 10(2)	63(1)–(3), 65
(3)	97(4)
(4)	100
paras. 23(4), 32	Sch. 5, Pt. VI, para. 3(1)– (3)
Sch. 14,	
para. 1	Sch. 7, para. 2(1)
para. 6	Sch. 5, Pt. III, paras. 1(1) (3), 3(1)(3), Pt. IV, para. 1(1)

THE HOUSING RENTS AND SUBSIDIES ACT 1975

1975	1985
s.6	ss.41(1), 54(1)
Sch. 5,	
para. 7(1)	103
para. 12	93(2)
para. 13	60(2)

THE HOUSING RENTS AND SUBSIDIES (SCOTLAND) ACT 1975

1975	1985
s.12	ss.41(1), 54(1)
Sch. 3,	
para. 13	60(2)

THE STATUTORY CORPORATIONS (FINANCIAL PROVISIONS) ACT 1975

1975	1985
Sch. 4,	
para. 8	s.92(3)

THE DEVELOPMENT OF RURAL WALES ACT 1976

1976	1985
Sch. 7,	
para. 12	s.90(2)

THE RENT ACT 1977

1977	1985
s.15(5)	s.2

THE HOME PURCHASE ASSISTANCE AND HOUSING GUARANTEE ACT 1978

1978	1985	1978	1985
s.5(1)(2)	s.83(3)(4)	Sch.	
Sch.		para. 9	Sch. 2,
paras. 6, 7,			para. 2(4)
8	106(1)(2),		
	Sch. 2,		
	para. 2(4)		

INTERPRETATION ACT 1978

1978	1985
Sch. 1	s.101

THE HOUSING ACT 1980

1980	1985	1980	1985	1980	1985
s.74(2)	s.2	s.127(1) to		Sch. 17,	
92	Sch. 2,	(3)	s.4(3)	para. 1	s.28(1)
	paras.	128	9(4)	para. 2	(2)(5)
	1(1)(2),	(1)(a),		para. 3(a) ..	30(1)
	2(1)(3),	(2)	6(4)	(b) ..	(5)
	3(1)–(6),	130(1)	43	(c) ...	(4)
	8(1)(2)	(2)	48(3)	paras. 4, 5 ..	18(1), 31(1)
111	s.106(1)(2)	(3)	106(1)(2)	paras. 6(a) .	31(1)
(1)	84(1)(4)	131(1)	53(1)	(b) ..	18(2), 28(2),
(3)	(2)	(2)	(2)		30(1)
(4)	(3)	(3)	(3)	(c)(d)	31(3)
(5)	(4)(5)	(3)	(4)	(e) ...	29(2)
(6)	(5)	(4)	(4)(5)	para. 7	18(3), 31(2)
(7)		(5)	(6)	para. 8	17(4)
"building		(6)	(7)	para. 9	30(6)
society"	101	132	19(2)–(4)	Sch. 18,	
111(8)	84(6)	133(1)	38	para. 1	42(2), (3)
120(1)	93(2)	(2)	54(5),	para. 2	47(5)
(2)	(4)		106(1)(2)	para. 3	41(1)(2)
121(1)	95	137(1)	9(3), 12	para. 4	49(1) to (4)
(2)	87(1)–(3)	(2)	12	para. 5	50(1), (2)
(3)	87(4)	151(1), (3) ..	24(5), 48(4)	para. 6	52(1)(2)
122(1) to		155(2)	28(6)	para. 9	
(3)	8(1)–(3)	Sch. 11, Pt. II	13(3)	"housing	
(4)–(6) ..Sch. 2		Sch. 16, Pt. I,		activities"	106(1)(2)
123(2)	s.9(2)	para. 1(1)(2)Sch. 3,		para. 9(a) ..	54(1)
(3)	10(1)		para. 1(1)(2)	paras.	
(4)	(2)	para. 2(1)(2)	para. 2(1)(2)	9(b)(i),	
(5)	(3)	para. 3(1)–		10(b)	56(1)
(6)	9(3)	(4)	para. 3(1)–	para.	
(7)	2		(4)	9(b)(ii)	(2)
"secure		para. 4(1)(2)	para. 4(1)(2)	para.	
tenancy"	39	para. 5(1)(2)	para. 5	9(b)(iii)	(3)
124(1)	24(1)	(3)(4)	para. 6	para. 9(c) ...	54(5)
(2)	(3)	para. 6	para. 7	(e) ...	54(4)
(3)	(4)	Pt. II ....ss.14(1)(2),		(f) ...	57(1) to (3)
(4)	25		15(1)–(3)	para. 10(a) .	55(1)
(5)	26			(b) .	56(1)(2)
(6)	24(2)	"co-opted		(d) .	55(5)
(7)	(5)	member" ...	37	(e) .	(6)
125(1)	27(1)			(f) .	57(1) to (3)
(2)	(2)				
(3)	(3)				
(4)	(4)				

THE HOUSING ACT 1980—*continued*

1980	1985	1980	1985	1980	1985
Sch. 25,		Sch. 25,		Sch. 25,	
para. 13 .....Sch. 6,		para. 24 ..... s.90(3)		para. 25 ..... 13(2)	
	para. 9(1)				

THE TENANTS RIGHTS ETC. (SCOTLAND) ACT 1980

1980	1985
s.31 .... s.86	

THE NEW TOWNS ACT 1981

1981	1985
Sch. 12,	
para. 13(*a*) .ss.90(2),	
	106(1)(2)

THE ACQUISITION OF LAND ACT 1981

1981	1985
Sch. 4,	
para. 1 ...... s.88(3)	

THE CRIMINAL JUSTICE ACT 1982

1982	1985
s.37 ....ss.28(3), 30(6)	
(1)	27(2)
46(1)	28(3), 30(6)
(2)	27(2)
54	28(3), 30(6)
74(1)	64

THE MISCELLANEOUS FINANCIAL PROVISIONS ACT 1983

1983	1985
s.4 .... s.94(1)	

THE HOUSING AND BUILDING CONTROL ACT 1984

1984	1985	1984	1985	1984	1985
s.18(3) ....ss.85(4),		s.20(4)(*a*) ..... s.84(4)		s.20(7) .... s.84(6)	
	106(1)(2)	(*b*)	(5)	24(1)	81
"urban		(5)		33(1)	44(1)
development		"local		(2)	(2)
corporation" s.106(1)(2)		authority" ..	106(1)(2)	34(1)	52(1)
18(4)	85(4)	"recognised		(2)	(3)
"long lease"	(5)	body"	85(2)	(3)	(4)
20(1)	84(1)	"relevant		35(1)	45(1), (2)
(2)	(2)	advance" ...	(4)	(2)	(3)
(3)	(3)	20(6)	(3)	(3)	(4)
				(4)	(3)

THE HOUSING AND BUILDING CONTROL ACT 1984—*continued*

THE COMPANIES CONSOLIDATION (CONSEQUENTIAL PROVISIONS) ACT 1985

THE LOCAL GOVERNMENT ACT 1985

REPORT ON CONSOLIDATION OF THE HOUSING ACTS (CMND. 9515) RECOMMENDATIONS

THE ISLES OF SCILLY (HOUSING) ORDER 1972

THE ISLES OF SCILLY (HOUSING) (NO. 2) ORDER 1973

THE HOUSING ACT 1974 (COMMENCEMENT NO. 4) ORDER 1975

THE ISLES OF SCILLY (HOUSING) ORDER 1975

THE HOUSING CORPORATION ADVANCES (INCREASE OF LIMIT) ORDER 1983

1983   **1985**
S.I. 1983
No. 664 ..... s.93(2)

THE HOUSING ASSOCIATION GRANT (DISPOSAL OF DWELLINGS) ORDER 1984

1984   **1985**
S.I. 1984
No. 1803 .... s.48(3)

LANDLORD AND TENANT ACT 1985*

(1985 c.70)

Tables of derivations and destinations can be found at the end of the Act.

---

* Annotations by Andrew Arden, LL.B., Barrister, and Siobhan McGrath, B.A., Barrister.

38. Minor definitions.
39. Index of defined expressions.

Final provisions

40. Short title, commencement and extent.

An Act to consolidate certain provisions of the law of landlord and tenant formerly found in the Housing Acts, together with the Landlord and Tenant Act 1962, with amendments to give effect to recommendations of the Law Commission.   [30th October 1985]

PARLIAMENTARY DEBATES
Hansard: H.L. Vol. 463, col. 531; Vol. 464, col. 170; Vol. 466, cols. 322, 864; Vol. 467, cols. 1560 to 1569; H.C. Vol. 84, cols. 116, 974.

Information to be given to tenant

Disclosure of landlord's identity

1.—(1) If the tenant of premises occupied as a dwelling makes a written request for the landlord's name and address to—
  (*a*) any person who demands, or the last person who received, rent payable under the tenancy, or
  (*b*) any other person for the time being acting as agent for the landlord, in relation to the tenancy,
that person shall supply the tenant with a written statement of the landlord's name and address within the period of 21 days beginning with the day on which he receives the request.

(2) A person who, without reasonable excuse, fails to comply with subsection (1) commits a summary offence and is liable on conviction to a fine not exceeding level 4 on the standard scale.

(3) In this section and section 2—
  (*a*) "tenant" includes a statutory tenant; and
  (*b*) "landlord" means the immediate landlord.

DEFINITIONS
  "address": s.38.
  "dwelling": s.38.
  "landlord": s.36.
  "statutory tenant": s.37.
  "tenant": s.36.

GENERAL NOTE
  First introduced in 1974 (Housing Act 1974, s.121(1)), this section, together with the next, seeks to meet the problem of the "secret landlord", where the letting has been by *e.g.* an agent or a housekeeper. See also s.3 below for the duty to inform the tenant of an assignment of the landlord's interest. See also as to liability for offences, s.33 below.
  The provisions apply only to (a) tenancies, not licences (*cf.* ss.4–7 below), of (b) residential accommodation (note that part only of a building may qualify, but see generally the definition of "dwelling" in s.38, below), but (c) *not* including an assured tenancy (see s.32, excluding tenancies to which Pt.II, Landlord and Tenant Act 1954 applies, which includes assured tenancies by reason of s.58 and Sched. 5, Housing Act 1980).
  For weekly tenancies, see also s.4 below.
  For the distinction between tenancy/licence see most recently *Street* v. *Mountford* [1985] A.C. 809, 17 H.L.R. 402, H.L., reaffirming the traditional view that a grant of a dwelling house with exclusive possession at a rent creates a tenancy despite any label to the contrary attached thereto. *Street* v. *Mountford* does not affect the position of lodgers and expressly excludes agreements where on a true construction of the effect there has been no grant of exclusive possession or where there has been no intention to create legal relations, and envisages other situations where there may be no tenancy despite the fact that the agreement

fulfils the usual prerequisites, *e.g.* occupancy under a contract for sale of land or pursuant to a contract of employment. A lodger for this purpose is one the terms of whose occupation include the provision of services or attendances which require the landlord or his employees to exercise unrestricted access to and use of the premises.

The tenant's *request* must, as the reply, be in writing.

Subs. (2)

Failure to comply with the requirement is punishable by a fine of up to level 4 on the standard scale under s.37, Criminal Justice Act 1982, currently £1,000, by S.I. 1984 No. 447.

Disclosure of directors, &c. of corporate landlord

2.—(1) Where a tenant is supplied under section 1 with the name and address of his landlord and the landlord is a body corporate, he may make a further written request to the landlord for the name and address of every director and of the secretary of the landlord.

(2) The landlord shall supply the tenant with a written statement of the information requested within the period of 21 days beginning with the day on which he receives the request.

(3) A request under this section is duly made to the landlord if it is made to—

(*a*) an agent of the landlord, or

(*b*) a person who demands the rent of the premises concerned;

and any such agent or person to whom such a request is made shall forward it to the landlord as soon as may be.

(4) A landlord who, without reasonable excuse, fails to comply with a request under this section, and a person who, without reasonable excuse, fails to comply with a requirement imposed on him by subsection (3), commits a summary offence and is liable on conviction to a fine not exceeding level 4 on the standard scale.

DEFINITIONS

"address": s.38.

"landlord": s.36.

"tenant": s.36.

GENERAL NOTE

This section is ancillary to s.1, above, and enables a request for information under s.1 which is answered with the name of a body corporate to be followed up with a request for the names and addresses of directors and the secretary of such a body. As with the initial request, the further request must be in writing. As to liability for offences, see also s.33, below. For weekly tenancies, see also s.4, below.

Subs. (4)

The offence is punishable by a fine of up to level 4 on the standard scale under s.37, Criminal Justice Act 1982, currently £1,000, by S.I. 1984 No. 447.

Duty to inform tenant of assignment of landlord's interest

3.—(1) If the interest of the landlord under a tenancy of premises which consist of or include a dwelling is assigned, the new landlord shall give notice in writing of the assignment, and of his name and address, to the tenant not later than the next day on which rent is payable under the tenancy or, if that is within two months of the assignment, the end of that period of two months.

(2) If trustees constitute the new landlord, a collective description of the trustees as the trustees of the trust in question may be given as the name of the landlord, and where such a collective description is given—

(*a*) the address of the new landlord may be given as the address from which the affairs of the trust are conducted, and

(*b*) a change in the persons who are for the time being the trustees of the trust shall not be treated as an assignment of the interest of the landlord.

(3) A person who is the new landlord under a tenancy falling within subsection (1) and who fails, without reasonable excuse, to give the notice required by that subsection, commits a summary offence and is liable on conviction to a fine not exceeding level 4 on the standard scale.

(4) In this section—

(*a*) "tenancy" includes a statutory tenancy, and

(*b*) references to the assignment of the landlord's interest include any conveyance other than a mortgage or charge.

DEFINITIONS
"address": s.38.
"dwelling": s.38.
"landlord": s.36.
"statutory tenancy": s.37.
"tenancy": s.36.

GENERAL NOTE

This is an important provision. As with ss.1 and 2, it was introduced by the Housing Act 1974 and imposes a positive obligation on a landlord of premises let under a *tenancy* (not a licence *cf.* ss.4–7 below), to inform the tenant, in writing, of an assignment, and of the name and address of the new landlord, either by the next rent day, or a period of two months, (whichever is the *later*. The provisions do not include assured tenancies (see s.32, below), but do include a statutory tenancy (see s.37, below). A change in the identity of trustees does not, however *per se* amount to an assignment.

For weekly tenancies, see also s.4 below.

Subs. (3)

An offence is punishable by a fine of up to level 4 on the standard scale under s.37, Criminal Justice Act 1982, currently £1,000, by S.I. 1984 No. 447.

Subs (4)

This widens the scope of the word assignment, to include any conveyance of land *e.g.* by creation of a leasehold interest from a freehold, or where an individual landlord conveys the interest in land to a company of which he is a director. The important factor is that there is a change of landlord, other than a mere change of trustee (subs. (2)(*b*)).

Provision of rent books

Provision of rent books

4.—(1) Where a tenant has a right to occupy premises as a residence in consideration of a rent payable weekly, the landlord shall provide a rent book or other similar document for use in respect of the premises.

(2) Subsection (1) does not apply to premises if the rent includes a payment in respect of board and the value of that board to the tenant forms a substantial proportion of the whole rent.

(3) In this section and sections 5 to 7—

(*a*) "tenant" includes a statutory tenant and a person having a contractual right to occupy the premises; and

(*b*) "landlord", in relation to a person having such a contractual right, means the person who granted the right or any successor in title of his, as the case may require.

DEFINITIONS
"landlord": s.36.
"statutory tenant": s.37.
"tenant": s.36.

GENERAL NOTE

This section applies to *premises*, as distinct from a *dwelling*, so that the requirement for a 'separate dwelling' is not applicable (*cf.* notes to s.38, below). Further evidence of the breadth of this provision is to be found in the definition in subs. (3), expanding landlord and tenant in their s.36 meanings to include licensor and licensee.

"Payable weekly" is not the same as a "weekly rent". The test is how the rent is to be paid, not how it is calculated, so that an annual rent payable weekly brings the premises within the section (*cf.* the Y.W.C.A. "scheme" described at 1978 L.A.G. Bulletin 129). But equally a rent calculated by the week but payable at less frequent intervals, would not be within the section: see also *R.* v. *Ewing* (1977) 65 Cr.App.R. 4, in which it was held that payment on such a basis did not fall within s.126 Rent Act 1977, otherwise prohibiting a landlord under a regulated tenancy charging a weekly tenant more than one week in advance.

In *Moses* v. *Lovegrove* [1952] 2 Q.B. 533, C.A., rent books were described as not in themselves creating an interest in land, but merely as books acknowledging payment of weekly sums and where appropriate evidencing terms.

As to the *content* of a "rent book or other similar document", see s.5 below. As to company landlord companies, see s.6 below. As to offences see ss.7 and 33.

A failure to comply with the requirement does not however, excuse the tenant from paying rent: *Shaw* v. *Groom* [1970] 2 Q.B. 504, C.A.

Subs. (2)

Occupiers excluded by this subsection will be excluded from (a) Rent Act full protection, and (b) Rent Act restricted protection (*Rent Tribunal jurisdiction*): see notes to s.38, below.

No statutory definition is offered of "board", which has been called a common and well understood word (*Wilkes* v. *Goodwin* [1923] 2 K.B. 86, C.A.). Doubtless the legislature has daily meals in mind—some food for consumption by the tenant on the premises. As to substantial proportion, see also notes to s.38, below.

In assessing whether a payment is in respect of board it is contractual entitlement to such, rather than whether or not such is provided (*Artillery Mansions* v. *Mabartney* [1947] 1 K.B. 164, C.A. and *Palser* v. *Grinling* [1948] A.C. 291, H.L.).

Information to be contained in rent books

5.—(1) A rent book or other similar document provided in pursuance of section 4 shall contain notice of the name and address of the landlord of the premises and—

(a) if the premises are occupied by virtue of a restricted contract, particulars of the rent and of the other terms and conditions of the contract and notice of such other matters as may be prescribed;

(b) if the premises are let on or subject to a protected or statutory tenancy, notice of such matters as may be prescribed.

(2) If the premises are occupied by virtue of a restricted contract or let on or subject to a protected or statutory tenancy, the notice and particulars required by this section shall be in the prescribed form.

(3) In this section "prescribed" means prescribed by regulations made by the Secretary of State, which—

(a) may make different provision for different cases, and

(b) shall be made by statutory instrument which shall be subject to annulment in pursuance of a resolution of either House of Parliament.

DEFINITIONS
"address": s.38.
"landlord": ss.4(3), 36.
"protected tenancy": s.38.
"restricted contract": s.38.
"statutory tenancy": s.37.

GENERAL NOTE
This section details what the "rent book or other similar document" required by s.4 is to contain. The forms of notice to be inserted in the rent book are now prescribed by the Rent Book (Form of Notice) Regulations 1982 (S.I. 1982 No. 1474), made under the Landlord and Tenant Act 1962, but retained in force by s.2, Housing (Consequential Provisions) Act 1985. Additional requirements concerning overcrowding are to be found in Housing Act 1985, s.332. As to offences see ss.7, 33 below.

Information to be supplied by companies

6.—(1) Where the landlord of premises to which section 4(1) applies (premises occupied as a residence at a weekly rent) is a company, and the tenant serves on the landlord a request in writing to that effect, the landlord shall give the tenant in writing particulars of the name and address of every director and of the secretary of the company.

(2) A request under this section is duly served on the landlord if it is served—

    (*a*) on an agent of the landlord named as such in the rent book or other similar document, or

    (*b*) on the person who receives the rent of the premises;

and a person on whom a request is so served shall forward it to the landlord as soon as may be.

DEFINITIONS
"address": s.38.
"landlord": ss.4(3), 36.
"tenant": ss.4(3), 36.

GENERAL NOTE
This section repeats the effect of s.2 above, where the occupier is informed in the rent book that the landlord is a company, but is not entirely superfluous because (a) s.2 applies by way of *further* request, and (b) a wider class of occupier is within this series of sections than within ss.1, 2. As to offences see ss.7, 33 below.

Offences

7.—(1) If the landlord of premises to which section 4(1) applies (premises occupied as a residence at a weekly rent) fails to comply with any relevant requirement of—

    section 4 (provision of rent book),

    section 5 (information to be contained in rent book), or

    section 6 (information to be supplied by companies),

he commits a summary offence and is liable on conviction to a fine not exceeding level 4 on the standard scale.

(2) If a person demands or receives rent on behalf of the landlord of such premises while any relevant requirement of—

    section 4 (provision of rent book), or

    section 5 (information to be contained in rent book),

is not complied with, then, unless he shows that he neither knew nor had reasonable cause to suspect that any such requirement had not been complied with, he commits a summary offence and is liable to a fine not exceeding level 4 on the standard scale.

(3) If a person fails to comply with a requirement imposed on him by section 6(2) (duty to forward request to landlord), he commits a summary offence and is liable on conviction to a fine not exceeding level 4 on the standard scale.

(4) If a default in respect of which—

    (*a*) a landlord is convicted of an offence under subsection (1), or

    (*b*) another person is convicted of an offence under subsection (3),

continues for more than 14 days after the conviction, the landlord or other person commits a further offence under that subsection in respect of the default.

DEFINITIONS
"landlord": ss.4(3), 36.

GENERAL NOTE

This section makes it an offence for a landlord to fail to provide a rent book under s.4, to fail to include in the rent book the information required by s.5, or to fail to provide particulars about the officers of a company landlord under s.6. In the case of any offence by a corporate body any officer who consented to or connived at the offence is liable: s.33. A person who demands or receives rent while ss.4 and 5 are not being complied with is also guilty of an offence, subject to the defence that he did not know and did not have reasonable cause to suspect that the requirements were not being complied with. Finally, an offence is commited by failure of such a person to pass on to the landlord a request for information under s.6(2).

Standard Scale.

Offences are punishable by a fine of up to level 4 on the standard scale under s.37, Criminal Justice Act 1982, currently £1,000, by S.I. 1984 No. 447.

Implied terms as to fitness for human habitation

Implied terms as to fitness for human habitation

8.—(1) In a contract to which this section applies for the letting of a house for human habitation there is implied, notwithstanding any stipulation to the contrary—

(*a*) a condition that the house is fit for human habitation at the commencement of the tenancy, and

(*b*) an undertaking that the house will be kept by the landlord fit for human habitation during the tenancy.

(2) The landlord, or a person authorised by him in writing, may at reasonable times of the day, on giving 24 hours' notice in writing to the tenant or occupier, enter premises to which this section applies for the purpose of viewing their state and condition.

(3) This section applies to a contract if—

(*a*) the rent does not exceed the figure applicable in accordance with subsection (4), and

(*b*) the letting is not on such terms as to the tenant's responsibility as are mentioned in subsection (5).

(4) The rent limit for the application of this section is shown by the following Table, by reference to the date of making of the contract and the situation of the premises:

TABLE

Date of making of contract	*Rent limit*
Before 31st July 1923.	In London: £40. Elsewhere: £26 or £16 (see Note 1).
On or after 31st July 1923 and before 6th July 1957.	In London: £40. Elsewhere: £26.
On or after 6th July 1957.	In London: £80. Elsewhere: £52.

NOTES

1. The applicable figure for contracts made before 31st July 1923 is £26 in the case of premises situated in a borough or urban district which at the date of the contract had according to the last published census a population of 50,000 or more. In the case of a house situated elsewhere, the figure is £16.

2. The references to "London" are, in relation to contracts made before 1st April 1965, to the administrative county of London and, in relation to contracts made on or after that date, to Greater London exclusive of the outer London boroughs.

(5) This section does not apply where a house is let for a term of three years or more (the lease not being determinable at the option of either party before the expiration of three years) upon terms that the tenant puts the premises into a condition reasonably fit for human habitation.

(6) In this section "house" includes—

(a) a part of a house, and

(b) any yard, garden, outhouses and appurtenances belonging to the house or usually enjoyed with it.

DEFINITIONS

"fit for human habitation": s.10.
"lease": s.36.
"tenancy": s.36.
"tenant": s.36.

GENERAL NOTE

This section applies in relation to a house which, by subs. (6), means a house or part of a house: see notes below. It applies in relation to lettings at very low rents indeed: see subs. (4). It does not apply where the contract is for a term of three years or more (and, therefore, is applicable where the term is periodic, even although it may well last for more than three years), *and* the occupier is under an obligation to put the premises into a condition reasonably fit for human habitation. The "policy" of the requirement (*cf.* notes below), *i.e.* that landlords should bear principal responsibility for the condition of rented accommodation, is now represented by ss.11–16, below. As to enforcement of the provision, see also s.17, below.

Under Pts. VI and IX, Housing Act 1985, if property is unfit for human habitation— defined in relation to this section in s.10, below, and in relation to that Act by s.604, Housing Act 1985, but in identical terms—the local housing authority will be bound to take action either to cause the property to be repaired, or to close it to human habitation, if necessary by demolition. The property will be subject to repairs procedure under Pt VI if repairable at a reasonable expense within s.206, Housing Act 1985. As to the mandatory nature of those procedures, see *R.* v. *Kerrier District Council, ex parte Guppys (Bridport) Ltd.* (1977) 32 P. & C.R. 411, C.A.

If the property is part of an area of unfit housing, it may also be subject to clearance area procedure under Pt. IX. In the case of either class of Pt. IX procedure (individual action where not repairable at reasonable expense, or clearance), the authority are entitled to purchase the property for temporary housing use, in which case the provisions of this section will cease to apply: Housing Act 1985, s.302. A local authority landlord is not otherwise exempt from the provisions, even although the individual house action of Pts. VI and IX are normally inapplicable to their own properties: *R.* v. *Cardiff City Council, ex parte Cross* (1982) 6 H.L.R. 1, C.A., affirming (1981) 1 H.L.R. 54, Q.B.D.

Notwithstanding the language of the section, it would seem that it is applicable only to *tenants*, not also *licensees*: *cf.* s.9, below dealing with agricultural tied workers ("by reason only of the house not being let to him"), see also *Bomford* v. *South Worcestershire Assessment Committee* [1947] 1 All E.R. 299, C.A.

Subs. (1)
Common Law

At common law, there is no implied term that premises will either be fit for human habitation at the commencement of a term, or rendered so fit (see *Hart* v. *Windsor* (1844) 12 M. & W. 68, *Cruse* v. *Mount* [1933] Ch. 278, *Sleafer* v. *London Borough of Lambeth* [1960] 1 Q.B. 43), save (a) in the case of a furnished letting (*Wilson* v. *Finch Hatton* (1877) 2 Ex.D. 336), and (b) in the case of a lease or agreement for a lease entered into while a house or other premises is still under construction. In such a case it is implied that the house will be fit at the commencement of the lease (*Perry* v. *Sharon Development Co.* (1937) All E.R. 390).

In each of these cases, the term does not extend to an undertaking to *keep* the premises fit for human habitation throughout the letting, but is confined to their state at the outset: *Hart* v. *Windsor* (1844) 12 M. & W. 68, *Sarsons* v. *Roberts* (1895) 2 Q.B. 395. The proposition as it related to furnished accommodation was that "every person who undertakes to let a ready-furnished house or apartment is bound to take care that the premises are free from nuisance . . . If a man lets a house, he does so under an implied contract that it is fit for the reception of a family; and it is his duty to take care that it is so, and that it is in a comfortable and tenantable state . . . ." (*Smith* v. *Marrable* (1943) 11 M. & W. 5).

On appeal, Lord Abinger C.B. added: "It is plain good common sense, that if a man lets a house, it shall be fit for the purposes of occupation . . ." (*ibid.*). The apparent applicability of this to *all* lettings for residential accommodation was restricted to *furnished* lettings in a series of later cases: see *Sutton* v. *Temple* (1843) 12 M. & W. 52, *Hart* v. *Windsor* (1844) 12 M. & W. 68, *Cruse* v. *Mount* [1933] Ch. 278, *Sleafer* v. *London Borough of Lambeth* [1960] 1 Q.B. 43. Further, while it has been held that the furniture restriction is as applicable to flats as houses (*Cruse* v. *Mount*), this decision was without reference to an earlier, conflicting authority: *Sarsons* v. *Roberts* [1895] 2 Q.B. 395.

Amongst the matters which have been considered to amount to unfitness for human habitation at common law are: inadequate drainage (*Wilson* v *Finch Hatton* (1877) 2 Ex.D. 336), infestation by bugs or pests (*Smith* v. *Marrable* (1843 11 M. & W. 5), infection (*Bird* v. *Greville* (1844) C. & E. 317, *Collins* v. *Hopkins* [1923] 2 K.B. 617, *Hart* v. *Windsor* (1844) 12 M. & W. 68, *Sutton* v. *Temple* (1843) 12 M. & W. 52), premises unsafe for occupation (*Edwards* v. *Etherington* (1825) 7 Dow. & Ry. K.B. 117, *Cruse* v. *Mount* [1933] Ch. 278), and insufficiency of water supplies (*Chester* v. *Powell* (1885) 52 L.T. (N.S.) 722).

Statute

Since the Artizans and Labourers Dwellings Act 1868, the Housing Acts have been using the term "unfit for human habitation", when repairs notices under what is now s.189, Housing Act 1985, or demolition orders under *ibid.*, s.265, were introduced. In the Artizans and Labourers Dwellings Improvement Act 1887, it was used in relation to what are now clearance areas under *ibid.*, s.289. The present section was introduced in s.12, Housing of the Working Classes Act 1885, as 'in any contract made after the passing of this Act for letting for habitation by persons of the working classes a house or part of a house, there shall be implied a condition that the house is at the commencement of the holding in all respects reasonably fit for human habitation".

Lettings for the working classes meant lettings below specified rent levels. By s.12, Housing of the Working Classes Act 1903, the condition was to be take effect "notwithstanding any agreement to the contrary, and any such agreement made after the passing of this Act shall be void". The rent limits were extended by s.14, Housing, Town Planning etc. Act 1909, and by *ibid.*, s.15, the condition was extended to cover *keeping* in repair throughout the letting: see now, subs. (1)(*b*) of this section.

The term "unfit for human habitation" continued to mean "in all respects reasonably fit for human habitation", otherwise unqualified, until the Housing Repairs and Rents Act 1954 when, by s.9, the definition now to be found in s.10, below, was introduced, without "internal arrangement" but with facilities for "storage" as well as for preparation and cooking of food. The addition of internal arrangement, and the elimination of food storage facilities (the latter on account of powers now to be found in s.70, Building Act 1984, permitting the authority to require their introduction), were effected by s.71, Housing Act 1969. See, further, notes to s.10, below.

Notice of breach

The condition and the undertaking must be read as part of the contract. It is a condition precedent to the liability of a landlord under a repairing obligation that notice of latent as well as patent defects should have been given to him by the tenant, regardless of the landlord's right to inspect the premises: *Morgan* v. *Liverpool Corporation* [1927] 2 K.B. 131, C.A., a case decided on similar wording in the Housing Act, 1925, s.1(1), approved in *McCarrick* v. *Liverpool Corporation* [1947] A.C. 219, H.L. The same point has been restated in relation to s.11, below, see notes thereto; see, especially, *O'Brien* v. *Robinson* [1973] A.C. 912, 13 H.L.R. 7, H.L., and the description thereof as "unfortunate" in *McGreal* v. *Wake* (1984) 13 H.L.R. 107, C.A.

However, *actual* notice is enough, and notice does not need to come from the tenant, *i.e.* it could come from another source, *e.g.* the local authority: *ibid.* Where a husband and wife were driven from their bed by fleas in a house that had been recently decorated and disinfected, the point was not argued that the landlord had no knowledge of the defect and judgment was given for the husband: *Thompson and Wife* v. *Arkell* (1949) 99 L.J. 597 (a county court decision).

Where a tenant gave the landlord notice of a bulge in the ceiling and then occupied for eight months before the ceiling fell, the landlord was held liable: *Porter* v. *Jones* (1942) 112 L.J.K.B. 173, C.A.

Where, for want of notice, there is no actionable breach, the tenant may nonetheless be able to sue in tort under the Defective Premises Act 1972, s.4.

Remedies for breach

Where the house is not fit for human habitation at the commencement of the tenancy, the tenant may sue the landlord for damages for resultant injuries: *Walker and Wife* v. *Hobbs & Co.* (1889) 23 Q.B.D. 458. The tenant may also repudiate the contract—*ibid.*

Damages may be recovered for personal injury or damage to property or for such other loss as is occasioned by the breach: *Horrex* v. *Pidwell* [1958] C.L.Y. 1461. In *John Waterer, Sons & Crisp* v. *Huggins* (1931) 47 T.L.R. 305, where a closing order had been made as a result of the landlord's failure to keep the house fit for human habitation, the tenant failed to recover damages for the loss of a controlled tenancy.

See further on remedies, notes to s.11, below.

Rights of third parties

As the obligation is contractual, it has been held that a stranger to the tenancy agreement could not sue upon it: *Ryall* v. *Kidwell* [1914] 3 K.B. 135. But this was in effect reversed by the Occupiers' Liability Act 1957, s.4, and, now, the Defective Premises Act 1972, s.4.

Subs. (4)

Rent means the actual rent contracted to be paid by the tenant to the landlord for the use of the house, without any deductions in respect of rates or other outgoings which the landlord may have agreed to pay: *Rousou* v. *Photi* [1940] 2 K.B. 379.

The annual rent is ascertained by multiplying the weekly rent by 52: *Whitcombe* v. *Pollock* [1956] J.P.L. 896; 106 L.J. 554l [1956] C.L.Y. 3928.

Subs. (6)

As to appurtenances, see notes to s.38, below.

The s.38 definition of "dwelling" is somewhat different than the term "house", used here: see notes thereto and, particularly, note that the reference in that section is to "building", not "house", although in each case a part is included.

The word "house" has fallen for consideration on a number of occasions, both under and not under Housing Acts. The approach of the courts is not merely to consider the word in relation to the Housing Acts, but, indeed, particular parts of the Housing Acts: "As usual, though the matter is so very clear to my mind on the facts and on the Act . . ., it has been embarrassed by a reference to a number of authorities . . ." (*per* Jessel M.R., *Duke of Bedford* v. *Dawson* (1875) L.R. 20 Eq. 353 at p.357, cited by Browne L.J. in *Sovmots Investments Ltd.* v. *Secretary of State for the Environment* at the Court of Appeal, [1979] A.C. 144, C.A. and H.L.)

In *Quillotex Co. Ltd.* v. *Minister of Housing and Local Government* [1966] 1 Q.B. 704, Salmon L.J. adopted the view of Sir George Jessel M.R. in *Attorney-General* v. *Mutual Tontine Westminster Chambers Association Ltd.* (1876) 1 Ex. D. 469, C.A., that no real help can be gained as to the meaning of a word in Statute A by reference to its meaning in Statute B, C or D. "What is the ordinary natural meaning of the word within the context of the section in which it appears?" And: "In construing the language of any statutory enactment, it is important to look at it in its context and to consider, amongst other things, the mischief at which it is aimed . . ."

In *Annicola Investments Ltd.* v. *Minister of Housing and Local Government* [1968] 1 Q.B. 631, it was said "that the word has a distinct fluidity of meaning, and that it is best construed in relation to the context in which it is found, and in relation to the objects and purposes of the Act or of the section of the Act in which it is used". In *In Re Butler, Camberwell (Wingfield Mews) No. 2 Clearance Order 1936* [1939] 1 K.B. 570, C.A., Sir Wilfred Greene M.R. said that "whether a particular building does or does not fall under that word is a mixed question of fact and law; fact in so far as it is necessary to ascertain all the relevant facts relating to the building, and law in so far as the application of the word "houses" to those facts involves the construction of the Act.

"However, as so frequently happens in dealing with Acts of Parliament, words are found used—and very often the commoner the word is, the greater doubt it may raise—the application of which to individual cases can only be settled by the application of a sense of language in the context of the Act, and if I may say so, a certain amount of common sense in using and understanding the English language in a particular context . . ."

It is also clear that the fact that there may be provisions in another part of an Act which treat issues differently will not be conclusive. ". . . It is dangerous to interpret one Part by reference to the provisions of another Part" (*per* Woolf J, in *R.* v. *Cardiff City Council, ex parte Cross* (1981) 1 H.L.R. 54, Q.B.D., upheld on appeal (1982) 6 H.L.R. 1, C.A.). "Comparative" construction was also considered and rejected in *Okereke* v. *London Borough of Brent* [1967] 1 Q.B. 42, C.A. Accordingly, no importance should be attached to the difference between the definition in this section, and in s.38, below, which derives not from any deliberate policy, but simply from the different statutory origins of many of the provisions of this Act.

It has been said that "house" has no very precise meaning: the word can cover many types of building (*Quillotex* v. *Minister of Housing and Local Government* [1966] 1 Q.B. 704, C.A. See also *Critchell* v. *Lambeth Borough Council* [1957] 2 Q.B. 535, C.A.—a house means what is commonly called a house, *i.e.* a separate structure, but in this Part it of course includes flats by virtue of the definition in this section). In *Howard* v. *Ministry of Housing and Local Government* (1967) 65 L.G.R. 257, it was said that the word "house" in the Housing Act 1957 from which this section is derived had the same meaning as "dwelling house" in the previous (1936) legislation.

A house is "a building for human habitation; especially a building that is the ordinary dwelling place of a family", according to the *Oxford English Dictionary* as quoted by Pearson L.J. in *Reed* v. *Hastings Corporation* (1964) 62 L.G.R. 588, C.A. In *Ashbridge Investments Ltd.* v. *Ministry of Housing and Local Government* [1965] 1 W.L.R. 1320, C.A., a greengrocer's shop with a rear living room and scullery, three first floor rooms and an outside lavatory, was considered within what could properly be held a house: "It is apparent that a 'house'. . . means a building which is constructed or adapted for use as or for the purposes of a dwelling" (*per* Lord Denning M.R. at p.1324).

In *In Re Butler, Camberwell (Wingfield Mews) No. 2 Clearance Order 1936* [1939] 1 K.B. 570, C.A. a structure consisting of a garage or workshop with a dwelling above was held to be a house (see also *Re Hammersmith (Bergham Mews) Clearance Order, 1936* [1937] 3 All E.R. 539). Where a building is used partly for residential purposes, and partly for other purposes, the building has to be looked at as a whole to ascertain whether, as a question of degree, it can properly be described as a house: *Annicola Investments Ltd.* v. *Minister of Housing and Local Government* [1968] 1 Q.B. 631, C.A. It need not be shown that all of the rooms in a building are used for residential purposes: *Premier Garage Co.* v. *Ilkeston Corporation* (1933) 97 J.P. 786.

Although original construction of a building is an important consideration (*In Re Butler, Camberwell (Wingfield Mews) No. 2 Clearance Order 1936* [1939] 1 K.B. 570, C.A.) regard may be had to the use of a building at the time the question falls to be determined (*ibid.*; see also *Grosvenor* v. *Hampstead Junction Railway* [1857] L.J. Ch. 731), so that something not built as a house but used as such may qualify. An unfinished house may qualify as a house: *Alexander* v. *Crystal Palace Railway* (1862) 30 Beav. 556. A building constructed as a house but used for other purposes has been held to remain a house: *Howard* v. *Ministry of Housing and Local Government* (1967) 65 L.G.R. 257.

A hostel or a building used for multiple occupation or as a lodging-house may itself qualify as a house: *London County Council* v. *Rowton Houses Ltd.* (1897) 62 J.P. 68; *Re Ross and Leicester Corporation* (1932) 96 J.P. 459; *R.* v. *London Borough of Southwark, ex parte Lewis Levy Ltd.* (1983) 8 H.L.R. 1, Q.B.D.; *R.* v. *London Borough of Camden, ex parte Rowton (Camden Town) Ltd.* (1983) 10 H.L.R. 28, Q.B.D.

Similarly, a building subdivided into flats can remain a house, whether so constructed or not: *Annicola Investments Ltd.* v. *Minister of Housing and Local Government* [1968] 1 Q.B. 631, *Quillotex Co. Ltd.* v. *Minister of Housing and Local Government* [1966] 1 Q.B. 704, *Benabo* v. *Wood Green Borough Council* [1946] 1 K.B. 38, *Critchell* v. *London Borough of Lambeth* [1957] 2 Q.B. 535, C.A., *Okereke* v. *London Borough of Brent* [1967] 1 Q.B. 42, C.A.

In *Lake* v. *Bennett* [1970] 1 Q.B. 663, C.A., under the Leasehold Reform Act 1967, Lord Denning M.R. doubted that a tower block could reasonably be called a house, but Salmon L.J. emphasised that the decision did not necessarily affect the Housing Acts, and the wording of the 1967 Act refers to a house "reasonably so called".

Application of s.8 to certain houses occupied by agricultural workers

9.—(1) Where under the contract of employment of a worker employed in agriculture the provision of a house for his occupation forms part of his remuneration and the provisions of section 8 (implied terms as to fitness for human habitation) are inapplicable by reason only of the house not being let to him—

    (*a*) there are implied as part of the contract of employment, notwithstanding any stipulation to the contrary, the like condition and undertaking as would be implied under that section if the house were so let, and (*b*) the provisions of that section apply accordingly, with the substitution of "employer" for "landlord" and such other modifications as may be necessary.

(2) This section does not affect any obligation of a person other than the employer to repair a house to which this section applies, or any remedy for enforcing such an obligation.

(3) In this section "house" includes—
    (*a*) a part of a house, and
    (*b*) any yard, garden, outhouses and appurtenances belonging to the house or usually enjoyed with it.

DEFINITIONS
"fit for human habitation": s.10.

GENERAL NOTE
This section extends the benefit of section 8 to tied cottages occupied by agricultural workers. This provision is required because such person may be occupying as licensee and not as tenant (*Bomford* v. *South Worcestershire Assessment Committee* [1947] 1 All E.R. 299, C.A.), so that there is no contract for letting within the meaning of s.8.

Subs. (3)
See notes to s.8(6), above.

Fitness for human habitation

10. In determining for the purposes of this Act whether a house is unfit for human habitation, regard shall be had to its condition in respect of the following matters—
    repair,
    stability,
    freedom from damp,
    internal arrangement,
    natural lighting,
    ventilation,
    water supply,
    drainage and sanitary conveniences,
    facilities for preparation and cooking of food and for the disposal of waste water;
and the house shall be regarded as unfit for human habitation if, and only if, it is so far defective in one or more of those matters that it is not reasonably suitable for occupation in that condition.

GENERAL NOTE
This section is in identical terms to s.604, Housing Act 1985, with reference to the provisions of Pts. VI and IX of that Act: see notes to s.8, above.

The term "unfit for human habitation" meant "in all respects reasonably fit for human habitation", otherwise unqualified, until the Housing Repairs and Rents Act 1954 when, by s.9, the present definition was introduced, without "internal arrangement" but with facilities for "storage" as well as for preparation and cooking of food. The addition of internal arrangement, and the elimination of food storage facilities (the latter on account of powers now to be found in s.70, Building Act 1984, permitting the authority to require their introduction), were effected by s.71, Housing Act 1969.

Earlier cases on the statutory definition must accordingly be read subject to the "all respects reasonably fit" general definition, as distinct from the present requirement that premises are not "reasonably suitable for occupation", having regard to whether or not "they are so far defective in one or more of" the specified schedule: *Critchell* v. *Lambeth Borough Council* [1957] 2 Q.B. 535, C.A. But this does not mean that unfitness must be attributable to each of the matters specified, as it were in turn and in isolation. The question to be asked is whether the property suffers from any one or more of those defects, and then whether or not the totality of the defects, taken in the round, means that the property is not reasonably suitable for occupation: *E.A. Wyse* v. *Secretary of State for the Environment and Borough of Newcastle-under-Lyme* [1984] J.P.L. 256, Q.B.D.

Nonetheless, the earlier cases retain some relevance. Thus, in *Jones* v. *Green* [1925] 1 K.B. 659, D.C., it was said that a high standard of proof is not required: "it is only required that the place must be decently fit for human beings to live in". It is a standard of repair lower than that of "good and tenantable repair": *ibid.* In *Hall* v. *Manchester Corporation* (1915) L.J. Ch. 732, H.L., it was said that the standard was that of the "ordinary reasonable man". In *Summers* v. *Salford Corporation* [1943] A.C. 283, the House of Lords adopted the minority judgment of Atkin L.J. (as he then was) in *Morgan* v. *Liverpool Corporation* [1927] 2 K.B. 131, C.A.: "If the state of repair of a house is such that by ordinary user damage may naturally be caused to the occupier, either in respect of personal injury to life or limb or injury to health, then the house is not in all respects reasonably fit for human habitation".

Repair remains, of course, one of the defects which may mean that premises are not "reasonably suitable for occupation", and it is difficult to see a basis for distinguishing the proposition. Similarly, *Summers* was a case of a broken sash-cord to the window of one of two bedrooms in the house, out of a total of four rooms. The House of Lords was in no doubt that this rendered the whole house unfit, because it would be difficult to confine the effects of inadequate ventilation to one room alone. Ventilation remains a specified defect. The question of unfitness has been said to be one of fact, to be determined in a judicial spirit: *Hall* v. *Manchester* (1915) L.J. Ch. 732, H.L.

It is the *effect* of the defect which matters: 'One is rather inclined to associate the idea of a house being unfit for human habitation with its being in such a condition, structurally or otherwise, as to call for demolition . . . At the first blush it seemed to me difficult to say that the existence of a broken sash-cord in the window of one of the four rooms of the appellant's house cased the house not to be "in all respects reasonably fit for human habitation", but a closer consideration has convinced me that the respondents have committed a breach of the undertaking . . ." (*i.e.* the statutorily implied condition—at that time, under s.2, Housing Act 1936, now s.8, above). "The result of such a state of affairs was that the window could not be put to its normal use, namely, being opened and shut for the purpose of ventilation or cleaning, without danger to the operator" (*per* Lord Russell of Killowen, in *Summers*).

The effect of the defect must be measured in terms of the whole of the property in question: *Hall* v. *Manchester Corporation* (1915) 84 L.J. Ch. 732, H.L.; see also *Estate and Trust Agencies (1927) Ltd.* v. *Singapore Improvement Trust* [1937] A.C. 898, P.C.; *Summers* v. *Salford Corporation* [1943] A.C. 283, H.L. But it is only the property, not, *e.g.*, common parts, such as stairs: *Dunster* v. *Hollis* [1918] 2 K.B. 795.

A fall of plaster from the ceiling has been held to be a breach of the implied condition to keep premises fit: *Walker* v. *Hobbs & Co.* (1889) 23 Q.B.D. 458, *Fisher* v. *Walters* [1926] 2 K.B. 315, *Porter* v. *Jones* [1942] 112 L.J. K.B. 173; so has a defective lavatory and guttering: *Horrex* v. *Pidwell* [1958] C.L.Y. 1461.

Infestation with rats, as distinct from an *occasional* (*i.e.* from time to time) invasion, was considered a breach in *Stanton* v. *Southwick* [1920] 2 K.B. 642 (but it is hard to imagine that this distinction would now be applied, at least once the number of times on which the "visits" occurred were sufficient to make clear that it is the property which is the attraction). Where a tenant and his wife were driven from their bed by fleas, the house was held not to be reasonably fit for human habitation: *Thompson* v. *Arkell* (1949) 99 L.J. 597, C.C. Defective stairs were held to make a house unfit in *McCarrick* v. *Liverpool Corporation* [1947] A.C. 219, H.L.

Principal government guidance on the provisions—for the purpose of their application under Parts VI and IX, Housing Act 1985 (*cf.* notes to s.8, above), is to be found in M.H.L.G. Circular 69/67:

(1) Repair. "To be satisfactory, any part of the structure must function in the manner in which it was intended. Any disrepair that may exist in the house and its curtilage should not be a threat to the health of, or cause any serious inconvenience to the occupants. A multiplicity of items may well cause serious inconvenience.

"Consideration must be given to the condition of all parts of the fabric of the house and to the fixtures normally provided by a landlord. It is not expected that disrepair of outbuildings, of boundary walls and of the surfaces of yards and paths will be sufficient, in the absence of defects in the house itself, to render it unfit but disrepair of these items should be taken into account in assessing the unfitness of the whole house". (M.H.L.G. Circular 69/67, Appendix, paragraph 2).

Internal decorative conditions will not normally be taken into account: *ibid;* see also *Ellis Copp* v. *Richmond London Borough Council* (1976) 3 H.L.R. 55, C.A., and *Adams* v. *Tuer* (1923) 130 L.T. 218. However, these can be a valid indicator of structural conditions.

(2) Stability. "Evidence of instability is only significant if it indicates the probability of further movement which would constitute a threat to the occupants of the house". (M.H.L.G. Circular 69/67, Appendix, paragraph 2).

(3) Freedom from Damp. "Any dampness should not be so extensive or so pervasive as to be a threat to the health of the occupants. Such items as a small patch of damp caused by defective pointings around window reveals or door jambs or by a defective rain water pipe are due to disrepair rather than inherent dampness. Care must also be taken not to be misled by temporary condensation". (M.H.L.G. Circular 69/67, Appendix, paragraph 2).

Nonetheless, in cases under Part III, Public Health Act 1936 (statutory nuisances) it has been established that condensation dampness can be dangerous to health, and further that this may be attributable to the construction (original or by adaptation) of the property: see *Dover District Council* v. *Farrar* (1980) 2 H.L.R. 32, D.C., explained in *Greater London Council* v. *London Borough of Tower Hamlets* (1983) 15 H.L.R. 54, D.C. Indeed, given that ventilation is a consideration under this section, and that condensation dampness is closely related to the degree of ventilation available, there is all the more reason to treat condensation as a symptom of statutory unfitness.

In *Tower Hamlets,* the flat had been constructed with an open solid fuel fire in the living room. Subsequently, because the flues were found to be defective, they were blocked up, and the open fire place removed and replaced with an electric heater. The result was that the advantages of a fire which would have been kept in for most of the day, and its considerable ventilating effect, were lost. The Greater London Council put in one storage heater, which was insufficient to combat the condensation that might be anticipated following the blocking up of the flues. Subsequently, even this storage heater was removed by them. Griffiths L.J. said:

"If the construction of a building is so unusual that there has to be some special form of heating to combat condensation, it is reasonable that the landlord should be expected to instal items such as storage heaters to provide that warmth. Of course, if the tenant does not choose to use the facilities provided, he will have no cause for complaint if the result is that condensation makes the place uninhabitable.

"A landlord is required to apply his mind to the necessity of ventilation and, if need be, to insulation and heating. The landlord must provide a combination of these factors to make a house habitable for the tenant. However, once the landlord has provided the facilities, the tenant must use them. If it is shown in any further inquiry into condensation in this flat that the landlord has done everything reasonable and the cause of the continuing condensation is that the tenant is unwilling to use the appliances or any reasonable alternative means of heating the flat, then the landlord cannot be held responsible for the ensuing state of the premises."

While the issues of liability to which Griffiths L.J. was addressing himself are not apparently relevant to the question of whether or not premises are so far defective as regards freedom from damp, or ventilation, as to be unfit, it is submitted that the test will serve equally well to determine whether or not *premises* are defective, as distinct from a *use* of premises which results in a defect. This would not seem to be affected by the decision of the Court of Appeal in *Quick* v. *Taff Ely Borough Council* [1985] 3 All E.R. 321, 18 H.L.R., C.A., see notes to s.11, below, in which dicta suggests that premises ordinary use of which leads to condensation would qualify as unfit.

(4) Internal Arrangements. M.H.L.G. Circular 68/69, Appendix, paragraph 23, suggests that "internal bad arrangement is any feature which prohibits the safe or unhampered passage of the occupants in the dwelling, *e.g.* narrow, steep or winding staircases, absence of hand rails, inadequate landings outside bedrooms, ill-defined changes in floor levels, a bedroom entered only through another bedroom, and also includes a W.C. opening directly from a living room or kitchen."

(5) Natural Lighting. "There should be sufficient natural lighting in all rooms intended for sleeping, sitting or the consumption of meals to enable domestic work to be done without the use of artificial light under good weather conditions". (M.H.L.G. Circular, Appendix, para. 2.)

(6) Ventilation. "There should be adequate ventilation of all habitable rooms and working kitchens to the external air. For example, windows should be capable of being opened to such an extent that fresh air can readily circulate to all parts of the room. Windows, satisfactory in themselves, may be made unsatisfactory by external obstructions." (*Ibid.*) See also the comments on ventilation causing condensation, under (3) Dampness, above.

(7) Water Supply. "There must be an adequate and wholesome water supply within the house. Whilst one tap may be adequate a polluted supply would, and an intermittent supply could alone be a sufficiently serious defect to render the house unfit." (*Ibid.*) The supply need only be judged, however, for the purposes of domestic use: *Re Willesden Corporation and Municipal Mutual Insurance Ltd.'s Arbitration* [1944] 2 All E.R. 600.

(8) Drainage and Sanitary Conveniences. "There should be a readily accessible water closet for the exclusive use of the occupants of the dwelling in a properly lighted and

ventilated compartment . . . The water closet and bath or shower (if any) should be connected to an efficient disposal system, *i.e.* a public sewerage system, septic tank or cesspool capable of dealing with the normal discharge. There should be adequate means for the disposal of water from roof surfaces and yard pavings. Gutter and disposal pipes should be of a capacity capable of dealing with the normal discharge." (M.H.L.G. Circular 67/69, Appendix, paragraph 2.)

(9) Facilities for Preparation and Cooking of Food and Disposal of Waste Water. "There should be a sink, with an impervious surface, located beneath the piped water supply and connected to a suitable disposal system. There should be either a suitable fixed solid fuel or oil fired cooking appliance or provision for the installation of a gas or electric cooker. Generally the disposition of these facilities should make the preparation and cooking of food capable of being carried out in a convenient and hygenic manner." (*Ibid.*) The repeal by s.71, Housing Act 1969, of the former reference to food storage facilities was considered not to make any substantial difference to the operation of the provisions, in M.H.L.G. Circular 68/69, Appendix, paragraph 11.

Repairing obligations

Repairing obligations in short leases

11.—(1) In a lease to which this section applies (as to which, see sections 13 and 14) there is implied a covenant by the lessor—

  (*a*) to keep in repair the structure and exterior of the dwelling-house (including drains, gutters and external pipes),

  (*b*) to keep in repair and proper working order the installations in the dwelling-house for the supply of water, gas and electricity and for sanitation (including basins, sinks, baths and sanitary conveniences, but not other fixtures, fittings and appliances for making use of the supply of water, gas or electricity), and

  (*c*) to keep in repair and proper working order the installations in the dwelling-house for space heating and heating water.

(2) The covenant implied by subsection (1) ("the lessor's repairing covenant") shall not be construed as requiring the lessor—

  (*a*) to carry out works or repairs for which the lessee is liable by virtue of his duty to use the premises in a tenant-like manner, or would be so liable but for an express covenant on his part,

  (*b*) to rebuild or reinstate the premises in the case of destruction or damage by fire, or by tempest, flood or other inevitable accident, or

  (*c*) to keep in repair or maintain anything which the lessee is entitled to remove from the dwelling-house.

(3) In determining the standard of repair required by the lessor's repairing covenant, regard shall be had to the age, character and prospective life of the dwelling-house and the locality in which it is situated.

(4) A covenant by the lessee for the repair of the premises is of no effect so far as it relates to the matters mentioned in subsection (1)(*a*) to (*c*), except so far as it imposes on the lessee any of the requirements mentioned in subsection (2)(*a*) or (*c*).

(5) The reference in subsection (4) to a covenant by the lessee for the repair of the premises includes a covenant—

  (*a*) to put in repair or deliver up in repair,

  (*b*) to paint, point or render,

  (*c*) to pay money in lieu of repairs by the lessee, or

  (*d*) to pay money on account of repairs by the lessor.

(6) In a lease in which the lessor's repairing covenant is implied there is also implied a covenant by the lessee that the lessor, or any person authorised by him in writing, may at reasonable times of the day and on giving 24 hours' notice in writing to the occupier, enter the premises

comprised in the lease for the purpose of viewing their condition and state of repair.

DEFINITIONS
"dwelling house": s.16.
"lease": s.16.
"lessor": s.16.

GENERAL NOTE
This section derives from the well-known s.32, Housing Act 1961 (hence the provision in s.13 that it applies only to a lease or tenancy granted after October 24 1961). It remains the principal statutory repairing obligation (designed originally to replace s.6, Housing Act 1957, now s.8 of this Act). The burden imposed on landlords by this section is to maintain the structure and exterior of premises and also the installations for sanitation, water, electricity and gas. The obligation is "triggered" by the landlord's receipt of actual notice.

The term applies to all tenancies and leases for a term of less than seven years (see s.13, below), other than an assured tenancy within the provisions of Part II, Landlord and Tenant Act 1954: see s.32, below. It applies whether what is let is a whole building, or part only of a building (see s.16, below). The covenant does not extend so far as to make the landlord liable for works for which the tenant is responsible under the implied covenant to use the premises in a tenant like manner. Nor does it oblige the landlord to rebuild or reinstate the premises in the case of destruction or damage by fire, or by "tempest, flood or other inevitable accident" (subs. (2)(*b*)). While the provisions are as applicable to public sector as to other tenants, lettings *to* public landlords are outside the provisions: see s.14, below.

The section does not apply to licences: see notes to s.1, above. However if the repairing obligation under a licence lies upon the occupier, this may well be a good indication that what has been granted is in fact tenancy (*Addiscombe Garden Estate Ltd.* v. *Crabbe* [1958] 1 Q.B. 513, C.A.). Under a licence there will in any event be implied such terms as are necessary to give business efficacy to the contract, and the lack of legal interest in the property on the part of a licensee would suggest that placing an obligation on him to repair would normally run counter to good business sense if indeed not business efficacy see *The Moorcock* (1889) 14 P.D. 64; see also *Smith* v. *Nottinghamshire County Council, The Times*, Nov 13, 1981 C.A. and *Western Electric Ltd* v. *Welsh Development Agency* [1983] Q.B. 766. (Naturally these considerations would not be applicable where the disrepair is at the heart of the reason why the arrangement is licence only *i.e.* short-life licence of property scheduled for redevelopment, whether or not under Housing Act 1985, s.79 and Sched. 2, para. 3.)

Note that the section will cease to apply for a period, where an item of disrepair is subject to tenant's exercise of the "right to repair" under s.96, Housing Act 1985, and S.I. 1985 No. 1493; *see also* D.O.E. Circular 23/85.

Subs (1)
The covenant to "keep in repair" means an obligation to "put and keep in repair," for that which is not put into repair cannot be kept in repair. (see *Proudfoot* v. *Hart* (1890) 25 Q.B.D. 42 and *Liverpool City Council* v. *Irwin* [1977] A.C. 239, 13 H.L.R. 38, H.L.). There is no difference in principle in the interpretation of the covenant when implied by the statute from when it appears in a lease.

What is Repair?
It is necessary to bear in mind that the covenant concerns "repair." What is a repair has been the subject of much recent judicial consideration. The question is to be regarded as a question of fact and degree, having regard in particular to the cost of a particular job, relative to the value of the property: *Ravenseft Properties Ltd.* v. *Davstone Holdings Ltd.* [1980] Q.B. 12; see also *Smedley* v. *Chumley & Hawkes Ltd.* (1981) 261 E.G. 775, C.A., *Halliard Property Co. Ltd.* v. *Nicholas Clarke Investments Ltd.* (1983) 269 E.G. 1257, Q.B., and *Elmcroft Developments Ltd.* v. *Tankersley-Sawyer* (1984) 15 H.L.R. 63, C.A.

These recent cases have made a considerable impact in this area of the law. Until *Ravenseft*, it was thought that repair must always be distinguished from improvement, using the latter term to mean the provision of something different in quality, or in kind, from that which was demised under a lease or tenancy, and this was sometimes accompanied by, and sometimes assimilated into, another proposition, that to cure an inherent (*e.g.* design, construction) meant improvement rather than repair. Thus, classically, while damp might have to be treated as a repair, if premises lack a damp-proof course only a right to require improvement could be used to secure its installation, even where installation is the most modern, convenient, efficient or even economic means of treating the damp: *Pembery* v. *Lamdin* [1940] 2 All E.R. 434, C.A.

Similarly, it had been thought that if underpinning was needed to save an old house from falling down, and was the only means of preventing destruction of the house, such works would be works of improvement, and as such not qualifying as repair: *Sotheby* v. *Grundy* [1947] 2 All E.R. 761, *Collins* v. *Flynn* [1963] 2 All E.R. 1068, *Lurcott* v. *Wakeley* [1911] 1 K.B. 905, *Brew Brothers* v. *Snax (Ross) Ltd.*[1970] 1 Q.B. 612.

All of these older cases were reviewed in *Ravenseft*. Tenants were under an obligation to repair a block of flats, clad in stone, mounted on a concrete frame. As built, the construction lacked expansion joints, to retain the stone cladding once the frame expanded. In consequence, when expansion started, the stone cladding threatened to tumble from the frame. The fault was clearly a design fault.

As a professional proposition, no competent engineer would permit rectification of the fault without the introduction of expansion joints, even though to do so meant to introduce a modern method of construction. The court held that such works *could* be required by the repairing covenant. The court rejected the concept of "inherent defect" constituting improvement, or that works of construction could not fall within a repairing covenant. Each one of the earlier cases could be construed as a decision as to fact and degree. Of particular relevance is the question of cost of works, relative to value of property. Even if the works were done, it could not be said that the landlord's reversion was now in something different from that which had been demised.

It would now seem to be open, to refer back to the earlier cases, to consider the modern costs of a damp-proof course, or underpinning, and current value of premises. This line of argument derives much support from the second of the recent cases, *Smedley* v. *Chumley & Hawkes Ltd.* (1981) 261 E.G. 775, C.A. This case concerned a restaurant constructed at a river's edge. The restaurant was built on a raft, or pier. The pier lacked adequate underpinning. The restaurant was beginning to sink. The question was whether works could be required within the landlord's repairing obligation, and the Court of Appeal held that they could.

A distinction was here drawn between old houses, and new properties, and the approach adopted was that of construction of covenant in lease, *i.e.* construction in context, or intention. In *Elmcroft Developments Ltd.* v. *Tankersley-Sawyer* (1984) 15 H.L.R. 63, C.A., a county court finding that rising damp attributable to an ineffectual damp-proof course constituted a breach of a covenant to repair was upheld, even though the remedy found by the court to be necessary was replacement of the course by a different and modern method of protection.

The Court of Appeal followed *Ravenseft* in approaching the issue as one of fact and degree. Referring to *Pembery* v. *Lamdin* [1940] 2 All E.R. 434, the Court of Appeal considered it to be "of no assistance at all. It does not involve the letting of a flat. It involved a letting of premises that contained this cellar in a building which was built some 100 years before the court considered the problems. That must be round about 1840. We are concerned with a letting a few years ago of what was built as a separate self-contained flat and a flat in a high-class fashionable residential area in the centre of London. I entirely agree with what Forbes J. said in the *Ravenseft* case—'that this was a decision arrived at by considering the question as one of degree' . . . "

The Court of Appeal added, having regard to the test in subs. (3), and to the description of the premises by the county court judge, that the premises were "very probably unfit for any tenant." (" . . . Due to rising and penetrating damp the condition of this flat is appalling. It feels and smells very damp . . . She has been unable to use the living room since 1979 . . . The bedroom is exceptionally damp and she has to use an electric blanket constantly to keep the bed clothes dry and is unable to keep the majority of her clothing in that room; she is unable to put the hall area to any use now owing to its dampness . . . The lavatory, bathroom and kitchen are all badly affected by mainly rising damp . . .")

On the main point, the Court of Appeal cited *Lurcott* v. *Wakely* [1911] 1 K.B. 905, C.A. ("it follows that the question of repair is in every case one of degree, and the test is whether the act to be done is one which in substance is the renewal or replacement of defective parts, or the renewal or replacement of substantially the whole . . . " *per* Buckley L.J. at p.924), *Wates* v. *Rowland* [1952] 2 Q.B. 12 ("Between the two extremes, it seems to be largely a matter of degree, which in the ordinary case the county court judge would decide as a matter of fact, applying a common-sense, man-of-the-world view . . . " *per* Lord Evershed M.R. at p.23), and *Brew Bros. Ltd* v. *Snax (Ross) Ltd.* [1970] 1 Q.B. 612, C.A.

Ravenseft was also followed in *Halliard Property Co. Ltd.* v. *Nicholas Clarke Investments Ltd.* (1983) 269 E.G. 1257, Q.B.D. It was held, as a question of fact and degree, that a repairing obligation did not extend to a requirement to rebuild a back-addition warehouse or storehouse, at a cost representing more than a third of the cost of rebuilding the whole premises, although still a cost less than that for which the premises could be sold. The rebuilding of what was described as an "unstable jerry-built structure" would involve handing back on the expiry of the lease an entirely different edifice.

In another recent decision, however, *Pembery* was still being applied: *Wainwright* v. *Leeds City Council* (1984) 13 H.L.R. 117, C.A., decided under what is now this section. That case concerned a back-to-back terraced house in a poor part of Leeds, built in the early part of the century. It suffered from damp, some of which was attributable to the absence of a damp-proof course. The Court of Appeal decided that a house with a damp-proof course was a different "thing" from a house without, following *Pembery* as binding *as to* facts (as distinct from as to degree), and that accordingly the introduction of a damp-proof course did not fall within this section.

Neither *Ravenseft,* nor *Smedley,* nor *Halliard* was cited in *Wainwright*; nor, most relevantly, was *Elmcroft,* not only similar on its facts, but also a *prior* decision of the Court of Appeal (unlike *Ravenseft,* in the High Court)—*Elmcroft* was not, however, *reported* until shortly after judgment in *Wainwright. Wainwright* appears to have proceeded on an argument—which was unsurprisingly rejected—that in the construction of the covenant implied by this section, local authority landlords should be held to apply a higher standard than others. In *Quick* v. *Taff Ely Borough Council* [1985] 3 All E.R. 321, 18 H.L.R., C.A., the Court of Appeal accordingly did not consider that *Wainwright* affected the authority of the *Ravenseft* approach, and adopted *Ravenseft* instead.

Structure and Exterior

Disrepair has to be *to* the structure and exterior. In *Quick* v. *Taff Ely Borough Council* [1985] 3 All E.R. 321, 18 H.L.R., C.A., the Court of Appeal considered the problem of condensation caused by design or inherent defects: cold bridging from window lintels because no insulating material, sweating from single glazed metal windows, and inadequate heating both in respect of the system and of the occupier not maintaining a high enough thermostat setting. While not disapproving the *Ravenseft* line of cases, and even although the property was virtually unfit for human habitation in the winter months, it was held necessary to show that there is disrepair related to the *physical condition* of the structure and/or exterior, *e.g.* walls, windows; internal damage *resulting from* a condition not amounting to physical harm did not qualify within the implied covenant.

In another context (reduction of rateable value under Housing Act 1974, Sched. 8, for the purposes of Leasehold Reform Act 1967) the Court of Appeal has adopted a wide view of what is meant by "structural". It is something appertaining to the fabric of the building so as to be part of the complete whole. A house is a complete unity. Structure implies concern with the constituent or material parts of that unity. That involves more than the load bearing elements, such as walls, roof and foundations. Rather it is that which pertains to basic fabric and parts, as distinguished from decoration and fittings. See *Pearlman* v. *Keepers and Governors of Harrow School* [1979] 1 Q.B. 56 *per* Eveleigh L.J. at 79.

Exterior includes the partition wall between a house and the adjoining house (*Green* v. *Eales* (1841) 2 Q.B. 225; *Pembery* v. *Lamdin* [1940] 2 All E.R. 434. It does not include nearby premises or installations which are not demised (*Peters* v. *Prince of Wales Theatre (Birmingham)* [1943] K.B. 73).

Structure and exterior will include windows (although *cf.* subs. (2)(*a*), so that window breakages owing to tenant–default will not fall within the landlord's obligations): see *Ball* v. *Plummer, The Times*, June 17, 1879, *Boswell* v. *Crucible Steel Co.* [1925] 1 K.B. 119 and *Quick* v. *Taff Ely Borough Council* [1985] 3 All E.R. 321, 18 H.L.R., C.A., but *cf. Holiday Fellowship* v. *Hereford* [1959] 1 W.L.R. 211.

The phrase "structure and exterior" does not include the back yard of the house or means of access to the back yard: *Hopwood* v. *Cannock Chase D.C.* [1975] 1 W.L.R. 373; 13 H.L.R 31, C.A., but the essential means of access to the house is included in the "exterior" *Brown* v. *Liverpool Corporation* [1969] 3 All E.R. 1345; 13 H.L.R. 1, C.A.

In the case of a block of flats the implied covenant applies to anything which can be regarded as part of the structure or exterior of the particular flat, and not of the block as a whole: *Campden Hill Towers* v. *Gardner* [1977] Q.B. 823; 13 H.L.R. 64, C.A. The matter is to be determined with reference to the ordinary use of words, rather than to the question of what has been demised. Thus, the external wall of the block will not in itself form part of the structure and exterior of individual flats, but *parts* of it will form part of the structure and exterior of individual flats, just as the internal dividing walls, and floors and ceilings, will form part of the structure and exterior of flats.

"The paragraph applies to the outside wall or walls of the flat; the outside of inner party walls of the flat; the outer sides of horizontal divisions between . . . flats above and below;

the structural framework and beams directly supporting floors, ceilings and walls of the flat . . . " (*per* Megaw L.J. at p. 834).

Campden Hill Towers was followed in *Douglas-Scott* v. *Scorgie* [1984] 1 W.L.R. 716, 13 H.L.R. 97 (C.A.), in which it was held that the roof of a block of flats, or building converted into flats or other units, could constitute part of the exterior of a top floor flat or unit, even although it remained in the landlord's possession. The crucial question was held to be whether the roof of the premises would, in the ordinary use of words, be regarded as a part of the structure or of the exterior of the top floor flat, when that flat is regarded as a separate part of the building.

If the ceiling and roof of a particular top floor dwelling all form part of one inseparable, structural unit, prima facie the roof and ceiling would be regarded as part of the structure or exterior of that dwelling; on the other hand, it does not follow that the roof, or part of a roof, lying above *any* so-called top floor flat will necessarily fall within the term. In the instant case, the decision below had been on a preliminary point of law, that because the roof was within the landlord's possession and control, it would not fall within the phrase "structure or exterior," and the Court of Appeal accordingly remitted the matter to the county court for decision on the facts:

"In the present case we have been told that the roof of the plaintiff's flat is not a flat roof, that it has a valley gutter and that there is a gap between the roof and the ceiling of the flat . . . These points . . . may conceivably provide some ammunition for the [landlord] when he seeks to argue that the roof of these particular premises cannot, in the ordinary use of words, be regarded as part of the structure, or of the exterior, of this particular top floor flat . . . On the other hand, the [tenant] will no doubt argue that, notwithstanding these points, the roof is still an "essential integral part of the flat," viewed as a separate dwelling-house, to echo the words of Megaw L.J." (*per* Slade L.J.).

But in principle, the section does not apply to common parts so that *e.g.* a central heating boiler situated in the common parts is not within its ambit: *Campden Hill Towers*. Note, however, that in *Liverpool City Council* v. *Irwin* [1977] A.C. 239; 13 H.L.R. 38, H.L., it was held that a local authority owning multi-storey blocks of dwellings and retaining control of the common parts of the building were, by necessary implication, under an obligation to take reasonable care to maintain the common stairs and their lighting, the lifts and communal rubbish chutes in reasonable repair and that this obligation could only be avoided by express exclusion in the contract of letting.

Implied term was also held applicable—following *Liverpool City Council* v. *Irwin*—in *Gordon* v. *Selico* (1984) 275 E.G. 899, Ch.D., in which landlords failed to cure dry rot in the common parts of a house containing flats; it was considered, following *Booth* v. *Thomas* [1926] Ch. 397, that such a failure could also constitute breach of the covenant for quiet enjoyment.

Installations and Pipes

A landlord is not obliged to lag internal water pipes under this provision: *Wycombe Area Health Authority* v. *Barnett* (1982) 5 H.L.R. 840 C.A.

A pipe which is choked has been held to be out of repair (*Bishop* v. *Consolidation London Properties* (1933) 102 L.J.K.B. 257).

For a case of a local authority being held liable for damage from a burst water tank in a council house, see *Sheldon* v. *West Bromwich Corporation* (1973) 13 H.L.R. 23 C.A.

As regards "proper working order", even a design defect may be caught by the covenant: see *Liverpool City Council* v. *Irwin* (above) a case of a defective water cistern. Again the obligation to "keep" installations in repair and proper working order is to be construed as a covenant to "put and keep".

Notice

A landlord's liability to repair only arises after he has had notice or actual knowledge of a defect: *O'Brien* v. *Robinson* [1973] A.C. 912, 13 H.L.R. 7, H.L.; *Sheldon* v. *West Bromwich Corporation* (1973) 13 H.L.R. 23, C.A.; *Uniproducts (Manchester)* v. *Rose Furnishers* [1956] 1 W.L.R. 45; *Griffin* v. *Pillet* [1926] 1 K.B. 17. This is so even if the covenant to repair contains no requirement that the tenant first give notice of the disrepair *Makin* v. *Watkinson* (1870) L.R. 6E.24 *Torrens* v. *Walker* (1906) 2 Ch. 166.

However, this precondition of notice applies only to those premises or parts of premises demised to a tenant, and not in relation to those parts retained in the landlord's own possession and control (*Melles & Co.* v. *Holme* [1918] 2 K.B. 100, *Bishop* v. *Consolidation London Properties Ltd.* (1933) 102 L.J.K.B.).

The decision in *O'Brien* was described as "unfortunate" in *McGreal* v. *Wake* (1984) 13 H.L.R. 107, C.A., because it was said to penalise the conscientious landlord and reward the absentee. Notice need not be in writing, nor need it be given by the tenant to the landlord, so that liability can arise as a result of information given to the landlord by a third party, as in *McGreal* where liability was "triggered" by a notice under what is now s.189, Housing Act 1985. All that is needed is enough information as would put a reasonable man upon inquiry as to whether works of repair are needed: *O'Brien, Sheldon.*

The Master of the Rolls stressed in *McGreal's* case how important it is that tenants should notify their landlords of disrepair, observing that if the item in question was not the responsibility of the landlord no harm was done, while without notice no liability would arise. Notice can be given to an employee of the landlord. Thus, in *Sheldon*, notice by way of inspection by plumbers employed by the landlord authority was held adequate.

Compare the position under the Defective Premises Act 1972, s.4 where liability will arise if the landlord knew *or ought to have known* of the defect: see *Smith* v. *Bradford M.D.C.* (1982) 4 H.L.R. 86, C.A. Consider, too, the position at common law, in negligence, where the landlord has also designed and/or constructed the premises: *Rimmer* v. *Liverpool City Council* (1983) 12 H.L.R. 23, C.A.

The basis for the notice requirement is that the landlord does not have any other means of establishing whether or not there is disrepair. But it applies even if the landlord has the right of entry to inspect or repair, or the tenant has agreed that he may enter to inspect (*Morgan* v. *Liverpool Corporation* [1927] 2 K.B. 131; *McCarrick* v. *Liverpool Corporation* [1947] A.C. 219, H.L.). The requirement for notice applies even when the defects existed at the time of letting (*Uniproducts (Manchester)* v. *Rose Furnishers* [1956] 1 W.L.R. 45). The requirement applies even where the landlord is, and the tenant is not, in a position to establish whether or not there is a defect (*Hugall* v. *McLean* (1885) 53 L.T. 94). It applies in the case of a latent as well as a patent defect *Morgan* v. *Liverpool Corporation* (above).

What constitutes notice is a question of fact. Notification of a ceiling bulge was held to be enough notice of defect to found liability when the ceiling fell some eight months later in *Porter* v. *Jones* (1942) 112 L.J.K.B. 173. Discoloration of a water tank was enough to put a landlord on notice that works of repair were needed, even though the tank had not begun to weep: *Sheldon* v. *West Bromwich* (above). But a lapse of several years effectively vitiated the notice in *O'Brien* v. *Robinson* (above), although only in the context of some repairs having been carried out, and no further notice given thereafter.

The tenant is not, however, obliged to identify the degree or extent of disrepair, but must simply give enough information to put the landlord on enquiry and require him to follow the matter up: *Griffin* v. *Pillet* (above). Put another way, the landlord must have enough information about the existence of the defect as would put a reasonable man on enquiry as to whether repairs were needed. *O'Brien* v. *Robinson* (above); *Sheldon* v. *West Bromwich* (above).

There is no requirement that notice be in writing, although this is clearly evidentially preferable. Once notice has been given, liability arises, so that a change of ownership should make no difference to the tenant, the purchaser of the landlord's interest having recourse against the vendor to the extent that he administered appropriate enquiries and failed to receive satisfactory responses.

Damages

On the subject of damages for breach of a landlord's repairing covenant, see the recent review in *Calabar Properties Ltd.* v. *Stitcher* [1984] 1 W.L.R. 287, 11 H.L.R. 20, C.A. The case approved *Hewitt* v. *Rowlands* (1924) 93 L.J.K.B. 1080, that the correct calculation is of diminution in value of premises, for the purpose of putting the tenant in the position he would have been in had the breach not occurred. This will normally involve calculation of cost of alternative accommodation, cost of redecoration, and an amount of compensation for discomfort, inconvenience, ill-health, etc., will be added where appropriate, along with any special damages (which must be specifically pleaded).

Calabar concerned the tenant under a 99-year lease of a flat on the top floor of a block built by the plaintiffs during the 1960s. The defendant became the tenant by assignment in 1975, at which time she redecorated the flat. In January 1976, she was complaining of water penetration, and damage to the walls, following weeks of delay after a visit by the landlords' representative. The landlord took the view that dampness was caused by condensation, not water penetration, notwithstanding a report they had obtained which confirmed the tenant's complaints. Proceedings were issued by the landlords, and the tenant counterclaimed for breach of repairing obligation. On the issue of liability, the court found in favour of the tenant, from which finding there was no appeal.

The court below awarded damages to the tenant in two amounts: (*a*) £4,606.44 (cost of making good and redecorating interior of flat), plus 10 per cent. for supervision, plus VAT, making £6,909.67 in all; and (*b*) £3,000 for disappointment, discomfort, loss of enjoyment and bouts of ill-health suffered by the tenant's husband. The first sum had not been claimed by way of special damages, but was awarded, in the absence of acceptable evidence of diminution in value, as an appropriate alternative basis, when coupled to an order requiring external repairs to be carried out, on which to determine difference in value. This amount, however, was arrived at at first instance by reducing actual costs by an element of betterment.

In addition, the tenant claimed, but did not plead, and the court did not award, amounts for (c) rates, rents, running costs and service charges for the period when the flat was rendered uninhabitable by disrepair, and (d) a further sum for loss of use, based on reduction in capital value of lease, or alternatively reduction in rack rental value of lease. The court below rejected the second of these additional heads as too remote, and the first on the grounds that it was comparable to expenses incurred in taking alternative accom-modation, considered irrecoverable following *Green* v. *Eales* (1841) 2 Q.B. 225. The tenant appealed the refusal to award these sums, but did not appeal the reduction for betterment.

The Court of Appeal dismissed the appeal. It would have been open to the tenant to challenge the reduction for betterment, but she had not done so. The decision in *Green* v. *Eales* was confined to the facts of that case, or was not binding on the Court of Appeal, or was wrongly decided, and there is no principle that the costs of alternative accommodation cannot be claimed; however, the running costs had not been pleaded and quantified. The claim based upon diminution in capital or rack rental value had not been pleaded and quantified, and as the tenant had no intention of selling the property, such a basis for damages would be wholly unreal.

The correct approach was to seek to put the tenant in the position she would have been in if the landlords had performed their covenant to repair, and there was held to be no one set of rules as to how this should be calculated; in a case such as the present, damages should be awarded (a) for the cost of alternative accommodation while the premises were uninhabitable, (b) for the cost of redecorating, and (c) for discomfort, loss of enjoyment and ill-health. Any special damages must, however, be specifically pleaded.

Calabar was followed in *McGreal* v. *Wake* (1984) 13 H.L.R. 107, C.A. In that case, the plaintiff was the tenant of a house in disrepair. Between 1976 and 1977, she spent £1,172 on the house, and subsequently wrote asking the defendant to pay a share of this. It was, however, agreed that neither this nor dealings with the landlord's agent constituted notice of disrepair. But in November 1979, the local authority served notice under what is now the Housing Act 1985, s.189, requiring the execution of works, and this gave the landlord knowledge of defects, which defects fell within the provisions of this section.

As the landlord did not comply with the notice, the local authority carried out the works in default. They did not, however, clear up debris or clean up after the works had been done, or redecorate. The tenant was obliged to move her property into storage, and to take alternative accommodation for herself, while the works were being executed. She was able to move back in at the end of July 1980.

The tenant claimed damages for (a) disrepair between notice of defects and completion of works, (b) cost of alternative accommodation during works, (c) cost of storage, (d) work involved in clearing up after works, and (e) redecorating. Her action was dismissed on the grounds that the delay between November 1979 and the completion of works was negligible and that the landlord was not liable for incidental expenses. The tenant appealed.

The Court of Appeal allowed her appeal. The landlord was in breach from a reasonable period after receiving notice, which in the present case was from January 1, 1980. For some months from January 1, 1980, the tenant had to live in an unrepaired house and was entitled to damages therefor. A landlord's obligation to repair carries with it an obligation to make good any consequential damage to decorations; there should be no reduction of the plaintiff's reasonable expenditure on redecoration on the grounds of betterment, if as seemed to be the case the redecoration could not have been carried out without betterment. The tenant was also entitled to damages for her efforts in clearing up debris and cleaning the premises.

In addition, the tenant was entitled to damages for the cost of alternative accommodation, if the expenditure flowed from the landlord's breach of covenant (*Saner* v. *Bilton* (1978) 7 Ch.D. 815). A landlord's right of entry to carry out repairs pursuant to his obligations is limited to such entry and occupation as is strictly necessary in order to do the works of repair, which does not amount to an obligation to give him exclusive occupation, nor to permit him access to all parts of the house at the same time, unless either is essential.

In the present case, it did not seem to be necessary for the tenant to move out while works were done, but the works would have taken longer, and been more expensive, if she had remained in occupation. If the tenant had done the works herself, she would have been entitled to do them by moving herself and her furniture out, in mitigation of damage, and the position was no different where the local authority had caused the works to be executed;

she was, accordingly, entitled to damages for the costs of storage and alternative accommodation.

In *Bradley* v. *Chorley Borough Council* (1985) 17 H.L.R. 305, C.A., the Court of Appeal held that *McGreal* was as applicable where the landlord had not failed to carry out works after notice, but required a landlord to make good—or pay damages for failing to make good—internal decorations arising from works which had to be carried out (to wiring) in order to comply with their obligations under this section. A landlord, then, is always bound to make good damage consequential on compliance.

The court rejected a finding by the county court judge that the previous decorations had been almost non-existent, and did not accept that a covenant imposed on the tenant to maintain the property in a clean condition, or that a covenant for the tenant to be responsible for internal repairs, could extend to making good after landlord's works. The court also rejected a proposition in the court below that the tenant's rent arrears amounted to a forfeiture of his entitlement to rely on the section, although they could be taken into account in calculating damages.

In *McCoy & Co.* v. *Clark* (1982) 13 H.L.R. 87 (C.A.), the court was principally concerned with reduction in value. A flat was damp, on account of water penetration, and the tenant had been complaining since 1977. Repairs were not carried out until 1981. The property was in a worse state for the last two years of this period. The tenant would not seem to have been excluded from any part of the flat as a whole, *e.g.* one or more rooms.

The county court judge took the view that the tenant did not spend a great deal of time at home, and that the house was not of great importance to him, being used mainly as a place to sleep. The Court of Appeal did not accept this as a basis for calculating reduction in value: the tenant was entitled to the reduction in value calculated in proportion to that for which he was paying, *i.e.* as distinct from how he was using the flat. The award of 10 per cent. of the rent for the first two years, and 20 per cent. for the second two years, was considered "much too low," and was doubled in the Court of Appeal.

The Court of Appeal also doubled an award of £100 (reduced by 50 per cent. for contributory causation by tenant) to £200 (also reduced by 50 per cent.), for pneumonia, resulting in part from the conditions in the flat and leading to pain, about nine days in hospital, and five to six weeks feeling ill. The judge had been wrong to take into account that the tenant had a comfortable time in hospital: "I daresay he did: I daresay his hospital bed was more comfortable than that at his flat. . . . "

See further *Taylor* v. *Knowsley Borough Council* (1985) 17 H.L.R. 376, C.A., in which a tenant's appeal against an award of £159 in respect of (a) interruption to hot water supply for five months (£100), and (b) leaking bathroom ceiling for eight months (£59), was dismissed on the grounds that the amount was not "obviously wrong". The tenant was a young man with relations in the neighbourhood, but the Court of Appeal considered that different considerations might have applied if the tenant had a young family.

It has been held in the county court that no allowance should be made because premises may in any event have been let at less than market rental, *e.g.* because they are local authority lettings: *Devereux* v. *Liverpool C.C.* [1978] L.A.G. Bull. 266 C.C., *cf. Daftan* v. *Tully* [1978] L.A.G. Bull. 266 C.C. See also *Taylor* v. *Liverpool Corporation* [1939] 3 All E.R. 329: "The motive of the corporation . . . was wholly admirable, and *their* purpose . . . beneficent. I do not think, however, that the propriety of their motives can or does affect their legal liability." *per* Stable J. at 331.

A tenant is entitled to claim damages on behalf of himself and those others, *e.g.* family, for whose benefit the contract of tenancy was made: *Jackson* v. *Horizon Holidays* [1975] 1 W.L.R. 1468, C.A. The tenant can also claim for loss of enjoyment, disappointment, distress, inconvenience and unfulfilled expectations: *Jarvis* v. *Swan Tours* (1973) 1 Q.B. 233, C.A. The application of these principles, developed in cases involving holidays, to the law of landlord and tenant was specified in the case of *McCall* v. *Abelesz* [1976] Q.B. 585, C.A.

In some cases, a tenant will, having given his landlord notice of breach, go ahead and execute works in default himself, withholding rent on account. In such circumstances, he will wish to allege that he has set-off such expenditure against his rent, and defend any subsequent action for rent arrears on this basis. A tenant is entitled to discharge his landlord's obligations in this way, provided the obligation has arisen, *e.g.* provided notice has been given: *Lee-Parker* v. *Izzett* [1971] 1 W.L.R. 1688. It is considered a significant element of such an action, although probably not an essential prerequisite, that the tenant warn the landlord that if he does not comply with his covenants, he proposes to proceed in this way: *Asco Developments Ltd.* v. *Lowes, Lewis & Gordon* [1978] L.A.G. Bull. 293, Ch.D. The set-off may be against not only future rents, but also against rent arrears already accrued. (*ibid.*)

It is of the essence of set-off, however, that the nature of the matter giving rise to the landlord's liability be directly connected with the nature of the matter giving rise to the landlord's claims (*The Teno* [1977] 2 Lloyd's Rep. 289), so that the set-off could not be used because the landlord had acquired liability against his tenant in some matter unrelated to, or unconnected with, the tenancy. But subject to this, set-off is available "where the party seeking the benefit of it can show some equitable ground for being protected against his adversary's demands": *Rawson* v. *Samuel* (1841) 1 Cr. & Ph. 161.

Until recently, it was thought that such proceeding could only be applied to quantified sums, either directly expended on discharge of the landlord's covenants, or, at the most, quantified sums expended in consequence of the breach: *Hanak* v. *Green* [1958] 2 Q.B. 9. It would appear, however, that the older authorities which seem to achieve this effect (*Taylor* v. *Beal* (1591) Cro. Eliz. 222; *Waters* v. *Weigall* (1795) 2 Anst. 575) are not to be so considered, and that even unquantified sums may be set-off against rent owing, and stand as a defence to an action for rent arrears: *British Anzani (Felixstowe) Ltd.* v. *International Marine Management (U.K.) Ltd.* [1980] Q.B. 137; *Melville* v. *Grapelodge Developments* (1978) 254 E.G. 1193.

It also used to be thought that a claim for unquantified damages could only be used to confront an action for rent arrears, by way of counterclaim: *Hart* v. *Rogers* [1916] 1 K.B. 646; *Taylor* v. *Webb* [1937] 2 K.B. 283. It now appears to be accepted that the distinction is artificial, and anachronistic, and that fair dealing between parties (*Federal Commerce and Navigation Co. Ltd.* v. *Molena Alpha Incorporated* [1978] Q.B. 927) entitles the tenant both to set-off quantified sums, whether consequential on the breach, or expended in discharge of the landlord's obligations, and unquantified general damages for the breach: *British Anzani (Felixstowe) Ltd.* v. *International Marine Management (U.K.) Ltd.; Melville* v. *Grapelodge Developments.* A counterclaim may, however, be necessary or advisable, if the amount of damages, whether quantified or unquantified, is, or even may be, in excess of the amount claimed in rent arrears.

Subs. (2)

"tenant like manner." See *Warren* v. *Keen* [1954] 1 Q.B. 15, C.A., as to the tenant's obligation to avoid or repair wilful or negligent damage and to do the minor acts necessary to keep the premises in a reasonable state:

"It can, I think, best be shown by some illustrations. The tenant must take proper care of the place. He must, if he is going away for the winter, turn off the water and empty the boiler. He must clean the chimneys, when necessary, and also the windows. He must mend the electric light when it fuses. He must unstop the sink when it is blocked by his waste. In short, he must do the little jobs about the place which a reasonable tenant would do. In addition, he must, of course not damage the house, wilfully or negligently; and he must see that his family and guests do not damage it: and if they do, he must repair it. But apart from such things, if the house falls into disrepair through fair wear and tear or lapse of time, or for any reason not caused by him, then the tenant is not liable to repair it."

In *Wycombe Area Health Authority* v. *Barnett* (1982) 5 H.L.R. 84, C.A., a tenant who left the house during a cold spell, without turning off the stop-cock and draining the system, without leaving the house heated, and knowing that water pipes were unlagged, was held not to have failed to use the premises in a tenant-like manner. The distinction is between leaving the house for the winter, as in *Warren* v. *Keen,* and for a relatively short period.

Subs. (3)

The standard of repair required is to be determined having regard to the age, character and prospective life of the property, and the locality in which it is situated. The phrase "age, character and locality" is derived from *Proudfoot* v. *Hart* (1890) 25 Q.B.D. 42; see also *Jacquin* v. *Holland* [1960] 1 W.L.R. 258. The phrase "prospective life" was considered in *London Borough of Newham* v. *Patel* (1978) 13 H.L.R. 77, C.A., in which the Court of Appeal upheld the finding of the county court that there was no breach of this section even though the property in question was—or appeared to be—unfit for human habitation (see s.10 above) having regard to the likely future of the property.

But the appropriate criteria will be the age, character and locality at the commencement of the tenancy, rather than the time of action: *Calthorpe* v. *McOscar* [1924] 1 K.B. 716. There is no reason for construing this covenant in such a way as to impose a higher obligation on a local authority landlord than on a private landlord: *Wainwright* v. *Leeds C.C.* (1984) 13 H.L.R. 117, C.A.

Subs. (4)

When the section applies to a tenancy, the landlord has the right to enter, himself or through any person authorised by him in writing, after giving not less than 24 hours' notice in writing to the occupier, at reasonable times of the day, to view the condition of the premises and their state of repair.

In addition to the statutory provision, a right or duty to repair carries with in an implied licence to enter and do the works involved, for such reasonable time as they may take: *Saner* v. *Bilton* (1878) 7 Ch.D. 815. The right is subject to a requirement that the landlord give notice of his intention so to enter: *Granada Theatres* v. *Freehold Investment (Leyton-stone)* [1959] 1 W.L.R. 570. A tenant who refuses permission to his landlord so to enter will be unable to take action over the breach: *ibid.*

The landlord's right of entry to carry out repairs pursuant to his obligations is, however, limited to such entry and occupation as is strictly necessary in order to do the works of repair, which does not amount to an obligation to give him exclusive occupation, nor to permit him access to all parts of the house at the same time, unless either is essential: *McGreal* v. *Wake* (1984) 13 H.L.R. 107, C.A.

Specific Performance
See as to this, s.17, below.

Restriction on contracting out of s.11

12.—(1) A covenant or agreement, whether contained in a lease to which section 11 applies or in an agreement collateral to such a lease, is void in so far as it purports—

> (*a*) to exclude or limit the obligations of the lessor or the immunities of the lessee under that section, or
>
> (*b*) to authorise any forfeiture or impose on the lessee any penalty, disability or obligation in the event of his enforcing or relying upon those obligations or immunities,

unless the inclusion of the provision was authorised by the county court.

(2) The county court may, by order made with the consent of the parties, authorise the inclusion in a lease, or in an agreement collateral to a lease, of provisions excluding or modifying in relation to the lease, the provisions of section 11 with respect to the repairing obligations of the parties if it appears to the court that it is reasonable to do so, having regard to all the circumstances of the case, including the other terms and conditions of the lease.

DEFINITIONS
"lease": s.16.
"lessee": s.16.
"lessor": s.16.

GENERAL NOTE
Contracting out of s.11 is normally ineffective, but the county court has power, on the joint application of both parties to the tenancy, to authorise contracting-out. This power is only to be used if it appears reasonable to the court, having regard to the other terms and conditions of the lease or tenancy, and to all other circumstances of the case. Unless the county court exercises its discretion to authorise contracting out, any term of the lease or tenancy which is contrary to the effect of the provisions, is void. Nor can the landlord evade the effect of the provisions by imposing any fine or charge in relation to items contained in the covenant.

See also note on "right repair" in General Note to s.11, above.

Leases to which s.11 applies: general rule

13.—(1) Section 11 (repairing obligations) applies to a lease of a dwelling-house granted on or after 24th October 1961 for a term of less than seven years.

(2) In determining whether a lease is one to which section 11 applies—

> (*a*) any part of the term which falls before the grant shall be left out of account and the lease shall be treated as a lease for a term commencing with the grant,

(*b*) a lease which is determinable at the option of the lessor before the expiration of seven years from the commencement of the term shall be treated as a lease for a term of less than seven years, and

(*c*) a lease (other than a lease to which paragraph (*b*) applies) shall not be treated as a lease for a term of less than seven years if it confers on the lessee an option for renewal for a term which, together with the original term, amounts to seven years or more.

(3) This section has effect subject to—

section 14 (leases to which section 11 applies: exceptions), and

section 32(2) (provisions not applying to tenancies within Part II of the Landlord and Tenant Act 1954).

DEFINITIONS

"dwelling house": s.16.
"lease": s.16.
"lessee": s.16.
"lessor": s.16.

GENERAL NOTE

This section applies the provisions of s.11 to tenancies of a dwelling house, granted after the passing of the Housing Act 1961 for terms of less than seven years, but note the exclusion of assured tenancies, by s.32, below. The reference to October 24, 1961, is to the commencement of the Housing Act 1961, when what is now s.11 was first introduced. See also s.14, below, for "second" leases and other exclusions.

A lease which is determinable by the lessor in less than seven years is treated as a lease for less than seven years, but conversely where the lessee has an option for a renewal which will bring the total term to seven years or more, the lease is not for less than seven years and the term is not implied.

In *Brikom Investments* v. *Seaford* [1981] 1 W.L.R. 863, 1 H.L.R. 21, C.A., it was held: (a) delivery of a lease at a later date (from which date there was less than seven years to run) did not stop the exclusion of s.11—time runs from the date when the tenant is legally entitled to take up occupation under the lease or agreement for the lease (see also *Roberts* v. *Church Commissioners for England* [1972] 1 Q.B. 278); but (b) the landlord was estopped from denying the applicability of s.11 where the rent officer had registered a rent on the assumption that it applied, which registration had not been rectified or challenged, so that the landlord had been receiving rent at the (higher) level which accounted for its putative repairing obligation.

The decision means that where a tenancy entered into before October 24, 1961, has been subject to a rent registration on the assumption that s.11 applies, such a tenancy will also now fall within the scope of these statutory provisions, unless or until the landlord applies for rectification of the register.

In *Cottage Holiday Associates Ltd.* v. *Customs & Excise Commissioners* [1983] 1 Q.B. 735 construing the period of tenancy in a "time share" agreement it was held that there was a distinction between the 80-year lease creating the interest and the interest itself which was merely for 80 one week periods and that it was within the contemplation of the legislature that s.11 might be applicable to such an interest.

By s.15 the county court has jurisdiction to make a declaration as to the applicability/non-applicability of s.11 whether or not other relief is sought and whatever the rateable value of the property.

See also note on "right to repair" in General Note to s.11 above.

Leases to which s.11 applies: exceptions

14.—(1) Section 11 (repairing obligations) does not apply to a new lease granted to an existing tenant, or to a former tenant still in possession, if the previous lease was not a lease to which section 11 applied (and, in the case of a lease granted before 24th October 1961, would not have been if it had been granted on or after that date).

(2) In subsection (1)—

"existing tenant" means a person who is when, or immediately before, the new lease is granted, the lessee under another lease of the dwelling-house;

"former tenant still in possession" means a person who—

(*a*) was the lessee under another lease of the dwelling-house which terminated at some time before the new lease was granted, and

(*b*) between the termination of that other lease and the grant of the new lease was continuously in possession of the dwelling-house or of the rents and profits of the dwelling-house; and

"the previous lease" means the other lease referred to in the above definitions.

(3) Section 11 does not apply to a lease of a dwelling-house which is a tenancy of an agricultural holding within the meaning of the Agricultural Holdings Act 1948.

(4) Section 11 does not apply to a lease granted on or after 3rd October 1980 to—

a local authority,

a new town corporation,

an urban development corporation,

the Development Board for Rural Wales,

a registered housing association,

a co-operative housing association, or

an educational institution or other body specified, or of a class specified, by regulations under section 8 of the Rent Act 1977 (bodies making student lettings).

(5) Section 11 does not apply to a lease granted on or after 3rd October 1980 to—

(*a*) Her Majesty in right of the Crown (unless the lease is under the management of the Crown Estate Commissioners), or

(*b*) a government department or a person holding in trust for Her Majesty for the purposes of a government department.

DEFINITIONS

"co-operative housing association": s.38.
"dwelling house": s.16.
"lease": s.16.
"lessor": s.16.
"lessee": s.16.
"local authority": s.38.
"new town corporation": s.38.
"registered housing association": s.38.
"urban development corporation": s.38.

GENERAL NOTE

This section contains three types of exemption: (a) exemption for former tenants whose tenancies were not within s.11 (subss. (1)–(2)), (b) tenancies of agricultural holdings (subs. (3)), and (c) tenancies *to* public bodies (subss. (4)–(5)).

Subss. (1), (2).

A tenant under a lease to which s.11 did not apply, who at the coming to an end of that lease becomes a tenant under a new lease to which s.11 would otherwise have applied is deemed not to take a lease to which s.11 will apply. The subsection applies as an exception whether the new lease is granted immediately on the determination of the previous lease or whether the old lease determined at some time prior to the grant of the new lease, as long as the tenant has remained in possession in the interval. However, this is not so if the sole reason why the former tenancy was not subject to s.11 is that it was granted prior to October 24, 1961.

Subss. (4)–(5)

The purpose of these provisions is to enable public or quasi-public landlords to *take* tenancies of property scheduled for development for subletting on "short-life" licences. The reference to October 3, 1980, is to the date when the relevant provisions of the Housing Act 1980, which introduced this class of exception, commenced. Occupiers under such agreements will not be secure tenants within Pt. IV, Housing Act 1985: see s.79 and Sched. 1, para. 3, thereof. The reference to educational institutions specified is to regulations under which certain bodies can be exempted from the provisions of the Rent Act 1977, in order to let to students: see Rent Act 1977, s.8, and S.I.s 1974 No. 1366 and 1976 No. 905.

Jurisdiction of county court

15. The county court has jurisdiction to make a declaration that section 11 (repairing obligations) applies, or does not apply, to a lease—
  (*a*) whatever the net annual value of the property in question, and
  (*b*) notwithstanding that no other relief is sought than a declaration.

GENERAL NOTE
  This provision is additional to County Courts Act 1984, s.22, which permits application to the county court for a declaration, notwithstanding that no other relief is sought, which relates to the use, enjoyment, possession or occupation of land, but is limited to property within the rateable value jurisdiction of the county court for the time being.

Meaning of "lease" and related expressions

16. In sections 11 to 15 (repairing obligations in short leases)—
  (*a*) "lease" does not include a mortgage term;
  (*b*) "lease of a dwelling-house" means a lease by which a building or part of a building is let wholly or mainly as a private residence, and "dwelling-house" means that building or part of a building;
  (*c*) "lessee" and "lessor" mean, respectively, the person for the time being entitled to the term of a lease and to the reversion expectant on it.

GENERAL NOTE
  As to dwelling-house, see also notes to s.38, below.

Specific performance of landlord's repairing obligations

17.—(1) In proceedings in which a tenant of a dwelling alleges a breach on the part of his landlord of a repairing covenant relating to any part of the premises in which the dwelling is comprised, the court may order specific performance of the covenant whether or not the breach relates to a part of the premises let to the tenant and notwithstanding any equitable rule restricting the scope of the remedy, whether on the basis of a lack of mutuality or otherwise.
  (2) In this section—
  (*a*) "tenant" includes a statutory tenant,
  (*b*) in relation to a statutory tenant the reference to the premises let to him is to the premises of which he is a statutory tenant,
  (*c*) "landlord", in relation to a tenant, includes any person against whom the tenant has a right to enforce a repairing covenant, and
  (*d*) "repairing covenant" means a covenant to repair, maintain, renew, construct or replace any property.

DEFINITIONS
  "dwelling": s.38.
  "landlord": s.36.
  "statutory tenant": s.37.
  "tenant": s.36.

GENERAL NOTE
  This provision is not confined to the repairing obligations statutorily implied under this Act (ss.8, 11). It applies to *any* repairing obligation in *any* tenancy (other than one to which Pt. II, Landlord and Tenant Act 1954 applies (see s.32), which includes an assured tenancy

under s.56 Housing Act 1980, see *ibid.* s.58. Note the wide definition of repairing obligation contained in subs. (2). See also distinction between repair and improvement in notes to s.11, above. But note, too, the extension to parts of premises not even let to the tenant, *i.e.* common parts (also see notes to s.11, above).

Since the introduction of this provision by Housing Act 1974, s.125, there has ceased to be any practical distinction to be drawn between an order for specific performance of the landlord's repairing covenant, and a mandatory injunction compelling him to comply, so that a review of the technical limitations on the latter remedy should be superfluous. Specific performance was in any event available against a landlord (*Jeune* v. *Queen's Cross Properties* [1974] Ch. 97).

The remedy is available, even if the landlord can show want of financial capacity to comply (*Francis* v. *Cowcliffe* (1976) 239 E.G. 977). The remedy is available in the county court if the property is within the rateable values for the time being: County Courts Act 1984 s.22. The remedy remains available, even if there has been a forfeiture and proceedings for relief are pending, as the covenants in the lease are still potentially good: *Peninsular Maritime Ltd.* v. *Padseal Ltd.* (1981) 259 E.G. 860.

Where the landlord cannot be found, it may be possible for a receiver to be appointed, to fulfil his obligations, by application to the High Court. In *Hart* v. *Emelkirk* [1983] 1 W.L.R. 1289, 9 H.L.R. 114, Ch.D., the defendants claimed to have disposed of their interest in a mansion block, and for two or three years, no efforts had been made to collect rent or to perform repairing or service obligations, resulting in serious deterioration and damp, threatening reasonably comfortable occupation.

In the course of action to compel the defendants to comply with the landlord's covenants, the plaintiff tenants successfully issued motions to appoint a named receiver to receive the rents and profits, and to manage the properties in accordance with the rights and obligations of the freeholders, until trial or further order. The order was made under the Supreme Court Act 1981, s.37: "The High Court may by Order (whether interlocutory or final) . . . appoint a receiver in all cases in which it appears to the court to be just and convenient to do so . . . "

Hart was followed in *Daiches* v. *Bluelake Investments Ltd.* (1985) 17 H.L.R. 543, Ch.D., in the appointment of a receiver and manager of a block of flats which had fallen into a dangerous structural condition which needed urgent works, which the landlord, in breach of the covenants under the leases, was refusing to carry out. The important point of distinction is that the landlord in *Hart* had simply walked out and was not even collecting the rents, while in the present case, the landlord was collecting rents and performing some of his duties, and some of them well. Nevertheless, in view of the urgency of the repairs and the lack of any possible prejudice to the landlord, it was just and convenient to appoint a receiver under s.37(1), Supreme Court Act 1981.

In *Parker* v. *Camden London Borough Council, Newman* v. *Camden London Borough Council* (1985) 17 H.L.R. 380, C.A., however, the Court of Appeal refused applications by tenants for receiving orders against the authority, when hot water and heating were not working because the authority's boilermen were on strike and the authority were not willing to employ private contractors for fear of escalating the industrial dispute.

Following *Gardner* v. *London Chatham and Dover Railway Co. (No.1)* [1867] 2 Ch.App. Cas. 201, the Court of Appeal held that when Parliament expressly conferred powers and duties and responsibilities on particular bodies, it was improper for the court by the appointment of a receiver or manager to assume those powers and duties. In this case, management powers were conferred by statute (then, Housing Act 1957, now, Housing Act 1985) on the authority. The Court of Appeal did, however, in the exceptional circumstances of the case, grant mandatory injunctions.

In *Regan & Blackburn Ltd.* v. *Rogers* [1985] 2 All E.R. 180, Ch.D., it was held that an action for breach of a landlord's repairing obligations, even if coupled to a claim for an order for specific performance to carry out repairs, is not a "pending land action" within s.17, Land Charges Act 1972, because it does not amount to an interest in land, merely an action to enforce contractual obligations; accordingly it cannot be protected by entry of a caution in the Land Registry.

Service charges

Meaning of "service charge" and "relevant costs"

18.—(1) In the following provisions of this Act "service charge" means an amount payable by a tenant of a flat as part of or in addition to the rent—

(*a*) which is payable, directly or indirectly, for services, repairs, maintenance or insurance or the landlord's costs of management, and

(*b*) the whole or part of which varies or may vary according to the relevant costs.

(2) The relevant costs are the costs or estimated costs incurred or to be incurred by or on behalf of the landlord, or a superior landlord, in connection with the matters for which the service charge is payable.

(3) For this purpose—

(*a*) "costs" includes overheads, and

(*b*) costs are relevant costs in relation to a service charge whether they are incurred, or to be incurred, in the period for which the service charge is payable or in an earlier or later period.

DEFINITIONS

"flat": s.30.

"landlord": s.30.

"tenant": s.30.

GENERAL NOTE

This section defines the "service charges" which are to be the subject of protection in the following sections (down to and including s.30). Service charges are only protected under this Act in respect of a *flat*, defined in s.30 to mean a separate set of premises, forming part of a building, divided horizontally from some other part of the building, and constructed or adapted for use for a dwelling, and occupied wholly or mainly as a private dwelling. There is *some* protection against analogous charges in respect of *houses*, under Housing Act 1985, ss.45–51, and applicable where the house in question was formerly owned by a "public sector authority" within *ibid.*, s.45(6) (including a registered housing association).

Public sector *tenants,* as opposed to long leaseholders and owners, are exempt from the provisions of this series of sections (see s.26, below), but otherwise, those who have exercised the "right to buy" under Part V, Housing Act 1985, in respect of a flat will (with the exception of s.25, below, making failure to comply with certain of these provisions a criminal offence) be as much within this protection as any other leaseholder. Private sector tenants will be within this protection, *unless* there is a rent registered by the Rent Officer, *and* that rent is *not* a "variable" rent, *i.e.* variable with the cost of services: see s.27, below. There is no provision limiting the application of this protection by reference to length of lease, so that even a statutory tenant may be included: see s.30, below.

Prior to Housing Act 1980, Sched. 19, which this series of sections replaces, service charge protection (Housing Finance Act 1972, as amended by Housing Act 1974) did not permit the landlord to recover costs of management. Note, however, that the word used is "costs," not "charges," which seems to mean that no element of profit to the landlord can be built into those costs: *Regis Property Co.* v. *Dudley* [1958] 1 Q.B. 346, affirmed [1959] A.C. 370, H.L.

See also *Russell* v. *Laimond Properties Ltd.* (1983) 269 E.G. 947: "In my judgment, in both the lease and the schedule, cost means cost; that is to say money laid out and does not mean lost revenue or income, whether it be gross or not, which is foregone. But, cost, in the sense that I take it to mean, money laid out, might well include either interest paid or a reasonable return on the capital employed . . . " It was held in that case that "annual rental value" of a flat provided to a resident porter was not the right method for determining the costs, *inter alia,* of the porter's services.

It must be remembered that this definition of service charge does not give a right to recover in respect of all of the matters referred to, *additional* to rights in the lease, *i.e.* the landlord's entitlement starts with the lease. In *Embassy Court Residents Association Ltd.* v. *Lipman* (1984) 271 E.G. 545, C.A., an entitlement to charge for management costs was implied, although the case was one of a Management Company (the residents' association,) with an intervening leasehold interest. The same would not seem to follow in the case of an "ordinary" landlord's interest, where "no doubt . . . it is necessary for the landlord to spell out specifically in the terms of the lease, and in some detail a sufficient description of every financial obligation imposed upon the tenant in addition to the tenant's obligation for rent . . . "

Where the terms of a lease or tenancy are no longer relevant, because the relevant premises have undergone major alterations, the courts have asserted a power—independently of the provisions considered below—to fix charges that are "fair and reasonable" (see *Pole*

Properties Ltd. v. *Feinberg* (1981) 43 P. & C.R. 121, C.A., see also *O'May* v. *City of London Real Property* [1983] 2 A.C. 736, H.L.).

The words "subject to the lessee paying" a service charge do not mean that payment is a condition precedent to the landlord's obligations: *Yorkbrook Investments Ltd.* v. *Batten* (1985) 276 E.G. 545, 18 H.L.R., C.A. Note that a covenant by the landlord to provide a supply of hot water and/or heating will require him to replace obsolete or antiquated and unserviceable equipment, for it is the *supply* which must be maintained: *ibid.*

Limitation of service charges: reasonableness

19.—(1) Relevant costs shall be taken into account in determining the amount of a service charge payable for a period—

(*a*) only to the extent that they are reasonably incurred, and

(*b*) where they are incurred on the provision of services or the carrying out of works, only if the services or works are of a reasonable standard;

and the amount payable shall be limited accordingly.

(2) Where a service charge is payable before the relevant costs are incurred, no greater amount than is reasonable is so payable, and after the relevant costs have been incurred any necessary adjustment shall be made by repayment, reduction or subsequent charges or otherwise.

(3) An agreement by the tenant of a flat (other than an arbitration agreement within the meaning of section 32 of the Arbitration Act 1950) is void in so far as it purports to provide for a determination in a particular manner, or on particular evidence, of any question—

(*a*) whether costs incurred for services, repairs, maintenance, insurance or management were reasonably incurred,

(*b*) whether services or works for which costs were incurred are of a reasonable standard, or

(*c*) whether an amount payable before costs are incurred is reasonable.

(4) A county court may make a declaration—

(*a*) that any such costs were or were not reasonably incurred,

(*b*) that any such services or works are or are not of a reasonable standard, or

(*c*) that any such amount is or is not reasonable,

notwithstanding that no other relief is sought in the proceedings.

DEFINITIONS
"flat": s.30.
"relevant costs": s.18.
"service charge": s.18.
"tenant": s.30.

GENERAL NOTE
This is the principal, substantive protection afforded in respect of service charges: they are only recoverable to the extent that they are reasonable and only so far as works or services are to a reasonable standard. As to additional protection by way of prior estimates for building works above specified levels, see s.20, below; as to obtaining information about how service charges are calculated, see s.21, below; as to exemptions for (a) public tenants, and (b) protected and statutory tenants under the Rent Act 1977 whose rents are registered with a fixed, as distinct from variable, service element, see ss.26, 27.

Subs. (1)
Sub-para. (*b*) is similar to the common law test discussed in *Re Davstone Estates Ltd's Lease* [1969] 2 Ch. 378, and *Finchbourne Ltd.* v. *Rodrigues* [1976] 3 All E.R. 581, C.A. In *Parkside Knightsbridge Ltd.* v. *Horwitz* (1983) 268 E.G. 49 (C.A.) decided under the Housing Finance Act 1972 provisions (*cf.* notes to s.18, above), which also required that charges be reasonable, evidence was admitted of quotations for services from other agents. When the county court judge misunderstood or wrongly applied or adapted such evidence, the landlords were accordingly able successfully to appeal. To assist in the interpretation of these provisions, the county court is given a specific jurisdiction to make declarations in relation to them, even though no other relief is sought in the proceedings (subs. (4)).

If works or services are not to a reasonable standard, a proportionate deduction may be applied; the wording does not require an "all or nothing" approach: *Yorkbrook Investments Ltd.* v. *Batten* (1985) 276 E.G. 545, 18 H.L.R., C.A. The court should not ignore inadequate or non-provision on a *de minimis* approach save in exceptional circumstances, for though small in quantum, the matter may be of considerable importance to the tenants: *ibid.*

Subs. (2)

This was designed to overturn the effect of *Frobisher* (*Second Investments*) *Ltd.* v. *Kiloran Trust Co. Ltd.* [1980] 1 W.L.R. 425, Ch.D, that a service charge could only be levied in respect of work, the cost—or, possibly, the liability for the cost—of which had already been incurred. A reasonable charge may now be recovered before the costs are incurred, but only to a reasonable amount, and subject to a requirement for adjustment after the expenditure has been incurred.

Subs. (3)

S.32 Arbitration Act 1950 requires that an arbitration agreement must be in writing and provide that present or future differences will be referred to arbitration. The parties must have bilateral rights of reference in the provided manner (*Baron* v. *Sutherland Corp.* [1966] 2 Q.B. 56). There must be an intention to hold a judicial inquiry in a judicial manner to settle differences as distinct from a forum to prevent differences from arising (*Re Hammond and Waterton* (1890) 62 L.T. 808).

Subs. (4)

As an alternative and in addition to any agreement for arbitration the parties may refer disputes to the county court for a declaration whether or not other relief is sought in the action (*cf.* notes to s.15, above).

Limitation of service charges: estimates and consultation

20.—(1) Where relevant costs incurred on the carrying out of works on a building exceed the limit specified in subsection (2), the excess shall not be taken into account in determining the amount of a service charge unless—

    (*a*) the requirements of subsection (3) as to estimates and consultation have been complied with, or

    (*b*) those requirements have been dispensed with by the court in accordance with subsection (5);

and the amount payable shall be limited accordingly.

(2) The limit is whichever is the greater of—

    (*a*) £25, or such other amount as may be prescribed by order of the Secretary of State, multiplied by the number of flats in the building, or

    (*b*) £500, or such other amount as may be so prescribed.

(3) The requirements are:—

    (*a*) At least two estimates for the works shall be obtained, one of them from a person wholly unconnected with the landlord.

    (*b*) A notice accompanied by a copy of the estimates shall be given to each of the tenants concerned or shall be displayed in the buildings so as to be likely to come to the notice of all those tenants; and, if there is a recognised tenants' association for the building, the notice and copy of the estimates shall also be given to the secretary of the association.

    (*c*) The notice shall describe the works to be carried out and invite observations on them and on the estimates and shall state the name and the address in the United Kingdom of the person to whom the observations may be sent and the date by which they are to be received.

    (*d*) The date stated in the notice shall not be earlier than one month after the date on which the notice is given or displayed as required by paragraph (*b*).

    (*e*) The landlord shall have regard to any observations received in pursuance of the notice; and unless the works are urgently required they shall not be begun earlier than the date specified in the notice.

(4) For the purposes of subsection (3) the tenants concerned are all the landlord's tenants of flats in the building by whom a service charge is payable to which the costs of the proposed works are relevant.

(5) In proceedings relating to a service charge the court may, if satisfied that the landlord acted reasonably, dispense with all or any of the requirements of subsection (3).

(6) An order under this section—

(*a*) may make different provision with respect to different cases or descriptions of case, including different provision for different areas, and

(*b*) shall be made by statutory instrument which shall be subject to annulment in pursuance of a resolution of either House of Parliament.

DEFINITIONS

"flat": s.30.

"landlord": s.30.

"service charge": s.18.

"tenant": s.30.

"tenants' association": s.29.

GENERAL NOTE

The protection afforded by this section is more specific than the last. It is, of course, the cost of building works that causes the most potential difficulty. Even though they may be "relevant", and even though the works may have been carried out to a "reasonable standard", those costs which exceed the prescribed amount shall not be taken into account unless certain requirements are satisfied. The "prescribed amount" is £25 multiplied by the number of flats in the building, or £500, whichever is larger. The Secretary of State has power to vary either amount. The requirements are:

(i) at least two estimates for the works are to be obtained, one from a person "wholly unconnected" with the landlord (*cf. Finchbourne Ltd.* v. *Rodrigues* [1976] 3 All E.R. 581, C.A., where a landlord's agent was held not to be "independent" of the landlord);

(ii) a copy of these estimates are either to be supplied to each of the "landlord's tenants" (see subs. (4), those tenants liable to pay a part of the charge in question), of flats in the building or shall be displayed in the building "so as to be likely to come to the notice of all those tenants";

(iii) if there is a "recognised tenants' association" (see s.29) for the building, a copy must also be supplied to its secretary;

(iv) the notice must describe the works to be carried out and invite observation on them and on the estimates and shall state the name and address in the United Kingdom of the person to whom such observations may be sent and the date by which they are to be received;

(v) the date stated in the notice must not be earlier than one month after the date on which it was originally given or displayed;

(vi) the landlord must "have regard" to any observation received;

(vii) unless the works are urgently required, they shall not be begun before the date specified on the notice. However, in any proceedings relating to a service charge, the court may dispense with any or all of the above requirements if satisfied that the landlord acted reasonably (subs. (5)), which clearly will permit *genuinely* urgent works to be carried out without compliance.

Request for summary of relevant costs

21.—(1) A tenant may require the landlord in writing to supply him with a written summary of the costs incurred—

(*a*) if the relevant accounts are made up for periods of twelve months, in the last such period ending not later than the date of the request, or (*b*) if the accounts are not so made up, in the period of twelve months ending with the date of the request,

and which are relevant costs in relation to the service charges payable or demanded as payable in that or any other period.

(2) If there is a recognised tenants' association for the building and the tenant consents, the request may be made by the secretary of the association instead of by the tenant and may then be for the supply of the summary to the secretary.

(3) A request is duly served on the landlord if it is served on—

(*a*) an agent of the landlord named as such in the rent book or similar document, or

(*b*) the person who receives the rent on behalf of the landlord;

and a person on whom a request is so served shall forward it as soon as may be to the landlord.

(4) The landlord shall comply with the request within one month of the request or within six months of the end of the period referred to in subsection (1)(*a*) or (*b*) whichever is the later.

(5) The summary shall set out the costs in a way showing how they are or will be reflected in demands for services charges.

(6) If there are more than four flats in the building or the costs also relate to another building, the summary shall be certified by a qualified accountant as—

(*a*) in his opinion a fair summary complying with the requirement of subsection (5), and

(*b*) being sufficiently supported by accounts, receipts and other documents which have been produced to him.

DEFINITIONS

"flat": s.30.
"landlord": s.30.
"qualified accountant": s.28.
"service charge": s.18.
"tenant": s.30.
"tenant's association": s.29.

GENERAL NOTE

This is how tenants can find out how claims for service charges are calculated, with a view perhaps to challenge under s.19. See also s.25 for offences.

The tenant may make a written request of the landlord to supply a written summary of the costs which have been incurred in the "relevant period" (subs. (1)), which relate to the service charges which are payable or have been demanded in that or any other period. The summary must be provided within six months of the end of the period, or one month of the request, whichever is the later (subs. (4)). If there is a "recognised tenants' association" (see s.29) for the building, and the tenant consents, the request for information may be made by the association's secretary, and must be supplied to him (subs. (2)). The summary must show how those costs are or will be reflected in demands for service charges (subs. (5)).

If there are more than four flats in the building, the summary must be certified by a "qualified accountant" (s.28) as being, in his opinion, a fair summary, which complies with the requirement of showing how the costs are or will be reflected in demands for service charges, and which has been supported by accounts receipts and other documentation that may have been produced to him (subs. 6).

See also s.22, below, for access to supporting documentation, and s.23, below, where a superior landlord is involved. Under s.24, an assignment does not affect the validity of the request for information, but the landlord is only obliged to provide the information once. Under s.25, it is a criminal offence to fail to comply with a request under this section, within the time specified in subs. (4).

Subs. (3)

Any request described above shall be deemed to be served on the landlord, if it is served on any agent of the landlord named in a rent book "or similar document"; or on anyone who receives the rent for the landlord. A person thus receiving a request who is not the landlord must forward it, as soon as possible, to the landlord.

Request to inspect supporting accounts, &c.

22.—(1) This section applies where a tenant, or the secretary of a recognised tenants' association, has obtained such a summary as is referred to in section 21(1) (summary of relevant costs), whether in pursuance of that section or otherwise.

(2) The tenant, or the secretary with the consent of the tenant, may within six months of obtaining the summary require the landlord in writing to afford him reasonable facilities—

(*a*) for inspecting the accounts, receipts and other documents supporting the summary, and

(*b*) for taking copies or extracts from them.

(3) A request under this section is duly served on the landlord if it is served on—

(*a*) an agent of the landlord named as such in the rent book or similar document, or

(*b*) the person who receives the rent on behalf of the landlord;

and a person on whom a request is so served shall forward it as soon as may be to the landlord.

(4) The landlord shall make such facilities available to the tenant or secretary for a period of two months beginning not later than one month after the request is made.

DEFINITIONS
"tenant": s.30.
"tenant's association": s.29.
"landlord": s.30.
"summary": s.21.

GENERAL NOTE
Once the summary under s.21 above has been obtained, the tenant (or secretary of tenant's association with the tenant's consent) may, within six months of obtaining it, write to the landlord, and require him to afford the tenant/secretary reasonable facilities for inspecting the accounts, receipts and documents supporting the summary, and for taking copies or extracts therefrom. These facilities are to be made available for two months beginning not later than one month from the date when the request was made. (subs. (4)).

See s.23, below, where a superior landlord is involved. By s.24, below, an assignment does not affect the validity of the request but the landlord is only obliged to make the facilities available once. Under s.25, below, a failure to comply with the requirements of this section is a criminal offence.

Subs. 3
See notes to s.21(3) above.

Request relating to information held by superior landlord

23.—(1) If a request under section 21 (request for summary of relevant costs) relates in whole or in part to relevant costs incurred by or on behalf of a superior landlord, and the landlord to whom the request is made is not in possession of the relevant information—

(*a*) he shall in turn make a written request for the relevant information to the person who is his landlord (and so on, if that person is not himself the superior landlord),

(*b*) the superior landlord shall comply with that request within a reasonable time, and

(*c*) the immediate landlord shall then comply with the tenant's or secretary's request, or that part of it which relates to the relevant costs incurred by or on behalf of the superior landlord, within the time allowed by section 21 or such further time, if any, as is reasonable in the circumstances.

(2) If a request under section 22 (request for facilities to inspect supporting accounts, &c.) relates to a summary of costs incurred by or on behalf of a superior landlord—

    (*a*) the landlord to whom the request is made shall forthwith inform the tenant or secretary of that fact and of the name and address of the superior landlord, and

    (*b*) section 22 shall then apply to the superior landlord as it applies to the immediate landlord.

DEFINITIONS
"flat": s.30.
"landlord": s.30.
"relevant costs": s.18.
"tenant": s.30.

GENERAL NOTE
There may be cases where the relevant costs have been incurred by or on behalf of a superior landlord, so that the tenant's immediate landlord is not in possession of the relevant information. In such a case, if the immediate landlord receives a request for a summary of costs, under s.21, above, he must in turn request such a summary from the superior landlord, who must comply with the request "within a reasonable time": subs. (1)(*b*). Once the immediate landlord has that information he must forward it to the tenant/secretary within the relevant time limits, or within such further time as is reasonable in the circumstances: subs. (1)(*c*) and s.21.

Similarly, if the tenant or secretary of tenant's association, wishes to have access to the documents supporting the summary, under s.22, above, the immediate landlord is to inform the tenant or secretary that the costs were incurred by or on behalf of a superior landlord, and provide him with the name and address of that superior landlord. The tenant or secretary is then entitled to the same facilities for access as under s.22.

An assignment does not affect the validity of a request under this section, although the landlord or superior landlord is only obliged to comply the one time: s.24, below. Failure to comply with the obligations under this section is a criminal offence under s.25, below.

Effect of assignment on request

24. The assignment of a tenancy does not affect the validity of a request made under section 21, 22 or 23 before the assignment; but a person is not obliged to provide a summary or make facilities available more than once for the same flat and for the same period.

GENERAL NOTE
The validity of requests is not affected by any assignment of the tenancy; but a person is not obliged to provide a summary or make facilities available more than once for the same flat and same period.

Failure to comply with s.21, 22 or 23 an offence

25.—(1) It is a summary offence for a person to fail, without reasonable excuse, to perform a duty imposed on him by section 21, 22 or 23.

(2) A person committing such an offence is liable on conviction to a fine not exceeding level 4 on the standard scale.

GENERAL NOTE
A failure to comply under ss.21–23, above, is a criminal offence, punishable by a fine of up to level 4 on the standard scale under s.37, Criminal Justice Act 1982, currently £1,000, by S.I. 1984 No. 447. Public sector landlords are, however, exempt from this section: see s.26, below. See also s.33 below for liability of officers etc.

Exception: tenants of certain public authorities

26.—(1) Sections 18 to 25 (limitation on service charges and requests for information about costs) do not apply to a service charge payable by a tenant of—

a local authority,

a new town corporation, or

the Development Board for Rural Wales,

unless the tenancy is a long tenancy, in which case sections 18 to 24 apply but section 25 (offence of failure to comply) does not.

(2) The following are long tenancies for the purposes of subsection (1), subject to subsection (3)—

    (*a*) a tenancy granted for a term certain exceeding 21 years, whether or not it is (or may become) terminable before the end of that term by notice given by the tenant or by re-entry or forfeiture;

    (*b*) a tenancy for a term fixed by law under a grant with a covenant or obligation for perpetual renewal, other than a tenancy by sub-demise from one which is not a long tenancy;

    (*c*) any tenancy granted in pursuance of Part V of the Housing Act 1985 (the right to buy).

(3) A tenancy granted so as to become terminable by notice after a death is not a long tenancy for the purposes of subsection (1), unless—

    (*a*) it is granted by a housing association which at the time of the grant is registered,

    (*b*) it is granted at a premium calculated by reference to a percentage of the value of the dwelling-house or the cost of providing it, and

    (*c*) at the time it is granted it complies with the requirements of the regulations then in force under section 140(4)(*b*) of the Housing Act 1980 (conditions for exclusion of shared ownership leases from Part I of Leasehold Reform Act 1967) or, in the case of a tenancy granted before any such regulations were brought into force, with the first such regulations to be in force.

DEFINITIONS

    "local authority": s.38.

    "new town corporation": s.38.

    "service charge": s.18.

    "tenant": s.30.

GENERAL NOTE

This and the following section set out the exceptions to s.18–25 above.

The provisions do not apply to service charges payable by tenants of certain public authorities unless the tenancy is a "long tenancy". If the tenancy is a "long tenancy" then ss.18–24 apply, but s.25 (offence of failure to comply) does not.

A "long tenancy" means a tenancy granted for a term certain exceeding 21 years. The fact that the lease may be determinable before the period of 21 years has expired, by re-entry or forfeiture, or by notice given *by* the tenant, does not prevent the lease being a long lease (incorporating the common law rule, see *Quinlan* v. *Avis* (1933) 149 L.T. 214).

The definition includes a tenancy for a term fixed by law under a grant with a covenant or obligation for perpetual renewal, unless it is a tenancy by way of sub-demise from one which is not itself a long tenancy. A grant for a covenant or obligation for permanent renewal takes effect as a lease for 2,000 years (Law of Property Act 1922, s.145, Sched. 15; Law of Property Act 1925, s.202), although if granted by way of sub-lease it takes effect as a grant for a term one day less than the term out of which it was granted (Law of Property Act 1922, s.145 and Sched. 15). The effect in this Act is that all grants with a covenant or obligation for perpetual renewal are long leases, save where the grant is of a sub-lease and the superior lease is not a long lease. But a tenancy determinable by notice after death is expressly not a long lease, *unless* the lease constitutes a shared ownership tenancy. (subs. (3)).

A shared ownership tenancy is one (a) granted by a housing association registered under the Housing Associations Act 1985; (b) granted at a premium calculated by reference to a percentage of the value of the dwelling-house or of the cost of providing it; and (c) at the time of the grant it complies with the regulations in force under s.140, Housing Act 1980, or, if granted before such regulations are brought into force, it complies with the first such regulations brought into force.

S.140 governs the exclusion of certain long leases, under shared ownership tenancies, from the provisions of the Leasehold Reform Act 1967, although the leaseholders of flats will not in any event benefit from the provisions of that Act. The regulations are the Housing (Exclusion of Shared Ownership Tenancies from the Leasehold Reform Act 1967) Regulations 1982, S.I. 1982 No. 62.

Exception: rent registered and not entered as variable

27. Sections 18 to 25 (limitation on service charges and requests for information about costs) do not apply to a service charge payable by the tenant of a flat the rent of which is registered under Part IV of the Rent Act 1977, unless the amount registered is, in pursuance of section 71(4) of that Act, entered as a variable amount.

DEFINITIONS
 "flat": s.30.
 "service charge": s.18.
 "tenant": s.30.

GENERAL NOTE
 The provisions of ss.18–25 do not apply to tenants whose rents have been registered under Pt. IV of the Rent Act 1977, unless that amount has been registered as "variable", *i.e.* "varying according to the cost from time to time of—(a) any services provided by the landlord or a superior landlord, or (b) any works of maintenance or repair carried out by the landlord or superior landlord" (1977, s.71(4)).
 Tenants whose rents are registered under Pt. 1V of the 1977 Act are private sector, protected or statutory tenants (*cf.* notes to s.38, below). Registration of a rent as "variable" is only an available option when the Rent Officer is (or, on appeal, Rent Assessment Committee are), satisfied that the "terms as to the variation are reasonable" (1977, s.71(4)). As the provisions of these sections may be taken into account (*cf. Wigglesworth* v. *Property Holding & Investment Trust PLC* (1984) 270 E.G. 555, *Betts* v. *Vivamat Properties Ltd.* (1983) 270 E.G. 849), and, in any event, it is to be presumed that a service charge provision will be operated fairly and reasonably (*Firstcross Ltd.* v. *Teasdale* (1982) 265 E.G. 305), this is an option many landlords will be able to seek. However, the choice is one for Rent Officer/Rent Assessment Committee ("may . . . be entered as an amount variable in accordance with those terms").

Meaning of "qualified accountant"

28.—(1) The reference to a "qualified accountant" in section 21(6) (certification of summary of information about relevant costs) is to a person who, in accordance with the following provisions, has the necessary qualification and is not disqualified from acting.
 (2) A person has the necessary qualification if he is a member of one of the following bodies—
    the Institute of Chartered Accountants in England and Wales,
    the Institute of Chartered Accountants in Scotland,
    the Association of Certified Accountants,
    the Institute of Chartered Accountants in Ireland, or
    any other body of accountants established in the United Kingdom and recognised by the Secretary of State for the purposes of section 389(1)(*a*) of the Companies Act 1985,
or if he is a person who is for the time being authorised by the Secretary of State under section 389(1)(*b*) of that Act (or the corresponding provision of the Companies Act 1948) as being a person with similar qualifications obtained outside the United Kingdom.
 (3) A Scottish firm has the necessary qualification if each of the partners in it has the necessary qualification.
 (4) The following are disqualified from acting—
 (*a*) a body corporate, except a Scottish firm;
 (*b*) an officer or employee of the landlord or, where the landlord is a company, of an associated company;

70–37

(c) a person who is a partner or employee of any such officer or employee.

(5) For the purposes of subsection (4)(b) a company is associated with a landlord company if it is (within the meaning of section 736 of the Companies Act 1985) the landlord's holding company, a subsidiary of the landlord or another subsidiary of the landlord's holding company.

(6) Where the landlord is a local authority, a new town corporation or the Development Board for Rural Wales—

(a) the persons who have the necessary qualification include members of the Chartered Institute of Public Finance and Accountancy, and

(b) subsection (4)(b) (disqualification of officers and employees of landlord) does not apply.

DEFINITIONS
"landlord": s.30.
"local authority": s.38.
"new town corporation": s.38.

GENERAL NOTE
This section defines qualified accountants who may certify a summary under s.21, above. Note the inclusion of C.I.P.F.A. members where the landlord is a public authority (subs. (6)).

Meaning of "recognised tenants' association"

29.—(1) A recognised tenants' association is an association of tenants of flats in a building which is recognised for the purposes of the provisions of this Act relating to service charges either—

(a) by notice in writing given by the landlord to the secretary of the association, or

(b) by a certificate of a member of the local rent assessment committee panel.

(2) A notice given under subsection (1)(a) may be withdrawn by the landlord by notice in writing given to the secretary of the association not less than six months before the date on which it is to be withdrawn.

(3) A certificate given under subsection (1)(b) may be cancelled by any member of the local rent assessment committee panel.

(4) In this section the "local rent assessment committee panel" means the persons appointed by the Lord Chancellor under the Rent Act 1977 to the panel of persons to act as members of a rent assessment committee for the registration area in which the building is situated.

(5) The Secretary of State may by regulations specify the matters to which regard is to be had in giving or cancelling a certificate under subsection (1)(b).

(6) Regulations under subsection (5)—

(a) may make different provisions with respect to different cases or descriptions of case, including different provision for different areas, and

(b) shall be made by statutory instrument which shall be subject to annulment in pursuance of a resolution of either House of Parliament.

DEFINITIONS
"flat": s.30.
"landlord": s.30.
"service charge": s.18.
"tenant": s.30.

GENERAL NOTE
Tenant's associations have a role under ss.20–24. They are defined as associations of tenants of flats in a building recognised, for present purposes, either by notice in writing

given by the landlord to the secretary, or by a certificate given by one of the Lord Chancellor's appointees to rent assessment panels for the registration area in which the building is located. Where notice of recognition has been given by the landlord, he may withdraw it on giving six months' notice; and once a certificate has been given, it may be cancelled by any of the persons entitled to give it. The Secretary of State has power to specify in regulations (not thus far made) matters to which regard must be had when granting or cancelling certificates.

Meaning of "flat", "landlord" and "tenant"

30. In the provisions of this Act relating to service charges—
"flat" means a separate set of premises, whether or not on the same floor, which—
   (*a*) forms part of a building,
   (*b*) is divided horizontally from some other part of the building, and
   (*c*) is constructed or adapted for use for the purposes of a dwelling and is occupied wholly or mainly as a private dwelling;
"landlord" includes any person who has a right to enforce payment of a service charge;
"tenant" includes
   (*a*) a statutory tenant, and
   (*b*) where the flat or part of it is sub-let, the sub-tenant.

DEFINITIONS
"service charge": s.18.
"statutory tenant": s.37.

GENERAL NOTE
"Landlord". In *Adelphi (Estates) Ltd.* v. *Christie* (1983) 269 E.G. 221, C.A., the court considered the term "lessor" in a lease. The tenant was obliged to pay a fixed percentage of "the lessor's" annual expenditure on maintenance. The tenant in residence, and the plaintiffs, had been granted concurrent leases, so that the tenant's immediate landlord was the plaintiff company. *Their* expenditure on maintenance was no more than the share attributable to the one flat, and the tenant accordingly argued that she was obliged to pay no more than the percentage stated in the lease applied to the amount charged by the superior landlords to her landlords.

The court held that the term lessor in the lease was wide enough to include the superior landlord, *i.e.* the expenditure incurred by the superior landlords. The court below had derived some assistance from the definition of landlord in what is now this section, which the Court of Appeal, otherwise upholding the decision, held irrelevant. But in principle it seems that the same circumstances would be likely to lead to the same result on the words of this provision as in that case.

Miscellaneous

Reserve power to limit rents

31.—(1) The Secretary of State may by order provide for—
   (*a*) restricting or preventing increases of rent for dwellings which would otherwise take place, or
   (*b*) restricting the amount of rent which would otherwise be payable on new lettings of dwellings;
and may so provide either generally or in relation to any specified description of dwelling.
   (2) An order may contain supplementary or incidental provisions, including provisions excluding, adapting or modifying any provision made by or under an enactment (whenever passed) relating to rent or the recovery of overpaid rent.
   (3) In this section—

"new letting" includes any grant of a tenancy, whether or not the premises were previously let, and any grant of a licence;

"rent" includes a sum payable under a licence, but does not include a sum attributable to rates or, in the case of dwellings of local authorities or new town corporations, to the use of furniture, or the provision of services;

and for the purposes of this section an increase in rent takes place at the beginning of the rental period for which the increased rent is payable.

(4) An order under this section shall be made by statutory instrument which shall be subject to annulment in pursuance of a resolution of either House of Parliament.

DEFINITIONS
"dwelling": s.38.
"local authority": s.38.
"new town corporation": s.38.
"tenancy": s.36.

GENERAL NOTE
Although inapplicable to assured tenancies (see s.32, below), this provision is available in respect of licences as much as tenancies (*cf.* notes to s.1, above). The provision derives from s.11 Housing Rents and Subsidies Act 1975. The reserve power applies to private sector and public sector rents. In moving the second reading of the 1975 Bill in the Commons, the Secretary of State said of the reserve power "This is not framed in such a way that the Government could make an order controlling the rents of individual local authorities, or individual dwellings". (*Hansard* H.C. Vol. 881, col. 906.)

Supplementary provisions

Provisions not applying to tenancies within Part II of the Landlord and Tenant Act 1954

32.—(1) The following provisions do not apply to a tenancy to which Part II of the Landlord and Tenant Act 1954 (business tenancies) applies—

sections 1 to 3 (information to be given to tenant),
section 17 (specific performance of landlord's repairing obligations).

(2) Section 11 (repairing obligations) does not apply to a new lease granted to an existing tenant, or to a former tenant still in possession, if the new lease is a tenancy to which Part II of the Landlord and Tenant Act 1954 applies and the previous lease either is such a tenancy or would be but for section 28 of that Act (tenancy not within Part II if renewal agreed between the parties).

In this subsection "existing tenant", "former tenant still in possession" and "previous lease" have the same meaning as in section 14(2).

(3) Section 31 (reserve power to limit rents) does not apply to a dwelling forming part of a property subject to a tenancy to which Part II of the Landlord and Tenant Act 1954 applies; but without prejudice to the application of that section in relation to a sub-tenancy of a part of the premises comprised in such a tenancy.

DEFINITIONS
"tenancy": s.36.

GENERAL NOTE
"Assured tenants" were introduced by Part 11, Housing Act 1980, and represent an attempt to revive "building for rent" by exempting newly built property from Rent Act 1977 protection; instead, such tenants are taken into the Landlord and Tenant Act 1954, Pt. II, *i.e.* the protection afforded to business tenants, but subject to adaptation of those provisions—see Housing Act 1980, ss.56–58 and Sched. 5. This section either disapplies or modifies provisions of this Act in relation to assured tenancies.

Liability of directors, &c. for offences by body corporate

33.—(1) Where an offence under this Act which has been committed by a body corporate is proved—

(*a*) to have been committed with the consent or connivance of a director, manager, secretary or other similar officer of the body corporate, or a person purporting to act in any such capacity, or

(*b*) to be attributable to any neglect on the part of such an officer or person,

he, as well as the body corporate, is guilty of an offence and liable to be proceeded against and punished accordingly.

(2) Where the affairs of a body corporate are managed by its members, subsection (1) applies in relation to the acts and defaults of a member in connection with his functions of management as if he were a director of the body corporate.

GENERAL NOTE

This general application of what is now considered the common form approach to offences is pursuant to Law Commission Recommendations (Cmnd. 9515), No. 28.

Power of local housing authority to prosecute

34. Proceedings for an offence under any provision of this Act may be brought by a local housing authority.

DEFINITIONS

"local housing authority": s.38.

Application to Isles of Scilly

35.—(1) This Act applies to the Isles of Scilly subject to such exceptions, adaptations and modifications as the Secretary of State may by order direct.

(2) An order shall be made by statutory instrument which shall be subject to annulment in pursuance of a resolution of either House of Parliament.

GENERAL NOTE

This method of dealing with the Isles of Scilly is pursuant to Law Commission Recommendations (Cmnd. 9515), No. 29.

Meaning of "lease" and "tenancy" and related expressions

36.—(1) In this Act "lease" and "tenancy" have the same meaning.

(2) Both expressions include—

(*a*) a sub-lease or sub-tenancy, and

(*b*) an agreement for a lease or tenancy (or sub-lease or sub-tenancy).

(3) The expressions "lessor" and "lessee" and "landlord" and "tenant", and references to letting, to the grant of a lease or to covenants or terms, shall be construed accordingly.

Meaning of "statutory tenant" and related expressions

37. In this Act—

(*a*) "statutory tenancy" and "statutory tenant" mean a statutory tenancy or statutory tenant within the meaning of the Rent Act 1977 or the Rent (Agriculture) Act 1976; and

(*b*) "landlord", in relation to a statutory tenant, means the person who, apart from the statutory tenancy, would be entitled to possession of the premises.

GENERAL NOTE

The general definition of statutory tenant as including statutory tenants under the Rent (Agriculture) Act 1976 means that s.17, above, now applies to them as to the Rent Act 1977 statutory tenants, pursuant to Law Commission Recommendations (Cmnd. 9515), No. 14.

"Statutory Tenancy", "Statutory Tenant". Under either Act, this means a former protected tenant or occupier, *i.e.,* after the termination of the contractual arrangement. In each case, however, a statutory tenancy will last only so long as the premises are occupied as a residence. As to protected tenant under the Rent Act 1977, see notes to s.38, below.

Under the Rent (Agriculture) Act 1976, a person is a "protected occupier" if he has:

(1) A relevant licence or tenancy of a dwelling-house or part of a house; and

(2) At some time during the subsistence of the relevant licence or tenancy the house has been in qualifying ownership; and

(3) The occupier is, or at any time during the subsistence of the licence or tenancy has been, a qualifying worker (Rent (Agriculture) Act 1976, ss.2(1), 34(3)).

A relevant licence is one which, whether or not for any consideration, confers exclusive occupation of premises for use as a residence (*ibid.*, s.34(1)) and which, if it had been a tenancy, would have been a protected tenancy under the Rent Act 1977 given certain modifications of that Act (*ibid.*, Sched. 2, para. 1).

A relevant tenancy is one which, not being a tenancy to which the Landlord and Tenant Act 1954 (*i.e.* business tenancy *or* assured tenancy—see notes to s.32, above) applies, and not being a tenancy of an agricultural holding within the Agricultural Holdings Act 1948, as amended by the Agricultural Holdings Act 1984, would be a protected tenancy under the Rent Act 1977, again given modification (Rent (Agriculture) Act 1976, Sched. 2, para. 2). Tenancy includes sub-tenancy (*ibid.*, s.34(1)).

The modifications of the Rent Act 1977 (*cf.* notes to s.38, below) are:

(i) Occupation will be included even though the occupier pays no rent or pays only a low rent, or even although the tenancy or licence is of a dwelling-house comprised in an agricultural holding;

(ii) Occupation will be excluded from protection if it is a bona fide term of the letting that the landlord provides the occupier with board or attendance, *excluding* meals given in the course of employment, and attendances where the value to the occupier is not substantial (*cf.* notes to s.38, below).

Note that where a tenant/licensee has the right to exclusive occupation of some part of his accommodation, but shares another part (with someone other than his landlord, for he will be excluded from protection if there is a resident landlord, *i.e.* because he would not be protected under the Rent Act 1977—see notes to s.38, below), a protected occupancy is still available on the basis of the separate accommodation (*ibid.*, ss.23(1), 34(1), (2)), unless the separate accommodation consists of only one room and, at the time of the grant, at least three other similar rooms were let or available for letting (*ibid.*, s.23(2)), *i.e.* hostels for agricultural workers are excluded.

Qualifying ownership means that either the occupier's employer is the landlord under the letting, or that the dwelling has been let by some person with whom the occupier's employer has made arrangements for the premises in question to be used for persons employed by him in agriculture: Rent (Agriculture) Act 1976, Sched. 3, para. 3(1). Employer includes one of a number of joint employers: *ibid.*, para. 3(2). Employment in agriculture includes dairy farming, livestock keeping and breeding, arable farming, market gardening and forestry: *ibid.*, s.1(1). Gamekeepers have been held outside this definition: *Glendyne* v. *Rapley* (1978) E.G. 573, C.A.; *Earl of Normanton* v. *Giles* [1980] 1 W.L.R. 28, H.L.

A qualifying worker is a person who has worked whole–time in agriculture, or has worked in agriculture as a permit–worker for not less than 91 out of the previous 104 weeks: Rent (Agriculture) Act 1976, Sched. 3, para. 1. A person works whole-time if he works not less than the standard number of hours in agriculture: *ibid.*, para. 4. A permit-worker is one who has been granted a permit under s.5, Agricultural Wages Act 1948: *ibid.*, paras. 5, 7. There are provisions to protect a worker against loss of qualifying time by reason of injury or disease, holiday entitlement, or if the worker is absent with the consent of his employer: *ibid.*, para. 4(3)–(5), para. 5(3)–(4).

Minor definitions

38. In this Act—

"address" means a person's place of abode or place of business or, in the case of a company, its registered office,

"co-operative housing association" has the same meaning as in the Housing Associations Act 1985;

"dwelling" means a building or part of a building occupied or intended to be occupied as a separate dwelling, together with any yard, garden, outhouses and appurtenances belonging to it or usually enjoyed with it;

"housing association" has the same meaning as in the Housing Associations Act 1985;

"local authority" means a district, county or London borough council, the Common Council of the City of London or the Council of the Isles of Scilly and in sections 14(4), 26(1) and 28(6) includes the Inner London Education Authority and a joint authority established by Part IV of the Local Government Act 1985;

"local housing authority" has meaning given by section 1 of the Housing Act 1985;

"new town corporation" means—

(*a*) a development corporation established by an order made, or treated as made, under the New Towns Act 1981, or

(*b*) the Commission for the New Towns;

"protected tenancy" has the same meaning as in the Rent Act 1977;

"registered", in relation to a housing association, means registered under the Housing Associations Act 1985;

"restricted contract" has the same meaning as in the Rent Act 1977;

"urban development corporation" has the same meaning as in Part XVI of the Local Government, Planning and Land Act 1980.

GENERAL NOTE

"Dwelling". Any building—not only a house (*cf.* notes to s.8, above)—qualifies. However, the dwelling must be occupied or intended to be occupied as a separate dwelling. Because of the inclusion of actual occupation, caselaw on the purpose of a letting will be less relevant here than under s.1, Rent Act 1977, or s.79, Housing Act 1985, when defining protected (below) or secure tenancies. But the letting must still be as "a" separate dwelling. In *St. Catherine's College* v. *Dorling* [1980] 1 W.L.R. 66, C.A., a college took the tenancy of a flat, already subdivided into separate living units, for sub-leasing to their own students. As against the college, the students could not enjoy full Rent Act protection (*cf.* 1977 Act, s.8, below), and as against the landlord, the college could not avail itself of a statutory tenancy following the contractual arrangement, for a corporate body cannot as such "reside" (*cf.* notes to s.37, above). The college sought, however, to avail itself of the provisions of Pt. IV of the 1977 Act, governing the registration of rents.

It was held that the letting was not as *a* separate dwelling but, indeed, as several separate dwellings: see also *Whitty* v. *Scott-Russell* [1950] 2 K.B. 32, C.A., *Horford Investments* v. *Lambert* [1976] Ch. 39, C.A., *Regalian Securities Ltd.* v. *Ramsden* (1980) 254 E.G. 1191, C.A.

But two or more dwellings may be let for use as one: *Langford Property Co. Ltd.* v. *Goldrich* [1949] 1 K.B. 511, C.A., *Whitty* v. *Scott-Russell* [1950] 2 K.B. 32, C.A., *Lower* v. *Porter* [1956] 1 Q.B. 325, C.A. Similarly, several lettings at different times may add up to one letting, as one dwelling: *Verity* v. *Waring* [1953] C.P.L. 423, C.A. And while a letting of a unit already subdivided into several separate living units for use as such, will not be let as *a* dwelling, a letting of one unit subsequently subdivided into living units, *e.g.* into bedsitting rooms, does not cease to be a letting as a separate dwelling on that account: *Sissons Cafe Ltd.* v. *Barber* (1929) E.G.D. 117, D.C.

The essence of "separate" is that the premises in question must be capable of use on their own, as a dwelling, even if they comprise no more than a single room (see, *e.g.* *Curl* v. *Angelo* [1948] 2 All E.R. 189, C.A.), so that there is and needs be no sharing with another of "living accommodation". The term "living accommodation" is a judicial creation, and does not extend to the sharing of a bathroom or lavatory: *Cole* v. *Harris* [1945] K.B. 474, C.A. A bathroom or lavatory is accommodation not used for living in, but merely visited for occasional, specific purposes, as distinct from a room used for the primary purposes of living, or one in which a person spends a significant part of his time: see also *Curl, Goodrich* v. *Paisner* [1957] A.C. 65, H.L., *Marsh* v. *Cooper* [1969] 1 W.L.R. 803, C.A.

For these purposes, the primary living purposes may be considered as sleeping, cooking and feeding (*Wright* v. *Howell* (1947) 92 S.J. 26, C.A., *Curl* v. *Angelo* [1948] 2 All E.R. 189, C.A.), but *not*, as noted, sanitary activities.

But a kitchenette, even though too small to eat in and only available to cook or wash up in, has been held to constitute living accommodation (*Winters* v. *Dance* [1949] L.J.R. 165, C.A.), as also has a normal kitchen: *Neale* v. *Del Soto* [1945] K.B. 144, C.A., *Sharpe* v. *Nicholls* (1945) 147 E.G. 177, C.A. So if the letting comprises premises together with shared user of such living accommodation, there is, prima facie, no use as a "separate dwelling": *Winters* v. *Dance, Neale* v. *Del Soto, Goodrich* v. *Paisner* [1957] A.C. 65, H.L.

Sharing with one's own sub-tenant, or sub-licensee, does not prevent use as a separate dwelling: *Baker* v. *Turner* [1950] A.C. 401, H.L. And sharing living accommodation must be distinguished from a letting which leaves someone else, *e.g.* another occupier or even the landlord, with a defined or limited right merely to *use* part of the accommodation which has been let, *e.g.* the right to come in and make a morning cup of tea as in *James* v. *James* [1952] C.L.Y. 2948, C.C., a right of passage as in *James* v. *Coleman* [1949] E.G.D. 122, C.C., a right to use a bath sited in a kitchen as in *Trustees of the Waltham Abbey Baptist Church* v. *Stevens* (1950) E.G. 294, C.C., and a right to draw and boil water weekly as in *Hayward* v. *Marshall* [1952] 2 Q.B. 89, C.A.

In each case, the whole of the circumstances must be looked at in order to ascertain whether a person has the right to use a separate dwelling, or something less: *Goodrich* v. *Paisner* [1957] A.C. 65, H.L. In Rent Act law, the fact that a sharing right is not exercised does not bring the tenant back into full protection (*Stanley* v. *Compton* [1951] 1 All E.R. 859, C.A., *Kenyon* v. *Walker* [1946] 2 All E.R. 595, C.A.) although it has been thought that a clear abandonment of the right might do so: *Stanley* v. *Compton*.

The question is to be determined as at the date when it is relevant, rather than as at the date of letting: *Baker* v. *Turner* [1950] A.C. 401, H.L.

Finally, there is the term "dwelling", as it were "within" the definition. This has been defined as something in which all the major activities of life, such as sleeping, cooking and feeding, are carried out: *Wright* v. *Howell* (1947) 92 S.J. 26, C.A., *Curl* v. *Angelo* [1948] 2 All E.R. 189, C.A., *Metropolitan Properties* v. *Barder* [1968] 1 All E.R. 536. Premises not used for sleeping cannot be in use as a dwelling: *Wimbush* v. *Cibulia* [1949] 2 K.B. 564, C.A. But use need not be by the person to whom the premises are let: *Whitty* v. *Scott-Russell* [1950] 2 K.B. 32, C.A., *Edgware Estates Ltd.* v. *Coblentz* [1949] 2 K.B. 717, C.A., *Carter* v. *S.U. Carburetter Co.* [1942] 2 K.B. 288, C.A., *Watson* v. *Saunders-Roe Ltd.* [1947] K.B. 437, C.A., *Anspach* v. *Charlton SS Co. Ltd.* [1955] 2 Q.B. 21, C.A.

In addition, "any yard, garden, outhouses and appurtenances belonging to . . . or usually enjoyed with" the dwelling are to be considered part of the dwelling. This extended definition of dwelling—or, in the Housing Act 1985 and in ss.8, 9, above, of "house"—dates as far back as the Artizans' and Labourers' Dwellings Act 1868, and has been maintained since (see, *e.g.,* s.29, Housing of the Working Classes Act 1890, s.135, Housing Act 1925, s.188, Housing Act 1936).

In *Trim* v. *Sturminster Rural District Council* [1938] 2 K.B. 508, decided under the last of these provisions, 10 acres of grassland were let together with a cottage, and the question arose whether they were appurtenant to the cottage. It was held, following *Bryan* v. *Wetherhead* (1623) Cro. Cas. 17, that the word "appurtenances" was used in its well established legal sense of including only such matters as outhouses, yards and gardens, but not the land itself, although it might in certain cases be competent to pass incorporeal hereditaments. How much of the ten acres ought to be included depended on the facts of the case, which had to be a question for the county court judge, but it would certainly be less than the full ten acres in issue.

In *Clymo* v. *Shell-Mex & B.P. Ltd.* (1963) 10 R.R.C. 85, C.A., under the Rating and Valuation Act 1925, open land surrounded by depot buildings was held to be appurtenant to the buildings, on the basis that had there been a conveyance or demise it would have passed without specific mention:

"The word 'appurtenance' is one of the oldest words in use in the history of English law, and we would not attempt to define it in any way; whether land is properly described as an appurtenance to one or more buildings must depend very much on the particular facts and circumstances of each case, and it does not seem possible to try to lay down any tests to determine whether land ought to be regarded as an appurtenance [for the purposes of the section]. Each case must be decided entirely on its own facts, and no doubt there may in practice be a number of difficult and borderline cases . . .

"It must be remembered that in law the grant of buildings automatically passes everything that can properly be described as an appurtenance belonging thereto. In strictness of law, it may be doubted whether the use of the word appurtenance [in the section] added anything to what would otherwise pass . . . but no doubt the words which follow were wisely added to prevent any argument on that matter". The same would seem applicable under this section. In *Methuen-Campbell* v. *Walters* [1979] Q.B. 525, under the Leasehold Reform Act

1967, it was held that land cannot ordinarily be appurtenant to land, but the ordinary and strict meaning of the word may yield to a wider meaning if the context so requires.

In *Hansford* v. *Jago* [1921] 1 Ch. 322, a right of way was held to pass with the word appurtenances. In *Sovmots Investments Ltd.* v. *Secretary of State for the Environment* [1979] A.C. 144, H.L., it was held that appurtenances could not include rights of way and other ancillary rights not yet defined or in some cases even in existence, although this decision was overturned by s.13, Local Government (Miscellaneous Provisions) Act 1976, so far as compulsory purchase by local authorities is concerned.

In *F.F.F. Estates Ltd.* v. *Hackney London Borough Council* [1981] Q.B. 503, 3 H.L.R. 107, C.A., the court, considering the meaning of dwelling under what is now Pt. VII, Housing Act 1985, defining dwelling with this "appurtenant" extension, did not "find any real help" in caselaw considering rights passing on a conveyance, and it would certainly seem at the least arguable that—as with the word "house" itself, see notes to s.8, above— the word should always be construed as a mixed question of fact and law, *i.e.* applying the relevant section to the facts of each case: see in particular the quotation from *In Re Butler, Camberwell (Wingfield Mews) No. 2 Clearance Order 1936* [1939] 1 K.B. 570, C.A., in the notes to s.8, above.

"Protected Tenancy". A protected tenancy is a regulated (*i.e.* contractual) tenancy within the full protection of the Rent Act 1977: see s.1 thereof. In outline, it is the letting as a separate dwelling, under a tenancy (not licence, *cf.* notes to s.1, above), which is not excluded from protection under any of the provisions of Part 1 of the 1977 Act. The exclusions are:

(1) High rated property—1977, s.4;

(2) Low rented tenancies—1977, s.5;

(3) Lettings together with land exceeding 2 acres (other than agricultural land)—1977, ss.6 and 26;

(4) Tenancies under which board to any value, or attendances to a value to the tenant which represents a substantial proportion of the rent, are provided—1977, s.7; as to substantial proportion, see note on Restricted Contract, below;

(5) Specified student lettings—1977, s.8;

(6) Holiday lettings—1977, s.9;

(7) Agricultural holdings—1977, s.10;

(8) Licensed premises—1977, s.11;

(9) Tenancies from a resident landlord—1977, s.12;

(10) Crown tenancies not under the management of the Crown Estate Commissioners— 1977, s.13;

(11) Tenancies from local authorities and development corporations—1977, s.14;

(12) Tenancies from registered housing associations and housing trusts—1977, s.15;

(13) Tenancies from a housing co–operative under s.27, Housing Act 1985, *i.e.* "management co-operative"—1977, s.16;

(14) Assured tenancies under Part II, Housing Act 1980—1977, s.16A (*cf.* notes to s.32, above);

(15) Business tenancies—1977, s.24.

Notwithstanding that the premises are not let as a separate dwelling, they may be the subject of a protected or statutory tenancy if the only sharing is with other tenants (1977, s.22), although if the sharing is with the landlord, the tenancy will be a restricted contract, even if it would not otherwise so qualify (1977, s.21). A tenancy from a resident landlord is similarly a restricted contract, even if it would not otherwise so qualify: 1977, s.20.

"Restricted Contract". A restricted contract is a tenancy *or licence* under which one person grants to another, in consideration of a rent which includes payment for rent or services, the right to occupy a dwelling as a residence: 1977, s.19(2). Services for this purpose includes attendances (*e.g.* room cleaning, changing sheets, porterage), provision of heating or lighting, supply of hot water, and any other privilege or facility connected with the occupation, *other* than those merely of access, or cold water supply or sanitary accommodation: 1977, s.19(8). There must be exclusive occupation of some part of the dwelling, but the letting can still be a restricted contract even if, in addition to an exclusive part, there is sharing of other accommodation: 1977, s.19(6).

Holiday lettings are excluded: s.19(7). So are high rated dwellings (s.19(3), (4)), regulated tenancies (above), lettings from local authorities and development corporations, lettings from the Crown other than when the property is under the management of the Crown Estate Commissioners, a protected occupancy under the Rent (Agriculture) Act 1976, a *tenancy* (but not a licence) from a registered housing association, housing trust or the Housing Corporation within s.86, Rent Act 1977, and a letting under which the rent includes payment for board, and the value of the board to the occupier forms a substantial proportion of the whole rent (1977, s.19(5)).

"Substantial proportion" is usually taken as from 15 per cent. or 20 per cent. of the rent: see *Palser* v. *Grinling* [1948] A.C. 291, H.L.; see also *Woodward* v. *Docherty* [1974] 1 W.L.R. 966, C.A.; "board" means more than a mere early morning cup of tea—see *Wilkes* v. *Goodwin* [1923] 2 K.B. 86, C.A. Partial board would seem to suffice but it is the value to the tenant which must be taken into account. The rent to which the value is to be compared is the whole rent.

Index of defined expressions

39. The following Table shows provisions defining or otherwise explaining expressions used in this Act (other than provisions defining or explaining an expression in the same section):

address	section 38
co-operative housing association	section 38
dwelling	section 38
dwelling-house (in the provisions relating to repairing obligations)	section 16
fit for human habitation	section 10
flat (in the provisions relating to service charges)	section 30
housing association	section 38
landlord—	
(generally)	section 36(3)
(in sections 1 and 2)	section 1(3)
(in the provisions relating to rent books)	section 4(3)
(in the provisions relating to service charges)	section 30
(in relation to a statutory tenancy)	section 37(*b*)
lease, lessee and lessor—	
(generally)	section 36
(in the provisions relating to repairing obligations)	section 16
local authority	section 38
local housing authority	section 38
new town corporation	section 38
protected tenancy	section 38
qualified accountant (for the purposes of section 21(6))	section 28
registered (in relation to a housing association)	section 38
recognised tenants' association	section 29
relevant costs (in relation to a service charge)	section 18(2)
restricted contract	section 38
service charge	section 18(1)
statutory tenant	section 37(*a*)
tenancy and tenant—	
(generally)	section 36
(in sections 1 and 2)	section 1(3)
(in the provisions relating to rent books)	section 4(3)
(in the provisions relating to service charges)	section 30
urban development corporation	section 38

Final provisions

Short title, commencement and extent

40.—(1) This Act may be cited as the Landlord and Tenant Act 1985.

(2) This Act comes into force on 1st April 1986.

(3) This Act extends to England and Wales.

TABLE OF DERIVATIONS

1. The following abbreviations are used in this Table:—

Acts of Parliament

1957	=	The Housing Act 1957 (c.56).
1961	=	The Housing Act 1961 (c.65).
1962	=	The Landlord and Tenant Act 1962 (c.50).
1963 (c.33)	=	The London Government Act 1963.
1968 (c.23)	=	The Rent Act 1968.
1969	=	The Housing Act 1969 (c.33).
1972 (c.70)	=	The Local Government Act 1972.
1974	=	The Housing Act 1974 (c.44).
1975	=	The Housing Rents and Subsidies Act 1975 (c.6).
1976 (c.80)	=	The Rent (Agriculture) Act 1976.
1977 (c.42)	=	The Rent Act 1977.
1980	=	The Housing Act 1980 (c.51).
1980 (c.65)	=	The Local Government, Planning and Land Act 1980.
1981 (c.64)	=	The New Towns Act 1981.
1982 (c.48)	=	The Criminal Justice Act 1982.
1985 (c.9)	=	The Companies Consolidation (Consequential Provisions) Act 1985.
1985 (c.51)	=	The Local Government Act 1985.

Subordinate legislation

S.I. 1975/512 = The Isles of Scilly (Housing) Order 1975.

2. The Table does not show the effect of Transfer of Functions Orders.

3. The letter R followed by a number indicates that the provision gives effect to the Recommendation bearing that number in the Law Commission's Report of the Consolidation of the Housing Acts (Cmnd. 9515).

4. The entry "drafting" indicates a provision of a mechanical or editorial nature affecting the arrangement of the consolidation; for instance, a provision introducing the provisions which follow or introducing a definition to avoid undue repetition of the defining words.

Provision	Derivation
1(1)	1974 s.121(1).
(2)	1974 s.121(1); 1980 s.144; 1982 (c.48) ss.37, 46(1).
(3)	1974 s.121(9).
2(1),(2)	1974 s.121(2).
(3)	1974 s.121(4).
(4)	1974 s.121(5); 1980 s.144; 1982 (c.48) ss.37, 46(1).
3(1)	1974 s.122(1), (2).
(2)	1974 s.122(4).
(3)	1974 s.122(5); 1980 s.144; 1982 (c.48) ss.37, 46(1).
(4)	1974 s.122(8), (9)(*a*).
4(1)	1962 s.1(1).
(2)	1962 s.1(2).
(3)	1962 ss.1(1), 6(1)(*a*).
5(1)	1962 s.2(1); 1976 (c.80) Sch. 8 para. 9; 1977 (c.42) Sch. 23 para. 31(*a*), (*b*).
(2)	1962 s.2(1); 1968 (c.23) Sch. 15.
(3)	1962 s.6(1)(*b*).
6(1)	1962 s.3(1).
(2)	1962 s.3(2).
7(1),(2)	1962 s.4(1), (3); 1982 (c.48) ss.37, 46(1), Sch. 3.
(3)	1962 s.4(2), (3); 1982 (c.48) ss.37, 46(1), Sch.3.
(4)	1962 s.4(4).
8(1), (2)	1957 s.6(2), (3).
(3)	1957 s.6(1), (2).
(4)	1957 s.6(1); 1963 (c.33) Sch. 8 para. 2.

Provision	Derivation
(5)	1957 s.6(2) proviso.
(6)	1957 s.189(1) "house" (*a*).
9(1), (2)	1957 s.7.
(3)	1957 ss.7, 189(1) "house" (*a*).
10	1957 s.4(1); 1969 s.71.
11(1)	1961 s.32(1).
(2)	1961 s.32(2).
(3)	1961 s.32(3).
(4)	1961 s.32(1), (2).
(5)	1961 s.32(1).
(6)	1961 s.32(4).
12(1)	1961 s.33(7).
(2)	1961 s.33(6).
13(1)	1961 s.33(1).
(2)	1961 s.33(2), (5).
14(1), (2)	1961 s.33(3).
(3)	1961 s.33(4).
(4)	1977 (c.42) ss.14, 15(3); 1980 s.80(1)(*a*)–(*c*), (2), (3); 1980 (c.65) s.155(1); 1981 (c.64) Sch. 12 para. 24.
(5)	1980 s.80(1)(*d*), (*e*).
15	1961 s.33(8).
16	1961 s.32(5).
17(1)	1974 s.125(1).
(2)	1974 s.125(2); R.14(i).
18(1)–(3)	1980 Sch. 19 para. 1(1).
19(1)	1980 Sch. 19 paras. 2, 3.
(2)	1980 Sch. 19 para. 2.
(3)	1980 Sch. 19 para. 11.
(4)	1980 Sch. 19 para. 12.
20(1)	1980 Sch. 19 paras. 2, 4(1).
(2)	1980 Sch. 19 para. 4(2).
(3)	1980 Sch. 19 para. 5(1)–(6).
(4)	1980 Sch. 19 para. 5(7).
(5)	1980 Sch. 19 para. 6.
(6)	1980 s.151(1), (3).
21(1)	1980 Sch. 19 para. 7(1), (5).
(2)	1980 Sch. 19 para. 7(2).
(3)	1980 Sch. 19 para. 9.
(4)	1980 Sch. 19 para. 7(1).
(5), (6)	1980 Sch. 19 para. 7(3).
22(1), (2)	1980 Sch. 19 para. 7(4).
(3)	1980 Sch. 19 para. 9.
(4)	1980 Sch. 19 para. 7(4).
23(1), (2)	1980 Sch. 19 para. 8(1), (2).
24	1980 Sch. 19 para. 10.
25(1), (2)	1980 Sch. 19 para. 13(1); 1982 (c.48) ss.37, 46(1).
26(1)	1980 s.50(1) "development corporation", "local authority", Sch. 19 para. 14(1), (2)(*a*).
(2), (3)	1980 Sch. 3 para. 1(2), (2A), (3), Sch. 19 para. 14(1); 1984 Sch. 1 para. 12, Sch. 11 para. 33(1).
27	1980 Sch. 19 para. 15.
28(1)	drafting.
(2)	1980 Sch. 16 para. 3(2), Sch. 19 para. 17(1); 1985 (c.9) Sch. 2.
(3)	1980 Sch. 16 para. 3(4), Sch. 19 para. 17(1).
(4)	1980 Sch. 19 para. 17(2).
(5)	1980 Sch. 19 para. 17(2)(*b*); 1985 (c.9) Sch. 2.
(6)	1980 Sch. 19 para. 14(1), (2)(*b*).
29(1)	1980 Sch. 19 para. 20.
(2), (3)	1980 Sch. 19 para. 21(1).
(4)	1980 Sch. 19 para. 20(*b*).
(5)	1980 Sch. 19 para. 21(2).
(6)	1980 s.151(1), (3).

Provision	Derivation
30	
"flat"	1980 Sch. 19 para. 16.
"landlord"	1980 Sch. 19 para. 18.
"tenant"	1980 Sch. 19 para. 19.
31(1)	1975 ss.11(1), 15(1), (5).
(2)	1975 ss.11(2), 15(5).
(3)	1975 s.11(10), (11).
(4)	1975 ss.11(3), 15(1).
32(1)	1974 ss.121(9), 122(8), 125(2).
(2)	1961 s.33(3).
(3)	1975 s.11(11) "dwelling".
33(1)	1962 s.4(6); 1974 ss.121(6), 122(6); 1980 Sch. 19 para. 13(2).
(2)	1974 ss.121(7), 122(7); 1980 Sch. 19 para. 13(3); R.28.
34	1962 s.5(2); 1968 (c.23) Sch. 15; 1972 (c.70) s.222(1); 1974 s.121(8); 1977 (c.42) s.149(2), Sch. 23 para. 32, Sch. 24 para. 30.
35(1), (2)	1972 s.103; 1975 s.17(11), Sch. 5 para. 7(1); S.I. 1972/1204; S.I. 1975/512; R.29.
36	1961 s.32(5); 1974 ss.121(9), 125(2); 1975 s.11(11) "new letting"; drafting.
37	1962 s.6(1)(*a*); 1974 ss.121(9), 122(8), 125(2); 1976 (c.80) Sch. 8 para. 31; 1977 (c.42) Sch. 23 para. 66; 1980 Sch. 19 para. 18; R.14(i).
38	
"address"	1962 s.6(2); 1974 ss.121(3), 122(3), Sch. 13 para. 9.
"co-operative housing association"	1977 (c.42) s.15(3)(*d*); 1980 s.80(1)(*b*); drafting.
"dwelling"	1974 s.129(1) "dwelling"; 1975 s.16(1) "dwelling".
"housing association"	1977 (c.42) s.15(3)(*a*); 1980 s.80(1)(*b*).
"local authority"	1975 ss.11(11), 16(1) "local authority"; 1977 (c.42) s.14(1)(*a*)–(*c*); 1980 s.80(1)(*c*); 1985 (c.51) Sch. 13 para. 21, Sch 14 paras. 56, 58(h).
"local housing authority"	1962 s.5(2); 1968 (c.23) Sch. 15; 1974 s.121(8); S.I. 1975/512; 1977 (c.42) s.149(2), Sch. 23 para. 32, Sch. 24 para. 30; 1980 s.50(1) "local authority", Sch. 19 para. 14(1)(*a*).
"new town corporation"	1977 (c.42) s.14(*d*), (*e*); 1980 ss.50(1) "development corporation, 80(1)(*c*), Sch. 19 para. 14(1)(*a*), (*c*); 1981 (c.64) Sch. 12 para. 24; drafting.
"protected tenancy"	1962 s.2(1); 1968 (c.23) Sch. 15; 1977 (c.42) Sch. 23 para. 31(*b*), Sch. 24 para. 30.
"registered"	1977 (c.42) s.15(3)(*a*); 1980 s.80(1)(*b*).
"restricted contract"	1962 s.2(1); 1977 (c.42) Sch. 23 para. 31(*a*).
"urban development corporation"	1977 (c.42) s.14(1)(*g*); 1980 s.80(1)(*c*); 1980 (c.65) s.155(1).
39	drafting.
40	drafting.

TABLE OF DESTINATIONS

The Housing Act 1957

1957	1985
s.4(1)	s.10
6(1)	8(3)(4)
6(2)	8(1) to (3)
6(2) proviso	8(5)
6(3)	8(1), (2)
7	9(1) to (13)
189(1)	
"house" (*a*) ...ss.8(6), 9(3)	

The Housing Act 1961

1961	1985	1961	1985
s.32(1)	s.11(1)(4)(5)	s.33(3) ....ss.14(1), (2),
32(2)	11(2)(4)		32(2)
32(3)	11(3)	33(4)	14(3)
32(4)	11(6)	33(5)	13(2)
32(5)	16, 36	33(6)	12(2)
33(1)	13(1)	33(7)	12(1)
33(2)	13(2)	33(8)	

The Landlord and Tenant Act 1962

1962	1985	1962	1985	1962	1985
s.1(1)	s.4(1)(3)	s.3(1)	s.6(1)	s.5(2) ss.34, 38
1(2)	4(2)	3(2)	6(2)		"local housing
2(1)	5(1)(2), 38	4(1)	7(1), (2)		authority"
	"protected	4(2)	7(3)	6(1)(*a*)	4(3), 37
	tenancy",	4(3)	7(1) to (3)	6(1)(*b*)	5(3)
	"restricted	4(4)	7(4)	6(2)	38
	contract"	4(6)	33(1)		"address"

The London Government Act 1963

1963	1985
Sch. 8,	
para. 2	s.8(4)

The Rent Act 1968

1968	1985
Sch. 15 ....ss.5(2), 34, 38
	"local housing
	authority",
	"protected
	tenancy"

The Housing Act 1969

1969	1985
s.71	s.10

The Local Government Act 1972

1972	1985
s.222(1)	s.34
103	35(1), (2)

THE HOUSING ACT 1974

1974	1985
s.121(1)	s.1(1)(2)
121(2)	2(1), (2)
121(3)	38
	"address"
121(4)	2(3)
121(5)	2(4)
121(6)	33(1)
121(7)	33(2)
121(8)	34, 38
	"local housing authority"

1974	1985
s.121(9)	s.1(3), 32(1), 36, 37
122(1)	3(1)
122(2)	3(1)
122(3)	38
	"address"
122(4)	3(2)
122(5)	3(3)
122(6)	33(1)
122(7)	33(2)
122(8)	3(4), 32(1), 37

1974	1985
s.122(9)(a) ..	s.3(4)
125(1)	17(1)
125(2)	17(2), 32(1), 36, 37
129(1)	
"dwelling"	38
	"dwelling"
Sch. 13,	
para. 9	38
	"address"

THE HOUSING RENTS AND SUBSIDIES ACT 1975

1975	1985
s.11(1)	s.31(1)
11(2)	31(2)
11(3)	31(4)
11(10)	31(3)
11(11)	31(3)
11(11)	
"dwelling"	32(3)
11(11)	

1975	1985
"local authority"	s.38
	"local authority"
s.11(11)	
"new letting" .	36
15(1)	31(1)(4)

1975	1985
s.15(5)	s.31(1)(2)
16(1)	
"dwelling"	s.38
	"dwelling"
17(11)	35(1), (2)
Sch. 5,	
para. 7(1) ..	35(1), (2)

THE RENT (AGRICULTURE) ACT 1976

1976	1985
Sch. 8,	
para. 9	s.5(1)
para. 31	37

THE RENT ACT 1977

1977	1985
s.14	s.14(4)
14(d)(e)	38
	"new town corporation"
14(1)(a) to	
(c)	38
	"local authority"
14(1)(g)	38
	"urban development"
15(3)	14(4)
15(3)(a)	38
	"housing association" "registered"

1977	1985
s.15(3)(d) ...	s.38
	"co-operative housing association"
80(1)(c)	38
	"new town corporation"
149(2)	34, 38
	"local housing authority"
Sch. 19,	
para. 14(1)(a)(c)	

1977	1985
Sch. 23,	
para. 31(a) .	s.5(1), 38
	"restricted contract"
Sch. 23,	
para. 31(b) .	5(1), 38
	"protected tenancy"
para. 32 .....ss.34, 38	
	"local housing authority"
para. 66	37
Sch. 24,	
para. 30	34, 38
	"protected tenancy"

THE HOUSING ACT 1980

1980	1985
s.50(1)	
"development corporation" ..ss.26(1), 38	
	"new town corporation"
50(1)	
"local authority"	26(1), 38
	"local housing authority"
s.80(1)(a)	14(4)
80(1)(b)	14(4), 38
	"co-operative housing association", "housing association" "registered"

1980	1985
s.80(1)(c)	s.14(4), 38
	"local authority" "urban development"
80(1)(d)	14(5)
80(1)(e)	14(5)
80(2)	14(4)
80(3)	14(4)
144	1(2), 2(4), 3(3)
151(1)	20(6), 29(6)
151(3)	20(6), 29(6)
Sch. 3,	
para. 1(2) ..	26(2), (3)
para. 1(3) ..	26(2), (3)
para. 1(2A)	26(2), (3)

1980	1985
Sch. 16,	
para. 3(2) ..	s.28(2)
para. 3(4) ..	28(3)
Sch. 19,	
para. 1(1) ..	18(1) to (3)
para. 2	19(1)(2), 20(1)
para. 3	19(1)
para. 4(1) ..	20(1)
para. 4(2) ..	20(2)
para. 5(1) to	
(6)	20(3)
para. 5(7) ..	20(4)
para. 6	20(5)
para. 7(1) ..	21(1)(4)
para. 7(2) ..	21(2)
para. 7(3) ..	21(5), (6)

THE HOUSING ACT 1980

1980	1985
para. 7(4)	.. s.22(1), (2), (4)
para. 7(5)	.. 21(1)
para. 8(1)	.. 23(1), (2)
para. 8(2)	.. 23(1), (2)
para. 9	...... 21(3), 22(3)
para. 10	 24
para. 11	..... 19(3)
para. 12	..... 19(4)
para. 13(1)	. 25(1), (2)
para. 13(2)	. 33(1)
para. 13(3)	. 33(2)
para. 14(1)	. 26(1) to (3), 28(6)

1980	1985
para. 14(1)(*a*)	s.38 "local housing authority"
para. 14(2)(*a*)	.... 26(1)
Sch. 19, para. 14(2)(*b*)	.... 28(6)
Sch. 19, para. 15	 27
para. 16	..... 30 "flat"

1980	1985
para. 17(1)	. s.28(2)(3)
para. 17(2)	. 28(4)
para. 17(2)(*b*)	.... 28(5)
para. 18	..... 30 "landlord", 37
para. 19	..... 30 "tenant"
para. 20	..... 29(1)
para. 20(*b*)	. 29(4)
para. 21(1)	. 29(2), (3)
para. 21(2)	. 29(5)

THE LOCAL GOVERNMENT PLANNING AND LAND ACT 1980

1980	1985
s.155(1)	.......ss.14(4), 38 "urban development"

THE NEW TOWNS ACT 1981

1981	1985
Sch. 12, para. 24	.....ss.14(4), 38 "new town corporation"

THE CRIMINAL JUSTICE ACT 1982

1982	1985
ss.37, 46(1)	...ss.1(2), 2(4), 3(3), 7(1)(3), 25(1)(2)
Sch. 3	.... 7(1) to (3)

THE COMPANIES CONSOLIDATION (CONSEQUENTIAL PROVISIONS) ACT 1985

1985	1985
Sch. 2	.... s.28(2)(5)

THE LOCAL GOVERNMENT ACT 1985

1985	1985
Sch. 13, para. 21	..... s.38 "local authority"

1985	1985
Sch. 14, paras. 56, 58(*h*)	.... s.38 "local authority"

LAW COMMISSION'S REPORT OF THE CONSOLIDATION OF THE HOUSING ACTS (CMND. 9515) RECOMMENDATIONS

1974	1985
R.14(i)	.... s.17(2)
R.28	.... 33(2)

Destinations for Statutory Instruments

THE ISLES OF SCILLY (HOUSING) ORDER 1985

1975	1985
S.I. 1975 No. 512	.... s.38 "local housing authority"

HOUSING (CONSEQUENTIAL PROVISIONS) ACT 1985

(1985 c.71)

An Act to make provision for repeals, consequential amendments, transitional matters and savings in connection with the consolidation of enactments in the Housing Act 1985, the Housing Associations Act 1985 and the Landlord and Tenant Act 1985.

[30th October 1985]

Meaning of "the consolidating Acts"

1. In this Act "the consolidating Acts" means—
the Housing Act 1985,
the Housing Associations Act 1985, and
the Landlord and Tenant Act 1985,
and this Act in so far as it reproduces the effect of provisions repealed by this Act.

Continuity of the law

2.—(1) The re-enactment of provisions in the consolidating Acts, and the consequent repeal of those provisions by this Act, does not affect the continuity of the law.

(2) Anything done (including subordinate legislation made), or having effect as done, under a provision reproduced in the consolidating Acts has effect as if done under the corresponding provision of the consolidating Acts.

(3) References (express or implied) in the consolidating Acts or any other enactment, instrument or document to a provision of the consolidating Acts shall, so far as the context permits, be construed as including, in relation to times, circumstances and purposes before the commencement of those Acts, a reference to corresponding earlier provisions.

(4) A reference (express or implied) in an enactment, instrument or other document to a provision reproduced in the consolidating Acts shall be construed, so far as is required for continuing its effect and subject to any express amendment made by this Act, as being, or as the case may require including, a reference to the corresponding provision of the consolidating Acts.

Repeals

3.—(1) The enactments specified in Schedule 1 are repealed to the extent specified.

(2) The repeals include repeals, in accordance with Recommendations of the Law Commission and the Scottish Law Commission, of provisions which are obsolete or no longer of practical utility or whose repeal is otherwise desirable for the purpose of achieving a satisfactory consolidation of the enactments reproduced in the consolidating Acts.

(3) The repeals have effect subject to any relevant savings in—
    Schedule 4 to this Act (miscellaneous and general savings), or
    Schedule 15, 18 or 19 to the Housing Act 1985 or Schedule 5 to the
        Housing Associations Act 1985 (which relate to certain
        superseded financial provisions).

Consequential amendments

4.—(1) The enactments specified in Schedule 2 have effect with the amendments specified.

(2) The amendments have effect subject to any relevant transitional provisions in Schedule 3.

Transitional provisions and savings

5.—(1) Schedule 3 has effect with respect to transitional matters in connection with the coming into force of the consolidating Acts and the consequential amendments made by this Act.

(2) Schedule 4 contains savings in connection with the repeals made by this Act (including savings for repealed transitional provisions and repealed savings).

(3) The provisions of Schedule 4 do not affect the general operation of section 16 of the Interpretation Act 1978 (general savings to be implied on a repeal).

Short title, commencement and extent

6.—(1) This Act may be cited as the Housing (Consequential Provisions) Act 1985.

(2) This Act comes into force on 1st April 1986.

(3) The following provisions of this Act extend to England and Wales—
    sections 1 to 6,
    Part I of Schedule 1,
    in Schedule 2, paragraphs 1 to 9, 11, 12, 14, 15, 18 to 24, 26, 28 to
        36, 38, 43, 44, 46 to 50, 52 to 58, 60 and 61.
    Schedules 3 and 4.

(4) The following provisions of this Act extend to Scotland—
    sections 1 to 6,
    Part II of Schedule 1,
    in Schedule 2, paragraphs 2, 5, 6, 7(3), 8, 10, 15 to 18, 20, 21, 25 to
        29, 31, 37, 39 to 43, 45, 48, 52, 54 and 59,
    in Schedule 4, paragraphs 1, 2, 4, 15 and 16.

(5) The following provisions of this Act extend to Northern Ireland—
    sections 1 to 4 and 6,
    Part III of Schedule 1,
    in Schedule 2, paragraphs 13, 51, and 52.

SCHEDULES

SCHEDULE 1

REPEALS

PART I

ENGLAND AND WALES

Act	Short title	Extent of repeal
62 & 63 Vict. c.44.	Small Dwellings Acquisition Act 1899.	The whole Act.
4 & 5 Geo. 5. c.31.	Housing Act 1914.	The whole Act.
9 & 10 Geo. 5. c.35.	Housing, Town Planning, &c. Act 1919.	The whole Act, so far as unrepealed.
13 & 14 Geo. 5. c.24.	Housing, &c. Act 1923.	The whole Act, so far as unrepealed.
15 & 16 Geo. 5. c.5.	Law of Property (Amendment) Act 1924.	In paragraph 5 of Schedule 9, the words "The Small Dwellings Acquisition Act 1899 and other".
25 & 26 Geo. 5. c.40.	Housing Act 1935.	The whole Act, so far as unrepealed.
26 Geo. 5. & 1 Edw. 8. c.49.	Public Health Act 1936.	Part IX.
12 & 13 Geo. 6. c.60.	Housing Act 1949.	Sections 44 and 50.
5 & 6 Eliz. 2. c.56.	Housing Act 1957.	The whole Act.
6 & 7 Eliz. 2. c.42.	Housing (Financial Provisions) Act 1958.	The whole Act.
7 & 8 Eliz. 2. c.33.	House Purchase and Housing Act 1959.	The whole Act.
7 & 8 Eliz. 2. c.34.	Housing (Underground Rooms) Act 1959.	The whole Act.
7 & 8 Eliz. 2. c.53.	Town and Country Planning Act 1959.	Section 26(5)(*a*). Section 58(4). In Schedule 7, the amendments of the Housing Act 1957.
9 & 10 Eliz. 2. c.33.	Land Compensation Act 1961.	Section 8(7)(*d*). In Schedule 4, paragraphs 9 and 10.
9 & 10 Eliz. 2. c.62.	Trustee Investments Act 1961.	In Schedule 4, paragraph 6.
9 & 10 Eliz. 2. c.65.	Housing Act 1961.	The whole Act.
10 & 11 Eliz. 2. c.50.	Landlord and Tenant Act 1962.	The whole Act.
1963 c.33.	London Government Act 1963.	Section 21. Schedule 8.
1964 c.56.	Housing Act 1964.	Parts I and IV. Sections 96, 102, 103 and 106. In section 108— (*a*) subsection (1)(*a*); (*b*) in subsection (4) the words "subject to the following subsection"; (*c*) subsection (5). Schedules 1 to 4.
1965 c.25.	Finance Act 1965.	Section 93.

Act	Short title	Extent of repeal
1965 c.56.	Compulsory Purchase Act 1965.	In section 4, the words from "For the purposes" to the end. In section 11(2), the second paragraph. Sections 34 and 35. In Schedule 7, the entry relating to the Housing Act 1957.
1965 c.81.	Housing (Slum Clearance Compensation) Act 1965.	The whole Act.
1967 c.29.	Housing Subsidies Act 1967.	The whole Act.
1967 c.88.	Leasehold Reform Act 1967.	In section 30(7)(*b*), the words from "including" to "1961". In Schedule 5, paragraph 8(4).
1968 c.13.	National Loans Act 1968.	In section 6(1), the references to section 92(2) of the Housing Act 1935 and section 7(2)(*a*) of the Housing Act 1961. In Schedule 1, the entries relating to the Housing (Financial Provisions) Act 1958, the House Purchase and Housing Act 1959 and the Housing Act 1961.
1968 c.42.	Prices and Incomes Act 1968.	The whole Act so far as unrepealed.
1969 c.33.	Housing Act 1969.	Parts II, IV and V. Sections 70 to 72, 75, 84 to 90. In section 91— (*a*) subsections (2) to (4); (*b*) in subsection (5) the words "except sections 78 and 79". Schedules 4 to 9.
1970 c.42.	Local Authority Social Services Act 1970.	In Schedule 1, the entry relating to section 9(1)(*b*) of the Housing (Homeless Persons) Act 1977.
1970 c.23.	Courts Act 1971.	In Schedule 9, the entry relating to s.14(5) of the Housing Act 1957.
1970 c.76.	Housing Act 1971.	The whole Act.
1971 c.78.	Town and Country Planning Act 1971.	In Schedule 23— (*a*) in Part I, the entry relating to the London Government Act 1963; (*b*) in Part II, the amendment of section 21(4)(*a*)(i) of the London Government Act 1963 and the entry relating to the Housing Act 1969.
1972 c.11.	Superannuation Act 1972.	In Schedule 6, paragraph 47.
1972 c.47.	Housing Finance Act 1972.	The whole Act.
1972 c.70.	Local Government Act 1972.	In section 131(2), paragraphs (*i*), (*jj*) and (*l*). Sections 193 and 194. In Schedule 13, paragraph 21(*b*). Schedule 22.
1972 c.71.	Criminal Justice Act 1972.	Section 32.
1973 c.5.	Housing (Amendment) Act 1973.	The whole Act.
1973 c.26.	Land Compensation Act 1973.	In section 37(2), the words from "In this subsection" to the end. In section 39, subsections (5) and (8A) In section 73(4), the words "paragraph 2 of".
1974 c.7.	Local Government Act 1974.	Section 1(5)(*c*). Section 37.

Act	Short title	Extent of repeal
1974 c.39.	Consumer Credit Act 1974.	In Schedule 4, paragraph 18.
1974 c.44.	Housing Act 1974.	Part I, except section 11. Parts II to VIII. Sections 105 to 117, 121 to 130. In section 131— (*a*) subsection (2); (*b*) in subsection (5), the words from the beginning to "VIII and", from "105" to "110 to" and "124, 125 and 126". Schedules 1 to 7 and 9 to 12. In Schedule 13, paragraphs 3 to 11, 19 to 21, 24, 30 to 32, 35, 36 and 40(6). Schedules 14 and 15.
1974 c.49.	Insurance Companies Act 1974.	In Schedule 1, the entry relating to the Housing Subsidies Act 1967.
1975 c.6.	Housing Rents and Subsidies Act 1975.	The whole Act.
1975 c.18.	Social Security (Consequential) Provisions Act 1975.	In Schedule 2, paragraph 49.
1975 c.45.	Finance (No. 2) Act 1975.	In section 69(3)(*e*), the words "housing society". In section 71(3), the words from " 'housing society' " to "1964".
1975 c.55.	Statutory Corporations (Financial Provisions) Act 1975.	In Schedule 4, paragraph 8.
1975 c.67.	Housing Finance (Special Provisions) Act 1975.	The whole Act.
1975 c.72.	Children Act 1975.	In Schedule 3, paragraphs 15, 66 and 83.
1975 c.76.	Local Land Charges Act 1975.	In Schedule 1, the entries relating to the Housing Act 1961 and the Housing Act 1974.
1976 c.57.	Local Government (Miscellaneous Provisions) Act 1976.	Sections 9 and 10.
1976 c.75.	Development of Rural Wales Act 1976.	In Schedule 3, paragraph 30(4). In Schedule 7, paragraphs 8, 9, and 12 to 15.
1976 c.80.	Rent (Agriculture) Act 1976.	In Schedule 8, paragraphs 4 to 6, 9 to 11 and 27 to 31.
1977 c.42.	Rent Act 1977.	Section 118. Section 145. In section 149(1)(*a*)(iii), the words ", and section 136". In Schedule 23, paragraphs 22 to 28, 31 to 36, 47, 48, 55, 59 to 66, 69 and 70.
1977 c.48.	Housing (Homeless Persons) Act 1977.	The whole Act.
1978 c.27.	Home Purchase Assistance and Housing Corporation Guarantee Act 1978.	The whole Act.
1978 c.44.	Employment Protection (Consolidation) Act 1978.	In Schedule 16, paragraph 31.
1978 c.48.	Homes Insulation Act 1978.	The whole Act.
1979 c.37.	Banking Act 1979.	In Schedule 6, Part I, paragraph 11.

SCHEDULE 1—*continued*

Act	Short title	Extent of repeal
1980 c.9.	Reserve Forces Act 1980.	In Schedule 9, paragraph 13.
1980 c.43.	Magistrates' Courts Act 1980.	In Schedule 1, paragraph 25. In Schedule 7, paragraph 22.
1980 c.48.	Finance Act 1980.	In section 97(3), paragraph (*g*).
1980 c.51.	Housing Act 1980.	Part I. Section 80. In section 81(1), the words "secure tenancies,". In section 83, the words "a secure tenant," and "for the purposes of Chapter II of Part I of this Act or, as the case may be,". In section 85(1), the words "in Chapter II of Part I of this Act or" and "that Chapter or, as the case may be,". Section 87. Parts V to VIII. Sections 134 to 137, 139, 144 to 147 and 149. In section 150, the definitions of "the 1957 Act", "the 1969 Act", "the 1972 Act", "the 1974 Act", "the 1975 Act" and "the 1984 Act". In section 151(1), the words "22(1), 33(2),", "or paragraph 11 of Schedule 3" and "8(5),". Section 151(4). Section 153(1) and (2). In section 153(3) the words from "90 to" to "137 to". Section 154(2). Schedules 1 to 4A. In Schedule 10, paragraph 1(3). Schedules 11 to 13, 16 to 20, 23 and 24. In Schedule 25, paragraphs 7 to 9, 11 to 13, 18 to 31, 34, 62, 69, 71, 74 and 76.
1980 c.65.	Local Government, Planning and Land Act 1980.	In section 47— (*a*) in subsection (4)(*b*) the words "6(2) and (3) and"; (*b*) subsection (4)(*c*); (*c*) subsection (6)(*b*). Section 54(5)(*b*) and (6)(*c*). Section 68(3) and (6). Section 156(1) and (2). In section 159(1)(*b*), the words "or IX (common lodging houses)". In Schedule 6, paragraphs 7 to 9 and 17 to 20. In Schedule 27, paragraph 14. In Schedule 33, paragraphs 6 and 8.
1981 c.54.	Supreme Court Act 1981.	In Schedule 5, the amendment of the Small Dwellings Acquisition Act 1899.
1981 c.64.	New Towns Act 1981.	Section 50(4) to (6) and (8). Section 80(4)(*a*). In Schedule 10, paragraph 3(3)(*d*). In Schedule 11, paragraphs 9 and 10. In Schedule 12, paragraphs 7, 8, 13, 14, 25 and 27(*a*), (*b*) and (*d*).
1981 c.65.	Trustee Savings Banks Act 1981.	In Schedule 6, the entry relating to the Home Purchase Assistance and Housing Corporation Guarantee Act 1978.

Act	Short title	Extent of repeal
1981 c.67.	Acquisition of Land Act 1981.	In Schedule 4— (a) in the Table in paragraph 1, the entries relating to the Housing Act 1957, the Housing Act 1969 and the Housing Act 1974; (b) paragraph 10; (c) in paragraph 14(7), the reference to section 34(1) of the Compulsory Purchase Act 1965.
1982 c.24.	Social Security and Housing Benefits Act 1982.	In section 35(1), in the definition of "Housing Revenue Account rebate", the words "(within the meaning of the Housing Finance Act 1972)". In Schedule 4, paragraph 6(2) to (4).
1982 c.39.	Finance Act 1982.	Section 153(3).
1982 c.48.	Criminal Justice Act 1982.	In Schedule 3, the entries relating to provisions of the Housing Act 1957, the Landlord and Tenant Act 1962 and the Housing Act 1980.
1982 c.50.	Insurance Companies Act 1982.	In Schedule 5, paragraph 4.
1983 c.29.	Miscellaneous Financial Provisions Act 1983.	In Schedule 2 the entry relating to the Housing Act 1974.
1984 c.12.	Telecommunications Act 1984.	In Schedule 4, paragraph 35.
1984 c.22.	Public Health (Control of Disease) Act 1984.	In Schedule 2, paragraph 2.
1984 c.28.	County Courts Act 1984.	In Schedule 2, paragraphs 27 and 28.
1984 c.29.	Housing and Building Control Act 1984.	Sections 1 to 38. Schedules 1 to 7. In Schedule 11, paragraphs 1 to 3, and 6 to 34.
1984 c.50.	Housing Defects Act 1984.	The whole Act.
1984 c.55.	Building Act 1984.	Section 89(2). In Schedule 5, in paragraph 2, the words "and the Housing Act 1957". In Schedule 6, paragraph 6.
1985 c.9.	Companies Consolidation (Consequential Provisions) Act 1985.	In Schedule 2, the entries relating to the Housing Act 1964, the Housing Subsidies Act 1967, the Housing Act 1974, the Housing Act 1980 and the Housing and Building Control Act 1984.
1985 c.51.	Local Government Act 1985.	In Schedule 8, paragraphs 12(1) and (3) to (5) and 14(3). In Schedule 13, in paragraph 21, the words "and section 80(1)(c) of the Housing Act 1980". In Schedule 14, paragraphs 58(a) to (d) and (f) to (h), 64 and 65.

SCHEDULE 1—*continued*

PART II

SCOTLAND

Act	Short title	Extent of repeal
7 & 8 Eliz. 2. c.33.	House Purchase and Housing Act 1959.	Section 1.
1964 c.56.	Housing Act 1964.	Part I.
1965 c.25.	Finance Act 1965.	Section 93.
1966 c.49.	Housing (Scotland) Act 1966.	In section 1, the words "section 152 of this Act and". Section 152. Section 156. Section 158.
1968 c.31.	Housing (Financial Provisions) (Scotland) Act 1968.	Sections 23 and 24.
1972 c.11.	Superannuation Act 1972.	In Schedule 6, paragraph 47.
1972 c.46.	Housing (Financial Provisions) (Scotland) Act 1972.	Sections 51 to 59.
1972 c.47.	Housing Finance Act 1972.	Section 77(2).
1973 c.65.	Local Government (Scotland) Act 1973.	In Schedule 12, paragraphs 4 and 10.
1974 c.44.	Housing Act 1974.	Part I, except section 11. Part II, except section 18(2) to (6) and Schedule 3. Part III. In Schedule 13, paragraphs 21 and 23(2) to (4). In Schedule 14, paragraphs 1, 2 and 6.
1975 c.28.	Housing Rents and Subsidies (Scotland) Act 1975.	Section 12. In Schedule 3, paragraphs 12 and 13.
1975 c.45.	Finance (No. 2) Act 1975.	In section 69(3)(*e*), the words "housing society". In section 71(3), the words from " 'housing society' " to "1964".
1977 c.48.	Housing (Homeless Persons) Act 1977.	In section 6— (*a*) in subsection (1)(*a*), the words "Part V of the Housing Act 1957 or"; (*b*) in subsection (2), the words "section 113(2) of the Housing Act 1957 or". Section 7(11)(*a*). In section 10, the words "section 111 of the Housing Act 1957 or". In section 13— (*a*) in subsections (2), (3), (5) and (6), the words "or the Greater London Council"; (*b*) in subsection (4) the words "nor the Greater London Council"; (*c*) in subsections (5) and (7) the words "as the case may be"; (*d*) in subsection (10) the words "the Housing Finance Act 1972 and". In section 19(1)— (*a*) in the definition of "development corporation" paragraph (*a*); (*b*) in the definition of "housing authority" the words from "as respects England and Wales" to "Scotland";

Schedule 1—*continued*

Act	Short title	Extent of repeal
1977 c.48— *cont.*	Housing (Homeless Persons) Act 1977—*cont.*	(*c*) in the definition of "relevant authority", paragraphs (*b*) and (*d*); (*d*) the definition of "social services authority". Section 20(2). In section 21— (*a*) in subsection (2), the words from the beginning to "Scotland"; (*b*) in subsection (3), the words from "(*a*) in England" to "in Scotland".
1978 c.14.	Housing (Financial Provisions) (Scotland) Act 1978.	In Schedule 2, paragraph 3.
1978 c.27.	Home Purchase Assistance and Housing Corporation Guarantee Act 1978.	Sections 4 and 5. Section 6(2).
1978 c.48.	Homes Insulation Act 1978.	In section 1(8)— (*a*) paragraphs (*a*) and (*b*); (*b*) in paragraph (*c*), the words "in Scotland". Section 3.
1980 c.51.	Housing Act 1980.	Part VIII. In Schedule 16, Part II. In Schedule 17, paragraphs 1, 2 and 3. Schedule 18. In Schedule 25— (*a*) in paragraph 11 the words from "and in paragraph 3(2)(*a*)" to the end; (*b*) paragraphs 12, 13, 24, 25 and 70.
1980 c.52.	Tenants' Rights &c. (Scotland) Act 1980.	Section 9. In section 31— (*a*) in subsection (1) the words "or the Housing Corporation" and "or, as the case may be, the Housing Corporation"; (*b*) in subsection (2) the words "or, as the case may be, the Housing Corporation"; (*c*) in subsection (4) the words "with the Housing Corporation and".

SCHEDULE 1—*continued*

PART III

NORTHERN IRELAND

Act	Short title	Extent of repeal
1975 c.45.	Finance (No. 2) Act 1975.	In section 69(3)(*e*), the words "housing society". In section 71(3), the words from " 'housing society' " to "1964".
1978 c.27.	Home Purchase Assistance and Housing Corporation Guarantee Act 1978.	Section 4. Section 6(3).
1978 c.48.	Homes Insulation Act 1978.	Section 3.
1980 c.51.	Housing Act 1980.	Section 111(8). Sections 152(1), 153 and 155. In Schedule 25, paragraphs 11, 12, 18 and 19.

Section 4

SCHEDULE 2

CONSEQUENTIAL AMENDMENTS

Brine Pumping (Compensation for Subsidence) Act 1891 (c.40)

1.—(1) Notwithstanding anything in section 50 of the Brine Pumping (Compensation for Subsidence) Act 1891 (persons excluded from right to compensation), a local authority is entitled to compensation in accordance with the provisions of that Act in respect of any injury or damage to houses belonging to them which were provided under a housing scheme towards the losses on which the Secretary of State, or any predecessor of his, was liable to contribute under the Housing, Town Planning, &c. Act 1919 at any time before 10th August 1972.

(2) In sub-paragraph (1) "local authority" means a county council, district council or London borough council, the Common Council of the City of London or the Council of the Isles of Scilly.

Coal Mining (Subsidence) Act 1957 (c.59)

2.—(1) The Coal Mining (Subsidence) Act 1957 is amended as follows.

(2) In section 1(4) (cases in which NCB may make payment instead of executing remedial works)—

(*a*) in paragraph (*b*) (dwelling-houses likely to be acquired for clearance) for "Part III of the Housing Act 1936" substitute "Part IX of the Housing Act 1985" and for "subsection (2) or (3) of section forty of the said Act of 1936" substitute "section 587 of the said Act of 1985";

(*b*) in paragraph (*c*) (clearance orders) for "either of the said Parts III" substitute "the said Part III";

(*c*) in the passage following paragraph (*c*) for "either of the said Parts III" in the first place where it occurs substitute "under Part IX of the said Act of 1985 or Part III of the said Act of 1950" and in the second place where it occurs substitute "the said Part III";

(*d*) in paragraph (ii) of the proviso (consultation with relevant local authority) for "the local authority for the purposes of Part II of the Housing Act 1936" substitute "the local housing authority within the meaning of the Housing Act 1985" and after "Scotland" insert "the local authority".

(3) In Schedule 1 (obligations of NCB as regards houses rendered uninhabitable)—

(*a*) in paragraph 2(1)(*a*)(i) (standard of alternative accommodation) for "the local authority for the purposes of Part V of the Housing Act 1936" substitute "the

local housing authority within the meaning of the Housing Act 1985" and after "or, as the case may be," insert "the local authority";
(*b*) in the proviso to paragraph 5(3) (limit on rent payable) for "the local authority for the purposes of Part V of the Housing Act 1936 or" substitute "the local housing authority within the meaning of the Housing Act 1985 or the local authority".

(4) In Schedule 2 (determination of amount of depreciation), in paragraph 2(1) (determination of value of property)—
(*a*) in the passage following paragraph (*c*) for the words from "a closing order" to "1953" substitute "a closing order under section 266 of the Housing Act 1985";
(*b*) in paragraph (i) of the proviso for the words from "a demolition order" to "1953" substitute "a demolition or closing order under section 266 of the Housing Act 1985";
(*c*) in the same provision for "section one of the Slum Clearance Act 1956" substitute "Part I of Schedule 24 to the Housing Act 1985" and for "within the meaning of the said Act of 1956" substitute "as defined in paragraph 4(2)(*a*) of that Part of that Schedule".

Town and Country Planning Act 1959 (c.53)

3. In section 26 of the Town and Country Planning Act 1959 (consents to disposal of land by certain authorities), in subsection (5) (exceptions)—
(*a*) omit paragraph (*a*);
(*b*) after that paragraph insert—
"(*aa*) to a disposal for which consent is required under section 32 or 43 of the Housing Act 1985 (disposal of land held for housing purposes);".

Land Compensation Act 1961 (c.33)

4. For Schedule 2 to the Land Compensation Act 1961 (acquisition of houses as being unfit for human habitation) substitute—

"SECOND SCHEDULE

ACQUISITION OF HOUSES AS BEING UNFIT FOR HUMAN HABITATION

Acquisitions to which this Schedule applies

1.—(1) This Schedule applies to a compulsory acquisition of a description mentioned in sub-paragraph (2) where the land in question comprises a house which in the opinion of the local housing authority is unfit for human habitation and not capable at reasonable expense of being rendered so fit.
(2) The compulsory acquisitions referred to above are—
(*a*) an acquisition under section 6 of the Town Development Act 1952;
(*b*) an acquisition under Part VI of the Town and Country Planning Act 1971;
(*c*) an acquisition in pursuance of Part IX of that Act;
(*d*) an acquisition of land by an acquiring authority under the new towns code within the meaning of the Development of Rural Wales Act 1976;
(*e*) an acquisition by the Land Authority for Wales under section 104 of the Local Government, Planning and Land Act 1980;
(*f*) an acquisition by means of an order under section 141 of that Act vesting land in an urban development corporation;
(*g*) an acquisition by such a corporation under section 142 of that Act;
(*h*) an acquisition of land within the area designated by an order under section 1 of the New Towns Act 1981 as the site of a new town;
(*i*) an acquisition by a development corporation or local highway authority or the Secretary of State under the New Towns Act 1981 or under any enactment as applied by any provision of that Act;
(*j*) an acquisition under the provisions of Part VIII of the Housing Act 1985 relating to general improvement areas.

Procedure for declaring house to be unfit

2.—(1) The local housing authority may make and submit to the Minister an order, in the prescribed form, declaring the house to be in the state referred to in paragraph 1(1).

(2) Before doing so, they shall serve on every owner and, so far as it is reasonably practicable to ascertain such persons, on every mortgagee of the land or any part of it. a notice in the prescribed form—

(a) stating the effect of the order and that it is about to be submitted to the Minister, and

(b) specifying the time within which and the manner in which objection to the order can be made.

(3) If no objection is duly made by any of the persons on whom notices are required to be served, or if all the objections so made are withdrawn, the Minister may, if he thinks fit, confirm the order.

(4) In any other case he shall, before confirming the order, consider any objection not withdrawn and shall, if either the person by whom the objection was made or the local housing authority so desires, afford to that person and the authority an opportunity of appearing before and being heard by a person appointed by the Minister for the purpose.

The site value rule and its qualifications apply

3.—(1) If the order is confirmed by the Minister—

(a) either before or concurrently with the confirmation of a compulsory purchase order for the acquisition of the land, or

(b) after the date on which notice to treat is deemed to have been served, in such a case as is mentioned in sub-paragraph (2), or

(c) either before or concurrently with the coming into force of an order under section 141 of the Local Government, Planning and Land Act 1980 for the vesting of the land in an urban development corporation,

the site value provisions, that is, the provisions of sections 585 to 592 of the Housing Act 1985, including the provisions of Schedules 23 and 24 to that Act (supplementary payments), apply as they apply in the case of a house which is made the subject of a compulsory purchase order under section 290 of that Act (acquisition of land for clearance) as being unfit for human habitation.

(2) The cases referred to in sub-paragraph (1)(b) are where the acquisition is in pursuance of a notice to treat deemed to have been served in consequence of the service of a notice under—

(a) section 180 of the Town and Country Planning Act 1971, or the provisions of that section as applied by or under any other enactment, or

(b) any other provision of Part IX of that Act,

and the order is made before the date on which the notice to treat is deemed to have been served.

4. The site value provisions as applied by paragraph 3 have effect with the following further adaptations—

(a) substitute for references to the local housing authority in provisions requiring the authority to make a payment, or enabling the Secretary of State so to direct, references to the acquiring authority;

(b) substitute for the reference in paragraph 3(1) of Schedule 23 to the compulsory purchase order being confirmed a reference to the condition in paragraph 3(1)(a), (b) or (c) above being fulfilled;

(c) substitute for the reference in paragraph 7(3) of Schedule 23 (period of notification of amount payable) to the notice under paragraph 3(3) of Schedule 22 to that Act a reference to the notice under paragraph 2(2) above;

(d) substitute for the reference in paragraph 8(2) of Schedule 23 (period for appealing) to the compulsory purchase order a reference to the order under paragraph 2 above; and

(e) the "relevant date" for the purposes of Parts I and II of Schedule 24 is the date on which the order under paragraph 2 above was made.

Interpretation

5. This Schedule shall be construed as one with Part XVII of the Housing Act 1985.".

Trustee Investments Act 1961 (c.62)

5.—(1) Schedule 1 to the Trustee Investments Act 1961 (permitted investments) is amended as follows.

(2) In paragraph 12 of Part II and paragraph 2 of Part III (loans to or deposits and shares in certain building societies), for "designated under section 1 of the House Purchase and Housing Act 1959" substitute "designated for the purposes of this Act".

(3) After paragraph 3 of Part IV insert—

"3A.—(1) The Registrar may designate for the purposes of this Act a permanent building society which he is satisfied fulfils such requirements as to its assets and liabilities, liquid funds, reserves and other matters as the Treasury may by regulations prescribe.

(2) The Registrar shall publish in the London, Edinburgh and Belfast Gazettes notice of any such designation made by him and of the revocation of such a designation.

(3) If a person knowingly or recklessly makes, or causes or procures another person to make, a false or misleading statement in connection with any information which the Registrar may request for the purposes of this paragraph, he commits an offence and is liable—

(*a*) on summary conviction, to a fine not exceeding the statutory maximum or imprisonment for a term not exceeding three months, or both;

(*b*) on conviction on indictment, to a fine or imprisonment for a term not exceeding two years, or both.

(4) In this paragraph—

"building society" means a building society within the meaning of the Building Societies Act 1962 or the Building Societies Act (Northern Ireland) 1967 and "permanent", in relation to such a society, has the meaning given by section 1(2) of that Act;

"Registrar" means—

(*a*) in relation to a building society within the meaning of the 1962 Act, the Chief Registrar of Friendly Societies, and

(*b*) in relation to a building society within the meaning of the 1967 Act, the officer appointed to perform in Northern Ireland the functions of registrar of building societies.

(5) Regulations under this paragraph shall be made by statutory instrument which shall be subject to annulment in pursuance of a resolution of either House of Parliament.

(6) Regulations and designations made, and any other thing done, under or for the purposes of section 1 of the House Purchase and Housing Act 1959 before the repeal of that section by the Housing (Consequential Provisions) Act 1985 shall have effect as if made or done under or for the purposes of this paragraph.".

Building Societies Act 1962 (c.37)

6.—(1) Schedule 3 to the Building Societies Act 1962 (permitted classes of additional security) is amended as follows.

(2) In paragraph 3(1) for "local authorities" there shall continue to be substituted "bodies".

(3) In paragraph 3(2)(*a*) (guarantees given under certain enactments: England and Wales) for "section 111 of the Housing Act 1980" substitute "section 442 of the Housing Act 1985, section 84 of the Housing Associations Act 1985, section 111 of the Housing Act 1980".

(4) In paragraph 3(2)(*b*) (guarantees given under certain enactments: Scotland) after "Scotland" insert "section 86 of the Housing Associations Act 1985".

(5) In paragraph 3(2)(*c*) (guarantees given under certain enactments: Northern Ireland) for the words from "any statutory provision" to "1980" substitute "any statutory provision for the time being in force in Northern Ireland and made for purposes corresponding to those of section 442 of the Housing Act 1985, section 84 of the Housing Associations Act 1985 or section 111 of the Housing Act 1980".

(6) For paragraph 14 substitute—

"14.—(1) An agreement under section 442 of the Housing Act 1985, section 84 of the Housing Associations Act 1985 or section 111 of the Housing Act 1980 (agreement by local authority or Housing Corporation to indemnify building society in respect of mortgagor's default).

(2) An agreement under any statutory provision for the time being in force in Northern Ireland and made for purposes corresponding to those of the provisions referred to in sub-paragraph (1).".

(7) In paragraph 15 after "1980" insert "or section 86 of the Housing Associations Act 1985".

Pipelines Act 1962 (c.58)

7.—(1) The Pipelines Act 1962 is amended as follows.

(2) In section 28(4) (recovery of expenses incurred in executing demolition order)—

    (*a*) for "Subsections (2) to (5) of section twenty-three of the Housing Act 1957" substitute "The provisions of section 272 of the Housing Act 1985";

    (*b*) for "Part II" in each place where it occurs substitute "Part IX".

(3) In section 30 (recovery of possession of building to be demolished)—

    (*a*) in subsection (1) for "Section seventy-three of the Housing Act 1957" substitute "Section 286 of the Housing Act 1985";

    (*b*) in subsection (2) for "section seventy-three of the said Act of 1957" substitute "section 286 of the said Act of 1985";

    (*c*) in subsections (1) and (2) for "Part III" wherever occurring substitute "Part IX".

Industrial and Provident Societies Act 1965 (c.12)

8. In section 6(1) of the Industrial and Provident Societies Act 1965 (maximum share-holding in society), in paragraph (*b*) (exception for certain local authority holdings) for the words from "section 119(3)" to the end substitute "section 58(2) or 59(2) of the Housing Associations Act 1985".

Compulsory Purchase Act 1965 (c.56)

9. In section 27 of the Compulsory Purchase Act 1965 (acquiring authority to make good deficiency in rates), in subsection (1) (excepted cases) for "an acquisition of land under the Housing Act 1957" substitute "an acquisition of land under any Part of the Housing Act 1985 other than Part VIII (area improvement)".

Housing (Scotland) Act 1966 (c.49)

10.—(1) The Housing (Scotland) Act 1966 is amended as follows.

(2) Sections 162, 165, 177, 178, 186, 193 and 194 (general provisions with respect to housing functions of local authorities) apply in relation to sections 59 and 61 of the Housing Associations Act 1985 (functions of local authorities in relation to housing associations) as they apply in relation to provisions of the 1966 Act.

(3) In section 175(2) (compulsory purchase by Scottish Special Housing Association at request of Housing Corporation), for "section 3(5) of the Housing Act 1974" substitute "section 88(5) of the Housing Associations Act 1985".

(4) In section 208(1) (general interpretation), for the definition of "housing association" substitute—

    " 'housing association' has the same meaning as in the Housing Associations Act 1985;".

General Rate Act 1967 (c.9)

11. In Schedule 13 to the General Rate Act 1967 (determination whether premises used as a private dwelling), in paragraph 2(1) hereditaments used for letting of rooms)—

    (*a*) in paragraph (*b*) after "the Act" insert "or in accordance with applications approved under section 18 of the Housing Act 1969";

    (*b*) in paragraph (*c*) after "that Act" insert "or in respect of which grants or contributions have been made to a housing association under Part I of the Housing Act 1969".

Leasehold Reform Act 1967 (c.88)

12. In section 3(1) of the Leasehold Reform Act 1967 (meaning of "long tenancy"), in paragraph (*b*) of the proviso for "otherwise than by virtue of section 37A of the Housing Act 1980 (assignments by way of exchange)", substitute "otherwise than by virtue of section 92 of the Housing Act 1985 (assignments by way of exchange)".

Building Societies Act (Northern Ireland) 1967 (c.31) (N.I.)

13.—(1) Schedule 3 to the Building Societies Act (Northern Ireland) 1967 (permitted classes of additional security) is amended as follows.

(2) In paragraph 3(2)(*b*) (guarantees given under certain enactments: England and Wales) for "section 111 of the Housing Act 1980" substitute "section 442 of the Housing Act 1985, section 84 of the Housing Associations Act 1985, section 111 of the Housing Act 1980".

(3) In paragraph 3(2)(*c*) (guarantees given under certain enactments: Scotland) after "Scotland" insert "section 86 of the Housing Associations Act 1985.".

(4) For paragraph 14 substitute—

"14. An agreement under section 442 of the Housing Act 1985, section 84 of the Housing Associations Act 1985 or section 111 of the Housing Act 1980 (agreement by local authority or Housing Corporation to indemnify building society on mortgagor's default).".

(5) In paragraph 15 after "1980" insert "or section 86 of the Housing Associations Act 1985".

Greater London Council (General Powers) Act 1967 (c.xx)

14. In section 15 of the Greater London Council (General Powers) Act 1967 (application of provisions of Compulsory Purchase Act 1965 to acquisition by agreement of land for certain housing purposes), in subsection (1) for "Part V of the Act of 1957", in both places where it occurs, and for "the said Part V", substitute "Part II of the Housing Act 1985".

National Loans Act 1968 (c.13)

15. In Schedule 4 to the National Loans Act 1968 (local loans), in paragraph 3 (certain loans for housing purposes) for the words from "or section 47" to the end substitute ", section 451 of the Housing Act 1985 or section 67 or 68 of the Housing Associations Act 1985 (certain loans for housing purposes)".

Housing (Financial Provisions) (Scotland) Act 1968 (c.31)

16.—(1) Section 25 of the Housing (Financial Provisions) (Scotland) Act 1968 (advances to Scottish Special Housing Association) is amended as follows.

(2) In subsection (1)(*d*) (advances where Association act as agent for Housing Corporation) for "section 11(1) of the Housing Act 1964" substitute "section 100 of the Housing Associations Act 1985.".

(3) For subsection (4) (application of financial and accounting provisions) substitute—

"(4) The Treasury may issue to the Secretary of State out of the National Loans Fund such sums as are necessary to enable him to make advances under this section; and any sums received by the Secretary of State in repayment of such advances shall be paid into the National Loans Fund.

(4A) The Secretary of State shall—

(*a*) prepare in respect of each financial year an account, in such form and manner as the Treasury may direct, of sums issued to him for advances under this section, and of sums received by him under this section, and of the disposal by him of those sums respectively, and

(*b*) send it to the Comptroller and Auditor-General not later than the end of November in the following financial year;

and the Comptroller and Auditor-General shall examine, certify and report on the account and lay copies of it, together with his report, before each House of Parliament.".

Housing (Scotland) Act 1969 (c.34)

17. In section 59 of the Housing (Scotland) Act 1969 (exchequer contributions towards expenditure in improving residential areas), in subsection (8) (definitions: "housing associ-ation") for "Housing Act 1974" substitute "Housing Associations Act 1985".

Income and Corporation Taxes Act 1970 (c.10)

18.—(1) The Income and Corporation Taxes 1970 is amended as follows.

(2) In section 341 (co-operative housing associations), in subsection (6)(i) for "the Housing Act 1957, the Housing (Scotland) Act 1950" substitute "the Housing Associations Act 1985".

(3) In section 341A (self-build societies), in subsection (11) for "Part I of the Housing Act 1974" substitute "the Housing Associations Act 1985".

(4) In section 342 (disposals of land between the Housing Corporation and housing societies)—

(*a*) after "section 5 of the Housing Act 1964" insert "or paragraph 5 of Schedule 7 to the Housing Associations Act 1985";

(*b*) for "housing society" and "society", wherever occurring, substitute "housing associ-ation" and "association";

(c) for "Part I of the Housing Act 1964" substitute "the Housing Associations Act 1985".

(5) In section 342A (disposals by certain housing associations)—

    (a) in subsection (1) for "Part II of the Housing Act 1974" substitute "Part I of the Housing Associations Act 1985".

    (b) in subsection (2) for "Part I of the Housing Act 1974" substitute "the Housing Associations Act 1985".

Local Authority Social Services Act 1970 (c.42)

19. In Schedule 1 to the Local Authority Social Services Act 1970 (enactments conferring functions assigned to Social Services Committee) at the end add—

| "Housing Act 1985, section 72(b) | Co-operation in relation to homeless persons and persons threatened with homelessness". |

Chronically Sick and Disabled Persons Act 1970 (c.44)

20. For section 3 of the Chronically Sick and Disabled Persons Act 1970 (duties of housing authorities) substitute—

"Duties of housing authorities

    3.—(1) A local housing authority in discharging their duty under section 8 of the Housing Act 1985 to consider housing conditions in their district and the needs of their district with respect to the provision of further housing accommodation shall have regard to the special needs of chronically sick or disabled persons.

    (2) A local authority for the purposes of Part VII of the Housing (Scotland) Act 1966 in discharging their duty under section 137 of that Act to consider housing conditions in their district and the needs of their district with respect to the provision of further housing accommodation shall have regard to the special needs of chronically sick or disabled persons; and any proposals prepared and submitted to the Secretary of State by the authority under that section for the provision of new houses shall distinguish any houses which the authority propose to provide which make special provision for the need of such persons.".

Fire Precautions Act 1971 (c.40)

21.—(1) Section 36 of the Fire Precautions Act 1970 (loans to meet expenditure on certain alterations) is amended as follows.

(2) For subsection (8) (terms of loan) substitute—

    "(8) The local authority's offer may in particular include provision—

    (a) for the advance to be made by instalments from time to time as the alterations progress;

    (b) for repayment either by instalments of principal or by an annuity of principal and interest combined;

    (c) that in the event of any of the conditions subject to which the advance is made not being complied with, the balance for the time being unpaid shall become repayable on demand by the local authority;

    (d) that the balance for the time being unpaid may be repaid on one of the usual quarter days by the person for the time being entitled to the equity of redemption after one month's written notice of intention to repay has been given to the local authority.".

(3) In subsection (9) (application to Scotland) for paragraph (d) substitute—

    "(d) in subsection (8) for 'on one of the usual quarter days' there shall be substituted 'at any term of Whitsunday or Martinmas' and for 'the person for the time being entitled to the equity of redemption' there shall be substituted 'the debtor'.".

Town and Country Planning Act 1971 (c.78)

22.—(1) The Town and Country Planning Act 1971 is amended as follows.

(2) In section 192 (scope of planning blight provisions), in paragraph (h) (land proposed to be acquired for purposes of general improvement area) for the words from "sections 31" to the end substitute "section 257 of the Housing Act 1985 as land which a local authority propose to acquire in the exercise of their powers under the provisions of Part VIII of that Act relating to general improvement areas".

(3) In section 197 (blight notices: land in clearance areas)—

(*a*) for "Part III of the Housing Act 1957" substitute "section 290 of the Housing Act 1985 (acquisition of land for clearance)";

(*b*) for "Part III of the said Act of 1957" substitute "the said Act of 1985".

Local Government Act 1972 (c.70)

23. In section 131(2) of the Local Government Act 1972 (saving for special provisions regulating land transactions), after paragraph (*l*) insert—

"(*m*) the Housing Act 1985".

Land Compensation Act 1973 (c.26)

24.—(1) The Land Compensation Act 1973 is amended as follows.

(2) In section 29 (home loss payments)—

(*a*) in subsection (1)(*b*) (improvement notices) for "Part VIII of the Housing Act 1974" substitute "Part VII of the Housing Act 1985";

(*b*) for subsection (1)(*d*) (improvement &c. by certain housing associations) substitute—

"(*d*) the carrying out of any improvement to the dwelling or of redevelopment on the land by a housing association which has previously acquired the land and at the date of the displacement is registered under the Housing Associations Act 1985";

(*c*) at the end of subsection (2) (but not as part of paragraph (*b*)) there shall continue to be the words "and in a case within subsection (1)(*d*) above, unless the displacement occurred on or after 31st July 1974 (on which date the Housing Act 1974 was passed)";

(*d*) for subsection (7) substitute—

"(7) In this section "a housing order or undertaking" means—

(*a*) a demolition, or closing order, or an obstructive building order, under Part IX of the Housing Act 1985 (slum clearance);

(*b*) a closing order under section 368(4) of that Act (closing of multi-occupied house with inadequate means of escape from fire);

(*c*) an undertaking accepted under section 211, 264 or 368 of that Act (undertaking in lieu of improvement notice or housing order).".

(3) In section 37 (disturbance payments)—

(*a*) in subsection (1)(*b*) (improvement notices) for "Part VIII of the Housing Act 1974" substitute "Part VII of the Housing Act 1985";

(*b*) for subsection (1)(*d*) (improvement &c. by certain housing associations) substitute—

"(*d*) the carrying out of any improvement to a house or building on the land or of re-development on the land by a housing association which has previously acquired the land and at the date of the displacement is registered under the Housing Associations Act 1985;";

(*c*) in subsection (2)(*b*)(ii) (exclusion where full compensation paid) for a "site value provision" substitute "section 585 of the Housing Act 1985 (site value for unfit houses)" and after "owner-occupier's supplement" insert "under Part I of Schedule 24 to that Act";

(*d*) after subsection (2)(*c*) there shall continue to be—

"(*d*) in a case within subsection (1)(*d*) above, unless the displacement occurred on or after 31st July 1974 (on which date the Housing Act 1974 was passed).".

(4) In section 39 (duty to rehouse residential occupiers)—

(*a*) in subsection (1)(*d*) (improvement notices) for "Part VIII of the Housing Act 1974" substitute "Part VII of the Housing Act 1985";

(*b*) in subsection (4)(*b*) (exclusion of person with local authority mortgage) after "1958" insert "or section 435 of the Housing Act 1985";

(*c*) for subsection (7) (definition of relevant authority) substitute—

"(7) Subject to subsection (8) below, the 'relevant authority' for the purposes of this section is the local housing authority within the meaning of the Housing Act 1985.".

(5) In section 42 (duty of displacing authority to indemnify rehousing authority)—

(*a*) in subsection (1)(*b*) for "Part V of the Housing Act 1957" substitute "Part II of the Housing Act 1985";

(*b*) in subsection (2)(*a*) for "Part V of the said Act of 1957" substitute "Part II of the said Act of 1985";

(c) in subsection (2)(b) for "the said Part V" substitute "the said Part II";

(d) for subsection (6) (provision for construction as one with Housing Finance Act 1972) substitute—

"(6) In subsection (2)—

'Housing Revenue Account dwelling' means a dwelling which is within the authority's Housing Revenue Account (within the meaning of Part XIII of the Housing Act 1985) and is not—

(a) a dwelling for the time being let on a long tenancy at a low rent within the meaning of the Leasehold Reform Act 1967, or

(b) a dwelling no longer owned by the authority;

'year' means financial year.".

(6) In section 52 (right to advance payment of compensation), in subsection (11) for the words from "section 98" to "that Act" substitute "section 583 of the Housing Act 1985".

(7) In section 57(3) (application of provisions as to notice of entry in respect of part of agricultural holding) for the words from "section 101" to "that Act)" substitute "section 584 of the Housing Act 1985 (power to enter and determine short tenancies of land acquired or appropriated for certain purposes of that Act)".

(8) In section 73 (planning blight: land affected by slum clearance resolution)—

(a) in subsection (1) for "section 42 of the Housing Act 1957" substitute "section 289 of the Housing Act 1985" and for "section 43 of that Act" substitute "section 290 of that Act";

(b) in subsection (3) for "section 43 of the Housing Act 1957" substitute "section 290 of the Housing Act 1985";

(c) in subsection (4) for "section 59(2) of the said Act of 1957" substitute "section 585 of the Housing Act 1985";

(d) in subsection (5)(a) for "section 60 of, and Part I of Schedule 2 to, the said Act of 1957" substitute "Part I of Schedule 24 to the Housing Act 1985" and for "Part III" substitute "section 290";

(e) in section (5)(b) for the words from "Part II" to "1969" substitute "Part II of that Schedule" and for "Part III" substitute "section 290";

(f) in the closing words of subsection (5) for "the said Schedules 2 and 5" substitute "that Schedule".

(9) In section 87 (general interpretation) for the definitions of "housing association" and "registered" substitute—

" 'housing association' has the same meaning as in the Housing Associations Act 1985 and 'registered', in relation to a housing association, means registered under that Act;".

Housing Act 1974 (c.44)

25.—(1) The Housing Act 1974 is amended as follows.

(2) In section 18(2) (certain housing association tenancies within the Rent (Scotland) Act 1984) for "subsection (1) above" substitute "section 5(4) of the Rent (Scotland) Act 1984".

(3) In Schedule 3 (provisions supplementary to section 18), in paragraphs 13(1)(c) and 14(1)(a) and in paragraph 16, in the definition of "the previous housing association tenancy," for "section 18(1) of this Act" substitute "section 5(4) of the Rent (Scotland) Act 1984".

Friendly Societies Act 1974 (c.46)

26. In section 51 of the Friendly Societies Act 1974 (power of friendly society to invest in housing association), in subsection (4) (definition of "housing association") for the words from "means" to the end substitute "has the same meaning as in the Housing Associations Act 1985".

Housing Rents and Subsidies (Scotland) Act 1975 (c.28)

27. In section 5 of the Housing Rents and Subsidies (Scotland) Act 1975 (agreements for exercise by housing co-operatives of local authority housing functions), for subsection (4) substitute—

"(4) A housing association is not entitled under the Housing Associations Act 1985 to housing association grant, revenue deficit grant or hostel deficit grant in respect of land comprised in an agreement to which this section applies.".

Finance (No. 2) Act 1975 (c.45)

28. In section 71 of the Finance (No. 2) Act 1975 (interpretation of provisions relating to payments to sub-contractors in construction industry), in subsection (3) (definition of certain housing bodies)—

(a) for the definition of "housing association" substitute—
    " 'housing association' has the same meaning as in the Housing Associations Act 1985 or the Housing (Northern Ireland) Order 1981", and

(b) in the definition of "housing trust" for "Housing Act 1957" substitute "Housing Associations Act 1985".

Airports Authority Act 1975 (c.78)

29. In section 19(5) of the Airports Authority Act 1975 (housing enactments for purposes of which the Airports Authority are statutory undertakers) for "Part III of the Housing Act 1957" substitute "sections 283, 296 and 611 of the Housing Act 1985".

Greater London Council (General Powers) Act 1975 (c.xxx)

30.—(1) Section 7 of the Greater London Council (General Powers) Act 1975 (byelaws as to parking, &c. on housing estates) is amended as follows.

(2) In subsection (1) (extension of power to make byelaws)—

(a) for "subsection (1) of section 112 of the Housing Act 1957" substitute "section 23(1) of the Housing Act 1985", and

(b) for "Part V" substitute "Part II".

(3) In subsection (2) (extension of ancillary provisions) for "the said section 112" substitute "section 23(1) of the Housing Act 1985".

Finance Act 1976 (c.40)

31. In section 62 of the Finance Act 1976 (exceptions from general charge on benefits provided by employer), in subsection (4) (certain repairs to living accommodation) for "section 32 of the Housing Act 1961" substitute "section 11 of the Landlord and Tenant Act 1985".

Development of Rural Wales Act 1976 (c.75)

32. In section 8 of the Development of Rural Wales Act 1976 (assistance from public authorities and others), in subsection (4) for the words from "the Housing Act 1974" to the end substitute "the Housing Associations Act 1985."

Rent (Agriculture) Act 1976 (c.80)

33.—(1) The Rent (Agriculture) Act 1976 is amended as follows.

(2) In section 5 (no statutory tenancy where landlord's interest belongs to certain authorities or bodies), in subsection (4) (certain housing associations) for the words from "belong to a housing association" to the end substitute—
    "belong to a housing association which—

(a) is registered under the Housing Associations Act 1985, or

(b) is a co-operative housing association within the meaning of that Act.".

(3) In section 27 (rehousing: application to housing authority), for subsection (3) substitute—
    "(3) In this Act the 'housing authority concerned' is the local housing authority within the meaning of the Housing Act 1985.".
in which case it is the Greater London Council.".

(4) In Schedule 4 (grounds for possession of dwelling-house)—

(a) in paragraph 4 of Case I (alternative accommodation privately provided: accommodation unsuitable if overcrowded), and

(b) in Case XIII (dwelling-house overcrowded),
for "the Housing Act 1957" substitute "Part X of the Housing Act 1985".

(5) In Schedule 5 (terms of statutory tenancy)—

(a) in paragraph 6(1) (landlord's repairing obligations) and in paragraph 12(4)(b) (variation of statutory tenancy) for "section 32 of the Housing Act 1961" substitute "section 11 of the Landlord and Tenant Act 1985";

(b) in paragraph 6(2) for "the said section 32" substitute "the said section 11".

Agricultural Holdings (Notices to Quit) Act 1977 (c.12)

34. In Schedule 1A to the Agricultural Holdings (Notices to Quit) Act 1977 (suitable alternative accommodation)—

(a) in paragraph 4 (overcrowding) for "the Housing Act 1957" substitute "Part X of the Housing Act 1985";

(b) for paragraph 6(1) (meaning of "housing authority") substitute—
    "(1) In this Schedule 'housing authority', and 'district' in relation to such an authority, mean a local housing authority and their district within the meaning of the Housing Act 1985.".

Rent Act 1977 (c.42)

35.—(1) The Rent Act 1977 is amended as follows.

(2) In section 15 (certain housing association tenancies), for subsection (3) (associations to which the section applies) substitute—
    "(3) A housing association falls within this subsection if—
    (a) it is registered under the Housing Associations Act 1985, or
    (b) it is a co-operative housing association within the meaning of that Act.".

(3) In section 16 (certain housing co-operative tenancies) for the words from "as defined in paragraph 1 of Schedule 20" to the end substitute "within the meaning of section 27 of the Housing Act 1985 (exercise of local authority housing management functions by co-operatives) and the dwelling-house is comprised in an agreement under that section".

(4) In section 78 (powers of rent tribunals on reference of restricted contract) in subsection (5) (meaning of "housing authority") for the words from "means a council" to the end substitute "means a local housing authority within the meaning of the Housing Act 1985".

(5) In section 86 (meaning of "housing association tenancy" for purposes of Part VI)—
    (a) in subsection (3) (definition of "housing association") for the words from "has the meaning assigned" to the end substitute "has the same meaning as in the Housing Associations Act 1985";
    (b) in subsection (3A) (definition of "co-ownership tenancy") for "falls within section 15(3)(d) of this Act" substitute "is a co-operative housing association within the meaning of the Housing Associations Act 1985".

(6) In section 88 (rent limit for certain housing association tenancies), in subsection (7) (conditions imposed under certain enactments to be disregarded in determining rent limit)—
    (a) for paragraph (b) substitute—
        "(b) paragraph 2 of Part II of Schedule 15 to the Housing Act 1985, or any corresponding earlier enactment";
    (b) for paragraph (d) substitute—
        "(d) section 33 of the Housing Act 1985, or any corresponding earlier enactment;".
    (c) for the words from "(which impose" to "houses)" substitute "which imposes a rent limit in respect of the dwelling-house".

(7) In section 92 (conversion of housing association tenancies), in subsection (5) (definition of "housing association") for "section 189(1) of the Housing Act 1957" substitute "the Housing Associations Act 1985".

(8) For section 101 (overcrowded dwelling-houses) substitute—
    "Overcrowded dwelling-houses
        101. At any time when a dwelling-house is overcrowded within the meaning of Part X of the Housing Act 1985 in such circumstances as to render the occupier guilty of an offence, nothing in this Part of this Act shall prevent the immediate landlord of the occupier from obtaining possession of the dwelling-house."

(9) In section 116 (power of court to authorise carrying out of works without consent of statutory tenant)—
    (a) in subsection (3)(a) (works approved for grant) for "Part VII of the Housing Act 1974" substitute "Part XV of the Housing Act 1985";
    (b) in subsection (3)(b) (works likely to be approved for grant) for "a local authority" substitute "the local housing authority within the meaning of that Act";
    (c) in subsection (5) (compliance with conditions as to time) for "local authority under section 82(1) of the Housing Act 1974" substitute "local housing authority under section 512(2) of the Housing Act 1985".

(10) In section 149(1) (powers of local authorities to provide information), for sub-paragraph (a)(i) substitute—
    "(i) sections 4 to 7 (provision of rent books) and sections 18 to 30 (service charges) of the Landlord and Tenant Act 1985,".

(11) In Schedule 15, Part IV (determination whether suitable alternative accommodation is or will be available)—
    (a) for "housing authority" wherever occurring substitute "local housing authority";
    (b) in paragraph 6 (overcrowding) for "the Housing Act 1957" substitute "Part X of the Housing Act 1985";

(*c*) for paragraph 8 (meaning of "housing authority" and "district") substitute—

"8. In this Part 'local housing authority' and 'district' in relation to such an authority have the same meaning as in the Housing Act 1985.".

(12) In Schedule 16 (further grounds for possession of dwelling-houses let to agricultural workers)—

(*a*) for the "the housing authority concerned" wherever occurring substitute "the local housing authority";

(*b*) in paragraph 4 of Case I (overcrowding) for "the Housing Act 1957" substitute "Part X of the Housing Act 1985";

(*c*) for paragraph 7 of Case I (definition of "the housing authority concerned") substitute—

"7. In this Case and in Case II below "the local housing authority" has the same meaning as in the Housing Act 1985.";

(*d*) in paragraph 4 of Case II for "housing authority's offer" substitute "local housing authority's offer".

Criminal Law Act 1977 (c.45)

36. In section 7 (offence of adverse possession of premises) in subsection (5) (authorities whose prospective tenants are protected intending occupiers) for paragraph (*c*) substitute—

"(*c*) a registered housing association within the meaning of the Housing Associations Act 1985.".

Housing (Homeless Persons) Act 1977 (c.48)

37.—(1) The Housing (Homeless Persons) Act 1977, as it continues to apply in Scotland, is amended as follows.

(2) In section 1(1) (definition of homelessness) after "if there is no accommodation" insert "in Scotland, England or Wales".

(3) In section 3(3) (inquiries as to local connection with another housing authority) after "housing authority" insert "in Scotland, England or Wales".

(4) In section 5(1)(*a*) (grounds for referral of application to another housing authority), in sub-paragraph (ii) for "another housing authority's area" substitute "the area of another housing authority in Scotland, England or Wales".

(5) In section 9(1) (co-operation between authorities)—

(*a*) in paragraph (*a*) after "another housing authority" insert "in Scotland, England or Wales";

(*b*) in paragraph (*b*) for "social services authority or a social work authority" substitute "social work authority in Scotland, England or Wales".

(6) After section 18 insert—

"**Application of this Act to cases arising in England and Wales**

18A.—(1) Section 5(3), (4) and (7) to (11) above (notification of application to another housing authority and duties to persons whose applications are so notified) apply—

(*a*) to applications notified by an authority in England or Wales in pursuance of section 67 of the Housing Act 1985, and

(*b*) to persons whose applications are so notified,

as they apply to cases arising under this Act.

(2) Section 9 above (duty of authorities to co-operate with housing authority) applies to a request by a local housing authority in England or Wales under section 72 of the Housing Act 1985 as it applies to a request by a housing authority in Scotland.

(3) In this Act, in relation to England and Wales—

(*a*) "housing authority" means a local housing authority within the meaning of section 1 of the Housing Act 1985, and references to the area of such an authority are to their district within the meaning of section 2 of that Act, and

(*b*) "social work authority" means a local authority for the purposes of the Local Authority Social Services Act 1970, as defined in section 1 of that Act;

and in section 9(1)(*c*) (requests for co-operation) "development corporation" includes a development corporation established under the New Towns Act 1981.".

(7) In section 19(1) (general interpretation), in the definition of "registered housing association" for the words from "registered in" to the end substitute "registered under the Housing Associations Act 1985".

(8) In section 21 (citation and extent), for subsection (4) substitute—

"(4) This Act extends to Scotland only.".

National Health Service Act 1977 (c.49)

38.—(1) The National Health Service Act 1977 is amended as follows.

(2) In section 28A (payments by health authorities towards expenditure on community services), in subsection (2) (authorities to whom, and functions in respect of which, payments may be made)—

(a) for paragraph (d) substitute—

"(d) to a local housing authority within the meaning of the Housing Act 1985, towards expenditure incurred or to be incurred by them in connection with their functions under Part II of that Act (provision of housing); and";

(b) in paragraph (e) for sub-paragraph (i) substitute—

"(i) a registered housing association within the meaning of the Housing Associations Act 1985;".

(3) In section 28B (payments by Secretary of State towards community services in Wales), in subsection (1)(b) for sub-paragraph (i) substitute—

"(i) a registered housing association within the meaning of the Housing Associations Act 1985;".

(4) In section 123(1) (arrangements for housing of persons displaced by health service development), for paragraphs (a) to (c) substitute—

"(a) a local housing authority within the meaning of section 1 of the Housing Act 1985",

(b) a housing association or housing trust within the meaning of the Housing Associations Act 1985,".

Housing (Financial Provisions) (Scotland) Act 1978 (c.14)

39.—(1) The Housing (Financial Provisions) (Scotland) Act 1978 is amended as follows.

(2) In section 5 (financial assistance to voluntary organisations), in subsection (2) for the words from "in the register" to "1974" substitute "under the Housing Associations Act 1985".

(3) In section 7 (restriction on certain exchequer payments)—

(a) in subsection (7) (housing association grant) for "section 29 of the Housing Act 1974" substitute "Part II of the Housing Associations Act 1985";

(b) in subsection (8) (hostel deficit grants) for "section 33 of the Housing Act 1974" substitute "section 55 of the Housing Associations Act 1985".

Home Purchase Assistance and Housing Corporation Guarantee Act 1978 (c.27)

40.—(1) The Home Purchase Assistance and Housing Corporation Guarantee Act 1978, as it continues to apply in Scotland, is amended as follows.

(2) In section 2(5) (exclusion of Restrictive Trade Practices Act 1976) after "this Act" insert ", or the corresponding English or Northern Ireland provisions,".

(3) In section 3 (modifications of building society law), after "under this Act", wherever occurring, insert ", or the corresponding English or Northern Ireland provisions,".

(4) After section 3 insert—

"Corresponding English or Northern Ireland provisions

3A. The references in this Act to the corresponding English or Northern Ireland provisions are to, respectively, sections 445 to 449 of the Housing Act 1985 and Part IX of the Housing (Northern Ireland) Order 1981.".

(5) For section 6(3) substitute—

"(3) This Act extends to Scotland only.".

(6) In the Schedule (recognised lending and savings institutions)—

(a) in paragraph 1 (building societies) for "designated under section 1 of the House Purchase and Housing Act 1959" substitute "designated for the purposes of the Trustee Investments Act 1961";

(b) in paragraph 13 (savings institutions recognised under other provisions) for the words from "legislation" to the end substitute "the corresponding English or Northern Ireland provisions".

National Health Service (Scotland) Act 1978 (c.29)

41. In section 16A of the National Health Service (Scotland) Act 1978 (payments by Health Boards towards expenditure on community services), in subsection (2) (payments to certain bodies towards expenditure on provision of housing accommodation) for paragraph (a) substitute—

"(a) a registered housing association within the meaning of the Housing Associations Act 1985;".

Homes Insulation Act 1978 (c.48)

42. In the Homes Insulation Act 1978, as it continues to apply in Scotland, for section 4(2) substitute—
"(2) This Act extends to Scotland only.".

Finance Act 1980 (c.48)

43. In section 97 of the Finance Act 1980 (stamp duty: certain shared ownership leases to be stamped as conveyances), in subsection (3) (bodies granting leases to which the section applies) for paragraphs (*a*) and (*b*) substitute—
"(*a*) a local authority within the meaning of the Housing Act 1985;
(*b*) a housing association registered under the Housing Associations Act 1985 or Article 124 of the Housing (Northern Ireland) Order 1981;".

Housing Act 1980 (c.51)

44.—(1) The Housing Act 1980 is amended as follows.
(2) In section 86 (jurisdiction of county court), for subsections (1) and (2) substitute—
"(1) A county court has jurisdiction to determine any question arising under Part III of this Act (tenant's improvements) and to entertain any proceedings brought thereunder.
(2) The jurisdiction conferred by this section includes jurisdiction to entertain proceedings on any question whether any consent required by section 81 was withheld or unreasonably withheld, notwithstanding that no other relief is sought than a declaration.".
(3) In section 140 (exclusion of shared ownership tenancies from Leasehold Reform Act 1967), in subsection (6) (definition of "registered housing association") for "section 13 of the Housing Act 1974" substitute "the Housing Associations Act 1985".
(4) In Schedule 9 (provisions consequential on amendment of definition of "housing trust" in the Rent Act 1977)—
(*a*) in paragraphs 2 and 4 for "Chapter II of Part I of this Act" substitute "Part IV of the Housing Act 1985 (secure tenancies)";
(*b*) in paragraph 5 for "Section 33 of this Act" substitute "Section 83 of the Housing Act 1985 (notice of proceedings for possession)".

Tenants' Rights, &c. (Scotland) Act 1980 (c.52)

45.—(1) The Tenants' Rights, &c. (Scotland) Act 1980 is amended as follows.
(2) In section 1(10) (landlords relevant to qualifying period for right to purchase and discount), in paragraph (*e*) (certain housing co-operatives) for "paragraph 9 of Schedule 1 to the Housing Rents and Subsidies Act 1975" substitute "section 27 of the Housing Act 1985".
(3) In section 10(2) (landlord condition for secure tenancies), in paragraph (*e*) (registered housing associations) for "the Housing Act 1974" substitute "the Housing Associations Act 1985".
(4) For section 11 (special provision for certain housing associations) substitute—
"Special provision for certain housing associations
11.—(1) A tenancy shall not be a secure tenancy at any time when the interest of the landlord belongs to a registered housing association which is a co-operative housing association.
(2) This Part of this Act (with the exception of sections 16, 17 and 21 to 25) shall apply to a tenancy at any time when the interest of the landlord belongs to a housing association which is a co-operative housing association and is not registered.
(3) If a registered housing association which is a co-operative housing association ceases to be registered, it shall notify those of its tenants who thereby become secure tenants.
(4) Notice under subsection (3) shall be given in writing to each tenant concerned, within the period of 21 days beginning with the date on which the association ceases to be registered.
(5) In this section—
(*a*) references to registration in relation to a housing association are to registration under the Housing Associations Act 1985, and
(*b*) "co-operative housing association" has the same meaning as in that Act.".

Local Government, Planning and Land Act 1980 (c.65)

46.—(1) The Local Government, Planning and Land Act 1980 is amended as follows.

(2) In section 152(1)(*c*) (power to confer on urban development corporations functions with respect to home insulation), for "section 1 of the Homes Insulation Act 1978" substitute "section 521 of the Housing Act 1985".

(3) In section 153(1) (power to confer local authority housing functions on urban development corporation) for the words from "the Housing Acts 1957 to 1975 and the Housing Act 1980" substitute "the Housing Act 1985 or the Housing Associations Act 1985".

(4) In Schedule 12 (prescribed expenditure for purposes of controls on capital expenditure), in paragraph 1(*e*) (certain expenditure on land) for "Part V of the Housing Act 1957" substitute "Part II of the Housing Act 1985".

Highways Act 1980 (c.66)

47. In section 36(2) of the Highways Act 1980 (general definition of highways maintainable at the public expense), in paragraph (*b*) (highways constructed by local authorities under housing powers)—

   (*a*) for "Part V of the Housing Act 1957" substitute "Part II of the Housing Act 1985";
   (*b*) for "the said Part V", in each place where it occurs, substitute "the said Part II".

Finance Act 1981 (c.35)

48. In section 107 of the Finance Act 1981 (stamp duty: sale of houses at discount by local authorities, &c.), in subsection (3) (authorities to whose dispositions the section applies)—

   (*a*) in paragraph (*b*) for "local authority within the meaning of Part V of the Housing Act 1957" substitute "local housing authority within the meaning of the Housing Act 1985";
   (*b*) in paragraph (*f*) for "section 13 of the Housing Act 1974" substitute "the Housing Associations Act 1985".

New Towns Act 1981 (c.64)

49.—(1) The New Towns Act 1981 is amended as follows.

(2) In sections 47(6) and (7) and 50(7) (transfer of housing to district council) for "Part V of the Housing Act 1957" substitute "Part II of the Housing Act 1985".

(3) In section 50(3) (financial arrangements as to transfer schemes)—

   (*a*) for "paragraph 3(1)(*a*) of Schedule 1 to the Housing Finance Act 1972" substitute "item 1 in Part II of Schedule 14 to the Housing Act 1985";
   (*b*) for "Part V of the Housing Act 1957" substitute "Part II of the Housing Act 1985".

(4) In section 57 (interpretation of Part III) in the definition of "Housing Act dwelling" for "Part V of the Housing Act 1957" substitute "Part II of the Housing Act 1985".

Greater London Council (General Powers) Act 1981 (c.xvii)

50.—(1) Part IV of the Greater London Council (General Powers) Act 1981 (control of overcrowding in certain hostels) is amended as follows.

(2) In section 9(1) (overcrowding notices), in the proviso (cases where similar restrictions are in force), for the words from "applied" to the end substitute "for the time being applied to the premises by a registration scheme under section 346 of the Housing Act 1985, a direction under section 354 of that Act, or an overcrowding notice under section 358 of that Act".

(3) In section 12(1) (penalties), in the proviso (exclusion where a person previously convicted under other similar provisions), for the words from "section 90(13)" to the end substitute "section 355(2) or 358(4) of the Housing Act 1985".

(4) In section 16 (premises exempted from controls)—

   (*a*) in paragraph (*e*) (registered common lodging houses), for "section 238 of the Act of 1936" substitute "Part XII of the Housing Act 1985";
   (*b*) in paragraph (*l*) (premises run by registered housing associations), for "Part II of the Housing Act 1974" substitute "the Housing Associations Act 1985".

Housing (Northern Ireland) Order 1981 (S.I.1981/156)(N.I.3)

51.—(1) The Housing (Northern Ireland) Order 1981 is amended as follows.

(2) In Article 155 (modifications of building society law in relation to financial assistance for first-time buyers)—

(*a*) in paragraph (1) for the words from "the Home Purchase Assistance and Housing Corporation Guarantee Act 1978" to "Act of 1978' " substitute "sections 445 to 449 of the Housing Act 1985 or the Home Purchase Assistance and Housing Corporation Guarantee Act 1978 (in this Article and Article 155A referred to as 'the corresponding English or Scottish provisions')";

(*b*) in paragraph (2) for "the Act of 1978" substitute "the corresponding English or Scottish provisions";

(*c*) in paragraph (3) for "the Act of 1978" substitute "the corresponding English or Scottish provisions";

(*d*) in paragraph (4) for "the Act of 1978" substitute "the corresponding English or Scottish provisions".

(3) After that Article insert—

"Exclusion of Restrictive Trade Practices Act 1976

155A. Section 16(3) and (5) of the Restrictive Trade Practices Act 1976 (recommendations by services supply associations to members) do not apply to recommendations made to lending and savings institutions about the manner of implementing Articles 153 and 154, or the corresponding English or Scottish provisions, provided that the recommendations are made with the approval of the Department of the Environment for Northern Ireland, or, as the case may be the Secretary of State, which may be withdrawn at any time on one month's notice".

(4) In Article 156 (indemnity agreements with building societies), at the end add—

"(7) Section 16(3) and (5) of the Restrictive Trade Practices Act 1976 (recommendations by services supply associations) do not apply to a recommendation made about the making of agreements under this Article, or under the corresponding provisions in England and Wales (namely, section 442 of the Housing Act 1985 and section 84 of the Housng Associations Act 1985), provided that the recommendations are made with the approval of the Department of the Environment for Northern Ireland, or, as the case may be, of the Secretary of State, which may be withdrawn at any time on one month's notice.".

(5) In Schedule 10 (institutions recognised for purposes of the scheme for assisting first-time buyers)—

(*a*) in Part I (lending institutions), in paragraph 1 (building societies) for "designated under section 1 of the House Purchase and Housing Act 1959" substitute "designated for the purposes of the Trustee Investments Act 1961";

(*b*) In Part II (savings institutions) in paragraph 12 after "section 1 of the Home Purchase Assistance and Housing Corporation Guarantee Act 1978" insert "or section 446 of the Housing Act 1985".

Civil Aviation Act 1982 (c.16)

52. In paragraph 4 of Schedule 2 to the Civil Aviation Act 1982 (enactments for purposes of which the Civil Aviation Authority are statutory undertakers) for "Part III of the Housing Act 1957" substitute "sections 283, 296 and 611 of the Housing Act 1985".

Social Security and Housing Benefits Act 1982 (c.24)

53. In section 35(1) of the Social Security and Housing Benefits Act 1982 (interpretation of Part II)—

(*a*) before the definition of "Housing Revenue Account rebate" insert—

" 'Housing Revenue Account dwelling', in relation to a local authority means a dwelling which is within the authority's Housing Revenue Account (within the meaning of Part XIII of the Housing Act 1985) and is not—

(*a*) a dwelling for the time being let on a long tenancy at a low rent within the meaning of the Leasehold Reform Act 1967, or

(*b*) a dwelling no longer owned by the authority;";

(*b*) in the definition of "Housing Revenue Account rebate" omit the words "(within the meaning of the Housing Finance Act 1972)".

Finance Act 1982 (c.39)

54.—(1) The Finance Act 1982 is amended as follows.

(2) In section 29 (mortgage interest relief: application of provisions to certain housing associations), in paragraph (*b*) (self-build societies) for "Part I of the Housing Act 1974" substitute "the Housing Associations Act 1985".

(3) In Schedule 12 (capital allowances for dwelling-houses let on assured tenancies), in paragraph 3(3)(*b*) (exclusion of premises if landlord is, inter alios, a self-build society) for "Part I of the Housing Act 1974" substitute "the Housing Associations Act 1985".

Greater London Council (General Powers) Act 1982 (c.i)

55. In section 4 of the Greater London Council (General Powers) Act 1982 (removal of vehicles illegally parked on housing estates)
   (*a*) in subsection (1) for the words from "subsection (1)" to "Housing Act 1957" substitute "section 23(1) of the Housing Act 1985 (byelaws for regulation of authority's houses)";
   (*b*) in the same subsection for "Part V of the said Act of 1957" substitute "Part II of the Housing Act 1985";
   (*c*) in subsection (2) for "the said section 112" substitute "section 23(1) of the Housing Act 1985".

Matrimonial Homes Act 1983 (c.19)

56.—(1) The Matrimonial Homes Act 1983 is amended as follows.
(2) In section 1(6) (occupation under the Act by one spouse to be treated as occupation by the other) for "for the purposes of Chapter II of Part I of the Housing Act 1980" substitute "for the purposes of Part IV of the Housing Act 1985 (secure tenancies)".
(3) In Schedule 1 (transfer of certain tenancies on divorce, &c.)—
   (*a*) in paragraph 1(1)(*c*) for "within the meaning of section 28 of the Housing Act 1980" substitute "within the meaning of section 79 of the Housing Act 1985";
   (*b*) in paragraph 2(1) for "within the meaning of the Housing Act 1980" substitute "within the meaning of the Housing Act 1985";
   (*c*) in paragraph 2(3) for "within the meaning of Chapter II of Part I of the Housing Act 1980" substitute "within the meaning of Part IV of the Housing Act 1985.".

County Courts Act 1984 (c.28)

57.—(1) The County Courts Act 1984 is amended as follows.
(2) In section 66(1) (trial by jury: cases for trial without jury), in paragraph (*c*) (housing appeals) for "the Housing Act 1957" substitute "the Housing Act 1985".
(3) In section 77 (appeals), in subsection (6) (restriction of appeal on question of fact where court has unfettered discretion whether or not to order possession), in paragraph (*e*) for "section 34(3)(*a*) of the Housing Act 1980" substitute "section 84(2)(*a*) of the Housing Act 1985".

Building Act 1984 (c.55)

58.—(1) The Building Act 1984 is amended as follows.
(2) In section 76(7) (power to act in respect of defective building notwithstanding that authority might have proceeded under housing powers) for "section 9 of the Housing Act 1957" substitute "Part VI of the Housing Act 1985 (repair notices)".
(3) In section 80(1)(*a*) and section 81(1)(*a*), (3)(*b*) and (4)(*b*) (which relate to demolition orders) for "the Housing Act 1957" substitute "Part IX of the Housing Act 1985".

Rent (Scotland) Act 1984 (c.58)

59.—(1) The Rent (Scotland) Act 1984 is amended as follows.
(2) In section 5 (no protected or statutory tenancy where landlord's interest belongs to certain authorities), in subsection (4) (certain housing associations) for the words from "belongs to" to the end substitute—
   "belongs to a housing association which—
      (*a*) is registered under the Housing Associations Act 1985, or
      (*b*) is a co-operative housing association within the meaning of that Act;
   nor shall a person at any time be a statutory tenant of a dwelling-house if the interest of his immediate landlord belongs at that time to such a housing association".
(3) In section 61(1) (interpretation of Part VI), in the definition of "housing association" for the words from "meaning" to the end substitute "same meaning as in the Housing Associations Act 1985".
(4) In section 63(4) (lessors excluded from Part VII), in paragraph (*e*) (registered housing associations), for "Housing Act 1974" substitute "Housing Associations Act 1985".

Greater London Council (General Powers) Act 1984 (c.xxvii)

60.—(1) The Greater London Council (General Powers) Act 1984 is amended as follows.

(2) In section 10 (registration of certain sleeping accommodation: buildings to which the provisions apply), in subsection (2) (exceptions)—

   (*a*) in paragraph (*h*) (premises run by registered housing association), for "Part II of the Housing Act 1974" substitute "the Housing Associations Act 1985";

   (*b*) in paragraph (*m*) (registered common lodging houses), for "section 238 of the Public Health Act 1936" substitute "Part XII of the Housing Act 1985".

(3) In section 39 (occupants removed from buildings to have priority housing need), for "the Housing (Homeless Persons) Act 1977" substitute "Part III of the Housing Act 1985 (housing the homeless)".

Local Government Act 1985 (c.51)

61. In Schedule 13 to the Local Government Act 1985 (provisions with respect to residuary bodies) for paragraphs 22 and 23 (application of certain housing enactments) substitute—

   "22. A residuary body shall be treated as a local authority for the purposes of the following provisions of the Housing Act 1985—

      sections 43 and 44 (consent required for certain disposals of houses),

      sections 45 to 51 (restrictions on recovery of service charges after disposal of house),

      Parts IV and V (secure tenancies and the right to buy),

      sections 442 (so far as relates to agreements within subsection 1(*b*)), 443, 444, 452 and 453 (provision in connection with local authority mortgages), and

      Part XVI (assistance for owners of defective premises disposed of by local authorities and others).

   23. A residuary body shall be treatd as a local authority for the purposes of sections 84(5)(*b*) and 85(4) of the Housing Associations Act 1985 (consultation on forms of agreement and meaning of "relevant advance").

   24. A residuary body shall be treated as a local authority for the purposes of the following provisions of the Landlord and Tenant Act 1985—

      section 14(4) (exclusion of implied repairing obligations), and

      sections 18 to 30 (service charges).".

Section 5(1)   SCHEDULE 3

TRANSITIONAL PROVISIONS

The general rule

1.—(1) The general rule is that the provisions of the consolidating Acts apply, in accordance with section 2 of this Act (continuity of the law), to matters arising before the commencement of those Acts as to matters arising after that commencement.

(2) The general rule has effect subject to any express provision to the contrary, either in this Schedule or in connection with the substantive provision in question.

(3) The general rule does not mean that the provisions of the consolidating Acts apply to cases to which the corresponding repealed provisions did not apply by virtue of transitional provision made in connection with the commencement of the repealed provisions (such transitional provisions, if not specifically reproduced, are saved by paragraph 1 of Schedule 4).

(4) The general rule does not apply so far as a provision of the consolidating Acts gives effect to an amendment (in pursuance of a Recommendation of the Law Commission and, in some cases, the Scottish Law Commission).

Specific transitional provisions

2. The provisions of the consolidating Acts listed below apply only in the cases specified; in other cases the corresponding repealed provisions continue to apply.

Provision of consolidation	*Cases to which applicable*
Part V of the Housing Act 1985 (the right to buy)	Where the tenant's notice claiming to exercise the right to buy is served on or after 1st April 1986.

Sections 421 to 427 of that Act (housing subsidy)	The year 1986–87 and subsequent years.

3. The amendment in paragraph 35(8) of Schedule 2 to this Act substituting a new section 101 in the Rent Act 1977 (landlord's right to recover possession if dwelling-house is overcrowded) applies only where the tenant (or statutory tenant) occupies the dwelling-house under (or by virtue of) a tenancy granted on or after 1st April 1986.

Delayed operation of certain provisions

4. The provisions of section 589(4) to (6) of, and paragraph 11 of Schedule 13 to, the Housing Act 1985 (which relate to apportionment by reference to gross rateable values) apply only for rate periods, within the meaning of the General Rate Act 1967, beginning on or after the first date after 1st April 1986 on which new valuation lists come into force under section 68(1) of that Act.

Commencement of the Local Government Act 1985 (c.51)

5.—(1) The consolidating Acts and the Local Government Act 1985 shall be construed and have effect as if the consolidating Acts had come into force immediately after that Act.

(2) References to a local authority in provisions of the consolidating Acts which confer powers, duties, rights or immunities by reference to things done by or in relation to a local authority before 1st April 1986 include references to the councils abolished by the Local Government Act 1985.

(3) Sub-paragraph (2) applies in particular to the following provisions—
> section 45(2)(*b*) of the Housing Act 1985 (restriction on service charges payable after disposal of house by local authority),
> section 444(4) of that Act and section 85(4) of the Housing Associations Act 1985 (power to agree to indemnify mortgagee of property disposed of by local authority),
> section 573(1) of the Housing Act 1985 (definition of public sector authority for the purposes of assistance for persons having acquired defective housing from such an authority),
> paragraph 7(1) of Schedule 4 to that Act (public sector landlords for purposes of qualifying period for the right to buy),
> section 41(2) of the Housing Associations Act 1985 (approval of programme for purposes of housing association grant), and
> section 14(4) of the Landlord and Tenant Act 1985 (exclusion of implied repairing obligation in case of lease granted by local authority).

Section 5(2)   SCHEDULE 4

SAVINGS

General saving for old transitional provisions

1. The repeal by this Act of a provision relating to the coming into force of a provision reproduced in the consolidating Acts does not affect the operation of that provision, in so far as it is not specifically reproduced in the consolidating Acts but remains capable of having effect, in relation to the corresponding provision of the consolidating Acts.

General saving for old savings

2.—(1) The repeal by this Act of an enactment previously repealed subject to savings does not affect the continued operation of those savings.

(2) The repeal by this Act of a saving made on the previous repeal of an enactment does not affect the operation of the saving in so far as it is not specifically reproduced in the consolidating Acts but remains capable of having effect.

(3) Sub-paragraph (2) does not apply to the repeal of paragraph 23(3) of Schedule 1 to the Housing Rents and Subsidies Act 1975 (saving for orders under section 80 of the Housing Finance Act 1972).

Savings relating to the Common Council of the City of London

3.—(1) The repeal by this Act of any provision not specifically reproduced in the consolidating Acts does not affect the powers of the Common Council of the City of London.

(2) Sub-paragraph (1) applies in particular to the repeal of the following provisions (which as regards local authorities in general are superseded by provisions of the Local Government Act 1972 not applying to the Common-Council)—

    section 47 of the Housing Act 1957 (treatment of land acquired for clearance), so far as it confers powers of appropriation and disposal, and section 26(5)(a) of the Town and Country Planning Act 1959 (consents to disposals) so far as it relates to that section,

    section 137 of that Act (borrowing for purposes of housing operations outside authority's area),

    section 138 and Schedule 8 of that Act (power to issue local housing bonds), and

    section 35 of the Housing Act 1969 (restriction on disposal of land at an undervalue).

(3) Section 112(3) of the Housing Act 1957 (confirming authority for byelaws) continues to apply in relation to byelaws made under section 23 of the Housing Act 1985 by the Common Council.

(4) Sections 166 to 169 of the Housing Act 1957 (authentication and service of documents) continue to apply in relation to the Common Council.

(5) A reference in a provision of the consolidating Acts to the "proper officer" of a local authority shall be construed in relation to the Common Council of the City of London as a reference to any specific officer of that Council referred to in the corresponding provision repealed by this Act.

Saving for certain powers of existing companies and associations

4.—(1) The repeal by this Act of—

    (a) section 127 of the Housing Act 1957 (power of certain companies, &c. to provide housing for their employees), or

    (b) section 47(4) of the Housing (Financial Provisions) Act 1958 or section 24(3) of the Housing (Financial Provisions) (Scotland) Act 1968 (power of certain companies, &c. to borrow from Public Works Loan Commissioners),

does not affect the powers of any company, association or society in relation to which the provision in question applied before 1st April 1986.

(2) The repeal by this Act of section 47(8) of the Housing (Financial Provisions) Act 1958 (quasi-incorporation of certain bodies for certain housing purposes) does not affect the status of any company, association or society in relation to which the provision applied before 1st April 1986.

(3) The repeal by this Act of section 47(9) of the Housing (Financial Provisions) Act 1958 (borrowing powers of certain housing associations) does not affect the power of any housing association to which that provision applied before 1st April 1986 to raise money on loan at a rate of interest not exceeding that determined by the Treasury for the purposes of the definition of "housing association" in section 1 of the Housing Associations Act 1985.

Options granted by local authorities
before 8th August 1980

5. The limitations on a local authority's statutory power to dispose of houses acquired or appropriated for the purposes of Part V of the Housing Act 1957 shall not be taken to have prevented a local authority, at any time before 8th August 1980 (when the power of disposal conferred by section 91 of the Housing Act 1980 came into force), from granting to the tenant of a house an option to purchase the freehold of, or any other interest in, the house.

Conditions imposed under section 104 of the Housing Act 1957
before 8th August 1980

6. A condition imposed under section 104 of the Housing Act 1957 before 8th August 1980 which by virtue of paragraph 69(1) of Schedule 25 to the Housing Act 1980 was a local land charge immediately before the commencement of this Act continues to be a local land charge notwithstanding the repeal of that paragraph.

Transfers under section 14 of the Housing (Homeless Persons)
Act 1977

7.—(1) The repeal by this Act of section 14 of the Housing (Homeless Persons) Act 1977 (transfers of property and staff) does not affect the operation of any order previously made under that section.

(2) The transfer of an employee in pursuance of such an order shall be treated—

(*a*) for the purposes of section 94 of the Employment Protection (Consolidation) Act 1978 (redundancy payments) as occurring on a change in the ownership of a business;

(*b*) for the purposes of Schedule 13 to that Act (continuity of employment) as occurring on the transfer of an undertaking.

Operation of section 37 of the Housing Act 1980, as originally enacted

8.—(1) Section 37 of the Housing Act 1980 (effect of assignment of subletting, &c.) as originally enacted shall be deemed never to have applied in relation to the assignment of secure tenancies.

(2) Sub-paragraph (1) does not affect—

(*a*) in the case of a periodic tenancy, the operation of a notice to quit served on the tenant before 26th August 1984;

(*b*) in the case of a tenancy for a term certain, any proceedings for forfeiture in pursuance of a notice served on the tenant before that date.

Modifications of conveyances and grants in consequence of the Housing and Building Control Act 1984

9.—(1) This paragraph applies to a conveyance or grant executed in pursuance of Chapter I of Part I of the Housing Act 1980 (the right to buy) before 26th August 1984, when Part I of the Housing and Building Control Act 1984 came into force.

(2) Where the conveyance or grant contains the covenant required by section 8(1) of the 1980 Act (repayment of discount on early disposal), the covenant has effect with such modifications as may be necessary to bring it into conformity with the amendments made by section 5 of the 1984 Act.

(3) Where the conveyance or grant contains such a covenant as was mentioned in section 19(1) of the 1980 Act (restriction on disposal of dwelling-houses in National Parks, &c.), the covenant—

(*a*) is binding not only on the purchaser and any successor in title of his but also on any person deriving title under him or any such successor, and

(*b*) has effect with such modifications as may be necessary to bring it into conformity with the amendments made by section 8 of the 1984 Act.

10.—(1) This paragraph applies to a conveyance grant or assignment executed in pursuance of section 104 of the Housing Act 1957 or section 122 of the Housing Act 1980 (voluntary disposals by local authorities or registered housing associations) before 26th August 1984, when Part I of the Housing and Building Control Act 1984 came into force.

(2) Where the conveyance, grant or assignment contains the covenant required by section 104B(2) of the 1957 Act (repayment of discount on early disposal), the covenant has effect with such modifications as may be necessary to bring it into conformity with the amendments made by paragraph 1 of Schedule 6 to the 1984 Act.

(3) Where the conveyance grant or assignment contains such a covenant as was mentioned in section 104C(1) of the 1957 Act (restriction on disposal of dwelling-houses in National Parks, &c.), the covenant—

(a) is binding not only on the purchaser and any successor in title of his but also on any person deriving title under him or any such successor, and

(b) has effect with such modifications as may be necessary to bring it into conformity with the amendments made by paragraph 2 of Schedule 6 of the 1984 Act.

Section 35 of the Housing Act 1957

11. The provisions of Part IX of the Housing Act 1985 (slum clearance) apply in relation to a closing order made under section 35 of the Housing Act 1957 (retention of houses needed to support other buildings) as they apply to a closing order made under the proviso to section 17 of the 1957 Act.

Telecommunication apparatus in clearance area

12. Paragraph 33 of Schedule 3 to the British Telecommunications Act 1981 (provision for protection of certain telecommunication apparatus) continues to have effect in relation to any order under section 64 of the Housing Act 1957 (extinguishment of rights over land acquired for clearance) coming into force before the appointed day for the purposes of the Telecommunications Act 1984.

Definition of multiple occupation

13.—(1) Any statutory provision passed or made before 25th August 1969 referring (in whatever terms) to a house which, or part of which, is let in lodgings or which is occupied by members of more than one family shall continue to have effect as if it referred to a house which is occupied by persons who do not form a single household.

(2) In sub-paragraph (1) "statutory provision" means any provision contained in an Act of Parliament or in any order or other instrument made under an Act of Parliament.

Houses in multiple occupation : undertakings accepted, &c.
before 27th October 1980

14.—(1) The repeal by this Act of section 147 of the Housing Act 1980 does not affect the operation of any enactment in relation to a notice served, undertaking given or order made under section 16 of the Housing Act 1961 or section 60 of the Housing Act 1969 (houses in multiple occupation: means of escape from fire) before 27th October 1980.

(2) In relation to a breach of an undertaking accepted under section 60 of the Housing Act 1969 before that date, the maximum fine under subsection (3) of that section is level 2 on the standard scale (within the meaning of section 75 of the Criminal Justice Act 1982).

(3) Sub-paragraph (2) does not affect the provisions of section 60(3) of the Housing Act 1969 as to continuing offences.

Certain arrangements, &c. with housing associations

15.—(1) The repeal by this Act of section 7 of the Housing Act 1961 or section 23 of the Housing (Financial Provisions) (Scotland) Act 1968 (advances to housing associations providing housing accommodation) does not affect the continued operation of that section in relation to advances or arrangements made before the repeal.

(2) The repeal by this Act of section 34 of the Housing Act 1974 (transfer to Housing Corporation of rights of Secretary of State in relation to certain advances) does not affect the rights and obligations transferred by that section.

Use of existing forms, &c.

16. Any document made, served or issued on or after 1st April 1986 which contains a reference to an enactment repealed by this Act shall be construed, except so far as a contrary intention appears, as referring or, as the context may require, including a reference to the corresponding provision of the consolidating Acts.

WEIGHTS AND MEASURES ACT 1985

(1985 c.72)

Tables of derivations and destinations can be found at the end of the Act.

63. Instructions by inspectors.

Miscellaneous

64. Disclosure of information.
65. Power to modify Part V.
66. Regulations under Part V.
67. Service of documents.
68. Interpretation of Part V.

PART VI

ADMINISTRATION

Local administration

69. Local weights and measures authorities.
70. Annual reports by local weights and measures authorities.
71. Inspection of local weights and measures arrangements.

Inspectors of weights and measures

72. Appointment of inspectors.
73. Certificate of qualification to act as inspector.
74. Performance by inspectors of additional functions.
75. Offences in connection with office of inspector.

Fees

76. Fees for performance of community obligations.
77. Reduction of fees.
78. Fees received by inspectors.

PART VII

GENERAL

Enforcement and legal proceedings

79. General powers of inspection and entry.
80. Obstruction of inspectors.
81. Failure to provide assistance or information.
82. Offences by corporations.
83. Prosecution of offences.
84. Penalties.
85. Determination of certain questions by Secretary of State.

Miscellaneous and supplementary

86. Regulations and orders.
87. Secretary of State to report to Parliament.
88. Application to Crown.
89. Saving for use of certain units in wholesale transactions.
90. Saving for certain rights in City of London.
91. Validity of contracts.
92. Spelling of "gram," etc.
93. Powers under other Acts with respect to marking of food.
94. General interpretation.
95. Application to Northern Ireland.
96. Transitional provisions and savings.
97. Consequential amendments.
98. Repeals and revocations.
99. Short title and commencement.
    SCHEDULES:

    Schedule 1—Definitions of units of measurement.
        Part I—Measurement of length.
        Part II—Measurement of area.
        Part III—Measurement of volume.

An Act to consolidate certain enactments relating to weights and measures.

[30th October 1985]

Parliamentary Debates

Hansard: H.L. Vol. 465, cols. 10, 955, vol. 466, col. 1206, Vol. 467, cols. 1560 to 1569, H.C. Vols. 84, col. 120, 566.

PART I

UNITS AND STANDARDS OF MEASUREMENT

Units of measurement

1.—(1) The yard or the metre shall be the unit of measurement of length and the pound or the kilogram shall be the unit of measurement of mass by reference to which any measurement involving a measurement of length or mass shall be made in the United Kingdom; and—

(*a*) the yard shall be 0.9144 metre exactly;

(*b*) the pound shall be 0.453 592 37 kilogram exactly.

(2) Schedule 1 to this Act shall have effect for defining for the purposes of measurements falling to be made in the United Kingdom the units of measurement set out in that Schedule; and for the purposes of any measurement of weight falling to be so made, the weight of any thing may be expressed, by reference to the units of measurement set out in Part V of that Schedule, in the same terms as its mass.

(3) Subject to subsection (4) below, the Secretary of State may by order amend Schedule 1 to this Act by adding to or removing from Parts I to VI of that Schedule any unit of measurement of length, of area, of volume, of capacity, or of mass or weight, as the case may be.

(4) An order under subsection (3) above shall not remove—

(*a*) from Part I of Schedule 1, the mile, foot or inch, or

(*b*) from Part IV of that Schedule, the gallon or pint,

but this subsection is without prejudice to section 8(6)(*b*) below.

(5) An order under subsection (3) above may contain such transitional or other supplemental or incidental provisions as appear to the Secretary of State expedient.

United Kingdom primary standards and authorised copies of the primary standards

2.—(1) The Secretary of State shall cause to be maintained standards of the yard, pound, metre and kilogram which shall be the standards (in this Act referred to as "United Kingdom primary standards") by reference to which, in the United Kingdom, all other standards of those units and of any other unit of measurement derived wholly or partly from any of those units shall be maintained.

(2) The Secretary of State shall from time to time as may appear to him expedient cause—

(*a*) the value of each of the United Kingdom primary standards to be determined or redetermined, and

(*b*) any authorised copy of any of those standards to be compared with, and its value determined or redetermined by reference to, that standard,

in such manner as he may direct.

(3) The United Kingdom primary standards shall be—

(*a*) in the case of the yard, the bar described in Part I of Schedule 2 to this Act;

(*b*) in the case of the pound, the cylinder described in Part II of that Schedule;

(*c*) in the case of the metre, the bar described in Part III of that Schedule;

(*d*) in the case of the kilogram, the cylinder described in Part IV of that Schedule.

(4) The copies of the United Kingdom primary standards of the yard and pound which are described in Part V of Schedule 2 to this Act and deposited as mentioned in that Part shall for the purposes of this Act be authorised copies of those standards.

Department of Trade and Industry secondary, tertiary and coinage standards

3.—(1) The Secretary of State shall maintain secondary, tertiary and coinage standards in accordance with the provisions of this section, which shall be known collectively as the Department of Trade and Industry standards.

(2) The secondary standards shall consist of standards of all the measures set out in Parts I and IV and all weights set out in Part V of Schedule 3 to this Act other than capacity measures of more than one gallon or ten litres; and any such standard shall be constructed and, while it remains in use, from time to time at intervals not exceeding five years have its value or values redetermined, by reference to such one or more of the United Kingdom primary standards or any authorised copies of those standards as may appear to the Secretary of State to be appropriate.

(3) The tertiary standards shall consist of such standards of such of the measures or weights set out in Parts I, IV and V of Schedule 3 to this Act as may from time to time appear to the Secretary of State to be necessary or expedient; and any such standard shall be constructed and, while it remains in use, from time to time at intervals not exceeding two years have its value or values redetermined, by reference to such one or more of the secondary standards as may appear to the Secretary of State to be appropriate.

(4) The coinage standards shall consist of such standards of the weight of each coin of the realm for the time being authorised by or under the enactments relating to the coinage as may from time to time appear to the Secretary of State to be necessary or expedient; and any such standard shall be constructed and, while it remains in use, from time to time at intervals not exceeding two years have its value redetermined, by reference to such one or more of the secondary standards as may appear to the Secretary of State to be appropriate.

(5) Department of Trade and Industry standards shall be provided or replaced by the Secretary of State from time to time as may appear to him necessary or expedient and shall be in such form and of such material, and be kept under his control at such place or places, as he may think fit.

(6) A secondary or tertiary standard of any linear or capacity measure may—

    (*a*) be provided either as a separate standard or by means of divisions marked on a standard of a larger measure, and

    (*b*) either be marked in whole or in part with subdivisions representing any smaller unit of measurement or multiples or fractions of such a unit or have no such markings,

as the Secretary of State thinks fit.

Local standards

4.—(1) There shall be maintained by each local weights and measures authority such standards (in this Act referred to as "local standards") of such of the measures and weights set out in Schedule 3 to this Act as the Secretary of State may from time to time approve or require in the case of that authority as being proper and sufficient for the purposes of this Act.

(2) Local standards—

    (*a*) shall be provided and replaced by the local weights and measures authority from time to time as may appear to the authority to be necessary or expedient or as the Secretary of State may require,

    (*b*) shall be of material and form approved by the Secretary of State,

    (*c*) shall be kept in such manner and under such conditions as the Secretary of State may direct at premises provided by the authority, and

    (*d*) shall not be used elsewhere than at those premises or at other premises which appear to the authority to be appropriate.

(3) A local standard of any linear or capacity measure—

    (*a*) shall be provided either as a separate standard or by means of divisions marked on a standard of a larger measure, and

    (*b*) shall either be marked in whole or in part with sub-divisions representing any smaller unit of measurement or multiples or fractions of such a unit or have no such markings,

as the Secretary of State may from time to time direct.

(4) No article shall be used as a local standard unless there is for the time being in force a certificate of its fitness for the purpose issued by the Secretary of State.

(5) The Secretary of State shall cause any article submitted to him for certification under this section to be compared with such one or more of the tertiary standards as may appear to him to be appropriate and, if it falls within the prescribed limits of error and satisfies any other requirements of the Secretary of State, shall issue a certificate of its fitness for use as a local standard which, if the authority so request, shall include a statement of the amount of any error in it.

(6) Subject to paragraph 9 of Schedule 11 to this Act, a certificate issued under subsection (5) above shall cease to be in force at the end of the prescribed period.

(7) The Secretary of State shall keep a record of all certificates issued under subsection (5) above.

(8) Any comparison of an article with the tertiary standards in pursuance of subsection (5) above shall be carried out—

    (*a*) if the article is not for the time being a local standard, at such place as the Secretary of State may direct; or

    (*b*) if the article is for the time being a local standard, at the premises where it is kept or at other premises approved in that behalf by the Secretary of State.

(9) The Secretary of State may charge on any occasion on which an article is submitted to him for certification under this section such fee as he may from time to time with the approval of the Treasury determine.

Working standards and testing and stamping equipment

5.—(1) Subject to subsection (3) below, each local weights and measures authority shall provide for use by the inspectors appointed for the authority's area, and maintain or from time to time replace—

    (*a*) such standards (in this Act referred to as "working standards") of such of the measures and weights set out in Schedule 3 to this Act,

    (*b*) such testing equipment, and

    (*c*) such stamping equipment,

as are proper and sufficient for the efficient discharge by those inspectors of their functions in the authority's area.

(2) An authority may—

    (*a*) provide a particular working standard or item of equipment as required by subsection (1) above by making arrangements with another person for the standard or item to be made available by him, and

    (*b*) make arrangements with another person for standards or equipment provided by the authority under subsection (1) above, except stamping equipment, to be made available to the other person.

(3) If a local weights and measures authority are of opinion—

    (*a*) that any particular description of testing equipment is proper and sufficient for the efficient discharge of the functions of the inspectors appointed for the authority's area, but

    (*b*) that, having regard to the expenditure involved and the frequency with which such equipment is likely to be used by those inspectors, it would not be reasonable for the authority to provide and maintain such equipment,

the authority may request the Secretary of State to provide and maintain such equipment and to make it available for hire to the authority.

(4) The terms of hire of equipment under subsection (3) above shall be such as the Secretary of State may determine.

(5) Working standards and testing and stamping equipment provided under subsection (1) above shall be of material and form approved by the Secretary of State.

(6) Except so far as may be necessary for the purposes of their use elsewhere, such working standards and testing and stamping equipment shall be kept, subject to subsection (7) below, at premises provided by the local weights and measures authority.

(7) Subsection (6) above shall not apply to things which are the subject of arrangements under subsection (2)(*a*) above.

(8) A working standard of a linear or capacity measure—

    (*a*) shall be provided either as a separate standard or by means of divisions marked on a standard of a larger measure, and

    (*b*) shall either be marked in whole or in part with sub-divisions representing any smaller unit of measurement or multiples or fractions of such a unit or have no such markings.

as the Secretary of State may from time to time direct.

(9) The Secretary of State shall by regulations make provision—

    (*a*) for working standards to be from time to time tested by comparison with, and if necessary adjusted to within such limits of error as may be specified in the regulations by reference to, the local standards or other working standards more recently tested, and

    (*b*) with respect to the testing, adjustment and limits of error of testing equipment provided under subsection (1) above.

(10) No article shall be used by an inspector as a working standard or as testing equipment provided under subsection (1) above unless the relevant requirements of regulations under subsection (9) above are for the time being satisfied with respect to it.

(11) Nothing in subsection (2) above prejudices the operation of—

    (*a*) the Local Authorities (Goods and Services) Act 1970,

    (*b*) section 101 of the Local Government Act 1972, or

    (*c*) section 56 of the Local Government (Scotland) Act 1973,

(which among other things enable a local authority to arrange for the provision of goods or services and the discharge of its functions by another local authority).

Testing of other standards and equipment

6.—(1) The Secretary of State may, if he thinks fit, on the application of any government or person, accept for testing as to accuracy or compliance with any specification and for report—

(*a*) any article used or proposed to be used as a standard of a unit of measurement of mass, length, capacity, area or volume, or as a standard of the weight of any coin,

(*b*) any weighing or measuring equipment,

(*c*) any other metrological equipment, and

(*d*) any article for use in connection with equipment mentioned in paragraph (*b*) or (*c*) above,

submitted by that government or person for the purpose at such place as the Secretary of State may direct.

(2) The Secretary of State may charge, in respect of any article or equipment accepted by him in pursuance of subsection (1) above, a fee of an amount ascertained in such manner as he may determine with the approval of the Treasury.

PART II

WEIGHING AND MEASURING FOR TRADE

General

Meaning of "use for trade"

7.—(1) In this Act "use for trade" means, subject to subsection (3) below, use in Great Britain in connection with, or with a view to, a transaction falling within subsection (2) below where—

(*a*) the transaction is by reference to quantity or is a transaction for the purposes of which there is made or implied a statement of the quantity of goods to which the transaction relates, and

(*b*) the use is for the purpose of the determination or statement of that quantity.

(2) A transaction falls within this subsection if it is a transaction for—

(*a*) the transferring or rendering of money or money's worth in consideration of money or money's worth, or

(*b*) the making of a payment in respect of any toll or duty.

(3) Use for trade does not include use in a case where—

(*a*) the determination or statement is a determination or statement of the quantity of goods required for despatch to a destination outside Great Britain and any designated country, and

(*b*) the transaction is not a sale by retail, and

(*c*) no transfer or rendering of money or money's worth is involved other than the passing of the title to the goods and the consideration for them.

(4) The following equipment, that is to say—

(*a*) any weighing or measuring equipment which is made available in Great Britain for use by the public, whether on payment or otherwise, and

(*b*) any equipment which is used in Great Britain for the grading by reference to their weight, for the purposes of trading transactions by reference to that grading, of hens' eggs in shell which are intended for human consumption,

shall be treated for the purposes of this Part of this Act as weighing or measuring equipment in use for trade, whether or not it would apart from this subsection be so treated.

(5) Where any weighing or measuring equipment is found in the possession of any person carrying on trade or on any premises which are used for trade, that person or, as the case may be, the occupier of those premises shall be deemed for the purposes of this Act, unless the contrary is proved, to have that equipment in his possession for use for trade.

Units of measurement, weights and measures lawful for use for trade

8.—(1) No person shall—
    (*a*) use for trade any unit of measurement which is not included in Parts I to V of Schedule 1 to this Act, or
    (*b*) use for trade, or have in his possession for use for trade, any linear, square, cubic or capacity measure which is not included in Schedule 3 to this Act, or any weight which is not so included.
(2) No person shall use for trade—
    (*a*) the ounce troy, except for the purposes of transactions in, or in articles made from, gold, silver or other precious metals, including transactions in gold or silver thread, lace or fringe, or
    (*b*) the carat (metric), except for the purposes of transactions in precious stones or pearls, or
    (*c*) a capacity measure of 125, 150 or 175 millilitres, except for the purposes of transactions in intoxicating liquor.
(3) Subsection (1)(*a*) above shall not apply to the prescribing of, or the dispensing of a prescription for, drugs.
(4) A person who contravenes subsection (1) or (2) above shall be guilty of an offence, and any measure or weight used, or in any person's possession for use, in contravention of that subsection shall be liable to be forfeited.
(5) The preceding provisions of this section have effect subject to—
    (*a*) sections 9 and 89 below, and
    (*b*) regulation 9 of the Units of Measurement Regulations 1980 (which authorises the use for trade of supplementary indications).
(6) The Secretary of State may by order—
    (*a*) amend Schedule 3 to this Act by adding to or removing from it any linear, square, cubic or capacity measure, or any weight;
    (*b*) add to, vary or remove from subsection (2) above any restriction on the cases or circumstances in which, or the conditions subject to which, a unit of measurement, measure or weight may be used for trade or possessed for use for trade.
(7) An order under subsection (6) above may contain such transitional or other supplemental or incidental provisions as appear to the Secretary of State expedient.
(8) In this section "unit of measurement" means a unit of measurement of length, area, volume, capacity, mass or weight.

Dual marking and conversion charts

9.—(1) The Secretary of State may make regulations—
    (*a*) requiring or authorising a person who uses a metric unit for trade to afford, for explanatory purposes, information giving the equivalent in the imperial system of the relevant quantity in the metric system, and
    (*b*) specifying the manner in which the information is to be given, and in particular specifying the cases in which any obligation to give information in metric units is to be extended to include the same information in imperial units.

(2) The Secretary of State may make regulations requiring or authorising the display on premises where metric units are used for trade of conversion tables or other material for converting metric units into imperial units.

(3) Regulations under this section—

(*a*) may prescribe the form and manner in which any information or other material is to be given or displayed,

(*b*) may prescribe appropriate conversion factors by reference to which, in prescribed cases or circumstances, an amount expressed in imperial units is to be treated as equivalent to a given amount expressed in metric units,

(*c*) may prescribe the persons to whom, and the cases and circumstances in which, the regulations apply and may make different provision for different persons, cases or circumstances,

(*d*) may contain such consequential, incidental or supplementary provisions as appear to the Secretary of State to be expedient.

(4) A person contravening regulations made under this section shall be guilty of an offence.

(5) In this section "unit" in the expressions "metric unit" and "imperial unit" means any unit of measurement of length, area, volume, capacity, mass or weight.

(6) Regulations under this section imposing obligations apply whether or not the relevant imperial unit may lawfully be used for trade, and regulations authorising, but not requiring, anything to be done authorise it to be done notwithstanding that the relevant imperial unit may not be lawfully used for trade, but do not in any other respect authorise what is unlawful.

Multiples and fractions of measures and units

10.—(1) Except as may be prescribed, and subject to any regulations made under section 15 below,—

(*a*) a linear measure specified in Part I of Schedule 3 to this Act may be marked in whole or in part with divisions and sub-divisions representing any shorter length or lengths; but

(*b*) no capacity measure specified in Part IV of that Schedule shall be used for trade by means of any division or sub-division marked on it as a capacity measure of any lesser quantity.

(2) Any person who contravenes paragraph (*b*) of subsection (1) above shall be guilty of an offence, and any measure used, or in any person's possession for use, in contravention of that paragraph, shall be liable to be forfeited.

(3) The Secretary of State may by regulations prescribe what may be treated for the purposes of use for trade as the equivalent of, or of any multiple or fraction of, any unit of measurement included in Schedule 1 to this Act in terms of any other such unit.

(4) Nothing in any regulations under subsection (3) above shall apply to any transaction in drugs.

(5) The Secretaries of State respectively concerned with health in England, in Wales and in Scotland acting jointly may by regulations, which shall have effect notwithstanding anything in, or in any instrument made under, any other enactment—

(*a*) prescribe what may be treated for the purposes of dealings with drugs as the equivalent of, or of any multiple or fraction of, any unit of measurement which—

(i) is included in Schedule 1 to this Act, or

(ii) was included in Schedule 1 to the Weights and Measures Act 1963 on 31st January 1964 (the date of the commencement of section 10 of that Act), in terms of any other such unit; and

(*b*) require that any person carrying out any such dealing with drugs as is specified in the regulations for the purposes of which the quantity of the drugs is expressed in terms of any such unit which is so specified shall carry out that dealing in terms of such equivalent quantity prescribed under paragraph (*a*) above as is so specified.

Weighing or measuring equipment for use for trade

Certain equipment to be passed and stamped by inspector

11.—(1) The provisions of this section shall apply to the use for trade of weighing or measuring equipment of such classes or descriptions as may be prescribed.

(2) No person shall use any article for trade as equipment to which this section applies, or have any article in his possession for such use, unless that article, or equipment to which this section applies in which that article is incorporated or to the operation of which the use of that article is incidental,—

(*a*) has been passed by an inspector as fit for such use, and

(*b*) except as otherwise expressly provided by or under this Act, bears a stamp indicating that it has been so passed which remains undefaced otherwise than by reason of fair wear and tear.

(3) If any person contravenes subsection (2) above, he shall be guilty of an offence and any article in respect of which the offence was committed shall be liable to be forfeited.

(4) Any person requiring any equipment to which this section applies to be passed as fit for use for trade shall submit the equipment, in such manner as the local weights and measures authority may direct, to an inspector who (subject to the provisions of this Act and of any regulations under section 15 below) shall—

(*a*) test the equipment by means of such local or working standards and testing equipment as he considers appropriate or, subject to any conditions which may be prescribed, by means of other equipment which has already been tested and which the inspector considers suitable for the purpose,

(*b*) if the equipment submitted falls within the prescribed limits of error and by virtue of subsection (10) below is not required to be stamped as mentioned in paragraph (*c*) of this subsection, give to the person submitting it a statement in writing to the effect that it is passed as fit for use for trade, and

(*c*) except as otherwise expressly provided by or under this Act, cause it to be stamped with the prescribed stamp.

(5) There shall be charged in respect of any test carried out under subsection (4) above such reasonable fees as the local weights and measures authority may determine.

(6) An inspector shall keep a record of every test carried out by him under subsection (4) above.

(7) Except as otherwise expressly provided by or under this Act, no weight or measure shall be stamped as mentioned in subsection (4)(*c*) above unless it has been marked in the prescribed manner with its purported value.

(8) Subject to subsection (9) below, where any equipment submitted to an inspector under subsection (4) above is of a pattern in respect of which a certificate of approval granted under section 12 below is for the time being in force, the inspector shall not refuse to pass or stamp the equipment on the ground that it is not suitable for use for trade.

(9) If the inspector is of opinion that the equipment is intended for use for trade for a particular purpose for which it is not suitable, he may

refuse to pass or stamp it until the matter has been referred to the Secretary of State, whose decision shall be final.

(10) The requirements of subsections (2), (4) and (7) above with respect to stamping and marking shall not apply to any weight or measure which is too small to be stamped or marked in accordance with those requirements.

(11) Where a person submits equipment to an inspector under this section, the inspector may require the person to provide the inspector with such assistance in connection with the testing of the equipment as the inspector reasonably considers it necessary for the person to provide and shall not be obliged to proceed with the test until the person provides it; but a failure to provide the assistance shall not constitute an offence under section 81 below.

(12) If an inspector refuses to pass as fit for use for trade any equipment submitted to him under this section and is requested by the person by whom the equipment was submitted to give reasons for the refusal, the inspector shall give to that person a statement of those reasons in writing.

(13) In the case of any equipment which is required by regulations made under section 15 below to be passed and stamped under this section only after it has been installed at the place where it is to be used for trade, if after the equipment has been so passed and stamped it is dismantled and reinstalled, whether in the same or some other place, it shall not be used for trade after being so reinstalled until it has again been passed under this section.

(14) If any person—

    (a) knowingly uses any equipment in contravention of subsection (13) above, or

    (b) knowingly causes or permits any other person so to use it, or

    (c) knowing that the equipment is required by virtue of subsection (13) above to be again passed under this section, disposes of it to some other person without informing him of that requirement,

he shall be guilty of an offence and the equipment shall be liable to be forfeited.

(15) Subject to subsection (13) above, a stamp applied to any equipment under this section shall have the like validity throughout Great Britain as it has in the place in which it was originally applied, and accordingly that equipment shall not be required to be re-stamped because it is used in any other place.

(16) If at any time the Secretary of State is satisfied that, having regard to the law for the time being in force in Northern Ireland, any of the Channel Islands or the Isle of Man, it is proper so to do, he may by order provide for any equipment to which this section applies duly stamped in accordance with that law, or treated for the purposes of that law as if duly stamped in accordance with it, to be treated for the purposes of this Act as if it had been duly stamped in Great Britain under this section.

Approved patterns of equipment

12.—(1) Where any pattern of weighing or measuring equipment is submitted by any person to the Secretary of State for the purpose in such manner as may be prescribed, the Secretary of State shall examine in such manner as he thinks fit the suitability for use for trade of equipment of that pattern, having regard in particular to the principle, materials and methods used or proposed to be used in its construction, and—

    (a) may require the person to provide such assistance as the Secretary of State thinks fit in connection with the examination (and shall not be obliged to proceed with the examination until the person provides it), and

(b) may require the person to pay in respect of the examination a fee of an amount ascertained in such manner as the Secretary of State may determine with the approval of the Treasury.

(2) Subsection (1) above applies to a pattern consisting of an approved pattern with modifications as it applies to other patterns, and in this subsection "approved pattern" means a pattern in respect of which a certificate of approval under this section is in force.

(3) If the Secretary of State is satisfied that any equipment in respect of which a pattern is submitted to him under subsection (1) above is suitable for use for trade, then, subject to subsection (4) and section 14(2) below, he shall issue a certificate of approval of that pattern (in this section referred to as "a certificate of approval") and shall cause particulars of the pattern to be published.

(4) Where the Secretary of State is satisfied as mentioned in subsection (3) above, he may require the person submitting the pattern of equipment to deposit with the Secretary of State parts of equipment of that pattern or a model or drawings of such equipment or parts of it and may withhold a certificate of approval of that pattern or, as the case may be, a declaration in pursuance of section 14(2) below in respect of the pattern, until the person complies with the requirement.

(5) A certificate of approval may be granted subject to such conditions as the Secretary of State thinks fit.

(6) Without prejudice to the generality of subsection (5) above, a certificate of approval may be granted subject to a condition under which it ceases to be in force at the end of a specified period of less than ten years.

(7) Subject to any condition imposed under subsection (6) above, a certificate of approval, unless previously revoked, shall cease to be in force at the end of the period of ten years beginning with the date when it was granted.

(8) A certificate of approval may be renewed by the Secretary of State on an application made in such manner and during such period as may be prescribed and on payment, except in such cases as the Secretary of State may determine, of a fee of an amount ascertained in such manner as the Secretary of State may determine with the approval of the Treasury; and subsections (5) to (7) above apply in relation to the renewal of a certificate of approval as they apply in relation to the grant of such a certificate.

(9) Where application has been made to the Secretary of State in accordance with subsection (8) above for the renewal of a certificate of approval, the certificate shall remain in force until the Secretary of State gives to the applicant, in such manner as may be prescribed, notice of the Secretary of State's decision with respect to the application.

(10) The Secretary of State, after consultation with such persons appearing to him to be interested as he thinks fit, may at any time revoke any certificate of approval (including a certificate remaining in force by virtue of subsection (9) above) and shall cause notice of any such revocation to be published.

(11) Where a certificate of approval—

(a) expires (whether at the end of a period or by virtue of a notice under subsection (9) above), or

(b) is revoked in a case where the notice of revocation published under subsection (10) above states that this subsection and section 13(2) below are to apply with respect to the revocation,

the certificate shall remain in force in relation to any equipment of the pattern in question which was used for trade at a time when the certificate was in force otherwise than by virtue of this subsection; and the power of revocation under subsection (10) above includes power to revoke a certificate remaining in force by virtue of this subsection.

(12) Any equipment of a pattern in respect of which a certificate of approval has been granted may, and in such cases as may be prescribed shall, be marked in the prescribed manner so as to identify it with the pattern in question.

Offences in connection with approved patterns of equipment

13.—(1) Where one or more conditions are imposed by the Secretary of State on the grant or renewal of a certificate of approval, then if any person—

    (*a*) knowing that a condition, other than such a condition as is mentioned in section 12(6) above, has been imposed with respect to any equipment, uses, or causes or permits any other person to use, that equipment in contravention of that condition, or

    (*b*) knowing that any condition has been imposed with respect to any equipment, disposes of that equipment to any other person in a state in which it could be used for trade without informing that other person of that condition,

he shall be guilty of an offence and the equipment shall be liable to be forfeited.

(2) Where a certificate of approval in respect of any pattern of equipment—

    (*a*) expires (whether at the end of a period or by virtue of a notice under section 12(9) above), or

    (*b*) is revoked in a case falling within section 12(11)(*b*) above,

then if any person, knowing that the certificate has expired or has been so revoked, supplies to another person any equipment of the pattern in question which is marked with a stamp and which was not used for trade at a time when the certificate was in force otherwise than by virtue of section 12(11) above, he shall be guilty of an offence and the equipment supplied shall be liable to be forfeited.

(3) Where a certificate of approval in respect of any pattern of equipment is revoked in a case not falling within section 12(11)(*b*) above, then if any person, knowing that the certificate has been so revoked (and except as may be permitted by any fresh certificate granted in respect of that pattern)—

    (*a*) uses for trade, or has in his possession for such use, any equipment of that pattern,

    (*b*) causes or permits any other person to use any such equipment for trade, or

    (*c*) disposes of any such equipment to any such person in a state in which it could be used for trade without informing that other person of the revocation,

he shall be guilty of an offence and the equipment shall be liable to be forfeited.

(4) In this section "certificate of approval" means a certificate of approval of a pattern of weighing or measuring equipment granted under section 12 above; and subsections (1) and (3) above have effect in relation to a certificate of approval remaining in force by virtue of subsection (9) or (11) of section 12 above as they have effect in relation to other certificates of approval.

General specifications of equipment

14.—(1) The Secretary of State may by regulations prescribe general specifications for the construction of equipment to which section 11 above applies and, subject to subsection (4) below, while any such specification is for the time being so prescribed no equipment which does not conform with it shall be passed or stamped by an inspector under that section unless it is of a pattern in respect of which a certificate of approval under section 12 above is in force.

(2) If the Secretary of State is satisfied that any pattern submitted to him under section 12(1) above conforms with any general specification for the time being prescribed under this section he may, instead of issuing a certificate of approval under that section, cause to be published a declaration to that effect together with particulars of that pattern.

(3) Where a specification prescribed by regulations under this section is varied or revoked by further regulations under this section, then if any person—

(*a*) uses for trade any equipment which conformed with that specification but which to his knowledge no longer conforms with any specification prescribed by regulations under this section,

(*b*) has any such equipment in his possession for use for trade,

(*c*) causes or permits any other person to use any such equipment for trade, or

(*d*) disposes of any such equipment to any other person in a state in which it could be used for trade without informing that other person that it no longer conforms with any specification prescribed by regulations under this section,

he shall be guilty of an offence and the equipment shall be liable to be forfeited.

(4) Where, in the case of any particular equipment, the Secretary of State is of opinion that there are special circumstances which make it impracticable or unnecessary for that equipment to comply with any particular requirement of any specification prescribed under this section, the Secretary of State may exempt that equipment from that requirement subject to compliance with such conditions, if any, as he thinks fit.

(5) If any person knowingly contravenes any condition imposed with respect to any equipment by virtue of subsection (4) above, he shall be guilty of an offence and the equipment shall be liable to be forfeited.

(6) If any difference arises between an inspector and any other person as to the interpretation of any specification prescribed under this section, or as to whether or not any equipment conforms with such a specification, that difference may with the consent of that other person, and shall at the request of that other person, be referred to the Secretary of State, whose decision shall be final.

Miscellaneous

Regulations relating to weighing or measuring for trade

15.—(1) The Secretary of State may make regulations with respect to—

(*a*) the materials and principles of construction of weighing or measuring equipment for use for trade,

(*b*) the inspection, testing, passing as fit for use for trade and stamping of such equipment, including—

(i) the prohibition of the stamping of such equipment in such circumstances as may be specified in the regulations,

(ii) the circumstances in which an inspector may remove or detain any such equipment for inspection or testing,

(iii) the marking of any such equipment found unfit for use for trade,

(*c*) the circumstances in which, conditions under which and manner in which stamps may be destroyed, obliterated or defaced, (*d*) where any stamp on weighing or measuring equipment is lawfully destroyed, obliterated or defaced, the circumstances in which, and conditions subject to which, the equipment may be used for trade without contravening section 11(2) above,

(*e*) the purposes for which particular types of weighing or measuring equipment may be used for trade,

(*f*) the manner of erection or use of weighing or measuring equipment used for trade,

(*g*) the abbreviations of or symbols for units of measurement which may be used for trade, and

(*h*) the manner in which the tare weight of road vehicles, or of road vehicles of any particular class or description, is to be determined.

(2) Regulations under subsection (1) above with respect to the testing of equipment may provide—

(*a*) that where a group of items of equipment of the same kind is submitted for testing and prescribed conditions are satisfied with respect to the group, the testing may be confined to a number of items determined by or under the regulations and selected in the prescribed manner, and

(*b*) that if items so selected satisfy the test other items in the group shall be treated as having satisfied it.

Subject to subsection (5) below, if any person contravenes any regulation made by virtue of subsection (1)(*e*), (*f*), (*g*), or (*h*) above, he shall be guilty of an offence, and any weighing or measuring equipment in respect of which the contravention was committed shall be liable to be forfeited.

(4) If any difference arises between an inspector and any other person as to the interpretation of any regulations made under this section or as to the method of testing any weighing or measuring equipment, that difference may with the consent of that other person, and shall at the request of that other person, be referred to the Secretary of State, whose decision shall be final.

(5) Where in the special circumstances of any particular case it appears to be impracticable or unnecessary that any requirement of any regulations made under this section should be complied with, the Secretary of State may if he thinks fit dispense with the observance of that requirement subject to compliance with such conditions, if any, as he thinks fit to impose; and if any person knowingly contravenes any condition imposed with respect to any equipment by virtue of this subsection he shall be guilty of an offence and the equipment shall be liable to be forfeited.

Offences in connection with stamping of equipment

16.—(1) Subject to subsection (2) below, any person who, in the case of any weighing or measuring equipment used or intended to be used for trade—

(*a*) not being an inspector or a person acting under the instructions of an inspector, marks in any manner any plug or seal used or designed for use for the reception of a stamp,

(*b*) forges, counterfeits or, except as permitted by or under this Act, in any way alters or defaces any stamp,

(*c*) removes any stamp and inserts it into any other such equipment,

(*d*) makes any alteration in the equipment after it has been stamped such as to make it false or unjust, or

(*e*) severs or otherwise tampers with any wire, cord or other thing by means of which a stamp is attached to the equipment,

shall be guilty of an offence.

(2) Paragraphs (*a*) and (*b*) of subsection (1) above shall not apply to the destruction or obliteration of any stamp, plug or seal, and paragraph (*e*) of that subsection shall not apply to anything done, in the course of the adjustment or repair of weighing or measuring equipment by, or by the duly authorised agent of, a person who is a manufacturer of, or regularly engaged in the business of repairing, such equipment.

(3) Any person who uses for trade, sells, or exposes or offers for sale any weighing or measuring equipment which to his knowledge—

> (*a*) bears a stamp which is a forgery or counterfeit, or which has been transferred from other equipment, or which has been altered or defaced otherwise than as permitted by or under this Act, or
>
> (*b*) is false or unjust as the result of an alteration made in the equipment after it has been stamped,

shall be guilty of an offence.

(4) Any weighing or measuring equipment in respect of which an offence under this section is committed, and any stamp or stamping implement used in the commission of the offence, shall be liable to be forfeited.

Offences relating to false or unjust equipment or fraud

17.—(1) If any person uses for trade, or has in his possession for use for trade, any weighing or measuring equipment which is false or unjust, he shall be guilty of an offence and the equipment shall be liable to be forfeited.

(2) Without prejudice to the liability of any equipment to be forfeited, it shall be a defence for any person charged with an offence under subsection (1) above in respect of the use for trade of any equipment to show—

> (*a*) that he used the equipment only in the course of his employment by some other person, and
>
> (*b*) that he neither knew, nor might reasonably have been expected to know, nor had any reason to suspect, the equipment to be false or unjust.

(3) If any fraud is committed in the using of any weighing or measuring equipment for trade, the person committing the fraud and any other person party to it shall be guilty of an offence and the equipment shall be liable to be forfeited.

PART III

PUBLIC WEIGHING OR MEASURING EQUIPMENT

Keepers of public equipment to hold certificate

18.—(1) No person shall attend to any weighing or measuring by means of weighing or measuring equipment available for use by the public, being a weighing or measuring demanded by a member of the public and for which a charge is made, other than a weighing or measuring of a person, unless he holds a certificate from a chief inspector that he has sufficient knowledge for the proper performance of his duties.

(2) Any person refused such a certificate by a chief inspector may appeal against the refusal to the Secretary of State, who may if he thinks fit direct the chief inspector to grant the certificate.

(3) Any person who contravenes, or who causes or permits any other person to contravene, subsection (1) above shall be guilty of an offence.

Provision of public equipment by local authorities

19.—(1) Without prejudice to any functions conferred or imposed by any other enactment, any local authority who are for the time being, or have at any time been, a local weights and measures authority under this Act or the Weights and Measures Act 1963 may provide and maintain within their area for use by the public such weighing or measuring equipment as may appear to the authority to be expedient.

(2) Without prejudice to the provisions of any other Act, and subject to section 18 above, a local authority may employ persons to attend to any weighing or measuring by means of equipment provided by that authority for use by the public.

(3) Except in the case of a weighing or measuring for which, under any other Act, the charge falls to be regulated from time to time by some other person, a local authority by whom any weighing or measuring equipment is provided for use by the public may make such charges for any weighing or measuring by means of that equipment as they may from time to time think fit.

Offences in connection with public equipment

20.—(1) Subsection (2) below shall apply where any article, vehicle (whether loaded or unloaded) or animal has been brought for weighing or measuring by means of weighing or measuring equipment which is available for use by the public and is provided for the purpose of weighing or measuring articles, vehicles or animals of the description in question.

(2) If any person appointed to attend to weighing or measuring by means of the equipment in question—

(a) without reasonable cause fails to carry out the weighing or measuring on demand,

(b) carries out the weighing or measuring unfairly,

(c) fails to deliver to the person demanding the weighing or measuring or to his agent a statement in writing of the weight or other measurement found, or

(d) fails to make a record of the weighing or measuring, including the time and date of it and, in the case of the weighing of a vehicle, such particulars of the vehicle and of any load on the vehicle as will identify that vehicle and that load,

he shall be guilty of an offence.

(3) If in connection with any such equipment as is mentioned in subsection (1) above—

(a) any person appointed to attend to weighing or measuring by means of the equipment delivers a false statement of any weight or other measurement found or makes a false record of any weighing or measuring, or

(b) any person commits any fraud in connection with any, or any purported, weighing or measuring by means of that equipment,

he shall be guilty of an offence.

(4) If, in the case of a weighing or measuring of any article, vehicle or animal carried out by means of any such equipment as is mentioned in subsection (1) above, the person bringing the article, vehicle or animal for weighing or measuring, on being required by the person attending to the weighing or measuring to give his name and address, fails to do so or gives a name or address which is incorrect, he shall be guilty of an offence.

(5) The person making any weighing or measuring equipment available for use by the public (in this section referred to as "the responsible person") shall retain for a period of not less than two years any record of any weighing or measuring by means of that equipment made by any person appointed to attend to the weighing or measuring.

(6) An inspector, subject to the production of his credentials if so requested, may require the responsible person to produce any such record as is mentioned in subsection (5) above for inspection at any time while it is retained by him.

(7) If the responsible person fails to retain any such record as is mentioned in subsection (5) above in accordance with that subsection or fails to produce it in accordance with subsection (6) above, he shall be guilty of an offence.

(8) If any person wilfully destroys or defaces any such record as is mentioned in subsection (5) above before the expiration of two years from the date when it was made, he shall be guilty of an offence.

PART IV

REGULATION OF TRANSACTIONS IN GOODS

Transactions in particular goods

Transactions in goods mentioned in Schedules 4 to 7

21. Schedules 4, 5, 6 and 7 to this Act (which relate to transactions in the goods mentioned in those Schedules) shall have effect.

Orders relating to transactions in particular goods

22.—(1) The Secretary of State may by order make provision with respect to any goods specified in the order for all or any of the following purposes, that is to say, to ensure that, except in such cases or in such circumstances as may be so specified, the goods in question—

(*a*) are sold only by quantity expressed in such manner as may be so specified,

(*b*) are pre-packed, or are otherwise made up in or on a container for sale or for delivery after sale, only if the container is marked with such information as to the quantity of the goods as may be so specified,

(*c*) are pre-packed, or are otherwise made up for sale or for delivery after sale, only in or on a container of a size or capacity so specified,

(*d*) are sold, or are pre-packed, or are otherwise made up in or on a container for sale or for delivery after sale, or are made for sale, only in such quantities as may be so specified,

(*e*) are not sold without the quantity sold expressed in such manner as may be so specified being made known to the buyer at or before such time as may be so specified,

(*f*) are sold by means of, or are offered or exposed for sale in, a vending machine only if there is displayed on or in the machine—

    (i) such information as to the quantity of the goods in question comprised in each item for sale by means of that machine as may be so specified, and

    (ii) a statement of the name and address of the seller,

(*g*) are carried for reward only in pursuance of an agreement made by reference to the quantity of the goods in question expressed in such manner as may be so specified,

(*h*) in such circumstances as may be so specified, have associated with them in such manner as may be so specified in a document containing a statement of the quantity of the goods in question expressed in such manner, and a statement of such other particulars, if any, as may be so specified, or

72–20

    (*i*) when carried on a road vehicle along a highway are accompanied by a document containing such particulars determined in such manner as may be so specified as to the weight of the vehicle and its load apart from the goods in question.

(2) An order under subsection (1) above may be made with respect to any goods, including goods to which any of the provisions of Schedule 4, 5, 6 or 7 to this Act applies, and may—

    (*a*) make provision for any of the purposes mentioned in subsection (1) above in such manner, whether by means of amending, or of applying with or without modifications, or of excluding the application in whole or in part of, any of the provisions of this Act (except Part V) or of any previous order under subsection (1) or otherwise,

    (*b*) make such, if any, different provision for retail and other sales respectively, and

    (*c*) contain such consequential, incidental or supplementary provision, whether by such means as mentioned in paragraph (*a*) above or otherwise,

as may appear to the Secretary of State to be expedient, and may in particular make provision in respect of contraventions of the order for which no penalty is provided by this Act for the imposition of penalties not exceeding those provided by section 84(6) below for an offence under this Act.

(3) Without prejudice to the generality of the powers conferred by paragraph (*c*) of subsection (1) above, an order made by virtue of that paragraph—

    (*a*) may require a container to be marked with such information concerning it or its contents as is specified in the order, and

    (*b*) in order to prevent size or capacity from giving a false impression of the quantity of the goods in a container, may prescribe a minimum quantity for the goods in a container of a given capacity.

(4) The minimum quantity referred to in subsection (3)(*b*) above may be expressed in the order by weight or volume, by percentage of the capacity of the container or in any other manner.

Regulations as to information

    23.—(1) The Secretary of State may make regulations—

    (*a*) as to the manner in which any container required by any of the provisions of Schedule 4, 5, 6 or 7 to this Act or of any order under section 22(1) above to be marked with information (including in particular information as to quantity or capacity) is to be so marked,

    (*b*) as to the manner in which any information required by any such provision to be displayed on or in a vending machine is to be so displayed,

    (*c*) as to the conditions which must be satisfied in marking with information as to the quantity of goods made up in it the container in or on which any goods are made up for sale (whether by way of pre-packing or otherwise) where those goods are goods on a sale of which (whether any sale or a sale of any particular description) the quantity of the goods sold is required by any such provision to be made known to the buyer at or before a particular time,

    (*d*) as to the units of measurement to be used in marking any such container or machine with any information,

    (*e*) for securing, in the case of pre-packed goods, that the container is so marked as to enable the packer to be identified, (*f*) as to the method by which and conditions under which quantity is to be determined in connection with any information relating to quantity required by or under section 21 or 22 above, and

(*g*) permitting, in the case of such goods and in such circumstances as may be specified in the regulations, the weight of such articles used in making up the goods for sale as may be so specified to be included in the net weight of the goods for the purposes of this Part of this Act.

(2) Any person who contravenes any regulation made under subsection (1) above otherwise than by virtue of paragraph (*f*) or (*g*) of that subsection shall be guilty of an offence.

Exemption from requirements imposed under sections 21 to 23

24.—(1) The Secretary of State may by order grant, with respect to goods or sales of such descriptions as may be specified in the order, exemption, either generally or in such circumstances as may be so specified, from all or any of the requirements imposed by or under sections 21 to 23 above.

(2) Until otherwise provided by an order under subsection (1) above, the following shall be exempted from all requirements imposed by or under sections 21 to 23 above, that is to say—

(*a*) goods made up in or on a container for sale only for use by Her Majesty's forces or by a visiting force within the meaning of any of the provisions of Part I of the Visiting Forces Act 1952 and not sold or offered, exposed or in any person's possession for sale for any other use,

(*b*) any sale of goods in the case of which the buyer gives notice in writing to the seller before the sale is completed that the goods are being bought—

(i) for despatch to a destination outside Great Britain and any designated country, or

(ii) for use as stores within the meaning of the Customs and Excise Management Act 1979 in a ship or aircraft on a voyage or flight to an eventual destination outside the United Kingdom and the Isle of Man,

(*c*) any goods sold for, or offered, exposed or in any person's possession for sale only for, use or consumption at the premises of the seller, not being intoxicating liquor, and

(*d*) any assortment of articles of food pre-packed together for consumption together as a meal and ready for such consumption without being cooked, heated or otherwise prepared.

Offences relating to transactions in particular goods

25.—(1) Subject to section 44 below, where any goods are required, when not pre-packed, to be sold only by quantity expressed in a particular manner or only in a particular quantity, any person shall be guilty of an offence who—

(*a*) whether on his own behalf or on behalf of another person, offers or exposes for sale, sells or agrees to sell, or

(*b*) causes or suffers any other person to offer or expose for sale, sell or agree to sell on his behalf,

those goods otherwise than by quantity expressed in that manner or, as the case may be, otherwise than in that quantity.

(2) Any person shall be guilty of an offence who—

(*a*) whether on his own behalf or on behalf of another person, has in his possession for sale, sells or agrees to sell, (*b*) except in the course of carriage of the goods for reward, has in his possession for delivery after sale, or

(*c*) causes or suffers any other person to have in his possession for sale or for delivery after sale, sell or agree to sell on behalf of the first-mentioned person,

any goods to which subsection (3) below applies, whether the sale is or is to be, by retail or otherwise.

(3) This subsection applies to any goods—

(*a*) which are required to be pre-packed only in particular quantities but are not so pre-packed,

(*b*) which are required to be otherwise made up in or on a container for sale or for delivery after sale only in particular quantities but are not so made up,

(*c*) which are required to be made for sale only in particular quantities but are not so made,

(*d*) which are required to be pre-packed only if the container is marked with particular information but are pre-packed otherwise than in or on a container so marked,

(*e*) which are required to be otherwise made up in or on a container for sale or for delivery after sale only if the container is marked with particular information but are so made up otherwise than in or on a container so marked,

(*f*) which are required to be pre-packed only in or on a container of a particular description but are not pre-packed in or on a container of that description, or

(*g*) which are required to be otherwise made up in or on a container for sale or for delivery after sale only in or on a container of a particular description but are not so made up in or on a container of that description.

(4) In the case of any sale where the quantity of the goods sold expressed in a particular manner is required to be made known to the buyer at or before a particular time and that quantity is not so made known, the person by whom, and any other person on whose behalf, the goods were sold shall be guilty of an offence.

(5) Where any goods required to be sold by means of, or to be offered or exposed for sale in, a vending machine only if certain requirements are complied with are so sold, offered or exposed without those requirements being complied with, the seller or person causing the goods to be offered or exposed shall be guilty of an offence.

(6) The preceding provisions of this section have effect subject to sections 33 to 37 below.

(7) For the purposes of this section the quantity of the goods in a regulated package (as defined by section 68(1) below) shall be deemed to be the nominal quantity (as so defined) on the package.

(8) In this section "required" means required by or under this Part of this Act.

Quantity to be stated in writing

Quantity to be stated in writing in certain cases

26.—(1) Subject to section 27 below, the provisions of this section shall have effect on any sale of goods—

(*a*) which is required by or under this Part of this Act to be a sale by quantity expressed in a particular manner,

(*b*) in the case of which the quantity of the goods sold expressed in a particular manner is so required to be made known to the buyer at or before a particular time, or (*c*) which, being a sale by retail not falling within paragraph (*a*) or (*b*) above, is, or purports to be, a sale by quantity expressed in a particular manner other than by number.

(2) Subject to subsections (4) to (6) below, unless the quantity of the goods sold expressed in the manner in question is made known to the buyer at the premises of the seller and the goods are delivered to the buyer at those premises on the same occasion as, and at or after the time when, that quantity is so made known to him, a statement in writing of that quantity shall be delivered to the consignee at or before delivery of the goods to him.

(3) If subsection (2) above is contravened then, subject to sections 33 to 37 below, the person by whom, and any other person on whose behalf, the goods were sold shall be guilty of an offence.

(4) If at the time when the goods are delivered the consignee is absent, it shall be sufficient compliance with subsection (2) above if the statement is left at some suitable place at the premises at which the goods are delivered.

(5) Subsection (2) above shall not apply to any sale otherwise than by retail where, by agreement with the buyer, the quantity of the goods sold is to be determined after their delivery to the consignee.

(6) Where any liquid goods are sold by capacity measurement and the quantity sold is measured at the time of delivery and elsewhere than at the premises of the seller, subsection (2) above shall not apply but, unless the quantity by capacity measurement of the goods sold is measured in the presence of the buyer, the person by whom the goods are delivered shall immediately after the delivery hand to the buyer, or if the buyer is not present leave at some suitable place at the premises at which the goods are delivered, a statement in writing of the quantity by capacity measurement delivered, and if without reasonable cause he fails so to do he shall be guilty of an offence.

Exemption from requirements of section 26

27.—(1) The Secretary of State may by order grant, with respect to goods or sales of such descriptions as may be specified in the order, exemption, either generally or in such circumstances as may be so specified, from all or any of the requirements of section 26 above.

(2) Until otherwise provided by an order under subsection (1) above, nothing in section 26 above shall apply to—

(*a*) a sale by retail from a vehicle of—

(i) any of the following in a quantity not exceeding 224 pounds, that is to say, any solid fuel within the meaning of Schedule 5 to this Act, and wood fuel, or

(ii) any of the following in a quantity not exceeding five gallons, that is to say, liquid fuel, lubricating oil, and any mixture of such fuel and oil,

(*b*) a sale by retail of bread within the meaning of the Weights and Measures Act 1963 (Miscellaneous Foods) Order 1984,

(*c*) goods made up for sale (whether by way of pre-packing or otherwise) in or on a container marked with a statement in writing with respect to the quantity of the goods expressed in the manner in question, being a container which is delivered with the goods,

(*d*) a sale of goods in the case of which a document stating the quantity of the goods expressed in the manner in question is required to be delivered to the buyer or consignee of the goods by or under any other provision of this Part of this Act,

(*e*) any such goods or sales as are mentioned in section 24(2)(*a*) to (*d*) above,

(*f*) a sale of intoxicating liquor for consumption at the premises of the seller,
(*g*) a sale by means of a vending machine, or
(*h*) goods delivered at premises of the buyer by means of an installation providing a connection of a permanent nature between those premises and premises of the seller.

General offences

Short weight, etc.

28.—(1) Subject to sections 33 to 37 below, any person who, in selling or purporting to sell any goods by weight or other measurement or by number, delivers or causes to be delivered to the buyer—
(*a*) a lesser quantity than that purported to be sold, or
(*b*) a lesser quantity than corresponds with the price charged,
shall be guilty of an offence.
(2) For the purposes of this section—
(*a*) the quantity of the goods in a regulated package (as defined by section 68(1) below) shall be deemed to be the nominal quantity (as so defined) on the package, and
(*b*) any statement, whether oral or in writing, as to the weight of any goods shall be taken, unless otherwise expressed, to be a statement as to the net weight of the goods.
(3) Nothing in this section shall apply in relation to any such goods or sales as are mentioned in section 24(2)(*a*) or (*b*) above.

Misrepresentation

29.—(1) Subject to sections 33 to 37 below, any person who—
(*a*) on or in connection with the sale or purchase of any goods,
(*b*) in exposing or offering any goods for sale,
(*c*) in purporting to make known to the buyer the quantity of any goods sold, or
(*d*) in offering to purchase any goods,
makes any misrepresentation whether oral or otherwise as to the quantity of the goods, or does any other act calculated to mislead a person buying or selling the goods as to the quantity of the goods, shall be guilty of an offence.
(2) Subsection (2) of section 28 above shall have effect for the purposes of this section as it has effect for the purposes of that section.
(3) Nothing in this section shall apply in relation to any such goods or sales as are mentioned in section 24(2)(*a*) or (*b*) above.

Quantity less than stated

30.—(1) If, in the case of any goods pre-packed in or on a container marked with a statement in writing with respect to the quantity of the goods, the quantity of the goods is at any time found to be less than that stated, then, subject to sections 33 to 37 below—
(*a*) any person who has those goods in his possession for sale shall be guilty of an offence, and
(*b*) if it is shown that the deficiency cannot be accounted for by anything occurring after the goods had been sold by retail and delivered to, or to a person nominated in that behalf by, the buyer, any person by whom or on whose behalf those goods have been sold or agreed to be sold at any time while they were pre-packed in or on the container in question, shall be guilty of an offence.
(2) If—

(*a*) in the case of a sale of or agreement to sell any goods which, not being pre-packed, are made up for sale or for delivery after sale in or on a container marked with a statement in writing with respect to the quantity of the goods, or

(*b*) in the case of any goods which, in connection with their sale or an agreement for their sale, have associated with them a document containing such a statement,

the quantity of the goods is at any time found to be less than that stated, then, if it is shown that the deficiency cannot be accounted for by anything occurring after the goods had been delivered to, or to a person nominated in that behalf by, the buyer, and subject to sections 33 to 37 below and paragraph 10 of Schedule 4 to this Act, the person by whom, and any other person on whose behalf, the goods were sold or agreed to be sold shall be guilty of an offence.

(3) Subsections (1) and (2) above shall have effect notwithstanding that the quantity stated is expressed to be the quantity of the goods at a specified time falling before the time in question, or is expressed with some other qualification of whatever description, except where—

(*a*) that quantity is so expressed in pursuance of an express requirement of this Part of this Act or any instrument made under this Part, or

(*b*) the goods, although falling within subsection (1) or subsection (2)(*a*) above—

(i) are not required by or under this Part of this Act to be pre-packed as mentioned in subsection (1) or, as the case may be, to be made up for sale or for delivery after sale in or on a container only if the container is marked as mentioned in subsection (2)(*a*), and

(ii) are not goods on a sale of which (whether any sale or a sale of any particular description) the quantity sold is required by or under any provision of this Part of this Act other than section 26, to be made known to the buyer at or before a particular time, or

(*c*) the goods, although falling within subsection (2)(*b*) above, are not required by or under this Part of this Act to have associated with them such a document as is mentioned in that provision.

(4) In any case to which, by virtue of paragraph (*a*), (*b*) or (*c*) of subsection (3) above, the provisions of subsection (1) or (2) above do not apply, if it is found at any time that the quantity of the goods in question is less than that stated and it is shown that the deficiency is greater than can be reasonably justified on the ground justifying the qualification in question, then, subject to sections 33 to 37 below—

(*a*) in the case of goods such as are mentioned in subsection (1) above, if it is further shown as mentioned in that subsection, then—

(i) where the container in question was marked in Great Britain, the person by whom, and any other person on whose behalf, the container was marked, or

(ii) where the container in question was marked outside Great Britain, the person by whom, and any other person on whose behalf, the goods were first sold in Great Britain, shall be guilty of an offence;

(*b*) in the case of goods such as are mentioned in subsection (2) above, the person by whom, and any other person on whose behalf, the goods were sold or agreed to be sold shall be guilty of an offence if, but only if, he would, but for paragraph (*a*), (*b*) or (*c*) of subsection (3) above have been guilty of an offence under subsection (2).

(5) Subsection (2) of section 28 above shall have effect for the purposes of this section as it has effect for the purposes of that section.

(6) Nothing in this section shall apply in relation to any such goods or sales as are mentioned in section 24(2)(*a*) or (*b*) above.

Incorrect statements

31.—(1) Without prejudice to section 30(2) to (4) above, if in the case of any goods required by or under this Part of this Act to have associated with them a document containing particular statements, that document is found to contain any such statement which is materially incorrect, any person who, knowing or having reasonable cause to suspect that statement to be materially incorrect, inserted it or caused it to be inserted in the document, or used the document for the purposes of this Part of this Act while that statement was contained in the document shall be guilty of an offence.

(2) Subsection (2) of section 28 above shall have effect for the purposes of this section as it has effect for the purposes of that section.

(3) Nothing in this section shall apply in relation to any such goods or sales as are mentioned in section 24(2)(*a*) or (*b*) above.

Offences due to default of third person

32. Where the commission by any person of an offence under this Part of this Act or an instrument made under this Part is due to the act or default of some other person, the other person shall be guilty of an offence and may be charged with and convicted of the offence whether or not proceedings are taken against the first-mentioned person.

Defences

Warranty

33.—(1) Subject to the following provisions of this section, in any proceedings for an offence under this Part of this Act or any instrument made under this Part, being an offence relating to the quantity or pre-packing of any goods, it shall be a defence for the person charged to prove—

(*a*) that he bought the goods from some other person—
    (i) as being of the quantity which the person charged purported to sell or represented, or which was marked on any container or stated in any document to which the proceedings relate, or
    (ii) as conforming with the statement marked on any container to which the proceedings relate, or with the requirements with respect to the pre-packing of goods of this Part of this Act or any instrument made under this Part,
    as the case may require, and

(*b*) that he so bought the goods with a written warranty from that other person that they were of that quantity or, as the case may be, did so conform, and

(*c*) that at the time of the commission of the offence he did in fact believe the statement contained in the warranty to be accurate and had no reason to believe it to be inaccurate, and

(*d*) if the warranty was given by a person who at the time he gave it was resident outside Great Britain and any designated country, that the person charged had taken reasonable steps to check the accuracy of the statement contained in the warranty, and

(*e*) in the case of proceedings relating to the quantity of any goods, that he took all reasonable steps to ensure that, while in his possession, the quantity of the goods remained unchanged and, in the case of such or any other proceedings, that apart from any change in their quantity the goods were at the time of the commission of the offence in the same state as when he bought them.

(2) A warranty shall not be a defence in any such proceedings as are mentioned in subsection (1) above unless, not later than three days before the date of the hearing, the person charged has sent to the prosecutor a copy of the warranty with a notice stating that he intends to rely on it and specifying the name and address of the person from whom the warranty was received, and has also sent a like notice to that person.

(3) Where the person charged is the employee of a person who, if he had been charged, would have been entitled to plead a warranty as a defence under this section, subsection (1) above shall have effect—

> (a) with the substitution, for any reference (however expressed) in paragraphs (a), (b), (d) and (e) to the person charged, of a reference to his employer, and
>
> (b) with the substitution for paragraph (c) of the following—
>
>> "(c) that at the time of the commission of the offence his employer did in fact believe the statement contained in the warranty to be accurate and the person charged had no reason to believe it to be inaccurate,".

(4) The person by whom the warranty is alleged to have been given shall be entitled to appear at the hearing and to give evidence.

(5) If the person charged in any such proceedings as are mentioned in subsection (1) above wilfully attributes to any goods a warranty given in relation to any other goods, he shall be guilty of an offence.

(6) A person who, in respect of any goods sold by him in respect of which a warranty might be pleaded under this section, gives to the buyer a false warranty in writing shall be guilty of an offence unless he proves that when he gave the warranty he took all reasonable steps to ensure that the statements contained in it were, and would continue at all relevant times to be, accurate.

(7) Where in any such proceedings as are mentioned in subsection (1) above ("the original proceedings") the person charged relies successfully on a warranty given to him or to his employer, any proceedings under subsection (6) above in respect of the warranty may, at the option of the prosecutor, be taken either before a court having jurisdiction in the place where the original proceedings were taken or before a court having jurisdiction in the place where the warranty was given

(8) For the purposes of this section, any statement with respect to any goods which is contained in any document required by or under this Part of this Act to be associated with the goods or in any invoice, and, in the case of goods made up in or on a container for sale or for delivery after sale, any statement with respect to those goods with which that container is marked, shall be taken to be a written warranty of the accuracy of that statement.

Reasonable precautions and due diligence

34.—(1) In any proceedings for an offence under this Part of this Act or any instrument made under this Part, it shall be a defence for the person charged to prove that he took all reasonable precautions and exercised all due diligence to avoid the commission of the offence.

(2) If in any case the defence provided by subsection (1) above involves an allegation that the commission of the offence in question was due to the act or default of another person or due to reliance on information supplied by another person, the person charged shall not, without the leave of the court, be entitled to rely on the defence unless, before the beginning of the period of seven days ending with the date when the hearing of the charge began, he served on the prosecutor a notice giving

such information identifying or assisting in the identification of the other person as was then in his possession.

Subsequent deficiency

35.—(1) This subsection applies to any proceedings for an offence under this Part of this Act, or any instrument made under this Part, by reason of the quantity—

(*a*) of any goods made up for sale or for delivery after sale (whether by way of pre-packing or otherwise) in or on a container marked with an indication of quantity,

(*b*) of any goods which, in connection with their sale or an agreement for their sale, have associated with them a document purporting to state the quantity of the goods, or

(*c*) of any goods required by or under this Part of this Act to be pre-packed, or to be otherwise made up in or on a container for sale or for delivery after sale, or to be made for sale, only in particular quantities,

being less than that marked on the container or stated in the document in question or than the relevant particular quantity, as the case may be.

(2) In any proceedings to which subsection (1) above applies, it shall be a defence for the person charged to prove that the deficiency arose—

(*a*) in a case falling within paragraph (*a*) of subsection (1) above, after the making up of the goods and the marking of the container,

(*b*) in a case falling within paragraph (*b*) of that subsection, after the preparation of the goods for delivery in pursuance of the sale or agreement and after the completion of the document,

(*c*) in a case falling within paragraph (*c*) of that subsection, after the making up or making, as the case may be, of the goods for sale,

and was attributable wholly to factors for which reasonable allowance was made in stating the quantity of the goods in the marking or document or in making up or making the goods for sale, as the case may be.

(3) In the case of a sale by retail of food, other than food pre-packed in a container which is, or is required by or under this Part of this Act to be, marked with an indication of quantity, in any proceedings for an offence under this Part of this Act or any instrument made under this Part, by reason of the quantity delivered to the buyer being less than that purported to be sold, it shall be a defence for the person charged to prove that the deficiency was due wholly to unavoidable evaporation or drainage since the sale and that due care and precaution were taken to minimise any such evaporation or drainage.

(4) If in any proceedings for an offence under this Part of this Act or any instrument made under this Part, being an offence in respect of any deficiency in the quantity of any goods sold, it is shown that between the sale and the discovery of the deficiency the goods were with the consent of the buyer subjected to treatment which could result in a reduction in the quantity of those goods for delivery to, or to any person nominated in that behalf by, the buyer, the person charged shall not be found guilty of that offence unless it is shown that the deficiency cannot be accounted for by the subjecting of the goods to that treatment.

Excess due to precautions

36. In any proceedings for an offence under this Part of this Act or any instrument made under this Part, being an offence in respect of any excess in the quantity of any goods, it shall be a defence for the person charged to prove that the excess was attributable to the taking of measures reasonably necessary in order to avoid the commission of an offence in respect of a deficiency in those or other goods.

Provisions as to testing

37.—(1) If proceedings for an offence under this Part of this Act, or any instrument made under this Part, in respect of any deficiency or excess in the quantity—

(a) of any goods made up for sale (whether by way of pre-packing or otherwise) in or on a container marked with an indication of quantity, or

(b) of any goods which have been pre-packed or otherwise made up in or on a container for sale or for delivery after sale, or which have been made for sale, and which are required by or under this Part of this Act to be pre-packed, or to be otherwise so made up, or to be so made, as the case may be, only in particular quantities,

are brought with respect to any article, and it is proved that, at the time and place at which that article was tested, other articles of the same kind, being articles which, or articles containing goods which, had been sold by the person charged or were in that person's possession for sale or for delivery after sale, were available for testing, the person charged shall not be convicted of such an offence with respect to that article unless a reasonable number of those other articles was also tested.

(2) In any proceedings for such an offence as is mentioned in subsection (1) above, the court—

(a) if the proceedings are with respect to one or more of a number of articles tested on the same occasion, shall have regard to the average quantity in all the articles tested,

(b) if the proceedings are with respect to a single article, shall disregard any inconsiderable deficiency or excess, and

(c) shall have regard generally to all the circumstances of the case.

(3) Subsections (1) and (2) above shall apply with the necessary modifications to proceedings for an offence in respect of the size, capacity or contents of a container as they apply to proceedings for an offence in respect of the excess or deficiency in the quantity of certain goods.

(4) Where by virtue of section 32 above a person is charged with an offence with which some other person might have been charged, the reference in subsection (1) above to articles or goods sold by or in the possession of the person charged shall be construed as a reference to articles or goods sold by or in the possession of that other person.

Powers of inspectors

Special powers of inspectors with respect to certain goods

38.—(1) Subsection (2) below applies where any person—

(a) makes in any manner any representation as to the quantity of any goods offered or exposed for sale by him, or

(b) has in his possession or charge awaiting or in the course of delivery to the buyer any goods which have been sold or agreed to be sold, and the sale is, or purports to be, or is required by or under this Part of this Act to be, by quantity expressed in a particular manner, or is such that the quantity of the goods sold is required by or under any provision of this Part other than section 26 to be made known to the buyer at or before a particular time, or

(c) has in his possession or charge for sale, or awaiting or in the course of delivery to a buyer after they have been sold or agreed to be sold—

(i) any goods pre-packed or otherwise made up in or on a container for sale or for delivery after sale which are required by or under this Part of this Act to be pre-packed, or to be otherwise so made up, as the case may be, only in particular quantities or only if the container is marked with particular information, or

(ii) any goods pre-packed in or on a container marked with an indication of quantity, or

(iii) any goods required by or under this Part of this Act to be made for sale only in particular quantities, or

(*d*) has in his possession or charge for sale, or awaiting or in the course of delivery to a buyer after they have been sold or agreed to be sold, any goods subject to a requirement imposed by virtue of section 22(1)(*c*) above.

(2) Where this subsection applies, the powers of an inspector under section 79 below shall, subject to subsection (4) below, include power to require the person referred to in subsection (1) above either to do in the presence of the inspector, or to permit the inspector to do, all or any of the following things, that is to say—

(*a*) weigh or otherwise measure or count the goods,

(*b*) weigh or otherwise measure any container in or on which the goods are made up,

(*c*) in the case of goods within subsection (1)(*d*) above, do anything else as respects the goods or container which is reasonably necessary to ascertain whether the requirement there mentioned is complied with, and which does not damage or depreciate the goods or container,

(*d*) if necessary for any of the purposes of paragraphs (*a*) to (*c*) above, break open any container of goods, or open any vending machine in which goods are offered or exposed for sale,

and, in the case of any of the goods which are not already sold, power to require that person to sell any of them to the inspector.

(3) Where any container of goods is broken open under subsection (2) above and all requirements of, and of any instrument made under, this Part of this Act which are applicable to those goods are found to have been complied with, then—

(*a*) if the container can be resealed without injury to the contents, the inspector may reseal it with a label certifying that all such requirements have been complied with, and

(*b*) if he does not so reseal it or it cannot be so resealed without injury to the contents, the inspector shall at the request of the person referred to in subsection (1) above buy the goods on behalf of the local weights and measures authority.

(4) The powers conferred by subsection (2) above shall not be exercisable in relation to milk within the meaning of the Weights and Measures Act 1963 (Miscellaneous Foods) Order 1984 except while the milk is on premises for the time being registered in pursuance of Milk and Dairies Regulations made under the Food Act 1984 or in pursuance of section 7 of the Milk and Dairies (Scotland) Act 1914.

Powers of inspectors with respect to certain documents

39.—(1) An inspector, subject to the production if so requested of his credentials, may require the person in charge of any document required by or under this Part of this Act to be associated with any goods to produce that document for inspection.

(2) If the inspector has reasonable cause to believe that any document produced to him under subsection (1) above contains any inaccurate statement, he may either—

(*a*) seize and detain the document, giving in exchange a copy with an endorsement signed by him certifying that the original has been seized and giving particulars of any inaccuracy alleged, or

(b) without prejudice to any proceedings which may be taken by reason of any inaccuracy alleged, make on the document an endorsement signed by him giving particulars of any such inaccuracy;

and, except where the context otherwise requires, any reference in this Part of this Act to any such document includes a reference to a copy given in pursuance of paragraph (a) above.

Powers of inspectors with respect to goods carried on road vehicles

40.—(1) Subsection (2) below applies where, in the case of any goods being carried on a road vehicle,—

(a) the whole of the vehicle's load is being carried for sale to, or for delivery after sale to, the same person, and

(b) any document produced in pursuance of section 39(1) above by the person in charge of the vehicle purports, or is required by or under this Part of this Act, to state the quantity of the goods.

(2) Where this subsection applies, the inspector may, for the purpose of the exercise of his powers under section 38(2) above do all or any of the following things, that is to say—

(a) require the goods to which the document relates to be unloaded from the vehicle;

(b) require the vehicle to be taken to the nearest suitable and available weighing or measuring equipment;

(c) require the person in charge of the vehicle to have it check-weighed.

(3) The powers conferred by subsection (2) above shall be exercised only to such extent as may appear to the inspector reasonably necessary in order to secure that the provisions of this Act (apart from Part V) and of any instrument made under those provisions are duly observed.

Miscellaneous and supplementary

Check-weighing of certain road vehicles

41. Where any road vehicle is loaded with goods for sale by weight to a single buyer of the whole of the vehicle's load, or for delivery to the buyer after they have been so sold, the buyer or seller of the goods, or any inspector who shows that he is authorised so to do by the buyer or seller of the goods, may require the person in charge of the vehicle to have it check-weighed, and if that person fails without reasonable cause to comply with any such requirement he shall be guilty of an offence.

Power to make test purchases

42. A local weights and measures authority shall have power to make, or to authorise an inspector to make on their behalf, such purchases of goods as may appear expedient for the purpose of determining whether or not the provisions of this Part of this Act and any instrument made under this Part, and the provisions of Parts II and III of this Act and any instrument made under either of those Parts, are being complied with.

Beer and cider

43.—(1) In ascertaining the quantity of any beer or cider for any of the purposes of section 25 or sections 28 to 31 above, or of the Weights and Measures Act 1963 (Intoxicating Liquor) Order 1984, the gas comprised in any foam on the beer or cider shall be disregarded and, for the purposes of this subsection, "beer" and "cider" have the meanings given by section 1 of the Alcoholic Liquor Duties Act 1979.

(2) This section shall come into force on such date as the Secretary of State may by order appoint, and different dates may be appointed for different purposes.

Selling by quantity

44. Where any goods are required by or under this Part of this Act to be sold only by quantity expressed in a particular manner—

(*a*) it shall be a sufficient compliance with that requirement in the case of any sale of, or agreement to sell, any such goods if the quantity of the goods expressed in the manner in question is made known to the buyer before the purchase price is agreed; and

(*b*) no person shall be guilty of an offence under section 25(1) above by reason of the exposing or offering for sale of such goods at any time if both the quantity of the goods expressed in the manner in question and the price at which they are exposed or offered for sale are made known at that time to any prospective buyer.

Making quantity known to a person

45.—(1) For the purposes of this Part of this Act, without prejudice to any other method of making known to a person the quantity of any goods expressed in a particular manner, that quantity shall be taken to be made known to that person—

(*a*) if the goods are weighed or otherwise measured or counted, as the case may require, in the presence of that person,

(*b*) if the goods are made up in or on a container marked with a statement in writing of the quantity of the goods expressed in the manner in question and the container is readily available for inspection by that person, or

(*c*) upon such a statement in writing being delivered to that person.

(2) The Secretary of State may by order provide that subsection (3) below shall apply, in the case of such goods in such circumstances as are specified in the order, to any requirement so specified of, or of any instrument made under, this Part of this Act with respect to the making known to the buyer of the quantity by weight of such goods sold by retail.

(3) In any case to which this subsection applies, the requirement specified in the order shall be taken to be satisfied if the goods are bought at premises at which weighing equipment of such description as may be prescribed—

(*a*) is kept available by the occupier of those premises for use without charge by any prospective buyer of such goods for the purpose of weighing for himself any such goods offered or exposed for sale by retail on those premises, and

(*b*) is so kept available in a position on those premises which is suitable and convenient for such use of the equipment, and

(*c*) is reserved for use for that purpose at all times while those premises are open for retail transactions,

and a notice of the availability of the equipment for such use is displayed in a position on the premises where it may be readily seen by any such prospective buyer.

Weighing in presence of a person

46. For the purposes of this Part of this Act, a person shall not be taken to weigh or otherwise measure or count any goods in the presence of any other person unless he causes any equipment used for the purpose to be so placed, and so conducts the operation of weighing or otherwise measuring or counting the goods, as to permit that other person a clear and unobstructed view of the equipment, if any, and of the operation, and of any indication of quantity given by any such equipment as the result of that operation.

PART V

PACKAGED GOODS

Quantity control

Duty of packers and importers as to quantity

47.—(1) It shall be the duty of a person who is the packer or importer of regulated packages to ensure that when a group of the packages marked with the same nominal quantity is selected in the prescribed manner and the packages in the group or such a portion of the group as is so selected are tested in the prescribed manner by an inspector—

(*a*) the total quantity of the goods shown by the test to be included in the packages tested divided by the number of those packages is not less than the nominal quantity on those packages, and

(*b*) the number of non-standard packages among those tested is not greater than the number prescribed as acceptable in relation to the number tested.

(2) It is hereby declared that a person discharges the duty imposed on him by subsection (1) above in respect of a group of packages if the quantity of goods in each package is or exceeds the nominal quantity on the package.

(3) Regulations in pursuance of subsection (1) above with respect to the manner of selecting or testing packages may, without prejudice to the generality of the powers to make regulations conferred by that subsection or to the generality of section 66(*b*) below, make provision by reference to a document other than the regulations (which may be or include a code of practical guidance issued by the Secretary of State).

(4) Where, as a result of a test in respect of a group of packages which is carried out when the packages are in the possession of the packer or importer of the packages or another person, it is shown that the packer or importer of the packages has failed to perform the duty imposed on him by subsection (1) above in respect of the packages, then, without prejudice to the liability of the packer or importer under section 50(1) below in respect of the failure, it shall be the duty of the person in possession of the packages to keep them in his possession—

(*a*) except so far as he is authorised by or under regulations to dispose of them, or

(*b*) if he is the packer or importer of them, until he has performed his duty under subsection (1) above in respect of the group.

Duty of packers and importers as to marking of containers

48.—(1) It shall be the duty of a person who is the packer or importer of a regulated package to ensure that the container included in the package is marked before the prescribed time and in the prescribed manner with—

(*a*) a statement of quantity in prescribed units either of weight or of volume, as regulations require, and

(*b*) his name and address or a mark which enables his name and address to be readily ascertained by an inspector, or—

(i) if he is the packer of the package, the name and address of a person who arranged for him to make up the package or a

mark which enables that name and address to be readily ascertained by an inspector,

(ii) if he is the importer of the package, the name and address
of the packer of the package or of the person who arranged for
the packer to make up the package or a mark which enables the
name and address of the packer or that person to be readily
ascertained by an inspector, and

(c) if regulations so provide, a mark allocated to him by a scheme in
pursuance of section 58 below for the purpose of enabling the place
where the package was made up to be ascertained.

(2) If at the time when a regulated package is made up or imported the
container included in the package is not marked with such a statement as
is mentioned in paragraph (a) of subsection (1) above, it shall be the duty
of the packer or, as the case may be, the importer of the package—

(a) to decide what statement he proposes to mark on the container in
pursuance of that paragraph, and

(b) to make at that time, and to maintain for the prescribed period, a
record of the statement.

(3) Until the time mentioned in subsection (1) above or any earlier
time at which the container is actually marked in the prescribed manner
in pursuance of paragraph (a) of that subsection, it shall be treated for
the purposes of this Part of this Act as marked with the statement in the
record.

(4) A statement applied to a package in pursuance of subsection (1)(a)
above shall be deemed not to be a trade description within the meaning
of the Trade Descriptions Act 1968.

Duties as to equipment, checks and documentation

49.—(1) It shall be the duty of a person who makes up packages
either—

(a) to use suitable equipment of the prescribed kind in an appropriate
manner in making up the packages, or

(b) to carry out at the prescribed time a check which is adequate to
show whether he has performed the duty imposed on him by
section 47(1) above in respect of the packages and—

(i) to use suitable equipment of the prescribed kind in an
appropriate manner in carrying out the check, and

(ii) to make, and to keep for the prescribed period, an
adequate record of the check.

(2) It shall be the duty of a person who is the importer of regulated
packages—

(a) to carry out at the prescribed time such a check as is mentioned in
paragraph (b) of subsection (1) above and to comply with sub-
paragraphs (i) and (ii) of that paragraph in connection with the
check, or

(b) to obtain before the prescribed time, and to keep for the prescribed
period, documents containing such information about the packages
as is adequate to show that the person is likely to have complied
with his duty under section 47(1) above in relation to the packages.

(3) Without prejudice to the generality of the powers to make regulations conferred by subsection (1) or (2) above or to the generality of
section 66 below, regulations may provide—

(a) for equipment not to be suitable equipment for the purposes of the
subsection in question unless it is made from materials and on
principles specified in the regulations and is inspected, tested and
certified as provided by the regulations.

(b) for questions as to the suitability of equipment, the appropriate
manner of using equipment and the adequacy of checks, records

and information to be determined for those purposes by reference to documents other than the regulations (which may be or include codes or parts of codes of practical guidance issued or approved by the Secretary of State), and

(c) that the use and the possession for use, for the purposes of subsection (1) or (2) above, of a thing which is suitable equipment for the purpose of the subsection in question shall not constitute a contravention of section 8(1)(b) above.

(4) Where regulations made by virtue of subsection (3)(a) above provide for inspection, testing and certification of equipment, a local weights and measures authority may charge such reasonable fees as they may determine for the inspection, testing and certification of the equipment.

Enforcement of control

Offences, etc.

50.—(1) A person who fails to perform a duty imposed on him by section 47, 48 or 49 above shall be guilty of an offence.

(2) If a person purports to comply with his duty under—

(a) sub-paragraph (ii) of subsection (1)(b) of section 49 above, or

(b) that sub-paragraph as applied by subsection (2)(a) of that section,

by making a record which he knows is false in a material particular, he shall be guilty of an offence.

(3) If a person purports to comply with his duty under section 49(2)(b) above by reference to a document containing information which he knows is false in a material particular, he shall be guilty of an offence.

(4) If a person, with intent to deceive, alters—

(a) any record kept for the purposes of section 48(2) or 49(1)(b)(ii) above or section 49(1)(b)(ii) above as applied by section 49(2)(a) above, or

(b) any document kept for the purposes of section 49(2)(b) above,

he shall be guilty of an offence.

(5) If a person has in his possession for sale, agrees to sell or sells a regulated package which is inadequate and either—

(a) he is the packer or importer of the package, or

(b) he knows that the package is inadequate,

he shall be guilty of an offence.

(6) If the packer of a regulated package which is inadequate and which was made up by him in the course of carrying out arrangements with another person for the packer to make up packages delivers the package to or to the order of a person to whom it falls to be delivered in pursuance of the arrangements, the packer shall be guilty of an offence.

(7) No action shall lie in respect of a failure to perform a duty imposed by section 47, 48 or 49 above.

Defences to certain charges under section 50

51.—(1) Where a person is charged with an offence under section 50(1) above of failing to perform the duty imposed on him by section 47(1) above in respect of any packages, it shall be a defence to prove that the test in question took place when the packages were not in his possession and by reference to a nominal quantity which was not on the packages when they were in his possession.

(2) Where the importer of packages is charged with an offence under section 50(1) above of failing to perform the duty imposed on him by section 47(1) above in respect of the packages, it shall be a defence to prove—

(*a*) that in respect of the packages the accused performed the duty imposed on him by paragraph (*b*) of section 49(2) above, and

(*b*) that within the prescribed period after obtaining the documents mentioned in that paragraph relating to the packages he took all reasonable steps to verify the information contained in the documents and that when the relevant test in pursuance of section 47(1) above began he believed and had no reason to disbelieve that the information was true, and

(*c*) that before the beginning of the period of seven days ending with the date when the hearing of the charge began he served on the prosecutor a copy of the said documents and a notice which stated that the accused intended to rely on them in proving a defence under this subsection, and

(*d*) that he took all reasonable steps to ensure that the quantity of goods in each of the packages did not alter while the packages were in his possession.

(3) Where a person is charged with an offence under section 50(1) above of failing to perform the duty imposed on him by paragraph (*b*) of section 48(1) above in respect of a package, it shall be a defence to prove—

(*a*) that the container included in the package was marked at the time and in the manner mentioned in that subsection with a mark as to which he had, before that time, given notice to an inspector stating that the mark indicated a name and address specified in the notice, and

(*b*) that at that time the name and address were such as are mentioned in relation to him in that paragraph.

(4) Where a person is charged with—

(*a*) an offence under subsection (1) of section 50 above, or

(*b*) an offence alleged to have been committed by him, as the packer or importer of a package, under subsection (5) or (6) of that section,

it shall be a defence to prove that he took all reasonable precautions and exercised all due diligence to avoid the commission of the offence.

Enforcement of Part V by local weights and measures authority

52.—(1) It shall be the duty of a local weights and measures authority to enforce the provisions of this Part of this Act within the area of the authority.

(2) Nothing in subsection (1) above authorises a local weights and measures authority to institute proceedings in Scotland for an offence.

Powers of inspectors and local weights and measures authority under Part V

53. Schedule 8 to this Act shall have effect.

Special provision for certain packages

Special provision for certain packages

54.—(1) Subsections (2) to (7) below apply only to packages containing goods of a prescribed quantity, and references to packages in those subsections shall be construed accordingly.

(2) If in the course of carrying on a business—

(*a*) a person marks a package with the EEC mark and is neither the packer nor the importer of the package nor a person acting on behalf of the packer or importer of the package, or (*b*) a person marks a package with a mark so closely resembling the EEC mark as to be likely to deceive,

he shall be guilty of an offence.

(3) For the purposes of this Part of this Act a person who brings a package marked with the EEC mark into the United Kingdom does not import the package if he shows that the package is from a member State of the Economic Community in which it was liable to be tested under a law corresponding to section 47(1) above and, except in such cases as are determined by or under regulations, has not since leaving that State been in a country which is not such a member State.

(4) Subject to subsection (6) below, it shall be the duty of—

    (*a*) the packer of packages which are marked with the EEC mark and which he intends to export from the United Kingdom,

    (*b*) a person who intends to import packages which are so marked and to export them from the United Kingdom to a place in another member State of the Economic Community, and

    (*c*) a person who intends to import packages, to mark them with the EEC mark and to export them as mentioned in paragraph (*b*) above,

to give before the prescribed time and in the prescribed manner, to the local weights and measures authority for the area in which the packages were packed or, as the case may be, in which the place of intended import is situated, a notice containing such information about the packages as is prescribed and, in the case of a person who has given such a notice in pursuance of paragraph (*b*) or (*c*) above, such further information about the packages in question as an inspector may specify in a notice served on the person by the inspector.

(5) A person who fails without reasonable cause to perform a duty imposed on him by subsection (4) above shall be guilty of an offence.

(6) Regulations may enable an inspector to give notice to any person providing that, until an inspector informs the person in writing that the notice is cancelled, any paragraph of subsection (4) above which is specified in the notice shall not apply to the person or shall not apply to him as respects packages of a kind specified in the notice or a place so specified.

(7) In this section "the EEC mark" means such mark as may be prescribed; and, without prejudice to the generality of section 66 below, regulations prescribing a mark in pursuance of this subsection—

    (*a*) may contain such provisions as the Secretary of State considers appropriate with respect to the dimensions of the mark and the manner and position in which it is to be applied to the container included in a package, and

    (*b*) may provide for a mark which is not in accordance with those provisions to be disregarded for the purposes of prescribed provisions of this section.

Co-ordination of control

The National Metrological Co-ordinating Unit

55.—(1) There shall continue to be a body corporate called the National Metrological Co-ordinating Unit (in this Part of this Act referred to as "the Unit"), which shall consist of not less than five persons and not more than fifteen persons appointed by the Secretary of State.

(2) A person shall not be qualified for appointment under subsection (1) above unless he is a member of a local authority; and it shall be the duty of the Secretary of State, before he makes such an appointment, to consult an organisation which in his opinion represents such local authorities as he considers appropriate in connection with the appointment.

(3) In subsection (2) above "local authority" means—
  (a) the council of a county or a district in England or Wales,
  (b) the council of a region or an islands area in Scotland,
  (c) the council of a London borough,
  (d) the Common Council of the City of London, and
  (e) the Council of the Isles of Scilly.
(4) Schedule 9 to this Act shall have effect with respect to the Unit.
(5) The Secretary of State may, out of money provided by Parliament, make payments to the Unit from time to time for the purpose of enabling the Unit to defray the whole or part of its expenses.
(6) It is hereby declared that the Unit is not to be regarded as the servant or agent of the Crown or as enjoying any status, privilege or immunity of the Crown or as exempt from any tax, duty, rate, levy or other charge whatsoever, whether general or local, and that its property is not to be regarded as property of or held on behalf of the Crown.

General duties of Unit

56.—(1) It shall be the duty of the Unit—
  (a) to keep under review the operation of this Part of this Act and to carry out such research in connection with the review as the Unit considers appropriate;
  (b) to make available, to local weights and measures authorities and to packers and importers of packages, such information as the Unit considers appropriate in connection with the operation of this Part of this Act;
  (c) to give advice to local weights and measures authorities—
      (i) about arrangements to be made by them for the purpose of enforcing this Part of this Act within their area; and
      (ii) about such other matters as the Unit considers appropriate in connection with the operation of this Part of this Act;
  (d) to seek to collaborate, with any authority in a place outside Great Britain appearing to the Unit to have functions which correspond to those of the Unit or to those conferred on a local weights and measures authority by this Part of this Act, about matters which are connected with packages and are of interest to the Unit and the authority;
  (e) to give advice to the Secretary of State about such documents as are mentioned in section 49(3)(b) above which are prepared by persons appearing to the Secretary of State to represent the interests of packers or importers of packages;
  (f) to make and maintain a record of the names and addresses of packers and importers of packages and of—
      (i) the kinds of packages which they make up or import, and
      (ii) the marks of which particulars have been furnished by them in pursuance of section 57 below;
  (g) to make and maintain a record of the names and addresses of persons who make measuring container bottles in any member State of the Economic Community and of the marks put on the bottles for the purpose of enabling the makers of them to be identified;
  (h) to perform any duty conferred on the Unit by paragraphs (a) to (g) above in accordance with any directions given to the Unit by the Secretary of State.

(2) In this section—

"measuring container bottle" has the same meaning as in the 1977 Regulations or, if regulations so provide, such other meaning as is prescribed, and

"the 1977 Regulations" means the Measuring Container Bottles (EEC Requirements) Regulations 1977.

Power of Unit to require packers and importers to furnish particulars of marks

57.—(1) The Unit may serve, on any person carrying on business as a packer or importer of packages, a notice requiring him—

(*a*) to furnish the Unit from time to time with particulars of the kind specified in the notice of any marks which, otherwise than in pursuance of section 48(1)(*c*) above, are applied from time to time to packages made up or as the case may be imported by him, for the purpose of enabling the place where the packages were made up to be ascertained, and

(*b*) if he has furnished particulars of a mark in pursuance of the notice and the mark ceases to be applied for that purpose to packages made up or imported by him, to give notice of the cesser to the Unit;

but a notice given by the Unit in pursuance of this subsection shall not require a person to furnish information which he does not possess.

(2) A person who without reasonable cause fails to comply with a notice served on him in pursuance of subsection (1) above shall be guilty of an offence.

Duty of Unit to prepare scheme allocating marks

58. It shall be the duty of the Unit—

(*a*) if the Secretary of State so directs, to prepare a scheme which—

(i) allocates, to persons carrying on business as packers or importers of packages, marks from which there can be ascertained the places where packages made up or imported by them were made up, and

(ii) specifies the kinds of packages to which each mark is to be applied;

(*b*) to make from time to time such alterations of the scheme as the Unit considers appropriate and the Secretary of State approves;

(*c*) to give, to each person to whom a mark is for the time being allocated by the scheme, a notice which specifies the mark, states that it has been allocated to him in pursuance of the scheme and specifies the kinds of packages to which it is to be applied.

Supervision by Unit of certain functions of inspectors

59.—(1) The Unit may serve on any local weights and measures authority a notice requiring the authority—

(*a*) to furnish the Unit with information of such a kind as is specified in the notice (and, if the notice so provides, relating only to persons so specified or packages or measuring container bottles of a kind so specified) with respect to relevant functions which inspectors appointed by the authority have performed or propose to perform during a period so specified, or

(*b*) to arrange for the performance by an inspector, in relation to persons, premises or equipment specified in the notice or packages or measuring container bottles of a kind so specified and during a period so specified, of such relevant functions as are so specified and to make to the Unit a report containing information of a kind so specified about the results of complying with the notice;

and, subject to subsection (4)(*b*)(ii) below, it shall be the duty of the authority to comply with the requirements of the notice.

(2) In subsection (1) above "relevant functions" means—

   (*a*) the function of carrying out a test in pursuance of section 47(1) above,

   (*b*) functions conferred on an inspector—

       (i) by paragraphs 1 and 5 of Schedule 8 to this Act, and

      (ii) by regulation 8(1) of the 1977 Regulations (inspection for the purposes of those regulations), and

   (*c*) such other functions conferred on an inspector by this Part of this Act as are prescribed.

(3) In relation to a notice served in pursuance of subsection (1)(*b*) above the inspector in question shall be treated as having such reasonable cause as is mentioned in paragraph 1(*a*) and (*b*) of Schedule 8 to this Act and regulation 8(1)(*b*) of the 1977 Regulations.

(4) If the Unit is of the opinion that a local weights and measures authority has not complied with a requirement contained in a notice served on the authority in pursuance of subsection (1) above, the Unit may refer the matter to the Secretary of State who, if he is also of that opinion, may—

   (*a*) serve a notice on the authority requiring it to comply with the requirement within a period specified in the notice; or

   (*b*) in the case of a requirement in pursuance of subsection (1)(*b*) above—

       (i) make such arrangements as the Secretary of State considers appropriate for securing that the requirement is complied with by persons acting on his behalf,

      (ii) serve on the authority a notice stating that he proposes to make the arrangements and prohibiting the authority from complying with the requirement,

     (iii) by an instrument in writing appoint a person specified in the instrument to be an inspector for the purpose of carrying out the arrangements and to exercise accordingly for that purpose any power which by virtue of this Part of this Act or the 1977 Regulations is conferred on an inspector, and

     (iv) recover from the authority the reasonable cost of making and carrying out the arrangements.

(5) In this section "measuring container bottle" and "the 1977 Regulations" have the meanings given by section 56(2) above.

Annual reports by Unit

60.—(1) It shall be the duty of the Unit to make in each year a report to the Secretary of State on the performance during the preceding year of its functions, and it shall be the duty of the Secretary of State to publish, in such manner as he thinks fit, each report received by him in pursuance of this subsection.

(2) In preparing a report under subsection (1) above the Unit shall have regard to the need for excluding, so far as it is practicable to do so, any matter which relates to the private affairs of an individual or which relates specifically to the affairs of a particular person where the publication of that matter would, in the opinion of the Unit, seriously and prejudically affect the interests of that individual or person.

(3) For the purposes of the law of defamation every publication of a report made under subsection (1) above shall be absolutely privileged.

Accounts and audit

61.—(1) It shall be the duty of the Unit—

    (*a*) to keep proper accounts and proper records in relation to the accounts,

    (*b*) to prepare in respect of each accounting year a statement of those accounts, and

    (*c*) to send the statement to the auditors for the time being appointed in pursuance of this subsection and to do so within six months beginning with the last day of the accounting year to which the statement relates;

and the accounts kept and the statements prepared in pursuance of this subsection shall be audited by auditors appointed by the Unit.

(2) A person shall not be qualified to be so appointed unless he is a member of one or more of the following bodies—

    the Institute of Chartered Accountants in England and Wales,

    the Institute of Chartered Accountants of Scotland,

    the Association of Certified Accountants,

    the Institute of Chartered Accountants in Ireland,

    any other body of accountants established in the United Kingdom and for the time being recognised for the purposes of section 389(1)(*a*) of the Companies Act 1985 by the Secretary of State;

but a Scottish firm may be so appointed if each of the partners in the firm is qualified to be so appointed.

(3) It shall be the duty of the Unit to include, in the first report it makes under section 60 above after the accounts and statement of accounts of the Unit for any accounting year have been audited, a copy of the statement and of any report made by the auditors on the statement or the accounts.

(4) In this section "accounting year" means the period of twelve months ending with 31st March in any year except that a particular accounting year shall, if the Secretary of State so directs, be such other period not longer than two years as is specified in the direction.

Power to extend or transfer Unit's functions and to abolish Unit

62.—(1) The Secretary of State may by order confer on the Unit such functions as he thinks fit in addition to the functions conferred on the Unit by this Act.

(2) The Secretary of State may by order—

    (*a*) transfer any functions of the Unit to himself;

    (*b*) establish a body and transfer to it any function of the Unit and any function transferred by virtue of paragraph (*a*) above;

    (*c*) where all the functions of the Unit are transferred by virtue of paragraphs (*a*) and (*b*) above, abolish the Unit.

(3) An order made by virtue of this section may—

    (*a*) make such modifications—

        (i) of section 55(1) to (4) and (6) above and Schedule 9 to this Act, and

        (ii) of references to the Unit in any provision of this Act except section 55,

    as the Secretary of State considers appropriate in connection with the conferring or transfer of any function, the establishment of a body or the abolition of the Unit in pursuance of this section;

(b) contain such supplemental and transitional provisions as the Secretary of State considers appropriate in that connection.

(4) The Secretary of State may make payments out of money provided by Parliament to any body established by virtue of this section for the purpose of enabling the body to defray its expenses.

Instructions by inspectors

Instructions by inspectors

63.—(1) If an inspector has reasonable cause to believe that a person has failed to perform the duty imposed on him by section 47(1) above in relation to a group of packages, the inspector may give to the person in possession of the packages instructions in writing—

(a) specifying the packages, and

(b) requiring that person to keep the packages at a place specified in the instructions and at the disposal of the inspector for the period of twenty-four hours beginning with the time when the inspector gives him the instructions or for such shorter period as the inspector may specify.

(2) If an inspector has reasonable cause to believe that a person has failed to perform the duty imposed on him by section 49(1) or (2) above, the inspector may give to that person such instructions in writing as the inspector considers appropriate with a view to ensuring that that person does not subsequently fail to perform that duty.

(3) Instructions given to a person by an inspector under subsection (2) above shall not come into force until the expiration of the prescribed period beginning with the day when the instructions are given to him and, if during that period that person gives notice to the inspector that he objects to the instructions, they shall not come into force except as agreed in writing by that person or as directed by the Secretary of State.

(4) Where under subsection (3) above a person gives to an inspector notice of objection to instructions, it shall be the duty of the inspector to refer the instructions to the Unit and it shall be the duty of the Unit to seek to obtain the persons's agreement in writing to the instructions either without modifications or with such modifications as the Unit considers acceptable.

(5) If at the expiration of the prescribed period beginning with the day when the instructions are received by the Unit, the Unit considers that it has not obtained the agreement of the person in question as mentioned in subsection (4) above, it shall be the duty of the Unit to refer the instructions to the Secretary of State.

(6) Where instructions are referred to the Secretary of State in pursuance of subsection (5) above, it shall be his duty—

(a) to invite representations in writing about the instructions from the Unit, from the inspector who gave them and from the person to whom they were given,

(b) to consider any representations made in response to the invitations within the periods specified in the invitations,

(c) to direct that the instructions shall come into force, without modifications or with modifications specified in the direction, on a day so specified or that they shall not come into force, and

(d) to give notice of the direction to the Unit, to the inspector and to the person in question.

(7) Where—

(a) instructions have been given to a person under subsection (1) above, or

(b) instructions given to a person under subsection (2) above have come into force (or have come into force with modifications) in accordance with subsections (3) to (6) above,

he shall be guilty of an offence if without reasonable cause he fails to comply with those instructions (or, as the case may require, those instructions with modifications).

Miscellaneous

Disclosure of information

64.—(1) If a person discloses information which—

(*a*) relates to a trade secret or secret manufacturing process, and

(*b*) was obtained by him by virtue of this Part of this Act when he was—

(i) a member of the Unit,

(ii) a person employed by the Unit,

(iii) an inspector,

(iv) a person who accompanied an inspector by virtue of paragraph 3(1) of Schedule 8 to this Act, or

(v) a person appointed by the Secretary of State in pursuance of section 59(4)(*b*)(iii) above,

he shall be guilty of an offence unless the disclosure was made in the performance of his duty as a member, inspector or other person mentioned in paragraph (*b*) above, or, in the case of an inspector, was made to the Unit in consequence of a request by the Unit.

(2) For the purposes of subsection (1) above information disclosing the identity of the packer of a package or the identity of the person who arranged with the packer of a package for the package to be made up shall be treated as a trade secret unless the information has previously been disclosed in a manner which made it available to the public.

Power to modify Part V

65. Regulations may provide—

(*a*) that in relation to packages of a prescribed kind the provisions of this Part of this Act, except this section, shall have effect with prescribed modifications;

(*b*) for the said provisions to apply, with prescribed modifications, to goods of a prescribed kind which are not comprised in packages.

Regulations under Part V

66. Without prejudice to section 86(1) below, any power to make regulations conferred by this Part of this Act includes power—

(*a*) to make provision relating only to specified circumstances,

(*b*) to make provision by reference to documents which do not form part of the regulations, and

(*c*) to include in the regulations such supplemental and incidental provisions as the Secretary of State considers appropriate.

Service of documents

67.—(1) Any document required or authorised by virtue of this Part of this Act to be served on a person may be so served—

(*a*) by delivering it to him or by leaving it at his proper address or by sending it by post to him at that address, or

(*b*) if the person is a body corporate, by serving it in accordance with paragraph (*a*) above on the secretary or clerk of that body, or

(*c*) if the person is a partnership, by serving it in accordance with paragraph (*a*) above on a partner or on a person having the control or management of the partnership business.

(2) For the purposes of subsection (1) above and of section 7 of the Interpretation Act 1978 (which relates to the service of documents by post) in its application to that subsection, the proper address of any person on whom a document is to be served by virtue of this Part of this Act shall be his last known address except that—

(*a*) in the case of service on a body corporate or its secretary or clerk, it shall be the address of the registered or principal office of the body, and

(*b*) in the case of service on a partnership or a partner or a person having the control or management of a partnership business, it shall be the principal office of the partnership;

and for the purposes of this subsection, the principal office of a company registered outside the United Kingdom or a partnership carrying on business outside the United Kingdom is its principal office within the United Kingdom.

Interpretation of Part V

68.—(1) In this Part of this Act—

"container" includes any wrapping;

"goods", in relation to a package, excludes the container included in the package;

"importer", in relation to a package, means, subject to section 54(3) above, the person by whom or on whose behalf the package is entered for customs purposes on importation;

"modifications" includes additions, omissions and alterations;

"nominal quantity", in relation to a package, means the units of weight or volume prescribed for the package and the number of them in the statement of quantity marked on the container included in the package (any other matter in the statement being disregarded);

"notice" means notice in writing;

"package" means, subject to section 54(1) above, a container containing prescribed goods together with the goods in the container in a case where—

(*a*) the goods are placed for sale in the container otherwise than in the presence of a person purchasing the goods, and

(*b*) none of the goods can be removed from the container without opening it;

"packer" means, in relation to a package, the person who placed in the container included in the package the goods included in it;

"regulated package" means any package which—

(*a*) was made up in the United Kingdom on or after the date on which the goods in the package became prescribed goods, or

(*b*) was imported on or after that date;

"regulations" means regulations made by the Secretary of State by virtue of this Part of this Act;

"the Unit" means the National Metrological Co-ordinating Unit.

(2) For the purposes of this Part of this Act a package—

(*a*) is non-standard if the quantity of the goods it contains is less by more than a prescribed amount than the nominal quantity on the package, and

(*b*) is inadequate if the quantity of the goods it contains is less by more than twice that amount than the nominal quantity on the package.

(3) Regulations may make provision, in relation to a package which contains more than one container or goods of more than one kind, as to which of the containers or goods shall be disregarded for the purposes of prescribed provisions of this Part of this Act.

(4) If two or more different nominal quantities are marked on a package, each of those quantities except the one which indicates the larger or largest quantity shall be disregarded for the purposes of this Part of this Act.

PART VI

ADMINISTRATION

Local administration

Local weights and measures authorities

69.—(1) In England, the local weights and measures authority shall be—

(a) for each non-metropolitan county, metropolitan, district and London borough, the council of that county, district or borough,

(b) for the City of London and the Inner and Middle Temples, the Common Council of the City of London, and

(c) for the Isles of Scilly, the Council of the Isles of Scilly.

(2) In Wales, the local weights and measures authority for each county shall be the county council.

(3) In Scotland, the local weights and measures authority for each region or islands area shall be the regional or islands council.

(4) The Secretary of State, after consultation with any local weights and measures authority appearing to him to be concerned, may by order provide that the area of any local weights and measures authority specified in the order shall, for the purposes of their functions as such an authority, be deemed to include such area consisting of inland waters or of territorial waters of the United Kingdom adjacent to any part of Great Britain as may be so specified, being an area which would otherwise not fall within the area of any local weights and measures authority.

(5) A local weights and measures authority may make, or assist in the making of, arrangements to provide advice to or for the benefit of consumers of goods and services within the area of the authority.

(6) Until 1st April 1986, subsection (1)(a) above shall have effect with the substitution for the words "non-metropolitan county, metropolitan district and London borough, the council of that county, district" of the words "county and London borough, the council of that county".

Annual reports by local weights and measures authorities

70.—(1) Each local weights and measures authority shall, in respect of each financial year of the authority, make to the Secretary of State by such date as he may direct a report on the operation during that year of the arrangements made to give effect in that authority's area—

(a) to the purposes of this Act, and

(b) to functions relating to weights and measures which are conferred on the authority otherwise than by or under this Act and which are specified, in a notice in writing given to the authority by the Secretary of State and not withdrawn, as functions to which this paragraph applies.

(2) Any report under subsection (1) above shall be in such form and contain such particulars of such matters as the Secretary of State may direct.

(3) Any report made to the Secretary of State under this section may be published by the local weights and measures authority by whom it is made.

(4) The Secretary of State may include the whole or any part of, or any information contained in, any such report, whether published or not, in any statement which may be made or published by the Secretary of State with respect to such arrangements as are mentioned in subsection (1) above either generally or in any particular area.

Inspection of local weights and measures arrangements.

71.—(1) The Secretary of State may from time to time cause an inspection to be made of, or of any part of, any such arrangements as are mentioned in section 70 above.

(2) Any such inspection shall be carried out by an officer of the Secretary of State authorised in that behalf by the Secretary of State.

(3) The officer—

   (*a*) may examine any equipment or records kept in connection with those arrangements,

   (*b*) may require any inspector having duties under those arrangements to give such assistance and information as the officer may reasonably specify, and

   (*c*) may make reasonable enquiries of any person who appears to the officer likely to be able to give him information concerning the operation of those arrangements.

(4) The officer by whom any inspection under this section is made shall report its results in writing to the Secretary of State.

(5) The Secretary of State shall send a copy of the report to any local weights and measures authority concerned and to any chief inspector responsible for the operation of all or any of the arrangements inspected.

(6) The Secretary of State may, if he thinks fit, publish any such report in whole or in part.

Inspectors of weights and measures

Appointment of inspectors

72.—(1) Each local weights and measures authority shall from time to time appoint from among persons holding certificates of qualification under section 73 below, and reasonably remunerate—

   (*a*) a chief inspector of weights and measures, and

   (*b*) such number of other inspectors of weights and measures, if any (who may, if the authority so desire, include a deputy chief inspector), as may be necessary for the efficient discharge in the authority's area of the functions conferred or imposed on inspectors by or under this Act.

(2) Any person appointed under subsection (1) above shall hold office during the pleasure of the authority by whom he was appointed.

(3) A chief inspector shall be responsible to the local weights and measures authority for the custody and maintenance of the local standards, working standards and testing and stamping equipment provided for the area for which he was appointed and generally for the operation of the arrangements made to give effect in that area to the purposes of this Act.

(4) A deputy chief inspector may perform any functions of the chief inspector for the area for which he was appointed in any case where it appears to the local weights and measures authority to be desirable or

necessary in the interests of the efficient operation of the said arrangements to authorise him so to do, and when so authorised shall have all the powers of a chief inspector.

Certificate of qualification to act as inspector

73.—(1) The Secretary of State shall provide for the holding of examinations for the purpose of ascertaining whether persons possess sufficient skill and knowledge for the proper performance of the functions of an inspector, and for the grant of certificates of qualification to persons who pass such examinations.

(2) The Secretary of State may if he thinks fit arrange with some other person for that person to hold examinations for the purpose mentioned in subsection (1) above.

(3) The Secretary of State shall not grant a certificate of qualification to any person while he is under twenty-one years of age.

(4) There shall be charged in respect of any examination which is held by the Secretary of State under this section such fees as the Secretary of State may from time to time with the approval of the Treasury determine.

Performance by inspectors of additional functions

74.—(1) The arrangements made by a local weights and measures authority to give effect in their area to the purposes of this Act may include the provision under the supervision of the chief inspector for their area of a service for the adjustment of weights and measures, but not of other weighing or measuring equipment.

(2) Where a service is provided under subsection (1) above, the local weights and measures authority shall charge such reasonable fees as they may determine in connection with it.

(3) No person holding office as an inspector who is employed in the inspection of weighing or measuring equipment for the purposes of its use for trade shall also undertake, whether as part of a service provided under subsection (1) above or otherwise, the adjustment for those purposes of weighing or measuring equipment of any description.

(4) Without prejudice to the functions of local weights and measures authorities or inspectors under any other provision of this Act, a local weights and measures authority may make arrangements whereby an inspector may, at the request of any person and subject to payment by that person of such fee, if any, as the authority may think fit, carry out and submit to that person a report on—

    (*a*) a weighing or other measurement of any goods submitted for the purpose by that person at such place as the authority may direct or approve;

    (*b*) a test of the accuracy of any weighing or measuring equipment so submitted.

Offences in connection with office of inspector

75.—(1) Any inspector who—

    (*a*) stamps any weighing or measuring equipment in contravention of any provision of this Act or of any instrument made under this Act or without duly testing it, or

    (*b*) derives any profit from, or is employed in, the making, adjusting or selling of weighing or measuring equipment, or

    (*c*) knowingly commits any breach of any duty imposed on him by or under this Act or otherwise misconducts himself in the execution of his office,

shall be guilty of an offence.

(2) If any person who is not an inspector acts or purports to act as an inspector, he shall be guilty of an offence.

Fees

Fees for performance of Community obligations

76. A local weights and measures authority may charge such reasonable fees as they may determine—
>   (*a*) for services or facilities provided by them, or by the inspectors appointed for their area, in pursuance of a Community obligation, and
>   (*b*) for authorisations, certificates or other documents issued by the authority or any such inspector in pursuance of a Community obligation.

Reduction of fees

77. Where a person gives assistance in connection with the inspection, testing or stamping of weighing or measuring equipment by an inspector, the local weights and measures authority may reduce, by a sum which the authority considers is reasonable by reference to the assistance, the amount of any payment falling to be made by that person to the inspector in respect of the inspection, testing or stamping.

Fees received by inspectors

78. Every inspector shall, at such times as the local weights and measures authority may direct, account for and pay over to that authority or as they may direct all fees taken by him for the performance of his duties.

PART VII

GENERAL

Enforcement and legal proceedings

General powers of inspection and entry

79.—(1) Subject to the production if so requested of his credentials, an inspector may, within the area for which he was appointed inspector, at all reasonable times—
>   (*a*) inspect and test any weighing or measuring equipment which is, or which he has reasonable cause to believe to be, used for trade or in the possession of any person or upon any premises for such use,
>   (*b*) inspect any goods to which any of the provisions of Part IV of this Act or any instrument made under that Part for the time being applies or which he has reasonable cause to believe to be such goods, and
>   (*c*) enter any premises at which he has reasonable cause to believe there to be any such equipment or goods, not being premises used only as a private dwelling-house.

(2) Subject to the production if so requested of his credentials, an inspector may at any time within the area for which he was appointed inspector seize and detain—
>   (*a*) any article which he has reasonable cause to believe is liable to be forfeited under Part II or IV of this Act, and
>   (*b*) any document or goods which the inspector has reason to believe

may be required as evidence in proceedings for an offence under this Act (except an offence under Part V).

(3) If a justice of the peace, on sworn information in writing—

(*a*) is satisfied that there is reasonable ground to believe that any such equipment, goods, articles or documents as are mentioned in subsection (1) or (2) above are on any premises, or that any offence under this Act or any instrument made under it (except an offence under Part V or any instrument made under that Part) has been, is being or is about to be committed on any premises, and

(*b*) is also satisfied either—

(i) that admission to the premises has been refused, or a refusal is apprehended, and that notice of the intention to apply for a warrant has been given to the occupier, or

(ii) that an application for admission, or the giving of such a notice, would defeat the object of the entry, or that the case is one of urgency, or that the premises are unoccupied or the occupier temporarily absent,

the justice may by warrant under his hand, which shall continue in force for a period of one month, authorise an inspector to enter the premises, if need be by force.

(4) In the application of subsection (3) above to Scotland, "justice of the peace" includes a sheriff.

(5) An inspector entering any premises by virtue of this section may take with him such other persons and such equipment as may appear to him necessary.

(6) An inspector who leaves premises which he has entered by virtue of a warrant under subsection (3) above and which are unoccupied or from which the occupier is temporarily absent shall leave the premises as effectively secured against trespassers as he found them.

(7) If any inspector or other person who enters any workplace by virtue of this section discloses to any person any information obtained by him in the work-place with regard to any secret manufacturing process or trade secret, he shall, unless the disclosure was made in the performance of his duty, be guilty of an offence.

(8) In exercising his functions under this Act at any mine of coal, stratified ironstone, shale or fire-clay, an inspector shall so exercise those functions as not to impede or obstruct the working of the mine.

(9) Nothing in this Act shall authorise any inspector to stop any vehicle on a highway.

Obstruction of inspectors

80. Any person who wilfully obstructs an inspector acting in pursuance of this Act shall be guilty of an offence.

Failure to provide assistance or information

81.—(1) Any person who—

(*a*) wilfully fails to comply with any requirement properly made of him by an inspector under section 38, 39 or 40 above, or

(*b*) without reasonable cause fails to give to any inspector acting in pursuance of this Act any other assistance or information which the inspector may reasonably require of him for the purposes of the performance by the inspector of his functions under Part II, III, IV or VI of this Act or under this Part of this Act,

shall be guilty of an offence.

(2) If any person, in giving to an inspector any such information as is mentioned in subsection (1) above, gives any information which he knows to be false, he shall be guilty of an offence.

(3) Nothing in this section shall be construed as requiring a person to answer any question or give any information if to do so might incriminate him.

(4) Subsection (1) of section 14 of the Civil Evidence Act 1968 (which relates to the privilege against self-incrimination) shall apply to the right conferred by subsection (3) above as it applies to the right described in subsection (1) of that section; but this subsection does not extend to Scotland.

Offences by corporations

82.—(1) Where an offence under, or under any instrument made under, this Act which has been committed by a body corporate is proved to have been committed with the consent or connivance of, or to be attributable to any neglect on the part of, any director, manager, secretary or other similar officer of the body corporate, or any person who was purporting to act in any such capacity, he as well as the body corporate shall be guilty of that offence and shall be liable to be proceeded against and punished accordingly.

(2) In subsection (1) above "director" in relation to any body corporate established by or under any enactment for the purpose of carrying on under national ownership any industry or part of an industry or undertaking, being a body corporate whose affairs are managed by its members, means a member of that body corporate.

Prosecution of offences

83.—(1) Subject to subsection (2) below, in England and Wales, proceedings for any offence under this Act or any instrument made under this Act, other than proceedings for an offence under section 64, shall not be instituted except by or on behalf of a local weights and measures authority or the chief officer of police for a police area.

(2) Proceedings for an offence under section 57(2) above shall not be instituted in England or Wales except by or on behalf of the Director of Public Prosecutions or the National Metrological Co-ordinating Unit.

(3) Proceedings for an offence under any provision contained in, or having effect by virtue of, Part IV or V of this Act, other than proceedings for an offence under section 33(6), 57(2) or 64 or proceedings by virtue of section 32, shall not be constituted—

(*a*) unless there has been served on the person charged a notice in writing of the date and nature of the offence alleged and, except in the case of an offence under section 50, 54 or 63 or Schedule 8, where the proceedings are in respect of one or more of a number of articles of the same kind tested on the same occasion, of the results of the tests of all those articles; or

(*b*) except where the person charged is a street trader, unless the said notice was served before the expiration of the period of thirty days beginning with the date when evidence which the person proposing to institute the proceedings considers is sufficient to justify a prosecution for the offence came to his knowledge; or

(*c*) after the expiration of the period—
> (i) of twelve months beginning with the date mentioned in paragraph (*a*) above, or
> (ii) of three months beginning with the date mentioned in paragraph (*b*) above,
> whichever first occurs.

(4) Such a notice as is mentioned in subsection (3)(*a*) above may be served on any person either by serving it on him personally or by sending it to him by post at his usual or last known residence or place of business in the United Kingdom or, in the case of a company, at the company's registered office.

(5) For the purposes of subsection (3) above—

    (*a*) a certificate of a person who institutes proceedings for an offence mentioned in that subsection which states that evidence came to his knowledge on a particular date shall be conclusive evidence of that fact; and

    (*b*) a document purporting to be a certificate of such a person and to be signed by him or on his behalf shall be presumed to be such a certificate unless the contrary is proved.

Penalties

84.—(1) A person guilty of an offence under any of the provisions of this Act specified in subsection (2) below shall be liable on summary conviction to a fine not exceeding level 3 on the standard scale.

(2) The provisions of this Act to which subsection (1) above refers are—

    section 8(4);
    section 9(4);
    section 10(2);
    section 11(3);
    section 11(14);
    section 13(1);
    section 13(2);
    section 13(3);
    section 14(3);
    section 14(5);
    section 15(3);
    section 15(5);
    section 18(3);
    section 20(2);
    section 20(4);
    section 20(7);
    section 20(8);
    paragraphs 4 and 5 of Schedule 4;
    paragraph 28(3) of Schedule 5.

(3) A person guilty of an offence under paragraph 24(4) of Schedule 5 to this Act shall be liable on summary conviction to a fine not exceeding £2,000.

(4) A person guilty of an offence—

    (*a*) under section 17(3), 20(3)(*b*) or 50(2), (3) or (4) above, or

    (*b*) under paragraph 10 of Schedule 5 to this Act,

shall be liable on summary conviction to a fine not exceeding level 5 on the standard scale or to imprisonment for a term not exceeding six months or to both.

(5) A person guilty of an offence under section 64 or 79(7) above shall be liable, on summary conviction, to a fine not exceeding the statutory maximum and, on conviction on indictment, to imprisonment for a term not exceeding two years or to a fine or to both.

(6) A person guilty of an offence under any provision of this Act other than those mentioned in subsections (1) to (5) above shall be liable on summary conviction to a fine not exceeding level 5 on the standard scale.

(7) The Secretary of State may by order alter the penalty imposed by subsection (3) above but such an order shall not impose any penalty exceeding that provided by subsection (6) above.

Determination of certain questions by Secretary of State

85.—(1) Where in any proceedings for an offence under this Act or any instrument made under it, except proceedings for an offence under Part V or any instrument made under that Part, any question arises as to the accuracy of any weighing or measuring equipment, the court shall at the request of any party to the proceedings, and may if it thinks fit without any such request, refer the question to the Secretary of State, whose decision shall be final.

(2) Except where in any particular proceedings the Secretary of State waives his rights under this subsection, any expenses incurred by the Secretary of State in making any test for the purpose of determining any question referred to him under subsection (1) above shall be paid by such of the parties to the proceedings as the court may by order direct.

Miscellaneous and supplementary

Regulations and orders

86.—(1) Any power to make orders or regulations conferred on the Secretary of State by this Act shall be exercisable by statutory instrument, and any such order or regulations may make different provision for different circumstances.

(2) Before making—
- (a) an order under any provision of this Act except sections 11(16), 43(2), 62, 69(4) or 94(2) or paragraph 7 of Schedule 11, or
- (b) regulations under section 9 or Part V of this Act,

the Secretary of State shall consult such organisations as appear to him to be representative of interests substantially affected by the order or regulations.

(3) In the case of an order made under section 1(3) or 8(6) above which relates to imperial units, measures or weights, the Secretary of State in acting under subsection (2) above shall have particular regard to the need to consult organisations representative of the interests of consumers.

(4) Before making an order under section 62 above, the Secretary of State shall consult an organisation which in his opinion represents such local authorities (within the meaning of section 55(3) above) as he considers appropriate in connection with the proposal.

(5) An order under any provision of this Act except section 11(16), 43(2), 69(4) or 94(2) or paragraph 7 of Schedule 11 shall not be made unless a draft of the order has been laid before, and approved by a resolution of, each House of Parliament.

(6) Any statutory instrument containing regulations made under this Act shall be subject to annulment in pursuance of a resolution of either House of Parliament.

Secretary of State to report to Parliament

87. The Secretary of State shall from time to time, and in any event not less than once in every five years, lay before each House of Parliament a report on the exercise of his functions under this Act, except Part V.

Application to Crown

88.—(1) Her Majesty may by Order in Council provide for the application to the Crown of such of the provisions of this Act or of any instrument made under it as may be specified in the Order, with such exceptions, adaptations and modifications as may be so specified.

(2) Without prejudice to the generality of subsection (1) above, an Order in Council under this section may make special provision for the enforcement of any provisions applied by the Order, and, in particular, as to the person liable to be proceeded against for any offence under any such provision.

(3) A statutory instrument containing an Order in Council made under this section shall be subject to annulment in pursuance of a resolution of either House of Parliament.

Saving for use of certain units in wholesale transactions

89.—(1) Except as the Secretary of State may by order otherwise provide, and subject to subsection (2) below, nothing in this Act shall make unlawful the use in any transaction, by agreement between the parties to that transaction, of any unit of measurement which—

(*a*) was customarily used for trade in the like transactions immediately before 31st July 1963, and

(*b*) is not inconsistent with anything for the time being contained in Schedule 1 to this Act.

notwithstanding that the unit in question is not included in Parts I to V of that Schedule.

(2) Subsection (1) above shall not apply in relation to—

(*a*) any retail transaction, or

(*b*) any transaction with respect to which provision to the contrary effect is made by or under Part IV of this Act.

Saving for certain rights in City of London

90.—(1) Subject to subsection (2) below, nothing in this Act shall affect any rights of the mayor and commonalty and citizens of the City of London or of the Lord Mayor of the City of London for the time being with respect to the stamping or sealing of weights and measures, or with respect to the gauging of wine or oil or other gaugeable liquors.

(2) A person using weighing or measuring equipment within the City of London shall not be required to have that equipment passed or stamped by more than one authority.

Validity of contracts

91. No contract for the sale or carriage for reward of any goods shall be void by reason only of a contravention of any provision contained in or made under this Act with respect to any document which is, or is required by that provision to be, associated with the goods.

Spelling of "gram", etc

92. No provision contained in or made under this or any other Act prevents the use of "gram" or "gramme" as alternative ways of spelling that unit, and the same applies for other units in the metric system which are compounds of "gram".

Powers under other Acts with respect to marking of food

93. Any power to make provision by statutory instrument with respect to the marking of any food which is conferred on any person other than the Secretary of State by any Act passed before 31st July 1963 or by the Food Act 1984 shall not extend to the marking of such food with a statement of its quantity by weight or other measurement or by number.

General interpretation

94.—(1) Except where the context otherwise requires, in this Act—

"capacity measurement" means measurement in terms of a unit of measurement included in Part IV of Schedule 1 to this Act;

"check-weighed", in relation to any vehicle, means weighed with its load by means of the nearest suitable and available weighing equipment, and weighed again after it has been unloaded by means of the same or other suitable weighing equipment;

"chief inspector" means a chief inspector of weights and measures appointed under section 72(1) above;

"container" except in Part V, includes any form of packaging of goods for sale as a single item, whether by way of wholly or partly enclosing the goods or by way of attaching the goods to, or winding the goods round, some other article, and in particular includes a wrapper or confining band;

"contravention", in relation to any requirement, includes a failure to comply with that requirement, and cognate expressions shall be construed accordingly;

"credentials", in relation to an inspector, means authority in writing from the local weights and measures authority who appointed him for the exercise by that inspector of powers conferred on inspectors by this Act;

"Department of Trade and Industry standards" means the secondary, tertiary and coinage standards maintained by the Secretary of State under section 3 above;

"drugs" and "food" have the same meanings respectively as for the purposes of the Food Act 1984 or, in Scotland, the Food and Drugs (Scotland) Act 1956;

"gross weight", in relation to any goods, means the aggregate weight of the goods and any container in or on which they are made up;

"indication of quantity", in relation to any container in or on which goods are made up, means a statement in writing to the effect that those goods are of, or of not less than, a specified quantity by net weight, gross weight or other measurement or by number, as the case may require;

"industrial use", in relation to any goods, means the use of those goods in the manufacture of, or for incorporation in, goods of a different description in the course of the carrying on of a business;

"inspector" means an inspector of weights and measures appointed under section 72(1) above;

"intoxicating liquor" means spirits, beer, wine, made-wine or cider as defined in section 1 of the Alcholic Liquor Duties Act 1979;

"local standard" means a standard maintained under section 4 above;

"mark" includes label;

"occupier", in relation to any stall, vehicle, ship or aircraft or in relation to the use of any place for any purpose, means the person for the time being in charge of the stall, vehicle, ship or aircraft or, as the case may be, the person for the time being using that place for that purpose;

"premises", except in section 45 above, includes any place and any stall, vehicle, ship or aircraft;

"pre-packed" means made up in advance ready for retail sale in or on a container;

"prescribed" means prescribed by the Secretary of State by regulations;

"secondary standard" means a standard maintained under section 3(2) above;

"ship" includes any boat and any other description of vessel used in navigation;

"stamp" means a mark for use as evidence of the passing of weighing or measuring equipment as fit for use for trade, whether applied by impressing, casting, engraving, etching, branding, or otherwise, and cognate expressions shall be construed accordingly;

"standard scale" has the meaning given by section 75 of the Criminal Justice Act 1982;

"statutory maximum" has the meaning given by section 74 of that Act;

"tertiary standard" means a standard maintained under section 3(3) above;

"testing equipment" means testing equipment maintained under section 5 above;

"United Kingdom primary standard" means a standard maintained under section 2 above;

"use for trade" shall be construed in accordance with section 7 above;

"weighing or measuring equipment" means equipment for measuring in terms of length, area, volume, capacity, weight or number, whether or not the equipment is constructed to give an indication of the measurement made or other information determined by reference to that measurement;

"working standard" means a standard maintained under section 5 above.

(2) In any provision of this Act "designated country" means such, if any, of the following, that is to say, Northern Ireland, any of the Channel Islands and the Isle of Man, as the Secretary of State, having regard to the law for the time being in force there, thinks it proper to designate for the purposes of that provision by order.

(3) On any premises where articles of any description are—

(a) made up in advance ready for retail sale in or on a container, or

(b) kept or stored for sale after being so made up,

any article of that description found made up in or on a container shall be deemed to be pre-packed unless the contrary is proved; and it shall not be sufficient proof of the contrary to show that the container has not been marked in accordance with the requirements of this Act or any instrument made under it with respect to the pre-packing of such articles.

(4) Except where the context otherwise requires, any reference in this Act to any person, other than a reference to an inspector, shall be construed as a reference to that person or some other person acting on his behalf in the matter in question.

Application to Northern Ireland

95. Schedule 10 to this Act shall have effect in relation to Northern Ireland but, except as provided in that Schedule, this Act shall not extend to Northern Ireland.

Transitional provisions and savings

96.—(1) Schedule 11 to this Act (which contains transitional provisions and savings) shall have effect.

(2) The re-enactment—

(a) in section 84(3) of, and Part IV of Schedule 5 to, this Act, of provisions contained in the Weights and Measures (Solid Fuel) (Carriage by Rail) Order 1966, and

(*b*) in paragraphs 12 to 17, 22 and 25 of Schedule 11 to this Act, of provisions contained in the Units of Measurement Regulations 1978 and the Units of Measurement Regulations 1980,

shall be without prejudice to the validity of those provisions; and any question as to the validity of any of those provisions shall be determined as if the re-enacting provision of this Act were contained in a statutory instrument made under the powers under which the original provision was made.

(3) The provisions of Schedule 11 to this Act are without prejudice to the operation of sections 16 and 17 of the Interpretation Act 1978 (which relate to the effect of repeals).

Consequential amendments

97. Schedule 12 to this Act shall have effect.

Repeals and revocations

98.—(1) The enactments specified in Part I of Schedule 13 to this Act are hereby repealed to the extent specified in the third column of that Schedule.

(2) The instruments specified in Part II of Schedule 13 to this Act are hereby revoked to the extent specified in the third column of that Schedule.

Short title and commencement

99.—(1) This Act be cited as the Weights and Measures Act 1985.

(2) Except as provided by section 43(2) above, this Act shall come into force at the end of the period of three months beginning with the day on which it is passed.

SCHEDULES

Sections 1(2), 8(1)   SCHEDULE 1

DEFINITIONS OF UNITS OF MEASUREMENT

PART I

MEASUREMENT OF LENGTH

Imperial units

Mile	= 1760 yards.
YARD	= 0·9144 metre.
Foot	= 1/3 yard.
Inch	= 1/36 yard.

Metric units

Kilometre	= 1000 metres.
METRE	= is the length of the path travelled by light in vacuum during a time interval of 1/299 792 458 of a second.
Decimetre	= 1/10 metre.
Centimetre	= 1/100 metre.
Millimetre	= 1/1000 metre.

PART II

MEASUREMENT OF AREA

Imperial units

Acre	= 4840 square yards.
SQUARE YARD	= a superficial area equal to that of a square each side of which measures one yard.
Square foot	= 1/9 square yard.

Metric units

Hectare	= 100 ares.
Decare	= 10 ares.
Are	= 100 square metres.
SQUARE METRE	= a superficial area equal to that of a square each side of which measures one metre.
Square decimetre	= 1/100 square metre.
Square centimetre	= 1/100 square decimetre.
Square millimetre	= 1/100 square centimetre.

PART III

MEASUREMENT OF VOLUME

Metric units

CUBIC METRE	= a volume equal to that of a cube each edge of which measures one metre.
Cubic decimetre	= 1/1000 cubic metre.
Cubic centimetre	= 1/1000 cubic decimetre.
Hectolitre	= 100 litres.
LITRE	= a cubic decimetre.
Decilitre	= 1/10 litre.
Centilitre	= 1/100 litre.
Millilitre	= 1/1000 litre.

PART IV

MEASUREMENT OF CAPACITY

Imperial units

GALLON	= 4·546 09 cubic decimetres.
Quart	= 1/4 gallon.
Pint	= 1/2 quart.
Gill	= 1/4 pint.
Fluid ounce	= 1/20 pint.

Metric units

Hectolitre	= 100 litres.
LITRE	= a cubic decimetre.
Decilitre	= 1/10 litre.
Centilitre	= 1/100 litre.
Millilitre	= 1/1000 litre.

PART V

MEASUREMENT OF MASS OR WEIGHT

Imperial units

POUND	=	0·453 592 37 kilogram.
Ounce	=	1/16 pound.
Ounce troy	=	12/175 pound.

Metric units

Tonne, metric tonne	=	1000 kilograms.
KILOGRAM	=	is the unit of mass; it is equal to the mass of the international prototype of the kilogram.
Hectogram	=	1/10 kilogram.
Gram	=	1/1000 kilogram.
Carat (metric)	=	1/5 gram.
Milligram	=	1/1000 gram.

PART VI

DEFINITIONS OF CERTAIN UNITS WHICH MAY NOT BE USED FOR TRADE

MEASUREMENT OF LENGTH

Furlong	=	220 yards.
Chain	=	22 yards.

MEASUREMENT OF AREA

Square mile	=	640 acres.
Rood	=	1210 square yards.
Square inch	=	1/144 square foot.

MEASUREMENT OF VOLUME

Cubic yard	=	a volume equal to that of a cube each edge of which measures one yard.
Cubic foot	=	1/27 cubic yard.
Cubic inch	=	1/1728 cubic foot.

MEASUREMENT OF CAPACITY

Bushel	=	8 gallons.
Peck	=	2 gallons.
Fluid drachm	=	1/8 fluid ounce.
Minim	=	1/60 fluid drachm.

MEASUREMENT OF MASS OR WEIGHT

Ton	=	2240 pounds.
Hundredweight	=	112 pounds.
Cental	=	100 pounds.
Quarter	=	28 pounds.
Stone	=	14 pounds.
Dram	=	1/16 ounce.
Grain	=	1/7000 pound.
Penny weight	=	24 grains.
Ounce apothecaries	=	480 grains.
Drachm	=	1/8 ounce apothecaries.
Scruple	=	1/3 drachm.
Metric ton	=	1000 kilograms.
Quintal	=	100 kilograms.

PART VII

MEASUREMENT OF ELECTRICITY

1. (*a*) AMPERE — is that constant current which, if maintained in two straight parallel conductors of infinite length, of negligible circular cross-section and placed 1 metre apart in vacuum, would produce between these conductors a force equal to 2×10^{-7} newton per metre of length.

(*b*) OHM — is the electric resistance between two points of a conductor when a constant potential difference of 1 volt, applied between the two points, produces in the conductor a current of 1 ampere, the conductor not being the seat of any electromotive force.

(*c*) VOLT — is the difference of electric potential between two points of a conducting wire carrying a constant current of 1 ampere when the power dissipated between these points is equal to 1 watt.

(*d*) WATT — is the power which is one second gives rise to energy of 1 joule.

2. Kilowatt = 1000 watts.
   Megawatt = one million watts.

Section 2(3)   SCHEDULE 2

EXISTING UNITED KINGDOM PRIMARY STANDARDS AND AUTHORISED COPIES

PART I

DESCRIPTION OF UNITED KINGDOM PRIMARY STANDARD OF THE YARD

A solid bronze bar, about 38 inches long and about 1 inch square in transverse section, marked "Copper 16 oz. Tin 2½ Zinc 1 Mr. Baily's Metal No. 1 STANDARD YARD at 62°·00 Faht. Cast in 1845 Troughton & Simms, LONDON." and having near to each end a cylindrical hole sunk to the depth of about ½ inch at the bottom of which is inserted in a smaller hole a golden plug about one-tenth of an inch in diameter with, cut upon its surface, three fine lines about one hundredth of an inch apart transverse, and two fine lines about three hundredths of an inch apart parallel, to the axis of the bar, measurement being made of the mean interval between the two plugs on their respective middle transverse lines between their respective longitudinal lines when the bar is at the temperature of 62° Fahrenheit and supported on bronze rollers placed under it in such manner as best to avoid flexure of the bar and to facilitate its free expansion and contraction from variations of temperature.

PART II

DESCRIPTION OF UNITED KINGDOM PRIMARY STANDARD OF THE POUND

A platinum cylinder about 1.35 inches in height and about 1.15 inches in diameter marked "PS 1844 1 lb", having its edges rounded off and a groove about 0.34 inch below the top of the cylinder.

PART III

DESCRIPTION OF UNITED KINGDOM PRIMARY STANDARD OF THE METRE

The British copy of the prototype metre, being a bar about 102 centimetres long with a cross-section of modified X-form and made of platinum-iridium alloy (90 per cent. platinum, 10 per cent. iridium), bearing at one end the markings "0°C & 20°C", "A.16 SIP GENEVE 1956" and (on the cross-section) "1" and at the other end the markings "B.16" and (on the cross-section) "2", and having engraved on the exposed neutral plane—

(*a*) near each end and also at the centre, two parallel longitudinal lines about 0.12 millimetre apart;

(*b*) near the end marked "1" and at the centre, one transverse line; and

(*c*) near the end marked "2", two transverse lines about 0.17 millimetre apart, measurement being made of the mean interval between the portions of the most widely separated transverse lines which are between the respective longitudinal lines when the bar is at the temperature of 0° Celsius, is subjected to an atmospheric pressure of 1013.250 millibars, and is supported on two rollers at least one centimetre in diameter placed symmetrically 571 millimetres apart in the same horizontal plane.

PART IV

DESCRIPTION OF UNITED KINGDOM PRIMARY STANDARD OF THE KILOGRAM

The British copy of the prototype kilogram, being a solid cylinder marked "18" of height equal to its diameter made of platinum-iridium alloy (90 per cent. platinum, 10 per cent. iridium).

PART V

AUTHORISED COPIES OF UNITED KINGDOM PRIMARY STANDARDS OF THE YARD AND POUND

Copies of the bar and cylinder described in Parts I and II respectively of this Schedule of the same construction and form as that bar and cylinder are respectively marked and deposited as follows—

 (*a*) a bronze bar marked "Copper 16 oz. Tin 2½ Zinc 1 Mr. Baily's Metal No. 2 STANDARD YARD at 61°·94 Faht. Cast in 1845 Troughton & Simms, LONDON.", and a platinum cylinder marked "No. 1 PC 1844 1 lb", deposited at the Royal Mint;

 (*b*) a bronze bar marked "Copper 16 oz. Tin 2½ Zinc 1 Mr. Baily's Metal No. 3 STANDARD YARD at 62°·10 Faht. Cast in 1845 Troughton & Simms, LONDON.", and a platinum cylinder marked "No 2 PC 1844 1 lb", deposited at the premises of the Royal Society;

 (*c*) a bronze bar marked "Copper 16 oz. Tin 2½ Zinc 1 Mr. Baily's Metal No. 5 STANDARD YARD at 62°·16 Faht. Cast in 1845 Troughton & Simms, LONDON.", and a platinum cylinder marked "No. 3 PC 1844 1 lb", deposited at the Royal Greenwich Observatory;

 (*d*) a bronze bar marked "Copper 16 oz. Tin 2½ Zinc 1 Mr. Baily's Metal No. 4 STANDARD YARD at 61°·98 Faht. Cast in 1845 Troughton & Simms, LONDON.", and a platinum cylinder marked "No 4 PC 1844 1 lb", immured in the Palace of Westminster;

 (*e*) a bronze bar marked "Copper 16 oz. Tin 2½ Zinc 1. BAILY'S METAL. PARLIA-MENTARY COPY (VI) OF THE IMPERIAL STANDARD YARD. 41 & 42 VICTORIA, CHAPTER 49. STANDARD YARD AT 62° FAHT. CAST IN 1878. Troughton & Simms. London. H.J.C.", and a platinum-iridium cylinder marked "P.C. 5 1879" deposited at the National Weights and Measures Laboratory of the Department of Trade and Industry.

Section 8(1)   SCHEDULE 3

MEASURES AND WEIGHTS LAWFUL FOR USE FOR TRADE

PART I

LINEAR MEASURES

Imperial system

1. Measures of—

100 feet	5 feet
66 feet	4 feet
50 feet	1 yard
33 feet	2 feet
20 feet	1 foot
10 feet	6 inches
8 feet	1 inch
6 feet	

Metric system

2. Measures of—

50 metres	2 metres
30 metres	1·5 metres
20 metres	1 metre
10 metres	0·5 metre
5 metres	1 decimetre
3 metres	1 centimetre

PART II

SQUARE MEASURES

Imperial system

1. Measures of, or of any multiple of, 1 square foot.

Metric system

2. Measures of, or of any multiple of, 1 square decimetre.

PART III

CUBIC MEASURES

Metric system

1. Measures of, or of any multiple of, 0·1 cubic metre.
2. Measures of—
   any multiple of 10 litres

10	litres	100	millilitres
5	litres	50	millilitres
2·5	litres	25	millilitres
2	litres	20	millilitres
1	litre	10	millilitres
500	millilitres	5	millilitres
250	millilitres	2	millilitres
200	millilitres	1	millilitre

PART IV

CAPACITY MEASURES

Imperial system

1. Measures of—
   any multiple of 1 gallon

1 gallon	1 gill
½ gallon	4 fluid ounces
1 quart	½ gill
1 pint	$\frac{2}{5}$ gill
½ pint	$\frac{1}{3}$ gill
8 fluid ounces	¼ gill
⅓ pint	⅕ gill
6 fluid ounces	¹/₆ gill

Metric system

2. Measures of—
   any multiple of 10 litres

10	litres	125	millilitres
5	litres	100	millilitres
2·5	litres	50	millilitres
2	litres	25	millilitres
1	litres	20	millilitres
500	millilitres	10	millilitres
250	millilitres	5	millilitres
200	millilitres	2	millilitres
175	millilitres	1	millilitre
150	millilitres		

PART V

WEIGHTS

Imperial system

1. Weights of—

	any of the following multiples or fractions of 1/7000 pound that is to say:—
56 pounds	
50 pounds	
28 pounds	
20 pounds	100
14 pounds	50
10 pounds	30
7 pounds	20
5 pounds	10
4 pounds	5
2 pounds	3
1 pound	2
8 ounces	1
4 ounces	0·5
2 ounces	0·3
1 ounce	0·2
$\frac{1}{2}$ ounce	0·1
$\frac{1}{4}$ ounce	0·05
$\frac{1}{8}$ ounce	0·03
$\frac{1}{16}$ ounce	0·02
$\frac{1}{32}$ ounce	0·01

2. Weights of—

500 ounces troy	0·4 ounce troy
400 ounces troy	0·3 ounce troy
300 ounces troy	0·2 ounce troy
200 ounces troy	0·1 ounce troy
100 ounces troy	0·05 ounce troy
50 ounces troy	0·04 ounce troy
40 ounces troy	0·03 ounce troy
30 ounces troy	0·025 ounce troy
20 ounces troy	0·02 ounce troy
10 ounces troy	0·01 ounce troy
5 ounces troy	0·005 ounce troy
4 ounces troy	0·004 ounce troy
3 ounces troy	0·003 ounce troy
2 ounces troy	0·002 ounce troy
1 ounce troy	0·001 ounce troy
0·5 ounce troy	

Metric system

3. Weights of—

25 kilograms	3 grams
20 kilograms	2 grams
10 kilograms	1 gram
5 kilograms	500 milligrams
2 kilograms	400 milligrams
1 kilogram	300 milligrams
500 grams	200 milligrams
200 grams	150 milligrams
100 grams	100 milligrams
50 grams	50 milligrams
20 grams	20 milligrams
15 grams	10 milligrams
10 grams	5 milligrams
5 grams	2 milligrams
4 grams	1 milligram

4. Weights of—

500 carats (metric)	1 carat (metric)
200 carats (metric)	0·5 carat (metric)
100 carats (metric)	0·25 carat (metric)
50 carats (metric)	0·2 carat (metric)
20 carats (metric)	0·1 carat (metric)
10 carats (metric)	0·05 carat (metric)
5 carats (metric)	0·02 carat (metric)
2 carats (metric)	0·01 carat (metric)

Section 21   SCHEDULE 4

SAND AND OTHER BALLAST

PART I

GENERAL PROVISIONS

1. In this Schedule, "ballast" means any of the following materials, that is to say—
   (a) sand, gravel, shingle, ashes and clinker of any description,
   (b) broken slag, slag chippings, granite chippings, limestone chippings, slate chippings and other stone chippings (including such materials which have been coated with tar, bitumen or cement),
   (c) any other material commonly used in the building and civil engineering industries as a hardcore or an aggregate, and
   (d) any other material commonly known in those industries as ballast.

2. Subject to paragraphs 3 and 11 below, ballast shall be sold only by volume in a multiple of 0·2 cubic metre or by net weight.

3. There shall be exempted from the requirements of paragraph 2 above—
   (a) ballast in a quantity both less than 2240 pounds and less than one cubic metre,
   (b) any sale with a view to its industrial use of ballast of any description mentioned in paragraph 1(b), (c) or (d) above,
   (c) any sale in the case of which the buyer is to take delivery in or from a ship,
   (d) any sale as a whole of ballast produced in the demolition or partial demolition of a building where the buyer is responsible for the removal of the ballast from the site of the building, and
   (e) any sale in the state in which it was produced of clinker or ashes produced as a by-product, or of any other ballast produced as a casual product, of the carrying on of an industrial process on any premises or of the mining of coal where the buyer is responsible for the removal of the ballast from those premises or, as the case may be, from the colliery tip.

4. Without prejudice to section 15 of this Act, no article shall be used for trade as a cubic measure of ballast other than a receptacle (which may, if so desired, form part of a vehicle) which conforms with such requirements as to form, capacity, calibration and other matters as may be prescribed; and any person who uses for trade, or has in his possession for use for trade, as a cubic measure of ballast any article other than such a receptacle shall be guilty of an offence.

5. In measuring any ballast against a calibration mark on such a receptacle as mentioned in paragraph 4 above, the ballast shall be filled into all parts of the receptacle as far as, and be levelled off against, that calibration mark as nearly as the nature of the ballast will permit; and where any ballast is measured for the purposes of trade in such a receptacle, any person who—
   (a) being the person carrying out the measuring, fails so to level off the ballast when it is loaded into the receptacle, or
   (b) causes or permits a heaped load to be sent out in the receptacle,
shall be guilty of an offence.

PART II

CARRIAGE OF BALLAST BY ROAD

6. This Part of this Schedule shall have effect with respect to the carriage of ballast by a road vehicle on a journey any part of which is along a highway.

7.—(1) If any of the ballast is being carried for delivery to a buyer in pursuance of, or of an agreement for, its sale and paragraph 2 above applies to the sale, the following provisions of this paragraph shall have effect with respect to that ballast.

(2) There shall, before the journey begins, be delivered to the person in charge of the vehicle a document signed by or on behalf of the seller (in this paragraph referred to as "the delivery document") stating—

(*a*) the name and address of the seller,

(*b*) the name of the buyer, and the address of the premises to which the ballast is being delivered,

(*c*) the type of the ballast,

(*d*) subject to sub-paragraph (4) below, the quantity of the ballast either by net weight or by volume,

(*e*) sufficient particulars to identify the vehicle, and

(*f*) the place, date and time of the loading of the ballast in the vehicle.

(3) Where the quantity of the ballast is stated in the delivery document by volume, the ballast shall be carried on the vehicle only in such a receptacle as is mentioned in paragraph 4 above.

(4) The statement referred to in sub-paragraph (2) (*d*) above shall not be required at any time while the vehicle is travelling between the place where it was loaded and the nearest suitable and available weighing equipment if the whole of the vehicle's load is being delivered to the same person at the same premises and the delivery document states that the quantity of the ballast is to be expressed by net weight determined by means of that equipment and specifies the place at which the equipment is situated.

(5) In any case to which sub-paragraph (4) above applies, the person in charge of the vehicle at the time when the net weight of the ballast is determined shall forthwith add to the delivery document a statement of that net weight, and if he fails so to do he shall be guilty of an offence.

(6) If any of the provisions of sub-paragraph (2) or (3) above is contravened, the seller shall be guilty of an offence.

(7) If the vehicle is carrying ballast as mentioned in sub-paragraph (1) above for delivery to each of two or more persons, sub-paragraphs (1) to (3) above shall apply separately in relation to each of those persons; but this sub-paragraph shall not be construed as prohibiting the use of the same receptacle such as is mentioned in sub-paragraph (3) above for the carriage of ballast for delivery to two or more different persons.

8.—(1) Subject to sub-paragraph (2) below, if all or any of the ballast on the vehicle is being carried in such circumstances that paragraph 7 above does not apply to it, there shall before the journey begins be delivered to the person in charge of the vehicle a document containing a statement to that effect signed by or on behalf of the person causing that ballast to be carried and giving the name and address of the last-mentioned person, and if this paragraph is contravened the last-mentioned person shall be guilty of an offence.

(2) Sub-paragraph (1) above shall not apply where all the ballast in the vehicle is being carried in such circumstances that paragraph 7 does not apply to it and is being so carried in a container which does not form part of the vehicle.

9. Any document required by paragraph 7 or 8 above shall at all times during the journey be carried by the person for the time being in charge of the vehicle and shall be handed over by him to any other person to whom he hands over the charge of the vehicle in the course of the journey; and in the case of any document such as is mentioned in paragraph 7 above, on the unloading of the ballast to which the document relates at the premises to which that ballast is to be delivered—

(*a*) before any of that ballast is so unloaded, the document shall be handed over to the buyer, or

(*b*) if the document cannot be so handed over by reason of the absence of the buyer, it shall be left at some suitable place at those premises;

and if at any time any of the provisions of this paragraph is contravened without reasonable cause, the person in charge of the vehicle at that time shall be guilty of an offence.

10. In the case of any document such as is mentioned in paragraph 7 above, if at any time during the journey or on unloading at the place of delivery the quantity of the ballast to which the document relates is found to be less than that stated in the document, the

statement shall nevertheless be deemed for the purposes of this Act to be correct if, but only if, it is proved that the deficiency is solely attributable to the draining away of normal moisture from, or the consolidation of, the ballast during the journey.

PART III

APPLICATION TO SCOTLAND

11.—(1) In Scotland, paragraph 2 above and Part II of this Schedule shall have effect only in such areas as the Secretary of State may by order specify.

(2) In relation to any area specified by order under sub-paragraph (1) above, a sale of ballast in a quantity both less than 4480 pounds and less than 2 cubic metres shall be exempted from the requirements of paragraph 2 above if the sale is effected, and the ballast is situated, in Scotland.

<table>
<tr><td>**Section 21**</td><td align="center">SCHEDULE 5</td></tr>
</table>

SOLID FUEL

PART I

GENERAL

Introductory

1. This Schedule applies to goods of any of the following descriptions (in this Schedule referred to as "solid fuel"), that is to say—
    (*a*)   coal,
    (*b*)   coke, and
    (*c*)   any solid fuel derived from coal or of which coal or coke is a constituent.

Sales by net weight

2.—(1) Subject to sub-paragraphs (2) and (3) below, solid fuel shall be sold only by net weight.

(2) There shall be exempted from the requirements of sub-paragraph (1) above—
    (*a*)   briquettes in a quantity not exceeding 14 pounds, and
    (*b*)   any solid fuel pre-packed in a securely closed container marked with an indication of quantity by net weight.

(3) In the case of any area in Scotland which the Secretary of State may by order specify for the purposes of this sub-paragraph, solid fuel for delivery in that area may be sold by volume in a quantity of 0·2 cubic metre or a multiple of 0·2 cubic metre.

Quantities in containers

3.—(1) Solid fuel shall be made up in a container for sale, or for delivery after sale, only if it is made up in one of the quantities by net weight specified in the following Table—

TABLE

Imperial	*Metric*
7 pounds	25 kilograms
14 pounds	50 kilograms
28 pounds	Any multiple of 50 kilograms.
56 pounds	
112 pounds	
140 pounds	
Any multiple of 112 pounds.	

(2) This paragraph shall not apply to any solid fuel pre-packed in a quantity not exceeding 30 kilograms in a securely closed container.

(3) References in this Schedule to solid fuel made up in an imperial quantity are references to solid fuel made up in one of the imperial quantities specified in the Table in sub-paragraph (1) above, and references to solid fuel made up in a metric quantity shall be construed in a corresponding way.

72–66

(4) This paragraph and paragraphs 4, 5 and 6 below have effect subject to the exemptions in paragraph 7.

Indication of quantity

4.—(1) This paragraph applies to solid fuel made up in a container for sale, or for delivery after sale, except where it is made up in a metric quantity in a container which is not securely closed.

(2) The solid fuel shall be made up in a container for sale, or for delivery after sale, only if the container is marked with an indication of quantity by net weight.

Loads on vehicles

5.—(1) Solid fuel made up in containers in the quantity of 140 pounds shall be carried on a road vehicle on a highway for sale, or for delivery after sale, only if all solid fuel carried on the vehicle which is made up in containers is so made up in that quantity.

(2) Solid fuel made up in metric quantities in containers which are not securely closed shall be carried on a road vehicle on a highway for sale, or for delivery after sale, only if all solid fuel carried on the vehicle in containers which are not securely closed is made up in metric quantities.

(3) If this paragraph is contravened the seller shall be guilty of an offence.

Information about containers made up in metric quantities

6.—(1) This paragraph applies where solid fuel is carried on a road vehicle on a highway for sale, or for delivery after sale, and is made up in metric quantities in containers which are not securely closed or is delivered from the vehicle in such containers in any metric quantity.

(2) There shall be displayed on the vehicle—

    (*a*) an indication of the quantity, or quantities, by net weight of the fuel comprised in the containers (other than any securely closed containers) on, or delivered from, the vehicle, and

    (*b*) a statement of the name and address of the seller.

(3) Regulations under section 23 of this Act may prescribe the manner in which the information required by sub-paragraph (2) above is to be displayed, and a person who contravenes any such regulation shall be guilty of an offence.

(4) If this paragraph is contravened, the seller, and any other person who is in charge of the vehicle at the time of the contravention, shall each be guilty of an offence.

Exemptions

7. There shall be exempted from all the requirements of paragraphs 3, 4, 5 and 6 above—

    (*a*) solid fuel supplied under arrangements made in the coal industry for the supply of solid fuel to persons who are or have been employed in that industry or to the dependants of such persons;

    (*b*) solid fuel made up in a container only for ease of handling as part of the load of a vehicle or ship where the whole of that load so far as it consists of solid fuel is being delivered to a single buyer.

Vending machines

8. Solid fuel shall be sold by means of, or offered or exposed for sale in, a vending machine only if there is displayed on or in the machine—

    (*a*) an indication of the quantity by net weight of the fuel comprised in each item for sale by means of that machine; and

    (*b*) except where the machine is on premises at which the seller carries on business, a statement of the name and address of the seller.

Byelaws

9. A local weights and measures authority may make byelaws, subject to the confirmation of the Secretary of State,—

(a) for securing that on any premises within their area on or from which solid fuel available for purchase in a quantity of 224 pounds or less is sold or kept or exposed for sale there is displayed a notice specifying the price of the fuel,

(b) prohibiting the sale on or from any such premises of any such fuel at a higher price than that so displayed in relation to that fuel, and

(c) prescribing penalties not exceeding level 2 on the standard scale for any offence under such byelaws.

Damping of fuel

10. Any person who with intent to defraud or deceive damps any solid fuel shall be guilty of an offence.

Sale of fuel from vehicles

11.—(1) This paragraph applies to any vehicle which is used on highways for carrying solid fuel for sale, or for delivery after sale; and in this paragraph "container" means any container in which solid fuel is carried on such a vehicle, or is delivered from such a vehicle.

(2) The Secretary of State may by order make provision—

(a) for securing the display on any such vehicle of an indication of the quantities in which solid fuel is made up in containers;

(b) for requiring all containers carried on or delivered from any one vehicle to be made up in the same quantity, or for regulating in any other way the quantities in which they are made up;

(c) for imposing any requirement as to the loading of the vehicle, or the delivery of solid fuel from the vehicle, which appears to the Secretary of State appropriate for securing that purchasers are not misled as to the quantity of fuel they purchase.

(3) An order under sub-paragraph (2) above may—

(a) make provision for any of the purposes mentioned in that sub-paragraph by means of amending, or of applying with or without modifications, or of excluding the application in whole or in part of, any of the preceding paragraphs of this Schedule;

(b) contain such consequential, incidental or supplementary provision, whether of such kinds as aforesaid or otherwise, as appear to the Secretary of State to be expedient;

(c) may in particular make provision, in respect of contraventions of the order for which no penalty is provided by this Act, for the imposition of penalties not exceeding those provided by section 84(6) of this Act for an offence under this Act.

12. An order under section 22 of this Act may amend or repeal any of the preceding paragraphs of this Schedule.

Part II

Weighing of Solid Fuel at Buyer's Request

13. If in the case of any solid fuel sold otherwise than by means of a vending machine the buyer so requests—

(a) with respect to any of that fuel the delivery of which has not at the time of the request been completed, or

(b) if the request is made before the departure from the premises at which the fuel is delivered of the person delivering it, with respect to any of that fuel the delivery of which has been completed but which is still capable of identification,

the seller shall cause the fuel to be weighed by means of suitable weighing equipment in the presence of the buyer and, in the case of any fuel such as is mentioned in sub-paragraph (a) of this paragraph, before the delivery of that fuel is completed; and if this paragraph is contravened, the seller shall be guilty of an offence.

14. Where a request under paragraph 13 above is made in respect of the whole load of a vehicle, the requirements of that paragraph shall be deemed to be satisfied, notwithstanding that the weighing is not done in the presence of the buyer, if the seller causes the vehicle to be check-weighed and the statements of the weights found by the person or persons attending to the check-weighing to be delivered to the buyer.

15. Where after any weighing in pursuance of a request under paragraph 13 above the weight of the solid fuel is found to be not less than that marked on any container in which the fuel was made up or than that stated by the seller in any document delivered to the buyer at or before the delivery of the fuel to him, the buyer shall be liable to repay to the seller all costs reasonably incurred by the seller in connection with the weighing.

PART III

CARRIAGE OF SOLID FUEL BY ROAD

16. This Part of this Schedule shall have effect with respect to the carriage by a road vehicle on a journey any part of which is along a highway of any solid fuel required by paragraph 2 above to be sold only by net weight (in this Part of this Schedule referred to as "relevant goods").

17.—(1) If the vehicle is carrying any relevant goods for delivery to a buyer in pursuance of, or of an agreement for, a sale of a quantity exceeding 224 pounds, then, subject to sub-paragraph (6) below, there shall before the journey begins be delivered to the person in charge of the vehicle a document signed by or on behalf of the seller (in this paragraph referred to as "the delivery document") stating—

 (*a*) the name and address of the seller,
 (*b*) the name of the buyer and the address of the premises to which the goods to which the document relates are being delivered,
 (*c*) the type of those goods,
 (*d*) subject to sub-paragraph (2) below, the aggregate net weight of those goods, and
 (*e*) where any of those goods are made up in containers—
       (i) the number of those containers, and
       (ii) except where the whole of the relevant goods carried on the vehicle are for delivery to a single buyer, and except where the whole of the vehicle's load consists of such solid fuel as is mentioned in paragraph 7(*a*) above, the net weight of the goods in each of those containers;

and if this sub-paragraph is contravened the seller shall be guilty of an offence.

(2) Where the whole of the vehicle's load consists of relevant goods not made up in containers and is being delivered to the same person at the same premises, the statement referred to in sub-paragraph (1)(*d*) above shall not be required at any time while the vehicle is travelling between the place where it was loaded and the nearest suitable and available weighing equipment if the delivery document states that the quantity of the relevant goods is to be expressed by net weight determined by means of that equipment and specifies the place at which the equipment is situated.

(3) In any case to which sub-paragraph (2) above applies, the person in charge of the vehicle at the time when the net weight of the relevant goods is determined shall forthwith add to the delivery document a statement of that net weight, and if he fails so to do he shall be guilty of an offence.

(4) Subject to sub-paragraph (5) below, if the vehicle is carrying relevant goods to which sub-paragraph (1) above applies for delivery to each of two of more buyers—

 (*a*) that sub-paragraph shall apply separately in relation to each of those buyers, and
 (*b*) the relevant goods for delivery to each respectively of those buyers shall be carried on the vehicle made up separately in containers or in separate compartments;

and if paragraph (*b*) of this sub-paragraph is contravened the seller shall be guilty of an offence.

(5) Sub-paragraph (4)(*b*) above shall not apply where the vehicle is constructed or adapted for the mechanical making up in containers of the fuel carried thereon and incorporates weighing equipment approved by the Secretary of State for that purpose.

(6) Sub-paragraph (1) above shall not apply to any goods which to the knowledge of the seller are to be loaded into a ship before their delivery to the buyer.

18.—(1) Subject to sub-paragraph (2) below, if all or any of the relevant goods on the vehicle are being carried in such circumstances that paragraph 17(1) above does not apply, there shall, before the journey begins, be delivered to the person in charge of the vehicle a document signed by or on behalf of the person causing the goods to be carried giving the name and address of the last-mentioned person and containing a statement to the effect that all or part of the relevant goods on the vehicle are goods to which paragraph 17(1) above does not apply, and if this paragraph is contravened the last-mentioned person shall be guilty of an offence.

(2) Sub-paragraph (1) above shall not apply where the total quantity of the relevant goods carried on the vehicle does not exceed 224 pounds.

19. Any document required by paragraph 17 or 18 above shall at all times during the journey be carried by the person for the time being in charge of the vehicle and shall be handed over by him to any other person to whom he hands over the charge of the vehicle in the course of the journey; and in the case of any document such as is mentioned in paragraph 17 above, on the unloading of the goods to which the document relates at the premises to which those goods are to be delivered—

(a) before any of those goods are so unloaded, the document shall be handed over to the buyer, or

(b) if the document cannot be so handed over by reason of the absence of the buyer, it shall be left at some suitable place at those premises;

and if at any time any of the requirements of this paragraph is contravened without reasonable cause, the person in charge of the vehicle at that time shall be guilty of an offence.

Part IV

Carriage of Solid Fuel by Rail

20. Where any seller of solid fuel causes that fuel to be loaded into a rail vehicle by way of, or for the purpose of, the delivery of that fuel to, or to a person nominated in that behalf by, the buyer, and the fuel is not carried on the vehicle made up in containers, then, except where at the time of loading it is known to the seller that before the fuel is delivered to the consignee it is to be loaded into a ship, paragraphs 21 to 25 below shall apply in relation to that vehicle.

21. Subject to paragraphs 22 and 28 below, the vehicle shall not be loaded until its tare weight has been determined or redetermined by means of suitable weighing equipment at the place of loading.

22.—(1) Paragraph 21 above shall not apply to any rail vehicle which forms part of or is intended to form part of a train conveying only fuel destined for a particular generating station, gas works or other industrial undertaking if—

(a) the vehicle is loaded by equipment which weighs the fuel and discharges it directly into the vehicle, or

(b) the buyer has agreed with the seller that the weight of the load shall be ascertained at the vehicle's destination, or

(c) the buyer has agreed to accept as the tare weight of the vehicle a tare weight ascertained not more than three months before the time of loading and the vehicle has marked upon it in durable lettering a statement of the weight so ascertained and of the date and place at which it was ascertained, or

(d) all the vehicles comprised in the train are coupled together in such a manner that they may be weighed while in motion by equipment designed to determine the total weight of the train, and the buyer has agreed with the seller that the total net weight of fuel carried in the train shall be ascertained by deducting the total weight of the train so determined before loading from the total weight thereof so determined when loaded.

(2) Nothing in sub-paragraph (1)(c) above shall afford any exemption from the requirements of paragraph 21 above in the case of a vehicle which has undergone repairs or modification or has suffered substantial damage since its tare weight was last ascertained and marked as mentioned in that sub-paragraph.

23. Subject to paragraph 24 below, as soon as the loading has been completed and the seller has ascertained the weight of the vehicle with its load and the identity of the consignee, the seller shall cause to be attached to the vehicle a document stating—

(a) the name of the seller and the place and date of weighing,

(b) the name of the consignee and the destination of the vehicle,

(c) sufficient particulars to identify the vehicle,

(d) the tare weight of the vehicle as determined or redetermined in pursuance of paragraph 21 above or, if by virtue of paragraph 28 below paragraph 21 does not apply to the vehicle, the tare weight of the vehicle expressed to be as estimated by the seller,

(e) the weight attributed to the solid fuel in the vehicle by the seller for the purpose of calculating its purchase price, and

(f) the type of that fuel.

72–70

24.—(1) Paragraph 23 above shall not apply to any vehicle forming part or intended to form part of any such train as is mentioned in paragraph 22 above, but the seller shall before the departure of the train which includes that vehicle deliver to the authority responsible for railway traffic at the place of loading for carriage on that train a document (in this paragraph and paragraph 25 below referred to as "a train bill") giving the information specified in sub-paragraph (2) below or, in the case of any such train as is mentioned in paragraph 22(1)(*d*) above, sub-paragraph (3) below.

(2) Except in a case to which sub-paragraph (3) below applies, the train bill shall contain the following information—

(*a*) the names of the seller and of the consignee and the destination of the train,

(*b*) sufficient particulars to identify each vehicle in the train,

(*c*) the date and place of loading of each vehicle,

(*d*) a statement of the type of fuel in each vehicle,

(*e*) except in the case of fuel which a buyer has agreed shall be weighed at the train's destination, the weight attributed by the seller to the fuel in each vehicle for the purpose of calculating its purchase price,

(*f*) where any vehicle is not exempted from paragraph 21 above, the tare weight of that vehicle,

(*g*) where any vehicle has been loaded by equipment which weighs fuel and discharges it directly into vehicles, a statement as to the vehicle which has been so loaded,

(*h*) where any vehicle is loaded with fuel the weight of which is to be ascertained at the train's destination, a statement as to the vehicle so loaded,

(*i*) where any vehicle is exempted from paragraph 21 above by reason of paragraph 22(1)(*c*) above, a statement of the tare weight and related particulars marked upon that vehicle, and

(*j*) where any vehicle is so exempt by reason of any certificate or direction under paragraph 28 below, a weight stated to be the seller's estimate of the tare weight of that vehicle.

(3) In the case of any such train as is mentioned in paragraph 22(1)(*d*) above, the train bill shall contain the following information—

(*a*) the names of the seller and the consignee and the destination of the train,

(*b*) the date and place of loading of the train,

(*c*) the number of vehicles in the train,

(*d*) the total net weight of fuel carried in the train,

(*e*) a statement of the type of fuel carried in the train, and

(*f*) a statement that the buyer has agreed that the total net weight of fuel carried in the train shall be ascertained in the manner mentioned in paragraph 22(1)(*d*) above.

(4) If the requirements of sub-paragraph (1) above are contravened, the seller shall be guilty of an offence.

25.—(1) The following provisions of this paragraph apply—

(*a*) in a case where by virtue of paragraph 24 above a train bill is carried, when the train reaches its destination, and

(*b*) in any other case, when the vehicle in question reaches its destination.

(2) The authority responsible for railway traffic at the destination of the train or vehicle, as the case may be, shall—

(*a*) permit the consignee and, subject to the production if so requested of his credentials, any inspector to inspect the document required by paragraph 23 or, as the case may be, 24 above,

(*b*) permit the consignee either to take possession of that document after the train or vehicle is unloaded or to make a copy of the particulars stated therein, and

(*c*) if so requested by the consignee with respect to any such copy which the authority is satisfied is accurate, certify the accuracy thereof,

and if any of the provisions of this sub-paragraph is contravened the authority shall be guilty of an offence.

(3) Subject to sub-paragraphs (5) and (6) below, any of the following persons, that is to say—

(*a*) any inspector, subject to the production if so requested of his credentials, or

(*b*) the consignee, subject to his undertaking to pay any cost reasonably incurred,

may require the vehicle to be weighed either before or after or both before and after it is unloaded, and the vehicle shall be weighed accordingly unless it is certified by or on behalf of the authority mentioned in sub-paragraph (2) above that in the circumstances of the particular case the carrying out of the weighing would cause undue dislocation of railway traffic at the vehicle's destination; and any inspector who is present at any such weighing shall if so requested certify the weight found.

(4) If when the fuel is unloaded from the vehicle it is weighed accurately with accurate weighing equipment in the presence of an inspector, the inspector shall if so requested certify that it was so weighed and state in his certificate the weight found.

(5) Where by virtue of paragraph 24 above a train bill is carried and the buyer has agreed that the weight of the fuel in any vehicle is to be ascertained at the train's destination, sub-paragraph (3) above shall not apply in relation to that vehicle.

(6) In a case falling within paragraph 22(1)(*d*) above, sub-paragraph (3) above shall have effect—

> (*a*) with the omission of paragraph (*b*), and
> (*b*) as if any reference to a vehicle were a reference to a train.

26. Where, in the case of any rail vehicle used on a journey to carry solid fuel which is not made up in containers, paragraphs 21 to 25 above do not apply, the consignor shall cause to be attached to the vehicle before it starts on the journey a document stating the name of the consignor and the place of loading of the vehicle.

27.—(1) If paragraph 21 or 23 above is contravened, the seller shall be guilty of an offence.

(2) If paragraph 26 above is contravened, the consignor shall be guilty of an offence.

(3) If, in the case of any rail vehicle used on a journey to carry solid fuel—

> (*a*) the authority responsible for railway traffic at the place of loading or any person employed by that authority wilfully prevents or impedes the attachment to the vehicle of the document required by paragraph 23 or 26 above, or
> (*b*) any person, being a person concerned in the sale, carriage or delivery of that fuel, wilfully removes, defaces or alters any such document attached to the vehicle,

that authority or person shall be guilty of an offence.

28.—(1) Paragraph 21 above shall not apply to any rail vehicle loaded at a mine of coal with respect to which it is certified by or on behalf of the National Coal Board—

> (*a*) that in no year is the aggregate amount of solid fuel loaded as mentioned in paragraph 20 above likely to exceed 224 million pounds; or
> (*b*) that owing to a shortage of rail vehicles compliance with paragraph 21 above would for the time being cause undue dislocation of the working of the mine.

(2) If any seller of solid fuel who uses any place, other than a mine to which sub-paragraph (1) above applies, for causing solid fuel to be loaded as mentioned in paragraph 20 above makes representations to the Secretary of State that the provision at that place of weighing equipment suitable for determining the tare weight of rail vehicles is not reasonably practicable or would be unjustified on economic grounds and the Secretary of State is satisfied that there are grounds for those representations, the Secretary of State may direct, that subject to such conditions and for such period as may be specified in the direction, paragraph 21 above shall not apply to any vehicle loaded at that place.

(3) The National Coal Board shall cause notice in writing to be given forthwith to the local weights and measures authority within whose area the mine in question is situated of the issue or withdrawal of any certificate such as is mentioned in sub-paragraph (1)(*b*) above, and if without reasonable cause they fail so to do they shall be guilty of an offence.

Section 21   SCHEDULE 6

                    MISCELLANEOUS GOODS OTHER THAN FOODS

                                   PART I

                          LIQUID FUEL AND LUBRICANTS

1. This Part of this Schedule applies to—

> (*a*) liquid fuel, lubricating oil and any mixture of such fuel and oil, and
> (*b*) lubricating grease.

2. Subject to paragraph 3 below, goods to which this Part of this Schedule applies—

> (*a*) unless pre-packed, shall be sold only by net weight or by capacity measurement,
> (*b*) shall be pre-packed only if the container is marked with an indication of quantity either by net weight or by capacity measurement, and
> (*c*) in the case of lubricating oil in a quantity of one quart or less, shall be made up

in a container for sale otherwise than by way of pre-packing only if the container is marked with an indication of quantity by capacity measurement.

3. Notwithstanding anything in paragraph 2 above, liquid fuel—

    (a) when not pre-packed may be sold by volume, and

    (b) may be pre-packed in a container marked with an indication of quantity by volume,

being in either case the volume of the gas which would be produced from the fuel in question at such temperature and such atmospheric pressure as are specified in regulations made by the Secretary of State with respect to fuel of the type in question or, if no such regulations are in force, as may be made known by the seller to the buyer before he pays for or takes possession of the fuel; and there shall be exempted from all requirements of paragraph 2 above goods of any description in a quantity of less than half a pound or of less than half a pint.

Part II

Ready-Mixed Cement Mortar and Ready-Mixed Concrete

4. This Part of this Schedule applies to ready-mixed cement mortar and ready-mixed concrete.

5.—(1) Subject to the following provisions of this Part of this Schedule, any goods to which this Part of this Schedule applies shall be sold only by volume in a multiple of 0·1 cubic metre.

(2) There shall be exempted from the requirements of this paragraph any goods in a quantity of less than one cubic metre.

6. Part II of Schedule 4 to this Act, except sub-paragraph (3) of paragraph 7, shall apply for the purposes of this Part of this Schedule as if—

    (a) any reference in the said Part II to ballast included a reference to goods to which this Part of this Schedule applies; and

    (b) the reference in sub-paragraph (1) of paragraph 7 to paragraph 2 of Schedule 4 were a reference to paragraph 5 of this Schedule.

7. Paragraphs 5 and 6 above shall not have effect in any area in Scotland specified by the Secretary of State by order.

Part III

Agricultural Liming Materials, Agricultural Salt and Inorganic Fertilisers

8. This Part of this Schedule applies—

    (a) to agricultural liming materials, other than calcareous sand,

    (b) to agricultural salt,

    (c) to, and to any mixture consisting mainly of, inorganic fertilisers, other than such fertilisers or such a mixture made up into pellets or other articles for use as individual items, and

    (d) to any mixture of any of the foregoing.

9.—(1) Goods to which this Part of this Schedule applies which are not pre-packed, other than liquid fertilisers, shall be sold only by quantity, being—

    (a) quantity by net weight; or

    (b) if the goods are sold in a container which does not exceed the permitted weight and the gross weight of the goods is not less than fifty-six pounds, quantity either by net weight or by gross weight; or

    (c) quantity by volume.

(2) Goods to which this Part of this Schedule applies shall be pre-packed only if the container is marked with an indication of quantity, being—

    (a) in the case of liquid fertilisers, quantity by capacity measurement;

    (b) in any other case, quantity by net weight or, if the container does not exceed the permitted weight and the gross weight of the goods is not less than fifty-six pounds, quantity either by net weight or by gross weight.

(3) In this paragraph, "the permitted weight" means a weight at the rate of twenty-four ounces per 112 pounds of the gross weight.

(4) There shall be exempted from all requirements of this paragraph any sale of goods with a view to their industrial use.

10. Paragraphs 4 and 5 of Schedule 4 to this Act shall have effect as if any reference in those paragraphs to ballast included a reference to any goods to which this Part of this Schedule applies.

PART IV

WOOD FUEL

11. Subject to paragraphs 12 and 13 below—
> (*a*) wood fuel which is not made up in a container for sale shall be sold by retail only by net weight;
> (*b*) in the case of a sale by retail of wood fuel made up in a container for sale, the quantity by net weight of the fuel sold shall be made known to the buyer before he pays for or takes possession of it.

12.—(1) Paragraph 11 above shall not have effect in any area unless the local weights and measures authority for that area so direct by byelaw.

(2) Not less than one month before making any byelaw by virtue of this paragraph, the local weights and measures authority shall give public notice of their intention to make it by advertisement in one or more newspapers circulating in the area to which the byelaw is to apply.

(3) The local weights and measures authority by whom any byelaw is made by virtue of this paragraph shall give notice of the making of the byelaw to the Secretary of State.

13. There shall be exempted from the requirements of paragraph 11 above any sale of wood fuel in a quantity which does not exceed fourteen pounds or which exceeds 1120 pounds.

14. Paragraphs 9 and 10 of Schedule 5 to this Act shall have effect as if any reference in those paragraphs to solid fuel included a reference to wood fuel.

PART V

PERFUMERY AND TOILET PREPARATIONS

15. This Part of this Schedule applies to goods of any of the following descriptions, that is to say—
> (*a*) perfumes and toilet waters,
> (*b*) other toilet preparations for use on the hair or scalp of human beings,
> (*c*) other toilet preparations for external use on any other part of the human body, and
> (*d*) dentifrices other than dentifrices pre-packed in tubes,

whether in liquid, solid or any other form, including any such goods which are medicated but are not pharmaceutical preparations, but excluding soap in any form.

16.—(1) Subject to sub-paragraph (2) below, goods to which this Part of this Schedule applies shall be pre-packed only if the container is marked with an indication of quantity either by net weight or by volume.

(2) There shall be exempted from the requirements of sub-paragraph (1) above—
> (*a*) any goods such as are mentioned in sub-paragraph (*a*) of paragraph 15 above in a quantity not exceeding twelve grams or not exceeding twenty cubic centimetres,
> (*b*) any goods such as are mentioned in sub-paragraph (*b*) of paragraph 15 above in a quantity not exceeding twenty grams or not exceeding twenty cubic centimetres, and
> (*c*) any goods such as are mentioned in sub-paragraph (*c*) or (*d*) of paragraph 15 above in a quantity not exceeding twelve grams or not exceeding twelve cubic centimetres.

PART VI

SOAP

17. Subject to paragraph 18 below—
> (*a*) soap in the form of a cake, tablet or bar shall be pre-packed only if the container is marked with an indication of quantity by net weight,
> (*b*) liquid soap shall be pre-packed only if the container is marked with an indication of quantity by capacity measurement, and
> (*c*) soap in any other form—

(i) unless pre-packed, shall be sold by retail only by net weight, and

(ii) shall be pre-packed only if the container is marked with an indication of quantity by net weight.

18. There shall be exempted from the requirements of this Part of this Schedule—

    (*a*) liquid soap in a quantity of less than five fluid ounces, and

    (*b*) soap in any other form in a quantity of less than one ounce.

Part VII

Miscellaneous Goods to be Sold by or Marked with Length

19. This Part of this Schedule applies to goods of any of the following descriptions, that is to say, bias binding, elastic, ribbon, tape and sewing thread.

20. Subject to paragraph 21 below, goods to which this Part of this Schedule applies—

    (*a*) unless pre-packed, shall be sold by retail only by length, and

    (*b*) shall be pre-packed only if the container is marked with an indication of quantity by length.

21. There shall be exempted from all requirements of paragraph 20 above goods of any description in a quantity of less than one yard.

Part VIII

Miscellaneous Goods to be Sold by or Marked with Net Weight

22. This Part of this Schedule applies to—

    (*a*) distemper,

    (*b*) articles offered as feed for household pets, being manufactured feed or bird feed, other than animal feed in biscuit or cake form pre-packed in a quantity by number not exceeding sixteen,

    (*c*) nails,

    (*d*) paste paint,

    (*e*) seeds, other than pea or bean seeds, and

    (*f*) rolled oats.

23. Subject to paragraphs 24 and 25 below, goods to which this Part of this Schedule applies—

    (*a*) unless pre-packed, shall be sold by retail only by net weight, and

    (*b*) shall be pre-packed only if the container is marked with an indication of quantity by net weight.

24. There shall be exempted from all requirements of this Part of this Schedule—

    (*a*) any of the following in a quantity of less than half a pound, that is to say, distemper and paste paint,

    (*b*) bird seed in a quantity of less than four ounces, and other seeds in a quantity of less than half an ounce,

    (*c*) nails in a quantity of less than half an ounce, and

    (*d*) any other goods in a quantity of less than one ounce.

25. Notwithstanding anything in paragraph 24 above, nails—

    (*a*) when not pre-packed may be sold by retail by number, and

    (*b*) may be pre-packed in or on a container marked with an indication of quantity by number.

Part IX

Miscellaneous Goods to be Marked when Pre-Packed with Net Weight

26. This Part of this Schedule applies to—

    (*a*) Portland cement,

    (*b*) cleansing powders and scouring powders,

    (*c*) detergents, other than liquid detergents, and

    (*d*) paint remover, other than liquid paint remover.

27. Subject to paragraph 28 below, goods to which this Part of this Schedule applies shall be pre-packed only if the container is marked with an indication of quantity by net weight.

28. There shall be exempted from the requirements of this Part of this Schedule goods of any description in a quantity of less than one ounce.

Part X

Miscellaneous Goods to be Sold by or Marked with Capacity Measurement

29. This Part of this Schedule applies to antifreeze fluid for internal combustion engines, linseed oil, paint (other than paste paint), paint thinner, turpentine, turpentine substitute, varnish, and wood preservative fluid (including fungicides and insecticides).

30. Subject to paragraph 31 below, goods to which this Part of this Schedule applies—
   (a) unless pre-packed, shall be sold by retail only by capacity measurement, and
   (b) shall be pre-packed only if the container is marked with an indication of quantity by capacity measurement.

31. There shall be exempted from all requirements of this Part of this Schedule goods of any description in a quantity of less than five fluid ounces.

Part XI

Miscellaneous Goods to be Marked when Pre-Packed with Capacity Measurement

32. This Part of this Schedule applies to enamel, lacquer, liquid detergents, liquid paint remover, petrifying fluid and rust remover.

33. Subject to paragraph 34 below, goods to which this Part of this Schedule applies shall be pre-packed only if the container is marked with an indication of quantity by capacity measurement.

34. There shall be exempted from the requirements of this Part of this Schedule goods of any description in a quantity of less than five fluid ounces.

Part XII

Miscellaneous Goods to be Sold by or Marked With Net Weight or Capacity Measurement

35. This Part of this Schedule applies to—
   (a) polishes,
   (b) dressings, analogous to polishes, and
   (c) pea seeds and bean seeds.

36. Subject to paragraph 37 below, goods to which this Part of this Schedule applies—
   (a) unless pre-packed, shall be sold by retail only by net weight or by capacity measurement, and
   (b) shall be pre-packed only if the container is marked with an indication of quantity either by net weight or by capacity measurement.

37. The following shall be exempted from all the requirements of this Part of this Schedule, that is to say—
   (a) pea or bean seeds in a quantity of less than half a pound or of less than half a pint, and
   (b) any other goods in a quantity of less than one ounce or of less than one fluid ounce.

Part XIII

Miscellaneous Goods to be Marked When Pre-Packed With Quantity by Number

38. This Part of this Schedule applies—
   (a) to cheroots, cigarettes and cigars,
   (b) to postal stationery, that is to say, paper or cards for use in correspondence, and envelopes,
   (c) to, and to any mixture consisting mainly of, inorganic fertilisers, being such fertilisers or such a mixture made up into pellets or other articles for use as individual items, and
   (d) to manufactured animal feed in biscuit or cake form pre-packed in a quantity by number of sixteen or less.

39. Subject to paragraphs 40 and 41 below, goods to which this Part of this Schedule applies shall be pre-packed only if the container is marked with an indication of quantity by number.

40. In relation to postal stationery, the reference to number in paragraph 39 above shall be construed as a reference to the number of sheets of paper, cards or envelopes, as the case

may be, in the pad, confining band or other form of container; and postal stationery shall be exempted from the requirements of that paragraph if pre-packed as part of a collection of articles made up for sale together and including any article other than postal stationery and blotting or other paper.

41. There shall be exempted from the requirements of this Part of this Schedule any goods in a quantity by number of one.

SCHEDULE 7

COMPOSITE GOODS AND COLLECTIONS OF ARTICLES

1.—(1) This paragraph applies to any goods which, not being pre-packed, and not themselves being goods—
  (a) required by or under Part IV of this Act, except this paragraph, to be sold (whether on any sale or on a sale of any particular description) only by quantity expressed in a particular manner, or
  (b) on a sale of which (whether any sale or a sale of any particular description) the quantity of the goods sold expressed in a particular manner is required by or under Part IV of this Act, except this paragraph, to be made known to the buyer at or before a particular time, or
  (c) expressly exempted by or under Part IV of this Act, except this paragraph, from all such requirements as mentioned in paragraph (a) or (b) above which would otherwise apply to them,
consist of a mixture constituted wholly or mainly of goods of one or more descriptions to which there applies any such requirement made by reference to any of the following (whether exclusively or otherwise), that is to say, weight, capacity measurement or volume.

(2) Subject to paragraph 5 below, goods to which this paragraph applies shall be sold only by net weight or by capacity measurement or by volume.

2.—(1) This paragraph applies to any goods which, not being aerosol products and not themselves being goods—
  (a) required by or under Part IV of this Act, except this paragraph, to be pre-packed only if the container is marked with an indication of quantity, or
  (b) in the case of which when sold pre-packed (whether on any sale or on a sale of any particular description) the quantity of the goods sold expressed in a particular manner is required by or under Part IV of this Act, except this paragraph, to be made known to the buyer at or before a particular time, or
  (c) expressly exempted by or under Part IV of this Act, except this paragraph, from all such requirements as mentioned in paragraph (a) or (b) above which would otherwise apply to them,
consist of a mixture constituted wholly or mainly of goods of one or more descriptions to which there applies any such requirement made by reference to any of the following (whether exclusively or otherwise), that is to say, weight, capacity measurement or volume.

(2) Subject to paragraph 5 below, goods to which this paragraph applies shall be pre-packed only if the container is marked with an indication of quantity either by net weight or by capacity measurement or by volume.

3.—(1) This paragraph applies to aerosol products containing any goods required by or under Part IV of this Act, except this paragraph, to be pre-packed only if the container is marked with an indication of quantity expressed in a particular manner.

(2) Subject to paragraph 5 below, any aerosol product to which this paragraph applies shall be pre-packed only if the container is marked with an indication of the quantity by net weight of the entire contents of the container.

4.—(1) This paragraph applies to any collection of two or more items which, not itself being—
  (a) required by or under Part IV of this Act, except this paragraph, to be pre-packed only if the container is marked with particular information, or
  (b) expressly exempted by or under Part IV of this Act, except this paragraph, from any such requirement which would otherwise apply to it,
contains one or more articles to which any such requirement applies.

(2) Any collection to which this paragraph applies shall be pre-packed only if—
  (a) the container in which the collection is pre-packed is marked with an indication of the quantity of each of any such articles as mentioned in sub-paragraph (1) above contained in it, or
  (b) each of any such articles contained in the container is made up in an individual container marked with an indication of quantity,

being in either case the like indication of the quantity of each respectively of those articles as would have been required if that article had itself been pre-packed.

5. There shall be exempted from any requirement of paragraph 1, 2 or 3 above food of any description in a quantity of less than five grams or of less than five millilitres and goods of any other description in a quantity of less than one ounce or of less than one fluid ounce.

Section 53   SCHEDULE 8

POWERS OF INSPECTORS AND LOCAL WEIGHTS AND MEASURES AUTHORITY UNDER PART V

Powers of entry and inspection

1. An inspector may, within the area for which he is appointed an inspector and on production if so requested of his credentials, at all reasonable times—
   (*a*) enter any premises (except premises used only as a private dwelling-house) as to which he has reasonable cause to believe that packages are made up on the premises or that imported packages belonging to the importer of them are on the premises or that regulated packages intended for sale are on the premises;
   (*b*) inspect and test any equipment which he has reasonable cause to believe is used in making up packages in the United Kingdom or in carrying out a check mentioned in subsections (1) and (2) of section 49 of this Act;
   (*c*) inspect, and measure in such manner as he thinks fit, any thing which he has reasonable cause to believe is or contains or is contained in a package and, if he considers it necessary to do so for the purpose of inspecting the thing or anything in it, break it open;
   (*d*) inspect and take copies of, or of any thing purporting to be, a record, document or certificate mentioned in section 48(2) and subsections (1) to (3) of section 49 of this Act;
   (*e*) require any person on premises which the inspector is authorised to enter by virtue of paragraph (*a*) of this paragraph to provide such assistance as the inspector reasonably considers necessary to enable the inspector to exercise effectively any power conferred on him by paragraphs (*a*) to (*d*) above;
   (*f*) require any person to give to the inspector such information as the person possesses about the name and address of the packer and of any importer of a package which the inspector finds on premises he has entered by virtue of this paragraph or paragraph 2 below.
2. If a justice of the peace, on sworn information in writing—
   (*a*) is satisfied that there is reasonable ground to believe that—
         (i) a package or a thing containing a package, or
         (ii) any such equipment, record, document or certificate as is mentioned in paragraph 1 above,
      is on any premises or that an offence under section 50 or 63 of this Act is being or is about to be committed on any premises, and
   (*b*) is also satisfied either—
         (i) that admission to the premises has been refused or that a refusal is apprehended and that notice of the intention to apply for a warrant has been given to the occupier, or
         (ii) that an application for admission or the giving of such a notice would defeat the object of the entry or that the premises are unoccupied or that the occupier is temporarily absent and it might defeat the object of the entry to await his return,
the justice may by warrant under his hand, which shall continue in force for a period of one month, authorise an inspector to enter the premises if need be by force.
   In the application of this paragraph to Scotland "justice of the peace" includes a sheriff.
3.—(1) An inspector entering any premises by virtue of paragraph 1 or 2 above may take with him such other persons and such equipment as he considers necessary.
   (2) It shall be the duty of an inspector who leaves premises which he has entered by virtue of paragraph 2 above and which are unoccupied or from which the occupier is temporarily absent to leave the premises as effectively secured against trespassers as he found them.

Power of seizure

4. Where an inspector has reasonable cause to believe that an offence under section 50, 54 or 63 of this Act or this Schedule has been committed and that any equipment, record,

document, package or thing containing or contained in a package may be required as evidence in proceedings for the offence he may seize it and detain it for as long as it is so required.

Power to require information

5.—(1) An inspector may serve, on any person carrying on business as the packer or importer of packages in the area for which the inspector is appointed an inspector, a notice requiring that person—
  (a) to furnish the inspector from time to time with particulars of the kind specified in the notice of any marks which, otherwise than in pursuance of section 48(1)(c) of this Act, are applied from time to time to packages made up in that area by that person or (as the case may be) to packages imported by him, for the purpose of enabling the place where the packages were made up to be ascertained, and
  (b) if the person has furnished particulars of a mark in pursuance of the notice and the mark ceases to be applied to such packages for that purpose, to give notice of the cesser to the inspector.
(2) A notice given by an inspector under this paragraph shall not require a person to furnish information which he does not possess.

Purchase of goods

6.—(1) A local weights and measures authority shall have power to purchase goods, and to authorise any of its officers to purchase goods on behalf of the authority, for the purpose of ascertaining whether an offence under section 50, 54(2) or 63 of this Act has been committed.
(2) If an inspector breaks open a package in pursuance of paragraph 1(c) above otherwise than on premises occupied by the packer or importer of the package and the package is not inadequate, it shall be the duty of the inspector, if the owner of the package requests him to do so, to buy the package on behalf of the local weights and measures authority for the area in which he broke it open.

Failure to provide assistance or information

7. Any person who without reasonable cause fails to comply with a requirement made of him in pursuance of paragraph 1(e) or (f) or 5 above shall be guilty of an offence.

Section 55(4)   SCHEDULE 9

Provisions Relating to constitution of National Metrological Co-ordinating Unit

Tenure of members

1.—(1) Subject to paragraph 2 below, a member shall hold office as a member until the Secretary of State gives him notice that his appointment as a member is terminated.
(2) Without prejudice to the generality of the Secretary of State's power to give notices in pursuance of sub-paragraph (1) above, it shall be his duty to give a member such a notice if the Secretary of State is satisfied that the member is no longer a member of any local authority.
2. A person may at any time resign his office as a member by giving to the Secretary of State a notice signed by that person and stating that he resigns that office.

Proceedings

3. The quorum of the Unit and the arrangements relating to meetings of the Unit shall be such as the Unit may determine.
4. The validity of any proceedings of the Unit shall not be affected by any vacancy among the members or by any defect in the appointment of a member.

Chairman

5. The Unit may appoint a member to be the chairman of the Unit and may terminate an appointment made in pursuance of this paragraph.

6. A person shall cease to hold office as the chairman of the Unit if he ceases to be a member.

Staff

7. The Unit may employ, on such terms as are applicable to comparable employment in the service of a local authority, such persons as are needed to assist the Unit in the performance of its functions.

Instruments

8. The fixing of the common seal of the Unit shall be authenticated by the signature of the chairman or of any other member authorised by the Unit to authenticate it.

9. A document purporting to be duly executed under the seal of the Unit shall be received in evidence and shall, unless the contrary is proved, be deemed to be so executed.

Interpretation

10. In this Schedule—

"member", except in relation to a local authority, means member of the Unit; and

"local authority" has the meaning given by section 55(3) of this Act.

Section 95   SCHEDULE 10

PROVISIONS RELATING TO NORTHERN IRELAND

PART I

PROVISIONS OF THIS ACT EXTENDING TO NORTHERN IRELAND

1. The following provisions of this Act shall extend to Northern Ireland—

(*a*) sections 1 and 2,

(*b*) section 3 so far as it relates to the coinage standards,

(*c*) section 92,

(*d*) section 93 so far as it relates to regulations under section 7 of the Food Act 1984 which, by virtue of sections 7(3) and 135 of that Act, apply to Northern Ireland,

(*e*) Schedules 1 and 2,

(*f*) so much of any other provision of this Act as relates to the interpretation of the provisions mentioned in paragraphs (*a*) to (*e*) above or to the making, variation or revocation of any order under this Act which by virtue of this paragraph extends to Northern Ireland,

(*g*) section 95 and this Schedule,

(*h*) paragraph 22 of Schedule 11 and section 96 so far as it relates to that paragraph,

(*i*) paragraph 10 of Schedule 12 and section 97 so far as it relates to that paragraph,

(*j*) section 98(1) and Part I of Schedule 13 so far as they relate to enactments which extend to Northern Ireland,

(*k*) section 98(2) and Part II of Schedule 13 so far as they relate to —

(i) regulation 13 of, and Schedule 4 to, the Units of Measurement Regulations 1980, or

(ii) regulation 4 of the Units of Measurement Regulations 1985, and

(*l*) section 99.

PART II

STANDARDS IN NORTHERN IRELAND

2.—(1) The Department of Economic Development for Northern Ireland may by order direct that there shall be standards for Northern Ireland of the yard, pound, metre and kilogram which shall be, and shall be known as, the Northern Ireland primary standards.

(2) No order shall be made under this paragraph unless a draft of the order has been laid before, and approved by a resolution of, the Northern Ireland Assembly.

3. For the purposes of providing the Northern Ireland primary standards in pursuance of such an order, the Department of Economic Development for Northern Ireland shall cause

to be made, in such manner as the Department may direct, copies in such form and of such material as the Department may think fit of the United Kingdom primary standards, and those copies shall be the Northern Ireland primary standards.

4. The Secretary of State shall from time to time as the Department of Economic Development for Northern Ireland may think it expedient to require, and at the expense of the Department, cause any Northern Ireland primary standard to be compared with, and its value redetermined by reference to, the corresponding United Kingdom primary standard in such manner as the Secretary of State may direct.

5. Any Northern Ireland primary standard maintained under this Part of this Schedule shall be in the custody of the Department of Economic Development for Northern Ireland.

Section 96(1)   SCHEDULE 11

Transitional Provisions and Savings

General

1. In this Schedule—
    "the 1963 Act" means the Weights and Measures Act 1963;
    "the commencement of this Act" means the commencement of the provisions of this Act other than section 43.

2. Any reference, whether express or implied, in any enactment, instrument or document (including this Act and any enactment amended by Schedule 12 to this Act) to, or to things done or falling to be done under or for the purposes of, any provision of this Act shall, if and so far as the context permits, be construed as including, in relation to times, circumstances and purposes before the commencement of this Act, a reference to, or to things done or falling to be done under or for the purposes of, the corresponding provision repealed by this Act.

3. Any reference, whether express or implied, in any enactment, instrument or document to, or to things done or falling to be done under or for the purposes of, any provision reproduced in this Act shall be construed, so far as is required for retaining for the enactment, instrument or document the same force and effect as it would have had but for the passing of this Act (and subject to any express amendment made by this Act) as being, or as the case may require including, a reference to, or to things done or falling to be done under or for the purposes of, the corresponding provision of this Act.

4. Where a period of time specified in an enactment repealed by this Act is current at the commencement of this Act, this Act has effect as if the corresponding provision of this Act had been in force when that period began to run.

Acts passed before 31st July 1963

5. In any Act passed before 31st July 1963—
    (*a*) any reference to local authorities for the purposes of the Weights and Measures Acts 1878 to 1963 shall continue to be construed as a reference to local weights and measures authorities, and
    (*b*) any reference to an inspector of weights and measures shall continue to be construed as a reference to an inspector within the meaning of this Act.

6. Any local Act passed before 31st July 1963 shall continue to be construed—
    (*a*) as not making unlawful the use for trade, as equipment to which section 11 of this Act applies, of any article of which such use is not unlawful under that section, and
    (*b*) as not requiring any such article to be stamped otherwise than as required by that section.

7. Where an enactment contained in any local Act passed before 31st July 1963 appears to the Secretary of State to have been superseded by, or to be inconsistent with, any of the provisions of the 1963 Act re-enacted in this Act, or any instrument made under those provisions, the Secretary of State may by order, a draft of which shall be laid before Parliament, specify that enactment for the purposes of this paragraph and, without prejudice to the operation in the meantime of any rule of law relating to the effect on any such enactment of any such provision, any enactment specified in the order shall be repealed as from the date of the making of the order.

Standards, etc.

8. Any standard which immediately before the commencement of this Act was deemed by virtue of subsection (6) of section 3 of the 1963 Act to be a secondary, tertiary or coinage

standard provided under that section shall be deemed to be a secondary, tertiary or coinage standard, as the case may be, for the purposes of this Act.

9. A certificate of fitness for use as a local standard issued under section 4(4) of the 1963 Act which was in force both on 4th October 1979 and immediately before the commencement of this Act shall cease to be in force at the expiration of the period of ten years from the date of issue of the certificate.

Stamping of equipment

10. Any equipment to which section 11 of this Act applies which immediately before the commencement of this Act was treated as having been duly stamped under section 11 of the 1963 Act by virtue of subsection (7) of that section shall for the purposes of this Act be treated as having been duly stamped under section 11 of this Act.

Approved patterns of equipment

11.—(1) Each of the following instruments, namely—
   (a) a certificate of approval granted under section 12 of the 1963 Act before 4th April 1979 and in force immediately before the commencement of this Act,
       (b) an authorisation of modifications granted under that section before 4th April 1979 and in force immediately before the commencement of this Act,
       (c) a certificate which was deemed by virtue of section 12(5) of the 1963 Act to be a certificate of approval granted under section 12 and which was in force immediately before the commencement of this Act,

shall continue to have effect as if it were a certificate of approval granted under section 12 of the 1963 Act on 4th April 1979 and, in the case of a certificate of approval actually granted subject to a condition relating to a specified period, as if that condition had been imposed under section 12A(1)(*b*) of the 1963 Act and provided for the certificate to cease to be in force at the end of a period equal to that period and beginning with the day when the certificate was actually granted.

(2) The power conferred by section 12(10) of this Act to revoke a certificate of approval of a pattern shall, in the case of a certificate in respect of which an authorisation of modifications has effect by virtue of sub-paragraph (1) above as if it were a further certificate of approval, include power to revoke the original certificate as it has effect apart from the modifications without revoking it as it has effect with the modifications.

Weighing equipment passed etc. before 27th April 1978

12.—(1) Weighing equipment (including weights) which weighs wholly or partly in drams may continue to be used for trade if it was first passed as fit for use for trade and stamped in accordance with the 1963 Act before 27th April 1978.

(2) Nothing in sub-paragraph (1) above shall be taken as authorising the continued use for trade of the dram except in so far as the weight of the goods in drams or partly in drams is treated as having been made known to a prospective buyer by virtue of sections 45(1)(*a*) and 46 of this Act.

(3) Products and equipment necessary to complete or replace components or parts of equipment the continued use of which is authorised by sub-paragraph (1) above may be manufactured, placed on the market and used after the commencement of this Act, but this sub-paragraph shall not permit the replacement of weights, whether or not the weights form part of other weighing equipment.

(4) Without prejudice to sub-paragraphs (1) and (2) above, every pattern of weighing equipment—
       (a) the certificate of approval in respect of which was, or is deemed to have been, granted under section 12 of the 1963 Act and was in force immediately before 27th April 1978, and
       (b) which provides for weighing to be made wholly or partly in drams,
(including a pattern modified in accordance with an authorisation for the time being in force under that section) shall continue to be deemed modified to the extent necessary to require equipment of that pattern to weigh in fractions of an ounce in substitution for drams and fractions of a dram.

Products and equipment used etc. before 1st December 1980

13.—(1) Nothing in section 8 of this Act shall prevent any of the units of measurement mentioned in sub-paragraph (2) below being used for products or equipment which were placed on the market or used before 1st December 1980, other than weighing or measuring equipment (including weights).

(2) The units of measurement referred to in sub-paragraph (1) above are the chain, furlong, rood, square mile, square inch, cubic yard, cubic foot, cubic inch, ton, hundredweight, cental, quarter, stone, dram, grain and quintal.

14.—(1) Weighing equipment (including weights) which weighs wholly or partly in grains, stones, quarters, hundredweights or tons may continue to be used for trade if, in the case of equipment prescribed for the purposes of section 11 of this Act, it was first passed as fit for use for trade and where necessary stamped in accordance with the 1963 Act before 1st December 1980 or if, in the case of equipment not so prescribed, it was placed on the market and used before that date.

(2) Measuring equipment measuring in square inches, cubic inches or cubic feet may continue to be used for trade if it was placed on the market and used before 1st December 1980.

(3) Nothing in sub-paragraph (1) above shall be taken as authorising the continued use for trade of the grain, stone, quarter, hundredweight or ton except in so far as the weight of the goods in those units or partly in those units is treated as having been made known to a prospective buyer by virtue of sections 45(1)(*a*) and 46 of this Act.

15. Paragraphs 12(1) and 14(1) and (2) above have effect notwithstanding regulation 3 of the Units of Measurement Regulations 1978 (under which certain units are not authorised for use in certain circumstances on or after 27th April 1978) and regulation 8 of the Units of Measurement Regulations 1980 (under which certain units are not authorised for use in certain circumstances on or after 1st September 1980).

16.—(1) Nothing in section 8 of this Act shall prevent any unit of measurement being used for components and parts of products and of equipment necessary to supplement or replace components or parts of products and equipment referred to in paragraph 13(1) or 14(1) or (2) above.

(2) Nothing in regulation 3 of the Units of Measurement Regulations 1978 or in regulation 8 of the Units of Measurement Regulations 1980 shall prevent any unit of measurement being used for components and parts of products and of equipment necessary to supplement or replace components or parts of products and equipment referred to in paragraph 14(1) or (2) above.

17.—(1) This paragraph applies to any pattern of weighing equipment—

(*a*) the certificate of approval in respect of which was, or is deemed to have been, granted under section 12 of the 1963 Act and was in force immediately before 1st December 1980, and

(*b*) which provides for weighing to be made wholly or partly in grains, stones, quarters, hundredweights or tons,

including a pattern modified in accordance with an authorisation of the Secretary of State granted or deemed to have been granted under that section before 4th April 1979 and for the time being in force.

(2) Without prejudice to paragraph 14 above, every pattern of weighing equipment to which this paragraph applies shall continue to be deemed modified to the extent necessary to require equipment of that pattern—

(*a*) to weigh in pounds with scale intervals in the form 1×10^n, 2×10^n or 5×10^n pounds, the index n being a positive or negative whole number or zero, in substitution for stones, quarters, hundredweights or tons or fractions thereof and to have its capacity expressed in pounds, or

(*b*) to weigh in multiples or fractions of an ounce troy in substitution for grains or fractions thereof and to have its capacity expressed in ounces troy.

Joint local weights and measures authorities in Greater London

18.—(1) This paragraph applies to any agreement which—

(*a*) was made under section 37 of the 1963 Act before 1st April 1974 by two or more local weights and measures authorities for areas within Greater London, and

(*b*) was in force immediately before the commencement of this Act.

(2) The repeal by this Act of section 37 of the 1963 Act, and of the provisions enabling an agreement under that section to relate to functions of a local weights and measures authority under the Trade Descriptions Act 1968, section 25 of the Agriculture Act 1970 and Part II of the Fair Trading Act 1973, shall not affect any agreement to which this paragraph applies.

(3) The parties to an agreement to which this paragraph applies shall cause notice in writing to be given to the Secretary of State of any variation from time to time made in the agreement and, if the agreement ceases to have effect, of its cessation.

(4) Where an agreement to which this paragraph applies has effect in relation to functions of a local weights and measures authority under sections 4, 5 or 72 of this Act, any reference in that section to a local weights and measures authority shall be construed subject to the terms of the agreement.

(5) Where—

(a) two or more local weights and measures authorities are parties to an agreement to which this paragraph applies, and

(b) the agreement relates to all their functions under this Act and to any functions specified in a notice given to them under section 70(1)(b) of this Act and not withdrawn,

those authorities may make a joint report to the Secretary of State under section 70(1) of this Act in respect of any financial year during the whole of which the agreement was in operation.

Relaxation of Ministerial controls

19. Subsection (3) of section 35 of the Local Government Act 1974 (power of Secretary of State to remove or relax control conferred on any Minister etc. on functions of local authorities) shall continue to apply to any such control as is mentioned in that subsection which was conferred on the Board of Trade (subsequently becoming exercisable by the Secretary of State) by any enactment contained in the 1963 Act and re-enacted in this Act.

National Metrological Co-ordinating Unit

20. Any reference to the Secretary of State in the Measuring Container Bottles (EEC Requirements) Regulations 1977 which by virtue of section 7(5) of the Weights and Measures Act 1979 was immediately before the commencement of this Act to be construed as a reference to the National Metrological Co-ordinating Unit shall continue to be construed as a reference to the Unit.

Inspectors

21.—(1) Any person who, immediately before the commencement of section 46 of the 1963 Act, was an inspector of weights and measures appointed under section 43 of the Weights and Measures Act 1878 shall, if immediately before the commencement of this Act he was acting as an inspector for the purposes of the 1963 Act, be deemed to have been appointed an inspector under section 72 of this Act, and any certificate of qualification granted to him under section 8 of the Weights and Measures Act 1904 shall be deemed to be a certificate granted to him under section 73 of this Act.

(2) Nothing in this Act shall prevent any person who immediately before the commencement of this Act was, with the sanction of a local weights and measures authority, acting for any of the purposes of the 1963 Act by virtue of section 46(2) of that Act from continuing to act, with that sanction, for the corresponding purposes of this Act; and so far as may be necessary for the purposes of his so acting any reference in this Act (except Part V)—

(a) to credentials shall, in relation to such a person, be construed as a reference to written authority for him so to act from that authority; and

(b) to an inspector shall, in relation to such a person and except in section 79(3), be construed as a reference to that person while so acting.

"Gallon" and "litre"

22. Nothing in the definition of "gallon" or "litre" in Schedule 1 to this Act affects any contract or agreement entered into before 1st November 1976, notwithstanding that it relates to the delivery of goods after that date.

Byelaws

23. Any byelaws made by a local authority for any of the purposes mentioned in paragraph 9 of Schedule 5 to this Act which immediately before the commencement of this Act were in force by virtue of sub-paragraph (2) of paragraph 5 of Schedule 6 to the 1963 Act shall notwithstanding the repeal by this Act of that sub-paragraph continue in force by virtue of this paragraph; and any authority which immediately before the commencement of this Act had power to revoke any such byelaws to any extent shall continue to have that power.

24. Any provision contained in a byelaw made under paragraph 5 of Schedule 6 to the 1963 Act (including that paragraph as extended to wood fuel by paragraph 4 of Part IV of Schedule 7 to that Act) which—

. (a) immediately before 17th July 1978 (the date of the commencement of section

31(3) of the Criminal Law Act 1977 and section 289C(3) of the Criminal Procedure (Scotland) Act 1975) specified £20 as the maximum fine which might be imposed on summary conviction in respect of a contravention of, or an offence under, any byelaw mentioned in that provision, and

(b) immediately before the commencement of this Act had effect by virtue of either of those sections as if it specified £50 instead,

shall continue to have effect as if it specified £50.

25. Where any byelaw having effect under paragraph 5 of Schedule 6 to, or paragraph 2 or 4 of Part IV of Schedule 7 to, the 1963 Act immediately before the commencement of this Act refers to any of the following units of measurement namely ton, hundredweight, quarter or stone, that reference shall continue to be treated as a reference to the equivalent number of pounds in relation to that unit referred to in Part VI of Schedule 1 to this Act.

SCHEDULE 12

CONSEQUENTIAL AMENDMENTS

The Petroleum (Consolidation) Act 1928

1. In section 20(1) of the Petroleum (Consolidation) Act 1928, for the words "may from time to time prescribe" there shall be substituted the words "may from time to time with the approval of the Treasury determine".

The Agriculture Act 1967

2. In section 8(3) of the Agriculture Act 1967, for paragraph (b) there shall be substituted the following—
"(b) conferring powers of entry on inspectors appointed under section 72 of the Weights and Measures Act 1985,".

The Trade Descriptions Act 1968

3. In section 22(1) of the Trade Descriptions Act 1968—
(a) for the words "Weights and Measures Act 1963" there shall be substituted the words "Weights and Measures Act 1985";
(b) in sub-paragraph (a) for the words "subsection (2) of section 51 of the said Act of 1963" there shall be substituted the words "subsection (3) of section 83 of the said Act of 1985"; and
(c) in sub-paragraph (b) for the words "subsections (2), (3) and (5) to (7) of section 26 of the said Act of 1963" there shall be substituted the words "sections 35, 36 and 37(1) and (2) of the said Act of 1985".

4.—(1) In section 32 of the Trade Descriptions Act 1968—
(a) in paragraph (a) for the words "section 21(5)(b) of the Weights and Measures Act 1963" there shall be substituted the words "section 24(2)(b) of the Weights and Measures Act 1985"; and
(b) for paragraph (d) there shall be substituted the following—
"(d) for industrial use within the meaning of the Weights and Measures Act 1985 or for constructional use;"

(2) At the end of that section there shall be inserted the following—
"(2) In this section "constructional use", in relation to any goods, means the use of those goods in constructional work (or, if the goods are explosives within the meaning of the Explosives Acts 1875 and 1923, in mining, quarrying or demolition work) in the course of the carrying on of a business;".

The Greater London Council (General Powers) Act 1972

5. In section 17(5)(b) of the Greater London Council (General Powers) Act 1972, for the words "Weights and Measures Act 1963" there shall be substituted the words "Weights and Measures Act 1985".

The Fair Trading Act 1973

6. In section 3(5)(b) of the Fair Trading Act 1973, for the words "Weights and Measures Act 1963" there shall be substituted the words "Weights and Measures Act 1985".

The Weights and Measures &c. Act 1976

7.—(1) Section 12 of the Weights and Measures &c. Act 1976 shall be amended as follows.
(2) In subsection (1), for paragraph (*d*) there shall be substituted the following—
"(*d*) section 21, 22 or 23 of the 1985 Act;".
(3) In subsection (9)(*c*), for the words "the 1963 Act" there shall be substituted the words "the 1985 Act".
8. In section 14 of the Weights and Measures &c. Act 1976, for the definition of "the 1963 Act" there shall be substituted the following—
" "the 1985 Act" means the Weights and Measures Act 1985;".
9. In Schedule 6 to the Weights and Measures &c. Act 1976, for paragraph 5 there shall be substituted the following—

"Weights and Measures Act 1985

5.—(1) This paragraph applies where the relevant requirement took effect under or by virtue of the 1985 Act.
(2) The following provisions of that Act—
(*a*) sections 25 to 31 (offences),
(*b*) sections 32 to 37 (liability of third parties and defences),
(*c*) sections 38 to 42 and 44 to 46 (powers of inspectors, etc.), and
(*d*) sections 79 to 83 (further powers of inspectors and prosecution of offences),
shall apply as if the substituted requirement were imposed under Part IV of the Act."

The Weights and Measures (Northern Ireland) Order 1981

10.—(1) The Weights and Measures (Northern Ireland) Order 1981 shall be amended as follows.
(2) In Article 1(3), for the words from "and Article 54(2)" to the end there shall be substituted the words "shall come into operation on such date or dates as may be appointed by the Secretary of State under subsection (2) of section 43 of the Act of 1985 for the coming into force of that section".
. (3) In Article 2(2)—
(*a*) for the definition of "the Act of 1963" there shall be substituted the following—
" "the Act of 1985" means the Weights and Measures Act 1985;", and
(*b*) in the definition of "capacity measurement", for the words "Act of 1963" there shall be substituted the words "Act of 1985".
(4) In Articles 3(3), 4(6), 10(8) and 53(1), for the words "Act of 1963", wherever they occur, there shall be substituted the words "Act of 1985".
(5) In Article 8—
(*a*) in paragraph (3), for the words "Schedule 1 to the Act of 1963" there shall be substituted the words "Schedule 1 to the Act of 1985" and for the words "section 10(6) of the Act of 1963" there shall be substituted the words "section 10(3) of the Act of 1985", and
(*b*) in paragraph (5)(*a*), for the words "which is or on 25th October 1967 was included in Schedule 1 to the Act of 1963", there shall be substituted the words "which is included in Schedule 1 to the Act of 1985 or was on 25th October 1967 included in Schedule 1 to the Weights and Measures Act 1963".
(6) In Article 12(5), for the words "section 13 of the Act of 1963" there shall be substituted the words "section 14 of the Act of 1985".

The Local Government Act 1985

11. In paragraph 15 of Schedule 8 to the Local Government Act 1985—
(*a*) in sub-paragraph (4), after the words "this paragraph" there shall be inserted the words "and section 69(1)(*a*) of the Weights and Measures Act 1985",
(*b*) in sub-paragraph (5), for the words "(1) to (3) above" there shall be substituted the words "(2) and (3) above and the said section 69(1)(*a*)", and
(*c*) at the end of sub-paragraph (6), there shall be inserted the words "and the said section 69(1)(*a*)".

Section 98

SCHEDULE 13

REPEALS AND REVOCATIONS

PART I

REPEALS

Chapter	Short title	Extent of repeal
1963 c.31.	The Weights and Measures Act 1963.	The whole Act.
1968 c.29.	The Trade Descriptions Act 1968.	In section 26(1), the words from "and section 37" to the end.
1970 c.40.	The Agriculture Act 1970.	In section 25, in subsection (3), the words from "and section 37" to "that Act" and, in subsection (5), the words from "shall have effect" to "1963 but".
1972 c.70.	The Local Government Act 1972.	Section 112(4)(*d*). Section 201.
1973 c.41.	The Fair Trading Act 1973.	In section 27(1), the words from "and section 37" to the end.
1973 c.65.	The Local Government (Scotland) Act 1973.	Section 64(5)(*d*). Section 149. In Schedule 25, paragraphs 29, 30 and 31.
1974 c.7.	The Local Government Act 1974.	In Schedule 6, paragraph 15.
1975 c.21.	The Criminal Procedure (Scotland) Act 1975.	Section 289C(2)(*b*).
1976 c.77.	The Weights and Measures &c. Act 1976.	The whole Act, except sections 12 to 14 and 15(1) to (3) and Schedule 6.
1977 c.45.	The Criminal Law Act 1977.	Section 31(2)(*b*).
1979 c.2.	The Customs and Excise Management Act 1979.	In Schedule 4, in paragraph 12, in the Table, the entry relating to the Weights and Measures Act 1963.
1979 c.4.	The Alcoholic Liquor Duties Act 1979.	In Schedule 3, paragraphs 3 and 4.
1979 c.45.	The Weights and Measures Act 1979.	The whole Act.
1980 c.43.	The Magistrates' Courts Act 1980.	In Schedule 7, paragraphs 188 and 189.
1980 c.65.	The Local Government, Planning and Land Act 1980.	In section 1(4), the words "weights and measures and to". In Schedule 4, paragraphs 2 to 9 and 11 and 12.
1984 c.30.	The Food Act 1984.	In Schedule 10, paragraphs 4 and 5.
1985 c.9.	The Companies Consolidation (Consequential Provisions) Act 1985.	In Schedule 2, the entry relating to the Weights and Measures Act 1979.
1985 c.51.	The Local Government Act 1985.	In Schedule 8, paragraph 15(1).

PART II

REVOCATIONS

Number	Title	Extent of revocation
S.I. 1966/238.	The Weights and Measures (Solid Fuel) (Carriage by Rail) Order 1966.	The whole order.
S.I. 1970/1708.	The Weights and Measures Act (Amendment of Schedules 5 and 7) Order 1970.	The whole order.
S.I. 1974/874.	The Weights and Measures Act 1963 (Dentifrices) Order 1974.	Article 2.
S.I. 1978/484.	The Units of Measurement Regulations 1978.	Regulation 4(2) and (3). Regulation 5. Regulation 8.
S.I. 1979/955.	The Weights and Measures (Solid Fuel) (Carriage by Rail) (Amendment) Order 1979.	The whole order.
S.I. 1979/1753.	The Weights and Measures Act 1963 (Solid Fuel) Order 1979.	The whole order.
S.I. 1980/1070.	The Units of Measurement Regulations 1980.	In regulation 9(1), 10(1) and 11, the words "or in Part IV of these Regulations". Regulation 10(2) to (4). In regulation 11, the words "to (3)". Regulation 12. Regulation 13. Regulation 16. Schedule 4. In Schedule 5, the amendments of the Weights and Measures Act 1963.
S.I. 1980/1742.	The Units of Measurement (No. 2) Regulations 1980.	Regulations 2 and 3.
S.I. 1983/1077.	The Weights and Measures Act 1963 (Amendment of Schedule 3) Order 1983.	The whole order.
S.I. 1984/1314.	The Weights and Measures Act 1963 (Intoxicating Liquor) Order 1984.	Article 2.
S.I. 1984/1315.	The Weights and Measures Act 1963 (Cheese, Fish, Fresh Fruits and Vegetables, Meat and Poultry) Order 1984.	Article 3.
S.I. 1984/1316.	The Weights and Measures Act 1963 (Miscellaneous Foods) Order 1984.	Articles 3 and 17.
S.I. 1985/435.	The Weights and Measures (Solid Fuel) (Carriage by Rail) (Amendment) Order 1985.	The whole order.
S.I. 1985/777.	The Units of Measurement Regulations 1985.	Regulations 4.

TABLE OF DERIVATIONS

Notes:
(1) This Table does not take into account transfers of Ministerial functions under the provisions from which the Act is derived.
(2) The following abbreviations are used in this Table:—

1963	=	The Weights and Measures Act 1963 (c.31).
1972 c.70	=	The Local Government Act 1972.
1973 c.36	=	The Northern Ireland Constitution Act 1973.
1973 c.65	=	The Local Government (Scotland) Act 1973.
1974 c.7	=	The Local Government Act 1974.
1975 c.21	=	The Criminal Procedure (Scotland) Act 1975.
1976	=	The Weights and Measures &c. Act 1976 (c.77)
1977 c.45	=	The Criminal Law Act 1977.
1979 c.2	=	The Customs and Excise Management Act 1979.
1979 c.4	=	The Alcoholic Liquor Duties Act 1979.
1979	=	The Weights and Measures Act 1979 (c.45).
1980 c.43	=	The Magistrates' Courts Act 1980.
1980 c.65	=	The Local Government, Planning and Land Act 1980.
1982 c.48	=	The Criminal Justice Act 1982.
1984 c.30	=	The Food Act 1984.
1985 c.9	=	The Companies Consolidation (Consequential Provisions) Act 1985.
1985 c.51	=	The Local Government Act 1985.
S.I. 1966/238	=	The Weights and Measures (Solid Fuel) (Carriage by Rail) Order 1966.
S.I. 1970/1708	=	The Weights and Measures Act (Amendment of Schedules 5 and 7) Order 1970.
S.I. 1974/874	=	The Weights and Measures Act 1963 (Dentifrices) Order 1974.
S.I. 1978/484	=	The Units of Measurement Regulations 1978.
S.I. 1979/955	=	The Weights and Measures (Solid Fuel) (Carriage by Rail) (Amendment) Order 1979.
S.I. 1979/1753	=	The Weights and Measures Act 1963 (Solid Fuel) Order 1979.
S.I. 1980/1070	=	The Units of Measurement Regulations 1980.
S.I. 1980/1742	=	The Units of Measurement (No. 2) Regulations 1980.
S.I. 1983/1077	=	The Weights and Measures Act 1963 (Amendment of Schedule 3) Order 1983.
S.I. 1984/1316	=	The Weights and Measures Act 1963 (Miscellaneous Foods) Order 1984.
S.I. 1985/435	=	The Weights and Measures (Solid Fuel) (Carriage by Rail) (Amendment) Order 1985.
S.I. 1985/777	=	The Units of Measurement Regulations 1985.

Provision	Derivation
1(1)	1963 s.1(1).
(2)	1963 s.1(2).
(3)	1963 ss.1(3), 9A(3)(*a*), (8); 1976 ss.1(1), 2(1).
(4)	1963 s.9A(4); 1976 s.2(1).
(5)	1963 s.9A(5); 1976 s.2(1).
2	1963 s.2.
3	1963 s.3.
4(1)	1963 s.4(1).
(2)(3)	1963 s.4(2); 1973 c.65 Sch. 25 para. 29; 1974 c.7 Sch. 6 para. 15(1).
(4)(5)	1963 s.4(3), (4).
(6)	1963 s.4(5); 1979 Sch. 5 para. 1.
(7)	1963 s.4(5).
(8)(9)	1963 s.4(6)(7).

Provision	Derivation
5(1)	1963 s.5(1); 1980 c.65 Sch. 4 para. 2.
(2)	1963 s.5(1A); 1979 Sch. 5 para. 2.
(3)(4)	1963 s.5(2), (2A); 1980 c.65 Sch. 4 para. 4.
(5)(6)	1963 s.5(3).
(7)	1963 s.5(1A); 1979 Sch. 5 para. 2.
(8)	1963 s.5(3).
(9)(10)	1963 s.5(4).
(11)	1963 s.5(1A); 1979 Sch. 5 para. 2.
6	1963 s.6(1); 1979 Sch. 5 para. 3.
7(1)–(4)	1963 s.9.
(5)	1963 s.17.
8(1)	1963 s.9A(1); 1976 s.2(1).
(2)	1963 Sch. 1A Part VI, Sch. 3 Part VI, S.I. 1980/1070 reg. 13(1) Sch. 4; S.I. 1983/1077 art. 2(2).
(3)	1963, s.10(7); 1976 s.2(3)(*a*).
(4)	1963 s.9A(2); 1976 s.2(1).
(5)	1963 s.9A(7); 1976 s.2(1); S.I. 1980/1070 reg. 9(1).
(6)	1963 s.9A(3)(*b*)(*c*); 1976 s.2(1).
(7)	1963 s.9A(5); 1976 s.2(1).
(8)	1963 s.9A(8); 1976 s.2(1).
9	1963 s.9B; 1976 s.2(1).
10(1)–(3)	1963 s.10(4)–(6).
(4)(5)	1963 s.10(7).
11(1)	1963 s.11(1).
(2)(3)	1963 s.11(2).
(4)	1963 s.11(3); 1979 s.16(1).
(5)	1963 s.11(3); 1980 c.65 Sch. 4 para. 5.
(6)(7)	1963 s.11(3).
(8)(9)	1963 s.11(4).
(10)	1963 s.11(5).
(11)(12)	1963 s.11(5A), (5B); 1979 s.16(1).
(13)(14)	1963 s.11(6); 1979 s.16(1).
(15)	1963 s.11(7).
(16)	1963 s.11(9).
12(1)	1963 ss.12(1), 12A(3); 1979 s.17(3).
(2)	1963 s.12(1A); 1979 s.17(1).
(3)	1963 s.12(1).
(4)	1963 s.12A(3); 1979 s.17(3).
(5)	1963 s.12(2); 1979 s.17(1).
(6)(7)	1963 s.12A(1); 1979 s.17(3).
(8)	1963 ss.12(2), 12A(1); 1979 s.17(1), (3).
(9)	1963 s.12A(2); 1979 s.17(3).
(10)	1963 ss.12(3), 12A(7); 1979 s.17(3).
(11)	1963 s.12A(4), (7); 1979 s.17(3).
(12)	1963 s.12(4).
13(1)	1963 s.12(2); 1979 s.17(1).
(2)	1963 s.12A(4); 1979 s.17(3).
(3)	1963 s.12(3), (3A); 1979 s.7(1), (3).
(4)	1963 s.12A(7); 1979 s.17(3).
14	1963 s.13.
15(1)	1963 s.14(1); 1976 s.5.
(2)	1963 s.14(1A); 1979 s.16(3).
(3)	1963 s.14(1).
(4)(5)	1963 s.14(2), (3).
16(1)	1963 s.15(1); 1979 Sch. 5 para. 5.
(2)	1963 s.15(1); 1979 Sch. 5 para. 5.
(3)(4)	1963 s.15(2), (3).
17	1963 s.16.
18	1963 s.18.
19	1963 s.19.
20	1963 s.20.

Provision	Derivation
21	1963 s.21(1).
22(1)	1963 s.21(2); 1976 s.6(1).
(2)	1963 s.21(3).
(3)	1963 s.21(3A), (3B); 1976 s.6(2).
(4)	1963 s.21(3B); 1976 s.6(2).
23(1)	1963 s.21(4); 1976 s.6(3).
(2)	1963 s.21(4).
24	1963 s.21(5); 1979 c.2 Sch. 4 para. 12.
25(1)	1963 s.22(1).
(2)(3)	1963 s.22(2); 1976 s.7(1).
(4)(5)	1963 s.22(3)(4).
(6)	1963 s.22(1)–(4).
(7)	1979 s.2(6).
(8)	1963 s.22(1)–(4).
26(1)	1963 s.23(1).
(2)–(5)	1963 s.23(2).
(6)	1963 s.23(3).
27(1)	1963 s.23(4).
(2)	1963 s.23(4); S.I. 1980/1070 Sch. 5.
28(1)	1963 s.24(1)
(2)	1963 s.24(8); 1979 s.2(6).
(3)	1963 s.24(9).
29(1)	1963 s.24(2).
(2)	1963 s.24(8); 1979 s.2(6).
(3)	1963 s.24(9).
30(1)–(4)	1963 s.24(3)–(6).
(5)	1963 s.24(8); 1979 s.2(6).
(6)	1963 s.24(9).
31(1)	1963 s.24(7).
(2)	1963 s.24(8); 1979 s.2(6).
(3)	1963 s.24(9).
32	1963 s.27(2); 1979 Sch. 5 para. 8.
33	1963 s.25.
34(1)	1963 s.26(1); 1979 Sch. 5 para. 7.
(2)	1963 s.27(1); 1979 Sch. 5 para. 8.
35(1)(2)	1963 s.26(2).
(3)	1963 s.26(3).
(4)	1963 s.26(5).
36	1963 s.26(6).
37(1)(2)	1963 s.26(7).
(3)	1963 s.26(8); 1976 s.7(2).
(4)	1963 s.27(3); 1979 Sch. 5 para. 8.
38(1)(2)	1963 s.29(1); 1976 s.7(3).
(3)	1963 s.29(2); 1976 s.7(4).
(4)	1963 s.29(3); 1984 c.30 Sch. 10 para. 4.
39	1963 s.30(1), (2).
40	1963 s.30(3).
41	1963 s.31.
42	1963 s.32.
43(1)	1979 s.19.
(2)	1979 s.24(3)(*b*).
44	1963 s.33(1).
45(1)	1963 s.33(2).
(2)(3)	1963 s.33(3).
46	1936 s.33(4).
47(1)	1979 s.1(1).
(2)	1979 s.15(7).
(3)(4)	1979 s.1(2)(3).
48(1)	1979 s.1(4).
(2), (3)	1979 s.1(5).
(4)	1979 s.15(6).

Provision	Derivation
49(1)–(3)	1979 s.1(6)–(8).
(4)	1979 s.1(9); 1980 c.65 Sch. 4 para. 11(2).
50(1)	1979 s.2(1).
(2)–(4)	1979 s.2(4).
(5)(6)	1979 s.2(5).
(7)	1979 s.2(7).
51(1)	1979 s.3(4).
(2)	1979 s.3(5).
(3)	1979 s.3(6).
(4)	1979 s.3(7).
52(1)	1979 s.4(1).
(2)	1979 s.4(4).
53	1979 s.4(2).
54(1)–(3)	1979 s.5(1)–(3).
(4)(5)	1979 s.5(4).
(6)(7)	1979 s.5(5), (6).
55	1979 s.6.
56(1)	1979 s.7(1).
(2)	1979 s.7(6).
57(1)(2)	1979 s.7(2), (3).
58	1979 s.7(4).
59(1)–(4)	1979 s.8.
(5)	1979 s.7(6).
60	1979 s.9.
61(1)	1979 s.10(1), (3).
(2)	1979 s.10(1A), (3); 1985 c.9 Sch. 2.
(3)	1979 s.10(2), (3).
(4)	1979 s.10(5).
62(1)–(3).	1979 s.11(1)–(3).
(4)	1979 s.11(5).
63(1)	1979 s.2(2).
(2)	1979 s.2(3).
(3)	1979 Sch. 1 para 1.
(4)(5)	1979 Sch. 1 para 2.
(6)	1979 Sch. 1 para 3.
(7)	1979 s.2(2), (3).
64	1979 s.12(1)(2).
65	1979 s.13.
66	1979 s.15(2).
67	1979 s.15(4), (5).
68	1979 s.14(1)–(4).
69(1)	1972 c.70 s.201(2); 1985 c.51 Sch. 8 para. 15(1).
(2)	1972 c.70 s.201(2).
(3)	1963 s.36; 1973 c.65 s.149(1).
(4)	1963 s.35(3).
(5)	1972 c.70 s.201(8); 1973 c.65 s.149(6).
(6)	1985 c.51 ss.1, 2.
70(1)	1963 s.38(1); 1979 s.4(3), Sch. 5 para. 10.
(2)	1963 s.38(1).
(3)(4)	1963 s.38(2).
71(1)–(3)	1963 s.39(1).
(4)–(6)	1963 s.39(2).
72	1963 s.41.
73(1)	1963 s.42(1).
(2)	1963 s.42(1A); 1979 Sch. 5 para. 11.
(3)	1963 s.42(2).
(4)	1963 s.42(3); 1979 Sch. 5 para. 11.
74(1)	1963 s.43(1).
(2)	1963 s.43(1); 1980 c.65 Sch. 4 para. 8.
(3)	1963 s.43(1).
(4)	1963 s.43(2).

Provision	Derivation
75(1)	1963 s.45(1); 1979 s.4(3).
(2)	1963 s.45(2).
76	1963 s.47A; 1976 s.9; 1980 c.65 Sch. 4 para. 9.
77	1963 s.44(1); 1979 Sch. 5 para. 12.
78	1963 s.44(2).
79(1)	1963 s.48(1).
(2)	1963 s.48(2); 1979 Sch. 5 para. 13(1).
(3)(4)	1963 s.48(3).
(5)(6)	1963 s.48(4).
(7)	1963 s.48(5); 1979 Sch. 5 para. 13(2).
(8)(9)	1963 s.48(6)(7).
80	1963 s.49(1)(*a*); 1979 Sch. 2 para. 6.
81(1)	1963 s.49(1)(*b*)(*c*).
(2)(3)	1963 s.49(2)(3).
(4)	Civil Evidence Act 1968 (c.64) s.14(2).
82	1963 s.50; 1979 ss.3(3), 5(7), 7(3), Sch. 2 para. 6.
83(1)	1963 s.51(1); 1979 ss.3(2), 5(7), Sch. 2 para. 6.
(2)	1979 s.7(3).
(3)	1963 s.51(2); 1979 ss.3(2), 5(7), Sch. 2 para. 6, Sch. 5 para. 14.
(4)	1963 s.51(3).
(5)	1963 s.51(4); 1979 ss.3(2), 5(7), Sch. 2 para. 6, Sch. 5 para. 14.
84(1)(2)	1963 s.52(1); 1975 c.21 s.289G; 1976 s.2(3)(*b*); 1979 ss.17(4), 18(1)(*b*); 1982 c.48 ss.46, 54.
(3)	S.I. 1966/238 art. 5; S.I. 1985/435.
(4)	1963 s.52(3); 1975 c.21 s.289G; 1979 s.3(1)(*a*); 18(3); 1982 c.48 ss.46, 54.
(5)	1963 s.52(3); 1975 c.21 s.289B; 1977 c.45 Sch. 11 para. 5; 1979 ss.12(3), 18(3); 1980 c.43 s.32(2).
(6)	1963 s.52(2); 1975 c.21 s.289G; 1979 ss.3(1)(*b*), 7(3), 18(2); 1982 c.48 ss.46, 54.
(7)	1963 ss.21, 54(4).
85	1963 s.53.
86(1)	1963 s.54(1); 1979 ss.11(6), 15(2).
(2)	1963 s.54(2); 1976 ss.2(3)(*d*), 3, Sch. 4 para. 3(1); 1979 s.15(3).
(3)	1963 s.54(2A); 1976 s.2(4).
(4)	1979 s.11(4).
(5)	1963 s.54(3); 1976 Sch. 4 para. 3(2); 1979 s.11(6).
(6)	1963 s.54(5); 1979 s.15(2).
87	1963 s.55.
88	1963 s.57; 1979 s.15(1).
89	1963 s.62(1).
90	1963 s.62(3), (6).
91	1963 s.62(2).
92	1976 s.1(4).
93	1963 s.63(4).
94(1)	1963 s.58(1); 1979 ss.12(3), 14(1), Sch. 5 para. 15; 1979 c.4 Sch. 3 para. 3; 1982 c.48 ss.74, 75; 1984 c.10 Sch. 10 para. 4.
(2)(3)	1963 s.58(1).
(4)	1963 s.58(2).
95–99	—
Sch. 1	1963 Sch. 1, Sch. 1A; S.I. 1980/1070 reg. 13, Sch. 4; S.I. 1985/777 reg. 4.
Sch. 2	1963 Sch. 2.
Sch. 3	1963 Sch. 3; S.I. 1980/1070 reg. 13, Sch. 4; S.I. 1983/1077 art. 2.
Sch. 4	
para. 1	1963 Sch. 5 para. 1.
2	1963 Sch. 5 para. 2; S.I. 1970/1708 art. 2.
3	1963 Sch. 5 para. 5; S.I. 1970/1708 art. 3; S.I. 1980/1070 Sch. 5.
4–10	1963 Sch. 5 paras. 4–10.
11	1963 Sch. 5 para. 11; S.I. 1970/1708 art. 4; S.I. 1980/1070 Sch. 5.

Provision	Derivation
Sch. 5	
para. 1	1963 Sch. 6 para. 1.
2	1963 Sch. 6 para. 2; S.I. 1980/1070 Sch. 5.
3	1963 Sch. 6 para. 3; 1976 Sch. 4, para. 1; S.I. 1979/1753 art. 2; S.I. 1980/1070 Sch. 5.
4	1963 Sch. 6 para. 3A; 1976 Sch. 4 para. 1.
5	1963 Sch. 6 para. 3B; 1976 Sch. 4 para. 1; S.I. 1980/1070 Sch. 5.
6, 7	1963 Sch. 6 paras. 3C, 3D; 1976 Sch. 4 para. 1.
8	1963 Sch. 6 para. 4.
9	1963 Sch. 6 para. 5(1); 1975 c.21 ss.289C(2)(3), 289G; 1977 c.45 s.31(2)(3); Sch. 11 para. 5; 1980/1070 Sch. 5; 1982 c.48 ss.46, 54.
10	1963 Sch. 6 para. 6.
11, 12	1963 Sch. 6 paras. 6A, 6B; 1976 Sch. 4 para. 2.
13–16	1963 Sch. 6 paras. 7–10.
17, 18	1963 Sch. 6 paras. 11, 12; S.I. 1980/1070 Sch. 5.
19	1963 Sch. 6 para. 13.
20	1963 Sch. 6 para. 14.
21	1963 Sch. 6 para. 15.
22	S.I. 1966/238 art. 1; S.I. 1979/955 art. 3.
23	1963 Sch. 6 para. 16.
24(1)	S.I. 1966/238 art. 2; S.I. 1985/435 art. 2.
(2)	S.I. 1966/238 art. 3; S.I. 1979/955 art. 4.
(3)	S.I. 1966/238 art. 3A; S.I. 1979/955 art. 5.
(4)	S.I. 1966/238 art. 5.
25(1)	1963 Sch. 6 para. 17(1); S.I. 1966/238 art.4.
(2)	1963 Sch. 6 para. 17(2); S.I. 1966/238 art. 4.
(3)(4)	1963 Sch. 6 para. 17(3)(4).
(5)	S.I. 1966/238 art. 4.
(6)	S.I. 1966/238 art. 4; S.I. 1979/955 art. 6.
26	1963 Sch. 6 para. 18.
27	1963 Sch. 6 para. 19.
28(1)	1963 Sch. 6 para. 20(1); S.I. 1980/1070 Sch. 5.
(2)	1963 Sch. 6 para. 20(1).
(3)	1963 Sch. 6 para. 20(2).
Sch. 6	
para. 1–3	1963 Sch. 7 Pt. I.
4	1963 Sch. 7 Pt. II para. 1.
5	1963 Sch. 7 Pt. II para. 2; S.I. 1970/1708 art. 5.
6	1963 Sch. 7 Pt. II para. 3.
7	1963 Sch. 7 Pt. II para. 4; S.I. 1970/1708 art. 6.
8–10	1963 Sch. 7 Pt. III; S.I. 1980/1070 Sch. 5.
11–14	1963 Sch. 7 Pt. IV; S.I. 1980/1070 Sch. 5.
15	1963 Sch. 7 Pt. V para. 1; S.I. 1974/874 art. 2.
16	1963 Sch. 7 Pt. V para. 2.
17, 18	1963 Sch. 7 Pt. VI.
19–21	1963 Sch. 7 Pt. VII.
22	1963 Sch. 7 Pt. VIII para. 1; 1979 Sch. 5 para. 21.
23–25	1963 Sch. 7 Pt. VIII paras. 2, 3.
26–41	1963 Sch. 7 Pts. IX–XIII.
Sch. 7	
para. 1–4	1963 Sch. 8 paras. 1–4
5	1963 Sch. 8 para. 5; S.I. 1984/1316 art. 17.
Sch. 8	
para. 1	1979 Sch. 2 para. 1(1).
2, 3	1979 Sch. 2 paras. 2, 3.
4	1979 Sch. 2 para. 4.
5	1979 Sch. 2 para. 1(2).
6, 7	1979 Sch. 2 paras. 5, 6.

Provision	Derivation
Sch. 9	1979 Sch.3.
Sch. 10	
para. 1	1963 Sch. 10 para. 1; 1976 s.15(3); 1984 c.30 Sch. 10 para. 5.
2–5	1963 Sch. 10 paras. 7–10; 1973 c.36 Sch. 5.
Sch. 11	
para. 1–4	
5	1963 ss.46(1), 63(1).
6	1963 s.11(8).
7	1963 s.63(2).
8	1963 s.3(6).
9	1979 Sch. 5, para. 1.
10	1963 s.11(7).
11	1963 s.12A(5), (6); 1979 s.17(3).
12(1)	S.I. 1978/484 reg. 4(2).
(2)	S.I. 1978/484 reg. 4(3).
(3)	S.I. 1978/484 reg. 5.
(4)	S.I. 1978/484 reg. 8.
13	S.I. 1980/1070 reg. 10(1).
14(1)	S.I. 1980/1070 reg. 10(2).
(2)	S.I. 1980/1070 reg. 10(3).
(3)	S.I. 1980/1070 reg. 10(4).
15	S.I. 1978/484 reg. 4(2); S.I. 1980/1070 reg. 10(2), (3); S.I. 1980/1742 regs. 2, 3.
16	S.I. 1980/1070 reg. 11.
17	S.I. 1980/1070 reg. 12.
18	1963 ss.37, 38(1); Trade Descriptions Act 1968 (c.29) s.26(1); Agriculture Act 1970 (c.40) s.25(3); 1972 c.70 s.201(5); Fair Trading Act 1973 (c.41) s.27(1).
19	1974 c.7 s.35(3).
20	1979 s.7(5).
21	1963 s.46.
22	S.I. 1980/1070 reg. 13(3).
23	1963 Sch. 6 para. 5(2); 1973 c.65 s.149(5).
24	1975 c.21 s.289C(2)(*b*), (3); 1977 c.45 s.31(2)(*b*), (3), Sch. 11 para. 4.
25	S.I. 1980/1070 reg. 16; S.I. 1980/1742 reg. 3.
Schs. 12, 13	—

TABLE OF DESTINATIONS

The Weights and Measures Act 1963

1963	1985
s.1(1)	s.1(1)
1(2)	1(2)
1(3)	1(3)
9A(3)(*a*), (8)	1(3)
9A(4)	1(4)
9A(5)	1(5)
2	2
3	3
3(6)	Sch. 11, para. 8
4(1)	s.4(1)
(2)	(2)(3)
(3), (4)	(4)(5)
(5)	(6)(7)
(6)(7)	(8)(9)
5(1)	5(1)
(1A)	(2)(7), (11)
(2), (2A)	(3)(4)
(3)	(5)(6)(8)
(4)	(9)(10)
6(1)	6
9	7(1)–(4)
9A(1)	8(1)
(2)	(4)
(3)(*b*)(*c*)	(6)
(5)	(7)
(7)	(5)
(8)	(8)
9B	9
10(4)–(6)	10(1)–(3)
(7)	ss.8(3), 10(4)(5)
11(1)	s.11(1)
(2)	(2)(3)
(3)	(4)(5)(6)(7)
(4)	(8)(9)
(5)	(10)
(5A), (5B)	(11), (12)
(6)	(13)(14)
(7)	(15), Sch. 11, para. 10
(8)	Sch. 11, para. 6
(9)	(16)
12(1)	s.12(1), (3)
(1A)	(2)
(2)	(5), (8), 13(1)
(3)	(10)
(3), (3A)	13(3)
(4)	12(12)
12A(1)	(6)(7), (8)
(2)	(9)
(3)	(1), (4)
(4)	(11), 13(2)
(5), (6)	Sch. 11, para. 11
(7)	s.12(10), (11), 13(4)
13	14
14(1)	15(1)(3)
(1A)	(2)
(2), (3)	(4)(5)
15(1)	16(1)(2)
(2), (3)	(3)(4)
16	17
17	7(5)

1963	1985
s.18	s.18
19	19
20	20
21	84(7)
(1)	21
(2)	22(1)
(3)	(2)
(3A)	(3)
(3B)	(3)(4)
(4)	23(1), (2)
(5)	24
22(1)	25(1)(6)(8)
(2)	(2)(3)(6)(8)
(3)(4)	(4)(5)(6)(8)
23(1)	26(1)
(2)	(2)–(5)
(3)	(6)
(4)	27(1)(2)
24(1)	28(1)
(2)	29(1)
(3)–(6)	30(1)–(4)
(7)	31(1)
(8)	28(2), 29(2), 30(5), 31(2)
(9)	28(3), 29(3), 30(6), 31(3)
25	33
26(1)	34(1)
(2)	35(1)(2)
(3)	(3)
(5)	(4)
(6)	36
(7)	37(1)(2)
(8)	(3)
27(1)	34(2)
(2)	32
(3)	37(4)
29(1)	38(1)(2)
(2)	(3)
(3)	(4)
30(1), (2)	39
(3)	40
31	41
32	42
33(1)	44
(2)	45(1)
(3)	(2)(3)
(4)	46
35(3)	69(4)
36	(3)
37	Sch. 11, para. 18
38(1)	s.70(1), (2), Sch. 11, para. 18
(2)	70(3)(4)
39(1)	71(1)–(3)
(2)	(4)–(6)
41	72
42(1)	73(1)
(1A)	(2)
(2)	(3)
(3)	(4)
43(1)	74(1), (2), (3)

1963	1985
s.43(2)	s.74(4)
44(1)	77
(2)	78
45(1)	75(1)
(2)	(2)
46	Sch. 11, para. 21
46(1)	Sch. 11, para. 5
47A	s.76
48(1)	79(1)
(2)	(2)
(3)	(3)(4)
(4)	(5)(6)
(5)	(7)
(6)(7)	(8)(9)
49(1)(*a*)	80
(1)(*b*)(*c*)	81(1)
(2)(3)	(2)(3)
50	82
51(1)	83(1), 84(1), (2)
(2)	(3)
(3)	(4)
(4)	(5)
52(1)	84(1)(2)
(2)	(6)
(3)	(4)
(3)	(5)
53	85
54	86(1)
(2)	(2)
(2A)	(3)
(3)	(5)
(4)	84(7)
(5)	86(6)
55	87
57	88
58(1)	94(1), (2), (3)
(2)	(4)
62(1)	89
(2)	91
(3), (6)	90
63(1)	Sch. 11, para. 5
(2)	para. 7
(4)	s.93
Sch. 1,	
Sch. 1A	Sch. 1
Sch. 1A,	
Pt. VI,	
Sch. 3, Pt. VI	s.8(2)
Sch. 2	Sch. 2
Sch. 3	Sch. 3
Sch. 5,	
para. 1	Sch. 4, para. 1
para. 2	para. 2
paras. 4–10	paras. 4–10
para. 5	para. 3
para. 11	para. 11
Sch. 6,	
para. 1	Sch. 5, para. 1
para. 2	para. 2

THE WEIGHTS AND MEASURES ACT 1963

1963	1985
Sch. 6 ....Sch. 5	
para. 3	para. 3
para. 3A	para. 4
para. 3B	para. 5
paras. 3C,	
3D	paras. 6, 7
para. 4	para. 8
para. 5(1) ..	para. 9
para. 5(2) ..Sch. 11,	
	para. 23
para. 6 ......Sch. 5,	
	para. 10
paras. 6A,	
6B .... Sch. 5,	
	paras. 11, 12
paras. 7–10 .	paras. 13–16
Sch. 6,	
paras. 11, 12	paras. 17, 18
para. 13	para. 19
para. 14	para. 20
para. 15	para. 21

1963	1985
Sch. 6 ....Sch. 5	
para. 16	paras. 16, 23
para. 17(1) .	para. 25(1)
para. 17(2) .	para. 25(2)
para.	
17(3)(4) ..	para. 25(3)(4)
para. 18	para. 26
para. 19	para. 26
para. 20(1) .	para. 28(1), (2)
para. 20(2) .	para. 28(3)
Sch. 7,	
Pt. 1 ....Sch. 6,	
	paras. 1–3
Pt. II,	
para. 1 ...	para. 4
para. 2 ...	para. 5
para. 3 ...	para. 6
para. 4 ...	para. 7
Pt. III	paras. 8–10

1963	1985
Sch. 7 ....Sch. 6	
Pt. IV	paras. 11–14
Pt. V,	
para. 1 ...	para. 15
para. 2 ...	para. 16
Pt. VI	paras. 17, 18
Pt. VII	paras. 19–21
Pt. VIII,	
para. 1 ...	para. 22
paras. 2, 3	paras. 23–25
Pts. IX–XIII	paras. 26–41
Sch. 8,	
paras. 1–4 ..Sch. 7,	
	paras. 1–4
para. 5	para. 5
Sch. 10,	
para. 1 ......Sch. 10,	
	para. 1
paras. 7–10 .	paras. 2–5

TRADE DESCRIPTIONS ACT 1968

1968	1985
s.26(1) ....Sch. 11,	
	para. 18

CIVIL EVIDENCE ACT 1968

1968	1985
s.14(2) ....s.81(4)	

AGRICULTURE ACT

s.25(3) ....Sch. 11,	
	para. 18

THE LOCAL GOVERNMENT ACT 1972

1972	1985
s.201(2) ....s.69(1), (2)	
201(5) ....Sch. 11,	
	para. 18
(8) .... 69(5)	

THE NORTHERN IRELAND CONSTITUTION ACT 1973

1973	1985
Sch. 5 ....Sch. 10,	
	paras. 2 to 5

FAIR TRADING ACT 1973

1973	1985
s.27(1) ....Sch. 11,	
	para. 18

THE LOCAL GOVERNMENT (SCOTLAND) ACT 1973

1973	1985
s.149(1) ....s.69(3)	
(5) ....Sch. 11,	
	para. 23
(6) .... 69(4), (5)	
Sch. 25,	
para. 29 ..... 4(2)(3)	

THE LOCAL GOVERNMENT ACT 1974

1974	1985
s.35(3) ....Sch. 11,	
	para. 19
Sch. 6,	
para. 15(1) .s.4(2)(3)	

THE CRIMINAL PROCEDURE (SCOTLAND) ACT 1975

1975	1985
s.289B ....s.84(5)	
289C(2)(3) ..Sch. 5, para. 9	
(2)(*b*),	
(3) ...Sch. 11,	
	para. 24
289G ....s.84(1), (2),	
	(4), (6),
	Sch. 5, para. 9

THE WEIGHTS AND MEASURES &c. ACT 1976

1976	1985	1976	1985	1976	1985
s.1(1) ....s.1(3)		s.5 ....s.15(1)		s.15(3) ....Sch. 10,	
(4) 92		6(1) .... 22(1)			para. 1
2(1) .... 1(3), (4), (5),		(2) .... (3), (4)		Sch. 1,	
	8(1) to (8), 9	(3) .... 23(1)		para. 3 ......s.63(6)	
(3)(*a*) .... 8(3)		7(1) .... 25(2)(3)		Sch. 4,	
(3)(*b*) .... 84(1)(2)		(2) .... 37(3)		para. 1 ......Sch. 5,	
(3)(*d*) .... 86(2)		(3) .... 38(1)(2)			paras. 3–7
(4) .... (3)		(4) .... (3)		para. 2 ...... paras. 11, 12	
3 .... (2)		9 76		para. 3(1) ..s.86(2)	
				para. 3(2) .. (5)	

THE CRIMINAL LAW ACT 1977

1977	1985
s.31(2)(*b*), (3) Sch. 11,	
	para. 24
(2)(3) ......Sch. 5, para. 9	
Sch. 11,	
para. 4 ......Sch. 11,	
	para. 24
para. 5 ......s.84(5),	
	Sch. 5, para. 9

THE CUSTOMS AND EXCISE MANAGEMENT ACT 1979

1979	1985
Sch. 4,	
para. 12 .....s.24	

THE ALCOHOLIC LIQUOR DUTIES ACT 1979

1979	1985
Sch. 3,	
para. 3 ......s.94(1)	

THE WEIGHTS AND MEASURES ACT 1979

1979	1985	1979	1985	1979	1985
s.1(1) ....s.47(1)		s.2(6) ....s.25(7), 28(2),		s.3(7) ....s.51(4)	
(2)(3) .... (3)(4)			29(2), 30(5),	4(1) .... 52(1)	
(4) .... 48(1)			31(2)	(2) 53	
(5) .... (2), (3)		(7) .... 50(7)		(3) .... 70(1)	
(6)–(8) ...... 49(1)–(3)		3(1)(*a*) .... 84(4)		(3) .... 75(1)	
(9) .... (4)		(1)(*b*) .... (6)		(4) .... 52(2)	
2(1) .... 50(1)		(2) .... 83(1), (3), (5)		5(1)–(3) ...... 54(1)–(3)	
(2) .... 63(1), (7)		(3) 82		(4) .... (4)(5)	
(3) .... (2), (7)		(4) .... 51(1)		(5), (6) ..... (6)(7)	
(4) .... 50(2)–(4)		(5) .... (2)		(7) 82,	
(5) .... (5)(6)		(6) .... (3)			83(1)(3)(5)

The Weights and Measures Act 1979

The Magistrates' Courts Act 1980

The Local Government, Planning and Land Act 1980

The Criminal Justice Act 1982

The Food Act 1984

The Companies Consolidation (Consequential Provisions) Act 1985

The Local Government Act 1985

DESTINATIONS FOR STATUTORY INSTRUMENTS

THE WEIGHTS AND MEASURES (SOLID FUEL) (CARRIAGE BY RAIL) ORDER 1966

1966	**1985**
S.I. No. 238,	
art. 1 ....Sch. 5, para. 22	
art. 2 .... para. 24(1)	
art. 3 .... para. 24(2),	
	(3)
art. 4 .... 25(1), (2),	
	(5), (6)
art. 5 .... 84(3), Sch. 5,	
	para. 24(4)

THE WEIGHTS AND MEASURES ACT (AMENDMENT OF SCHEDULES 5 AND 7) ORDER 1970

1970	**1985**
S.I. No. 1708,	
art. 2 ....Sch. 4, para. 2	
art. 3 .... para. 3	
art. 4 .... para. 11	
art. 5 ....Sch. 6, para. 5	
art. 6 .... para. 7	

THE WEIGHTS AND MEASURES ACT 1963 (DENTIFRICES) ORDER 1974

1974	**1985**
S.I. No. 874,	
art. 2 ....Sch. 6, para. 15	

THE UNITS OF MEASUREMENT REGULATIONS 1978

1978	**1985**
S.I. No. 484,	
reg. 4(2) ....Sch. 11,	
	paras. 12(1),
	15
reg. 4(3) .... 12(2)	
reg. 5 ....Sch. 11, 12(3)	
reg. 8 .... para. 12(4)	

THE WEIGHTS AND MEASUES ACT 1963 (SOLID FUEL) ORDER 1979

1979	**1985**
S.I. No. 1753,	
art. 2 ....Sch. 5, para. 3	
art. 3 ....Sch. 5,	
	para. 22
art. 4 ....Sch. 5,	
	para. 24(2)
art. 5 ....Sch. 5,	
	para. 24(3)
art. 6 ....Sch. 5, 25(6)	

THE UNITS OF MEASUREMENT REGULATIONS 1980

1980	1985	1980	1985	1980	1985
S.I. No. 1070,		reg. 11 ...... para. 16		Sch. 5 .... 27(2),	
reg. 9(1) .... 8(5)		reg. 12 ...... para. 17			Sch. 4,
reg. 10(1) ...Sch. 11,		reg. 13 ......Schs. 1, 3			paras. 3, 11,
	para. 13	reg. 13(1) ... 8(2)			Sch. 5
reg. 10(2) ... paras. 14(1),		reg. 13(3) ...Sch. 11,			paras. 2, 3, 5,
	15		para. 22		9, 17, 18,
reg. 10(3) ... paras. 14(2),		reg. 16 ...... para. 25			28(1),
	15	Sch. 4 .... 8(2),			Sch. 6,
reg. 10(4) ... para. 14(3)			Schs. 1, 3		paras. 8 to 14

THE UNITS OF MEASUREMENT (NO. 2) REGULATIONS 1980

1980	1985
S.I. 1980 No. 1742,	
reg. 2 ....Sch. 11,	
	para. 15
reg. 3 .... paras. 15, 25	

THE WEIGHTS AND MEASURES ACT 1963 (AMENDMENT OF SCHEDULE 3) ORDER 1983

1983	1985
S.I. 1983 No. 1077,	
art. 2 ....Sch. 3	
art. 2(2) .....s.8(2)	

THE WEIGHTS AND MEASURES ACT 1963 (MISCELLANEOUS FOODS) ORDER 1984

1984	1985
S.I. 1984 No. 1316,	
art. 17 ....Sch. 7, para. 5	

THE WEIGHTS AND MEASURES (SOLID FUEL) (CARRIAGE BY RAIL) (AMENDMENT) ORDER 1985

1985	1985
S.I. 1985 No. 435 .....s.84(3)	
art. 2 ....Sch. 5,	
	para. 24(1)

THE UNITS OF MEASUREMENT REGULATIONS 1985

1985	1985
S.I. 1985 No. 777,	
reg. 4 ....Sch. 1	

LAW REFORM (MISCELLANEOUS PROVISIONS) (SCOTLAND) ACT 1985*

(1985 c. 73)

ARRANGEMENT OF SECTIONS

---

* Annotations by J. M. Thomson, LL.B., Professor of Law, University of Strathclyde.

An Act to amend the law of Scotland in respect of certain leases, other contracts and obligations; certain courts and their powers; evidence and procedure; certain criminal penalties; the care of children; the functions of the Commissioner for Local Administration; solicitors; and certain procedures relating to crofting and the valuation of sheep stocks; and to make, as respects Scotland, certain other miscellaneous reforms of the law.

[30th October 1985]

PARLIAMENTARY DEBATES
   Hansard: H.C. Vol. 68, col. 1118, Vol. 78, col. 423; Vol. 84, col. 200; H.L. Vol. 465, col. 1018; Vol. 467, cols. 168, 503, 1008, 1570.
   The Bill was considered by the first Scottish Standing Committee (January 15 to March 28, 1985).

Provisions relating to leases

Limitation on use of property held on long lease not to apply to property held on certain renewable leases

1. In subsection (4) of section 8 of the Land Tenure Reform (Scotland) Act 1974 (property on long lease not to be used as private dwelling house) in the definition of "long lease" there shall be inserted at the end of the following—

"but, in relation to a lease granted before 1st September 1974, does not include its renewal (whether before or after the commencement of section 1 of the Law Reform (Miscellaneous Provisions) (Scotland) Act 1985) in implement of an obligation in or under it."

GENERAL NOTE

Under s.8 of the Land Tenure Reform (Scotland) Act 1974 a lease of residential property, granted after August 31, 1974, cannot exceed 20 years. The question has arisen whether s.8 would prohibit the renewal of a lease entered into before the 1974 Act came into operation, under which the tenant has a right to have the lease renewed for a period of more than 20 years (a Blairgowrie lease). S.1 provides that the tenant's right to have the lease renewed is not affected by the 1974 Act. It does so, by excluding the renewal of the lease from the definition of "long lease" in the 1974 Act.

"in relation to a lease granted before September 1, 1974"

The right to have the lease renewed must be in a lease granted before the 1974 Act came into operation.

"(whether before or after the commencement of section 1 of the Law Reform (Miscellaneous Provisions) (Scotland) Act 1985)

The section is retrospective in the sense that it renders valid renewals of leases for more than 20 years made before the commencement of the 1985 Act but after the commencement of the 1974 Act.

"in implement of an obligation in or under it"

The obligation to renew the lease must be in the original lease.

Power of sheriff to grant renewals of certain long leases

2. After section 22 of the Land Registration (Scotland) Act 1979 there shall be inserted the following section—

"Power of sheriff to grant renewals of certain long leases

22A—(1) Where a landlord has failed to renew a long lease in implement of an obligation in or under it, the sheriff may, on summary application by the tenant, make an order directing the sheriff clerk to execute a renewal of the lease instead of the landlord.

(2) On making an order under subsection (1) above, the sheriff may require the tenant to consign in court such amount (whether by way of rent or expenses or otherwise) in respect of the lease and its renewal as appears to the sheriff to be lawfully due and payable or appears to him would have been so due and payable had the landlord duly renewed the lease.

(3) A renewal executed under this section shall have the like force and effect as if it were executed by the landlord.

(4) Without prejudice to subsection (7)(*a*) below, a landlord shall be regarded, for the purposes of subsection (1) above, as having failed to renew a lease in implement of an obligation in or under it if, having been given written notice in accordance with subsection (5) below by the tenant that he requires the landlord, in implement of the obligation, to renew the lease, the landlord has failed to do so when he was obliged to and continues so to fail.

(5) Notice is in accordance with this subsection if it is given not less than 3 months before the lodging of the summary application.

(6) Subsection (4) above is subject to subsection (7)(*b*) below and to any provision in or under the lease for earlier, or a longer period of, notice requiring renewal of the lease than that mentioned in subsection (5) above.

(7) If the sheriff is satisfied that a landlord is unknown or cannot be found, he may—

(*a*) in a case where the tenant is thereby prevented from bringing the landlord, in accordance with the lease, under an obligation to renew it, order that the landlord shall be regarded, for the purposes of subsection (1) above, as having failed to renew the lease in implement of an obligation under it; and

(b) in any other case, dispense with notice under subsection (4) above.

(8) The sheriff may, on the application of any party, order the investment, payment of distribution of any sums consigned in court under subsection (2) above, and in so doing the sheriff shall have regard to the respective interests of any parties appearing to have a claim on such sums.

(9) The sheriff's power under subsection (8) above extends to ordering that any award of expenses of the application under this section be paid out of any sums consigned in court under subsection (2) above.".

GENERAL NOTE

The purpose of this section is to amend s.22 of the Land Registration (Scotland) Act 1979 to provide a procedure whereby a sheriff may make an order directing the sheriff clerk to execute the renewal of a lease in lieu of a landlord, when the landlord has failed to implement his obligation to renew a long lease, or is unknown. The renewal shall have the like force and effect as if it were executed by the landlord.

New subs. 22A(1)
"*long lease*"
The sheriff's power only extends to long leases.

"*in implement of an obligation in or under it*"
The obligation to renew the lease must be in the original lease.

New subs. 22A(2)
"*(whether by way of rent or expenses or otherwise) in respect of the lease or its renewal*"
The amount to be consigned is to cover rent that is due under the lease, expenses that are due under the lease and the conveyancing fees arising from the renewal. It is not intended to cover the general expenses of the application when the ordinary rules as to expenses apply.

New subs. 22A(4)
A landlord is to be taken as having failed to renew the lease, if the tenant has given written notice that he requires the landlord to renew the lease in accordance with his obligation under the lease and the landlord has failed to do so.

New subs. 22A(5)
In order to qualify as written notice for the purposes of s.22A(4), the notice must be given not less than three months before the tenant lodges the summary application under s.22A(1).

New subs. 22A(6)
Where the lease provides for an earlier, or a longer, period of notice requiring renewal than that provided in s.22A(5), then the provision in the lease is to prevail.

New subs. 22A(7)
"*landlord is unknown or cannot be found*"
This section only applies when the landlord is unknown or cannot be found. When this is so, the notice provisions in s.22A(4) do not apply, and the situation is governed by s.22A(7)(a) or (b).

New subs. 22A(7)(a)
This deals with the situation where under the original lease, the landlord's obligation to renew is activated only when the tenant asks him to do so. When the landlord is unknown or cannot be found, the tenant will obviously be unable to give written notice to renew and therefore the landlord cannot be said to have failed in his obligation under the lease.

S.22A(7)(*a*) provides that in this situation, *i.e.* where the landlord is unknown or cannot be found, the sheriff can order that the landlord be taken as having failed to renew the lease in implement of an obligation thereunder, and can make an order directing the sheriff clerk to execute a renewal of the lease under s.22A(1).

New subs. 22A(7)(b)
This deals with the situation where the landlord is simply obliged under the lease to renew and has failed to do so. Where the landlord is unknown or cannot be found, the sheriff can dispense with the requirement of notice under s.22A(4), and proceed to make an order directing the sheriff clerk to execute a renewal of the lease under s.22A(1).

New subs. 22A(8)
This subsection empowers the sheriff on the application of any party, to invest, pay or distribute any sums consigned under s.22A(2). In doing so, the sheriff must have regard to the respective interests of any parties—including the tenant—who appear to have a claim on any such sums.

New subs. 22A(9)
While the sums consigned under s.22A(2) are not prima facie intended to cover the expenses of the application, nevertheless the sheriff's powers under s.22A(8) extend to ordering that an award of expenses *vis-à-vis* the application can be paid out of the sums so consigned. This could mean, for example, that a tenant who has incurred the expenses of the application because of a landlord's refusal to implement his obligation to renew the lease, may be able to offset his expenses against the sums which he has consigned in court.

Creation of real conditions in assignations of certain long leases

3. Section 3 of the Registration of Leases (Scotland) Act 1857 (assignations of recorded leases) shall be renumbered as subsection (1) of that section and after that subsection there shall be inserted the following subsections—

"(2) Notwithstanding—
 (*a*) any restriction imposed by subsection (1) above on the power under that subsection to assign such a lease; or
 (*b*) any rule of law to the contrary,
it shall be, and shall be deemed always to have been, competent in an assignation under this section to impose conditions and make stipulations which, upon the recording of such assignation or the registration under the Land Registration (Scotland) Act 1979 of the assignee's interest, shall be as effectual against any singular successor of the assignee in the subjects assigned as if such assignee had been a grantee of the lease and it had been duly recorded or, as the case may be, the grantee's interest had been so registered.

(3) Nothing in subsection (2) above makes effectual against any successor of the assignee any obligation of periodical payment other than a payment—
 (*a*) of rent or of an apportionment of rent;
 (*b*) in defrayal of a contribution towards some continuing cost related to the lands and heritages subject to the lease assigned; or
 (*c*) under a heritable security.

(4) A provision in an assignation which purports to make effectual against any successor of the assignee any obligation of periodic payment other than one specified in paragraphs (*a*) to (*c*) of subsection (3) above shall not render the deed void or unenforceable, but the assignation shall have, and shall be deemed always to have had, effect only to the extent (if any) that it would have had effect if it had not imposed such obligation.

(5) Section 32 of the Conveyancing (Scotland) Act 1874 (which enables reservations, conditions, covenants etc. affecting lands to be

effectually imported into one deed by reference to another) and section 17 of the Land Registration (Scotland) Act 1979 (which provides that certain obligations in deeds of conditions shall become real obligations upon the recording of the deed or registration of the obligation) shall, with the necessary modifications, respectively apply for the purposes of enabling conditions and stipulations to be effectually imported into any assignation under this section and enabling land obligations in a deed of conditions relating to the land subject to the assignation to become real obligations affecting the land.

In this subsection "land obligation" has the meaning assigned to it by section 1(2) of the Conveyancing and Feudal Reform (Scotland) Act 1970."

GENERAL NOTE

At common law, a lease is essentially a personal contract binding the original landlord and original tenant and their representatives. If the lease is assignable, however, its conditions remain binding in a question between the original landlord and the tenant's assignees and successors. But if leasehold property is split up by assignations of parts of the property, there does not appear to be any way at common law in which the assignor can validly create conditions in the assignation which are binding upon the singular successors of the assignees. One solution was to proceed by way of a sub-lease imposing fresh conditions in the sub-lease. This option was effectively removed by the Land Tenure Reform (Scotland) Act 1974 which prohibits the creation of both leases and sub-leases of residential property of more than 20 years. Moreover, it was extremely doubtful whether it was possible to use the facility of a deed of conditions to get round the problem because, while s.32 of the Conveyancing (Scotland) Act 1874 allows a proprietor of lands to use such a deed, the definition of "lands" in the 1874 Act is restricted to heritable property held on feudal tenure.

With the advent of Registration of Title, it was discovered that, in spite of the doubtful validity of the practice, it had become quite common when leasehold property was split up to attempt to create conditions either in assignations or in separate deeds of conditions.

The purpose of s.3 is to add new subsections to the Registration of Leases (Scotland) Act 1857, retrospectively to regularise both of these practices thus ensuring that the real conditions therein remain binding on the singular successors of the assignees.

New subs. 3(2)

This provision allows conditions to be effectual against the singular successors of the assignee, upon recording or registration of the assignation.

"shall be, and shall be deemed always to have been"

The provision has retrospective effect, and thus regularises the practice which although its validity was doubtful, had become common before the commencement of this section.

New subss. 3(3) and (4)

Any condition obliging the assignee to make a periodical payment other than one of those listed in (*a*) (*b*) or (*c*), is not effectual as a result of s.3(2). However, the presence of such a condition does not render other real conditions in the assignation ineffectual: s.3(4).

New subs. (5)

This allows real conditions and land obligations to be imported into assignations through the facility of a deed of conditions.

"any assignation under this section"

This can be an assignation made before as well as after the commencement of this section: see s.3(2). Thus it retrospectively regularises the practice which although its validity was doubtful, had become common before the commencement of this section.

Irritancy clauses etc. relating to monetary breaches of lease

4.—(1) A landlord shall not, for the purpose of treating a lease as terminated or terminating it, be entitled to rely—

(*a*) on a provision in the lease which purports to terminate it, or to enable him to terminate it, in the event of a failure of the tenant to pay rent, or to make any other payment, on or before the due date therefor or such later date or within such period as may be provided for in the lease; or

(*b*) on the fact that such a failure is, or is deemed by a provision of the lease to be, a material breach of contract,

unless subsection (2) or (5) below applies.

(2) This subsection applies if—

(*a*) the landlord has, at any time after the payment of rent or other payment mentioned in subsection (1) above has become due, served a notice on the tenant—

(i) requiring the tenant to make payment of the sum which he has failed to pay together with any interest thereon in terms of the lease within the period specified in the notice; and

(ii) stating that, if the tenant does not comply with the requirement mentioned in sub-paragraph (i) above, the lease may be terminated; and

(*b*) the tenant has not complied with that requirement.

(3) The period to be specified in any such notice shall be not less than—

(*a*) a period of 14 days immediately following the service of the notice; or

(*b*) if any period remaining between the service of the notice and the expiry of any time provided for in the lease or otherwise for the late payment of the sum which the tenant has failed to pay is greater than 14 days, that greater period.

(4) Any notice served under subsection (2) above shall be sent by recorded delivery and shall be sufficiently served if it is sent to the tenant's last business or residential address in the United Kingdom known to the landlord or to the last address in the United Kingdom provided to the landlord by the tenant for the purpose of such service.

(5) This subsection applies if the tenant does not have an address in the United Kingdom known to the landlord and has not provided an address in the United Kingdom to the landlord for the purpose of service.

GENERAL NOTE

In *Dorchester Studios (Glasgow) Ltd.* v. *Stone and Another*, 1975 S.L.T. 153, the House of Lords refused to allow a conventional irritancy, incurred by the tenant's failure to pay an instalment of rent on the due date required by the lease, to be purged by an offer of payment of the arrears in full made shortly after that date and before the action to enforce the irritancy was brought. The harshness of this decision is obvious. Although, the landlord's rights were subject to the equitable power of the court to relieve a tenant in cases of abuse or oppressive use of an irritancy, the Scottish courts have been reluctant to exercise this power: see *Lucas's Exrs.* v. *Demarco*, 1968 S.L.T. 89; *H.M.V. Fields Properties Ltd.* v. *Skirt 'n' Slack Centre of London Ltd.*, 1982 S.L.T. 477. The matter was referred to the Scottish Law Commission who recommended a softening of the remedy of irritancy (Scot. Law Com. No. 75). The Commission's recommendations are implemented in ss.4–7. The purpose of this section is to introduce a mandatory notice procedure in respect of termination based on the tenant's failure to make a monetary payment due under the lease.

Subs. (1)

The effect of this subsection is to compel a landlord to give notice to the tenant when, in the event of non-payment of rent or other monetary payment under the lease, the landlord is relying on (a) a conventional irritancy clause or (b) the tenant's material breach, to terminate the lease.

"lease"

A lease of land used wholly or mainly for residential purposes or comprising an agricultural holding, a croft, the subject of a cottar or the holding of a landholder or a statutory small tenant, is *excluded* from the scope of the provision *i.e.* s.4 is only concerned with leases of commercial or industrial property: see s.7. The provisions apply, however, to leases entered into before or after the commencement of the section.

Subs. (2)
   This sets out the details of the notice procedure. The notice is served after the payment has become due. The notice must state that the landlord requires payment—with interest—by a specified period and that if the tenant does not comply with that requirement, the lease may be terminated. In order to obtain protection, the tenant must comply with the requirement: if he does not, the landlord will be able to terminate the lease: ss.(2)(*b*).

Subs. (3)
   This sets out the minimum periods for payment of arrears which is to be specified in the notice. The minimum is a period of 14 days immediately following the service of the notice or, where days of grace are permitted, the period remaining between the service of the notice and the expiry of the time for late payment, provided that period is more than 14 days.

Subs. (4)
"shall be sent by recorded delivery"
   This provision requires notices to be served by recorded delivery to the tenant's last business or residential address (including an address for service) in the United Kingdom known to the landlord.

Subs. (5)
   The effect of this subsection, when read with ss.(1), is to exempt the landlord from the requirement to observe the notice procedure in the exceptional case where the tenant has no known address for service in the United Kingdom.

Irritancy clauses etc not relating to monetary breaches of leases

   5.—(1)   Subject to subsection (2) below, a landlord shall not, for the purpose of treating a lease as terminated or terminating it, be entitled to rely—

   (*a*) on a provision in the lease which purports to terminate it, or to enable the landlord to terminate it, in the event of an act or omission by the tenant (other than such a failure as is mentioned in section 4(1)(*a*) of this Act) or of a change in the tenant's circumstances; or

   (*b*) on the fact that such act or omission or charge is, or is deemed by a provision of the lease to be, a material breach of contract,

if in all the circumstances of the case a fair and reasonable landlord would not seek so to rely.

   (2) No provision of a lease shall of itself, irrespective of the particular circumstances of the case, be held to be unenforceable by virtue of subsection (1) above.

   (3) In the consideration, for the purposes of subsection (1)(*a*) or (*b*) above, of the circumstances of a case where—

   (*a*) an act, omission or change is alleged to constitute a breach of a provision of the lease or a breach of contract; and

   (*b*) the breach is capable of being remedied in reasonable time,

regard shall be had to whether a reasonable opportunity has been afforded to the tenant to enable the breach to be remedied.

GENERAL NOTE
   The purpose of this section is to establish the test of the fair and reasonable landlord as a means of regulating a landlord's powers of termination when they arise form non-monetary breaches of the lease by the tenant.

Subs. (1)
   The effect of this subsection is to prevent a landlord, in circumstances other than those covered in s.4, from exercising his power to terminate a lease as the result of (a) a

conventional irritancy clause or (b) the tenant's material breach, unless in all the circumstances of the case a fair and reasonable landlord would do so.

"lease"

A lease of land used wholly or mainly for residential purposes or comprising an agricultural holding, a croft, the subject of a cottar or the holding of a landholder or a statutory small tenant, is *excluded* from the scope of the provision *i.e.* s.5 is only concerned with leases of commercial or industrial property: see s.7. The provisions apply, however, to leases entered into before or after the commencement of the section.

"in all the circumstances of the case"

This phrase is deliberately wide to allow the court no little discretion in determining whether or not a fair and reasonable landlord would terminate the lease. However, by virtue of subs. (3), where the breach is capable of being remedied in a reasonable time, the court must consider whether a reasonable opportunity has been afforded the tenant to remedy the breach. If a fair and reasonable landlord would have done so, then the landlord cannot terminate the lease if he has not done so. However, there can be circumstances, for example, where the tenant has allowed the premises to fall into serious disrepair, when a fair and reasonable landlord would decline to allow the tenant an adequate time to remedy the breach. In short, in cases of a remediable breach, the absence of providing an opportunity to remedy the breach will be an important but not necessarily a conclusive factor in determining whether a fair and reasonable landlord would terminate the lease. In cases of an irremediable breach, there could be circumstances, for example, where the breach was of a very trivial nature, when a fair and reasonable landlord might not terminate the lease. It is to be hoped that the uncertainty surrounding the "fair and reasonable landlord" test will not be the occasion for prolonged litigation.

Subs. (2)

The validity of a conventional irritancy clause as such is not open to question: the fair and reasonable landlord test applies only to the purported exercise by the landlord of his power to terminate the lease in the particular circumstances of the case.

Subs. (3)

See note to subs. (1).

Supplementary and transitional provisions relating to sections 4 and 5

6.—(1) The parties to a lease shall not be entitled to disapply any provision of section 4 or 5 of this Act from it.

(2) Where circumstances have occurred before the commencement of sections 4 and 5 of this Act which would have entitled a landlord to terminate a lease in reliance on a provision in the lease or on the ground that the circumstances constitute a material breach of contract, but the landlord has not before such commencement given written notice to the tenant of his intention to terminate the lease in respect of those circumstances, he shall, after such commencement, be entitled to terminate the lease in respect of those circumstances only in accordance with the provisions of section 4 or 5 (as the case may be) of this Act.

(3) Nothing in section 4 or 5 of this Act shall apply in relation to any payment which has to be made, or any other condition which has to be fulfilled, before a tenant is entitled to entry under a lease.

Subs. (1)

The effect of this subsection is to prevent parties from contracting out of the new protection afforded to tenants under ss.4 and 5.

Subs. (2)

The provisions of ss.4 and 5 apply to all relevant leases regardless of their date and regardless of when the tenant's breach occurred. However, where a landlord has, prior to the commencement of ss.4 and 5, given *written* notice to the tenant of his intention to terminate the lease, whether on the basis of a conventional irritancy clause or the latter's material breach of contract, ss.4 and 5 do *not* apply.

Subs. (3)

The effect of this subsection is to restrict ss.4 and 5 to irritancy during the currency of a relevant lease. Any action taken by landlords in respect of conditions requiring to be fulfilled prior to entry being taken is not affected by the provisions of ss.4 and 5.

Interpretation of sections 4 to 6

7.—(1) In sections 4 to 6 of this Act "lease" means a lease of land, whether entered into before or after the commencement of those sections, but does not include a lease of land—

(*a*) used wholly or mainly for residential purposes; or

(*b*) comprising an agricultural holding, a croft, the subject of a cottar or the holding of a landholder or a statutory small tenant.

(2) In subsection (1) above—

"agricultural holding" has the same meaning as in section 1 of the Agricultural Holdings (Scotland) Act 1949;

"cottar" has the same meaning as in section 28(4) of the Crofters (Scotland) Act 1955;

"croft" has the same meaning as in section 3 of the Crofters (Scotland) Act 1955; and

"holding" (in relation to a landholder or statutory small tenant), "landholder" and "statutory small tenant" have the same meanings as in the Small Landholders (Scotland) Acts 1886 to 1931.

See notes to ss.4(1) and 5(1) *supra.*

Provisions relating to other contracts and obligations

Rectification of defectively expressed documents

8.—(1) Subject to section 9 of this Act, where the court is satisfied, on an application made to it, that—

(*a*) a document intended to express or to give effect to an agreement fails to express accurately the common intention of the parties to the agreement at the date when it was made; or

(*b*) a document intended to create, transfer, vary or renounce a right, not being a document falling within paragraph (*a*) above, fails to express accurately the intention of the grantor of the document at the date when it was executed,

it may order the document to be rectified in any manner that it may specify in order to give effect to that intention.

(2) For the purposes of subsection (1) above, the court shall be entitled to have regard to all relevant evidence, whether written or oral.

(3) Subject to section 9 of this Act, in ordering the rectification of a document under subsection (1) above (in this subsection referred to as "the original document"), the court may, at its own instance or on an application made to it, order the rectification of any other document intended for any of the purposes mentioned in paragraph (*a*) or (*b*) of subsection (1) above which is defectively expressed by reason of the defect in the original document.

(4) Subject to section 9(4) of this Act, a document ordered to be rectified under this section shall have effect as if it had always been so rectified.

(5) Subject to section 9(5) of this Act, where a document recorded in the Register of Sasines is ordered to be rectified under this section and the order is likewise recorded, the document shall be treated as having been always so recorded as rectified.

(6) Nothing in this section shall apply to a document of a testamentary nature.

(7) It shall be competent to register in the Register of Inhibitions and Adjudications a notice of an application under this section for the rectification of a deed relating to land, being an application in respect of which authority for service or citation has been granted; and the land to which the application relates shall be rendered litigious as from the date of registration of such a notice.

(8) A notice under subsection (7) above shall specify the names and designations of the parties to the application and the date when authority for service or citation was granted and contain a description of the land to which the application relates.

(9) In this section and section 9 of this Act "the court" means the Court of Session or the sheriff.

GENERAL NOTE

If the written expression of a concluded agreement or other juristic act is defective, there is no general remedy in Scots law under which the written document can be rectified. If the defect is patent, it can be corrected by sensitive construction of the document: but if it is latent, a decree of reduction must be sought in the Court of Session followed by a declarator of the parties' rights and obligations. See, for example, *Anderson* v. *Lambie*, 1954 S.L.T. 73 *per* Lord Reid at p.80; *Hudson* v. *Hudson's Trs.*, 1978 S.L.T. 88: *cf.* the approach taken in *Krupp* v. *Menzies*, 1907 S.C. 903. The matter was considered by the Scottish Law Commission and ss.8 and 9 implement the Commission's recommendations (Scot. Law Com. No. 79) by introducing into Scots law a remedy of rectification to simplify the "cumbersome" process which existed before.

Subs. (1)
"Subject to section 9 of this Act"
S.9 is concerned with the protection of the interests of third parties who have relied upon the non-rectified document. See *infra* notes to s.9.
"the court"
I.e. the Court of Session or the sheriff: see s.8(9).

Subs. (1)(a)
"a document intended to express or to give effect to an agreement"
This provision is concerned with the written expression of bilateral or mutual obligations created by convention or agreement.
"fails to express accurately the common intention of the parties to the agreement at the date it was made"
The new remedy is simply concerned with the narrow circumstances where a written document does not accurately express the common intention of the parties to a concluded agreement. Rectification cannot be used when there is no concluded agreement, for example, because of the existence of *error in substantialibus*.

Subs. (1)(b)
"a document intended to create, transfer, vary or renounce a right"
This is widely drawn to cover the whole range of unilateral juristic acts, where the intention of the grantor has been expressed in a deed: however, documents of a testamentary character are excluded: see s.8(6). Again rectification cannot be used where the grantor's original intention was defective, for example, because of the existence of error *in substantialibus*. The court is only concerned with the narrow circumstances where the document does not accurately reflect the grantor's intention at the date it was executed. In other words, the power to rectify a document in s.8(1)(*a*) and (*b*) is only to enable the deed to give effect to the parties' or grantor's intentions: the courts cannot formulate new terms for the parties.

Subs. (2)
This makes a further exception to the parole evidence rule by empowering the court to examine all relevant evidence extrinsic to the document.

Subs. (3)
This provides the court with an ancillary power to rectify any document which is defectively expressed as a consequence of the defect in the original document which as a result of an

application under s.8(1), the court is in the course of rectifying. The reference to "any other document intended for any of the purposes mentioned in paragraph (*a*) or (*b*) of subsection (1) above", limits the class of documents subject to the court's ancillary power to the same categories of documents subject to its original power of rectification.

Subs. (4)

The effect of this provision is that a document ordered to be rectified "shall have effect as if it had always been so rectified". Thus, as a general rule, rectification has retroactive effect, going back to the date of the execution of the document, thus restoring the parties to the position originally intended. This is, however, subject to s.9(4), by virtue of which, for the purpose of protecting the interests of third parties, the court may order that the rectification take effect at a later date.

Subs. (5)

When a document which has been recorded in the Register of Sasines is ordered to be rectified, then when the order is recorded, the document will be treated as having been always so recorded as rectified. Thus, again, the general rule is that rectification has retroactive effect. This is subject to s.9(5), by virtue of which, for the purpose of protecting the interests of third parties the court may order that the document as rectified be treated as recorded at a later date.

Subs. (6)

This excludes documents of a testamentary nature from the scope of the new remedy.

Subs. (7)
"a deed relating to land"

This section is only concerned with an application for rectification of a deed relating to land. It enables a notice of litigiosity to be registered in the Register of Inhibitions and Adjudications, thus prohibiting the voluntary alienation of land which could be effected by an order for rectification. Similar powers currently exist in relation to actions of reduction.

Subs. (8)

This provision requires the notice to give the names and designations of the parties to the application and the date when authority for service or citation was granted. However, in order to facilitate searches in the register, the notice must also contain a description of the land to which the application relates. This will be particularly useful where the name of a party is a common one, or where he owns several pieces of land other than the one to which the application relates.

Provisions supplementary to section 8: protection of other interest

9.—(1) The court shall order a document to be rectified under section 8 of this Act only where it is satisfied—

    (*a*) that the interests of a person to whom this section applies would not be adversely affected to a material extent by the rectification; or

    (*b*) that that person has consented to the proposed rectification.

(2) Subject to subsection (3) below, this section applies to a person (other than a party to the agreement or the grantor of the document) who has acted or refrained from acting in reliance on the terms of the document or on the title sheet of an interest in land registered in the Land Register of Scotland being an interest to which the document relates, with the result that his position has been affected to a material extent.

(3) This section does not apply to a person—

    (*a*) who, at the time when he acted or refrained from acting as mentioned in subsection (2) above, knew, or ought in the circumstances known to him at that time to have been aware, that the document or (as the case may be) the title sheet failed accurately to express the common intention of the parties to the agreement or, as the case may be, the intention of the grantor of the document; or (*b*) whose reliance on the terms of the document or on the title sheet was otherwise unreasonable.

(4) Notwithstanding subsection (4) of section 8 of this Act and without prejudice to subsection (5) below, the court may, for the purpose of protecting the interests of a person to whom this section applies, order that the rectification of a document shall have effect as at such date as it may specify, being a date later than that as at which it would have effect by virtue of the said subsection (4).

(5) Notwithstanding subsection (5) of section 8 of this Act and without prejudice to subsection (4) above, the court may, for the purpose of protecting the interests of a person to whom this section applies, order that a document as rectified shall be treated as having been recorded as mentioned in the said subsection (5) at such date as it may specify, being a date later than that as at which it would be treated by virtue of that subsection as having been so recorded.

(6) For the purposes of subsection (1) above, the court may require the Keeper of the Registers of Scotland to produce such information as he has in his possession relating to any persons who have asked him to supply details with regard to a title sheet mentioned in subsection (2) above; and any expense incurred by the Keeper under this subsection shall be borne by the applicant for the order.

(7) Where a person to whom this section applies was unaware, before a document was ordered to be rectified under section 8 of this Act, that an application had been made under that section for the rectification of the document, the Court of Session, on an application made by that person within the time specified in subsection (8) below, may—

(*a*) reduce the rectifying order; or

(*b*) order the applicant for the rectifying order to pay such compensation to that person as it thinks fit in respect of his reliance on the terms of the document or on the title sheet.

(8) The time referred to in subsection (7) above is whichever is the earlier of the following—

(*a*) the expiry of 5 years after the making of the rectifying order;

(*b*) the expiry of 2 years after the making of that order first came to the notice of the person referred to in that subsection.

GENERAL NOTE

This provision is supplementary to s.8. It provides for the protection of third parties whose interests may be adversely affected to a material extent by the rectification and who have not consented to the proposed rectification.

Subs. (1)

This provision protects a third party who has relied on a defectively expressed document, or an entry in the Land Register related to such a document, where his interests would be adversely affected to a material extent by the rectification and he has not consented to the proposed rectification. It does so by providing that the court cannot order a document to be rectified unless satisfied that the interests of the third party would not adversely affected to a material extent *or* that he has consented to the proposed rectification.

Subs. (2)

This defines the person protected by subs. (1) as being a person other than a party to the agreement or the grantor of the document, who has acted or refrained from acting in reliance on the terms of the document or the title sheet of an interest in land registered in the Land Register of Scotland being an interest to which the document relates, with the result that his position has been affected to a material extent. It is necessary that the person has acted or refrained from acting in reliance on the document. This subsection is, however, subject to subs. (3).

Subs. (3)

Parties are excluded from the protection of this section if they were in bad faith *i.e.* knew or in all the circumstances ought to have known of the defective expression in the document.

Moreover subs. 3(*b*) provides that a person, although acting in good faith, will be excluded from protection if his reliance on the document was unreasonable.

Subs. (4)

While, as a general rule, rectification has retroactive effect, back to the date of execution of the document (s.8(4)) the court is given a discretion by this subsection to order the rectification to have effect from a later date, to protect the interests of a third party to which this section applies. This is without prejudice to its powers under s.9(5).

Subs. (5)

While, as a general rule, when a document recorded in the Register of Sasines is rectified, it is to be treated as having always been so recorded as rectified (s.8(5)), the court is given a discretion by this subsection to order that a document as rectified should be treated as having been so recorded at a later date, in order to protect the interests of a third party to whom this section applies. This is without prejudice to its powers under s.9(4).

Subs. (6)

This provision gives the court the power to require the keeper of the Registers of Scotland to produce such information he has in his possession regarding any persons who have consulted a title sheet of an interest in land which may be subject to rectification as the result of rectification of a document. Thus the court will be able to assess the interests of all relevant third parties.

Subs. (7)

This provision is designed to protect a relevant third party who was unaware that an application for rectification was being made and whose interests were not taken into account before the order was made. In these circumstances, the Court of Session may either reduce the rectifying order or order the applicant for the rectifying order to pay such compensation to the third party as it thinks fit in respect of his reliance on the terms of the document or the sheet. This is, however, subject to the time limits in s.9(8).

Subs. (8)

The earlier of two limitation periods applies for bringing an application for reduction or compensation under s.9(7):
  (a) the period of five years after the making of the rectifying order; or
  (b) the period of two years after the third party first had notice that the rectifying order had been made.

It was thought unreasonable that if the third party had notice of the rectification order shortly after it was made, he should have up to five years in order to challenge it; consequently the shorter limitation period was introduced which is applicable when the rectification order has come to the notice of the third party.

Negligent misrepresentation

10.—(1) A party to a contract who has been induced to enter into it by negligent misrepresentation made by or on behalf of another party to the contract shall not be disentitled, by reason only that the misrepresentation is not fraudulent, from recovering damages from the other party in respect of any loss or damage he has suffered as a result of the misrepresentation; and any rule of law that such damages cannot be recovered unless fraud is proved shall cease to have effect.

(2) Subsection (1) applies to any proceedings commenced on or after the date on which it comes into force, whether or not the negligent misrepresentation was made before or after that date, but does not apply to any proceedings commenced before that date.

GENERAL NOTE

It is accepted that in Scots law there is general liability for culpa arising from a negligent misrepresentation: *John Kenway* v. *Orcantic Ltd.*, 1980 S.L.T. 46. But this does not apply in the case where the negligent misrepresentation induced the pursuer to enter into a contract with the person who made the representation: *Eastern Marine Services (and Supplies) Ltd.* v. *Dickson Motors Ltd.*, 1981 S.C. 355; *Twomax Ltd.* v. *Dickson, McFarlane*

& *Robinson*, 1983 S.L.T. 98. The reason for this anomalous situation is the decision of the Inner House in *Manners* v. *Whitehead* (1898) 1 F. 171, where it was held that a person who has been induced to enter into a contract as a result of a misrepresentation made by the other party to the contract, could seek rescission of the contract and restitution but could not obtain damages *in delict* unless he could prove fraud *cf.* negligence. Even though the rationale of the decision in *Manners* would appear inconsistent with the general principles of liability for negligent misrepresentation laid down by the House of Lords in *Hedley Byrne & Co.* v. *Heller & Partners* [1964] A.C. 465, and accepted as part of Scots law, the Scottish courts have hitherto refused to apply the maxim *cessante ratione cessat ipsa lex* to free themselves from the case, though to be fair, they have kept its effect within the narrowest of bounds: see *Ferguson* v. *Mackay*, 1985 S.L.T. 94.

The rule in *Manners* v. *Whitehead* did nevertheless prevent the logical development of liability for culpa in the area of negligent misrepresentation and professional negligence. The matter was considered by the Scottish Law Commission which recommended that the rule should be abolished (Scot Law No. 92). S.10 implements this recommendation. The effect of s.10 is that a person who has been induced to enter into a contract as a result of a negligent misrepresentation made by or on behalf of another party to the contract, shall no longer be disentitled to recover damages in delict merely because the misrepresentation is not fraudulent. The pursuer will, of course, have to prove *inter alia* that, in the circumstances, the defender owed him a duty of care and that the misrepresentation was, in fact, made negligently. Where a professional man induces a person to enter a contract with him, this is surely the paradigm situation where a duty of care should be owed: see *Esso Petroleum Co. Ltd.* v. *Mardon* [1976] Q.B. 801 *per* Lord Denning M.R. at p.820. The difficulties of proving negligence can be eased by judicious use of the *res ipsa loquitur* doctrine. Thus the way is now open for the rational development of negligent misrepresentation in the Scots law of delict.

Subs. (1)
"A party to a contract"
The rule in *Manners* v. *Whitehead* was restricted to the situation where the pursuer was a party to the contract which he had been induced to enter as a result of a misrepresentation made by or on behalf of the defender. Before *Hedley Byrne & Co.* v. *Heller & Partners* [1964] A.C. 465, it was doubtful whether a defender owed a duty of care to a pursuer who had been induced to enter into a contract with a third party as a result of the defender's misrepresentation: see, *Robinson* v. *National Bank of Scotland*, 1916 S.C. (H.L.) 154 *cf.* T. B. Smith, *A Short Commentary on the Law of Scotland*, p.676 at note 19. When *Hedley Byrne & Co.* v. *Heller & Partners* [1964] A.C. 405 opened up the possibility of liability in these circumstances, the rule in *Manner* v. *Whitehead* became anomalous: see GENERAL NOTE *supra*.

"made by or on behalf of another party to the contract"
The scope of the rule in *Manners* v. *Whitehead* included misrepresentations made by the defender or his agent, which had induced the pursuer to enter into contract with the defender.

"shall not be disentitled by reason only that the misrepresentation is not fraudulent"
The section merely removes the disability to sue as a result of the rule in *Manners* v. *Whitehead, i.e.* that the misrepresentation was not actionable in delict unless the pursuer could establish fraud. Although this disability is now removed the onus rests on the pursuer to establish culpa on the part of the defender arising from the misrepresentation. It is left to the judges to continue to develop the law relating to delictual actions in respect of misrepresentation resulting in economic loss to the pursuer.

"and any rule of law that such damages cannot be recovered unless fraud is proved shall cease to have effect"
This provision in effect abolishes the rule in *Manners* v. *Whitehead*.

Subs. (2)
This provides that the rule in *Manners* v. *Whitehead* cannot be relied upon in any proceedings commenced on or after s.10(1) came into force: it is irrelevant that the negligent misrepresentation was made before that date. However, it will continue to apply in proceedings commenced before s.10(1) came into operation.

Amendment of Bills of Exchange Act 1882 as respects countermanded cheques

11. In the Bills of Exchange Act 1882—

    (*a*) at the beginning of section 53(2) (which provides as to the effect of presentment of a bill of exchange) there shall be inserted the words "Subject to section 75A of this Act,"; and

    (*b*) after section 75 there shall be inserted the following section—

        "75A.—(1) On the countermand of payment of a cheque, the banker shall be treated as having no funds available for the payment of the cheque.

        (2) This section applies to Scotland only.".

GENERAL NOTE

  This section is designed to remove a difficulty which has arisen in relation to cheques. If a person stops a cheque, the amount for which the cheque is drawn is transferred by the bank to a non-interest-bearing suspense account. The funds remain there until the dispute giving rise to the countermand is settled or there is a court action to unfreeze them or until the prescriptive period of five years has elapsed. The reason why this is done is that it is a fundamental principle of Scots law that where the drawee of a bill, *i.e.* the banker has in his hands funds available for the payment thereof, the bill operates as an assignation of the sum for which it is drawn in favour of the holder from the time when the bill is presented to the drawee: s.53(2) of the Bills of Exchange Act 1882. The amendments to the 1882 Act remove the current injustice in relation to stopped cheques by the simple expedient of providing that on the countermand of payment of a cheque, the banker is deemed to have no funds available for the payment of the cheque; thus, s.53(2) will not operate in relation to countermanded cheques. For an important discussion on the legal issues raised by counter-manded cheques in Scots law, see G. L. Gretton, *The Stopped Cheque*, (1983) 28 J.L.S.S. pp.333 and 389.

New subs. 75A(1)
"On the countermand of payment of a cheque"
  S.75A only applies in relation to cheques.

"the banker shall be treated as having no funds available for the payment of the cheque"
  The general principle is that presentment of a bill of exchange operates as an assignation of funds in favour of the payee *provided the drawee has funds available to make payment.* S.75A, by deeming that the banker, *i.e.* the drawee, has no funds available, thus provides a solution to the particular problems arising from countermanded cheques, without over-turning the general principle in s.53(2) of the Bills of Exchange Act 1882.

New subs. 75A(2)
"This section applies to Scotland only"
  In England a bill, of itself, does not operate as an assignment of funds in the hands of the drawee which are available to make payment: see s.53(1) of the Bills of Exchange Act 1882.

Limitation of defamation and other actions

12.—(1) The Prescription and Limitation (Scotland) Act 1973 shall be amended in accordance with the following provisions of this section.

  (2) After section 18 of that Act there shall be inserted the following section—

    "Limitation of defamation and other actions

    18A—(1) Subject to subsections (2) and (3) below and section 19A of this Act, no action for defamation shall be brought unless it is commenced within a period of 3 years after the date when the right of action accrued.

    (2) In the computation of the period specified in subsection (1) above there shall be disregarded any time during which the person alleged to have been defamed was under legal disability by reason of nonage or unsoundness of mind.

(3) Nothing in this section shall affect any right of action which accrued before the commencement of this section.

(4) In this section—

(*a*) "defamation" includes *convicium* and malicious falsehood, and "defamed" shall be construed accordingly; and

(*b*) references to the date when a right of action accrued shall be construed as references to the date when the publication or communication in respect of which the action for defamation is to be brought first came to the notice of the pursuer."

(3) In section 19A(1) of that Act (power of court to override time limits) after "18" there shall be inserted the words "and 18A".

(4) In section 22(2) of that Act (assigned rights of action) for the words "or 18" there shall be substituted the words ", 18 or 18A" and for the words ", as the case may be, 18" there shall be substituted the words "of the said section 18 or, as the case may be, subsection (4)(*b*) of the said section 18A".

(5) In Schedule 1 to that Act, in paragraph 2 (obligations to which the five year prescription does not apply) after subparagraph (*g*) there shall be inserted the following—

"(*gg*) to any obligation to make reparation or otherwise make good in respect of defamation within the meaning of section 18A of this Act;".

GENERAL NOTE

The purpose of this provision is to reduce the limitation period for defamation actions from five to three years. The amendments to the Prescription and Limitation (Scotland) Act 1973 will bring the limitation period for actions of defamation into line with that for personal injury claims: see s.17 of the 1973 Act.

However, the new s.18A is subject to s.19A of the 1973 Act whereby a court has discretion to allow an action outwith the three-year period, if it is equitable to do so.

Subs. (2)
New subs. 18A(2)
"legal disability by reason of non-age or unsoundness of mind"

Following the principle in ss.17(3) and 18(3) of the 1973 Act (as substituted by ss.2 and 3 of the Prescription and Limitation (Scotland) Act 1984), even if time has begun to run, any period during which the person alleged to have been defamed was under legal disability by reason of non-age or unsoundness of mind is to be left out of account.

It would appear that non-age means simply that the person has not reached the age of majority, *i.e.* 18. (This was certainly the view of the Scottish Law Commission on the basis of whose Report the 1984 Act was enacted: see Scot. Law Com. No. 74, paras. 3.35–42.) *Cf.* the view of the Under Secretary of State for Scotland who thought it was 16! (Report of the First Scottish Standing Committee, January 24, 1985, col. 133.)

New subs. 18A(3)

This subsection makes it clear that the new limitation period is not retrospective, *i.e.* it does not apply where any right of action has accrued before the commencement of the section.

New subs. 18A(4)(a)

Defamation is not restricted to the delict defamation *strictu senso* but includes *convicium* and malicious falsehood. It therefore covers all three aspects of verbal injury as understood by Walker *viz.*:

". . . verbal injury is the genus, and it comprises three species, *convicium*, defamation (or libel or slander), and malicious or injurious falsehood" *Delict* (2nd ed., 1981), p.732.

New subs. 18A(4)(b)

The date when a right of action accrued is to be the date when the publication or communication in respect of which the action for defamation is to be brought "*first came to the notice of the pursuer*". Thus time will only begin to run when the defamatory material is communicated to the pursuer.

Subs. (3)

This provides that s.18A is subject to s.19A whereby a court can override the three-year limitation period, "if it seems equitable to do so".

Subs. (4)

Where an assignee is suing, the three-year limitation period runs from the date when the publication or communication in respect of which the action for defamation is brought first came to the notice of the assignor, not the assignee. It should be noticed, moreover, that s.18A(2) operates in favour of the person alleged to have been defamed only and not to the assignee.

Subs. (5)

This adds the obligation to make reparation in respect of defamation to the list of obligations to which the prescriptive period of five years under s.6 of the Prescription and Limitation (Scotland) Act 1973 does not apply.

Amendments of Matrimonial Homes (Family Protection) (Scotland) Act 1981

13.—(1) The Matrimonial Homes (Family Protection) (Scotland) Act 1981 shall be amended in accordance with the following provisions of this section.

(2) In section 1(1)(*a*) of that Act (right of occupying spouse not to be excluded from matrimonial home), for the words from "not" to the end there shall be substituted the words "to continue to occupy the matrimonial home;".

(3) After section 1 of that Act there shall be inserted the following subsection—

"(1A) The rights conferred by subsection (1) above to continue to occupy or, as the case may be, to enter and occupy the matrimonial home include, without prejudice to their generality, the right to so so together with any child of the family.".

(4) In section 1(6) of that Act (renunciation of occupancy rights to be sworn or affirmed before notary public) at the end there shall be added the following—

"In this subsection, "notary public" includes any person duly authorised by the law of the country (other than Scotland) in which the swearing or affirmation takes place to administer oaths or receive affirmations in that other country.".

(5) In section 4(1) of that Act after the words "either spouse" there shall be inserted the words "whether or not that spouse is in occupation at the time of the application.".

(6) In section 6 of that Act (continued exercise of occupancy rights after dealings with the matrimonial home)—

(*a*) the word "or" occurring immediately after subsection (3)(*d*) shall be omitted;

(*b*) in subsection (3)(*e*)—

(i) for the words "purchase of a matrimonial home by" there shall be substituted the words "a sale to";

(ii) after the word "at" there shall be inserted the words "or before";

(iii) for the words from "entitled spouse", where first occurring, the word "spouse", where thirdly occurring, there shall be substituted the words—

"seller—

(i) an affidavit sworn or affirmed by the seller declaring that the subjects of sale are not a matrimonial home in relation to which a spouse of the seller has occupancy rights;" and

(iv) at the end there shall be added the words—
> "For the purposes of this paragraph, the time of the dealing, in the case of the sale of an interest in heritable property, is the date of delivery to the purchaser of the deed transferring title to that interest.";

(*c*) after subsection (3)(*e*) there shall be added—
> "; or

(*f*) the entitled spouse has permanently ceased to be entitled to occupy the matrimonial home, and at any time thereafter a continuous period of 5 years has elapsed during which the non-entitled spouse has not occupied the matrimonial home.".

(7) In section 8(2) of that Act (protection of interests of heritable creditors) after the word "apply" there shall be inserted the words "to secured loans in respect of which the security was granted prior to the commencement of section 13 of the Law Reform (Miscellaneous Provisions) (Scotland) Act 1985".

(8) After section 8(2) of that Act there shall be inserted the following subsections—
> "(2A) This section shall not apply to secured loans in respect of which the security was granted after the commencement of section 13 of the Law Reform (Miscellaneous Provisions) (Scotland) Act 1985 unless the third party in granting the secured loan acted in good faith and at or before the granting of the security there was produced to the third party by the grantor—
>
> (*a*) an affidavit sworn or affirmed by the grantor declaring that the security subjects are not a matrimonial home in relation to which a spouse of the grantor has occupancy rights; or
>
> (*b*) a renunciation of occupancy rights or consent to the granting of the security which bears to have been properly made or given by the non-entitled spouse.
>
> (2B) For the purposes of subsections (2) and (2A) above, the time of granting a security, in the case of a heritable security, is the date of delivery of the deed creating the security.".

(9) In section 18 of that Act (occupancy rights of cohabiting couples)—
(*a*) in subsection (1) for the word "3" there shall be inserted the word "6"; and
(*b*) in subsection (6), in the definition of "occupancy rights"—
(i) in paragraph (a) for the words from "not" to the end there shall be substituted the words "to continue to occupy the house;" and
(ii) at the end there shall be inserted the words—
> "and, without prejudice to the generality of these rights, includes the right to continue to occupy or, as the case may be, to enter and occupy the house together with any child residing with the cohabiting couple".

(10) In section 22 of that Act in the definition of "matrimonial home" there shall be added at the end the following—
> "but does not include a residence provided or made available by one spouse for that spouse to reside in, whether with any child of the family or not, separately from the other spouse.".

(11) Any—
(*a*) affidavit lawfully sworn or affirmed before the commencement of this section in pursuance of paragraph (*e*) of subsection (3) of section 6 or subsection (2) of section 8 of that Act;
(*b*) consent lawfully given before such commencement in pursuance of the said subsection (2),

shall have effect for the purposes of the said subsection (3) as amended by this section or, as the case may be, section 8(2A) of that Act as if it had been duly sworn, affirmed or, as the case may be, given in pursuance of the said paragraph (*e*) as so amended or, as the case may be, the said section 8(2A).

GENERAL NOTE

The purpose of this section is to make amendments to the Matrimonial Homes (Family Protection) (Scotland) Act 1981. The amendments seek to strengthen the right of occupation of the non-entitled spouse and to remove some of the conveyancing difficulties which have been experienced in operating the 1981 Act.

Subs. (2)

Under s.1(1) of 1981 Act, a non-entitled spouse had two rights,
>   (a) if in occupation, a right not to be excluded from the matrimonial home or any part of it by the entitled spouse;
>   (b) if not in occupation, a right to enter into and occupy the matrimonial home.

It is not clear from the wording of s.1(1)(*a*) whether the non-entitled spouse's right is merely not to be excluded from the matrimonial home or is a positive right to occupy the home, with all the rights implicit in the right to occupy, such as the right to invite others into the house.

The effect of the amendment to s.1(1)(*a*) is to make it clear that a non-entitled spouse has a positive right under s.1(1)(*a*) to occupy the matrimonial home *viz.* "if in occupation, a right to continue to occupy the matrimonial home".

Subs. (3)

On a strict interpretation of s.1(1) of the 1981 Act, the statutory rights are rights enjoyed by the non-entitled spouse alone. In some cases, where a wife was the non-entitled spouse who had left the home with her children, her statutory rights were frustrated because her husband, the entitled spouse, was prepared to allow her to re-enter the matrimonial home but not to allow the children to return. The effect of the new s.1(1A) is to make it clear that the statutory rights to occupy the matrimonial home includes the right to do so "together with any child of the family".

"child of the family"

This is defined in s.22 of the 1981 Act as including "any child or grandchild of either spouse, and any person who has been brought up or accepted by either spouse as if he or she were a child of that spouse, whatever the age of such a child, grandchild or person may be".

There is no age limit, but where a child is an adult, that will be a factor which the courts will take into account when regulating the statutory rights of occupation: see ss.3(3)(*c*) and 4(3)(*a*) of the 1981 Act. Where an adult child is suffering from a physical or mental disability, this will, of course, be a particularly important factor to be taken into account.

Subs. (4)

A non-entitled spouse may renounce in writing his or her occupancy rights (s.1.(5)) but must swear or affirm before a notary public that it was made freely and without coercion of any kind (s.1(6)). The question has arisen whether s.1(6) would be satisfied if a non-entitled spouse swore or affirmed in a country other than Scotland, before a person who was authorised to administer oaths or receive affirmations by the law of that country. The effect of the amendment is to enable a non-entitled spouse to do so, without having to come to Scotland. This is achieved by extending the definition of notary public for the purpose of s.1(6) to include any person authorised to administer oaths or receive affirmations by the law of the country where the non-entitled spouse swears or affirms.

Subs. (5)

By s.4 of the 1981 Act, a spouse may apply for an exclusion order or interim exclusion order, suspending the occupancy rights of the non-applicant spouse. The court shall make such an order if it appears to the court "necessary" for the protection of the applicant or any child of the family from the conduct or reasonably apprehended conduct of the non-applicant spouse which is or would be injurious to the physical or mental health of the applicant or child.

In the case of *Bell* v. *Bell*, 1983 S.L.T. 224, the Inner House considered that it was not "necessary" to make an exclusion order where the applicant had obtained an interim interdict against her husband against molesting her and had left the matrimonial home to live in temporary accommodation. As there was no evidence that the husband had broken the interdict, an exclusion order was not necessary and her application under s.4 failed. This "high and severe" test for "necessary" was approved by the Inner House in *Smith* v. *Smith* 1983 S.L.T. 275.

This decision led to the fear that the courts would refuse an applicant an exclusion order whenever he or she had left the matrimonial home. However, in *Colagiacomo* v. *Colagia-como*, 1983 S.L.T. 559, the Lord Justice Clerk (Wheatley) attempted to remove these fears.

"If there is any misconception that following *Bell* v. *Bell* an interim exclusion order will only be granted if the parties are both occupying the matrimonial home, the sooner that misconception is removed the better. The fact that only one of the parties is occupying the matrimonial home is a factor to be taken into account but it is not *per se* to be regarded as a conclusive one" (*ibid.* at p. 562).

Thus, provided the necessity criterion is established, an applicant can obtain an exclusion order, even though not living in the matrimonial home at the time of the application: see for example, *Ward* v. *Ward*, 1983 S.L.T. 472; *Brown* v. *Brown*, 1985 S.L.T. 376.

While the fears raised by *Bell* v. *Bell* and *Smith* v. *Smith* have now been resolved as a result of these later decisions, nevertheless, the opportunity was taken to put beyond doubt that a spouse may apply under s.4 even although he or she has left the matrimonial home at the time of the application. This is done by amending s.4(1) so that it states expressly that, "either spouse, whether or not that spouse is in occupation at the time of the application, may apply to the court for an order".

Subs. (6)

The non-entitled spouse's statutory rights of occupation are prima facie effective against third parties. This is achieved by s.6(1) of the 1981 Act which provides that the statutory rights "shall not be prejudiced by reason only of any dealing of the entitled spouse relating to that home".

S.6(3) provides exceptions. The most important is s.6(3)(*e*). In its original form it read as follows:—

"The dealing comprises the purchase of a matrimonial home by a third party who has acted in good faith, if, at the time of the dealing, there is produced to the third party by the entitled spouse—

(i) an affidavit sworn or affirmed by the entitled spouse declaring that there is no non-entitled spouse; or

(ii) a renunciation of occupancy rights or consent to the dealing which bears to have been properly made or given by the non-entitled spouse".

The present wording has proved unsatisfactory and this subsection *inter alia* amends s.6(3)(*e*) in order to "tidy up" some of the difficulties.

Subs. (b)(i)

In its original form, for s.6(3) to apply the dealing must comprise "the purchase of a matrimonial home by a third party". The obvious construction of this phrase is that the bona fide purchaser is buying the entitled spouse's matrimonial house. However, it could be construed to mean that the bona fide purchaser must himself purchase the property for use as a matrimonial home. If so, this would limit the protection of s.6(3)(*e*) to bona fide purchasers who were buying the property for use as a matrimonial home.

To remove any doubts, the phrase, "a sale to" a third party is substituted for the phrase "a purchase of a matrimonial home by" a third party, making it clear that the protection is not limited to bona fide third parties who purchase the property for use as a matrimonial home.

Subs. (b)(ii) and (iv)

In its original form, s.6(3)(*e*) states that the affidavit must be produced "at the time of the dealing". This phrase was not defined and there was therefore doubt as to its meaing. These doubts are removed by the amendment in subs. (*b*)(iv) which provides that the time of the dealing is the date of delivery to the purchaser of the title deeds. Moreover the phrase is amended by subs. (*b*)(ii) to read "at *or before* the time of the delivery" so that it is sufficient if the affidavit has been produced earlier in the conveyancing process.

Subs. (b)(iii)

It its original form, s.6(3)(*e*)(i) provides that the entitled spouse must swear or affirm an affidavit that there is no non-entitled spouse. This form of affidavit is unsatisfactory in two situations:

(a) Where the property to be sold is not a matrimonial home. The seller may well be married and have a non-entitled spouse who has a statutory right in the house which is the matrimonial home. To declare that there is no non-entitled spouse in these circumstances is a lie.

(b) Where the person who is selling the property is not married. As s.6(3)(*e*)(i) specifically states that the affidavit is sworn or affirmed by the entitled spouse, an unmarried person cannot strictly take advantage of this provision as he or she is not an entitled *spouse.*

To remove these difficulties the word "seller" is substituted for "entitled spouse" and the affidavit takes the form of a declaration that the property is "not a matrimonial home in relation to which a spouse of the seller has occupancy rights".

Subs. (c)

This adds a further exception to the general principle that a non-entitled spouse's statutory rights are prima facie effective against third parties. This amendment to s.6(3) provides that when the entitled spouse has permanently ceased to be entitled to occupy the matrimonial home, for example, by selling it, the non-entitled spouse's rights cease to be exercisable against a third party if the non-entitled spouse has, at any time thereafter, not occupied the property for a continuous period of five years.

"ceased to be entitled to occupy the matrimonial home"

This phrase is deliberately wide. It will cover not only the sale of the property but also the assignation of a lease or the compulsory sale of the property when the entitled spouse was granted a security over it but has defaulted.

Subs. (7) and (8)

In it original form, s.8 of the 1981 Act provided that the interests of a heritable creditor are not prejudiced by the statutory rights of a non-entitled spouse, *provided* the heritable creditor acted in good faith and, before the granting of the loan the entitled spouse produced an affidavit declaring that there is no non-entitled spouse (s.8(2)(*a*)) or a renunciation or consent purporting to be made by the non-entitled spouse.

The form of the affidavit in s.8(2)(*a*) suffered from the same defects discussed above in the context of s.6(3)(*e*)(i): see notes to subs. (*b*)(i), (ii), (iii), and (iv) *supra*. The effect of subsections (7) and (8) is to provide a new form of affidavit which will remove the difficulties which have been experienced in a similar way to the amendments to s.6(3)(*e*). However, the new form of affidavit only applies to secured loans granted after the date of the commencement of this section: subs. (7).

New subs. 8(2A)
"This section shall not apply"

S.8(1) provides that the rights of a heritable creditor will not be prejudiced, but it will not apply unless the heritable creditor acted in good faith and received an affidavit or renunciation in accordance with s.8(2A).

"after the commencement of section 13 of the Law Reform (Miscellaneous Provisions) (Scotland) Act 1985"

The new form of affidavit only applies to loans granted after the commencement of this section. For loans granted before that date, the form of affidavit in s.8(2) must still be used.

"the grantor"

This phrase is used instead of "entitled spouse" to avoid the difficulties discussed in note to subs. (*b*)(iii) *supra*. Thus an unmarried person can swear the affidavit.

"at or before the granting of the security"

The affidavit or renunciation can be produced at or before the granting of the security, *i.e.* the delivery of the deeds creating the security: see new s.8(2B). Where s.8(2) is still applicable it should be noted that the affidavit or renunciation must be produced "before" the *granting* of the loan.

"the security subjects are not a matrimonial home"

This enables the grantor who is married and has a non-entitled spouse to use the affidavit in respect of property which is not the matrimonial home.

New subs. 8(2B)

This makes it clear that for the purposes of ss.8(2) and (2A) the time of granting a heritable security is the date of delivery of the deed creating the security. The reference to s.8(2) is necessary because of the amendment to s.8(2) made by subs. (7): see note to subs. (7) and (8).

Subs. (9)(a)

In its original form, s.18(1) of the 1981 Act provided that where a couple were cohabiting as husband and wife, the non-entitled partner could apply for occupancy rights and the court could "grant occupancy rights therein to the applicant for such period, not exceeding three months, as the court may specify". The court could, however, extend this initial period for a further period or periods of up to six months with no overall limit. In practice, it has been found that the initial period of three months is too short to enable applicants to examine the options available in regard to their housing needs, for example, the transfer of the tenancy under s.13 of the 1981 Act. Accordingly, to save the need for applications for extensions, the maximum length of the initial period of occupancy rights is raised from three to six months.

Subs. (9)(b)

The effect of this provision is to amend the definitions of the occupancy rights of cohabiting couples in s.18(6) of the 1981 Act. The changes correspond to those made by ss.13(2) and (3) *supra*, in relation to the occupancy rights of spouses.

Subs. (10)

Where a couple have separated, and one spouse has provided or made available, for example, by transferring the tenancy of the existing home, a house for the other to live in (with or without a child of the family), the effect of this amendment to s.22 of the 1981 Act is to exclude that property from the definition of a matrimonial home. Accordingly, the spouse who provided or made the residence available will no longer have statutory rights of occupation in respect of it and the other spouse will be able to reside there without fear that the other may turn up at any time and insist on resuming occupation.

Subs. (11)

This is a transitional provision. It provides that any affidavit lawfully sworn or affirmed under s.6(3)(*e*) or s.8(2) as originally drafted or any consent lawfully given under s.8(2), if done so before the commencement of this section, shall have effect for the purposes of the amended s.6(3)(*e*) and the new s.8(2A) as if they had been duly sworn, affirmed or given in pursuance of the new provisions. Thus there will be no need to produce a fresh affidavit or consent at or before the dealing or the granting of the security, if this takes place after the commencement of the section.

Provisions relating to civil jurisdiction and procedure

Remit from Court of Session to sheriff

14. The Court of Session may in relation to an action before it which could competently have been brought before a sheriff remit the action (at its own instance or on the application of any of the parties to the action) to the sheriff within whose jurisdiction the action could have been brought, where, in the opinion of the Court, the nature of the action makes it appropriate to do so.

GENERAL NOTE

This section gives the Court of Session the right to remit an action which could competently have been brought before a sheriff, to the sheriff within whose jurisdiction it could have been brought.

"at its own instance or on the application of any of the parties to the action"

Not merely does the power exist when an application for the remit is made by either party to the action, but the court may remit the action at its own instance. However, it is unlikely that a Court of Session judge would order a remit without having fully considered the views of the parties. Moreover, there are the usual rights of appeal against his decision.

"the nature of the action makes it appropriate to do so"

It is not intended that this section should be used to transfer whole categories of actions from the Court of Session to the sheriff court. Instead it is envisaged that a remit would only be made when in the circumstances of the particular case it would be appropriate to do so, for example, if there were other related proceedings currently before the sheriff court and for reasons of efficiency and convenience of the parties, it would be desirable that both sets of proceedings should be dealt with in one court: see the views of the Lord Advocate H.L. Vol. 467, col. 194.

Withdrawal of privilege against self-incrimination in certain proceedings relating to intellectual property

15.—(1) In any proceedings to which this subsection applies a person shall not be excused, by reason that to do so would tend to expose him to proceedings for a related offence or for the recovery of a related penalty—

> (a) from answering any questions put to him in the first-mentioned proceedings; or
>
> (b) from complying with any order made in those proceedings.

(2) Subsection (1) above applies to civil proceedings in the Court of Session or the sheriff court—

> (a) for infringement of rights pertaining to any intellectual property or for passing off;
>
> (b) brought to obtain disclosure of information relating to any infringement of such rights or to any passing off; and
>
> (c) brought to prevent any apprehended infringement of such rights or any apprehended passing off.

(3) The proceedings referred to in subsection (2) above include—

> (a) proceedings on appeal arising out of these proceedings;
>
> (b) proceedings under section 1(1) of the Administration of Justice (Scotland) Act 1972 (provision in relation to the power of the court to order inspection of documents and other property etc.) which relate to civil proceedings falling within subsection (2) above which are likely to be brought.

(4) No statement or admission made by a person—

> (a) in answering a question put to him in any proceedings to which subsection (1) applies; or
>
> (b) in complying with any order made in such proceedings,

shall in proceedings for any related offence, or for the recovery of any related penalty, be admissible in evidence against him;

Provided that this subsection shall not render any such statement or admission inadmissible against him in proceedings for perjury or contempt of court.

(5) In this section—

> "intellectual property" means any patent, trade mark, copyright, registered design, technical or commercial information or other intellectual property;
>
> "related offence", in relation to any proceedings to which subsection (1) above applies, means—
>
>> (a) in the case of proceedings within subsection (2)(a) or (b)—
>>
>>> (i) any offence committed by or in the course of the infringement or passing off to which those proceedings relate; or

      (ii) any offence not within sub-paragraph (i) commit-
          ted in connection with that infringement or passing
          off, being an offence involving fraud or dishonesty;
    (*b*) in the case of proceedings within subsection (2)(*c*), any
      offence revealed by the facts on which the pursuer relies
      in those proceedings.
"related penalty", in relation to any proceedings to which subsection
(1) above applies, means—
    (*a*) in the case of proceedings within subsection (2)(*a*) or (*b*),
      any penalty incurred in respect of anything done or
      omitted in connection with the infringement or passing
      off to which those proceedings relate;
    (*b*) in the case of proceedings with subsection (2)(*c*), any
      penalty incurred in respect of any act or omission revealed
      by the facts on which the pursuer relies in those
      proceedings.

GENERAL NOTE

S.1 of the Administration of Justice (Scotland) Act 1972 empowers the court to order the
production and recovery of documents and other property prior to the raising of any
proceedings on the application of a person who appears to the court to be likely to be a
party to or minuter in proceedings which are likely to be brought. In addition an order can
be made for "the inspection, photographing, preservation, custody and detention of
documents and other property . . . which appear to the court to be property as to which any
question may relevently arise . . . in civil proceedings which are likely to be brought". The
order can be made ex parte, in order that the respondent does not have time to destroy the
relevant material.

This provision is of extreme importance in copyright infringement cases. In a case of
video "piracy", for example, the main concern of the copyright owner is to discover the
whereabouts of the master tapes. In order to trace these, it is often necessary to take
proceedings against the retailer. If a s.1 order is made in respect of the retailer's property,
for example, invoices and delivery notes, it will often be possible to trace the supplier.
However, the retailer will often have committed an offence in relation to the "piracy". In
British Phonographic Industry Ltd. v. *Cohen, Cohen, Kelly, Cohen & Cohen Ltd.* 1983
S.L.T. 137, the Inner House held (at pp. 138–9) ". . . that where what the respondents in
a petition such as this [*i.e.* under s.1 of the 1972 Act] are alleged to have done would
constitute a criminal offence the court should consider carefully whether compliance with
the order under s.1 of the Act would, if it were granted, require the respondents to
incriminate themselves. In such a case, ... , the proper course will be to refuse to grant the
application". This decision would seem correct as s.1(4) of the 1972 Act expressly preserves
the privileges of witnesses and havers. The effect of this development was, of course,
drastically to restrict the utility of s.1 proceedings in relation to copyright infringement cases:
see, generally, H. L. MacQueen, *A Copyright Anomaly Revealed,* 1983 S.L.T. (News) 133.

In England, the equivalent of a s.1 order is the Anton Piller order. But in *Rank Film
Distributors Ltd.* v. *Video Information Centre* [1982] A.C. 380, the House of Lords held that
the making of such an order was subject to the privilege against self incrimination. However,
s.72 of the Supreme Court Act 1981 overruled this case and withdrew the privilege against
self incrimination in certain proceedings in relation to intellectual property. But s.72 of the
1981 Act did not apply to Scotland.

S.15, which is modelled on s.72 of the Supreme Court Act 1981, now largely brings Scots
law into line with the current position in England. The privilege against self incrimination
is removed in civil proceedings relating to the protection of intellectual property and the
prevention of passing off, including proceedings under s.1(1) of the Administration of Justice
(Scotland) Act 1972 where an order is sought in relation to impending civil proceedings
concerned with intellectual property. Thus, the major difficulty in obtaining an order under
s.1 of the 1972 Act in copyright infringement cases is removed and the copyright owner's
attempt to trace the suppliers pirated material is thereby facilitated. However, the information so obtained from a person, while admissible in civil proceedings, is, whether
incriminating or not, not admissible in evidence in criminal proceedings related to the misuse
of the intellectual property concerned.

Subs. (1)

This withdraws the privilege against self incrimination but only in so far as it would expose the person to proceedings for a *related* offence or for the recovery of a *related* penalty *i.e.* offences and penalties arising from the misuse of intellectual property.

Subs. (2)

The proceedings concerned cover the whole range of civil proceedings related to the protection of intellectual property and the prevention of passing off.

Subs. (3)

The relevant proceedings in subs. (2) include appeals and most importantly, proceedings under s.1(1) of the 1972 Act which relate to civil proceedings falling within subs. (2) *"which are likely to be brought"*. This, in effect, reverses *British Phonograph Industry Ltd.* v. *Cohen, Cohen, Kelly, Cohen & Cohen Ltd.* 1983 S.L.T. 137, in so far as it applies to intellectual property cases. However, s.1 of the 1972 Act is not, of course, restricted to intellectual property proceedings, and, accordingly, in other areas an order may not be granted if this infringes the respondent's privilege against self incrimination.

Subs. (4)

"No statement or admission"

The statement or admission need not be incriminating: any statement or admission so obtained is not admissible in evidence against the person in criminal proceedings for any related offence or the recovery of a related penalty. An exception is made for perjury or contempt of court.

Subs. (5)

Related offence and related penalty

These are widely defined to cover the wide range of criminal offences and penalties arising from the misuse of intellectual property.

Power of sheriff to interdict removal of child

16. In section 13 of the Matrimonial Proceedings (Children) Act 1958 (which makes provision as to prohibiting the removal of a child from Scotland or from the person having control of him)—

    (*a*) in subsection (1) for the words "Court of Session" and "Court" there shall be substituted the words "appropriate court" and "court" respectively; and

    (*b*) after subsection (1) there shall be inserted the following subsection.

        "(1A) In subsection (1) above, "appropriate court" means—

        (*a*) the Court of Session (where the action in connection with which the court would have jurisdiction to make orders with respect to the custody, maintenance and education of a child is an action before the Court of Session);

        (*b*) the Court of Session or the sheriff (where the action in connection with which the court would have that jurisdiction is an action before the sheriff).".

GENERAL NOTE

Where an action has commenced in which the Court of Session or the sheriff court has jurisdiction to make orders with respect to the custody, maintenance and education of a child, s.13 of the Matrimonial Proceedings (Children) Act 1958 provided that either party to the action, the guardian of the child, or any person who has or wishes to obtain the custody or care of the child, can apply to the Court of Session to grant interim interdict prohibiting the removal of the child furth of Scotland. If the Court was satisfied that there was a likelihood that the child would be removed, it had the power to grant interim interdict accordingly.

Now that the sheriff court has jurisdiction in divorce, there has been an increase of cases in the sheriff court where the custody, maintenance and education of children will be an issue. It was therefore anomalous that the sheriff did not have power to grant interim interdict to prevent the child at the centre of those proceedings from being "kidnapped", and that resort still had to be made to the Court of Session. S.16 removes this anomaly by amending s.13 of the 1958 Act to the effect that where an action has commenced in the sheriff court, the sheriff has also the power to grant interim interdict prohibiting the removal of the child furth of Scotland.

New subs. 13(1A)(a)
Where the action has commenced in the Court of Session, only the Court of Session may grant interim interdict.

New subs. 13(1A)(b)
Where the action has commenced in the sheriff court, both the Court of Session and the sheriff may grant interim interdict. Thus the amendment merely increases the sheriff's powers: it does not affect the existing powers of the Court of Session.

Power of sheriff to order sheriff clerk to execute deeds relating to heritage

17. After section 5 of the Sheriff Courts (Scotland) Act 1907 there shall be inserted the following section—

> **"Power of sheriff to order sheriff clerk to execute deeds relating to heritage**
> 5A.—(1) This section applies where—
> (*a*) an action relating to heritable property is before the sheriff; or
> (*b*) it appears to the sheriff that an order under this section is necessary to implement a decree of a sheriff relating to heritable property.
> (2) Where the grantor of any deed relating to the heritable property cannot be found or refuses or is unable or otherwise fails to execute the deed, the sheriff may—
> (*a*) where subsection (1)(*a*) above applies, on application;
> (*b*) where subsection (1)(*b*) above applies, on summary application,
> by the grantee, make an order dispensing with the execution of the deed by the grantor and directing the sheriff clerk to execute the deed.
> (3) Where in pursuance of an order under this section a deed is executed by the sheriff clerk, it shall have the like force and effect as it it had been executed by the grantor.
> (4) In this section—
> "grantor" means a person who is under an obligation to execute the deed; and
> "grantee" means the person to whom that obligation is owed.".

GENERAL NOTE
This section adds a new provision to s.5 of the Sheriff Courts (Scotland) Act 1907 whereby the sheriff may order the sheriff clerk to execute deeds relating to heritage.

New subs. 5A(1)
This section applies where an action relating to heritable property is before the sheriff or it appears that an order is necessary to implement a decree of the sheriff relating to heritable property. It is therefore restricted to the execution of deeds relating to heritable property.

New subs. 5A(2)
"may"
The sheriff has a discretion to make an order dispensing with the execution of the deed by the grantor and directing the sheriff clerk to execute the deed, when the grantor of the deed cannot be found or refuses or is unable to execute the deed or has failed to execute the deed for any other reason.

New subs. 5A(4)
"Grantor" is used not in its normal sense of a person who grants a deed, but refers to a person who is under an obligation to grant a deed but has not done so. "Grantee" is not

used in its normal sense of a person who has obtained a deed in his favour, but refers to a person who is entitled in law to be granted the deed.

Small claims

18.—(1) For subsection (2) of section 35 of the Sheriff Courts (Scotland) Act 1971 (summary causes) there shall be substituted the following subsections—

"(2) There shall be a form of summary cause process, to be known as a "small claim", which shall be used for the purposes of such descriptions of summary cause proceedings as are prescribed by the Lord Advocate by order.

(3) No enactment or rule of law relating to admissibility or corroboration of evidence before a court of law shall be binding in a small claim.

(4) An order under subsection (2) above shall be by statutory instrument but shall not be made unless a draft of it has been approved by a resolution of each House of Parliament.".

(2) After section 36 of that Act (procedure in summary causes) there shall be inserted the following sections—

"**Further provisions as to small claims**
36A. Where the pursuer in a small claim is not—
(*a*) a partnership or a body corporate; or
(*b*) acting in a representative capacity,
he may require the sheriff clerk to effect service of the summons on his behalf.

Expenses in small claims
36B.—(1) No award of expenses shall be made in a small claim in which the value of the claim does not exceed such sum as the Lord Advocate shall prescribe by order.

(2) Any expenses which the sheriff may award in any other small claim shall not exceed such sum as the Lord Advocate shall prescribe by order.

(3) Subsections (1) and (2) above do not apply to a party to a small claim—
(*a*) who being a defender—
(i) has not stated a defence; or
(ii) having stated a defence, has not proceeded with it; or
(iii) having stated and proceeded with a defence, has not acted in good faith as to its merits; or
(*b*) on whose part there has been unreasonable conduct in relation to the proceedings or the claim;
nor do they apply in relation to an appeal to the sheriff principal.

(4) An order under this section shall be by statutory instrument but shall not be made unless a draft of it has been approved by a resolution of each House of Parliament.".

(3) In section 37 of that Act (remits)—
(*a*) after subsection (2A) there shall be inserted the following subsections—
"(2B) In the case of any small claim the sheriff at any stage—
(*a*) may, if he is of the opinion that a difficult question of law or a question of fact of exceptional complexity is involved, of his own accord or on the motion of any party to the small claim;
(*b*) shall, on the joint motion of the parties to the small claim,

direct that the small claim be treated as a summary cause
(not being a small claim) or ordinary cause, and in that case
the small claim shall be treated for all purposes (including
appeal) as a summary cause (not being a small claim) or
ordinary cause as the case may be.

(2C) In the case of any cause which is not a small claim
by reason only of any monetary limit applicable to a small
claim or to summary causes, the sheriff at any stage shall,
on the joint motion of the parties to the cause, direct that
the cause be treated as a small claim and in that case the
cause shall be treated for all purposes (including appeal) as
a small claim and shall proceed accordingly."; and

(b) in subsection (3)(a) after "(2A)" there shall be inserted the
words "(2B) or (2C)".

(4) In section 38 of that Act (appeal in summary causes) for the words
from "any summary cause" to "(b)" there shall be substituted the
words—

"—

(a) any summary cause an appeal shall lie to the sheriff principal
on any point of law from the final judgment of the sheriff; and

(b) any summary cause other than a small claim an appeal shall
lie".

GENERAL NOTE

The need for a small claims procedure in Scotland has been recognised for a long time.
The literature on the subject is extensive: for a comprehensive survey, see Paterson and
Bates, *The Legal System of Scotland*, pp. 17–23. The provisions of s.18 are of an enabling
nature: the detailed provisions on such important matters as the upper limits of small claims
are left for subordinate legislation. The broad structure of the procedure is clear. There is
to be a form of summary cause process in the sheriff court to be known as a "small claim".
In general, every summary cause whose subject-matter falls within the prescribed description
for small claims—which, it is thought will be in the region of £500–£1,000—will proceed as
a small claim, irrespective of whether a defence has been stated. The normal rules of
evidence shall not apply in small claims, but all the existing remedies for execution of a
summary cause decree will be available. Where the pursuer is not a partnership or a body
corporate or acting in a representative capacity, he can require the sheriff clerk to effect the
summons on his behalf.

New s.35(2)

This provision sets out the broad structure of the small claim procedure. The descriptions
of summary causes which are to be treated as small claims and the financial limit for the new
procedure will be prescribed by the Lord Advocate by order. The orders are subject to the
affirmative resolution procedure in each House of Parliament. This procedure was thought
more appropriate than the negative resolution procedure because of the general importance
and interest of the subject-matter of the orders. The term "small claim" was finally settled
at the Committee stage in the House of Lords: H.L. Vol. 467, col. 195.

New s.35(3)

The normal rules of evidence do not apply to a small claim.

New subs. 36B(1)

The effect of this subsection is that no expenses are to be awarded when the value of the
claim does not exceed a sum to be prescribed by the Lord Advocate.

New subs. 36B(2)

Where a small claim exceeds the sum prescribed by the Lord Advocate, but is still a small
claim, the expenses awarded shall be limited to a sum to be prescribed by order of the Lord
Advocate: the orders are subject to the affirmative resolution procedure: see new subs.
36B(4).

New subs. 36B(3)

This provides exceptions to the limitations on the award of expenses in small claims.

Subs. (3)(a)

A defender will be liable to pay expenses if he has not stated a defence (s.36B(*a*)(i)) or has not proceeded with a defence (s.36B(3)(*a*)(ii)). This is to deal with the situation where the small claims are brought by major utilities and other enterprises for debt collection. If the no expenses rule were to be applied universally, this might encourage debtors to avoid paying bills and cause financial hardship to pursuers who would have to meet their own expenses. However, in order to prevent debtors proceeding with defences simply to get the benefit of the no expenses rule, s.36B(*a*)(iii), provides that expenses will be payable if the defender has not acted in good faith as to the merits of the defence.

Subs. (3)(b)

This is a general provision that expenses will be awarded if either party to the proceedings has acted unreasonably in relation to either the proceedings or the claim itself. Expenses will be awarded in relation to an appeal to the sheriff principal.

New subs. 37(2B)

This provides that at any stage the sheriff may, if he is of the opinion that a difficult question of law or an exceptionally complex question of fact is involved, of his own accord or on the motion of any party to the small claim, direct that the small claim be treated as a summary or ordinary cause: the sheriff is obliged to do so, on the joint motion of the parties to the proceedings.

New subs. 37(2C)

This deals with the converse case. Where any cause is not a small claim only because it is above the monetary limit applicable to a small claim, the sheriff must direct the cause to be treated as a small claim, on the joint motion of the parties to the cause. It should be noted that the sheriff does not have the power of his own accord to treat the cause as a small claim: *cf.* his powers under s.37(2B) *supra*.

Subs. (4)

The effect of this amendment of s.38 of the Sheriff Courts (Scotland) Act 1971 is to provide that there will be an appeal to the sheriff principal on a point of law only from the final judgment of the sheriff in a small claim.

Disclosure of names in certain proceedings

19. In section 1 of the Administration of Justice (Scotland) Act 1972 (which makes provision in relation to the powers of the court to order inspection of documents and other property) after subsection (1) there shall be inserted the following subsection—

> "(1A) Without prejudice to the existing powers of the Court of Session and of the sheriff court, those courts shall have power, subject to subsection (4) of this section, to order any person to disclose such information as he has as to the identity of any persons who appear to the court to be persons who—
>
> (*a*) might be witnesses in any existing civil proceedings before that court or in civil proceedings which are likely to be brought; or
>
> (*b*) might be defenders in any civil proceedings which appear to the court to be likely to be brought.".

GENERAL NOTE

S.1 of the Administration of Justice (Scotland) Act 1972 empowers the court to order the production and recovery of documents and other property prior to the raising of any proceedings on the application of a person who appears to the court to be likely to be a party or minuter in proceedings which are likely to be brought. It is thus only concerned with property. It was therefore doubtful whether the court could order the respondent to disclose information as to the identity of any person who might be a witness or defender in existing or future civil proceedings. While there was some authority that such a power might exist at common law, the position was unsatisfactory. See on this point, H. L. MacQueen, *A Copyright Anomaly Revealed,* 1983 S.L.T.(News) 133.

S.19 amends s.1 of the 1972 Act to empower the court to order the respondent to disclose such information. This will be particularly important in copyright infringement cases, where, for example, a retailer can now be ordered to disclose the identity of the supplier of the pirated material.

New subs. 1(1A)
"Without prejudice to the existing powers of the Court of Session and of the sheriff court"
The nature and extent of these powers are controversial. The court has a general common law power to order a party to proceedings to disclose the names and addresses of potential witnesses: see *Henderson* v. *Patrick Thomson Ltd.,* 1911 S.C. 246; *Clarke* v. *Edinburgh & District Tramway & Co.,* 1914 2 S.L.T. 39 and *Halloran* v. *Greater Glasgow Passenger Transport Executive,* 1976 S.L.T. 77. The difficulty was whether the power extended to ordering disclosure so that proceedings could be brought against the persons whose identity was disclosed: there was some authority that it could. See *De Duca* v. *Sillitoe* (1936) 52 Sh.Ct.Rep. 18. The matter is discussed fully in H. L. MacQueen, *op. cit.* at pp. 136–7.

"subject to subsection (4) of this section"
S.1(4) of the 1972 Act provides that the rules of law and practice relating to the privileges of witnesses and havers, confidentiality of communications and withholding or non-disclosure of information on the grounds of public interest, remain unaffected by the courts powers in ss.1(1) and (1A). This includes the respondent's privilege against self-incrimination: *British Phonographic Industry Ltd.* v. *Cohen, Cohen, Kelly, Cohen & Cohen Ltd.,* 1983 S.L.T. 137. However the privilege against self-incrimination has been withdrawn in respect of proceedings relating to intellectual property by s.15 of the present Act. Accordingly, this proviso will not inhibit the utility of s.1(1A) in copyright infringement cases.

New subs. (1A)(a)
The power extends to the disclosure of persons who might be witnesses in existing civil proceedings or civil proceedings likely to be brought.

New subs. (1A)(b)
The power extends to the disclosure of persons who might be defenders in any civil proceedings "which might *appear to the court*" to be likely to be brought. It is this power which will be important for copyright owners seeking the identity of the suppliers of pirated material in order to bring civil proceedings against them. However, the power is general and applies to all types of civil proceedings.

Other provisions relating to courts

Removal of prohibition of sheriffs' principal and sheriffs' accepting appointment to certain offices

20. Section 6(1)(*b*) of the Sheriff Courts (Scotland) Act 1971 (prohibition of sheriffs' principal and sheriffs' accepting appointment to certain offices) shall cease to have effect.

GENERAL NOTE
S.6(1)(*b*) of the Sheriff Courts (Scotland) Act 1971 provides that a sheriff principal or a sheriff shall not "accept appointment to any office, except such office as may by statute be attached to the office of sheriff principal or sheriff, as the case may be". In spite of this prohibition, sheriffs in the past have sought permission of the Lord Advocate, officials of the Scottish courts' administration or the sheriff principal to accept appointments in order to play a role in the public life of their sheriffdoms. However, the scope of the restriction was uncertain. For example, would appointment as deputy lieutenant or as trustee of a public body such as the National Galleries of Scotland be a breach of the section? After representations from both the Sheriffs' association and the sheriffs principal it was decided that the restriction should be removed. This is done by s.20.

Additional court holidays

21. In section 10 of the Bail etc. (Sotland) Act 1980 (which, amongst other things, empowers the sheriff principal to prescribe up to 10 days as court holidays)—

(*a*) in subsection (2) at the end there shall be added—
   "; and may in the like manner prescribe as an additional court holiday any day which has been proclaimed, under section 1(3) of the Banking and Financial Dealings Act 1971, to be a bank holiday either throughout the United Kingdom or in a place or locality in the United Kingdom within his jurisdiction."; and
(*b*) in subsection (3) at the end there shall be added—
   "; and he may, after such consultation, prescribe as an additional holiday any day which has been proclaimed, under section 1(3) of the said Banking and Financial Dealings Act 1971, to be a bank holiday either throughout the United Kingdom or in a place or locality in the United Kingdom within his jurisdiction.".

GENERAL NOTE

By s.10(2) of the Bail etc. (Scotland) Act 1980, a sheriff prinicipal may prescribe in respect of criminal business not more than 10 days (other than Saturdays and Sundays) in a calendar year as court holidays in the sheriff courts within his jurisdiction. By s.10(3) of the 1980 Act he may, after consultation with the appropriate district or islands council, prescribe not more than 10 days (other than Saturdays and Sundays) in a calendar year as court holidays in the district courts within his jurisdiction. The purpose of s.21 is to amend ss.10(2) and 10(3) respectively to allow the sheriff principal to prescribe as an additional court holiday any day that has been proclaimed to be a bank holiday under s.1(3) of the Banking and Financial Dealings Act 1971. S.1(3) provides that "Her Majesty may from time to time by proclamation appoint a special day to be, either in the United Kingdom or in any place or locality in the United Kingdom, a bank holiday under this Act". It is therefore restricted to the proclamation of a bank holiday in respect of a special event, for example, a Royal wedding or State funeral. As these events are rare, there are unlikely to be too many additional court holidays. Should, however, there be a large number of proclamations in one year, the sheriff principal has discretion whether or not to prescribe the bank holidays as court holidays.

S.21(a)

This applies in respect of the sheriff courts.

S.21(b)

This applies in respect of the district courts.

Re-employment of retired judges

22.—(1) If it appears to the Lord President of the Court of Session that it is expedient as a temporary measure to make an appointment under this section in order to facilitate the disposal of business in the Court of Session or the High Court of Justiciary he may, with the consent of the Secretary of State, appoint a person who—
   (*a*) has held office as a judge of the Court of Session; or
   (*b*) has held office as a Lord of Appeal in Ordinary and who, at the time of his appointment as a Lord of Appeal in Ordinary, was eligible for appointment as a judge in the Court of Session,
and, in either case, has not reached the age of 75 years, to act as a judge of the Court of Session and High Court of Justiciary during such period or on such occasions as the Lord President thinks fit but, subject to subsection (4) below, a period during which or occasion on which a person may so act, shall not extend beyond or be after he reaches the age of 75 years.

(2) A person while acting under this section shall, subject to subsection (3) below, be treated for all purposes as, and accordingly may perform any of the functions of, a judge of the Court in which he is acting.

(3) A person shall not, by virtue of subsection (2) above, be treated as a judge of the Court of Session or the High Court of Justiciary for the purposes of any statutory provision or rule of law relating to—

(*a*) the appointment, retirement, removal or disqualification of judges of that Court (including, without prejudice to the foregoing generality, any statutory provision or rule of law relating to the number of judges who may be appointed);

(*b*) the tenure of office and oaths to be taken by such judges;

(*c*) the remuneration, allowances or pensions of such judges.

(4) Notwithstanding the expiry of any period for which a person is appointed by virtue of subsection (1) above to act as a judge of the Court of Session and High Court of Justiciary—

(*a*) he may attend at the Court for the purpose of continuing to deal with, giving judgement in, or dealing with any matter relating to, any case begun before him while acting as a judge of that Court; and

(*b*) for that purpose, and for the purpose of any proceedings arising out of any such case or matter, he shall be treated as being or, as the case may be, having been, a judge of that Court.

(5) The Secretary of State may pay to, or in respect of, a person appointed under subsection (1) above such remuneration or allowances as he may, with the consent of the Treasury, determine.

GENERAL NOTE

The purpose of this section is to enable the Lord President of the Court of Session with the consent of the Secretary of State, as a temporary measure to recall a retired judge, under the age of 75, to facilitate the disposal of the civil or criminal business of the Court of Session or the High Court of Justiciary. It is envisaged that should the power be exercised, the judges recalled would be used to provide temporary assistance in appellate cases.

Subs. (1)

"it is expedient as a temporary measure"

It should be emphasised that the new power is perceived as a temporary measure when the pressure of business in the Court of Session or the High Court of Justiciary is such that the Lord President considers an appointment desirable. The appointment is made by the Lord President with the consent of the Secretary of State.

"has not reached the age of 75 years"

Only those judges who have retired from the bench but have not yet reached the age of 75, *i.e.* the statutory retirement age for judges, are eligible to be re-employed. The number of retired judges thus eligible is very small.

"such period or on such occasions as the Lord President thinks fit"

The extent of the period for which the judge may act is at the discretion of the Lord President. However, it cannot extend beyond or after he reaches the age of 75.

Subss. (2) and (3)

While the re-employed judge is to be treated for all purposes as, and may perform any of the functions of, a judge of the Court in which he is acting, he is not to be treated as a judge of the Court of Session or the High Court of Justiciary for the purposes of any statutory provision or rule of law relating to a number of important matters including, appointment, retirement, removal, tenure of office and oaths to be taken by such judges and the remuneration, allowances or pensions of such judges.

Subs. (4)

This provides a limited exception to the general principle in subs. (1) that a judge so appointed cannot act after he reaches 75. The exception relates to allowing the judge to continue beyond the age of 75 for the purpose of continuing to deal with, giving judgment in, or dealing with any matter relating to a case which had begun before him while acting as a judge.

Subs. (5)

Under subs. (3), a person appointed a judge under this section is not treated as a judge for the purpose of statutory provisions relating to remuneration, allowances or pensions of such judges. However, subs. (5) provides that he shall receive such remuneration or allowances as the Secretary of State may, with the consent of the Treasury, determine.

Replacement of general jury book by lists of men and women eligible for jury service

23.—(1) In section 3 of the Jurors (Scotland) Act 1825 (sheriff principal to maintain the general jury book), for the words from "a book" to "that book" there shall be substituted the words, "in such form as may be approved by the Lord Justice-General, two lists (to be known as the "lists of potential jurors") containing the names, designations and dates of birth of such number as the sheriff principal considers appropriate of—
   (*a*) in the first list, men; and
   (*b*) in the second list, women
within the district who appear to him to be qualified and liable to serve as jurors; and those lists".

(2) Section 10 of the said Act of 1825, section 4 of the Juries (Scotland) 1826 and sections 88 to 91 and 98 of the Criminal Procedure (Scotland) Act 1975 shall have effect subject to the amendments to these enactments specified in Schedule 2 to this Act; and for any other reference, however expressed, in any enactment passed before this Act to the general jury book maintained under section 3 of the Jurors (Scotland) Act 1825 there shall be substituted a reference to the lists of potential jurors.

GENERAL NOTE

This section amends s.3 of the Jurors (Scotland) Act 1825 to replace the general jury book by lists of men and women eligible for jury service. By removing the statutory requirement that the lists should be entered in a book, the way is open to store the lists on computer. The form the lists will take is to be approved by the Lord Justice-General.

Subs. (1)

There is a statutory requirement dating from the Jurors (Enrolment of Women) (Scotland) Act 1920 that the names and designation of male and female potential jurors should be kept in separate lists. Moreover para. 1(*b*), Sched. 3 to the Criminal Procedure (Scotland) Act 1975 stipulates that the returns of jurors for criminal trials must contain as nearly as possible, an equal number of women and men grouped separately. There is thus a practical reason for the retention of separate lists of men and women.

Subs. (2)

This provides for consequential amendments arising from the amendment of s.3 of the Jurors (Scotland) Act 1825.

Provisions relating to the care of children

Power to increase size of Children's Panel Advisory Committees

24. After paragraph 3 of Schedule 3 to the Social Work (Scotland) Act 1968 there shall be inserted the following paragraph—
   "3A. The Secretary of State may, at the request of the local authority provide for an increase in the membership of the Children's Panel Advisory Committee for the area of the authority by such number, not exceeding 5, of additional members as the authority specify in relation to their request, the additional members to be nominated as follows—
      (*a*) the first, second and fourth additional members, by the Secretary of State;
      (*b*) the third and fifth additional members, by the local authority".

GENERAL NOTE

The Children's Panel Advisory Committees (C.P.A.C.) have many duties: to recommend new members to children's panels, to ensure that both new and existing members of

children's panels undergo training programmes, to monitor the performance of members of
children's panels in order to have evidence to decide whether or not to recommend their
re-appointment, and to sit in on some hearings in order to keep themselves acquainted with
the performance of the panel and the changing needs of the children coming before them.
Currently, Strathclyde C.P.A.C. has ten members, the other C.P.A.C.'s five members.
Difficulty has been experienced by members, particularly in relation to C.P.A.C.'s in remote
areas, in fulfilling all their functions as well as attending the meetings of the C.P.A.C. The
new section enables each C.P.A.C. to increase its membership by up to five members, in
order that the C.P.A.C. can better fulfil its various tasks.

New para. 3A
"at the request of the local authority"
   The local authority makes the request to the Secretary of State after the C.P.A.C. has
decided that it requires additional members. The initiative does not come from the Secretary
of State.

"not exceeding 5"
   The maximum increase in membership is 5.

New para. 3A(a) and (b)
   At present of the ten members of the Strathclyde C.P.A.C., six are nominees of the
Secretary of State, four of the local authority: in relation to the other C.P.A.C.'s, three are
nominees of the Secretary of State and two of the local authority, *i.e.* a ratio of 3 to 2. In
order to keep a fair balance between the local authority's members and the Secretary of
State's appointees, this formula was devised for the nomination of the additional members.
The current ratio will, of course, be disturbed if less than the maximum increase in
membership is made.

Amendment of provisions about detention of children

25.—(1) In section 42(3) of the Social Work (Scotland) Act 1968
(which, amongst other things, limits to 7 days the period of detention,
pending disposal of the case, of a child who has failed to attend before
the sheriff in an application to him in respect of the grounds of referral of
the child to a children's hearing) for the words from "for", where last
occurring, to the end there shall be substituted the words "after whichever
is the earlier of the following—
   (a) the expiry of 14 days beginning with the day on which he was first
         detained;
   (b) the disposal of the application by the sheriff.".
   (2) In section 42(6) of the Social Work (Scotland) Act 1968 (remission
of case from sheriff to reporter where the sheriff is satisfied that grounds
of referral have been established)—
   (a) after the word "established" there shall be inserted "(a)"; and
   (b) after the word "case", where secondly occurring, there shall be
         inserted "; and
      (b) if he is satisfied that detention of the child is necessary in his
            own interest or has reason to believe that the child will run
            away before the children's hearing sit to consider the case, he
            may issue a warrant requiring the detention of the child until
            the children's hearing sit to consider the case, but a child shall
            not be detained under this subsection after whichever is the
            earlier of the following—
               (i) the expiry of 3 days beginning with the day on which
               he was first detained;
               (ii) the consideration of his case by the children's
               hearing."

GENERAL NOTE
   When a child or his parents do not accept the grounds stated by the reporter for the
referral to a children's hearing that a child is in need of compulsory measures of care, the

children's hearing must direct the reporter to make application to a sheriff for a finding whether the grounds for the referral are established: ss.42(1) and (2) of the Social Work (Scotland) Act 1968. Where a child fails to attend the hearing of the application, the sheriff may issue a warrant for the apprehension of the child which is authority for bringing him before the sheriff and for his detention in a place of safety until the sheriff can hear the application. However, the child could only be detained in a place of safety for a period not exceeding seven days or, if the sheriff has disposed of the application within a shorter period, after the sheriff has disposed of the application: s.42(3) of the 1968 Act. S.25(1) amends s.42(3) of the 1968 Act to allow the child to be detained for up to 14 days or the disposal of the application by the sheriff, whichever is earlier.

If the sheriff finds that the grounds are established, he must remit the case to the reporter to make arrangements for a children's hearing for consideration and determination of the case: s.42(6) of the 1968 Act. S.25(2) amends s.42(6) of the 1968 Act, to empower the sheriff, if he is satisfied that the detention of the child is necessary in his own interest or he has reason to believe that the child will run away before the children's hearing sits to consider his case, to issue a warrant requiring the detention of the child until the children's hearing sits to consider the case. However the child may only be detained for up to three days or the consideration of his case by the children's hearing, whichever is earlier.

Subs. (2)
"detention"

While s.42(3) expressly states that the child is to be detained "in a place of safety", this phrase does not appear in the new subs. 42(6)(*b*). It is thought, however, that since the section must be interpreted as a whole, it is to be implied that the detention is to be in a place of safety. "A place of safety" is defined in s.94 of the 1968 Act as "any residential or other establishment provided by a local authority, a police station, or any hospital, surgery or other suitable place, the occupier of which is willing temporarily to receive a child". In practice, it will often be a foster home. It will be for the social workers to decide what accommodation is suitable for the child so detained. However, when issuing a warrant under ss.46(3) or (6), the sheriff can, if satisfied with regard to the criteria in s.58A(3) of the 1968 Act, order the child to be detained in secure accommodation in a named residential establishment: s.58E of the 1968 Act.

Amendment of power to detain children in secure accommodation

26. In the Social Work (Scotland) Act 1968—

   (*a*) in section 58B(3) (power to detain child in secure accommodation) for the words from "authorise" to the end there shall be substituted the words "order that, pending the determination of his case in accordance with section 42(5) or (6) of this Act, the child shall be liable to be placed and kept in secure accommodation in a named residential establishment at such times as the person in charge of that establishment with the agreement of the director of social work of the local authority for the area of the children's hearing, considers necessary.".

   (*b*) In section 58E(1) (warrant to detain child in secure accommodation) for the words from "authorise" to the end there shall be substituted the words "order that the child shall be liable to be placed and kept in secure accommodation in a named residential establishment at such times as the person in charge of that establishment, with the agreement of the director of social work of the local authority, considers necessary. The local authority referred to in this subsection is, in the case of a warrant issued or renewed by the sheriff, the local authority for the area of the children's hearing which was dealing with the child in respect of whom the warrant was issued and, in the case of a warrant issued or renewed by a children's hearing, the local authority for the area of that children's hearing."

GENERAL NOTE

By s.58A(3) the Social Work (Scotland) Act 1968 a children's hearing may, if a child is likely to abscond and his welfare will be at risk or he is likely to be a danger to himself or others, make it a condition of a supervision requirement that the child be liable to be placed and kept in secure accommodation in a named residential establishment. But, it is expressly stated in the subsection that the child is to be kept in secure accommodation for "such times as the person in charge of that establishment, with the agreement of the director of social work of the local authority required to give effect to the supervision requirement, considers it necessary that he do so".

But the Act also provides that a children's hearing can issue warrants for the interim detention of a child in secure accommodation pending the disposal of his case: see ss.37(4) and (5), (5A) and (5B) (warrant authorising the detention of a child already in a place of safety pending the disposal of his case by a children's hearing), ss.40(4) and (5) (warrant authorising the detention of a child to ensure his appearance at a children's hearing). A sheriff, too, can issue warrants for the interim detention of a child in secure accommodation pending the disposal of his case: see ss.37(5A) and (5B) (warrant authorising further renewal of interim detention of a child already in a place of safety pending the disposal of his case), ss.40(8A) and (8B) (warrant authorising further renewal of interim detention of a child pending the disposal of his case by a children's hearing), s.42(3) (warrant authorising the detention of a child pending a hearing of an application before a sheriff). This is the effect of s.58E of the 1968 Act. Moreover, s.58B(3) expressly provides that a children's hearing has the power to authorise the detention of a child in secure accommodation pending the application to the sheriff and the final disposal of his case by the children's hearing if the grounds are established.

Unlike s.58(3), in none of these provisions relating to interim detention, is it expressly stated that it is for the person in charge of the residential establishment to determine the periods during which the child should be kept in secure accommodation. And in at least one unreported case, it has been held that such interim detention is mandatory, *i.e.* the social work authorities have no discretion in relation to the care of the child and must keep him in secure accommodation for the duration of the interim detention.

The purpose of s.26 is to amend the provisions of the 1968 Act in relation to warrants and orders for interim detention in secure accommodation, including the sheriff's new powers in s.42(6) (see *supra* note to s.25), so that the time actually spent in secure accommodation is that considered by the person in charge of the residential establishment, with the agreement of the director of social work of the relevant local authority, to be necessary. As the Shadow Secretary of State said on Report, "It is wise for the law to authorise that the child be kept in secure accommodation, but it should not demand that he is": H.C. Vol. 78, col. 517.

S.26(a)

This amends s.58B(3) of the 1968 Act to ensure that when a children's hearing orders the detention of a child in secure accommodation pending an application to a sheriff and the final disposal of his case by a children's hearing if the grounds are established, the time actually spent by the child in the secure accommodation is that considered to be necessary by the person in charge of the residential establishment, with the agreement of the director of social work of the local authority for the area of the children's hearing.

S.26(b)

This amends s.58E(1) of the 1968 Act to ensure that when a children's hearing or a sheriff issues or renews warrants for the interim detention of a child in secure accommodation, by virtue of their powers under ss.37, 40 and 42 of the Act, the time actually spent by the child in the secure accommodation is that considered to be necessary by:
  (a) in the case of a warrant issued or renewed by a sheriff, the person in charge of the residential establishment with the agreement of the director of social work of the local authority for the area of the children's hearing which was dealing with the child in respect of whom the warrant was issued; and
  (b) in the case of a warrant issued or renewed by a children's hearing, the person in charge of the residential establishment with the agreement of the director of social work of the local authority for the area of that children's hearing.

Requirement of children's hearing for pre-adoptive supervision not to constitute making arrangements for adoption for purposes of Adoption (Scotland) Act 1978

27. In section 65(3) of the Adoption (Scotland) Act 1978 (which deems certain actings to constitute the making of arrangements for the adoption of a child, the making of such arrangements being, in certain circumstances, an offence under section 11 of that Act) there shall be inserted at the end the following—"but the making, under section 44 of the Social Work (Scotland) Act 1968, by a children's hearing of a supervision requirement which, in respect that it provides as to where he is to reside, facilitates his being placed for adoption by an adoption agency, shall not constitute the making of such arrangements.".

GENERAL NOTE

The purpose of this provision is to facilitate the adoption of children who are subject to a supervision requirement. By s.11 of the Adoption (Scotland) Act 1978 it is an offence for a person other than an adoption agency to make arrangements for the adoption of a child. By s.65(3) of the 1978 Act a person is deemed to make arrangements for the adoption of a child, if "he enters into or makes any agreement or arrangement for, or for facilitating, the adoption of the child . . . or if he initiates or takes part in any negotiations of which the purpose or effect is the conclusion of any agreement or the making of any arrangement therefore, or if he causes another person to do so". S.27 amends s.65(3) of the 1978 Act to exclude from the scope of such an arrangement the situation where a supervision requirement is made which facilitates the child being placed for adoption by an adoption agency by stipulating that he is to reside in a particular place, *e.g.* with potential adopting parents. Thus, a barrier is removed which would have impeded children's hearings from making pre-adoption placements.

Child subject to supervision requirement to be regarded as in the care of the local authority for the purposes of his being freed for adoption under section 18 of the Adoption (Scotland) Act 1978

28. In section 44(5) of the Social Work (Scotland) Act 1968 (which, amongst other things, provides that, for the purposes of the enactments set out there, a child subject to a supervision requirement shall be in the care of the local authority) after the word "Act", where first occurring, there shall be inserted the words "and section 18 of the Adoption (Scotland) Act 1978 (which, amongst other things, provides that an application by an adoption agency to dispense with parental agreement to the freeing of a child for adoption is competent only where the child is in the care of the agency).".

GENERAL NOTE

An adoption agency can only apply for an order freeing the child for adoption (*a*) if each parent or guardian agrees to the making of an adoption order or (*b*) the adoption agency is applying for the dispensation of the agreement of each parent or guardian, and the child is *in the care* of the adoption agency: see s.18(2) of the Adoption (Scotland) Act 1978.

Where a child was subject to a supervision requirement, he was not deemed to be in the care of the local authority for the purpose of s.18 of the 1978 Act. Accordingly, the local authority, as adoption agency, could not make an application for an order under s.18(2)(*b*). S.28 remedies this situation by amending s.44(5) of the Social Work (Scotland) Act 1968 to the effect that a child who is subject to a supervision requirement shall be deemed to be in the care of the local authority for the purposes of s.18 of the Adoption (Scotland) Act 1978, thereby enabling the local authority, as adoption agency, to apply for an order freeing the child for adoption. The decision to dispense with the agreement of the parent or guardian to the order remains, of course, a matter for the court and is only possible if a ground for dispensation of agreement in s.16 of the 1978 Act exists.

Reporter's power to arrange review by children's hearing of supervision requirement

29. In section 48 of the Social Work (Scotland) Act 1968 (review by children's hearing of supervision requirements) after subsection (4) there shall be inserted the following subsection—

"(4A) If a supervision requirement has not been reviewed under this section during the period of nine months following the date when it was made or last reviewed (whichever is the later), the reporter may arrange for it to be reviewed.".

GENERAL NOTE

The purpose of this section is to place beyond doubt the power of reporters to children's panels to call for a review of the case of a child whose supervision requirement is due to lapse. Although it has been their practice to do so, nevertheless, reporters are not among those mentioned in s.48 of the Social Work (Scotland) Act 1968 who can, on their own initiative, ask for a review, though the local authority can do so.

New subs. 48(4A)
"during the period of nine months following the date when it was made or last reviewed (whichever is later)"
A supervision requirement cannot last more than a year unless it is reviewed and renewed. By giving a reporter the right to arrange for the review of a case which has not been reviewed for nine months, there is time for the case to be prepared thoroughly so that the children's hearing has adequate material on which to base its decision whether the supervision requirement should be renewed or allowed to lapse.

Procedures relating to crofting tenure and the valuation of sheep stocks

Interest on awards of compensation by Scottish Land Court

30.—(1) In section 12 of the Crofters (Scotland) Act 1955, after subsection (1) (which provides, amongst other things, for compensation of a crofter whose croft, or part thereof, has been resumed by the landlord) there shall be inserted the following subsection—

"(1A) A sum awarded as compensation under subsection (1) above shall, if the Land Court so determine, carry interest as from the date when such sum is payable at the same rate as would apply (in the absence of any such statement as is provided for in Rule 66 of the Act of Sederunt (Rules of Court, consolidation and amendment) 1965) in the case of decree or extract in an action commenced on that date in the Court of Session if interest were included in or exigible under that decree or extract;

Provided that this subsection shall not affect any case in which the hearing has begun before the coming into force of section 30 of the Law Reform (Miscellaneous Provisions) (Scotland) Act 1985.".

(2) In section 9 of the Crofting (Reform) (Scotland) Act 1976 (which entitles a crofter whose croft, or part thereof, has been resumed by the landlord to a share in the value of the land so resumed) after subsection (5) there shall be inserted the following subsection—

"(5A) A sum awarded under this section shall, if the Land Court so determine, carry interest as from the date when such sum is payable at the same rate as would apply (in the absence of any such statement as is provided for in Rule 66 of the Act of Sederunt (Rules of Court, consolidation and amendment) 1965) in the case of a decree or extract in an action commenced on that date in the Court of Session if interest were included in or exigible under that decree or extract:

Provided that this subsection shall not affect any case in which the hearing has begun before the coming into force of section 30 of the Law Reform (Miscellaneous Provisions) (Scotland) Act 1985.".

GENERAL NOTE

This provision empowers the Scottish Land Court to provide for the payment of interest on compensation awarded by the court to a crofter on the resumption of his land by a landlord. The rate of interest will be the same as in the Court of Session. Because the Scottish Land Court is a creature of statute, it did not have the right to impose interest on awards unless Parliament gave it that right. The Scottish Land Court, it appears, requested these powers.

New subs. 12(1A)
This amends s.12 of the Crofters (Scotland) Act 1955, to allow interest on awards of compensation made by the Land Court under s.12(1) of the 1955 Act. By s.12(1) the Land

Court can award compensation to a crofter whose landlord requires the crofter to surrender his, or part of his, croft. The compensation can take the form of the landlord letting to the crofter other land of equivalent value in the neighbourhood or an adjustment of rent. Compensation in money is usually small.

New subs. 9(5A)

This amends s.9 of the Crofting (Reform) (Scotland) Act 1976, which provides that where the Land Court has authorised the resumption of a croft by a landlord under s.12 of the 1955 Act, the crofter is entitled to receive from the landlord, in addition to any compensation under s.12 of the 1955 Act, a share in the value of the land so resumed. A formula for calculating the share of the value of the land is provided in the 1976 Act: see ss.3 and 12. By virtue of the amendment, the Land Court can provide for the payment of interest on such a sum. These sums can be considerable. The prospect of having to pay interest will therefore encourage landlords to make the payment to the crofter.

Restriction of duty to record notice of cesser of conditions relating to croft

31. In section 22(4)(*e*) of the Crofters (Scotland) Act 1955 (by virtue of which the Secretary of State must, when appropriate, record in the Register of Sasines, a notice of cesser of the conditions which applied to a croft in respect of which financial assistance had been given) after the word "apply", where thirdly occurring, there shall be inserted the words "by virtue of such a payment to the Secretary of State as is referred to in paragraph (*c*) above,".

GENERAL NOTE

By s.22(2) of the Crofters (Scotland) Act 1955, the Secretary of State may, in accordance with arrangements made by him with the approval of the Treasury, *inter alia*, provide assistance by way of grants towards "the erection or improvement or rebuilding of dwelling houses and other buildings for crofters". By s.22(4) of the 1955 Act, the Secretary of State is empowered to make regulations which specify conditions of the grant in relation to the occupation and maintenance of the new or improved buildings. These conditions are binding on the recipient and his successors in the tenancy for a period stipulated in the grant. The Secretary of State is obliged to record the conditions of the grant—including the time for which the grant period and conditions run—in the Register of Sasines. When the conditions cease to apply to the dwelling house or building the Secretary of State must record a notice of cesser in the Register: s.24(4)(*e*). This is important where, for example, the tenant repays the grant or a proportion thereof before the period of the grant has expired, thereby prematurely freeing the buildings from the conditions: see s.22(4)(*c*). But under s.24(4)(*e*) the Secretary of State is bound to register a notice of cesser even where the conditions have ceased to apply because the period stipulated in the grant for their operation has expired. This serves little purpose as the date of the expiry of the conditions will have already been given when the original notice of conditions was registered. The purpose of s.31 is to amend s.22(4)(*e*) of the 1955 Act to limit the Secretary of State's obligation to record a notice of cesser to the situation where the conditions cease to apply before the expiry of the period of the grant as a result of repayment under s.22(4)(*c*). The Secretary of State is therefore no longer obliged to register a notice of cesser when the grant conditions cease because they have become time expired, *i.e.* the period during which the conditions are to apply has passed. This should prevent the Register becoming cluttered with unnecessary notices of cesser.

Rules as to valuations of sheep stocks

32. In section 28 of the Hill Farming Act 1946 (which makes provision as to the valuation of sheep stocks in Scotland) after subsection (1) there shall be inserted the following subsections—

"(1A) The Secretary of State may by order made by statutory instrument subject to annulment in pursuance of a resolution of either House of Parliament, vary the provisions of the said Schedule.

(1B) A variation made under subsection (1A) above shall not apply for the purposes of a valuation made in respect of a lease entered into before the variation was made.".

GENERAL NOTE

S.28 of the Hill Farming Act 1946 provides that in fixing the value of sheep stock to be taken over at the termination of a tenancy at Whitsunday or Martinmas, in any arbitration the arbiter shall use the criteria set out in Pts. I and II of the Second Schedule to the Act respectively. The Act is almost 40 years old and both sides of the industry are agreed that the Schedule is so outdated as to be almost impossible to operate in modern conditions. The amendment to s.28 enables the Secretary of State to vary the provisions of the Schedule by statutory instrument under the negative resolution procedure.

New subs. 28(1B)

The existing provisions for valuation of sheep stock in Schedule 2 to the Hill Farming Act 1946 continue to apply on the termination of a lease entered into before any variation of the Schedule is made by statutory instrument.

Criminal courts, procedure, evidence and justice

Establishment and disestablishment of district courts

33. After section 1 of the District Courts (Scotland) Act 1975 there shall be inserted the following section—

"Further provision as to establishment and disestablishment of district courts

1A.—(1) Where it appears to the Secretary of State that—

(*a*) there is insufficient business for the district court in a particular commission area; and

(*b*) such insufficiency of business is likely to continue,

he may by order provide that the district court for that area cease to exist on a specified date.

(2) Where it appears to the Secretary of State that, in a commission area in which there is no district court, there is likely to be a sufficient business to justify the establishment of such a court, he may by order provide for the establishment of such a court in that area on a specified date.

(3) An order under subsection (1) or (2) above may contain all such provisions as appear to the Secretary of State to be necessary or expedient for rendering the order of full effect and any incidental, supplemental or consequential provisions which appear to him to be necessary or expedient for the purposes of the order, including, but without prejudice to the generality of the foregoing words, provisions amending, repealing or revoking any enactment (whether passed or made before or after the commencement of this enactment).

(4) Before making an order under subsection (1) or (2) above, the Secretary of State shall consult the district or islands council for the area concerned, and such other persons as appear to him to have an interest in the proposed order.

(5) Orders under subsection (1) or (2) above shall be made by statutory instrument, which shall be subject to annulment in pursuance of a resolution of either House of Parliament.".

GENERAL NOTE

The purpose of this section is to amend the District Courts (Scotland) Act 1975, to empower the Secretary of State to establish or disestablish district courts where the volume, and likely volume, of business makes this desirable after consultation with the district or islands council and other interested persons. The amendment derives directly from the recommendation of the Montgomery Committee's Inquiry into the Function and Powers of the Islands Councils of Scotland (Cmnd. 9216) that the Secretary of State should have the power to disestablish district courts where there was insufficient business. The opportunity was also taken in the Act, however, to give the Secretary of State the power to establish a new district court if it is shown that the area has enough business to merit one. The initiation for changes will, in practice, come from the district or islands council. Hitherto, there has been no power to alter the pattern of district courts established by the 1975 Act.

New subs. 1A(4)
"such other persons as appear to him to have an interest in the proposed order"
Before making an order disestablishing or establishing a district court, the Secretary of State must consult the district or islands council for the area concerned and "such other persons as appear to him to have an interest in the proposed order". These would include, for example, the justices' committee, local Bar interest, community councils and the sheriff principal.

New subs. 1A(5)
The order disestablishing or establishing a district court will be made by statutory instrument under the negative resolution procedure.

Power of Secretary of State to remove justices etc.

34. In the District Courts (Scotland) Act 1975—
    (*a*) at the end of subsection (7) of section 11 (which relates to ex officio justices) there shall be inserted the words "and, notwithstanding that he remains a duly nominated member of the authority, may be removed from office in like manner as a justice appointed under that section.";
    (*b*) in subsection (2) of section 15 (which relates to the supplemental list of justices), at the end of paragraph (*a*) there shall be inserted— .
        "(*aa*) that by reason of the justice's conduct it is expedient that he should cease to exercise judicial functions as a justice for the area; or"

GENERAL NOTE
The purpose of paragraph (*a*) is to amend the District Courts (Scotland) Act 1975 to clarify the power of the Secretary of State to remove from office ex officio justices of the peace. At present, the vast majority of justices of the peace are appointed in the name of the Crown by instrument under the hand of the Secretary of State and can be removed from office in like manner. However, some justices of the peace are ex officio justices who are nominated by local authorities. There were no provisions in the 1975 Act to enable the Secretary of State to remove these justices. The effect of para. (*a*) is to give the Secretary of State the same power to remove ex officio justices, as he has justices appointed by instrument.
The purpose of para. (*b*) is to add a new ground for the removal of a justice from bench duty to the supplemental list, to those already in s.15 of the 1975 Act. At present the grounds include, *inter alia*, age (70 or over), incapacity due to age or infirmity, circumstances existing in his area, neglect of judicial function and failure to attend courses of instruction. The amendment adds the ground of conduct. The provisions of s.15 apply to all justices, *i.e.* justices ex officio and those appointed by instrument.

para. (a)
While the purport of the amendment is clear, there are no statutory criteria on how the Secretary of State should exercise his power to remove justices. However, assurances were given during the Committee Stage of the Bill that a justice would only be removed entirely from bench duty and the supplemental list, if he was guilty of a serious criminal offence, such as dishonesty. Where a justice was convicted of a minor offence, he would be removed from bench duty to the supplemental list under the Secretary of State's new power to do so under s.15(2)(*aa*) of the Act: see s.34(*b*) *supra*: First Scottish Standing Committee February 26, 1985, col. 466.

Provisions as to persons arrested in respect of terrorism

35. After section 3 of the Criminal Justice (Scotland) Act 1980 there shall be inserted the following sections—

"Rights of persons arrested or detained in connection with terrorism

3A.—(1) A person who has been arrested or detained under the terrorism provisions and who is in detention in a police station or other premises shall be entitled to have intimation of his detention and of the place where he is being detained sent without delay to a solicitor and to another person reasonably named by him:

Provided that a police officer not below the rank of superintendent may authorise a delay (not extending longer than the period of 48 hours from the start of the detention) where, in his view, such delay is necessary on one of the grounds mentioned in section 3C(3) of this Act.

(2) Where a person arrested or detained under the terrorism provisions requests that the intimation be made, there shall be recorded the time when such request is—

(*a*) made; and

(*b*) complied with.

(3) A person arrested or detained under the terrorism provisions shall be entitled to consult a solicitor at any time, without delay:

Provided that a police officer not below the rank of superintendent may authorise a delay (not extending longer than the period of 48 hours from the start of the detention) where, in his view, such delay is necessary on one of the grounds mentioned in section 3C(3) of this Act.

(4) Subject to section 3C of this Act the consultation provided for in subsection (3) above shall be private.

Provisions as to children detained in connection with terrorism

3B.—(1) Subject to the provisions of this section the provisions of section 3A of this Act apply to children as they apply to adults.

(2) Without prejudice to—

(*a*) subsection (3) of this section, or

(*b*) his entitlement, in terms of section 2A(1), to have intimation of his detention and of the place where he is being detained sent to a solicitor—

a person arrested or detained under the terrorism prevention provisions who appears to a constable to be a child shall not be entitled to have such intimation sent to any other person named by him.

(3) Where it appears to a constable that a person arrested or detained under the terrorism provisions is a child, he shall, subject to subsection (4), without delay—

(*a*) send intimation of the arrest or detention and of the place where the child is being held to his parent (if known); and

(*b*) allow such parent access to the child.

(4) A police officer not below the rank of superintendent may authorise—

(*a*) a delay in compliance with the duty mentioned in subsection (3)(*a*) above;

(*b*) non-compliance with the duty mentioned in subsection (3)(*b*) above,

where such delay or, as the case may be, non-compliance is, in his view, necessary on one of the grounds mentioned in section 3C(3) of this Act:

Provided that any such delay in compliance with the duty mentioned in subsection (3)(*a*) shall not extend longer than the period of 48 hours from the start of the detention.

(5) There shall be recorded the time at which the intimation mentioned in subsection (3)(*a*) is made.

(6) Subject to section 3C of this Act the access mentioned in subsection (3)(*b*) above shall be private.

(7) Where a child is, by virtue of any enactment, in the care either of a local authority or of a voluntary organisation, the intimation shall be either to the authority or organisation or to the parent, and the right of access shall be exercisable both by an officer of the authority or organisation and by the parent; and subsections (4) and (6) above and section 3C of this Act shall apply in relation to intimation and access under this subsection as they apply to intimation and access under subsection (3) above.

Provisions relating to consultations and access in connection with terrorism

3C.—(1) An officer not below the rank of Assistant Chief Constable may direct that the consultation or access mentioned in sections 3A(3) and 3B(3) of this Act respectively be in the presence of a uniformed officer not below the rank of inspector if it appears to the officer giving the direction to be necessary on one of the grounds mentioned in subsection (3) below.

(2) A uniformed officer directed to be present during a consultation or, as the case may be, access shall be an officer who, in the opinion of the officer giving the direction, has no connection with the case.

(3) The grounds mentioned in sections 3A(1), 3A(3) and 3B(4) of this Act and in subsection (1) above are that it is in the interests of the investigation or prevention of crime, or of the apprehension, prosecution or conviction of offenders.

(4) Where delay or non-compliance is authorised in the exercising of any of the rights or, as the case may be, the carrying out of any of the duties, mentioned in sections 3A(1), 3A(3), and 3B(3) of this Act, there shall be recorded the reason for such delay or non-compliance.

Interpretation and effect of sections 3A to 3D

3D.—(1) In sections 3A to 3C and this section of this Act—
    (*a*) "terrorism provisions" means—
        (i) section 12(1) of the Prevention of Terrorism (Temporary Provisions) Act 1984; or
        (ii) any provisions conferring a power of arrest or detention and contained in an order under section 13 of that Act; and
    (*b*) "child" and "parent" have the same meanings as in section 3 of this Act.

(2) The provisions of sections 3A to 3C and this section of this Act shall have effect, in relation to persons arrested or detained under the terrorism provisions, in place of any enactment or rule of law under or by virtue of which a person arrested or detained may be entitled to communicate or consult with any other person.".

GENERAL NOTE

The purpose of this provision is to give suspects arrested or detained under ss.12 and 13 of the Prevention of Terrorism (Temporary Provisions) Act 1984, the right to have someone informed (subject to delay in certain circumstances) and to have an interview with a solicitor. The provisions were enacted in the light of the recommendations of the Jellicoe Review of the Operation of the Prevention of Terrorism (Temporary Provisions) Act 1976, Cmnd. 8803. It takes the form of adding a new section to s.3 of the Criminal Justice (Scotland) Act 1980, which provides similar—but less extensive—rights to persons arrested or detained on suspicion of having committed a criminal offence. In practice, the police had already provided persons arrested on suspicion of terrorist offences, the rights under s.3. The amendment puts this on a statutory footing, setting out the rights in detail.

New subs. 3A(1)
"terrorism provisions"
By s.3D(*a*) these mean
    (a) s.12(1) of the Prevention of Terrorism (Temporary Provisions) Act 1984 *viz.*:
        (i) the arrest of a person suspected of having committed an offence under ss.1, 9 or 10 of the 1984 Act (membership and support of prescribed organisations, s.1; offences relating to an exclusion order, s.9; and contributions towards acts of terrorism, s.10);
        (ii) the arrest of a person who is or has been concerned in the commission, preparation or instigation of acts of terrorism; and
        (iii) the arrest of a person subject to an exclusion order.
    (b) the arrest or detention of persons as a result of powers of arrest or detention contained in an order under s.13 of the 1984 Act.

"without delay"
Intimation of detention and of the place where the suspect is detained must be sent immediately to a solicitor *and* to another person reasonably named by the suspect. However, this can be subject to a delay not exceeding 48 hours, where a police officer, not below the rank of superintendent considers delay is necessary on one of the grounds mentioned in s.3C(3).

New subs. 3A(3)
The suspect has also the right to consult a solicitor at any time, without delay. However this is subject to a delay of up to 48 hours, in the same way as the right to have intimation of his detention under s.3A(1). Subject to s.3C, the consultation should be in private: s.3A(4).

New subs. 3B
The provisions of s.3A apply to children as well as adults who are arrested or detained under the terrorism provisions. But, in relation to children, these are subject to important modifications.

New subs. 3B(2) and (3)
While a child retains the right under s.3A to have intimation of his arrest or detention sent to a solicitor, he does not have the right to have such intimation sent to "another person reasonably named by him". Instead, when it appears to a constable that the person arrested or detained is a child, the constable must send intimation of the arrest or detention and the place where the child is being held, to the child's parent (if known) and allow the parent access to the child.

"child"
"child" is defined as a person under 16 years of age: s.3D(*b*) which incorporates the definition of "child" in s.3(5) of the 1980 Act.

"parent"
"parent" is defined as including "guardian" and any person who has the actual custody of a child: s.3D(*b*) which incorporates the definition of "parent" in s.3(5) of the 1980 Act as amended by para. 21 of Sched. 2 to the current statute.

New subs. 3B(4)
The right to have intimation to a parent is subject to a delay of up to 48 hours, when a police officer not below the rank of superintendant considers delay necessary on one of the grounds in s.3C(3) of the Act. Moreover, if it is thought necessary on one of the grounds in s.3C(3), the duty to allow the parent immediate access need not be complied with. Subject to s.3C, access shall be in private: s.3B(6).

New subs. 3B(7)
Where the child is in the care of a local authority or a voluntary organisation, intimation can be to the local authority or the voluntary organisation or the parent. The right of access, however, is exercisable by both an officer of the local authority or organisation *and* the parent. These rights are subject to the restrictions in ss.3B(4), 3B(6) and s.3C.

New subs. 3C(1) and (2)

If it appears necessary on one of the grounds in s.3C(3), an officer not below the rank of Assistant Chief Constable may direct that both the consultation with a solicitor (s.3A(3)) and access by a parent (s.3B(3)) must take place in the presence of a uniformed officer not below the rank of inspector, who in the opinion of the officer making the direction, has no connection with the case: s.3C(2).

New subs. 3C(3)

It has been noted that the rights of the person arrested or detained are subject to modification if it is thought necessary on one of the grounds listed in this subsection *viz.* the interests of the investigation, or prevention of crime, or of the apprehension, prosecution or conviction of offenders. These are much more general than the grounds recommended in para. 111 of the Jellicoe Report. The effectiveness of the new rights will therefore greatly be determined by how wide these grounds are interpreted.

New subs. 3C(4)
"there shall be recorded the reason for such delay or non-compliance"

The only safeguard provided in the Act against abuse of the power to delay or non-compliance in ss.3A(1), 3A(3) and 3B(3), is that the reason for the delay or non-compliance must be recorded. The word "reason" is used, not "ground". Accordingly, it is insufficient simply to state the ground in s.3C(3) which has been relied upon: instead, specific reasons arising from the facts and circumstances of the particular case must be recorded which can justify that delay or non-compliance is necessary on one of the grounds in s.3C(3).

New subs. 3D(2)

The provisions of s.3A to 3C have effect in relation to persons arrested or detained under the terrorism provisions, in place of any other statutory or common law rights that a person arrested or detained has to communicate or consult with any other person: *e.g.* under s.3 of the Criminal Justice (Scotland) Act 1975.

Evidence in trials of certain sexual offences

36.—(1) After section 141 of the Criminal Procedure (Scotland) Act 1975 there shall be inserted the following sections—

"Evidence in relation to sexual offences

141A.—(1) In any trial of a person on any charge to which this section applies, subject to section 141B, the court shall not admit, or allow questioning designed to elicit, evidence which shows or tends to show that the complainer—

(a) is not of good character in relation to sexual matters;

(b) is a prostitute or an associate of prostitutes; or

(c) has at any time engaged with any person in sexual behaviour not forming part of the subject matter of the charge.

(2) This section applies to a charge of committing or attempting to commit any of the following offences, that is to say

(a) rape;

(b) sodomy;

(c) assault with intent to rape;

(d) indecent assault;

(e) indecent behaviour (including any lewd, indecent or libidinous practice or behaviour);

(f) an offence under section 106(1)(a) or 107 of the Mental Health (Scotland) Act 1984 (unlawful sexual intercourse with mentally handicapped female or with patient);

(g) an offence under any of the following provisions of the Sexual Offences (Scotland) Act 1976—

   (i) section 2 (procuring by threats etc.);

   (ii) section 3 (unlawful sexual intercourse with girl under 13);

   (iii) section 4 (unlawful sexual intercourse with girl under 16);

(iv) section 5 (indecent behaviour towards girl between 12 and 16);

(v) section 8 (abduction of girl under 18);

(vi) section 9 (unlawful detention of female); or

(*h*) an offence under section 80(7) of the Criminal Justice (Scotland) Act 1980 (homosexual offences).

(3) In this section "complainer" means the person against whom the offence referred to in subsection (2) above is alleged to have been committed.

(4) This section does not apply to questioning, or evidence being adduced, by the Crown.

Exceptions to prohibition

141B.—(1) Notwithstanding the terms of section 141A, in any trial of a person on any charge to which that section applies, where the court is satisfied on an application by that person—

(*a*) that the questioning or evidence referred to in section 141A(1) above is designed to explain or rebut evidence adduced, or to be adduced, otherwise than by or on behalf of that person,

(*b*) that the questioning or evidence referred to in section 141A(1)(*c*) above—

(i) is questioning or evidence as to sexual behaviour which took place on the same occasion as the sexual behaviour forming the subject-matter of the charge, or

(ii) is relevant to the defence of incrimination, or

(*c*) that it would be contrary to the interests of justice to exclude the questioning or evidence referred to in section 141A(1) above,

the court shall allow such questioning or, as the case may be, admit such evidence.

(2) Where questioning or evidence is or has been allowed or admitted under this section, the court may at any time limit as it thinks fit the extent of that questioning or evidence.

(3) Any application under this section shall be made in the course of the trial but in the absence of the jury, the complainer, any person cited as a witness and the public.".

(2) After section 346 of the said Act there shall be inserted the following sections—

"Evidence in relation to sexual offences

346A.—(1) In any trial of a person on any charge to which this section applies, subject to section 346B, the court shall not admit, or allow questioning designed to elicit, evidence which shows or tends to show that the complainer—

(*a*) is not of good character in relation to sexual matters;

(*b*) is a prostitute or an associate of prostitutes; or

(*c*) has at any time engaged with any person in sexual behaviour not forming part of the subject matter of the charge.

(2) This section applies to a charge of committing or, in the case of paragraphs (*b*) to (*g*), attempting to commit any of the following offences, that is to say—

(*a*) attempted rape;

(*b*) sodomy;

(*c*) assault with intent to rape;

(*d*) indecent assault;

(*e*) indecent behaviour (including any lewd, indecent or libidinous practice or behaviour);

    (*f*) an offence under any of the following provisions of the Sexual
        Offences (Scotland) Act 1976—
          (i) section 2 (procuring by threats, etc.);
         (ii) section 3(2) (unlawful sexual intercourse with girl under
             13);
       (iii) section 4 (unlawful sexual intercourse with girl under 16);
       (iv) section 5 (indecent behaviour towards girl between 12
            and 16);
        (v) section 8 (abduction of girl under 18);
       (vi) section 9 (unlawful detention of female); or
    (*g*) an offence under section 80(7) of the Criminal Justice (Scot-
        land) Act 1980 (homosexual offences).

    (3) In this section. "complainer" means the person against whom
the offence referred to in subsection (2) above is alleged to have been
committed.

    (4) This section does not apply to questioning, or evidence being
adduced, by the Crown.

Exceptions to prohibition

    346B.—(1) Notwithstanding the terms of section 346A above, in
any trial of a person on any charge to which that section applies,
where the court is satisfied on an application by that person—
    (*a*) that the questioning or evidence referred to in section 346A(1)
        above is designed to explain or rebut evidence adduced, or to
        be adduced, otherwise than by or on behalf of that person,
    (*b*) that the questioning or evidence referred to in section
        346A(1)(*c*) above—
          (i) is questioning or evidence as to sexual behaviour which
             took place on the same occasion as the sexual behaviour
             forming the subject matter of the charge, or
         (ii) is relevant to the defence of incrimination, or
    (*c*) that it would be contrary to the interests of justice to exclude
        the questioning or evidence referred to in section 346A(1)
        above, the court shall allow such questioning or, as the case
        may be, admit such evidence.
        (2) Where questioning or evidence is or has been allowed or
admitted under this section, the court may at any time limit as
it thinks fit the extent of that questioning or evidence.
        (3) Any application under this section shall be made in the
course of the trial but in the absence of the complainer, any
person cited as a witness and the public.".

    The purpose of this provision is to provide new rules of evidence in relation to rape and
other sexual offences. At common law, the complainer in a rape trial can be cross-examined
and evidence may be led to establish her bad moral character: *Dickie* v. *H.M.A.* (1897) 2
Adam. 331. This is considered relevant to her credibility but it is doubtful whether such
evidence is admissible if consent is not at issue. However, evidence of bad character can
only be adduced if it relates, or is continuously linked to the time of the alleged offence:
H.M.A. v. *Reid* (1861) 4 Irv. 124. But the common law does not permit the cross-
examination nor the leading of evidence as to specific acts of intercourse with third parties
unless the evidence was part of the *res gestae*. Evidence of previous sexual intercourse with
the panel is not permitted unless it relates to sexual relations which took place, "a short time
before the alleged sexual attack". These rules, apart from the admissibility of bad character,
have been described by a recent commentator as "not merely adequate but thoroughly
enlightened": J. Temkin, "Evidence in Sexual Assault Cases: The Scottish Proposal and
Alternatives" (1984) 47 M.L.R. 625 at p.630.

However, it would appear that the common law rules have not been observed in recent cases and the Scottish Law Commission advised reform (Scot. Law Com. No. 78). This section to a large extent implements the Commission's recommendations.

New subss. 141A, 141B, subss. 346A, 346B
Ss.141A and B are concerned with solemn procedure; ss.346A and B are concerned with summary procedure.

New subss. 141A(1) and subs. 346A(1)
"on any charge to which this section applies"
While the controversy surrounding the law of evidence has been concerned with the crime of rape, the new provisions apply to the full range of sexual offences listed in s.141A(2) and s.346A(2).

"subject to section 141B": "subject to section 346B"
The general prohibition of evidence relating to the complainer is subject to the exceptions listed in s.141B and s.346B.

"the complainer"
This is defined in s.141A(3)and s.346A(3) as the person against whom the sexual offence is alleged to have been committed.

"is not of good character in relation to sexual matters"
In the Bill as originally drafted, it was proposed that there should be a ban on questioning and evidence which showed that the complainer in a sexual offence case was not of good character: but the prohibition was not to apply to questioning or evidence which the court was satisfied related wholly or mainly to the question of the truthfulness of the complainer's evidence or any statement or representation of the complainer to be put in evidence. This exception caused widespread alarm as it was considered to be a loophole which might have undermined the whole purpose of the new provision. After a lengthy debate in Committee, the exception was abandoned and the clause was redrafted so as only to exclude evidence or questioning which showed that the complainer was not of good character *in relation to sexual matters*. Accordingly, it is still possible for the defence to attack the general character of the complainer with, of course, the risk of possible retaliation.

New subs. 141A(4) and subs. 346A(4)
The prohibition of evidence in s.141A(1) and s.346A(1) only applies to questioning or evidence being adduced by the defence. It does not apply to questioning or evidence being adduced by the Crown. Cases where the Crown would wish to engage in such questioning or adduce such evidence will be rare.

New subs. 141B(1) and subs. 346B(1)
"Notwithstanding the terms of section 141A"; "Notwithstanding the terms of section 346A"
S.141B(1) and s.346B(1) provide exceptions to the prohibitions in s.141A(1) and s.346A(1).

"on an application"
The panel must make an application to the court to allow the evidence on one of the grounds listed in s.141B(1) or s.346B(1). The application is made in the course of the trial but in the absence of the jury, the complainer, any person cited as a witness and the public: see s.141B(3) and s.346B(3).

New subs. 141B(1)(a) and subs. 364B(1)(a)
This exception allows such questioning or the admission of such evidence if it is designed to explain or rebut evidence adduced or to be adduced by someone other than the panel, for example, medical or scientific evidence.

New subs. 141B(1)(b) and subs. 346B(1)(b)
Questioning or evidence that the complainer has engaged in sexual behaviour not forming part of the subject matter of the charge may be allowed or admitted under this exception if it relates to matters forming part of the *res gestae*, for example, if it was maintained that the alleged rape was simply an incident in some sort of group orgy. An exception is also made where the questioning or evidence is relevant to the defence of incrimination.

New subs. 141B(1)(c) and subs. 346B(1)(c)

This exception allows such questioning or the admission of such evidence if it would be contrary to the interests of justice to exclude the questioning or evidence. Concern has been expressed as to the potential width of this exception. The Solicitor-General for Scotland has stressed that before questioning or evidence can be allowed under this exception the court must be satisfied that *not* to allow it "would be contrary to the interests of justice. That takes account not only of the concept of fairness to the accused but of the interests of the complainer and the public at large": First Scottish Standing Committee, col. 944. It remains to be seen whether the courts will exercise their discretion in this way or whether the provision will be widely construed and so frustrate the primary aim of the legislation which is to exclude evidence of the sexual history of the complainer. The way in which the common law rules were applied in recent practice, must give cause for concern on this point.

Evidence in replication

37. In each of sections 149A and 350A of the Criminal Procedure (Scotland) Act 1975 (evidence in replication), in subsection (1)(*a*), for the words "led by the defence" there shall be substituted the words "given by any defence witness".

GENERAL NOTE

By ss.149A and 350A of the Criminal Procedure (Scotland) Act 1975, the judge may permit the prosecutor to lead additional evidence for the purpose, *inter alia*, of contradicting evidence "led by the defence" which could not reasonably have been anticipated by the prosecutor. In *Sandlan* v. *H.M. Adv.*, 1983 S.L.T. 519, it was argued that the trial judge had been wrong to allow the prosecutor to lead evidence in replication when the evidence sought to be contradicted had not been "led by the defence" in the evidence in chief of the defence witnesses but had been elicited in cross-examination. It was, however, unnecessary to determine the point in the case. The effect of this amendment is to substitute the phrase "given by any defence witness" for the words "led by the defence" in ss.149A and 350A of the 1975 Act. This removes any ambiguity and confirms the approach of the trial judge in the *Sandlan* case.

It should be noted that the accused will be treated as a defence witness for the purpose of ss.149A and 350A of the 1975 Act, as a result of ss.141 and 346 of that Act which provide that, "the accused shall be a competent witness for the defence at every stage of the case".

Corroboration not required in relation to vehicle licensing offences

38. In the Road Traffic Regulation Act 1984, in section 120 (which relaxes the requirement of corroboration in relation to certain road traffic and vehicle licensing offences), after subsection (2)(*e*) there shall be added—

"or,

(*f*) by its being used or kept on a public road within the meaning of the Vehicle (Excise) Act 1971 without there being in force a licence under that Act for the vehicle within the meaning of section 8 of that Act".

GENERAL NOTE

S.120 of the Road Traffic Regulations Act 1984 relaxes the requirement of corroboration in relation to certain road traffic offences including that of a vehicle "being used or kept on a public road within the meaning of the Vehicles (Excise) Act 1971 without a licence under that Act being exhibited on the vehicle in the manner prescribed under that Act". One consequence of the relaxation was that when a traffic warden who was operating singly discovered that a vehicle was not displaying a licence, while he or she could deal with the lesser offence of failure to display, if it was discovered that the vehicle did not have a valid excise licence, the more serious charge of using or keeping an unlicensed vehicle on a public road could not be dealt with as there was no corroboration of the vital fact that the vehicle was on a public road at the relevant time.

S.38 which was introduced at the request of the Department of Transport, amends s.120 of the 1984 Act, to extend the offences where it shall be lawful to convict the accused on the evidence of one witness to include the offence of using or keeping a vehicle on a public road without a valid licence.

Fines in respect of drug offences

39. After section 193A of the Criminal Procedure (Scotland) Act 1975 there shall be inserted the following section—

"Offences relating to controlled drugs

193B.—(1) Without prejudice to section 395(1) of this Act (as applied to solemn proceedings by section 194), where a person is—

(*a*) convicted on indictment of an offence to which this section relates, and

(*b*) sentenced in respect of that offence to a period of imprisonment or detention,

the Court shall, unless it is satisfied that for any reason it would be inappropriate to do so, also impose a fine.

(2) In determining the amount of a fine imposed pursuant to subsection (1), the Court shall have regard to any profits likely to have been made by the offender from the crime in respect of which he has been convicted.

(3) This section relates to any of the offences mentioned in paragraphs (*a*) to (*c*) of subsection (4) or any offence mentioned in paragraphs (*d*) to (*g*) of that subsection where such latter offence involves a controlled drug as defined in section 2(1)(*a*) of the Misuse of Drugs Act 1971 ("the 1971 Act").

(4) The offences are those created by—

(*a*) section 4(2) of the 1971 Act (production, or being concerned in the production of, a controlled drug);

(*b*) section 4(3) of the 1971 Act (supply, or offer to supply, or being concerned in the supply, of a controlled drug);

(*c*) section 5(3) of the 1971 Act (possession of a controlled drug with intent to supply);

(*d*) section 50(2) and (3) of the Customs and Excise Management Act 1979 ("the 1979 Act") (importation etc. of prohibited goods);

(*e*) section 68(2) of the 1979 Act (exportation etc. of prohibited goods);

(*f*) section 170(1) of the 1979 Act (possessing or dealing with prohibited goods); and

(*g*) section 170(2) of the 1979 Act (being concerned in evasion or attempt at evasion of a prohibition).

(5) Where a fine has been imposed pursuant to subsection (1) in respect of an offence to which this section relates, and the offender is sentenced to a period of imprisonment or detention because he has not paid that fine, that period of imprisonment or detention shall be served consecutively upon—

(*a*) the period of imprisonment or detention in respect of the offence, and

(*b*) any period of imprisonment or detention imposed in respect of any other offence dealt with in the same proceedings,

unless either of the latter periods is one of life imprisonment or detention for life.".

GENERAL NOTE

The increase in drug abuse is one of the most serious contemporary social problems in Scotland. The purpose of this section is to deprive drug traffickers of the profits of their crime. Where a person is convicted on indictment for an offence related to a controlled drug and is sentenced to a period of imprisonment or detention, the court must, unless it is satisfied that it would be inappropriate to do so, also impose a fine. In determining the amount of the fine imposed, the court "shall have regard to any profits likely to have been made by the offender from the crime in respect of which he has been convicted". If the fine is not paid, any period of imprisonment or detention for non-payment is to be served consecutively upon the initial sentence.

New subs. 193B(1)
"without prejudice to section 395(1) of this Act"
S.395(1) provides a general rule that a court must take into account the means of the accused in determining the amount of the fine. This provision is applicable to solemn proceedings as a result of s.194.

"convicted on indictment of an offence to which this section relates"
The offences to which the section relates are these listed in s.193B(4) whenever a restricted substance is involved, *i.e.* Class A, B, or C controlled drugs: see s.193B(3).

"sentenced in respect of that offence to a period of detention or imprisonment"
Before a fine must be imposed under this section the panel must be convicted on indictment and sentenced to a period of detention or imprisonment.

"unless it is satisfied that for any reason it would be inappropriate to do so"
A fine in addition to the sentence of detention or imprisonment is mandatory unless the court is satisfied that it would be inappropriate in the particular facts and circumstances of the case.

New subs. 193B(2)
"profits likely to have been made by the offender from the crime in respect of which he has been convicted"
In determining the amount of the fine, the court shall have regard to the profits likely to have been made by the offender from the crime in respect of which he has been convicted. It appears from the debates in the First Scottish Standing Committee that it is the government's intention that "what is considered is the crime of which evidence has been given and of which the court has found the accused guilty. The size of the fine will be decided on the likely profits from that crime". Two points should, however, be noticed. First, it is only the profits likely to have been made by the particular offender from the crime which is relevant, not, for example, the profits which a co-accused is likely to obtain by committing it: often the offender may only receive drugs for his part in the offence. Secondly, it is only the likely profits of that particular crime which are relevant. Thus, it would appear that profits from previous drug trafficking—even if known—are excluded. There will also be difficulty in assessing what profits were "likely" to have been made from the crime.

New subs. 193B(5)
Where the fine has not been paid, any period of imprisonment or detention imposed for non-payment of the fine is to be served consecutively upon the initial sentence, unless the initial sentence is one of life imprisonment or detention for life.

Further provision as to fines

40. In the Criminal Procedure (Scotland) Act 1975, in section 407(1A) (periods of imprisonment for non-payment of fines)—
   (a) after "£10,000" there shall be inserted "but not exceeding £20,000";
   (b) after "12 months" there shall be added—
     "Exceeding £20,000 but not exceeding £50,000 ....18 months
     Exceeding £50,000 ....2 years.".

GENERAL NOTE
The effect of this provision is to increase the periods of imprisonment for non-payment of fines as laid down in s.407(1A) of the Criminal Procedure (Scotland) Act 1975 (as amended by the Increase of Criminal Penalties (Scotland) Order 1984 (S.I. 1984 No. 526)). Seen in the context of the new s.193B(5) of the 1975 Act, it shows the extent of the government's determination to take strong measures against drug traffickers: see note to s.39 *supra*.

Penalties under food and drugs legislation

41. In the Food and Drugs (Scotland) Act 1956—
- (a) in subsection (1)(a) of section 40 (which relates to penalties) the words from "or to imprisonment" to "offence is continued" shall cease to have effect;
- (b) in subsection (1)(b) the words from "and", where it occurs for the second time, to the end shall cease to have effect;
- (c) in subsection (8A) of section 56 (which specifies certain maximum penalties)—
    - (i) in paragraph (a) the words "or imprisonment for a term not exceeding 6 months or both" shall cease to have effect; and
    - (ii) in paragraph (b)(i) the words "or imprisonment for a term not exceeding 6 months or both" shall cease to have effect.

GENERAL NOTE

The purpose of this section is to amend the penalties in respect of offences under the Food and Drugs (Scotland) Act 1956. These offences include the incorrect description of food on labels or in advertising, the preparation of injurious or adulterated food and drugs and the sale of food that is unfit for human consumption. In the original clause, it had been intended to increase the imprisonment penalty on indictment from one year to two years: however, this was successfully defeated in the First Scottish Standing Committee, February 28, col. 479.

para. (a)

This restricts the penalty on summary conviction to a fine, by removing the alternative of six months imprisonment and, in the case of continuing offence, of further fines for every day the offence is continued.

para. (b)

This restricts the penalties on conviction on indictment to a fine or to imprisonment for a term not exceeding one year, by removing the power, in the case of a continuing offence, of further fines for every day the offence is continued.

para. (c)

This amends s.56(8A) of the 1956 Act which lists maximum penalties for breaches of regulations made under the 1956 Act, by providing that in relation to convictions triable only summarily, or on summary conviction when an offence is triable summarily or on indictment, that the only penalty is a fine. S.56(8A) is to be found in para. 8 of Sched. 15 to the Criminal Justice Act 1982.

Amendments of Prisons (Scotland) Act 1952

42. In the Prisons (Scotland) Act 1952—
- (a) section 7(2) (which relates to the appointment of women to visiting committees) shall cease to have effect;
- (b) for subsections (1) and (1A) of section 16 (which relates to the discharge of prisoners) there shall be substituted—
    - "(1) Where a prisoner would, but for this subsection, be discharged on a Saturday or Sunday, he shall be discharged on the preceding Friday";
- (c) for subsection (2) of section 17 (which relates to allowances to prisoners on discharge) there shall be substituted—
    - "(2) The Secretary of State may make such payments to or in respect of persons released or about to be released from prisons as he may, with the consent of the Treasury, determine.";
- (d) in section 34 (which relates to the temporary detention of

young offenders) after the word "institution" there shall be
inserted the words ", remand centre,"; and
(e) section 35(5)(b) (which relates to special treatment for persons
convicted of sedition) shall cease to have effect.

GENERAL NOTE
This section makes various amendments to the Prisons (Scotland) Act 1952.

para. (a)
This removes the statutory requirement that the rules for the constitution of visiting
committees to prisons should prescribe a certain number of women, and that the Secretary
of State should have the power to appoint women where their number fell below that
prescribed. This was a fall back power enjoyed by the Secretary of State, as members to the
committees were prima facie appointed by the regional islands and district councils. Because
of the increasing number of women on these councils and the decline in the number of
women in Scottish prisons it was considered that it was no longer necessary to prescribe a
minimum number of women for membership of visiting committees and that it should be left
to the good sense of the councils to appoint a reasonable proportion of women to visiting
committees.

para. (b)
This provides that where a prisoner who is serving a sentence would, but for this
subsection, be discharged on a Saturday or Sunday, he shall be discharged on the preceding
Friday. Ss.16(1) and (1A) provided different rules where a prisoner was serving a sentence
of 31 days or less (s.16(1)) and more than 31 days (s.16(1A)). These are replaced by the new
s.16(1), which applies the same rule to short term prisoners as formerly applied only to long
term prisoners.

para. (c)
The purpose of the new s.17(2) is to put on a statutory basis the present administrative
arrangements for discharge grants. These are reviewed annually after consultation with the
D.H.S.S. The grant is to enable homeless ex-offenders to obtain immediate accommodation
without the need to apply and wait for money from the D.H.S.S.

para. (d)
S.34 of the 1952 Act provides that a person who is required to be taken to a young
offenders institution or a detention centre, can temporarily be detained elsewhere—in
practice a local prison—until arrangements have been made for taking him to the institution
or centre. The effect of this provision is to extend the scope of s.34 to include a person who
is required to be taken to a remand centre. At present there is no remand centre in Scotland,
but the opportunity was taken to make the amendment which would be useful should a
remand centre ever be built in Scotland.

para. (e)
This deletes s.35(5)(b) which provides for special Rules for persons serving a sentence on
conviction of sedition.

Detention of young offenders

43. In each of sections 207 and 415 of the Criminal Procedure (Scotland)
Act 1975 (detention of young offenders)—
(a) in subsection (5)(a), after the word "shall" there shall be inserted
the words ", subject to subsection (5A) below,"; and
(b) after the said subsection (5) there shall be inserted—
"(5A) Where dention in a detention centre would be required
by subsection (5) above but the accused has already served such
a sentence, the court shall order that the detention be in a young
offenders institution, unless it appears to the court that, in the
particular circumstances of the case, and having regard to the
character of the offender, it would be more appropriate for the
detention to be served in a detention centre.".

General Note

There has been widespread criticism of the "short, sharp, shock" treatment of young offenders in a detention centre. Under the Criminal Procedure (Scotland) Act 1975, it was possible for a person who had served a period of detention in a detention centre to be sentenced to serve detention there for a second or third time. This was, of course, to defeat the purpose of such detention. The purpose of s.43 is to amend the Criminal Procedure (Scotland) Act 1975 to ensure that young offenders who have served one term of detention in a detention centre will normally serve any subsequent custodial centre in a young offenders institution. However, the courts will retain discretion to send an offender to a detention centre for a second or subsequent time, if, in the circumstances of the case, this is considered to be the more appropriate place of detention.

S.207 of the 1975 Act is concerned with the court's power to impose detention on conviction after solemn proceedings: s.415 is concerned with the court's power to impose detention on conviction after summary proceedings.

New subs. 207(5A) and 415(5A)

"would be required by subsection 5 above"

Normally detention must be served in a detention centre if the court has imposed a sentence of detention on a male person for a period of at least 28 days but not exceeding four months. However, the detention is not required to be served in a detention centre if the convicted person is physically or mentally unfit to be detained there, or there is a special reason why a young offenders institution is more appropriate: s.207(6) and 415(6) of the 1975 Act.

"shall order"

If the accused has already served a sentence in a detention centre, prima facie the court will order the detention to be served in a young offenders institution.

"unless it appears"

This enables the court in exceptional cases to order that detention should be served in a detention centre in spite of the fact that the accused has already served detention there. Detention in a detention centre must be more appropriate than in a young offenders institution in the particular circumstances of the case and having regard to the character of the offender.

Functions of Parole Board for Scotland and local review committees in relation to children detained on conviction on indictment

44.—(1) Section 59 of the Criminal Justice Act 1967 shall be amended in accordance with this section.

(2) In subsection (3) of that section (duty of Parole Board for Scotland to advise Secretary of State on release from imprisonment and recall of certain persons)—

 (*a*) in paragraph (*a*)—
  (i) after the word "61" there shall be inserted the words "of this Act or section 206 of the Criminal Procedure (Scotland) Act 1975 (detention and release of children convicted on indictment)"; and
  (ii) after the word "Act" there shall be inserted the words "section 12 of the Criminal Justice (Scotland) Act 1963 or section 206 or 206A of the Criminal Procedure (Scotland) Act 1975";
 (*b*) in paragraph (*c*) for the word "applies" there shall be substituted the words "or the said section 206 applies or the recall of persons to whom the said section 12 or the said section 206A applies".

(3) In subsection (5) of that section (Board to be given any written representations made by person whose release or recall is under consideration)—

 (*a*) in paragraph (*a*) after the word "Act" there shall be inserted the words "or section 206 of the Criminal Procedure (Scotland) Act 1975"; and
 (*b*) in paragraph (*b*) after the word "Act" there shall be inserted the

words "section 12 of the Criminal Justice (Scotland) Act 1963 or section 206 or 206A of the Criminal Procedure (Scotland) Act 1975".

(4) In subsection (6) of that section (establishment and functions of local review committees), in paragraph (*a*), after the words "of this Act" there shall be inserted the words "or section 206 of the Criminal Procedure (Scotland) Act 1975".

GENERAL NOTE
The purpose of this section is to amplify the statement of duties of the Parole Board and the local review committees which is contained in s.59 of the Criminal Justice Act 1967.

At present the statutory duties of the Board and local review committees do not extend to giving advice to the Secretary of State on the release, on licence, under s.206 of the Criminal Procedure (Scotland) Act 1975 of the small number of children convicted on indictment, or the recall of persons so released. In practice, however, they already give this advice. The effect of s.42(2) is simply to make it their statutory duty to do so. This will not lead to any great increase in their tasks: in 1983, for example, only eight cases concerning such children were considered.

Secondly, s.59 of the Criminal Justice Act 1967 is amended to take into account the duties given to the Parole Board as a result of s.206 of the 1975 Act and s.45 of this Act. These are to make recommendations to the Secretary of State on the recall of persons released on supervision under s.206 or s.206A of the 1975 Act or under s.12 of the Criminal Justice (Scotland) Act 1963 and to consider the representations in writing of persons so recalled: see notes to s.45 *infra*.

Supervision of children released after detention

45.—(1) After section 206 of the Criminal Procedure (Scotland) Act 1975 there shall be inserted the following section—

"Supervision of children after release
    206A.—(1) A child released after detention under section 206 who has not been released on licence during the period of detention may be required, by notice given by the Secretary of State on his release, to be under the supervision of such officer as may be specified in the notice, and to comply, while the notice is in force, with such conditions as may be specified.

(2) Subject to subsection (5) below, the supervision requirement shall not continue after the expiry of the period of 12 months from the date of release.

(3) The Secretary of State may, on giving notice to the person concerned, at any time vary or cancel a requirement or condition specified under subsection (1) above.

(4) A period of supervision required under subsection (1) above shall not extend beyond the date on which the person under supervision attains the age of 23 years.

(5) Where, before a supervision requirement expires, the Secretary of State is satisfied that the person to whom it relates has failed to comply with its terms and either—
    (*a*) the Parole Board for Scotland so recommends; or
    (*b*) it appears to him to be in the public interest to do so before consultation with the Board is practicable, he may recall the person to detention for a period not exceeding 3 months; and a person at large after such recall shall be deemed to be unlawfully at large.

(6) The Secretary of State shall inform a person recalled under subsection (5) above of the reasons for his recall, so that the person may make representations in writing with respect to his recall to the Parole Board for Scotland; and the Board may, on receipt of such representations, require the Secretary of State to release him forthwith.

(7) The Secretary of State may at any time release a person detained by virtue of subsection (5) above.

(8) The powers conferred by subsection (5) above may be exercised as often as it appears to the Secretary of State that the person concerned has failed to comply with the supervision requirement; but no person may be recalled to detention for periods totalling more than 3 months by virtue of that subsection.

(9) A recall under subsection (5) above may continue beyond the date of expiry of the supervision requirement unless the person to whom it relates is not in custody at that date.".

(2) In section 12 of the Criminal Justice (Scotland) Act 1963 (supervision of persons released from young offenders' institution)—

   (*a*) in subsection (7) after the word "above", where first occurring, there shall be inserted "and either—
      (*a*) the Parole Board for Scotland so recommends; or
      (*b*) it appears to him to be in the public interest to do so before consultation with the Board is practicable,";

   (*b*) after that subsection there shall be inserted the following subsection.
      "(7A) The Secretary of State shall inform a person recalled under subsection (7) above of the reasons for his recall, so that the person may make representations in writing with respect to his recall to the Parole Board for Scotland; and the Board may, on receipt of such representations, require the Secretary of State to release him forthwith."; and

   (*c*) in subsection (9)—
      (i) for the words "that person" there shall be substituted the words "a person released under subsection (7A) above or this subsection"; and
      (ii) after the word "under", where secondly occurring, there shall be inserted the words "subsection (7A) above or".

GENERAL NOTE

By s.206 of the Criminal Procedure (Scotland) Act 1975, where a child who has been convicted on indictment, is released before the expiry of his sentence, he is released on licence which lasts 12 months. This enables the child to be supervised during the period of the licence. When s.206 of the 1975 Act was revised by s.44 of the Criminal Justice (Scotland) Act 1980, it had been intended that children who had been convicted on indictment should be subject to supervision, whether or not they had been released on licence before the expiry of their sentence. However, the drafting of s.206 was such that it did not provide the powers for supervision of those few children, convicted on indictment, who were not released on licence before the expiry of their sentence. But, ironically, a child who cannot safely be released on licence before the end of his sentence, is precisely the child who has most need to keep in touch with a social worker. The purpose of s.45(1) is to amend s.206 of the Criminal Procedure (Scotland) Act to allow supervision of children, convicted on indictment, who have not been released on licence before the expiry of their sentence. A child released on supervision may be recalled by the Secretary of State on the recommendation of the Parole Board or if it appears to the Secretary of State that it is in the public interest to do so. However, the child so recalled can make representations to the Parole Board, which can order his immediate release. The purpose of s.45(2) is to apply a similar system of recall to young persons released on supervision under s.12 of the Criminal Justice (Scotland) Act 1963.

S.45(1)
New subs. 206A(1)
"who has not been released in licence"
   S.206A deals with the supervision of the small number of children, *convicted on indictment*, who are not released on licence before the expiry of their sentences.

"by notice given by the Secretary of State"

It is the Secretary of State who is empowered to give notice that the child on release will be under the supervision of a social worker.

New subs. 206A(2)

The supervision requirement does not extend beyond 12 months after the date of release. However, this is subject to subs. 206A(5).

New subs. 206A(4)

The age limit of 23 is quite arbitrary. It is possible for a child to serve a very long sentence. If there was no age limit, he could be subject to supervision whatever his age on release. Accordingly the age limit of 23 was chosen to draw to a conclusion a concept which was intended for supervising young people rather than adults.

New subs. 206A(5)
"before a supervision requirement expires"

This gives the Secretary of State the power to recall the child to detention if he fails to comply with the terms of the supervision requirement and either (a) the Parole Board for Scotland so recommends or (b) it appears to the Secretary of State, before consultation with the Parole Board is practicable, that it is in the public interest to do so. However the supervision requirement must not have expired. While the detention cannot exceed three months, it does not matter if it has the effect of extending the period during which the child is in fact supervised beyond 12 months. If, for example, the child was recalled during the eleventh month of the supervision requirement, he can be kept in detention for 3 months, with the result that the total supervision would have been 14 not 12 months: subs. 206A(2) is expressly made subject to this subsection.

"unlawfully at large"

When the child is unlawfully at large, he can be placed in detention for three months if he is caught before the expiry of the supervision requirement.

New subs. 206A(6)

It is the duty of the Secretary of State to inform the person subject to the recall of the reasons for the recall. The person recalled can then make written representations to the Parole Board, which can order the Secretary of State to release him immediately.

New subs. 206A(8)

The power of recall can be used more than once but the total period(s) spent in detention must not exceed three months.

New subs. 206A(9)

A recall can continue beyond the date of expiry of the supervision requirement: see note to subs. 206A(5). However if a child who is subject to a recall has eluded custody at the date when the supervision requirement expires, the recall lapses.

S.45(2)

The effect of these amendments to the Criminal Justice (Scotland) Act 1963 is to provide that the Parole Board of Scotland be similarly involved in the recall of young offenders released on supervision under s.12 of the 1963 Act (as substituted by para. 2 of Sched. 5 to the Criminal Justice (Scotland) Act 1980).

S.45(2)(a)

The Secretary of State may only recall a young person released on supervision either (a) if the Parole Board so recommends or (b) it appears to the Secretary of State, before consultation with the Parole Board is practicable, that it is in the public interest to do.

New subs. 12(7A)

It is the duty of the Secretary of State to inform the person subject to recall of the reasons for his recall. The person can then make written representations to the Parole Board, which can order the Secretary of State to release him immediately.

Post-release supervision of service offenders

46.—(1) In section 71AA of the Army Act 1955 and the Air Force Act 1955 respectively and section 43AA of the Naval Discipline Act

1957(custodial orders), after subsection (6A) in each case there shall be inserted the following subsection—

"(6B) Section 12 of the Criminal Justice (Scotland) Act 1963 (supervision of young offenders following release) shall apply to persons released from a term of detention under a custodial order as it applies to those released from a term of detention imposed under section 207 or section 415 of the Criminal Procedure (Scotland) Act 1975.".

(2) In paragraph 10 of Schedule 5A to the Army Act 1955 and to the Air Force Act 1955 respectively and Schedule 4A to the Naval Discipline Act 1957 (custodial orders), after sub-paragraph (6A) in each case there shall be inserted the following sub-paragraph—

"(6B) Section 12 of the Criminal Justice (Scotland) Act 1963 (supervision of young offenders following release) shall apply to persons released from a term of detention under a custodial order as it applies to those released from a term of detention imposed under section 207 or section 415 of the Criminal Procedure (Scotland) Act 1975.".

GENERAL NOTE

This section is concerned with persons under the age of 21 who are sentenced under the Armed Forces Acts to detention under custodial orders for six months or more. The amendments provide that where the detention ordered by the military court is to be served in Scottish penal institutions, the service offender once he enters the penal system will be treated in the same way as a civilian young offender, and can consequently be made subject to supervision following release: see s.12 of the Criminal Justice (Scotland) Act 1963 (as substituted by para. 2 of Sched. 5 to the Criminal Justice (Scotland) Act 1980).

Miscellaneous and general

Transfer of sheriff clerks and procurators fiscal

47. In section 1 of the Sheriff Clerks and Legal Officers (Scotland) Act 1927 (appointment of sheriff clerk and procurator fiscal)—

(*a*) in subsection (3), after the words "foregoing subsections" there shall be inserted the words "but subject to subsections (4) and (5) below"; and

(*b*) after subsection (3) there shall be added the following subsections—

"(4) The right vested—

(*a*) in the Secretary of State under subsection (1) above shall include the right to transfer the sheriff clerk of one sheriff court district to an office, whether of sheriff clerk or (however styled) or sheriff clerk depute, in another sheriff court district;

(*b*) in the Lord Advocate under subsection (2) above shall include the right to transfer the procurator fiscal of one district to an office, whether of procurator fiscal or (however styled) of procurator fiscal depute, in another district,

where in the opinion of the Secretary of State or, as the case may be, of the Lord Advocate the transfer is for the purpose of securing efficient organisation and administration.

(5) It is hereby declared that, for the purposes of subsection (3) above, a transfer under subsection (4) above is not a removal from office.".

GENERAL NOTE

By s.1(3) of the Sheriff Clerks and Legal Officers (Scotland) Act 1927, ". . . no sheriff clerk or procurator fiscal shall be removed from his office except upon a report of the Lord President of the Court of Session and the Lord Justice Clerk".

This provision is important for the independence of sheriff clerks and procurators fiscal as it prevents arbitrary dismissal from office. However, there has grown up a view that s.1(3) not only prevents arbitrary dismissal from office but also prevents a sheriff clerk or a procurator fiscal at a particular grade being moved within the service. The purpose of s.47 is to remove the doubts which have arisen about the scope of s.1(3). The 1927 Act is amended to make it clear that the Secretary of State has the right to transfer sheriff clerks and the Lord Advocate the right to transfer procurators fiscal from one district to another when of the opinion that "the transfer is for the purpose of securing efficient organisation and administration". Such transfers are not removals from office for the purposes of s.1(3).

New subs. 1(4)

The power to transfer includes the right to transfer a sheriff clerk in one sheriff court district to the post of sheriff clerk depute in another sheriff court district and transfer a procurator fiscal in one district to the post of procurator fiscal depute in another district. In so far as this may amount to down grading, it is nevertheless within the powers of the Secretary of State and the Lord Advocate *provided* it was considered that the transfer is for the purpose of securing efficient organisation and administration.

New subs. 1(5)

This provision makes it clear that a transfer under s.1(4) is not a removal from office for the purposes of s.1(3) of the 1927 Act, which is therefore limited to arbitrary dismissal from office.

Power of Lord Advocate and Secretary of State in relation to research into law

48. The Lord Advocate or the Secretary of State may assist (whether financially or otherwise) other persons in conducting research into any matter connected with the law (other than research into any matter referred to in section 75(1) of the Criminal Justice (Scotland) Act 1949).

GENERAL NOTE

It is the practice of the Lord Advocate and the Secretary of State to fund research into law by outside bodies. But apart from matters relating to the cause of delinquency and the treatment of offenders—which is authorised by s.75(1)(*b*) of the Criminal Justice (Scotland) Act 1949—there is no specific statutory authority to do so. This section provides that authority. It thus implements the recommendation of the Public Accounts Committee that where continuing functions are exercised by governmental departments, particularly when they involve financial liabilities which extend beyond a given year, there should be statutory authority to do so.

Arrestment of National Savings Bank deposits

49. In section 46 of the Crown Proceedings Act 1947 (which makes provision as to arrestment in the hands of the Crown)—

(*a*) after paragraph (*a*) of the proviso there shall be inserted the word "or";

(*b*) paragraph (*c*) of the proviso (which precludes arrestment of money payable on account of a deposit in the National Savings Bank) and the word "or" which precedes that paragraph shall cease to have effect.

GENERAL NOTE

By s.46(*c*) of the Crown Proceedings Act 1947 it was incompetent for a creditor to place arrestments on "any money payable by the Crown to any person on account of a deposit in the National Savings Bank". The corresponding provision for England in s.27 of the Act was amended by s.139 of the Supreme Court Act 1981, to allow attachment of funds on deposit in the National Savings Bank. This led to the anomalous situation "that in Scotland a creditor remained unable to place arrestments with the National Savings Bank as regards sums at credit of deposit accounts whereas his English counterpart, as a result of the 1981 Act, was free to attach funds at credit of his debtor's deposit account with that bank"—even although the bank's principal office is in Glasgow!: see *Brooks Associates Incorp.* v. *Basu*

[1984] 2 W.L.R. 141; I. S. Dickinson, *Some Legislative Fragments* 1985 S.L.T. (News) 145 at p. 146.

S.49 removes this anomaly by providing that s.46(*c*) is to cease to have effect. In the original clause, the Lord Advocate was given a "long stop" order-making power to disapply the arrestment provisions and so prevent arrestments being placed, a power enjoyed by the Lord Chancellor in the corresponding section of the Supreme Court Act 1981. The necessity for this power was questionable, and it was removed from the clause on Report in the Commons H.C. Vol. 78, col. 521.

Registration of divorces and declarators of nullity of marriage

50.—(1) After section 28 of the Registration of Births, Deaths and Marriages (Scotland) Act 1965 there shall be inserted the following section—

"Part IIIA

Registration of divorces and declarators of nullity of marriage

28A.—(1) The Registrar General shall maintain at the General Register Office a register of decrees of divorce and of declarator of nullity of marriage (which register shall be known as the "Register of Divorces").

(2) The Registrar General shall cause to be made and kept at the General Register Office an alphabetical index of the entries in the Register of Divorces (in this section referred to as "the index").

(3) The Register of Divorces shall be in such form as may be prescribed.

(4) On payment to him of such fee or fees as may be prescribed, the Registrar General shall, at any time when the General Register Office is open for that purpose—

(*a*) cause a search of the index to be made on behalf of any person or permit that person to search the index himself;

(*b*) issue to any person an extract of any entry in the Register of Divorces which that person may require.

(5) An extract of an entry in the Register of Divorces shall be sufficient evidence of the decree of divorce or, as the case may be, of declarator of nullity of marriage to which it relates.

(6) The Registrar General may delete or amend any entry in the Register of Divorces or substitute another for it.

(7) In this section, references to decrees of divorce are references to decrees thereof of the Court of Session or the sheriff and references to decrees of declarator of nullity of marriage are references to decrees thereof of the Court of Session.".

(2) In section 48 of the said Act of 1965 (decrees altering status to be notified to Registrar General) after the words "be made", where secondly occuring, there shall be inserted—

"(*a*) where the decree is of divorce or of declarator of nullity of marriage, in the Register of Divorces; and

(*b*) in any other case,".

(3) Any entry made in the Register of Corrections Etc. between 1st May 1984 and the date of the coming into force of this section which could have been made after the latter date in the Register of Divorces shall be treated as an entry in the Register of Divorces.

GENERAL NOTE

Since May 1, 1984, the Registrar General has operated a register of divorces as part of the Register of Corrections Etc., which was established by s.44 of the Registration of Births, Deaths and Marriages (Scotland) Act 1965. The purpose of this section is to provide statutory authority for the establishment of a Register of Divorces in which to record decrees of divorce and declarator of nullity. It does so by adding a new Part IIIA to the 1965 Act.

New subs. 28A(1)
"register of decrees of divorce and of declarator of nullity"
Although the new register is to be known as the "Register of Divorces", decrees of declarator of nullity as well as decrees of divorce are to be recorded there.

New subs. 28A(5)
An extract of an entry in the Register of Divorces is to be sufficient evidence of the decree of divorce or decree of declarator of nullity of marriage to which it relates. An extract may therefore by sufficient to satisfy s.3(1)(*a*) of the Marriage (Scotland) Act 1977, whereby when submitting a notice of intention to marry, a person who has previously been married must also produce "a copy of the decree of divorce, dissolution or annulment".

Subs. (2)
S.48 of the 1965 Act provides that decrees of court altering status are to be notified to the Registrar General who will cause an appropriate entry to be made in the Register of Corrections Etc. This amendment to s.48 provides that in the case of decrees of divorce and declarator of nullity the entry should be made in the Register of Divorces.

Subs. (3)
This is a transitional provision. It provides that decrees of divorce or declarator of nullity recorded in the Register of Corrections Etc. from May 1, 1984, until the date when this section comes into force, will be treated as entries in the Register of Divorces. Thus the Registrar General can continue to record decrees in the Register of Corrections Etc. until the new Register of Divorces is operational.

Amendments to Mental Health (Scotland) Act 1984 as respects hospital orders

51.—(1) The Mental Health (Scotland) Act 1984 shall be amended in accordance with the following provisions of this section.
(2) In each of sections 21 (approval of applications by the sheriff: hospital) and 40 (approval of applications by the sheriff: guardianship)—
  (*a*) the words "for his approval" shall be omitted from subsection (1);
  (*b*) in subsection (2), after the word "considering" there shall be inserted the words "whether to approve".

GENERAL NOTE
Both an application for admission of a patient to a hospital and an application for reception of a patient into guardianship must be approved by a sheriff: s.21 of the Mental Health (Scotland) Act 1984 (hospital), s.40 of the Mental Health (Scotland) Act 1984 (guardianship). In both sections it is provided that the application must be submitted to the sheriff "*for his approval* within seven days of the last date on which the patient was examined for the purposes of any medical recommendation accompanying the application". The wording is unfortunate as it can be taken to mean that not only must the application be submitted in the seven day period but that the sheriff's *approval* of the application must also be obtained within that period. This is clearly not what was intended by Parliament, as both sections empower the sheriff to make extensive inquiries and, in certain circumstances, give the nearest relative and the mental health officer the right to be heard in the proceedings. To present an effective case will often take more than seven days.
The effect of s.53 is to amend ss.21 and 40 of the 1984 Act to put beyond doubt that it is the submission of the application rather than the sheriff's approval of the application which is subject to the seven day limit.

Application of certain liquor licensing appeal provisions to certain appeals under the Lotteries and Amusements Act 1976

52. In section 133(4) of the Licensing (Scotland) Act 1976 (application of certain provisions relating to appeals in respect of liquor licensing to certain appeals in respect of certain betting and gaming permits and licences)—
  (*a*) after the word "1968", where first occurring, there shall be inserted the words "and paragraph 12 of Schedule 3 to the Lotteries and Amusements Act 1976"; and

(*b*) for the words "and 1968", there shall be substituted the words "1968 and 1976".

GENERAL NOTE
The purpose of this provision is to amend s.133(4) of the Licensing (Scotland) Act 1976 so that ss.39(3) to (6) of the 1976 Act apply to appeals to the sheriff from the refusal of an appropriate authority to grant or renew a permit for commercial provision of amusements with prizes: see para. 12 of Sched. 3 to the Lotteries and Amusements Act 1976. Accordingly, the appeal procedure in respect of liquor licensing, in so far as it concerns time limits for the appeal, grounds of appeal, evidence, and the powers of the sheriff on upholding the appeal, applies to these appeals under the Lotteries and Amusements Act 1976.

Amendment of definition of "alcoholic liquor".

53. In section 139(1) of the Licensing (Scotland) Act 1976, in the definition of "alcoholic liquor"—
  (*a*) after the word "include" there shall be inserted "(*a*)"; and
  (*b*) at the end there shall be inserted—
    "(*b*) perfumes;
    (*c*) flavouring essences recognised by the Commissioners as not being intended for consumption as or with dutiable alcoholic liquor;
    (*d*) spirits, wine or made-wine so medicated as to be, in the opinion of the Commissioners, intended for use as a medicine and not as a beverage.".

GENERAL NOTE
The purpose of this is to exclude from the definition of alcoholic liquor perfumes, flavouring essences and medicines. Accordingly, a liquor licence will no longer be required for the sale of these products. Hitherto, a liquor licence was necessary unless the products had a limited alcoholic content.

New subs. 139(1)(d)
The most common example of a product envisaged by the subsection is cough mixture: "made wine" is defined in s.1 of the Alcoholic Liquor Duties Act 1979.

Clarification of investment powers of Scottish Hospital Trust and Scottish Hospital Endowments Research Trust

54.—(1) In sub-paragraph (*b*) of paragraph 4 of Schedule 6 to the National Health Service (Scotland) Act 1978 and in paragraph 4 of Schedule 7 to that Act (which provisions respectively enable the Scottish Hospital Trust and the Scottish Hospital Endowments Research Trust to invest as therein provided) after "1921" there shall be inserted the words "and the Trustee Investments Act 1961".
  (2) In the said paragraph 4 of the said Schedule 6 there shall be inserted at the end—
    "It is hereby declared, for the avoidance of doubt, that the Trust has at all times had the power referred to in subparagraph (*b*) above to invest in any security in which trustees are authorised to invest under or in pursuance of the Trustee Investments Act 1961.".
  (3) In the said paragraph 4 of the said Schedule 7 there shall be inserted at the end—
    "It is hereby declared, for the avoidance of doubt, that the Research Trust has at all times had the power referred to in this paragraph to invest in any security in which trustees are authorised to invest under or in pursuance of the Trustee Investment Act 1961.".

GENERAL NOTE
The Scottish Hospital Trust was established under the Hospital Endowments (Scotland) Act 1971, now consolidated as Sched. 6 to the National Health Service (Scotland) Act 1978,

for the purpose of bringing hospital endowment funds in Scotland—previously administered by regional hospital boards—under central management. The 1971 Act sought to give the Trust the powers to invest up to half the endowment funds in wider-range investments but did so by reference to the Trusts (Scotland) Act 1921. Some sections of that Act had been repealed and replaced by the Trustee Investment Act 1961. Although the 1961 Act contained provisions to ensure that the wider powers of investment introduced by the Act extended to bodies on which the powers under the 1921 Act had been conferred, these were not applicable to the Scottish Hospital Trust as it was established ten years after the 1961 Act was passed.

In spite of the doubts surrounding their powers, it appears that the trustees have invested substantially in wider-range investments. The effect of s.54 is firstly to amend Sched. 6 to the National Health Service (Scotland) Act 1978 so that the Trust has power to invest in wider-range investments as authorised under or in pursuance of the Trustee Investment Act 1961. Secondly, the Trust is declared to have had at all times the power to invest in wider-range investments. This is a remarkable, if justifiable, example of retrospective legislation.

Although the same doubts did not apply to the sister body, the Scottish Hospital Endowments Research Trust, the opportunity was taken to clarify the position of its wider-range investments in the same way.

Power of Commissioner for Local Administration to investigate Scottish Special Housing Association and new town development corporations

55.—(1) In section 23 of the Local Government (Scotland) Act 1975 (authorities subject to investigation)—

(*a*) in subsection (1) there shall be added at the end of the words—

"(*g*) the Scottish Special Housing Association;

(*h*) subject to subsection (2A) below, any development corporation established under an order made, or having effect as if made under the New Towns (Scotland) Act 1968 (in this section and section 24 of this Act referred to as a "new town development corporation");"; and

(*b*) after subsection (2) there shall be added the following subsection—

"(2A) The application of this Part of this Act to any new town development corporation by virtue of subsection (1)(*h*) above extends only to the Corporation's functions in relation to housing.".

(2) In section 24 of that Act (matters subject to investigation)—

(*a*) after subsection (3) there shall be inserted the following subsection—

"(3A) Subsections (2) and (3) above do not apply in relation to the Scottish Special Housing Association or a new town development corporation."; and

(*b*) in subsection (4) after the word "concerned" there shall be inserted the words "or, in the case of the Scottish Special Housing Association or a new town development corporation, to the Commissioner".

GENERAL NOTE

Under Pt. II of the Local Government (Scotland) Act 1975, the Commissioner for Local Administration in Scotland has the power to investigate complaints of maladministration by local authorities. Many of these complaints have been concerned with local authority housing. However, the Commissioner's powers do not extend to the Scottish Special Housing Association or new town development corporations. The purpose of this section is to amend the 1975 Act to enable the Commissioner to investigate complaints of maladministration in relation to the housing functions of these two authorities.

New s.23(2A)

This provision makes it clear that the Commissioner's powers only extend to the housing functions of new town development corporations.

S.56(2)
By s.24(2) and (3) of the 1975 Act, a complaint must be made in writing to a member of the authority concerned, or of any other authority, which is then referred by him, with the consent of the complainant, to the Commissioner. If the member refuses to refer the complaint, the Commissioner may dispense with the referral procedure. The effect of the new s.24(3A) is that the usual referral procedure is not to apply to complaints against the Scottish Special Housing Association or a new town development corporation. Instead, complaints against these authorities can be made directly to the Commissioner. However, as a result of the amendment to s.24(4), the complaint must be made to the Commissioner within twelve months from the day on which the complainant first had notice of the matters alleged in the complaint.

Amendments of enactments relating to solicitors

56. The enactments specified in Schedule 1 to this Act (Part I of which Schedule contains amendments relating to the incorporation of solicitors' practices and Part II amendments relating to other matters relating to solicitors) shall have effect subject to the amendments to these enactments there set out.

GENERAL NOTE
See notes to Pts. I and II of Sched. 1 to this Act.

Power to pay extra-parliamentary Commissioners for service on inquiries under the Private Legislation Procedure (Scotland) Act 1936

57. In section 5 of the Private Legislation Procedure (Scotland) Act 1936 (which provides, amongst other things, as to the appointment of Commissioners for inquiries under the Act) there shall be added at the end of the following subsection—
"(9) The Secretary of State may pay Commissioners taken from the extra-parliamentary panel such fees or other amounts in respect of the performance of their duties under this Act as he may, with the approval of the Treasury, determine.".

GENERAL NOTE
When the Secretary of State directs that an inquiry should be held into a petition for a Provisional Order which has been submitted to him, Commissioners must be appointed to serve on the inquiry. There are four Commissioners on each inquiry. Usually the Commissioners are two MPs, appointed by the Chairman of Ways and Means and two members of the House of Lords, appointed by the Chairman of Committees. However, very occasionally, the Chairmen are unable to appoint four parliamentary Commissioners. In these circumstances, Commissioners for the inquiry are appointed from the extra-parliamentary panel, which consists of 20 persons qualified by their experience of affairs who are nominated by the Chairmen, acting jointly with the Secretary of State: see generally ss.3–6 of the Private Legislation Procedure (Scotland) Act 1936.
While s.14 of the 1936 Act provides for travelling and subsistence allowances for all Commissioners, there was no provision for the payment of a fee to the extra-parliamentary Commissioners, who may well spend months on an inquiry. This section amends s.5 of the 1936 Act to enable the Secretary of State to pay the extra-parliamentary Commissioners a fee or reimburse them for loss of earnings through service as a Commissioner. The provision is only concerned with payments to Commissioners appointed from the extra-parliamentary panel.

New subs. 5(9)
"with the approval of the Treasury"
The level of "the fees or other amounts" is not indicated: it is left to the Secretary of State. However, he must obtain the approval of the Treasury.

Finance

58. There shall be paid out of money provided by Parliament—
   (*a*) any expenses incurred by the Secretary of State under section

22(5) of this Act or section 5(9) of the Private Legislation
Procedure (Scotland) Act 1936 or by the Secretary of State or
the Lord Advocate under section 48 of this Act; and
  (*b*) any increase attributable to this Act in the sums which, under
  any other Act, are payable out of money so provided.

Amendment and repeal of enactments

59.—(1) The enactments specified in Schedule 2 to this Act shall have
effect subject to the amendments to these enactments there set out.
  (2) The enactments specified in Schedule 4 to this Act are hereby
repealed to the extent there set out.

GENERAL NOTE
See notes to Sched. 2 of this Act.

Citation, transitional provisions, commencement and extent

60.—(1) This Act may be cited as the Law Reform (Miscellaneous
Provisions) (Scotland) Act 1985.
  (2) Schedule 3 to this Act shall have effect for the purpose of making
transitional provision.
  (3) This Act shall come into force as follows—
  (*a*) sections 26 to 29, 54, this section, paragraphs 28 to 30 and 32
  of Schedule 2 and so much of section 59(1) as relates to these
  paragraphs, when it is passed;
  (*b*) sections 14, 15, 18, 19 and 36 and paragraphs 8, 12, 13 and 24
  of Schedule 2 and so much of section 59(1) as relates to these
  paragraphs, on such day as the Lord Advocate may by order
  appoint;
  (*c*) sections 35 and 50, on such day as the Secretary of State may
  by order appoint; and
  (*d*) the remaining provisions, at the end of the period of two
  months beginning with the day on which it is passed.
  (4) Different days may be appointed under subsection (3)(*b*) and (*c*)
above for the different provisions specified therein.
  (5) An order under this section shall be made by statutory instrument.
  (6) This Act applies to Scotland only.

SCHEDULES

Section 56   SCHEDULE 1

PART I

INCORPORATION OF SOLICITORS' PRACTICES

Solicitors (Scotland) Act 1980 c.46

1. In section 16(1) (appeal to Court of Session against decisions of Council in relation to
practising certificates)—
  (*a*) after the word "where" there shall be inserted "(*a*)"; and
  (*b*) after the word "applicant" there shall be inserted ";
    (*b*) the Council refuse to recognise a body corporate as being suitable in terms of
    section 34(1A)(*b*), the body corporate".
2. In section 18 (suspension of practising certificates)—
  (*a*) after subsection (1) there shall be inserted the following subsection—
    "(1A) If—
      (*a*) an administration or winding-up order, or an appointment of a

provisional liquidator, liquidator, receiver or judicial factor has been made in relation to the incorporated practice; or

(*b*) a resolution has been passed for the voluntary winding-up of an incorporated practice (other than a resolution passed solely for the purposes of reconstruction or amalgamation of the incorporated practice with another incorporated paractice),

the recognition under section 34(1A) of the incorporated practice shall be thereby revoked.";

(*b*) after subsection (3) there shall be inserted the following subsection—

"(3A) On the occurrence of the circumstances mentioned in—

(*a*) paragraph (*a*) of subsection (1A), the administrator, provisional liquidator, liquidator, receiver or, as the case may be, judicial factor appointed in relation to the incorporated practice;

(*b*) paragraph (*b*) of subsection (1A), the incorporated practice

shall immediately intimate that fact to the Council.".

3. In section 21(3) (definition of "consultant" in relation to requirement upon consultants to hold practising certificates)—

(*a*) after the word "who" there shall be inserted "(*a*)";

(*b*) after the word "name", where thirdly occurring, there shall be inserted—

"(*b*) not being a director of an incorporated practice, causes or permits his name to be associated with that incorporated practice,".

4. In section 26 (offence for solicitors to act as agents for unqualified persons)—

(*a*) in subsection (1)—

(i) after the word "who" there shall be inserted the words "or incorporated practice which";

(ii) in each of paragraphs (*b*) and (*d*) after the word "his" there shall be inserted "or, as the case may be, its";

(*b*) in subsection (3) there shall be inserted at the end the words "but "unqualified person" does not include an incorporated practice".

5. In section 27 (offence for solicitors to share fees with unqualified person)—

(*a*) in subsection (1)—

(i) after the word "solicitor" there shall be inserted the words "or incorporated practice";

(ii) after the word "him" there shall be inserted the words "or, as the case may be, it";

(*b*) in subsection (2)—

(i) after the word "solicitor", where first occurring, there shall be inserted the words "or incorporated practice";

(ii) in paragraph (*a*) after the word "him" there shall be inserted the words "or, as the case may be, to it" and after the word "business", where secondly occurring, there shall be inserted the words "or former director of the incorporated practice";

(iii) in paragraph (*b*), after the word "business", where first occuring, there shall be inserted the words "or, as the case may be, a director or member of the incorporated practice" and after the word "he" there shall be inserted the words "or, as the case may be, it";

(iv) in paragraph (*c*) after the word "him" there shall be inserted the words "or, as the case may be, it".

6. In section 28 (disqualified solicitors not to seek employment without informing employer)—

(*a*) after the word "practice" where thirdly occurring, there shall be inserted the words "or by an incorporated practice";

(*b*) after the word "him" there shall be inserted the words "or, as the case may be, it".

7. In section 30 (liability for fees of another solicitor)—

(*a*) after the word "solicitor", where first occurring, there shall be inserted the words "or an incorporated practice";

(*b*) after that word, where secondly and thirdly occurring, there shall be inserted the words "or incorporated practice";

(*c*) after the word "he" in each place where it occurs, there shall be inserted the words "or, as the case may be, it";

(*d*) after the word "solicitor's" there shall be inserted the words "or incorporated practice's".

8. Section 31 (offence for unqualified persons to pretend to be solicitors or notaries public) shall be renumbered as subsection (1) of that section and—

(*a*) in that subsection (as so renumbered) there shall be inserted at the end the following—

"In this section, 'unqualified person' does not include an incorporated practice";

(*b*) after that subsection there shall be inserted the following subsections—

"(2) Any person (including a body corporate) who either by himself or together with others, wilfully and falsely—

(*a*) pretends to be an incorporated practice;

(*b*) takes or uses any name, title, addition or description implying that he is an incorporated practice,

shall be guilty of an offence.

(3) Where an offence under this section which has been committed by a body corporate is proved to have been committed with the consent or connivance of, or to be attributable to any neglect on the part of the director, manager, secretary or other similar officer of the body corporate, or any person purporting to act in any such capacity, he as well as the body corporate shall be guilty of the offence and shall be liable to be proceeded against and punished accordingly.".

9. In section 32(2) (persons to whom offence of preparing certain documents does not apply) there shall be inserted at the end the following—"; or

(*e*) an incorporated practice.".

10. In section 33 (unqualified persons not entitled to fees etc) there shall be inserted at the end—

"This section does not apply to an incorporated practice.".

11. After section 33 there shall be inserted the following section—

"Privilege of incorporated practices from disclosure etc.

33A.—(1) Any communication made to or by an incorporated practice in the course of its acting as such for a client shall in any legal proceedings be privileged from disclosure in like manner as if the body had at all material times been a solicitor acting for the client.

(2) Any enactment or instrument making special provision in relation to a solicitor or other legal representative as to the disclosure of information, or as to the production, seizure or removal of documents, with respect to which a claim to professional privilege could be maintained, shall, with any necessary modifications, have effect in relation to an incorporated practice as it has effect in relation to a solicitor.".

12. In section 34 (rules as to professional practice, conduct and discipline)—

(*a*) in subsection (1) at the end there shall be inserted the words "and incorporated practices";

(*b*) after subsection (1) there shall be inserted the following subsection—

"(1A) Rules made under this section may—

(*a*) provide as to the management and control by—

(i) solicitors holding practising certificates or their executors;

(ii) other incorporated practices

of bodies corporate carrying on business consisting of the provision of professional services such as are provided by individuals and firms practising as solicitors being bodies the membership of which is restricted to such solicitors, executors and other incorporated practices;

(*b*) prescribe the circumstances in which such bodies may be recognised by the Council as being suitable to undertake the provision of any such services;

(*c*) prescribe the conditions which (subject to any exceptions provided by the rules) must at all times be satisfied by bodies corporate so recognised if they are to remain so recognised (which bodies, when and for so long as so recognised, are in this Act referred to as "incorporated practices";

(*d*) regulate the conduct of the affairs of incorporated practices; and

(*e*) provide—

(i) for the manner and form in which applications for recognition under this section are to be made, and for the payment of fees in connection with such applications;

(ii) for regulating the names that may be used by incorporated practices;

(iii) as to the period for which any recognition granted under this section shall (subject to the provisions of this Act) remain in force;

(iv) for the revocation of any such recognition on the grounds that it was granted as a result of any error or fraud;

(v) for the keeping by the Society of a list containing the names and places of business of all incorporated practices and for the information contained in any such list to be available for inspection;

(vi) for rules made under any provision of this Act to have effect in relation to incorporated practices with such additions, omissions or other modifications as appear to the Council to be necessary or expedient;

(vii) for empowering the Council to take such steps as they consider necessary or expedient to ascertain whether or not any rules applicable to incorporated practices by virtue of this section are being complied with.

(*c*) after subsection (4) there shall be inserted the following subsections—

"(4A) A certificate purporting to be signed by an officer of the Society and stating that any body corporate is or is not an incorporated practice shall, unless the contrary is proved, be sufficient evidence of that fact.

(4B) Subject to the provisions of this Act, the Secretary of State may, by order made by statutory instrument subject to annulment in pursuance of a resolution of either House of Parliament, provide for any enactment or instrument passed or made before the commencement of section (1A) above and having effect in relation to solicitors to have effect in relation to incorporated practices with such additions, omissions, or other modifications as appear to him to be necessary or expedient.".

13. In section 35(1) (accounts rules) after the word "solicitors", in each place where it occurs, there shall be inserted the words "and incorporated practices".

14. In section 36 (interest on client's money)—

(*a*) in subsection (1)—

(i) after the word "solicitor,", where first occurring, there shall be inserted the words "or an incorporated practice";

(ii) after the word "his" there shall be inserted the words "or, as the case may be, by the incorporated practice in its";

(iii) after the word "solicitor's" there shall be inserted the words "or, as the case may be, the incorporated practice's";

(*b*) in subsection (2) after the word "solicitor" there shall be inserted the words "or incorporated practice";

(*c*) in subsection (3)—

(i) after the word "solicitor", where first occurring, there shall be inserted the words "or incorporated practice";

(ii) after the word "solicitor", where lastly occurring, there shall be inserted the words "or, as the case may be, the incorporated practice";

(iii) after the word "his" there shall be inserted the words "or, as the case may be, its";

(*d*) in subsection (4) after the word "client" there shall be inserted the words "or an incorporated practice and its client".

15. In section 37 (accountant's certificates)—

(*a*) in subsection (2) after the word "solicitor" there shall be inserted the words "and incorporated practice";

(*b*) in subsection (3) after the word "firm" there shall be inserted the words "or of an incorporated practice";

(*c*) in subsection (5)—

(i) in paragraph (*a*) after the word "who" there shall be inserted the words "or incorporated practice which", after the word "firm" there shall be substituted the words "or, as the case may be, of the incorporated practice" and after the word "them" there shall be inserted the words "or, as the case may be, it";

(ii) in paragraph (*b*), after the word "solicitor" there shall be inserted the words "or incorporated practice" and after the word "practice" there shall be inserted the words "or, as the case may be, it has not";

(*d*) in subsection (6)—

(i) in paragraph (*a*)(iii) after the word "solicitors" there shall be inserted the words "or incorporated practices";

(ii) after the word "he" there shall be inserted the words "or, as the case may be, an incorporated practice which satisfies the Council that it";

    (*e*) in subsection (7)—

        (i) after the word "solicitor" there shall be inserted the words "or incorporated practice";

        (ii) after the word "him" there shall be inserted the words "or, as the case may be, it".

16. In section 38 (powers of Council where dishonesty alleged)—

    (*a*) in subsection (1)—

        (i) after the word "his", where first occurring, there shall be inserted the words "or an incorporated practice or any employee thereof";

        (ii) after the word "firm" there shall be inserted the words "or, as the case may be, such incorporated practice";

    (*b*) in subsection (2)—

        (i) in paragraph (*a*), there shall be inserted at the end the words "or, as the case may be, such incorporated practice";

        (ii) in paragraph (*b*), there shall be inserted at the end the words "or, as the case may be, of which the incorporated practice or one of its employees is a sole trustee or it is a co-trustee only with one or more of its employees.".

17. In section 39 (Council's powers where delay alleged)—

    (*a*) in subsection (1)—

        (i) after the word "solicitor" there shall be inserted the words "or an incorporated practice";

        (ii) after the word "firm" there shall be inserted the words "or, as the case may be, it";

      (iii) after the word "employees" there shall be inserted the words "or, as the case may be, the incorporated practice or one of its employees was the sole trustee or it was a co-trustee only with one or more of its employees",

      (iv) after the word "solicitor" where secondly occurring, there shall be inserted the words "or, as the case may be, incorporated practice";

    (*b*) in subsection (2)—

        (i) after the word "solicitor", where first and lastly occurring there shall be inserted the words "or, as the case may be, incorporated practice";

        (ii) after the word "he" there shall be inserted the words "or, as the case may be, it";

      (iii) after the word "firm" there shall be inserted the words "or, as the case may be, to that incorporated practice.".

18. In section 40 (Council's powers where failure to comply with accounts rules etc.)—

    (*a*) in subsection (1)—

        (i) after the word "solicitor", where first occurring, there shall be inserted the words "or incorporated practice";

        (ii) after the word "solicitor", where secondly and thirdly occurring, there shall be inserted the words "or, as the case may be, incorporated practice";

      (iii) after the word "his" there shall be inserted the words "or, as the case may be, its";

      (iv) after the word "section", where lastly occurring, there shall be inserted "(*a*);

       (v) for the words "and the certificate" there shall be substituted the following "; or, as the case may be—

    (*b*) withdraw the practising certificate or certificates of any or all of the solicitors who are directors of the incorporated practice,

and a certificate so withdrawn";

    (*b*) in subsection (2)—

        (i) after the word "he" there shall be inserted the words "or as the case may be. by the incorporated practice that it";

        (ii) after the word "solicitor" where secondly occurring, there shall be inserted the words "or, as the case may be, the incorporated practice",

      (iii) for the words from "and" onward there shall be substituted the words "or solicitors concerned and shall restore to him or them any practising certificate or certificates held by him or them for the practice year then current.";

    (*c*) in subsection (3) for the word "the", where secondly occurring, there shall be substituted the word "a".

19. In section 41 (appointment of judicial factor)—
    (*a*) after the word "solicitor", where first occurring, there shall be inserted the words "or an incorporated practice";
    (*b*) after the word "solicitor" where secondly occurring, there shall be inserted the words "or, as the case may be, the incorporated practice";
    (*c*) for the words "in connection with his practice as a solicitor" there shall be substituted the words ", in the case of a solicitor, in connection with his practice as such";
    (*d*) after the word "arise" there shall be inserted the following "; or
        (*c*) that, in the case of an incorporated practice, either—
                (i) its liabilities exceed its assets, or
                (ii) its books, accounts and other documents are in such a condition that it is not reasonably practicable to ascertain definitely whether its liabilities exceed its assets, or
                (iii) there is a reasonable ground for apprehending that a claim on the guarantee fund may arise";
    (*e*) after the word "solicitor", where fourthly occurring, there shall be inserted the words "or, as the case may be, of the incorporated practice";
    (*f*) after the word "solicitor", where fifthly occurring, there shall be inserted the words "or, as the case may be, the incorporated practice";
    (*g*) for the words "the solicitor's" there shall be substituted the word "such".
20. In section 42 (distribution of sums in client bank account)—
    (*a*) in subsection (1)—
        (i) after the word "(2)" there shall be inserted the words "or (2A)";
        (ii) after the word "solicitor", where first occurring, there shall be inserted the words "or an incorporated practice";
        (iii) after the word "him", where first and thirdly occurring, there shall be inserted the words "or, as the case may be, by it";
        (iv) after the word "clients", where firstly occurring, there shall be inserted the words "or, as the case may be, by it on behalf of its clients";
        (v) after the word "solicitor", where secondly occurring, there shall be inserted the words "or, as the case may be, the incorporated practice";
        (vi) after the word "behalf", where secondly occurring, there shall be inserted the words "or, as the case may be, by it on their behalf";
        (vii) after the word "him", where lastly occurring, there shall be inserted the words "or, as the case may be, by it";
    (*b*) after subsection (2) there shall be inserted the following subsection—
        "(2A) The events to which subsection (1) applies are in relation to any incorporated practice—
                (*a*) the making of an administration or winding up order or the appointment of a provisional liquidator, liquidator, receiver or judicial factor; or
                (*b*) the passing of a resolution for voluntary winding up (other than one passed solely for the purposes of reconstruction or amalgamation with another incorporated practice)";
    (*c*) in subsection (3)—
        (i) after the word "solicitor", where first occurring, there shall be inserted the words "or an incorporated practice";
        (ii) after the word "his", where first occurring, there shall be inserted the words "or, as the case may be, its";
        (iii) after the word "client", where secondly occurring, there shall be inserted the words "or, as the case may be, by the incorporated practice on that behalf";
        (iv) after the word "him" there shall be inserted the words "or, as the case may be, by it";
        (v) after the word "name" there shall be inserted the words "or, as the case may be, by the incorporated practice in its own name".
21. In section 43 (Guarantee Fund)—
    (*a*) in subsection (2) after the words "part of" there shall be inserted "(*a*)" and at the end there shall be inserted "; or
        (*b*) any incorporated practice or any director, manager, secretary or other employee of an incorporated practice, notwithstanding that subsequent to the commission of that act it may have ceased to be recognised under section 34(1A) or have been wound up";

    (*b*) in subsection (3), after paragraph (*c*), there shall be added the following—

        "(*cc*) to an incorporated practice or any director or member thereof in respect of a loss suffered by it or him by reason of dishonesty on the part of any director, manager, secretary or other employee of the incorporated practice in connection with the practice";

    (*c*) in subsection (7)(*c*) there shall be inserted at the end the following "or in the employment of an incorporated practice".

22. In section 44 (professional indemnity)—

    (*a*) in subsection (1)—

        (i) after the word "solicitors", where secondly occurring, there shall be inserted the words "and incorporated practices";

        (ii) in paragraph (*c*) after the words "solicitors", where secondly occurring, there shall be inserted the words "and incorporated practices or any specified class thereof";

    (*b*) in subsection (3)—

        (i) in each of paragraphs (*b*) and (*c*) after the word "solicitors", where secondly occurring, there shall be inserted the words "and incorporated practices or any class of incorporated practices";

        (ii) in paragraph (*f*) after the word "solicitor" there shall be inserted the words "or incorporated practice" and after each of the words "he" and "him" there shall be inserted the words "or, as the case may be, it";

        (iii) in paragraph (*g*) after the word "solicitors" there shall be inserted the words "and incorporated practices";

    (*c*) in subsection (5) there shall be inserted at the end the words "and, as respects incorporated practices, means any liability incurred by it which if it had been incurred by a solicitor would constitute such civil liability".

23. In section 45 (safeguarding interests of clients of solicitors struck off or suspended)—

    (*a*) in subsection (1) at the end there shall be inserted the words "and, in relation to any incorporated practice, the recognition under section 34(1A) of which is revoked";

    (*b*) in subsection (2)—

        (i) at the beginning there shall be inserted the words "in the case of a solicitor,";

        (ii) after the words "solicitors" there shall be inserted the words "or incorporated practice";

    (*c*) after subsection (2) there shall be inserted the following subsection—

        "(2A) In the case of an incorporated practice, it shall within 21 days of the material date satisfy the Council that it has made suitable arrangements for making available to its clients or to some other solicitor or solicitors or incorporated practice instructed by its clients or itself—

           (*a*) all deeds, wills, securities, papers, books of accounts, records, vouchers and other documents in its possession or control which are held on behalf of its clients or which relate to any trust of which it is sole trustee or co-trustee only with one or more of its employees; and

           (*b*) all sums of money due from it or held by it on behalf of its clients or subject to any trust as aforesaid.";

    (*d*) in subsection (3)—

        (i) after the word "solicitor" in both places where it occurs, there shall be inserted the words "or, as the case may be, incorporated practice";

        (ii) after the word "he" there shall be inserted the words "or, as the case may be, any director, manager, secretary or other employee of the incorporated practice";

    (*e*) in subsection (5), after the word "practice" there shall be inserted the words "or, as the case may be, the recognition under section 34(1A) is revoked.".

24. In section 47 (restriction on employing solicitor struck off or suspended)—

    (*a*) in subsection (1)—

        (i) after the word "solicitor", where secondly occurring, there shall be inserted the words "and, unless it has such permission, an incorporated practice shall not";

        (ii) after the word "his", where first occurring, there shall be inserted the words "or, as the case may be its";

(b) in subsection (3) after the word "solicitor" there shall be inserted the words "or, as the case may be, incorporated practice";

(c) in subsection (4) at the end there shall be inserted the words "and if any incorporated practice so acts its recognition under section 34(1A) shall be revoked.".

25. In section 49 (investigation by lay observer of Society's treatment of complaints), in subsection (1) after the word "solicitor". where secondly occurring, there shall be inserted the words "or about an incorporated practice or an employee thereof".

26. In section 51(2) (complaints to Discipline Tribunal) after the words "client" there shall be inserted the words "or an incorporated practice may have failed to comply with any provision of this Act or of rules made under this Act applicable to it".

27. In section 52(1) (procedure and powers of Discipline Tribunal) there shall be inserted at the end "or incorporated practice".

28. In section 53 (powers of Discipline Tribunal)—

(a) in subsection (1) there shall be inserted at the end—
"; or
(c) an incorporated practice has been convicted by any court of an offence, which conviction the Tribunal is satisfied renders it unsuitable to continue to be recognised under section 34(1A); or
(d) after holding an inquiry into a complaint, the Tribunal is satisfied that an incorporated practice has failed to comply with any provision of this Act or of rules made under this Act applicable to it.".

(b) in subsection (2) (powers of Discipline Tribunal)—
(i) in paragraphs (c) and (d) after the word "solicitor" there shall be inserted the words "or, as the case may be, the incorporated practice".
(ii) in paragraph (e) after the word "him" there shall be inserted the words "or, as the case may be, it".
(iii) after paragraph (e) there shall be added the following— "or
(f) order that the recognition under section 34(1A) of the incorporated practice be revoked".

(c) after subsection (6) (effective date of striking off or suspension of solicitor) there shall be inserted the following subsection—
"(6A) Where the Tribunal order that the recognition under section 34(1A) of an incorporated practice be revoked, the Tribunal shall direct that the order shall take effect on such date as the Tribunal specifies, being a date not earlier than 60 days after its order is intimated to the incorporated practice, and such order shall take effect accordingly.".

(d) in subsection (7) after the word "(6)" there shall be inserted the words "or (6A)" and for the words "that subsection" there shall be substituted the words "subsection (6) or, as the case may be, subsection (6A)".

29. In section 54 (appeals by solicitors from decisions of the Discipline Tribunal)—

(a) in subsection (1) for the word "him" there shall be substituted the words "that person";

(b) in subsection (2)—
(i) after the word "where" there shall be inserted "(a)";
(ii) after the word "effect", where secondly occurring, there shall be inserted—
";
(b) the Tribunal has ordered the revocation of the recognition under section 34(1A) of an incorporated practice, the incorporated practice may within 21 days of the date when the order is intimated to it apply to the court for an order varying (subject to the limit of 60 days referred to in subsection (6A) of section 53) the direction under that subsection;"

30. In section 60 (offence for notaries public to act for unqualified persons) in subsection (2) there shall be inserted at the end the words "but "unqualified person" does not include an incorporated practice".

31. In section 61 (protection of banks)—

(a) in each of subsections (1) and (2) after the word "solicitor" there shall be inserted the words "or an incorporated practice";

(b) in subsection (3) after the word "solicitor", where first occurring, there shall be inserted the words "or an incorporated practice" and after that word, where secondly occurring, there shall be inserted the words "or, as the case may be, the incorporated practice".

32. In section 64 (service of notices) there shall be inserted at the end the words "or, in the case of an incorporated practice, if it is left at, or delivered or sent by post to, its registered office".

33. In section 65(1) (interpretation) after the definition of "functions" there shall be inserted the following—

"incorporated practice" has the meaning given by section 34(1A)(c);"

34. In Schedule 3 (The Scottish Solicitors' Guarantee Fund)—

    (*a*) in paragraph 1—

        (i) after sub-paragraph (2) there shall be inserted the following sub-paragraphs—

            "(2A) Sub-paragraphs (1) and (2) do not apply to solicitors who are directors of incorporated practices.

            (2B) Subject to the provisions of this Act, there shall be paid to the Society on behalf of the Guarantee Fund by every incorporated practice in respect of each year during which, or part of which, it is recognised under section 34(1A) a contribution (hereafter referred to as an "annual corporate contribution") in accordance with the scale of such contributions referred to in sub-paragraph (3).

        (ii) in sub-paragraph (3) there shall be inserted at the end the words "and the scale of the annual corporate contributions to be so paid, which scale shall be fixed by reference to factors which shall include the number of solicitors who are directors or employees of each of the incorporated practices to which the scale relates.";

        (iii) in sub-paragraph (4) after the word "solicitor" there shall be inserted the words "and no annual corporate contribution by an incorporated practice";

        (iv) in sub-paragraph (5) for the words "a special", where secondly occurring, there shall be substituted the words "upon every incorporated practice a contribution (hereafter referred to as a "special corporate contribution") in accordance with a scale of such contributions fixed by the Council as under sub-paragraph (3), and a special or special corporate";

        (v) in paragraph 1(8) after the word "solicitors" there shall be inserted the words "or of an incorporated practice";

    (*b*) in paragraph 3(2), after the word "solicitors", where first occurring, there shall be inserted the words "and incorporated practices" and after that word, where secondly occurring, there shall be inserted the words "or incorporated practice or practices";

    (*c*) in paragraph 4(2) after the word "employee" there shall be inserted the words "or the incorporated practice in question or its employee".

    (*d*) in paragraph 5(2) after the word "solicitor" there shall be inserted the words "or incorporated practice".

35. In Schedule 4 (constitution, procedure and powers of Tribunal)—

    (*a*) in paragraph 9—

        (i) after the word "solicitor", where first and secondly occurring, there shall be inserted respectively, the words "or an incorporated practice" and "or the incorporated practice"; and

        (ii) after the word "him" there shall be inserted the words "or, as the case may be, it";

        (iii) after the word "solicitor" where thirdly and lastly occurring there shall be inserted, in each case, the words "or, of failure on the part of the incorporated practice to comply with any provision of this Act or of rules made under this Act";

    (*b*) in paragraph 10 (duty of Discipline Tribunal to give respondent solicitor notice of complaint)—

        (i) after the word "solicitor" there shall be inserted the words "or incorporated practice";

        (ii) after the words "him" and "his" there shall be inserted respectively the words "or, as the case may be, it" and "or, as the case may be, its".

    (*c*) In paragraph 16—

        (i) in each of paragraphs (*c*) and (*d*) after the word "solicitor" there shall be inserted the words "or an incorporated practice";

(ii) after paragraph (*d*) there shall be added—
"or
(*e*) order that the recognition under section 34(1A) of an incorporated practice be revoked";
(iii) for "(*d*)" where secondly occurring, there shall be substituted "(*e*)";
(iv) after the word "court", where secondly occurring, there shall be inserted the words "or under section 53(6A) which has not been varied by the court";
(v) after the word "roll", where secondly occurring, there shall be inserted the words "or as to revoking the recognition under section 34(1A) of an incorporated practice".

Building Societies Act 1962 (c.37)

36. In section 34(4) (restriction on commissions for introduction of business) after the word "solicitor" there shall be inserted the words "(including that of an incorporated practice within the meaning of the Solicitors (Scotland) Act 1980".

Legal Aid (Scotland) Act 1967 (c.43)

37. In section 6(3)(*a*) (exclusion of certain solicitors from giving legal aid) the word "or" immediately preceding sub-paragraph (iii) shall be omitted and after that sub-paragraph there shall be inserted the following—
"or—
(iv) in the case of a director of an incorporated practice, such conduct on the part of any person who is for the time being a director of the incorporated practice.".

Income and Corporation Taxes Act 1970 (c.10)

38. In sections 481(3) and 490(3) (savings for solicitors in relation to certain requirements to furnish information to Inland Revenue) any reference to a solicitor shall include a reference to an incorporated practice within the meaning of the Solicitors (Scotland) Act 1980 and any reference to a solicitor's client shall, in relation to a solicitor who is a director, manager, secretary or employee of such a practice, be construed as a reference to a client of that practice.

Legal Advice and Assistance Act 1972 (c.50)

39. In section 5(2) (definition of "the solicitor" for purposes of rules relating to payment of certain charges or fees), after the word "solicitors", where first occurring, there shall be inserted the words "or by an incorporated practice (within the meaning of the Solicitors (Scotland) Act 1980") and after that word, where secondly occurring, there shall be inserted the words ",incorporated practice".

Estate Agents Act 1979 (c.38)

40. In section 1(2)(*a*) (disapplication of Act to practising solicitors and their employees) after the word "him" there shall be inserted the words "or by an incorporated practice (within the meaning of the Solicitors (Scotland) Act 1980) or a person employed by it".

Finance Act 1980 (c.48)

41. In section 30(5) (savings for solicitors in relation to requirement to furnish certain information to Inland Revenue) any reference to a solicitor shall include a reference to an incorporated practice and any reference to a solicitor's client shall, in relation to a solicitor who is a director, manager, secretary or employee of an incorporated practice within the meaning of the Solicitors (Scotland) Act 1980, be construed as a reference to a client of that practice.

GENERAL NOTE

The purpose of these amendments is to permit Scottish solicitors to incorporate themselves into companies—"incorporated practices"—instead of being able to practice only as individuals or in partnership. Detailed provisions relating to such important matters as the management and control of incorporated practices and their recognition by the Council of the Law Society of Scotland are to be the subject of rules made by the Council: see s.34(1A) of the Solicitors (Scotland) Act 1980: para. 12(*b*) of Part I of this Schedule. However, the opportunity was taken to amend the provisions of the Solicitors (Scotland) Act 1980, making clear to what extent they are to apply to the new incorporated practices. This accounts for the length and number of the amendments.

The shareholders and directors of the incorporated practice will generally have to be practising solicitors and will therefore be persons who are subject to professional discipline as individuals. It will be an offence to pretend to be an incorporated practice: this can also lead to personal *criminal* liability on the part of an officer of the company: para. 8. The incorporated practice will itself be subject to the same disciplinary procedures and rules as individual solicitors: see, for example, para. 17 (where delay alleged), para. 18 (failure to comply with accounts rules) paras. 26–29 (complaints to and powers of the Discipline Tribunal). Incorporated practices will have to be covered by indemnity insurance (para. 22) and make contributions to the Scottish Solicitors' Guarantee Fund (para. 34). The intention is that there should be no diminution in the protection afforded to solicitors' clients as a result of the introduction of incorporated practices.

The recognition of an incorporated practice is automatically revoked if (a) an administration or winding up order, or an appointment of a provisional liquidator, liquidator, receiver or judicial factor has been made or (b) a resolution has been made for the voluntary winding up of the incorporated practice: para. 2.

PART II

AMENDMENTS OF LEGAL AID AND SOLICITORS (SCOTLAND) ACT 1949 AND SOLICITORS (SCOTLAND) ACT 1980

Legal Aid and Solicitors (Scotland) Act 1949 (c.63)

1. Section 25 (provisions as to taking apprentices) is hereby repealed.

Solicitors (Scotland) Act 1980 (c.46)

2. In section 6 (admission as solicitor)—
    (a) in subsection (1)(b) the words "by affidavit or otherwise" are hereby repealed.
    (b) after subsection (3) there shall be inserted the following subsections—
        "(3A) The Council may petition the court for the admission as a solicitor of an applicant who has compiled with the requirements of subsection (1) above; and, where it does so it shall lodge the petition not later than one month after the applicant has first so complied.
        (3B) The Court shall, on a petition being made to it under subsection (3A) above, make an order admitting the applicant as a solicitor.".

3. Section 15(2)(a) (Council to have discretion as to issue of practising certificates where applicant still has to serve post-qualifying year of practical training) is hereby repealed.

4. In section 35(1) (power to make accounts rules)—
    (a) the word "and" immediately preceding paragraph (d) shall be omitted;
    (b) after that paragraph there shall be added the following—
        "; and
    (e) as to the recovery from solicitors of fees and other costs incurred by the Council in ascertaining whether or not a solicitor who has failed to comply with the accounts rules has remedied that failure and is complying with the rules.".

5. Section 48 (restriction on number of apprentices) is hereby repealed.

6. After section 62 there shall be inserted the following section—

"Council's power to recover expenses incurred under section 38, 45 or 46

62A.—(1) Without prejudice to the Society's entitlement under section 46(4) to recover expenses, the Council shall be entitled to recover from a solicitor or incorporated practice in respect of whom it has taken action under section 38, 45, or 46, any expenditure reasonably incurred by it in so doing.

(2) Expenditure incurred in taking action under section 38 is recoverable under subsection (1) above only where notice has been served under paragraph 5(2) of Schedule 3 in connection with that action and—
    (a) no application has been made in consequence under paragraph 5(4) of that Schedule; or
    (b) the Court, on such an application, has made a direction under paragraph 5(5) of that Schedule.".

7. In Schedule 1 (constitution etc. of the Law Society of Scotland)—

(*a*) for paragraph 6 (subscriptions) there shall be substituted the following paragraphs—

"6. Subject to paragraph 7, every member of the Society shall, for each year, pay to the Society such subscription as may be fixed from time to time by the Society in general meeting.

6A. The subscription payable under paragraph 6 by a practising member (or the proportion of it so payable calculated by reference to the number of months remaining in the practice year) shall be paid at the time of submission of his application for a practising certificate.";

(*b*) in paragraph 7 (subscription in first three years of enrolment)—

(i) the word "annual", in both places where it occurs, is hereby repealed;

(ii) after the word "year" there shall be inserted the words "or part thereof"; and

(iii) there shall be added at the end of the words "(reduced, in the case of a solicitor first included in the roll for only part of a year, in that year proportionately)"; and

(*c*) after the said paragraph 7 there shall be inserted the following paragraphs—

"7A. The Society shall have power, subject to paragraphs 7B to 7D, to impose in respect of any year a special subscription on all members of the Society of such amount and payable at such time and for such specified purpose as it may determine.

7B. The Society may determine that an imposition under paragraph 7A shall not be payable by any category of member or shall be abated as respects any category of member.

7C. An imposition under paragraph 7A or a determination under that paragraph or paragraph 7B may be made only in general meeting.

7D. No imposition may be made under paragraph 7A above unless a majority of those members entitled to attend and vote at the general meeting at which it is proposed has, whether by proxy or otherwise, voted in favour of its being made.".

8. In Schedule 3 (the Scottish Solicitors Guarantee Fund)—

(*a*) in paragraph 1(1) (annual contributions to Guarantee Fund) the words "not exceeding the sum of £25" are hereby repealed.

(*b*) in paragraph 1(3) (Council to fix amount of contributions for each year by previous 31 July) for the words "31 July" there shall be substituted the words "30 September"; and

(*c*) paragraph 1(7) (limit to special contributions to Guarantee Fund) is hereby repealed.

GENERAL NOTE

This is a far reaching series of amendments dealing largely with the powers of the Law Society of Scotland.

para. 1

This provision removes the reference in the 1949 Act to "apprentices": since the introduction of the traineeship scheme, s.25 is redundant.

para. 2(a) and (b)

At present when a person qualifies as a solicitor and seeks admission, this is done by petition to the Court of Session. Each person has to petition individually and has to sign the petition. Before doing so, he must obtain a certificate from the Council that he has complied with the regulations and is a fit and proper person to be a solicitor. To obtain the certificate he has to produce evidence to the Council that he has complied with the regulations. This is done by affidavit. The effect of para. 2(*a*) is to remove the need for formal proof that he has satisfied the regulations and should make for easier administration.

New subs. 6(3A) and 3(B)

This enables the Council to petition the court for the admission of an applicant as a solicitor. At present, the applicant must himself petition the Court. The effect of these amendments will allow the Council to petition the court to admit several applicants at the same time, and thus reduce the number of individual petitions to the court. They have the approval of the Lord President of the Court of Session.

para. 3

This repeals a provision in relation to apprentices which is now redundant as a result of the introduction of the traineeship scheme.

para. 4

Where there has been some form of default or irregularity and as a result there have to be subsequent and regular inspections of a solicitor's books, there is at present no provision for recovering the costs of those subsequent inspections. The effect of this amendment is to allow the Council to recover the fees and other costs arising from its investigations.

para. 5

This repeals a provision in relation to apprentices which is now redundant as a result of the introduction of the traineeship scheme.

para. 6

The Council has power to intervene in a solicitor's practice where there have been allegations of dishonesty (s.38), to safeguard the interests of the client of a solicitor struck off or suspended (s.45) and to safeguard the interests of clients in other circumstances, for example where a sole solicitor is incapacitated by illness (s.46). The new s.62A enables the Council to recover outlays and expenditure incurred as a result of such intervention.

paras. 7(a) and (b)

The practice year runs from November to November. At present, a solicitor who applies for a practising certificate must pay the full annual subscription, irrespective of the months remaining in the practice year. The effect of this amendment is to introduce a degree of flexibility to enable a solicitor to pay a partial subscription proportionate to the number of months remaining in the practice year.

para. 7(c)

At present, the Society can merely increase the annual subscription, but any such increase continues indefinitely. The new paras. 7A, 7B, 7C and 7D empower the Law Society to impose a special "one-off" subscription to enable the Society to raise money for a project in one particular year.

para. 8

The Scottish Solicitors Guarantee Fund exists to enable the Society to make good losses suffered by a client through the dishonesty of a solicitor in manipulating the client's account. It is funded by an annual contribution by all practising solicitors which is fixed at a maximum £25 per annum: there is a provision for a special contribution but it is also fixed at a maximum of £25 per annum. The effect of these amendments is to remove the maximum limit of £25 in both the annual contribution and the special contribution on the grounds that these had become "unrealistic".

Sections 23 and 59   SCHEDULE 2

AMENDMENT OF ENACTMENTS

The Jurors (Scotland) Act 1825 (c.22)

1. In section 10 (order in which names or jurors are to be taken for civil proceedings) for the words "in the said jury books" and "general jury book" there shall be substituted respectively the words "of potential jurors" and "lists".

The Juries (Scotland) Act 1826 (c.8)

2. In section 4 (names of dead and disqualified jurors not to be included in returns of jurors) for the words "said general jury book", in both places where these occur, there shall be substituted the words "list of potential jurors".

Lyon King of Arms Act 1867 (c.17)

3. In section 10 the words from "Provided also" to the end of the section shall cease to have effect.

Titles to Land Consolidation (Scotland) Act 1868 (c.101)

4. In section 159 (litigiosity not to begin before the date of registration in Register of Inhibitions and Adjudications of notice of summons) after the word "summons", where thirdly occurring, there shall be inserted the words "and contain a description of the lands to which the summons relates".

5. In Schedule RR (form of notice of summons) after the word "*signeting*]" there shall be inserted the words "The summons relates to [*insert description of lands*].".

Conveyancing (Scotland) Act 1924 (c.27)

6. In section 44 (limitation of effect of entries in Register of Inhibitions)—
    (*a*) in subsection (2)(*a*)—
           (i) after the words "unless and until" there shall be inserted "—
                (i)"; and
           (ii) at the end there shall be inserted—
                "; or
           (ii) a notice of an application under section 8 of the Law Reform (Miscellaneous Provisions) (Scotland) Act 1985 has been registered in the said register.".
    (*b*) in subsection (3)(*a*) for the words "and notices of litigiosity" there shall be substituted the words, notices of litigiosity and notices of applications under section 8 of the Law Reform (Miscellaneous Provisions) (Scotland) Act 1985".

7. Section 46 shall be renumbered as subsection (1) thereof and after that subsection there shall be inserted the following subsection—
    "(2) This section shall apply to the rectification of a document by an order under section 8 of the Law Reform (Miscellaneous Provisions) (Scotland) Act 1985 as it applies to the reduction of a deed but with the substitution of any reference to the decree of reduction of the deed with a reference to the order rectifying the document.".

Administration of Justice (Scotland) Act 1933 (c.41)

8. In section 16 (power to regulate procedure by Act of Sederunt)—
    (*a*) after paragraph (*g*) there shall be inserted the following paragraph—
        "(*gg*) to regulate the expenses which may be awarded to parties in causes before the Court;"; and
    (*b*) after paragraph (*h*) there shall be inserted the following paragraph—
        "(*hh*) to regulate the days on which and times at which the Court shall sit;".

The Social Work (Scotland) Act 1968 (c.49)

9. In section 21(2) (mode pof provision of accommodation and maintenance of child in care of local authority) for the words "the last foregoing section" there shall be substituted the words "section 20 of this Act".

10. In section 58B(3) for the word "child's" there shall be substituted the word "children's".

The Conveyancing and Feudal Reform (Scotland) Act 1970 (c.35)

11. In section 41 (restriction on effect of reduction of certain discharges of securities) at the end there shall be inserted the following subsection—
    "(5) This section shall apply to an order under section 8 of the Law Reform (Miscellaneous Provisions) (Scotland) Act 1985 rectifying a discharge as it applies to a decree of reduction of a discharge"."

Sheriff Courts (Scotland) Act 1971 (c.58)

12. In section 32(1) (power of Court of Session to regulate civil procedure in sheriff court)—
    (*a*) after paragraph (*h*) there shall be inserted the following paragraph—
        "(i) regulating the expenses which may be awarded by the sheriff to parties in proceedings before him:"; and
    (*b*) in paragraph (i) of the proviso after the word "Act" there shall be inserted the words "(as amended by the Law Reform (Miscellaneous Provisions) (Scotland) Act 1985".

13. In section 33(4) (appointment of secretary of Sheriff Court Rules Council) the words "whole-time sheriff clerk as" shall cease to have effect.

14. In section 35 (summary causes) after subsection (1) there shall be inserted the following subsection—

"(1A) For the avoidance of doubt it is hereby declared that nothing in subsection (1) above shall prevent the Court of Session from making different rules of procedure and practice in relation to different descriptions of summary cause proceedings.".

Administration of Justice (Scotland) Act 1972 (c.59)

15. In subsection (2) of section (1) (extended power of court to order inspection of documents and other property etc.) after the words "subsection (1)" there shall be inserted the words "or (1A)".

The Criminal Procedure (Scotland) Act 1975 (c.21)

16. In sections 88 to 91 (jurors in criminal proceedings) for each of the expressions "general jury roll", "jury book" where first occurring, "lists in the said jury books" and "said general jury book", in each place where it occurs, there shall be substituted the words "lists of potential jurors".

17. In section 98 (citation of jurors) for the words "roll of" there shall be substituted the words "lists of potential".

18. In subsection (1) of section 108 (which relates to the competency of certain objections for the word "sheriff" there shall be substituted the word "court".

19. In section 271 (forms relating to appeals), for the words "shall cause any such notice" to the end there shall be substituted the words ", if any prisoner in his custody so requests, shall cause any such intimation, note or notice given by that prisoner to be forwarded on the prisoner's behalf to the Clerk of Justiciary".

20. In subsection (1)(*a*) of section 447 (which relates to the preparation of draft stated cases) for the words from "the justice" to "may be required" there shall be substituted the words "the clerk of court".

The Land Registration (Scotland) Act 1979 (c.33)

21. In section 9 (rectification of the register)—

    (*a*) at the end of subsection (3)(*b*) there shall be added the words—

        "or the rectification is consequential on the making of an order under section 8 of the Law Reform (Miscellaneous Provisions) (Scotland) Act 1985.".

    (*b*) after subsection (3) there shall be inserted the following subsection—

        "(3A) Where a rectification of an entry in the register is consequential on the making of an order under section 8 of the said Act of 1985, the entry shall have effect as rectified as from the date when the entry was made;

Provided that the court, for the purpose of protecting the interests of a person to whom section 9 of that Act applies, may order that the rectification shall have effect as from such later date as it may specify."

22. At the end of section 12(3) (exclusion of indemnity) there shall be added the following paragraph—

    (*p*) the loss arises from a rectification of the register consequential on the making of an order under section 8 of the Law Reform (Miscellaneous Provisions) (Scotland) Act 1985.".

The Criminal Justice (Scotland) Act 1980 (c.62)

23. In section 3(5) (which defines the terms "parent" and "child") after the word "guardian" there shall be inserted the words "and any person who has the actual custody of a child".

Civil Jurisdiction and Judgements Act 1982 (c.27)

24. In section 28 (application of section 1 Administration of Justice (Scotland) Act 1972 after "1972" there shall be inserted the words "as amended by the Law Reform (Miscellaneous Provisions (Scotland) Act 1985".

The Cinematograph (Amendment) Act 1982 (c.33)

25. The entry in Schedule 2 relating to paragraph 4 of Schedule 7D to the Criminal Procedure (Scotland) Act 1975 shall be treated as never having been enacted.

The Transport Act 1982 (c.49)

26. In section 42 (which relates to fixed penalties)—
    (*a*) in subsections (2)(*c*)(i) and (7), for the word "tenders" there shall be substituted the word "makes";
    (*b*) in subsection (11), for the word "applies" there shall be substituted the words "and section 43 below apply.".
27. In section 43 (which relates to the endorsement of licences)—
    (*a*) in subsection (2), for the words "the fixed penalty is paid" there shall be substituted the words "payment of the fixed penalty is tendered";
    (*b*) after subsection (2) there shall be inserted the following subsections—
        "(2A) Where it appears to a clerk of court that there is an error in an endorsement made by virtue of this section on a licence he may amend the endorsement so as to correct the error; and the amended endorsement shall have effect and shall be treated for all purposes as if it has been correctly made on acceptance of the fixed penalty.
        (2B) On amending an endorsement under subsection (2A) above, the clerk of court shall send notice of the amendment to the Secretary of State.
        (2C) Subject to subsection (2D) below, where a cheque tendered in payment is subsequently dishonoured—
            (*a*) any endorsement made by a clerk of court in terms of subsection (2) above shall remain effective, notwithstanding that the licence-holder is still liable to prosecution in respect of the alleged offence to which the endorsement relates, and
            (*b*) the clerk of the court shall, upon the expiry of the period specified in the conditional offer or, if the period has expired, forthwith notify the procurator fiscal who made the offer that no payment has been made.
        (2D) When proceedings are brought against a licence-holder after notification has been made in terms of subsection (2C)(*b*) above the court—
            (*a*) shall order the removal of the fixed penalty endorsement from the licence, and
            (*b*) may, on finding the licence-holder guilty, make any competent order of endorsement or disqualification, and pass any competent sentence.

        (2E) The clerk of the court shall send to the Secretary of State notice of any order made by a court under subsection (2D)(*a*) above.".

The Rent (Scotland) Act 1984 (c.58)

28. In section 56(2) (registration of housing association and Housing Corporation rents), after the word "Sections", where first occurring, there shall be inserted the words "22 to 27.".
29. In subsection (5) of Section 106 (compulsory entry to carry out works on substandard houses), for the words from "has" where first occurring, to the end there shall be substituted the words "and 'tolerable standard' have the meaning respectively assigned to them by section 49(3) of the said Act of 1974".
30. In Schedule 9 (savings and transitional provisions), at the end, there shall be inserted the following paragraph—
    "7. The amendments to this Act made by Schedule 2 to the Law Reform (Miscellaneous Provisions) (Scotland) Act 1985 shall be deemed to have had effect from the commencement of this Act.".

The Family Law (Scotland) Act 1985 (c.37)

31. In section 27(1) (interpretation) in the definition of "matrimonial home" there shall be added at the end the words "as amended by section 13(10) of the Law Reform (Miscellaneous Provisions) (Scotland) Act 1985".

The Representation of the People Act 1985 (c.50)

32. In Schedule 4, in paragraph 61(*b*) (amendments of the Representation of the People Act 1983 relating to the time limit for prosecutions) after the word "without" there shall be inserted the word "undue".

paras. 1 and 2
These are consequential amendments arising from s.23.

para. 3
On April 1, 1985, the vote-related responsibilities for the office of the Lord Lyon were transferred from the Treasury to the Scottish Courts Administration. This amendment is consequential on the new arrangements and removes the responsibility that hitherto fell on the Treasury to provide accommodation for the Lyon King of Arms and his staff which will now be provided on the same basis as other Departments.

paras. 4 and 5
These amendments provide that notices of litigiosity under the 1868 Act, must give a description of the land to which the summons mentioned in the notice relates. This will facilitate searches of the register, particularly where the name of a party is a common one, or where he owns several pieces of land other than the one to which the application relates. For registration of notices of an application for rectification of a deed relating to land, see ss.8(7) and (8) *supra.*

para. 6
These are consequential amendments arising from s.8(7) which allows registration in the Register of Inhibitions and Adjudications of a notice of an application for the rectification of a deed relating to land.

para. 7
This amendment provides that an extract of an order rectifying a deed recorded in the Register of Sasines or registered in the Land Register of Scotland should be recorded or registered in the appropriate Register and shall not be pleadable against a third party who shall in bona fide onerously acquire rights to the land, lease or heritable security, prior to the recording or registration of the extract.

para. 8
These amendments give the Court of Session power, by Act of Sederunt, to regulate the award of expenses in cases before the Court of Session and to regulate its sittings.

para. 9
This is a drafting amendment. In s.21(2) of the 1968 Act, there is a reference to "the last foregoing section": this is no longer accurate after the insertion of a new s.20A by the Children Act 1975.

para. 10
This removes the spurious reference in s.58B(3) of the expression "child's hearing" when it was clearly intended to refer to a "children's hearing".

para. 11
This amendment extends the protection provided to a bona fide purchaser for value by s.41 of the Conveyancing and Feudal Reform (Scotland) Act 1970, in respect of reduction of discharges, to include orders for rectification of discharges. After five years from the date of recording of the discharge, his title shall not be challengeable by reason only of recording an extract of an order of rectification of the discharge, as well as an extract of a decree of reduction of the discharge.

para. 12
This gives the Court of Session the power, by Act of Sederunt, to regulate the award of expenses in cases in the Sheriff Court. The power will, however, be subject to the provisions in s.36B of the Sheriff Courts (Scotland) Act 1971, relating to expenses in small claims.

para. 13
By s.33(4) of the 1971 Act, the office of secretary of the Sheriff Court Rules Council is to be held by a "whole-time sheriff clerk". But the incumbent spends at least half his time on his secretarial duties. Accordingly, it is doubtful whether he can properly be described as a "whole-time sheriff clerk". In practice, the post is filled by a member of the staff of the Scottish Courts Administration, who has in the past held a commission as a full time sheriff clerk, though he does not do so during his time at the Scottish Courts Administration. The

removal of the statutory requirement that the incumbent be a "whole-time sheriff clerk" regularises current practice.

para. 14

The power of the Court of Session, by Act of Sederunt, to regulate the procedure and practice in civil proceedings in the Sheriff Court, cannot derogate from the provisions of ss.35–38 relating to summary causes: s.32(1)(*i*). The new s.35(1A), however, makes it clear that nothing in s.35(1) is to prevent the Court of Session making different rules of procedure and practice in relation to different descriptions of summary cause proceedings.

para. 15

This is a consequential amendment arising from s.19.

paras. 16 and 17

These are consequential amendments arising from s.23.

para. 18

This is a drafting amendment. S.108(1) applies to proceedings in both the High Court and Sheriff Court; the reference to "sheriff" only in s.108 is therefore inaccurate and is removed and replaced by the word "court".

para. 19

At present, prison standing orders take the view that s.271 obliges a governor of a prison to submit notices of appeal to the Clerk of Justiciary, even where the prisoner wishes his solicitor to handle his case. The purpose of this amendment is to put beyond doubt that governors have a duty to forward notices of appeal only when a prisoner requests the governor to do so. If the prisoner does ask the governor to forward the appeal, he must, of course, make arrangements to do so.

para. 20

The effect of this amendment is that in appeals from a district court to the High Court, the draft stated case will be prepared by the district clerk of court rather than the justice of the peace presiding in the case. The stated case will be drafted by the clerk of the court or the deputy clerk who was present in the case. A clerk of court or deputy must be a solicitor or barrister and will therefore have had legal training. The desire for the change came from a departmental working group of district court clerks and the central advisory committee on J.P.s. It replaces the current practice where the justice drafts the stated case with the advice of the clerk.

para. 21

This is a consequential amendment arising from ss.8 and 9.

para. 22

This adds a further ground of exclusion of indemnity: *viz.* loss arising from the rectification of the Register as a result of an order for rectification.

para. 23

This extends the definition of parent to include any person who has the actual custody of a child, for the purpose of receiving intimation of the child's arrest or detention under the terrorism provisions, and access to the child; see s.3B of the Criminal Justice (Scotland) Act 1980 and note to s.35 *supra.*

para. 24

This is a consequential amendment arising from s.19.

para. 26(a)

This provision makes amendments to s.42 which is concerned with fixed penalty offences. Where the procurator has sent a conditional offer to the alleged offender, then in the original wording of s.42, he will be discharged if he "tenders" payment within 28 days and in the case of an offence involving obligatory endorsement, delivers his driving licence to the clerk of court, and the clerk accepts payment. The amendment substitutes the word "makes" for "tenders", to ensure that s.42 will only operate, in a case where payment is made by cheque, if the cheque is honoured.

para. 26(b)
This amendment makes it clear that both ss.42 and 43 apply to offences committed in Scotland only.

para. 27
New subss. 43(2A) and (2B)
This new subsection empowers the clerk of court to correct any error in an endorsement made in relation to the new fixed penalty endorsements. Such a power already exists for court endorsements but it did not exist for the new fixed penalty endorsements.

New subss. 43(2D) and (2E)
These new subsections deal with the situation where a cheque tendered in payment of a fixed penalty is subsequently dishonoured. It provides that any endorsement shall remain effective, even though the licence holder is still liable to prosecution in respect of the alleged offence. In the later proceedings, the court shall order the removal of the fixed penalty endorsement, and if the licence holder is found guilty, make any competent order of endorsement or disqualification and pass any competent sentence. Para. 27(*a*) is a consequential amendment of s.43(2) arising from these new subsections.

para. 28
The purpose of this amendment is to remove any doubts which could arise from the original drafting of s.56(2), whether housing association tenants continue to enjoy the protection of ss.27–27 of the Rent (Scotland) Act 1984 in respect of harassment or eviction without due process of law. The amendment makes it clear that housing association tenants continue to enjoy their rights under ss.22–27 of the 1984 Act.

para. 29
This corrects an error in the original s.106(5) where the definitions of the expressions "standard amenities" and "the tolerable standard" for the purposes of the 1984 Act were applied by reference to the meaning of those expressions given respectively in the Housing (Financial Provisions) (Scotland) Act 1968 and the Housing (Scotland) Act 1969. It had been overlooked that these definitions had been superseded by new definitions in the Housing (Scotland) Act 1974. The amendment corrects this error.

para. 30
As these amendments will not become effective until this Act becomes law, this amendment provides that they shall be deemed to have had effect since the 1984 Act came into force, thus covering the transitional period.

para. 31
This amends the definition of matrimonial home for the purpose of the Family Law (Scotland) Act 1985 so that it has the same meaning as the definition in the Matrimonial Homes (Family Protection) (Scotland) Act 1981, which was amended by s.13(10): see note to s.13(10) *supra*.

para. 32
Para. 61(*b*) of Sched. 4 to the Representation of the People Act 1985 substitutes a new subs. (2) in s.176 of the Representation of the People Act 1983. The new s.176(2) referred in its application to Scotland, to the execution of a warrant "without delay" instead of "without undue delay", which is the wording in s.331 of the Criminal Procedure (Scotland) Act 1975, from which s.176 was derived. The effect of para. 32 is to convert the reference to "without *undue* delay" in s.176(2) so that it is now consistent with the wording in the 1975 Act.

Section 60   SCHEDULE 3

TRANSITIONAL PROVISIONS

Section 36

1. Sections 141A, 141B, 346A and 346B of the Criminal Procedure (Scotland) Act 1975 do not apply in relation to a trial which has commenced before the coming into force of

those sections; and, for the purposes of this paragraph, a trial shall be taken to commence—

(*a*) in the case of solemn proceedings, when the oath is administered to the jury;

(*b*) in the case of summary proceedings, when the first witness is sworn.

Section 38

2. The amendment to section 120 of the Road Traffic Regulation Act 1984 effected by section 38 of this Act has no effect in relation to proceedings in which the complaint was served on the accused before the coming into force of section 38 of this Act.

Section 39

3. Section 193B of the Criminal Procedure (Scotland) Act 1975 shall not affect the punishment for an offence committed before the coming into force of section 39 of this Act.

Section 40

4. The amendments to section 407(1A) of the Criminal Procedure (Scotland) Act 1975 effected by section 40 of this Act have no effect in relation to fines imposed in respect of offences committed before the coming into force of section 40 of this Act.

GENERAL NOTE

Ss.36 and 38 change the rules on the admissibility of evidence. The effect of these transitional provisions provide that s.36 will not apply to trials, and s.38 will not apply to proceedings, commenced before these sections come into force. Similarly, ss.39 and 40 which change penalties do not apply to offences committed before these sections come into force.

Section 59   SCHEDULE 4

Repeals

Chapter	Short title	Extent of repeal
1825 c.22.	The Jurors (Scotland) Act 1825.	Sections 11 and 14.
1830 c.37.	The Criminal Law (Scotland) Act 1830.	Section 11.
1867 c.17.	The Lyon King of Arms Act 1867.	In section 10, the words from "Provided also" to the end of the section.
1920 c.53.	The Jurors (Enrolment of Women) (Scotland) Act 1920.	The whole Act.
1947 c.44.	The Crown Proceedings Act 1947.	In section 46, paragraph (*c*) of the proviso and the word "or" which precedes it.
1949 c.63.	The Legal Aid and Solicitors (Scotland) Act 1949.	Section 25.
1952 c.61.	The Prisons (Scotland) Act 1952.	Section 7(2). Section 18(4) and (5). Section 35(5)(*b*).
1965 c.22.	The Law Commissions Act 1965.	Section 2(5).
1971 c.10.	The Vehicles (Excise) Act 1971.	In subsection 9(5) (as it applies to Scotland) the words "convicted on indictment of, or is", the words "Part I or", and the words from "the conviction on" to "as the case may be,".
1971 c.58.	The Sheriff Courts (Scotland) Act 1971.	In section 6, in subsection (1) paragraph (*b*) and the word "or" which precedes it. In section 33(4), the words "whole-time sheriff clerk as".
1975 c.20.	The District Courts (Scotland) Act 1975.	Section 19.

Chapter	Short title	Extent of repeal
1975 c.21.	The Criminal Procedure (Scotland) Act 1975.	In section 448(2C)(*b*), the words "to the draft case".
1976 c.32.	The Lotteries and Amusements Act 1976.	In Schedule 3, paragraph 14.
1980 c.45.	The Water (Scotland) Act 1980.	Section 96.
1980 c.46.	The Solicitors (Scotland) Act 1980.	In section 6(1)(*b*), the words "by affidavit or otherwise". Section 15(2)(*a*). In section 35(1), the word "and" immediately preceding paragraph (*d*). In Schedule 1, in paragraph 7 the word "annual" in both places where it occurs. In Schedule 3, in paragraph 1(1), the words "not exceeding the sum of £25" and paragraph 1(7).

CONSOLIDATED FUND (No. 3) ACT 1985

(1985 c.74)

An Act to apply certain sums out of the Consolidated Fund to the service of the years ending on 31st March 1986 and 1987.

[19th December 1985]

PARLIAMENTARY DEBATES
   Hansard: H.C. Vol. 89, col. 391; H.L. Vol. 469, col. 900.

Issue out of Consolidated Fund for the year ending 31st March 1986.

1. The Treasury may issue out of the Consolidated Fund of the United Kingdom and apply towards making good the supply granted to Her Majesty for the service of the year ending on 31st March 1986 the sum of £1,622,416,000.

Issue out of the Consolidated Fund for the year ending 31st March 1987

2. The Treasury may issue out of the Consolidated Fund of the United Kingdom and apply towards making good the supply granted to Her Majesty for the service of the year ending on 31st March 1987 the sum of £43,136,812,000.

Short title

3. This Act may be cited as the Consolidated Fund (No. 3) Act 1985.

EUROPEAN COMMUNITIES (SPANISH AND PORTUGUESE ACCESSION) ACT 1985

(1985 c.75)

An Act to extend the meaning in Acts, Measures and subordinate legislation of "the Treaties" and "the Community Treaties" in connection with the accession of the Kingdom of Spain and the Portuguese Republic to the European Communities.

[19th December, 1985]

PARLIAMENTARY DEBATES
  Hansard: H.L. Vol. 468, cols. 21, 497, 735 and 797; H.C. VOL. 88, COLS. 313 and 859.

Extended meaning of "the Community Treaties"

1. In section 1(2) of the European Communities Act 1972, in the definition of "the Treaties" and "the Community Treaties", after paragraph (*f*) (inserted by the European Communities (Finance) Act 1985) there shall be inserted the words "and

(*g*) the treaty relating to the accession of the Kingdom of Spain and the Portuguese Republic to the European Economic Community and to the European Atomic Energy Community, signed at Lisbon and Madrid on 12th June 1985; and

(*h*) the decision, of 11th June 1985, of the Council relating to the accession of the Kingdom of Spain and the Portuguese Republic to the European Coal and Steel Community;".

Short title

2. This Act may be cited as the European Communities (Spanish and Portuguese Accession) Act 1985.

NORTHERN IRELAND (LOANS) ACT 1985

(1985 c.76)

An Act to increase the limit imposed by section 1 of the Northern Ireland (Loans) Act 1975.

[19th December 1985]

PARLIAMENTARY DEBATES
Hansard: H.C. Vol. 86, col. 118; Vol. 87, col. 977; Vol. 88, col. 388; H.L. Vol. 468, col. 1524; col. 489; col. 906.

Increase of limit

1.—(1) In subsection (2) of section 1 of the Northern Ireland (Loans) Act 1975 (which imposes an overall limit, increased from £800 million to £1,000 million by the Northern Ireland Loans (Increase of Limit) Order 1984, on certain loans to the Consolidated Fund of Northern Ireland) for "£1,000 million" there shall be substituted "£1,700 million".

(2) Subsection (5) of that section shall apply in relation to the limit set by virtue of subsection (1) above as it applied in relation to the limit set by subsection (2) of that section as originally enacted, but with the substitution of "£300 million" for "£200 million".

(3) The Order of 1984 is hereby revoked.

Short title

2. This Act may be cited as the Northern Ireland (Loans) Act 1985.

CURRENT LAW
STATUTE CITATOR 1985

This edition of the Current Law Statute Citator covers the period January to December 1985.

It comprises in a single table:
  (i) Statutes passed between January 1 and December 31, 1985;
 (ii) Statutes affected during this period by Statutory Instrument;
(iii) Statutes judicially considered during this period;
 (iv) Statutes repealed and amended during this period.

(S.) Amendments relating to Scotland only.

ACTS OF THE PARLIAMENT OF SCOTLAND

CAP.
18. Bankruptcy Act 1621.
repealed: 1985, c.66, sch. 8.

CAP.
5. Bankruptcy Act 1696.
repealed: 1985, c.66, sch.8.

ACTS OF THE PARLIAMENTS OF ENGLAND, GREAT BRITAIN, AND THE UNITED KINGDOM

CAP.

37 Geo. 3 (1797)

127. Meeting of Parliament Act 1797.
ss. 3–5, repealed: 1985, c.50, s.20, sch. 5.

6 Geo. 4 (1825)

22. Jurors (Scotland) Act 1825.
s. 3, amended: 1985, c.73, s.23.
s. 10, amended: *ibid.*, sch. 2.
ss. 11, 14, repealed: *ibid.*, sch. 4.

120. Court of Session Act 1825.
s. 10, see *Johnston* v. *Johnston* (O.H.), July 29, 1983.

7 Geo. 4 (1826)

8. Juries (Scotland) Act 1826.
s. 4, amended: 1985, c.73, s.23, sch. 2.

11 Geo. 4 & 1 Will. 4 (1830)

37. Criminal Law (Scotland) Act 1830.
s. 11, repealed: 1985, c.73, sch. 4.

3 & 4 Will. 4 (1833)

41. Judicial Committee Act 1833.
s. 24, order 85/1635.

7 Will. 4 & 1 Vict. (1837)

26. Wills Act 1837.
s. 18A, see *Sinclair (Dec'd), Re, Lloyds Bank* v. *Imperial Cancer Research Fund* [1985] 1 All E.R. 1066, C.A.

1 & 2 Vict. (1837–38)

110. Judgments Act 1838.
s. 17, amended: order 85/437.
114. Debtors (Scotland) Act 1838.
s. 27, see *Aalco Glasgow* v. *Harska Engineering,* 1985 S.L.T.(Sh.Ct) 65.

6 & 7 Vict. (1843)

86. London Hackney Carriages Act 1843.
s. 23, repealed in pt.: 1985, c.54, sch. 27.
s. 25, amended: 1985, c.67, sch. 7.

7 & 8 Vict. (1844)

69. Judicial Committee Act 1844.
s. 1, orders 85/445, 450, 1199.

8 & 9 Vict. (1845)

118. Inclosure Act 1845.
s. 163, repealed in pt.: 1985, c.54, sch. 27.

10 & 11 Vict. (1847)

14. Markets and Fairs Clauses Act 1847.
see *Halton Borough Council* v. *Cawley* [1985] 1 W.L.R. 15, Blackett-Ord V.C.

89. Town Police Clauses Act 1847.
s. 37, repealed in pt.: 1985, c.67, sch. 8.
s. 38, see *R.* v. *Bournemouth Borough Council* (1985) 83 L.G.R. 622, Mann J.
s. 46, amended: 1985, c.67, sch. 7.

12 & 13 Vict. (1849)

16. Justices Protection (Ireland) Act 1849.
repealed: 1985, c.61, sch. 8.

17 & 18 Vict. (1854)

91. Lands Valuation (Scotland) Act 1854.
s. 42, see *Assessor for Orkney* v. *Post Office,* 1982 S.C. 32; *Assessor for Lothian Region* v. *B.P. Oil Grangemouth Refinery,* 1985 S.L.T. 453.

CAP.

19 & 20 Vict. (1856)

60. Mercantile Law Amendment (Scotland) Act 1856.
s. 9, see *The Royal Bank of Scotland* v. *Welsh* (O.H.), 1985 S.L.T. 439.

20 & 21 Vict. (1857)

26. Registration of Leases (Scotland) Act 1857.
s. 3, amended: 1985, c.73, s.3.
43. Summary Jurisdiction Act 1857.
s. 6, see *Maydew* v. *Flint* (1985) 80 Cr.App.R. 49, D.C.
60. Irish Bankrupt and Insolvent Act 1857.
ss. 73–75, 259 (in pt.), 305 (in pt.), 312 (in pt.), 320 (in pt.), 370 (in pt.), 410 (in pt.), repealed: 1985, c.65, sch. 10.
72. Police (Scotland) Act 1857.
s. 29, see *Cormack* v. *The Crown Estate Commissioners*, 1985 S.L.T. 181.

24 & 25 Vict. (1861)

86. Conjugal Rights (Scotland) Amendment Act 1861.
ss. 6 (in pt.), 9 (in pt.), 15, 16, repealed: 1985, c.37, sch. 2.
94. Accessories and Abettors Act 1861.
s. 8, see *R.* v. *Hollinshead* [1985] 1 All E.R. 850, C.A.; *R.* v. *Calhaem* [1985] 2 W.L.R. 826, C.A.
100. Offences against the Person Act 1861.
s. 18, see *R.* v. *Pearman* [1985] R.T.R. 39, C.A.; *R.* v. *Gibson*; *R.* v. *Gibson* (1985) 80 Cr.App.R. 24, C.A.; *R.* v. *Hamand* (1985) 82 L.S.Gaz. 1561, C.A.; *R.* v. *Bryson, The Times*, June 28, 1985, C.A.
s. 20, see *R.* v. *Bird (Debbie), The Times*, March 28, 1985, C.A.; *R.* v. *Gibson*; *R.* v. *Gibson* (1985) 80 Cr.App.R. 24, C.A.
s. 24, see *R.* v. *Hill* [1985] Crim.L.R. 384, C.A.
ss. 32–34, see *R.* v. *Criminal Injuries Compensation Board, ex p. Webb, The Times*, March 28, 1985, C.A.
s. 34, see *R.* v. *Criminal Injuries Compensation Board, ex p. Warner* [1985] 2 All E.R. 1069, D.C.
s. 42, see *R.* v. *Harrow JJ., ex p. Osaseri* [1985] 3 All E.R. 185, D.C.
ss. 44, 45, see *Saeed* v. *Inner London Education Authority* [1985] I.C.R. 638, Popplewell J.
s. 47, see *R.* v. *Harrow JJ., ex p. Osaseri* [1985] 3 All E.R. 185, D.C.

25 & 26 Vict. (1862)

97. Salmon Fisheries (Scotland) Act 1862.
ss. 18, 19, 24, see *Cormack* v. *The Crown Estate Commissioners*, 1985 S.L.T. 181.

28 & 29 Vict. (1865)

90. Metropolitan Fire Brigade Act 1865.
amended: 1985, c.51, sch. 11.

CAP.

29 & 30 Vict. (1866)

122. Metropolitan Commons Act 1866.
s. 25, repealed in pt.: 1985, c.51, sch. 17.
sch. 1, amended: *ibid.*, sch. 8; repealed in pt.: *ibid.*, sch. 17.

30 & 31 Vict. (1867)

17. Lyon King of Arms Act 1867.
s. 10, repealed in pt. (S.): 1985, c.73, schs. 2, 4.

31 & 32 Vict. (1868)

101. Titles to Land Consolidation (Scotland) Act 1868.
s. 148, repealed: 1985, c.66, sch. 8.
s. 159, Sch. RR, amended: 1985, c.73, sch. 2.
123. Salmon Fisheries (Scotland) Act 1868.
ss. 6, 13, see *Cormack* v. *The Crown Estate Commissioners*, 1985 S.L.T. 426 (H.L.).

32 & 33 Vict. (1869)

115. Metropolitan Public Carriage Act 1869.
s. 9, orders 85/933, 1023.

33 & 34 Vict. (1870)

52. Extradition Act 1870.
s. 2, orders 85/751, 1634, 1637, 1989–1993.
s. 8, see *R.* v. *Bow Street Magistrates' Court, ex p. Van Der Holst, The Times*, November 20, 1985, D.C.
s. 14, see *R.* v. *Secretary of State for the Home Office, ex p. Rees, The Times*, March 18, 1985, D.C.
s. 17, orders 85/751, 1634, 1637, 1989–1993.
s. 18, order 85/167.
s. 21, orders 85/1634, 1637, 1989–1993.
sch. 1, amended: 1985, c.38, s.3.

34 & 35 Vict. (1871)

50. Bankruptcy Disqualification Act 1871.
repealed: 1985, c.65, sch. 10.
78. Regulation of Railways Act 1871.
s. 6, S.R. 1985 No. 10.
96. Pedlars Act 1871.
ss. 3, 5, see *Murphy* v. *Duke* [1985] 2 W.L.R. 773, Forbes J.
s. 5, amended: order 85/2027.

35 & 36 Vict. (1872)

58. Bankruptcy (Ireland) Amendment Act 1872.
ss. 2 (in pt.), 40–42, repealed: 1985, c.65, sch. 10.
s. 53, see *Industrial Design and Manufacture, Re* [1984] 10 N.I.J.B., Carswell J.
ss. 65, 121, repealed in pt.: 1985, c.65, sch. 10.
94. Licensing Act 1872.
s. 12, see *Neale* v. *R. M. J. E. (A Minor)* (1985) 80 Cr.App.R. 20, D.C.

CAP.

37 & 38 Vict. (1874)

42. Building Societies Act 1874.
s. 32, repealed in pt.: 1985, c.65, sch. 10.

38 & 39 Vict. (1875)

17. Explosives Act 1875.
ss. 15, 18, 21, amended: regs. 85/1108.
s. 67, amended: 1985, c.51, sch. 11.

55. Public Health Act 1875.
s. 149, see *Russell* v. *Barnet London Borough Council* [1985] 83 L.G.R. 152, Tudor Evans J.

86. Conspiracy and Protection of Property Act 1875.
s. 7, see *R.* v. *Bonsall* (1985) Crim.L.R. 150, Derby Crown Court; *Thomas* v. *National Union of Mineworkers* [1985] 2 All E.R. 1, C.A.

41 & 42 Vict. (1878)

71. Metropolitan Commons Act 1878.
s. 2, amended: 1985, c.51, sch. 8.

77. Highways and Locomotives (Amendment) Act 1878.
s. 26, amended: 1985, c.51, sch. 4.

42 & 43 Vict. (1879)

11. Bankers' Books Evidence Act 1879.
see *R.* v. *Nottingham Justices, ex p. Lynn* (1984) 79 Cr.App.R. 238, D.C.
s. 9, repealed in pt.: 1985, c.58, sch. 4.

58. Public Offices Fees Act 1879.
s. 2, orders 85/1783, 1784.
ss. 2, 3, orders 85/358, 359, 372; S.Rs. 1984 Nos. 419, 420.

43 & 44 Vict. (1880)

4. Judicial Factors (Scotland) Act 1880.
s. 3, amended: 1985, c.66, sch. 7.

44 & 45 Vict. (1881)

21. Married Women's Property (Scotland) Act 1881.
s. 1, repealed in pt.: 1985, c.66, sch. 8.
ss. 1–5, 8, sch., repealed: 1985, c.37, sch. 2.

45 & 46 Vict. (1882)

15. Commonable Rights Compensation Act 1882.
sch., amended: 1985, c.51, sch. 8.

43. Bills of Sale Act (1878) Amendment Act 1882.
s. 11, amended: 1985, c.65, sch. 8.

56. Electric Lighting Act 1882.
s. 17, see *Christian Salvesen (Properties)* v. *Central Electricity Generating Board* (1984) 48 P. & C.R. 465, Lands Tribunal, V.G. Wellings Esq., Q.C.

61. Bills of Exchange Act 1882.
s. 53, amended (S.): 1985, c.73, s.11.
s. 75A, added (S.): *ibid.*

75. Married Women's Property Act 1882.
s. 17, see *Thompson* v. *Thompson, The Times*, February 14, 1985, C.A.; *Hamlin* v. *Hamlin, The Times*, May 9, 1985, C.A.

CAP.

45 & 46 Vict. (1882)—cont.

77. Citation Amendment (Scotland) Act 1882.
s. 4, see *McCormick* v. *Martin*, 1985 S.L.T.(Sh.Ct.) 57.

46 & 47 Vict. (1883)

1. Consolidated Fund (Permanent Charges Redemption) Act 1883.
s. 2, repealed in pt.: 1985, c.58, sch. 4.

3. Explosive Substances Act 1883.
s. 4, see *R.* v. *Berry* [1984] 3 W.L.R. 1274, H.L.

52. Bankruptcy Act 1883.
s. 32, amended (S.): 1985, c.66, sch. 7.
ss. 32–34, repealed in pt.: 1985, c.65, sch. 10.
s. 34A, added (S.): 1985, c.66, sch. 7.

50 & 51 Vict. (1887)

40. Savings Banks Act 1887.
s. 10, repealed in pt.: 1985, c.58, sch. 4.

54. British Settlements Act 1887.
orders 85/444, 449.

52 & 53 Vict. (1889)

39. Judicial Factors (Scotland) Act 1889.
s. 2, amended: 1985, c.66, sch. 7.
s. 5, repealed in pt.: *ibid.*, sch. 8.
ss. 11A, 11B, added: *ibid.*, sch. 7.
ss. 14 (in pt.), 15, 16, 22, repealed: *ibid.*, sch. 8.

63. Interpretation Act 1889.
s. 1, see *Worthing Rugby Football Club Trustees* v. *I.R.C.* [1985] 1 W.L.R. 409, Peter Gibson J.

69. Public Bodies Corrupt Practices Act 1889.
s. 1, see *R.* v. *Parker* [1985] Crim.L.R. 589, C.A.

53 & 54 Vict. (1890)

39. Partnership Act 1890.
s. 28, see *Ferguson* v. *Mackay* (O.H.), 1985 S.L.T. 94.
s. 33, see *William S. Gordon & Co.* v. *Mrs. Mary Thomson Partnership*, 1985 S.L.T. 122.

71. Bankruptcy Act 1890.
s. 9, repealed: 1985, c.65, sch. 10.

54 & 55 Vict. (1891)

39. Stamp Act 1891.
ss. 8, 10, repealed: 1985, c.54, sch. 27.
ss. 13, 75, see *Ingram* v. *I.R.C., The Times*, November 18, 1985, Vinelott J.
s. 58, amended: 1985, c.54, s. 82.
s. 59, repealed in pt.: *ibid.*, sch. 27.
sch. 1, repealed in pt.: *ibid.*, s.85, schs. 24, 27.

55 & 56 Vict. (1892)

6. Colonial Probates Act 1982.
s. 2, rules 85/1232.

57 & 58 Vict. (1894)

30. Finance Act 1894.
s. 8, amended: orders 85/561, 562.

(3)

CAP.

57 & 58 Vict. (1984)—cont.

60. Merchant Shipping Act 1894.
s. 36, repealed: 1985, c.65, sch. 10; c.66, sch. 8(S.).
s. 427, amended: 1985, c.3, sch.
s. 735, order 85/1636.
s. 738, order 85/1197.

58 & 59 Vict. (1895)

14. Courts of Law Fees (Scotland) Act 1895.
s. 2, order 85/825–827.

59 & 60 Vict. (1896)

35. Judicial Trustees Act 1896.
s. 1, amended: 1985, c.61, s.50.
44. Truck Act 1896.
ss. 1, 2, 4, see *Bristow* v. *City Petroleum* [1985] 3 All E.R. 463, D.C.
48. Light Railways Act 1896.
s. 3, order 85/747.
ss. 7, 9–11, orders 85/725, 747, 810, 844, 1578.
s. 12, orders 85/747, 1578.
s. 18, orders 85/747, 810, 844.
s. 24, order 85/810.

61 & 62 Vict. (1898)

36. Criminal Evidence Act 1898.
s. 1, see *R.* v. *Naudeer* [1984] 3 All E.R. 1036, C.A.; *R.* v. *Rowson* [1985] Crim.L.R. 307, C.A.; *R.* v. *Powell, The Times*, November 18, 1985, C.A.
43. Metropolitan Commons Act 1898.
repealed: 1985, c.51, sch. 17.

62 & 63 Vict. (1899)

9. Finance Act 1899.
s. 12, repealed: 1985, c.54, s.88, sch. 27.
sch., repealed: *ibid.*, sch. 27.
44. Small Dwellings Acquisition Act 1899.
repealed: 1985, c.71, sch. 1.

2 Edw. 7 (1902)

8. Cremation Act 1902.
s. 7, regs. 85/153; 820(S.).

6 Edw. 7 (1906)

41. Marine Insurance Act 1906.
s. 1, see *Continental Illinois National Bank & Trading Company of Chicago* v. *Bathurst, The Times*, February 12, 1985, Mustill J.
s. 17, see *Black King Shipping Corp.* v. *Massie, The Times*, December 17, 1984, Hirst J.
48. Merchant Shipping Act 1906.
s. 80, order 85/1200.
50. National Galleries of Scotland Act 1906.
s. 3, amended: 1985, c.16, s.16.
s. 4, substituted: *ibid.*
ss. 4A–4D, added: *ibid.*
s. 7, amended: *ibid.*, sch. 2.
sch., added: *ibid.*, s.17.
55. Public Trustee Act 1906.
s. 9, order 85/373.
s. 41, rules 85/132.

CAP.

7 Edw. 7 (1907)

13. Finance Act 1907.
s. 7, amended: 1985, c.54, s.85.
s. 77, repealed in pt.: *ibid.*, s.86.
29. Patents and Designs Act 1907.
s. 91A, orders 85/173, 456, 457.
51. Sheriff Courts (Scotland) Act 1907.
s. 3, see *W. Jack Baillie Associates* v. *Kennedy*, 1985 S.L.T.(Sh.Ct.) 53.
s. 4, see *Banque Indo Suez* v. *Maritime Co. Overseas*, 1985 S.L.T. 117.
s. 5, amended: 1985, c.37, sch. 1.
s. 5A, added: 1985, c.73, s.17.
s. 40, Acts of Sederunt 85/544, 759.
sch. 1, see *Hardy* v. *Robinson; Johnstone* v. *W. Y. Walker*, 1985 S.L.T.(Sh.Ct.) 40; *McCormick* v. *Martin*, 1985 S.L.T.(Sh.Ct.) 57.
55. London Cab and Stage Carriage Act 1907.
s. 1, orders 85/933, 1023.

8 Edw. 7 (1908)

36. Small Holdings and Allotments Act 1908.
s. 61, repealed in pt.: 1985, c.51, sch. 17.
44. Commons Act 1908.
s. 1, amended: 1985, c.51, sch. 8.
69. Companies (Consolidation) Act 1908.
s. 93, see *Welsh Irish Ferries, Re, Financial Times*, June 5, 1985, Nourse J.

9 Edw. 7 (1909)

30. Cinematograph Act 1909.
repealed: 1985, s.13, sch. 3.
s. 1, see *British Amusement Catering Trades Association* v. *G.L.C.* [1985] 2 All E.R. 535, Mervyn Davies J.
43. Revenue Act 1909.
s. 9, repealed: 1985, c.54, sch. 27.

10 Edw. 7 & 1 Geo. 5 (1910)

8. Finance (1909–10) Act 1910.
s. 74, see *Berkeley* v. *Comrs. of Inland Revenue* [1984] 13 N.I.J.B., Murray J.
s. 74, repealed: 1985, c.54, s.82, sch. 27.
ss. 77–79, repealed in pt.: *ibid.*, sch. 27.

1 & 2 Geo. 5 (1911)

6. Perjury Act 1911.
s. 1, see *R.* v. *Millward (Neil)* [1985] 1 W.L.R. 532, C.A.
s. 9, repealed: 1985, c.23, s.28, sch. 2.
28. Official Secrets Act 1911.
s. 2, see *R.* v. *Loat* [1985] Crim.L.R. 154, Dudley Crown Court; *R.* v. *Ponting* [1985] Crim.L.R. 318, C.C.C., McCowan J.
46. Copyright Act 1911.
see *Butterworth & Co.* v. *Ng Sui Nam, Financial Times*, March 5, 1985, High Ct. Republic of Singapore; *Geographia* v. *Penguin Books* [1985] F.S.R. 208, Whitford J.
s. 21, see *Barson Computers (N.Z.)* v. *Gilbert (John) & Co.* [1985] F.S.R. 489, New Zealand H.C.

CAP.

1 & 2 Geo. 5 (1911)—cont.

49. Small Landholders (Scotland) Act 1911.
ss. 26, 32, see *Representatives of the late Hugh Matheson* v. *Master of Lovat*, 1984 S.L.C.R. 82.

3 & 4 Geo. 5 (1913)

20. Bankruptcy (Scotland) Act 1913.
repealed: 1985, c.66, sch. 8.
s. 29, see *The Royal Bank of Scotland* v. *Aitken*, 1985 S.L.T.(Sh.Ct.) 13.
ss. 41, 97, 107, see *Cook's Tr., Petr.* (O.H.), 1985 S.L.T. 33.
s. 189, repealed in pt.: 1985, c.54, sch. 27.

27. Forgery Act 1913.
s. 7, see *R.* v. *Hagan* [1985] Crim.L.R. 598, C.A.
s. 16, see *Reynolds* v. *Comr. of Police of the Metropolis* [1984] Crim.L.R. 688, C.A.

4 & 5 Geo. 5 (1914)

30. Injuries in War Compensation Act 1914.
s. 1, schemes 85/299, 1566.

31. Housing Act 1914.
repealed: 1985, c.71,sch. 1.

47. Deeds of Arrangement Act 1914.
ss. 3, 11, 13–16, amended: 1985, c.65, sch. 8.
s. 9, amended: *ibid.*; repealed in pt.: *ibid.*, sch. 10.
s. 23, amended: *ibid.*, sch. 8.
ss. 24 (in pt.), 27, repealed: *ibid.*, sch. 10.
s. 30, amended: *ibid.*, sch. 8.

59. Bankruptcy Act 1914.
repealed: 1985, c.65, sch. 10.
s. 4, see *Hastings (A Bankrupt), Re* [1985] 1 All E.R. 885, D.C.
s. 26, see *Waldron (A Bankrupt), Re, ex p. The Bankrupt* v. *The Official Receiver* [1985] F.L.R. 164, C.A.
s. 33, repealed in pt.: 1985, c.58, sch. 4.
ss. 56, 83, 100, see *Debtor, A, Re (No. 26A of 1975)* [1984] 3 All E.R. 995, Scott J.
ss. 82, 105, see *Colgate, Re (A Bankrupt), The Times*, November 12, 1985, C.A.
ss. 121–123, repealed: 1985, c.65, sch. 10.
s. 133, order 85/1783.
s. 148, repealed in pt.: 1985, c.54, sch. 27.

61. Special Constables Act 1914.
s. 1, S.R. 1985 No. 255.

5 & 6 Geo. 5 (1914–15)

90. Indictments Act 1915.
see *R.* v. *Noe* [1985] Crim.L.R. 97, Snaresbrook Crown Court.
ss. 5 (in pt.), 6, repealed: 1985, c.23, sch. 2.

6 & 7 Geo. 5 (1916)

31. Police, Factories, etc. (Miscellaneous Provisions) Act 1916.
s. 5, see *Meaden* v. *Wood* [1985] Crim.L.R. 678, D.C.

CAP.

7 & 8 Geo. 5 (1917–18)

31. Finance Act 1917.
s. 30, repealed in pt.: 1985, c.54, sch. 27.

64. Representation of the People Act 1918.
repealed: 1985, c.50, sch. 5.
s. 21, repealed in pt.: *ibid.*, s.28.

9 & 10 Geo. 5 (1919)

35. Housing, Town Planning, etc. Act 1919.
repealed: 1985, c.71, sch. 1.

100. Electricity (Supply) Act 1919.
s. 22, see *Christian Salvesen (Properties)* v. *Central Electricity Generating Board* (1984) 48 P. & C.R. 465, Lands Tribunal, V. G. Wellings Esq., Q.C.

10 & 11 Geo. 5 (1920)

53. Jurors (Enrolment of Women) (Scotland) Act 1920.
repealed: 1985, c.71, sch. 4.

64. Married Women's Property (Scotland) Act 1920.
repealed: 1985, c.37, sch. 2.
s. 5, repealed in pt.: 1985, c.66, sch. 8.

75. Official Secrets Act 1920.
s. 4, repealed: 1985, c.56, s. 11.

81. Administration of Justice Act 1920.
s. 14, order 85/1994.

11 & 12 Geo. 5 (1921)

32. Finance Act 1921.
sch. 3, repealed in pt.: 1985, c.54, sch. 27; c.58, sch. 4.

49. War Pensions Act 1921.
s. 1, order 85/1544.

12 & 13 Geo. 5 (1922).

35. Celluloid and Cinematograph Film Act 1922.
s. 2, amended: 1985, c.13, sch. 2.
s. 9, amended: 1985, c.51, sch. 11.

13 & 14 Geo. 5 (1923)

8. Industrial Assurance Act 1923.
s. 43, regs. 85/338.

24. Housing, etc. Act 1923.
repealed: 1985, c.71, sch. 1.

14 & 15 Geo. 5 (1924)

27. Conveyancing (Scotland) Act 1924.
s. 6, repealed in pt.: 1985, c.54, sch. 27.
s. 44, amended: 1985, c.66, sch. 7; c.73, sch. 2; repealed in pt.: 1985, c.66, sch. 8.
s. 46, amended: 1985, c.73, sch. 2.

15 & 16 Geo. 5 (1924–25)

5. Law of Property (Amendment) Act 1924.
sch. 9, repealed in pt.: 1985, c.71, sch. 1.

18. Settled Land Act 1925.
s. 103, amended: 1985, c.65, sch. 8.

19. Trustee Act 1925.
s. 54, rules 84/2035.
s. 57, see *Thompson* v. *Thompson, The Times*, February 14, 1985, C.A.

CAP.
15 & 16 Geo. 5 (1924–25)—cont.

20. Law of Property Act 1925.
s. 30, see *Thompson* v. *Thompson, The Times*, February 14, 1985, C.A.; *Singh* v. *Singh* (1985) 15 Fam.Law 97, Anthony Lincoln J.
ss. 34–36, see *Goodman* v. *Gallant, The Times*, November 7, 1985, C.A.
s. 46, see *Stearn* v. *Twitchell* [1985] 1 All E.R. 631, C.A.
s. 52, amended: 1985, c.65, sch. 8.
s. 53, see *Midland Bank* v. *Dobson* (1985) 135 New L.J. 751, C.A.
ss. 56, 62, 78, see *Pinemain* v. *Welbeck International* (1984) 272 E.G. 1166, Mr.
. E. G. Nugee, Q.C.
s. 65, see *Wiles* v. *Banks* (1985) 50 P. & C.R. 81, C.A.
s. 110, repealed in pt.: 1985, c.65, sch. 10.
s. 146, see *Official Custodian for Charities* v. *Mackey* [1985] 49 P. & C.R. 242, Scott J.; *Expert Clothing Service & Sales* v. *Hillgate House* [1985] 3 W.L.R. 359, C.A.; *British Petroleum Pension Trust* v. *Behrendt* (1985) 276 E.G. 199, C.A.; *South Buckinghamshire County Council* v. *Francis*, October 1, 1985, Slough County Ct., P. S. J. Langan Q.C.; *Church Comrs. for England* v. *Nodjoumi* (1985) 135 New L.J. 1185, Hirst J.
s. 172, repealed: 1985, c.65, sch. 10.
ss. 193, 194, amended: 1985, c.51, sch. 8.

21. Land Registration Act 1925.
s. 42, amended: 1985, c.65, sch. 8.
ss. 61, 62, amended: *ibid.*; repealed in pt.: *ibid.*, sch. 10.
s. 70, see *Celsteel* v. *Alton House Holdings* [1985] 1 W.L.R. 204, Scott J.; *Kling* v. *Keston Properties* (1985) 49 P. & C.R. 212, Vinelott J.; *Paddington Building Society* v. *Mendelsohn* (1985) 50 P. & C.R. 244, C.A.
s. 82, see *Argyle Building Society* v. *Hammond* (1985) 49 P. & C.R. 148, C.A.
s. 100, repealed in pt.: 1985, c.51, sch. 17.
s. 110, see *Walia* v. *Naughton (Michael)* [1985] 1 W.L.R. 1115, Judge John Finaly Q.C.
s. 112, amended: 1985, c.65, sch. 8.
s. 112A, amended: *ibid.*; repealed in pt.: *ibid.*, sch. 10.
s. 120, order 85/1999.
ss. 144, 145, order 85/359.

23. Adminstration of Estates Act 1925.
s. 34, sch. 1, repealed in pt.: 1985, c.65, sch. 10.

38. Performing Animals (Regulation) Act 1925.
s. 5, amended: 1985, c.51, sch. 8.

45. Guardianship of Infants Act 1925.
s. 3, amended (S.): 1985, c.37, sch. 1; repealed in pt. (S.): *ibid.*, sch. 2.
ss. 5 (in pt.), 8, repealed (S.): *ibid.*

CAP.
15 & 16 Geo. 5 (1924–25)—cont.

49. Supreme Court of Judicature (Consolidation) Act 1925.
s. 45, see *House of Spring Gardens* v. *Waite* [1985] F.S.R. 173, C.A.
s. 51, see *Rohrberg* v. *Charkin, The Times*, January 30, 1985, C.A.

73. National Library of Scotland Act 1925.
s. 2, amended: 1985, c.16, s.18; repealed in pt.: *ibid.*, s.18, sch. 2.
s. 2A, added: *ibid.*, s.18.
s. 10, repealed: *ibid.*, sch. 2.
sch., amended: *ibid.*, s.18.

16 & 17 Geo. 5 (1926)

7. Bankruptcy (Amendment) Act 1926.
repealed: 1985, c.65, sch. 10.

26. Chartered Associations (Protection of Names and Uniforms) Act 1926.
s. 1, order 85/611.

51. Electricity (Supply) Act 1926.
s. 35, amended: 1985, c.51, sch. 4.

59. Coroners (Amendment) Act 1926.
s. 13, see *R.* v. *West Yorkshire Coroner, ex p. National Union of Mineworkers (Yorkshire Area), The Times*, October 22, 1985, D.C.
ss. 26, 27, rules 85/1414.

60. Legitimacy Act 1926.
s. 10, see *Dunbar of Kilconzie, Petr.*, 1985 S.L.T.(Lyon Ct.) 6; 1985 S.L.T. 158.

17 & 18 Geo. 5 (1927)

10. Finance Act 1927.
s. 56, repealed: 1985, c.54, sch. 27.

35. Sheriff Courts and Legal Officers (Scotland) Act 1927.
s. 1, amended: 1985, c.73, s. 47.

36. Landlord and Tenant Act 1927.
s. 23, see *Italica Holdings SA* v. *Bayadea* (1985) 273 E.G. 888, French J.

18 & 19 Geo. 5 (1928)

32. Petroleum (Consolidation) Act 1928.
s. 2, amended: 1985, c.51, sch. 11.
s. 20, amended: 1985, c.72, sch. 12.

43. Agricultural Credits Act 1928.
s. 5, repealed in pt.: 1985, c.58, sch. 4.
s. 7, amended: 1985, c.65, sch. 8.
s. 8, repealed in pt.: *ibid.*, sch. 10.
s. 9, order 85/372.

44. Rating and Valuation (Apportionment) Act 1928.
s. 5, see *B.P. Oil Grangemouth Refinery* v. *Assessor for Lothian Region*, 1985 S.L.T. 228.

19 & 20 Geo. 5 (1929)

13. Agricultural Credits (Scotland) Act 1929.
s. 9, repealed in pt.: 1985, c.58, sch. 4.

29. Government Annuities Act 1929.
s. 22, repealed in pt.: 1985, c.54, sch. 27.
s. 51, repealed in pt.: 1985, c.58, sch. 4.
s. 58, repealed in pt.: 1985, c.54, sch. 27.

CAP.

20 & 21 Geo. 5 (1929–30)

25. Third Party (Rights against Insurers) Act 1930.
see *Pioneer Concrete (U.K.)* v. *National Employers Mutual General Insurance Association* [1985] 2 All E.R. 395; [1985] 1 Lloyd's Rep. 274, Bingham J.; *Aluminium Wire and Cable Co.* v. *Allstate Insurance Co.* [1985] 2 Lloyd's Rep. 280, N. Collier Q.C. (sitting as deputy judge).
s. 1, amended: 1985, c.65, sch. 8, c.66, sch. 7(S.).
ss. 2, 3, amended: 1985, c.65, sch. 8.
s. 4, amended (S.): 1985, c.66, sch. 7; repealed in pt. (S.): *ibid.*, schs. 7, 8.

33. Illegitimate Children (Scotland) Act 1930.
ss. 1, 2 (in pt.), 3, 5, repealed: 1985, c.37, sch. 2.

43. Road Traffic Act 1930.
s. 101, repealed in pt.: 1985, c.67, schs. 7, 8.
s. 121, repealed in pt.: 1985, c.51, sch. 7; c.67, sch. 8.

21 & 22 Geo. 5 (1930–31)

28. Finance Act 1931.
s. 35, repealed in pt.: 1985, c.54, s.89, sch. 27.

22 & 23 Geo. 5 (1931–32)

47. Children and Young Persons (Scotland) Act 1932.
s. 73, repealed in pt.: 1985, c.37, sch. 2.
51. Sunday Entertainments Act 1932.
ss. 1, 4 (in pt.), 5 (in pt.), repealed: 1985, c.13, sch. 3.

23 & 24 Geo. 5 (1932–33)

12. Children and Young Persons Act 1933.
s. 1, see *R.* v. *Gibson; R.* v. *Gibson* (1985) 80 Cr.App.R. 24, C.A.
s. 12, amended: 1985, c.13, sch. 2; c.51, sch.8; repealed in pt.: 1985, c.13, sch. 3.
ss. 50, 53, see *R.* v. *F. (A Child), The Times*, March 20, 1985, C.A.; *R.* v. *F (A Child), The Times*, April 20, 1985, C.A.
s. 53, see *R.* v. *Nightingale* (1984) 6 Cr.App.R.(S.) 65, C.A.; *R.* v. *Storey (Stephen)* (1984) 6 Cr.App.R.(S.) 104, C.A.; *R.* v. *Butler (M.P.)* (1984) 6 Cr.App.R.(S) 236, C.A.
sch. 2, amended: order 85/1383; 1985, c.61, s. 61.

36. Administration of Justice (Miscellaneous Provisions) Act 1933.
s. 2, repealed in pt.: 1985, c.23, sch. 2.
41. Administration of Justice (Scotland) Act 1933.
s. 4, Act of Sederunt 85/317.
s. 16, Acts of Sederunt 85/227, 500, 555, 760, 1178, 1426, 1600.
s. 16, amended: 1985, c.73, sch. 2.

CAP.

24 & 25 Geo. 5 (1933–34)

41. Law Reform (Miscellaneous Provisions) Act 1934.
see *Wilson* v. *Stag, The Times*, November 27, 1985, C.A.

25 & 26 Geo. 5 (1935)

30. Law Reform (Married Women and Tortfeasors) Act 1935.
s. 6, see *Southern Water Authority* v. *Lewis and Duvivier (No. 2)* (1984–85) 1 Const.L.J. 74, H.H. Judge Smout, Q.C., O.R.; *Harper* v. *Gray & Walker* [1985] 2 All E.R. 507, Judge John Newey, Q.C.
40. Housing Act 1935.
repealed: 1985, c.71, sch. 1.

26 Geo. 5 & 1 Edw. 8 (1935–36)

49. Public Health Act 1936.
see *Perry* v. *Tendring District Council; Thurbon* v. *Same* [1985] C.I.L.L. 145, H.H. Judge John Newey, Q.C., O.R.; *Greater London Council* v. *Tower Hamlets, London Borough of* (1983) 15 H.L.R. 57, D.C.
s. 21, amended: 1985, c.51, sch. 4.
s. 32, repealed in pt.: *ibid.*, sch. 17.
s. 66, see *R.* v. *West Devon Borough Council, ex p. North East Essex Building Co.* [1985] J.P.L. 391, Mann J.
ss. 72, 73, see *Craven District Council* v. *Brewer Properties, The Times*, May 7, 1985, Kennedy J.
s. 87, repealed in pt.: 1985, c.51, sch. 17.
s. 92, see *Wivenhoe Port* v. *Colchester Borough Council* [1985] J.P.L. 175, Chelmsford Crown Court.
ss. 93, 94, 99, 289, see *Warner* v. *Lambeth, London Borough of* (1984) 15 H.L.R. 42, D.C.
s. 226, amended: 1985, c.13, sch. 2.
Pt. IX (ss.235–248), repealed: 1985, c.71, sch. 1.
52. Private Legislation Procedure (Scotland) Act 1936.
s. 5, amended: 1985, c.73, s.57.

1 Edw. 8 & 1 Geo. 6 (1936–37)

6. Public Order Act 1936.
s. 5, see *Nicholson* v. *Gage* (1985) 80 Cr.App.R. 40, D.C.; *Joyce* v. *Hertfordshire Constabulary* (1985) 80 Cr.App.R. 298, D.C.
37. Children and Young Persons (Scotland) Act 1937.
s. 23, repealed in pt.: 1985, c.13, sch. 3.
43. Public Records (Scotland) Act 1937.
s. 7, amended and repealed in pt.: 1985, c.16, s.19.
s. 10, Act of Sederunt 85/1815.
s. 11A, added: 1985, c.16, s.19.
s. 12, amended: *ibid.*

CAP.

1 & 2 Geo. 6 (1937–38)

22. Trade Marks Act 1938.
ss. 4, 8, see *Parker Knoll* v. *Knoll Overseas* [1985] F.S.R. 349, Whitford J.
ss. 9, 17, see *Coca Cola Trade Marks* [1985] F.S.R. 315, C.A.
s. 40, rules 85/921, 1099.
s. 41, rules 85/921.
s. 68, see *Coca Cola Trade Marks* [1985] F.S.R. 315, C.A.

2 & 3 Geo. 6 (1938–39)

4. Custody of Children (Scotland) Act 1939.
s. 1, repealed in pt.: 1985, c.37, sch. 2.
21. Limitation Act 1939.
s. 2A, see *Farmer* v. *National Coal Board, The Times,* April 27, 1985, C.A.
s. 26, see *Waldron (A Bankrupt), Re, ex p. The Bankrupt* v. *The Official Receiver, The Times,* February 12, 1985, C.A.
44. House to House Collections Act 1939.
ss. 1, 11, see *Murphy* v. *Duke* [1985] 2 W.L.R. 773, Forbes J.
69. Import, Export and Customs Powers (Defence) Act 1939.
s. 1, orders 85/34, 148, 849, 1085, 1293, 1294.
82. Personal Injuries (Emergency Provisions) Act 1939.
ss. 1, 2, scheme 85/1313.

5 & 6 Geo. 6 (1941–42)

21. Finance Act 1942.
s. 44, repealed: 1985, c.54, sch. 27.
s. 47, regs. 85/1146.

6 & 7 Geo. 6 (1942–43)

39. Pensions Appeal Tribunals Act 1943.
sch., amended: 1985, c.61, s.59.

7 & 8 Geo. 6 (1943–44)

31. Education Act 1944.
s. 39, see *Jarman* v. *Mid-Glamorgan Education Authority, The Times,* February 11, 1985, D.C.; *Rogers* v. *Essex County Council* [1985] 2 All E.R. 39, C.A.
ss. 71, 76, see *R.* v. *Secretary of State for Education and Science, ex p. Talmud Torah Machzikei Hadass School Trust, The Times,* April 12, 1985, D.C.
s. 81, see *R.* v. *Hampshire County Council, The Times,* December 5, 1985, Taylor J.
s. 100, regs. 85/684.
sch. 1, see *R.* v. *Brent London Borough Council, ex p. Gunning, The Times,* April 30, 1985, Hodgson J.

8 & 9 Geo. 6 (1944–45)

28. Law Reform (Contributory Negligence) Act 1945.
s. 1, see *A.B. Marintrans* v. *Comet Shipping Co., The Times,* March 19, 1985,

CAP.

8 & 9 Geo. 6 (1944–45)—cont.

28. Law Reform (Contributory Negligence) Act 1945—cont.
Neill J.; *James* v. *I.M.I. (Kynoch)* [1985] I.C.R. 155, C.A.; *Lancashire Textiles (Jersey)* v. *Thomson Shepherd & Co. (O.H.),* November 29, 1984.
s. 4, see *A.B. Marintrans* v. *Comet Shipping Co., The Times,* March 19, 1985, Neill J.
42. Water Act 1945.
s. 23, orders 84/2050, 2051; 85/72, 73, 88, 93, 96, 121, 231, 240, 513, 709, 716, 815, 819, 990, 1668, 1706, 1725.
s. 32, orders 85/60, 81, 121, 266, 513, 709, 716, 990, 1677.
s. 33, orders 85/74, 240, 513, 716, 1677.
s. 50, orders 85/60, 81, 96, 240, 266, 716, 990, 1677.
sch. 1, amended: 1985, c.51, sch. 8.

9 & 10 Geo. 6 (1945–46)

7. British Settlements Act 1945.
orders 85/444, 449.
22. Dock Workers (Regulation of Employment) Act 1946.
s. 1, see *Gibbons* v. *Associated British Ports* [1985] I.R.L.R. 376, Tudor Price J.
35. Building Restrictions (War Time Contraventions) Act 1946.
ss. 3, 4, see *R.* v. *Secretary of State for the Environment, ex p. Bulk Storage* [1985] J.P.L. 35, McCullough J.
58. Borrowing (Control and Guarantees) Act 1946.
ss. 1, 3, order 85/1150.
64. Finance Act 1946.
s. 57, see *Arbuthnot Financial Services* v. *I.R.C.* [1985] S.T.C. 211, Walton J.
s. 57, repealed in pt.: 1985, c.54, sch. 27.
s. 66, repealed in pt.: 1985, c.64, sch. 4.
73. Hill Farming Act 1946.
s. 20, amended: 1985, c.32, s.1.
s. 28, amended (S.): 1985, c.73, s.32.

10 & 11 Geo. 6 (1946–47)

14. Exchange Control Act 1947.
sch. 4, amended: 1985, c.65, sch. 8; c.66, sch. 7(S.); repealed in pt.: 1985, c.65, sch. 10.
41. Fire Services Act 1947.
s. 4, amended: 1985, c.51, sch. 11.
s. 8, amended: 1985, c.43, sch. 2.
s. 17, regs. 85/930.
s. 18, regs. 85/1176.
s. 26, order 85/318.
ss. 30, 31, see *R.* v. *Eastbourne Justices, ex p. Kisten, The Times,* December 22, 1984, D.C.
44. Crown Proceedings Act 1947.
s. 10, see *Smith* v. *Ministry of Defence,* January 25, 1985, Woolf J.; *Bell* v. *Secretary of State for Defence, The Times,* June 29, 1985, C.A.

CAP.
10 & 11 Geo. 6 (1946–47)—cont.
44. Crown Proceedings Act 1947—*cont.*
  s. 40, see *R. v. Secretary of State for Foreign and Commonwealth Affairs, ex p. Trawnick, The Times,* April 18, 1985, D.C.; *Trawnick* v. *Lennox (Gordon)* [1985] 2 All E.R. 368, C.A.
  s. 46, amended (S.): 1985, c.73, s.49; repealed in pt. (S.): *ibid.,* sch. 4.
47. Companies Act 1947.
  s. 91, repealed: 1985, c.65, sch. 10; c.66, sch. 8 (S.).
  ss. 92, 99, repealed: 1985, c.65, sch. 10.
  s. 115, repealed (S.): *ibid.,* c.66, sch. 8.
  ss. 121, 123, repealed: 1985, c.65, sch. 10.
48. Agriculture Act 1947.
  s. 109, see *Jones* v. *Metropolitan Borough of Stockport* (1985) 50 P. & C.R. 299, C.A.

11 & 12 Geo. 6 (1947–48)
29. National Assistance Act 1948.
  ss. 21, 24, see *R.* v. *Waltham Forest London Borough Council, ex p. Vale, The Times,* February 25, 1985, Taylor J.
  s. 22, reg. 85/1317, 1530(S.).
  s. 26, regs. 85/1530 (S.).
37. Radioactive Substances Act 1948.
  s. 5, regs. 85/1729.
38. Companies Act 1948.
  repealed: 1985, c.9, sch. 1.
  s. 12, see *South India Shipping Corp.* v. *Bank of Korea* [1985] 1 W.L.R. 585, C.A.
  s. 54, see *Charterhouse Investment Trust* v. *Tempest Diesels, Financial Times,* June 28, 1985, Hoffmann J.
  ss. 66, 68 see *Jupiter House Investments (Cambridge), Re,* [1985] 1 W.L.R. 975, Harman J.; *Grosvenor Press, Re* [1985] 1 W.L.R. 980, Nourse J.
  s. 95, see *Clough Mill* v. *Martin* [1984] 3 All E.R. 982, C.A.; *Welsh Irish Ferries, Re* [1985] 3 W.L.R. 610, Nourse J.; *Oriel, Re* [1985] 3 All E.R. 216, C.A.
  ss. 95, 96, see *Foster, Re; Foster* v. *Crusts* (1985) 129 S.J. 333, Judge Finlay Q.C. sitting as a High Court Judge.
  s. 98, see *R.* v. *Registrar of Companies, ex p. Esal (Commodities) (in liquidation), The Times,* November 26, 1984, Mervyn Davies J.
  s. 106, see *Oriel, Re* [1985] 3 All E.R. 216, C.A.
  s. 108, see *Wilkes (John) (Footwear)* v. *Lee International (Footwear), The Times,* July 20, 1985, C.A.
  s. 174, see *Westminster Property Group, Re* [1985] 1 W.L.R. 676, C.A.
  s. 188, see *R.* v. *Corbin* (1984) 6 Cr.App.R.(S.) 17, C.A.; *R.* v. *Austin* (1985) 82 L.S. Gaz. 2499, C.A.
  s. 207, see *Minster Assets, Re* [1985] P.C.C. 105, Harman J.
  s. 210, see *London School of Electronics, Re* [1985] 3 W.L.R. 474, Nourse J.
  s. 218, repealed in pt.: 1984, c.9, s.28.

CAP.
11 & 12 Geo. 6 (1947–48)—cont.
38. Companies Act 1948—*cont.*
  s. 222, see *Teague, Petr.* (O.H.), May 15, 1984.
  ss. 231, 319, see *Memco Engineering, Re* [1985] 3 All E.R. 267, Mervyn Davies, J.
  s. 322, see *Mace Builders (Glasgow)* v. *Lunn* [1985] 3 W.L.R. 456, Ch.D., Scott, J.
  s. 323, see *Potters Oils, Re* [1985] P.C.C. 148, Harman J.
  s. 327, see *Manley, Petr.* (O.H.), 1985 S.L.T. 42.
  s. 332, see *Rossleigh* v. *Carlaw* (O.H.) January 11, 1985; *Augustus Barnett & Son, Re, The Times,* December 7, 1985, Hoffman J.
  ss. 357–359, repealed: 1984, c.9, s.28.
  s. 365, order 85/574; rules 85/95.
  ss. 382, 384, 385, 394, repealed in pt.: 1984, c.9, s.28.
  ss. 398, 399, see *Nourse Self Build Association, Re* (1985) 82 L.S. Gaz. 1709, Harman J.
  ss. 424 (in pt.), 434 (in pt.), 450, repealed: 1985, c.9, s.28.
  s. 454, regs. 84/1859, 1860; 85/805.
  s. 455, repealed in pt.: 1984, c.9, s.28.
39. Industrial Assurance and Friendly Societies Act 1948.
  s. 2, repealed in pt.: 1985, c.65, sch. 10; c.66, sch. 8(S.).
44. Merchant Shipping Act 1948.
  s. 5, regs. 85/1607.
45. Agriculture (Scotland) Act 1948.
  sch. 6, see *Luss Estates Co.* v. *Firkin Farm Co.,* 1984, S.L.C.R. 1.
56. British Nationality Act 1948.
  s. 7, see *Gowa* v. *Att.-Gen.* [1985] 1 W.L.R. 1003, H.L.
59. Laying of Documents before Parliament (Interpretation) Act 1948.
  s. 1, see *R.* v. *Secretary of State for the Environment, ex p. Leicester City Council* (1985) 25 R.V.R. 31, Woolf J.
63. Agricultural Holdings Act 1948.
  s. 2, see *Lampard* v. *Barker* (1984) 272 E.G. 783, C.A.; *Collier* v. *Hollinshead* (1984) 272 E.G. 941, Scott J.
  ss. 58, 70, 92, see *Lady Hallinan* v. *Jones & Jones,* November 13, 1984, Mr. Assistant Recorder Langdon Davies, Aberystwyth County Ct.
  s. 68, amended: 1985, c.65, sch. 8; repealed in pt.: *ibid.,* sch. 10.
  s. 77, order 85/1829.
64. National Service Act 1948.
  repealed: 1985, c.17, sch. 5.

12, 13 & 14 Geo. 6 (1948–49)
10. Administraton of Justice (Scotland) Act 1948.
  s. 2, Acts of Sederunt 80/1928; 83/119; 84/61; 85/317.
42. Lands Tribunal Act 1949.
  s. 3, rules 85/581(S.).

CAP.

12, 13 & 14 Geo. 6 (1948–49)—cont.

43. Merchant Shipping (Safety Convention) Act 1949.
s. 33, regs. 85/936, 1607.
s. 36, amended: regs. 85/212.

47. Finance Act 1949.
sch. 8, repealed in pt.: 1985, c.54, sch. 27.

54. Wireless Telegraphy Act 1949.
s. 2, regs. 85/490.
s. 10, regs. 85/807, 808.

60. Housing Act 1949.
ss. 40, 50, repealed: 1985, c.71, sch. 6.

63. Legal Aid and Solicitors (Scotland) Act 1949.
s. 25, repealed: 1985, c.73, schs. 1, 4.

66. House of Commons (Redistribution of Seats) Act 1949.
s. 3, order 85/1776.

74. Coast Protection Act 1949.
ss. 2, 5, 8, sch. 2, repealed in pt.: order 85/442.

75. Agricultural Holdings (Scotland) Act 1949.
s. 20, see *Coats* v. *Logan* (O.H.), 1985 S.L.T. 221.
s. 21, see *Morrison-Low* v. *Paterson* (H.L.), 1985 S.L.T. 255; *Coats* v. *Logan* (O.H.), 1985 S.L.T. 221.
ss. 25, 26, see *McRobbie* v. *Halley,* 1984 S.L.C.R. 10.
s. 26, see *Peace* v. *Peace,* 1984 S.L.T. (Land Ct.) 6.
s. 28, see *Luss Estates Co.* v. *Firkin Farm Co.,* 1984 S.L.C.R. 1.
s. 75, see *Aberdeen Endowments Trust* v. *Will,* 1985 S.L.T.(Land Ct.) 23; *Earl of Seafield* v. *Stewart,* 1985 S.L.T.(Land Ct.) 35.
sch. 6, see *Earl of Seafield* v. *Stewart,* 1985 S.L.T.(Land Ct.) 35.

87. Patents Act 1949.
s. 13, see *Sevcon* v. *Lucas Cav* [1985] F.S.R. 545, C.A.
s. 31, see *Dow Chemical Co.* v. *Ishihara Sangyo K.K.* [1985] F.S.R. 4, Whitford J.
s. 32, see *Reckitt & Colman Products* v. *Biorex Laboratories* [1985] F.S.R. 94, Falconer J.
s. 35, see *R.* v. *Comptroller-General of Patents, Designs and Trade-Marks, ex p. Gist-Brocades N.V., The Times,* August 5, 1985, H.L.
s. 51, see *Monsanto* v. *Stauffer Chemical Co.* [1985] F.S.R. 55, Falconer J.
s. 66, see *Reckitt & Colman Products* v. *Biorex Laboratories* [1985] F.S.R. 94, Falconer J.

88. Registered Designs Act 1949.
ss. 1, 3, 5, 8, 11, rules 84/1989.
s. 13, orders 85/173, 456, 457.
ss. 17–23, 31, 32, rules 84/1989.
s. 36, rules 84/1989; 85/1099.
s. 39, rules 84/1989.
s. 40, rules 84/1989; 85/784.

94. Criminal Justice (Scotland) Act 1949.
s. 2, see *McPherson* v. *Henderson,* 1984 S.C.C.R. 294.

CAP.

14 Geo. 6 (1950)

12. Foreign Compensation Act 1950.
s. 4, instrument 85/697.
s. 7, order 85/168.

27. Arbitration Act 1950.
s. 3, amended: 1985, c.65, sch. 8.
s. 4, see *Turner & Goudy (A Firm)* v. *McConnell* [1985] 2 All E.R. 34, C.A.
s. 10, amended: 1985, c.61, s.58.
s. 17, see *Mutual Shipping Corp. of New York* v. *Bayshore Shipping Co. of Monrovia; Montan, The* [1985] 1 All E.R. 520, C.A.
s. 22, see *Mutual Shipping Corp. of New York* v. *Bayshore Shipping Co. of Monrovia, Montan, The* [1985] 1 All E.R. 520, C.A.; *Shield Properties & Investments* v. *Anglo-Overseas Transport Co.* (1985) 273 E.G. 69, Bingham J.; *Learmonth Property Investment Co.* v. *Hinton (Amos) & Sons* (1985) 274 E.G. 725, Walton J.
s. 23, see *Top Shop Estates* v. *C. Danino; Same* v. *Tandy Corp.* (1985) 273 E.G. 197, Leggatt J.; *Shield Properties Investments* v. *Anglo-Overseas Transport Co.* (1985) 273 E.G. 69, Bingham J.; *Cook International Inc.* v. *B.V. Handelmaat Schappij Jean Devaux, The Times,* April 10, 1985, Leggatt J.; *Agromet Motoimport* v. *Maulden Engineering Co. (Beds.)* [1985] 2 All E.R. 436, Otton J.; *Tracomin S.A.* v. *Gibbs Nathaniel (Canada) and Bridge (George Jacob)* [1985] 1 Lloyd's Rep. 586, Staughton J.; *Zermat Holdings S.A.* v. *Nu-Life Upholstery Repairs* (1985) 275 E.G. 1134, Bingham J.
s. 27, see *Casillo Grani* v. *Napier Shipping Co.* [1984] 2 Lloyd's Rep. 481, Neill J.; *Tote Bookmakers* v. *Development and Property Holding Co.* [1985] 2 W.L.R. 603, Peter Gibson J.; *Davies (Graham) (U.K.)* v. *Rich (Marc) & Co., The Times,* August 5, 1985, C.A.
s. 32, see *Excomm* v. *Ahmed Abdul-Qawi Bamaodah; the St. Raphael* [1985] 1 Lloyd's Rep. 403, C.A.

28. Shops Act 1950.
s. 22, amended: 1985, c.13, sch. 2; order 85/39.
s. 47, see *Lewis* v. *Rogers; Gardner* v. *Duffell* (1984) 82 L.G.R. 670, D.C.
ss. 49, 57, see *York City Council* v. *The Little Gallery, The Times,* December 2, 1985, D.C.
s. 71, see *R.* v. *North West Leicestershire District Council, ex p. Dakin* [1985] Crim.L.R. 390, D.C.
s. 74, see *Lewis* v. *Rogers; Gardner* v. *Duffell* (1984) 82 L.G.R. 670, D.C.
s. 74, amended: 1985, c.13, sch. 2.
sch. 5, amended: order 85/39.

37. Maintenance Orders Act 1950.
ss. 6, 7, repealed in pt. (S.): 1985, c.37, sch. 2.
s. 16, amended: *ibid.,* sch. 1.
s. 16, amended (S.): *ibid.*

CAP.

14 Geo. 6 (1950)—cont.

39. Public Utilities Street Works Act 1950.
s. 26, see *Yorkshire Electricity Board* v. *British Telecommunications, Financial Times*, May 24, 1985, C.A.

14 & 15 Geo. 6 (1950–51)

10. Reinstatement in Civil Employment Act 1950.
repealed: 1985, c.17, sch. 5.

26. Salmon and Freshwater Fisheries (Protection) (Scotland) Act 1951.
s. 7, see *Corbett* v. *MacNaughton*, 1985 S.L.T. 312.

60. Mineral Workings Act 1951.
repealed (exc. ss.28, 32, 40 (in pt.)–42 (in pt.), 43): 1985, c.12, s.1, sch. 2.
s. 41, amended: *ibid.*, s.6.

65. Reserve and Auxiliary Forces (Protection of Civil Interests) Act 1951.
sch. 1, amended: 1985, c.17, sch. 4.

15 & 16 Geo. 6 & 1 Eliz. 2 (1951–52)

10. Income Tax Act 1952.
s. 510, see *Scorer* v. *Olin Energy Systems, The Times*, March 29, 1985, H.L.

33. Finance Act 1952.
s. 30, repealed in pt.: 1985, c.9, sch. 1; c.65, sch. 10; c.66, sch. 8(S.).

39. Motor Vehicles (International Circulation) Act 1952.
s. 1, order 85/459.

41. Affiliation Orders Act 1952.
repealed (S.): 1985, c.37, sch. 2.

47. Rating and Valuation (Scotland) Act 1952.
ss. 3, 5, order 85/62.
s. 6, Act of Sederunt 85/499.

52. Prison Act 1952.
s. 13, see *R.* v. *Moss; R.* v. *Hartle, The Times*, June 20, 1985, C.A.
s. 39, see *Nicoll* v. *Catron, The Times*, January 25, 1985; [1985] Crim.L.R. 223, D.C.; *R.* v. *Moss; R.* v. *Hartle, The Times*, June 20, 1985, D.C.
s. 42, see *R.* v. *Moss; R.* v. *Hartle, The Times*, June 20, 1985, C.A.
s. 47, see *R.* v. *Secretary of State for the Home Department, ex p. Broom* [1985] 3 W.L.R. 778, Kennedy J.

54. Town Development Act 1952.
ss. 4, 7, 10, amended: 1985, c.51, sch.8.

61. Prisons (Scotland) Act 1952.
s. 7, rules 84/2058.
s. 7, repealed in pt.: 1985, c.73, s.42, sch. 4.
ss. 16, 17, amended: *ibid.*, s.42.
s. 18, repealed in pt.: *ibid.*, sch. 4.
s. 34, amended: *ibid.*, s.42.
s. 35, rules 84/2058.
s. 35, repealed in pt.: 1985, c.73, s.42, sch. 4.

66. Defamation Act 1952.
s. 5, see *Pamplin* v. *Express Newspapers, The Times*, March 18, 1985, C.A.
sch., amended: 1985, c.43, sch. 2.

CAP.

15 & 16 Geo. 6 & 1 Eliz. 2 (1951–52)—cont.

67. Visiting Forces Act 1952.
s. 1, amended: 1985, c.3, sch.
sch., amended; 1985, c.38, s.3.

68. Cinematograph Act 1952.
repealed: 1985, c.13, sch. 3.

1 & 2 Eliz. 2 (1952–53)

14. Prevention of Crime Act 1953.
s. 1, see *O'Rourke* v. *Lockhart*, 1984 S.C.C.R. 322; *R.* v. *Russell (Raymond)* [1985] Crim.L.R. 231, C.A.

20. Births and Deaths Registration Act 1953.
ss. 1, 11, regs. 85/1133, 1134.
ss. 22, 39, regs. 85/568, 569, 1133, 1134.
s. 58, amended: 1985, c.56, s.11.

33. Education (Miscellaneous Provisions) Act 1953.
ss. 5–7, see *R.* v. *Hampshire County Council, The Times*, December 5, 1985, Taylor J.

37. Registration Service Act 1953.
s. 6, see *Miles* v. *Wakefield Metropolitan District Council* [1985] 1 All E.R. 905, C.A.

49. Historic Buildings and Ancient Monuments Act 1953.
ss. 5, 6, 8, amended (S.): 1985, c.16, s.21.

2 & 3 Eliz. 2 (1953–54)

14. National Museum of Antiquities of Scotland Act 1954.
repealed: 1985, c.16, sch. 2.

17. Royal Irish Constabulary (Widows' Pensions) Act 1954.
s. 1, regs. 85/1319.

56. Landlord and Tenant Act 1954.
s. 23, see *Simmonds* v. *Egyed*, February 12, 1985, Bloomsbury County Ct.; *Christina* v. *Seear* (1985) 275 E.G. 898, C.A.; *Linden* v. *Secretary of State for Social Services, The Times*, November 21, 1985, Scott J.
s. 24A, see *Halberstam* v. *Tandalco Corp. N.V.* (1985) 274 E.G. 393, C.A.
s. 25, see *Italica Holdings SA* v. *Bayadea* (1985) 273 E.G. 888, French J.; *Southport Old Links* v. *Naylor* (1985) 273 E.G. 767, C.A.; *Earthcare Cooperative* v. *Troveworth*, May 13, 1985; Durham County Ct.; *Hogg Bullimore & Co.* v. *Co-operative Insurance Society* (1985) 50 P. & C.R. 105, Whitford J.; *Trustees of National Deposit Friendly Society* v. *Beatties of London* (1985) 275 E.G. 55, Goulding J.
s. 29, see *Riley (E. J.) Investments* v. *Eurostile Holdings* [1985] 3 All E.R. 181, C.A.
s. 30, see *Botterill* v. *Bedfordshire County Council* (1985) 273 E.G. 1217, C.A.; *Europark (Midlands)* v. *Town Centre Securities* (1985) 274 E.G. 289, Warner J.; *Trustees of the National Deposit Friendly Society* v. *Beatties of London*

CAP.

2 & 3 Eliz. 2 (1953–54)—cont.

56. Landlord and Tenant Act 1954—*cont.*
(1985) 275 E.G. 55, Goulding J.; *Morar v. Chauhan* [1985] 3 All E.R. 493, C.A.
s. 33, see *CBS (U.K.) v. London Scottish Properties* (1985) 275 E.G. 718, H.H. Judge Micklem.
s. 34, see *Halberstam v. Tandalco Corp. N.V.* (1985) 274 E.G. 393, C.A.; *Brett v. Brett Essex Golf Club* (1985) 49 P. & C.R. 315, Judge John Finlay, Q.C.
s. 37, order 84/1932.
s. 41, see *Morar v. Chauhan* [1985] 3 All E.R. 493, C.A.
s. 42, amended: 1985, c.9, sch. 2.
s. 56, see *Linden v. Secretary of State for Social Services, The Times,* November 21, 1985, Scott J.
s. 57, amended: order 85/39.
s. 69, amended: 1985, c.51, sch. 14; order 85/1884.

57. Baking Industry (Hours of Work) Act 1954.
s. 11, repealed in pt.: 1985, c.9, sch. 2.

64. Transport Charges etc. (Miscellaneous Provisions) Act 1954.
s. 1, repealed: 1985, c.67, schs. 7, 8.
ss. 12, 13, repealed in pt.: *ibid.,* sch. 8.

65. National Gallery and Tate Gallery Act 1954.
sch. 1, amended and repealed in pt. (S.): 1985, c.16, sch. 2.

70. Mines and Quarries Act 1954.
s. 22, amended: regs. 85/2023.
ss. 108, 109, see *English v. Cory Sand & Ballast Company, The Times,* April 2, 1985, Stocker J.
s. 123, amended: regs. 85/2023.

3 & 4 Eliz. 2 (1954–55)

18. Army Act 1955.
continued in force: order 85/1196.
s. 71AA, amended (S.): 1985, c.73, s.46.
s. 225, amended: 1985, c.3, sch.
sch. 5A, amended (S.): 1985, c.73, s.46.

19. Air Force Act 1955.
continued in force: order 85/1196.
s. 13, see *R. v. Garth* [1985] 2 W.L.R. 569, C.A.
s. 71AA, amended (S.): 1985, c.73, s.46.
s. 223, amended: 1985, c.3, sch.
sch. 5A, amended (S.): 1985, c.73, s.46.

21. Crofters (Scotland) Act 1955.
s. 3, see *Representatives of the Late Hugh Matheson v. Master of Lovat,* 1984 S.L.C.R. 82; *MacLaren v. MacLaren,* 1984 S.L.C.R. 43.
s. 12, see *Secretary of State for Scotland v. Sutherland,* 1984 S.L.C.R. 53.
s. 12, amended: 1985, c.73, s.30.
ss. 16, 16A, see *Steven v. Crofters Commission,* 1984 S.L.C.R. 30.
s. 22, amended: 1985, c.73, s.31.
sch. 2, see *MacLaren v. MacLaren,* 1984 S.L.C.R. 43.

26. Public Service Vehicles (Travel Concessions) Act 1955.
repealed: 1985, c.67, sch. 8.

CAP.

4 & 5 Eliz. 2 (1955–56)

16. Food and Drugs Act 1955.
s. 2, see *R. v. Uxbridge JJ., ex p. Gow, The Times,* October 17, 1985, D.C.; *Shearer v. Rowe* (1985) 4 Tr.L. 206, D.C.
Pt. III (ss.49–61), see *Halton Borough Council v. Cawley* [1985] 1 W.L.R. 15, Blackett-Ord V.C.
s. 108, see *R. v. Harvey, ex p. Select Livestock Producers* [1985] Crim.L.R. 510, D.C.; *R. v. Uxbridge JJ., ex p. Gow, The Times,* October 17, 1985, D.C.
s. 113, see *R. v. Uxbridge JJ., ex p. Gow, The Times,* October 17, 1985, D.C.

20. Agriculture (Improvement of Roads) Act 1955.
ss. 1, 3, amended: 1985, c.51, sch. 4.

30. Food and Drugs (Scotland) Act 1956.
s. 4, regs. 85/1438.
ss. 4, 7, regs. 85/1068, 1222.
s. 13, regs. 84/1885; 85/913, 1068, 1222.
s. 16, regs. 85/1068.
s. 26, regs. 85/913.
s. 40, repealed in pt.: 1985, c.73, s.41.
s. 56, regs. 84/1885; 85/913, 1068, 1222, 1438.
s. 60, regs. 85/1068.

46. Administration of Justice Act 1956.
s. 1, see *Gatoil International v. Arkwright–Boston Manufacturers Mutual Insurance Co.* [1985] 2 W.L.R. 74, H.L.
s. 36, repealed in pt.: 1965, c.65, sch. 10.
s. 40, amended: *ibid.,* sch. 8; repealed in pt.: *ibid.,* schs. 8, 10.
s. 47, see *Gatoil International v. Arkwright–Boston Manufacturers Mutual Insurance Co.* [1985] 2 W.L.R. 74, H.L.; *William Batey & Co (Exports) v. Kent* (O.H.), June 11, 1985.

52. Clean Air Act 1956.
s. 11, orders 85/315 (S.), 864.
ss. 33, 34, regs. 85/1812.

60. Valuation and Rating (Scotland) Act 1956.
ss. 13, 42, order 85/62.

69. Sexual Offences Act 1956.
s. 22, see *R. v. Morris-Lowe* [1985] 1 W.L.R. 29, C.A.
s. 30, see *R. v. Grant* [1985] Crim.L.R. 387, C.A.
s. 31, see *R. v. Hanton, The Times,* February 14, 1985, C.A.
sch. 2, amended: 1984, c.44, s.3.

74. Copyright Act 1956.
s. 1, see *Infabrics v. Jaytex* [1985] F.S.R. 75, Jeffs Q.C.; *Evans (C.) & Sons v. Spritebrand* [1985] 1 W.L.R. 317, C.A.; *Barson Computers (N.Z.) v. Gilbert (John) & Co.* [1985] F.S.R. 489, New Zealand H.C.
s. 2, see *Express Newspapers v. Liverpool Daily Post and Echo* [1985] F.S.R. 306; [1985] 1 W.L.R. 1089, Whitford J.
s. 3, see *Smith v. Greenfield* [1984] 6 N.I.J.B., Murray J.; *Geographia v. Penguin Books* [1985] F.S.R. 208, Whitford J.

CAP.
4 & 5 Eliz. 2 (1955–56)—cont.
74. Copyright Act 1956—*cont.*
s. 5, see *Infabrics* v. *Jaytex* [1985] F.S.R. 75, Jeffs Q.C.
s. 9, see *Merlet* v. *Mothercare, The Times*, November 6, 1985, C.A.
s. 10, see *Smith* v. *Greenfield* [1984] 6 N.I.J.B., Murray J.
s. 11, see *Wiseman* v. *Wiedenfeld & Nicolson and Donaldson* [1985] F.S.R. 525, Whitford J.
s. 13, amended: 1985, c.21, s.7; repealed in pt.: *ibid.*, s.7, sch. 2.
s. 16, see *Barson Computers (N.Z.)* v. *Gilbert (John) & Co.* [1985] F.S.R. 489, New Zealand H.C.
s. 17, see *Goswami* v. *Hammons* (1985) 129 S.J. 653, C.A.
ss. 17, 18, see *Infabrics* v. *Jaytex* [1985] F.S.R. 75, Jeffs Q.C.
s. 18, see *Staver Co.* v. *Digitext Display* [1984] F.S.R. 512, Scott J.
s. 31, orders 84/1987; 85/1985–1988.
s. 32, orders 84/1987; 85/1777.
s. 47, orders 84/1987; 85/1777, 1985–1988.
s. 48, see *Express Newspapers* v. *Liverpool Daily Post and Echo* [1985] 1 W.L.R. 1089, Whitford J.
s. 49, see *Smith* v. *Greenfield* [1984] 6 N.I.J.B., Murray J.; *Barson Computers (N.Z.)* v. *Gilbert (John) & Co.* [1985] F.S.R. 489, New Zealand H.C.

5 & 6 Eliz. 2 (1957)
11. Homicide Act 1957.
s. 2, see *R.* v. *Seers* (1984) 79 Cr.App.R. 261, C.A.
42. Parish Councils Act 1957.
s. 5, amended: 1985, c.51, sch. 4.
53. Naval Discipline Act 1957.
continued in force: order 85/1196.
s. 43AA, amended (S.): 1985, c.73, s.46.
s. 135, amended: 1985, c.3, sch.
sch. 4A, amended (S.): 1985, c.73, s.46.
55. Affiliation Proceedings Act 1957.
s. 2, see *Willett* v. *Wells* [1985] 1 W.L.R. 237, Hollings J.; *T.* v. *B., The Times*, November 30, 1985, D.C.
ss. 4, 5, see *R.* v. *Harrow Magistrates Court, ex p. Weiser* (1985) 15 Fam. Law 153, Webster J.
56. Housing Act 1957.
repealed: 1985, c.71, sch. 1.
s. 9, see *Pollway Nominees* v. *Croydon London Borough Council* [1985] 3 W.L.R. 564, C.A.; *Kenny* v. *Kingston-upon-Thames Royal London Borough Council* (1985) 274 E.G. 395, C.A.
ss. 16, 27, see *Barber* v. *Shah, The Times* August 2, 1985, Watkins L.J.
s. 27, see *Wrekin District Council* v. *Shah* (1985) 149 J.P. 703, D.C.
ss. 37, 39, see *Pollway Nominees* v. *Croydon London Borough Council* [1985] 3 W.L.R. 564, C.A.

CAP.
5 & 6 Eliz. 2 (1957)—cont.
56. Housing Act 1957—*cont.*
s. 93, repealed in part: 1985, c.51, sch. 17
s. 111, see *Parker* v. *Camden London Borough Council* [1985] 2 All E.R. 141, C.A.
s. 146, amended: 1985, c.51, sch. 8.
s. 166, repealed in pt.: *ibid.*, sch. 17.
s. 189, amended: *ibid.*, sch. 8.
57. Agriculture Act 1957.
s. 1, order 85/63.
ss. 5, 9, order 85/64.
s. 35, orders 85/63, 64.
59. Coal Mining (Subsidence) Act 1957.
s. 1, schs. 1, 2, amended: 1985, c.71, sch. 2.

6 & 7 Eliz. 2 (1957–58)
32. Opticians Act 1958.
s. 7, order 85/2024.
s. 15, order 85/1580.
s. 20A, order 85/856.
ss. 21, 30, see *Smith* v. *Mackeith*, 1985 S.C.C.R. 164.
s. 25, order 85/203.
s. 27, amended: 1985, c.9, sch. 2.
sch., order 85/664.
33. Disabled Persons (Employment) Act 1958.
s. 3, repealed in pt.: 1985, c.51, sch. 17.
39. Maintenance Orders Act 1958.
ss. 3, 4, see *Allen* v. *Allen* [1985] 2 W.L.R. 65, Booth J.
40. Matrimonial Proceedings (Children) Act 1958.
ss. 7, 9, repealed in pt.(S.): 1985, c.37, sch. 2.
s. 13, amended (S.): 1985, c.73, s.16.
42. Housing (Financial Provisions) Act 1958.
repealed: 1985, c.71, sch. 1.
44. Dramatic and Musical Performers' Protection Act 1958.
s. 2, see *Rickless* v. *United Artists Corp., The Times*, June 17, 1985, D.C.
45. Prevention of Fraud (Investments) Act 1958.
ss. 2, 12, 14, 16, 26, amended: 1985, c.9, sch. 2.
ss. 3, 21, regs. 85/974.
s. 4, repealed in pt.: 1985, c.65, sch. 10.
47. Agricultural Marketing Act 1958.
s. 2, sch. 1, order 85/312.
sch. 2, amended: 1985, c.9, sch. 2.
49. Trading Representations (Disabled Persons) Act 1958.
s. 1, see *Murphy* v. *Duke* [1985] 2 W.L.R. 773, Forbes J.
s. 1, repealed in pt.: 1985, c.51, sch. 17.
51. Public Records Act 1958.
sch. 1, amended: order 85/39.
69. Opencast Coal Act 1958.
ss. 35, 49, orders 84/1903; 85/187, 1130.
71. Agriculture Act 1958.
s. 10, sch. 1, repealed in pt.: 1985, c.12, sch. 2.

CAP.

7 & 8 Eliz. 2 (1958–59)

5. Adoption Act 1958.
s. 13, see *H. (A Minor) (Adoption), Re* (1985) 15 Fam. Law 133, C.A.
s. 29, see *Gatehouse* v. *R., The Times,* October 31, 1985, D.C.
ss. 29, 57, see *S (A Minor) (Adoption), Re* (1985) 15 Fam. Law 132, C.A.

22. County Courts Act 1959.
s. 191, see *Di Palma* v. *Victoria Square Property Co.* [1985] 2 All E.R. 676, C.A.

24. Building (Scotland) Act 1959.
s. 4, regs. 85/1272.
s. 13, sch. 6, see *Howard* v. *Hamilton District Council,* 1985 S.L.T.(Sh.Ct.) 42.

25. Highways Act 1959.
s. 44, see *Bartlett* v. *Department of Transport* (1984) 83 L.G.R. 579, Boreham J.; *McKenna* v. *Scottish Omnibuses and Northumberland County Council,* March 13, 1985, C.A.
s. 82, see *Russell* v. *Barnet London Borough Council* [1985] 83 L.G.R. 152, Tudor Evans J.

33. House Purchase and Housing Act 1959.
repealed: 1985, c.71, sch. 1.
s. 1, repealed (S.): *ibid.*

34. Housing (Underground Rooms) Act 1959.
repealed: 1985 c.71, sch. 1.

40. Deer (Scotland) Act 1959.
s. 23A, order 85/1168.

53. Town and Country Planning Act 1959.
s. 22, repealed in pt.: 1985, c.12, sch. 2.
s. 26, amended: 1985, c.71, sch. 2; repealed in pt.: *ibid.,* schs. 1, 2.
s. 58, sch. 7, repealed in pt.: *ibid.,* sch. 1.

54. Weeds Act 1959.
s. 5, amended: 1985, c.51, sch. 8.

66. Obscene Publications Act 1959.
s. 2, see *R.* v. *Bristol Crown Court, ex p. Willets, The Times,* January 25, 1985, D.C.; *R.* v. *Skirving*; *R.* v. *Grossman (Beth)* [1985] 2 W.L.R. 1001, C.A.
s. 2, amended: 1985, c.13, sch. 2.
s. 3, see *R.* v. *Croydon Metropolitan Stipendiary Magistrate, ex p. Richman, The Times,* March 8, 1985, D.C.; *R.* v. *Snaresbrook Crown Court, ex p. Comr. of Police for the Metropolis* (1984) 79 Cr.App.R. 184, D.C.

73. Legitimacy Act 1959.
s. 2, see *Dunbar of Kilconzie, Petr.,* 1985 S.L.T. 158.

8 & 9 Eliz. 2 (1959–60)

16. Road Traffic Act 1960.
s. 104, see *McPherson* v. *Henderson,* 1984 S.C.C.R. 294.

22. Horticulture Act 1960.
s. 14, amended: 1985, c.9, sch. 2.

30. Occupiers' Liability (Scotland) Act 1960.
s. 2, see *Johnstone* v. *Sweeney,* 1985 S.L.T. (Sh.Ct.) 2; *Johnstone* v. *City of Glasgow District Council,* First Division, March 29, 1985.

CAP.

8 & 9 Eliz. 2 (1959–60)—cont.

33. Indecency with Children Act 1960.
s. 2, amended: 1985, c.44, s.5; repealed in pt.: *ibid.,* sch.

34. Radioactive Substances Act 1960.
s. 2, orders 85/1047–1049.
s. 4, order 85/1049.
ss. 6, 7, 20, orders 85/1047–1049.
s. 19, amended: order 85/1884; repealed in pt.: 1985, c.51, sch. 17.
sch. 1, amended: regs. 85/708.

37. Payment of Wages Act 1960.
s. 7, repealed in pt.: 1985, c.58, sch. 4.

46. Corporate Bodies' Contracts Act 1960.
s. 2, amended: 1985, c.9, sch. 2.

57. Films Act 1960.
repealed: 1985, c.21, s.1, sch. 2.

58. Charities Act 1960.
ss. 8, 30, amended: 1985, c.9, sch. 2.
s. 19, order 85/1935.
sch. 2, order 84/1976.

62. Caravan Sites and Control of Development Act 1960.
s. 1, sch. 1, see *Holmes* v. *Cooper* [1985] 1 W.L.R. 1060, C.A.
ss. 14, 17, see *Hereford City Council* v. *Edmunds* (1985) 274 E.G. 1030, D.C.

66. Professions Supplementary to Medicine Act 1960.
sch. 1, amended: 1985, c.9, sch. 2.

67. Public Bodies (Admissions to Meetings) Act 1960.
s. 1, see *R.* v. *Brent Health Authority, ex p. Francis* [1984] 3 W.L.R. 1317, Forbes J.
s. 1, amended: 1985, c.43, sch. 2; repealed in pt.: *ibid.,* sch. 3.
s. 2, repealed in pt.: *ibid.,* schs. 2, 3.
sch., amended: *ibid.,* sch. 2; c.51, sch. 14; order 85/1884; repealed in pt.: 1985, c.43, schs. 2, 3.

9 & 10 Eliz. 2 (1960–61)

27. Carriage by Air Act 1961.
s. 4, orders 85/229, 1428.

33. Land Compensation Act 1961.
s. 5, see *Harrison & Hetherington* v. *Cumbria County Council* (1985) 275 E.G. 457, H.L.
s. 8, repealed in pt.: 1985, c.71, sch. 1.
s. 17, see *Sutton* v. *Secretary of State for the Environment* (1985) 50 P. & C.R. 147, McCullough J.
s. 32, regs. 84/1967; 85/157, 1131.
sch. 2, repealed in pt.: 1985, c.51, sch. 17; substituted: 1985, c.71, sch. 2.
sch. 4, repealed in pt.: *ibid.,* sch. 1.

34. Factories Act 1961.
ss. 13, 16, see *Boyes* v. *Carnation Foods* (O.H.), 1986 S.L.T. 145.
s. 14, see *Jayes* v. *I.M.I. (Kynoch)* [1985] I.C.R. 155, C.A.; *Walker* v. *Dick Engineering Co. (Coatbridge)* (O.H.), 1985 S.L.T. 465.
s. 29, see *Rice* v. *Central Electricity Generating Board, The Times,* February 23,

9 & 10 Eliz. 2 (1960–61)—cont.

34. Factories Act 1961—cont.
1985, Pain J.; *Darby* v. *G. K. N. Screws and Fasteners*, March 12, 1985, Peter Pain J., Birmingham.
ss. 82, 140 (in pt.), repealed: 85/2023.

39. Criminal Justice Act 1961.
s. 22, see *Nicoll* v. *Catron* [1985] Crim.L.R. 223, D.C.

40. Consumer Protection Act 1961.
ss. 1, 2, regs. 85/1279, 2043, 2047.
sch. 1, regs. 85/2047.

46. Companies (Floating Charges) (Scotland) Act 1961.
s. 7, repealed: 1985, c.9, sch. 1.

50. Rivers (Prevention of Pollution) Act 1961.
s. 14, repealed in pt.: 1985, c.51, sch. 17.

57. Trusts (Scotland) Act 1961.
s. 1, see *Morris, Petr.*, 1985 S.L.T. 252.

62. Trustee Investments Act 1961.
s. 11, amended: 1985, c.51, sch. 14; order 85/1884; repealed in pt.: 1985, c.51, sch. 17.
s. 12, order 85/1780.
s. 17, repealed in pt.: 1985, c.58, sch. 4.
sch. 1, amended: 1985, c.71, sch. 2; order 85/1780.
sch. 4, repealed in pt.: 1985, c.71, sch. 1.

64. Public Health Act 1961.
s. 14, see *Hertsmere Borough Council* v. *Dunn Alan Building Contractors* [1985] Crim.L.R. 726, D.C.
s. 73, amended: 1985, c.51, sch. 11.
s. 81, repealed in pt.: *ibid.*, sch. 17.

65. Housing Act 1961.
repealed: 1985, c.71, sch. 1.
s. 32, see *Wainwright* v. *Leeds City Council* (1984) 82 L.G.R. 657, C.A.; *McCoys & Co.* v. *Clark* (1982) 13 H.L.R. 89, C.A.; *Bradley* v. *Chorley Borough Council* (1985) 17 H.L.R. 305; (1985) 83 L.G.R. 623, C.A.; *Quick* v. *Taff Ely Borough Council* [1985] 3 All E.R. 321, C.A.; *Taylor* v. *Knowsley Borough Council* (1985) 17 H.L.R. 376, C.A.
s. 33, see *Bradley* v. *Chorley Borough Council* (1985) 83 L.G.R. 623, C.A.

10 & 11 Eliz. 2 (1961–62)

12. Education Act 1962.
s. 1, see *R.* v. *Hertfordshire County Council, ex p. Cheung, The Times,* July 15, 1985, McNeill J.
s. 1, regs. 85/1126.
s. 3, regs. 85/741, 1220, 1883.
s. 4, regs. 85/741, 1126, 1220, 1883.
sch. 1. regs. 85/1126.

35. Shops (Airports) Act 1962.
s. 1, orders 85/654, 1739.

37. Building Societies Act 1962.
ss. 22, 50, 55, amended: 1985, c.9, sch. 2.
s. 34, amended (S.): 1985, c.73, sch. 1.
s. 59, repealed in pt.: 1985, c.58, sch. 4.
ss. 86, 92, 103, amended: 1985, c.9, sch. 2.
s. 117, repealed in pt.: 1985, c.54, sch. 27.
s. 123, regs. 85/339.

10 & 11 Eliz. 2 (1961–62)—cont.

37. Building Societies Act 1962—cont.
sch. 1, amended: 1985, c.9, sch. 2.
sch. 3, amended: *ibid.*; c.71, sch. 2.

46. Transport Act 1962.
s. 3, amended: 1985, c.67, sch. 7.
s. 4, repealed in pt.: *ibid.*, sch. 8.
s. 4A, added: *ibid.*, s. 118.
s. 24, amended: 1985, c.9, sch. 2.
s. 57, repealed in pt.: 1985, c.67, sch. 8.
s. 67, see *Khan* v. *Evans* [1985] R.T.R. 33, D.C.
s. 92, amended: 1985, c.9, sch. 2; repealed in pt.: 1985, c.67, sch.8.
sch. 10, repealed: *ibid.*

50. Landlord and Tenant Act 1962.
repealed: 1985, c.71, sch. 1.

56. Local Government (Records) Act 1962.
s. 2, amended: 1985, c.51, schs. 8, 14.
s. 8, amended: *ibid.,* sch. 14; repealed in pt.: *ibid.,* sch. 17.

58. Pipe-lines Act 1962.
s. 18, repealed: 1985, c.51, sch. 17.
ss. 28, 30, amended: 1985, c.71, sch. 2.

11 Eliz. 2 (1962)

4. Foreign Compensation Act 1962.
s. 3, order 85/168.

1963

2. Betting, Gaming and Lotteries Act 1963.
ss. 5 (in pt.), 6 (in pt.), 7, repealed: 1985, c.18, sch.
s. 12, amended: 1985, c.53, s.25.
s. 16, amended: 1985, c.18, s.2; repealed in pt.: *ibid.,* sch.
s. 24, amended: 1985, c.53, s.25.
s. 55, regs. 85/1513(S.).
s. 55, sch. 2, amended: 1985, c.9, sch. 2.
sch. 3, amended: 1985, c.51, sch. 8; repealed in pt.: *ibid.,* schs. 8, 17.
sch. 5, regs. 85/1476, 1513(S.).

12. Local Government (Financial Provisions) (Scotland) Act 1963.
s. 9, order 85/94; regs. 85/246.
s. 10, order 85/101.

18. Stock Transfer Act 1963.
ss. 1, 2, amended: 1985, c.9, sch. 2.

22. Sheriff Courts (Civil Jurisdiction and Procedure) (Scotland) Act 1963.
s. 3, order 85/626.
s. 3, substituted: 1985, c.37, s.23.

24. British Museum Act 1963.
s. 10, order 85/462.
sch. 3, amended: *ibid.*

25. Finance Act 1963.
ss. 64, 67 (in pt.), repealed: 1985, c.54, sch. 24.

31. Weights and Measures Act 1963.
repealed: 1985, c.72, sch.13.
s. 11, regs. 85/209, 1532.
s. 12, regs. 85/209.
s. 14, regs. 85/209, 1532.
s. 21, orders 85/778, 988; 1980.
s. 26, see *Westminster City Council* v. *Turner, Gow* (1984) 4 Tr.L. 130, D.C.

1963—*cont.*

31. Weights and Measures Act 1963—*cont.*
s. 51, see *Baker Boy (Hot Bread)* v. *Barnes* (1985) 4 Tr.L. 52, D.C.
s. 54, regs. 85/209, 1532; orders 85/435, 778, 988, 1980.
s. 58, regs. 85/209, 1532.

33. London Government Act 1963.
ss. 2, 4, repealed in pt.: 1985, c.51, sch. 17.
s. 5, amended: *ibid.*, sch. 14; order 85/1884; repealed in pt.: 1985, c.51, sch. 17.
ss. 7, 9 (in pt.), 19 (in pt.), repealed: *ibid.*
s. 21, repealed: 1985, c.71, sch. 1.
s. 22, repealed: 1985, c.51, sch. 17.
s. 23, see *Fleming* v. *Wandsworth London Borough Council* (1984) 83 L.G.R. 277.
s. 23, orders 85/828, 993.
s. 23, amended: 1985, c.51, sch. 8; repealed in pt.: *ibid.*, sch. 17.
ss. 30, 31, 40, 43, 47, 48, repealed in pt.: *ibid.*
ss. 49, 50 (in pt.), 51 (in pt.), repealed: *ibid.*
s. 52, repealed in pt.: 1985, c.13, sch. 3.
ss. 53, 55, 57–60, 62, repealed in pt.: 1985, c.51, sch. 17.
s. 66, amended: *ibid.*, s.83; repealed in pt.: *ibid.*, sch. 17.
ss. 71, 72, repealed: *ibid.*
s. 73, amended: *ibid.*, sch. 16.
s. 75, amended: *ibid.*, sch. 14; order 85/1884; repealed in pt.: 1985, c.51, sch. 17.
ss. 78, 81 (in pt.), 82, 83 (in pt.), repealed: *ibid.*
s. 80, order 85/1999.
s. 84, orders 85/828, 993.
ss. 84, 85, see *Fleming* v. *Wandsworth London Borough Council* (1984) 83 L.G.R. 277.
ss. 85, 87, 89, repealed in pt.: 1985, c.51, sch. 17.
s. 90, orders 85/828, 993, 1999.
sch. 8, repealed: 1985, c.71, sch. 1.
sch. 11, amended: 1985, c.51, sch. 5; repealed in pt.: *ibid.*, sch. 17.
sch. 12, amended: *ibid.*, sch. 8; repealed in pt.: 1985, c.13, sch. 3.
schs. 14, 17, repealed in pt.: 1985, c.51, sch. 17.

37. Children and Young Persons Act 1963.
sch. 2, amended: 1985, c.61, s.61.

38. Water Resources Act 1963.
s. 133, order 85/1469.

39. Criminal Justice (Scotland) Act 1963.
s. 12, amended: 1985, c.73, s.45.

41. Offices, Shops and Railway Premises Act 1963.
s. 52, amended: 1985, c.51, sch. 8.
s. 84, amended: 1985, c.3, sch.
s. 90, amended: 1985, c.13, sch. 2.

51. Land Compensation (Scotland) Act 1963.
ss. 12, 25, see *Edmonstone* v. *Central Regional Council*, 1985 S.L.T. (Lands Tr.) 57.

51. Land Compensation (Scotland) Act 1963—*cont.*
ss. 14, 22, 24, sch. 1, see *James Miller & Partners* v. *Lothian Regional Council (No. 2)*, 1984 S.L.T. (Lands Tr.) 2.
s. 40, regs. 84/1968; 85/158, 1132.

1964

14. Plant Varieties and Seeds Act 1964.
ss. 1, 2, 4, 6, see *Moulin Winter Wheat* [1985] F.S.R. 283, Plant Varieties and Seeds Tribunal.
ss. 1, 3, 5, schemes 85/1090, 1091, 1093–1097.
s. 7, schemes 85/1090, 1091, 1096, 1097.
s. 9, regs. 85/357, 1092.
s. 11, regs. 85/1092.
s. 16, regs. 84/1872, 1873; 85/356, 385(S.), 438; 975–981, 1529.
s. 17, regs. 85/975–979.
ss. 24, 26, regs. 85/980.
s. 36, regs. 84/1872, 1873; 85/357, 975–980, 1092.
sch. 2, see *Moulin Winter Wheat* [1985] F.S.R. 283, Plant Varieties and Seeds Tribunal.
sch. 2, order 85/1098.
sch. 3, schemes 85/1090, 1091, 1093–1097.

19. Married Women's Property Act 1964.
repealed (S.): 1985, c.37, sch. 2.

24. Trade Unions (Amalgamations, etc.) Act 1964.
s. 7, regs. 85/300.

26. Licensing Act 1964.
s. 2, order 85/1383.
ss. 3–6, see *R.* v. *Licensing JJ. for the City of London, ex p. Davys of London Wine Merchants* (1985) 149 J.P. 507, MacPherson J.
ss. 8, 10, amended: 1985, c.65, sch. 8.
s. 70, repealed in pt.: 1985, c.40, s.1.
s. 74, see *R.* v. *Doncaster Justices, ex p. Langfield* (1985) 149 J.P. 26, Nolan J.
s. 76, repealed in pt.: 1985, c.40, s.1.
s. 77, see *Young* v. *O'Connell, The Times,* May 25, 1985, Glidewell J.
s. 87, orders 85/653, 1730.
s. 169, see *Woby* v. *B, The Times,* October 8, 1985, D.C.
s. 198, order 85/1730.

40. Harbours Act 1964.
ss. 9, 10, repealed: 1985, c.30, sch.
s. 14, orders 84/1878, 1974; 85/992, 1026, 1251, 1449, 1473, 1554, 1667, 1678, 1803.
s. 15A, order 85/1504.
s. 42, amended: 1985, c.9, sch. 2.
ss. 45, 46, repealed in pt.: 1985, c.30, sch.

41. Succession (Scotland) Act 1964.
s. 14, see *Morrison-Low* v. *Paterson* (H.L.), 1985 S.L.T. 255.
s. 16, see *Morrison-Low* v. *Paterson* (H.L.), 1985 S.L.T. 255; *Coats* v. *Logan* (O.H.), 1985 S.L.T. 221.
s. 33, amended: 1985, c.37, sch. 1.

CAP.

1964—cont.

42. Administration of Justice Act 1964.
s. 37, repealed in pt.: 1985, c.51, sch. 17.

47. Merchant Shipping Act 1964.
ss. 3, 5, 20, amended: regs. 85/212.

48. Police Act 1964.
s. 1, amended: 1985, c.51, sch. 11.
s. 2, amended: *ibid.*; repealed in pt.: *ibid.*, schs. 11, 17.
s. 2A, added: *ibid.*, sch. 11.
s. 3, amended: 1985, c.43, sch. 2.
ss. 8, 11, 31, amended: 1985, c.51, sch. 11.
ss. 33, regs. 85/130, 131, 518, 519, 885, 1045, 1577, 1808.
s. 35, regs. 85/686, 1909.
s. 44, regs. 85/809, 1531(S.).
s. 46, regs. 85/130, 131, 518, 519, 1045, 1808.
s. 49, see *Conerney* v. *Jacklin* [1985] Crim.L.R. 234, C.A.; *R.* v. *Comr. of Police of the Metropolis, ex p. Ware, The Times,* July 31, 1985, Forbes J.
sch. 5, rules 85/576.
sch. 5, amended: 1985, c.51, sch. 11.

52. Films Act 1964.
repealed: 1985, c.21, s.1, sch. 2.

55. Perpetuities and Accumulations Act 1964.
s. 1, see *Green's Will Trusts, Re* [1985] 3 All E.R. 455, Nourse J.

56. Housing Act 1964.
Pts. I (ss. 1–12), IV (ss. 64–91), 96, 102, 103, 106, 108 (in pt.), schs. 1–4, repealed: 1985, c.71, sch. 1.
Pt. I (ss.1–12), repealed (S.): *Ibid.*

63. Law of Property (Joint Tenants) Act 1964.
s. 1, amended: 1985, c.65, sch. 8.

71. Trading Stamps Act 1964.
s. 1, amended: 1985, c.9, sch. 2.

74. Obscene Publications Act 1964.
s. 1, see *R.* v. *Bristol Crown Court, ex p. Willets, The Times,* January 25, 1985, D.C.; *R.* v. *Skirving; R.* v. *Grossman (Beth), The Times,* March 9, 1985, C.A.

81. Diplomatic Privileges Act 1964.
sch. 1, see *R.* v. *Lambeth Justices, ex p. Yusufu* [1985] Crim. L.R. 510, D.C.

84. Criminal Procedure (Insanity) Act 1964.
s. 4, see *R.* v. *Metropolitan Stipendiary Magistrate, ex p. Anufowsi, The Times,* August 5, 1985, Div.Ct.

89. Hairdressers (Registration) Act 1964.
s. 13, amended: 1985, c.9, sch. 2.

95. Travel Concessions Act 1964.
repealed: 1985, c.67, sch. 8.

1965

3. Remuneration of Teachers Act 1965.
s. 1, see *R.* v. *Burnham Primary and Secondary Committee, ex p. Professional Association of Teachers, The Times,* March 30, 1985, MacPherson J.
s. 1, order 85/1663.
ss. 2, 7, orders 84/2043; 85/38, 495, 944, 1248.

12. Industrial and Provident Societies Act 1965.
s. 1, amended: 1985, c.9, sch. 2.

CAP.

1965—cont.

12. Industrial and Provident Societies Act 1965—*cont.*
s. 6, amended: 1985, c.71, sch. 2.
ss. 52, 53, 55, amended: 1985, c.9, sch. 2.
s. 55, see *Nourse Self Build Association, Re* (1985) 82 L.S.Gaz. 1709, Harman J.
ss. 70, 71, regs. 85/344, 345.
s. 74, amended: 1985, c.9, sch. 2.

14. Cereals Marketing Act 1965.
s. 13, order 85/1013.
s. 21, amended: 1985, c.19, sch. 2.

17. Museum of London Act 1965.
s. 1, repealed in pt.: 1985, c.51, sch. 17.
s. 9, amended: *ibid.*, s.43; repealed in pt.: *ibid.*, sch. 17.
ss. 14, 15, amended: *ibid.*, s.43.
sch., amended: *ibid.*; repealed in pt.: *ibid.*, sch. 17.

19. Teaching Council (Scotland) Act 1965.
sch. 1, amended: 1985, c.9, sch. 2.

22. Law Commissions Act 1965.
s. 2, repealed in pt. (S.): 1985, c.73, sch. 2.

24. Severn Bridge Tolls Act 1965.
s. 2, order 85/726.

25. Finance Act 1965.
s. 19, see *Worthing Rugby Football Club Trustees* v. *I.R.C.* [1985] 1 W.L.R. 409, Peter Gibson J.; *Craven* v. *White* [1985] 1 W.L.R. 1024, D.C.
s. 22, see *Golding* v. *Kaufman* [1985] S.T.C. 152, Ch.D.; *Worthing Rugby Football Club Trustees* v. *I.R.C.* [1985] 1 W.L.R. 409, Peter Gibson J.; *Zim Properties* v. *Procter* [1985] S.T.C. 90, D.C.; *Mashiter* v. *Pearmain* [1985] S.T.C. 165, C.A.; *Anders Utkilens Rederi A/S* v. *O/Y Lovisa Stevedoring Co. A/B; The Golfstraum* [1985] 2 All E.R. 669, Goulding J.; *Bell* v. *I.R.C.,* 1985 S.L.T. (Lands Tr.) 52.
s. 23, see *Larner* v. *Warrington* [1985] S.T.C. 442, Nicholls J.
s. 56, see *Ellis* v. *B.P. Oil Northern Ireland Refinery and Related Appeals* [1985] S.T.C. 722, Walton J.
s. 90, amended: 1985, c.54, s.82; repealed in pt.: *ibid.*, sch. 27.
s. 92, regs. 85/1886.
s. 92, amended: 1985, c.67, s.110; repealed in pt.: *ibid.*, s.110, sch. 8.
s. 93, repealed (S.): 1985, c.71, sch.1.
s. 93, repealed: 1985, c.71, sch. 1.
sch. 6, see *Mashiter* v. *Pearmain* [1985] S.T.C. 165, C.A.; *Passant* v. *Jackson* [1985] S.T.C. 133, Vinelott J.
sch. 7, see *Golding* v. *Kaufman* [1985] S.T.C. 152, Ch.D.; *Reed* v. *Nova Securities* [1985] 1 W.L.R. 193, H.L.; *Craven* v. *White* [1985] 1 W.L.R. 1024; [1985] S.T.C. 531, D.C.
sch. 10, repealed in pt.: 1985, c.65, sch. 10; c.66, sch. 8(S.).
sch.17, see *Bell* v. *I.R.C.,* 1985 S.L.T. (Lands Tr.) 52.

CAP.

1965—cont.

32. Administration of Estates (Small Payments) Act 1965.
ss. 5, 6, repealed in pt.: 1985, c.58, sch. 4.

36. Gas Act 1965.
s. 28, repealed in pt.: 1985, c.51, sch. 17.

49. Registration of Births, Deaths and Marriages (Scotland) Act 1965.
s. 28A, added: 1985, c.73, s.50.
ss. 38, 43, 47, 54, regs. 85/268.
s. 48, amended: 1985, c.73, s.50.

51. National Insurance Act 1965.
s. 36, amended: order 85/1245.

56. Compulsory Purchase Act 1965.
ss. 4,11, repealed in pt.: 1985, c.71, sch. 1.
s. 27, amended: *ibid.*, sch. 2.
s. 30, see *Fagan* v. *Knowsley Metropolitan Borough* (1985) 275 E.G. 717, C.A.
ss. 34, 35, repealed: 1985, c.71, sch. 1.
sch. 6, repealed in pt.: 1985, c.12, sch. 2.
sch. 7, repealed in pt.: 1985, c.71, sch. 1.

57. Nuclear Installations Act 1965.
s. 28, orders 85/752, 1985.

64. Commons Registration Act 1965.
s. 2, amended: 1985, c.51, sch. 8.
ss. 5, 6, see *West Anstey Common, Re* [1985] 1 All E.R. 618, C.A.
s. 22, repealed in pt.: 1985, c.51, sch. 17.

69. Criminal Procedure (Attendance of Witnesses) Act 1965.
s. 2, see *Day* v. *Grant*; *R.* v. *Manchester Crown Court, ex p. Williams* [1985] R.T.R. 299, C.A.; *R.* v. *Skegness Magistrates' Court, ex p. Cardy*; *R.* v. *Manchester Crown Court, ex p. Williams* [1985] R.T.R. 49, D.C.

81. Housing (Slum Clearance Compensation) Act 1965.
repealed: 1985, c.71, sch. 1.

82. Coal Industry Act 1965.
s. 1, amended: 1985, c.9, sch. 2.

1966

8. National Health Service Act 1966.
s. 8, amended: 1985, c.9, sch. 2.

13. Universities (Scotland) Act 1966.
s. 12, amended: 1985, c.9, sch. 2.

18. Finance Act 1966.
s. 46, repealed: 1985, c.54, sch. 27.
sch. 6, repealed in pt.: 1985, c.9, sch. 1.

19. Law Reform (Miscellaneous Provisions) Act 1966.
s. 7, see *Docherty* v. *McGlynn* (O.H.), 1985 S.L.T. 237.
s. 8, amended: 1985, c.37, sch. 1.

29. Singapore Act 1966.
sch., repealed in pt.: 1985, c.9, sch. 1; c.21, sch. 2.

34. Industrial Development Act 1966.
s. 8, repealed in pt.: 1985, c.23, sch. 2.

36. Veterinary Surgeons Act 1966.
s. 11, order 84/2009.

38. Sea Fisheries Regulation Act 1966.
ss. 1–3, 17, 19, sch. 3, amended: 1985, c.51, sch. 8.
s. 5, regs. 85/1785(S.).

CAP.

1966—cont.

42. Local Government Act 1966.
s. 11, amended: 1985, c.51, sch. 14.
ss. 35, 40, order 85/2027.
s. 41, repealed in pt.: 1985, c.51, sch. 17.
sch. 3, order 85/2027.
sch. 3, repealed in pt.: 1985, c.13, sch. 3.

45. Armed Forces Act 1966.
s. 2, regs. 85/1819, 1820, 2003.

49. Housing (Scotland) Act 1966.
ss. 1 (in pt.), 152, 156, 158, repealed: 1985, c.71, sch. 1.
ss. 175, 208, amended: 1985, c.71, sch. 2.

51. Local Government (Scotland) Act 1966.
s. 2, order 85/94.
ss. 3, 4, orders 85/94, 556, 1705.
s. 15, see *Bustin* v. *Assessor for Strathclyde Region*, 1985 S.L.T. 204.
s. 45, orders 85/94, 556, 1705.
sch. 1, orders 85/94, 1705.
sch. 4, repealed in pt.: 1985, c.13, sch. 3.

1967

1. Land Commission Act 1967.
s. 25, repealed in pt.: 1985, c.54, sch. 27.

7. Misrepresentation Act 1967.
s. 2, see *Sharneyford Supplies* [1985] 1 All E.R. 976, Mervyn Davies J.

8. Plant Health Act 1967.
s. 2, orders 84/1871, 1892; 85/873, 1230.
s. 3, orders 84/1871, 1892; 85/242, 637(S), 873, 1230.

9. General Rate Act 1967.
s. 7, see *Investors in Industry Commercial Properties* v. *Norwich City Council* [1985] 3 W.L.R. 711, C.A.
s. 9, see *R.* v. *Tower Hamlets London Borough Council, ex p. Chetnik Developments* (1985) 25 R.V.R. 87, Mann J.
s. 12, amended: 1985, c.51, s.68; repealed in pt.: *ibid.*, sch. 17.
s. 16, see *Locker* v. *Stockport Metropolitan Borough Council* (1985) 83 L.G.R. 652, Glidewell J.
s. 17, see *London Merchant Securities* v. *Islington London Borough Council* (1985) 25 R.V.R. 87, Judge Morder Q.C.; *Camden London Borough Council* v. *Bromley Park Gardens Estates, The Times*, October 7, 1985, McPherson J.; *Hastings Borough Council* v. *Tarmac Properties* (1985) 83 L.G.R. 629, C.A.
s. 26, see *Hayes* v. *Loyd* [1985] 1 W.L.R. 714, H.L.
s. 32A, amended: 1985, c.9, sch. 2.
ss. 38, 44, repealed in pt.: 1985, c.51, sch. 17.
ss. 76, 77, see *Electricity Supply Nominees* v. *Sharma (V.O.)* (1985) 276 E.G. 299, C.A.
s. 79, see *Hastings Borough Council* v. *Tarmac Properties* (1985) 83 L.G.R. 629, C.A.
s. 85, amended: 1985, c.51, sch. 14; order 85/1884; repealed in pt.: 1985, c.51, sch. 17.
s. 90, amended: 1985, c.65, sch. 8.

CAP.

1967—cont.

9. General Rate Act 1967—cont.
s. 91, amended: 1985, c.51, s.14.
s. 94, repealed in pt.: *ibid.*, sch. 17.
s. 113, rules 85/6, 1486.
s. 115, see *Westminster City Council* v. *Hailbury Investments, The Times,* December 24, 1984, D.C.
sch. 1, see *Debenhams* v. *Westminster City Council* (1985) 274 E.G. 826, Hodgson J.; *Hastings Borough Council* v. *Tarmac Properties* (1985) 274 E.G. 925; (1985) 83 L.G.R. 629, C.A.; *Hailbury Investments* v. *Westminster City Council* (1985) 273 E.G. 733; [1985] 83 L.G.R. 383, C.A.; *London Merchant Securities* v. *Islington London Borough Council* (1985) 25 R.V.R. 87, Judge Morder Q.C.; *Camden London Borough Council* v. *Bromley Park Gardens Estates* (1985) 276 E.G. 928, McPherson J.; *Investors in Industry Commercial Properties* v. *Norwich City Council* [1985] 3 W.L.R. 711, C.A.
sch. 1, regs. 85/258.
sch. 1, amended: 1985, c.51, sch. 14; repealed in pt.: *ibid.*, sch. 17.
sch. 13, amended: 1985, c.71, sch. 2.

10. Forestry Act 1967.
s. 1, amended: 1985, c.31, s.4.
s. 9, regs. 85/1572, 1958.
s. 9, amended: regs. 85/1958.
s. 32, regs. 85/1572, 1958.

19. Private Places of Entertainment (Licensing) Act 1967.
s. 2, repealed in pt.: 1985, c.13, sch. 3.
sch., amended: 1985, c.51, sch. 8; repealed in pt.: *ibid.*, sch. 17.

22. Agriculture Act 1967.
s. 8, amended: 1985, c.72, sch. 12.
s. 19, amended: 1985, c.9, sch. 2.
ss. 61, 62, scheme 85/334.

24. Slaughter of Poultry Act 1967.
s. 3, regs. 84/2056.

27. Merchant Shipping (Load Lines) Act 1967.
s. 26, regs. 85/1607.

29. Housing Subsidies Act 1967.
repealed: 1985, c.71, sch. 1.
s. 32, amended: 1985, c.9, sch. 2.

32. Development of Inventions Act 1967.
s. 12, amended: 1985, c.9, sch. 2.

43. Legal Aid (Scotland) Act 1967.
s. 2, see *Johnston* v. *Johnston* (O.H.), 1985 S.L.T. 510.
s. 6, amended: 1985, c.73, sch. 1.
s. 14A, regs. 85/337, 554, 557.
s. 15, regs. 85/337, 554, 557, 1628.

48. Industrial and Provident Societies Act 1967.
s. 3, substituted: 1985, c.9, s.26.
ss. 4, 5, amended: *ibid.*

52. Tokyo Convention Act 1967.
s. 2, order 85/1993.

54. Finance Act 1967.
s. 40, order 85/563.

CAP.

1967—cont.

58. Criminal Law Act 1967.
s. 2, see *R.* v. *Jackson (Kenneth)* [1985] R.T.R. 257, C.A.; *R.* v. *Richards*; *R.* v. *Leeming* (1985) 81 Cr.App.R. 125, C.A.
s. 3, see *R.* v. *Jackson (Kenneth)* [1985] R.T.R. 257, C.A.

66. Welsh Language Act 1967.
s. 2, regs. 85/36, 713.
ss. 2, 3, regs. 85/1133, 1134.

68. Fugitive Offenders Act 1967.
sch. 1, amended: 1985, c.38, s.3.

75. Matrimonial Homes Act 1967.
sch. 2, see *Lewis* v. *Lewis* [1985] 2 W.L.R. 962, H.L.

76. Road Traffic Regulation Act 1967.
s. 55, see *West* v. *Buckinghamshire County Council* (1985) 83 L.G.R. 449, Caulfield J.
ss. 71, 72, see *Spittle* v. *Kent County Constabulary* [1985] Crim.L.R. 744, D.C.

77. Police (Scotland) Act 1967.
s. 26, regs. 85/111, 1325, 1733.
s. 27, regs. 84/2029.

80. Criminal Justice Act 1967.
s. 11, see *R.* v. *Rossborough* [1985] Crim.L.R. 372; (1985) 81 Cr.App.R. 139, C.A.
s. 32, amended: 1985, c.23, sch. 1; repealed in pt.: *ibid.*, schs. 1, 2.
s. 59, amended (S.): 1985, c.73, s.44.
s. 62, see *R.* v. *Secretary of State for the Home Department, ex p. Gunnell* [1985] Crim.L.R. 105, C.A.

81. Companies Act 1967.
repealed (exc. Pt. II (ss.58–108) (in pt.)): 1985, c.9, sch. 1.
s. 35, see *Highfield Commodities, Re* [1984] 3 All E.R. 884, Megarry V.C.
s. 90, substituted: 1985, c.9, sch. 3.

83. Sea Fisheries (Shellfish) Act 1967.
s. 1, order 85/847.

84. Sea Fish (Conservation) Act 1967.
s. 1, order 85/100.
s. 5, order 84/1935.
ss. 15, 20, orders 84/1935; 85/100.

88. Leasehold Reform Act 1967.
see *Johnson* v. *Duke of Westminster* (1984) 17 H.L.R. 136, C.A.
s. 2, see *Cresswell* v. *Duke of Westminster* (1985) 275 E.G. 461, C.A.
s. 3, amended: 1985, c.71, sch. 2.
s. 4, see *Duke of Westminster* v. *Johnson* (1985) 275 E.G. 241, C.A.
ss. 8, 20, see *Collins* v. *Duke of Westminster* [1985] 1 All E.R. 463, C.A.
s. 28, amended: orders 85/39, 1884; 1985, c.51, sch. 14; repealed in pt.: *ibid.*, sch. 17.
s. 30, repealed in pt.: 1985, c.71, sch.
sch. 3, see *Cresswell* v. *Duke of Westminster* (1985) 275 E.G. 461, C.A.
sch. 5, repealed in pt.: 1985, c.71, sch. 1.

1968

2. Provisional Collection of Taxes Act 1968.
s. 1, amended: 1985, c.54, s.97.

1968—cont.

3. Capital Allowances Act 1968.
s. 68, amended: 1985, c.54, s.62; repealed in pt.: *ibid.*, s.62, sch. 27.
s. 82, repealed in pt.: *ibid.*, s.56, sch. 27.
s. 91, see *Gaspet* v. *Elliss* [1985] 1 W.L.R. 1214; [1985] S.T.C. 572, Gibson J.
ss. 91, 92, amended: 1985, c.54, s.63.
s. 94, repealed in pt.: *ibid.*, sch. 27.

5. Administration of Justice Act 1968.
s. 1, order 85/1213 (S.); amended: *ibid.* (S.).

7. London Cab Act 1968.
s. 1, orders 85/933, 1023.

13. National Loans Act 1968.
s. 6, repealed in pt.: 1985, c.71, sch. 1.
s. 14, rules 85/1147.
sch. 1, repealed in pt.: 1985, c.71, sch. 1.
sch. 4, amended: *ibid.*, sch. 2.

14. Public Expenditure and Receipts Act 1968.
s. 5, order 85/202, 281(S.), 1960.

16. New Towns (Scotland) Act 1968.
s. 1A, added: 1985, c.5, s.10.
ss. 18A–18C, added: *ibid.*, sch. 3.
sch. 1A, added: *ibid.*, s.10, sch. 1.

18. Consular Relations Act 1968.
ss. 1, 3, order 84/1978.
s. 12, order 84/1977.
s. 14, orders 84/1977, 1978.

19. Criminal Appeal Act 1968.
s. 2, see *R.* v. *Tonner; R.* v. *Evans (Ronald)* [1985] 1 W.L.R. 344, C.A.; *R.* v. *Drew* [1985] 1 W.L.R. 914, C.A.
s. 3, see *R.* v. *Tonner; R.* v. *Evans (Ronald)* [1985] 1 W.L.R. 344, C.A.
s. 11, see *R.* v. *Sandwell* [1985] R.T.R. 45, C.A.
ss. 18, 31, see *R.* v. *Suggett, The Times*, April 24, 1985, C.A.
sch. 2, repealed in pt.: 1985, c.23, sch. 2.

22. Legitimation (Scotland) Act 1968.
ss. 2, 7, 8, see *Dunbar of Kilconzie, Petr.*, 1985 S.L.T. 158.

23. Rent Act 1968.
s. 3, see *Hampstead Way Investments* v. *Lewis-Weare* [1985] 1 W.L.R. 164, H.L.

27. Firearms Act 1968.
ss. 30, 44, see *R.* v. *Acton Crown Court, ex p. Varney* [1984] Crim.L.R. 683, D.C.

29. Trade Descriptions Act 1968.
s. 1, see *Simmons* v. *Ravenhill* [1984] R.T.R. 412, D.C.; *Davis* v. *Allan, The Times*, February 11, 1985, D.C.; *Cavendish Woodhouse* v. *Wright, The Times*, March 8, 1985, D.C.; *R.* v. *Beaconsfield Justices, ex p. Johnston and Sons, The Times*, March 23, 1985, D.C.; *Cahaine* v. *Croydon London Borough Council, The Times*, March 20, 1985, D.C.; *Norman (Alec) Garages* v. *Phillips* [1985] R.T.R. 164, D.C.; *Lewin* v. *Bland* [1985] R.T.R. 171, D.C.; *Newham London Borough* v. *Co-operative Retail Services* (1984) 149 J.P. 421, D.C.; *Queensway Discount Warehouses* v. *Burke, The Times*, October 14, 1985,

1968—cont.

29. Trade Descriptions Act 1968—*cont.*
D.C.; *Olgeirsson* v. *Kitching, The Times*, November 16, 1985, D.C.
ss. 1–3, see *Corfield* v. *Sevenways Garage* [1985] R.T.R. 109, D.C.
s. 3, see *Simmons* v. *Ravenhill* [1984] R.T.R. 412, D.C.
s. 4, see *Norman (Alec) Garages* v. *Phillips* [1985] R.T.R. 164, D.C.
s. 14, see *Dixons* v. *Roberts* (1984) 82 L.G.R. 689, D.C.; *Cahalne* v. *Croydon London Borough* (1985) 4 Tr.L. 199, D.C.
s. 19, see *Newham London Borough* v. *Co-operative Retail Services* (1984) 149 J.P. 421, D.C.; *R.* v. *Beaconsfield JJ., ex p. Johnston & Sons* (1985) 4 Tr.L. 212, D.C.; *R.* v. *Pain, Jory and Hawkins, The Times*, November 11, 1985, C.A.
s. 20, see *Lewin* v. *Bland* [1985] R.T.R. 171, D.C.
s. 22, amended: 1985, c.72, sch. 12.
s. 23, see *Hicks* v. *Grewal* (1985) 4 Tr.L. 92, D.C.; *Olgeirsson* v. *Kitching, The Times*, November 16, 1985, D.C.
s. 24, see *Simmons* v. *Ravenhill* [1984] R.T.R. 412, D.C.; *Davis* v. *Allen, The Times*, February 11, 1985, D.C.; *Norman (Alec) Garages* v. *Phillips* [1985] R.T.R. 164, D.C.; *Hicks* v. *Grewal* (1985) 4 Tr.L. 92, D.C.; *Amos* v. *Melcon (Frozen Foods)* (1985) 149 J.P.N. 667, D.C.
s. 26, repealed in pt.: 1985, c.72, sch. 13.
s. 32, amended: *ibid.*, sch. 12.

31. Housing (Financial Provisions) (Scotland) Act 1968.
ss. 23, 24, repealed: 1985, c.71, sch. 1.
s. 25, order 85/926.
s. 25, amended: 1985, c.71, sch. 2.

41. Countryside Act 1968.
s. 6, repealed in pt.: 1985, c.51, sch. 17.

42. Prices and Incomes Act 1968.
repealed: 1985, c.71, sch. 1.

46. Health Services and Public Health Act 1968.
s. 63, amended: order 85/39; repealed in pt.: 1985, c.51, sch. 17.
s. 64, amended: order 85/39.
s. 65, repealed in pt.: 1985, c.51, sch. 17.

47. Sewerage (Scotland) Act 1968.
s. 1, see *James Miller & Partners* v. *Lothian Regional Council (No. 2)*, 1984 S.L.T. (Lands Tr.) 2.

48. International Organisations Act 1968.
s. 1, orders 84/1980–1982; 85/750, 753.
s. 10, orders 85/446, 451, 750, 753.

49. Social Work (Scotland) Act 1968.
Pts. II (ss.12–29), III (ss.30–58), see *Central Regional Council* v. *B.*, 1985 S.L.T. 413.
ss. 15, 16, see *Central Regional Council* v. *B.*, 1985 S.L.T. 413.
s. 16, amended: 1985, c.60, s.25.
s. 18A, Act of Sederunt 85/780.

CAP.

1968—cont.

49. Social Work (Scotland) Act 1968—*cont.*
s. 21, amended: 1985, c.73, s.24.
s. 34A, rules 85/843; Act of Sederunt 85/781.
s. 35, rules 84/1867; 85/843.
s. 42, amended: 1985, c.73, s.25.
s. 44, see *D.* v. *Strathclyde Regional Council*, 1985 S.L.T. 114; *Central Regional Council* v. *B.*, 1985 S.L.T. 413.
s. 44, amended: 1985, c.73, s.28.
s. 48, amended: *ibid.*, s.29.
s. 58B, amended: *ibid.*, s.26, sch. 2.
s. 58E, amended: *ibid.*, s.26.
s. 78, Act of Sederunt 85/780.
ss. 90, 93, order 85/1514.
sch. 3, amended: 1985, c.73, s.24.
sch. 7, order 85/1514.

50. Hearing Aid Council Act 1968.
s. 12, amended: 1985, c.9, sch. 2.

52. Caravan Sites Act 1968.
ss. 6, 9, see *R.* v. *Secretary of State for the Environment, ex p. Lee & Bond* [1985] J.P.L. 724, Mann J.
ss. 6, 12, amended: 1985, c.51, sch. 8.
s. 12, orders 84/1958, 1959, 1964; 85/324, 382, 407, 1652, 1764, 1795, 1885.

54. Theatres Act 1968.
s. 18, amended: 1985, c.51, sch. 8.

55. Friendly and Industrial and Provident Societies Act 1968.
ss. 7, 8, amended: 1985, c.9, sch. 2.

60. Theft Act 1968.
ss. 1, 6, see *R.* v. *Lloyd (Sidney)*; *R.* v. *Bhuee*; *R.* v. *Ali (Chaukal)* [1985] 3 W.L.R. 30, C.A.
s. 9, see *R.* v. *Brown (Vincent)* [1985] Crim.L.R. 212, C.A.
s. 12, see *R.* v. *Marchant* (1985) 80 Cr.App.R. 361, C.A.
s. 15, see *R.* v. *Zemmel; R.* v. *Mecik* [1985] Crim.L.R. 213, C.A.
s. 20, see *R.* v. *Beck* [1985] 1 W.L.R. 22, C.A.
s. 22, see *R.* v. *Cash (Noel)* C.A.; *R.* v. *Hall (Edward), The Times*, March 14, 1985, C.A.; *Anderton* v. *Ryan, The Times*, May 13, 1985, H.L.; *R.* v. *Hall* [1985] Crim.L.R. 376, C.A.
s. 25, see *R.* v. *Cooke; R.* v. *Sutcliffe* [1985] Crim.L.R. 215, C.A.
s. 27, see *R.* v. *Perry* [1984] Crim.L.R. 680, C.A.
sch. 2, repealed in pt.: 1985, c.65, sch. 10.

64. Civil Evidence Act 1968.
ss. 2, 4, see *P.* v. *D., The Times*, December 13, 1985, Wood J.

65. Gaming Act 1968.
ss. 1, 5, 8, 34, see *Brown* v. *Plant*, 1985 S.L.T. 371.
ss. 20, 31, orders 85/575, 641(S.); amended: order 85/576.
s. 44, repealed in pt.: 1985, c.51, sch. 17.
s. 51, orders 85/575, 641(S.).
sch. 1, amended: 1985, c.53, s.25.

CAP.

1968—cont.

65. Gaming Act 1968—*cont.*
sch. 9, see *Westminster City Council* v. *Lunepalm, The Times*, December 10, 1985 (and correction December 13, 1985), Woolf J.

67. Medicines Act 1968.
Commencement order: 85/1539.
s. 16, order 85/1539.
s. 40, regs. 85/1533.
s. 51, order 85/1540.
s. 57, orders 84/1861; 85/310, 857, 1823.
s. 58, see *Pharmaceutical Society of Great Britain* v. *Storkwain* [1985] 3 All E.R. 4, D.C.
s. 58, orders 84/1862; 85/309.
s. 59, orders 84/1862; 85/309, 1288.
s. 72, amended: 1985, c.65, sch. 8.
ss. 75, 76, regs. 84/1886; 85/1878.
ss. 85, 91, regs. 85/1558, 2008.
s. 86, regs. 85/2008.
s. 103, regs. 85/803, 804; S.R. 1985 No. 131.
s. 105, order 85/1403.
s. 112, see *Mistry* v. *Norris, The Times*, October 16, 1985, D.C.
ss. 112, 113, 115, modified: regs. 85/273.
s. 117, regs. 85/273.
s. 129, regs. 84/1886; 85/1558, 1878; orders 84/1861, 1862; 85/309, 310, 857, 1288, 1403, 1539, 1540, 1823.

68. Design Copyright Act 1968.
see *Smith* v. *Greenfield* [1984] 6 N.I.J.B., Murray J.

69. Justices of the Peace Act 1968.
s. 1, see *R.* v. *Kingston-upon-Thames Crown Court, ex p. Guarino, The Times*, November 27, 1985, C.A.

73. Transport Act 1968.
s. 9, amended: 1985, c.67, ss. 57, 58, sch. 3; repealed in pt.: *ibid.*, s.57, schs. 3, 8.
ss. 9A, 9B, added: *ibid.*, 57.
s. 9B, amended (prosp.): *ibid.*, s.58.
s. 10, amended: *ibid.*, schs. 3, 7; repealed in pt.: *ibid.*, schs. 3, 8.
s. 11, repealed in pt.: *ibid.*
s. 12, amended: *ibid.*, sch. 3; repealed in pt.: *ibid.*, schs. 3, 8.
s. 13, substituted: *ibid.*, sch. 3.
s. 14, amended: 1985, c.9, sch. 2; 1985, c.67, sch. 3; repealed in pt.(S): *ibid.*, schs. 3, 8.
s. 15, amended: *ibid.*, schs. 3, 7; repealed in pt.: *ibid.*, schs. 3, 8; repealed in pt.(S): *ibid.*, schs. 3, 8.
s. 15A, repealed in pt.: *ibid.*
s. 16, amended: *ibid.*, schs. 3, 7; repealed in pt.: *ibid.*, schs. 3, 8.
ss. 17–19, repealed: *ibid.*
s. 20, amended: *ibid.*, sch. 3; repealed in pt.: *ibid.*, schs. 3, 8.
ss. 21, 22 (in pt.), repealed: *ibid.*
s. 23, amended: *ibid.*, sch. 3.
s. 24, amended: *ibid.*, s.113, sch. 3; repealed in pt.: *ibid.*, s.113, sch. 8.
s. 29, repealed in pt.: *ibid.*, sch. 8.

CAP.

1968—cont.

73. Transport Act 1968—*cont.*
s. 34, amended: *ibid.*, sch. 7; repealed in pt.: *ibid.*, schs. 3, 8; repealed in pt.(S.): *ibid.*
s. 36, repealed: *ibid.*, sch. 8.
s. 54, amended: *ibid.*, s.123, sch. 3; repealed in pt.: *ibid.*, s.123, sch. 8.
s. 56, amended: 1985, c.51, sch. 12; c.67, sch. 7.
s. 59, amended: *ibid.*, s.3; repealed in pt.: *ibid.*, sch. 8.
s. 63, repealed in pt.: 1985, c.51, sch. 17.
s. 69, amended: 1985, c.9, sch. 2.
s. 86, amended: 1985, c.65, sch. 8.
ss. 88, 90, repealed: 1985, c.67, sch. 8.
s. 91, regs. 84/1835; 85/30.
s. 92, amended: 1985, c.9, sch. 2.
s. 96, see *Licensing Authority for Goods Vehicles in Metropolitan Traffic Area* v. *Coggins, The Times*, February 28, 1985, D.C.
s. 96, amended: 1985, c.67, sch. 2.
s. 97, see *R.* v. *Scott (Thomas) & Sons Bakers* [1984] R.T.R. 337, European Ct. of Justice; *D.P.P.* v. *Hackett (Sidney) (Nos. 91/84 and 92/84)* [1985] R.T.R. 209, European Ct.
ss. 98, 99, amended: 1985, c.67, sch. 2.
s. 103, amended: *ibid.*; repealed in pt.: *ibid.*, sch. 8.
ss. 115, 123, 124, repealed in pt.: 1985, c.51, sch. 17.
s. 121, order 85/1578.
ss. 134, 137, amended: 1985, c.67, sch. 3.
s. 138, repealed: *ibid.*, sch. 8.
s. 141, amended: *ibid.*, sch. 3.
s. 159, amended: *ibid.*, sch. 1, repealed in pt.: *ibid.*, sch. 8.
s. 160, amended: *ibid.*, sch. 3.
sch. 5, amended: *ibid.*; repealed in pt.: *ibid.*, schs. 3, 8.
sch. 6, repealed: *ibid.*, sch. 8.
sch. 8, repealed in pt.: 1985, c.23, sch. 2.
sch. 10, repealed in pt.: 1985, c.67, sch. 8.

1969

2. Local Government Grants (Social Need) Act 1969.
s. 1, amended: 1985, c.51, sch. 14.
10. Mines and Quarries (Tips) Act 1969.
s. 11, amended: 1985, c.51, s.11.
32. Finance Act 1969.
s. 52, repealed in pt.: 1985, c.58, sch. 4.
sch. 19, see *Worthing Rugby Football Club Trustees* v. *I.R.C.* [1985] 1 W.L.R. 409, Peter Gibson J.
33. Housing Act 1969.
ss. 39 (in pt.), 40, repealed: 1985, c.51, sch. 17.
Pts. II (ss.28–42), IV (ss.58–64), V (ss.65–69), repealed: 1985, c.71, sch. 1.
s. 59, amended: *ibid.*, sch. 2.
ss. 70–72, 75, 84–91 (in pt.), schs. 4–9, repealed: *ibid.*
35. Transport (London) Act 1969.
s. 30, repealed: 1985, c.51, sch. 17.

CAP.

1969—cont.

46. Family Law Reform Act 1969.
s. 7, see *L. (A Minor) Re, The Times*, November 2, 1984, Hollings J.; *M.* v. *Lambeth London Borough Council (No. 2), The Times*, December 20, 1984, Sheldon J.; *W. (A Minor), Re* (1985) 129 S.J. 523, Sheldon J.
s. 21, see *Hodgkiss* v. *Hodgkiss and Walker* (1985) 15 Fam. Law 87, C.A.
s. 22, regs. 85/1416.
48. Post Office Act 1969.
s. 7, amended: 1985, c.67, sch. 3, 7; repealed in pt.: *ibid.*, schs. 7, 8.
s. 86, amended: 1985, c.9, sch. 2.; c.51, sch. 14; order 85/1884; repealed in pt.: 1985, c.51, sch. 17.
sch. 4, repealed in pt.: 1985, c.65, sch.10; c.66, sch. 8(S.).
sch. 5, amended: 1985, c.56, s.11.
51. Development of Tourism Act 1969.
s. 14, amended: 1985, c.9, sch. 2.
54. Children and Young Persons Act 1969.
s. 1, see *R.* v. *F. (A Child), The Times*, April 20, 1985, C.A.; *M.* v. *Westminster City Council* (1985) 15 Fam. Law 93, D.C.; *A.-R.* v. *Avon County Council, The Times*, April 25, 1985, Div. Ct.; *W. (A Minor) (Wardship Jurisdiction), Re* [1985] 2 W.L.R. 892, H.L.; *sub nom. W.* v. *Hertfordshire C.C.* [1985] 2 All E.R. 301, H.L.
s. 3, amended: 1985, c.23, s.27.
s. 7, see *W.* v. *Heywood, The Times*, March 15, 1985, D.C.; *R.* v. *F. (A Child), The Times*, April 20, 1985, C.A.
s. 17, amended: 1985, c.60, s.25.
s. 20A, see *R.* v. *F. (A Child), The Times*, March 20, 1985, C.A.; *R.* v. *F. (A Child), The Times*, April 20, 1985, C.A.
s. 21, see *R.* v. *Tower Hamlets Juvenile Justices, ex p. London Borough of Tower Hamlets* (1984) 14 Fam. Law 307, Bush J.
s. 23, see *R.* v. *Leicester Juvenile Court, ex p. K.D.C.* (1985) 80 Cr.App.R. 320, D.C.
s. 32A, see *R.* v. *Wandsworth West Juvenile Court, ex p. S.* (1984) 14 Fam. Law 303, C.A.; *A.-R.* v. *Avon County Council* [1985] 3 W.L.R. 311, D.C.
57. Employers' Liability (Compulsory Insurance) Act 1969.
s. 3, amended: 1985, c.51, sch. 14; order 85/1884; repealed in pt.: 1985, c.51, sch. 17.

1970

8. Insolvency Services (Accounting and Investment) Act 1970.
s. 1, repealed in pt.: 1985, c.9, sch. 1.
s. 4, amended: *ibid.*, sch. 2; c.65, sch. 8.
9. Taxes Management Act 1970.
see *Baker* v. *Superite Tools, The Times*, July 19, 1985, E.A.T.

CAP.

1970—cont.

9. Taxes Management Act 1970—*cont.*

s. 29, see *Honig* v. *Sarsfield* [1985] S.T.C. 31, Gibson J.; *Duchy Maternity* v. *Hodgson* [1985] S.T.C. 764, Walton J.

s. 31, repealed in pt.: 1985, c.54, sch. 27.

s. 32, see *Bye* v. *Coren* [1985] S.T.C. 113, D.C.

s. 36, see *Kovak* v. *Morris* [1985] S.T.C. 183, C.A.

s. 38, amended: 1985, c.54, sch. 25.

s. 40, see *Honig* v. *Sarsfield* [1985] S.T.C. 31, Gibson J.

s. 40, amended: 1985, c.54, sch. 25.

s. 41, see *R.* v. *Comr. for the Special Purposes of the Income Tax Acts, ex p. Stipple Choice* [1985] 2 All E.R. 465, C.A.

s. 50, see *Owton Fens Properties* v. *Redden* [1984] S.T.C. 618, D.C.; *Banin* v. *MacKinlay (Inspector of Taxes)* [1985] 1 All E.R. 842, C.A.; *Duchy Maternity* v. *Hodgson* [1985] S.T.C. 764, Walton J.

s. 54, see *Scorer* v. *Olin Energy Systems, The Times*, March 29, 1985, H.L.

s. 56, see *Valleybright (In Liquidation)* v. *Richardson* [1985] S.T.C. 70, Ch.D.; *Hughes (Inspector of Taxes)* v. *Viner* [1985] 3 All E.R. 40; [1985] S.T.C. 235, Walton J.; *Furniss* v. *Ford* (1981) 55 T.C. 561, D.C.

s. 70, amended: 1985, c.54, sch. 25.

s. 78, amended: *ibid.*, s.50.

s. 89, order 85/563.

s. 98, amended: 1985, c.54, ss.38, 40, schs. 13, 22, 23; repealed in pt.: *ibid.*, sch. 27.

ss. 100, 103, see *Willey* v. *I.R.C.* [1985] S.T.C. 56, Scott J.

s. 103, see *Carco Accessories* v. *I.R.C.* [1985] S.T.C. 518, C.A.

s. 108, amended: 1985, c.9, sch. 2.

sch. 8, see *Worthing Rugby Football Club Trustees* v. *I.R.C.* [1985] 1 W.L.R. 409, Peter Gibson J.

10. Income and Corporation Taxes Act 1970.

s. 8, amended: order 85/430; 1985, c.54, s.36.

ss. 30, 33, repealed: *ibid.*, sch. 27.

s. 49, see *Reed (Inspector of Taxes)* v. *Clark* [1985] 3 W.L.R. 142; [1985] S.T.C. 323, Nicholls J.

s. 64, amended: 1985, c.9, sch. 2.

s. 108, see *Reed (Inspector of Taxes)* v. *Clark* [1985] 3 W.L.R. 142, Nicholls J.

s. 109, see *Parkside Leasing* v. *Smith (Inspector of Taxes)* [1985] 1 W.L.R. 310, Scott J.

s. 114, see *MacPherson* v. *Bond* [1985] 1 W.L.R. 1157; [1985] S.T.C. 675, Vinelott J.

ss. 119, 120, see *Moore* v. *Austin* [1985] S.T.C. 673, Browne-Wilkinson V.-C.

s. 130, see *Watkis* v. *Ashford Sparkes and Harward (A Firm)* [1985] 1 W.L.R. 994; [1985] S.T.C. 451, Nourse J.

CAP.

1970—cont.

10. Income and Corporation Taxes Act 1970—*cont.*

s. 168, see *Reed* v. *Young* [1984] S.T.C. 25, C.A.

s. 177, amended: 1985, c.54, s.60.

s. 181, see *Richardson* v. *Worrall; Westall* v. *McDonald* [1985] S.T.C. 693, Scott J.

s. 204, see *Clarke* v. *Oceanic Contracts Incorporated* (1982) 56 T.C. 183, H.L.

s. 204, regs. 84/1858; 85/350.

s. 242, amended: 1985, c.9, sch. 2.

s. 247, see *R.* v. *Comr. for the Special Purposes of the Income Tax Acts, ex p. Stipple Choice* [1985] 2 All E.R. 465, C.A.

s. 247, amended: 1985, c.9, sch. 2.

s. 250, see *Owton Fens Properties* v. *Redden* [1984] S.T.C. 618, D.C.

s. 263, amended: 1985, c.54, sch. 9; repealed in pt.: *ibid.*, schs. 9, 27.

s. 265, amended: 1985, c.9, sch. 2.

s. 270, amended: 1985, c.54, s.67; repealed in pt.: *ibid.*, sch. 27.

s. 272, amended: 1985, c.9, sch. 2.

s. 274, see *Coates (Inspector of Taxes)* v. *Arndale Properties* [1984] 1 W.L.R. 1328, H.L.; *Reed* v. *Nova Securities* [1985] 1 W.L.R. 193, H.L.

s. 280, amended: 1985, c.9, sch. 2.

ss. 313, 316, amended: 1985, c.54, sch. 25.

s. 333, repealed in pt.: *ibid.*, s.41, sch. 27.

s. 334, amended: *ibid.*, s.41; repealed in pt.: *ibid.*, s.41, sch. 27.

s. 335, repealed in pt.: *ibid.*

s. 337, amended: *ibid.*. s.41; repealed in pt.: *ibid.*, s.41, sch. 27.

ss. 341, 341A, 342, 342A, amended: 1985, c.71, sch. 1.

s. 343, amended: 1985, c.9, sch. 2; c.54, sch. 9; repealed in pt.: *ibid.*, schs. 9, 27.

s. 378, amended: 1985, c.54, s.64; repealed in pt.: *ibid.*, s.4, sch. 27.

s. 379, repealed: *ibid.*, s.64, sch. 27.

s. 385, amended: *ibid.*, s.64.

s. 386, amended: *ibid.*, s.65; repealed in pt.: *ibid.*, s.65, sch. 27.

s. 387, repealed in pt.: *ibid.*, sch. 27.

s. 388, amended: *ibid.*, s.64.

s. 393, amended: *ibid.*, s.41.

s. 411, amended: *ibid.*, s.43.

s. 437, see *Harvey (Inspector of Taxes)* v. *Sivyer* [1985] 3 W.L.R. 261, Nourse J.; *I.R.C.* v. *Craw* [1985] S.T.C. 512, Ct. of Session; First Division, June 5, 1985.

s. 444, see *Harvey (Inspector of Taxes)* v. *Sivyer* [1983] 3 W.L.R. 261; [1985] S.T.C. 434, Nourse J.

s. 457, see *Watson* v. *Holland (HMIT)* [1985] 1 All E.R. 290, Gibson J.

s. 457, amended: 1985, c.54, s.49.

s. 460, see *R.* v. *I.R.C., ex p. Preston* [1985] 2 W.L.R. 836, H.L.; *Bird* v. *I.R.C.* [1985] S.T.C. 584, Vinelott J.

s. 481, amended (S.): 1985, c.73, sch. 1.

s. 482, amended: 1985, c.9, sch. 2.

s. 490, amended (S.): 1985, c.73, sch.1.

CAP.

1970—cont.

10. Income and Corporation Taxes Act 1970—*cont.*
s. 497, orders 84/1825, 1826; 85/1996–1998.
sch. 1, amended: 1985, c.54, s.41, sch. 10.
sch. 15, repealed in pt.: 1985, c.65, sch. 10;
c.66, sch. 8(S.).

24. Finance Act 1970.
s. 16, amended: 1985, c.51, sch. 8, repealed in pt.: 1985, c.67, sch. 8.
s. 30, order 85/561.
sch. 7, repealed in pt.: 1985, c.54, sch. 27.

26. Films Act 1970.
repealed: 1985, c.21, s.1, sch. 2.

27. Fishing Vessels (Safety Provisions) Act 1970.
s. 6, regs. 85/1607.

31. Administration of Justice Act 1970.
s. 36, see *Bank of Scotland* v. *Grimes* [1985] 2 All E.R. 254, C.A.
s. 37, see *National Westminster Bank* v. *Oceancrest, The Times*, April 24, 1985, C.A.
s. 44, order 85/437.
sch. 9, amended: 1985, c.23, sch. 1; repealed in pt.: *ibid.*, schs. 1, 2.

35. Conveyancing and Feudal Reform (Scotland) Act 1970.
s. 1, see *Lothian Regional Council* v. *George Wimpey & Co.*, 1985 S.L.T. (Lands Tr.) 2; *Grampian Regional Council* v. *Viscount Cowdray*, 1985 S.L.T. (Lands Tr.) 6; *Hughes* v. *Frame*, 1985 S.L.T.(Lands Tr.) 12; *George T. Fraser* v. *Aberdeen Harbour Board*, 1985 S.L.T. 314.
ss. 26, 27, see *Halifax Building Society* v. *Smith*, 1985 S.L.T. (Sh. Ct.) 25.
s. 27, see *Sowman* v. *City of Glasgow District Council*, 1984 S.L.T. 65.
s. 41, repealed: 1985, c.73, sch. 2.
sch. 3, amended: 1985, c.65, sch. 8; c.66, sch. 7.

36. Merchant Shipping Act 1970.
s. 9, regs. 85/340.
s. 43, regs. 85/1306.
s. 58, rules 85/1001.
s. 68, regs. 85/1306, 1828.
s. 84, regs. 85/1607, 1727.
s. 89, order 85/174.
s. 99, regs. 85/340, 1306.

39. Local Authorities (Goods and Services) Act 1970.
s. 1, amended: 1985, c.51, sch. 14; order 85/1884; repealed in pt.: 1985, c.51, sch. 17.

40. Agriculture Act 1970.
s. 13, order 85/311.
ss. 20, 24, amended: 1985, c.9, sch. 2.
s. 25, repealed in pt.: 1985, c.72, sch. 13.
ss. 28, 29, schemes 84/1923; 85/1029.
s. 38, repealed in pt.: 1985, c.51, sch. 17.
s. 66, regs. 85/1119, S.R.S. 1985 No. 194.
s. 67, amended: 1985, c.51, sch. 8.
ss. 75–77, 84, regs. 85/1119, S.R. 1985 No. 194.
s. 86, S.R. 1985 No. 194.

CAP.

1970—cont.

41. Equal Pay Act 1970.
s. 1, see *Hayward* v. *Cammell Laird Shipbuilders* [1985] I.C.R. 71, Industrial Tribunal; *Rainey* v. *Greater Glasgow Health Board*, 1985, S.L.T. 518.
s. 6, see *Newstead* v. *Department of Transport and H.M. Treasury* [1985] I.R.L.R. 299, E.A.T.

42. Local Authority Social Services 1970.
s. 5, amended: 1985, c.67, sch. 7.
sch. 1, amended: 1985, c.71, sch. 2; repealed in pt.: *ibid.*, sch. 1.

44. Chronically Sick and Disabled Persons Act 1970.
s. 3, substituted: 1985, c.71, sch. 2.
s. 21, amended: 1985, c.51, sch. 4.

55. Family Income Supplements Act 1970.
ss. 1, 4, see *Chief Adjudication Officer* v. *Hogg, The Times*, June 11, 1985, C.A.; *Lowe* v. *The Adjudication Officer, The Times*, June 11, 1985, C.A.
s. 2, see *Chief Adjudication Officer* v. *Hogg, The Times*, June 11, 1985, C.A.
ss. 2, 3, regs. 85/1188.
s. 4, regs. 85/1946.
s. 6, regs. 84/1991.
s. 10, regs. 84/1991; 85/1188.
s. 14, see *Rowe* v. *Rigby* [1985] 2 All E.R. 903, C.A.

1971

3. Guardianship of Minors Act 1971.
ss. 9, 14, see *O. (A Minor), Re* (1985) 15 Fam. Law 135, C.A.

10. Vehicles (Excise) Act 1971.
s. 2, amended: 1985, c.54, s.4.
s. 7, order 85/722.
s. 8, see *Cummings* v. *Tudhope*, 1985 S.C.C.R. 125; *Chief Constable of Kent* v. *Mather, The Times*, August 1, 1985, D.C.
s. 9, see *Chief Constable of Kent* v. *Mather, The Times*, August 1, 1985, D.C.
s. 9, repealed in pt. (S.): 1985, c.73, sch. 4.
s. 13, amended: 1985, c.54, s.9.
s. 16, amended: *ibid.*, s.4.
ss. 23, 37, regs. 85/610.
s. 37, amended: 1985, c.54, s.9.
s. 39, sch. 1, regs. 85/610.
schs. 1–5, amended: 1985, c.54, s.4, sch. 2.

11. Atomic Energy Authority Act 1971.
s. 14, amended: 1985, c.9, sch. 2.

16. Coal Industry Act 1971.
s. 10, amended: 1985, c.9, sch. 2.

19. Carriage of Goods by Sea Act 1971.
order 85/443.

23. Courts Act 1971.
s. 9, see *Investors in Industry Commercial Properties* v. *Norwich City Council* (1985) 83 L.G.R. 64, Hodgson J.
s. 11, see *R.* v. *Iqbal* (1985) 81 Cr.App.R. 145, C.A.

1971—cont.

23. Courts Act—*cont.*
s. 56, sch. 8, see *R.* v. *Skegness Magistrates' Court, ex p. Cardy; R.* v. *Manchester Crown Court, ex p. Williams* [1985] R.T.R. 49, D.C.; *Day* v. *Grant; R.* v. *Manchester Crown Court, ex p. Williams* (1985) R.T.R. 299, C.A.
sch. 9, repealed in pt.: 1985, c.71, sch. 1.
26. Betting, Gaming and Lotteries (Amendment) Act 1971.
repealed: 1985, c.18, sch.
27. Powers of Attorney Act 1971.
s. 1, see *T.C.B.* v. *Gray, Financial Times,* November 27, 1985, Browne-Wilkinson V.-C.
s. 10, see *Walia* v. *Naughton (Michael)* [1985] 1 W.L.R. 1115, Judge John Finlay Q.C.
29. National Savings Bank Act 1971.
s. 2, regs. 85/342.
ss. 2 (in pt.), 13, 14, 27 (in pt.), repealed: 1985, c.58, sch. 4.
32. Attachment of Earnings Act 1971.
s. 24, amended: 1985, c.53, sch. 4.
34. Water Resources Act 1971.
s. 1, orders 85/320, 633, 816, 1472.
38. Misuse of Drugs Act 1971.
s. 2, order 85/1995.
s. 4, see *R.* v. *Dempsey, The Times,* November 22, 1985, C.A.
s. 5, see *Murray* v. *MacNaughton,* 1984 S.C.C.R. 361; *Donnelly* v. *H.M. Advocate,* 1984 S.C.C.R. 419; *Varley* v. *H.M. Advocate,* 1985 S.C.C.R. 55.; *R.* v. *Hunt, The Times,* October 24, 1985, C.A.
s. 23, see *R.* v. *Forde (James)* [1985] Crim.L.R. 323; (1985) 81 Cr.App.R. 19, C.A.; *Carmichael* v. *Brannan,* 1985 S.C.C.R. 234.
s. 28, see *H.M. Advocate* v. *Bell,* 1985 S.L.T. 349.
ss. 30, 31, regs. 85/138; S.R. 1985 No. 32.
s. 38, S.R. 1985 No. 32.
sch. 2, see *Murray* v. *MacNaughton,* 1984 S.C.C.R. 361.
sch. 2, amended and repealed in pt.: order 85/1995.
sch. 4, amended: 1985, c.39, s.1.
40. Fire Precautions Act 1971.
s. 12, amended: 1985, c.13, sch. 3; repealed in pt.: *ibid.,* sch. 3.
s. 36, amended: 1985, c.71, sch. 2.
45. Redemption of Standard Securities (Scotland) Act 1971.
s. 2, amended: 1985, c.9, sch. 2.
48. Criminal Damage Act 1971.
s. 1, see *R.* v. *Hardie* [1984] 3 All E.R. 848, C.A.; *R.* v. *R. (S. M.)* (1984) 79 Cr.App.R. 334, C.A.
51. Investment and Building Grants Act 1971.
s. 1, amended: 1985, c.9, sch. 2.
53. Recognition of Divorces and Legal Separations Act 1971.
ss. 2, 6, see *Chaudhary* v. *Chaudhary* [1984] 3 All E.R. 1017, C.A.

1971—cont.

53. Recognition of Divorces and Legal Separations Act 1971—*cont.*
ss. 3, 7, see *Lawrence* v. *Lawrence* [1985] 3 W.L.R. 125, C.A.
s. 8, see *Chaudhary* v. *Chaudhary* [1984] 3 All E.R. 1017, C.A.; *Mamdani* v. *Mamdani* (1985) 15 Fam. Law 122, C.A.; *Sabbagh* v. *Sabbagh* (1985) 15 Fam. Law 187, Balcombe J.
56. Pensions (Increase) Act 1971.
sch. 2, amended: 1985, c.51, s.61; repealed in pt.: *ibid.,* sch. 17.
sch. 3, amended: *ibid.,* s.61; c.67, sch. 3.
57. Pool Competitions Act 1971.
continued in force: order 85/1069.
s. 8, order 85/1069.
58. Sheriff Courts (Scotland) Act 1971.
s. 6, repealed in pt.: 1985, c.73, s.20, sch. 4.
s. 32, Acts of Sederunt 85/821, 1427.
s. 32, amended: 1985, c.73, sch. 2.
s. 33, repealed in pt.: *ibid.,* schs. 2, 4.
s. 35, amended: *ibid.,* s.18, sch. 2.
ss. 36A, 36B, added: *ibid.*
ss. 37, 38, amended: *ibid.*
ss. 38, 45, see *W. Jack Baillie Associates* v. *Kennedy* 1985 S.L.T.(Sh.Ct.) 53.
59. Merchant Shipping (Oil Pollution) Act 1971.
s. 18, order 85/1197.
60. Prevention of Oil Pollution Act 1971.
s. 15, repealed in pt.: 1985, c.9, sch. 2.
61. Mineral Workings (Offshore Installations) Act 1971.
s. 6, regs. 85/1612.
62. Tribunals and Inquiries Act 1971.
s. 8, amended: 1985, c.65, sch. 1.
s. 9, repealed: 1985, c.17, sch. 5.
s. 10, rules 84/1989; 85/785, 921; regs. 85/967, 980, 1092.
s. 13, amended: 1985, c.65, sch. 1.
s. 40, rules 85/784.
sch. 1, amended: 1985, c.17, sch. 4; c.65, sch. 1; c.67, schs. 2, 7.
68. Finance Act 1971.
s. 31, amended: 1985, c.9, sch. 2.
s. 32, amended: order 85/430; 1985, c.54, s.34.
s. 41, amended: *ibid.,* s.55; repealed in pt.: *ibid.,* s.55, sch. 27.
s. 43, order 84/2060.
s. 44, amended: 1985, c.54, s.55, sch. 14; repealed in pt.: *ibid.,* s.55, sch. 27.
s. 46, amended: *ibid.,* s.54, sch. 14.
s. 50, repealed in pt.: *ibid.,* s.56, sch. 27.
s. 64, schs. 6, 7, repealed in pt.: *ibid.,* sch. 27.
sch. 8, amended: *ibid.,* s.59, schs. 14, 16; repealed in pt.: *ibid.,* s.58, schs. 14, 27.
sch. 10, see *Magnavox Electronics Co.* v. *Hall* [1985] S.T.C. 260, Nicholls J.
69. Medicines Act 1971.
ss. 1, 129, regs. 85/1231.
71. Mineral Workings Act 1971.
repealed: 1985, c.12, s.1, sch. 2.

CAP.

1971—cont.

72. Industrial Relations Act 1971.
ss. 96, 101, 116, 167, see *General Aviation Services (U.K.)* v. *Transport and General Workers Union* [1985] I.C.R. 615, H.L.

76. Housing Act 1971.
repealed: 1985, c.71, sch. 1.

77. Immigration Act 1971.
see *R.* v. *Secretary of State for the Home Department, ex p. Bugdaycay, The Times,* November 12, 1985, C.A.
s. 1, see *W. (A Minor) (Adoption: Non-Patrial), Re, The Times,* July 27, 1985, C.A.; *R.* v. *Immigration Appeal Tribunal, ex p. Hoque, The Times,* November 27, 1985, D.C.
ss. 2, 3, see *R.* v. *Chief Immigration Officer, ex p. Brahmbhatt, The Times,* December 12, 1984, C.A.
s. 3, see *R.* v. *Immigration Appeal Tribunal, ex p. Nashouki, The Times,* October 17, 1985, C.A.
s. 8, see *Tusin* v. *Secretary of State for the Home Department* [1984] Imm.A.R. 42, Imm.A.T.
s. 8, order 85/1809.
s. 9, order; 85/1854.
s. 14, see *R.* v. *Secretary of State for the Home Department, ex p. Musisi, The Times,* June 8, 1985, C.A.; *Tusin* v. *Secretary of State for the Home Department* [1984] Imm.A.R. 42, Imm.A.T.
s. 18, see *R.* v. *Immigration Appeal Tribunal, ex p. Hubbard, The Times,* July 16, 1985, D.C.
s. 18, regs. 84/2040.
s. 19, see *R.* v. *Immigration Appeal Tribunal, ex p. Wirdestedt, The Times,* December 12, 1984, C.A.
s. 20, see *Tusin* v. *Secretary of State for the Home Department* [1984] Imm.A.R. 42, Imm.A.T.
s. 22, rules 84/2041.
s. 26, see *R.* v. *Secretary of State for the Home Department, ex p. Addo, The Times,* April 18, 1985, D.C.; *R.* v. *Clarke (Ediakpo)* [1983] 3 W.L.R. 113, H.L.
s. 32, order; 85/1854.
sch. 2, rules 84/2041.

78. Town and Country Planning Act 1971.
s. 1, amended: 1985, c.51, s.3.
s. 5, repealed: *ibid.,* sch. 17.
s. 9, see *Barham* v. *Secretary of State for the Environment; Pye* v. *Secretary of State for the Environment, The Times,* May 25, 1985, Farquharson J.
s. 22, see *Lydcare* v. *Secretary of State for the Environment* (1985) 83 L.G.R. 33, C.A.; *North Warwickshire Borough Council* v. *Secretary of State for the Enviroment* (1985) 50 P. & C.R. 47, Woolf J.
s. 23, see *Carmichael* v. *Brannan,* 1985 S.C.C.R. 234.
s. 24, orders 85/1011, 1012, 1579.

1971—cont.

78. Town and Country Planning Act 1971— *cont.*
s. 26, see *R.* v. *Torfaen Borough Council, ex p. Jones,* September 2, 1985, Woolf J.
s. 27, see *Main* v. *Swansea City Council* (1985) 49 P. & C.R. 26, C.A.
s. 28, amended: 1985, c.51, sch. 2.
s. 29, see *R.* v. *Royal County of Berkshire, ex p. Mangnall* [1985] J.P.L. 258, Nolan J.
s. 33, see *R.* v. *Hammersmith and Fulham London Borough Council, ex p. Greater London Council, The Times,* October 16, 1985, C.A.
s. 35, see *Sir Brandon Meredith Rhys Williams* v. *Secretary of State for Wales and the Welsh Water Authority and Taff Ely Borough Council* [1985] J.P.L. 29, C.A.
s. 52, see *Avon County Council* v. *Millard* (1985) 274 E.G. 1025; (1985) 50 P. & C.R. 275, C.A.
s. 53, see *Trustees of the Earl of Lichfield's Estate* v. *Secretary of State for the Environment and Stafford Borough Council* [1985] J.P.L. 251, McNeill J.
s. 54, see *Debenhams* v. *Westminster City Council* (1985) 274 E.G. 826, Hodgson J.
ss. 54, 54A, amended: 1985, c.51, sch. 2.
s. 55, see *Cotswold District Council* v. *Secretary of State for the Environment and Pearson* [1985] J.P.L. 407, David Widdicombe Q.C.
s. 58, amended: 1985, c.51, sch. 2.
s. 58A, added: *ibid.*
s. 62, amended: 1985, c.52, s.1.
s. 87, see *Lydcare* v. *Secretary of State for the Environment* (1985) 83 L.G.R. 33, C.A.; *R.* v. *Greenwich London Borough Council, The Times,* July 5, 1985, C.A.; *Balco Transport Services* v. *Secretary of State for the Environment, The Times,* August 8, 1985, C.A.
s. 88, see *R.* v. *Smith (Thomas George)* (1984) 48 P. & C.R. 392, C.A.; *Dover District Council* v. *McKeen* (1985) 50 P. & C.R. 250, D.C; *R.* v. *Greenwich London Borough Council, The Times,* July 5, 1985, C.A.; *Lenlyn* v. *Secretary of State for the Environment; R.* v. *Secretary of State for the Environment, ex p. Lenlyn* (1985) 50 P. & C.R. 129, Hodgson J.; *R.* v. *Secretary of State for the Environment, ex p. Crossley (Theresa)* [1985] J.P.L. 632, Webster J.
s. 89, see *R.* v. *Smith (Thomas George)* (1984) 48 P. & C.R. 392, C.A.; *R.* v. *Greenwich London Borough Council, The Times,* July 5, 1985, C.A.; *Prosser* v. *Sharp* (1985) 274 E.G. 1249, D.C.
s. 91, see *R.* v. *Greenwich London Borough Council, The Times,* July 5, 1985, C.A.
ss. 92, 93, see *Prosser* v. *Sharp* (1985) 274 E.G. 1249, D.C.

CAP.

1971—cont.

78. Town and Country Planning Act 1971—
cont.

s. 92A, amended: 1985, c.51, s.3; repealed in pt.: *ibid.*, sch. 17.

s. 99B, added: *ibid.*, sch. 2.

s. 100, repealed in pt.: *ibid.*, sch. 17.

s. 101, amended: *ibid.*, sch. 2.

s. 109, see *Preston* v. *British Union for the Abolition of Vivisection, The Times,* July 24, 1985, Mann J.

ss. 114, 115, 117, 126, amended: 1985, c.51, sch. 2.

ss. 164, 165, see *Jones* v. *Metropolitan Borough of Stockport* (1985) 50 P. & C.R. 299, C.A.

ss. 165, 169, amended: 1985, c.19, s.1.

s. 177, see *Sample (Warkworth)* v. *Alnwick District Council* (1984) 48 P. & C.R. 474, Lands Tribunal.

s. 178A, regs. 85/698.

s. 180, see *Balco Transport Services* v. *Secretary of State for the Environment* (1985) 276 E.G. 447, C.A.

s. 192, amended: 1985, c.51, sch. 1; c.71, sch. 2.

s. 194, see *Mancini* v. *Coventry City Council* (1985) 49 P. & C.R. 127, C.A.

s. 194, amended: 1985, c.51, sch. 1.

s. 197, amended: 1985, c.71, sch. 2.

s. 209, amended: 1985, c.51, sch. 4; repealed in pt.: *ibid.*, sch. 17.

s. 215, amended: *ibid.*, sch. 14; repealed in pt.: *ibid.*, sch. 17.

s. 216, amended: *ibid.*, sch. 4.

s. 242, see *G.L.C.* v. *Secretary of State for the Environment, The Times,* July 18, 1985, Woolf J.

s. 242, amended: 1985, c.51, sch. 1.

s. 243, see *R.* v. *Smith (Thomas George)* (1984) 48 P. & C.R. 392, C.A.; *R.* v. *Greenwich London Borough Council, The Times,* July 5, 1985, C.A.; *Prosser* v. *Sharp* (1985) 274 E.G. 1249, D.C.

s. 244, see *Barham* v. *Secretary of State for the Environment; Pye* v. *Secretary of State for the Environment, The Times,* May 25, 1985, Farquharson.

s. 244, amended: 1985, c.51, sch. 1.

s. 245, see *Nash* v. *Secretary of State for the Environment and Epping Forest District Council* [1985] J.P.L. 474, Widdicombe Q.C.

s. 246, see *Rhymney Valley District Council* v. *Secretary of State for Wales and G. Isaac* [1985] J.P.L. 27, Nolan J.; *Lenlyn* v. *Secretary of State for the Environment; R.* v. *Secretary of State for The Environment, ex p. Lenlyn* (1985) 50 P. & C.R. 129, Hodgson J.; *Gabbitas* v. *Secretary of State for the Environment and Newham Borough Council* [1985] J.P.L. 630, Judge Dobry Q.C.; *London Parachuting* v. *Secretary of State for the Environment, The Times,* November 20, 1985, D.C.

s. 246, amended: 1985, c.51, sch. 2.

CAP.

1971—cont.

78. Town and Country Planning Act 1971—
cont.

s. 250, regs. 85/1152.

ss. 255, 266, amended: 1985, c.51, sch. 1.

ss. 277, 277A, amended: *ibid.*, sch. 2.

s. 280, amended: *ibid.*, schs. 1, 2.

s. 283, see *Lenlyn* v. *Secretary of State for the Environment; R.* v. *Secretary of State for the Environment, ex p. Lenlyn* (1985) 50 P. & C.R. 129, Hodgson J.

s. 284, see *R.* v. *Greenwich London Borough Council, The Times,* July 5, 1985, C.A.

s. 287, regs. 85/1152; orders 85/1011, 1012, 1579.

s. 290, see *North Warwickshire Borough Council* v. *Secretary of State for the Environment* (1985) 50 P. & C.R. 47, Woolf J.

s. 290, amended: 1985, c.51, sch. 1; repealed in pt.: *ibid.*, sch. 17.

schs. 3, 4 (in pt.), 6 (in pt.), 7 (in pt.), repealed: *ibid.*, sch. 17.

sch. 11, amended: *ibid.*, sch. 2; repealed in pt.: *ibid.*, sch. 17.

sch. 20, amended: *ibid.*, sch. 14; repealed in pt.: *ibid.*, sch. 17.

sch. 22, amended: *ibid.*, sch. 4; repealed in pt.: *ibid.*, sch. 17.

sch. 23, repealed in pt.: 1985, c.71, sch. 1.

1972

11. Superannuation Act 1972.

s. 1, order 85/1855.

s. 5, amended: 1985, c.65, sch. 8; c.66, sch. 7 (S.).

s. 7, regs. 85/489, 1515, 1920, 1922.

s. 8, regs. 85/1922.

s. 9, regs. 84/2028 (S.); 85/1844.

s. 10, regs. 84/1970 (S.); 85/1492, 1626.

s. 12, regs. 84/1970 (S.), 2028 (S.); 85/489, 1492, 1515, 1626, 1844, 1920, 1922.

s. 24, regs. 85/1181, 1659.

sch. 1, amended (S.): 1985, c.16, sch. 1 (S.); order 85/1855.

sch. 3, regs. 85/1492, 1626, 1659, 1844.

sch. 6, repealed in pt.: 1985, c.71, sch. 1.

sch. 6, repealed in pt. (S.): *ibid.*

18. Maintenance Orders (Reciprocal Enforcement) Act 1972.

s. 5, see *Horn* v. *Horn* (1985) Fam. Law 260, Wood J.

s. 31, amended: 1985, c.37, sch. 1; repealed in pt.: *ibid.*, schs. 1, 2.

s. 39, amended: *ibid.*, sch. 1.

19. Sunday Cinema Act 1972.

repealed: 1985, c.13, sch. 3.

20. Road Traffic Act 1972.

s. 1, see *R.* v. *Krawec* [1985] R.T.R. 1, C.A.

ss. 1, 2, see *R.* v. *Boswell* (1984) 6 Cr.App.R.(S.) 257, C.A.

s. 2, see *R.* v. *Bell (David)* [1984] 3 All E.R. 842, C.A.; *Frame* v. *Lockhart,* 1985 S.L.T. 193.

1972—cont.

20. Road Traffic Act 1972—cont.

s. 3, see *Dunlop* v. *Allan*, 1984 S.C.C.R. 329; *R.* v. *Krawec* [1985] R.T.R. 1, C.A.; *Donaldson* v. *Aitchison*, 1985 S.C.C.R. 43; *Melville* v. *Lockhart*, 1985 S.C.C.R. 242.

s. 5, see *Kenny* v. *Tudhope*, 1984 S.C.C.R. 290.

s. 6, see *Howard* v. *Hallett* [1984] R.T.R. 353, D.C.; *Lodwick* v. *Brow* [1984] R.T.R. 394, D.C.; *Brown* v. *Braid*, 1985 S.L.T. 37; *R.* v. *Skegness Magistrates' Court, ex p. Cardy*; *R.* v. *Manchester Crown Court, ex p. Williams* [1985] R.T.R. 49, D.C.; *Anderton* v. *Lythgoe* [1985] 1 W.L.R. 222, D.C.; *R.* v. *Burley Magistrates, ex p. Dixon (Allan Timothy)* [1984] Crim.L.R. 759, D.C.; *Wright* v. *Taplin, The Times*, February 13, 1985, D.C.; *Owen* v. *Chesters* [1985] Crim.L.R. 156; [1985] R.T.R. 191, D.C.; *Morgan* v. *Lee, The Times*, April 17, 1985, D.C.; *Anderton* v. *Royle* [1985] R.T.R. 91, D.C.; *Sparrow* v. *Bradley* [1985] R.T.R. 122, D.C.; *Over* v. *Musker* [1985] R.T.R. 84, D.C.; *Gatens* v. *Wilson*, 1985 S.C.C.R. 47; *Snelson* v. *Thompson* [1985] R.T.R. 220, D.C.; *Hughes* v. *McConnell* [1985] R.T.R. 244, D.C.; *Chief Constable of Surrey* v. *Wickens* [1985] R.T.R. 277, D.C.; *Tudhope* v. *Craig*, 1985 S.C.C.R. 214; *Stepniewski* v. *Comr. of Police of the Metropolis* [1985] R.T.R. 330, D.C.; *MacDonald* v. *Skelt* [1985] R.T.R. 321, D.C.; *R.* v. *Fox* [1985] 1 W.L.R. 1126, H.L.; *Lockhart* v. *Deighan*, 1985 S.L.T. 549; *Rowan* v. *Chief Constable of Merseyside, The Times*, December 10, 1985, D.C.

s. 7, see *Anderton* v. *Royle* [1985] R.T.R. 91, D.C.; *Woon* v. *Maskell* [1985] R.T.R. 289, D.C.

s. 8, see *Cotter* v. *Kamil* [1984] R.T.R. 371, D.C.; *Castle* v. *Cross* [1984] 1 W.L.R. 1372, D.C.; *Howard* v. *Hallett* [1984] R.T.R. 353, D.C.; *Tudhope* v. *Quinn*, 1984 S.C.C.R. 255; *Stewart* v. *Aitchison*, 1984 S.C.C.R. 357; *Reeves* v. *Enstone, The Times*, January 15, 1985, D.C.; *R.* v. *Skegness Magistrates' Court, ex p. Cardy*; *R.* v. *Manchester Crown Court, ex p. Williams* [1985] R.T.R. 49, D.C.; *Hayward* v. *Eames* [1985] R.T.R. 12, D.C.; *Anderton* v. *Lythgoe* [1985] 1 W.L.R. 222, D.C.; *Pritchard* v. *Jones* [1985] Crim.L.R. 52, D.C.; *Smith* v. *Nixon*, 1985 S.L.T. 192; *Morgan* v. *Lee, The Times*, April 17, 1985, D.C.; *Anderton* v. *Royle* [1985] R.T.R. 91, D.C.; *Sparrow* v. *Bradley* [1985] R.T.R. 122, D.C.; *Spalding* v. *Paine, The Times*, May 21, 1985, D.C.; *Knox* v. *Lockhart*, 1985 S.L.T. 248; *Owen* v. *Chesters* [1985] R.T.R. 191, D.C.; *Kelly* v. *MacKinnon*, 1985 S.C.C.R. 97; *Chief*

1972—cont.

20. Road Traffic Act 1972—cont.

Constable of Avon and Somerset Constabulary v. *Creech, The Times*, August 5, 1985, C.A.; *Nichols* v. *Bulman* [1985] R.T.R. 236, D.C.; *Hughes* v. *McConnell* [1985] R.T.R. 244, D.C.; *Pine* v. *Collacott* [1985] R.T.R. 282, C.A.; *Woolman* v. *Lenton* [1985] Crim.L.R. 516, D.C.; *Chief Constable of West Yorkshire Metropolitan Police* v. *Johnson, The Times*, August 27, 1985, D.C.; *Oldfield* v. *Anderton, The Times*, October 9, 1985, D.C.; *Green* v. *Lockhart*, 1985 S.C.C.R. 257; *Reid* v. *Tudhope*, 1985 S.C.C.R. 268; *Stepniewski* v. *Comr. of the Police of the Metropolis* [1985] R.T.R. 330, D.C.; *Chief Constable of Gwent* v. *Dash* [1985] Crim.L.R. 674, D.C.; *Gull* v. *Scarborough, The Times*, November 15, 1985, D.C.; *R.* v. *Fox* [1985] 1 W.L.R. 1126, H.L.; *Archbold* v. *Jones* [1985] Crim.L.R. 740, D.C.; *Lockhart* v. *Deighan*, 1985, S.L.T. 549; *McCormick* v. *Hitchins, The Times*, December 10, 1985, D.C.

s. 9, see *Franklin* v. *Jeffries, The Times*, March 11, 1985, D.C.; *Over* v. *Musker* [1985] R.T.R. 84, D.C.; *Nichols* v. *Bulman* [1985] R.T.R. 236, D.C.

s. 10, see *Howard* v. *Hallett* [1984] R.T.R. 353, D.C.; *Reeves* v. *Enstone, The Times*, January 15, 1985, D.C.; *Walton* v. *Rimmer, The Times*, February 11, 1985, D.C.; *Hayward* v. *Eames* [1985] R.T.R. 12, D.C.; *Patterson* v. *Charlton* [1985] Crim.L.R. 449, D.C.; *Anderton* v. *Kinnard, The Times*, February 13, 1985, D.C.; *Annan* v. *Crawford*, 1984 S.C.C.R. 382; *McNamee* v. *Tudhope*, 1984 S.C.C.R. 423; *Owen* v. *Chesters* [1985] Crim.L.R. 156; [1985] R.T.R. 191, D.C.; *Donoghue* v. *Allan*, 1985 S.C.C.R. 93; *McDerment* v. *O'Brien*, 1985 S.C.C.R. 50; *Snelson* v. *Thompson* [1985] R.T.R. 220, D.C.; *Hughes* v. *McConnell* [1985] R.T.R. 244, D.C.; *Chief Constable of Surrey* v. *Wickens* [1985] R.T.R. 277, D.C.; *Temple* v. *Botha* [1985] Crim.L.R. 517, D.C.; *Allan* v. *Miller*, 1985 S.C.C.R. 227; *Reid* v. *Tudhope*, 1985 S.C.C.R. 268.

s. 12, see *Castle* v. *Cross* [1984] 1 W.L.R. 1372, D.C.; *Anderton* v. *Waring, The Times*, March 11, 1985, D.C.; *Anderton* v. *Royle* [1985] R.T.R. 91, D.C.; *Snelson* v. *Thompson* [1985] R.T.R. 220, D.C.; *Hughes* v. *McConnell* [1985] R.T.R. 244, D.C.; *Stepniewski* v. *Comr. of Police of the Metropolis* [1985] R.T.R. 330, D.C.

s. 25, see *Britton* v. *Mackenzie*, 1985 S.C.C.R. 115; *R.* v. *Jackson (Kenneth)* [1985] R.T.R. 257, C.A.

s. 31, amended: 1985, c.51, sch. 5.

s. 32, amended: 1985, c.28, s.1.

s. 33, amended: 1985, c.51, sch. 5.

1972—cont.

20. Road Traffic Act 1972—*cont.*
s. 33A, amended: 1985, c.34, s.1.
ss. 33AA, regs. 85/1593.
ss. 33AA, 35, amended: 1985, c.51, sch. 5.
s. 36A, repealed in pt.: *ibid.*, sch. 17.
s. 38, amended: *ibid.*, sch. 5.
s. 40, see *Streames* v. *Copping, The Times*, February 25, 1984, D.C.; *Target Travel (Coaches)* v. *Roberts, The Times*, June 20, 1985, D.C.
s. 40, regs. 85/91, 730, 1363, 2039.
s. 42, order 85/745.
s. 43, regs. 85/834, 1923.
s. 43, repealed in pt.: 1985, c.51, sch. 17.
s. 44, regs. 85/45.
s. 45, regs. 85/1525.
s. 47, regs. 85/46, 1651.
s. 50, regs. 85/46, 1651, 1656.
s. 60, see *Streames* v. *Copping, The Times*, February 25, 1984, D.C.
s. 63, regs. 85/113.
s. 68, see *Gatens* v. *Wilson*, 1985 S.C.C.R. 47.
ss. 68, 78, 81, see *R.* v. *Derby Crown Court, ex p. Sewell* [1985] R.T.R. 251, D.C.
s. 85, regs. 85/1161.
s. 93, see *White* v. *Metropolitan Police Comr.* [1984] Crim.L.R. 687, Snaresbrook Crown Court; *Vaughan* v. *Dunn* [1984] R.T.R. 376, D.C.; *Lodwick* v. *Brow* [1984] R.T.R. 394, D.C.; *R.* v. *Lazzari* (1984) 6 Cr.App.R.(S.) 83, C.A.; *R.* v. *Sandwell* [1985] R.T.R. 45, C.A.; *Smith* v. *Nixon*, 1985 S.L.T. 192; *Pridige* v. *Gant* [1985] R.T.R. 196, D.C.; *Thompson* v. *Diamond* [1985] R.T.R. 316, D.C.
ss. 96, 99, see *Smith* v. *Allan*, 1985 S.L.T. 565.
s. 99, see *R.* v. *Sandwell* [1985] R.T.R. 45, C.A.
s. 101, see *Anderson* v. *Allan*, 1985 S.C.C.R. 262; *Johnston* v. *Over* [1985] R.T.R. 240, D.C.
s. 107, regs. 85/1161.
s. 110, orders 85/65, 1461.
s. 113, amended: 1985, c.67, sch. 2.
s. 114, regs. 84/1925.
ss. 115, 116, 118, see *Bennington* v. *Peter* [1984] R.T.R. 383, Woolf J.
s. 119, regs. 84/1925; 85/832.
s. 120, regs. 85/832.
ss. 123, 124, amended: 1985, c.67, sch. 2.
s. 124, regs. 84/1925; 85/832.
s. 127, amended: 1985, c.51, sch. 5.
ss. 128, 131, 133, regs. 84/1834; 85/577.
s. 137, amended: 1985, c.34, s.1.
s. 142, regs. 84/1834; 85/577.
s. 143, see *Reid* v. *McLeod*, 1984 S.C.C.R. 333; *Cooper* v. *Motor Insurers' Bureau* [1985] 2 W.L.R. 248, C.A.; *Johnston* v. *Over* [1985] R.T.R. 240, D.C.
s. 144, amended: 1985, c.51, sch. 14; order 85/1884; repealed in pt.: 1985, c.51, sch. 17.

1972—cont.

20. Road Traffic Act 1972—*cont.*
s. 145, see *Cooper* v. *Motor Insurers' Bureau* [1985] 2 W.L.R. 248, C.A.
s. 150, amended: 1985, c.65, sch. 8.
sch. 7(S.); repealed in pt. (S.): *ibid.*, schs. 7, 8.
c.66, schs. 7, 8.
ss. 154, 155, amended: order 85/202.
s. 159, see *Lodwick* v. *Sanders* [1985] 1 W.L.R. 382, D.C.; *Gatens* v. *Wilson*, 1985 S.C.C.R. 47.
ss. 161, 162, amended: 1985, c.34, s.1.
s. 196, amended: 1985, c.51, sch. 5.
s. 199, regs. 85/45, 46, 91, 113, 713, 730, 832, 834, 1161, 1363, 1525, 1651, 1656.
sch. 4, see *Vaughan* v. *Dunn* [1984] R.T.R. 376, D.C.; *Lodwick* v. *Brow* [1984] R.T.R. 394, D.C.; *R.* v. *Krawec* [1985] R.T.R. 1, C.A.; *R.* v. *Sandwell* [1985] R.T.R. 45, C.A.; *McLellan* v. *Tudhope*, 1984 S.C.C.R. 397; *Pridige* v. *Gant* [1985] R.T.R. 196, D.C.; *Johnston* v. *Over* [1985] R.T.R. 240, D.C.; *Thompson* v. *Diamond* [1985] R.T.R. 316, D.C.

38. Matrimonial Proceedings (Polygamous Marriages) Act 1972.
s. 2, amended (S.): 1985, c.37, sch. 1.

41. Finance Act 1972.
s. 2, see *Lord Advocate* v. *Largs Golf Club* [1985] S.T.C. 226, Ct. of Session.
s. 31, see *Lord Advocate* v. *Johnston*, 1985 S.L.T. 533; *Lord Advocate* v. *Johnson* [1985] S.T.C. 527, Ct. of Session.
s. 33, see *Lord Advocate* v. *Johnson*, 1985 S.L.T. 533.
s. 38, see *R.* v. *Asif, The Times*, May 24, 1985, C.A.; *R.* v. *Gamer; R.* v. *Bullen; R.* v. *Howard, The Times*, August 10, 1985, C.A.
s. 45, see *Lord Advocate* v. *Largs Golf Club* [1985] S.T.C. 226, Ct. of Session.
s. 67, repealed in pt.: 1985, c.54, sch. 27.
sch. 9, see *Hughes (Inspector of Taxes)* v. *Viner* [1985] 3 All E.R. 40; [1985] S.T.C. 235, Walton J.
sch. 16, amended: 1985, c.9, sch. 2; c.54, s.49, sch. 25.

42. Town and Country Planning (Amendment) Act 1972.
s. 3, see *Barham* v. *Secretary of State for the Environment; Pye* v. *Secretary of State for the Environment, The Times*, May 25, 1985, Farquharson J.

45. Trading Representations (Disabled Persons) Amendment Act 1972.
s. 1, sch., repealed in pt.: 1985, c.51, sch. 17.

46. Housing (Financial Provisions) (Scotland) Act 1972.
s. 23A, see *City of Edinburgh District Council* v. *Secretary of State for Scotland*, 1985 S.L.T. 551.
s. 23A, order 85/3.
ss. 51–59, repealed: 1985, c.71, sch. 1.

CAP.

1972—cont.

47. Housing Finance Act 1972.
repealed: 1985, c.71, sch. 1.
s. 77, repealed in pt. (S.): *ibid.*
s. 104, repealed in pt.: 1985, c.51, sch. 17.

48. Parliamentary and other Pensions Act 1972.
ss. 7, 110, order 84/1909.

50. Legal Advice and Assistance Act 1972.
s. 4, regs. 85/1628 (S.).
s. 5, amended (S.): 1985, c.73, sch. 1.
s. 11, regs. 85/1628 (S.)

52. Town and Country Planning (Scotland) Act 1972.
s. 21, order 85/1014.
s. 60, amended: 1985, c.52, s.2.
ss. 84, 88, see *Midlothian District Council v. Stevenson*, 1985 S.L.T. 424.
ss. 154, 158, amended: 1985, c.19, s.2.
s. 181, order 85/291.
s. 273, orders 85/291, 1014.

59. Administration of Justice (Scotland) Act 1972.
s.1, see *Yau v. Ogilvie & Co.* (O.H.), 1985 S.L.T. 91; *Smith, Petr.* (O.H.), 1985 S.L.T. 461.
s. 1, amended: 1985, c.73, s.19, sch. 2.
s. 4, Act of Sederunt 85/1179.

60. Gas Act 1972.
s. 21, regs. 85/1149.
s. 23, amended: 1985, c.9, sch. 2.
s. 31, see *Mackenzie v. Brougham,* 1985 S.L.T. 276.
s. 39, repealed in pt.: 1985, c.51, sch. 17.
s. 48, amended: 1985, c.9, sch. 2.

61. Land Charges Act 1972.
s. 3, amended and repealed in pt.: 1985, c.9, sch. 2.
s. 5, repealed in pt.: 1985, c.65, schs. 8, 10.
ss. 5, 17, see *Regan & Blackburn v. Rogers* [1985] 2 All E.R. 180, Scott J.
s. 6, amended: 1985, c.65, sch. 8; repealed in pt.: *ibid.*, schs. 8, 10.
s. 16, order 85/358.
s. 16, amended: 1985, c.65, sch. 8.

62. Agriculture (Miscellaneous Provisions) Act 1972.
s. 20, orders 84/1871, 1892; 85/637(S.).

63. Industry Act 1972.
s. 10, amended: 1985, c.9, sch. 2.

65. National Debt Act 1972.
s. 11, regs. 85/146, 861, 891, 1035, 1479.

66. Poisons Act 1972.
s. 7, rules 85/1077.
s. 11, amended: 1985, c.51, sch. 8.

67. Companies (Floating Charges and Receivers) (Scotland) Act 1972.
repealed: 1985, c.9, sch. 1.
ss. 1, 13, see *Ross v. Taylor*, 1985 S.L.T. 387.
s. 15, see *Manley, Petr.* (O.H.), 1985 S.L.T. 42.

68. European Communities Act 1972.
s. 1, orders 84/1820; 85/1198, 1772.
s. 1, amended: 1985, c.64, s.1; c.75, s.1.

CAP.

1972—cont.

68. European Communities Act 1972—cont.
ss. 1, 2, see *R.* v. *H.M. Treasury, ex p. Smedley* [1985] 2 W.L.R. 576, C.A.
s. 2, regs. 84/1787, 1885 (S.), 1902, 1917, 1918, 1922, 1927, 2005, 85/67, 71, 216, 306, 475, 498(S.), 509, 615, 777, 913 (S.), 1025, 1068 (S.), 1072, 1154, 1155, 1266, 1271, 1279, 1310, 1377, 1851, 1857, 1968; orders 85/749, 1027, 1773, 1774, 1801; S.Rs. 1984 No. 407; 1985 Nos. 4, 63, 81, 120, 123, 175, 352.
s. 5, orders 84/1969; 85/12, 118, 1299, 1630.
s. 6, order 85/135.
s. 8, repealed: 1985, c.21, sch. 2.
s. 9, see *T.C.B.* v. *Gray, Financial Times*, November 27, 1985, Browne-Wilkinson V.-C.
s. 9, repealed: 1985, c.9, sch. 1.
s. 11, repealed in pt.: 1985, c.23, sch. 2.
sch. 2, order 85/2020.

70. Local Government Act 1972.
ss. 2, 6, amended: 1985, c.51, sch. 16.
s. 7, order 85/59.
s. 7, amended: 1985, c.51, sch. 16.
s. 8, repealed in pt.: *ibid.*, sch. 17.
s. 47, orders 84/1906; 85/1891.
s. 47, amended: 1985, c.51, schs. 9, 16; repealed in pt.: *ibid.*, sch. 17.
s. 48, amended: *ibid.*, sch. 16.
s. 50, amended: *ibid.*, sch. 9.
s. 51, orders 84/1906, 1944; 85/139, 140, 219, 264, 335, 336, 402, 634, 1753, 1891, 1892, 2048–2050.
s. 58, order 85/265.
s. 60, amended: 1985, c.51, sch. 9.
s. 62, amended: *ibid.*, sch. 16.
s. 67, regs. 85/110; orders 84/1875, 1906, 1930, 1944, 2023, 2049; 85/59, 89, 129, 219, 264, 265, 335, 336, 1753, 1763, 1816, 1892, 2048–2050.
s. 67, amended: 1985, c.51, sch. 9.
s. 68, repealed in pt.: *ibid.*, sch. 17.
s. 70, amended: *ibid.*, sch. 14; order 85/1884.
s. 77, repealed: *ibid.*, 1985, c.51, sch. 17.
s. 78, amended: *ibid.*, sch. 9.
s. 79, amended: *ibid.*, sch. 14.
s. 80, amended: *ibid.*; order 85/1884; repealed in pt.: 1985, c.67, sch. 8.
s. 81, amended: 1985, c.65, sch. 8; repealed in pt.: 1985, c.51, sch. 17.
s. 82, amended: *ibid.*, sch. 14; order 85/1884.
s. 83, amended: 1985, c.51, sch. 14; repealed in pt.: *ibid.*, sch. 17.
ss. 84–86, amended: *ibid.*, sch. 14; order 85/1884.
ss. 87, 88, amended: 1985, c.51, sch. 14.
s. 89, amended: 1985, c.50, s.19; c.51, sch. 14; repealed in pt.: *ibid.*, schs. 14, 17.
ss. 90, 92, amended: *ibid.*, sch. 14; order 85/1884.
s. 93, repealed: 1985, c.51, sch. 17.
s. 98, order 85/1781.

1972—cont.

70. Local Government Act 1972—*cont.*
ss. 98, 99, amended: 1985, c.51, sch. 14; order 85/1884.
s. 100, amended: 1985, c.43, sch. 2; repealed in pt.: *ibid.*, schs. 2, 3.
ss. 100A–100K, added: *ibid.*, s.1.
s. 100J, amended: order 85/1884.
s. 101, see *R.* v. *Secretary of State for the Environment, ex p. Hillingdon London Borough Council, The Times*, November 20, 1985, D.C.
s. 101, order 85/1781.
s. 101, amended: 1985, c.51, sch. 14; order 85/1884; repealed: 1985, c.51, sch. 17.
s. 111, see *R.* v. *Greater London Council, ex p. Westminster City Council, The Times*, December 27, 1984, Glidewell J.
s. 112, see *R.* v. *Hertfordshire County Council, ex p. National Union of Public Employees; R.* v. *Sussex County Council, ex p. National Union of Public Employees* [1985] I.R.L.R. 258, C.A.
s. 112, repealed in pt.: 1985, c.51, sch. 17; c.72, sch. 13.
s. 131, amended: 1985, c.71, sch. 2, repealed in pt.: *ibid.*, sch. 1.
s. 140B, repealed in pt.: 1985, c.51, sch. 17.
s. 141, amended: *ibid.*, sch. 16.
s. 142, see *R.* v. *I.L.E.A., ex p. Westminster City Council, The Times*, December 31, 1984, Glidewell J.; *R.* v. *Greater London Council, ex p. Westminster City Council, The Times*, December 27, 1984, Glidewell J.; *R.* v. *Greater London Council, ex p. Westminster City Council, The Times*, January 22, 1985, Nolan J.
s. 144, repealed in pt.: 1985, c.51, sch. 17.
s. 146A, added: *ibid.*, sch. 14; amended: order 85/1884.
ss. 148, 149, repealed in pt.: 1985, c.51, sch. 17.
s. 153, amended: *ibid.*; order 85/1884.
s. 173, regs. 85/426.
s. 173A, amended: order 85/1884.
s. 176, amended: 1985, c.51, sch. 14; order 85/1884.
s. 177, amended: 1985, c.51, sch. 14; repealed in pt.: *ibid.*, sch. 17.
s. 177A, regs. 85/426.
s. 177A, amended: 1985, c.51, sch. 14; repealed in pt.: *ibid.*, sch. 17.
s. 181, repealed in pt.: *ibid.*
s. 182, amended: *ibid.*, s.3, sch. 3.
s. 184, amended: *ibid.*, sch. 3.
s. 186, repealed in pt.: 1985, c.67, sch. 8.
ss. 193, 194, repealed: 1985, c.71, sch. 1.
s. 201, amended: 1985, c.51, sch. 8; repealed: 1985, c.72, sch. 13.
s. 202, amended: 1985, c.51, sch. 12; repealed in pt.: 1985, c.67, schs. 3, 8.
s. 204, repealed in pt.: 1985, c.13, sch. 3; c.51, sch. 17.
s. 206, repealed in pt.: *ibid.*, sch. 17.

1972—cont.

70. Local Government Act 1972—*cont.*
s. 220, amended: *ibid.*, s.13; repealed in pt.: *ibid.*, sch. 17.
s. 222, see *Runnymede Borough Council* v. *Ball, The Times*, July 23, 1985, C.A.; *R.* v. *North West Leicestershire District Council, ex p. Dakin* [1985] Crim.L.R. 390, D.C.; *London Docklands Development Corp.* v. *Rank Hovis McDougall, The Times*, July 25, 1985, C.A.
ss. 223–225, amended: 1985, c.51, sch. 14; order 85/1884.
s. 226, amended: 1985, c.51, sch. 8.
s. 228, see *Russell-Walker* v. *Gimblett, The Times*, March 14, 1985, D.C.
s. 228, amended: 1985, c.51, schs. 2, 14; order 85/1884.
ss. 229–234, amended: 1985, c.51, sch. 14; order 85/1884.
ss. 236, 238, amended: 1985, c.51, sch. 14.
s. 239, amended: *ibid.*; order 85/1884.
s. 243, amended: 1985, c.50, s.19; c.51, sch. 14; repealed in pt.: 1985, c.50, s.19, sch. 5.
s. 264, repealed: 1985, c.51, sch. 17.
s. 266, orders 85/402, 634.
s. 270, see *London Docklands Development Corporation* v. *Rank Hovis McDougall, The Times*, July 25, 1985, C.A.
s. 270, amended: 1985, c.51, schs. 14, 16; repealed in pt.: *ibid.*, sch. 17.
sch. 2, repealed in pt.: *ibid.*
sch. 10, orders 84/1875, 1930, 2049; 85/89, 129, 1763, 1816.
sch. 11, amended: 1985, c.51, sch. 9; repealed in pt.: *ibid.*, sch. 17.
sch. 12, amended: *ibid.*, sch. 14; order 85/1844; repealed in pt.: 1985, c.51, sch. 17.
sch. 12A, added: 1985, c.43, s.1, sch. 1.
sch. 13, regs. 85/1148.
sch. 13, amended: 1985, c.51, s.70; repealed in pt.: *ibid.*, c.71, sch. 1.
sch. 14, amended: 1985, c.51, sch. 6; order 85/1844; repealed in pt.: 1985, c.51, sch. 17.
sch. 16, amended: *ibid.*, sch. 3; repealed in pt.: *ibid.*, sch. 17.
sch. 17, amended: *ibid.*, sch. 3.
sch. 22, repealed: 1985, c.71, sch. 1.
sch. 24, repealed in pt.: 1985, c.67, schs. 3, 8.
schs. 27, 29, repealed in pt.: 1985, c.51, sch. 17.

71. Criminal Justice Act 1972.
s. 31, see *York City Council* v. *The Little Gallery, The Times*, December 2, 1985, D.C.
s. 32, repealed: 1985, c.71, sch. 1.
s. 36, amended: 1985, c.23, sch. 1.

73. Museums and Galleries Admission Charges Act 1972.
s. 1, amended (S.): 1985, c.16, sch. 2.

CAP.

1973

5. Housing (Amendment) Act 1973.
repealed: 1985, c.71, sch. 1.

8. Coal Industry Act 1973.
s. 12, amended: 1985, c.9, sch. 2.

13. Supply of Goods (Implied Terms) Act 1973.
ss. 10, 12, see *McCann* v. *Patterson* [1984]
16 N.I.J.B., Lord Lowry L.C.J.

14. Costs in Criminal Cases Act 1973.
repealed: 1985, c.23, sch. 2.
s. 2, see *R.* v. *Scunthorpe Justices ex p.
Holbrey, The Times*, May 24, 1985,
D.C.

15. Administration of Justice Act 1973.
s. 8, see *Bank of Scotland* v. *Grimes* [1985]
2 All E.R. 254, C.A.
s. 17, repealed in pt.: 1985, c.23, sch. 2.
sch. 1, repealed in pt.: 1985, c.51, sch. 17.

16. Education Act 1973.
s. 3, regs. 85/1160.

17. Northern Ireland Assembly Act 1973.
ss. 2, 5, order 85/1268.

18. Matrimonial Causes Act 1973.
ss. 1, 2, see *Newman* v. *Newman*; *McLean*
v. *McLean*; *Jones* v. *Jones (Queen's
Proctor Intervening)* (1985) 15 Fam.Law
52, Sir John Arnold P.
s. 3, see *Nota* v. *Nota* (1984) 14 Fam.Law
310, C.A.
s. 9, see *Newman* v. *Newman*; *McLean* v.
McLean; *Jones* v. *Jones (Queen's Proctor Intervening)* (1985) 15 Fam.Law 52,
Sir John Arnold P.
s. 23, see *Banyard* v. *Banyard* (1985) 15
Fam.Law 120, C.A.; *Sandford* v. *Sandford* (1985) 15 Fam.Law 230, Ewbank
J.; *Davies* v. *Davies, The Times*, November 2, 1985, C.A.
s. 24, see *Banyard* v. *Banyard* (1985) 15
Fam.Law 120, C.A.; *Thompson* v.
Thompson [1985] 2 All E.R. 243, C.A.;
Teschner v. *Teschner* (1985) 15
Fam.Law 250, C.A.
s. 24A, see *Thompson* v. *Thompson* [1985]
2 All E.R. 243, C.A.
s. 25, see *Jenkins* v. *Livesey (Formerly
Jenkins)* [1985] 2 W.L.R. 47, H.L.;
Leadbeater v. *Leadbeater* (1985) 15
Fam.Law. 280, Balcombe J.
s. 31, see *Morris* v. *Morris, The Times*,
June 17, 1985, C.A.; *Thompson* v.
Thompson [1985] 2 All E.R. 243, C.A.;
Sandford v. *Sandford* (1985) 15
Fam.Law 230, Ewbank J.; *Whitfield* v.
Whitfield (1985) 15 Fam.Law 226, Wood
J.; *Morley-Clarke* v. *Jones* [1985] 3 All
E.R. 193, C.A.
s. 37, see *Hamlin* v. *Hamlin* [1985] 2 All
E.R. 1037, C.A.
s. 39, amended: 1985, c.65, sch. 8.
s. 41, see *Yeend* v. *Yeend* (1984) 14 Fam.
Law 314, C.A.
ss. 43, 44, repealed in pt.: 1985, c.51, sch.
17.

CAP.

1973—cont.

18. Matrimonial Causes Act 1973—*cont.*
s. 49, see *Bradley* v. *Bradley (Queen's
Proctor Intervening), The Times*, June
15, 1985, Eastham J.
s. 50, rules 85/144, 1315.

26. Land Compensation Act 1973.
s. 19, amended: 1985, c.51, sch. 4.
s. 29, see *G.L.C.* v. *Holmes, The Times*,
December 10, 1985, C.A.
s. 29, amended: 1985, c.71, sch. 2.
ss. 29, 37, see *Newery* v. *Liverpool City
Council* (1982) 14 H.L.R. 75.
s. 37, amended: 1985, c.71, sch. 2;
repealed in pt.: *ibid.*, sch. 1.
s. 39, amended: *ibid.*, sch. 2; repealed in
pt.: 1985, c.51, sch. 17; c. 71, sch. 1.
ss. 42, 52, 57, amended: *ibid.*, sch. 2.
s. 73, amended: *ibid.*; repealed in pt.:
ibid., sch. 1.
s. 87, amended: *ibid.*, sch. 2.

33. Protection of Wrecks Act 1973.
s. 1, orders 84/1963; 85/699.

35. Employment Agencies Act 1973.
s. 13, amended: 1985, c.51, sch. 14; order
85/1884; ; repealed in pt.: 1985, c.51,
sch. 17.

36. Northern Ireland Constitution Act 1973.
s. 38, orders 85/169, 454.
sch. 3, repealed in pt.: 1985, c.58, sch. 4.

37. Water Act 1973.
ss. 11, 14, 16, repealed in pt.: 1985, c.51,
sch. 17.
s. 25, repealed: *ibid.*
s. 29, orders 84/1995; 85/1805.
s. 30, see *South West Water Authority* v.
Rumble's [1985] 2 W.L.R. 405, H.L.
s. 34, order 85/914.
ss. 34, 38, repealed in pt.: 1985, c.51, sch.
17.
sch. 3, amended: 1985, c.9, sch. 2.
sch. 6, order 85/914.
sch. 8, repealed in pt.: 1985, c.51, sch. 17.

38. Social Security Act 1973.
s. 65, order 85/1975.
ss. 66, 89, amended: 1985, c.53, sch. 5.
s. 99, sch. 16, regs. 85/1323, 1926.
sch. 16, amended: 1985, c.53, sch. 5;
repealed in pt.: *ibid.*, s.1, sch. 6.
sch. 27, repealed in pt.: 1985, c.9, sch. 1.

41. Fair Trading Act 1973.
s. 3, amended: 1985, c.72, sch. 12.
s. 27, repealed in pt.: *ibid.*, sch. 13.
s. 50, order 84/1887.
s. 92, amended: 1985, c.9, sch. 2.
s. 137, amended: *ibid.*, c.67, s.116.
sch. 4, amended: 1985, c.61, s.60.
sch. 5, amended: 1985, c.67, s.114.

43. Hallmarking Act 1973.
sch. 4, amended: 1985, c.9, sch. 2.

**45. Domicile and Matrimonial Proceedings Act
1973.**
s. 5, see *Kapur* v. *Kapur* (1985) 15 Fam.
Law 22, Bush J.
s. 16, see *Chaudhary* v. *Chaudhary* [1984]
3 All E.R. 1017, C.A.

CAP.

1973—cont.

45. Domicile and Matrimonial Proceedings Act 1973—*cont.*
sch. 1, see *Gadd* v. *Gadd* [1984] 1 W.L.R. 1435, C.A.; *Thyssen-Bornemisza* v. *Thyssen-Bornemisza* [1985] 1 All E.R. 328, C.A.
sch. 2, amended (S.): 1985, c.37, sch. 1; repealed in pt. (S.): *ibid.*, sch. 2.

48. Pakistan Act 1973.
sch. 3, repealed in pt.: 1985, c.9, sch. 1.

49. Bangladesh Act 1973.
sch., repealed in pt.: 1985, c.21, sch. 2.

51. Finance Act 1973.
s. 16, see *Bosanquet* v. *Allen*; *Carver* v. *Duncan* [1985] 2 W.L.R. 1010, H.L.
s. 38, see *Clarke* v. *Oceanic Contracts Incorporated* (1982) 56 T.C. 183, H.L.
s. 47, amended: 1985, c.9, sch. 2.
s. 49, repealed in pt.: 1985, c.54, sch. 27.
s. 56, regs. 85/307, 386, 852, 1656; S.R. 1985 No. 14.
sch. 19, repealed in pt.: 1985, c.9, sch. 1.

52. Prescription and Limitation (Scotland) Act 1973.
s. 6, see *McPhail* v. *Cunninghame District Council, William Loudon & Son* v. *Cunninghame District Council* (O.H.), 1985 S.L.T. 149; *Hobday* v. *Kirkpatrick's Trs.* (O.H.), 1985 S.L.T. 197; *East Hook Purchasing Corporation* v. *Ben Nevis Distillery (Fort William)* (O.H.), 1985, S.L.T. 442.
s. 9, amended: 1985, c.9, sch. 2; c.66, sch. 7.
s. 11, see *Dunfermline District Council* v. *Blyth & Blyth Associates* (O.H.), 1985 S.L.T. 345.
ss. 11, 13, see *McPhail* v. *Cunninghame District Council, William Loudon & Son* v. *Cunninghame District Council* (O.H.), 1985 S.L.T. 149.
s. 17, see *Meek* v. *Milne* (O.H.), 1985 S.L.T. 318.
s. 18A, added: 1985, c.73, s.12.
ss. 19A, 22, sch. 1, amended: *ibid.*

56. Land Compensation (Scotland) Act 1973.
s. 28, order 85/292.

57. Badgers Act 1973.
ss. 1, 2, amended: 1985, c.31, s.1.

62. Powers of Criminal Courts Act 1973.
s. 14, see *Walsh* v. *Barlow*; *Thorpe* v. *Griggs* [1985] 1 W.L.R. 90, D.C.
s. 21, see *R.* v. *Cardiff JJ., ex p. Salter* (1985) 149 J.P. 619, D.C.
s. 35, see *R.* v. *Swann (Alan) and Webster (Alan)* (1984) 6 Cr.App.R.(S.) 22, C.A.; *R.* v. *Chappell* (1985) 80 Cr.App.R. 31, C.A.; *R.* v. *Horsham JJ., ex p. Richards* [1985] 1 W.L.R. 986, D.C.
s. 39, amended: 1985, c.65, sch. 8; repealed in pt.: *ibid.*, sch. 10.
s. 41, repealed: *ibid.*.
s. 43, see *R.* v. *Bramble* (1984) 6 Cr.App.R.(S.) 80, C.A.
s. 51, repealed in pt.: 1985, c.51, sch. 17.

CAP.

1973—cont.

62. Powers of Criminal Courts Act 1973—*cont.*
s. 54, order 85/1084, 1156, 1759, 1870, 1964, 1965, 2004.
sch. 2, repealed: 1985, c.65, sch. 10.
sch. 3, orders 85/1084, 1156, 1506, 1759, 1870, 1964, 1965, 2004.
sch. 3, repealed in pt.: 1985, c.51, sch. 17.

63. Government Trading Funds Act 1973.
ss. 1, 6, order 85/927.

65. Local Government (Scotland) Act 1973.
s. 17, orders 84/1855, 1856, 1938–1941, 2030.
s. 31, amended: 1985, c.65, s.31.
s. 44, repealed: 1985, c.43, sch. 3.
ss. 45, 49A, 50, regs. 85/395.
ss. 50A–50K, added: 1985, c.43, s.2.
s. 64, repealed in pt.: 1985, c.72, sch. 13.
s. 105, regs. 85/267.
s. 111, regs. 85/246.
s. 149, repealed: 1985, c.72, sch. 13.
ss. 150 (in pt.), 151, repealed: 1985, c.67, schs. 3, 8.
s. 188, repealed in pt.: 1985, c.13, sch. 3.
s. 197, repealed in pt.: 1985, c.43, sch. 3.
s. 215, see *McPhail* v. *Cunninghame District Council, William Loudon & Son* v. *Cunninghame District Council* (O.H.), 1985 S.L.T. 149.
s. 225, orders 84/1926, 85/1629.
s. 233, regs. 85/246.
sch. 7A, added: 1985, c.43, s.2, sch. 1.
sch 12, repealed in pt.: 1985, c.71, sch. 1.
sch. 18, repealed in pt.: 1985, c.67, schs. 3, 7, 8.
sch. 24, repealed in pt.: 1985, c.13, sch. 3.
sch. 25, repealed in pt.: 1985, c.72, sch. 13.

67. Fuel and Electricity (Control) Act 1973.
ss. 1–8, continued in force: order 85/1639.
s. 10, order 85/1639.

1974

4. Legal Aid Act 1974.
s. 1, regs. 85/1614.
s. 1, amended: 1985, c.61, s.45; regs. 85/1614.
s. 3, regs. 85/1840.
s. 4, regs. 85/1694; amended: *ibid.*
s. 6, regs. 84/1838, 85/1615.
s. 6, amended: regs. 85/1615.
s. 8, see *Littaur* v. *Steggles Palmer* [1985] 1 W.L.R. 1208, Sir Neil Lawson.
s. 9, see *Curling* v. *The Law Society* [1985] 1 All E.R. 705, C.A.
s. 12, amended: 1985, c.61, sch. 7; repealed in pt.: *ibid.*, s.40, sch. 8.
s. 13, see *Lee* v. *South West Thames Regional Health Authority (No. 2), The Times*, July 22, 1985, C.A.
s. 20, regs. 84/1838; 85/1491, 1614, 1615, 1694, 1840, 1879, 1880.
s. 22, amended: 1985, c.61, sch. 7.
s. 30, amended: *ibid.*, s.46.

CAP.

1974—cont.

4. Legal Aid Act 1974—cont.
s. 38, amended: *ibid.*, sch. 7; repealed in pt.: *ibid.*, s.40, sch.8.
s. 39, regs. 85/333, 1632.
sch. 3, amended: regs. 85/1694.

7. Local Government Act 1974.
s. 1, repealed in pt.: 1985, c.71, sch. 1.
s. 6, amended: 1985, c.51, s.8; repealed in pt.: *ibid.*, sch. 17.
s. 7, amended: *ibid.*, sch. 3.
s. 15, see *Norwich City Council* v. *Investors in Industry Commercial Properties, The Times*, August 5, 1985, C.A.
s. 19, order 85/102.
s. 21, see *Wright, Re*; *Maudsley, Re*; *Smith, Re, The Times*, January 16, 1985; (1985) 274 E.G. 717, C.A.
ss. 25, 26, amended: 1985, c.51, sch. 14; order 85/1884.
s. 34, repealed in pt.: 1985, c.51, sch. 17.
s. 37, repealed: 1985, c.71, sch. 1.
sch. 4, amended: 1985, c.51, sch. 8.
sch. 6, repealed in pt.: 1985, c.12, sch. 2; c.67, sch.8; c.72, sch.13.

9. Pensions (Increase) Act 1974.
s. 6, repealed in pt.: 1985, c.58, sch. 4.

20. Dumping at Sea Act 1974.
repealed: 1985, c.48, s.15.

24. Prices Act 1974.
s. 2, order 85/995.

28. Northern Ireland Act 1974.
Commencement orders: 85/60; S.Rs. 1984 Nos. 300, 422.
s. 1, order 85/1054.
sch. 1, orders 84/1821, 1822, 1983, 1984, 1986; 85/60, 170, 171, 452, 453, 754–756, 957–959; S.Rs. 1984 Nos. 300, 422; 1985 Nos. 82, 136, 188, 218, 247.

30. Finance Act 1974.
s. 17, repealed in pt.: 1985, c.54, schs. 14, 17.
s. 27, amended: *ibid.*, s.41.
ss. 38–47, 57 (in pt.), repealed: *ibid.*, sch. 27.
sch. 1, see *Hughes (Inspector of Taxes)* v. *Viner* [1985] 3 All E.R. 40; [1985] S.T.C. 235, Walton J.
sch. 2, see *Cooke* v. *Blacklaws* [1985] S.T.C. 1, Gibson J.
sch. 3, repealed: 1985, c.54, sch. 27.
sch. 4, see *Furniss* v. *Ford* (1981) 55 T.C. 561, D.C.
schs. 4, 6–10, repealed: 1985, c.54, sch. 27.

37. Health and Safety at Work etc. Act 1974.
s. 2, see *Dutton & Clark* v. *Daly* [1985] I.R.L.R. 363, E.A.T.
s. 4, see *Westminster City Council* v. *Select Management* [1985] 1 All E.R. 897, C.A.
s. 11, regs. 84/1890, 1902; 85/279, 910, 1107, 1108, 1333, 1601, 2023.
s. 15, regs. 84/1890, 1902; 85/910, 1107, 1108, 1333, 1601, 2023.
s. 18, regs. 85/1107.

CAP.

1974—cont.

37. Health and Safety at Work Act 1974—cont.
s. 28, amended: 1985, c.51, sch. 14; order 85/1884.
s. 43, regs. 84/1890, 1902; 85/279, 1333.
s. 50, regs. 84/1890, 1902; 85/910, 1107, 1108, 1333, 1601, 2023.
s. 52, regs. 85/1333.
s. 53, see *Westminster City Council* v. *Select Management* [1985] 1 All E.R. 897, C.A.
s. 53, repealed in pt.: 1985, c.51, sch. 17.
s. 79, repealed: 1985, c.9, sch. 1.
s. 80, regs. 85/1333.
s. 82, regs. 84/1890, 1902, 1333.
sch. 3, regs. 84/1890, 1902; 85/910, 1333, 2023.
sch. 10, repealed in pt.: 1985, c.51, sch. 17.

38. Land Tenure Reform (Scotland) Act 1974.
s. 8, amended: 1985, c.73, s.1.

39. Consumer Credit Act 1974.
s. 16, orders 85/620, 757, 1736, 1918.
s. 20, regs. 85/1192.
s. 43, order 85/621.
ss. 44, 52, regs. 85/619.
ss. 70, 73, 75, 141, Act of Sederunt 85/705.
s. 143, S.R. 1985 No. 102.
ss. 145, 170, 174, see *Brookes* v. *Retail Credit Card, The Times*, October 19, 1985, D.C.
ss. 151, 152, regs. 85/619.
s. 178, S.R. 1985 No. 90.
s. 180, regs. 85/666.
s. 182, orders 85/620, 757, 1736; regs. 85/619, 666, 1192, 1918.
s. 189, regs. 85/619, 666.
s. 189, repealed in pt.: 1985, c.51, sch. 17.
s. 191, S.R. 1985 No. 90.
sch. 4, repealed in pt.: 1985, c.65, sch. 10; c.71, sch. 1.

40. Control of Pollution Act 1974.
Commencement order: 85/70.
ss. 2, 5, 11–13, amended: 1985, c.51, sch. 6; order 85/1884.
s. 14, amended: *ibid.*
s. 30, regs. 85/708.
s. 30, amended: 1985, c.51, sch. 6; order 85/1884; repealed in pt.: *ibid.*.
ss. 31, 32, amended: 1985, c.48, s.15.
s. 36, repealed in pt.: 1985, c.51, sch. 17.
s. 40, regs. 85/5.
ss. 41, 55, regs. 85/813.
s. 56, regs. 85/178(S.), 507, 708.
s. 62, see *Tower Hamlets London Borough Council* v. *Creitzman* (1985) 83 L.G.R. 72, D.C.
s. 71, orders 84/1992; 85/145(S.).
ss. 75, 77, regs. 85/1728.
s. 98, amended: order 85/1448; repealed in pt.: 1985, c.51, sch. 17.
s. 100, regs. 85/2011.
s. 104, orders 84/1992; 85/70, 145(S.); regs. 85/5, 813, 2011.
s. 109, order 85/70.

CAP.

1974—cont.

43. Merchant Shipping Act 1974.
s. 1, orders 85/230, 1430.
s. 2, amended: 1985, c.9, sch. 2.
s. 5, order 85/1665.
s. 17, regs. 85/1607.
s. 20, order 85/1197.
sch. 5, regs. 85/1607.

44. Housing Act 1974.
Pts. I (ss.1–12) (exc. s.11), II–VIII (ss.13–104), repealed: 1985, c.71, sch. 1.
Pts. I (ss.1–12) (exc. s.11), II (ss.13–28) (exc. s.18), III (ss. 29–35), repealed (S.): *ibid.*
s. 5, repealed in pt.: 1985, c.51, sch. 17.
s. 12, amended: 1985, c.9, sch. 2.
s. 18, amended: 1985, c.71, sch. 2.
s. 19, see *Ashby* v. *Ebdon* [1984] 3 All E.R. 869, Warner J.
ss. 22, 24, 25, amended: 1985, c.9, sch. 2.
ss. 30, 43, 49, repealed in pt.: 1985, c.51, sch. 17.
s. 56, see *R.* v. *Kerrier District Council, ex p. Guppys (Bridport)* (1985) 274 E.C. 924, C.A.
ss. 59, 78, order 84/1880.
s. 84, amended: 1985, c.51, sch. 8; repealed in pt.: *ibid.*, sch. 17.
s. 99, repealed in pt.: 1985, c.51, sch. 17.
ss. 105–117, repealed: 1985, c.71, sch. 1.
s. 121, repealed in pt.: 1985, c.51, sch. 17.
sch. 121–130, repealed: 1985, c.17, sch. 1.
s. 128, order 84/1880.
s. 131 (in pt.), schs. 1–7, repealed: 1985, c.71, sch. 1.
sch. 3, amended: *ibid.*, sch. 2; repealed (S.): *ibid.*, sch. 1.
sch. 5, repealed in pt.: 1985, c.51, sch. 17.
sch. 8, see *Johnston* v. *Duke of Devonshire* (1984) 272 E.G. 661, C.A.; *Mayhew* v. *Governors of Harrow Road Trust*, December 14, 1984, Judge Wild, Bloomsbury County Court; *Johnson* v. *Duke of Westminster* (1984) 17 H.L.R. 136, C.A.
schs. 9–12, 13 (in pt.), 14, 15, repealed: 1985, c.71, sch. 1.
schs. 13, 14, repealed in pt. (S.): *ibid.*

45. Housing (Scotland) Act 1974.
ss. 3, 10A, 48, order 85/297.

46. Friendly Societies Act 1974.
s. 7, repealed in pt.: 1985, c.54, s.41, sch. 27.
s. 36, amended: 1985, c.9, sch. 2.
s. 46, repealed in pt.: 1985, c.58, sch. 4.
s. 51, amended: 1985, c.71, sch. 2.
s. 59, repealed in pt. (S.): 1985, c.66, sch. 8.
s. 64, amended: 1985, c.54, s.41.
s. 87, amended: 1985, c.9, sch. 2.
s. 104, regs. 85/343.
s. 105, repealed in pt.: 1985, c.54, sch. 27.
s. 111, amended: 1985, c.9, sch. 2.
sch. 9, repealed in pt.: 1985, c.54, sch. 27.

47. Solicitors Act 1974.
s. 3, amended: 1985, c.61, sch. 1.
ss. 7, 8, repealed in pt.: *ibid.*, schs. 1, 8.

CAP.

1974—cont.

47. Solicitors Act 1974—*cont.*
s. 11, amended: 1985, c.23, s.4; c.61, sch. 1.
s. 12, amended: 1985, c.61, s.4; c.65, sch. 8; repealed in pt.: *ibid.*, sch. 10.
s. 13, amended: 1985, c.61, sch. 1.
s. 13A, added: *ibid.*, s.5; repealed in pt.: 1985, c.65, sch. 10.
s. 21, amended: 1985, c.61, sch. 1.
s. 22, amended: *ibid.*, s.6.
s. 23, substituted: *ibid.*, s.7.
ss. 24, 28, 34, amended: *ibid.*, sch. 1.
s. 43, amended: *ibid.*; repealed in pt.: *ibid.*, schs. 1, 8.
s. 44A, added: *ibid.*, s.1.
s. 44B, added: *ibid.*, s.2.
s. 45, amended: *ibid.*, s.3.
s. 46, rules 85/226.
s. 47, amended: 1985, c.61, s.44, sch. 7.
s. 47A, added: *ibid.*, s.3.
ss. 48, 49, amended: *ibid.*, sch. 7.
s. 50, see *McKernan's Application, Re, The Times,* October 26, 1985, C.A.
s. 70, see *Symbol Park Lane* v. *Steggles Palmer (A Firm)* [1985] 1 W.L.R. 668, C.A.
s. 79, amended: 1985, c.61, sch. 1.
s. 87, amended: *ibid.*; repealed in pt.: 1985, c.58, sch. 4.
s. 88, amended: 1985, c.23, s.4.
sch. 1, amended: 1985, c.61, sch. 1.
sch. 2, amended: 1985, c.23, s.4, repealed in pt.: 1985, c.61, schs. 1, 8.

49. Insurance Companies Act 1974.
sch. 1, repealed in pt.: 1985, c.71, sch. 1.

52. Trade Union and Labour Relations Act 1974.
s. 2, see *Hughes* v. *Transport and General Workers' Union* [1985] I.R.L.R. 382, Vinelott J.
ss. 2–4, amended: 1985, c.9, sch. 2.
s. 8, regs. 85/300.
s. 13, see *Thomas* v. *National Union of Mineworkers* [1985] 2 All E.R. 1, C.A.; *Shipping Company Uniform Inc.* v. *International Transport Workers Federation* [1985] I.C.R. 245, Staughton J.
ss. 18, 30, see *Gibbons* v. *Associated British Ports* [1985] I.R.L.R. 376, Tudor Price J.
s. 29, see *Cleveland County Council* v. *Springett* (1985) I.R.L.R. 131, E.A.T.
s. 30, sch. 2, amended: 1985, c.9, sch. 2.

53. Rehabilitation of Offenders Act 1974.
s. 9, see *X.* v. *Commissioner of Police of the Metropolis* [1985] 1 W.L.R. 420, Whitford J.

1975

3. Arbitration Act 1975.
s. 1, see *S.L. Sethia Liners* v. *State Trading Corp. of India, The Times,* October 19, 1985, C.A.

CAP.

1975—cont.

3. Arbitration Act 1975—*cont.*
s. 3, see *Agromet Motoimport* v. *Maulden Engineering Co. (Beds.)* [1985] 2 All E.R. 436, Otton J.
s. 7, order 85/455.

6. Housing Rents and Subsidies Act 1975.
repealed: 1985, c.71, sch. 1.
s. 16, repealed in pt.: 1985, c.51, sch. 17.

7. Finance Act 1975.
s. 14, repealed in pt.: 1985, c.54, schs. 14, 27.
s. 19, see *Clore (Deceased) (No. 3); Re I.R.C.* v. *Stype Trustees (Jersey)* [1985] S.T.C. 394, Walton J.
s. 20, see *Macpherson* v. *I.R.C.* [1985] S.T.C. 471, D.C.
s. 48, amended: 1985, c.9, sch. 2.
sch. 4, see *Finch* v. *I.R.C.* [1985] Ch. 1, C.A.; *Clore (Deceased) (No. 3), Re; I.R.C.* v. *Stype Trustees (Jersey)* [1985] 2 All E.R. 819; [1985] S.T.C. 394, Walton J.
sch. 5, see *Macpherson* v. *I.R.C.* [1985] S.T.C. 471, D.C.
sch. 7, see *Minden Trust (Cayman)* v. *I.R.C.* [1985] S.T.C. 758, C.A.

8. Offshore Petroleum Development (Scotland) Act 1975.
s. 5, repealed in pt.: 1985, c.30, sch.
s. 18, amended and repealed in pt.: 1985, c.48, s.15.

14. Social Security Act 1975.
s. 1, order 84/1904.
s. 1, amended: 1985, c.53, sch. 5.
s. 4, regs. 85/1398.
s. 4, amended: 1985, c.53, ss.7, 8.
s. 7, amended: *ibid.*, s.7.
s. 7A, regs. 85/397.
s. 7A, amended: regs. 85/1398.
s. 8, regs. 85/397.
s. 8, amended: 1985, c.53, s.7; regs. 85/1398.
s. 11, regs. 85/398, 399.
s. 13, regs. 85/1398, 1417.
s. 13, amended: 1985, c.53, sch. 5.
s. 15A, added: *ibid.*, s.18.
s. 16, amended: *ibid.*, s.9.
s. 17, regs. 85/1571.
s. 18, amended: 1985, c.53, sch. 5.
s. 20, amended: *ibid.*, s.10.
s. 22, amended: *ibid.*, sch. 4.
s. 24, see *Burns* v. *Secretary of State for Social Services*, 1985 S.L.T. 351.
s. 27, see *Decision No. R(P) 2/85.*
s. 27, regs. 85/600.
s. 28, amended: 1985, c.53, s.9; repealed in pt.: *ibid.*, sch. 6.
s. 29, amended: *ibid.*, s.9.
s. 30, amended: order 85/1245.
s. 36, amended: 1985, c.53, sch. 4.
s. 37A, see *Lees* v. *Secretary of State for the Social Services* [1985] 2 W.L.R. 805, H.L.; *Decision No. R(M) 1/85.*
s. 37A, order 85/1245.
s. 38, regs. 85/1327.

CAP.

1975—cont.

14. Social Security Act 1975—*cont.*
s. 39, amended: 1985, c.53, s.12; repealed in pt.: *ibid.*, s.12, sch. 6.
s. 41, order 85/1570; amended: *ibid.*
s. 45, regs. 85/1190.
s. 45, amended: 1985, c.53, s.13; repealed in pt.: *ibid.*, sch. 6.
ss.45A, 46, 47, regs. 85/1190.
ss. 45A, 46, 47, amended: 1985, c.53, s.13.
s. 49, regs. 85/1190, 1618.
s. 50, see *Nancollas* v. *Insurance Officer; Ball* v. *Insurance Officer* [1985] 1 All E.R. 833, C.A.
s. 58, regs. 85/1571.
s. 59, amended: 1985, c.53, s.9.
s. 60, see *Smith (John Michael)* v. *Insurance Officer*, October 16, 1984, C.A.
s. 60, amended: 1985, c.53, s.14.
s. 64, order 85/1570; amended: *ibid.*
s. 66, regs. 85/1190.
ss. 76, 77, regs. 85/159, 967.
s. 78, regs. 85/967.
s. 79, repealed in pt.: 1985, c.53, sch. 6.
s. 80, regs. 85/600.
s. 82, repealed in pt.: 1985, c.53, sch. 6.
s. 83, substituted: *ibid.*, sch. 5.
s. 84, regs. 85/1505.
s. 84, amended: 1985, c.53, s.13.
s. 90, repealed in pt.: *ibid.*, sch. 6.
s. 104, see *Decision No. R(M) 1/85.*
s. 112, regs. 84/1991.
s. 113, regs. 85/159, 967.
ss. 114, 115, regs. 84/1991.
s. 122, amended: 1985, c.53, sch. 5.
s. 123A, added: *ibid.*, s.7.
s. 124, order 85/1245.
s. 124, amended: 1985, c.53, sch. 5.
s. 125, order 85/1245.
s. 125, amended: 1985, c.53, ss.15, 16; repealed in pt.: *ibid.*, s.16, sch. 6.
s. 126A, order 85/1245.
s. 126A, repealed in pt.: 1985, c.53, s.16, sch. 6.
s. 129, regs. 85/143, 400.
s. 131, regs. 85/1571.
s. 134, amended: 1985, c.53, sch. 5.
s. 143, orders 84/1817; 85/1202.
s. 152, repealed in pt.: 1985, c.65, s.216, sch. 10.
s. 153, repealed: *ibid.*, sch. 10.
s. 155, regs. 85/967.
s. 165A, regs. 85/1250.
s. 165A, added: 1985, c.53, s.17.
s. 166, regs. 85/677, 1305, 1327, 1570, 1618.
s. 167, order 84/1904.
s. 167, amended: 1985, c.53, sch. 5.
s. 168, regs. 84/1921; 85/397–399, 600, 1398, 1926–1931.
sch. 1, regs. 85/396, 399, 1411.
sch. 1, amended: 1985, c.53, sch. 5.
sch. 2, amended: 1985, c.54, s.42.
sch. 4, amended: order 85/1245.
sch. 4, repealed in pt.: 1985, c.53, sch. 6.
sch. 13, regs. 84/1991.

1975—cont.

14. Social Security Act 1975—*cont.*
sch. 14, regs. 85/1571.
sch. 18, amended: 1985, c.19, sch. 2; repealed: 1985, c.65, sch. 10; c.66, sch. 8(S.).
sch. 20, regs. 84/1921, 1991; 85/397, 398, 600, 967, 1190, 1305, 1323, 1327, 1398, 1618, 1926–1931.
sch. 20, amended: 1985, c.53, sch. 5.

15. Social Security (Northern Ireland) Act 1975.
s. 1, S.R. 1984 No. 425.
s. 4, S.R. 1985, No. 260.
ss. 7A, 8, 11, S.R. 1985 No. 61.
s. 13, S.Rs. 1985 Nos. 260, 263.
s. 17, S.R. 1985 No. 278.
s. 27, S.R. 1985 No. 92.
s. 36, see *Insurance Officer* v. *McCaffrey* [1984] 1 W.L.R. 1353, H.L.
s. 38, S.R. 1985 No. 227.
s. 41, S.R. 1985 No. 281.
ss. 45, 45A, 46, 47, S.R. 1985 No. 229.
s. 49, S.Rs. 1985 Nos. 229, 300.
s. 58, S.R. 1985 No. 278.
s. 64, S.R. 1985 No. 281.
s. 66, S.R. 1985 No. 229.
ss. 76, 77, S.R. 1985 No. 41.
s. 79, see *Insurance Officer* v. *McCaffrey* [1984] 1 W.L.R. 1353, H.L.
ss. 80, 81, S.R. 1985 No. 92.
s. 84, S.R. 1985 No. 229.
s. 113, S.R. 1985 No. 41.
ss. 114, 115, S.R. 1984 No. 445.
s. 120, S.R. 1984 No. 424; S.R. 1985 No. 230.
s. 124, S.Rs. 1985 Nos. 25, 61.
s. 126, S.R. 1985 No. 278.
s. 134, S.R. 1984 No. 449; S.R. 1985 No. 205.
s. 154A, S.R. 1985 No. 226.
s. 155, S.Rs. 1985 No. 227, 229.
s. 157, S.Rs. 1984 No. 444; 1985 No. 41.
sch. 1, S.Rs. 1985 Nos. 59, 61, 257.
sch. 2, amended: 1985, c.54, s.42.
sch. 13, S.R. 1984 No. 445.
sch. 14, S.R. 1985 No. 278.
sch. 17, S.Rs. 1984 No. 444; 1985 No. 41.

16. Industrial Injuries and Diseases (Old Cases) Act 1975.
ss. 2,4, scheme 85/1446.
ss. 2, 7, amended: order 85/1245.
s. 5, scheme 85/491.

17. Industrial Injuries and Diseases (Northern Ireland Old Cases) Act 1975.
ss. 2, 4, S.R. 1985 No. 253.

18. Social Security (Consequential Provisions) Act 1975.
sch. 2, repealed in pt.: 1985, c.9, sch. 1; c.65, sch. 10; c.66, sch. 8(S.); c.71, sch. 1.

20. District Courts (Scotland) Act 1975.
s. 1A, added: 1985, c.73, s.33.
ss. 11, 15, amended: *ibid.*, s.34.
s. 19, repealed: *ibid.*, sch. 4.

1975—cont.

21. Criminal Procedure (Scotland) Act 1975.
s. 20A, see *H.M. Advocate* v. *Cafferty*, 1984 S.C.C.R. 444; *Walker* v. *H.M. Advocate*, 1985 S.C.C.R. 150.
s. 70, see *McAllister* v. *H.M. Advocate*, 1985 S.L.T. 399.
s. 78, see *H.M. Advocate* v. *Cafferty*, 1984 S.C.C.R. 444; *H.M. Advocate* v. *Graham*, 1985 S.L.T. 498.
ss. 88–91, 98, amended: 1985, c.73, s.23, sch. 2.
s. 101, see *H.M. Advocate* v. *Brown*, 1984 S.C.C.R. 347; *McGinty* v. *H.M. Advocate*, 1985 S.L.T. 25; *Farrell* v. *H.M. Advocate*, 1985 S.L.T. 58.
s. 108, see *H.M. Advocate* v. *Cafferty*, 1984 S.C.C.R. 444; *McAllister* v. *H.M. Advocate*, 1985 S.L.T. 399.
s. 108, amended: 1985, c.73, sch. 2.
s. 114, Act of Adjournal 85/1534.
ss. 141A, 141B, added, 1985, c.73, s.36.
s. 149A, amended: *ibid.*, s.37.
s. 193B, amended: *ibid.*, s.45.
s. 206A; added: *ibid.*, s.45.
s. 207, amended: *ibid.*, s.43.
s. 252, see *McCadden* v. *H.M. Advocate*, 1985, S.C.C.R. 282.
s. 271, amended: 1985, c.73, sch. 2.
s. 282, Acts of Adjournal 85/316, 1565.
s. 289C, repealed in pt.: 1985, c.72, sch. 13.
s. 289D, amended: 1985, c.13, sch. 2.
s. 311, see *Aitchison* v. *Wringe*, 1985 S.L.T. 449.
s. 312, see *Dyce* v. *Aitchison*, 1985 S.C.C.R. 184; *Smith* v. *Allan*, 1985, S.L.T. 565.
s. 316, see *Aitchison* v. *Wringe*, 1985 S.L.T. 449.
s. 334, see *Aitchison* v. *Wringe*, 1985 S.L.T. 449.
s. 335, see *Mackenzie* v. *Brougham*, 1985 S.L.T. 276; *Dyce* v. *Aitchison*, 1985 S.C.C.R. 184.
ss. 346A, 346B, added: 1985, c.73, s.36.
s. 350A, amended: *ibid.*, s.37.
s. 357, see *Anderson* v. *Allan*, 1985 S.C.C.R. 262.
s. 396, see *Dunlop* v. *Allan*, 1984 S.C.C.R. 329.
s. 407, amended: 1985, c.73, s.40.
s. 415, amended: *ibid.*, s.43.
s. 439, see *Tudhope* v. *Senatti Holdings*, 1984 S.C.C.R. 251.
s. 447, amended: 1985, c.73, sch. 2.
s. 448, see *Berry, Petr.*, 1985 S.C.C.R. 106.
s. 448, repealed in pt.: 1985, c.73, sch. 4.
s. 457, Acts of Adjournal 84/1955; 85/43, 316, 1565.

22. Oil Taxation Act 1975.
s. 2, sch. 3, see *R.* v. *Att.-Gen., ex p. I.C.I., The Financial Times*, January 29, 1985, Woolf J.
s. 5A, amended: 1985, c.54, s.90.

CAP.

1975—cont.

22. Oil Taxation Act 1975—*cont.*
s. 9, amended: *ibid.*, s.91.
s. 14, amended: *ibid.*, s.53.

23. Reservoirs Act 1975.
Commencement order: 85/176.
s. 2, amended: 1985, c.51, s.11.
ss. 2, 3, regs. 85/177.
s. 4, regs. 84/1874; 85/175, 1086.
s. 5, regs. 84/1874; 85/175, 177, 548, 1086.
s. 11, regs. 85/177, 548.
s. 12, regs. 84/1874.
s. 29, order 85/176.

24. House of Commons Disqualification Act 1975.
s. 5, order 85/1212.
sch. 1, amended: 1985, c.17, sch. 4; c.51, sch. 13; c.56, sch. 1; c.62, schs. 1, 4; c.65, sch. 1; order 85/1212; repealed in pt.: order 85/1212.

25. Northern Ireland Assembly Disqualification Act 1975.
sch. 1, amended: 1985, c.17, sch. 4; c.62, schs. 1, 4; c.65, sch. 1; repealed in pt.: 1985, c.21, sch. 2.

26. Ministers of the Crown Act 1975.
s. 1, orders 84/1814, 1818; 85/166, 442, 1778, 1779.
s. 2, order 85/1778.

27. Ministerial and Other Salaries Act 1975.
s. 1, order 85/1214.

28. Housing Rents and Subsidies (Scotland) Act 1975.
s. 5, amended: 1985, c.71, sch. 2.
s. 12, sch. 3 (in pt.), repealed: *ibid.*, sch. 1.

30. Local Government (Scotland) Act 1975.
s. 2, see *B.P. Oil Grangemouth Refinery* v. *Assessor for Lothian Region*, 1985 S.L.T. 228.
s. 6, see *Assessor for Orkney* v. *Post Office*, 1982 S.C. 32.
ss. 6, 35, orders 85/193–200, 588.
ss. 23, 24, amended: 1985, c.73, s.55.

34. Evidence (Proceedings in Other Jurisdictions) Act 1975.
s. 2, see *R.* v. *Rathbone, ex p. Dikko* [1985] 2 W.L.R. 375, Forbes J.; *Asbestos Insurance Coverage Cases. Re, The Financial Times*, March 6, 1985, H.L.
s. 3, see *R.* v. *Rathbone, ex p. Dikko* [1985] 2 W.L.R. 375, Forbes J.

35. Farriers Registration Act 1975.
sch. 1, amended: 1985, c.9, sch. 2.

45. Finance (No. 2) Act 1975.
s. 36, amended: 1985, c.9, sch. 2.
s. 38, see *Brady* v. *Hart (trading as Jaclyn Model Agency)* [1985] S.T.C. 498, D.C.
ss. 47, 48, order 85/563.
s. 49, repealed in pt.: 1985, c.54, schs. 14, 27.
s. 58, repealed in pt.: *ibid.*, sch. 27.
s. 69, regs. 85/158, 351.
s. 69, repealed in pt.: 1985, c.71, sch. 1.
s. 69, repealed in pt. (S.): *ibid.*
s. 70, regs. 84/2008; 85/185, 351.

CAP.

1975—cont.

45. Finance (No. 2) Act 1975—*cont.*
s. 71, amended: 1985, c.71, sch. 2; repealed in pt.: 1985, c.65, sch. 10; c.71, sch. 1.
s. 71, repealed in pt. (S.): 1985, c.66, sch. 8; c.71, sch. 1.
sch. 9, repealed: 1985, c.54, sch. 27.
sch. 12, regs. 84/2008.
sch. 12, amended: 1985, c.9, sch. 2; repealed in pt.: *ibid.*, schs. 1, 2.

47. Litigants in Person (Costs and Expenses) Act 1975.
s. 1, see *MacBeth Currie & Co.* v. *Matthew*, 1985 S.L.T.(Sh.Ct.) 44.

51. Salmon and Freshwater Fisheries Act 1975.
s. 28, sch. 3, order 85/783.
sch. 3, amended: 1985, c.51, sch. 8.

52. Safety of Sports Grounds Act 1975.
s. 1, orders 85/1063, 1064.
ss. 3–5, 10, 11, 17, amended: 1985, c.51, sch. 8.
s. 18, orders 85/1063, 1064.

55. Statutory Corporations (Financial Provisions) Act 1975.
sch. 4, repealed in pt.: 1985, c.71, sch. 1.

60. Social Security Pensions Act 1975.
s. 1, regs. 85/1726.
s. 1, amended: 1985, c.53, sch. 5.
s. 4, regs. 85/397.
s. 6, regs. 85/1417.
s. 6, amended: 1985, c.53, sch. 5; order 85/1245.
s. 21, order 85/688.
s. 21, amended: 1985, c.53, sch. 3.
s. 26, repealed in pt.: *ibid.*, sch. 6.
ss. 27, 28, amended: *ibid.*, sch. 5.
s. 32, regs. 85/1323.
s. 34, repealed in pt.: 1985, c.53, sch. 6.
s. 35, regs. 85/1417, 1930.
s. 35, amended: 1985, c.53, sch. 3.
s. 36, amended: *ibid.*, sch. 5.
s. 38, regs. 85/1323.
s. 41, amended: 1985, c.53, sch. 5.
ss. 41A, 41B, amended: *ibid.*, s.6, sch. 5; repealed in pt.: *ibid.*, sch. 6.
s. 41B, regs. 85/1927.
s. 41C, regs. 84/1921; 85/1925.
s. 41C, amended: 1985, c.53, sch. 3.
s. 41D, repealed in pt.: *ibid.*, sch. 6.
ss. 42, 43, amended: *ibid.*, schs. 3, 5.
ss. 43, 44, regs. 85/1323.
s. 44, amended: 1985, c.53, schs. 3, 5.
s. 44A, regs. 85/1928.
s. 44D, added: 1985, c.53, sch. 1.
s. 45, amended: *ibid.*, schs. 3, 5.
ss. 46–48, amended: *ibid.*, sch. 5.
s. 52, regs. 85/1928.
ss. 52A–52D, added: 1985, c.53, sch. 1.
s. 52C, regs. 85/1929.
s. 55, amended: 1985, c.53, sch. 5.
ss. 56A–56N, added: *ibid.*, sch. 5.
s. 58, amended: 1985, c.65, sch. 8; c.66, sch. 7(S.).
s. 59, order 85/1575.
s. 59, repealed in pt.: 1985, c.53, schs. 5, 6.

CAP.

1975—cont.

60. Social Security Pensions Act 1975—*cont.*
s. 60, amended: *ibid.*, sch. 5.
s. 62, regs. 85/1323, 1929.
s. 66, regs. 84/1921.
s. 66, repealed in pt.: 1985, c.53, sch. 6.
s. 68, amended: *ibid.*, sch. 5.
sch. 1, amended: *ibid.*, s.9.
sch. 1A, regs. 85/1930, 1931.
sch. 1A, added: 1985, c.53, sch. 1.
sch. 2, regs. 85/1323, 1928.
sch. 3, amended: 1985, c.53, sch. 5; c.65,
sch. 8; c.66, sch. 7(S.).
sch. 4, repealed in pt.: 1985, c.9, sch. 1;
c.53, sch. 6; c.65, sch. 10; c.66,
sch. 8(S.).

61. Child Benefit Act 1975.
ss. 6, 7, 11, regs. 84/1960.
s. 22, regs. 84/1960; 85/1243.
s. 24, regs. 85/1243.

63. Inheritance (Provision for Family and Dependants) Act 1975.
see *F. (decd.) Re, The Times*, February
11, 1985, Balcombe J.
ss. 1, 2, see *Leach (decd.), Re* [1985] 2 All
E.R. 754, C.A.
ss. 1, 3, 6, see *Stead* v. *Stead* (1985) 15
Fam.Law 154, C.A.
s. 4, see *Freeman (decd.), Re* [1984] 3 All
E.R. 906, H.H. Judge Thomas.

65. Sex Discrimination Act 1975.
s. 1, see *Porcelli* v. *Strathclyde Regional
Council* [1985] I.C.R. 177, E.A.T.;
Hayes v. *Malleable Working Men's Club
and Institute, The Times*, June 19, 1985;
Newstead v. *Department of Transport
and H.M. Treasury* [1985] I.R.L.R. 299,
E.A.T.; *Rainey* v. *Greater Glasgow
Health Board*, 1985 S.L.T. 518; *Kidd* v.
D.R.G. (U.K.) [1985] I.C.R. 405,
E.A.T.
ss. 3, 5, see *Kidd* v. *DRG (UK)* [1985]
I.C.R. 405, E.A.T.
s. 6, see *Porcelli* v. *Strathclyde Regional
Council* [1985] I.C.R. 177, E.A.T.;
Newstead v. *Department of Transport
and H.M. Treasury* [1985] I.R.L.R. 299,
E.A.T.
s. 23, see *R.* v. *Secretary of State for
Education and Science, ex p. Keating,
The Times*, December 3, 1985, Taylor J.
s. 28, repealed in pt.: 1985, c.47, s.4.
s. 56A, order 85/387.
s. 82, see *Mirror Group Newspapers* v.
Gunning, The Times, November 6,
1985, C.A.

66. Recess Elections Act 1975.
s. 1, amended: 1985, c.65, sch. 8; repealed
in pt.: *ibid.*, sch. 10.
s. 5, repealed in pt.: *ibid.*

**67. Housing Finance (Special Provisions) Act
1975.**
repealed: 1985, c.71, sch. 1.

68. Industry Act 1975.
s. 37, schs. 1, 2, amended: 1985, c.9, sch.
2.

CAP.

1975—cont.

69. Scottish Development Agency Act 1975.
s. 25, sch. 1, amended: 1985, c.9, sch. 2.

70. Welsh Development Agency Act 1975.
s. 27, sch. 1, amended: 1985, c.9, sch. 2.
sch. 3, amended: 1985, c.25, s.5.

71. Employment Protection Act 1975.
s. 8, regs. 85/300.
ss. 99, 101, see *Jowett (Angus) & Co.* v.
*National Union of Tailors and Garment
Workers* [1985] I.R.L.R. 326; [1985]
I.C.R. 646, E.A.T.; *Transport and General Workers Union* v. *Ledbury Preserves* (1928) [1985] I.R.L.R. 412,
E.A.T.
sch. 16, repealed in pt.: 1985, c.21, sch. 2.

72. Children Act 1975.
Commencement orders: 85/779, 1557 (S.).
s. 3, see *R.* v. *Tower Hamlets Juvenile
Justices, ex p. London Borough of
Tower Hamlets* (1984) 14 Fam. Law 307,
Bush J.; *P.B. (A Minor) (Application to
Free for Adoption), Re* (1985) 15 Fam.
Law 198, Sheldon J.
s. 8, see *M., Re, The Times*, May 9, 1985,
C.A.
s. 9, see *S. (A Minor) (Adoption), Re*
(1985) 15 Fam. Law 132, C.A.; *Y.
(Minors) (Adoption: Jurisdiction), Re*
[1985] 3 W.L.R. 601, Sheldon J.
s. 12, see *K. (A Minor), Re, The Times*,
March 7, 1985, C.A.; *V. (Adoption:
Parental Consent), Re* (1985) 15 Fam.
Law 56, C.A.; *C. (A Minor), Re, The
Times*, July 22, 1985, C.A.; *P.B. (A
Minor) (Application to Free for Adoption), Re* (1985) 15 Fam. Law 198, Sheldon J.; *A.B.* v. *C.B.*, 1985 S.L.T. 514.
s. 14, see *Adoption Application No.
118/1984, Re, The Times*, February 15,
1985, *sub nom, M.* v. *Berkshire C.C.*
(1985) 15 Fam.Law 161, C.A.; *W. (A
Minor) (Wardship Jurisdiction), Re*
[1985] 2 W.L.R. 892, H.L.; *sub nom.
W.* v. *Hertfordshire C.C.* [1985] 2 All
E.R. 301, H.L.; *P.B. (A Minor) (Application to Free for Adoption), Re*, (1985)
15 Fam.Law 198, Sheldon J.
s. 18, see *Y. (Minors) (Adoption: Jurisdiction), Re* [1985] 3 W.L.R. 601,
Sheldon J.
s. 28, see *S (A Minor) (Adoption), Re*
(1985) 15 Fam.Law 132, C.A.
s. 40, regs. 85/792, 1494.
s. 67, see *R.* v. *Leicester Juvenile Court,
ex p. K.D.C.* (1985) 80 Cr.App.R. 320,
D.C.
s. 103, regs. 85/1556 (S.).
s. 107, see *Y. (Minors) (Adoption: Jurisdiction), Re* [1985] 3 W.L.R. 601,
Sheldon J.
s. 107, repealed in pt.: 1985, c.51, sch. 17.
s. 108, orders 85/779, 1557 (S.).
sch. 3, repealed in pt.: 1985, c.71, sch. 1.

**74. Petroleum and Submarine Pipe-lines Act
1975.**
s. 1, repealed (prosp.): 1985, c.62, sch. 4.

CAP.

1975—cont.

74. Petroleum and Submarine Pipelines Act 1975—*cont.*
Pt. I (ss.1–16), repealed (except s.1, sch. 1): *ibid.*
s. 10, amended: 1985, c.9, sch. 2.
s. 31, regs. 85/1051.
s. 45, amended: 1985, c.48, s.15.
s. 46, repealed in pt.: 1985, c.62, sch. 4.
s. 48, amended: 1985, c.9, sch. 2; repealed in pt.: 1985, c.62, sch. 4.
sch. 1, repealed (prosp.): *ibid.*

75. Policyholders Protection Act 1975.
s. 5, amended: 1985, c.9, sch. 2; repealed in pt.: 1985, c.65, sch. 10.
ss. 15, 16, 20, 27, 29, sch. 1, amended: 1985, c.9, sch. 2.

76. Local Land Charges Act 1975.
s. 14, rules 85/221.
sch. 1, repealed in pt.: 1985, c.71, sch. 1.

78. Airports Authority Act 1975.
s. 8, amended: 1985, c.9, sch. 2.
s. 19, amended: 1985, c.71, sch. 2.
s. 23, repealed in pt.: 1985, c.51, sch. 17.

83. Northern Ireland (Loans) Act 1975.
s. 1, order 84/1915.
s. 1, amended: 1985, c.76, sch. 1.

1976

1. National Coal Board (Finance) Act 1976.
s. 2, order 85/522; amended: *ibid.*

9. Water Charges Act 1976.
s. 2, see *South West Water Authority* v. *Rumble's* [1985] 2 W.L.R. 405, H.L.

13. Damages (Scotland) Act 1976.
s. 1, see *Prentice* v. *Chalmers*, Second Division, July 24, 1984.

15. Rating (Caravan Sites) Act 1976.
s, 3A, order 84/1881.

21. Crofting Reform (Scotland) Act 1976.
s. 9, see *Enessy Co. S.A.* v. *Shareholders in Tarbert Common Grazings*, 1984 S.L.T.(Land Ct.) 7; *Highland Regional Council* v. *Macaulay*, 1984 S.L.C.R. 70; *Galson Estate* v. *Saunders*, 1984 S.L.C.R. 74.
s. 9, amended: 1985, c.73, s.30.

22. Freshwater and Salmon Fisheries (Scotland) Act 1976.
s. 1, order 85/384.

24. Development Land Tax Act 1976.
repealed: 1985, c.54, sch.,27.
ss. 1, 7, sch. 2, see *Lowe* v. *Comr. of Inland Revenue*, 1985 S.L.T.(Lands Tr.) 12.
ss. 28, 33, see *Worthing Rugby Football Club Trustees* v. *I.R.C.* [1985] 1 W.L.R. 409, Peter Gibson J.
s. 42, repealed: 1985, c.65, sch. 10; repealed in pt. (S.): 1985, c.66, sch. 8.

27. Theatres Trust Act 1976.
sch., amended: 1985, c.9, sch. 2.

28. Congenital Disabilities (Civil Liability) Act 1976.
s. 4, order 85/752.

CAP.

1976—cont.

30. Fatal Accidents Act 1976.
see *Robertson* v. *Lestrange* [1985] 1 All E.R. 950, Webster J.

32. Lotteries and Amusements Act 1976.
ss. 2, 14, see *Express Newspapers* v. *Liverpool Daily Post and Echo* [1985] 1 W.L.R. 1089, Whitford J.
s. 16, see *Brown* v. *Plant*, 1985 S.L.T. 371.
ss. 18, 24, orders 85/262, 263, 480(S.), 481(S.).
s. 23, repealed in pt.: 1985, c.51, sch. 17.
sch. 3, repealed in pt. (S.): 1985, c.73, sch. 4.

34. Restrictive Trade Practices Act 1976.
s. 9, order 84/2031.
ss. 11, 14, order 85/2044.
s. 19, see *Association of British Travel Agents Agreement (No. 2), Re* [1985] I.C.R. 122, Restrictive Practices Court.
s. 20, amended: 1985, c.67, s.116.
ss. 33, 43, amended: 1985, c.9, sch. 2.
s. 42, order 85/2044.
sch. 1, amended: 1985, c.61, s.60; c.65, s.217.

35. Police Pensions Act 1976.
ss. 1, 3, 4, regs. 85/156.
s. 1, 3, 5, regs. 85/1318.

39. Divorce (Scotland) Act 1976.
s. 1, see *Hastie* v. *Hastie* (O.H.), 1985 S.L.T. 146.; *Matthews* v. *Matthews*, 1985, S.L.T.(Sh.Ct.) 68; *Duncan* v. *Duncan* (O.H.), 1986 S.L.T. 17.
s. 5, see *Bryan* v. *Bryan* (O.H.), 1985 S.L.T. 444; *Elder* v. *Elder* (O.H.), 1985 S.L.T. 471; *Finlayson* v. *Finlayson's Exrx.* (O.H.), 1986 S.L.T. 19.
ss. 5–8, repealed: 1985, c.37, sch. 2.

40. Finance Act 1976.
s. 62, amended: 1985, c.71,sch. 2.
s. 64, order 85/1598; amended: *ibid.*
s. 64A, order 85/1599; amended: *ibid.*
s. 129, repealed: 1985, c.54, sch. 27.
sch. 5, see *Payne* v. *Barratt Developments (Luton), The Times*, December 17, 1984, H.L.; *Fraser* v. *London Sports Car Centre, Financial Times*, July 17, 1985, C.A.; *Pobjoy Mint* v. *Lane* [1985] S.T.C. 314, C.A.; *General Motors Acceptance Corp. (U.K.)* v. *I.R.C.* [1985] S.T.C. 408, Walton J.
sch. 7, amended: order 85/1598.
sch. 10, see *Finch* v. *I.R.C.* [1985] Ch. 1, C.A.

47. Stock Exchange (Completion of Bargains) Act 1976.
ss. 1–4, repealed: 1985, c.9, sch. 1.
s. 7, amended: *ibid.*, sch. 2; repealed in pt.: *ibid.*, sch. 1.

50. Domestic Violence and Matrimonial Proceedings Act 1976.
s. 1, see *Thurley* v. *Smith* (1985) 15 Fam. Law 31, C.A.; *Wooton* v. *Wooton* (1985) 15 Fam. Law 31, C.A.; *Galan* v. *Galan* (1985) 15 Fam.Law 256, C.A.

53. Resale Prices Act 1976.
s. 27, amended: 1985, c.9, sch. 2.

CAP.

1976—cont.

55. Agriculture (Miscellaneous Provisions) Act 1976.
s. 18, order 85/997.
ss. 18, 20, see *Trinity College Cambridge* v. *Caines* (1984) 272 E.G. 1287, C.A.
ss. 18, 20, 21 see *Wilson* v. *Earl Spencer's Settlement Trustees* (1985) 274 E.G. 1254, Hodgson J.

57. Local Government (Miscellaneous Provisions) Act 1976.
ss. 9, 10, repealed: 1985, c.71, sch. 1.
s. 19, amended: 1985, c.51, sch. 14.
s. 35, repealed in pt.: *ibid.*, sch. 17.
s. 42, amended: 1985, c.48, s.15; repealed in pt.: 1985, c.30, sch.
s. 44, amended: 1985, c.51, sch. 14; order 85/1884; repealed in pt.: 1985, c.51, sch. 17.
s. 46, amended: 1985, c.67, sch. 7.
s. 48, see *R.* v. *Bournemouth Borough Council* (1985) 83 L.G.R. 662, Mann J.
s. 63, amended: 1985, c.67, sch. 1.
s. 75, repealed in pt.: *ibid.*, schs. 7, 8.
s. 80, amended: *ibid.*, sch. 7.

58. International Carriage of Perishable Foodstuffs Act 1976.
ss. 1–4, 20, regs. 85/1071.

60. Insolvency Act 1976.
ss. 1, 2, repealed: 1985, c.65, sch. 10.
s. 3, amended: 1985, c.9, sch. 2; c.65, sch. 8.
ss. 4, 5 (in pt.), 6–8, repealed: 1985, c.65, sch. 10.
s. 5, repealed (S.): 1985, c.66, sch. 8.
s. 9, repealed: 1985, c.9, sch. 1.
s. 10, rules 85/95.
ss. 10, 11, 12 (in pt.), repealed: 1985, c.65, sch. 10.
s. 14, repealed in pt.: 1985, c.9, sch. 1; c.65, sch. 10.
sch. 1, repealed: *ibid.*
sch. 1, repealed in pt. (S.): 1985, c.66, sch. 8.
sch. 2, repealed in pt.: 1985, c.9, sch. 2.

63. Bail Act 1976.
ss. 3, 4, sch. 1, see *R.* v. *Mansfield Justices, ex p. Sharkey* [1984] 3 W.L.R. 1328, D.C.
sch. 2, repealed in pt.: 1985, c.23, sch. 2.

66. Licensing (Scotland) Act 1976.
s. 6, see *Tuzi* v. *City of Edinburgh District Licensing Board* (O.H.), 1985 S.L.T. 477.
s. 10, see *Tevan* v. *Motherwell District Licensing Board (No. 1),* 1985 S.L.T.(Sh.Ct.) 14.
s. 18, see *R. W. Cairns* v. *Busby East Church Kirk Session,* 1985 S.L.T. 493.
s. 38, see *Allied Breweries (U.K.)* v. *City of Glasgow District Licensing Board* (O.H.), 1985 S.L.T. 307.
s. 39, see *R. W. Cairns* v. *Busby East Church Kirk Session,* 1985 S.L.T. 493; *Botterills of Blantyre* v. *Hamilton District Licensing Board,* Second Division, 1986 S.L.T. 14.

CAP.

1976—cont.

66. Licensing (Scotland) Act 1976—*cont.*
s. 92, amended: 1985, c.67, sch. 7.
s. 133, amended: 1985, c.73, s.52.
s. 139, see *Tuzi* v. *City of Edinburgh District Licensing Board* (O.H.), 1985 S.L.T. 477; *Chief Constable, Northern Constabulary* v. *Lochaber District Licensing Board,* 1985 S.L.T. 410.
s. 139, amended: 1985, c.73, s.53.
sch. 1, see *Chief Constable, Northern Constabulary* v. *Lochaber District Licensing Board,* 1985 S.L.T. 410.
sch. 4, see *R. W. Cairns* v. *Busby East Church Kirk Session,* 1985 S.L.T. 493.

69. Companies Act 1976.
repealed: 1985, c.9, sch. 1.

70. Land Drainage Act 1976.
s. 2, amended: 1985, c.51, sch. 7; repealed in pt.: *ibid.*, sch. 17.
s. 3, repealed in pt.: *ibid.*
s. 5, amended: *ibid.*, sch. 7, repealed in pt.: *ibid.*, sch. 17.
s. 11, orders 85/58, 210, 505, 681, 1124, 1393, 1559.
ss. 16, 24, amended: 1985, c.51, sch. 7.
s. 25, order 84/2064.
s. 28, amended: 1985, c.51, sch. 7.
s. 32, repealed in pt.: *ibid.*, sch. 17.
s. 45, amended: *ibid.*, sch. 7.
ss. 92, 97, repealed in pt.: *ibid.*, sch. 17.
s. 98, amended: *ibid.*, sch. 7; repealed in pt.: *ibid.*, sch. 17.
s. 99, amended: *ibid.*, sch. 7.
s. 101, repealed: *ibid.*, sch. 17.
s. 109, orders 84/2064; 85/681, 1393.
s. 110, amended: 1985, c.51, sch. 7; repealed in pt.: *ibid.*, sch. 17.
s. 116, amended: *ibid.*, sch. 7.
sch. 1, amended: 1985, c.65, sch. 8.

71. Supplementary Benefits Act 1976.
see *Decision No. R(SB) 17/85.*
s. 1, regs. 85/613, 1835.
s. 2, regs. 84/1991, 2034; 85/613, 614, 1136, 1246, 1247, 1835.
s. 3, regs. 85/1247.
s. 4, regs. 85/1016.
s. 6, see *Chief Supplementary Benefit Officer* v. *Cunningham* [1985] I.C.R. 660, C.A.
s. 14, regs. 85/1016.
ss. 17, 25, see *Meikle* v. *Annan,* 1984 S.C.C.R. 270.
s. 27, see *R.* v. *Secretary of State for Social Services, ex p. Child Poverty Action Group and G.L.C., The Times,* August 8, 1985, C.A.; *Decision No. R(SB) 27/85.*
s. 33, regs. 84/2034; 85/613, 614, 1136, 1246, 1247, 1835.
s. 34, regs. 84/1991, 2034; 85/613, 614, 1136, 1246, 1247, 1835.
sch. 1, see *Chief Supplementary Benefit Officer* v. *Leary* [1985] 1 W.L.R. 84, C.A.

CAP.

1976—cont.

71. Supplementary Benefits Act 1976—*cont.*
sch. 1, regs. 84/2034; 85/613, 614, 1136, 1246, 1247, 1835.
sch. 5, repealed in pt.: 1985, c.51, sch. 17.

72. Endangered Species (Import and Export) Act 1976.
ss. 3, 11, order 85/1502.

74. Race Relations Act 1976.
s. 1, see *Orphanos* v. *Queen Mary College* [1985] 2 All E.R. 233, H.L.; *Singh* v. *British Rail Engineering, The Times,* August 6, 1985, E.A.T.; *R.* v. *Commission for Racial Equality, ex p. Westminster City Council* [1985] I.R.L.R. 426, C.A.
ss. 1, 3, see *Raval* v. *D.H.S.S. and The Civil Service Commission* [1985] I.R.L.R. 370, E.A.T.
s. 4, see *Kingston* v. *British Railways Board* [1984] I.C.R. 781, C.A.; *De Souza* v. *Automobile Association, The* [1985] I.R.L.R. 87, E.A.T.; *Raval* v. *D.H.S.S. and The Civil Service Commission* [1985] I.R.L.R. 370, E.A.T.; *R.* v. *Commission for Racial Equality, ex p. Westminster City Council* [1985] I.R.L.R. 426, C.A.; *Wadi* v. *Cornwall and Isles of Scilly Family Practitioner Committee* (1985) I.C.R. 492, E.A.T.
ss. 20, 21, see *Alexander* v. *Home Office,* December 20, 1984, Judge Smithers, Southampton County Ct.
s. 32, see *Kingston* v. *British Railways Board* [1984] I.C.R. 781, C.A.; *Wadi* v. *Cornwall & Isles of Scilly Family Practitioner Committee* [1985] I.C.R. 492, E.A.T.
ss. 57, see *Orphanos* v. *Queen Mary College* [1985] 2 All E.R. 233, H.L.
s. 58, see *R.* v. *Commission for Racial Equality, ex p. Westminster City Council* [1985] I.R.L.R. 426, C.A.
s. 71, see *Wheeler* v. *Leicester City Council* [1985] 3 W.L.R. 335, H.L.
s. 71, amended: 1985, c.51, sch. 14; order 85/1884.
s. 72, see *Orphanos* v. *Queen Mary College* [1985] 2 All E.R. 233, H.L.
s. 75, regs. 1309, 1757.
s. 78, see *Wadi* v. *Cornwall and Isles of Scilly Family Practitioner Committee* [1985] I.C.R. 492, E.A.T.

75. Development of Rural Wales Act 1976.
s. 8, amended: 1985, c.71, sch. 2.
s. 13A, added: 1985, c.5, sch. 2.
s. 31, repealed: 1985, c.54, sch. 27
schs. 3, 7, repealed in pt.: 1985, c.71, sch. 1.

76. Energy Act 1976.
sch. 1, amended: 1985, c.67, sch. 1, repealed in pt.: *ibid.*, schs. 1,8.

77. Weights and Measures etc. Act 1976.
repealed, except ss. 12–14, 15 (in pt.), sch. 6: 1985, c.72, sch. 13.
ss. 12, 14, sch. 6, amended: *ibid.*, sch. 12.

CAP.

1976—cont.

78. Industrial Common Ownership Act 1976.
s. 2, amended: 1985, c.9, sch. 2.

79. Dock Work Regulation Act 1976.
sch. 1, amended: 1985, c.9, sch. 2.

80. Rent (Agriculture) Act 1976.
s. 5, amended: 1985, c.51, sch. 14; c.71, sch. 2; order 85/1884; repealed in pt.: 1985, c.51, sch. 17.
s. 27, amended: 1985, c.71, sch. 2; repealed in pt.: 1985, c.51, sch. 17.
schs. 4, 5, amended: 1985, c.71, sch. 2.
sch. 8, repealed in pt.: *ibid.*, sch. 1.

82. Sexual Offences (Amendment) Act 1976.
s. 1, see *R.* v. *Breckenridge* (1984) 79 Cr.App.R. 244, C.A.; *R.* v. *Taylor (R.P.)* (1985) 80 Cr.App.R. 327, C.A.; *R.* v. *Haughian* (1985) 80 Cr.App.R. 334, C.A.

86. Fishery Limits Act 1976.
ss. 2, 6, sch. 3, order 85/244.

1977

3. Aircraft and Shipbuilding Industries Act 1977.
s. 3, amended: 1985, c.9, sch. 2.
s. 11, order 85/327; amended: *ibid.*
ss. 17, 23, 56, amended: *ibid.*

5. Social Security (Miscellaneous Provisions) Act 1977.
s. 5, repealed in pt.: 1985, c.53, sch. 6.
s. 12, order 85/1201.
s. 21, regs. 85/1323.
s. 21, amended: 1985, c.53, sch. 3.
s. 22, regs. 85/1323.
s. 22, repealed in pt.: 1985, c.53, sch. 6.
s. 24, regs. 85/1323.

7. Nuclear Industry (Finance) Act 1977.
s. 3, amended: 1985, c.9, sch. 2.

8. Job Release Act 1977.
s. 1, continued in force: order 85/1128.

12. Agricultural Holdings (Notice to Quit) Act 1977.
s. 2, see *Featherstone* v. *Staples* (1985) 273 E.G. 193; (1985) 49 P. & C.R. 273, Nourse J.
s. 12, amended: 1985, c.65, sch. 8.
sch. 1, repealed in pt.: 1985, c.12, sch. 2.
sch. 1A, amended: 1985, c.71, sch. 2.

22. Redundancy Rebates Act 1977.
s. 2, S.R. 1985 No. 146.

24. Merchant Shipping (Safety Convention) Act 1977.
s. 1, amended: regs. 85/212.

36. Finance Act 1977.
ss. 5 (in pt.), 6 (in pt.), 55, repealed: 1985, c.54, sch. 27.
sch. 7, see *Varnam* v. *Deeble* [1985] S.T.C. 308, C.A.

37. Patents Act 1977.
s. 2, see *Furr* v. *Truline (C.D.) (Building Products)* [1985] F.S.R. 553, Falconer J.
s. 32, rules 85/1166.
ss. 37, 39, see *Reiss Engineering Co.* v. *Harris* [1985] I.R.L.R. 232, Falconer J.

CAP.

1977—cont.

37. Patents Act 1977—cont.
s. 46, see *Allen & Hanburys* v. *Generics (U.K.), Gist-Brocades N.V.* v. *Beecham Group, Financial Times,* June 7, 1985, C.A.
s. 60, see *Monsanto* v. *Stauffer Chemical Co. and Stauffer Chemical, Financial Times,* June 18, 1985, C.A.; *Furr* v. *Trueline (C.D.) (Building Products)* [1985] F.S.R. 553, Falconer J.
s. 65, see *Brupat* v. *Smith* [1985] F.S.R. 156, Court of Session.
s. 68, see *Christian Salvesen (Oil Services)* v. *Odfjell Drilling and Consulting Co. (U.K.)* (O.H.), 1985 S.L.T. 397.
s. 71, see *Reckitt & Colman Products* v. *Biorex Laboratories* [1985] F.S.R. 94, Falconer J.
s. 74, see *Dow Chemical Co.* v. *Ishihara Sangyo K.K.* [1985] F.S.R. 4, Whitford J.; *Reckitt & Colman Products* v. *Biorex Laboratories* [1985] F.S.R. 94, Falconer J.
s. 84, amended: 1985, c.61, s.60.
s. 88, amended: 1985, c.9, sch. 2.
s. 90, orders 85/173, 456, 457.
s. 102, amended: 1985, c.61, s.60.
s. 105, see *Santa Fe International Corporation* v. *Napier Shipping S.A.* (O.H.) 1985 S.L.T. 481.
s. 114, amended: 1985, c.9, sch. 2; c.61, s.60.
s. 123, rules 85/785, 1099, 1166.
s. 127, see *Santa Fe International Corporation* v. *Napier Shipping S.A* (O.H.), 1985 S.L.T. 481.
s. 130, amended: 1985, c.61, s.60.
s. 131, amended: 1985, c.9, sch. 2.
sch. 1, see *Reckitt & Colman Products* v. *Biorex Laboratories* [1985] F.S.R. 94, Falconer J.; *Allen & Hanburys* v. *Generics (U.K.), Gist-Brocades N.V.* v. *Beecham Group, Financial Times,* June 7, 1985, C.A.; *R.* v. *Comptroller-General of Patents, Designs and Trade Marks, ex p. Gist-Brocades N.V., The Times,* August 5, 1985, H.L.
sch. 2, see *Santa Fe International Corporation* v. *Napier Shipping S.A.* (O.H.), 1985 S.L.T. 481.
sch. 4, see *Reckitt & Colman Products* v. *Biorex Laboratories* [1985] F.S.R. 94, Falconer J.
sch. 4, rules 85/785, 1099.

39. Coal Industry Act 1977.
s. 6, amended: 1985, c.27, s.2.
s. 7, order 85/558.
s. 7, amended: 1985, c.27, s.3.
s. 14, amended: 1985, c.9, sch. 2.

42. Rent Act 1977.
see *Sopwith* v. *Stutchbury* (1984) 17 H.L.R. 50, C.A.
s. 1, see *R.* v. *Rent Officer of Nottingham Registration Area, ex p. Allen,* (1985) 275 E.G. 251, Farquharson J.

CAP.

1977—cont.

42. Rent Act 1977—cont.
s. 2, see *Hampstead Way Investments* v. *Lewis-Weare* [1985] 1 W.L.R. 164, H.L.; *Kavanagh* v. *Lyroudias* [1985] 1 All E.R. 560, C.A.
s. 12, see *Cooper* v. *Tait* (1984) 48 P. & C.R. 460, C.A.
s. 14, amended: 1985, c.51, sch. 14; order 85/1884; repealed in pt.: 1985, c.51, sch. 17.
ss. 15, 16, amended: 1985, c.71, sch. 2.
s. 24, see *Simmonds* v. *Egyed*, February 12, 1985, Bloomsbury County Court.
s. 62, amended and repealed in pt.: 1985, c.51, sch. 8.
s. 63, amended: *ibid.*
ss. 70, 71, see *Perseus Property Co.* v. *Burberry* (1985) 273 E.G. 405, Nolan J.
ss. 78, 86, 88, 92, amended: 1985, c.71, sch. 2.
s. 98, see *Pazgate* v. *McGrath* (1984) 272 E.G. 1069, C.A.; *R.* v. *Bloomsbury and Marylebone County Court, ex p. Blackburne* (1985) 275 E.G. 1273, C.A.
s. 101, substituted: 1985, c.71, sch. 2.
s. 116, amended: *ibid.*
ss. 118, 145, repealed: *ibid.*, sch. 1.
s. 137, see *Patoner* v. *Lowe* (1985) 275 E.G. 540, C.A.
s. 149, amended: 1985, c.71, sch.2; repealed in pt.: *ibid.*, sch. 1.
sch. 15, see *Pazgate* v. *McGrath* (1984) 272 E.G. 1069, C.A.; *R.* v. *Bloomsbury and Marylebone County Court, ex p. Blackburne* (1984) 14 H.L.R. 56, Glidewell J.; *Perseus Property Co.* v. *Burberry* (1985) 273 E.G. 405, Nolan J.; *Naish* v. *Curzon* (1985) 273 E.G. 1221, C.A.; *Bradshaw* v. *Baldwin-Wiseman* (1985) 274 E.G. 285; 49 P. & C.R. 382, C.A.; *Alexander* v. *Mohamadzadeh, The Times,* November 21, 1985, C.A.
sch. 15, amended: 1985, c.24, s.1; c.71, sch.2.
sch. 16, amended: *ibid.*; repealed in pt.: 1985, c.51, sch. 17.
sch. 23, repealed in pt.: 1985, c.71, sch.1.

43. Protection from Eviction Act 1977.
see *Ashgar* v. *Ahmed* (1984) 17 H.L.R. 25, C.A.
s. 1, see *R.* v. *Yuthiwattana* (1985) 80 Cr.App.R. 55, C.A.; *R.* v. *A.M.K. (Property Management)* [1985] Crim.L.R. 600, C.A.

45. Criminal Law Act 1977.
Commencement order: 85/579.
s. 1, see *R.* v. *Tonner; R.* v. *Evans (Ronald)* [1985] 1 W.L.R. 344, C.A.; *R.* v. *Zemmel; R* v. *Mecik* [1985] Crim.L.R. 213, C.A.; *R.* v. *Cooke; R.* v. *Sutcliffe* [1985] Crim.L.R. 215, C.A.; *R.* v. *Lloyd; R.* v. *Bhuee; R.* v. *Ali* [1985] 3 W.L.R. 30, C.A.; *R.* v. *Hollinshead* [1985] 3 W.L.R. 159, H.L.; *R.* v. *Anderson (William Ronald)* [1985] 3 W.L.R. 268, H.L.

CAP.

CAP.

1977—cont.

45. Criminal Law Act 1977—*cont.*
 s. 5, see *R. v. Tonner; R. v. Evans
 (Ronald)* [1985] 1 W.L.R. 344, C.A.; *R.
 v. Zemmel; R. v. Mecik* [1985]
 Crim.L.R. 213, C.A.; *R. v. Hollinshead*
 [1985] 3 W.L.R. 159, H.L.
 s. 7, amended: 1985, c.71, sch. 2.
 s. 31, repealed in pt.: 1985, c.72, sch. 13.
 s. 38, repealed in pt.: 1985, c.65, sch. 10.
 s. 48, rules 85/601.
 ss. 50, 65, see *R. v. Krawec* [1985] R.T.R.
 1, C.A.
 s. 53, repealed in pt.: 1985, c.13, sch. 3.
 s. 65, order 85/579.
 sch. 12, see *R. v. Krawec* [1985] R.T.R. 1,
 C.A.

46. Insurance Brokers (Registration) Act 1977.
 ss. 11, 29, amended: 1985, c.9, sch. 2.
 ss. 27, 28, order 85/1804.

48. Housing (Homeless Persons) Act 1977.
 repealed: 1985, c.71, sch. 1.
 see *R. v. Exeter City Council, ex p. Glid-
 don and Draper* (1984) 14 H.L.R. 103,
 Woolf J.; *R. v. Southampton City Coun-
 cil, ex p. Ward* (1984) 14 H.L.R. 119,
 McCullough J.; *R. v. Woodspring Dis-
 trict Council, ex p. Walters* (1984) 16
 H.L.R. 75, D.C.; *R. v. Surrey Heath
 Borough Council, ex p. Li* (1984) 16
 H.L.R. 83, D.C.; *R. v. Ryedale District
 Council, ex p. Smith* (1984) 16 H.L.R.
 69, D.C.; *R. v. Hambleton District
 Council, ex p. Geoghan (Thomas)* [1985]
 J.P.L.394, Forbes J.; *R. v. Preseli Dis-
 trict Council, ex p. Fisher* (1984) 17
 H.L.R. 147, D.C.; *City of Gloucester* v.
 Miles (1985) 17 H.L.R. 292, C.A.; *R. v.
 West Dorset District Council, ex p. Phil-
 lips* (1984) 17 H.L.R. 336, Hodgson J.
 s. 1, see *R. v. South Herefordshire District
 Council, ex p. Miles* (1983) 17 H.L.R.
 82, D.C.; *R. v. Hillingdon London Bor-
 ough Council, ex p. Pulhofer* (1985) New
 L.J. 983, C.A.; *R. v. Borough of
 Dinefwr, ex p. Marshall* (1984) 17
 H.L.R. 130, McCullough J.; *McAlinden
 v. Bearsden and Milngavie District
 Council* (O.H.), September 6, 1985;
 Hynds v. *Midlothian District Council*
 (O.H.), 1986 S.L.T. 54.
 s. 1, amended (S.): 1985, c.71, sch. 2.
 s. 2, see *Noble* v. *South Herefordshire District Council* (1983) 17 H.L.R. 80, C.A.;
 *R. v. Bath City Council, ex p. Sanger-
 mano* (1984) 17 H.L.R. 94; *Hynds* v.
 Midlothian District Council (O.H.),
 1986 S.L.T. 54.
 s. 3, see *City of Gloucester Council* v.
 Miles (1985) 17 H.L.R. 292, C.A.; *Eastleigh Borough Council* v. *Walsh* [1985]
 2 All E.R. 112, H.L.
 s. 3, amended (S.): 1985, c.71, sch. 2.
 s. 4, see *R. v. Exeter City Council, ex p.
 Gliddon* [1985] 1 All E.R. 493, Woolf
 J.; *R. v. Hammersmith and Fulham
 London Borough Council, ex p.*

1977—cont.

48. Housing (Homeless Persons) Act 1977—
 cont.
 O'Brian, (1985) 17 H.L.R. 471, Glidewell J.; *Kensington and Chelsea Royal
 Borough Council* v. *Hayden* (1984) 17
 H.L.R. 114, C.A.; *R. v. Ealing London
 Borough Council, ex p. McBain, The
 Times*, October 10, 1985, C.A.; *Hynds*
 v. *Midlothian District Council* (O.H.),
 1986 S.L.T. 54.
 s. 5, see *R. v. Hammersmith and Fulham
 London Borough Council, ex p. O'Brian*
 (1985) 17 H.L.R. 471, Glidewell J.; *R.
 v. Vale of the White Horse District Council, ex p. Smith* (1985) 83 L.G.R. 437,
 Woolf J.: *Hynds* v. *Midlothian District
 Council* (O.H.), 1986 S.L.T. 54.
 s. 5, amended (S.): 1985, c.71, sch. 2.
 ss. 6, 7, repealed (S.): *ibid.*, sch. 1.
 s. 9, see *R. v. South Herefordshire District
 Council, ex p. Miles* (1983) 17 H.L.R.
 82, D.C.
 s. 9, amended (S.): 1985, c.71, sch. 2.
 ss. 10, 13, repealed (S.): *ibid.*, sch. 1.
 s. 16, see *R. v. Wimborne District Council,
 ex p. Curtis, The Times*, October 15,
 1985, Mann J.
 s. 17, see *R. v. Reigate and Banstead Borough Council* (1985) 15 Fam.Law 28,
 McCullough J.; *R. v. Exeter City Council, ex p. Gliddon* [1985] 1 All E.R. 493,
 Woolf J.; *R. v. South Herefordshire District Council, ex p. Miles* (1983) 17
 H.L.R. 82, D.C.; *R. v. Hillingdon
 London Borough Council, ex p. Puhlhofer* (1985) New L.J. 983, C.A.; *R. v.
 Ealing London Borough Council, ex p.
 McBain, The Times*, October 10, 1985,
 C.A.: *R. v. Gloucester City Council, ex
 p. Miles* (1985) 83 L.G.R. 607, C.A.
 s. 18, see *R. v. Vale of White Horse District
 Council, ex p. Smith* (1985) 83 L.G.R.
 437, Woolf J.
 s. 18A, added (S.): 1985, c.71, sch. 2.
 s. 19, see *R. v. Hillingdon London Borough Council, ex p. Pulhofer* (1985) New
 L.J. 983, C.A.
 s. 19, amended (S.): 1985, c.71, sch. 2;
 repealed in pt. (S.): *ibid.*, sch. 1.
 s. 20, repealed in pt. (S.): *ibid.*
 s. 21, amended (S.): *ibid.*, sch. 2; repealed
 in pt. (S.): *ibid.*, sch. 1.

49. National Health Service Act 1977.
 s. 8, orders 85/25, 26, 369, 370.
 s. 10, orders 84/1946; 85/301.
 s. 11, orders 85/996, 1345, 1877.
 s. 12, regs. 85/1876.
 ss. 13, 14, regs. 85/304.
 s. 16, regs. 85/213.
 s. 18, repealed in pt.: order 85/39.
 s. 22, order 85/305.
 ss. 28A, 28B, amended: 1985, c.71, sch. 2.
 s. 29, regs. 85/290, 540, 803, 1053, 1712.
 ss. 29–36, amended: order 85/39.
 s. 32, regs. 85/1353.
 ss. 35–37, regs. 85/1336.

1977—cont.

49. National Health Service Act 1977—cont.
ss. 38, 39, regs. 85/298.
ss. 38, 39, amended: order 85/39.
ss. 41, 42, regs. 85/290, 540, 805, 955, 1053, 1712.
ss. 41–43, amended: order 85/39.
s. 43, regs. 85/290, 803, 955.
ss. 46, 54–56, amended: order 85/39.
s. 49, regs. 85/1671.
s. 77, regs. 85/326.
s. 78, regs. 85/298, 352.
s. 79, regs. 85/352.
s. 83, regs. 85/326.
s. 119, repealed in pt.: order 85/39.
s. 121, regs. 85/371, 508.
s. 123, amended: 1985, c.71, sch. 2.
s. 126, orders 85/26, 301, 370.
s. 128, repealed in pt.: 1985, c.51, sch. 17.
s. 130, order 85/149.
sch. 5, see *Wadi* v. *Cornwall and Isles of Scilly Family Practitioner Committee* [1985] I.C.R. 492, E.A.T.
sch. 5, regs. 85/47, 213, 1067, 1876; orders 85/66, 303, 369.
sch. 5, amended and repealed in pt.: order 85/39.
sch. 7, regs. 85/304.
sch. 12, regs. 85/298, 326, 352.

50. Unfair Contract Terms Act 1977.
ss. 1, 2, 11, 13, see *Phillips Products* v. *Hyland (T.) and Hamstead Plant Hire Co.* (1985) 4 Tr.L. 98, C.A.
s. 11, see *Stevenson* v. *Nationwide Building Society* (1984) 272 E.G. 663, Mr. J. Wilmers, Q.C.
ss. 17, 20, see *Border Harvesters* v. *Edwards Engineering (Perth)* (O.H.), 1985 S.L.T. 128.
s. 20, see *Landcatch* v. *Marine Harvest* (O.H.), 1985 S.L.T. 478.
s. 28, orders 85/230, 1430.

1978

1. Participation Agreements Act 1978.
s. 1, amended: 1985, c.9, sch. 2.
2. Commonwealth Development Corporation Act 1978.
s. 9A, amended: 1985, c.9, sch. 2.
3. Refuse Disposal (Amenity) Act 1978.
s. 1, amended: 1985, c.51, sch. 6; order 85/1884; repealed in pt.: order 85/1884.
s. 3, amended: 1985, c.51, sch. 6; order 85/1884; repealed in pt.: 1985, c.51, sch. 17.
s. 4, order 85/1661.
s. 4, amended: 1985, c.51, sch. 6; order 85/1884.
s. 5, order 85/1661.
s. 5, amended: 1985, c.51, sch. 6; order 85/1884; repealed in pt.: 1985, c.51, sch. 17.
ss. 6, 7, repealed in pt.: *ibid.*
s. 11, amended: order 85/1884.

1978—cont.

5. Northern Ireland (Emergency Provisions) Act 1978.
temporary provisions continued in force (exc. 12, sch. 1): orders 85/40, 1083.
ss. 11, 31, see *McKee* v. *Chief Constable of Northern Ireland* [1984] 1 W.L.R. 1358, H.L.
s. 33, order 85/40.
6. Employment Subsidies Act 1978.
s. 1, continued in force: order 85/1959.
s. 3, order 85/1959; S.R. 1985 No. 324.
10. European Assembly Elections Act 1978.
s. 3, see *Prince* v. *Secretary of State for Scotland* (O.H.), 1985 S.L.T. 74.
11. Shipbuilding (Redundancy Payments) Act 1978.
s. 1, amended: 1985, c.9, sch. 2.
s. 2, repealed in pt.: 1985, c.14, s.1.
14. Housing (Financial Provisions) (Scotland) Act 1978.
ss. 1, 2, orders 85/185, 186.
s. 3, order 85/185.
ss. 5, 7, amended: 1985, c.71, sch. 2.
sch. 2, repealed in pt.: *ibid.*, sch. 1.
17. Internationally Protected Persons Act 1978.
ss. 3, 4, order 85/1990.
19. Oaths Act 1978.
s. 5, see *R.* v. *Bellamy, The Times*, October 4, 1985, C.A.
21. Co-operative Development Agency Act 1978.
sch. 2, amended: 1985, c.9, sch. 2.
22. Domestic Proceedings and Magistrates' Courts Act 1978.
Commencement order: 85/779.
ss. 2, 3, see *Vasey* v. *Vasey* (1985) 15 Fam.Law 158, C.A.
s. 20, see *Whitton* v. *Devizes JJ,* (1985) 15 Fam.Law 125, Anthony Lincoln J.
s. 29, see *Fletcher* v. *Fletcher* [1985] 2 All E.R. 260, D.C.
s. 60, repealed in pt.: 1985, c.37, sch. 2.
s. 89, order 85/779.
sch. 2, repealed in pt. (S.): 1985, c.37, sch. 2.
23. Judicature (Northern Ireland) Act 1978.
s. 55, S.Rs. 1985 Nos. 170, 347.
s. 62, see *Monteith* v. *Western Health and Social Services Board* [1984] 13 N.I.J.B., Carswell J.
s. 70, repealed in pt.: 1985, c.61, c.62, sch. 8.
s. 103, amended: *ibid.*, s.62.
s. 116, S.Rs. 1984 Nos. 419, 420.
27. Home Purchase Assistance and Housing Corporation Guarantee Act 1978.
repealed: 1985, c.71, sch. 1.
ss. 1, 2, order 85/937.
ss. 2, 3, amended (S.): 1985, c.71, sch. 2.
s. 3A, added (S.): *ibid.*
ss. 4, 5, repealed (S.): *ibid.*, sch. 1.
s. 6, amended (S.): *ibid.*, sch. 2; repealed in pt.: *ibid.*, sch. 1.
sch., repealed in pt.: 1985, c.51, sch. 17; c.58, sch. 4.

1978—cont.

28. Adoption (Scotland) Act 1978.
s. 65, amended: 1985, c.73, s.27.

29. National Health Service (Scotland) Act 1978.
s. 16A, amended: 1985, c.71, sch. 2.
s. 19, regs. 85/296, 534, 804, 1625, 1713.
s. 25, regs. 85/1552.
s. 26, regs. 85/355.
s. 27, regs. 85/296, 534, 804, 1713.
s. 28, regs. 85/296, 534, 804.
s. 69, regs. 85/353.
s. 70, regs. 85/354, 355.
s. 71, regs. 85/354.
s. 75, regs. 85/353.
s. 98, regs. 85/383.
s. 108, regs. 85/296, 353–355, 383, 534, 804, 1625, 1713.
sch. 1, regs. 85/208.
schs. 6, 7, amended: 1985, c.73, s.54.
sch. 11, regs. 85/353–355.

30. Interpretation Act 1978.
s. 7, see *Lenlyn* v. *Secretary of State for the Environment; R.* v. *Secretary of State for the Environment, ex p. Lenlyn* (1985) 50 P. & C.R. 129, Hodgson J.
s. 12, see *Wilson* v. *Colchester Justices* [1985] 2 All E.R. 97, H.L.

31. Theft Act 1978.
s. 3, see *R.* v. *Allen (Christopher)* [1985] 3 W.L.R. 107, H.L.

33. State Immunity Act 1978.
s. 21, see *R.* v. *Secretary of State for Foreign and Commonwealth Affairs, ex p. Trawnik, The Times*, April 18, 1985, D.C.
s. 23, order 85/1642.

38. Consumer Safety Act 1978.
see *R.* v. *Secretary of State for Trade and Industry, ex p. Ian Kynaston Ford* (1985) 4 Tr.L. 150, Woolf J.
s. 1, regs. 85/1191, 2042, 2043, 2045, 2047.
ss. 1, 7, regs. 85/99, 127, 128.
s. 2, regs. 85/2045.
s. 11, regs. 85/2043.
sch. 2, regs. 85/99, 2043, 2047.

40. Rating (Disabled Persons) Act 1978.
s. 4, order 85/245.

42. Finance Act 1978.
s. 39, repealed in pt.: 1985, c.54, sch. 27.
s. 54, amended: *ibid.*, s.45; repealed in pt.: (prospectively): *ibid.*, s.45, sch. 27.
s. 56, amended: *ibid.*, s.45.
sch. 2, repealed in pt.: *ibid.*, sch. 27.

44. Employment Protection (Consolidation) Act 1978.
see *Gorictree* v. *Jenkinson* [1985] I.C.R. 51, E.A.T.
s. 15, orders 84/2019; 85/2032; amended: orders; 84/2019; 85/2032.
s. 18, order 85/1270.
s. 19, order 85/1787.
s. 28, see *Wignall* v. *British Gas Corp.* [1984] I.C.R. 716, E.A.T.
s. 29, amended: order 85/39.

1978—cont.

44. Employment Protection (Consolidation) Act 1978—*cont.*
ss. 33, 34, see *Secretary of State for Employment* v. *Cox* [1984] I.C.R. 867, E.A.T.
s. 53, see *Gilham* v. *Kent County Council (No. 1)* [1985] I.C.R. 227, C.A.
s. 54, see *Hughes* v. *Department of Health and Social Security; Coy* v. *D.H.S.S.; Jarnell* v. *Department of the Environment* [1985] 2 W.L.R. 866, H.L.
s. 55, see *Crank* v. *Her Majesty's Stationery Office* [1985] I.C.R. 1, E.A.T.; *Newham London Borough Council* v. *Ward, The Times*, July 19, 1985, C.A.; *North Yorkshire County Council* v. *Fay* [1985] I.R.L.R. 247, C.A.; *Shepherd (F. C.) & Co.* v. *Jerrom* [1985] I.R.L.R. 275, E.A.T.; *Delabole Slate* v. *Berriman* [1985] I.R.L.R. 305, C.A.; *Dutton & Clark* v. *Daly* [1985] I.R.L.R. 363, E.A.T.: *Norwest Holst Group Administration* v. *Harrison* [1985] I.C.R. 668, C.A.
s. 57, see *Kingston* v. *British Railways Board* [1984] I.C.R. 781, C.A.; *Smith* v. *City of Glasgow District Council*, 1985 S.L.T. 138; *Hotson* v. *Wisbech Conservative Club* [1984] I.C.R. 859, E.A.T.; *Yusuf* v. *Aberplace* [1984] I.C.R. 850, E.A.T.; *Murphy* v. *Epsom College* [1985] I.C.R. 80, C.A.; *Gilham* v. *Kent County Council (No. 2)* [1985] I.C.R. 233, C.A.; *North Yorkshire County Council* v. *Fay* [1985] I.R.L.R. 247, C.A.; *Shepherd (F. C.) & Co.* v. *Jerrom* [1985] I.R.L.R. 275, E.A.T.; *Neale* v. *County Council of Hereford and Worcester* [1985] I.R.L.R. 281, E.A.T.; *West Midlands Co-operative Society* v. *Tipton* [1985] I.C.R. 444, C.A.: *Greenall Whitley* v. *Carr* [1985] I.C.R. 451, E.A.T.; *McGrath* v. *Rank Leisure* [1985] I.C.R. 527, E.A.T.; *Stacey* v. *Babcock Power, The Times*, November 1, 1985, E.A.T.; *Berriman* v. *Delabole Slate* [1985] I.C.R. 546, C.A.
s. 58, see *Home Delivery Services* v. *Shackcloth* [1958] I.C.R. 147, E.A.T.; *Sakals* v. *United Counties Omnibus Co.* [1984] I.R.L.R. 474, E.A.T.; *McGhee* v. *Midland British Road Services* [1985] I.R.L.R. 503, E.A.T.
s. 59, see *Henry* v. *Ellerman Lines* [1985] I.C.R. 57, C.A.; *Cross International* v. *Reid* [1985] I.R.L.R. 387, C.A.
s. 62, see *Hindle Gears* v. *McGinty* [1985] I.C.R. 111, E.A.T.; *Highlands Fabricators* v. *McLaughlin* [1984] I.C.R. 183, E.A.T.
s. 64, see *Hughes* v. *Department of Health and Social Security; Coy* v. *D.H.S.S.; Jarnell* v. *Department of the Environment* [1985] 2 W.L.R. 866, H.L.; *Hyland* v. *Barker (J.H.) (North West)* [1985] I.R.L.R. 403, E.A.T.

1978—cont.

44. Employment Protection (Consolidaton) Act 1978—*cont.*
s. 64, amended: order 85/782.
s. 64A, see *Cox* v. *ELG Metals* [1985] I.C.R. 310, C.A.
s. 64A, amended: order 85/782.
s. 67, *Crank* v. *Her Majesty's Stationery Office* [1985] I.C.R. 1, E.A.T.
s. 68, see *Freemans* v. *Flynn* [1984] I.C.R. 874, E.A.T.
s. 69, see *Freemans* v. *Flynn* [1984] I.C.R. 874, E.A.T.; *Lilley Construction* v. *Dunn* [1984] I.R.L.R. 483, E.A.T.; *Electronic Data Processing* v. *Wright, The Times*, March 7, 1985, E.A.T.
s. 71, see *Freemans* v. *Flynn* [1984] I.C.R. 874, E.A.T.
s. 73, orders 84/2021, 2033; amended: orders 84/2021, 2033.
s. 74, see *Morris* v. *Acco. Co.* [1985] I.C.R. 306, E.A.T.; *Shepherd (F.C.) & Co.* v. *Jerrom* [1985] I.R.L.R. 275, E.A.T. ; *Finnie* v. *Top Hat Frozen Foods* [1984] I.R.L.R. 365, E.A.T.
s. 75, order 84/2020; amended: *ibid.*
s. 75A, orders 84/2021; 85/2033; amended: order 85/2033.
s. 81, see *Pink* v. *White, The Times*, December 29, 1984, E.A.T.; *Secretary of State for Employment* v. *Cheltenham Computer Bureau, The Times*, January 24, 1985, E.A.T.; *Murphy* v. *Epsom College* [1985] I.C.R. 80, C.A.; *Macfisheries* v. *Findlay* [1985] I.C.R. 160, E.A.T.; *Birch* v. *University of Liverpool* [1985] I.C.R. 470, C.A.; *North Yorkshire County Council* v. *Fay* [1985] I.R.L.R. 247, C.A.; *Morley* v. *Morley (C.T.)* [1985] I.C.R. 499, E.A.T.
s. 82, see *Gloucestershire County Council* v. *Spencer* [1985] I.R.L.R. 393, C.A.
s. 83, see *Birch* v. *University of Liverpool* [1985] I.C.R. 470, C.A.
s. 88, see *Allinson* v. *Drew Simmons Engineering* [1985] I.C.R. 488, E.A.T.
s. 91, see *Secretary of State for Employment* v. *Cheltenham Computer Bureau, The Times*, January 24, 1985, E.A.T.
s. 94, see *Jeetle* v. *Elster, The Times*, December 17, 1984, E.A.T.
s. 104, see *Secretary of State for Employment* v. *Cheltenham Computer Bureau* [1985] I.C.R. 381, E.A.T.
s. 106, amended: 1985, c.65, sch. 8; c.66, sch.7(S.).
s. 121, see *Jowett (Angus) & Co.* v. *National Union of Tailors and Garment Workers* [1985] I.R.L.R. 326, E.A.T.
s. 121, repealed: 1985, c.65, sch. 10; repealed in pt.: (S.): 1985, c.66, sch. 8.
s. 122, see *Morris* v. *Secretary of State for Employment* [1985] I.C.R. 522, E.A.T.; *Jowett (Angus) & Co.* v. *National Union of Tailors and Garment Workers* [1985] I.R.L.R. 326, E.A.T.

1978—cont.

44. Employment Protection (Consolidation) Act 1978—*cont.*
s. 122, orders 84/2019; 85/2032.
s. 122, amended: 1985, c.9, sch. 2; c.65, s.218, sch. 8; c.66, sch. 7(S.); orders 84/2019; 85/2032.
s. 123, amended: 1985, c.65, sch. 8.
s. 124, see *Morris* v. *Secretary of State for Employment* [1985] I.C.R. 522, E.A.T.
s. 125, amended: 1985, c.9, sch. 2; c.65, sch. 8; c.66, sch. 7(S.); repealed in pt.: 1985, c.65, sch. 10.
s. 136, see *Medallion Holidays* v. *Birch* [1985] I.R.L.R. 406, E.A.T.
s. 140, see *Igbo* v. *Johnson Matthey Chemicals, The Times*, February 9, 1985, E.A.T.; *Hennessey* v. *Craigmyle & Co., The Times*, July 11, 1985, E.A.T.
s. 144, see *Goodeve* v. *Gilson's (A Firm)* [1985] I.C.R. 401, C.A.
s. 148, orders 84/2019; 85/2032.
s. 149, orders 85/782, 1872.
s. 151, see *Jeetle* v. *Elster* [1985] I.R.L.R. 227, E.A.T.
s. 153, see *Poparm* v. *Weekes* [1984] I.R.L.R. 388, E.A.T.; *Hair Colour Consultants* v. *Mena* [1984] I.R.L.R. 386, E.A.T.; *Capron* v. *Capron, The Times*, February 5, 1985, White J.; *Hughes* v. *Department of Health and Social Security; Coy* v. *D.H.S.S.; Jarnell* v. *Department of the Environment* [1985] 2 W.L.R. 866, H.L.; *Jeetle* v. *Elster* [1985] I.R.L.R. 227, E.A.T.
s. 154, orders 84/2019–2021; 85/782, 2032, 2033; amended: order 85/2033.
sch. 1, amended: order 85/1787.
schs. 4, 6, see *Secretary of State for Employment* v. *Cheltenham Computer Bureau, The Times*, January 24, 1985, E.A.T.
sch. 5, amended: order 85/39.
sch. 6, order 85/260; amended: *ibid.*
sch. 9, regs. 85/16, 17(S.).
sch. 11, see *Medallion Holidays* v. *Birch* [1985] I.R.L.R. 406, E.A.T.
sch. 11, rules 85/29.
sch. 13, see *Jeetle* v. *Elster* [1985] I.C.R. 389, E.A.T.
sch. 13, amended: 1985, c.17, sch. 4; repealed in pt.: *ibid.*, sch. 5.
sch. 14, orders 84/2019; 85/2032; amended: orders 84/2019; 85/2032.
sch. 16, repealed in pt.: 1985, c.71, sch. 1.
48. Homes Insulation Act 1978.
repealed: 1985, c.71, sch. 1.
s. 1, amended: 1985, c.51, sch. 8; repealed in pt.(S.): 1985, c.71, sch. 1.
s. 2, repealed in pt.: 1985, c.51, sch. 17.
s. 3, repealed (S.): 1985, c.71, sch. 1.
s. 4, amended (S.): *ibid.*, sch. 2.
55. Transport Act 1978.
ss. 1–4, repealed: 1985, c.67, sch. 8.
56. Parliamentary Pensions Act 1978.
s. 11, order 84/1907.

1979

2. Customs and Excise Management Act 1979.
s. 22, order 85/1730.
s. 93, regs. 85/252, 1627.
s. 114, order 85/252.
s. 170, see *R.* v. *Shivpuri* [1985] 2 W.L.R. 29, C.A.
sch. 1, amended: 1985, c.39, s.1.
sch. 4, repealed in pt.: 1985, c.72, sch. 13.

3. Customs and Excise Duties (General Reliefs) Act 1979.
s. 1, orders 84/2006; 85/19, 112.
s. 4, orders 84/2006; 85/135, 283, 989.
s. 7, order 85/1378.
s. 13, orders 85/1375, 1376.

4. Alcoholic Liquor Duties Act 1979.
s. 2, regs. 85/1627.
s. 3, regs. 85/252, 1627.
s. 5, amended: 1985, c.54, s.1.
ss. 13, 14, amended: *ibid.*, sch. 3.
s. 36, amended: *ibid.*, s.1.
s. 38, amended: *ibid.*, sch. 3.
ss. 43, 46, 49, regs. 85/252, 1627.
s. 49, amended: 1985, c.54, sch. 3.
s. 50, regs. 85/1627.
s. 52, amended: 1985, c.54, sch. 3.
s. 54, see *Cinzano (U.K.)* v. *Customs and Excise Comrs.* [1985] 1 W.L.R. 484, H.L.
s. 54, amended: 1985, c.54, s.4.
s. 56, regs. 85/403, 404.
ss. 61, 62, regs. 85/404.
s. 62, amended: 1985, c.54, s.1.
s. 71A, regs. 85/1627.
s. 71A, added: 1985, c.54, sch. 3.
s. 72, repealed in pt. (prospectively): *ibid.*, schs. 3, 27.
sch. 1, amended: *ibid.*, s.1, sch. 1.
sch. 3, repealed in pt.: 1985, c.72, sch. 13.

5. Hydrocarbon Oil Duties Act 1979.
s. 6, amended: 1985, c.54, s.3.
s. 20, substituted: *ibid.*, sch. 4.
s. 20A, regs. 85/1450.
s. 20A, added: 1985, c.54, sch. 4.
s. 21, regs. 85/1450.
s. 24, regs. 85/1033, 1450.
s. 27, amended: 1985, c.54, sch. 4.
sch. 3, repealed in pt.: *ibid.*, schs. 4, 27.

7. Tobacco Products Duty Act 1979.
sch. 1, amended; 1985, c.54, s.2.

9. Films Act 1979.
repealed: 1985, c.21, s.1, sch. 2.

10. Public Lending Right Act 1979.
s. 2, order 85/201; amended: *ibid.*
s. 3, orders 84/1847; 85/1581.

14. Capital Gains Tax Act 1979.
s. 5, order 85/428.
s. 9, amended: 1985, c.9, sch. 2.
ss. 19, 62, 63, see *Spencer-Nairn* v. *I.R.C.*, 1985 S.L.T. (Lands Tr.) 46.
s. 27, see *Lyon* v. *Pettigrew* [1985] S.T.C. 369, Walton J.
ss. 65, 66, repealed in pt.: 1985, c.54, sch. 27.
s. 67, repealed in pt.: *ibid.*, s.67, sch. 27.
ss. 68–70, repealed in pt.: *ibid.*, sch. 27.

1979—cont.

14. Capital Gains Tax Act 1979—*cont.*
s. 84, amended: *ibid.*, s.67; repealed in pt.: *ibid.*, sch. 27.
s. 114, repealed: *ibid.*
s. 120, amended: *ibid.*, s.70.
ss. 124, 125, repealed: *ibid.*, s.69, sch. 27.
s. 126, amended: *ibid.*, s.70.
s. 137, amended: *ibid.*, s.72.
s. 147, amended: *ibid.*, s.95.
s. 149, amended: 1985, c.9, sch. 2.
s. 151, repealed: 1985, c.54, sch. 27.
s. 155, amended: *ibid.*, s.72.
sch. 2, order 84/1966.
sch. 4, amended: 1985, c.54, s.70.
sch. 7, repealed in pt.: *ibid.*, sch. 27.

17. Vaccine Damage Payments Act 1979.
s. 1, order 85/1249.
s. 1, amended: 1985, c.53, s.23.

18. Social Security Act 1979.
sch. 1, repealed in pt.: 1985, c.53, s.11, sch. 6.

31. Prosecution of Offences Act 1979.
repealed: 1985, c.23, sch. 2.
s. 6, see *R.* v. *Elliott* (1985) 81 Cr.App.R. 115, C.A.
ss. 8, 9, regs. 85/243.

33. Land Registration (Scotland) Act 1979.
Commencement order: 85/501.
ss. 2, 9, see *Hughes* v. *Frame*, 1985 S.L.T.(Lands Tr.) 12.
s. 9, amended: 1985, c.73, sch. 2.
s. 12, amended: 1985, c.37, sch. 1; c.66, sch. 7; c. 73, sch. 2.
s. 22A, added: 1985, c.73, s.2.
s. 30, order 85/501.

34. Credit Unions Act 1979.
s. 6, amended: 1985, c.9, sch. 2.
s. 31, repealed in pt.: 1985, c.58, sch. 4.

36. Nurses, Midwives and Health Visitors Act 1979.
Commencement order: 85/789.
s. 1, order 85/789.
s. 11, order 85/1852.
s. 11, amended: order 84/1975.
sch. 4, amended: 1985, c.9, sch. 2.

37. Banking Act 1979.
Commencement order: 85/797.
s. 1, see *SCF Finance* v. *Masri, The Times,* July 20, 1985, Leggatt J.
s. 2, regs. 85/564, 572, 1845.
s. 6, amended: 1985, c.9, sch. 2; c.65, sch. 8.
s. 17, amended: 1985, c.9, sch. 2.
s. 18, amended: *ibid.*, c.65, s.219.
s. 19, amended: 1985, c.9, sch. 2; c.65, s.219; repealed in pt.: *ibid.*, sch. 10.
s. 20, amended: 1985, c.9, sch. 2.
Pt. II (ss.21–33), order 84/1990.
s. 28, amended: 1985, c.9, sch. 2; 1985, c.65, sch. 8; c.66, sch. 7(S.); repealed in pt. (S.): *ibid.*, schs. 7, 8.
s. 31, amended: 1985, c.9, sch. 2; c.65, sch. 8.
s. 34, regs. 85/220.
s. 36, amended: 1985, c.9, sch. 2; repealed in pt.: 1985, c.58, sch. 4.

CAP.
1979—cont.

37. Banking Act 1979—cont.
ss. 40, 48, 49, amended: 1985, c.9, sch. 2.
s. 50, amended: *ibid.*; repealed in pt.: 1985, c.58, sch. 4.
s. 52, order 85/797.
sch. 1, repealed in pt.: 1985, c.58, sch. 4.
schs. 3, 5, amended: 1985, c.9, sch. 2.
sch. 6, repealed in pt.: 1985, c.71, sch. 1.

38. Estate Agents Act 1979.
s. 1, amended (S.): 1985, c.73, sch. 1.
s. 14, amended: 1985, c.9, sch. 2.
s. 23, amended: 1985, c.65, sch. 8; c.66, sch. 7(S.).

39. Merchant Shipping Act 1979.
Commencement order: 85/1827.
s. 21, order 85/2002.
s. 21, regs. 85/211, 512, 659–661, 663, 855, 936, 1193, 1194, 1216–1218.
s. 22, regs. 85/211, 212, 512, 659–661, 663, 855, 936, 1193, 1194, 1217, 1218, 1664.
s. 52, order 85/1827.
sch. 3, orders 85/230, 1430.

41. Pneumoconiosis etc. (Workers' Compensation) Act 1979.
s. 1, regs. 84/1972; order 85/2034.
ss. 1, 4, amended: 1985, c.53, s.24.
s. 4, regs. 84/1972; 85/1645.
s. 5, regs. 85/1645.
s. 7, regs. 84/1972; 85/1645.

42. Arbitration Act 1979.
s. 1, see *Pera Shipping Corp.* v. *Petroship S.A.*; *Pera, The, The Times*, May 7, 1985, Lloyd J.: *National Westminster Bank* v. *Arthur Young McClelland Moores & Co.* [1985] 2 All E.R. 817, C.A.

43. Crown Agents Act 1979.
s. 17, order 84/2036.
ss. 22, 31, amended: 1985, c.9, sch. 2.

45. Weights and Measures Act 1979.
repealed: 1985, c.72, sch. 13.
s. 10, amended: 1985, c.9, sch. 2.
s. 15, regs. 85/573.

46. Ancient Monuments and Archaeological Areas Act 1979.
ss. 33, 34, amended: 1985, c.51, sch. 2.
s. 61, repealed in pt.: *ibid.*, sch. 17.
sch. 2, amended: *ibid.*, sch. 2.

47. Finance (No. 2) Act 1979.
s. 22, repealed: 1985, c.62, sch. 4.
s. 24, sch. 4 (in pt.), repealed: 1985, c.54, sch. 27.

48. Pensioners' Payments and Social Security Act 1979.
s. 4, order 85/1189.

50. European Assembly (Pay and Pensions) Act 1979.
s. 4, order 85/1116.

53. Charging Orders Act 1979.
s. 4, repealed: 1985, c.65, s. 10.

54. Sale of Goods Act 1979.
ss. 13, 14, see *Border Harvesters* v. *Edwards Engineering (Perth)* (O.H.), 1985 S.L.T. 128.

CAP.
1979—cont.

54. Sale of Goods Act 1979—cont.
s. 14, see *Lancashire Textiles (Jersey)* v. *Thomson Shepherd & Co.* (O.H.), 1986 S.L.T. 41.
s. 25, see *Archivent Sales & Development* v. *Strathclyde Regional Council,* 1985 S.L.T. 154; [1984] 27 Build.L.R. 98, Court of Session (Outer House) Lord Mayfield.
s. 51, see *Allen* v. *W. (Burns) (Tractors)* (O.H.), 1985 S.L.T. 252.
s. 55, see *Landcatch* v. *Marine Harvest* (O.H.), 1985 S.L.T. 478.
s. 61, repealed in pt.: 1985, c.65, sch. 10; c.66, sch. 8(S.).

55. Justices of the Peace Act 1979.
s. 2, repealed in pt.: 1985, c.51, sch. 17.
ss. 4, 12, 19, 22, amended: *ibid.*, s.12.
s. 23, orders 85/1078, 1117, 1633, 1673, 1796, 1863, 1961.
s. 23, amended: 1985, c.51, s.12.
s. 24, orders 85/1078, 1117.
s. 24, amended: 1985, c.51, s.12; repealed in pt.: *ibid.*sch. 17.
s. 52, see *R.* v. *Waltham Forest JJ., ex p. Solanke* [1985] 3 W.L.R. 788, Woolf J.
s. 57, amended: 1985, c.51, s.2; order 85/1383; repealed in pt.: 1985, c.51, sch. 17.
s. 58, amended: *ibid.*, s.60.
s. 59, amended: *ibid.*, s.12.
s. 60, repealed: *ibid.*, sch. 17.
s. 64, amended: *ibid.*, sch. 14; order 85/1884; repealed in pt.: 1985, c.51, sch. 17.
sch. 2, repealed in pt.: *ibid.*

1980

4. Bail etc. (Scotland) Act 1980.
s. 1, see *MacNeill* v. *Milne*, 1984 S.C.C.R. 427.
ss. 2, 3, see *H. M. Advocate* v. *Crawford*, 1985 S.L.T. 242.
s. 10, amended: 1985, c.73, s.21.

5. Child Care Act 1980.
s. 2, see *W.* v. *Hertfordshire C.C.* [1985] 2 All E.R. 301, H.L.
s. 5, amended and repealed in pt.: 1985, c.60, s.25.
s. 12, see *Hereford and Worcester County Council* v. *E.H.* (1985) 15 Fam.Law 229, Wood J.
ss. 12A–12G, see *M.* v. *Berkshire C.C.* (1985) 15 Fam.Law 161, C.A.
s. 12B, see *R.* v. *Bolton Metropolitan Borough Council, ex p. B.* (1985) 15 Fam.Law 193, Wood J.
s. 12C, see *R.* v. *Slough Justices, ex p. B.* (1985) 15 Fam.Law 189, Wood J.; *Y.* v. *Kirklees Borough Council, The Times,* February 23, 1985, Waterhouse J.; *Southwark London Borough Council* v. *H.* [1985] 1 W.L.R. 861, D.C.; *Devon County Council* v. *C., The Times*, May 18, 1985, C.A.

1980—cont.

5. Child Care Act 1980—*cont.*
s. 18, see *M.* v. *Lambeth London Borough Council (No. 2), The Times,* December 20, 1984, Sheldon J.
s. 21, see *R.* v. *F. (A Child), The Times,* March 20, 1985, C.A.; *R.* v. *F. (A Child), The Times,* April 20, 1985, C.A.; *S.* v. *Walsall Metropolitan Borough Council* [1985] 3 All E.R. 294, C.A.
s. 21A, see *K. (A Minor), Re, The Times,* December 20, 1984, Heilbron J.; *L. (A Minor), Re, The Times,* November 2, 1984, Hollings J.; *M.* v. *Lambeth Borough Council (No. 2), The Times,* December 20, 1984, Sheldon J.; *M.* v. *Lambeth Borough Council* (1985) 83 L.G.R. 185, Balcombe J.; *R.* v. *Northampton Juvenile Court, ex p. Hammersmith and Fulham London Borough* (1985) 15 Fam.Law 124, Ewbank J.
Pt. IA (ss.21A–21G), see *Devon County Council* v. *C., The Times,* February 21, 1985, Sheldon J.; *M. (A Minor), Re* [1985] 1 All E.R. 745, C.A.

9. Reserve Forces Act 1980.
s. 145, amended: 1985, c.17, sch. 4.
sch. 9, repealed in pt.: 1985, c.71, sch. 1.

10. Police Negotiating Board Act 1980.
s. 2, regs. 85/130, 686, 885, 1045.

18. Betting, Gaming and Lotteries (Amendment) Act 1980.
repealed: 1985, c.18, sch.

20. Education Act 1980.
s. 7, see *R.* v. *Surrey County Council Education Committee, ex p. H.* (1985) 83 L.G.R. 219, C.A.
s. 12, see *R.* v. *Secretary of State for Education and Science, ex p. Birmingham City Council* (1985) 83 L.G.R. 79, McCullough J.
s. 17, regs. 85/685.
s. 18, regs. 85/830.
s. 35, regs. 85/685, 830.

21. Competition Act 1980.
s. 2, order 84/1919.
s. 11, amended: 1985, c.9, sch. 2; c.67, s.114.
s. 12, amended: 1985, c.9, sch. 2.
s. 26, see *Association of British Travel Agents Agreement (No. 2), Re* [1985] I.C.R. 122, Restrictive Practices Court.

22. Companies Act 1980.
repealed: 1985, c.9, sch. 1.
ss. 29–43, see *Precision Dippings* v. *Precision Dippings Marketing* [1985] 3 W.L.R. 812, C.A.
s. 75, see *London School of Electronics* [1985] 3 All E.R. 523, Nourse J.; *Bird Precision Bellows, Re* [1985] 3 All E.R. 523, C.A.

23. Consular Fees Act 1980.
s. 1, orders 84/1979; 85/1984.

26. British Aerospace Act 1980.
ss. 3, 4, 9, amended: 1985, c.9, sch. 2.

1980—cont.

29. Concessionary Travel for Handicapped Persons (Scotland) Act 1980.
ss. 1, 2, amended: 1985, c.67, sch. 7; repealed in pt.: *ibid.,* schs. 7, 8.

30. Social Security Act 1980.
s. 3, repealed in pt.: 1985, c. 53, sch. 6.
s. 9, amended: *ibid.,* sch. 5.

33. Industry Act 1980.
ss. 2, 3, amended: 1985, c.9, sch. 2.

34. Transport Act 1980.
ss. 47, 48, amended: 1985, c.9, sch. 2.
s. 64 amended: 1985, c.67, sch. 7.
sch. 5, repealed in pt.: *ibid.,* sch. 8.

39. Social Security (No. 2) Act 1980.
s. 6, see *Decisions Nos. R(SB) 17/85; R/(SB) 29/85.*
s. 6, order 85/1454; amended: *ibid.*

41. Films Act 1980.
repealed: 1985, c.21, s.1, sch. 2.

42. Employment Act 1980.
s. 4, see *National Graphical Association* v. *Howard* [1985] I.C.R. 97, C.A.; *Howard* v. *National Graphical Association* [1985] I.C.R. 101, E.A.T.; *Goodfellow* v. *NATSOPA* [1985] I.C.R. 187, E.A.T.; *McGhee* v. *Midland British Road Services; Same* v. *Transport and General Workers' Union* [1985] I.R.L.R. 198, E.A.T.; *Du Cheur Clark* v. *National Society of Operative Printers Graphical and Media Personnel, The Times,* July 31, 1985, E.A.T.
s. 5, see *Howard* v. *National Graphical Association* [1985] I.C.R. 101, E.A.T.
s. 16, see *Thomas* v. *National Union of Mineworkers (South Wales), The Times,* February 18, 1985, Scott J.
s. 17, see *Shipping Co. Uniform Inc.* v. *International Transport Workers Federation, Allen, Ross and Davies* [1985] 1 Lloyd's Rep. 173, Staughton J.; *Thomas* v. *National Union of Mineworkers* [1985] 2 All E.R. 1, C.A.
sch. 1, repealed in pt.: 1985, c.65, sch. 10.

43. Magistrates' Courts Act 1980.
ss. 2, 6, see *R.* v. *Cambridgeshire Justices, ex p. Fraser* [1984] 1 W.L.R. 1391, D.C.
s. 12, amended: 1985, c.23, sch. 1.
ss. 18–20, see *R.* v. *Birmingham Justices, ex p. Hodgson* [1985] 2 W.L.R. 630, D.C.
s. 19, amended: 1985, c.23, sch. 1.
s. 25, see *R.* v. *Cambridgeshire Justices, ex p. Fraser* [1984] 1 W.L.R. 1391, D.C.; *R.* v. *Dudley Magistrates' Court, ex p. Gillard, The Times,* November 13, 1985, H.L.; *sub nom. Gillard, Re* (1985) 135 New L.J. 1139, H.L.
s. 25, amended: 1985, c.23, sch. 1; repealed in pt.: *ibid.,* sch. 2.
s. 30, repealed in pt.: *ibid.*
s. 49, see *R.* v. *Tottenham JJ., ex p. L (A Minor), The Times,* November 11, 1985, D.C.; *R.* v. *Marylebone Magistrates'*

1980—cont.

43. Magistrates' Courts Act 1980—*cont.*
    Court and the Commissioner of Police for the Metropolis, ex p. Ryser [1985] Crim.L.R. 735, D.C.
    s. 63, see *Tilmouth* v. *Tilmouth* (1985) 15 Fam.Law 92, D.C.; *Thomason* v. *Thomason* (1985) 15 Fam.Law 91, D.C.
    s. 77, see *Wilson* v. *Colchester JJ.* [1985] 2 All E.R. 97, H.L.
    s. 82, see *R.* v. *Steyning Magistrates' Court, ex p. Hunter, The Times*, November 22, 1985, D.C.
    s. 93, see *R.* v. *Waltham Forest Justices, ex p. Solanke, The Times*, January 12, 1985, Woolf J.
    s. 95, see *Allen* v. *Allen* [1985] 2 W.L.R. 65, Booth J.; *Fletcher* v. *Fletcher* [1985] 2 All E.R. 260, D.C.
    s. 97, see *R.* v. *Barking Justices, ex p. Goodspeed* [1985] R.T.R. 70, D.C.; *R.* v. *Skegness Magistrates' Court, ex p. Cardy*; *R.* v. *Manchester Crown Court, ex p. Williams* [1985] R.T.R. 49, D.C.; *R.* v. *Coventry Magistrates' Court, ex p. Perks* [1985] R.T.R. 74, D.C.
    s. 111, see *Streames* v. *Copping, The Times*, February 25, 1984, D.C.; *Fletcher* v. *Fletcher* [1985] 2 All E.R. 260, D.C.
    s. 115, see *Chief Constable of the Surrey Constabulary* v. *Ridley and Steel* [1985] Crim. L.R. 725, D.C.; *Howley* v. *Oxford* [1985] Crim.L.R. 724, D.C.
    s. 123, see *R.* v. *Eastbourne Justices, ex p. Kisten, The Times*, December 22, 1984, D.C.
    s. 127, see *Y.* v. *Kirklees Borough Council, The Times*, February 23, 1985, Waterhouse J.; *R.* v. *Dacorum Magistrates Court, ex p. Gardner (Michael)* [1985] Crim.L.R. 394, D.C.; *Hertsmere Borough Council* v. *Dunn Alan Building Contractors* [1985] Crim.L.R. 726, D.C.
    s. 143, amended: 1985, c.13, sch. 2.
    s. 144, rules 85/601, 1695, 1944, 1945.
    s. 145, rules 85/1944.
    sch. 1, repealed in pt.: 1985, c.71, sch. 1.
    sch. 6, amended: 1985, c.13, sch. 2.
    sch. 7, repealed in pt.: 1985, c.71, sch. 1; c.72, sch. 13.

44. Education (Scotland) Act 1980.
    s. 22, see *Deane* v. *Lothian Regional Council*, 1986 S.L.T. 22.
    s. 35, see *Neeson* v. *Lunn*, 1985 S.C.C.R. 102.
    s. 49, regs. 85/1120.
    ss. 73, 74, regs. 85/506, 1183.
    s. 75A, 75B, regs. 85/1076.
    s. 77, regs. 85/543, 679, 866, 1163, 1164.
    s. 86, see *Neeson* v. *Lunn* 1985 S.C.C.R. 102.
    s. 111, amended: 1985, c.9, sch. 2.
    s. 135, regs. 85/542, 678.

45. Water (Scotland) Act 1980.
    s. 96, repealed: 1985, c.73, sch. 4.

1980—cont.

46. Solicitors (Scotland) Act 1980.
    s. 6, amended: 1985, c.73, sch. 1; repealed in pt.: *ibid.*, schs. 1, 4.
    s. 15, repealed in pt.: *ibid.*, schs. 1, 4.
    ss. 16, 18, 21, 26–28, 30–32, amended: *ibid.*, sch. 1.
    s. 33A, added: *ibid.*
    s. 34, amended: *ibid.*
    s. 35, amended: *ibid.*; repealed in pt.: 1985, c.58, sch. 4; c.73, sch. 4.
    ss. 36–45, 47, amended: *ibid.*, sch. 1.
    s. 48, repealed: *ibid.*
    ss. 51–54, 60, 61, amended: *ibid.*
    s. 62A, added: *ibid.*
    ss. 64, 65, amended: *ibid.*
    sch. 1, amended: *ibid.*; repealed in pt.: *ibid.*, sch. 4.
    sch. 3, amended: *ibid.*, sch. 1; repealed in pt.: *ibid.*, schs. 1, 4.
    sch. 4, amended: *ibid.*, sch. 1.

47. Criminal Appeal (Northern Ireland) Act 1980.
    ss. 14, 25, see *R.* v. *McGrady* [1984] 8 N.I.J.B., C.A.

48. Finance Act 1980.
    s. 7, repealed in pt.: 1985, c.54, sch. 27.
    s. 24, order 85/430.
    s. 30, amended (S.): 1985, c.73, sch. 1.
    s. 57, repealed in pt.: 1985 c.54, sch. 27.
    s. 64, order 84/2060.
    s. 65, amended: 1985, c.54, sch. 14; repealed in pt.: *ibid.*, schs. 14, 27,
    s. 71, repealed in pt.: *ibid.*
    s. 79, amended: *ibid.*, s.70.
    s. 97, amended: 1985, c.71, sch. 2; repealed in pt.: *ibid.*, sch. 1.
    ss. 99, 110–116, repealed: 1985, c.54, sch. 27.
    s. 117, see *Combined Technologies Corp.* v. *I.R.C.* [1985] S.T.C. 348, Vinelott J.
    s. 118, sch. 6, repealed in pt.: 1985 c.54, sch. 27.
    sch. 10, amended: 1985, c.9, sch. 2.
    sch. 15, see *Combined Technologies Corp.* v. *I.R.C.* [1985] S.T.C. 348, Vinelott J.
    sch. 18, repealed in pt.: 1985, c.54, sch. 27.

50. Coal Industry Act 1980.
    s. 3, order 84/1888.
    s. 7, order 84/1889.

51. Housing Act 1980.
    Pt. I (ss.1–27), repealed: 1985, c.71, sch. 1.
    s. 8, order 85/1979.
    s. 16, see *Sutton London Borough Council* v. *Swann, The Times*, November 30, 1985, C.A.
    s. 19, amended: 1985, c.51, sch. 14; order 85/1884.
    s. 19, amended: 1985, c.51, sch. 14.
    s. 22, regs. 85/36.
    s. 28, amended: 1985, c.51, sch. 14.
    s. 30, see *Harrogate Borough Council* v. *Simpson* (1985) 25 R.V.R. 10, C.A.

1980—cont.

51. Housing Act 1980—cont.

s. 33, see *South Buckinghamshire County Council* v. *Francis*, October 1, 1985, Slough County Ct., P. S. J. Langan Q.C.

s. 34, see *Enfield London Borough Council* v. *French* (1985) 49 P. & C.R. 223, C.A.

s. 41A, regs. 85/1493.

s. 48, see *Kensington and Chelsea Royal Borough Council* v. *Hayden* (1984) 17 H.L.R. 114, C.A.

s. 50, see *Harrogate Borough Council* v. *Simpson* (1985) 25 R.V.R. 10, C.A.

s. 50, repealed in pt.: 1985, c.51, sch. 17.

s. 56, orders 85/812, 1311, 1312.

s. 66, see *Bradshaw* v. *Baldwin-Wiseman, The Times*, January 24, 1985, C.A.

ss. 80, 81 (in pt.), 83 (in pt.), 85 (in pt.), repealed: 1985, c.71, sch. 1.

s. 86, amended: *ibid.*, sch. 2.

s. 87, repealed: *ibid.*, sch. 1.

Pts. V–VIII (ss.90–133), repealed: *ibid.*

ss. 105, 108, repealed in pt.: 1985, c.51, sch. 17.

ss. 110, 111, amended: *ibid.*, sch. 14; repealed in pt.: *ibid.*, sch. 17.

Pt. VIII (ss.120–133), repealed (S.): 1985, c.71, sch. 1.

s. 124, order 84/1833.

ss. 134–137, repealed: 1985, c.71, sch. 1.

s. 135, repealed in pt.: 1985, c.51, sch. 17.

s. 139, repealed: 1985, c.71, sch. 1.

s. 140, amended: 1985, c.51, sch. 14; c.71, sch. 1.

ss. 144–147, 149, 150 (in pt.), repealed: *ibid.*

s. 151, order 84/1833; regs. 85/36.

ss. 151, 153, 154, repealed in pt.: 1985, c.71, sch. 1.

schs. 1, 1A, amended: 1985, c.51, sch. 14; order 85/1884.

schs. 1–4A, repealed: 1985, c.71, sch. 1.

sch. 3, see *Eastleigh Borough Council* v. *Walsh* [1985] 2 All E.R. 112, H.L.; *Kensington and Chelsea Royal Borough Council* v. *Hayden* (1984) 17 H.L.R. 114, C.A.

sch. 4, see *Enfield London Borough Council* v. *French, The Times*, January 2, 1985; (1985) 49 P. & C.R. 223, C.A.

sch. 7, see *Bradshaw* v. *Baldwin-Wiseman, The Times*, January 24, 1985, C.A.

sch. 9, amended: 1985, c.71, sch. 2.

schs. 10 (in pt.), 11–13, repealed: *ibid.*, sch. 1.

sch. 16, amended: 1985, c.9, sch. 2; repealed in pt. (S.): 1985, c.71, sch. 1.

schs. 16–20, repealed: *ibid.*

schs. 17 (in pt.), 18, repealed (S.): *ibid.*

sch. 19, amended: 1985, c.9, sch. 2; c.51, sch. 14.

schs. 23, 24, 25 (in pt.), repealed: 1985, c.71, sch. 1.

sch. 25, repealed in pt. (S.): *ibid.*

1980—cont.

52. Tenants' Rights, etc. (Scotland) Act 1980.

s. 1, see *Graham* v. *Motherwell District Council; Robertson* v. *The Same*, 1985 S.L.T.(Lands Tr.) 44; *Murdoch* v. *Gordon District Council*, 1985 S.L.T.(Lands Tr.) 42; *Docherty* v. *City of Edinburgh District Council*, 1985 S.L.T.(Lands Tr.) 61.

s. 1, amended: 1985, c.71, sch. 2.

ss. 2, 3, sch. 1, see *Stevenson* v. *West Lothian District Council*, 1985 S.L.T.(Lands Tr.) 9.

ss. 2, 7, see *Thomson* v. *Stirling District Council*, 1985 S.L.T. (Lands Tr.) 4.

s. 7, see *Murdoch* v. *Gordon District Council*, 1985 S.L.T.(Lands Tr.) 42.

s. 9, repealed: 1985, c.71, sch. 1.

s. 10, see *Docherty* v. *City of Edinburgh District Council*, 1985 S.L.T.(Lands Tr.) 61.

s. 10, amended: 1985, c.71, sch. 2.

s. 11, substituted: *ibid.*

s. 31, repealed in pt.: *ibid.*, sch. 1.

sch. 1, see *Docherty* v. *City of Edinburgh District Council*, 1985 S.L.T.(Lands Tr.) 61.

53. Health Services Act 1980.

s. 1, order 85/305.

sch. 1, repealed in pt.: order 85/39.

55. Law Reform (Miscellaneous Provisions) (Scotland) Act 1980.

s. 1, see *H.M. Advocate* v. *Leslie*, 1985 S.C.C.R. 1.

s. 12, repealed: 1985, c.66, sch. 8.

58. Limitation Act 1980.

s. 2, see *Sevcon* v. *Lucas Cav* [1985] F.S.R. 545, C.A.

s. 4A, added: 1985, c.61, s.57.

s. 7, see *Agromet Motoimport* v. *Maulden Engineering Co. (Beds.)* [1985] 2 All E.R. 436, Otton J.

s. 8, see *Collin* v. *Duke of Westminster* [1985] 1 All E.R. 463, C.A.

s. 11, see *Pattison* v. *Hobbs, The Times*, November 11, 1985, C.A.

s. 14, see *Davis* v. *Ministry of Defence, The Times*, August 7, 1985, C.A.

s. 28, amended: 1985, c.61, s.57.

s. 32A, added: *ibid.*

s. 33, see *Eastman* v. *London County Bus Services, The Times*, November 23, 1985, C.A.

s. 36, amended: 1985, c.61, s.57.

60. Civil Aviation Act 1980.

ss. 4, 5, amended: 1985, c.9, sch. 2.

s. 6, see *H.M. Advocate* v. *Cafferty*, 1984 S.C.C.R. 444.

62. Criminal Justice (Scotland) Act 1980.

s. 3, amended: 1985, c.73, s.35.

ss. 3A–3D, added: *ibid.*

s. 6, see *Walker* v. *H.M. Advocate*, 1985 S.C.C.R. 150.

s. 9, see *Cirignaco* v. *Lockhart*, 1985 S.C.C.R. 157.

s. 20, see *Tudhope* v. *Senatti Holdings*, 1984 S.C.C.R. 251.

1980—cont.

62. Criminal Justice (Scotland) Act 1980—cont.
s. 26, see *Smith* v. *Allan*, 1985 S.L.T. 565.
s. 58, see *Carmichael* v. *Siddique*, 1985 S.C.C.R. 145.
s. 68, order 85/1224.
ss. 68, 69, 77, amended: 1985, c.57, s.10.
s. 78, see *Black* v. *Allen*, 1985 S.C.C.R. 11; *MacDougall* v. *Yuk-Sun Ho*, 1985 S.C.C.R. 199.
sch. 4, see *H.M. Advocate* v. *Cafferty*, 1984 S.C.C.R. 444.

63. Overseas Development and Co-operation Act 1980.
s. 4, orders 85/592, 1289.

64. Broadcasting Act 1980.
s. 17, see *R.* v. *Broadcasting Complaints Commission, ex p. Owen, The Times*, January 26, 1985, D.C.

65. Local Government, Planning and Land Act 1980.
s. 1, repealed in pt.: 1985, c.72, sch. 13.
s. 2, amended: 1985, c.51, sch. 14; order 85/1884; repealed in pt.: 1985, c.51, sch. 17.
s. 4, repealed in pt.: 1985, c.67, sch. 8.
ss. 5, 16, repealed in pt.: 1985, c.51, sch. 14.
s. 20, see *Inner London Education Authority* v. *Department of the Environment* (1985) 83 L.G.R. 24, C.A.; *Wilkinson* v. *Doncaster Metropolitan District Council, The Times*, July 23, 1985, C.A.
s. 20, amended: 1985, c.51, sch. 14; order 85/1884; repealed in pt.: 1985, c.51, sch. 17.
s. 47, repealed in pt.: 1985, c.71, sch. 1.
s. 51, order 84/1863.
s. 53, amended: 1985, c.51, s.69; repealed in pt.: *ibid.*, s.69, sch. 17.
s. 54, amended: 1985, c.51, s.69; repealed in pt.: 1985, c.71, sch. 1.
s. 55, amended: 1985, c.51, s.69; repealed in pt.: *ibid.*, sch. 17.
s. 56, amended: *ibid.*, sch. 16; repealed in pt.: *ibid.*, sch. 17.
s. 59, see *R.* v. *Secretary of State for the Environment, ex p. London Borough of Hackney, The Times*, May 11, 1985, C.A.; *Nottinghamshire County Council* v. *Secretary of State for the Environment; City of Bradford Metropolitan Council* v. *The Same, Financial Times*, December 13, 1985, H.L.
s. 59, amended: 1985, c.51, s.69; repealed in pt.: *ibid.*, sch. 17.
s. 60, see *R.* v. *Secretary of State for the Environment, ex p. Leicester City Council* (1985) 25 R.V.R. 31, Woolf J.
s. 63, see *R.* v. *Secretary of State for Education and Science, ex p. ILEA, The Times*, June 20, 1985, D.C.
s. 63A, added: 1985, c.51, s.83.
s. 67, regs. 85/23.
s. 68, amended: 1985, c.51, s.69; repealed in pt.: 1985, c.71, sch. 1.

1980—cont.

65. Local Government, Planning and Land Act 1980—cont.
s. 71, amended: 1985, c.51, sch. 14; order 85/1884.
s. 72, regs. 85/257.
s. 72, amended: 1985, c.51, sch. 14.
s. 75, regs. 85/257.
s. 81, repealed: 1985, c.51, sch. 17.
s. 82, amended: *ibid.*, sch. 14; c.67, sch. 3; repealed in pt.: *ibid.*, schs. 3, 8.
s. 84, regs. 85/257.
s. 86, repealed in pt.: 1985, c.51, sch. 17.
s. 87, regs. 85/1180(S.), 1182.
s. 99, amended: 1985, c.51, sch. 14; order 85/1884; repealed in pt.: 1985, c.51, sch. 17.
s. 100, amended: 1985, c.9, sch. 2.
s. 116, repealed in pt.: 1985, c.51, sch. 17.
s. 136, see *London Docklands Development Corp.* v. *Rank Hovis McDougall, The Times*, July 25, 1985, C.A.
s. 141, amended: 1985, c.9, sch. 2.
ss. 152, 153, amended: 1985, c.71, sch. 2.
ss. 156, 159, repealed in pt.: *ibid.*, sch. 1.
s. 165, repealed in pt.: 1985, c.51, sch. 17.
s. 170, amended: 1985: c.9, sch. 2.
sch. 4, repealed in pt.: 1985, c.67, sch. 3.
sch. 6, repealed in pt.: 1985, c.71, sch. 1.
sch. 10, see *R.* v. *Secretary of State for Education and Science, ex p. ILEA, The Times*, June 20, 1985, D.C.
sch. 12, amended: 1985, c.71, sch. 2.
schs. 13–15, repealed in pt.: 1985, c.51, sch. 17.
sch. 16, amended: *ibid.*, sch. 14; order 85/1884; repealed in pt.: 1985, c.51, sch. 17.
sch. 22, regs. 84/2048.
sch. 27, repealed in pt.: 1985, c.71, sch. 1.
sch. 31, amended: 1985, c.5, s.12; c.9, sch. 2.
sch. 32, order 85/137.
sch. 32, repealed in pt.: 1985, c.51, sch. 17.
sch. 33, repealed in pt.: 1985, c.71, sch. 1.

66. Highways Act 1980.
s. 1, amended: 1985, c.51, sch. 4; repealed in pt: *ibid.*, sch. 17.
ss. 2, 4, amended: *ibid.*, sch. 4.
s. 6, amended: *ibid.*: repealed in pt.: *ibid.*, schs. 4, 17.
s. 7, repealed: *ibid.*, sch. 17.
s. 8, amended: *ibid.*, sch. 4.
ss. 11 (in pt.), 15, 18 (in pt.), repealed: *ibid.*, sch. 17.
s. 20, amended: *ibid.*, sch. 4.
ss. 24, 25, repealed in pt.: *ibid.*, sch. 17.
s. 31, see *Gloucestershire County Council* v. *Farrow* [1985] 1 All E.R. 878, C.A.
ss. 31, 34, 35, amended: 1985, c.51, sch. 4.
s. 36, amended: *ibid.*, c.71, sch. 2.
s. 38, repealed in pt.: 1985, c.51, sch. 17.
ss. 39, 40, 42, 43, 50, 61, amended: *ibid.*, sch. 4.
s. 62, repealed in pt.: *ibid.*, sch. 17.

CAP.   CAP.

1980—cont.

66. Highways Act 1980—*cont.*

s. 64, amended: *ibid.*, sch. 4; repealed in pt.: *ibid.*, sch. 17.

s. 66, amended: *ibid.*, sch. 4.

ss. 67, 69, repealed in pt.: *ibid.*, sch. 17.

ss. 79, 80. amended: *ibid.*, sch. 4; repealed in pt.: *ibid.*, sch. 17.

ss. 90A, 90B, repealed in pt.: *ibid.*

.s. 95, amended: *ibid.*, sch. 4; repealed in pt.: *ibid.*, sch. 17.

s. 100, amended: *ibid.*, sch. 4.

s. 106, instrument 84/1864.

s. 114, amended: 1985, c.51, sch. 4.

ss. 115H, 116, amended: *ibid.*; repealed in pt.: *ibid.*, sch. 17.

s. 117, repealed in pt.: *ibid.*

s. 134, amended: *ibid.*, sch. 4.

s. 137, see *Waite* v. *Taylor* (1985) 82 L.S.Gaz 1092, D.C.

s. 139, regs. 84/1933.

s. 143, amended: 1985, c.51, sch. 4.

s. 144, repealed in pt.: *ibid.*, sch. 17.

ss. 146, 147, amended: *ibid.*, sch. 4.

s. 151, amended: *ibid.*; repealed in pt.: *ibid.*, sch. 17.

s. 154, amended: *ibid.*, sch. 4.

s. 156, amended: *ibid.*; repealed in pt.: *ibid.*, sch. 17.

ss. 157–159, repealed: *ibid.*

s. 160, amended: *ibid.*, sch. 4; repealed in pt.: *ibid.*, sch. 17.

s. 170, repealed in pt.: *ibid.*

ss. 172, 175, 186, 188–200, 203, 205, 210, amended: *ibid.*, sch. 4.

s. 219, repealed in pt.: *ibid.*, sch. 17.

ss. 220, 223, 230, amended: *ibid.*, sch. 4.

s. 254, amended: *ibid.*; repealed in pt.: *ibid.*, sch. 17.

s. 263, amended: *ibid.*, sch. 4.

s. 264, amended: *ibid.*: repealed in pt.: *ibid.*, sch. 17.

s. 269, repealed: *ibid.*

s. 271, amended: *ibid.*, sch. 4.

s. 285, amended: 1985, c.51, sch. 4; repealed in pt.: *ibid.*, sch. 17.

s. 287, repealed in pt.: *ibid.*

s. 298, amended: *ibid.*, sch. 4; repealed in pt.: *ibid.*, sch. 17.

ss. 326, 329, repealed in pt.: *ibid.*

s. 330, amended: *ibid.*, sch. 4.

sch. 1, repealed in pt.: *ibid.*, sch. 17.

sch. 7, amended: *ibid.*, sch. 4.

sch. 9, repealed in pt.: *ibid.*, sch. 17.

schs. 12, 15, amended: *ibid.*; repealed in pt.: *ibid.*, sch. 17.

1981

13. English Industrial Estates Corporation Act 1981.

s. 2, amended: 1985, c.25, s.1.

s. 3, amended: *ibid.*, sch.

s. 4, amended: *ibid.*, s.2.

s. 6, amended: *ibid.*, s.3; repealed in pt.: *ibid.*, sch.

s. 7, amended: 1985, c.9, sch.2; c.25, s.4.

1981—cont.

14. Public Passenger Vehicles Act 1981.

ss. 1 (in pt.), 2, repealed: 1985, c.67, sch. 8.

s. 3, amended: *ibid.*, sch. 2.

ss. 4, 5, substituted: *ibid.*, s.3.

s. 5, amended: 1985, c.51, sch. 5.

s. 8, amended: 1985, c.67, sch. 7.

s. 9, amended: *ibid.*, schs. 2, 7.

s. 9A, added: *ibid.*, s.33.

ss. 12, 14, amended: *ibid.*, schs. 1, 2.

s. 14A, added: *ibid.*, s.25.

s. 15, amended: *ibid.*, schs. 1, 2.

s. 16, regs. 85/1905.

s. 16, amended: 1985, c.67, s.24, schs. 2, 7; repealed in pt.: *ibid.*, sch. 8.

s. 17, amended: *ibid.*, schs. 2, 7.

s. 17A, added: *ibid.*, s.5.

s. 18, amended: *ibid.*, s.24, sch. 2.

s. 19, amended: 1985, c.65, sch. 8; c.67, sch. 2.

s. 20, amended: *ibid.*, s.29, sch. 2.

s. 21, amended: *ibid.*, sch. 2.

s. 22, regs. 85/214, 833.

s. 22, amended: 1985, c.67, schs. 1, 7.

s. 23, amended: *ibid.*, sch. 2.

s. 28, repealed: *ibid.*, s.32, sch. 8.

Pt. III (ss.30–41), repealed: 1985, c.67, s.1, sch. 8.

s. 31, regs. 85/1907.

s. 31, amended: 1985, c.51, sch. 5; repealed in pt.: *ibid.*, sch. 17.

s. 35, repealed in pt.: *ibid.*

s. 37, regs. 85/1907.

ss. 38, 40, amended: 1985, c.51, sch. 5.

ss. 42–45, repealed: 1985, c.67, sch. 8.

s. 46, repealed in pt.: *ibid.*, schs. 1, 8.

s. 47, order 85/1010.

s. 47, amended: 1985, c.51, sch. 5.

ss. 47, 48, repealed: 1985, c.67, s.32, sch. 8.

s. 49, repealed: *ibid.*, sch. 8.

s. 50, regs. 85/1907.

ss. 50, 51, substituted: 1985, c.67, s.31.

s. 52, regs. 85/214, 833, 1905.

s. 52, amended: 1985, c.67, sch. 2; repealed in pt.: *ibid.*, schs. 1, 8.

s. 53, amended: *ibid.*, sch. 1; repealed in pt.: *ibid.*, sch. 8.

s. 54, substituted: *ibid.*, s.4.

s. 55, substituted: *ibid.*, s.4.

s. 55, amended: *ibid.*, sch. 2.

s. 56, amended: *ibid.*, schs. 2, 7; repealed in pt.: *ibid.*, sch. 8.

s. 57, amended: *ibid.*, sch. 2; repealed in pt.: *ibid.*, schs. 1, 8.

s. 58, regs. 85/1906.

s. 58, repealed in pt.: 1985, c.67.

s. 59, regs. 85/214, 1905, 1907.

s. 59, repealed in pt.: 1985, c.67, schs. 1, 8.

s. 60, regs. 85/214, 833, 1905, 1907.

s. 60, amended: 1985, c.67, s.134, schs. 2, 7; repealed in pt.: *ibid.*, s.134, sch. 8.

s. 61, regs. 85/833, 1906.

s. 61, repealed in pt.: 1985, c.67, s.135, sch. 8.

1981—cont.

14. Public Passenger Vehicles Act 1981
—cont.
ss. 62, 65 (in pt.), 66 (in pt.), 67 (in pt.):
repealed in pt.: *ibid.*, sch. 8.
s. 68, amended: *ibid.*, sch. 1; repealed in
pt.: *ibid.*, sch. 8.
s. 69, amended: *ibid.*, sch. 2; repealed in
pt.: *ibid.*, sch. 8.
ss. 70–72, 74, 76, repealed in pt.: *ibid.*,
sch. 8.
s. 78, order 85/1477.
s. 79, amended: 1985, c.67, sch. 7.
s. 81, repealed in pt.: *ibid.*, schs. 1, 8.
ss. 81, 82, regs. 85/1905.
s. 82, amended: 1985, c.67, sch. 2;
repealed in pt.: *ibid.*, schs. 1, 8.
s. 83, repealed in pt.: *ibid.*
s. 87, amended: *ibid.*, sch. 7.
sch. 1, amended: 1985, c.51, sch. 5; c.67,
sch. 1; repealed in pt.: *ibid.*, sch. 8.
sch. 2, substituted: *ibid.*, s.3, sch. 2.
sch. 3, amended: *ibid.*, sch. 2.
sch. 4, amended: 1985, c.51, sch. 5.
schs. 4, 5, repealed: 1985, c.67, sch. 8.

**15. National Film Finance Corporation Act
1981.**
s. 1, order 85/1943.
s. 7, amended: 1985, c.9, sch. 2.
s. 9, order 85/1942.
sch. 1, order 85/1943.
sch. 1, repealed in pt.: 1985, c.21, s.3,
sch. 2.
sch. 2, amended: 1985, c.9, sch. 2.

16. Film Levy Finance Act 1981.
sch. 1, amended: 1985, c.9, sch. 2.

20. Judicial Pensions Act 1981.
s. 21, order 85/1691; amended: *ibid.*

21. Ports (Financial Assistance) Act 1981.
s. 1, amended: 1985, c.30. s.2.

22. Animal Health Act 1981.
s. 1, orders 84/1943, 2063(S.); 85/24, 328,
1174, 1542, 1765, 1766.
s. 7, orders 84/1943, 2063(S.); 85/24, 1174.
s. 8, orders 84/1943, 2063(S.); 85/328,
1542, 1765, 1766.
s. 10, orders 84/1943, 2063(S.).
ss. 10, 34, sch. 2, see *R.* v. *Secretary of
State for Agriculture, Fisheries and
Food, ex p. Avi Centre (London), The
Times*, May 22, 1985, Kennedy J.
s. 11, order 85/217.
s, 15, orders 84/1943, 2063(S.); 85/328.
s. 17, orders 85/328, 1542.
s. 23, orders 85/24, 328, 1174, 1542.
s. 25, orders 84/1943, 2063(S.); 85/328,
1542.
s. 28, order 85/328.
s. 32, orders 84/1943, 2063(S.).
s. 50, amended: 1985, c.51, sch. 8.
s. 72, order 84/2063(S.).
s. 83, orders 84/1943, 2063(S.).
s. 86, order 84/2063(S.).
s. 87, orders 84/1943, 2063(S.); 85/1765,
1766.
s. 87, amended: 85/1765.

1981—cont.

22. Animal Health Act 1981—*cont.*
s. 88, orders 84/1943, 2063(S.); 85/328,
1765, 1766.
s. 88, amended: orders 85/1765, 1766.

25. Industrial Diseases (Notification) Act 1981.
s. 1, regs. 85/568, 569, 1133, 1134.

**28. Licensing (Alcohol Education and
Research) Act 1981.**
s. 10, amended: 1985, c.9, sch. 2.

29. Fisheries Act 1981.
ss. 15, 18, scheme 84/1879; 85/987.
s. 30, orders 84/1956; 85/215, 313, 487.

33. Social Security Act 1981.
sch. 2, repealed in pt.: 1985, c.53, sch. 6.

35. Finance Act 1981.
ss. 7, 8, 41, repealed in pt.: 1985, c.54,
sch. 27.
s. 55, amended: 1985, c.9, sch. 2.
s. 107, amended: 1985, c.71, sch. 2;
repealed in pt.: 1985, c.54, sch. 27.
s. 111, amended: *ibid.*, s.91.
ss. 129–133, repealed: *ibid.*, sch. 27.
s. 135, amended: *ibid.*, sch. 25.

**36. Town and Country Planning (Minerals) Act
1981.**
s. 2, repealed in pt.: 1985, c.51, sch. 17.

37. Zoo Licensing Act 1981.
s. 3, repealed in pt.: 1985, c.51, sch. 17.

38. British Telecommunications Act 1981.
s. 67, repealed in pt.: 1985, c.58, sch. 4.
s. 85, amended: 1985, c.9, sch. 2.
sch. 4, repealed in pt.: 1985, c.65, sch. 10.

**41. Local Government and Planning (Amend-
ment) Act 1981.**
s. 87, see *Hughes (H.T.)* v. *Secretary of
State for the Environment and Fareham
Borough Council* [1985] J.P.L. 486,
Hodgson J.

42. Indecent Displays (Control) Bill 1981.
s. 1, amended: 1985, c.13, sch. 2.

45. Forgery and Counterfeiting Act 1981.
ss. 1, 10, see *R.* v. *Campbell* (1985) 80
Cr.App.R. 47; [1984] Crim.L.R. 683,
C.A.
s. 3, see *R.* v. *Tobierre, The Times*, November 18, 1985, C.A.

47. Criminal Attempts Act 1981.
s. 1, see *R.* v. *Shivpuri* [1985] 2 W.L.R.
29, C.A.; *R.* v. *Pearman* [1985] R.T.R.
39, C.A.; *Anderton* v. *Ryan* [1985] 2
W.L.R. 968, H.L.

49. Contempt of Court Act 1981.
ss. 2, 7, see *Peacock* v. *London Weekend
Television, The Times*, November 27,
1985, C.A.
s. 8, see *McCadden* v. *H.M. Advocate*,
1985 S.C.C.R. 282.
s. 11, see *R.* v. *Arundel Justices, ex p.
Westminster Press* [1985] 1 W.L.R. 708,
D.C.
s. 12, see *R.* v. *Havant Justices, ex p.
Palmer, The Times*, May 15, 1985.
s. 14, see *Lee* v. *Walker, The Times*,
December 14, 1984, C.A.

1981—cont.

49. Contempt of Court Act 1981—*cont.*

sch. 1, see *Peacock* v. *London Weekend Television, The Times,* November 27, 1985, C.A.

sch. 1, amended: 1985, c.23, sch. 1.

53. Deep Sea Mining (Temporary Provisions) Act 1981.

s. 3, order 85/2000.

s. 16, amended: 1985, c.48, s.15.

54. Supreme Court Act 1981.

s. 18, see *Hall* v. *Wandsworth Health Authority, The Times,* February 16, 1985, Tudor Price J.; *Bonalumi* v. *Secretary of State for the Home Department* [1985] 1 All E.R. 797, C.A.; *Marshall* v. *Levine* [1985] 2 All E.R. 177, C.A.; *McCarney* v. *McCarney, The Times,* July 27, 1985, C.A.; *Thompson* v. *Fraser* [1985] 3 All E.R. 511, C.A.; *Day* v. *Grant; R.* v. *Manchester Crown Court, ex p. Williams* [1985] R.T.R. 299, C.A.

s. 20, see *Samick Lines* v. *Owners of the Antonis P. Lemos* [1985] 2 W.L.R. 468, H.L.

s. 21, see *Stephan J, The* [1985] 2 Lloyd's Rep. 344, Sheen J.

s. 28, see *Smalley, Re* [1985] 2 W.L.R. 538, H.L.; *Westminster City Council* v. *Lunepalm, The Times,* December 10, 1985 (and correction December 13, 1985), Woolf J.

s. 29, see *R.* v. *Chichester Crown Court, ex p. Abodunrin* (1984) 79 Cr.App.R. 293, D.C.; *Smalley, Re* [1985] 2 W.L.R. 538, H.L.

s. 31, see *Hall* v. *Wandsworth Health Authority, The Times,* February 16, 1985, Tudor Price J.; *R.* v. *Beverley County Court, ex p. Brown, The Times,* January 25, 1985, C.A.; *R.* v. *West Devon Borough Council, ex p. North East Essex Building Co.* [1985] J.P.L. 391, Mann J.

s. 33, see *Hall* v. *Wandsworth Health Authority, The Times,* February 16, 1985, Tudor Price J.

s. 35A, see *Allied London Investments* v. *Hambro Life Assurance* (1985) 274 E.G. 148, C.A.; *Fansa* v. *American Express International Banking Corp., The Times,* June 26, 1985, Russell J.

s. 37, see *Hill Samuel & Co.* v. *Littaur* (1985) 135 New L.J. 57, Bingham J.; *House of Spring Gardens* v. *Waite* [1985] F.S.R. 173, C.A.; *Parker* v. *Camden London Borough Council* [1985] 2 All E.R. 141, C.A.; *Ainsbury* v. *Millington, The Times,* August 12, 1985, C.A.; *Daiches* v. *Bluelake Investments* (1985) 275 E.G. 462, Harman J.; *Peacock* v. *London Weekend Television, The Times,* November 27, 1985, C.A.

s. 40A, amended: 1985, c.9, sch. 2; c.61, s.51; c.65, sch. 8; repealed in pt.: 1985, c.61, s.51, sch. 8.

1981—cont.

54. Supreme Court Act 1981—*cont.*

s. 42, see *Rohrberg* v. *Charkin, The Times,* January 30, 1985, C.A.

s. 51, see *Aiden Shipping Co.* v. *Interbulk, Financial Times,* October 16, 1985, C.A.

s. 52, amended: 1985, c.23, sch. 1.

s. 54, see *Coldunell* v. *Gallon, The Times,* November 21, 1985, C.A.

s. 56, see *Day* v. *Grant; R.* v. *Manchester Crown Court, ex p. Williams* [1985] R.T.R. 299, C.A.

s. 77, amended: 1985, c.23, sch. 1; repealed in pt.: *ibid.,* sch. 2.

s. 84, rules 85/69, 846.

s. 99, order 85/511.

s. 106, repealed in pt.: 1985, c.61, s.51, sch. 8.

s. 127, rules 85/1232.

s. 150, order 85/1197.

sch. 5, repealed in pt.: 1985, c.9, sch. 1; c.65, sch. 10; c.71, sch. 1.

55. Armed Forces Act 1981.

s. 1, order 85/196.

56. Transport Act 1981.

ss. 11, 13, 14, amended: 1985, c.9, sch. 2.

s. 19, see *Pender* v. *Keane,* 1984 S.C.C.R. 325; *R.* v. *Sandwell* [1985] R.T.R. 45, C.A.; *Luongo* v. *King* [1985] R.T.R. 186, D.C.; *Johnston* v. *Over* [1985] R.T.R. 240, D.C.; *North* v. *Tudhope,* 1985 S.C.C.R. 161; *R.* v. *Yates, The Times,* November 11, 1985, C.A.

s. 25, see *Cotter* v. *Kamil* [1984] R.T.R. 371, D.C.; *Howard* v. *Hallett* [1984] R.T.R. 353, D.C.; *Vaughan* v. *Dunn* [1984] R.T.R. 376, D.C.; *Hayward* v. *Eames* [1985] R.T.R. 12, D.C.; *Anderton* v. *Royle* [1985] R.T.R. 91, D.C.; *R.* v. *Skegness Magistrates' Court, ex p. Cardy; R.* v. *Manchester Crown Court, ex p. Williams* [1985] R.T.R. 49, D.C.; *Owen* v. *Chesters* [1985] R.T.R. 191, D.C.; *Snelson* v. *Thompson* [1985] R.T.R. 220, D.C.; *Hughes* v. *McConnell* [1985] R.T.R. 244, D.C.; *Chief Constable of Surrey* v. *Wickens* [1985] R.T.R. 277, D.C.; *Pine* v. *Collacott* [1985] R.T.R. 282, D.C.; *Stepniewski* v. *Comr. of Police of the Metropolis* [1985] R.T.R. 330, D.C.; *Woon* v. *Maskell* [1985] R.T.R. 289, D.C.

s. 30, see *Johnston* v. *Over* [1985] R.T.R. 240, D.C.

sch. 6, repealed in pt.: 1985, c.30, sch.

sch. 7, see *R.* v. *Sandwell* [1985] R.T.R. 45, C.A.; *Johnston* v. *Over* [1985] R.T.R. 240, D.C.

sch. 8, see *Tudhope* v. *Quinn,* 1984 S.C.C.R. 255; *Stewart* v. *Aitchison,* 1984 S.C.C.R. 357; *Cotter* v. *Kamil* [1984] R.T.R. 371, D.C.; *Howard* v. *Hallett* [1984] R.T.R. 353, D.C.; *Vaughan* v. *Dunn* [1984] R.T.R. 376, D.C.; *Reeves* v. *Enstone, The Times,* January 15, 1985, D.C.; *Walton* v. *Rimmer, The*

CAP.

1981—cont.

56. Transport Act 1981—*cont.*

Times, February 11, 1985, D.C.; *Hayward* v. *Eames* [1985] R.T.R. 12, D.C.; *Anderton* v. *Waring*, *The Times*, March 11, 1985, D.C.; *Annan* v. *Crawford*, 1984 S.C.C.R. 382; *Morgan* v. *Lee*, *The Times*, April 17, 1985, D.C.; *Anderton* v. *Royle* [1985] R.T.R. 91, D.C.; *R.* v. *Skegness Magistrates' Court, ex p. Cardy*; *R.* v. *Manchester Crown Court, ex p. Williams* [1985] R.T.R. 49, D.C.; *Owen* v. *Chesters* [1985] R.T.R. 191, D.C.; *Kelly* v. *MacKinnon*, [1985] S.C.C.R. 97; *McDerment* v. *O'Brien*, 1985 S.C.C.R. 50; *Snelson* v. *Thompson* [1985] R.T.R. 220, D.C.; *Hughes* v. *McConnell* [1985] R.T.R. 244, D.C.; *Chief Constable of Surrey* v. *Wickens* [1985] R.T.R. 277, D.C.; *Pine* v. *Collacott* [1985] R.T.R. 282, D.C.; *Tudhope* v. *Craig*, 1985 S.C.C.R. 214; *Allan* v. *Miller*, 1985 S.C.C.R. 227; *Reid* v. *Tudhope*, 1985 S.C.C.R. 268; *Green* v. *Lockhart*, 1985 S.C.C.R. 257; *Stepniewski* v. *Comr. of Police of the Metropolis* [1985] R.T.R. 330, D.C.; *Woon* v. *Maskell* [1985] R.T.R. 289, D.C.; *Gull* v. *Scarborough*, *The Times*, November 15, 1985, D.C.; *McCormick* v. *Hitchins*, *The Times*, December 10, 1985, D.C.

    sch. 9, see *McLellan* v. *Tudhope*, 1984 S.C.C.R. 397; *Johnstone* v. *Over* [1985] R.T.R. 240, D.C.

59. Matrimonial Homes (Family Protection) (Scotland) Act 1981.

s. 1, amended: 1985, c.73, s.13.

s. 4, see *Brown* v. *Brown*, Second Division, 1985 S.L.T. 376.

s. 4, amended: 1985, c.73, s.13.

s. 6, amended and repealed in pt.: *ibid.*

s. 7, see *Longmuir* v. *Longmuir*, 1985, S.L.T.(Sh.Ct.) 33.

s. 7, repealed in pt.: 1985, c.37, sch. 2.

s. 8, amended: 1985, c.73, s.13.

s. 10, repealed: 1985, c.66, sch. 8.

s. 13, see *McGowan* v. *McGowan* (O.H.), 1986 S.L.T. 312.

s. 13, amended: 1985, c.37, sch. 1.

s. 14, see *Brown* v. *Brown*, 1985 S.L.T. 376.

s. 18, see *McAlinden* v. *Bearsden and Milngavie District Council* (O.H.), September 6, 1985.

ss. 18, 22, amended: 1985, c.73, s.13.

60. Education Act 1981.

s. 1, see *R.* v. *Hampshire County Council*, *The Times*, December 5, 1985, Taylor J.

61. British Nationality Act 1981.

s. 41, regs. 85/1574.

sch. 3, amended: 1985, c.3, sch.

sch. 8, see *Gowa* v. *Att.-Gen.* [1985] 1 W.L.R. 1003, H.L.

62. Companies Act 1981.

repealed: 1985, c.9, sch. 1.

s. 38, substituted: regs. 84/2007.

CAP.

1981—cont.

62. Companies Act 1981—*cont.*

s. 41, regs. 84/2007.

s. 72, regs. 85/622.

ss. 74, 77, see *Lloyd (F.H.) Holdings, Re*, [1985] P.C.C. 268, Nourse J.

63. Betting and Gaming Duties Act 1981.

s. 6, order 85/515.

s. 21, amended: 1985, c.54, sch. 5.

s. 21A, amended: *ibid.*; repealed in pt.: *ibid.*, schs. 5, 27.

s. 22, amended: *ibid.*, sch. 5.

s. 23, amended: *ibid.*; repealed in pt.: 1985, schs. 5, 27.

ss. 24, 26, amended: *ibid.*, sch. 5.

s. 30, repealed: 1985, c.65, sch. 10; c.66, sch. 8 (S.).

ss. 33, 35, sch. 4, amended: 1985, c.54, sch. 5.

64. New Towns Act 1981.

ss. 1, 5, repealed in pt.: 1985, c.5, sch. 4.

s. 7, amended; 1985, c.51, sch. 8.

ss. 17, 35, amended: 1985, c.5, sch. 3.

s. 36, amended: *ibid.*, s.1, sch. 3; repealed in pt.: *ibid.*, s.1, sch. 4.

s. 37, amended: *ibid.*, s.1, sch. 3; repealed in pt.: *ibid.*, sch. 4.

s. 39, amended: *ibid.*, sch. 3.

s. 41, orders 85/321–323, 1951.

s. 44, amended: 1985, c.5, s.3; repealed in pt.: *ibid.*, s.3, sch. 4.

s. 45, amended: 1985, c.51, sch. 8.

s. 47, amended: 1985, c.5, s.3; 1985, c.71, sch. 2.

s. 48, repealed: 1985, c.5, sch. 4.

s. 50, amended: *ibid.*, sch. 3; c.71, sch. 2; repealed in pt.: *ibid.*, sch. 1.

s. 51A, added: 1985, c.5, s.4.

s. 54, regs. 85/274.

s. 54, repealed in pt.: 1985, c.5, s.5, sch. 4.

s. 56, amended: *ibid.*, sch. 2; repealed in pt.: *ibid.*, schs. 2, 4.

s. 57, amended: *ibid.*, s.3; 1985, c.71, sch. 2.

s. 58, amended: 1985, c.5, sch. 3; repealed in pt.: *ibid.*, sch. 4.

s. 58A, added: *ibid.*, s.6.

s. 60, amended: *ibid.*, s.7.

s. 61, repealed in pt.: *ibid.*, schs. 3, 4.

ss. 62A, 62B, added: *ibid.*, s.8.

s. 63, repealed in pt.: *ibid.*, sch. 4; repealed (S.): *ibid.*, sch. 3.

s. 64, amended: *ibid.*, repealed in pt.: *ibid.*, schs. 3, 4; repealed (S.): *ibid.*, sch. 3.

s. 66, repealed in pt.: *ibid.*, sch. 4; repealed (S.): *ibid.*, sch. 3.

s. 67, amended: *ibid.*, s.9.

s. 68, amended: 1985, c.9, sch. 2.

s. 74, amended: 1985, c.5, sch. 3.

s. 77, amended: *ibid.*, s.8, sch. 3; repealed in pt.: *ibid.*, schs. 3, 4.

s. 80, amended: 1985, c.5, sch. 3; repealed in pt.: *ibid.*, c.71, sch. 1.

s. 82, amended: 1985, c.5, sch. 3, repealed in pt.: *ibid.*, schs. 3, 4.

CAP.

1981—cont.

64. New Towns Act 1981—*cont.*
sch. 2, amended: *ibid.*, sch. 3; repealed in pt.: *ibid.*, schs. 3, 4.
sch. 4, amended and repealed in pt.: order 85/442.
sch. 9, amended: 1985, c.5, s.2.
sch. 10, orders 85/321–323, 1951.
sch. 10, amended: 1985, c.5, sch. 3; repealed in pt.: 1985, c.71, sch. 1.
schs. 11, 12, repealed in pt.: *ibid.*

65. Trustee Savings Banks Act 1981.
repealed: 1985, c.58, sch. 4.
sch. 5, orders 84/1971; 85/798, 1274, 1501, 1830.
sch. 6, repealed in pt.: 1985, c.65, sch. 10; c.71, sch. 1.

67. Acquisition of Land Act 1981.
s. 17, amended: 1985, c.51, sch. 14; order 85/1884; repealed in pt.: 1985, c.51, sch. 14.
sch. 4, repealed in pt.: 1985, c.12, sch. 2; c.71, sch. 1.

68. Broadcasting Act 1981.
ss. 2, 4, 53–56, see *R.* v. *Broadcasting Complaints Commission, ex p. Owen, The Times*, January 26, 1985, D.C.
s. 4, see *R.* v. *Independent Broadcasting Authority, ex p. Whitehouse, The Times*, April 4, 1985, C.A.
s. 12, amended: 1985, c.9, sch. 2.
s. 18, repealed in pt.: 1985, c.51, sch. 17.
s. 42, amended: 1985, c.9, sch. 2.
ss. 54, 55, see *R.* v. *Broadcasting Complaints Commission, ex p. Owen* [1985] 2 W.L.R. 1025, D.C.
s. 63, sch. 7, amended: 1985, c.9, sch. 2.

69. Wildlife and Countryside Act 1981.
s. 27, repealed in pt.: 1985, c.51, sch. 17.
s. 28, amended: 1985, c.31, s.2; repealed in pt.: *ibid.*; c.59, s.1.
s. 34, amended: 1985, c.51, sch. 3.
s. 36, repealed in pt.: *ibid.*, sch. 17.
s. 39, amended: *ibid.*, sch. 3; repealed in pt.: *ibid.*, sch. 17.
s. 42, amended: *ibid.*, sch. 3.
s. 43, amended: 1985, c.31, s.3; c.51, sch. 3.
ss. 44, 51, 52, 66, amended: *ibid.*
s. 70A, added: 1985, c.59, s.1.
s. 72, schs. 14, 15, amended: 1985, c.51, sch. 3.

1982

2. Social Security (Contributions) Act 1982.
sch. 1, repealed in pt.: 1985, c.53, sch. 6.

4. Stock Transfer Act 1982.
sch. 2, repealed in pt.: 1985, c.9, sch. 1.

7. New Towns Act 1982.
repealed: 1985, c.5, sch. 4.

9. Agricultural Training Board Act 1982.
s. 5, amended: 1985, c.36, s.1.
s. 7A, added: *ibid.*, s.2.
s. 8, amended: 1985, c.9, sch. 2; c.36, s.1.

10. Industrial Training Act 1982.
s. 3, order 85/1662.
s. 8, amended: 1985, c.9, sch. 2.

CAP.

1982—cont.

16. Civil Aviation Act 1982.
ss. 15, 23, amended: 1985, c.9, sch. 2.
s. 60, orders 84/1988; 85/458, 1643.
s. 61, orders 85/458, 1643.
ss. 73, 74, regs. 84/1916, 1920; 85/160, 349, 510, 1916, 1917.
ss. 77, 101, order 85/1643.
s. 102, orders 84/1988; 85/458, 1643.
s. 105, amended: 1985, c.9, sch. 2; repealed in pt.: 1985, c.15, sch. 17.
sch. 2, amended: 1985, c.71, sch. 2.

23. Oil and Gas (Enterprise) Act 1982.
ss. 1–7, repealed: 1985, c.62, sch. 4.
s. 10, amended: 1985, c.9, sch. 2.
s. 21, orders 84/1870, 1895–1901, 1911–1914, 1947, 1948, 1999–2001, 2011; 85/13, 22, 82–87, 106–109, 114–117, 141, 188, 189, 280, 346–348, 391–394, 469–473, 483, 484, 514, 516, 517, 523–527, 603–609, 628–632, 690–692, 763–773, 790, 791, 793–795, 869, 870, 894–903, 928, 929, 946–954, 968–971, 1017–1022, 1041–1043, 1060–1062, 1080, 1081, 1225–1229, 1331, 1332, 1334, 1335, 1379–1382, 1385–1389, 1431–1437, 1462–1464, 1495–1498, 1509–1512, 1522–1524, 1647–1649, 1692, 1693, 1720–1723, 1750–1752, 1767–1771, 1810, 1811, 1813, 1814, 1824, 1825, 1867–1869, 1894, 1895, 1984–1950, 1972–1974.
s. 32, repealed in pt.: 1985, c.62, sch. 4.
s. 33, amended: *ibid.*, s.7; repealed in pt.: *ibid.*, sch. 4.
s. 36, sch. 3, repealed in pt.: *ibid.*

24. Social Security and Housing Benefits Act 1982.
see *R.* v. *Secretary of State for Health and Social Security, ex p. Sheffield City Council, The Times*, August 2, 1985, Forbes J.
s. 1, see *Palfrey* v. *Greater London Council* [1985] I.C.R. 437, D.C.
s. 1, regs. 85/126.
s. 2, amended: 1985, c.53, s.18.
s. 3, amended: *ibid.*, s.18, sch. 4.
s. 5, amended: *ibid.*, s.18; repealed in pt.: *ibid.*, s.18, sch. 6.
s. 7, order 84/2037; amended: *ibid.*
s. 9, regs. 85/1411.
s. 9, amended: 1985, c.53, s.19.
s. 17, regs. 85/1604.
s. 17, amended: 1985, c.53, s.19.
s. 20, amended: *ibid.*, sch. 5.
s. 24, repealed: *ibid.*, schs. 4, 6.
s. 25, regs. 84/1965.
s. 26, amended: 1985, c.53, sch. 4.
s. 28, see *R.* v. *Secretary of State for Social Services, ex p. Association of Metropolitan Authorities* (1985) 17 H.L.R. 487, Webster J.
s. 28, regs. 85/368, 677, 1100, 1244, 1445.
s. 29, regs. 85/1244.
s. 32, order 85/440.
s. 32, amended: 1985, c.53, s.22; repealed in pt.: 1985, c.51, sch. 17.

CAP.
1982—cont.

24. Social Security and Housing Benefits Act 1982—*cont.*
s. 34, repealed in pt.: *ibid.*
s. 35, amended: 1985, c.71, sch. 2; repealed in pt.: 1985, c.51, sch. 17; c.71, sch. 2.
s. 36, see *R. v. Secretary of State for Social Services, ex p. Association of Metropolitan Authorities* (1985) 17 H.L.R. 487, Webster J.
s. 36, order 85/440.
s. 45, regs. 85/677.
sch. 1, repealed in pt.: 1985, c.53, sch. 6.
sch. 2, amended: *ibid.*, s.18; repealed in pt.: *ibid.*, schs. 4, 6; c.65, sch. 10.
sch. 4, repealed in pt.: 1985, c.71, sch. 1.

25. Iron and Steel Act 1982.
s. 19, order 85/1079; amended: *ibid.*
s. 24, amended: 1985, c.9, sch. 2.
s. 36, order 85/1079.
s. 37, sch. 4, amended: 1985, c.9, sch. 2.
sch. 6, repealed in pt.: 1985, c.12, sch. 2.

26. Food and Drugs (Amendment) Act 1982.
see *R. v. Uxbridge JJ., ex p. Gow, The Times,* October 17, 1985, D.C.

27. Civil Jurisdiction and Judgments Act 1982.
s. 18, amended: 1985, c.65, sch. 8; repealed in pt.: *ibid.*, sch. 10.
s. 28, amended (S.): 1985, c.73. sch. 2.
sch. 5, amended: 1985, c.9, sch. 2.
sch. 9, repealed in pt.: 1985, c.37, sch. 2.

28. Taking of Hostages Act 1982.
ss. 3, 5, order 85/751.
s. 5, order 85/1992.

29. Supply of Goods and Services Act 1982.
s. 12, order 85/1.

30. Local Government (Miscellaneous Provisions) Act 1982.
s. 1, amended: 1985, c.13, sch. 2.
s. 2, see *R. v. Birmingham City Council v. ex p. Quietlynn* (1985) 83 L.G.R. 471, Forbes J.; *Tunbridge Wells Borough Council v. Quietlynn; South Tyneside Borough Council v. Private Alternative Birth Control information and Education Centres; Watford Borough Council v. The Same* [1985] Crim.L.R. 594, D.C.
s. 19, see *Dodds v. Spear, The Times,* October 31, 1985, D.C.
s. 29, repealed in pt.: 1985, c.51, sch. 17.
s. 33, amended: *ibid.*; sch. 14; order 85/1884; repealed in pt.: 1985, c.51, sch. 17.
s. 40, see *Sykes v. Holmes, The Times,* July 16, 1985, D.C.
s. 41, amended: 1985, c.51, sch. 14; order 85/1884.
sch. 1, see *R. v. North Hertfordshire District Council, ex p. Cobbold* [1985] 3 All E.R. 486, Mann J.
sch. 1, amended: 1985, c.13, sch. 2.
sch. 3, see *Westminster City Council v. Croyalgrange* [1985] 1 All E.R. 740, D.C.; *R. v. Birmingham City Council, ex p. Quietlynn* (1985) 83 L.G.R. 461, Forbes J.; *Tunbridge Wells Borough*

CAP.
1982—cont.

30. Local Government (Miscellaneous Provisions) Act 1982—*cont.*
Council v. Quietlynn; South Tyneside Borough Council v. Private Alternative Birth Control Information and Education Centres; Watford Borough Council v. The Same [1985] Crim. L.R. 594, D.C.; *Lambeth London Borough Council v. Grewal, The Times,* November 26, 1985, C.A.
sch. 3, amended: 1985, c.13, sch. 2.

32. Local Government Finance Act 1982.
s. 5, repealed in pt.: 1985, c.51, sch. 17.
s. 8, see *R. v. Secretary of State for the Environment, ex p. Hammersmith and Fulham London Borough Council, The Times,* May 18, 1985, D.C.; *R. v. Secretary of State for the Environment, ex p. London Borough of Hackney, The Times,* May 11, 1985, C.A.
s. 12, amended: 1985, c.51, s.72.
s. 18, amended: 1985, c.43, sch. 2.
s. 31, amended: 1985, c.9, sch. 2; c.67, sch. 7.
s. 36, amended: *ibid.*

33. Cinematograph (Amendment) Act 1982.
repealed: 1985, c.13, sch. 3.
s. 2, sch. 1, see *British Amusement Catering Trade Association v. G.L.C.* (1985) 129 S.J. 400, Mervyn Davies J.
sch. 2, repealed in pt. (S.): 1985, c.73, sch. 2.

34. Forfeiture Act 1982.
ss. 2, 7, see *K. (decd.), Re* [1985] 3 W.L.R. 234, C.A.

36. Aviation Security Act 1982.
ss. 9, 39, order 85/1989, 1991.

37. Merchant Shipping (Liner Conferences) Act 1982.
Commencement order: 85/182.
ss. 2, 3, 13, regs. 85/405, 406.
s. 15, orders 85/182, 447, 448.

39. Finance Act 1982.
s. 29, regs. 85/1252.
s. 29, amended: 1985, c.71, sch. 2.
s. 58, repealed in pt.: 1985, c.54, sch. 27.
s. 72, amended: 1985, c.21, s.6; repealed in pt.: *ibid.*, s.6, sch. 2.
ss. 86–88, amended: 1985, c.54, sch. 18; repealed in pt.: *ibid.*, schs. 18, 27.
s. 89, repealed: *ibid.* schs. 18, 27.
s. 129, repealed in pt.: *ibid.*, sch. 27.
s. 134, see *R. v. Att.-Gen., ex p. I.C.I., The Financial Times,* January 29, 1985, Woolf J.
s. 146, repealed: 1985, c.62, sch. 4.
s. 153, repealed in pt.: 1985, c.71, sch. 1.
s. 155, sch. 6 (in pt.), repealed: 1985, c.54, sch. 27.
sch. 7, orders 84/1945; 85/1697.
sch. 7, amended: 1985, c.54, s.37; c.58, sch. 2.
sch. 9, amended: 1985, c.9, sch. 2.
sch. 12, amended: 1985, c.71, sch. 2; repealed in pt.: 1985, c.54, sch. 27.

CAP.

1982—cont.

39. Finance Act 1982—cont.
sch. 13, amended: *ibid.*, sch. 18; c.58, sch. 2; repealed in pt.: 1985, c.54, schs. 18. 27.
sch. 18, see *R.* v. *Att.-Gen., ex p. I.C.I., The Financial Times*, January 29, 1985, Woolf J.

41. Stock Transfer Act 1982.
Commencement order: 85/1137.
s. 1, regs. 85/1145.
s. 3, regs. 85/1144.
s. 6, order 85/1137.
sch. 1, amended: 1985, c.51, sch. 14; order 85/1884; repealed in pt.: 1985, c.51, sch. 17.

42. Derelict Land Act 1982.
s. 1, orders 85/1102–1104.
s. 1, repealed in pt.: 1985, c.51, sch. 17.

44. Legal Aid Act 1982.
s. 1, regs. 85/1880.
s. 7, regs. 85/1632.
s. 13, repealed in pt.: 1985, c.23, sch. 2.

45. Civic Government (Scotland) Act 1982.
s. 10, amended: 1985, c.67, sch. 7.
s. 18, amended: *ibid.*, schs. 2, 7.
ss. 20, 21, amended: *ibid.*, sch. 7.
s. 41, amended: 1985, c.13, sch. 2.
s. 46, see *White* v. *Allan*, 1985 S.C.C.R. 85.
s. 136, sch. 1, see *Seath* v. *City of Glasgow District Council*, 1985 S.L.T. 407.

46. Employment Act 1982.
s. 1, repealed: 1985, c.9, sch. 1.
s. 15, see *Express and Star* v. *National Graphical Association, Financial Times*, June 25, 1985, Skinner J.
sch. 3, repealed in pt.: 1985, c.65, sch. 10.

47. Duchy of Cornwall Management Act 1982.
s. 9, amended: 1985, c.9, sch. 2.

48. Criminal Justice Act 1982.
s. 7, see *R.* v. *Iqbal* (1985) 81 Cr.App.R. 145, C.A.
s. 9, see *Howley* v. *Oxford* [1985] Crim.L.R. 724, D.C.; *Chief Constable of the Surrey Constabulary* v. *Ridley and Steel* [1985] Crim.L.R. 725, D.C.
s. 12, see *R.* v. *Secretary of State for the Home Department, ex p. H, The Times*, August 21, 1985, D.C.
s. 22, see *R.* v. *F. (A Child), The Times*, March 20, 1985, C.A.; *R.* v. *F. (A Child), The Times*, April 20, 1985, C.A.
s. 46, repealed in pt.: 1985, c.9, sch. 1.
s. 72, see *R.* v. *Tonner; R.* v. *Evans (Ronald)* [1985] 1 W.L.R. 344, C.A.
sch. 3, repealed in pt.: 1985, c.71, sch. 1.

49. Transport Act 1982.
Pt. I (ss. 1–7), repealed: 1985, c.67, sch. 8.
ss. 7, 13, amended: 1985, c.9, sch. 2.
ss. 28, 35, amended: 1985, c.34, s.1.
ss. 42, 43, amended (S.): 1985, c.73, sch. 2.
s. 70, order 84/1996; amended: *ibid.*
s. 73, repealed in pt.: 1985, c.67, sch. 8.

50. Insurance Companies Act 1982.
amended: 1985, c.9, sch. 2.

CAP.

1982—cont.

50. Insurance Companies Act 1982—cont.
ss. 2, 5, 7, regs. 85/1419.
s. 7, amended: 1985, c.9, sch. 2.
s. 9, regs. 85/1419.
s. 10, amended: 1985, c.9, sch. 2.
s. 15, regs. 85/1419.
s. 21, amended: 1985, c.9, sch. 2.
ss. 32, 33, 35, regs. 85/1419.
ss. 47A, 47B, added: 1985, c. 9, s.25.
ss. 48–50, 53, 54, amended: *ibid.*
ss. 55, 56, amended: 1985, c. 65, sch. 8.
s. 57, amended: *ibid.*; repealed in pt.: *ibid.*, sch. 10.
s. 59, rules 85/95.
s. 59, amended: 1985, c.9, sch. 2; c.65, sch. 8.
ss. 60–62, regs. 85/1419.
s. 71, amended: 1985, c.9, sch. 2.
ss. 72, 74, 75, 78, regs. 85/1419.
ss. 87, 89, amended: 1985, c.9, sch. 2.
s. 90, regs. 85/1419.
s. 94A, added: 1985, c.46, s.1.
s. 96, amended: 1985, c.9, sch. 2.
s. 97, regs. 85/1419.
s. 100, amended: 1985, c.9, sch. 2.
sch. 4, repealed in pt.: *ibid.*, sch. 1.
sch. 5, repealed in pt.: 1985, c.71, sch. 1.

52. Industrial Development Act 1982.
s. 5, orders 84/1843, 1846.
s. 16, repealed in pt.: 1985, c.25, s.4, sch.

53. Administration of Justice Act 1982.
Commencement order: 85/858.
ss. 7–9, see *Denheen* v. *British Railways Board* (O.H.), June 26, 1984.
s. 21, see *Williams (decd.), Re* [1985] 1 All E.R. 964, Nicholls J.
s. 63, see *R.* v. *Elliott* [1985] Crim.L.R. 310; (1985) 81 Cr.App.R. 115, C.A.
s. 67, see *R.* v. *Horsham JJ., ex p. Richards, The Times*, May 25, 1985, D.C.
s. 71, repealed: 1985, c.61, s.64, sch. 8.
s. 76, order 82/858.

1983

2. Representation of the People Act 1983.
s. 1, see *Hipperson* v. *Newbury District Electoral Registration Officer* [1985] 3 W.L.R. 61, C.A.
s. 3, amended: 1985, c.50, sch. 4.
s. 5, see *Hipperson* v. *Newbury District Electoral Registration Officer* [1985] 3 W.L.R. 61, C.A.
ss. 9, 10, amended: 1985, c.50, s.4.
s. 11, amended: *ibid.*, sch. 4.
s. 12, amended: *ibid.*, s.4.
s. 15, amended: *ibid.*, sch. 4.
s. 18, amended: *ibid.*; repealed in pt.: *ibid.*, s.4, schs. 4, 5.
ss. 19, 20, repealed: 1985, c.50, sch. 5.
*s. 21, repealed: *ibid.*; repealed in pt.: 1985, c.54, sch. 27.
*s. 22, repealed: 1985, c.50, sch. 5; amended: 1985, c.51, sch. 16.
ss. 26, 28, amended: 1985, c.50, sch. 4.

1983—cont.

2. Representation of the People Act 1983— *cont.*

s. 31, amended: 1985, c.51, sch. 9; repealed in pt.: *ibid.*, sch. 17.

ss. 32–34, repealed: 1985, c.50, sch. 5.

s. 35, amended: 1985, c.51, schs. 9, 16; repealed in pt.: *ibid.*, sch. 17.

s. 36, rules 85/1848.

s. 36, amended: 1985, c.50, s.17; c.51, sch. 9; repealed in pt.: *ibid.*, sch. 17.

s. 37, amended: *ibid.* s.18.

s. 38, repealed: *ibid.*, schs. 4, 5.

s. 39, amended: *ibid.*, s.19; c.51, sch. 9; repealed in pt.: 1985, c.50, schs. 4, 5; c.51, sch. 17.

s. 40, amended: 1985, c.50, ss.16, 19; c.51, sch. 9; repealed in pt.: c.50, s.19, sch. 5.

s. 43, amended: *ibid.*, s.19, repealed in pt.: *ibid.*, sch. 5.

s. 44, repealed: *ibid.*, schs. 4, 5.

s. 47, amended: 1985, c.51, sch. 9.

s. 49, amended: 1985, c.50, s.4; repealed in pt.: *ibid.*, schs. 4, 5.

s. 51, repealed: *ibid.*, schs. 4, 5.

s. 52, amended: *ibid.*, sch. 4; repealed in pt.: *ibid.*, schs. 4, 5.

s. 53, amended: *ibid.*, sch. 4; repealed in pt.: *ibid.*, sch. 5.

s. 54, amended: *ibid.*, sch. 4.

s. 55, repealed: *ibid.*, schs. 4, 5.

s. 56, amended: *ibid.*, schs. 2, 4; repealed in pt.: *ibid.*, schs. 4, 5.

s. 58, amended: *ibid.*, sch. 4.

s. 61, amended: *ibid.*, sch. 2; repealed in pt.: *ibid.*, schs. 2, 5.

s. 62, amended: *ibid.*, schs. 3, 4.

s. 63, substituted: *ibid.*, sch. 4.

ss. 65, 66, amended: *ibid.*, sch. 3.

ss. 67, 70, amended: *ibid.*, sch. 4.

ss. 73, 74, amended: *ibid.*, s.14.

s. 75, amended: *ibid.*, s.14, sch. 4.

s. 76, amended: 1985, c.51, sch. 9; repealed in pt.: 1985, c.50, schs. 4, 5; c.51, sch. 17.

s. 76A, added: 1985, c.50, s.14.

ss. 78, 81, amended: *ibid.*, sch. 4.

s. 82, amended: *ibid.*; c.51, sch. 9; repealed in pt.: *ibid.*, sch. 17.

ss. 85–89, amended: 1985, c.50, sch. 4.

s. 90, amended: *ibid.*, s.14.

ss. 91, 93–95, amended: *ibid.*, sch. 4.

s. 96, substituted: *ibid.*

s. 97, amended: *ibid.*

ss. 99, 100, amended: *ibid.*, sch. 3.

s. 103, repealed in pt.: *ibid.*, schs. 4, 5.

s. 104, repealed in pt.: *ibid.*, sch. 5.

ss. 106, 108, repealed in pt.: *ibid.*, schs. 4, 5.

s. 110, amended: *ibid.*, sch. 3.

s. 118, amended: *ibid.*, sch. 4.

s. 119, amended: *ibid.* s.19.

s. 122, amended: *ibid.*, sch. 4.

ss. 124, 125, repealed in pt.: *ibid.*, schs. 4, 5.

s. 126, amended: *ibid.*, sch.4; repealed in pt.: *ibid.*, sch. 5.

1983—cont.

2. Representation of the People Act 1983— *cont.*

s. 127, see *Gilham* v. *Tall,* July 24, 1985, Mr. Bruce Loughland, Q.C., The Election Court.

s. 36, rules 85/1278.

ss. 136, 140, amended: 1985, c.50, sch. 4; repealed in pt.: *ibid.*, schs. 4, 5.

ss. 141 (in pt.), 142, repealed: *ibid.*

s. 148, repealed in pt.: *ibid.*, sch. 5.

s. 149, amended: *ibid.*, sch. 3.

s. 156, amended: *ibid.*, sch. 4, repealed in pt.: *ibid.*, schs. 4, 5.

s. 160, amended: *ibid.*, sch. 4; repealed in pt.: *ibid.*, schs. 4, 5.

ss. 161–163, amended: *ibid.*, sch. 4; repealed in pt.: *ibid.*, sch. 5.

s. 167, amended: *ibid.*, sch. 4.

s. 168, amended: *ibid.*, sch. 3; repealed in pt.: *ibid.*, schs. 4, 5.

s. 169, amended: *ibid.*, sch. 3; repealed in pt.: *ibid.*, sch. 5.

ss. 171, 172, 173 (in pt.), repealed: *ibid.*, schs. 4, 5.

s. 176, amended: *ibid.*, sch. 4; repealed in pt.: *ibid.*, schs. 4, 5.

s. 178, substituted: *ibid.*, sch. 4.

s. 181, amended: *ibid.*; sch. 4; repealed in pt.: 1985, c.23, sch. 2; c.50, schs. 4, 5.

s. 182, rules 85/1278; Acts of Sederunt 85/1426, 1427.

s. 187, amended: 1985, c.50, sch. 4; repealed in pt.: *ibid.*, schs. 4, 5.

s. 190, repealed: *ibid.*, schs. 4, 5.

s. 191, amended: *ibid.*, sch. 4; repealed in pt.: *ibid.*, sch. 5.

ss. 192, 196 (in pt.), repealed: *ibid.*

s. 197, amended: *ibid.*, sch. 4.

s. 199, repealed: *ibid.*, s.22, sch. 5.

ss. 200, 201, amended: *ibid.*, sch. 4.

s. 202, amended: *ibid.*, s.4, sch. 2; repealed in pt.: *ibid.*, schs. 4, 5.

s. 203, amended: *ibid.*, sch. 4; c.51, sch. 9; repealed in pt.: 1985, c.50, schs. 4, 5; c.51, sch. 17.

s. 205, amended: 1985, c.50, sch. 4.

sch. 1, amended: 1985, c.2, ss.1, 2 (N.I.); c.50, ss.4, 13, 19, schs. 2, 4; repealed in pt.: *ibid.*, s.19, schs. 2, 4, 5; c.51, sch. 17.

sch. 2, amended: 1985, c.50, s.4, schs. 2–4; repealed in pt.: *ibid.*, schs. 2, 4, 5.

sch. 3, amended: *ibid.*, sch. 4.

sch. 4, amended: *ibid.*, s,14, sch. 4.

sch. 7, amended: *ibid.*, sch. 4; repealed in pt.: *ibid.*, schs. 4, 5.

sch. 8, repealed in pt.: *ibid.*, sch. 5.

5. Consolidated Fund (No. 2) Act 1983.
repealed: 1985, c.55, sch. (C).

8. British Fishing Boats Act 1983.
s. 10, order 85/1203.

10. Transport Act 1983.
s. 1, amended: 1985, c.51, sch. 12; c.67, sch. 3.

1983—*cont.*

10. Transport Act 1983—*cont.*
s. 3, amended: 1985, c.67, s.102, sch. 3; repealed in pt.: 1985, c.51, schs. 12, 17; c.67, s.102, sch. 8.
s. 4, amended: *ibid.*, s.102; repealed in pt.: 1985, c.51, schs. 12, 17.
s. 5, repealed in pt.: *ibid.*
s. 6, amended: *ibid.*, sch. 12; repealed in pt.: *ibid.*, schs. 12, 17.
s. 9, repealed in pt.: 1985, c.67, schs. 3, 8.

11. Civil Aviation (Eurocontrol) Act 1983.
Commencement order: 85/1915.
s. 4, order 85/1915.

12. Divorce Jurisdiction, Court Fees and Legal Aid (Scotland) Act 1983.
sch. 1, repealed in pt.: 1985, c.37, sch. 2.

13. Merchant Shipping Act 1983.
s. 5, sch., regs. 85/1727.
s. 8, order 84/1985.

14. International Transport Conventions Act 1983.
s. 11, order 85/612.

16. Level Crossings Act 1983.
s. 1, repealed in pt.: 1985, c.51, sch. 17.

19. Matrimonial Homes Act 1983.
s. 1, see *Summers* v. *Summers, The Times*, July 31, 1985, C.A.
s. 1, amended: 1985, c.71, sch. 2.
s. 2, repealed in pt.: 1985, c.65, sch. 10.
sch. 1, amended: 1985, c.71, sch. 2.

20. Mental Health Act 1983.
see *Crompton* v. *General Medical Council (No. 2)* (1985) 82 L.S.Gaz. 1864, P.C.
s. 37, see *R.* v. *Ramsgate JJ, ex p. Kazmarek* (1985) 80 Cr.App.R. 366, D.C.
ss. 37, 47, 49, 50, see *R.* v. *Castro, The Times*, March 19, 1985, C.A.
ss. 72, 73, 78, see *Bone* v. *Mental Health Review Tribunal* [1985] 3 All E.R. 330, Nolan J.
s. 95, see *E. (Mental Health Patient), Re* [1985] 1 W.L.R. 245, C.A.
ss. 106–108, rules 84/2035.
s. 139, see *Waldron, Re, The Times*, October 8, 1985, C.A.; *Winch* v. *Jones* [1985] 3 W.L.R. 729, C.A.

21. Pilotage Act 1983.
s. 3, order 85/251.
s. 4, amended: 1985, c.9, sch. 2.
s. 9, order 85/831.

25. Energy Act 1983.
s. 26, repealed in pt.: 1985, c.51, sch. 17.
s. 33, order 85/752.

27. Appropriation Act 1983.
repealed: 1985, c.55, sch. (C).

28. Finance Act 1983.
ss. 29, 34 (in pt.), 46 (in pt.), repealed: 1985, c.54, sch. 27.
sch. 3, repealed in pt.: *ibid.*, sch. 25.
sch. 5, amended: 1985, c.9, sch. 2; c.54, s.44.
sch. 6, amended: *ibid.*, sch. 19.

29. Miscellaneous Financial Provisions Act 1983.
sch. 2, repealed in pt.: 1985, c.62, sch. 4; c.71, sch. 1.

1983—*cont.*

30. Diseases of Fish Act 1983.
s. 7, order 85/1391.

34. Mobile Homes Act 1983.
ss. 1, 2, 5, see *Balthazar* v. *Mullane, The Times*, July 25, 1985, C.A.

35. Litter Act 1983.
s. 1, repealed in pt.: 1985, c.51, sch. 17.
ss. 4, 6, amended: *ibid.*, sch. 6.

37. Importation of Milk Act 1983.
s. 1, regs. 85/1089, 1167(S.), 1324(S.).

40. Education (Fees and Awards) Act 1983.
ss. 1, 2, regs. 85/219, 1223(S.).

41. Health and Social Services and Social Security Adjudications Act 1983.
Commencement order: 85/704.
s. 32, order 85/704.
sch. 1, see *Southwark London Borough Council* v. *H., The Times*, April 6, 1985, D.C.

44. National Audit Act 1983.
sch. 4, amended: 1985, c.62, s.7; repealed in pt.: *ibid.*, sch. 4.

45. County Courts (Penalties for Contempt) Act 1983.
s. 1, see *Lee* v. *Walker, The Times*, December 14, 1984, C.A.

47. National Heritage Act 1983.
s. 30, order 85/1818.
ss. 30, 31, order 84/1850.
sch. 3, amended: 1985, c.9, sch. 2.

48. Appropriation (No. 2) Act 1983.
repealed: 1985, c.55, sch.(C.).

49. Finance (No. 2) Act 1985.
s. 7, repealed in pt.: 1985, 54, sch. 27.
s. 14, repealed: *ibid.*
s. 15, amended: *ibid.*, s.82; repealed in pt.: *ibid.*, sch. 27.

50. Companies (Beneficial Interests) Act 1983.
repealed: 1985, c.9, sch. 1.

52. Local Authorities (Expenditure Powers) Act 1983.
s. 1, order 85/547.

53. Car Tax Act 1983.
ss. 3, 5, 7, 8, sch. 1, regs. 85/1737.
sch. 1, amended: 1985, c.9, sch. 2; repealed in pt.: *ibid.*, sch. 1; c.65, sch. 10; c.66, sch. 8(S.).

54. Medical Act 1983.
s. 17, amended: order 85/1774.
s. 37, see *Crompton* v. *General Medical Council (No. 2)* [1985] 1 W.L.R. 885, P.C.
sch. 1, amended: 1985, c.9, sch. 2.
sch. 2, amended: order 85/1774.

55. Value Added Tax Act 1983.
s. 3, order 85/1646.
s. 5, regs. 85/866.
s. 7, regs. 85/866; order 85/799.
s. 14, regs. 85/886; order 85/919.
s. 15, regs. 85/105.
s. 16, regs. 85/105, 866, 1650; orders 85/18, 431, 799, 919.
s. 17, orders 85/432, 1900.
s. 19, regs. 85/693, 886, 1384, 1646.
s. 20, order 85/1101.
s. 20, repealed in pt.: 1985, c.51, sch. 17.

CAP.

1983—cont.

55. Value Added Tax Act 1983—*cont.*
s. 22, substituted: 1985, c.54, s.32; amended (S.): 1985, c.66, sch. 7.
s. 24, regs. 85/886.
s. 25, regs. 85/105, 886.
s. 29, amended: 1985, c.9, sch. 2.
s. 31, regs. 85/886, 1650.
s. 31, amended: 1985, c.54, s.31.
s. 33, regs. 85/886.
s. 34, order 85/1046.
s. 35, regs. 85/886.
s. 39, see *Aikman* v. *White*, 1985 S.L.T. 535.
s. 39, amended: 1985, c.54, sch. 6; repealed in pt.: *ibid.*, s.12, schs. 6, 27.
s. 40, amended: *ibid.*, s.24.
s. 41, regs. 85/886.
s. 45, order 85/1646.
s. 45, amended: 1985, c.54, s.27.
s. 48, regs. 85/886; orders 85/18, 431, 432, 799, 919, 1900.
sch. 1, regs. 85/886, 1650; order 85/433; amended: order 85/433.
sch. 3, amended: order 85/799.
sch. 5, amended: orders 85/18, 431, 799, 919; repealed in pt.: 1985, c.54, s.11, sch. 27; order 85/799.
sch. 6, amended: 1985, c.54, sch. 26; order 85/432.
sch. 7, see *Aikman* v. *White*, 1985 S.L.T. 535.
sch. 7, regs. 85/105, 886; 1650.
sch. 7, amended: 1985, c.9, sch. 2; c.54, s.23, sch. 7; repealed in pt.: 1985, c.9, sch. 1; c.54, s.23, schs. 7, 27; c.65, sch. 10; c.66, sch. 8(S.).
sch. 8, amended: 1985, c.54, ss.27, 28, sch. 8; repealed in pt.: *ibid.*, s.27, schs. 8, 27.

56. Oil Taxation Act 1983.
ss. 8, 15, sch. 2, amended: 1985, c.54, s.92.

57. Consolidated Fund (No. 3) Act 1983.
repealed: 1985, c.55, sch.(C.).

1984

5. Merchant Shipping Act 1984.
s. 13, order 84/1985.

8. Prevention of Terrorism (Temporary Provisions) Act 1984.
continued in force: order 85/378.
s. 17, order 85/378.

11. Education (Grants and Awards) Act 1984.
s. 1, regs. 85/2028.
ss. 1, 3, regs. 85/1070.

12. Telecommunications Act 1984.
ss. 7, 8, orders 85/694, 882.
s. 9, orders 85/788, 822, 998, 999, 1594–1597.
s. 28, orders 85/717, 718, 1031.
s. 29, orders 85/719, 1030.
s. 45, substituted: 1985, c.56, s.11, sch. 2.
s. 60, order 85/496.
ss. 60, 61, amended: 1985, c.9, sch. 2.
s. 65, order 85/496.

CAP.

1984—cont.

12. Telecommunications Act 1984—*cont.*
ss. 66, 68, 70, 73, amended: 1985, c.9, sch. 2.
s. 97, repealed in pt.: 1985, c.51, sch. 17.
s. 98, order 85/61.
s. 104, orders 85/61, 496, 788, 822, 998, 999, 1594–1597.
sch. 4, orders 85/1011, 1014(S.).
sch. 4, repealed in pt.: 1985, c.13, sch. 3; c.71, sch. 1.
sch. 5, amended: 1985, c.9, sch. 2.

13. Road Traffic (Driving Instruction) Act 1984.
Commencement order: 85/578.
s. 5, order 85/578.

15. Law Reform (Husband and Wife) (Scotland) Act 1984.
sch. 1, repealed in pt.: 1985, c.37, sch. 2.

16. Foreign Limitation Periods Act 1984.
Commencement order: 85/1276.
s. 7, order 85/1276.

22. Public Health (Control of Disease) Act 1984.
ss. 2–4, order 85/707.
s. 8, repealed in pt.: 1985, c.51, sch. 17.
s. 13, regs. 85/434.
sch. 2, repealed in pt.: 1985, c.71, sch. 2.

24. Dentists Act 1984.
s. 29, order 85/172.
s. 45, regs. 85/1850.
sch. 2, repealed: order 85/1774.
sch. 3, order 84/2010.

26. Inshore Fishing (Scotland) Act 1984.
Commencement order: 85/961.
s. 1, order 85/1569.
s. 11, order 85/961.

27. Road Traffic Regulation Act 1984.
s. 1, amended: 1985, c.51, sch. 5.
s. 3, repealed in pt.: 1985, c.67, sch. 8.
s. 6, amended: 1985, c.51, sch. 5.
s. 7, amended: 1985, c.67, sch. 1.
s. 9, amended: 1985, c.51, sch. 5.
s. 10, amended: *ibid.*, c.67, sch. 1.
ss. 12, 15, 19, amended: 1985, c.51, sch. 5.
s. 23, amended: *ibid.*; repealed in pt.: *ibid.*, sch. 17.
s. 26, amended: *ibid.*, sch. 5.
s. 28, regs. 85/713.
s. 29, amended: 1985, c.51, sch. 5.
s. 30, amended: *ibid.*; repealed in pt.: *ibid.*, sch. 17.
s. 31, amended: *ibid.*, sch. 5.
s. 32, repealed in pt.: *ibid.*, sch. 17.
ss. 36, 37, amended: *ibid.*, sch. 5.
s. 38, amended: 1985, c.67, sch. 2.
ss. 39, 43, amended: 1985, c.51, sch. 5; repealed in pt.: *ibid.*, sch. 17.
s. 44, amended: *ibid.*, sch. 5.
s. 45, amended: *ibid.*; repealed in pt.: *ibid.*, sch. 17.
s. 47, repealed in pt.: *ibid.*
s. 50, repealed: *ibid.*
s. 51, amended: *ibid.*, sch. 5; repealed in pt.: *ibid.*, sch. 17.
s. 53, amended: *ibid.*, sch. 5.

CAP.

1984—cont.

27. Road Traffic Regulation Act 1984—*cont.*
s. 55, amended: *ibid.*; repealed in pt.: sch. 17.
ss. 58, 59, 61, amended: *ibid.*, sch. 5.
s. 64, regs. 85/463, 713.
s. 65, regs. 85/713.
s. 67, regs. 85/463.
ss. 73, 74, 78, amended: 1985, c.51, sch. 5.
s. 79, repealed in pt.: *ibid.*, sch. 17.
s. 91, amended: *ibid.*, sch. 5.
s. 94, substituted: *ibid.*
s. 100, amended: *ibid.*; repealed in pt.: *ibid.*, sch. 17.
ss. 101, 102, regs. 85/1661.
s. 102, amended: 1985, c.51, sch. 5.
s. 104, regs. 85/1660.
s. 106, amended: 1985, c.51, sch. 5.
s. 112, repealed in pt.: *ibid.*, sch. 17.
s. 120, amended (S.): 1985, c.73, 38.
s. 122, see *R.* v. *Secretary of State for Transport ex p. G.L.C., The Times,* October 31, 1985, C.A.
s. 122, amended: 1985, c.51, sch. 5; repealed in pt.: *ibid.*, sch. 17.
s. 123, repealed: *ibid.*
s. 125, amended: *ibid.*, sch. 5.
s. 129, amended: *ibid.*: repealed in pt.: *ibid.*, sch. 17.
s. 134, regs. 85/463, 713.
s. 142, amended: 1985, c.51, sch. 5; c.67, sch. 1; repealed in pt.: 1985, c.51, sch. 17.
sch. 4, amended: 1985, c.51, sch. 5; repealed in pt.: *ibid.*, sch. 17.
sch. 9, see *R.* v. *Secretary of State for Transport, ex p. G.L.C., The Times,* October 31, 1985, C.A.
sch. 9, amended: 1985, c.51, sch. 5; c.67, schs. 1, 2, 3.
sch. 10, orders 84/1936(S.); 85/464.
sch. 13, repealed in pt.: 1985, c.67, sch. 8.

28. County Courts Act 1984.
s. 32, substituted: 1985, c.61, s.51.
s. 33, amended: *ibid.*, sch. 7; repealed in pt.: *ibid.*, schs. 7, 8.
s. 38, see *Lee* v. *Walker* [1985] 1 All E.R. 781, C.A.
ss. 38, 39, see *Bush* v. *Green* [1985] 1 W.L.R. 1143, C.A.
s. 58, amended: 1985, c.61, sch. 7; repealed in pt.: *ibid.*, schs. 7, 8.
s. 60, amended: 1985, c.51, sch. 14; order 85/1884; repealed in pt.: 1985, c.51, sch. 17.
s. 66, amended: 1985, c.71, sch. 2.
s. 69, see *Ward* v. *Chief Constable of Avon and Somerset, The Times,* July 17, 1985, C.A.
s. 73, regs. 85/1807.
s. 73, amended: 1985, c.61, sch. 54.
s. 73A, added: *ibid.*
s. 75, rules 85/1269.
s. 77, amended: 1985, c.71, sch. 2.
s. 98, amended: 1985, c.9, sch. 2; c.65, sch. 8.

CAP.

1984—cont.

28. County Courts Act 1984—*cont.*
s. 102, amended: *ibid.*
s. 109, see *Webb (Gerry) Transport* v. *Brenner (T/A Russell Brenner Metals and Midland Bank),* April 16, 1985, H.H. Judge Barr, Brentford County Court.
s. 109, amended: 1985, c.61, s.52; c.65, sch. 8; repealed in pt.: 1985, c.61, s.52, sch. 8.
s. 112, amended: 1985, c.65, s.220.
s. 113, repealed in pt.: 1985, c.61, sch. 8.
s. 115, amended: 1985, c.65, s.220.
s. 128, orders 85/574, 1834.
s. 138, see *Gadsby and Mitchell* v. *Price and Harrison,* April 19, 1985, H.H. Judge Taylor, Harlow County Court; *Di Palma* v. *Victoria Square Property Co., The Times,* May 7, 1985, C.A.
s. 138, amended: 1985, c.61, s.55; repealed in pt.: *ibid.*, s.55, sch. 8.
s. 139, amended: *ibid.*, s.55.
sch. 2, repealed in pt.: 1985, c.65, sch. 10; c.71, sch. 1.

29. Housing and Building Control Act 1984.
ss. 1–38, repealed: 1985, c.71, sch. 1.
s. 16, regs. 85/758
s. 18, amended: 1985, c.51, sch. 14.
s. 20, order 85/1978.
s. 20, amended: 1985, c.51, sch. 14; repealed in pt.: *ibid.*, sch. 17.
schs. 1–7, 11 (in pt.), repealed: 1985, c.71, sch. 1.
sch. 4, amended: 1985, c.9, sch. 2, c.51, sch. 14.

30. Food Act 1984.
see *R.* v. *Uxbridge JJ., ex p, Gow, The Times,* October 17, 1985, D.C.
s. 2, see *R.* v. *Uxbridge JJ., ex p. Co-operative Retail Services, The Times,* October 23, 1985, D.C.
s. 4, regs. 85/912.
s. 13, regs. 84/1917, 1918: 85/216.
ss. 33, 34, regs. 85/68.
ss. 38, 45, regs. 85/530.
s. 51, amended: 1985, c.9, sch. 2.
s. 68, order 85/308.
s. 71, amended: 1985, c.51, sch. 8.
s. 74, regs. 85/530.
s. 100, see *R.* v. *Uxbridge JJ., ex p. Co-operative Retail Services, The Times,* October 23, 1985, D.C.
s. 118, regs. 84/1917, 1918; 85/68, 216, 530, 912.
s. 135, regs. 84/1917.
sch. 10, repealed in pt.: 1985, c.72, sch. 13.

32. London Regional Transport Act 1984.
ss. 7, 10, repealed in pt.: 1985, c.51, sch. 17.
s. 13, order 85/165.
s. 28, repealed in pt.: 1985, c.67, sch. 8.
s. 30, repealed in pt.: 1985, c.51, sch. 17.
s. 35, amended: 1985, c.67, sch. 7.
ss. 43–45, repealed: *ibid.*, sch. 8.

CAP.

1984—cont.

32. London Regional Transport Act 1984—cont.
s. 49, see *R.* v. *Secretary of State for Transport, ex p. G.L.C.* [1985] 3 W.L.R. 574, McNeill J.
s. 49, amended: 1985, c.10, s.1.
s. 50, repealed in pt.: 1985, c.51, sch. 17; c.67, sch. 8.
s. 55, amended: *ibid.*, sch. 7.
s. 68, repealed in pt.: *ibid.*, schs. 7. 8.
sch. 5, amended: *ibid.*, schs. 2, 7; repealed in pt.: *ibid.*, schs. 7, 8.
sch. 6, repealed in pt.: *ibid.*, s.114, sch. 8.

33. Rates Act 1984.
s. 1, orders 85/147, 256.
s. 1, amended: 1985, c.51, s.68; repealed in pt. *ibid.*: sch. 17.
s. 2, orders 85/823, 863.
s. 2, amended: orders 895/823, 863; 1985, c.51, s.68; repealed in pt.: *ibid.*, s.68, sch. 17.
s. 4, see *R.* v. *Secretary of State for the Environment, ex p. Leicester City Council* (1985) 25 R.V.R. 31, Woolf J.
s. 4, order 85/147, 256.
s. 5, repealed in pt.: 1985, c.51, sch. 17.
s. 6, order 85/32.
ss. 6, 7, repealed in pt.: 1985, c.51, sch. 17.
s. 14, rules 85/1486.
s. 15, rules 85/6, 1486.

35. Data Protection Act 1984.
Commencement order: 85/1055.
ss. 6, 8, 40, regs. 85/1465.
s. 42, order 85/1055.
sch. 3, rules 85/1568.

36. Mental Health (Scotland) Act 1984.
ss. 21, 40, amended: 1985, c.73, s.15; repealed in pt.: *ibid.*

39. Video Recordings Act 1984.
Commencement orders: 85/883, 904(S.), 1264.
s. 3, amended: 1984, c.13, sch. 2.
s. 8, regs. 85/911.
s. 23, orders 85/883, 904(S.), 1264, 1265(S.).

40. Animal Health and Welfare Act 1984.
Commencement order: 85/1267.
s. 10, regs. 85/1861, 1862.
s. 17, order 85/1267.

41. Agricultural Holdings Act 1984.
Commencement order 85/1644.
s. 8, regs. 85/1967.
s. 11, orders 85/1644, 1829.
sch. 5, order 85/1829.

42. Matrimonial and Family Proceedings Act 1984.
Commencement order: 85/1316.
s. 6, see *Morris* v. *Morris, The Times*, June 17, 1985, C.A.
s. 29A, added: 1985, c.37, sch. 1.
s. 30, amended: *ibid.*
s. 47, order 85/1316.

43. Finance Act 1984.
ss. 4, 29, 34, repealed: 1985, c.54, sch. 27.
s. 26, order 85/1836.

CAP.

1984—cont.

43. Finance Act 1984—cont.
s. 62, repealed in pt.: 1985, c.21, sch. 2.
ss. 73 (in pt.), 99 (in pt.), repealed: 1985, c.54, sch. 27.
s. 111, see *Ingram* v. *I.R.C., The Times*, November 18, 1985, Vinelott J.
ss. 118–123, repealed: 1985, c.54, sch. 27.
s. 126, order 85/1172.
s. 126, amended and repealed in pt.: 1985, c.54, s.96.
schs. 2, 7, repealed in pt.: *ibid.*, sch. 27.
sch. 8, regs. 85/1696, 1702.
sch. 8, amended: 1985, c.54, s.38.
sch. 9, amended: *ibid.*, sch. 11; repealed in pt.: *ibid.*, sch. 27.
sch. 11, amended: *ibid.*, s.70.
sch. 13, amended; *ibid.*, s.67; repealed in pt.: *ibid.*, sch. 27.
sch. 15, amended: *ibid.*, s.51.
sch. 16, amended: *ibid.*, sch. 14.
sch. 21, repealed in pt.: *ibid.*, sch. 27.

46. Cable and Broadcasting Act 1984.
s. 2, order 84/1994.
s. 13, order 84/1993.
s. 36, repealed in pt.: 1985, c.51, sch. 17.
sch. 5, repealed in pt.: 1985, c.13, sch. 3.

47. Repatriation of Prisoners Act 1984.
Commencement order: 85/550.
s. 9, order 85/550.

48. Health and Social Security Act 1984.
s. 5, orders 85/39, 302, 497.
s. 7, see *R.* v. *Secretary of State for Social Services, ex p. Westhead, The Times*, October 17, 1985, D.C.
s. 22, regs. 85/126.
s. 26, amended: 1985, c.53, sch. 5.
s. 28, regs. 85/298, 355(S.).
sch. 7, regs. 85/126.
sch. 7, repealed in pt.: 1985, c.53, sch. 6.

49. Trade Union Act 1984.
s. 10, see *Shipping Co. Uniform Inc.* v. *International Transport Workers Federation, Allen, Ross and Davies* [1985] 1 Lloyd's Rep. 173; [1985] I.C.R. 245, Staughton J.
s. 11, see *Austin Rover Group* v. *Amalgamated Union of Engineering Workers (TASS)* [1985] I.R.L.R. 162, Hodgson J.

50. Housing Defects Act 1984.
repealed: 1985, c.71, sch. 1.
sch. 4, amended: 1985, c.51, sch. 14.

51. Capital Transfer Tax Act 1984.
s. 2, repealed: 1985, c.54, sch. 27.
s. 8, order 85/429.
ss. 13, amended: 1985, c.9, sch. 2.
ss. 18–29, amended: 1985, c.54, s.95.
ss. 30, 31, amended: *ibid.*, s.95, sch. 26.
s. 32, amended; *ibid.*; repealed in pt.: *ibid.*, schs. 26, 27.
s. 32A, added: *ibid.*, sch. 26.
ss. 33–35, amended: *ibid.*, s.95, sch. 26.
ss. 36–42, 76, amended: *ibid.*, s.95.
ss. 78, 79, amended: *ibid.*, sch. 26.
s. 103, amended: 1985, c.9, sch. 2.
ss. 207, 216, 226, amended: 1985, c.54, sch. 26.

CAP.
1984—cont.

51. Capital Transfer Tax Act 1984—*cont.*
s. 233, order 85/560.
s. 233, amended; 1985, c.54, sch. 26.
s. 234, amended: 1985, c.9, sch. 2.
sch. 1, substituted: order 85/429.
sch. 3, amended: 1985, c.16, sch. 2(S.); c.54, s.95.
sch. 4, amended: *ibid.*, s.95, sch. 26.
sch. 5, amended: *ibid.*, s.95.
sch. 6, amended: *ibid.*, sch. 26.
sch. 8, repealed in pt.: *ibid.*, sch. 27.

52. Parliamentary Pensions etc. Act 1984.
ss. 1, 2, 4, order 84/1909.
s. 5, order 84/1908.

53. Local Government (Interim Provisions) Act 1984.
Commencement order: 85/2.
repealed (except ss.4, 6 (in pt.), 10, 11, 13): 1985, c.51, sch. 17.
s. 1, order 85/2.
s. 6, see *R.* v. *Secretary of State for the Environment, ex p. Greater London Council* [1985] J.P.L. 543, Taylor J.
s. 6, order 85/176.
s. 7, see *R.* v. *District Auditor, ex p. West Yorkshire Metropolitan County Council, The Times,* July 25, 1985, D.C.

54. Roads (Scotland) Act 1984.
s. 143, regs. 85/1165; order 85/1471.
s. 144, regs. 85/1165.
s. 154, order 85/1471.

55. Building Act 1984.
Commencement orders: 85/1602, 1603.
s. 1, regs. 85/488, 1065, 1066, 1576.
s. 3, regs. 85/1065, 1576.
s. 8, regs. 85/1065.
ss. 11, 12, repealed in pt.: 1985, c.51, sch. 17.
s. 14, regs. 85/1936.
s. 16, regs. 85/1066, 1576; order 85/1603.
s. 17, regs. 85/1066.
s. 18, repealed in pt.: 1985, c.51, sch. 17.
s. 30, order 85/1603.
s. 34, regs. 85/1576.
s. 35, regs. 85/1066, 1576.
ss. 47, 49–54, 56, regs. 85/1066.
s. 68, repealed in pt.: 1985, c.51, sch. 17.
ss. 76, 80, 81, amended: 1985, c.71, sch. 2.
s. 88, repealed in pt.: 1985, c.51, sch. 17.
s. 89, repealed in pt.: 1985, c.71, sch. 1.
s. 91, repealed in pt.: 1985, c.51, sch. 17.
s. 120, orders 85/1602, 1603.
s. 126, amended: 1985, c.51, sch. 8; repealed in pt.: *ibid.*, sch. 17.
sch. 1, regs. 85/488, 1065, 1066, 1576.
sch. 3, amended: 1985, c.51, sch. 8; repealed in pt.: *ibid.*, sch. 17.
sch. 4, regs. 85/1066.
schs. 5, 6, repealed in pt.: 1985, c.71, sch. 1.

57. Co-operative Development Agency and Industrial Development Act 1984.
Commencement order: 84/1845.
s. 7, order 84/1845.

CAP.
1984—cont.

58. Rent (Scotland) Act 1984.
s. 1, order 85/314.
s. 5, amended: 1985, c.71, sch. 2.
s. 56, amended: 1985, c.73, sch. 2.
ss. 61, 63, amended: 1985, c.71, sch. 2.
s. 64, order 85/314.
s. 106, amended: 1985, c.73, sch. 2.
sch. 2, amended: 1985, c.24, s.1.
sch. 9, amended: 1985, c.72, sch. 2.

59. Ordnance Factories and Military Services Act 1984.
s. 10, order 84/2022.
s. 15, order 85/927.

60. Police and Criminal Evidence Act 1984.
Commencement orders: 84/2002; 85/623, 1934.
s. 24, repealed in pt: 1985, c.44, sch. 5.
s. 26, amended: 1985, c.50, s.25.
s. 27, regs. 85/1941.
s. 67, order 85/1937.
s. 77, amended: order 85/1800.
s. 87, regs. 85/673.
s. 89, regs. 85/520, 673.
s. 94, regs. 85/518, 519.
s. 99, regs. 85/520, 671, 672.
s. 100, regs. 85/520, 671–673.
s. 101, regs. 85/518, 519.
s. 102, regs. 85/518.
s. 113, orders 85/1881, 1882.
s. 114, order 85/1800.
s. 121, orders 84/2002; 85/623, 1934.
sch. 7, repealed in pt.: 1985, c.50, sch. 5.

1985

1. Consolidated Fund Act 1985.
Royal Assent, January 24, 1985.

2. Elections (Northern Ireland) Act 1985.
Royal Assent, January 24, 1985.
Commencement order: 85/1221.
s. 3, amended: 1985, c.50, s.25.
s. 7, order 85/1221.

3. Brunei and Maldives Act 1985.
Royal Assent, March 11, 1985.

4. Milk (Cessation of Production) Act 1985.
Royal Assent, March 11, 1985.

5. New Towns and Urban Development Corporations Act 1985.
Royal Assent, March 11, 1985.

6. Companies Act 1985.
Royal Assent, March 11, 1985.
s. 3, regs. 85/805.
s. 6, regs. 85/854.
s. 8, regs. 85/805, 1052.
ss. 10, 12, 21, 30, 43, 49, 51, 53, 54, 65, 72, 77, 88, 97, regs. 85/854.
s. 112AA, added: 1985, c.65, s.215.
ss. 117, 122, 123, 128, 129, 139, 147, regs. 85/854.
s. 153, amended: 1985, c.65, sch. 6.
ss. 155–157, 169, 173, 176, regs. 85/854.
s. 178, repealed in pt.: 1985, c.65, sch. 10.
s. 185, order 85/806.
s. 190, regs. 85/854.

1985—cont.

6. Companies Act 1985—*cont.*

ss. 196, 216, 222, amended: 1985, c.65, sch. 6.

ss. 224, 225, regs. 85/854.

s. 225, modified: 1985, c.65, sch. 6.

ss. 241, 242, 266, 272, 273, 287, 288, regs. 85/854.

s. 295, amended: 1985, c.65, sch. 6.

s. 297, see *Arctic Engineering, Re, Financial Times*, October 30, 1985, Hoffman J.

s. 300, repealed: 1985, c.65, sch. 10.

s. 301, regs. 85/829.

s. 301, amended: 1985, c.65, sch. 6.

s. 302, repealed in pt.: *ibid.*, sch. 10.

s. 318, regs. 85/854.

s. 324, regs. 85/802.

ss. 325, 353, 362–364, 386, 395, regs. 85/854.

s. 395, amended: 1985, c.65, sch. 6.

ss. 397, 398, 400, 401, 403, 405, 409, 410, regs. 85/854.

s. 410, amended: 1985, c.65, sch. 6.

ss. 413, 416, 417, 419, 424, regs. 85/854.

ss. 425, 426, amended: 1985, c.65, sch. 6.

ss. 428, 429, regs. 85/854.

ss. 441, 449, 461, 463, 464, amended: 1985, c.65, sch. 6.

s. 466, regs. 85/854.

s. 467, repealed: 1985, c.65, sch. 10.

s. 469, regs. 85/854.

s. 469, amended: 1985, c.65, s.56.

s. 470, regs. 85/854.

s. 470, repealed: 1985, c.65, sch. 10.

s. 471, amended: *ibid.*, s.57; repealed in pt.: *ibid.*, s.57, sch. 10.

s. 473, amended: *ibid.*, s.58; repealed in pt.: *ibid.*, s.58, sch. 10.

ss. 475, 476, amended: *ibid.*, sch. 6.

s. 477, amended: *ibid.*, s.59; repealed in pt.: *ibid.*, s.59, sch. 10.

s. 478, amended: *ibid.*, s.60, sch. 6.

s. 479, substituted: *ibid.*, s.61.

s. 481, regs. 85/854.

s. 481, substituted: 1985, c.65, s.62.

s. 482, regs. 85/854.

s. 482, substituted: 1985, c.65, s.63.

s. 482A, added: *ibid.*, s.64.

s. 482B, added: *ibid.*, s.65.

ss. 485, 486, 495–498, regs. 85/854.

ss. 495–497, repealed: 1985, c.65, sch. 10.

ss. 501–504, repealed in pt.: *ibid.*

s. 507, amended: *ibid.*, sch. 6.

s. 511, repealed in pt.: *ibid.*, sch. 10.

ss. 512, 515, amended: *ibid.*, sch. 6; repealed in pt.: *ibid.*, sch. 10.

s. 517, see *Palmer Marine Surveys, Re, The Times*, October 26, 1985, Hoffman J.

ss. 518, 519, amended: 1985, c.65, sch. 6; repealed in pt.: *ibid.*, sch. 10.

s. 525, amended: *ibid.*, sch. 6.

ss. 526–531, 533, 534, repealed: *ibid.*, sch. 10.

s. 535, substituted: *ibid.*, sch. 6.

s. 536, repealed: *ibid.*, sch. 10.

1985—cont.

6. Companies Act 1985—*cont.*

s. 539, amended: *ibid.*, sch. 6; repealed in pt.: *ibid.*, schs. 6, 10.

ss. 540 (in pt.), 541–548, 551; repealed: *ibid.*, sch. 10.

s. 552, amended: *ibid.*, sch. 6.

ss. 553 (in pt.), 556, 560 (in pt.), 561, repealed: *ibid.*, sch. 10.

s. 562, amended: *ibid.*, sch. 6.

ss. 563, 564, 565 (in pt.), repealed: *ibid.*, sch. 10.

s. 567, amended: *ibid.*, sch. 6.

ss. 568, 570, 571 (in pt.), repealed: *ibid.*, sch. 10.

s. 577, amended: *ibid.*, sch. 6.

ss. 580 (in pt.), 582 (in pt.), 583, repealed: *ibid.*, sch. 10.

s. 584, amended: *ibid.*, sch. 6.

ss. 586, 588, repealed: *ibid.*, sch. 10.

s. 589, amended: *ibid.*, sch. 6.

ss. 590, 591, amended: *ibid.*; repealed in pt.: *ibid.*, sch. 10.

s. 593, amended: *ibid.*, sch. 6.

s. 598, amended: *ibid.*; repealed in pt.: *ibid.*, sch. 10.

s. 600, regs. 85/854.

ss. 601, 604 (in pt.), Pt. XX, Chap. IV (ss.606–610), 611–618, 619 (in pt.), 620, repealed: 1985, c.65, sch. 10.

s. 613, amended(S.): 1985, c.66, sch. 7.

ss. 615A, 615B, added(S.): *ibid.*

s. 622, amended: 1985, c.65, sch. 6; repealed in pt.: *ibid.*, sch. 10.

s. 623, amended(S.): 1985, c.66, sch. 7.

s. 624, amended: 1985, c.65, sch. 6.

ss. 625, 626, amended: *ibid.*; repealed in pt.: *ibid.*, sch. 10.

ss. 628, 629, repealed in pt.: *ibid.*

s. 630, amended: *ibid.*, sch. 6; repealed in pt.: *ibid.*, sch. 10.

s. 631, repealed: *ibid.*

s. 632, amended: *ibid.*, sch. 6; repealed in pt.: *ibid.*, sch. 10.

ss. 634, 637 (in pt.), repealed: *ibid.*

s. 638, repealed in pt.: 1985, c.54, sch. 27.

ss. 640, 642, repealed: 1985, c.65, sch. 10.

s. 643, amended(S.): 1985, c.66, sch. 7.

s. 645, see *Palmer Marine Surveys, Re, The Times*, October 26, 1985, Hoffmann J.

ss. 651, 657, 658, 659, amended: 1985, c.65, sch. 6.

ss. 660–663, repealed: *ibid.*, sch. 10.

s. 663, order 85/1784.

s. 664, amended: 1985, c.65, sch. 6; repealed in pt.: *ibid.*, sch. 10.

s. 665, repealed in pt.: 1985, c.58, sch. 4; c.65, sch. 10, c.66, sch.(S.).

s. 666, repealed in pt.: 1985, c.58, sch. 4; c.65, sch. 10.

ss. 667–669, amended: *ibid.*, sch. 6.

s. 671, repealed in pt.: *ibid.*, sch. 10.

ss. 680, 681, 684–686, 690–692, 694, 698, 700, 701, regs. 85/854.

s. 718, regs. 85/680.

s. 723, regs. 85/725.

1985—cont.

6. Companies Act 1985—cont.
s. 726, see *Jenred Properties* v. *Ente Nazionale Italiano per il Turismo, Financial Times*, October 29, 1985, C.A.
s. 733, amended: 1985, c.65, sch. 6.
s. 744, regs. 85/854.
s. 744, repealed in pt.: 1985, c.65, sch. 10.
sch. 12, amended: *ibid.*, sch. 6; repealed in pt.: *ibid.*, sch. 10.
schs. 13, 14, regs. 85/854.
schs. 16 (in pt.), 17–19, 20 (in pt.), repealed: 1985, c.65, sch. 10.
sch. 22, regs. 85/680.
sch. 24, amended: 1985, c.65, sch. 6; repealed in pt.: *ibid.*, sch. 10.

7. Business Names Act 1985.
Royal Assent, March 11, 1985.

8. Company Securities (Insider Dealing) Act 1985.
Royal Assent, March 11, 1985.

9. Companies Consolidation (Consequential Provisions) Act 1985.
Royal Assent, March 11, 1985.
ss. 2, 4, regs. 85/854.
sch. 2, repealed in pt.: 1985, c.65, sch. 10; c.71, sch. 1; c.72, sch. 13.

10. London Regional Transport (Amendment) Act 1985.
Royal Assent, March 11, 1985.

11. Consolidated Fund (No. 2) Act 1985.
Royal Assent, March 27, 1985.

12. Mineral Workings Act 1985.
Royal Assent, March 27, 1985.
s. 8, regs. 85/814.

13. Cinemas Act 1985.
Royal Assent, March 27, 1985.
ss. 17, 18, 21, amended: 1985, c.51, sch. 8.

14. Shipbuilding Act 1985.
Royal Assent, March 27, 1985.

15. Hong Kong Act 1985.
Royal Assent, April 4, 1985.

16. National Heritage (Scotland) Act 1985.
Royal Assent, April 4, 1985.
Commencement order: 85/851.
s. 25, order 85/851.

17. Reserve Forces (Safeguard of Employment) Act 1985.
Royal Assent, May 9, 1985.
s. 13, repealed: 1985, c.65, sch. 10.
s. 13, repealed in pt.(S.): 1985, c.66, sch. 8.

18. Betting, Gaming and Lotteries (Amendment) Act 1985.
Royal Assent, May 9, 1985.
Commencement order: 85/1475.
s. 3, order 85/1475.

19. Town and Country Planning (Compensation) Act 1985.
Royal Assent, May 9, 1985.

20. Charities Act 1985.
Royal Assent, May 23, 1985.
Commencement order: 85/1583.
s. 7, order 85/1583.

21. Films Act 1985.
Royal Assent, May 23, 1985.
s. 2, order 85/811.

1985—cont.

21. Films Act 1985—cont.
s. 3, order 85/1943.
s. 6, order 85/2001.
sch. 1, regs. 85/994; orders 85/960, 2001.

22. Dangerous Vessels Act 1985.
Royal Assent, May 23, 1985.

23. Prosecution of Offences Act 1985.
Royal Assent, May 23, 1985.
Commencement order: 85/1849.
s. 3, orders 85/1956, 2010.
ss. 11, 29, regs. 85/1846.
s. 31, order 85/1849.

24. Rent (Amendment) Act 1985.
Royal Assent, May 23, 1985.

25. Industrial Development Act 1985.
Royal Assent, June 13, 1985.

26. Intoxicating Substances (Supply) Act 1985.
Royal Assent, June 13, 1985.

27. Coal Industry Act 1985.
Royal Assent, June 13, 1985.

28. Motor-Cycle Crash-Helmets (Restriction of Liability) Act 1985.
Royal Assent, June 13, 1985.

29. Enduring Powers of Attorney Act 1985.
Royal Assent, June 26, 1985.

30. Ports (Finance) Act 1985.
Royal Assent, June 26, 1985.
Commencement order: 85/1153.
s. 7, order 85/1153.

31. Wildlife and Countryside (Amendment) Act 1985.
Royal Assent, June 26, 1985.
s. 2, repealed in pt.: 1985, c.59, s.1.

32. Hill Farming Act 1985.
Royal Assent, June 26, 1985.

33. Rating (Revaluation Rebates) (Scotland) Act 1985.
Royal Assent, June 26, 1985.
s. 1, order 85/1170.

34. Road Traffic (Production of Documents) Act 1985.
Royal Assent, July 16, 1985.

35. Gaming (Bingo) Act 1985.
Royal Assent, July 16, 1985.

36. Agricultural Training Board Act 1985.
Royal Assent, July 16, 1985.

37. Family Law (Scotland) Act 1985.
Royal Assent, July 16, 1985.
s. 14, amended: 1985, c.66, sch. 7.
s. 27, amended: 1985, c.73, sch. 2.

38. Prohibition of Female Circumcision Act 1985.
Royal Assent, July 16, 1985.

39. Controlled Drugs (Penalties) Act 1985.
Royal Assent, July 16, 1985.

40. Licensing (Amendment) Act 1985.
Royal Assent, July 16, 1985.

41. Copyright (Computer Software) Amendment Act 1985.
Royal Assent, July 16, 1985.

42. Hospital Complaints Procedure Act 1985.
Royal Assent, July 16, 1985.

43. Local Government (Access to Information) Act 1985.
Royal Assent, July 16, 1985.

1985—cont.

44. Sexual Offences Act 1985.
Royal Assent, July 16, 1985.
45. Charter Trustees Act 1985.
Royal Assent, July 16, 1985.
46. Insurance (Fees) Act 1985.
Royal Assent, July 16, 1985.
47. Further Education Act 1985.
Royal Assent, July 16, 1985.
Commencement order: 85/1429.
s. 7, order 85/1429.
48. Food and Environment Protection Act 1985.
Royal Assent, July 16, 1985.
Commencement orders: 85/1390, 1698.
s. 7, order 85/1699.
s. 16, order 85/1516; regs. 85/1517.
s. 27, orders 85/1390, 1698.
sch. 5, regs. 85/1517.
49. Surrogacy Arrangements Act 1985.
Royal Assent, July 16, 1985.
50. Representation of the People Act 1985.
Royal Assent, July 16, 1985.
Commencement order: 85/1185.
s. 8, repealed in pt.: 1985, c.54, sch. 27.
s. 29, order 85/1185.
sch. 4, amended: 1985, c.73, sch.2.
51. Local Government Act 1985.
Royal Assent, July 16, 1985.
Commencement orders: 85/1175, 1177, 1263, 1283, 1285, 1286, 1295, 1342, 1362, 1408.
s. 10, order 85/1884.
s. 13, order 85/1933.
s. 15, orders 85/1408, 1409.
ss. 18, 23, order 85/1283.
ss. 24, 25, rules 85/1184.
s. 42, repealed in pt.: 1985, c.67, sch. 8.
s. 57, orders 85/1175, 1263, 1285, 1286, 1295, 1342, 1362.
s. 85, regs. 85/1302, 1303.
s. 98, order 85/1341.
s. 101, order 85/1320, 1383, 1410, 1506.
sch. 4, order 85/1177.
sch. 8, amended: 1985, c.72, sch. 12; repealed in pt.: 1985, c.71, sch. 1; c.72, sch. 13.
sch. 12, repealed in pt.: 1985, c.67, sch. 8.
sch. 13, amended: 1985, c.71, sch. 2; repealed in pt.: *ibid.*, sch. 1.
sch. 14, repealed in pt.: 1985, c.67, sch. 8; c.71, sch. 1.
52. Town and Country Planning (Amendment) Act 1985.
Royal Assent, July 22, 1985.
53. Social Security Act 1985.
Royal Assent, July 22, 1985.
Commencement orders: 85/1125, 1364.
s. 6, regs. 85/1927; order 85/1622.
s. 7, regs. 85/1398, 1417.
s. 13, regs. 85/1305.
s. 17, regs. 85/1250.
s. 27, regs. 85/1190.
s. 32, orders 85/1125, 1364; regs. 85/1398, 1417.

1985—cont.

54. Finance Act 1985.
Royal Assent, July 25, 1985.
Commencement orders: 85/1451, 1622.
s. 7, order 85/1451.
s. 96, order 85/1172.
55. Appropriation Act 1985.
Royal Assent, July 25, 1985.
56. Interception of Communications Act 1985.
Royal Assent, July 25, 1985.
57. Sporting Events (Control of Alcohol etc.) Act 1985.
Royal Assent, July 25, 1985.
s. 9, order 85/1151.
58. Trustee Savings Banks Act 1985.
Royal Assent, July 25, 1985.
s. 7, orders 85/1210, 1211.
59. Wildlife and Countryside (Service of Notices) Act 1985.
Royal Assent, July 25, 1985.
60. Child Abduction and Custody Act 1985.
Royal Assent, July 25, 1985.
61. Administration of Justice Act 1985.
Royal Assent, October 30, 1985.
s. 16, amended: 1985, c.65, sch. 8; repealed in pt.: *ibid.*, sch. 10.
s. 17, repealed in pt.: *ibid.*
62. Oil and Pipelines Act 1985.
Royal Assent, October 30, 1985.
Commencement orders: 85/1748, 1749.
s. 3, order 85/1749.
s. 8, order 85/1748.
63. Water (Fluoridation) Act 1985.
Royal Assent, October 30, 1985.
64. European Communities (Finance) Act 1985.
Royal Assent, October 30, 1985.
65. Insolvency Act 1985.
Royal Assent, October 30, 1985.
66. Bankruptcy (Scotland) Act 1985.
Royal Assent, October 30, 1985.
67. Transport Act 1985.
Royal Assent, October 30, 1985.
Commencement order: 85/1887.
ss. 66, 71, order 85/1902.
s. 73, order 85/1901.
ss. 90, 91, order 85/1921.
s. 129, order 85/1903.
s. 140, order 85/1887.
sch. 6, regs. 85/1904.
68. Housing Act 1985.
Royal Assent, October 30, 1985.
s. 4, amended: order 85/1884.
s. 121, repealed in pt.: 1985, c.65, sch. 10.
sch. 18, amended: *ibid.*, sch. 8.
69. Housing Associations Act 1985.
Royal Assent, October 30, 1985.
70. Landlord and Tenant Act 1985.
Royal Assent, October 30, 1985.
s. 38, amended: order 85/1884.
71. Housing (Consequential Provisions) Act 1985.
Royal Assent, October 30, 1985.
72. Weights and Measures Act 1985.
Royal Assent, October 30, 1985.

INDEX

References, e.g. 6/44 are to the Statutes of 1985, Chapter 6, section 44.

[1]

Index

Index